1941

1942

1942

1943

DICTIONARY

OF

AMERICAN NAVAL FIGHTING SHIPS

1944

1955

1955

1959

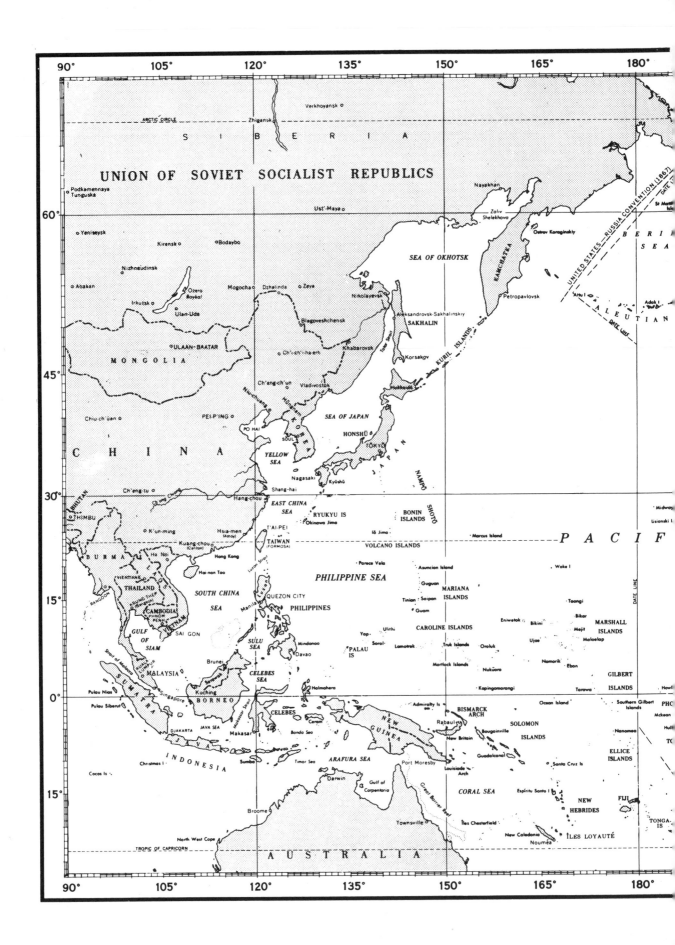

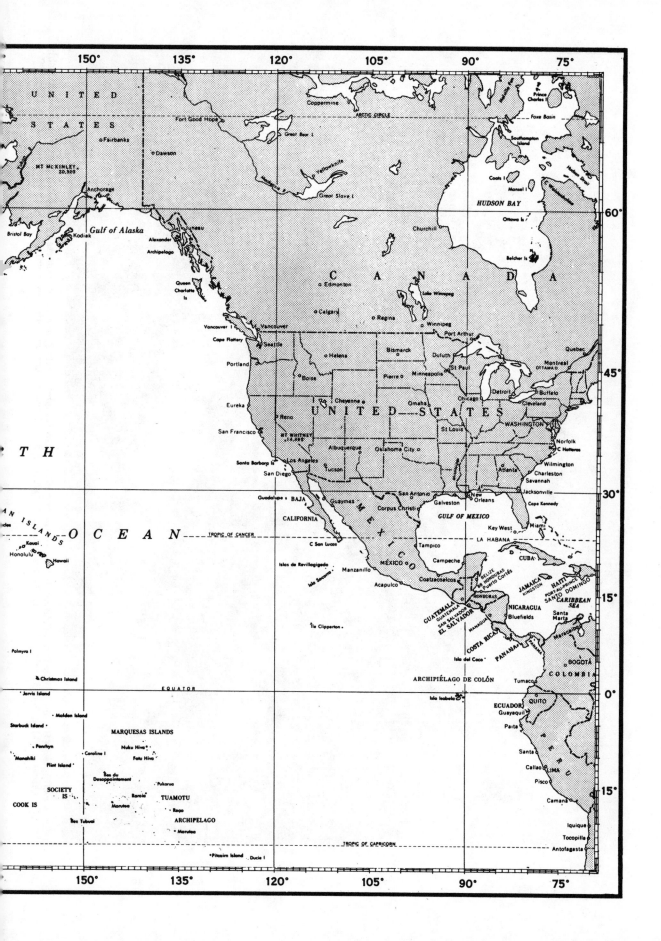

USS *Washington* (BB–56). In action off Guadalcanal on the night of 14–15 November, 1942, her gunfire mortally wounded the Japanese battleship *Kirishima*, making *Washington* the only American capital ship to defeat one of her own kind in a ship-to-ship action. (80–G–704128)

Dictionary of

American Naval

Fighting Ships

VOLUME VIII

Historical Sketches—Letters W through Z

JAMES L. MOONEY, Editor

In association with Commander Richard T. Speer, United States Navy, Retired

WITH A FOREWORD BY

EDWARD HIDALGO, SECRETARY OF THE NAVY

AND AN INTRODUCTION BY

REAR ADMIRAL JOHN D. H. KANE, JR., United States Navy, Retired,
THE DIRECTOR OF NAVAL HISTORY

NAVAL HISTORICAL CENTER
DEPARTMENT OF THE NAVY
WASHINGTON: 1981

L.C. CARD 60–60198

UNITED STATES

GOVERNMENT PRINTING OFFICE

WASHINGTON, D.C.

FOREWORD

This volume concludes the Naval History Division's series, the Dictionary of American Naval Fighting Ships. The project, unique among the navies of the world, goes back over 20 years to 1959 when Volume I was published. Included within its eight volumes are the histories of the almost 10,000 ships which have served the United States Navy and its forebear, the Continental Navy. Large or small; wind, steam, or nuclear-propelled; these ships, and the sailors who manned them, are our naval heritage. Their story is truly the story of our Navy from its infancy to its present preeminence.

Within the pages of these volumes, the reader can discern the continuity of spirit and the tradition of service which have animated the American Navy since the Continental Congress first authorized its establishment over two centuries ago. The succinct biographies of the famous naval leaders who have served as namesakes for many of the ships provide inspiring examples of the special kind of fighting men who have served in our men-of-war. The various appendices lend insight into the immense diversity and technological growth which have characterized the Fleet, particularly in the present century. The rich and varied illustrations provide a graphic representation of the steady evolution of our ships--from smooth bore cannon to Poseidon missiles, from wooden hulls to high-tensile steel, and from sail to atom as motive power.

In years to come, there will be supplementary volumes to this work as the Navy amasses new history; but, as any re-reading of these pages which have gone before will show, that history will be but a continuum of the lofty spirit and tradition which have preceded it.

Edward Hidalgo
Secretary of the Navy

THE DICTIONARY OF AMERICAN NAVAL FIGHTING SHIPS

James L. Mooney, Editor

In association with Richard T. Speer, Commander, United States Navy (Retired)

PRINCIPAL WRITERS

Robert J. Cressman
Christopher N. Kennedy
Roland S. Kennerly
Suzanne MacFarlane
Raymond A. Mann
Luann Parsons
Barbara A. Ponsolle
John C. Reilly, Jr.
Theresa M. Schuster

SECRETARY OF THE NAVY'S ADVISORY COMMITTEE ON NAVAL HISTORY

Richard W. Leopold (Chairman)

Francis L. Berkeley, Jr.
James A. Field
Captain Joy Bright Hancock, USN (Ret.)
Caryl P. Haskins
Jim Dan Hill

John H. Kemble
Augustus P. Loring
Forrest C. Pogue
Gordon B. Turner

**DIRECTOR OF NAVAL HISTORY AND
CURATOR FOR THE NAVY DEPARTMENT**

INTRODUCTION

This volume--which completes the DANFS project--was originally planned to be a part of Volume VII. However, in an effort to flesh out the historical sketches with more data, the manuscript grew in size until, shortly before publication date, it seemed wise to publish it in two parts. Accordingly, Volume VII contains the histories of ships beginning with the letters "T" through "V" together with a comprehensive appendix devoted to tank landing ships, and Volume VIII completes the alphabet. It is our hope that the reader will welcome the additional details contained in the individual sketches.

In the introduction to Volume VII, I acknowledged the generous contributions of the many persons associated with the project, either directly or indirectly, which made its publication possible. My remarks there are equally applicable to this volume, of course.

With the launching of Volume VIII, the DANFS fleet is finally complete. I wish its readers well as they explore unknown waters of naval history. May tomorrow's sailors and friends of the Navy find strength and inspiration in its pages.

JOHN D. H. KANE, JR.
Rear Admiral, USN (Ret.)

1 October 1980

CONTENTS

CONTENTS

A NOTE ON ILLUSTRATIONS

Negatives for many of the photographs used in this volume are held by the National Archives or the Naval Photographic Center. Negative numbers for those illustrations are included in parentheses at the end of their captions.

Prints of photographs bearing negative numbers with 80–G, 19–N, or 26–G prefixes can be purchased from the Audiovisual Archives Division, National Archives, Washington, D.C. 20408. Those with USN, NH, NR&L, K, or KN prefixes can be purchased from the Command-ing Officer, Naval Photographic Center, Washington, D.C. 20374 (ATTN: Still Pictures).

Unless otherwise specified, all the ships illustrated in this volume are commissioned ships of the U.S. Navy with their names preceded by the identification United States Ship (USS). Ships of the Military Sealift Command are civilian-manned and designated U.S. Naval Ship (USNS). Coast Guard vessels are identified as U.S. Coast Guard Cutter (USCGC).

ABBREVIATIONS AND SYMBOLS

A—alternating current generator.
a.—armament.
AA—antiaircraft.
AB—crane ship.
ABD—advance base dock.
ABDA—American–British–Dutch–Australian Command.
ABSD—advance base section dock.
A/C—Allis–Chalmers Mfg. Co., Milwaukee, Wis.
AC—collier.
ac.—aircraft.
ACM—auxiliary mine layer.
ACR—armored cruiser.
ACV—auxiliary aircraft carrier; or tender.
Act.—acting.
AD—destroyer tender.
ADG—degaussing ship.
AE—ammunition ship.
A.E.F.—American Expeditionary Force (World War I); or Allied Expeditionary Force (World War II).
AEW—airborne early warning (radar picket system).
AF—store ship.
AFD—auxiliary floating dock.
AFDB—large auxiliary floating dry dock (nsp.)
AFDL—small auxiliary floating dry dock (nsp.)
AFDM—medium auxiliary floating dry dock (nsp.)
AFS—combat store ship.
AG—miscellaneous auxiliary.
AGB—icebreaker.
AGC—general communications vessel; or amphibious force flagship (now LCC).
AGD—seagoing dredge.
AGDE—escort research ship.
AGDS—deep submergence support ship.
AGEH—hydrofoil research ship.
AGER—environmental research ship.
AGF—miscellaneous command ship.
AGL—lighthouse tender.
AGM—missile range instrumentation ship.
AGMR—major communications relay ship.
AGOR—oceanographic research ship.
AGP—motor torpedo boat tender.
AGR—radar picket ship.
AGS—surveying ship.
AGSC—coastal survey ship.
AGSL—satellite launching ship.
AGSS—auxiliary submarine.
AGTR—technical research ship.
AH—hospital ship.
AHP—evacuation hospital ship.
AK—cargo ship.
AKA—attack cargo ship (now LKA).
AKD—cargo ship, dock; or deep-hold cargo ship.
AKI—general stores issue ship.
AKL—light cargo ship.
AKN—net cargo ship.
AKS—stores issue ship.
AK(SS)—cargo submarine.
AKV—cargo ship and aircraft ferry.
AKR—vehicle cargo ship.
AL—lightship.
ALCo—American Locomotive Co., Auburn, N.Y.
AM—minesweeper.
AMh—minesweeper, harbor.
AMc—coastal minesweeper

Am–Int—American International Shipbuilding Corp., Hog Island, Pa.
AMS—motor minesweeper.
AMCU—coastal minesweeper (underwater locator); or mine hunter.
AN—net laying ship (now ANL).
ANL—net laying ship (formerly AN).
ANZAC—Australian–New Zealand Force.
AO—oiler; or fuel oil tanker.
AOG—gasoline tanker.
AOE—fast combat support ship.
AOR—replenishment oiler.
AOSS—submarine oiler.
AP—transport.
APA—attack transport (now LPA); or animal transport.
APB—self-propelled barracks ship; or artillery barge.
APb—base repair ship.
APC—cavalry transport; or small coastal transport (formerly APc).
APD—high-speed transport.
APF—administrative flagship.
APG—supporting gunnery ship.
APH—transport fitted for evacuation of wounded.
APL—barracks craft (nsp.).
APM—mechanized artillery transport.
APN—nonmechanized artillery transport.
APP—troop barge, class A.
APR—rescue transport.
APS—mine laying submarine; or transport, submarine.
APSS—transport, submarine.
APT—troop barge, class B.
APV—transport and aircraft ferry.
APY—giant "Y" boat.
AR—repair ship.
ARB—battle damage repair ship.
ARC—cable repairing ship.
ARD—auxiliary repair dock (nsp.).
ARDC—auxiliary repair dock, concrete.
ARDM—medium auxiliary repair dry dock (nsp.).
ARG—internal combustion engine repair ship.
ARH—heavy-hull repair ship.
ARL—landing craft repair ship.
ARM—heavy machinery repair ship.
ARS—salvage ship.
ARSD—salvage lifting ship.
ARST—salvage craft tender.
ARV—aircraft repair ship.
ARVA—aircraft repair ship (aircraft).
ARVE—aircraft repair ship (engine).
ARVH—aircraft repair ship (helicopter).
AS—submarine tender.
ASPB—assault support patrol boat.
ASR—submarine rescue ship.
ASROC—antisubmarine rocket.
ASSA—cargo submarine.
ASSP—transport submarine.
ASW—antisubmarine warfare.
AT—ocean tug.
ATA—auxiliary ocean tug.
ATC—armored troop carrier.
ATF—fleet ocean tug.
ATL—tank landing craft.
Atlas—Atlas Imperial Diesel Engine Co., Mattoon, Ill.
ATO—ocean tug, old.

ATR—rescue tug.
ATS—salvage tug.
aux.—auxiliary.
AV—seaplane tender.
AVB—advance aviation base ship.
AVC—large catapult lighter.
AVD—seaplane tender (destroyer).
AVG—aircraft escort vessel.
avgas—aviation gasoline.
AVM—guided missile ship.
AVP—small seaplane tender.
AVR—aircraft rescue vessel.
AVS—aviation supply ship.
AVT—auxiliary aircraft transport.
AW—distilling ship.
AWK—water tanker.
AZ—airship tender (lighter than air).
B—The letter "B" used as a prefix to a hull number indicates that the ship was built by the United States for a British Comonwealth Navy.
b.—beam.
BAK—British cargo ship.
BB—battleship.
BBG—guided missile capital ship.
bbls.—barrels.
B.C.—British Columbia.
BLM—ballistic intercontinental missile.
BDE—British escort ship.
Beth–Alam—Bethlehem–Alameda Shipyard, Inc., Alameda, Calif.
Beth–Fair—Bethlehem–Fairfield Shipyard, Inc., Baltimore, Md.
Beth–Hing—Bethlehem–Hingham Shipyard, Inc., Hingham, Mass.
BethPac–SanP—Bethlehem Pacific Coast Steel Corp., San Pedro, Calif.
BethPac–SanF—Bethlehem Pacific Coast Steel Corp., San Francisco, Calif.
BethSb–Wilm—Bethlehem Shipbuilding Corp., Wilmington, Del.
Beth–Spar—Bethelem–Sparrows Point Shipyard, Inc., Sparrows Point, Md.
BethSt–Balt—Bethlehem Steel Co., Shipbuilding Div., Baltimore, Md.
Beth–Bklyn—Bethlehem Steel Co., Shipbuilding Div., Brooklyn, N.Y.
BethSt–Quin—Bethlehem Steel Co., Shipbuilding Div., Quincy, Mass.
BethSt–Stat—Bethlehem Steel Co., Shipbuilding Div., Staten Island, N.Y.
Bg—barge.
bhp.—brake horsepower.
blr.—breach-loading rifle.
BM—monitor.
bom—"builders old measurement."
bp.—between perpendiculars (length).
BPDSMS—Basic point defense surface missile system.
Bt.—boat.
btry—battery.
Buda—Buda Diesel Engine Co.
BUEXP—Bureau Express Boiler.
Buff–B—Buffalo Shipbuilding Co., Buffalo, N.Y.
Buff–E—Buffalo Shipbuilding Co., Erie, Pa.
BUMODT—Bureau-modified Thorneycroft boiler.
BUR4DR—Bureau-4-Drum Boiler.
Busch—Busch Sulzer Brothers Diesel Engine Co., St. Louis, Mo.
BUSHIPS—Bureau of Ships (now NSSC).
BW—Babcock & Wilcox Co., Boiler Div., Barberton, Ohio.
BWA—Babcock & Wilcox Co., header-type boiler.
BWA3DR—Babcock & Wilcox 3-drum express-type boiler.
BWHDR—Babcock & Wilcox header-type boiler.
B.W.I.—British West Indies.
BWSHC—Babcock & Wilcox superheat control boiler.
BWSX—Babcock & Wilcox sectional express boiler.

BW2DR—Babcock & Wilcox 2-drum boiler.
BW2DRD—Babcock & Wilcox 2-drum D-type boiler.
BW2DSU—Babcock & Wilcox 2-drum single-uptake boiler.
C—protected cruiser; commanding officer.
CA—heavy cruiser.
CAG—guided missile heavy cruiser.
cal.—caliber.
CAP—combat air patrol.
car.—carronade.
CB—large cruiser.
C/B—Cooper Bessemer.
CBC—large tactical command ship.
CC—battle cruiser; or command ship.
C/C—controlled-circulation boiler.
CCB—command and control boat.
CCS—Combined Chiefs of Staff.
C/E—Combustion Engineering Co., Chattanooga, Tenn.
CED—Combustion Engineering D-type boiler.
CEH—Cummins Engine Co., Inc.
CEHDR—Combusion Engineering header-type boiler.
CENTO—Central Treaty Organization.
CE2DR—Combustion Engineering 2-drum boiler.
CE2DRD—Combustion Engineering 2-drum D-type boiler.
CF—flying-deck cruiser.
CFC—controlled forced circulation.
CG—guided missile cruiser.
CGC—Coast Guard cutter.
CGN—guided missile cruiser (nuclear propulsion).
CH—Cutler–Hammer.
Char—Naval Shipyard, Charleston, S.C. (formerly Navy Yard, Charleston).
Chry—Chrysler Corp.
CIC—Command Information Center.
CinCLant—Commander in Chief, U.S. Atlantic Fleet.
CinCPac—Commander in Chief, U.S. Pacific Fleet.
CIW—Columbian Iron Works, Baltimore, Md.
CL—light cruiser.
cl.—class.
CLAA—Antiaircraft light cruiser.
ClBt—canal boat.
CLC—tactical command ship.
CLG—guided missile light cruiser.
CLK—cruiser hunter-killer ship.
CM—minelayer.
CMc—coastal minelayer.
CMC—Continental Motors Corp.
CNO—Chief of Naval Operations.
C.O.—commanding officer.
compos.—composite drive (2 diesel engines, electric drive; 2 diesel engines, geared drive; hydraulic couple).
const.—construction.
cont.—continued.
Cor.—corvette.
CortRon—escort squadron.
cpl.—complement.
Craig—Craig Shipbuilding Co., Long Beach, Calif.
Cramp—Wm. Cramp & Sons Ship & Engine Building Co., Philadelphia, Pa.
Cres—Crescent Shipyard, Elizabethport, N.J.
CS—scout cruiser.
CSA—Confederate States Army.
CSN—Confederate States Navy.
CSS—Confederate States Ship.
CTB—coastal torpedo boat.
CTF—Commander Task Force.
CTG—Commander Task Group.
Ctr.—cutter.
CTU—Commander Task Unit.
Cur.—Curtis-type turbine.
CV—aircraft carrier.
CVA—attack aircraft carrier.
CVAN—attack aircraft carrier (nuclear propulsion).
CVB—large aircraft carrier.
CVE—escort aircraft carrier.
CVHA—assault helicopter aircraft carrier.

CVL—small aircraft carrier.
CVS—antisubmarine warfare support aircraft carrier; or seaplane carrier.
CVT—training aircraft carrier.
CVU—utility aircraft carrier.
Cwt.—hundred weight.
C.Z.—Canal Zone.
DANFS—Dictionary of American Naval Fighting Ships.
DASH—drone antisubmarine helicopter.
dc.—depth charge.
dcp.—depth charge projector.
dcp. (hh.)—depth charge projector (hedgehog-type).
dct.—depth charge track.
DD—destroyer.
dd.—dry dock.
d/d—diesel direct.
DDC—corvette.
ddd.—diesel direct drive.
DDE—antisubmarine destroyer.
DDG—guided missile destroyer.
DDR—radar picket destroyer.
DE—escort ship.
d/e—diesel electric.
DEC—control escort vessel.
ded.—diesel electric drive.
DEG—guided missile escort ship.
DeL—De Laval Steam Turbine Co., Trenton, N.J.
DeL–FB—De Laval & Farrel–Birmingham.
DeL–Falk—De Laval & Falk.
DeL–GE—De Laval & General Electric.
DeL–Wes—De Laval & Westinghouse.
DER—radar picket escort ship.
de/r—diesel-electric reduction.
derd.—diesel electric reduction drive.
des.—design.
Des—destroyer.
DesDiv—Destroyer Division.
DesRon—Destroyer Squadron.
det.—diesel electric tandem motor drive.
DEW—Distant Early Warning System (a radar network across upper North America).
dgd.—diesel geared drive.
Diehl—Diehl Manufacturing Co., Bridgeport, N.Y.
div.—division.
DL—frigate.
DLG—guided missile frigate.
DLGN—guided missile frigate (nuclear propulsion).
dlt.—double reduction-locked train.
DM—destroyer minelayer; or light minelayer (now MMD).
DMS—high-speed minesweeper; or destroyer minesweeper.
DMZ—Demilitarized Zone.
dp.—displacement; or dual purpose (guns).
dph.—depth of hold.
dr.—draft.
D.r.—Dahlgren rifle.
drd.—diesel reduction drive.
D.sb.—Dahlgren smoothbore.
EAG—experimental miscellaneous auxiliary.
EBCo—Electric Boat Co., Groton, Conn.
ED—Electric Dynamic Co., Bayonne, N.J.
ehp.—estimated horsepower.
EIWHDR—Edgemoor Iron Works header-type boiler.
Ell—Elliot Motor Co., Jeannette, Pa.
EllMach—Ellicott Machine Corp., Baltimore, Md.
ElSpecCo—Electric Specialty Co., Stamford, Conn.
eng.—engine.
enl.—enlisted.
Enter—Enterprise Engine and Foundry Co., San Francisco, Calif.
ew.—extreme width of flight deck.
ex—former.
Exide—Exide Electric Storage Battery Corp., Philadelphia, Pa.
exp.—expansion.
f.—full load (displacement).

Falk–DeL—Falk & De Laval.
Falk–FB—Falk & Farrel–Birmingham.
Falk–GE—Falk & General Electric.
Falk–Wes—Falk & Westinghouse.
FAST—Fast At Sea Transfer equipment.
FB—Farrel–Birmingham Co., N.Y.
FB–Falk—Farrel–Birmingham & Falk.
FB–Wes—Farrel–Birmingham & Westinghouse.
FBM—fleet ballistic missile.
FDL—fast deployment logistics ship.
Fed—Federal Shipbuilding & Drydock Co., Kearny, N.J.
Fiat—Fiat–San Giorgio, Ltd., Turin, Italy.
Flot—flotilla.
FltBtry—floating battery.
FM—Fairbanks Morse diesel, reverse gear drive (manufactured by Fairbanks Morse & Co., Beloit, Wis.).
Fore—Fore River Ship and Engine Co., Quincy, Mass.
Fr.—Frigate.
FRAM—Fleet Rehabilitation And Modernization.
FSch.—F. Schichau, Gmbh., Elbing, Germany.
f.t.—fire-tube (Scotch-type boiler).
FW—Foster Wheeler Corp., Mountaintop, Pa.
FWA3DR—Foster Wheeler 3-Drum Express-Type Boiler.
FWH—Foster Wheeler Header-Type Boiler.
FWPFS—Foster Wheeler Pressure-Fixed Supercharged Boiler.
FWSFD—Foster Wheeler Single-Furnace D-Type Boiler.
FWSHC—Foster Wheeler Superheat Control Boiler.
FW2DR—Foster Wheeler 2-Drum Boiler.
FW2DRS—Foster Wheeler 2-Drum Superheat Control Boiler.
gal.—gallon.
Gbt.—gunboat.
gd.—gundeck.
GDEB—Grot—General Dynamics Corp., Electric Boat Div., Groton, Conn.
GDEB—Quin—General Dynamics Corp., Electric Boat Div., Quincy, Mass.
GE—General Electric Co., Schenectady, N.Y.
gen.—generator.
G.g.—Gatling gun.
GM—General Motors Corp., Cleveland Diesel Division, Cleveland, Ohio.
Gond—gondola.
Gould—Gould Storage Battery Co., Trenton, N.J.
gr.—gross (tonnage).
Gulf—Gulf Shipbuilding Corp., Chickasaw, Ala.
Gy—galley.
Hall-S—Hall–Scott.
HBM—His (Her) Britannic Majesty's.
helo.—helicopter.
Herc—Hercules Motor Co., Canton, Ohio.
HH—Harlan and Hollingsworth Corp., Wilmington, Del.
HIJMS—His Imperial Japanese Majesty's Ship.
HL—R. L. Hawthorne, Leslie and Co., Ltd., Newcastle-on-Tyne, England.
HMAS—His (Her) Majesty's Australian Ship.
HMCS—His (Her) Majesty's Canadian Ship.
HMNZS—His (Her) Majesty's New Zealand Ship.
HNMS—Her Netherlands Majesty's Ship.
HORC—Hooven, Owens, Renschler Co., Hamilton, Ohio.
hor3—horizontal triple-expansion.
how.—howitzer.
hp.—horsepower.
HT—Humphreys and Tenant, Ltd., London, England.
HUK—Hunter/Killer; offensive ASW.
Hw—Hunter-wheel.
HwGbt—Hunter-wheel gunboat.
HwStr—Hunter-wheel steamer.
IFS—inshore fire support ship (now LFR).
ihp.—indicated horsepower.
ip.—intermediate pressure.
int.—international.
Irc—ironclad.
IrcFltBtry—ironclad floating battery.

IrcGbt—ironclad gunboat.
IrcRam—ironclad ram.
IrcSlp—ironclad sloop.
IrcStr—ironclad steamer.
IrcStFltBtry—ironclad steam floating battery.
IX—unclassified miscellaneous auxiliary ship.
JCS—Joint Chiefs of Staff.
JHendy—Joshua Hendy.
JTF—Joint Task Force.
k.—knots.
KA—contraction of AKA (attack cargo ship).
Kopp—Koppers Manufacturing Co.
kw.—kilowatts.
l.—length.
LBP—personnel landing boat.
lbp.—length between perpendiculars.
LBS—support landing boat.
LBV—vehicle landing boat.
LCA—assault landing craft.
LCAP—local combat air patrol.
LCB—landing craft, vehicle.
LCC—amphibious comand ship (formerly AGC).
LCC(1)—landing craft, control Mk I.
LCC(2)—landing craft, control Mk II.
LC(FF)—landing craft, infantry (gunboat).
LCI(L)—landing craft, infantry (large).
LCI(M)—landing craft, infantry (mortar).
LCI(R)—landing craft, infantry (rocket).
LCM—landing craft, mechanized.
LCM(2)—landing craft, mechanized, Mk II.
LCM(3)—landing craft, mechanized, Mk III.
LCM(6)—landing craft, mechanized, Mk VI.
LCM(8)—landing craft, mechanized, Mk VIII.
LCPL—landing craft, personnel (large).
LCP(N)—landing craft, personnel (nested).
LCPR—landing craft, personnel, ramped.
LCR(L)—landing craft, inflatable boat (large).
LCR(S)—landing craft, inflatable boat (small).
LCSL—landing craft, infantry (support).
LCSR—landing craft, swimmer reconnaissance.
LCS(S)(1)—landing craft, support (small) Mk I.
LCS(S)(2)—landing craft, support (small) Mk II.
LCT—landing craft, tank.
LCU—landing craft, utility.
LCV—landing craft, vehicle.
LCVP—landing craft, vehicle, personnel.
LFR—inshore fire support ship (formerly IFS, LSMR).
Lht.—lighthouse tender.
LFS—amphibious fire support ship.
LHA—amphibious assault ship (general purpose).
lim.—limiting.
LKA—amphibious cargo ship (formerly AKA).
Loran—long range navigation [system].
lp.—low pressure.
LPA—amphibious transport (formerly APA).
LPD—amphibious transport dock.
LPH—amphibious assault ship.
LPR—amphibious transport, small (formerly APD).
LSD—dock landing ship.
LSFF—flotilla flagship (amphibious).
LSI—landing ship, infantry (giant "Y" boat).
LSI(G)—landing ship, infantry (gunboat).
LSI(L)—landing ship, infantry (large).
LSI(M)—landing ship, infantry (mortar).
LSI(R)—landing ship, infantry (rocket).
LSM—medium landing ship.
LSM(R)—medium landing ship (rocket), (now LFR).
LSS(L)—support landing ship (large) Mk III.
LST—tank landing ship.
LSTH—landing ship, tank (casualty evacuation).
LSTS—landing ship (utility).
LSU—landing ship (utility).
LSV—landing ship, vehicle.
LT—large tug (Army).
lt—light (displacement).
Lufkin—Lufkin Foundry & Machine Co.
LVA—assault landing vehicle.
LVT—landing vehicle, tracked.

LWT—amphibious warping tug.
M—Marine.
M.—mortar.
MAC—Military Airlift Command.
MarAd—Maritime Administration.
MAP—Military Assistance Program.
MB—motor boat.
M.C.—Maritime Commission.
M.C.E.—Maritime Commission Emergency Ship Program ("Liberty" ships).
MSC—mine countermeasures ship.
M.C.V.—Maritime Commission Victory Ship Program ("Victory" ships).
M.D.A.P.—Mutual Defense Assistance Program.
Mfr.—manufacturer.
mg.—machine gun.
MHA—minehunter, auxiliary.
MHC—minehunter, coastal.
MinDiv—mine division.
MinFlot—mine flotilla.
MinLant—Mine Force Atlantic.
MinPac—Mine Force Pacific.
MinRon—mine squadron.
mis.—missile.
mis. ln.—missile launcher.
mk.—mark.
mlr.—muzzle-loading rifle.
MM—minelayer, fleet.
mm.—millimeter.
MMA—minelayer, auxiliary.
MMC—minelayer, coastal.
MMD—minelayer, fast (formerly DM).
MMF—minelayer, fleet.
Mon—monitor.
MON—monitor (new riverine warfare type).
Moran—Moran Brothers Co., Seattle, Wash.
Mssh.—Mosher-type boiler.
mot—motor generator.
mph—miles per hour.
MS—motor ship.
MSA—minesweeper, auxiliary.
MSB—minesweeping boat.
M.S.C.—Military Sealift Command (formerly MSTS).
MSC—minesweeper, coastal (nonmagnetic).
MSCO—minesweeper, coastal (old).
MSD—minesweeper, drone.
MSF—minesweeper, fleet (steel hull).
MSI—minesweeper, inshore.
MSL—minesweeping launch.
MSM—minesweeper, river.
MSO—minesweeper, ocean (nonmagnetic).
MSR—minesweeper, patrol.
MSS—minesweeper, special (device).
MSTS—Military Sea Transportation Service (now Military Sealift Command).
n.—normal (displacement).
NAR—Naval Auxiliary Reserve.
NASA—National Aeronautics and Space Administration.
NaSuCo—National Supply Co.
NATO—North Atlantic Treaty Organization.
NaTran—National Transit Pump & Machine Co., Oil City, Pa.
NATS—Naval Air Transport Service.
NavSea—Naval Sea Systems Command (formerly NSSC and Naval Ordnance Systems Command).
NavSyd—naval shipyard.
NavSyd–Bos—Boston Naval Shipyard, Boston, Mass. (formerly Boston Navy Yard).
NavSyd–Bklyn—New York Naval Shipyard, Brooklyn, N.Y. (formerly New York Navy Yard).
NavSyd–Charl—Charleston Naval Shipyard, Charleston, S.C. (formerly Charleston Navy Yard).
NavSyd–Hunt—Hunters Point Div., San Francisco Bay Naval Shipyard, San Francisco, Calif.
NavSyd–LBeach—Long Beach Naval Shipyard, Long Beach, Calif.

NavSyd–MI—Mare Island Naval Shipyard, Vallejo, Calif.

NavSyd–Norfolk—Norfolk Naval Shipyard, Norfolk, Va. (formerly Norfolk Navy Yard).

NavSyd–Pearl—Pearl Harbor Naval Shipyard, Pearl Harbor, Hawaii (formerly Pearl Harbor Navy Yard).

NavSyd–Phil—Philadelphia Naval Shipyard, Philadelphia, Pa. (formerly Philadelphia Navy Yard).

NavSyd–Ports—Portsmouth Naval Shipyard, Portsmouth, N.H. (formerly Portsmouth Navy Yard).

NavSyd–Puget—Puget Sound Naval Shipyard, Bremerton, Wash. (formerly Puget Sound Navy Yard).

Neafie—Neafie and Levy Ship and Engine Building Co., Philadelphia, Pa.

N.E.I.—Netherlands East Indies.

Nfld.—Newfoundland.

N.G.—New Guinea.

N.I.—Northern Ireland.

NICB—Niclausse-type boiler (built by the Stirling Co., Barberton, Ohio).

Niles—Niles Tool Works Div., General Machinery Corp.

NLSE—New London Ship and Engine Co., Groton, Conn.

NN—Newport News Shipbuilding and Dry Dock Co., Newport News, Va.

NNV—National Naval Volunteers.

NOB—Naval Operating Base.

NOR—Normand-type boiler.

Nordb—Nordberg Manufacturing Co., Milwaukee, Wis.

NOTS—Naval Overseas Transportation Service.

NR—submersible research vehicle (nuclear propulsion).

NROTC—Naval Reserve Officers Training Corps.

N.S.—Nova Scotia.

nsp.—non-self-propelled.

NSSC—Naval Ship Systems Command (formerly BUSHIPS, now part of NavSea).

N.W.I.—Netherlands West Indies.

NYd—Navy yard.

NYd–Pensa—Pensacola Navy Yard, Pensacola, Fla.

NYd–Wash—Washington Navy Yard, Washington, D.C.

NYSb—New York Shipbuilding Corp., Camden, N.J.

off.—officer(s).

OIC—Officer in Charge.

OTC—Officer in Tactical Command.

PA—contraction of APA (attack transport).

PACV—patrol air cushion vehicle.

Palm—N. F. Palmer, Jr., and Co., New York, N.Y.

PARPRO—Peacetime Aerial Reconnaissance Program.

PBM—twin-engine patrol bomber seaplane, known as "Mariner," manufactured by Glenn L. Martin Co.

PBR—river patrol boat.

PBY—twin-engine patrol bomber seaplane, known as "Catalina," manufactured by Consolidated–Vultee Aircraft Corp.

PC—submarine chaser (173').

PCC—control submarine chaser (173').

PCE—patrol escort.

PCEC—control escort (180').

PCER—patrol rescue escort.

PCF—patrol craft, inshore.

PCH—patrol craft (hydrofoil).

PCS—patrol craft, submarine.

PCSC—control submarine chaser (136').

pdr.—pounder.

PE—eagle boat.

PF—patrol escort; or frigate.

PG—patrol gunboat.

PGH—patrol gunboat (hydrofoil).

PGM—motor gunboat.

Phib—amphibious.

PhibRon—amphibious squadron.

P.I.—Philippine Islands.

PIRAZ—positive identification and radar advisory zone.

Pol.—Polaris missile system.

P.Q.—Province of Quebec.

PR—river gunboat.

P.R.—Puerto Rico.

P.r.—Parrott rifle.

PT—motor torpedo boat.

PTC—motor boat subchaser.

PTF—fast patrol craft.

Pusey—Pusey & Jones, Wilmington, Del.

PY—patrol vessel converted yacht.

PYc.—patrol vessel converted yacht (coastal).

QIW—Quintard Iron Works, New York, N.Y.

quad.—quadruple.

quint.—quintuple.

R and R—rest and rehabilitation.

r.—rifle.

r. pivt.—rifled pivot gun.

RAF—Royal Air Force.

RAAF—Royal Australian Air Force.

RAN—Royal Australian Navy.

RC—revenue cutter.

RCAF—Royal Canadian Air Force.

RCN—Royal Canadian Navy.

RCS—Revenue Cutter Service.

recip3—reciprocating, triple expansion.

Reg.—Regulus missile system.

rf.—rapid fire.

Rich—Richmond Locomotive Works, Richmond, Va.

Ridg—Ridgeway Dynamo and Electric Co., Ridgeway, Pa.

rkt.—rocket launcher.

RN—Royal Navy.

RNN—Royal Netherlands Navy.

RNZN—Royal New Zealand Navy.

Roach—John Roach and Sons, Chester, Pa.

ROK—Republic of Korea.

RON—squadron.

RU—Reciprocating (Skinner Unaflow).

s.—speed.

sa.—semiautomatic.

SACEUR—Supreme Allied Commander, Europe.

SACLANT—Supreme Allied Commander, Atlantic.

SACMED—Supreme Allied Commander, Mediterranean.

SAR—Search and Rescue, sea air rescue.

sat.—saturated.

sb.—smooth bore.

SC—submarine chaser (110'); or cruiser submarine.

Sc—screw.

SCAJAP—Shipping Control Administrator, Japan.

SCC—control submarine chaser (110').

ScFr—screw frigate.

ScGbt—screw gunboat.

Sch—schooner.

SchBg—schooner barge.

SCOTCH—Scotch fire tube boiler. (All others are water-tube.)

ScSlp—screw sloop-of-war.

ScStr—screw steamer.

ScTug—screw tug.

SEAL—Sea Air and Land (Naval Special Forces).

SEATO—Southeast Asia Treaty Organization.

seabee—construction battalion.

SF—fleet submarine.

Sg.—shell gun.

s-g—single & double reduction gears.

sgl.—single.

SHAEF—Supreme Headquarters Allied Expeditionary Forces.

SHAPE—Supreme Headquarters Allied Powers, Europe.

shp.—shaft horsepower.

SINS—Ships Inertial Navigational System.

SL—ship-of-the-line.

Slp—sloop.

SlpW—sloop-of-war.

SlvBg—salvage barge.

SM—mine laying submarine.

SNAP—anti-snooper air patrol.

SP—motor patrol boat.

sp—self-propelled.
sr—single reduction gears.
S.r.—Sawyer rifle.
SS—submarine; or merchant steamship.
SSA—cargo submarine.
SSB—fleet ballistic missile submarine.
SSBN—fleet ballistic missile submarine (nuclear powered).
SSC—cruiser submarine.
SSG—guided missile submarine.
SSGN—guided missile submarine (nuclear powered).
SSK—antisubmarine submarine.
SSN—submarine (nuclear powered).
SSO—submarine oiler.
SSP—submarine transport.
SSR—radar picket submarine.
SSRN—radar picket submarine (nuclear powered).
SSS—strike support ship.
SST—target and training submarine (sp.).
St—steam.
StBrig—steam brig.
StBt—steamboat.
stbd.—starboard.
StFr.—steam frigate.
Str—steamer.
StRam—steam ram.
StTBt—steam torpedo boat.
StTug—steam tug.
Stw—stern wheel.
StwGbt—stern wheel gunboat.
StwRam—stern wheel ram.
StwStr—stern wheel steamer.
SubDiv—submarine division.
SubFlot—submarine flotilla.
subm.—submerged.
SUBROC—submarine rocket.
SubRon—submarine squadron.
Sun—Sun Shipbuilding and Dry Dock Co., Chester, Pa.
Sup—Superior Marine Manufacturing Co., Milwaukee, Wis.
surf.—surface.
Sw—side wheel.
SwGbt—side wheel gunboat.
SwStr—side wheel steamer.
SwRam—side wheel ram.
SwTug—side wheel tug.
Syd—shipyard.
t.—tonnage.
T.—Maritime Commission standard type.
T—prefix indicating M.S.C. (MSTS) ship.
Tal.—Talos missile system.
Tar.—Tartar missile system.
TB—torpedo boat.
TBS—talk between ships.
td.—turbine direct drive.
ted.—turbine electric drive.
Ter.—Terrier missile system.
terd.—turbine electric reduction drive.
TF—Task Force.
TG—Task Group.
THORN—Thornycroft-type boiler.
Tk—tanker.
tl.—trial (speed).
TLL—tank lighter.
TLLW—tank lighter (medium tank-well type).
torp.—torpedo(es).
TR—geared turbine drive.
Tr—trawler.
Trans—transport.
TransRon—transport squadron.
Trigg.—Wm. R. Trigg Co., Richmond, Va.
Troy—Troy Engine & Machine Co.
trp.—troop capacity.
tt.—torpedo tubes.
TU—Task Unit.
tur.—turbine.
UDT—underwater demolition team.
UIW—Union Iron Works, San Francisco, Calif.

UIWHDR—Union Iron Works header-type boiler.
U.K.—United Kingdom.
UN—United Nations.
UN-CR—Universal Cruiser.
unrep.—underway replenishment.
USA—United States Army.
USAAC—United States Army Air Corps.
USAAF—United States Army Air Forces.
USAF—United States Air Force.
USAMC—United States Army Medical Corps.
USANF—United States Auxiliary Naval Force.
USAT—United States Army Transport.
USCG—United States Coast Guard.
USCGR—United States Coast Guard Reserve.
USCGS—United States Coast and Geodetic Survey.
USCS—United States Coast Survey.
USMC—United States Marine Corps.
USMCR—United States Marine Corps Reserve.
USMCWR—United States Marine Corps Women's Reserve.
USN—United States Navy.
USNA—United States Naval Academy.
USNR—United States Naval Reserve.
USNRF—United States Naval Reserve Forces.
USNS—United States Naval Ship.
USRCS—United States Revenue Cutter Service.
USRM—United States Revenue Marine.
USS—United States Ship.
USSB—United States Shipping Board.
VB—Navy bombing plane; Navy dive bombing squadron.
VBF—Navy bombing-fighting aircraft; Navy bomber-fighter squadron.
VBT—bombing, torpedo plane.
VC—composite aircraft squadron.
VD—photographic squadron (aircraft).
vert.—vertical.
VF—Navy fighter plane; Navy fighter squadron.
VFB—fighter bombing plane.
VF(M)—fighter plane (two engine).
VF(N)—Navy night fighter squadron.
VG—light transport plane (single engine).
VGF—escort-fighting squadron.
VGS—escort-scouting squadron.
VH—ambulance plane; Navy rescue squadron.
V.I.—Virgin Islands.
VJ—utility plane; Navy utility squadron.
VMB—Marine medium and heavy patrol bomber squadron (land based and seaplane).
VMBF—Marine fighter bomber squadron.
VMD—Marine photographic squadron.
VMF—Marine fighter squadron.
VMF(N)—Marine fighter squadron (night).
VMJ—Marine utility squadron.
VMO—Marine observation squadron.
VMO(AS)—Marine observation squadron (artillery spotting).
VN—training squadron.
VO—observation plane; Navy battleship observation squadron.
VOG—Navy observation plane squadron.
Vog—Henry Vogt Machine Co., Louisville, Ky.
VOGHDR—Vogt header-type boiler.
VP—patrol plane; Navy patrol squadron.
VPB—patrol-bombing plane; Navy medium and heavy patrol bomber squadron (land based and sea based).
VPT—patrol-torpedo plane.
VR—transport plane; Navy transport squadron.
VS—scouting plane; Navy shore based scouting squadron.
VSB—scout-bombing plane.
VSO—scout observation plane.
VT—torpedo plane; Navy torpedo bomber squadron.
VTB—torpedo bombing plane.
VT(N)—Navy night torpedo bomber squadron.
vt2—vertical double-expansion.
vt3—vertical triple-expansion.

vt4—vertical quadruple-expansion.
WAVES—Women Accepted for Voluntary Emergency Service.
Wes—Westinghouse.
Wes–Del—Westinghouse & De Laval.
Wes–Falk—Westinghouse & Falk.
Wes–FB—Westinghouse & Farrel–Birmingham.
WestPac—Western Pacific.
WFB—White–Forster-type boiler (manufactured by Babcock and Wilcox Co.).
Wint—Winton Engine Corp., Cleveland, Ohio.
WIW—Washington Iron Works, Seattle, Wash.
WL—water line.
WM—White and Middleton Co., Springfield, Ohio.
WSA—War Shipping Administration.
wt.—water-tube boiler.
WTDF—water-tube single-furnace boiler.
WWI—World War I.
WWII—World War II.
X—submersible craft (sp.).
XMAP—sweeper device.
YA—ash lighter.
YAG—miscellaneous auxiliary (service craft).
YAGR—ocean radar station ship.
YAR—Yarrow-type boiler.
YC—open lighter (nsp.).
YCD—fueling barge.
YCF—car float (nsp.).
YCK—open cargo lighter.
YCV—aircraft transportation lighter (nsp.).
YD—floating crane (nsp.).
Yd—Yard (Navy).
YDG—district degaussing vessel.
YDT—diving tender (nsp.).
YE—amunition lighter.
YF—covered lighter (sp.); or freight lighter.
YFB—ferryboat or launch (sp.).
YFD—yard floating dry dock (nsp.).
YFN—covered lighter (nsp.).
YFNB—large covered lighter (nsp.).
YFND—dry dock companion craft (nsp.).
YFNG—covered lighter (special purpose) (later YFNX).
YFNX—lighter (special purpose (nsp.) (formerly YFNG).
YFP—floating power barge (nsp.).
YFR—refrigerated covered lighter (sp.).
YFRN—refrigerated covered lighter (nsp.).
YFRT—covered lighter (range tender).
YFT—torpedo transportation lighter.
YFU—harbor utility craft (sp.).
YG—garbage lighter (sp.).

YGN—garbage lighter (nsp.).
Y-gun—Y-type depth charge projector.
YH—ambulance boat.
YHB—house boat.
YHLC—salvage lift craft, heavy (nsp.).
YHT—scow, heating.
YLA—open landing lighter.
YLLC—salvage lift craft, light (sp.).
YM—dredge (sp.).
YMLC—salvage lift craft, medium (nsp.).
YMP—motor mineplanter.
YMS—auxiliary motor minesweeper.
YMT—motor tug.
YN—net tender (boom).
YNG—gate craft (nsp.).
YNT—district net tender.
YO—fuel oil barge (sp.).
YOG—gasoline barge (sp.).
YOGN—gasoline barge (nsp.).
YON—fuel oil barge (nsp.).
YOS—oil storage barge (nsp.).
YP—patrol craft (sp.).
YPD—floating pile driver (nsp.).
YPK—pontoon stowage barge.
YR—floating workshop (nsp.).
YRB—repair and berthing barge (nsp.).
YRBM—repair, berthing, and messing barge (nsp.).
YRBM(L)—submarine repair, berthing, and messing barge (large).
YRC—submarine rescue chamber.
YRDH—floating dry dock workshop (hull) (nsp.).
YRDM—floating dry dock workshop (machine) (nsp.).
YRL—covered lighter (repair).
YRR—radiological repair barge (nsp.).
YRST—salvage craft tender (nsp.).
YS—stevedoring barge.
YSD—seaplane wrecking derrick (sp.).
YSR—sludge removal barge (nsp.).
YSP—stowage pontoon.
YT—harbor tug.
YTB—large harbor tug.
YTL—small harbor tug.
YTM—medium harbor tug.
YTT—torpedo testing barge.
YV—drone aircraft catapult control craft (sp.); or seaplane barge.
YVC—catapult lighter.
YW—water barge (sp.).
YWN—water barge (nsp.).
ZR—rigid airship.
ZRS—rigid airship (scouting).

HISTORICAL SKETCHES

W. A. Edwards

The name, *W. A. Edwards*, was used frequently in place of *Wilbert A. Edwards* (SP–315) (*q.v.*).

W. F. Babcock

(Seagoing Barge: t. 2,128 (gross); l. 240'10''; b. 43'9''; dr. 25'8'' (mean); dph. 19'4''; cpl. 6; a. none)

W. F. Babcock—a wooden-hulled, schooner-rigged barge launched in 1882 at Bath, Maine, by A. Sewall and Co.—was acquired by the Navy from the Luckenbach Steamship Co. on 18 October 1917. Given Id. No. 1239 and commissioned on 8 November, *W. F. Babcock* operated as a collier at the 5th Naval District until 8 August 1918, when she was assigned to the Naval Overseas Transportation Service. Plying the eastern seaboard between New England and Norfolk, *W. F. Babcock* served as a coastwise collier through the end of World War I. Reassigned to the 1st Naval District on 15 August 1919, she was struck from the Navy list on 20 November 1919 and simultaneously sold to Reinhard and Hall. Her name disappeared from the shipping registers about that time.

W. F. Marty

(MB: l. 40'0''; b. 10'0''; dr. 3'0'' (aft); s. 11.0 k.)

W. F. Marty—a wooden-hulled motorboat built in 1917 for W. F. Marty of Olney, Pa.—was inspected by the Navy, in the 4th Naval District, in 1917 for possible use as a section patrol vessel. She was assigned the classification SP–1145.

Little is known, however, of any actual service. Listed as "delivered" on 6 October 1917 and "enrolled" 10 days later, *W. F. Marty* was subsequently returned to her owner on 28 January 1918 and struck from the Navy list on 5 February, indicating that her service—if any—was of short duration. There are no records to indicate whether or not the boat was ever placed in commission. Her eventual fate is also unrecorded.

W. L. Bartlett

(Sch.)

W. L. Bartlett—a wooden-hulled Chesapeake Bay schooner—was acquired by the Navy on 13 August 1861 at Baltimore, Md. It was planned to use *W. L. Bartlett* and 21 other similar craft as blockships at entrances to inlets leading to the North Carolina sounds. The project—the Navy's first "stone fleet" venture—ultimately failed; no record of *W. L. Bartlett*'s ultimate fate has been found.

W. L. Messick

(ScStr.: t. 237 (gross); l. 145'0''; b. 23'0''; dr. 9'0'' (mean); cpl. 36; a. 1 6-pdr.)

W. L. Messick—a wooden-hulled, screw steamer built in 1911 at Norfolk, Va., by Smith and McCoy—was purchased by the Navy on 7 April 1917 from Joseph H. Bellows of Reedville, Va. Commissioned simultaneously, *W. L. Messick*—classified as SP–322—was assigned to the 5th Naval District and served as a minesweeper in the Virginia capes area for the duration of World War I. She was subsequently decommissioned and sold on 27 August 1919 to her former owner.

W. L. Steed

(Tanker: dp. 13,000; l. 431'10''; b. 56'0''; dr. 25'6'' (mean); s. 10.5 k.; cpl. 96; a. 1 6'', 1 3'')

W. L. Steed—a steel-hulled tanker built in 1918 at Quincy, Mass., by the Fore River Shipbuilding Co., under a United States Shipping Board (USSB) contract—was inspected by the Navy on 10 August 1918, assigned Identification Number 3449, and was commissioned at Boston, Mass., on 18 September 1918, Lt. Comdr. John Charlton, USNRF, in command.

Assigned to the Naval Overseas Transportation Service (NOTS), *W. L. Steed* departed Boston on 28 September and proceeded to Philadelphia, where she took on a cargo of oil. She sailed for New York on 8 October, whence she headed for Nova Scotia on the 17th. The tanker departed Sydney six days later, bound for Devonport, England, but developed a steering gear casualty en route and put into St. John's, Newfoundland, for repairs, on 30 October.

She departed that port on 10 November and was at sea when the armistice—ending World War I—was signed at Compiegne, France, on the 11th. *W. L. Steed* made port at New York on the 13th and entered drydock for repairs which lasted through the remainder of November.

W. L. Steed got underway again on 1 December, bound for France, and arrived at Le Havre three days before Christmas of 1918. Discharging her oil cargo in two days, the tanker subsequently departed Le Havre on 26 December, bound for the Gulf of Mexico.

After touching at Bermuda, she arrived at New Orleans on 18 January 1919; took on another cargo of oil; and left the Mississippi delta on 4 February 1919, bound again for France. She never completed the voyage, however, for she was damaged en route and put into New York on 18 February. After inventories of all equipment were taken and repairs were completed, *W. L. Steed* was decommissioned, struck from the Navy list, and simultaneously returned to the USSB on 26 March 1919.

Acquired by the Pan-American Petroleum and Transport Co. in 1922, *W. L. Steed* was subsequently acquired by the Standard Oil Co. of New Jersey in 1937. Following some two years of operation with Standard Oil, the ship was in need of repairs and docked at Constable Hook, Bayonne, N.J., on 30 June 1939. She remained there through August and departed Bayonne shortly after the outbreak of war in Europe with orders to proceed to Mariner's Harbor, Staten Island, N.Y., for repairs at the Bethlehem Steel Co. yard there.

Upon completion of the necessary repairs and alterations, *W. L. Steed* departed New York on 4 October, bound for Texas. Making port at Aransas Pass a short time later, the bulk oil tanker took on a cargo of

68,169 barrels of west Texas crude oil—the first of five such cargoes she would carry in 1939. Once the crude was safely aboard, *W. L. Steed* cast off for New York.

During 1940 and 1941, *W. L. Steed* performed primarily coastwise duties for Standard Oil of New Jersey, although she occasionally included Havana, Cuba; Aruba, Dutch West Indies; and Cartagena, Colombia, among her ports-of-call. She made 17 voyages in 1940 and 22 in 1941, carrying bulk oil cargoes of 1,053,261 and 1,396,278 barrels, respectively.

W. L. Steed departed Norfolk, Va., under the command of her master, Harold G. McVenia, on 14 January 1942. She made port at Cartagena one week later and there loaded a cargo of 65,396 barrels of oil in two days, departing that port on 23 January. She subsequently called at Key West for Navy orders before transiting the Florida Straits.

The voyage proceeded uneventfully until early on the afternoon of 30 January, when a lookout spotted what he thought was a small fishing craft on the port bow. Capt. McVenia, soon ascertaining the strange ship to be a submarine lying low on the surface, sounded the general alarm and radioed for help. All hands except the "black gang"—below in the engine spaces—manned their boat stations, donned life preservers, and stood by for the worst.

The submarine soon disappeared, probably because of *W. L. Steed*'s radio message that brought a Navy patrol plane out to take a look. Over the next two days, though, the weather worsened, making protective aircraft operations particularly difficult. *W. L. Steed* plodded through the Atlantic swells, occasionally shipping heavy seas that damaged her decks.

By 2 February, visibility had shrunk to about two miles, and snow was falling. Shortly after noon, when *W. L. Steed* was between 80 and 90 miles off the coast of New Jersey, *U–103*—already a high scorer in the German U-boat arm with over 30 ships to her credit—poked up her periscope and tracked the plodding tanker. One torpedo soon leapt from the bow tubes, sped inexorably toward *W. L. Steed*, and hit the tanker on her starboard side, forward of the bridge, and in number 3 tank. The explosion touched off a fire in the oil drums stored there.

W. L. Steed sent out a hurried SOS and radioed her plight to any ship within hearing; the entire crew— 38 men—abandoned ship into the vessel's four life boats. *U–103* surfaced soon thereafter and closed the burning tanker as she slowly sank by the bow. The Germans soon manned their deck gun and commenced firing, pumping 17 shells into the stern of the tanker to hasten her demise while her crew watched from the nearby boats. After *W. L. Steed* slipped beneath the chill waves of the North Atlantic, *U–103* stood briefly toward the survivors before shaping a course away in a southwesterly direction.

The U-boat's departure left the four boats alone in the frigid waters. They drifted apart and, one by one, the ill-clad sailors began to succumb to the cold. *W. L. Steed* had been abandoned with such haste that hardly any of the men had had time to enter the boats prepared to face the bitter winter snowstorm and the biting northeasterly winds.

One boat was never found. The British steamer *Hartlepool* rescued two men from the second on 4 February, but one later died; the Canadian armed merchant cruiser HMCS *Alcantara* picked up three men from the third boat two days later, including the senior surviving officer, 2d Mate Sydney Wayland. On 12 February, the British merchantman *Raby Castle* came across the last of *W. L. Steed*'s boats, containing four men, but of whom only one was alive, suffering much from exposure. Brought aboard *Raby Castle*, that man—2d Assistant Engineer Elmer E. Maihiot, Jr.—died three days later, and was buried at sea.

W. L. Steed was the second Standard Oil tanker sunk during World War II; her loss was ultimately avenged when Allied aircraft pounding the port of Gdynia, Poland, sank *U–103* on 15 April 1945.

W. S. Cahill

Winfield S. Cahill (SP–493) (*q.v.*) was sometimes referred to in official documents as *W. S. Cahill*.

W. S. Sims

See *Sims* for biography.

(DE–1059: dp. 2,887 (f.); l. 438'; b. 47'; dr. 25'; s. 27 k.; cpl. 245; a. 1 5", 4 15.5" tt., ASROC, BPDSMS; cl. *Knox*)

W. S. Sims (DE–1059) was laid down on 10 April 1967 by Avondale Shipyards, Inc., Westwego La.; launched on 5 January 1969; sponsored by Mrs. Robert H. Hopkins; and commissioned on 3 January 1970, Comdr. C. M. Plumly in command.

Following an extended fitting-out period at the Charleston Naval Shipyard and a restricted availability at Jacksonville Shipyards for correction of minor construction faults, *W. S. Sims* became fully operational in June of 1970 and proceeded to Guantanamo Bay, Cuba, for shakedown training. After a two and one-half month post-shakedown availability at the Charleston Naval Shipyard to correct deficiencies uncovered during shakedown and to install additional equipment, *W. S. Sims* put to sea in November to evaluate the feasibility of installing the LAMPS (Light Airborne Multi-Purpose System). She was the first ship of her class to have a manned helicopter land on her deck; and, during the next four days, she successfully demonstrated the capability of these fine new ships to operate manned helicopters. Upon completion of the testing, the escort proceeded to her home port, Mayport, Fla., for the holiday season.

On 11 January 1971, *W. S. Sims* left Mayport with personnel from the Key West Testing and Evaluation Detachment embarked. The project consisted of six cruises, numbered 0 to 5, where *W. S. Sims* operated with various types of submarines in order to determine the capabilities and limitations of the installed long range underwater sound detection equipment. The tests continued throughout the year and took the escort to such ports as New Orleans; Fredriksted, St. Croix; San Juan, Puerto Rico; and Nassau, New Providence, Bahama Islands.

The ship returned to Mayport in time for Thanksgiving and, between 22 November and 31 December 1971, was involved in a fleet standdown period during which officials representing the squadron, flotilla, and type commanders conducted a series of inspections.

The final cruise for the Key West testing project began on 4 January 1972. *W. S. Sims* returned to Mayport on 15 January and spent the next month preparing for operations with the 6th Fleet.

On 15 February 1972, the ocean escort sailed for the Caribbean to participate in "LantFltRedEx 2–72" and then proceeded on to the Mediterranean. On 10 March, *W. S. Sims* inchopped to the 6th Fleet and took part in various antisubmarine exercises besides visiting Barcelona, Spain, and Naples, Italy. From 27 March to 6 April, the destroyer escort and *William V. Pratt* (DLG–13) maintained a close surveillance of Soviet naval units in the south central Mediterranean.

W. S. Sims visited Gaeta, Italy, and Golfe Juan, France, before taking part in Operation "Quickdraw," a combined United States and Italian naval exercise held on 17 April. A visit to San Remo, Italy, and tender availability at Naples followed the exercise.

On 8 May 1972, the ship joined in a combined naval exercise, Operation "Dawn Patrol," with British, French, and Italian warships. After visiting Sfax, Tunisia, *W. S. Sims* conducted special surveillance operations on Soviet submarines from 23 May to 10 June. The ship then participated in Operation "Good Friendship" with the Turkish Navy and a second Operation "Quick Draw" with the Italian Navy. During August, the crew enjoyed leave at San Remo, Italy; Barcelona, Spain; and Theoule, France. When *Vreeland* (DE-1068) relieved *W. S. Sims* late that month, the latter headed home and returned to Mayport on 5 September.

Upon completing a month-long standdown period, the ship commenced an extended availability at the Jacksonville Shipyards, Jacksonville, Fla., which lasted through the end of the year and the first three months of 1973. The ship then carried out post-availability sea trials. The discrepancies which the testing uncovered were corrected by 9 April. The following day, the ocean escort steamed south to Roosevelt Roads, Puerto Rico, and joined the surface missile fleet in gunfire support exercises conducted at the Atlantic Fleet weapons range, Culebra Island.

On 8 May 1973, *W. S. Sims* arrived at Guantanamo Bay, Cuba, for refresher training, but an engineering casualty soon forced her to return to Mayport for repairs. When the corrections had been made, she returned to Cuba and conducted refresher training from the end of May to mid-June. Upon returning to Mayport, the ship executed a LAMPS workup from 17 June to 9 July.

From 12 to 26 July, *W. S. Sims* participated in "LantRedEx 1–74" in the Caribbean. As her next assignment, the ship evaluated the basic point defense missile. The ocean escort returned to her home port on 10 August, enabling the crew to enjoy a period of leave and liberty.

W. S. Sims sailed for North Atlantic and Mediterranean operations on 14 September. Upon arrival, the ship held a LAMPS demonstration for the Royal Netherlands Navy in Amsterdam. At the time of *W. S. Sims'* inchop to the 6th Fleet, the Middle East was in a state of war. For the first month and one-half, the ocean escort's duties involved operations in support of United States interests in the Middle East crisis. From 26 to 30 November, *W. S. Sims* guarded the King of Morocco embarked on the French luxury liner *Roussilion* en route to the Arab oil conference held in Algiers, Algeria. The King, as a gesture of gratitude, sent the officers and men a gift of three tons of oranges, tangerines, sardines, and orange juice. After visiting Naples, Italy, and Rota, Spain, *W. S. Sims* spent the 1973 holiday season at Valencia, Spain.

On 4 January 1974, *W. S. Sims* stood out of Valencia harbor to operate with *Independence* (CVA–42). After a visit to Rota and exercises with *America* (CVA–66), the escort ship participated in a search for survivors of a small British trawler; and four of six missing sailors were recovered. On 25 January, she proceeded via Gibraltar to Casablanca, Morocco, where she arrived on 1 February. The following day, the Soviet military attache came on board for a special tour of the ship. After brief stops at Rota and at Bermuda, *W. S. Sims* arrived at Mayport on 14 February.

During March and April, the ship took part in interim-sea-control ship-evaluation operations in waters between Jacksonville and Charleston. She returned to her home port on 27 April and underwent various inspections. The escort ship commenced tender availability on 6 May. On 1 July 1975, *W. S. Sims* was reclassified a frigate and redesignated FF-1059.

On 7 August, *W. S. Sims* sailed for the Portsmouth (N.H.) Naval Shipyard for repairs in drydock. She returned to Mayport on 19 September and spent the rest of the year and the first part of 1975 in training and in improving the physical condition of the ship.

On 15 April 1975, the frigate joined in Fleet Exercise "Agate Punch" which involved naval air, surface, subsurface, and land forces. The exercise ended on the 27th, and *W. S. Sims* proceeded to the naval weapons station where she offloaded weapons in preparation for going into the shipyard in June.

The ship suffered an engineering casualty on 30 April and was towed to Charleston for repairs. Upon her arrival back at Mayport on 8 May, *W. S. Sims* commenced a month-long tender availability. The escort ship got underway on 11 June for Philadelphia for a nine-month overhaul. The ship went into drydock on 21 June and remained there until 8 December; and, after she was refloated, work renewing the ship continued into the spring of 1976.

After tests and sea trials in the Virginia capes area, the ship returned to Mayport on 14 April 1976. From the 23d to the 27th of that month, *W. S. Sims* was moored at Port Everglades and then got underway for Andros Island and trials to evaluate new antisubmarine warfare equipment. She next returned to Mayport and conducted operations in the Jacksonville area.

W. S. Sims arrived at Guantanamo Bay, Cuba, on 23 May and spent the next five weeks in intensive training. After an operational readiness evaluation and gunfire support qualifications at Roosevelt Roads, Puerto Rico, the ship returned to Mayport on 2 July. Tender availability occupied the month of July and continued into August. After completing several inspections, *W. S. Sims* got underway on 2 September for a North Atlantic crossing.

En route, she participated in Operation "Joint Effort," a series of exercises conducted in a task group environment. On 14 September, *W. S. Sims* was 700 yards aft of *John F. Kennedy* (CV–67) when *Bordelon* (DD–881) collided with that carrier and searched the nearby waters for any men who might have been thrown overboard.

The North Atlantic cruise was divided into four separate operations. "Joint Effort," conducted during the crossing, was a workup phase. "Teamwork 76" was a major NATO exercise involving the forces of the United States, Great Britain, Belgium, Denmark, West Germany, the Netherlands, and Norway. It included a show of strength in the North Cape area. "Baltic Operations" was conducted in the Baltic Sea and was an exercise in fleet steaming in a confined area. "Bonded Item," the final exercise, was an exercise designed around an amphibious assault at Jutland.

On 27 October 1976, *W. S. Sims* departed Edinburgh, Scotland; headed home; and arrived at Mayport on 9 November. The ship spent the remainer of 1976 and January 1977 in availability. Shipyard work and underway training occupied February. On 1 March, a propulsion examining board embarked; and the ship passed in all respects. During the remainder of the month, the escort ship prepared for an upcoming deployment.

W. S. Sims departed Mayport on 30 March, bound for Lisbon, Portugal, and a six and one-half month Mediterranean deployment. A severe storm with 20- to 30-foot seas, encountered en route, damaged the main mast to the point where it had to be supported by riggings of mooring lines. As a result, the ship arrived in Rota rather than Lisbon and remained there from 12 April to 13 May undergoing repairs.

The destroyer escort then conducted operations in the areas of Crete, Greece, Tunisia, and Sicily. *W. S. Sims* arrived at Alexandria, Egypt, on 8 August and, during her visit there, was visited by the American consul general, the Governor of Alexandria, and the Commander in Chief of the Egyptian Navy. She then departed for Augusta Bay, Sicily.

"National Week XXIII" began on 15 August and consisted of intensive war games involving both 6th Fleet task groups, elements of the Italian Navy, and American Air Force planes. The exercise concluded on 22 August when the fleet anchored off Taranto, Italy, for debriefing.

The crew enjoyed a port visit to Palma de Mallorca, Spain, before going to sea for "Bystander" operations near Gibraltar. After a tender availability at Naples, *W. S. Sims* joined the NATO Exercise "Display Determination"—already in progress—on 24 September. When the exercise ended, the escort ship acted as the sole escort for *Independence* (CV–62) as they visited Malaga and Rota, Spain. On 14 October, *W. S. Sims*, along with *Independence* and several other ships, departed Rota and arrived at Mayport on the 21st.

The ship spent most of November undergoing tender availability and, on the 28th, participated in Operation "Marcot," a joint operation with the Canadian Navy.

On 3 December, while operating near Bermuda, the ship lost all power due to an engineering failure. The ship had no power to any equipment except those powered by batteries. An aircraft responded to distress flares and contacted surface ships in the area. *Ainsworth* (DE–1090) responded and came alongside, "skin to skin" on the high seas, with all lines tripled. In the midst of six-foot swells, there began heavy movement between the two ships causing frequent contact, buckling several frames in the midships section, and causing considerable superficial damage to the starboard side. After temporary repairs were made, all lines were cleared, and *W. S. Sims* returned to home port for repairs. The year 1977 ended with the destroyer escort in restricted availability, conducting repairs on both diesels and structural repairs to the starboard side.

W. S. Sims remained in restricted availability into March 1978. On the 8th, she joined units of the 2d Fleet in the Caribbean for Exercise "Safepass '78." The ship then proceeded north to provide services for *Hammerhead* (SSN–663). After refueling at New London, Conn., *W. S. Sims* arrived back at Mayport on 24 March and began an upkeep period until 6 April.

After successfully undergoing an operational propulsion plant exam, the frigate got underway for the Caribbean and Exercise "Comptuex;" then headed up the Cooper River to moor at the Charleston Naval Station on 27 April. After onloading weapons, the ship returned to her home port for availability and upkeep which lasted through 5 June.

W. S. Sims conducted tests and inspections at sea, followed by an inport period from 13 to 28 June during which she completed preparations for the upcoming Mediterranean cruise. On 29 June, the frigate sailed for her fourth and longest Mediterranean cruise. Following her Atlantic crossing, the ship arrived in Malaga on 9 July. After a brief run to Naples, she received on board Admiral H. E. Shear, Commander in Chief, Allied Forces, Southern Europe.

The ship got underway on 29 July for Augusta Bay, Sicily, and for operations in the Ionian Sea. "National Week XXV" was held from 23 July to 5 August. After visiting ports in Greece, she participated in "Anti-Aircraft Warfare Week" and returned to Naples on 21 August. During the last week of August, the Chief of Naval Operations, Admiral Thomas B. Hayward, paid a visit to tour the ship.

The month of September found *W. S. Sims* taking part in Operation "Ocean Missilex" in the eastern Mediterranean; Operation "Display Determination-78," a combined NATO operation; and conducting antisubmarine warfare exercises with a Greek destroyer squadron and an opposing Greek submarine. The end of the month found *W. S. Sims* conducting tests with French submarine *Daphne* and NATO's oceanographic research ship *Maria Paola Gee*.

Upon returning to La Spezia, Italy, on 2 November 1978, the ship took part in "Antisubmarine Warfare Week" from 7 to 14 November and then underwent intermediate maintenance availability at Cartagena, Spain. The frigate arrived at Toulon, France, on 9 December for a 10-day visit. *W. S. Sims* spent the holiday season from 21 December until the year ended in Alicante, Spain.

Late in January 1979, *W. S. Sims* departed Malaga; and she arrived at Mayport in February. She remained at her home port through May preparing for an upcoming shipyard period. After a brief visit to Portland, Maine, *W. S. Sims* reported to the Bath Iron Works, Bath, Maine, on 7 May 1979 for an overhaul.

She was scheduled to return to Mayport in March 1980 and resume operations.

W. T. James

(TR: t. 267 (gross); l. 150′; b. 22′; dr. 8′5″ (mean); s. 13 k.; cpl. 38; a. 1 3″, 2 .30-cal. mg.)

W. T. James—a "Menhaden fisherman" built in 1912 at Wilmington, Del., by Harlan and Hollingsworth—was acquired by the Navy in the spring of 1917 from the Taft Fish Co., of Tappahannock, Va.; ordered delivered on 1 April; and accepted on 28 May for service as a minesweeper. Navy General Order No. 314 shortened the ship's name to *James* on 28 July, and the erstwhile fishing craft was commissioned in the 5th Naval District on 10 August 1917, Ens. E. R. Burr, USNRF, in command.

Designated SP–429, *James* was fitted out for "distant service" at the Norfolk Navy Yard and, near the end of August, departed the Tidewater area, bound for Boston. There, with other sister ships which had made the passage from Hampton Roads, *James* prepared for the voyage to European waters. Accordingly, after shifting from Boston to Provincetown, Mass., on 25 August, *James* got underway for the Azores two days later, on the first leg of the Atlantic crossing.

Reaching Ponta Delgada, Azores, on 6 September, *James* and her sister ships remained for five days, awaiting the tardy arrival of coal and water. On 11 September, the group departed the Azores on the last leg of the passage.

Disbanded as a mine squadron almost immediately after arriving at Brest, France, on 18 September, the vessels of the group soon were busy escorting convoys into and out of port. Between these missions, they spent long weeks awaiting delivery of winches and French minesweeping gear. In November, the mine squadron was reconstituted under the command of Capt. Thomas P. Magruder. *James*, among the second group to be fitted out for minesweeping service, soon shifted to Lorient, France, where she would base for the remainder of the war.

From Lorient, *James* not only conducted minesweeping operations but covered coastal convoys, cleared important passages near Belle Isle, undertook night antisubmarine patrols using her crude listening gear, and assisted vessels in distress in her area. In July 1918, *James* and two sister ships swept a minefield south of Belle Isle and, despite the heavy weather in which the ships were forced to operate, accomplished their mission in such exemplary fashion that the three mine vessels received commendations from Vice Admiral Aubry, the French *Prefet Maritime*. During this operation, *James* cut out four mines in the space of 17 minutes.

James remained in European waters through the winter of 1918–1919. She departed Brest on 27 April 1919, bound for the United States, but soon began encountering "boisterous weather" with increasing northwesterly winds and a choppy sea. At 1422, the escort commander, in *Marietta* (Gunboat No. 15), ordered the group to return to Brest.

When it became evident that James was taking on more water than usual, she was directed to proceed to Brest without delay. Unfortunately, the "Menhaden fisherman" worked so much that her seams opened, allowing water to flood the engine rooms and affect the boiler fires—an occurrence that severely limited the ship's capacity to deal with the rising flood waters.

James—her predicament grave—signalled the nearby *MacDonough* (Torpedo Boat Destroyer No. 9) and *Rambler* (SP–211) for aid. The former closed swiftly and attempted—unsuccessfully—to take the foundering minecraft in tow. The tug *Penobscot* (SP–982) managed to get a towline across to *James* the following morning and towed the ship for about 20 minutes before the line parted.

By that point, the heavy seas were nearly swamping the ship. *Marietta* closed as close as was practicable in the gale and put over a line. Rigging up a ferry arrangement with a liferaft from *James*, the trawler's entire crew reached safety on board the gunboat by shortly after 0800 on 28 April. Two hours later, *James* sank, six miles off Armen Light.

W. W. Burns

(Sch.)

W. W. Burns—a wooden-hulled Chesapeake Bay schooner—was acquired by the Navy on 13 August 1861 at Baltimore, Md., for use as a stone-laden blockship. The purchase of *W. W. Burns* was one of 22 made at Baltimore in the summer of 1861, and she and the other 21 ships were slated to be loaded with stone, taken to the North Carolina coast, and sunk off the entrances to the major inlets leading to North Carolina sounds—Albemarle, Pamlico, and Okracoke. The project was the first of its nature undertaken by the Navy; and, due to delays and other problems, it failed. Some of the ships seem to have remained at their anchorages in Hampton Roads and deteriorated late that summer and into the autumn. *W. W. Burns'* ultimate fate as part of the first "stone fleet" venture is unrecorded.

Waban

A Nipmuc Indian, born about 1604 at Musketaquid, Mass., near the present town of Concord. Waban was one of the first Massachusetts Indians to profess Christianity. He maintained close and friendly relations with the white settlers and, in April 1675, reported to an English magistrate that trouble was brewing amongst the Wampanoags. Within two months, Waban's predictions came to pass when a Wampanoag named King Philip led his braves in an initially successful war. Philip's subsequent death in August 1678 signalled the end of the brief war; and the rebellion soon collapsed due to a lack of leadership. Nevertheless, Waban, falsely accused of being a conspirator, was imprisoned in October 1675. After a brief period of captivity, Waban was released the following spring and returned to his settlement of Natick, Mass., where he became a justice of the peace. While the exact date of his passing is not known, it is believed that Waban died either in late 1676 or early 1677.

(StwStr.: dp. 150; l. 85'; b. 17'6½''; dr. 8'; s. 13 k.; cpl. 13; a. 1 3'' blr.)

Confidence—an iron-hulled, stern-wheel steamer completed in 1880 at Philadelphia by William Cramp and Sons—was acquired by the Navy on 25 June 1898 from M. Revel for use during the Spanish-American War. Renamed *Waban*, the ship was commissioned on 25 July and assigned to the 6th Naval District.

Waban served with the Auxiliary Naval Force and was based at the 6th district headquarters at Port Royal, S.C., during the brief Spanish-American War. She was subsequently stationed at the Naval Station, Guantanamo Bay, Cuba, and remained in Cuban waters through 1901. She then shifted to Pensacola, Fla.

Transferred once more to Caribbean waters, *Waban* departed Pensacola on 17 October 1911, bound for Cuba, and arrived at Guantanamo Bay on 31 October. She remained there performing local tug and towing duties with the Fleet through World War I. Subsequently decommissioned, *Waban* was struck from the Navy list on 17 July 1919 and sold to Whiteman Bros., of New Orleans, La. She retained the name *Waban* in mercantile service and operated, first at New Orleans and later at Port Arthur, Tex., until 1924.

Wabaquasset

A tribe or band of Indians who formerly lived west of the Quinnebaug River, in what is now Windham County, Conn. Also the name of the village situated about six miles from the Quinnebaug River, south of the present city of Woodstock, Conn.

(YTB–724: t. 199; l. 94'3''; b. 25'0''; dph. 13'6''; cl. *YTB–331*; T. V2–ME–A1)

Port Hudson—a steel-hulled, metal arc-welded, large harbor tug—was laid down under a Maritime Commission contract (MC hull 440) on 31 December 1941, at Slidell, La., by the Canulette Shipbuilding Co., Inc.; launched on 17 June 1942; sponsored by Miss Jean Canulette; and delivered to the War Shipping Administration (WSA) on 26 April 1943.

On 24 March 1945, the name *Wabaquasset* and the designation YTB–724 were approved by the Navy for *Port Hudson*, but the ship was apparently not taken over for active service. Records indicate that *Wabaquasset* was in fact not included on Navy crafts' lists. One source indicates that while the WSA owned the ship, the Navy operated her; but this statement is not supported by the sketchy records. Another source indicates that the tug was returned to WSA on 7 June 1945. In any event, it seems probable that the harbor tug saw little, if any, naval service.

Wabanquot

A Chippewa Indian chief—born at Gull Lake, Minn., about 1830—succeeded to the office of chief at the death of his father, Wabojeeg. Wabanquot was considered by many to be the principal chief of the Mississippi bands of Chippewa. In 1868, he led his band to the White Earth reservation, where he lived until his death 30 years later.

(YTB–525: dp. 310 (f.); l. 101'0''; b. 28'0''; dr. 9'7''; s. 12.0 k.; cpl. 10; cl. *Hisada*)

Wabanquot (YTB–525) was laid down in May 1945 at Jacksonville, Fla., by the Gibbs Gas Engine Co.; launched on 9 August 1945; sponsored by Mrs. G. W. Scott, Jr.; and delivered to the Navy on 13 November 1945.

Since she was completed after hostilities ended in the Pacific, *Wabanquot* was assigned to the 11th Naval District, San Diego, Calif., rather than to the western Pacific. She was transferred to the Atlantic Fleet in 1947 and was placed in reserve status with the 16th Fleet.

In 1948, she was assigned to the 3d Naval District. The ship provided towing services and pilot assistance at New York from 1948 into 1976. During her tour, in February 1962, she was reclassified as a medium harbor tug and redesignated YTM–525. *Wabanquot* was struck from the Navy list in April 1976.

Wabash

A river that rises in Drake County, Ohio, near Fort Recovery and meanders westward across Indiana until it reaches Illinois at a point just southwest of Terre Haute. South of that point, it outlines the border between the two states until emptying into the Ohio a few miles west of Uniontown, Ky. Wabash is an abbreviation of the Miami Indian name for the stream, Wabashiki, which means "bright white" or "gleaming white." It refers to the limestone bed of the stream along its upper course.

I

(ScFr: dp. 4,808; l. 301'6''; b. 51'4''; dr. 23'; s. 9 k.; a. 2 10'' D. sb., 14 8'' D. sb., 24 9'' D. sb.; cl. *Colorado*)

The first *Wabash* was laid down on 16 May 1854 by

USS *Wabash* as a receiving ship; she is still fully rigged although her sails have been removed. Steam engines and heavy shell guns made the big steam frigates of the 1850s perhaps the most powerful seagoing warships afloat for the few years before the introduction of armor. (NR&L(0) 7680)

6

the Philadelphia Navy Yard; launched on 24 October 1855; sponsored by Miss Pennsylvania Grice; and commissioned there on 18 August 1856, Capt. Frederick K. Engle in command.

Wabash departed Philadelphia on 7 September 1856, stopping at Portsmouth, N.H., to embark President Franklin Pierce for passage to Annapolis, Md. She arrived at New York on 23 October 1856, sailing on 28 November 1856 to become flagship of Commodore Hiram Paulding's Home Squadron. The squadron was instrumental in foiling the expedition against Nicaragua underway by American filibusterer, William Walker, who had dreamed of uniting the nations of Central America into a vast military empire led by himself. Through insurrection, he became president of Nicaragua in 1855 only to have Cornelius Vanderbilt—who controlled the country's shipping lifelines—shut off supplies and aid. A revolt toppled Walker from power, and he was trying for a military comeback before he was captured in 1857 by the Home Squadron. Stateside controversy over the questionable legality of seizing American nationals in foreign, neutral lands prompted President James Buchanan to relieve Commodore Paulding of his command. *Wabash* was decommissioned on 1 March 1858 at the New York Navy Yard.

Wabash was recommissioned on 25 May 1858, Capt. Samuel Barron in command, and became the flagship of Commodore E. A. F. La Vallette's Mediterranean Squadron. The future naval hero of the Spanish-American War, George Dewey—then a midshipman—served in *Wabash* when she touched at her first port of call, Gibraltar, on 17 August 1858. *Wabash* returned to the New York Navy Yard on 16 December 1859 and decommissioned there on 20 December 1859.

With the outbreak of the Civil War, *Wabash* was recommissioned on 16 May 1861, Capt. Samuel Mercer in command, and departed New York on 30 May 1861 as flagship of the Atlantic Blockading Squadron under Rear Admiral Silas H. Stringham.

Wabash captured the brigantine *Sarah Starr* off Charleston, S.C., on 3 August 1861, and recaptured the American schooner *Mary Alice*, taken earlier by the CSS *Dixie*. By this date, she had also captured the brigantines *Hannah, Balch,* and *Solferino*, along with 22 Confederate prisoners from the four vessels.

On 26 August 1861, *Wabash* departed Hampton Roads, bound for Hatteras Inlet, N.C., to take part in the first combined amphibious assault of the war. *Wabash* accompanied *Monticello, Pawnee*, revenue cutter *Harriet Lane*, the tug *Fanny*, and two transports, carrying over 900 troops under Major General Butler. Union forces secured Hatteras Inlet with the capture of Forts Hatteras and Clark on 29 August 1861. The attack force suffered no casualties and took over 700 prisoners. Among these was Capt. Samuel Barron, CSN, the former commander in the United States Navy of *Wabash* when she served under Rear Admiral La Vallette. *Wabash* was later designated the flagship of Flag Officer Samuel F. Du Pont, the new commander of the South Atlantic Blockading Squadron, and was sent to the New York Navy Yard for repairs on 21 September 1861.

After refit, *Wabash* departed Fort Monroe on 29 October 1861 to spearhead the Federal assault on Port Royal, S.C. The assembled invasion fleet was the largest yet organized by the Navy, containing 77 vessels and 16,000 Army troops under Brigadier General Thomas W. Sherman. The combined force secured Port Royal Sound on 7 November 1861 after a furious four-hour battle. *Wabash* led the battle line in this major strategic Union victory.

Wabash now took up permanent station on the Charleston blockade, operating out of Port Royal. On 11 March 1862, a landing party led by ship's commanding officer, Comdr. C. R. P. Rodgers, occupied St. Augustine, Fla. A detachment of seamen and officers from *Wabash* landed and manned a battery which bombarded Fort Pulaski, Ga., on 10 and 11 April 1862 and was instrumental in forcing that Southern fort to surrender. A naval battery of three 12-pounder boat howitzers from *Wabash* supported Union troops at the Battle of Pocotaligo, S.C., on 22 October 1862.

Confederate vessels twice harassed *Wabash* while on duty in Port Royal Sound. On 5 August 1863, CSS *Juno*, a small steamer on picket duty below Fort Sumter, fired upon and ran down a launch from *Wabash*, capturing 10 sailors and drowning two. A "David" submarine torpedo boat also attacked *Wabash* on 18 April 1864. Ensign Charles H. Craven, officer of the deck, spotted the cigar-shaped vessel in time for *Wabash* to get underway. The "David" disengaged from the attack in the face of musket fire and round shot discharged from *Wabash*.

Wabash departed her station on 1 October, bound for the Norfolk Navy Yard and an overhaul. En route, she grounded briefly on Frying Pan Shoals, suffering minor damage to her rudder. Repairs and overhaul were completed by 16 December, in time for *Wabash* to join the North Atlantic Blockading Squadron and to participate in the first attack on Fort Fisher, N.C., on 24 and 25 December 1864. The failure of this initial attempt to take the fort necessitated a second, successful combined operation between 13 and 15 January 1865.

Wabash returned to Hampton Roads on 17 January 1865, receiving orders on 25 January 1865 to proceed to the Boston Navy Yard. *Wabash* was decommissioned at Boston on 14 February 1865. She was placed in ordinary from 1866 to 1869; overhauled during 1870 to 1871; and recommissioned on 24 October 1871, Capt. Robert W. Shufeldt commanding. *Wabash* departed the Boston Navy Yard on 17 November 1871 and served as the flagship of Rear Admiral James Alden, commanding the Mediterranean Squadron. She arrived at Cadiz, Spain, on 14 December 1871 and cruised throughout the Mediterranean until 30 November 1873 when she departed Gibraltar, bound for Key West, Fla. *Wabash* arrived in Key West on 3 January 1874. She was decommissioned on 25 April 1874 at the Boston Navy Yard. In 1875, she was placed in ordinary and served as a housed-over receiving ship from 1876 to 1912. *Wabash* was struck from the Navy list on 15 November 1912 and sold that same day to the Boston Iron and Metal Co., Boston, Mass.

II

(Freighter: dp. 10,475; l. 393'0''; b. 49'11''; dr. 26'0'' (mean); s. 11.4 k.; cpl. 93; a. 1 5'', 1 3'')

Wartburg—a single-screw, steel-hulled freighter completed in 1900 at Newcastle-on-Tyne, England, by Wigham Richardson and Co., Ltd., for service with the *Deutsche Dampferfahrts Gesellschaft*—was renamed *Tübingen* between 1906 and 1907 and owned by the *Norddeutscher Lloyd* line. She was interned by the United States Government at the onset of World War I. In April 1917, when the United States entered the conflict, the steamer was taken over by the United States Shipping Board (USSB). She was acquired by the Navy on 9 February 1918, at Hoboken, N.J., for use with the Naval Overseas Transportation Service. The cargo ship was renamed *Wabash*; designated Id. No. 1824; and commissioned on the same day, Lt. Comdr. Frank C. Seeley, USNRF, in command.

Loaded with construction iron and ammunition, *Wabash* departed New York City on 28 February, bound for France. After delivering her cargo at Paulliac, she returned to the United States on 22 April. She made four more voyages to St. Nazaire, France, and returned to New York from her last run on 6 April 1919. Decommissioned on 21 April, the freighter was returned to the USSB.

The ship subsequently home-ported at New York and operated under the flag of the North Atlantic and Western Steamship Co., until sometime in 1924 or 1925. She was then transferred to Italian registry.

III

(AOG–4: dp. 4,335; l. 310'9''; b. 48'6''; dr. 15'8''; s. 14 k.; cpl. 140; a. 4 3''; cl. *Patapsco*)

Wabash (AOG–4) was laid down on 30 June 1942 at Seattle, Wash., by the Seattle-Tacoma Shipbuilding Co.; launched on 28 October 1942; sponsored by Mrs. Louis A. Puckett; and was commissioned at the Puget Sound Navy Yard, Bremerton, Wash., on 10 May 1943, Lt. James F. Ardagh, USNR, in command.

Wabash departed Seattle on 26 May for Alaskan waters. After delivering a cargo of gasoline to Annette Bay and Yakutat, the gasoline tanker returned to Seattle on 5 June. She made four more voyages carrying fuel to Alaskan ports before 15 September, when she headed south for the last time to San Francisco, Calif.

Proceeding to Hawaii soon thereafter, *Wabash* was assigned to Service Squadron (ServRon) 8 upon her arrival at Pearl Harbor on 19 October. From then through the first half of 1944, she made runs in the Central Pacific carrying high-test aviation gasoline and lubricants to Palmyra Island, Canton, and Midway. Departing Pearl Harbor on 9 July, *Wabash* steamed in convoy for the Marshall Islands. Transferred to ServRon 10 upon her arrival at Eniwetok on 18 July, *Wabash* pumped gasoline and lubricants to station tanker *YOG–185*; tended small craft; and carried Marine Corps equipment to Roi Island before moving on to the Marianas.

Arriving at Saipan on 20 August 1944, she operated in the Marianas until sailing for the Volcano Islands on 5 March 1945 to support the American conquest of Iwo Jima. There, *Wabash* furnished fuel and lubricants to amphibious ships of Task Force 53, including minecraft and tank landing ships. On 14 March, she returned via Saipan to the Western Carolines and arrived at Ulithi on the 27th.

Wabash soon got underway again to support her second major Pacific operation, the battle for Okinawa. Soon after her arrival off Hagushi beach on 9 April, she began tending miscellaneous small craft at Okinawa through the cessation of hostilities and the first months following Japan's surrender.

On 28 November, she sailed for Hong Kong. From December 1945 to the summer of 1946, *Wabash* operated in the Far East supporting the Fleet in its occupation duties. She served as tender and fuel ship at Hong Kong; Hainan Island, French Indochina; Subic Bay, Philippines; and at Shanghai and Tsingtao, China.

Decommissioned at Tsingtao on 29 July 1946, *Wabash* was transferred to the Army Transportation Corps on that day and was struck from the Navy list on 23 April 1947.

Manned and officered by Japanese, the tanker operated for the Army out of Yokosuka, Japan, into 1950. With the onset of the Korean War, *Wabash* was reinstated òn the Navy list on 1 June 1950; enrolled in the Military Sea Transportation Service (MSTS); and designated T-AOG-4.

During the Korean conflict, the ship supported United Nations air operations with vital cargoes of jet fuel and gasoline through the year 1952. Manned by a mixed crew of Americans and Japanese, *Wabash* served MSTS through the Panmunjom armistice in the summer of 1953 and subsequently carried oil between Iwo Jima and South Korean and Japanese ports through the mid-1950's. Inactivated on 10 September 1957, *Wabash* was struck from the Navy list for the second time on 8 May 1958, placed in permanent custody of the Maritime Administration, and assigned to the National Defense Reserve Fleet at Suisun Bay, Calif. She remained there into the 1970's.

Wabash received two battle stars for her World War II service and two for service during the Korean conflict.

IV

(AOR–5: dp. 37,360 (f.); l. 659'; b. 96'; dr. 36'; s. 20 k.; cpl. 390; a. 4 3''; cl. *Wichita*)

Wabash (AOR–5) was laid down on 21 January 1970 Quincy, Mass., by the General Dynamics Corp.; launched on 6 February 1971; sponsored by Mrs. William G. Bray; and commissioned on 20 November 1971 at the Boston Naval Shipyard, Capt. Robert P. Chrisler in command.

Wabash sailed for the west coast on 5 January 1972, called at Rio de Janeiro, Brazil; transited the bleak Strait of Magellan; and visited Valparaiso, Chile; Callao, Peru; and Acapulco, Mexico, before arriving at her home port, Long Beach, Calif., on 3 March. She underwent shakedown from 22 May to 16 June and operated off the coast of southern California into the autumn.

The replenishment oiler commenced her first western Pacific (WestPac) deployment when she departed Long Beach on 9 November. After proceeding via Pearl Harbor, Hawaii, she arrived at Subic Bay, Philippine Islands, on 1 December and, assigned to Service

The gasoline tanker *Wabash* (AOG–4) at Kodiak in July 1943. Her dull gray finish offers little contrast to the background. (80-G-7989)

Squadron 9, assumed duties as flagship for Commander, Task Group (TG) 73.5.

That group sortied for Tonkin Gulf on 7 December. *Wabash* conducted 46 underway replenishments during her first tour on the "line" off the coast of Vietnam and celebrated Christmas at sea while returning to the Philippines. Arriving in Subic Bay on 28 December, *Wabash* soon headed back toward the line on 2 January 1973. She conducted two or three replenishments a day during the final phase of American combat operations in Vietnam.

In February, United States forces were withdrawn from combat. However, she made two more line deployments during her WestPac deployment, for—while combat operations had ceased—the vital job of supplying the ships of the Fleet still remained. On 21 May, *Wabash* departed Yokosuka, Japan, bound, via Pearl Harbor, for Long Beach.

The ship engaged in training exercises and underwent inspections into the summer. On 6 September 1973, her home port was changed to Alameda, Calif. The oiler conducted local operations out of Alameda through the end of the year and departed the west coast on 2 March 1974 for her second WestPac deployment. This lasted through the summer, with operations in Philippine and Japanese waters, before the ship departed Subic Bay on 25 September to return to the United States.

During this period of Alameda-based fleet support operations, *Wabash* participated in the multinational maneuvers "FleetEx 1–76." This operation, conducted off the southern California coast, lasted from 1 to 13 March 1976, and included units of the United States, British, Canadian, and New Zealand navies.

On 5 June 1976, *Wabash* again set sail for WestPac. En route, she collided with *Flint* (AE–32) during a towing exercise, but neither ship suffered damage curtailing her primary mission capabilities. No one was injured. After damage and voyage repairs at Subic Bay, *Wabash* commenced routine local operations in Philippine waters. On 9 July, however, she returned hurriedly to Subic Bay to load stores and cargo and departed the following day to conduct a "stern chase" of TG 77.7. This group was then headed for the Indian Ocean and a 30-day "show the flag" cruise. En route, *Wabash* rendezvoused with *Mars* (AFS–1) to load further supplies and stores, transited the Strait of Malacca, and entered the Indian Ocean on 17 July.

Wabash conducted underway replenishments with *Ranger* (CVA–61), *Preble* (DDG–46), *Goldsborough* (DDG–20), and *Ouellet* (FF–1077), as TF–77 "showed the flag" in the Indian Ocean as part of the American effort to balance a growing Soviet presence in that area of the globe. Her duties thus completed, *Wabash* returned to Subic Bay on 7 August and got underway nine days later to rejoin the *Ranger* task group to replenish them as they returned to the United States.

Completing her duties with the *Ranger* group soon thereafter, *Wabash* put into Guam, Mariana Islands, and prepared to provision the incoming *Enterprise* (CVN–65) task group. The replenishment ship subsequently conducted local operations in the Philippines in September and in Japanese waters in October—operating out of Sasebo—before visiting Pusan, Korea. Returning to Sasebo on 25 October, the ship headed for Yokosuka soon thereafter for repairs and upkeep prior to concluding her WestPac deployment. During this, her third WestPac tour, *Wabash* had steamed over 35,000 miles, conducted 100 underway replenishments, and had been at sea nearly 65 percent of the time. Departing Japanese waters on 10 November, *Wabash* arrived at her home port one day before Thanksgiving.

Completing the year 1976 in port at Alameda, *Wabash* spent the latter half of January 1977 undergoing a restricted availability at Alameda. During the period 17 February to 1 March, the ship engaged in Exercise "RIMPAC '77," a major fleet exercise involving ships from the United States, Australian, New Zealand, and Canadian navies. *Wabash* conducted 28 underway replenishments during this time. Refresher training continued throughout the spring until the replenishment ship entered Todd Shipyard, Alameda, on 15 June for the commencement of a regular overhaul.

With the overhaul completed on 9 June 1978, *Wabash* devoted the remainder of the year in shakedown and refresher training. January 1979 found *Wabash* in her home port of Alameda preparing to meet scheduled commitments for that year.

Waccamaw

A river in South Carolina, taking its name from a small tribe which formerly dwelt along the lower Pee Dee River and its branches in the Carolinas. Like other tribes of the region, the Waccamaw were probably incorporated with the Catawba tribe by late in the 19th century.

(AO–109: dp. 23,235; l. 553'; b. 75'; dr. 32'4"; s. 18.3 k.; cpl. 304; a. 1 5", 4 3", 8 40mm.; cl. *Cimarron*)

Waccamaw (AO–109) was laid down on 28 April 1945 by the Sun Shipbuilding and Drydock Co., Chester, Pa.; launched on 30 March 1946; sponsored by Miss Irene F. Long; and commissioned on 25 June 1946, Capt. Guy W. Stringer in command.

After completing shakedown and training at Norfolk and Guantanamo, *Waccamaw* spent her first two years engaged in transporting oil from the Persian Gulf to the United States. In September 1948, she was assigned to duty with the 6th Fleet in the Mediterranean and, in the spring of 1949, was transferred to the 2d Fleet for exercises in the Caribbean. A second tour of the Mediterranean followed in the early part of 1950 and a third in 1951, the latter extending to nine months.

After a shipyard overhaul at Boston, Mass., in 1952, *Waccamaw* participated in the development of the Thompson-Arwood method of fueling destroyers at sea in heavy weather. In 1953, the ship made her first midshipman cruise, which included a visit to Edinburgh, Scotland. During the summer of 1954, *Waccamaw* was again in the Mediterranean for her fourth tour with the 6th Fleet. This was followed by logistic services in the western Atlantic and Caribbean. On a second midshipman cruise in 1955, she visited Copenhagen and Edinburgh. In the fall of 1955, the ship entered the Philadelphia Naval Shipyard for overhaul and proceeded to the Caribbean for training the following spring. A third midshipman cruise was made in June and July of 1956, the visit this time being to Halifax, Nova Scotia. At the end of July, the ship departed for a fifth assignment to the 6th Fleet. This tour was extended until January 1957 because of the Suez crisis. During this period, *Waccamaw* provided logistic support to the ships engaged in the evacuation of Haifa, Israel; and Alexandria, Egypt.

After returning from the Mediterranean, *Waccamaw* operated in the Caribbean for two months, participated in the International Naval Review at Norfolk, Va., on 12 and 13 June 1957, and then departed on her fourth midshipman cruise which took her to Rio de Janeiro, Brazil; and Aruba, Dutch West Indies.

During September and October 1957, *Waccamaw*, as a member of the underway replenishment group, supported the international fleet participating in the NATO fall exercises. These exercises were designed to test the ability of the navies of the Atlantic community to cooperate in mutual defense. In the course of these operations, *Waccamaw* played a novel role in the rapidly developing character of the Fleet; she was the last oiler to fuel *Wisconsin* (BB–64), the last of the battleships, and the first to fuel the new super carriers, *Forrestal* (CVA–59) and *Saratoga* (CVA–60).

In the winter of 1957 and 1958, *Waccamaw* underwent a much-needed overhaul at Boston, followed by training at Guantanamo Bay, Cuba. During the spring

Waccamaw (AO–109) rides light in the water at Philadelphia, 16 July 1946.

of 1958, she provided logistic support to antisubmarine groups in the western Atlantic. Refitted and retrained, *Waccamaw* joined the 6th Fleet for a Mediterranean deployment, during which she participated in the operations connected with the United States landing in Lebanon. *Waccamaw* returned to Newport, R.I., her home port, in November 1958.

After a brief rest in December 1958, *Waccamaw* returned to her assigned mission by fueling Destroyer Flotilla 2 in January 1959 and then proceeded south to the Virgin Islands where she remained until the end of March.

On 20 April 1959, *Waccamaw* departed for another Mediterranean tour. This seventh tour, however, was shorter than those previous, and she returned to Newport in June. Upon her return, the ship continued her familiar role of logistic support to the antisubmarine forces in the western Atlantic. This continued until November when she began a period of overhaul at the Bethlehem Steel Shipyard, New York. Due to a labor-management dispute in January 1960, *Waccamaw* was moved by tugs to the New York Shipyard at Brooklyn, N.Y., to complete her overhaul in April.

After completing refresher training at Guantanamo Bay, the ship returned to Newport, R.I., and embarked 18 midshipmen from several eastern colleges for a cruise in Atlantic waters. After an eight-day tender availability at Newport, R.I., *Waccamaw* departed for an eighth tour with the 6th Fleet in the Mediterranean. During this deployment, *Waccamaw* was the first naval ship to visit the newly independent country of Cyprus. On 25 February 1961, she returned to Newport for a leave and upkeep period.

The spring months of 1961 were spent supporting the 2d Fleet and conducting a sixth midshipman cruise. During August, *Waccamaw* underwent a much-needed tender availability, and a one-day dependents' cruise was fitted into her busy September schedule. In October, *Waccamaw* supported the newly created antisubmarine warfare group operating in the eastern Atlantic. She arrived back in the United States just in time for Christmas after an 11,800-mile cruise. *Waccamaw* then commenced preparations for overhaul at the Bethlehem Steel Shipyard in Hoboken, New Jersey. Completing overhaul in April 1962, the ship sailed for refresher training at Guantanamo Bay.

In June 1962, *Waccamaw* again resumed support of the 2d Fleet; and, in August, she set sail for the Mediterranean on her ninth tour with the 6th Fleet. On the way, *Waccamaw* participated in Operation "Riptide," working in support of such ships as the nuclear carrier *Enterprise* (CVA(N)–65). The ship spent the holiday season at Golfe Juan, France, and gave a Christmas party for some 50 orphans. She returned to her home port, Newport, on 2 March 1963.

During the period from March through June, *Waccamaw* held a dependents' cruise; supported the

fruitless *Thresher* (SSN–593) search; and conducted two deployments which totalled five weeks with Canadian antisubmarine warfare forces. Late in July, *Waccamaw* departed Newport for six weeks in the Caribbean supporting Commander, ASW Forces, Atlantic Fleet, embarked in *Randolph* (CVS–15). *Waccamaw* fueled the carrier and her five escorting destroyers 10 times. Upon her return, she stopped at Norfolk, Va., for a successful operational readiness inspection.

Waccamaw spent most of the fall in Newport, with scattered brief commitments and type training periods underway. Much time was devoted to the administrative inspection for fiscal 1964 which was held in November. At the year's end, preparations were hard underway on board *Waccamaw* for the most extensive yard period in the ship's 17-year history. She was scheduled to enter the Puget Sound Bridge and Drydock Co. in Seattle on 29 February 1964.

On 27 January 1964, *Waccamaw* got underway for Seattle, Wash., and arrived on the 21st of February. During a seven-month yard period, she received the oiler equivalent of "framming", "jumbo conversion."

On 26 February 1965, the ship returned to the Puget Sound Naval Shipyard, Bremerton, Wash. At that time, her status was changed from "in commission, in reserve" to "in commission, active." Following a fitting out and ready-for-sea period, *Waccamaw* departed the Puget Sound area and proceeded to San Diego, Calif., arriving there on 23 April. After stopping at Acapulco, Mex., and Guantanamo Bay, Cuba, the ship returned to Newport, R.I., on 12 May 1965.

During the period between 14 May and 17 June, *Waccamaw* engaged in shakedown training at Guantanamo Bay; then proceeded to Norfolk, Va., her new home port, for a period of upkeep and acceptance trials. On 13 July, she sailed for the Boston Naval Shipyard for post-shakedown availability which lasted from 19 July through 9 November. On 14 November, *Waccamaw* returned to Norfolk and underwent type training and services before serving as a replenishment ship for the primary recovery group assigned to the Gemini VI and VII space missions. She returned to Norfolk on 19 December and spent the remainder of 1965 in type training and services.

Waccamaw got underway on 10 January 1966 for the Caribbean and Operation "Springboard." During this exercise, she refueled 42 ships and conducted gunnery exercises and other at-sea trials before returning to Craney Island on 4 February. Upon her return, she operated in the Virginia capes area and began making preparations for overseas deployment.

On 4 May 1966, *Waccamaw* departed Norfolk destined for the Mediterranean. She was the first "jumbo oiler" to operate with the 6th Fleet. During her Mediterranean cruise, she steamed in excess of 20,000 miles, refueled 256 ships, and pumped more than 32 million gallons of fuel oil. On 20 October, she returned to the Norfolk Naval Station, then proceeded to the Norfolk Naval Shipyard to repair the damage sustained in a minor collision with *Noa* (DD–841).

The ship took part in Exercise "Lantflex 66" in the Caribbean on 28 November. *Waccamaw* returned to the Norfolk Naval Station on 15 December and remained until the end of the year for tender availability and holiday leave.

After refueling ships of the 2d Fleet and lifting fuel at Craney Island, *Waccamaw* departed on 27 February 1967 to escort six destroyers to the Azores. She returned on 21 March, then got underway again on 10 April for Operation "Clovehitch III" which lasted through the end of the month. On 1 May, the ship returned to Norfolk for upkeep and tender availability.

On 12 June 1967, *Waccamaw* departed for a midshipman training cruise to the Caribbean and returned to Norfolk for upkeep. On 24 July, she took part in NATO Exercise "Lashout;" and, upon her return to Norfolk, she prepared for annual administrative and operational readiness inspections which were completed on 28 August and 12 September, respectively. From 6 to 27 October, the ship had tender availability at the Norfolk Naval Base.

Waccamaw departed on 13 November for her 11th Mediterranean cruise. At the close of 1967, *Waccamaw* was at Naples, Italy, for a holiday liberty and upkeep period. This cruise ended on 23 April 1968 when the ship arrived at Norfolk, Va. On 28 May, she participated in the search for the nuclear submarine *Scorpion* (SSN–589). This was followed by exercises in the Jacksonville, Fla., and Virginia capes operating areas and participation in NATO Exercise "Silvertower" with the British and Canadian Navies. During "Silvertower," *Waccamaw* refueled 69 ships before returning to Norfolk on 15 October. The ship then operated off the Virginia and Florida coasts until 21 November when she underwent tender availability at Craney Island, Va., and returned to Norfolk on 18 December 1968 to finish the year in liberty and upkeep.

Waccamaw began the year 1969 in her home port of Norfolk, Va., and, on 2 January, arrived at the Maryland Shipbuilding and Drydock Co., Baltimore, for routine hull maintenance followed by regular overhaul at Horne Bros. Shipyard, Newport News, Va. After conducting exercises in the Virginia capes operating area, she completed refresher training in Guantanamo Bay on 20 June. The next month was spent in operations off the Virginia and Florida coasts. On 21 August, the ship moved to the Norfolk Naval Shipyard, Portsmouth, Va., to make final preparations for deployment.

On 2 September 1969, *Waccamaw* got underway for deployment to the North Atlantic. From 17 to 23 September, she participated in NATO Exercise "Operation Peacekeeper." *Waccamaw* returned to the Naval Station, Norfolk, on 11 December and remained there until the end of 1969 for leave and upkeep.

During January and February of 1970, *Waccamaw* continued a period of tender availability. After a fuel lift at Craney Island, she departed on 5 March for a Mediterranean deployment. However, problems with her feed pumps forced *Waccamaw* to return to Norfolk. Repairs completed, she again set sail for the Mediterranean on 17 March and arrived at Rota, Spain, 12 days later. On 7 April, *Waccamaw* was honored by the visits of the Vice Chief of Naval Operations and the Commander, 6th Fleet. On 22 May, Admiral Zumwalt, Chief of Naval Operations, visited *Waccamaw*, highlining on board from *Julius A. Furer* (DEG–6).

The ship arrived at Rota, Spain, on 17 September. However, just four hours before outchop, she was notified that her deployment was to be extended due to the crisis in Jordan. Underway on the 18th, she returned to the Mediterranean. After visiting Athens, Greece, and Soudha Bay, Crete, *Waccamaw* again departed for Rota, Spain, and home. *Waccamaw* arrived at Norfolk, Va., on 31 October and spent the remainder of 1970 in leave and upkeep.

The year 1971 found *Waccamaw* in restricted availability status in Norfolk, Va. After sea trials on 10 February and a fuel lift at Craney Island on 16 February, *Waccamaw* got underway for operations on 20 February. Three days later, she collided with *Detroit* (AOE–4) during an underway replenishment but sustained very little damage. However, she returned to Norfolk for repairs which lasted from 24 February to 9 March.

During the next month, *Waccamaw* operated in the Jacksonville, Fla., operations area. Upon her return to Norfolk, the ship remained in port for repairs until 28 June.

On 28 June 1971, *Waccamaw* deployed to the North Atlantic to support the antisubmarine warfare group. Steering difficulties forced her to return home early on 29 August. *Waccamaw* spent the remainder of the year in port undergoing steering repairs and upkeep, except for sea trials on 20 September and services in the Virginia capes area from 2 to 24 November 1971.

Waccamaw departed on 3 January 1972 for refresher training at Guantanamo Bay, Cuba. She returned to Norfolk on 12 February, after having visited Port-au-Prince, Haiti, and Port Everglades, Fla. The ship spent the next month in port providing services for a naval reserve surface division. From 17 March through 30 May, *Waccamaw* conducted operations in the Virginia capes area and off the east coast of Florida and South Carolina.

On 30 May 1972, *Waccamaw* set sail from Norfolk, Va., for a nine-month deployment to Subic Bay, Philippines. On 21 June, the ship rounded the Cape of Good Hope and entered the Indian Ocean. Arriving on 11 July, she anchored in Subic Bay after a 41-day transit. Five days later, she got underway for her first "line swing" off the embattled coast of Vietnam. This duty consumed the rest of the year, with the exception of periodic rests and repairs at Hong Kong and Singapore.

Waccamaw found herself working again early in the new year. On 4 January 1973, a milestone was reached: *Waccamaw* refueled *Lang* (DE–1060), her last of 246 commitments off the coast of Vietnam. The ship returned to Subic Bay, thence to Pearl Harbor, the Panama Canal, and, finally, Norfolk, Va. She arrived at her home port on 17 February 1973, after circumnavigating the world.

On 9 April, *Waccamaw* got underway to provide services to NATO forces operating off the coast of Greenland. Upon her return to Norfolk, the ship underwent restricted availability from 4 May until 16 July. After extensive repairs, *Waccamaw* got underway on 8 December 1973 to operate off the coast of Virginia. She returned to Norfolk one week later and spent the last weeks of 1973 in her home port area.

On 8 January 1974, *Waccamaw* got underway for Mayport, Fla., and operated in the Jacksonville area. On 27 January, she arrived at Roosevelt Roads, Puerto Rico, and took part in Operation "Springboard-74," followed by a stop at Guantanamo Bay, Cuba, arriving on 18 February. *Waccamaw* departed on the 1st of March for Norfolk, Va., where she remained through April. On 3 May, the ship got underway for a Mediterranean cruise. This seven-month deployment took the ship to ports in Spain, Italy, France, Greece, Crete, and Turkey.

On 6 December 1974, *Waccamaw* returned to Norfolk, Va., where she prepared for decommissioning. The ship was decommissioned on 24 February 1975. *Waccamaw* is presently serving in the Military Sealift Command, where she is manned by a civilian crew.

Waccamaw received one award of the Meditorious Unit Commendation for participation in the Jordanian crisis of 1970 and a Meritorious Unit Commendation and one battle star for service in Vietnam.

Wachapreague

An inlet on the eastern shore of the state of Virginia.

(AGP–8: dp. 2,592; l. 310'9''; b. 41'1''; dr. 13'6'';
s. 18.2 k.; cpl. 246; a. 2 5'', 8 40mm., 8 20mm., 2
dct.; cl. *Oyster Bay*)

Wachapreague (AVP–56) was laid down on 1 February 1943 at Houghton, Wash., by the Lake Washington Shipyards; reclassified as a motor torpedo boat tender and redesignated AGP–8 on 2 February; launched on 10 July 1943; sponsored by Mrs. E. L. Barr; and commissioned on 17 May 1944, Lt. Comdr. Harold A. Stewart, USNR, in command.

Following her shakedown training out of San Diego, Calif., *Wachapreague* got underway on 18 July for Pearl Harbor, Hawaii, en route to the South Pacific. Soon thereafter, she stopped briefly at Espiritu Santo, New Hebrides, and called at Brisbane, Australia, on 17 August, before reaching her ultimate destination, Milne Bay, New Guinea, three days later.

She dropped anchor at Motor Torpedo Boat Base 21—at that time the largest PT boat operating base in the Pacific; reported to Commander, Motor Torpedo Boats, 7th Fleet; and commenced tending the 10 PT boats from Motor Torpedo Boat Squadron (MTBRon) 12. This unit had previously taken a heavy toll of Japanese barge traffic and had wreaked much havoc upon enemy shore installations, in almost nightly actions, during the New Guinea campaign. As Allied forces wrapped up the New Guinea operations, *Wachapreague* received an additional five boats from MTBRon 7 as the Navy prepared for operations to liberate the Philippine Islands.

On Friday, 13 October, *Wachapreague* sailed in company with *Half Moon* (AVP–26), two Army craft and two additional PT tenders, for Leyte—1,200 miles away. The 45 PT's were convoyed by the larger ships, refuelled while underway at sea, and successfully completed the voyage under their own power. Slowing to nine knots, *Wachapreague* fueled two boats simultaneously, one alongside to starboard and one astern—eventually replenishing the fuel supply of all 15 of her brood. A brief two-day respite at Kossol Roads, Palau Islands, for repairs and a further refueling of the PT's, preceded the final leg of the voyage.

While *Wachapreague* dropped anchor at northern San Pedro Bay off Leyte, her PT's—fresh and ready for action immediately—entered Leyte Gulf on 21 October, the day after the initial landings on Leyte. Three days later, the tender shifted to Liloan Bay, a small anchorage which scarcely afforded the ship room to swing with the tide. Soon after her arrival at this body of water off Panoan Island, 65 air miles south of San Pedro Bay, *Wachapreague* contacted the Philippine guerrilla radio network for a mutual exchange of information as to Japanese forces lurking in the area.

On the afternoon of the 24th, upon receipt of word that three powerful Japanese task forces were approaching from three directions, *Wachapreague*'s PT's sped to action stations. In the van of the southern enemy force steamed two battleships and a heavy cruiser, screened by four destroyers; 30 miles behind came the second group, consisting of three cruisers and four destroyers.

American PT's met the enemy's southern force headon; three coordinated destroyer torpedo attacks soon followed; while American battleships and cruisers under Rear Admiral Oldendorf deployed across the northern end of Surigao Strait to "cross the T." The devastation the American warships wreaked upon this enemy force was nearly total. Only one Japanese ship, *Shigure*, emerged from the fiery steel holocaust now known as the Battle of Surigao Strait.

PT's from MTBRon 12 then threw the second task group off balance at the head of the strait, slamming a torpedo into the side of light cruiser *Abukuma* and forcing the enemy ship out of the battle line, badly damaged. The Japanese flagship, heavy cruiser *Nachi*, collided with another ship in the melee and found her own speed reduced to 18 knots. This second echelon of Japanese ships, correctly surmising that the first had

fallen upon some hard times, then fled, hotly pursued by American planes which administered the *coup de grace* to sink the already-crippled *Abukuma* and destroyer *Shiranui*.

Meanwhile, to the north of the strait, Rear Admiral Sprague's escort carrier group held off a powerful Japanese battleship-cruiser force off Samar, while Admiral Halsey's 3d Fleet units crippled a Japanese battleship-carrier force off Cape Engaño. In these surface actions and in the ensuing air attacks, the Japanese lost a total of four carriers, a battleship, six cruisers and four destroyers, while suffering damage to three carriers, five cruisers, and seven destroyers. The Battle for Leyte Gulf sounded the death knell of the Japanese Navy. As Admiral Chester W. Nimitz later wrote: "Our invasion of the Philippines was not even slowed down, and the losses sustained by the Japanese reduced their fleet from what had once been a powerful menace to the mere nuisance level."

Yet, while the Japanese capacity for seaborne operations lessened, they nevertheless could still strike back from the skies. While *Wachapreague*'s ship's force labored mightily to repair the badly damaged *PT–194*, a Japanese plane attacked the ship, only to be driven off by a heavy antiaircraft barrage. Later on the 25th, the tender shifted to Hinunangan Bay for refueling operations that would enable her six PT's to return to San Pedro Bay. Japanese nuisance attacks from the air continued, however, and a dive bomber attacked *Wachapreague* as the tender was just completing fueling operations with *PT–134*. As the boat pulled away from the larger ship's side, a Japanese bomb landed some 18 feet from its stern, killing one man and wounding four on board *PT–134*. Moving out under cover of a smokescreen, *Wachapreague* vacated her anchorage just before 14 Japanese planes struck and, while clearing the bay, fired on three twin-motored "Betties," claiming two kills as one "Betty" crashed into the sea and a second, trailing a banner of smoke, crashed behind a nearby island.

Wachapreague arrived at San Pedro Bay late on the 26th and conducted tending operations at that site until 13 November. During this time, her PT's operated with devastating effect against Japanese shipping in the Ormoc Bay and Mindanao Sea areas. On the 13th, her task completed in these waters for the time being, *Wachapreague* sailed in company with *Willoughby* (AGP–9) for Mios Woendi. Returning two weeks later, *Wachapreague* now tended a total of 22 boats—from MTBRons 13, 16, and 28—as well as six more from MTBRon 36 and two from MTBRon 17, at San Pedro Bay. The tender remained at San Pedro until 4 January 1945, when she headed for Lingayen in company with MTBRons 28 and 36.

At noon on the day of departure, a Japanese suicide aircraft dived into a merchantman 100 yards ahead—a prelude to the dusk attack in which seven Japanese planes participated. In the latter action, one plane crashed in the sea some 100 yards ahead of the PT tender; another came under fire as it plunged toward SS *Kyle B. Johnson*; while a third headed for *Wachapreague*—only to be knocked into the sea by a heavy antiaircraft barrage. Later that evening, *PT–382* came alongside the tender and transferred two men who had been blown overboard from *Kyle B. Johnson* during the earlier heavy air action.

Wachapreague entered Lingayen Gulf on the 13th and anchored near the town of Damortis. Three days later, she shifted her anchorage to Port Sual to tend boats from MTBRons 28 and 36. These boats gradually extended their patrols northward to the coastal towns of Vigan and Aparri, wreaking havoc on enemy barge traffic and shipping along the northwest coast of Luzon—shelling shore installations and destroying some 20 barges. *Wachapreague* meanwhile continued to make all electrical and engine repairs for the squadron PT's and handled all major communications until she departed Lingayen on 12 March to replenish at Leyte.

The small seaplane tender *Wachapreague* (AVP–57) later served with the Coast Guard in the Atlantic under the name *McCulloch* (WAVP–386).

Underway again on 23 April, the tender accompanied MTBRon 36 to Dutch North Borneo and took part in the invasion of Tarakan Island. While the guns still pounded the shore and the invasion itself was underway, *Wachapreague* entered the bay on 1 May to establish an advance base for her boats. For the next four months, the motor torpedo boat tender operated from this bay, tending MTBRon 36 boats while they in turn conducted daily offensive runs up the coast of Borneo.

In the course of these operations, the PT's sought out and destroyed Japanese shipping at Tawao, Cowie Harbor, Noneokan, Dutch North Borneo, shelling and rocketing shore installations. As the Japanese later attempted evacuation by small boats and rafts, the PT's netted some 30 prisoners. In addition to these tasks, the PT's assisted LST retractions from the beachheads by speeding across the water astern of the landing ships and creating swells which enabled the LST's to back off and float free.

Wachapreague tended PT's after the end of the war, basing at Tarakan, until she headed home and arrived at San Francisco, Calif., on 5 December 1945. After upkeep at the Mare Island Naval Shipyard, *Wachapreague* got underway for the east coast on 20 March 1946 and reported at Boston on 6 April for inactivation. She was decommissioned on 10 May and transferred outright to the United States Coast Guard on the 27th. Her name was struck from the Navy list on 5 June 1946.

Renamed *McCulloch*—in honor of the financier, Hugh McCulloch (1808 to 1895), who served as Secretary of the Treasury for Presidents Abraham Lincoln, Andrew Johnson, and Chester A. Arthur—and designated WAVP–386, the ship initially operated out of Boston, and later into the 1970's out of Wilmington, N.C., as a weather patrol ship. Spending an average of 21 days per month at sea, *McCulloch* patrolled the direct line of air routes to Europe, relayed weather data to the United States Weather Bureau, and maintained an air-sea rescue station for overseas civilian and military flights. Subsequently redesignated WHEC–386, *McCulloch* remained engaged in these duties until more modern techniques of weather reporting and data gathering came into use and thus made the seagoing weather ships obsolete.

As one of the seven former *Barnegat*-class ships transferred by the Coast Guard to the South Vietna-

mese Navy in 1971 and 1972, *McCulloch* was renamed *Ngo Kuyen* (HQ–17). The former coast guard cutter served that Southeast Asian republic as one of the largest and most heavily armed units of its navy, on patrol and coastal interdiction duties during the Vietnam War against the communists. In the spring of 1975, with the fall of the Saigon government, *Ngo Kuyen*, heavily laden with refugees, fled to the Philippines. As she and her sisters had become ships without a country, the ship was acquired by the Philippine government in 1975, and the transfer was made formal on 5 April 1976. She was subsequently renamed *Gregorio de Pilar* (PS–8) and served under that name into 1979.

Wachapreague received four battle stars for her World War II service.

Wachusett

A mountain peak in north central Massachusetts eight miles southwest of Fitchburg, Mass. The word Wachusett is a Natick Indian term which means "near the mountain."

I

(ScSlp.: t. 1,032; l. 201'4"; b. 33'11"; dph. 16'; dr. 14'; s. 11.5 k.; a. 2 11" D. sb., 2 30-pdr. P.r., 1 20-pdr. P.r., 4 32-pdrs., 1 12-pdr. r.)

The first *Wachusett*—one of seven screw sloops-of-war authorized by Congress in February 1861—was laid down by the Boston Navy Yard, Mass., in June 1861; launched on 10 October; sponsored by Miss Mary C. Frothingham; and commissioned at the Boston Navy Yard on 3 March 1862, Comdr. John S. Missroon in command.

Wachusett's long and eventful career began on 10 March 1862 with her assignment to the North Atlantic Blockading Squadron. The warship left Boston two days later and arrived in Hampton Roads, Va., on the 16th. She was deployed in the York and James rivers, Va., and performed valuable service in support of Major General George B. McClellan's Peninsular Campaign of spring, 1862. On 4 May, a boat crew from *Wachusett* raised the Stars and Stripes at Gloucester Point, Va., following the Union occupation of Yorktown, Va.; and,

13

An artist's impression of USS *Wachusett*. Her forward pivot gun is mounted on a platform which raises it above her spardeck bulwarks. (Peabody Museum of Salem, Mass.) (NH 68681)

on the 6th and 7th, the vessel helped to land troops at West Point, Va., in the face of Confederate shore fire. Soon thereafter, the screw sloop moved to the James and, on the 15th, participated in the attack on Fort Darling, Drewry's Bluff, Va. She remained in the York and James rivers through August and later served with the Potomac Flotilla as Commodore Charles Wilkes' flagship from 29 August to 7 September.

On 8 September, *Wachusett* was designated flagship of a special "Flying Squadron" under Commodore Wilkes. This squadron of seven vessels was deployed in the West Indies with orders to search for the destructive and elusive Confederate commerce raiders CSS *Alabama* and *Florida*. On 18 January 1863, *Wachusett* and *Sonoma* captured the Southern merchant steamer *Virginia* off Mugueres Island, Mex., and took the British blockade runner *Dolphin* between Puerto Rico and St. Thomas Island on 25 March. However, all efforts to track down *Alabama* and *Florida* failed; and *Wachusett* returned to Boston in May for badly needed repairs. She was later decommissioned at the Philadelphia Navy Yard on 19 June 1863.

Repairs completed, *Wachusett* was recommissioned on 28 January 1864. On 4 February, she sailed for the coast of Brazil to protect American commerce from the Confederacy's "piratical cruisers," particularly *Alabama* and *Florida*. Many months passed tracking down fruitless leads as to the whereabouts of the two vessels. Finally, on 4 October, Comdr. Napoleon Collins of *Wachusett* sighted *Florida*, Lt. Charles M. Morris, CSN, entering Bahia harbor, Brazil. Comdr. Collins dared Lt. Morris to come out and fight, but the Confederate captain prudently declined. However, Collins was determined not to allow *Florida* to slip away. In the early morning darkness of the 7th, *Wachusett* got underway, steamed past the Brazilian gunboat anchored between his ship and *Florida*, and rammed the raider on her starboard quarter. After a brief exchange of cannon fire, Lt. Porter, commanding *Florida* in Morris's absence, surrendered the ship. Aroused by the commotion, the Brazilian coastal fort at Bahia opened fire on *Wachusett* as she towed her prize to sea. The two vessels

escaped unscathed, steamed north, and reached Hampton Roads on 11 November. Commander Collins was promptly court-martialed for the incident, but soon after was restored to his command by Secretary of the Navy Gideon Welles.

After undergoing repairs at the Boston Navy Yard, *Wachusett* got underway on 5 March 1865 and sailed, via the Cape of Good Hope, for the East Indies. There, she joined *Wyoming* and *Iroquois* in an effort to track down the Confederate commerce raider CSS *Shenandoah*. She remained in Chinese waters into 1867. Upon her return to the United States, she was decommissioned on 4 February 1868 and was placed in ordinary at the New York Navy Yard.

Recommissioned on 1 June 1871, *Wachusett* left New York a week later, bound for the Mediterranean where she cruised until November 1873. Returning home, she served along the Atlantic and gulf coasts for a year before she was decommissioned at Boston on 29 December 1874. *Wachusett* remained laid up at Boston for five years and was recommissioned on 26 May 1879. She sailed for the Gulf of Mexico on 5 June and visited New Orleans and Vicksburg to enlist seamen before returning to Boston in August.

On 2 October 1879, *Wachusett* left Boston for the South Atlantic Station where she cruised until May 1880. She then sailed for the Pacific, arriving off the coast of Chile in June. The vessel remained on the Pacific Station, cruising extensively until September 1885 when she was decommissioned at the Mare Island Navy Yard, Vallejo, Calif. *Wachusett* was sold there to W. T. Garratt & Co. on 30 July 1887.

II

(ScStr: dp. 9,200; l. 387'; b. 44'2''; dr. 24'8'' (aft); s. 10.7 k.; cpl. 30; a. none)

SS *Suevia*—a freighter built in 1896 by Blohm & Voss at Hamburg, Germany—was seized from the Hamburg-America Line in 1917 by customs officials for the United States Shipping Board; renamed *Wachusett* (Id. No.

1840); turned over to the War Department on 22 December 1917; chartered to the Navy on 26 December 1917; and commissioned at Hoboken, N.J., on 9 January 1918, Lt. Comdr Roy W. Look, USNRF, in command.

Assigned to the Naval Overseas Transportation Service as an Army account, she was fitted out for naval service as a cargo transport. She put to sea on 19 January, laden with a cargo of general Army supplies bound for Brest, France. On 23 January, urgent need for repairs to her radio and engine forced her out of her convoy and into port at Halifax, Nova Scotia. She completed those repairs on 9 February and resumed her transatlantic voyage that same day. Her convoy arrived in Brest on 24 February, and *Wachusett* discharged her cargo. On 18 March, the freighter set out on the return voyage and arrived in New York on 1 April.

Following a brief repair period, the ship loaded another Army cargo and departed New York, bound for Norfolk, Va., and refueling. She steamed out of Hampton Roads on 16 April and headed across the Atlantic in company with another convoy. She arrived at Le Havre, France, on 7 May, discharged her cargo and completed her turnaround on the 19th by putting to sea with a New York-bound convoy.

Wachusett entered New York harbor on 4 June and simultaneously began repairs and cargo loading. Eleven days after her arrival, she stood out of New York, bound southward to Norfolk where she coaled ship on the 15th before her departure the following day for England. Her convoy entered port at Southampton on 10 July, and she unloaded her 4,300 tons of supplies before heading for the United States on the 20th.

Back in New York on 8 August, she underwent voyage repairs while also loading cargo. Again, she steamed south to Norfolk to coal ship and join an eastbound convoy. She sailed from Norfolk on 21 August and pulled into Brest on 11 September. *Wachusett* left Brest on 31 September after a six-day delay during which she awaited the formation of a homeward-bound convoy. She returned to New York on 15 October, underwent the usual minor repairs, and loaded cargo for her last wartime Atlantic crossing. She stood out of New York on 24 October in convoy for Brest, where she arrived on 8 November. Three days later, the armistice ended hostilities. *Wachusett* remained in France for 10 more days and then headed back to the United States—for the first time unmenaced by the danger of enemy U-boats.

The end of the war, however, did not signal an end to *Wachusett*'s Navy career. After her arrival back in New York on 12 December, the cargoman loaded 4,445 tons of supplies and, on 22 January 1919, headed back across the Atlantic. She entered port at St. Nazaire, France, on 7 February and, after discharging her cargo, loaded ordnance material for return to the United States. Departing the French coast on 20 February, she made a brief stop in the Azores en route to New York. Diverted from her original destination, she arrived in Philadelphia on 14 March.

Wachusett loaded a partial cargo at Philadelphia and then moved to New York where she filled out her cargo and topped off her coal bunkers. On 10 April, she set sail from New York bound for Gibraltar. There, she received orders to continue her voyage—destination: Singapore. She reached the British colonial city in the Orient on 27 April and unloaded her cargo there. From Singapore, *Wachusett* set sail on 5 June for Java in the Netherlands East Indies. She visited the Javanese cities of Weltevreden in June and Batavia at the beginning of July. On 12 July, she headed back to Singapore and departed that British colony on the 22d. Steaming via the Suez Canal and the Mediterranean Sea, *Wachusett* refueled in the Azores on 8 September and arrived in New York on the 21st.

Following voyage repairs, *Wachusett* was placed out of commission on 6 October 1919 and was returned to the United States Shipping Board that same day. She was retained by the Shipping Board until late in 1923 or early in 1924, at which time all mention of her in mercantile registers ceased.

Wachusetts

(MB: t. 65 (gross); l. 101'; b. 16'6"; dr. 7' (f.); s. 12 k.; cpl. 6; a. 1 3-pdr., 2 .30-cal. mg.)

W.C.T.U. was built in 1916 by W. A. and S. D. Moss of Friendship, Maine. Acquired by the Navy in the spring of 1917 from the Howard Lumber Co. of Boston, Mass., the craft—renamed *Wachusetts* by that time—was taken over on 26 April 1917 and designated SP–548. As of 1 February 1918, *Wachusetts* was operating out of the section base at Boothbay, Maine, probably on local patrol duties, under the aegis of Commandant, 1st Naval District. Her commanding officer as of that time was Ens. J. B. Eckroll, USNRF.

The ship's name was apparently dropped somewhat later to avoid confusion with *Wachusett* (Id. No. 1840), and the boat became simply *SP–548*. Little is known of her activities because her deck logs have been lost. Further confusion exists as to her ultimate fate. She was struck from the Navy list on 25 October 1919 and reportedly transferred to the Bureau of Fisheries simultaneously. However, subsequent lists of vessels operated by that agency fail to account for her.

Wacissa

A river in the state of Florida.

(AOG–59: dp. 4,335 (f.); l. 310'9"; b. 48'6"; dr. 15'8"; s. 14 k.; cpl. 124; a. 4 3", 2 40mm.; cl. *Patapsco*)

Wacissa (AOG–59) was laid down on 11 November 1944 at Savage, Minn., by Cargill, Inc.; launched on 15 June 1945; sponsored by Mrs. Albert Ford; and completed on 20 May 1946. Declared surplus to Navy needs on 1 June 1946, the ship was authorized for disposal on the 5th. Struck from the Navy list on 23 April 1947, *Wacissa* was delivered to the Maritime Commission during the following summer and berthed with the Maritime Commission Reserve Fleet at Lake Charles, La. She was then placed on a list of ships slated for disposal via sale.

The Navy, however, requested that the gasoline tanker be taken off the sale list. She was accordingly transferred to the Naval Reserve Fleet berthing area at Orange, Tex., on 3 April 1948. However, as facilities for upkeep and preservation were minimal at Orange, *Wacissa* was towed to New Orleans, La., for a preservation process which would prepare the ship for retention in the Navy's inactive fleet. Towed back to Orange, Tex., the ship was reinstated on the Navy list on 30 April, inactivated on 2 May, and placed in reserve on the 3d.

The onset of the Korean War caused an expansion of the United States Navy. On 18 February 1952, *Wacissa* was transferred to the Military Sea Transportation Service (MSTS) and received the designation T–AOG–59. She took part in Operation "Sumac," exercises conducted in the North Atlantic from May through July 1952, and subsequently carried cargoes of high test aviation gasoline and lubricating oils to Goose Bay, Labrador, and Argentia, Newfoundland. She ran aground at Polaris Reef, Baffin Bay, on 9 October. Floated free on the 16th, the tanker then put into Halifax, Nova Scotia, for repairs which lasted from 25 October to 19 December. She then resumed her operations along the east coast and continued them into the spring of 1954.

On 25 May 1954, *Wacissa* was placed out of service, in reserve, and was assigned to the Florida Group, Atlantic Reserve Fleet. Berthed at the Mayport Basin of the Green Cove Springs facility, the gasoline tanker remained in reserve until returned to MSTS on 24 May 1956. She carried a cargo of gasoline and oils from

Aruba, Netherlands West Indies, to San Pedro and Long Beach, Calif., via the Panama Canal, and operated for a time off the west coast, stopping at Seattle, Wash., and San Francisco, Calif. She was then inactivated at the latter port and delivered to the Maritime Administration—the renamed Maritime Commission—and, on 16 October 1956, was delivered to the National Defense Reserve Fleet at Suisun Bay, Calif.

Remaining in custodial status from that date, she lay there inactive until 8 April 1957, when she was transferred back to MSTS to resume her lubricant and fuel carrying duties off the west coast. *Wacissa* was tarnsferred to the Department of the Air Force on 16 September 1957; but, soon thereafter, she was turned over to the Canadian government to operate with the Northern Transportation Co., Ltd.—the firm which had assumed responsibility for the annual resupplying of Distant Early Warning (DEW) line radar stations in the central Arctic.

The Canadian government operated the tanker in these northern climes until 1963, when *Wacissa* was returned to the United States Navy. Struck from the Navy list on 1 December 1963, she was transferred to the Maritime Administration in May 1964 and was then sold in the same month to the Nicolai Joffre Corp., of Beverly Hills, Calif., for scrapping.

Wacondah

(ScStr: t. 190 (gross); l. 177'; b. 17'; dr. 7'3'' (mean); s. 18 k.; cpl. 28; a. 2 6-pdrs., 2 mg.)

Revolution—a steel-hulled, screw steam yacht designed by Charles L. Seabury—was completed in 1901, at Morris Heights, N.Y., by the Charles L. Seabury Co. and the Gas Engine and Power Co., for mining engineer F. Augustus Heinze. One of the first American turbine-powered steam "express" yachts, *Revolution* was later acquired by Boston banker Charles Hayden in 1907 and renamed *Wacondah*.

When the United States entered World War I on 6 April 1917, the Navy soon began collecting ships and small craft from civilian owners to serve as auxiliaries and patrol craft. Inspected at the 3d Naval District, *Wacondah* was acquired by the Navy on 24 May 1917. Fitted out for wartime service, *Wacondah* was commissioned on 14 September 1917, Lt. (jg.) Samuel Wainwright, USNRF, in command.

By virtue of her light construction—built for speed rather than sea-keeping—*Wacondah* was restricted to "sheltered waters." Assigned to the 3d Naval District, she operated on local patrol duties out of New York harbor for the duration of the war. Decommissioned and struck from the Navy list on 21 August 1919, *Wacondah* was sold on 4 June 1920 to the International Steamship and Trading Co.

Waddell

James Iredell Waddell—born on 13 July 1824 in Pittsboro, N.C.—was appointed a midshipman on 10 September 1841—and began serving in ship-of-the-line *Pennsylvania* the following December. During the Mexican War, he took part in the blockade at Vera Cruz while assigned to the brig *Somers*; and he subsequently saw sea duty along the coast of South America in sloop-of-war *Germantown* and completed a tour of duty as an instructor at the Naval Academy. In July 1859, he reported on board *Saginaw* and later returned from a tour of duty in the Orient with the East Indies Squadron, in *John Adams*, shortly after the outbreak of the Civil War. As his sympathies lay with the Southern States, he resigned his commission in the Navy, and his name was struck from the Navy rolls on 18 January 1862.

Waddell secretly entered the service of the Confederacy by way of Baltimore, Md., and received an appointment as lieutenant in the Confederate States Navy on 27 May 1862. The Confederate Navy, however,

had few ships to which these officers could be assigned. Naval officers were, as a result, assigned to artillery units. Thus employed, Waddell participated in the attempt to stop the Federal Fleet from investing New Orleans; helped man a gun battery in repulsing the Union flotilla in the Battle of Drewry's Bluff, Va., and performed nearly identical service manning a gun battery in the defense of Charleston, S.C., until March of 1863. At that time, he sailed for France in a steamer acquired by Confederate naval agent James D. Bulloch.

On 19 October 1864, near Funchal, Madeira, Waddell took command of an iron-hulled screw steamer—*Sea King*—a Clyde-built merchantman which had earlier sailed, ostensibly, for Bombay, India, on a trading voyage. It was off Madeira, however, that *Sea King* underwent the transformation from merchantman to man-of-war. Fitted out secretly, *Sea King* was armed and renamed *Shenandoah*, and set course for the Pacific.

Under orders to concentrate on the previously unmolested Union whaling fleet in the Pacific, *Shenandoah* put five ships to the torch en route to the Cape of Good Hope, and bonded a sixth to carry prisoners to Bahia, Brazil. Proceeding through the Indian Ocean, Waddell paused at Melbourne, Australia, long enough to repair a defective propeller shaft in January 1865 and enlist the aid of 42 "stowaways" who appeared on deck soon after departure to swell the ranks of what had previously been an under-strength crew.

Shenandoah captured four Yankee whalers en route to the Sea of Okhotsk, and later operated in the Bering Sea—capturing two dozen prizes between 21 and 29 June. One of the latter prizes carried a choice find—relatively recent newspapers. But the news which the Southerners read was not good—General Robert E. Lee had surrendered at Appomattox Court House, Va., while President Jefferson Davis had issued his defiant "Danville Proclamation" calling for a continued vigorous prosecution of the war against the Union forces.

Waddell and his crew sighted no additional sails until 2 August 1865, when his ship fell in with British merchantman *Barracouta*. The Briton informed *Shenandoah* that the Confederacy had completely collapsed and that *Shenandoah* was thus no longer a man-of-war, but a "pirate" ship without a country. This made the erstwhile raider subject to seizure under international law.

A thousand miles west of Acapulco, Mex., and 13 days from San Francisco, Calif., Waddell disregarded advice to beach his ship or sail to the nearest British colonial port where his men would be forced to shift for themselves. Subsequently, courage and seamanship brought *Shenandoah* through a remarkable 17,000-mile voyage, via Cape Horn, to England. On 2 November 1865, *Shenandoah* stood proudly into Liverpool, England, where she was surrendered to British authorities for eventual turnover to the United States government.

Waddell remained in England until amnesty was offered in 1875. He then returned to his native land after an absence of nearly a decade and became a captain in the Pacific Mail Company steamship line. Given command of steamer *City of San Francisco*, Waddell sailed to the South Pacific near waters where, nearly 10 years before, his name and that of his ship had been feared. Calling at Honolulu in 1876, the arrival of the erstwhile raider-skipper went, apparently, unnoticed. Or so it seemed. As *City of San Francisco* stood out to sea the next day, the Royal Hawaiian Band played "Dixie"—farewell music with a different "twist." Waddell dipped his flag in salute!

Subsequently, the sea captain became commander of the Maryland State Flotilla for the policing of oyster beds. While thus employed, Waddell died at Annapolis, Md., on 15 March 1886.

(DDG–24: dp. 4,500 (f.); l. 435'; b. 47'; dr. 21'10''; s. 30 k.; cpl. 354; a. 2 5'', ASROC, 2 Mk. 32 tt., Tartar; cl. *Charles F. Adams*)

Waddell (DDG–24) was laid down on 6 February

1962 at Seattle, Wash., by Todd Shipyards Corp.; launched on 26 February 1963; sponsored by Mrs. Howard W. Cannon; and commissioned on 28 August 1964, Comdr. Carl J. Boyd in command.

Following trials from October 1964 to May 1965, the new guided missile destroyer conducted shakedown off the west coast into July, before she participated in antiaircraft and electronic warfare Exercise "Hot Stove" from 26 August to 3 September. During this time, while serving as plane-guard for *Ticonderoga* (CVA–14), *Waddell* rescued Comdr. C. H. Peters, whose plane had ditched off the coast of southern California.

On 28 September 1965, *Waddell*—in company with *Ticonderoga* and three destroyers, and acting as flagship for Commander, Destroyer Squadron (DesRon) 132—departed her home port, Long Beach, Calif., bound for her first tour of duty in the Western Pacific (WestPac). After stopping at Pearl Harbor, she proceeded on toward the Philippines.

While en route on 31 October, the American task group received a radio message reporting that Japanese merchantman *Tokei Maru* had suffered an explosion on board. Detached to render assistance, *Waddell* sped to the scene and lowered her motor whaleboat containing the squadron doctor. The ship's rescue party arrived on board to find three men of *Tokei Maru*'s complement already dead and another seriously burned. After providing medical assistance which saved the man's life and having left *Tokei Maru* a supply of medicine to suffice until the Japanese ship could make port, *Waddell* rejoined her consorts.

Only one day after reaching Subic Bay, *Waddell* got underway on 2 November for the coast of Vietnam and her first deployment to "Yankee Station" W–5, in the Tonkin Gulf. On station with Task Unit (TU) 77.0.2 until the 14th, the ship returned to Subic Bay for brief local operations before sailing back to the combat zone to take her post on the northern search and rescue station (SAR) from 29 November to 29 December.

On 7 December, *Waddell* steamed alongside *Sacramento* (AOE–1) conducting an underway replenishment on the oiler's port side; while *Brinkley Bass* (DD–887) replenish to starboard of the oiler. During the operation, *Brinkley Bass* reported a man overboard; and *Waddell* executed an emergency break-away and doubled back to pick up the man.

Upon completion of this SAR tour, the destroyer sailed via Sasebo to Buckner Bay, Okinawa. She conducted a missile shoot in Ryukyu waters and then visited Hong Kong. On 31 January 1966, she sailed for Danang, en route to a second deployment to the northern SAR area.

At 1410 on 3 February 1966, *Waddell* was notified that a pilot was possibly downed in their vicinity. While proceeding to investigate, the ship noted "surface action" to port and commenced shore bombardment at 1501. Communist guns replied 14 minutes later. *Waddell* then trained her guns on the communist batteries. At 1545, while still shelling the communist gun positions, *Waddell* was straddled by the enemy guns which had found the range. Radical maneuvers enabled the destroyer to retire without damage, and she emerged from the action unscathed.

The following day, after receiving fuel from *Sacramento* in an underway replenishment while on station, *Waddell* collided with *Brinkley Bass*. The damage which *Waddell* sustained forced her to return to the Philippines for repairs.

Back in Vietnamese waters in late February, *Waddell* provided gunfire support in the III Corps operating area from 27 February to 11 March, as part of TU 70.8.9. She then returned—via Subic Bay, Guam, Midway, and Pearl Harbor—to her home port, Long Beach, where she arrived on 8 April.

Following a yard period—during which the ship underwent structural repairs—*Waddell* participated in various fleet and independent exercises off the California coast. Two days after Christmas of 1966, the ship got underway for another WestPac deployment.

Early in 1967, *Waddell* was again busily engaged off the Vietnamese coastline. From 2 March to 21 May 1967, the ship displayed "exceptional readiness and effectiveness in all tasks assigned," including gunfire support off South Vietnam; interdiction of North Vietnamese supply traffic along the coast; and gunfire against selected targets in North Vietnam. Coming under hostile fire from shore on one occasion, *Waddell* returned the fire and inflicted maximum damage on enemy shore batteries while emerging without harm. During her second WestPac deployment in Vietnamese waters, the destroyer fired some 2,000 rounds of ammunition while winning the reputation of being "the busiest ship in the Tonkin Gulf" before heading home.

Waddell made port at Long Beach on 29 May 1967 and operated briefly off the southern California coast. She entered the Long Beach Naval Shipyard on 4 August and commenced an extensive overhaul which lasted through the end of the year 1967 and into February 1968.

She returned to WestPac that summer—with logistics stops at Pearl Harbor and Midway en route—and arrived at her new home port of Yokosuka, Japan, on 1 August 1968. She conducted three tours on the "gun line" off North and South Vietnam into the fall, as well as one tour as plane guard for the attack carrier strike group based around *Coral Sea* (CVA–43) and *Ranger* (CVA–61).

On 22 September while operating off the demilitarized zone (DMZ) in company with *St. Paul* (CA–73), *Waddell* participated in a SAR operation. At 0145, an attack bomber splashed near the ship. Both crew members had previously ejected from their stricken jet and parachuted to the sea. *Waddell* closed to within 5,000 yards of the mouth of the Cua Vet River and rescued the navigator/bombardier, while *St. Paul* picked up the pilot.

After completing an overhaul at Yokosuka toward the end of December 1968, *Waddell* got underway on 7 January 1969, bound for the "gun line." Between 17 and 30 January, she fired two gunfire support missions in the I Corps area for the Army's 101st Airborne Division and one for the 7th and 9th Divisions of the Republic of Vietnam (ARVN) units. After a quick trip via Buckner Bay to Yokosuka, *Waddell* sped back to the "gun line" in late February and resumed her gunfire support duties on 1 March. There, in the II Corps area, she fired 12 support missions with Task Force "South." She subsequently conducted 79 more gunfire support missions including 12 for Australian units, 11 for ARVN units, and 15 in support of Operation "Sheridan"—in which the United States Army 101st Airborne and an ARVN regiment participated.

During the first week of April, the downing by North Koreans of a Navy EC–121 Connie early-warning intelligence aircraft in the Sea of Japan greatly increased tension in the Far East. *Waddell* departed the "gun line" at 22 knots, refueled at Buckner Bay, and arrived in the Strait of Tsushima to screen aircraft carriers *Ticonderoga* and *Ranger*. She operated in the Sea of Japan until the crisis abated enabling her to head for Yokosuka on the afternoon of 28 April.

Returning to the "gun line," *Waddell* then lobbed shells at Viet Cong (VC) camps and infiltration points from waters off Phu Quoc Island in the Gulf of Siam in support of Operation "Javelin," before she was assigned to the Mekong Delta region. There, supporting two ARVN divisions, she conducted 19 bombardments against VC structures, bunkers, rest sites, and supply routes.

Subsequently returning to "Yankee Station," she screened *Enterprise* (CVAN–65) in June, as the big carrier conducted strike operations, and returned to waters near the DMZ in mid-July for gunnery support duties.

The guided-missile destroyer *Waddell* (DDG–24).

In 1970, *Waddell*'s home port was again changed—this time to San Diego, Calif. During her next WestPac deployment, the destroyer continued her busy task of supporting ground units and standing by as a plane guard and a picket destroyer on "Yankee Station." In addition, she conducted occasional surveillance missions, watching Russian warships operating near the American task forces on not-so-subtle intelligence gathering missions of their own. One such mission took place as the Russians conducted Operation "Okean" in the Philippine Sea.

Returning to the west coast in the late summer of 1970, the ship operated off southern California and participated in underway exercises and plane-guard details through the end of that year and into 1971. She underwent an extended period of refresher training through the summer of 1971, operating off Seal Beach, San Diego, and San Clemente Island, Calif., until she got underway on 12 November for Danang, South Vietnam.

Waddell returned to the "gun line" on 12 December near the DMZ to resume gunfire support operations in the southern half of the zone. She also performed interdiction and night harassment duties. Returning to Danang on 30 December, she got underway on the last day of the year to participate in TF 74's operations in the Indian Ocean.

Hostilities between India and Pakistan had caused the flurry of activity, as contingency plans were drawn up to rescue Americans caught in the area, if the need arose. However, the crisis soon passed; and *Waddell* returned to Subic Bay on 15 January 1972. Two days later, the ship was picked to represent the United States at the Imperial Ethiopian Navy Day celebration at Massawa, Ethiopia. After hasty preparations, *Waddell* stood out of Philippine waters and entered the Indian Ocean soon thereafter—for the second time in a fortnight.

After a brief stop at Colombo, Sri Lanka, on 28 January, *Waddell* arrived at Massawa on 4 February and fired the prescribed 21-gun salute while her crew smartly manned the rail. During the visit, *Waddell*'s athletic teams competed with those from visiting Russian, French, British, Sudanese, and Ethiopian ships. One high point of the brief stay was a visit by Emperor Haile Selassie. Another was a graduation exercise at which the Emperor requested an encore performance of *Waddell*'s precision drill team—which had been first formed and trained while en route to Massawa!

Waddell's respite from the war was a short one, for she returned to the "gun line" on 1 April. Although her tour was scheduled to end on the 14th, stepped-up communist ground activities resulted in her remaining into May.

From 3 to 9 April, *Waddell* encountered daily counterbattery fire from communist guns ashore. The ship's gunfire, in turn, was credited with knocking out several counterbattery sites. Most missions during this period fell in the area of the Cua Viet naval base and in Quang Tri province north of the Cua Viet River. At times, the range was so short that *Waddell* could observe her own fall of shot.

Late on the afternoon of 8 April, *Waddell* took a "high priority" target under fire, and received heavy counterbattery fire in return. A secondary explosion ashore attested to the fact that *Waddell*'s shells had hit something—but the enemy stubbornly kept up the fire, landing a shell very close to the destroyer's bow. A surface burst damaged the ship's ASROC launcher, and shrapnel littered the destroyer's deck.

On 9 and 10 April, the ship fired so many missions that she needed two underway replenishments of her ammunition. From the 11th through the 21st, the pace continued to be rapid. On one occasion, *Waddell* destroyed several sampans detected ferrying Viet Cong and North Vietnamese troops across the Ben Hai River. In addition, the ship's guns blasted antiaircraft sites and coastal gun emplacements.

After renewing her guns at Subic Bay—they had been so worn by combat operations during April—*Waddell* returned to Vietnamese waters to join TU 77.1.2 in Operation "Linebacker." For two weeks, *Waddell* made continuous gunnery strikes at night and sometimes encountered the fiercest return fire she had thus far experienced. She silenced some enemy batteries while picking up some shrapnel in return from near-misses by the communist guns—before she shifted to waters off the DMZ, where she supported ARVN operations until 26 June. Her final two weeks of this WestPac deployment were spent on "Yankee Station" planeguarding for *Coral Sea.*

After sailing back to the United States—via Yokosuka—the ship underwent an extensive yard period. She spent the waning days of 1972 preparing for another deployment to the Far East, one which was different from the previous ones. For by this point, American land, sea, and air forces were no longer committed in active combat roles in Vietnam. Thus, she conducted only training operations in the Gulf of Tonkin in February 1973, before she visited Beppu and Sasebo, Japan.

Waddell then took part in supervising parts of Operation "End Sweep," the clearance of minefields which had been planted in North Vietnamese coastal waters and off key ports. She conducted her first tour of "End Sweep" from 19 March to 13 April and was at sea again with "End Sweep" from 27 to 30 June. In between these deployments, *Waddell* performed screening duties for *Coral Sea* and *Constellation* (CVA–64) and visited Hong Kong; Subic Bay; Penang, Malaysia; and Singapore.

Returning to the west coast on 2 August, *Waddell* spent the remainder of the year in exercises and local operations off the southern California coast before again sailing for the Orient on 23 April 1974. Following the usual stops—Pearl Harobor, Guam, and Midway—

she arrived in the Philippines on 16 May to conduct local operations out of Subic Bay.

Subsequently, the ship participated in Exercise "Kangaroo I" near Shoalwater Bay, Australia, with units of the Royal Australian Navy. Following local operations out of Subic Bay and Kaohsiung, Taiwan, *Waddell* got underway for the west coast on 28 September 1974 and made port at San Diego on 18 October.

Remaining at San Diego until 22 January 1975, she was towed by *Tawasa* (ATF–92) to the Long Beach Naval Shipyard where she underwent an extensive overhaul from 24 January to 3 December. As of 1979, *Waddell* actively served with the Pacific Fleet.

Waddell received 11 engagement stars for her service in waters off Vietnam and two Navy Unit Commendations.

Wadena

A chief of the Minnesota Sioux Indians.

(ScStr: t. 246 (gross); l. 176′; b. 20′ 10′′; dr. 10′6′′; s. 13 k.; cpl. 66; a. 2 3′′, 2 .30-cal. Colt mg., 10 dc. Mk. I)

Wadena—a steel-hulled, screw steam, schooner-rigged yacht—was built in 1891 at Cleveland, Ohio, by the Cleveland Shipbuilding Co. In the spring of 1917, the Navy inspected *Wadena* and acquired her from J. H. Wade, of Cleveland, who delivered the ship to the 3d Naval District on 25 May 1917. Designated SP–158, *Wadena* was fitted out at the New York Navy Yard for "distant service." She was commissioned at New York on 14 January 1918, Lt. Comdr. Walter M. Falconer, USN (Ret.), in command.

In company with *Yacona* (SP–617) and the steam tug *Mariner* (SP–1136), *Wadena* shifted to New London, Conn., and remained there from 6 February to 24 February. *Wadena* then coaled at Newport, R.I.—a difficult and time-consuming process since it had to be done by handshovels—before she got underway for Bermuda on the 24th and rendezvoused with a convoy of 11 subchasers (SC's) soon thereafter.

As the little convoy made its way down the eastern seaboard, *Mariner* fell progressively astern. She briefly towed *SC–177* before the tug herself began to founder in the heavy southeasterly gale that sprang up on the 26th. At 1140 on that day, *Mariner* hoisted the breakdown flag, cast loose *SC–177*, and began fighting a losing battle against the sea. At 1400, *Mariner* sent a message: "We are sinking fast."

Wadena stood by the helpless tug, her log noting that the sea was "very rough and running high." *Wadena* sprayed oil on the water to calm the raging sea, and brought on board *Mariner*'s entire complement between 1550 and 1730, the last raft reaching the yacht's side at 1730 with the tug's commanding officer, Lt. (jg.) Martin Miller, USNRF, on board. *Wadena* later went off in search of *SC–177* after *Mariner* slipped beneath the waves, while the rest of the convoy continued on its passage. The yacht then took *SC–177* in tow and later caught up with the rest of the group shortly before reaching the British naval station at Hamilton, Bermuda, on 1 March.

Wadena returned to the east coast of the United States soon thereafter, reaching Charleston, S.C., on 10 March. She remained there until the 25th, when she escorted another convoy of subchasers to Bermuda, arriving there on the 29th. Assigned to the "special task force"—probably formed to safeguard the transatlantic passage of subchasers slated to operate in European waters—*Wadena* sailed on 15 April in company with seven SC's, the Army transport service tug *Knickerbocker*, and the tug *Lykens* (SP–876).

Making most of the passage under sail, *Wadena* reached Ponta Delgada, Azores, on the 27th. In company with *Yacona* and the fuel ship *Arethusa*, *Wadena* sailed for Bermuda on 4 May and reached the British admiralty dockyard there 10 days later. While at Bermuda, she was drydocked for repairs and the application of anticorrosive and antifouling paint to her hull. Underway again on 25 May, *Wadena* sailed for the Azores and returned to Bermuda—in company with *Undaunted* (SP–1950), *Goliath* (SP–1494), *Arctic* (SP–1158), and *Yacona*—on 20 June.

After subsequently taking part in another transatlantic movement of SC's from Bermuda to European waters, *Wadena* continued on via Ponta Delgada to Gibraltar in company with the Italian ship SS *Bronte* and three French SC's. Reaching Gibraltar on 31 July, the yacht operated with the patrol squadrons based at that port into the autumn.

She performed parol and escort duties beween Gibraltar and Funchal, Madeira; Ponta Delgada and the Canary Islands; and Tangiers and Safi, Morocco. On occasion, she also transported mail and personnel. After escorting the cargo vessel *Mount Shasta* from Ponta Delgada to Gibraltar between 16 and 21 October, *Wadena* remained at Gibraltar through the armistice. During the afternoon watch on 11 November, her log recorded the news: "At 1:00 (pm) received word that Germany had signed the armistice and that hostilities had ceased at 11:00 a.m."

While the ship was at Gibraltar, she was inspected by Rear Admiral Albert P. Niblack, Commander, Squadron 2, Patrol Force. Eventually getting underway on 11 December to return to the United States, she made part of the passage in company with *Sacramento* (Gunboat No. 19), *Paducah* (Gunboat No. 18), and the Coast Guard cutter *Manning*. *Wadena* used her sails again for most of the passage sailing via Ponta Delgada and Bermuda—and reached New London in company with *Manning* on 3 January 1919.

Placed in reserve, *Wadena* remained at New London through April of 1919. As squadron flagship, she departed that port on 5 May, bound for the New York Navy Yard, reaching there the following day in company with *Wanderer* (SP–132), *Corona* (SP–813), *Christabel* (SP–162), and *Emeline* (SP–175). Later that day, the process of removing her guns and other Navy equipment began. After shifting to the Marine Basin at Brooklyn a week later, *Wadena* was decommissioned on the afternoon of 19 May 1919. She was sold to S. H. Johnson of New York City on 12 July 1920.

Wadleigh

George Henry Wadleigh—born in Dover, N.H., on 28 September 1842—was appointed a midshipman on 27 September 1860 and graduated from the Naval Academy in May 1863. He reported to *Lackawanna* at New Orleans and participated in the Union blockade of the Confederacy's gulf coast, first in *Lackawanna* and later in *Richmond*.

Detached from the latter vessel on 11 July 1865, Wadleigh reported to *Ticonderoga* the following August. He had advanced to the rank of lieutenant commander by March 1868 and then served at the Naval Academy discharging duties in communications and torpedo work before sailing for the Brazil Station on 15 March 1871 as executive officer of *Shawmut*.

Subsequently serving in *Canonicus*, *Ohio*, *St. Mary's*, and *Pensacola*, he served briefly on shore duty at the Portsmouth (N.H.) Navy Yard in late 1878. Rising to the rank of commander on 13 March 1880, he received his first sea command, *Alliance*, on 6 June 1881 and remained in command of her until December 1882 when he returned to Portsmouth for a second tour.

Following service at the Boston Navy Yard and duty at sea commanding *Michigan* into the 1890's, Wadleigh again served ashore at Boston. On 19 July 1894, he rose to the rank of captain and commanded *Richmond* from that day until detached on 7 December of that year. Soon thereafter, he assumed command of *Minneapolis*. After filling the billets of president, General

Court Martial Board, at Norfolk, and captain of the yard at the Boston Navy Yard, Wadleigh successively commanded *Philadelphia* and *Wabash* before being appointed commandant of the Philadelphia Navy Yard on 18 January 1902.

Promoted to rear admiral on 9 February, he was detached from the Philadelphia Navy Yard on 26 April and became President of the Board of Inspection and Survey on 6 May. However, he held that post only until he was transferred to the retired list on 7 June 1902. Rear Admiral Wadleigh lived in retirement into the 1920's, and died in Dover, N.H., on 11 July 1927.

(DD–689: dp. 2,050; l. 376'5''; b. 39'7''; dr. 17'9''; s. 35.2 k.; cpl. 329; a. 5 5'', 10 40mm., 7 20mm., 10 21'' tt., 2 dct., 6 dcp.; cl. *Fletcher*)

Wadleigh (DD–689) was laid down on 5 April 1943 at Bath, Maine, by the Bath Iron Works; launched on 7 August 1943; sponsored by Miss Clara F. Wadleigh, daughter of Rear Admiral Wadleigh; and commissioned at the Boston Navy Yard on 19 October 1943, Lt. Comdr. Walter C. Winn in command.

Following shakedown training in the West Indies, *Wadleigh* rendezvoused in the mid-Atlantic with *Iowa* (BB–61), *Halsey Powell* (DD–686), and *Marshall* (DD–676). The three destroyers escorted the battleship as she carried President Franklin D. Roosevelt back to the United States from talks with other Allied leaders at Cairo, Egypt.

Soon after her return from this special escort duty, *Wadleigh* got underway from Hampton Roads, Va., on 3 January 1944 and steamed via Panama to Pearl Harbor.

Her baptism of fire came on 20 March 1944 during the Marshall Islands campaign. Assigned shore bombardment duties, *Wadleigh*—in company with *McCalla* (DD–488) and *Sage* (AM–111)—supported LCI's and LST's during the landings on Ailinglapalap and expended 478 rounds of 5-inch shells which destroyed an enemy-held village. Three days later, the new destroyer again took part in shooting up Japanese defenses, shelling a weather station and a radio station on Ebon Island, helping to clear the way for the 1,500 marines who soon took the island.

The ship returned to the Hawaiian Islands for further operational training in preparation for the upcoming conquest of the Marianas. Assigned to Task Group (TG) 52.4, *Wadleigh* arrived off Roi Island in the Marshalls on 10 June, five days before D-day for the invasion of Saipan Island. The day before the first landings, the warship closed Saipan and commenced fire early in the morning, beginning her part in the operations designed to "soften up" the enemy defenses.

On D-day, *Wadleigh* lay offshore, providing predawn gunfire support for underwater demolition teams (UDT) and for the initial waves of troops. After spending the day in shelling enemy positions, she retired seaward to conduct screening patrols. While thus engaged, *Wadleigh* and *Melvin* (DD–680) both picked up strong sonar contacts with a submarine west of Tinian. Both ships went to general quarters and attacked, dropping depth charges with deadly precision. A heavy explosion, followed by a widening slick of oil and debris, indicated that whatever had been down there had been heavily hit. Postwar accounting revealed that the two destroyers had teamed to sink the Japanese submarine *RO–114*.

Assigned to bombard Garapan, the capital city of Saipan, *Wadleigh* encountered heavy activity of all types in this area, from both friend and foe alike, while expending some 1,700 rounds of 5-inch shells against the Japanese-held island. Not only was *Wadleigh* fired on by a Japanese shore battery, but the doughty destroyer was also straddled by a stick of bombs from a Japanese plane, mistaken for a low-flying aircraft by American forces, and again taken under fire from shore—all within a hair-raising space of 15 minutes! During the latter days of the campaign,

Wadleigh shot enemy snipers out of caves, trees, and cliffs; picked up an occasional Japanese prisoner, and rescued downed American aircrews shot down near her position.

Following escort runs to Eniwetok and Guadalcanal, *Wadleigh* was assigned to support the invasion of the Palaus. On 15 September, she patrolled north of the islands on radar picket duty, standing ready to provide early warning if Japanese planes were sighted.

On the following day, *Wadleigh* steamed to Kossol Roads to begin assisting minesweepers in clearing the sealanes there. Floating mines swept up by the minesweepers provided the destroyers with "game," and *Wadleigh* destroyed 22 with 40-millimeter fire. The 23d, however, was deadly. While approaching one mine, the destroyer brushed horns with another, an unswept mine which burst amidships. The explosion ripped into the bowels of the ship, killing three men and injuring 20, while flooding three engineering compartments and one living space. As the crew raced to general quarters, the ship settled five feet by the stern, and listed seven degrees to starboard. *Wadleigh*—now sporting a 40-foot rent in her bottom—came to an even keel as the crew manhandled all moveable weight from starboard to port to correct the list.

Bennett (DD–473) passed a towline and towed the stricken destroyer out of danger. The crippled ship, now sagging noticeably amidships, "worked" noticeably in the swells, prompting initial fears that the ship was breaking in two. In addition, the shock of the blast snapped one radar antenna and jarred both 26-foot motor whaleboats from their blocks.

After temporary repairs, the ship painfully made her way back to Pearl Harbor and thence proceeded to the west coast to enter the Mare Island Navy Yard for repairs. Nearly rebuilt from the keel up, *Wadleigh* emerged from Mare Island on 20 February 1945 for speed trials and gunnery shoots. She departed San Diego, Calif., on 19 Apil and arrived at Pearl Harbor on the 25th, in company with *Charrette* (DD–581), to conduct type-training exercises in the Hawaiian Islands.

She departed Pearl Harbor on 3 May, bound for Ulithi, and arrived there after an 11-day passage. Rejoining her old unit—DesRon 54—the destroyer sortied with other 5th Fleet units on the 25th. After serving several tours on radar picket stations with the Fleet, *Wadleigh* weathered heavy typhoons from 5 to 7 June and subsequently accompanied *Alaska* (CB–1) and *Guam* (CB–2) in a shore bombardment mission to Minami Daito Shima (Rasa Island) on the 9th, demolishing radar installations and buildings.

After a rest period in the Philippines, *Wadleigh* sailed again for Japanese waters to screen the carriers as they continued to pound the Japanese home islands. On 10 July, the ship embarked a party of dignitaries— including Assistant Secretary of the Navy for Air, John L. Sullivan, and Vice Admiral Aubrey W. Fitch, for transportation to Iwo Jima.

Rendezvousing with *Ticonderoga* (CV–14) at Guam, she rejoined her task force on 21 July to support offensive operations off Japan's doorstep. While serving on occasion 50 miles from the enemy shore, *Wadleigh* rescued two downed Navy aircrewmen who had been shot down during a strike on Tokyo.

The destroyer slowed to destroy a derelict mine on 10 August, but excessive turbine vibrations forced the ship to shut down her starboard engine. Detached from the task force, *Wadleigh* limped back to Ulithi, in a convoy of replenishment ships and tankers, for repairs. While en route, she received word of the Japanese capitulation.

Departing Ulithi on 23 August and hoping to rejoin the Fleet in time for the triumphal entry into Tokyo Bay, *Wadleigh* stopped at Iwo Jima en route for passengers and mail and arrived 24 hours after the first ships had entered the bay. Ordered to proceed directly to Sagami Wan, *Wadleigh* went to general quarters in company with *Benevolence* (AH–13) as the ships passed

beneath the once-menacing shore batteries along the Urage Strait. They soon arrived at their destination, the Yokosuka Naval Base, on 29 August.

As the first American troops went ashore at Yokohama and Yokosuka, *Wadleigh* headed out to sea and rendezvoused with incoming carrier groups. She returned to her anchorage, near *Missouri* (BB–63), on 2 September—in time to be on hand when the official surrender accords were signed that day.

Back at sea with the carriers once more, *Wadleigh* patrolled off the Japanese coast for two weeks, before she departed Nipponese waters on 16 September and proceeded via Eniwetok to Saipan in company with *Bennington* (CV–20) and *Lexington* (CV–16) for air group replacements. The destroyer returned to Tokyo Bay after a week at Saipan and arrived on 13 October, escorting *Belleau Wood* (CVL–24) and *Lexington*.

Departing Japanese waters on 20 October, bound for the Hawaiian Islands, *Wadleigh* carried a load of men eligible for discharge upon their return to the United States. After a 48-hour layover in the Hawaiian Islands, she pressed on for San Francisco, arriving on 5 November 1945. She commenced a preinactivation overhaul on 5 December and sailed for San Diego, Calif., on 27 January 1946, for inactivation. The destroyer was placed out of commission, in reserve, in the San Diego group of the Pacific Reserve Fleet, in January 1947.

Wadleigh remained in reserve until she was reactivated during the Korean War. On 3 October 1951, *Wadleigh* was recommissioned at San Diego, Comdr. R. H. Pauli in command.

She departed San Diego on 4 January 1952, bound for duty with the Atlantic Fleet. She transited the Panama Canal on 14 January—in company with *Hazelwood* (DD–531), *Heermann* (DD–532), *Cassin Young* (DD–793), and *Cowell* (DD–547)—and, upon arrival at her new home port of Newport, R.I., became flagship for Commander, DesDiv 342.

After participating in various Fleet exercises, *Wadleigh* arrived at Pensacola, Fla., on 17 August, to commence four weeks of plane-guard duty for *Cabot* (CVL–28). She rescued three downed aviators from the Gulf of Mexico during this tour. Next, the destroyer sailed north for an overhaul at the Boston Naval Shipyard—during which time the ship received a battery of 3-inch guns—replacing the older 40-millimeter mounts.

On 3 May 1954, *Wadleigh* departed Newport, bound via the Panama Canal, Pearl Harbor, Midway, and Guam for the Western Pacific (WestPac), and arrived at Yokosuka, Japan, on 7 June 1954. After initially operating in the Philippine Islands, the destroyer shifted to the waters off the east coast of Korea, assisting in the supervision of Korean armistice agreements reached at Panmunjom the year before.

While in Subic Bay, *Wadleigh* was put on alert and ordered to rendezvous with TG 70.2. Once she joined with the group, TG 70.2 proceeded to the southern coast of Formosa in a precautionary move by the United States to forestall possible Chinese communist intentions towards the American-supported Nationalist Chinese regime on the island. While en route to Formosa, the ship struck an underwater object which inflicted minor damage to both screws. Returning to Subic Bay, the ship repaired the damage and sailed to rejoin the group. Once back on station, she spent 20 tense but uneventful days on patrol off Formosa and, soon thereafter, proceeded back to Sasebo, Japan, to prepare to return to the United States.

Wadleigh returned to Newport—via Hong Kong, Singapore, Colombo, and various Mediterranean ports— and arrived at her home port on 28 November 1954. Shifting to the Caribbean, she operated both in these waters and off the east coast, on antisubmarine warfare (ASW) exercises and local operations, through the end of 1955. She then deployed three times to the Mediterranean.

During the third of these deployments, in July 1958, tensions flared in Lebanon; and civil strife threatened

American lives and property. Accordingly, the United States landed troops to restore order. *Wadleigh* was among the first American ships to arrive on the scene, with another much-decorated *Fletcher*-class destroyer, *The Sullivans* (DD–537), arriving simultaneously. During the Lebanese crisis, she conducted eastern Mediterranean patrols as a unit of TF 61.

She returned to the east coast soon thereafter to operate along the Atlantic seaboard and into the Caribbean through the fall of 1958 before deploying to the Mediterranean for a fourth time in June of 1959. While homeward-bound to Newport in September of that year, she served as one of the chain of ships beneath the aerial route of President Dwight D. Eisenhower's return to the United States after his summit conferences in Europe.

During the period in which the ship continued to be based out of Newport, she conducted ASW exercises and local operations through the end of the year and into 1960. On 19 March 1960, *Wadleigh* sped to the scene of a collision between *Darby* (DE–218) and a Swedish tanker off Cape Henry. Commander, DesRon 20, embarked in *Wadleigh*, was on-scene commander and directed the succesful effort to take *Darby* under tow.

Returning to a schedule of local operations, *Wadleigh* conducted a midshipman's training cruise, ASW patrols, and exercises. During a deployment to European waters in the fall of 1960, she conducted NATO fall exercises in the North Sea and across the Arctic Circle.

Deploying to the Mediterranean for the fifth time, *Wadleigh* transited the Suez Canal and participated in CENTO Exercise "Midlink III," in which the naval forces of five nations participated. In November 1960, the ship returned to Mediterranean and western European waters, and took part in ASW Exercises "Haystrike" and "Jetstream" with French Navy units before returning to Newport on 15 December 1960.

She then conducted ASW exercises out of Mayport, Fla., and practiced recovery techniques for participation in Project "Mercury," the first American manned spaceflight program. Attached to TG 140.8, *Wadleigh* was on station on 5 May 1961 when Comdr. Alan Shepard conducted his history-making flight. A second participation by *Wadleigh* in the Project Mercury program came in August of that year, but unfavorable weather "scrubbed" the launch, and the destroyer was detached to return to Newport.

Late in the following fall, *Wadleigh* sailed for European waters once more and participated in Exercise "Line Jug II"—extensive ASW exercises with Royal Navy units. She topped this deployment with visits to ports in the British Isles like Londonderry and Southampton before returning to her home port on 22 February 1962. She conducted rotuine local operations until departing Newport on 22 June for Norfolk, Va. There, the ship was decommissioned and placed in reserve on 28 June 1962.

Transferred to Chile under the Military Aid Program in 1963, *Wadleigh* was renamed *Blanco Encalada* and was given identification number 14. She served with the Chilean Navy into 1979.

Wadleigh received six battle stars for her service in World War II.

Wadsworth

Alexander Scammel Wadsworth was born in 1790 at Portland, Maine. He was appointed a midshipman on 2 April 1804 and was promoted to lieutenant on 21 April 1810. Lt. Wadsworth was the first lieutenant on board *Constitution* during that famous frigate's successful engagement with *Guerriere* in the War of 1812. For this action, he received a silver medal and was included in the vote of thanks received by the commanding officer, Isaac Hull, and his officers. Wadsworth later served as first lieutenant of the corvette *Adams* during that ship's cruise in 1814 when she captured 10 prizes.

Promoted to master-commandant on 27 April 1816 for his services during the war, Wadsworth commanded the brig *Prometheus* in the Mediterranean Squadron after the Algerian War in 1816 and 1817 and later commanded the sloop *John Adams*. Under Wadsworth, *John Adams* conducted cruises in the West Indies in 1818 and 1819, and 1821 and 1822 for the suppression of piracy. Promoted to captain on 3 March 1825, he commanded frigate *Constellation* in the Mediterranean Squadron from 1829 to 1832. Wadsworth was commodore commanding the Pacific Squadron from 1834 to 1836, a member of the Board of Navy Commissioners from 1837 to 1840, and Inspector of Ordnance from 1841 to 1850. Commodore Wadsworth died at Washington, D.C., on 5 April 1851.

I

(Destroyer No. 60: dp. 1,060 (n.); l. 315'3"; b. 29'11" (wl.); dr. 10'¼"; s. 30.67 k. (tl.); cpl. 99; a. 4 4", 8 21" tt.; cl. *Tucker*)

The first *Wadsworth* (Destroyer No. 60) was laid down on 23 February 1914 at Bath, Maine, by the Bath Iron Works; launched on 29 April 1915; sponsored by Miss Juanita Doane Wells; and commissioned at the Boston Navy Yard on 23 July 1915, Lt. Comdr. Joseph K. Taussig in command.

After trials and torpedo firing drills out of Newport, R.I., the destroyer took up duty off the New England coast line in October. Her duty included patrols to insure America's neutrality vis-a-vis the year-old European war. On 7 January 1916, she departed Provincetown, Mass., to join in the annual Fleet maneuvers in the Caribbean. After a stop at Norfolk, she reached the West Indies at Culebra Island on 15 January and began a three-month round of war games, drills, and exercises. During her stay in the Caribbean, she visited Guantanamo Bay, Guacanayabo Bay, Manzanillo, and Santiago—all in Cuba. On 10 April, she left Guantanamo Bay to steam north, stopped at New York for a five-week stay, and returned to Newport on 21 May. *Wadsworth* resumed operations along the New England coast, and the succeeding year passed in much the same way as its predecessor—summer operations along the northeastern coast followed by Fleet maneuvers in the Caribbean.

At the completion of her second round of winter Fleet maneuvers in the spring of 1917, *Wadsworth* returned north as far as Hampton Roads. As America's entry into World War I approached, she and her sister destroyers began patrolling the Norfolk-Yorktown area to protect the naval bases and ships there against potential incursions by German submarines. Then, on 6 April 1917, while the warship rode at anchor with the rest of the Fleet at Yorktown, Va., the United States opted for the Allies in World War I. *Wadsworth* moved to New York almost immediately to prepare for the voyage to Europe and war service. On 24 April, she departed New York as the flagship of the first six-ship destroyer division dispatched to Great Britain. She led *Porter* (Destroyer No. 59), *Davis* (Destroyer No. 65), *Conyngham* (Destroyer No. 58), *McDougal* (Destroyer No. 54), and *Wainwright* (Destroyer No. 62) into Queenstown, Ireland, on 4 May and began patrolling the southern approaches to the Irish Sea the next day.

Wadsworth's first summer overseas proved to be the most eventful period of her wartime service. She sighted her first U-boat on 18 May, less than two weeks after she began patrols out of Queenstown. Though the destroyer sped to the attack, her adversary submerged and escaped. Three days later, *Wadsworth* picked up some survivors from HMS *Paxton* which had been torpedoed and sunk the preceding day. On 7 June, the destroyer caught a glimpse of another enemy submarine just before it submerged and escaped. Between 24 and 27 June, *Wadsworth* served as part of the escort for the first American troop convoy to reach Europe. Though she scored no definitely provable successes against German submarines, the destroyer made depth charge attacks on four separate occasions in July and a gunfire attack in one other instance. The first two depth-charge attacks—on the 10th and 11th—obtained no results whatsoever, and the gun attack—on the 20th—netted her the same. However, after sighting a double periscope the following day, she made a depth-charge attack. During that attack, one of the explosions seemed much stronger than those from the other charges she dropped. Moreover, a patch of reddish-brown material rose to the surface. Perhaps the destroyer had damaged a submarine, but no conclusive evidence was found to prove this possibility.

Wadsworth made her fourth depth charge attack on a U-boat on 29 July. At about 1725 that afternoon, she dropped several charges in what appeared to be the wake of a submarine proceeding submerged. The conjecture that a U-boat was damaged was supported by the appearance of a large amount of heavy oil on the surface following the attack. Just before 2300 that night, the warship attacked another supposed submarine wake. It was too dark to evaluate the results; but, not long thereafter, Trippe (Destroyer No. 33) struck a submerged metallic object which caused her to list 10 degrees temporarily. Later, Wadsworth's wireless operator intercepted messages sent by a German submarine over a period of about half an hour. While none of this evidence can be construed as definitive, it does suggest that she may have damaged a submarine. Early in August, the destroyer concluded her summer of peak activity by escorting the first United States merchant convoy on the last leg of its voyage to Europe. During the mission, on the 16th, the destroyer dropped a barrage on what was thought to be a submarine.

For the remainder of the war, her encounters with the enemy were infrequent. In fact, her next submarine contact did not occur until 17 December and, like those before, resulted in no definite damage to the enemy. Although the opening months of 1918 brought no new U-boat contacts, Wadsworth worked hard escorting convoys and patrolling British waters.

Early in March, she received a change in assignment. On the 4th, she arrived in Brest, France, whence she operated for the remainder of the war. During that assignment, she recorded only two scrapes with German submarines: the first on 1 June and the second on 25 October. In each case, she dropped depth charges, but could produce no solid proof of damage to the enemy. The war ended on 11 November 1918 when Germany accepted Allied armistice terms.

Almost two months later, on 31 December, Wadsworth stood out of Brest to return to the United States and reached Boston on 9 January 1919. Following an extended overhaul, she put to sea on 1 May to serve as one of the picket ships stationed at intervals across the ocean for the transatlantic flight of four Navy-Curtiss flying boats, one of which, NC–4, successfully completed the feat. The destroyer returned home and operated on the east coast through the summer of 1919. On 29 August, Wadsworth was placed in reduced commission at Philadelphia where she remained almost two years. On 9 May 1921, the destroyer returned to active service along the east coast. Just over a year later, on 3 June 1922, Wadsworth was decommissioned at the Philadelphia Navy Yard. The ship remained in reserve there until 7 January 1936 when her name was struck from the Navy list. She was sold for scrapping on 30 June 1936 and was broken up the following August.

II

(DD–516: dp. 2,050; l. 376'6''; b. 39'7''; dr. 13'0'' (mean); s. 37 k.; cpl. 273; a. 5 5'', 6 40mm., 8 20mm., 10 21'' tt., 2 dct., 6 dcp.; cl. Fletcher)

The second Wadsworth (DD–516) was laid down on 18 August 1942 at Bath, Maine, by the Bath Iron Works; launched on 10 January 1943; sponsored by Mrs. Rebecca Wadsworth Peacher, the great-great-granddaughter of Commodore Alexander S. Wadsworth; and commissioned at the Boston Navy Yard, on 16 March 1943, Comdr. John F. Walker in command.

Wadsworth departed Boston on 5 April and conducted exercises in Casco Bay, Maine, until the 15th, when she sailed for Cuban waters. After shakedown training out of Guantanamo Bay, the new destroyer steamed north for post-shakedown availability and voyage repairs in the Boston Navy Yard.

Putting to sea on 23 May, Wadsworth screened the carriers Princeton (CVL–23) and Yorktown (CV–10) out of Port of Spain, Trinidad, as they conducted training evolutions. Following that cruise, Wadsworth touched at Norfolk, Va., on 17 June and returned to Boston the following day.

After escorting Bunker Hill (CV–17) to Hampton Roads, Va., Wadsworth screened Cowpens (CVL–25) and planeguarded for that carrier as her air group trained off the Virginia capes. Following a return to Boston, the destroyer got underway again on 20 July to rendezvous with a task group formed around Lexington (CV–16), Princeton, and Belleau Wood (CVL–24). She met the carriers off the Delaware breakwater, and the warships then set a southerly course, bound for the Panama Canal.

Reaching Pearl Harbor on 9 August, Wadsworth spent 10 days in the Hawaiian operating area before heading for Canton Island in the screen for Prince William (CVE–31). Subsequently touching Espiritu Santo, in the New Hebrides Islands, Wadsworth reported to Rear Admiral Aubrey W. Fitch, Commander, Aircraft, South Pacific (ComAirSoPac), for duty.

On the last day of August 1943, Wadsworth cleared Espiritu Santo to hunt for the enemy submarine—later identified as I–20—that had torpedoed and damaged the tanker W. S. Rheem about 10 miles north of Bougainville Strait. Wadsworth made no contact with any submarines in the first area searched but then teamed with amphibious patrol planes to scour the seas to the south of Espiritu Santo and west of Nalekula Island.

Her diligence was soon rewarded. On 1 September, Wadsworth picked up an underwater sound contact and dropped seven patterns of depth charges and claimed unconfirmed damage to the submersible. I–20 may have survived that onslaught but never returned home. Records list her as "missing" as of 10 October 1943.

Putting into Havannah Harbor, Efate Island, on 6 September, Wadsworth then exercised with a task force formed around Saratoga (CV–3). The destroyer subsequently cleared that port on the 17th in company with Tracy (DM–19) and, over the ensuing days, escorted a convoy of supply ships to Kukum beach, Guadalcanal.

Returning to Efate with empty cargo ships on 30 September, Wadsworth took a screening station near South Dakota (BB–60) to escort that battlewagon to the west for a rendezvous with a cruiser-battleship striking force under the command of Rear Admiral Willis A. Lee. Wadsworth then patrolled off Meli Bay, Efate, to cover the entrance of convoys into Havannah Harbor.

Wadsworth subsequently joined other units of Destroyer Division (DesDiv) 45 as part of the protective screen for a dozen troop transports, Task Group (TG) 31.5, bound for the Solomons and the initial landings of men in Empress Augusta Bay, Cape Torokina, Bougainville. The expeditionary force arrived off the beach at Cape Torokina in the early morning darkness on 1 November. Then Wadsworth led in the initial force, a group of minesweepers, into Empress Augusta Bay.

At 0547, Wadsworth's 5-inch guns began to bark, and her shells destroyed enemy barges along the shoreline. For nearly two hours, the warship blasted targets behind the beaches, before she and sistership Sigourny (DD–643) took a patrol station to protect the transports which were landing troops. Suddenly, six enemy planes plunged out of the sun at the two destroyers, and the first of six bombs exploded only 25 yards to starboard of *Wadsworth*. Two other bombs burst within 500 yards of her beam, one to starboard and one to port. Then, a near-miss 20 feet from her port side sprayed the after section of the ship with fragments that killed two *Wadsworth* sailors and wounded nine others. On the other hand, the two destroyers each bagged two of the attackers.

Standing out of the unloading area on the night of 1 November, *Wadsworth* patrolled off Koli Point, Guadalcanal. Early in the morning a week later, the destroyer returned to Bougainville, escorting the second echelon of troop transports to Empress Augusta Bay. On this occasion, *Wadsworth* took a fighter-director station off the transport area and assisted in repelling a noon enemy air attack, her guns claiming one dive bomber and one torpedo plane.

Clearing Cape Torokina shortly before midnight, *Wadsworth* patrolled off Guadalcanal until the 10th, when she moved to Purvis Bay, Florida Island. However, she soon returned to Bougainville's coastal waters, escorting a troop convoy. The destroyer arrived off Cape Torokina near midnight on the 12th and, before dawn, had repelled two torpedo attacks with her radar-controlled 5-inch gunnery.

Wadsworth operated in support of the Bougainville occupation through the end of 1944, escorting troop-and supply-laden convoys from Kukum beach, Guadalcanal, to Empress Augusta Bay. From time to time, she also carried out shore bombardment missions. Three days after Christmas 1943, she blasted Japanese trenches and gun emplacements on both the south and north sides of the mouth of the Reini River, aided by air spot.

After returning to Purvis Bay from her last screening and escort missions in support of the Bougainville operation, *Wadsworth* departed the Solomons on 8 January 1944, bound for Pago Pago, Samoa, escorting a merchantman. She returned to Espiritu Santo shepherding *Shasta* (AE–6), before she steamed to Guadalcanal as part of the escort for *West Point* (AP–23). She then put into Blanche Harbor, Treasury Islands, on 1 February.

That day, *Wadsworth* conducted an antishipping sweep off the Buka Passage, trading shells with an enemy shore battery on Buka Island, before she entered Bougainville Strait in company with *Waller* (DD–466) and *Halford* (DD–480). Those three ships then proceeded to bombard the newly constructed Japanese airfield at Choiseul Island.

Subsequently taking on ammunition at Hawthorne Sound, New Georgia, *Wadsworth* left on the night of 1 February to exercise with motor torpedo boats off Rendova. The following day off Blanche Harbor, she joined the screen for a convoy of landing craft and cargo ships that had arrived off Cape Torokina on 4 February.

Near midnight, she helped to repel enemy air attacks on the Torokina beaches, before she left the area the next morning, screening *Patapsco* (AOG–1) to Purvis Bay.

Clearing Purvis Bay on 11 February, *Wadsworth* rendezvoused with destroyers and troop-laden LST's off Munda, New Georgia, bound for the Green Islands. Before dawn on the 15th, *Wadsworth*, acting as fighter-director ship, vectored night fighters toward an enemy raid of five planes that dropped flares off the formation. As a result of the destroyer's instructions, the prowling night fighters knocked down one enemy floatplane. At dawn, *Wadsworth* vectored fighters against another raid, during which they splashed three intruders and repelled the enemy without damage to any ship of the formation. *Wadsworth* then screened the transports as they disembarked their troops.

After putting into Purvis Bay on the night of 17 February, *Wadsworth* steamed to Kukum beach and joined a troop convoy earmarked for the Green Island

occupation. After her charges had safely delivered their troops to the objective on 20 February, *Wadsworth* returned to Purvis Bay the next afternoon.

Getting underway on 23 February, *Wadsworth* steamed via St. George's Channel to Kavieng, New Ireland, and to Rabaul, New Britain, for an antishipping sweep. A few minutes after midnight on the 24th, the destroyer opened fire and shelled a supply dump, stowage houses, and enemy troop concentrations in that area. One salvo of 5-inch shells started a fierce fire that lit up the entire target area. The flames from that blaze were still glowing as *Wadsworth* and the rest of the bombardment force stood down St. George's Channel three hours later.

With Purvis Bay as her base of operations, *Wadsworth* escorted supply convoys to Green Island and from Guadalcanal to Cape Torokina until 17 March. That day, the destroyer joined the screen for high-speed transports (APD's) setting course from Guadalcanal for the landings at Emirau Island.

On the morning of the 19th, *Wadsworth* took a patrol station near Emirau and remained in the vicinity, supporting the operation, until sunset on the 20th. She subsequently conducted two more Guadalcanal-to-Emirau runs—escorting troopships—that kept her busy through mid-April.

After a period of rest and recreation at Sydney, Australia, *Wadsworth* returned to Havannah Harbor on 10 May. Assigned to duty with Battleship Division (BatDiv) 3—comprised of *Idaho* (BB–42), *New Mexico* (BB–40), and *Pennsylvania* (BB–38)—*Wadsworth* engaged in battle maneuvers and training off the New Hebrides in preparation for the conquest of the Marianas. While his ship lay moored in Havannah Harbor on 31 May, *Wadsworth*'s commanding officer, Comdr. John F. Walsh, was given the additional duty of Commander, DesDiv 90, and broke his pennant in his ship.

On 2 June, *Wadsworth* and the other destroyers in her squadron and with BatDiv 3 formed TG 53.14 and cleared Havannah Harbor, bound for the Marianas. At 0430 on 14 June, the destroyer joined the screen of *Pennsylvania*, *Idaho*, and *Honolulu* (CL–48) for the bombardment of shore installations on eastern Tinian. She completed the initial phase of her operations in the Marianas on the 16th by screening bombardment-force cruisers and battleships off Guam.

After refuelling off Saipan, *Wadsworth* joined Vice Admiral Marc A. Mitscher's Task Force (TF) 58 on the afternoon of 17 June, becoming a part of TG 58.3, formed around the veteran aircraft carrier *Enterprise* (CV–6) in TF 58's bid to repel the First Japanese Mobile Fleet then on its way to the Marianas. On the morning of the 19th, TG 58.3 came under attack from Japanese carrier- and land-based aircraft during the beginning of what history would record as the Battle of the Philippine Sea.

Sometimes known as the "Great Marianas Turkey Shoot," that battle sounded the death knell for the Japanese Navy. During the action, the enemy lost 395 carrier planes and 31 floatplanes—about 92 percent and 72 percent of its total strength in those categories. At the end of its ill-fated effort to defend the Marianas, the Imperial Japanese Navy retained the operational use of only 35 carrier planes and 12 float planes. Besides the losses afloat, the Japanese lost some 50 land-based bombers as well.

During the two-day battle, Vice Admiral Mitscher's fliers had done well, turning back the enemy raids before they reached the American fleet. As TF 58 steamed westward to destroy the fleeing enemy on the 20th, Mitscher ordered further air strikes—attacks that sank the Japanese carrier *Hiyo*.

Mitscher had taken a calculated risk, however, launching the last strikes so late in the day. As the planes droned home in the gathering darkness, the admiral faced an agonizing decision. Many planes would be lost if they could not see their carriers. On the other hand, if the ships were illuminated, enemy submarines might also see the vital carriers. Mitscher ordered the lights turned on. Meanwhile, *Wadsworth* and other destroyers received orders to pick up any fliers who were forced to "ditch."

When TF 58 had reached a point some 300 miles off Okinawa, it abandoned further pursuit of the Japanese. *Wadsworth* then returned to the Marianas and patrolled off Saipan. On 5 July, her commanding officer was relieved of his collateral duties as ComDesDiv 90.

Two days later, *Wadsworth* joined a cruiser-destroyer force under Rear Admiral C. Turner Joy for the bombardment of Tinian. The destroyer and her mates soon shifted their attention to Guam and destroyed many shore installations and gasoline dumps at Apra Harbor and Agana Harbor, besides blasting enemy airstrips well in advance of the landings scheduled for that island. Terminating her bombardment duties off Guam on the afternoon of the 12th, *Wadsworth* joined the screen for the retiring carriers, *Coral Sea* (CVE-57) and *Corregidor* (CVE-58), and reached Eniwetok, in the Marshalls, on 15 July.

However, the respite provided by that in-port period was brief, for *Wadsworth* proceeded to sea on the 17th, as part of the escort for troop-laden transports slated to put their combat-garbed marines and soldiers ashore on Guam. *Wadsworth* patrolled off that isle as those men splashed ashore and, while engaged in that duty 26 miles offshore, picked up eight natives of Guam, who had escaped from the Japanese, on the morning of 22 July. The destroyer quickly transferred them to *George Clymer* (APA-37), because they possessed valuable intelligence information on Japanese dispositions ashore.

Wadsworth's guns again spoke in the invasion of Guam on the night of 24 and 25 July, before she took a radar picket station between Guam and Rota Islands. Relieved by *Hudson* (DD-475) on 2 August, *Wadsworth* then spent four days acting as primary fighter-director ship off Agana beach for two divisions of fighters based on *Belleau Wood*, *Langley* (CVL-27), and *Essex* (CV-9). Relieved of that duty on 6 August, *Wadsworth* departed Guam on the 10th, screening fleet oilers as they withdrew to Eniwetok.

Pressing on from the Marshalls for Hawaiian waters on 13 August as escort for a merchantman, *Wadsworth* reached Pearl Harbor on the 20th. She then operated off Oahu on radar picket patrols. She departed Hawaiian waters on 15 September as part of the escort for *Natoma Bay* (CVE-62) and *Manila Bay* (CVE-61), heading for the Marshalls. Arriving there on 25 September, the destroyer reported for duty with the 3d Fleet.

That tour of duty proved brief, however; for, soon thereafter, *Wadsworth* sailed for the west coast of the United States. Proceeding via Eniwetok, Ulithi, and Pearl Harbor, the destroyer arrived at the Mare Island Navy Yard on 25 October for a major overhaul and completed that period of repairs and alterations on 5 December.

Wadsworth—shifted from DesRon 45 to DesRon 24— then conducted refresher training evolutions at San Diego before departing San Francisco five days before Christmas and heading for the Hawaiian Islands as an escort for a convoy. The destroyer safely conducted her charges into Oahu's waters on 29 December 1944.

After local maneuvers out of Pearl Harbor—during which she rescued three aviators from the water on 2 January 1945—*Wadsworth* set course via Ulithi for the Kossol Passage, Palau Islands.

Reaching the Palaus on the 16th, *Wadsworth* relieved *Lansdowne* (DD-486) as tender for four minesweepers and two subchasers (SC's) engaged in patrols between Peleliu and Angaur Islands. In the early morning darkness two days later, she illuminated a target heading for the transport area and received information that there were no friendly small craft in the vicinity. *Wadsworth*'s searchlight continued to illuminate the small boat—a barge—as it beached, where Army searchlights ashore soon fixed their beams upon it. Men

began to debark from the craft, just as small arms fire began to crackle. Some 50 Japanese troops had attempted a daring raid to damage American aircraft on the ground and destroy ammunition, only to be foiled by *Wadsworth* and the Army troops ashore. The Japanese landing party was exterminated.

During the night of the 19th, *Wadsworth* provided illuminating gunfire support for troops on "Amber" beach, Peleliu, before she sailed on the 25th for Ulithi. There, she joined the screen of TG 51.1, a transport group slated to take part in the invasion of Iwo Jima.

Touching at Apra Harbor, Guam, between 8 and 16 February, *Wadsworth* arrived off Iwo Jima on the morning of the 19th. The destroyer then conducted antisubmarine patrols off the southern tip of the island until nightfall, when she joined a bombardment group. The next morning, *Wadsworth* took station in the fire support sector off Iwo Jima and blasted enemy tanks and mortar and rocket positions. She continued that action in support of the ground troops ashore until the afternoon of the 21st, when she resumed screening duty for transports carrying the occupation force which ultimately landed on 2 March.

Clearing Iwo Jima on 5 March, *Wadsworth* headed for the Philippines, arriving at Dulag anchorage, in Leyte Gulf, on the 9th. For most of the rest of March, *Wadsworth* operated locally in Philippine waters, conducting bombardment and fire support exercises in San Pedro Bay, off Leyte, until 27 March. On that day, the destroyer got underway, screening the sortie of a transport group bound for the Ryukyus.

Wadsworth arrived off Okinawa on the morning of 1 April 1945—Easter Sunday, April Fools' Day, and D day for that operation. At 0415, the destroyer completed an advance sweep ahead of the transports off the invasion beaches and then took a fire support station off the southern end of the island. For the next 15 days, *Wadsworth*'s guns blasted Japanese troop concentrations and gun emplacements, as well as caves where the fantical defenders had holed-up.

On 17 April, *Wadsworth* took on board a fighter-director team at Kerama Retto; and technicans from *Estes* (AGC-12) assisted the destroyer's ship's force in installing fighter-director equipment. She sailed later that day on her first radar picket assignment, part of the early warning network to provide the alarm of incoming Japanese aircraft. From 17 April to 24 June, *Wadsworth* carried out nine assignments on station, repelling 22 attacks by enemy aircraft, shooting down six, and assisting in the destruction of seven others. In addition, the combat air patrol fighters that she directed splashed 28 enemy aircraft.

During one day of that duty, on 28 April 1945, *Wadsworth* repelled six determined attacks by 12 enemy aircraft. The raids—which came from all points of the compass—commenced at sunset and continued for over three hours. One enemy torpedo plane closed fast on her port beam as *Wadsworth* skillfully maneuvered to keep the enemy on the beam to allow a heavy concentration of antiaircraft fire. Frustrated in his first attempt, the enemy pilot then brought the plane around a second time, circling to the right to commence an attack from directly astern, strafing as he came.

Wadsworth maneuvered to port as the plane went into a power dive that took him within 30 feet of the waves before he passed the destroyer to starboard at a distance of about 100 yards. The Japanese then zoomed sharply and turned to cross in front of *Wadsworth*. He then opened the range before boring in low and fast on the third attack.

Wadsworth's determined adversary then dropped a torpedo at 1,200 yards. The destroyer turned "left full" and the "fish" passed harmlessly by her starboard side. Meanwhile, under constant fire from every gun in *Wadsworth* that could be brought to bear, the enemy plane came on, attempting to crash into the ship.

The Japanese bore in through the flak-peppered skies. His wing struck the forward port 40-millimeter gun,

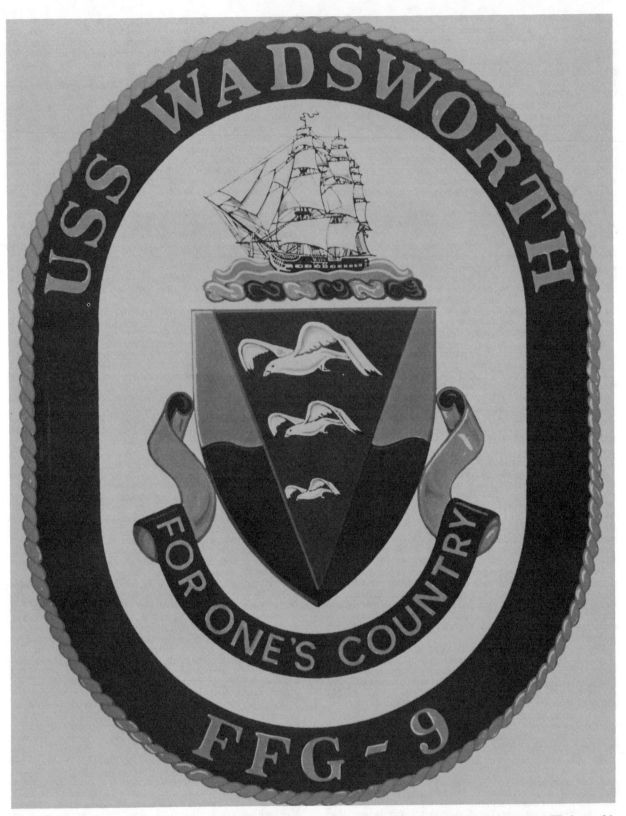

The insignia adopted by the missile frigate *Wadsworth* (FFG–9) recalls Commodore Alexander Wadsworth's service in USS *Constitution* and indicates that FFG–9 is the third ship to honor the name.

and the main body of the plane spun into the gig rigged outboard, carried away a life raft, and then smashed a 26-foot motor whaleboat before falling into the sea. Providentially, the enemy did not explode; the ship did, however, receive a shower of debris and gasoline. That had been the ship's second narrow escape. Only six days previous on 22 April, *Wadsworth*'s gunners had shot down a suicider that exploded in the sea only 20 feet from the ship, showering the ship with fragments. Fortunately, only minor hull damage resulted, and only one sailor was wounded.

At Hagushi anchorage on the morning of 24 June, *Wadsworth*, relieved of radar picket duty, put her fighter-director team ashore. Since her first arrival off Okinawa, she had sounded general quarters 203 times, detected and reported the approach of hundreds of enemy aircraft, and successfully fought off all that attacked her. Her exploits during that time earned her the Presidential Unit Citation.

Departing Okinawa on 24 June, *Wadsworth* anchored in San Pedro Bay, Leyte, on the 27th. She spent a fortnight in Philippine waters before getting underway with a group of heavy cruisers. The force touched at Okinawa on 16 July and then headed for the East China Sea for antishipping sweeps off the coast of China between the ports of Foochow and Wenchow. Returning to Okinawa on 29 July, that force made a similar sweep during the first week of August.

After "V-J Day" in mid-August, *Wadsworth* remained in the Far Eastern area, clearing Okinawa on 12 September. bound for Nagasaki, Japan, as escort for two LST's. Reaching that atomic bomb-devastated port two days later, *Wadsworth* assisted in the evacuation of Allied prisoners of war from that port. On the 18th, she received on board a total of 125 liberated men, American, British, Dutch, and Australian, and transported them to Okinawa, reaching Buckner Bay on 20 September.

Clearing Buckner Bay on 25 September, *Wadsworth* arrived at Sasebo, Japan, the next day. Soon thereafter, she commenced transport and occupation duties, carrying troops and escorting their vital supply ships between Sasebo, Wakayama, and Yokosuka—duties in which she remained engaged through mid-November.

Departing Sasebo on 17 November 1945, *Wadsworth* headed for the United States, her occupation service completed. Sailing via the Hawaiian Islands, the destroyer reached San Diego between 6 and 10 December and disembarked returning veterans at that port before she headed on for Panama. Transiting the Panama Canal soon thereafter, *Wadsworth* arrived at the Charleston (S.C.) Naval Shipyard two days before Christmas 1945 and reported for inactivation.

Decommissioned on 18 April 1946, *Wadsworth* was assigned to the Charleston Group of the Atlantic Reserve Fleet. The destroyer remained inactive until selected for transfer to the Federal Republic of Germany under the Military Assistance Program. In the summer of 1959, the German transfer crew assembled at Charleston, S.C., for indoctrination, while the ship herself was being prepared for turnover. On 6 October 1959, *Wadsworth* was turned over to the West Germans and simultaneously commissioned in their service as *Z-3* (D-172).

After its initial six-year loan period was extended, *Z-3* remained with the West German Navy into the 1970's. Struck from the United States Navy list on 1 October 1974, *Wadsworth* was sold to the Federal Republic of Germany on that date. She remained active with the West German Navy into 1980.

Wadsworth (DD-516) earned seven battle stars and the Presidential Unit Citation for her World War II service.

III

(FFG-9: dp. 3,600; l. 445'; b. 45'; dr. 24'6''; s. 28+ k.; cpl. 164; a. 1 mis. ln., Standard mis., Harpoon mis., 1 76mm., 6 15.5'' tt., LAMPS; cl. *Oliver Hazard Perry*)

The third *Wadsworth* (FFG-9) was laid down on 13 July 1977 at San Pedro, Calif., by the Los Angeles Division of the Todd Pacific Shipyards Corp.; launched on 29 July 1978; and sponsored by Mrs. Patricia P. Roberts, great-great-great-granddaughter of Commodore Alexander S. Wadsworth. The frigate was commissioned on 2 April 1980, Comdr. John C. Ruff in command, and has joined the Atlantic Fleet.

Wagner

William Daniel Wagner—born on 16 May 1924 at Cincinnati, Ohio—enlisted in the Naval Reserve on 7 February 1942 and attended the Navy Armed Guard School at Little Creek, Va. Attached to SS *Steel Navigator*'s armed guard crew, Seaman 2d Class Wagner was killed in action when his ship was torpedoed on 19 October 1942.

In the days before the sinking, his ship had been separated from its convoy—ON 137—and battered by a hurricane. The heavy seas and high winds forced a dangerous shift in ballast, which in turn caused a precarious 40-degree list to port. The Navy gun crew volunteered to go below and soon was hard at work performing the exhausting task of shifting ballast— sand and water—for the next 30 hours without relief, until the ship had momentarily passed out of danger.

However, a lurking German submarine, *U-610*, had spotted the straggler and closed at periscope depth. Upon sighting the submarine some 4,000 yards off her starboard beam, *Steel Navigator* went to general quarters, and her Navy armed guard manned their guns. Forced down by the furious gunfire drawn from the merchantmen, *U-610* temporarily abandoned her plans for attack. Later, however, at 1445, the U-boat stealthily closed the ship and sank her with torpedoes. Seaman Second Class Wagner was among the casualties from *Steel Navigator*'s crew.

(DER-539: dp. 1,350; l. 306'0''; b. 36'8''; dr. 9'5''; s. 24 k.; cpl. 210; a. 2 5'', 6 20mm., 1 dct., 1 dcp. (hh.); cl. *John C. Butler*)

Wagner (DE-539) was laid down on 8 November 1943 at Boston, Mass., by the Boston Navy Yard; launched on 27 December 1944; and sponsored by Mrs. Alfred Thomas. Due to adjustments of wartime priorities and postwar cutbacks, construction of *Wagner* was suspended on 17 February 1947, while the ship was 61.5 percent complete. Towed to the Naval Industrial Reserve Shipyard, Boston, the ship lay "mothballed" for the next seven years, until 1 July 1954. Chosen for completion as a radar picket escort ship, *Wagner* was towed to the Boston Naval Shipyard (the renamed Boston Navy Yard), where construction was resumed. Redesignated DER-539, *Wagner* was commissioned on 22 November 1955, Lt. Comdr. Edward A. Riley in command.

She departed Boston on 4 January 1956 for the Caribbean and conducted shakedown out of Roosevelt Roads, Puerto Rico. Returning north, *Wagner* joined Escort Squadron 18 and operated out of Newport, R.I. The ship conducted radar picket duty on the seaborne extension of the Distant Early Warning (DEW) line—the Eastern Contiguous Radar Coverage System and the Atlantic Barrier—into late 1959. Primarily operating in the North Atlantic, *Wagner* interrupted these lonely vigils in the Atlantic Barrier patrol system with visits to east coast ports and an occasional deployment to the warmer climes of the Caribbean for refresher training.

As more sophisticated systems diminished the need for these seaborne patrols, *Wagner* was placed "in commission, in reserve," on 31 March 1960 and arrived at Sabine Pass, Texas, on 1 April to commence lay-up preparations. Decommissioned in June 1960, *Wagner* lay in the Atlantic Fleet Reserve until struck from the Navy list on 1 November 1974. She was subsequently slated for use as a target.

Wahaka

A former Awami village at the base of the rock known as "The Three Brothers," in Yosemite Valley, Mariposa County, California. It is also the name of the rock itself.

(YTB–526: dp. 310 (f.); l. 101'0''; b. 28'0''; dr. 11'0''; s. 12 k.; cpl. 10; cl. *Sassaba*)

Wahaka (YTB–526) was laid down on 2 June 1945 at Jacksonville, Fla., by the Gibbs Gas Engine Co., Inc.; launched on 9 September 1945; sponsored by Mrs. Charles Strohmeyer, wife of Lt. Charles Strohmeyer, an officer who was attached to the Industrial Manager's Office, Jacksonville, Fla.; and completed on 3 December 1945.

Allocated to the 11th Naval District, San Diego, Calif., upon completion, *Wahaka* was briefly placed in reserve before being activated once more in December of 1947 for service in the 6th Naval District. She operated out of Charleston, S.C., through the 1950's, providing tug and tow service as well as pilot assistance. In 1962—the same year in which the ship was reclassified as a medium harbor tug (YTM–526)—the versatile workhorse harbor craft was assigned to Advanced Bases, Atlantic Area. She remained active in that assignment into 1979.

Wahkiakum County

A county in southwestern Washington state, established on 24 April 1854 and named for the Indian tribe which lived along the Columbia River. The tribe was discovered during the Lewis and Clark expedition of 1805 and 1806.

(LST–1162: dp. 5,777; l. 384'; b. 56'6''; dr. 10'6''; s. 14.5 k.; cpl. 153; trp. 366; a. 6 3''; cl. *LST–1156*)

Wahkiakum County (LST–1162) was laid down as *LST–1162* on 21 July 1952 at Pascagoula, Miss., by the Ingalls Shipbuilding Corp.; launched on 23 January 1953; sponsored by Mrs. Wilbur G. Dees; and commissioned on 13 August 1953, Lt. Comdr. I. W. Mathews in command.

Following shakedown in Guantanamo Bay, *LST–1162* operated out of the Atlantic Fleet's amphibious force base at Little Creek, Va., for the remainder of 1953, conducting local operations out of Little Creek and off the coast of Florida. In 1954, the LST participated in Atlantic Fleet amphibious maneuvers "NorAmEx" and "LantFlex"—and conducted operations with the Operational Development Force out of Key West, Fla., testing antisubmarine warfare gear. Later during the year, *LST–1162* visited Havana, Cuba, with embarked naval reservists. During March 1955, *LST–1162* operated off Bloodsworth Island, conducting gunfire tests and serving as range safety vessel at the Navy's gunnery practive areas there. On 1 July 1955, *LST–1162* was named *Wahkiakum County*.

For the next five years, *Wahkiakum County* pursued a regular schedule of operations off the east coast of the United States and into the Caribbean and Gulf of Mexico. Operating with the Atlantic Fleet's amphibious force, the LST served alternatively as a helicopter carrier—a precursor of the roles which other ships of her type would perform during the Vietnam war; as a shore bombardment safety vessel; an afloat gunnery training ship; and a transport for Navy construction battalions (CB's or "Seabees") and their equipment.

At the end of this period, she deployed to the Mediterranean and operated with the 6th Fleet from May to December 1960. She carried cargo and troops and participated in amphibious exercises with naval units of NATO powers in the Mediterranean. The ship underwent a major overhaul at Newport News, Va., in 1961, before she resumed active operations with a three-month Caribbean deployment.

Transferred to Amphibious Squadron (PhibRon) 12 on 1 July 1961, the LST participated in several amphibious landing exercises and contingency operations over the remainder of the year. During July and September, she transported midshipmen from Annapolis to Little Creek, Va., for annual summer training and began a three-month Caribbean deployment in September.

During the Cuban missile crisis in the autumn of 1962, *Wahkiakum County* embarked the 2d Battalion, 8th Marine Regiment, and operated in support of the blockade of Cuba from 24 October to 7 December 1962. She deployed to the Mediterranean in the spring of 1963, operating with the 6th Fleet Amphibious Task Force, and again to the Caribbean during the spring of 1964.

On 24 April 1965, supporters of the ousted Dominican Republic President Juan Bosch launched a coup d'etat in Santo Domingo, which soon degenerated into a civil war, with loyalists battling a rebel group backed by armed civilians. As the fighting threatened Americans there, the United States sent marines to protect and evacuate Americans. When it appeared that the revolt had been taken over by Castro's Cubans, the United States intervened with more men—paratroops of the 82d Airborne and marines. During the period from 9 to 17 May 1965, *Wahkiakum County* operated in support of this evacuation and intervention operation.

For the remainder of the 1960's and into 1970, *Wahkiakum County* operated on regular deployments to the Caribbean and Mediterranean.

Decommissioned at the Inactive Ship Facility, Orange, Tex., on 16 October 1970, *Wahkiakum County* was transferred to the Military Sealift Command (MSC) at Brooklyn, N.Y., on 10 April 1972. Reclassified as T–LST–1162, *Wahkiakum County* operated with MSC until struck from the Navy list on 11 January 1973. Transferred to the National Defense Reserve Fleet (NDRF) berthing area at Suisun Bay, Calif., soon thereafter, the LST disappeared from NDRF lists in 1974.

Wahneta

A variant spelling of Waneta, a Yanktonai Sioux Indian. Born about 1795 in what is now Brown County, S. Dak., he joined his father in siding with the British during the War of 1812. He fought at Fort Meigs and Sandusky and was wounded in the latter battle. After the war, the British rewarded Waneta for his loyalty by presenting him with a captain's commission. He subsequently visited England and remained sympathetic to the British until 1820, when an abortive expedition against Fort Snelling resulted in his change of heart. Thereafter, he gave wholehearted support to American interests. A dominant chief of the Sioux tribe, Waneta signed a trade treaty with the Americans on 25 July 1825; and, on 17 August of that year, he signed the Treaty of Prairie du Chien which fixed the boundaries of Sioux territory. He died in 1848 at the mouth of the Warreconne, the present Beaver Creek, in Emmons County, N. Dak.

I

(Yard Tug No. 1: dp. 192; lbp. 92'6''; b. 20'11½''; dr. 8'; s. 11.5 k.)

Wahneta (Yard Tug No. 1) was laid down in April 1891 at Boston, Mass., by the City Point Iron Works; launched on 3 March 1892 and subsequently was placed in service and assigned to the 5th Naval District.

Stationed at the Norfolk Navy Yard, the tug engaged in the unglamorous but vital tug, tow, and general harbor duties. In February 1893, she served as a seagoing observation platform off Port Royal, S.C. From her deck, observers watched test firings of "dynamite gun cruiser" *Vesuvius'* guns—15-inch pneumatic rifles. Returning to her routine work soon thereafter, the tug remained based at Norfolk from 1893 to 1922, through both the Spanish-American and First World Wars. On 17 July 1920, the ship was designated YT-1. Subsequently placed out of service at Norfolk on 4 August, the venerable yard craft was sold on 6 December 1922 to the Norfolk Lighterage Company.

II

(YT–134: dp. 250; l. 100'0''; b. 25'0''; dr. 10'0'')

Wahneta (YT–134) was laid down on 29 September 1938 at Mare Island Navy Yard, Vallejo, Calif.; and launched at midnight on 3 May 1939—as tide conditions were most favorable then—via an "aerial route." Large cranes hoisted her up from her building way, swung her out over the water, and then gently lowered her into the channel. Completed on 23 June 1939, and subsequently commissioned, *Wahneta* performed towing and fire-fighting duties in the busy 12th Naval District throughout World War II. During this service, she was redesignated YTM–134 on 15 May 1944. After the close of World War II, the yard craft was declared surplus to the Navy needs and was struck from the Navy list on 30 December 1946. She was transferred to the Maritime Commission on 2 June 1947 for disposal.

Wahoo

A dark blue food fish of Florida and the West Indies.

I

(SS–238: dp. 1,525 (surf.), 2,424 (subm.); l. 311'10''; b. 27'4''; dr. 15'2'' (mean); s. 20.25 k. (surf.), 8.75 k. (subm.); cpl. 60; a. 10 21'' tt., 1 3'', 2 .30-cal. mg., 2 .50-cal. mg.; cl. *Gato*)

The first *Wahoo* (SS–238) was laid down on 28 June 1941 by the Mare Island Navy Yard, Vallejo, Calif.; launched on 14 February 1942; sponsored by Mrs. William C. Barker, Jr.; and commissioned on 15 May 1942, Lt. Comdr. Marvin Granville Kennedy in command.

Following fitting out and initial training along the California coast which took the submarine as far south as San Diego, *Wahoo* departed San Francisco on 12 August, bound for Hawaii. She arrived at Pearl Harbor on 18 August and underwent exercise training until the 21st.

Two days later, the ship got underway for her first war patrol and stalked enemy shipping in waters near Truk, particularly in the area between the Hall Islands and the Namonuito Atoll. On 6 September, *Wahoo* fired three torpedoes at her first target, a lone freighter; but all probably missed, because the ship turned and headed for *Wahoo*. *Wahoo* "kept going," fearful of counterattack from the air. This retreat was a damaging blow for the crew. As one crew member put it, "After the exhausting months of drills, it was demoralizing to creep away submerged from that first target."

The submarine continued to patrol the Truk area until 20 September when she decided to leave the southwest part of the patrol area and explore south of the Namonuito Atoll. Under a bright moon and clear sky, the submarine sighted a freighter and her escort. *Wahoo* fired three torpedoes; all three missed. A fourth torpedo hit the target, which took a port list and settled bodily and by the stern. Four minutes later, a series of three underwater explosions racked the freighter. *Wahoo* was chased by the escort but escaped by radically changing course in a rain squall. Kennedy claimed a freighter of 6,400 tons, but postwar analysis of Japanese shipping records showed no sinking at this time or place.

Wahoo continued her patrol and sighted several airplanes, a patrol boat, and a tender but was unable to close on any possible targets. On 1 October 1942, the submarine extended her patrol to Ulul Island where she sighted several fishing boats. Within the next few days, Kennedy would miss two of the best targets of the war. The first was aircraft tender *Chiyoda*, which came along without an escort. Kennedy did not have time to get into position to shoot. On 5 October, *Wahoo* sighted an aircraft carrier which Kennedy believed to be *Ryujo*, sunk six weeks earlier in the Solomons. Whatever it was, it came into sight escorted by two destroyers. Due to an approach, which Kennedy later admitted lacked aggressiveness and skill, the target sailed away untouched. Two days later, *Wahoo* departed the patrol area. On 16 October, she made rendezvous with her escort and proceeded to Pearl Harbor.

Wahoo arrived at Hawaii on 17 October 1942 from her first war patrol and commenced refit the following day alongside *Sperry* (AS–12). She then shifted to the Submarine Base, Pearl Harbor, for overhaul. There a 4-inch gun and two 20-millimeter guns were installed. Overhaul was completed on 2 November; and, after a three-day training period, *Wahoo* was ready for sea.

On 8 November 1942, *Wahoo* got underway for her second war patrol in company with the small escort vessel *PC-23*. She arrived at her assigned area in the Solomon Islands and continued her patrol, keeping in sight of Bougainville and Buka Islands. On 30 November, the submarine spotted smoke at a distance of 8,000 yards. *Wahoo* sighted a lightly burdened freighter or transport with a destroyer escort on station on the port bow of the target. The submarine's approach was unsuccessful, and she proceeded east of Cape Hanpan.

Wahoo (SS–238) at Mare Island, 10 August 1942.

Having patrolled the Buka-Kilinailau Channel for 17 days, on 7 December, the submarine decided to patrol the direct route between Truk and the Shortlands for a few days. This proved fruitless, and *Wahoo* returned to her former hunting grounds, the Buka-Kilinailau Channel. On 10 December, while making her return trip, *Wahoo* ran across a convoy of three heavily loaded cargo ships escorted by a destroyer. She chose the largest tanker as the first target and fired a spread of four torpedoes at a range of 700 yards. Although three torpedoes hit, it took two hours for the *Kamoi Maru* to sink. The destroyer got too close, and *Wahoo* started down before another attack could be launched. The destroyer dropped approximately 40 depth charges which were fairly close aboard, causing minor damage. Kennedy was urged to mount a second attack. Using the new SJ radar, executive officer Mush Morton and Lt. Dick O'Kane argued, it would be easy to knock off the freighter and possibly the destroyer. However, Kennedy had had enough. *Wahoo* moved into a new area, and the convoy continued on to the northeast.

Four days later, a hospital ship was sighted headed for the Shortlands. *Wahoo* then sighted a submarine proceeding singly on the surface with the designation *I-2* painted on the side of the conning tower. *Wahoo* fired a divergent spread of three torpedoes at a range of 800 yards. The first torpedo hit 20 feet forward of the conning tower. The boat went down with personnel still on the bridge. In postwar records, however, *Wahoo* was not credited with this sinking. On 15 December, she left the area and looked into Kieta Harbor, Buka Island, and passed Moreton Light on the 26th for entrance into Brisbane, Australia, where she commenced refit the following day. On 31 December, Lt. Comdr. Marvin Granville Kennedy was relieved as commanding officer by Lt. Comdr. D. W. Morton.

Morton had served as executive officer of *Wahoo* during her first two patrols under Kennedy. Morton, endeared to his Annapolis classmates as "Mushmouth" (abbreviated "Mush") because of a knack for yarn-spinning, was an uncommonly talented submarine officer. Before *Wahoo* left Brisbane on her third war patrol, her first under "Mush" Morton, the skipper gave the crew a flaming pep talk. Morton said, "*Wahoo* is expendable. We will take every reasonable precaution, but our mission is to sink enemy shipping. . . . Now, if anyone doesn't want to go along under these conditions, just see the yeoman. I am giving him verbal authority now to transfer anyone who is not a volunteer. . . . Nothing will ever be said about your remaining in Brisbane." No one asked for a transfer, and this speech inspired a new spirit amongst the crew, a feeling of "confidence in the capabilities and luck" of *Wahoo* and the thought that she was "capable of performing miracles."

Of the many innovations Morton had put into effect on *Wahoo*, the most extraordinary was having the executive officer, Dick O'Kane, not the captain, man the periscope. George Grider, a junior officer, commented: "This," he explained, "left the skipper in a better position to interpret all factors involved, do a better conning job, and make decisions more dispassionately. There is no doubt it is an excellent theory, and it worked beautifully for him, but few captains other than "Mush" ever had such serene faith in a subordinate that they could resist grabbing the scope in moments of crisis." Thus evolved the successful and renowned duo of Morton and O'Kane.

Wahoo was ready for sea on ⸱⸱ January 1943. She commenced sound listening tests in Moreton Bay, then fell in with her escort, *Patterson* (DD–392), to begin her third war patrol. Three days later, the submarine passed into Vitiaz Strait en route to her patrol area. *Wahoo*'s orders were to reconnoiter Wewak, a Japanese supply base on the north coast of New Guinea. There was one large problem about reconnoitering Wewak: *Wahoo* had no charts of the harbor. However, it turned out that one of the motor machinists had bought a cheap school atlas while in Australia. It had a map of New Guinea with a small indentation labeled "Wewak." With that as a reference, Morton located the unmarked area on a large Navy chart and had a blowup made of the Navy chart with an ingenious device composed of a camera and signal lights. Then, to the crew's amazement, they learned that Morton's definition of "reconnoiter" meant to penetrate the harbor and sink whatever ships could be found.

On 24 January 1943, *Wahoo* dove two miles north of Kairiru Island and proceeded around the western end to investigate Victoria Bay. She sighted a destroyer with RO-class submarines nested around it. The destroyer was getting underway, so Morton fired a spread of three torpedoes at the moving target. They missed and were observed going aft. Another fish was fired which the destroyer avoided by turning away, then he circled right and headed for *Wahoo*. The submarine watched the ship come, and she kept her bow pointed at it. Morton delayed firing the fifth and last torpedo in the forward tubes until the destroyer had closed to a frightening distance of 800 yards. This torpedo clipped him amidships "and broke his back. The explosion was terrific." The topside was covered with Japanese on turret tops and in the rigging. Over 100 members of the crew must have been acting as lookouts. The target's bow was settling fast, and her boilers were heard to explode. *Wahoo* had no difficulty escaping the area. Morton was certain that the destroyer sank. However, he was not credited with a kill.

The next day, *Wahoo* changed base course for Palau. On 26 January, the submarine sighted the smoke of two freighters, obtained a position, and fired two torpedoes at the leading ship and, 17 seconds later, two at the second freighter. The first two torpedoes hit their points of aim in bow and stern. The third torpedo passed ahead of the second freighter, but the fourth torpedo was a hit. Upon observation of the damage, *Wahoo* discovered that there were two freighters, a huge transport, and a tanker. The leading freight was listing badly to starboard and sinking by the stern; the second ship was headed directly for *Wahoo*, but at a slow speed. *Wahoo* fired a three-torpedo spread at the transport; the second and third torpedoes hit and stopped him.

Turning her attention to the second target, *Fukuei Maru No. 2*, which was still headed for her, *Wahoo* fired two bow torpedoes "down the throat" to stop him. The second torpedo hit, but he kept coming and forced the submarine to turn hard left at full speed to avoid being rammed. There followed so many explosions that it was hard to tell what was happening. Coming to periscope depth, *Wahoo* observed that the first target had sunk; the second target was still moving, evidently with steering trouble; and the transport, *Buyo Maru*, was stopped but still afloat. *Wahoo* headed for the transport and fired a bow torpedo which passed directly under the middle of the ship but failed to explode. She then fired another torpedo which headed right for the stack and blew her midships section "higher than a kite." Troops jumped over her sides "like ants off a hot plate." Her stern went up, and *Buyo Maru* headed for the bottom. The submarine then headed for the crippled second target which had joined with a tanker. *Wahoo* decided to let these two ships get over the horizon, while she surfaced to recharge her batteries and to destroy the estimated 20 troop boats now in the water. The water was so thick with enemy soldiers that it was literally impossible to cruise through them without pushing them aside like driftwood.

Wahoo changed course to intercept the two fleeing ships. She decided to attack the tanker first since she was as yet undamaged. With only four torpedoes left, the submarine fired two at the tanker, the second hitting him just abaft of his midships, breaking his back. He went down almost instantly. *Wahoo* then turned her attention to the freighter and fired her last two torpedoes without a spread. They both hit; and 15 minutes later, the freighter sank. It had required four hits from three separate attacks to sink this ship. *Wahoo* then set a course for Fais Island. That night, Morton drafted a triumphant report for Pearl Harbor: "In ten-hour running gun and torpedo battle destroyed entire convoy of two freighters one transport one tanker . . . all torpedoes expended." However, postwar Japanese shipping records only credited *Wahoo* with three sinkings for this date: the transport, *Buyo Maru*, 5,300 tons; *Fukuei Maru*, 2,000 tons; and an unknown maru, 4,000 tons.

On 27 January 1943, *Wahoo* made contact with a convoy of eight ships, including two freighters and a tanker. However, efforts to gain a position were foiled by a persistent destroyer escort who dropped six depth charges. The submarine had no option but to retreat, since she had previously expended all torpedoes. The next day, *Wahoo* sighted Fais Island, and her plan to shell a phosphorite refinery was scrapped due to the untimely appearance of an inter-island steamer.

The submarine departed for Hawaii and arrived there on 7 February, 23 days after leaving Brisbane. For her entrance into Pearl Harbor, *Wahoo* had donned topside embellishments to celebrate her victory. There was a straw broom lashed to her periscope shears to indicate a clean sweep. From the signal halyard fluttered eight tiny Japanese flags, one for each Japanese ship believed to have been sunk in all three of *Wahoo*'s patrols. Morton was nicknamed "The One-Boat Wolf Pack" and awarded a Navy Cross. From Port Moresby, General MacArthur awarded Morton an Army Distinguished Service Cross.

Wahoo commenced refit by a tender relief crew and the ship's force. On 15 February, refit was completed, and the submarine was declared ready for sea on 17 February. She then conducted two days of training and was drydocked at the Submarine Base, Pearl Harbor, on 21 February.

On 23 February 1943, *Wahoo* got underway for Midway, where she arrived four days later, topped off, and headed for her patrol area. For *Wahoo*'s fourth patrol, Morton was assigned an area never before patrolled by United States submarines: the extreme northern reaches of the Yellow Sea, in the vicinity of the Yalu River and Dairen. One reason for this was that the water was extremely shallow, averaging 120 feet. But the "wading pond" barely fazed Morton; he welcomed virgin territory. From 27 February to 11 March, the submarine was en route to her patrol area, conducting training dives, fire control drills, and battle surface drills. She had the unique experience of making the entire passage to the China Sea without sighting a single aircraft; thus making the entire trip on the surface. On 11 March, *Wahoo* commenced a submerged patrol in her assigned area and along the Nagasaki-Formosa and Shimonoseki-Formosa shipping routes.

On 19 March 1943, the shooting began with a freighter identified as *Zogen Maru*. A single torpedo was fired, and it hit the after part of the ship, causing it to disintegrate upon impact. The forward part of the freighter sank two minutes later. There were no survivors. Four hours later, *Wahoo* sighted a new freighter, *Kowa Maru*, and fired two torpedoes. The first torpedo hit under the target's foremast with a terrific blast, but his bow remained intact. However, a tremendous hole on his side was visible. The second torpedo hit amidships, but it was a dud. Two more torpedoes were fired, but the freighter maneuvered and avoided them. That defective torpedo cost *Wahoo* a victim, plus the opportunity to shoot more targets at this location.

Wahoo then patrolled off the Korean coast, just south of Chinnampo. On 21 March, she sighted a large freighter identified as *Hozen Maru*. She fired three torpedoes, and the third torpedo hit the target amidships. The Japanese freighter was literally disemboweled. He went down by the bow, attaining a near vertical angle and was out of sight in four minutes, leaving approximately 33 survivors clinging to the debris.

Four hours later, *Wahoo* sighted the freighter *Nittsu Maru*. The submarine fired a spread of three torpedoes; two torpedoes hit the target, one under his bridge and the other under his mainmast. The ship went down vertically by the bow and was out of sight in three minutes. Four survivors remained who ignored all efforts to rescue them. After collecting a few souvenirs from the scattered wreckage, *Wahoo* commenced a surface patrol, heading for Shantung Promontory. On 22 March, the submarine headed for Laotiehshan Promontory, just around the corner from Port Arthur.

The following day, *Wahoo* patrolled Laotiehshan Channel, also known as "Sampan Alley;" the submarine was literally surrounded by them. *Wahoo* sighted a medium-size freighter and fired one torpedo. This hit collier *Katyosan Maru* just under the bridge immediately enveloping her in a screen of coal dust. She settled fast and slowed down; 13 minutes later, nothing was seen of her.

Morton set a course for a point to the northeast of Round Island, off Dairen. In the vicinity of the port's approaches, the deepest water is about 50 fathoms, with an average depth of around 20 fathoms. The Yellow Sea was no place for a submarine to be caught unawares. In water that shallow, depth charges would go off "like firecrackers in a birdbath."

On 24 March, at 1247, *Wahoo* sighted smoke and began to make her approach. At 1949, she fired a spread of three torpedoes at a large tanker which was fully loaded with fuel oil. The first two torpedoes exploded prematurely, and the third missed. *Wahoo* fired a fourth shot, and it, too, missed. The target commenced shooting at *Wahoo*. The submarine surfaced after 14 minutes of ducking shots, gained position ahead, and dove. She fired another three-torpedo spread. The torpedo hit the engine room and sank the ship in four minutes. The tanker was identified as *Takaosan Maru*.

The next day, *Wahoo* sighted freighter *Satsuki Maru*. She fired a spread of two torpedoes; but, when each exploded prematurely, Morton ordered a battle-surface. The submarine closed in on the target and raked him with 20-millimeter shells and holed him with almost 90 rounds of 4-inch. The target caught fire in several places and sank in about one hour.

Wahoo left on the following morning to investigate a ship on the horizon, which proved to be a small diesel-driven freighter. The submarine commenced firing with her 20-millimeter and 4-inch guns. The freighter tried to ram the submarine, but *Wahoo* had no trouble in keeping clear. She continued her gunfire and had the freighter blazing from stem to stern and dead in the water. The crew alternated looks through the periscope as the freighter sank.

Later that day, *Wahoo* sighted a 100-ton trawler and opened up with her 4-inch and 20-millimeter guns. When all three 20-millimeter guns jammed, Morton brought the submarine alongside the riddled trawler, and the *Wahoo* men hurled on board some homemade Molotov cocktails, gifts from the marines at Midway. *Wahoo* departed, leaving the ship in a wrecked condition, spouting flame and smoke. On 28 March, while conducting a surface patrol on the Shimonoseki-Formosa shipping route, *Wahoo* opened fire on two lighted motor sampans with two 20-millimeter guns. They did not sink but were also left in a wrecked condition.

The following day, the submarine sighted the freighter *Yamabato Maru* and fired two stern shots. The first torpedo hit at the point of aim under the mainmast and completely disintegrated everything abaft of the stack. The forward section sank in two minutes. The second torpedo was aimed at the foremast; it missed because the first torpedo stopped the freighter in its tracks.

Wahoo surfaced, transited Collnett Strait, and headed for her base, thus concluding a war patrol which topped the record to that date in number of ships sunk. When Morton reported his results to Pearl Harbor, the reply was: "Congratulations on a job well done . . . Japanese think a submarine wolf pack operating in Yellow Sea. All shipping tied up."

Meanwhile, the United States mounted its offensive against Attu, and Admiral Koga returned his major units from Truk to Tokyo Bay for the sortie to Alaska. Forewarned by codebreakers that the Japanese intended to counter the Attu invasion by a major sortie of the fleet, Lockwood sent his top skipper to the Kurils to intercept it; "Mush" Morton in *Wahoo.*

On 6 April 1943, *Wahoo* arrived at the Submarine Base, Midway Island, and commenced refit the following day. On the 21st and 22d of April, the submarine conducted training exercises underway and was declared ready for sea on 25 April.

Wahoo began her fifth war patrol on 25 April, departing Midway under air escort for patrol areas via the Kuril Islands. The following day, she commenced a surface patrol along the Kuril Islands and reconnoitered Matsuwa, taking photographs of the enemy installations there. The submarine explored the islands of the Kuril chain to the southwest and found them to be barren and completely covered with snow and ice.

On 4 May, *Wahoo* proceeded to reconnoiter the northeast tip of Etorofu Island; she found nothing and changed course to the southeast. Morton was positioned to intercept a seaplane tender, *Kamikawa Maru.* The submarine sighted the target and fired a divergent spread of three torpedoes. The first torpedo hit between the stack and bridge; the other two shots missed. *Kamikawa Maru* turned away and was making 11 knots, with a slight list. *Wahoo* continued on an easterly course, surfaced and continued her patrol of the Kuril chain southward.

Three days later, *Wahoo* submerged 12 miles off the Benten Saki coast and sighted two ships hugging the shoreline on a northerly course. She fired a spread of two torpedoes at the leading ship, followed immediately by a spread of four torpedoes at the escort. The first torpedo hit the leading ship, *Tamon Maru No. 5,* under the stack and broke her back; the second torpedo missed ahead. The escort successfully avoided all four torpedoes fired at her and escaped. *Tamon Maru,* 5,260 tons, sank, and *Wahoo* proceeded down the coast.

The submarine submerged one mile off Kobe Zaki and sighted a three-ship convoy consisting of two escort vessels and a large naval auxiliary. *Wahoo* fired a spread of three torpedoes; two exploded prematurely, and the third hit but failed to explode. This ship got away, and Morton was forced down by the escorts.

On 9 May 1943, *Wahoo* proceeded up the coast with the intention of closing Kone Saki. The radar operator picked up two targets, soon identified as a large tanker and a freighter in column. They were evidently making the night run between ports without an escort. The submarine fired a spread of three torpedoes at the tanker and immediately thereafter a three-torpedo spread at the freighter. *Wahoo* had two successful hits, and both ships went down, *Takao Maru,* 3,200 tons and *Jinmu Maru,* 1,200 tons.

Morton cleared the area to the northeast to patrol the Tokyo-Paramushiro route. *Wahoo* continued her patrol; and, on 12 May, she sighted two freighters. The submarine dove to gain position for a "two ship" shot where they would come by in column. She fired four torpedoes from 1,200 yards; only one was a hit. Then, Morton fired his last two remaining torpedoes. Nothing was seen of the first torpedo or its wake. The second shot hit under the bridge with a dull thud, much louder than the duds heard only on sound but lacking the "whacking" noise which accompanies a wholehearted explosion. It is considered that this torpedo had a low order detonation. The other freighter opened fire with heavy guns and charged *Wahoo.* The submarine was helpless to stop the two ships. Morton cleared the area to the east and set a course for Pearl Harbor.

Wahoo's fifth war patrol was again outstanding in aggressiveness and efficiency. In 10 action-packed days, *Wahoo* delivered 10 torpedo attacks on eight different targets. However, faulty torpedo performance cut positive results probably by as much as one-half.

This was "Mush" Morton's third patrol as commanding officer of *Wahoo.* These three patrols established a record not only in damage inflicted on the enemy for three successive patrols, but also for accomplishing this feat in the shortest time on patrol. *Wahoo* had sunk a total of 93,281 tons and damaged 30,880 more in only 25 patrol days.

Wahoo arrived at Pearl Harbor on 21 May 1943. The next day, Admiral Chester W. Nimitz, Commander in Chief, U.S. Pacific Fleet, came on board and made presentations of awards. A gold star, in lieu of a second Navy Cross, was presented to Comdr. Dudley W. Morton. On 23 May, the submarine departed for the Navy Yard, Mare Island, Calif., and she arrived six days later to commence overhaul. From 11 to 20 July, the submarine underwent intensive post-repair trials and training. On 20 July, Capt. John B. Griggs, Jr., came on board and made presentations of awards. The following day, *Wahoo* departed for Pearl Harbor, furnishing services for surface and air forces while en route. She arrived at Hawaii on 27 July 1943 and departed on 2 August for her patrol area. Four days later, *Wahoo* arrived at Midway but left the same day.

On 13 August, *Wahoo* entered the Sea of Okhotsk, having completed passage through the Etorofu Strait. She arrived in the Sea of Japan the following day and sighted three medium freighters headed south. The submarine fired one torpedo at the trailing ship, but it missed. On 15 August, *Wahoo* sighted a large freighter on a northerly course and broke off the chase on the three freighters. She commenced a surface tracking of the new target and dove for a submerged approach. Morton fired one torpedo which hit at the point of aim but was a dud and failed to explode. She fired two more torpedoes, and both missed. *Wahoo* then swung and headed directly for the target, which presented a good up-the-stern shot. The submarine fired another torpedo which missed and must have broached and exploded before the end of the run. *Wahoo* soon sighted an *Otori-*class torpedo boat and commenced evading. She decided to move over on the Hokkaido-Korea shipping route and spend the night and the following day.

On 16 August, *Wahoo* sighted a freighter headed south but made another contact in a better position for attack. Shifting targets, she fired one torpedo at a medium freighter; however, it missed. The next day, the scene was repeated with the same results. Morton decided not to chase this ship north but to wait for a loaded one heading south. However, *Wahoo* sighted a partially-loaded freighter heading north, and she commenced a submerged approach. *Wahoo* fired one torpedo which missed. Just as *Wahoo* fired, a southbound freighter and this target passed each other close aboard; still no hit. She then surfaced and chased the southbound freighter. While pursuing this ship, the submarine sighted another target well ahead and away from the coast, so she shifted targets. While tracking this new target, she passed two small northbound ships —one looked like a tug and the other resembled a tanker. *Wahoo* made a submerged approach and fired a torpedo at the medium-sized freighter. It was a miss. She fired again; still a miss, but this torpedo, probably broaching, exploded. The submarine surfaced and headed further away from the coast.

Wahoo had the worst possible luck with her torpedoes. Within four days, 12 Japanese vessels were sighted; nine were hunted down and attacked to no avail. Ten torpedoes broached, made erratic runs, or thumped against target hulls "like derelict motorboats." Morton wrote in wrath, "Damn the torpedoes!" He reported the poor torpedo performance to ComSubPac and received orders to return to base.

On 19 August, the submarine sighted a ship and commenced tracking. However, she withheld fire when she recognized the flag as Russian. *Wahoo* then headed for La Perouse Strait. The next day, she sighted a sampan and fired warning shots across the bow. When the sampan failed to stop, the submarine opened up on it with her 20-millimeter and 4-inch guns. The sampan was soon a wreck with no signs of life. However, six Japanese fishermen surrendered and were taken on board as prisoners of war. Eight hours later, *Wahoo* opened fire on two more sampans, enveloping the ships in flames. Members of the crews jumped overboard but showed no desire to be rescued. *Wahoo* completed the passage of Etorofu Strait and arrived at Midway on 25 August. She immediately got underway for Pearl Harbor and arrived there on 29 August.

"Mush" Morton, smarting from his last luckless patrol, asked to return to the Sea of Japan, and permission was granted. On 9 September, *Wahoo* got underway from Pearl Harbor, topped off at Midway on 13 September, and headed for La Perouse Strait. The plan was for Morton to enter the Sea of Japan first, on or about 20 September, with *Sawfish* (SS–276) following by a few days. At sunset on 21 October, *Wahoo* was supposed to leave her assigned area, south of the 43d parallel, and head for home. She was instructed to report by radio after she passed through the Kuril chain. Nothing further was ever heard from Morton in *Wahoo*.

On 5 October, the Japanese news agency, Domei, announced to the world that a steamer was sunk by an American submarine off the west coast of Honshu near Tsushima Strait, with the loss of 544 lives. This was the 8,000-ton *Konron Maru*. In addition, JANAC showed that Morton sank three other ships for 5,300 tons, making the total for this last patrol four ships amounting to about 13,000 tons. Japanese records also reported that, on 11 October, the date *Wahoo* was due to exit through La Perouse Strait, an antisubmarine aircraft found a surfaced submarine and attacked, dropping three depth charges. *Sawfish* had been depth-charged by a patrol boat while transiting the strait two days before, and the enemy's antisubmarine forces were obviously on the alert in that area. There could be little doubt that this attack fatally holed *Wahoo*, and that she sank, taking down "Mush the Magnificent" and all hands. *Wahoo* was announced overdue on 2 December 1943 and stricken from the Navy list on 6 December 1943.

The loss of Morton and *Wahoo* caused profound shock in the submarine force. All further forays into the Sea of Japan ceased, and it was not again invaded until June 1945, when special mine detecting equipment was available for submarines. Morton was posthumously awarded a fourth Navy Cross. When he died, his claimed sinkings exceeded those of any other submarine skipper: 17 ships for 100,000 tons. In the postwar accounting, this was readjusted to 19 ships for about 55,000 tons. This left Morton, in terms of individual ships sunk, one of the top three skippers of the war. So ended the career of one of the greatest submarine teams of World War II—*Wahoo* and "Mush" Morton.

Wahoo earned six battle stars for World War II service.

SS–518, projected as a *Corsair*-class fleet submarine, was originally assigned the name *Wahoo*. However, her construction was canceled on 29 August 1944; and the name *Wahoo* was reassigned to another projected *Corsair*-class fleet boat, SS–516.

Wahoo (SS–516), projected as a *Corsair*-class fleet submarine, was laid down on 15 May 1944 at the Mare Island Navy Yard, but the end of World War II obviated her completion. The contract for her construction was canceled on 7 January 1946.

II

(SS–565: dp. 1,560 (surf.), 2,260 (subm.); l. 269'2"; b. 27'2"; dr. 17'; s. 15.5 k. (surf.), 18.3 k. (subm.); cpl. 83; a. 8 21" tt.; cl. *Tang*)

The second *Wahoo* (SS–565) was laid down on 24 October 1949 by the Portsmouth (N.H.) Naval Shipyard; launched on 16 October 1951; sponsored by Mrs. Harry W. Hill; and commissioned on Memorial Day, 30 May 1952, Comdr. Eugene P. Wilkinson in command.

Following a shakedown cruise to the British West Indies and post-shakedown repairs at Portsmouth, N.H., *Wahoo* got underway for her home port, Pearl Harbor, on 1 December 1952. After a stop at New London, Conn., she proceeded to the Canal Zone, transited the Panama Canal, and then touched at San Diego before continuing on to Oahu. The submarine spent the entire year 1953 in training and evaluation exercises conducted in the Hawaiian Islands operating area. The warship also served as a target for surface and air units practicing their own antisubmarine warfare (ASW) tactics.

In January 1954, *Wahoo* embarked upon her first tour of duty with the 7th Fleet in the western Pacific. For about six months, she cruised Far Eastern waters with ships of the 7th Fleet conducting various exercises and visiting Oriental ports. She returned to Pearl Harbor in June and underwent her first shipyard overhaul before resuming local operations in the Hawaiian Islands. In March 1955, the submarine took time from her busy training schedule to visit Tahiti. At the conclusion of that voyage, she then resumed duty at Hawaii but, in November, embarked upon her second assignment with the 7th Fleet. The Oriental cruise brought port calls to Hong Kong; Kaohsiung, Taiwan; Apra Harbor, Guam; Yokosuka, Japan; and Manila and Subic Bay in the Philippines. Her deployment ended in May 1956 when she returned to Pearl Harbor to resume local operations and training exercises.

Such duty was broken in April by a yard overhaul which lasted until October 1957. In November, the ship made a shakedown voyage back to Tahiti. Soon after her return to Hawaii, *Wahoo* stood out of Pearl Harbor on her way back to the western Pacific. Normal training operations and a schedule of port visits occupied her time during the six-month assignment in the Far East. The warship returned to Pearl Harbor in June 1958 and, soon thereafter, she received the Battle "E" for Submarine Squadron (SubRon) 1 attesting to her overall operational and administrative superiority within the unit. She spent the ensuing year in the Hawaiian Islands conducting training operations for the most part. In November, she began a two-month repair period at the Pearl Harbor Naval Shipyard at the conclusion of which, in January 1959, she resumed local operations.

In June, the submarine transferred administratively from SubRon 1 to SubRon 7; and, in July, she headed west once more for a tour in the Far East. Again, training exercises predominated with *Wahoo* serving as target in ASW practice and participating in several fleet exercises. She returned to Oahu at the beginning of 1960 and, after two months of normal operations, once again entered the Pearl Harbor Naval Shipyard, this time for a major overhaul. Exiting the yard in late August, she conducted refresher training and then resumed her normal schedule of operations in the Hawaiian Islands.

That employment continued during the first three months of 1961. Late in March, she began a month-long battery renewal at the end of which, in late April, she began preparations for another overseas deployment. On 22 May, *Wahoo* departed Pearl Harbor and shaped a westward course. During that cruise with the 7th Fleet, she visited Yokosuka, Sasebo, and Hakodate in Japan, and stopped at Naha on the island of Okinawa. After six months of operations and exercises in the Far East, she headed home, returning to Pearl Harbor on 7 November. A year of normal operations in the Hawaiian group followed; and, in December 1962, she began preparations for another cruise to the western Pacific. The ship stood out of Pearl Harbor on 15 January 1963 to begin a six-month tour of duty during which she added Osaka to her ports of call in

Japan. That cruise ended on 15 July when she re-entered Pearl Harbor and resumed her nomal Hawaiian schedule of training operations, interrupted between October 1963 and April 1964 by a major overhaul.

During the summer of 1964, she returned to local operations out of Pearl Harbor. In August, however, the Gulf of Tonkin incident occurred and changed the complexion of her 7th Fleet deployments. When she returned to the Far East in November, the August occurrence had already spurred an increased American involvement in civil strife in Vietnam. As a consequence of that change, Wahoo was called upon to do two tours of duty in the waters off Vietnam during a deployment of extended duration.

She returned to Hawaii in June 1965 and remained in the vicinity until February of 1966. During her 1966 western Pacific cruise, which began on 17 February and ended on 29 August, she returned to the combat zone off Vietnam as well as fulfilling a schedule of 7th Fleet exercises and port visits. Upon her arrival back to Oahu, the submarine began an extended period of operations in the islands, broken by a major overhaul of 17 months' duration. That overhaul included radical modifications to her hull structure during which she was lengthened by 15 feet.

She completed her extended overhaul in the latter part of June 1968 and, following refresher training, she resumed local operations out of Pearl Harbor. On 11 February 1969, Wahoo departed Oahu on her way to the Far East for the eighth time in her career. That deployment brought only a very brief tour in the Vietnam combat zone; otherwise, she conducted a normal peacetime deployment visiting Oriental ports and participating in 7th Fleet training exercises.

She returned to Pearl Harbor on 14 August and took up her usual training routine in the Hawaiian Islands. Her ninth tour of duty in the western Pacific began on 1 April 1970. During the last week of the month, she again cruised briefly in the combat zone off Vietnam; but, as in the previous deployment, she spent the remainder engaged in a normal 7th Fleet schedule of operations. She returned to Pearl Harbor on 21 October and began an overhaul which was completed on 1 June 1971.

On the same day that she completed her overhaul, Wahoo departed Pearl Harbor and shaped a course for her new home port, San Diego, Calif. En route, she visited Portland, Oreg., and Vancouver, British Columbia. The submarine arrived at San Diego on 26 June and began type training and other local operations along the southern California coast. The change in home ports, however, did not signal an end to tours of duty in the western Pacific. Her next deployment brought with it a visit to Chinhae and Pusan in Korea and a period of combined operations with units of the South Korean Navy. Later in that cruise, she also visited Taiwan and participated in bilateral ASW exercises with units of the Taiwan Navy. She finally concluded the deployment at San Diego on 28 April 1972. After a series of brief exercises with ships and aircraft during the month of May, she entered Hunters Point Naval Shipyard for a three-month overhaul. Back at sea by the middle of September, she resumed local operations—type training, ASW exercises with surface units and aircraft, and torpedo and mine evaluation tests—for the remainder of the year.

On 16 February 1973, the submarine exited San Diego harbor to embark upon her 11th tour of duty with the 7th Fleet. Bilateral exercises with the South Korean and Nationalist Chinese navies again highlighted a normal peacetime deployment. This time, however, she also joined units of the Japanese Maritime Self Defense Force in ASW training operations. She returned to San Diego on 14 August and resumed operations in the southern California operating area which were highlighted by submarine against submarine exercises which included firing exercise torpedoes. Local operations occupied her through the end of 1973 and during the first five months of 1974. On 14 June 1974,

she entered the Mare Island Naval Shipyard for an extended overhaul which lasted until July 1975. Wahoo completed post-overhaul sea trials on 23 July and, after visiting Seattle for the 1975 "Sea Fair" and conducting weapons systems tests and electronics accuracy trials off the coast of the Pacific northwest, she returned to San Diego on 28 August. She then resumed local operations—including a tour as school ship for prospective commanding officers in November and refresher training in December—which kept her busy until the beginning of April 1976.

On 2 April, she stood out of San Diego to resume deployments with the 7th Fleet. During that assignment, she participated in 7th Fleet exercises, bilateral exercises with South Korean naval units, and SEAL team exercises with Marine Corps and South Korean naval personnel. She completed the tour of duty on 8 September and began the voyage home. She returned to San Diego at the beginning of October and resumed operations along the coast of southern California.

On 6 September 1977, she departed San Diego to transfer to the Atlantic Fleet. Steaming via the Panama Canal; Cartagena, Colombia; Miami, Fla.; and Savannah, Ga., she arrived at New London, Conn., on 15 October. On 1 November, she began training a crew from the Iranian Navy scheduled to take possession of her sister-ship Trout (SS–566) sometime the following year. That duty continued until the summer of 1978 and included a six-week Caribbean deployment early in 1978 in support of ReadEx 1–78. On 6 July 1978, the submarine began an extended overhaul at the Philadelphia Naval Shipyard, where she remained as of January 1979.

Wahoo earned three battle stars for service in the Vietnam conflict.

Wahpeton

A tribal division of the Dakota branch of the Sioux Indians noted for their hunting ability and warlike manner. The word itself means "dwellers among deciduous trees" and is commemorated by the town of Wahpeton, the county seat of Richland County, North Dakota.

I

(YTB–527: dp. 310 (f.); l. 101'0''; b. 28'0''; dr. 11'0''; s. 12 k.; cpl. 10; cl. Sassaba)

The first Wahpeton (YTB–527) was laid down on 23 June 1945 at Jacksonville, Fla., by the Gibbs Gas Engine Co., Inc.; launched on 29 September 1945; sponsored by Mrs. Emery H. Price, the wife of Congressman Price, a member of the Naval Affairs Committee; and completed on 2 January 1946.

Listed as "out of service" with the Texas group of the Reserve Fleet as of March 1946, Wahpeton was activated in August of 1946; assigned to the 6th Naval District; and placed in service at Charleston, S.C., soon thereafter. As of 1979, Wahpeten was still attached to the 6th Naval District, performing tug and tow assistance, providing pilot services, and standing ready to provide waterfront fire protection. During that long period of duty at Charleston, the ship was reclassified —to a medium harbor tug (YTM–527)—in February 1962, a classification that she retained into the late 1970's.

II

(YTM–757: dp. 310 (f.); l. 107'0''; b. 27'0''; dr. 12'0''; s. 12 k. (tl.); cpl. 16; cl. Chicopee)

The second Wahpeton (YTM–757)—oddly enough carried on the Navy list simultaneously with YTB–527 —was acquired by the Navy in April 1968 from the Army, which she had served as LT–2084. Renamed Wahpeton and classified as YTM–757, the tug was soon thereafter assigned to the 14th Naval District and served the Pacific Fleet into the 1970's. Subsequently taken out of service, *Wahpeton* was struck from the Navy list and sold in September of 1974.

Wahtah

An Indian word meaning "ship."

(YT–140: dp. 300; l. 100'9''; b. 27'10''; dr. 9'7''; cl. *Woban*)

Wahtah (YT–140) was laid down on 28 August 1939 at Portsmouth, Va., by the Norfolk Navy Yard; launched on 14 December 1939; sponsored by Miss Marie Yvonne Thornton; and soon thereafter was placed in service at the Washington Navy Yard. For the remainder of her active career, *Wahtah* remained attached to the Washington Navy Yard performing local tugging and towing operations, providing waterfront fire protection, and other related services. She was reclassified as a large harbor tug, YTB–140, on 15 May 1944. Struck from the Navy list on 15 October 1974, she was soon sold.

Wailaki

Wailaki (YTB–706)—a *Hisada*-class large yard tug —was slated to be built at Terminal Island, San Pedro, Calif., by the Bethlehem Steel Co.; but the contract for her construction was cancelled on 29 August 1945.

Wainwright

Comdr. Jonathan Mayhew Wainwright—born in New York City on 27 July 1821—was initially commissioned in the United States Navy on 30 June 1837 and served with distinction in the Civil War. Wainwright commanded *Harriet Lane*, Admiral David Dixon Porter's flagship, in an engagement with Forts Jackson and St. Philip and took part in operations below Vicksburg. He was killed in an attack upon Confederate forts in Galveston Harbor on 1 January 1863.

Master Jonathan Mayhew Wainwright, Jr., son of Commander Wainwright, was born in New York City on 29 January 1849 and graduated from the United States Naval Academy in 1867. He was promoted to master on 21 March 1870, while attached to *Mohican* in the Pacific Squadron. Shortly thereafter, Wainwright was wounded during a boat expedition under his command against the piratical steamer, *Forward*, lying-to in a lagoon at San Blas, Mexico. Succumbing to the effect of his wounds, he died on board *Mohican* on 19 June 1870.

Comdr. Richard Wainwright, a cousin of Comdr. Jonathan Mayhew Wainwright, was born in Charlestown, Mass., in 1817 and was commissioned in the United States Navy on 11 May 1831. Between 1841 and 1857, Wainwright served in the Coast Survey and on the Navy's Home Station. He cruised in *Merrimack* on special service from 1857 to 1860. Following the outbreak of the Civil War, Wainwright commanded *Hartford*, flagship of Admiral David G. Farragut's West Gulf Blockading Squadron. During the passage of forts below New Orleans on the night of 24 and 25 April 1861, he performed gallant service in extinguishing a fire on *Hartford* while continuing the bombardment of the forts. Commended by Admiral Farragut for his actions, Wainwright later participated in the squadron's operations below Vicksburg until taken ill with fever. He died in New Orleans on 10 August 1862.

Rear Admiral Richard Wainwright, son of Comdr. Richard Wainwright, was born on 17 December 1849 in Washington, D.C. Initially commissioned in the United States Navy on 28 September 1864, Wainwright was executive officer on board the battleship *Maine* when she blew up in the harbor of Havana, Cuba, on 15

February 1898. Surviving the explosion, he was assigned to command of the tender *Fern* and was in charge of the recovery of the bodies of the victims. He also assisted in the collection of information for the subsequent court of inquiry. Wainwright later commanded the wooden gunboat *Gloucester* at the battle of Santiago on 3 July 1898. In this engagement, *Gloucester* sank one Spanish torpedo boat and drove another on the beach. Wainwright was commended for his valor in this engagement. Later, promoted to rear admiral, he commanded the Second Division of the United States Atlantic Fleet during that fleet's historic voyage around the world from 1907 to 1909. Retired from active duty on 7 December 1911, Admiral Wainwright died in Washington, D.C., on 6 March 1926.

Comdr. Richard Wainwright, son of Admiral Wainwright, was born in Washington, D.C., on 15 September 1881. Graduating from the United States Naval Academy in 1903, he served on board battleship *Louisiana* during that ship's participation in the voyage of the Great White Fleet around the world from 1907 to 1909. Wainwright was awarded the Medal of Honor for his outstanding conduct in battle while commanding a landing force from battleship *Florida* at Vera Cruz, Mexico, on 21 and 22 April 1914. He retired from the Navy on physical disability on 3 March 1921 and died at Annapolis, Md., on 28 March 1944.

Wainwright (Destroyer No. 62) was named for Comdr. Jonathan Mayhew Wainwright, his son, Master Jonathan Mayhew Wainwright, Jr., and his cousin, Commander Richard Wainwright. *Wainwright* (DD–419) honored these three officers as well as Rear Admiral Richard Wainwright, the son of Commander Richard Wainwright. *Wainwright* (DLG–28) honored the previous four Wainwrights and Commander Richard Wainwright, the son of Admiral Wainwright.

I

(Destroyer No. 62: dp. 1,150 (n.); l. 315'3''; b. 29'11''; dr. 10'8¼'' (f.) (aft); s. 29.67 k. (tl.); cpl. 99; a. 4 4'', 8 21'' tt.; cl. *Tucker*)

The first *Wainwright* (Destroyer No. 62) was laid down on 1 September 1914 at Camden, N.J., by the New York Shipbuilding Co.; launched on 12 June 1915; sponsored by Miss Evelyn Wainwright Turpin; and commissioned at the Philadelphia Navy Yard on 12 May 1916, Lt. Fred H. Poteet in command.

After fitting out at Philadelphia, the destroyer rounded Cape May on 20 June and headed for Newport, R.I., to load torpedoes before joining Division 8 of the Atlantic Fleet Destroyer Flotilla. Following exercises near Eastport, Maine, she remained on the New England coast until mid-September when she headed south for gunnery tests and training off the Virginia capes. Upon the completion of a fortnight's gun drills, the ship then returned to Buzzard's Bay, Mass., on 2 October. Later that month, *Wainwright* operated out of Newport, practiced torpedo tactics near Vineyard Sound, and visited New York to pick up cargo for the flotilla's tender, *Melville* (Destroyer Tender No. 2). She returned to Newport on the 18th and, eight days later, resumed torpedo practice near Vineyard Sound for the remainder of the month. She put into Boston on 1 November for extensive repairs in the navy yard.

Refurbished, the destroyer got underway for the Caribbean on 8 January 1917. Steaming via Hampton Roads, she reached Culebra Island, near Puerto Rico, on the 14th and conducted war games exercises with the Atlantic Fleet. In the course of those operations, she visited the Dominican Republic as well as Guantanamo Bay and Santiago in Cuba. Later that month, *Wainwright* carried Assistant Secretary of the Navy Franklin D. Roosevelt, the Commandant of the Marine Corps, and the Chairman of the Civil Service Commission from Santiago to Port-au-Prince, Haiti. Following that assignment, she conducted torpedo exercises, patrols, and power trials near Guantanamo Bay until the beginning of March.

She returned to Boston on the 10th for a short period in the navy yard. On 31 March, she departed Boston for Hampton Roads where she arrived on 2 April.

The following morning, in response to the imminent threat of war with Germany, *Wainwright* began to ". . . search for submarines . . ." and to patrol Hampton Roads to protect the Fleet and naval bases. Two days later, other warships relieved her on patrol; and she anchored with the Fleet in the mouth of the York River. The next day, 6 April 1917, the United States entered World War I.

By the spring of 1917, the unrestricted submarine warfare campaign—which Germany had launched at the beginning of February—had so succeeded that the entire Allied war effort was endangered. Strong reinforcements to the Allied antisubmarine forces were desperately needed to avert defeat and needed at once. In response to a request from the Royal Navy for the service of American antisubmarine warfare ships in European waters, the United States Navy began sending destroyers eastward across the Atlantic.

Wainwright again briefly patrolled Hampton Roads before heading for the New York Navy Yard on the 14th. From there, the destroyer continued on to Boston where she arrived on 16 April to prepare for overseas duty. Eight days later, the destroyer departed Boston in company with *Wadsworth* (Destroyer No. 60), *Porter* (Destroyer No. 59), *Davis* (Destroyer No. 65), *Conyngham* (Destroyer No. 58), and *McDougal* (Destroyer No. 54), bound for the British Isles. This division—ably led by Comdr. Joseph K. Taussig—was the first American naval unit to be sent to Europe. The destroyers reached Queenstown on the southern coast of Ireland on 4 May and, after fueling, began patrolling the southern approaches to Liverpool and other British ports on the coast of the Irish Sea.

Wainwright reported her first scrape with a German submarine on 11 May. She sighted an abandoned lifeboat at about 0800. After investigating the drifting boat for occupants and finding none, she sank the boat with gunfire. At about 0815, a lookout reported that a torpedo had missed the destroyer some 150 yards astern. *Wainwright* then fired several rounds from her 4-inch guns at what was thought to be a periscope. The supposed submarine disappeared soon thereafter; and, despite a thorough investigation of the area, the destroyer could turn up no more evidence of the presence of a U-boat.

The summer of 1917 provided few opportunities for *Wainwright* to test her sub-killing techniques. On Independence Day, a member of the destroyer's crew spotted a purported periscope and soon thereafter others claimed that a torpedo was reported to have passed the ship, five feet astern. *Wainwright* depth-charged the last indicated position of the undersea raider but to no avail. On the morning of 20 August, after *Rowan* (Destroyer No. 64) brought up some oil with one of her depth charges, *Wainwright* dropped a couple of depth charges as she passed through the faint slick. A few minutes later, she joined other ships in some sporadic gunfire but failed to prove that a submarine was in the area.

The fall, on the other hand, brought *Wainwright* increased activity. After spending the first two weeks of September in repairs at Birkenhead, near Liverpool, she departed the yard at Laird Basin at about 0700 on the 14th to return to Queenstown. Three quarters of an hour into the afternoon watch, she received orders sending her to the scene of a submarine attack against an Allied merchantman some 15 miles southeast of Helvick Head, Ireland. *Wainwright* rang up full speed, made off for the reported location, and began a search for the U-boat in conjunction with a British dirigible and other surface units. Near the end of the second dog watch, she sighted the submarine's conning tower and bow about six miles off.

Wainwright charged to the attack, but the submarine submerged almost immediately. Upon reaching the spot where the submarine had been, the warship located an oil slick and began dropping depth charges which failed to achieve positive results. Approaching darkness and the necessity of escorting an Admiralty oiler forced *Wainwright* to break off her attack. After she shepherded the oiler to safety, she returned to the area of her attack and patrolled throughout the night, but the submarine had apparently retired from the neighborhood.

Four days later, while searching for a U-boat in the area of Connigbeh, the destroyer received word that the Connigbeh Lightship had rescued survivors from a fishing vessel. *Wainwright* rendezvoused with the craft to interview the four seamen of the smack *Our Bairn*. They revealed that the U-boat was of the latest type Germany had in action. The destroyer relieved the lighthouse vessel of the four fishermen and continued the search until dusk, when she headed back to Queenstown to land the rescued men.

For a month, she carried on conducting routine patrols—routine only in the sense that they brought no action with the enemy. The inhospitable Atlantic, on the other hand, severely taxed her crew. Action finally came on the morning of 18 October, when *Wainwright* again received orders to Helvick Head to hunt for an enemy submarine. She arrived at the designated location at about 1115 and searched for more than two hours for clues as to the U-boat's location. Then, at 1358, she sighted a submarine's conning tower about 1,500 yards off her starboard bow. The enemy appeared to be maneuvering into position for a torpedo attack but submerged the moment *Wainwright* charged to the attack. When the destroyer reached the estimated location of the U-boat, she dropped a depth charge and then a buoy to mark the spot. The warship followed that maneuver with a systematic, circular search out to a radius of 20 miles. Having found nothing by 0400 the following day, she gave up and shaped a course for Queenstown.

The ensuing six months brought no new encounters with U-boats. She scouted areas where submarines had been reported but neither sighted nor engaged the enemy. On one occasion, she collided with a merchantman, SS *Chicago City*, and had to enter the drydock at Spencer Jetty that same day, 24 November 1917, for repairs.

While steaming generally south on 29 April 1918, she sighted a sail bearing almost due west whose hull was down below the horizon. By the time the destroyer had swung around to an intercepting course, the sail had disappeared. While the destroyer steamed toward the estimated position of the sail, she searched for evidence of a submarine. After covering 10 miles to westward, she came upon an area marked by a number of small oil slicks. *Wainwright* chose the most promising of the slicks and dropped four depth charges. She then commenced another fruitless search which ended at midnight when she received orders to return to Queenstown.

Wainwright continued to operate out of Queenstown until June of 1918 when she was reassigned to United States naval forces in France. On the 8th, she reported for duty at Brest, the French port from which she conducted her patrols for the remainder of the war. Those patrols brought no further encounters with the enemy. Only two events of note occurred between June and November 1918. On the night of 19 and 20 October, she sighted what appeared to be a submarine running on the surface. However, upon closer inspection, the object proved to be a derelict carrying the crew of the 77-ton schooner *Aida* captured by a U-boat and sunk with explosive charges. *Wainwright* took on the survivors and saw them safely into port. Later, during the evening of 1 November, heavy winds at Brest caused the destroyer to drag anchor; and she struck the breakwater. After *Jarvis* (Destroyer No. 38) had failed to pull her loose, the tug *Concord* took over and finally managed to refloat the warship at 1920 and towed her into Brest.

Hostilities ended on 11 November 1918, and *Wainwright* returned home early in 1919 to resume duty with the Atlantic Fleet destroyers. She operated along the east coast and in the Caribbean until 19 May 1922 when she was decommissioned at Philadelphia. The destroyer remained in reserve until the spring of 1926. On 2 April, she was transferred to the Coast Guard; and her name was struck from the Navy list on the same day. She moved to Boston on 22 May and remained there until 27 July when she got underway for the Connecticut coast. She reached New London two days later; and, on the 30th, she was commissioned by the Coast Guard. The warship retained her name while serving with the Coast Guard's "Rum Patrol" to suppress the illegal importation of alcoholic beverages. She served at New London from the summer of 1926 until 1929. On 4 January 1929, she headed south to Charleston, S.C., whence she conducted gunnery practice until 4 February when she returned north to Boston. In January 1930, she headed south again for gunnery practice but this time at St. Petersburg, Fla. During each of the two succeeding years—in January 1931 and late in March 1932—she returned to St. Petersburg for a month of target practice and afterward resumed her duties along the New England coast.

In May 1933, her permanent duty station was changed to New York, and she reported there at the end of the first week in June. After a summer of normal operations, the warship began target practice at Hampton Roads, Va., on 7 September. That duty, however, was interrupted on the 9th by orders to report for duty with the Navy in the area of the Florida Strait during the series of revolts in Cuba which finally resulted in the beginning of Fulgencio Batista's 25-year dictatorship. On 6 November, *Wainwright* was released from duty with the Navy and was ordered back to New York. She arrived three days later and resumed duties with the Coast Guard until March 1934. On the 14th, she departed the station at Stapleton, New York, and arrived in Philadelphia the following day. She was decommissioned by the Coast Guard on 29 March; and, on 27 April, the Commandant, 4th Naval District, took possession of her for the Navy. Her name was reinstated on the Navy list briefly but was struck once again on 5 July 1934. On 22 August, she was sold to Michael Flynn, Inc., of Brooklyn, N.Y., for scrapping.

II

(DD-419: dp. 1,570; l. 347'8''; b. 35'6¾''; dr. 13'6''; s. 36 k.; cpl. 192; a. 4 5'', 8 21'' tt., 4 .50-cal. mg., 2 dct.; cl. *Sims*)

The second *Wainwright* (DD-419) was laid down on 7 June 1938 at the Norfolk Navy Yard; launched on 1 June 1939; sponsored by Mrs. Henry Meiggs; and commissioned on 15 April 1940, Lt. Comdr. Thomas L. Lewis in command.

Following shakedown, *Wainwright* began duty with the Atlantic Fleet in conjunction with the Neutrality Patrol which had been established by President Franklin D. Roosevelt soon after World War II broke out in Europe early in September of 1939 to keep hostilities from spreading to the Western Hemisphere. Just before the opening of hostilities between Japan and the United States, *Wainwright* embarked upon a mission which indicated an acceleration in America's gradual drift into the Allied camp. She departed Halifax, Nova Scotia, on 10 November, as a unit of the screen for Convoy WS–12X, an all-American ship convoy transporting British and Commonwealth troops via the Cape of Good Hope to Basra in the Near East. The convoy steamed first to Trinidad in the British West Indies, in order that the "short-legged" destroyers might refuel there before beginning the long South Atlantic leg of the voyage to Capetown. There, the convoy was to be turned over to the British Admiralty for orders and protection, and the destroyers were to turn around and head home.

The convoy reached Capetown on 9 December 1941, two days after the Japanese attack on Pearl Harbor and two days before Germany and Italy declared war on the United States. This change in the strategic picture caused changes in the destinations of the transports. Some went to Suez and thence to Australia while other carried reinforcements to the doomed "fortress" of Singapore. The escorting American destroyers headed back to the United States, but this time they put to sea as full-fledged belligerents.

Upon her return to the east coast, *Wainwright* resumed her patrols. Her assignment, however, took on a new complexion. No longer simply trying to prevent the spread of hostilities to the Western Hemisphere, she patrolled instead to protect America's shorelines and sea-going traffic along her coast from Germany's undersea fleet. That duty continued until mid-March 1942, when the warship received orders to join the British Home Fleet as part of an American force composed of *Wasp* (CV-7), *North Carolina* (BB-55), *Washington* (BB-56), *Tuscaloosa* (CA-37), *Wichita* (CA-45), and seven other destroyers. On 25 March, she departed Casco Bay, Maine, in company with *Wasp*, *Washington*, *Wichita*, *Tuscaloosa* and the destroyers of Destroyer Squadron (DesRon) 8 with ComDesRon 8 embarked. The task unit reached Scapa Flow, in the Orkney Islands north of the British Isles, on 3 April.

Until the fall of 1942, *Wainwright* participated in convoy operations between Iceland, the Orkneys, and northern Russia. During this period, she had frequent brushes with *Luftwaffe* planes and *Kriegsmarine* submarines. Her most famous and most successful encounter with the enemy came three months after she arrived in European waters while the destroyer was protecting the North Russia convoys. She was then part of the covering force for the ill-fated Convoy PQ–17, making the run from Iceland to Archangel. The force—built around HMS *London*, *Tuscaloosa*, *Wichita*, and HMS *Norfolk*, with *Wainwright*, *Rowan* (DD–405), and seven British destroyers in the screen—departed Seidisfjord, Iceland, on 1 July.

PQ–17 suffered *Luftwaffe* and submarine attacks on 2 and 3 July, but *Wainwright* did not get involved directly until the 4th. In mid-afternoon, the destroyer joined the convoy to refuel from the tanker *Aldersdale*. On her way to the rendezvous, the warship assisted the convoy in repulsing two torpedo-plane raids. During the first, her long-range fire kept the six enemy planes at a distance sufficient to make their torpedo drops wholly inaccurate. The second was a desultory, single-plane affair in which the warship easily drove off the lone torpedo bomber. During the ensuing dive-bombing attack, she evaded the enemy handily, the nearest bomb landing at least 150 yards away.

After that attack, a two-hour lull in the action allowed *Wainwright* to resume her original mission—refueling—but the enemy returned at about 1820. At the sight of 25 Heinkel 111's—each carrying two torpedoes—milling about on the southern horizon, the warship turned to port to clear the convoy. At that juncture, the Heinkels divided themselves into two groups for the attack—one on her starboard quarter and the other on her starboard bow. *Wainwright* took the group off her quarter under fire at extreme range—about 10,000 yards distant—and maintained her fire until it endangered the convoy. At that juncture, she shifted her attention to the more dangerous bow attack. Her fire on that group proved so effective that only one plane managed to penetrate her defenses to make his drop between *Wainwright* and the convoy. All the others prudently dropped their torpedoes about 1,000 to 1,500 yards from the destroyer. That resulted in a torpedo run to the convoy itself in excess of 4,000 yards. The ships in the convoy easily evaded the torpedoes ap-

37

proaching from the bow, but the torpedoes coming from the starboard quarter found their marks, liberty ship SS *William Hooper* and the Russian tanker SS *Azerbaidjan. Wainwright*, though, had put up a successful defense. Her antiaircraft gunners damaged three or four enemy planes and generally discouraged the raiders from pressing home their attack with the vigor necessary for greater success.

Not long after that attack, at about 1900, *Wainwright* parted company with convoy PQ–17 to rejoin her own task unit, then heading off to meet the supposed threat posed by the possible sortie of a German surface force built around battleship *Tirpitz*, pocket battleship *Scheer*, and cruiser *Hipper*. Convoy PQ–17, naked to the enemy after the Support Force withdrew to meet a danger which never materialized, scattered. Each ship tried to make it to northern Russia as best she could. *Luftwaffe* planes and *Kriegsmarine* submarines saw that few succeeded. After more than three weeks of individual hide-and-seek games with the Germans, the last groups of PQ–17 ships straggled into Archangel on 25 July. Operation *"Rosselsprung"* as the Germans dubbed the action, had proved an overwhelming success. It cost the Allies over two-thirds of the ships in PQ–17. However, *Wainwright's* brief association with the convoy probably saved several others from being added to the casualty list.

Wainwright continued to escort Atlantic convoys through the summer and into the fall of 1942. However, no action like that she encountered on 4 July occurred. It was not until the first large-scale amphibious operation of the European-African-Middle Eastern theater came along in November that she again engaged the enemy in deadly earnest.

For the invasion of French Morocco, *Wainwright* was assigned to the four-destroyer screen of the Covering Group (Task Group 34.1) built around *Massachusetts* (BB–59), *Tuscaloosa* (CA–37), and *Wichita* (CA–45). Assembled at Casco Bay, Maine, that group got underway on 24 October and, two days later, rendezvoused with the remainder of the Western Naval Task Force (Task Force 34) which had sortied from Hampton Roads. The task force reached the Moroccan coast on the night of 7 and 8 November. The invasion was scheduled for the pre-dawn hours of the following morning. The Covering Force drew the two-fold mission of protecting the transports in the event of a sortie by French heavy surface units based at Dakar and of preventing a sortie by the French light forces based at Casablanca.

For *Wainwright*, the action off Casablanca opened just before 0700 on the 8th when her antiaircraft gunners joined those of the other ships of the Covering Force in chasing away two Vichy French planes. Later that morning, Casablanca-based submarines, destroyers, and the light cruiser *Primauguet* sallied forth to oppose the landings, already in progress at Fedhala. *Wainwright* joined *Massachusetts*, *Tuscaloosa*, *Wichita* and the other three destroyers in stopping that attack. Their efforts cost the French heavily. Four Vichy destroyers and eight submarines were sunk while the light cruiser and two destroyer-leaders suffered crippling damage. In addition to her part in the engagement with the French warships, *Wainwright* also participated in the intermittent gun duels with batteries ashore.

For the next three days, *Wainwright* remained off the Moroccan coast supporting the invasion. The Army invested Casablanca by the night of the 10th, and the French capitulated late the following morning. On the 12th, the Covering Force—with *Wainwright* in the screen—sailed for home. The destroyer arrived in New York on 21 November and immediately began a two-week repair period.

Next, after a brief training period, the warship resumed duty with transatlantic convoys. For the next six months, she busied herself protecting merchant ships making the voyage to North African ports. During her stay in Casablanca after one such voyage, she played host to a group of Moroccan dignitaries including Sidi

Mohammed, the Sultan of Morocco. During another convoy operation, she helped screen Convoy UGS–6 which lost five of its 45 ships to U-boat torpedoes. When not engaged in Atlantic convoy duty, she trained with other ships of the Atlantic Fleet and underwent brief repairs in various American ports.

In June of 1943, *Wainwright* returned to North Africa for convoy duty between ports along the Mediterranean coast of North Africa which occupied her until the invasion of Sicily in July. For that operation, *Wainwright* was assigned to TG 80.2, the Escort Group. The force arrived off the Sicilian coast on the night of 9 and 10 July, and the assault troops went ashore the following morning. During the campaign, *Wainwright* protected the transports from enemy air and submarine activity. While she was patrolling off Palermo on 26 July, a formation of twin-engine Ju. 88 medium bombers attacked her group. Two near misses flooded both main engine rooms in sister-destroyer *Mayrant* (DD–402), and *Wainwright* joined in escorting the stricken warship into port under tow. Later, she supported the "leap-frog" amphibious moves employed by Major General George S. Patton in his rampage across northern Sicily to the Strait of Messina. During her stay in Sicilian waters, the destroyer also supported minesweeping operations and conducted antishipping sweeps. In mid-August, she returned to North Africa at Mersel-Kebir, Algeria, where she remained until early September. On the 5th, she resumed convoy duty—this time between North Africa and Sicily—frequently warding off *Luftwaffe* air raids. Italy proper had been invaded early in September; and, late in October, the warship was called upon to bombard enemy installations around Naples in support of the 5th Army's advance on that city.

She resumed convoy duty soon thereafter. Her next noteworthy contact with the enemy came on 13 December. While conducting an antisubmarine sweep 10 miles north of Algiers in company with *Niblack* (DD–424), *Benson* (DD–421), and HMS *Calpe*, she made contact with *U-593*. First *Wainwright* and then HMS *Calpe* attacked with depth charges. Those attacks brought the submarine to the surface, and *Wainwright's* gun crews went to work on her. In less than two minutes, the German crew began to abandon their vessel. *Wainwright* responded with a boarding party. The American sailors rescued survivors but failed to save the U-boat. After returning to Algiers and delivering her prisoners to British authorities there, she resumed convoy and patrol duties in North African waters. At the beginning of 1944, she provided support for the troops trying to break out of the beachheads at Anzio and Nettuno on the Italian mainland. Those duties occupied her until early February when she received orders to return to the United States. She steamed homeward in company with *Ariel* (AF–22) and *Niblack* via Ponta Delgada in the Azores, arrived at New York on 12 February, and entered the navy yard there for a three-week overhaul. When that chore was finished on 6 March, the destroyer began 13 months of escort and training duty along the eastern seaboard.

That routine ended on 27 April 1945 when she passed through the Panama Canal into the Pacific Ocean. After a stop at San Diego and exercises out of Pearl Harbor, the warship headed for the western Pacific. She reached Ulithi Atoll on 13 June and for the next two months sailed between various islands in the area. She visited Iwo Jima, Okinawa, Saipan, Guam, and Eniwetok. On 12 August, she departed the last-named atoll in company with TF 49 bound for the Aleutian Islands. While she was at sea, the Japanese capitulation ended hostilities. Four days later, the ship steamed into Adak. She remained there until the last day of the month when she got underway with TF 92, bound for Honshu, Japan. *Wainwright* arrived in Ominato Ko on 12 September and began a six-week tour of duty in support of the occupation forces. That duty ended on 30 October, and the warship headed back toward the United States.

After stops at Midway and Pearl Harbor, she pulled into San Diego on 16 December.

Wainwright remained at San Diego in an inactive status until the spring of 1946. At that time, she was designated a target ship for the atomic tests to be conducted at Bikini Atoll that summer. She survived both blasts at Bikini in July. On 29 August 1946, she was decommissioned. *Wainwright* remained at Bikini almost two years under intermittent inspection by scientists evaluating the effects of the Operation "Crossroads" tests. Finally, she was towed out to sea in July 1948 and sunk as a target on the 5th. Her name was struck from the Navy list on 13 July 1948.

Wainwright (DD–419) earned seven battle stars for World War II service.

III

(DLG–28: dp. 7,930 (f.); l. 547′; b. 55′; dr. 28′10′′; s. 30 k. (tl.); cpl. 418; a. 1 5′′, 2 3′′, 1 mis. ln., Terrier, 6 15.5′′ tt.; cl. *Belknap*)

The third *Wainwright* (DLG–28) was laid down on 2 July 1962 at Bath, Maine, by the Bath Iron Works Corp.; launched on 25 April 1965; sponsored by Mrs. Richard W. Wainwright; and commissioned on 8 January 1966 at the Boston Naval Shipyard, Capt. Robert P. Foreman in command.

Between January and May, the guided missile frigate completed her outfitting at Boston. On 21 May, she departed Boston, initially to test the Navy's newest sonar equipment and then to proceed to her home port, Charleston, S.C. During the months of June, July, and early August, she operated out of that port along the eastern seaboard and in the West Indies. During this period, she made six highly successful missile firings on the Atlantic Fleet weapon range and conducted a three-day search for an unidentified submarine contact. Though no positive identification of the submarine could be made, *Wainwright* did establish contact with her new long-range sonar and then tracked the vessel for a time.

On 13 August, the ship returned to Charleston for 15 days of upkeep in preparation for shakedown training, upon which she embarked on 28 August. At the conclusion of shakedown, she proceeded to Culebra Island for both gun and Terrier missile shoots. She returned to Charleston in October to prepare for the annual Atlantic Fleet exercise. On 28 November, the guided missile frigate stood out of Charleston for 17 days of drills, including replenishment exercises, weapon coordination drills, and formation steaming maneuvers and tactics. She returned home on 16 December and ended the year in a leave and upkeep status.

On 6 January 1967, *Wainwright* got underway for Boston and post-shakedown availability. She concluded that repair period and headed back to Charleston on 15 March. Following local operations there, the guided missile frigate embarked upon her first deployment to the western Pacific on 10 April. She transited the Panama Canal a week later and arrived in San Diego, Calif., on the 23d. For almost a month, she conducted exercises off the coast of southern California before heading west on 15 May. After brief stops at Pearl Harbor and Guam, *Wainwright* entered Subic Bay in the Philippines on 3 June.

Three days later, she arrived on station in the Tonkin Gulf and, on the 8th, took over positive identification radar advisory zone (PIRAZ) duties from *Long Beach* (CGN–9). In that capacity, *Wainwright* maintained constant radar and visual surveillance of the gulf and adjoining coasts for the purpose of identifying all aircraft in the zone and vectoring defensive forces to the interception of any possible airborne enemy intruders. Because of the relative immobility necessary to those duties, she also served as a reference point to guide American strike aircraft to their targets ashore. Since her duties afforded her a continual picture of the events occurring in the air over the zone, she also served as a base for search and rescue (SAR) helicopters. During that first line period, one SAR helicopter crashed *Wainwright*'s flight deck area; but the damage proved to be minimal, and the frigate was able to resume full-scale flight operations the following day.

After a three-week upkeep period at Sasebo, Japan, and a Terrier missile shoot at Okinawa, the warship resumed PIRAZ duty on 12 August. Her 27 days on station ended on 8 September when she cleared the gulf for a five-day visit to Hong Kong. On 15 Septem-

Wainwright (CG–28) firing a salute during bicentennial observances at New York, July 1976.

ber, she stood out of the British colony to return to Vietnamese waters. During that third and final tour, she served as a screen commander for two of the attack aircraft carriers operating on "Yankee Station" located in the southern reaches of the Tonkin Gulf as well as antiaircraft warfare command ship for all of Task Force (TF) 77. On 28 September, *Wainwright* completed her final assignment in the combat zone and departed the Tonkin Gulf. En route home, she visited Subic Bay; Sydney, Australia; Wellington, New Zealand; and Tahiti. The warship retransited the Panama Canal on 12 November and reentered Charleston four days later.

The guided missile frigate ended 1967 and began 1968 at Charleston. On 19 January 1968, she exited her home port and headed for Newport, R.I., where she served as school ship for the Destroyer School from 21 January to 3 February before returning to Charleston on the 5th. Her operations from her home port—including Operation "Rugby Match" exercises in the West Indies—lasted until she sailed for the western Pacific on 24 June. The warship transited the Panama Canal on 29 June, stopped briefly at Pearl Harbor from 11 to 15 July and at Guam on the 21st, and arrived at Subic Bay on the 26th. Four days later, she embarked upon the first tour of combat duty of her 1968 deployment. She stopped at Danang for briefings on 2 August and then relieved *Sterett* (DLG–31) on PIRAZ station on the 4th. During the following 41 days, she left her station only once—to evade a typhoon—and returned immediately after the storm passed. On 14 September, she turned PIRAZ duties back over to *Sterett* and steamed off for a month of port visits which included a brief upkeep period at Subic Bay followed by calls at Hong Kong and Yokosuka. On 13 October, she headed from Japan directly to the PIRAZ station and relieved *Sterett* once more. The 27 days of her second line period passed even more routinely than those of the first, and she cleared the Tonkin Gulf on 15 November for a four-day upkeep in Sasebo from the 19th to the 23d. Back on station on the 28th, *Wainwright* concluded the year as the Navy's air coordinator in the northern portion of the Tonkin Gulf.

The warship spent the first three days of 1969 winding up her third and final tour of duty as PIRAZ ship and then set a course for the Philippines, the first pause on her way home. After stopping at Subic Bay from 5 to 9 January, she continued her roundabout voyage to Charleston, stopping along the way at Sydney, Australia; Auckland, New Zealand; and Papeete, Tahiti. She passed back through the Panama Canal on 11 February, stopped at St. Thomas for a two-day visit on the 15th, and reached Charleston on the 21st.

Following a month of leave and upkeep, *Wainwright* underwent a whole series of inspections at Charleston that spring. During the middle of May, she steamed north to Norfolk where she participated in the Presidential Seapower Demonstration conducted in the Virginia capes operating area. At the conclusion of that event on 19 May, she headed south for the multifaceted combat exercise, "Exotic Dancer." For the first two weeks of June, *Wainwright* remained in the West Indies and participated in the NATO antisubmarine warfare exercise, "Spark Plug," along with ships of the navies of Canada, Great Britain, the Netherlands, and Portugual. That exercise ended on 11 June, and the frigate proceeded to Newport where she disembarked the Commander, Cruiser-Destroyer Flotilla 2. She returned to Charleston on 16 June and spent all but two days of the next two months in port. On 18 August, *Wainwright* entered the Charleston Naval Shipyard for her first regular overhaul.

On 16 February 1970, the ship returned to operational status. Training off the Florida coast followed by more of the same off the Virginia capes occupied her until mid-March. After three days in Charleston, *Wainwright* got underway for gunnery and missile shoots on the Atlantic Fleet weapons range near Puerto Rico. Refresher training out of Guantanamo

Bay followed in April, but it was interrupted by two special assignments. On 26 April, she received orders to intercept three Haitian Coast Guard vessels fleeing that country in the wake of an unsuccessful coup. The ship encountered one near the entrance to Guantanamo Bay; but, observing American port officials boarding the ship peacefully, she continued on her way. Later, *Wainwright* found the other two ships and escorted them back to Guantanamo Bay for temporary asylum. Later, on 10 May, she put to sea to intercept quite a different force—a Soviet task group. That night, she came upon two of the Russian ships, a guided missile cruiser and a guided missile destroyer. The following day, two submarines, an oiler, and a submarine tender rendezvoused with the first two ships; and all six entered port at Cienfuegos, Cuba, on the 14th. The next day, *Wainwright* returned to Guantanamo Bay to resume refresher training. Less than a month later, on 12 June, she moored at Charleston for two months of upkeep and training in preparation for her forthcoming deployment to the Far East.

On 25 August, the guided missile frigate stood out of Charleston, bound for her third and final deployment to the western Pacific in conjunction with the Vietnam conflict. Steaming via the Panama Canal and Pearl Harbor, she arrived in Yokosuka, Japan, on 21 September. For almost two months, she conducted operations in Japanese waters—primarily bilateral ASW exercises in the Sea of Japan with units of the Japanese Maritime Self Defense Force. Periodically, the warship put into Yokosuka and Sasebo for upkeep and liberty.

Wainwright departed Japan on 14 November and headed via the Taiwan Strait for the Tonkin Gulf. On the 20th, she relieved *Jouett* (DLG–29) on PIRAZ station and took up familiar duty as the American air coordinator in the northern part of the gulf. That assignment proved very brief for, on the following day, *Chicago* (CG–11) relieved *Wainwright*; and the guided missile frigate moved on to new duties as the coordinator ship assigned to the north SAR station. For almost a month, she alternated between north and south SAR stations, taking time briefly in mid-December to participate in Operation "Beacon Tower," a three-day exercise to test the readiness of American warships in the Tonkin Gulf to meet and deal with air and surface attacks. On 16 December, *Wainwright* left the combat zone, bound for Singapore, where she remained from 19 to 26 December. From there, she set a course for the Philippines and arrived in Subic Bay on the 29th.

The warship completed six days in port at Subic Bay on 4 January 1971 and got underway for Hong Kong. She returned briefly to Subic Bay, however, for repairs to one of her radar antennae but finally reached Hong Kong on the 11th. Following a four-day visit, she stood out of the British colony on her way to the Tonkin Gulf. She served 16 days in the gulf, dividing her time between PIRAZ duties and assignments as the northern SAR ship.

After a final two-day stop at Subic Bay, *Wainwright* began the long voyage back to Charleston which took her through the Indian Ocean, around the Cape of Good Hope, and across the southern Atlantic to complete her first circumnavigation of the globe. Along the way, she made a series of calls at African and South American ports, beginning with Djibouti in French Somaliland. From there, she headed for Massawa, Ethiopia, where she participated in the celebration of the Ethiopian Navy Day, during which she joined ships of other nations in observing the graduation of midshipmen from the Ethiopian Naval Academy and hosted then-Emperor Haile Selassie I on board. She rounded out her African itinerary with calls at Diego Suarez, Madagascar, and at Lourenco Marques, Mozambique, before rounding the cape and heading across the Atlantic toward Brazil. Visits to Rio de Janeiro and Recife in Brazil and at St. Thomas in the Virgin Islands preceded gunfire support training and a missile shoot at Culebra Island. On 2 April, *Wain-*

wright steamed into Charleston and began an extended standown period.

Upon completion of a 59-day post-deployment standdown, *Wainwright* resumed operations early in June as a unit of the Atlantic Fleet Cruiser-Destroyer Force. She spent much of June in the Caribbean undergoing gunnery and missile training and returned to Charleston on the 19th. Four days later, work began on the installation of a light airborne multipurpose system (LAMPS). Those modifications were completed by mid-July, and *Wainwright* occupied the following four months with operations along the eastern seaboard in conjunction with the initial evaluation of her LAMPS helicopter. A tender availability followed by the conversion of her propulsion plant to burn Navy distillate fuel brought the year to a close at Charleston. The warship completed the conversion on 11 January 1972 and had resumed operations at sea out of Charleston by the 24th. For the next nine months, she tested her new LAMPS installation, made port visits to Atlantic and gulf coast ports, and participated in the usual 2d Fleet exercises. Those duties took her from the southeastern coast of Texas to the West Indies and thence as far north as Maine. By late November, she was at Charleston preparing for her first tour of duty in the Mediterranean Sea.

On 1 December, *Wainwright* stood out of Charleston and set a course for Rota, Spain, where she arrived on the 10th. After changing operational control from the 2d to the 6th Fleet, the guided missile frigate departed Rota on the 11th and entered the Mediterranean. Conducting ASW and antiair warfare (AAW) exercises, the warship headed across the Mediterranean —stopping at Barcelona from 20 to 26 December and arriving in Naples, Italy, on the 30th. She departed that port on 6 January 1973, and headed for the Ionian Sea. During ASW exercises in Greek waters, *Wainwright* contacted, tracked, and positively identified four Soviet submarines in spite of their strenuous efforts to evade.

Upon completing those exercises, she headed for the southern coast of France, arriving in Marseille on the 17th for a two-day visit. More AAW exercises followed, as did port visits to Palma de Mallorca; Malaga, Spain; and Genoa, Italy. On 17 February, she joined Genoa in company with the Italian cruiser *Vittorio Veneto* to participate in National Week XV, a multinational naval exercise of broad scope conducted across the Central Mediterranean. In addition to the Americans and Italians, units of the Greek and Turkish navies also participated in drills and battle exercises extending westward from Crete to the Strait of Messina between Sicily and the toe of the Italian boot.

After National Week XV, *Wainwright* punctuated a series of 6th Fleet ASW and AAW exercises with visits to many of the ports already mentioned as well as at Athens, Greece; Civitavecchia and Livorno, Italy; and Golfe Juan, France. On 17 June, she steamed from Palma de Mallorca through the Strait of Gibraltar to Rota on the Atlantic coast of Spain. There, she turned her duties over to *Belknap* (DLG-26) on the 21st.

That same day, she departed Rota for Lisbon, Portugal, where she joined *Guam* (LPH-9) and *Bowen* (DE-1074) in preparation for a transatlantic exercise to test the concept of the sea control ship. The three warships departed Lisbon on the 28th. The exercise lasted from 28 June to 8 July, during which time *Wainwright* vectored *Guam*-based Harrier aircraft to the interception of two Soviet "Bear" aircraft. Just before the conclusion of the exercise on 8 July, *Wainwright* ventured across the Arctic Circle briefly before setting a course for Charleston. The guided misile frigate concluded her first Mediterranean deployment on 20 July and began her standdown period at Charleston. On 10 September, she entered the Charleston Naval Shipyard for her second regular overhaul.

Wainwright completed sea trials, the final phase of overhaul, between 10 and 14 June 1974 and officially rejoined the Atlantic Fleet on 20 June at the Charleston Naval Station. For the remainder of the year, the warship was busy with refresher training, a myriad of tests, qualifications, inspections, and evaluations, and other normal 2d Fleet operations conducted along the southern Atlantic coast and in the Caribbean. The beginning of 1975 brought another period in drydock—this time at the Norfolk Naval Shipyard—for repairs to her sonar dome. She returned to Charleston on 1 February 1975 and resumed tests and inspections in preparation for her second deployment to European waters.

On 5 March, she stood down the Cooper River on her way to Europe. En route to the Mediterranean, the guided missile frigate joined *Forrestal* (CV–59) and *Tunney* (SSN–682) in a series of ASW, surface, and air action drills, at the conclusion of which *Wainwright* continued on her way to Spain.

She changed operational control to the 6th Fleet while at Rota between 15 and 17 March. The warship entered the "middle sea" on the latter date and arrived in her first Mediterranean port of call—Naples, Italy —on the 22d. As during her previous Mediterranean cruise, she engaged in one training exercise after another, but interrupted that schedule almost as frequently for port calls all along the Mediterranean coast of Europe. Late in April, a missile-firing exercise was interrupted by a snoopy Soviet destroyer and had to be postponed until the following day.

June proved to be an important month in *Wainwright*'s history, for it was during the latter part of that month that she transited the Straits of the Bosphorus and the Dardanelles into the Black Sea and became the first American ship to visit Rumania— at the port city of Constanta—in 49 years. After concluding that visit on the 24th and passing back into the Mediterranean on the 25th, she conducted a brief surveillance of the Soviet helicopter carrier *Leningrad* before resuming her schedule of training exercises and port visits. On 30 June, *Wainwright* was redesignated a guided missile cruiser, CG–28. Her second tour of duty with the 6th Fleet lasted until late August. On the 22d, she made a one-day stop at Rota; then headed home. Nine days later, she moored at Charleston and, for the remainder of the year, resumed a routine of 2d Fleet operations, inspections, and upkeep.

Following a spring of special operations and underway training out of Charleston, *Wainwright* got underway on 30 June for New York and her big events for 1976—the International Naval Review and Operation "Sail," both in honor of the United States' Bicentennial birthday. To the guided missile cruiser went the signal honor of being the focal point of both events—serving as flagship for the naval review and as reviewing ship for Operation "Sail." During her service in those two capacities, she entertained Vice President Nelson D. Rockefeller, Secretary of State Kissinger, Secretary of Defense Rumsfeld, Admiral James L. Holloway, III, Chief of Naval Operations, and Admiral Shanahan, Commander, 2d Fleet. All too quickly, however, the celebration of 4 July 1976 ended. On 6 July, the ship departed New York and headed back to Charleston to resume her more mundane schedule of special operations and training cruises. That routine—spiced liberally with tests, inspections, evaluations, and certifications— saw her through the Bicentennial year and the first three months of 1977.

On 31 March 1977, *Wainwright* embarked upon her third deployment to the Mediteranean. She joined the 6th Fleet officially upon arrival in Rota on 12 April and actually entered the Mediterranean the following day. Port visits and an almost incessant schedule of training exercises—ASW drills, AAW practice, missile shoots, multinational and bilateral exercises—occupied her once again. During June, she visited the Black Sea once more, but otherwise, her routine was similar to that she had experienced in previous tours of duty with the 6th Fleet. She concluded her Mediterranean operations at Rota at the end of the first week in October and arrived back in Charleston on the 21st. For the remaining two months of 1977, typical 2d Fleet operations out of Charleston filled her schedule.

January 1978 was spent in grooming for a multi-threat training exercise, "READEX 1–78," which took place in February in the southern Florida and Caribbean operating areas. Returning to Charleston late in the month, *Wainwright* entered the Charleston Naval Shipyard on 23 February for the commencement of a scheduled 13-month overhaul which concluded in March 1979.

Wainwright received four battle stars for Vietnam service.

Wake

A small atoll in the northern Pacific, some 500 miles north-northwest of the Marshalls. Composed of three islets—Wake, Wilkes, and Peale—Wake was discovered by the British in 1796 but remained uninhabited until claimed by the United States in 1899. Pan American World Airways System developed a way-station for the transpacific "Clipper" flights there in 1935; and, in 1939, Congress belatedly voted appropriations to construct a Naval Air Station there which was captured in December 1941 by the Japanese and held until 4 September 1945—two days after Japan formally surrendered in Tokyo Bay.

(PG–43: dp. 350; l. 159'5''; b. 27'; dr. 5'3''; s. 14.5 k.; cpl. 59; a. 2 3'', 8 .30-cal. mg.)

Guam (PG–43) was laid down on 17 October 1926 at Shanghai, China, by the Kiangnan Dock and Engineering Works; launched on 28 May 1927; sponsored by Miss Louise Frances Bruce; and commissioned on 28 December 1927, Lt. Comdr. Robert K. Awtrey in command.

With Rear Admiral Yates Stirling, Jr., Commander, Yangtze Patrol (ComYangPat) embarked, *Guam* departed Shanghai on 19 January 1928 for shakedown training. She arrived at Hankow on 24 January and soon commenced her passage up the middle Yangtze River, bound for Chungking. On 1 February, *Guam* received her first first convoy-escort assignment, shepherding Standard Oil Co. vessels *Mei Lu* and *Mei Foo*—towing *Mei Yung* and *Mei Hung* respectively—through bandit-infested territory along the river. *Mei Foo*

grounded in the tricky current, but *Guam* came to the rescue and towed her out of danger. Within a few hours, *Guam* went to general quarters immediately after *Mei Hung* drew a few rounds of sniper fire from the riverbanks; but, before the gunboat's guns could reply, the snipers melted away into the hinterland.

The small warship completed the passage through the scenic Yangtze gorges and returned from Chungking to I'Chang by mid-July. Soon thereafter, the second gunboat of the "new six," *Tutuila* (PG–44), joined *Guam* at I'Chang, and the two convoyed merchantmen upriver past "bandit country" to Chungking. In the interim, the gunboat's designation was changed to PR–3 on 28 June.

At this juncture, inasmuch as the South China Patrol had been forced to "make-do" for years with antiquated ships, Commander, Asiatic Fleet (CINCAF), dispatched *Guam* southward to join the South China Patrol, and the gunboat got underway on 5 October 1928 for Hong Kong. Delayed by bad weather which forced her to turn back at Amoy, she made port at Hong Kong on 14 October.

With the arrival of *Mindanao* (PR–8) in mid-June 1929 to assume duties as flagship of the South China Patrol, *Guam* rejoined the Yangtze Patrol and resumed operations on that mighty river. On Independence Day 1930, *Guam* departed Changsha to investigate at Chenglin and Yochow, as a report had indicated that American nationals were endangered by the communists who held the cities.

As she neared Yochow, shots rang out from the riverbank, and *Guam* went to general quarters, manning her main battery of 3-inch and .30-caliber guns. The gunboat made five passes by the offending area, giving gunners on both sides of the ship a chance to fire. The 3-inch guns added a touch of bass to the orchestration which soon silenced the communist sniper fire—but not before one bluejacket in *Guam* had been killed.

The gunboat stood ready to protect American lives and property during the early 1930's, while Chiang Kai-shek sought to consolidate and centralize his power in China. Chiang also pursued a civil war against the communists. Chasing Red forces into the hills of Yenan removed them from the Yangtze, but the communists remained Chiang's "thorn in the flesh." However, his tactics of "buying time" by giving in to

The Yangtze River gunboat *Wake* (PR–3).

continued Japanese encroachment in the north earned him the enmity of many Chinese who felt that resistance to Japan was imperative.

When Chiang Kai-shek was kidnapped on 12 December 1936 and forced into an alliance with the communists—albeit into an association which proved to be temporary—the country's morale took an upswing. By the spring of 1937, it appeared to most western observers that China had found a hitherto unknown unity. At this juncture, Admiral Harry E. Yarnell, CINCAF, took a cruise up the Yangtze to inspect naval facilities and installations along the river. Yarnell subsequently shifted his flag from *Isabel* (PY–10) to the ill-fated *Panay* (PR–5) and thence later from *Panay* to *Guam* on 24 May for the return cruise downriver. However, before returning downsteam, he shifted his flag back to *Isabel* on 26 May.

Admiral Yarnell's cruise in *Guam* turned out to be the last peacetime passage by a CINCAF on the Yangtze, for, in the following summer, hostilities between Chinese and Japanese troops broke out at Marco Polo Bridge, outside of Peking. At first, little anxiety was felt for the safety of Americans on the Yangtze. In fact, the evacuation of Japanese nationals from Yangtze ports in late July and early August actually lessened the concern.

However, on 13 August, fighting broke out at Shanghai and soon spread upriver toward the Chinese national capital of Nanking. In September, upon receipt of warnings of heavy Nipponese air raids on the city, *Guam* and *Luzon* (PR–7) embarked members of the U.S. Embassy staff from Nanking. From this point on, the Yangtze Patrol gunboaters had grandstand seats on the Sino-Japanese "incident." *Guam* evacuated Americans from Nanking prior to the city's fall to Japanese forces in December. The perils of such neutral duty were amply illustrated when *Panay*—standing by at Nanking and evacuating the last Americans in the city—was attacked and sunk by Japanese bombers between Nanking and Wuhu on 12 December. The Japanese speedily settled this incident, which nearly sparked a war between the United States and Japan, by quickly apologizing, punishing the guilty aviators, and rapidly paying indemnities to the United States government.

By 1939, the Japanese controlled the Yangtze River. Third power commerce was at a standstill, and even neutral naval forces were restricted or hampered by the Japanese, who insisted that escorts were necessary at all times and to all places. *Guam*'s crew observed Japanese troop movements and sighted flights of Japanese bombers headed upstream to bomb the subsequent Chinese capitals at Hankow and, later, at Chungking.

On 23 January 1941, the gunboat was renamed *Wake* in order to clear the former name for new construction. She sailed downriver for Shanghai on 29 March and seved briefly as station ship there from 2 April to 5 May. She briefly returned upriver to Chinkiang before heading south to Shanghai, where she was inspected on 21 June by Rear Admiral William A. Glassford, Commander, Yangtze Patrol.

From 3 to 6 July, *Wake* headed back upriver to her old haunt at Nanking before mooring at her familiar berth at Hankow, where the German-owned *Norddeutscher Lloyd* (NDL) pontoon served as station ship. *Wake*'s crew found diversion ashore in rifle range and small bore practice, while lookouts on board the gunboat continued to log nearly round-the-clock flights of Japanese bombers northward for Chungking. Although Chungking lay beyond the reach of Japan's troops and ships, the city lay well within the reach of Japanese planes.

Wake remained at Hankow into the late fall, and frequent dreary weather did nothing to brighten her melancholy duty. On 25 November, the ship closed out the Navy warehouse at Hankow—liquidating the 80 tons of stores and supplies by distributing its supplies among Americans in Hankow. This done, the gunboat sailed for Shanghai.

Arriving at the port three days later, *Wake* found two of her near-sisters, *Luzon* and *Oahu* (PR–6), busy preparing for "deep water" operations. With the arrival of authorization from Washington to withdraw what ships he could, Admiral Thomas C. Hart, CINCAF, ordered *Luzon* and *Oahu* to Manila. *Tutuila*, upriver at Chungking, was trapped at the Nationalist capital, unable to run the gauntlet in time. *Wake*'s stores and crew were divided between *Luzon* and *Oahu*, and the ship was left under the care of a skeleton crew of 14 men—mostly reservist radiomen who were to maintain the ship as a communications link with American marines remaining in China. Chosen to command *Wake* was a former Yangtze River commercial pilot, Lt. Comdr. Columbus D. Smith, USNR.

That same day, 28 November, *Luzon* (with Rear Admiral Glassford embarked) and *Oahu* departed Shanghai for the last time and sailed for the Philippines. Pending the results of the cruise of these two gunboats—which were never designed for the open sea—*Mindanao* remained at Hong Kong.

After a typhoon-fraught passage through the Formosa Strait, the two gunboats eventually made the Philippines and safely arrived at Manila on 3 December. Two days later, Rear Admiral Glassford disestablished YangPat; and, in the meantime, *Mindanao* got underway for the Philippines.

Three days later, on 8 December (7 December east of the IDL), a radioman on duty in *Wake* picked up news of the Japanese attack on Pearl Harbor. Comdr. Smith, alerted by a phone call soon therefater, sped to the waterfront. His crew, however, had no time to react to the suddenness of war. A launch, carrying a detachment of Japan's Special Naval Landing Force, came alongside and the enemy swarmed on board, taking the ship intact—the only American man-of-war to be captured intact by the enemy in World War II.

Nearby, the British gunboat *Peterel*, further out in the stream of the Whangpoo River and downriver from *Wake*, stubbornly refused to surrender. Then, upon a pre-arranged signal, previously emplaced field guns opened fire and swiftly shelled the virtually defenseless British gunboat to a mass of flaming rubble. With her white ensign still flying bravely, *Peterel* sank soon thereafter. Of her crew of 14, only six survived.

The Japanese renamed *Wake*, *Tatara*; and the United States Navy struck the ship from the Navy list on 25 March 1942. The gunboat survived the war intact, was transferred to the Chinese Nationalists after the surrender of Japan, and subsequently fell to the communists in 1949. Her fate thereafter is, as yet, unknown.

Wake received one battle star for World War II service.

Wake Island

An atoll in the northern Pacific, consisting of three islands—Wake, Peale, and Wilkes—which became an American advanced base in 1941. At the time of the Japanese attack on Pearl Harbor on 7 December 1941 (8 December on Wake), all naval activities at the atoll were under Comdr. Winfield S. Cunningham, United States Navy; under his overall command were the 13 officers and 365 enlisted men of the 1st Defense Battalion, United States Marine Corps, commanded by Maj. James P. S. Devereaux, United States Marine Corps, whose heaviest guns were 5-inch/51-caliber rifles once mounted in old battleships. A Marine fighter squadron, dispatched at the "eleventh hour," reached Wake only a few days before the Japanese attack; that unit, consisting of 12 Grumman F4F–3 Wildcat fighters from Marine Fighter Squadron (VMF) 211, was commanded by Maj. Paul A. Putnam, USMC. Also on Wake were 1,000 civilian construction workers employed by Contractors, Pacific, Naval Air Bases, and a small Army communication detachment.

Although the atoll went to general quarters upon hearing of the Pearl Harbor attack, a combination of a lack of radar, loud surf noises (which made sound-detectors practically useless), and heavy cloud cover rendered it possible for the Japanese to achieve a surprise attack shortly before noon on 8 December. Twenty-seven planes emerged from the low-hanging clouds and bombed and strafed the airfield, destroying seven of VMF–211's F4F–3's and killing or wounding 62 percent of the aviation personnel on the island.

Over the next two weeks, the Japanese bombed Wake almost incessantly, softening up the atoll for invasion. The first attempt met with failure on 11 December, when shore batteries and VMF–211's remaining F4F–3's sank two Japanese destroyers, *Kisaragi* and *Hayate,* and damaged the light cruiser *Yubari,* the flagship of the invasion force.

The setback suffered on 11 December forced the Japanese to bring up reinforcements—including two of the homeward-bound Pearl Harbor striking force carriers—and carrier-based planes began hitting the atoll on 21 December. The following day, the last two flyable Wildcats—there had never been more than four operational over the two-week defense of Wake —went up to do battle with Japanese. One crippled Wildcat returned, so badly shot-up that it was unuseable.

With the aviation element now disposed of, the Japanese felt confident that they could land. Accordingly, at 0200 on 23 December 1941, the enemy managed to establish a beachhead, running two old destroyer-transports ashore in the process under heavy gunfire. After bitter fighting, the men of the Japanese Special Naval Landing Force managed to overcome the defending marines but not without sustaining heavy casualties. Wilkes was the last island to surrender, on the afternoon of the 23d.

(CVE–65: dp. 7,800; l. 512'3''; b. 65'; ew. 108'1''; dr. 22'6''; s. 19 k.; cpl. 860; a. 1 5'', 16 40mm., ac. 28; cl. *Casablanca*; T. S4–S2–BB3)

Wake Island (CVE–65) was laid down under a Maritime Commission contract (MC hull 1102) on 6 Februrary 1943 at Vancouver, Wash., by the Kaiser Shipbuilding Co., Inc.; launched on 15 September 1943; sponsored by Mrs. Frederick Carl Sherman, the wife of Rear Admiral Sherman; commissioned on 7 November 1943, Capt. Hames R. Tague in command.

Following commissioning, *Wake Island* received supplies, ammunition, and gasoline at Astoria, Oreg., and got underway on 27 November 1943 for Puget Sound and anchored the following day at Bremerton, Wash., where she continued to load supplies and ammunition. The escort carrier operated in the Puget Sound area conducting structural firing tests and making stops at Port Townsend, Sinclair Inlet, and Seattle before sailing south on 6 December. She arrived at San Francisco on 10 December; took on fuel; and, two days later, headed for San Diego, arriving there on 14 December for shakedown and availability. Before departing, the escort carrier took on board the personnel and planes of squadron VC–69.

On 11 January 1944, *Wake Island* got underway and steamed, via the Panama Canal, to Hampton Roads, Va., arriving at Norfolk on 26 January. Following availability, the escort carrier sailed on 14 February for New York in company with *Mission Bay* (CVE–59), *Swenning* (DE–394), and *Haverfield* (DE–393).

On 16 February—after loading supplies and embarking Army and Navy officers for transportation— *Wake Island* set course for Recife, Brazil, the first stop on her voyage to Karachi, India. She arrived at Recife on 1 March and made stops at Capetown, South Africa, and Diego Suarez Harbor, Madagascar, before arriving at Karachi on 29 March. The escort carrier began her return trip on 3 April and arrived back at Norfolk on 12 May.

She spent the remainder of May and part of June undergoing alterations and an overhaul. She then took on board the planes and personnel of VC–58 and, on 15 June, set course toward Bermuda for duty as the nucleus of Task Group (TG) 22.6, a combined, air-and-surface, antisubmarine, hunter-killer group. The highlight of her cruise came on 2 July, when one of the carrier's Avengers intercepted the surfaced *U–543* off the coast of Africa between the Canary and the Cape Verde Islands, making its way home after an unsuccessful patrol in the Gulf of Guinea. The torpedo bomber's pilot, Ens. Frederick L. Moore, USNR, braved heavy antiaircraft fire from the German submarine while making two bombing attacks which sank the U-boat. However, no evidence appeared to confirm the kill, so the escort carrier and her escorts spent the ensuing fortnight hunting the already-destroyed submarine.

Task Group (TG) 22.6 began her next serious encounter with the enemy two minutes before noon on 2 August, when *Howard* (DE–138) sighted a U-boat's conning tower some eight miles away. She and *Fiske* (DE–143) were detached to investigate, while all planes in the area were recalled. A "killer" TBM, armed with depth bombs, was catapulted at 1209. At 1235, a torpedo—apparently fired by a second submarine—hit *Fiske* midships and broke her in two. The ships of the group managed to maneuver clear of two more torpedoes which were fired at the force. The first report of casualties listed 4 dead, 26 missing, and 55 seriously injured. *Farquhar* (DE–139) was detached to support *Howard* and later to pick up survivors. As the group was preparing to avenge the loss of *Fiske,* heavy fog and rain stopped all operations.

On 4 August, TG 22.6 was dissolved and, four days later, *Wake Island* made rendezvous with Convoy UC–32 as it steamed westward. She left the convoy on the 11th and headed for Hampton Roads. She arrived at Norfolk on the 15th for alterations and repairs which lasted through the 25th. Following post-repair trials and a brief availability, the escort carrier sailed on 29 August for Quonset, R.I., to relieve *Mission Bay* on carrier aircraft qualification operation duty which lasted through 30 October.

The next day, the escort carrier sailed for Norfolk with *Lea* (DD–118) and *Babbitt* (DD–128) as escorts and arrived on 1 November for a period of availability. On the 11th, she stood out of Norfolk in company with *Shamrock Bay* (CVE–84) and escorts bound via the Panama Canal for the west coast. The escort carrier entered San Francisco Bay on 28 November and moored at the Naval Air Station, Alameda, Calif., where she embarked two new aircraft squadrons before heading for Hawaii the following day. She moored at Ford Island, Pearl Harbor, on 5 December; detached squadrons VC–9 and VPB–149; and disembarked personnel, planes, and equipment. Ten days later, *Wake Island*—her flight deck laden with cargo and unable to launch or receive planes—got underway for the Admiralty Islands with escorts *Rowell* (DE–403) and *O'Flaherty* (DE–340). She arrived at Manus on 27 December, discharged all cargo and passengers, sailed for the Palau Islands, and arrived at Kossol Reef Lagoon on New Year's Day 1945. Late that evening, she loaded ammunition from a barge and got underway at 0642, bound for the Philippines and the forthcoming invasion of Luzon, in company with a tremendous fleet which had gathered for the operation.

Two days later, *Wake Island* passed through Surigao Strait and launched both SNAP (antisnooper air patrol) and LCAP (local combat air patrol). On 4 January 1945, she was operating in the Sulu Sea and launched a three-hour SNAP. The American planes sighted a single-engine Japanese float plane on the water off the southeastern tip of Panay Island. It appeared to be in the hands of a salvage crew. Two of the scout planes made two strafing runs each and left the plane riddled and the salvage crew dispersed.

The Fleet entered Panay Gulf about 100 miles northwest of Manila. *Wake Island*'s surface search radar was jammed by enemy transmission, and the escort carrier went to general quarters at 1714. One minute later, a Japanese single-engine plane appeared overhead in a steep diving attack on *Ommaney Bay* (CVE–79), some 4,200 yards away. Fire immediately flared from that carrier's flight and hangar decks; and, after 20 minutes, her crew abandoned *Ommaney Bay* under a dense cloud of black smoke. She burned with explosions of ammunition and was finally scuttled astern of the Fleet by a torpedo from an American destroyer.

On 5 January, *Wake Island* received 19 survivors of *Ommaney Bay* who had been rescued by *Maury* (DD–401). The ship went to general quarters on bogies on the radar screen, but three threatened raids failed to develop. At 1502, eight LCAP fighters from *Wake Island* pounced upon a division of Japanese Army fighters. When the melee was over, the Americans claimed three certain kills and a probable without suffering any loss themselves. In all, *Wake Island* launched three LCAP's during daylight. At 1655, the ship again went to general quarters to repel an air attack and for the next hour was under severe attack. At one time, six single-engine planes were simultaneously diving on carriers off *Wake Island*'s port side. Five were knocked down by antiaircraft fire, narrowly missing their targets, but one managed a hit on *Manila Bay* (CVE–61). She caught fire and dropped behind, but her efficient damage control efforts enabled her to resume her position in the formation in only 51 minutes, with her flight deck out of commission. During the attack, at least 10 enemy planes splashed within 5,000 yards of *Wake Island*, and her own antiaircraft gunners claimed three.

On 13 January, two enemy planes attacked *Salamaua* (CVE–96), cruising about eight miles astern of *Wake Island*. One of the attackers was shot down, but the other scored a hit which briefly slowed that carrier. She soon regained speed and controlled a fire on her hanger deck without losing her position in the formation. Four days later, *Wake Island* was detached and left Lingayen Gulf in TG 77.14—a force consisting of eight escort carriers and their screen to retire to Ulithi, Caroline Islands. She anchored at Ulithi's southern anchorage from 23 to 31 January, undergoing availability and preparing for further operations. During this period, her home port was changed from Norfolk to Puget Sound, Bremerton, Washington.

On 10 February 1945, the escort carrier got underway to join TG 52.2, which had been established to provide air cover and support while escorting major units to the Volcano Islands and then to furnish naval gunfire, spotting, and direct air support for landing forces. The following day, she steamed to an area off Saipan-Tinian where rehearsals for the invasion took place. On 13 February, *Wake Island*'s commanding officer was designated OTC of Task Unit (TU) 52.2.1.

On 14 February, the escort carrier set course for Iwo Jima and, two days later, arrived at her operating area 49 miles from the southwestern top of Iwo. Shortly after daylight, the heavy bombardment group began shelling shore installations on the island. Planes from *Wake Island* flew spotting sorties, attacked defensive works with rocket fire, and flew local antisubmarine patrols and hydrographic observation flights over the beaches. D day for the invasion of Iwo Jima was 19 February; and, on that day, *Wake Island* operated as before, flying 56 spotting sorties and firing 87 rockets. *Bismarck Sea* (CVE–95), a carrier in her group, was sunk by enemy air attack on 21 February. The next day, *Wake Island* was detached and ordered to proceed to a rendezvous point east of Iwo Jima. There, she was refueled on 23 February and set course to return to the operating area east of Iwo Jima. The following day, she took station some 35 miles from the southern tip of Iwo Jima and flew 55 spotting sorties, expending 205 rockets. In the ensuing weeks, *Wake Island* continued her operations supporting the marines who paid

with pain and blood for each square foot of the bitterly defended island. On 5 March, she received a message of special interest from Commander, TU 52.2.1, Rear Admiral Clifton Sprague: "If your ship is as good as your Air Department and Squadron, it is a standout. I have seen nearly all the combat CVEs' work and I must say the *Wake* tops them all for efficiency, smoothness and good judgement. I hope we are together again."

After 24 consecutive days of operations, *Wake Island* retired on 8 March from her station off Iwo Jima and rendezvoused with *Saginaw Bay* (CVE–82) west of the island. The next day, they headed for Ulithi and arrived there on 14 March.

The escort carrier spent the next five days at anchor, preparing for another operation. She got underway on 21 March to supply air support for forces about to invade Okinawa. On 25 March, she arrived in the operating area roughly 60 miles south of Okinawa Jima and began sending flights over Kerama Retto beaches and Okinawa. *Wake Island* continued her support of the campaign through the initial landings at Okinawa on 1 April.

On the 3d, the escort carrier was operating southeast of Okinawa. At 1722, she completed the landing of her fifth spotting sortie, and all her planes were back on board. Eight minutes later, she went to general quarters, and enemy bogies were reported. At 1742, a violent wave hit the ship while planes were being moved for spotting on the flight deck. Two FM–2's were thrown off the flight deck into the water. Two fighters were flipped over on their backs, and two others received severe damage when tossed about.

At the same instant, two FM–2's broke loose from their lashings on the hangar deck and collided with major damage to both. At 1744, a Japanese single-engine plane plunged at the ship from a high angle and missed the port forward corner of the flight deck, exploding in the water abreast the forecastle. Thirty seconds later, a second similar plane whistled down on the starboard side at tremendous speed, narrowly missing the bridge structure and plunging into the water about 10 feet from the hull. The plane exploded after impact, ripping a hole in the ship's side below the waterline, about 45 feet long and about 18 feet from top to bottom and making many shrapnel holes. Parts of the plane were thrown onto the forecastle and into the gun sponsons. Various compartments were flooded, and the shell plating cracked between the first and second decks. Other shell plating buckled, and the main condensers were flooded with salt water, contaminating some 30,000 gallons of fresh water and 70,000 gallons of fuel oil. At 1824, salting made it necessary to secure the forward engine, and the ship proceeded on one propeller. Remarkably, there were no injuries; and, by 2140, corrective measures had been taken, and the ship was again steaming on both engines. The next day, *Wake Island* steamed to Kerama Retto anchorage with escorts *Dennis* (DE–405) and *Gross* (DE–444). While she remained there undergoing inspection by the fleet salvage officer, special precautions were taken to guard against possible Japanese suicide swimmers from islands of the cluster not yet secured.

The escort carrier set course for Guam on 6 April 1945 and, four days later, arrived at Apra Harbor for repairs in drydock which lasted through 20 May. The next day, the ship, in company with *Wantuck* (APD–125), headed for Okinawa where she resumed her mission of supporting the troops on the island.

Wake Island was then detached on 2 June and, escorted by *Ralph Talbot* (DD–390), proceeded to Kerama Retto for replenishment. At Kaika Harbor, Kerama Retto, she loaded bombs, rockets, and dry and fresh provisions, despite many enemy aircraft in the vicinity. The escort carrier made rendezvous with *Cowanesque* (AO–79) for refueling and, once her tanks were full, returned to the operating area off Okinawa on 6 June 1945.

The following day, *Wake Island*, as part of the task

unit, engaged in strikes on Sakashima Gunto. *Natoma Bay* (CVE–62) was hit by a suicide plane, and *Sargent Bay* (CVE–83) was attacked by a second. *Wake Island*'s support operations continued until 15 June when Rear Admiral Durgin landed on board the escort carrier for an official visit. In a ceremony held on the flight deck, he presented citations and awards to 16 pilots of VOC–1.

The following day, *Wake Island* and *Dennis* were detached, proceeded independently for Kerama Retto, and arrived there on 17 June. She was replenished and then returned to the area southwest of Okinawa to resume flight operations. Two days later, *Wake Island* received a message detaching her from TG 32.1 due to battle damage received on 3 April and a subsequent finding by the Bureau of Ships that "pending yardwork, this vessel is considered unsafe for operations in a forward area." She headed for Guam and conducted firing practices and launched LASP sorties en route. Upon her arrival at Port Apra on 24 June, all personnel of squadron VOC–1 were transferred to Naval Air Base, Agana.

Between 25 June and 3 July, *Wake Island*, loaded with nine Hellcats, 24 Corsairs, 11 Avengers, and two Piper Cubs, made a round-trip to Okinawa and delivered aircraft with 46 ferry pilots to Tactical Air Force, Yontan Field, Okinawa.

Arriving back at Guam, the escort carrier unloaded ammunition and aviation spares and took on board 300 sacks of United States mail along with 10 Corsair and 20 Helldiver duds for transportation, then sailed for Pearl Harbor in company with *Cape Esperance* (CVE–88) and *Bull* (APD–78). On July 10th, she detached *Bull* and *Cape Esperance* and proceeded independently to Hawaii. A week later, the ship arrived at Ford Island, Pearl Harbor, where she unloaded her cargo and took on board 138 enlisted men and 49 officers as passengers to the continental United States. On 18 July, *Wake Island* cleared the channel at Pearl Harbor, bound for southern California. She arrived at San Diego, Calif., on 25 July and discharged her passengers and planes.

While moored at North Island, San Diego, the escort carrier took on board six Avengers, 10 Wildcats, 53 officers, and 13 men of squadron VC–75 for training and carrier aircraft landing qualifications off San Nicholas Island. She continued to conduct flight qualifications through December 1945.

This period was distinguished on 5 November when the first jet-propelled landing on an aircraft carrier was made on *Wake Island*. Personnel of VF–41 and representatives of the Ryan Company came on board during the morning, and the escort carrier got underway from the Naval Air Station, San Diego, in company with *O'Brien* (DD–725). For two days, she conducted tests and landing qualifications for the jet-propelled FR–1's (Fireballs).

With the new year 1946, *Wake Island* prepared for inactivation. She was decommissioned on 5 April; struck from the Navy list on the 17th; and subsequently sold for scrap to the Boston Metals Co., Baltimore, Md., on 19 April 1946.

Wake Island earned three battle stars during World War II.

Wakefield

The birthplace of George Washington, located in Westmoreland County, Va.

(AP–21: dp. 33,560; l. 705'0''; b. 86'0''; dr. 30'9''; s. 21.5 k.; cpl. 934; a. 4 5'', 4 3'', 8 .50-cal. mg.)

Manhattan—a passenger liner built for the United States Lines at Camden, N.J., by the New York Shipbuilding Co.—was launched on 5 December 1931; and sponsored by Mrs. Edith Kermit Roosevelt, widow of former President Theodore Roosevelt.

After trials in and off the Delaware River, *Manhattan* departed New York City at midnight on 10 August 1932 for her maiden Atlantic crossing. Arriving at Hamburg 10 days later, she made the return voyage to New York in 5 days, 14 hours, and 28 minutes—a record for passenger liners. Proudly carrying the title of "the fastest cabin ship in the world," the liner continued to ply the North Atlantic from New York to Hamburg, via Cobh, Ireland; Southampton, England; and Le Havre, France, into the late 1930's. When Germany recalled her ships from the high seas during the Munich crisis in September 1938, *Manhattan* was en route to Hamburg but immediately came about and put into British and French ports instead, to bring back anxious American travelers who feared that they would be engulfed in a European war.

After war broke out a year later, she made voyages to Genoa and Naples, Italy. Following the Allied collapse in the lowlands of western Europe in the spring of 1940, she made a transatlantic crossing in July to repatriate American nationals from Portugal. With the European war endangering commercial shipping of neutral nations, *Manhattan* was then withdrawn from the once-lucrative transatlantic trade and placed in intercoastal service from New York to San Francisco, via the Panama Canal and Los Angeles.

In February 1941, during her third voyage to California, *Manhattan* ran aground off West Palm Beach, Fla., but was pulled free by tugs after the ship was lightened. After the ship was repaired at New York, the Government chartered her on 6 June 1941 for a two-year period and renamed her *Wakefield*. Converted to a troop transport at Brooklyn, N.Y., by the Robins Drydock Co., her costly furnishings and trappings of a luxury cruise liner were carefully removed and stored for future use. All of the ship's external surfaces were painted in Navy camouflage colors. On 15 June 1941, *Wakefield* was commissioned, with Comdr. W. N. Derby, USCG, in command.

On 13 July, *Wakefield* departed New York to participate in joint Navy-Marine-Army-Coast Guard amphibious training exercises at New River Inlet, N.C., in late July and early August. In early November, the troopship proceeded to Halifax, Nova Scotia, to take on board British troops. *Wakefield*, with 6,000 men embarked, and five other transports got underway on 10 November for Capetown, South Africa. Escorted by a strong screen—which, as far as Trinidad, included *Ranger* (CV–4)—the convoy arrived at Capetown on 8 December, the day after Japan bombed Pearl Harbor. This drastic change in the strategic situation prompted the convoy to be rerouted to the Far East. On 29 January, *Wakefield* and *West Point* arrived at Singapore to disembark troops doomed later to capture by the Japanese upon the fall of the city in the following month.

On 30 January, *Wakefield* commenced fueling at Keppel Harbor for the return voyage and awaited the arrival of some 400 British women and children who were being evacuated to Ceylon. At 1100, lookouts spotted two formations of Japanese bombers—27 planes in each—approaching the dock area at Keppel Harbor. Unhampered by antiaircraft fire or British fighter planes, the enemy bombers droned overhead and released a brief rain of bombs on the waterfront. One bomb hit 50 yards off *Wakefield*'s port quarter, and another blew up in the dock area 40 feet from the transport's bow before a third struck the ship's "B" deck and penetrated through to "C" deck where it exploded in the sick bay spaces. A fire broke out, but it was extinguished in less than one-half hour. Using oxygen masks, fire-fighting and damage control crews extricated five dead and nine wounded. Medical assistance soon came from *West Point*.

Completing her fueling, *Wakefield* embarked her passengers and got underway soon thereafter, burying her dead at sea at 2200 and pushing on for Ceylon. After disembarking her passengers at Colombo, the ship found that port authorities would not cooperate in arranging for repair of her damage. *Wakefield*, therefore, promptly sailed for Bombay, India, where she was able to effect temporary repairs and embark 336 American evacuees. Steaming home via Capetown, the transport reached New York on 23 March and then proceeded to Philadelphia for permanent repairs.

Underway on 11 May for Hampton Roads, *Wakefield* arrived at Norfolk two days later to load cargo in preparation for Naval Transportation Service Operating Plan "Lone Wolf." This provided for *Wakefield* to travel, for the most part, unescorted—relying on her superior speed to outrun or outmaneuver enemy submarines. On the 19th, she embarked 4,725 marines and 309 Navy and Army passengers for transportation to the South Pacific and moved to Hampton Roads to form up with a convoy bound for the Canal Zone. Arriving at Cristobal on the 25th, *Wakefield* was released from the convoy to proceed west. After *Borie* (DD–215) escorted her out of the Canal Zone, *Wakefield* proceeded independently to New Zealand and arrived at Wellington on 14 June. Departing one week later, the transport steamed via the Panama Canal and reached New York on 11 July.

On 6 August 1942, *Wakefield* departed New York with Convoy AT–18—the largest troop convoy yet assembled. A dozen troop transports made up the bulk of the convoy, escorted by 12 warships—cruisers and destroyers. After proceeding via Halifax to Great Britain, *Wakefield* received orders routing her and three other transports to the River Clyde, where they arrived without incident. On 27 August, *Wakefield* departed the Clyde estuary as part of Convoy TA–18, bound for New York.

While the transport was en route to her destination, on the evening of 3 September, fire broke out deep within the bowels of the ship and spread rapidly. In the port column of the formation, *Wakefield* swung to port to run before the wind while fire-fighting began immediately. Ready-use ammunition was thrown overboard to prevent detonation; code room publications were secured, and sick bay and brig inmates were released. *Mayo* (DD–422) and *Brooklyn* (CL–40) closed to windward to take off passengers, a badly-burned officer, and members of the crew not needed to man pumps and hoses. Other survivors were disembarked by boat and raft, to be picked up forthwith by the screening ships.

At 2100, *Brooklyn* again came alongside to remove the remainder of the crew, while a special salvage detail boarded the ship. On 5 September, towing operations commenced, and the big transport nosed aground at McNab's Cove, near Halifax, at 1740 on the 8th. When fire-fighting details arrived alongside to board and commence the mammoth operation, fires still burned in

three holds and in the crew's quarters on two deck levels. Four days later, the last flames had been extinguished, and the ship was refloated on the 14th.

While *Wakefield* was undergoing partial repairs in Halifax harbor, a torrential rainstorm threatened to fill the damaged ship with water and capsize her at her berth. Torrents of rain, at times in cloud-burst proportions, poured into the ship and caused her to list heavily. Salvage crews, meanwhile, cut holes in the ship's sides above the waterline, draining away the water to permit the ship to regain an even keel. For the next 10 days, the salvagers engaged in extensive initial repair work—cleaning up the ship, pumping out debris, patching up holes, and preparing the vessel for her voyage to the Boston Navy Yard for complete rebuilding.

Temporarily decommissioned, the charred liner proceeded for Boston with a four-tug tow, and was declared a "constructive total loss." The Government purchased the hulk from the United States Lines and stripped the vessel to the waterline. Construction began, and a virtually new *Wakefield* arose, Phoenix-like, from her ashes.

The repairs and alterations began in the fall of 1942, and lasted through 1943. On 10 February 1944, *Wakefield* was recommissioned at Boston, with Capt. R. L. Raney, USCG, in command. She departed Boston on 13 April, beginning the first of 23 round-trips in the Atlantic theater, and three in the Pacific. Between 13 April 1944 and 1 February 1946, *Wakefield* transported 110,563 troops to Europe and brought some 106,674 men back to America—a total of 217,237 passengers.

In many cases, *Wakefield* operated as a "lone wolf," except for air coverage a few miles out of a port. Her primary port of call in the European theater was Liverpool—visited so often in fact that the transport's crew nicknamed her "The Boston and Liverpool Ferry." The average round-trip voyage took 18 days.

After D day, 6 June 1944, *Wakefield* began the first of her trips as a casualty-evacuation ship, bringing home wounded GI's. On occasion, she also brought back German prisoners of war for internment in the United States. Sometimes she even carried both evacuees and prisoners on the same voyage. After 13 trips to Liverpool, *Wakefield* was sent to the Mediterranean theater to carry men and equipment to Italy. She made three visits to Naples and a run each to Marseilles, Oran, Taranto, Le Havre, and Cherbourg. Returning from her 22d voyage to Europe, the transport departed Boston on 4 December 1945 for Taku, China, and a "Magic Carpet" mission—returning to San Diego, Calif., on 1 February 1946. Two round trips to Guam, in February

Wakefield (AP–21) in dark wartime gray, with a small "trellis" mast supporting radar antennas. As a naval ship, she carries only a few small boats, but each side of her superstructure is lined with large life floats.

through April 1946, rounded out the ship's active service as a Navy transport.

Mooring at New York on 27 May 1946, *Wakefield* was decommissioned on 15 June—five years to the day since she first entered service. Laid up in reserve, out of commission, at New York, she remained there into the 1950's, until disposed of by the Navy in 1957. After a brief tour with the National Defense Reserve Fleet, *Wakefield* was struck from the Navy list in 1959 and scrapped in 1964.

Wakiva II

(Yacht: t. 853 (gross) ; l. 239'6''; b. 30'6''; dr. 15'0'' (mean) ; s. 15 k.; a. 4 3'', 2 .30-cal. mg.)

Wakiva II—a steel-hulled steam yacht built at Leith, Scotland, by Ramage and Ferguson—was launched on 3 February 1907 for Lamon V. Harkness. The graceful yacht served the Harkness family—first for Lamon V. and then for his son Harry—and ranged from the North Sea to the Netherlands East Indies in the halcyon days before the first World War. After the United States entered this conflict on the side of the Allies the Navy acquired *Wakiva II* on 20 July 1917 and commissioned her on 6 August at the Boston Navy Yard, Lt. Comdr. Thomas R. Kurtz in command.

While shipwrights were still laboring to complete the conversion of the erstwhile pleasure craft to a man-of-war for "distant service," Capt. Thomas P. Magruder hoisted his burgee pennant in *Wakiva II* as Commander, Squadron Four, Patrol Force, on 18 August. With the necessary alterations completed on the ship one week later, she set sail for Provincetown, Mass., in company with six French subchasers and the remainder of the squadron—a collection of converted fishing craft and patrol boats—and departed the east coast on 26 August for France.

Wakiva II paused at Ponta Delgada in the Azores from 6 to 11 September—towing *P. K. Bauman* (SP–377) part of the distance from the United States, due to a breakdown in the SP boat's propulsion system—and arrived at Brest on 18 September. Nine days later, Capt. Magruder hauled down his pennant to establish headquarters ashore. Released from this "flag" duty, *Wakiva II* soon commenced her convoy watchdog duties on the high seas on 28 September, putting to sea to meet a convoy 75 miles west of Ushant.

Wakiva II operated on patrol and escort duty out of Brest, France, from the fall of 1917 to her loss the following year. On 28 October 1917, when transport *Finland* was torpedoed, *Wakiva II* and *Alcedo* (SP–166) teamed to pick up survivors—standing towards the sinking ship soon after she was hit. *Wakiva II* lowered two boats and manned one of the transport's lifeboats—eventually rescuing 126 men before setting course for Brest. On 23 November, the yacht's lookouts sighted an object 500 yards distant which looked initially like a submarine's conning tower. Going to general quarters, the yacht sped towards the contact and commenced fire with her forward guns. After the warship had loosed seven shots, a closer investigation disclosed that the object of their attack—which resulted in the destruction of the object—was a convincingly painted target.

Her first actual head-to-head encounter with the enemy came within a week. *Wakiva II* sailed from St. Nazaire on 28 November to join up with a west-bound convoy. The passage proceeded uneventfully until oiler *Kanawha* fired off two Very pistol stars and sounded a loud blast on her siren. Thus alerted, *Wakiva II* sounded general quarters and rang down for full speed ahead. While *Noma* (SP–131) also closed to screen the vulnerable and valuable fuel carrier on the starboard side, *Wakiva II* took up station on the port beam. Thirty minutes of painstaking search revealed nothing to the hunters, however, and the three ships returned to the van of the convoy.

No sooner had the search been discontinued when *Noma* suddenly sounded another alarm and dropped a depth charge on what her lookouts felt was a submarine. Her crew at general quarters, *Wakiva II* sped to the scene to assist in the hunt and, at 1902, while still one and one-half miles from *Noma*, sighted a periscope 100 yards away. Putting over hard-a-port, *Wakiva II* commenced fire with her after guns—her third salvo was thought to have sheared the periscope. As the yacht passed over the suspected submarine the second time, she dropped a depth charge barrage—all of which exploded and sent oil and debris to the surface, indicating that they had heavily hit the enemy submersible. Two hits on the wreckage, fired from number one gun, added the coup de grace to what appeared to be a shattered submarine. *Wakiva II* made a third pass and sighted three men clinging to wreckage, but by the time the yacht had come full circle, all that remained was the heavy smell of fuel oil and bits and pieces of wreckage on the surface of the sea.

Wakiva II's commanding officer glowingly praised his crew's performance in the subsequent after action report, noting their work as a "perfect fighting unit." His men showed "admirable coolness and courage," and did not manifest any nervousness or inefficiency. *Wakiva II* —while receiving credit for only a "probably seriously damaged" submarine, by the Admiralty—was nonetheless commended by Vice Admiral Henry B. Wilson, commanding naval forces on the coast of France, and Admiral William S. Sims, commanding United States Naval Forces in European waters.

On 12 February 1918, *Wakiva II*, while in company with *Corsair* (SP–159) and *May* (SP–164), sighted a submarine running on the surface dead astern. Signalling the report of the sighting to the three merchantmen in the small convoy—*Munindies, Florence H.,* and *Thorwald Halvorsen*—*Wakiva II* commenced fire with number two and four 3-inch guns, checking fire momentarily to avoid hitting *Florence H.* which was steaming just beyond where the enemy submarine had suddenly appeared. The U-boat quickly submerged, and the yacht remained at the scene for 90 minutes before abandoning the search.

Wakiva II maintained a schedule of patrol and escort out of Brest through the late winter. On 21 May, she steamed in convoy with a group of eight ships on the port flank, heading eastward from the French coast. As fog set in shortly after sunset, speed was reduced. The ships crept along with *Wakiva II* taking station on the freighter *Wabash* (Id. No. 1824). Zigzagging ceased with the onset of the murky weather, and *Noma* sent a message to the convoy commodore, in *Black Arrow,* to this effect.

By 0300 on the 22d, visibility improved—but only briefly—before the convoy slipped into another fog bank. The sounds of whistles from the loosely assembled shipping pierced the gloomy dawn; and, at 0310, those on watch in *Wakiva II* distinctly heard *Wabash*'s whistle but could not see the ship. As another blast from the cargo vessel sounded even closer soon thereafter, Lt. Comdr. E. G. Allen, commanding the yacht, ordered the helm put over to port, one point, and the whistle sounded. Ten seconds later, *Wabash* loosed another blast, even closer.

Suddenly, the shape of the cargo vessel loomed out of the mist and bore down, inexorably, on *Wakiva II.* Ringing down full speed ahead, Allen ordered a turn to port—but before the helm could be put over, *Wabash*'s stem tore into the yacht's starboard quarter, just abaft the mainmast and forward of the after guns, and ripped a mortal gash in the ship's side from the main deck down to the propeller shaft. On board *Wakiva II,* there had been barely enough time to reach the general alarm. The collision threw both ships briefly on parallel courses, carrying away *Wabash*'s starboard boats. Both ships also hung together briefly before parting, with the cargo vessel slowly going astern.

While two men were lost on board the patrol vessel,

individual acts of heroism occurred simultaneously. Upon feeling the shock of the collision and hearing the general alarm, Chief Gunner's Mate Oliver P. Cooper, USNRF, ran aft to the fantail where the depth charges were secured, withdrew the bursting pins from the British mines stored there, and set the American depth charges on "safe." He reported that all was "secure" within five minutes of the collision.

Electrician Second Class Charles E. Kirkpatrick, UNSRF, on watch in the ship's radio room, remained at his post and sent out the SOS—remaining on board until abandoning at the last possible moment. Chief Boatswain's Mate Thomas Olson, USNRF, rigged out the motor whaleboat and rousted out men from below-decks, and then, along with the captain, inspected and cleared the ship. Below, as the engine room filled with water, Machinist Mate First Class Charles A. A. Smith began to start the pumps before realizing that at the rate at which the water was cascading in through the rent in the ship's side, the pumps could not hold their own.

As Wakiva II sank by the stern, the captain and his crew pulled clear in the ship's boats at 0330. The yacht disappeared beneath the waves six minutes later, as Wabash simultaneously lowered her undamaged boats and assisted in picking up survivors from the doughty yacht.

Wakonda

A term used by tribes of the Sioux family when praying. The word is also applied to objects or phenomena regarded as sacred or mysterious.

Wakonda (YTB–528)—a Hisada-class large harbor tug slated for construction at Jacksonville, Fla., by the Gibbs Gas Engine Co.—was cancelled in October 1945.

Wakulla

A river, a village, a county, and a group of springs—all located in Florida.

I

(Freighter: dp. 12,186; l. 423'9''; b. 54'0''; dph. 29'9''; dr. 24'2'' (mean); s. 11.5 k.; cpl. 62; a. 1 5'', 1 6-pdr.)

The first Wakulla—a steel-hulled, single-screw cargo vessel built under a contract from the United States Shipping Board (USSB) at Los Angeles, Calif., by the Los Angeles Shipbuilding and Drydock Co.—was launched on 14 January 1918; acquired by the United States Navy on 22 June 1918; and commissioned on 26 June, at San Francisco, Lt. Comdr. Albert J. McAlman, USNRF, in command.

Wakulla—designated Id. No. 3147—loaded a capacity cargo of flour and sailed for the east coast of the United States on 21 July. En route, the freighter underwent repairs at Balboa, Panama, from 11 to 18 August. Making port at New York on 27 August, Wakulla bunkered, underwent further repairs, and sailed for Sydney, Nova Scotia, on 7 September. Six days later, the cargo vessel joined a convoy bound for the British Isles and made arrival at Dublin, Ireland, on 29 September.

After unloading her cargo there, Wakulla shifted to Liverpool, England, late in October. Underway from Liverpool on 9 November, Wakulla was en route to New York when the armistice of 11 November stilled the guns of World War I.

Loading a cargo of foodstuffs earmarked for the French Government, Wakulla departed New York a week before Christmas of 1918, only to turn back for repairs, arriving back at New York on 21 December. She remained under repairs into 1919 before finally departing, sailing again for France on 28 January 1919. Arriving at Bordeaux on 19 February, Wakulla discharged her cargo; loaded 1,000 tons of Army ordnance materiel; and departed France on 29 March, bound for home. After arriving at New York on 13 April, she was decommissioned at Hoboken, N.J., on 18 April 1919 and simultaneously struck from the Navy list.

Returned to the USSB, Wakulla operated actively out of Los Angeles, Calif., until 1923, when she was laid up, in reserve. The cargo vessel remained in this status until abandoned, due to age and deterioration, during the first half of 1931.

II

(AOG–44: dp. 2,300; l. 221'0''; b. 37'0''; dph. 15'0''; s. 15.0 k.; cpl. 58; a. 1 3'', 6 20mm.; cl. Mettawee; T. T1–M–A2)

The second Wakulla (AOG–44) was laid down on 31 October 1944 under a Maritime Commission contract (MC hull 2070) at Bayonne, N.J., by the East Coast Shipyards, Inc.; launched on 17 December 1944; sponsored by Mrs. J. I. McClain; accepted by the Navy on 15 January 1945; converted to naval use at the builder's yard; and commissioned at the New York Navy Yard on 3 February 1945, Lt. Clifford G. Pickering in command.

Wakulla in "dazzle" camouflage during her brief World War I service. (NH 65036)

Following trials in Long Island Sound and shakedown out of Norfolk, Va., *Wakulla* got underway on 23 March 1945 for the Netherlands West Indies. She loaded a full cargo of diesel oil and high-octane gasoline at Aruba and shaped course westward. She passed through the Panama Canal from 5 to 7 April, arrived at San Diego on the 22d, and got underway for the Hawaiian Islands on the 30th. Assigned to Service Squadron (ServRon) 8 soon after her 11 May arrival at Pearl Harbor, *Wakulla* subsequently made one voyage to Canton Island in the Phoenix group and two to Johnston Island—each time with full cargoes of high-octane gasoline. During one of her cruises to Johnston, she interrupted unloading operations to put to sea and tow *LST–765* into port after a damaged screw and an inoperable rudder had left the tank landing ship adrift.

Wakulla served as yard oiler at Pearl Harbor through VJ-day. After ServRon 8 was disestablished in September, the gasoline tanker operated under the dual control of the Commandant, 14th Naval District, and Commander, Service Force, Pacific Fleet, into late 1945. She sailed for the west coast in January 1946 and was decommissioned at San Francisco, Calif., on 13 June 1946. *Wakulla* was struck from the Navy list on 19 July 1946 and transferred to the Maritime Commission on 14 November 1946.

Waldegrave

William Waldegrave—born on 9 July 1753—entered the Royal Navy as a midshipman in 1766 and served for three years in the Mediterranean on board *Jersey*. In ensuing years, he served in *Quebec*, *Montagu*, *Portland*, and was given his first command, sloop *Zephyr*, on 23 June 1775. Assignments of increasing responsibility followed. In 1778, he assumed command of *Pomona* and took her to the West Indies where he captured the renowned American privateer *Cumberland*.

His distinguished service as captain of *Courageux* off Toulon in 1793 helped to win him promotion to rear admiral in 1794. He became a vice admiral in the following year and was made peer in 1800 as the first Baron Radstock. Upon his retirement on 29 April 1802, he became admiral. He died on 20 August 1825.

(DE–570: dp. 1,300; l. 306'0''; b. 37'0''; dr. 9'0''; s. 26.0 k.; cpl. 200; a. 3 3'', 1 2-pdr., 2 40mm., 8 20mm., 2 dct., 6 dcp., 1 dcp. (hh.); cl. *Buckley*)

Waldegrave (DE–570) was laid down on 16 October 1943 at Hingham, Mass., by the Bethlehem-Hingham Shipyard; launched on 4 December 1943; and transferred to the Royal Navy under lend-lease on 25 January 1944, when she was commissioned for service under the white ensign as HMS *Waldegrave* (K.579). She served in the Royal Navy for the duration of World War II, garnering "battle honors" for her operations in the Atlantic and in the English Channel.

Returned to the United States after World War II, the ship was accepted on 3 December 1945 and was subsequently struck from the Navy list on 21 January 1946. Sold, three times in succession—first to the Atlas Steel and Supply Co. of Cleveland, Ohio; then to the Kulka Steel and Equipment Co. of Alliance, Ohio, and last to the Bristol Engineering Co. of Somerset, Mass., on 8 December 1946, the erstwhile "Captain-class" escort vessel was scrapped in June 1948.

Waldersee, see *Graf Waldersee*.

Waldo County

A county in southern Maine. It is centrally located on the state's Atlantic coast.

(LST–1163: dp. 2,440; l. 384'; b. 56'; dr. 17'; s. 13 k. (tl.); cpl. 567; a. 3 3''; cl. *LST–1156*)

Waldo County (LST–1163) was laid down in August 1952 at Pascagoula, Miss., by Ingalls Shipbuilding Corp. simply as *LST–1163*; launched on St. Patrick's Day 1953; sponsored by Mrs. C. Richard Shaeffner; and commissioned on 17 September 1953, Lt. Comdr. Robert H. Steinkellner in command.

LST–1163 departed Pascagoula on 14 October and steamed via Key West, Port Everglades, and Charleston to her permanent home port, the amphibious base at Little Creek, Va. She arrived at Little Creek on 25 October. Exercises and shakedown training occupied the remainder of 1953 and the first few months of 1954. On 14 June 1954, the tank landing ship departed Little Creek for Morehead City, N.C., to embark marines for amphibious exercises. She arrived at Morehead City on the 15th, loaded troops and equipment, and got underway on the 16th for Vieques Island located near Puerto Rico in the West Indies. The ship reached Vieques on 21 June and conducted amphibious training until 1 July when she headed back to Little Creek. She arrived at Little Creek on 5 July and remained there eight days before entering the Norfolk Naval Shipyard on 13 July. She left the shipyard on 6 August and returned to Little Creek to resume duty with the Amphibious Force, Atlantic Fleet. For the remainder of the year, *LST–1163* conducted a series of amphibious exercises, mostly at Vieques in the West Indies, but she also participated in one cold weather exercise at Hamilton Inlet on the coast of Labrador in November.

On 18 January 1955, she entered the Philadelphia Naval Shipyard for her first major overhaul. She emerged from the yard, revitalized, on 20 May and resumed duty with the Amphibious Force. On 1 July 1955, *LST–1163* became *Waldo County* (LST–1163). Through the summer of 1955, *Waldo County* remained close to or in Little Creek; however, on 24 August, she departed the Norfolk area for her first overseas deployment. After stops at Bordeaux in France, Port Lyautey in Morocco, and at Gibraltar, she joined the 6th Fleet in the Mediterranean late in September. For the next four months, she ranged the length and breadth of the "middle sea," conducting 6th Fleet amphibious exercises and making port visits. On 25 January 1956, she departed Port Lyautey on her way home. The ship returned to Norfolk on 6 February and resumed operations with the 2d Fleet.

In her first two years of active service, *Waldo County* established a pattern of operations which endured until the end of 1964. She alternated five Mediterranean deployments with periods of duty out of Little Creek conducting amphibious training at such places as Vieques Island, Onslow Beach in North Carolina, and at various locations in the Canadian maritime provinces. During her second Mediterranean deployment, which lasted from August of 1957 to February of 1958, she acted as a unit of the contingency force established in the eastern Mediterranean during the civil unrest in Lebanon. The remaining three deployments were more routine in nature, consisting only of training missions and port visits. Between her third and fourth deployments to the 6th Fleet, she earned the Armed Forces Expeditionary Medal in November and December of 1961 when she cruised Cuban waters as a part of another contingency force established in response to the wave of government terrorism which followed the abortive Bay of Pigs invasion. Otherwise, the periods between deployments consisted entirely of routine 2d Fleet operations, primarily amphibious training missions at the previously named locations.

Waldo County returned to Little Creek from her fifth and last Mediterranean cruise on 17 November 1964. At that point, she began a new phase of her career. No longer did she deploy to the 6th Fleet. For the remaining six years of her active career, the tank landing ship confined her operations to the Atlantic seaboard and the West Indies. The ubiquitous amphibious exercises predominated; but, on two occasions, she did perform special missions. In May and June of 1965, she again earned the Armed Forces Expeditionary Medal when she joined another contingency force in the West Indies during a period of extreme internal unrest in the Dominican Republic quelled by the intervention of forces of the Organization of American States. The following year, she qualified for that award again by returning to the island republic once more. From that time on, *Waldo County* broke her routine of Atlantic coast-West Indies operations only one time. In January 1970, she steamed to the Panama Canal and transited it for a brief series of landing exercises on the Pacific side of the isthmus. She retransited the canal on 2 February and resumed operations in the West Indies. Normal operations occupied her time until September at which time she began preparations for inactivation.

Waldo County was decommissioned sometime in October 1970, and she was berthed with the Atlantic Reserve Fleet at Orange, Tex. She remained there until May of 1972 at which time she was reactivated for service with the Military Sealift Command (MSC). Operated by a civil service crew in a non-commissioned status, USNS *Waldo County* served with MSC only briefly, about 18 months. Her name was struck from the Navy list on 1 November 1973, and she was transferred to the Maritime Administration for layup with its National Defense Fleet located at Suisun Bay, Calif. As of January 1980, she remained at Suisun Bay.

Waldron

John Charles Waldron—born on 24 August 1900 at Fort Pierre, South Dakota—received an appointment as midshipman from his home state on 16 June 1920 and graduated with the United States Naval Academy Class of 1924. Following his initial sea duty in *Seattle* (CA-11), Waldron went to Pensacola, Fla., where he received his wings in the summer of 1927.

Over the ensuing months, Waldron flew with Torpedo Squadrons (VT) 1S and 9S and received his commission as lieutenant (jg.) on 16 February 1928. He served at the Naval Academy from 24 May to 13 September 1929, where he instructed midshipmen in the field of aviation. Then, after duty as an instructor at the Naval Air Station (NAS), Pensacola, between October of 1929 and June of 1931, Waldron went to sea again, this time with Scouting Squadron (VS) 3B, based on board *Lexington* (CV-2), reporting for duty on 1 July 1931.

Waldron then flew observation aircraft off *Colorado* (BB-45), before he flew with Patrol Squadron (VP) 1B, Battle Force, for a brief period in late 1936. Subsequently flying from *Saratoga* (CV-3) with Fighter Squadron (VF) 3 until the early summer of 1939, he reported back to NAS, Pensacola, for further instructor's duty on 27 June 1939.

Waldron then served three successive tours of shore duty, all involving flying, at the Naval Proving Ground, Dahlgren, Va.; the Bureau of Ordnance, Washington, D.C.; and finally in the 3d Naval District, where he was appointed naval inspector of ordnance at the plant of Carl L. Norden, Inc., in New York—makers of the famed Norden bombsight.

Detached from the last-named duty in the summer of 1941, Lt. Comdr. Waldron reported for duty with the newly-formed VT-8, part of the embryonic air group being assembled to embark in the new fleet carrier *Hornet* (CV-8), then completing at Newport News, Va. The Pearl Harbor attack, though, meant that the training had to be intensive. Waldron molded what was initially a group of young men barely dry behind the ears in aviation into a confident team.

"Torpedo 8" did not get a chance to practice its trade, however, until nearly 10 months after it had been commissioned at Norfolk. Too late to take part in the

Battle of the Coral Sea, VT-8 would receive its brutal baptism of fire at the turning point of the Pacific war —the battle of Midway.

For the days previous to that battle, VT-8 led a relaxed existence on board the carrier as she steamed toward "Point Luck" from Pearl Harbor those first few days of June 1942. Finally, on the eve of battle, Commander Waldron called his men together and distributed a mimeographed plan of attack. He concluded by saying that if worst came to worst, he wanted each man to do his utmost to destroy the enemy. "If there is only one plane left to make a final run-in," he told his men, "I want that man to go in and get a hit. May God be with us all. Good luck, happy landings, and give 'em hell."

The next day, 4 June, the 15 Douglas TBD-1 Devastators of VT-8 launched from *Hornet*'s flight deck in search of the enemy. While the dive-bomber and fighter units from that carrier made a wrong turn and thus missed contact with the Japanese Fleet, Waldron found it and, grimly aware of the lack of fighter protection, resolutely decided to lead Torpedo 8 in to the attack—unprotected.

All of the planes fell to the murderous slashing attacks by the enemy's combat air patrol of Mitsubishi "Zero" fighters. Waldron and his gunner perished, as did 13 other pilots and 14 rear-seat men. Of the 30 men who set out to find the Japanese that morning, only one—Ens. George H. Gay, Jr., USNR—survived to tell the tale of Torpedo 8. Their sacrifice, however, had not been in vain. The vulnerable TBD's had drawn off the fighter cover for the Japanese carriers and forced the ships themselves to maneuver radically. With no fighters aloft and launching operations temporarily disrupted, the enemy lay open to the Douglas SBD Dauntlesses from *Yorktown* (CV-5) and *Enterprise* (CV-6) that dove to the attack and changed the course of the battle.

Torpedo 8 earned the Presidential Unit Citation; Lt. Comdr. Waldron received the Navy Cross posthumously, as well as a share of the unit citation.

(DD-699: dp. 2,200; l. 376'6''; b. 40'; dr. 15'8''; s. 34 k.; cpl. 336; a. 6 5'', 12 40mm., 11 20mm., 10 21'' tt., 6 dcp.; cl. *Allen M. Sumner*)

Waldron (DD-699) was laid down on 16 November 1943 at Kearny, N.J., by the Federal Shipbuilding & Drydock Co.; launched on 26 March 1944; sponsored by Miss Nancy Waldron; and commissioned at the New York Navy Yard on 7 June 1944, Comdr. George E. Peckham in command.

Waldron conducted shakedown in the vicinity of Bermuda during the early summer of 1944. She conducted post-shakedown availability at New York from 22 July until 6 August and then headed back to the Bermuda area for further training. The destroyer returned to New York in mid-September but got underway again on the 26th. Steaming via the Delaware capes, the warship arrived at the Panama Canal on 1 October. She transited the canal that same day and reported for duty with the Pacific Fleet. She departed Balboa on 4 October, stopped at San Pedro, Calif., from 12 to 14 October, and arrived in Pearl Harbor on 20 October. She remained in the Hawaiian Islands until 17 December, at which time she got underway for the western Pacific. She arrived in Ulithi lagoon on 28 December and reported for duty in the screen of the Fast Carrier Task Force (TF-38/58).

Waldron spent her entire World War II service with the fast carriers. She departed Ulithi with TF 38 on 30 December and protected the carriers while they launched their planes against enemy installations on 3 and 4 January 1945. On the 6th and 7th, her charges' aircraft pummeled targets on the island of Luzon. Both raids were part of the preparations for the amphibious assault on Luzon carried out at Lingayen Gulf on 9 January. While the troops stormed ashore there, however, *Waldron* and the carriers had returned north to suppress enemy air power on Formosa during the actual assault. That same day, she steamed through Bashi Channel into the South China Sea with TF 38 to begin a series of raids on Japan's inner defenses. First on the agenda came Camranh Bay in Indochina, where Admiral Halsey hoped to find battleships *Ise* and *Hyuga*. Unknown to the American Fleet, however, was the fact that the two Japanese warships had moved south to safer waters at Singapore. The raids went forward anyhow on 12 January, and the naval aviators still managed to rack up a stupendous score: 44 ships sunk, 15 of which were Japanese combatants and the remainder being merchant ships. After fueling on the 13th, TF 38, with *Waldron* still in the screen, carried out air attacks on Hainan Island and on Hong Kong. The following day, the planes of TF 38 returned to Formosa for antishipping sweeps and attacks on the Formosa airfields.

On 16 January, the carriers launched their planes against Hainan and Hong Kong once more. Late on the 20th, *Waldron*—on the antimine and antisubmarine patrol—led TF 38 out of the South China Sea through Balintang Channel and into the Philippine Sea. The destroyer and her charges returned to their base at Ulithi on the 26th after conducting strikes on Formosa and on Okinawa.

Waldron remained at Ulithi until 10 February at which time she got underway again with TF 58, this time to support the assault on Iwo Jima scheduled for the 19th. As a part of that support, the carriers planned to carry out the first carrier-based air strikes on Japan since the Halsey-Doolittle Raid of 1942. On 16 and 17 February, the carriers of TF 58 sent their aircraft aloft for raids on the Tokyo area of Honshu. The task force then began its retirement to Iwo Jima, there to provide air support for the following day's invasion.

On the night of 17 and 18 February, *Waldron*'s task group encountered several small Japanese patrol craft. One of the craft attacked *Dortch* (DD–670) with her 3-inch guns, killing three of the destroyer's crewmen. Due to darkness and the proximity of *Dortch* and *Charles S. Sperry* (DD–697), *Waldron* could not bring her battery to bear. Instead, she laid on a course for the enemy craft and charged her at 21 knots. At about 0509 on the 18th, *Waldron* rammed the Japanese picket boat amidships and cut her neatly in two. About four hours later, the destroyer received orders detaching her from TF 58 to head for Saipan and repairs to her bow.

The warship arrived at Saipan on 20 February, completed repairs quickly, and departed Saipan in the afternoon of the 23d. Upon arrival off Iwo Jima on the 25th, *Waldron* reported to TF 51 for temporary duty with the transport screen. During that assignment, she also provided naval gunfire support for the troops operating ashore on the 26th and 27th. On 27 February, the destroyer rejoined the screen of TG 58.3. After an air strike on Okinawa on 1 March, she headed back to Ulithi with the carriers, arriving there on 4 March.

Ten days later, *Waldron* exited the lagoon once again on her way back to the Japanese home islands with the fast carriers. She arrived in Japanese home waters on 18 March, and the carriers began launching strikes on Kyushu airfields that same day. Later that day, the enemy counterattacked with kamikazes and succeeded in crashing *Franklin* (CV–13). *Waldron* was one of the ships assigned to cover the severely damaged carrier during the initial stage of her retirement from action. Antiaircraft action continued throughout the three days *Waldron* provided escort for *Franklin*; and, on the night of 20 and 21 March, the destroyer scored a kill of her own when her radar-directed main battery brought down a Japanese "Judy." She took another intruder under fire briefly that night, but technical problems prevented a second kill. On 22 March, she rejoined the main carrier force and resumed her screen-

ing duties while the planes struck at Okinawa and Kyushu in preparation for the invasion of Okinawa.

For the next three months, *Waldron* continued to screen the carriers during their support missions for the Okinawa campaign. During that time, she was engaged in a number of antiaircraft actions and participated in two shore bombardments of air installations on Minami Daito Shima. The one antiaircraft action which resulted in a definite kill for the destroyer occurred on 14 May, although she claimed four sure assists in addition during that period. On 26 May, she cleared the Ryukyus with her task group and, on 1 June, arrived at San Pedro Bay, Leyte, for a much-needed availability. The destroyer remained at San Pedro Bay until 1 July at which time she returned to sea with TF 38.

For the remainder of World War II, she steamed with the fast carriers during the final strikes on the Japanese home islands. The 15 August cessation of hostilities found her still off the Japanese coast in company with TF 38. She screened the carriers while their aircraft covered the initial occupation of Japan. That duty lasted until 10 September, at which time she finally entered Tokyo Bay.

During the immediate postwar period, *Waldron* remained in the Far East in support of American occupation forces. In addition to Japan, she visited Saipan, Eniwetok, and Okinawa during the repatriation of Japanese—both military and civilian—back to Japan. On 4 November, she departed Okinawa, bound for home. After stops at Eniwetok and Pearl Harbor, the warship arrived at San Francisco on 20 January 1946. From there, she moved to Portland, Oreg., whence she departed on 4 February. The destroyer transited the Panama Canal on 14 February and arrived in Norfolk on the 19th.

Waldron operated along the east coast of the United States for about three months. Early in May, she began an extended repair period at the Boston Naval Shipyard and did not return to active service until the end of the year. During the first few months of 1947, the destroyer operated out of Charleston, S.C.; but, by June, she had been reassigned to New Orleans. For the next two years, she cruised the waters of the Gulf of Mexico and the West Indies as a training platform for reservists of the 8th Naval District. In August of 1949, she made a visit to Norfolk, Va., before getting underway for a deployment to European waters on 6 September. During the first part of that deployment, *Waldron* cruised northern European waters visiting British and western European ports. Midway through November, however, she transited the Straits of Gibraltar and entered the Mediterranean Sea. She cruised the length and breadth of the Mediterranean, making a number of port visits, until 28 January 1950 when she retransited the Straits of Gibraltar. She arrived back in Norfolk on 7 February but remained only until the 16th on which day she made the brief voyage to Charleston, S.C. Following preinactivation overhaul, *Waldron* was decommissioned on 17 May 1950 and was berthed with the Charleston Group, Atlantic Reserve Fleet.

Less than six weeks later, however, events in the Far East transpired which brought her back into active service before the end of the year. On 25 June, the forces of communist North Korea invaded the Republic of Korea to the south. The compelling need to send most available active combat ships to the Far East to support the United States' and United Nations' commitment to help the South Koreans meant that many others in reserve had to be reactivated to take their places. Accordingly, the decision to reactivate *Waldron* came on 17 August, just three months after her decommissioning.

On 20 November 1950, *Waldron* was recommissioned at Charleston, Comdr. James C. Shaw in command. She conducted shakedown training out of Guantanamo Bay, Cuba, from December 1950 to March 1951. After post-shakedown availability at Charleston, she moved to her new home port, Norfolk, in August. In September, she departed Norfolk for a 10-week cruise to northern European waters before entering the Mediterranean for duty with the 6th Fleet. Early in February 1952, the destroyer returned to Norfolk and resumed 2d Fleet operations from that base.

During the summer of 1952, *Waldron* voyaged to Europe once more with Naval Academy midshipmen embarked for their summer training cruise. She completed that voyage in September and returned to Atlantic Fleet duty out of Norfolk. In March 1953, the warship began an overhaul at the Charleston Naval Shipyard. She completed repairs in June and conducted refresher training in the Guantanamo Bay operating area before resuming normal operations out of Norfolk at the end of the month.

On 2 November, the destroyer departed Norfolk for a tour of duty in the Far East. She transited the Panama Canal on the 9th and continued her voyage west. She stopped at Pearl Harbor along the way and arrived in Yokosuka, Japan, on 9 December. Her duty in the Orient took her to Japanese and Korean ports, and she served as a unit of the United Nations security forces on patrol in the wake of the cessation of hostilities in Korea the previous summer. That assignment lasted until 7 April 1954, at which time she departed Sasebo for home. Steaming via Hong Kong, Singapore, Ceylon, the Suez Canal, the Mediterranean Sea, and the Atlantic Ocean, *Waldron* completed a circumnavigation of the globe at Norfolk on 4 June.

In July, the ship resumed normal operations along the east coast and in the West Indies. That duty continued until the spring of 1956. On 1 April, she stood out of Chesapeake Bay on her way to the Mediterranean for her second tour of duty with the 6th Fleet.

Over the next decade, *Waldron* alternated operations out of Norfolk with a series of deployments to the 6th Fleet in the "middle sea." In June of 1962, the destroyer began a fleet rehabilitation and modernization (FRAM) overhaul at the Norfolk Naval Shipyard to update her antisubmarine capabilities. At the conclusion of those alterations, the warship returned to normal operations and completed her decade of deployments and duty in home waters.

The summer of 1967, however, brought a different, though by no means new, type of assignment—duty in the Far East. On 5 July 1967, she stood out of Norfolk, bound for the Panama Canal. The destroyer transited the canal on 10 July. After stops at San Diego and Pearl Harbor, she arrived in Yokosuka on 10 August. She departed Yokosuka on 13 August and, after stops at Okinawa and Subic Bay, arrived in Vietnamese waters on the 24th. Patrolling near the 17th parallel, she provided gunfire support for the III Marine Amphibious Force (MAF) during operations ashore against communist forces. That first line period lasted until 17 September when she got underway for a port visit to Kaohsiung, Taiwan. She stopped at Kaohsiung from 20 September to 1 October and then moved on to Hong Kong, which port she visited between 2 and 6 October.

On the 9th, she resumed naval gunfire support duties in Vietnamese waters, this time off the coast of the II Corps tactical zone. During her second tour on the gunline, *Waldron*'s main battery supported troops of the Army's 1st Air Cavalry Division and of the South Vietnamese 40th Division. On 20 October, she concluded her assignments on the gunline and headed for Yankee Station to join the fast carriers of TF 77. Two days later, she rendezvoused with Task Group (TG) 77.8 for two weeks of planeguard duty with the carriers. She departed the war zone again on 3 November and, after a stop at Okinawa, arrived in Yokosuka on the 8th.

A week later, she headed back to Yankee Station with TG 77.8 but parted company with the group on the 18th for a stop at Subic Bay. *Waldron* returned to Vietnamese waters on 24 November and took up naval gun-

fire support duties once again off the coast of the II Corps zone. That assignment endured until 10 December when she cleared the war zone for the last time. She made a stop at Subic Bay and then arrived in Yokosuka on 22 December.

Four days later, the destroyer set out for the United States. After stops at Midway and Pearl Harbor, she arrived in San Francisco on 9 January 1968. From there, she headed via San Diego to the Panama Canal which she transited on the 25th. *Waldron* reentered Norfolk on 30 January.

Over the next two years, the destroyer resumed her schedule of Atlantic coast operations alternated with two more deployments to the Mediterranean. On 1 April 1970, *Waldron* was reassigned to Naval Reserve training under the control of the Commandant, 6th Naval District. Her new home port was Mayport, Fla. She arrived there on 7 May 1970 and began cruises along the Florida coast and in the West Indies training reservists. That duty lasted until the fall of 1973. On 30 October 1973, *Waldron* was decommissioned at Mayport. She was simultaneously transferred, by sale, to the Colombian Navy, in which she was commissioned as ARC *Santander* (DD–03). Her name was struck from the Navy list on 31 October 1973. As of the beginning of 1980, *Santander* was still active with the Colombian Navy.

Waldron earned four battle stars during World War II and one battle star for service during the Vietnam conflict.

Walke

Henry A. Walke—born on Christmas Eve 1809 in Princess Anne County, Va.—was appointed a midshipman on 1 February 1827 and reported for duty at the navy yard at Gosport, Va. (Norfolk). Walke received his initial naval training at Gosport and, from July 1827 to November 1828, cruised the West Indies in sloop *Natchez* in the campaign against pirates in that area. He made a voyage to the Mediterranean in *Ontario* between August 1829 and November 1831. Walke received his warrant as a passed midshipman on 12 July 1833 and, after several months of post-sea duty leave, transferred to duty ashore at the Philadelphia Navy Yard on 7 March 1834. Between January 1836 and June 1839, he cruised the Pacific Station in the 74-gun ship-of-the-line *North Carolina*, primarily along the western coast of South America protecting American commerce during a period of unrest caused by strained relations between the United States and Mexico and the war between Peru and Chile.

During service in the receiving ship at New York, Walke was promoted to lieutenant before reporting on board *Boston* on 5 October 1840. While Lt. Walke was assigned to that sloop of war, she made a cruise to the East Indies. Returning home in 1843, he went ashore for an extended leave before returning to sea in the brig *Bainbridge* in May 1844 for a cruise along the Brazilian coast.

He returned home early in 1846 and, after a year assigned to the receiving ship at New York, made an eight-month voyage in *Vesuvius* during which his ship participated in the Mexican War, blockading Laguna and supporting landings at Tuxpan and Tabasco. In October 1847, Lt. Walke went home for another extended leave after which he reported back to the receiving ship at New York on 22 September 1848.

On 23 June 1849, he returned to sea in *Cumberland* for a cruise to the Mediterranean which lasted until mid-January 1851. Following a post-voyage leave, he reported to the Naval Observatory on 22 April for a very brief tour before beginning further duty in the receiving ship at New York. That tour lasted three years, from 17 July 1851 to 17 July 1854, but consisted of two distinct periods separated by a very short tour of duty in *St. Mary's* during September of 1853.

In January 1861, as the American Civil War approached, Comdr. Walke found himself on board *Supply* at Pensacola, Fla. On the 12th, Capt. James Armstrong surrendered the navy yard to Confederate forces from Alabama and Florida. After providing temporary support for the defenders of Fort Pickens who refused to follow Armstrong's example, Walke took off some of the loyal sailors and navy yard employees and got underway for New York on the 16th. After arriving at New York on 4 February, the commander and his ship loaded supplies and reinforcements for Fort Pickens. *Supply* set sail on 15 March and anchored near the fort on 7 April and landed the troops and supplies.

Operations supporting the nascent Union blockade occupied the ship for the next month, at the end of which Walke received orders to New York to take command of one of the Navy's newly acquired steamers. Following that service—during the summer of 1861—and a four-day tour as lighthouse inspector for the 11th District early in September, Walke headed west in response to orders to special duty at St. Louis, Mo.

That assignment proved to be the command of *Tyler*, one of the river gunboats of the Army's Western Flotilla. In September and October, he took his gunboat downriver to bombard Confederate shore batteries at Hickman and Columbus in western Kentucky and traded a few shots with the Confederate gunboat *Jackson*. Early in November, his ship supported Grant's move on the Southern camp at Belmont, Mo., escorting troop transports, bombarding shore batteries and, finally, covering the withdrawal of Grant's mauled forces.

In mid-January 1862, Comdr. Walke assumed command of the ironclad gunboat *Carondelet*, also assigned to the Western Flotilla. In February 1862, during his tenure as *Carondelet*'s commanding officer, Walke led her during the captures of Forts Henry and Donelson which guarded the Tennessee and Cumberland Rivers, respectively. In April, he led her in the passing of heavily fortified Island No. 10 and in the attack on and spiking of shore batteries below New Madrid, Mo. From April through the end of June, his ship participated in the drawn-out series of operations against Plum Point Bend, Fort Pillow, and Memphis. On 15 July, Comdr. Walke almost met his match when the Confederate ironclad ram *Arkansas* made its move down the falling Yazoo River toward Vicksburg. *Carondelet* supported by *Queen of the West* and Walke's former command, *Tyler*, engaged the Southern ironclad. During the brisk opening exchange, *Carondelet* suffered heavy damage and was forced out of action in a disabled, though floating, condition. *Queen of the West* retreated immediately, leaving only little *Tyler* to face the powerful ram. The Southern warship, consequently, made it safely to the stronghold at Vicksburg.

On 4 August 1862, Walke was promoted to captain and assumed command of the ironclad ram *Lafayette* then under conversion from a river steamer at St. Louis. He put her in commission on 27 February 1863 and commanded her during the dash past Vicksburg on 6 April and during the duel with shore batteries at Grand Gulf on the 29th. That summer, his ship briefly blockaded the mouth of the Red River early in June.

Later, on 24 July, Capt. Walke was ordered back to the east coast to prepare the sidewheeler *Fort Jackson* for service. He put her in commission on 18 August 1863 at New York, but his command of that steamer proved brief. On 22 September, he was transferred to the screw sloop *Sacramento*, which he commanded through the final two years of the Civil War, cruising the South American coast in search of Confederate commerce raiders. On 17 August 1865, he was detached from *Sacramento* and returned home to await orders.

On 31 July 1866, Walke was promoted to Commodore. From 1 May 1868 until 30 April 1870, he commanded the naval station at Mound City, Ill. While waiting orders to his next assignment, Walke was promoted

to rear admiral on 20 July 1870. He was placed on the retired list on 26 April 1871. However, his service to the Navy did not end for, on that same day, he reported for some variety of special duty under the senior admiral of the Navy, Admiral David Dixon Porter. That tour lasted until 1 October at which time he was appointed to the Lighthouse Board. Detached on 1 April 1973, he retired to a life of writing and sketching until his death on 8 March 1896 at Brooklyn, N.Y.

I

(Destroyer No. 34: dp. 742 (n.); l. 293'10''; b. 26'1½'' (wl.); dr. 9'5'' (aft) (f.); s. 29.5 k.; cpl. 86; a. 5' 3'', 6 18'' tt.; cl. *Paulding*)

The first *Walke* (Destroyer No. 34) was laid down on 5 March 1910 at Quincy, Mass., by the Fore River Shipbuilding Co.; launched on 3 November 1910; sponsored by Miss Mildred Walke Walter, granddaughter of Rear Admiral Walke; and commissioned on 22 July 1911 at the Boston Navy Yard, Lt. Charles R. Train in command.

Upon commissioning, *Walke* was assigned to the 9th Division, Atlantic Torpedo Fleet. After fitting out at Boston, she moved to the Torpedo Station at Newport, R.I., where she loaded torpedoes for training with the Atlantic Torpedo Fleet. During the fall and winter, the destroyer conducted battle practice and torpedo-firing exercises with the destroyers and submarines of the torpedo fleet. In addition, she operated with the larger units of the Atlantic Fleet itself during training in more comprehensive combat drills. Those exercises covered the entire Atlantic coast from Cape Cod in the north to Cuba in the south.

Such operations occupied the destroyer until 1 November 1913, when she was placed in reserve at the New York Navy Yard. Though in reserve for the next 17 months, *Walke* never went out of commission. During her semi-retirement, the ship retained a commanding officer and at least a partial crew. Though not active with the Fleet, she did get underway periodically to keep her machinery in good working order while always remaining close to New York.

In July 1915, the destroyer returned to fully active service, first to participate in the Independence Day celebration at Perth Amboy, N.J., and then to visit Washington, D.C., for the Grand Army of the Republican celebration in late September. By 5 October, she found herself off Newport, R.I., with the Fleet conducting maneuvers. On 1 November 1915, *Walke* entered the Charleston Navy Yard for a major overhaul. Those repairs were completed at the end of February 1916; and, in March, the ship moved south to Key West to prepare for gunnery practice.

However, in May, revolutionary disorders broke out in the Dominican Republic; and *Walke* was dispatched to support the troops and marines landed there to restore order. Between 6 May—the day the warship departed Key West and headed for Hispaniola—and 19 June, she cruised along the coast of Hispaniola, leaving the area periodically for fuel or provisions at Ponce, Puerto Rico, or at Guantanamo Bay, Cuba. After a brief visit to Haiti, the republic occupying the western end of Hispaniola, *Walke* returned to Key West on 19 June. On 21 July, she arrived at the Norfolk Navy Yard to begin an eight-month overhaul.

The warship completed her overhaul in March 1917 and got underway on the 25th, bound for New York. She arrived at Staten Island the following day. By coincidence, *Walke* entered the New York Navy Yard on 6 April 1917, the day the United States declared war on Germany. Two weeks and four days later, she emerged from the yard ready to go into action. After patrols off New York, the destroyer voyaged to Charleston, S.C., where she arrived on 3 May. Following a 16-day visit to Charleston, she headed north and arrived back in New York on the 20th. Three days later, she put to sea bound for European waters. Because of her limited fuel capacity, the destroyer made the first three days of the voyage under tow by the collier, *Jupiter*. Steaming under her own power after 26 May, she arrived in Gironde, France, on 5 June. Following brief service there and at Brest, *Walke* moved to Queenstown on the southeastern coast of Ireland. From that port, she patrolled the western approaches to England and France, hunting for U-boats and escorting convoys into British and French ports until mid-November.

On 17 November, the warship headed back to the United States. Again after making the first leg of the transatlantic voyage under tow because of her limited range, *Walke* arrived in New York on 30 November. From there, she headed south to Charleston, where she entered the yard in mid-December 1917. She completed repairs in March 1918 and returned to New York on the 16th. For the remainder of World War I, *Walke* patrolled the coastal waters of the United States from New York north to Cape Cod and escorted incoming and departing convoys into and out of New York harbor.

Following the end of the war, *Walke* settled down to a routine of east coast operations and Atlantic Fleet exercises. Early in December 1918, she visited Baltimore and returned to New York on the 20th. In mid-January 1919, she moved south via Charleston to join in winter maneuvers held in the Cuba-Haiti area. Returning north by way of Key West and Miami, the destroyer reentered New York on 14 April. Between mid-April and mid-July, the warship cruised almost the entire Atlantic coast of the United States—from New York to Key West—conducting torpedo practice and various other exercises.

On 18 July, *Walke* arrived in Philadephia to begin preparations for inactivation. Decommissioned on 12 December 1919, *Walke* remained at the Philadelphia Navy Yard until the mid-1930's. She received the alphanumeric hull designation DD–34 on 17 July 1920 but lost her name 13 years later on 1 July 1933 when it was reassigned to DD–416. Known simply as *DD–34*, she was struck from the Navy list on 20 March 1935 and was scrapped at the Philadelphia Navy Yard on 23 April 1935 under the terms of the London Treaty on the Limitation of Naval Armaments.

II

(DD–416: dp. 1,960 (f.); l. 347'11''; dr. 11'5'' (mean); s. 35 k.; cpl. 192; a. 5 5'', 4 .50-cal. mg., 8 21'' tt., 2 dct.; cl. *Sims*)

The second *Walke* (DD–416) was laid down on 31 May 1938 at the Boston Navy Yard; launched on 20 October 1939; sponsored by Mrs. Clarence Dillon, grand-niece of the late Rear Admiral Walke; and commissioned on 27 April 1940, Lt. Comdr. Carl H. Sanders in command.

Following fitting-out and engineering trials, *Walke* took on board torpedoes, warheads, and exercise warheads at the Naval Torpedo Station, Newport, R.I., on 25 June and sailed for Norfolk, Va., on the following day. She reached Norfolk on the 27th and there embarked 2d Lt. Donald B. Cooley, USMC, and 47 enlisted marines for transportation to the heavy cruiser *Wichita* (CA–45)—then in South American waters. Later that same day, in company with *Wainwright* (DD–419), *Walke* got underway for Cuba.

After fueling at Guantanamo on 4 July, *Walke* got underway for Rio de Janeiro, Brazil, at 0658 on the 6th, again in company with *Wainwright*. En route, the destroyers were diverted to the mouth of the Surinam River, where *Walke* took on board an appendicitis patient from *Wainwright* for passage to Paramaribo for medical attention. After transferring the patient, Pvt. Lawrence P. Coghlan, USMC, ashore, *Walke* got underway for Para, Brazil, where she fueled before pushing on for Rio de Janeiro.

Walke and *Wainwright* reached Rio on 19 July; *Walke* then transferred her marine passengers—half of the heavy cruiser's marine detachment—to *Wichita* while *Wainwright* transferred hers to *Quincy* (CA–39). Due to unsettled conditions in the area, the two cruisers were in South American waters, "showing the flag" and evidencing strong American interest in the "good neighbors" south of the border.

Still operating in company with her sistership, *Walke* visited Rio Grande del Sol, Brazil; Buenos Aires, Argentina; Santos and Bahia, Brazil, and made a return call to Buenos Aires before rendezvousing with *Quincy* and *Wichita* on 15 August. *Walke* took on board mail, freight, and embarked passengers from *Wichita* before getting underway and steaming via Bahia and Guantanamo Bay to the Boston Navy Yard where she arrived on the morning of 4 September. *Walke* underwent post-shakedown repairs for the rest of that month and all of October before she joined the United States Fleet as a unit of Destroyer Division 4, Destroyer Squadron 2, Patrol Force. In mid-November, she served as the vehicle for degaussing tests under the auspices of the Naval Ordnance Laboratory at Solomons Island, Md. Returning to Norfolk upon the conclusion of those tests, *Walke* set her course southward on 2 December, bound once more for Guantanamo Bay.

Walke's active service had begun in the spring of 1940 when Germany was unleashing her military might in Norway and the lowlands of western Europe to turn the so-called "Phony War" into the blitzkrieg which swept across nothern France, driving British troops off the continent and knocking France out of the war. The resulting establishment of a new government in that country, more favorable to Germany, aroused fear in Allied and neutral circles that French fighting forces, particularly French warships, might be placed in German hands. *Walke* would have a role in seeing that this unfortunate development would never take place.

After fueling at San Juan on the 6th, the destroyer got underway on the afternoon of the following day on "Caribbean Patrol" in company with sistership *O'Brien* (DD–415). Rendezvousing with *Moffett* (DD–362) and *Sims* (DD–409) off Fort de France, Martinique, *Walke* and *O'Brien* patrolled the approaches to that port, keeping an eye on the movements of the Vichy French warships—the auxiliary cruisers *Barfleur* and *Quercy* and the aircraft carrier *Bearn*—through 14 December. *Walke* then visited Port Castries, British West Indies, on the 15th and embarked Comdr. Lyman K. Swenson, Commander, Destroyer Division 17, who hoisted his pennant in her that day.

Walke put into Guantanamo Bay on 19 December and remained there into the new year, 1941, moored in a nest with *Prairie* (AD–15), undergoing upkeep. In ensuing weeks, *Walke* operated in the Guantanamo Bay-Gonaives, Haiti, areas, conducting battle and torpedo practices, engaging in a full slate of the training exercises assigned such ships in those areas. She then shifted to Fajardo Roads, Puerto Rico, and operated from there through mid-March.

Walke then sailed north and arrived at Charleston, S.C., on 20 March for a period of repairs and alterations that lasted into May. She touched briefly at Norfolk between 10 and 13 May before reaching Newport, R.I.—her base for the better part of the year—on the following day.

Walke then patrolled off the Atlantic coast between Norfolk and Newport well into June, as the Atlantic Fleet's neutrality patrols were steadily extended eastward, closer to the European war zone. She departed Newport on 27 July and screened a convoy to Iceland, reaching Reykjavik on 6 August and turning toward Norfolk the same day, her charges safely delivered.

The destroyer subsequently returned to those northern climes in mid-September—after local operations in the Newport-Boston area—reaching Hvalfjordur on 14 September. She operated in Icelandic waters into late September, before she put into Argentia, Newfoundland, on 11 October, en route to Casco Bay, Maine. She began an overhaul at the Boston Navy Yard on 25 November and completed it on 7 December, the "day of infamy" on which Japan attacked Pearl Harbor and thrust the United States into war in the Pacific. Departing the yard on that day, *Walke* reached Norfolk on 12 December, via Casco Bay, and remained there until the 16th when she sailed for the Panama Canal and the Pacific.

After reaching San Diego, Calif., on 30 December, *Walke* sailed with the newly formed Task Force (TF) 17, bound for the South Pacific, on 6 January 1942, screening *Yorktown* (CV–5) as that carrier covered the movement of reinforcements for the Marine garrision on American Samoa. The convoy subsequently arrived at Tutuila on 24 January. However, TF 17 remained in Samoan waters for only a short time, for it soon sailed north for the Marshalls-Gilberts area to deliver the first offensive blow to the enemy, only eight weeks after the bombing of Pearl Harbor.

Walke served in the antisubmarine screen and plane-guarded for *Yorktown* as that carrier launched air strikes on suspected Japanese installations on the atolls of Jaluit, Makin, and Milli. Although Admiral Chester W. Nimitz, the Commander in Chief, Pacific Fleet (CinCPAC), considered the raids "well-conceived, well-planned, and brilliantly executed," the damage they actually caused was not as great as reported; and, outside of the boost they gave to American morale, the attacks were only a minor nuisance to the Japanese. Nevertheless, the American Fleet had finally taken the war to the enemy.

Returning to Hawaiian waters on 7 February, *Walke* trained in the Hawaiian area until 27 February, when she sailed for the Ellice Islands. She later exercised with TF 17 off New Caledonia in early March before she sailed, again screening *Yorktown*, for the New Guinea area, as part of the force put together to check Japanese expansion in that area.

By that time, the enemy advance to the southward, in the New Guinea-New Britain area, had gained considerable momentum with the occupation of Rabaul and Gasmata, New Britain; Kavieng, New Ireland; and on sites on Bougainville in the Solomons and in the Louisiades. By the end of February 1942, it seemed probable that the Japanese were planning to mount an offensive in early March. TF 11 and TF 17 were dispatched to the area. Vice Admiral Wilson Brown, in overall charge of the operation, initially selected Rabaul and Gasmata, in New Britain, and Kavieng, in New Ireland, as targets for the operation.

Walke then screened *Yorktown* as she launched air strikes on Tulagi in the Solomons on 4 May and later separated from that carrier with the "Support Force"—the Australian heavy cruiser HMAS *Australia*, a light cruiser HMAS *Hobart*, and the American destroyers *Farragut* (DD–348) and *Perkins* (DD–377)—to protect the southern mouth of the Jomard Passage. On the afternoon of 7 May, Japanese Aichi D3A1 "Val" dive-bombers attacked the formation, but the heavy antiaircraft fire thrown up by the ships caused the enemy to retire without scoring any hits.

An hour after the "Vals" departed, however, Japanese twin-engined bombers appeared and made a torpedo attack from dead ahead. Again, a heavy volume of antiaircraft fire from *Walke* and the other destroyers peppered the skies. Five bombers splashed into the sea, and no torpedoes found their mark on the Allied ships. Later, 19 high altitude bombers passed over, dropping sticks of bombs that splashed harmlessly into the water. Antiaircraft fire proved ineffective, due to the high altitude maintained by the planes. However, the last group of planes were apparently American planes. The force commander, Rear Admiral John G. Crace, Royal Navy, swore that the planes were B–26's; *Walke*'s commander, Comdr. Thomas E. Fraser, subsequently reported them to be B–17's. In any event, it was fortunate that the bombardiers were not too accurate.

On 7 March, Allied intelligence learned that a Japanese surface force—including transports—lay off Buna, New Guinea. On the following day, Japanese troops went ashore at Lae and Salamaua, New Guinea, and secured those places by noon.

Three days later, *Yorktown* and *Lexington* launched air strikes against the newly established Japanese beachheads at Lae and Salamaua. The attack took the enemy by surprise. The planes from the two American flattops came in from over the Owen Stanley Mountains and inflicted damage on ships, small craft, and shore installations, before they retired.

Walke remained at sea with the *Yorktown* task force into April. Detached to escort *Ramsay* (DM–16) and *Sumner* (AG–32), the destroyer reached Suva, in the Fiji Islands, on 19 April and got underway the next day, bound for the Tonga Islands. Reaching Tongatabu on the 22d, *Walke* fueled from *Kaskaskia* (AO–27) before she underwent boiler repairs and loaded depth charges prior to her return to TF 17.

Detached from the group because of a damaged starboard reduction gear, *Walke* headed to Australia for repairs and reached Brisbane on 12 May. Upon completion of the work on 29 May, the destroyer ran trials in the Brisbane River before being pronounced fit for service and sailed for New Caledonia on 9 June.

Arriving at Noumea on 13 June, *Walke* fueled there before proceeding via Tongatabu to Pago Pago, Samoa. Assigned to Task Group (TG) 12.1, the destroyer sailed on 26 June for Bora Bora in the Society Islands. With the dissolution of TG 12.1 on 11 July, *Walke* then reported for duty to Commander, TG 6.7—the commanding officer of *Castor* (AKS–1). She then escorted *Castor* to San Francisco, Calif., arriving there on 2 August.

On 7 August, while *Walke* was undergoing repairs and alterations at the Mare Island Navy Yard, the United States Navy wrested the initiative in the war from Japan by landing marines on Guadalcanal in the Solomon Islands. In ensuing months, the armed forces of the two nations struggled mightily for control of that island chain. The contest soon developed into a logistics race as each side tried to frustrate its opponent's efforts to reinforce and supply his forces fighting on Guadalcanal while doing all in his power to strengthen his own. *Walke*'s future was to be inextricably tied to the almost daily—and nightly—American air and naval attempts to best the Japanese in their thrusts down "The Slot," the strategic body of water which stretches between the two lines of islands which make up the Solomons chain and lead to Guadalcanal.

Completing the yard work on 25 August, *Walke* ran her trials in San Francisco Bay and that day received orders to proceed to San Pedro, Calif., to rendezvous with the oiler *Kankakee* (AO–39) and escorted her from the west coast of the United States—via Noumea, New Caledonia—to Tongatabu, arriving there on 9 September. The destroyer later escorted a convoy consisting of *Kankakee*, *Navajo* (AT–64), and *Arctic* (AF–7) from Tongatabu to Noumea, where she prepared for action in the Solomons.

About sunset on 13 November, the day after the Naval Battle of Guadalcanal began, *Walke* sortied with TF 64 which was built around the fast battleships *Washington* (BB–56) and *South Dakota* (BB–57) and —besides *Walke*—was screened by *Preston* (DD–377), *Gwin* (DD–433), and *Benham* (DD–397). By late in the forenoon on the 14th, TF 64 had reached a point some 50 miles south-by-west from Guadalcanal.

Sighted by the enemy—who reported them as one battleship, one cruiser, and four destroyers—the American warships spent most of the day on the 14th avoiding contact with enemy planes. From the information available in dispatches, the commander of the American task force, Rear Admiral Willis A. Lee, knew of the presence of three groups of enemy ships in the area, one of which was formed around at least two battleships.

Proceeding through the flat claim sea and disposed

in column formation with *Walke* leading, the American ships approached on a northerly course about nine miles west of Guadalcanal.

Lee's ships continued making their passage, picking up Japanese voice transmissions on the radio while the ships' radar "eyes" scanned the darkness. At 0006 on 15 November, *Washington* received a report that indicated the presence of three ships, rounding the north end of Savo Island, headed westward. Almost simultaneously the flagship's radar picked up two ships on the same bearing.

Ten minutes later, *Washington* opened fire with her 16-inch guns; and, within seconds, *South Dakota* followed suit. *Walke* opened fire at 0026, maintaining a rapid barrage at what probably was the Japanese light cruiser *Nagara*. After checking fire within a few minutes, the lead destroyer opened up again at a Japanese destroyer 7,500 yards to starboard and, later, at gunflashes off her port side near Guadalcanal.

Japanese shells straddled *Walke* twice, and then a "Long Lance" torpedo slammed into her starboard side at a point almost directly below mount 52. Almost simultaneously, a salvo of shells from one of the Japanese light cruisers hurtled down upon the hapless destroyer, a deluge of steel that struck home with devastating effect in the radio room, the foremast, below the gig davits, and in the vicinity of mount 53, on the after deckhouse. Meanwhile the torpedo had blown off the bow of the ship; and fire broke out as the forward 20-millimeter magazine blew up.

With the situation hopeless, Comdr. Thomas E. Fraser, *Walke*'s commanding officer, ordered the ship abandoned. As the destroyer sank rapidly by the bow, only two life rafts could be launched. The others had been damaged irreparably. After the crew made sure that the depth charges were set on safe, they went over the side just before the ship slipped swiftly under the surface.

As *Washington*—dueling with the Japanese battleship *Kirishima* and smaller ships—swept through the flotsam and jetsam of batle, she briefly noted *Walke*'s plight and that of *Preston*, which had also gone down under in a deluge of shells. At 0041—just a minute or so before *Walke*'s battered form sank beneath the waves of the waters off Savo Island into "Ironbottom Sound" —life rafts from the battleship splashed into the sea for the benefit of the survivors. Although the destroyer's depth charges had apparently been set to "safe," some depth charges went off, killing a number of swimming survivors and seriously injuring others. As the battle went on ahead of them, the able-bodied survivors placed their more seriously wounded comrades on rafts.

Walke's survivors were, at one point, in two groups —some clinging to the still-floating bow section and others clustered around the two rafts that ship had been able to launch. During the harrowing night, they were twice illuminated by enemy warships but not molested, before the enemy switched off his searchlights and moved on.

At dawn, however, *Walke*'s survivors—and those from *Preston*—witnessed the end of a quartet of Japanese transports beached during the night. Bombed and strafed by Army, Marine, and Navy planes—including aircraft from "The Big E"—*Enterprise* (CV–6)—the four Japanese ships received the *coup de grace* from *Meade* (DD–571) that morning, just before the destroyer altered course and picked up the destroyermen from *Walke* and *Preston*.

Meade rescued 151 men from *Walke*, six of whom later died after they were brought ashore at Tulagi. Six officers—including Comdr. Fraser—and 76 men had died in the ship's fiery end off Savo Island. She was struck from the Navy list on 13 January 1943.

Walke received three battle stars for her World War II service.

III

(DD–723: dp. 2,200; l. 376'6''; b. 41'1''; dr. 15'8''; s. 34 k.; cpl. 336; a. 6 5'', 11 20mm., 10 21'' tt., 6 dcp., 2 dct.; cl. *Allen M. Sumner*)

The third *Walke* (DD–723) was laid down on 7 June 1943 at Bath, Maine, by the Bath Iron Works; launched on 27 October 1943; sponsored by Mrs. Douglas Dillon; and commissioned at the Boston Navy Yard on 21 January 1944, Comdr. John C. Zahm in command.

After fitting out at the Boston Navy Yard, *Walke* got underway on 12 February for Washington, D.C., which she visited from the 14th to the 18th before heading for Bermuda and shakedown training. She returned to Boston on 19 March 1944 for availability before moving to Norfolk, Va., to conduct high-speed, over-the-stern fueling exercises with *Aucilla* (AO–56) under the auspices of the Bureau of Ships. From Hampton Roads, the destroyer moved to Key West, Fla., at the end of the first week in April to conduct antisubmarine warfare (ASW) tests on a new type of sound gear. She completed that duty on 17 April and headed to Norfolk where she arrived two days later

Walke (DD–723) after her FRAM modernization, with a variable-depth sonar (VDS) installation at her stern. The prominent flight deck and hangar abaft the second stack, designed for the unsuccessful drone antisubmarine helicopter (DASH), is characteristic of FRAMmed destroyers.

for almost a month of duty training nucleus crews for newly constructed destroyers.

On 12 May, *Walke* got underway for New York where she arrived the following day. On the 14th, she headed for European waters to participate in the Normandy invasion. She arrived in Greenock, Scotland, on the 24th. As a unit of Destroyer Division (DesDiv) 119, *Walke* participated in the Normandy invasion between 6 and 26 June. On the 7th and 8th, she conducted shore bombardments, destroying blockhouses and machine-gun positions as well as helping to repulse a counterattack mounted by German armored units. On the 23d and 24th, the warship supported minesweeping operations at Cherbourg and duelled with enemy shore batteries.

After the Allied ground forces had pushed the fighting front inland out of range of the destroyer's guns, *Walke* departed European waters on 3 July and arrived at the Boston Navy Yard on the 9th. Following repairs there and refresher training at Casco Bay, Maine, she sailed south and arrived at Norfolk on 26 August.

Four days later, the ship departed Norfolk in the screen of *Ticonderoga* (CV–14), bound ultimately for the western Pacific. Steaming via the Panama Canal and San Diego, Calif., the destroyer arrived in Pearl Harbor on 25 September. She conducted training exercises there for almost a month before departing the Hawaiian Islands on 23 October in the screen of *North Carolina* (BB–55). Steaming via Eniwetok and Manus, she arrived in Ulithi on 5 November. There, she became a unit of Task Group (TG) 38.4, of the fast carrier task force, with which she sortied that day for a series of air strikes on targets in the Philippines. The warship returned from that foray to Ulithi on 22 November and lay at anchor there until the 27th when she got underway with Destroyer Squadron (DesRon) 60 for the Philippines. She arrived in San Pedro Bay, Leyte, on the 29th and joined the screen of TG 77.2 operating in Leyte Gulf. She returned to the anchorage at San Pedro Bay on 4 December and remained there until the 6th when she departed with TG 78.3 to support landings from Ormoc Bay on the western coast of Leyte. The troops of the Army's 77th Infantry Division stormed ashore unopposed on the 7th, but the Japanese mounted heavy kamikaze attacks on the supporting ships in an attempt to foil the assault. During those air raids, *Walke* assisted *Mahan* (DD–364) when three kamikazes of a nine-plane raid succeeded in crashing into her. After rescuing a number of *Mahan*'s crewmen, *Walke* sent the stricken destroyer to the bottom with a torpedo and gunfire. The next day, en route back to San Pedro Bay, she helped to splash an attacking enemy aircraft. She safely reached her destination later that day and operated in Leyte Gulf and at San Pedro Bay until the 13th.

That day, she got underway with TG 77.3 to support the assault on Mindoro. She arrived off that island on 15 December as a part of Rear Admiral Berkley's close covering force, made up of one heavy cruiser, two light cruisers, *Walke*, and six other destroyers. Besides protecting the heavier elements from air and submarine attack, she destroyed by gunfire the grounded Japanese destroyer *Wakaba*. After completing that mission, she headed back to Leyte Gulf. En route, she drove off by antiaircraft fire several planes which approached her and arrived safely in San Pedro Bay on 18 December 1944.

The destroyer remained there until 2 January 1945 when she got underway for Lingayen Gulf and the invasion of Luzon. American minesweepers moved into the gulf on 6 January, and *Walke* steamed in with them to provide covering fire and antiaircraft defense. That day, four enemy "Oscars" approached the destroyer from her starboard side forward, low on the water. She opened fire and succeeded in splashing the first two attackers. The third plane pressed home his combination strafing run-suicide attack and, though hit

several times, managed to crash into *Walke*'s bridge on the port side and burst into flames. The destroyer lost all communications, radars, gyro repeaters, and electricity throughout the superstructure. She also suffered extensive damage to the bridge itself as well as to her gun and torpedo directors. The 250-pound bomb the plane carried fortunately did not explode but passed completely through the ship in the vicinity of the combat information center.

Two minutes after the first suicider crashed *Walke*, the last of the four "Oscars" began his death dive. As this attacker came in toward the destroyer's starboard quarter, he was subjected to fire from 5-inch mount number 3 in local control and from the starboard side 40- and 20-millimeter guns. Their concentrated fire saved the ship from a second crash when the plane burst into flames and splashed into the sea close aboard. Soon thereafter, control was shifted aft to secondary conn, and fires were under control within 15 minutes.

Throughout the action, though seriously wounded and horribly burned, the warship's commanding officer, Comdr. George F. Davis, continued to conn his ship and exhorted her crew to heroic efforts to save the ship. Only after he was certain that she would remain afloat and intact, did he consent to relinquish command to the executive officer and allowed himself to be carried below. Comdr. Davis succumbed to his wounds several hours later; but, for his gallant action, he was awarded the Medal of Honor, posthumously. He was further honored by having *Davis* (DD–937) (q.v.) named for him.

Amazingly, *Walke* continued to operate with TG 77.2 until after the landings on 9 January. The next day, she departed the gulf with Task Unit (TU) 78.4.2 and headed for Leyte. She arrived in San Pedro Bay on the 13th and remained there undergoing patching for two days before getting underway for the Admiralty Islands. She received further temporary repairs at Manus from 18 to 21 January and then resumed her voyage home, via Pearl Harbor. The ship reached the Mare Island Navy Yard on 6 February and began permanent repairs. The last of her extensive battle damage had been corrected by 4 April, when the ship set a course—via Pearl Harbor, Eniwetok, and Ulithi—for Okinawa where, on 10 May, she joined the campaign to capture that island. During the first part of her stay in the Ryukyus, she served as a support ship on radar picket stations around Okinawa. On 24 June, she was ordered to join the screen of Task Force (TF) 32, the Amphibious Support Force, with which she operated until 23 July. The following day, she departed the Ryukyus in the screen of a task unit, bound for Leyte, and underwent an availability at San Pedro Bay from 28 July to 14 August. On the latter day, *Walke* and *Barton* (DD–722) got underway to rendezvous at sea with TF 38. The destroyer joined the screen of TG 38.3 on 18 August—three days after hostilities ended. On 10 September, she switched to the screen of TG 38.1 and operated with the fast carriers.

The warship remained in Japanese waters until 30 September when she headed via Guam for the northwest coast of the United States. She arrived in Seattle on 24 October and operated along the western seaboard until the following spring. On 18 March 1946, the ship departed San Diego for a round-trip voyage to Pearl Harbor, returned to San Diego on 10 April, and remained there until 13 May. After steaming back into Pearl Harbor on the 19th, she departed that port again two days later, but this time she continued west toward the Marshall Islands. She reached Bikini Atoll on 26 May and, for the next two months, supported the atomic tests carried out there. She returned to Pearl Harbor on 15 August, remained overnight, and got underway for the west coast on the 16th. *Walke* entered San Diego on 22 August and then moved to the Mare Island Naval Shipyard for three months of repairs.

The warship returned to San Diego on 15 November

and remained there through the end of the year. On 6 January 1947, *Walke* departed San Diego for Pearl Harbor whence she operated with *Tarawa* (CV–40), and later with *Shangri-La* (CV–38), on special duty under the auspices of the Commander, Naval Air Force Pacific Fleet. That duty lasted until 1 May when she joined the unit sent to Sydney, Australia, to commemorate the Battle of the Coral Sea. The ship returned to San Diego in mid-June and was decommissioned there on the 30th.

Following a little over three years in the San Diego Group, Pacific Reserve Fleet, *Walke* was recommissioned on 5 October 1950, Comdr. Marshall F. Thompson in command. After shakedown training along the west coast, the destroyer departed San Diego on 2 January 1951 and set a course for the Far East and service in the six-month old Korean conflict. She repaired storm damage at Yokosuka, Japan, before joining TF 77 off the coast of Korea.

In addition to providing antisubmarine protection for the carriers of TF 77, she moved close to the Korean coast to bombard such places as Yondae Gap, Wonsan, Songjin, Chongjin, and Chuminjin as well as various other rail and road locations. On 12 June, while steaming some 60 miles off the Korean coast with TF 77, *Walke* struck a floating mine which severely damaged her hull on the port side, killed 26 men, and wounded another 40 sailors.

She made temporary repairs at Sasebo and then headed back to the United States where she entered the Mare Island Naval Shipyard in July for permanent repairs and a complete overhaul. *Walke* returned to the Korean combat zone in June of 1952 and resumed screening duty with TF 77 punctuated by shore bombardment missions. That combat cruise lasted until January 1953, when she arrived in Long Beach, Calif., and took up normal west coast operations. In July, the warship rejoined TF 77 off the Korean coast for another seven months of duty screening the fast carriers; but, by that time, the armistice had been signed ending the combat aspect of her duties.

Between the end of the Korean conflict in July of 1953 and the dramatic increase in American involvement in the Vietnamese civil war that began in August 1964, *Walke* settled into a routine which alternated peacetime deployments to the western Pacific with periods of normal west coast operations out of Long Beach. In that interval, she made six deployments to the Orient, on each occasion operating as a unit of the 7th Fleet and usually as a part of the ASW screen of the fast carriers of TF 77. She also did periodic duty as a unit of the Taiwan Strait patrol. The ship made frequent visits to such ports as Sasebo and Yokosuka in Japan, Hong Kong, and Subic Bay in the Philippines. On her return voyage from the 1956 to 1957 western Pacific cruise, *Walke* visited Brisbane, Australia, before steaming back to Long Beach on 28 April 1957.

When not deployed to the Far East, the destroyer operated along the west coast conducting ASW and gunnery training and independent ship's exercises. Much of the time spent in the United States also went to repairs and overhauls. For instance, in 1961, she received a complete fleet rehabilitation and modernization (FRAM II) overhaul.

In 1964 and 1965, however, events in South Vietnam conspired to make *Walke*'s final four deployments to the Far East combat tours. She departed Long Beach on 24 March 1965, steamed via Pearl Harbor, and arrived in Yokosuka, Japan, on 30 April. On 4 May, the destroyer headed for the Philippines. She entered Manila Bay on the 10th and joined ships of other SEATO navies. On the 12th, the warship sortied with them to participate in Exercise "Sea Horse" en route to Bangkok, Thailand. She arrived in Bangkok on 22 May and made a two-day liberty call. She returned to the Philippines, at Subic Bay, on the 28th. In June, the ship made a port call at Hong Kong and then headed to Sasebo,

Japan, for upkeep and then spent the rest of the month in operations out of Japanese ports. Early in July, *Walke* paid a visit to Kaohsiung, Taiwan, and then did a four-week tour of duty on the Taiwan Strait patrol.

The ship's first direct participation in the Vietnam conflict came in August when she served as ASW picket ship for TG 70.4 on Yankee Station in the Gulf of Tonkin. She left Vietnamese waters on the 17th for five days of upkeep at Subic Bay. She returned to Yankee Station on 27 August and resumed ASW picket duty with TG 70.4. On 4 September, the destroyer moved inshore to provide gunfire support for troops operating ashore. That duty lasted until 9 September when she rejoined TG 70.4 on Yankee Station. At Yokosuka on 19 September, she had a four-day upkeep period before heading back toward the United States on 23 September.

Walke spent the remainder of 1965 and the first five months of 1966 engaged in normal west coast operations—mostly ASW exercises. On 9 June 1966, she departed Long Beach for another deployment to the western Pacific. However, while she was passing the outer breakwater, a major fire broke out in her after fireroom. The destroyer's damage control efforts succeeded in putting the blaze out; but, while the ship was being towed back into Long Beach on the 10th, her towline parted, and she ran aground. Later that day, she finally entered the Long Beach Naval Shipyard for repairs to both her hull and her main propulsion plant.

She completed repairs on 18 July, loaded ammunition at Seal Beach, and set a course for the Far East. She reached Yokosuka on 3 August for a brief fuel stop and then continued on to Sasebo where she arrived on the 5th. She remained there until the 8th, when she got underway for Yankee Station to join the ASW screen of TG 77.9. On 16 August, she took leave of TG 77.9 and set a course for Kaohsiung, Taiwan, and a tour of duty on the Taiwan Strait patrol. On 12 September, she headed back to Yankee Station; but, three days later, a typhoon forced her into Subic Bay. She resumed duty with TG 77.9 on 17 September but remained only until the 22d when she headed for the waters near Luzon to participate in SEATO Exercise "Silverskate."

She returned to Vietnamese waters on 29 September and took up station just offshore to provide gunfire support for the troops ashore. That duty lasted until 4 October when she headed back to the Philippines for another SEATO exercise before entering Subic Bay for a nine-day tender availability alongside *Bryce Canyon* (AD–36). She stood out of Subic Bay on 18 October and reached Yankee Station on 20 October and served with the carriers there for eight days. After a visit to Hong Kong, she set a course for Taiwan and another four-week tour of duty on the Taiwan Strait patrol. She concluded that assignment on 1 December and headed for Yokosuka where she underwent an upkeep period from 6 to 9 December. On the 9th, the warship got underway to return home. She arrived in Long Beach on 20 December and began post-deployment standdown.

Walke devoted the next seven months to local operations out of Long Beach. For the most part, this duty consisted of ASW exercises conducted with aircraft carriers. On 17 August, the destroyer departed Long Beach and set a course for the western Pacific. Steaming via Pearl Harbor, the warship arrived in Yokosuka on 24 September. She operated out of Japanese ports conducting ASW exercises until 18 October at which time she got underway for Yankee Station. The destroyer joined TF 77 in the Gulf of Tonkin on 23 October and served in the ASW screen until 16 November when she retired to the Philippines. She arrived in Subic Bay on 14 November and remained there 10 days undergoing a tender availability. Following that, she put to sea to participate in another "Silverskate" ASW exercise which she completed on the 28th.

From there, the warship headed for the Gulf of Tonkin and duty with carriers on Yankee Station. That assignment lasted until 11 December at which time she moved inshore to provide gunfire support for troops operating ashore in the I Corps combat zone. On the 17th, she moved up the coast to the vicinity of the demilitarized zone between North Vietnam and South Vietnam to support troops fighting in that neighborhood. On 19 December, the ship departed Vietnamese waters and set a course for Sasebo where she arrived on the 23d.

On 3 January 1968, *Walke* departed Sasebo to return to Vietnam. She arrived in the combat zone on the 7th and spent the following month on the gunline providing gunfire support for troops fighting ashore. On 20 February, the warship shaped a course for Sasebo where she conducted an upkeep period. Following a series of ASW exercises in the Sea of Japan, she got underway on 24 March to return to the United States.

She arrived in Long Beach on 6 April and began post-deployment standdown. On 14 May, the destroyer entered the Long Beach Naval Shipyard for a four-month overhaul. At the conclusion of that repair period in September, she conducted shakedown training and then began normal west coast operations.

That duty continued until 29 March 1969 at which time she got underway for the final western Pacific tour of her career. Steaming by way of Pearl Harbor, she arrived in Yokosuka on 26 April. On the 30th, she set a course for the Tonkin Gulf. The destroyer joined the fast carriers on 5 May and provided ASW defense for them until the 15th when she headed for Subic Bay. Following upkeep at Subic Bay and a visit to Manila, she put to sea on the 26th to participate in SEATO Exercise "Sea Spirit." She returned to Subic Bay on 7 June, remained there until the 10th, and then headed back to Vietnam via Kaohsiung, Taiwan. The warship reached Yankee Station on the 19th and served in the ASW screen of TG 77.3 until July. She visited Kaohsiung again from 7 to 15 July and then headed for Sasebo where she arrived on the 17th.

The warship departed Sasebo on the 18th for Exercise "Sea King" before a brief return to Sasebo. *Walke* soon headed back toward Vietnam and reached Yankee Station on 25 July. She served there until 7 August and then headed back to Kaohsiung. She visited the Taiwanese port from 8 to 14 August and then made a call at Hong Kong from 15 to 22 August. She returned to Yankee Station on 25 August and served on the gunline until 21 September. She retired to Subic Bay on 23 September and, after five days, steamed back to Vietnam. She provided gunfire support in the I Corps combat zone and at Danang until 4 October when she shaped a course for Japan.

She conducted upkeep at Sasebo from 9 to 17 October and then got underway with *Constellation* (CVA–64) for exercises in the Sea of Japan. After a return visit to Sasebo and a stop at Okinawa, she returned to Yokosuka to prepare for the voyage home. On 6 November, the destroyer sailed for the west coast. She made stops at Midway Island and at Pearl Harbor before arriving at Long Beach on 21 November.

Walke spent her last year of active service operating along the west coast. On 30 November 1970, she was decommissioned at the Puget Sound Naval Shipyard and was berthed with the Columbia River Group, Pacific Reserve Fleet, until 1974. On 1 February 1974, her name was struck from the Navy list. She was sold to General Metals, of Tacoma, Wash., on 16 April 1975 for scrapping.

Walke (DD–723) earned six battle stars during World War II, four battle stars in the Korean conflict, and seven battle stars for Vietnam service.

Walker

John Grimes Walker—born in Hillsborough, N.H., on 20 March 1835—was appointed a midshipman on 5 October 1850 and graduated at the head of his class at the Naval Academy in 1856. He served in *Falmouth*

and *St. Lawrence* in 1858 and 1859; in *Susquehanna* in 1860 and 1861; in *Connecticut* in 1861; and in *Winona* in 1861 and 1862.

He distinguished himself under Farragut during the Mississippi River campaigns while serving in *Winona*, *Baron de Kalb* (which he commanded), and *Saco*. He participated in the engagements with Forts St. Philip and Jackson, as well as the Chalmette batteries during the operations which resulted in the fall of New Orleans. He later took part in the Navy's operations against Vicksburg. During the winter of 1862 and 1863, Walker participated in the thrusts against Haines Bluff and Arkansas Post. He also took part in the Yazoo Pass expedition, the attack on Fort Pemberton, and the capture of Yazoo City. At the siege of Vicksburg, Walker commanded the naval gun battery attached to the 15th Army Corps. His subsequent war service included operations which resulted in the capture of Fort Fisher, and he participated in the ensuing bombardments of Forts Anderson and Caswell on the Cape Fear (N.C.) River and in the capture of Wilmington, N.C.

Promoted to commander in 1866, Walker served as Assistant Superintendent of the Naval Academy from 1866 to 1869. After commanding *Sabine* in 1869 and 1870—during which time he took the ship to Europe on a midshipman training cruise—he served as secretary to the Lighthouse Board from 1873 to 1878. From 1881 to 1889, Walker held the post of Chief of the Bureau of Navigation before he went to sea commanding the White Squadron in 1889, with his flag in *Chicago*. Appointed rear admiral in 1894, he took the White Squadron to Hawaii in 1895 when a coup d'etat posed a threat to American interests. He received a commendation for his attitude of watchful waiting and his squadron's posture of readiness to respond to a possible emergency.

Upon his return to shore duty in 1896, he headed the Lighthouse Board and concurrently chaired the committee investigating locations for deep water harbors in southern California. Soon after retiring as a full admiral in 1897, Walker was chosen to serve as President of the Nicaraguan Canal Commission. Two years later, in 1899, he was appointed President of the Isthmian Canal Commission to look into possible routes for a canal across the Central American isthmus.

Admiral Walker died on 16 September 1907, at the age of 72, at Ogunquit, Maine.

I

(Destroyer No. 163: dp. 1,284; l. 314′4½″; b. 30′11½″; dr. 9′2″ (mean); s. 34.92 k.; cpl. 101; a. 4 4″, 2 1-pdrs., 12 21″ tt.; cl. *Wickes*)

The first *Walker* (Destroyer No. 163) was laid down on 19 June 1918 at Quincy, Mass., by the Fore River Shipbuilding Co. under contract from Bethlehem Steel Co.; launched on 14 September 1918; sponsored by Mrs. Francis Pickering Thomas; and commissioned at the Boston Navy Yard on 31 January 1919, Lt. Comdr. Harold A. Waddington in command.

Walker got underway on 20 February to rendezvous with transport *George Washington* as it returned from France with President Woodrow Wilson embarked. Upon completion of this duty, the new destroyer returned to Boston, where she was soon assigned to Division 18, Destroyer Force. She proceeded to Newport, R.I., and loaded her full allotment of torpedoes at the Naval Torpedo Station there. She sailed for the West Indies on 6 March and, soon after her arrival in the Caribbean, fell into the Fleet's regular schedule of exercises and maneuvers. *Walker* conducted tactical exercises off San Juan, Puerto Rico, and gunnery exercises out of Guantanamo Bay, Cuba, into the late winter and early spring of 1919 before she headed north.

After steaming into New York harbor on 14 April, the destroyer was sent to her base at Newport, R.I. Early the next month, she supported the Navy's NC-boat transatlantic flights. Initially stationed at

Trepassy Bay from 6 to 8 May, she later operated at sea from the 10th to the 17th, serving as one of the chain of picket ships to provide the NC flying boats with position reports and bearings. When this mission was completed, she returned to Newport on the 20th.

After calling at Annapolis in early June for a two-day visit during Naval Academy graduation exercises, *Walker* headed south and transited the Panama Canal on 24 July. She called briefly at Acapulco, Mex., for two days before pressing on for southern California, arriving at Coronado on 8 August.

Based at San Diego, *Walker* conducted local operations off the west coast into late 1919, when she was assigned to the Reserve Destroyer Flotilla. She embarked naval reservists for an indoctrination cruise on 27 October 1920 and remained in "rotating reserve" duty, conducting periodic target practices, full-power runs, and undergoing overhauls at the Mare Island Navy Yard. Decommissioned on 7 June 1922, as part of an austerity program, *Walker* was placed in reserve at San Diego, where she remained into the 1930's.

After 16 years on "Red Lead Row," the ship was struck from the Navy list on 28 March 1938 and slated for disposal by sale. Logistics requirements of west coast naval districts, however, resulted in the former destroyer being placed back on the list and earmarked for conversion to a water barge. Redesignated *YW–57* on 1 April 1939, the ship was undergoing conversion at the Mare Island Navy Yard when the Navy again decided to change the vessel's role. With the outbreak of war in Europe and the possibility of American involvement in the conflict, the ship was slated for use as a damage control hulk.

Designated *DCH–1* on 11 July 1940, the vessel was based at the Destroyer Base, San Diego, and used for training exercises in formulating and evolving new damage control techniques. In the following year, as the Pacific Fleet's base had been moved from San Diego to Pearl Harbor, plans were made to tow *DCH–1* (which had been stripped of propulsion machinery during the initial conversion work to *YW–57*) to the Hawaiian Islands. However, the ship—which had been redesignated *IX–44* on 17 February 1941—remained at San Diego until the Japanese attack on Pearl Harbor on 7 December 1941 filled the Pacific Fleet's need for practice damage control hulks. Accordingly, *IX–44* was taken to sea and scuttled on 28 December 1941. She was struck from the Navy list on 24 June 1942.

II

(DD–517: dp. 2,940; l. 376'5''; b. 39'4''; dr. 12'6''; s. 35.2 k.; cpl. 329; a. 5 5'', 10 40mm., 10 21'' tt.; cl. *Fletcher*)

The second *Walker* (DD–517) was laid down on 31 August 1942 by the Bath Iron Works Corp., Bath, Maine; launched on 31 January 1943; sponsored by Miss Sarah C. Walker; and commissioned on 3 April 1943, Comdr. O. F. Gregor in command.

The first seven months of *Walker*'s service took place in the Atlantic where she was engaged in Caribbean escort duty and training exercises in preparation for Pacific combat duty. The highlights of this period included the capture of 43 survivors of a Nazi U-boat which had been damaged by Navy air units off Cuba and the responsibility of escorting the Secretary of State, Cordell Hull, from San Juan, Puerto Rico, to Casablanca to participate in the Moscow Conference of October 1943.

Walker transited the Panama Canal on 1 November 1943 and proceeded to join the forces engaged in the conquest of Tarawa. After a month of operations in that area, the destroyer took part in the Marshall Islands campaign from 29 January through 8 February 1944. She joined forces at Funafuti for the invasion of Kwajalein; and, as part of a heavy cruiser bombardment unit, she participated in numerous neutralization bombardments at Wotje and Taroa. The only Japanese

resistance encountered came from shore batteries which failed to hit their mark.

From March through June 1944, *Walker* operated in the South Pacific escorting troops and transports from Guadalcanal to Bougainville and from various points in New Guinea. Other ports visited during this period were Purvis Bay, Tulagi; Empress Augusta Bay, Bougainville; Milne Bay and Buna, New Guinea.

The Marianas operation involved the invasion of Saipan, Tinian, and Guam by forces under Admiral Raymond A. Spruance. *Walker* began service assigned to an escort carrier unit providing air support for the amphibious forces headed for Guam. The group departed from Kwajalein in June; but, due to the bitterness of the campaign for Saipan, the Guam landings were postponed, and the ships returned to Eniwetok. After the need for further naval support had passed, *Walker* proceeded to Pearl Harbor for rehearsals of scheduled landings on Yap Island.

Leaving Pearl Harbor in September, *Walker* was transferred to the 7th Fleet as a fire support ship for the invasion of the Philippines. This group of transports and destroyers sailed from Manus and arrived at Leyte Gulf on 20 October. During this operation, *Walker* experienced her first air action and downed one enemy fighter plane as well as provided gunfire support in the Dulag area. The transports were rapidly unloaded and departed with *Walker* and other escorts prior to the arrival of the Japanese naval forces and the ensuing Battle of Leyte Gulf from 24 to 25 October 1944.

The group proceeded to Morotai to reload support troops for Leyte. At Morotai, nightly Japanese air attacks harassed the ships but caused little damage. The group then returned to Leyte and unloaded its troops. Suicide air attacks and torpedo bombers were encountered during this trip, but no damage was suffered. After a brief stop at Palau, *Walker* received orders to return home, and she reached the Mare Island Navy Yard, San Francisco, Calif., on Christmas Eve 1944.

The most memorable part of *Walker*'s combat service began in mid-March 1945 when, fresh from navy yard overhaul, she joined Admiral Marc Mitcher's famed Task Force (TF) 58 at Ulithi, Caroline Islands. This force proceeded to Kyushu and Honshu, Japan, for air strikes designed to neutralize and weaken Japanese air power.

Following these strikes, TF 58 proceeded to Okinawa to support the amphibious assault launched there on 1 April 1945. While alone on picket duty 12 miles from the main group, *Walker* was subjected to persistent Japanese kamikaze attacks. One suicider crashed dangerously close, its wing parting a lifeline on the forward portion of the ship. Another plane dropped a torpedo just after dark which passed close astern. During that night, *Walker*'s agile maneuvers and accurate guns beat off three more such attacks.

After 80 days at sea, the task group returned to port. During this period, *Walker* towed *Haggard* (DD–555) to Kerama Retto near Okinawa after she had been damaged by kamikaze hits.

The destroyer continued operations through July and August with the 3d Fleet and encountered no Japanese air opposition. *Walker* was among the ships which bombarded Kamaishi, Honshu, Japan, on 18 July and made a similar attack at Hammahatsu and a return trip to Kamaishi. The coming of peace resulted in *Walker* entering Tokyo after a period of air-rescue duty during the airborne phase of the occupation.

On 1 November 1945, *Walker* arrived from the forward area at San Pedro, Calif.; and, on 31 May 1946, she was placed out of commission, in reserve, at San Diego. The ship remained in "mothballs" until 15 September 1950 when she was recommissioned and converted to an escort destroyer. From the time of her recommissioning until 27 February 1951, *Walker* remained in yard overhaul.

Following a shakedown cruise, the escort destroyer

Walker (DD–517) in 1965. She retains her pole foremast, but her bridge has been enlarged and 3″/50 AA guns installed. A Weapon *Alfa* launcher has replaced her second forward 5-inch gun. (USN 1110825)

departed San Diego and participated in the atomic Exercise "Greenhouse" at Eniwetok until June 1951. The next month, the ship joined the newly formed Escort Destroyer Squadron 1 based at Pearl Harbor, Hawaii. She remained in Hawaii until November 1951 when she sailed for the western Pacific and joined the United Nations Blockading Force assisting UN ground troops in the Korean War. She escorted the fast carrier task forces which were supporting ground units with strategic air strikes. Thus ended *Walker*'s Korean War service.

Walker returned to Pearl Harbor during March 1952 and conducted type training and routine exercises for the next several months. On 2 June, the escort destroyer sailed for her second western Pacific deployment. From that time until 29 December 1963, *Walker* completed nine such deployments. These very active years were spent, for the most part, conducting anti-submarine warfare exercises and various operations with her task group and elements of the Republic of Korea Navy and the Japanese Maritime Self-Defense Force. *Walker*'s many "People to People" visits during this period helped to spread American good will abroad. Highlights of these years included assistance to the town of Koniya, Amami Oshima, which had suffered major damage from a raging fire in September 1958 and as a recovery ship for the space flight project "Mercury" on 28 September 1962.

On 4 January 1964, *Walker* commenced a two-week tender availability at Pearl Harbor with *Bryce Canyon*

(AD–36). On 31 January, the ship officially entered the Pearl Harbor Naval Shipyard for overhaul. The completion of yard overhaul on 30 April marked the commencement of local exercises in preparation for refresher training. On 19 May, *Walker* took part in the filming of the movie "None But The Brave" at the island of Kauai. After a month of refresher training and an administrative inspection, the escort destroyer underwent upkeep which took her through June.

The summer months found *Walker* engaged in local operations. On 17 August 1964, the ship continued her movie career with a supporting role in Otto Preminger's production of "In Harm's Way." During October and November, the escort destroyer underwent a pre-employment inspection and an operational readiness inspection which was concluded on 20 November, three days prior to departure for a western Pacific deployment.

On 3 December 1964, *Walker* arrived at Yokosuka, Japan, where she joined in Exercise "Tall Back" with the carrier *Yorktown*, (CVS–10), followed by duties on the junk patrol which combatted the infiltration of arms into South Vietnam from North Vietnam and communist China. During this period, the escort destroyer performed a month of uneventful duty on the Taiwan patrol.

Walker departed Vietnam waters on 27 April and, after a brief stop at Yokosuka, Japan, arrived at Pearl Harbor on the 13th of May. The remainder of May and June was spent in leave and upkeep. The escort destroyer spent the rest of the year in local operations. On 8 December, *Walker* was drydocked and spent the holiday season in leave and upkeep.

January 1966 saw the ship taking part in local operations and making preparations for an upcoming deployment. On 7 February, she commenced a six-month cruise, arriving at Yokosuka via Midway Island 10 days later. Duty in the South China Sea began on 28 February with assignments as a planeguard and as a naval gunfire support ship. *Walker's* first offensive actions of the Vietnam War occurred on 5 March in support of United States and Allied forces. This assignment was interrupted by patrol duty in the Taiwan Strait and rest and rehabilitation at Keelung, Taiwan; and Hong Kong.

Walker returned to Qui Nhon, South Vietnam, on 22 April and began support missions, shooting direct fire at the Vietcong coastal supply areas and troop concentrations. The second ship on station, *Walker* received sporadic machine gunfire from the enemy ashore while a gig was returning with spotters and advisors to the ship for a briefing. This was the first time since World War II that *Walker* had been subjected to hostile fire.

On 26 April 1966, the escort destroyer supplied direct, indirect, harassment, and interdiction support for Operation "Osage," a combined amphibious assault at Chu Lai. These duties were interrupted to escort a Marine Corps motor convoy from Danang to Phu Bai on 28 April. On the 1st of May, the ship detached and proceeded independently for repairs at Sasebo, Japan, via Buckner Bay, Okinawa.

Walker set course on 17 May for Manila Bay, Philippines, where she joined in SEATO antisubmarine warfare Exercise "Sea Imp" which lasted until 6 June. The ship next joined *Taylor* (DDE–458) for a month of patrol duty in the Taiwan Strait during which time she rescued a Nationalist Chinese fishing boat adrift for 48 hours. The escort destroyer returned to Yokosuka, Japan, on 8 July.

Instead of departing for home, *Walker* received orders to replace *Walke* (DD–723) in antisubmarine exercises in the Sea of Japan. These exercises included the Japanese Maritime Self-Defense Force and naval units of the Republic of Korea. On 24 July, a Soviet *Kotlin*-class destroyer was sighted as it commenced shadowing the Allied group. *Walker* was designated to shoulder the Russian destroyer, and she was successful in preventing the attempted penetration of the screen by the Russian ship and her replacement. *Walker* also assumed duty on 29 July as a shadow against the Soviet Elint (electronics intelligence) trawler *Izmeritel.*

On 1 August 1966, *Walker* detached and proceeded to Yokosuka from whence she began the transit to Hawaii. She arrived at Pearl Harbor on 10 August and made preparations for a yard overhaul. *Walker* entered the Pearl Harbor Naval Shipyard on 19 September and remained in overhaul status for the rest of calendar year 1966.

Regular overhaul was completed on 3 February 1967, and type training exercises, refresher training, and an operational readiness evaluation followed. On 18 April, *Walker* departed Pearl Harbor en route to Japan. From 4 to 17 May, the task group embarked on a transit of the Sea of Japan to demonstrate antisubmarine and antiair capabilities with the Japanese Maritime Self-Defense Force.

On 10 May 1967, *Walker* relieved *Taylor* (DDE–468) of screening duty for *Hornet* (CVS–12) from the Soviet *Kotlin*-class destroyer (DD–022) which was attempting to close *Hornet* and harass the task group. A collision occurred between the two ships with minor damage sustained by both ships. The next day, *Walker* was again involved in screening duties with a Soviet ship. Late in the afternoon, a Soviet *Krupnyy*-class destroyer (DDGS–025) began to maneuver in an attempt to close *Hornet; Walker* effectively maneuvered the ship away. The Soviet destroyer than signaled a left turn. *Walker* signaled "do not cross ahead of me." The Soviet ship came left and collided with *Walker* causing minor

damage to both ships. Following exercises with the Republic of Korea Navy, *Walker* returned to Sasebo, Japan, and held a news conference and interviews on board concerning the Sea of Japan incidents.

The escort destroyer arrived at the Gulf of Tonkin on 25 May 1967. *Walker* served in several capacities: providing call fire, harassment, and interdiction fire for airborne spotters; acting as a rescue destroyer for *Hornet* (CVS–12), *Bon Homme Richard* (CVA–31), and *Constellation* (CVA–64); and firing around-the-clock missions for numerous Army and Marine units.

On the evening of 15 July, while providing gunfire support south of Cape Batangan, *Walker* received notification that a North Vietnamese trawler (459) carrying arms was expected to attempt a landing in the vicinity. *Walker* provided gunfire support for the attack on the trawler and suppressed enemy fire from the beach. The trawler was beached by the crew and abandoned with large quantities of arms, ammunition, and demolition equipment recovered by American forces.

Walker joined Operation "Beacon Guide" as a naval gunfire support ship on 20 July and provided preparation fire for the amphibious and helicopter assault south of Hue. After a brief tender availability at Taiwan, *Walker* returned to the Tonkin Gulf on 9 August and operated with *Intrepid* (CVS–11) for a week prior to departure for Hong Kong.

The escort destroyer rejoined *Hornet,* and the task group arrived at Hong Kong on 16 August, then transited to Sasebo, Japan, for repairs. *Walker* returned to the Gulf of Tonkin on 7 September and was detached three days later to proceed to the Paracel Islands in the South China Sea and conduct surveillance and gather intelligence data about the Chinese communist-held islands.

Upon her return to the waters off Vietnam, *Walker* reported to *Coral Sea* (CVA–43) for duty as her escort and spent the majority of September in various antisubmarine warfare exercises. On 27 September, *Walker* rejoined *Hornet* and rescued four survivors of an aircaft which had plunged into the water after losing an engine during launch.

On 1 October 1967, the escort destroyer returned to antisubmarine warfare exercises, then headed for upkeep at Yokosuka prior to proceding to the eastern Pacific. *Walker* arrived at Pearl Harbor on the 23d of October and spent a month in post-deployment leave, type training, and a reserve cruise. Holiday leave commenced on 15 December.

Walker spent the first seven months of 1968 in her home port conducting type training and preparing for a final western Pacific deployment. On 5 August, the escort destroyer got underway on the fourth western Pacific deployment since the beginning of the Vietnam conflict. She arrived at Subic Bay, Philippines, via Midway Island and Guam on 18 August, then proceeded to Vietnam.

Planeguard duty with *America* (CVA–66) was *Walker's* first assignment. During her first night on station, she rescued a man overboard from *America.* On 13 November, *Walker* was relieved and proceeded to Subic Bay for upkeep. On 1 December, the escort destroyer arrived at the area north of Vung Tau for gunline duty which ended on 15 December.

After a fuel stop at Subic Bay, *Walker* continued to Cebu, Philippines, arriving on 18 December as part of Operation "Handclasp." The ship returned to Subic Bay on 22 December for a five-day tender availability alongside *Samuel Gompers* (AD–37). On 29 December, *Walker* returned to Vietnam for a week of planeguard duty with *Constellation* (CVA–64).

On 5 January 1969, the escort destroyer departed for visits to Hong Kong and Subic Bay. The ship joined three other destroyers and sailed for Australia and New Zealand. *Walker* and *Taylor* visited Wollongong and Melbourne, Australia; and Auckland, New Zealand, before arriving back at Pearl Harbor on the 28th of February. March was spent in leave; and, at the end of the month, *Walker* received word that she would be decommissioned.

May was spent in port at Pearl Harbor; but, on 2 June, *Walker* got underway for San Diego, the designated decommissioning site. On 2 July 1969, *Walker* was decommissioned and stricken from the Navy list. She was sold to the Italian Navy as *Fante* (D–516). *Fante* was retired from service in 1977.

Walker earned six battle stars for World War II engagements, two for service in Korea, and three for Vietnam service.

Walker, J. B., see *J. B. Walker*.

Walker, Nelson M., see *General Nelson M. Walker*.

Wallace L. Lind

Wallace Ludwig Lind, born on 18 June 1887 in Brainerd, Minn., was appointed a midshipman on 30 June 1905 and commissioned an ensign on 5 June 1911.

Ensign Lind served on *Stewart* (D–13), *Denver* (C–14), *Goldsborough* (TB–20), and *Cheyenne* (BM–10). On 31 August 1915, he departed *Cheyenne* and, one month later, arrived at the United States Naval Academy, Annapolis, Md., for a post-graduate course in steam engineering, following which he attended Columbia University for special instruction.

Lind served on board *Rhode Island* (BB–17) from 2 March to 12 July 1917 and was then detailed to New York, N.Y., for duty on board *President Lincoln* (Str) as engineering officer and, later, as executive officer. It was during this assignment that he was awarded the Navy Cross for heroism. On 4 May 1920, he reported to *Michigan* (BB–27) as first lieutenant followed by a tour as first lieutenant on *Arizona* (BB–39).

Lind assumed command of *Capella* (AK–13) on 5 June 1922 and, upon being detached from that ship, reported to the Naval Air Station, San Diego, Calif., on 18 April 1923 for duty as executive officer. Upon the completion of his duties there, he served as engineering officer of *Arizona*. This was followed by instruction at the Naval Unit, Edgewood Arsenal, Edgewood, Md., and at the Naval War College, Newport, R.I.

Into the 1930's, Lind served as executive officer of *Medusa* (AR–1), *Altair* (AD–11), and *Omaha* (CL–4); followed by shore duty at the Navy Yard, Boston, Mass. From 1935 to 1938, Commander Lind was assigned to the Office of the Chief of Naval Operations, Navy Department, Washington, D.C. During this period, he received his promotion to captain to rank from 30 June 1937. Captain Lind died on 12 April 1940 at Baltimore, Md.

(DD–703: dp. 2,200; l. 376′6″; b. 40′; dr. 15′8″; s. 34 k.; cpl. 336; a. 6 5″, 12 40mm., 11 20mm., 10 21″ tt., 6 dcp., 2 dct.; cl. *Sumner*)

Wallace L. Lind (DD–703) was laid down on 14 February 1944 by the Federal Shipbuilding and Dry Dock Co., Kearny, N.J.; launched on 14 June 1944; sponsored by Mrs. Wallace L. Lind; and commissioned at the New York Navy Yard on 8 September 1944, Comdr. G. DeMetropolis in command.

Shakedown, which took *Wallace L. Lind* from the New York Navy Yard to Bermuda and back, extended through 2 November 1944. Departing Virginia en route to the Pacific on 14 November, she transited the Panama Canal on the 27th and arrived at Pearl Harbor on 13 December and underwent upkeep and training exercises. *Wallace L. Lind* and *Tracy* (DM–19) took leave of Hawaii on 23 December, escorting *Enterprise* (CV–6) to Ulithi. *Tracy* left the formation and proceeded to Eniwetok, and she was replaced by *Frazier* (DD–607).

On 5 January 1945, the destroyer made rendezvous with Fast Carrier Task Force 38 under Admiral W. F. Halsey, Commander, 3d Fleet in *New Jersey* (BB–62). Air strikes against Luzon began on 6 January 1945 and were followed by strikes against Formosa, Saigon, the Pescadore Islands, and Hong Kong. Photo reconnaissance planes surveyed Okinawa Gunto in preparation for the upcoming invasion. On 23 January, *Wallace L. Lind* left the area north of Luzon and arrived at Ulithi three days later for upkeep.

The destroyer reported for duty with Task Force (TF) 58, a fast carrier task force, on 11 February 1945. On 16 February, carrier planes conducted raids in the Tokyo area and, the following afternoon, retired toward Iwo Jima, with the carrier planes conducting air searches en route.

On 19 February 1945, the carriers launched aircraft as cover for the initial landing of troops on Iwo Jima. These operations continued through 25 February when strikes again commenced against Tokyo. During the above actions, *Wallace L. Lind* was assigned to screen the carriers and to assist in mail deliveries and transfer of personnel.

Wallace L. Lind's destroyer group departed the Honshu area on 27 February and set course for Okinawa, arriving four days later. On 1 March, this vessel acted as a plane guard for strikes against Okinawa and Minami Daito. Upon recovery of the strike planes, the task group set course for Ulithi, Caroline Islands.

After a period of routine upkeep, drydock, and availability, *Wallace L. Lind* set course for Kyushu, where the first air strikes were launched on 18 March. Numerous enemy aircraft appeared sporadically throughout this first day. The second day saw strikes and sweeps against Kyushu targets, as well as a special sweep on Kii Suido. Two Japanese planes closed the formation, and the destroyer opened fire. Both planes were destroyed by gunfire.

Wallace L. Lind departed the area on 19 March. The destroyer temporarily joined a unit which proceeded to execute shore bombardment against Minami Daito on 28 March. The following day, strikes were launched against airfields on Kyushu. *Lind* exploded two floating mines and fired on an enemy torpedo plane which crashed shortly afterward. While commencing a southerly retirement, *Wallace L. Lind* executed a strike against Amami Gunto en route.

On 30 and 31 March 1945, strikes and sweeps over Okinawa Gunto provided cover for D day landing operations. The operations in that area continued, with intermittent strikes against Amami Gunto and refueling and rearming operations, throughout April. On 7 April, dawn search planes reported contact with units of the Japanese Fleet consisting of one battleship (later identified as *Yamato*), two light cruisers, and eight destroyers. All available planes of the three task groups, totalling 380, were launched to make the strike. Upon their return, they reported sinking the battleship, both cruisers, and three destroyers. During the month of April, *Wallace L. Lind* destroyed two enemy planes and made three assists.

The month of May was spent participating in strikes against Okinawa Gunto, Kyushu, and the Amami O'Shima-Kikai Jima area. *Wallace L. Lind* performed various duties ranging from screening the carriers to recovering downed pilots. During these operations, Japanese kamikaze planes dove on TF 58, hitting both *Enterprise* (CV–6) and *Bunker Hill* (CV–17). The destroyer participated in one shore bombardment, sank three mines, shot down three Japanese planes, and had two assists.

This marked the end of a period of continuous steaming from 14 March 1945 when *Wallace L. Lind* started from Ulithi with TF 58 in support of the Okinawa occupation. On 1 June, *Wallace L. Lind* arrived at San Pedro Bay, Philippines, and went alongside *Dixie* (AD–14) for availability through 12 June. The remainder of June was spent in various training exercises and getting the ship ready for sea.

On 1 July 1945, *Wallace L. Lind,* in company with ships of Destroyer Squadron (DesRon) 62, got underway from San Pedro Bay in advance of the heavy ships of Task Group (TG) 38.3 to provide an antisubmarine screen for their sortie. Nine days later, the vessel arrived at the area off the east coast of Honshu, Japan, and the task group launched strikes against the Tokyo plains area. *Wallace L. Lind* assumed duty as a picket station, then acted as a communication link between task groups. On 14 July 1945, she joined the carrier strikes on the east coast of Honshu and the northern Honshu-Hokkaido target area.

After refueling east of the Bonin Islands, *Wallace L. Lind* returned to the operating area off the east coast of Kyushu on 24 July. She was then in position to act as a picket in the "Able Day" strikes against the Kure area. On 30 July, the task group launched strikes at air installations in the Tokyo-Nagoya area. The next day, the ships retired on a southerly course for replenishment. On 8 August, planes hit northern Honshu and Hokkaido as well as the Tokyo plains area. *Wallace L. Lind* received official word that the war with Japan had ceased on 15 August 1945. The task group moved to the southeast of Tokyo with all ships taking precautions against attacking enemy aircraft which persisted, in some cases, despite the war's end.

On 1 September, the destroyer went alongside *Shangri-La* (CV–38) and took on board Vice Admiral John H. Towers and staff and then transported them to Tokyo Bay for the surrender ceremonies. Vice Admiral Towers shifted his flag from *Shangri-La* to *Wallace L. Lind* and, upon completion of the ceremonies the following day, returned to *Shangri-La.*

The destroyer took part in maintaining air patrols and searches over northern Japan in connection with the occupation; then, on 21 September, set course for Eniwetok. She underwent availability through 6 October and spent the remainder of the month in upkeep and training exercises in Tokyo Bay.

Wallace L. Lind and *John W. Weeks* (DD–701) departed Tokyo Bay on 31 October for Sasebo, Japan, where she spent the final months of 1945 operating between Sasebo and Okinawa. On 5 January 1946, the destroyer stopped briefly at Eniwetok before commencing her homeward journey. She arrived at her home port of Norfolk, Va., on 19 February 1946, after stopping at Pearl Harbor and San Francisco and transiting the Panama Canal.

From 9 March through 26 April, *Wallace L. Lind* underwent tender availability, a leave period, and training at Casco Bay, Maine. She then travelled to Charleston, S.C., where she underwent restricted availability and operated with *John W. Weeks* until 12 July when her home port was changed to New Orleans. *Wallace L. Lind* then commenced Naval Reserve training cruises in the Caribbean. This type of operations characterized her activity for the next several years.

On 7 January 1949, the destroyer returned to Norfolk, Va., and conducted operations out of that port until 6 September. The next day, she made rendezvous with TF 89 and commenced a Mediterranean cruise which lasted through 26 January 1950 when she returned to Norfolk, Va.

Wallace L. Lind spent the greater part of 1950 engaged in training operations and a cruise to the Caribbean. On 6 September, the destroyer sailed for the Far East and the Korean War. The ship arrived off the coast of Korea on 13 October and centered her movements around Wonsan Harbor, then under siege, with frequent interruptions for blockade patrol and bombardment missions in the vicinity of Songjin and Hungnam.

During the period 17 to 24 December, *Wallace L. Lind* took part as an active member of what was said by many to be one of the mightiest naval forces ever assembled in short range support of ground forces. This was in the defense of Hungnam and in the support of the eventual evacuation.

Throughout the entire month of January 1951, *Wallace L. Lind* operated as a member of the East Korea Blockade Group and attended to duties such as naval gunfire support and support of minesweeping operations.

The destroyer spent February conducting special intelligence missions which included shore bombardment, fire support, and screening duties in the area of Kangnung and placing intelligence teams ashore in the areas of Wonsan, Chaho, and Chongjin. The ship conducted many gunfire support missions against targets spotted by these intelligence teams. On 20 February, *Wallace L. Lind,* along with *Ozbourn* (DD–846) and *Charles S. Sperry* (DD–697), engaged in the rescue of a pilot who had crash-landed in Wonsan harbor. While the three ships were attempting rescue operations, shore batteries opened fire on them, and *Wallace L. Lind* successfully returned fire.

On 15 March 1951, a seven-ship naval bombardment of the Wonsan district resulted in reported enemy casualties of some 6,000. The following afternoon, shore batteries fired at the ships in the harbor, and counterbattery fire from the destroyers began in a matter of seconds. Gun positions were taken under fire, and several explosions were noted on the peninsula. On 17 March, *Wallace L. Lind* patrolled independently from Wonsan south along the coast. The ship took the city of Kosong under fire and exposed and silenced a camouflaged shore battery located south of Suwon Dan lighthouse.

Wallace L. Lind departed the Korean area on 9 May 1951 and arrived at Pearl Harbor 10 days later, having stopped at Yokosuka and Midway en route. She transited the Panama Canal and arrived at Norfolk, Va., on 9 June.

After a brief trip to New York, the destroyer departed Norfolk on 26 August 1952 for a Mediterranean deployment. She returned to Norfolk on 4 February 1953 and spent several months in her home port. On 19 November, the destroyer departed for refresher training at Guantanamo, returning on 14 December to spend the holiday season at Norfolk. On 4 January 1954, the ship returned to the Guantanamo area for the remainder of the month. On 31 January 1954, *Wallace L. Lind* returned to Norfolk where she remained through 10 May. Commencing 11 May, the destroyer operated off the Middle Atlantic coast and returned to her home port nine days later. On 1 June, she set course for Key West and operated in that area and the Gulf of Honduras until the 25th of June when she arrived back at Norfolk and remained there until 7 September. At that time, she again made a brief cruise off the Middle Atlantic coast before departing on a transatlantic voyage.

On 22 September, *Wallace L. Lind* arrived at Lisbon, Portugal. After a stay of five days, the destroyer departed for a brief stop at Bermuda before returning to Norfolk on 8 October. She took part in Operation "Lantflex 1–55" which ran from 20 to 29 October. On 1 November, the ship returned to Norfolk and remained at her home port through the 1st of May 1955.

On 2 May 1955, *Wallace L. Lind* got underway for a cruise to several European countries including England, Scotland, France, Germany, and Portugal as well as Reykjavik, Iceland. While in Germany, the crew had the pleasure of sailing through the Kiel Canal to participate in the International Sailing Regatta. The destroyer returned to Norfolk, Va., on 19 August and remained in port until 10 October when she set course for Philadelphia, Pa., where she underwent an extensive overhaul which lasted through 12 February 1956.

The destroyer then returned to her home port and spent several weeks before departing for Guantanamo and various training exercises which lasted through 23 March 1956. On 27 March, the ship returned to Norfolk and conducted operations in the Virginia capes area and as far north as New York. She arrived back at Norfolk on 21 June and stayed in port for approximately one month.

On 28 July 1956, *Wallace L. Lind* set course for the Middle East to screen the evacuation of American citizens during hostilities between Egypt and Israel. She arrived at Port Said and the Suez Canal on 13 August; and, for the next two months, she visited ports in Saudi Arabia, Iran, Iraq, Ethiopia, and Aden before departing the area on 14 September for Naples, Cannes, and Malta. The destroyer arrived at Phaleron Bay, Greece, on 15 October and remained through 27 October when she departed for home. On 4 December, *Wallace L. Lind* returned to Norfolk where she remained until 2 February 1957.

Departing Norfolk, the ship arrived at the operations area outside of San Juan, Puerto Rico, on 5 February. She conducted exercises through 11 February when she headed for Kingston, Jamaica, and Guantanamo before arriving back at Norfolk on 7 March 1957. *Wallace L. Lind* then operated along the east coast before finally departing Norfolk on 25 June for a Middle East deployment. The ship arrived at Norfolk on 20 November and remained there until 4 January 1958.

On 6 January 1958, *Lind* set out for a month of exercises in the Caribbean. The ship returned to Norfolk on 7 February and, one week later, went into the Norfolk Naval Shipyard for three months of overhaul. On 27 May, the destroyer returned to the naval base, then set course for Guantanamo and underwent refresher training through 18 July.

Upon her return to Norfolk, *Wallace L. Lind* conducted local operations until 24 October 1958 when she was deployed to the Mediterranean with the 6th Fleet. On 5 November, she reached Barcelona, Spain, then headed for the Middle East, making stops in the areas of the Suez Canal, Red Sea, Gulf of Aden, and the Persian Gulf. On 14 January 1959, the destroyer arrived at Livorno, Italy, and spent the remainder of the cruise operating between Italy and Spain. She made a brief stop at Cannes, France, before starting the trip homeward. *Wallace L. Lind* arrived at Norfolk, Va., on 8 April 1959 and participated in services and type training until July when she entered the Norfolk Naval Shipyard for an interim refitting and docking period. For the remainder of the year, she operated from her home port, making trips to Mayport, Fla., and Narragansett Bay, R.I., acting under the control of COMASWFORLANT for duty with the antisubmarine warfare hunter/killer forces.

Wallace L. Lind operated with these forces through 29 June 1960 when she took on board 27 NROTC midshipmen for their annual training cruise. The destroyer demonstrated her antisubmarine warfare proficiency during this six-week outing which included stops at Halifax, Nova Scotia, and New York City.

Throughout August and September, the destroyer prepared for NATO fall exercises in the North Atlantic. On 6 September, she sailed from Norfolk and spent four weeks operating at sea with NATO forces. It was during this cruise that she crossed the Arctic Circle, and all were initiated into the Royal Order of the Blue Noses.

After returning to Norfolk on 20 October, *Wallace L. Lind* kept occupied with type training and miscellaneous services until December when she rejoined COMASWFORLANT for a brief assignment with the hunter/killer forces.

Wallace L. Lind welcomed in the new year, 1961, while at sea with COMASWFORLANT. On 13 February, she sailed for the Caribbean and "Springboard 61." She returned to Norfolk, Va., conducted local operations, and underwent upkeep commencing on 26 May.

On 1 June 1961, *Wallace L. Lind*'s tender availability was interrupted when the destroyer was ordered to proceed, in company with other units of the 2d Fleet, to the Dominican Republic. After three weeks of carrier task group operations, antisubmarine warfare, and shore bombardment exercises, the international crisis in that area lessened, and the destroyer returned to Norfolk on 20 June.

Lind provided services as a DesLant Gunnery School ship at Newport, R.I., from 23 June until 7 July. While participating in "Lantflex 2–61," the destroyer spent the period between 17 and 27 July with midshipmen from the Naval Academy embarked on their summer cruise.

From 11 August until 22 September 1961, the ship participated in Project "Mercury" and was assigned to an area just south of the Canary Islands. She returned to Norfolk on 22 September and remained in upkeep status through 1 October.

On 16 October, *Wallace L. Lind* began a pre-FRAM availability; and, one month later, she underwent FRAM II conversion. This overhaul amounted to a complete renewal of her after superstructure, a new and modern combat information center, and modernization or complete overhaul of almost all machinery, weapons systems, and living accommodations. Changes to weapons systems involved adding to the previously installed Hedgehog mounts two new side torpedo racks amidships for current inventory torpedoes. Immediately aft of the torpedo deck on the 01 level of the new superstructure, a hangar area and flight deck, from which the new Drone Antisubmarine Helicopter (DASH) could operate, was installed. Also installed was a variable depth sonar rig adding coverage for submarine search at various depth levels.

Wallace L. Lind was declared ready for sea on 25 August 1962. On 7 September, she arrived at Guantanamo for refresher training. After successfully completing the final operational readiness inspection on 17 October, the destroyer departed Guantanamo for Culebra Island, thence to Key West. However, while en route to Florida, the Cuban Missile Crisis intervened; and, on 21 October, the ship returned to Guantanamo. When the immediate crisis had ended, *Wallace L. Lind* returned to Norfolk on 28 November and commenced a needed in-port period of upkeep and preparation for the final outfitting with DASH.

The destroyer followed a two-week visit to Key West as a Fleet Sonar School ship in March 1963 with a trip to Argentia, Newfoundland. This voyage north was interrupted by the tragic news of the loss of *Thresher* (SSN–593). *Wallace L. Lind*, which was in the immediate vicinity at the time, joined in the search.

The destroyer completed the year's competitive exercises in May and was occupied with rocket and missile firings in June. She participated in the development acceptance program incident to Polaris missile firings for *Lafayette* (SSBN–616) off Cape Kennedy. During this period, *Wallace L. Lind* hosted the Commander in Chief, Atlantic Fleet and Commander, Submarine Force, Atlantic Fleet as observers of the launches. She also hosted the Secretary of Defense, the Secretary of the Navy, and the Chairman of the Joint Chiefs of Staff. *Wallace L. Lind* became the first operationally qualified DASH destroyer in the Atlantic Fleet during trials in July of 1963.

In November 1963, the destroyer joined the operational forces of COMASWFORLANT and participated in an antisubmarine warfare demonstration for the American Helicopter Society in the Narragansett Bay area. During ensuing antisubmarine warfare operations with Task Group Bravo, *Wallace L. Lind* engaged fast nuclear submarines in hunter/killer operations and proved herself fully ready as a unit of the "HUK Team."

Upon completion of a Christmas leave and upkeep period in January 1964, *Wallace L. Lind* departed for antisubmarine warfare barrier operations in the Caribbean and participated in Operation "Springboard." In early March, the destroyer acted as the special project ship for the Gemini/Apollo test program. Large cranes were installed on the fantail for recovery of space cap-

The modernized *Wallace L. Lind* (DD–703) in the 1960s. (KN–22465)

sules, and *Lind* worked with NASA officials successfully recovering mock-up capsules.

During April and May, *Wallace L. Lind* joined Task Group Bravo for antisubmarine warfare operations; and, in April, she took part in Operation "Quick Kick," a large fleet exercise. Having undergone restricted availability for hull and bottom work at the Newport News Shipbuilding and Drydock Co., the ship spent the month of July in preparation for a forthcoming Mediterranean deployment.

On 3 August 1964, *Wallace L. Lind* departed for the Mediterranean and served as flagship for Capt. Maylon T. Scott, Commander, Destroyer Division 22. She participated in exercises as part of a fast carrier task force and conducted numerous community relations programs in the various ports visited. The destroyer returned to Norfolk, Va., three days before Christmas after earning a well-deserved leave and upkeep period.

Wallace L. Lind remained moored at the Naval Destroyer and Submarine Pier, Norfolk, Va., until 25 January when she got underway and exercised independently. On 29 January, she moored at the Naval Base, San Juan, Puerto Rico, and conducted local operations in the San Juan operating areas through 8 February. The destroyer arrived at Norfolk on 12 February and remained moored until late March when she got underway for refueling and rearming. She returned to the

Norfolk Naval Shipyard on 31 March for regular overhaul followed by drydock in May. On 28 June 1965, *Wallace L. Lind* got underway for two days of trials in the Virginia capes operating area. She returned to her berth at Norfolk and remained there for almost a month.

The ship got underway on 23 July for Key West, Fla., where she conducted various antiair and antisubmarine warfare exercises. She finished the month at Port Everglades, Fla. On 5 August, *Lind* arrived at Mayport, Fla., and, four days later, took departure for Guantanamo Bay, Cuba, arriving on 12 August.

Having successfully completed post-overhaul trials and shakedown, *Wallace L. Lind* departed Guantanamo on 25 September. The destroyer made stops at Culebra and Roosevelt Roads, Puerto Rico, as well as Charlotte Amalie, Saint Thomas. She returned to Norfolk on 1 October 1965. On 25 October, the ship got underway and finished the month conducting exercises in the Jacksonville, Fla., operating area.

Wallace L. Lind returned to Norfolk on 5 November and prepared for a transatlantic deployment which commenced on 27 November. She stopped briefly at Gibraltar on 8 December, then visited Livorno and Naples, Italy.

The New Year 1966 found *Wallace L. Lind* at Naples, the second of her Mediterranean cruise ports. The destroyer operated out of ports in Italy, France, and Spain and participated in a two-week search for a nuclear weapon lost off the coast of Spain. On 9 March, she joined Franco-American forces for an already-in-progress amphibious exercise off the coast of Santa Monza, Corsica. On 16 March, the ship began her homeward journey and arrived at Norfolk, Va., 10 days later.

From 18 April to 6 May, *Wallace L. Lind* conducted ASW operations with other units of DesRon 2 and three German destroyers. She then participated in the orientation of *Wasp* (CVS–18) at Guantanamo Bay; and, upon her return to Norfolk, she remained in port for almost a month. The summer months from June through September were spent working with Fleet Sonar School, Key West, Fla., and conducting a midshipmen summer cruise.

On 7 September, the destroyer headed for the Gemini Recovery Station off the Florida coast and was responsible for emergency recovery of the Gemini II astronauts should an abort of the mission occur within the first three minutes of flight. The remainder of the year was spent conducting various antisubmarine warfare exercises including "Aswex V" which was prematurely terminated by the collision of the *Essex* (CV–9) and *Nautilus* (SSN–571). The ship then underwent predeployment overhaul.

On 10 January 1967, *Wallace L. Lind* departed the Destroyer and Submarine Pier, Norfolk, and commenced a Mediterranean tour. During the eastward transit, *Wallace L. Lind* had a unique experience in antisubmarine warfare practice. The highlight of the cruise came when, after 25 hours of continuous tracking, the officers and crew of the destroyer, in coordination with other forces, successfully surfaced a Soviet "Foxtrot" submarine off the Straits of Gibraltar on 21 January.

The ship visited ports in Italy, Spain, and France before steaming from Naples on 30 March to rendezvous for Operation "Dawn Clear 67," a combined exercise with the NATO forces. *Wallace L. Lind* also participated in Operation "Spanex 1–67," an exercise with the Spanish Navy, and Operation "Fair Game V" with the French Navy. On 11 May, the destroyer began the journey home and arrived at Norfolk on 20 May 1967.

After several weeks of type training, the ship spent July, August, and September taking part in ASW Exercise "Fixwex Golf 67"; Operation "Lash Out," a NATO exercise which simulated an attack on the east coast; as well as various other exercises and tender availability. On 3 October, *Wallace L. Lind* arrived at the Boston Naval Shipyard to have a special sound source installed in place of the variable depth sonar. She then headed for the Bahama Islands to take part in Operation "Fixwex I," an exercise designed to measure submarine and task group noise levels. The destroyer spent the remainder of 1967 undergoing availability and in leave and upkeep. During this period, the special sound source was removed, and the ship was returned to her original configuration.

During January 1968, *Wallace L. Lind* participated in Operation "Springboard" in the Caribbean. The exercise was completed on 6 February; and, upon her return to Norfolk, the destroyer provided pro-submarine services for SUBLANT, followed by an extended period of availability and pre-deployment preparations.

The ship began an eight-month distant deployment on 9 April by steaming out of Norfolk for the Western Pacific (WestPac) via the Panama Canal. After stopping at Pearl Harbor and Guam, she reached Subic Bay, Philippine Islands, on 20 May. Five days later, *Wallace L. Lind* headed toward the Gulf of Tonkin acting as screen command for *America* (CVA–66). Upon arrival, she assumed duty as screen commander and plane guard destroyer for *Ticonderoga* (CVA–14), and also joined *Enterprise* (CVAN–65) for more plane guard duty. After a brief period of leave on 1 July, *Lind* returned to her station in the Gulf of Tonkin and served as plane guard for *Bonne Homme Richard*

(CVA–31), relieved *Steinaker* (DD–863) as southwest AAW picket, and again operated with *Ticonderoga*.

From 17 July through 9 October, the destroyer took three turns on the "Gunline" off the DMZ. During this period, she visited Subic Bay and Hong Kong for liberty. Departing the "Gunline" on 9 October, *Wallace L. Lind* stopped at Yokosuka, Japan, and made preparations for the return voyage across the Pacific. She arrived at Norfolk on 27 November 1968 and finished up the year in a period of leave, upkeep, and postdeployment repairs.

The year 1969 was devoted almost entirely to maintenance and training. On 27 January, *Wallace L. Lind* reported to the Norfolk Naval Shipyard, Portsmouth, Va., for regular overhaul which was completed on 10 June. The vessel spent a month in Norfolk preparing for "Project X–SI;" and, on 24 July, she set course for San Juan for testing her new additions. The destroyer returned to Norfolk for the final evaluation of the project on 14 August. On 17 September, the ship arrived at Guantanamo for refresher training which lasted through 20 November. During the month of October, *Wallace L. Lind's* home port was changed to Pearl Harbor effective on 1 January 1970.

The destroyer spent January and February of 1970 conducting a brief excursion in the Virginia capes-Florida areas. She arrived back at Norfolk on 8 March for tender availability. After a series of delays, extensions, and standbys, *Wallace L. Lind* made a colorful arrival in Hawaii on 18 April, having transited the Panama Canal and visited San Diego.

Throughout May and June, the destroyer qualified as a naval gunfire ship and participated in "Comtuex," an exercise in antisubmarine and antiair warfare and all facets of destroyer seamanship. She then conducted ASW operations with the Japanese Maritime Self-Defense Force submarine *Michishio* (SS–564) in preparation for "Aswex 1–70," a joint United States, Japanese, and British Commonwealth ASW exercise which lasted from 19 to 26 June. A period of tender availability followed.

On 12 August 1970, *Wallace L. Lind* sailed out of Pearl Harbor to commence deployment to WestPac. She arrived at Subic Bay, Philippines, on 27 August for type training and embarked COMDESDIV 252. The destroyer then made rendezvous with *America* (CVA–66) to act as a plane guard destroyer. From 14 to 17 September, *Lind* participated in antiair warfare Exercise "Beacon Tower" in the Gulf of Tonkin. On 21 September, she arrived at Okinawa for fuel and embarked a Beachjumper Unit. Two days later, the destroyer again made rendezvous with *America* for operations in the Sea of Japan, followed by upkeep at Yokosuka and Sasebo, Japan, where she debarked COMDESDIV 252.

On 19 October, *Wallace L. Lind* embarked three Japanese officers to act as observers for "ASWEX 5–70," a week-long exercise which got underway on 22 October. The destroyer arrived at Yokosuka, Japan, and underwent upkeep prior to departure for Taiwan on 9 November. After a brief Taiwan patrol and a stop at Subic Bay on 16 November, the destroyer got underway for "FIREX" and conducted typhoon evasion exercises.

On 28 November, *Wallace L. Lind* arrived at her station on the "Gunline" off the coast of South Vietnam. She conducted operations through 12 December when she departed for Hong Kong. Two days later, she arrived in the port of Hong Kong and relieved *Vernon County* (LST–1161) as SOPA.

Wallace L. Lind departed Hong Kong on 5 January 1971. The destroyer spent the month of January rotating plane guard duty among *Kitty Hawk* (CVA–63), *Wainwright* (DLG–28), *Chicago* (CLG–11), *Hollister* (DD–788), and *Ranger* (CVA–61). On 4 February, the destroyer performed amphibious operations off the coast of South Vietnam; then, on 11 February, she proceeded independently to Subic Bay, Philippines, to prepare for her return to Pearl Harbor. *Wallace L. Lind* arrived in Hawaii on the morning of 26 February 1971.

During March and April, the crew enjoyed a well-earned rest, and the ship received some necessary repairs. The destroyer conducted various exercises in the Hawaiian operating areas throughout May and June. On 27 July, *Wallace L. Lind* departed Pearl Harbor for Portland, Oreg., her new home port. Upon her arrival on 4 August, the destroyer assumed a new mission as a Naval Reserve ship responsible for the training of inactive duty reservists from the western United States. By 31 August, *Lind* had completed her transition to the Naval Reserve Force and embarked upon a cruise to the Washington-Oregon coastal area which lasted through 10 September. One month later, the destroyer underwent tender availability at San Diego, returned to Portland one month later, and tied up at Swan Island where she remained through the close of 1971.

January, February, and March of 1972 were spent undergoing repairs at Portland. On 25 March, *Wallace L. Lind* set to sea and conducted gunnery exercises off the coast of Washington, then sailed to San Francisco where she rearmed before returning to Portland. On 6 April, the destroyer got underway for Seattle, Washington, the first of six such trips that she would make in the next eight months. While in Washington, she attended the Daffodil Festival at Tacoma. *Wallace L. Lind* conducted a reservist training cruise to Pearl Harbor, arriving on 24 June. In August, the destroyer sailed north to Juneau, Alaska, for the Juneau Salmon Derby. She followed this trip with a transit of the Columbia River to the Astoria Regatta festival. During September, *Wallace L. Lind*'s only sea time was a three-day junket to Esquimalt, British Columbia, with her select reserve crew embarked for training purposes. On 24 October, she got underway for San Diego and a three-week availability. On 18 November, *Wallace L. Lind* set sail for her home port of Portland, Oreg., where she remained for the rest of the year.

The last year of her commissioned service saw *Wallace L. Lind* become active in the recruiting effort as well as in her duties as a Naval Reserve training ship. From 9 to 25 January 1973, the ship underwent restricted availability in Portland, and it was discovered that drydocking was necessary to correct some hull problems. On 12 February, the destroyer entered drydock for a nine-day period. After rearming at Bangor, Wash., she headed south and arrived at San Diego on 1 March. The destroyer conducted three days of local operations; then, along with *James C. Owens* (DD–776), cruised to Mazatlan, Mexico.

Wallace L. Lind returned to San Diego on 17 March and conducted a brief period of operations with a reserve crew. On 26 April, the ship cruised to Anchorage, Alaska, to participate in a mass recruiting effort which included conducting ship's visits and a "Go Navy" cruise. After a final INSURV inspection in May, *Lind* remained berthed at her home port until she cruised to Vancouver, Wash., to participate in the 4th of July celebration.

On 1 August, *Wallace L. Lind* departed Portland for Hawaii. However, two days out of San Francisco, she developed engine trouble and limped back to port. On 17 August, the ship steamed out of San Francisco and returned to Portland.

On 25 September, *Wallace L. Lind* passed the familiar Columbia lightship for the last time as she sailed for San Diego. After spending the weekend conducting tours, she moved to the naval station on 1 October. Work was then begun in earnest to prepare *Wallace L. Lind* for decommissioning and transfer to the Republic of Korea under the Military Assistance Program. The first contingent of Korean officers and men arrived on 16 November, with the majority arriving in San Diego on 29 and 30 November. *Wallace L. Lind* was decommissioned and stricken from the Navy list on 4 December 1973 and officially transferred on that date to the Republic of Korea. She served that navy as *Dae Gu* (DD–97) into 1980.

Wallace L. Lind earned four battle stars for World War II service, four for service in the Korean conflict, and three for her Vietnam service.

Wallacut

An Anglicized derivation of an Indian term which means "place of stones."

(YTB–420: dp. 345 (f.); l. 100'0''; b. 25'0''; dr. 9'7''; s. 12 k.; cpl. 8; cl. *Sassaba*)

Wallacut (YTB–420) was laid down on 14 August 1944 by the Coast Guard Yard at Curtis Bay, Md.; launched on 28 October 1944; sponsored by Miss Sally Koshorek; completed on 23 March 1945; delivered to the Navy and placed in service on 31 March 1945.

The large harbor tug departed Curtis Bay on 8 April 1945 and, after stops at Norfolk, Charleston, Miami, Key West, New Orleans, and Balboa in the Canal Zone, reached Eniwetok on 21 July. She remained there for two weeks; then moved on—via Guam and Saipan—to Okinawa where she arrived on 3 September, the day after Japan's formal surrender ceremony. She served at Okinawa until June 1947 when she headed, via Guam and Kwajalein, to Pearl Harbor where she was placed out of service, in reserve, in August.

Wallacut remained in reserve until American involvement in the Korean conflict increased the Navy's need for active ships. The tug returned to active service on 11 August 1950 and departed Pearl Harbor for the Far East on 3 October. After stops at Kwajalein, Guam, and Sasebo, the tug reached Korean waters on 16 November. She served at Hungnam in December during the evacuation of United Nations troops following the intervention of Chinese communist troops. At the completion of her part in that operation, the tug stopped over at Pusan briefly before returning to Sasebo on the 27th.

Records of her service for the period following December 1950 are almost nonexistent. All that is known is that she continued to be listed as an active unit of the 1st Fleet until 1960 when she was assigned to the Commander, Naval Forces, Far East. Perhaps she might have spent the interim in the Orient, her 1st Fleet assignment notwithstanding. Within a year, though, she was reassigned simply to the Pacific Fleet, and her duty location or locations are unrecorded. In February 1962, she was redesignated a medium harbor tug, YTM–420. As such, the tug continued to serve the Pacific Fleet until January 1973, when she was placed in reserve and berthed at Guam in the Marianas. After three years of inactivity at Guam, she was struck from the Navy list in June 1976. As of April 1977, she was slated to be sold sometime that summer.

Waller

Littleton Waller Tazewell Waller—born in York County, Va., on 26 September 1856—was appointed as a second lieutenant of Marines on 24 June 1880 and served initial tours of successive shore duty at the Marine Barracks in Norfolk, Va., and Washington, D.C. Going to sea in *Lancaster*, the flagship of the European Squadron, in 1881, Waller participated in the landing of a mixed bluejacket and marine landing force at Alexandria, Egypt, during a serious local uprising in the summer of 1882. The timely arrival of the ships of the European Squadron and their landing forces gave protection to the American consulate and to American citizens and interests and also afforded a refuge for the citizens of other nations who had been displaced from their homes or businesses.

Later—after tours of shore duty at Norfolk and Washington; and at sea in *Iroquois*, *Tallapoosa*, and

Lancaster—he served in *Indiana* (Battleship No. 1) during the Spanish-American War and was in that vessel during the Battle of Santiago on 3 July 1898. During this naval engagement, Spanish Admiral Cervera's fleet was totally destroyed by the American fleet waiting just outside the harbor. The Spanish-American War left the United States with a new colonial empire and increased the nation's responsibilities in world affairs. Waller played a part in America's colonial expansion into the second decade of the 20th century.

While stationed at the naval station at Cavite early in 1900, Waller was ordered to command a detachment of marines assigned to take part in the expedition mounted to relieve the siege of Tientsin. This city, with its enclave of foreign nationals, was besieged by a mixed force of "Boxers" and Chinese Imperial troops supporting them. Accordingly, Waller and his men arrived at Taku, China, on 19 June 1900, soon moved inland, and linked up with a Russian column of 400 men.

At 0200 on the 21st, this small combined force set out for Tientsin, arrayed against a Chinese contingent of some 1,500 to 2,000 men. Outnumbered from the start, the column came under heavy enemy fire and was forced to retreat, with the Russians in the lead. In a desperate rear-guard action, Waller and his marines—leaving their dead behind and dragging their wounded with them—fought off the numerically superior (but less aggressive) Chinese forces and reached safety.

Waller's detachment immediately returned to duty, attached to a British column led by Comdr. Christopher Craddock. At 0400 on the 24th, an international army —consisting of Italian, German, Japanese, Russian, British, and American forces—set out again for Tientsin. Finding the enemy at 0700, a bitter fight ensued until 1230, when the Allied force reached the city and broke the siege.

After participating in the final fighting for the city of Tientsin from 13 to 14 July, Waller and his men took possession of the American sector and brought order out of the havoc caused by the Chinese retreat. Promoted by brevet to lieutenant colonel and advanced two numbers in grade for his performance of duty at Tientsin, Littleton Waller was commended in 1903 by Brigadier General A. S. Daggett, U.S. Army, Ret., in his book, *America in the China Relief Expedition.* He recalled that the marine had ". . . participated willingly and energetically . . ." with the Allies ". . . in all movements against the enemy . . ." and that ". . . he and his officers and men . . . reflected credit upon American valor . . . ."

Remaining in the Far East for a short time more, Waller led a detachment of marines which defeated Philippine insurgents in a battle at Sohoton on 5 November 1901. Later, he led an expedition across the island of Samar, from 28 December 1901 to 6 January 1902—subduing Moro insurgents under great climatic hardships—his battalion returning to Cavite on 2 March.

Returning to the United States soon thereafter, Waller served in charge of recruiting in Pennsylvania, Delaware, and western New Jersey into 1903 and commanded, in succession, the Provisional Regiment of Marines on the Isthmus of Panama in 1904; the expeditionary forces on the island of Cuba from 1906 and rose to command the Provisional Brigade in Cuba by 1911. He later commanded the Marine Barracks at the Mare Island Navy Yard from 1911 to 1914 and the First Brigade of marines during service at Vera Cruz in Mexico in 1914 before being appointed to command marines in Haiti in 1915.

Waller's troops crushed all armed resistance to the American occupation of the country and restored some semblance of peace and order to Haiti. Promoted to brigadier general on 29 August 1916 and to major general on 29 August 1918, Waller closed out his active duty in the Marine Corps as Commander of the Advanced Base Force at Philadelphia from 8 January 1917 until his retirement in June 1920.

Major General Waller lived in retirement in Philadelphia until his death on 13 July 1926.

(DD–466: dp. 2,940 (f.); l. 376′5″; b. 39′7″; dr. 17′9″; s. 35.2 k.; a. 5 5″, 10 40mm., 7 20mm., 10 21″ tt., 6 dcp., 2 dct.; cl. *Fletcher*)

Waller (DD–466) was laid down on 12 February 1942, at Kearny, N.J., by the Federal Shipbuilding and Drydock Co.; launched on 15 August 1942; sponsored by Mrs. Littleton W. T. Waller, the widow of General Waller; and commissioned on 1 October 1942, Lt. Comdr. Lawrence H. Frost in command.

Into the fall of 1942, *Waller* conducted shakedown out of Casco Bay, Maine, and occasionally performed local escort duties for training submarines based at New London, Conn. On 31 November, *Waller* departed the New York Navy Yard, Brooklyn, N.Y., bound for the Pacific, via the Panama Canal and Pearl Harbor.

She arrived at Efate on 21 January 1943 and, six days later, sortied as part of the destroyer screen with Task Force (TF) 18. Rear Admiral Robert C. Giffen, commanding the force, flew his flag in *Wichita* (CA–45). The mission of TF 18 was to rendezvous, off Guadalcanal, with a transport force sent to resupply and reinforce the land-based forces there in their struggle to dislodge the Japanese from the key island. Intelligence reports indicated—wrongly, as it turned out—that the Japanese were mounting a big "push" to resupply their forces. As events would show, the enemy was, instead, massing his forces to evacuate his troops.

On the 29th, 50 miles to the north of Rennell Island, Japanese torpedo-carrying "Betty" bombers (Mitsubishi G4M–1's) came in low from the east—carefully avoiding silhouetting themselves against the afterglow of dusk. *Waller*, on the starboard beam of flagship *Wichita* and cruisers *Chicago* (CA–29) and *Louisville* (CA–28), came under machine gun fire from the lead "Betty" as it bore in on the attack. The American ships responded with heavy fire toward the first two planes, and one cartwheeled into the sea and exploded in a brilliant fireball.

Soon red, green, and white flares gave the scene an eerie, ghostly effect, as the Japanese set off pyrotechnics to illuminate the American force. At 1931, another flight of "Betties" appeared and pressed their attacks on the heavy cruisers steaming in the right van of the task force. One "Betty" splashed into the sea astern of *Waller*, before another enemy aircraft scored a torpedo hit on *Chicago* at 1945, holing the cruiser's starboard side, forward, and stopping three of the ship's four drive-shafts. A second torpedo soon struck home after the first, flooding number three fireroom and the forward engine room leaving *Chicago* dead in the water.

The attack momentarily subsided, giving the Americans a respite. *Louisville* took her crippled near-sister in tow and, by early on the 24th, the damaged cruiser was on her way to Espiritu Santo at four knots. At 1445, well after *Louisville* had passed the tow to *Navajo* (AT–64), 12 "Betties" were reported south of New Georgia heading for Rennell Island. Combat air patrol fighters from *Enterprise* (CV–6) splashed three of the attackers, but nine remained to attack *Chicago*. Seven of these went down to the antiaircraft fire from the task force and the slashing attacks by Wildcats from *Enterprise*. *Waller* claimed one "Betty" killed and two damaged.

Chicago, however, took two more torpedoes and was abandoned soon thereafter, sinking stern-first, at 1644. *Navajo, Sands* (APD–13), *Edwards* (DD–619), and *Waller* collected 1,049 survivors from the cruiser. In the melee, *La Vallette* (DD–448) was damaged and left the area, towed by *Navajo.* While retiring to Espiritu Santo, *Waller* located a submarine contact but could not develop it.

The Battle of Rennell Island, which resulted in the loss of one American cruiser and damage to a destroyer, succeeded in diverting Japanese intentions from the transports off Lunga Point and allowed vital American reinforcements to enter the final phase of the battle to drive the Japanese from Guadalcanal.

In early March 1943, Capt. Arleigh "31-knot" Burke broke his broad pennant in *Waller*. On the 5th, she led *Conway* (DD–507), *Montpelier* (CL–57), *Cleveland* (CL–55), *Denver* (CL–58), and *Cony* (DD–508) in a raid on the Japanese airfields at Vila, on the southern coast of New Georgia. Assigned to protect the larger ships, the destroyers drew the duty of silencing any hostile shore batteries which might try to interfere with the cruisers as they carried out the main bombardment.

Entering Kula Gulf shortly after midnight on the 5th, *Waller*'s radar detected two ships—later determined to be *Murasame* and *Mineguno*—at the eastern entrance to Blackett Strait and standing out at high speed, apparently unaware of the American ships' presence. *Waller* opened the action at about 0100, firing a five-tube spread of torpedoes at a range of three and one-half miles. A minute later, her gunners soon commenced fire with the main battery.

Taken by surprise, the two Japanese destroyers answered with ragged and inaccurate fire. Six minutes after action had commenced, *Murasame* broke in two from an "extremely violent" explosion, the victim of a combination of torpedoes and gunfire from *Waller* and her mates.

Minegumo, too, came in for her share of attention and was soon reduced to junk—although she stubbornly remained afloat for a short while. Leaving the Japanese in their wakes, the American force swung westward at 0114 and soon thereafter commenced their scheduled bombardment of Vila. The six American ships pounded the air strip for 16 minutes before breaking off action and leaving a number of fires burning brightly in the darkness. *Waller* was ordered to dispatch *Minegumo*, but the blazing wreck sank before the American destroyer could get to do the job.

The Vila raid evoked the praise of Admiral Chester W. Nimitz, who with glowing understatement called the exploit a "creditable performance." Nimitz cited the exemplary way in which TF 68 had picked up two enemy ships by radar, despite a close-by land background; promptly obtained a fire control set-up; sank the enemy vessels in a "businesslike manner" and then proceeded to conduct their planned bombardment mission approximately on schedule. "The Operation had all the precision of a well-rehearsed exercise by veteran ships—which these were not."

Waller continued her operations in the Solomons through the end of 1943 and into 1944. As the Japanese sought to resupply their trapped garrisons on islands like Vella Lavella, Arundel, and Kolombangara, they utilized destroyers as transports and supply ships in what became known as the "Tokyo Express." These ships clashed with American cruisers and destroyers in a series of sharp, bitter night actions.

The Americans, meanwhile, kept up the pressure on the Japanese, subjecting their islands to nearly continual harassment from the sea and from the air. On the night of 29 and 30 June 1943, *Waller*, in company with three other destroyers and four cruisers, bombarded Vila-Stanmore plantation, Kolombangara, and the Shortland Islands. Much of the firing was done in the teeth of a driving rainstorm which obscured visibility and precluded claims of damage to Japanese installations.

Soon thereafter, on 6 July, a task group of three cruisers and four destroyers under Rear Admiral W. L. "Pug" Ainsworth, tangled with 10 Japanese destroyers carrying troops and supplies to Kolombangara. In the fierce night action, two Japanese destroyers, *Niizuki* and *Nagatsuki*, were sunk as was *Helena* (CL–50) which fell victim to the dreaded "long lance" torpedoes.

During efforts to save *Helena*'s surviving crew, *Waller* served in the force covering *Woodworth* (DD–460) and *Gwin* (DD–433) which were engaged in the primary rescue operations. *Waller* detected a submarine by her radar and went in to try to seek out the enemy craft. A three-hour search netted a contact, and *Waller* dropped depth charges. Although the destroyer found no visible evidence that she had scored a kill, the Commander, TG 36.2, Rear Admiral A. S. "Tip" Merrill, commented that the probability of the submarine's destruction was good endorsement to *Waller*'s action report.

The warship continued supporting operations in the Solomons by escorting troop and supply convoys. While screening TG 31.2—four destroyers and four fast transports (APD's) bound for Enogai Inlet, New Georgia— a search plane picked up what looked like four enemy ships near Kolombangara Island and radioed a contact report. *Waller*, as part of the covering force, changed course to intercept and soon sighted three ships lying low off the jungle coastline.

Unbeknownst to *Waller*, these three "enemy" ships were, in reality, *PT–157*, *PT–159*, and *PT–160*, out on patrol, having unintentionally strayed north of their assigned patrol area. *Waller*, tracking as best she could, opened fire at 20,000 yards, and other ships in company reported that she straddled and hit the "enemy." Fortunately, she had not. The PT's, suddenly thrown into a bad situation, loosed torpedoes at the attacking "enemy" and sped off to the southward. Again fortunately, *Waller* and her mates did not pursue the fleeing "enemy" but broke off action and returned to their duties covering the departing APD's, apparently satisfied that one had made a hit on the "Japanese destroyer." In the subsequent action report written up on 29 July, *Waller*'s commanding officer wrote: "It has since been learned that these ships were probably our own PT boats."

No such case of mistaken identity occurred in *Waller*'s operations on 15 August, while covering the landings at Vella Lavella. At 0800, approximately 10 Japanese dive bombers appeared on the destroyer's radar, 38 miles distant. She fired an umbrella barrage at the approaching enemy to keep the attackers at "arm's length"—and claimed two "Vals."

Later in the day, *Waller* again battled persistent Japanese planes, picking up on her radar eight torpedo planes heading in at low level. Director-controlled gunfire from the main battery—5-inch—spat out fiery steel at the incoming "Kates" but knocked none down.

On the evening of 17 August, a Japanese air attack caused *Waller* and *Philip* (DD–498) to collide while undertaking evasive action; and *Waller* eventually steamed out of the combat area to undergo needed repairs. However, in October, she was back in the thick of the fighting.

On the night of 1 and 2 October, *Waller* entered waters off Vella Lavella in an attempt to cut off the evacuation of Japanese troops from the island. *Waller* shot up six landing barges that night and four on the following, wreaking heavy destruction, along with her mates, on the smaller-sized "Tokyo Express." All told during this period, 46 enemy craft of this type met destruction at the hands of American destroyers, cruisers, and PT boats.

Waller continued her convoy escort and support functions into the fall months. On 17 and 18 November, as American forces pushed towards Bougainville, *Waller* screened the 5th echelon of transports and supply ships. The total American force—consisting of six destroyers, eight APD's, a fleet tug, and eight LST's—was crossing Empress Augusta Bay, off the coast of Bougainville, when 10 Japanese torpedo planes swooped in low and fast at 0300. The ships quickly put up a tremendous barrage of antiaircraft fire to discourage the Japanese attackers.

Flares and float lights dropped by the Japanese planes lit up the scene with an eerie light. Destroyer gunfire sent tracer streaks across the night sky, and one "Betty" spun into the sea off the port bow of *Pringle* (DD–477). Another attacker, roaring in low and fast at 0330, flew into a veritable hail of flak and crashed, trailing flames into the sea astern of *Conway* (DD–507). The torpedoes launched by the doomed aircraft failed to hit their mark and sped off past the American ships. Two minutes later, however, another "Betty" drew blood from the American force by torpedoing *McKean* (APD–5), which later sank. When the smoke of battle had cleared, *Waller* picked up eight Japanese aviators.

The warship soon was back off Torokina, Bougainville, on the shore of Empress Augusta Bay, with the 7th echelon of support ships. On 23 November, she shelled Magine Island.

She and her sister ships bombarded enemy positions on Buka Island and in the Choiseul Bay area on 1 February 1944. At 0625, enemy shore batteries on Buka opened fire on the American men-of-war. *Waller* immediately served up a round of return fire at the Japanese guns which silenced one enemy battery. About a fortnight later, during the Green Island invasion, the ship set out, in company with *Saufley* (DD–465), *Renshaw* (DD–499), and *Philip*, to bombard the Japanese radar station at Cape St. George and the Borpop and Namatanai airfields. However, inclement weather hampered the spotting of shot, and it was impossible to ascertain the effectiveness of the raid.

Meanwhile, the Allied war effort continued to gain momentum; and, in June, American forces struck at the Marianas. *Waller*, having sailed to the Hawaiian Islands for a rest period, departed Pearl Harbor and passed the 180th Meridian on 5 June 1944. She escorted TG 51.18 via Kwajalein to Saipan. TG 51.18, an expeditionary force reserve whose mission was to support the occupation of the Marianas, was slated to land on whatever island the situation might dictate—Saipan, Guam, or Tinian.

Saipan was designated its target, and *Waller* began to bombard Japanese positions on that island. On the evening of 18 June, the warship received orders to give fire support in two areas to assist the marines in repelling an enemy tank attack. At 1755, in company with *Pringle*, she entered Magicienne Bay. *Waller* closed the beach to get a better view but was unable to distinguish any tanks—American or Japanese. At 1758, all engines were stopped to give the watch a better look at the shore. Suddenly, three minutes later, enemy shore guns opened up on the two destroyers.

Waller and *Pringle* both leapt ahead at full speed, heading in an easterly direction as their funnels belched forth a large amount of oily, black smoke. Splashes from near misses rose on both sides of the ships as they disappeared into the thick, boiling smoke. *Waller* fired several salvoes in return; but, as her action report noted, "possibly the terrain favored the Japanese, and no good point of aim was offered the director pointer."

American forces returned to Guam in the summer of 1944, and *Waller* took part in these operations by serving as screening unit for the forces landing on the island. She then conducted fire support and screening missions off Tinian as that island fell to the American naval steamroller in August. Following these operations, the ship returned to the west coast for a refit which lasted through the early fall of 1944.

She joined the 7th Fleet on 27 November for operations in the Philippine Islands. Shortly after noon that day, the Japanese seemingly celebrated *Waller*'s return to the battle zones by launching a suicide-plane raid by 15 planes. During the fracas, *Waller* shot down one intruder and assisted in splashing another.

On the night of 27 and 28 November, the destroyer led the four ships of DesDiv 43 in a night sweep into Ormoc Bay, preparatory to American landings there. Her mission was one of the first penetrations of these waters since the Americans had been forcibly ejected from the Philippines almost three years before. While bombarding Japanese troop concentrations, she kept on the lookout for whatever small Japanese coastal naval craft might be encountered.

The ships poured shells onto the shores around the bay for an hour, before they proceeded into the Camotes Sea in search of shipping. Shortly after midnight on the 27th, an Allied patrol plane radioed a message to the division noting that a surfaced Japanese submarine —later determined to be *I–46*—was south of Pacijan Island, heading for Ormoc Bay.

The division reversed course to intercept; and, at 0127, *Waller*'s radar picked up the target just off the northeast coast of Ponson Island. Firing all batteries that would bear, the destroyer steamed directly for the submarine—passing the word to "stand by to ram." Countermanding this order at the last minute because the submarine looked like she was already severely damaged, *Waller* instead continued to pump 40-millimeter and 5-inch shellfire into the enemy submersible, which attempted a weak and ineffective return fire with her deck guns. At 0145, as *Waller* doubled back for a second pass, the submarine's bow rose up towards the sky; and she sank, stern first.

Waller remained in the Leyte Gulf area until 2 December, after making a second sweep into the Camotes Sea on the night of 29 and 30 November in search of a reported 10-ship Japanese convoy. While she found no trace of the convoy, she nevertheless located and smashed six enemy barges with gunfire. Also during the Ormoc Bay raids, the ship came under Japanese air attack on both Ormoc Bay excursions—on one occasion, three bombs fell within a few hundred yards of the destroyer.

In mid-December, *Waller* participated in the invasion of Mindoro as a unit of the covering force of battleships, escort carriers, cruisers, and destroyers. On 15 December, this force repulsed a heavy kamikaze attack in the Sulu Sea. *Waller* again downed one and helped to destroy another Japanese attacker. One of the planes, a twin-engined "Betty," was attempting a suicide run on *Waller* before heavy antiaircraft fire splashed her.

Early in January 1945, *Waller* shifted the scene of her operations to Lingayen Gulf, as American forces were landing there. While thus engaged, she scored hits on two suicide boats and poured some 3,000 rounds of ammunition at both air and surface targets. While she did not down a single plane, she damaged a countless number at the height of the heavy Japanese suicide raids.

February and March of 1945 again found *Waller* escorting and screening the vital Allied transports and cargo vessels. When American forces splashed ashore at Basilan, *Waller* was off the beaches as flagship of the task group and received additional fire-support assignments at Tawi Tawi and Jolo, in the Sulu archipelago, during April.

A joint Australian-American effort against Borneo kept *Waller* busy from May to July. *Waller* participated in this campaign by escorting convoys to Tarakan Island, Brunei Bay, and Balikpapan, as well as by covering minesweeping operations in the Miri-Lulong area, below Brunei Bay. She then rejoined the 3d Fleet early in August to be in readiness for the projected invasion of the Japanese home islands. But while en route toward Honshu, escorting a convoy, *Waller* received the most welcome news that the Japanese had accepted the unconditional surrender terms of the Potsdam Declaration.

Returned to the 7th Fleet once more, *Waller* entered Shanghai, China, on 19 September for a tour with the reconstituted Yangtze Patrol force and was one of the first American warships to make port at that Chinese city. A fortnight later, the destroyer neutralized a Japanese suicide-boat garrison base when a 21-man landing force from the ship assisted local Chinese authorities in disarming an estimated 2,700 Japanese at Tinghai.

While returning to Shanghai on 9 October, *Waller* fouled a Japanese-moored "Shanghai"-type contact mine. Three officers and 22 men were wounded, and the ship sustained enough structural damage to warrant a dry-docking at Kiangnan Dock and Engineering Works at Shanghai. Following this period of repairs, the ship supervised minesweeping operations and supplied provisions and water to the ships engaged in the sweeps which netted some 60 mines. In addition, she provided Yangtze River pilots for incoming vessels and monitored all shipping traffic passing her patrol station in the Yangtze estuary. The ship departed Chinese waters on 12 December, bound for the United States, and—after a stop at Pearl Harbor—arrived at San Diego 18 days later.

Placed out of commission soon thereafter and attached to the 6th Naval District, *Waller* remained in reserve at Charleston, S.C., until the onset of the Korean War. Selected as one of the *Fletcher*-class units to be converted to escort destroyers, *Waller* was redesignated DDE–466 on 26 March 1949 and was recommissioned at Charleston on 5 July 1950. Following shakedown, she joined Escort Destroyer Squadron 2 as flagship on 28 January 1951.

On 14 May of that year, *Waller* headed west to participate in the Korean War and, upon arrival near the Land of the Morning Calm, immediately joined Task Force (TF) 95 as it was proceeding to Wonsan harbor. For 10 days, she fired shore bombardment missions against communist targets, hurling some 1,700 rounds of 5-inch shells on enemy positions. During the following summer, the destroyer acted as an escort for 7th Fleet units exercising in waters off Okinawa before returning to the seaborne blockade lanes in October 1951 for a two-week tour of duty before again returning to the United States.

From 1951 to late 1956, *Waller* participated in many ASW exercises off the east coast and made two extensive deployments to the Mediterranean and two to the Caribbean. She entered the Norfolk Naval Shipyard late in 1956 and was again modified—this time with extensive alterations in her ASW battery. She rejoined the Fleet soon thereafter and, after a Mediterranean deployment in 1957, joined DesRon 28, as a unit of ASW Task Force "Alpha."

Subsequently joining DesRon 36 on 1 July 1964, *Waller* made numerous Mediterranean deployments over the next four years. On 6 September 1968, the destroyer departed Norfolk with DesDiv 362 for Vietnamese waters. Arriving in October, she reported immediately to the "gunline" and took up patrol duties on Yankee Station, off Qui Nhon, South Vietnam.

Supporting Korean troops, her 5-inch gunfire did extensive damage to Viet Cong bunkers and storage areas, before she moved south to a station off Phan Thiet, where she supported the U.S. Army 173d Airborne Brigade. During this deployment, she destroyed numerous Viet Cong structures—rest camps and the like—as well as interdicted the movement of Viet Cong supply traffic by destroying trails.

After having fired 2,400 rounds and completing her gunline assignment, *Waller* received a "well done" from Commander, Task Unit 70.8.9: "*Waller*'s ability to meet all commitments is indeed noteworthy."

Proceeding to Yankee Station in the Gulf of Tonkin, *Waller* joined *Intrepid* (CVS–11) for attack carrier escort duties and, upon this carrier's departure, joined *Ranger* (CVA–61) to conduct similar missions. After 109 consecutive days of this duty, the veteran destroyer started for home on 2 March 1969. After a brief tour as a Naval Reserve training ship on the east coast, *Waller* was decommissioned and struck from the Navy list on 15 July 1969. She was authorized to be disposed of, as a target, on 2 February 1970.

Waller received 12 battle stars for her World War II service and two each for Korean and Vietnam service.

Walnut

A shade tree whose hard wood is used in making furniture and whose round nut is edible.

Walnut (YN–31) was renamed *Pepperwood* (*q.v.*) on 16 October 1940, nine days before the net tender's keel was laid down at Camden, N.J., by the John H. Mathis Co.

I

(WAGL–252: dp. 885; l. 174'10½''; b. 32'0''; dr. 11'3½''; s. 12 k.; a. none)

Walnut—a steel-hulled, twin-screw tender built for the Coast Guard in 1939 at Oakland, Calif.—apparently served at Detroit, Mich., into mid-1941. She came under naval control in November 1941, when the United States drew closer to war and performed tender services in the 14th Naval District during World War II. Sometime in early 1942, she was classified as "miscellaneous tender" and given the hull number WAGL–252. By the spring of 1942, her armament comprised two 3-inch guns; four 20-millimeter Oerlikon machine guns; and two depth charge tracks.

Resuming her peacetime pursuits with the Coast Guard after the cessation of hostiilties, *Walnut* apparently remained in the Hawaiian area into the early 1950's, although records of her service are sketchy at best. Departing Honolulu on 16 April 1952, she sailed for the west coast of the United States and reached San Francisco soon thereafter. *Walnut* subsequently operated in the Caribbean and Gulf of Mexico into the late 1950's. The quest for data concerning her subsequent career has been unsuccessful.

Walrus

A gregarious, aquatic mammal, related to the seal and found in Arctic waters. The walrus is a prime source of leather, oil, ivory, and food.

Walrus (Submarine No. 14) was renamed *K–4* (*q.v.*) on 17 November 1911.

The name *Walrus* was assigned to SS–431—a *Balao*-class submarine to be built at Philadelphia, Pa., by the Cramp Shipbuilding Co.—but the contract for her construction was cancelled on 29 July 1944.

Walrus (SS–437)—a *Balao-class* submarine—was laid down on 21 June 1945, at Groton, Conn., by the Electric Boat Co.; launched on 20 September 1946; and sponsored by Miss Winifred P. Nagle. However, work on the submarine was suspended on 7 January 1946 when the contract for her construction was cancelled. Her hull was assigned to the New London Group of the Atlantic Reserve Fleet on 9 December 1952. Her name was struck from the Navy list on 9 June 1958.

Walsh

Patrick Joseph Walsh—born on 19 January 1908 in New York City—accepted a commission in the Naval Reserve as a lieutenant, junior grade, on 4 May 1942. Receiving instruction at the Naval Training School, Boston, Mass., he later received more specialized training at the Armed Guard School, Little Creek, Va., from 16 June to 22 July.

As armed guard commander in SS *Patrick J. Hurley*, Lt. (jg.) Walsh was killed in a brief, one-sided engagement with a German U-boat in the North Atlantic. On the night of 12 September 1942, *U–512* stealthily surfaced and closed the merchantman, undetected, before she opened fire with devastating effect. Walsh fell severely wounded in the initial shelling, taking shrapnel in the throat. In spite of the withering machine-gun fire

The incomplete hull of *Walrus* (SS–437) goes into the water. At the end of World War II, some ships, whose hulls were substantially complete, were launched and inactivated for possible future completion. (NH 79756)

directed at his battle station on the bridge, Lt. (jg.) Walsh remained at his post, though weak from loss of blood. For displaying selfless gallantry in battle, Walsh was posthumously awarded the Purple Heart and Silver Star medals.

(APD–111: dp. 1,650; l. 306'0"; b. 37'0"; dr. 13'9"; s. 23.6 k.; cpl. 203; a. 1 5", 6 40mm., 6 20mm.; cl. *Crosley*)

Walsh (APD–111) was laid down on 27 February 1945 at Hingham, Mass., by the Bethlehem Steel Co.; launched on 27 April 1945; sponsored by Mrs. John J.

Walsh; and commissioned on 11 July 1945, Lt. Comdr. Philip J. Tiffany, USNR, in command.

After shakedown out of Guantanamo Bay, Cuba, from 1 to 29 August, *Walsh* visited Norfolk and then took part in smokescreen experiments in Chesapeake Bay as part of Task Group 23.19. On 4 October, the fast transport sailed north for training exercises in company with PT boats out of Melville, R.I. She later participated in Navy Day festivities at Portland, Maine, in late October, before departing Portland on 30 October, bound for Philadelphia.

Walsh secured her sonar gear at the Philadelphia Naval Shipyard and received hull repairs. She departed

Philadelphia on 13 November bound for Hampton Roads and arrived at Norfolk the following day. She then unloaded all ammunition and turned in registered publications before proceeding on to Jacksonville, Fla.

Later decommissioned on 26 April 1946 at Green Cove Springs, Fla., *Walsh* berthed initially with the Florida reserve group and, later, in the Texas group. She remained there until struck from the Navy list on 1 May 1966, and she was scrapped soon thereafter.

Walter A. Luckenbach

(ScStr.: dp. 17,170; l. 469'3''; b. 55'11''; dr. 30'7'' (mean); s. 14.0 k.; cpl. 70)

Walter A. Luckenbach (Id. No. 3171)—a steamer launched on 19 December 1917 by the Seattle Construction & Drydock Co. for the Luckenbach Steamship Co.—was taken over by the United States Shipping Board early in 1918; delivered to the Navy on 9 June 1918; and commissioned that same day at Seattle, Wash., Lt. Comdr. James A. McDonald, USNRF, in command.

Assigned to the Naval Overseas Transportation Service, *Walter A. Luckenbach* sailed from Seattle on 13 June; but an unsuccessful series of trials forced her to put into the Mare Island Navy Yard for further work and repairs. Those modifications were completed on 18 August, and she returned to sea. *Walter A. Luckenbach* entered Mejillones, Chile, and loaded 10,000 tons of nitrates. She departed the Chilean port on 10 September, transited the Panama Canal, and arrived at Norfolk, Va., on the 24th. After discharging her cargo and completing voyage repairs, the ship cleared Capes Henry and Charles on 7 October and headed for Philadelphia. There, she loaded Army supplies bound for Europe and, on 29 October, headed for France. After a stop at Gibraltar, *Walter A. Luckenbach* arrived in Marseille on 14 November—three days after the armistice was signed—discharged her cargo, and loaded ballast for the return voyage. She stood out of Marseille on 26 November, stopped briefly at Gibraltar once again, and arrived in New York on 11 December.

On the day of her arrival, *Walter A. Luckenbach* was detached from the Naval Overseas Transportation Service and was reassigned to the Transport Force. At New York, she was converted to a troop transport to help in the task of bringing home American troops from Europe. By 22 January 1919, the ship was ready to begin her role in that large movement of people. Between late January and early July, *Walter A. Luckenbach* made five round-trip voyages to France, two to Bordeaux and three to St. Nazaire. She returned to New York from her final voyage on 11 July; was decommissioned at Hoboken, N.J., on 28 July 1919; and was returned to the Luckenbach Steamship Co. that same day. She entered into mercantile service with that company and labored in its behalf until 1950. During that year, she changed hands and names twice. First, she was sold to the New Orleans Coal & Bisso Towboat Co., Inc., and briefly served the company as SS *A. L. Bisso*. Later in the year, the Turkish firm Marsa Ithalat-Ithracat, T.A.S., bought her and renamed her SS *Mardin*. She served that firm and under that name for the remainder of her mercantile career. By 1955, her name had been dropped from the merchant vessel lists.

Walter Adams

(ScStr.: t. 271; l. 137'0''; b. 24'3''; dr. 8'6'' (mean); s. 10.5 k.; cpl. 27; a. none)

Walter Adams—a wooden-hull fishing craft built in 1890 by Robert Palmer and Son, of Noank, Conn., and rebuilt in 1898—was chartered by the Navy on 23 June 1918 for service in the 6th Naval District. Commissioned on 1 October 1918, Lt. (jg.) Hugh G. Taylor in command, and assigned the designation SP–400, *Walter*

Adams operated locally out of Charleston through the end of World War I. There are no records indicating exactly what the ship did during her operational career, but it appears likely that she conducted practice minesweeping operations. She was decommissioned at the Customs House Dock, Wilmington, N.C., on 10 January 1919; struck from the Navy list the same day; and simultaneously returned to her owner.

Walter B. Cobb

Walter Benjamin Cobb—born on 8 September 1919 at Grays, Kentucky—enlisted in the Navy on 17 November 1937 and attained the rating of coxswain.

While assigned to *Mugford* (DD–389), Cobb served in the crew of that destroyer's number four 5-inch mount. On 7 August 1942, *Mugford* screened transports unloading troops off Guadalcanal on the first day of the landings. At 1457, lookouts spotted seven planes with distinctive fixed landing gear. *Mugford* rang up 30 knots and prepared for action—putting her helm over hard right. Four of the planes—identified now as "Vals"—dove toward the destroyer; and each, in quick succession, dropped its bomb. The first struck the water 25 yards off *Mugford*'s starboard propeller guard; the second splashed 25 yards to port, abreast her number four torpedo tube mount; the third hit the ship's after deckhouse, silencing her after 5-inch and 20-millimeter guns, as well as disabling her secondary conning and after radio stations; and the last missed to starboard, some 200 yards off the bridge. In return, *Mugford* splashed two "Vals."

The direct hit aft blew four men overboard—including Cobb, who was uninjured. After *Ralph Talbot* (DD–390) picked up the four displaced sailors, Cobb volunteered to join the crew of that destroyer's number four gun.

In the early morning darkness of 9 August, *Ralph Talbot* patrolled the waters to the northeast of Savo Island to protect the northern flank of the transport forces still unloading off Tulagi and Guadalcanal. Between the destroyer and the transports, steamed the northern force of Allied cruisers: *Vincennes* (CA–44), *Astoria* (CA–34), and *Quincy* (CA–39). Unbeknownst to the Americans, a strong force of Japanese cruisers steamed into these waters. With lightning-like speed, the Japanese torpedoed Australian heavy cruiser *Canberra* and *Chicago* (CA–29) further to the south. They also set *Canberra* afire in a flurry of shellfire. Then, turning north, Rear Admiral Gunichi Mikawa's force, led by cruiser *Chokai*, proceeded to subject the other three American cruisers to an avalanche of shellfire.

Ralph Talbot sighted the first gun flashes at 0200 and altered course to close. At 0217, *Tenryu* spotted the destroyer and, in company with *Yubari* and *Furutaka*, loosed seven salvoes at *Ralph Talbot*. One shell struck her number one torpedo tube mount. Thinking that she was under fire from friendly guns, *Ralph Talbot* called out her identity over TBS radio; flashed her recognition lights and drew a respite—but not for long. *Yubari*, bringing up the rear of Mikawa's force, opened fire and, on the second salvo, got the range. Illuminated by searchlights and skewered by the shaft of light like a bug on the end of a pin, *Ralph Talbot* staggered under the impact of the Japanese barrage. Four 5.5-inch salvos struck in quick succession—the last of which hit the American destroyer's number four gun mount, killing Cobb. For his gallantry Cobb was awarded the Silver Star.

(APD–106: dp. 1,650; l. 306'0''; b. 37'0''; dr. 13'9''; s. 23.6 k.; cpl. 203; a. 1 5'', 6 40mm., 6 20mm.; cl. *Crosley*)

Walter B. Cobb (DE–596) was laid down on 15 January 1944 at Hingham, Mass., by the Bethlehem Shipbuilding Co.; launched on 23 February 1944; sponsored by Mrs. Huey Cobb; reclassified as a high-speed transport and redesignated APD–106 on 15 July 1944; and commissioned on 25 April 1945, Lt. Comdr. R. E. Parker, USNR, in command.

Following shakedown in Guantanamo Bay, Cuba, *Walter B. Cobb* departed Hampton Roads, Va., on 24 June, bound for the California coast; emerged from the Panama Canal on 1 July; and arrived at San Diego a week later. She conducted amphibious training exercises out of that port into August, preparing for the assault on the Japanese home islands. Shifting to Oceanside, Calif., on the 13th, *Walter B. Cobb* embarked Underwater Demolition Team (UDT) 27. But the following day, 14 August, Japan capitulated, obviating further invasions.

There now remained the occupation of the erstwhile enemy's land. *Walter B. Cobb* got underway for Japan on the 17th, steamed via Pearl Harbor, and entered Tokyo Bay on 4 September. Her embarked UDT 27 reconnoitered beaches, marked and mapped landing areas, and generally helped to set the stage for the occupation landings in the Tokyo area. The ship then returned, via Guam and Eniwetok, to Pearl Harbor and joined in the massive sealift of demobilized military men, Operation "Magic Carpet."

Walter B. Cobb made a cruise between Pearl Harbor and San Diego before sailing on 30 October 1945 for the Philippines. Proceeding via Guam, she arrived at Manila on 13 November; later touched at Subic Bay, Samar, and Leyte; and made two other visits to Manila before departing the Philippines on 22 January 1946. She sailed to San Pedro, Calif., and thence moved south to the Canal Zone before making port at New York on 9 March. Decommissioned on 29 March 1946, at Green Cove Springs, Fla., the ship was subsequently towed to Mayport, Fla., in April 1948, for berthing. She remained in reserve there until the communist invasion of South Korea in the summer of 1950.

As a result of the Navy's increased need for ships, *Walter B. Cobb* was recommissioned on 6 February 1951, Lt. Comdr. William D. Craig, USNR, in command. The ship conducted shakedown in Guantanamo Bay before engaging in amphibious exercises off Little Creek, Va., her new home port. From 1951 to 1954, *Walter B. Cobb* was homeported at Little Creek, Va., and made two Mediterranean deployments, as well as three midshipmen's cruises—to England and Ireland; to Canada and Cuba; and to Brazil. After landing exercises at Little Creek and at Onslow Beach, N.C., *Walter B. Cobb* got underway from Little Creek on 30 November 1954, bound for the west coast.

Homeported at Long Beach, Calif., *Walter B. Cobb* spent her next tour of duty primarily deployed to the Far East—from the spring of 1955 through the summer of 1956. She conducted local operations and exercises out of Yokosuka, Sasebo, and Kure before she returned, via Pearl Harbor, to the west coast of the United States for decommissioning. On 15 May 1957, *Walter B. Cobb* was placed out of commission and in reserve at the Mare Island Naval Shipyard, Vallejo, Calif. Her name was struck from the Navy list on 15 January 1966.

Sold to Taiwan on 22 February 1966, *Walter B. Cobb* and *Gantner* (APD–42) were accepted by the Chinese Navy on 15 March. The Chinese dispatched tug *Ta Tung* to tandem-tow the two transports to Taiwan. While en route to the western Pacific, the two APD's collided on 21 April and both suffered heavy damage. *Gantner* was towed to Treasure Island, Calif., but *Walter B. Cobb*, however, listed progressively from 18 to 40 degrees while settling aft. At 2340 on 21 April, the former high-speed transport filled with water and sank, stern first, in 2,100 fathoms of water.

Walter C. Wann

Walter Carl Wann, Jr.—born at Goldendale, Wash., on 13 May 1921—enlisted in the Navy at Portland, Oreg. on 14 December 1939 and eventually received the rating of pharmacist's mate, 2d class (PhM2/c). While on duty with marines engaged in the attack on Gavutu and Tanambogo, Pharmacist's Mate Wann received the Silver Star medal for conspicuous gallantry and "intrepidity during action" on the night of 7 August 1942. Japanese machine guns, raking the causeway between Gavutu and Tanambogo Islands, pinned down the marines with heavy fire. Wann volunteered to cross the area to render aid and return casualties to the aid station. Ignoring the enemy fire and with complete disregard of his own life, he sprinted back and forth, carrying and rendering aid to wounded marines. He remained attached to Marine units in the Guadalcanal campaign until killed in action on 4 November 1942.

(DE–412: dp. 1,350; l. 306'0''; b. 36'8''; dr. 9'5''; s. 24 k.; cpl. 186; a. 2 5'', 4 40mm., 10 20mm., 2 dct., 8 dcp., 1 dcp. (hh.), 3 21'' tt.; cl. *Rudderow*)

Walter C. Wann (DE–412) was laid down on 6 December 1943 at Houston, Tex., by the Brown Shipbuilding Co.; launched on 19 January 1944; sponsored by Mrs. Walter C. Wann, Sr.; and commissioned on 2 May 1944, Lt. Comdr. John W. Stedman, Jr., USNR, in command.

Following her Caribbean shakedown from 25 May to 23 June, *Walter C. Wann* underwent availability at Boston from 24 June to 5 July and got underway on the 6th in company with *Abercrombie* (DE–343), bound for Hampton Roads, Va. Arriving at Norfolk on 7 July, *Walter C. Wann* and *Abercrombie* got underway on the 8th for the Dutch West Indies. She escorted four gasoline tankers (AOG's) to St. Nicholas Bay, Aruba, where they loaded petroleum cargoes from 13 to 15 July. The task unit proceeded thence to Cristobal, Canal Zone, and arrived on the 17th, whereupon the unit was dissolved, and the escorts were assigned to duty with the Panama Sea Frontier.

Walter C. Wann soon joined *Abercrombie* and *McCoy Reynolds* (DE–440) in antisubmarine patrols on the Aruba-Canal Zone tanker route as TU 05.3.2 as a result of increased U-boat activity in the vicinity. The destroyer escort departed for Guantanamo Bay, Cuba, on the 21st, in company with *McCoy Reynolds*. On the afternoon of the 22d, the two ships received orders to assist a downed Martin PBM Mariner approximately 200 miles away.

Ringing up flank speed, *Walter C. Wann* and her sister ship proceeded to the scene and sighted signal flares at 2224 on that day. Braving strong winds and high seas, the escorts picked up all 40 survivors; and *McCoy Reynolds* prepared to tow the plane to port, but the arrival of *SC–1281* on the scene obviated her undertaking that task. *Walter C. Wann* then proceeded to Kingston, Jamaica, to disembark the survivors and arrived at 2016 on the 23d. She proceeded back to sea on the following day, escorting two merchantmen to the Canal Zone, and arrived at Cristobal with her charges on the evening of 25 July. She transited the Panama Canal on the 26th and reported for duty with the Pacific Fleet on the following day.

Walter C. Wann, in company with *LeRoy Wilson* (DE–414) and *McCoy Reynolds*, departed Balboa on 29 July; proceeded to the California coast, and arrived at San Diego on 6 August. From 7 August to 4 September, the ship underwent major engineering repairs and received a new high pressure turbine, conducting sea trials for the new turbine. She then got underway for Hawaii on 5 September, proceeding independently, and arrived at Pearl Harbor six days later.

From 21 to 30 September, the ship escorted a 16-vessel convoy from Pearl Harbor to Eniwetok, Marshall Islands, before proceeding on toward the Admiralties—as part of TU 33.1.1 which consisted of four other destroyer escorts, *Preserver* (ARS–8), and *ATF–100*—and arriving at Seeadler Harbor, Manus, on 6 October.

Walter C. Wann sortied in the screen of TG 77.4—the escort carrier group commanded by Rear Admiral Thomas L. Sprague—and nicknamed "Taffy Two"—on 12 October, to support American landings at Leyte in the Philippine Islands. While en route to the launching areas off Leyte Gulf, a tropical disturbance of near-typhoon intensity struck the task group on 17 October.

Local combat air patrols (CAP) protected the carriers as they launched their air strikes against Japanese positions on Leyte; and, as a result, *Walter C. Wann* and her fellow escorts did not initially see any enemy air activity. Operating off Samar during the daytime, the group retired each evening to the eastward.

Arriving back off Samar on 25 October to commence the day's air strikes, TG 77.4 received reconnaissance reports indicating the closing presence of a large Japanese surface force; and, by 0700, the northern carrier group, TU 77.4.3, was under attack. *Walter C. Wann*, with the southern carrier group, screened her charges as they launched all available aircraft while retiring to the southeast. By 0900, the enemy forces—reported as consisting of three battleships, eight cruisers, and numerous destroyers—closed the southern group. On the horizon to the northward could be seen pilars of smoke from the death struggle of the northern group—four groups of shell splashes suddenly erupted astern of *Walter C. Wann* as the enemy dropped in their heavy shells and groped for the range. While the destroyers of the southern group prepared to make smoke and dash in, in a suicidal torpedo attack, *Walter C. Wann* and her sister ships formed a circular screen around the highly vulnerable escort carriers. Air strikes and torpedo attacks had by 1100 diverted the Japanese from the carriers, and the range opened to 40 miles, thus ending the immediate threat to the southern group.

After retiring to the Admiralties, *Walter C. Wann* anchored at Seeadler Harbor on 3 November. As if having a Japanese task force breathing down her neck at Samar had not been enough, *Walter C. Wann* again came close to being damaged at Manus on 10 November when *Mount Hood* (AE–10) blew up in a cataclysmic blast which atomized the ammunition ship and damaged many other ships in the immediate area. *Walter C. Wann*, 2,000 yards off the doomed ship's port quarter, found herself showered by debris from the exploding ammunition ship but fortunately sustained only minimal damage, and none of her men were hurt.

Back on escort duty on 27 November, the destroyer escort screened Transport Division 10 on its voyage to Cape Gloucester, New Britain, arriving at Borgen Bay on the 28th. She conducted antisubmarine screening off the entrance to the bay until proceeding independently to Manus on 30 November—anchoring at Seeadler Harbor on 1 December.

While at Manus, the ship received additional radio equipment, thus outfitting herself for her new duty of landing craft control ship during the Lingayen Gulf landings on the Philippine island of Luzon. A round-trip voyage to and from New Britain preceded her linking up with TG 79.6; and, on 15 December, Capt. E. A. Seay (Commander, TG 79.6, and Commander, LST Flotilla 14) embarked with his staff; *Walter C. Wann* then departed for training exercises and acted as flag and control ship. Capt. Seay then disembarked on the 22d and transferred to *LST–610*.

Two days after Christmas, 1944, *Walter C. Wann* got underway as part of TU 79.11.3, screening TG 79.5 and 79.6. On 2 January, she fell in astern of TG 78.5 and proceeded through Surigao Strait and into the Mindanao Sea on 5 January and into the Sulu Sea on the 6th. On 7 January, while the American force was in the Mindoro Strait, two "Oscars" attacked the disposition astern of *Walter C. Wann* at 1822. One dropped a bomb and was shot down by an LST, and the second attacked *Walter C. Wann*, only to be driven off by antiaircraft fire.

The destroyer escort reached Lingayen Gulf on 9 January and took station ahead of TG 79.6—Tractor Group Baker—as control ship, anchoring off Lingayen beach at 0737. Capt. Seay returned to *Walter C. Wann* and established his temporary headquarters on board.

While she lay anchored off Lingayen, *Walter C. Wann* provided antiaircraft fire in attempts to repel Japanese suicide plane attacks. However, despite the intense antiaircraft fire, one plane succeeded in crashing into *Columbia* (CL–56) some 1,500 yards ahead of the destroyer escort. Another suicider attempted to attack *Pennsylvania* (BB–38)—located off the destroyer escort's starboard beam—but was driven off, heavily damaged.

At 1530 on 9 January, *Walter C. Wann* got underway and moved in a further 1,800 yards toward Lingayen and dropped anchor off the town. CTG 79.6 shifted to *LST–610* soon thereafter, and the destroyer escort, thus relieved of her control-ship duties, got underway again to proceed through a heavy smoke screen and rendezvous as part of the screen for TU 79.14.1 which was proceeding to Leyte Gulf.

This task unit—consisting of kamikaze-damaged *Columbia*, *Louisville* (CA–28), and Australian heavy cruiser *Australia*, as well as transports, LSD's, LSV's—was attacked by a single plane on 10 January but drove off the attacker with gunfire. Two days later, the destroyer escort and *Jenkins* (DD–447) escorted *Kadashan Bay* (CVE–76) to the inner harbor of San Pedro Bay, Leyte, and anchored there at 1957 on the 12th. She spent the 14th on antisubmarine patrol before returning to her anchorage on the 15th for provisioning.

Walter C. Wann conducted local operations and convoy escort missions between Dutch New Guinea and Philippine waters into the late winter of 1944 and 1945. She got underway on 27 March in the screen for Transport Group "Easy," bound for Nansei Shoto in the Ryukyus. Approaching Okinawa Shima with the invasion force on the morning of D day, 1 April, her task unit was deployed to their respective screening stations—*Walter C. Wann* taking station A–29. At 0603 on 1 April, the destroyer escort took an "Oscar" under fire, but the pilot commenced evasive maneuvers and banked away from the ship. That evening, Transport Division 40, one of Transport Group "Easy," conducted night retirement, with *Walter C. Wann* among the escorts.

Upon conclusion of the night retirement evolutions, *Walter C. Wann* screened the transports at various stations and participated in a hunter/killer group operation. For the remainder of her first week off Okinawa and into the second, the ship observed considerable air raids—some taking heavy tolls on American light forces engaged in supporting the invasion of Okinawa.

At 1309 on 12 April, the Japanese launched a determined series of air strikes which lasted until 1720. During this time, at 1418, an Aichi "Val" began a suicide dive on *Walter C. Wann* from the starboard side. At about 500 yards away, the dive bomber faltered, pulled up slightly, and crossed the ship in a steep vertical bank before crashing 20 feet off the port bow. At 1500, a second attack occurred, another "Val" streaking in for *Walter C. Wann*. The destroyer escort's gunners set it afire; and, as it faltered, the "Val" was shot out of the sky by two American fighters.

Walter C. Wann remained on patrol off Okinawa until 14 April, when she sailed for Guam in company with *Nevada* (BB–36), *Maryland* (BB–46), and *Pensacola* (CA–24), as TU 51.29.14, escorting a convoy of transports. Arriving at Apra Harbor, Guam, on the 19th, *Walter C. Wann* effected battle damage repairs until 6 May, when she sailed for Saipan in the Marianas. She next escorted TU 94.19.18—AK's, LST's, LCI's and LSM's—in company with *Hemminger* (DE–746) and three SC's, arriving at Okinawa on 14 May. For the next several days following her arrival, *Walter C. Wann* was assigned to various patrol stations and, although frequent enemy air attacks sent the ship to an anxious succession of alerts at general quarters, she did not encounter any enemy aircraft herself. The destroyer escort remained on screening duty, supporting the Okinawa strike through June, escorting everything from landing ship docks (LSD's) to light cruisers. On 4 July, *Walter C. Wann* joined Vice Admiral Jesse B. Oldendorf's Task Force 32. TF 32 provided cover for the operations in the Ryukyus and for the minesweeping operations underway in the East China Sea (conducted by TG 39.11).

Walter C. Wann remained engaged in screening operations for the remainder of the war and was at anchor in Buckner Bay when word of the Japanese surrender first came through. The ship conducted training exercises and tactical drills into September, subsequently riding out four typhoons between July and October. During this time, the ship steamed to Wakayama, Honshu, Japan, standing in readiness to render support for the landings there should it be needed. The 6th Army landed without incident to occupy the key Osaka-Kyoto-Kobe area, and *Walter C. Wann* later rendered plane-guard duties for *Suwannee* (CVE–27) off the Hiroshima-Kure occupation zone.

Walter C. Wann continued her support duties for the American occupation of Japan through the late fall of 1945. On 4 November, in company with CortDiv 69, the destroyer escort got underway from Yokosuka, bound, via Pearl Harbor, for San Diego, Calif.

Assigned to the 19th Fleet (Pacific Reserve Fleet), *Walter C. Wann* was placed out of commission, in reserve, at San Diego, Calif., on 31 May 1946.

Her post-1946 records are sketchy. Some documents suggest that in November 1951 the ship may have joined reserve training exercises, although she is officially listed as being "in reserve, out of commission." Movement reports indicate that the ship was at San Diego from 8 November 1951 to 5 June 1956; at Long Beach from 5 to 22 June 1956; and at San Diego from 23 June 1956 to 10 June 1958. Further indications show the ship attached to the San Diego Reserve Group into 1960 and berthed at the Stockton Reserve Facility near Mare Island, Vallejo, Calif. In any event, *Walter C. Wann* was struck from the Navy list on 30 June 1968; acquired by the National Metal and Steel Co., of Terminal Island, Calif., in June 1969; and scrapped soon thereafter.

Walter C. Wann received four battle stars for World War II service.

Walter D. Munson

(ScStr.: dp. 8,375; l. 384'6''; b. 48'0'' (wl.); dr. 22'6''; s. 12 k.; cpl. 65; a. 1 5'', 1 3'')

Walter D. Munson (Id. No. 1510)—a freighter constructed in 1917 by the Bethlehem Steel Co. in its yard at Sparrows Point, Md.—was acquired by the United States Shipping Board from the Munson Steamship Lines early in 1918; turned over to the Navy on 15 April 1918; and commissioned on 19 April 1918 at New York City, Lt. Comdr. William J. Connors, USNRF, in command.

Assigned to the Naval Overseas Transportation Service, she loaded Army supplies at New York and put to sea on 25 April with a convoy bound for France. The ship concluded her first Atlantic crossing at Brest on 10 May and moved on to Gironde on the 13th, in which port she unloaded her cargo and took on ballast for the return voyage. On 27 May, *Walter D. Munson* departed Gironde with a New York-bound convoy. She entered New York on 7 June, completed voyage repairs, and loaded another Army cargo.

The freighter's second east-bound convoy sailed for Europe on 18 June and arrived in Brest on Independence Day 1918. This time, she unloaded a portion of her cargo at Brest before moving on to Gironde on the 6th. The cargoman completed her unloading at Gironde, took on ballast, and stood out to sea on 24 July. Her convoy arrived back in New York on 6 August, and

Walter D. Munson made voyage repairs before loading supplies in preparation for her third voyage to Europe and back.

Walter D. Munson departed New York on 15 August and entered Brest 15 days later. On the 31st, she was routed on to Le Havre where she discharged her cargo. Before setting out back across the Atlantic, the ship visited Plymouth, England, where she topped off her bunkers with coal. Her return convoy rendezvoused on 10 September and stood into New York on the 23d.

During a week at New York, *Walter D. Munson* completed another series of voyage repairs and loaded her fourth Europe-bound cargo. On 30 September, she departed New York in convoy for France. The ship arrived at Le Havre on 16 October, discharged her cargo there, and then headed back to the United States on the 24th, arriving home on 6 November. Though hostilities ceased on the 11th, she completed her turnaround and, four days later, started back across the Atlantic. *Walter D. Munson* reached France at Quiberon Bay on 27 November, discharged a portion of her cargo there, and then moved on to Nantes where she unloaded the remainder. The ship stood out of Nantes on 6 December and headed for Brest where she loaded a cargo of steel rails for return to the United States. She left Brest on 11 December and arrived in New York on Christmas Eve. After unloading the steel rails, *Walter D. Munson* took on a cargo of commissary supplies and gas. On 8 January, she set out upon her last round-trip voyage to Europe. The freighter entered Quiberon Bay on 24 January and, on the 29th, continued on to Nantes where she discharged her cargo. She returned to sea on 15 February and set a course for the Delaware capes.

She arrived at Philadelphia on 7 March and there received word of her imminent demobilization. *Walter D. Munson* was placed out of commission on 14 April 1919 and was simultaneously returned to her owners. She served with the Munson Steamship Lines until 1940 when she was sold to the Greek firm, Rethymnis & Kulukundis (Hellas) S.A. of Piraeus, Greece. Renamed SS *Mount Kyllene*, the ship remained in merchant service operating out of Piraeus, Greece, until 1960 at which time her name disappeared from mercantile lists.

Walter Forward

Walter Forward—born on 24 January 1786 at Old Granby (now East Granby), Conn.—spent the first 14 years of his life at the place of his birth. In 1800, he moved with his family to a farm near Aurora, Ohio; but, after three years of farming with his father, he moved to Pittsburgh where he studied law in the office of Henry Baldwin, one of the best-known attorneys in Pennsylvania. Admitted to the bar in 1806, Forward quickly established his reputation as an able trial lawyer. He served for years in the Pennsylvania State Legislature and, after Baldwin resigned from Congress, Forward was chosen to serve the remainder of his term, took his seat in the House of Representatives on 2 December 1822, and served in that chamber until 3 March 1825. He then returned to the practice of law but remained active in both state and national politics. He played an important role in the establishment of the Whig Party in the 1830's and took a prominent part in the Pennsylvania state constitutional convention of 1837 and 1838.

As a reward for his part in William Henry Harrison's successful bid for the Presidency in 1840, Forward was offered the office of United States district attorney for western Pennsylvania. He declined that appointment but accepted one as Comptroller of the Treasury, taking office on 6 April 1841. He held that position only five months for, on 13 September, he was appointed Secretary of the Treasury in the cabinet shuffle which followed Harrison's death and John Tyler's succession to the Presidency. Since constant friction with the new President marred his entire tenure as Secretary of the

Treasury, he left Tyler's cabinet on 28 February 1843, returned to Pittsburgh, and resumed the practice of law. On 8 November 1849, President Zachary Taylor appointed him chargé d'affaires to Denmark, and Forward served in that office until 10 October 1851. Soon after his return to the United States, Forward took over the post of president judge of the district court of Allegheny County; and he served on the bench until his death on 24 November 1852.

(RC: t. 150; a. 6 9-pdrs.)

Walter Forward—a schooner built in 1841 by William Easby at Washington, D.C., for service as a cutter in the Revenue Marine—was delivered to that service at Washington on 23 April 1842. Operating out of Baltimore, Md., she served with the Revenue Marine until 1846. On 16 May of that year, soon after hostilities broke out with Mexico, *Walter Forward* was ordered to sail to Philadelphia, make repairs there, and then to join the naval forces in the Gulf of Mexico as soon as possible. She set sail for the gulf on 23 May in company with another cutter, *Ewing*, and arrived at South West Pass of the Mississippi River on 19 June. There, General Zachary Taylor ordered the ship to blockade a stretch of the Mexican coast near Soto la Marina and capture any ships engaged in trade with the enemy. That and similar missions occupied her mid-summer. On 23 August, she received orders to report for duty with Commodore David Conner's naval squadron off Tampico. Four days later, she entered the anchorage at Anton Lizardo and began patrolling off Tampico. That assignment lasted until the middle of September, at which time she moved farther down the coast to join the blockade of Veracruz.

In mid-October, she joined a force commanded by Matthew Calbraith Perry. On the 15th, Perry's ships attempted to cross the bar at the mouth of the Alvarado River. The steamer *Vixen* led the way and succeeded in making her crossing, and *Walter Forward* followed, in tow of sister revenue cutter *McLane*. *McLane* grounded on the bar while the three ships towed fouled each other's towlines. *Vixen* engaged the Mexican batteries on shore but, when it became apparent that *McLane* would never succeed in getting across the bar, she and her tows retired. Luckily, *McLane* came off the bar, and all American ships retired.

The next day, however, *Walter Forward* set sail for a similar, but far more successful, operation at the mouth of the Tabasco River on the Yucatan peninsula. Successfully navigating the bar on the 23d, the force quickly seized the town of Frontera and took several prizes in the process. *Walter Forward* and the other small steamers attached to Perry's force then continued the foray, sailing 74 miles up the river through hostile territory to the town of Tabasco. There, they seized additional enemy shipping—before returning to the ocean on the 26th. However, *Walter Forward* remained at Frontera until late November, engaged in the destruction of the captured Mexican shipping. She departed the area on 21 November and returned to the base at Anton Lizardo on the 23d.

In December, the revenue cutter left the Mexican coast to carry dispatches to Belize City in British Honduras. She returned to blockade duty on 7 February 1847 and took station off Veracruz once again on the 9th. She continued routine blockade operations at various points along the eastern coast of Mexico until April. On the 15th, she received orders to set sail for Wilmington, Del. Voyaging by way of New Orleans, La., she reached her destination on 23 May.

She underwent repairs during the summer of 1847 and, that fall, transferred to the cognizance of the Coast Survey. *Walter Forward* completed that duty in mid-December and resumed service with the Revenue Marine at Wilmington. She performed routine Revenue Marine duty for most of the remainder of her active career. During the Civil War, *Walter Forward*

participated in troop transport convoys in the Chesapeake and took part in one small skirmish at the mouth of Wicomico River in Virginia. Her career ended soon after the end of that war. Her sale was ordered at Baltimore on 30 November 1865.

Walter Hardcastle

Walter Hardcastle—a steel-hulled tanker completed in 1912 at Toledo, Ohio, by the Toledo Shipbuilding Co. for the Sinclair Navigation Co.—was assigned Id. No. 2464 when the Navy was considering acquisition of the vessel for duty with the Naval Overseas Transportation Service. However, no records have been found indicating that the ship was ever taken over.

Walter S. Brown

Walter Scott Brown—born on 14 March 1916 at North Loup, Nebr.—enlisted in the Navy on 9 January 1940. Assigned to Patrol Squadron (VP) 24 on 9 October, Brown advanced to the rank of aviation machinists' mate 2d class on 1 November 1941.

Flying PBY Catalinas, VP-24 operated on patrol flights out of Naval Air Station Kaneohe Bay, Oahu, Hawaii. When Japanese carrier-based aircraft struck Pearl Harbor on 7 December, they also attacked other Navy and Army facilities on Oahu, including Kaneohe Bay. As the enemy planes bombed and strafed the seaplane base, Brown completely disregarded the danger to his own life as he attempted to repel the attack. Killed in action during the fight, Brown was commended by the Commander in Chief of the United States Fleet for his selfless bravery.

(DE–258: dp. 1,140; l. 289'5''; b. 35'1''; dr. 8'3''; s. 21 k.; cpl. 156; a. 3 3'', 4 1.1'', 9 20mm., 2 dct., 8 dcp., 1 dcp. (hh.); cl. *Evarts*)

Walter S. Brown (DE–258) was laid down on 10 January 1943 at Boston, Mass., by the Boston Navy Yard; launched on 22 February 1943; sponsored by Mrs. Garth Thomas; and commissioned on 25 June 1943, Lt. Comdr. W. L. Harmon in command.

Following shakedown in Casco Bay, Maine, *Walter S. Brown* joined Escort Division (CortDiv) 5 and began escorting convoys across the Atlantic to Gibraltar and North African ports. By the spring of 1944, she had completed four such round-trip voyages, keeping a vigilant watch for Axis submarines and aircraft as she shepherded the merchantmen. Interspersed between these voyages were periods of refresher training and availability.

On 20 April 1944, *Walter S. Brown* arrived at Hampton Roads, Va., to join the screen of UGS–40. Three days later, this group—which included some 65 merchantmen—sailed for the Mediterranean. The screen, led by *Campbell* (WPG–32), contained three elderly flush-decked, four-pipe destroyers, six American destroyer escorts from CortDiv 5, and two French destroyer escorts.

Due to the success of recent attacks by the German Luftwaffe against Allied convoys in the western Mediterranean, UGS–40 sailed with an elaborate air defense plan, formulated by the convoy's screen commander, Comdr. Jesse C. Sowell, in *Campbell*. Practiced in Hampton Roads prior to the convoy's departure and as it crossed the Atlantic, these tactics were designed to meet mass aerial attacks by German aircraft carrying a variety of weapons ranging from bombs, to torpedoes, to radio-controlled glider bombs. Only a short time before, such a complex attack had devastatingly mauled UGS–38.

Off Gibraltar, UGS–40 acquired additional escorts— British antiaircraft cruiser HMS *Caledon*, *Wilhoite* (DE–397), *Benson* (DD–421), and two American minesweepers carrying special apparatus to jam radar transmissions and thus confuse the German glider bombs. A British salvage tug brought up the rear of the reinforcements.

On 9 May, the convoy possed through the Straits of Gibraltar without incident but, two days later, detected German "snoopers" trailing the convoy. In the next few hours, 10 successive shore-based fighter interception sorties—even sorties conducted by British radar-equipped Bristol Beaufighters—failed to drive off the enemy reconnaissance aircraft. The Germans persistently maintained contact with the Allied ships.

First alerted by shore-based radar "eyes," the escort screen went to general quarters at 1316 on 11 May, beginning the first of five successive "on again—off again" alerts. *Walter S. Brown* took station on the starboard bow of the convoy, some 6,000 yards from the guide. In *Campbell*, the commander of the screen, Jesse Clyburn Sowell, enjoined his escorts to be especially vigilant and warned that a dusk attack was well within the realm of possibility. At 2025, radar noted the approach of enemy aircraft; and Sowell formed his charges into eight columns 1,000 yards apart to allow for plenty of maneuvering room. As UGS–40 went to general quarters at 2043 that evening, *Dobler* (DE–48) and *Ellis* (DD–154) took stations on *Walter S. Brown*'s flanks.

When the enemy was reported 70 miles north of Cape Corbelin, UGS–40 steered due east, through a smooth sea barely rippled by the light easterly airs, past Cape Bengut. Eleven minutes after sunset beneath a moonless, overcast sky—*Walter S. Brown* received orders to commence laying smoke.

The Germans—a mixed force of Junkers Ju.–88's, Heinkel He. 111's, and Dornier Do. 217's—approached from the stern of the convoy and broke into groups to attack from different points of the compass. Eight minutes after the initial sightings, the first German planes came in low and fast and entered *Walter S. Brown*'s defense sector. The destroyer escort trained her guns on two planes, but these targets quickly slipped out of range. Two more, however, then came into range. *Walter S. Brown* commenced fire with her forward 20-millimeter and 3-inch battery and scored hits on both planes. One climbed for a moment into a steep, almost vertical bank but then faltered and crashed astern of the ship.

Seconds later, a fifth plane bore in fast across the destroyer escort's bow and her starboard side and crossed over to port. Both *Walter S. Brown* and *Dobler* deluged the plane in a murderous cross fire of 20-millimeter and 1.1-inch guns that slapped it into the sea. "Almost immediately," wrote Lt. Comdr. Louis B. Burdette, USNR, in his action report, "another single plane was reported coming in from ahead." Again all forward guns swung about, tracked their target, and opened fire as the plane swung right to attempt to launch a torpedo at the lead escorts. Despite the fact that they could not hear the bearings being called out from the bridge over the sound-powered phones, the gunners manning the Oerlikons kept up a withering fire which forced the fifth enemy away.

When the smoke of battle cleared, the Allied force had emerged unscathed from the German gauntlet. *Walter S. Brown*, which had taken six enemy planes under fire during the seven-minute engagement, dropped astern at 2153—in company with *Evarts* (DE–5); British tug *Hengist*; and *Cimieterre*—to search for possible casualties. After a prolonged and thorough search in which they found nothing, the ships returned to the convoy for the remainder of the voyage.

Of UGS–40's defense, Comdr. Sowell had high praise for the men and ships of the convoy's screen; and he was especially complimentary in judging *Walter S. Brown*'s performance. "It is believed," he wrote, "that her performance, when coordinated with the other forces present, broke up the enemy's attack, disrupted his plans, and resulted in no Allied losses; whereas, the enemy suffered a heavy loss of planes."

For the remainder of the war in Europe, *Walter S.*

Brown continued to escort convoys on round trips from the east coast of the United States to North African ports. Then, in the summer of 1945, she operated briefly in training exercises with submarines off the northeast coast of the United States. Decommissioned at the New York Naval Shipyard on 4 October 1945, *Walter S. Brown* was struck from the Navy list on 24 October 1945. Her scrapping by the New York Naval Shipyard was completed by 12 July 1946.

Walter S. Brown received one battle star for her World War II service.

Walter S. Gorka

Walter Stanley Gorka—born on 24 March 1922 at Windsor Locks, Conn.—enlisted in the Naval Reserve at Hartford, Conn., on 15 May 1940 and eventually attained the rate of aviation ordnanceman, third class.

Attached to Escort Scouting Squadron (VGS) 27 which was embarked in the auxiliary carrier *Suwannee* (ACV–27) at the time of Operation "Torch"—the invasion of French North Africa—Gorka served as bombardier and gunner in the aircrew of a Grumman TBF–1 Avenger of that squadron.

On 8 November 1942—the first day of the landings—*Suwannee*'s air group bombed French ships and shore installations in the Casablanca area, including the immobile but formidable battleship *Jean Bart* and the coast defense and shore batteries at Table d'Aukasha. Two days later, Gorka went on an attack mission against a French submarine. The French antiaircraft fire proved deadly accurate, and Gorka's plane was shot down.

For his performance of duty with VGS–27 during "Torch," Gorka received the Air Medal posthumously.

(APD–114: dp. 1,650; l. 306'0''; b. 37'0''; dr. 13'9''; s. 23.6 k.; cpl. 221; a. 1 5'', 6 40mm., 6 20mm.; cl. *Crosley*)

Walter S. Gorka (APD–114) was laid down on 3 April 1945 at Hingham, Mass., by the Bethlehem Shipbuilding Co.; launched on 26 May 1945; sponsored by Mrs. Josephine B. Gorka; and commissioned on 7 August 1945, Comdr. R. G. Werner, USNR, in command.

Following fitting out, *Walter S. Gorka* conducted shakedown training in Guantanamo Bay, Cuba, from 2 to 27 September and subsequently carried some 140 officers and men to the United States. Upon her return, she was ordered to remain in commission, in reserve, at the St. John's River reserve group at Green Cove Springs, Fla. She served there as headquarters ship during the deactivation of several of her sister ships. The ship was decommissioned in January 1947 and struck from the Navy list in June 1960. *Walter S. Gorka* was subsequently acquired by the government of Ecuador for conversion and use as a floating power plant.

Walter X. Young

Walter Xavier Young was born in Chicago, Ill., on 22 October 1918. He enlisted in the Marine Corps Reserve on 6 January 1941 and, following training at the Marine Barracks, Quantico, Va., was commissioned a second lieutenant on 29 May 1941. After commissioning, Lt. Young received training at the Signal Corps School, Fort Monmouth, N.J., and was then assigned to the Marine Barracks, New River, N.C., into 1942.

Promoted to first lieutenant on 6 June 1942, he was communications officer of a Marine parachute battalion which took part in the attack upon Gavutu, Solomon Islands, on 7 August 1942. During the extremely dangerous initial landings on Gavutu, Lt. Young single-handedly assaulted a Japanese-held dugout commanding a portion of the dock on the island which was a key objective. While successfully penetrating and neutralizing the dugout, Young was wounded by rifle fire and died later that day. For his heroic action, Lt. Young was awarded the Navy Cross posthumously.

On 7 February 1944, the name *Walter X. Young* was approved for DE-723, a *Rudderow*-class destroyer escort slated to be built by the Dravo Corp., of Pittsburgh, Pa. However, before work on the ship began, the contract for her construction was cancelled on 12 March 1944 in order to free the Dravo yard for the building of landing craft.

I

(APD-131: dp. 1,650; l. 306'0''; b. 37'0''; dr. 12'7''; s. 23.6 k.; cpl. 201; tr. 162; a. 1 5'', 6 40mm., 6 20mm.; cl. *Crosley*)

Walter X. Young (DE-715) was laid down on 27 May 1944 at Bay City, Mich., by the Defoe Shipbuilding Co.; reclassified a high-speed transport and redesignated APD-131 on 15 July 1944; launched on 30 September 1944; sponsored by Mrs. John J. McGeeney; and commissioned on 1 May 1945, Lt. Comdr. Nicholas Biddle, USNR, in command.

After conducting shakedown in Guantanamo Bay, *Walter X. Young* interrupted her voyage to Norfolk when she transported an emergency appendectomy patient from *LSM-406* to Guantanamo Bay for medical attention. Upon the completion of this mission of mercy, she arrived at Hampton Roads on 10 June. Post-shakedown availability and training exercises preceded her sailing south for Fort Pierce, Fla., for specialized training with underwater demolition teams (UDT). She departed the east coast on 30 July for San Pedro, Calif.; transited the Panama Canal on 3 August; and, while en route up the Pacific coast of Mexico, received word of the atomic bomb detonation at Hiroshima on the 6th and, three days later, of a nuclear blast at Nagasaki, and of Russia's entry into the Pacific war the same day.

Two days after her arrival at San Diego on 12 August, further welcome news arrived, telling that Japan had accepted the unconditional surrender terms of the Potsdam Declaration and had capitulated. As a result of this development, *Walter X. Young*'s original orders—calling for her embarked UDT personnel to take part in the projected invasion of Japan—were cancelled. Instead, the ship received a different mission.

On 16 August, *Walter X. Young* embarked the 93 men of UDT 22 (Lt. Comdr. J. F. Chace, USNR, in command) and, after sunset on that date, sailed for the Hawaiian Islands. Arriving at Pearl Harbor on the morning of 22 August, she fueled and provisioned to capacity, loaded UDT explosives, and got underway on the afternoon of the 23d for Japan.

Her group steamed via the Marshall Islands, arrived in Tokyo Bay on 4 September, and reported to Vice Admiral Theodore S. "Ping" Wilkinson, Commander, 3d Amphibious Force. With the group now reconstituted as Task Group (TG) 32.2, as two further APD's and their embarked UDT's joined, they awaited their assignments. The dock areas at Yokohama—the scene for one of the major initial occupation landings—were found to be in good condition, suitable for immediate use. Thus, they did not require reconnoitering by the UDT's for possible mines or other obstructions. Midway through her stay in Tokyo Bay, *Walter X. Young* was buffeted about by a typhoon. With high winds and seas, she dragged her anchor and eventually shifted anchorage to the lee side of the bay. During the height of the tempest, the APD received word from *Topeka* (CL-67) that one of *Walter X. Young*'s boats—an LCPR—which had been loaned to the cruiser, had broken away and been lost. When the storm cleared, however, the "missing" craft was seen riding at a painter astern of the cruiser and later was recovered intact.

On the 20th, the ship's waiting period ended. In company with *Gantner* (APD-42), *Walter X. Young* got underway on that date for Aomori, on the northern end of Honshu, to conduct a reconaissance and beach survey and to clear any obstacles that might impede Army landings. The two APD's escorted *Catamount* (LSD-17) on this short voyage. While en route on the 21st, the American warships sighted a floating mine and sank it with rifle fire. Upon arrival at Mutsu Kaiwan on the 22d, *Gantner* proceeded to Ominato to pick up local Japanese officials to assist in the clearance program. Meanwhile, *Walter X. Young* proceeded to Aomori, where, with the aid of underwater sounding devices, she located the hulks of three sunken ships. Swimmers from UDT 22 then attached buoys to them, while a fourth wreck also located during the survey was found to have been already helpfully buoyed by the Japanese.

On the 23d, UDT 22 surveyed the beach and its approaches, as well as the available exits to the main highway which ran parallel to the beach itself, to the eastward of Aomori. They found nothing which required dynamiting but did attach buoys to some small wrecks at one end of the beach. They reported that the beach was suitable for all types of landing craft; was capable of supporting vehicles; and possessed several exits to the main road. Placing beach markers and drawing up maps of the area, *Walter X. Young*'s UDT conducted an additional survey the following day, thus preparing the way for the landings at Aomori which followed on the 25th and continued throughout the day. Detached on the evening of the 25th, *Walter X. Young* reported to Commander, TG 32.2, for orders.

Anchoring at Ominato on the evening of the 26th, the ship obtained information concerning Japanese minefields still extant in Tsugaru Strait and the next day got underway for Niigata, on the west coast of Honshu. Proceeding independently, the ship rendezvoused with a Japanese tug—the Japanese craft carrying two American Army officers who had travelled overland from Tokyo, several Japanese police, and a local pilot—off the port. In an ensuing conference, it was learned that although the Japanese claimed to have swept a channel into Niigata, the width of the channel was too narrow to provide a margin of safety for an occupation force of transports. However, some 15 miles north of Niigata lay Senami. *Walter X. Young*'s embarked UDT soon surveyed the beach and found it in excellent condition. Nevertheless, any landings should be conducted in calm weather or with a prevailing off-shore wind due to the beach's exposed position on the Sea of Japan. Marking and mapping the beach, UDT 22 reembarked in *Walter X. Young*, and the ship got underway for Tokyo Bay, stopping at Hakodate, Hokkaido, en route, to pick up an officer from UDT 22 who had served a tour of detached duty there.

Walter X. Young dropped anchor at Yokohama on 30 September. On 12 October, she got underway for the west coast of the United States and steamed homeward via Guam and Pearl Harbor. The ship arrived at San Diego on 2 November and immediately disembarked UDT 22. Ten days of availability at the Naval Repair Base, San Diego, preceded the ship's participation in coastwise transportation of Navy and Marine Corps dischargees within the 11th Naval District. The ship was decommissioned on 2 July 1946 and placed in reserve at Stockton, Calif.

Struck from the Navy list on 1 May 1962 and stripped of all militarily useful items and equipment, *Walter X. Young* was towed from her berth with the Stockton Reserve Group to her final duty station—the Naval Missile Center at Point Mugu, Calif. Subsequently converted to a test hulk, *Walter X. Young* was sunk in missile-firing tests on 11 April 1967.

Walton

Merrit Cecil Walton—born at St. Paul, Minn., on 18 December 1915—enlisted in the United States Marine Corps on 19 May 1937 at San Francisco, Calif., and initially served at San Diego, Calif., before going to the Asiatic Station that autumn. As a member of the 4th Marine Regiment—quartered in the International Settlement of Shanghai, China—Walton witnessed part of the bloody battle that raged for that key city between Chinese and Japanese forces and, as such, was an early observer of Japanese aggression in the Far East. During his tour in China, he received promotion to private, 1st class, on 10 May 1939.

Returning to the United States in the autumn of 1940, Walton served successive tours of duty at the Marine barracks at Mare Island, Vallejo, Calif.; the Naval Air Station, Lakehurst, N.J.; Quantico, Va.; and New River, N.C. He was promoted to sergeant on 1 August 1941 and platoon sergeant on 8 April 1942.

Platoon Sergeant Walton was serving in a parachute battalion as part of the 1st Marine Division (Reinforced) that was selected to land in the Solomons in August 1942. Companies A and B of that battalion landed on the island of Gavutu on the morning of 7 August 1942. The enemy, already alterted by the landings on Guadalcanal and Tulagi, met the marines' frontal assault with a withering fire.

Although fully aware of the danger involved, Platoon Sergeant Walton volunteered to reconnoiter the position of a troublesome Japanese machine gun nest threatening his platoon's right flank. Once he had spotted the weapon's location, he led a daring attack during which the leathernecks silenced the gun. Mortally wounded, however, Platoon Sergeant Walton died later that same day. Posthumous awards accorded the sergeant included the Navy Cross, the Purple Heart, and a share of the Presidential Unit Citation awarded the 1st Marine Division (Reinforced).

(DE–361: dp. 1,350; l. 306'0''; b. 36'8''; dr. 9'5'' (mean); s. 24 k.; cpl. 186; a. 2 5'', 4 40mm., 10 20mm., 3 21'' tt., 2 dct., 8 dcp. 1 dcp. (hh.); cl. John C. Butler)

Walton (DE–361) was laid down on 21 March 1944 at Orange, Tex., by the Consolidated Steel Corp.; launched on 20 May 1944; sponsored by Mrs. Clara Olson, the mother of the late Sergeant Walton; and commissioned on 4 September 1944, Lt. Comdr. Wilbur S. Wills, Jr., in command.

After she conducted her shakedown out of Great Sound Bay, Bermuda, Walton underwent post-shakedown availability at the Boston Navy Yard. The new destroyer escort subsequently sailed for Hampton Roads, Va., and arrived at Norfolk on 15 November. While in that vicinity, she served as a school ship, training nucleus crews for the other destroyer escorts then entering the fleet.

When Escort Division (CortDiv) 85 was established, Walton was assigned to it and sailed for the Pacific. She transited the Panama Canal on 7 December and arrived at Bora Bora, in the Society Islands, on the 22d. From there, the destroyer escort pushed on for the Solomon Islands, touching at Port Purvis, Florida Island, and moved thence to Seeadler Harbor, Manus, in the Admiralty Islands. While at Manus, the ship underwent repairs and alterations. During that refit, her after 40-millimeter twin Bofors mount was replaced by a quadruple-mount Bofors—a necessary augmentation of the ship's antiaircraft battery that reflected the growing concern over the destructive attacks of Japanese suicide planes "divine wind"—or kamikaze.

Walton began her first active wartime duty at Hollandia late in January of the following year. On 21 January 1945, the destroyer escort departed that port, bound for the Philippines as part of the escort for a large convoy of merchantmen, slow fleet auxiliaries, and amphibious vessels. Informed that those sea lanes had been, of late, patrolled by Japanese submarines and that enemy planes might be encountered, Walton and her fellow escorts alertly screened the important convoy bound for the Allies' westernmost outpost. After a 10-day voyage, the convoy arrived safely at its destination, San Pedro Bay, Leyte, on the last day of the month.

During February, March, and April, Walton escorted convoys between Hollandia and Lingayen Gulf, Philippines. She also made runs between Leyte and Kossol Roads, in the Palaus, as well as trips to Mangarin Bay, Mindoro, Philippines. During the later part of April, the destroyer escort patrolled the waters between Homonhon Island and Dinagat, at the mouth of Leyte Gulf.

In May, Walton visited Manila, Leyte, and Hollandia, before CortDiv 85 received orders to sail for Subic Bay to relieve another division of destroyer escorts that had been conducting antisubmarine sweeps along the west coast of Luzon. Those patrols had been instituted primarily to interdict the flow of enemy submarines from bases in China, Formosa, or the Japanese home islands themselves. Secondarily, Walton and her sisters were to train British and American submarines prior to their departure for extended war patrols and to escort them to and from a release point where they were starting or finishing such patrols.

During the course of those ensuing duties, Walton escorted Brill (SS–330) to Cape Calavite, Mindoro, where the fleet submarine torpedoed a beached and abandoned Japanese tanker. Walton salvaged all equipment of worth from the erstwhile enemy vessel and then stood off while Brill completed the demolition work with three torpedoes.

On 28 July, Walton departed Subic Bay in company with Rolf (DE–362) and later rendezvoused with Munro (DE–422) to form a hunter-killer group on the eastern coast of Luzon, off Casiguran Bay. They swept northeast of Luzon and across the convoy lanes between Leyte and Okinawa, without success, before Walton was relieved by Johnnie Hutchins (DE–360) off Aparri.

Walton spent the remainder of August at Subic Bay and was there when hostilities with Japan ceased in mid-month. As the fleet moved northward to Japanese waters to commence the occupation of the former enemy's homeland, its necessary train followed. Walton escorted Chepachet (AO–78) to a point where the oiler rendezvoused with a fast carrier task group at the end of August, before the destroyer escort put into Buckner Bay, anchoring there on 2 September 1945—the day of Japan's formal surrender.

Walton later departed Okinawa to escort hospital ship Mercy (AH–6) to Jinsen (now Inchon), Korea. En route, the ships kept a vigilant lookout for stray mines; and Walton exploded 11 of them as the ships passed through the Yellow Sea. Arriving at Jinsen on 8 September, Mercy soon commenced taking care of the many Allied prisoners of war and internees from a camp near the Korean port. Walton consequently found employment as a river pilot ship, leading vessels which did not have adequate anchorage or area charts—a necessary precaution due to the many narrow and shallow passages in the waters off Jinsen. On 26 September, while engaged in that duty, Walton suffered damage when an LCT—under tow by LST–557—collided with her port bow, opening a large hole and breaking several frames above the waterline.

Repaired alongside Jason (ARH–1), Walton subsequently escorted Geneva (APA–86) to Taku, China. Once there, the attack transport embarked internees from camps in North China and sailed from that port for the Shantung peninsula and South China. Walton stood by while Geneva embarked former civilian internees at Tsingtao, and she accompanied the transport on a voyage to Hong Kong. While en route, on 10 and 11 October, the ships rode out the outer edge of a typhoon swirling its way up the China coast. Walton—although buffeted by 30- and 40-foot waves and winds clocked at over 50 knots—sustained no materiel damage.

Arriving at Hong Kong on 13 October, *Walton* remained at that port until 4 November when she weighed anchor for Shanghai, China—where her namesake had served in the late 1930's—and escorted the stores issue ship *Iolanda* (AKS–14) to that port. *Walton* next returned to Jinsen, hunting for and sinking stray mines while acting as an escort.

At Jinsen on 20 November, *Walton* received the long-awaited homeward-bound orders and, in company with *Pratt* (DE–363), sailed for Okinawa. There, the two destroyer escorts embarked passengers—taking part in a phase of the Operation "Magic Carpet," the return home of discharge-bound veterans. On the 25th, they set out for the Hawaiian Islands, on the first leg of their voyage to the west coast of the United States. Arriving at San Pedro, Calif., nine days before Christmas of 1945, *Walton* subsequently shifted to San Diego, where she was decommissioned and placed in reserve on 31 May 1946.

The destroyer escort remained inactive until the Korean War. Recommissioned at San Diego on 26 January 1951, Lt. Comdr. John D. Brink in command, *Walton* operated off the coast of California, training and assisting in the training of submarines and sonar teams, into the spring of the next year.

The destroyer escort—her homeport officially changed from San Diego to Pearl Harbor on 4 November 1951—departed San Diego on 19 April 1952, bound for the Far East, in company with sister ships *Currier* (DE–700) and *Marsh* (DE–699). *McCoy Reynolds* (DE–440) rendezvoused with those three ships at Pearl Harbor to complete CortDiv 92. *Walton* arrived off Hungnam on 17 May and immediately assumed patrol and blockade duties off the Korean coast.

Over the next four months, *Walton* worked jointly with the naval units of other UN nations—Great Britain, Thailand, Colombia, and the Republic of Korea. During her patrols, the destroyer escort fired over 2000 rounds of 5-inch ammunition at communist shore targets; provided close gunfire support for minesweeping operations; worked in conjunction with carrier strikes on coastal targets; and, during the latter operations, rescued a ditched Navy pilot. On one occasion, the ship sent a raiding party to reconnoiter a harbor on the far northern coast of Korea. Enemy machine guns opened up on the party, but a heavy fusillade from *Walton*'s small boat silenced the gunners.

During that Far Eastern deployment, *Walton* also engaged in patrolling the Formosa Strait to keep communist China from attacking Nationalist China on the island of Formosa (Taiwan). Besides the ship's active patrol and combat operations, she participated in hunter-killer evolutions in waters south of Japan. As a result of her Korean service in 1952, *Walton* received the Korean Service Medal with one engagement star, the UN Service Medal, and the Republic of Korea Presidential Unit Citation.

Returning to Pearl Harbor on 29 August, *Walton* underwent a shipyard availability during September and, over the ensuing months, conducted a regular schedule of training operations in the Hawaiian operating area. After a major overhaul at Pearl Harbor, *Walton* got underway on 9 May 1953 sailing, via Midway, to the Far East. Subsequently based at Sasebo, Japan, *Walton* operated briefly out of Pusan, South Korea, and then patrolled near Cheju Do, an island off the southern coast of South Korea. In July, she made a passage to Beppu, Japan, for a period of repairs alongside a tender, before she operated as a screening vessel with TF 77. She returned to Pusan soon thereafter, before resuming her patrols out of Sasebo to the eastern coast of South Korea.

Even after the signing of the armistice on 27 July brought an uneasy peace to the "land of the Morning Calm," there was still work for *Walton* in Far Eastern waters. The ship participated in port visits to Hong Kong; underwent upkeep in Subic Bay, Philippines; visited Yokosuka, Sasebo, and Kobe, Japan; and operated in Korean waters again that November before sailing as part of a simulated convoy screen and reaching Pearl Harbor on 11 December 1953.

Walton remained in Hawaiian waters into the summer of 1954, conducting a varying slate of operations that included exercises in gunnery, communications, engineering, antisubmarine warfare, navigation, and tactics—broken from time to time by the usual upkeep and maintenance periods in port. She also participated in a hunter-killer exercise in May that helped to evaluate killer submarines.

Departing Pearl Harbor on 15 June, *Walton* began her third deployment to the Western Pacific (WestPac). On 9 July, she relieved the seaplane tender *Orca* (AVP–49) as station ship at Hong Kong and, outside of a brief period of upkeep at Subic Bay, performed station ship duties at the British Crown Colony into the autumn. During the deployment, the ship sortied twice to evade typhoons swirling their way toward Hong Kong—typhoon Ida from 28 to 30 August and typhoon Pamela from 5 to 7 November.

Walton departed Hong Kong on 8 November and proceeded back to Pearl Harbor, via the Philippines, Guam, and Midway, having to dodge two more typhoons (Ruby and Sally) while en route. The destroyer escort then spent the period from late November 1954 to early May 1955 in the Hawaiian Islands, training and undergoing needed upkeep.

On 11 May 1955, *Walton* set sail for the Marianas, on the first leg of her fourth WestPac voyage. While operating under the operational aegis of the Commander, Naval Forces, Marianas, *Walton* carried out surveillance operations at Rikar Atoll, Erikub Atoll, Kwajalein, Rongevik Atoll, and Ailingnac Atoll. In June and July, *Walton* alternated making surveillance voyages to the places mentioned above with performing duties as search and rescue (SAR) ship operating out of Guam.

During the latter part of July, *Walton* visited the northern Marianas, the Bonin and Volcano Islands, and Yokosuka, before she resumed SAR duties at Guam. She divided September between surveillance in the western Carolines and SAR at Guam before sailing on 22 September for Pearl Harbor. She arrived home, via Kwajalein, on 1 October.

Walton subsequently conducted two more WestPac deployments out of Pearl Harbor. During the fifth deployment, the ship visited Singapore, the Federated Malay States; Hong Kong; Kobe, Japan; the Marianas; and Chinhae, Korea; where she, in company with *Bream* (SS–243) and units of the ROK Navy, trained in antisubmarine warfare. Later, while en route from Japanese waters to Keelung, Taiwan, in company with *Foss* (DE–59), *Walton* conducted an unsuccessful search for an American plane that had ditched in the ocean. The two destroyer escorts sighted nothing during the two-day quest.

During the ship's sixth WestPac deployment, in 1957, the ship conducted five surveillance cruises in the Bonins; the Carolines; and the northern Mariana Islands. Also—in company wiith her sister ship *McGinty* (DE–365)—she visited Townsville, Australia—via Subic Bay and Manus—arriving "down under" on 19 August 1957. After five days of hearty Australian hospitality, the two escort vessels set out for Pago Pago, Samoa, on the first leg of their voyage back to Pearl Harbor where they arrived on 5 November.

Following a three-month overhaul at the Pearl Harbor Naval Shipyard, *Walton* conducted underway training evolutions and type training in the Hawaiian Islands through the spring of 1958. Ultimately, on 30 June 1958, *Walton* bid "aloha" to Pearl Harbor and, while en route to the United States, the destroyer escort was reassigned to Reserve CortRon 1, Reserve CortDiv 12. With her home port officially changed to San Francisco, *Walton* underwent a brief availability alongside *Bryce Canyon* (AD–36) at Long Beach before she pushed on for her ultimate destination—San Francisco. She arrived at her new home port on 20 July.

Walton's mission was now to train Naval Reserve personnel. Over the next three years, she operated out of San Francisco on reserve training cruises that took the ship to such places as Mazatlan, Mexico; San Diego and Treasure Island, Calif.; Pearl Harbor; Drakes Bay, Calif.; Monterey, Calif.; and Esquimalt, British Columbia. During the many two-week reserve cruises, she conducted a variety of operations including "live" antisubmarine warfare training and gunnery exercises, highline transfers, general quarters drills, and underway refuelings in order to bring reservists up to date on latest methods and equipment. During that time, *Walton* won the Battle Efficiency "E" for Reserve CortRon 1 in 1959 and 1960.

While at Long Beach on 1 October 1961, *Walton* received word that, in the words of her command history, "her shuttling about the west coast was ended for the time being." With her selected reserve crew of 70 men, the destroyer escort was recalled to active duty as part of the overall buildup of military force ordered by President John F. Kennedy to meet the communist threat in Berlin and, possibly, elsewhere.

Again homeported at Pearl Harbor, *Walton* departed the west coast on 23 October for the Hawaiian Islands. She arrived eight days later and immediately commenced underway training evolutions. She later underwent a two-week availability alongside *Hamul* (AD–20) before she resumed underway training. On 4 December, the ship entered the Pearl Harbor Naval Shipyard to commence an overhaul that lasted through the end of the year 1961.

After further underway training evolutions in Hawaiian waters, *Walton* departed Pearl Harbor on 22 June, bound for the Marianas, on the first leg of her seventh WestPac deployment. After stopping for a day at Guam, she arrived in Subic Bay on 6 February. Nine days later, she got underway for Danang, South Vietnam.

Walton arrived off Danang on 17 February and immediately began patrols in company with units of the small South Vietnamese Navy. Returning to Subic Bay briefly toward the middle of March, and after visiting Manila and Hong Kong, the destroyer escort resumed patrols off the coastline of South Vietnam, operating from Danang. For the remainder of her tour, the destroyer escort was almost constantly on the move, shifting to Subic Bay and Yokosuka; and patrolling the strait of Korea, before she returned via Yokosuka to Pearl Harbor on 5 June.

Following a brief stint of local operations out of Pearl Harbor, *Walton* sailed for the west coast on 11 July 1962. Arriving at San Francisco on 1 August, she soon resumed her Naval Reserve training role.

For the next five years, *Walton* operated off the west coast training reservists. Ultimately decommissioned on 20 September 1968, *Walton* was struck from the Navy list on 23 September 1968 and was sunk as a target on 7 August 1969.

Walton (DE–361) earned two battle stars for her Korean War service.

Walworth County

Counties in South Dakota and Wisconsin.

(LST–1164: dp. 2,590; l. 384'; b. 56'; dr. 17'; s. 14 k.; cpl. 160; trp. 376; a. 6 3"; cl. *LST–1156*)

LST–1164 was laid down on 22 September 1952 at Pascagoula, Miss., by the Ingalls Shipbuilding Corp.; launched on 15 May 1953; sponsored by Mrs. John A. Furr; and commissioned on 26 October 1953, Lt. F. Kay in command.

The new tank landing ship departed Pascagoula on 20 November 1953, bound for Norfolk, Va. She conducted shakedown in the Chesapeake Bay and became a unit of LST Division 23. The ship arrived at her home port of Little Creek, Va., on 3 December 1953. On 6 April 1954, *LST–1164* departed the amphibious base for a brief stop at the Naval Reserve training center at Jacksonville, Fla. On 19 April, the ship took part in simulated atomic warfare strikes and returned to Little Creek on 25 May 1954.

She spent June participating in amphibious exercises at Vieques Island, Puerto Rico. *LST–1164* returned to Little Creek on 11 July for voyage repairs in the Norfolk Naval Shipyard and towing exercises off Little Creek beach.

From 3 November 1954 through 24 March 1955, the ship participated in various exercises with the Marine Corps and the Army in the areas of Camp Pendleton, Va.; Onslow Beach, N.C.; and Vieques Island, Puerto Rico.

On 30 March, the LST entered the Philadelphia Naval Shipyard for a four-month overhaul. During that period, she was named *Walworth County* on 1 July 1955. She returned to Little Creek on 5 August and conducted exercises in the Chesapeake Bay. The ship put to sea on 21 September for atomic attack drills along the eastern seaboard; gunnery practice in operating areas out of Jacksonville, Fla.; and assault beaching runs with men of the 3d Marines and their vehicles and combat equipment on the coast of North Carolina. *Walworth County* returned to Little Creek on 8 November 1955 and spent the following months in local waters with trips to Guantanamo and the Caribbean.

Walworth County left Norfolk with a load of ammunition on 7 May 1956 and, two weeks later, arrived at the United States naval base at Port Lyautey, French Morocco. Two days later, she sailed for Greece and arrived at Piraeus on 30 May for operations with an amphibious task force of the 6th Fleet which took her to principal ports of the Mediterranean. *Walworth County* returned home to Little Creek on 26 September and spent the remainder of the year in local operating areas.

On 5 March 1957, the tank landing ship arrived at the Naval Base, Coco Solo, Canal Zone. From there, she took survey parties to beaching sites in the Chagres River and other places in preparation for Operation "Caribex" which tested the mobility of American forces in defending the Panama Canal. She returned to Little Creek from this cruise on 16 March and put to sea on 10 April to participate in a three-phase operation involving the Marine Corps, the Army, and the Air Force. The exercise—conducted on Vieques Island, Fort Lorenzo, Canal Zone, and Rio Hata—terminated on 28 April 1957; and *Walworth County* underwent extended upkeep in the New York Naval Shipyard from 14 May through 11 July. She returned to Little Creek the following day and began local operations which lasted until 14 November 1957. At that time, *Walworth County* undertook exercises with amphibious warfare forces that included practice assaults with marines on Vieques Island, Puerto Rico, and St. Thomas, Virgin Islands.

The ship returned to Little Creek on 25 March 1958 but a month later headed for Morehead City, N.C. There, she loaded marines and combat cargo in preparation for an amphibious training operation to be held in the Mediterranean with forces of the United Kingdom and Italy. She transited the Strait of Gibraltar on 14 May and visited the ports of Izmir, Turkey; Athens, Greece; and Suda Bay, Crete.

However, the operation was cancelled because of Middle East tensions, and *Walworth County* had the distinction of acting as a primary control ship in the initial landing of marines at Beirut, Lebanon, on 15 July. Her operations in this area continued until 1 October when she departed Beirut and sailed for the United States. She reached Morehead City on 19 October and became a unit of Amphibious Squadron 6.

From 12 December 1958 to 24 February 1959, *Walworth County* underwent an overhaul in the Charleston Naval Shipyard. The ship conducted local operations and visited Guantanamo before sailing for Spain. She arrived at Rota on 30 July and commenced her third Mediterranean tour which lasted until 9 February 1960. She returned to Morehead City and spent the following months conducting practice landings at Onslow Beach, making cruises to Halifax, Nova Scotia, and to Bermuda, and completing another tour of duty in the Caribbean Sea that included amphibious warfare practice in the waters of Puerto Rico and the Virgin Islands.

On 28 October 1960, *Walworth County* sailed from Little Creek with Amphibious Squadron 6 for a fourth Mediterranean deployment. The ship gave effective support to assault practice with Marine battalion landing teams at Augusta Bay, Sicily; with Greek Raider Teams at Navplion, Greece; and with both Amphibious Squadrons 6 and 4 and two Marine battalion landing teams at Portoscuso, Sardinia.

Walworth County returned to Little Creek on 19 May 1961 and underwent overhaul in the Norfolk Naval Shipyard through September 1961. She spent the remainder of the year in amphibious assault training on Onslow Beach and at Camp Pendleton where she took part in Army landing assault training.

Walworth County departed Little Creek on 17 January 1962, embarked marines at Morehead City, and headed for Guantanamo Bay to participate in Operation "Springboard 62." The ship made calls at several Caribbean ports and then disembarked the marines at Morehead City on 1 March. Four days later, she returned to Norfolk where she was placed on restricted availability status until 15 May 1962.

At that time, *Walworth County* embarked marines of "Foxtrot" Company, Battalion Landing Team 2/6 and, on 1 June, proceeded to tour the entire length of the Mediterranean from Alicante, Spain, to Marmaris, Turkey, where she operated with combined Turkish and Greek forces. After extensive exercises, including seven amphibious training assaults on various beaches, she sailed for her home port and arrived at Norfolk on 20 October 1962. The next day, she was called upon to participate in the Cuban blockade and operated in the Caribbean with the ready amphibious group until 4 December when she returned to the United States and debarked marines at Morehead City. *Walworth County* arrived at Norfolk the following day and spent the remainder of the year in leave and upkeep.

During the early part of 1963, *Walworth County* conducted local operations in the Little Creek area. After entering Gibbs Shipyard, Jacksonville, Fla., on 3 April, she completed her scheduled yard period and sea trials; then headed for Little Creek on 10 June. The ship took part in amphibious refresher training through July and August, followed by a three-week period of restricted availability. During the remainder of 1963, she participated in local operations; visited Rockland, Maine, to obtain tactical data for the LST–1156-class; and underwent overhaul.

In January 1964, *Walworth County* got underway for Panama where she spent more than four months, making 16 transits of the canal—including one round trip which she completed in less than 23 hours. Late in May, she returned to Little Creek and, after tender availability, took part in the "MEBLEX" and midshipman exercises. Following this, she made a call to New York for the World's Fair and returned to Little Creek on 11 August. While in port, *Walworth County* was used in the production of a Bureau of Medicine and Surgery mental health movie. In late August, LST–1164 again got underway for a lift to Guantanamo Bay, Cuba, and returned—via Miami, Fla.—on 13 September 1964.

Walworth County spent a short period in the yard before getting underway on 5 October for "Steel Pike I," the largest amphibious exercise since World War II. Besides carrying out her role in the operation, she called at Rota, Spain, and the Canary Islands before returning home on 28 November. *Walworth County*

spent the Christmas and New Year holidays undergoing tender availability.

In early February 1965, LST–1164 sailed for Vieques and took liberty in the Virgin Islands and at San Juan and Ponce, Puerto Rico. She arrived back at Little Creek on 8 March and then participated in exercises to train Army personnel in amphibious warfare. Following these training exercises, the ship conducted local operations and made preparations for an upcoming deployment.

Having completed all preparations, *Walworth County* got underway with Amphibious Squadron (PhibRon) 6 on 24 January 1966. She proceeded to Bermuda as an escort for minesweepers when the squadron was recalled. After spending one week in Bermuda, she returned to Little Creek. On 6 March, the ship got underway for her sixth Mediterranean tour. There, she joined in a combined NATO exercise and other amphibious assault operations. On 1 July, she became a part of PhibRon 8. *Walworth County* returned to the United States on 2 August, underwent a period of training and upkeep, and then spent the final weeks of August on a midshipman cruise and taking on board dependents of the crew for a day at sea.

On 1 September 1966, *Walworth County* got underway for Guantanamo Bay with marines embarked. After a short stay, she returned to her home port where she underwent training and upkeep. On 26 September, she headed for the Boston operating area with civilian technicians and representatives from the Naval Ordnance Testing Laboratory. The ship travelled to Ft. Lauderdale, Fla., to unload testing equipment before returning to Little Creek. On 18 October, *Walworth County* underwent a period of tender availability. Late in November, she participated in an exercise off Vieques and put into San Juan, Puerto Rico, for repairs. On 15 December, the LST got underway for Little Creek and spent the Christmas holidays at home.

The New Year, 1967, found *Walworth County* in the Norfolk Naval Shipyard for repairs to her propellers, but she returned to Little Creek on 20 March. After a short trip to New York, the ship got underway on 8 April and headed for the Caribbean to participate in the joint services exercise, "Clove Hitch III." She returned to Little Creek on 4 May and spent a month undergoing maintenance and post-repair training.

September and October were devoted to a goodwill tour off Deal Island, Maryland, and Operation "JCOC 37," an amphibious assault off Onslow Beach, N.C. From 27 October to 10 November 1967, *Walworth County* was deployed to the Caribbean. On the ship's return to Little Creek, she began an overhaul and then prepared for an upcoming Mediterranean tour.

On 3 January 1968, *Walworth County* got underway for Morehead City, where she embarked marines and loaded equipment. On 6 January, she rendezvoused with five minesweepers and began the voyage across the North Atlantic for her seventh Mediterranean cruise. She reached Rota, Spain, on 3 February and began a series of "Phiblex" exercises which took her to Sardinia and Corsica. Her crew enjoyed leave at Toulon, France; La Spezia and Naples, Italy; and Rota, Spain. On 27 April 1968, *Walworth County* took part in Operation "Dawn Patrol" involving 40 ships of five nations. The exercises were completed on 12 May at Timbakion, Crete. The ship then sailed for Rota, Spain, and steamed across the North Atlantic. *Walworth County* arrived at Morehead City, N.C., on 8 June 1968 and proceeded to Little Creek where she arrived the next day.

After a month of maintenance, *Walworth County* participated in a riverine exercise in the James River—which taught the fundamentals of river warfare and lessons learned in Vietnam—from 9 to 19 July. The ship then spent the remainder of July and most of August undergoing a tender availability.

The landing ship got underway on 23 September 1968 for a SOUTHCOM deployment as a member of LST Division 41. After a trip to the Canal Zone, she got underway on 9 October for a visit to Jamaica. Upon reaching Montego Bay, *Walworth County* was called back to Panama when an uprising overthrew the Panamanian government. She arrived in the Canal Zone on 14 October and, the next day, transited the canal to the Pacific. She remained at the Rodman Naval Station until 8 November 1968.

Loaded with Operation "Handclasp" material, *Walworth County* got underway for Equador that day and arrived at Guayaquil on 9 November 1968. She returned to Rodman on 17 November and—except for four amphibious landings and a round-trip transit of the canal —remained there until 9 January 1969.

From 1 March to 16 May, LST–1164 underwent upkeep at the Norfolk Shipbuilding and Drydock Corp. in Berkley, Va. The ship then began a period of upkeep at her home port. On 21 July, she started amphibious refresher training and then prepared for movement overseas. From 15 September through 25 November, the ship operated in the Caribbean Ready Group.

Upon her return to Little Creek, the tank landing ship began another period of leave and upkeep. Then, she conducted a training exercise from 12 to 16 January 1970. On 30 January, the ship began a month of tender availability by *Vulcan* (AR–5) which was moored at the Norfolk Navy Base. This work lasted until 20 February when *Walworth County* returned to Little Creek.

Following several months of local operations, *Walworth County* sailed independently on 8 July 1970 for South America. Her mission was primarily one of good will. She delivered earthquake relief supplies to Peruvian ports and carried Project "Handclasp" matefial to Ecuador. For the remainder of the deployment, LST–1164 carried out many and varied missions, ranging from being a home for Smithsonian scientists performing marine biology research to acting as a ferryboat for United States exhibits to a regional fair at Bocas del Toro, Panama. During her three-month deployment, *Walworth County* steamed over 9,000 miles,

and she received a letter of commendation from Admiral C. D. Nace, Commander, United States Naval Forces, Southern Command and Commandant, 15th Naval District. After a final transit of the Panama Canal, *Walworth County* headed homeward, arriving back at Little Creek on 23 October 1970.

Following the post-deployment leave periods, *Walworth County* commenced preparations for inactivation. On 4 January 1971, operational and administrative control of the ship was shifted from Amphibious Force, United States Atlantic Fleet to the Inactive Ship Maintenance Facility, Norfolk.

After three months of work by her crew, LST–1164 was decommissioned in April 1971. The ship was subsequently towed to Orange, Tex., where she arrived on 14 April 1971. She was drydocked on 11 May for the underwater phase of inactivation with the topside phase scheduled to commence upon completion of the drydock phase.

In May of 1972, *Walworth County* was scheduled for transfer to the Maritime Administration and layup at Suisun Bay, Calif.; but she served with the Military Sealift Command from May 1972 until stricken from the Navy list on 1 November 1973. On 19 June 1974, she was turned over to the Maritime Administration and berthed at Suisun Bay, Calif.

As of April 1979, *Walworth County* was still with the National Defense Reserve Fleet.

Wampanoag

An Indian tribe formerly occupying the territory extending from Narragansett Bay and the Pawtucket River, R.I., to the Atlantic Ocean, including Nantucket Island and Martha's Vineyard, Mass. The name means "eastern people."

I

(ScFr: dp. 4,215; l. 355'; b. 45'2''; dr. 19'; s. 18 k.; a. 10 8'' sb., 2 100-pdrs., 2 24-pdr. how., 2 12-pdr. how., 1 60-pdr. r. pivt.; cl. *Wampanoag*)

Wampanoag—a screw frigate—was laid down on 3

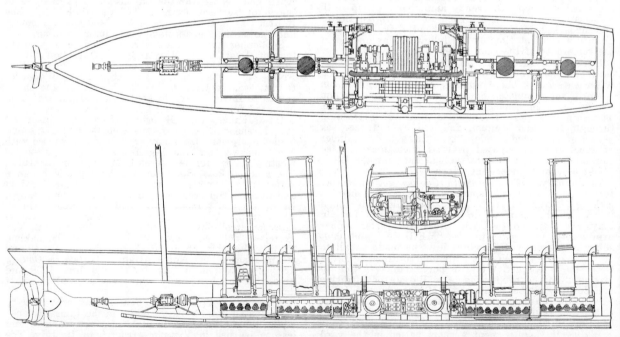

This drawing of the controversial steamer *Wampanoag* illustrates what was, for her time, the extraordinary amount of hull space devoted to machinery in this high-performance ship. Eight coal-burning fire-tube boilers, four of them with superheaters, are arranged in two boiler rooms; between them are two compound reciprocating engines which turn *Wampanoag*'s four-bladed 19-foot propeller. (Drawing from Frank M. Bennett, *The Steam Navy of the United States* (Pittsburgh, Pa., 1895))

August 1863 by the New York Navy Yard, N.Y.; launched on 15 December 1864; sponsored by Miss Case, daughter of Capt. Augustus Ludlow Case, second-in-command of the navy yard; and commissioned on 17 September 1867, Capt. J. W. A. Nicholson in command.

Commerce raiding by CSS *Alabama* and CSS *Florida*, both built in English yards, reached a point in 1863 where continued peaceful relations between the United States and Great Britain were seriously jeopardized. As a result, Congress responded by authorizing construction of a new class of screw frigates as part of the naval procurement bill of that year. These vessels, designed to be the fastest in the world, were intended for use in hit-and-run operations against British ports and commerce in the event of war. *Wampanoag* was the lead ship of this class.

Wampanoag contained numerous design features unprecedented in American naval construction. Her hull —designed by clipper ship architect B. F. Delano— was unusually long and tapered relative to the vessel's beam. Her machinery, developed by controversial Naval Engineer B. F. Isherwood, was unique for its geared steam engine in which slow-moving machinery coupled to fast-moving propulsion gear. Tremendous debate caused by this design delayed construction, preventing *Wampanoag* from being completed in time to serve in the Civil War.

The screw frigate finally left New York for sea trials on 7 February 1868. On 11 February, she commenced speed tests, running flat-out in rough weather from Barnegat Light, N.J., to Tybee Island, Ga. She covered the distance of 728 statute miles in 38 hours for an average sustained speed of 16.6 knots, at one point making 17.75 knots. Another naval vessel, American cruiser *Charleston*, did not equal this record for 21 years.

From 22 February 1868 to 8 April, *Wampanoag* was deployed as flagship of the North Atlantic Fleet. On 5 May 1868, she decommissioned at the New York Navy Yard. *Wampanoag* was renamed *Florida* on 15 May 1869.

The controversy generated by the frigate's unconventional design reached a peak in 1869 when a naval commission examined and condemned the vessel. Rear Admiral R. M. Goldsborough, Commodore Charles S. Boggs, and Engineers E. D. Robie, John W. Moore, and Isaac Newton judged the ship unacceptable for active duty in the Navy. They complained of her unusually large machinery spaces, heavy coal consumption, and found particular fault with her narrow breadth relative to her length. The commission said this caused inordinate rolling and straining of the vessel. As a result, *Florida* remained in ordinary at New York for five years before departing on 5 March 1874, bound for New London, Conn., to become a receiving and store ship at the naval station there.

Florida remained at New London, rotting, until February 1885. She was sold, at New York, on 27 February 1885 to Edwin LeBars.

II

(ATA–202: dp. 835 (tl.); l. 143'0''; b. 33'10''; dr. 13'2''; s. 13 k. (tl.); cpl. 45; a. 1 3''; cl. *ATA–170*)

ATA–202 was laid down on 24 August 1944 at Port Arthur, Tex., by the Gulfport Boiler & Welding Works; launched on 10 October 1944; and commissioned on 8 December 1944.

The auxiliary ocean tug completed her shakedown training during the latter half of December 1944 and proceeded via the Panama Canal to the Pacific. On 12 January 1945, she reported for duty with the Pacific Fleet and, by late April, had joined Service Squadron (ServRon) 10 in support of the Okinawa campaign. Late in May, she moved to Okinawa itself for a brief tour of duty and returned to her base at Ulithi in

mid-June. It is reasonable to assume that her round-trip voyage to the Ryukyus was for the purpose of towing battle-damaged ships back to Ulithi for repair. She continued her duty with ServRon 10 through the end of the war, returned to the United States in September, and began nine months of duty in the 11th Naval District at San Diego. She was reassigned to the Atlantic Reserve Fleet's Texas Group in March 1946 and actually reported to Orange, Tex., in July. On 27 February 1947, the tug was placed out of service there and berthed with the Texas Group, Atlantic Reserve Fleet. *ATA–202* was named *Wampanoag* on 16 July 1948.

Wampanoag remained in reserve until 25 February 1959 at which time she was loaned to the Coast Guard. A little over 10 years later, on 1 June 1969, she was transferred permanently to the Coast Guard, and her name was struck from the Navy list. During her Coast Guard service, the ship has served under the name *Comanche* (WMEC–202). As of 11 May 1979, she was stationed at Eureka, Calif.

Wampanoag (ATA–202) was awarded one battle star during World War II.

Wampatuck

A leader of the Mattakeesett tribe of the Massachusetts Indians—known to English settlers as Josiah Sagamore. An early friend of European settlers, he sold the British the land upon which the city of Boston was established. He was slain in 1669 when he led a force of his warriors in an attack upon the Mohawks.

(YT–337: dp. 473; l. 141'2''; b. 29'9½''; dph. 17'6¼''; a. 2 .50-cal. mg.)

Sea Ranger—a wooden-hulled, single-screw, steam harbor tug built at Oakland, Calif., by W. F. Stone and Son and completed in May 1921—was acquired by the Navy under a bareboat charter from the Foss Launch and Tug Co. of San Francisco on 28 October 1942 and renamed *Wampatuck* (YT–337). Placed in service at Pearl Harbor, Territory of Hawaii, on 22 December 1942, the ship served as a harbor tug and performed tow services at the vital Pacific Fleet base through the end of hostilities with Japan. During her tour of duty at Pearl Harbor, she was reclassified as a big harbor tug on 15 May 1944 and simultaneously redesignated YTB–337.

Subsequently shifting to the west coast, *Wampatuck* was placed out of service at San Francisco on 6 May 1946. Her name was struck from the Navy list on 21 May; and she soon resumed using her former name, *Sea Ranger*. Transferred to the Maritime Commission at Mare Island, Calif., on 16 August 1946, the tug was subsequently assigned to the National Defense Reserve Fleet and laid up at Suisun Bay, Calif., on 31 March 1948. The ship remained there until her name disappeared from the merchant shipping registers in 1955.

Wamsutta

A Wampanoag sachem (chief). Wamsutta was the eldest son of Massasoit, the chief of all the Indian tribes between the Charles River, Mass., and Narraganset Bay, R.I., including the tribes in eastern Rhode Island and eastern Massachusetts. Massasoit joined the English in an alliance soon after the arrival of white men in New England so that he might use them as a counter-weight to the hostile Pequots, Narragansetts, and Mohegans. The price of this alliance was English encroachment upon Indian land and interference in tribal affairs. In 1656, Wamsutta and his brother, Metacom, received the names "Alexander" and "Philip" from the colonists.

In 1661, Wamsutta succeeded his father. His efforts to maintain the alliance forged by Massasoit were not entirely successful. The English summoned Wamsutta to Duxbury, Mass., in 1662 for questioning concerning a rumored plot against the colonial settlements. Wamsutta fell ill during the questioning and soon died.

Metacom became sachem at Wamsutta's death. A hot-tempered, embittered individual, Metacom fanned smoldering Indian resentment of the colonists until the situation degenerated into open warfare lasting from June 1675 until Metacom's death on 12 August 1676. Called King Philip's War by the English, this was the bloodiest of all the confrontations between the colonists and Indians during the 17th century.

I

(ScGbt.: t. 270; l. 129'3''; b. 26'8''; dr. 11'; s. 9 k.; a. 1 20-pdr. P.r., 4 32-pdrs.)

Wamsutta—a screw steamer built in 1853 at Hoboken, N.J.—was purchased by the Navy on 20 September 1861 at New York City from H. Haldrege; and commissioned on 14 March 1862, Acting Volunteer Lieutenant William L. Stone in command.

Wamsutta was assigned to the South Atlantic Blockading Squadron and arrived in Port Royal harbor on 14 April 1862. The next day, she received orders to report to Comdr. Edmund Lanier, in *Alabama*, for blockade and reconnaissance duty in St. Simon's Sound, Ga. On 27 April, while on an expedition to destroy a brig believed to be near Dorchester, Ga., *Wamsutta* and *Potomska* engaged a company of dismounted Confederate cavalry on Woodville Island in the Riceboro River. The battle lasted 40 minutes. *Wamsutta* suffered two casualties and received superficial damage to her port side. On 8 May, again accompanied by *Potomska*, *Wamsutta* proceeded to Darien, Ga., to capture stored lighthouse machinery. However, a search of the town on the 9th found nothing, and the two gunboats withdrew that evening. *Wamsutta* remained off Darien, blockading Doboy Sound, Ga.

On 4 August 1862, *Wamsutta* departed Doboy Sound to blockade St. Catherine's Sound, Ga. There, she and *Braziliera* captured the schooner *Defiance* on 19 September. On 8 November, a broken air pump forced *Wamsutta* to Port Royal for repairs. Ultimately, she proceeded to the New York Navy Yard where she was decommissioned on 3 December 1862.

Wamsutta was recommissioned there on 2 February 1863 and returned to the South Atlantic Blockading Squadron, arriving off Port Royal on the 13th. Five days later, she proceeded to Doboy Sound to tow *Fernandina* into position to blockade the entrance to the sound. On the 28th, *Wamsutta* was ordered to Sapelo Sound, Ga., to relieve *Potomska* and remained until ordered to Wassaw Sound, Ga., on 29 March to relieve *Marblehead*. By 1 May, *Wamsutta* lay off Charleston, S.C., but spent the remainder of May and the first two weeks of June repairing and reprovisioning in Port Royal. *Wamsutta* arrived back off Sapelo Sound on 15 June 1863. Four days later, she was relieved by *Midnight* and ordered to proceed to Doboy Sound to relieve *Fernandina*. After serving there for most of the summer, *Wamsutta* headed north on 5 September for repairs in the Philadelphia Navy Yard. She was decommissioned there on 14 September 1863.

Wamsutta was reactivated on 24 April 1864 at Philadelphia and was ordered back to the South Atlantic Blockading Squadron. She arrived in Port Royal harbor on 6 May and was assigned to blockade duty off Georgetown, S.C. On 3 June, she chased the British steamer *Rose* aground there and burned the blockade runner. On 9 June, while reconnoitering Confederate island batteries scattered about Winjah Bay, S.C., she drew sporadic fire from shore batteries. On 14 July, *Wamsutta* returned to duty in Charleston and carried out frequent operations against Confederate vessels from her anchorage off Morris Island, S.C. On 22 October, she helped chase the blockade runner *Flora* aground

near Fort Moultrie, S.C. On 5 December 1864, she drove off an unidentified blockade runner attempting to slip into port. On 4 February 1865, *Wamsutta* and *Potomska* ran another schooner aground, but the crew of the potential prize burned the ship before the Federals could take possession of her. Finally, two days later, *Wamsutta* turned back a blockade runner attempting to reach Charleston.

Late in April, *Wamsutta* was reassigned to duty off St. Simon's Island, Ga. She remained there through May and sailed for the Portsmouth (N.H.) Navy Yard early in June. She was decommissioned at Portsmouth on 29 June 1865 and was sold at public auction there on 20 July to Otis Seabury.

Wanaloset

Possibly a variant spelling of *Wannalancet*.

Wanaloset—sometimes spelled *Wanalosett*—was a bark-rigged screw sloop-of-war—scheduled to be built at Baltimore, Md., by the firm of Hazelhurst and Wiegard. Although carried on the Navy list of January 1865, the ship's keel was apparently never laid down; and her hull was certainly never built. Her engines, however, were completed; and they were installed in the screw steamer *Pensacola*. The name *Wanaloset* was dropped from the Navy list about 1867.

Wanamassa

An Indian chief of the 17th century, whose name is commemorated by a town in New Jersey.

(YTB–820: dp. 346; l. 108'; b. 31'; dr. 14'; s. 12 k.; cpl. 12; cl. *Natick*)

Wanamassa (YTB–820) was laid down on 28 October 1972 at Marinette, Wis., by the Marinette Marine Corp.; launched on 4 May 1973; and delivered to the Navy on 28 July 1973.

Assigned to the 10th Naval District, *Wanamassa* operated out of San Juan, Puerto Rico, into 1980, aiding ships in berthing and docking maneuvers and standing ready to provide waterfront fire protection.

Wandank

I

(Fleet Tug No. 26: dp. 795; l. 156'8''; b. 30'; dr. 14'7'' (mean); s. 13 k.; cpl. 25; a. none; cl. *Algorma*)

The first *Wandank* (Fleet Tug No. 26) was laid down on 7 April 1919 at Buffalo, N.Y., by the Ferguson Steel and Iron Co.; launched on 21 October 1919; and commissioned on 23 March 1920, Boatswain O. Rhode in temporary command, pending the turnover to Lt. S. J. Drellishak in April.

Assigned to the 5th Naval District, *Wandank* operated out of Norfolk until placed out of commission on 31 March 1922. Recommissioned on 8 May of the same year, *Wandank* continued to provide tug services out of Norfolk for the Atlantic Fleet in the Hampton Roads-Virginia capes area until transferred to Boston on 8 October 1940 for special duty in the 1st Naval District.

She operated out of Boston on coastal towing duties throughout World War II. Her duties included towing yard oilers and other small craft and participating in the towing of *Wakefield* (AP–21) which had been severely damaged by fire in September 1942. On 15 May 1944, her designation was changed to ATO–26.

Decommissioned on 20 September 1946 and struck from the Navy list on 13 November of that year, she was transferred to the Maritime Commission on 17 July 1947 and simultaneously delivered to W. A. Bisso, of New Orleans, La. She served the New Orleans Coal and Bisso Towboat Co. as *W. A. Bisso* until 1971.

II

(ATA–204: dp. 860; l. 143'; b. 33'; dr. 14'; s. 14 k.; cpl. 46; a. 1 3''; cl. *ATA–121*)

The second *Wandank* (ATA–204)—originally projected as *ATR–131*, a steel-hulled rescue tug—was laid down as *ATA–204* on 25 September 1944 at Port Arthur, Tex., by the Gulfport Boiler and Welding Works; launched on 9 November 1944; and commissioned on 18 January 1945, Lt. (jg.) Vernon L. Ryan, USNR, in command.

Following her shakedown in the Caribbean, *ATA–204* got underway on 23 February for the Panama Canal, en route to the Pacific. The auxiliary ocean tug operated with the Pacific Fleet through the end of hostilities, performing services at locales ranging from Pearl Harbor, Hawaii, to the Marshall Islands. After hostilities ended, she returned to San Francisco, Calif., late in August 1945 and soon shifted to the Puget Sound Navy Yard, Bremerton, Wash. She operated in the 13th Naval District until she was decommissioned on 26 November 1947 and placed in reserve.

The onset of the Korean War gave the vessel a new lease on life, however, triggering the expansion of the United States Navy to maintain a posture of global readiness. *ATA–204* was reactivated on 17 April 1952 at Astoria, Oreg., for assignment to the 14th Naval District. Recommissioned at Pearl Harbor on 3 May 1952, Lt. William A. Walden in command, the auxiliary ocean tug received the name *Wandank* and retained her ATA–204 designation.

For the next three years, *Wandank* operated out of Pearl Harbor, providing tug and tow services for the Pacific Fleet, and occasionally deployed to Samoa and other Pacific isles with tows. On 9 September 1955, the tug was transferred to the Marianas. There, she towed

barges of supplies, stood ready to assist in search and rescue (SAR) operations, provided target services for gunnery and torpedo exercises, and conducted local surveillance missions out of Guam into the 1960's.

During this deployment, the ocean tug supported scientific operations in addition to her more routine duties. In January 1960, for example, *Wandank* served as communication relay and support ship for the bathyscaphe *Trieste* in Project "Nekton." She towed the underwater craft some 260 miles from Guam to the vicinity of the Challenger Deep, where, on 23 January, *Trieste* descended to 37,000 feet. Four years later, in November 1964, *Wandank* conducted a survey of the Solomon Islands in a joint project sponsored by the University of Hawaii's Institute of Geophysics and the Office of Naval Research. During the course of this operation, she measured the earth's gravity in the area.

On occasion, *Wandank*'s operations nonetheless assumed a dangerous character during tropical tempests. During one of these storms, which occurred late in 1963, *Wandank* was trapped between two typhoons while en route to her annual buoy maintenance duty at Chichi Jima in the Bonins. In the heavy seas, her tow line parted, leaving *YCV–18* adrift. During the ensuing recovery operations, the tug's first lieutenant, J. B. Clark, was knocked overboard by a heavy wave and swept from sight.

In July 1966, *Wandank* rendezvoused with Japanese merchantman *Yeiji Maru*, which had been experiencing engine trouble, and escorted the distressed ship to Guam. Later that year, she towed SS *Old Westbury* to a safe haven, relieving *Sunnadin* (ATA–197) which had run low on fuel on 11 November.

The year 1967 passed with much the same routine; and, in 1968, the ship participated in her first operations in connection with the Vietnam War. She towed a gasoline barge, *YOG–131*, from Guam to Danang, South Vietnam, from 3 to 15 January. After returning from Vietnamese waters, she performed island survey

USS *Wandank* (ATA–204) in 1966–67.

duties in the Western Carolinas and subsequently helped to search for floating drydock *AFDM–6* which had broken loose from her civilian tow vessel. *Wandank* next participated in special operations into the summer before making a second voyage to Vietnamese waters, towing *APL–30* to Vung Tau, Vietnam, from 16 August to 1 September.

Wandank commenced the year 1969 with more island surveillance missions in the central Carolinas, sending a landing party ashore from her crew to ascertain the needs of the islanders who lived under the care and protection of the Trust Territories. She conducted a training mission to Yokosuka, Japan, in February and March before returning to a schedule of surveillance operations in the northern Marianas. She trained for possible participation in Project "Apollo" in April before she towed three barges from Sattahip, Thailand, to Vung Tau, from 13 April to 8 May.

Upon returning to the vicinity of the Marianas and Carolinas soon thereafter, she conducted local operations through the end of the year. *Wandank* interrupted this duty only long enough to tow *LCU–1483* to Ponape Island and *LCU–1497* to Majuro, from 25 November to 4 December. During her final full year of naval service, 1970, the ship conducted local operations out of her home port of Apra Harbor, Guam.

She got underway from Guam on 20 January 1971 for Hong Kong and then escorted three *Asheville*-class patrol gunboats to Subic Bay and Camranh Bay, serving as a communication back-up vessel. She later escorted two gunboats from Camranh Bay to Hong Kong before returning to island surveillance duties.

Decommissioned at Guam on 1 July 1971, *Wandank* was simultaneously turned over to the Department of the Interior for service in the Trust Territories, her old habitat. Returned to the Navy on 22 May 1973, *Wandank* was adjudged unfit for further service and accordingly struck from the Navy list on 1 August 1973. Subsequently returned to the Interior Department, she serves in the Trust Territories on island surveillance and local towing duties.

Wandank was awarded three battle stars for her Vietnam War service.

Wandena

(MB: t. 38 (gross); l. 65'0''; b. 13'0''; dr. 3'6'' (mean); s. 11.0 k.; cpl. 10; a. 2 1-pdrs.)

Chipper—a wooden-hulled motorboat—was built in 1913 at the New York Yacht, Launch, and Engine Co., Morris Heights, N.Y. Subsequently renamed *Wandena* and acquired by the Navy from J. B. Nichols, the motorboat—assigned the classification SP–354—was delivered to the Navy on 28 June 1917. She was commissioned at the New York Navy Yard on 5 November 1917, Boatswain H. A. Rudolph, USNRF, in command.

For the duration of World War I, *Wandena* performed local section patrol duties in the 3d Naval District, out of Section Base No. 10. She probably ceased such defensive patrols on 24 November 1918 as specified by the order that date to all naval districts. Struck from the Navy list on 24 April 1919 and decommissioned on 7 May 1919, *Wandena* was sold on 10 September 1919.

Wanderer

I

(Sch.: dp. 300; l. 106'; b. 25'6''; dr. 9'6''; s. 20 k.; a. 1 20-pdr. P.r., 2 24-pdr. D.how.)

The first *Wanderer*—a schooner-rigged yacht built in 1857 in the shipyard of Joseph Rowland at Setauket, Long Island, N.Y., by Thomas B. Hawkins—was originally owned by Col. John Johnson of New York City and Louisiana. After a cruise down the Atlantic coast and to the Gulf of Mexico in which she visited Charleston, S.C.; Brunswick, Ga.; Key West, Fla.; and New Orleans, *Wanderer* returned to New York where she was soon sold to William C. Corrie of Charleston, S.C. Her new owner had several alterations made to the ship, some of which—particularly the installation of tanks which could hold 15,000 gallons of fresh water—suggested that *Wanderer* was being fitted out as a slave ship. As she was attempting to leave New York harbor, she was seized as a suspected slaver on 9 June 1858 by the steam revenue cutter *Harriet Lane* and towed back to Manhattan Island and anchored near the battery. The next morning, Federal officials inspected the schooner and found that—while her extremely fast lines and her equipment and provisions would be valuable assets should she enter the "black gold" trade—there was no conclusive evidence of evil intent on the part of her owner, her master, or crew.

The yacht was thus free to clear port, and she sailed for Charleston where she arrived on 25 June. There, her fitting out as a slave ship was completed before she got underway for Port of Spain, Trinidad, on 3 July. After a pleasant visit, she left that port on the 27th, crossed the Atlantic, and entered the Congo River on 16 September. Braving an epidemic of yellow fever which was then raging in the Congo, she took on board some 500 blacks and sailed for North America on 18 October. She was briefly chased by USS *Vincennes* as she left the mouth of the river but quickly outdistanced her American pursuer. At the end of a six-week voyage in which many of the captives died, *Wanderer* arrived at Jekyll Island on 28 November and delivered her human cargo.

Word of *Wanderer*'s arrival quickly spread, and a great deal of litigation ensued—both civil and criminal—but resulted in no convictions. During the next two years, ownership of the vessel changed several times and, on one occasion, the ship was stolen and taken to sea on a piratical and slaving voyage. Near the coast of Africa, the first mate led a mutiny and left the pirate captain at sea in a small boat before bringing the ship back to Boston on Christmas Eve 1859 and turning her over to authorities there.

A week before the outbreak of the Civil War, *Wanderer* arrived in Key West, Fla., from Havana, Cuba, under Southern registry on 5 April 1861. She was caught in that port during the bombardment of Ft. Sumter on 12 April 1861 and confiscated in May 1861 to prevent her from being used by the Confederacy as a privateer. Operating out of Key West from 27 June, she carried wood, coal, water, and mail to the vessels of the Gulf Blockading Squadron. On 30 November, she stopped the British schooner *Telegraph* off Key Vaccas, Fla. Upon examination of that vessel's papers, *Wanderer* released the British schooner, but the incident nevertheless prompted a diplomatic protest from the British on 8 March 1862.

When Union naval forces were divided on 20 January 1862, *Wanderer* was assigned to the newly formed East Gulf Blockading Squadron. She continued provisioning and dispatch duties, operating between Tortugas, Fla., and Havana and Cape San Antonio, Cuba. In early July 1862, *Wanderer* patrolled off Indian River and Jupiter Inlet, Fla., in search of possible blockade running activity but found none. In October 1862, she was assigned to the blockade of St. Andrew Bay, Fla. She had returned to Key West by 1 January 1863 for recoppering and cruised between Saint Marks and Cedar Keys, Fla., in early March. Accompanied by *Ezilda*, she captured the sloop *Ranger* off Cedar Keys on 25 March. *Wanderer* also captured the schooner *Annie B.* and her cargo of cotton on 17 April 1863 off Egmont Key, Fla. On 30 April, *Wanderer* proceeded to Key West for extensive repairs to her hull and spars.

Meanwhile, legal action against the ship was slowly taking place in the North; and the schooner was condemned by the Philadelphia prize court in May 1863 and was simultaneously purchased by the Union Navy.

Wanderer left Key West early in May for patrol duty

The schooner *Wanderer* during her wartime naval service, with two merchantmen in the background. (NR&L(0) 17832)

west of Tortugas. She stopped in Tampa Bay, Fla., in June and had returned to Key West by 15 July for refit as a hospital ship. She remained in ordinary through the fall and winter undergoing alterations to prepare her for this new role, and she was ready in the spring. However, hot and humid weather brought an epidemic of yellow fever to Key West during June and July 1864. All crewmen on board *Wanderer* sickened, and one died. The vessel spent the remaining months of 1864 at Key West as a guard ship.

Wanderer deteriorated rapidly during her relative inactivity. On 1 June 1865, shortly after the end of hostilities, Rear Admiral Cornelius K. Stribling, commanding the East Gulf Blockading Squadron, advised that *Wanderer* not be sent north for disposal because of her unseaworthy condition. She was sold at public auction on 28 June 1865, at Key West, by A. Patterson to Packer & Watson. She subsequently entered the banana trade and operated in mercantile service until lost off Cape Maisi, Cuba, on 21 January 1871.

II

(MB: t. 5; l. 33'6"; b. 9'0"; dr. 2'6" (mean); s. 9.5 k.)

The second *Wanderer*—a motor boat built in 1913 at Norfolk, Va., by Craig Bros., and owned by R. F. Barret of Norfolk—was acquired by the Navy for service as a section patrol boat. Inspected at the 5th Naval District on 13 April 1917 and designated SP-2440, *Wanderer* was placed in commission on the same day. She operated on local and section patrol duties for the duration of the war and was returned to her owner on 30 December 1918.

III

(Yacht: t. 362 (gross); l. 197'; b. 24'2"; dr. 13'0" (aft); s. 12 k.; cpl. 56; a. 2 3", 2 mg.)

Kethailes—a steam yacht built in 1897 at Leith,

Scotland, by Ramage & Ferguson—was acquired by the Navy from Mr. H. A. C. Taylor of New York City on 10 June 1917; renamed *Wanderer* (SP–132); and commissioned at New York on Bastille Day 1917, Lt. Pierre L. Wilson in command.

A fortnight later, the converted yacht departed New York for a brief shakedown before she joined the rest of her division at St. John's, Newfoundland, where she arrived on 9 August. *Wanderer* and six other yachts cleared St. John's on 12 August, bound for Ponta Delgada in the Azores, where they made a four-day stop between 19 and 24 August. Late in the evening of the 29th, the little band of yachts anchored off the breakwater at their destination, Brest, France. The following morning, she and her division mates entered the port itself and tied up to mooring buoys.

Wanderer was assigned to antisubmarine patrol and coastal convoy escort duties along the north Bay of Biscay coast. Her duty there was enlivened by the weather which was known for its severity. The little yacht—designed as a pleasure craft, not as sturdy as a warship—had less to fear from German U-boats than from mines, weather, and the rocky, foggy shore. She operated initially on the Brest-to-Quiberon Bay leg of the coastal convoy route. To add to the danger, the Americans initially adopted the French-British system of running their coastal and channel convoys at night.

The darkness, however, did not hide *Wanderer*'s convoy on the night of 28 and 29 November when a submarine successfully sank one of the ships in the convoy and made good her escape. The darkness that was supposed to conceal the convoy actually covered the U-boat's retirement and foiled attempts to hunt the submerged enemy.

Nevertheless, the French and British stuck stubbornly to their guns on the question of night versus daylight convoys. It was not until the evening of 7 January 1918—when another *Wanderer*-escorted convoy lost four ships to a lurking U-boat—that the Allies

USS *Wanderer* (SP-132).

grudgingly acquiesced to American demands for daylight convoys supported by patrolling aircraft.

The theory behind sending convoys through dangerous waters during daylight was the belief that it is better to find and attack the enemy than try to conceal shipping from him. The very next week, *Wanderer's* first daylight convoy—also one of the first so conducted —helped to prove the validity of the concept. On 12 January, while escorting that convoy from Brest to Quiberon Bay in daylight, the warship rescued 10 survivors from the French ship SS *Chateau Faite* which had stubbornly stuck to the defensive tactics of the night transit. "Penmarch Pete"—as the U-boat usually stationed off Point Penmarch was nicknamed—exacted his toll. By contrast, *Wanderer's* own convoy accompanied by converted yachts and aircraft made the passage unmolested.

On 8 February 1918, *Wanderer's* portion of the coastal convoy route was extended. From then on, instead of simply making the single-day passage from Brest to Quiberon Bay, she laid over for the night at Quiberon Bay and continued south with the convoy to the mouth of the Gironde River and thence into Bordeaux. On the night of 22 and 23 April, during the layover at Quiberon Bay on the return trip from Bordeaux to Brest, she witnessed the explosion of the ammunition-laden SS *Florence H*. Though in reasonably close proximity to the ill-fated ship, *Wanderer* was prevented from approaching the floating conflagration by the large quantity of high explosives she carried to use against U-boats. Instead, she was forced to leave the rescue operations to the destroyers and smaller craft in the bay.

The little warship continued her escort and patrol service on the French coast through the end of the war. It appears that she made no further noteworthy encounters, because the German submarine war gradually waned with the approach of fall, the collapse of the German army, and the armistice of 1918. *Wanderer* departed Brest on 5 December 1918, sailed via the Azores and Bermuda, and reached New London, Conn., on 30 December. The following April, she moved to New York City and was placed out of commission. Her name was struck from the Navy list on 24 April 1919, and she was sold on 22 July 1920 to Mr. J. S. Webster, of Baltimore, Md.

Wanderlust

(MB: t. 48; l. 83'0''; b. 13'1''; dr. 3'8½'' (mean); s. 12.0 k.; cpl. 13; a. 2 1-pdrs., 1 mg.)

Faalua—a wooden-hulled screw launch designed by F. D. Lawley and built by George Lawley and Sons, of Neponset, Mass., for George G. Peters of Boston— was subsequently owned in turn by Sherburn M. Becker and E. J. Steiner, both of New York City, prior to World War I. Apparently Steiner purchased the yacht in 1913 and renamed her *Wanderlust*, the name she carried at the time of her acquisition by the Navy in the summer of 1917 and carried during her naval service. Delivered to the Navy on 26 August 1917, *Wanderlust* was designated SP-923 and was commissioned at the Charleston Navy Yard, Charleston, S.C., on 12 September 1917, Lt. (jg.) J. P. Smith, USNRF, in command.

Wanderlust operated on section patrol duties in the 6th Naval District well into 1918, although she appears to have spent much time, initially, undergoing repairs for her temperamental engines. Her ports of call included Parris Island, Port Royal, and Charleston, S.C.; Savannah, Ga.; and Jacksonville, Fla. When on patrol duty, *Wanderlust* stopped and boarded fishing craft, ascertaining whether or not they carried proper navigational equipment and licenses that were in order.

Wanderlust conducted night harbor patrols at Brunswick, Ga., from April into the late autumn of 1918. The ship's deck logs cease on 30 September 1918 when the ship was at Brunswick. The 1918 edition of *Ship's Data: U.S. Naval Vessels* lists the craft as serving on section patrol duties as of 1 November 1918.

In the absence of solid data, it must be assumed that, like many other district patrol craft, if she was in active service in mid-to-late November of 1918, she would have ceased defensive patrolling on 24 November, nearly two weeks after the armistice stilled the guns on the western front. She may have lain in reserve or performed dispatch services between 30 September 1918 (when her deck logs end) and 2 February 1919, the date upon which the erstwhile patrol craft was struck from the Navy list.

Wanderlust retained her name into the 1920's under a succession of owners—including Irving E. Raymond of Stamford, Conn., and Mrs. Marguerite Park of New York City—before she was acquired in 1927 by William Sternfeld of New York City, who renamed her *Diana*.

She disappears from the *Lloyd's List of American Yachts* between 1929 and 1931.

Wando

The first *Wando* was probably named for a river in South Carolina that flows southwest between Charleston and Berkeley Counties before it empties into Charleston harbor.

The second *Wando* (Tug No. 17) was named for a tribe of Indians of the Muskhogean language Indian group who lived in South Carolina on the banks of the Cooper River.

I

(SwStr: t. 645; l. 230'; b. 26'; dr. 7'; a. 1 20-pdr. P.r., 1 12-pdr., 1 12-pdr. r.)

Wando—a side-wheel steamer built in 1864 at Glasgow, Scotland—was captured at sea off Cape Rosmain, S.C., by Union side-wheel steamer *Fort Jackson* on 21 October 1864 as she attempted to slip away from the Confederate coast laden with cotton. The former blockade runner had sailed under British colors as *Let Her Rip* until May 1864 when the Chicora Import & Export Co. of Charleston, S.C., had purchased the vessel and renamed her *Wando*. The Navy purchased the ship from the Boston prize court on 5 November 1864; and commissioned her at the Boston Navy Yard on 22 December 1864, Acting Master Frederick T. King in command.

Late in December, *Wando* proceeded south for duty with the South Atlantic Blockading Squadron. She arrived at Port Royal on 5 January 1865 and was stationed on blockade duty off Charleston in February.

Wando departed Charleston on 11 February and joined in amphibious operations against the Confederate fort and batteries at Andersonville, Bull's Bay, S.C., lasting from 13 to 17 February. The fort and batteries were silenced, prompting the evacuation of Charleston on the 18th. In March, *Wando* joined the blockading force off Georgetown, S.C., and then returned to Charleston in April.

Wando remained at Charleston until ordered north to the New York Navy Yard on 28 July 1865. She was decommissioned there on 10 August 1865 and was sold at public auction on 30 November 1865 to H. Allen.

II

(Tug No. 17: dp. 575 (n.); l. 123'6½''; b. 26'8''; dr. 11'6'' (mean); cpl. 23; a. 2 3-pdrs.; cl. *Wando*)

The second *Wando* (Tug No. 17) was laid down on 14 June 1915 by the Charleston (S.C.) Navy Yard; launched on 7 March 1916; and commissioned on 3 April 1917, Boatswain J. W. Bettens in command.

Wando remained at Charleston until 15 April, when she got underway for New England waters and, with the ferryboat *Wave* in tow, steamed north, via Lynnhaven Roads, Va., and the New York Navy Yard, arriving at Newport six days later. Shifting to Boston, Mass.—via the Cape Cod Canal—soon thereafter, the tug towed a coal barge to the New York Navy Yard on 25 and 26 April and subsequently towed the cruiser *Salem* from Philadelphia to the Boston Navy Yard before she returned, via Philadelphia, to Charleston on 19 May, towing the torpedo boat *Barney*.

After brief tours of duty at Georgetown, S.C., and Jacksonville, Fla., *Wando* sailed for Hampton Roads, Va., anchoring with the Fleet in the York River on 11 June. Through the summer, the tug performed various utility duties—mostly towing targets and lighters; shifting target rafts and planting buoys—out of Tangier Sound and Yorktown, Va. During that time, she assisted the grounded battleship *Louisiana* (Battleship No. 19) on 6 July.

In mid-August, *Wando* underwent repairs at the Norfolk Navy Yard and there received a "minesweeping outfit." She departed Norfolk on 23 August, heading for New York waters, and reached "Base 10"—Port Jefferson, Long Island—on the morning of the 25th. From there, the tug shifted to New London, Conn., where she received additional minesweeping gear from *Baltimore*. On the evening of 8 September, *Wando* embarked Capt. Reginald R. Belknap, Commander, Mine Force, and transported him to Newport, R.I., arriving there later that evening. The tug subsequently per-

The tug *Wando* at Charleston, 4 June 1917. (NH 48474)

formed buoy and net-tending functions off the Cornfield Light Vessel from 10 to 13 September.

Wando returned to New London on the 16th and the following day had more minesweeping gear installed. She again transported Capt. Belknap as a passenger, from New London to Newport, before heading for Norfolk. For the remainder of September, *Wando* operated at "Base One," Tangier Sound, mooring target rafts, working on target moorings, and conducting brief trips for repairs or supplies at the Norfolk Navy Yard. *Wando* subsequently remained in the Chesapeake Bay–Hampton Roads–Tangier Sound region through the autumn months and into the winter.

Detached from her duty with the Mine Force on 19 November 1917, *Wando* resumed her operations with the Atlantic Fleet Train. However, she continued to perform the same basic duties, serving as target/net tender and delivering mail and dispatches through the end of March 1918. She subsequently towed targets for battleships engaging in gunnery exercises off the southern drill grounds, off the Virginia capes, and later laid buoys at the Potomac River Torpedo Range, off the mouth of the St. Mary's River.

Wando was deployed in the Caribbean for the first time in early 1919. Underway from Norfolk on 6 February 1919, the tug arrived at Guantanamo Bay on 14 February, with Pontoon No. 23 in tow. She performed her unglamorous service functions for the Fleet—towing targets, lighters, barges, and delivering men and mail—in Cuban waters (Guantanamo Bay, Guacanayabo Bay, and Manzanillo Bay) until 17 April, when she headed home.

Reaching New York on the 18th, *Wando* subsequently shifted to Hoboken, N.J., where she underwent repairs over the first few days of May. Returning to Norfolk on 6 May, *Wando* towed targets and performed general utility service with the Atlantic Fleet Train through mid-July and then operated in waters off the northern part of the eastern seaboard, out of Newport, New London, and New York. She remained at New York City from 10 August 1919 to 10 January 1920.

Underway for Norfolk on the latter day, *Wando* arrived there the next day but, on the 14th, sailed south for Charleston and reached that port on the 16th. Detached from the Atlantic Fleet Train on 26 January 1920, *Wando* was simultaneously assigned duties as a yard craft at the Charleston Navy Yard, her crew reduced to 14 men. While on active duty at Charleston, she was classified AT–17 on 17 July 1920, during the fleet-wide assignment of alphanumeric hull numbers.

Wando operated in the 6th Naval District, out of Charleston, until 18 April 1922, when she was decommissioned and placed in reserve.

Recommissioned at the Mare Island Navy Yard, Vallejo, Calif., on 15 March 1933, *Wando* was reclassified on 27 February 1936 from a seagoing tug (AT) to a harbor tug, YT–123. On 15 April 1944, she was reclassified again to a large harbor tug, YTB–123—a classification she carried for the remainder of her active naval service.

Assigned to the 13th Naval District after her recommissioning to operate at the Puget Sound Navy Yard, Bremerton, Wash., *Wando* performed her vital but unsung tug services from the late 1930's through World War II. Ultimately placed out of commission and out of service on 3 July 1946, *Wando* was delivered to the Maritime Commission's War Shipping Administration for disposal. Her name was struck from the Navy list on 30 December 1946, and she was acquired by the Puget Sound Tug and Barge Co. on 28 April 1947.

Waneta

Probably a variant spelling of *Wahneta* (q.v.).

(YT–384: dp. 218; l. 101'0''; b. 25'0''; dr. 10'0''; s. 11 k.; cpl. 10; cl. *Pessacus*)

Waneta (YT–384) was laid down on 8 September 1943 at Brooklyn, N.Y., by Ira S. Bushey and Sons; launched on 24 December 1943; and completed and delivered to the Navy on 25 April 1944.

Reclassified a large harbor tug, YTB–384, on 15 May 1944, *Waneta* was initially allocated to the Pacific Fleet's service force and operated actively in her designed role until placed out of service, in reserve, in March 1946. Berthed at San Diego, Calif., *Waneta* remained inactive until placed in service once again in October 1953 for duty in the 6th Naval District, Charleston, S.C.

Waneta performed tug and tow services and stood ready to provide waterfront fire protection and pilotage, at Charleston, into the.1970's. Inactivated and placed out of service early in 1974, *Waneta* was struck from the Navy list on 1 April of that year and was sold in February 1975. During her nearly two decades of service in the 6th Naval District, the ship was reclassified a medium harbor tug, YTM–384, in February 1962 and carried that classification for the rest of her active service.

Wanka

(MB: l. 48'0''; b. 9'6'')

Wanka—a wooden motor boat—is virtually unchronicled in the records of the U.S. Navy. Her place of construction is unknown, but it is believed that she was built about 1901. She is carried on the lists of the period from 1912 to 1919 under "miscellaneous craft." She served with the Louisiana Naval Militia in the pre-World War I years and operated in the New Orleans vicinity, probably for her entire career. On 1 July 1920, she is dropped from the Navy list, and her subsequent fate—like her origin—is unrecorded.

Wannalancet

Wannalancet—probably born sometime in or near 1619—was a sagamore of the Penacook Indian Confederacy; he became chief of his tribe upon the death of his father Passaconaway. Wannalancet, at the deathbed wish of his father, resolved never to fight the English settlers and refused to participate in King Philip's War in 1675. He was invited to attend a meeting with English settlers and, after he arrived, was treacherously imprisoned. After he was eventually released, he returned home but, despairing of the marauding white men in the environs of New Hampshire and Maine, took his people to Canada.

(YTB–385: dp. 218; l. 100; b. 25'; dr. 10'; s. 12 k.; cpl. 10; cl. *Pessacus*)

Wannalancet (YTB–385)—originally projected as YT–385—was launched on 12 January 1944 at Brooklyn, N.Y., by Ira S. Bushey and Sons and was completed in May 1944. Assigned to Service Force, Pacific Fleet, soon thereafter, the ship operated, in service, until placed in reserve in March of 1946 at San Diego. Reclassified as YTM–385 in February 1962, *Wannalancet* was transferred, on loan, to the Venezuelan Government in January 1963. Renamed *Fabrio Gallipoli* (R–14), she served with the Venezuelan Navy into the late 1970's. As of November 1978, she was slated for sale.

Wantuck

John Joseph Wantuck—born on 23 November 1923 in Elmira, N.Y.—enlisted in the United States Marine Corps on 6 January 1942. After basic training at the Marine barracks at Parris Island, S.C., he served at Guantanamo Bay, Cuba, from 30 June 1942 until late in the year.

By 5 December, Private Wantuck was serving in the Solomon Islands where, on 30 June 1943, he went ashore with other marines at Zanana beach on the island of New Georgia. For two weeks, the troops tried to dislodge the Japanese defenders farther inland near Munda while Wantuck served with the beachhead and supply depot antiaircraft defense unit. On 17 July, the Japanese mounted a major offensive at the severed and disoriented American forces.

Though eventually stymied in their attempt, they managed to reach the perimeter of the beachhead and Private Wantuck's position. Using a light machine gun salvaged from the discard pile, Wantuck stuck to his position through the night. The following morning, after the enemy offensive had been repulsed, Private Wantuck was found dead at his gun with evidence in front of him that he had killed 18 to 20 of the enemy and had probably wounded many more. For his gallant defense and supreme sacrifice Private Wantuck was awarded the Navy Cross, posthumously.

(APD–125: dp. 1,650 (tl.); l. 306'0"; b. 37'0"; dr. 12'7"; s. 23.6 k. (tl.); cpl. 204; trp. 162; a. 1 5", 6 40mm., 6 20mm., 2 dct.; cl. *Crosley*)

Wantuck (APD–125) was laid down on 17 August 1944 at Quincy, Mass., by the Bethlehem Shipbuilding Co.; launched on 25 September 1944; sponsored by Miss Mary Wantuck; and commissioned at the Boston Navy Yard on 30 December 1944, Lt. Comdr. Richard Bensen, USNR, in command.

Wantuck conducted shakedown training along the New England coast and then in the vicinity of Bermuda until 18 February 1945, when she arrived in Hampton Roads, Va. Three days later, she departed Norfolk, bound—via the Panama Canal, San Diego, and Pearl Harbor—for the western Pacific. She arrived at Oahu on 21 March but got underway again on 2 April. The high-speed transport stopped at Eniwetok on the night of 10 and 11 April and then resumed her voyage. She touched at Guam in the Marianas on 14 April and then pushed on to the lagoon at Ulithi. There, the ship joined a convoy bound for the Ryukyu Islands and arrived in Kerama Retto near Okinawa on 21 April. She remained at Okinawa screening the American ships there until the last day of April when she got underway in the screen of a convoy containing 16 other ships bound for Saipan in the Marianas. However, after seeing them safely out of the Ryukyus, she returned to Okinawa and resumed her duty screening the ships remaining at Kerama Retto. On 4 May, she helped repulse an enemy air attack but claimed no kills or assists for herself. Later that day, when a kamikaze crashed *Birmingham* (CL–62), *Wantuck* went to the aid of the stricken cruiser. The following day, she departed Okinawa in company with damaged *Birmingham* and *Rodman* (DMS–21) and set a course for Ulithi. En route, however, the ships received orders diverting them to Guam in the Marianas and, for the next two months, the high-speed transport made regular shuttle runs escorting convoys between Guam and Okinawa. That particular routine ended on 5 July when she departed Guam for Leyte in the Philippines. She entered San Pedro Bay on 8 July and then headed back to Okinawa.

After more than a month of further service in the Ryukyus—during which hostilities ended on 15 August —she embarked troops for the planned occupation of Japan and joined the 3d Fleet on the 18th. The warship entered Tokyo Bay on the 27th and disembarked her share of the occupation force. On 30 August, she moved to the Yokosuka Naval Station where she began loading Allied prisoners of war from the hospital ship *Benevolence* (AH–13). During the first week of September, she made calls at various Japanese ports embarking former Allied prisoners of war. On the 7th, she transferred her passengers to *Lansdowne* (DD–486). On the 9th, *Wantuck* took several British prisoners on board and the next day transferred them to a Royal Navy destroyer. She continued to shuttle former prisoners of war between locations in Japan until 2 October at which time she headed for the Marianas.

The ship arrived at Guam on 5 October and remained there until the 19th when she headed back to Yokosuka. The ship reached Yokosuka on 22 October but got underway again on the 30th. Steaming via Guam, she arrived at Manus in the Admiralty Islands on 8 November but that same day headed for Rabaul where she arrived on 9 November. On the 18th she began a circuitous voyage back to the United States.

After stops at Manus, Guam, Eniwetok, and Pearl Harbor, the warship reached San Francisco on 21 December. On 3 January 1946, *Wantuck* entered the Mare Island Naval Shipyard for an overhaul which she completed on 10 March.

That same day, she sailed for her new home port, San Diego. For almost a year, the high-speed transport operated out of San Diego, primarily conducting amphibious warfare exercises at San Clemente Island. On 24 February 1947, *Wantuck* departed San Diego for a three-month voyage to the western Pacific. Her ports of call included Pearl Harbor, Kwajalein, Manus, and Guam. She returned to San Diego on 19 June and resumed normal operations out of that port which she continued until the beginning of the following year.

On 15 January 1948, the warship again stood out of San Diego for a voyage to the western Pacific. After stops at Pearl Harbor, Kwajalein, and Guam, she arrived in Tsingtao, China, on 15 February. For the next six months, she cruised along the China coast observing conditions during the latter stages of civil war in China and transported Chinese Nationalist troops to various locations in support of their efforts against the Chinese Communists. On 16 August, *Wantuck* departed Tsingtao to return to the United States. She made stops at Guam, Kwajalein, and Pearl Harbor before reentering San Diego on 9 September and resumed normal west coast operations.

Early in 1950, the warship made a round-trip voyage to Alaskan waters and back to San Diego before departing that port on 1 May to deploy overseas once more. She stopped at Pearl Harbor from 9 to 12 May and then continued her voyage west. After stops in the Mariana and Philippine Islands, *Wantuck* arrived at Hong Kong on 7 June.

While she remained at Hong Kong, war erupted in Korea when communist North Korean troops invaded South Korea on 25 June. Whether or not this event prompted *Wantuck's* unusually long stay—three months —in a liberty port for a warship is not clear from the documents. However, she did not leave Hong Kong until 6 September. From there, the ship moved to Sasebo where they arrived on 8 September.

Two days later, the high-speed transport was in the Korean combat zone at the port of Pusan preparing for the amphibious assault at Inchon. She departed Pusan on 13 September with elements of the 3d Battalion, 5th Marines, embarked. Early on the morning of the 15th, the warship was off Wolmi Do, an island just off Inchon. Her troops stormed ashore on the island and quickly consolidated their position in preparation for the second phase of the operation, the invasion of Inchon itself scheduled for that afternoon. *Wantuck* remained at Inchon supporting the consolidation and expansion of the beachhead until 26 September at which time she returned to Yokosuka, Japan.

The high-speed transport returned to Korea early in October with Royal Marine Commandos embarked. In cooperation with *Bass* (APD–124) and supported by *De Haven* (DD–727), she executed a series of raids near Wonsan to disrupt North Korean transportation facilities—primarily rail lines—to support a scheduled amphibious attack on Wonsan. However, that operation was obviated by the fact that Republic of Korea (ROK) troops entered the city from landward on 11 October. The day before that event, *Wantuck* returned to Japan. She did not arrive back in Korean waters again until the 20th—once again at Wonsan. By that time, however, United Nations efforts to reopen the port were well advanced, and the transport saw no further combat duty during that deployment. She returned to Yokosuka on 25 November and, three days later, headed back to the United States. After stops at Midway and Pearl Harbor, the fast transport arrived in San Diego on 15 December 1950.

Wantuck spent almost eight months conducting normal operations along the west coast out of San Diego. On 23 July 1951, she pointed her bow westward once again and set a course for the Far East. Following calls at Pearl Harbor and at Midway Island, the fast transport arrived in Yokosuka on 22 August. By the time of *Wantuck*'s return to the Korean conflict, that war had degenerated into a stalemate on land with the principals locked in armistice negotiations and jockeying for military advantage at the bargaining table. At sea, the naval war had become almost purely one of fast carrier operations with planes interdicting communist supply routes and hitting strategic targets in North Korea. *Wantuck* resumed duty with TF 90, the Amphibious Force, and consequently took little active part in the conflict from that point. In fact, during the 1951 to 1952 deployment, she did not even qualify for the Korean Service Medal, though she did visit Korean ports on occasion—particularly Inchon and Pusan. The fast transport departed Yokosuka late in March 1952; and, after a stop at Oahu along the way, she reentered San Diego on 19 April.

The ship remained on the west coast for almost a year. A paucity of movements on her part—limited to one move to San Francisco in September for a three-month stay before returning to San Diego in December—suggests a period of extensive repairs probably including an overhaul. In any event, she departed San Diego again on 7 March 1953 and steamed via Pearl Harbor to the Far East. The warship arrived in Yokosuka on 30 March and, though she patrolled extensively in Korean waters, her operations were essentially as peaceful as they had been during the previous deployment. That summer, the signing of the armistice made those conditions permanent, and *Wantuck* contented herself with patrols, training exercises, and port visits for the remainder of the deployment. On 9 November, she departed Yokosuka to return to the United States. En route home, the warship stopped at Midway and Pearl Harbor before arriving back in San Diego on 25 November.

Over the remaining four years of her active career, *Wantuck* made two more cruises to the Orient—one in 1954 and another in 1955. In 1956 and 1957, her zone of operations centered in two areas, the California coast and the waters around Alaska. The warship was decommissioned at San Diego on 15 November 1957 and berthed there with the Pacific Reserve Fleet. Her name was struck from the Navy list on 4 March 1958, and she was sold on 27 October 1958 to the Sundfelt Equipment Co., Inc., of Wilmington, Calif. Presumably she was scrapped.

Wantuck earned one battle star during World War II and five battle stars during the Korean conflict.

Wapakoneta

The seat of Auglaize County, Ohio, a city founded in 1833 and named for the Shawnee Indian chief of the same name. The city is the hometown of Neil Armstrong, who, in July 1969, became the first man to walk on the surface of the Moon.

I

(PC–579: dp. 450 (f.); l. 173'8''; b. 23'0''; dr. 10'10'' (mean); cpl. 65; s. 20.2 k.; a. 2 3'', 5 20mm., 2 dct., 2 dcp., 2 mousetrap; cl. PC–461)

More than two decades after she was built, the first *Wapakoneta* (PC–579) was given that name on 15 February 1956 while she was resting in the Atlantic Reserve Fleet at Norfolk, Va. She was originally laid down as the unnamed *PC–579* on 5 January 1942 at Portland, Oreg., by the Albina Engine and Machinery Works, Inc.; launched on 29 April 1942; sponsored by Mrs. S. M. Rovang; and commissioned on 25 August 1942, Lt. Grinnel Lewis, USNR, in command.

After fitting out at the Puget Sound Navy Yard, Bremerton, Wash., *PC–579* reported for duty to the Commander, Western Sea Frontier, on 18 September 1942. She operated locally, on patrol and escort missions, into the autumn of the following year, before she sailed for Hawaii. From mid-November 1943, *PC–579* operated under the aegis of Commander, Hawaiian Sea Frontier, performing more escort and patrol missions locally in the Hawaiian Islands, principally around Oahu and Pearl Harbor, through the end of World War II and into March 1946.

Assigned to the Atlantic Fleet in the spring of 1946, *PC–579* arrived at the Charleston Navy Yard, Charleston, S.C., via the Panama Canal on 20 April 1946. After an overhaul there, *PC–579* departed Charleston on 8 July, bound for Norfolk, Va., arriving there the following day. She remained there until 14 August, when she headed northward for Narragansett Bay, reaching Newport, R.I., on the 15th.

PC–579 served briefly as a training ship under the aegis of Commander, Training Command, Atlantic Fleet, based at Newport into the spring of 1947. During that time, the patrol craft was homeported at Newport and visited Salem, Mass., from 25 to 28 October 1946 and New London, Conn., from 27 March to 7 April 1947. Completing that tour of temporary duty on 23 May 1947, *PC–579* departed Newport and sailed for Fort Pierce, Fla.

Working out of Fort Pierce and Mayport, Fla., the patrol craft again operated in a training capacity—primarily in the Banana River region—into the summer. On 1 August, she departed Mayport, bound for Narragansett Bay, and reached Newport on 3 August. She then underwent repairs alongside the repair ship *Vulcan* (AR–5) from 4 to 18 August before she sailed to Warren, R.I., on the 22d, to take part in observances marking the 200th anniversary of the founding of that town.

PC–579 continued training evolutions off the eastern seaboard until "immobilized" on 1 November 1947. Thereafter, the patrol craft conducted "limited operations" out of Newport into the autumn of the following year, 1948, making only comparatively short cruises—to such ports as Bangor and East Boothbay, Maine, and Newburyport and Gloucester, Mass.

Apparently restored to full operational status in mid-1948, *PC–579* shifted her area of operations southward to warmer climes. The ports she visited and operated from, between late 1948 and late 1955, included Baltimore, Md.; Key West, St. Petersburg, and Jacksonville, Fla.; Charleston, S.C.; Norfolk; Port-au-Prince, Haiti; and the Cuban ports of Guantanamo Bay and Havana.

Placed in reserve at Norfolk on 17 October 1955, *PC–579* was decommissioned on 17 December of the same year. Although named *Wapakoneta* (retaining her PC–579 classification) on 15 February 1956, the patrol craft never served actively under that name, remaining in the Atlantic Reserve Fleet until struck from the Navy list on 1 July 1960. The exact nature of her ultimate disposal is not recorded.

II

(YTB–766: dp. 356 (f.); l. 109'0''; b. 31'0''; dph. 14'0''; s. 12.0 k.; cpl. 12; cl. *Natick*)

The second *Wapakoneta* (YTB–766) was laid down on 1 August 1962 at Slidell, La., by the Southern Shipbuilding Corp.; launched on 11 June 1963; and delivered to the Navy on 25 July 1963.

Soon thereafter, *Wapakoneta* was placed in service in the 5th Naval District, Norfolk, Va. Since October

1963, she has performed unglamorous, but vital, duties in those waters, providing tug and tow services, pilot assistance, and stand-by waterfront fire protection. As of 1 January 1979, she was still active at Norfolk.

Wapasha

The name of a succession of Mdewakanton Sioux chiefs whose lineage extends forward from time immemorial into the 20th century. Wapasha I (1718–1799) formed a friendship with the governing British and served them during the American Revolution; Wapasha II (d. 1855), on the other hand, formed a friendship with the fledgling American nation and, although nominally allied with the British during the War of 1812, did not take part in hostilities; Wapasha III (also named Joseph Wapasha) led his people to the Sioux reservation at the head of the Minnesota River; and Wapasha IV (also known as Napoleon Wapasha) became a United States citizen in 1909.

(YN–45: t. 200; l. 94′4½″; b. 25′0″; dr. 8′6″; s. 13 k.; a. 2 .30-cal. mg.)

William J. Moran—a steel-hulled, single-screw tug completed in September 1938 at Bay City, Mich., by the Defoe Boat and Motor Works, Inc.—was acquired by the Navy from the Moran Towing and Transportation Co., of New York City, on 9 December 1940. The tug was classified as a net tender, renamed *Wapasha*, and designated YN–45 on 25 December 1940. Converted for naval use at the New York Navy Yard, *Wapasha* was placed in service on 27 January 1941.

After shifting to her home port, Boston, Mass., on 1 February, she took up her net tending duties in Narragansett Bay, based at the naval training station. During her service there—which lasted into 1947—she was twice reclassified: on 8 April 1942, *Wapasha* was reclassified a tug-class net tender and redesignated YNT–13; and, on 4 August 1945, she was reclassified a large harbor tug and redesignated YTB–737.

Placed out of service on 11 February 1947, *Wapasha* was struck from the Navy list on 11 March and turned over to the Maritime Commission for disposal on 16 May. Acquired by Tug Anne Moran, Inc., of New York, N.Y., the vessel was renamed *Anne Moran* and performs harbor tug services in New York harbor into 1977.

Wapato

An Indian word for a bulbous root resembling a potato. Wapato is also the name of a city in Yakima County, Wash.

(YTB–788: dp. 356; l. 109′; b. 31′; dr. 14′; s. 12 k.; cpl. 12; cl. *Natick*)

Wapato (YTB–788) was laid down on 14 January 1966 at Marinette, Wis., by the Marinette Marine Corp.; launched on 18 April 1966; and completed two months later.

Assigned to the 10th Naval District, *Wapato* has operated out of San Juan, Puerto Rico, into 1980, assisting warships in the harbor there and providing waterfront fire protection.

Wapello

Wapello—the head chief of the Fox tribe—was born in 1787 at Prairie du Chien, in the present state of Wisconsin. Short and stout in physical stature, with a kindly visage, Wapello entertained friendly relations with white settlers throughout his life, signing treaties with them at Fort Armstrong on 3 September 1822; at Prairie du Chien on 15 July 1830; again at Fort Armstrong on 21 September 1832; at Dubuque, Iowa,

on 28 September 1836; and at Washington, D.C., on 21 October 1837.

In 1829, he led his tribe to Muscatine Slough on the west bank of the Mississippi River and later settled near the present site of the town of Wapello, Iowa. In 1837, Wapello accompanied the renowned chief, Keokuk, and Indian agent General James M. Street on a tour of northeastern and mideastern states. During this trip, Wapello made an eloquent speech at Boston, wherein he expressed friendly sentiments towards white settlers and raffirmed his desire to continue harmonious relations with them.

While on a hunting trip near Ottumwa, Iowa, Wapello died on 15 March 1842. He was later buried in accordance with his oft-expressed wish that he be laid to rest alongside his good friend General Street.

(YN–56: l. 102′2″; b. 24′0″; dr. 9′6″)

R. K. Evans was completed in April 1941 at Port Arthur, Tex., by the Gulfport Boiler and Welding Works, for the General Motors Corp., of Cleveland, Ohio. Acquired by the Navy for service as a net tender, renamed *Wapello*, and designated YN–56, the ship was placed in service on 9 June 1941. Six days later, the ship arrived at the naval station at Key West, Fla., for conversion and fitting-out.

On 26 June, *Wapello* set sail for Cuba, in company with *Umpqua* (AT–25), and arrived at Guantanamo Bay three days later. Escorted by *Vega* (AK–17) from Guantanamo Bay to San Diego and by *Ramapo* (AO–12) from the west coast to the Hawaiian Islands, *Wapello* arrived at Pearl Harbor on 27 August.

While attached to the 14th Naval District, the ship tended harbor nets through the Japanese attack on 7 December and the remainder of the crucial year, 1941. She remained at Pearl Harbor for the duration of hostilities, engaged in unglamorous but vital tasks. The ship was reclassified YNT–24 on 7 April 1942. With the end of the war in the Pacific, the need for the ship's services decreased rapidly, and *Wapello* was declared surplus. Placed out of service at Bremerton, Wash., on 23 October 1946 and struck from the Navy list on 21 November 1946, the ship was turned over to the War Shipping Administration for disposal on 3 May 1947.

War Bug

(MB: t. 28.89 (gross); l. 62′4″; b. 10′11″; dr. 2′9″ (mean); s. 20 k.; cpl. 9; a. 1 1-pdr.)

War Bug—a wooden-hulled motor boat completed in 1917 at Bristol, R.I., by the Herreshoff Manufacturing Co.—was purchased by the Navy from Felix Warburg of New York City on 6 November 1917.

Designated SP–1795 and commissioned on 17 November 1917, *War Bug* was assigned to the 1st Naval District and served in waters near Boston through the end of World War I. Decommissioned on 28 December 1918, she was sold on 30 June 1919 to E. Atkins and Co., of Boston.

War Hawk

(AP–168: dp. 13,910; l. 459′2″; b. 63′0″; dr. 23′0″; s. 16.5 k.; cpl. 276; trp. 1,575; a. 1 5″, 4 3″; cl. *La Salle*; T. C2–S–B1)

War Hawk was laid down under a Maritime Commission contract (MC hull 1154) on 24 December 1942 at Oakland, Calif., by the Moore Dry Dock Co.; launched on 3 April 1943; sponsored by Miss Jeanette Thomson; acquired by the Navy under a bareboat charter on 9 March 1944; designated AP–168; and commissioned at San Francisco, Calif., on the same day, Comdr. S. H. Thompson, USNR, in command.

War Hawk got underway for Hawaii on 21 April and, upon her arrival at Pearl Harbor on the 27th, joined the 5th Fleet Amphibious Force. Assigned initially to Transport Division (TransDiv) 18, the transport conducted practice landings in the Hawaiian Islands before sailing on 30 May to participate in the initial phase of Operation "Forager," the conquest of the Marianas. After pausing at Eniwetok Atoll en route, the ship arrived off Saipan on 15 June. *War Hawk* landed troops and equipment of the 2d Marine Division at Saipan during daylight and retired from the battle area each evening. During her sojourn off the beachheads, she helped to ward off two air attacks before embarking 11 badly wounded Japanese prisoners of war and getting underway for Hawaii on 23 June.

After embarking elements of the Army 77th Infantry Division at Pearl Harbor, *War Hawk* participated in the final phase of "Forager," landing her troops at Guam between 21 and 29 July, before sailing for Pearl Harbor on the latter date. She spent a month at Oahu, conducting further practice landings, before she took on board the men of the Army's 96th Infantry Division for transport to Yap. However, the invasion of that island was cancelled while the transport was steaming toward the Carolines, and she was routed via Eniwetok to Manus in the Admiralties.

On 14 October, the transport got underway for the Philippines to take part in the initial landings on Leyte. After she had put her troops ashore there, she sailed for Dutch New Guinea to pick up a field hospital unit for passage to Leyte. She subsequently returned south to Cape Gloucester, New Britain, to embark troops of the Army's 40th Infantry Division. She travelled thence to Manus and New Guinea before returning to Seeadler Harbor on 10 December. On New Year's Eve, 1944, *War Hawk* got underway for Luzon.

The warship arrived off the beaches of Lingayen Gulf on 9 January 1945, D day, to find that the Japanese were determined to use all their forces available against the invading American forces—every weapon from kamikazes to suicide motorboats. At 0410 on 10 January 1945, *War Hawk* suddenly shuddered heavily as a Japanese suicide motorboat, laden with explosives and going full-throttle, crashed into her port side, tearing a 25-foot hole in number three hold and killing 61 men. The ship lay without power as an engine room began to flood, and repair crews, below decks in stifling heat with only dim emergency lights and with little, if any, ventilation, worked to restore power and to patch the gash in the ship's side.

Meanwhile, *War Hawk*'s gunners fought to repel the Japanese air attacks. The transport then gamely disembarked her remaining troops and began unloading her embarked mechanized equipment. Christened the "sitting duck" by her crew, *War Hawk* remained off Lingayen until 11 January, when she began her creeping trek to Leyte Gulf. On the 13th, while en route, her gunners splashed a kamikaze dead ahead of the ship. Before it crashed in a ball of fire, the plane, trailing gasoline and flames, liberally sprinkled burning gasoline on the bow of the transport but did not succeed in starting any serious fires.

Despite nightly air raids, San Pedro Bay, Leyte Gulf, seemed peaceful in comparison to the hectic and dangerous Lingayen Gulf area. Temporary repairs effected at San Pedro Bay enabled the ship to get underway for Manus, where she arrived on 30 January and entered the floating drydock there. On 22 February, *War Hawk* headed for home and passed beneath the Golden Gate bridge on 19 March, entering her builder's yard soon thereafter for extensive repairs and a major overhaul.

After getting underway for San Diego on 29 May, *War Hawk* embarked troops there and loaded cargo for the Marianas and proceeded to Guam where she discharged her passengers and cargo. Following her return to San Francisco, she reloaded with naval replacements and got underway for Leyte Gulf, via Eniwetok and Ulithi. En route, the ship received the welcome news that Japan, twice struck by atomic bombs and hammered by task forces off her very doorstep,

accepted the unconditional surrender terms of the Potsdam Declaration on 15 August 1945.

Disembarking her troops and unloading her cargo at Leyte and at Samar, *War Hawk* returned home on "Magic-Carpet" duties with 1,800 discharged sailors embarked. On 6 September, the ship departed Ulithi with Convoy UE–129 on the first leg of the 17-day voyage to the west coast of the United States and arrived at San Francisco on 23 September. "Welcome Home" signs and blaring bands were very much in evidence. During her brief west coast stay, from 23 September to 5 October, the first draft of demobilized members of *War Hawk*'s crew left the ship.

War Hawk stood out of the Golden Gate on 5 October, bound for China. Calling at Pearl Harbor and Buckner Bay, Okinawa, en route, the transport arrived at Shanghai, China, on 8 November before getting underway on the 12th for Taku with Chinese Nationalist government officials embarked. She arrived at her destination late on the 12th and lay offshore after an uneventful passage. Prospects for the crew to enjoy liberty in North China ports were not good, however, as local tensions between the communists and Nationalists jockeying for control in the formerly Japanese-occupied territorites had frequently erupted into bloodshed.

En route to the west coast of the United States once more, *War Hawk* called at Manila from 26 to 28 November before getting underway for San Francisco on that day with homeward-bound Army veterans. On 16 December, the transport reached Los Angeles, Calif. *War Hawk* subsequently conducted three voyages between the west coast and the Orient into the summer of 1946, calling at such ports as Shanghai, Taku, Tsingtao, Nagoya, Yokohama, and Hong Kong, as well as pausing at Pearl Harbor and Midway while en route.

Decommissioned on 12 August 1946, at Seattle, Wash., *War Hawk* was returned to the Maritime Commission on 13 August at Olympia, Wash. Struck from the Navy list on 8 October 1946, the transport was converted for mercantile service and was subsequently acquired by the Waterman Steamship Corp., of Mobile, Ala., which operated her on freight and cargo-carrying duties until 1954. Acquired that year by the Ocean Transportation Co., Inc., of New York, the erstwhile transport was renamed *Ocean Dinny*. She retained this name while serving with Ocean Clippers, Inc., of New York, until 1966, when she acquired her third name, *Overseas Dinny*, and served with new owners, the Overseas Carrier Corp., until she was dropped from the *American Shipping Board Register* in 1970.

War Hawk received three battle stars for her World War II service.

Warbler

A small, brightly colored songbird.

I

(Minesweeper No. 53: dp. 950; l. 187'10"; b. 35'6"; dr. 9'9½" (mean); s. 14 k.; cpl. 85; a. none; cl. *Lapwing*)

The first *Warbler* (Minesweeper No. 53) was laid down on 24 April 1919 by the Philadelphia Navy Yard; launched on 30 July 1919; sponsored by Miss Alice Kempff, the daughter of Capt. C. S. Kempff, the Captain of the Yard; and commissioned on 22 December 1919, Lt. Daniel J. O'Connell in command.

After brief service with the Train of the Atlantic Fleet, *Warbler* was decommissioned on 16 June 1920 and simultaneously transferred, on loan, to the United States Shipping Board. The ship operated with a civilian crew under the aegis of Merritt, Chapman, and Scott, a New York-based salvage firm. On 13 September 1941, the Navy reclassified *Warbler* a salvage vessel and designated her ARS–11.

During World War II, she continued to operate with a civilian crew under a contract with the Naval Salvage Service. She was based at the Merritt, Chapman, and Scott salvage depot at Key West, Fla., and worked primarily in the Gulf of Mexico and the Caribbean, towing disabled ships; assisting stranded or grounded vessels; escorting coastwise convoys; and conducting salvage operations.

After the war ended, the Navy designated *Warbler* for disposal on 29 March 1946 and declared her surplus on 13 January 1947. She was struck from the Navy list on 10 June 1947.

II

(MSC–208: dp. 412'; l. 145'; b. 28'; dr. 12' (max.); s. 12.8 k.; cpl. 40; a. 1 20mm., 2 .50-cal. mg., 1 81mm. M.; cl. *Redwing*)

The second *Warbler* (AMS–208) was laid down on 15 October 1953 at Bellingham, Wash., by the Bellingham Shipyards Co.; launched on 18 June 1954; sponsored by Mrs. S. A. Blythe; redesignated MSC–208 on 7 February 1955; and commissioned at the Naval Station, Tacoma, Wash., on 26 July 1955, Lt. (jg.) James S. Elfelt in command.

Following shakedown training, *Warbler* reported to Commander, Mine Force, Pacific Fleet, and operated locally out of Long Beach for the next year. In August 1956, in company with *Whippoorwill* (MSC–207), the minesweeper set sail for the Far East to assume duties as flagship for Mine Division 32. Homeporting at Sasebo, Japan, *Warbler* would remain in the Far East over the next 14 years, participating in numerous mine exercises with the navies of other friendly Far Eastern nations such as South Korea, Nationalist China, the Philippines, and Japan.

Highlighting the ship's deployment to the western Pacific, *Warbler* conducted numerous tours of duty on "Market-Time" patrols off the coast of Vietnam. A small wooden craft especially designed for coastal minesweeping operations and deployments lasting from a few days to several weeks, *Warbler* and her sister minesweepers filled the gap between the heavier units of the fleet, like the destroyers and destroyer escorts, and the small craft used for patrol work, until built-for-the-purpose patrol craft could enter the fray. During her "Market-Time" cruises, *Warbler* boarded many junks, ascertaining cargo and destination; investigated contacts of steel-hulled vessels picked up on radar; and endured what at times appeared to be "fearfully strong weather that seemed bent on total destruction" of the ship. At times, boarding of junks was an impossibility because of the vagaries of monsoon-type weather.

During one "Market-Time" patrol in the spring of 1968, *Warbler* conducted a joint salvage evolution with the salvage vessel *Conserver* (ARS–39). She located a downed aircraft, an F-100 Super Sabre fighter, and a wayward box of hypodermic needles. The ship also conducted extensive searches for an A–6 Intruder, a medevac (medical evacuation) helicopter, and two target drones. The minesweeper then cruised off the delimitarized zone (the DMZ) before heading home to Sasebo via the Nationalist Chinese port of Kaohsiung.

With 45 days of "Market-Time" patrols under her belt in 1968, *Warbler* returned to the coast of Vietnam in January of 1969 and patrolled briefly near the port of Vung Tau.

Later that autumn, *Warbler*, in company with her sistership *Whippoorwill*, departed Sasebo on 5 September, bound for Taiwan and Mine Exercise "Canned Heat." Unfortunately beset with mechanical difficulties, the ship went dead in the water in Formasa Strait after attempted repairs at Keelung, Taiwan, had proved ineffective. Eight hours after the ship stopped, *Schofield* (DEG–3) answered *Warbler*'s call for assistance and passed a tow to the heavily rolling minecraft. By 10 September, after rapid repairs at Kaohsiung, *Warbler* was ready for sea and participated in the scheduled

slate of exercises. At the close of the year, the ship received counter-insurgency practice by tracking high-speed patrol boats sent out for exercise purposes by Commander, Mine Flotilla 1.

The ship's last "Market-Time" patrols in 1970 were similar to the ones she had conducted in past years, as she operated off the coast of Vietnam to aid in the interdiction campaign to cut off the flow of arms and munitions to the Viet Cong in South Vietnam. For two months in 1970, *Warbler* patrolled between Camranh Bay and Nha Trang, investigating suspicious contacts —none of which proved hostile. "Our greatest excitement during this patrol," her comanding officer later wrote, "was provided by an occasional Soviet Merchantman that would steam through our area and find himself shadowed and photographed by the mighty *Warbler*."

Whippoorwill consequently relieved *Warbler* of "Market-Time" duties on 19 July 1970, and the latter got underway from Camranh Bay for the succession of port visits. However, two days after leaving the bay, the ship received a message directing her to return to the United States for decommissioning.

Departing Sasebo on 17 August and sailing via Pearl Harbor for an overnight refueling stop, *Warbler* reached the west coast of the United States on 17 September in company with *Catskill* (MCS–1), *Vireo* (MSC–205), and *Widgeon* (MSC–208). On 1 October 1970, *Warbler* was decommissioned.

Simultaneously placed in service as a Naval Reserve training (NRT) ship and homeported at Seattle, Wash., *Warbler* commenced her new duties soon thereafter. She trained reservists out of Seattle into the mid-1970's and was placed on the sale list in July 1975. On 14 October 1975, she was sold to the government of Fiji.

Warbler (MSC–206) was awarded seven engagement stars for her important services on "Market-Time" patrols.

Ward

Born on 25 September 1806, at Hartford, Conn., James Harmon Ward received his early educational training in Connecticut common schools before attending the American Literary Scientific and Military Academy at Norwich, Vermont. After graduating in 1823, Ward accepted an appointment as a midshipman in the Navy on 4 March 1823. Subsequently, he sailed in frigate *Constitution* on a four-year Mediterranean cruise and then received a year's leave of absence for scientific studies at Washington College, Hartford, Conn.

When Ward returned to sea, he served once more in the Mediterranean and then saw duty off the African coast in interdicting the slave trade. He next served in the West Indies helping to prevent a resurgence of piracy.

Upon his return to the United States, he taught courses in ordnance and gunnery at the Naval School at Philadelphia, Pa. These popular courses were later published as *An Elementary Course of Instruction in Ordnance and Gunnery*.

On 10 October 1845, the new Naval Academy opened at Annapolis, Md.; and Lt. Ward was a member of the faculty—one of the first line officers to pass along the benefits of his own experience to young midshipmen. One of the most scholarly officers of the Navy of his day, Ward held the office of executive officer (a post which later became that of the Commandant of Midshipmen), with collateral duties as instructor of gunnery and steam engineering.

The advent of the war with Mexico prompted many naval officers and men to seek assignment to ships serving in Mexican waters. Detached from the Academy, Ward took comand of *Cumberland* in 1847 and served in that capacity for the duration of the war. After a period spent waiting for orders, he was given command of steamer *Vixen* in 1848 and remained in her through 1850.

After intermittent periods awaiting orders and serving at the Washington and Philadelphia Navy Yards, Ward took command of *Jamestown* and took her to the African coast to hunt down slave ships trafficking in human flesh. During this time, in his off-duty hours, he proceeded to work on another textbook—*A Manual of Naval Tactics*—a scholarly work which one day would run into four editions after its initial publication in 1859.

In 1860, as war clouds gathered over the United States, Ward served at the New York Navy Yard, where he wrote a popular treatise on steam egineering, entitled *Steam for the Million.* In the spring of 1861, with the Southern states leaving the Union and Confederate forces mounting a siege at Fort Sumter, S.C., Gideon Welles summoned Ward to Washington to plan for a relief expedition for Sumter. Ward volunteered to lead it but opposition, notably from General Winfield Scott (who perceived it as being futile), forced cancellation of the plans.

Ward pressed for front line service, proposing that a "flying squadron" be established in the Chesapeake Bay for use against Confederate naval and land forces threatening that area south of the Union capital. The idea proved acceptable, and the squadron took shape. With steamer *Thomas Freeborn* serving as Ward's flagship, the steamers *Freelance, Alliance,* and three coast survey ships made up the flotilla.

The newly composed unit—later known as the Potomac Flotilla—saw its first action on 1 June, when guns from Ward's ships silenced Confederate shore batteries at Aquia Creek. On 27 June, Ward sent a landing party ashore to dislodge Southern forces from another battery at Matthias Point, in St. Mary's County, but encountered heavy resistance. The Federals gave up the attack and retired, under heavy sniper and cannon fire, to their ships. Sizing up the situation, Ward brought his flotilla in close to the shoreline to provide gunfire support for the returning Union forces. As he sighted the bow gun in his flagship, *Thomas Freeborn,* Comdr. James Harmon Ward took a bullet in his abdomen and fell to the deck, mortally wounded. He died within the hour, the first officer of the United States Navy killed during the tragic Civil War.

(Destroyer No. 139: dp. 1,247; l. 314'4''; b. 30'11''; dr. 9'10''; s. 35.0 k.; cpl. 231; a. 4 4'', 2 3'', 12 21'' tt.; cl. *Wickes*)

Ward (Destroyer No. 139) was laid down on 15 May 1918 by the Mare Island Navy Yard; launched

in a record 15 days on 1 June 1918; sponsored by Miss Dorothy Hall Ward; and commissioned on 24 July 1918, Comdr. Milton S. Davis in command.

Following shakedown and training, *Ward* cleared the west coast on 2 December 1918. As flagship of Destroyer Division (DesDiv) 18, the ship took part in the annual winter maneuvers in the Guantanamo Bay area. In May 1919, *Ward* provided navigational aids and lifeguard station services as NC-1, NC-3, and NC-4 set out on their transatlantic flight. *Ward* served on station off Newfoundland and supported the first leg of the passage from Newfoundland to the Azores, while stationed 50 miles from sister ships, *Boggs* (Destroyer No. 136) and *Palmer* (Destroyer No. 161).

In July 1919, *Ward* was among the first "nest" of destroyers which passed through the Panama Canal locks as the Fleet took passage from the Atlantic to the Pacific. Following this canal transit, *Ward* proceeded north and called at Acapulco, Mexico. For the remainder of July and into August, she visited such California ports as San Diego, San Pedro, San Luis Obispo, Monterey, San Francisco, and Eureka, before heading north to Portland, Oreg. On 13 September 1919, *Ward* was among the ships of the Fleet reviewed by President Woodrow Wilson at Seattle, Wash.

The destroyer then returned south to San Diego to operate off the west coast for the remainder of 1919 and into 1920. On 17 July 1920, during the sweeping Navywide assignment of hull numbers, *Ward* was assigned the designation DD–139. With DesDiv 18 through the late spring of 1921, *Ward* subsequently joined many of her sisters in reserve when she was decommissioned on 21 July 1921 and placed in "Red Lead Row" at San Diego.

As the Axis challenge of Germany, Italy, and Japan threatened peace and the security of the democratic nations in the latter half of the 1930's, the United States Navy began to rearm. While new ships joined the fleet, a number of older ones—*Ward* among them—were recommissioned. Some went to the Atlantic to take part in the *de facto* war with German U-boats as the year 1941 progressed. Others went to local district defense duties, and the latter role was *Ward's* new assignment.

Ward was recommissioned on 15 January 1941 at the Naval Destroyer Base, San Diego, Lt. Comdr. Hunter Wood, Jr., in command. After provisioning and fueling, the warship set out into the Pacific, bound for Hawaii, and rolled and pitched heavily as soon as she hit the open sea on 28 February. She managed to struggle through and arrived at Pearl Harbor on 9 March and joined the 14th Naval District local defense forces and

The new *Ward* (DD–139). One of the relatively few "flushdeck" destroyers completed before the armistice of 1918, she wears pattern camouflage, and a censor has obliterated the hull number painted in small characters just below the bridge. (19–N–13752)

DesDiv 80. Consisting of four destroyers—two of *Ward*'s sisters and a World War I veteran, *Allen* (DD–66)—DesDiv 80's job was to patrol the channel entrance off Pearl Harbor—a large job for such a small and antiquated force and an important one since the Pacific Fleet was to base at Pearl Harbor as a deterrent to the rising imperialistic ambitions of Japan in the Far East.

Throughout 1941, *Ward* conducted routine antisubmarine patrols in the Hawaiian area, as did *Chew* (DD–106), *Schley* (DD–103), and *Allen*, and the three Coast Guard cutters and a handful of coastal minecraft that made up the rest of Comdr. John B. Wooley's Inshore Patrol command. As tensions with Japan increased following the oil embargo in July 1941 and again at the accession of the Tojo cabinet in October, Washington, late in November 1941, dispatched a "war warning" to the force commanders in the Hawaiian and Philippine Island areas to be on the alert for possible Japanese hostile action.

Accordingly, Commander in Chief, Pacific Fleet, Admiral Husband E. Kimmel, ordered his inshore patrol to depth-charge suspicious submarine contacts operating in the defensive sea areas. Given orders, in effect to "shoot to kill," Ward and her consorts continued as before, with the exception that they were now to be on a wartime footing. Equipped with listening gear, *Ward* continued vigilant patrols in the inshore operating zones, cutting routine figure-eights back and forth within a two-mile radius of the channel-entrance buoys.

One of the old four-pipers had the duty each weekend. Soon it came to be *Ward*'s turn—but she went to sea this particular weekend with a new commanding officer. Lt. William W. Outerbridge took command from Lt. Comdr. Wood on 5 December; and, at 0628 on the 6th, Outerbridge took his first sea command out for a routine entrance patrol.

At 0408 on 7 December, the old destroyer went to general quarters to search for a suspected submarine detected by *Condor* (AMc–14), but came up with nothing. Meanwhile, *Antares* (AKS–14), flagship of Training Squadron 8, plodded back from Palmyra Island with a target raft in tow. She anchored off the harbor entrance to await a favorable tide and the opening of the boom-net defenses. Exchanging calls with *Antares* as she subsequently headed for the channel, at 0506, *Ward* continued her early morning vigil until lookouts on the destroyer's bridge noticed a small feather wake astern of the auxiliary, between *Antares* and the raft.

Within moments, *Ward* was a ship alive—the general quarters alarm routed the men from their bunks and sent them on the double to their action stations. Outerbridge, who had retired to a makeshift bunk rigged up in the charthouse, was on the bridge in seconds, pulling a life jacket on over a kimono and pajamas, and a World War I style "tin helmet" on his head.

Ward charged at the submarine like a terrier; and, for a moment, Outerbridge thought it looked like his ship was going to run down the little intruder. Number one four-inch mount trained around, and her gunners tried to draw a bead on the elusive target. The first shot of the Pacific war barked from *Ward*'s gun at 0645 and splashed harmlessly beyond the small conning tower. As *Ward* pounded past at 25 knots, number three gun atop the galley deckhouse amidships commenced fire—its round passed squarely through the submersible's conning tower. As the Japanese midget wallowed lower in the water and started to sink, the destroyer swiftly dropped four depth charges—signalled by four blasts on the ship's whistle. Black water gushed upwards in the ship's boiling wake as the bombs went off—sealing the submarine's doom.

Outerbridge radioed a terse action report to Commandant, 14th Naval District headquarters, and to distinguish this attack from the numerous sightings that had plagued local patrol forces, added that he had sighted and fired upon an unidentified submarine in the defensive sea area. Delays in seeking confirmation and a reluctance to heed the warning resulted in the message's slow transmission through tortuously slow communication channels. *Ward* echo-ranged for further contacts—and soon latched on to another one, dropping depth charges but not coming up with concrete results.

Subsequently, as the day dawned upon the purple and verdant hillsides of Oahu, *Ward* headed for home—her date with destiny kept. She soon spotted a Japanese fishing sampan—one of many that was a familiar sight in the waters in the Hawaiian archipelago. A fisherman suddenly started waving a white flag—perhaps he had seen the determined depth-charge attacks and thought that the Americans would bomb anything that moved. *Ward* slowed and closed to investigate and took the small craft in tow to turn her over to the Coast Guard for disposition.

Nearing the harbor entrance around 0800, those on deck heard the sound of gunfire and explosions, as smoke began to boil into the skies over Pearl Harbor. Soon a strafing Japanese plane convinced the doubters that there indeed was a war on.

On that Sunday morning, *Ward* had the distinction of firing the first American gun in anger during the Pacific war. For the remainder of the year, the venerable destroyer continued her routine district patrols and—for a time—anything that moved beneath the waters was fair game. As Outerbridge recalled years later, *Ward* and her sisters must have killed a lot of fish. But as newer and more modern destroyers began joining the fleet, as well as built-for-the purpose subchasing craft, some of the old "flush-decked, four-pipers" began to be assigned to other duties: tending seaplanes, laying or sweeping mines, or—for a newer innovation in modern warfare—carrying fully equipped troops for assault landings as fast transports.

Accordingly, *Ward* sailed to Bremerton, Wash., for conversion to a high-speed transport at the Puget Sound Navy Yard. During the ensuing months, the old "four-piper" began to take on an altered appearance. Her forward funnels were removed, as the forward boiler and fire rooms were converted to accommodate troops. Antiaircraft guns—3-inch/50s and 20-millimeter Oerlikons—replaced the antiquated "iron-sighted" single-purpose 4-inch guns and the .50-caliber machine guns, and she acquired four sets of davits and four 36-foot landing craft to put her embarked troops ashore. Thus outfitted, *Ward* was designated APD–16 and got underway for the South Pacific on 6 February 1943.

Based at Espirito Santo, *Ward* performed a variety of duties—antisubmarine patrols, escort duties, and transport service—while she worked up as a fast transport. Soon after completing a run to the Russell Islands, *Ward* neared Tulagi on the afternoon of 7 April 1943, as Japanese aircraft swept overhead in Admiral Isoroku Yamamoto's last planned Operation "I"—the air strike designed to cripple American seapower in the Solomons in the wake of Japan's evacuation from Guadalcanal.

At 1510, *Ward* went to general quarters and opened fire, charging out of the harbor, eager for action. In the confused melee of gunfire, the ship helped splash two Japanese planes. When the final score was tallied on the American side, the Navy had lost *Aaron Ward* (DD–483) and *Kanawha* (AO–9), while *Adhara* (AK–71) and *Tappahannock* (AO–43) had suffered damage.

The following day, *Ward* headed for Espiritu Santo—as escort for five merchantmen and in company with *Taylor* (DD–468), *Farenholt* (DD–491), and *Sterett* (DD–407)—and arrived there on 10 April. The fast transport then underwent a tender overhaul through the 17th. She then embarked men of the 4th Marine Battalion, 1st Marine Raider Regiment, for a practice landing at Powell Point, New Hebrides, and for night landing exercises. Upon the conclusion of these maneuvers, she reembarked troops and conducted antisubmarine screening.

Continuing her escort and transport operations into June, *Ward* helped to beat off a Japanese air attack in the Guadalcanal area on the 16th, her gunners claiming four attacking aircraft. Seven days later, on 23 June, *Ward* steamed in the screen of a convoy on escort duty. On that day, Japanese submarine *RO-103*, commanded by Lt. Rikinosuke Ichimura, slipped past the screen and torpedoed and sank two cargo ships—*Aludra* (AK–72) and *Deimos* (AK–78), which proved to be Ichimura's only "kills" of the war.

Ward arrived at Milne Bay, New Guinea, on 17 December for duty with Task Force (TF) 76. She engaged in practice exercises off Cape Sudest, British New Guinea, with Companies "I" and "L" of the 3d Battalion, 7th Marine Regiment, from 22 to 23 December. On the 24th, she embarked 140 officers and men of Companies "I" and "M" of the 3d Battalion, 7th Regiment, and set out for Cape Gloucester, New Britain, as part of TU 76.1.21 with the eight-ship formation in double column order.

The group approached the landing area on the 26th, in a single column and at a speed of five knots. At 0600, a cruiser bombardment heralded the Americans' approach; and *Ward* disembarked her troops at 0653, launching her Higgins boats off beach "Yellow One" and then retiring to wait the return of her brood. Army heavy bombers droned over enemy positions at 0705, and Army medium bombers then commenced both bombing and strafing enemy defenses some 19 minutes later. *Ward*'s boats returned by 0845; and, an hour later, the ship got underway for Buna, British New Guinea. After what her war diary termed an "uneventful return trip," *Ward* dropped anchor off Buna at 2259 on 26 December.

Two days later, at 1140, *Ward* embarked 200 officers and men of Company "B," 1st Battalion, 5th Marines, bound for Cape Gloucester as a part of TU 76.1.21. Underway at 1427, the ship went to general quarters at 1933 as numerous planes were reported in the vicinity. However, none came near; and the ship stood down from quarters at 2018 that night.

The following day, 29 December, *Ward* and her sister fast transports approached the landing area at 15 knots and disembarked marines at 0655, standing out to await the return of her boats. During the landings, Army medium bombers pounded the airfield and other targets of opportunity while the destroyer transports stood out to sea to recover landing craft later. All *Ward*'s boats had returned by 0815, and all the other transports except *Noa* (APD–24) had recovered theirs by 0900. Soon thereafter, the warships returned to Buna.

Operating as part of Transport Division 22, *Ward* got underway at 0601 on 1 January 1944 for Cape Sudest. That afternoon, she joined up with the Western Assault Group bound for Saidor, New Guinea, and got underway for British New Guinea. At 0615 the following day, *Ward* approached the transport area, while escorting destroyers opened fire on beach targets and enemy defenses 30 minutes later. Disembarking Company "L," 126th Army Infantry Regiment, 32d Division, *Ward* stood by off shore. Destroyer bombardment ceased at 0717; and, one minute later, the landing craft approaching the beach strafed the beach-front jungle with machine guns and automatic weapons fire. Those off shore in *Ward* were unable to see the actual landing due to the heavy pall of smoke and dust caused by the bombardment.

After returning from the Cape Sudest landings to Buna, *Ward* conducted local operations out of Espiritu Santo into February 1944. She then carried out practice landing exercises with embarked marines and New Zealand troops off Juno River, Vella Lavella, Solomon Islands, before getting underway late on 14 February to take part in the Nissan Island landings.

Screened by *Fullam* (DD–474), *Halford* (DD–480), in which Commander, Task Unit (CTU) 31.1.4 rode, *Guest* (DD–472), *Hudson* (DD–475), and *Bennett* (DD–473), *Ward* arrived in the vicinity of Nissan Island as several enemy aircraft were reported flying nearby. Approaching the transport area at 0512, she disembarked her landing craft at beach "Blue One" and soon noted Japanese aircraft attacking LCI and LST formations. During the melee, *Ward* counted six Japanese aircraft, but friendly fighters took care of the enemy formations—downing two, while "heavy and moderately accurate" gunfire from the surface ships below helped to drive away the others. Ashore, the troops encountered no opposition and soon took their objective. *Ward*, her job completed, headed for the Russell Islands to embark men of the 33d Navy Construction Battalion on the 20th for passage to Nissan Island.

Upon landing her embarked seabees on "Beach Red," *Ward* patrolled offshore, screening a dozen LST's as they got underway for Guadalcanal, before she headed for Espiritu Santo to dock in *ARD–5* to repair sound gear damaged during the second phase of the ship's Nissan Island operations.

The following month, the durable fast transport took part in the landings at Emirau Island, with "B" Company, 1st Battalion, 4th Marines, embarked. She disembarked 208 troops and 22 tons of stores in four hours and subsequently joined the antisubmarine screen protecting the still-unloading transports and dock-landing ships. Refuelling soon thereafter en route to Purvis Bay, *Ward* anchored at her destination on 23 February to undergo a needed upkeep period for the remainder of the month.

Conducting practice landings at Cape Cretin, with officers and men of the 163d Army Regimental Combat Team in early April, *Ward* embarked these troops for transportation to Aitape, New Guinea, and got underway at 1617 on 18 April with TG 77.1. Going to general quarters at 0430 on 22 April, the transport lay to at 0537 off the landing area and, after disembarking her troops, proceeded to a fire support station off Tumleo Island. For one-half hour, *Ward* conducted a shore bombardment with her 3-inch main battery before shifting gunfire to what initially appeared to be a beached Japanese landing craft, but which later investigation proved to be a small reef.

Subsequently screening off the transport area, *Ward* transferred a wounded man from a landing craft to *Kilty* (APD–15) for evacuation and medical treatment. After picking up her landing boats, *Ward* later escorted reinforcements to Aitape on the 22d. The following day saw a continuation of her troop-carrying and fire-support duties, as her boats embarked troops from *Ormsby* (APA–49) to transport them to the beach, while *Ward*'s 3-inch gunfire again aided the troops ashore.

Shifting to Cape Cretin on the 25th and to Buna on the 26th, *Ward* conducted antisubmarine screening duties with transports headed to Saidor, New Guinea, before returning to Aitape. She screened and patrolled near the unloading transports and, after refuelling, escorted *Henry T. Allen* (AP–30) and Australian transports *Kanimbla*, *Manoora*, and *Westralia* to Humboldt Bay where they unloaded their embarked troops. Steaming back to Cape Sudest and Cape Cretin, *Ward* provisioned ship on 10 May and underwent a tender overhaul alongside *Dobbin* (AD–3) at Port Harvey, British New Guinea, on the 14th. Subsequently returning to Humboldt Bay in company with *Herbert* (APD–22), *Ward* anchored at Humboldt Bay on 24 May and embarked troops of the Army 186th Infantry Regiment for transport to Bosnik, Biak Island, in the Schoetens. The operation, commencing on the 27th, went off without a hitch; and all troops landed without opposition on the beaches. Forming up in open column order, *Ward* and her sister fast transports sailed for Hollandia and Humboldt Bay.

Ward conducted routine antisubmarine patrol operations off Humboldt Bay and in the New Guinea area into late June. She underwent a tender overhaul with *Dobbin* at Manus, in the Admiralties, from 24 June to 4 July, before proceeding to Cape Cretin where she exchanged her landing boats with those from sister ship *Schley* (APD–14). Sailing later for Milne Bay, the ship conducted local transport duties in the New Guinea area through July. *Ward* subsequently served as picket ship and navigational guide for a Humboldt Bay-to-

Maffin Bay convoy, in local New Guinean waters, before conducting a practice landing east of Toem, New Guinea.

Embarking troops of Companies "E" and "F" of the 1st Army Infantry Regiment, 6th Division, as well as a combat photographic unit and three Australian war correspondents, *Ward* got underway on 27 July for Cape Sansapor. She arrived at the transport area off Warsai at 0626 on the 30th and immediately commenced disembarkation. The first wave of troops to land encountered no opposition, and the ships returned to Humboldt Bay.

During August, *Ward* conducted local transport operations and then sailed to Australia for an overhaul. En route, on the morning of 9 August, heavy seas ripped a 3-inch ready-use locker from the deck forward and tore a small hole in the main deck. After completing temporary repairs later that day, *Ward* arrived at Port Jackson, Sydney, on the 12th and remained there for 10 days. While steaming for Milne Bay, the ship and her companions—*Herbert, Schley, Crosby,* and *Kilty*—reduced speed to five knots due to an emergency appendectomy being performed in *Schley* but eventually resumed their normal speed and made Milne Bay at 0800 on 27 August.

Ward conducted transport and practice landing exercises early in September before getting underway on 10 September for Morotai, as part of TU 77.3.2. She landed six officers and 151 enlisted men from Company "A," 124th Infantry Regiment, 31st Division, 6th Army, United States Army, and then recovered all of her landing craft and screened an LCI flotilla before commencing antisubmarine patrol.

The high-speed transport anchored off Cape Sansapor on the 16th and, three days later, got underway for Humboldt Bay as part of the screen for LCI Flotilla 8. At 1143 that day, she observed an Army Air Force Lockheed P–38 Lightning crash and sent a landing boat to rescue the pilot, 1st Lt. Edgar B. Scott. *Ward* arrived at Humboldt Bay at 0512 on the 22d and immediately commenced repairs alongside *Dobbin* to correct a defective reduction gear.

With that work completed by 1 October, *Ward* shifted to Cape Cretin where she loaded stores, ammunition, and seven officers and 140 enlisted men of the Companies "E" and "F" of the 6th Army Ranger Battalion for transportation to the Philippines. She got underway on the 12th with British minelayer-transport HMS *Ariadne* as fleet guide; proceeded via Humboldt Bay; and, as they approached Dinagat Island on the 17th, went to general quarters at 0558, when a Japanese aircraft dropped a white flare—which vividly outlined every ship in the formation in the ghostly white glare. Commencing evasive action, the fast transport headed for the troop disembarkation points while *Lang* (DD–399) and *Bisbee* (PF–46) commenced shore bombardment.

Once they had been launched, the boats encountered difficulties. High winds and seas and dangerous coral reefs all presented obstacles for their crews, as there was no lee behind which to lie and the winds blew directly towards the beach. After landing, all boats from *Ward* returned to *Ariadne* to embark troops, while *Schley*'s boats came alongside to be filled with Ranger Company "F" from *Ward*. Meanwhile, Ward was having difficulty remaining in the swept channel, as strong tidal currents, with high winds and seas, frequently almost caused the ship to drag anchor.

All but one of *Ward*'s boats then became stranded on the beach. One of these three was pulled off by boats from *Schley*; but the others remained there overnight. The fourth of *Ward*'s boat group, unable to get back to her own ship, was hoisted on board *Schley* before night retirement; and *Schley*'s boat—which had helped to refloat one of *Ward*'s boats, was taken on board *Ward*. Returning to the troop transport area the next morning, *Ward* continued unloading supplies for Army rangers. While engaged in this task, the ship sighted two Japanese "Val's" coming over the hills of Dinagat

Island. The ship quickly went to general quarters and commenced firing. One plane made a strafing run on the transports but was driven off, while the second plane remained at 3,000 feet and, upon seeing his comrade's failure, soon withdrew without making an attack.

While proceeding to Kossol Roads, in the Palaus, tragedy struck *Ward* when a lifeline gave way, and two men fell overboard. Turning to starboard, *Ward* heeled about to make the rescue, as men on deck threw life-jackets to the men in the water. *Herbert*, steaming in company, drew near, and one of her men dove over the side and rescued one of the *Ward* sailors. The other *Ward* bluejacket vanished. As *Ward*'s war diary noted ominously: "sharks were seen in the vicinity." Giving up the search at 1645, *Ward* sailed on, listing the man as "presumed lost."

While refueling at Kossol Roads, *Ward* was assigned to join *Kilty* in escorting three LST's to the Philippines. Proceeding via Morotai, *Ward*, her sister ship, and their charges arrived in Leyte Gulf at 0045 on 12 November. The ship went to general quarters at 0454, detached the LST's which proceeded to Dulag Bay anchorage, and observed antiaircraft fire over San Pedro Bay, as a Japanese air attack swept in upon the invading American fleet.

As yet disengaged, *Ward* watched as a Japanese plane was hit by antiaircraft fire from an LST and, trailing a column of smoke, plunged into the sea, nearly in the path of the recently detached and now beach-bound LST's. The retaliatory strikes tapered off for a time; but *Ward*—in response to a report that 50 to 60 Japanese aircraft were winging their way towards the transport area—returned to general quarters from 0708 to 0750. After an "all clear" sounded, *Ward* stood down from general quarters but returned to that condition at 1335, as several Japanese aircraft returned to attack American shipping.

Intense antiaircraft fire downed two enemy planes almost instantly; two more crashed into repair ships—*Egeria* (ARL–8) and *Achilles* (ARL–41). That evening, *Ward* was ordered to escort a convoy to Hollandia, and she left the area.

Returning to San Pedro Bay in a five-column, 15-ship convoy on 28 November, *Ward* remained at anchor on the 29th and 30th of the month in Leyte Gulf preparing to take part in the scheduled landings at Mindoro. Although there were numerous air raid alerts signalled, *Ward*'s log records that she saw no enemy planes.

Continual air raid alerts during this period made life difficult for men of the Fleet engaged in the landing operations, with nearly round-the-clock watches. *Ward* embarked four officers and 104 enlisted men of the Army's 77th Division on 6 December and sortied for Ormoc Bay, Leyte Island, at 1237 with TG 78.3. Since enemy aircraft had been reported in the area, *Ward* went to general quarters while en route to Ormoc Bay.

At 0153, the ship observed a large group of flares west of Himuquitan Island on the west coast of Leyte. At 0445, they sighted another flare, ahead of the convoy. Antiaircraft fire criss-crossed the sky as what appeared to be a Japanese floatplane passed down the starboard side of the group and emerged unscathed despite heavy fire. More flares which were dropped around the convoy just before sunrise pointed to the possibility of an attack, but no Japanese planes came over. At 0630, the escorting destroyers left the screen to commence shore bombardment; and, 12 minutes later, *Ward* began disembarking her troops for the beach into her LCP(R)'s.

On screening patrol between Pomson Island and Leyte from 0825, *Ward* sighted a formation of nine twin-engined "Betties" coming in from the north over Leyte at an altitude between 4,000 and 5,000 feet. Commencing high-speed evasive maneuvers, the ship went into action with guns blazing but did not make any observable hits. Shortly before 1000, *Mahan* (DD–364) came under attack from another group of planes; and *Ward*'s lookouts noted that the unfortunate destroyer was emitting large quantities of grey and black smoke.

Ward now came under a concentrated attack by "Betties" and "Oscars," and both *Mahan* and the fast transport fought for their lives against the onslaught. Army P–38's and Curtiss P–40's streaked over to intercept the attackers and engaged the Japanese over the unfortunate *Mahan*. The formation of nine "Betties," again flying over the destroyer, soon broke, as three headed for *Ward* in a loose vee formation. *Ward*'s gunners opened fire with 3-inch and 20-millimeter batteries, sprinkling the sky with puffs of flak. The center plane was hit by the barrage, wavered, and crashed the ship at the waterline at 0956, entering the forward part of the boiler room and the after part of the lower troopspace. One of the plane's two engines continued on through the ship, exiting at the waterline on the starboard side. An instant later, a "Betty" passed low over *Ward*'s forecastle, strafing the ship en route, and crashed into the water 200 yards off the starboard bow, slapped into the sea by *Ward*'s gunfire.

The third attacker which had singled the transport out also joined her partners, splashing 600 yards off the starboard quarter. In the meantime, the bomber which had crashed the ship had blown up, starting uncontrollable fires in the troopspaces—fortunately unoccupied at the time—and in the fireroom. Boiler fires flared back and the forced draft blower, dislodged from its mounting, fell into the fireroom.

Ceasing fire at 0957, all hands started to fight the fires as the air attack abruptly ended. In the distance, *Mahan*, too, burned fiercely—the victim of a heavy and devastating attack. Men in the forward part of *Ward* could not contact those in the aft, since the fires amidships had severed all communications. Thick smoke boiled out of the mortal wound in the fast transport amidships.

Several minutes after the explosion, water pressure dropped to below 100 pounds, making it nearly impossible to train water on the fires to attempt to put them out. The ship soon lost way as the fire amidships burned fiercely. The thick smoke boiling from the damaged troopspace and fireroom area made the suction hoses for the gasoline-driven handy billies as well as asbestos suit stowage—located amidships—inaccessible. In an effort to dissipate the smoke, the awning over the well-deck was cut away. This reduced the density of the smoke but did not make the area amidships any more accessible. Two boats were lowered in an attempt to fight the fires through the holes in the hull made by the entrance and exit of the "Betty" on its death run. The handy billies carried in the LCP(R)'s unfortunately proved inadequate to deal with the raging gasoline-fed fires.

At 1015, *O'Brien* (DD–725), *Saunter* (AM–295), *Scout* (AM–296), and *Crosby* stood towards *Ward*. *Scout* and *Crosby* lowered boats to pick up survivors. In the meantime, with main communications systems out of commission, a report was made via battery-powered radio to the other ships. *Ward*'s commanding officer, Lt. R. E. Farwell, USNR, announced the intention of abandoning if the fires could not be brought under control. *O'Brien*—commanded by Lt. Comdr. Outerbridge, the same man who had commanded *Ward* during her historic encounter with the Japanese midget submarine three years to the day before—moved close aboard to port and commenced fire fighting operations 1018.

By this time, however, fires raged in the troopspaces —igniting both fuel tanks and the diesel oil storage; the fireroom filled with black smoke, and it proved impossible to regain steam pressure to get underway. Flames rose and extended along the main deck in the vicinity of the 20-millimeter ready use ammunition lockers. The danger posed by the explosion of fuel tanks, ready-use ammunition and magazines, at 1024 caused Farwell to order "abandon ship"—less than one-half hour after the Japanese plane had crashed into the ship. Almost miraculously, only one man had been injured, and all hands left the ship to board other vessels.

Saunders joined *O'Brien* in trying to put out the blaze, but the fire defied all attempts to extinguish it. Commander, TG 78.3, ordered *O'Brien* to sink the blazing fast transport with gunfire. Accordingly, the ships stood away, and *O'Brien* commenced firing. From the bridge of *O'Brien*, Lt. Comdr. Outerbridge watched as that destroyer's guns sank *Ward*, his first sea command. Years later, he recalled that there was little emotion involved in the task: "it just was somehing that had to be done." *Ward* sank at 1130 on 7 December 1944, in Ormoc Bay between Poro Island and Apali Point. Her name was struck from the Navy list on 20 January 1945.

Ward received one battle star for World War II services as a destroyer and eight as a fast transport.

Ward, Aaaron, see *Aaron Ward*.

Ward, J. Richard, see *J. Richard Ward*.

Ware, Charles R., see *Charles R. Ware*.

Warren

Joseph Warren—born on 11 June 1741 at Roxbury, Mass.—graduated with distinction from Harvard College in 1759. After a year as headmaster of the Roxbury Grammar School, he entered the medical profession and later practiced as a physician in Boston. There, he became interested in politics and formed an early association with the firebrand Samuel Adams.

As the break in relations between the colonies and Great Britain approached, Warren abandoned his medical practice to enter military service. While still in Boston, he dispatched William Dawes and Paul Revere on their famous nocturnal rides to warn John Hancock and Samuel Adams of approaching British troops on 18 April 1775.

Elected a major general by the provincial congress on 14 June, Warren went out to Bunker Hill to look over the defenses shortly before the British attack on the afternoon of 17 June 1775. Although he consistently refused to take command, claiming that he would take part in the battle only as a volunteer, Warren eventually tried to exert leadership in rallying the colonial militia at Breed's Hill. Unfortunately, he was shot and killed by a British soldier while engaged in the attempt.

I

(Sch.: t. 64; cpl. 50; a. 4 4-pdrs., 10 swivels)

The first *Warren* was originally the fishing schooner *Hawk*, probably built at Marblehead, Mass., and owned by John Twisdon at the time of her appraisal by Colonel Jonathan Glover and Edward Fettyplace on 12 October 1775. Hurriedly fitted out as the fourth vessel of the fledgling seagoing force assembled by General George Washington to intercept Boston-bound British supply ships, *Warren* was commissioned at Beverly late in October 1775. Under the command of Capt. Winborn Adams, the armed schooner sailed from Beverly on 31 October 1775, on her maiden voyage under Continental colors.

Warren cruised north of Cape Ann and captured a small wood schooner before bagging a Boston-bound supply ship, the schooner *Rainbow*, around 27 November.

The Continental schooner continued to cruise north of Cape Ann until she came across the brig *Sally* on Christmas Eve, 1775. Bound from Lisbon to New York with 153 quarter casks of wine, the brig had been captured by HMS *Niger* earlier in the month, placed under a prize crew, and ordered taken to Boston. *Warren* captured *Sally* and took her into Marblehead as a "Christmas present" for General Washington.

After returning to port and undergoing repairs into January 1776, *Warren* was placed under the command of William Burke. The schooner set sail from Boston on 25 March 1776 to intercept a convoy of transports but was frustrated by the weather in her attempt to pick off any strays while sailing in company with the Continental schooner *Franklin*. The schooners then sailed their separate ways, with *Warren* going to the familiar waters north of Cape Ann.

After another refit and recruiting new crewmen, *Warren* joined *Lynch* and *Lee* in an attempt to get to sea on 27 May, but that day they could not slip past the British frigate HMS *Milford* patrolling outside Cape Ann harbor. When *Warren* did manage to get to sea, she scoured the waters of the bay near Cape Ann but did not score any successes that summer. In June, she tangled with the British troopship *Unity*, bound for Halifax with Hessian troops embarked, but met with a hot reception from the troopers' carriage guns and musket fire. While the schooner was disengaging, some powder stored on *Warren*'s quarterdeck exploded, killing three and wounding seven.

Returning to Beverly for repairs, *Warren*, still under the luckless Burke, put to sea again in late August 1776 to patrol the supply lanes between Nova Scotia and Boston. Before dawn on 26 August, *Warren* and *Lynch* encountered HMS *Liverpool* patrolling. The two schooners separated to flee, and the British frigate chose to follow *Warren*.

The ensuing engagement was one-sided, and *Liverpool* had little difficulty forcing *Warren* to strike her colors before noon. Burke and his crew were transferred to *Liverpool*, which kept *Warren* as a tender until 4 September. On that day, *Liverpool* rendezvoused with *Milford* off Cape Ann, transferred the Continental schooner's guns to that frigate, and sent *Warren* to Halifax.

Condemned by a British prize court, *Warren* subsequently served as a tender to *Milford* until the erstwhile Continental ship ran aground in a storm near Portsmouth, N.H., and was destroyed around Christmas of 1776.

II

(Fr: l. 132′1″; b. 24′5¼″; dph. 11′0″; a. 32 guns)

The second *Warren*—one of the 13 frigates authorized by the Continental Congress on 13 December 1775—was given that name on 6 June 1776. Built at Providence, R.I., by Sylvester Bowers, *Warren* was probably one of the first two of the 13 frigates to be completed. The other was the Rhode Island-built frigate *Providence*. However, difficulties in manning the two ships and the British occupation of Newport made the tricky task of getting the vessels out doubly difficult.

Although the ship was bottled up in the Providence River, Commodore Esek Hopkins broke his pennant in *Warren* early in December of 1776. Ordered to prepare for sea as soon as possible to cruise the upper half of the eastern seaboard to interdict British troop and logistics shipping traveling the Rhode Island to Virginia route, Hopkins' flagship nevertheless remained anchored in the Providence River for nearly a year afterward. As a result, Hopkins was suspended by the Marine Committee of the Continental Congress for his lethargic performance. *Warren*, blockaded in Narragansett Bay, did no cruising.

Aided by favorable weather, *Warren* finally slipped through the British blockade on or about 8 March 1778 and escaped into the open sea at last. *Warren* took two prizes in her first cruise: the ship *Neptune*—bound from Whitehaven, England, to Philadelphia—with a cargo of provisions; and another supply vessel, before the Continental frigate put into Boston on 23 March. She apparently conducted a second cruise off the eastern seaboard in the autumn, as records indicate that she cruised for a time in company with the Massachusetts State Navy ship *Tyrannicide* in September.

Warren remained at Boston into the winter of 1778 and apparently did not sortie again until 13 March 1779. The frigate, under the command of Commodore John B. Hopkins, departed in company with *Queen of France* and *Ranger* for a cruise off the northeastern coast. The squadron took the armed schooner *Hibernia* as a prize on 6 April, and good fortune smiled upon them even more the following day, because at 0400, American lookouts sighted two "fleets" of ships. One contained 10 vessels and the other, nine.

Warren and her two consorts set upon the nine-ship group to windward and, by 1400, had captured seven of the nine. The British convoy had been bound from New York to Georgia. The catch included two ships, four brigs, and a schooner. Most of the prizes were richly laden with provisions for the British Army. *Warren* towed the brig *Patriot* from 10 April, bringing her triumphantly into port.

Initially, Congress expressed great pleasure with Hopkins' exploit, but its satisfaction soon soured. The Marine Committee charged Hopkins with violating his orders, maintaining that he had returned to port too soon and had not sent his prizes to the nearest port. As a disciplinary measure, the Committee relieved Hopkins, suspended him from the Navy, and gave his command to Capt. Dudley Saltonstall—a move which would have sad repercussions for both ship and her new commander.

While *Warren* lay at Boston, fitting out for further operations, the British established a base on the Bagaduce peninsula, near the present site of Castine, Maine, in mid-June 1779. This British intrusion into the figurative back yard of the Massachusetts colony could not go unchallenged. Thus a large—but unfortunately uncoordinated—force was assembled in hope of evicting the newly established British. Saltonstall became the naval commander, in *Warren*, and was given 19 armed vessels and some 20 transports with which to project the Continental invasion.

On 19 July 1779, the Continental armada sailed from Boston, bound for Penobscot Bay. The expedition turned out to be a dismal failure. First, the fleet was unfit for the work and was primarily composed of privateers. The military forces—as in the seagoing ones—lacked decisive leadership; and the land forces lacked artillery and necessary equipment and supplies. Cooperation between military and naval forces was entirely lacking, with the obvious end result that the entire expedition collapsed in disaster like a house of cards.

Warren and the other vessels of the American fleet were consequently burned to prevent their capture by the British. *Warren* was probably set afire by her crew on either 14 or 15 August 1779 in the Bagaduce River, above the Bagaduce peninsula. Later that autumn, Saltonstall was tried by court martial on board the frigate *Deane* in Boston harbor and was summarily dismissed from the Continental Navy.

III

(SlpW: t. 385; cpl. 160; a. 20 guns)

The third *Warren*—a copper-sheathed sloop-of-war—was built at Newburyport, Mass. On 6 July 1799, while she was still under construction, the Secretary of the Navy, Benjamin Stoddert, ordered Master Commandant Timothy Newman to take command of *Warren*. The ship was fitted out there, into the winter, and was probably commissioned in either November or December of 1799.

Assigned the duty of protecting American commerce in Cuban waters against the possible incursions of French warships or privateers during the "Quasi War" with France, *Warren* set sail for Havana, Cuba, on 31 December 1799, escorting the schooner *Trio*. The latter was laden with stores for the American men-of-war on the Havana station. As the ships stood out of Nantasket Roads, near Boston, Sailing Master Joseph Whitmore, in *Warren*, penned fervently in his journal,

"God send us safe to our orders End in our Lawfull (sic) Ways in supporting our Independence."

Trio was separated from the sloop-of-war about 4 or 5 January 1800, and *Warren* proceeded on independently. The passage proved uneventful until the 17th, when six men came to Master Commandant Newman's cabin door at half-past six in the evening, swearing that "they would not do Duty and . . . would go aboard the first British Man-of-War they could see." According to Sailing Master Whitmore's journal, one of the men wielded the cook's hatchet and all apparently "used other Mutenous (sic) language." As a reward for their behavior, the six were promptly clapped in irons, to stand trial later.

At 1300 on 19 January, *Warren* spoke with the sloop *Mary*, 18 days out of Philadelphia and bound for Cuba. That vessel needed assistance, and *Warren* provided her with rigging and the ship's foretopmast stay sail. Three hours later, *Warren* met the schooner *Lucy*, 25 days out of Providence, R.I., and took her into the convoy. *Warren* later passed a hawser to *Mary* and took her in tow. The three ships remained in company for five days, before the sloop-of-war lost sight of the merchantmen.

Warren reached Havana early in the afternoon of 29 January, almost a month out of Nantasket Roads. Over ensuing days, she supplied the brig *Norfolk* and assisted the brig *Fanny*, of Salem, on 11 February. On the morning of 16 February, she got underway in company with *Norfolk* to escort a convoy of 19 merchantmen out of the coastal waters off Havana. *Warren* remained at sea until 8 March, when she dropped anchor at Matanzas, Cuba, for upkeep and to take on fresh water. She returned to patrol duties off the coast of Cuba at sunrise on 13 March.

After a week at sea, *Warren* returned to Havana on the 20th and waited for a fleet of merchantmen to emerge from the harbor and form a convoy. That evening, a dozen ships sailed; and *Warren* joined them as they emerged from the harbor and gave them routing instructions as they headed for the United States. *Warren* remained at sea, on patrol, for another week thereafter, and returned to Havana on the 28th. She stood out to sea again on the morning of 2 April and proceeded to Matanza where she arrived on the 5th.

Warren joined *Ganges* and a convoy of 22 merchantmen on 21 April and sailed with them for a time before returning to Havana early in the following month. Sailing again on 5 May, the sloop-of-war patrolled off the Cuban coast until she arrived back at Havana on the 23d.

Warren operated locally between Havana and the pan of Matanza until mid-June and anchored in Havana harbor on the 15th of that month. Nine days later, the ship's doctor sent Quarter Gunner William Dogget ashore to the hospital at Havana, the man suffering from a fever. Ominously, Dogget's case signified only the beginning of what would become a terrible ordeal for the sloop-of-war *Warren*.

During *Warren*'s stay at Havana, her crew—hitherto "in general, healthy, and robust"—began to have "evident symptoms of an increasing universal debility." *Warren*, departing Havana in company with the frigate *General Greene* and 12 merchantmen, sailed for Veracruz, Mexico, on 26 June.

Gunner Dogget, convalescent in the hospital at Havana, was spared seeing the agony of many of his shipmates. For the remainder of the month of June, an average of 15 men per day were incapacitated for performing ship's work. The first fatality occurred shortly before dawn on 30 June, when young Midshipman Jonathan Greenleaf died. Nineteen men, recorded Whitmore—who survived the yellow fever epidemic—were then down with "the fever."

Thirteen more, including the doctor's mate, died before the ship reached Veracruz on 13 July. *Warren* sent 20 men ashore there, but four died in the ensuing days. *Warren* ultimately departed Veracruz on the 23d, having had an average of 20 to 24 sick men ashore

in the hospital and 25 on board unfit for duty. Sailing Master Whitmore noted on 25 July that two dozen men were sick but noted optimistically that there were "many mending."

Warren headed back to Havana; two men died on 27 July, three on the 28th, and one on 1 August. The following day at 1000 in the morning, the captain's only son, John Newman along on the voyage as a midshipman, "departed this life." *Warren* subsequently anchored at Havana on 15 August, dropping her hook at 1100 that morning. Four hours later, Master Commandant Newman succumbed to the illness that had decimated his crew and killed his only son, when he, too, died. His remains were accordingly sent ashore and interred at Havana.

Lt. Joseph Strout then took command and, soon thereafter, took the ship northward, bound for the United States.

Meanwhile, as *Warren* sailed homeward, Secretary Stoddert ordered Capt. James Barron to take command of the ship as soon as possible after she arrived, with expressed instructions to "relieve the sick; recruit men to fill the deficiency; cleanse, reprovision, rewater, and prepare her for another cruise with the most dispatch." Stoddert later instructed Barron to provide "all the protection in your power to the vessels which sail under your convoy, and see that as many as may be practicable to their destined ports."

Warren apparently arrived at Boston in the autumn of 1800. She subsequently fitted out for another cruise and sailed for the West Indies, where she operated, on patrol and escort duties primarily off St. Martin's and St. Bartholomew's Islands, near Guadalupe and Haiti, until the "Quasi-War" with France ended early the following year. *Warren* returned to the United States that spring and was sold by 1 June 1801 at Boston.

IV

SlpW: t. 697; lbp. 127'0''; b. 33'9''; dph. 15'6''; cpl. 190; a. 20 32-pdrs.)

The fourth *Warren*, a 2d class sloop-of-war, was built at the Boston Navy Yard between 1825 and 1827 and was commissioned at her builders on 14 January 1827, Master Commandant Lawrence Kearny in command.

Warren sailed for the Mediterranean on 22 February 1827 to stop Greek-flag pirates from victimizing American merchantmen. Unsettled conditions in the Near East and the Greek fight for independence had resulted in some excesses against third parties, notably American flag merchantmen. The piracy caused the American Mediterranean Squadron to establish a regular convoy system from Malta to Smyrna.

Warren sailed with a convoy of American vessels on 25 September 1827 and separated from them some 200 miles west of Cerigo. On 4 October, Kearny's command bagged her first "piratical boat" and its crew of five. Later that same day, *Warren* captured a brig "peerced (sic) for 16 guns" flying the Greek flag. For the next three weeks, *Warren* cruised between Cape Matapan and Carabusa, touching occasionally to contact outward-bound American merchantmen.

While off Melo on 25 October, Kearny learned of recent pirate attacks on the American ships *Cherub* and *Rob Roy*. That same day, *Warren* chased a 10-gun pirate brig ashore at the island of Argenteero; but the brigands escaped to the nearby hills. *Warren*'s men cut away the masts of the erstwhile pirate ship and stripped them of their sails, leaving the rigging submerged in the waters offshore.

Three days later, *Warren* came across *Cherub* and took possession of her. That evening, the brig *Lexington* arrived and assumed protective guard over *Cherub* while *Warren* returned to the pirate-hunt. They did not have far to go nor long to wait to see further evidence of the freebooters' handiwork. The next day, between

Tino and Miconi, *Warren* fell in with the Austrian brig *Silence* "robbed of everything." The American sloop-of-war towed *Silence* to Syra, where she left her in care of *Lexington*.

Cruising around the island of Mykonos, *Warren* captured a large *tratta* "capable of rowing 40 oars," before she put in to Mykonos harbor on 1 November. The following day, Kearny and his men recovered sails and some property taken from *Cherub* and two cases of opium taken from the brig *Rob Roy*, as well as the sails and rigging from *Silence*. The local inhabitants turned over four men accused of being pirates while a landing party of *Warren* men picked up a fifth man from the mountains. Kearny and his men also took possession of a boat belonging to pirates living at Mykonos and later burned it.

Returning to Syra on the 7th, Kearny restored the goods to *Cherub* and the sails and rigging from the Austrian ship. *Cherub*, escorted by *Lexington*, set sail for Smyrna. That evening, *Warren* put to sea, bound for the reputed pirate lair of the island of Andros.

A boat expedition, led by Lt. William L. Hudson, departed the ship to circle Andros Island. While Hudson's party was thus engaged, a brig with a convoy of some 20 to 30 boats opened fire on them in the darkness. Although shot went through the sails of *Warren*'s boats and through the clothing of some of her sailors, no one was hurt. After this action—which probably occurred because he and his expedition had been mistaken for pirates—Hudson continued on, undaunted. Near the south end of the town of Andros, *Warren*'s men brought out one "piratical craft" and burned another in a small bay nearby. At the head of that bay, the American sailors blew up a house believed to have been owned by a pirate and raised and took possession of a boat which had been sunk by pirates to avoid detection by the Americans. *Rob Roy*'s master later identified the boat as the craft in which pirates had attacked his vessel.

Kearny, in *Warren*, remained in the vicinity of Andros and Jura until 14 November. The people of Andros again cooperated and produced a pirate boat which contained a 12-pound carronade and some tools from *Cherub*.

Four days later, *Warren* made port at Milos and tarried there into late November. On the 27th of that month, the American brig *Sarah and Esther* and six other vessels arrived. Three days later, that convoy sailed for Smyrna under *Warren*'s protection. They arrived at their destination, without incident, on 6 December.

For the next two years, *Warren* remained in the Mediterranean guarding American commerce in the western end of that historic sea. She returned to the United States in the summer of 1830, arriving at Norfolk, Va., on 30 August. Decommissioned for repairs, on 10 September, *Warren* was recommissioned on 2 September 1831, Master Commandant Benjamin Cooper in command, for service on the Brazil Station. After two years in the South Atlantic, the sloop-of-war headed northward and reached Philadelphia on 31 October 1833.

Warren then made three successive tours in the West Indies, protecting American commerce in deployments that began in 1836, 1839, and 1841. On 19 October 1843, *Warren* sailed for the Pacific and served on the western coast of the North American continent for the remainder of her naval career.

During the war with Mexico, *Warren* acted as a guardship at Monterey and eventually moved to San Francisco for duty as a stores and receiving ship. On 13 November 1846, the former sloop-of-war's launch, in charge of Acting Master William H. Montgomery, departed the ship with $900.00 to pay bills accrued by the Navy for supplies, bound for Sutter's Fort, up the Sacramento River. By the end of the month, when no word came from the launch's crew, *Warren*'s commanding officer felt "great anxiety" and sent out a hired boat with some men from his ship to hunt for the

missing craft and its crew. On 18 December, the search party—having combed the river and inlets as far as Fort Sacramento—returned and reported finding no sign of the launch or of the crew.

Eventually, the fate of *Warren*'s launch came to light. The officers had been murdered—their throats cut—and their bodies thrown overboard. The men divided the money and split up, some returning overland across the North American continent to the east; others remained in California to pan for "washing gold." Records do not indicate whether or not the guilty men were ever found and brought to trial. However, they do show that orders were issued that valid discharges were to be shown by all naval personnel returning overland to prove that they were not deserters.

Thereafter, *Warren* was solely a stores ship. She was sold at Panama on 1 January 1863. Her eventual fate is unrecorded, although records indicate that the erstwhile sloop-of-war was used as a coal hulk by the Pacific Mail Steamship Co. as late as 1874.

V

(APA–53: dp. 13,910; l. 468'8"; b. 63'0"; dr. 13'3" (lim.); s. 16.5 k.; cpl. 658; trp. 1,400; a. 2 5", 8 1.1", 10 20mm.; cl. *Sumter*; T. C2–S–E1)

Jean Lafitte—named for the legendary pirate of Barataria, La., who assisted General Andrew Jackson in defending New Orleans against the British in 1815—was a C2–S–E1-type merchant ship laid down under a Maritime Commission contract (MC hull 415) on 19 April 1942 at Chickasaw, Ala., by the Gulf Shipbuilding Co.; launched on 7 September 1942; sponsored by Mrs. F. L. Leatherbury; renamed *Warren* and classified a transport, AP–98; redesignated as an attack transport, APA–53, on 1 February 1943; and placed in commission, in ordinary, on 19 February 1943. Taken to the Key Highway plant of the Bethlehem Steel Corp. soon thereafter, the ship was decommissioned on 10 March 1943; and was recommissioned on 2 August 1943, Comdr. William A. McHale, USNR, in command.

Warren soon sailed south to the Norfolk Navy Yard, where the work converting her to an attack transport was completed and she was fitted out for service. She next conducted her shakedown and type training in the waters of Chesapeake Bay. In intensive exercises, the ship practiced the amphibious tactics and techniques that she would soon be putting into practice.

On 1 November 1943, *Warren* departed Hampton Roads and headed for Panama, reaching the Canal Zone on the 5th after a brief stop at Guantanamo Bay, Cuba, en route. Following her transit of the Panama Canal, *Warren* pushed on for San Diego and reached that California port on 17 November. The ship subsequently underwent repairs and a drydocking at Long Beach before she returned to San Diego for more amphibious training. From 26 November 1943 to 13 January 1944, *Warren* landed troops of the 4th Marine Division in practice assaults at Aliso Canyon and San Clemente Island.

On the latter day, Friday the 13th, of January 1944, *Warren* sailed for the Central Pacific with men of the 1st Battalion, 25th Regiment, 4th Marine Division, embarked. Steaming via the Hawaiian Islands, the attack transport arrived off the northern islets of Kwajalein Atoll in the Marshalls at dawn on 31 January. The marines embarked in *Warren* were assigned the task of taking two small islands in the atoll, nicknamed "Ivan" and "Jacob." Those isles lay to the south of Roi and Namur, two heavily fortified areas of the atoll. Her marines were to secure both a guarded passage into the lagoon and artillery bases from which to soften up the defenses on the main islands, Roi and Namur, in support of the landings slated to take place the following day. The initial men ashore encountered minor opposition, and the casualties sustained were very light.

Warren eased into the lagoon on 1 February and continued the process of discharging munitions and

Warren (APA–53) at Hampton Roads on 23 August 1943, her decks crowded with a landing craft and antiaircraft guns. (80-G-78655)

cargo for her troops ashore. After a channel had been blasted through the coral, the attack transport's beach party supervised the arrival of supplies on "Ivan." *Warren* herself remained in the lagoon with other ships from her division for the next five days.

Warren departed Kwajalein on 4 February, leaving the island still smoking "and reeking with the stench of unburied dead." As the ship's commanding officer later wrote, "we knew now the horror of war."

Sailing southward, the attack transport reached Funafuti in the Ellice Islands on 9 February, before she continued onward, arriving at Noumea, New Caledonia, on 19 February. She ultimately weighed anchor from New Caledonian waters on 7 March and got underway for Guadalcanal—the scene of once-bitter fighting. She arrived off Lunga Point on the morning of the 10th and spent the majority of her days over the next three months in the Guadalcanal-Tulagi area. The only exceptions were trips to Kwajalein to pick up marines from the 22d Marine Regiment and to Cape Gloucester—where she landed the troops from elements of the Army's 40th Division and returned to the Russells with men of the 1st Marine Division embarked.

At the end of May, *Warren* completed the loading of the men of the 3d Battalion, 3d Regiment, 3d Marine Division, and headed north in convoy—her objective, Guam, where she was to debark the marines after their comrades had landed at Saipan in the Marianas.

However, because of the fierceness of the Japanese resistance on Saipan, *Warren*'s mission was aborted; and she therefore spent over a week cruising off that island, standing by with her marines forming a reserve force. Ultimately, however, *Warren*'s leathernecks were not needed, and the ship returned to Eniwetok, to commence a three-week stay in the Marshall Islands.

Warren finally received the nod to go into action once more, and she accordingly sailed for Guam, sending boatloads of marines from the 3d Marine Division ashore on 20 July. Over the ensuing five days, *Warren* remained off the bitterly contested beaches, her beach party lying pinned-down in their foxholes ashore. "So perilous was the position on the *Warren* beach—the left flank of the assault," wrote *Warren*'s commanding officer, "that supplies could not be landed there." Time and time again, *Warren*'s hospital corpsmen exposed themselves to enemy fire, evacuating wounded marines, and the ship's boat crews went to the reef's edge to pick up the precious cargo of human lives beneath the enemy's mortar fire.

After departing Guam on 25 July, *Warren* evacuated marine casualties to Espiritu Santo. She then shifted to the Russell Islands in the Solomons, where she embarked men of the 1st Battalion, 1st Regiment, 1st Marine Brigade—combat veterans of the Guadalcanal campaign. The attack transport then took those combat-hardened marines to the island of Peleliu in the Palaus. Despite the carrier-based air strikes and intense bombardment which preceded the initial landings of 15 September, the marines who went ashore that day still met fierce resistance from the Japanese defenders. The enemy, firmly entrenched in caves and tunnels that honeycombed the hills overlooking the beach and the strategic airfield, proved difficult to dislodge.

Again, *Warren*'s beach party worked to keep the supplies flowing from the ship to shore where they were needed, providing the necessary supplies and ammunition for the hard-pressed marines. Meanwhile, as the casualties began coming back to the ship, the attack transport's medical department worked diligently to save the wounded. Among the first ships to discharge her cargo, *Warren* remained offshore in the ensuing days, becoming a floating hospital, as doctors and corpsmen worked to sustain lives of men evacuated from "the flaming hell of Peleliu."

The routine remained almost the same during the days and nights that *Warren* lay off the beachhead. Each night there would be more burials at sea while the crew waited at battle stations for what became almost a regular visit by snooping Japanese planes. It was not until 22 September that *Warren* departed Pelelieu, bound for New Guinea.

She arrived at Hollandia on 25 September and stayed there until 15 October, when she embarked the men and equipment of the 52d Field Artillery, 24th Division Artillery, 24th Division, USA. As part of TG 78.6 she subsequently sailed for the Philippine Islands, as General Douglas MacArthur made good his pledge to return—this time well-backed by ships, men, and planes—to the islands from which he had been so unceremoniously ejected in 1942.

On 22 October—two days after the initial landings on Leyte commenced—*Warren* discharged her cargo and disembarked her troops before pulling out of the area that evening. *Warren* returned to Leyte on 14 November, this time with six Red Cross nurses as passengers in addition to the 1st Battalion, 127th Regiment, 32d Division, USA. The attack transport's commanding officer later recounted: "We all recalled that old superstition of the sea—'women on board ship bring bad luck'—when a Jap torpedo plane came close to hitting us with its deadly charge the afternoon before we sailed into Leyte Gulf." *Warren* relied on more than luck to enable her to escape damage—it was the straight-shooting of the after 5-inch gun that did the trick.

The enemy aircraft, a torpedo-carrying "Jill," bore in at the attack transport while flak blossomed about it. Only at the last instant, a 5-inch shell blew the right wing off the "Jill," sending the plane sliding past *Warren*'s fantail and into the sea. Later that day, the attack transport witnessed other air attacks in her vicinity and watched while an Army Air Force Lockheed P-38 Lightning darted daringly through the flak to explode a Japanese fighter in mid-air with a burst from her machine guns.

Leyte was still a hot target, so *Warren*'s unloading was efficient and rapid, discharging her cargo within a few hours and getting underway that evening and then slipping away in the darkness, bound for New Guinea. After stopping at Manus, in the Admiralties, and Oro Bay, *Warren* reached Milne Bay, New Guinea, on 27 November. The attack transport remained at Milne Bay through Christmas Day.

Underway on 26 December 1944, *Warren* picked up her convoy at Manus and then set out for Leyte again on 2 January 1945. Nine days later, she reached Lingayen Gulf off Luzon where the ship lost the first members of her crew to enemy action.

The first boat to leave the ship during the landings carried half of *Warren*'s beach party, along with several members of the Army shore party embarked. Due to the heavy smoke screen and a faulty boat compass, the landing craft landed on a Japanese-held beach near the town of Damortis. It was a fatal mistake. Before it could get underway, the boat came under artillery, mortar, and machine gun fire, wrecking the vessel, killing several men, and wounding others. The remaining men abandoned the craft and began to swim away from the beach, but the Japanese automatic weapons opened up on them as they struggled to get out of range. Only 17 men out of 28 survived the deadly hail of fire. It was two hours before the survivors—many of them badly wounded—were picked up.

By their firing on *Warren*'s boat, the Japanese gave away positions that pre-attack bombardments and bombings had not reached. Accordingly, *Russell* (DD–414) and two fast transports moved in close and joined Army heavy artillery in bombarding the area until all opposition was silenced completely.

On the 13th, a Japanese plane came out of the clouds off the ship's port bow, apparently intent on crashing into *Warren*. Antiaircraft fire reached up and blossomed in the sky around the intruder. While still several hundred yards away from the attack transport, the plane levelled off, swooped directly over *Warren* and headed for *Zeilin* (APA–3).

As *Warren*'s men watched, horror-stricken, the drama unfolded before their eyes, as the kamikaze plunged headlong into *Zeilin*. *Warren* herself was raked by machine gun fire from a "friendly" ship. Shells coming from the port quarter pounded the attack transport's port side. One man of her boat group, manning a gun in the cockpit in one of the ship's landing craft, was killed outright. On the flying bridge alone, there were 22 casualties.

Warren completed her unloading on 15 January and returned. Ultimately, the attack transport completed one last voyage carrying troops, landing the men of the 1st Battalion, 163d Regiment, 41st Division, USA, at Mindoro in the Philippines, after lifting them from Biak Island, New Guinea. Later discharging all surplus supplies and all but two of her landing craft, *Warren* steamed eastward via Eniwetok and stopped at Pearl Harbor on 18 March before heading on toward the west coast of the United States on 20 March.

Reaching Portland, Oreg., on the 27th, *Warren* underwent an overhaul there, lasting into June of 1945. Subsequently shifting to San Diego and then to San Francisco, the attack transport departed the west coast on 24 June, bound for the Marshalls, and arrived at Eniwetok on 6 July. From there she sailed via Ulithi to Okinawa and arrived off that island on 23 July. Over the next few days, *Warren* unloaded the men and material of the 66th Construction Battalion ("Seabees"), undergoing nearly constant air raid alerts as the enemy maintained its pressure on the invading Americans.

From 1 to 3 August, *Warren* steamed in circles off Okinawa, riding on the outer edge of a typhoon, and sailed for Ulithi on the 6th. Arriving at her destination soon thereafter, *Warren* lay at anchor in Ulithi lagoon when the word of Japan's capitulation was received.

Warren put into Cebu harbor to load units of the Army's Americal Division; but, before she embarked those troops, her orders were changed. Instead, she was to proceed to Manila. There, she embarked the troops of the Army's 43d Division and headed for Tokyo Bay, reaching that body of water on 13 September, less than two weeks after the formal surrender ceremony on board the battleship *Missouri* (BB–62).

The attack transport subsequently sailed for Okinawa, where she embarked men of the 1st Battalion, 5th Regiment, 1st Marine Division, and their equipment. She sailed from Okinawan waters on 29 September and reached the mouth of the Taku River—the approaches to the city of Tientsin, China—on 2 October. She thus completed the second of her occupation tasks, disembarking the marines over the ensuing days.

Warren departed Taku Bar on 11 October and reached Manila a few days later. She then left Philippine waters for a three-day voyage across the South China Sea to the Gulf of Tonkin. Reaching Haiphong on 26 October, *Warren* embarked 1,800 troops of the Chinese 52d Army before she departed that port, bound for Manchuria.

However, because of unsettled conditions between Chinese Communist and Nationalist forces in Manchuria—a part of the brewing civil war that would reach its climax in the expulsion of the Nationalists from mainland China to Formosa in 1949—*Warren* sailed instead to Chinwangtao, China, the seaport at the base of the Great Wall. There, she debarked her passengers on 7 November. Two days later, *Warren* dropped down the coast for her second visit to Taku and Tientsin.

On 16 November, *Warren* sailed for Manila and participation in the mass movement of men back to the continental United States, Operation "Magic Carpet."

After lifting a contingent of "seabees" to Guam at the end of November, *Warren* streamed a "homeward bound" pennant on 1 December and set her course for the California coast.

Reaching San Francisco on 17 December, *Warren* remained at that west coast port until 14 January 1946, when she got underway for New Orleans. Transiting the Panama Canal soon thereafter, *Warren* pushed on to the coast of the Gulf of Mexico. Decommissioned on 14 March 1946, *Warren* was struck from the Navy list on 17 April 1946 and turned over to the War Shipping Administration on 1 August of the same year at Mobile, Ala.

Subsequently acquired by the Waterman Steamship Corp., the ship apparently kept her original name, *Jean LaFitte*, for only a short time. Renamed *Arizpa* in 1947, the former attack transport was converted for merchant service and operated under the Waterman house flag until 1966, when she appeared on contemporary merchant vessels registers as operating with Litton Industries Leasing Corp. of Wilmington, Del. *Arizpa* operated with Litton until 1976, when she was transferred to the Reynolds Leading Corp., also of Wilmington. She remained with that firm until she disappeared from merchant registers in 1979.

Warren received four battle stars for World War II service.

Warren J. Courtney

(ScStr.: t. 276 (gross); l. 155'0''; b. 23'3''; dr. 12'0'' (mean); s. 12.0 k.; cpl. 36; a. 2 3'', 2 mg.)

Warren J. Courtney—a wooden-hulled steam fishing craft of the "Menhaden Fisherman" design built in 1912 by Jackson and Sharpe, boatbuilders, of Wilmington, Del.—was acquired by the Navy from the C. E. Davis Packing Co. of Reedville, Va., on 28 May 1917. Before *Warren J. Courtney*—designated SP–375—entered commissioned service, the Navy shortened her compound name to the surname only under the terms of General Order No. 314 promulgated on 28 July 1917. The erstwhile fishing craft thus became *Courtney* (SP–375).

Commissioned at the Norfolk Navy Yard, Portsmouth, Va., on 10 August 1917, for service as a convoy escort and patrol craft for "distant service," *Courtney* was fitted out and then sailed for France. She convoyed and escorted transports and supply ships, operating out of Brest, France, as a unit of the Patrol Force, until operational difficulties—unseaworthiness—resulted in the restriction of the "Menhaden" trawlers to minesweeping and coastal duties. Proved unfit for the role for which she had been acquired, *Courtney* operated as a minesweeper for the rest of her career and through the end of World War I. While operating off the coast of France in the spring of 1919, she foundered and sank on 27 April 1919. She was struck from the Navy list the same day.

Warrick

A county in southwestern Indiana, established on 1 April 1813, whose name honors Capt. Jacob Warrick, an officer killed at the Battle of Tippecanoe on 7 November 1811.

(AKA–89: dp. 13,910; l. 473'1''; b. 63'0''; dr. 26'4'' (lim.); s. 16.5 k.; cpl. 366 a. 1 5'', 8 40mm., 18 20mm.; cl. *Andromeda*; T. C2–S–B1)

Warren J. Courtney served the Navy as *Courtney* (SP–375). Ships and craft of many types and of every size have been acquired for temporary use in time of war. (NH 87961)

Warrick (AKA–89)—originally named *Black Prince* —was laid down under a Maritime Commission contract (MC hull 1189) on 7 April 1944 at Oakland, Calif., by the Moore Dry Dock Co.; launched on 29 May 1944; sponsored by Mrs. C. Wells Maren; and acquired and simultaneously commissioned by the Navy on 30 August 1944, at the Moore Dry Dock Company's west yard, Lt. Comdr. Ernest J. Grey, USNR, in command.

After loading stores at the Naval Supply Depot, Oakland, *Warrick* underwent a two-week shakedown out of San Pedro, Calif., concluding that necessary period of familiarization and training on 25 September. She subsequently conducted practice landings at San Clemente Island before undergoing repairs and alterations between 13 and 20 October. Taking on cargo at Wilmington, Calif., on the 24th, *Warrick* departed the west coast at 1430 the following day, bound for Manus in the Admiralties.

The ship visited Manus; Hollandia, Finschhafen, and Langemak Bay, New Guinea; and Manus a second time before she returned to Hollandia to offload the 333 tons of general Army cargo. She then again shifted to Finschafen, arriving at 1635 on 1 December. There, she loaded 1,137 tons of Army equipment—mostly vehicles— and, on the day after Christmas, embarked 17 officers and 210 enlisted men (Army) at Langemak Bay. After fueling on the 27th, *Warrick* sailed for Manus, joined *Tryon* (APH–1) en route, and rendezvoused with Task Group (TG) 77.9 on the 28th.

Warrick stopped at Manus from 29 December 1944 to 2 January 1945, before getting underway on the latter day for Lingayen Gulf, on the northern coast of the island of Luzon, in the Philippines. En route, her convoy's escorts picked up three submarine contacts and depth charged them without obtaining results. No air attacks came the way of TG 77.9, fortunately, as American amphibious forces converged on Lingayen Gulf.

Warrick reached her destination at 0500 on 11 January and came to anchor at 0830. One hour later, she commenced offloading her cargo, some two days after the first of the Army troops under the overall command of General Douglas MacArthur had splashed ashore at Lingayen. *Warrick* continued her unloading of cargo over the next day. Landing craft, LCVP's and LCM's, from *Warren* (APA–53) assisted in the unloading, continuing that task until 2200, when the operation ceased due to two factors: contact with her beach party had been lost and the beach itself was reportedly coming under shellfire.

After resuming the unloading on the 13th, *Warrick* completed her assigned duties by 1015. Taking the boats on board from 1040, *Warrick* got underway for Leyte Island, joining Task Unit (TU) 78.11.3 formed around *Mt. McKinley* (AGC–7) at 1745. She reached Leyte on the 16th.

The attack cargo ship took on board two LCVP's from the attack transport *Oconto* (APA–187) to replace boats which she had lost at Lingayen Gulf on the 17th. She departed the Philippines on the 19th, bound for the Carolines.

Reaching Ulithi on 23 January, *Warrick* fueled from *Merrimack* (AO–37) on 1 February, five days before she headed for the Marianas. Arriving at Guam on 8 February, the attack cargo ship began loading cargo and embarking troops two days later. Her load was a varied one: a transportation company, a tractor-trailer platoon, an engineer company, a war dog platoon, medical companies, ordnance repair units, replacement drafts of personnel, plus water, fuel, rations, and other supplies. With elements of the 3d Marine Division thus embarked, *Warrick* got underway for Iwo Jima on 17 February.

As part of TU 51.1.1, the attack cargo ship participated in the Iwo Jima assault as part of TG 51.1, the Joint Expeditionary Force Reserve. Screened by four destroyers and two destroyer escorts, *Warrick* sailed for that soon-to-be-famous island in company with Transport Divisions 31 and 33. She arrived at point

"Equity" on the 19th and, during ensuing days, cruised in operating area "Porch" in keeping with her reserve status. She moved in closer to Iwo Jima on the 22d, but was still lying to, awaiting orders, on the following day. The attack cargo ship finally commenced unloading operations on the 24th in the transport area four miles off the southeastern coast of Iwo Jima.

Warrick hoisted out her boats at 0750 and commenced lowering them soon thereafter. She dispatched all of her LCM's to assist in the unloading of nearby attack transports. She soon learned over the voice radio, however, that the smaller LCVP's were showing a tendency to broach and break up on the steep beaches. Beachmasters were accordingly waving off the LCVP's so that the beaches would not become fouled with the wrecks of numerous landing craft, thus impeding the flow of supplies necessary to keep the marines advancing against the stubborn Japanese defenders. Thus, with no lighterage, *Warrick* did not start unloading her own cargo until the following day.

After returning from the night retirement area, the attack cargo ship hoisted out her boats at 0810 on the 25th. At that time, *Warrick* was noting that a strong sea was running with moderate to heavy swells, which, in connection with a good breeze, made unloading conditions decidedly unfavorable. *LST–731* came alongside at 1245 but, on her attempt, carried away two debarkation ladders and stove in some of *Warrick's* hull plating at two spots on her starboard side. At 1315, on her second attempt, *LST–731* secured alongside and commenced taking on cargo.

Over the next two days, beach conditions remained the same, with the small landing craft suffering considerably in the heavy swells, leading to many bans on craft the size of LCM's and LCVP's being waived off from the beachhead. Accordingly, LST's and LSM's were utilized as lighters for the cargo. Over the next few days, the ship offloaded her cargo to *LCT–692* and *LST–731*. On 2 March, *Warrick* dispatched three LCM's to help unload ammunition from SS *Columbia Victory*. She then completed discharging cargo in ensuing days to *LSM–266* and *LSM–238*. In addition, she embarked 23 Marine casualties from the beach and later transferred them to *Doyen* (APA–1). On 6 March, after transferring smoke pots to *LST–646*, *Warrick* cleared Iwo Jima, bound for the Marianas.

Sailing from thence to the Solomon Islands, the attack cargo ship reached Tulagi on 18 March. For the remainder of hostilities, *Warrick* performed her vital but unglamourous support role. She transported boats from Guam and Manus to Florida Island and New Guinea; lifted Army cargo and troops from Noumea, New Caledonia, and Manila to Leyte, Cebu, and Manila, in the Philippines; and took return passengers to Manus. The end of hostilities in mid-August found the ship at Finschhafen, New Guinea.

Between the end of World War II in the Pacific and the onset of the Korean War—a time span of a little under five years—*Warrick* operated primarily in the western Pacific and in the Far East. Soon after the Japanese surrender, the attack cargo ship made two trips from the Philippines to Honshu, Japan, touching at the ports of Aomori, Sasebo, and Yokosuka, carrying men and materiel to support the occupation of the erstwhile enemy's homeland. She participated in Operation "Magic Carpet"—the return of discharged sailors, marines, airmen, and soldiers to the United States—and later supported the occupation of China and Korea, visiting ports that ranged from Tsingtao to Hong Kong; and Shanghai to Sasebo. In addition, during those "interwar" years, the attack cargo ship lifted cargo to such places as Johnston Island, Tarawa, Ponape, and Kwajalein. Besides performing her vital logistics functions, the ship also took part in exercises with the Fleet.

When elements of the North Korean People's Army crossed the 38th parallel into South Korean territory at 0400 on 25 June 1950, they triggered the Korean

War. At that time, *Warrick* was in port at San Francisco. She sailed for the Marshalls on 1 July and made port at Eniwetok on the 14th. She subsequently returned, via Pearl Harbor, to the west coast of the United States on 8 August. On 16 July, while deployed to the western Pacific, she received orders to berth at the Naval Supply Center, Oakland, to load as fleet issue ship for the western Pacific.

Moored at the supply center from 10 to 24 August, *Warrick* loaded balanced dry provisions sufficient for 20,000 men for 90 days; ships' store stock; clothing and small stores; general stores material; and a deck load of bottled gasses. When the task was complete, she sailed for the Far East, leaving San Francisco behind on 24 August.

Diverted to Sasebo, Japan, en route, *Warrick* arrived at that port on 9 September and, from 10 to 23 September, carried out duties of fleet issue supply ship. Attached to TF 79 on 11 September, the attack cargo ship sailed for the newly secured port of Inchon, North Korea, on 23 September, less than 10 days after American amphibious forces had attacked that port.

After performing her stores issue duties at Inchon from 25 September to 1 October, the attack cargo ship got underway to replenish ships of TF 77. Making contact with the fast carrier task force built around the carrier *Valley Forge* (CV–45), *Warrick* received the flattop alongside at 1143 on 2 October and commenced transferring cargo 12 minutes later. After delivering fleet freight, mail, napalm and drop tanks, *Warrick* set course to rendezvous with other men-of-war in the operating area off Korea's western coast.

After issuing stores to the veteran destroyer *Fletcher* (DDE–445) from 2335 on 2 October to 0040 on the 3d, *Warrick* set a return course for Sasebo and arrived at that port on 4 October. She carried out her duties as stores issue ship there from 5 to 8 October before returning to Inchon to provide round-the-clock replenishment services to the ships of TF 90 from 11 to 14 October. "For performing an efficient job under adverse conditions," *Warrick*'s commander wrote later, "*Warrick* received a 'well done.'"

Returning once more to Sasebo, the busy supply ship then proceeded to Buckner Bay, Okinawa, where she arrived on the 24th. She replenished stores of the seaplane tender *Salisbury Sound* (AV–17) before getting underway for Keelung, Formosa, on the 25th. Shifting to the Pescadores on the 28th, she arrived on the 29th to replenish the small seaplane tender *Floyds Bay* (AVP–40) at Shochi Wan anchorage. Underway for Okinawa at 1326 on 29 October, the ship received radio reports en route of the progress of typhoon "Ruby." Warned of the critical area, the attack cargo ship remained in the Formosa Strait into the early hours of the 30th, trying to ascertain the progress of the storm. When she had accurately plotted the typhoon's course—revealing her to be apparently out of danger—the ship resumed her voyage to her original destination.

Taking on board cargo at Buckner Bay, *Warrick* returned to Sasebo, making port on 3 November. She unloaded the cargo lifted from Okinawa and discharged the remnants of her fleet issue stores at Sasebo before she got underway on 16 November, bound, once more, for the west coast of the United States.

There was little rest for *Warrick*, however. No sooner had she reached home than she received orders to prepare for yet another Korean deployment. She accordingly loaded provisions, clothing and small stores; ship store items; general stores; and consigned cargo between 3 and 23 December and embarked 135 Army and Air Force personnel for transportation to Sasebo. Departing San Francisco two days before Christmas 1950, *Warrick* reached Sasebo on 9 January 1951, mooring alongside *Pollux* (AKS–4) upon arrival.

Warrick remained at Sasebo, performing her duties as fleet issue ship, into mid-February. After taking on board approximately 800 tons of empty brass shell casings for shipment back to the United States, and unloading her dry provisions and clothing stores at Yokosuka from 16 to 18 February, *Warrick* sailed for the United States on 19 February.

Over the next four years, *Warrick*'s routine changed little. She operated in the western Pacific in regular deployments, carrying fleet freight, and touched at the familiar ports such as Sasebo and Yokosuka, as well as Hong Kong and Manila. In between, there were the usual stops at Pearl Harbor and San Francisco in the course of the ship's transpacific voyages.

After having spent her entire active career with the Pacific Fleet, *Warrick* commenced her last cruise to the

Warrick (AKA–89) at Mare Island, 21 January 1946. Guns and heavy-lift equipment for handling landing craft and assault cargo do not obscure the basic outline of the Maritime Commission C2 cargo ship from which she was converted. (19–N–95003)

Orient when she departed San Francisco on 28 January 1957. Her itinerary on the voyage included Yokosuka, Hong Kong, Sasebo, and Subic Bay, before she returned to San Francisco on 30 March. Placed in reserve at Astoria, Oreg., on 4 August 1957, the workhorse cargo ship was decommissioned on 3 December 1957.

Struck from the Navy list on 1 July 1961, *Warrick* was transferred to the Maritime Administration (MarAd) for lay-up at the MarAd reserve site at Olympia, Wash. Reacquired by the Navy on 20 April 1971 for use as a target to destruction, the ship was torpedoed and sunk by *Trigger* (SS-564) 100 miles off Cape Flattery, Wash., in 1400 fathoms of water, on 28 May 1971.

Warrick (AKA-89) received two battle stars for her World War II service and one for Korea.

Warrington

Lewis Warrington—born on 3 November 1782 at Williamsburg, Va.—attended the College of William and Mary briefly before accepting an appointment as a midshipman in the Navy on 6 January 1800. His first duty, in the frigate *Chesapeake*, took him to the West Indies where his ship cruised with a squadron during the last year of the Quasi-War with France. His ship appears to have engaged in one action near the end of the cruise. On New Year's Day 1801, she took the French privateer *La Jeune Creole*.

Following the cessation of hostilities with France, Midshipman Warrington remained in the Navy. His ship spent most of 1801 in ordinary at Norfolk. The following year, Warrington was transferred to the frigate *President* for service in the Mediterranean against the Barbary pirates. Over the next five years, he remained with the Mediterranean Squadron, serving successively in *President*, *Vixen*, and *Enterprise*. Promoted to lieutenant in 1805, he returned home to Va. in 1807 to assume command of a gunboat at Norfolk, Va. In 1809, Lt. Warrington voyaged to Europe in *Siren* as a dispatch courier. He next served a tour of duty in *Essex*.

When the war with England began in June of 1812, Warrington was in *Congress* serving as the frigate's first lieutenant while she patrolled the North Atlantic. During his tour of duty in that warship, she made two successful war cruises, capturing nine prizes off the east coast of the United States during the first and four off the Atlantic seaboard of South America during the second.

Promoted to master commandant in July 1813, he took command of the sloop-of-war *Peacock* later in the year. On 12 March 1814, he put to sea with his new command bound for the naval station at St. Mary's, Ga. After delivering supplies to that installation, he encountered the British brig *Epervier* off Cape Canaveral, Fla. *Peacock* emerged victorious from a brisk 45-minute exchange with that opponent, inflicting 10 times her own losses on the enemy. For his role in the victory, Warrington received the thanks of Congress in the form of a gold medal, and of the state of Virginia in the form of a gold-hilted sword.

Warrington took his prize into Savannah, Ga., and then embarked upon his second cruise on 4 June. On that voyage—which took him to the Grand Banks, the Irish coast, the Shetland Islands, and the Faroe Islands —he took 14 prizes.

After returning via the West Indies to New York, Warrington took *Peacock* on her third and final war cruise. His sloop-of-war stood out of New York with *Hornet* and *Tom Bowline* on 23 January 1815, sailed around the Cape of Good Hope, and entered the Indian Ocean. Unaware that peace had been concluded in December 1814 at Ghent, Belgium, Warrington led his little force on another successful foray against British commerce. After taking three prizes in the Indian Ocean, he entered the East Indies in search of more game. On 30 June, he encountered the East India Company cruiser *Nautilus* in the Sunda Strait and

attacked her. After a sharp action which cost the British ship 15 men including her first lieutenant, she surrendered to Warrington and his force. At this point, Warrington learned of the peace, and he therefore released the prize and started for home. *Peacock* arrived back in New York on 30 October 1815.

In 1816, he commanded *Macedonian* briefly for a voyage to Cartagena, Spain, to convey there Christopher Hughes, the representative of the United States at negotiations over the release of some Americans imprisoned by Spanish authorities. In 1819 and 1820, Capt. Warrington commanded *Java*, followed by *Guerriere* in 1820 and 1821. Each ship was assigned to the Mediterranean Squadron during his tenure as her commanding officer. Capt. Warrington returned home and received orders to duty at the Norfolk Navy Yard. In February 1825, he relieved Porter as commander of the West Indian Squadron during the latter stages of the piracy suppression campaign and thereafter bore the title, commodore.

In 1826, Warrington returned home and served ashore for the remainder of his career. After four years in Washington—1826 to 1830—as one of three commissioners on the Navy Board, a body charged with the administration of naval materiel, Warrington returned to Norfolk for a decade as commandant of the navy yard. In 1840, he was reassigned to Washington for another two years as commissioner on the Navy Board. After the 1842 reorganization of the Navy Department, Warrington became Chief of the Bureau of Yards and Docks.

On 28 February 1844, he took over temporarily the duties of the Secretary of the Navy after Secretary Thomas W. Gilmer died as a result of wounds received when the large cannon "Peacemaker" exploded during a firing demonstration on board *Princeton* at Washington. Near the end of March, Warrington relinquished those duties to the new secretary, John W. Mason, and resumed his former assignment. In 1846, he became Chief of the Bureau of Ordnance, which office he held until his death on 12 October 1851.

I

(Destroyer No. 30: dp. 742 (n.); l. 293'10''; b. 26'1½'' (wl.); dr. 9'5'' (aft) (f.); s. 30 k. (tl.); cpl. 89; a. 5 3'', 6 18'' tt., 3 .30-cal. mg.; cl. *Roe*)

The first *Warrington* (Destroyer No. 30) was laid down on 21 June 1909 at Philadelphia by the William Cramp & Sons Ship & Engine Building Co.; launched on 18 June 1910; sponsored by Mrs. Richard Hatton; and commissioned on 20 March 1911, Lt. Walter M. Hunt in command.

After fitting out at the Philadelphia Navy Yard, *Warrington* moved on 5 August to the Torpedo Station at Newport, R.I., where she loaded torpedoes in preparation for training with the Atlantic Torpedo Fleet. During most of the fall and early winter, the warship conducted battle drills and practice torpedo firings with the submarines and destroyers of the torpedo fleet. She also joined the cruisers and battleships of the Atlantic Fleet for training in broader combat maneuvers. Those training evolutions took her as far north as Cape Cod, Mass., and as far south as Cuba.

On 27 December 1911, the destroyer departed Charleston, S.C., in company with the ships of Destroyer Divisions 8 and 9, bound for Hampton Roads. At about 1240 the following morning, the two divisions of destroyers reached the vicinity of the Virginia capes. Suddenly, an unidentified schooner knifed her way through the darkness and mist, struck *Warrington* aft, and sliced off about 30 feet of her stern. The collision deprived her of all propulsion and forced her to anchor at sea some 17 miles off Cape Hatteras. *Sterett* (Destroyer No. 27) responded to her distress call first; but, soon, *Walke* (Destroyer No. 34) and *Perkins* (Destroyer No. 26) joined the vigil. The three ships struggled through the morning and forenoon watches to pass a towline to their stricken sister, but it was not until the revenue cutter *Conondaga* arrived at 1300 that the latter ship succeeded in taking *Warrington* in tow. The revenue cutter towed her into the Norfolk Navy Yard where she was placed in reserve while undergoing repairs which were not completed until 2 December 1912.

Upon her return to active service, *Warrington* resumed operations with the torpedo forces assigned to the Atlantic Fleet, by then designated the Atlantic Torpedo Flotilla. For a little over four years, she plied the eastern coastal waters of the United States, participating in various gunnery drills and torpedo-firing practices with the torpedo flotilla as well as in fleet maneuvers and battle problems with the assembled Atlantic Fleet. During part of that interlude, the destroyer was based at Newport and worked out of Boston during the remainder.

When the United States entered World War I on 6 April 1917, *Warrington* began patrols off Newport to protect the harbor from German submarines. After six weeks of such duty and preparations for service overseas, she stood out of Boston on 21 May, bound for Europe. After a stop at Newfoundland en route, she arrived at Queenstown, on the southern coast of Ireland, on 1 June. There, she began six months of service patrolling the southern approaches to British ports on the Irish Sea and escorting convoys on the final leg of their voyage across the Atlantic to the British Isles. The destroyer operated out of Queenstown until late November 1917 when she was ordered to France.

She reached Brest, her new base of operations, on 29 November and resumed a grueling schedule of patrols and escort missions. Records indicate that she experienced only one apparent brush with a U-boat. On the morning of 31 May 1918, while escorting a convoy along the French coast, she received a distress call from the Navy transport *President Lincoln* which, earlier that morning, had been torpedoed by *U–90* well out to sea. The destroyer parted company with her coastal convoy immediately and raced to rescue the sinking ship's crew. She did not reach the area of the sinking until late that night but succeeded in rescuing 443 survivors just after 2300. *Smith* (Destroyer No. 17) took on all but one of the remaining 688 survivors of *President Lincoln*. That single exception, Lt. Isaacs, had the dubious honor of being rescued by *U–90*. On 1 June, during the voyage back to Brest, *Warrington* and *Smith* depth-charged the *U–90*. Lt. Isaacs, the captured naval officer who later escaped from a German prison camp, reported that the charges shook the submarine severely. However, no evidence of any success appeared on the surface; and the two destroyers, conscious of the importance of landing their human cargo, abandoned the attack and continued on to Brest. They entered that port the following day, disembarked the *President Lincoln* survivors, and resumed their patrol and escort missions.

Through the end of the war, *Warrington* operated out of Brest, patrolling against enemy submarines. However, the threat posed by the U-boats diminished considerably after the failure of Germany's last offensive in July and an Allied offensive had made their bases on the Belgian coast untenable. Late in October, Germany discontinued unrestricted submarine warfare and, early in November, sued for peace.

The armistice was concluded on 11 November 1918, but *Warrington* continued to serve in European waters until the spring of 1919. On 22 March, she stood out of Brest in the screen of a convoy of subchasers and tugs. After visiting the Azores and delivering her charges safely at Bermuda, the warship headed for Philadelphia. She reached the Delaware capes early in May and remained in the navy yard at League Island until decommissioned on 31 January 1920. *Warrington* lay at Philadelphia in reserve until 1935. On 20 March 1935, her name was struck from the Navy list. She was sold to M. Black & Co., Norfolk, Va., on 28 June 1935 for scrapping in accordance with the terms of the London Treaty for the Limitation and Reduction of Naval Armaments.

II

(DD–383: dp. 1,850; l. 381'; b. 36'7''; dr. 17'; s. 35 k.; cpl. 294; a. 8 5'', 2 .50-cal. mg., 8 21'' tt., 2 dct.; cl. *Somers*)

The second *Warrington* (DD–383) was laid down on 10 October 1935 at Kearny, N.J., by the Federal Shipbuilding & Drydock Co.; launched on 15 May 1937; sponsored by Miss Katherine Taft Chubb; and commissioned at the New York Navy Yard on 9 February 1938, Comdr. Leighton Wood in command.

Following a shakedown cruise to the West Indies during April and May, the destroyer returned to New York on 24 May, underwent post-shakedown availability, and then conducted tactical training off Cape Cod and the Virginia capes. She also participated in maneuvers with the boats of Submarine Division 4 in waters near New London. In October, she headed south for refresher training in Cuban waters.

On 4 December, the warship headed north to Newport, R.I., where she became a unit of Destroyer Division (DesDiv) 17, Destroyer Squadron (DesRon) 9. *Warrington* operated along the east coast and made a cruise to the Caribbean in a task group built around *Enterprise* (CV–6) and *Yorktown* (CV–5) to participate in Fleet Problem XX.

In mid-February 1939, she reported to Key West to serve as an escort for *Houston* (CA–30), the cruiser in which President Franklin D. Roosevelt and Chief of Naval Operations Admiral William D. Leahy embarked to observe the concluding phase of the 1939 annual Fleet exercise. The destroyer concluded that assignment upon her arrival at Charleston, S.C., on 3 March where Roosevelt and Leahy left *Houston* to return to Washington. After three months of operations along the coast between New York and Norfolk, the destroyer moored at Fort Hancock, N.J., on the morning of 9 June to embark King George VI and Queen Mary of Great Britain for passage to Manhattan.

Warrington departed Norfolk on the 26th, transited the Panama Canal on 3 July and arrived in her new home port, San Diego, soon thereafter. Assigned to the Battle Force, United States Fleet, the destroyer conducted operations along the California coast for the next nine months. At the beginning of April 1940, she departed San Diego with the ships of Battle Force to participate in Fleet Problem XXI, conducted in Hawaiian waters. Though nominally retaining San Diego as her home port, *Warrington* was based at Pearl Harbor for most of her remaining peacetime service. Between April 1940 and April 1941, she returned to the west coast only twice, once in June 1940 for repairs after the conclusion of the Fleet exercise and again in late November and early December of that year.

After 12 months of training out of Pearl Harbor—frequently with submarines engaged in torpedo practice—*Warrington* departed Hawaii on 18 April 1941 to augment the forces engaged in the so-called "Neutrality Patrol." After passing back through the Panama Canal on 7 May, she continued on to Guantanamo Bay, Cuba. There, she became part of a patrol force composed of *Cincinnati* (CL–6), *Memphis* (CL–13), and *Davis* (DD–395). Her area of operations encompassed the eastern Caribbean and the western Atlantic from the West Indies south to about 12 degrees south latitude. In addition to patrolling, she later began intermittent escort duties; and, in fact, her last assignment during the "Neutrality Patrol" period consisted of a voyage in company with *Milwaukee* (CL–5) to escort SS *Acadia* from Recife, Brazil, to Puerto Rico. She arrived at San Juan on 3 November; then headed north for a two-day visit at Norfolk; and entered the Charleston Navy Yard on the 9th for repairs.

Still moored at Charleston on 7 December when word arrived that the Japanese attack on Pearl Harbor had catapulted the United States into World War II, *Warrington* put to sea the following day to conduct war patrols along the Atlantic coast from Norfolk to Newport. Late in December, she rendezvoused with HMS *Duke of York* and escorted the British battleship into Norfolk on the 21st. For another three weeks, the destroyer patrolled the eastern seaboard as far north as the Massachusetts coast and then headed south on her way to a new area of operations. On 17 January 1942, the warship arrived in Balboa at the Pacific terminus of the Panama Canal where she reported for duty with the Southeast Pacific Force.

Based at Balboa, she operated with the other ships of the Southeast Pacific Force—three cruisers and another destroyer—for the next 16 months. She had two primary missions to perform: escorting merchant, supply, and troop ships between Panama and the Society Islands and patrolling for submarines in the southeastern Pacific as far south as Callao, Peru. Secondary assignments included duty as target and training ship for submarines preparing to enter the war zone and for Army patrol bombers getting ready to do the same. After the Guadalcanal landings on 7 August, her runs to the Society Islands took on new meaning because the bulk of the ships she escorted after that date carried supplies and reinforcements to support America's first offensive in the Pacific.

On 10 and 11 December, she had the honor of escorting *South Dakota* (BB–57)—heavily damaged in the Naval Battle of Guadalcanal in mid-November—into Balboa on her way to repairs at New York. She continued her patrol and escort duties with the Southeast Pacific Force until early June 1943. On 23 May, she stood out of Balboa on her last mission with that organization, to escort a convoy to the Society Islands. Upon arrival at Bora Bora on 4 June, she received orders to report for duty to the Commander in Chief, Pacific Fleet.

At that juncture, the southwestern Pacific became *Warrington*'s area of operations. Upon reaching Noumea, New Caledonia, she began a five-week stretch of convoy duty that took her to such diverse places as Australia, Samoa, Hawaii, Guadalcanal, and the New Hebrides Islands. On 1 October, she departed Espiritu Santo in the last-named island group to escort *Prince William* (CVE–31) to Samoa, whence the destroyer headed to Pearl Harbor for repairs and to pick up a convoy.

Warrington returned to Espiritu Santo on 30 October but, by 6 November, had arrived off Koli Point, Guadalcanal, where she joined up with the second echelon of the Bougainville invasion force. At daybreak two days later, she escorted the troop ships charged to her protection into Empress Augusta Bay, Bougainville. She patrolled to seaward while the transports landed reinforcements and supplies on the beaches to the east and southeast of Cape Torokina.

Near noon, the air raid warning sounded. Both troop and cargo ships got underway to evade the action; and *Warrington* joined the antiaircraft defenses for the anchorage and beachhead. At four minutes after noon, the destroyer opened fire on two Japanese planes crossing her stern. The first began smoking almost immediately and crashed dead astern. The second came under fire from the other ships as well; shuddered under the impact of the combined fire of the ships and then, trailing pieces from his fuselage, splashed down, too. *Warrington* claimed sole credit for downing the first plane and a part in getting the second. The enemy withdrew at about 1225; and, six minutes later, the transports resumed their tasks at Cape Torokina. That night, she escorted the empty transports back to Guadalcanal.

For the next month, *Warrington* made escort runs between Guadalcanal and Espiritu Santo. On 14 March, she became a part of the antisubmarine screen for an escort carrier task group operating in support of Task Force (TF) 37 which, in turn, was striking at Kavieng, a large Japanese base located on the northwestern tip of New Ireland. Later that month, she escorted the third convoy of troopships to Emirau Island, arriving there on the 28th. On 6 April, the destroyer returned to the New Hebrides, stopping briefly at Espiritu Santo before continuing on to Efate where she discharged passengers. On 9 April, she reentered the port at Espiritu Santo for an 11-day availability.

On the 20th, she rejoined TF 37 at Efate and, four days later, headed south to Sydney, Australia, where she arrived on the 29th. After a week in the Australian port, *Warrington* headed back to Efate with TF 37, entering Havannah Harbor on 10 May.

There, she and *Balch* (DD–363) were detached from the task force and ordered to New Guinea. The two destroyers reached Milne Bay on 13 May and reported for duty with the 7th Fleet. Two days later, *Warrington* stood out of Milne Bay bound for Capes Sudest and Cretin. At the latter place, she joined the antisubmarine screen of a Hollandia-bound convoy of LST's. She escorted her charges into Humboldt Bay on 22 May and remained there for three days. She and *Balch* got underway together again on the 25th to conduct a shore bombardment mission at Wakde Island in support of the advancing troops of the 6th Army.

She began her first mission early on the 26th. Dense foliage precluded the identification of specific targets, so *Warrington* contented herself with an area bombardment, firing more or less uniformly throughout the designated sector. On the 27th, she and *Balch* returned for a repeat performance, at the conclusion of which they received a message from the general commanding ashore lauding their ". . . superb cooperation . . ." and indicating that their gunfire had been ". . . of great assistance . . ." to the troops ashore. That same day, the two destroyers headed back to Humboldt Bay.

The return to Hollandia, however, proved brief. *Warrington* entered the bay on the 28th but departed again late that afternoon to escort an echelon of LST's to a convoy rendezvous point. Upon her arrival, she joined the convoy's antisubmarine screen and set course to escort it to Biak Island. The convoy reached Biak at 0725 on 30 May, and *Warrington* received orders instructing her to report to shore fire control group no. 1 to deliver call-fire in support of American ground forces advancing toward Mokmer airstrip. About an hour later, she received instructions from the commanding general ashore to patrol west of the beachhead to keep the Japanese from moving reinforcements in from that direction. After a singularly uneventful morning and afternoon, the destroyer quit her patrols and assumed responsibility as fighter director ship when *Swanson* (DD–443) left the unit that night.

The following day, she retired from Biak with TG 77.8 and arrived back at Humboldt Bay the same day. Between 3 and 5 June, she made another voyage to Biak during which she provided gunfire support briefly on the 5th before departing to escort the empty LST's back to Humboldt Bay.

Following a voyage that took her to Manus in the Admiralties and back to Espiritu Santo in the New Hebrides, *Warrington* departed the latter port on 19 June in company with *Balch* to return to the United States. Steaming via Bora Bora, the two destroyers transited the Panama Canal on 8 July, stopped briefly at Colon, and arrived in New York on the 15th. She immediately entered the New York Navy Yard and began repairs.

She completed her yard period at New York early in August, conducted maneuvers at Casco Bay, Maine, and then entered the Norfolk Navy Yard for additional alterations. On 10 September, she departed Norfolk in company with *Hyades* (AF–28) and set her course for Trinidad.

Two days out of Norfolk, along the Florida coast, the two ships encountered heavy weather. In the afternoon, *Warrington* received word that she was steaming directly into a hurricane. Later that evening, the storm forced the destroyer to heave to while *Hyades* continued on her way alone. Keeping wind and sea on her port bow, *Warrington* rode relatively well through most of the night. Wind and seas, however, continued to build during the early morning hours of the 13th. *Warrington* began to lose headway and, as a result, started to ship water through the vents to her engineering spaces.

The water rushing into her vents caused a loss of electrical power which set off a chain reaction. Her main engines lost power, and her steering engine and mechanism went out. She wallowed there in the trough of the swells—continuing to ship water. She regained headway briefly and turned upwind, while her radiomen desperately, but fruitlessly, tried to raise *Hyades*. Finally, she resorted to a plain-language distress call to any ship or shore station. By noon on the 13th, it was apparent that *Warrington*'s crewmen could not win the struggle to save their ship, and the order went out to prepare to abandon ship. By 1250, her crew had left *Warrington*; and she went down almost immediately. A prolonged search by *Hyades*, *Frost* (DE–144), *Huse* (DE–145), *Inch* (DE–146), *Snowden* (DE–246), *Swasey* (DE–248), *Woodson* (DE–359), *Johnnie Hutchins* (DE–360), *ATR–9*, and *ATR–62* rescued only 5 officers and 68 men of the destroyer's 20 officers and 301 men. *Warrington*'s name was struck from the Navy list on 23 September 1944.

Warrington earned two battle stars during World War II.

III

(DD–843: dp. 2,425; l. 390'6''; b. 40'10''; dr. 18'6''; s. 34.6 k. (tl.); cpl. 345; a. 6 5'', 16 40mm., 20 20mm., 5 21'' tt., 6 dcp., 2 dct.; cl. *Gearing*)

The third *Warrington* (DD–843) was laid down on 14 May 1945 at Bath, Maine, by the Bath Iron Works Corp.; launched on 27 September 1945; sponsored by Mrs. Katherine Chubb Sheehan; and commissioned at the Boston Naval Shipyard on 20 December 1945, Comdr. Don W. Wulzen in command.

Warrington conducted shakedown training and winter exercises in the West Indies during February and early March and then returned to Boston for duty in Destroyer Division (DesDiv) 82, Destroyer Squadron (DesRon) 8. During the next year, the destroyer cruised almost the length of the eastern seaboard planeguarding for carriers such as *Ranger* (CV–4). Late in the spring of 1946, she joined *Little Rock* (CL–91) in an extended cruise to Europe and visited ports in England, Scotland, Sweden, Denmark, Belgium, Portugal, and the Netherlands before entering the Mediterranean for her first tour of duty with the 6th Fleet. That assignment ended on 8 February 1947 when she passed through the Strait of Gibraltar on her way back home. *Warrington* arrived at New York on 19 February and entered the naval shipyard there for voyage repairs.

At the conclusion of the yard work on 8 March, she steamed to her new home port, Newport, R.I., and for two years cruised along the east coast, serving primarily as gunnery training ship for the Atlantic Destroyer Force. In April 1949, the ship was reassigned to DesDiv 222, which she served as flagship, and to DesRon 22. Late that summer, she departed the New England coast for a two-month training voyage to the West Indies. After a brief stop at Norfolk at the conclusion of those maneuvers, *Warrington* headed north at the end of October for cold weather training near the Arctic Circle, returning to Newport on 20 November.

On 3 January 1950, the destroyer sailed from Newport in company with her squadron and *Wright* (CVL–49) for hunter/killer exercises along the east coast and in the vicinity of Bermuda. The following month, she conducted antisubmarine warfare (ASW) exercises with *Dogfish* (SS–350) out of Newport News, Va., before returning to that port for a brief yard availability.

The ship next returned north to Newport for a tour of duty with the Operational Development Force detachment during which her division tested ASW tactics in company with *Saipan* (CVL–48) along the coast of Newfoundland and in the waters around Iceland. That assignment lasted from 10 July to 8 August, at which time she returned to Newport to prepare for her second deployment to the Mediterranean. That tour of duty lasted only two months and one day. The destroyer returned to Newport on 10 November and resumed normal east coast operations.

In January 1951, *Warrington* changed from DesDiv 222 to DesDiv 142 for which she served as flagship. Over the next eight years, the destroyer settled into a fairly repetitive routine, alternating four deployments to the 6th Fleet with operations out of Newport. Her Mediterranean cruises came in the spring of 1952, the summers of 1954 and 1956, and in the spring of 1957. Her 2d Fleet duties consisted primarily of ASW training in company with Atlantic Fleet aircraft carriers and took her from the coast of New England south to the Caribbean and the West Indies.

In May 1959, *Warrington* was reassigned to DesDiv 102. In June, she embarked Naval Academy midshipmen at Annapolis for a unique training cruise. Instead of Europe or the West Indies, the area of activity for that voyage was the Great Lakes. *Warrington* passed through the newly constructed St. Lawrence Seaway and participated in the opening ceremonies for the waterway led by Queen Elizabeth II of Great Britain and President Dwight D. Eisenhower of the United States. At the conclusion of those ceremonies—held at Montreal, Canada, on 26 June—*Warrington* continued on her mission, visiting a series of American ports on the Great Lakes, including Chicago, Detroit, and Sault Ste. Marie among others before returning to Newport on 4 August.

During the next 22 months, she performed her normal duties out of Newport. Exercises along the east coast occupied her for the remainder of 1959 and the beginning of 1960. On 21 March, she began another cruise with the 6th Fleet which also included a six-week assignment with the Middle East Force between 16 June and 28 July. She concluded her Mediterranean deployment at Rota, Spain, on 7 October and reentered Newport on the 15th. East coast operations—broken only by a visit to Washington, D.C., in January 1961 for the inauguration of President John F. Kennedy and duty as a recovery ship for a Project "Mercury" test in February—dominated her schedule until late in the spring of 1961.

On 12 May, the destroyer entered the New York Naval Shipyard for major alterations during her Mark I Fleet Rehabilitation and Modernization (FRAM I) overhaul. Those modifications reflected the enormous technological advances registered in antisubmarine warfare since the end of World War II and might be considered the beginning of the final phase in the shift of mission for destroyers from a surface-attack role to that of a submarine hunter.

Her superstducture silhouette changed markedly as she received a larger combat information center (CIC) and sonar control as well as an antisubmarine rocket (ASROC) launcher, a torpedo magazine, and a hangar and flight deck for a drone antisubmarine helicopter (DASH). The new ASROC launcher was installed between the stacks in the space formerly held by her 21-inch torpedo tubes which, in turn, were replaced by two 15.5-inch triple torpedo tube mounts located in the waist at the after stack—one to port and the other to starboard. The DASH flight deck and hangar replaced her after 5-inch double mount, reducing her main surface battery to four 5-inch, 38-caliber guns in two twin mounts forward.

Warrington's FRAM conversion took eight days short of a year. She emerged from the New York Naval Shipyard on 4 May 1962 and began various post-conversion qualifications and tests which culminated in

USS *Warrington* (DD–843).

refresher training in the Guantanamo Bay area during June and July. After two weeks at the Fleet Sonar School at Key West, she returned to Newport on 12 August to begin duty with the Atlantic Fleet's ASW forces.

Over the next 27 months, *Warrington*'s east coast operations routine—annual "Springboard" operations in the Caribbean and ASW training evolutions out of Newport—was spiced up by a series of special assignments. On 19 September 1962, she got underway to serve as a unit of the recovery group for Lt. Comdr. Walter Schirra's "Sigma Seven" space flight which took place on 3 October. Later that month, when the Cuban missile crisis occurred, the destroyer joined a special ASW task group which, though it did not participate in the actual quarantine, performed a support role for the ships so engaged.

During early April 1963, the warship helped to conduct the unsuccessful search-and-rescue attempt prompted by the loss of the nuclear-powered submarine *Thresher* (SSN–593) during deep-submergence tests. After a summer of operations out of Newport, *Warrington* got underway for the Indian Ocean on 1 October. Steaming via the Atlantic and the Mediterranean, she arrived in Karachi, Pakistan, at the end of the first week in November. For the next fortnight, the destroyer joined other United States and CENTO powers' ships in Operation "Midlink VI." She began the voyage home on 23 November and, after stops at several ports, returned to Newport on 23 December.

The first eight months of 1964 brought 2d Fleet operations, broken only by a repair period at Norfolk and another later one at Boston following her collision with *Barry* (DD–933) on 25 July. Between 8 September and 18 December, the ship made another brief deployment to the Mediterranean, highlighted by Operation "Masterstroke" and NATO Exercise "Teamwork" during the outbound voyage. While conducting the latter operation, *Warrington* briefly ventured north of the Arctic Circle.

Warrington returned to Newport on 18 December 1964 and began almost two years of operations along the east coast—primarily ASW training evolutions—as well as occasional cruises to the Caribbean area for "Springboard" operations, gunnery drills, and refresher training. That duty ended late on 4 October 1966 when the destroyer stood out of Newport to deploy to the Far East. She transited the Panama Canal on 9 October, stopped at Pearl Harbor on 24 October, and arrived at Yokosuka, Japan, on 10 November. That same day, she headed for the Tonkin Gulf in company with *Manley* (DD–940) and *Keppler* (DD–765). On 21 November, she relieved *Reeves* (DLG–24) on "Traffic Cop" station off the coast of North Vietnam. Operation "Traffic Cop," soon to be redesignated Operation "Sea Dragon," was an ongoing patrol to interdict waterborne logistics to the insurgents in South Vietnam. After 13 days of "Traffic Cop" duty, *Warrington* put into Danang on 3 December before sailing later that same day for Kaohsiung, Taiwan. There she spent another 13 days undergoing a tender availability alongside *Isle Royal* (AD–29) before getting underway for Hong Kong on the 19th.

On 26 December 1966, she departed Hong Kong to return to the Gulf of Tonkin, this time for plane guard duty with the fast carriers on Yankee Station. She continued that assignment until 19 January 1967 when she steamed south to the II Corps area of South Vietnam to provide naval gunfire support for troops of the 1st Cavalry Division conducting Operation "Thayer II" ashore. She completed that mission on 25 January and headed for Kaohsiung for another tender availability.

Following a visit to Hong Kong and another repair period—at Subic Bay in the Philippines—the destroyer resumed plane guard duty in the Gulf of Tonkin on 27

February. On 10 March, she parted company with the carrier *Ticonderoga* (CV–14) to conduct a gunfire support mission in the III Corps zone near Rung Sat. She completed that task early on 24 March and set a course for Subic Bay. There, the warship rendezvoused with *Keppler*, *Manley*, and *Newman K. Perry* (DD–883) for the voyage home. The four destroyers began their journey home on 26 March, heading west across the Indian Ocean rather than east back across the Pacific. On their way, they stopped at Singapore and Massawa in Ethiopia, transited the Suez Canal, steamed across the Mediterranean Sea, and visited Ponta Delgada in the Azores before arriving back in Newport on 8 May.

The ensuing six years brought a return to the familiar routine of east coast operations alternated with deployments to the 6th Fleet in the Mediterranean. After eight months of training, readiness inspections, and the other normal evolutions of duty out of Newport, *Warrington* departed the United States in mid-February 1968, bound for a four-month tour of duty with the 6th Fleet. During that assignment, she also visited a number of northern European ports as well as those along the Mediterranean littoral. The destroyer returned to the United States on 14 June and operated out of Newport until October. On the 18th, she entered the Boston Naval Shipyard for a five-month overhaul.

She completed her post-overhaul sea trials between 27 March and 3 April 1969 and returned to Newport on 5 April. Between 10 April and 27 June, the warship voyaged to the West Indies to conduct gunnery drills at Culebra Island and refresher training out of Guantanamo Bay, Cuba. She returned to Newport on 27 June and spent the major portion of the summer and the entire fall in an extended upkeep and in preparations for overseas movement.

On 2 November, the destroyer stood out of Newport and headed back to the Mediterranean. During that assignment, her primary mission was to observe units of the Soviet Navy operating in the eastern Mediterranean. However, she also made goodwill visits and liberty calls at ports all along the Mediterranean coastline. On 13 May 1970, *Warrington* completed her tour of duty with the 6th Fleet and began her journey home. She reentered Newport on 22 May and began post-deployment leave and upkeep. Following a month of repairs at Boston late in July and early in August, the warship spent most of the remainder of the year in Newport, though she did get underway for two brief periods at sea—once in September for the America's Cup yachting race and again in October to escort *Forrestal* (CVA–59) during the carrier's post-repair acceptance trials. On 14 January, *Warrington* embarked upon a two-month cruise to the Mediterranean to participate in 6th Fleet ASW exercises. She returned to Newport on 3 March and resumed her 2d Fleet routine. Her duties included two tours as school ship for the Destroyer School and the ever-present ASW training operations. Regular overhaul commenced on 15 September 1971 and ended on 16 January 1972.

Following overhaul and a brief visit to Newport, *Warrington* put to sea on 23 January for post-overhaul gunnery drills and refresher training in the Caribbean. She completed those evolutions on 21 March and headed back to Newport for a brief period of local operations before her second deployment to the Far East. Departing Newport on 5 June, *Warrington* headed, via the Panama Canal and Pearl Harbor, for the Mariana Islands. Arriving at Guam on 30 June, she departed Apra Harbor the following day, bound for Subic Bay. She left the Philippines on 6 July and reached Vietnamese waters the same day. During her first period on the gunline, the destroyer conducted gunfire support missions all up and down the coast of the I Corps zone of South Vietnam. On 15 July, she put into port at Danang briefly and then headed for the coast of North

Vietnam to participate in Operation "Linebacker." On 16 July, she relieved *Hamner* (DD–718) of "Linebacker" duty and began her primary mission—the destruction of North Vietnamese small craft and observation of communist Chinese merchant shipping. The following morning, while operating in company with *Hull* (DD–945) and *Robinson* (DDG–12), *Warrington* came under the rapid and heavy fire of enemy shore batteries; but she took prompt evasive action and avoided damage.

That same afternoon, however, luck abandoned her. At 1316, two underwater explosions close aboard her port side rocked the destroyer. She suffered severe damage in her after fireroom, after engine room, and in the main control room. Her crew rose to the occasion, and their efforts enabled her to retire from the area at 10 knots. Later, the damage forced her to shut down her propulsion plant and ask *Robinson* for a tow. Through the night of 17 and 18 July, her crew struggled against flooding caused by ruptured fuel oil and fresh water tanks, but she remained afloat the next morning when *Robinson* turned her over to *Reclaimer* (ARS–42) for the first leg of the trip to Subic Bay. *Tawakoni* (ATF–114) took over from *Reclaimer* on the 20th and towed *Warrington* safely into Subic Bay on the 24th. Throughout the six-day voyage, *Warrington*'s ship's company worked magnificently to keep their ship afloat.

For a month after her arrival, *Warrington* received the special attention of the ship repair facility at Subic Bay to improve her habitability and insure watertight integrity. However, at the end of August, a board of inspection and survey found her to be unfit for further naval service. Accordingly, on 30 September 1972, *Warrington* was decommissioned at Subic Bay, and her name was struck from the Navy list. On 24 April 1973, she was sold to the Taiwan Navy for cannibalization and scrapping.

Warrington (DD–843) received two battle stars for service in the Vietnam conflict.

Wasaka III

(MB: l. 53'0''; b. 10'0''; s. 9.0 k.; cpl. 6; a. 1 1-pdr., 1 Colt mg.)

Wasaka III—a wooden-hulled motorboat—was built at Lynn, Mass., by Britt Brothers, boat builders. Acquired by the Navy in the spring of 1917 from Mr. John J. Martin of Boston under a free-lease agreement, *Wasaka III* was apparently manned on 22 April 1917, as her deck log indicates that the first men—the most senior rating being a Machinist's Mate 2d Class A. Rowbottom, USNRF—reported on board on that day. There is no record of a commissioning, and the deck log does not start until 1 June 1917.

Initially, *Wasaka III*—classified SP–342—operated from the Commonwealth Pier, Boston, Mass. On 26 September 1917, she shifted to the Bumkin Island section base, whence she operated for the duration of the war and into 1919. Her log ends on 31 March 1919, and she was returned to her owner on 18 April of the same year.

Wasatch

A mountain chain in central Utah.

(AGC–9: dp. 12,750; l. 459'2''; b. 63'; dr. 24'; s 16.4 k.; cpl. 612; a. 2 5'', 4 40mm., 18 20mm.; cl. *Mount McKinley*; T. C2–S–AJ1)

Fleetwing was laid down under a Maritime Commission contract (MC hull 1349) on 7 August 1943 at Wilmington, N.C., by the North Carolina Shipbuilding Corp.; launched on 8 October 1943; sponsored by Mrs. P. A. Wilson; and acquired by the Navy on 31 December 1943 for conversion to an amphibious command ship (AGC). Renamed *Wasatch* and designated AGC–9, the ship was converted for naval use at the Norfolk Navy Yard, Portsmouth, Va., and commissioned there on 20 May 1944, Capt. Alford M. Granum in command.

Following sea trials in Chesapeake Bay, *Wasatch* sailed for the Pacific on 26 June—in company with *Stafford* (DE–411) and *La Prede* (DE–409)—and transited the Panama Canal on 3 July, bound for New Guinea. The general communications vessel reached Milne Bay at 1725 on 31 July and, 10 days later, embarked Rear Admiral William M. Fechteler from *Blue Ridge* (AGC–2). On 7 September, Rear Admiral Daniel E. "Uncle Dan" Barbey, who commanded Task Force (TF) 76, embarked in *Wasatch*; and the ship got underway for Aitape to join other units of the Morotai-bound task force.

On 15 September, air strikes and surface bombardments softened up the invasion beaches; and American troops splashed ashore to occupy the island. Meanwhile, *Wasatch* stood off shore and served as the nerve center of the operation. At 1800, she retired to seaward to await the dawn when she would again close the beach to direct the landing operations. Retaliatory air strikes did not come near the command ship on this occasion, although her war diary notes that a plane was downed ahead in the next group.

Anchoring off Doeroba at 0830 on the 17th, Admiral Barbey directed operations from *Wasatch* until he shifted his flag to *Russell* (DD–414) to orchestrate the proceedings from there, from 1809. A half-hour later, *Wasatch*, in company with *McKee* (DD–575), got underway for Humboldt Bay.

The AGC remained at Humboldt and prepared for upcoming operations into early October. On the 14th, Vice Admiral Thomas C. Kincaid broke his flag in *Wasatch*, as Commander, Task Unit (TU) 77.1.1. On the following day, the ship—with Lt. Gen. Walter Krueger embarked—got underway for the Philippines, to participate in the first act of the dramatic "return" to the Philippine archipelago.

Entering Surigao Strait at 0455 on the 20th, *Wasatch* proceeded up Leyte Gulf. Battleships, cruisers, and destroyers commenced bombarding the Leyte beachhead at 0920 that morning and, some 40 minutes later, the first landing craft were churning towards the beach. Throughout the day, *Wasatch* stood offshore in a position from which the landings could be observed and served as the nerve center for the operation. From the 20th through the 23d, the ship retired to sea nightly, in company with *Nashville* (CL–43), *Ammen* (DD–527), and *Mullany* (DD–528).

Enemy air retaliation materialized swiftly in the wake of the American landings; and *Wasatch*'s gunners stood at their weapons, ready to augment the heavy volume of antiaircraft fire from other Allied ships that fought off the attackers. Anchored off "white beach" early on the morning of the 25th, those on watch topside in *Wasatch* saw lightning-like flickerings of gunfire in the distance to the southward, as Rear Admiral Jesse B. Oldendorf's battleships and cruisers crossed the "T" of the Japanese "Southern Force" and in short order annihilated the enemy warships in the Battle of Surigao Strait.

However, the "Southern Force" was not the only one that the Japanese threw against the Allied forces to contest the Leyte invasion. The enemy's "Center Force" —consisting of four battleships and five cruisers, had passed into the Philippine Sea during the night of 24 and 25 October. That group suddenly appeared to Rear Admiral Clifton A. F. Sprague's "Taffy 3" escort carrier task group off Samar.

Sprague's six escort carriers and their attending screen fought bravely against overwhelming odds in what became known as the Battle off Samar. While the destroyers and destroyer escorts hurled themselves at the Japanese capital ships and cruisers in suicidal attacks, the "jeep carriers" launched planes. Capt. Richard F. Whitehead—embarked in *Wasatch*

as Commander, Support Aircraft—immediately ordered all American planes not attacking Japanese shore positions in support of the landings to strike the Japanese ships of the "Center Force." Six Avengers and 20 Wildcats from the CVE's nearby responded to the summons and, together with the planes launched from "Taffy 3" under fire, bore in at 0830 for their first attack.

Ultimately, the heroic defense forced the Japanese "Center Force" to withdraw without damaging the vulnerable transports still unloading off the Leyte beachhead. The victory had not been won without cost. The American forces lost *Gambier Bay* (CVE–73), destroyers *Johnston* (DD–557) and *Hoel* (DD–533), and the destroyer escort, *Samuel B. Roberts* (DE–413). They had given their lives to buy time.

At 1310 on the 25th, the AGC's gunners splashed a Japanese aircraft and helped to down two additional planes the following day. On the 29th, the command ship got underway for New Guinea, in company with a powerful battleship-cruiser force, and, although buffeted by 80-knot winds en route, completed a safe passage to Humboldt Bay at 1218 on 2 November. Admiral Kinkaid disembarked upon arrival and shifted his flag to headquarters ashore. Rear Admiral Arthur D. Struble, commanding Amphibious Group 9, embarked in *Wasatch* on 3 November and remained in the command ship until transferring to *Mount McKinley* (AGC–7).

On 20 November, Admiral Kinkaid again embarked in *Wasatch*, and, escorted by *Lough* (DE–536) and *Daniel E. Joy* (DE–595), proceeded to Leyte and anchored in San Pedro Bay on the 25th. There, while intense planning sessions were occurring on board—in preparation for the Lingayen landings in January of the following year—Rear Admiral J. L. Kauffman embarked to establish his temporary headquarters in *Wasatch* as Commander, Philippine Sea Frontier, from 29 November to 2 December.

While *Wasatch* was in San Pedro Bay, enemy nuisance air attacks kept all hands constantly on the alert. On 6 January 1945, escorted by *Smith* (DD–378), *Wasatch* got underway for Lingayen Gulf, Luzon. Japanese suicide aircraft materialized off the coast near Manila; and, as she had done earlier, *Wasatch* put up a heavy barrage of antiaircraft fire from every gun in her battery from 20-millimeter to 5-inch. Japanese kamikazes and suicide motorboats flung themselves at the American ships; but, in three days, the fury had largely spent itself.

As American troops consolidated their beachhead at Lingayen, *Wasatch*, in company with *Kimberly* (DE–521), departed the area on 27 January, bound for Mindoro where she anchored at 0530 on the 29th. Vice Admiral Kinkaid shifted his flag ashore on 4 February, leaving the command ship temporarily bereft of an embarked flag officer. Rear Admiral Fechteler—who had been the first flag officer who utilized *Wasatch* as his headquarters—again hoisted flag in the AGC from 7 to 16 March. Then, Rear Admiral Arthur G. Noble broke his flag in her on the 22d.

Wasatch weighed anchor on 31 March, in company with USCGC *Campbell* (WAGC–5), *Newman* (APD–59), and *Cofer* (APD–62) and departed Leyte Gulf for Mindoro. On 11 April, Rear Admiral Noble directed a mock landing before directing the "real thing" six days later, as American forces went ashore on sparsely garrisoned Mindanao, while *Wasatch* stood by at anchor in Polluc Harbor, from the 17th.

Rear Admiral Noble shifted to *Spencer* on 1 May for landings in southern Mindanao and later used *Wasatch* as his base when he travelled to and from Manila on important conferences through the end of the month. Shifting to Morotai, the scene of the ship's baptism of fire, *Wasatch* took part in the staging operations which led to the landings on North Borneo. On 26 June, the command ship, with Rear Admiral Noble embarked, cleared Morotai; and she arrived off the target beachhead on 1 July. While General Douglas MacArthur observed from *Cleveland* (CL–55) and Rear Admiral Barbey watched from *Phoenix* (CL–43), the first wave of Australian troops splashed ashore to encounter light opposition.

Wasatch subsequently returned to Morotai, where Admiral Noble shifted his flag to *Spencer* on 3 July. Shifting to Humboldt Bay once more, and then to Seeadler Harbor, Manus, in the Admiralties, *Wasatch* was undergoing general repairs and an overhaul when she received word on 15 August of Japan's surrender.

After VJ-day, *Wasatch* took part in the occupation of Wakayama and Nagoya, Japan, and Taku, China, into the fall of 1945. Underway from Taku on 7 November 1945, the AGC sailed for the United States, via Pearl Harbor, and arrived at San Francisco on 10 December 1945.

Decommissioned at San Diego, Calif., on 30 August 1946, *Wasatch* was placed in the San Diego group of the reserve fleet in April 1947. Struck from the Navy list on 1 January 1960, the ship was transferred to the Maritime Administration and sold for scrapping to the National Metal and Steel Corp., of Terminal Island, Calif.

Wasatch received two battle stars for her World War II service.

Washakie

A Shoshone chief of mixed Shosone and Umatilla blood. Born about 1804, Washakie died in 1900 and was noted for his friendship for the white man and for his valor as a warrior against tribal enemies, the Blackfoot and Crow. Later in life, he served as a scout for the United States Army during the campaigns against the Cheyenne, Sioux, Arapaho, Ute, and other hostile tribes. Fort Washakie, Wyo., bears his name and is his burial place.

(YTB–386: dp. 218; l. 100'0''; b. 25'0''; dr. 10'0''; s. 11 k. (tl.); cl. *Iwana*)

Washakie (YTB–386) was laid down on 13 October 1943 at Brooklyn, N.Y., by Ira S. Bushey & Sons as YT–386; launched on 13 February 1944; reclassified a large harbor tug and redesignated YTB–386 on 15 May 1944; delivered to the Navy on 30 June 1944; and placed in service on 1 July 1944.

The tug steamed from New York, transited the Panama Canal, and served the Service Force, Pacific Fleet, for the duration of World War II. During the last year of hostilities, she served at various forward bases in the Central Pacific but finally ended up at Okinawa. She remained active at Okinawa even after the Japanese capitulation in mid-August 1945. When a typhoon struck Okinawa in October, *Washakie* was one of several ships grounded or otherwise damaged by the storm. As a result of that damage, she was placed out of service on 16 October 1945. Soon refloated, she was returned to the United States sometime in November and, after completing inactivation overhaul, was placed in reserve with the San Diego Group, Pacific Reserve Fleet.

In May 1953, *Washakie* came out of reserve, retransited the Panama Canal, and reported for duty at Mayport, Fla. There she remained for the next 22 years, serving under the auspices of the Commandant, 6th Naval District. In February 1962, she was reclassified a medium harbor tug and received the new designation YTM–386. Apparently, she was placed out of service and her name struck from the Navy list sometime between 1 October 1975 and 1 January 1976, for her name appears in the *Naval Vessel Register* for 1975 but not in that for 1976. Presumably, she was sold.

Washakie received one battle star for World War II service.

Washburn

A county in northwestern Wisconsin.

(AKA–108: dp. 13,910 (tl.); l. 459'2''; b. 63'0''; dr. 26'4'' (lim.); s. 16.5 k. (tl.); cpl. 425; a. 1 5'', 8 40mm., 16 20mm.; cl. *Tolland*; T. C2–S–AJ3)

Washburn (AKA–108) was laid down on 24 October 1944 at Wilmington, N.C., by the North Carolina Shipbuilding Co. under a Maritime Commission contract (MC hull 1801); launched on 18 December 1944; sponsored by Maj. K. A. Towle, USMCR; delivered to the Navy in an incomplete state on 30 December 1944; and completed at the Todd-Hoboken shipyard at Hoboken, N.J., where she was commissioned on 17 May 1945, Comdr. W. C. Jackson, USNR, in command.

Following two weeks of shakedown training in the Virginia capes area, *Washburn* departed Norfolk, Va., en route to the Mediterranean coast of France. She arrived in Marseille on the 26th and began loading Army troops and supplies bound for the Philippines. She stood out of Marseille on 11 July and arrived in Manila on 24 August, nine days after the cessation of hostilities. With the war ended, the attack cargo ship unloaded her passengers and cargo at Manila and began service in support of the occupation of former Japanese holdings in the Far East. She moved to Lingayen in northern Luzon to load soldiers of the 6th Army's 33d Division for transportation to the Japanese home islands and occupation duty. She departed the Philippines soon thereafter and arrived at Wakayama on the island of Honshu, Japan, and disembarked her passengers.

For the remainder of the year, the cargo ship carried passengers and equipment between various locales in the western Pacific in continued support of the American occupation. From January to March 1946, she conducted amphibious and fleet training in the eastern Pacific before returning to the Far East to resume her support missions for the occupation forces. In April, *Washburn* headed back east to resume her training schedule. That employment—broken only by a voyage to Alaskan waters in July 1948 for a resupply mission —lasted until November 1948.

At that point, the ship returned to the Orient once more for almost a year of duty in support of the occupation forces. During that time, she visited Okinawa, Iwo Jima, Pearl Harbor, and Tsingtao in China. During the fall of 1949, she returned to the west coast to participate in Operation "Miki," a large-scale, joint-service exercise staged out of Puget Sound, Wash., which simulated the invasion and defense of the Hawaiian Islands.

In February 1950, she transited the Panama Canal to return to the Atlantic for the first time since her maiden voyage. She participated in Operation "Portrex," an Atlantic Fleet Amphibious Forces assault exercise held at a small island near Puerto Rico. After a liberty call at San Juan, Puerto Rico, at the operation's conclusion, she retransited the Panama Canal and resumed duty with the Pacific Fleet.

That summer, the outbreak of hostilities in Korea called her back to the Far East. Following a resupply mission to Point Barrow, Alaska, *Washburn* turned west toward Japan; and, for about 18 months, she plied the waters between Japan and Korea keeping the flow of supplies and reinforcements to bolster the United Nations forces. She participated in the Inchon and Wonsan landings in September and, afterward, resumed her supply and reinforcement shuttles. In June of 1951, she returned to the role for which she was designated by participating in the diversionary landings staged at Kangmung, Korea. After a resumption of Japan-to-Korea runs, which she conducted from July to November, she headed back to the United States, arriving on the west coast on 16 December 1951. Eastern Pacific operations, including another resupply run to Point Barrow in Alaska during June of 1952, occupied her time until the spring of 1953. In March, she again voyaged to the Far East, visiting Nagoya and Sasebo in

USS *Washburn* (AKA-108), 1968.

Japan and Pusan and Inchon in Korea. She stopped at the latter port during her participation in Operation "Big Switch," the mutual repatriation of prisoners of war at the end of the Korean conflict. In October, *Washburn* returned to the United States and resumed west coast operations.

In October 1954, the attack cargo ship set out upon an eight-month deployment to the Orient. She stopped at many already familiar ports—Nagoya, Sasebo, Pusan, Inchon, and Okinawa—and added some new ones to her itinerary—Yokosuka in Japan, Subic Bay in the Philippines, the island of Taiwan, and, most notably, the Tachen Islands. The last-named group of islands came into her sphere of operations because of their proximity to mainland China and the consequent communist threat to their Nationalist Chinese populations and garrisons. Early in February 1955, *Washburn* and the other ships of Rear Admiral Sabin's Amphibious Evacuation Force, TF 76, brought 15,627 civilians and 11,120 military men as well as 8,630 tons of equipment, 166 artillery pieces, and 128 vehicles out of the Tachens to Taiwan while the carriers of TF 77 and the gun ships of TF 75 stood guard.

For almost another decade, *Washburn* continued alternating western Pacific deployments of varying length with normal operations along the west coast. Periodically, crises occurred and took her to some of the world's trouble spots. In January 1962, she showed up at Na-

tionalist Chinese-held offshore islands once again in support of naval forces sent there as a show of force in response to communist Chinese shelling of Quemoy and Matsu islands. By the following fall, she found herself halfway around the world in the West Indies supporting the Navy's quarantine of Cuba called by President Kennedy to rid that island of offensive Russian missiles. Otherwise, the decade between 1955 and 1965 proved relatively normal, made up of the usual resupply voyages, amphibious and fleet exercises, port visits, and ever-recurring overhauls.

Near the end of 1964, however, the attack cargo ship entered a geographic region that dominated her western Pacific deployments for the remainder of her career —Vietnam. In December of that year, she began hauling supplies and equipment there for use by the South Vietnamese government in its struggle with communist insurgents. Thereafter, she cruised off the coast with marines embarked as part of a contingency force. That duty lasted until 8 March 1965 when she landed troops near Danang. She returned to amphibious operations in mid-April, landing reinforcements for the defense of the airfield near Danang and Phu Bai in the so-called Hue landings, and again early in May when three battalion landing teams (BLT's) and a mobile construction battalion went ashore near Chu Lai to extend the perimeter and construct an airfield. She departed the Vietnamese coast at the end of May for more routine

7th Fleet duties but returned for one more brief tour of duty in the combat zone before heading home early in September.

Almost a year later, in August 1966, the attack cargo ship returned to the Far East and, late in September, to Vietnamese waters. Her duty again consisted of transporting troops and supplies to, from, and between points in Vietnam. Each month, from September 1966 to February 1967, brought duty off the coast of Vietnam. Between each tour in the combat zone, she visited ports elsewhere in the Orient, calling frequently at places in Japan, on Okinawa, and in the Philippines.

Early in February 1967, she completed her last mission in the combat zone and headed home. Steaming via Okinawa and Yokosuka, Japan, she arrived in San Diego on 15 March. She conducted normal operations until the end of July when she entered the Todd Shipyard at Seattle, Wash., for a three-month overhaul. Washburn returned to San Diego on 2 November and began refresher training on the 20th.

Early in 1968, she headed back to the Far East and, by late February, returned to the coast of Vietnam. During her 1968 deployment, Washburn spent four extended tours of duty off Vietnam again carrying troops and supplies to and from operational areas throughout the southern half of the country.

That fall, she resumed normal operations out of San Diego; but, late the following spring, she headed back to the western Pacific. From May to October, the ship cruised the coast of Vietnam, departing periodically to transport marines to Okinawa, to make liberty calls at various ports in the Far East, and to replenish in Japan and in the Philippines. She finished the last of four tours in the combat zone on 3 October and, after stopping at Okinawa to participate in an amphibious exercise, headed back to the United States on 9 October.

She arrived in San Diego on 26 October and resumed local operations. That employment continued until 16 May 1970 at which time she was decommissioned. Soon thereafter, Washburn was placed in the National Defense Reserve Fleet at Suisun Bay, Calif. On 1 September 1971, she was transferred permanently to the custody of the Maritime Administration. On 1 October 1976, Washburn's name was struck from the Navy list, and she was sold for scrapping.

Washburn earned five battle stars during the Korean War and six battle stars for Vietnam service.

Washington

Washington, the 42d state, was admitted to the Union on 11 November 1889. The first six Washingtons were named for George Washington; the seventh and eighth, for Washington state. See General Washington, Vol. III, page 65, for biography.

I

(Brigantine: t. 160; cpl. 74; a. 6 6-pdrs., 4 4-pdrs., 10 swivels)

The first Washington—while never part of the Continental Navy—was a 160-ton schooner named Endeavor acquired by General George Washington in early October of 1775 from George Erving and Capt. Benjamin Wormwell of Plymouth, Mass. Renamed Washington, the schooner was fitted out at Plymouth and was re-rigged as a brigantine at the behest of her prospective commanding officer, a Continental Army officer from Rhode Island, Capt. Sion Martindale. On 3 November 1775, Washington's charter was consummated, and she was authorized to operate off the New England coast between Cape Cod and Cape Ann in the hope of disrupting British shipping.

Washington sailed in company with the schooner Harrison on 23 November. No more than three leagues from shore, both Continental ships came across the British frigate HMS Tartar and two forage-laden transports. The British ships scared off and separated Washington and Harrison and chased the former until well after nightfall.

Although Washington spent most of 25 November looking for Harrison, she did not find her. Soon thereafter, she captured the provision-laden, 80-ton sloop Britannia and turned her over to Continental authorities before returning to sea on the 28th. However, stormy weather and a poorly disciplined crew caused Washington to head back to port the next day. Back at Plymouth, it was ascertained that some of the men's grumblings had been occasioned by their contention that they had enlisted to serve in the army—not as sailors. Moreover, a lack of winter clothing demoralized the crew. They were quickly supplied with suitable winter outfits, and the ship returned to sea on Sunday, 3 December 1775. Late the next day, the British 6th rate, 20-gun frigate HMS Fowey, cruising Massachusetts Bay on the lookout for "rebel cruisers," in company with HMS Lively, sighted Washington and gave chase.

Just before nightfall, Fowey reached gun range and fired a warning shot. Seven subsequent rounds brought the brigantine to, and she lowered her colors. Taken to Boston, Washington, upon inspection by the Royal Navy, was deemed unsuitable for operations on the high seas; she eventually rotted away at Boston.

II

(Gy: cpl. 60; a. 1 18-pdr.)

In the autumn of 1775, the Rhode Island General Assembly ordered the construction of two row galleys, Washington and Spitfire, and in January 1776 appointed John Grimes commodore of galleys. During the winter and spring of 1776, these galleys operated in Narragansett Bay, protecting the colony's shipping, carrying troops, and covering foraging parties seeking supplies.

In July, the galleys were sent to New York to join the tiny flotilla George Washington was fitting out on the Hudson River and apparently came under Continental control. On the afternoon of 3 August, Washington served as flagship for Lt. Col. Benjamin Tupper as that officer led an attack on the Royal Navy's warships Phoenix and Rose. As the galleys approached, Phoenix opened fire on the American boats to begin an action at grapeshot range which lasted some two hours before the Americans retired to Dobb's Ferry.

During the engagement, four Americans were killed, and 14 others were wounded. On the British side, Phoenix was hulled twice and suffered substantial damage.

After the British captured Manhattan Island late in the summer, Washington and her sister galleys vanished in the mists of unrecorded history.

The 32-gun frigate Washington—one of the 13 authorized by the Continental Congress on 13 December 1775—was built above Philadelphia, Pa., by Manuel, Jehu, and Benjamin Eyre. Launched on 7 August 1776, the ship lay under construction into the following year. However, the British occupied Philadelphia on 26 September 1777 forcing the local Continental forces to strip and sink Washington on 2 November 1777 to prevent her falling into enemy hands intact.

Although the still-incomplete frigate was apparently raised by the spring of 1778, she was never completed. On 7 May 1778, both Washington and Effingham were destroyed, by fire, where they lay, below Bordentown, N.J. Washington's remains were later salvaged and sold at Philadelphia.

III

(Gy: t. 123; l. 72'4"; b. 19'7"; dph. 6'2"; cpl. 80; a. 8–10 guns)

The third Washington—a lateen-rigged, two-masted galley—was built on Lake Champlain at Skenesboro,

N.Y., in the autumn of 1776. On 6 October 1776, the galley joined the small fleet established and commanded by Brigadier General Benedict Arnold.

Washington—commanded by Brigadier General David Waterbury, Arnold's second in command—was among Arnold's ships that anchored in the lee of Valcour Island to await the expected English move. When that lakeward push began, Capt. Thomas Pringle, RN, led a 25-ship fleet past Valcour Island on 11 October. Pringle sighted the American fleet after he had passed it and attacked from leeward. In the ensuing action, *Washington* suffered the heaviest damage of any ship in Arnold's fleet; Waterbury, her commander, subsequently reported that she was ". . . so torn to pieces that it was almost impossible to keep her above water."

Arnold regrouped his shattered fleet and slipped past the British on 12 October with muffled oars, the Americans slipping noiselessly past Pringle's fleet in a desperate attempt at escape. However, after a long chase, the British caught the retreating Continental force the following day, on 13 October, at Split Rock near Crown Point.

Arnold managed to beach and destroy four of the galleys and his own flagship, *Congress*, while most of the remaining ships escaped upriver. Only *Washington* —at the rear of the van—was captured by the enemy; she struck her colors, as Arnold reported later, ". . . after receiving a few broadsides."

Washington was eventually taken into British service, apparently retaining her name, and was re-rigged as a brig. Her subsequent fate, however, is unrecorded.

IV

(SL: t. 750; lbp. 190'10''; b. 54'7½''; dph. 19'9''; dr. 24'4''; cpl. 750; a. 74 guns)

The fourth *Washington*—a 74-gun ship-of-the-line— was authorized by Congress on 2 January 1813 and was laid down in May of that year at the Portsmouth (N.H.) Navy Yard under a contract with the shipbuilders, Hartt and Badger. The ship was launched on 1 October 1814 and was commissioned at Portsmouth on 26 August 1815, Capt. John O. Creighton in command.

After fitting out, *Washington* sailed for Boston on 3 December 1815. In the spring of the following year, the ship-of-the-line shifted to Annapolis, Md., and arrived there on 15 May 1816. Over the ensuing days, the man-of-war welcomed a number of distinguished visitors who came on board to inspect what was, in those days, one of the more powerful ships afloat. The guests included Commodore John Rodgers and Capt. David Porter; Col. Franklin Wharton, the Commandant of the Marine Corps; and President and Mrs. James Madison. The Chief Executive and his lady came on board "at half past meridian, to visit the ship, on which occasion yards were manned and they were saluted with 19 guns and three cheers."

Washington then sailed down Chesapeake Bay and embarked William Pinckney and his "suite" on 5 June. On 8 June, the ship of the line set sail for the Mediterranean flying the broad pennant of Commodore

The ship-of-the-line *Washington* in the Bay of Naples as Commodore Chauncey's flagship, with his broad pendant flying at the main. This artist's rendition depicts *Washington* in an unusual color scheme, with a single white or yellow streak between the upper and lower gun decks.

Isaac Chauncey, the commander of the fledgling United States Navy's Mediterranean Squadron. *Washington* reached Gibraltar on 2 July, en route to her ultimate destination, Naples.

Washington made port at Naples on 25 July, and Pickney debarked to commence his special mission—to adjust the claims of American merchants against the Neapolitan authorities. The talks ensued well into August. At the end of the month, the demands of diplomacy apparently satisfied, *Washington* set sail.

For the next two years, the ship-of-the-line operated in the Mediterranean as flagship of the American squadron, providing a display of force to encourage the Barbary states to respect American commerce. Dignitaries that visited the American man-of-war during this Mediterranean cruise included General Nugent, the commander in chief of Austrian forces (on 5 August 1817) and Prince Henry of Prussia (on 12 August 1817).

On 1 February 1818, Commodore Charles Stewart relieved Commodore Chauncey as commander of the American Mediterranean Squadron, at Syracuse harbor, after which time *Washington* cruised to Messina and the Barbary Coast. She set sail for home on 23 May 1818—convoying 40 American merchantmen—and reached New York on 6 July 1818. The next day, the Vice President of the United States, Daniel D. Tompkins, visited the ship; and the warship blocked her colors at half-mast on the 8th, in honor of the interment of the remains of General Richard Montgomery, who had been killed leading the Continental assault against Quebec in 1775.

Washington did little cruising thereafter, remaining at New York as Commodore Chauncey's flagship until 1820. Placed "in ordinary" that year, the ship-of-the-line remained inactive until broken up in 1843.

V

(RC: a. 4 12-pdrs.)

The fifth *Washington*—a revenue cutter completed at New York in 1833—initially operated out of Mobile, Ala. She shifted to Key West, Fla., as her base of operations and spent a brief period of time at Charleston, S.C., undergoing repairs, before returning to Key West on 20 May 1835 and remaining based there for the remainder of the year.

Around Chirstmas of 1835, two companies of regular Army troops under the command of Major Francis L. Dade, USA, were massacred by Seminole Indians. One badly wounded survivor managed to make a difficult 60-mile trek to the head of Tampa Bay, where he reported the disaster to the garrison commander at Fort Brooke, Fla., Capt. Francis S. Belton, USA. Fearing for the safety of his post, Belton immediately dispatched a request for reinforcements via the sloop *Motto*.

Belton's message reached Key West early in January. Meanwhile in the Federal capital, Levi Woodbury, the Secretary of the Treasury—who had also heard of Dade's disaster—directed Capt. Ezekiel Jones, commanding *Washington*, to place his ship under Navy control "until otherwise directed." Interestingly enough, Jones did not receive this order—issued on 6 January 1836—until he had already begun operations in cooperation with the Army and Navy.

Word of the massacre reached Jones on or about 11 January. *Washington* soon got underway and proceeded via Tampa Bay to Charlotte Harbor and arrived at Fort Brooke on 25 January. At 1700 that afternoon, the revenue cutter landed a pair of 12-pounder guns—with sufficient powder and shot for 35 rounds—along with 10 seamen under the command of Lt. L. B. Childs and a Lieutenant Clark, to cooperate with the Army garrison troops. Belton, expecting an imminent attack by the Seminoles, took the precaution of ordering noncombatants—mostly women and children—to take refuge on board the merchant ships in the harbor.

Washington, meanwhile, lay to with springs to her anchors and her decks cleared for battle. At that juncture, the sloop-of-war *Vandalia*, Master Commandant Thomas T. Webb, USN, in command, sailed from Pensacola escorting a small merchantman carrying a detachment of 57 marines under 1st Lt. Nathaniel S. Waldron, USMC. *Vandalia* and her mercantile consort reached Fort Brooke on 28 January.

With the arrival of *Vandalia* and Waldron's marines, *Washington* withdrew her landing force from the beach on 1 February. Three days later, the revenue cutter received orders to reconnoiter Charlotte Harbor, south of Tampa Bay; got underway on the 5th, and arrived at her assigned destination on the 8th.

Under the command of Lt. Childs, a party of 13 men in two boats landed at 0800 on the island of Sanibel in search of Seminole dependents reported there. Finding none, however, they withdrew but sighted three canoes and 10 men on the opposite shore at 1500 that day. Going ashore again on the 10th, *Washington*'s landing force ascertained that the 10 men and three canoes had been in the employ of a local friendly Spaniard that lived in the vicinity.

After the men returned to the ship, *Washington* shifted back to her previous anchorage near Fort Brooke, reaching there on 13 February. At 1230, men in the revenue cutter heard the reports of heavy guns to the southeast side of the bay and spotted two canoes full of Indians "who appeared to be retreating from the scene of action." *Washington* made sail and gave chase, firing a 12-pounder loaded with round shot. Anchoring at 1230, *Washington* dispatched all of her boats, with crews, to overtake the Indians, who eventually hove to under the threats of superior force. They turned out to be friendly, though, and were allowed to go on their way.

Capt. Jones brought *Washington* back to Key West on 19 February to repair his ship. Such were the vagaries of long-distance communication that Jones only then received Secretary Woodbury's instructions of 6 January. The following day, Jones reported to the Secretary, "I have been cooperating since January 11th, having half my battery and crew on shore at Fort Brook (sic) a part of the time and have rendered such service as the emergency of the case required. I shall sail again for Tampa as soon as I can effect some necessary repairs."

On 16 March, Master Commandant Webb, the local senior officer present, afloat, directed *Washington* to reconnoiter a reported Indian encampment in the neighborhood of the Manatee River. Late in the afternoon of that same day, 16 March, Jones landed a force of 25 men under the command of Lt. William Smith, USN, of *Vandalia*. By nightfall, the men had located the site of an encampment but found neither Indians nor cattle. Returning on board that evening, *Washington* again put the landing force on the beach on the morning of the 17th. With competent Indian guides, the party followed a fresh Indian and cattle trail 10 miles into the interior before they returned to the ship, again empty-handed.

Almost simultaneously, Seminole forces were reported to be in retreat in boats down the Pease River. Webb ordered *Washington* to Charlotte Harbor to blockade the river "so as to cut off most effectually all retreat to or communication with the glades of the south."

Sailing to that locale, *Washington* examined St. Joseph's Bay, Costa Islands, Mullett Key, and sundry other places in and about Tampa Bay. She also examined Charlotte Harbor and Charlotte Bay, together with the neighboring keys and inlets. On 28 and 29 March, a boat expedition in the charge of Lt. Smith saw an Indian encampment some 30 miles from the mouth of Tampa Bay. Hoping to learn the whereabouts of "hostiles," Smith and his two friendly Indian guides landed and invited a parley. Smith and his guides returned to the ship safely with no information as to any local Seminole strongholds in the area.

Washington, her sister revenue cutters *Dallas* and *Dexter*, and the sloop-of-war *Vandalia* continued to perform valuable services in cooperation with Army units against the Seminoles, on patrol duties into the spring of 1836. *Washington* subsequently sailed for Sarasota, Fla., and arrived there on 11 May, anchoring at the mouth of the bay. She dispatched a cutter—in charge of Lt. Childs—and brought out two Spaniards and about 20 women and children, all fleeing from hostile Seminoles in that area.

Washington and *Dallas* subsequently cruised off the coast of Florida in the Gulf of Mexico during most of June. *Washington* later carried dispatches from Governor Call to Master Commandant M. P. Mix in *Concord*—the ship that had relieved *Vandalia*—in early July, before she transported a company of Army volunteers from Pensacola to St. Marks. She also surveyed the rivers, inlets, and bars along that stretch of the Florida seaboard.

After operating in Pensacola Bay and Tampa Bay during most of August and September, *Washington* accompanied *Vandalia* from Pensacola to Key West, departing on 2 October 1836 for Cape Florida and New River. Their mission was to surprise and, if possible, to capture some 200 Seminoles—braves, women, and children.

Embarked in *Washington*—now commanded by Capt. Robert Day, United States Revenue Marine—were 50 seamen under the command of Lt. Smith and four midshipmen, as well as 95 marines under the command of Lt. Waldron and 2d Lt. McNeill. To carry this expeditionary force, six boats and two schooners were employed with *Washington* and *Vandalia* to carry the force. Sent to Tampa Bay on 4 November after the expedition had gotten underway, *Washington* delivered provisions from Tampa Bay to Cape Sable on 15 November. The revenue cutter subsequently sailed for Key West, arriving on 8 December.

A party of men from *Washington*, under the command of the indefatigable Lt. Levin M. Powell, USN—the man who conceived of vigorous riverine warfare concepts—surveyed the coast around New River from Cape Sable to Charlotte Harbor and, while he penetrated 15 miles into the trackless Everglades, found no Indians during their trip. Commodore Alexander Dallas, in overall command of the naval forces operating in the Seminole War, highly commended Powell and his men, citing their "perseverance and exertions under circumstances of privation and exposure . . . in open boats."

Eventually, by the spring of 1837, the pace of operations began to tell upon *Washington*, and she was released by Commodore Dallas to receive extensive repairs at Key West, Fla. Although ordered to Norfolk and, later, to Baltimore, on 22 May 1837, *Washington* apparently remained in southern waters, eventually returning to her original duty station, Mobile, Ala., where she was sold on 26 June 1837.

VI

(RC: a. 10 guns)

The sixth *Washington*—a revenue cutter of unknown dimensions—was the second cutter of that name to serve the Navy. Authorized on 6 July and named on 1 August of 1837, *Washington* was apparently built quickly, as orders were issued on 11 November for the ship to conduct "winter cruising" off the eastern seaboard between New York and the Virginia capes. She sailed on 18 December on her first cruise. In ensuing years, the ship cruised that stretch of sea in the winters and conducted sounding and surveying operations off the coast in the summers of 1838 and 1839. She was rerigged from a schooner to a brig during that period—apparently at Baltimore, Md.

While sounding between Gardiner's Point and Montauk Point, N.Y., in the summer of 1839, the cutter encountered evidence of a grim event at sea. On 26 August, *Washington* sighted a "suspicious-looking vessel" at anchor. The brig's commander, Lt. Thomas R. Gedney, USN, sent an armed party to board the craft.

The men found the suspicious ship to be the schooner *Armistad*, of and from Havana, Cuba. She had set sail from the coast of Africa two months or so before, carrying two white passengers and 54 slaves, bound for Guanaja, Cuba. Four days out of port, the slaves rose and murdered the captain and his crew, saving the two passengers to navigate the ship back to Africa. During the next two months, in which *Armistad* had drifted at sea, nine of the slaves had died.

Washington apparently never encountered a similar event again. She was transferred to the Coast Survey—the forerunner of today's National Oceanic and Atmospheric Administration—on 23 April 1840. For the next 12 years, the brig operated under the aegis of the Navy, off the eastern seaboard of the United States on surveying and sounding duties. All was not entirely tranquil, however, for there were storms to be contended with. While stationed in Chesapeake Bay in 1846, *Washington* was dismasted in a severe gale. Battered and worn but still afloat, the cutter limped to port. She had lost 11 men overboard in the tempest, including Lt. George M. Bache, the ship's commanding officer.

When the United States went to war in Mexico, *Washington* served with Commodore Matthew C. Perry's forces. Under the command of Lt. Comdr. S. P. Lee, *Washington* took part in the capture of Tobasco on 16 June 1847 and contributed six officers and 30 men to a force under the comand of Capt. S. L. Breese that formed part of the 1,173-man landing force that attacked and captured the Mexican stronghold at Tuxpan.

Returned to the Treasury Department on 18 May 1852, *Washington* underwent extensive repairs at New York which lasted into the early winter. Alterations were completed on 9 December 1852, but *Washington* remained in the New York area where she operated locally for the next six years. The cutter participated in the search for the foundering steamer *San Francisco* in the second week of January 1854. *Washington*, along with five other revenue cutters, sailed almost simultaneously from their home ports—ranging from New London, Conn., to Wilmington, Del., and from Norfolk to New York; but, unfortunately, none of the ships fell in with *San Francisco*.

Ordered to the Gulf of Mexico in the spring of 1859 to relieve *Robert McClelland*, *Washington* apparently arrived at Southwest Pass, La., soon thereafter. She apparently remained there into 1861; and—although slated to be relieved, in turn, by *Robert McClelland*—the outbreak of the War Between the States caught the brig at New Orleans where she was taken over by authorities of Louisiana soon after that state seceded from the Union on 31 January 1861. Little is known of the ship thereafter. In June 1861, Comdr. David Dixon Porter reported that the ship was being fitted out at New Orleans and was almost ready for sea, but no clues to the ship's subsequent career thereafter have been found.

VII

(Armored Cruiser No. 11: dp. 15,712; l. 504'5''; b. 72'10''; dr. 25'0''; s. 22.0 k.; cpl. 887; a. 4 10'', 16 6'', 22 3'', 12 3-pdrs., 2 1-pdrs., 4 18'' tt.; cl. *Tennessee*)

The seventh *Washington* (Armored Cruiser No. 11) was laid down on 23 September 1903 at Camden, N.J., by the New York Shipbuilding Co.; launched on 18 March 1905; sponsored by Miss Helen Stewart Wilson, daughter of United States Senator John L. Wilson of Washington state; and commissioned at the Philadelphia Navy Yard on 7 August 1906, Capt. James D. Adams in command.

Washington was fitted out there until 1 November when she got underway for Hampton Roads, Va., whence she departed a week later as an escort for *Louisiana* (Battleship No. 19) which was then carrying President Theodore Roosevelt to Panama for an inspection of progress of work constructing the Panama Canal. During that voyage, the armored cruiser touched at Hampton Roads and Piney Point, Va.; Colon, Panama; Chiriqui lagoon; and Mona Passage before she returned to Newport News on 26 November. She headed back toward the Delaware capes on 8 December, arrived at the Philadelphia Navy Yard on the 11th, and remained there undergoing repairs into the spring of 1907.

Washington departed League Island on 11 April and arrived at Hampton Roads the next day. She remained there into May participating in festivities of the Jamestown Tercentenary Exposition which commemorated the founding of Jamestown in 1607, the first permanent settlement of Anglo-Saxon people in America. She returned northward soon thereafter, spending most of May undergoing docking and tests at the New York Navy Yard. She then shook down off Tompkinsville, Staten Island, N.Y., from 28 May to 5 June before she returned to Hampton Roads for further observances at the Jamestown Exposition.

Washington departed Hampton Roads on 11 June and proceeded via Bradford, R.I., to Newport where she joined *Tennessee* (Armored Cruiser No. 10) before heading across the Atlantic on the 14th, bound for European waters. The sisterships visited the French ports of Royan, Ile d'Aix, La Pallice, and Brest between 23 June and 25 July, before returning to Tompkinsville in August to run speed trials.

Following those trials and a period of yard work at the New York Navy Yard, *Washington* set sail for the Pacific Station, again in company with *Tennessee*. The two armored cruisers subsequently called at Hampton Roads; Port-of-Spain, Trinidad; British West Indies; Rio de Janeiro, Brazil; Montevideo, Uruguay; Punta Arenas, Chile; Callao, Peru; Acapulco, Mexico; and Pichilinque Bay, Mexico; before they joined the Pacific Fleet in time to fire target practices with them at Magdalena Bay, Mexico, from late December 1907 into January 1908. *Washington* subsequently operated both in company with the Fleet and on independent tactical exercises out of Magdalena Bay into March, operating also off Santa Barbara, San Francisco, and San Diego, as well as San Pedro, Calif. Other ports visited by the

armored cruiser into the summer of 1908 included Redondo Beach, Venice, Monterey, Angel Island, Calif.; and Port Townsend, Port Angeles, Seattle, Tacoma, and Bremerton, Wash. She was among the units of the Fleet reviewed by the Secretary of the Navy at San Francisco between 6 and 17 May.

Washington operated off the west coast into 1909 before she made preparations to sail in company with the Armored Cruiser Squadron to "show the flag" in the Far East. She accordingly got underway from San Francisco on 5 September 1909 and called, in succession, at Honolulu, Hawaii, from 10 to 20 September; and Nares Harbor, Admiralty Islands—where she coaled ship between 17 and 25 October—before she arrived at Manila, Philippine Islands, on 30 October.

After visiting Woosung (near Shanghai), China, from 14 to 30 December 1909, *Washington* and her sisters called at Yokohama, Japan, from 3 to 20 January 1910, and Honolulu from 31 January to 8 February, before returning to the west coast. *Washington* made port back at San Francisco via Port Discovery and Bremerton, Wash., on 3 March. She then returned to Bremerton where she commenced a period of repairs on 21 March.

Washington next operated off the west coast into the autumn of 1910, holding target practices off Santa Cruz, Calif., before returning to San Francisco. She coaled ship at Tiburon, Calif., on 7 and 8 August before shifting to San Francisco to prepare for her next deployment. On 14 August, she departed San Francisco, bound for South America on the first leg of her voyage to the east coast to join the Atlantic Fleet. With the ships of the 1st Division of the Pacific Fleet, *Washington* visited Valparaiso, Chile, and took part in the observances of the Chilean Centennial Celebration from 10 to 23 September. She then resumed her voyage around South America, touching at Talcahuano and Punta Arenas, Chile; Rio de Janeiro; Carlisle Bay, Barbados; and St. Thomas, Danish West Indies; before she arrived at Culebra, Puerto Rico, on 2 November to prepare for target practice with the Fleet.

Washington's next area of operations was the Tidewater area of Virginia—especially Hampton Roads and Lynnhaven Bay—before the armored cruiser underwent repairs at the Norfolk Navy Yard from 20 December 1910 to 2 January 1911. The armored cruiser subsequently underwent another period of repairs at the Portsmouth (N.H.) Navy Yard before heading south with stores and material for delivery to the 5th

Washington (Armored Cruiser No. 11) at Seattle in 1908, with the Olympic Mountains in the background. Her four tall stacks underscore the emphasis on speed in the design of the armored cruiser, predecessor of the battle cruiser of World War I. (NH 63652)

Division of the Fleet in Cuban waters. She arrived at Guantanamo Bay on 20 March and remained there into the summer, conducting trials and exercises with the 5th Division. She then returned northward and stopped at Hampton Roads from 21 to 24 June before pushing on to New York, where she arrived on the 25th.

The armored cruiser operated off the northeastern seaboard through the summer, holding exercises and maneuvers in areas ranging from Cape Cod Bay to Hampton Roads. During that time, she cruised briefly with the Naval Militia from 19 to 21 July 1911; acted as a reference ship for torpedo practice off Sandwich Island, Mass., on 2 August; witnessed the *Delaware* (Battleship No. 28) as that man-of-war fired at the target hulk *San Marcos* on 27 and 28 August; and then conducted battle practice with the Fleet off the southern drill grounds. In early November, *Washington* was among the ships of the Fleet reviewed by President William H. Taft.

The cruiser then participated in a search problem out of Newport, R.I., from 9 to 18 November before she sailed for the West Indies in company with *North Carolina* (Armored Cruiser No. 12), arriving at Santo Domingo, Dominican Republic, on 26 November. *Washington* subsequently returned home to Hampton Roads in company with her sistership and went into drydock at the Norfolk Navy Yard three days before Christmas of 1911.

After returning to the Fleet and participating in maneuvers in Guantanamo Bay, Cuba, in late January and early February 1912, *Washington* steamed back to the Norfolk Navy Yard where, between 13 and 19 February, she underwent special preparations to embark the Secretary of State and his party. The armored cruiser then shifted to Key West where she embarked the Secretary on 23 February. In the ensuing weeks, *Washington* carried the honorable Philander C. Knox and his guests to such ports as Colon, Panama; Port Limon, Costa Rica; Puerto Barrios, Guatemala; La Guaira, Venezuela; Santo Domingo; St. Thomas; Puerto Cabalo, Venezuela; San Juan; Port-au-Prince; Guantanamo Bay; Kingston, Jamaica; and Havana; before disembarking her distinguished guests at Piney Point, Md., on 16 April.

The high point of the spring of 1912 for *Washington* was her service as temporary flagship for the Commander in Chief, Atlantic Fleet, while she was at the Philadelphia Navy Yard between 19 April and 3 May. The warship subsequently paused at New York from 9 to 12 May and at the Portsmouth (N.H.) Navy Yard for an inspection by the Board of Inspection and Survey for ships before she conducted maneuvers out of Provincetown and Newport and then received Rear Admiral Hugo Osterhaus—the Commander in Chief, Atlantic Fleet—on board on 26 May. After shifting to Hampton Roads, *Washington* embarked a detachment of additional marines on 27 May; took on stores; and set out that day for Key West. There, she awaited further orders between 30 May and 10 June, while President Taft concentrated a strong naval force there to prepare for possible action which might be required by internal problems in Cuba.

In the late spring and early summer, a rebellion on that Caribbean island occasioned a show of force by the United States. *Washington* accordingly departed Key West on 10 June and arrived at Havana later that day. She remained there on "duty in connection with the Cuban rebellion" until 1 July when she shifted to Guantanamo. The rebellion on the island was put down by the Cuban Government, resulting in the withdrawal of the American naval and marine representation there. Accordingly, *Washington* sailed to Hampton Roads, where she discharged her marines and equipment and went into "first reserve" at the Portsmouth (N.H.) Navy Yard on 9 July.

She remained inactive until 8 October when she sailed for New York to participate in the naval review

held there between 10 and 15 October and then resumed her reserve status at Portsmouth on 17 October. Shifted subsequently from Portsmouth to the New York Navy Yard—via President Roads, Mass., and Tompkinsville, Staten Island—*Washington* was assigned duty as receiving ship at the navy yard on 20 July.

The armored cruiser was placed in commission again on 23 April 1914, Capt. Edward W. Eberle in command. Later that spring, the armored cruiser took on board drafts of men from Norfolk and Port Royal, S.C., on 30 May and 2 April; touched at Key West, Fla.; and proceeded to Santo Domingo.

Once again there was unrest in the Dominican Republic. A revolution in the northern province of Santiago, against the rule of Provisional President Jose Bordes Valdes, had been quelled; but one in the province of Puerto Plata—near the capital of Santo Domingo itself—continued unchecked and was marked by severe fighting—fighting so severe that "marked apprehension" existed in Washington.

On 1 May, the gunboat *Petrel* had been ordered to Dominican waters, but a further show of force seemed to be in order. Accordingly, *Washington* was chosen to "show the flag" in those troubled waters. She departed Key West on 4 May and arrived at the beleaguered city of Puerto Plata on 6 May to protect American interests, joining the gunboat *Petrel*. Six days later, Capt. Eberle invited representatives of both warring parties—the insurgents and the government—out to his ship, in an attempt to persuade both sides to come to an amicable settlement.

Unfortunately, the attempt failed, and the fighting continued. The insurgents were aided by a recent large consignment of guns and ammunition smuggled across the Haitian border that had given them new blood. The revolutionaries soon recaptured the key city of Le Vega and were successfully holding Puerto Plata. Government forces, laying siege to that port and shelling the insurgents, clearly endangered the lives of the neutral citizens still living in the city. Capt. Eberle objected to the bombardment and warned President Valdes repeatedly.

Washington departed Puerto Plata on 6 June with the conflict between the insurgents and the government of President Valdes still unresolved. Her place had been taken by *Machias* (Gunboat No. 5). *Washington* coaled ship and took on stores at Guantanamo Bay from 7 to 10 June before she sailed for Veracruz, Mexico. She then remained in Mexican waters between 14 and 24 June before she shifted to Cape Haitien, Haiti, to protect American interests there during an outbreak of violence that summer.

Washington remained at Cape Haitien into July. In the meantime, the situation in the Dominican Republic had worsened when government shellings of rebel positions in Puerto Plata resulted in an inevitable "incident." On 26 June, a stray shell killed an English woman in Puerto Plata causing the gunboat *Machias* to shift to a berth in the inner harbor and shell one of President Valdes' batteries, silencing it with a few well-placed shots. During early July, *Machias* again fired her guns in anger when stray shots hit the ship.

In view of those developments, *Washington* returned to Puerto Plata on 9 July and remained there into the autumn, keeping a vigil to protect American lives and property and standing by to land her landing force if the situation required it. That August, Capt. Eberle's attempts to bring about a conference finally bore fruit. The United States government sent a commission—consisting of J. F. Fort, the former governor of New Jersey; James M. Sullivan, the American Minister to Santo Domingo; and Charles Smith, a New Hampshire lawyer—to mediate a peace in the Dominican Republic.

Both sides ultimately accepted the American suggestions which provided for the establishment of a constitutional government and the institution of elections under United States "observation."

Washington left Santo Domingo on 20 November; but, later that month, continued high feelings over the closely contested election resulted in further unrest— unrest met by the dispatch of additional marines to Santo Domingo. For *Washington*, however, her part in the Dominican intervention of 1914 was over. She sailed for home and arrived at Philadelphia on 24 November and became flagship of the Cruiser Squadron.

Following an overhaul at the Portsmouth (N.H.) Navy Yard from 12 December 1914 to 11 January 1915, *Washington* sailed—via President Roads, Mass. (where she took on ammunition on 11 January)—for Hampton Roads, arriving there on 14 January. After a five-day visit, during which she took on stores and provisions and an expeditionary force of marines, *Washington* sailed for the Caribbean once more.

Two revolutions had rocked Haiti in 1914; a third, in January 1915, led by General Vilbrun Guillaume Sam, had resulted only in further unrest for that troubled nation. *Washington* arrived at Cape Haitien on 23 January, a week after General Sam's troops had invested it. The armored cruiser, flying the flag of Rear Admiral Caperton and commanded by Capt. Edward L. Beach— the father of the future naval officer who would win fame as a famous submariner and author—stayed in port there until the 26th, investigating "political conditions" before she shifted to the Haitian capital, Port-au-Prince, on 27 January. There, she again observed local political conditions in the wake of General Sam's takeover of the government before sailing via Guantanamo for Mexican waters.

Washington conducted sub-caliber practices, observed political conditions, and conducted torpedo practices off the ports of Tampico, Tuxpan, Progreso, and Veracruz into the summer. Receiving provisions and stores from the supply ship *Celtic* off Progreso on 26 and 27 June, the armored cruiser sailed for Guantanamo where she coaled and took on water on 30 June. She sailed the same day for Cape Haitien, as all reports from the American minister there indicated that yet another crisis was brewing.

While *Washington* awaited further developments at Cape Haitien, events in Port-au-Prince deteriorated, moving American Charge d'Affaire Davis to send a telegram on 27 July to the Secretary of State, Robert Lansing, reporting the troubled conditions. He reported that President Sam and some of his men had been surrounded in the presidential palace and that the presence of American war vessels was desirable.

In accordance with that message, the Navy dispatched *Washington* to that port. Meanwhile, Sam took refuge in the French legation where he hoped that diplomatic immunity would prevail. The mobs of angry Haitians, however, were not concerned with such international niceties: they invaded the legation at 1030 on 28 July 1915, forcibly removed former President Sam, killed and dismembered him, and paraded portions of his body on poles around the city.

Washington arrived at Port-au-Prince that day. Upon reviewing the situation, Admiral Caperton acted quickly. He ordered marines and a landing force ashore from his flagship to protect not only American interests but those of other foreign nations as well. *Washington* remained at Port-au-Prince into the winter. During that time, the United States effectively ran Haiti. On 12 August, Philippe Sudra Dartinguenave was elected president; and his government was recognized by the United States on 17 September 1915.

Ending that lengthy in-port period, *Washington* departed Port-au-Prince on 31 January 1916 and arrived at Guantanamo the following day. There, she transferred passengers and stores to other ships of the Fleet and later transferred a company of marines to Norfolk soon after her arrival in Hampton Roads on 5 February. The armored cruiser steamed north via New York and Boston; reached Portsmouth, N.H., on 29 February; and began an overhaul in the navy yard

there which lasted until the end of Mach. Then, on 31 March, she was placed in reserve.

On 9 November 1916, *Washington* was renamed *Seattle* (retaining her classification as Armored Cruiser No. 11). She was simultaneously taken out of reserve and recommissioned for duty as flagship of the Destroyer Force.

Seattle's peacetime duties as flagship for the Destroyer Force were short. On 6 April 1917, the United States, after attempting patiently but futilely to remain neutral, despite repeated incidents on the high seas, finally entered World War I.

Seattle arrived at New York on 3 June 1917 to be fitted out at the New York Navy Yard for war service. She sailed on 14 June as an escort for the first American convoy to European waters and as flagship for Rear Admiral Albert Gleaves. At 2215 on 22 June, she encountered her first enemy submarines in latitude 48–00 N, longitude 25–50 W.

Shortly before the convoy was attacked, *Seattle*'s helm jammed; and she sheered out of formation sharply, sounding her whistle to warn the other vessels. A few minutes later, the ship was brought back on course. Soon lookouts noted a white streak in the water 50 yards ahead of the vessel, crossing from starboard to port at right angles to *Seattle*'s course. Admiral Gleaves, asleep in the charthouse at the time, awoke and was on the bridge in time to see the armored cruiser's gun crews manning their weapons and the transport *De Kalb* opening fire on the U-boat.

Subsequently, the destroyer *Wilkes* (Destroyer No. 67) attacked an enemy submersible but failed to sink the German submarine. Later information indicated that the enemy, probably aware of the approach of the first American expeditionary forces, had dispatched a pair of submarines to lie in wait for it. The attack, conducted under "ideal" conditions, was, fortunately for the Americans, unsuccessful. Admiral Gleaves, in his report to the Commander in Chief, Atlantic Fleet, on 12 July 1917, reported unequivocally: "their [the enemy's] failure to score hits was probably due to the attack being precipitated by the fortuitous circumstances of the *Seattle*'s helm jamming and the sounding of her whistle, leading the enemy to suppose he had been discovered."

Seattle operated on comparatively uneventful escort duties for the remainder of World War I, completing her ninth round-trip voyage at New York on 27 October 1918. After the armistice of 11 November 1918, *Seattle*—like many other ships—was fitted with extra accommodations to enable her to function as a transport, and she brought back doughboys from France until 5 July 1919. Later, after all of her special troop fittings had been removed, *Seattle* sailed for the west coast to join the Pacific Fleet.

Reviewed by President Woodrow Wilson on 12 September at her namesake city—Seattle—the armored cruiser shifted to the Puget Sound Navy Yard where she was placed in "reduced commission." While in that inactive status, *Seattle* was reclassified a heavy cruiser, CA–11, on 17 July 1920.

Placed in full commission again on 1 March 1923, Capt. George L. P. Stone in command, *Seattle* became the flagship for the Commander in Chief, United States Fleet. In that role, over the next four years, she wore the four-starred flags of a succession of officers: Admiral Hilary P. Jones, Admiral Robert E. Koontz, Admiral Samuel S. Robison (who was embarked in the ship at the time of the Australian cruise of 1925), and Admiral Charles F. Hughes. During that time, the armored cruiser operated from Seattle to Hawaii and from Panama to Australia.

Subsequently returning to the Atlantic in June of 1927, *Seattle* passed in review before President Calvin Coolidge on 3 June 1927. After a cruise along the east coast, the ship arrived at New York on 29 August to assume duties as the receiving ship at that port. On

1 July 1931, the ship's designation was changed to "unclassified."

As receiving ship, *Seattle* served as a floating barracks—a "clearance house for personnel"—at New York into the 1940's. Ships and stations transferred men to her for attending various schools in the 3d Naval District; she provided men for tugs and other district craft, as well as naval escorts for patriotic functions (parades and funerals, etc.) and, on board her, crews for ships preparing to go into commission were assembled. Among those ships was the light cruiser *Honolulu* (CL–48).

On 17 February 1941, the erstwhile armored cruiser was reclassified as IX–39. She was ultimately placed out of commission at New York on 28 June 1946 and was struck from the Navy list on 19 July of the same year. Sold on 3 December 1946 to Hugo Neu, of New York City, the former flagship of the United States Fleet and receiving ship at New York was subsequently scrapped.

(Battleship No. 47: dp. 32,600; l. 624'0"; b. 97'6"; dr. 30'6"; s. 21 k.; cpl. 1,354; a. 8 16", 20 5", 8 3" (AA); cl. *Colorado*)

Washington (Battleship No. 47) was laid down on 30 June 1919 at Camden, N.J., by the New York Shipbuilding Corp.; reclassified BB–47 on 17 July 1920; launched on 1 September 1921; and sponsored by Miss Jean Summers, the daughter of Congressman J. W. Summers of Washington state. However, on 8 February 1922, two days after the signing of the Washington Treaty for the Limitation of Naval Armaments on 6 February 1922, all construction work ceased on the 75.9 percent completed dreadnought. Ultimately, her incompleted hulk was towed out to sea, where she was sunk as a gunnery target on 25 November 1924.

VIII

(BB–56: dp. 35,000; l. 729'; b. 108'; dr. 38'; s. 27 k.; cpl. 1,880; a. 9 16", 20 5", 16 1.1" mg.; cl. *North Carolina*)

The eighth *Washington* (BB–56) was laid down on 14 June 1938 at the Philadelphia Navy Yard; launched on 1 June 1940; sponsored by Miss Virginia Marshall, of Spokane, Wash., a direct descendant of former Chief Justice Marshall; and commissioned at the Philadelphia Navy Yard on 15 May 1941, Capt. Howard H. J. Benson in command.

Her shakedown and underway training ranged along the eastern seaboard and into the Gulf of Mexico and lasted through American entry into World War II in December 1941. Sometimes operating in company with her sistership *North Carolina* (BB–55) and the new aircraft carrier *Hornet* (CV–8), *Washington* became the flagship for Rear Admiral John W. Wilcox, Commander, Battleship Division (ComBatDiv) 6, and Commander, Battleships, Atlantic Fleet.

Assigned duty as flagship for Task Force (TF) 39 on 26 March 1942 at Portland, Maine, *Washington* again flew Admiral Wilcox' flag as she sailed for the British Isles that day. Slated to reinforce the British Home Fleet, the battleship, together with the carrier *Wasp* (CV–7) and the heavy cruisers *Wichita* (CA–45) and *Tuscaloosa* (CA–37), headed for Scapa Flow, the major British fleet base in the Orkney Islands.

While steaming through moderately heavy seas the following day, 27 March, the "man overboard" alarm sounded on board *Washington*, and a quick muster revealed that Admiral Wilcox was missing. *Tuscaloosa*, 1,000 yards astern, maneuvered and dropped life buoys while two destroyers headed for *Washington*'s wake to search for the missing flag officer. Planes from *Wasp*, despite the foul weather, also took off to aid in the search.

Lookouts in the destroyer *Wilson* (DD–408) spotted Wilcox' body in the water, face down, some distance away, but could not pick it up. The circumstances surrounding Wilcox being washed overboard from his flagship have never been fully explained to this day; one school of thought has it that he had suffered a heart attack.

At 1228 on the 27th, the search for Wilcox was abandoned, and command of the task force devolved upon the next senior officer, Rear Admiral Robert C. Giffen, whose flag flew in the cruiser *Wichita*. On 4 April, the task force reached Scapa Flow, joining the British Home Fleet under the overall command of Sir John Tovey, whose flag flew in the battleship HMS *King George V.*

Washington engaged in maneuvers and battle practice with units of the Home Fleet, out of Scapa Flow, into late April, when TF 39 was redesignated as TF 99 with *Washington* as flagship. On the 28th, the force got underway to engage in reconnaissance for the protection of the vital convoys running lend-lease supplies to Murmansk in the Soviet Union.

During those operations, tragedy befell the group. On 1 May 1942, HMS *King George V* collided with a "Tribal"-class destroyer. HMS *Punjabi*, cut in two, sank quickly directly in the path of the oncoming *Washington*. Compelled to pass between the halves of the sinking destroyer, the battleship proceeded ahead, *Punjabi*'s depth charges exploding beneath her hull as she passed.

Fortunately for *Washington*, she suffered no major hull damage nor developed any hull leaks from the concussion of the exploding depth charges. She did, however, sustain damage to some of her delicate fire control systems and radars; and a diesel oil tank suffered a small leak.

Two destroyers, meanwhile, picked up *Punjabi*'s captain, four other officers and 182 men; HMS *King George V* then proceeded back to Scapa Flow for repairs. *Washington* and her escorts remained at sea until 5 May, when TF 99 put into the Icelandic port of Hvalfjordur to provision from the supply ship *Mizar* (AF–12). While at Hvalfjordur, the American and Danish ministers to Iceland called upon Admiral Giffen and inspected his flagship on 12 May.

Task Force 99 subsequently sortied on the 15th to rendezvous with units of the Home Fleet and returned to Scapa Flow on 3 June. The next day, Admiral Harold R. Stark, Commander, Naval Forces, Europe, came on board and broke his flag in *Washington*, establishing a temporary administrative headquarters on board. The battleship played host to His Majesty, King George VI, at Scapa Flow on the 7th, when the King came on board to inspect the ship.

Soon after Admiral Stark left *Washington*, the battleship resumed her operations with the Home Fleet, patrolling part of the Allied shipping lanes leading to Russian ports. On 14 July 1942, Admiral Giffen hauled down his flag in the battleship at Hvalfjordur and shifted to *Wichita*. That same day, *Washington*, with a screen of four destroyers, upped-anchor and put to sea, leaving Icelandic waters in her wake. She reached Gravesend Bay, N.Y., on 21 July; two days later, she shifted to the New York Navy Yard, Brooklyn, N.Y., for a thorough overhaul.

Upon completion of her refit, *Washington* sailed for the Pacific on 23 August, escorted by three destroyers. Five days later, she transited the Panama Canal and, on 14 September, reached Nukualofa Anchorage, Tongatabu, Tonga Island. On that day, Rear Admiral Willis A. "Ching" Lee, Jr., broke his flag in *Washington* as Commander, Battleship Division (BatDiv) 6, and Commander, Task Group 12.2.

The next day, 15 September, *Washington* put to sea bound for a rendezvous with TF 17, the force formed around the aircraft carrier *Hornet*. *Washington* then proceeded to Noumea, New Caledonia, and supported the ongoing Solomons campaign, providing escort services for various reinforcement convoys proceeding to and from Guadalcanal. During those weeks, the battleship's principal bases of operation were Noumea and Espiritu Santo, New Hebrides.

By mid-November, the situation in the Solomons was far from good for the Allies, who were now down to one aircraft carrier—*Enterprise* (CV-6)—after the loss of *Wasp* in September and *Hornet* in October, and Japanese surface units were subjecting Henderson Field on Guadalcanal to heavy bombardments with disturbing regularity. Significantly, however, the Japanese only made their moves at night, since Allied planes controlled the skies during the day. That meant that the Allies had to move their replenishment and reinforcement convoys into Guadalcanal during the daylight hours.

Washington performed those vital duties into mid-November of 1942. On 13 November, she learned that three groups of Japanese ships—one consisting of about 24 transports, with escort—were steaming toward Guadalcanal. One enemy force sighted that morning was reported as consisting of two battleships, a light cruiser, and 11 destroyers.

At sunset on the 13th, Rear Admiral Lee took *Washington*, *South Dakota* (BB-57), and four destroyers and headed for Savo Island—the scene of the disastrous night action of 8 and 9 August—to be in position to intercept the Japanese convoy and its covering force. Lee's ships, designated as TF 64, reached a point about 50 miles south-by-west from Guadalcanal late in the forenoon on the 14th and spent much of the remainder of the day trying—unsuccessfully—to avoid being spotted by Japanese reconnaissance planes.

Approaching on a northerly course, nine miles west of Guadalcanal, TF 64—reported by the Japanese reconnaissance planes as consisting of a battleship, a cruiser, and four destroyers—steamed in column formation. *Walke* (DD-416) led, followed by *Benham* (DD-397), *Preston* (DD-377), *Gwin* (DD-433), and the two battleships, *Washington* and *South Dakota*.

As the ship steamed through the flat calm sea beneath the scattered cirrus cumulus clouds in the night sky, *Washington*'s radar picked up a contact, bearing to the east of Savo Island, at 0001 on 15 November. Fifteen minutes later, at 0016, *Washington* opened fire with her 16-inch main battery. The fourth battle of Savo Island was underway.

The Japanese force proved to be the battleship *Kirishima*, the heavy cruisers *Atago* and *Takao*, the light cruisers *Sendai* and *Nagara*, and a screen of nine destroyers escorting four transports. Planning to conduct a bombardment of American positions on Guadalcanal to cover the landing of troops, the Japanese force ran head-on into Lee's TF 64.

For the next three minutes, *Washington*'s 16-inchers hurled out 42 rounds, opening at 18,500 yards range, her fire aimed at the light cruiser *Sendai*. Simultaneously, the battleship's 5-inch battery was engaging another ship also being engaged by *South Dakota*.

As gunflashes split the night and the rumble of gunfire reverberated like thunder off the islands nearby, *Washington* continued to engage the Japanese force. Between 0025 and 0034, the ship engaged targets at 10,000 yards range with her 5-inch battery.

Most significantly, however, *Washington* soon engaged *Kirishima*, in the first head-to-head confrontation of battleships in the Pacific war. In seven minutes, tracking by radar, *Washington* sent 75 rounds of 16-inch and 107 rounds of 5-inch at ranges from 8,400 to 12,650 yards, scoring at least nine hits with her main battery and about 40 with her 5-inchers, silencing the enemy battleship in short order. Subsequently, *Washington*'s 5-inch batteries went to work on other targets spotted by her radar "eyes."

The battle, however, was not all one-sided. Japanese gunfire proved devastating to the four destroyers of TF 64, as did the dreaded and effective "long lance" torpedoes. *Walke* and *Preston* both took numerous hits of all calibers and sank; *Benham* sustained heavy damage to her bow, and *Gwin* sustained shell hits aft.

South Dakota had maneuvered to avoid the burning *Walke* and *Preston* but soon found herself the target of the entire Japanese bombardment group. Skewered by searchlight beams, *South Dakota* boomed out salvoes at the pugnacious enemy, as did *Washington* which was proceeding, at that point, to deal out severe punishment upon *Kirishima*—one of *South Dakota*'s assailants.

South Dakota, the recipient of numerous hits, retired as *Washington* steamed north to draw fire away from her crippled sister battleship and the two crippled destroyers, *Benham* and *Gwin*. Initially, the remaining ships of the Japanese bombardment group gave chase to *Washington* but broke off action when discouraged by the battleship's heavy guns. Accordingly, they withdrew under cover of a smokescreen.

After *Washington* skillfully evaded torpedoes fired bᵞ the retiring Japanese destroyers in the van of the enemy force, she joined *South Dakota* later in the morning, shaping course for Noumea. In the battleship action, *Washington* had done well and had emerged undamaged. *South Dakota* had not emerged unscathed, however, sustaining heavy damage to her superstructure; 38 men had died; 60 lay wounded. The Japanese had lost the battleship *Kirishima*. Left burning and exploding, she later had to be abandoned and scuttled. The other enemy casualty was the destroyer *Ayanami*, scuttled the next morning.

Washington remained in the South Pacific theater, basing on New Caledonia and continuing as flagship for Rear Admiral "Ching" Lee. The battleship protected carrier groups and task forces engaged in the ongoing Solomons campaign until late in April of 1943, operating principally with TF 11, which included the repaired *Saratoga* (CV-3), and with TF 16, built around *Enterprise*.

Washington departed Noumea on 30 April 1943, bound for the Hawaiian Islands. While en route, TF 16 joined up; and, together, the ships reached Pearl Harbor on 8 May. *Washington*, as a unit of, and as flagship for, TF 60, carried out battle practice in Hawaiian waters until 28 May 1943, after which time she put into the Pearl Harbor Navy Yard for overhaul.

Washington resumed battle practice in the Hawaiian operating area upon conclusion of those repairs and alterations and joined a convoy on 27 July to form Task Group (TG) 56.14, bound for the South Pacific. Detached on 5 August, *Washington* reached Havannah Harbor, at Efate, in the New Hebrides, on the 7th. She then operated out of Efate until late in October, principally engaged in battle practice and tactics with fast carrier task forces.

Departing Havannah Harbor on the last day of October, *Washington* sailed as a unit of TG 53.2—four battleships and six destroyers. The next day, the carriers *Enterprise*, *Essex* (CV-9), and *Independence* (CVL-22), as well as the other screening units of TG 53.3, joined TG 53.2 and came under Rear Admiral Lee. The ships held combined maneuvers until 5 November, when the carriers departed the formation. *Washington*, with her escorts, steamed to Viti Levu, in the Fiji Islands, arriving on the 7th.

Four days later, however, the battleship was again underway, with Rear Admiral Lee—by that point Commander, Battleships, Pacific—embarked, in company with other units of BatDivs 8 and 9. On the 15th, the battlewagons and their screens joined Rear Admiral C. A. "Baldy" Pownall's TG 50.1, Rear Admiral Pownall flying his two-starred flag in *Yorktown* (CV-10), the namesake of the carrier lost at Midway. The combined force then proceeded toward the Gilbert Islands to join in the daily bombings of Japanese positions in the Gilberts and Marshalls—softening them up for impending assault.

On the 19th, the planes from TG 50.1 attacked Mili and Jaluit in the Marshalls, continuing those strikes through 20 November, the day upon which Navy, Marine, and Army forces landed on Tarawa and Makin in the Gilberts. On the 22d, the task group sent its planes against Mili in successive waves; subsequently, the group steamed to operate north of Makin.

Washington rendezvoused with other carrier groups that composed TF 50 on 25 November and, during the reorganization that followed, was assigned to TG 50.4, the fast carrier task group under the command of Rear Admiral Frederick C. "Ted" Sherman. The carriers comprising the core of the group were *Bunker Hill* (CV-17) and *Monterey* (CVL-26); the battleships screening them were *Alabama* (BB-50) and *South Dakota*. Eight destroyers rounded out the screen.

The group operated north of Makin, providing air, surface, and antisubmarine protection for the unfolding unloading operations at Makin, effective on 26 November. Enemy planes attacked the group on the 27th and 28th but were driven off without inflicting any damage on the fast carrier task forces.

As the Gilbert Islands campaign drew to a close, TG 50.8 was formed on 6 December, under Rear Admiral Lee, in *Washington*. Other ships of that group included sistership *North Carolina* (BB-55), *Massachusetts* (BB-59), *Indiana* (BB-58), *South Dakota*, and *Alabama* (BB-60) and the Fleet carriers *Bunker Hill* and *Monterey*. Eleven destroyers screened the heavy ships.

The group first steamed south and west of Ocean Island to take position for the scheduled air and surface bombardment of the island of Nauru. Before dawn on 8 December, the carriers launched their strike groups while the bombardment force formed in column; 135 rounds of 16-inch fire from the six battleships fell on the enemy installations on Nauru; and, upon completion of the shelling, the battleships' secondary batteries took their turn; two planes from each battleship spotted the fall of shot.

After a further period of air strikes had been flown off against Nauru, the task group sailed for Efate, where they arrived on 12 December. On that day, due to a change in the highest command echelons, TF 57 became TF 37.

Washington tarried at Efate for less than two weeks. Underway on Christmas Day, flying Rear Admiral Lee's flag, the battleship sailed in company with her sistership *North Carolina* and a screen of four destroyers to conduct gunnery practice, returning to the New Hebrides on 7 January 1944.

Eleven days later, the battleship departed Efate for the Ellice Islands. Joining TG 37.2—carriers *Monterey* and *Bunker Hill* and four destroyers—en route, *Washington* reached Funafuti, Ellice Islands, on 20 January. Three days later, the battleship, along with the rest of the task group, put to sea to make rendezvous with elements of TF 58, the fast carrier task force under the overall command of Vice Admiral Marc A. "Pete" Mitscher. Becoming part of TG 58.1, *Washington* screened the fast carriers in her group as they launched air strikes on Taroa and Kwajalein in the waning days of January 1944. *Washington*, together with *Massachusetts* and *Indiana*, left the formation with four destroyers as screen and shelled Kwajalein Atoll on the 30th. Further air strikes followed the next day.

On 1 February, however, misfortune reared her head; *Washington*, while maneuvering in the inky darkness, rammed *Indiana* as she cut across *Washington*'s bow while dropping out of formation to fuel escorting destroyers. Both battleships retired for repairs; *Washington* having sustained 60 feet of crumpled bow plating. Both ships put into the lagoon at Majuro the next morning. Subsequently, after reinforcing the damaged bow, *Washington* departed Majuro on 11 February, bound for the Hawaiian Islands.

With a temporary bow fitted at the Pearl Harbor Navy Yard, *Washington* continued on for the west coast of the United States. Reaching the Puget Sound Navy Yard, Bremerton, Wash., the battleship received a new bow over the weeks that followed her arrival. Joining BatDiv 4 at Port Townsend, Wash., *Washington* embarked 500 men as passengers and sailed for Pearl

Harbor, reaching her destination on 13 June and disembarking her passengers.

Arriving back at Majuro on 30 May, *Washington* again flew Admiral Lee's flag as he shifted on board the battleship soon after her arrival. Lee, now a vice admiral, rode in the battleship as she headed out to sea again, departing Majuro on 7 June and joining Mitscher's fast carrier TF 58.

Washington supported the air strikes pummeling enemy defenses in the Marianas on the islands of Saipan, Tinian, Guam, Rota, and Pagan. Task Force 58's fliers also attacked twice and damaged a Japanese convoy in the vicinity on 12 June. The following day, Vice Admiral Lee's battleship-destroyer task group was detached from the main body of the force and conducted shore bombardment against enemy installations on Saipan and Tinian. Relieved on the 14th by two task groups under Rear Admirals J. B. Oldendorf and W. L. Ainsworth, Vice Admiral Lee's group retired momentarily.

On 15 June, Admiral Mitscher's TF 58 planes bombed Japanese installations on Iwo Jima in the Volcano Islands and Chichi Jima and Haha Jima in the Bonins. Meanwhile, marines landed on Saipan under cover of intensive naval gunfire and carrier-based planes.

That same day, Admiral Jisaburo Ozawa, commanding the main body of the Japanese Fleet, was ordered to attack and destroy the invasion force in the Marianas. The departure of his carrier group, however, came under the scrutiny of the submarine *Redfin* (SS-272), as it left Tawi Tawi, the westernmost island in the Sulu Archipelago.

Flying Fish (SS-229) also sighted Ozawa's force as it entered the Philippine Sea. *Cavalla* (SS-244) radioed a contact report on an enemy refueling group on 16 June and continued tracking it as it headed for the Marianas. She again sighted Japanese Combined Fleet units on 18 June.

Admiral Raymond A. Spruance, commanding the 5th Fleet, had meanwhile learned of the Japanese movement and accordingly issued his battle plan. Vice Admiral Lee's force formed a protective screen around the vital fleet carriers. *Washington*, six other battleships, four heavy cruisers, and 14 destroyers deployed to cover the flattops; on 19 June, the ships came under attack from Japanese carrier-based and land-based planes as the Battle of the Philippine Sea commenced.

The tremendous firepower of the screen, however, together with the aggressive combat air patrols flown from the American carriers, proved too much for even the aggressive Japanese. The heavy loss of Japanese aircraft, sometimes referred to as the "Marianas Turkey Shoot," caused serious losses in the Japanese naval air arm. During four massive raids, the enemy launched 373 planes—only 130 returned.

In addition, 50 land-based bombers from Guam fell in flames. Over 300 American carrier planes were involved in the aerial action; their losses amounted to comparatively few: 23 shot down and six lost operationally without the loss of a single ship in Mitscher's task force.

Only a few of the enemy planes managed to get through the barrage of flak and fighters, one scoring a direct hit on *South Dakota*—killing 27 and wounding 23. A bomb burst over the flight deck of the carrier *Wasp* (CV-18), killing one man, wounding 12, and covering her flight deck with bits of phosphorus. Two planes dove on *Bunker Hill*, one scoring a near miss and the other a hit that holed an elevator, knocking out the hanger deck gasoline system temporarily; killing three and wounding 73. Several fires started were promptly quenched. In addition, *Minneapolis* (CA-36) and *Indiana* also received slight damage.

Not only did the Japanese lose heavily in planes; two of their carriers were soon on their way to the bottom—*Taiho*, torpedoed and sunk by *Albacore* (SS-218); and *Shokaku*, sunk by *Cavalla*. Admiral Ozawa, his flagship, *Taiho*, sunk out from under him, transferred his flag to *Zuikaku*.

As the Battle of the Philippine Sea proceeded to a close, the Japanese Mobile Fleet steamed back to its bases, defeated. Admiral Mitscher's task force meanwhile retired to cover the invasion operations proceeding in the Marianas. *Washington* fueled east of that chain of islands and then continued her screening duties with TG 58.4 to the south and west of Saipan, supporting the continuing air strikes on islands in the Marianas, the strikes concentrated on Guam by that point.

On 25 July, aircraft of TG 58.4 conducted air strikes on the Palaus and on enemy shipping in the vicinity, continuing their schedule of strikes through 6 August. On that day, *Washington*, with *Iowa* (BB–61), *Indiana*, *Alabama*, the light cruiser *Birmingham* (CL–62), and a destroyer screen, was detached from the screen of TG 58.4, forming TG 58.7, under Vice Admiral Lee.

That group arrived at Eniwetok Atoll in the Marshalls to refuel and replenish on 11 August and remained there for almost the balance of the month. On 30 August, that group departed, headed for, first, the Admiralty Islands, and ultimately, the Palaus.

Washington's heavy guns supported the taking of Peleliu and Angaur in the Palaus and supported the carrier strikes on Okinawa on 10 October, on northern Luzon and Formosa from 11 to 14 October, as well as the Visayan air strikes on 21 October. From 5 November 1944 to 17 February 1945, *Washington*, as a vital unit of the fast carrier striking forces, supported raids on Okinawa, in the Ryukyus; Formosa; Luzon; Camranh Bay, French Indochina; Saigon, French Indochina; Hong Kong; Canton; Hainan Island; Nansei Shoto; and the heart of the enemy homeland—Tokyo itself.

From 19 to 22 February 1945, *Washington*'s heavy rifles hurled 16-inch shells shoreward in support of the landings on Iwo Jima. In preparation for the assault, *Washington*'s main and secondary batteries destroyed gun positions, troop concentrations, and other ground installations. From 23 February to 16 March, the fast battleship supported the unfolding invasion of Iwo Jima, including a carrier raid upon Tokyo on 25 February. On 18, 19, and 29 March, *Washington* screened the Fleet's carriers as they launched airstrikes against Japanese airfields and other installations on the island of Kyushu. On 24 March, and again on 19 April, *Washington* lent her support to the shellings of Japanese positions on the island of Okinawa.

Anchoring at San Pedro Bay, Leyte, on 1 June 1945 after an almost ceaseless slate of operations, *Washington* sailed for the west coast of the United States on 6 June, making stops at Guam and Pearl Harbor before reaching the Puget Sound Navy Yard on 23 June.

As it turned out, *Washington* would not participate in active combat in the Pacific theater again. Her final wartime refit carried on through V–J Day in mid-August of 1945 and the formal Japanese surrender in Tokyo Bay on 2 September. She completed her post-repair trials and conducted underway training out of San Pedro, Calif., before she headed for the Panama Canal, returning to the Atlantic Ocean. Joining TG 11.6 on 6 October, with Vice Admiral Frederick C. Sherman in overall command, she soon transited the Panama Canal and headed for Philadelphia, the place where she had been "born." Arriving at the Philadelphia Naval Shipyard on 17 October, she participated in Navy Day ceremonies there on the 27th.

Assigned to troop transport duty on 2 November 1945—as part of the "Magic Carpet" operations—*Washington* went into dockyard hands on that day, emerging on the 15th with additional bunking facilities below and a crew that now consisted of only 84 officers and 835 men. Sailing on 15 November for the British Isles, *Washington* reached Southampton, England, on 22 November.

After embarking 185 army officers and 1,479 enlisted men, *Washington* sailed for New York. She completed that voyage and, after that brief stint as a transport,

was placed out of commission, in reserve, on 27 June 1947. Assigned to the New York group of the Atlantic Reserve Fleet, *Washington* remained inactive through the late 1950's, ultimately being struck from the Navy list on 1 June 1960. The old warrior was sold on 24 May 1961 to the Lipsett Division, Luria Bros., of New York City, and was scrapped soon thereafter.

Washington (BB–56) earned 13 battle stars during World War II in operations that had carried her from the Arctic Circle to the western Pacific.

Washington, George, see *George Washington.*

Washington, Martha, see *George Washington.*

Washoe County

A county in northwestern Nevada.

(LST–1165: dp. 2,590; l. 384'; b. 56'6''; dr. 16'1''; s. 14.5 k.; cpl. 153; a. 6 3''; cl. *LST–1156*)

LST–1165 was laid down on 1 December 1952 at Pascagoula, Miss., by the Ingalls Shipbuilding Corp.; launched on 14 July 1953; sponsored by Mrs. Ralph K. James; and commissioned on 30 November 1953, Lt. Comdr. Robert R. Davis in command.

In January 1954, the tank landing ship joined the Atlantic Fleet and became part of the Atlantic Amphibious Force. After completing training in the vicinity of Hampton Roads in early spring, *LST–1165* became very active in naval reserve training and made cruises to Miami; Boston; New York; and Havana, Cuba.

During 1955, the ship participated in many Atlantic Fleet exercises which took her from Labrador to the Caribbean. She also took part in the filming of the motion picture "Away All Boats" at Vieques Island, Puerto Rico. On 1 July of that year, she was named *Washoe County.* On 5 November, the ship arrived at Little Creek, Va., where she spent the remainder of the year.

Washoe County completed underway preparations at Little Creek on 20 February 1956 and—after a brief stop at Morehead City, N.C.—sailed on 25 February for refresher training at Guantanamo Bay, Cuba. She conducted exercises in the Caribbean until 29 April when she returned to Miami, Fla. For the next few months, *Washoe County* worked along the east coast taking part in various operations.

Washoe County departed Norfolk on 27 August and headed for the Mediterranean and her first tour with the 6th Fleet. She also visited ports in Spain, Morocco, France, and Tunisia before returning to Hampton Roads on 5 February 1957.

The next three months of 1957 found *Washoe County* operating in the Norfolk area. On 28 March, the ship headed for the Caribbean and operations at Barbados, St. Thomas, and Puerto Rico. She returned to Morehead City on 14 April and spent the remainder of 1957 in local operations in the Chesapeake Bay area.

Washoe County departed Little Creek on 6 January 1958; stopped briefly at Guantanamo Bay, Cuba; then transited the Panama Canal; arrived at San Diego, Calif., on 27 January; and remained there for the next five months. On 10 June, the ship began supply runs to Seal Beach, Port Hueneme, and San Nicolas Island, Calif.

Washoe County returned to San Diego on 26 June for a month's rest before sailing for Pearl Harbor on 23 July. The ship returned to San Diego on 20 August 1958 and spent the rest of the year in operations off the California coast.

During the early months of 1959, *Washoe County* was at San Diego preparing for an upcoming Western Pacific (WestPac) deployment. She set course for

Japan on 15 April and arrived at Sasebo on 7 May. Except for a visit to Hong Kong during June, the tank landing ship operated between Okinawa and Japan into the autumn. She returned to San Diego on 26 November 1959 and conducted local operations in waters off the California coast through the end of the year.

During the first half of 1960, *Washoe County* conducted various operations along the west coast, including operations: "Swan Dive" off Cape Pendleton; "Bay Island" off Tacoma, Wash., with the Army and Air Force; and "Shark Bite" at San Francisco with Marine reservists. On 1 July 1960, the ship's home port was changed to Yokosuka, Japan. One month later, she sailed for WestPac; stopped at Pearl Harbor; and arrived at Iwakuni, Japan, on 3 September. The ship spent September and October carrying Marine Corps troops and vehicles with stops in Naha and Buckner Bay, Okinawa, and Numazu, Japan. *Washoe County* completed a restricted availability on 17 October and, after a visit to Hong Kong, took part in Operation "Packboard" off Okinawa from 11 to 19 November. On 7 December 1960, the ship commenced an overhaul at Yokosuka which lasted into the new year.

Washoe County finished her yard work on 8 February 1961 and began training. She then made a visit to Tokyo and remained there until 22 March. The months of April and May were occupied with operations off Vietnam in the South China Sea, and she returned to Japan late in the spring for local operations. From 2 to 14 August, *Washoe County* participated in Operation "Sharp Edge" off Korea. The ship ended the year by taking part in Operation "Fiesta" at San Jose, Mindoro, Philippines, commemorating the 17th anniversary of the landing of United States forces in the Philippines in World War II.

On 17 February 1962, *Washoe County* began her participation in the large-scale SEATO exercise—"Tulungan"—in the Philippine area which lasted through 20 April. The ship then devoted the remainder of the year to visiting the ports of Keelung, Taiwan; Subic Bay, Philippines; Hong Kong; and Beppu and Kyushu, Japan. During July and August, she joined in Operation "Seven Seas" off Korea. On 8 December 1962, the LST entered the shipyard at Yokosuka for an overhaul.

She devoted the major portion of 1963 to routine operations and training and from 12 to 30 June participated in her only operation of the year, Operation "Flagpole." On 30 September, *Washoe County* rescued 15 men from the foundering Japanese fishing boat, *Shoyo Maru No. 10*, near Miyako Jima.

The year 1964 began with the tank landing ship moored at Yokohama. From 3 to 27 January, she underwent upkeep at Yokosuka. An administrative inspection of the ship held on 3 February was followed by preparations for the upcoming Exercise "Back Pack" which she conducted from 26 February to 16 March.

Washoe County lifted ammunition from Sasebo to Numazu, Japan, from 10 to 17 April. The ship participated in Operation "Ligtas" from 29 May to 8 June; then sailed to Hong Kong for a port visit. She spent July undergoing another physical security inspection plus sea trials.

During August and September, *Washoe County* conducted special operations in the South China Sea off the coast of Vietnam. Following routine operations and training, *Washoe County* visited Beppu, Japan, from 2 to 4 December and, after a force medical inspection and an operational readiness inspection, spent the Christmas holidays at Yokohama.

Washoe County spent the first three quarters of 1965 making shuttle trips between Okinawa, Japan, and Vietnam in support of American forces in Vietnam. The loads she carried during the year included Marine Corps, Naval Beach Group, Naval Beach Jumper, and Amphibious Construction Battalion equipment and personnel. Most of the year's last quarter was devoted to a yard overhaul at Yokosuka which began on 16 September and ended on 10 December. On 27 December,

the ship commenced refresher training which continued into 1966.

The ship departed Yokosuka loaded with pontoon barge sections destined for Danang, South Vietnam. Following a short stop in Okinawa, the ship arrived at Danang on 22 February. She then proceeded to Chu Lai and discharged the remainder of the cargo.

After hauling cargo to Danang, Chu Lai, Camranh Bay, and Phan Rang, *Washoe County* joined with an amphibious ready group whose mission was to conduct an amphibious raid, Operation "Jackstay," against Viet Cong southeast of Saigon. She served in a pioneering role as an advance base providing gunfire support, arms, ammunition, rations, and water to assault boat groups.

Washoe County returned to Yokosuka on 28 May for a brief period of repairs and rehabilitation. On the 18th of June, the ship sailed for Okinawa to reload supplies; then made a visit to Hong Kong before resuming her duties as a cargo carrier along the Vietnamese coast.

In mid-August, she steamed through the Inland Sea of Japan and Shimonoseki Strait on her way to Korea. After a week of training with the Republic of Korea Navy, *Washoe County* returned to Iwakuni, Japan, and embarked marines and cargo. Before returning to Yokosuka at the end of October, the ship made two more lifts to Vietnam, carrying cargo to Chu Lai and Qui Nhon and returning equipment from Danang to Naha, Okinawa.

The year 1967 began with *Washoe County* in the port of Naha, Okinawa, loading cargo. She spent the month of January engaged in shuttle runs carrying cargo and personnel along the South Vietnamese coast and Okinawa and then enjoyed a rest and recreation visit to Hong Kong. The ship spent most of February conducting intra-coastal logistic support lifts along the South Vietnam coast. On 20 February, *Washoe County* participated in Operation "De Soto," in which material was offloaded by Marine helicopters operating off the ship's main deck. The operation was concluded on 8 March, and the tank landing ship underwent an upkeep period lasting from 20 March to 11 April.

From 15 April to 2 June 1967, *Washoe County* made shuttle runs with cargo and troops to Chi Lung, Taiwan; Danang and Chu Lai, South Vietnam; Naha, Okinawa; Yokosuka, Japan; and Inchon, Korea. The ship then returned to Yokosuka for upkeep from 7 to 22 June, during which time *Washoe County* became the flagship for Landing Squadron 9.

The crew enjoyed liberty at Hong Kong from 11 to 16 July; then debarked the commodore and his staff at Buckner Bay, Okinawa, and took Army personnel to Pusan, Korea, before returning to Yokosuka on 3 August for upkeep which was completed on 7 September. In mid-September, the ship arrived at Danang and participated in three major operations: "Fortress Sentry," "Formation Leader," and "Badger Hunt," from 14 September to 2 December.

Washoe County retired to Subic Bay on 5 December and soon sailed to Okinawa for training exercises with marines. She returned to Yokosuka on 18 December for upkeep which lasted into 1968.

On 1 March 1968, *Washoe County* sailed for Danang, South Vietnam, in company with *Terrell County* (LST–1157) and *Westchester County* (LST–1167), carrying causeway sections to be used at Wunder Beach, South Vietnam. The sections were splashed and moved into place on 17 March. While engaged in the causeway installation, *Washoe County*'s port shaft was damaged; and she underwent repairs at Subic Bay from 21 to 25 March. She then returned to Vietnam, but further problems with the port shaft developed, necessitating more extensive repairs at Subic Bay which lasted until 29 April. The ship then successfully completed sea trials and got underway for Japan and arrived at Yokosuka on 5 May.

Washoe County underwent upkeep at Yokosuka which was not finished until early June. On the 3d, she began loading Marine equipment at Naha, and she delivered it at Subic Bay on the 8th. Following a visit to Hong Kong from the 14th to the 19th, she headed for South Vietnam. En route on 20 June, *Washoe County* embarked two injured personnel from the American freighter, SS *John C.*, after that ship had run aground on the north reef of the Paracel Islands.

The next day, *Washoe County* returned to Danang and resumed duties with the amphibious ready group. With the exception of upkeep from 10 to 20 July, the ship served in the combat zone continuously through July and much of August. On the 24th, *Washoe County* headed for her home port and arrived at Yokosuka on 12 September.

Washoe County began her last deployment of 1968 off the coast of South Vietnam at the Ca Mau peninsula for Operation "Market Time," sealing off the coastline of South Vietnam and adjacent waterways from communist infiltration. From 27 October to 9 December, the tank landing ship functioned as an emergency helicopter landing pad in evacuating eight Navy and Coast Guardsmen wounded in action and the body of one Coast Guardsman who had been killed in action ashore. She also dispensed fuel, food, water, and ammunition to 134 patrol boats and fired 42 naval gunfire support missions.

Washoe County arrived back at Yokosuka on 19 December and celebrated the holidays in her home port.

Washoe County began 1969 preparing for the cyclical yard overhaul period which commenced on 19 January and continued through 10 April. From 20 April to 6 June, the ship conducted refresher training and amphibious refresher training. On 12 June, *Washoe County* got underway for the first deployment of the year as a support ship for Operation "Seafloat/Tran Hung Dao III" in the Ca Mau peninsula of South Vietnam. "Seafloat" was a floating advanced tactical support base primarily for psychological warfare missions conducted in the Cua Lon River at the southernmost tip of South Vietnam. During this period, *Washoe County* served as a helicopter platform and provided logistics and communications support.

On 10 August, after 46 days on station, *Washoe County* sailed via Subic Bay to Hong Kong for a two-week assignment as station ship. She got underway on 4 September for Yokosuka but was diverted by a trip from Okinawa to Danang and finally arrived at her home port on 23 September. She remained there until 9 October when she transported a detachment of marines and equipment from Okinawa to Numazu, Japan.

Departing Japan on 28 October, the ship participated in Operation "Keystone Cardinal," a major troop redeployment lift from Vietnam. During November, *Washoe County* steamed more than 7,000 miles bringing troops and equipment from Vietnam to Okinawa before returning to Yokosuka on 3 December for annual inspections and the holiday season.

The ship took station as a "Seafloat" support vessel from 20 January 1970 to 12 March and again from 17 May to 2 August. Between these two deployments, *Washoe County* served as station ship in Hong Kong from 18 to 27 March 1970.

On 12 August, *Washoe County* arrived at Osaka, Japan, to enjoy four days at the World's Fair, "Expo 70." From 19 August to 19 September, the ship underwent upkeep at Yokosuka and then made a visit to Hong Kong.

After stopping at Chu Lai, Vietnam, and Subic Bay, Philippines, to load cargo on board, *Washoe County* headed for the California coast, via Pearl Harbor, arriving at San Diego on 10 November. The ship offloaded Marine cargo at Camp Pendleton on 13 November, then made a port visit to San Francisco.

On 24 November 1970, *Washoe County* arrived at Bremerton, Wash.; and, the following day, her status changed to "in commission, in reserve." On 25 March 1971, the ship was decommissioned. She served with the Military Sealift Command from January 1973 until

stricken from the Navy list on 1 November 1973. At that time, she was transferred to the Maritime Administration for layup at Suisun Bay, Calif., where she still remained into 1980.

Washoe County earned 12 battle stars for Vietnam service.

Washtenaw County

A county in southeastern Michigan.

(LST–1166: dp. 5,777 (f.); l. 384'; b. 56'6''; dr. 17'; s. 14.5 k.; cpl. 600; a. 6 3''; cl. *LST–1156*)

LST–1166 was laid down on 29 November 1951 at Sturgeon Bay, Wis., by the Christy Shipbuilding Corp.; launched on 22 November 1952; sponsored by Miss Dorothy Christenson; and commissioned at the New Orleans Naval Station on 29 October 1953, Lt. Comdr. Mack D. Ellis in command.

The tank landing ship (LST) departed New Orleans on 28 November to join Landing Ship Flotilla 2, Atlantic Fleet, based at Little Creek, Va. There, she first joined the Amphibious Operational Training Element for seven weeks of shakedown training, following which she participated in amphibious operations at Vieques Island near Puerto Rico as a unit of LST Squadron 4. Routine operations out of the amphibious base at Little Creek occupied her time through the summer of 1954 and into the fall. In October, she began an extended repair period at the Philadelphia Naval Shipyard to correct vibration problems. She returned to active operations in March 1955. On 1 July 1955, *LST–1166* was named *Washtenaw County*. Between July and November, she operated out of Little Creek and then began preparations for her first overseas deployment.

On 9 January 1956, *Washtenaw County* stood out of Norfolk for a cruise with the 6th Fleet in the Mediterranean. That deployment proved to be a quiet one, and the most notable events in which she participated were exercises and visits to a long itinerary of ports along the Mediterranean littoral. At the conclusion of that assignment, she headed back to Norfolk, where she arrived on 4 June. Following repairs at the Norfolk Naval Shipyard, she resumed operations with the Atlantic Amphibious Force out of Little Creek. That November, the amphibious exercise in which she was scheduled to participate were cancelled because of the Suez Canal crisis. *Washtenaw County* remained in port through the end of the year on alert status ready to leave port on 24 hours notice. By January 1957, however, the crisis subsided, and the ship moved north to Staten Island, N.Y., for an overhaul, followed by a month of refresher training in April. In June and July, she joined in a series of exercises in preparation for the NATO exercises which followed that fall.

On 6 January 1958, the ship departed Little Creek in conjunction with her transfer to the Pacific Fleet Amphibious Force as a unit of PhibRon 1. She transited the Panama Canal on the 15th and headed north in company with *Vernon County* (LST-1161), *Washoe County* (LST-1165), *Westchester County* (LST-1167), and *Windham County* (LST-1170). The landing ships reached San Diego on 27 January and began a period of upkeep and local operations. In May, *Washtenaw County* participated in two amphibious exercises with marines from Camp Pendleton and, in June, joined *Thomaston* (LSD-28) for another one. In July and August, the crises which broke out in Lebanon and Taiwan, respectively, caused *Washtenaw County* to be alerted once again. In August, she embarked upon an emergency deployment to the Far East. The tank landing ship made it only as far as Pearl Harbor before the trouble in the Orient abated sufficiently to allow her to head back to the west coast. There, she resumed her schedule of normal operations and exercises with PhibRon 1 until 3 October when she entered the Mare Island Naval Shipyard for a two-month overhaul. Upon completion of the yard work, the ship returned to San Diego on 7 December for refresher training and preparations for her first deployment to the Far East.

On 15 April 1959, she cleared San Diego in company with *Terrell County* (LST–1157) and *Washoe County*. After stops at Sasebo, Japan, and Buckner Bay, Okinawa, *Washtenaw County* got underway with the other ships of PhibRon 1 for SEATO Exercise "Saddle Up"—conducted along the coast of British North Borneo. After 19 days of drills, she departed Borneo for a liberty visit to the British crown colony at Hong Kong. *Washtenaw County*'s first western Pacific assignment lasted until September. In the period of time between Exercise "Saddle Up" and the end of the tour, she participated in a number of routine exercises, transported troops and equipment, and visited such ports as Sasebo, Numazu, and Yokosuka, in Japan; Naha, Okinawa; and Keelung, Taiwan. On 10 September, the tank landing ship was again placed on alert in response to the tense situation in Laos. At the time, it was felt that troops might be required there under the aegis of the United Nations. However, the situation never developed to full crisis proportions, and ships such as *Washtenaw County* were not needed to lift troops into the area. Consequently, the tank landing ship ended her deployment on schedule, returned to the west coast in November, and resumed normal operations out of San Diego.

Late in June 1960, *Washtenaw County* bade farewell to the United States for the last time. Though her Navy career was destined to continue for another 13 years, the tank landing ship would never return to American shores. After a peaceful transit of the Pacific Ocean, she reached her new home port, Yokosuka, Japan, on 12 July. A brief period for voyage repairs followed, and then she was off to join the 7th Fleet in training operations in the Philippines near Manila.

Washtenaw County's final 13 years of service divide easily into two phases—the period before America's buildup in Vietnam and the period of that involvement. The first phase was characterized by routine operations in support of the 7th Fleet Amphibious Force and encompassed the period from 1960 to 1964. During that time, she carried troops and equipment to various bases in the Far East—including a trip or two to Vietnam during the initial stages of the American presence there. More often, however, she engaged in amphibious exercises—both unilateral and with units of foreign navies—as well as goodwill missions to Far Eastern ports. The tank landing ship's itinerary of foreign ports during those four years would read like a travel guide of the Orient, ranging from Korean and Japanese ports in the north to Philippine harbors in the south and across to cities on both coasts of the Southeast Asian peninsula.

Not long after the Tonkin Gulf incident in the summer of 1964, however, she began to concentrate increasingly upon the waters around Southeast Asia, though not to the exclusion of other areas. Initially, her efforts in regard to the Vietnam conflict centered around logistics and troop transportation. During the buildup, the ship carried troops and supplies into Vietnam and took on equipment headed for other American bases. When not engaged in that duty, *Washtenaw County* continued her routine of amphibious training at Okinawa and in the Philippines with Marine Corps battalion landing teams based at Numazu, Japan.

Throughout the first four years of America's involvement in Vietnam, *Washtenaw County*'s contact with that war remained one of brief visits, though with one notable exception. In January 1967, she helped to pioneer some of the techniques which later became the basis of the doctrines used by the River Patrol and Mobile Riverine Forces. In Operation "Deckhouse V," she joined *Coconino County* (LST–603) and *St. Francis River* (LSMR–525) in conducting the first seaward penetration of the Co Chien River to support an assault launched by the 7th Marines against enemy forces in the area. Otherwise, she made only brief visits to bring in troops and supplies.

It was not until 1968 that *Washtenaw County* began a more intimate association with the war in Vietnam. That phase of her service began as a result of her duty in support of the Mobile Riverine Force operating in the Mekong Delta area of South Vietnam. She departed Yokosuka on 8 January, stopped at Danang in South Vietnam to unload cargo on the 15th and 16th, and then continued on to the mouth of the Cua Tien River in the Mekong Delta where she arrived on the 17th. The tank landing ship anchored there for the night and, the next morning, crossed the bar and headed upriver to join Task Force 117, the Mobile Riverine Force. She relieved *Westchester County* as support ship for the boats and monitors of the riverine force on 27 January. For three months, she served as a mobile home for 200 Army troops and 170 sailors of the force—a joint Army-Navy organization charged with the mission to control the many waterways in the Mekong Delta. In addition to providing berthing space for men, she also served as a mobile, floating supply depot transporting and issuing tons of ammunition, rations, and other supplies to the gunboats and river monitors operating in the delta.

Washtenaw County ended her assignment in the Mekong Delta on 27 March and headed for Bangkok, Thailand. There, her crew enjoyed five days of rest and relaxation before departing with a Saigon-bound cargo of steel. After a brief stop at Sattahip—also in Thailand—to embark an Army signal company, she reached Saigon on 11 April, unloaded the steel, and then continued on—via Naha, Okinawa—to Japan. The tank landing ship arrived in Yokosuka on 22 April and began 37 days of upkeep, inspections, and repairs.

On 29 May, she departed Yokosuka on what was supposed to be a round-trip voyage to Subic Bay and back to her home port. However, two days out, she received a change in orders sending her back to Vietnam at the completion of her mission to the Philippines. On 20 June, the ship arrived at Can Tho in the Mekong Delta and relieved *Vernon County* as the support LST for the Mobile Riverine Force. This time, she remained only one month and made just nine river transits before *Whitfield County* (LST–1169) relieved her on 20 July. After a visit to Kaohsiung, Taiwan, and another to Naha, the tank landing ship reentered Yokosuka on 5 August. Another period of repairs, upkeep, and inspections followed as well as a training exercise with units of the Republic of Korea (ROK) Navy at Chin Hae late in September.

At the completion of those exercises, the tank landing ship returned to Yokosuka on 7 October to prepare for another tour of duty in Vietnam. Ten days later, she put to sea again for the combat zone. Before joining the riverine forces, however, she completed a brief assignment at Vung Tau. She arrived there on 26 October and began a two-week assignment in support of Operation "Bold Dragon VIII," an amphibious search-and-destroy mission conducted at Phu Quoc Island by TF 115, the Coastal Surveillance Force. *Washtenaw County* joined *Weiss* (APD–125) and two Cobra gunships in providing naval gunfire support for Navy SEAL teams engaged in the actual operation. She completed her assignment with TF 115 on 7 November and headed on to Dong Taw to join TF 117. She arrived on the 10th and relieved *Westchester County*, heavily damaged below the waterline by a bomb planted by a Viet Cong swimmer. Her emergency assignment to the riverine forces lasted less than a month, though, because *Whitfield County* took over as support LST on 2 December and released *Washtenaw County* for a liberty call at Hong Kong followed by a return to Yokosuka on 20 December.

She remained at Yokosuka for about a month, departing again on 21 January 1969 for minor repairs at Subic Bay and thence returned to Vietnam. After loading ammunition at Baie de Binh Ba and Vung Tau on 2 and 3 February, she relieved *Terrell County* (LST–1157) as support LST for the Coastal Surveillance

Force's "Market Time" operations. For the next six weeks, she served as a mobile supply ship for the smaller patrol craft engaged in the interdiction of enemy coastwise logistics efforts. On one occasion, 20 February, she entered the fray herself, when her 3-inch guns were called upon to support the smaller craft with naval gunfire. On 23 March, *Westchester County* relieved her as support ship, and *Washtenaw County* moved out for Yokosuka by way of Keelung, Taiwan. She reached her home port on 3 April and began an extended overhaul which lasted until late August.

On 26 August, she put to sea again—this time to join Amphibious Ready Group "Alfa" at Danang, Vietnam. She reached her destination on 3 September and spent the next two days loading marines and equipment for the first phase of Operation "Defiant Stand." Before dawn on 7 September, *Washtenaw County* debarked her complement of marines which made up the first and second waves of the first phase. Over the next three days, the tank landing ship embarked troops of the 5th and 6th Companies of the ROK Marine Brigade for the second phase of the amphibious operation, conducted on 11 September. That landing marked the first joint American-Korean combat operation since the end of the Korean War in 1953. After a five-day Hong Kong visit and an 11-day upkeep period at Subic Bay, *Washtenaw County* rejoined Amphibious Ready Group "Alfa" at Danang on 19 October. A month later, she was reassigned to Amphibious Ready Group "Bravo" for a short time before heading for a visit at Manila. From there she steamed to Naha, Okinawa, to pick up marines for transportation to Japan. Upon her arrival there, she disembarked the marines at Numazu and returned to Yokosuka, where she spent the remainder of the year.

Washtenaw County made a brief visit to Vietnam in late February to participate in Operation "Keystone Blue Jay" but spent most of her time during the first part of 1970 conducting amphibious exercises. While entering Hong Kong on 18 May, the tank landing ship suffered extensive damage when a merchant steamer, SS *Kota Selatan*, struck her. She continued into the harbor where temporary repairs were made during the next 11 days. She then departed the British colony for Yokosuka where she entered drydock for permanent repairs on 12 June.

Washtenaw County completed repairs and left drydock on 22 July. Two days later, she embarked marines at Numazu for transportation to Okinawa. Following that voyage, she returned to Yokosuka where she remained until mid-August. When not in port at Yokosuka, during the rest of the year, the tank landing ship supported 7th Fleet training activities. Most frequently, her training took her to the Philippines where she operated out of Subic Bay. The major exercise scheduled for that fall—Operation "Fortress Light," a joint Philippine-American amphibious exercise set for the last half of October—had to be cancelled due to heavy typhoon activity in the area. While the rest of her task force headed south to assist victims of storm damage, *Washtenaw County* debarked Philippine Navy men and picked up elements of the "aggressor force" positioned earlier at Paluan Bay for the exercise. After returning those troops to Manila, the ship headed for Taiwan where she made a five-day visit to Kaohsiung. Following that, she steamed back to Subic Bay for 11 days of upkeep during the second week in November. On the 16th, she got underway for Okinawa to transport marines there from the Philippines. She reached her destination on the 20th, disembarked her troops and cargo, and picked up 261 marines bound for Japan. She departed the Ryukyus on 25 November, delivered her passengers to Numazu on 1 December, and then returned to Yokosuka where she remained through the end of the year.

The year 1971 brought a resumption of duty in the embattled Republic of South Vietnam. Upon completion of a restricted availability at Yokosuka in January, *Washtenaw County* departed Japan to rejoin TF 115,

the Coastal Surveillance Force, off the coast of Vietnam. For almost three months, the ship provided logistics support for "Market Time" operations, the interdiction of enemy coastal and coastwise logistics operations, in the vicinity of Vung Tau and Danang. In mid-April, the tank landing ship headed back to Japan where she spent several weeks undergoing extensive repairs. Following that, she was engaged in a number of logistic lifts as well as amphibious training at Okinawa. She also managed a visit each to Hong Kong and Kaohsiung before entering another period of restricted availability in preparation for her return to the Vietnamese combat zone. On 27 September she stood out of Yokosuka for South Vietnam. There, she resumed logistic support duties for Operation "Market Time" as well as some shore bombardment and patrol assignments. At the conclusion of her deployment in December, she loaded troops and equipment upriver on the Cua Tien and departed Vietnam for Yokosuka by way of Subic Bay. The ship reached Japan on 20 December and began post-deployment standdown.

Washtenaw County began the year 1972 at Yokosuka and departed her home port on 31 January for Iwakuni where she embarked marines for training at Okinawa. During the next two months, she made two such voyages between Japanese ports and Okinawa to carry marines to the Ryukyus for training exercises. She concluded the second round trip at Yokosuka on 19 March. After a six-week availability, she departed Japan for her only Vietnam deployment of the year. She made a stop at Subic Bay to load ammunition desperately needed by 7th Fleet ships which were fighting hard to stem a major enemy offensive in Vietnam. She reached Danang on 21 May, unloaded the ammunition, and then headed for Qui Nhon. During this tour of duty in Vietnam, the tank landing ship served at Qui Nhon until 10 July as a mobile helicopter platform in support of coastal radar stations engaged in "Market Time" operations.

Relieved of that duty on 10 July, she made a brief stop at Vung Tau on the 11th before continuing on to Bangkok, Thailand, for a four-day port visit. From there, she moved to Singapore and thence to Keelung, Taiwan, via Subic Bay. From Keelung, *Washtenaw County* headed back to Yokosuka, arriving there on 12 August. For the remainder of the year, the ship steamed from port to port in the Far East making goodwill visits and transporting marines between Japan and Okinawa. By 22 November, she was back in Yokosuka to begin an extended period of repairs and modifications.

Those modifications continued into 1973. On 9 February 1973, *Washtenaw County* (LST–1166) was decommissioned at Yokosuka after completing conversion to a special minesweeper and became *Washtenaw County* (MSS–2). That same day, she departed Yokosuka for Subic Bay where she underwent a restricted availability in preparation for minesweeping operations to be conducted along the coast of North Vietnam. On 2 April, the ship stood out of Subic Bay, bound for Haiphong harbor in North Vietnam. She reached that port on 6 April and joined TF 78, the force assigned to sweep up the mines following the termination of hostilities between the United States and North Vietnam.

Washtenaw County served as a special type of auxiliary craft to check the channels for mines. Specially configured for that purpose over the previous two months and manned by a volunteer skeleton crew, she was to make several transits of the mined areas to ascertain whether or not sweeping operations had to be made. She made her first six runs on 14 April, thereby becoming the first American ship to enter Haiphong in over a decade. She was scheduled to make an additional six transits the next day; but, after the first two, political complications in the negotiations between the United States and North Vietnam caused an interruption in minesweeping operations. Ultimately, *Washtenaw*

County took a 50-day break in operations at Subic Bay while the negotiators resolved the political difficulties.

On 15 June, she departed Subic Bay once more and reached Haiphong again on the morning of 20 June. She completed her assignments in Operation "End Sweep" and departed Haiphong. She returned to Subic Bay in July to await the completion of other phases of the operation. On 24 July, she headed for Yokosuka with *Westchester County* and reached that port on 30 July. *Washtenaw County* completed final deactivation work during the following month, and her name was struck from the Navy list on 30 August 1973.

Washtenaw County earned 13 battle stars, two Presidential Unit Citations, two Navy Unit Commendations, and four Meritorious Unit Commendations for Vietnam service.

Washtucna

A Palouse Indian chief whose name is commemorated by the small town in Adams County, Wash.

(YTB–826: dp. 356 (f.); l. 109'; b. 31'; dr. 14' (max.); s. 12.0 k.; cpl. 12; cl. *Natick*)

Washtucna (YTB–826) was laid down on 1 May 1973 at Marinette, Wis., by the Marinette Marine Corp.; launched on 9 October 1973; and delivered to the Navy on 11 December 1973. Placed in service at San Diego, Calif., soon thereafter, *Washtucna* performed local and coastal towing tasks for the 11th Naval District into 1978.

Wasmuth

Henry Wasmuth—born in Germany but later a naturalized American citizen—enlisted in the United States Marine Corps on 11 June 1861. Ultimately attached to the Marine detachment of the sidewheeler *Powhatan*, Wasmuth took part in the assault on Fort Fisher, N.C., on 21 January 1865.

During the battle, Ens. Robley D. "Fighting Bob" Evans fell wounded from a Confederate sharpshooter's bullet. Private Wasmuth picked up the seriously wounded young officer and carried him to a place of comparative safety—a shell hole on the beach. The private stayed with the future admiral, ignoring the latter's urgings to take cover, until a sharpshooter's bullet pierced Wasmuth's neck, cutting the jugular vein. Within a few minutes, Wasmuth dropped in the edge of the surf and died. Evans later wrote: "He was an honor to his uniform."

(DD–338: dp. 1,215 (n.); l. 314'4½''; b. 30'11½''; dr. 9'4'' (mean); s. 35.0 k.; cpl. 122; a. 4 4'', 1 3'', 12 21'' tt.; cl. *Clemson*)

Wasmuth (Destroyer No. 338) was laid down on 12 August 1919 at the Mare Island Navy Yard, Vallejo, Calif.; designated DD–338 on 17 July 1920; launched on 15 September 1920; sponsored by Miss Gertrude E. Bennet, stepdaughter of Lieutenant Colonel R. H. Davis, USMC, an officer on duty at Mare Island; and commissioned on 16 December 1921, Comdr. W. P. Gaddis in command.

Wasmuth was fitted out at Mare Island until 27 February 1922, when she sailed for Richmond, Calif., to commence her shakedown cruise. Operating off Sausalito and Mare Island, Calif., the new destroyer completed her trials on 14 March, putting into her builder's yard on that day for post-shakedown repairs.

She sailed for San Francisco on 1 May and calibrated her sound signal apparatus at that port until the 4th, when she shifted to San Pedro. *Wasmuth* then spent the next month operating in connection with battleship torpedo practices, a duty broken on 7 May by dispatch service to San Diego. Returning to that port from San Pedro on 8 June, she commenced preparations for decommissioning soon thereafter.

Placed out of commission at San Diego on 26 July 1922, *Wasmuth* remained in reserve for nearly eight years during the financially tight 1920's, when treaty restrictions and cuts in operating funds reduced the Navy's active seagoing forces. Recommissioned on 11 March 1930, Lt. Comdr. I. C. Sowell in command, *Wasmuth* operated as a destroyer for the next decade, participating in an intensive slate of tactical exercises and maneuvers, varying that routine with upkeep and training. She also operated with the Battle Force's Destroyer Flotilla 2 from the western seaboard into the Caribbean. Only for one brief period, in the autumn of 1934, was *Wasmuth* not fully active—being then assigned to Rotating Reserve Squadron 10.

With the construction of newer, more heavily armed and far-ranging destroyers, the need for the old "flush-deckers" in their designed destroyer role diminished. While, of course, a great many of those World War I–authorized ships lay in reserve on both coasts, the Navy was expanding as the 1930's had progressed and, in view of ominous developments in Europe and the Far East, was broadening its operational horizons. Aviation-oriented and mine-warfare types of ships—seaplane tenders and fast minesweepers and minelayers—were needed.

Accordingly, some of the old "flush-deckers" were converted to other roles. *Wasmuth*, a unit of the fleet in Hawaiian waters since the permanent basing of the ships there in April 1940, was among the *Clemson*-class ships chosen for conversion to high-speed minesweepers of the *Chandler*-class.

Wasmuth—reclassified as DMS–15 on 19 November 1940—underwent the metamorphosis at the Pearl Harbor Navy Yard. Retaining her full four-gun main battery and an antiaircraft battery of .50-caliber machine guns, as well as depth-charge tracks, the ship lost her torpedo capability when minesweeping gear replaced her dozen 21-inch torpedo tubes.

Upon completion of that conversion at the Pearl Harbor Navy Yard on 5 April 1941, *Wasmuth* sailed for Palmyra Island and operated there until 19 April, when she set course to return to Pearl Harbor. The high-speed minesweeper subsequently remained in Hawaiian waters until 10 June, when she sailed for the west coast of the United States.

Returning to Hawaii in early July, *Wasmuth* operated out of Pearl Harbor through the autumn of 1941, as tensions increased in the Far East with each passing day. She operated on local patrol and minesweeping exercises during that time, as the fleet maintained an intensive training schedule to enable it to be ready for the hostilities with Japan that most in higher echelons feared inevitable.

Those fears, however, were realized quite unexpectedly—shortly before 0800 on 7 December 1941, planes from six Japanese aircraft carriers swept down upon the fleet units present at Pearl Harbor, in a surprise attack. *Wasmuth*—among the ships in port that Sunday—lay at buoys D–7 and D–7S inboard in a nest with three sisterships of Mine Division (MineDiv) 4: *Trever* (DMS–16), *Zane* (DMS–14), and *Perry* (DMS–17), at the mouth of Pearl Harbor's Middle Loch and just off Pearl City.

Wasmuth went to general quarters at once, and Lt. (jg.) J. R. Grey—in the absence of both the commander and executive officer—assumed command of the ship. Within three minutes, her gunners had all of the .50-caliber Browning machine guns ready for action while the "black gang" below prepared the ship to get underway. Inside the nest, however, the high-speed minesweeper could only bring her aftermost machine guns to bear against the approaching planes.

Shortly after 0900, about midway through horizontal bomber attacks (carried out by Mitsubishi B5N bombers), Aichi D3A–1's (later code-named "Vals") began glide- and dive-bombing attacks on the ships and shore installations, kicking off the fourth phase of the raid. Those planes, coming from a westerly direction, proved to be good targets for the eager gunners in the minesweepers and minelayers moored in Middle Loch. *Wasmuth's* gunners (who expended 6,000 rounds of .50-caliber ammunition that December morn) opened fire whenever the planes came within range. One man, Seaman 1st Class James P. Hannon, was given credit for a "kill"—shooting down an Aichi that crashed on Waipio Peninsula, near Middle Loch. The ship managed to score hits on several other planes as they came by.

Lt Comdr. L. M. LeHardy—*Zane's* commanding officer and the senior officer present of MineDiv 4—ordered the ships to get underway, *Trever* leading the pack at 0932. Five minutes later, Lt. J. W. Leverton, *Wasmuth's* executive officer, arrived as his ship edged out of Middle Loch, and took command, relieving Lt. (jg.) Grey who had fought the ship since the outset of the attack. Shortly thereafter, *Trever's* commander reported on board too, since his own ship was steaming down the channel without him.

Proceeding out of her harbor herself soon thereafter, *Wasmuth* took up patrols off the channel entrance. Meanwhile, while the attack itself had ceased, jittery sailors, marines, and soldiers were not so sure. At sea, the forces searching for the retiring Japanese suspected the presence of enemy submarines—real or otherwise.

At 1023, *Wasmuth* dropped one depth charge "on suspicious water" but came up with only a negative result. At 1036, the high-speed minesweeper dropped another depth charge, but only achieved the same result as the first attack—nothing. Although it brought up "large quantities of oil," there was no wreckage.

Later that afternoon, *Wasmuth* and *Zane* swept the Pearl Harbor entrance channel before the former anchored at the coal docks when her sweep wire parted. After she retrieved the sweep gear, she headed back to the open sea, where her commanding officer, Lt. Comdr. J. L. Wilfong, reported aboard. *Trever's* commanding officer, Lt. Comdr. D. M. Agnew, rejoined his own ship at 1635. MineDiv 4 soon resumed its patrol operations.

Wasmuth operated in the Hawaiian chain between Johnston Island and Pearl Harbor into the spring of 1942. She departed Pearl Harbor on 31 May 1942, and escorted Convoy 4111 to San Francisco, Calif., reaching her destination on 10 June. Departing "Frisco" on the last day of July, *Wasmuth* returned to Pearl Harbor with Convoy 2113, arriving on 12 August.

Departing Pearl Harbor on the 14th, *Wasmuth* left Hawaii in her wake for the last time, bound for the Aleutians. Reaching Kodiak, Alaska, on 20 August, the high-speed minesweeper spent the remainder of her career in those inhospitable northern climes as part of Task Force 8, performing screen and escort duties for the supply ships necessary to bear the "beans, bullets, and black oil" to that theater. In the course of her operations that autumn and winter, the ship visited such picturesquely named places as Women's Bay, Dutch Harbor, Chernofski, Nome, Kodiak, and Point Mush.

Two days after Christmas of 1942, *Wasmuth* was escorting a convoy through a heavy Alaskan storm when two depth charges were wrenched from their tracks by the pounding sea, fell over the side, and exploded beneath the ship's fantail. The blasts carried away part of the ship's stern and the ship began to founder; in the gale, the pumps could not make headway against the inexorably rising water below.

Despite the heavy sea, *Ramapo* (AO–12) came alongside the crippled and foundering *Wasmuth* in a display of seamanship and daring. For three and one-half hours, the tanker remained with the sinking high-speed minesweeper, battling the waves while proceeding with the ticklish business of transferring the latter's officers and men (134) and two passengers. After completing that heroic rescue, *Ramapo* pulled away; *Wasmuth*

eventually sank early on 29 December. Her name was struck from the Navy list on 3 September 1943.

Wasmuth (DMS–15) received one battle star for her part in the defense of the Fleet at Pearl Harbor on 7 December 1941.

Wasp

Any of numerous winged hymenopterus insects possessing smooth, slender bodies, and an abdomen attached by a narrow stalk. They have well developed wings, biting mouthparts, and often administer painful stings.

I

(Sch.: a. 8 2-pdrs., 6 swivel guns)

Scorpion, a merchant schooner built at Baltimore, was purchased by the Continental Navy late in 1775; renamed *Wasp*; outfitted at Baltimore during the winter of 1775 and 1776; and commissioned in December 1775 or January 1776, Capt. William Hallock in command.

Wasp set sail from Baltimore on 14 January 1776 in company with *Hornet* and a convoy of ships bound for the Delaware capes. By virtue of their voyage to meet Commodore Esek Hopkins' squadron at the Delaware capes, *Wasp* and *Hornet* appear to be the first ships of the Continental Navy to get to sea. They joined Hopkins' squadron on 13 February; and, four days later, the first American squadron to put to sea began its maiden voyage. Interpreting his orders rather liberally by ignoring those portions which related to operations in the Chesapeake Bay and along the southern coast of the colonies, Hopkins led his fleet directly to the Bahamas. The ships, minus *Hornet* and *Fly*, arrived at Abaco in the Bahamas on 1 March, and Hopkins began laying plans for the raid on New Providence. The fleet ran in to attempt a landing at the port of Nassau but failed to achieve surprise. The landing, therefore, went forward several miles to the east of the town. *Wasp* and *Providence* covered the marines as they went ashore, but their guns never fired because the landing was not opposed. That afternoon, the landing force took Fort Montague and the following day captured the town of Nassau and Fort Nassau. They took a large quantity of cannon, close to 90 pieces, and 15 brass mortars, but the governor had managed to foil the mission in its primary objective by spiriting away the bulk of the gunpowder which had been stored there. Hopkins had to settle for 24 casks of powder out of the 174 originally stored there. The cannon and other military stores captured, however, more than justified the enterprise.

The fleet remained at Nassau for about two weeks loading the booty of war. So large was the take that several local ships had to be pressed into service to carry the materiel back to North America. Hopkins' squadron finally hoisted sail on 17 March and set course for New England. *Wasp*, however, parted with the main fleet and made her way independently back to the Delaware capes and thence into port at Philadelphia, where she arrived on 4 April.

After repairs at Philadelphia, *Wasp* returned to duty in the Delaware River and Bay. On 5 May, two British men-of-war, the 44-gun *Roebuck* and the 28-gun *Liverpool*, entered the bay with several prizes. In the face of these two formidable enemies, *Wasp* retreated into Christiana Creek but came out again on the 8th to join a force of galleys in attacking *Roebuck* after she had run aground. During the ensuing engagement, the Continental schooner captured the British brig *Betsey* and took her into Philadelphia where the British officers were placed in jail. The schooner continued to operate on the Delaware River and Bay and along the nearby Atlantic coast for the remainder of her career. Near the end of the year, she took three more prizes—*Leghorn Galley* late in October, *Two Brothers* in December, and an unnamed sloop that same month. She also recaptured *Success*, an American ship previously taken by HMS *Roebuck*.

Into the fall of 1777, *Wasp* continued her operations in the vicinity of the Delaware capes until November when she and four other ships unsuccessfully engaged the British force under Admiral Sir Richard ("Black Dick") Howe. Philadelphia had already fallen to Admiral Howe's brother, General Sir William Howe, late in September, but American forces retained control of the river below the city until losing that engagement. Following the clash, *Wasp* was run aground, set afire, and destroyed when her gunpowder exploded.

II

(SlpW: t. 450; lbp. 105′7″; b. 30′1″; dph. 14′1⅝″; cpl. 140; a. 2 12-pdrs., 16 32-pdr. car.)

The second *Wasp*, a sloop of war constructed in 1806 at the Washington Navy Yard, was commissioned sometime in 1807, Master Commandant John Smith in command. *Wasp*'s movements in 1807 and 1808 remain unrecorded; but, by 1809, she was cruising the eastern seaboard of the United States. By the close of 1810, she was operating from the ports of Charleston, S.C., and Savannah, Ga., presumably concentrating on the waters along the southern portion of the country's eastern coast. In 1811, she moved to Hampton Roads, Va., where she and brig *Nautilus* joined frigates *United States* and *Congress* in forming a squadron commanded by Commodore Stephen Decatur.

She continued to operate along the coast of the middle states after the United States went to war with Great Britain in June of 1812. Her single action of that war came in October 1812. On the 13th, she exited the mouth of the Delaware River and, two days later, encountered a heavy gale which carried away her jib

Huzza for "Free Trade and Sailor's Rights."

John Bull stung to agony by the Wasp and Hornet.

A cartoon, *circa* 1813, celebrates the early accomplishments of the sloops-of-war *Wasp* and *Hornet* during the War of 1812, with punning allusions to the victories of Isaac Hull and William Bainbridge. (New York Historical Society)

boom and washed two crewmen overboard. The following evening, *Wasp* came upon a squadron of ships and, in spite of the fact that two of their number appeared to be large men-of-war, made for them straight away. She finally caught the enemy convoy the following morning and discovered six merchantmen under the protection of a 22-gun sloop-of-war, HBM brig *Frolic*. At half past eleven in the morning, *Wasp* and *Frolic* closed to do battle, commencing fire at a distance of 50 to 60 yards. In a short, but sharp, fight, both ships sustained heavy damage to masts and rigging, but *Wasp* prevailed over her adversary by boarding her. Unfortunately for the gallant little ship, a British 74-gun ship-of-the-line, *Poictiers*, appeared on the scene, and *Frolic*'s captor became the final prize of the action. *Wasp*'s commanding officer, Master Commandant Jacob Jones, had to surrender his small ship to the new adversary because he could neither run nor hope to fight such an overwhelming opponent. *Wasp* served briefly in the Royal Navy as *Peacock* but was lost off the Virginia capes in 1813.

III

(Sch.: t. 55; l. 59'; b. 17'3''; dr. 6'3''; cpl. 40; a. 1 long 6-pdr.)

The third *Wasp*—a schooner built in 1810 at Baltimore, Md.—received a privateer's warrant from the United States government in July 1812 when she put to sea for a privateering foray into the West Indies. During that cruise, she stopped three British merchantmen, allowed one to continue due to the fact that she carried nothing of value, and took the other two as prizes. While putting a prize crew on board the last of the three, the schooner *Dawson*, *Wasp* was surprised by the British sloop-of-war *Garland*. Both captor and prize hoisted full sail and got underway. The prize crew easily took *Dawson* to safety at Savannah, Ga., because HMS *Garland* chose to chase *Wasp*. The latter managed to outsail her would-be captor and, after sailing through a hurricane which cost her both her masts, finally returned to Baltimore on 28 November 1812.

At Baltimore, her owners sold her to a group of businessmen who refitted and rearmed her with a long 9-pounder and then chartered her to the United States Navy as a dispatch boat during the summer of 1813. She passed her brief period of naval service without incident, and the Navy returned her to her owners that autumn. On 1 October 1813, she was sold at auction at Baltimore. The two merchants who purchased her, Mr. Joseph Lane and Mr. Thomas White, refitted her, rearmed her with a long 4-pounder, and sent her to sea as a privateer. Her second cruise appears to have met with even less success than her first for the last reference to her career was an advertisement the *Baltimore American* ran on 4 August 1814 which called her owners to a meeting on the 11th to settle accounts. Presumably, she was sold.

IV

(Slp.: a. 2 12-pdrs.)

The fourth *Wasp*, a sloop chartered on Lake Champlain late in the summer of 1813, served as a tender for Commodore Thomas Macdonough's fleet during the latter part of 1813 and into 1814. Small and a poor sailer, *Wasp* saw no combat. She was returned to her owners early in 1814; and her battery was transferred to the newly launched schooner, *Ticonderoga*.

V

(SlpW: t. 509; lbp. 117'11''; b. 31'6''; dph. 14'6''; cpl. 173; a. 2 long 12-pdrs., 20 32-pdr. car.)

The fifth *Wasp*—a ship-rigged sloop-of-war constructed in 1813 at Newburyport, Mass., by Cross & Merrill—was commissioned early in 1814, Master Commandant Johnston Blakeley in command. She remained at Portsmouth, N.H., until late spring awaiting sailing orders and, upon receipt of them, put to sea on 1 May 1814 for a war cruise to the western approaches to the English Channel. She captured her first vessel, the 207-ton bark *Neptune*, on 2 June; embarked her crew as prisoners; and burned the prize at sea. Eleven days later, she took *William*, a 91-ton brig, and burned her as well. *Wasp* encountered the 131-ton, armed brig, *Pallas*, on the 18th and captured her—apparently without resistance—and scuttled her. Her fourth victim—which she took on the 23d—the 171-ton galiot *Henrietta*, was given up to the prisoners she had thus far taken. Three days later, she captured and scuttled the 325-ton ship *Orange Boven*.

On 28 June, she came upon the 21-gun sloop-of-war *Reindeer* some 225 miles west of Plymouth and brought her to battle. The fight lasted only 19 minutes; but, during that brief span of time, the two ships traded a murderous fire of grape and solid shot. Several times, *Reindeer*'s crew tried to board *Wasp*; but the American crew repulsed them on each occasion. In the end, *Wasp*'s own ship's company boarded *Reindeer* and carried the day. *Wasp* suffered six hits in her hull, and some of her rigging was shot away, but she remained sailable. After taking prisoners on board, setting fire to *Reindeer*, and watching her explode, *Wasp* set course for L'Orient, France. En route, she took two more prizes, the 112-ton brig *Regulator* on Independence Day and the 151-ton schooner *Jenny* two days later. Not long thereafter, she entered L'Orient for repairs, provisions, and care for her wounded.

Wasp remained in L'Orient until she again put to sea on 27 August. On her third day underway, she captured the brig *Lettice* and, the following day, took another, *Bon Accord*. Early in the morning of 1 September, she encountered a convoy of 10 ships escorted by the 74-gun ship-of-the-line *Armada*. *Wasp* made for the convoy and singled out the brig *Mary* which she quickly took as a prize, carrying off her crew as prisoners and burning her. The American sloop then attempted to take another ship in the convoy, but *Armada* chased her off.

That evening, she spied another sail on the horizon and gave chase. By 2130, she had the brig under her lee bow and opened fire. The enemy returned fire until 2200 at which time her battery seemed to cease fire. When *Wasp* did the same and called for the stranger's surrender, the British ship answered with another cannonade. *Wasp* again opened fire on the ship, now known to have been the 18-gun, 477-ton brig *Avon*. Some broadsides later, *Avon*'s guns fell silent once more, and *Wasp* repeated the call for surrender. *Avon*, at this point a battered hulk, had no choice but to comply.

However, just as *Wasp* began to lower the boat for the prize crew, the lookout sighted another enemy brig standing toward the two adversaries. *Wasp*'s crew manned their battle stations immediately in hope of taking the newcomer as well. Just then, two more British ships appeared on the horizon; and *Wasp* was forced to give up the destruction of *Avon* and see to her own salvation. The lead British ship, however, failed to engage *Wasp*. Instead, she hauled in close to *Wasp*'s stern and loosed a broadside into the American's rigging which damaged sails, sheets, and braces considerably and then came about to rendezvous with the other two ships following her and the sinking *Avon*. Although the Americans didn't know it at the time, *Avon* sank soon after *Wasp* left her.

The American warship continued her ravages of the British merchant marine. On 12 September, she encountered *Three Brothers*, a brig, and scuttled her. Two days later, she sank the brig *Bacchus*. On the 21st, an eight-gun brig, *Atlanta*, ran afoul of *Wasp*, and she, too, suffered the ignominy of capture. Deemed too valuable to destroy, *Atlanta* was placed under the command of Midshipman Geisinger and was sent home to the United States. She entered Savannah, Ga., safely on 4 November. From the time *Wasp* and *Atlanta* parted company, nothing was heard from the former. She was last seen by a Swedish merchantman bound from Rio de Janeiro to Falmouth, England, about three weeks after the *Atlanta* capture and was said to be headed for the Caribbean. *Wasp* apparently sank in a storm.

VI

(SwGbt.: t. 521; l. 212'0''; b. 25'2''; dph. 10'0''; dr. 6'0''; a. 1 30-pdr. P. r., 2 24-pdr. how.)

Emma Henry, an iron-hulled sidewheel steamer, was captured at sea in December of 1864 attempting to run the Union blockade of the Confederacy; purchased from the New York prize court on 13 January 1865; and commissioned on 11 May 1865.

At Norfolk, *Emma Henry* joined the squadron commanded by Acting Rear Admiral Sylvanus W. Godon which had been established to search for the Confederate ram *Stonewall*. She departed Hampton Roads with the rest of the squadron on 17 May. On the 22d, she carried Acting Rear Admiral Godon into Charleston harbor to confer with Rear Admiral Dahlgren before the squadron continued on its way. During that interlude, she collided with another ship and, after returning Godon to his flagship *Susquehanna*, headed north for repairs at Philadelphia.

On 13 June 1865, while undergoing repairs, she was renamed *Wasp*. As soon as she completed repairs, the ship rejoined Rear Admiral Godon's squadron, designated the Brazil Squadron and based at Rio de Janeiro. The original reason for the squadron's dispatch, CSS *Stonewall*, had long since ceased to pose a problem. The former Confederate ironclad had surrendered to Spanish authorities in Cuba on 19 May just as *Wasp* had begun her repairs at Philadelphia. Thus, she and her squadron-mates took up a different duty—watching out for American interests in South America and along the eastern coast of Africa.

The latter location, however, *Wasp* left to her larger sisters while she concentrated upon the vicinity of the La Plata and Uruguay Rivers during the war between Paraguay and the coalition of Brazil, Argentina, and Uruguay which had begun when the Paraguayan dictator, Francisco Solano Lopez, invaded Brazil on the day after Christmas 1864. The war lasted until mid-1870, peace coming only after the complete reduction of Paraguay and the death of Lopez at the hands of Brazilian lancers following a protracted guerrilla campaign. In the meantime, *Wasp* patrolled the area to protect Americans and their interests in the combat zone. As frequently on the rivers in the interior as she was at sea, she ascended Rio de La Plata and its tributaries, the Uruguay Parana and Paraguay Rivers.

After the war ended in June 1870, *Wasp* continued to operate out of Montevideo in Uruguay on the aforementioned rivers, ascending them as far as Asuncion, Uruguay. Her duty consisted of transporting diplomats and generally watching out for American interests. She continued to be so employed until surveyed early in 1876 when she was found to be unfit for further naval service. Decommissioned that same spring, *Wasp* was sold to Mr. L. B. Scheiner of Montevideo on 5 June 1876.

VII

(Yacht: dp. 630; l. 180'0'' (wl.); b. 23'0''; dr. 12'0'' (mean); s. 16.5 k.; cpl. 55; a. 4 6-pdrs., 2 Colt mg.)

Columbia—a steam yacht built in 1898 at Philadelphia by William Cramp & Sons—was acquired by the Navy from Mr. J. H. Ladew; renamed *Wasp*; and commissioned at New York on 11 April 1898, Lt. Aaron Ward in command.

The converted yacht departed New York on 26 April and headed south for duty blockading Cuba. She stopped at Key West, Fla., from 1 to 7 May and arrived off Havana on the latter day. From there, she moved west along the northern coast to Bahia Honda, also arriving there on the 7th. On 12 May, while cruising on blockade station off the Cuban coast between Havana and Bahia Honda, *Wasp* joined a small convoy escorted by the revenue cutter *Manning* and made up of the merchantman SS *Gussie* and the tugs *Triton* and *Dewey*. *Gussie* carried two companies of Army troops scheduled to land at Bahia Honda while *Triton* and *Dewey* carried representatives of the press.

Just before 1500 that afternoon, some of the soldiers from *Gussie* went ashore near Cabanas—purportedly the first American troops to land on Cuban soil. They formed a skirmish line and started their advance through dense underbrush. At about 1515, Spanish forces counterattacked the American troops and opened fire on the ships in the bay. *Wasp* returned fire with her portside six pounders, carefully avoiding the area occupied by friendly forces. At that point, she received word that the 100 or so soldiers fighting ashore were heavily outnumbered and outflanked to the west. The only course of action open to them was to disengage the enemy and reembark in *Gussie*. During that operation, *Wasp* joined *Manning* and recently arrived *Dolphin* in providing covering gunfire for the evacuation. When another landing, scheduled for the following day, did not occur, *Wasp* lobbed a few shells at an adobe watchtower from which Spanish riflemen had taken the ships under fire, and then she resumed her patrol station off the coast.

Two days later, the converted yacht departed the Cuban coast to return to Florida. She arrived at Key West that same day and remained in the Keys—either at Key West or Sand Key—almost until the end of May. *Wasp* returned to the blockade, at Cienfuegos, briefly on the 29th but was back at Key West on the 31st. During June, the yacht moved from blockade station to blockade station, returning periodically to the Florida Keys for necessities. From 9 to 11 June, she stood off Havana. After a three-day return to Key West, *Wasp* took station off the southeastern coast of Cuba on 20 June patrolling between Santiago de Cuba and Guantanamo Bay.

At the beginning of July, she paid a five-day visit to Key West, returning to the Santiago area again on 10 July. On the 19th, the converted yacht cleared Guantanamo Bay for Nipe Bay on Cuba's northeastern coast. She arrived at Nipe Bay late on the morning of the 21st and, on orders to reconnoiter the bay in company with *Leyden*, started in toward Port Nipe. Upon entering, *Wasp* sighted a Spanish warship at anchor some four miles up the bay. She fired several shots at the signal station located at the entrance; then sped forward to engage the enemy ship. At 1244, the Spanish ship opened fire at extreme range, and *Wasp* returned fire immediately. *Leyden*, followed by *Annapolis* and *Topeka*, quickly joined in. As the range decreased, American gunfire became more accurate, and all four ships began scoring telling hits on the enemy. Finally, at 1312, the Spaniard's colors disappeared. *Wasp* and her three colleagues ceased fire and watched their quarry, the cruiser *Don Jorge Juan*, sink at 1342. After making a complete reconnaissance of the southern and western portions of the bay, *Wasp* anchored there for the night.

On 23 July, the ship departed Cuba, bound for Puerto Rico, and arrived off Fajardo that same day. For the next seven weeks, she cruised the coasts of Puerto Rico in company with *Dixie*, *Annapolis*, and *Gloucester*. Throughout the entire period, only one noteworthy event occurred. On 27 July, the four ships encountered three Spanish brigantines at Ponce but evaluated them as too insignificant even to take as prizes. On 8 September, *Wasp* departed San Juan to return to the United States. After a five-day stop at Charleston, she continued her voyage north on the 18th and entered the Norfolk Navy Yard on the 21st. On 27 September, she was decommissioned there and laid up.

On 15 December, the yacht was loaned to the Florida Naval Militia for training purposes. That tour of duty lasted until 21 June 1899 at which time she was returned to the Navy. She resumed her retirement to serve as station ship at Port Royal, S.C. In July 1902, she returned to Norfolk to be decommissioned once again on the 23d.

However, on 2 October, she went into commission again and received orders to the 8th Naval District. During her service there as a district tender, she made infrequent cruises in the Gulf of Mexico and the West Indies. In 1906, she moved from the Gulf of Mexico to Newport, R.I., for a tour of duty at the Torpedo Station. In 1907, she visited east coast, gulf, and Mississippi River ports during a cruise to spur enlistments in the Navy. The following year, *Wasp* began a nine-year assignment, again training naval militiamen, this time on loan to the New York Naval Militia.

That duty ended early in 1917, as the United States moved closer to war. On 7 April, the day after the American declaration of war on the German Empire, she began patrolling the coast of Long Island. Throughout the first year of the war, the yacht cruised the coastal waters of the 3d Naval District as a unit of, and later as flagship for, Squadron 8, Patrol Force. In April 1918, *Wasp* received orders detaching her from the 3d Naval District and assigning her to duty at Annapolis, Md. She arrived in Annapolis on 9 May and, but for periodic runs to Norfolk, remained there for the remainder of her naval career. Struck from the Navy list on 13 November 1919, *Wasp* was formally decommissioned at Norfolk on 1 December 1919. On 20 September 1921, she was sold to Mr. Halsted P. Layton of Georgetown, Del.

(MB: l. 40'0''; b. 9'0''; dr. 2'9'' (mean); s. 12.0 k.; cpl. 5; a. 1 1-pdr.)

Wasp—a steel-hulled motorboat built in 1910 at the Superior Shipbuilding Co.—was owned by W. S. Pattison of Duluth, Minn., in 1917, when the Navy inspected the ship, in the 9th Naval District, for possible service. She was assigned the classification SP-1159 but was never listed in the *Naval Vessel Register*. However, records indicate that *Wasp* was acquired by the Navy on a free-lease basis on 29 June 1917 and was used as a patrol craft by the 9th Naval District. She operated on

the Great Lakes until returned to her owner on 3 November 1917.

VIII

(CV-7: dp. 14,700; l. 741'4''; b. 80'8''; ew. 109'0''; dr 19'11'' (mean); s. 29.5 k.; cpl. 2,367; a. 8 5'', 16 1.1'' 16 .50-cal. mg.; ac. 80; cl. *Wasp*)

The eighth *Wasp* (CV-7) was laid down on 1 April 1936 at Quincy, Mass., by the Bethlehem Shipbuilding Co.; launched on 4 April 1939; sponsored by Mrs Charles Edison, the wife of the Assistant Secretary of the Navy, Charles Edison; and commissioned on 25 April 1940 at the Army Quartermaster Base, South Boston, Mass., Capt. John W. Reeves, Jr., in command

Wasp remained at Boston through May, fitting out before she got underway on 5 June 1940 for calibration tests on her radio direction finder gear. After further fitting out while anchored in Boston harbor, the new aircraft carrier steamed independently to Hampton Roads, Va., anchoring there on 24 June. Four days later she sailed for the Caribbean in company with *Morris* (DD-417).

En route, she conducted the first of many carrier qualification tests. Among the earliest of the qualifiers was Lt. (jg.) David T. McCampbell, who later became the Navy's top-scoring "ace" in World War II. *Wasp* arrived at Guantanamo Bay in time to "dress ship" in honor of Independence Day.

Tragedy marred the carrier's shakedown. On 9 July one of her Vought SB2U-2 Vindicators crashed two miles from the ship. *Wasp* bent on flank speed to close as did the planeguarding destroyer *Morris*. The latter's boats recovered items from the plane's baggage compartment, but the plane itself had gone down with its crew of two.

Wasp departed Guantanamo Bay on 11 July and arrived at Hampton Roads four days later. There, she embarked planes from the 1st Marine Air Group and took them to sea for qualification trials. Operating off the southern drill grounds, the ship and her planes honed their skills for a week before the marines and their planes were disembarked at Norfolk; and the carrier moved north to Boston for post-shakedown repairs

While civilian workmen from the Bethlehem Steel Co.

USS *Wasp* (CV-7) in 1942, escorted by a camouflaged *Gleaves* (DD-423)-class destroyer. (80-G-12240)

came on board the ship to check their workmanship and to learn how it had stood up under the rigors of shake-down, *Wasp* lay alongside the same pier at which she had been commissioned. While at Boston, she fired a 21-gun salute and rendered honors to President Franklin D. Roosevelt, whose yacht, *Potomac* (AG-25), stopped briefly at the Boston Navy Yard on 10 August.

Wasp departed the Army Quartermaster Base on the 21st to conduct steering drills and full-power trials. Late the following morning, she got underway for Norfolk. For the next few days, while *Ellis* (DD-154) operated as plane guard, *Wasp* launched and recovered her aircraft: fighters from Fighter Squadron (VF) 7, and scout-bombers from Scouting Squadron (VS) 72. The carrier put into the Norfolk Navy Yard on 28 August for repair work on her turbines—alterations which kept the ship in dockyard hands into the following month. Drydocked during the period from 12 to 18 September, *Wasp* ran her final sea trials in Hampton Roads on 26 September 1940.

Ready now to join the fleet and assigned to Carrier Division (CarDiv) 3, Patrol Force, *Wasp* shifted to Naval Operating Base (NOB), Norfolk, from the Norfolk Navy Yard on 11 October. There, she loaded 24 P-40's from the 8th Army Pursuit Group and nine O-47A's from the 2d Observation Squadron, as well as her own spares and utility unit Grumman J2F's on the 12th. Proceeding to sea for maneuvering room, *Wasp* flew off the Army planes in a test designed to compare the take-off runs of standard Navy and Army aircraft. That experiment, the first time that Army planes had flown from a Navy carrier, foreshadowed the use of the ship in the ferry role that she performed so well in World War II.

Wasp then proceeded on toward Cuba in company with *Plunkett* (DD-431) and *Niblack* (DD-424). The carrier's planes flew routine training flights, including dive-bombing and machine gun practices, over the ensuing four days. Upon arrival at Guantanamo, *Wasp's* saluting batteries barked out a 13-gun salute to Rear Admiral Hayne Ellis, Commander, Atlantic Squadron, embarked in *Texas* (BB-35), on 19 October.

For the remainder of October and into November, *Wasp* trained in the Guantanamo Bay area. Her planes flew carrier qualification and refresher training flights while her gunners sharpened up their skills in short-range battle practices at targets towed by the new fleet tug *Seminole* (AT-65). While operating in the Culebra, Virgin Islands, area, *Wasp* again teamed with the aviators of the 1st Marine Air Wing, giving the flying leathernecks practice in carrier take-offs and landings.

Her work in the Caribbean finished, *Wasp* sailed for Norfolk and arrived shortly after noon on 26 November. She remained at the Norfolk Navy Yard through Christmas of 1940. Then, after first conducting degaussing experiments with *Hannibal* (AG-1), she steamed independently to Cuba.

Arriving at Guantanamo Bay on 27 January 1941, *Wasp* conducted a regular routine of flight operations into February. With *Walke* (DD-416) as her plane guard, *Wasp* operated out of Guantanamo and Culebra, conducting her maneuvers with an impressive array of warships—*Texas*, *Ranger* (CV-4), *Tuscaloosa* (CA-37), *Wichita* (CA-45) and a host of destroyers. *Wasp* ran gunnery drills and exercises, as well as routine flight training evolutions, into March. Underway for Hampton Roads on 4 March, the aircraft carrier conducted a night battle practice into the early morning hours of the 5th.

During the passage to Norfolk, heavy weather sprang up on the evening of 7 March. *Wasp* was steaming at standard speed, 17 knots, a pace that she had been maintaining all day. Off Cape Hatteras, a lookout in the carrier spotted a red flare arcing into the stormy black night skies at 2245. The big ship swung around to head in the direction of the distress signal while a messenger notified the captain, who reached the bridge

in an instant. Capt. Reeves himself took the conn, as a second set of flares was seen at 2259.

Finally, at 2329, with the aid of her searchlights probing the wet night, *Wasp* located the stranger in trouble. She proved to be the lumber schooner *George E. Klinck*, bound from Jacksonville, Fla., to Southwest Harbor, Maine.

The sea, in the meantime, worsened from a state 5 to a state 7. *Wasp* lay to, maneuvering alongside at 0007 on 8 March. At that time, four men from the schooner clambered up a swaying jacob's ladder buffetted by gusts of wind. Then, despite the raging tempest, *Wasp* lowered a boat, at 0016, and brought the remaining four men aboard from the foundering 152-foot schooner.

Later that day, *Wasp* disembarked her rescued mariners and immediately went into drydock at the Norfolk Navy Yard. The ship received vital repairs to her turbines. Port holes on the third deck were welded over to provide better watertight integrity, and steel splinter shielding around her 5-inch and 1.1-inch batteries was added. After those repairs and alterations were finished, *Wasp* got underway for the Virgin Islands on 22 March, the carrier arriving at St. Thomas three days later. She soon shifted to Guantanamo Bay and loaded marine stores for transportation to Norfolk.

Returning to Norfolk on 30 March, *Wasp* conducted routine flight operations out of Hampton Roads over the ensuing days, into April. In company with *Sampson* (DD-394), the carrier conducted an abortive search for a downed patrol plane in her vicinity on 8 April. For the remainder of the month, *Wasp* operated off the eastern seaboard between Newport, R.I., and Norfolk, conducting extensive flight and patrol operations with her embarked air group. She shifted to Bermuda in mid-May, anchoring at Grassy Bay on the 12th. Eight days later, the ship got underway in company with *Quincy* (CA-39), *Livermore* (DD-429), and *Kearny* (DD-432) for exercises at sea before returning to Grassy Bay on 3 June. *Wasp* sailed for Norfolk three days later with *Edison* (DD-439) as her antisubmarine screen.

After a brief stay in the Tidewater area, *Wasp* headed back toward Bermuda on 20 June. *Wasp* and her escorts patrolled the stretch of the Atlantic between Bermuda and Hampton Roads until 5 July, as the Atlantic Fleet's neutrality patrol zones were extended eastward. Reaching Grassy Bay on that day, she remained in port a week before returning to Norfolk, sailing on 12 July in company with *Tuscaloosa* (CA-37), *Grayson* (DD-435), *Anderson* (DD-411), and *Rowan* (DD-405).

Following her return to Norfolk on the 13th, *Wasp* and her embarked air group conducted refresher training off the Virginia capes. Meanwhile, the situation in the Atlantic had taken on a new complexion, with American participation in the Battle of the Atlantic only a matter of time, when the United States took another step toward involvement on the side of the British. To protect American security and to free British forces needed elsewhere, the United States made plans to occupy Iceland. *Wasp* played an important role in the move.

Late on the afternoon of 23 July, while the carrier lay alongside Pier 7, NOB Norfolk, 32 Army Air Force (AAF) pilots reported on board "for temporary duty." At 0630 the following day, *Wasp's* crew watched an interesting cargo come on board, hoisted on deck by the ship's cranes: 30 Curtiss P-40C's and three PT-17 trainers from the AAF 33d Pursuit Squadron, 8th Air Group, Air Force Combat Command, home-based at Mitchell Field, N.Y. Three days later, four newspaper correspondents—including the noted journalist Fletcher Pratt—came on board.

The carrier had drawn the assignment of ferrying those vital army planes to Iceland because of a lack of British aircraft to cover the American landings. The American P-40's would provide the defensive fighter cover necessary to watch over the initial increment of American occupying forces. *Wasp* consequently cast off from Pier 7 and slipped out to sea through the swept channel at 0932 on 28 July, with *O'Brien* (DD–415) and *Walke* as plane guards. *Vincennes* (CA–44) later joined the formation at sea.

Within a few days, *Wasp's* group joined the larger Task Force (TF) 16—consisting of *Mississippi* (BB–41), *Quincy*, *Wichita*, five destroyers, *Semmes* (AG–24), *American Legion* (AP–35), *Mizar* (AF–12), and *Almaack* (AK–27). Those ships, too, were bound for Iceland with the first occupation troops embarked. On the morning of 6 August, *Wasp*, *Vincennes*, *Walke*, and *O'Brien* parted company from TF 16. Soon thereafter, the carrier turned into the wind and commenced launching the planes from the 33d Pursuit Squadron. As the P–40's and the trio of trainers droned on to Iceland, *Wasp* headed home for Norfolk, her three escorts in company. After another week at sea, the group arrived back at Norfolk on 14 August.

Underway again on 22 August, however, *Wasp* put to sea for carrier qualifications and refresher landings off the Virginia capes. Two days later, Rear Admiral H. Kent Hewitt, Commander, Cruisers, Atlantic Fleet, shifted his flag from *Savannah* (CL–42) to *Wasp*, while the ships lay anchored in Hampton Roads. Underway on the 25th, in company with *Savannah*, *Monssen* (DD–436) and *Kearny*, the aircraft carrier conducted flight operations over the ensuing days. Scuttlebutt on board the carrier had her steaming out in search of a German heavy cruiser, *Admiral Hipper*, which was reportedly roaming the western Atlantic in search of prey. Suspicions were confirmed for many on the 30th when the British battleship HMS *Rodney* was sighted some 20 miles away, on the same course as the Americans.

In any event, if they had been in search of a German raider, they did not make contact with her. *Wasp* and her escorts anchored in the Gulf of Paria, Trinidad, on 2 September, where Admiral Hewitt shifted his flag back to *Savannah*. The carrier remained in port until 6 September, when she again put to sea on patrol "to enforce the neutrality of the United States in the Atlantic."

While at sea, the ship received the news of a German U-boat unsuccessfully attempting to attack the destroyer *Greer* (DD–145). The United States had been getting more and more involved in the war; American warships were now convoying British merchantmen halfway across the Atlantic to the "mid-ocean meeting point" (MOMP).

Wasp's crew looked forward to returning to Bermuda on 18 September, but the new situation in the Atlantic meant a change in plans. Shifted to the colder climes of Newfoundland, the carrier arrived at Placentia Bay on 22 September and fueled from *Salinas* (AO–19) the following day. The respite in port was a brief one, however, as the ship got underway again, late on the 23d, for Iceland. In company with *Wichita*, four destroyers, and the repair ship *Vulcan* (AR–5), *Wasp* arrived at Hvalfjordur, Iceland, on the 28th. Two commands earlier, Admiral Harold R. Stark, the Chief of Naval Operations, had ordered American warships to do their utmost to destroy whatever German or Italian warships they found. The "short-of-war" operations were drawing frightfully close to the real thing!

With the accelerated activity entailed in the United States Navy's conducting convoy escort missions, *Wasp* put to sea on 6 October in company with *Vincennes* and four destroyers. Those ships patrolled the foggy, cold, North Atlantic until returning to Little Placentia Bay, Newfoundland, on the 11th, anchoring during a fierce gale that lashed the bay with high winds and stinging spray. On 17 October, *Wasp* set out for home—Norfolk—patrolling en route, and arrived at her destination on the 20th. The carrier soon sailed for Bermuda and conducted qualifications and refresher training flights en route. Anchoring in Grassy Bay on 1

November, *Wasp* operated on patrols out of Bermud for the remainder of the month.

October had seen the incidents involving America and German warships multiplying on the high sea *Kearny* was torpedoed on 17 October; *Salinas* took "fish" on the 28th; and in the most tragic incident tha autumn, *Reuben James* (DD–245) was torpedoed an sunk with heavy loss of life on 30 October. Meanwhile in the Pacific, tension between the United States an Japan increased almost with each passing day.

Wasp slipped out to sea from Grassy Bay on 3 December and rendezvoused with *Wilson* (DD–408). Whil the destroyer operated as plane guard, *Wasp's* ai group flew day and night refresher training mission In addition, the two ships conducted gunnery drills be fore returning to Grassy Bay two days later.

Wasp lay at anchor on 7 December 1941, observing "holiday routine"—it being a Sunday. In the Pacific the Japanese broke the Sunday morning peace in devastating surprise attack on the Pacific Fleet at Pear Harbor. Their daring attack plunged the United State into World War II in both oceans. On 11 December Germany and Italy followed Japan into war against the United States.

Meanwhile, naval authorities felt considerable anxiety that French warships in the Caribbean and West Indie were prepared to make a breakout and attempt to ge back to France. Accordingly, *Wasp*, *Brooklyn* (CL–40) and two destroyers, *Sterett* (DD–407) and *Wilson*, de parted Grassy Bay and headed for Martinique. Faulty intelligence gave American authorities in Washingto the impression that the Vichy French armed merchan cruiser *Barfleur* had gotten underway for sea. The French were accordingly warned that the auxiliary cruiser would be sunk or captured unless she returne to port and resumed her internment. As it turned out *Barfleur* had not departed after all, but had remaine in harbor. The tense situation at Martinique eventually dissipated, and the crisis abated.

With tensions in the West Indies lessened consider ably, *Wasp* departed Grassy Bay and headed for Hamp ton Roads three days before Christmas, in compan with *Long Island* (AVG–1), and escorted by *Stac* (DD–406) and *Sterett*. Two days later, the carrie moored at the Norfolk Navy Yard to commence a overhaul that would last into 1942.

After departing Norfolk on 14 January 1942, *Was* headed north and touched at Argentia, Newfoundland and Casco Bay, Maine, while operating in those north ern climes. On 16 March, as part of Task Group (TG 22.6, she headed back toward Norfolk. During th morning watch the next day, visibility lessened con siderably; and, at 0550, *Wasp's* bow plunged int *Stack's* starboard side, punching a hole and completel flooding the destroyer's number one fireroom. *Stac* was detached and proceeded to the Philadelphia Navy Yard, where her damage was repaired.

Wasp, meanwhile, made port at Norfolk on the 21s without further incident. Shifting back to Casco Bay three days later, she sailed for the British Isles on 2 March, with Task Force (TF) 39 under the comman of Rear Admiral John W. Wilcox, Jr., in *Washingto* (BB–56). That force was to reinforce the Home Flee of the Royal Navy. While en route, Rear Admira Wilcox was swept overboard from the battleship an drowned. Although hampered by poor visibility con ditions, *Wasp* planes took part in the search. Wilcox body was spotted an hour later, face down in th raging seas, but it was not recovered.

Rear Admiral Robert C. Giffen, who flew his fla in *Wichita*, assumed command of TF–39. The America ships were met by a force based around the ligh cruiser HMS *Edinburgh* on 3 April. Those ships es corted them to Scapa Flow in the Orkney Islands.

While the majority of TF 39 joined the British Hom Fleet—being renumbered to TF 99 in the process— to cover convoys routed to North Russia, *Wasp* de parted Scapa Flow on 9 April, bound for the Clyd stuary and Greenock, Scotland. On the following day, he carrier sailed up the Clyde River, past the John Brown Clydebank shipbuilding facilities. There, shipyard workers paused long enough from their labors to accord Wasp a tumultuous reception as she passed. Wasp's impending mission was an important one—one upon which the fate of the island bastion of Malta hung. That key isle was then being pounded daily by German and Italian planes. The British, faced with the loss of air superiority over the island, requested the use of a carrier to transport planes that could wrest air superiority from the Axis aircraft. Wasp drew ferry duty once again.

Having landed her torpedo planes and dive bombers, Wasp loaded 47 Supermarine "Spitfire" Mk. V fighter planes at the King George Dock, Glasgow, on 13 April, before she departed the Clyde estuary on the 14th. Her screen consisted of Force "W" of the Home Fleet—a group that included the battlecruiser HMS Renown and antiaircraft cruisers HMS Cairo and HMS Charybdis. Madison (DD–425) and Lang (DD–399) also served in Wasp's screen.

Wasp and her consorts passed through the Straits of Gibraltar under cover of the pre-dawn darkness on 19 April, avoiding the possibility of being discovered by Spanish or Axis agents. At 0400 on 20 April, Wasp spotted 11 Grumman F4F–4 Wildcat fighters on her deck and quickly launched them to form a combat air patrol (CAP) over Force "W". Meanwhile, the "Spitfires" were warming up their engines in the hangar deck spaces below. With the Wildcats patrolling overhead, the Spitfires were brought up singly on the after elevator, spotted for launch, and then given the go-ahead to take off. One by one, they roared down the deck and over the forward rounddown, until each Spitfire was aloft and winging toward Malta.

When the launch was complete, Wasp retired toward England, having safely delivered her charges. Unfortunately, those "Spitfires," which flew in to augment the dwindling numbers of "Gladiator" and "Hurricane" fighters, were tracked by efficient Axis intelligence and their arrival pinpointed. The unfortunate "Spitfires" were decimated by heavy German air raids which caught many planes on the ground.

As a result, it looked as if the acute situation required a second ferry run to Malta. Accordingly, Prime Minister Winston Churchill, fearing that Malta would be "pounded to bits," asked President Roosevelt to allow Wasp to have "another good sting." Roosevelt responded in the affirmative. Rising to the occasion, Wasp loaded another contingent of "Spitfire" V's and sailed for the Mediterranean on 3 May. Again, especially vigilant for submarines, Wasp proceeded unmolested. This time, the British aircraft carrier HMS Eagle accompanied Wasp; and she, too, carried a contingent of Spitfires bound for the "unsinkable aircraft carrier," Malta.

The two Allied flattops reached their launching points early on Saturday, 9 May, with Wasp steaming in column ahead of Eagle at a distance of 1,000 yards. At 0630, Wasp commenced launching planes—11 F4F–4's of VF–71 to serve as CAP over the task force. The first "Spitfire" roared down the deck at 0643, piloted by Sergeant-Pilot Herrington, but lost power soon after takeoff and plunged into the sea. Both pilot and plane were lost.

Undaunted by the loss of Herrington, the other planes flew off safely and formed up to fly to Malta. Misfortune, however, again seemed to dog the flight, when one pilot accidentally released his auxiliary fuel tank as he cimbed to 2,000 feet. He obviously could not make Malta, as the slippery tank fitted beneath the belly of the plane had increased the range of the plane markedly. With that gone, he had no chance of making the island. His only alternatives were to land back on board Wasp or to ditch and take his chances in the water.

Sergeant-Pilot Smith chose the former. Wasp bent on full speed and recovered the plane at 0743. The "Spitfire" came to a stop just 15 feet from the forward edge of the flight deck, making what one Wasp sailor observed to be a "one wire" landing. With her vital errand completed, the carrier set sail for the British Isles while a German radio station broadcast the startling news that the American carrier had been sunk! Most in the Allied camp knew better, however; and, on 11 May, Prime Minister Churchill sent a witty message to the captain and ship's company of Wasp: "Many thanks to you all for the timely help. Who said a Wasp couldn't sting twice?"

While Wasp was conducting those two important missions to Malta, a train of events far to the westward beckoned the carrier to the Pacific theater. Early in May, almost simultaneously with Wasp's second Malta run—Operation "Bowery"—the Battle of the Coral Sea had been fought. That action turned back the Japanese thrust at Port Moresby. One month later, from 4 to 6 June, an American carrier force smashed its Japanese counterpart in the pivotal Battle of Midway. These two victories cost the United States two precious carriers: Lexington (CV–2) at Coral Sea and Yorktown (CV–5) at Midway. While the Japanese had suffered the damaging of two at Coral Sea and the loss of four carriers at Midway, the United States could scarcely afford to be left with only two operational carriers in the western and central Pacific—Enterprise (CV–6) and Hornet (CV–8). Saratoga (CV–3) was still undergoing repairs and modernization after being torpedoed off Oahu in early January 1942.

To prepare to strengthen the American Navy in the Pacific, Wasp was hurried back to the United States for alterations and repairs at the Norfolk Navy Yard. During the carrier's stay in the Tidewater region, Capt. Reeves—who had been promoted to flag rank—was relieved by Capt. Forrest P. Sherman on 31 May. Departing Norfolk on 6 June, the last day of the critical Battle of Midway, Wasp sailed with TF 37 which was built around the carrier and the new battleship North Carolina (BB–55) and escorted by Quincy (CA–39) and San Juan (CL–54) and a half-dozen destroyers. The group transited the Panama Canal on 10 June, at which time Wasp and her consorts became TF 18, the carrier flying the two-starred flag of Rear Admiral Leigh Noyes.

Arriving at San Diego on 19 June, Wasp embarked the remainder of her complement of aircraft, Grumman TBF–1's and Douglas SBD–3's—10 of the former and 12 of the latter conducting their carrier qualification on 22 and 23 June, respectively—the latter replacing the old Vindicators. On 1 July, she sailed for the Tonga Islands as part of the convoy for the five transports that had embarked the 2d Marine Regiment.

While TF 18 and the transports were en route to Tongatabu, Wasp received another congratulatory message—this time from Admiral Noyes, embarked in the ship. "During the two weeks my flag has been in Wasp I have been very favorably impressed by the fine spirit of her ship's company and the way that all hands have handled their many problems. Since we have been at sea, every day has shown marked improvement in operations. I am sure that when our opportunity comes to strike the enemy in this ocean, Wasp and her squadrons will add more glory to the name she bears." Noyes' hopes were to be realized, but for all too brief a time.

Four days out of Nukualofa harbor, Wasp developed serious engine trouble. The ship's "black gang," however, worked diligently to do the preliminary work in lifting, repairing, and replacing the ship's starboard high-pressure turbine. The work done en route substantially helped enough to allow speedy completion of the repairs after the ship dropped her hook at Tongatabu on 18 July.

Meanwhile, preparations to invade the Solomon Islands were proceeding apace. Up to that point, the Japanese had been on the offensive, establishing their defensive perimeter around the edge of their "Greater East Asia Co-Prosperity Sphere."

On 4 July, while *Wasp* was en route to the South Pacific, the Japanese landed on Guadalcanal. Allied planners realized that if the enemy operated land-based aircraft from that key island, then it immediately imperiled Allied control of the New Hebrides and New Caledonia area. Rather than wait until the Japanese were firmly entrenched, they proposed to evict the Japanese before they got too deeply settled. Vice Admiral Robert L. Ghormley—who had attained a sterling record in London as Special Naval Observer—was detailed to take command of the operation; and he established his headquarters at Auckland, New Zealand. Since the Japanese had gotten a foothold on Guadalcanal, time was of the essence. Preparations for the invasion proceeded apace with the utmost secrecy and speed.

Wasp—together with the carriers *Saratoga* and *Enterprise*—was assigned to the Support Force under Vice Admiral Frank Jack Fletcher. Under the tactical command of Rear Admiral Noyes, embarked in *Wasp*, the carriers were to provide air support for the invasion.

Wasp and her airmen worked intensively practicing day and night operations to hone their skills to a high degree. Pilot qualification and training, necessitated by the ship's recent operations in the Atlantic and by the re-equipment of her air group and newer types of planes, proceeded at an intensive pace and, by the time the operations against Guadalcanal were pushed into high gear, Capt. Sherman was confident that his airmen could perform their mission. "D-day" had originally been set for 1 August, but the late arrival of some of the transports carrying marines pushed the date to 7 August.

Wasp, screened by *San Francisco* (CA-38), *Salt Lake City* (CA-25), and four destroyers, steamed westward toward Guadalcanal on the evening of 6 August until midnight. Then, she changed course to the eastward to reach her launch position 84 miles from Tulagi one hour before the first rays of sunlight crept over the horizon. A fresh breeze whipped across the carrier's darkened flight deck as the first planes were brought up to prepare for launch. The night offshore was bright, but clouds hung heavily over the assigned objective. So far, so good. No Japanese patrols had been spotted.

At 0530, the first planes from *Wasp*'s air group barreled down the deck: 16 F4F-4's under Lt. Comdr. Courtney Shands. Then, 15 SBD-3's under Lt. Comdr. John Eldridge, Jr. and the TBF-1 flown by the air group commander, Lt. Comdr. Wallace M. Beakley—fitted with a larger gasoline tank in its bomb bay to lengthen its time in the air—followed seven minutes later. At 0557, the first combat air patrol fighter took off.

The early flights of F4F's and SBD's were assigned specific targets: Tulagi, Gavutu, Tanambogo, Halavo, Port Purvis, Haleta, Bungana, and the radio station dubbed "Asses' Ears." After taking off, the 16 Wildcats split up into sections and raced off to their respective hunting areas. At about 0600, the planes passed over the transport area off Lunga Point, as the ships were preparing to disembark their troops. In the pre-dawn darkness, the ships were almost invisible until the fighters passed directly over them. Soon, the fourth division of Shands' flight climbed to 5,000 feet above Tulagi to serve as CAP for the strafers. The third division broke off and headed for their target—Haleta—before Shands took three planes around the northwest tip of Tulagi.

Shands and his wingman, Ens. S. W. Forrer, then swung down the north coast toward Gavatu. The other two headed for Tanambogo, to work over the seaplane facilities there. The Japanese appeared to be caught flat-footed, and the Grummans, arriving simultaneously at daybreak, shot up all of the patrol planes and fighter-seaplanes that were in the area. Fifteen Kawa-

nishi flying boats and seven Nakajima floatplane fighters—the seaplane derivative of the Mitsubishi "Zero"—were destroyed by Shands' fighters that flew almost "on the deck." Shands himself bagged at least four Nakajima single-float fighter seaplanes and one four-engined flying boat. His wingman, Forrer, bagged three floatplane fighters and one patrol plane; Lt. Wright and Ens. Kenton bagged three patrol planes apiece and destroyed a motorboat apparently attempting to tend the flying boats; Ensigns Reeves and Conklin each bagged two and shared a fifth patrol plane between them. In addition, the strafing F4F's destroyed an aviation fuel truck and a truck loaded with spare parts.

The SBD's, too, laid their bombs "on the money." Post-attack assessment estimated that the antiaircraft and shore battery sites pinpointed by intelligence had been destroyed by the dive bombers in their first attack. So complete was the enemy's unpreparedness that none of *Wasp*'s planes was shot down. Only one plane from the 16 Grummans failed to return; and, in that case, its pilot, Ensign Reeves, put her down on board *Enterprise* after having run low on fuel.

That was not all, however. At 0704, 12 Grumman TBF-1's, led by Lt. H. A. Romberg, rolled ponderously down the deck, loaded with bombs for use against land targets. Having encountered resistance, the initial landing forces called for help. Romberg's dozen Avengers blasted enemy troop concentrations east of the nob of land known as Hill 281, in the Makambo-Sasapi sector, and the prison on Tulagi Island. "All enemy resistance," the official report later stated, was "apparently effectively silenced by this flight."

The first day's operations against Guadalcanal had proved successful. Some 10,000 men had been put ashore there and met only slight resistance. On Tulagi, however, the Japanese resisted stoutly, retaining about one-fifth of the island by nightfall. *Wasp*, *Saratoga*, and *Enterprise*, with their screens, retired to the southward at nightfall.

Wasp returned the next morning, 8 August, to maintain a continuous CAP over the transport area until noon. These fighters were led by Lt. C. S. Moffett. Meanwhile, she also launched a scouting flight of 12 SBD-3's led by Lt. Comdr. E. M. Snowden. The Dauntlesses searched a sector to a radius of 220 miles from their carrier, extending it to include all of the Santa Isabel Island and the New Georgia group.

The Dauntless pilots sighted nothing that morning and made no contact with the enemy during their two hours in the air. But that was soon to change for the flight leader. At 0815, Snowden sighted a "Rufe" some 40 miles from Rekata Bay and gave chase. The Japanese airman, seeing that he had been spotted, had no stomach for a fight. He pulled up and attempted to use the clouds for cover. Each time the dogged dive bomber pilot gunned the SBD-3 after him: twice the "Rufe" headed for the clouds. Snowden finally pulled within close range, and, using his two fixed .50-caliber guns, fired a short burst that hit home, causing the "Rufe" to spin into the Solomon Sea.

Meanwhile, a large group of Japanese planes approached from Bougainville, apparently bent upon attacking the transports off Lunga Point. Upon learning of their approach, Rear Admiral Richmond K. Turner ordered all transports to get underway and to assume cruising disposition. The Americans accordingly cleared the decks for action. *Wasp*'s planes took part in the melee that followed—some planes by accident.

Lt. Comdr. Eldridge—again leading a formation of SDB-3's from VS-71—had led his planes against Mbangi Island, off Tulagi, the site of some still fierce Japanese resistance. Eldridge's rear seat gunner, Aviation Chief Radioman L. A. Powers, suddenly spotted a formation of planes coming in from the northeast: but, thinking them to be a relief flight, Eldridge continued on his present course. The Americans did a double-ake, however, and discovered that the planes were, in fact, enemy. At that instant, six "Zeroes" showed up and bounced the first section, but showed remarkably little skill in the attack, for they made 12 firing passes but could not down any of the Dauntlesses.

Meanwhile, the leader of the last section of VS–71, Lt. (jg.) Robert L. Howard, spotted a cluster of twin-engined G4M1 "Betty" bombers heading for the American transports. Howard dove to the attack; but, in his excitement, failed to flip his armament switch to "on." After two runs during which his guns had failed to fire—thinking that the guns needed to be recharged—he discovered his error—but too late to do anything about the Mitsubishi bombers. At that moment, four "zeroes," escorts for the bombers, attacked the single SBD.

Howard's rear gunner, Seaman 2d Class Lawrence P. Lupo, handled his twin 30-caliber mount magnificently and kept the enemy fighters at arm's length, his bullets scoring several hits on them as well. After about eight passes, one "Zero" veered up sharply and made a head-on run that Howard met with simultaneous fire from his fixed .50's. The "Zero" caught fire like a flying tinder box, passed close aboard the Dauntless' left wing, and crashed in flames amidst the American landing craft far below. At the same time Howard was downing the "Zero" ahead, Seaman Lupo was firing on another "Zero" making an attack from the stern. Lupo kept the enemy away, but he had to shoot through his own plane's vertical stabilizer to do it. Eventually, the enemy tired of sporting with the SBD and retired to leave Howard and his squadron mates in VS–71 to return safely to their carrier.

At 1807 on 8 August, Vice Admiral Frank Jack Fletcher recommended to Ghormley, at Noumea, that the air support force be withdrawn. Fletcher, concerned by the large numbers of enemy planes that had attacked on the 8th, reported that he had only 78 fighters left (he had started with 99) and that fuel for the carriers was running low. Ghormley approved the recommendation, and *Wasp* joined *Enterprise* and *Saratoga* in retiring from Guadalcanal. By midnight on 8 August, the landing had been a success, having attained the immediate objectives of the landing. All Japanese resistance—but a few snipers—on Gavutu and Tanombogo had been overcome. Early on 9 August, a Japanese surface force engaged an American one off Savo Island and retired at very little cost to themselves. The Allied force suffered loss of four heavy cruisers off Savo Island, including two that had served with *Wasp* in the Atlantic: *Vincennes* and *Quincy*. The early and unexpected withdrawal of the support force, including *Wasp*, when coupled with Allied losses in the Battle of Savo Island, jeopardized the success of the operation in the Solomons.

After the initial day's action in the Solomons campaign, the carrier spent the next month engaged in patrol and covering operations for convoys and resupply units headed for Guadalcanal. The Japanese, while reacting sluggishly to the initial thrust at Guadalcanal, soon began pouring reinforcements down to contest the Allied forces.

Wasp was ordered south by Vice Admiral Fletcher to refuel and did not participate in the Battle of Eastern Solomons on 24 August 1942. That engagement cost the American force the use of the valuable *Enterprise*. *Saratoga* was torpedoed a week later and departed the South Pacific war zone for repairs as well. That left only two carriers in the southwest Pacific: *Hornet*—which had been in commission for only a year—and *Wasp*.

On Tuesday, 15 September, those two carriers and *North Carolina*—with 10 other warships—were escorting the transports carrying the 7th Marine Regiment to Guadalcanal as reinforcements. *Wasp* had drawn the job of ready-duty carrier and was operating some 150 miles southeast of San Cristobal Island. Her gasoline system was in use, as planes were being refueled and rearmed for antisubmarine patrol missions; and *Wasp* had been at general quarters from an hour before sunrise until the time when the morning search returned to the ship at 1000. Thereafter, the ship was in condition 2, with the air department at flight quarters. There was no contact with the enemy during the day, with the exception of a Japanese four-engined flying boat downed by a *Wasp* Wildcat at 1215.

About 1420, the carrier turned into the wind to launch eight fighters and 18 SBD–3's and to recover eight F4F–3's and three SBD's that had been airborne since before noon. The ship rapidly completed the recovery of the 11 planes; she then turned easily to starboard, the ship heeling slightly as the course change was made. The air department at flight quarters, as they had done in earlier operations, worked coolly at refueling and respotting the ship's planes for the afternoon mission. Suddenly, at 1444, a lookout called out, "three torpedoes . . . three points forward of the starboard beam!"

A spread of four torpedoes, fired from the tubes of the Japanese submarine *I-19*, churned inexorably closer. *Wasp* put over her rudder hard-a-starboard, but it was too late. Two torpedoes smashed home in quick succession while a fourth passed ahead. Both hit in the vicinity of gasoline tanks and magazines.

In quick succession, fiery blasts ripped through the forward part of the ship. Aircraft on the flight and hangar decks were thrown about as if they were toys and dropped on the deck with such force that landing gears snapped. Planes triced up in the hangar overheads fell and landed upon those on the hangar deck; fires broke out almost simultaneously in the hangar and below decks. Soon, the heat of the intense gasoline fires detonated the ready ammunition at the forward antiaircraft guns on the starboard side; and fragments showered the forward part of the ship. The number two 1.1-inch mount was blown overboard and the corpse of the gun captain was thrown onto the bridge where it landed next to Capt. Sherman.

Water mains in the forward part of the ship proved useless, since they had been broken by the force of the explosions. There was no water available to fight the conflagration forward; and the fires continued to set off ammunition, bombs, and gasoline. As the ship listed to starboard between 10 and 15 degrees, oil and gasoline, released from the tanks by the torpedo hit, caught fire on the water.

Sherman slowed to 10 knots, ordering the rudder put to port to try to get the wind on the starboard bow; he then went astern with right rudder until the wind was on the starboard quarter, in an attempt to keep the fire forward. At that point, some flames made central station untenable, and communication circuits went dead. Soon, a serious gasoline fire broke out in the forward portion of the hanger; within 24 minutes of the initial attack, three additional major gasoline vapor explosions occurred. Ten minutes later, Capt. Sherman consulted with his executive officer, Comdr. Fred C. Dickey. The two men saw no course but to abandon, as all fire-fighting was proving ineffectual. The survivors would have to be gotten off quickly if unnecessary loss of life was not to be incurred.

Reluctantly, after consulting with Rear Admiral Noyes, Capt. Sherman ordered "abandon ship" at 1520. All badly injured men were lowered into rafts or rubber boats. Many unwounded men had to abandon from aft because the forward fires were burning with such intensity. The departure, as Capt. Sherman observed it, looked "orderly," and there was no panic. The only delays occurred when many men showed reluctance to leave until all the wounded had been taken off. The abandonment took nearly 40 minutes; and, at 1600—satisfied that no one was left on deck, in the galleries, or in the hangar aft—Capt. Sherman swung over the lifeline on the fantail and slid into the sea.

Although the submarine hazard caused the accompanying destroyers to lie well clear or to shift position, the "tin cans" carried out the rescue efforts with persistence and determination until *Laffey* (DD–459), *Lansdowne* (DD–486), *Helena* (CL–50), and *Salt Lake City* had 1,946 men embarked. The abandoned ship drifted with her crew of remaining dead. The fires greedily traveled aft; four more violent explosions boomed as night began to fall. *Lansdowne* drew the duty of destruction, and she fired five torpedoes into the dying ship's fire-gutted hull. Three hit, but she remained afloat. By now, the orange flames had enveloped the stern. The carrier literally floated in a burning pool of gasoline and oil. She sank at 2100 by the bow.

Wasp received two battle stars for her World War II service.

IX

(CV–18: dp. 27,100; l. 872'0''; b. 93'0''; ew. 147'6''; dr. 28'7''; s. 32.7 k.; cpl. 3,448; a. ac. 80 to 100, 12 5'', 40 40mm., 55 20mm.; cl. *Essex*)

The ninth *Wasp* (CV–18) was laid down as *Oriskany* on 18 March 1942 at Quincy, Mass., by the Bethlehem Steel Co.; renamed *Wasp* on 13 November 1942; launched on 17 August 1943; sponsored by Miss Julia M. Walsh, the sister of Senator David I. Walsh of Massachusetts; and commissioned on 24 November 1943, Capt. Clifton A. F. Sprague in command.

Following a shakedown cruise which lasted through the end of 1943, *Wasp* returned to Boston for a brief yard period to correct minor flaws which had been discovered during her time at sea. On 10 January 1944, the new aircraft carrier departed Boston; steamed to Hampton Roads, Va.; and remained there until the last day of the month, when she sailed for Trinidad, her base of operations through 22 February. She returned to Boston five days later and prepared for service in the Pacific. Early in March, the ship sailed south; transited the Panama Canal; arrived at San Diego, Calif., on 21 March; and reached Pearl Harbor on 4 April.

Following training exercises in Hawaiian waters, *Wasp* steamed to the Marshall Islands and at Majuro Rear Admiral Alfred E. Montgomery's newly formed Task Group (TG) 58.6 of Vice Admiral Marc A. Mitscher's Fast Carrier Task Force (TF 58). On 14 May, she and her sister carriers of TG 58.6, *Essex* (CV–9) and *San Jacinto* (CV–30), sortied for raids on Marcus and Wake Islands to give the new task group combat experience; to test a recently devised system of assigning—before takeoff—each pilot a specific target; and to neutralize those islands for the forthcoming Marianas campaign. As the force neared Marcus, it split, sending *San Jacinto* north to search for Japanese picket boats while *Wasp* and *Essex* launched strikes on the 19th and 20th, aimed at installations on the island. American planes encountered heavy antiaircraft fire but still managed to do enough damage to prevent Japanese forces on the island from interfering with the impending assault on Saipan.

When weather canceled launches planned for the 21st, the two carriers rejoined *San Jacinto* and steamed to Wake. Planes from all three carriers pounded that island on the 24th and were sufficiently effective to neutralize that base. However, the system of preselecting targets for each plane fell short of the Navy's expectations; and, thereafter, tactical air commanders resumed responsibility for directing the attacks of their planes.

After the strike on Wake, TG 58.6 returned to Majuro to prepare for the Mariana campaign. On 6 June, *Wasp*—reassigned to TG 58.2 which was also commanded by Rear Admiral Montgomery—sortied for the invasion of Saipan. During the afternoon of the 11th, she and her sister carriers launched fighters for strikes against Japanese air bases on Saipan and Tinian. They were challenged by some 30 land-based fighters which they promptly shot down. Antiaircraft fire was heavy, but the American planes braved it as they went on to destroy many Japanese aircraft which were still on the ground.

During the next three days, the American fighters—now joined by bombers—pounded installations on Saipan to soften up Japanese defenses for American assault troops who would go ashore on the 15th. That day and thereafter until the morning of the 17th, planes from TG 58.2 and TG 58.3 provided close air support for marines fighting on the Saipan beachhead.

The fast carriers of those task groups then turned over to escort carriers responsibility for providing air support for the American ground forces, refueled, and steamed to rendezvous with TG 58.1 and 58.4 which were returning from strikes against Chichi Jima and Iwo Jima to prevent Japanese air bases on those islands from being used to launch attacks against American forces on or near Saipan.

Meanwhile, Japan—determined to defend Saipan, no matter how high the cost—was sending Admiral Jisaburo Ozawa's powerful First Mobile Fleet from the Sulu Islands to the Marianas to sink the warships of Admiral Spruance's 5th Fleet and to annihilate the American troops who had fought their way ashore on Saipan. Soon after the Japanese task force sortied from Tawi Tawi on the morning of 13 June, American submarine *Redfin* (SS–272) spotted and reported it. Other submarines—which from time to time made contact with Ozawa's warships—kept Spruance posted on their progress as they wended their way through the Philippine Islands, transited San Bernardino Strait, and entered the Philippine Sea.

All day on the 18th, each force sent out scout planes in an effort to locate its adversary. Because of their greater range, the Japanese aircraft managed to obtain some knowledge of Spruance's ships, but American scout planes were unable to find Ozawa's force. Early the following morning, 19 June, aircraft from Mitscher's carriers headed for Guam to neutralize that island for the coming battle and, in a series of dogfights, destroyed many Japanese land-based planes.

During the morning, carriers from Ozawa's fleet launched four massive raids against their American counterparts; but all were thwarted almost completely. Nearly all of the Japanese warplanes were shot down while failing to sink a single American ship. They did manage to score a single bomb hit on *South Dakota* (BB–57), but that solitary success did not even put the tough Yankee battleship out of action.

That day, Mitscher's planes did not find the Japanese ships, but American submarines succeeded in sending two enemy carriers to the bottom. In the evening, three of Mitscher's four carrier task groups headed west in search of Ozawa's retiring fleet, leaving only TG 58.4 and a gun line of old battleships in the immediate vicinity of the Marianas to cover ground forces on Saipan. Planes from the American carriers failed to find the Japanese force until mid-afternoon on the 20th when an Avenger pilot reported spotting Ozawa almost 300 miles from the American carriers. Mitscher daringly ordered an all-out strike even though he knew that night would descend before his planes could return.

Over two hours later, the American aviators caught up with their quarry. They damaged two oilers so severely that they had to be scuttled; sank carrier *Hiyo*; and scored damaging but non-lethal hits on carriers *Ryuho*, *Junyo*, and *Zuikaku* and several other Japanese ships. However, during the sunset attack, the fuel gauges in many of the American planes registered half empty or more, presaging an anxious flight back to their now distant carriers.

When the carriers spotted the first returning plane at 2030 that night, Rear Admiral J. J. Clark bravely defied the menace of Japanese submarines by ordering all lights to be turned on to guide the weary fliers home.

After a plane from *Hornet* landed on *Lexington*, Mitscher gave pilots permission to land on any available deck. Despite these unusual efforts to help the Navy's airmen, a good many planes ran out of gasoline before they reached the carriers and dropped into the water.

When fuel calculations indicated that no aircraft which had not returned could still be aloft, Mitscher ordered the carriers to reverse course and resume the stern chase of Ozawa's surviving ships—more in the hope of finding any downed fliers who might still be alive and pulling them from the sea than in the expectation of overtaking Japan's First Mobile Fleet before it reached the protection of the Emperor's land-based planes. During the chase, Mitcher's ships picked up 36 pilots and 26 crewmen.

At mid-morning of the 21st, Admiral Spruance detached *Wasp* and *Bunker Hill* from their task group and sent them with Admiral Lee's battleships in Ozawa's wake to locate and destroy any crippled enemy ships. The ensuing two-day hunt failed to flush out any game, so this ad hoc force headed toward Eniwetok for replenishment and well-earned rest.

The respite was brief; for, on 30 June, *Wasp* sortied in TG 58.2—with TG 58.1—for strikes at Iwo Jima and Chichi Jima. Planes from the carriers pounded those islands on 3 and 4 July and, during the raids, destroyed 75 enemy aircraft, for the most part in the air. Then, as a grand finale, cruisers from the force's screen shelled Iwo Jima for two and one-half hours. The next day, 5 July, the two task groups returned to the Marianas and attacked Guam and Rota to begin more than a fortnight's effort to soften the Japanese defenses there in preparation for landings on Guam. Planes from *Wasp* and her sister carriers provided close air support for the marines and soldiers who stormed ashore on the 21st.

The next day, *Wasp's* task group, TG 58.2, sortied with two other groups of Mitscher's carriers, headed southwest toward the Western Carolines, and launched raids against the Palaus on the 25th. The force then parted, with TG 58.1 and TG 58.3 steaming back north for further raids to keep the Bonin and Volcano Islands neutralized while *Wasp* in TG 58.2 was retiring toward the Marshalls for replenishment at Eniwetok which she reached on 2 August.

Toward the end of *Wasp's* stay at that base, Admiral Halsey relieved Admiral Spruance on 26 August and the 5th Fleet became the 3d Fleet. Two days later, the Fast Carrier Task Force—redesignated TF 38—sortied for the Palaus. On 6 September, *Wasp*—now assigned to Vice Admiral John S. McCain's TG 38.1—began three days of raids on the Palaus. On the 9th, she headed—with her task group, TG 38.2, and TG 38.3—for the southern Philippines to neutralize air power there during the American conquest of Morotai, Peleliu, and Ulithi—three islands needed as advanced bases during the impending campaign to liberate the Philippines. Planes from these carriers encountered little resistance as they lashed Mindanao airfields that day and on the 10th. Raids against the Visayan Islands on the 12th and 13th were carried out with impunity and were equally successful. Learning of the lack of Japanese air defenses in the southern Philippines enabled Allied strategists to cancel an invasion of Mindanao which had been scheduled to begin on 15 November. Instead, Allied forces could go straight to Leyte and advance the recapture of Philippine soil by almost a month.

D day in the Palaus, 15 September, found *Wasp's* TG 38.1 some 50 miles off Morotai, launching air strikes. It then returned to the Philippines for revisits to Mindanao and the Visayas before retiring to the Admiralties on 29 September for replenishment at Manus in preparation for the liberation of the Philippines.

Ready to resume battle, she got underway again on 4 October and steamed to the Philippine Sea where TF 38 reassembled at twilight on the evening of 7 October, some 375 miles west of the Marianas. Its mission was to neutralize airbases within operational air distance of the Philippines to keep Japanese warplanes out of the air during the American landings on Leyte scheduled to begin on 20 October. The carriers steamed north to rendezvous with a group of nine oilers and spent the next day, 8 October, refueling. They then followed a generally northwesterly course toward the Ryukyus until the 10th when their planes raided Okinawa, Amami, and Miyaki. That day, TF 38 planes destroyed a Japanese submarine tender, 12 sampans, and over 100 planes. But for Lt. Col. Doolittle's Tokyo raid from *Hornet* (CV-8) on 18 April 1942 and the daring war patrols of Pacific Fleet submarines, this carrier foray was the United States Navy's closest approach to the Japanese home islands up to that point in the war.

Beginning on the 12th, Formosa—next on the agenda—received three days of unwelcome attention from TF 38 planes. In response, the Japanese Navy made an all-out effort to protect that strategic island, even though doing so meant denuding its remaining carriers of aircraft. Yet, the attempt to thwart the ever advancing American Pacific Fleet was futile. At the end of a three-day air battle, Japan had lost more than 500 planes and 20-odd freighters. Many other merchant ships were damaged as were hangars, barracks, warehouses, industrial plants, and ammunition dumps. However, the victory was costly to the United States Navy, for TF 38 lost 79 planes and 64 pilots and air crewmen,

USS *Wasp* as an antisubmarine carrier (CVS–18).

while cruisers *Canberra* and *Houston* and carrier *Franklin* received damaging, but non-lethal, bomb hits.

From Formosa, TF 38 shifted its attention to the Philippines. After steaming to waters east of Luzon, *Wasp*'s TG 58.1 began to launch strikes against that island on the 18th and continued the attack the following day, hitting Manila for the first time since it was occupied by the Japanese early in the war.

On the 20th, the day the first American troops waded ashore on Leyte, *Wasp* had moved south to the station off that island whence she and her sister carriers launched some planes for close air support missions to assist MacArthur's soldiers, while sending other aircraft to destroy airfields on Mindanao, Cebu, Negros, Panay, and Leyte. Task Group 38.1 refueled the following day and, on the 22d, set a course for Ulithi to rearm and provision.

While McCain's carriers were steaming away from the Philippines, great events were taking place in the waters of that archipelago. Admiral Soemu Toyoda, the Commander in Chief of Japan's Combined Fleet, activated plan *Sho-Go-1*, a scheme for bringing about a decisive naval action off Leyte. The Japanese strategy called for Ozawa's carriers to act as a decoy to lure TF 38 north of Luzon and away from the Leyte beachhead. Then—with the American fast carriers out of the way—heavy Japanese surface ships were to debouch into Leyte Gulf from two directions: from the south through Surigao Strait and from the north through San Bernardino Strait. During much of the 24th, planes from Halsey's carrier task groups still in Philippine waters pounded Admiral Kurita's powerful Force "A," or Center Force, as it steamed across the Sibuyan Sea toward San Bernardino Strait. When darkness stopped their attack, the American aircraft had sunk superbattleship *Musashi* and had damaged several other Japanese warships. Moreover, Halsey's pilots reported that Kurita's force had reversed course and was moving away from San Bernardino Strait.

That night, Admiral Nishimura's Force "C", or Sourthern Force, attempted to transit Surigao Strait but met a line of old battleships commanded by Rear Admiral Jesse B. Oldendorf. The venerable American men-of-war crossed Nishimura's "T" and all but annihilated his force. Admiral Shima—who was following in Nishimura's wake to lend support—realized that disaster had struck and wisely withdrew.

Meanwhile, late in the afternoon of the 24th—after Kurita's Center Force had turned away from San Bernardino Strait in apparent retreat—Halsey's scout planes finally located Ozawa's carriers a bit under 200 miles north of TF 38. This intelligence prompted Halsey to head north toward Ozawa with his Fast Carrier Task Force. However, at this point, he did not recall McCain's TG 58.1 but allowed it to continue steaming toward Ulithi.

After dark, Kurita's Center Force again reversed course and once more headed for San Bernardino Strait. About half an hour past midnight, it transited that narrow passage; turned to starboard; and steamed south, down the east coast of Samar. Since Halsey had dashed north in pursuit of Ozawa's carriers, only three 7th Fleet escort carrier groups and their destroyer and destoyer escort screens were available to challenge Kurita's mighty battleships and heavy cruisers and to protect the American amphibious ships which were supporting the troops fighting on Leyte.

Remembered by their call names, "Taffy 1," "Taffy 2," and "Taffy 3," these three American escort-carrier groups were deployed along Samar's east coast with "Taffy 3"—commanded by *Wasp*'s first captain, Rear Admiral Clifton A. F. Sprague—in the northernmost position, about 40 miles off Paninihian Point. "Taffy 2" was covering Leyte Gulf, and "Taffy 1" was still farther south watching Surigao Strait.

At 0645, lookouts on "Taffy 3" ships spotted bursts of antiaircraft fire blossoming in the northern sky, as Center Force gunners opened fire on an American anti-

submarine patrol plane. Moments later, "Taffy 3" made both radar and visual contact with the approaching Japanese warships. Shortly before 0700, Kurita's guns opened fire on the hapless "baby flattops" and their comparatively tiny but incredibly courageous escorts. For more than two hours, "Taffy 3's" ships and planes—aided by aircraft from sister escort-carrier groups to the south—fought back with torpedoes, guns, bombs, and consummate seamanship. Then, at 0911, Kurita—shaken by the loss of three heavy cruisers and thinking that he had been fighting TF 38—ordered his remaining warships to break off the action.

Meanwhile, at 0848, Admiral Halsey had radioed McCain's TG 58.1—then refueling en route to Ulithi—calling that carrier group back to Philippine waters to help "Taffy 3" in its fight for survival. *Wasp* and her consorts raced toward Samar at flank speed until 1030 when they began launching planes for strikes at Kurita's ships which were still some 330 miles away. While these raids did little damage to the Japanese Center Force, they did strengthen Kurita's decision to retire from Leyte.

While his planes were in the air, McCain's carriers continued to speed westward to lessen the distance of his pilots' return flight and to be in optimum position at dawn to launch more warplanes at the fleeing enemy force. With the first light of the 26th, TG 38.1 and Rear Admiral Bogan's TG 38.2—which finally had been sent south by Halsey—launched the first of their strikes that day against Kurita. The second left the carriers a little over two hours later. These fliers sank light cruiser *Noshiro* and damaged, but did not sink, heavy cruiser *Kumano*. The two task groups launched a third strike in the early afternoon, but it did not add to their score.

Following the Battle for Leyte Gulf, which ended the Japanese Fleet as a serious challenge to American supremacy at sea in the Far East, TG 38.1 operated in the Philippines for two more days providing close air support before again heading for Ulithi on the 28th. However, the respite—during which Rear Admiral Montgomery took command of TG 38.1 when McCain fleeted up to relieve Mitscher as CTF 38—was brief since Japanese land-based planes attacked troops on the Leyte beachhead on 1 November. *Wasp* participated in raids against Luzon air bases on the 5th and 6th, destroying over 400 Japanese aircraft, for the most part on the ground. After a kamikaze hit *Lexington* during the operation, McCain shifted his flag from that carrier to *Wasp* and, a short time later, returned in her to Guam to exchange air groups.

Wasp returned to the Philippines a little before mid-month and continued to send strikes against targets in the Philippines—mostly on Luzon—until the 25th when the Army Air Force assumed responsibility for providing air support for troops on Leyte. TF 38 then retired to Ulithi. There, the carriers received greater complements of fighter planes and, in late November and early December, conducted training exercises to prepare them better to deal with Japan's new threat to the American warships, kamikazes or suicide planes.

Task Force 38 sortied from Ulithi on 10 and 11 December and proceeded to a position east of Luzon for round-the-clock strikes against air bases on that island from the 14th through the 16th to prevent Japanese fighter planes from endangering landings on the southwest coast of Mindoro scheduled for the 15th. Then, while withdrawing to a fueling rendezvous point east of the Philippines, TF 38 was caught in a terribly destructive typhoon which battered its ships and sank three American destroyers. The carriers spent most of the ensuing week repairing storm damage and returned to Ulithi on Christmas Eve.

But the accelerating tempo of the war ruled out long repose in the shelter of the lagoon. Before the year ended, the carriers were back in action against airfields in the Philippines, on Sakishima Gunto, and on Okinawa. These raids were intended to smooth the way for General MacArthur's invasion of Luzon through the Lingayen Gulf. While the carrier planes were unable to knock out all Japanese air resistance to the Luzon landings, they did succeed in destroying many enemy planes and thus reduced the air threat to manageable proportions.

On the night after the initial landings on Luzon, Halsey took TF 38 into the South China Sea for a week's rampage in which his ships and planes took a heavy toll of Japanese shipping and aircraft before they retransited Luzon Strait on the 16th and returned to the Philippine Sea. Bad weather prevented Halsey's planes from going aloft for the next few days; but, on the 21st, they bombed Formosa, the Pescadores, and the Sakishimas. The following day, the aircraft returned to the Sakishimas and the Ryukyus for more bombing and reconnaissance. The overworked Fast Carrier Task Force then headed for Ulithi and entered that lagoon on the 25th.

While the flattops were catching their breath at Ulithi, Admiral Spruance relieved Halsey in command of the Fleet, which was thereby transformed from the 3d to the 5th. The metamorphosis also entailed Mitscher's replacing McCain and Clark's resuming command of TG 58.1—still *Wasp*'s task group.

The next major operation dictated by Allied strategy was the capture of Iwo Jima in the Volcano Islands. Iwo was needed as a base for Army Air Force fighter planes which were to protect Mariana-based B–29 bombers during raids against the Japanese home islands and as an emergency landing point for crippled warplanes. Task Force 58 sortied on 10 February, held rehearsals at Tinian, and then headed for Japan.

Fighter planes took off from the carriers before dawn on the 16th to clear the skies of Japanese aircraft. They succeeded in this mission, but *Wasp* lost four of her fighters during the sweep. Bombing sorties, directed primarily at aircraft factories in Tokyo, followed; but clouds hid many of these plants, forcing some planes to drop their bombs on secondary targets. Bad weather, which also hampered Mitscher's fliers during raids the next morning, prompted him to cancel strikes scheduled for the afternoon and head the task force west.

During the night, Mitscher turned the carriers toward the Volcano Islands to be on hand to provide air support for the marines who would land on beaches of Iwo Jima on the morning of the 19th.

For the next few days, planes from the American carriers continued to assist the marines who were engaged in a bloody struggle to wrest the island from its fanatical defenders. On the 23d, Mitscher led his carriers back to Japan for more raids on Tokyo. Planes took off on the morning of the 25th; but, when they reached Tokyo, they again found their targets obscured by clouds. Moreover, visibility was so bad the next day that raids on Nagoya were called off, and the carriers steamed south toward the Ryukyus to bomb and reconnoiter Okinawa, the next prize to be taken from the Japanese Empire. Planes left the carriers at dawn on 1 March; and, throughout the day, they hammered and photographed the islands of the Ryukyu group. Then, after a night bombardment by surface ships, TF 58 set a course for the Carolines and anchored in Ulithi lagoon on the 4th.

Damaged as she was, *Wasp* recorded—from 17 to 23 March—what was often referred to as the busiest week in flattop history. In these seven days, *Wasp* accounted for 14 enemy planes in the air, destroyed six more on the ground, scored two 500-pound bomb hits on each of two Japanese carriers, dropped two 1,000-pound bombs on a Japanese battleship, put one 1,000-pounder on another battleship, hit a heavy cruiser with three 500-pound missiles, dropped another 1,000-pound bomb on a big cargo ship, and heavily strafed "and probably sank" a large Japanese submarine. During this week, *Wasp* was under almost continuous attack by shore-based aircraft and experienced several close kamikaze attacks. The carrier's gunners fired

more than 10,000 rounds at the determined Japanese attackers.

On 13 April 1945, *Wasp* returned to the Puget Sound Navy Yard, Bremerton, Wash., and had the damage caused by the bomb hit repaired. Once whole again, she steamed to Hawaii and, after a brief sojourn at Pearl Harbor, headed toward the western Pacific on 12 July 1945. *Wasp* conducted a strike at Wake Island and paused briefly at Eniwetok before rejoining the rampaging Fast Carrier Task Force. In a series of strikes, unique in the almost complete absence of enemy airborne planes, *Wasp* pilots struck Yokosuka Naval Base near Tokyo, numerous airfields, and hidden manufacturing centers. On 9 August, a suicide plane swooped down at the carrier; but a *Wasp* pilot flying above the ship forced the enemy to splash into the sea.

Then, on 15 August, when the fighting should have been over, two Japanese planes tried to attack *Wasp*'s task group. Fortunately, *Wasp* pilots were still flying on combat air patrol and sent both enemies smoking into the sea. This was the last time *Wasp* pilots and gunners were to tangle with the Japanese.

On 25 August 1945, a severe typhoon, with winds reaching 78 knots, engulfed *Wasp* and stove in about 30 feet of her bow. The carrier, despite the hazardous job of flying from such a shortened deck, continued to launch her planes on missions of mercy or patrol as they carried food, medicine, and long-deserved luxuries to American prisoners of war at Narumi, near Nagoya.

The ship returned to Boston for Navy Day, 27 October 1945. On 30 October, *Wasp* got underway for the naval shipyard in New York for a period of availability to have additional facilities installed for maximum transportation of troops. This work was completed on 15 November 1945 and enabled her to accommodate some 5,500 enlisted passengers and 400 officers.

After receiving the new alterations, *Wasp* was assigned temporary duty as an Operation "Magic Carpet" troop transport. On 17 February 1947, *Wasp* was placed out of commission in reserve, attached to the Atlantic Reserve Fleet.

In the summer of 1948, *Wasp* was taken out of the reserve fleet and placed in the New York Naval Shipyard for refitting and alterations to enable her to accommodate the larger, heavier, and faster planes of the jet age. Upon the completion of this conversion, the ship was recommissioned on 10 September 1951.

Wasp reported to the Atlantic Fleet in November 1951 and began a period of shakedown training which lasted until February 1952. After returning from the shakedown cruise, she spent a month in the New York Naval Shipyard preparing for duty in distant waters.

On 26 April 1952, *Wasp* collided with destroyer minesweeper *Hobson* (DD–464) while conducting night flying operations en route to Gibraltar. *Hobson* lost 176 of the crew, including her skipper. Rapid rescue operations saved 52 men. *Wasp* sustained no personnel casualties, but her bow was torn by a 75-foot saw-tooth rip.

The carrier proceeded to Bayonne, N.J., for repairs and, after she entered drydock there, the bow of aircraft carrier *Hornet* (CV–12)—then undergoing conversion—was removed and floated by barge from Brooklyn, N.Y., and fitted into position on *Wasp*, replacing the badly shattered forward end of the ship. This remarkable task was completed in only 10 days, enabling the carrier to get underway to cross the Atlantic.

On 2 June 1952, *Wasp* relieved *Tarawa* (CV–40) at Gibraltar and joined Carrier Division (CarDiv) 6 in the Mediterranean Sea. After conducting strenuous flight operations between goodwill visits to many Mediterranean ports, *Wasp* was relieved at Gibraltar on 5 September by *Leyte* (CV–32).

After taking part in NATO Exercise "Mainbrace" at Greenock, Scotland, and enjoying a liberty period at Plymouth, England, *Wasp* headed home and arrived at Norfolk early on the morning of 13 October 1952.

On 7 November 1952, *Wasp* entered the New York Naval Shipyard to commence a seven-month yard period to prepare her for a world cruise which was to bring her into the Pacific Fleet once more. After refresher training in the Caribbean, *Wasp* departed Norfolk on 16 September 1953.

After transiting the Panama Canal and crossing the Pacific, the carrier made a brief visit to Japan and then conducted strenuous operations with the famed TF 77. While operating in the western Pacific, she made port calls at Hong Kong, Manila, Yokosuka, and Sasebo.

On 10 January 1954, China's Generalissimo Chiang Kai-shek spent more than four hours on board *Wasp* watching simulated air war maneuvers in Formosan waters. On 12 March, President Ramon Magsaysay of the Republic of the Philippines came on board to observe air operations as a guest of American Ambassador Raymond A. Spruance. *Wasp* operated out of Subic Bay, Philippines, for a time, then sailed for Japan; where, in April 1954, she was relieved by *Boxer* (CV–21) and sailed for her new home port of San Diego, Calif.

Wasp spent the next few months preparing for another tour of the Orient. She departed the United States in September 1954 and steamed to the Far East visiting Pearl Harbor and Iwo Jima en route. She relieved *Boxer* in October 1954 and engaged in air operations in the South China Sea with Carrier Task Group 70.2. *Wasp* visited the Philippine Islands in November and December and proceeded to Japan early in 1955 to join TF 77. While operating with that naval organization, *Wasp* provided air cover for the evacuation of the Tachen Islands by the Chinese Nationalists.

After the Tachen evacuation, *Wasp* stopped at Japan before returning to San Diego, Calif., in April. She entered the San Francisco Naval Shipyard in May for a seven-month conversion and overhaul. On 1 December, the carrier returned to duty displaying a new canted flight deck and a hurricane bow. As 1955 ended, *Wasp* had returned to San Diego and was busily preparing for another Far Eastern tour.

After training during the early months of 1956, *Wasp* departed San Diego, Calif., on 23 April for another cruise to the Far East with Carrier Air Group 15 embarked. She stopped at Pearl Harbor to undergo inspection and training and then proceeded to Guam where she arrived in time for the Armed Forces Day ceremonies on 14 May. En route to Japan in May, she joined TF 77 for Operation "Sea Horse," a five-day period of day and night training for the ship and air group. The ship arrived at Yokosuka on 4 June; visited Iwakuni, Japan; then steamed to Manila for a brief visit. Following a drydock period at Yokosuka, *Wasp* again steamed south to Cubi Point, Philippine Islands, for the commissioning of the new naval air station there. Carrier Air Group 15 provided an air show for President Ramon Magsaysay of the Philippines and Admiral Arthur Radford. During the third week of August, *Wasp* was at Yokosuka enjoying what was scheduled to be a fortnight's stay, but she sailed a week early to aid other ships in searching for survivors of a Navy patrol plane which had been shot down on 23 August off the coast of communist China. After a futile search, the ship proceeded to Kobe, Japan, and made a final stop at Yokosuka before leaving the Far East.

Wasp returned to San Diego on 15 October and while there was reclassified an antisubmarine warfare aircraft carrier, CVS–18, effective on 1 November 1956. She spent the last days of 1956 in San Diego preparing for her transfer to the east coast.

Wasp left San Diego on the last day of January 1957, rounded Cape Horn for operations in the South Atlantic and Caribbean Sea, then proceeded to Boston where she arrived on 21 March. The carrier came into Norfolk, Va., on 6 April to embark members of her crew from the Antisubmarine Warfare School. The carrier spent the next few months in tactics along the

eastern seaboard and in the waters off Bermuda before returning to Boston on 16 August.

On 3 September, *Wasp* got underway to participate in NATO Operations "Seaspray" and "Strikeback," which took her to the coast of Scotland and simulated nuclear attacks and counterattacks on 130 different land bases. The carrier returned to Boston on 23 October 1957 and entered the Boston Naval Shipyard for a major overhaul which was not completed until 10 March 1958 when she sailed for antisubmarine warfare practice at Guantanamo Bay, Cuba. Upon returning to Boston on 29 April and picking up air squadrons at Quonset Point, R.I., on 12 May, she became the hub of TF 66, a special antisubmarine group of the 6th Fleet.

The carrier began her Atlantic crossing on the 12th of May and sailed only a few hundred miles when trouble flared in Lebanon. *Wasp* arrived at Gibraltar on the 21st of May and headed east, making stops at Souda Bay, Crete; Rhodes, and Athens. *Wasp* next spent 10 days at sea conducting a joint Italian-American antisubmarine warfare exercise in the Tyrrhenian Sea off Sardinia. On 15 July, the carrier put to sea to patrol waters off Lebanon. Her Marine helicopter transport squadron left the ship five days later to set up camp at the Beirut International Airport. They flew reconnaissance missions and transported the sick and injured from Marine battalions in the hills to the evacuation hospital at the airport. She continued to support forces ashore in Lebanon until 17 September 1958 when she departed Beirut Harbor, bound for home. She reached Norfolk on 7 October, unloaded supplies, and then made a brief stop at Quonset Point before arriving in her home port of Boston on 11 October.

Four days later, *Wasp* became flagship of Task Group Bravo, one of two new antisubmarine defense groups formed by the Commander in Chief of the Atlantic Fleet. *Wasp*'s air squadrons and seven destroyers were supported by shore-based seaplane patrol aircraft. She sailed from Quonset Point on 26 November for a 17-day cruise in the North Atlantic. This at-sea period marked the first time her force operated together as a team. The operations continued day and night to coordinate and develop the task group's team capabilities until she returned to Boston on 13 December 1958 and remained over the Christmas holiday season.

Wasp operated with Task Group Bravo throughout 1959, cruising along the eastern seaboard conducting operations at Norfolk, Va., Bermuda, and Quonset Point, R.I. On 27 February 1960, she entered the Boston Naval Shipyard for overhaul. In mid-July, the carrier was ordered to the South Atlantic where she stood by when civil strife broke out in the newly independent Congo and operated in support of the United Nations airlift. She returned to her home port on 11 August 1960 and spent the remainder of the year operating out of Boston with visits to Guantanamo Bay, Cuba, for refresher training and exercises conducted in the Virginia capes operating areas and the Caribbean operating areas. The carrier returned to Boston on 10 December 1960 and remained in port there into the New Year.

On 9 January 1961, *Wasp* sailed for the Virginia capes operating area and devoted the first half of 1961 to exercises there; at Narragansett Bay, R.I., and at Nova Scotia. On 9 June, *Wasp* got underway from Norfolk, Va., for a three-month Mediterranean cruise. The ship conducted exercises at Augusta Bay, Sicily; Barcelona, Spain; San Remo and La Spezia, Italy; Aranci Bay, Sardinia; Genoa, Italy; and Cannes, France; and returned to Boston on 1 September. The carrier entered the Boston Naval Shipyard for an interim overhaul and resumed operations on 6 November 1961.

After loading food, clothing, and equipment, *Wasp* spent the period from 11 to 18 January 1962 conducting antisubmarine warfare exercises and submarine surveillance off the east coast. After a brief stop at

Norfolk, the ship steamed on to further training exercises and anchored off Bermuda from 24 to 31 January. *Wasp* then returned to her home port.

On 17 February, a delegation from the Plymouth Plantation presented a photograph of the *Mayflower II* to Captain Brewer who accepted this gift for *Wasp*'s "People to People" effort in the forthcoming European cruise.

On 18 February, *Wasp* departed Boston, bound for England, and arrived at Portsmouth on 1 March. On 16 March, the carrier arrived at Rotterdam, Netherlands, for a week's goodwill visit.

From 22 to 30 March, *Wasp* travelled to Greenock, Scotland, thence to Plymouth, England. On 17 April, Capt. Brewer presented Alderman A. Goldberg, Lord Mayor of Plymouth, England, a large picture of *Mayflower II* as a gift from the people of Plymouth, Mass. On 5 May, *Wasp* arrived at Kiel, West Germany, and became the first aircraft carrier to ever visit that port. The ship made calls at Oslo, Norway; Reykjavik, Iceland; and Argentia, Newfoundland; before returning to Boston, Mass., on 16 June.

From August through October, *Wasp* visited Newport, R.I., New York, and Earle, N.J., then conducted a dependents' cruise, as well as a reserve cruise, and visitors cruises. The 1st of November gave *Wasp* a chance to use her capabilities when she responded to a call from President Kennedy and actively participated in the Cuban blockade. After tension relaxed, the carrier returned to Boston on 22 November for upkeep work; and, on 21 December, she sailed to Bermuda with 18 midshipmen from Boston area universities. *Wasp* returned to Boston on 29 December and finished out the year there.

The early part of 1963 saw *Wasp* conducting antisubmarine warfare exercises off the Virginia capes and steaming along the Caribbean coast of Costa Rica in support of the presidential visit. On 21 March, President Kennedy arrived at San Jose for a conference with presidents of six Central American nations. After taking part in Fleet exercises off Puerto Rico, the carrier returned to Boston on 4 April. From 11 to 18 May, *Wasp* took station off Bermuda as a backup recovery ship for Major Gordon Cooper's historic Mercury space capsule recovery. The landing occurred as planned in the mid-Pacific near Midway Atoll, and carrier *Kearsage* (CVA–33) picked up Cooper and his *Faith 7* space craft. *Wasp* then resumed antisubmarine warfare exercises along the Atlantic seaboard and in the Caribbean until she underwent overhaul in the fall of 1963 for FRAM (Fleet rehabilitation and modernization) overhaul in the Boston Naval Shipyard.

In March 1964, the carrier conducted sea trials out of Boston. During April, she operated out of Norfolk and Narragansett Bay, R.I. She returned to Boston on 4 May and remained there until 14 May when she got underway for refresher training in waters between Guantanamo Bay, Cuba, and Kingston, Jamaica, before returning to her home port on 3 June 1964.

On 21 July 1964, *Wasp* began a round-trip voyage to Norfolk and returned to Boston on 7 August. She remained there through 8 September when she headed, via the Virginia capes operating area, to Valencia, Spain. She then cruised the Mediterranean, visiting ports in Spain, France, and Italy, and returned home on 18 December 1964.

The carrier remained in port until 8 February 1965 and sailed for fleet exercises in the Caribbean. Operating along the eastern seaboard, she recovered the Gemini IV astronauts White and McDivitt with their spacecraft on 7 June. During the summer, the ship conducted search and rescue operations for an Air Force C–121 plane which had gone down off Nantucket. Following an orientation cruise for 12 congressmen on 20 to 21 August, *Wasp* participated in joint training exercises with German and French forces. From 16 to 18 December, the carrier recovered the astronauts of Gemini VI and VII, and then returned to Boston on 22 December to finish out the year.

On 24 January 1966, *Wasp* departed Boston for fleet exercises off Puerto Rico. En route, heavy seas and high winds caused structural damage to the carrier. She put into Roosevelt Roads, Puerto Rico, on 1 February to determine the extent of her damages and effect as much repair as possible. Engineers were flown from Boston who decided that the ship could cease "Springboard" operations early and return to Boston. The ship conducted limited antisubmarine operations from 5 to 8 February prior to leaving the area. She arrived at Boston on 18 February and was placed in restricted availability until 7 March, when her repair work was completed.

Wasp joined in exercises in the Narragansett Bay operating areas. While the carrier was carrying out this duty, a television film crew from the National Broadcasting Company was flown to *Wasp* on 21 March and stayed on the ship during the remainder of her period at sea, filming material for a special color television show to be presented on Armed Forces Day.

The carrier returned to Boston on 24 March 1966 and was moored there until 11 April. On 27 March, Doctor Ernst Lemberger, the Austrian Ambassador to the United States, visited the ship. On 18 April, the ship embarked several guests of the Secretary of the Navy and set courses for Guantanamo Bay, Cuba. She returned to Boston on 6 May.

A week later, the veteran flattop sailed to take part in the recovery of the Gemini IX spacecraft. Embarked in *Wasp* were some 65 persons from NASA, the television industry, media personnel, an underwater demolition recovery team, and a Defense Department medical team. On 6 June, she recovered astronauts Lt. Col. Thomas P. Stafford and Lt. Comdr. Eugene Cernan and flew them to Cape Kennedy, Fla. *Wasp* returned their capsule to Boston.

Wasp participated in "ASWEX III," an antisubmarine exercise which lasted from 20 June through 1 July 1966. She spent the next 25 days in port at Boston for upkeep. On the 25th, the carrier got underway for "ASWEX IV." During this exercise, the Soviet intelligence collection vessel, *Agi Traverz*, entered the operation area necessitating a suspension of the operation and eventual repositioning of forces. The exercise was terminated on 5 August. She then conducted a dependents' day cruise on 8 and 9 August, and orientation cruises on 10, 11, and 22 August. After a two-day visit to New York, *Wasp* arrived in Boston on 1 September and underwent upkeep until the 19th. From that day to 4 October, she conducted hunter/killer operations with the Royal Canadian Navy aircraft embarked.

Following upkeep at Boston, the ship participated in the Gemini XII recovery operation from 5 to 18 November 1966. The recovery took place on 15 November when the space capsule splashdown occurred within three miles of *Wasp*. Capt. James A. Lovell and Maj. Edwin E. Aldrin were lifted by helicopter hoist to the deck of *Wasp* and there enjoyed two days of celebration. *Wasp* arrived at Boston on 18 November with the Gemini XII spacecraft on board. After offloading the special Gemini support equipment, *Wasp* spent 10 days making ready for her next period at sea.

On 28 November, *Wasp* departed Boston to take part in the Atlantic Fleet's largest exercise of the year, "Lantflex-66," in which more than 100 United States ships took part. The carrier returned to Boston on 16 December where she remained through the end of 1966.

Wasp served as carrier qualification duty ship for the Naval Air Training Command from 24 January to 26 February 1967 and conducted operations in the Gulf of Mexico and off the east coast of Florida. She called at New Orleans for Mardi Gras from 4 to 8 February, at Pensacola on the 11th and 12th, and at Mayport, Fla., on the 19th and 20th. Returning to Boston a week later, she remained in port until 19 March when she sailed for "Springboard" operations in the Caribbean. On 24 March, *Wasp* joined *Salamonie*

(AO–26) for an underway replenishment but suffered damage during a collision with the oiler. After making repairs at Roosevelt Roads, she returned to operations on 29 March and visited Charlotte Amalie, St. Thomas, United States Virgin Islands, and participated in the celebration from 30 March to 2 April which marked the 50th anniversary of the purchase of the Virgin Islands by the United States from Denmark. *Wasp* returned to Boston on 7 April, remained in port four days, then sailed to Earle, N.J., to offload ammunition prior to overhaul. She visited New York for three days, then returned to the Boston Naval Shipyard and began an overhaul on 21 April 1967 which was not completed until early 1968.

Wasp completed her cyclical overhaul and conducted post-repair trials throughout January 1968. Returning to the Boston Naval Shipyard on the 28th, the ship made ready for two months of technical evaluation and training which began early in February.

The 28th of February marked the beginning of almost five weeks of refresher training for *Wasp* under the operational control of Commander, Fleet Training Group, Guantanamo Bay, Cuba. On 30 March, *Wasp* steamed north and was in Boston from 6 to 29 April for routine upkeep and minor repairs. She then departed for operations in the Bahamas and took part in "Fixwex C," an exercise off the Bermuda coast. The carrier set course for home on 20 May but left five days later to conduct carrier qualifications for students of the Naval Air Training Command in the Jacksonville, Fla., operations area.

On 12 June, *Wasp* and *Truckee* (AO–147) had a minor collision during an underway replenishment. The carrier returned to Norfolk where an investigation into the circumstances of the collision was conducted. On 20 June, *Wasp* got underway for Boston, where she remained until 3 August when she moved to Norfolk to take on ammunition.

On 15 June, *Wasp*'s home port was changed to Quonset Point, R.I., and she arrived there on 10 August to prepare for overseas movement. Ten days later, the carrier got underway for a deployment in European waters. The northern European portion of the cruise consisted of several operational periods and port visits to Portsmouth, England; Firth of Clyde, Scotland; Hamburg, Germany; and Lisbon, Portugal. *Wasp*, as part of TG 87.1, joined in the NATO Exercise "Silvertower," the largest combined naval exercise in four years. "Silvertower" brought together surface, air, and subsurface units of several NATO navies.

On 25 October 1968, the carrier entered the Mediterranean and, the following day, became part of TG 67.6. After a port visit to Naples, Italy, *Wasp* departed on 7 November to conduct antisubmarine warfare exercises in the Tyrrhenian Sea, Levantine Basin, and Ionian Basin. After loading aircraft in both Taranto and Naples, Italy, *Wasp* visited Barcelona, Spain, and Gibraltar. On 19 December, the ship returned to Quonset Point, R.I., and spent the remainder of 1968 in port.

Wasp began 1969 in her home port of Quonset Point. Following a yard period which lasted from 10 January through 17 February, the carrier conducted exercises as part of the White Task Group in the Bermuda operating area. The ship returned to Quonset Point on 6 March and began a month of preparations for overseas movement.

On 1 April 1969, *Wasp* sailed for the eastern Atlantic and arrived at Lisbon, Portugal, on 16 April. From 21 to 26 April, she took part in joint Exercise "Trilant" which was held with the navies of the United States, Spain, and Portugal. One of the highlights of the cruise occurred on 15 May as *Wasp* arrived at Portsmouth, England, and served as flagship for TF 87, representing the United States in a NATO review by Queen Elizabeth and Prince Phillip in which 64 ships from the 11 NATO countries participated.

After conducting exercises and visiting Rotterdam, Oslo, and Copenhagen, *Wasp* headed home on 30 June and, but for a one-day United Fund cruise on 12 Au-

gust, remained at Quonset Point until 24 August. The period from 29 August to 6 October was devoted to alternating operations between Corpus Christi, Tex., for advanced carrier qualifications, and Pensacola for basic qualifications, with inport periods at Pensacola.

A period of restricted availability began on 10 October and was followed by operations in the Virginia capes area until 22 November. In December, *Wasp* conducted a carrier qualification mission in the Jacksonville operations area which lasted through 10 December. The ship arrived back at Quonset Point on 13 December and remained there for the holidays.

The carrier welcomed the year 1970 moored in her home port of Quonset Point but travelled over 40,000 miles and was away from home port 265 days. On 4 January, she proceeded to Earle, N.J., and offloaded ammunition prior to entering the Boston Naval Shipyard for a six-week overhaul on 9 January.

The carrier began a three-week shakedown cruise on 16 March but returned to her home port on 3 April and began preparing for an eastern Atlantic deployment. *Wasp* reached Lisbon on 25 May 1970 and dropped anchor in the Tagus River. A week later, the carrier got underway to participate in NATO Exercise "Night Patrol" with units from Canada, the Netherlands, Portugal, the United Kingdom, and West Germany. On 8 June, *Wasp* proceeded to the Naval Station, Rota, Spain, to embark a group of midshipmen for a cruise to Copenhagen. During exercises in Scandinavian waters, the carrier was shadowed by Soviet naval craft and aircraft. The ship departed Copenhagen on 26 June and, three days later, crossed the Arctic Circle.

On 13 July 1970, *Wasp* arrived at Hamburg, Germany, and enjoyed the warmest welcome received in any port of the cruise. A Visitors' Day was held, and over 15,000 Germans were recorded as visitors to the carrier. After calls at Edinburgh and Glasgow, Scotland, *Wasp* got underway on 10 August for operating areas in the Norwegian Sea. The carrier anchored near Plymouth, England, on 28 August and, two days later, sailed for her home port.

Wasp returned to Quonset Point on 8 September and remained there through 11 October when she got underway to offload ammunition at Earle, N.J., prior to a period of restricted availability at the Boston Naval Shipyard beginning on 15 October. The work ended on 14 December; and, after reloading ammunition at Earle, *Wasp* returned to Quonset Point on 19 December to finish out the year 1970.

On 14 January 1971, *Wasp* departed Quonset Point, R.I., with Commander, ASWGRU 2, CVSG–54 and Detachment 18 from Fleet Training Group, Guantanamo Bay, Cuba, embarked. After refresher training at Bermuda, she stopped briefly at Rota, Spain, then proceeded to the Mediterranean for participation in the "National Week VIII" exercises with several destroyers for the investigation of known Soviet submarine operating areas. On 12 February, Secretary of the Navy John Chafee, accompanied by Commander, 6th Fleet, Vice Admiral Isaac C. Kidd, visited the carrier.

Wasp detached early from the "National Week" exercise on 15 February to support *John F. Kennedy* (CVA–67) as she steamed toward Gibraltar. Soviet ships trailed *Wasp* and *John F. Kennedy* until they entered the Strait of Sicily when the Soviets departed to the east. After a brief stop at Barcelona, Spain, *Wasp* began her homeward journey on 24 February and arrived at Quonset Point on 3 March.

After spending March and April in port, *Wasp* got underway on 27 April and conducted a nuclear technical proficiency inspection and prepared for the forthcoming "Exotic Dancer" exercise which commenced on 3 May. Having successfully completed the week-long exercise, *Wasp* was heading home on 8 May when an American Broadcasting Co. television team embarked and filmed a short news report on carrier antisubmarine warfare operations.

On 15 May, the veteran conducted a dependents' day cruise and, one month later, participated in Exercise

Rough Ride" at Great Sound, Bermuda, which took her to Halifax, Nova Scotia.

Wasp returned to Quonset Point on 2 July 1971 and spent the next two months in preparation and execution of Exercise "Squeeze Play IX" in the Bermuda operating area. During August, the ship conducted exercises with an east coast naval reserve air group while proceeding to Mayport, Fla. She returned to her home port on 26 August and spent the next month there. On 23 September, *Wasp* got underway for Exercise "Lantcortex 1–72" which terminated on 6 October. For the remainder of the month, the carrier joined in a crossdeck operation which took her to Bermuda, Mayport, and Norfolk. She arrived back at Quonset Point on 4 November.

Four days later, the carrier set her course for the Newport News Shipbuilding and Drydock Co. where she was in drydock until 22 November. She then returned to Quonset Point and remained in her home port for the remainder of the year preparing for decommissioning.

On 1 March 1972, it was announced that *Wasp* would be decommissioned and stricken from the Navy list. Decommissioning ceremonies were held on 1 July 1972. The ship was sold on 21 May 1973 to the Union Minerals and Alloys Corp., of New York City, and subsequently scrapped.

Wasp earned eight battle stars for her World War II service.

Wassaic

A village in Dutchess County, N.Y. The word wassaic is an Indian term meaning "difficult" or "hard work."

(Freighter: dp. 12,186; l. 423'9''; b. 54'; dph. 29'9''; dr. 24'2'' (mean); s. 11.5 k.; cpl. 82; a. 1 5'', 1 3'')

Wassaic—a steel-hulled, single-screw freighter built under a Shipping Board contract—was launched on 14 April 1918 at Los Angeles, Calif., by the Los Angeles Shipbuilding and Drydock Co. Subsequently taken over by the Navy for use by the Naval Overseas Transportation Service (NOTS) and given Id. No. 3230, *Wassaic* was commissioned at New Orleans, La., on 14 October 1918, Lt. Comdr. George H. Cooke, USNRF, in command.

Wassaic loaded 7,468 tons of Army supplies and got underway for Bordeaux, France, on 10 November—the day before the armistice was signed, ending World War I. En route to Europe, *Wassaic* encountered mechanical difficulties and was obliged to put into New York on the 16th for repairs. Underway 13 days later, on the 29th, the freighter—rerouted in light of the war's end—sailed for Brest, France, instead of Bordeaux.

Arriving on 13 December, the ship spent Christmas there before getting underway for the United States on the last day of the year. After a stop at Corona, Spain, for repairs to her damaged propeller, *Wassaic* got underway from that port on 6 January 1919. Following stops at the Azores and Bermuda, the freighter made port at Newport News, Va., on 7 February.

The ship took on a cargo of railroad supplies and departed the east coast on her second NOTS voyage on 10 March, bound for La Pallice, France. Arriving there on the 23d, she discharged her cargo and returned to the United States, heavily ballasted partly with a cargo of steel rails. Putting briefly into Norfolk on 22 April, *Wassaic* sailed for New Orleans on the following day, arriving on the 29th. Discharging her cargo of steel there, the freighter shifted to New York. There, after final repairs and inventories, *Wassaic* was decommissioned, struck from the Navy list, and returned to the Shipping Board, all on 29 May 1919.

Wassaic remained in Shipping Board ownership until she was abandoned due to age and deterioration in 1931 or 1932.

Wassuc

A mountain range in Nevada some 250 miles northwest of Las Vegas. Commonly spelled Wassuk, the term is of Paiute origin, and its meaning is unclear.

(Mon.: dp. 1,175: l. 225'; b. 45'; dr. 6'; s. 9 k.; a. 2 11'' D. sb.; cl. *Casco*)

Wassuc—a single-turreted, twin-screw monitor—was laid down in June 1863 at Portland, Maine, by George W. Lawrence & Co.; launched on 25 July 1865; and completed on 28 October 1865.

Wassuc was a *Casco*-class monitor intended for service in the shallow bays, rivers, and inlets of the Confederacy. These warships sacrificed armor plate for shallow draft and were fitted with a ballast compartment designed to lower them in the water during battle.

However, when the first ships of the class were launched in the spring of 1864, the Navy discovered that serious errors had been made in calculating their displacements. They proved to have barely three inches of freeboard—even without turret, guns, and stores. Therefore, the Navy Department ordered on 24 June 1864 that *Wassuc*'s deck be raised 22 inches to provide sufficient freeboard. Upon delivery, the monitor was laid up at the Boston Navy Yard; and she saw no commissioned service. She was renamed *Stromboli* on 15 June 1869 but resumed the name *Wassuc* on 10 August 1869. *Wassuc* was sold for scrapping on 9 September 1875.

I

(CMc–3: dp. 1,830 (f.); l. 230'6''; b. 42'; dr. 10' (max.); s. 13 k.; cpl. 85; a. 1 3'', 4 .50-cal. mg.; cl. *Wassuc*)

The first *Wassuc* (CMc–3)—originally a steel-hulled, coastal passenger vessel built in 1924 at Elizabethport, N.J., by the New Jersey Drydock and Transportation Corp. of New York City as SS *Yale*—was acquired by the Navy on 20 December 1940. *Yale* then began conversion to a coastal minelayer at the New York Navy Yard. Classified CMc–3 on 30 December 1940 and renamed *Wassuc* on 10 January 1941, the ship was commissioned at the New York Navy Yard on 15 May 1941.

After commissioning, *Wassuc* proceeded south; touched at Norfolk; and then sailed back northward to the Washington Navy Yard where she arrived on 4 June. She subsequently moved to the Mine Warfare School at Yorktown, Va., on 23 June, where she relieved *Cormorant* (AM–40), freeing that minesweeper to begin an overhaul. During her service at Yorktown, *Wassuc* participated in experimental mine work under the aegis of the Bureau of Ordnance (BuOrd).

Completing that tour in mid-August, *Wassuc* moved to the Marine Basin at Brooklyn, N.Y., for extensive alterations that were not completed until after the Japanese attack on Pearl Harbor had plunged the United States into World War II. Two days after Christmas of 1941, *Wassuc* departed Tompkinsville, Staten Island, N.Y., bound for Yorktown to receive mine warfare instruction duties and further work under the auspices of BuOrd.

Wassuc spent the next two years operating in the 5th Naval District, primarily plying the waters of the Chesapeake Bay region and occasionally ranging as far north as the Washington Navy Yard and as far south as Cape Hatteras. She operated principally in BuOrd testing programs at the Naval Mine Warfare Proving Grounds at Solomon's Island, Md., and at Yorktown. She also served two tours of duty as a training ship, providing instruction for officers in the compensation of magnetic compasses. Although her duties appear to have been largely experimental and test-oriented, records indicate that the ship laid a small minefield off Cape Hatteras on 22 May 1942.

The single-turret monitors *Shawnee* (left) and *Wassuc* (right) "mothballed" at the Boston Navy Yard, *circa* 1871–72. At the right is the larger monitor *Miantonomoh*, housed over and used for accommodations. (NH 85969)

By 1944, *Wassuc* was the only coastal minelayer on the Navy inventory. The Army held primary responsibility for defensive coastal minelaying, and submarines and aircraft were proving superbly capable of carrying mine warfare to enemy shores. Nevertheless, *Wassuc* continued her undramatic but vital experimental and test work, far from the limelight of the far-flung battlefronts. She continued her coastwise routine, ranging from Provincetown, Mass., and Cape May, N.J., to New York and Norfolk, as well as Solomon's Island, through the end of World War II.

Decommissioned at the Norfolk Navy Yard on 8 November 1945 and struck from the Navy list on 28 November 1945, the Navy's last coastal minelayer was sold to the Patapsco Scrap Corp. on 3 August 1948 for scrapping.

Watauga

A river in the Blue Ridge mountains of North Carolina that passes into eastern Tennessee. The river's name probably honors the Watauga Indian tribe, Cherokee Indians that lived in northeastern Tennessee.

Although she was projected as a screw frigate and was first carried on Navy lists in 1864, *Watauga* was never laid down, and the contract for her construction was cancelled in 1866.

Watch

After several months of service with the Potomac Flotilla and the James River Flotilla, *A. C. Powell*, a steamer purchased by the Navy on 3 October 1861, was renamed *Alert* (*q.v.*) during the summer of 1862. On 2 February 1865, her name was again changed, on this occasion to *Watch*.

Watchman

(AGR–16: dp. 10,760 (f.): l. 441'6''; b. 57'; dr. 24'; s. 12.5 k.; cpl. 154; cl. *Guardian*; T. Z–EC2–S–C5)

SS *Vernon S. Hood* was laid down under a Maritime Commission contract (MCE hull 2343) on 17 January 1945 at the Wainwright yard of the J. S. Jones Construction Co. in Panama City, Fla.; launched on 20 February 1945; sponsored by Mrs. Inez Bulifant; and delivered to the Maritime Commission on 7 March 1945.

Following a shakedown cruise in the Gulf of Mexico, the freighter was turned over to the Overlakes Freight Corp. to be operated by that firm under a contract with the Maritime Commission. During her brief period of active operations with the Maritime Commission, 1945 to 1947, she also served under contract with the Moore-McCormack Lines. Later that year, she was placed out of service and was berthed with the National Defense Reserve Fleet at James River, Va.

The ship remained there until mid-1958 when she was taken over by the Navy and converted to a radar picket ship at the Charleston (S.C.) Naval Shipyard. During conversion, she was renamed *Watchman* and received the designation YAGR–16. However, that designation was changed to AGR–16 before she completed her conversion late in the year. On 5 January 1958, *Watchman* was placed in commission at Charleston, Lt. Comdr. Irvin Boaz in command.

Watchman conducted shakedown training in the Guantanamo Bay operating area during February. Following post-shakedown availability at Charleston from 5 to 18 March, she completed repairs and got underway for the west coast. After transiting the Panama Canal and visiting Acapulco, Mexico, she arrived in her new home port—San Francisco, Calif.—on 11 April. Assigned to the Continental Air Defense Command, she served as one of several radar picket ships operating as seaborne extensions of the command's contiguous radar coverage system. She operated from her base at San Francisco during her entire naval career, spending an average of 200 days per year actually at sea engaged in picket patrols. That routine continued until 1 September 1965, at which time she and the remaining AGR's were placed out of commission. Her name was struck from the Navy list that same day, and she was returned to the Maritime Administration for lay up with the National Defense Reserve Fleet at Suisun Bay, Calif. She remained there until 3 October 1974 when she was sold to American Ship Dismantlers for scrapping.

Water Lily

(MB: dp. 29; l. 61'0''; b. 11'0''; dr. 2'11''; s. 9 k.; cpl. 5)

Water Lily—a motor launch constructed for the United States Lighthouse Service in 1895 at Morris Heights, N.Y.—was transferred to the Navy in April 1917 along with the entire Lighthouse Service. She operated in the 6th Naval District during America's participation in World War I and for several months thereafter. *Water Lily* resumed her prewar duties on 1 July 1919 when the Navy returned control of the Lighthouse Service to the Department of Commerce.

Water Witch

I

(Str.: l. 100'; b. 21'; s. 6½ k.)

The first *Water Witch*, a steamer built in 1844 and 1845 at the Washington Navy Yard, saw little active service. She was originally constructed to serve as a water supply vessel for the Norfolk station, but she was not used for that purpose because her draft was too deep for her to pass through the locks of the Dismal Swamp Canal to obtain fresh water. Consequently, she was fitted as a harbor vessel and tug.

However, her unique, but poorly conceived, propulsion system caused her to fail in that mission as well. In order to rid steamers of their vulnerable above-water paddle wheel housings and to increase their broadside weight, Lt. W. W. Hunter had devised and patented a system of placing the wheels inside the hull of the ship at a right angle to the keel making their rotations horizontal rather than vertical. The paddles extended their full length outside of the hull for maximum contact with the water for propulsive purposes; and, inside the hull, they were encased by a cofferdam which kept the water from entering the ship proper. Unfortunately for Lt. Hunter, the wheels lost much of their power pushing water through the encased area inside the hull, forfeiting between 50 and 70 percent of their potential power.

That fact was recognized before the ship had served

a year, so she was condemned and sent to Philadelphia where she had arrived sometime before 21 November 1845. Her modifications there were so extensive that, in spite of the fact that she retained her name, the new creation is regarded as a second, distinct ship.

II

(Str.: t. 255; l. 131'; b. 21'10''; dr. 7'3''; s. 9 k.; cpl. 54; a. 1 8'' shell gun, 2 32-pdrs.)

The second *Water Witch* was a modification of the hull of the first. She entered the Philadelphia Navy Yard late in 1845; had her hull lengthened by some 30 feet; and had all her machinery removed and replaced with a new power plant to drive a Loper propeller. However, that configuration, after some months of experimentation, also proved unsatisfactory and; in 1847, she again traded her propulsion plant for an inclined condensing engine driving conventional sidewheels. She probably was not finally commissioned until 21 August 1847, Lt. George M. Totten in command.

In any event, the war with Mexico took her to blockade duty in the Gulf of Mexico where she arrived late in October 1847. At Anton Lizardo, she joined the squadron under Commodore Matthew C. Perry. Late in November and early in December, she cruised to reconnoiter the Mexican ports of Alvarado, Coatzacoolcos, Tabasco, Carmen, and Campeche in company with *Mississippi* and *Scorpion*. She served with the blockading forces in the Gulf of Mexico through the end of the Mexican War in February 1848.

Thereafter, *Water Witch* served in American waters with the Home Squadron. Her much repaired hull prevented her from seeing overseas service, but her career continued until 1851. During the spring of that year, she sailed from Norfolk on a coastal voyage but broke down on her first day out and was towed back to port. She was placed out of commission on 25 April 1851. Her machinery was removed at Washington for use in the third *Water Witch*, and her hull became a target for gunnery practice.

III

(SwStr.: t. 378; l. 150'0''; b. 23'0''; dr. 9'0''; dph. 11'6'')

The third *Water Witch*—a wooden-hulled, sidewheel gunboat—was launched by the Washington Navy Yard in 1851 and was commissioned during the winter of 1852 and 1853, Lt. Thomas Jefferson Page in command.

On 8 February 1853, the gunboat set sail from Norfolk, Va., for an extended exploration and survey voyage along the Atlantic coast of the southern portion of South America and of the rivers which drain that part of the continent. Over the next few years, she conducted surveys of the rivers in Paraguay, Argentina, and Uruguay. In February 1855, while the little steamer was surveying the La Plata River, she was fired upon by a Paraguayan fort. The bombardment killed one member of her crew and ended her surveying mission on the river. The gunboat, however, continued her mission in other areas of the southeastern coast of South America until 1856. On 8 May 1856, she returned to the Washington Navy Yard for repairs and went out of commission on the 12th.

The ship recommissioned briefly during the summer of 1858, but her next real active service came after yet another recommissioning on 17 September of that same year. She headed for the coast of South America with a force of warships under Flag Officer W. B. Shubrick to exact an apology and an indemnity from Paraguay over the incident which had occurred in 1855. In January 1859, *Water Witch* and *Fulton* arrived in Asuncion, the capital of Paraguay; and, backed by the warships, an American commissioner, Mr. Bowlin, began negotiations with the Paraguayans. As a result of that expedition, Paraguay extended a satisfactory apology to the

The sidewheel steamer *Water Witch*. (NH 60353)

United States, indemnified the family of the slain *Water Witch* crewman, and granted the United States a new and highly advantageous commercial treaty.

After the resolution of the difficulties with Paraguay, *Water Witch* resumed her survey missions in that region of the world. That employment, punctuated by periods out of commission in the United States, lasted until the fall preceding the outbreak of the Civil War. She was again decommissioned at Philadelphia for repairs on 1 November 1860. She returned to active duty on 10 April 1861, two days before General Beauregard's bombardment of Fort Sumter opened hostilities between the North and the South. Steaming via Key West, Fla., she joined the Gulf Blockading Squadron off Pensacola, Fla., on 2 May. There, her initial duty consisted of dispatch service and shuttling mail between the blockaders and their base at Key West. She also carried mail to Havana, Cuba.

However, later that summer, her duty station was changed to the area around the mouth of the Mississippi River. That duty lasted until the beginning of 1862. During the intervening months, she made several reconnaissance runs into the mouth of the Mississippi, missions, for which her shallow draft made her an ideal ship. During one such incursion, ships of the Federal Fleet were attacked by the Confederate ram *Manassas* and the converted gunboat *Ivy*. *Water Witch* engaged *Ivy* briefly but never encountered the ram which zeroed in on and damaged *Richmond*. The Union ships recrossed the bar; and the Confederates retired upriver, *Manassas* having suffered damage to her ram.

On 20 January 1862, the Gulf Blockading Squadron was divided in two to create the West Gulf Blockading Squadron and the East Gulf Blockading Squadron. *Water Witch* was assigned to the latter organization, and her area of operations became the gulf coasts of Alabama and Florida. She served most frequently off Mobile and Pensacola but also performed the familiar duty of dispatch vessel and mail packet. On 5 March 1862, the gunboat pursued the Confederate Schooner, *William Mallory*, for five hours before finally capturing the blockade runner late in the day. In April,

she began another period of repairs that lasted until September. On 6 September, she was recommissioned and ordered to join Rear Admiral Samuel F. Du Pont's South Atlantic Blockading Squadron. She arrived at Port Royal, S.C., on 18 September and, by the end of the month, was on blockade station in the St. John's River in northeastern Florida.

On 1 October, *Water Witch*, *Cimarron*, and *Uncas* moved up the river as far as St. John's Bluff to reconnoiter Confederate batteries situated on the heights. They traded some shots with the heavy caliber battery but soon retired because of well-directed fire from the Southerners. The following day, Federal troops landed and moved inland to isolate the Confederates manning the batteries on the bluff. Thereupon, the Southerners abandoned their guns in haste, and *Water Witch* participated in the unopposed occupation of the former Confederate positions late on the 3d. Over the next few days, the warship participated in a foray farther up the river to destroy shipping and river barges.

On 17 October, she returned to Port Royal to resume her role as a dispatch vessel again. She continued to serve with the South Atlantic Blockading Squadron until February of 1863 when she broke down and had to be towed north for repairs.

She completed repairs late that spring and returned to Port Royal on 14 June. She performed blockade duty at several points along the coasts of South Carolina, Georgia, and northern Florida, but most frequently at Ossabaw Sound between Ossabaw Island and the Georgia mainland about 15 miles due south of Savannah. That remained her primary duty station well into 1864. On the night of 3 June of that year, a Confederate boat force under the command of First Lieutenant Thomas P. Pelot, CSN, succeeded in boarding and capturing *Water Witch* in Ossabaw Sound after a brief scuffle which cost the Union ship two killed and 12 wounded.

The prize was subsequently taken into the Confederate Navy in which she retained the name *Water Witch*. Lt. W. W. Carnes, CSN, commanded the ship during her service for the South. Plans were being made to move her to Savannah for some special assignment, but she remained at White Bluff, Ga., until 19 December 1864 when the Confederates burned her to prevent capture.

Wateree

I

(SwGbt.: t. 974; l. 205'0''; b. 35'0''; dph. 11'6''; s. 10 k.; a. 2 100-pdr. P.r., 4 9'' D.sb., 4 24-pdr. how., 2 13-pdrs., 2 12-pdr. r.)

The first *Wateree*, a sidewheel gunboat, was built at Chester, Pa., by Reany Son & Archbold; launched on 12 August 1863; and commissioned at the Philadelphia Navy Yard on 20 January 1864, Comdr. F. E. Murray in command.

Assigned to the Pacific Squadron, *Wateree* departed Philadelphia soon after commissioning. During the next 10 months, she made the arduous voyage around Cape Horn to the Pacific. In addition to struggling against the heavy weather for which the Cape region is noted, the warship experienced difficulty acquiring fuel. That problem necessitated her making numerous stops along the way to acquire wood for her boilers; and, as a result, *Wateree* did not reach San Francisco, Calif., until mid-November 1864.

Upon her arrival there, the ship entered the Mare Island Navy Yard for repairs to damage she suffered during her arduous voyage and for a hull scraping. She did not leave San Francisco until late February 1865 when she put to sea to patrol the coast of Central America. During 1866, American naval forces in the Pacific were divided into a North Pacific Squadron and a South Pacific Squadron. *Wateree* was assigned to the latter unit, whose patrol area extended south from Panama to Cape Horn and west to Australia. For the remaining two years of her brief naval career, *Wateree* patrolled the coasts of Central and South America, protecting American interests in that region.

On 15 August 1868, while she was in port at Arica, Peru, a devastating earthquake struck the city subjecting *Wateree* and the other ships in the harbor to several massive tidal waves. The last wave broke the side-wheeler gunboat's anchor chains and drove her ashore almost 500 yards inland from the normal high water mark. Too badly damaged for economical repair, the ship was sold to Mr. William Parker on 21 November 1868. Apparently her hulk was converted to living spaces ashore, and the former warship served as an inn for some years thereafter.

II

(ATF-117: dp. 1,589 (tl.); l. 205'0''; b. 38'6''; dr. 15'4''; s. 16.5 k. (tl.); cpl. 85; a. 1 3'', 2 40mm.; cl. *Abnaki*)

The second *Wateree* (ATF-117) was laid down on 22 September 1943 at Alameda, Calif., by the United Engineering Co. as an ocean tug, AT-117; redesignated a fleet ocean tug, ATF-117, on 15 May 1944; launched on 14 June 1944; sponsored by Mrs. Henry B. Wagner; and commissioned on 17 February 1945 at San Francisco, Calif., Lt. Gilbert E. Perry in command.

After fitting out at San Francisco, *Wateree* got underway for San Pedro on 4 March. She reported for duty at the Small Craft Training Center on 6 March and, for the next 25 days, trained strenuously. During the first week in April, she conducted more training, this time out of San Diego. From 6 to 13 April, the tug underwent repairs at the San Diego repair base. She arrived back at San Francisco on 15 April and, on the 23d, got underway towing three pontoon barges to the forward areas. The ship arrived in Pearl Harbor on 10 May and conducted voyage repairs. On the 22d, she put to sea to rescue a disabled freighter; found the ship on the 24th; took her in tow; and arrived

back in Pearl Harbor on the 26th. On 30 May, she stood out of the port once again towing the three pontoon barges. After a month's voyage, which included a five-day stop at Eniwetok between 18 and 23 June and a brief pause at Guam on the 30th, *Wateree* delivered the barges to Okinawa on 12 July. Two days later, she headed back to Eniwetok, where she arrived on 25 July. She remained there until 15 August, first undergoing some repairs and then providing harbor tug services in the anchorage.

The tug's departure coincided with Japan's capitulation ending hostilities in the Pacific. She steamed to Kwajalein where she took *ARD-29* in tow, bound via Guam for Okinawa. She and her charge departed Kwajalein on 24 August, stopped at Guam from 2 to 15 September, and arrived at Okinawa on 23 September. Six days later, she assisted several tugs with tows in trouble between the Philippines and Okinawa. On 1 October, she encountered *Cinnabar* (IX-162) adrift with *ATR-29* standing by. *Wateree* took both ships in tow and arrived back in Buckner Bay on 4 October.

When it was ascertained that a typhoon would soon strike the anchorage at Buckner Bay, the tug received orders on 7 October to stand by to render assistance to any ships which got into trouble during the storm. *Wateree* herself, however, fell victim to the storm when it hit the anchorage on 9 October. At about 1220, her starboard anchor was carried away by one of the many ships and barges cast about by the storm. In order to ease the strain on her remaining port anchor chain, she started her engines. Soon, however, she had to weigh anchor in an effort to avoid all the vessels adrift in the anchorage. The wind blew her afoul the anchor buoy for *APL-28*, and she was drawn in toward that ship. She and *APL-28* collided, but the damage was repaired quickly, and she untangled herself from the anchor buoy. Between 1515 and 1558, she cleared the APL and attempted to drop her port anchor again. The anchor machinery failed; and, at 1528, the wind blew her onto a reef and battered out her starboard side before she could be brought clear. At about 1555, the order to abandon ship went out; and, by 1610, all crewmen had gone over the side. Soon thereafter, *Wateree* sank in about 8 fathoms of water. The ship's commanding officer, her executive officer, and six enlisted men were lost. *Wateree*'s name was struck from the Navy list on 1 November 1945.

III

(ATA-174: dp. 835 (tl.); l. 143'0''; b. 33'10''; dr. 13'2'' (f.); s. 13 k. (tl.); cpl. 45; a. 1 3''; cl. *ATA-121*)

The third *Wateree* (ATA-174) was laid down on 5 October 1943 at Orange, Tex., by the Levingston Shipbuilding Co. as the unnamed rescue tug *ATR-101*; launched on 18 November 1943; redesignated an auxiliary ocean tug, *ATA-174*, and commissioned on 20 July 1944, Lt. A. J. Vetro in command.

ATA-174 departed Orange on 4 August and arrived in Norfolk on the 11th. Over the next 10 days, she conducted shakedown training in the Chesapeake Bay and then underwent an eight-day, post-shakedown repair period before heading for New York on 2 September. The tug remained at Staten Island for five days and then took departure for the Panama Canal with three open lighters in tow. She made an unscheduled three-day stop in mid-September to evade a hurricane but finally arrived in Cristobal on 26 September. On the 27th, she transited the canal and reported to the Pacific Fleet for duty. The tug departed Balboa on 10 October towing *YC-1131* and *YC-1137* to San Diego where she arrived on 26 October after a voyage complicated by a steering control failure. Following repairs at San Diego, the ship moved north to San Pedro making the voyage on 10 and 11 November. She remained there until the 19th on which day she took the three open lighters in tow and set a course for Pearl Harbor. *ATA–174* arrived in Pearl Harbor on 3 December, remained there for 10 days, and then got underway for the Marshall Islands on the 13th. After a 16-day voyage plagued by mishaps in her main propulsion plant, the tug arrived at Eniwetok Atoll on 29 December. Between 1 and 3 January 1945, she towed *YSR–4* from Eniwetok to Kwajalein and, after a six-day stopover, continued on to Manus in the Admiralty Isands where she arrived on 18 January.

On the 22d, she stood out to sea from Manus and set a course for Noumea, New Caledonia. En route, however, she received orders diverting her to Guadalcanal. The tug arrived at her new destination on 26 January. She served in the southern Solomons for almost two months. Early in February, she conducted diving operations on the sunken wreck of *Serpens* (AK–97) during the investigation of her explosion and sinking. In mid-February, she salvaged six bulldozers from 110 feet of water off Lunga Point. Later, she pulled two grounded submarine chasers off reefs in Skylark Channel. She concluded her duty at Guadalcanal on 22 March when she took *ARD–18* in tow for Hollandia, New Guinea. She stopped at Hollandia from 30 March to 2 April and then continued her voyage towing *ARD–18* to Ulithi where she arrived on 7 April. After an overnight stop, the tug departed Ulithi on the 8th and set a course for Manus. She reached Manus on the 12th but departed again the next day. The ship made Guadalcanal on the 17th and remained two days. From there, she voyaged via Espiritu Santo to Tutuila, Samoa, arriving at the latter island on 27 April.

She made emergency repairs until 1 May on which day she shaped a course for the Russell Island subgroup of the Solomons with *AFD–20* in tow. In the Russells, she added a pontoon barge to the tow and continued on to Manus where she arrived on 20 May. On the 24th, *ATA–174* resumed her voyage, this time to Leyte in the Philippines where she arrived on 2 June. The tug remained at Leyte for 15 days and then got underway for Guadalcanal on the 17th. She reached her destination on 27 June but departed again the next day towing *E. A. Poe* (IX–103) via Tulagi to Leyte. After a stop in the Russell Islands and another at Manus, she and her charge arrived in San Pedro Bay on 19 July. On the 23d, *ATA–174* left Leyte and set sail for Espiritu Santo in the New Hebrides where, after a diversion back to the Russell Islands, she arrived on 10 August. The tug remained at Espiritu Santo until 14 August when she set sail to return to Leyte with *YC–812* and *YF–366* in tow. She arrived in Leyte on 29 August, delivered her charges, and remained there for a little over a week. On 8 September, the tug headed back to the Solomons by way of Manus. She arrived at Guadalcanal on the 19th and began duty as an air-sea rescue vessel and towing diesel fuel barges between Tulagi and the Russells. That assignment lasted a little more than a month. On 26 October, she took a former LST in tow for Leyte and arrived there on 8 November. She departed Leyte 11 days later and, after stops at Eniwetok and Pearl Harbor, arrived in San Francisco on 1 January 1946.

For the next month, the tug operated along the west coast, visiting San Diego, Astoria, Portland, and Seattle. On 18 February, she reported for duty at the naval station at Astoria, Oreg. After almost 9 months of active service with the Columbia River Group, Pacific Reserve Fleet, she was placed out of commission on 16 January 1947. Berthed with the Columbia River Group, she remained inactive at Astoria until the summer of 1953. During that period, she received the name *Wateree* on 16 July 1948. On 2 June 1953, she departed Astoria to be transferred to the Commandant, 13th Naval District, who in turn transferred her to the Military Sea Transportation Service (MSTS) for duty in Alaskan waters. She was placed in service on 13 August 1953 and served with the MSTS in Alaska and the Pacific Northwest until the spring of 1955. On

14 March 1955, *Wateree* rejoined the Columbia River Group. She remained inactive until November 1961 at which time she was sold to Peru. She served the Peruvian Navy as *Uranue* (ATA–136) until 1977. Sometime between late 1977 and early 1978, the Peruvians disposed of her.

Waterford

A town in Connecticut.

(ARD–5: l. 485′8″; b. 71′0″; dr. 32′6″ (max.); cpl. 112; cl. *ARD–2*)

Waterford (ARD–5) was originally the unnamed, steel-hulled, auxiliary repair drydock *ARD–5*. She was completed in June of 1942 at San Diego, Calif., by the Pacific Bridge Co., and at the end of World War II was serving at the navy yard at Mare Island, Calif. She remained there until shifting to the east coast to serve the repair needs of the Atlantic Fleet. *ARD–5* was named *Waterford* on 17 November 1976. She remained active, "in service" with the Atlantic Fleet into 1979.

Waterman

Andrew Kenneth Waterman—born in Lewis County, Ky., on 20 December 1913—enlisted in the Navy on 21 November 1932 at Buffalo, N.Y. After instruction at the Naval Training Station, Newport, R.I., he served successive tours of sea duty in *Nitro* (AE–2), *New Mexico* (BB–40), and *Relief* (AH–2) before he underwent aviation training at the Fleet Air Base, Coco Solo, Canal Zone. After he attained the rate of aviation machinist's mate 3d class in December 1935 and extended his enlistment in November 1936, Waterman served with Utility Squadron 1 into mid-1939.

Transferred to Patrol Squadron (VP) 21 in August 1939, Waterman joined that unit in time to make the transpacific flight from Hawaii to the Philippines of VP–21's PBY–4's to reinforce the Asiatic Fleet's patrols out of Cavite and Olongapo. For his role in that movement, Waterman received a commendation from Commander, Patrol Wing (PatWing) 2, Rear Admiral Arthur L. Bristol, Jr., on 2 October 1939. The admiral praised Waterman's "through planning, attention to detail, and exceptional ability" that indicated a "high degree of efficiency" instrumental in the success of that important mission.

Transferred to VP–1 in September 1940—three months before the establishment of PatWing 10 on 16 December 1940—Waterman remained with the Asiatic Fleet's air arm for the rest of his life. PatWing 10 flew reconnaissance and patrol missions from Cavite's Sangley Point seaplane base or from tender-supported Olongapo up to the outbreak of war with Japan on 8 December 1941. After that day—with the Asiatic Fleet on the defensive against the relentless pressure applied by the invading Japanese—PatWing 10's lumbering PBY's conducted their reconnoitering and patrol missions in the face of increasingly heavy antiaircraft fire and fighter opposition.

On occasion, the PBY's were pressed into service as bombers; and it was on such a mission that Waterman was killed. Before midnight on 26 December 1941, a six-plane attack group of PBY's from VP–101 (the redesignated VP–1) departed their advance base at Ambon, Netherlands East Indies, and set course for the Philippines. The Catalina flying boats were slated to hit Japanese shipping reportedly in the harbor at the island of Jolo, in the Sulu Archipelago. Waterman—who had by that time advanced to the rate of aviation machinist's mate 1st class—was flying as waist gunner and first mechanic in the PBY–4 flown by Ens. Elwyn L. Christman, USNR.

Soon after the PBY's arrived over Jolo Harbor, antiaircraft fire from shore emplacements greeted them

—fire assessed by Ens. Christman as "very accurate." Gunfire from the enemy ships below proved less troublesome, but soon the guns stopped firing when attacking Japanese fighter aircraft hove into view. Waterman and Aviation Machinist's Mate 2d Class Joseph Bangust, the waist gunners, stood by their machine guns and downed the first attacker.

While in a 60-degree dive aimed at a cruiser below, Christman released his bombs at 5,000 feet before heading the lumbering PBY westward to clear the area. One fighter, however, pursued doggedly.

In the ensuing running fight, the PBY fared badly. On one pass, the fighter's cannon shells tore into the plane's gasoline tank; and the volatile fuel spilled from the ruptured area. On another pass, the fighter's fire ignited the gasoline and set the *Catalina* ablaze. Christman headed for the water to land and abandon ship; two men, Radiomen 2 Class Landers and Bangust, bailed out at 300 feet while Christman and his second and third pilots rode the plane down. Waterman, after manning his single .30-caliber machine gun with great dexterity, had been mortally wounded, probably in the fighter's last pass.

The burning PBY made a landing, and the remaining living crewman abandoned the aircraft and struck out for shore. There was no time to extricate Waterman's body from the blazing Catalina.

Waterman was awarded a posthumous Navy Cross for "extraordinary heroism and courage" as plane captain of Christman's PBY. His citation noted his "loyal and conscientious devotion to duty" during the engagement in which he lost his life in the service of his country.

(DE–740: dp. 1,240; l. 306′0″; b. 36′8″; dr 8′9″ (mean); s. 21 k.; cpl. 186; a. 3 3″, 2 40mm., 8 20mm., 3 21″ tt., 2 dct., 8 dcp., 1 dcp. (hh.); cl. *Cannon*)

Waterman (DE–740) was laid down on 24 February 1943 at San Pedro, Calif., by the Western Steel and Pipe Co.; launched on 20 June 1943; sponsored by Mrs. June M. Waterman, the widow of Aviation Machinist's Mate 1st Class Waterman; and commissioned on 30 November 1943, Lt. Comdr. W. B. Hinds, USNR, in command.

After shakedown out of San Diego and post-shakedown availability at her builder's yard, *Waterman* departed San Pedro on 12 February 1944 and proceeded independently to Pearl Harbor, where she arrived six days later. Once in Hawaiian waters, the new escort vessel underwent further training in antisubmarine warfare and gunnery.

Waterman departed Pearl Harbor on 6 March and screened the escort carrier *Nassau* (CVE–16) as she ferried replacement aircraft, passengers, and cargo to Kwajalein, Majuro, Tarawa, and Makin in the Marshalls and Gilberts. The destroyer escort returned to Pearl Harbor on 24 March.

Continuing in her role as an escort vessel, *Waterman* sailed from Hawaiian waters on 9 April, bound again for the Marshalls in company with *Bowers* (DE–637) and escorting Convoy 4152–A which was made up of merchant tankers. *Waterman* arrived at Majuro one week later and then performed local escort missions out of that base through May.

On 1 June, *Waterman* joined Task Group (TG) 50.17, a fleet service group made up of vital support ships—particularly fleet oilers, tugs, ammunition ships, supply ships, and the like—that allowed the fast carrier task forces to remain at sea for prolonged periods of time. Those ships provided the carriers and their escorts with the vital necessities of life—food, fuel, ammunition, mail, etc.—anything the fleet needed to keep up the pressure on the Japanese.

Waterman's first assignment in that role was operating in support of the Marianas operation. She departed Majuro on 6 June and protected the task group for a fortnight before completing her mission at Eniwetok on the 20th. She then steamed to the

Marianas and picked up an oiler at Saipan—while fighting was still in progress ashore—and screened her back to the Marshalls.

Underway again from Eniwetok on 26 July, *Waterman* rendezvoused with the fleet service group east of the Marianas and protected the oilers as they refuelled the ships supporting the landings on Guam.

After returning to the Marshalls, the destroyer escort sailed from Eniwetok on 26 August, bound for the Admiralties, and arrived at Manus five days later. Soon thereafter, she returned to the open sea with a Service Force unit, TU 30.8.7, supporting the invasion of the Western Carolines. During that time, the destroyer escort operated west of the Philippine Islands, supporting carrier strikes. *Waterman*—operating out of Manus through September—weighed anchor on 4 October and stood out to sea, escorting the fleet service group to points east of the Philippines, where they replenished carriers launching air strikes smashing Japanese positions on the island of Leyte.

After escorting Service Force units which were supporting the Leyte landings, *Waterman* operated between 2 November and 23 December with TG 30.8—the task group servicing carrier forces operating east of the Philippine Islands; planes from those fast carriers largely neutralized Japanese air and sea power in the Philippines and Formosa.

While operating with TG 30.8, *Waterman* encountered the worst weather of her career—the infamous typhoon of 18 December 1944. For approximately 36 hours, the fierce storm battered Admiral Halsey's fleet—large and small ships alike. Winds of 120 knots threw almost solid clouds of spume and spray and whipped up waves of about 80 feet in height, making life aboard *Waterman* decidedly "uncomfortable." Upon occasion, the ship rolled as much as 65 degrees. As her commanding officer recounted: "This day was a never to be forgotten one and was indelibly impressed in the minds of the crew."

Before the typhoon had spent itself, three ships—all lightly-loaded destroyers, low on fuel—had been sunk and others damaged. On 23 December, two days before Christmas, *Waterman* steamed back to Ulithi "somewhat battered but in much better condition than a majority of the larger ships."

One week later, the destroyer escort was at sea again, bound for Guam. From 4 January 1945 to 3 March, *Waterman* saw continuous service screening the fleet service group. She spent much of January supporting the occupation of Luzon from the fueling areas east of the Philippines and, in February, escorted the vital auxiliaries to a rendezvous with the fleet that soon commenced the preinvasion bombardment of Iwo Jima.

While thus engaged, *Waterman* distinguished herself. On 17 February, an internal explosion ripped through the forward section of the oiler *Patuxent* (AO–44), leaving gaping holes in her bow and fires that raged over the forward part of the ship, endangering part of the cargo of volatile aviation gas. *Waterman* promptly left her screening station and was the first of two escorts to come alongside and lend a hand. She closed the endangered ship from one side while *Dewey* (DD–349) approached her from the other. The destroyer escort's repair parties, operating under extremely hazardous conditions, streamed thousands of gallons of water on *Patuxent*'s blaze and finally extinguished it. For his part in directing the destroyer escort's effort, Lt. Comdr. J. H. Stahle, USNR, the ship's commanding officer, received the Bronze Star Medal.

After upkeep and logistics back at Ulithi, *Waterman* departed the Carolines on 22 March for a fueling area east of Okinawa. During the first two weeks of April, *Waterman* escorted *Attu* (CVE–102) as she ferried replacement planes to the fast carrier task forces on two round trips between Okinawa and Guam.

For the remainder of the war in the Pacific, *Waterman* screened Fleet Service Force units steaming a few hundred miles off the Japanese homeland while the fleet's carriers, battleships, and cruisers carried out devastating attacks on the enemy's very doorstep.

On 21 August, less than a week after Japan capitulated, *Waterman* was assigned to TG 35.80, a special support group set up to enter Tokyo Bay as part of the initial occupation force. With their "battle colors" flying, she and *Kyne* (DE–774)—the first destroyer escorts to reach Sagami Wan—entered that body of water just southwest of the erstwhile enemy's capital city of Tokyo on 28 August and dropped anchor less than a mile off shore from the town of Katase. On 31 August, she moved into Tokyo Bay proper and, two days later, hauled down her "battle flag" as surrender terms were signed on board the battleship *Missouri* (BB–63).

On 4 September, *Waterman* was assigned to TG 30.6, whose duty it was to evacuate Allied prisoners of war (POW's) from nearby prison camps. That afternoon, the destroyer escort entered the harbor at Yokohama and transported POW's to nearby hospital ships, receiving ships, and Kizarazu airfield. *Waterman* continued that work of mercy until 10 September, when she departed the Tokyo area with TU 30.6.3—four LSM's and sister ship *Weaver* (DE–741)—bound for Shiogama, on the eastern coast of Honshu, through which port the POW's from the Sendai camp were being evacuated.

The following morning, *Waterman* entered Shiogama harbor and joined other units of TG 30.6 who were already in the process of evacuating the Allied POW's there. On 14 September, the destroyer escort sailed for Kamaishi, arriving there the following morning for further evacuation of POW's.

Upon completion of that operation, TG 30.6 returned to Tokyo Bay where it was dissolved; *Waterman* was assigned to escort duties with TG 16.5 (of Service Squadron 6) for duty. In that role, the destroyer escort remained moored in Yokosuka harbor from 19 to 29 September.

On the afternoon of 29 September, *Waterman* received homeward-bound orders after 20 months of duty in the Pacific war zone; and she stood out of Tokyo Bay on 2 October.

After steaming via Pearl Harbor, she arrived at San Pedro, Calif., on 20 October and remained there until 6 November, when she got underway for the Canal Zone and Philadelphia. Arriving there on 22 November, the ship remained at Philadelphia until 10 December, undergoing availability. Soon thereafter, *Waterman* shifted to Green Cove Springs, Fla., where she was laid-up in reserve at the Atlantic Reserve Fleet berthing area on 31 May 1946.

Waterman never again saw active service under the Stars and Stripes. She was transferred to the government of Peru on 21 February 1952 under the Mutual Defense Assistance Pact (MDAP) and was struck from the Navy list on 18 April of that same year. Arriving in Peruvian waters on 24 May 1952, *Waterman* was renamed *Aguirre* and classified as a destroyer, D–2. Reclassified a destroyer escort, DE–2 in 1959 and DE–62 in 1960, *Aguirre* served the Peruvian Navy until she was disposed of in 1974.

Waterman (DE–740) received eight battle stars for her World War II service.

Waters

Daniel Waters, born on 20 June 1731 at Charlestown, Mass., was one of the "minute men" who engaged the British at the onset of the Revolutionary War. Later placed in charge of a small gunboat during the American investment of Boston, Waters was appointed by General George Washington to command the schooner *Lee* on 20 January 1776. He was soon actively engaged in the ensuing assault upon British communications, capturing one enemy vessel in February and another in May. Aided by *Warren*, *Lee* seized an

armed troopship with 94 Scottish Highlander troops on board in early June. Later in the month, Waters and *Lee* shared with other vessels the capture of transports *Howe* and *Annabella*.

Again at the recommendation of Washington, Waters was appointed a captain in the Continental Navy on 15 March 1777 and given command of the frigate *Fox*. Shortly thereafter, Waters and *Fox*, along with *Hancock*, were forced to surrender to superior British forces off Halifax, Nova Scotia. Following exchange in 1778, Waters made a cruise to the West Indies in the spring of 1779 in the Continental sloop *General Gates*. He then commanded the Massachusetts ship *General Putnam* in an ill-fated expedition against Castine, Maine, in which the American ships were destroyed in the mouth of the Penobscot River to prevent their capture.

Waters' most famous exploit occurred on Christmas Day, 1779, when he led the Boston privateer *Thorn* in a successful, two-hour action against two enemy privateers of about equal armament but more heavily manned. In the fierce fight, during which *Governor Tryon* and *Sir William Erskine* were captured, Waters was wounded. John Adams was to write of this engagement: "There has not been a more memorable action this war."

Waters' last cruise was in the Massachusetts privateer *Friendship*, to which he was appointed in January 1781. Following the war, Waters retired to his farm in Malden, Mass., where he died on 26 March 1816.

(Destroyer No. 115: dp. 1,154; l. 314'4½''; b. 30'11¼'' (wl.); dr. 9'10¼'' (f.) (aft); s. 35.2 k. (tl.); cpl. 122; a. 4 4'', 2 3'', 12 21'' tt., 2 .30-cal. mg., 2 dct., 1 Y-gun; cl. *Wickes*)

Waters (Destroyer No. 115) was laid down on 26 July 1917 at Philadelphia, Pa., by William Cramp & Sons; launched on 3 March 1918; sponsored by Miss Mary Borland Thayer; and commissioned at the Philadelphia Navy Yard on 8 August 1918, Lt. Comdr. Charles F. Russell in command.

Though her active service began late in World War I, *Waters* still managed to get in two round-trip voyages to the British Isles and one to the Azores before the armistice in November 1918. On 11 August, she joined a convoy at Tompkinsville, N.Y., and put to sea for England. She escorted her charges safely into Davenport on 23 August and stood out again four days later in the screen for four ships headed home.

The destroyer delivered the small convoy at New York on 6 September and, following a three-day layover, departed once again—this time bound for Ireland. Eleven days later, she entered the port at Buncrana. She remained there for eight days before again putting to sea. On 8 October, *Waters* arrived in New York and, but for a run to Newport, R.I., on 31 October and 1 November, remained there until she put to sea with a convoy again on 4 November. This one was made up of 11 merchantmen bound for the Azores. *Waters* and her convoy were still three days steaming time from Ponta Delgada on 11 November 1918, when the armistice brought hostilities in Europe to a close. She entered the Portuguese island port with the convoy on the 14th. Eight days later, *Waters* headed west again and arrived at New York on the 28th.

The destroyer remained there under repairs until mid-January 1919. On the 15th, she put to sea for another voyage to the Azores. *Waters* stayed in Ponta Delgada from her arrival on 21 January until 17 February when she headed back to the United States. She reached Boston on 25 February and moved to Philadelphia early in March for another series of repairs. On 3 April, she got underway for a brief run, via New York, to Guantanamo Bay, Cuba.

The destroyer returned to New York on the 14th and remained there through the end of the month. On 1 May, she stood out of port—in company with destroyers *Craven*, *Dent*, *Hopewell*, *Philip Roper*, and *Stockton*—

An early photo of *Waters* (DD–115). (NH 48477)

to take up station as part of the picket of destroyers dotting the path of the transatlantic flight to be conducted by Navy flying boats. After an overnight stop at Trepassey Bay, Newfoundland, on 4 and 5 May, *Waters* dropped anchor off Santa Cruz in the Azores on the 10th.

On the 17th, she got underway at 0643 and arrived at her station, located between the islands of Corvo and Flores, at 0750. There, she lay to await the passage of the three seaplanes attempting the flight. Finally, at about 1112, her crew heard the drone of the engines of a single seaplane as NC–4, the only one of the three seaplanes to successfully complete the flight, passed overhead.

That afternoon, the warship left her station to search for NC–1 which had made a forced landing at sea. During the search, she received word that the third plane, NC–3, was also lost in the fog. Just after noon the following day, she received word that NC–1 had been found and its crew rescued by SS *Ionia*. Accordingly, *Waters* returned to her anchorage off Santa Cruz that night.

Early the next morning, she weighed anchor to participate in the search for NC–3; however, she soon learned that NC–3 had been sighted off Ponta Delgada, navigating on the surface, and heading for that port under its own power. That same day, 19 May, the warship departed the Azores and shaped a course for Newport, R.I., where she arrived on 23 May.

The destroyer operated out of Newport and New York until mid-July. She was among the destroyers which escorted *Pennsylvania* (Battleship No. 38) out to sea on 8 July when Secretary of the Navy Josephus Daniels embarked in the battleship to meet *George Washington* off New York harbor and to welcome President Woodrow Wilson as he returned home from the peace negotiations in Europe.

On 14 July, *Waters* sailed from New York, via Hampton Roads and the Panama Canal, to the west coast. She pulled into San Diego on 5 August and, after six weeks of operations which included a voyage to the Hawaiian Islands, was placed in reserve at San Diego on 21 September 1919.

On 24 February 1920, *Waters* came out of reserve and moved to Bremerton, Wash., where she began a nine-month overhaul preparatory to her return to active service. While the destroyer was at Puget Sound, the Navy adopted the alphanumeric system of hull designations, and *Waters* became DD–115 on or about 17 July 1920. She completed her reconditioning on 30 November and returned to San Diego at the end of the first week in December.

During the first few months of 1921, she operated as a unit of Division X, a special organizational unit —to which *Dorsey* (DD–117) and *Dent* (DD–116) were also attached—pending the reconstitution of Division 14 in its entirety. In January and February, she made a cruise to Central and South America. She stopped in the Canal Zone on her way south and visited Valparaiso and Mejillones Bay in Chile during the first two weeks of February and then returned to Panama for nine days of battle practice with the Fleet. On 23 February, she headed home and, after visits to Costa Rica and Salvador, reached San Diego on 11 March.

Waters remained there until 21 June when she got underway north and, following brief stops at San Pedro and Mare Island, entered Bremerton, Wash., on 27 June to prepare at the Puget Sound Navy Yard for duty in the Far East. Almost a month later, she returned south to San Francisco, whence she sailed for the Far East on 21 July. After stops at Pearl Harbor, Midway, and Guam, *Waters* steamed into Manila Bay on 24 August and reported for duty with the Asiatic Fleet at the Cavite Navy Yard.

The destroyer remained in the vicinity of Luzon through most of her tour of duty in the Orient. She visited Olongapo and Manila frequently and conducted combat training and torpedo exercises off the northwestern shores of the island in Lingayen Gulf. On 3 June 1922, she departed the Philippines and headed north for the Asiatic Fleet's usual summer cruise to Chinese waters. She arrived at Shanghai three days later and, for the remaining seven weeks of her tour in the Orient, visited Chinese ports such as Chefoo and Chinwangtao.

On 25 August, the warship weighed anchor at Chefoo to return to the United States. She stopped at Nagasaki in Japan, Midway Island, and Pearl Harbor en route to

San Francisco, where she finally arrived on 3 October. After a week of repairs at Mare Island Navy Yard, *Waters* steamed south and, upon her arrival at San Diego on 23 October, immediately began preparations for inactivation. On 28 December 1922, *Waters* was decommissioned there and was laid up at the destroyer base.

On 4 June 1930, following more than seven years of inactivity, *Waters* was recommissioned at San Diego, Lt. Comdr. Conrad Ridgely in command. After a month of refurbishing, she began operations along the west coast on 18 July and continued that routine for the next 18 months.

On 1 February 1932, she departed the west coast for the first time since her return from the Far East in 1922. She arrived in Lahaina Roads in the Hawaiian Islands on 12 February and took part in a landing exercise as a unit of the antisubmarine screen. The destroyer spent most of her time in Lahaina Roads but managed brief visits to Oahu and Hilo.

Waters returned to San Diego on 21 March and resumed normal operations until late January 1933. On the 24th, the warship arrived at Mare Island where she was placed in Rotating Reserve Squadron 20. She passed the next six months idly, moored to pierside at Mare Island with a severely reduced crew on board

Early in July 1933, *Waters* returned to active service as a unit of Destroyer Division (DesDiv) 5, Destroyer Squadron (DesRon) 2, Battle Force Destroyers. She left Mare Island on 10 July, arrived at San Diego two days later, and resumed operations along the west coast. After more than eight months of such activity, the warship put to sea from San Diego on 9 April 1934 for an extended voyage to the Atlantic.

Waters reached Balboa in the Canal Zone on the 22d, transited the canal three days later, and was moored at Cristobal for a fortnight. On 5 May, she sailed for the gunnery range at Culebra Island near Puerto Rico. For the next three weeks, *Waters* participated in maneuvers in conjunction with Fleet Problem XV, a three-phased exercise which encompassed an attack upon and defense of the Panama Canal, the capture of advanced bases, and a major fleet engagement. On 25 May, the destroyer shaped a course north to Rhode Island. After a stop at New York City, she stood into Newport on 6 July and conducted tactical exercises out of Newport for two months.

On 7 September, she embarked upon a leisurely voyage back to San Diego. Along the way, she stopped at Hampton Roads; Tampa, Fla.; and Guantanamo Bay, Cuba. Consequently, the warship did not transit the canal until 25 October. She reached San Diego on 8 November and went back into the Rotating Reserve on 19 December.

The warship returned to active duty in May 1935 and resumed operations along the west coast as a unit of DesDiv 19. Late in April 1936, she steamed south to the Panama Canal where she again joined in the maneuvers associated with the annual fleet concentrations which were conducted on the Pacific side of the isthmus. She returned to San Diego at the end of the first week in June and conducted normal operations for a month before leaving the west coast on 6 July.

Her voyage to Hawaii came as a result of DesDiv 19's assignment to the Submarine Force in conjunction with sonar tests. Sometime during the first half of the year, *Waters* and her sisters in the division had received the latest sound gear—high frequency directional sonar which allowed a destroyer to locate a submarine more accurately. Previously, sonar could at best indicate the presence of a submarine somewhere near the destroyer. The new equipment enabled submarine hunters to estimate the interloper's bearing and distance and therefore increased the probability of success of the destroyer's depth charge attacks. From July 1936 until late June 1939, *Waters* and her division mates cooperated with units of the Submarine Force in experiments to develop the techniques which trans-

lated the theoretical potential of the new technological developments into efficient antisubmarine warfare doctrine. *Waters* departed Hawaii for the west coast on 20 June 1939. She reached San Diego 10 days later and was assigned to the Underwater Sound Training School. Between that time and America's entry into World War II, the destroyer continued to develop the Navy's antisubmarine warfare capability by teaching techniques which she had developed to sonar operators and officers assigned to the Fleet.

When the Japanese launched their surprise attack on Pearl Harbor, *Waters* was in port at San Diego and still operating with the Sound School. She received word of the hostilities at 1125 and immediately began preparations to put to sea. That afternoon, the destroyer made a three-hour antisubmarine sweep of the approaches to San Diego. On 8 December, she departed San Diego in the screen of Hawaii-bound *Saratoga* (CV-3). Six days later, the carrier and her screen, DesDiv 50, entered Pearl Harbor. During her 10 days at Oahu, *Waters* periodically conducted patrols of the sea approaches to the harbor. Two days before Christmas, she got underway homeward with a task unit built around *St. Louis* (CL-49), *Helena* (CL-50), and *Raleigh* (CL-7). She escorted the cruisers into San Francisco on the 29th and returned to San Diego on the 30th.

After a month patrolling the California coast, *Waters* slipped her moorings at San Diego on 31 January 1942 and headed north for duty with the defense forces of the 13th Naval District. She arrived at Bremerton, Wash., on 5 February and, six days later, continued north to Alaska. For the next 10 months, the destroyer escorted supply ships from Seattle, Wash., to and between the bases along the Alaskan coast and through the Aleutians chain. She was later assigned to the forces of the Northwestern Sea Frontier as a unit of Task Force 8, the Alaskan defense force. Her mission, however, remained the same as she plied the cold waters of the northeastern Pacific between such ports as Kodiak, Dutch Harbor, Chernofski, Adak, and Sitka—returning periodically to Seattle.

The exigencies of the campaign for Guadalcanal—where neither side enjoyed the overwhelming local naval and air supremacy which insured victory in every other amphibious operation of the war—necessitated an increase in the number of high-speed transports. These hybrid warships combined the functions of transports and of destroyers into one. The concept of the high-speed transport embodied sufficient armament for the ship to defend herself against smaller warships and to support the troops she carried with sufficient speed to enable her to outrun more heavily armed ships. Overage flushdeck destroyers such as *Waters* were the first ships to be so converted to fill this role.

Waters entered the Puget Sound Navy Yard on 19 December 1942 to begin conversion and later that month was redesignated APD-8. During the modifications, her forward boilers were removed to make room for the troops she would carry while her torpedo tubes came off to accommodate landing craft and their davits. Though the ship retained her four-gun main battery configuration, she swapped her obsolete single-purpose 4-inch guns for more up-to-date dual-purpose 3-inch guns. Her antiaircraft defenses were further augmented by the addition of several single 20-millimeter mounts. She completed conversion in February and returned to San Diego on the 10th.

On 17 February, *Waters* stood out of San Diego, bound for the South Pacific. After a five-day stop at Pearl Harbor, she resumed her voyage and reported for duty with the South Pacific Amphibious Force at Noumea, New Caledonia, on 21 March. Five days later, she got underway for Espiritu Santo where she arrived the following day. For the next three weeks, the high-speed transport conducted amphibious training at Espiritu Santo with units of the 4th Marine Raider Battalion. On 18 April, *Waters* headed for the Fiji Islands. She arrived at Suva two days later, embarked men and equipment of Carrier Air Group 11, and proceeded via Espiritu Santo to the Solomons. She arrived off Guadalcanal on 25 April, disembarked her passengers, unloaded cargo, and departed the same day.

During the next nine days, she made a circuitous voyage that took her first to Efate, thence to the Fijis, and from there back to Espiritu Santo where she arrived on 4 May. Eleven days later, the warship exited Segond Channel and set a course for Pago Pago in American Samoa where she stopped from 19 to 23 May. The next stop on her itinerary was Auckland, New Zealand, where she laid over from 29 May to 5 June while her crew enjoyed their last real shore leave for quite some time. *Waters* returned to Noumea on 8 June and got underway the following day with a convoy bound for the southern Solomons. She and her charges arrived off Guadalcanal on 14 June, and the high-speed transport began patrolling the anchorage off Koli Point.

With her arrival in the Solomons, *Waters* began almost a year engaged in the type of operations for which ships of her type were ideally suited. The battered remnants of the Japanese defense forces had evacuated Guadalcanal over three months before; and the American Navy, Marine Corps, and Army possessed relatively secure bases—at that island and across Ironbottom Sound at Florida Island—from which to begin the climb up the Solomons staircase toward the Bismarcks and Rabaul. Operating from Purvis Bay at Florida Island, *Waters* shuttled troops and supplies north to the invasions of various central and northern Solomon islands—New Georgia, Vella Lavella, Bougainville, Treasury Island, and the Green Islands subgroup. After the move toward the Bismarcks began in earnest, she supported both initial invasions and consolidation operations.

New Georgia, the center island of a cluster which, with Vella Lavella, made up the southern branch of the Solomon Archipelago, constituted the second rung on the ladder to Rabaul. While *Waters* waited for the assault on that island, scheduled for the end of June, she patrolled the anchorages between Guadalcanal and Florida Island. On 16 June, she fought her first action when attacking Japanese planes dropped a stick of bombs close aboard. She returned the compliment more accurately than her adversaries, as her antiaircraft battery splashed two of the offending bombers.

Four days later, she received orders to move to Guadalcanal to embark five officers and 187 men of the 4th Marine Raider Battalion, part of a force hastily collected to occupy Segi Point on the southern coast of New Georgia. The Japanese were then moving in on a coastwatcher named Kennedy who held the plantation on the point, and Rear Admiral Turner decided to advance the date of the opening of the Segi Point phase of the New Georgia operation in order to keep possession of the beachhead which for all intents and purposes was already established there and to protect Kennedy and his native guerrillas. *Waters* and *Dent* (APD–9) transited the Slot during the night of 20 and 21 June and, early the next morning, threaded their way through the uncharted shoal water between New Georgia and Vangunu to Segi Point. In less than two hours, the two former flushdeckers disembarked their passengers and stood out to sea again. After a daylight passage back down the Slot, *Waters* and her sister ship returned to Guadalcanal late that afternoon and thence moved to Port Purvis without incident.

On 25 June, *Waters* moved to Guadalcanal to embark more troops, this time the "Barracudas" scout troops of the Army's 172d Infantry. Until the 29th, she practiced amphibious landings at Purvis Bay; then headed north for the landings on Rendova, a small island south of New Georgia and directly opposite Munda, the main objective of the operation. The troops she carried were to have led the assault on Rendova and to have secured a beachhead for the main invasion force. However, heavy weather obscured the beacon fires which were to have guided them ashore, and the "Barracudas" landed some 10 miles down the coast from their objective. By the time they reembarked and moved up the coast, the troops were able to land unopposed across a beachhead already established by units of the main invasion force. *Waters* completed disembarkation and unloading operations without further incident and, by 0855, stood down Blanche Channel in company with *Dent* to return to Purvis Bay, where she anchored that afternoon.

Rendova had been taken primarily as a stepping-stone to the main objective—Munda—as well as its airstrip—and to provide locations for supporting heavy artillery and its observation posts. By the time troops began shuttling from Rendova to Zanana—located to the east of Munda Point—for the planned occupation, *Waters* had picked up more troops at Guadalcanal and had landed them on the opposite coast of New Georgia. She departed Guadalcanal on Independence Day and, the following morning, sent them ashore at Rice Anchorage on the northern coast of the island. The force she landed, a mixture of Marine Corps and Army units, succeeded in isolating and reducing the Japanese garrisons at Bairoko and on Enogai Inlet while the troops in the south concentrated upon the seizure of Munda without fear of interference from the north.

During the next 10 days, she made two more runs to New Georgia carrying reinforcements and supplies to Rendova and returning to Guadalcanal with casualties. On the morning of 13 July, in the aftermath of the naval battles of Kula Gulf and Kolombangara, she escorted the damaged cruisers *Honolulu* (CL–48) and *St. Louis* into Purvis Bay. Two days later, she received orders to head for Vella Lavella—located northwest of New Georgia—to pick up survivors from *Helena* which had been sunk during the Battle of Kula Gulf. She embarked three war correspondents at Koli Point and cleared Guadalcanal at 1325 on the 15th. At 2258 that night, she hauled in sight of her destination and began searching for the *Helena* sailors. At 0159 on the 16th, she lowered her boats to enter Paraso Bay. Later, she moved to Lambu Lambu cove, where her boats picked up 40 officers and men from the sunken cruiser. She completed rescue operations at 0450 and departed Vella Lavella for Guadalcanal. She disembarked the 40 survivors at Tulagi just after 1300 and anchored in Purvis Bay an hour later.

For the next month, *Waters* transported supplies, reinforcements, and garrison troops from Guadalcanal to Rendova and New Georgia and evacuated casualties in support of the mopping up of New Georgia and the capture of the remainder of the smaller islands of the group. During these operations, she served both as a transport and as escort for the slower and less well-armed LST's and LCI's which were used so extensively for transportation throughout the campaigns in the southwestern Pacific.

In mid-August, while the troops she had ferried to New Georgia over the previous seven weeks continued to mop up that island and the smaller ones surrounding it, *Waters* trained her sights on a new objective. Though Kolombangara, the big round island just to the northwest of New Georgia, appeared to be the next step in the ascent to Rabaul, American commanders had become intrigued with the possibility of by-passing, or "leapfrogging," its strong garrison and isolating it by occupying Vella Lavella, the next island above it on the southern arm of the Solomons chain.

Accordingly, *Waters* and six other fast transports loaded troops and equipment at Guadalcanal on 13 and 14 August. Two other transport groups, both composed of slower ships—LST's and LCI's—departed ahead of her and her sisters who cleared Guadalcanal just before 1600 on the 14th. On the way up the Slot, the faster transports took over the lead from the tank landing ships and landing craft and arrived off Vella Lavella at 0529 the following morning. Since there was no organized Japanese garrison on the island, troops from *Waters* and the other fast transports established and consolidated their beachhead quickly. By 0730, she was steaming back down the Slot toward Guadalcanal and Purvis Bay. During the first hour of the passage, planes from the enemy air raids which halfheartedly contested the Vella Lavella landings attacked the transports. *Waters'* antiaircraft battery engaged the attackers, but neither side scored. The remainder of the trip proved uneventful, and *Waters* dropped anchor in Purvis Bay at 2133 that night.

Over the next two months, *Waters* transported replacement troops, reinforcements, and supplies to New Georgia and Vella Lavella. On the return trips, she evacuated casualties and later, after both islands had been secured and garrison forces had moved in, began evacuating the combat-weary veterans of the campaign. These operations signaled the close of the central Solomons phase of the campaign to isolate Rabaul. Future operations centered upon Bougainville, the northernmost major island in the Solomons. In preparation for the invasion of that island, *Waters* participated in simulated amphibious landings at Kukum Beach on Guadalcanal on 26 October. Later that day, she embarked New Zealand troops and laid a course up the Slot to the Treasury Islands, a small pair located not far south of Bougainville and ideally suited as a staging base for small craft and PT boat patrols. The warship landed her portion of the Treasuries assault force expeditiously on the 27th and returned south to Purvis Bay on the 28th.

Waters remained at Purvis Bay for the remainder of October and into the first week of November. Consequently, she missed the 1 November landings on Bougainville at Cape Torokina. However, she moved to Guadalcanal on the 4th, loaded elements of the second echelon, and stood out toward Bougainville. She entered Empress Augusta Bay at 0609 on 6 November and disembarked her passengers by 0733. She then stood out of the bay and took up patrol position outside and helped to screen the entrance to the bay until the following day when she steamed back toward Purvis Bay.

For the following two weeks, *Waters* shuttled troops and equipment back and forth between Guadalcanal and Bougainville. All but the last of those trips were relatively peaceful affairs which began with troop embarkation at Guadalcanal, disembarkation at Empress Augusta Bay after passage up the Slot, and a return voyage with casualties bound for Guadalcanal. During the last voyage, however, enemy dive bombers attacked her convoy just as it arrived off Cape Torokina at 0755 on the 17th. The warship's antiaircraft batteries quickly engaged the intruders and scored a kill on a Japanese "Val." During a lull in the attacks, *Waters* disembarked her troops, but another air raid at 0615 delayed the embarkation of wounded, and she did not complete the operation until 0845. She lay to off Cape Torokina until 1819 when she formed up with a south-bound convoy and headed back to Guadalcanal. On 19 November, she disembarked the casualties at Kukum Beach and returned to Purvis Bay at about 1330.

After 11 days in port at Purvis Bay, *Waters* departed the Solomons for the first time since her arrival the previous June. On 1 December, she stood out of Purvis Bay for Noumea, where she arrived on the 3d. Two days later, she weighed anchor again to escort merchantmen SS *Amy Lowell* and SS *Juan Cabrillo* as far as Lady Elliott Island and then continued independently to Australia. She reached Sydney on 10 December and began nine days of shore leave and repairs.

On the morning of 20 December, she sailed for New Caledonia. On the 23d, she received orders to rendezvous with another merchantman, SS *Walter Colton*, and to escort that ship into Noumea. The warship reached the rendezvous point on Christmas Eve Day and began a fruitless two-day search for SS *Walter Colton*. Early in the evening of Christmas Day, she gave up the search and entered Noumea alone.

Four days later, *Waters* returned to sea and, on 30 December 1943, joined the screen of a Guadalcanal-bound convoy. En route back to the Solomons, *Waters*

received orders detaching her from the convoy and instructions to rendezvous with SS *Sea Barb* and see that ship safely to Auckland, New Zealand. She made the rendezvous that same day, 5 January 1944, escorted her to her destination, and came about to return to Noumea. *Waters* arrived in Noumea on 9 January and, a week later, entered drydock for three days. On 20 January, the day after she left the dock, the fast transport headed back to the Solomons and, two days later, arrived in Purvis Bay.

After a brief excursion as target ship for TF 38 on 24 and 25 January, she moved to Guadalcanal on the 28th and embarked a reconnaissance party for the initial raid on the Green Islands, a small pair north of Buka and Bougainville. She departed Guadalcanal the same day and headed up the Slot. En route, she stopped at Vella Lavella on the 29th to embark a further 112 officers and men, all members of the 30th Battalion, New Zealand Commando Force. That evening, the fast transport and the embarked raiders rehearsed the landing at Vella Lavella. The next morning, she started out on the last leg of the journey. The landing force reached the Green Islands around 2400 that night, and the commandos landed, unopposed, on Nissan, the larger of the two islands. At 0120 on the 31st, *Waters* received word that the landing had succeeded. Late that evening, she moved in toward the Nissan transport area to recover the reconnaissance party which had completed its mission. She completed reembarkation before dawn on 1 February and steamed back down the Slot. Later that day, she and *Hudson* parted company with the rest of the task group to return the New Zealanders to Vella Lavella. Afterward, she continued on toward Guadalcanal, where she arrived on 2 February.

After debarking her remaining passengers at Guadalcanal, *Waters* returned to Purvis Bay for an 11-day stay. On the 13th and 14th, the fast transport retraced her steps of two weeks before. On the 13th, she embarked troops at Guadalcanal and steamed northwest up the Slot. The following day, she stopped at Vella Lavella and took on additional troops, mostly members of the 207th Battalion, 3d New Zealand Division, before continuing on to the Green Islands for the actual occupation. At 0625 on 15 February, the task force arrived off Nissan and began landing the occupation force. The miniscule enemy garrison did not oppose the landing and *Waters* completed her part of the mission and cleared the area by 0846. She returned to Florida Island on the 16th. Between 18 and 21 February, the warship made another round-trip voyage to the Green Islands to ferry a mixed bag of Navy, Army, and New Zealand forces before reentering Purvis Bay for the remainder of the month.

During the first half of March, she made two more voyages to the Green Islands—via Bougainville—before returning to Purvis Bay on the 16th to prepare for the occupation of Emirau Island. At 0630 on St. Patrick's Day, she shifted from Florida Island to Guadalcanal, where she embarked units of the newly reconstituted 4th Marines. At 1800, she passed through Indispensible Strait with the Emirau invasion force and laid in a course to the northwest of the Solomons and New Ireland. At 0615, she arrived in the St. Matthias Islands and began disembarking troops for the invasion of Emirau, the southernmost island of the group. Once again, *Waters'* troops made their landing unopposed. The fast transport completed unloading by 1030 and took up station to patrol the transport area against enemy submarines. Finally, at 1930 that evening, she formed up with the other ships of the force and headed back to the southern Solomons. On the evening of the 22d, the force retransited Indispensible Strait and, the next morning, broke up off Savo Island to return to their various anchorages. *Waters* reentered Purvis Bay at 1130 and let go her anchor.

The fast transport remained in Purvis Bay for the remainder of March and the first week in April. On the 8th, she stood out of the anchorage, picked up passengers at Guadalcanal, and took departure for

Pearl Harbor in company with *Stringham* (APD–6). She made a brief stop at Funafuti, in the Ellice Islands, on 11 April and moored at the DE docks in Pearl Harbor on the 18th. The warship completed repairs by 1 May and began amphibious training at Kauai to prepare for the Marianas operation.

On 21 May while *Waters* was in Pearl Harbor, an LST moored near her exploded. The resulting fire quickly spread to ships moored nearby. Though *Waters* was unable to get underway immediately and clear the area, her crew responded quickly by manning the fire-fighting equipment and wetting down the decks. Further explosions occurred during the afternoon, showering her with debris and injuring one of her crewmen, but the warship sustained relatively minor damage—a few sprung doors, cut cables, some sprung bulkheads, a bent yardarm brace, and a slightly damaged hull frame. Later, her crew responded to the emergency by launching the ship's boats and rescuing 75 survivors from the oil and fire-covered waters surrounding the stricken LST's. The fires smoldered for two days after the incident, and fire-fighting parties were called away intermittently. However, *Waters* soon completed repairs of the damage caused on the 21st and resumed amphibious exercises in preparation for Operation "Forager."

On 28 May, *Waters* stood out of Pearl Harbor for Kawaihae Bay, where she embarked marines the following day. That same day, she joined TF 51 and departed the Hawaiian Islands en route to Eniwetok Atoll, the staging point for the invasion of Saipan. She entered Eniwetok Lagoon at 0900 on 8 June and remained at anchor there for three days. On the 11th, TF 52—the Northern Attack Force—sortied from Eniwetok and headed for the Marianas. *Waters* served as flagship for both TransDiv 12 and TG 52.8, the Eastern Landing Group, administrative and operational organizations, respectively; the same six fast transports made up both organizations.

As she led her task group on the approach to Saipan late in the evening of 14 June, *Waters* made sonar contact with a submarine. She attacked with depth charges around 2200 and was unable to reestablish the contact after the barrage. Though the evidence did not support crediting her with a confirmed kill, her crew observed an oil slick which suggested that she had at least damaged an enemy submarine. She resumed her place in formation just before 2300 and continued to close Saipan, the northernmost of the Marianas islands.

At 0510, she went to general quarters in anticipation of the landing and moved into the transport area off the lower portion of Saipan's western coast. She received orders to patrol 2,000 yards to seaward of the transport area, and she led TransDiv 12 to that station at around 0715. The assault force hit the beaches at about 0845, but *Waters'* complement of marines remained embarked throughout the day and the night of 15 and 16 June while she screened the transport area. She closed the transports once—at 1835—to help repel an air attack and, later, screened them during night retirement.

A little after 0800 on the 16th, *Waters* and the other APD's of TransDiv 12 closed the Charon Kanoa beaches and disembarked their troops—members of the 1st Battalion, 2d Marine Regiment—originally intended for a secondary landing on the eastern coast at Magicienne Bay but landed at the main beachhead because of unexpectedly stiff resistance ashore and an impending battle at sea. She completed debarking marines by 0858 and formed her division in column to take up screening station for the transports. The fast transport reached her assigned position at 1330 and relieved *Bagley* (DD–386).

She remained off Saipan until late June, shepherding the transports of TF 51. During that time, she helped repel several air attacks but did not actually participate in the great air battle of the Philippine Sea fought on 19 and 20 June 1944. Before departing the Marianas on 2 July, the warship also made two unsuccessful

attacks on enemy submarines and bombarded Japanese positions on Tinian.

On 2 July, the fast transport cleared the Marianas to escort TG 51.4 to Eniwetok. She reached her destination two days later and, after a 48-hour layover, exited the lagoon to return to the Marianas. *Waters* resumed patrols of the transport area off Saipan upon her arrival there on the 12th. That night, she delivered night illumination and harrassment fire on Tinian near Tinian Town, probably to discourage any attempt by the Japanese on that island to reinforce their comrades in the Saipan garrison. She resumed antisubmarine patrols on the 13th; and, on the 14th, she departed the Marianas once more—this time to escort *Patuxent* (AO–44) and SS *Sea Cat* to Eniwetok. After reaching Eniwetok on 17 July, the warship spent the next 11 days undergoing repairs and then stood out of the lagoon on the 28th to screen another task unit on its voyage to Saipan. She arrived in the Marianas two days later, parted company with the task unit, and entered the anchorage off Guam, which American forces had invaded while the fast transport was at Eniwetok.

Following three days of screening transports in Agat Bay, she joined a task unit built around battleships *Colorado* (BB–45) and *Pennsylvania* (BB–38). *Waters* reached Eniwetok on the 6th, remained overnight, and then steamed out of the lagoon to escort *Colorado* to Pearl Harbor.

Waters arrived in Pearl Harbor on 12 August but departed again six days later. On the 22d, she entered San Francisco. After six weeks of repairs and modifications, the fast transport left San Francisco on 7 October to return to Hawaii. Upon arrival in Pearl Harbor on the 14th, she began additional repairs in preparation for training with underwater demolition teams (UDT) which she began at the end of October. She completed that training by the beginning of January 1945 and, on the 10th, departed Pearl Harbor with TG 52.11, built around *Texas* (BB–35) and *Nevada* (BB–36). The task group reached Ulithi Atoll on the 23d, and *Waters* remained until 10 February when she got underway to join in the assault on Iwo Jima. She arrived in the Marianas on the 12th, conducted rehearsals at Saipan and Tinian, and continued on to the Bonin-Volcano group on the 14th.

She arrived off Iwo Jima on the morning of 16 February as part of the screen for the fire support group. During the three days before the actual invasion, *Waters* protected the bombardment battleships from enemy submarines and supported the UDT's in their preinvasion reconnaissance of Iwo Jima's beaches. On the day of the assault, she joined the transports and screened them during the landings. The warship remained in the vicinity of Iwo Jima until the first week in March, supporting UDT operations and patrolling against Japanese submarines. On 5 March, the high-speed transport cleared the area with TransDiv 33 and a four-ship screen and headed for Guam. She remained at Guam for a day and a night, arriving there early on the 8th and departing again on the 9th. She entered Ulithi again on the 11th and began preparations for the last campaign of World War II—Operation "Iceberg," the assault on Okinawa.

Following 10 days in Ulithi lagoon, *Waters* steamed out of the atoll on 21 March and joined TG 54.2, part of Rear Admiral M. L. Deyo's Gunfire and Covering Force, for the voyage to the Ryukyus. During the approach for the preinvasion bombardment on 26 March, *Waters* fired upon a Japanese "Val" dive bomber which tried to crash into *Gilmer* (APD–11). Though she claimed no kill, *Waters'* antiaircraft battery was probably instrumental in deflecting that kamikaze's aim and causing him to miss his target by a mere 75 yards. Over the four days before the landings, she screened the "old" battleships while they softened up Okinawa's defenses and supported UDT reconnaissance missions and demonstrations along the Okinawa coastline. Late on the 31st, she joined Tractor Group "Fox" to cover its approach to the beaches on the following morning.

During the first week of the assault, she conducted patrols off those same beaches. On 6 April, she teamed up with *Morris* (DD–417) to splash a "Betty" twin-engine bomber. Early that evening, a suicide plane crashed *Morris*, and *Waters* rushed to her assistance, helping to control the fires that blazed on board the destroyer for two hours. Two days later, *Waters* entered Kerama Retto for fuel and to await reassignment. The following day, she received orders to screen Mine Squadron (MinRon) 3 and, for the remainder of the month, supported minesweeping operations. On 3 May, she took up famiilar duty protecting the transport area from submarines, but that assignment proved to be a brief one.

The following day, she joined the escort of a Ulithi-bound convoy. On 6 May, she and *Herbert* (APD–22) were diverted to Leyte Gulf, where they arrived on the 8th. There, they picked up a convoy of LST's and shepherded them back to Okinawa, arriving on the 15th. After four days at Okinawa—punctuated by frequent Japanese air attacks, she departed once again in the escort of a convoy bound for Saipan. The fast transport reached her destination on the 24th, underwent repairs, and shifted to Guam on 5 June to unload her UDT equipment. From Guam, she moved to Ulithi for another week of repairs from 6 to 13 June. On the 17th, the warship returned to Okinawa with another convoy and, after two days at Kerama Retto, cleared the Ryukyus for the last time.

During this voyage, which ultimately took her home, she fired her last shot in anger on 24 June when she dropped a barrage of depth charges on an underwater sound contact. Following the attack, she lost contact and continued on her way. After stops at Saipan, Eniwetok, and Pearl Harbor, the warship finally hauled into San Pedro, Calif., on 21 July. Soon after her arrival, she began an extensive overhaul at the Western Steel & Pipe Co. On 2 August, she resumed her former classification as a destroyer and became DD–115 once again. The war ended on 14 August while she was still in the yard; and, in September, she was moved to Terminal Island, and the overhaul became preinactivation preparations. On 12 October 1945, the veteran of two world wars was decommissioned at Terminal Island. Her name was struck from the Navy list on 24 October 1945, and she was sold for scrapping on 10 May 1946.

Waters received seven battle stars for service during World War II.

Watertown

Cities and towns in the states of Connecticut, Massachusetts, New York, South Dakota, and Wisconsin.

(T–AGM–6: dp. 15,200 (f.); l. 455.3'; b. 62.2'; dr. 28.6'; s. 17.0 k.; cpl. 56; cl. *Range Tracker*)

Niantic Victory was laid down on 12 February 1944 at Portland, Oreg., by the Oregon Shipbuilding Corp. under a Maritime Commission contract (MCV hull 100); launched on 25 April 1944; sponsored by Mrs. Marvin Owen; and delivered to the Maritime Commission on 18 May 1944. From 1944 until 1957, *Niantic Victory* was operated for the Maritime Commission by a succession of contractor firms, beginning with the American-Hawaiian Steamship Line and ending with the Isbrandtsen Co. in 1957. Her activities between 1957 and 1960 are a mystery. She was listed in the *American Bureau of Shipping Record* as still belonging to the Maritime Commission, but no operator was listed. Furthermore, she was dropped from the active list of Maritime Commission ships in the April 1957 issue of *Merchant Vessel Register*. All of this suggests that she went out of service early in 1957. This speculation, however, cannot be corroborated, because her name does not appear in any of the lists of ships in National Defense Reserve Fleet berthing areas.

In any event, *Niantic Victory* was turned over to the Navy Department in 1960 and assigned to the Military Sea Transportation Service on 11 August for conversion to a range instrumentation ship. On 27 November, she was renamed *Watertown* and designated AGM–6. For the next 11 years, she served in the Pacific in support of the National Aeronautics and Space Administration and the Air Force on the latter service's Western Missile Test Range. She operated as a mobile tracking station, recording test data from missiles and satellites out of range of land-based stations. In February 1972, the Air Force decided that it no longer required *Watertown*'s services. Her name was struck from the Navy list on 16 February 1972, and she was returned to the Maritime Administration at its berthing facility at Suisun Bay, Calif., on 23 March. She was probably sold for scrap soon thereafter.

Waterway

Waterway (LSD–15)—formerly *Tomahawk*—was renamed *Shadwell* (q.v.) on 6 April 1944.

Wathena

An American Indian chief of the Kickapoo tribe who lived on land which is now the site of the city in Doniphan County, Kansas, which now bears his name.

I

(Freighter: dp. 12,225; l. 417'9½''; b. 54'0''; dph. 32'9''; dr. 25'6''; s. 11 k.; cpl. 70; a. none)

The first *Wathena*—a steel-hulled, single-screw freighter built for the United States Shipping Board (USSB) in 1918 at Bristol, Pa., by the Merchants' Shipbuilding Corp.—was taken over by the Navy on 1 February 1919 for operation by the Naval Overseas Transportation Service (NOTS), assigned Id. No. 3884, and was placed in commission at Philadelphia on the same day, Lt. Comdr. Percy E. Crosby, USNRF, in command.

Wathena conducted only one round-trip voyage for NOTS. Her holds loaded with 5,754 tons of cargo, she departed Philadelphia on 13 February, bound for the British Isles. After arriving at London, England, on 1 March, she discharged her cargo in the ensuing days, underwent voyage repairs, and sailed on the 17th to return to the United States.

She arrived back at Philadelphia on 3 April and was placed in line for demobilization soon thereafter. Decommissioned and struck from the Navy list on 10 April 1919, *Wathena* was simultaneously turned over to the USSB. She remained in the ownership of the USSB through the 1920's. Eventually laid up, the freighter deteriorated so much that she was abandoned in 1933 due to "age and deterioration."

II

(YTB–825: dp. 356; l. 109'0''; b. 31'0''; dph. 14'; s. 12 k.; cpl. 12; cl. *Natick*)

The second *Wathena* (YTB–825) was laid down on 4 April 1973 at Marinette, Wis., by the Marinette Marine Corp.; launched on 6 September 1973; and delivered to the Navy on 16 October 1973. Placed in service soon thereafter at Norfolk, Va., in the 5th Naval District, *Wathena* served that district into 1980, providing assistance and towing services in that locale.

Watonwan

A county and river in south central Minnesota.

(Freighter: dp. 12,200; l. 417'9½''; b. 54'2''; dr. 25'6'' (mean); dph. 32'10''; s. 8.9 k.; cpl. 70; a. 1 4'', 1 3'')

Watonwan—a single-screw, steel-hulled freighter

built in 1918 for the United States Shipping Board (USSB) at Bristol, Pa., by the Merchants' Shipbuilding Co.—was taken over by the Navy for use with the Naval Overseas Transportation Service (NOTS), assigned Id. No. 4296, and commissioned at Philadelphia on 4 February 1919, Lt. Comdr. Arnold H. Lewis, USNRF, in command.

After loading 7,087 tons of flour, *Watonwan* departed Philadelphia on 19 February, bound for the British Isles, and arrived in Falmouth, England, on 5 March. After discharging a part of her cargo there, she departed that port on the 12th and called at Plymouth and Gibraltar before sailing from the latter port on 22 March for Italy. Reaching Genoa on 26 March, the ship discharged the last of her cargo of flour there, loaded 1,250 tons of stone ballast, and sailed via Gibraltar for the United States.

Watonwan tarried briefly at Norfolk, arriving on the 26th and departing the next day, before moving on to New Orleans, La. She arrived there on 8 May and was decommissioned on 14 May. She was simultaneously struck from the Navy list and turned back to the Shipping Board. Laid up in 1923, *Watonwan* was eventually abandoned, due to age and deterioration, in 1931.

Watseka

Possibly a variant spelling of Watsaghika, a former village of the Iruwaitsu Shasta Indian tribe of northern California, at the extreme west end of Scott Valley.

(YT–387: l. 100'0''; b. 25'0''; dr. 10'0'')

Watseka (YT–387) was purchased in 1943 from Ira S. Bushey and Sons, of Brooklyn, N.Y., and assigned to the 8th Naval District, New Orleans, La. On 15 May 1944, her designation was changed to YTB–387. Placed in reserve, out of service, and berthed with the Columbia River, Oreg., Group of the Pacific Reserve Fleet from March 1946, she was subsequently sold on 1 July 1972.

Watson

John Crittenden Watson—born in Frankfort, Ky., on 24 August 1842—graduated from the Naval Academy on 15 June 1860. After tours in *Susquehanna* and *Richmond*, Watson was promoted to master on 19 September 1861 and joined *Sabine*. He distinguished himself in this ship when she went to the aid of the chartered government transport *Governor* off the coast of South Carolina on the night of 2 and 3 November 1861. Watson managed the cables and hawsers which held the two ships together in spite of a violent gale, allowing some 500 men—marines and crew—to clamber from the foundering *Governor* to safety in *Sabine*. His commanding officer, Capt. Cadwalader Ringgold, praised Watson for his "indefatigable exertions" and "utmost skill and efficiency" in keeping the two ships lashed together.

Promoted to lieutenant in July 1862, Watson later served as flag lieutenant to Rear Admiral Farragut, who flew his flag in the steam sloop *Hartford*, and participated in the Battle of Mobile Bay. He was later wounded by a shell fragment during an engagement with a Confederate battery at Warrington.

Watson served in a number of sea and shore billets into the 1880's, including duty as executive officer of the steam sloop *Alaska*; the post of inspector of ordnance at the Mare Island Navy Yard, Vallejo, Calif.; command of *Wyoming* when that warship carried the American exhibit to the Paris Exposition of 1878; and governor of the Naval Home at Philadelphia, Pa.

As a commodore, he hoisted his broad pennant in *Newark* (Cruiser No. 1) as Commander, Eastern Fleet, on 10 June 1898, shifting later to *Oregon* (Battleship No. 3). The battleship served as his flagship during the subsequent Battle of Santiago, Cuba, on 3 July 1898, in which the Spanish squadron under Admiral Cervera was destroyed. Promoted to Rear Admiral in 1899, he served as Commander in Chief, Asiatic Fleet, from 20 June 1899 into 1900 before returning to the United States to serve as President of the Naval Examining Board. Watson represented the United States at the coronation of King Edward VII of England in 1902.

Placed on the retired list in 1904, Rear Admiral Watson lived in retirement until he died at Washington, D.C., on 14 December 1923.

Watson (DD–482)—planned as a modified *Fletcher*-class destroyer to be built at Kearny, N.J., by the Federal Shipbuilding and Drydock Co.—was to be powered by an experimental diesel propulsion system. However, due to more pressing wartime destroyer construction programs, the ship was never laid down, and her construction was cancelled on 7 January 1946.

Watson, R. E. & A. H., see *R. E. & A. H. Watson.*

Watts

Little is known about John Watts other than the fact that he was an American merchant captain at the end of the eighteenth century and the beginning of the nineteenth. Probably born about 1778, location unknown but most likely in Virginia, he was captain of the 18-gun, armed merchantman *Planter* in 1799. He is remembered for an action between *Planter* and a 22-gun French privateer which took place on 10 July 1799 in the eastern Atlantic during the Quasi War with France. During that five-hour engagement, he and *Planter*'s 43-man crew successfully fought off two concerted attacks by the more heavily armed Frenchman and thwarted the privateer's attempt to take the American ship. Watts and his crew received a generous reward for their efforts from Lloyd's Coffee House in London, the forerunner of the world-famous insurance company Lloyd's of London. Watts presumably continued in merchant service after the adventure with the French privateer, but he never served in the United States Navy. John Watts died in 1823, again location unknown.

(DD–567: dp. 2,050; l. 376'5''; b. 39'7''; dr. 17'9''; s. 35.2 k. (tl.); cpl. 329; a. 5 5'', 10 40mm., 7 20mm., 10 21'' tt., 6 dcp., 2 dct.; cl. *Fletcher*)

Watts (DD–567) was laid down on 26 March 1943 at Seattle, Wash., by the Seattle-Tacoma Shipbuilding Corp.; launched on 31 December 1943; sponsored by Mrs. Judith Bundick Gardner; and commissioned on 29 April 1944, Comdr. Joseph B. Maher in command.

Following two weeks of testing and calibrating equipment in Puget Sound. *Watts* embarked upon her first voyage on 17 May. She headed for San Diego and a month of shakedown training. She returned to Bremerton on 26 June and underwent three weeks of post-shakedown availability. On 12 July, she departed Bremerton in company with battleships *Mississippi* (BB–41) and *West Virginia* (BB–48) bound for San Diego. The destroyer remained at San Diego until the 22d, at which time she put to sea in the screen of a Hawaii-bound convoy of troop transports. She arrived in Pearl Harbor on 29 July and remained only until 3 August when she stood out with Destroyer Division (DesDiv) 113 and shaped a course for Aleutian waters. On 8 August, *Watts* led her division mates into port at Adak, Alaska.

During the next seven months, the destroyer operated with the other units of DesDiv 113 as a part of the Navy's North Pacific Force. Since her assignment there came well after America had consolidated her hold on the Aleutians chain, the bulk of *Watts*' duties consisted of patrols and supply convoy-escort missions between the various outposts scattered across the fog and snow-bound archipelago. On the other hand, she and her division mates did, on occasion, conduct offensive operations against the Japanese Empire—primarily against the northern Kuril Islands.

Her first attempt came after more than two months of operations which might be characterized as routine—as much so as possible in the stormy northern Pacific. On 14 October, she departed Massacre Bay, Attu, for her first bombardment mission with the cruisers and destroyers of the North Pacific Force. Bad weather foiled that mission and the next which began on 24 October. Late in November, however, she departed Attu for her third attempt at bombarding the Kurils. That one proved successful; and, on the night of 23 and 24 November, her guns joined those of the other warships of the force in pounding airfields and installations on Matsuwa To. During the retirement from the Kurils, heavy seas lashed the task force. Fortunately, the same storms which buffeted *Watts* and her sister ships kept enemy air power grounded, and the bombardment group arrived safely back at Attu on 25 November. After two weeks of badly needed repairs at Dutch Harbor, she returned to Attu on 21 December, following a brief stop at Adak.

On 3 January 1945, the destroyer steamed out of Massacre Bay for another sweep of the waters surrounding the northern Kurils. The climax of that operation came on 5 January when she joined in successful shelling of the Suribachi area of Paramushiro. After a brief stop at Attu, *Watts* moved on to Dutch Harbor with the rest of DesDiv 113. The following month, February, brought two more forays into the waters around the Kurils. However, only the second, which began on 16 February, ended with a bombardment. That one—on the 18th—hit installations in the Kurabi Zaki area of Paramushiro.

After a brief return to Attu, *Watts* departed the Aleutians on 22 February and headed for Hawaii with *Jarvis* (DD–799). The two destroyers reached Pearl Harbor on 1 March and began a fortnight of training and voyage repairs. On the 15th, *Watts* stood out of Pearl Harbor and headed back to the Aleutians for less than a month of operations. On 18 April, DesDiv 113 left the northern Pacific for good. From there, *Watts* and her division mates headed for Hawaii and three weeks of training in preparation for duty in the recently launched Okinawa invasion. On 5 May, she cleared the Hawaiian Islands and steamed west by way of Eniwetok and Ulithi.

On 21 May, when she arrived at Okinawa, the campaign had been in progress for almost two months, but the Japanese still hung on tenaciously. The members of the Kamikaze Corps continued to hurl themselves at the ships supporting the troops ashore. *Watts* proved to be a lucky ship while on radar picket station. Not only did her guns help to shoot down six aerial attackers, but she suffered only one really close call. A suicide plane almost managed to crash into her port side forward, but accurate 20-millimeter fire splashed him at the last possible instant, only 10 yards off the destroyer's port bow.

Mercifully, her stay at Okinawa proved brief. In mid-June, she received orders to join the screen of TF 38 at Leyte Gulf, where she arrived on 17 June. For the remainder of the war, *Watts* screened the fast carriers of TF 38 while their planes flew their last series of sorties against the Japanese home islands. Ranging from Hokkaido in the north to Kyushu in the south, those planes helped to decimate enemy shipping, land communications, and military and manufacturing installations. On 23 July, *Watts* made her own personal contribution to the destruction visited upon the enemy when her guns joined in a bombardment of the outpost island, Chichi Jima, in the Bonins.

The Japanese capitulation on 15 August 1945 found the ship steaming in Japanese waters screening TF 38.

A bit under a month later, on 10 September, she entered Tokyo Bay to begin participation in the occupation of Japan. She remained on that duty until mid-November; then headed back to the United States. After brief stops at Pearl Harbor and San Diego, the destroyer transited the Panama Canal on 7 December and headed for Philadelphia on the 18th. *Watts* arrived at the Philadelphia Naval Shipyard on 23 December and began a three-month inactivation overhaul. In mid-March, she shifted to the Charleston Naval Shipyard, where she was placed out of commission on 12 April 1946. There, she remained, in reserve until—to bolster the Navy during the Korean conflict—she was recommissioned on 6 July 1951, Comdr. George L. Block in command.

During the first 42 months of the second phase of her career, *Watts* operated with the Destroyer Force, Atlantic Fleet. In the late summer and fall of 1951, the warship was fitted out, conducted shakedown, and made a cruise to Guantanamo Bay, Cuba. The spring of 1952 brought a round of exercises, notably "Convex III." That summer, she went into the yard at Philadelphia for overhaul. Refresher training at Guantanamo Bay followed, and then the destroyer resumed normal operations which she continued until the beginning of 1953.

On 7 January, she put to sea from Norfolk for her first deployment with the 6th Fleet in the Mediterranean Sea. That May, after visits to northern European ports, *Watts* returned to Norfolk and began operations in the western Atlantic. Her assignment for almost a year centered upon antisubmarine warfare training with the Hunter/Killer Force, Atlantic Fleet. During that time, she made at least one cruise to the West Indies and visited Kingston, Jamaica, and San Juan, Puerto Rico. Her tour of duty with the Hunter/Killer Force ended on 12 April 1954 when she entered the Norfolk Naval Shipyard for another overhaul. The destroyer completed that yard period on 7 July and conducted refresher training in the vicinity of Guantanamo Bay from late July to mid-September, when she resumed duty out of Norfolk.

That assignment continued until December at which time *Watts* was reassigned to the Cruiser-Destroyer Force, Pacific Fleet. After a voyage which took her to Guantanamo Bay and Havana, Cuba, as well as through the Panama Canal, she arrived in her new home port—Long Beach, Calif.—on 28 January 1955. Between January 1955 and December 1957, the destroyer alternated three deployments to the western Pacific with operations out of Long Beach along the western coast of the United States. During each of her tours of duty with the 7th Fleet, *Watts* divided her time between escort duty with the carriers of TF 77 and assignments with the Taiwan Strait patrol. Overhauls, type training, and refresher training filled her schedule when she returned to the west coast.

In December 1957, the destroyer entered the Long Beach Naval Shipyard for what was to have been her decommissioning overhaul. In June 1958, however, a reprieve arrived in the form of orders to shift home port to Seattle, Wash., and become a Naval Reserve training ship as the flagship of Reserve Escort Squadron (ResCortRon) 1. *Watts* served with the reserve training program for almost four years, from June 1958 to March 1962. Throughout the entire period, the Seattle-Tacoma area remained her base of operations. She provided a platform upon which naval reservists could reacquaint themselves with the intricacies of and skills necesary to constructive Navy service. During her more than three years of reserve training cruises, she ranged the length of the western coast of the United States from San Diego in the south to the Canadian border. She also cruised farther north to make goodwill calls at Canadian ports such as Victoria in British Columbia. During the summer of 1959, she became the first Naval Reserve training ship to participate in a regular Fleet exercise with her reserve crew embarked. In December 1961, the destroyer was undergoing a yard period when the Berlin crisis developed in Europe. Her reserve crew was called to active duty; and, upon completing the overhaul on 8 January 1962, she departed Puget Sound to return to Long Beach. She completed refresher training out of San Diego on 1 March and departed the west coast for a tour of duty with the 7th Fleet in the Orient. During that cruise, she participated in at least one training operation, a combined antiaircraft-antisubmarine exercise, and visited Guam, Hong Kong, Kobe, Sasebo, and Yokosuka. The easing of tensions in Europe late that spring allowed her to head home at the end of June. The destroyer arrived back in Long Beach on 9 July and, on 16 July, she resumed Naval Reserve training duty at Tacoma.

Watts completed another 30 months training reservists out of the Seattle-Tacoma area. In mid-1963, one of her training cruises took her to Hawaii; but, for the most part, she operated just off the west coast. In December 1964, *Watts* was decommissioned and placed in reserve at Bremerton. She remained there for almost a decade. On 1 February 1974, her name was struck from the Navy list, and she was sold on 5 September 1974 to General Metals Co., of Tacoma, Wash., for scrapping.

Watts earned three battle stars for her World War II service.

Waubansee

A chief of the Potawatomi Indians.

(YTB–366: dp. 345 (f.); l. 100′0″; b. 25′0″; dr. 9′7″ (f.); s. 12.0 k.; cpl. 14; cl. *Sassaba*)

Waubansee (YTB–366) was laid down on 24 April 1944 at Morris Heights, N.Y., by the Consolidated Shipbuilding Corp.; reclassified as YTB–366 on 15 May 1944; launched on 10 June 1944; and completed and placed in service at the New York Navy Yard, Brooklyn, N.Y., on 11 October 1944.

After initial service at the Boston Navy Yard, *Waubansee* was reassigned to the Portsmouth (N.H.) Naval Shipyard on 30 April 1953. Reclassified as a medium harbor tug and redesignated YTM–366 in February 1962, *Waubansee* operated in the 1st Naval District, providing tug and tow services, as well as pilot assistance, into the late 1970's. Taken out of service and placed in reserve in August 1977, the medium harbor tug was berthed at Portsmouth, Va. In the spring of 1979, *Waubansee* was being prepared for reactivation.

Waubesa

One of the "Four Lakes" of Dane County, southern Wisconsin; located four miles southeast of Madison.

(ScStr: dp. 12,225; l. 419′½″; b. 54′0″; dr. 25′2″ (mean); dph. 32′10″; s. 11.0 k.; cpl. 89)

Waubesa—a steel-hulled, single-screw freighter built under a United States Shipping Board contract in 1918 by the Merchants' Shipbuilding Corp. of Bristol, Pa.—was inspected by the Navy in the 4th Naval District, designated Id. No. 3955, and earmarked for possible service as a collier in the Naval Overseas Transportation Service (NOTS). An order dated 13 August 1918 specified that, upon completion, the ship was to be turned over to the Navy for operation in NOTS (Army account). She is listed in the 1918 issue of *Ship's Data, U.S. Naval Vessels*, but the succeeding volume (1919) states that the ship was not, in fact, taken over.

Waukegan

A city in the extreme northeastern corner of Illinois on the shore of Lake Michigan. It is the seat of government for Lake County and derives its name from an Indian word meaning "little foot."

(YTM–755: dp. 390 (f.); l. 107′; b. 27′; dr. 13′; s. 12 k. (tl.); cpl. 16; cl. *Chicopee*)

Waukegan (YTM–755), a medium harbor tug, was acquired by the Navy in September 1964 from the Army for which she had served as *LT–1968*. Named *Waukegan* and designated YTM–755, she was assigned to the 10th Naval District at San Juan, Puerto Rico. The tug was based there for her entire 11-year naval career, serving ships in the 10th Naval District. In September 1975, she was placed out of service; and her name was struck from the Navy list. She was subsequently disposed of by sale.

Waukesha

A county in southeastern Wisconsin, noted for its abundant dairy and farm lands and many resort lakes. Waukesha County also contains the Cushing Memorial State Park within its boundaries.

(AKA–84: dp. 13,910; l. 459′2″; b. 63′0″; s. 16.5 k.; cpl. 357; a. 1 5″, 8 40mm., 16 20mm.; cl. *Tolland*; T. C2–S–AJ3)

Waukesha (AKA–84) was laid down under a Maritime Commission contract (MC hull 1395) on 3 July 1944, at Wilmington, N.C., by the North Carolina Shipbuilding Co.; launched on 6 September 1944; sponsored by Mrs. H. V. Mason; converted to an attack cargo ship by the Todd-Erie Shipyard of New York City; and commissioned at the New York Navy Yard, Lt. Comdr. John S. Herold, USNR, in command.

Following shakedown in Chesapeake Bay, *Waukesha* got underway for the Pacific on 27 March 1945. She transited the Panama Canal in company with *Vinton* (AKA–83) on 2 April and arrived at Pearl Harbor on the 17th. She conducted exercises and maneuvers in the Hawaiian area before getting underway on 11 May and proceeding via Eniwtok and Ulithi to Okinawa.

The cargo ship arrived at Buckner Bay on 13 July, with Convoy OKU-17, dropped anchor, and commenced unloading her cargo. Twice the operation was interrupted by fierce typhoons which whirled into Buckner Bay and forced the ships at anchor to get underway and make for the relative safety of the open sea. In addition, Japanese nuisance raids continued nightly, keeping all hands at general quarters for long periods.

Her next orders—to proceed to Pearl Harbor—were cancelled when the ship received news that the Japanese were entertaining thoughts of surrender in the aftermath of the explosions of two atomic bombs. The attack cargo ship instead steered a course for Guam and arrived at Apra Harbor on the 12th. Two days later, she embarked men and material of the 14th Marine Regiment. She was ready for sea on the following day, 15 August 1945, the day on which the Japanese accepted the terms of the Potsdam Declaration.

"VJ Day" only marked the beginning of another phase of *Waukesha*'s brief Navy career—the occupation of the Japanese home islands. She rendezvoused with units of the 3d Fleet off Honshu and entered Tokyo Bay on the 27th, anchoring off the bomb-scarred Yokosuka Naval Base on the 30th to commence offloading her men and equipment to support the occupation.

Waukesha returned to Saipan on 5 September and embarked men of the 2d Marine Division; transferred some of her own men to other ships for transportation back to the United States; and took on supplies for a second trip to Japanese ports. She arrived at Nagasaki and tied up at Dejima Wharf on the 24th, to disembark her marines of the occupation force.

Underway for the Philippines four days later, the ship transferred four landing boats to *Oconto* (APA–187) at Subic Bay on 4 October and then obtained five boats from the Army Boat Pool in Lingayen Gulf before moving to Manila. Loading cargo occupied the ship in the Philippines before she sailed for Japan for her third and final visit to that country's ports, carrying cargo to Honshu and reaching Kii Suido on 23 October.

Shifting to Nagoya on 1 November, *Waukesha* embarked demobilized sailors, soldiers, and marines to transport them home in Operation "Magic Carpet." After departing Nagoya on the 9th, she made port at Seattle, Wash., on the 21st and unloaded her passengers before proceeding south for San Francisco. The ship later made more Far Eastern cruises and called at Okinawa en route to Tsingtao, China, where she arrived on 2 March 1946. Remaining until 8 March, the attack cargo ship set course, via Okinawa, for San Diego, Calif., which she reached on 15 April 1946.

Waukesha departed San Diego on 30 April and steamed, via the Panama Canal, to the east coast. She arrived at Norfolk, Va., on 24 May. Decommissioned and returned to the Maritime Commission's War Shipping Administration on 10 July 1946, the attack cargo ship was struck from the Navy list on 31 July 1946.

Acquired by the Luckenbach Steamship Co. of New York City in 1947, the erstwhile warship was renamed *Mary Luckenbach* and operated with that firm until 1959, when the ship was renamed *Bayou State*. She sailed under the flag of the States Marine Lines, Inc., of New York, until 1970, when her name disappeared from the merchant registers.

Waupaca

A river in the east central part of the state of Wisconsin and a tributary of the larger Wolf River. A city and a county in Wisconsin also bear the name.

(AOG–46: dp. 2,300; l. 221'0''; b. 37'0''; dph. 15'0''; s. 15.0 k.; cpl. 61; a. 1 3'', 6 20mm.; cl. *Mettawee*; T. T1–M–A2)

Waupaca (AOG–46) was laid down under a Maritime Commission contract (MC hull 2072) on 23 November 1944, at Bayonne, N.J., by the East Coast Shipyard, Inc.; launched on 4 January 1945; sponsored by Miss Muriel A. Porter; and commissioned at Marine Basin, Brooklyn, N.Y., on 9 February 1945, Lt. William G. Brown, USNR, in command.

Waupaca got underway on 7 March for Norfolk, Va. After conducting shakedown in Chesapeake Bay, the tanker proceeded to the Netherlands West Indies. She arrived at Aruba on 16 April and completed loading a cargo of diesel oil and aviation gasoline the following day. Underway on the 17th, she transited the Panama Canal on the 22d, en route to southern California.

After discharging her cargo upon arrival at San Diego, she underwent repairs in dry dock before she proceeded to Los Angeles. Soon after her arrival there, she loaded a cargo of diesel and lubricating oil, got underway for Hawaii on 22 May, and arrived at Pearl Harbor on 7 June.

Assigned to Service Squadron 8 upon arrival, *Waupaca* got underway for the Marshalls on 26 June. She arrived at Eniwetok Atoll on 8 July and reported for duty with Service Division (ServDiv) 102. Based at Eniwetok, the tanker fueled many types of ships—mainly amphibious craft, PC's, and minecraft—from 8 July through the end of hostilities in the Pacific.

After the surrender of Japan, ServDiv 102 received orders to Tokyo Bay to fuel smaller units of the occupation forces. With a full cargo of diesel and lubricating oils, *Waupaca* got underway on 7 September, as part of Task Unit (TU) 30.9.21, and proceeded for Tokyo Bay. En route, lookouts sighted a floating, drifting, horn-type mine and notified the Officer in Tactical Command (OTC) of TU 30.9.21, who dispatched a patrol craft to investigate—*PC–825* soon sank the navigational hazard with gunfire.

Waupaca anchored off Yokosuka, Japan, on the 21st,

and shifted alongside the damaged Japanese battleship *Nagato* on the 30th to serve as a fueling station. The tanker remained in the Tokyo Bay area into the winter and returned to San Francisco, Calif., on 18 January 1946. Decommissioned on 26 March, *Waupaca* was struck from the Navy list on 1 May, and she was delivered to the Maritime Commission on 1 July 1946.

Purchased by the Standard-Vacuum Oil Co., of New York, N.Y., in 1947 and renamed *Mei Shan*, the tanker sailed under the Stars and Stripes until acquired by the Canadian-based firm of Oriental Trade and Transport Co., Ltd., in 1948. Successively renamed *Stanvac 312* and *Stanvac Mei Foo*, she served under the British flag until 1954, when the Philippine subsidiary of Standard-Vacuum Oil Co., based at Manila, purchased the ship and renamed her *Stanvac Visayas II*. In 1963, she was acquired by Mobil Oil, Philippines, Inc., and renamed *Mobil Visayas*; and, in 1970, she was sold and again renamed, this time *Lapu-Lapu Carrier*, by Del Mar Carriers, Inc., under which name she served, under Philippine registry, into 1977.

Wauseon

A village in northwestern Ohio about 32 miles west of Toledo. It is the seat of government for Fulton County.

(PC–1229: dp. 280; l. 173'8''; b. 23'0''; dr. 10'10''; s. 20.2 k. (tl.); cpl. 65; a. 1 3'', 1 40mm., 2 dcp. (mousetrap), 2 dct.; cl. *PC–461*)

PC–1229 was laid down on 7 September 1942 by the Leatham D. Smith Shipbuilding Co. at Sturgeon Bay, Wis.; launched on 19 December 1942; sponsored by Mrs. C. D. Brower; and moved to New Orleans, La., where she was commissioned on 11 June 1942, Lt. Gordon A. Weller, USNR, in command.

She departed New Orleans on 23 June for her shakedown cruise and antisubmarine warfare (ASW) training out of Miami and Key West, Fla. Upon completion of training, she began duty with the forces attached to the Gulf Sea Frontier which occupied her until late December. Her primary responsibilities centered on protecting coastwise convoys travelling between gulf coast and West Indian ports from Galveston, Tex., as far east as Guantanamo Bay, Cuba.

By the end of 1943, the major U-boat danger in the Gulf of Mexico had passed, and *PC–1229* received orders to join the Pacific Fleet. She arrived in the Canal Zone on 23 December, transited the canal sometime between then and 9 January 1944, and then continued her voyage west. Heading by way of the South Pacific, she made a brief stop at Bora Bora in the Society Islands on 1 February, another at Tongatabu in the Friendly Islands on the 8th, and arrived in Noumea, New Caledonia, on the 13th. The subchaser served at Noumea for almost a year, guarding the harbor and anchorage against a possible Japanese submarine attack.

In December 1944, she embarked upon a voyage which took her to the southern Solomons at mid-month and to Sydney, Australia, in mid-January 1945. From Sydney, she returned to Purvis Bay in the southern Solomons and thence voyaged to Espiritu Santo in the New Hebrides group where she arrived on 17 February. She served at Espiritu Santo for about seven weeks, returning to Noumea on 6 April. There, she remained until late July when she moved to the Fiji Islands for duty at Suva during August and September. During this assignment, the war in the Pacific ended; and, by 2 October, she returned to Guadalcanal in the Solomons.

On 3 November, the subchaser returned to Noumea. After almost three months at Noumea, *PC–1229* headed home on 26 January 1946. Steaming via Tutuila, Samoa, and Palmyra Island, the ship arrived in Pearl Harbor on 12 February. She remained in Hawaii for five weeks, resuming her voyage east on 19 March. She stopped at San Pedro, Calif., for three weeks, from 27 March to

19 April, before resuming her journey home by way of the Panama Canal to the east coast. The subchaser arrived in Key West, Fla., on 10 May and served there until 21 June when she got underway for Green Cove Springs, Fla., and inactivation. *PC-1229* was decommissioned on 7 August 1946 and was berthed with the Atlantic Reserve Fleet at Green Cove Springs. There, she remained for the rest of her Navy career. On 15 February 1956, she was named *Wauseon*, a name she carried only 19 months. On 5 September 1957, her name was struck from the Navy list. She was sold to the Boston Metals Co., of Baltimore, Md., on 1 July 1958 for scrapping.

Wautaga

In the summer of 1863, the building of *Wautaga*—a large steam frigate—was projected, but the Civil War ended before work on her was begun; and her construction was cancelled.

Wautauga

An alternate spelling of Watauga, a river about 75 miles in length which rises on Grandfather Mountain in the Blue Ridge Mountains of northwestern North Carolina and flows northwest into Tennessee, around the south end of the Stone Mountains, eventually merging with the south fork of the Holston River.

(AOG–22: dp. 2,700 (f.); l. 220'6''; b. 37'0''; dr. 13'1''; s. 10 k.; cpl. 62; a. 1 3'', 2 40mm., 3 20mm.; cl. *Sequatchie*; T. T1–M–A2)

Wautauga (AOG–22)—formerly *Conroe*—was laid down on 14 June 1943 under a Maritime Commission contract (MC hull 791) at Galveston, Tex., by the Todd-Galveston Dry Dock Co.; launched on 10 January 1944; sponsored by Mrs. E. R. Cox; converted for naval use by the Todd-Houston Shipbuilding Corp.; and commissioned on 28 September 1944 at Galveston, Lt. Robert E. McAllister, USNR, in command.

Following shakedown, *Wautauga* got underway on 20 October for the west coast and remained in the Canal Zone for a week before resuming her voyage on the 29th and proceeding via San Diego, Calif., to the Hawaiian Islands. She eventually arrived at Pearl Harbor on 2 December and joined Service Squadron 8.

Wautauga remained at Pearl Harbor through the end of the year 1944 and got underway on 13 January 1945 for the western Pacific, arriving at Eniwetok 12 days later. She sailed from the Marshalls on 7 February and reached Saipan on the 11th—where she remained, performing fueling and fuel carrier services until 22 May. Underway with Convoy SIW (Saipan to Iwo Jima) 28, she transported a cargo of fuel to Iwo Jima, arriving there on 25 May for a six-day stay, before returning to Saipan with Convoy IWS (Iwo Jima to Saipan) 22.

Continuing to work out of Saipan between June 1945 and March of 1946, *Wautauga* made two more fuel-carrying voyages to Iwo Jima; two to Marcus, and one to Guam. She returned to Pearl Harbor on 23 April and remained there, performing local oiler duties, until departing on 26 October to transport a cargo of aviation gasoline and lubricants to Canton Island. Returning to Pearl Harbor from Canton on 26 November, the gasoline tanker carried cargoes of gasoline and oil to Palmyra and Guam en route to the Philippines.

Arriving at Manila on 25 March 1947, *Wautauga* departed on 1 April for Subic Bay, where she arrived on the 2d to commence inactivation proceedings. Decommissioned on 26 April 1947, *Wautauga* was turned over to the Chinese Navy on 15 June 1948 and struck from the Navy list on 13 July 1948. She served as *Yu Chuan* (AO–303) until scrapped in 1959.

Wauwatosa

A city in southeastern Wisconsin located five miles west of Milwaukee. Its name is of Indian origin, but the meaning is obscure.

(YTB–775: dp. 356 (f.); l. 109'; b. 31'; dr. 14'; s. 12 k. (tl.); cpl. 12; cl. *Natick*)

Wauwatosa (YTB–775) was laid down in August 1964 at Marinette, Wis., by Marinette Marine; launched in May 1965; and placed in service in June 1966. Since that time, the harbor tug has served with the Pacific Fleet at advanced bases in the western Pacific. As of January 1980, she remained active with the Pacific Fleet.

Wave

I

(Sch.: 1 gun)

The first *Wave*—a schooner-rigged yacht built in 1832 in New York City by Brown & Bell—was purchased by the Navy in 1836 for use in the Seminole Indian insurrection. In that campaign, she cruised the Florida coast in support of Army operations until 1840. After that time, she served as a surveying vessel along the Atlantic seaboard under the command of Lt. J. R. Goldsborough. In his *History of the American Sailing Navy*, Howard I. Chapelle suggests that she was sold in 1846. However, no evidence has been found to corroborate or refute that assertion.

II

(SwStr.: t. 229; a. 6 guns)

Argosy No. 2, a sidewheel steamboat built in 1863 at Monongahela, Pa., was acquired by the Navy on 14 November 1863, renamed *Wave*, and converted to a "tinclad" gunboat. Early in 1864, she was assigned to the West Gulf Blockading Squadron and took up her initial station off New Orleans, La. On 15 April, she received orders to shift to Calcasieu Pass at the mouth of the Calcasieu River in southwestern Louisiana. She arrived there on 24 April and entered the mouth of the river in company with *Granite City* to collect Confederate renegades for service in the Navy and to round up all the arms, saddles, and harness in the area that could be utilized for military purposes by the Confederacy. At daybreak on 6 May, while riding at anchor in the river, the two ships were surprised by the entire Sabine Pass garrison. *Granite City* surrendered about 45 minutes later, but *Wave* fought on for another 45 minutes until, her engines and moveable guns disabled and eight of her crew wounded, she found herself unable to continue the struggle. Accordingly, her crew destroyed documents and war materiel on board, and her commanding officer surrendered *Wave* to the Southerners. The Confederates employed the vessel as a cargo steamer. Her ultimate disposition is unknown, but she was probably destroyed by retreating Confederate forces.

III

(Ferryboat: l. 105'0''; b. 30'0'')

The third *Wave*—a steel-hulled ferryboat—was either purchased at or built by the Charleston Navy Yard in 1916. Soon after being placed in service, she was assigned to the Torpedo Station at Newport, R.I. That may have been her only assignment since the few records of her service extant suggest that she served in the 2d Naval District—which contained Newport until it was disbanded—and then in the 1st—which inherited Newport—throughout the remainder of her active career. In July 1920, she received the alphanumeric hull designation YFB–10. Her name was struck from the Navy list on 20 January 1938, but no record of her subsequent fate has been uncovered.

(ScStr: dp. 450 (n.); l. 119'8"; b. 22'6"; dr. 12'9" (mean); s. 10.0 k. (tl.))

Wave (SP–1706)—a fishing vessel owned by the Bay State Fishing Co. and built in 1913 at Quincy, Mass., by the Fore River Shipbuilding Co.—was inspected by representatives of the Commandant, 1st Naval District, during the spring of 1917. Though ordered delivered and slated for assignment to the 1st Naval District as a minesweeper, *Wave* was never taken over by the Navy.

Waverly

Towns in Iowa, New York, Ohio, and Tennessee.

(PC–1225: dp. 280; l. 173'8"; b. 23'0"; dr. 10'10"; s. 20.2 k. (tl.); cpl. 65; a. 1 3", 1 40mm., 2 dcp. (mousetrap), 2 dct.; cl. *PC–461*)

PC–1225 was laid down on 10 June 1942 at Sturgeon Bay, Wis., by the Leathem D. Smith Shipbuilding Co.; launched on 7 September 1942; sponsored by Mrs. Jean Hellber; delivered to the Navy on 2 January 1943; and commissioned on 12 January 1943 at New Orleans, La., Lt. A. J. McCrudden, USNR, in command.

Following shakedown in the Gulf of Mexico early in 1943, she guarded convoys on the New York to Guantanamo Bay run. That duty lasted until 5 January 1944 at which time she headed for Great Britain to begin preparations for the invasion of Normandy scheduled for June. She spent the ensuing months operating along the southern coast of England patrolling and practicing for the invasion.

During the 6 June assault, *PC–1225* anchored two miles off Omaha beach and served as an amphibious control ship helping guide the landing craft to their proper beaches. After D-day, she began escorting cross-channel troop and supply convoys and conducted patrols off the French ports of Le Havre, Cherbourg, Granville, and St. Malo. While performing that duty, she participated in two rescue operations. On 2 July 1944, SS *Empire Broadsword* struck an air-dropped mine; and *PC–1225* picked up 70 survivors from the wreck. Later in the year—on Christmas Eve Day 1944—she screened rescuers as they picked up survivors from SS *Leopoldville*, a British troopship torpedoed near Cherbourg. For the first months of 1945, she patrolled near the still-occupied Channel Islands and, on one occasion, drew fire from the German garrison isolated on Guernsey. In May, after the Germans had surrendered, the subchaser was part of the contingent which reoccupied the Channel Islands for the Allies.

She participated in a naval gun salute at Omaha beach on the first anniversary of D-day, 6 June 1945, and later that day departed European waters, bound for home. Steaming by the way of the Azores and Bermuda, the little warship arrived in Key West on 21 June. She soon began repairs at Charleston, S.C., in preparation for her scheduled reassignment to the Pacific theater. However, the end of the war with Japan caught her still undergoing repairs at Charleston, S.C.

On 10 September, the ship received instructions to air-sea rescue duty with the Atlantic Fleet. On the 30th, she arrived in Argentina, Newfoundland, to begin that assignment. Early in 1946, she served briefly with the Operational Development Force before reporting in April for her preinactivation overhaul. *PC–1225* was placed out of commission on 18 July 1946 and was berthed at Green Cove Springs, Fla. She remained there for over a decade. In mid-February 1956, she was named *Waverly*; however, she carried that name only briefly. On 5 September 1957, her name was struck from the Navy list. She was sold to F&A Transportation of New Jersey on 1 July 1958.

Wawasee

A chief of the Potawatomi Indians.

(YTB–367: dp. 345 (f.); l. 100'0"; b. 25'0"; dr. 9'7" (f.); s. 12.0 k.; cpl. 14; cl. *Sassaba*)

Wawasee (YT–367) was laid down on 24 April 1944 at Morris Heights, N.Y., by the Consolidated Shipbuilding Corp.; reclassified YTB–367 on 15 May 1944; launched on 10 June 1944; and completed and placed in service on 27 October 1944.

Wawasee—reclassified as YTM–367 in February 1962—operated at Boston, Mass., performing tug and tow services in the waters of the 1st Naval District for her entire career. She was taken out of service and struck from the Navy list in May 1974.

Waxahachie

A town in Texas.

(YTB–814: dp. 356 (f.); l. 109'0"; b. 31'0"; dph. 14'0"; s. 12.0 k.; cpl. 12; cl. *Natick*)

Waxachachie (YTB–814)—sometimes misspelled *Waxahatchie*—was laid down on 1 April 1971 at Sturgeon Bay, Wis., by Peterson Builders, Inc., and lanuched on 9 September 1971. The large harbor tug was accepted by the Navy on 4 January 1972 at Pearl Harbor, Hawaii, and assigned to the 14th Naval District. She continued to serve the fleet actively, providing tug and tow services, as well as pilot assistance, at the busy Pacific Fleet base at Pearl Harbor into 1980.

Waxahatchie

An erroneous spelling of *Waxahachie* (q.v.), the name assigned to YTB–814.

Waxbill

A bird of the weaverbird family that has a bill with a waxy appearance; many, such as the Java sparrow, the amadavat, and the strawberry finch, are "cage" birds.

(AMc–15: dp. 195; l. 83'2"; b. 20'11"; dr. 5'0"; dph. 10'0"; s. 10.0 k.; cpl. 11; a. 1 .30-cal. mg.)

Leslie J. Fulton—a wooden-hulled purse seiner built in 1936 at Antioch, Calif., by F. L. Fulton—was purchased by the Navy on 19 November 1940 for eventual conversion to a coastal minesweeper. Taken over that day at Yerba Buena, San Francisco, Calif., the ship was placed in commission as *AMc–15* on 26 November, Ens. Edward L. Holtz, USNR, in command. The name *Waxbill* first appears as the ship's name the following day.

Not yet fully equipped or manned, *Waxbill* operated in the 12th Naval District's waters, training naval reservists through the end of 1940. Attached to the inshore patrol forces of the district as of 1 January 1941, *Waxbill* entered the General Engineering and Drydock Co. yard at Alameda, Calif., on 20 January, for conversion to a coastal minesweeper (AMc). While at Alameda, the ship was decommissioned and simultaneously placed in service on 19 February 1941.

Waxbill operated locally in the 12th Naval District attached, successively, to Patrol Force, Local Defense Forces and the Mine Force for the district until she was assigned to the Western Sea Frontier Force in August 1942. Reassigned to local defense forces of the district on 12 March 1943, she was eventually taken out of service on 12 September 1944 and was struck from the Navy list on 14 October 1944.

Transferred to the Maritime Commission's War Shipping Administration on 6 January 1945, the erstwhile minecraft was simultaneously sold to her original owner, F. L. Fulton.

II

(YMS–479: dp. 320; l. 136'0''; b. 24'6''; dr. 6'1'' (max.); s. 12 k.; cpl. 33; a. 1 3'', 2 20mm.; cl. YMS–1)

The second *Waxbill* (MHC–50) was originally the wooden-hulled, unnamed motor minesweeper YMS–479. Laid down as PCS–1456 on 28 April 1943 at Tacoma, Wash., by the Mojean and Ericson Shipbuilding Corp., the ship was reclassified as a motor minesweeper, YMS–479, on 27 September 1943. Launched on 30 September 1943, YMS–479 was commissioned at the Mojean and Ericson yard on 20 July 1944, Lt. Richard A. Woods, USNR, in command.

After fitting out at the Todd Pacific Shipyard, Tacoma, Wash., the new minecraft departed the Seattle area on 13 August. Making port at Long Beach, Calif., on the 17th, she conducted shakedown out of that port until 8 September, when she shifted to San Diego for training in antisubmarine warfare tactics. She departed San Diego on 25 September, when she sailed with YMS–59 as screen for a group of three LST's—LST–627, LST–1030, and LST–926—bound for the Hawaiian Islands.

After arriving at the Section Base, Pearl Harbor, on 6 October, YMS–479 had begun patrolling off Kauai by the end of the month. She operated in the Hawaiian chain through February 1945, providing local escort services for ships conducting maneuvers and exercises off Maui, Kauai, or Oahu, ranging from attack transports (APA's) to LST's. During that time, she also carried out patrols and periodically tested her sweep gear.

Assigned to the Pacific Fleet on 6 March, the motor minesweeper departed Pearl Harbor on the 23d, bound for the Marshall Islands. She subsequently operated out of Eniwetok, Kwajalein, and Majuro through the end of the war in the Pacific in mid-August 1945.

Departing Kwajalein on 10 December, YMS–479 arrived at Pearl Harbor on Christmas Day and subsequently operated in the Hawaiian Islands into 1946. Departing Pearl Harbor on 20 February in company with *Sheldrake* (AM–62), YMS–479 arrived at San Francisco on 1 March and began preparations for inactivation. YMS–479 was accordingly decommissioned on 6 August 1946 and was placed in the San Diego group of the Reserve Fleet.

Named *Waxbill* and reclassified as AMS–39 on 18 February 1947 while still in reserve, the minecraft was taken out of "mothballs" on 5 January 1949; and work began to ready her to resume duty. On 19 January, *Waxbill* was placed "in service" and, within a week, she was assigned to the 13th Naval District. She served as a Naval Reserve training ship, attached to the Navy and Marine Corps Training Center at Seattle where she served through the spring of 1950.

With the onset of the Korean War in June and consequent American support for the United Nations intervention to aid the embattled South Koreans, the Navy expanded accordingly. *Waxbill* was recommissioned, albeit "in reserve," on 1 September 1950. Ultimately, she was placed in full commission on 25 September, Lt. (jg.) F. J. Crozier in command.

Duty in the inhospitable Korean waters soon beckoned *Waxbill*. The minecraft departed San Diego on 27 February 1951, bound for the Far East. After stopovers at Pearl Harbor and the Japanese ports of Sasebo and Yokosuka, *Waxbill* commenced her tour of Korean War service on 12 May in operation area "S". She participated in combat minesweeping operations off Wonsan, Pusan, Inchon, Kyoshin Tan, and To Jang Po into 1953. Her operations took her to both coasts of the Korean peninsula—east and west—and she swept over 40 mines, earning the Korean Presidential Unit Citation for her often hazardous and unsung minesweeping chores. During that time, she operated out of Sasebo and, in between deployments to Korean waters, visited such Japanese ports as Kobe, Nagasaki, Yokosuka, Moji, and Fukuoka.

Waxbill remained in the Far East even after hostilities in Korea ceased. She was reclassified as a coastal minehunter, AMCU–50, on 1 February 1955, and, only six days later, again reclassified MHC–50. After her conversion to a coastal minehunter, she departed Yokosuka on 10 August, bound for the United States.

Sailing via Midway, Pearl Harbor, and Long Beach, *Waxbill* made port at San Francisco on 8 September. She operated off the coast of southern California into 1958, visiting, in the course of that deployment, such ports as Santa Cruz, San Francisco, and San Diego. Placed "in commission, in reserve," status on 1 May 1958, *Waxbill* was placed in the Stockton, Calif., group of the Pacific Fleet reserve, on 16 May, and was ultimately placed out of commission, in reserve, on 30 June 1958.

While exact details of the ship's ultimate fate are lacking, it is known that *Waxbill* was struck from the Navy list on 1 November 1959.

Waxbill received six battle stars for Korean War service.

On 27 April, 1945, a contract for construction of AM–414, an *Admirable*-class minesweeper, was awarded to the Defoe Shipbuilding Co. of Bay City, Mich. The sweeper was named *Waxbill* on 16 May 1945. However, the end of World War II resulted in the cancellation of *Waxbill's* contract on 11 August 1945, before the ship's keel had been laid down.

Waxsaw

An Indian tribe that lived during the 17th century in an area which now constitutes Lancaster County, S.C., and Union and Mecklenburg Counties, N.C. The Waxsaws, more commonly referred to as Waxhaws, were famous for their custom of artificially flattening the heads of their children during infancy.

(Mon: dp. 1,175; l. 225'; b. 45'; dr. 6'; s. 9 k.; a. 2 11'' D. sb.; cl. *Casco*)

Waxsaw—a single-turreted, twin-screw monitor—was laid down in March 1863 at Baltimore, Md., by A. & W. Denmead & Son; launched on 4 May 1865; and completed on 21 October 1865.

Waxsaw was a *Casco*-class, light-draft monitor intended for service in the shallow bays, rivers, and inlets of the Confederacy. These warships sacrificed armor plate for shallow draft and were fitted with a ballast compartment designed to lower them in the water during battle.

Numerous design modifications and contract disputes delayed the launching of the first ships of the class until the spring of 1864. The Navy then discovered that the monitors floated with a scant three inches of freeboard, even without their turret, guns, and stores.

As a result of this discovery, the Navy Department ordered on 24 June 1864 that *Waxsaw's* deck be raised 22 inches to provide sufficient freeboard. Upon delivery, the monitor was laid up at the Philadelphia Navy Yard; and she saw no commissioned service.

She was renamed *Niobe* on 15 June 1869. *Waxsaw* was broken up at New York City by John Roach on 25 August 1875.

(AN–91: d. 785; l. 168'6''; b. 33'10''; dr. 10'10''; s. 12.3 k.; cpl. 46; a. 1 3''; cl. *Cohoes*)

Waxsaw (AN–91)—originally classified as YN–120 —was laid down on 31 May 1944 at Duluth, Minn., by the Zenith Dredge Co.; launched on 15 September 1944; sponsored by Mrs. J. L. Conlon, wife of the general manager of the Zenith Dredge Co. shipyard; and commissioned on 6 May 1945, Lt. Kearny R. Garrison, USNR, in command.

The new netlaying ship sailed for Boston, Mass., on 11 May, and arrived there on the 29th, after steaming via Cleveland, Ohio; Ogdensburg, N.Y.; the St. Lawrence Seaway; Cornwall, Ontario; Montreal and Quebec, Quebec Province; and Halifax, Nova Scotia. Following shakedown out of Melville, R.I., from 13 to 30 June, the netlayer put into Boston for post-shakedown availability.

Waxsaw headed for the Panama Canal on 10 July, expecting her ultimate destination to be Pearl Harbor in the Hawaiian Islands. However, upon her arrival at the Small Craft Training Center, San Pedro, Calif., she was ordered to the Naval Net Depot and Training School, Tiburon Bay, Calif., for 18 days of refresher training. Arriving there on 10 August, the ship remained in the San Francisco region on temporary duty in connection with the removal of the net line protecting San Francisco after the Japanese surrender in mid-August. Completing that duty on 24 September, *Waxsaw* underwent an availability at Alameda, Calif., before she was assigned to the Atlantic Fleet.

On 12 October 1945, the netlayer headed for the east coast in company with sistership *Tunxis* (AN–90). Attached to Service Force, Atlantic Fleet, on 3 November, *Waxsaw* operated at Green Cove Springs, Fla.,

establishing moorings at the St. John's River area for the Reserve Fleet units until late in 1949, when she was shifted to her new home port of Norfolk, Va.

Based there at the time of the outbreak of the Korean War in the summer of 1950, *Waxsaw* not only took part in extensive netlaying operations in Hampton Roads but also towed targets and participated in various training exercises in ensuing months.

For the next nine years, *Waxsaw* operated with the Atlantic Fleet off the eastern seaboard of the United States, ranging from Nova Scotia to Key West. Her home ports during this time included Norfolk, Key West, and Charleston. During those years, *Waxsaw* performed a variety of service functions; participated in mine-hunting exercises; laid nets and buoys during Atlantic Fleet amphibious exercises including amphibious maneuvers off Onslow Beach, N.C.; cleared objects from the channel entrance at Hampton Roads; and even briefly operated at Charleston as a salvage vessel equipped with compressors, a recompression chamber, and other deep-sea diving gear. She also took part in NATO exercises off Nova Scotia and served at the Mine Defense Laboratory at Panama City, Fla.

Decommissioned on 23 March 1960, *Waxsaw* was ultimately transferred under the Mutual Defense Assistance Program to Venezuela in October 1963. Renamed *Puerto Miranda* (H–30), the netlayer served with the Venezuelan Navy as a survey ship into the late 1970's. Struck from the Navy list in December 1977, the ship was deleted from the Venezuelan Navy list apparently soon thereafter.

Waxwing

Any of several American and Asiatic songbirds which are for the most part brown and are characterized by predominant crests and velvety plumage.

Waxwing (AM–389) in the early 1950s. She has new search-radar antennas at her masthead, and 20-millimeter guns have been removed; she is, otherwise, little changed from her wartime appearance. (United States Naval Institute)

(AM–389: dp. 890; l. 221'1''; b. 32'2''; dr. 10'9''; s. 18.1 k.; cpl. 117; a. 1 3'', 2 40mm.; cl. *Auk*)

Waxwing (AM–389) was laid down on 24 May 1944 by the American Shipbuilding Co., Lorain, Ohio; launched on 10 March 1945; and commissioned on 6 August 1945, Lt. Comdr. J. F. Rowe in command.

Commissioned a little over a week before Japan capitulated, *Waxwing* was too late to participate in World War II. Nevertheless, she was valuable to the Navy during the postwar period, particularly in clearing the minefields which had been planted in Far Eastern waters during the war. The ship set out on Lake Erie, transited the Welland Canal into Lake Ontario, and sailed down the Saint Lawrence River; stopped at Quebec; and then continued on to the Atlantic. The minesweeper was fitted out at Boston and then conducted shakedown in nearby waters. On 28 September, she arrived at the Norfolk operating area to prepare for service in the Pacific Fleet.

Waxwing transited the Panama Canal; and, on 2 January 1946, the minesweeper arrived in Pearl Harbor where she spent a month before heading on for Japan. She arrived at Sasebo, Japan, on 24 February and conducted operations through most of the year. During the period from May through July, *Waxwing* observed and supported Japanese sweeping operations codenamed "guinea pig." *Waxwing* sailed for home on 6 December and reached San Francisco on Christmas Day 1946. She spent the next several months preparing for inactivation, was decommissioned on 12 May 1947, and placed in the Pacific Reserve Fleet.

Following the outbreak of Korean hostilities, the vessel was reactivated and recommissioned on 19 March 1952 at San Diego. From May to November, the ship conducted type training between Long Beach and San Diego. On 1 December 1952, *Waxwing* sailed for the Far East. Her minesweeping duties took her to both coasts of Korea and were broken by periods of rest and upkeep in Sasebo and Yokosuka, Japan. These operations continued until 9 June 1953 when the ship sailed for home. She reached Long Beach, Calif., on 8 July 1953.

From 20 August to 28 October 1953, *Waxwing* underwent an overhaul at the Mare Island Naval Shipyard followed by refresher training, type training, and independent ship exercises until 10 February 1954. The ship celebrated Washington's Birthday at San Francisco, then spent the remainder of February and half of March engaged in "Pactraex 54R," a full scale invasion exercise conducted in the Santa Cruz Channel and the coastal area from Santa Cruz to Long Beach, Calif., which utilized nearly all types of ships and aircraft.

The ship then prepared for Far East deployment. On 18 April 1954, *Waxwing* departed Long Beach, bound for Sasebo, Japan. After reaching the Orient, she patrolled the Korean coasts. During August, *Waxwing* enjoyed a rest and recreation visit to Hong Kong. She then engaged in an air-sea rescue mission taking her 200 miles south of Japan where she aided in salvaging a downed United States Air Force plane and returned with six of its survivors on board.

Waxwing completed her tour of duty in the Far East on 3 November 1954; departed Sasebo, Japan, bound for home; and arrived at Long Beach on 24 November. Shortly after returning, the minesweeper served as a salvage ship for divers examining the wreckage of an experimental jet plane that had crashed off Laguna Beach, Calif. Her work at Laguna won the ship a letter of commendation. In the latter half of March 1955, *Waxwing* took part in "Pactraex 55P," a full dress, combined Navy-Marine "invasion" at San Simeon Cove, Calif. The ship then proceeded to San Diego and underwent three weeks of intensive training under simulated battle conditions followed by a visit to Astoria, Oreg., from 18 to 29 August for participation in the sesquicentennial celebration of the arrival of the Lewis and Clark Expedition at the mouth of the Columbia River. For the remainder of the year and through February 1956, *Waxwing* conducted local operations along the California coast. In 1955, *Waxwing* was redesignated as a fleet minesweeper, MSF–389.

On 1 March 1956, *Waxwing* set course for the western Pacific as part of the 7th Fleet force in Sasebo, Japan. After four months of operations and training in Japan, Korea, and Taiwan, the minesweeper began an extended cruise that touched many ports in the East Indies, Australia, and the South Pacific. She returned to Long Beach, Calif., on 9 October 1956 and prepared to become part of the "mothball" fleet at Astoria. On 15 January 1957, *Waxwing* arrived at Astoria and was placed in commission in reserve with inactivation scheduled to be completed by May 1957.

While laid up in reserve, *Waxwing* was modified to become an antisubmarine escort ship; and she was transferred to Nationalist China on 14 October 1965 and served the Nationalist Chinese Navy as *Chu Yung* (PCE–67).

Wayne

Counties in 16 states.

(APA–54: dp. 13,910; l. 468'8''; b. 63'0''; dr. 13'3''; s. 16.5 k.; cpl. 535; tr. 1,433; a. 2 5'', a 1.1'', 18 20mm.; cl. *Sumter*; T. C2–S–E1)

Afoundria was laid down under a Maritime Commission contract (MC hull 476) on 20 April 1942 at Chickasaw, Ala., by the Gulf Shipbuilding Corp.; renamed *Wayne* and classified as a transport, AP–99, on 26 October 1942; launched on 6 December 1942; sponsored by Mrs. N. G. Nicolson; reclassified an attack transport, APA–54, on 1 February 1943; acquired by the Navy on 30 April 1943; delivered to the Navy the following day, 1 May 1943, and simultaneously placed in commission "in ordinary." Taken to the Bethlehem Steel Co. Key Highway Yard, Baltimore, Md., *Wayne* was converted for naval service.

Decommissioned on 11 May 1943 for the duration of the conversion work, *Wayne* (APA–54) was recommissioned at Baltimore on 27 August 1943, Comdr. T. V. Cooper in command. *Wayne* departed Baltimore on 1 September and headed down the eastern seaboard to Norfolk, Va., where she arrived the following day to take on fuel, stores, equipment, and a full complement of landing craft. After shakedown training in Chesapeake Bay, *Wayne* departed Hampton Roads on 4 October, bound for New York.

Upon finishing loading at New York, she put to sea on 13 October and, escorted by *Doran* (DD–634) and *Canfield* (DE–262), headed for the Pacific. The attack transport transited the Panama Canal on 21 and 22 October and arrived at San Diego at the end of the month. For the remainder of 1943, *Wayne* operated out of San Diego on training exercises with various battalion landing teams of the 4th Marine Division.

On 13 January 1944, *Wayne* got underway with marines of the 3d Battalion (Reinforced), 24th Marines embarked and steamed in convoy for the Hawaiian Islands. She arrived at Lahaina Roads, Maui, Territory of Hawaii, on the 21st. There, she fueled from *Tallulah* (AO–50) and took on stores from *Pastores* (AF–16). She departed Hawaiian waters two days later, bound for the Marshall Islands.

Arriving off Kwajalein on 30 January as part of the northern landing force, *Wayne* transferred her marines to LST's which then carried them inside the lagoon to the beachhead. After retiring to the open sea at night, the attack transport returned to the transport area the next morning, lowered her boats, and commenced unloading cargo. On the afternoon of 1 February, *Wayne* left the Marshalls and put in at Funafuti, in the Ellice Islands, on the 9th. Fueling there, *Wayne* and *Elmore* (APA–42) were detached from the homeward-bound convoy on the 17th, near Efate, in the New Hebrides, and anchored in Havannah Harbor. Nine days later, *Wayne* and her consort shifted to Guadalcanal.

Wayne trained with marines in the Solomons before she moved to Noumea, New Caledonia, on 21 March. Subsequently, after discharging naval passengers at Guadalcanal, she shifted to Emirau, St. Matthias Islands. *Wayne* disembarked marine replacements for the garrison there on the 11th of April. That same day, she stood out of Emirau harbor on a return run to Guadalcanal with the 1st Battalion, 4th Marine Division, embarked.

Wayne performed a similar reinforcement mission to New Britain where American forces had been fighting to push back Japanese troops since the previous December. At the time the attack transport arrived there, Allied troops had established a line about half-way across the island toward Rabaul and were awaiting more aid before continuing the push. On 18 April, *Wayne* began embarking men of the 213th Field Artillery Battalion, 4th Marine Division, and on the 20th stood out to relieve the 1st Marine Division on New Britain, arriving on 23 April. *Wayne* then began a complicated cargo and man-handling task. While troops and equipment of the 213th Field Artillery Battalion were being disembarked and unloaded on one side of the ship, men of the 4th Battalion, 11th Marines, were being embarked on the other. Completing that assignment on the 25th, *Wayne* sailed to the Russells, where she unloaded cargo and disembarked more troops on the 28th before moving on to Guadalcanal the same day.

From 10 May to 3 June, *Wayne* trained at Guadalcanal. On 4 June, the attack transport stood out for Kwajalein—the staging area for the forthcoming Marianas campaign—and, from the 9th to the 12th, participated in staging and rehearsal operations. On the latter day, *Wayne* got underway for the Marianas. Her embarked marines—1st Battalion, 21st Marines, 3d Marine Division—were earmarked to land at Guam if not needed at Saipan.

On 15 June, transports under Vice Admiral R. K. Turner landed marines under the command of Lt. General Holland M. Smith, USMC, on Saipan, covered by intensive naval gunfire and carrier-based air support. *Wayne* steamed offshore for several days after the initial assault. During the Battle of the Philippine Sea, which took place between the 19th and the 21st, *Wayne* remained on station about 250 miles east of Guam while the action was taking place some 500 miles to the west of the island. On 25 June, her troops as yet unused, the attack transport—part of Task Group (TG) 53—was ordered to retire to the Marshalls to await further orders.

Wayne remained at anchor in Eniwetok lagoon from the end of June through mid-July. Underway on 17 July, the attack transport proceeded to Guam, where she arrived three days later. There, she witnesesd part of the intensive preinvasion shelling by the gunfire support ships in the task force under Rear Admiral R. L. Conolly. Carrier-based air attacks also assisted in the "softening-up" process. At 0828 on 21 July, *Wayne*'s embarked marines headed for shore in the first wave of the invasion.

The attack transport completed her unloading of equipment on the morning of the 23d. During her stay, she received 177 wounded troops from the beaches, and her medical department rendered sterling work in the care and treatment of those men. *Wayne* stood by for two additional days after finishing her unloading before departing the Marianas on the 25th and carrying 165 wounded fighting men to Espiritu Santo, in the New Hebrides. Putting into Espiritu Santo on 5 August, *Wayne* discharged her disabled passengers and stood by to await further orders.

The attack transport remained at anchor in the New Hebrides until 14 August, when she shifted to Guadalcanal, en route to Renard Sound, in the Russell Islands, where the 1st Marine Division was encamped. From the 17th to the 26th, *Wayne* carried out practice landings in preparation for the next operation, the assault on the Palau Islands. On 26 August, the attack transport sailed with TG 32.3 and devoted the ensuing days of the voyage to drills and briefings for the upcoming landings.

On the morning of 15 September, marines of the 1st Marine Division moved ashore at Peleliu. *Wayne*'s troops were among those who landed that morning. They were later followed by boatloads of high-priority cargo: ammunition and medical supplies. By 1100, three and one-half hours after the initial waves waded ashore, the first of the casualties began to arrive back on the ship for medical treatment, evidence of the intense and bloody struggle going on ashore. Japanese guns swept the beaches and waters offshore with deadly accuracy. Casualties among the marines and boat crews were high.

In the days that followed, *Wayne* kept up a steady pace of discharging cargo and receiving casualties during the day and retiring seaward at night. On the night of 20 September, she was ordered to move close inshore to serve as casualty evacuation ship, 1,000 yards off the reef. As the attack transport closed the island, enemy artillery opened up, lobbing two shells over the ship. Later during the night, machine gun fire from Japanese guns passed ovehead.

Wayne retired from the Palaus on 21 September and proceeded to Humboldt Bay, New Guinea. Between 1 and 12 October, *Wayne* participated in staging operations, including loading troops of the 2d Battalion, 19th Infantry, 24th Division, USA, and their equipment on the 8th and a practice landing at Sko Skai beach, eight miles east of Humboldt Bay, on the 12th. On the morning of the 13th, the attack transport got underway for Leyte, in the Philippine Islands, and arrived off the town of Palo on the 20th, the first day of the invasion. An enemy plane, a twin-engined "Nick," passed by the ship and was taken under fire by *Wayne*'s 5-inch battery for a brief time before it dove steeply over friendly ships astern.

As the ship's commanding officer later recounted, the landings on Leyte were "accomplished with surprising ease." The beach upon which *Wayne* had landed her troops and equipment had been ". . . lightly defended at best . . .," facilitating a rapid unloading. The operation was not without cost to the ship, however, as a Japanese gun scored a direct hit on one of the ship's LCVP landing craft, killing some of the Army personnel embarked and slightly wounding the boat's coxswain.

By 1600 on the afternoon of D-day, all cargo and troops had been unloaded, and *Wayne* got underway for Humboldt Bay—but only to return to Leyte with troops of the 1st Battalion, 128th Infantry, 32d Division, together with their cargo. Departing Dutch New Guinean waters on 9 November, the attack transport arrived off Leyte on the 13th.

While no enemy planes made an appearance close to *Wayne* that morning, a solitary "Jill," carrying a torpedo, attacked the convoy to which she was attached. At 1700, the enemy aircraft appeared forward of the convoy, briefly took a parallel course to it, and then, when aft of *Wayne*'s position, banked to starboard and began a low-altitude run on *Catskill* (LSV-1). The torpedo missed, but *Catskill*'s gunners did not; and the raider splashed into the sea. Later that day, more enemy aircraft appeared in the vicinity, prompting the ships to go to general quarters, but did not come close enough to draw fire. By the time the word came to secure from general quarters, the convoy was in approach disposition in Leyte Gulf.

At 0735 on the 14th, *Wayne*'s lookouts observed three "Zeke" fighters forward of the ship at a range of 7,000 yards. The planes maneuvered back and forth, closing the range steadily and drawing fire from the ships of the convoy. *Wayne*'s forward 5-inch gun managed to get off one round to include in the scattered gunfire. Apparently the antiaircraft barrage sufficed to force the enemy to stay out of range. Attracted by the firing,

American P-38's soon showed up and downed two of the "Zekes."

The third "Zeke," however, returned to the area, going into a strafing dive. At a range of 400 yards, the plane swooped low at 150 feet altitude. *Wayne's* starboard guns opened fire and tracers began striking the plane. The "Zeke" changed course, crossing *Wayne's* bow at 200 yards. The attack transport's port batteries now commenced firing, scoring hits. Flames burst from the fuselage, and the "Zeke" executed a fatal wingover and spun out of control into the sea.

Within the space of a day, *Wayne* unloaded her cargo and disembarked her troops and, by 1630 on the 14th, was ready for sea, her boats hoisted on board and secured. Departing that day, the attack transport moved to Seeadler Harbor, at Manus, in the Admiralties. Provisioning and taking on fuel after her arrival there on the 20th, *Wayne* departed on 30 November, bound for Aitape, British New Guinea.

Arriving there on 1 December, *Wayne* remained at anchor through Christmas. Loading cargo on the 17th, the attack transport had fueled on Christmas Eve and, on the 26th, took the main body of troops—from the 3d Battalion, 172d Infantry, 43d Division, United States Army—on board. After landing exercises at Aitape on the 27th, *Wayne* departed British New Guinea the following day, as part of the San Fabian Attack Group, bound for Lingayen Gulf.

As the ship's commanding officer later recalled, "the most memorable feature of the assault on Luzon, from the standpoint of the transports involved, was the long and difficult journey which the ships were forced to make through enemy waters between Leyte and Luzon." The convoy passed through the Surigao Strait into the Mindanao Sea on 5 January 1945 and entered the Sulu Sea west of the islands of Panay and Mindoro on the 6th.

On 9 January, Army forces landed at Lingayen Gulf under cover of gunfire from ships offshore and carrier-based aircraft overhead. *Wayne* disembarked her troops in her fifth assault landing and remained in the transport area offshore until the evening of 10 January. Air activity was heavier than the ship had encountered in any previous operation. The Japanese often attacked at dawn and at dusk, frequently utilizing single planes. *Wayne* had opened fire on a low flying twin-engined "Dinah" but scored no hits. Later that day, at 1835, a twin-engined "Frances" flew over the transport area, dropping a stick of bombs that fell near *Wayne*. The danger of heavy antiaircraft fire laid down in the vicinity of "friendly" ships was amply demonstrated when two men in *Wayne's* crew were wounded by fragments from "friendly" gunfire.

Wayne departed the transport area on the 10th and, upon receipt of an enemy plane alert at 1905, went to general quarters. At 1914, a single enemy aircraft, under fire from the ships in column on both flanks of *Wayne*, crashed into the port side of *Du Page* (APA–41), the column leader directly ahead of *Wayne*. An explosion followed, and *Du Page* was rapidly shrouded in smoke.

Wayne sheared out of the column to port; but *Du Page* held her course and speed in column, prompting *Wayne* to move back into formation astern. The following morning, she transferred two medical officers and eight corpsmen to *Du Page* to treat casualties caused by the suicide plane.

On the afternoon of 15 January, *Wayne* reached Leyte Island, and anchored off Taytay Point, receiving on board an advance detail of the 1st Battalion, 128th Infantry, 32d Division—the same battalion that she had brought to Leyte almost three months before. Almost nightly air raid alerts enlivened the ship's ensuing stay at Tacloban, Leyte, and the ship's company became accustomed to almost nightly "red alerts."

USS *Wayne* (APA-54), 13 September 1943. (80-G-81701)

On 24 January, *Wayne* departed Leyte; en route back to Luzon, her convoy came under attack by Japanese torpedo planes. One succeeded in hitting the dock landing ship *Shadwell* (LSD–15), just astern of *Wayne* in the steaming disposition. *Shadwell*, able to proceed on one engine, consequently veered out of formation and returned to Leyte. *Wayne*, meanwhile, continued onward with the rest of the convoy and reached Lingayen Gulf with her embarked reinforcements on the 27th.

Between 0830 and 1331, *Wayne* unloaded her troops and cargo and got underway to return to Leyte at 1817 that evening. By 2100 on the 30th, the attack transport was back off Taytay Point. There was little rest for the ship, however, for she soon received orders directing her to Guadalcanal, as part of Transport Squadron (TransRon) 12. Departing Leyte on 2 February, *Wayne* arrived at Tulagi harbor on the 11th.

Assigned to carry the 2d Battalion, 22d Marines, of the 6th Marine Division, *Wayne* spent a bit over a month fueling, provisioning, loading cargo, and carrying out the inevitable training exercises. Early on the morning of 15 March, TransRon 12 got underway, bound, via the Carolines, for the Ryukyus.

A week later, *Wayne* arrived at Ulithi, the staging point for the invasion of Okinawa. There, a number of the marines and sailors embarked at Tulagi were transferred to tank landing ships (LST's). On the afternoon of 27 March, *Wayne* and the other ships of the invasion force set sail for Okinawa itself.

"All hands anticipated that the attack on Okinawa would be a difficult and dangerous undertaking," wrote *Wayne*'s chronicler. Her troops went ashore on D day—Easter Morning, 1 April 1945—on a small beach dominated by high ground and protected by a reef. The actual landing, gratifyingly, seemed "puzzlingly easy" to observers in *Wayne*. Her embarked troops went ashore against slight resistance.

During the day, unloading progressed until 1745, when *Wayne* and her consorts headed seaward in night retirement disposition. Red alerts, however, continued throughout the night—alerts that had resulted in the ship's being called repeatedly to general quarters. At 0543 on the 2d, *Wayne* returned to the transport area and observed heavy antiaircraft fire from other ships in the vicinity, as well as enemy planes attacking ships close to the beaches.

By evening, *Wayne* had made satisfactory progress in the unloading and then was ordered to move closer inshore. She anchored for the night close to the beach and completed unloading the remainder of her cargo before standing out to sea at 0015 on the morning of 3 April.

However, instead of being ordered from the area, *Wayne* was directed instead to put into Kerama Retto, by way of "Point Oboe." She consequently loaded empty brass shell casings from *Salt Lake City* (CA–25) before she moved into Kerama Retto to take on more brass and to receive on board casualties from other ships that had been sunk or damaged during the nearly incessant Japanese air raids.

Wayne remained at Kerama Retto from 5 April to 9 April, spending much of that time moored alongside the battle-battered attack transport *Hinsdale* (APA–120) that had been damaged by a suicide plane on 31 March. *Wayne* fed the crew of that ship and provided her with power.

Red alerts and air raids continued almost without letup; "more than once enemy planes were observed making suicide attacks on other ships in the vicinity." Loaded with empty brass, survivors, and casualties, *Wayne* weighed anchor on 9 April and headed for the Marianas. She anchored in Saipan harbor on the 13th before she shifted to the Marshalls, arriving at Eniwetok on the 18th. From there, the attack transport steamed on to Hawaii, arriving at Pier 8, Honolulu, on the morning of 27 April.

Proceeding independently from Hawaii to the west coast of the United States, *Wayne* departed Pearl Harbor on 29 April and reached San Francisco on 6 May. After disembarking casualties and survivors from the Okinawa crucible there, she sailed north to Astoria, Oreg., on 12 May for an overhaul. Completing repairs late in July, *Wayne* departed Astoria on the 27th, bound for San Diego, and arrived there soon thereafter.

On 10 August, *Wayne* sailed for the Marianas with naval and marine passengers—replacements bound for the forward areas of the Pacific theater. The end of the war in mid-August found *Wayne* at sea, steaming to the western Pacific. She made a fuel stop at Eniwetok on 26 August and reached Guam shortly thereafter where she unloaded her cargo and disembarked her passengers.

Wayne embarked men of the 3d Battalion, 6th Marines, at Saipan and, on 18 September, got underway for Japan. She disembarked the marines at Nagasaki on 23 September and then proceeded to the Philippines, touching at Manila first and later at Mindoro.

The attack transport departed the Philippines in late October, stopped at Guam for fuel on the 21st, and arrived at San Diego on 6 November. Between 21 November 1945 and 7 January 1946, *Wayne* made one similar trip to the Philippine Islands, returning Navy veterans to the United States in Operation "Magic Carpet."

Subsequently visiting Seattle and San Diego, she cleared the latter port on 26 January 1946 and transited the Panama Canal on 6 February. Making port at New Orleans on the 11th, *Wayne* later shifted to Mobile and thence moved to her building site at the Gulf Shipbuilding Corp. where she was decommissioned on 16 March 1946. Her name was struck from the Navy list on 17 April 1946; and, on 1 August of the same year, she was transferred to the War Shipping Administration.

Reverting to her original name, *Afoundria*, soon thereafter, the ship was acquired by the Waterman Steamship Corp., of Mobile, Ala., and renamed *Beauregard* in about 1947. She operated with the Waterman firm into the late 1950's. The erstwhile attack transport retained the name *Beauregard* as she operated into the 1970's with a succession of firms: with the Wilmington, Del.-based Beauregard, Inc.; the Litton Industries Leasing Corp., and the Reynolds Leasing Corp.—operating with the last two corporations as a container ship. She disappeared from the American Bureau of Shipping Register in 1978.

Wayne (APA–54) received seven battle stars for her World War II service.

Waynesburg

Borough in the southwestern corner of Pennsylvania about 26 miles west of Uniontown. It is the county seat of Greene County.

(PC–777: dp. 280; l. 173'8''; b. 23'0''; dr. 10'10''; s. 20.2 k. (tl.); cpl. 65; a. 1 3'', 1 40mm., 2 dct., 2 dcp.; cl. PC–461)

PC–777 was laid down on 7 September 1942 at Portland, Oreg., by the Commercial Iron Works; launched on 12 November 1942; sponsored by Miss Eleanor Whitgrove; and commissioned on 8 April 1943, Lt. Coleman H. Smith, USNR, in command.

Immediately following her commissioning, PC–777 got underway for San Pedro, Calif., where she reported for duty with the Small Craft Training Center at Terminal Island. Following shakedown training, she became a school ship attached to the training center. For the remainder of World War II, she prepared crews for various types of small craft—patrol craft, small minecraft, and certain types of yard craft. In addition to her primary duty as a school ship, PC–777 also served in Task Groups 14.2 and 14.3. In the first instance, she conducted air-sea rescue operations and, in the second, investigated reports of possible enemy submarine activity off the California coast.

Late in September 1945, PC–777 departed San Pedro

with orders to report to the Atlantic Fleet for inactivation at St. John's River, Fla. She steamed via the Panama Canal and Key West and reached the Jacksonville area on 25 November. She remained at the St. John's River facility while the authorities contemplated what would happen to the great surfeit of ships in the immediate postwar period. At different times between November 1945 and June 1946, she was slated for decommissioning and assignment to the Reserve Fleet at Green Cove Springs, then for an active assignment training reservists in the 9th Naval District. The records are unclear, but it appears that *PC-777* was decommissioned on 26 April 1946 and retained "in service." Ultimately, however, she received orders to duty as a reserve training ship for the 6th Naval District. She began that duty at Charleston, S.C., in July 1946, but, by December, had been shifted to the reserve battalion at Savannah, Ga.

For the remainder of her active career, *PC-777* conducted training cruises out of Savannah for members of the Naval Reserve. During the next three years, she visited ports along the east coast as far north as New York, but she called most frequently at Charleston and Savannah. Early in 1950, she received orders to report to Norfolk, Va., for inactivation and assignment to the Atlantic Reserve Fleet. She began inactivation overhaul at the Norfolk Naval Shipyard on 6 March 1950 and was placed out of service on 28 April. She was berthed with the Norfolk Group, Atlantic Reserve Fleet, and remained there for nine years. On 15 February 1956, she was named *Waynesburg*. On 1 April 1959, her name was struck from the Navy list. Presumably, she was subsequently sold for scrapping.

Weasel

(Sch.: t. 53; cpl. 31; a. 3 guns)

Weasel, a schooner, was purchased at Baltimore, Md., late in 1822 for service with Commodore David Porter's "Mosquito Fleet" which was established to eradicate piracy in the West Indies. Her outfitting was probably completed at Norfolk late in the year; and the schooner was commissioned early in 1823, Lt. Beverly Kennon in command.

Weasel—one of eight shallow-draft schooners built at Baltimore for mercantile service in the Chesapeake Bay —was acquired by the Navy because her shallow draft suited the ship ideally for pursuing priates into their refuges in the shoals and shallows of the various islands in the Caribbean Sea and the Gulf of Mexico. She departed Hampton Roads in company with the rest of the squadron on 15 February 1823. She stopped briefly at St. Thomas on 4 March and, the next day, continued on to her patrol area. For the next two years, *Weasel* alternated duty searching for pirates and escorting merchant convoys with return voyages to the United States to obtain repairs and to combat two outbreaks of yellow fever.

The first return home came in the fall of 1823 after six or seven months of relatively successful action against the pirates. The first outbreak of yelow fever struck at that time, laying low a large portion of the squadron's crews and making the depot at Key West untenable. *Weasel* spent the waning months of 1823 at home undergoing repairs and recruiting replacements for her decimated crew. The schooner returned to the West Indies early in 1824 and resumed duty protecting merchant traffic against the pirates. That tour continued until the summer of 1824 when yellow fever broke out again. Once more, the bulk of the squadron retired north to healthier climates. That fall, the epidemic subsided; and *Weasel* and her compatriots resumed their campaign to eradicate piracy in the West Indies.

By the middle of 1825, the campaign had markedly reduced the depredations of the pirates—though sporadic flare-ups and isolated events recurred until the

1840's. Thus, the Navy began to dispose of the ships of the squadron. *Weasel* was sold sometime in 1825. However, the identity of her purchaser and the purpose to which she was put remain mysteries.

Weatherford

Cities in Oklahoma and Texas.

(PC-618: dp. 280; l. 173'8''; b. 23'0''; dr. 10'10''; s. 20.2 k. (tl.); cpl. 65; a. 1 3'', 1 40mm., 2 dcp. (mousetrap), 2 dct.; cl. *PC-461*)

PC-618 was laid down on 29 April 1942 by George Lawley & Sons, Inc., at Neponset, Mass.; launched on 1 August 1942; and commissioned on 7 September 1942, Lt. Stewart in command.

Following two weeks of shakedown training in the coastal waters between Boston and New York, *PC-618* entered New York on 19 September to begin a tour of duty escorting coastwise convoys under the auspices of the Commander, Eastern Sea Frontier. She drew the New York to Key West run and, over the next six months, made eight round-trip voyages between the two locations. On 31 March 1943, she returned to New York from the last of these voyages and immediately began intensive training for a new assignment. She and her sister ship *PC-617* trained as the deceptive escort for the mystery- or Q-ship *Big Horn*, a former tanker armed and specially outfitted for her unique duty. They completed their preparations in time to sail with Convoy UGS-7A on 14 April. Upon reaching the waters around the Azores—believed to be heavily infested by U-boats— the decoy straggled behind the convoy in an attempt to bait U-boats into an imprudent attack while *PC-618* and her sister waited just over the horizon. On 3 May, a German submarine closed the decoy and received a hedgehog attack from *Big Horn*. The two patrol craft charged to the attack as well, but the U-boat easily evaded all attacks and slipped away. Later that month, after a brief visit to Bermuda, *Big Horn* and her escorts returned to New York empty-handed.

On 27 July, *PC-618* put to sea with *Big Horn* and *PC-617* as part of Convoy UGS-13 in hopes of a more successful U-boat hunt. Again, however, she and her associates failed to make a kill. The decoy ship *Big Horn* again straggled about 50 miles behind the convoy while the two patrol craft waited just over the horizon. On one occasion, *Big Horn* sighted a submarine, and one of the escorts attacked the U-boat, unsuccessfully, with her mousetrap battery. Otherwise, the cruise proved uneventful, and *PC-618* returned to New York in August with no submarines to her credit. After another hunting cruise in the vicinity of Recife, Brazil, conducted in the latter half of August and the month of September, *PC-618* returned to New York early in October for additional training. In November, the *Big Horn* decoy/killer group was reconstituted for one final, but also unsuccessful, cruise in the area around Bermuda. That assignment ended late in December at Boston, and the group was dissolved for the last time.

During the first three months of 1944, *PC-618* conducted antisubmarine patrols along the coast between her base at New York and the coast of Maine. On 13 January—while escorting a convoy to Guantanamo Bay, Cuba—she attacked a submerged sound contact and claimed a probable hit. However, no evidence ever corroborated that claim. The subchaser returned to New York at the end of the month and resumed her patrols in that area. When not conducting those patrols, she practiced her ASW technique with friendly submarines. Fruitless submarine searches and training exercises occupied her until April, when she departed the United States for European waters in preparation for the upcoming invasion at Normandy.

Initially based at Dartmouth, England, *PC-618* briefly conducted antisubmarine patrols between that port and Plymouth before concentrating all her energies on training and preparing for the invasion of France. During repeated practice landings along the southern coast of England, she rehearsed and re-rehearsed her role for the upcoming amphibious landing. Before dawn on 6 June 1944, *PC–618* took station near the middle of a three-mile stretch off the Normandy coast dubbed "Omaha Beach." There, the subchaser served as a control ship for the boats which landed units of the Army's 116th Regimental Combat Team (RCT) in sector Easy Green, located just west of center on Omaha Beach opposite the Les Moulins defile. In addition to guiding the landing craft ashore all day, the little warship provided close-in gunfire support for the hard-pressed and artillery-poor troops of the 116th RCT, on one occasion destroying an enemy position which had been harassing the soldiers.

As soon as the troops began their move inland late on the 6th, *PC–618* resumed antisubmarine patrols. Though she was scheduled to be based at Cherbourg, France, the stubborn German resistance in that port city forced her to conduct her patrols from the base at Dartmouth until Cherbourg fell on the night of 29 and 30 June.

At midsummer, she moved her base of operations to Cherbourg and, for the next 11 months, conducted antisubmarine patrols and guarded cross-channel traffic in support of the Anglo-American lunge across France and Belgium to Germany. On 7 May 1945, 11 months and one day after the D day landings, the Germans capitulated. One month later, *PC–618* started the voyage home where she was to be overhauled in preparation for the planned final assault on Japan. After stops at Fayal in the Azores and at Bermuda, the ship arrived in Miami, Fla., where she began extensive repairs. On 14 August, with *PC–618*'s repairs less than half complete, the Japanese capitulation removed the urgency of their completion and obviated the ship's voyage to the western Pacific. She completed her availability early in October and moved, under tow, to Key West, Fla., for duty with Service Force, Atlantic Fleet.

Further material casualties however, postponed her active utilization. After successive repair periods at Key West, Port Everglades, and Norfolk, she finally resumed active duty at Key West with the Operational Development Force in March 1946. However, due to a shortage of officers, she had ceased all operations by early summer; and she was recommended for disposal by the Commander, Operational Development Force. By August, she was completely immobilized and, in September, inspected by a board of inspection and survey. Probably as a result of that inspection, the decision was made to transfer "special ordnance gear" from *PC–576* to *PC–618*, to refurbish her fully, and activate her as an experimental subchaser with the Operational Development Force. Those alterations were completed at the Charleston Naval Shipyard during the winter of 1946 and 1947. By late spring of 1947, *PC–618* had resumed active duty with the Operational Development Force testing antisubmarine warfare equipment and techniques. Based at Key West, she ranged the waters of the Gulf of Mexico, the West Indies, and along the southeastern coast of the United States. In the fall of 1955, she added the New England coast to her itinerary when she moved to New London, Conn., to conduct experimental operations from that port for a brief period of time. The ship returned to Key West early in December and resumed her routine from that base.

For the remainder of her active career, the ship conducted experimental operations along the east coast and in the Gulf of Mexico, out of both Key West and New London. On 14 February 1956, *PC–618* was named *Weatherford*. She changed operational control from Commander, Operational Development Force, Atlantic Fleet, on 10 February 1959. On 1 November 1965, after almost six years of Atlantic coast operations with the Atlantic Fleet Service Force, *Weatherford* was decommissioned, and her name was struck from the Navy list. For the next three years, the former patrol craft served the Navy as a salvage training hulk. On 1 November 1968, she was sunk as a target.

PC–618 earned one battle star during World War II.

Weaver

Luther Dayton Weaver, born on 14 July 1920 at Morrilton, Ark., enlisted in the Navy at San Diego, Calif., on 12 July 1940. After basic training, apparently also at San Diego, Seaman Weaver was assigned to Patrol Wing (PatWing) 2 on 19 September. He was advanced to seaman first class on 1 August 1941. When the Japanese attacked the American bases in Hawaii on 7 December, Seaman Weaver was assigned to the Naval Air Station, Kaneohe Bay. He lost his life while trying to defend his base against the enemy attack. For his ". . . prompt and efficient action and utter disregard of personal danger in the effort to repel the attack on the Naval Air Station, Kaneohe Bay . . . ," Seaman Weaver received the commendation of the Commander in Chief, Pacific Fleet.

(DE–741: dp. 1,240; l. 306'0''; b. 36'7''; dr. 11'8'' (mean); s. 20.9 k. (tl.); cpl. 216; a. 3 3'', 2 40mm., 8 20mm., 3 21'' tt., 8 dcp., 1 dcp. (hh.), 2 dct.; cl. *Cannon*)

Weaver (DE–741) was laid down on 13 March 1943 at Los Angeles, Calif., by the Western Pipe & Steel Co.; launched on Independence Day 1943; sponsored by Mrs. John Franklin Weaver; and commissioned on 31 December 1943; Lt. Comdr. R. S. Paret, USNR, in command.

Weaver conducted shakedown training along the California coast during the first two months of 1944. On 2 March, she stood out of San Francisco Bay, bound for the western Pacific. The destroyer escort made an overnight stop at Pearl Harbor on 14 and 15 March and then continued her voyage west via Kwajalein. She arrived in Majuro later that month and joined the screen of Task Group (TG) 50.17, the 5th Fleet replenishment and refueling group. *Weaver* operated as a unit of the screen of the 5th/3d Fleet logistics group throughout her World War II service. Operating from the base at Majuro, she escorted the oilers to refueling rendezvous with the fast carriers during their raids on Truk, Satawan, and Ponape in late April and early May. Moving forward to the base at Eniwetok soon thereafter, she continued to protect the logistics group during the assault on Saipan in June. Later that summer, she and her charges kept the carriers in action during the invasion of the Western Carolines and the Palaus. Following that operation, the logistics group moved forward again operating briefly out of Seeadler Harbor at Manus in the Admiralty Islands and then out of Ulithi in the Western Carolines for the remainder of the war. Ulithi served as the base for TF 58/38 during the last year of the war in the Pacific. *Weaver* escorted the oilers to Ulithi where they replenished their storage tanks and then back to sea to refill the carriers' oil bunkers. Thus, in 1945, she helped to keep the pressure on the Japanese during the Luzon landings, the Iwo Jima assault, and during the Okinawa campaign. The latter phases of her service also included escort missions in support of the fast carrier raids on the Japanese home islands during the summer of 1945.

When the Japanese capitulated on 15 August 1945, the destroyer escort was at sea with TG 30.8 keeping the carriers in fuel. On 28 August, she carried a prize crew from *Proteus* (AS–19) to the surrendered Japanese submarine *I–400* and then entered Sagami Wan, Japan, to begin duty with the occupation forces. For the next month, the warship assisted in the evacuation of former Allied prisoners of war from Japan. On 2 October, however, she concluded her duty in Japan and set sail from Yokusuka, bound for home. Steaming via Pearl Harbor, San Pedro, and the Panama Canal, she arrived in Philadelphia on 22 November to begin preparations for inactivation. Late in December, she moved south to Green Cove Springs, Fla., where, though technically still in commission, she joined the Atlantic Reserve Fleet. *Weaver* was not finally decommissioned until 29 May 1947. She remained at Green Cove Springs until 21 February 1952 at which time she was sold to

Peru. Her name was struck from the Navy list on 18 April 1952. She served the Peruvian Navy as *Rodriguez* (DE–163); and, as of the beginning of 1980, she was still in service as a submarine accommodation ship.

Weaver earned nine battle stars during World War II.

Weazel

A small, carnivorous animal—found in Europe, Asia, and North America—which is a bold and often savage hunter, preying chiefly on small mammals.

Commencing with a sloop which entered service in 1704, 12 ships named *Weazle,* or *Weasel,* served in the Royal Navy.

(BAT–14: dp. 763; l. 143'0''; b. 33'0''; dr. 13'6''; s. 14 k.; cpl. 34; a. 1 3'', 4 20mm.; cl. *BAT*)

Weazel (BAT–14)—Gulfport Hull No. 208—was laid down on 30 October 1942, at Port Arthur, Tex., by the Gulfport Boiler and Welding Works; launched on 21 February 1943; and delivered to the United Kingdom on 10 April 1943 and commissioned in the Royal Navy on the same day.

Weazel served under the White Ensign through both V–E and V–J days, apparently ending up her service days in the Royal Navy with the British Pacific Fleet. Transferred back to the United States Navy at Subic Bay, Philippines, on 11 March 1946, the salvage and rescue tug was struck from the Navy list on 12 April 1946. Transferred to the Foreign Liquidation Commission for disposal soon thereafter, the ship was purchased by Bosey on 17 September 1946. One source indicates that she was to be converted for mercantile service, but records of this service, if any, cannot be found.

Weber

Frederick Thomas Weber—born on 4 February 1916 at Des Moines, Iowa—attended college at Knox College in Galesburg, Ill., in 1933 and 1934 before transferring to Drake University in Des Moines in 1935. He graduated from the latter school during the summer of 1938 and enlisted in the United States Naval Reserve on 30 August of that year. During the ensuing winter, Seaman 2d Class Weber successfully completed elimination flight training at the Naval Reserve Aviation Base, Kansas City, Kansas; and, on 27 July 1939, he was appointed an aviation cadet in the Naval Reserve. After 10 months of training at the Naval Air Station, Pensacola, Fla., Weber was appointed a naval aviator on 10 May 1940. A little over a month later, he concluded his training and, on 12 June 1940, received his commission as an ensign in the Naval Reserve. That same day, he received orders to report for duty with Bombing Squadron (VB) 6 attached to the carrier *Enterprise* (CV–6).

Enterprise and VB–6 proved to be Ens. Weber's only assignment during his brief naval career. During the remainder of 1940 and for 11 of the 12 months of 1941, he served with his ship and squadron operating out of San Diego, and later out of Pearl Harbor. His duties consisted entirely of training in aerial warfare in preparation for the conflict with Japan expected to erupt at any time.

At the end of the first week in December 1941, he was at sea with *Enterprise* which was returning from Wake Island where she had just delivered Marine Fighting Squadron (VMF) 211. Foiled in their attempt to locate the Japanese striking force on 7 December, Weber and his colleagues rode their carrier into devastated Pearl Harbor on the 8th. The following morning, they put to sea in *Enterprise* and began defensive patrols of the area to assure that no enemy invasion force was on its way to Hawaii.

In January 1942, Weber's ship guarded reinforcement convoys on their way to the southern Pacific. In February, he participated in the carrier raids on Japanese-held islands in the Central Pacific. In April, his ship served as an escort for *Hornet* (CV–8) during the Halsey-Doolittle bomber raid on Tokyo and returned to Oahu on 25 April. Dispatched too late to join in the Battle of the Coral Sea, his ship returned to Pearl Harbor on 26 May to prepare for what would be an even more important strategic battle—the first real defeat of Japanese naval airpower during the struggle over Midway Island.

On 28 May, Weber's ship steamed out of Pearl Harbor, accompanied by *Hornet* and the cruisers and destroyers of Task Force 16, to lie in ambush north of Midway. Swiftly repaired *Yorktown* (CV–5) followed two days later. On the morning of 4 June, land-based patrol planes from Midway made contact with the advancing Japanese force spearheaded by four of the six carriers that had attacked Pearl Harbor. While Midway defended itself against enemy air attacks and land-based air unsuccessfully tried to pierce the Japanese defenses, Weber and his comrades in VB–6 took to the air to begin a long gruelling search. By 0730, the entire attack group was aloft and streaking off toward the enemy's reported position. Lt. Comdr. Clarence "Wade" McClusky, the *Enterprise* air group commander, led the squadron himself as the formation winged on toward Vice Admiral Chuichi Nagumo's Carrier Striking Force.

At 0920, the squadron arrived at the supposed location of the enemy. Gazing down, the aircrewman strained for a glimpse of the threatening carriers but saw only empty seas. At that juncture, the air group commander made a hard decision. His planes had already consumed a great deal of fuel; and, were they to initiate a search, some would surely fail to return as a result. On the other hand, if they returned for fuel, Midway might fall or, even worse, the enemy might find and sink or severely damage one or more of the Pacific Fleet's three remaining carriers. Therefore, the importance of stopping Nagumo's carriers at almost any cost dictated the course of action. The American pilots ignored their fuel gauges and started hunting for the Japanese.

At 1005, Weber and his colleagues were rewarded for their perseverance and determination. On the horizon to the northwest loomed a task force composed of three large carriers and numerous escorts. Initially, some Americans believed that they had inadvertently circled back to their ships, but pagoda masts and yellow flight decks of the carriers below quickly dispelled that fear.

Though originally intending to attack *Akagi,* the squadron leader noticed that Scouting 6 had only near-missed *Kaga,* so he switched targets at the last minute and headed for the latter. Ens. Weber followed his squadron leader in on carrier *Kaga* as the third plane in the first section. The Bombing 6 *Action Report* states that ". . . at least three 1,000-pound bomb hits were observed on that target and it became a mass of flame and smoke." Since only the three Bombing 6 planes which participated in the attack on that carrier carried that size bomb, Weber and his two squadron mates all apparently scored direct hits on the target. Hence Weber contributed as much as anyone to the sinking of *Kaga.*

Pulling out of his dive, Weber formed on his leader, and the squadron headed home to refuel and rearm. At least one Japanese carrier remained intact, *Hiryu,* whose position far ahead of the other three saved her momentarily.

That afternoon, Weber took off from *Enterprise* with a composite attack group made up of the remnants of the several groups decimated earlier. At about 1545, planes from Scouting 6 and 14 of *Yorktown*'s Bombing 3 joined with the four operational aircraft remaining to Bombing 6 and sped off in chase of the remaining carrier. Unfortunately, the American fighters still extant had to remain with the carriers as combat air patrol so the attack group was denuded of fighter cover.

About an hour later, the American hunters found their quarry. The American planes climbed to 19,000 feet and maneuvered their way up sun of *Hiryu* and her escorts. During the jockeying for position, Japanese fighters jumped the unprotected dive bombers. Before reaching the "push over" point, Ens. Weber's plane fell victim to the enemy fighters. He and his aircrewman, Aviation Ordnanceman 3d Class E. L. Hilbert, spiraled into the sea and to their deaths. For his part in sinking *Kaga* and for his supreme sacrifice in assisting his colleagues to sink the remaining enemy carrier, Ens. Weber was promoted retroactively to lieutenant (junior grade) and was awarded the Navy Cross posthumously.

(DE–675: dp. 1,400; l. 306'0"; b. 36'10"; dr. 9'5" (mean) ; s. 24 k.; cpl. 186; a. 3 3", 4 1.1", 8 20mm., 8 dcp., 1 dcp. (hh.), 2 dct.; cl. *Buckley*)

Weber (DE–675) was laid down on 22 February at Quincy, Mass., by the Bethlehem Shipbuilding Co.; launched on 1 May 1943; sponsored by Mrs. Matt A. Walsh; and commissioned on 30 June 1943, Comdr. Rollo N. Norgaard in command.

The destroyer escort completed fitting out and then departed Provincetown, Mass., on 23 July for Bermuda. At the conclusion of shakedown training in waters surrounding those islands, she returned north and arrived in Boston, Mass., on 21 August. Following post-shakedown availability, the new warship left Boston for several days of additional training—in antisubmarine warfare tactics—out of New London, Conn. Upon completing that assignment, *Weber* entered New York harbor to prepare for her first combat duty.

On 5 September, the warship stood out of New York in the screen of a transatlantic convoy. Following a relatively uneventful voyage, she and her charges entered port at Londonderry, Northern Ireland, on the 16th. There, she remained until the 21st, when she headed back across the Atlantic with a return convoy. She ended that voyage at St. John's, Newfoundland, on 1 October but, soon thereafter, moved to New York for a 10-day availability at the navy yard at Brooklyn.

In mid-October, *Weber* escorted a convoy from New York to the Dutch island of Curacao, off the coast of Venezuela. She arrived in Willemstad on 24 October and remained there five days awaiting the formation of a transatlantic convoy. This group of Allied ships departed Curacao on 29 October and set a course for the British Isles and arrived in Londonderry on Armistice Day 1943.

At that point, *Weber* settled into a routine of escorting convoys between Londonderry and New York which lasted until August of 1944. By that time, she had made six more round-trip voyages between those ports. On many occasions during the period, she and her consorts in the screen made sonar and radar contacts on unidentified ships. While on such occasions they frequently attacked the strangers with depth charges, *Weber* and her sister escorts directed their greatest efforts to diverting their transports and cargo ships from the paths of U-boats. When doing so, they informed nearby hunter/killer groups of the location of the contacts and delegated to them primary responsibility for offensive antisubmarine warfare. As a result, confirmed U-boat kills eluded *Weber*; but she and the other escorts in the screens accomplished their primary mission of shepherding the convoys safely across the ocean.

On 7 August, she departed Londonderry for the last time. Her convoy arrived safely in New York on the 20th and, after voyage repairs, the warship began preparations to embark upon a new but brief phase in her wartime career. After the Allied forces which invaded Europe in June established control over the coast of France, convoys no longer needed to travel the long northern route around Ireland to avoid enemy aircraft and submarines based on that coast. Instead, they now could use the shorter and more economical route around the southern coast of England directly to the French channel ports primary among which was Cherbourg. In September, *Weber* made one round-trip voyage to Cherbourg; then returned to the United States via that route and arrived back at New York near the end of the month.

After a 10-day availability and four days of exercises, the ship proceeded to Norfolk to join a convoy bound for North Africa and the Mediterranean Sea. She departed Norfolk with the convoy on 21 October. En route to Gibraltar, she rescued the crew of a Portuguese fishing vessel damaged badly in a collision with *Weber* during an investigation of the then-unidentified vessel. Soon after the rescue, the Portuguese vessel sank. After landing the fishermen at Gibraltar, *Weber* continued on to Bizerte, Tunisia, where she stopped on 12 November, and thence proceeded to Palermo, Sicily, for repairs to damage sustained in the collision with the Portuguese trawler. She rejoined her escort group at Oran, Algeria, and embarked upon the return voyage on 23 November. *Weber* escorted one section of the attached convoy into Philadelphia on 10 December.

Five days after her arrival in Philadelphia, *Weber* was redesignated a high-speed transport and received a new hull number, APD–75. Conversion work on her began immediately. During the following three months, she exchanged her 3-inch battery for a new 5-inch, dual-purpose gun which had proven highly effective both for antiaircraft defense and for bombardment work. In addition, her relatively weak antiaircraft battery was beefed up substantially. Her spaces were modified to provide a place for underwater demolition teams (UDT) and their equipment. Her conversion indicated an impending reassignment to the Pacific theater where the UDT men played an important role in the initial stages of amphibious operations. She completed her conversion in mid-March 1945.

During the latter part of the month, she moved to Norfolk where she practiced shore bombardments and antiaircraft defense. On 14 April, she departed Norfolk. Arriving at Panama on the 19th, she transited the canal the following day and reported for duty with the Pacific Fleet. Continuing her voyage, the warship stopped briefly at San Diego and then headed for the Hawaiian Islands. She arrived in Pearl Harbor on 8 May and underwent a brief period of voyage repairs. During the middle part of May, she conducted reconnaissance and demolition exercises at Kahoolawe, Maui, with members of UDT 23. After a short series of refresher training and antisubmarine warfare exercises, she departed Oahu on the 24th for the western Pacific. She entered the lagoon at Eniwetok on 1 June, remained for a day due to a fueling delay, and then continued on to Ulithi where she arrived on 6 June.

On 13 June, *Weber* departed Ulithi to escort *California* (BB–34) to Okinawa where the battleship was needed to render gunfire support to American forces subduing the defenders on the southern portion of the island. The task unit arrived off the island four days later. Following a short time at Hagushi anchorage, *Weber* put into the roadstead at Kerama Retto for fuel. On 25 June, she was assigned to a surface force built around battleships *California* and *West Virginia* (BB–48), and cruisers *Wichita* (CA–45), *Tuscaloosa* (CA–37), *San Francisco* (CA–38), *St. Louis* (CL–49), and *Chester* (CA–27). Serving as antisubmarine and mine escort for that unit, she patrolled the waters around Okinawa until 1 July, protecting communications and supply lines. She returned to Hagushi for a week on 1 July and departed the Ryukyus on the 8th in the screen of a convoy bound for the Marianas. Delivering her charges safely at Saipan on July 12th, she continued her voyage the following day and arrived at San Pedro Bay, Leyte, on the 17th. She spent the remaining weeks of World War II at Leyte engaged in training exercises in preparation for the expected invasion of the Japanese home islands. Fortunately, the Japanese agreed to surrender terms on 15 August, making that operation unnecessary.

Soon after the cessation of hostilities, *Weber* returned

Weber (APD–75) in reserve, her 40-millimeter gun mounts covered with plastic domes for dehumidification. The large davit abaft her stack is designed to carry and launch two LCVP. The masts on each side of the davit belong to a radar-picket escort ship (DER) moored behind *Weber*.

to Okinawa to prepare for the occupation of territory remaining in Japanese hands. She arrived back in the Ryukyus on 21 August and reported for duty with Task Force (TF) 95. She trained briefly with that task organization at Okinawa until 7 September when she reported for duty with TF 55. On 10 September, she departed the Ryukyus with Task Unit (TU) 55.7.1 bound for Japan. She and her colleagues arrived at Nagasaki the following day and began two weeks of service evacuating and caring for former Allied prisoners of war held in Japan. She completed that assignment on 23 September and returned to Okinawa on the 25th. On 7 October, the warship put to sea once more, this time bound for Tsingtao and Taku in northern China with a convoy carrying marines for duty ashore there. A severe typhoon, however, scattered the little flotilla and damaged some of the ships, forcing *Weber* to return to Okinawa as an escort for the more severely damaged ones. She rejoined the remainder of the convoy just before mid-month and escorted a portion of it into Taku on 16 October. The next day, she got underway for the Philippines with two American merchant ships which she saw safely to Okinawa before breaking off and continuing on to Luzon. The ship arrived in Manila on 23 October and, after discharging about 100 passengers, headed back to China. During the month of November, she shuttled Nationalist Chinese troops from Hong Kong to strife-torn northern China.

She concluded that duty at Tsingtao on 25 November and sailed for the east coast of the United States that same day. Steaming via Okinawa, Guam, and Eniwetok, she arrived in Pearl Harbor on 13 December. On the 16th, she resumed her voyage home and arrived in San Diego on the 22d. Following a week's layover, she left San Diego and set course for the Panama Canal. The warship transited the canal between 7 and 9 January 1946 and headed for New York on the latter date. She entered the New York Naval Shipyard on 15 January, discharged passengers, and began her preinactivation overhaul. On 18 February, she departed New York and, after a two-day stop at Norfolk, Va., arrived in Green Cove Springs, Fla., on the 23d. There, she reported to the Atlantic Reserve Fleet for layup. Placed out of commission by directive in January 1947, *Weber* remained inactive for more than 15 years. Her name was struck from the Navy list on 1 June 1960; and, a little over two years later, she was sunk as a target on 15 July 1962 by "Bullpup" air-launched missiles.

Weber earned one battle star during World War II.

Webster

Walter Wynne Webster—born on 28 July 1888 in Fargo, North Dakota—was appointed a midshipman on 6 July 1907 and graduated from the Naval Academy with the Class of 1911. He spent his initial tours of sea duty in the battleship *North Dakota* and the tender *Panther* before he began post-graduate studies at the Naval Academy in 1913. He then took a course of instruction in naval architecture at the Massachusetts Institute of Technology.

Later commissioned as an assistant naval constructor, with the rank of lieutenant (junior grade), on 15 May 1914, Webster served in the hull divisions at the Puget Sound Navy Yard, Bremerton, Wash., and at the New York Navy Yard, Brooklyn, N.Y., before he went to Washington, D.C., for his first tour of duty in the Bureau of Aeronautics. In the years that followed, he became known as one of the pioneers of naval aviation, expending his energies in the development of better naval aircraft for the nation's fledgling naval air arm.

Commissioned as naval constructor, with the rank of lieutenant commander, on 6 June 1922 and given his naval observer's wings on 22 July of the same year, Webster was detached from his duty in Washington on 25 September 1925 for "duty involving flying" at the Naval Aircraft Factory, Philadelphia Navy Yard, where he arrived on 2 November 1925. He subsequently returned to Washington in the summer of 1929 for another tour in the Bureau of Aeronautics.

Subsequently taking instruction at the Naval Air Station, Pensacola, Fla., in heavier-than-air flight from 30 October 1933 to 20 June 1934, Webster went briefly to the Bureau of Aeronautics once more from 26 October to 19 November, before he became Force Materiel Officer on the staff of Rear Admiral H. V. Butler, Commander, Aircraft, Battle Force, on 21 December 1934. He later became manager of the Naval Aircraft Factory at Philadelphia, reporting for duty on 25 June 1936, a post in which he served until his detachment on 24 June 1940.

After another brief Washington tour, Webster resumed his duties as manager of the Naval Aircraft Factory on 26 December 1941, less than a month after the Japanese attack on Pearl Harbor. While serving in that post, Webster was killed in a plane crash outside of Chester, Pa., on 16 March 1943.

I

(ARV–2: dp. 14,350; l. 441'6"; b. 56'11"; dr. 22'0"; s. 12.5 k.; cpl. 578; a. 1 5", 8 40mm., 6 20mm.; cl. *Chourre*; T. EC2–S–C1)

On 30 March 1944, prior to the beginning of work on her construction, *Masbate* (ARG–1) was renamed *Webster* and reclassified ARV–2. The ship's keel was laid down under a Maritime Commission contract (MCE hull 2666) on 1 July 1944 at Baltimore, Md., by the Bethlehem Fairfield Shipyard, Inc. Sponsored by Mrs. Walter W. Webster, the widow of the ship's namesake, the ship was launched on 5 August 1944 and commissioned at Baltimore on 17 March 1945, Capt. Jesse G. Johnson in command.

After fitting out, *Webster* departed Baltimore on 22 March 1945 and arrived at Norfolk later that day. There, the aircraft repair ship loaded supplies and provisions into the second week of April, when she got underway for shakedown and training in Chesapeake Bay. After subsequent minor repairs and alterations at the Norfolk Navy Yard from 21 April to 8 May, *Webster* joined Convoy No. 507 on 12 May, transited the Panama Canal eight days later, and arrived at the Naval Air Station (NAS), Alameda, Calif., on 6 June.

After further repairs and alterations, the ship departed Alameda on 16 June, bound for the Hawaiian Islands. She arrived at Pearl Harbor on the 24th and docked at NAS Ford Island, where she stayed for four days before she shifted to the navy yard for armament alterations. Shifting subsequently to a berth alongside *Ozark* (LSV–2) on the 28th, *Webster* remained in Hawaiian waters through most of July.

The ship got underway for the Marshalls on the 31st; arrived at Eniwetok Atoll on 10 August; and remained there through mid-September. During her stay at Eniwetok, Japan surrendered, bringing World War II to a close. Meanwhile, the ship, herself, serviced the fleet carriers *Wasp* (CV–18), *Antietam* (CV–36), *Intrepid* (CV–11); the light fleet carrier *Cabot* (CVL–28), and a half-dozen CVE's, overhauling aviation equipment and returning it to stock for reissue. The material that could not be stored on board—bulky items such as drop tanks and the like—was stored ashore in a depot on Parry Island.

The end of the war had removed the necessity for the replenishment of fast carrier task forces in the fleet anchorage in the Marshalls and Gilberts advanced base sites, but there still remained the occupation of the former enemy's homeland. *Webster* accordingly departed Eniwetok on 13 September, bound via Guam for Tokyo Bay, where she arrived on the 26th. There, *Webster* serviced all naval aviation activities in the Tokyo Bay area, including the carriers *Yorktown* (CV–10), *Shangri-La* (CV–38), *Bon Homme Richard* (CV–31), *Boxer* (CV–21), *Munda* (CVE–104), and *Hoggatt Bay* (CVE–75); the aviation units of battleships *New Jersey* (BB–62), *Tennessee* (BB–43), *California* (BB–46); those of the heavy cruisers *St. Paul* (CA–73) and *Quincy* (CA–71); and finally the planes of 10 light cruisers. In addition, the aircraft repair ship serviced the planes from Marine Air Group 21 and assisted the board headed by Rear Admiral Frederick W. Pennoyer in its investigations into the development of Japanese aircraft and aircraft engine design in World War II.

Webster remained in Tokyo Bay from 6 October to 3 November. During that time, Rear Admiral Clifton A. F. Sprague visited the ship on 20 October and conferred the Presidential Unit Citation to, among others, Capt. Johnson, the ship's commanding officer, for his service in the escort carrier *Guadalcanal* (CVE–60) in the Atlantic. The aircraft repair ship ultimately departed Tokyo Bay at 1400 on 3 November.

Webster, transporting men homeward-bound for discharge, made Guam at 0825 on 9 November, and tarried only until 1748 on the 10th, when she got underway for the Marshalls. Six days later, she reached Roi Island, Kwajalein Atoll and, on the 18th, got underway at 1843 for the Hawaiian Islands.

Webster disembarked her passengers upon her arrival at Pearl Harbor on 27 November and stood out of Hawaiian waters on the 30th, bound for Panama. She reached the Pacific entrance of the Panama Canal at 0746 on 20 December, transited the canal later that day. and moored at Coco Solo at 1708.

The aircraft repair ship then pushed on for Norfolk, Va., at 0915 on 22 December, arrived at Norfolk seven days later, and remained in the Tidewater area through mid-January of the following year. On 25 January 1946, *Webster* departed Norfolk and arrived at Philadelphia at 1241 the following day, mooring alongside the heavy cruiser *Portland* (CA–33).

Berthed alongside a succession of ships—*Fomalhaut* (AK–22), *Tranquility* (AH–14), *Sanctuary* (AH–17), *Dithmarschen* (IX–301), *Okanagan* (APA–220), and *Augusta* (CA–31)—*Webster* awaited her decommissioning. At 1047 on 28 June 1946, her commissioning pennant came down for the last time. Struck from the Navy list on 1 September 1962, she was simultaneously transferred to the Maritime Administration for lay up. She was subsequently scrapped.

Hobart Victory—a "Victory ship"—was laid down under a Maritime Commission contract (MCV hull 705) on 20 April 1945 at Richmond, Calif., by the Permanente Metals Corp.; launched on 25 May 1945; sponsored by Mrs. Tom Connally; and delivered to her initial owners, the Black Diamond Steamship Co., on 25 July 1945. On 24 January 1966, the name *Webster* and classification T–AG–190 were assigned to her after she and 14 sister ships had been earmarked to become "Special Project Ships" for the Military Sea Transportation Service (MSTS). However, only three of the 15 vessels were actually taken over by MSTS, and *Hobart Victory* was not one of them, so she never served in the Navy.

Instead, *Hobart Victory* retained her "Victory" name and operated under an MSTS charter during the Vietnam conflict, carrying supplies to Southeast Asian ports. She was ultimately laid up in the James River, in the Maritime Administration (MarAd) berthing facility there, where she remained into 1979.

Webster, Daniel, see *Daniel Webster* (SSBN–626).

Wedderburn

Charles Foster Wedderburn was born in Chicago, Ill., on 2 October 1892 but grew up in Washington, D.C. Appointed a midshipman at the Naval Academy on 7 July 1911, he graduated and received his commission on 5 June 1915. Ens. Wedderburn served in *Brooklyn* (Cruiser No. 3) from graduation to the end of 1915. In December 1915, he transferred to *Chauncey* (Destroyer No. 3) assigned to the Asiatic Fleet and based at Cavite in the Philippines. He was promoted to lieutenant (junior grade) on 1 July 1917; and, a month later, his ship departed Cavite with orders to the coast of France. Based at St. Nazaire, his ship escorted convoys in the eastern Atlantic. While on such a mission about 110 miles west of Gibraltar, *Chauncey* was involved in a fatal collision with the British merchantman, SS *Rose*, on the night of 18 and 19 November. The destroyer sank at about 0317 on the morning of the 19th taking Wedderburn and 20 of his comrades to their deaths.

(DD–684: dp. 2,050; l. 376'5"; b. 39'7"; dr. 17'9"; s. 35.2 k. (tl.); cpl. 329; a. 5 5", 10 40mm, 7 20mm., 10 21" tt., 6 dcp., 2 dct.; cl. *Fletcher*)

Wedderburn (DD–684) was laid down on 10 January

1943 at San Francisco, Calif., by the Bethlehem Steel Co.; launched on 1 August 1943; sponsored by Mrs. Gertrude F. Wedderburn; and commissioned on 9 March 1944, Comdr. John L. Wilfong in command.

Following shakedown training along the west coast and post-shakedown availability back at the Bethlehem Steel Co., *Wedderburn* departed San Francisco on 21 June in company with *Fieberling* (DE–640). The two warships arrived in Pearl Harbor six days later, and *Wedderburn* joined Task Unit (TU) 19.3.2 with which she served briefly on plane guard and antisubmarine duty. On 1 July, the destroyer continued her voyage west to Eniwetok in the Marshall Islands where she joined Task Force (TF) 53 for the second assault of the Marianas operation, Guam.

She stood out of Eniwetok on 17 July in company with Task Group (TG) 53.4, the Southern Transport Group. She arrived off Guam on 22 July, the day after the initial assault on that island and, for the next three weeks, performed yeoman service protecting the invasion fleet—upon which the battle ashore depended—from the threat of Japanese submarine attack. Her service in the Marianas ended on 10 August when she shaped a course back to Eniwetok.

Wedderburn reentered the lagoon at Eniwetok on 14 August. There, she was reassigned to the antisubmarine screen of a fast carrier task group, TG 38.2, built around *Intrepid* (CV–11), *Hancock* (CV–19), *Bunker Hill* (CV–17), *Cabot* (CVL–28), and *Independence* (CVL–22). She sailed from Eniwetok on 29 August in company with the entire fast carrier task force to conduct a major sweep of Japanese-held islands including the Philippines, the Palaus, and Yap Island. *Wedderburn* screened the carrier from enemy submarine attacks while they sent their planes against targets on Mindanao and Leyte and, later, the Visayas sub-group. They also provided initial aerial bombardment for the Palau invasion and for the Morotai operation. Those missions took up almost the entire month of September, and the destroyer did not enter a "port" until the 28th when TG 38.2 arrived at Saipan. On 1 October, she and TG 38.2 moved on to recently captured Ulithi where the ships arrived the next day. *Wedderburn*, however, soon returned to sea. Task Force 38 rendezvoused about 375 miles west of the Marianas on 7 October to open the preliminaries to the invasion of Leyte. *Wedderburn* continued her antisubmarine vigil while the carriers she protected launched their aircraft first against Okinawa, then Formosa, and finally Philippine targets, striking enemy air bases on Luzon and the Visayas to give the United States dominance in the air over Leyte when the invasion began on 20 October.

Wedderburn continued to guard the fast carriers while they operated off the northeastern shore of Luzon providing distant air support for the Leyte invasion. By the 24th, it had become apparent that the Japanese planned to dispute the landing with some variety of naval force. The result was the four-phase Battle for Leyte Gulf. That same day, planes from *Wedderburn*-protected carriers opened the battle striking at the enemy's Center Force, commanded by Vice Admiral Takeo Kurita—while it traversed the Sibuyan Sea toward the San Bernardino Strait. Late that evening, after having sunk battleship *Musashi* and damaged other Japanese ships, the fast carriers raced northward to take the bait offered by a force of almost planeless aircraft carriers which Vice Admiral Ozawa was using as a decoy force. Thus, *Wedderburn* was far north when the Surigao Strait and Samar phases were fought on the night of 24 and 25 October and the morning of the 25th, respectively. Instead, she participated in the final phase of the battle, against Ozawa's force, though her role remained one of support for the carriers—whose planes did most of the damage—which she screened against submarine attack while she rescued their downed aviators.

After the Battle for Leyte Gulf, the destroyer continued to operate off Luzon with TG 38.2 while the carriers' planes provided additional air cover for the troops fighting to capture Leyte. That duty lasted until 5 November when engine trouble forced her to set a course for Ulithi. The warship arrived at that advanced base on 10 November, quickly completed repairs, and rejoined TG 38.2 off Luzon just after mid-month. Her return, however, proved brief; for, on 23 November, she received orders to return to Ulithi to join TG 38.1. At Ulithi, she conducted exercises until 10 December when she departed the atoll with TG 38.1 to support the landings on Mindoro. During that operation, TF 38 passed through the infamous typhoon of December 1944 which damaged many ships in the force and sank three. *Wedderburn*, however, suffered only minor damage and participated in the search for survivors of *Hull* (DD–350), *Monaghan* (DD–354), and *Spence* (DD–513) though she did not engage in any actual rescue operations. The damage caused by the typhoon necessitated a return to Ulithi for repairs. The destroyer and the other ships of TF 38 entered the lagoon on Christmas Eve and remained there six days, resuming operations on 30 December 1944.

The return to sea brought TF 38 into active participation in support of the Luzon invasion of Lingayen. The fast carriers sought to keep Japanese reinforcements—airborne, naval, and land—from entering the fray against the invading forces by keeping enemy airpower grounded and by sinking as much of his shipping as possible. Thus, *Wedderburn* resumed her role as guardian of the carriers while their planes made up the offensive arm of the 3d Fleet. On 3 and 4 January 1945, fast carrier aircraft hit air installations and shipping at Formosa and Okinawa. They went after targets on Luzon itself on the 6th and 7th and, on the day of the initial landings, the 9th, returned to Formosa for air suppression duty while troops were going ashore. Following that assignment, she moved through Bashi Channel with TF 38 for two weeks of air raids on Japanese-held southern China and French Indochina which included an antishipping sweep of the South China Sea. On the return voyage, TF 38 planes struck at the Nansei Shoto, a group of islands near Okinawa, on the 21st and 22d before reentering Ulithi Lagoon on the 25th.

Soon thereafter, the 3d Fleet became the 5th Fleet when Admiral Raymond A. Spruance relieved Admiral William F. Halsey. The change in designation reflected change of command only, and all else remained substantially as it was. *Wedderburn* continued to provide antisubmarine protection for her task group, redesignated TG 58.2. Early on 10 February, the fast carriers again stood out of Ulithi to provide air support for the assault on Iwo Jima in the Volcano Islands. On 16 February, they launched planes for a strike against air installations around Tokyo, the first air raid on the Japanese capital since 1942 when the Fast Carrier Task Force commander, Vice Admiral Marc A. Mitscher—then captain of *Hornet* (CV–8)—launched Lt. Col. James Doolittle's B–25 bombers on their famous raid. During the current two-day attack, the American planes made 138 sorties in which their pilots claimed to have sunk three picket boats and an escort carrier as well as to have destroyed over 700 enemy aircraft. Following the raid, *Wedderburn* escorted the carriers south to Iwo Jima where she participated in shore bombardments and patrolled against submarines in TF 51's transport area. On 23 February, she departed Iwo Jima and rejoined TG 58.2 as it headed off north with the rest of TF 58 for another round of strikes on the Japanese home islands. Foul weather, however, forced the cancellation of those strikes; and, after a refuelling rendezvous, the carriers and their escorts reentered the lagoon at Ulithi on 4 March.

After 10 days of refueling, rearming, and repairing, TF 58 left Ulithi and shaped a course for Japan. Their first targets were the airfields on Kyushu, located within striking range of Okinawa, the 5th Fleet's next objective. The carriers launched planes on 18 March, but the enemy struck back with fighters, bombers, and kamikazes. In the ensuing battle, near misses damaged *Enterprise* (CV–6), *Yorktown* (CV–10), and *Intrepid* (CV–11). The next day, *Franklin* (CV–13) received a direct bomb hit; and the enemy scored one on *Wasp* (CV–18) as well. However, on a more positive side, *Wedderburn* gunners claimed two of the attacking enemy planes. After TF 58 sustained the damage of 18 and 19 March, it was reorganized somewhat. *Wedderburn's* TG 58.2 became a task group made up of damaged carriers *Enterprise*, *Franklin*, and *Wasp*, and gave up a number of its screening units to the similarly reformed TG 58.1.

Wedderburn was one of those escorts so reassigned and consequently remained with TF 58 while the task group of cripples retired to base. She continued to screen the carriers as they launched air strikes on Okinawa during the last week in March and the week following the 1 April landings. Throughout the entire period, the Japanese launched air attacks at them incessantly.

It was not until the 6th, however, that sighting reports made it apparent that the enemy planned a suicidal surface attack with the remnants of their fleet. Superbattleship *Yamato*, screened by a cruiser and eight destroyers, started south to contest the landings. The fast carriers continued to steam on station off Okinawa protected by *Wedderburn* and her colleagues but, on 7 April, launched a series of search and attack sorties which ultimately sent the mighty Japanese battleship to the bottom along with light cruiser *Yahagi* and four of the escorting destroyers.

After that scrape, TF 58 concentrated its efforts on supporting the troops ashore and defending itself and the invasion force from the final onslaught of Japanese air power. *Wedderburn* remained in the vicinity of the Ryukyu Islands for another 20 days until TG 58.1 headed for Ulithi on 27 April. On 18 May, the destroyer departed Ulithi to escort *Missouri* (BB–63) to Guam to pick up Admiral William F. Halsey who was scheduled to take command of the naval forces off Okinawa later that month. She then escorted *Missouri* back to the Ryukyus and reentered the fray at Okinawa at the beginning of the final week of May.

Halsey took over from Spruance on 27 May; and— now that Admiral Halsey was back in overall command —*Wedderburn* and her associates became units of the 3d rather than of the 5th Fleet. For the remainder of World War II, she screened various task groups of TF 38 first while they continued support for the Okinawa operation and, later that summer, when they went on their final rampage in the Japanese home islands. The Japanese capitulation on 15 August found her in the screen of TG 38.4 while the carriers were preparing for yet another air strike—one which they did not launch.

Immediately following the war, the destroyer served with the occupation forces around Tokyo Bay, escorting Japanese merchant ships, supervising mine-clearing operations, and making hydrographic surveys. On 31 October, she shaped a course back to the United States. After a stop at Pearl Harbor from 9 to 13 November, she resumed her voyage and arrived at the Puget Sound Naval Shipyard on 19 November. Following repairs at Puget Sound, she was placed out of commission in March 1946 and was berthed at San Diego.

However, in August of the same year, she returned to semi-activity when she began training naval reservists until 21 November 1950 when she was recommissioned, Comdr. Richard B. Franklin in command.

The newly recommissioned destroyer joined the Pacific Fleet Destroyer Force in January 1951; completed her reactivation work at Hunters Point Naval Shipyard; and, in May, finished underway training. On 18 June, she departed the west coast for her first tour of duty in the Korean conflict. Though assigned operationally to the Blockading and Escort Force (TF 95), she also served periodically as a plane guard for the fast

carriers of TF 77 as well as on the Taiwan Strait patrol (TF 72). For the most part, though, her duties consisted of blockading the coastline of Korea and providing gunfire support for the United Nations troops operating ashore. She concluded her first tour of duty in the Far East with the Taiwan Strait patrol and returned to the United States in February 1952.

After an overhaul at the San Francisco Naval Shipyard and several weeks of training, the warship headed back to Korea in August 1952. Once again, she divided her time between blockading and gunfire support missions along the Korean coast and escort duty with the fast carriers as well as short periods with the Taiwan Strait patrol. *Wedderburn* concluded her second Korean War deployment and returned to San Diego in March 1953.

During the next seven months, the destroyer conducted normal west coast operations out of San Diego. The Korean conflict ended with the armistice of 27 July 1953 right near the mid-point of *Wedderburn's* seven months of 1st Fleet operations. When she returned to the Far East in October, she began the first essentially peacetime deployment of her career.

In the decade between 1954 and 1964, the warship continued to alternate deployments to the western Pacific with tours of duty along the coast of southern California. For the most part, the seven tours she made to the Far East consisted of port visits and training exercises. During the 1958 deployment, she visited Sydney, Australia, in addition to her usual ports of call farther north and participated in the multinational SEATO exercise, Operation "Ocean Link." That deployment also saw her on patrol in the Taiwan Strait during the American show of force over the Quemoy and Matsu bombardment by the Chinese communists. The remainder of her deployments were more routine in nature consisting of plane guard duty with TF 77, port visits, training exercises, and periods of time with the Taiwan Strait patrol. When not in the Orient, she conducted type training, upkeep, and periodic overhauls on the west coast.

The warship departed San Diego on 5 August 1964 to begin her 11th deployment to the Far East. Four days before, the Gulf of Tonkin incident occurred, signalling a stepped-up American involvement in the strife in South Vietnam. That involvement dictated the nature of *Wedderburn's* 7th Fleet assignments for the remainder of her active career. During the fall of 1964, she operated off the Vietnamese coast as plane guard and escort for TF 77, duplicating her service during World War II and the Korean War. She also provided sporadic gunfire support for units ashore in the Mekong Delta area. She departed the newly established combat zone in November for a SEATO weapons demonstration and then put into Subic Bay in the Philippines for upkeep.

After Christmas liberty at Yokosuka, Japan, she returned to active operations in the South China Sea in January 1965. At the conclusion of that duty, late in the month, she set course for home, arriving in San Diego on 6 February. She spent the remainder of 1965 in the eastern Pacific. After a month of post-deployment standdown followed by four weeks of local operations out of San Diego, she entered the Long Beach Naval Shipyard for a month-long availability. In June and July, she embarked NROTC midshipmen for their summer cruise, during which she visited San Francisco and the islands of Kauai and Oahu in Hawaii. Returning to San Diego on 4 August, the warship conducted three weeks of repairs and then resumed training operations which continued until she began preparations for another Far Eastern cruise in November.

On 7 January 1966, *Wedderburn* departed San Diego in company with *Worden* (DLG–18), *Richard B. Anderson* (DD–786), and *Bausell* (DD–845). After stops at Oahu, Midway, and Guam, she arrived in Subic Bay on 28 January. On 1 February, she headed for the South China Sea where she became a unit of TG 77.5 and served as escort and plane guard for the carriers until 28 February. Following a brief return to Subic Bay, she visited Sasebo, Japan, and Okinawa early in March. She returned to the Vietnam combat zone on 12 March as a unit of TG 77.7 and again served as escort and plane guard for carriers conducting air strikes in North Vietnam. She continued in that role until 2 April when she was detached and reassigned to TU 70.8.9 to conduct gunfire support missions near Danang and Quang Tri. On the 6th, the warship resumed her former assignment with TG 77.7. On 24 April, she joined a different unit, TU 77.0.3, to conduct trawler surveillance in the Gulf of Tonkin. On 2 May, she returned to gunfire support duty, this time near Chu Lai, until 8 May. On that day, the destroyer resumed duty with TF 77 as a search and rescue (SAR) vessel on the southern SAR station. On 15 May, she concluded her last combat assignment of the 1966 deployment. After a week's liberty call at Hong Kong and repairs at Yokosuka, Wedderburn headed home on 3 June and arrived in San Diego 10 days later. Following local operations, the destroyer entered the Long Beach Naval Shipyard on 11 August for a three-month overhaul. She completed sea trials on 20 November and resumed normal operations on the 21st.

During the first two months of 1967, Wedderburn conducted extensive refresher training exercises and, during March and early April, made preparations for overseas movement. On 8 April, she stood out of San Diego once more in company with Worden, Brush (DD–745), and Lyman K. Swenson (DD–729). She stopped at Pearl Harbor from 14 to 17 April and arrived in Yokosuka on the 27th. Three days later, she got underway for Okinawa whence she continued on to Yankee Station in the Gulf of Tonkin where she conducted plane guard duty with TG 77.6. Five days later, she shifted to shore bombardment duty near the demilitarized zone (DMZ). That assignment lasted until 27 May when she returned to the carriers on Yankee Station. She left the combat zone on 5 June and arrived in Subic Bay two days later.

She made repairs and embarked two NROTC midshipmen and then departed the Philippines on 10 June to return to the Gulf of Tonkin. There, she divided her time between plane guard duty for Hancock (CVA–19) and ASW exercises with Bronstein (DE–1037) and Catfish (SS–339). She visited Kaohsiung, Taiwan, from 25 June to 10 July and underwent repairs alongside Delta (AR–9). On her return to the coast of Vietnam, she rejoined TU 70.8.9 for a series of gunfire support missions in the I Corps zone of operations. Her guns helped the marines ashore complete Operation "Bear Chain," an amphibious assault by Special Landing Force "Bravo" near Quang Tri City. On 21 July, she headed back to Subic Bay for a week of repairs and upkeep.

She did not return to the Vietnamese coast for a month due to repairs to her evaporator system. However, on 20 August, she headed back to the combat zone where, on the 22d, she resumed gunfire support duty for troops in the II Corps zone. Relieved by Eaton (DD–510) on 26 August, she rejoined TF 77 in the Gulf of Tonkin and served as escort for the carriers until 3 September. She departed the Gulf of Tonkin late on the 3d and shaped a course for Okinawa, arriving there on the 7th. From there, she moved on to Yokosuka for a 10-day layover before getting underway for home on the 21st. Wedderburn reached San Diego on 6 October and began the normal post-deployment standdown. In mid-November, she resumed normal operations in the southern California operating area. That routine continued until she began repairs at Long Beach on 19 April 1968. She returned to San Diego on 24 May and resumed normal operations out of her home port.

Wedderburn embarked upon the final western Pacific deployment of her career on 30 September. Steaming in company with Hornet (CVS–12), she stopped at Oahu for nine days in mid-October and then continued her voyage to Yokosuka, where she arrived on the 27th. On the 30th, she accompanied Hornet out of Yokosuka, and together, they laid course for the Tonkin Gulf. They arrived in the gulf on 3 November; but, two days later, Wedderburn became an escort for Constellation (CVA–64) for two days. After that, she rejoined her old colleague, Hancock. On 17 November, a recurring sonar problem forced the destroyer to head for Subic Bay, where she remained until 9 December. She returned to duty in the Tonkin Gulf on 11 December but remained on station only until the 31st when steam leaks forced her back to Subic Bay.

She completed repairs late in January 1969 and returned to the combat zone soon thereafter. The warship remained on station, dividing her time between gunfire support, carrier escort, and Soviet trawler surveillance, until mid-March. After a brief return to Subic Bay, she began her final tour of duty on the gunline on 22 March. Wedderburn served as a gunfire support ship for about a month before beginning her homeward voyage on 20 April. En route, she made stops at Yokosuka, Japan, and Buckner Bay, Okinawa; and arrived back in San Diego on 12 May. She remained in port throughout the summer of 1969 due to a casualty to her propulsion plant and, in September, received word that she was going to be decommissioned. On 1 October 1969, Wedderburn was placed out of commission at San Diego, and her name was struck from the Navy list. On 25 January 1972, she was sold to Dhon's Iron & Steel Co., Ltd., for scrapping.

Wedderburn earned seven battle stars for World War II service, four battle stars for Korean War service, and six battle stars for service in the Vietnam conflict.

Weeden

Carl Alfred Weeden—born on 14 April 1916 in Trinidad, Colo.—grew up in Colorado and was appointed a midshipman at the Naval Academy on 22 June 1936. He graduated from the Naval Academy in June 1940 and reported for duty in Arizona (BB–39) on 9 June 1940. Ens. Weeden spent his entire but brief naval career in Arizona. He was killed during the Japanese attack on Pearl Harbor on 7 December 1941 which sank Arizona at the outset. Ens. Weeden was awarded the Purple Heart Medal posthumously.

(DE–797; dp. 1,400; l. 306'0''; b. 37'0''; dr. 13'6''; s. 23.6 k. (tl.); cpl. 213; a. 3 3'', 4 1.1'', 8 20mm., 8 dcp., 1 dcp. (hh.), 2 dct.; cl. Buckley)

Weeden (DE–797) was laid down on 18 August 1943 at Orange, Tex., by the Consolidated Steel Corp.; launched on 27 October 1943; sponsored by Mrs. Alice N. Weeden; and commissioned on 19 February 1944, Lt. Comdr. C. F. Tillinghast, Jr., in command.

After a fitting-out period complicated by the necessity for repairs to her power plant, the destroyer escort departed Galveston, Tex., on 30 March for her shakedown cruise. Arriving at Bermuda on 5 April, she spent the rest of the month in training exercises; left Bermuda on 1 May; and arrived in Boston on the 6th. She completed voyage repairs on the 14th and moved to Provincetown, Mass., where she served for a month as target ship for the Atlantic Fleet Torpedo Squadron Training School. Near the end of June, she reported for duty in Escort Division (CortDiv) 56.

On 4 July, she departed Boston in the screen of a convoy bound for Bizerte, Tunisia. The entire round-trip voyage, during which she escorted convoys in both directions, occupied her time until 18 August when she reentered Boston. After training exercises at Casco Bay, Maine, she rendezvoused with another Bizerte-bound convoy near Norfolk in mid-September. About half way across the ocean, CortDiv 56 received orders to part company with the convoy and head for Plymouth, England, where they picked up a convoy of LST's bound for the United States. Arriving home on

25 October, she again completed voyage repairs and conducted antisubmarine warfare (ASW) exercises at Casco Bay. On 17 November, she joined another transatlantic convoy at Norfolk. That voyage took her via Gibraltar to Oran, Algeria, thence back to the United States at Boston where she arrived at the end of the last week in December. She completed repairs in the navy yard at Charlestown early in January 1945 and then moved to Norfolk where she served briefly as a school ship.

On 28 January, the destroyer escort departed Norfolk for duty with the Pacific Fleet. She transited the Panama Canal on 7 February and laid in a course for Manus in the Admiralty Islands where she arrived late in the month.

After a week of repairs at Manus, the warship received orders assigning her to the Philippine Sea Frontier and got underway for Leyte. From March to September, she served under that command, escorting convoys both among the various islands of the Philippines and between the Philippines and American bases in other island groups. Her first escort assignment was a round-trip voyage to Ulithi and back to Leyte. In April, she saw a convoy safely to Hollandia, New Guinea, and returned to Leyte with a formation of tugs.

Early in May, she made a high-speed mail delivery on the Philippine circuit—visiting Zamboanga, Mindoro, Iloilo, Manila, and Subic Bay. For the remainder of May and the entire month of June, she operated in the Philippines—either patrolling the entrance to San Pedro Bay, Leyte; escorting convoys from Leyte to Manila; or making the inter-island mail run. In July, *Weeden* made two round-trip voyages escorting convoys between Leyte and Ulithi. At the conclusion of the second run, she steamed to Subic Bay where she joined the escort of a convoy bound for Okinawa. She departed Subic Bay on 27 July with a large group of LST's and LSM's and, after evading a typhoon, arrived at Okinawa on 4 August. Three days later, the destroyer escort started back to Leyte. During her return voyage, the atomic bomb fell on Japan; and, soon after her arrival at Leyte, the Japanese capitulated.

Over the next few weeks, *Weeden* completed escort missions in support of the developing occupation of former Japanese territory. Late in August, she made a round-trip voyage to Okinawa and back to Manila. Following that, the destroyer escort screened a British escort carrier to Nagasaki, where the latter ship picked up former Allied prisoners of war for repatriation. On the return voyage, *Weeden* herself carried 70 Dutch former prisoners as far as Okinawa and then continued on to Subic Bay for repairs.

En route, she received orders to assume plane guard duty on a station located about 100 miles north of Luzon. She performed that duty for four days and then resumed her voyage to the Philippines. She arrived in Subic Bay on 26 September and remained there, undergoing repairs, until 10 November.

After a stop at Manila from the 10th to the 26th, *Weeden* got underway to return to the United States. En route she stopped at Eniwetok and Pearl Harbor before arriving in San Pedro, Calif., on 17 December. After five months of inactivity, she was finally placed out of commission on 9 May 1946 and was berthed with the San Diego Group, Pacific Reserve Fleet.

In November of 1946, *Weeden* resumed activity though she remained out of commission. On the 20th, she reported for duty training naval reservists in the 11th Naval District. After almost four years at that duty, she changed status once more when she was placed in commission, in reserve, on 26 May 1950. Almost three months later, *Weeden* reported for duty with the Pacific Fleet, though her mission, Naval Reserve training in the 11th Naval District, appears to have remained the same. Over the next seven years her training cruises took her north to British Columbia, south as far as Callao, Peru, and west to the Hawaiian Islands. Her center of operations, however, remained the coast of California.

On 26 November 1957, *Weeden* began inactivation overhaul at Portland, Oreg. She was decommissioned on 26 February 1958 and was berthed at Astoria, Oreg., with the Columbia River Group, Pacific Reserve Fleet. She remained there just over a decade until 30 June 1968, at which time her name was struck from the Navy list. She was sold to Zidell Explorations, Inc., of Portland, Oreg., on 27 October 1969 for scrapping.

Weehawken

A township in Hudson County, N.J., seven miles northeast of Jersy City. The name was originally an Algonquin Indian term and later changed by folk-usage to a pseudo-Dutch form. Its exact meaning is unclear, but variously translated as "place of gulls," "rocks that look like trees," "maize land," "at the end" (of the Palisades) and "field lying along the Hudson." Weehawken was the site of the duel between Alexander Hamilton and Aaron Burr on 11 July 1804.

I

(Mon: dp. 1,875; l. 200'; b. 46'; dr. 10'6''; s. 5 k.; cpl. 75; a. 1 15'' D.sb., 1 11'' D.sb.; cl. *Passaic*)

The first *Weehawken*—a single-turreted monitor—was launched on 5 November 1862 at Jersey City, N.J., by Zeno Secor & Co.; sponsored by Miss Nellie Comstock; and commissioned on 18 January 1863, Capt. John Rodgers in command.

The *Passaic*-class *Weehawken* was an improved and enlarged version of *Monitor*. Accompanied by *Iroquois* and towed by *Boardman*, she departed New York on 18 January 1863, bound for Port Royal, S.C., and duty with the South Atlantic Blockading Squadron. The three vessels encountered gale force winds and high seas off the New Jersey coast on 20 January. *Iroquois* and *Boardman* headed for sheltered waters; but Rodgers pressed on in *Weehawken*. The *Passaic* ironclads differed from the original *Monitor* in having less deck overhang and a rounded lower hull. This enabled *Weehawken*, unlike her famous prototype, to ride out a heavy sea with relative ease. Rodgers reported that "the behavior of the vessel was easy, buoyant, and indicative of thorough safety." *Weehawken* put into Norfolk for minor repairs, leaving on 1 February 1863 in tow of screw steamer *Lodona*. She arrived at Port Royal on 5 February 1863, and deployed in the blockade off Charleston, S.C.

On 7 April 1863, *Weehawken* led the Union fleet in the first major naval assault against Confederate installations in Charleston harbor. The attack failed miserably, and the fleet withdrew after only 40 minutes. During the action, *Weehawken* took 53 hits and had a torpedo explode beneath her keel without suffering serious damage. Shortly after the attack, Rear Admiral John A. Dahlgren replaced Rear Admiral Samuel F. DuPont as commander of the squadron.

After repairs, *Weehawken* proceeded to Wassaw Sound, Ga., on 10 June 1863 to block the expected sortie of ironclad CSS *Atlanta*. The Confederate ram and two escort steamers showed themselves early on the morning of 17 June 1863. *Weehawken* and *Nahant* weighed anchor to meet *Atlanta* which ran hard aground only moments after entering the sound. *Weehawken* commenced firing at 0515 and ceased a quarter of an hour later when the Confederate vessel surrendered. With only five shots, Rodgers blew the roof off *Atlanta*'s pilothouse and pierced the grounded ram's casemate, putting two gun crews out of action. News of the capture electrified the North. Capt. Rodgers became a national hero and received commendations from Secretary of the Navy Gideon Welles, President Abraham Lincoln, and Congress. He was promoted to commodore and ordered north to command the new ironclad *Dictator*. Both *Weehawken* and *Atlanta* returned to Port Royal.

An artist's rendition of the monitor *Weehawken* in heavy weather, with a wooden steam warship in the background. With their shallow draft and low freeboard, monitors were well suited for river and coastal operations but were never intended to fight at sea. (NH 75618)

Weehawken resumed operations against Confederate strongholds in and around Charleston harbor. On 10 and 11 July 1863, Union ironclads *Catskill, Montauk, Nahant,* and *Weehawken* shelled Confederate batteries at Fort Wagner on Morris Island, S.C., to cover an Army amphibious landing under Brigadier General Quincy A. Gillmore. Despite additional bombardments on 18 and 24 July, the monitors failed to silence the fort, leaving General Gillmore's troops pinned down on the beach caught between a murderous hail of cross fire. Fort Wagner was finally reduced during a naval bombardment of Forts Gregg, Sumter, and Moultrie on 17 August 1863.

Weehawken, Montauk, Nahant, Passaic, and *Patapsco* now took aim at Fort Sumter, pounding it to rubble during two separate bombardments on 23 August and 1 and 2 September 1863. Admiral Dahlgren demanded Sumter's surrender on 7 September and ordered *Weehawken* to deploy in a narrow channel between the fort and Cumming's Point on Morris Island. There, *Weehawken* grounded, taking concentrated gunfire from Fort Moultrie and Sullivan's and James Island. The vessel was refloated with the help of tugs on 8 September, and received a "Well done!" from Admiral Dahlgren for outstanding defensive gunnery while aground. *Weehawken* repaired at Port Royal until 4 October 1863, then returned to Charleston for routine patrol duty in the harbor.

The next two months were uneventful, and *Weehawken* lay anchored off Morris Island during a moderate gale early on the morning of 6 December 1863. Suddenly, the ironclad signalled for assistance and appeared to observers ashore to be sinking. Attempts to beach the vessel failed, and she sank bow first five minutes later in 30 feet of water. A court of inquiry found that *Weehawken* had recently taken on a considerable amount of heavy ammunition in her forward compartments. This change excessively reduced her forward freeboard, causing water to rush down an open hawse pipe and hatch during the storm. As the bow sank, and the stern rose, water could not flow aft to the pumps and the vessel foundered.

Four officers and 27 enlisted men drowned aboard *Weehawken.*

II

(CM–12: dp. 6,525 (f.) ; l. 350'0'' ; b. 57'0'' ; dr. 17'6'' ; s. 12.0 k. (tl.) ; cpl. 290 ; a. 3 3'', 4 20mm.)

SS *Estrada Palma*—a car ferry built in 1920 by William Cramp & Sons at Philadelphia, Pa.—was acquired by the Navy on 15 June 1942; renamed *Weehawken* on 18 July 1942; converted to a minelayer by the Bethlehem Steel Co. at Hoboken, N.J.; designated CM–12; and commissioned on 30 September 1942, Lt. Comdr. Ralph E. Mills, USNR, in command.

On 6 October, *Weehawken* moved to Bayonne, N.J., and, two days later, to Tompkinsville, N.Y. On the 10th, she departed the latter port for the Naval Mine Depot at Yorktown, Va. She arrived in Yorktown the following day and began drills and exercises in the lower Chesapeake Bay. The minelayer stood out of the Chesapeake Bay on 5 November, bound for New York, and arrived at Brooklyn the following day. A week later, she put to sea with Mine Division (MinDiv) 50 and a convoy headed for French Morocco.

The minelayer dropped anchor in Casablanca harbor on 1 December. She remained in port until the 27th when she left to lay a defensive minefield off Casablanca. *Weehawken* returned to port that evening and then repeated the procedure the following day. On New Year's Eve, the *Luftwaffe* ushered in 1943 by subjecting Casablanca and the ships assembled there to a night of intermittent air raids. Fortunately, *Weehawken* suffered no damage during those raids and during the encore performed the following evening. Between 6 and 10 January, she made a round-trip voyage to Gibraltar and back to deliver minelaying equipment. Upon her return, the warship remained at Casablanca until 20 January, when she sailed for New York.

She arrived in New York with the convoy on 7 February and sailed the following day for Hampton Roads. The ship anchored in the roadstead late on the 9th, unloaded mines at Yorktown on the 10th, and entered the Norfolk Navy Yard on the 11th. Following a seven-week repair period, *Weehawken* exited the shipyard on St. Patrick's Day 1943 and moored at the Naval Operating Base for almost a week before returning to Yorktown on 23 March to load mines. For the next 11 weeks, *Weehawken* conducted minelaying drills and gunnery exercises in the lower reaches of the Chesapeake Bay. Throughout that span of time, she returned to Yorktown and Norfolk frequently for liberty, provisions, repairs, and the like.

On 9 June, the minelayer weighed anchor and departed Yorktown and headed for New York. There, she joined a convoy bound for Algeria. During the crossing, a German U-boat apparently attacked the convoy on 22 June, for SS *Gulf Stream* sank rapidly after suffering an explosion. However, *Weehawken's* good fortune held; and she arrived in Oran safely on Independence Day 1943. Two days later, she joined a convoy off Oran and set a course for Sicily where she arrived on the 11th, the day following the initial Allied invasion.

Throughout that day and most of the next, she laid defensive minefields around the invasion beaches at Gela on the southern coast of the island. On both days, the *Luftwaffe* appeared and dropped their explosive greetings to the invasion force. Between 2150 and 2345 on the 11th, *Weehawken's* group underwent a series of heavy attacks; however, the minelayer came through unscathed save for some fragments from a stick of bombs which exploded just off her starboard bow. On the 12th, she continued operations off Gela; and, around 1740 in the afternoon, German planes returned. The ship's war diary recorded these as "*Stuka's*," which indicates that they were probably Junkers Ju. 87 dive bombers. After making a great deal of noise, both the United States Navy and the German *Luftwaffe* emerged from that altercation unharmed.

Later that evening, *Weehawken* departed Sicily to return to North Africa. After stops at Bizerte, Tunisia, and Algeria, she returned to Oran on 17 July. Five days later, the minelayer shifted to Mers el-Kebir where she remained until 6 September when she sailed for Bizerte. The ship stayed at the Tunisian port from 8 to 14 September and returned to Mers el-Kebir on the 17th.

After another three weeks at Mers el-Kebir, *Weehawken* got underway on 7 October to return to the United States. She reached New York on 26 October. After 11 days in port, the warship put to sea on 6 November for Yorktown where she arrived the following day. For the next five months, she conducted battle practice, minelaying exercises, gunnery drills, and other training evolutions in the lower Chesapeake Bay and at Yorktown as well as repairs at the Norfolk Navy Yard.

On 20 April 1944, *Weehawken* received word that MinDiv 50 had been dissolved and that she was to be assigned to the Pacific Fleet to transport cargo, mines, and equipment to Pacific bases. On the 30th, she completed the availability which she had been undergoing at Norfolk since the 15th and returned to Yorktown. She loaded mines and cargo from 7 to 9 May and then cleared Hampton Roads on the 11th.

The minelayer entered the Panama Canal on 20 May, reported for duty with the Pacific Fleet, and joined Service Squadron 6. Completing her transit of the canal in the same day, she continued her voyage up the west coast to San Diego where she arrived on 1 June. Four days later, *Weehawken* headed west toward Hawaii. After arriving in Pearl Harbor on 14 June, she unloaded her cargo and spent 11 days at Oahu before heading back to the west coast on 25 June.

On Independence Day 1944, the warship reached San Francisco and immediately began alterations at the General Engineering & Drydock Co. located at Alameda. She completed the modifications—which included the removal of mine tracks from the after section of her mine deck—on 1 August. After embarking passengers and loading cargo, she departed San Francisco on 8 August and shaped a course for the South Pacific. During the last two days of August, she passed through the Solomon Islands and stopped at Florida Island and

Tulagi from 31 August to 5 September to disembark passengers and unload some cargo. She made Espiritu Santo in the New Hebrides on 8 September and began unloading the remainder of her cargo. She embarked another group of passengers and got underway on 10 September for Pearl Harbor. After a 12-day voyage, she passed though the antisubmarine nets at Oahu and moored in Pearl Harbor.

She spent eight days in Hawaii before embarking upon an extended voyage to the Central Pacific during which she visited a number of islands and bases. On 1 and 2 October, she embarked passengers bound for Saipan in the recently won Mariana Islands and, on the latter date, passed Diamond Head and set course for the Central Pacific. *Weehawken* made a brief overnight stop at Eniwetok Atoll in the Marshall Islands on 13 and 14 October and made Saipan on the 18th. Between 18 and 28 October, she unloaded mines, embarked passengers, and loaded cargo. From 28 October to 1 November, she steamed from Saipan to Kossol Roads—in the Palau Islands—where she embarked additional passengers and resumed her voyage. On 4 November, she sailed into the lagoon at Ulithi Atoll in the western Carolines. She spent the next two weeks at the atoll.

After disembarking her passengers and riding out a typhoon, *Weehawken* departed Ulithi on the 18th bound for the Marianas. She reached Guam the next day, took on passengers, and departed again by the 21st. Two days later, the minelayer reentered Ulithi. Early in December, she made a round-trip voyage to the Palaus, returning to Ulithi on the 10th. Five days later, the warship put to sea with a convoy bound for Saipan. She arrived in Saipan on the 17th and remained there five days before returning to sea—bound via Eniwetok to Pearl Harbor where she arrived on 8 January 1945.

Four days after her arrival, *Weehawken* shifted berths to the navy yard to begin another series of alterations and repairs. On 21 February, the ship stood out of Pearl Harbor once again and headed west. The minelayer arrived in Eniwetok on 4 March and, the following day, took leave of the convoy, and departed Eniwetok for Ulithi in company with *Facility* (AM-233). The two warships entered the lagoon at Ulithi on the 11th, and *Weehawken* began duty as a tender for motor minesweepers.

Almost a month later on 5 April, the minelayer exited the anchorage at Ulithi in convoy with *Monadnock* (CM-9), *Mona Island* (ARG-9), and *Clemson* (APD-31). The convoy passed Okinawa during the mid-morning hours of 10 April and anchored in Kerama Retto just before 1400. *Weehawken* immediately began providing logistic support, tender, and other services to the minesweeping units operating in the 10-day-old occupation of Okinawa. For the next three months, she remained anchored in Kerama Retto except for two occasions—4 June and 11 June—when she left the anchorage to evade typhoons. In both cases, she resumed her duties in Kerama Retto immediately after the storm passed.

Over that span of time, frequent air alerts called her crew to general quarters as Japanese kamikazes attempted to drive the American Navy from Okinawa. Though her gunners frequently fired on enemy planes and witnessed their spectacular crashes into other ships, *Weehawken* continued to lead a charmed life. On 28 April, a kamikaze bore in on her; but, at the last minute, antiaircraft fire from a nearby destroyer persuaded him to seek easier prey. Instead, he crashed into *Pinckney* (APH-2)—anchored nearby—and *Weehawken* dispatched rescue parties and medical assistance to the mortally wounded hospital evacuation transport. Three days later, she was called upon to render medical assistance again when a suicide plane smashed into minelayer *Terror* (CM-5). Her gunners tried unsuccessfully to bring down two other kamikazes, one which struck *St. George* (AV-16) on 6 May and another which exploded on *Curtiss* (AV-4) on 21 June.

The converted minelayer *Weehawken* (CM–12) at Norfolk, 5 March 1943. Her boxy ferryboat configuration made her a logical choice to carry and plant mines. The eight tracks visible at *Weehawken's* stern give an idea of her capacity.

In the latter instance, *Weehawken* rushed fire and rescue parties to the aid of the stricken warship.

On 7 July 1945, *Weehawken* stood out of the Kerama Retto roadstead and anchored in Buckner Bay. There, she resumed her support duties for the minesweeping forces. Ten days later, she departed Buckner Bay with a mixed force of auxiliaries and motor minesweepers for a brief operation near Unken Ko. She returned to Buckner Bay early in the morning of 22 July and remained there, either anchored or moored near Tsuken Shima, through the end of the war and into September 1945.

On 16 September, a typhoon hit the Okinawa area. Late that evening, *Weehawken* tried to get underway and to take on the crews of Coast Guard cutters moored nearby. During the operation, she collided with several of the cutters and with buoy tender *Woodbine* (WAGL–289). After several additional collisions with the cutters and *Woodbine*, *Weehawken* began to drag anchor toward Tsuken Shima at 2330. At 0440 on 17 September, she struck a reef off Tsuken Shima. Fortunately, the typhoon began to subside, and she was towed out of shoal water later that day by *ARS–22*. She suffered little damage in that scrape and resumed her duties off Tsuken Shima soon thereafter.

Following three weeks of routine operations, *Weehawken* battled another typhoon. Early in the morning of 9 October, steadily increasing winds forced her to use her engines to relieve the strain on her anchor chains. Through the morning, the winds rose steadily to gale force and, by 1400, reached 80 knots. *Weehawken* fought the raging seas; but, at 1522, the chain to the mooring buoy snapped in two. While playing out the port anchor chain to 95 fathoms and making precautionary preparations to abandon ship, the minelayer collided with a net tender broadside to port. The two ships parted with no apparent damage, and *Weehawken's* crewmen continued their struggle to keep her headed into the wind and relieve the strain on the anchor chain.

In spite of their efforts, she continued to drag anchor toward shoal water. At 1550, she collided with *LCI–31*

but again escaped without major damage. By 1600, the winds reached 125 knots; and *Weehawken* sailed out of control—broadside to the wind—and dragged anchor. At 1700, she ran hard aground and took on a list. She immediately flooded compartments below to return to even keel and rested firmly on the bottom. There, she remained through the night battered by wind and sea and with her crew ready to abandon ship at a moment's notice.

The following morning, the winds began to slacken and the sea to abate. Between 10 and 12 October, the minelayer unloaded the bulk of her provisions and transferred the majority of her crew to *Benson* (APA–120). On 16 October, her hull began to break in two, but a skeleton crew remained on board salvaging equipment. On the 31st, a board of inspection and survey convened in *Weehawken* to look her over and found her hull to be a complete loss. The board recommended that she be decommissioned, stripped, and destroyed. Accordingly, *Weehawken* was decommissioned on 11 December 1945, and her name was struck from the Navy list on 3 January 1946.

Weehawken earned two battle stars during World War II.

III

(YTB–776: dp. 356 (f.); l. 109'; b. 31'; dr. 14'; s. 12 k.; cpl. 12; cl. *Natick*)

The third *Weehawken* (YTB–776) was laid down in August 1964 at Marinette, Wis., by the Marinette Marine Corp.; launched on 8 June 1965; delivered to the 9th Naval District in July 1965; and placed in service in the 14th Naval District during November 1965.

Weehawken has spent her entire Navy career serving the 14th Naval District which is comprised of the Hawaiian Islands and surrounding smaller islets. She has conducted routine towing operations between those islands and has rendered assistance to ships entering and clearing Pearl Harbor. As of December 1979, she was still active in the 14th Naval District.

Weeks

John Wingate Weeks—born on 11 April 1860 near Lancaster, N.H.—served Presidents Harding and Coolidge as Secretary of War. See *John W. Weeks* for biography.

The order for the construction of *Weeks* (DE–285)—projected as a *Rudderow*-class destroyer escort to be built by the Charleston (S.C.) Navy Yard—was cancelled on 10 June 1944.

Weeks, John J., see *John J. Weeks*.

Weemootah

In official documents, *Wemootah* (SP–201) (*q.v.*) was frequently, but erroneously, rendered as *Weemootah*.

Weems, Mason L., see *Mason L. Weems*.

Weepoose

(MB: t. 24 (gross); l. 60'0"; b. 12'3"; dr. 3'6" (mean); s. 10.0 k.; cpl. 6; a. 1 1-pdr., 1 mg.)

Weepoose—a wooden-hulled motorboat built at Salisbury, Md., in 1911 by the Salisbury Marine Construction Co.—was acquired by the Navy from C. S. Thorne on 2 July 1917; designated SP–405; and placed in commission on 22 October 1917.

Little is known of the ship's active naval career other than the fact that she served on net patrol in the 3d Naval District, based (at least as of 1 February 1918) at Rosebank, Staten Island, N.Y. Like other vessels similar to her, she probably performed these duties up to the discontinuance of defensive "military patrols" on 24 November, less than two weeks after the armistice. No record has been found of the craft's decommissioning or even of her being struck from the Navy list. She was transferred to the Department of Agriculture on 28 September 1920, but no trace of her subsequent fate has been found.

Wego

(MB: l. 34'5"; b. 9'0"; dr. 2'9" (aft); s. 10.0 k.; cpl. 4; a. 1 mg.)

Wego (sometimes spelled *We-go*)—a wooden-hulled motorboat built by the Camden Anchor Rockland Machine Co.—was acquired by the Navy under free-lease from Mrs. R. B. Fuller of New York City; assigned the classification SP–1196; and was listed as "delivered and commissioned" as of 9 August 1917.

Apparently assigned to local patrol duties in the 1st Naval District, *Wego* presumably operated in such activities into the autumn of 1918. However, little is known for certain about the boat's actual routine because no deck logs are extant. While no records of her decommissioning or of her strike dates have been found, the *Ship's Data, U.S. Naval Vessels* 1918 edition contains the notation that the craft was "returned to owner" as of 1 October 1918.

Weigel, William, see *General William Weigel*.

Weight

(ARS–35: dp. 1,500; l. 183'3"; b. 38'2"; dr. 13'11"; s. 11.5 k.; cpl. 65; a. 1 3", 2 20mm.; cl. *Weight*)

Plymouth Salvor—a wooden-hulled salvage vessel originally earmarked for transfer to Great Britain under lend-lease and classified as BARS–7—was laid down on 7 April 1942 at Wilmington, Del., by the American Car and Foundry Co.; reclassified ARS–35 on 11 January 1943 and named *Weight* on 15 March 1943. The ship was launched on 21 April 1943; sponsored by Mrs. H. E. Haven, the wife of the Supervsor of Shipbuilding at the Dravo Corp. of Wilmington; and commissioned at her builder's yard on 14 August 1943, Lt. Frederick J. Leamond, USNR, in command.

Weight shifted to the Philadelphia Navy Yard on 16 August, where she fitted out prior to moving to Cape May, N.J., en route to New York City. Reaching New York late on the 23d, the salvage vessel remained there until the 27th, when she sailed for Norfolk in company with *Extricate* (ARS–16). After touching at Annapolis, Md., en route on the 29th, the salvage ships reached Norfolk later that day.

Following a brief shakedown, the ship was fitted out at the Norfolk Navy Yard from 5 to 13 September and remained in the Hampton Roads vicinity until late in the month. She departed her anchorage on 25 September and joined Convoy UGS–19, bound for North Africa.

Reaching Bizerte, Tunisia, on the 16th, *Weight* sailed for Italy on the 27th and reached Naples on the 29th. For almost the next three months, the salvage ship performed harbor clearance and salvage operations, an existence frequently interrupted by air raid alerts, and by air raids themselves, and the results of those attacks. Late on 5 November, soon after reaching Naples, she was called upon to turn her monitors (fire-fighting equipment) upon a serious warehouse blaze. While the ship was maneuvering to get into the best possible position to fight the fire, her starboard propeller struck some submerged wreckage, bending one blade out of alignment and curling the others about three inches each. By 0415 on the 6th, the blaze was controlled.

Moored to the wreckage of the Italian ship SS *Nirvo*, *Weight* performed salvage operations on that vessel through mid-November, before she shifted berths alongside the wrecks of SS *Irish Monarch* and SS *Silvano*. She also raised sunken LCVP's and fought a fire that had started in cargo carried by *LCT–309*, spending much of her time on New Year's Eve fighting that blaze.

On 2 January 1944, *Weight* shifted to a berth alongside the wreck of the former German merchantman SS *Resolute* where, over the next few days, she tended to the mine damage suffered by the British merchant vessel SS *Largs Bay*. *Weight* later provided fresh water to *YMS–69*, repairs to *LST–361*, *LCT–233*, and freed the port screw of *LCI–337*. She also conducted salvage and wreckage clearance operations on a sunken Italian destroyer and towed HMS *Thruster* off a nearby beach where she had gone aground.

Weight sailed from Naples at 0755 on 28 January and, reaching the Anzio beachhead the next day, observed German bombers making direct hits on the British destroyer HMS *Spartan* and the American merchantman SS *Samuel Huntington*. *Weight* commenced salvage operations on the stranded *LCT–223* while explosions from the burning *Samuel Huntington* shook the area.

After dragging *LCT–233* clear, *Weight* got underway to fight the blaze on the wrecked Liberty ship, *Samuel Huntington*. The salvage vessel trained both monitors—large deck-mounted water guns—and a 2½-inch hose on the wreck and, between 1605 and 1745, fought the fire that ravaged the freighter. Securing at 1745, *Weight* moved briefly away with the wreck still smoking but returned at 2207 to anchor alongside and renew her efforts to contain the flames.

However, *Weight*'s work off the Anzio beaches was not yet done. In company with the British salvage vessel HMS *Weazel* and aided by bulldozers ashore, she attempted to salvage the grounded British tank landing craft, *LCT–542*. Weight's divers cleared the fouled screws of *SC–497*, and the ship's force repaired *LCT–*

288 and again fought fires on *Samuel Huntington*. *Weight* finally departed Anzio at 0845 on 5 February and returned to Naples later that day.

Weight continued her vital but unglamorous salvage routine at Naples well into April. Between 10 and 25 February, she assisted and repaired HMS *Kempenfelt*, the damaged minesweeper *Pilot* (AM–104), and *LCI–2*, as well as HMS *Weazel*. On the 26th, she got underway for the beach off Bagnoli, Italy, to tow off stranded ships.

Heavy seas and high winds proved a nemesis to the salvors. Shortly after 2000 on 26 February, *Weight* attempted to pass a line to a grounded Army tug but, in the initial attempt to do so, used up three spools of line. The second try ended also in failure when the boat went too close to shore and broached, pitching two men into the surf. Fortunately, all of the six men from *Weight*'s motor launch reached shore safely, but the boat itself was smashed by the heavy surf.

Weight again attempted to tow off the Army tug— alone on the next day and in company with HMS *Barholm* on the 28th. Nevertheless, even after the joint attempt, the Army tug remained hard aground and defied all of the salvors' efforts; and the American salvage vessel subsequently returned to Naples to resume work on *Pilot*.

In early March, *Weight* salvaged HMS *Boxer* and HMS *Quantock*, and fought a fire that broke out on a nearby wreck. In the latter operation, the salvors had to cut holes in the deck to pass hoses. Late on 30 March, coal gas ignited on board SS *Richard Stockton*, causing a serious fire and injuries to three men. *Weight* got underway at 2220 and went to the aid of the burning merchantman.

Weight moved in close and brought her hoses to bear, using them to cool the side plates of the cargo vessel. She also took on board three injured men from *Richard Stockton* and later transferred them to an Army hospital ashore. At 0430 on 31 March, *Weight* labored to beach the stricken merchantman to help extinguish the fires by flooding the forward section of the blazing ship. *Weight* resumed fighting the fires at 0630 and, by 1356, finally had the blaze "under control." After continuing salvage operations and unbeaching the ship, *Weight* returned to Naples on 1 April.

Following a month of local salvage operations there, *Weight* departed Naples at 1139 on 1 May, in company with SS *Carillo* and *SC–561*, and headed for the coast of Morocco. She arrived at Algiers on 4 May and, the next day, entered drydock at Oran for repairs to her hull and propellers.

Shortly after noon on 29 May, *Weight* sailed in company with Convoy KMS–51. Steaming as last ship in the second column of the convoy, *Weight* received orders at 2310 on 30 May to make smoke. Shortly thereafter, she observed sporadic antiaircraft fire up ahead and at 2320 went to general quarters. At 0012 on the 31st, the convoy ceased making smoke; but, two minutes later, a white flare appeared overhead and brought the ship back to general quarters. An ensuing brief period of uneasy quiet was suddenly broken at 0020 by numerous flares—both red and white—which began dotting the sky above and began drifting down, illuminating the waters below.

The torpedo planes—probably Junkers 88's—succeeded in hitting two ships. At 0030, *Weight* intercepted a radio dispatch reporting that two ships had been torpedoed and that survivors from one were already in the water. *Weight* immediately altered course, initiating a search for the men.

At 0037, the salvage vessel sighted some survivors and proceeded into the midst of them, commencing rescue operations. After four survivors had been hauled from the water, lookouts heard a plane approaching the ship from her starboard quarter. When the target became visible approximately 300 yards away, two 20-millimeter guns immediately swung around and commenced firing. *Weight*'s heavy antiaircraft barrage managed to dissuade the German pilot from attempting

a strafing run on the survivors; and the plane, *sans* torpedo, swung away from the convoy. Soon thereafter, a second Ju 88 attacked, dropping a torpedo nearby that passed ahead of the rescue ship. *Weight*'s Oerlikons again forced the Germans to clear the area.

Although the area was still brightly lighted by numerous flares, *Weight* continued rescue operations, picking up four more men from the water. Soon the British tug HMRT *Henquist* neared the salvage vessel and informed her that she would pick up the rest of the survivors. *Weight* learned that the men she had rescued were from the British merchantman SS *Nordeflinge*, which had taken an aerial torpedo amidships and gone down in two minutes.

After giving the survivors medical care, food, and clothing, *Weight* transferred the eight to the British "Flower"-class corvette HMS *Nettle* (K 212).

Soon after reaching Augusta, Sicily, on the morning of 3 June, *Weight* shifted to Naples, reaching that port on the 5th. She spent a month engaged in local ship repair and salvage jobs and then shifted briefly to Palermo, Sicily, before returning to Naples, where she operated into early August.

Departing Naples on 5 August, *Weight* reached the Bay of Ajaccio, Corsica, late on the 6th. During the ensuing weeks, the salvage vessel supported the invasion of southern France, earning her second battle star performing her vital but unsung salvage and repair deeds on ships ranging from landing craft to patrol vessels. She remained at Corsica for much of August, before she towed *LST–690* to Palermo, en route to Naples. Reaching that port on 1 September, in company with *PC–1594* and *PC–1596*, *Weight* departed Naples on 6 September.

Arriving at St. Tropez on the 9th, the salvage vessel shifted to Toulon, France, on the 13th, arriving the next day. There, she commenced salvage operations on the sunken French "super-destroyer" *Vauban* on the 14th and continued them for a fortnight, moored astern of the sunken ship. After a brief trip to Dellys, Algeria, *Weight* returned to Toulon, where she performed salvage and repair operations on the mine-damaged SS *Eleanor Wylie* over ensuing days.

Departing Toulon at the end of October, the salvage vessel shifted to Marseille before moving down to Oran and Mers el-Kebir. She returned briefly to the Bay of Ajaccio, Corsica, before she put into Leghorn, Italy, to unload salvage gear there. Returning briefly to Naples and then to Arzew, Algeria, *Weight* departed Oran on 27 January 1945 and headed home.

She overtook Convoy GUS–68 on the 29th. The ship arrived at Fayal, Horta, in the Azores, on 4 February, and over the next two weeks' time, performed salvage operations on the damaged destroyer escort *Fogg* (DE–57). She ultimately departed the Azores on the 23d, bound for Boston.

Following an overhaul at Norfolk, Va., *Weight* sailed for the Pacific on 7 May. She then operated out of San Francisco and Pearl Harbor through the end of hostilities with Japan in mid-August 1945. Ultimately decommissioned at the Mare Island Naval Shipyard, Vallejo, Calif., on 29 March 1946, *Weight* was struck from the Navy list on 1 May.

Subsequently transferred to the United States Maritime Commission, the ship was sold and, on 24 July 1947, was delivered to her purchaser, Mr. David Davidoff, at Suisun Bay, Calif.

Weight won two battle stars for her World War II service.

Weiss

Carl Walter Weiss—born on 27 March 1915 in Detroit, Mich.—enlisted in the United States Marine Corps on 18 December 1939. After completing basic training at Parris Island, S.C., he served successively at Quantico, Va.; and at Philadelphia, Pa.; during the early part of 1940. On 1 March 1940, he reported to

Ft. Mifflin for duty which lasted for over a year. He returned to the base at Quantico briefly in June 1941 before going to sea in *McCawley* (AP–10) at the end of the first week in July for a month's assignment. Promoted to corporal while in that transport, Weiss returned ashore at Portsmouth, Va., on 14 August 1941 and, from there, moved on to duty at New River, N.C., in September. Weiss was promoted to sergeant in March 1942 and, by the following summer, had been assigned to the Pacific theater in preparation for the Solomon Islands operation.

During that campaign, Sgt. Weiss conducted himself with distinction. During a battle on 1 November with Japanese forces near Matanikau River, Guadalcanal, he charged an enemy machine gun position and destroyed it with a hand grenade. Returning to his own machine gun, Weiss directed his gunners in repulsing three fanatical bayonet charges. When one of his men received a wound and fell forward of the emplacement, Sgt. Weiss "crawled forward and dragged his comrade to safety." The next day, he again inched forward over the crest of the hill toward another enemy machine gun. Though the position opened fire on him, he continued forward and lobbed a grenade at the offending weapon. He then attempted to toss another grenade to finish the job begun by the first but was felled, mortally wounded by enemy fire. For "his great personal valor, aggressiveness and fine spirit of self sacrifice," Sgt. Weiss was awarded the Navy Cross, posthumously.

Weiss (DE–378)—a *John C. Butler*-class destroyer escort—was cancelled on 5 June 1944 before completion, and her materials were scrapped. The name *Weiss*, however, was concurrently reassigned to DE–719 which became *Weiss* (APD–135) on 17 July 1944.

I

(APD–135: dp. 2,130 (lim.) ; l. 306'0''; b. 37'0''; dr. 12'7'' (lim.) ; s. 23.6 k. (tl.) ; cpl. 204; trp. 162; a. 1 5'', 6 40mm., 6 20mm., 2 dct.; cl. *Crosley*)

Weiss (APD–135) was laid down on 4 October 1944 at Bay City, Mich., by the Defoe Shipbuilding Co.; launched on 17 February 1945; sponsored by Mrs. Anna Weiss; and commissioned at New Orleans on 7 July 1945, Lt. Comdr. Thomas D. Morris in command.

The warship departed New Orleans on 20 July to conduct shakedown training in the vicinity of Guantanamo Bay, Cuba. She was still engaged in those operations on 14 August when she received word of the end of hostilities in World War II. Thereafter, she continued her shakedown training but with a lesser sense of urgency.

Following a post-shakedown overhaul at Norfolk, she sailed on 4 September for Melville, R.I., where for the next two months she served as a training ship. On 29 October, the high-speed transport returned to Norfolk, where she remained until mid-January 1946. On the 14th of that month, she began a ten-week cruise to the West Indies, returning to the United States at Moorehead City, N.C., on the last day of March. In April, she visited Washington, D.C., and underwent repairs, first at Charleston in early May and later at the New York Naval Shipyard in June.

In August, the high-speed transport served as an escort for *Williamsburg* (AGC–369) when President Harry S. Truman voyaged in her to Bermuda for a vacation. *Williamsburg* returned the President to Washington on 2 September, and *Weiss* resumed east coast duty. Based at Norfolk, she spent the next 19 months operating from that port. On 2 May 1949, the warship was decommissioned at Charleston and then towed to Green Cove Springs, Fla., to be berthed with the Atlantic Reserve Fleet.

On 25 June 1950, communist North Korea launched an invasion of South Korea. The United Nations Security Council—taking advantage of the Soviet boycott—decided to provide military assistance to South Korea against the aggressor. The United Nations took on the majority of the responsibility for carrying out the Security Council's operations, particularly with regard to naval forces. That required the reactivation of many ships in the Reserve Fleet. *Weiss* was moved out of her berth at Green Cove Springs, quickly readied for action, and recommissioned on 14 October 1950, Lt. Comdr. W. H. Bargeloh in command.

Following shakedown training out of Guantanamo Bay, Cuba, *Weiss* set sail for the Pacific on 15 March 1951. She stopped at San Diego for two weeks of maintenance and upkeep and then continued her voyage west, arriving in Korean waters on 3 May.

The high-speed transport spent the bulk of her first Korean War tour in bombardment and UDT missions. She also conducted training and exercises with the UDT men as well as with other units of the 7th Fleet. She concluded her assignment in the Far East on 17 October when she set a course to return to the United States.

Following a period of upkeep and training on the west coast during the winter of 1951 and 1952, *Weiss* headed back to the Far East in the summer and arrived in Korean waters on 2 July. Once again, bombardment missions and UDT support duty occupied the majority of her time. The high-speed transport completed her second tour of Korean War service on 1 April 1953 and arrived in San Diego on 2 July.

Less than a month after *Weiss*' return to the United States, the armistice of 27 July 1953 effectively ended hostilities on the Korean peninsula. Consequently, the high-speed transport settled into a peacetime routine of deployments to the western Pacific alternated with upkeep and training periods along the west coast of the United States. Between July 1953 and December 1957, she made three deployments to the Far East. Port visits, training missions, and providing evidence of American military presence in Asian waters proved to be her major responsibilities during these initial post-Korean War tours with the 7th Fleet.

On 2 March 1958, *Weiss* was placed out of commission once again. She was berthed with the Pacific Reserve Fleet at Treasure Island, Calif., for the next four years. On 20 November 1961, *Weiss* was placed back in commission at San Diego, Comdr. Merritt D. Tuel in command.

The warship conducted shakedown and amphibious training during the winter of 1961 and 1962 and then settled into a normal west coast routine, operating out of San Diego. That duty lasted until 16 October 1962, at which time she departed San Diego on her first tour of duty in the western Pacific following her recommissioning. During that deployment, she operated from the base at Subic Bay in the Philippines and engaged in training missions with UDT men. Early in the assignment, the ship visited Sattahip, Thailand, with UDT men embarked. There, she participated in bilateral UDT exercises with members of the Royal Thai Navy. The high-speed transport returned to Subic Bay on 17 December and remained there through the beginning of the new year. During the latter stages of her western Pacific tour, in February and March of 1963, the warship earned the Armed Forces Expeditionary Medal for a tour of duty in Vietnamese waters.

She returned to the United States later that spring and resumed normal operations until commencing a Fleet Rehabilitation and Modernization (FRAM) overhaul late in the year. She completed her FRAM II conversion early in 1964 and resumed local operations out of San Diego. On 18 June 1964, she stood out of San Diego for another tour of duty in the western Pacific. En route, the warship stopped at Oahu for about a month of operations out of Pearl Harbor and then continued on to Okinawa.

During the night of 26 and 27 July, Typhoon "Flossie" struck her anchorage at Okinawa, parted her anchor chain, and drove the high-speed transport into uncharted waters. Efforts to maneuver back into known waters failed; and, at 2042, *Weiss* ran aground. On the 27th, tug *Tawasa* (ATF–92), while attempting to refloat *Weiss*, also grounded on an uncharted reef. *Safeguard* (ARS–25) then came to the aid of both stricken ships. Finally at about 2000 hours, *Weiss* eased off the reef into deeper water. Interestingly enough, *Tawasa* was refloated early on the 28th and departed Okinawa that same day, bound for Sasebo with *Weiss* in tow. The high-speed transport completed repairs by late August and joined a contingency force sent to Vietnamese waters as a result of the Gulf of Tonkin "incident" earlier that month. She remained there from 25 August to 28 September. After spending most of October in the Philippines, *Weiss* returned to Vietnamese waters briefly in November. On 28 November, she departed Subic Bay to return to San Diego where she arrived on 18 December.

Following the usual holiday leave and an upkeep period, *Weiss* commenced operations along the coast of southern California. Those missions consisted of exercises in cooperation with Marine Corps reconnaissance units and Navy underwater demolition teams. Such duty occupied her time until mid-summer 1965 when she entered the Long Beach Naval Shipyard for a two-month availability. She completed repairs on 30 August and returned to San Diego for refresher training. On 18 October, *Weiss* left San Diego for another tour of duty in the Far East with the 7th Fleet. She made an overnight stop at Pearl Harbor on 26 and 27 October and arrived in Subic Bay on 12 November. On the 23d, she departed the Philippines for her first tour of combat duty off the coast of Vietnam.

Her first actual combat mission came on 30 November and 1 December when she landed marines near Lang Ke Ga, South Vietnam, as part of Operation "Dagger Thrust IV." Her second such mission occurred on the 5th and 6th when her embarked marines made a search-and-destroy landing near Phu Tu as a part of Operation "Dagger Thrust V." On the evening of the 6th, she reembarked the troops and retired toward Subic Bay for a rest and relaxation period. However, on the 8th, she was recalled to assist in a salvage operation near Phu Tu. She completed her part in that mission on the 9th and resumed her voyage to Subic Bay where she arrived on the 13th.

In January 1966, *Weiss* did two tours of duty in Vietnamese waters conducting surveys of the coast and river mouths. She returned to the Philippines from the second Vietnam tour of the year on 1 February and embarked American UDT men and a Philippine under-

water operations unit to participate in bilateral reconnaissance exercises near Legaspi, Luzon, between 3 and 9 February. A visit to Hong Kong, availability at Subic Bay, and another survey tour off Vietnam followed in late February and early March. Her last combat operation of the deployment began on 20 March when she came under the operational control of the amphibious ready group for Operation "Jackstay," a combined surface and helicopter-borne amphibious assault on Viet Cong guerrillas in the Rung Sat Special Zone. The operation began on 26 March and continued through 6 April at which time *Weiss* headed back to Subic Bay for upkeep. Later that month, she departed the Philippines and headed home. She made a stop at Pearl Harbor along the way and arrived in San Diego on 14 May.

The ship remained in port for the next five weeks engaged in the usual post-deployment leave and upkeep. On 28 June, she stood out of San Diego and shaped a course for San Francisco where she began regular overhaul at the Bethlehem Steel shipyard. She remained there until 9 November when labor problems in the civilian yard forced her to shift to the San Francisco Bay Naval Shipyard to ensure timely completion of the overhaul. Repairs completed, the warship exited the yard on 9 December and headed back to San Diego, whence she operated until late February 1967.

On 24 February, she departed San Diego for the western Pacific. After stops at Pearl Harbor and at Guam, the ship entered Subic Bay on 20 March. *Weiss* operated in the Philippines for almost two months conducting surveys and reconnaissance training. In mid-May, she made a liberty call at Hong Kong and then returned to Subic Bay late in the month. On the 28th, she departed the Philippines with a detachment of UDT–11 embarked and set a course for South Vietnam. She arrived at Vung Tau on 31 May. Following briefings there and at An Thoi, *Weiss* began a series of coastal surveys to determine suitable landing beaches and canal entrances for amphibious operations. That duty lasted until 10 June at which time she headed back to Subic Bay. She remained in the Philippines from 10 to 21 June and then once more got underway for Vietnam. She conducted another series of coastal surveys until 3 July and returned to Subic Bay for a week's rest and relaxation. The warship arrived back in Vung Tau on 15 July and began her final series of surveys, completing them on the 31st. Following that, she made stops at Bangkok, Subic Bay, and Yokosuka before heading back to the United States on 26 August. She stopped at Pearl Harbor along the way and arrived

The high-speed transport *Weiss* (APD–135) at Yokosuka, 1954. Compare this photograph with that of the inactivated *Weber*. *Weiss'* low bridge identifies her as having been converted from a *Rudderow*-class DE.

in San Diego on 16 September. Post-deployment stand-down and an interim availability at a civilian yard occupied the remainder of 1967.

Weiss completed her availability and post-deployment standdown early in 1968 and began normal west coast operations out of San Diego. That employment lasted until 1 August at which time she headed back to the western Pacific. The warship stopped at Pearl Harbor from 9 to 11 August and then continued her voyage to Yokosuka, Japan, where she arrived on the 23d. A week later, the ship sailed for Subic Bay, where she remained from 3 to 9 September. From Subic Bay, she moved on to the coast of Vietnam to resume coast survey missions in support of 7th Fleet amphibious operations. She returned to Subic Bay on 24 September and stayed over until 2 October. Back off the coast of South Vietnam early in October, *Weiss* provided over-the-horizon support for Navy SEAL teams participating in Operations "Bold Dragon VII" and "Bold Dragon VIII" carried out in the IV Corps tactical zone. During these operations, the warship fired her guns in anger for the first time since the Korean conflict. She returned to Subic Bay on 11 November and remained until the 20th when she got underway for Hong Kong and a liberty call. Back in Vietnamese waters early in December, she again provided support for Navy SEAL teams engaged in Operation "Bold Dragon IX." That mission carried her into 1969. She departed the Far East early in the spring of 1969 and returned to San Diego. For the remainder of the year, she conducted normal west coast operations out of San Diego and began preparations for decommissioning. *Weiss* was placed out of commission in January 1970 and was berthed with the Atlantic Reserve Fleet at Orange, Tex. On 15 September 1974, her name was struck from the Navy list. *Weiss* was sold to J. R. Steel, Inc., on 24 June 1975 for scrapping.

Weiss earned three battle stars during the Korean conflict and seven battle stars for service in Vietnamese waters.

Welborn C. Wood

Welborn Cicero Wood—born in Georgia on 15 January 1876—was appointed to the United States Naval Academy on 6 September 1895. He served as a midshipman in the battleship *Texas* during the war with Spain in 1898, before graduating with the class of 1899, and later joined *Oregon* (Battleship No. 3) on the Asiatic Station to serve part of the two years required by law before commissioning. Subsequently given command of the gunboat *Urdaneta*—then operating in the Philippines during the Insurrection—Naval Cadet Wood was killed in action on 17 September 1899, when his ship ran aground in the Orani River, near Manila, and was overwhelmed by insurgent troops who enfiladed the gunboat with a withering fire from the shoreline.

(DD–195: dp. 1,215; l. 314'4½''; b. 30'11½''; dr. 9'4'' (mean); s. 35 k.; cpl. 111; a. 4 4'', 3 3'', 1 .30-cal. mg., 12 21'' tt.; cl. *Clemson*)

Welborn C. Wood (DD–195) was laid down on 24 September 1918 at Newport News, Va., by the Newport News Shipbuilding and Drydock Co.; launched on 6 March 1920; sponsored by Miss Virginia Mary Tate; designated DD–195 during the assignment of alpha-numeric hull number designations on 17 July 1920; and commissioned at the Norfolk Navy Yard on 14 January 1921, Lt. (jg.) Leon W. Mills in temporary command pending the arrival of Lt. (jg.) Brady J. Dayton 11 days later.

Welborn C. Wood operated off the eastern seaboard with the Atlantic Fleet, on a routine schedule of exercises and maneuvers until decommissioned at Philadelphia on 8 August 1922. During the ship's ensuing sojourn in reserve, the establishment of Prohibition gave rise to smuggling of illicit liquor into the United States. To deal with this problem, 25 older destroyers

were transferred by the Navy to the Treasury Department for service with the Coast Guard in enforcing Prohibition. Some began to show signs of wear and tear after the often arduous pace of operations on the "rum patrol" and required replacement. Accordingly, five of the newer "flush deck" destroyers were transferred to the Treasury Department in 1930 and 1931.

Welborn C. Wood was transferred to the Coast Guard on 1 October 1930 and was simultaneously struck from the Navy list. Reconditioned at Philadelphia, the destroyer soon bore a new hull number—CG–19—on her bows and was commissioned on 15 April 1931 at Philadelphia. She arrived at New London, Conn., a week later, for service out of her permanent station there. She operated on the "rum patrol" out of New London, trailing rumrunners and keeping a weather eye on them. Shifting south to Florida waters for target practice soon thereafter, she returned to New London upon the conclusion of her exercises and operated out of that port into the autumn of 1932.

After another period of routine patrols off the eastern seaboard, *Welborn C. Wood* operated with the Navy in Cuban waters, off Nueva Gerona, in September and October 1933, interrupting her scheduled target practices. Released from this duty on 6 November, she sailed north for New York that day.

Arriving at Stapleton, N.Y., on 10 November, *Welborn C. Wood* shifted to New London soon thereafter. Subsequently decommissioned at Philadelphia on 21 May 1934, *Welborn C. Wood* resumed her sojourn in reserve with the Navy, as the repeal of Prohibition in late 1933 had obviated the need for the destroyer's service in law enforcement duties.

While the warship lay in reserve, she was reinstated on the Navy list with many of her sisters in Philadelphia's reserve basin as the world situation slowly worsened. One crisis after another abroad in the late 1930's seemed to steadily erode what security the United States held by virtue of its self-imposed isolation from world affairs. On 1 September 1939, German forces invaded Poland, triggering a chain reaction on the part of Poland's allies, Great Britain and France, who rushed to her aid.

President Roosevelt swiftly ordered a Neutrality Patrol to sea to safeguard American coastlines. The Atlantic Squadron found itself hard pressed to meet the initial demands of the patrol and found itself needing more ships. Accordingly, 77 light minelayers and destroyers on both coasts (San Diego and Philadelphia) were recommissioned for duty on the Neutrality Patrol to augment the units already at sea.

On 4 September 1939, *Welborn C. Wood* was recommissioned at Philadelphia, Lt. Comdr. Robert E. Cronin in command. She was fitted out for sea and soon sailed to join the Neutrality Patrol. The destroyer conducted these operations interspersed with accelerated training evolutions off the eastern seaboard and into the Caribbean and gulf regions. Meanwhile, the situation in Europe continued to worsen, as Hitler's German legions overran western Europe and forced England's back to the wall by the late spring of 1940.

British destroyer forces had suffered heavily since the outbreak of war—primarily in the disastrous Norwegian campaign of May 1940. In addition, the entrance of Italy into the war in June meant that British escort forces would be thinly spread to protect not only the North Atlantic convoys but also the Mediterranean ones as well. Accordingly, British Prime Minister Winston Churchill shaped a plea for help from the United States—to which President Roosevelt answered affirmatively.

Welborn C. Wood became one of the first of the 50 over-age destroyers to be transferred to the British government in return for 99-year leases on important base sites in the Western Hemisphere. She and the rest of her division, Destroyer Division 67, arrived at Halifax, Nova Scotia, on 6 September 1940. Her crew instructed the Britishers slated to man the ship in the brief few days preceding the turnover ceremonies. On

9 September, *Welborn C. Wood*'s commissioning pennant came down; her American crew mustered ashore and marched off to board a train waiting to take them back to the United States; and the British officers and ratings assigned to the "flush decker" manned the destroyer. *Welborn C. Wood* was subsequently struck from the Navy list on 8 January 1941.

Commissioned into the Royal Navy simultaneously, the destroyer became HMS *Chesterfield* (I.28). Initially, her new crew must have found the ship difficult to handle, as she twice rammed HMS *Churchill* (I.45) (formerly *Haraden*, DD–138) which was lying alongside a pier, fitting out, before she sailed for the British Isles. As part of the first "Town" flotilla—so called because each British ship bore the name of a town common to both Great Britain and the United States (the Canadian vessels—six of them—bore names of common rivers)—*Chesterfield* sailed for Belfast, Northern Ireland, and arrived at her destination on 18 November. Shifting to Plymouth on the 22d, the destroyer underwent a refit at Chatham before joining the 11th Escort Group, Western Approaches Command, based at Greenock.

From 1941 to 1943, *Chesterfield* escorted convoys in the North Atlantic. Screening Convoy HX–222 on 17 January 1943, the destroyer attacked *U–268* with a depth charge barrage, only to suffer damage from her own charges. Limping to Plymouth for repairs soon thereafter, the ship remained there until November 1943.

Allocated to the 5th Western Approaches Command for duty as a target vessel for aircraft, she remained engaged in this vital, but unglamorous, duty through 1944. Subsequently placed in reserve at Grangemouth, Firth of Forth, on 17 January 1945 *Chesterfield* was eventually broken up for scrap in 1947.

Welch

A city in southern West Virginia. It is the seat of government for McDowell County.

I

(PC–817: dp. 280; l. 173'8''; b. 23'0''; dr. 10'10''; s. 20.2 k. (tl.); cpl. 65; a. 1 3'', 1 40mm., 2 dct., 2 dcp.; cl. *PC–461*)

PC–817 was laid down at Portland, Oreg., by the Albina Engine & Machinery Works on 8 January 1943; launched on 4 March 1943; sponsored by Mrs. H. O. McAlpine; and commissioned on 13 July 1943, Lt. H. L. Martin, USNR, in command.

PC–817 completed fitting out at Portland until 6 August when she shifted south to San Pedro, Calif. After shakedown training out of San Pedro between 18 August and 30 September, the patrol craft was assigned to the Western Sea Frontier. She served along the California coast—escorting coastwise convoys and conducting antisubmarine patrols—until 1 December when she arrived at the Naval Station, Seattle, for repairs incident to her imminent transfer to the Alaska Sea Frontier. On the 16th, she departed Seattle and arrived at Ketchikan four days later.

For the next 11 months, *PC–817* steamed between the sundry American bases along the Aleutians chain, escorting supply convoys, transporting passengers and mail, and conducting surveys. On 5 November 1944, the patrol vessel departed Shemya to escort SS *Griffco* to Seattle, Wash. After stops at Adak, Dutch Harbor, and Ketchikan, she arrived in Seattle on 29 November.

At the Puget Sound Navy Yard, she began a major overhaul that lasted until April 1945. On 18 April, the patrol vessel took leave of Puget Sound and headed—via San Francisco—to her last wartime assignment—the Hawaiian Islands. She reached Pearl Harbor on 1 May and conducted patrols among and escorted ships between the islands through the end of the war.

On 11 September, she headed back to the west coast, arriving in San Pedro on the 20th. From there, she steamed to the Panama Canal and thence proceeded via Key West, Fla., to Jacksonville, Fla., where she arrived on 28 November.

PC–817 was to have undergone inactivation overhaul at Jacksonville and then was to have been decommissioned and berthed with the Florida Group, Atlantic Reserve Fleet. However, her inactivation was never completed. She remained at Jacksonville until April 1946 when she moved north to Charleston, S.C., for disposal by the Commandant, 6th Naval District. However, while at Charleston, she received a reprieve by way of assignment as Naval Reserve training ship for the 9th Naval District. On 4 June, she headed north from Charleston. After a visit to New York City and port calls at American and Canadian ports along the St. Lawrence waterway, she arrived at Toledo, Ohio, on 11 July. Though placed out of commission on 22 July, *PC–817* remained active—in an "in service" capacity—as a Naval Reserve training ship for the 9th Naval District. After over three years of service training naval reservists on the Great Lakes, *PC–817* began her last voyage on 14 November 1949. From Chicago, she steamed down the Des Plaines and Illinois river system to the Mississippi River just above St. Louis, and thence moved south to New Orleans, where she arrived on 29 November. A week later, she continued her voyage—via Pensacola, St. Petersburg and Key West—and arrived in Philadelphia on 19 December.

On the 21st, she began inactivation overhaul at the Philadelphia Naval Shipyard. In March 1950, she was shifted south to Norfolk, Va., and was berthed with the Norfolk Group, Atlantic Reserve Fleet. She remained there for the next nine years; and, during that time, she received a name. On 15 February 1956, *PC–817* became *Welch* (PC–817). On 1 April 1959, her name was struck from the Navy list. She was probably sold for scrapping soon thereafter.

II

(PG–93: dp. 247 (f.); l. 165'; b. 24'; dr. 5'; s. 37.5 k.; cpl. 28; a. 1 3'', 1 40mm., 4 .50-cal. mg.; cl. *Asheville*)

The second *Welch* (PG–93) was laid down on 8 May 1967 by Peterson Builders, Inc., at Sturgeon Bay, Wis.; launched on 25 July 1968; sponsored by Mrs. Roy G. Anderson; and commissioned at the Boston Naval Shipyard on 8 September 1969, Lt. Paul F. Woods in command.

The gunboat completed her outfitting at Boston on 13 October 1969 and sailed for her first home port, San Diego, Calif. She arrived there on 12 November and, after about a month of upkeep, began operations in the southern California operating area for the remainder of the year. *Welch*'s service at San Diego proved to be brief. On 1 August 1970, she departed the continental United States and, in company with *Piedmont* (AD–17) and *Tacoma* (PG–92), headed for the Marianas. She paused at Pearl Harbor from 8 to 15 August and then continued on to Guam, where she arrived on the 28th.

Welch operated from the base at Guam for the next four years. During the first two, she alternated duty patrolling the Trust Territories in the Central Pacific and with combat assignments along the coast of Vietnam. After two weeks at Guam, she departed the island on 12 September for her first tour of combat duty. En route, trouble with one of her main engines forced her to remain at Subic Bay in the Philippines until 24 October. She finally reached the coast of Vietnam on the 28th and began three months of operations with Task Force (TF) 115, the Coastal Surveillance Force. Her main mission was the interdiction of communist coastwise logistics operations—dubbed Operation "Market Time." *Welch* completed her first Vietnam tour on 31 January 1971 and, after stops at Hong Kong and

Subic Bay, reentered Apra Harbor on 20 February 1971. She began her first regular overhaul on 1 March and completed it on the last day of May. From then until early July, she completed sea trials and a restricted availability at Guam.

On her way back toward Vietnam, *Welch* had to return to Guam to evade a typhoon. She finally reached Subic Bay on 30 July and remained there until 18 August. On the 20th, she relieved *Gallup* (PG–85) at Camranh Bay, South Vietnam, and resumed "Market Time" patrols with TF 115. Those operations—broken once by a visit to Bangkok, Thailand, early in October—lasted until 29 November. On that day, *Asheville* (PG–84) relieved her of "Market Time" duty. *Welch*'s voyage back to her base took her to Singapore, to Zamboanga and Subic Bay in the Philippines, and to Koror in the Palau Islands, before she arrived in Guam on 10 January 1972. Between 18 and 22 January she and *Marathon* (PG–89) conducted a surveillance patrol in the Marshall Islands and then resumed local operations out of Guam.

On 22 April, *Welch* departed Guam in company with *Crockett* (PG–88) and *Impervious* (MSO–449), bound initially for Subic Bay and ultimately the coast of South Vietnam. After almost two months of operations in the Philippines, the gunboat departed Subic Bay on 16 June and arrived off the coast of South Vietnam three days later. Instead of "Market Time" patrols, *Welch* spent the first 25 days on station in the Gulf of Tonkin, testing the gunboat's capabilities for sustained operations at sea. After a two-day voyage south, she resumed her "Market Time" assignments on 17 July. Her ensuing three months of service laboring to stop the flow of communist supplies were broken but once when she departed Vietnamese waters for a three-day visit to Bangkok. On 25 October, the gunboat departed Vietnam for visits to Singapore and Davao in the Philippines before reentering Apra Harbor on 16 November. In the following month, *Welch* conducted a surveillance patrol in the northern Marianas between 11 and 18 December and then ended the year in port at Apra Harbor.

Early in February 1973, the warship deployed to the Philippines where she spent the middle of the month engaged in high-speed missile boat attack exercises with larger ships of the Pacific Fleet. She departed Subic Bay on 20 February for a three-day visit to Hong Kong after which she put to sea to return to the Philippines. En route, she joined *Tacoma* in another series of high-speed missile boat exercises before reentering Subic Bay on the 26th. On 1 March, the gunboat headed back to Guam, arriving there on the 6th. Six days later, she entered the Naval Ship Repair Facility at Guam for an overhaul. Problems with her gas turbine engine, found during this repair period, affected her operations for most of the remainder of the year. She completed the overhaul—save repairs to her gas turbine—on 20 May.

In order to be available upon arrival of the parts needed to repair her gas turbine, *Welch* remained in the immediate vicinity of Guam until the end of October, but for three brief interruptions. On 24 May, she put to sea to rescue *Yukiko Maru* and towed the disabled Japanese ship into Apra Harbor the following day. A week later, she began a week-long, round-trip voyage to Ulithi Atoll in the Carolines for a public affairs visit. The last of these three periods away from Guam came between 30 July and 5 August when she made another surveillance patrol of the northern Marianas. The parts for her gas turbine finally arrived in mid-October, and *Welch*'s repairs were completed early in November. On the 5th, she got underway for her first extended cruise of 1973—a three-week surveillance patrol of the Pacific Trust Territories in the Central Pacific. She returned to Guam on the 24th but, after two weeks of upkeep, departed again for another brief patrol of the northern Marianas. She reentered Apra Harbor on 15 December and remained in the immediate vicinity for the remainder of the year.

Late January and early February 1974 brought interim refresher training in preparation for a four-month deployment. On 11 February, the gunboat departed Apra Harbor in company with two of her sister ships, *Tacoma* and *Marathon*. En route to Subic Bay, the three ships participated in a high-speed missile boat attack exercise with *Midway* (CV–41) and her escorts. They then joined the carrier's task group to observe air operations. On 18 February, *Welch* entered Subic Bay and, while there, put to sea briefly for another missile boat exercise, this time with the *Oriskany* (CV–34) task group. On 4 March, *Welch* departed Subic Bay with *Tacoma* for a month of diplomatic port visits in southeast Asia. On her itinerary were Singapore, Port Klang and Penang in Malaysia, and Bandar Seri Begewan on the island of Borneo. On 2 April, she returned to Subic Bay whence she participated in a series of training exercises during April. She got underway from Subic on 4 May bound for Taiwan to visit at Kaohsiung and Keelung. She reentered Subic Bay on the 15th, but she headed back toward Guam on the 21st and arrived there on the 27th.

On 21 June, *Welch* departed the Mariana Islands, bound for her new home port, Little Creek, Va. After stops at Pearl Harbor, San Diego, Acapulco, and Rodman in the Canal Zone, she transited the Panama Canal on 21 August and headed for Guantanamo Bay, Cuba. She made a one-night stop at Guantanamo Bay on 24 and 25 August and resumed her voyage. Following brief stops at Port Everglades and Mayport in Florida, she reached Little Creek on 2 September. During the remainder of 1974, she operated out of that base undergoing various inspections and availabilities in preparation for her assignment to Naval Reserve training duty. Early in 1975, she began Naval Reserve training operations out of Little Creek. Interrupted only by an overhaul in the summer—that duty continued until 1 November. At that time, she was designated a training ship for the joint American-Saudi Arabian program for the expansion of the Royal Saudi Navy. Since then, *Welch* has served as a training ship for officers and men of the Royal Saudi Navy. She has continued to operate from Little Creek with an American training crew and Saudi students.

Welch (PG–93) earned two battle stars and the Meritorious Unit Commendation for service in the Vietnam conflict.

Welcome

(MB: t. 4; l. 40′0′′; b. 8′0′′; dr. 2′6′′ (mean); s. 18.0 k. (max.); cpl. 6; a. none)

Welcome—a motorboat built in 1914 at St. Paul, Minn.—was acquired by the Navy on 7 August 1917 under a free lease from R. H. Wilcox of Detroit, Mich., and was placed in commission on 17 August 1917. Assigned the designation SP–1175, *Welcome* operated on patrol duties on the Great Lakes for the duration of World War I until November 1918. Subsequently decommissioned, *Welcome* was returned to her owner on 7 March 1919 and was simultaneously struck from the Navy list.

Welles

Gideon Welles—born on 1 July 1802 in Glastonbury, Conn.—became editor and part-owner of the *Hartford Times* in 1826 and remained its editor until he resigned a decade later. Elected to the Connecticut legislature in 1827, he served until 1835, before he was thrice elected state comptroller—in 1835, 1842, and 1843. He served as the Hartford, Conn., postmaster from 1836 to 1841.

Welles was appointed chief of the Navy's Bureau of Provisions and Clothing in 1846. During his three years in that office, he acquired valuable administrative experience and made enduring friendships. After an unsuccessful bid in 1850 for a Senate seat, Welles devoted his energies and considerable talents as a journalist to the fight against slavery. He broke with the Democratic party over this burning issue and helped organize the Republican party in Connecticut. In 1856, Welles was defeated in a bid for the governorship; but he became a Republican national committeeman that year. Staunchly supporting President Abraham Lincoln's policies, Welles became Lincoln's Secretary of the Navy on 7 March 1861.

At the onset of the Civil War in the spring of 1861, the Union Navy was in poor shape, with its ships scattered on various stations throughout the world. Some of its officers, feeling strong ties to their states, resigned their commissions. Welles, however, soon turned the situation around. A man of unusual energy, he rapidly doubled the size of the Navy and took an active part in the direction of the naval war against the South. Early in the conflict, he established a blockade of the Confederate coast with the limited number of ships available, and he constantly strengthened it until the South was almost completely sealed off from the rest of the world. Welles early recognized the need for ironclad warships and vigorously pushed their development, improvement, and construction. His ideas influenced the designs of ordnance, machinery, and armor. He urged improvement in navy yards—both existing and planned. He not only contributed to governmental policies but administered them as well.

Shrewd, methodical, and knowledgeable, the Union's remarkable Secretary of the Navy remained poised and calm throughout the tempestuous times engendered by the Civil War. Following Lincoln's death by assassination in April 1865, Welles remained in the cabinet as Secretary of the Navy under Andrew Johnson. After the new President ran into difficulties, Welles loyally and enthusiastically supported him throughout the impeachment proceedings. At the end of Johnson's administration, Welles returned to private life; and, although he never again occupied public office, he remained politically active and wrote prolifically until his death on 11 February 1878. C. A. Dana, in *Recollections of the Civil War*, wrote of Welles that he was "a very wise, strong man . . . he understood his duty and did it efficiently, continually, and unvaryingly."

I

(Destroyer No. 257: dp. 1,190; l. 314'4½''; b. 30'11½''; dr. 9'4''; s. 34.33 k.; cpl. 120; a. 4 4'', 2 3'', 12 21'' tt.; cl. *Clemson*)

The first *Welles* (Destroyer No. 257) was laid down on 13 November 1918—two days after the signing of the armistice that ended World War I—at Quincy, Mass., by the Bethlehem Shipbuilding Company's Fore River plant; launched on 8 May 1919; sponsored by Miss Alma Freeman Welles, the granddaughter of Gideon Welles; and commissioned at the Boston Navy Yard on 2 September 1919, Lt. Comdr. George N. Reeves, Jr., in command.

After her final sea trials off the east coast, *Welles* joined Squadron 2, Destroyer Force, Pacific Fleet, based at San Diego, Calif. She operated out of San Diego, "showing the flag" and training, until decommissioned there on 15 June 1922. Meanwhile, the destroyer was classified as DD–257 during the fleet-wide assignment of alphanumeric hull numbers on 17 July 1920.

Welles remained in "Red Lead Row" at San Diego into the 1930's, as crises multiplied in Europe and the Far East. On 1 September 1939, German forces invaded Poland, triggering World War II. In response to the European conflict, President Roosevelt proclaimed the neutrality of the United States and instructed the Navy to establish a Neutrality Patrol off the eastern seaboard, out of Guantanamo Bay, and at the eastward approaches of the Panama Canal.

To carry out the patrol, the Navy recommissioned 77 destroyers and light minelayers to augment fleet units already at sea that had assumed their patrol stations in September 1939, soon after the outbreak of

fighting in Poland. *Welles* was recommissioned at San Diego on 6 November 1939, Lt. Comdr. Clifton G. Grimes in command. She was fitted out at San Diego and then moved to the Mare Island Navy Yard, Vallejo, Calif., to undergo alterations and a drydocking that started a few days before Christmas and extended into the new year, 1940.

Following the yard work, *Welles* arrived back at San Diego in company with *Williams* (DD–108) and later departed the area on 5 February, bound for Panama. She transited the Panama Canal on the 16th and stopped at the Submarine Base at Coco Solo on the following day. There, she embarked six enlisted men for transportation to Guantanamo Bay, Cuba, and arrived there on 25 February.

After patrolling the approaches to Guantanamo Bay for nearly two weeks, *Welles*—transporting 10 enlisted men—sailed for Norfolk, Va., with the remainder of her division (Destroyer Division (DesDiv) 67)— *Welborn C. Wood* (DD–195), *Abel P. Upshur* (DD–193), and division flagship *Herndon* (DD–198)—on 14 March. Mooring at the navy yard and discharging her passengers on the 17th, the destroyer proceeded to sea on 6 April, bound for the Caribbean.

Arriving at San Juan, Puerto Rico, four days later, *Welles* departed the same evening. She joined *Omaha* (CL–4) on the following morning, and the two ships sailed in company on Neutrality Patrol and conducted exercises until 17 April, when the destroyer returned to San Juan.

Welles patrolled the waters near San Juan from 19 to 23 April before taking part in a battle problem and undergoing her annual military inspection on the 26th. The warship subsequently visited Charlotte Amalie, St. Thomas, Virgin Islands, on 1 May. She remained there for two weeks before returning to San Juan.

Proceeding to sea again on 8 June, *Welles* conducted exercises en route to Cuban waters and subsequently operated out of Guantanamo Bay over the next few days. During this time, the ship conducted a short-range battle practice. Shifting to Cay Lobos, Great Bahamas, on 20 June, *Welles* then transported 56 men and one officer from *Crowninshield* (DD–134) to Guantanamo, debarking the men to *George E. Badger* (AVP–16). *Welles* then remained at Guantanamo until she sailed for the Canal Zone on 27 July. Anchoring in Limon Bay, Canal Zone, on the 28th, *Welles* later transited the Panama Canal on 10 August, dropping anchor in Panama Bay on the 12th. She performed target services and conducted exercises and maneuvers with Submarine Division 11 until 16 August, when the destroyer retransited the canal, east-bound, and arrived at Coco Solo that day.

Welles sailed for Norfolk on 22 August with the rest of DesDiv 67, proceeded via Guantanamo Bay, and arrived six days later. At that time, *Welles* and 49 of her sister ships were slated to be transferred to the British government as a result of an agreement reached between President Roosevelt and the British Prime Minister, Winston Churchill. After suffering heavy destroyer losses in the Atlantic convoys and from the evacuation of Norway and France, the hard-pressed British desperately needed escort vessels. The United States needed advance base sites to strengthen her defenses. Accordingly, the two national leaders decided upon a bargain—the United States, in return for the transfer of 50 "overage" destroyers to the British, would receive 99-year leases on strategic base sites.

Welles loaded service ammunition at Norfolk before she sailed for Newport, R.I., where she then exchanged older torpedoes for ones of a later mark on 1 September. *Welles* soon shifted to the Boston Navy Yard, where she was drydocked, before she sailed—in company with *Russell* (DD–414) and *Herndon* on 5 September—for Halifax, Nova Scotia, the designated turn-over point. Arriving on the 6th as one of the first eight ships to be transferred, *Welles* soon took on board the prospective crew—six British officers and 120 enlisted men—for familiarization. Three days later, on 9 September, *Welles* was decommissioned and turned over to the Royal Navy. Her American name was struck from the United States Navy list on 8 January 1941.

Simultaneously, the destroyer was renamed HMS *Cameron* (I.05) and placed under the command of Lt. Comdr. P. G. Merriman, Royal Navy. Initially, the warship suffered problems with a faulty generator which delayed her sailing for the British Isles. After finally getting underway for England, the destroyer made port at Plymouth on 13 November, after a stop-over at Belfast, Northern Ireland. Shifting to Portsmouth three days later, *Cameron* was slated to receive her first major overhaul since coming under the White Ensign. However, she was fated never to finish this; as, on 5 December 1940, Luftwaffe bombers struck Portsmouth while *Cameron* lay defenseless in drydock no. 8. A high explosive bomb severely damaged the ship, capsizing her.

Deemed unsuitable for return to active sea service, *Cameron* was eventually refloated on 23 February 1941 and allocated for use as a hulk. United States Navy experts consequently subjected the ship to close scrutiny to derive damage control measures which could be applicable to ships of her type still in service with the Navy. As such, she presented them with what John Alden, in his book, *Flush Decks and Four Pipes*, termed the most extreme case of hull damage seen by Americans until *Cassin* (DD–372) and *Downes* (DD–375) were blasted by Japanese bombs at Pearl Harbor on 7 December 1941.

Admiralty records indicate that *Cameron* fulfilled a useful purpose. The Admiralty Committee on Shock in Ships conducted shock tests on the hulk between July 1942 and September 1943. "Paid off" on 5 October 1943, *Cameron* remained in dockyard hands at Portsmouth until towed to Falmouth in November 1944, where she was subsequently broken up for scrap.

II

(DD–628: dp. 1,630; l. 348'3''; b. 36'1''; dr. 17'5''; s. 37.4 k. (tl.); cpl. 276; a. 4 5'', 4 40mm., 7 20mm., 5 21'' tt., 2 dct., 6 dcp.; cl. *Gleaves*)

The second *Welles* (DD–628) was laid down on 27 September 1941 at Seattle, Wash., by the Seattle-Tacoma Shipbuilding Corp.; launched on 7 September 1942; sponsored by Mrs. Suzanne Dudley Welles Brainard; and commissioned on 16 August 1943, Lt. Comdr. Doyle M. Coffee in command.

Following shakedown training along the west coast of the United States, *Welles* returned to Puget Sound on 26 October. After post-shakedown availability there, she got underway on 15 November in company with two British escort carriers which she escorted as far as San Diego, Calif. Continuing on her way, the destroyer transited the Panama Canal on 28 November and set a course for New York. She stopped along the way at Norfolk and, upon her arrival at New York on 4 December, joined Destroyer Division (DesDiv) 38. Ordered farther north, the warship departed New York on 26 December and arrived in Boston harbor the following day. On the 28th, she and her division mates got underway for the western Pacific in the screen of *New Jersey* (BB–62). The task unit stopped briefly at Norfolk where *New Jersey*'s sister battleship, *Iowa* (BB–61), joined it for the voyage to the Pacific. The unit transited the Panama Canal during the first week in January 1944 and continued its voyage west on the 8th.

Welles and her travelling companions arrived at Funafuti in the Ellice Islands on 21 January and remained there for a week before getting underway for New Guinea. The destroyer arrived at Milne Bay on 5 February and joined the 7th Fleet. Later in the month, she escorted a convoy of LST's to Cape Gloucester on the island of New Britain. On 29 February, *Welles* provided gunfire support for elements of the Army's 1st Cavalry then landing on Los Negros Island in the Admiralties. During that operation, the destroyer came under fire from enemy automatic weapons and at least one field gun but sustained no damage. After completing her portion of the mission, she moved out to the transport area to provide antisubmarine defense. Periodically, she returned close to shore to provide call fire for American troops fighting ashore.

In March, she returned south to the area around Buna to prepare for operations to capture the remainder of the northern coast of New Guinea. During the Hollandia assault, the first of five leap frog steps to the Vogelkop, *Welles* was assigned to Task Group (TG) 77.2, the Central Attack Group which mounted its assault at Humboldt Bay on 22 April. About a month later, on 18 May, she supported the landings at Wakde Island and at Sarmi on the New Guinea mainland. From there, the warship continued with General MacArthur's amphibious jump to Biak Island where she provided gunfire support during the landings and consolidation operations from 27 May to 2 June. During that time, she destroyed several Japanese barges, harassed enemy ground forces, silenced a shore battery or two and helped to repel several air attacks.

Leaving Biak on 2 June, the warship screened logistics convoys along the New Guinea coast for about a month before arriving off Noemfoor Island—located just west of Biak—to support the capture of that island. At the end of July, she participated in the last amphibious operation in New Guinea when troops went ashore at Cape Sansapor on the Vogelkop.

She returned to Aitape early in August and then moved from there down the coast to Finschhafen whence she departed on 23 August, bound for the Solomon Islands. *Welles* arrived at Florida Island on 26 August and became a unit of the 3d Fleet. She immediately plunged into preparations for the impending Palau attack. For the assault on Peleliu and Angaur, the destroyer initially screened the carriers providing air support. After the mid-September landings on the two islands, she was detached from the carriers and moved into the transport area to provide antisubmarine defense and to guard against any attempts to reinforce the two islands. At the conclusion of her participation in the Palau operation, she joined TG 77.2 and began preparations for the invasion of the Philippines at Leyte.

She moved into Leyte Gulf on 18 October—two days before the actual landings—to cover preinvasion minesweeping and underwater demolition team operations. Her 5-inch shells also contributed to the preinvasion bombardment of the objective. After the 20 October landings, the warship delivered call fire in support of the troops advancing ashore and defended the invasion fleet against the heavy enemy air attacks launched against it. In the latter role, she claimed one unassisted kill. When the Japanese launched their three-pronged surface attack to break up the Leyte assault, *Welles* joined the screen of Vice Admiral Oldendorf's line of old battleships which virtually annihilated the enemy force which attempted to push through the Surigao Strait south of Leyte on the night of 24 and 25 October. Soon thereafter, she concluded her part in the Philippine operation and retired to Ulithi Atoll where she joined the screen of the Fast Carrier Task Force.

For the remainder of her participation in the war, *Welles* cruised with either the fast carriers or with their logistics unit as the flattops launched air strikes on Japan's inner defenses and supported—from a distance—the invasions at Luzon, Iwo Jima, and Okinawa.

In June 1945, she retired to Leyte for rest and upkeep. On the 21st of that month, she received orders to return to the United States for a major overhaul. Steaming via Eniwetok and Oahu, the destroyer arrived in Bremerton, Wash., on 16 July. She remained there through the end of hostilities in August and until late September.

On 29 September, she got underway for the east

coast. After a stop at San Pedro, Calif., she transited the Panama Canal on 14 October and headed for New York where she arrived on the 20th. In November, the ship moved south to Charleston, S.C., where she was placed out of commission on 4 February 1946. *Welles* was berthed with the Charleston Group, Atlantic Reserve Fleet, until 10 February 1968 at which time her name was struck from the Navy list. On 18 July 1969, she was sold to the Union Minerals & Alloy Corp. for scrapping.

Welles earned eight battle stars during World War II.

Wemootah

(MB: dp. 20.58; l. 70'; b. 13'; dr. 4'3'' (aft); s. 13 mph.; cpl. 13; a. 1 3-pdr., 2 mg.)

Wemootah (SP-201)—a motor boat constructed in 1916 at Morris Heights, N.Y., by the Gas Engine & Power Co. and the Charles L. Seabury Co.—was purchased by the Navy from A. Gardner Cooper of New York City on 16 June 1917; armed at New York; and placed in commission on 7 July 1917. Operating from the Rosebank Section Base on Staten Island, *Wemootah* served in New York harbor as a patrol craft and net tender through the end of World War I. In January 1919, her battery was removed; and the boat was put up for sale. Her name was struck from the Navy list on 13 June 1919; and she was sold to Mr. W. O. Graves of New York City on 10 October 1919.

Wenatchee

A tribe of Indians of the Salishan language group, who lived in the area that is now central Washington state, principally around Lake Chelan.

I

(ATF-118: dp. 1,330; l. 205'; b. 38'6''; dr. 14'3'' (mean); s. 16 k.; cpl. 85; a. 1 3'', 2 40mm.; cl. *Abnaki*)

The first *Wenatchee* (AT-118) was laid down on 12 January 1944 at Alameda, Calif., by the United Engineering Co.; reclassified from AT-118 to ATF-118 on 15 May 1944; launched on 7 September 1944; sponsored by Mrs. Hart A. Aaron, the wife of Lt. Comdr. H. A. Aaron, USNR, and commissioned on 24 March 1945.

Wenatchee conducted her shakedown training in the San Pedro-San Diego-San Francisco, Calif., area, before departing the west coast on 15 May, bound for the Hawaiian Islands. Reaching Pearl Harbor on 30 May, the fleet tug remained there through mid-June and then sailed for the Marshalls. She reached Eniwetok on 5 July.

The fleet tug performed ocean towing and screening duties supporting the 3d Fleet's drive against the Japanese homeland and, after hostilities ended, participated in the initial occupation of Japan. She was present in Tokyo Bay on 2 September, the day of Japan's formal surrender. That autumn, she engaged in salvage work at the former Japanese naval base at Yokosuka.

Wenatchee operated there through the end of 1945 and into the following year, finally departing that port in company with *Conserver* (ARS-39) on 20 February 1946, bound for Hawaiian waters. Reaching Pearl Harbor on 3 March, *Wenatchee* stayed there for over a month before she sailed for Bikini atoll on 13 April to take part in Operation "Crossroads."

As part of Task Unit 1.8.1, a repair and service unit, *Wenatchee* supported the atomic test operations there into the summer and then left Kwajalein on 20 August and headed for Pearl Harbor, reaching that port on 5 September. The fleet tug subsequently towed *AFDB-7* from Pearl Harbor to San Francisco, reaching the west coast in late October.

After transiting the Panama Canal in mid-December and reporting for duty with Service Force, Atlantic Fleet, *Wenatchee* reached New Orleans on 21 January 1947. Shifting to Orange, Tex., in mid-March, the fleet tug was decommissioned and placed in reserve there on 19 May 1947.

Struck from the Navy list on 1 September 1962, the ship was transferred to the Maritime Administration for lay up and preservation. Berthed at Beaumont, Tex., she remained there into the late 1970's, awaiting final disposition.

Wenatchee (ATF-118) earned one battle star for her World War II operations supporting the 3d Fleet.

II

(YTB-808: dp. 344 (f.); l. 109'; b. 29'; dr. 14'; s. 12 k. (tl.); cpl. 16; cl. *Natick*)

The second *Wenatchee* (YTB-808), a large harbor tug, was laid down on 24 November 1969 at Sturgeon Bay, Wis., by Pedersen Builders, Inc.; launched on 7 July 1970; and placed in service on Christmas Day 1970.

The tug was assigned to the 11th Naval District and, since going into service, has operated at San Diego, Calif. As of 1 January 1979, she was still active at San Diego.

Wendy

(MB: t. 24 (gross); l. 55'; b. 11'6''; dr. 3'6'' (aft); s. 9 k.; cpl. 9; a. 1 1-pdr., 1 mg.)

Wendy (SP-448)—a motorboat built in 1913 by the Jahncke Navigation Co.—was acquired by the Navy from Mr. C. A. Sporl in July 1917 for duty with the section patrol. Commissioned at New Orleans, La., on 3 August 1917, *Wendy* patrolled the waters around New Orleans during World War I. She was placed out of commission on 9 December 1918 and was returned to her owner that same day.

Wenonah

I

(SP-165: dp. 470 (approx.); l. 163'; b. 22'10''; dr. 10'6'' (aft); s. 12 k.; cpl. 65; a. 2 3'', 2 mg.)

The first *Wenonah* (SP-165)—a steam yacht built in 1915 at Neponset, Mass., by George Lawley & Sons—was acquired by the Navy from Mr. Walter G. Ladd on 8 June 1917; converted for naval service; and commissioned on 22 October 1917, Lt. Henry G. Fuller, NNV, temporarily in command.

The armed yacht was fitted out for distant service and departed Newport, R.I., on 4 November 1917 in company with tender *Hannibal* and yachts *Helenita* (SP-210), *Margaret* (SP-527), *May* (SP-164), *Rambler* (SP-211), and *Utowana* (SP-951). Each yacht towed a French-manned, American-made submarine chaser. In spite of a breakdown apiece for *Helenita*, *Margaret*, *May*, and *Utowana*, the flotilla of yachts and submarine chasers reached their first port of call—Hamilton, Bermuda—on 9 November. *Wenonah* remained at Hamilton for nine days and then departed in tow of *May* along with *Hannibal*, *Margaret*, *Rambler*, *Artemis* (SP-593), *Cythera* (SP-575), *Lydonia* (SP-700), and the six submarine chasers on the 18th for the next leg of the voyage, from Bermuda to the Azores. She reached the Azores on 5 December and, after two days at Horta, moved on to Ponta Delgada where she remained from 8 to 19 December. From there, the yacht continued on across the eastern Atlantic and arrived at Gibraltar on Christmas Day. On 15 January 1918, she began escorting convoys between Gibraltar and Bizerte, Tunisia. That duty continued uninterrupted through the end of hostilities in November 1918.

203

Wenonah (PY–11) in heavy seas, seen from *Margaret* (P–527) while en route from Bermuda to the Azores in November 1917. (NH 48479)

Wenonah's logs reveal only a single variation to that routine—a run to Genoa and back in July 1918. During the Gibraltar-to-Genoa leg of that voyage, the armed yacht engaged in her only combat action of the war. At about 1924 on the evening of the 23d, one of the ships she was escorting, SS *Messidor*, was torpedoed. *Wenonah* dropped a single depth charge in the vicinity of the sinking ship then busied herself with rescue operations. She dropped rafts and buoys for the survivors of SS *Messidor* and returned to her station with the convoy.

Several hours later, just before 0100 on the 24th as she zigzagged on patrol astern of the convoy, *Wenonah* spied a flare ahead and learned that another unit of the convoy, SS *Rutherglen*, had also run afoul of an enemy torpedo and was settling slowly by the stern. She dropped a single depth charge near the sinking ship, but it failed to detonate. After her inauspicious antisubmarine maneuver, the yacht turned to rescue work and, by 0123, had taken 38 survivors on board.

After a lull during the daylight hours of the 24th, action resumed that evening. Just before 2100, she made another unsuccessful attack on a suspected submarine contact. Again, her British depth charge failed to function. Near chaos followed on the heels of that attack. Almost immediately every ship in the convoy began to steer various courses to avoid the unseen "enemy." For almost an hour, they cruised the area in a highly disorganized manner, firing guns and dropping depth charges at almost anything that suggested the presence of a U-boat.

Finally, at 2150, the convoy reformed and moved off in some semblance of order. Two alarms occurred that night; and, during the second, *Wenonah* fired a single 3-inch shell at what proved to be a porpoise. Save for another porpoise masquerading as a U-boat the following day, the excitement abated, and the convoy completed the voyage in a more routine fashion.

A week after the armistice, *Wenonah* made a trip from Gibraltar to Lisbon, Portugal, and back. Then, on 7 December, she departed Gibraltar to return to the United States. Steaming in company with *Druid* (SP–321), *Wheeling* (Gunboat No. 14), and the Coast Guard cutter *Yamacraw*, she stopped first at Ponta Delgada. Then, on her way from the Azores to Bermuda, she lost her navigation officer overboard during a battle with a force 10 gale early on the morning of 23 December 1918. On 3 January 1919, the yacht entered port at New London, Conn. On 14 March, she moved to the New York Navy Yard, where she was placed out of commission on 12 April and transferred to the United States Coast and Geodetic Survey. The yacht served with that agency on the west coast until October 1922 when the Department of Commerce returned her to the Navy in the custody of the Commandant, 13th Naval District. *Wenonah* was reinstated on the Navy list and received the hull designation PY–11 on 22 September 1923. However, the yacht remained inactive; and her name was again struck from the Navy list on 20 January 1928. The yacht was sold to H. W. Goodall of Santa Barbara, Calif., on 15 May 1929.

II

(YT–148: dp. 218; l. 100'0"; b. 25'0"; dr. 9'7" (f.); s. 12 k. (tl.); cpl. 12; cl. *Woban*)

Wenonah (YT–148)—a harbor tug constructed during the winter of 1940 and 1941 at Morris Heights, N.Y., by the Consolidated Shipbuilding Corp.—was placed in service soon after her completion in June of 1941. *Wenonah* served in the 11th Naval District throughout her entire Navy career. She was initially based at San Diego; but, during her 33 years of service, she also operated at and visited various other ports on the California coast. On 15 May 1944, she was redesignated a large harbor tug with the hull designation, YTB–148. Some 18 years later, she again changed designation and became YTM–148, a medium harbor tug. In April 1974, she concluded her long career and went out of service. Her name was struck from the Navy list, and she was sold for scrapping. The identity of her purchaser is unrecorded.

Wesson

Morgan Wesson—born on 19 December 1918 in Longmeadow, Mass.—was commissioned an ensign in the United States Naval Reserve on 17 June 1941. He reported to the United States Naval Academy, Annapolis, Md., on 19 August 1941 for instruction in communications. Upon completion of that training, he reported to the Federal Shipbuilding and Dry Dock Company, Kearny, N.J., on 29 December 1941 for duty in connection with fitting out *Atlanta* (CL–51). After that cruiser was placed in commission, he served in her and was promoted to lieutenant (junior grade) on 15 June 1942. He was killed in action when *Atlanta* was sunk in the Battle of the Solomon Islands on 13 November 1942.

(DE–184: dp. 1,240; l. 306'0"; b. 36'7"; dr. 11'8"; s. 20.9 k.; cpl. 216; a. 3 3", 2 40mm., 8 20mm., 2 dct., 8 dcp., 1 dcp. (hh.), 3 21" tt.; cl. *Cannon*)

Wesson (DE–184) was laid down on 29 July 1943 at Newark, N.J., by the Federal Shipbuilding and Drydock Co.; launched on 17 October 1943; sponsored by Mrs. Eleanor Wesson; and commissioned on 11 November 1943, Comdr. H. Reich in command.

Wesson departed New York on 28 November for shakedown off Bermuda. She returned to New York on 28 December 1943 for post-shakedown availability which lasted until 9 January 1944 when she sailed for the Canal Zone. After transiting the Panama Canal, *Wesson* departed Balboa on the 19th, bound for Hawaii in company with *Riddle* (DE–185), and arrived at Pearl Harbor on 1 February. Following minor repairs and training exercises, the destroyer escort joined the screen of a westward-bound convoy. On 18 February, the convoy split; and *Wesson* headed for Kwajalein Atoll in the Marshall Islands. She arrived at Roi the following day and began patrolling the entrance to the harbor. On 22 February, *Wesson* sighted and fired upon a Japanese cutter, killing six of the enemy and bringing five prisoners on board. She later turned them over to the island commander at Roi.

The destroyer escort set course for Majuro, also in the Marshalls, on 4 March 1944 and, in company with *Steele* (DE–8), sailed for Oahu three days later, screening *Cambria* (APA–36). *Wesson* arrived at Pearl Harbor on 13 March and spent a week there undergoing minor repairs and receiving fuel, stores, and provisions. On 20 March, she got underway to escort SS *Meteor* to the Gilbert Islands and arrived at Tarawa on the 31st. After a one-day stop, *Wesson* again set her course for Hawaii as an escort for *Pecos* (AO–65). She arrived at Pearl Harbor on 10 April and conducted torpedo and antisubmarine exercises until 29 April when she received orders sending her to Majuro as an escort for *Preble* (DM–20).

Wesson returned to Hawaii on 13 May and received repairs and conducted antisubmarine exercises before getting underway on 27 May to escort a convoy to Majuro. Having moored at Majuro harbor on 3 June, *Wesson* departed three days later for a rendezvous with Task Group (TG) 58.1 to conduct fueling operations. On 12 June, she made rendezvous with *Copahee* (CVE–12) and *Evans* (DD–552); and, two days later, the destroyer escort took position in the screen while fueling operations were in progress. She continued to support fueling operations until 16 June when she set her course for Eniwetok Atoll in the Marshall Islands. After a brief stop there, the ship received orders to make a round-trip voyage to the Marianas and back, escorting three oilers. She returned to Eniwetok on 11 July and, five days later, put to sea to support several fuelings and mail transfers. On 31 July, *Wesson* arrived off Saipan Island screening *Patuxent* (AO–44).

On 1 August 1944, *Wesson* steamed for the Marshalls and arrived at Eniwetok on 5 August for upkeep and availability. From 29 to 30 August, the ship was drydocked to repaint her underwater hull. On 2 September, *Wesson* got underway to rendezvous with *Sitkoh Bay* (CVE–86) and *Barnes* (CVE–20) and proceed in company with the escort carriers to Manus in the Admiralty Islands. The force arrived at Seeadler Harbor, Manus, on 10 September and, four days later, sortied for a rendezvous off the Palau Islands in the Western Carolines. During flight operations, *Wesson* rescued three airmen who had crashed upon launching. The destroyer escort screened *Sitkoh Bay* as the escort carrier headed back to the Admiralty Islands for repairs to her catapult. On 22 September, she and *Mitchell* (DE–43) left Seeadler Harbor, Manus Island, escorting *Guadalupe* (AO–32) to a fueling area in the Palau Islands; but, on 29 September, *Wesson* received orders to return to Manus.

The first three days of October found *Wesson* anchored in Seeadler Harbor. On the 4th, she got underway as part of a task unit centered around *Nehenta Bay* (CVE–74), *Steamer Bay* (CVE–87), *Sitkoh Bay* (CVE–86), and *Nassau* (CVE–16). During fueling operations in the Philippine Sea, *Wesson* assumed plane guard duty. On 22 October—two days after American forces returned to the Philippine Islands with landings on Leyte—*Wesson* got underway to escort *Sitkoh Bay* to Manus, and they arrived back in Seeadler Harbor on 26 October. *Wesson* remained there undergoing availability for the remainder of the month.

On 1 November 1944, the ship left the Admiralties to escort *Armadillo* (IX–111) to Ulithi Atoll, where she arrived on 5 November. After conducting firing practice and fueling exercises, *Wesson* departed Ulithi on the 16th with a group of oilers to rendezvous with the fast carrier Task Force (TF) 38 for fueling in the western Philippine Sea. Following the successful conclusion of that operation, the destroyer escort returned to Ulithi on 29 November. On 10 December, *Wesson*, as part of a supply group, again made rendezvous with TF 38 for fueling and aircraft replacement. On 20 December, the destroyer escort received orders to escort *Kwajalein* (CVE–98) to Guam and, after completing that task, returned to Ulithi and spent the remainder of 1944 in drydock for repairs to her sonar gear.

During the first week of January 1945, *Wesson* underwent repairs and inspections. On the 7th, the ship got underway, with a task unit consisting of five oilers and three escorts, for a rendezvous east of the Philippines. On the 13th, *Wesson* proceeded to Leyte Gulf to procure charts and instructions. The next day, she received orders to escort *Housatonic* (AO–35) to the Lingayen Gulf off Luzon. On 15 January, having been detached from the oiler, *Wesson* returned to San Pedro Bay, Leyte. On the 19th, she got underway to escort *Housatonic* to Ulithi. After screening the oiler's entrance into Mugai Channel on 26 January, the destroyer proceeded independently to Ulithi Atoll and remained there into February.

On the 5th, *Wesson*—as part of Escort Division 44—set her course for the Marianas and made stops at Apra Harbor, Guam; Saipan; and Tanapag. The ship then departed the Marianas for duty supporting the invasion of Iwo Jima. On 16 February, the carriers began air strikes against the island. The destroyer escort served in the screen protecting the carriers for 10 days. She then returned to Ulithi Atoll and, on 21 March, got underway to escort TF 54 to Okinawa. The ship arrived off Kerama Retto on 25 March and took station in a circular screen. The next day, *Wesson* and *Barton* (DD–599) helped to protect *Tennessee* (BB–43), *Nevada* (BB–36), *Birmingham* (CL–62), *St. Louis* (CL–49), and *Wichita* (CA–45) while they shelled southern Okinawa.

On 26 March, *Wichita* sighted a torpedo wake and a periscope. After *Wesson* maneuvered and dropped a 13 depth charge pattern, an antisubmarine patrol plane observed an oil slick. However, no other evidence appeared to confirm that an enemy submarine had been destroyed or damaged. The next day, the formation came under attack by Japanese planes. *Wesson* fired at three of the raiders; and one plane took several hits in the fuselage just above the wing before bursting into flame and crashing astern of the screen. Enemy air attacks continued for the next two days. On 30 March, *Wesson* proceeded on orders west of Zampa Misaki and destroyed four mines by gunfire en route. She then reported mines in an unswept area north and east of Zampa Misaki. Her formation came under air attack every day until 5 April. The next day at 0307, the enemy struck with a sizeable formation of planes, and the action continued incessantly until dawn. From 1400 to 1800, there were so many enemy planes darting in and out of clouds that the ship maneuvered continuously in tight turns of up to 180 degrees. Scattered clouds provided the enemy planes with extremely effective cover. All enemy planes were considered to be suiciders. One plane attacked *Wesson* but was turned back by repeated fire. It then attempted to crash into a destroyer on the port side but missed and splashed into the water.

On 7 April, *Wesson* relieved *Sterett* (DD–407) north of Ie Shima and the Motobu Peninsula and took station screening *LCI–452* and *LCI–558*. At 0340, the destroyer escort fought off a small enemy air attack which lasted until dawn. At 0917, *Wesson* opened fire on three enemy planes crossing her bow and then engaged a plane diving from the clouds to starboard. The plane crashed into the destroyer escort's torpedo tubes amidships. Five men died instantly, one was missing, and 25 were wounded, two of whom died later. *Wesson* lost and regained power several times and suffered a fire on the boat deck, as well as flooding in the engineering spaces. All power was lost aft, propulsion was lost on the port shaft, and the rudder jammed full right. *Lang* (DD–399) came alongside and transferred a submersible pump and gasoline, then took *Wesson* under tow. The tow line parted at 1133, and *Wesson* steamed into Kerama Retto under her own power with *Lang* screening.

Despite enemy air attacks, the destroyer escort completed emergency repairs on 10 April. The next day, she got underway en route for the Marianas and arrived at Saipan on 17 April. A week later, *Wesson* sailed for San Francisco, where—from 17 May to 25 June—she received an overhaul while her battle damage was being repaired. On 3 July, the ship set course for San Diego and 10 days of refresher training before returning to Pearl Harbor on 21 July.

After conducting various exercises in Hawaiian waters through 14 August, the destroyer escort received orders to proceed, via Eniwetok, to the Philippines. She arrived at Eniwetok on 22 August; then escorted three attack transports to Ulithi and entered the lagoon of that atoll through Mugai Channel on the 28th. That same day, she pressed on for Leyte, escorting a convoy of eight ships. On 1 September, the convoy was dissolved; and *Wesson* proceeded independently into Leyte

Gulf. Four days later, *Wesson* departed San Pedro Bay, Leyte, bound for Okinawa and entered Buckner Bay on 8 September. On 16 September, *Wesson* and *Foreman* (DE–633) sailed to waters west of Okinawa to avoid a typhoon and returned to Buckner Bay the following day. On 20 September, *Wesson* set course for Japan and arrived at Wakayama, Honshu, two days later.

On 24 September 1945, the ship—with *Alvin C. Cockrell* (DE–366) and *Cecil J. Doyle* (DE–368)—got underway to screen a unit of TF 51 built around *Makin Island* (CVE–93) and *Santee* (CVE–29). *Wesson* took station in the screen operating in Kii Suido. After supporting two days of flight operations and exploding several mines, the destroyer escort returned to Wakanoura Wan after the task unit had been dissolved.

October 1945 began with *Wesson* and *McGinty* (DE–365) escorting *California* (BB–44), *Tennessee* (BB–43), *Makin Island* (CVE–93), and *Lunga Point* (CVE–94) to Tokyo Bay. On 7 October, the ship left Tokyo Bay and stopped at Kii Suido, Bungo Suido, and Okino Shima before arriving at Yokosuka, Japan, on 26 October. She returned to Wakanoura Wan before setting her course for Okinawa on 31 October. On 3 November, *Wesson* got underway for Naha Ho, then proceeded to escort two merchant ships and an Army transport to Jinsen, Korea. She returned to Buckner Bay, Okinawa, on 10 November, embarked passengers for Guam and Pearl Harbor, then sailed the next day, escorting the former *Stewart*, DD–224. *Wesson* took DD–224 in tow due to an engineering casualty and arrived at Apra harbor, Guam, on 17 November. Three days later, *Wesson* headed for Hawaii and arrived at Pearl Harbor on 28 November. There, she took on board passengers, pushed on, and arrived at San Diego on 6 December. *Wesson* transited the Panama Canal and reached Charleston, S.C., on 23 December where she spent the remaining days of 1945.

Wesson shifted to the inactive fleet berthing area at Green Cove Springs, Fla., to prepare for eventual inactivation. She was decommissioned there on 24 June 1946 and placed in reserve. *Wesson* was transferred to Italy on 10 January 1951 as *Andromeda* (F–592) and struck from the Navy list on 26 March 1951. In January 1972, she was struck from the Italian Naval Register and scrapped.

Wesson earned seven battle stars for her World War II service.

West Alsek

(Freighter: dp. 12,226; l. 423'9"; b. 54'0"; dph. 29'9"; dr. 24'2" (mean); s. 10.5 k.; cpl. 99; a. 1 4", 1 6-pdr.)

West Alsek—a single-screw, steel-hulled freighter built under a United States Shipping Board contract at Seattle, Wash., by Skinner and Eddy Corp.—was launched on 4 May 1918; acquired by the Navy for duty with the Naval Overseas Transportation Service; assigned Id. No. 3119; and commissioned on 4 June 1918, Lt. Comdr. J. S. Gibson, USNRF, in command.

West Alsek departed the Pacific Northwest on 15 June, with 7,067 tons of flour on board, for New York, where she arrived on 16 July. Soon after her arrival, she formed up with Convoy HB–8, eastbound for French ports, and got underway on 1 August. On the 15th, two weeks out of New York, German U-boats *U–90* and *U–107* singled out *Montanan* and *West Bridge* (Id. No. 2888), respectively, and torpedoed them—the former sank the following day, but the latter, after great feats of navigation and seamanship, reached Brest under tow on the 22d. Meanwhile, *West Alsek* and the remaining cargo vessels in convoy continued on to France —arriving at Verdon-sur-mer on 18 August—and unloaded their cargo before heading back to the United States.

Arriving at New York soon thereafter, *West Alsek* departed again on 27 October with a slow convoy for

Quiberon and Nantes, France. She remained at Nantes unloading her cargo from 15 November to 30 December 1918 before sailing on 30 December for the American east coast.

West Alsek reached New York on 19 January 1919 and was soon in line for demobilization. On 27 January, the cargo vessel was decommissioned and returned to the Shipping Board—in whose custody she remained until abandoned in 1933.

West Apaum

(Freighter: dp. 12,226; l. 423'9''; b. 54'0''; dph. 29'9''; dr. 24'2¼'' (mean); s. 10.5 k.; cpl. 81; a. 1 4'', 1 3'')

West Apaum—a single-screw, steel-hulled freighter built under a United States Shipping Board contract at Seattle, Wash., by Skinner and Eddy Corp.—was launched on 23 May 1918 and commissioned at the Puget Sound Navy Yard on 20 June 1918, Lt. Comdr. Thomas P. Dorris, USNRF, in command.

West Apaum departed Bremerton, Wash., on 27 June and sailed south to Arica, Chile, where she loaded a cargo of nitrates for transport, via the Panama Canal, to the United States. Arriving at Savannah, Ga., on 9 September, the cargo vessel proceeded to Hampton Roads where she made port on 10 October. Eight days later, *West Apaum* departed Norfolk, bound for France with a cargo of steel rails, rolling stock, and general Army supplies. Delayed by a stop at Halifax to repair a damaged propeller, she did not reach La Pallice until 22 November.

The war was then over, but the job of supplying the American Army in France continued. *West Apaum* unloaded her railway goods, took on 2,214 tons of return Army cargo, and got underway for home on 13 December. Arriving back in Hampton Roads three days into the new year, 1919, *West Apaum* made two more voyages to French ports. On her final trip, she transported airplane materials to the French and returned to New York on 11 July with 5,000 tons of Army ordnance material. Two weeks later, on 25 July 1919, *West Apaum* was decommissioned and returned to the Shipping Board, which retained custody of the freighter until abandoning her in 1933.

West Arrow

West Arrow—a single-screw, steel-hulled freighter built under a United States Shipping Board contract at Seattle, Wash., by the Skinner and Eddy Corp.— was launched on 23 May 1918. Although designated Id. No. 2585 and inspected by the Navy at the 13th Naval District for possible duty with the Naval Overseas Transportation Service, she was never taken over by the Navy.

West Avenal

(Freighter: dp. 12,200; l. 427'0''; b. 54'0''; dph. 29'9''; dr. 23'6'' (mean); s. 10.5 k.; cpl. 70; a. none)

West Avenal—a single-screw, steel-hulled freighter built in 1918 under a United States Shipping Board contract at San Francisco, Calif., by the Western Steel and Pipe Co.—was taken over by the Navy on 1 February 1919; designated Id. No. 3871; and commissioned the same day at San Francisco, Lt. Comdr. Franz Patterson, USNRF, in command.

West Avenal conducted one voyage for the Naval Overseas Transportation Service. She departed San Francisco on 17 February 1919 with a cargo of flour; transited the Panama Canal; and arrived at Norfolk, Va., on 4 April. The next day, the ship was placed out of commission and returned to the Shipping Board, in whose custody she remained until abandoned in late 1928.

West Bridge

(Freighter: dp. 12,200; l. 423'9''; b. 54'0''; dph. 29'9''; dr. 24'1'' (mean); s. 10.5 k.; cpl. 88; a. 1 4'', 1 3'')

West Bridge—a single-screw, steel-hulled freighter built under a United States Shipping Board contract at Seattle, Wash., by J. F. Duthie and Co.—was launched on 24 April 1918; acquired by the Navy on 26 May 1918; designated Id. No. 2888; and commissioned at the Puget Sound Navy Yard, Lt. Comdr. Mortimer Hawkins, USNRF, in command.

Assigned to the Naval Overseas Transportation Service (NOTS), *West Bridge* got underway on 10 June bound for the east coast with a cargo of flour. Developing engine trouble as she steamed toward the Panama Canal, the freighter put into Balboa, Canal Zone, for repairs which took until 4 July before she resumed her voyage. The ship reached New York on 16 July, replenished her fuel, and sailed for France with Convoy HB–8 on 1 August.

Escorted by *Noma* (SP–131) and French cruiser *Marseille*, the convoy plodded across the Atlantic. By

West Apaum (SP–3221) as delivered by her builders. "Dazzle" camouflage patterns were extensively used on warships and merchantmen alike during World War I for protection against submarines.

mid-August, the Allied ships entered the danger zone where U-boats had been highly active of late. In fact, two German submarines, *U–90* and *U–107*, were then lurking in the path of the convoy.

At 1740 on the 15th, *West Bridge*'s turbine broke down and defied all attempts at repair. As the ship dropped back within the convoy, Lt. Comdr. Hawkins notified the convoy commodore of *West Bridge*'s plight. He also signalled *Marseille* that his ship needed a tow.

Meanwhile, the convoy continued on its way, when suddenly—shortly before 1800 and four miles ahead of the now drifting *West Bridge*—German submarine *U–90* torpedoed *Montanan*.

At this juncture, Hawkins ordered general quarters and directed all hands to keep a sharp lookout, while also reducing the crew in the engine spaces to a minimum. *Noma* closed *West Bridge* and stood by the disabled freighter. On *Noma*'s orders, *West Bridge* darkened ship and prepared for the worst.

Meanwhile, *U–107* approached unseen and launched two torpedoes. One hit *West Bridge* forward near number 3 hold and the other amidships abreast of the engine room. A warning about torpedo tracks, shouted from the pilot house, was too late; and, almost simultaneously with the general alarm, the deadly "fish" struck their mark. The stricken freighter immediately took on water and commenced to sink, initially listing to starboard. Hawkins ordered "abandon ship," and the crew took to the boats. Hawkins and two crewmen remained behind until they felt sure that all the survivors were off and then joined the rest of the men in the water as waves began lapping over the gunwales onto the well deck.

Noma sped off in the direction from which the torpedoes had come and subjected the U-boat to a heavy depth charge barrage. The doughty patrol craft also sent out an "SOS" for *West Bridge*, since the shock of the initial explosion had disabled the freighter's wireless. In the interim, *West Bridge*'s boats pulled about one mile away from the sinking ship, where the survivors watched the ship slowly settle.

West Bridge remained afloat for the rest of the night, and the dawn revealed the cargo vessel extremely low in the water but on an even keel. *Noma* returned from her submarine hunt and signalled that help was on the way. She herself had just rescued the survivors of the torpedoed *Montanan*.

One hour later, *Burrows* (Destroyer No. 29) appeared on the scene and picked up *West Bridge*'s crew. A head count showed that four men were missing but turned up two women stowaways. After boarding *Burrows*, Commander Hawkins consulted with the destroyer's commanding officer and requested that he and his executive officer be allowed to return to *West Bridge* to determine whether or not the ship could be saved. Accordingly, they were boated back to the freighter and boarded her. They found that both her well decks were awash, her engineering spaces were flooded, and at least three holds were totally inundated. Deeming the situation hopeless, Hawkins advised *Burrows*' commander that to stand by the drifting hulk would only endanger the lives of *Burrows*' crew and of *West Bridge*'s survivors. Accordingly, *Burrows* proceeded for Brest, leaving *Smith* (Destroyer No. 17) to stand by the still floating *Montanan* (which soon sank) and *West Bridge*.

A volunteer work-and-salvage party from *Smith*, led by Lt. Richard L. Conolly, boarded *West Bridge*, while four tugs—two French, one British, and one American —set out from the French coast to assist. Soon thereafter, *Isabel* (Patrol Yacht No. 10) joined the convoy which arrived at Brest on 22 August. After being towed 400 miles in this condition, *West Bridge* had made it to port with only one-percent bouyancy remaining!

After extensive repairs which were completed in March 1919, *West Bridge* served with NOTS until 1 December when the cargo vessel was decommissioned and returned to the United States Shipping Board. She

remained in the custody of that agency until abandoned in 1928.

West Carnifax

(Freighter: dp. 12,211; l. 427'; b. 54'; dr. 24'1'' (mean); s. 10.5 k.; cpl. 83; a. none)

West Carnifax—a single-screw, steel-hulled freighter built in 1918 under a United States Shipping Board contract at San Francisco, Calif., by the Southwestern Shipbuilding Co.—was taken over by the Navy for duty with the Naval Overseas Transportation Service; and commissioned at San Pedro, Calif., on 31 December 1918, Lt. Comdr. Robert H. Cowan, USNRF, in command.

West Carnifax got underway on 31 January 1919 bound for Norfolk, Va., with a cargo of foodstuffs. Transiting the Panama Canal soon thereafter, the cargo vessel arrived at Hampton Roads on 15 March. Four days later, she stood out to sea, bound for Europe.

While originally routed to Danzig, via Falmouth, England, and the Hook of Holland, *West Carnifax* was diverted to Hamburg, Germany, where she unloaded her cargo from 31 March to 2 April. The freighter returned via Plymouth, England, to New Orleans, La., on 5 May. On 9 May 1919, *West Carnifax* was decommissioned and returned to the Shipping Board, in whose custody she remained until acquired by the Export Steamship Corp., of New York, N.Y., in late 1927 or early 1928.

West Caruth

West Caruth—a steel-hulled, single-screw cargo vessel built under a United States Shipping Board contract at San Pedro, Calif., by the Southwestern Shipbuilding Co., and completed in 1919—was inspected at the 12th Naval District on 18 February 1919 for possible Navy use as a service collier. Although assigned the Navy identification number, Id. No. 3850, she was never taken over by the Navy.

West Cheswald

(Freighter: dp. 12,200; l. 423'9''; b. 54'0''; dr. 24'1'' (mean); dph. 29'9'; s. 10.5 k.; cpl. 60)

West Cheswald—a single-screw, steel-hulled freighter completed in 1919 at Porland, Oreg., by the Northwest Steel Co.—was inspected by the Navy at the 13th Naval District, deemed suitable for service as a naval collier, and assigned the Id. No. 4199. However, due to the fact that World War I ended long before the ship was completed, she was not taken over by the Navy.

Nevertheless, she did receive an armed guard detachment (Navy) during World War II, while under the ownership of the United States Maritime Commission's War Shipping Administration. This detachment received two battle stars for the ship's World War II service: the first for taking part in convoy runs to North Russian ports in the spring of 1942 and the second for participating in the Normandy landings in June of 1944. On 16 July 1944, she was deliberately sunk to form part of the breakwater off the San Lorenzo, France, beachhead.

West Coast

(Freighter: dp. 12,200; l. 423'9''; b. 54'0''; dph. 29'9''; dr. 24'½'' (mean); s. 10.5 k.; cpl. 99; a. none)

West Coast—a steel-hulled, single-screw freighter built under a United States Shipping Board contract at Portland, Oreg., by the Columbia River Shipbuilding

Co.—was launched on 6 July 1918, and commissioned on 9 August 1918, Lt. Comdr. Robert Crabb, USNRF, in command.

West Coast departed the Pacific Northwest on 15 August, bound for Chile to take on a load of guano. The ship burned out a thrust-bearing in her turbine, however, and was forced to put into San Francisco on the 17th for extensive repairs which lasted until 7 December. Meanwhile, the armistice ended World War I and curtailed the Allies' need for nitrates. Hence *West Coast*'s voyage to Chile was cancelled, and the cargo vessel was ordered to proceed via the Panama Canal to Norfolk.

She entered Hampton Roads on the last day of 1918 and sailed for France on 6 January 1919. Arriving at Bordeaux on 21 January, *West Coast* discharged her cargo, loaded 1,994 tons of Army return cargo, and got underway for the United States on 16 February.

The cargo vessel reached Newport News, Va., and unloaded. She departed Hampton Roads on 18 March and arrived at New Orleans on the 26th. After loading a cargo of cotton, she sailed on 3 April and returned briefly to Norfolk, before getting underway for England on the 10th. She unloaded her cotton cargo in Falmouth and Liverpool and departed the British Isles on 30 May.

Calling at Norfolk from 12 to 15 June, *West Coast* proceeded for the Gulf of Mexico and made port at Galveston, Tex., on 22 June. Four days later, the cargo vessel was decommissioned and her name struck from the Navy list. Returned to the Shipping Board, she remained in its custody until abandoned in 1933 or 1934.

West Cobalt

(Freighter: dp. 12,424; l. 423'9''; b. 54'0''; dph. 29'9''; dr. 24'2'' (mean); s. 10.0 k.; cpl. 78; a. none)

West Cobalt—a steel-hulled, single-screw freighter built in 1918 under a United States Shipping Board contract at Portland, Oreg., by the Columbia River Shipbuilding Co.—was taken over by the Navy for use by the Naval Overseas Transportation Service (NOTS); designated Id. No. 3836; and commissioned at Puget Sound Navy Yard, Bremerton, Wash., on 29 December 1918, Lt. Comdr. Andrew Patterson, USNRF, in command.

Following sea trials, *West Cobalt* sailed on 11 January 1919 for San Pedro, Calif., where she loaded a full cargo of grain consigned to the Northern Food Relief for a Shipping Board account. On 17 January, the cargo vessel got underway for Norfolk, Va., and arrived at Hampton Roads on 10 February. Nine days later, *West Cobalt* got underway for Danzig, via Plymouth, England, and the Hook of Holland. She soon discharged her cargo—the needed grain going to feed the hungry in the aftermath of the World War—and sailed for the United States on 8 April.

West Cobalt reached New York City on 24 April, was decommissioned on 5 May, and returned to the Shipping Board. Eventually purchased by the Lykes Bros., Ripley Steamship Co., Inc., and homeported at New Orleans, La., and Galveston, Tex., into early 1940, the freighter was then acquired by the British government. Renamed *Empire Miniver*, she was torpedoed and sunk on 18 October 1940 by *U–99*—the U-boat commanded by *Korvettenkapitän* Otto Kretschmer, who went on to become the top-scoring German submariner in World War II.

West Cohas

(Freighter: dp. 12,225; l. 423'9''; b. 54'0''; dph. 29'9''; dr. 24'2'' (mean); s. 10.5 k.; cpl. 73; a. 1 4'', 1 3'')

West Cohas—a single-screw, steel-hulled freighter built under a United States Shipping Board contract at Seattle, Wash., by the Skinner and Eddy Corp., and launched on 4 June 1918—was taken over by the Navy

for use with the Naval Overseas Transportation Service (NOTS); designated Id. No. 3253; and commissioned at the Puget Sound Navy Yard, Bremerton, Wash., on 29 June 1918, Lt. Comdr. W. F. Andrews, USNRF, in command.

Following her sea trials off the northwest coast, *West Cohas* sailed for Chile; loaded a cargo of nitrates; and departed the port of Arica on 29 July, bound for Charleston, S.C. Sailing via the Panama Canal, the cargo vessel unloaded at her east coast destination and proceeded on to Norfolk, Va., where she arrived on 25 September. There, she loaded a full cargo of Army supplies for the American Expeditionary Force in France and departed the east coast on 9 October. Making port at Brest on the 28th, she discharged her cargo and departed on 21 November to return home for further Army supplies. She conducted two postwar voyages to La Pallice, France.

Returning to Norfolk on 5 May 1919, *West Cohas* was decommissioned and returned to the Shipping Board on 9 May. She remained in custody of the Board until 1932 or 1933, when she was sold to the Lykes Bros., Ripley Steamship Co. *West Cohas* operated out of New Orleans into 1940, when her name disappeared from the various registers of merchant vessels.

West Compo

(Freighter: dp. 12,185; l. 429'9''; b. 54'0''; dph. 29'9''; dr. 24'½'' (mean); s. 10 k.; cpl. 88; a. none)

West Compo—a steel-hulled, single-screw cargo freighter built in 1918 under a United States Shipping Board contract at Portland, Oreg.,—by the Northwest Steel Co.—was taken over by the Navy on 3 February 1919 for duty with the Naval Overseas Transportation Service; designated Id. No. 3912; and commissioned at Portland on the same day, Lt. Comdr. Charles A. A. Modeer, USNRF, in command.

West Compo took on board a cargo of flour and sailed for the east coast on 12 February. The cargo vessel transited the Panama Canal on 1 and 2 March and reached Norfolk, Va., on 11 March. Three days later, she got underway for the Mediterranean and arrived at Trieste, on the Adriatic, on 9 April and spent the next 10 days discharging her cargo. She then took on sand ballast, got underway, and proceeded via Gibraltar to the east coast of the United States.

She arrived at Philadelphia on 15 May 1919 and was decommissioned on 22 May 1919. Returned to the Shipping Board, she remained in the custody of that agency until 1933, when she was abandoned.

West Conob

West Conob—a steel-hulled, single-screw freighter completed in 1919 at San Pedro, Calif., by the Los Angeles Shipbuilding and Drydock Co.—was inspected by the Navy in the 12th Naval District for possible naval service. However, although the ship was assigned the Navy identification number Id. No. 4033, she was never taken over by the Navy.

Instead, *West Conob* entered merchant service—first with the United States Shipping Board and then with the United States Maritime Commission after that agency's establishment in the 1930's. Operated by the Matson Navigation Line, which renamed her *Golden Eagle* in 1934 and *Mauna Loa* in 1940, the ship was chartered by the War Department on 18 November 1941 to carry supplies to Manila.

Re-routed to Australian waters as the Japanese invasion of the Philippines had made the islands untenable, *Mauna Loa* subsequently arrived at Brisbane. Then, when ordered to Port Darwin, the ship's master filed a protest with the American consul in Brisbane and got underway, "under protest." The freighter loaded elements of the United States Army 148th Field Artillery Regiment and sailed in convoy on 15 February

West Conob (SP-4033) in the color scheme of her postwar mercantile service.

1942 for Timor with three other merchantmen and four escorts.

The Japanese soon pin-pointed the convoy's position through the persistent efforts of a four-engined flying boat—a "Mavis"—which spotted the convoy on the day they sailed. Before drawing away, the "Mavis" dropped a stick of bombs, all of which missed. Another "Mavis" returned the next day, continued the snooping, and called for more help. It soon arrived, in the form of 36 twin-engined bombers and nine flying boats from Kendari in the recently secured Celebes.

Houston (CA-30) put up a terrific barrage of anti-aircraft fire which, to one eyewitness, resembled "a sheet of flame." So effective was Houston's gunnery, that the Japanese succeeded in making only one hit —on Mauna Loa. Two men were wounded—one of whom later died.

In the meantime, a lightning-quick thrust by the Japanese resulted in the fall of Timor. Its mission thus aborted, the Allied convoy was turned back to Port Darwin, where it arrived on the 18th.

The return of the convoy had strained the port facilities, as its premature return had not been expected. Thus, Port Darwin, primitive in terms of port facilities and communications but singularly important as the northernmost Allied base of any size on the Australian continent, lay as an inviting target to the rampaging Japanese.

Accordingly, a heavy air strike arrived over Darwin on the morning of 19 February. Allied sources claim that some 108 enemy planes took part in the raid; Japanese records state that the number was 188— the entire air group strength of four Japanese carriers under the command of Vice Admiral Chuichi Nagumo. The attackers scattered the defending P-40 fighters and, unhampered by relatively ineffective gunfire from the ships and port defense guns, laid waste to much of the port, sinking eight ships and damaging nine. Mauna Loa was struck by two bombs which broke her back. The crew abandoned ship without loss, leaving her to sink in Darwin harbor.

West Corum

(Freighter: dp. 12,424; l. 424'; b. 54'; dr. 24'0" (mean) ; s. 10 k.; cpl. 82; a. none)

West Corum—a steel-hulled, single-screw freighter built under a United States Shipping Board contract at Portland, Oreg., by the Columbia River Shipbuilding Corp.—was taken over by the Navy on 10 February 1919; and commissioned that same day, Lt. Comdr. Alfred G. Thompson, USNRF, in command.

West Corum departed the Pacific Northwest on 24 February, bound for the east coast with a cargo of flour. She transited the Panama Canal and arrived in Hampton Roads on 19 March. The cargo ship then proceeded on to the Near East; arrived at Constantinople, Turkey, on 18 April; and unloaded her cargo.

She got underway again on 1 May and headed home via Gibraltar. Arriving at Norfolk on 6 June, the ship was placed out of commission on 9 June 1919 and returned to the Shipping Board the same day. She operated under the Board's flag until scrapped in 1949.

West Cressey

(Freighter: dp. 12,225; l. 423'9"; b. 54'0"; dph. 29'9"; dr. 23'2" (mean) ; s. 11 k.; cpl. 81; a. none)

West Cressey—a single-screw, steel-hulled cargo freighter completed in 1918 under a United States Shipping Board contract (Government hull 36) at Seattle, Wash., by the Skinner and Eddy Corp.—was taken over by the Navy on 17 December 1918 and commissioned on the same day at the Puget Sound Navy Yard, Lt. Comdr. Charles Lyons, USNRF, in command.

West Cressey soon loaded a cargo of flour for shipment to the Near East and got underway for the east coast on 12 January 1919. Proceeding via the Panama Canal, she arrived at Norfolk, Va., on 2 February. Following alterations and repairs, the ship sailed 10 days later for the Mediterranean.

Calling at Gibraltar en route, West Cressey reached Constantinople, Turkey, on 10 March and discharged her cargo. After taking on board a large quantity of opium to be used for medicinal purposes and filling out her cargo with tobacco, the cargo vessel headed home on 27 March and was moored at New York City on 28 April.

West Cressey was decommissioned on 13 May 1919 and returned to the Shipping Board. She remained in the custody of this agency until abandoned in 1933.

West Ekonk

(Freighter: dp. 12,225; l. 423'9''; b. 54'0''; dph. 29'9'';
dr. 24'2¼'' (mean); s. 11.5 k.; cpl. 107; a. 1 5'',
1 3'')

West Ekonk—a steel-hulled, single-screw cargo vessel
built under a United States Shipping Board contract at
Seattle, Wash., by the Skinner and Eddy Corp.—was
launched on 22 June 1918; was taken over by the Navy
on 13 July 1918 for use by the Naval Overseas Transportation Service (NOTS); assigned Id. No. 3313; and
commissioned at Seattle on the same day, Lt. Richard
Willowden, USNRF, in command.

West Ekonk sailed for Port Costa on 24 July with a
cargo of flour—en route, via the Panama Canal, to the
east coast. The cargo ship reached New York on 27
August and soon joined an east-bound convoy for
France. Departing New York on 5 September, she
arrived at Brest on 19 September, discharged her
cargo, and headed home on the 30th. The ship subsequently conducted two cargo-carrying voyages for
NOTS to Genoa, Italy, with goods consigned to the
Italian government. While en route to the Mediterranean on the first of these two voyages, *West Ekonk*
was at sea when the armistice, ending hostilities in
World War I, was signed on 11 November. Returning
to New York from the second voyage on 3 April 1919,
West Ekonk was decommissioned on 9 April 1919.

Returned to the Shipping Board the same day, the
freighter was subsequently sold to the Lykes Brothers
and Ripley Steamship Co., Inc., and homeported at
Houston, Tex. Acquired by the British government and
renamed *Empire Wildebeeste*, the freighter was torpedoed and sunk by *U-106* in the North Atlantic at
39°30'N/59°54'W on 24 January 1942. *Lang* (DD-399)
—dispatched from Bermuda—subsequently rescued 34
survivors from the sunken freighter.

West Elcajon

(Freighter: dp. 12,225; l. 423'9''; b. 54'0''; dph. 29'
9''; dr. 24'2'' (mean); s. 11.5 k.; cpl. 70; a. none)

West Elcajon—a steel-hulled, single-screw freighter
built in 1918 under a United States Shipping Board
contract at Seattle, Wash., by the Skinner and Eddy
Corp.—was taken over by the Navy for duty with the
Naval Overseas Transportation Service (NOTS) and
commissioned at the Puget Sound Navy Yard, Bremerton, Wash., on 18 January 1919, Lt. Comdr. Roy W.
Look, USNRF, in command.

West Elcajon sailed on 1 February for Norfolk, Va.,
laden with 7,282 tons of flour consigned to the United
States Food Administration for transport to the needy
hungry left in the aftermath of the World War. The
ship proceeded through the Panama Canal and arrived
at Hampton Roads on 5 March. She moved to Baltimore on the same day and replenished her fuel supply
for the transatlantic voyage to come. She got underway on 12 March, bound via Gibraltar for the Adriatic.
Arriving at Trieste on 8 April, she unloaded part of
her cargo. Shifting later to Palermo, Italy, she delivered the remainder of her cargo and sailed for New
York on the 26th.

On 15 May, *West Elcajon* arrived at New York and
was decommissioned 11 days later. Returned to the
Shipping Board, she remained in its custody until
sold to the Oceanic and Oriental Navigation Co. in 1928.
Homeported in San Francisco and renamed *Golden
Kauri*, the freighter served that company until hoisting
the flag of the Matson Navigation Line in 1939.

Renamed *Waipio*, the ship carried on in the freight
and cargo trade through World War II, still homeported in San Francisco. In 1946, the veteran cargo carrier again changed hands, this time to the *Compania
Paralos de Vapores, S.A.*, of Panama. Her name

changed for the third time, and she became *Paralos II*,
operating under Panamanian registry into the mid-
1950's when she ceased to be listed in merchant vessel
registers.

West Elcasco

(Freighter: dp. 12,200; l. 423'9''; b. 54'0''; dph. 29'9'';
dr. 24'2'' (mean); s. 11.25 k.; cpl. 70; a. none)

West Elcasco—a steel-hulled, single-screw freighter
built in 1918 under a United States Shipping Board
contract at Seattle, Wash., by Skinner and Eddy Corp.
—was acquired by the Navy on 23 October 1918 for use
with the Naval Overseas Transportation Service
(NOTS); designated Id. No. 3661; and commissioned
the same day, Lt. Comdr. Lt. T. Ward, USNRF, in command.

Laden with a cargo of flour, *West Elcasco* departed
Seattle on 31 October, bound for the east coast. After
stopping briefly at San Pedro, she transited the Panama
Canal and arrived at New York on 2 December. With
her cargo consigned to European food relief, she got
underway for Europe on 8 December and arrived at
Gibraltar on the last day of 1918. From the strait, she
proceeded to the Adriatic Sea and arrived at Trieste
on 11 January 1919. After discharging part of her
cargo there, *West Elcasco* shifted to Gallipoli, on the
Dardanelles, where she delivered the remainder of her
cargo. She then took on a cargo of depth charges and
headed home on 15 February.

After her arrival at Philadelphia on 7 March, she
shifted to Boston and loaded a cargo of foodstuffs for
France. She got underway on 8 April for France and
delivered her cargo after arriving at Verdon-sur-mer.
Returning from Europe, via New York, to Boston on 9
June, *West Elcasco* was decommissioned on 14 June.
Transferred to the Shipping Board on that day, the
freighter was sold in 1930 to the Mississippi Shipping
Co. and homeported at New York. In 1943, the United
States Army Quartermaster Corps acquired the ship
and renamed her *Major General Henry Gibbins*. She
served under that name until she disappeared from
vessel registers in 1949.

West Eldara

(Freighter: dp. 12,200; l. 423'9''; b. 54'0''; dph. 29'9'';
dr. 24'2½'' (mean); s. 11.5 k.; cpl. 84; a. none)

West Eldara—a steel-hulled, single-screw cargo vessel built under a United States Shipping Board contract in 1918 at Seattle, Wash., by the Skinner and
Eddy Corp.—was taken over by the Navy for use by
the Naval Overseas Transportation Service (NOTS);
and, on 23 November 1918, 12 days after the armistice
ended World War I, was commissioned at the Puget
Sound Navy Yard, Lt. Comdr. John P. Tibbetts,
USNRF, in command.

West Eldara sailed on 8 December for San Francisco, Calif., and entered the Mare Island Navy Yard
six days later for repairs to her steering gear. Four
days after Christmas, the cargo vessel got underway
from the west coast, bound—via the Panama Canal—
for the east coast and, on 14 January 1919, arrived at
New York. Laden with flour and lard, *West Eldara*
got underway for Europe on the 24th. Upon her arrival at Gibraltar, the cargo ship was routed on to the
Near East. On 12 February, she headed for Constantinople and on the 22d—Washington's Birthday—arrived
at that fabled city which sits astride the strategic
Bosporus.

After off-loading her foodstuffs, *West Eldara* returned via Gibraltar to the United States and arrived
in New York on 7 April. The ship loaded Army supplies and sailed on 16 April for a European voyage

which would take her to the Hook of Holland and to Antwerp before she reached Plymouth, England. She discharged the last of her cargo there before departing the British Isles on 12 May 1919. Arriving at New York on the 29th, *West Eldara* was decommissioned on 4 June 1919 and was returned to the United States Shipping Board on the same day. Sold to the A. H. Bull Steamship Co., Inc., in 1937 and renamed *Mae*, the freighter operated in merchant service out of New York. The onset of war in 1939 brought the specter of war again close to American shores; and, by late 1941, the United States was fully involved. Through these troubled years, *Mae* continued to ply the freight trade and steamed, unescorted on cargo-carrying missions. On her last voyage, her path crossed with that of German submarine *U–515*, off British Guayana. Commanded by *Kapitänleutnant* Werner Henke, that U-boat had already sunk five merchantmen. On 16 September 1942, *Mae* lurched and lost way under the impact of straight-running torpedoes from *U–515*. As the freighter took on water and settled, *U–515* surfaced, unlimbered her deck gun, and finished off the damaged merchantman with gunfire.

Western Port

Screw steamer *Western Port* was renamed *Wyandotte* (*q.v.*) on 14 June 1859.

West Florida

In September 1779, *West Florida*—a British sloop—was taken as a prize in "a very severe conflict" with the Continental armed schooner *Morris*—Capt. William Pickles, commanding—on Lake Ponchartrain, La. Oliver Pollock, the commercial agent of the Continental Congress stationed at New Orleans, subsequently fitted out *West Florida*, with the aid of the Spanish governor, Bernardo de Galvez, and commissioned her into Continental service. The sketchy records available indicate that the armed sloop operated against the small British forces in the gulf for a comparatively short time, under the command of the man whose ship first captured her, Capt. Pickles. In 1780, she was taken to Philadelphia, Pa., where she was sold as unserviceable.

West Galeta

(Freighter: dp. 12,287; l. 423'9"; b. 54'0"; dph. 29'9"; dr. 24'1" (mean); s. 10.5 k.; cpl. 70; a. 12 rifles)

West Galeta—a steel-hulled, single-screw freighter built under a United States Shipping Board (USSB) contract was launched on 4 July 1918 at Los Angeles, Calif., by the Los Angeles Shipbuilding and Drydock Co.—and was taken over by the Navy for operation by the Naval Overseas Transportation Service (NOTS) and assigned Id. No. 3330. After fitting out, *West Galeta* was commissioned on 4 September 1918 at the USNRF Training Center, San Pedro, Calif., Lt. Comdr. William H. Curtis, USNRF, in command.

West Galeta departed San Pedro on 8 September, bound for Chile. Less than a week out of port, she ran into a heavy storm with accompanying torrential rains and hurricane force winds that flooded some living compartments and caused minor damage to the entire ship. After effecting repairs en route, *West Galeta* arrived at Arica, Chile, on 3 October and shifted to the port of Mejillones on the 5th. There, she loaded a cargo of nitrates, completing that chore by the 11th. She transited the Panama Canal on 24 October and arrived at New York City on 4 November, just a week before the armistice ended World War I.

Unloading the nitrates—an ingredient used in the making of explosives—*West Galeta* hoisted on board 4,112 tons of "general cargo" at New York that included a deck load of cars and trucks. Departing New York on 30 November, the ship ran into a heavy storm shortly after noon on 6 December. Waves battered the lashed-down automobiles and trucks as the ship rolled heavily and deeply in the gale.

West Galeta, steaming alone, labored through the heavy seas in her battle against Neptune's fury, the ship's deck cargo shifting each time she rolled. Although the crew had attempted to lash down the wheeled cargo, the waves that continued to pound the ship over the ensuing days frustrated and nullified much of that effort. By the morning of 8 December, some of the automobiles were in such bad shape that they had to be jettisoned over the side by that afternoon. Aft, the cargo was reported to be "smashed to pieces." Forward, as the ship's log noted, the cargo was "in bad shape." Eventually, by late in the afternoon of the 9th, the storm gave some sign of abating. The weary crew finally succeeded in corralling the cars and trucks on deck—but not before a total of six had been lost in the seas and the remainder badly damaged.

Although somewhat battered and soaked but still afloat, *West Galeta* steamed into the Verdon Roads anchorage on the evening of 15 December. Shifting to Bordeaux soon thereafter, the freighter unloaded and prepared to take on board 3,086 tons of "return Army cargo." She spent Christmas and New Year's at Bordeaux. An interesting highlight of her stay was the posting of armed guards on her holds on 27 December to stop looting by the stevedores.

Departing Bordeaux on 8 January 1919, *West Galeta* arrived at New York City on the 28th. There she unloaded, subsequently loaded 4,626 tons of locomotives and "general cargo," and departed on 17 February for her second voyage to France. Arriving at Quiberon on 3 March, the cargo vessel shifted to St. Nazaire soon thereafter and unloaded there.

West Galeta departed St. Nazaire with 643 tons of return Army cargo and 1,600 tons of ballast, on 29 March, but was forced to put in to Brest after one blade from her propeller worked itself loose and fell off not long out of St. Nazaire. The cargo vessel remained at Brest from 29 March to 9 April undergoing repairs. Once seaworthy, she departed Brest on 9 April and arrived at New York on the 27th.

After discharging her final NOTS cargo, *West Galeta* was decommissioned, struck from the Navy list, and simultaneously returned to the USSB on 9 May 1919. She remained in government hands, laid up, until abandoned due to age and deterioration, in 1933.

West Galoc

(ScStr: dp. 12,186.5; l. 423'9"; b. 54'; dr. 25'2" (aft); s. 10.5 k.; cpl. 70; a. 1 5", 1 6-pdr.)

West Galoc (Id. No. 3347)—a freighter constructed for the United States Shipping Board in 1918 by the Los Angeles Shipbuilding & Drydock Co.—was acquired by the Navy on 21 August 1918 for duty with the Naval Overseas Transportation Service and was commissioned that same day at San Pedro, Calif., Lt. Comdr. Charles Clarkson, USNRF, in command.

Following trials, the steamer departed San Pedro on 24 September, bound for Arica, Chile. There, she loaded a cargo of nitrates and set course via the Panama Canal for the east coast of the United States. The ship arrived in Philadelphia on 31 October and delivered her nitrates. After repairs, she took on a general Army cargo destined for France. The freighter stood out of Philadelphia on 23 November and joined a transatlantic convoy. She arrived in Nantes on 9 December, unloaded, picked up an outbound cargo, and returned to sea on the 31st. The need for emergency repairs forced a stop at Gibraltar on 7 January 1919 and a week's delay before she could resume her voyage. *West Galoc* reached Baltimore on 1 February and immediately began preparations for a return voyage to France. After repairs and loading operations, she again sailed for Europe on 22 February. On 12 March, the freighter steamed into Verdon, France, and began unloading. At the conclusion of that task, she filled her cargo holds for return to the United States and left Verdon on 31 March. The ship arrived in Newport News, Va., at the end of a 17-day voyage. After unloading, she began preparations for demobilization. On 24 April 1919, she was placed out of commission and was returned to the United States Shipping Board. *West Galoc* served with the Shipping Board until 1931 when her name disappeared from all mercantile registers.

West Gambo

(Freighter: dp. 12,225; l. 423'9''; b. 54'0''; dph. 29'9''; dr. 24'2'' (mean); s. 10.5 k.; cpl. 103; a. none)

West Gambo—a steel-hulled, single-screw freighter built under a United States Shipping Board contract at Seattle, Wash., by Skinner and Eddy Corp.—was launched on 4 July 1918; acquired by the Navy on 20 July 1918 for use with the Naval Overseas Transportation Service (NOTS); designated Id. No. 3220; and commissioned the same day at Seattle, Lt. Comdr. H. E. Knight, USNRF, in command.

West Gambo departed Seattle on 30 July bound for Port Costa, where she loaded a full cargo of flour consigned to the Red Cross. After transiting the Panama Canal, she arrived at New York on 31 August. The ship sailed in convoy for Russian waters on 18 September and reached Archangel on 12 October. The cargo vessel was unloaded by 2 November and, on that day, headed via Glasgow, Scotland, for the United States.

She made port at New York on 13 December and was soon placed in line for demobilization. Decommissioned and returned to the Shipping Board on 17 January 1919, the freighter remained in the custody of that agency until sold to the Lykes Brothers Steamship Co. in late 1936 or early 1937.

Sometime in 1941, the British government acquired the ship and renamed her *Empire Hartlebeest*, in response to the island nation's need for merchantmen to replace ships sunk in the Battle of the Atlantic. On 20 September 1942, while steaming in company with Convoy SC–100, *Empire Hartlebeest* was torpedoed and sunk by *U–596*.

West Gate

(Freighter: dp. 12,185; l. 423'9''; b. 54'; dph. 29'9''; dr. 24'1'' (mean); s. 10.5 k.; cpl. 74; a. 1 5'', 1-6pdr.)

West Gate (Id. No. 3216)—a steel-hulled, single-screw freighter built at Portland, Oreg., by the Columbia River Shipbuilding Corp., for the Cunard Steamship Line—was launched on 27 January 1918; taken over by the Navy for duty with the Naval Overseas Transportation Service (NOTS); assigned Identification Number 3216; and commissioned at Norfolk, Va., on 29 May 1918, Lt. Comdr. Alexander Watson, USNRF, in command.

West Gate loaded 6,700 tons of cargo at New York—locomotives, steel rails, and general Army supplies—and sailed in convoy on 28 June for France. She had not gone far before she developed engine trouble—a frequent occurrence in ships of her type—and headed for Newfoundland, for temporary engine repairs.

While steaming toward St. John's, through moderate seas and beneath a cloudy sky, *West Gate* came under attack by two German submarines at 1915 on 3 July. One U-boat broached dead ahead and crossed the cargo ship's bow to starboard, while the second *Unterseeboot* showed her conning tower one point to starboard as *West Gate* turned to port to evade the first enemy submersible.

Sending out a quick "SOS" on her wireless, the armed freighter unlimbered her main battery and opened fire. The speed and accuracy of the doughty cargo vessel's salvoes surprised the Germans—who perhaps had not anticipated such a hot and accurate reception. As the cargo ship's six-pounder and five-inch gun thundered and barked out shells which bracketed the pair of U-boats, the Germans wisely beat a hasty retreat and submerged, choosing to leave the fighting *West Gate* alone. Unmolested for the remainder of the passage, *West Gate* made port at St. John's at 1800 on 7 July.

Concluding her repairs by the 11th, the cargo ship again got underway for France and arrived at the Gironde estuary on the 22d. Three days later, she moved to St. Nazaire, discharged her cargo, and sailed on 21 August for Newport News, Va. Arriving off the Virginia capes on 10 September, *West Gate* shifted north to New York City to undergo major engine repairs later in the month. *West Gate* then loaded 7,187 tons of general Army supplies and got underway in convoy for Bordeaux on 4 October.

Escorted by *Denver* (Cruiser No. 14), the convoy ran into a particularly dark and rainy evening on the night of 6 October. *West Gate* steamed in the first column, to the starboard of guide ship *Sagua* (Id. No. 1627) with *American* (Id. No. 2292) astern off *West Gate*'s port quarter. Flashing side lights in the nocturnal gloom helped the ships to stay on station as best they could, but the task proved difficult in the murk.

At 0228 on 7 October, the officer of the watch in *West Gate* reported that her steering gear engine had jammed at hard-a-port. Putting engines at half-speed ahead, *West Gate* attempted to drop out of the convoy to effect repairs, as her chief engineer and his assistant went aft to ascertain the damage. Men on the bridge, however, soon sighted the tell-tale red light of an oncoming ship, *American*, on the starboard beam at 0230.

The bridge watch rang down "full speed ahead," but *West Gate* could not respond quickly enough to escape. *American*'s sharp stem cut deeply into the freighter's starboard side, aft, near her poop deck. Stopping engines and sounding "general quarters," *West Gate* settled and sounded "Abandon ship," as *American* backed away.

West Gate's crew now manned the boats while others voluntarily remained behind to insure that as many men as possible could get over the side. Wielding a flashlight, Seaman Bernard B. Sederquist, USNRF, led shipmates who had been asleep in an after berthing compartment to safety before he jumped to lifeboat number six. Belowdecks, Lt. Spencer, USNRF, the engineer officer, and Lt. (jg.) Hillery, USNRF, his assistant, remained in the machinery spaces until all others had left. The two men secured the boilers—putting out the fires and turning safety valves to prevent an explosion—before the bulkhead separating the after hold from the engine room gave way to the force of onrushing waters.

Spencer and Hillery both arrived on deck in time to enter lifeboat number two, which had been held until the last to accommodate its assigned occupants who manned the after gun and the engine rooms. Chief Gunner's Mate Wallrath stayed on deck as the last boat was lowered away, making sure that every boat had left the ship before he himself departed. Going over the side, he was pulled into boat number six, just as a wave capsized the craft and tossed its occupants into the water. Two men—one of them Seaman Sederquist—drowned before the remainder, including Wallrath, could be pulled from the sea by other boats. A later head count revealed that five more men perished in the tragedy—probably killed during the collision.

Meanwhile, as his men exhibited conspicuous heroism, the ship's commanding officer, Lt. Comdr. R. B. Vandervoort, USNRF, heroically remained on board until he felt assured that all men had gone over the side. He then climbed atop the amidships deckhouse to cut adrift a life raft and found six men huddled there. Vandervoort stayed with this group as the ship sank beneath them but was soon swept off by the vortex caused by the sinking ship and sucked under. Eventually struggling to the surface, Vandervoort, after clinging to floating wreckage for two hours, was picked up by the same raft from which he had been swept earlier. At 0600, the captain and the six men on the raft were rescued by a lifeboat from *American*.

West Gotomska

(Freighter: dp. 12,225; l. 423′9″; b. 54′; dph. 29′9″; dr. 24′1″ (mean); s. 11.0 k.; cpl. 70; a. 1 5″, 1 3″)

West Gotomska (Id. No. 3322)—a steel-hulled, single-screw freighter built under a United States Shipping Board contract at Seattle, Wash., by Skinner and Eddy Corp.—was launched on 17 July 1918; taken over by the Navy for use by the Naval Overseas Transportation Service (NOTS); assigned Identification Number 3322; and commissioned at Seattle on 7 August 1918, Lt. Comdr. C. J. O'Brien, USNRF, in command.

West Gotomska got underway on 17 August for Arica, Chile, and, upon arrival, loaded a full cargo of guano for shipment via the Panama Canal to New Orleans, La. Making port at New Orleans on 11 October, *West Gotomska* discharged her cargo of nitrates and loaded a full cargo of Army supplies earmarked for American troops. She sailed for France on 10 November and arrived at Quiberon Bay on the 25th. After unloading, she headed back to the United States with 2,100 tons of Army return cargo four days before Christmas of 1918.

Following her arrival at Norfolk, Va., on 6 January 1919, *West Gotomska* unloaded and took on board 5,182 tons of fuel oil and sailed on the 25th for La Pallice, France. Following this voyage, the freighter conducted a second run to La Pallice with Army cargo before returning, via the Azores and Philadelphia, to Hampton Roads, Va.

Decommissioned and struck from the Navy list on 6 June 1919, *West Gotomska* subsequently operated out of Seattle, under the aegis of the Shipping Board, into the 1920's and 1930's, when the Maritime Commission was established. Her documentary trail runs cold in 1942, and there is no record as to her final fate. One source does indicate, however, that the ship—armed and assigned a Navy gun crew—served in the arduous Russian convoy runs between December 1941 and February 1943 and, in fact, received one battle star for this service.

West Grama

(Freighter: dp. 12,225; l. 423′9″; b. 54′; dph. 29′9″; dr. 24′2″ (mean); s. 10.5 k.; cpl. 70; a. none)

West Grama—a steel-hulled, single-screw cargo vessel built at Los Angeles, Calif., under a United States Shipping Board contract by the Los Angeles Shipbuilding and Drydock Co.—was launched on 4 July 1918; was taken over by the Navy on 9 January 1919 at San Pedro, Calif., for operation by the Naval Overseas Transportation Service (NOTS); and was commissioned there on the same day, Lt. Comdr. Eugene McCarthy, USNRF, in command.

After boiler repairs at the Union Iron Works, San Francisco, *West Grama* loaded a cargo of flour and departed San Francisco on 28 January, bound for Norfolk, Va. She transited the Panama Canal on 14 February and, after a four-day layover in the Canal Zone, resumed her voyage on the 19th. Six days later, on the 25th, she sighted a waterlogged vessel, altered course to investigate, and soon found the half-sunken American schooner *Nettie Shipman*; *West Grama* passed close aboard, saw no signs of life, and continued her voyage, eventually reaching Hampton Roads, Va., three days later. After undergoing general repairs and

replenishing her fuel, *West Grama* got underway on 13 March and headed for the Mediterranean. She paused at Gibraltar before moving on to the Near East. She discharged part of her cargo of flour at Constantinople, Turkey, and unloaded the remainder at Varna, Bulgaria, before returning via Gibraltar to the United States. On the return passage, she carried a mixed cargo of 13 depth charges and 218 tons of miscellaneous items which she delivered after her arrival at Norfolk on 11 June.

Decommissioned there on 16 June, *West Grama* was returned to the Shipping Board that same day, and her name was simultaneously struck from the Navy list. After brief active service under the auspices of the Shipping Board, *West Grama* was laid up in reserve in the mid-1920's. She was later converted to burn oil fuel instead of coal and returned to active service in the late 1930's as a motor ship, under the auspices of the Shipping Board's successor agency, the United States Maritime Commission.

Armed and given a Navy guard detachment during World War II, *West Grama* supported the war effort into 1944 and received a battle star for her service during the Normandy landings in June 1944. After having apparently lived out her usefulness, the erstwhile NOTS cargo vessel and merchantman was sunk as a block ship at San Lorenzo, France, on 16 July 1944.

West Haven

(Freighter: dp. 12,191; l. 423′9″; b. 54′0″; dr. 24′1¼″ (mean); dph. 29′9″; s. 11.0 k.; cpl. 86; a. 1 5″, 1 6-pdr.)

West Haven—sometimes referred to as *Westhaven*—was a steel-hulled, single-screw freighter built as *War Flame* at Seattle, Wash., for the United States Shipping Board (USSB) and was launched by the Skinner and Eddy Corp. on 1 November 1917. The cargo ship was taken over by the Navy for operation with the Naval Overseas Transportation Service (NOTS); renamed *West Haven* and assigned Id. No. 2159; and commissioned at New Orleans, La., on 18 June 1918, Lt. William M. Tonken, USNRF, in command.

Laden with general Army supplies, *West Haven* departed New Orleans on 3 July and steamed to Norfolk, Va., where she joined a convoy sailing for Europe. She arrived at Bordeaux, France, on 12 August 1918 and unloaded her cargo over the ensuing days. She departed Bordeaux on the 21st and reached New York on 5 September. After shifting to Philadelphia the same day, the vessel there took on board 5,125 tons of general Army supplies before leaving that port on 17 September and moving to Norfolk, whence she got underway on 23 September in a convoy bound for France.

After discharging her cargo at Brest, *West Haven* departed that French port on 3 November. While the ship was steaming home, the armistice was signed on 11 November 1918 ending World War I. However, the return of peace did not change the ship's duties, as there remained the postwar task of reconstructing Europe which had been devastated by the war.

Following a brief layover in New York, *West Haven* loaded 7,075 tons of general Army cargo at Baltimore and sailed on 5 December, bound for France. The ship made La Pallice on 2 January 1919, discharged her cargo over the ensuing days, picked up a return Army cargo, and sailed for Norfolk on the 26th. En route home, she ran low on fuel and was forced to reduce her speed to three and one-half knots. She finally reached Bermuda on 28 February.

After topping off her bunkers, *West Haven* arrived at Norfolk on 4 March to load cargo for her third and last voyage for NOTS. Between 28 March and 12 April, she transported 673 tons of general cargo to La Pallice before picking up 2,306 tons of return cargo and 375 tons of steel rail ballast and departing French waters on 17 May, bound for home.

Soon after arriving at New York on 8 June, the ship was placed in line for demobilization. She was accordingly decommissioned on 21 January 1919 and simultaneously struck from the Navy list and returned to the USSB. Sold to the Los Angeles Steamship Co. in 1929, the ship was renamed *Marian Otis Chandler* and operated under that name until she was purchased by the Matson Navigation Line in 1939 and given the name *Onomea*. Acquired by the British Ministry of War Transport in 1940 to alleviate the shipping shortage caused by sinkings at the hands of German U-boats in the Battle of the Atlantic, the ship was renamed *Empire Leopard*. Over two years later, the erstwhile NOTS freighter was steaming from Sydney, Nova Scotia, in Convoy SC–107, bound for the British Isles, when she was torpedoed and sunk by *U–402* at 0803 on 2 November 1942, south of Greenland.

West Hobomac

(Freighter: dp. 12,225; l. 423'9''; b. 54'0''; dph. 29'9''; dr. 24'1¼'' (mean); s. 11.0 k.; cpl. 29; a. none)

West Hobomac—a steel-hulled, single-screw freighter built under a United States Shipping Board (USSB) contract—was launched on 27 July 1918 at Seattle, Wash., by the Skinner and Eddy Corp. Acquired by the Navy on 17 August 1918 for operation by the Naval Overseas Transportation Service (NOTS), *West Hobomac* was assigned Id. No. 3335 and commissioned on the same day at Portland, Oreg., Lt. Comdr. Peter F. Johnson, USNRF, in command.

Departing Portland on 26 August 1918 with 7,928 tons of coal in her holds, *West Hobomac* arrived at Iquique, Chile, on 23 September. She discharged her cargo there before loading 824 tons of nitrates for shipment to New York. Departing Iquique on 19 October, the freighter steamed north up the Pacific coast of South America, transited the Panama Canal, and arrived at New York on 8 November 1918, three days before the armistice was signed ending World War I. At New York, when the war ended, *West Hobomac* received repairs to her engines and steering gear; underwent alterations to her crew's quarters; bunkered; and discharged the nitrate cargo.

West Hobomac departed New York on 30 November, bound for France with a cargo of Army supplies, and arrived at Brest nine days before Christmas. The ship discharged her cargo there, loaded 226 tons of Army return cargo and additional ballast, and sailed on 18 January 1919 for home. After making port at New York on 6 February, the ship remained there for nearly two weeks, unloading and taking on board 6,392 tons of cargo for transport to Holland.

Reaching Rotterdam on 11 March, *West Hobomac* unloaded and departed that port, in ballast, on the 23d, bound for the United States. Following her arrival at New York, she loaded 5,252 tons of foodstuffs and relief supplies and sailed on 23 April for Belgium. She unloaded the cargo within four days of her mooring at Antwerp on 12 May and sailed for the United States on the 16th. Arriving at Newport News, Va., on 5 June, the cargo vessel was decommissioned there on 10 June 1919 and simultaneously struck from the Navy list and returned to the USSB for disposition.

The freighter remained active with the USSB, ranging as far as the Mediterranean Sea, until acquired by the Lykes Brothers, Ripley Steamship Co. in 1933. The vessel was acquired by French interests in 1940—but apparently operated under the British flag—and renamed *Ile De Batz*. Torpedoes and gunfire from *U–68* sank the freighter off the west coast of Africa at 0635 on 17 March 1942.

West Honaker

West Honaker—a single-screw, steel-hulled freighter built at San Pedro, Calif., by the Los Angeles Shipbuilding and Drydock Co., and completed in 1920—was inspected by the Navy on 13 December 1921 for possible use as a service collier. Although assigned the Navy identification number, Id. No. 4455, she was never taken over by the Navy.

During World War II, *West Honaker* conducted cargo-carrying voyages with a Navy armed guard crew on board and received one battle star for her operations between 5 and 24 June 1944 during the Allied landings on Normandy beachheads.

West Hosokie

(Freighter: dp. 12,100; l. 423'9''; b. 54'; dph. 29'9''; dr. 24' (mean); s. 11.5 k.; cpl. 70)

West Hosokie—a single-screw, steel-hulled freighter

West Hosokie (SP–3695) at Philadelphia, 11 March 1919. (NH48486)

built under a United States Shipping Board contract at Seattle, Wash., by Skinner and Eddy Corp., and launched on 15 August 1918—was taken over by the Navy for duty with the Naval Overseas Transportation Service; assigned the identification number 3695; and commissioned on 29 August 1918, Lt. Comdr. Charles A. Wilson, USNRF, in command.

West Hosokie sailed on 7 September for Arica, Chile, where she loaded a cargo of guano upon arrival and sailed for the Gulf of Mexico. Reaching New Orleans on 12 November, via the Panama Canal, the freighter got underway on 20 November for Newport News, Va. There, she was partially loaded with Army cargo earmarked for the American Army in France and proceeded to Baltimore where she finished loading prior to sailing for France on 15 December.

After unloading at Verdon-sur-mer, *West Hosokie*, laden with Army return cargo, headed home on 14 February 1919, paused briefly at the Azores for provisions and fuel, and pushed on to Philadelphia, where she arrived on 10 March. She then discharged the Army return cargo, moved to New York, loaded more Army supplies slated for French ports, and sailed for France on 10 April.

Discharging her cargo upon her arrival at St. Nazaire, *West Hosokie* took on board Army ordnance materials, sailed for home soon thereafter, and reached Newport News on 20 June. Placed out of commission and struck from the Navy list on 2 July, *West Hosokie* was turned over to the Shipping Board on the same day. She subsequently operated out of Seattle, on the freight-carrying trade, until acquired, late in 1928 or early in 1929, by the Los Angeles Steamship Co., of Los Angeles, Calif.

Renamed *Constance Chandler* when acquired by the Matson Steamship Line in 1934 or 1935, she was later renamed *Liloa* in 1938 or 1939. She served in Matson livery until 1944, when she was turned over, by the War Shipping Administration, to the Soviet government. Renamed *Belorussia*, her subsequent activities under the Soviet flag are unrecorded; and she disappears into figurative mists in 1955.

West Humhaw

(Freighter: dp. 12,225; l. 423'9"; b. 54'; dph. 29'9"; dr. 24'2" (mean); s. 11.5 k.; cpl. 94; a. 1 5", 1 3")

West Humhaw (Id. No. 3718)—a steel-hulled, single-screw freighter built under a United States Shipping Board contract at Seattle, Wash., by Skinner and Eddy Corp.—was launched on 28 August 1918 and was taken over by the Navy for use by the Naval Overseas Transportation Service (NOTS) at the Puget Sound Navy Yard, Bremerton, Wash., on 13 September. Assigned Identification Number 3718, *West Humhaw* was commissioned on 16 September at Seattle, Lt. Comdr. Arthur Ravens, USNRF, in command.

Loading a full cargo of flour, *West Humhaw* departed Seattle on 5 October, bound for the east coast. Proceeding via the Panama Canal, she arrived at New York City on the 31st and got underway for France on 12 November 1918. Reaching La Pallice two weeks later, she shifted to Bordeaux soon thereafter for unloading and sailed for home on 21 December.

Arriving at New York on 12 January 1919, *West Humhaw* was decommissioned on 27 January and struck from the Navy list and returned to the Shipping Board the same day.

Operating out of Seattle under the Shipping Board from 1919 and into late 1928 or early 1929, the freighter was then acquired by the American-West African Line. She carried freight for this New York-based firm through the 1930's and into World War II. While in company with Convoy ON–143, she was torpedoed and sunk by *U–163* in the North Atlantic on 8 November 1942.

West Indian

(Freighter: dp. 12,100; l. 423'9"; b. 54'; dph. 29'9"; dr. 24' (mean); s. 10.5 k.; cpl. 74; a. none)

War Indian—formerly *War Diamond*, a single-screw, steel-hulled freighter built at Portland, Oreg., by the Columbia River Shipbuilding Corp., for the Cunard Steamship Line, and launched on 27 February 1918—was taken over by the Navy for duty with the Naval Overseas Transportation Service; assigned Identification Number 3120; and commissioned at Portland on 22 May 1918, Lt. Comdr. Oliver P. Rankin, USNRF, in command.

Decommissioned on 5 September after defective propulsion machinery frustrated two attempts to sail for the east coast, *West Indian* underwent enough repairs to convince the Shipping Board that the ship was again seaworthy, and she was recommissioned at New York City on 7 November. Taking on cargo, *West Indian* sailed for England on 14 November and reached the River Clyde on 12 December. Discharging her cargo and loading a return cargo of 510 tons of Navy stores (as well as 530 tons of gravel ballast), *West Indian* headed for the United States on 28 January 1919.

Making port on 11 February, the freighter was decommissioned, struck from the Navy list, and returned to the Shipping Board on 1 March 1919. She operated on the freight trade under the aegis of the Shipping Board until her documentary trail runs cold in 1939–1940.

West Kyska

(Freighter: dp. 12,200; l. 423'9"; b. 54'0"; dph. 29'9"; dr. 24'½" (mean); s. 9.0 k.; cpl. 86; a. none)

West Kyska—a steel-hulled, single-screw freighter built in 1918 at Portland, Oreg., by the Northwest Steel Co., under a United States Shipping Board (USSB) contract—was taken over by the Navy for operation by the Naval Overseas Transportation Service (NOTS) and commissioned on 22 November 1918, Lt. Comdr. Henry J. Hobbs, USNRF, in command.

West Kyska made one cargo-carrying voyage for NOTS. Laden with 8,130 tons of flour in her holds, the freighter departed Seattle on 7 December 1918, bound for the Mediterranean. Proceeding via the Panama Canal to the east coast of the United States, the freighter stopped at New York for repairs from 11 January to 2 February 1919 before resuming her journey to Europe. Stopping at the Azores for fuel and at Gibraltar for onward-routing instructions, the cargo vessel arrived at Trieste, Italy, on 27 February. After discharging her cargo there, she returned to the United States in ballast, arriving back at New York City on 17 April.

Decommissioned on 3 May 1919, *West Kyska* was simultaneously struck from the Navy list and returned to the USSB. Remaining in government ownership until 1932, the freighter was subsequently owned and operated by the Waterman Steamship Corp., of Mobile, Ala., until again acquired by the government in 1944. She remained under government ownership for the second time until she disappeared from the merchant vessel lists in 1949.

West Lashaway

(Freighter: dp. 11,390; l. 423'9"; b. 54'; dr. 24'2"; dph. 29'9"; s. 11 k.; cpl. 70; a. none)

West Lashaway—a steel-hulled, single-screw cargo freighter built for the United States Shipping Board—was launched on 12 September 1918 at Seattle, Wash., by the Skinner and Eddy Corp.; acquired by the Navy on 30 September 1918; and commissioned at the Puget Sound Navy Yard, Bremerton, Wash., Lt. Werner Anderson, USNRF, in command.

Assigned to the Naval Overseas Transportation Service (NOTS), *West Lashaway* conducted sea trials off the northwest Pacific coast before she loaded 7,790 tons of flour and sailed for the east coast on 17 October. Arriving at New York, via the Panama Canal, on 11 November—the day upon which the armistice ending World War I was signed—the freighter underwent a few minor repairs before sailing for the Adriatic Sea. Departing New York City on 29 November, *West Lashaway* arrived at Trieste, Italy, three days before Christmas of 1918. There, she unloaded the cargo of flour and subsequently returned to New York City, arriving there on 30 January 1919, to undergo general repairs.

After simultaneously bunkering and loading 5,144 tons of Quartermaster's and YMCA supplies, the cargo vessel got underway for France on 19 February. Arriving at Nantes on 7 March, *West Lashaway* loaded return cargo—which included 300 tons of Army ordnance materials—and sailed for New York City on 20 March. Unloading and undergoing general repairs after her arrival at New York on 4 April, *West Lashaway* was decommissioned and struck from the Navy list on 12 April 1919.

Simultaneously returned to the Shipping Board, *West Lashaway* was eventually acquired under a bareboat charter by the American-West African Line, Inc. (Barber Steamship Lines, Inc.). She operated with this firm on the North Atlantic to West African trade routes through the 1930's. *West Lashaway* was torpedoed and sunk in the North Atlantic on 30 August 1942 by *U-66*.

West Lianga

(Freighter: dp. 12,191; l. 423'9''; b. 54'; dr. 24'1½'' (mean); dph. 29'9''; s. 11 k.; cpl. 113; a. 1 5'', 1 6-pdr.)

West Lianga—a steel-hulled, single-screw cargo freighter built under a contract with the United States Shipping Board—was launched on 22 April 1918 at Seattle, Wash., by the Skinner and Eddy Corp. Taken over by the Navy for use by the Naval Overseas Transportation Service (NOTS), *West Lianga* was commissioned at Brooklyn, N.Y., on 19 August 1918, Lt. Comdr. Louis Laverge, USNRF, in command.

West Lianga—designated Id. No. 2758—loaded 6,882 tons of general Army cargo and a deck load of 32 trucks at New York and got underway in a convoy for France on the first of what would be four voyages for NOTS. Arriving at Bordeaux, the freighter off-loaded her cargo and returned to the United States, making port back in New York on 16 October. Undergoing repairs there, the ship bunkered and took on 6,685 tons of supplies consigned to the Army Quartermaster Corps for transportation to Europe. Departing New York on 3 November, the ship was at sea on 11 November when the armistice—ending World War I—was signed.

The cargo vessel discharged her cargo at St. Nazaire and took on 1,700 tons of return cargo. She departed France five days before Christmas and arrived at New York four days into the new year, 1919.

Shifting to New Orleans soon thereafter, *West Lianga* subsequently transported cargo from that gulf port to Brest, France. She loaded steel rails and sand for ballast and returned to the United States, arriving at Newport News, Va., on 21 March. The cargo vessel took on railroad supplies consigned to the Army Quartermaster Corps and sailed for La Pallice, France, on 4 April.

West Lianga returned to the east coast on 10 June, when she made port at New York. On 24 June 1919, the Navy decommissioned the ship, struck her from the Navy list, and returned her to the Shipping Board.

Shifted to the west coast, *West Lianga* was homeported at Seattle for a brief period before being placed in reserve and laid up about 1922 or 1923. The Los Angeles Steamship Co. acquired the freighter in late 1927 or early 1928.

West Lianga retained this name until 1938 when the Los Angeles Steamship Company became the Matson Navigation Line. At that time, she was renamed *Helen Whittier*. Again renamed *Kalani* in 1940—while under the Matson house flag—the cargo vessel subsequently came under the ownership of the United Kingdom's Ministry of War Transport—in late 1941. Britain's urgent need for merchant vessels had resulted in her acquisition, and she served under the "Red Duster"—the British commercial ensign—into late 1942. During this time, she was twice renamed—first to *Empire Cheetah* and then to *Hobbema*.

While sailing with Convoy SC–107 from Sydney, Nova Scotia, to the United Kingdom, *Hobbema* was torpedoed and sunk by *U–132* during the predawn hours of 4 November 1942.

West Loquassuck

(Freighter: dp. 12,225; l. 423'9''; b. 54'; dph. 29'9''; dr. 24'2½'' (mean); s. 11.5 k.; cpl. 70; a. none)

West Loquassuck—a single-screw, steel-hulled cargo freighter constructed under a Shipping Board contract at Seattle, Wash., by the Skinner and Eddy Corp.—was launched on 21 September 1918. Taken over by the Navy for duty with the Naval Overseas Transportation Service (NOTS) and assigned the identification number Id. No. 3638, *West Loquassuck* was placed in commission at the Puget Sound Navy Yard, Bremerton, Wash., on 15 October 1918, Lt. B. I. Joyce, USNRF, in command.

West Loquassuck sailed for Chile soon after completing her sea trials to load guano for shipment to Charleston, S.C. Departing Iquique, Chile, on 4 December, she steamed up the Pacific coast of South America, transited the Panama Canal, and put into Charleston two days before Christmas of 1918. After discharging her cargo, she shifted to Savannah, Ga., to fill her holds with cotton. Underway for the British Isles, *West Loquassuck* made port at Falmouth, England, on 17 February 1919 and departed on 25 March. Returning in ballast to Boston, Mass., the freighter was decommissioned, struck from the Navy list, and returned to the Shipping Board on 17 April 1919. She remained under Shipping Board ownership until abandoned due to age and deterioration sometime in the latter half of 1933.

West Madaket

(Freighter: dp. 12,225; l. 423'9''; b. 54'0''; dph. 29'9''; dr. 24'2'' (mean); s. 11.5 k.; cpl. 94; a. none)

West Madaket—a single-screw, steel-hulled freighter built under a United States Shipping Board contract at Seattle, Wash., by the Skinner and Eddy Corp.—was acquired by the Navy for duty with the Naval Overseas Transportation Service (NOTS); designated Id. No. 3636; and was commissioned on 31 October 1918 at the Puget Sound Navy Yard, Lt. Comdr. B. U. Heald, USNRF, in command.

Completing her sea trials too late to see wartime service with NOTS, *West Madaket* sailed for the east coast one week after the signing of the armistice, on 18 November, laden with a cargo of flour consigned to European food relief. Voyaging via the Panama Canal, the cargo vessel arrived at New York on 16 December and departed three days before Christmas, bound for Europe. She made port at Falmouth, England, on 5 January 1919 and pushed on, that same day, for Rotterdam, Holland, where she busied herself discharging her 7,031 tons of flour until 23 January.

Returning to New York on 9 February, *West Madaket* loaded 6,841 tons of general cargo and conducted one more voyage for NOTS—to Verdon-sur-mer, France—before arriving back at New York on 28 April. Decommissioned on 8 May at Newport News, Va., and returned to the Shipping Board on the same day, *West Madaket* remained in the custody of that agency until the establishment of the Maritime Commission, and she continued with the commission on freight-carrying voyages into World War II. On 5 May 1943, while steaming with Convoy ONS-5, the venerable cargo vessel was sunk in the Atlantic by torpedoes from German submarine *U-707*.

West Mahomet

(Freighter: dp. 12,225; 1. 423'9"; b. 54'0"; dph. 29'9"; dr. 24'2" (mean); s. 11.5 k.; cpl. 76; a. none)

West Mahomet—a steel-hulled, single-screw freighter built under a United States Shipping Board (USSB) contract by the Skinner and Eddy Corp. of Seattle, Wash.—was turned over to the Navy on 13 November 1918 for operation by the Naval Overseas Transportation Service (NOTS) and commissioned the same day, Lt. Comdr. Raymond O. Demarest, USNRF, in command.

The cargo ship departed Seattle on 29 November with a cargo of 7,886 tons of flour. After proceeding via the Panama Canal, she reached New York on 28 December and sailed for the Near East on New Year's Day 1919. Upon her arrival at Constantinople on 5 February, she began discharging her cargo and then loaded 970 bales of tobacco and 1,470 tons of water ballast before getting underway for home on 5 March.

Following the discharge of her cargo at New York, *West Mahomet* took on board 5,513 tons of general Army cargo for transportation to Europe, got underway for Belgium on 26 April, and arrived at Antwerp on 12 May. Four days later, the ship headed back toward the United States; and she reached Newport News, Va., on 2 June 1919.

Simultaneously decommissioned, struck from the Navy list, and returned to the USSB on 3 June 1919, *West Mahomet* remained under government ownership into the 1930's, laid up for the latter part of that period. She was eventually abandoned, due to age and deterioration, in or near 1933.

West Maximus

West Maximus—a single-screw, steel-hulled freighter built at Seattle, Wash., by Skinner and Eddy Corp. in 1919 for the United States Shipping Board (USSB)—was inspected by the Navy for duty with the Naval Overseas Transportation Service and was designated Id. No. 3924; but she was never taken over.

Serving under the USSB and its successor, the United States Maritime Commission, *West Maximus* operated in the mercantile trade and eventually flew the flag of the Moore-McCormack shipping lines of Baltimore, Md. While in the service of this line, she operated into World War II as part of the vital lifeline of ships to Britain.

While filling this role, she left Milford Haven, Wales, in ballast on 23 April 1943 bound for New York with Convoy ONS-5. On the night of 4 and 5 May, the convoy ran into a trap set by an exceptionally large group of U-boats. German submarine *U-264* drew a bead on the lumbering merchantman and launched a torpedo which struck the ship on the port side, aft, at 2308. The missile blew away much of the stern, demolished the living quarters, aft, and disabled the after guns.

U-264 struck again at 0110 and at 0130 on the 5th. The latter attack gave *West Maximus* the coup de grace which sent her under, bow-first, at 0140. Of the 62 men on board, 56 were rescued by trawler HMS *Northern Spray*.

West Mead

(Freighter: dp. 12,175; 1. 423'9"; b. 54'0"; dph. 29'9"; dr. 24'11¼" (mean); s. 10.5 k.; cpl. 113; a. none)

West Mead—sometimes referred to as *Westmead*—was a steel-hulled, single-screw, coal-burning cargo vessel built in 1918 at Seattle, Wash., under a United States Shipping Board contract with the Ames Shipbuilding and Drydock Co. Inspected by the Navy in the 13th Naval District on 26 October 1918, *West Mead* was assigned Id. No. 3550 and commissioned on 29 October 1918, Lt. Comdr. N. A. Nelson, USNRF, in command.

Assigned to the Naval Overseas Transportation Service (NOTS), *West Mead* loaded 6,865 tons of flour, departed the Pacific Northwest on 15 November, and proceeded via the Panama Canal to New York where she arrived on 14 December after a stop at Balboa, Canal Zone, en route. She underwent a few minor repairs, bunkered, and sailed in convoy for the British Isles on Christmas Eve. *West Mead* made port at Falmouth, England, on 9 January 1919.

She shifted to Rotterdam, Holland, on the 24th, and there unloaded her cargo of flour. She sailed for home, in ballast, and arrived at New York on 3 March. *West Mead* then proceeded to Savannah, Georgia, where she took on board a cargo of cotton and lumber and got underway for her second voyage to the British Isles on 2 April. She reached Liverpool on the 21st, discharged her cargo there, and returned to Savannah, arriving on 7 June 1919.

Decommissioned on 9 June 1919, *West Mead* was simultaneously struck from the Navy list and returned to the USSB. Apparently operating under the name *Westmead*, the erstwhile NOTS ship wore the flag of the USSB until she was laid up in the late 1920's. Eventually acquired by the Babcock Steamship Co., and renamed *Willanglo*, the ship operated with that firm until about 1929, when she was acquired by the Pacific-Atlantic Steamship Co., of Portland, Oreg., and renamed *San Angelo*. In response to the need caused by German U-boat activity in the North Atlantic convoy routes early in World War II, the British government acquired a number of former USSB ships in both American private and government ownership; *San Angelo* was among them. She was carried on the *Lloyd's Register of Shipping* as belonging to the Ministry of Transport in 1940–1941 but disappears from the list thereafter. Her fate is unrecorded.

West Milton

A village in Saratoga County, New York—the site of an early nuclear reactor important in the development of the Navy's nuclear propulsion plants.

(ARD-7: 1. 485'8"; b. 71'0"; dr. 32'6" (max.), 5'1" (light); cpl. 112; cl. ARD-2)

West Milton (ARD-7) was originally built as the unnamed, steel-hulled, auxiliary repair drydock *ARD-7*. She was completed at the Pacific Bridge Co. works at San Diego, Calif., in June of 1943 and, by the end of the war in the Pacific, was in service at the Pearl Harbor Navy Yard. Capable of operating either at pierside or offshore, the floating drydrock of the ARD-2-class has a lifting capacity of some 22,000 tons and contains shops for matters ranging from hull repairs to welding and electrical repairs. On 18 May 1976, she received the name *West Milton*. As of late 1978, *West Milton* is serving the repair needs of the Atlantic Fleet.

West Mount

(Freighter: dp. 12,175; 1. 423'9"; b. 54'0"; dph. 29'9"; dr. 23'11¼"; s. 9.5 k.; cpl. 75; a. 13")

West Mount—sometimes referred to as *Westmount*—was a steel-hulled, single-screw cargo vessel built under a United States Shipping Board contract for the *Compagnie Generale* of France. Constructed at Seattle, Wash., by the Ames Shipbuilding and Drydock Co. and launched on 16 April 1918, *West Mount* was taken over by the United States Navy for operation by the Naval Overseas Transportation Service (NOTS), assigned Id. No. 3202, and commissioned at Seattle on 21 May 1918.

West Mount—with a cargo of flour in her holds—departed Seattle on 23 May, bound for the east coast through the Panama Canal. After arriving at New York on 2 July, the freighter underwent repairs and sailed for France on the 13th. She made port at Bordeaux on the 29th, discharged her cargo, and sailed homeward with 1,000 tons of iron ore. She arrived at New York on 9 October.

The cargo vessel commenced her second wartime voyage for NOTS on 24 October and made port at Brest, France, on 8 November. Three days later, the armistice that stilled the guns on the Western Front was signed. *West Mount* subsequently departed Brest on 12 December, spent Christmas at sea, and arrived at New York on New Year's Day, 1919.

West Mount remained there long enough to load a cargo of flour and milk consigned to the Food Administration and got underway on 22 January 1919, bound via Gibraltar, for the Near East. After reaching Turkey, *West Mount* delivered her foodstuff at Constantinople and eventually returned home with 2,785 tons of return cargo for the Shipping Board. She arrived at Phildelphia on 1 May.

Decommissioned there on 31 May, *West Mount* was simultaneously struck from the Navy list and turned over to the Shipping Board. Subsequently referred to in mercantile lists as *Westmount*, the ship remained under government ownership into the late 1920's, after which time her name disappears from contemporary merchant ship registers.

West Nilus

West Nilus—a steel-hulled, single-screw freighter built under a United States Shipping Board contract at San Pedro, Calif., by the Southwestern Shipbuilding Co. and completed in 1920—was considered for Navy service as a collier and assigned the Navy identification number, Id. No. 4445. However, she was not taken over and soon entered merchant service with the Matson Navigation Company of San Francisco, Calif.

During World War II, *West Nilus* was armed and received a Navy armed guard gun crew. She earned two battle stars for her participation in convoy and armed guard actions. The first was awarded the merchantman for her part in Russian convoy runs between December 1941 and February 1943. She won the second while operating with Convoy UGS–6 from 16 to 18 April 1943. *West Nilus* was sunk as a block ship off the San Lorenzo, France, beachhead, on 16 July 1944.

West Nohno

West Nohno—a steel-hulled, single-screw freighter built under a United States Shipping Board contract by the Northwest Steel Corp., of Seattle, Wash., and completed in 1919—was inspected by the Navy for possible use by the Naval Overseas Transportation Service. She was found suitable for naval service and was assigned the Navy identification number, Id. No. 4029. However, she was never taken over.

After a career in merchant service between the World Wars, *West Nohno* was armed and assigned a Navy armed guard gun crew. She received one battle star for her service between 5 and 25 June 1944 in support of the Allied landings on the Normandy coast of France. *West Nohno* was sunk as a block ship off the San Lorenzo, France, beachhead on 16 July 1944.

West Point

A military post in New York state, located on the west bank of the Hudson River below Poughkeepsie. West Point is the site of the United States Military Academy.

I

(Id. No. 3254; dp. 12,459; l. 423'0''; b. 54'0''; dph. 29'9''; dr. 24'1'' (mean); s. 10 k.; cpl. 124; a. 1 6'', 1 6-pdr.)

The first *West Point* (Id. No. 3254)—a steel-hulled freighter built in 1918 at Portland, Oreg., by J. F. Duthie—was acquired by the Navy from the United States Shipping Board (USSB) on 5 August and commissioned at Brooklyn, N.Y., three days later, Lt. Comdr. Horace A. Arnold, USNRF, in command.

Laden with 6,884 tons of general cargo for the Army in France, *West Point* departed New York on 21 August for her first voyage under the aegis of the Naval Overseas Transportation Service (NOTS). She arrived at Brest on the 7th and pushed on for Paulliac the same day to unload her cargo. Returning to New York on 23 October, she loaded 5,532 tons of general Army supplies and sailed on 4 November for Verdon-sur-mer, France. During the crossing, the signing of the armistice on 11 November ended the World War.

Arriving at Verdon-sur-mer on 23 November, she unloaded and headed for the east coast of the United States on 6 December. The ship subsequently made one more voyage with cargo for Europe. She departed Boston on 18 January; unloaded her cargo from 2 to 12 February at Brest, took on 1,620 tons of steel rails, and reached Newport News, Va., on 13 March.

Shifting to Boston soon thereafter, *West Point* was decommissioned on 24 April 1919 and returned to the USSB.

II

(AP–23: dp. 35,400; l. 723'; b. 93'3''; dr. 32'9''; s. 17.5 k.; cpl. 969; trp. 7,678; a. 4 5'', 4 3'', 8 .50-cal. mg.; cl. *West Point*)

America was laid down under a Maritime Commission contract (MC hull 1) on 22 August 1938, at Newport News, Va., by the Newport News Shipbuilding and Drydock Co.; launched on 31 August 1939; sponsored by Mrs. Franklin Delano Roosevelt, wife of the President of the United States; and entered service as the flagship of the United States Lines on 22 August 1940, when she commenced her maiden voyage.

Although initially slated for the North Atlantic trade, *America* was deployed instead on the New York to West Indies cruise routes, because the war in Europe had resulted in the invocation of the Neutrality Act banning American ships from trade in the war zones. She made several voyages to the West Indies and two to California into the spring of 1941. Hurriedly recalled from a pleasure cruise in late May 1941, *America* moored at Norfolk and was acquired by the Navy on 1 June 1941 for conversion to a troop transport. Renamed *West Point* and designated AP–23, the erstwhile cruise ship which had once been the "last word" in luxurious ocean travel, entered her builder's yards on 6 June for conversion. On 15 June, "in a brief and simple ceremony on the after sun deck," *West Point* was commissioned at Newport News, Capt. Frank H. Kelley, Jr., in command.

West Point soon proceeded to New York City and, while anchored off the Staten Island quarantine station on 16 July, took on board 137 Italian citizens and 327 Germans from the consulates of those nations in the United States which had been closed. *West Point* got underway at 1455 on the 16th, bound for Portugal, and arrived at Lisbon on the 23d. While there, the ship was visited by Portuguese naval and diplomatic dignitaries; and she transferred supplies to the Coast Guard cutter

Ingham, the "station ship" at Lisbon. After her final Italian passenger had been debarked on the 23d and the last German on the 24th, *West Point* commenced taking on 321 Americans and 67 Chinese—consular staffs and their families—on the 26th.

Returning to New York on 1 August, *West Point* discharged her passengers and headed south for an overhaul at Portsmouth, Va. She then participated in tactical exercises off the Virginia capes from 26 to 29 August in company with *Wakefield* (AP–21) and *Mount Vernon* (AP–22).

On 3 November, she sailed from Carolina waters and arrived at Halifax, Nova Scotia, on the 5th. There, on 8 and 9 November, she embarked 241 officers and 5,202 men of the 55th Brigade, Hertfordshire and Bedfordshire Battalions, and 100 men of an American Army Field Service company. On the 10th, *West Point*—in company with five other transports: *Wakefield, Mount Vernon, Orizaba* (AP–24), *Leonard Wood* (AP–25), and *Joseph T. Dickman* (AP–25)—got underway for India as Convoy HS–124. En route, they were joined by *Ranger* (CV–4), *Vincennes* (CA–44), *Quincy* (CA–39), and a division of destroyers.

Reaching Capetown on 9 December, *West Point* and *Wakefield* were detached on 23 December to form Task Group (TG) 14.1, while *Leonard Wood* and *Joseph T. Dickman* formed TG 14.2. Escorted by the British heavy cruiser HMS *Dorsetshire*, the convoy proceeded uneventfully toward India until 0700 on the 27th, when TG 14.1 was detached to speed up and arrive at Bombay ahead of the other ships.

Wakefield commenced discharging her embarked troops at 1900 at the Ballard Piers, completed her unloading, and shifted berths the next morning. *West Point* took *Wakefield*'s former berth while *Joseph T. Dickman* moored to unload her equipment and troops. Having completed her discharge by 31 December 1941, *West Point* anchored in the stream on the morning of 2 January 1942 and awaited further orders until 4 January, when British authorities asked Capt. Kelley, of *West Point*, if his ship and *Wakefield* could be brought under 30-foot draught to make passage for Singapore. Kelley responded that it could be done, but this would entail discharging ballast and expanding some of the ship's fresh water supply—thus endangering the ship's stability.

Due to prevailing low-water conditions at Bombay at this point, neither *West Point* nor *Wakefield* could go alongside piers in the harbor to either load equipment or troops. Thus, the embarkation and loading procedures had to be carried out by the tedious process of embarking troops and loading supplies from smaller ships and lighters brought alongside. *Wakefield* embarked—almost to a man—the troops which she had brought from Halifax, a total of 4,506, while *West Point* embarked two-thirds of the troops which she had transported, in addition to some which had come out in other ships. All told, she carried some 5,272 men.

West Point sailed for Singapore at 1300 on 9 January, in a "15-knot" convoy, with Capt. Kelley as the convoy's commodore. In addition to the two American ships, three British transports—*Duchess of Bedford, Empress of Japan*, and *Empire Star*—made up the remainder of the van. Escorted by British light cruiser HMS *Caledon* until this ship was relieved by light cruiser HMS *Glasgow* at 1630 on the 22d, the convoy's escort soon swelled to three cruisers and four destroyers as the convoy neared Java. Japanese submarine activities near the Indonesian archipelago prompted concern for the safe arrival of the valuable ships, hence a 200-mile detour through the shallow, coral-studded Sunda Strait.

Led by British cruiser HMS *Exeter*, the ships slowed to 10 knots, and, streaming paravane gear, began the passage. An escorting destroyer steamed between each transport, as they steamed in single-column order. It was a ticklish business, for the least divergence from the charted course could mean a disastrous grounding.

During the passage, Dutch Consolidated PBY Catalinas patrolled overhead. No enemy aircraft were spotted until 1152, when a lone Japanese plane passed over at six to eight thousand feet. It dropped a stick of bombs which straddled the ships at the rear of the column. Although the ships opened fire, the range had soon opened enough to make this return fire ineffective.

The screen's commander, Capt. Oliver L. Gordon, R.N., commanding *Exeter*, desired to arrive at Singapore with as many ships as possible by dawn on 29 January, and thus split the convoy up, sending the

The transport *West Point* (AP–23) in a form of light North Atlantic pattern camouflage. (80–G–71251)

faster vessels—*West Point, Wakefield,* and *Empress of Japan*—ahead at increased speed under escort of cruisers HMS *Exeter, Durban, Dragon,* and destroyers *Express* and *Electra.* Proceeding to Singapore via Berhala Strait, Durian Strait, and Philips Channel, the group steamed through these bodies of water in bright moonlight which made navigational aids unnecessary. Upon their arrival off Singapore, the ships lay to in an exposed position, beyond the range of shore-based anti-aircraft guns, until pilots could be obtained to bring the ships in. Since the naval base came under daily heavy air raids, the transports thence proceeded to Keppel Harbor—the commercial basin—where they could discharge their troops and cargo.

Securing abreast godowns (warehouses) 52, 53, and 54, *West Point* commenced off-loading equipment and disembarking her troops. All but 670 engineer troops—who had been ordered retained on board—were ashore before nightfall. Air raids, meanwhile, continued until midnight as the Japanese steadily pounded Singapore from the air. At each alert, the coolies working dockside would vanish, taking to the shelters and leaving the vital cargo still unloaded. As a result, the unloading was carried out by the crew of *West Point,* her embarked troops, and 22 coolies who were brought aboard to assist.

At about 0940 on 30 January, seven Japanese bombers appeared over the city and were engaged by British Brewster Buffalo fighters. As the alert continued, 30 more Japanese planes appeared overhead, on course over Keppel Harbor. Several bombs fell on shore, eastward of *West Point*'s moorings, while another stick fell in the water to the southward. In the interim, bombs hit other targets. A small tanker moored near *Wakefield* was sunk at dockside; bombs fell abreast *Empress of Japan*; and *Wakefield* took a direct hit forward which destroyed her sick bay, killed five men, and wounded nine. The last bombs in this stick straddled *West Point* and showered her with shrapnel. As the raid lifted, *West Point* sent two medical officers and 11 corpsmen on board *Wakefield,* at the latter's request, to render medical assistance.

Later that morning, Capt. Kelley attended a conference with British authorities, who informed him that his ship was to be used to carry a contingent of Australian troops from Suez to Singapore and to transport refugees and evacuees to Ceylon. With the emergency "acute," Kelley agreed to take on board up to one thousand women and children and such additional men as the British desired to send. With the abandonment of the naval dockyard, untenable in the face of increasingly heavier Japanese bombardments from artillery and aircraft, several dockyard naval and civilian personnel and their families were assigned to *West Point* for evacuation. Most carried only hand baggage; had little, if any, money; but were all fortunate enough to escape the doomed city before its fall to the onrushing Japanese troops of General Yamashita. All told, some 1,276 naval officers, their families, dockyard civilians, civilian evacuees, a 16-man Royal Air Force (RAF) contingent, and 225 naval ratings made up the 1,276 people embarked by 1800 on the 30th.

Clearing Singapore, *West Point* and *Wakefield* headed due west, escorted by HMS *Durban.* Overcast and squally weather covered their departure and permitted them to transit the Banka Strait unmolested by the seemingly omnipresent Japanese aircraft. Routed to Batavia, Java, to embark more refugees, *West Point* led *Wakefield* and *Durban* through the minefields and anchored in Batavia Roads at 0305 on 31 January. HMS *Electra*—which would be lost in the Battle of the Java Sea at the end of the month—came alongside eight hours later and transferred 20 naval dockyard personnel, three women, five naval officers' wives, one Free French officer, and an RAF officer to *West Point* for passage to Ceylon.

At 1240 on 1 February, *West Point*—in company with *Wakefield* and under escort of *Exeter, Encounter,* and HMAS *Vampire*—got underway. The destroyers eventually went off to perform other duties, and *Exeter* as

well soon dropped away to escort another convoy, leaving the two big troopships on their own. While they were en route, disconcerting news came over the radio. Japanese I-boats (identified after the war as *I–162* and *I–153*) had been active in the vicinity, sinking six ships between them.

On the other hand, heavy seas and rain squalls aided the ships. *West Point* acquired an extra passenger while en route; for, at 1325 on 4 February, a baby boy was born on board.

Colombo Harbor, Ceylon—where they arrived on the 6th—was so crowded that British authorities could not permit *Wakefield* to repair her damage there. The passengers, in turn, experienced much difficulty in arranging for suitable transportation ashore. In addition, neither transport could fully provision.

British authorities requested the American ships to evacuate personnel to Bombay. Accordingly, *West Point* took on board eight men, 55 women, and 53 children, as well as 670 troops, for passage to India. *Wakefield,* despite her weakened condition caused by the direct hit on 29 January, embarked two naval ratings, six RAF personnel, and 25 men and one officer of a British Bofors gun detachment. The two ships departed Colombo on 8 February and, escorted by the Greek destroyer *Queen Olga,* proceeded at 20 knots. Capt. Kelley later highly praised the operations of this sole escort. Although heavy weather was encountered en route, the elderly Greek destroyer acquitted herself well, continuing to patrol her station "at all times at high speed ahead of our zig-zag."

After discharging her evacuees at Bombay, *West Point* parted company with *Wakefield* and proceeded to Suez where she picked up Australian troops who were being withdrawn from the North African front to fight the Japanese in southeast Asia. Meanwhile, one disaster after another had plagued the Allied forces. Singapore fell on 15 February; Java on 4 March. *West Point* carried her embarked troops to Australia and disembarked them at Adelaide and Melbourne before heading across the Pacific toward San Francisco.

As the Allies built up for the long road back, *West Point* participated in the effort to aid America's allies in the southwest Pacific with massive contingents of troops. Accordingly, the transport carried men to Wellington, New Zealand, and arrived on 30 May. There, she received orders to return to New York; and she got underway from Melbourne on 8 June, bound for the Panama Canal. She entered the Atlantic on 26 June and arrived at New York on 2 July.

After two voyages to the United Kingdom, *West Point* sailed for India, via the South Atlantic route, and arrived at Bombay on 29 November, before pushing on for Auckland, New Zealand, the following month. The transport returned via Noumea, New Caledonia, to San Francisco on 31 January 1943. She remained on the west coast until 16 February, when she got underway for the South Pacific and retraced her route to Wellington, New Zealand, and Australian ports. She then continued west—calling at Bombay, Massawa, Aden, and Suez—and stopped briefly at Capetown en route to Rio de Janeiro, Brazil. Eventually arriving at New York on 4 May, the ship subsequently made two voyages to Casablanca, French Morocco, before sailing for Bombay via the southern Atlantic route. Calling at Rio de Janeiro and Capetown en route, the big transport continued, via Bombay and Melbourne, on for the west coast of the United States.

Soon thereafter, *West Point* began transporting troops to Australia and continued making voyages there and to Allied bases in the Central and South Pacific through the end of 1943.

In 1944, the transport continued her vital workhorse duties, departing San Francisco on 12 January, bound for Noumea and Guadalcanal; and from San Pedro, Calif., on 22 February, bound for Noumea and Milne Bay. She sailed from the latter port and steamed via the Panama Canal to Boston, Mass., where she arrived on 12 June. She conducted five successive voyages to the United Kingdom before departing Boston on 6 December 1944 for Oran, Algeria; Casablanca, French Morocco; and Marseille, France. The transport left the Mediterranean one day after Christmas and proceeded to Norfolk, Va.

In 1945, *West Point* voyaged to Italian and French ports, via Oran or Gibraltar, staging from Hampton Roads, Va., Boston, or New York. After Germany surrendered, she took part in some of the initial "Magic Carpet" voyages, bringing home American troops from the European battlefronts. Following her last European voyage—to Le Havre, France—*West Point* was transferred to the Pacific Fleet. She departed Boston on 10 December 1945, transited the Panama Canal, and proceeded to Manila, Philippines, via Pearl Harbor. Retracing the same route, she returned to New York on 7 February 1946 and soon got underway for Hampton Roads, where she was released from troop-carrying service on 22 February, Washington's Birthday. Six days later, the ship was decommissioned and transferred to the Maritime Commission's War Shipping Administration. *West Point* was struck from the Navy list on 12 March 1946.

Carrying a total of over 350,000 troops during her naval service, *West Point* had the largest capacity of any Navy troopship in service during World War II. On one voyage in August 1944, she carried, including ship's company, a total of 9,305 people. In addition to troops, she had carried Red Cross workers; United Nations officials; children; civilians; prisoners of war; and U.S.O. entertainers.

Returning to her builder's yard at Newport News, *West Point* reacquired her old name—*America*—and immediately began conversion back to her original passenger-carrying configuration. She was returned to the United States Lines on 31 October 1946 and departed New York on 10 November to begin her maiden postwar crossing of the Atlantic. The liner continued to carry passengers between New York and Southhampton, England, into 1964.

With the advent of stiffer international competition in the transoceanic shipping business and the launching of the new United States Lines' flagship—the larger, more luxurious *United States*—*America* was sold to the Chandris Shipping Line, a Greek firm, in October 1964. Renamed *Australis*, the erstwhile transport and flagship of the United States Lines operated as a passenger liner into 1977 on cruises to the Far East and South Pacific. Acquired by an American cruise ship firm in early 1978, the ship's maiden voyage for her new owners was financially unsuccessful, and the ship began a major refit soon thereafter.

West Shore

(Freighter: dp. 12,000; l. 423'9''; b. 54'2''; dph. 27'8''; dr. 24'½'' (mean); s. 10.5 k.; cpl. 70; a. 1 5'', 1 3'')

West Shore—a steel-hulled, single-screw freighter originally named *War Archer*—was launched on 13 January 1918 at Portland, Oreg., by the Northwest Steel Co., under a United States Shipping Board (USSB) contract; taken over by the Navy and assigned the Id. No. 3170; and was commissioned at New York on 7 August 1918, Lt. Comdr. Harry R. Swift, USNRF, in command.

The freighter soon shifted to Norfolk, Va., where she loaded 6,753 tons of cars and trucks for transportation to France. Returning to New York, the freighter sailed in convoy for European waters on 23 September and arrived at Brest on 12 October. *West Shore* unloaded her cargo and sailed on 6 November 1918—with 1,500 tons of iron pyrites as ballast—for the east coast of the United States. While the ship was making the return leg of her voyage, the armistice was signed on 11 November 1918 ending World War I.

Arriving back at New York on 26 November, *West Shore* loaded 7,714 tons of flour and foodstuffs. She

sailed for Europe on 18 December; touched at Falmouth, England; and made port at Rotterdam, Holland, on 3 January 1919. Departing Rotterdam in ballast on 21 January, the cargo vessel arrived back at New York on 5 February 1919. Less than a month later, on 4 March 1919, *West Shore* was simultaneously decommissioned, struck from the Navy list, and returned to the USSB.

Eventually laid up by the USSB in the mid-1920's and listed in contemporary merchant ship lists as *Westshore*, the freighter subsequently deteriorated until she was abandoned in either late 1929 or early 1930.

West View

(Freighter: t. 5,508; l. 428'; b. 54'; dr. 24'½''; dph. 29'9''; s. 10 k.; cpl. 82)

West View—a steel-hulled, single-screw freighter completed in 1918 at Portland, Oreg., by the Northwest Steel Co., for the United States Shipping Board (USSB)—was acquired by the Navy for use by the Naval Overseas Transportation Service (NOTS). Taken over and commissioned at the Puget Sound Navy Yard, Bremerton, Wash., on 21 November 1918, *West View* conducted only one voyage for NOTS. She carried a cargo of 7,200 tons of flour from the west coast via the Panama Canal to New York City where she arrived on 12 January 1919. Decommissioned there on 20 January 1919, the ship was simultaneously returned to the USSB and struck from the Navy list. She remained in the hands of the USSB and its successor, the Maritime Commission, and lay in reserve in the James River into the late 1930's. Her name does not appear in any listing of American merchantmen after 1938, suggesting that she was probably broken up due to age and deterioration.

West Virginia

At the outbreak of the Civil War, 40 western counties of Virginia remained loyal when the rest of the state seceded. West Virginia was admitted to the Union as the 35th state on 20 June 1863.

I

West Virginia (Armored Cruiser No. 5) was renamed *Huntington* (q.v.) on 11 November 1916, in order to free the name *West Virginia* for Battleship No. 48.

II

(BB–48: dp. 33,590 (f.); l. 624'0''; b. 97'3½''; dr. 30'6'' (mean); s. 21.0 k.; cpl. 1,407; a. 8 16'', 12 5'', 8 3'', 4 6-pdrs., 2 21'' tt.; cl. *Colorado*)

The second *West Virginia* (Battleship No. 48) was laid down on 12 April 1920 by the Newport News Shipbuilding and Drydock Co. of Newport News, Va.; reclassified to BB–48 on 17 July 1920; launched on 17 November 1921; sponsored by Miss Alice Wright Mann, daughter of Issac T. Mann, a prominent West Virginian; and commissioned on 1 December 1923, Capt. Thomas J. Senn in command.

The most recent of the "super-dreadnoughts," *West Virginia* embodied the latest knowledge of naval architecture; the water-tight compartmentation of her hull and her armor protection marked an advance over the design of battleships built or on the drawing boards before the Battle of Jutland.

In the months that followed, *West Virginia* ran her trials and shakedown and underwent post-commissioning alterations. After a brief period of work at the New York Navy Yard, the ship made the passage to Hampton Roads, although experiencing trouble with her steering gear while en route. Overhauling the troublesome gear thoroughly while in Hampton Roads,

West Virginia put to sea on the morning of 16 June 1924. At 1010, while the battleship was steaming in the center of Lynnhaven Channel, the quartermaster at the wheel reported that the rudder indicator would not answer. The ringing of the emergency bell to the steering motor room produced no response; Capt. Senn quickly ordered all engines stopped, but the engine room telegraph would not answer—it was later discovered that there was no power to the engine room telegraph or the steering telegraph.

The captain then resorted to sending orders down to main control via the voice tube from the bridge. He ordered full speed ahead on the port engine; all stop on the starboard. Efforts continued apace over the ensuing moments to steer the ship with her engines and keep her in the channel and, when this failed, to check headway from the edge of the channel. Unfortunately, all efforts failed; and, as the ship lost headway due to an engine casualty, *West Virginia* grounded on the soft mud bottom. Fortunately, as Comdr. (later Admiral) Harold R. Stark, the executive officer, reported: ". . . not the slightest damage to the hull had been sustained."

The court of inquiry, investigating the grounding, found that inaccurate and misleading navigational data had been supplied the ship. The legends on the charts provided were found to have indicated uniformly greater channel width than actually existed. The findings of the court thus exonerated Capt. Senn and the navigator from any blame.

After repairs had been effected, *West Virginia* became flagship for the Commander, Battleship Divisions, Battle Fleet, on 30 October 1924, thus beginning her service as an integral part of the "backbone of the fleet"—as the battleships were regarded. She soon proved her worth under a succession of commanding officers—most of whom later attained flag rank. In 1925, for example, under Capt. A. J. Hepburn, the comparative newcomer to battleship ranks scored first in competitive short range target practices. During Hepburn's tour, *West Virginia* garnered two trophies for attaining the highest merit in the category.

The ship later won the American Defense Cup—presented by the American Defense Society to the battleship obtaining the highest merit with all guns in short-range firing—and the Spokane Cup, presented by that city's Chamber of Commerce in recognition of the battleship's scoring the highest merit with all guns at short range. In 1925, *West Virginia* won the Battle Efficiency Pennant for battleships—the first time that the ship had won the coveted "Meatball." She won it again in 1927, 1932, and 1933.

During this period, *West Virginia* underwent a cycle of training, maintenance, and readiness exercises, taking part in engineering and gunnery competitions and the annual large-scale exercises, or "Fleet Problems." In the latter, the Fleet would be divided up into opposing sides, and a strategic or tactical situation would be played out, with the lessons learned becoming part and parcel of the development of doctrine that would later be tested in the crucible of combat.

During 1925, the battleship took part in the joint Army-Navy maneuvers to test the defenses of the Hawaiian Islands and then cruised with the Fleet to Australia and New Zealand. In fleet exercises subsequent to the 1925 cruise, *West Virginia* ranged from Hawaii to the Caribbean and the Atlantic, and from Alaskan waters to Panama.

In order to keep pace with technological developments in ordnance, gunnery, and fire control—as well as engineering and aviation—the ship underwent modifications designed to increase the ship's capacity to perform her designed function. Some of the alterations effected included the replacement of her initial 3-inch antiaircraft battery with 5-inch/25-caliber dual-purpose guns; the addition of platforms for .50-caliber machine guns at the foremast and maintop; and the addition of catapults on her quarterdeck, aft, and on her number III, or "high" turret.

In the closing years of the decade of the 1930's, however, it was becoming evident to many that it was only a matter of time before the United States became involved in yet another war on a grand scale. The United States Fleet thus came to be considered a grand deterrent to the country's most probable enemy—Japan. This reasoning produced the hurried despatch of the Fleet to Pacific waters in the spring of 1939 and the retention of the Fleet in Hawaiian waters in 1940, following the conclusion of Fleet Problem XXI in April.

As the year 1941 progressed, *West Virginia* carried out a schedule of intensive training, basing on Pearl Harbor and operating in various task forces and groups in the Hawaiian operating area. This routine continued even through the unusually tense period that began in late November and extended into the next month. Such at-sea periods were usually followed by in-port upkeep, with the battleships mooring to masonry "quays" along the southeast shores of Ford Island in the center of Pearl Harbor.

On Sunday, 7 December 1941, *West Virginia* lay moored outboard of *Tennessee* (BB-43) at berth F-6 with 40 feet of water beneath her keel. Shortly before 0800, Japanese planes, flying from a six-carrier task force, commenced their well-planned attack on the Fleet at Pearl Harbor. *West Virginia* took five 18-inch aircraft torpedoes in her port side and two bomb hits—those bombs being 15-inch armor-piercing shells fitted with fins. The first bomb penetrated the superstructure deck, wrecking the port casemates and causing that deck to collapse to the level of the galley deck below.

USS *West Virginia* (BB-48), *circa* 1935. (80-G-462964)

Four casemates and the galley caught fire immediately, with the subsequent detonation of the ready-service projectiles stowed in the casemates.

The second bomb hit further aft, wrecking one Vought OS2U Kingfisher floatplane atop the "high" catapult on Turret III and pitching the second one on her top on the main deck below. The projectile penetrated the 4-inch turret roof, wrecking one gun in the turret itself. Although the bomb proved a dud, burning gasoline from the damaged aircraft caused some damage.

The torpedoes, though, ripped into the ship's port side; only prompt action by Lt. Claude V. Ricketts, the assistant fire control officer who had some knowledge of damage control techniques, saved the ship from the fate that befell Oklahoma (BB-37) moored ahead. She, too, took torpedo hits that flooded the ship and caused her to capsize.

Instances of heroic conduct on board the heavily damaged battleship proliferated in the heat of battle. The ship's commanding officer, Capt. Mervyn S. Bennion, arrived on his bridge early in the battle, only to be struck down by a bomb fragment hurled in his direction when a 15-inch "bomb" hit the center gun in Tennessee's Turret II, spraying that ship's superstructure and West Virginia's with fragments. Bennion, hit in the abdomen, crumpled to the deck, mortally wounded, but clung tenaciously to life until just before the ship was abandoned, involved in the conduct of the ship's defense up to the last moment of his life. For his conspicuous devotion to duty, extraordinary courage, and complete disregard of his own life, Capt. Bennion was awarded a Medal of Honor, posthumously.

West Virginia was abandoned, settling to the harbor bottom on an even keel, her fires fought from on board by a party that volunteered to return to the ship after the first abandonment. By the afternoon of the following day, 8 December, the flames had been extinguished. The garbage lighter, YG-17, played an important role in assisting those efforts during the Pearl Harbor attack, remaining in position alongside despite the danger posed by exploding ammunition on board the battleship.

Later examination revealed that West Virginia had taken not five, but six, torpedo hits. With a patch over the damaged areas of her hull, the battleship was pumped out and ultimately refloated on 17 May 1942. Docked in Drydock Number One on 9 June, West Virginia again came under scrutiny, and it was discovered that there had been not six, but seven torpedo hits.

During the ensuing repairs, workers located 70 bodies of West Virginia sailors who had been trapped below when the ship sank. In one compartment, a calendar was found, the last scratch-off date being 23 December. The task confronting the nucleus crew and shipyard workers was a monumental one, so great was the damage on the battleship's port side. Ultimately, however, West Virginia departed Pearl Harbor for the west coast and a complete rebuilding at the Puget Sound Navy Yard at Bremerton, Wash.

Emerging from the extensive modernization, the battleship that had risen, Phoenix-like, from the destruction at Pearl Harbor looked totally different from the way she had appeared prior to 7 December 1941. Gone were the "cage" masts that supported the three-tier fire-control tops, as well as the two funnels, the open-mount 5-inch/25's and the casemates with the single-purpose 5-inch/51's. A streamlined superstructure now gave the ship a totally new silhouette; dual-purpose 5-inch/38-caliber guns, in gunhouses, gave the ship a potent antiaircraft battery. In addition, 40-millimeter Bofors and 20-millimeter Oerlikon batteries studded the decks, giving the ship a heavy "punch" for dealing with close-in enemy planes.

West Virginia remained at Puget Sound until early July 1944. Loading ammunition on the 2d, the battleship got underway soon thereafter to conduct her sea trials out of Port Townsend, Wash. She ran a full power trial on the 6th, continuing her working-up until the 12th. Subsequently returning to Puget Sound for last-minute repairs, the battleship headed for San Pedro and her post-modernization shakedown.

Finally ready to rejoin the Fleet from which she had been away for two years, West Virginia sailed for the Hawaiian Islands on 14 September. Escorted by two destroyers, she made landfall on Oahu on the 23d. Ultimately pushing on for Manus, in the Admiralities, in company with the fleet carrier Hancock (CV-19), West Virginia, as a unit of Battleship Division (Bat Div) 4, reached Seeadler Harbor on 5 October. The next day, she again became a flagship when Rear Admiral Ruddock shifted his flag from Maryland (BB-46) to the "Wee Vee" as Commander, BatDiv 4.

Underway on 12 October to participate in the invasion of the Philippine Islands, West Virginia sailed as part of Task Group (TG) 77.2, under the overall command of Rear Admiral Jesse B. Oldendorf. On 18 October, the battle line passed into Leyte Gulf, West Virginia steaming astern of California (BB-44).

At 1645, California cut loose a mine with her paravanes; West Virginia successfully dodged the horned menace, it being destroyed a few moments later by gunfire from one of the destroyers in the screen. On 19 October, West Virginia steamed into her assigned station in San Pedro Bay at 0700 to stand by off shore and provide shore bombardment against targets in the Tacloban area of Leyte. Retiring to sea that evening, the battleship and her consorts returned the next morning to lay down heavy gunfire on Japanese installations in the vicinity of the town of Tacloban.

On the 19th, West Virginia's gunners sent 278 16-inch and 1,586 5-inch shells against Japanese installations, silencing enemy artillery and supporting the UDT (underwater demolition teams) preparing the beaches for the assault that came on the 20th. On the latter day, enemy planes made many apearances over the landing area. West Virginia took those within range under fire but did not down any.

On the 21st, as she was proceeding to her fire support area to render further gunfire support for the troops still pouring ashore, West Virginia touched bottom, slightly damaging three of her four screws. The vibrations caused by the damaged blades limited sustained speeds to 16 knots—18 in emergencies.

For the next two days, West Virginia, with her augmented antiaircraft batteries, remained off the beachhead during the daylight hours, retiring to seaward at night, providing antiaircraft covering fire for the unfolding invasion operations. Meanwhile, the Japanese, seeing that American operations against Leyte were on a large scale, decided to strike back. Accordingly, the enemy, willing to accept the heavy risks involved, set out in four widely separated forces to destroy the American invasion fleet.

Four carriers and two "hermaphrodite" battleship-carriers (Ise and Hyuga) sailed toward the Philippine Sea from Japanese home waters; a small surface force under Admiral Shima headed for the Sulu Sea; two striking forces consisting of battleships, cruisers, and destroyers sortied from Lingga Roads, Sumatra, before separating north of Borneo. The larger of those two groups, commanded by Admiral Kurita, passed north of the island of Palawan to transit the Sibuyan Sea.

American submarines Darter (SS-247) and Dace (SS-227) drew first blood in what would become known as the Battle for Leyte Gulf on 23 October when they sank, respectively, two of Kurita's cruisers—Maya and Atago. Undeterred, Kurita continued the transit, his force built around the giant battleship Musashi.

The smaller of the two forces, under Admiral Nishimura, turned south of Palawan and transited the Sulu Sea to pass between the islands of Mindanao and Leyte. Shima's forces obediently followed Nishimura's, heading for Leyte Gulf as the southern jaw of a pincer designed to hit the assemblage of amphibious ships and transports unloading off the Leyte beachhead.

Detailed to deal with the force heading in his direction, Admiral Oldendorf accordingly deployed his sizeable force—six battleships, eight cruisers, and 28 destroyers—across the northern end of Surigao Strait. The American men-of-war steamed along their assigned courses, their bows cleaving through the smooth sea.

At 2236 on 24 October 1944, the American PT boats deployed in the strait and its approaches made radar contact with Nishimura's force, conducting a harassing attack that annoyed, but did not stop, the oncoming enemy. Well into the strait by 0300 on the 25th, Nishimura took up battle formation when five American destroyers launched a well-planned torpedo attack. Caught in the spread of torpedoes, the battleship *Fuso* took hits and dropped out of the formation; other spreads of "fish" dispatched a pair of Japanese destroyers and crippled a third.

Fuso's sistership *Yamashiro*, meanwhile, had taken one hit and was slowed down, only to be hit again within 15 minutes' time. *Fuso* herself, apparently ravaged by fires ignited by the torpedo hits, blew up with a tremendous explosion at 0338.

West Virginia, meanwhile, was maintaining her position ahead of *Maryland*, *Mississippi* (BB-41), *Tennessee*, *California*, and *Pennsylvania* (BB-38)—four of these ships, like *West Virginia*, veterans of Pearl Harbor. From 0021 on the 25th, the battleship had picked up reports on the PT boat and destroyer attacks; finally at 0316, *West Virginia*'s radar picked up Nishimura's force at a range of 42,000 yards. She tracked them as they approached in the pitch black night.

At 0352, *West Virginia* unleashed her 16-inch main battery; she fired 16 salvoes in the direction of Nishimura's ships as Oldendorf crossed the Japanese "T" and thus achieved the tactical mastery of a situation that almost every surface admiral dreams of. At 0413, the "Wee Vee" ceased fire; the Japanese remnants proceeded in disorder down the strait from whence they had come. Several burning Japanese ships littered the strait; *West Virginia* had contributed to *Yamashiro*'s demise, thus averaging her own crippling in the Pearl Harbor attack.

West Virginia had thus taken part in the last naval engagement fought by line-of-battle ships and, on the 29th, departed the Philippines for Ulithi, in company with *Tennessee* and *Maryland*. Subsequently heading for Espiritu Santo, in the New Hebrides, after Admiral Ruddock had shifted his flag back from *West Virginia* to *Maryland*, the former underwent a period of upkeep in the floating drydock, ABSD-1, for her damaged screws.

The "Wee Vee" returned to the Philippines, via Manus, on 25 November, resuming her patrols in Leyte Gulf and serving as part of the antiaircraft screen for the transports and amphibious ships. At 1139 on the 27th, *West Virginia*'s antiaircraft guns splashed a suicider and assisted in downing others while on duty the next day.

Rear Admiral Ruddock shifted back on board on the 30th, *West Virginia* maintaining her operations off Leyte until 2 December, when the battleship headed for the Palaus. The battlewagon was then made the flagship for the newly formed TG 77.12 and proceeded toward the Sulu Sea to cover the landings made by the Southwest Pacific Force on the island of Mindoro. Entering Leyte Gulf late on the evening of 12 December, *West Virginia* transited the Surigao Strait on the 13th and steamed into the Sulu Sea with a carrier force to provide cover for the transports in TG 78.3.

She subsequently covered the retirement of the transports on 15 December, later fueling in Leyte Gulf before she returned to Kossol Roads, Palaus, at mid-day on the 19th. There, *West Virginia* spent the Christmas of 1944.

There was more work to be done, however, for the battleship, as the "return" to the Philippines continued apace. On New Year's Day, Rear Admiral Ingram C. Sowell relieved Rear Admiral Ruddock as Commander, BatDiv 4, and the ship got underway for Leyte Gulf as part of TG 77.2.

Entering the gulf during the pre-dawn hours of 3 January, *West Virginia* proceeded into the Sulu Sea. Japanese air opposition, intensifying since the early part of the Philippine campaign, was becoming more deadly. *West Virginia*'s men saw evidence of that when a twin-engined "Frances" crashed the escort carrier *Ommaney Bay* (CVE-79) at 1712 on the 4th. Fires and explosions ultimately forced the "jeep carrier's" abandonment, her survivors being picked up by other ships in the screen. *Burns* (DD-588) dispatched the blazing CVE with torpedoes.

Taking on board survivors from *Ommaney Bay* from the destroyer *Twiggs* (DD-591), *West Virginia* entered the South China Sea on the morning of the following day, 5 January 1945, defending the carriers during the day from Japanese air attacks. Subsequently, the battleship moved close inshore with the carriers outside to carry out a bombardment mission on San Fernando Point. *West Virginia* hammered Japanese installations ashore with her 16-inch rifles.

Suiciders, however, kept up their attacks in the face of heavy antiaircraft barrages and combat air patrol (CAP) fighters. Losses among Allied shipping continued to mount; kamikazes claimed damage to HMAS *Australia* and the battleships *California* and *New Mexico* (BB-40) on the 5th. *West Virginia* participated in putting up volumes of antiaircraft fire during those attacks, emerging unscathed herself.

West Virginia—in addition to the *Ommaney Bay* sailors on board—soon took on board another group of survivors from yet another ship: the men from the high-speed minesweeper *Hovey* (DMS-11) which had been sunk by a Japanese torpedo on the 6th. Before she could transfer the escort carrier's and minesweeper's sailors elsewhere, though, she had to carry out her assigned tasks first. Accordingly, *West Virginia*'s 16-inch rifles again hammered Japanese positions ashore at San Fabian on the 8th and 9th, as troops went ashore on the latter day. It was not until the night of 9 January that the battleship finally transferred her passengers off the ship.

After providing call fire support all day on the 10th, *West Virginia* patrolled off Lingayen Gulf for the next week before proceeding to an anchorage where she replenished her ammunition. During her shore bombardment tours off San Fabian, *West Virginia* had proved herself most helpful, covering UDT operations, destroying mortar positions, entrenchments, gun emplacements, and leveling the town of San Fabian. In addition, "Wee Vee" destroyed ammunition dumps, railway and road junctions, and machine gun positions and warehouses. During that time, the ship expended 395 16-inch shells and over 2,800 5-inch projectiles.

Underway again at 0707 on the 21st, *West Virginia* commenced call-fire support duties at 0815, operating in readiness for cooperation with the Army units ashore in the vicinity of the towns of Rosario and Santo Tomas. After a few more days of standing ready to provide call-fire support when needed, *West Virginia* anchored in Lingayen Gulf on 1 February.

Subsequently, as part of TG 77.2, *West Virginia* protected the shipping arriving at the Lingayen beachheads and stood ready to provide call-fire for the Army when needed. She later departed Lingayen Gulf, her duty completed there, on 10 February, bound for Leyte Gulf. Before her departure, she received 79 bags of United States mail—the first she had received since the day before Christmas.

After touching first at San Pedro Bay, Leyte, *West Virginia* arrived at Ulithi on 16 February, reporting for duty with the 5th Fleet upon arrival. Ordered to prepare in all haste for another operation, the battleship provisioned and refueled with the highest priority. The ship completed loading some 300 tons of stores by 0400 on the 17th. At 0730 on the 17th, *West Virginia* got underway, bound for Iwo Jima in company with the destroyers *Izard* (DD-589) and *McCall* (DD-400). As she headed off to Iwo Jima to join TF 51, *West Virginia* received a "Well-done" from Admiral Chester W.

Nimitz for the manner in which she had readied herself for her new duty after being released from the 7th Fleet such a short time before.

West Virginia sighted Iwo Jima at a range of 32 miles at 0907 on 19 February. As she drew nearer, she saw several ships bombarding the isle from all sides and the initial landings taking place. At 1125, she received her operations orders, via dispatch boat and, 20 minutes later, proceeded to her fire support station off the volcanic sand beaches. At 1245, her big guns bellowed to lend support to the marines ashore—gun positions, revetments, blockhouses, tanks, vehicles, caves and supply dumps—all came under her heavy guns. On 21 February, the ship returned and, at 0800, commenced her support duties afresh.

Her 16-inch shells sealed caves, destroyed antiaircraft gun positions and blockhouses; one salvo struck an ammunition or fuel dump, explosions occurring for about two hours thereafter. On the 22d, a small-caliber shell hit the battleship near turret II, wounding one enlisted man. That same day, another significant event occurred ashore—marines took Mount Suribachi, the prominent landmark on one end of Iwo Jima. From their position offshore, *West Virginia*'s sailors could see the flag flying from the top.

For the remainder of February, *West Virginia* continued her daily fire-support missions for the marines ashore. Again, Japanese positions felt the heavy blows of the battleship's 16-inch shells. She hit troop concentrations and trucks, blockhouses, trenches, and houses. During the course of that time spent off the beaches on 27 February, she spotted a Japanese shore battery firing upon *Bryant* (DD–665). *West Virginia* closed the range and, when about 600 yards from shore, opened fire with her secondary (5-inch) battery, silencing the enemy guns.

Replenishing her depleted ammunition stocks early on 28 February, *West Virginia* was back on the line again that afternoon, firing continuous night harassing and interdiction rounds, silencing enemy batteries with air bursts from her secondary batteries. For the first three days of March, *West Virginia* continued her fire-support missions, primarily off the northeastern shore of Iwo Jima. Finally, on 4 March, the ship set sail for the Caroline Islands, reaching Ulithi on 6 March.

Joining TF 54 for the invasion of the Okinawa Gunto area, *West Virginia* sailed on 21 March, reaching her objective four days later on the 25th. In fire support section one, *West Virginia* spent the ensuing days softening up Okinawa for the American landings slated to commence on 1 April. At 1029 on 26 March, lookouts reported a gun flash from shore, followed by a splash in the water some 5,000 yards off the port bow. Firing her first salvoes of the operation, *West Virginia* let fly 28 rounds of 16-inch gunfire against the pugnacious Japanese batteries.

The following day, the "Wee Vee" fought against enemy air opposition, taking a "Frances" under fire at 0520. The twin-engined bomber crashed off the battleship's port quarter—the victim of *West Virginia*'s antiaircraft guns. Over the days that followed, enemy opposition continued in the form of suicide attacks by Japanese planes. Mines, too, began making themselves felt; one sank the minesweeper *Skylark* (AM–63), 3,000 yards off *West Virginia*'s port bow at 0930 on the 28th.

After taking on ammunition at Kerama Retto—the island seized to provide an advance base for the armada massing against Okinawa—*West Virginia* sailed for Okinawa to give direct gunfire support to the landings. Scheduled to fire at 0630, the battleship headed for her assigned zone off the Okinawa beaches. While en route, though, at 0455, she had to back down all engines when an unidentified destroyer stood across her bow, thus avoiding a collision.

As she prepared to commence her bombardment, *West Virginia* spotted a Japanese plane off her port quarter; her antiaircraft batteries tracked the target and opened fire, downing the enemy aircraft 200 yards away. Four more enemy planes passed within her vicinity soon thereafter—*West Virginia* claimed one of them.

Finally, at 0630, *West Virginia* opened fire as landing craft dotted the sea as far as the eye could reach, all heading for the shores of Okinawa. *West Virginia*'s sailors, some 900 yards off the beaches, could see the craft heading shoreward like hundreds of tadpoles; at 0842, lookouts reported seeing some of the first troops going ashore. The battle for Okinawa was underway.

West Virginia continued her bombardment duties throughout the day, on the alert to provide counter-battery fire in support of the troops as they advanced rapidly inland. There appeared to be little resistance on 1 April, and *West Virginia* lay to offshore, awaiting further orders. At 1903, however, an enemy plane brought the war down on *West Virginia*.

The battleship picked up three enemy planes on her radar and tracked them as they approached; flak peppered the skies but still they came. One crossed over the port side and then looped over and crash-dived into *West Virginia*, smashing into a superstructure deck just forward of secondary battery director number two. Four men were killed by the blast, and seven were wounded in a nearby 20-millimeter gun gallery. The bomb carried by the plane broke loose from its shackle and penetrated to the second deck. Fortunately, it did not explode and was rendered harmless by the battleship's bomb disposal officer. Although her galley and laundry looked hard-hit, *West Virginia*—reporting her damage as repairable by ship's force—carried on, rendering night illumination fire to the marines ashore.

West Virginia buried her dead at sea in the wake of the kamikaze attack of 1 April and resumed her gunfire support duties soon thereafter. In the course of her tour offshore in early April, she shot down a "Val" on the 6th,

In early April, the Japanese attempted to strike at the invasion fleet in a last-gasp offensive formed around the super-battleship *Yamato*. On the night of 7 and 8 April, *West Virginia* steamed north and south in the waters west of Okinawa ready to intercept and engage the Japanese surface force headed her way. The next morning, 8 April, Commander, TF 58, reported that most of the ships in that enemy force had been sunk—including *Yamato*, whose last sortie had been made with enough fuel to get her to Okinawa—but not to return. Thus, the Japanese Navy's largest kamikaze perished—many miles short of her objective.

For *West Virginia*, however, her duties went on, providing illumination and counterbattery fire with both main and secondary batteries and giving her antiaircraft gunners a good workout due to the heavy presence of many suiciders. Her TBS crackled with reports of ships under attack and damaged—*Zellars* (DD–777), *Tennessee*, *Salt Lake City* (CA–24), *Stanley* (DD–478) —and others, all victims of the "divine wind," or kamikaze. Her shore bombardments elicited nothing but praise from those enjoying the benefits of the ship's firing; one spotter reported happily on 14 April: "You're shooting perfectly, you could shoot no better, no change, no change," and, "Your shooting is strictly marvelous. I cannot express just how good it is." She delivered sterling support fire for the 6th Marines upon that occasion; later, she continued in that fine tradition for the 10th Army and the XXIVth Army Corps.

West Virginia continued fire support for the Army until 20 April, at which point she headed for Ulithi, only to turn back to Okinawa, hurriedly recalled because of *Colorado*'s (BB–45) suffering damage when a powder charge exploded while she was loading powder at Kerama Retto. Returning to Hagushi beach, *West Virginia* fired night harassment and interdiction fire for the 10th Army and the XXIVth Army Corps. Ultimately, *West Virginia* sailed for Ulithi, in company with *San Francisco* (CA–38) and *Hobson* (DD–464), reaching her destination—this time without a recall en route—on 28 April.

Returning to Okinawa after a brief sojourn at

Ulithi, *West Virginia* remained in support of the Army and the Marines on the embattled island into the end of June. There were highlights of the tour—on 1 June, she sent her spotting plane aloft to locate a troublesome enemy blockhouse reportedly holding up an Army advance. A couple of rounds hurled in the enemy's direction produced no results; she had to settle for obliterating some of the enemy's motor transport and troop concentrations during the day instead. The next day, 2 June, while in support of the Army's XXIVth Corps, *West Virginia* scored four direct hits and seven near-misses on the blockhouse that had been hit the day before.

West Virginia then operated off the southeast coast of Okinawa, breaking up Japanese troop concentrations and destroying enemy caves. She also disrupted Japanese road traffic by scoring a direct hit on a road intersection and blasted a staging area. On 16 June, she was firing an assignment for the 1st Marines off southwestern Okinawa when her spotting plane, a Vought OS2U Kingfisher, took hits from Japanese antiaircraft fire and headed down in flames, her pilot and observer bailing out over enemy-held territory. Within a short time, aided by *Putnam* (DD–757) and an LCI, *West Virginia* closed and blasted enemy guns in an attempt to rescue her plane crew who had "dug in for the day" to await the arrival of the rescuers. The attempt to recover her aircrew, however, was not successful. Loaned a Kingfisher from *Tennessee*, *West Virginia* kept up her gunfire support activities for the balance of June.

Shifting to San Pedro Bay, Leyte, at the end of June, the battleship reached her destination on 1 July, escorted by *Connolly* (DE–306). There, on the morning of 5 July, she received her first draft of replacements since Pearl Harbor in 1944. After loading ammunition, *West Virginia* commenced training in the Philippine area, an activity she carried out through the end of July.

Sailing on 3 August for Okinawa, *West Virginia* reached Buckner Bay on the 6th, the same day that the first atomic bomb was dropped on the city of Hiroshima. Thee days later, a second bomb obliterated the greater part of the city of Nagasaki. Those two events hastened Japan's collapse. On 10 August, at 2115, *West Virginia* picked up a garbled report on radio that the Japanese government had agreed to surrender under the terms of the Potsdam Declaration, provided that they could keep the Emperor as their ruler. The American ships in Buckner Bay soon commenced celebrating—the indiscriminate use of antiaircraft fire and pyrotechnics (not only from the naval vessels in the bay but from marines and Army troops ashore) endangering friendly planes. Such celebrations, however, proved premature—at 2004 on 12 August, *West Virginia* sailors felt a heavy underwater explosion; soon thereafter, at 2058, the battleship intercepted a radio dispatch from *Pennsylvania* (BB–38) reporting that she had been torpedoed. *West Virginia* sent over a whaleboat at 0023 on the 13th with pumps for the damaged *Pennsylvania*.

The war ended on 15 August 1945. *West Virginia* drilled her landing force in preparation for the upcoming occupation of the erstwhile enemy's homeland and sailed for Tokyo Bay on the 24th as part of TG 35.90. She reached Tokyo Bay on the last day of August and was thus present at the time of the formal surrender on 2 September 1945. For that occasion, five musicians from *West Virginia*'s band were transferred temporarily to *Missouri* (BB–63) to play at the ceremonies.

West Virginia played her part in the occupation, remaining in Tokyo Bay into September of 1945, weathering a storm on the 15th that had winds clocked at 65 knots at one point. On 14 September, she received on board 270 passengers for transportation to the west coast of the United States. She got underway at midnight on the 20th, bound for Okinawa as part of TG 30.4. Shifting to Buckner Bay on the 23d, the battleship sailed for Pearl Harbor soon thereafter, reaching her destination on 4 October.

There, the crew painted ship and kept on board only those passengers slated for transportation to San Diego, Calif. Bound for that port on the 9th, *West Virginia* moored at the Navy Pier at San Diego at 1328 on 22 October. Two days later, Rear Admiral I. C. Sowell hauled down his flag as Commander, BatDiv 4.

On Navy Day—27 October—25,554 visitors (more the next day) came on board the ship. Three days later, on the 30th, she got underway for Hawaiian waters to take her place as part of the "Magic Carpet" operation returning veteran soldiers, sailors, marines, and airmen home to the states. After one run between San Diego and Pearl Harbor, *West Virginia* made another, the second time embarking Rear Admiral William W. Smith, who broke his flag in the battleship for the return voyage to San Francisco, Calif.

After making yet another run between the west coast and Hawaii, *West Virginia* reached San Pedro, Calif., on 17 December. There, she spent Christmas debarking her third draft of passengers. The veteran battlewagon upped-anchor on 4 January 1946 and sailed for Bremerton, Wash. She reached her distination on the 12th and commenced inactivation soon thereafter, shifting to Seattle, Wash., on the 16th, where she moored alongside sistership *Colorado*.

West Virginia entered her final stages of inactivation in the latter part of February 1946 and was decommissioned on 9 January 1947 and placed in reserve, as part of the Pacific Reserve Fleet. She never again received the call to active duty, remaining inactive until struck from the Navy list on 1 March 1959. On 24 August 1959, she was sold for scrapping to the Union Minerals and Alloys Corp. of New York City.

West Virginia (BB–48), although heavily damaged at Pearl Harbor and missing much of the war, nevertheless earned five battle stars.

West Wauna

(ScStr: dp. 12,185 (n.) lbp. 410'5½''; b. 54'0''; dr. 24'1½''; s. 10 k.)

West Wauna (Id. No. 3856)—a freighter constructed in 1918 at Portland, Oreg., by the Northwest Steel Co. under the supervision of the United States Shipping Board—was acquired by the Navy from the Shipping Board on 14 January 1918 and commissioned that same day, Lt. Comdr. William Mayne, USNRF, in command.

Assigned to the Naval Overseas Transportation Service, *West Wauna* made only one round-trip voyage to Europe during her brief Navy career. She loaded a cargo of flour at Portland and put to sea on 1 February bound for the east coast on the first leg of her journey to Europe. After transiting the Panama Canal at midmonth, she arrived in Norfolk, Va., on 1 March. Following eight days of repairs and refueling, she set out across the Atlantic. The freighter arrived in Falmouth, England, on 26 March; and, after unloading her cargo, she sailed for the gulf coast of the United States. She entered port at Galveston, Tex., on 13 May. Six days later, she was placed out of commission and was returned to the Shipping Board.

West Wauna continued to operate in mercantile service, out of Portland, under the auspices of the Shipping Board and then of the Maritime Commission. That service continued until the early stages of World War II. In 1941, she was transferred to British ownership and served through the war years as SS *Empire Grebe*. Still under British registry, she was renamed SS *Inchmark* in 1947 when she was acquired by the Inchmark Steamship Co., Ltd., of Hong Kong. On 29 May 1949, the freighter suffered mortal damage when she ran aground on Schildpat Island Reef, Indonesia.

227

West Wood

(Freighter: dp. 12,175; l. 423'9"; b. 54'; dr. 23'11¼"
(mean); dph. 29'9"; s. 10.5 k.; cpl. 75; a. 1 6", 1 3")

West Wood—a steel-hulled, single-screw freighter built under a United States Shipping Board (USSB) contract at Seattle, Wash., by the American Shipbuilding and Drydock Co.—was launched on 12 January 1918. Inspected by the Navy at the 13th Naval District on 9 March, the cargo vessel was acquired for duty with the Naval Overseas Transportation Service (NOTS) on 12 July—apparently after the ship had voyaged from the west coast to the east—and commissioned on 14 July 1918 at New York City, Lt. Comdr. Clyde F. Parker, USNRF, in command.

The day after she was commissioned, *West Wood*—assigned Id. No. 2812—departed New York for Norfolk, Va. There, she loaded 6,500 tons of general cargo for shipment to France, before she shifted back to New York to join a France-bound convoy. After sailing for the Gironde on 9 August, she discharged her cargo there and returned home, eventually arriving at Norfolk on 10 October.

The ship departed the Tidewater area on 3 November with a cargo of supplies earmarked for the Army and bound for La Pallice, France. *West Wood* was a little over a week out of Hampton Roads when the armistice of 11 November stilled the guns on the Western Front. The freighter arrived at La Pallice on the 20th, discharged her cargo, bunkered with fuel oil for the return trip, and headed for the United States on 6 December.

West Wood made port at New York two days before Christmas of 1918. Over the ensuing weeks, she underwent voyage repairs, bunkered, loaded 6,910 tons of general cargo, and finally sailed again for La Pallice on 19 January 1919. Following her return to New York on 18 March, the ship lifted 6,666 tons of Army cargo to France and then carried 1,007 tons of ammunition and 1,487 tons of steel rails on the voyage back home which ended on 13 June at New York.

After completing four voyages for NOTS, *West Wood* was selected for decommissioning. After final inventories, the ship was placed out of commission at New York on 26 June 1919 and returned to the USSB the same day. Her name was simultaneously struck from the Navy list.

Carried on subsequent lists of American merchant vessels as *Westwood*, the cargo vessel apparently remained operational with the USSB into 1922. After that time, she appears to have been laid up on the west coast, where she gradually deteriorated. She was consequently "abandoned," due to age and deterioration, in 1933.

West Zeda

(Freighter: t. 8,800 (gross); l. 423'9"; b. 54'; dr. 24'1½" (mean); s. 9 k.; cpl. 90; a. none)

West Zeda—a steel-hulled, single-screw freighter built under a United States Shipping Board (USSB) contract at Portland, Oreg., by the Northwest Steel Co.—was completed late in 1918 and taken over by the Navy for operation by the Naval Overseas Transportation Service (NOTS); assigned Id. No. 3801; and commissioned on 23 December 1918 at the Puget Sound Navy Yard, Bremerton, Wash., Lt. Richard Willowden, USNRF, in command.

After trials, *West Zeda* loaded 7,444 tons of flour earmarked for shipment to the Near East and departed the west coast on 4 January 1919. She transited the Panama Canal and touched briefly at New York and Gibraltar before arriving at Constantinople, Turkey, on 6 March. After discharging her cargo and taking on 1,998 tons of water ballast and a small cargo of medicinal opium, *West Zeda* sailed for home on 13 April. She

proceeded through the Strait of Gibraltar and reached New York on 17 May. The freighter was decommissioned at New York on 26 May and simultaneously was struck from the Navy list. She was returned to the USSB the following day.

West Zeda operated under the aegis of the United States Shipping Board into the late 1920's when she was placed in reserve and laid up on the west coast. With the onset of World War II, the ship operated under government ownership—the United States Maritime Commission—until torpedoed and sunk by *U–129* off the coast of Venezuela on 22 February 1942.

West Zucker

(Freighter: dp. 12,186; l. 423'9"; b. 54'; dr. 24'2" (mean); s. 10.5 k.; cpl. 75; a. none)

West Zucker—a steel-hulled, single-screw cargo freighter built under a United States Shipping Board (USSB) contract at Los Angeles, Calif., by the Los Angeles Shipbuilding and Drydock Co.—was completed late in 1918; inspected by the Navy on 4 November 1918; assigned the Id. No. 3584; and commissioned at San Pedro, Calif., on 20 November 1918, Lt. Comdr. Roy W. Look, USNRF, in command.

Following sea trials, *West Zucker* loaded a full cargo of flour and sailed for the east coast on 4 January 1919. Arriving at Hampton Roads, Va., on 22 March, via the Panama Canal, *West Zucker* unloaded her cargo and was decommissioned on 29 March. Simultaneously struck from the Navy list and transferred to the USSB on that day, the freighter remained in the hands of the Board until abandoned, due to age and deterioration, in 1933.

West Zula

(Freighter: dp. 12,287; l. 423'9"; b. 54'; dr. 24'2"; s. 10.5 k.; cpl. 71; a. none)

West Zula—a steel-hulled, single-screw freighter built under a United States Shipping Board contract and launched on 4 July 1918 at San Pedro, Calif., by the Los Angeles Shipbuilding and Drydock Co.—was acquired by the Navy on 26 September 1918 and commissioned at San Pedro on the same day, Lt. Walter E. Manning, USNRF, in command.

Assigned to the Naval Overseas Transportation Service (NOTS) and designated Id. No. 3501, *West Zula* conducted sea trials and then sailed for Chile. She loaded a cargo of guano at Arica, got underway on 22 November, and proceeded via the Panama Canal toward New York. Re-routed to the Florida coast soon thereafter, the ship unloaded her cargo of nitrates at Jacksonville before steaming on to Philadelphia for repairs which lasted until the end of January 1919. Shifting to New York City on the final day of the month, *West Zula* underwent further repairs before she was decommissioned and returned to the Shipping Board on 24 February 1919. Simultaneously struck from the Navy list, *West Zula* was berthed in the Shipping Board's reserve fleet at Norfolk, Va. While she was laid up, the freighter deteriorated until she was abandoned in 1933.

Westchester

(Freighter: dp. 12,185; l. 423'9"; b. 54'0"; dph. 29'9"; dr. 24'0" (mean); s. 11.5 k.; cpl. 88; a. 1 6", 1 6-pdr.)

Westchester—a single-screw, steel-hulled cargo vessel built as *War Ally* under a United States Shipping Board contract at Portland, Oreg., by the Northwest Steel Co.—was launched on 5 December 1917; acquired by the Navy on 9 August 1918; designated Id. No. 3122; and commissioned at Norfolk, Va., on the same day, Lt. Comdr. Thomas W. Sheridan. USNRF, in command.

Assigned to the Naval Overseas Transportation Service, *Westchester* got underway on 27 August from Newport News with general Army cargo and a deck load of 25 trucks. Arriving in New York two days later, she joined a convoy bound for Europe. She reached Le Havre, France, on 15 September and moved on to Davenport, England, before discharging her cargo.

Westchester was at sea, heading for the United States, when the armistice ended World War I. She made port at Newport News on 15 November, loaded 7,800 tons of Army cargo for shipment to France, and stood out of Hampton Roads on 19 December. She lost a propeller blade a few days out, however, and was obliged to put back into Norfolk for repairs. She set out on 3 January 1919, but another propeller casualty forced *Westchester* into New York eight days later.

Her third attempt to reach France succeeded, though, and she made port at Quiberon, France, on 2 March. With a return cargo of Army ordnance material, she set sail on 23 March. Arriving at New York on 7 April, *Westchester* discharged her cargo and was decommissioned on 25 April 1919. Returned to the Shipping Board, she remained in the custody of that agency until abandoned in 1933.

II

(Tug: dp. 56; l. 42′7′′; b. 14.1′; dr. 7′ (aft); s. 6 k.)

The second *Westchester* (Id. No. 3103), often but erroneously spelled *West Chester*—a tug built in 1896 by Russell at Long Island City, N.Y.—was acquired by the Navy from the Red Star Towing & Transport Co. on a charter basis on 4 September 1918 and commissioned at New York on 11 September 1918. She served in the 3d Naval District as a tug through the end of World War I in November 1918 and remained in service during the first four months of 1919. On 25 April 1919, *Westchester* was placed out of commission at New York and was delivered to the United States Shipping Board at Brooklyn, N.Y., for disposal. On 14 August 1919, the tug was returned to her owners, and, simultaneously, her name was struck from the Navy list.

The name *Westchester* and the designation AK–219 were assigned to the projected C1–M–AV1 cargo vessel *Coastal Defender* on 25 February 1945. The ship was laid down under a Maritime Commission contract (MC hull 2173) on 21 March 1945 at Sturgeon Bay, Wis., by the Leathem D. Smith Shipbuilding Co.; launched on 3 June 1945; sponsored by Mrs. Henry Steinbrenner; and completed on 27 June 1945. However, due to the end of the war in the Pacific, the Navy cancelled the contract for the acquisition of the completed vessel in August. The ship thus commenced operations later in 1945 with her original intended owners, the shipping firm of Smith and Johnson.

Westchester County

A county in southeastern New York.

(LST–1167: dp. 2,590; l. 384′; b. 56′6′′; dr. 17′; s. 14.5 k.; cpl. 153; a. 6 3′′; cl. *LST–1156*)

LST–1167 was laid down on 11 January 1952 by the Christy Corp., Sturgeon Bay, Wis.; launched on 18 April 1953; sponsored by Mrs. Robert E. Wood; and commissioned on 10 March 1954, Lt. Comdr. Leamond F. Lacy in command.

The tank landing ship departed New Orleans on 8 April 1954 and reached the Naval Amphibious Base at Little Creek, Va., on 14 April. The remainder of the year was spent in ampribious warfare exercises in the Chesapeake Bay.

On 14 February 1955, *LST–1167* sailed from Little Creek to embark 205 marines and equipment for exercises in the Caribbean. These exercises were re-

peated in April, and the ship returned to Little Creek on 6 May 1955. On 1 July, *LST–1167* was named *Westchester County*. *Westchester County* spent the remaining months of 1955 engaged in operations along the east coast with the majority of the time being spent in local training.

After loading marines and equipment at Morehead City, N.C., the tank landing ship sailed for exercises in the Caribbean on 11 January 1956. She returned to Norfolk on 6 February and made another training cruise to the Caribbean from 20 February to 24 March. Upon returning to Little Creek, Va., the ship conducted local operations until the Fourth of July which she spent at Yonkers, N.Y. She visited Trenton, N.J., and Washington, D.C., then went into overhaul on 21 September at the Brewer Dry Dock Company of Staten Island, N.Y. After a two-month yard period, the ship conducted local operations to finish out the year.

On 28 February 1957, *Westchester County* embarked personnel and equipment at Morehead City, N.C., and sailed to the Caribbean for amphibious training exercises, returning to Norfolk on 13 May. She conducted local operations until 28 August when she sailed for a Mediterranean deployment, joining the 6th Fleet at Messina, Sicily, on 15 September. The ship conducted exercises off Turkey, Greece, and Spain. On 4 November, the ship departed Alicante, Spain, for Little Creek, Va., where she spent the remainder of the year in local operations.

Westchester County began the year 1958 departing Norfolk for San Francisco via the Panama Canal. She arrived at the San Francisco Naval Shipyard on 31 January for overhaul which was completed on 2 April. The ship put to sea from San Diego on 7 June for her first tour of duty in the Far East. She reached Sasebo, Japan, on 5 July for amphibious warfare maneuvers and assault landing practice in Buckner Bay, Okinawa; Subic Bay, Philippines; and Tsoying, Taiwan; where she engaged in joint operations with Chinese Underwater Demolition Teams embarked. She returned to San Diego on 10 December 1958 and there finished the year.

The first eight months of 1959 were spent in amphibious training along the California coast. On 24 August, *Westchester County* embarked marines and vehicles for Kaneohe, Hawaii, and amphibious landings. On 6 October, she returned to California, off-loaded the marines and returned to San Francisco. On 30 November, *Westchester County* entered the Todd Shipyard, Alameda, Calif., for overhaul until 12 February 1960.

She resumed her training schedule out of San Diego until 1 August 1960 when she shifted to Port Hueneme to load cargo and take on fuel. The next day, she set course for her new home port of Yokosuka, Japan, via the Hawaiian Islands and Okinawa. The ship beached at Numazu, Japan, on 5 September 1960 to commence a series of large scale amphibious exercises with SEATO forces. From 1 to 31 December, *Westchester County* underwent overhaul at the Yokosuka Naval Base.

The year 1961 was spent making logistic runs between Subic Bay, Philippines; Okinawa; and North Borneo. *Westchester County* spent November and December 1961 in upkeep at her home port.

Westchester County got underway on 18 January 1962 for sea trials and refresher training. On 10 March, she rendezvoused with other units of the Pacific Fleet and departed for Mindoro, Philippines, for amphibious warfare maneuvers. The ship returned to Yokosuka, Japan, on 20 April and resumed a normal training schedule. The communist threat in Vietnam interrupted this training period; and, on 13 May, *Westchester County* was underway for Subic Bay, Philippines, with a combat load of marines.

On 15 June 1962, the tank landing ship returned to Yokosuka, Japan, for upkeep and in-port training. She then conducted operations at Keelung, Taiwan; Subic Bay, Philippines; Bangkok, Thailand; and Naha, Okinawa. During October, the ship participated in amphibious Exercise "Lone Eagle." This exercise was delayed in Okinawa due to the Cuban crisis, which put United States ships on a world-wide alert. On 12 November, *Westchester County* returned to her home port of Yokosuka, Japan, where she spent Christmas. On 28 December 1962, she departed for a New Year's visit to Tokyo, Japan.

The year 1963 began with a cold weather operation in Korea which commenced on 16 January. *Westchester County* spent the time until 24 May shuttling marine personnel and equipment to Naha, Okinawa; Tsoying, Taiwan; and Numazu, Japan, with interspersed upkeep periods at Yokosuka, Japan. On 24 May, she sailed from Naha, Okinawa, to transport Korean soldiers from Pusan to Pohang, Korea. After a brief upkeep at Sasebo, Japan, *Westchester County* took part in Operation "Flagpole," a joint amphibious exercise with the Republic of Korea Navy and Marines which concluded on 29 June. July and August were spent in upkeep at Yokosuka, followed by Exercise "Bayonet Beach" on 5 September at Tong Po Pi, Korea.

Westchester County returned to Yokosuka on 19 September for inspections and amphibious training. On 7 October, the ship sailed for Okinawa where she sustained damage to her bow ramp which required repairs at Sasebo, Japan, until 29 October. After a brief Marine lift to Okinawa, *Westchester County* returned to Yokosuka on 9 November for regular overhaul. The ship went into drydock on 27 December 1963 and thus ended the year.

Westchester County remained in drydock until 31 January 1964 and underwent sea trials, refresher training, and amphibious refresher training at Yokosuka, Japan, until 8 May. She departed Yokosuka on 19 May for Naha, Okinawa, and the first of many Marine lifts between Okinawa, Japan, and the Philippines which occupied the ship until 9 August.

At that time, due to the Tonkin Gulf crisis, *Westchester County* departed Naha, Okinawa, for extended operations off Vietnam in the South China Sea. She returned to Subic Bay, Philippines, on 2 October and began a series of Marine lifts between Naha and Buckner Bay, Okinawa; Tsoying, Taiwan; and Yokosuka, Japan. On 19 November, the ship returned to Yokosuka, Japan, and underwent upkeep and underway training until 24 December when she visited Tokyo, Japan. *Westchester County* departed Tokyo on 28 December 1964 and returned to Yokosuka.

Westchester County started 1965 with two marine lifts between Okinawa and Japan. February was spent at Okinawa; and, on 3 March, the ship transported marines and vehicles to Subic Bay, Philippines. Between 17 March and 15 April, the tank landing ship completed two Marine lifts to Danang, South Vietnam. On 29 April, she departed Buckner Bay, Okinawa, for the first amphibious landing at Chu Lai, South Vietnam. This operation was the largest in the Pacific since the Korean War. From 11 May to 24 May, the ship made two turnaround trips between Naha, Okinawa, and Chu Lai.

Following upkeep at Yokosuka, Japan, *Westchester County* spent the period from 22 June to 15 August making marine lifts to Danang and Chu Lai, South Vietnam. She returned to Yokosuka for upkeep until 30 September when she transported marines from Naha, Okinawa, to Numazu, Japan, for cold weather operations.

After reloading at Yokosuka, *Westchester County* transported Korean troops from Pusan, Korea, to Qui Nhon, South Vietnam. From 7 to 21 November, she joined in Operation "Blue Marlin," making two landings at Tam Ky, South Vietnam. These landings were followed by stops at Camranh Bay, Phan Rang, and Danang, South Vietnam. She arrived at Yokosuka, Japan, on 16 December and spent Christmas at her home port. On 26 December, she put to sea to load cargo at Iwakuni, Japan, arriving on the 28th and departing for Naha, Okinawa, the next day. On 31 December 1965, she arrived at Naha and there celebrated the New Year.

During 1966, *Westchester County* served extensively in carrying cargo to the Republic of Vietnam in support of American forces ashore. On 24 January, the ship joined in Operation "Double Eagle," an amphibious assault at Cap Mai, Vietnam. From February throughout August, *Westchester County* transported troops and equipment to Qui Nhon, Chu Lai, and Danang, Vietnam. This duty was interspersed with port visits to Hong Kong and repairs at Subic Bay and Yokosuka.

On 1 September 1966, *Westchester County* anchored at Vung Tau, Vietnam, to begin operations as the support ship for Operation "Market Time." Until 4 October, the ship steamed continuously on station off the Ca Mau Peninsula; refueling, replenishing, and serving as a base for the boats and crews who patrolled the coast of Vietnam to prevent infiltration by sea. After returning to Yokosuka, the ship spent the period from 16 October through 31 December undergoing upkeep interspersed with a short training visit to Okinawa and port visits to Keelung, Taiwan, and Hiroshima, Japan.

From 3 January to 15 March 1967, *Westchester County* transported troops and supplies between Okinawa and Vietnam. The tank landing ship went into overhaul on 15 March at Yokosuka, Japan, followed by refresher training which lasted through 5 August. *Westchester County* spent the remaining months of 1967 carrying marines and equipment between Yokosuka, Okinawa, and Vietnam. The LST served as a Mobile Riverine Force support ship in the Mekong Delta from 24 October through 31 December 1967.

Westchester County spent the early weeks of 1968 continuing service as a Mobile Riverine support ship. On 26 January, the tank landing ship began a series of lifts from Okinawa, Japan, and the Philippines to Vietnam. She underwent repair availability and training exercises from 16 July through 22 September.

The tank landing ship resumed duty with the Mobile Riverine Forces on 22 September. Tragedy struck on 1 November while *Westchester County* lay anchored in the vicinity of My Tho, Vietnam. Two giant underwater explosions ripped *Westchester County*, killing 26 men. The enemy mines had been attached to the hull about amidships on the starboard side causing ruptured berthing compartments and fuel and storage tanks. The day following the explosion, the entire Mobile Riverine Force moved from My Tho to Dong Tam. After beaching at Dong Tam for temporary repairs, she returned to Yokosuka, Japan, via Subic Bay, Philippines, on 26 November. *Westchester County* went into drydock at the United States Naval Ship Repair Facility where it remained until 5 February 1969.

Upon completion of refresher training and upkeep, the ship got underway on 10 March 1969 for Operation "Market Time" off the Vietnam coast. From 5 July through 23 August, *Westchester County* joined in the first phase of Vietnam troop withdrawal. The remainder of 1969 was spent carrying personnel and equipment from Korea, Japan, and Okinawa to Vietnam with intermittent periods of repair and liberty.

The beginning of the 1970's found *Westchester County* operating off the northern coast of Vietnam. During February, she conducted troop and equipment withdrawal from South Vietnam, then underwent restricted availability at Yokosuka beginning on 4 March.

April through July were spent transporting personnel and cargo from Japan and Okinawa to Vietnam. On 2 August, she relieved *Washoe County* (LST–1165) off the Ca Mau peninsula for Operation "Solid Anchor," which consisted of fueling boats and helicopters. Nine of *Westchester County*'s sailors received the Combat Action Ribbon when they withstood enemy small arms and rocket fire while transiting the Bo De River.

Following a restricted availability at Yokosuka which commenced on 30 October, *Westchester County* made stops at Camranh Bay, Danang, Hong Kong, Okinawa, and Iwakuni, Japan, before departing on 17 November for a vehicle lift from Chinhae, South Korea, to Okinawa. *Westchester County* spent the first half of December involved in landing rehearsals and gunnery exercises. She then transited to Singapore to enjoy a Christmas visit. The ship closed out the year en route to Subic Bay, Philippines.

During January 1971, *Westchester County* sailed between Hong Kong and Subic Bay, Philippines. On 2 February, she departed Subic Bay en route to the Gulf of Tonkin in support of "Lamson III," the Cambodian operation which lasted until 7 March. After restricted availability and training at Okinawa and Yokosuka, the ship returned to Vietnam on 21 June and continued operations.

From 6 August through 1 September, *Westchester County* assumed the administrative duties as SOPA (senior officer present afloat) in Hong Kong. Following restricted availability at Yokosuka, the ship lifted personnel and equipment of an Army security agency for transit to Pusan, Korea, and returned them to Okinawa on 6 December. During this period, she transported marines from Japan to Okinawa, departing Okinawa on 24 November to spend Thanksgiving at Yokosuka. Following the off-load of Army personnel on 6 December, *Westchester County* returnd to Yokosuka for the holiday season, arriving on 10 December.

Westchester County completed a restricted availability on 17 January 1972 and set out for a lift to Subic Bay, Philippines. The tank landing ship spent February at Subic Bay undergoing repairs and local operations. After SOPA duties at Hong Kong from 15 to 31 March, the ship resumed personnel and cargo transits to the Gulf of Tonkin, Vietnam, until 30 August 1972. During this period, the tank landing ship underwent a seven-week restricted availability followed by refresher training at Yokosuka, Japan.

From 7 September through 1 October 1972, *Westchester County* operated in logistic suport of Mine Flotilla 1. She returned to Yokosuka on 15 October for availability and inspection. The ship made a brief transit to Okinawa, departing on 30 November. She returned to Yokosuka on 5 December 1972 and enjoyed the Christmas holidays while in upkeep status.

On 27 January 1973, with the signing of the Vietnam Cease Fire in Paris, the ship was underway for Subic Bay, Philippines, to transport mine counter-measures equipment and Commander, Mine Flotilla One to the Gulf of Tonkin. Due to a breakdown in the cease-fire negotiations, the tank landing ship was ordered to a rendezvous point near Danang. Departing the vicinity on 3 March, she continued to work in support of Operation "End Sweep."

After availability and shore bombardment exercises at Subic Bay which commenced on 14 March, *Westchester County* returned to Vietnam in support of Operation "End Sweep" which was completed on 18 July. The ship made stops at Subic Bay, Philippines, and Okinawa before finally arriving at Yokosuka, Japan, on 30 July.

Westchester County was decommissioned on 30 August 1973 and arrived at the Inactive Ship Facility, Puget Sound Naval Shipyard, Bremerton, Wash., on 30 November of that year. On 27 August 1974, she was turned over to the Turkish Navy and commissioned as *Serdar* (L–402).

Westchester County earned 16 battle stars for Vietnam service.

Westerdijk

A Dutch name that means "western dike."

(Freighter: dp. 17,050; l. 475'; b. 55'; dr. 31'9''; s. 14.7 k.; cpl. 52; a. 1 5'', 1 4'')

Westerdijk—a steel-hulled, single-screw cargo vessel built at West Hartlepool, England, by Irvine's Shipbuilding and Drydock Co., Ltd.—was completed in 1913 and operated by the Dutch *Holland Amerika Lijn* in the transatlantic trade before World War I. The freighter was chartered by the United States Government on 30 March 1918. *Westerdijk*—listed as *Westerdyk* in the 1918 *Ship's Data, U.S. Naval Vessels*—was designated Id. No. 2514 and commissioned at New York on 27 March 1918, Lt. Comdr. Harold L. Thompson, USNRF, in command.

Assigned to the Naval Overseas Transportation Service (NOTS), *Westerdijk* commenced her first transatlantic cargo-carrying voyage on 9 April, departing New York with a load of general Army cargo. She conducted four voyages in all before the armistice ended World War I on 11 November 1918. Returning in ballast to New York from her fourth voyage, *Westerdijk* underwent repairs into 1919. She departed New York on 19 January 1919, proceeded via the Panama Canal, and arrived at Rosario, Chile, soon thereafter. Taking on a general commercial cargo, the freighter lifted this load of goods to New York before heading south to load another cargo at New Orleans late in June 1919. There, she took on 8,153 tons of goods consigned to the United States Shipping Board and sailed via Norfolk, Va., to European waters.

Westerdijk arrived at Liverpool on 29 July; unloaded her cargo; and sailed for Rotterdam, Holland, on 21 September. Arriving at her prewar home port two days later, the cargo vessel underwent a final inspection and inventory and was decommissioned on 25 September 1919. Simultaneously struck from the Navy list, *Westerdijk* was returned to her owners, the *Holland Amerika Lijn*, the same day. Renamed *Eschersheim*, the freighter soon resumed commercial service under the Dutch flag.

Westerly

A town in Washington County, Rhode Island, located on the Pawcatuck River near the Connecticut state line.

(PC–1198: dp. 280; l. 173'8''; b. 23'0''; dr. 10'10''; s. 20.2 k. (tl.); cpl. 65; a. 1 3'', 1 40mm., 3 20mm., 2 dct., 4 dcp. (K-guns), 2 dcp. (Mousetrap); cl. PC–461)

PC–1198 was laid down on 3 October 1942 at Morris Heights, N.Y., by the Consolidated Shipbuilding Corp.; launched on 12 December 1942; sponsored by Miss Dorothy Given; and placed in commission on 3 May 1943 at the New York Navy Yard, Lt. A. E. Lind in command.

After completing a month of shakedown training out of Miami, Fla., *PC–1198* reported for duty with the Caribbean Sea Frontier on 22 June. The submarine chaser was assigned duty escorting convoys between various islands in the West Indies and specialized in shepherding ships laden with petroleum products from Curaçao and Aruba on the initial legs of their voyages. She steamed most frequently between those two islands and American bases at Guantanamo Bay, Cuba, and Trinidad where other ships took over escort responsibility.

The end of the war in Europe in May 1945, however, brought a change to her duty. With the U-boat menace gone, the little warship took up air-sea rescue responsibilities and participated in mine removal operations in the West Indies. During these operations, she added Jamaica, Puerto Rico, and St. Thomas to her itinerary. Air-sea rescue duty in the Caribbean continued until June of 1946. At that time, she steamed north to New York where she reported to the Commandant, 3d Naval District, for duty training naval reservists. For the next three years, she plied the coastal waters between New York City and Portland, Maine, calling frequently at Portsmouth, N.H., Bridgeport and New Haven, Conn.; Provincetown, Mass.; and Portland, Maine. In July 1948, she voyaged farther north to visit the Canadian ports at Halifax and Yarmouth in the province of Nova Scotia. Later that year, she added Boston, Nantucket, and Gloucester, Mass., to her itinerary as well as New London and New Bedford, Mass. In May of 1949, she sailed south and visited Charleston, S.C., and St. Augustine, Fla., before returning to New York in June. On 11 January 1950, *PC–1198* entered Boston to begin inactivation. On 15 March 1950, she was placed out of commission, in reserve, and was berthed with the Boston Group, Atlantic Reserve Fleet. On 15 February 1956, while still in reserve, she was named *Westerly*. She never performed any active service under her new name before she was struck from the Navy list on 1 April 1959.

Western Ally

(Freighter: dp. 12,370; l. 426'6''; b. 54'0''; dph. 31'7''; dr. 25'6''; s. 12.3 k.; cpl. 70)

Western Ally—a single-screw, steel-hulled cargo vessel constructed as *War Hector* under a United States Shipping Board (USSB) contract, at Seattle, Wash., by the Ames Shipbuilding and Drydock Co.—was launched on 9 November 1918; designated Id. No. 3815; taken over by the Navy on 15 January 1919; and commissioned at the Puget Sound Navy Yard, Bremerton, Wash., Lt. Comdr. William E. Abernathy, USNRF, in command.

Assigned to the Naval Overseas Transportation Service, the cargo ship sailed for Norfolk laden with foodstuffs on 2 February. Proceeding via the Panama Canal, she arrived at Hampton Roads on 4 March. The cargo vessel headed for Gibraltar on 8 April, and thence got underway for the eastern Mediterranean on 25 April. After arriving at Constantinople on 3 May, she speedily discharged her goods and headed west on the following day.

After a brief stop at Gibraltar to repair her damaged screw, *Western Ally* arrived at Philadelphia, Pa., on 20 July. Decommissioned there on 23 July, *Western Ally* was returned to the USSB and remained in its custody until 1929 when she was abandoned due to age and deterioration.

Western Belle

(Freighter: dp. 12,100; l. 423'9''; b. 54'0''; dph. 29'9''; dr. 24'½'' (mean); s. 10.5 k.; cpl. 88; a. none)

Western Belle—a single-screw, steel-hulled cargo vessel completed in 1918 under a United States Shipping Board (USSB) contract, at Portland, Oreg., by the Columbia River Shipbuilding Corp.—was commissioned on 22 November 1918 at Bremerton, Wash., in the Puget Sound Navy Yard, Lt. Comdr. Olaf Breiland, USNRF, in command.

Taken over by the Navy for use with the Naval Overseas Transportation Service (NOTS), *Western Belle*—classified Id. No. 3551—sailed from Puget Sound on 22 December with a cargo of 6,818 tons of flour for delivery to New York, N.Y. Proceeding via the Panama Canal, she arrived at New York on 7 January 1919 and bunkered with coal prior to heading for Gibraltar on 18 January. After a brief stay at Gibraltar from 3 to 8 February, she was routed on to Deringe, France, where she off-loaded her cargo. On 20 March, she got underway for home with 924 tons of Army cargo.

Arriving at New York on 20 April, *Western Belle* was decommissioned on 3 May 1919 and returned to the USSB, which retained custody of her until 1932. The ship was then purchased by Merritt, Chapman, and Scott. She was abandoned the following year.

Western Chief

(Freighter: dp. 12,185; l. 423'9''; b. 54'0''; dph. 29'9''; dr. 24'2'' (mean); s. 10.5 k.; cpl. 99; a. 1 5'', 1 3'')

Western Chief—a single-screw, steel-hulled cargo vessel constructed under a United States Shipping Board

(USSB) contract for the *Compagnie Generale* of France, at Portland, Oreg., by the Northwest Steel Co.—was launched on 20 April 1918. Taken over by the Navy on 3 July 1918, the cargo ship was commissioned at Portland on the same day, Lt. Comdr. Thomas H. Thompson, USNRF, in command.

Designated Id. No. 3161 and assigned to the Naval Overseas Transportation Service, *Western Chief* departed the Pacific Northwest on 12 July with 7,170 tons of flour on board as cargo. Proceeding via the Panama Canal, she arrived at New York on 15 August; unloaded the flour; loaded 20 trucks, and got underway from Norfolk on the 22d in a convoy bound for France. She made port at Brest on 11 September and remained until 8 October when she sailed for the United States. Reaching New York on the 24th, she proceeded the same day to Newport News, Va., to prepare for another voyage.

Western Chief then conducted three more round-trip cargo runs to Europe. She was at sea on the first of these voyages en route to La Pallice on 11 November 1918, the day the armistice ending World War I was signed. On 16 April 1919, *Western Chief* got underway for Europe with a full cargo of flour on her last cruise under NOTS. Her final voyage embraced calls at the Hook of Holland; Dartmouth, England; Danzig, Poland; and Copenhagen, Denmark, before she returned home to Baltimore on 25 June 1919.

Western Chief was decommissioned, struck from the Navy list, and returned to the Shipping Board on 28 June 1919. She subsequently operated on mercantile service and was acquired by the British government when England's need for merchantmen became pressing during World War II. While steaming with Convoy SC–24, *Western Chief* was torpedoed at 1307 on 14 March 1941 by Italian submarine *Emo* and sunk in the North Atlantic, south of Iceland.

Western Comet

(Freighter: dp. 12,185; l. 423'9''; b. 54'0''; dph. 29'9''; dr. 24'0'' (mean); s. 10.5 k.; cpl. 109; a. 1 4'', 1 3'')

Western Comet—a single-screw, steel-hulled freighter built under a United States Shipping Board contract under the name *Argonne* for the French *Compagnie Generale*—was launched on 23 July 1918 at Portland, Oreg., by the Northwest Steel Co.; acquired by the Navy on 22 September 1918 and designated Id. No. 3569; and commissioned, Lt. Comdr. Walter Tinn, UNSRF, in command.

Assigned to the Naval Overseas Transportation Service, *Western Comet* got underway on 2 October for the east coast with a cargo of flour. Proceeding via the Panama Canal, she arrived at New York on 31 October and loaded 24 trucks. Getting underway again on 11 November—the day the armistice was signed ending hostilities in World War I—the cargo vessel reached Le Havre, France, on 28 November. There, she took on board 1,400 tons of Army cargo and sailed for home on New Year's Day 1919. En route to New York, she was forced to put into Bermuda on 19 January to correct turbine trouble. The cargo vessel got underway once more on 5 February and proceeded in company with *Mohave* (Tug No. 15) to New York on 7 February.

Decommissioned at New York on 1 March 1919, *Western Comet* was returned on the same day to the Shipping Board which retained custody of the vessel until she was abandoned in 1933.

Western Front

(Freighter: dp. 11,500; l. 423'0''; b. 54'0''; dph. 29'9''; dr. 24'1½'' (mean); s. 12.0 k.; cpl. 98; a. 1 4'', 1 6-pdr.)

Western Front—a steel-hulled, single-screw freighter, formerly named *Nikkosan Maru* and *Indiana* and built under a United States Shipping Board contract—was launched on 15 September 1917 at Seattle, Wash., by the Skinner and Eddy Corp. The ship subsequently proceeded to New York, where she was inspected by the Navy on 16 January 1918 and acquired soon thereafter for duty with the Naval Overseas Transportation Service (NOTS). Designated Id. No. 1787, *Western Front* was commissioned on 11 May 1918, Lt. Comdr. John Burns, USNRF, in command.

The cargo vessel soon took on board a cargo of steel rails, ordnance equipment, and 10 locomotives, and got underway for France on 17 May with Convoy HH–69, which was escorted by *Galveston* (Cruiser No. 17). Six days out, *Western Front* collided with and sank British merchantman *Clan Matheson*. She, herself, was forced to turn homeward for repairs at New York.

Western Front got underway again on 6 June and arrived at her original destination, St. Nazaire, on the 22d. She discharged her cargo and returned to New York, this time for drydocking and permanent repairs at the Robbins Drydock, Brooklyn, N.Y. The cargo vessel subsequently made four more voyages carrying cargoes for NOTS to the French ports of Bordeaux, La Pallice, Quiberon, and Brest. On one run, she carried 26 Army tanks and delivered these armored vehicles to New York in the spring of 1919. Returning from her last voyage on 2 August 1919, *Western Front* was decommissioned on 15 August at Newport News, Va., and returned to the Shipping Board on the same day. She remained in the custody of the Shipping Board until she disappeared from merchant vessel registers in 1922.

Western Hope

(Freighter: dp. 12,170; l. 423'9''; b. 54'0''; dr. 24'2''; dph. 29'9''; s. 9.5 k.; cpl. 102; a. none)

Western Hope—originally named *War Ruby* and slated to be built for the British Cunard Steamship Line—was a single-screw, steel-hulled freighter launched on 29 July 1918 at Seattle, Wash., by the shipbuilding firm of J. F. Duthie and Co. Acquired by the Navy from the United States Shipping Board (USSB) for use by the Naval Overseas Transportation Service (NOTS), *Western Hope* was commissioned at Seattle on 25 September 1918, Lt. Comdr. Andrew G. King, USNRF, in command.

After loading a cargo of flour, *Western Hope* sailed for the east coast on 8 October. She transited the Panama Canal en route and arrived at New York City on 7 November 1918, four days before the armistice stilled the guns of World War I. The freighter departed New York on the 17th, bound for Europe, and, after reaching Gibraltar, was routed on to Italy on 7 December.

Repairing an engine casualty at Taranto en route, *Western Hope* eventually arrived at Trieste and discharged her cargo of flour there. After departing that Adriatic port on 16 March 1919, she retransited the Straits of Gibraltar and arrived at Newport News, Va., on 21 April, ending her sole voyage for NOTS.

Decommissioned on 5 May 1919 at Newport News, *Western Hope* was simultaneously struck from the Navy list and returned to the USSB. The cargo vessel was laid up in 1923 and remained there until abandoned 10 years later due to age and deterioration.

Western Knight

Western Knight—a single-screw, steel-hulled freighter constructed in 1918 as *War Helen* at Seattle, Wash., by the Ames Shipbuilding and Drydock Co.—was built under a United States Shipping Board (USSB) contract for Navy use in the Naval Overseas Transportation Service but was never acquired by the Navy.

Western Light

(Freighter: dp. 12,185; l. 423'9''; b. 54'0''; dph. 29'9''; dr. 24'1'' (mean); s. 10.5 k.; cpl. 116; a. 1 4'', 1 3'')

Western Light—a steel-hulled, single-screw cargo ship built in 1918 at Portland, Oreg., by the Northwest Steel Co., for the United States Shipping Board (USSB) and completed in 1918—was taken over by the Navy at Portland on 30 July 1918 and was commissioned the same day, Lt. Comdr. Claude Smith, USNRF, in command.

Designated Id. No. 3300, she sailed for Chile in August, took on a cargo of nitrate at Arica, and got underway on 17 September for home. Proceeding through the Panama Canal, she arrived at Philadelphia on 7 October and discharged her cargo. She then shifted to New York to join an east-bound convoy on 4 November for the first of her three transatlantic voyages, carrying cargo to European ports for American forces in France.

Her ports of call included Verdon-sur-mer, France; Falmouth, England; and Rotterdam, Holland—carrying a total of 17,540 tons of hay, oats, flour, and lard, in addition to other varied Army supplies. Returning to New York from Rotterdam on 8 May 1919, *Western Light* was placed out of commission on 14 May and returned to the USSB. She remained in the custody of the USSB until abandoned in 1933.

Western Maid

(Freighter: dp. 12,185; l. 423'9''; b. 54'0''; dph. 29'9''; dr. 24'½'' (mean); s. 10.5 k.; cpl. 70; a. none)

Western Maid—a steel-hulled, single-screw freighter built as *Aisne* under a United States Shipping Board contract at Portland, Oreg., by the Northwestern Steel Co.—was launched on 8 July 1918; acquired by the Navy on 17 August 1918; designated Id. No. 3703; and commissioned on the same day, Lt. E. O. Smith, USNRF, in command.

Assigned to the Naval Overseas Transportation Service, *Western Maid* departed Portland on 21 August, bound for Chile with a full cargo of flour. Loading a consignment of nitrate soon after her arrival at Arica, the cargo vessel sailed, via the Panama Canal, for the Gulf of Mexico and arrived at New Orleans on 23 October. *Western Maid* subsequently sailed for New York, N.Y., on 11 November, the day fighting stopped in Europe.

The cargo vessel arrived at New York on the 17th with 6,082 tons of general Army cargo on board. She sailed in convoy for northern Europe on 10 January, but engine trouble forced her to return to New York for repairs. She got underway again on the 14th. After visits to Plymouth and Falmouth, England, and to Rotterdam, Holland, *Western Maid* returned to the east coast, arriving at Baltimore, Md., on 12 March 1919. *Western Maid* was decommissioned on 20 March and returned to the Shipping Board, in whose custody she remained until abandoned in 1933.

Western Ocean

(Freighter: dp. 12,185; l. 423'9''; b. 54'0''; dph. 29'9''; dr. 24'½'' (mean); s. 12.5 k. (max.); cpl. 91; a. 2 3'')

Western Ocean (Id. No. 3151)—a steam turbine, steel-hulled cargo ship originally listed as owned by the *Compagnie Generale* of France, and named *Joffre* —was completed on 31 May 1918 at Portland, Oreg., by the Willamette Iron Works; was taken over by the Navy on 17 June 1918 from the United States Shipping Board (USSB); and commissioned the same day at Portland, Lt. Comdr. J. M. Silversteen, USNRF, in command.

Ten days later, *Western Ocean* sailed on her maiden voyage, bound for the Hawaiian Islands. Arriving at

Hilo on 8 July, the cargo vessel loaded 8,800 tons of sugar and got underway again on the 13th bound, via the Panama Canal, for the east coast of the United States. She arrived at Philadelphia on 15 August, unloaded her cargo, and promptly took on board 6,830 tons of general Army cargo for American troops on the western front. She then sailed for New York to join an east-bound convoy, which sailed for Europe on 10 September.

Arriving in France on 27 September, *Western Ocean* unloaded her goods and sailed on 24 October for Newport News, Va., on what turned out to be her last wartime voyage. She arrived at Newport News on 11 November, the day the armistice ended hostilities. But the work of supplying United States forces still in France remained, and the ship made two more voyages carrying cargo to La Pallice, France. She arrived at Norfolk, Va., on 18 May; was decommissioned on 22 May 1919; and returned to the USSB on the same day. She remained in the custody of that agency and of its successor, the United States Maritime Commission, until late 1941 when she was transferred to the United Kingdom to serve the Ministry of War Transportation under management of G. Heyl & Sons, Ltd., as *Empire Opossum*. She served under this name until scrapped in 1949.

Western Plains

(Freighter: t. 12,185; l. 423'9"; b. 54'0"; dph. 29'9"; dr. 24'1½" (mean); s. 10.5 k.; cpl. 70)

Western Plains—a single-screw, steel-hulled cargo vessel constructed in 1918 under a United States Shipping Board contract at Portland, Oreg., by the Columbia River Shipbuilding Corp.—was taken over by the Navy for service with the Naval Overseas Transportation Service (NOTS); designated Id. No. 3741; and commissioned on 17 October 1918, Lt. Comdr. David C. Austin, USNRF, in command.

Western Plains took on board 7,296 tons of flour, got underway for the east coast on 25 October, transited the Panama Canal, and reached New York exactly one month later. After she unloaded her consignment of flour at New York, she pressed on for Gibraltar where she took on cargo for shipment to Turkey and arrived at Constantinople on 25 January 1919. *Western Plains* delivered her goods; loaded 2,500 tons of Turkish tobacco; sailed for the United States on 24 February; touched at the Azores; and arrived at Philadelphia on 10 April. *Western Plains* was decommissioned there on 30 April 1919 and returned to the Shipping Board on the same day. She remained in the custody of that agency until abandoned in 1933.

Western Sea

(Freighter: dp. 12,200; l. 423'9"; b. 54'0"; dph. 29'9"; dr. 24'1" (mean); s. 10.5 k.; cpl. 92)

Western Sea—a single-screw freighter built under a United States Shipping Board (USSB) contract at Seattle, Wash., by J. F. Duthie and Co.—was launched on 25 May 1918; taken over by the Navy for service with the Naval Overseas Transportation Service; and commissioned on 29 June 1918, Lt. Comdr. C. E. Stewart, USNRF, in command.

Laden with a cargo of 6,812 tons of flour, *Western Sea* sailed for the east coast on 7 July; transited the Panama Canal; and arrived at New York on 11 August. She off-loaded her consignment of flour and took on board general cargo—including 14 trucks—for the American Army in France and got underway for Europe.

After reaching Brest, France, the ship moved to Bordeaux where she speedily unloaded her cargo and took on 1,000 tons of pyrites for her voyage home. Proceeding via Halifax, Nova Scotia, she reached

New York on 24 November. She remained there only long enough to deliver the pyrites and pick up 7,516 tons of general Army stores. Following a stop at Falmouth, England, she reached Rotterdam, Holland, on 25 January and unloaded her cargo. On 7 February 1919, *Western Sea* headed for home and arrived at New York on 1 March. She was placed out of commission there two months later, on 9 May 1919, and was returned to the USSB on the same day. She remained in the custody of that agency until the early 1930's.

Western Spirit

(Freighter: dp. 12,185; l. 423'9"; b. 54'0"; dph. 29'9"; dr. 24'1½" (mean); s. 10.5 k.; cpl. 97; a. 1 4", 1 3")

Western Spirit—a single-screw, steel-hulled freighter constructed under a United States Shipping Board (USSB) contract at Portland, Oreg., by the Northwestern Steel Co.—was launched on 6 May 1918; was taken over by the Navy on 19 July 1918; designated Id. No. 3164; and commissioned at Portland on 30 July 1918, Lt. Comdr. Howard H. Rees, USNRF, in command.

Assigned to the Naval Overseas Transportation Service (NOTS), *Western Spirit* departed Portland on 26 July for Arica, Chile. There she loaded a cargo of nitrates and proceeded via the Panama Canal to Louisiana. The cargo vessel arrived at New Orleans on 11 September; unloaded; and sailed on the 23d for Hampton Roads, Va. Soon after arriving at Norfolk, she onloaded some 4,000 tons of general Army supplies and sailed on 13 October for New York to join an east-bound convoy for France.

Underway on the 16th, *Western Spirit* developed engine trouble and was forced to put in to Halifax, Nova Scotia, for emergency repairs which delayed her until 2 November. Arriving at Verdon-sur-mer on the 20th, the cargo vessel discharged her cargo, took on a return Army equipment cargo, and got underway on 18 December for the United States.

Returning to Norfolk on 7 January 1919, *Western Spirit* conducted one more cargo-carrying voyage for NOTS. She departed Norfolk on 19 February, carrying railroad supplies and a cargo of goods consigned to the Army Quartermaster Corps, and arrived at La Pallice, France, on 10 March. On the 23d, the cargo vessel departed French waters, bound for home, and reached Norfolk on 11 April.

Western Spirit was decommissioned on 17 April 1919 and returned to the USSB. She remained in the custody of that agency until abandoned, due to age and deterioration, in 1933.

Western Star

(Freighter: dp. 12,185; l. 423'9"; b. 54'0"; dph. 29'9"; dr. 24'0" (mean); s. 12.0 k.; cpl. 98; a. none)

Western Star—a single-screw, steel-hulled freighter constructed under a United States Shipping Board contract for the French *Compagnie Generale* at Portland, Oreg., by J. F. Duthie and Co.—was launched on 4 July 1918; was taken over by the Navy on 28 August 1918; designated Id. No. 4210; and commissioned on the same day, Lt. Comdr. Richard E. Tull, USNRF, in command.

Assigned to the Naval Overseas Transportation Service, *Western Star* arrived at Union Bay, British Columbia, on 5 September, where she loaded a cargo of coal for shipment to Chile and was thoroughly searched for possible bombs or explosives. Departing Union Bay on the 15th, she arrived at Iquique on 13 October and unloaded her coal cargo before shifting to Caleta Buena, where she loaded a cargo of nitrates.

After getting underway from Chile on 4 November, *Western Star* proceeded north, transited the Panama Canal, and made port at Savannah, Ga., on 5

December. She unloaded the nitrates and proceeded to Tompkinsville, N.Y., where she arrived on the last day of 1918. The cargo ship was decommissioned there on 1 March and returned to the Shipping Board on the same day. *Western Star* remained in the custody of that agency until abandoned in 1933.

Western World

(ScStr.: t. 441; l. 178'; b. 34'3''; s. 7 k.; a. 1 30-pdr. P.r., 2 32-pdr. P.r.)

Western World—a screw steamer built in 1856 at Brooklyn, N.Y.—was purchased by the Navy on 21 September 1861 at New York City from S. Schuyler; and commissioned on 3 January 1862 at the New York Navy Yard, Acting Master Samuel B. Gregory in command.

On 2 January 1862, *Western World* was ordered to Port Royal, S.C., to join the South Atlantic Blockading Squadron. On the 26th, she participated in a major reconnaissance sweep of the Savannah River, Ga., and its tributaries. The force included the gunboats *Ottawa* and *Seneca*; armed steamers *Isaac Smith, Potomska,* and *Ellen;* and transports *Cosmopolitan, Delaware,* and *Boston* carrying over 2,400 troops under the command of Brigadier General H. G. Wright. The Union flotilla repulsed an attack by five Confederate vessels on 28 January and the next day completed invaluable survey work. On 14 February 1862, *Western World* and *E. B. Hale* drove off four Confederate vessels which attempted to break the Union blockade of the Mud and Wright's Rivers, tributaries of the Savannah. This restricted Confederate activity upon the Savannah River and protected the newly installed Federal battery at Venus Point. After remaining off the Savannah through May, *Western World* returned to Port Royal on 2 June.

On the 6th, *Western World* called briefly at St. John's River, Fla., to reprovision Union ships on blockade duty there. She immediately returned to Port Royal and was dispatched on the 10th to the blockade off Georgetown, S.C., commanded by Comdr. G. A. Prentiss on board *Albatross*.

On 25 June 1862, *Western World, Andrew,* and *E. B. Hale* entered the North Santee River, S.C., intending to destroy an important railroad bridge inland. En route, parties from the warships set fire to several plantations and took over 400 slaves on board the steamers. During an expedition in Winyah Bay, S.C., *Western World* captured the British schooner *Volante* on 2 July. However, intense shore fire and the sharp, unnavigable bends of the river prompted Comdr. Prentiss to abandon the expedition the following day. On the 25th, *Western World* sailed for Port Royal carrying contraband. However, she soon left the squadron base for blockade duty off Doboy Sound, Ga., which occupied the ship until the end of October when she sailed north to the New York Navy Yard for extensive overhaul.

Western World departed New York on 16 February 1863 and arrived at Newport News on 11 March for duty with the North Atlantic Blockading Squadron. A week later, she towed *General Putnam* to Baltimore for repairs. Structural problems forced *Western World,* herself, to the Philadelphia Navy Yard late in the month; but she departed Philadelphia on 1 April for Yorktown, Va., and blockade duty between the Piankatank River and Fort Monroe, Va.

Through the spring and summer, *Western World* participated actively in operations along the Virginia coast and in the Chesapeake Bay. On 19 April, she and *Commodore Morris* escorted transport units of the Army of the Potomac up the York as far as the Pamunkey River. Together with *Samuel Rotan,* she captured schooners *Martha Ann* and *A. Carson* off Horn Harbor, Va., on the 24th. With *Crusader,* she destroyed two abandoned schooners in Milford Haven, Va., on 1 May 1863. On the 27th, she captured two large sailboats, took two prisoners, and confiscated Confederate coin and currency

in Stokes Creek, Va. On 13 June 1863, *Western World* proceeded north to search for Confederate commerce raider *Tacony*. However, she lost her rudderhead during a storm and returned to the Norfolk Navy Yard for repairs on 17 June 1863.

Western World was back in action within a week. Beginning on 23 June 1863, with gunboats *Commodore Barney, Commodore Morris, Morse, Smith Briggs,* and *Jesup,* she escorted and covered a troop landing at White House, Va. During the week-long operation, *Western World* brought up and landed nearly 300 cavalry. On 1 July 1863, she was deployed in the Pamunkey River, Va. Late in the month, *Western World* returned to Hampton Roads where she picked up mail for delivery to blockade ships off Wilmington, N.C. On the voyage to North Carolina waters, she also carried 150 seamen to Beaufort for blockade duty in the sounds. On 10 September 1863, the worn-out vessel proceeded to the Washington Navy Yard for repairs.

Repairs completed, *Western World* was assigned on 2 February 1864 to the Second Division of the Potomac Flotilla but, a week later, was transferred to the First Division and assigned to patrol duty from Piankatank River to Blakistone Island. However, the ship returned to the Washington Navy Yard on 1 April for more repairs and remained there until early November.

Western World was assigned to the North Atlantic Blockading Squadron on 10 November 1864. She patrolled the Virginia coast between the Nansemond River and Lawn's Creek and, on 15 December 1864, helped to refloat the grounded monitor *Saugus*. On 5 March 1865, she arrived in the Rappahannock River to support the Army of the Potomac in operations against Fredericksburg. Later transferred to White House, Va., she sailed on 21 March for St. Inigoes, Md., and duty in the Potomac Flotilla. *Western World* was deployed in Virginia's Mobjack Bay on 6 April and, on 5 May, proceeded to the Washington Navy Yard. She was decommissioned there on 26 May 1865 and was sold at public auction on 24 June 1865 to H. R. Hazelhurst.

Westerner

(Freighter: dp. 12,200; l. 423'9''; b. 54'0''; dph. 29'9''; dr. 24'1'' (mean); s. 10.5 k.; cpl. 87; a. 1 5'')

Westerner—a steel-hulled, single-screw cargo vessel built under a United States Shipping Board (USSB) contract—was launched on 4 November 1917 at Seattle, Wash., by J. F. Duthie and Co. and delivered to the Navy for operation by the Naval Overseas Transportation Service (NOTS) at Norfolk, Va., on 20 June 1918. Commissioned on that date, with Lt. Comdr. Henry W. Lyon, Jr., in command, *Westerner* departed Norfolk for New York on 10 July 1918 with a cargo of Army supplies in her holds.

Joining up with a France-bound convoy, *Westerner* departed New York on 24 July. An engine casualty en route forced the ship to spend three days at Halifax, Nova Scotia, before she resumed her voyage. Making port at Brest on 17 August, the cargo vessel soon shifted to St. Nazaire where she discharged her load. Departing St. Nazaire on 22 September, the ship arrived at Norfolk on 10 October to load another cargo of army supplies.

Westerner subsequently conducted three additional cargo-carrying voyages for NOTS: two to La Pallice, France (on one occasion lifting supplies consigned to the French government), and one to Trieste, Italy, via Gibraltar. After her final NOTS voyages, *Westerner* made port at New York on 6 August 1919.

Decommissioned on 21 August 1919, the cargo vessel was simultaneously struck from the Navy list and turned back to the USSB. Laid up in the late 1920's, *Westerner* was abandoned, due to age and deterioration, in either late 1932 or early 1933.

235

Westfield

A city in Hampden County in southwestern Massachusetts.

(SwStr: t. 822; l. 215'0''; b. 35'0''; dph. 13'6''; a. 1 100-pdr. P.r., 1 9'' D.sb., 4 8'' D.sb.)

Westfield, a sidewheel steam ferryboat, was purchased by the Navy from Cornelius Vanderbilt on 22 November 1861; outfitted at New York by J. A. Westervelt; and commissioned in January 1862, Comdr. William B. Renshaw in command.

Westfield departed New York on 22 February 1862, bound for Key West, Fla., to join Comdr. David D. Porter's Mortar Flotilla. That unit, however, departed Key West on 3 March before *Westfield*'s arrival. She, therefore, did not join the flotilla until her arrival at the Passes of the Mississippi on 18 March. For the next three weeks, she assisted *Mississippi* and *Pensacola* in their efforts to cross the bar at Pass à Outre and enter the Mississippi River.

That mission succeeded finally on 8 April, and *Westfield* began duty covering a coastal survey party developing more precise maps of the lower Mississippi for the assault on Forts Jackson and St. Philip. On 13 April, she received orders to proceed upriver and engage two Confederate gunboats. After two shots from her Parrott rifle, the two Southern ships retired to the protection of the guns of Fort Jackson where they joined six other Confederate gunboats. Undaunted, *Westfield* closed range and opened fire once more. That brief cannonade broke the shaft of CSS *Defiance* and damaged her so severely that her crew later had to abandon and sink her.

Between 14 and 24 April, she supported Porter's Mortar Flotilla during the bombardment of the two Confederate forts in preparation for Flag Officer David Glasgow Farragut's run between them to New Orleans. That event occurred on the 24th, but *Westfield* did not participate directly. Rather, she remained with the mortar boats and continued to support them and supply ammunition. Early in the summer of 1862, *Westfield* moved upriver with the Mortar Flotilla—to a point just below Vicksburg, Miss. There she resumed her duties in support of the mortars during the first campaign against the Confederate stronghold.

Late in July and early in August, the ship made her way back down the Mississippi via Baton Rouge and New Orleans to the Gulf of Mexico. She then took up duty blockading the coast of Texas as a unit of the West Gulf Blockading Squadron. On 4 October, *Westfield* led a unit composed of *Harriet Lane*, *Owasco*, *Clifton*, and *Harry James* in a successful assault on the city of Galveston, Tex., which capitulated formally on the 9th. She remained at Galveston until 1 January 1863 when, during the successful Confederate recapture of the city, she was attacked by two Southern warships. She was blown up to forestall her almost certain capture.

Westford

(Freighter: dp. 12,175; l. 423'9''; b. 54'0''; dph. 29'9''; dr. 23'11¼'' (mean); s. 9.0 k.; cpl. 89; a. 1 5'', 1 3'')

Westford—sometimes referred to as *West Ford*—was a steel-hulled, single-screw freighter launched under a U.S. Shipping Board (USSB) contract on 2 July 1918 at Seattle, Wash., by the Ames Shipbuilding and Drydock Co. She was taken over by the Navy for operation by the Naval Overseas Transportation Service (NOTS), assigned Id. No. 3198, and commissioned on 2 July 1918 Lt. Comdr. Louis C. Drewson, USNRF, in command.

Departing Seattle on 25 July with 6,982 tons of flour in her five holds, *Westford* sailed for the east coast of the United States. She transited the Panama Canal en route, and stopped briefly at Norfolk for voyage repairs before pushing on, in convoy, for France, on 7 September. Arriving at Le Havre, on 26 September, the freighter shifted to Devonport, England, on the 11th. After discharging the remainder of her cargo there, she took on board 763 barrels of lube oil and 2,000 tons of Army return cargo and departed the British Isles on 15 October.

Westford arrived at New York on 1 November, 10 days before the armistice ended World War I. Loading with Army supplies over the ensuing weeks, *Westford* departed New York on 16 November. She arrived at Marseilles on 5 December, discharged her cargo, and took on board 2,000 tons of return Army cargo for the voyage back to New York.

Underway four days before Christmas, the freighter stopped briefly at the Azores for fuel before proceeding on toward home. Arriving at New York on 28 January

The Civil War steamer *Westfield*. The walking beam of her steam engine stands out prominently abaft her stack. (NH 48488)

919, *Westford* soon took on board 4,961 tons of food-stuffs and flour and subsequently sailed for Rotterdam on 16 February. Making port on 7 March, the ship unloaded her cargo and subsequently departed the key Dutch seaport on 29 March for New York.

Arriving at that destination on 13 April, *Westford* was decommissioned, returned to the Shipping Board, and struck from the Navy list on 21 April 1919. She remained under government ownership, laid up until abandoned due to age and deterioration in 1933.

Westmoreland

Counties in Pennsylvania and Virginia.

The name *Westmoreland* was assigned to APR–11 on 13 August 1942. However, the contract of the projected rescue transport was cancelled on 12 March 1943.

I

(APA–104: dp. 11,760; l. 492'0"; b. 69'6"; dr. 23'3"; s. 18.4 k.; cpl. 576; tr. 1,226; a. 2 5", 8 40mm., 18 20mm.; cl. *Bayfield*; T. C2–S–A2)

Westmoreland (APA–104) was laid down under a Maritime Commission contract (MC hull 872) on 8 December 1943 at Pascagoula, Miss., by the Ingalls Shipbuilding Co.; launched on 28 April 1944; sponsored by Mrs. V. H. Hoagland; and placed in commission, for ferrying purposes, on 12 July 1944. Shifted to the Todd Shipyards Corp., Hoboken, N.J., for conversion to an attack transport, the ship was decommissioned on 22 July for the duration of the yard period. Once the task of fitting the ship out as an attack transport was completed, *Westmoreland* was placed in commission on 18 January 1945, Capt. James M. Hicks in command.

After spending most of February on shakedown in Chesapeake Bay, *Westmoreland* sailed for the Pacific on 22 February and arrived at the eastern entrance to the Panama Canal on the 27th. After transiting the canal, the attack transport pushed on for the Hawaiian Islands and reached Pearl Harbor on 14 March.

After training in Hawaiian waters, the ship returned to the west coast at the end of May for voyage repairs at San Pedro, Calif. In mid-June, she shifted northward to load troops and cargo at Portland, Oreg., for transportation to Hawaii. *Westmoreland* subsequently conducted one round-trip voyage between Pearl Harbor and San Francisco in July and then spent most of the first half of the month of August on exercises and further training in Hawaiian waters. During that time, the Japanese, worn down by ceaseless Allied pounding from the air and from the sea, surrendered on 15 August 1945.

Although *Westmoreland* had been commissioned too late to participate in combat against the Japanese in the Pacific, she nevertheless did take part in the massive reverse movement of men back to the United States, Operation "Magic Carpet." The attack transport subsequently called at Manila, in the Philippines; and Sasebo, Japan, operating with Transport Squadron 22; and brought back troops to Portland, before she returned to the Philippines once more. She carried a draft of troops from Samar to San Francisco before heading for the east coast of the United States.

She transited the Panama Canal on 8 April 1946 and arrived at Norfolk five days later. *Westmoreland* was decommissioned there on 5 June 1946 and was struck from the Navy list on 19 June. Acquired by the Isthmian Steamship Co. (later called Isthmian Lines) in July 1947, *Westmoreland* was renamed *Steel King*. The former attack transport carried general cargo for her company until about 1974, when her name disappeared from contemporary shipping registers.

Westover

(Freighter: dp. 12,205; l. 423'9"; b. 54'0"; dph. 29'9"; dr. 24'1" (mean); s. 10.5 k.; cpl. 92; a. 1 5", 1 6-pdr.)

Westover (Id. No. 2687)—a steel-hulled, single-screw freighter built as *War Sun* at Seattle, Wash., by J. F. Duthie and Co., for the Cunard Steamship Line—was launched on 17 February 1918; and inspected by the Navy on 9 April, nine days prior to her completion. Soon thereafter, she sailed for the east coast where she was taken over by the Navy for use by the Naval Overseas Transportation Service. Assigned identification number 2687, *Westover* was commissioned at Newport News, Va., on 22 May 1918.

Shifting to New York City, *Westover* took on a capacity cargo of general Army supplies and got underway in convoy on 27 May for France. However, the freighter developed engine troubles en route to St. Nazaire and fell astern of the convoy. *Westover* plodded resolutely onward but ran afoul of prowling German submarine U–92—12 days out of her base at Kiel—which made a submerged approach and lined up the crippled cargo ship in her periscope sights. At 0730 on 11 July 1918, U–92 torpedoed the luckless *Westover* and sent her to the bottom of the Atlantic, with the loss of 11 American sailors.

Westpool

(Freighter: dp. 12,170; l. 410'5¼"; b. 54'0"; dph. 29'9"; dr. 24'1" (mean); s. 11.5 k.; cpl. 103; a. none)

Westpool—sometimes referred to as *West Pool*—was a steel-hulled, single-screw freighter built under a United States Shipping Board (USSB) contract. She was completed in 1918 at Seattle, Wash., by J. F. Duthie and Co.; was inspected by the Navy; given the Id. No. 3675; was acquired by the Navy on 2 November 1918; and was commissioned the same day, Lt. Comdr. W. H. Harstedt, USNRF, in command.

Departing Puget Sound on 8 November, *Westpool* subsequently loaded cargo in the Canal Zone for the Panama Railroad Co. before resuming her voyage to New York City on 9 December, less than a month after the armistice ended World War I. After arriving there on the 20th, she delivered her cargo before loading 5,002 tons of Army cargo. Departing New York City on 1 February 1919, *Westpool* sailed for European waters.

Upon her arrival at Antwerp, Belgium, on 18 February, the freighter discharged part of her cargo there before shifting to Swansea, Wales, late in February to unload the remainder. Having completed this task between 1 and 5 March, *Westpool* departed the British Isles on 5 March and headed for the United States. *Westpool* put into New York harbor on 23 March and was decommissioned there eight days later, on 31 March 1919. Simultaneously struck from the Navy list and returned to the USSB, *Westpool* subsequently remained under government ownership, in and out of active service, through the 1930's.

Acquired by the British government to alleviate shipping shortages caused by German U-boats preying on transatlantic convoys, *Westpool* was eventually torpedoed and sunk by U–74 on 3 April 1941, while with Convoy SC–26.

Westport

A summer resort and residential city in Connecticut on Long Island Sound at the mouth of the Saugatuck River.

(Freighter: dp. 12,175; l. 423'9"; b. 54'0"; dph. 29'9"; dr. 23'11¼" (mean); s. 10.0 k.; cpl. 97; a. none)

Westport—a steel-hulled, single-screw freighter built under a United States Shipping Board (USSB) contract at Seattle, Wash., by the Ames Shipbuilding and Dry-dock Co.—was completed in 1918 and taken over by the Navy at Seattle on 10 September 1918 for operation by the Naval Overseas Transportation Service (NOTS); assigned identification no. 3548; and commissioned on the same day, Lt. Comdr. Gustaf F. Swanson, USNRF, in command.

Soon thereafter, *Westport* departed Seattle, bound for Chile on her maiden voyage. Upon her arrival at Arica, she loaded a cargo of nitrates and got underway again on 8 November 1918—three days before the armistice ended World War I. Sailing via the Panama Canal, the ship arrived at Baltimore, Md., on 28 November and discharged her cargo. She then took on board railroad supplies for shipment to the American Army in France and departed Baltimore on New Year's Day 1919.

The freighter made port at Brest on the 21st and unloaded. She then took on board 1,438 tons of Army return cargo before sailing on 15 February for home. Reaching Baltimore on 14 March, *Westport* discharged her cargo there before heading for New York City on 24 March. Arriving at New York two days later, *Westport* was subsequently decommissioned, struck from the Navy list, and returned to the USSB on 31 March 1919.

Westward Ho

A novel published by Charles Kingsley in 1855.

(Freighter: dp. 12,185; l. 423'9''; b. 54'0''; dr. 24'½'' (mean); dph. 29'9''; s. 10.5 k.; cpl. 60; a. 1 5'', 1 3'')

Westward Ho—a steel-hulled, single-screw freighter built under a United States Shipping Board (USSB) contract and launched on 20 November 1917 at Portland, Oreg., by the Columbia River Shipbuilding Corp.—was inspected in the 13th Naval District on 4 February 1918; she apparently sailed for European waters soon thereafter.

Assigned Id. No. 3098, *Westward Ho* was taken over by the Navy and commissioned at Brest, France, on 19 October 1918 for operation by the Naval Overseas Transportation Service (NOTS). Her first commanding officer was Lt. Comdr. Mortimer Hawkins, USNRF, whose previous ship, *West Bridge* (Id. No. 2888) had

been severely damaged that summer by two torpedoes from *U–107* on 15 August 1918.

Five days after the signing of the armistice, the freighter departed Brest on 16 November, bound for the United States, and arrived at New York City on 12 December. After drydocking for general repair, *Westward Ho* loaded general supplies and foodstuffs and got underway on 26 January 1919 and headed for European waters. In the course of her postwar voyage for NOTS, *Westward Ho* touched at Falmouth, England; the free city of Danzig; Copenhagen, Denmark; and Plymouth, England. She departed the latter port, in ballast, on 25 March 1919, bound for New York. She arrived there on 9 April 1919 and, 10 days later, was decommissioned and struck from the Navy list.

Simultaneously returned to the USSB, *Westward Ho* was laid up by that agency in the late 1920's, probably because of the onset of the Depression. She is carried on a period merchant vessel register as being "abandoned due to age and deterioration" in 1933 but was apparently saved from the scrapper's torch when acquired by the Japanese firm of *Kokoku Kisen K. K.* in the late 1930's. Homeported at Kobe, Japan, the merchantman was renamed *Westward Ho Maru* in 1937 and *Izan Maru* in 1938. She survived the crippling American submarine onslaught against her nation during World War II and operated with her prewar owner until about 1949, as Japan began the road to recovery from wartime devastation.

Westwind

(AGB-6: dp. 5,300; l. 269'0''; b. 63'6''; dr. 25'9''; s. 12 k.; cpl. 195; a. 4 5'', 12 40mm.; cl. *Wind*)

Westwind (AGB–6)—a steel-hulled, twin-screw ice-breaker—was launched on 31 March 1943 at San Pedro, Calif., by the Western Steel and Pipe Co., and transferred to the Soviet Navy on 21 February 1945 at Seattle, Wash., under the lend-lease program. Renamed *Severny Polyus* by the Russians, the icebreaker remained in Soviet hands through the end of World War II. She was returned to the United States Navy on 19 December 1951 at Bremerhaven, Germany.

Commissioned as *Westwind* (AGB–6) on 1 February

The icebreaker *Westwind* (AGB–6), with heavy wartime gun armament and a Grumman J2F utility amphibian bi-plane on her deck amidships.

1952, the icebreaker departed Bremerhaven on 12 February, bound for the United States, and arrived at the Boston Naval Shipyard on 25 February. Decommissioned on 13 March 1952 and turned over to the Boston Naval Shipyard for custody on that day, *Westwind* was transferred to the United States Coast Guard on 19 March. *Westwind* (AGB–6) was struck from the Navy list on 8 September 1952.

Redesignated as WAGB–281, *Westwind* subsequently operated in the waters off Greenland and Newfoundland in the 1950's. Eventually shifted to the Great Lakes, *Westwind* continued in Coast Guard service into 1979 on those bodies of water.

Wexford

A county in the state of Michigan.

Coastal Crusader—a C1–M–AV1 cargo vessel—was laid down under a Maritime Commission contract (MC hull 2174) on 12 April 1945 at Sturgeon Bay, Wis., by the Leathem D. Smith Shipbuilding Co.; launched on 24 June 1945; sponsored by Mrs. DeForrest Colburn; and completed on 26 July 1945.

On 25 February 1945, the Navy had assigned the name *Wexford* and the designation AK–220 to the projected ship; but the contract for her acquisition by the Navy was cancelled in August 1945 because of the cessation of hostilities in the Pacific. *Coastal Crusader* thus entered mercantile service, never having borne the name *Wexford*.

Wexford County

A county in the state of Michigan.

(LST–1168: dp. 2,590; l. 384'; b. 55'6''; dr. 16'2''; s. 14 k.; cpl. 157; a. 6 3''; cl. *LST–1156*)

LST–1168 was laid down on 27 February 1952 by the Christy Corp., Sturgeon Bay, Wis.; launched on 28 November 1953; sponsored by Mrs. Philip K. Wrigley; and commissioned on 15 June 1954, Lt. Comdr. Victor Vansant in command.

Following commissioning, *LST–1168* was assigned to the Atlantic Fleet with a home port at Norfolk, Va. She spent the remainder of 1954 in training, shakedown, upkeep, and independent ship exercises.

On 14 February 1955, she departed Norfolk for a three-month tour of duty in the Caribbean, operating from the island of Vieques, Puerto Rico. While in the Caribbean, the ship visited San Juan and Ponce, Puerto Rico; and St. Thomas, Virgin Islands. Upon returning to Norfolk in May, she engaged in exercises and spent the summer of 1955 on reserve cruises and midshipmen training exercises. The tank landing ship received the name *Wexford County* on 1 July 1955.

In late 1955, *Wexford County* entered the shipyard at Philadelphia for overhaul and remained there into April 1956. She completed overhaul and arrived back at Little Creek on 4 April. The ship then participated in east coast operations until July, when she deployed for the Caribbean. After stops at Vieques and Roosevelt Roads, Puerto Rico, she returned briefly to Little Creek, then set out for the west coast via the Panama Canal. *Wexford County* arrived at Long Beach, Calif., on 2 September 1956 and spent the year conducting routine operations off the California coast.

In January 1957, the ship reported to Long Beach for overhaul and remained there until April. She departed for San Francisco on 4 April and entered an upkeep period which lasted until 20 June. She returned to San Diego on 22 July 1957, where the tank landing ship continued operations along the California coast.

Wexford County departed for Pearl Harbor and her first deployment to the western Pacific on 23 January 1958 en route to Yokosuka, Japan. From Yokosuka, the ship made stops in Hong Kong; Sasebo, Japan; and Inchon, Korea. On 24 June 1958, she left for San Diego and arrived there on 18 August. After several months of activity, she went into upkeep on 5 December at Long Beach.

On 29 January 1959, *Wexford County* departed for Yokosuka again via Hong Kong and Okinawa. She arrived at Yokosuka on 24 March 1959. The ship made several shuttles between Yokosuka and Sasebo, Japan; and Naha, Okinawa. She left Yokosuka for San Diego, arriving there on 7 June 1959. The remainder of the year was spent in exercises off the coast and routine upkeep.

During the next several years, *Wexford County* was involved in numerous routine operations along the California coast. A highlight of these years was a deployment to Guam, for which she departed San Diego on 2 January 1962. After steaming 5,480 miles, she arrived on 23 January. The ship conducted operations for reconnaissance and installation of weather stations in the eastern Caroline Islands. The ship returned to San Diego on 1 September 1962. On 10 July 1963, she commenced overhaul at Bethlehem Steel, Long Beach, Calif., which lasted through late November.

The first two months of 1964 found *Wexford County* engaged in training. She was in a restricted availability status during March and April 1964. In May, she participated in Exercise "Pine Tree," in which *Wexford County* served as a secondary control ship. During July 1964, the ship was in type training. This was followed by Exercise "Sea Bar," held near Fort Lewis, Wash., in conjunction with the United States Army. In this exercise, *Wexford County* acted as primary control ship. Returning to San Diego in mid-September, *Wexford County* entered upkeep for several weeks. She then took part in amphibious exercises with Marine forces. Upon completion of various training exercises, the ship entered a holiday upkeep period.

In early 1965, *Wexford County* took part in Operations "Bubble Ops" and "Silver Lance," which were at that time the largest peacetime amphibious operations ever conducted in the Pacific. Shortly after, she departed for Okinawa and Yokosuka, Japan. Following a brief stay, the ship sailed in early May for San Diego. During June and July 1965, she carried out local operations. In August, *Wexford County* again deployed for the western Pacific and spent September in Danang, Vietnam. Subsequent stops were made in Chu Lai and Qui Nhon, Vietnam; and Hong Kong. In December 1965, *Wexford County* returned to San Diego for the duration of the year.

Wexford County was involved in local operations for the first four months of 1966 and provided services for the Amphibious School, Coronado, Calif. In late April, the LST steamed to Newport, Oreg., to participate in that community's Loyalty Day celebration. On 1 May 1966, *Wexford County* returned to San Diego. On 12 July, she arrived at the Long Beach Naval Shipyard for overhaul. The ship returned to San Diego on 9 November and began underway and refresher training on 27 November. This training period ended on 16 December 1966.

Amphibious training for the tank landing ship commenced on 16 January 1967 and continued through 27 January. She briefly returned to Long Beach for further repair; then continued on to Hawaii to participate in landing exercises on Molokai and to lift Marine forces to San Diego. In June 1967, *Wexford County* sailed to San Francisco, Portland, and Seattle to embark Marine troops bound for training at Camp Pendleton, Calif. She participated in various operations during July; and, in late August, she repeated her stops along the west coast to return Marine units to their respective home ports.

After returning to San Diego in September, *Wexford County* began a tender availability period. Amphibious exercises and deployment preparations lasted through October. In early November 1967, the ship sailed for

Vietnam by way of Pearl Harbor and Yokosuka. In December, *Wexford County* reached Vietnam and assumed her duties.

On 4 January 1968, *Wexford County* arrived in Subic Bay to off-load cargo and departed on 14 January to return to Vietnam. She remained on station until 13 March, at which time she left for Subic Bay, arriving there on 16 March. She returned to Vietnam, via Hong Kong, on 5 April to rejoin forces off Vietnam.

Wexford County left Vietnam in early May and returned to San Diego via Taiwan, Yokosuka, and Pearl Harbor. She arrived in San Diego on 26 June 1968, after approximately seven and one-half months overseas. For the next two months, the ship was in a restricted availability status.

On 28 August, the ship got underway for South Bend, Wash., to help celebrate the city's Labor Day festival. She returned to San Diego on 6 September. Throughout September and October, *Wexford County* carried out operations along the California coast. On 15 November 1968, she entered drydock at San Diego.

Wexford County got underway on 12 January 1969 with a task group headed for Mazatlan, Mexico, arriving on 18 January. She spent two weeks there involved in various training exercises. In February and March, *Wexford County* was again in San Diego for routine maintenance. She departed for exercises at Treasure Island, Calif., on 14 April. She sustained heavy damage to a main engine and spent May undergoing repairs at San Diego.

A midshipmen cruise occupied the months of June and July. August and September 1969 were devoted to exercises, and *Wexford County* spent the rest of the year in overhaul at San Diego.

The yard period ended on 20 February 1970. Inspections, training, and preparations for deployment occurred from March through May; and, on 2 June 1970, the ship left for Pearl Harbor and Guam. *Wexford County* reached Guam on 25 June; and, after taking on new cargo, she left for Subic Bay, Philippines, and then to Vietnam. After unloading a construction battalion and their equipment, she departed for Hong Kong, arriving there on 30 July.

From 2 September 1970 through early November, *Wexford County* was involved in numerous troop lifts, cargo transports, and exercises between Okinawa and Yokosuka and Numazu, Japan. On 2 November, she detached and began the voyage back to San Diego via Subic Bay; Guam; Ponape, Caroline Islands; and Pearl Harbor. She arrived at San Diego on 22 December 1970.

Wexford County spent the year 1971 in preparation for transfer to Spain. The ship was decommissioned on 29 October 1971 and transferred to the Spanish Navy that same date where she served as *Martin Alvarez* (L 12) into 1980.

Wexford County earned five battle stars for her service in Vietnam.

Whale

An extremely large, aquatic mammal which is fish-like in form. True air-breathing, warm-blooded mammals, whales are nearing extinction due to man's pursuit for oil and whalebone.

I

(SS–239: dp. 1,525 (surf.), 2,415 (subm.); l. 311'8"; b. 27'3"; dr. 15'3"; s. 20.25 k. (surf.), 8.75 k. (subm.); cpl. 80; a. 10 21" tt., 1 3", 1 .50-cal. mg.; cl. *Gato*)

The first *Whale* (SS–239) was laid down on 28 June 1941 by the Mare Island Naval Shipyard, Vallejo, Calif.; launched on 14 March 1942; sponsored by Mrs. A. D. Denny, wife of Capt. A. D. Denny, the commanding officer of the shipyard; and commissioned on 1 June 1942, Lt. Comdr. J. B. Azer in command.

Dock trials and initial shakedown training commenced on 30 July. The submarine—escorted by *Kilty* (DD–137)—departed San Francisco on 4 August and arrived at San Diego two days later. Between 30 July and 9 September, she conducted type training in the San Diego and San Francisco areas.

Whale got underway from San Francisco on 23 September and arrived at Pearl Harbor four days later. The submarine departed Hawaii on 9 October 1942, headed via Midway for Japanese home waters, and conducted training dives and battle surface drills en route. She arrived at her assigned patrol area off Kii Suido on 25 October and began to reconnoiter the vicinity which had been designated for a mine plant. Her original plans had called for the submarine to lay mines 20 miles offshore. However, after sighting several outbound freighters about one mile from the coast, executive officer Fritz Harlfinger convinced Azer that the mines be planted as close in as possible. Hence, *Whale*'s first war patrol was conducted "within spitting distance" of the Japanese beach. *Whale* was the first American submarine to plant mines in Japan's home waters. During the war, no one on the American side knew how effective these mines proved to be; but a postwar analysis of Japanese shipping records credited *Whale*'s minefield with sinking five enemy ships.

The following day, *Whale* arrived at Seto Saki hoping to intercept some inbound freighter traffic. By the light of a full moon, she sighted a large freighter directly ahead and fired a three-torpedo spread at the target. Two torpedoes hit the cargo ship, and she went down by the bow with her screws emerging. *Whale* sighted a second target astern of the freighter, fired three torpedoes, and observed the target listing slightly to port and heading for the beach. *Whale* fired a stern shot at a third freighter and heard a heavy torpedo explosion after 43 seconds.

From 27 to 29 October, *Whale* patrolled the entrance to Bungo Suido. On the 30th, 10 miles off Ichie Saki, *Whale* spotted two freighters and a torpedo boat escort; she fired two torpedoes at each of the ships, scoring only one hit. The torpedoes alerted the escort which bore down on the submarine and attacked her with depth charges. A 17-hour chase ensued in which *Whale*, although badly damaged, managed to shake the torpedo boat three times.

After an unsuccessful search for a disabled sampan, *Whale* made rendezvous with an escort and proceeded to Pearl Harbor where she underwent repairs from 10 November 1942 through 2 January 1943. The next day, *Whale* got underway from the Submarine Base, Pearl Harbor, bound for the Marshall Islands. After conducting training dives and drills en route, she arrived in the Wotje and Kwajalein area on 10 January for two days' patrol off those atolls.

On 13 January 1943, *Whale* began cruising the shipping lane from Kwajalein to Truk. She sighted a freighter and pursued her quarry for 117 miles before finally managing to work into position dead ahead of the target. She then fired four torpedoes. The first hit struck the freighter aft and broke off about 100 feet of the stern; the second struck just forward of the bridge; and the fourth also exploded on target. Within six minutes, 3,550-ton *Iwashiro Maru* sank; and *Whale* resumed her voyage toward Truk, running submerged.

Whale conducted surface patrols on the Truk-Empire shipping lanes until 17 January when she sighted a passenger-freighter bringing in troop reinforcements. Through the periscope, *Whale* observed hundreds of uniformed soldiers crowding the decks. She fired nine torpedoes and scored eight direct hits which were necessary to sink the 9,815-ton *Heiyo Maru*. The cargo must have been of such a nature as to prevent her from sinking more rapidly.

The next seven days were spent patrolling the Caroline Islands. On 25 January while on a surface patrol along the Truk-Empire line, *Whale* sighted smoke in the bright moonlight and fired a three-torpedo spread rom the stern tubes at the target; only one torpedo scored a hit. The tanker, *Syoyo Maru*, sent up a flare which summoned an escort to her rescue. *Whale* went deep and sustained light damage from several depth charges.

The following evening, *Whale* sighted the smoke of a steamer about 16 miles on her starboard bow. She closed and fired one torpedo. A dull thud was heard throughout the boat, and no explosion occurred. On the morning of the 27th, the submarine fired a three-torpedo spread but heard no explosions. A fourth torpedo failed to explode, and the target, *Shoan Maru*, turned away and presented a 180-degree angle. *Whale* fired a fifth and sixth torpedo and the latter passed directly below the target's stern and must have run under its full length without detonating. The Japanese ship then began dropping depth charges as she drew away. *Whale* fired the last remaining torpedo which hit the target just abaft her stack, causing her to lose power. Apparently, *Shoan Maru* sank as a result of this attack, for *Whale* was credited with the kill. After this action, *Whale* set her course for Midway where she arrived on 2 February 1943 and commenced preparations for her next patrol.

Refitting was completed on the 16th. Four days later, Lt. Comdr. John B. Azer was relieved of command by Lt. Comdr. Albert C. Burrows. On the last day of the month, after various test dives and underway tests, *Whale* got underway for the Marianas on her third war patrol. She arrived off Tanapag Harbor, Saipan Island, on 10 March and began patrolling the shipping lanes between the Marianas and Japan.

On the evening of the 19th, *Whale* sighted two large freighters and one torpedo boat or destroyer escort. Just after daylight the next morning, the submarine finally worked into a favorable attack position; fired six torpedoes—a spread of three at each freighter—and hit both. The first target—tentatively identified as *Mogamigawa Maru*—sank rapidly by the stern. The second—a cargoship resembling *Arizona Maru*—was plagued by several heavy internal explosions following a second torpedo hit. *Whale*, mistaking these secondary explosions for bombs, went deep. Upon discovering the mistake, she started to surface but was greeted by a barrage of depth charges from the escort. She dove again but again came under attack—this time from the air—when she attempted to return to examine the wreckage. The submarine suffered extensive damage during this attack—which prevented her learning the fate of her targets—her closest escape, by far.

Nevertheless, *Whale* continued to patrol shipping lanes to Kobe and Tokyo and, while off Tanapag Harbor on the evening of 22 March, she sighted the masts of two ships and the smoke of a third, all leaving the harbor. *Whale* tried to close but lost contact. The next morning, *Whale* gained a position ahead of two freighters and fired two spreads of three torpedoes each. Two hits were observed on each target, one under each stack and a second under each stern. The closer freighter, *Kenyo Maru*, blew up with a tremendous, deep-roaring explosion and sank in four minutes leaving no survivors. Part of the stern of the farther ship blew 60 feet into the air, and she appeared to be sinking slowly by the stern as she signalled rapidly with a blinker light.

Fearing the approach of an escort, *Whale* fired a fourth torpedo which ran "hot, straight and normal" for one minute; then circled, heading back in the direction of *Whale*. "We went to 120 feet and prayed," the commanding officer later reported. The erratic torpedo changed its mind after reaching *Whale's* beam and headed back for the freighter, finally exploding. The target was awash from stern to stack and on fire forward. At morning twilight, the ship was still burning with her bow up and her stern under.

The submarine spent the next two days patrolling Kobe-Saipan, Empire-Truk shipping routes. On the morning of the 25th, she sighted the smoke of a small freighter and pursued it throughout that entire day

and the next, firing seven torpedoes at the target, all misses. Either the target's draft had been overestimated or the torpedoes ran too deep, or both. This poor torpedo performance was bitterly disappointing to the submarine's crew. "The thought of the fuel expended," her commanding officer lamented, "on the long, end-around runs, coupled with the loss of the torpedoes themselves, made 'heartbreaking' but an inadequate euphemism."

On 28 March, *Whale* was on the surface, intending to cross the Saipan-Truk route, when she spotted the smoke of a small freighter headed for Truk. She fired a three-torpedo spread; the target made an unanticipated zig, and all three torpedoes missed. A lack of fuel forced *Whale* to abandon her quarry, and she headed north along the Empire-Truk route.

Whale headed homeward on 31 March, and she arrived at Midway on 6 April. She refueled there, had her last torpedo removed, and sailed for Hawaii the following day conducting daily training of gun crews and test dives for radio reception en route. She arrived at Pearl Harbor on 11 April and underwent refitting, subsequent tests, and then training. *Whale* got underway westward again on 5 May and arrived at Midway four days later to undergo repairs to her hydraulic system and her air search radar. *Whale* departed Midway to begin her fourth war patrol on 10 May.

Whale was ordered to take station 30 miles east of Wake at 0500, on 16 May, to assist in guiding in the Army Liberator bombers to that island for a bombing attack and to pick up the crews from any shot-down or seriously damaged planes. She arrived on 15 May and was ordered to remain on the surface until released by the Bombardment Group Commander or attacked by the enemy. *Whale* sat surfaced in broad daylight until 0945 waiting for the bombing to commence. At that time, observers on the submarine saw a flight of seven Liberator bombers heading for Wake; and the attack began. Radar picked up a contact at 11 miles and coming in fast. As *Whale* submerged, a bomb exploded 500 yards astern of the submarine, causing no damage. At 1922, *Whale* received a message releasing her from duty, and she proceeded to the Saipan area.

From 20 to 24 May, *Whale* patrolled the shipping lanes between Japan, Truk, and Saipan. On the latter day, she conducted a search for a submarine base reportedly on Rota; found nothing; then surfaced and headed for Guam.

The following day, *Whale* sighted the masts of three ships in the harbor at Apra, Guam, anchored in such a way as to be protected by reef islands. A retriever-type sampan appeared to be the only antisubmarine measure. Waiting outside the harbor, *Whale* sighted and then tracked the 3,580-ton freighter *Shoei Maru*. At 0014 on the 26th, *Whale* fired her first torpedo which hit with a blinding, orange flash midway between the stack and bow of the freighter. The explosion blew the ship's entire bow away, and she sank in four minutes with no survivors.

On 5 June, *Whale* sighted the masts of a seaplane tender, and she tracked and closed the target. The submarine fired four torpedoes, scoring three hits. The target's screws stopped instantly, and powerful, rumbling explosions came from the target. However, the tender must have managed to limp to port since postwar study of Japanese records did not confirm a kill. An escort was "running wild" toward *Whale*, so she went deep and eluded her pursuer.

The submarine spent the next three days patrolling the Saipan area and, on 8 June, set a course for the Empire-Truk route through the Marianas. The next day, she sighted the masts and kingposts of two large freighters about 800 to 1,000 yards abeam of each other with an escort ahead of and between them. *Whale* fired three torpedoes at the first freighter, scoring two hits. She then shifted to the second freighter and fired the fourth, fifth, and sixth torpedoes. Tremendous explosions from the first ship were followed by two more explosions. The submarine commander concluded that one or more of the latter spread of torpedoes—aimed at the second freighter—hit the first, already damaged target. *Whale* fired another three-torpedo spread at the second freighter and soon heard two heavy explosions followed by a deep, rumbling detonation with the accompanying water noises which suggested that a ship was breaking up. *Whale* then headed eastward and touched at Midway on 17 June, before continuing on toward Hawaii. She arrived at Pearl Harbor on 21 June and commenced refitting.

After almost a month there, *Whale* returned to Midway, completed her refitting, and sailed for the Tokyo-Truk shipping lanes to begin her fifth war patrol. Stormy weather, heavy seas, and poor visibility persisted from 4 to 6 August. A wave came over and covered the entire bridge structure, and large amounts of water flooded into the conning tower and down to the control room and the pump room. *Whale* headed southwest, to the east of the Bonin Islands. The continual pounding in heavy seas had cracked a number of battery jars, bringing the total of disabled cells to 10 forward and 13 aft.

On 7 August 1943, *Whale* covered the Tokyo-Truk lane east of the Bonins. The following day, *Whale*'s periscope watch sighted a large aircraft ferry and her escort. When everything was set to fire a spread of straight bow shots, the forward gyro regulator failed, and it was necessary to shift to manual operation of the gyro regulator. After one torpedo hit, 7,149-ton *Naruto Maru* stopped dead in her tracks, listed to starboard and started going down slowly by the stern. *Whale* fired another torpedo which hit amidships and prodded the ship into sinking faster. The submarine escaped aircraft bombs and set course for the Tokyo-Truk route.

From 9 August through the 19th, she patrolled the Tokyo-Truk route, the Bonin area, and the East China Sea where, on the 20th, she was caught in a typhoon. She weathered the three-day storm with her only severe problem being a low main storage battery. On the 24th, *Whale* positioned herself 20 miles west of Kusakaki Shima and intercepted an enemy convoy headed for Nagasaki. *Whale* fired a salvo of four torpedoes and, other than hearing four explosions, did not manage to ascertain their effect. The ships were last seen going over the horizon, and pursuit was impractical due to the submarine's proximity to Nagasaki and the condition of her battery.

Whale was en route to Midway when she sighted two large cargo ships and a destroyer escort. She fired a salvo of three torpedoes, followed by a fourth stern shot. All four shots missed, and *Whale* continued toward her home port, touching at Midway on 2 September and pushing on toward Hawaii the following day. *Whale* arrived at Pearl Harbor on 7 September and commenced a major overhaul which lasted until 7 December.

Whale arrived at Midway on 25 December 1943 and departed for her sixth war patrol. For two weeks, *Whale* patrolled the Tokyo-Truk shipping lanes, Minami Shima, and the Marianas, Nansei and Bonin Islands areas. On 14 January 1944, she received a dispatch from *Seawolf* stating that a convoy was headed in *Whale*'s direction. *Seawolf* attacked the convoy the next day and sank a tanker, expending all of her torpedoes. Nevertheless, *Seawolf* continued to trail the convoy; and *Whale* made radar contact on the 16th. *Whale* fired three torpedoes and sank the larger of the freighters, *Denmark Maru*. However, she suffered minor damage from an ensuing barrage of depth charges. *Seawolf* verified the sinking and reported that the last freighter headed south alone. Since she lacked torpedoes, *Seawolf* unsuccessfully tried to engage the freighter with gunfire. However, she assisted *Whale* by driving the freighter in *Whale*'s direction and by passing along the target's zig plan and speed. *Whale* fired four straight bow shots with one hit observed between the bow and stack. Four other explosions were heard and assumed to be either internal explosions or the torpedoes. The target seemed undamaged except for a slight trim down by the bow, and it was imperative that the ship be sunk expeditiously in order to avoid further depth charges by the escorts. *Whale* fired another stern shot which hit squarely under the stack, and the target, *Tarushima Maru*, started down by the bow while *Whale* filmed her sinking. However, a postwar analysis of Japanese losses does not credit *Whale* with this kill.

Whale patrolled the Mariana Islands and the Bonin Islands from 18 to 23 January. On the 24th, she made contact with an enemy submarine and attempted an end-around; but her maneuver was thwarted by a fire in the trim pump which filled the control room with smoke, forcing *Whale* to surface. Two days later, *Whale*—low on fuel—headed for Midway. She arrived there on 3 February for refitting. Lt. Comdr. John B. Grady relieved Comdr. Albert C. Burrows as commanding officer on 9 February. A casualty to the starboard propeller necessitated a trip to Pearl Harbor, and it was not until 13 March that *Whale* returned to Midway, the staging port for her seventh patrol.

The next day, *Whale* got underway for a rendezvous point where she joined submarine *Pollack* on the 23d and patrolled along a likely shipping route east of Tori Shima and the Bonin Islands. On the 25th, *Whale* changed course, passed between Tokara Shima, entered the East China Sea on 29 March, and conducted patrols off the western coast of Kyushu, including Quelpart Island and Iki Shima. On 8 April, she torpedoed an unescorted freighter, *Honan Maru*, which exploded and sank within 15 seconds. Nine days later, *Whale* made contact with two small destroyers or torpedo boats but was unable to close. She headed toward Nagasaki and patrolled uneventfully until 23 April when she was detected by a patrol boat 12 miles east of Asuseki Shima. *Whale* "turned tail at high speed and soon lost contact." She proceeded toward the Bonin Islands and made rendezvous with escort *Fair* (DE–35) on 2 May. The following day, she entered Majuro for refitting and a three-day training period.

Ready for sea, *Whale* departed on 28 May for her eighth war patrol with *Cassin* (DD–372) as escort. She released the destroyer the following day and proceeded to the Japanese home islands. On 7 June, she made contact with a convoy travelling in two parallel columns: four freighters in the starboard column and two in the port. They were screened by three escorts. *Whale* chose the largest ship, a transport of about 10,000 tons, as her first target. She fired a three-torpedo spread; then shifted to a second freighter and fired another three-torpedo spread. A hit under the stack of the first target was followed by two timed hits on the second target. Immediately, depth charges began to drop; *Whale* cleared the area to the southeast and later received a report of a crippled freighter in tow 120 miles north of her.

From 12 June to 4 July 1944, *Whale* patrolled off the southern coasts of Japan. She sighted several Japanese aircraft and a properly lighted hospital ship. On 5 July, *Whale* surfaced and set course for Midway where she arrived on the 11th. She pushed on toward Hawaii the following day and arrived at Pearl Harbor after a four-day passage. An extensive refitting lasted until 12 August and was followed by training exercises.

Whale got underway on 24 August for her ninth patrol. Shortly before, Admiral Halsey had requested a sizable force of submarines to form a reconnaissance line between the western Carolines and the Philippines to act as offensive scouts during Operation "Stalemate," the invasion of the Palaus. This flotilla, nicknamed the "Zoo," consisted of nine submarines organized into three wolfpacks under the overall command of Capt. Charles W. ("Weary") Wilkins in *Seahorse*. *Whale* and *Segundo* joined Wilkins' own pack which was known as the "Bears."

Whale arrived at Tanapag Harbor, Saipan, on 3 September and the next day got underway in company with the other "Bears" and *Heed* (AMC–100) which acted as their escort. She proceeded to a rendezvous with *Barbero* (SS–317) on 8 September about 45 miles from Samar Island, Philippines. She spent the next eight days making emergency repairs and conducting training dives, patrolling on station, and submerging to avoid detection by unidentified aircraft.

On 17 September, the position of the "Bear Pit" was changed to the southeast of Formosa; and *Whale* arrived on station on the 20th. Four days later, she received orders to disband and proceed as a coordinated attack group of four submarines called the "Bears" to "Convoy College," the north end of the South China Sea, between Luzon, Formosa, and the Chinese mainland. She entered those strategic waters on the 25th and, the following day, she surfaced in Bashi Channel, 41 miles from Y'Ami Island of the Batan Islands, and proceeded to her patrol station south of Garan Bi, Formosa. On the 27th, *Whale* evaded a small patrol craft and the next day submerged for a periscope patrol 60 miles south of Formosa. On 29 September, she made rendezvous with *Seahorse*; received written instructions for conducting the remainder of the patrol; and set her course for a new station southwest of Formosa. The submarine arrived on station on 3 October and submerged some 60 miles north of Cape Borjeador, Luzon, and patrolled around Calayan and Dalupiri islands in the Babuyan group.

"Wilkins' Bears" searched the Luzon Strait on 6 October and found a convoy of at least nine ships. Using a high periscope, *Whale* could see two large tankers, a large tender, and two *Hibiki*-class destroyers patrolling ahead of the tanker. *Whale* fired six bow tube shots at the tanker; then submerged quickly to avoid detection. The escorts dropped 34 depth charges, none of which was uncomfortably close. Meanwhile, *Seahorse* verified the sinking of *Whale*'s target, *Akane Maru*, and sank a destroyer herself that was picking up survivors from the tanker.

The next day, *Whale* received a message extending her patrol for seven days and ordering her to rendezvous with *Aspro* (SS–309) and *Cabrilla* (SS–288) in the area northwest of Luzon on the 9th and 10th, respectively. On the 16th, *Whale* was harrassed throughout the day by plane contacts and ordered to take a new station at the southwest end of Nansei Shoto in anticipation of a Japanese fleet sortie which never occurred. Three days later, *Whale* was ordered to head for Midway for refitting, and she arrived there on 29 October.

Whale got underway on 21 November for her 10th war patrol. She reached the Ryukyus on 4 December and operated off those islands through the end of the year. On 22 December, she sighted eight twin engine planes and three trawlers. She fired four torpedoes without scoring a hit and then cleared the area. The following day, while submerged 12 miles southeast of Nakano Jima, *Whale* sighted four trawlers. She went to gun-action stations and fired at the ships using 4-inch and .50-caliber guns. None of the fishing vessels fought back, and all were sunk within 80 minutes.

On 4 and 5 January 1945, *Whale* and *Kingfish* searched unsuccessfully in the waters near Sufu Gan for a life raft containing 11 survivors of a downed B–29. There were heavy seas and visibility was only 500 yards, and the B–29 did not answer calls on the lifeguard frequency. Its failure greatly hampered the rescue operation. On 6 January, *Whale* received orders to proceed via Midway to Hawaii, arriving at Pearl Harbor on the 15th. She soon pushed on to the west coast and entered the Mare Island Navy Yard, Vallejo, Calif., on 26 January 1945 for an overhaul.

Returning to Pearl Harbor, via San Francisco, the submarine's hydraulic plant required an overhaul and delayed departure on patrol for one month. Meanwhile, Lt. Comdr. Freeland H. Carle, Jr., relieved Comdr. James B. Grady. On 15 June, fully loaded with provisions and torpedoes, *Whale* commenced her 11th war patrol. En route to the Marianas, *Whale* conducted training drills—emphasizing evasive dives from aircraft—and battle surface drills. She arrived at Saipan on 21 June and, the next day, commenced patrolling across the Japan to Wake Island supply lines until 30 June when she headed for Guam. She arrived at Guam on 6 July and got underway the following day for lifeguard duty. From 8 to 23 July, *Whale* conducted lifeguard patrols in the areas of Nanpo Shoto, Mariana Islands, and Bungo Suido. *Whale* sighted several American B–29 and B–24 bombers overhead. She also encountered a few freighters afloat but could not get in position to attack. On occasion at night, she spotted Japanese planes that were searching the water for lights. Fortunately throughout this period, *Whale* rescued 15 downed aviators, saving several under adverse conditions. For example, on 26 July, while going in close for a rescue, *Whale* sighted 43 floating mines in 20 minutes, many close aboard. As a result of this lifeguard duty, *Whale* discovered many flaws in the air-sea rescue doctrine and made several noteworthy recommendations to improve future operations.

Whale commenced patrol east of Okino Shima on 30 July and ran into heavy seas: "Couldn't hold our own with this current, so took soundings ables half hour." On 4 August, she submerged for patrol off Bungo Suido and, four days later, made rendezvous with *Dragonet* (SS–293) to take on board a rescued pilot. On 9 August, *Whale* received 16 aviators and one patient who were transferred from *Blackfish* (SS–291), using a rubber boat with lines on bow and stern for propulsion. On 11 August, *Whale* received orders to proceed to Saipan for fuel and to Midway for refitting. She arrived at Saipan on 14 August. The next day, President Truman announced the final Japanese capitulation. *Whale* sailed in company with *Scabbardfish* (SS–397) for Hawaii and arrived at Pearl Harbor on 25 August 1945.

Whale departed Pearl Harbor on 30 August, bound for the Panama Canal, and arrived there on 14 September. After a three-day stay, *Whale* sailed for New York and arrived at Tompkinsville, Staten Island, on 23 September. In October, she moved north via Newport, R.I. and entered Boston harbor on the 23d for the Navy Day celebration. She arrived at New London, Conn., on 30 October 1945 to prepare for inactivation. *Whale* was decommissioned in January 1947, berthed in New London, and placed in the Atlantic Reserve Fleet. She was towed to Portsmouth, N.H., where she arrived on 8 April 1948. *Whale* made several visits to Portsmouth and New London during the summer, and she finally came to rest at New London on 11 September 1948. The submarine was partially activated from 14 November to 14 December 1956 in order to replace *Tarpon* (SS–175). *Whale* departed New London on 12 January 1957 and, on the 22d, arrived at New Orleans where she was recommissioned upon arrival. *Whale* was decommissioned for the last time in September 1957 and was struck from the Navy list on 1 March 1960. While at New Orleans, she was sold for scrap.

Whale earned 11 battle stars during World War II.

II

(SSN–638: dp. 3,860 (surf.), 4,640 (subm.); l. 292'3''; b. 31'8''; dr. 29'; s. 15+ k. (surf.), 20+ k. (subm.); cpl. 107; a. 4 21'' tt., SUBROC; cl. *Sturgeon*)

The second *Whale* (SSN–638)—a nuclear-powered attack submarine—was laid down on 27 May 1964 at Quincy, Mass., by the General Dynamics Corp., Quincy Division; launched on 14 October 1966; sponsored by Mrs. Russell B. Long; and commissioned on 12 October 1968, Comdr. William M. Wolff in command.

Whale arrived in her first home port, Charleston, on 2 November and, after a week in port, put to sea for shakedown training which the nuclear attack submarine completed in November and December, along with a

The nuclear-powered attack submarine *Whale* (SSN–638). Her hull form, designed for optimum submerged performance, gives her a distinct resemblance to the powerful ocean mammal she bears as her ship's insignia (inset). (General Dynamics PQ348-2)

series of post-commissioning tests, trials, and qualifications. In January 1969, she began normal operations out of Charleston with type training along the southeastern coast of the United States.

On 18 March, she stood out of Charleston on her way to operations north to the Arctic Circle. She reached the North Pole on 6 April and surfaced there in commemoration of the 60th anniversary of Rear Admiral Robert E. Peary's arrival there. Following that event, she completed her mission under the polar ice cap and then headed south. After a visit to Faslane, Scotland, she voyaged home to Charleston, where she arrived on 9 May.

Following two months of local operations out of Charleston, *Whale* sailed for Groton, Conn., and her post-shakedown repair period. After three months in the Electric Boat Division's yard, she started back to Charleston on 16 October. She arrived back in her home port on the 20th and conducted local operations for the remainder of the year.

During the first half of 1970, *Whale* continued operations out of Charleston. In late January, she participated in tests with a Navy Underwater Demolition Team and, in February and March, took part in three major Fleet exercises. In April, she headed north for a brief tour of duty as training ship for the Prospective Commanding Officers' School at New London, Conn. She returned to Charleston at the end of the first week in May and spent the remainder of the month conducting acoustic trials.

Whale departed Charleston on 27 July for an over-

seas deployment which she concluded in mid-September with visits to Faslane and Holy Loch in Scotland. While *Whale* visited Scotland, the Jordanian crisis—precipitated by civil war between the Jordanian Government and the Palestinian Liberation Organization (PLO) and aggravated by the incursion into northern Jordan by Syrian tanks—necessitated a show of American strength in the eastern Mediterranean. Thus, *Whale* received orders to join the 6th Fleet and did so near the end of September. She remained in the Mediterranean through October and into November. When the crisis abated, she headed for Charleston, arriving home on 18 November.

Three Fleet exercises and local operations out of Charleston occupied the submarine during the first half of 1971. Late in July, she deployed once more for special operations in the Atlantic, concluding that cruise late in September at Bremerhaven, Germany. She returned to Charleston on 12 October and resumed local operations upon arrival. That routine continued until 20 March 1972, when she departed once again for another special operations cruise in the Atlantic. At the end of that voyage, *Whale* made a brief call at Holy Loch before returning to Charleston on 9 June.

Almost two months after her return to the United States, *Whale* left Charleston and headed north to Groton, Conn., her new home port. She entered the yard at the Electric Boat Division on 7 August for a 46-week overhaul and remained there undergoing repairs until 27 October 1973.

She completed post-overhaul shakedown and refresher

training in November and December and began preparations for another deployment to the Mediterranean in response to the Middle Eastern crisis brought about by the Arab-Israeli War in October 1973. Late in January 1974, however, she received notification that her deployment had been delayed until May. During the interim, she conducted normal operations out of Groton —including submarine ASW exercises, type training, and a major fleet exercise, Operation "Safe Passage." On 3 May, she departed Groton en route to the Mediterranean Sea. Nine days later, she changed operational control from 2d Fleet to 6th Fleet.

While in the Mediterranean, *Whale* participated in two NATO exercises, "International Week" and "Dale Falcon," with units of the Greek and Italian navies as well as several ASW exercises with other units of the 6th Fleet. She passed through the Strait of Gibraltar and changed operational control back to the Commander, Submarines, Atlantic Fleet, on 18 October. During the voyage home, *Whale* participated in a Fleet ASW exercise which she completed on 28 October, two days before she reentered Groton.

Whale spent the next 11 months engaged in operations out of Groton. Various tests and evaluations occupied January and the first half of February 1975. Between then and June, the submarine provided training services for various units of the Atlantic Fleet and for prospective commanding officers. *Whale* also served as a training platform for midshipmen during indoctrination cruises held late in the summer. On 29 September, she stood out of Groton for another deployment with the 6th Fleet. During that cruise, she took part in a major 2d Fleet exercise, "Ocean Safari," and, after joining the 6th Fleet in the Mediterranean Sea, took part in a succession of unilateral, bilateral, and multilateral exercises with units of the navies of Greece, France, Italy, and the Netherlands. She completed her tour of duty with the 6th Fleet during the second week in March 1976 and arrived back in Groton on the 25th.

She resumed normal east coast operations until 9 September when she entered the Portsmouth (N.H.) Naval Shipyard for a refueling overhaul. That overhaul concluded on 7 July 1978. *Whale* then spent the remainder of the year in refresher training for the purpose of obtaining certification throughout the full range of her weapons system.

Wharton

Franklin Wharton—born in Philadelphia on 23 July 1767—was commissioned a captain of marines on 3 August 1798. He served in frigate *United States* during the Quasi-War with France and subsequently commanded the Marine Barracks at Philadelphia. On 7 March 1804, Wharton took office as the third Commandant of the Marine Corps. During this early period, Wharton's principal task was furnishing Marine detachments for the increasing number of warships being fitted out to fight the Barbary pirates.

When American naval strength combined with diplomacy to eliminate this longstanding problem, Congress cut back on the Navy's warships and men. During the early lean years of Wharton's tenure as Commandant, the new Marine Barracks and the Commandant's quarters in Washington, D.C., were completed, mostly by the labor of marines.

He made substantial contributions to the Corps. Under his leadership, uniforms and military equipment were standardized for the first time; and military practices became uniform throughout the Corps. During his time in office, the Marine Band was established and began winning the national reputation which it still maintains. While still Commandant, Wharton died in New York on 1 September 1818.

(AP-7: dp. 21,900; l. 535'2''; b. 72'0''; dr. 31'3''; s. 16.5 k.; cpl. 566; a. 4 6'', 8 .50-cal. mg.)

Southern Cross—a passenger-cargo liner built for the

Muson Steamship Line at Camden, N.J., by the New York Shipbuilding Corp., and completed in September 1921—operated in the South American trade until acquired by the Navy from the Maritime Commission on 8 November 1939. Two days later, the ship was renamed *Wharton* and designated AP-7. She was converted to a troop transport by the Todd Shipbuilding Corp., in the Robbins Drydock in Erie Basin at Brooklyn, N.Y. The transport was commissioned at the New York Navy Yard on 7 December 1940, Capt. Ernest L. Vanderkloot in command.

Wharton departed Brooklyn on 7 January 1941, bound for Guantanamo Bay, Cuba, where she conducted shakedown before proceeding on through the Panama Canal to her home port, Mare Island, Calif. Assigned to the Naval Transportation Service, *Wharton* transported service personnel and their families, as well as cargo, on triangular runs from San Francisco, San Diego, and Pearl Harbor. She also made one trip to Midway Island.

When the Japanese struck Pearl Harbor, Hawaii, on 7 December 1941, *Wharton* was undergoing overhaul at the Mare Island Navy Yard, Vallejo, Calif. On 6 January 1942, the transport sailed from the west coast for her first wartime voyage to the Hawaiian Islands. A series of runs followed in which *Wharton* transported service families and dependents home to the west coast on her eastbound passages and troops and cargo to Hawaii on her westbound trips.

From June through September, *Wharton* made three voyages to the Southwest Pacific theater—loading and unloading at such ports as Pago Pago, Samoa; Auckland, New Zealand; Espiritu Santo, New Hebrides; Noumea, New Caledonia; Canton Island, and Suva, Fiji Islands—before returning to the west coast for an overhaul which lasted into October. The troop transport then began a series of trips to the Aleutians which lasted from December 1942 to February 1943, carrying troops from Seattle, Wash., to Kodiak and Dutch Harbor and returning with civilians, troops, and patients. For the remainder of the year, *Wharton* made five more trips to the Southwest Pacific, during which she revisited Pago Pago, Noumea, Suva, Espiritu Santo, and Wellington, while adding Apia, British Samoa; Guadalcanal, Solomons; and Efate, New Hebrides; to her itinerary.

In January 1944, *Wharton* joined Transport Division 30 for the Marshall Islands operation. Equipped with seven manned LCVP's, *Wharton* sortied from Pearl Harbor in Task Group 51.1 on 23 January 1944, bound for Kwajalein and Eniwetok, with 526 Army Headquarters troops embarked. The group operated off the island of Bigej in Kwajalein Atoll from 31 January to 2 February, during the shore bombardment phase of the operation and the initial landings, before moving into the lagoon and anchoring there on 2 February. *Wharton* remained in the lagoon until she headed for Eniwetok on the 15th. Following her arrival there two days later, the troop transport, while disembarking her troops and unloading her cargo, took on additional duty as a hospital ship. She received on board 85 patients for treatment and subsequently transferred them all to other facilities prior to sailing for Kwajalein on 25 February.

On 29 February, *Wharton* got underway for the Ellice Islands to embark the 11th and 58th Construction Battalions ("Seabees") for transportation to the Admiralties. At 1700 on 17 April, while entering Seeadler Harbor at Manus, she ran aground due to an inaccurate chart and poor placement of buoys marking the channel. After the ship had been refloated at 0100 on the 18th, a quick check revealed no damage to her hull or machinery.

Wharton later transported 1,782 men of the Royal New Zealand Army from Green Island to Noumea before sailing for Espiritu Santo and Guadalcanal. At the latter island—the scene of bitter struggles from August 1942 to February 1943—the ship participated in training exercises with Transport Division 8. After two weeks of practice landings, *Wharton* sailed for Kwajalein with 1,587 troops of the 2d Battalion of the 12th Marines and the 1st Battalion of the 3d Marines embarked. At Kwajalein, she transferred the latter unit to LST's for the impending operations against the Japanese-held Marianas.

She got underway for Guam on 12 June and spent 17 days at sea before returning to Kwajalein, because fierce Japanese resistance on Saipan had forced Admiral Nimitz to postpone American landings on Guam. Underway again on 17 July, the transport made landfall off Guam four days later and soon disembarked her assault troops. That night, she retired to sea until midnight, when she reversed course to return to the beachhead for her role as casualty evacuation ship.

On the day that followed, she continued this pattern of operations. Although not designed for such work, *Wharton* performed yeoman service off the beaches. Two of the ship's lifeboats were kept ready in their davits for instant deployment, and litters containing casualties were brought alongside in landing craft and transferred to these boats which were then hoisted up to the promenade deck level to be rushed to emergency dressing stations in the passenger officers' wardroom spaces. During the landing operations, some 723 patients were logged into *Wharton*'s sick bay, most of them coming on board by way of this improvised "lifeboat elevator." Operating in company with *Rixey* (APH–3), *Wharton* returned to the transport area each morning for eight successive days to receive casualties and send an occasional beach party ashore. These latter groups worked on the off-shore reef, unloading supplies and ammunition from LCM's—which could not cross the coral to waiting amphibious tractors which carried the cargo to the beachhead. Working often in 24-hour stretches, these men on occasion came under enemy mortar fire. On 29 July, her part in the Guam operation completed, *Wharton* headed for Eniwetok with 519 patients embarked.

Following the Marianas operation, *Wharton* returned to the United States, reaching San Francisco on 25 August. After two months of repairs, the ship resumed her transport duties and made a voyage to Guadalcanal, Espiritu Santo, and Noumea before returning to the United States late in the year.

On 7 January 1945, *Wharton* got underway for the Philippine Islands, carrying troops and cargo in support of the operations to wrest the islands from the Japanese. She disembarked 1,386 troops and 131 tons of cargo at Samar on 14 February and, two days later, unloaded 134 tons of cargo and 869 more troops at Leyte Island. Underway for home on the 17th, the transport stopped at Ulithi before pressing on eastward and arriving at San Francisco on 12 March.

Wharton next participated in the operations against Okinawa, arriving offshore on 19 May. The transport soon disembarked 2,118 troops (including 30 Army nurses) in LCM's sent from shore, as *Wharton* ordinarily carried no landing craft of her own. Several times, the ship went to general quarters and was screened by smoke, but she emerged from the campaign unscathed by kamikazes that had taken such a dreadful toll from American ships. On 22 May, the transport departed for the Caroline Islands, with 273 troops and 29 casualties embarked, and arrived at Ulithi on the 28th.

Wharton took part in no further combat operations and returned home—via Seeadler Harbor, Guadalcanal, Espiritu Santo, Noumea, and Suva—to San Francisco on 25 June. The ship remained there until 3 August, when she moved to Seattle, Wash., before returning to Pearl Harbor.

Hostilities had then ended, but the gigantic job of returning troops from the far-flung bases and islands nonetheless remained. *Wharton* conducted three voyages to the western Pacific—calling at Eniwetok, Guam, Saipan, Samar, Tacloban, and Puerto Princessa through the end of 1945 to pick up Army, Navy, and Marine Corps veterans and return them to the United States in Operation "Magic Carpet."

In the spring of 1946, *Wharton* participated in Operation "Crossroads"—transporting observers to Bikini Atoll for the atomic bomb tests which were to be conducted there in July. She remained there until the completion of her duties on 27 August. She made one round-trip cruise from San Francisco to Guam and one from San Francisco to the Far East, adding Yokohama and Sasebo, Japan; and Shanghai, China; to her list of ports of call.

The transport returned to the United States on 28 January, when she made port at San Francisco prior to heading north to Seattle, and arrived there on 9 Feb-

USS *Wharton* (AP–7).

ruary 1947. On 11 March, the Secretary of the Navy declared *Wharton* "surplus to Navy needs" and accordingly authorized her disposal. Decommissioned on 26 March 1947, *Wharton* was struck from the Navy list on 4 April 1947.

Wharton was awarded three battle stars for her World War II service.

Wheatear

A small northern bird related to the stonechat and whinchat.

(AM–390: dp. 890; l. 221'1''; b. 32'2''; dr. 10'9'' (mean); s. 18.1 k. (tl.); cpl. 117; a. 1 3'', 2 40mm.; cl. *Auk*)

Wheatear (AM–390) was laid down on 29 May 1944 at Cleveland, Ohio, by the American Shipbuilding Co.; launched on 21 April 1945; sponsored by Mrs. H. P. Isham; and commissioned on 3 October 1945, Lt. Comdr. George M. Estep, USNR, in command.

Wheatear departed Cleveland on 8 October and arrived in Boston on the 20th. There, she completed the fitting-out process and its attendant exercises. On 23 November, she got underway and headed south, arriving at Little Creek, Va., on the 27th. She began shakedown training which lasted until 14 January 1946 when she became an active unit of Mine Division (MinDiv) 10. Following post-shakedown availability, *Wheatear* began training operations in the Chesapeake Bay from her base in Norfolk. That employment continued until 24 June when she received orders to proceed to Charleston, S.C., where she went into an inactive status due to a severe shortage of crew members. She continued in that status until 31 October. On 1 November, she returned to sea for a training cruise to the Panama Canal, during which voyage she also visited Orange, Tex., and Miami, Fla. For almost two years, the minesweeper operated out of Charleston as a unit of the Atlantic Fleet Mine Force.

In August 1948, she was reassigned to the Operational Development Force, based at Panama City, Fla. For almost five years, she supported the force's developmental work. Based at Panama City, she cruised the waters of the Gulf of Mexico and in the West Indies, operating frequently in the Guantanamo Bay operating area and infrequently making cruises along the Atlantic seaboard as far north as Argentia, Newfoundland. On 15 April 1953, *Wheatear* rejoined the active Mine Force at Charleston as a unit of MinDiv 81; however, less than a month later on 1 May, she transferred to MinDiv 85. For the remainder of her brief career, the warship operated along the Atlantic coast and in the West Indies carrying out training missions with the Atlantic Fleet. The only exception to that routine came on 19 September of 1953 when she departed Charleston on her only deployment. She served with the 6th Fleet in the Mediterranean until January of 1954 when she headed home. The minesweeper arrived in Charleston on 5 February 1954 and resumed her duties with the Mine Force. In June, she began preparations for inactivation. On 17 November 1954, *Wheatear* was decommissioned at Orange, Tex., and berthed with the Orange Group, Atlantic Reserve Fleet. On 7 February 1955, she was redesignated MSF–390. The warship remained in reserve at Orange until 1 July 1972 at which time her name was struck from the Navy list. On 20 December 1973, she was sold to the Southern Scrap Material Co., Ltd., of New Orleans, for scrapping.

Wheatland

A county in south central Montana.

(AKA–85: dp. 13,910 (tl.); l. 459'2''; b. 63'0''; dr. 26'4'' (lim.); s. 16.5 k. (tl.); cpl. 425; a. 1 5'', 8 40mm., 16 20mm.; cl. *Tolland*; T. C2–S–AJ3)

Wheatland (AKA–85) was laid down on 17 July 1944 at Wilmington, N.C., by the North Carolina Shipbuilding Co. under a Maritime Commission contract (MC hull 1397); launched on 21 September 1944; sponsored by Miss Shirley B. Anderson; transferred to the Navy on 6 October 1944; converted to an attack cargo ship in New York by the Atlantic Basin Iron Works; and commissioned on 3 April 1945, Comdr. Attilio A. Vischio, USNR, in command.

Commissioned two days after the beginning of the last amphibious operation of World War II, the Okinawa invasion, *Wheatland* never saw service in the role for which she had been converted. Instead of operating as an attack cargo ship during amphibious assaults, she spent her brief Navy career laboring as a conventional cargo ship and as a troop transport in support of the occupation of former Japanese possessions.

Following shakedown training and amphibious exercises at Hampton Roads, Va., and post-shakedown availability at the Norfolk Navy Yard, the ship departed the Chesapeake Bay on 7 May with 5,038 tons of dry cargo. Steaming in company with *Begor* (APD–127), *Cavallaro* (APD–128), *Lee Fox* (APD–45), and *Roberts* (APD–94), she set a course for Hawaii. Parting company with the high-speed transports at Panama, she transited the canal on 14 May and continued her voyage to Oahu independently. She arrived in Pearl Harbor on the 28th and immediately unloaded her cargo. The ship remained in the Hawaiian Islands for three weeks, during which she conducted a series of amphibious exercises at the island of Maui.

On 21 June, she departed Pearl Harbor with elements of the Army's 9th Corps embarked. After stops at Eniwetok and Ulithi, she arrived at Leyte in the Philippine Islands on 7 July. There, she disembarked the troops and unloaded much of her cargo. On 9 July, she moved to Samar Island, where she discharged the remainder of her cargo. From there, she moved to the Palau Islands, departing Samar on the 16th and arriving at Angaur on the 18th. She spent the next two days loading a Marine Corps antiaircraft unit and, on the 21st, got underway to return to Oahu.

After a brief stop at Eniwetok for fuel on 26 July, she arrived in Pearl Harbor on 1 August. She discharged her cargo and disembarked her passengers and then began an availability which lasted until 22 August. On the 23d, she moved to Hilo where she began embarking elements of the 5th Marine Division. She returned to Pearl Harbor on the 27th and remained there until 1 September when she got underway for Sasebo, Japan, in company with a 34-ship convoy. She made a three-day stop at Saipan along the way and arrived at Sasebo early on the 22d. She discharged her cargo over the next three days and departed Sasebo on the 25th.

Wheatland entered Subic Bay in the Philippines on 30 September and, the next afternoon, moved to Lingayen Gulf where she loaded men and equipment of the Army's 32d Division for transportation to Japan. On 9 October, she stood out of Lingayen Gulf on her way to Kyushu, Japan. The attack cargo ship arrived in Sasebo early in the morning of 16 October and began disembarking the troops later in the day. Returning to the United States via Okinawa and Guam, *Wheatland* arrived in Seattle, Wash., on 13 November. Later that month, she visited San Francisco for two weeks before embarking upon a voyage to the Marianas on 13 December. She arrived at Guam on the 28th and later visited Saipan whence she departed the Marianas on 22 January 1946. Steaming via the Panama Canal, the ship arrived in Norfolk, Va., on 21 February. She made one more voyage in her naval career—a round trip to New York and back to Norfolk between 28 February and 5 March—before beginning inactivation preparations at Norfolk. *Wheatland* was placed out of commission at Norfolk on 25 April 1946, and custody was transferred to the War Shipping Administration. Her name was struck from the Navy list on 8 May 1946.

Wheeling

A city on the Ohio border of West Virginia's panhandle. Wheeling is the seat of government for Ohio County.

I

(Gunboat No. 14: dp. 990 (n.); l. 189'7''; b. 34'0'' (wl.); dr. 12'10'' (aft); s. 12.88 k.; cpl. 140; a. 6 4'', 4 6-pdr. rf., 2 1-pdr. rf., 1 Colt mg.; cl. *Wheeling*)

The first *Wheeling* (Gunboat No. 14) was laid down on 11 April 1896 at San Francisco, Calif., by the Union Iron Works; launched on 18 March 1897; sponsored by Miss Lucie S. Brown; and commissioned on 10 August 1897, Comdr. Uriel Sebree in command.

Following a cruise to the Hawaiian Islands in the fall of 1897, *Wheeling* reported for duty in the northern Pacific and spent the entire period of the Spanish-American War patrolling the Alaskan coast and the Aleutian Islands.

In the spring of 1899, the gunboat was ordered to the Far East to reinforce the American fleet supporting operations to suppress the Philippine Insurrection. Until the spring of 1900, the gunboat parolled the islands, enforced the blockade, convoyed troop transports, and helped the Army maintain communications between its units operating on various islands of the archipelago. When the Boxer Rebellion broke out in March 1900, *Wheeling* departed the Philippines to patrol the northern coast of China. From 23 March to 9 May, she cruised the Chinese coast observing conditions in that strife-torn nation as she attempted to persuade Chinese officials to respect and protect foreigners resident in China. She and ships of European navies with similar missions spent most of their time at Taku, essentially the port city for Tientsin and Peking.

On 9 May, she departed Taku and headed home, via Yokohama, Japan. The gunboat laid over at Yokohama from the 13th to the 22d and then headed back across the Pacific to North America. From early June to late August, she operated in the Aleutian Islands out of Dutch Harbor. On 25 August, she departed Dutch Harbor for a leisurely cruise south. Along the way, she visited a number of Alaskan ports and did not reach Bremerton, Wash., until 11 December. By 19 December, *Wheeling* was at Mare Island, Calif., conducting oceanographic surveys in that vicinity.

The gunboat operated at Mare Island until the beginning of 1902, at which time she received orders to American Samoa for duty as station ship. After a cruise to Hawaii and the Philippines, *Wheeling* arrived in Samoa late in May. From that time until mid-year 1904, the gunboat cruised the Samoan group—erecting signal installations, performing survey work, and transporting passengers between the islands. On one occasion in January 1903, she transported Dr. Wilhelm Solf—then governor of German Samoa and later foreign minister of Germany in Prince Max von Baden's interim government at the end of World War I —and his staff from Pago Pago to Apia. The warship continued her duties in the Samoan islands until 15 June 1904 at which time she set course for the United States. On 1 July, she was decommisioned at Bremerton, Wash., and was berthed at the Puget Sound Navy Yard.

After almost six years of inactivity, *Wheeling* was recommissioned at Puget Sound on 3 May 1910, Comdr. Edward W. Eberle in command. In June, she made a brief cruise in Alaskan waters before starting on a voyage to Portsmouth, N.H., in company with *Petrel*. During that voyage, she nearly circumnavigated the globe. Departing the west coast on 17 June, *Wheeling* sailed via Yokohama, Japan, and Singapore to the southern terminus of the Suez Canal. After transiting the canal, she steamed westward across the Mediterranean Sea, stopping at Genoa, Italy, and at the British colony at Gibraltar. On her way across the

Atlantic, *Wheeling* made one stop—at Hamilton, Bermuda—before arriving in Portsmouth, N.H., on 2? November.

Following voyage repairs, the gunboat embarked upon almost six years of duty patrolling the troubled waters of the West Indies and the Gulf of Mexico. By mid January 1911, she was operating along the Centra American coast. During 1911 and 1912, she made numerous port visits in the Caribbean Sea while engaging in training operations. On 15 July 1913, the gunboat anchored in the vicinity of Vera Cruz and Tampico Mexico, to investigate reports of violence against Americans living there and remained to protect American property. From 15 February to 7 March 1914, she plied waters off the Republic of Haiti to protect American citizens against guerrilla terrorists fighting the government, and from 7 to 13 March she was at Puerto Plata, Santo Domingo, with the President of Santo Domingo on board. When the threat of violence against Americans loomed at Vera Cruz once again in mid-1914 *Wheeling* sailed to that port and landed a force to protect Americans during the period 25 April to 30 June. Upon being detached from duty in Mexico, *Wheeling* proceeded to Portsmouth, N.H., for repairs.

She returned to the West Indies in mid-October 1914 and took station off the Republic of Haiti. During the year 1915, *Wheeling* cruised between Haiti, Cuba, and Mexico showing the American flag for the benefit of various political groups in each country which were attempting to terrorize resident Americans. She patrolled the Mexcan coast near Vera Cruz from 23 March to 16 June 1916 to aid Americans in case of any disturbances, and put in at Puerto Mexico, Mexico, or 17 June to embark American refugees driven from their homes by bandits. *Wheeling* remained in port six days and then sailed to Carmen, Mexico, where she anchored from 25 to 29 June and took on board more displaced Americans. The gunboat joined United States Army transport *Sumner* at Vera Cruz on 29 June 1916 and transferred her passengers to that ship. Between 9 October and 16 December 1916, *Wheeling* returned to the waters off Vera Cruz to provide naval gunfire support to Army units operating ashore against Mexican bandits.

The beginning of 1917 found the warship still cruising the Mexican coast. When the United States entered World War I on 6 April, she rode at anchor at Vera Cruz. Later that month, she moved to Tampico, continuing her service with the Mexican patrol force until early in July. On the 10th, she headed for New Orleans, La., where she arrived on the 13th. After two weeks of extensive preparations for overseas service, the gunboat stood out of New Orleans on 31 July. After a stop at Key West, Fla., on 2 August, she continued her voyage to Hampton Roads, Va., where she arrived on the 6th. *Wheeling* cleared Hampton Roads on the 8th and shaped a course for Ponta Delgada in the Azores. Two days out to sea, she suffered a severe battering while trying to ride out a hurricane. The damage forced her return to the United States for repairs, and she entered the New York Navy Yard on 11 August.

Following 18 days of repairs, she put to sea again, bound for Lewes, Delaware. *Wheeling* rendezvoused with destroyers *Truxtun* (Destroyer No. 14) and *Whipple* (Destroyer No. 15) there, and together, the three warships headed east on the 31st. The little group of ships stopped at Bermuda from 3 to 8 September then continued their voyage to Ponta Delgada where they arrived on the 16th. For the next seven months, the gunboat operated out of Ponta Delgada with the Patrol Force Azores Detachment. For the most part, she conducted uneventful patrols and convoyed Allied shipping between the Azore Islands and the Madeira Islands. On 15 April 1918, she stood out of Ponta Delgada bound for Gibraltar. After a brief stop in the Canary Islands on the 19th, *Wheeling* arrived at the great British naval base on 22 April.

For the remainder of the war, she operated out of

Gibraltar escorting convoys between that place, Bizerte in North Africa, and Genoa in Italy. On 11 May, the convoy she was escorting lost one ship, SS *Susette Fraisinette*, to a torpedo fired by *UB–52*, which, in turn, was later sunk by the British submarine *H–4* while attempting to return to her base at Cattaro. Six days later on 17 May, another of her convoy's ships was lost to the combined efforts of *U–39* and *UB–50*. The first hint of trouble came at about 1848 that evening when SS *Sculptor* exploded, the victim of a torpedo from *U–39*. *Wheeling* went to general quarters immediately and rang up full speed. Initially, she concentrated on collecting the ships of the convoy, all of which had scattered in panic. At about 1915, a lookout reported a submarine off the starboard bow, and *Wheeling* charged to the attack. She circled to the spot at which the supposed U-boat had last been seen and marked the location with a calcium light. From there, she circled outward dropping a total of six depth charges—two of which failed to detonate.

While *Wheeling* had been engaged in hunting *U–39* and in collecting the scattered convoy, *UB–50* joined the fracas. At about 2016, the American warship witnessed a flash, then heard a report, to her port side, as *UB–50*'s torpedo slammed into SS *Mavisbrook*. The gunboat stopped her engines and began rescue operations. Over the side went two Franklin life buoys, two balsam rafts, and a dozen life belts. Just as she prepared to lower one of her boats to continue rescue duty, *Surveyor* appeared on the scene, assumed rescue duty, and released *Wheeling* to resume protection and collection of the convoy. For the remainder of the night, *Wheeling* listened to shots being fired sporadically but did not leave station. Unknown to the gunboat, *UB–50* also scored a hit on SS *Elswick Grange*, but the English steamer succeeded in making port under her own power. The convoy continued its voyage to Bizerte unmolested and reached port on 21 May. Upon arrival, *Wheeling* learned that severe damage had forced one of the two submarines which had attacked the convoy, *U–39*, to intern herself at Cartagena, Spain. Originally, the gunboat claimed that her depth charges had caused the damage, but that conclusion seems unlikely. German reports of the action make no mention of a depth charge attack and attribute all the damage to an attack by two British planes which occurred the following day.

Wheeling spent the month of June at Gibraltar undergoing repairs. On Independence Day 1918, she stood out of the harbor in the escort of a Bizerte-bound convoy which arrived safely on the 9th. She arrived back at Gibraltar with a return convoy on 14 July. Six days later, the gunboat started out on another escort mission which she completed uneventfully at Bizerte on the 24th. On the return voyage, her convoy once more ran afoul of *UB–50* when the U-boat sank SS *Magellan* early in the evening of the 25th.

Compared to the events of May and July, the remainder of her wartime service proved tame and routine. On 5 August, she left Gibraltar with 21 merchantmen and three other escorts for Genoa. Six days later, the group arrived in port; and, on 12 August, she put to sea with 12 steamers bound for Gibraltar. She made three voyages to Genoa during August, September, and October, followed by a final voyage to Bizerte before the war ended. *Wheeling* was in Gibraltar on 11 November when the armistice was signed; and, 19 days later, she left that port and headed for Lisbon, Portugal, where she anchored on 2 December.

Leaving Lisbon the following day, *Wheeling* returned to Gibraltar on 5 December and, two days later, sailed for the United States. She stopped at Ponta Delgada, Azores, between 12 and 17 December and spent the night of 27 and 28 December coaling at St. George in the British West Indies. Operating once again in the Caribbean Sea, *Wheeling* received orders in mid-1919 to proceed to New Orleans, La., where she was decommissioned on 18 October 1919. On 31 December of the

same year, she was assigned to the 8th Naval District for the training of naval reservists. *Wheeling* received the designation PG–14 on 17 July 1920; and, on the 17th, she was commissioned in the reserve fleet. Her classification was changed on 1 July 1921 to IX–28; and, on 21 January 1923, she received orders to the 3d Naval District to be used as the training vessel for the 6th Naval Reserve Battalion. *Wheeling* reached her new home port, New York, on 14 July 1923 and remained there until after World War II.

The warship was assigned to the Secretary of the Navy on 17 February 1941 for disposition, and the Navy solicited bids on her scrapping. However, on 28 December 1942, the order allowing her disposition was temporarily suspended, and the ship was ordered to be used as a berthing barge for motor torpedo boat crews manning newly built PT's in the New York area. On 13 February 1946, *Wheeling* was placed out of service; and on 8 March, she was declared ready for sale. Her name was struck from the Navy list on 28 March 1946; and, on 5 October 1946, she was sold for scrap.

II

(T–AGM–8: dp. 11,500; l. 455.3'; b. 62.2'; dr. 28.6'; s. 17.0 k.; cpl. 56; cl. *Range Tracker*; T. VC2–S–AP3)

The second *Wheeling* was laid down on 10 April 1945 as *Seton Hall Victory* by the Oregon Shipbuilding Corp. under a Maritime Commission contract (MCV hull 686); launched on 22 May 1945; sponsored by Mrs. Ross McIntyre; and delivered to the Maritime Commission on 21 June 1945. From July 1945 to September 1957, *Seton Hall Victory* was operated for the Maritime Commission by a succession of civilian contractors, beginning with the Olympic Steamship Line and ending with Pope & Talbot, Inc. In September 1957, she was placed out of service and was berthed in Virginia's James River with the National Defense Reserve Fleet.

Late in 1962, she was turned over to the Navy Department for conversion to a range instrumentation ship. On 19 March 1963, she was renamed *Wheeling* and designated AGM–8. On 28 May 1964, *Wheeling* was assigned to the Military Sea Transportation Service to be operated by a civil service crew in support of operations on the Navy's Pacific Missile Range. She has spent the intervening years as a mobile tracking station recording data on missiles and satellites that were out of range of land-based stations. As of 1 April 1978, *Wheeling* continued in active service on the Pacific coast.

Whetstone

Named for Whetstone Point, Md., first fortified in 1776. Those beginnings ultimately became Fort McHenry, the strongpoint that defended Baltimore, Md., harbor from a determined British assault during the War of 1812. The equally determined and successful resistance put up by the defenders of Fort McHenry inspired a young lawyer, Francis Scott Key, to pen the words for a song that eventually became the National Anthem: "The Star-Spangled Banner."

(LSD–27: dp. 9,375 (f.); l. 457'9''; b. 72'2''; dr. 18'0'' (max.); s. 15 k.; cpl. 326; trp. 284; a. 1 5'', 12 40 mm., 24 20mm.; cl. *Cas Grande*)

Whetstone (LSD–27) was laid down on 7 April 1945 at the Boston Navy Yard; launched on 18 July 1945; sponsored by Mrs. Worthington S. Bitler, the wife of Capt. W. S. Bitler on duty at the Boston Navy Yard; and commissioned on 12 February 1946, Comdr. G. R. Keating in command.

Following the ship's shakedown, *Whetstone* underwent post-shakedown availability at the Norfolk Naval Shipyard before heading for the Pacific. Transiting the

Panama Canal between 26 and 30 April 1946, the new dock landing ship reached San Diego on 11 May.

For the next few months, *Whetstone*—attached to Transport Division 11, Transport Squadron 1—operated in the waters of the Pacific Northwest and Alaska, conducting intra-area lifts of boats and equipment between Kodiak, Dutch Harbor, Adak, Sitka, Seattle and San Francisco. In addition, she also called at Port Angeles, Wash., and San Diego during that time.

She subsequently departed San Francisco on 18 February 1947 bound for the Far East. Reaching Shanghai, China, on 9 March, the LSD remained at that Chinese port until the 22d, when she got underway to shift down the coast to Hong Kong. *Whetstone* supported the American occupation and assistance efforts in not only Chinese waters but Japanese as well, the ship touching at Shanghai once more, as well as at Sasebo and Kobe, Japan, before she set course for the Palaus on 15 April 1947.

Whetstone returned to the waters off the Asian mainland, however, via Peleliu and Manus, the next time visiting the waters of North China—reaching Tsingtao, China on 15 July. She subsequently departed that port on the 22d, conducting voyages between Guam, Yokosuka, and Iwo Jima before setting course for Pearl Harbor via the Marshalls. After taking aboard a pair of seaplane wrecking derricks, *YSD-40* and *YSD-62*, at Kwajalein, *Whetstone* headed for Hawaii.

Reaching Pearl Harbor on 12 September, *Whetstone* remained there only long enough to drop off the two self-propelled derricks and take aboard a garbage lighter, *YG-54*, before she was underway again; her destination: San Diego. After delivering her charge, *Whetstone* operated off the west coast of the United States into late 1948, frequenting the waters off the coast of California. She participated in exercises and maneuvers off Oceanside, Calif., the site of the Marine Corps base at Camp Pendleton. She was soon to be a victim of the post-World War II reduction of military strength. On 20 October 1948, *Whetstone* was decommissioned and placed in reserve at San Diego.

Her sojourn in mothballs was a short one, though, for the North Korean assault on South Korea, hurled across the 38th parallel on 25 June 1950, caused a drastic naval build-up. Many World War II-vintage men-of-war were taken out of reserve and activated for service; some ships whose postwar careers had been very short—like *Whetstone*—were also placed on active duty. Accordingly, *Whetstone* was recommissioned on 2 December 1950.

During the Korean conflict, *Whetstone* proved her worth in support of UN operations in that war, conducting two deployments to Korean waters—first from April to November of 1951 and second from December of 1952 to the end of the hostilities in July 1953.

In the first deployment, she took part in a notable operation—the recovery of a Soviet-built MiG 15 fighter. On 9 July, word was received in the upper echelons that a MiG had been downed in the shoal waters off the mouth of the Chongchon River. The initial plot proved inaccurate, however, and planes from the British aircraft carrier HMS *Glory* sighted the MiG a few miles offshore, 33 miles north of the estuary of the Taedong River.

"Risky and navigationally difficult" to reach, the site lay less than 10 minutes' flight time from enemy air bases. Nevertheless, the risks to be run seemed acceptable—especially in view of the fact that no MiG's had thus been available for inspection to see what made them "tick." *Whetstone* loaded a special crane-equipped utility craft (LCU) at Inchon—the port at which the LSD had arrived, from Sasebo, Japan, on 12 June—and sailed for Cho Do Island on the 19th of July. The multinational effort proceeded apace, despite the initial grounding of the LCU on a sand bar and, by the evening of the 22d, had proceeded to a successful conclusion. *Whetstone*'s sistership *Epping Forest* (LSD-4) took the LCU and its precious cargo aboard and sailed for Inchon.

Whetstone remained in Korean waters, operating out of Sasebo, into September and returned again to those climes twice in November. She sailed for the United States on 5 December and reached San Diego, Calif., via Wake Island, two days before Christmas of 1951.

The tank landing ship remained at San Diego undergoing post-deployment availability until 5 February, when she shifted to Port Hueneme. She operated locally in southern Californian waters—touching at San Diego, Aliso Canyon, Long Beach, San Pedro and Port Hueneme—into the summer of 1952. Visiting Bangor, Wash., from 14 July to 7 October, *Whetstone* departed that port on the latter day, bound for San Diego.

She lingered on the west coast until 1 December, when she set sail for the western Pacific. Touching briefly at Pearl Harbor en route, *Whetstone* reached Yokosuka, Japan, on 22 December and spent Christmas in that port before she shifted to Sasebo on the 28th, reaching her destination on the last day of the year 1952.

Whetstone subsequently returned to Inchon two days into the new year, 1953, and remained there until the 8th, when she got underway to shift to Cho Do. The dock landing ship shuttled between Japan and Korean ports, frequenting Sasebo, Yokosuka, Wonsan, Inchon, Tokchokto, Nagoya, and the operating areas off the western coast of Korea through the summer of 1953 and the armistice that ended hostilities.

Whetstone operated in the Far East into late September 1953; she sailed for the west coast of the United States on 30 September and, after stopping at Kwajalein and Pearl Harbor en route, reached San Diego on 26 October. There, she spent the remainder of the year.

During her next Western Pacific (WestPac) tour, *Whetstone* returned to the Far East, touching at familiar ports. She also took part in Operation "Passage to Freedom," the movement of North Vietnamese to the South after the partition of the country in observance of the Geneva accords that ended the French-Viet Minh hostilities. For that evolution, the dock landing ship departed Yokosuka on 14 August and reached Haiphong on the 22d. She subsequently touched at Saigon and Tourane, as well as Haiphong—the first-named port four times, the second twice, and the last-named six.

Completing her participation in that humanitarian operation on Armistice Day (11 November) 1954, *Whetstone* departed Haiphong on that date, bound for Hong Kong and Subic Bay in the Philippines.

For the remainder of the 1950's and into the 1960's, *Whetstone* deployed regularly to the Far East and WestPac areas, there participating in numerous amphibious exercises, maintaining herself in a high state of readiness. During those years, non-military events highlighted her tours both at home and afar. In April 1961, for example, she rescued two San Diego businessmen from their capsized sailboat off Point Loma, Calif.; that July, she went to the aid of the burning merchantman SS *Steel Traveler* in Inchon harbor. In the latter, the efforts of the dock landing ship's fire and rescue party saved the crippled ship.

In February 1962, *Whetstone* deployed to Christmas Island to participate in operations with Joint Task Force (JTF) 8. Upon completion of that deployment, the ship returned home and conducted refresher training out of San Diego. Later that year, in October, November, and December, *Whetstone* deployed to the Atlantic and Caribbean areas, participating in the "quarantine" operations ordered in the wake of the discovery of offensive Soviet missiles on Cuban soil. During that time, she served in Task Forces 53 and 128. Upon the abating of the crisis, *Whetstone* resumed normal operations; she deployed once again on a WestPac tour that December.

Over the next few years, *Whetstone*'s regular WestPac tours were enlivened by operations that reflected the increasing tempo of American involvement in the

This view of the dock landing ship *Whetstone* (LSD–27) emphasizes the mass of her bulky hull. (United States Naval Institute)

war in Vietnam. During her 1964 deployment, the Gulf of Tonkin incident occurred, ushering in a new phase of the conflict. It would not be long before Americans —heretofore employed only as advisors—would be taking active combat roles on a large scale against the communist insurgents (Viet Cong) and their North Vietnamese allies.

From 7 August to 2 October, *Whetstone* steamed as part of TF 76 in the South China Sea, earning the Armed Forces Expeditionary Medal for her contingency operations. As the Vietnam buildup continued into 1965, the veteran dock landing ship was called upon to help transport men and materiel across the Pacific.

Whetstone departed San Diego on 11 February 1965, bound, ultimately, for Vietnam with elements of the 3d Marine Division (3d MarDiv) embarked for transportation to Okinawa. She arrived at her destination on 8 March, disembarked her passengers, and sailed for Japan, touching briefly at Yokosuka before she returned to Okinawa to embark elements of the 5th MarDiv for transportation to Vietnam.

Reaching Chu Lai on 27 March, *Whestone* offloaded her passengers brought from Okinawa and embarked different Marine elements for transport up the Vietnamese coast to the Hue-Phu Bai area of operations. After offloading at Hue, the dock landing ship shifted to Danang, where she soon commenced what was to become a six-week tour of duty as "boat haven" for Naval Support Activities (NavSuppAct), Danang, arriving on the last day of the month of March.

During her six-week stay, *Whetstone* made good use of her drydocking capability, performing major repairs on 41 small boats and craft—mostly LCM (Landing Craft, Medium) and LCU (Landing Craft, Utility). Those craft served as the keys to keeping open the flow of logistics onto the beach from the many merchant ships at anchor in Danang harbor.

Leaving Danang in her wake on 13 May, *Whetstone* arrived at Subic Bay for liberty and upkeep two days later, but Typhoon "Irma" forced the ship to execute a change in plans: five out of her allotted ten-day period was spent riding out "Irma's" fury. Departing Subic Bay on the 25th, *Whetstone* visited Hong Kong for five days of "rest and recreation" slated to start on the 27th. Unfortunately, the proximity of yet another typhoon—"Judy"—caused the dock landing ship to put to sea on the 28th and 29th to evade the storm. The

ship left Hong Kong on 1 June—it had been an abbreviated port visit!

Whetstone returned to the waters of Vietnam, dropping anchor at Qui Nhon to start two months as "boat haven" in support of the U.S. Army's Qui Nhon Support Command. Two boat repair divisions—consisting of *Whetstone* sailors and Army soldiers—worked 12-hour shifts, 24 hours a day, to repair Army landing craft in *Whetstone*'s capacious well-deck aft. The display of Army-Navy cooperation facilitated the vital offloading of ships delivering cargo to Qui Nhon. At the end of the time spent at the port, *Whetstone* received a plaque, commemorating her hard work, from the U.S. Army's 1st Logistical Command.

Whetstone hauled a load of Army LCM's to Camranh Bay on 31 July and then headed for Japanese waters, reaching Sasebo on 7 August for an eight-day port visit. The dock landing ship then returned briefly to Hong Kong—the weather proved more favorable that time than previously—before she sailed for Danang to commence the last major assignment of that WestPac tour.

Whetstone took part in the lift of elements of the combat veterans of the 5th MarDiv from Danang to Okinawa. For the leathernecks, most of them coming straight from action in the field to the ship, the hot meals and bunks on board *Whestone* proved a welcome change from life in the field. The ship subsequently arrived at Okinawa on 6 September to offload her troops.

Reaching Yokosuka on 11 September, *Whetstone* underwent six days of upkeep there before her departure from WestPac. She sailed for home on 17 September and reached Pearl Harbor on the 27th. Pushing on, two days later, the dock landing ship reached her home port of San Diego on 6 October—thus ending a deployment of 238 days' duration.

For the remainder of 1966, *Whetstone* remained in port, preparing for a shipyard overhaul slated to commence in January.

Shifting subsequently to Seattle, Wash., *Whetstone* spent four and one-half months undergoing an extensive yard overhaul. Major changes were effected to her communications facilities, while her engineering plant received extensive repairs. Upon returning to her home port later that spring on 26 May 1967, *Whetstone* was prepared for a summer of hard training in preparation for her deployment to WestPac in the autumn. Refresher training followed—evolutions that apparently revealed defects in the ship's propulsion systems; the ship underwent further yard work, this time at Long Beach. Following her return to San Diego on 2 September, the dock landing ship completed the remainder of her refresher and amphibious training and prepared for her WestPac deployment date of 31 October 1967.

Arriving in WestPac in early December, *Whetstone* lifted 11 Marine helicopters from Okinawa to Danang before she joined Task Group 76.5, Amphibious Ready Group (ARG) "Bravo." Embarking units of the Marine Special Landing Force (SLF), composed of men from the 3d Battalion, 1st Marine Regiment, *Whetstone* participated in two major amphibious operations during that deployment.

The first was "Fortress Ridge" (21–24 December 1967)—SLF "Bravo" made an unopposed landing and swept through the marshy, sandy region north of the city of Cua Viet. Encountering several pockets of enemy resistance, the marines called in air strikes, naval gunfire support and the fire from helicopter gunships—as well as artillery—to subdue the resistors. Killing 10 communist soldiers in the operation, the marines suffered the loss of 10 men and the wounding of 28.

Later in the deployment, *Whetstone* took part in Operation "Badger Catch," from 23 to 26 January 1968. Members of SLF "Bravo" went ashore from landing craft and helicopters to clear the Cua Viet River region of the enemy troops that had recently preyed upon Navy coastal convoys resupplying Marine activities along the coasts. After the landing—unopposed, as in "Fortress Ridge"—"Bravo" units teamed with elements of the 3d MarDiv in a sweep inland. At the cost of 32 leathernecks dead and 146 wounded, the marines succeeded in bagging at least 100 dead by the end of January.

Besides the amphibious operations, *Whetstone* made two hazardous coastwise supply runs—one to Hue and the other to Dong Ha—utilizing LCM's embarked in the ship's well deck. Ultimately, on 16 March, *Thomaston* (LSD–28) relieved *Whetstone* as an element of the ARG, releasing the latter for further support operations in the form of lifts of war materiel from support bases to various areas further inland.

The versatile *Whetstone* subsequently served one more deployment in Vietnamese waters in 1969, rounding out nearly two decades of naval service before returning to the United States. Decommissioned on 2 April 1970, *Whetstone* was struck from the Navy list on 1 September 1971 following transfer to the Maritime Administration (MarAd) for custody and lay up in July 1970. The dock landing ship remained in the National Defense Reserve Fleet, in MarAd custody, into the mid-1970's. As of 1 October 1979, the erstwhile amphibious craft was awaiting disposition, via a cash Navy sale. She had been on the sale list since April 1976.

Although *Whetstone* was built too late to participate in World War II, she earned four battle stars for Korean service and seven for Vietnam.

Whidbey

An island in Puget Sound, Wash., discovered in 1792 by Lt. James Whidbey, a member of the English expedition under Capt. George Vancouver.

(AG–141: dp. 540; l. 176'0''; b. 33'0''; dr. 10'0''; s. 10.0 k.; cpl. 24; a. none; cl. *Whidbey*)

FS–395—an inter-island freighter and cargo vessel completed for the United States Army on 2 January 1945 at Decatur, Ala., by the Ingalls Shipbuilding Corp.—was subsequently inspected by the Navy and accepted for service at the Naval Operating Base (NOB), Subic Bay, Philippine Islands, on 22 February

1947. *FS–395* was later given the name *Whidbey* and classified a miscellaneous auxiliary, AG–141; she was commissioned at NOB, Guam, while moored alongside SS *Hamilton Victory* on 8 August 1947, Chief Boatswain J. W. Jamieson in command.

Later assigned to Service Division 51, Service Force, Pacific Fleet, *Whidbey* initially performed service under the auspices of the Commander in Chief, Pacific Fleet, who was given the collateral duty of High Commisioner of the Trust Territories of the Pacific Islands, assigned by the United Nations to the United States after World War II. *Whidbey* carried passengers, provisions, and mail to the islands in the territories, returning to Guam with copra and other native products.

A highlight of *Whidbey's* first year in commission occurred shortly before Christmas of 1947. At 0945 on 22 December, the ship began doubling up all lines in anticipation of an approaching storm, while she was moored alongside the district oiler, YO–104, at Tomil Harbor, Yap Island; and at 1605 got underway for Guam, standing out to sea as the wind and sea began to rise menacingly. By 2200, the ship was maneuvering at various courses and speeds to keep headed into the wind; by 2330 the situation looked critical—all hands were ordered to don life jackets!

Whidbey fought the sea into the next morning. At 0042, a fire broke out in the bilges. Shutting down the port main engine, the auxiliary's crew battled the small fire for only a short time before they succeeded in putting it out, while, topside, heavy seas carried away one of the ship's lifeboats. The craft's port engine came to life only briefly before it had to be secured—leaving the ship operating on only one engine.

By 0413, heavy waves were breaking over the port and starboard sides of the ship; changing course at that instant, *Whidbey* suddenly ground onto a reef at 0418. All hands manned their abandon ship stations to prepare for any eventuality should the ship have foundered; but soundings were taken, and it looked as if the ship was on an even keel and not taking any water.

Whidbey remained aground off the east coast of Yap, with no hope in sight until the afternoon of Christmas day, when *Tawakoni* (ATF–114) hove in sight at 1229. After spending the afternoon in trying to pull *Whidbey* off the reef, *Tawakoni* secured salvage operations that evening, but resumed them the next morning. Ultimately, *Tawakoni* succeeded in her task, towing *Whidbey* approximately 22 feet and moving her astern on the 27th. On the 28th, the fleet tug set out for Guam at 1836 with the crippled auxiliary in tow. The little convoy arrived safely at Guam on the afternoon of the 31st.

Once repaired, *Whidbey* received a new task—a humanitarian mission. In an effort to look into the health and welfare of the inhabitants of all of the populated islands within the two and one-half million square miles of the Trust Territory, the Navy began a medical survey of those isles in 1948.

Converted from a small cargo vessel to a specially equipped floating clinic, *Whidbey's* medical technicians "surveyed" thousands of islanders—men, women, and children—conducting parasitology tests, providing dental care, and taking blood tests and X-rays. Her medical teams not only provided those services on board ship, but also ashore as well, visiting the sick and the aged. *Whidbey's* performance of duty enabled the Navy to ascertain a complete picture of both the common and the rare diseases that occurred in the territories.

Whidbey's duties as a floating clinic came to an end with the completion of her last survey in late April 1951. Not only had *Whidbey* performed significant and helpful medical services to and for the islanders of the Trust Territories, but she had also gathered useful hydrographic data in the course of her cruises throughout the many isles of the territories.

When the Navy relinquished its administrative duties to the Department of the Interior, *Whidbey's* role changed; her operations took on a different complexion in light of the Korean War that had broken out in the summer of 1950. *Whidbey*, the value of her past service as a mini-hospital ship proved by experience in the Trust Territories, was overhauled at Yokosuka and converted from a medical survey vessel to a Fleet epidemiological disease control ship, becoming, in effect, a modern floating laboratory, with equipment and trained technicians capable of analyzing the most minute organism.

Deployed to Yokosuka, Japan, a port through which marines were being rotated back to the United States from the combat zones in Korea, *Whidbey*'s embarked Fleet Epidemiological Disease Control Unit No. 2 processed the homeward-bound marines for dysentery, malaria, or any other parasites contracted at the front. After the ship's medical team had obtained the samples, the marines sailed for the United States.

Working almost 24-hour shifts to obtain the results in minimum time, *Whidbey*'s technicians then dispatched a report of results to the port of embarkation for each individual processed. As each transport arrived at her destination, quarantine officials there would thus be ready to treat whatever parasitical disease any marine had brought back from Korea. That process enabled those who had contracted malaria or any dormant infections to be cured before they returned to stateside posts or civilian life.

On 3 January 1952, *Whidbey* sailed for Taiwan (formerly Formosa) and carried out port visits to Keelung and Kaohsiung. She then shifted to the Nationalist Chinese naval base at Tsoying where, as "an ambassadress of good will and good health" she remained from 28 January to 5 May, her doctors working with those of the Chinese Navy. After touching at the Chinese naval base in the Pesadores, at Makung, until 15 May, *Whidbey* stopped briefly at Kaohsiung before she visited Hong Kong, en route to Sasebo. *Whidbey* again operated at Nationalist Chinese naval installations on Taiwan that summer.

Whidbey remained in the Far East, principally at Kobe and Yokosuka, through December 1953 and, placed in reserve on 1 July 1954, was assigned to the Pacific Reserve Fleet for overhaul and inactivation. She was decommissioned on 15 November 1954. Placed in the Columbia River group of the Pacific Reserve Fleet, she remained there into the late 1950's. Struck from the Navy list on 1 May 1959, the unique craft was sold to Albert Heller on 31 May 1960 and subsequently scrapped.

Whippet

I

(MB: dp. 21; l. 72'; b. 12'; dr. 3'3" (aft); s. 23 k.; cpl. 11; a. 1 1-pdr., 1 mg.)

The first *Whippet* (SP–89)—a motorboat built in 1917 by the Greenport Basin & Construction Co. at Greenport, Long Island—was acquired by the Navy on 9 July 1917 from Mr. O. C. Jennings of New York City and was placed in commission on 24 July 1917. *Whippet* conducted antisubmarine and coastal defense patrols in the 2d Naval District during World War I. On 11 January 1919, she was decommissioned, struck from the Navy list, and returned to her owner.

II

(IX–129: dp. 15,425; l. 441'6"; b. 57'; dr. 27'8⅞"; s. 11 k.; cpl. 109; a. 1 5", 1 3", 8 20mm.)

The second *Whippet* (IX–129) was laid down on 31 October 1943 at New Orleans, La., by the Delta Shipbuilding Co. under a Maritime Commission contract (MCE hull 1933); launched on 15 December 1943; sponsored by Mrs. Will Camp Sealy; delivered to the Navy on 13 January 1944; and commissioned on 14 January 1944, Lt. Comdr. R. Parmenter in command.

Following shakedown out of New Orleans, *Whippet* got underway late in January for duty in the South Pacific. She arrived at Bora Bora in the Society Islands on 27 February and remained there until 9 March when she continued her voyage. Two days later, the ship arrived at Funafuti and served there as station tanker until the beginning of the second week in May. On 10 May, *Whippet* headed for Oahu and, after a nine-day voyage, arrived in Pearl Harbor. Late in June, she had returned west of the International Dateline, arriving at Eniwetok on 24 June. For the next nine months, she served as station tanker at various forward bases in the Central Pacific—Eniwetok during the Marianas campaign and Ulithi during the struggles for the Palaus and the Philippines. By the spring of 1945, the tanker had moved to Saipan in the Marianas to prepare for the Okinawa assault.

On 27 March, she departed Saipan and, on 2 April, entered the anchorage at Kerama Retto in the Ryukyus to the west of Okinawa. There she remained, serving again as station tanker until well after organized resistance on Okinawa ceased. On 25 July, she departed the Ryukyus and steamed via Ulithi to Leyte where she arrived on 7 August.

Whippet remained there until 12 October when she got underway for Manila. The tanker arrived at Manila the following day and served there until near the end of the second month of 1946. On 24 February, she returned to Leyte briefly before continuing on to the Marianas. After spending the month of March in the Marianas, she returned to the Philippines at Subic Bay at the end of the second week in April. The ship stayed there until the end of the month at which time she received orders to return to the United States at Norfolk. She stopped at Pearl Harbor from 7 to 20 May and arrived in San Francisco on the 29th. Instead of returning to Norfolk, however, she remained on the west coast. On 1 July 1946, she was decommissioned at San Francisco, and returned to the War Shipping Administration for layup with the National Defense Reserve Fleet at Suisun Bay, Calif. Her name was struck from the Navy list on 19 July 1946.

Whippet received two battle stars for World War II service.

Whipple

Abraham Whipple—born on 26 September 1733, near Providence, R.I.—chose to be a seafarer early in his life and embarked upon a career in the lucrative West Indies trade. In the French and Indian War period, he became a privateersman and commanded privateer *Game Cock* from 1759 to 1760. In one six-month cruise, he captured 23 French ships.

As American colonists began to resist what they considered unfair oppression by the British crown—acts of defiance became more and more prevalent. One such occurrence happened on 18 June 1772, when Whipple led 50 Rhode Islanders in the capture and burning of British revenue cutter *Gaspee*, which had run aground off Pawtucket while chasing the packet *Hannah*.

Three years later, the Rhode Island Assembly appointed Whipple commodore of two ships fitted out for the defense of the colony's trade. On the day the sea captain received his commission, 15 June 1775, he led his men to capture the tender to frigate HMS *Rose*. After cruising in the vicinity of Narragansett Bay, he headed south to Bermuda to procure gunpowder for use by the colony and, on the return voyage, transported naval recruits to Philadelphia. Upon her arrival there, his ship, *Katy*, was taken over by agents of the Continental Congress and was fitted out as sloop-of-war *Providence*.

Whipple was commissioned a captain in the Continental Navy on 22 December and was given command of 24-gun frigate *Columbus*. During the period from 17 February to 8 April 1776, he commanded that ship

253

during the first American Navy-Marine Corps amphibious expedition—the cruise to New Providence, in the Bahamas, to seize essential military supplies from the British garrison at Nassau.

After returning north to New England, Whipple captured five British prizes before 27 March 1778, when his ship ran aground off Judith Point. After stripping the ship, the wily captain and his crew abandoned her and escaped capture ashore.

Next assigned to command 28-gun frigate *Providence*, Whipple ran the British blockade on the night of 30 April 1778, damaging HMS *Lark* and outrunning another Britisher during the escape. Tacking for France, Whipple's *Providence* crossed the Atlantic unmolested, bearing important dispatches relating to agreements between France and the American colonies, and reached Paimboeuf. After acquiring needed guns and supplies for the Continental Army, *Providence* and *Boston* sailed home to the colonies, taking three prizes en route.

Upon his return, Whipple received command of a small squadron—*Providence*, *Ranger*, and *Queen of France*. On one occasion in mid-July 1779, this group of ships encountered a large British convoy in dense fog off the Newfoundland Banks. Whipple cagily concealed his guns and ran up the British flag. Like a wolf among sheep, he cut 11 prizes out of the convoy—eight of which contained spoils of war valued together at over one million dollars—easily one of the richest captures of the entire war.

Following this adventure, Whipple cruised off Bermuda before arriving at Charleston, S.C., on 23 December 1779. British forces threatened that key Continental port, causing the guns and crews from the Continental Navy ships in port to be moved on shore to reinforce the land batteries to repulse the expected British assault.

However, after a rugged four-month siege, the overwhelming pressure of British arms forced the Continental forces to surrender on 12 May 1780. Whipple remained a prisoner of the British until he was paroled to Chester, Pa., and he took no further part in the war. Upon the conclusion of hostilities, Whipple took up farming near Cranston, R.I.

For the remainder of his life, he remained a farmer, with the exception of two spells of seafaring as master of merchantmen, first of *General Washington* and then of *St. Clair*. With the formation of the Ohio Company in 1788 and the initial westward migration into that territory, Whipple and his family became pioneers on the American frontier and were among the founders of the town of Marietta, Ohio. Granted a pension by Congress in recognition of his distinguished service in helping to win American independence, Whipple died at Marietta on 27 May 1819.

I

(Destroyer No. 15: dp. 600; l. 259'6''; b. 23'3''; dr. 6' (mean); s. 28.24 k.; cpl. 73; a. 2 3'', 6 6-pdrs., 2 18'' tt.; cl. *Bainbridge*)

The first *Whipple* (Destroyer No. 15) was laid down on 13 November 1899 at Sparrows Point, Md., by the Maryland Steel Co.; launched on 15 August 1901; sponsored by Miss Elsie Pope; and commissioned on 17 February 1903, Lt. Jehu V. Chase in command.

After training in Chesapeake Bay, *Whipple* was assigned to the 2d Torpedo Flotilla, Atlantic Fleet, and was based at Norfolk. The destroyer periodically served as flagship of the flotilla and operated off the east coast and in the Caribbean until she was placed in reserve at Norfolk on 5 September 1905.

Returning to active service on 16 July 1906, the ship conducted tactical exercises and routine training operations through November of 1907. On 2 December, *Whipple* stood out of Hampton Roads and headed south toward the Caribbean for goodwill visits—"showing the flag."

Subsequently following in the wake of the 16 battle-ships of the Great White Fleet, *Whipple* and her flotilla-mates called at Rio de Janeiro; rounded Cape Horn for ports on the Chilean and Peruvian coasts; and conducted target practice at Magdalena Bay, Mexico. After participating in a fleet review at San Francisco on 8 May 1908, *Whipple* remained on the west coast, based at San Diego, as a unit of the Pacific Torpedo Flotilla.

Departing San Francisco at the end of a towline on 24 August, the destroyer subsequently took part in fleet battle problems in Hawaiian waters. Upon completion of the exercises, she steamed back to the west coast via Samoa and Magdalena Bay, Baja California, before arriving at San Diego on 1 December.

For the next six years, the destroyer operated off the west coast between San Diego and Magdalena Bay and made one cruise to Alaskan waters for maneuvers. The ship received the Mexican Service Medal for service off the Mexican coast in 1914 and 1916. While that country suffered in the throes of revolution and civil strife, the destroyer conducted patrols and stood ready to protect American lives and property.

On 6 April 1917, America entered World War I on the side of Britain, France, and Italy. *Whipple* soon commenced patrols off the approaches to the vital Panama Canal before departing the Canal Zone on 5 July.

Refitted for "distant service," the destroyer put to sea on 28 August, bound for the Atlantic war zone, and put into the Azores on 17 September. *Whipple* operated on escort duties, convoying ships to and from the strategic islands for the next three months.

She then received orders to report at Brest, France. Antisubmarine patrols and convoy escort duties occupied *Whipple* through the early spring of 1918. On 17 April, munition ship *Florence H.* blew up off Quiberon Bay. Braving flying debris from the exploding ship, *Whipple* joined *Stewart* (Destroyer No. 13) and *Truxtun* (Destroyer No. 14) in rescuing 32 men of the 77-man crew of that doomed vessel.

Whipple carried out her routine wartime patrol duties through the end of hostilities. On 9 December, the destroyer departed the French coast and headed homeward, touching at the Azores and Bermuda before making port at Philadelphia on 3 January 1919.

The destroyer was decommissioned at the Philadelphia Navy Yard on 7 July 1919, and her name was struck from the Navy list on 15 September. On 3 January 1920, J. G. Hitner, of Philadelphia, purchased the ship for scrapping.

II

(Destroyer No. 217: dp. 1,308; l. 314'4½''; b. 30'11½''; dr. 9'4'' (mean); s. 35.0 k.; cpl. 101; a. 4 4'', 1 3'', 2 .30-cal. mg., 12 21'' tt.; cl. *Clemson*)

The second *Whipple* (Destroyer No. 217) was laid down on 12 June 1919 at Philadelphia, Pa., by William Cramp and Sons; launched on 6 November 1919; sponsored by Mrs. Gladys V. Mulvey, great-great-great granddaughter of Abraham Whipple; and commissioned on 23 April 1920, Lt. Richard F. Bernard in command.

Following shakedown training out of Guantanamo Bay, Cuba, *Whipple* returned to Philadelphia for post-shakedown availability. The destroyer sailed for the Near East on 29 May 1920 and arrived at Constantinople, Turkey, on 13 June. For the next eight months, she operated in the region of the Black Sea and eastern Mediterranean, under the overall command of Admiral Mark L. Bristol, Commander, U.S. Naval Detachment in Near Eastern Waters. At this time, the entire Near East simmered in a state of ferment, due to changes wrought by, and in the wake of, World War I.

Whipple delivered mail to *Chandler* (Destroyer No. 209) at Samsoun, Turkey, on 16 June and landed British and American Tobacco Co. representatives whom the destroyer had transported from Constantinople. She next visited Sevastopol, in the Russian Crimea, and Constanta, Romania. Unexpectedly ordered to

Batum, Russia, *Whipple* departed Samsoun on 6 July and made 30 knots to reach her destination the next day. There, she attended the peaceful birth of the Georgian Republic, as British and French troops turned over the city to White Russian forces.

Whipple then shifted south for a brief cruise along the Levantine coast during which she visited Beirut and Damascus, Syria; and Port Said, Egypt, before she returned to Constantinople on 18 August. While she was making this cruise, the sweeping Navy-wide designation of hull numbers took place; and *Whipple* was classified as DD-217 on 17 July 1920. The destroyer next resumed her previous routine on the Black Sea route, carrying mail between ports (including dispatches for consulates and the like), and observing conditions prevailing at the ports visited in Romania, Russia, and Asiatic Turkey.

While underway on 19 October, *Whipple* sighted distress signals from Greek steamer *Thetis* and proceeded to the stricken vessel's assistance, as she lay aground off Constanta. After 10 hours of exertion, the destroyer succeeded in freeing *Thetis* from her predicament and earned a commendation from her division commander. The citation lauded Lt. Comdr. Bernard's display of initiative and his excellent handling of the ship in shoal waters with a heavy sea running. "The whole affair," the citation concluded, ". . . reflected great credit on the *Whipple* and the United States Naval Service."

In the meantime, while *Whipple* conducted her patrols, the situation in Russia worsened materially. *Whipple* convoyed the disabled American steamer SS *Haddon* into Constantinople and later fueled at Constanta where she learned that Russian Bolshevik troops threatened the Crimea. Baron General Peter N. Wrangel, commanding the White Russian forces in the area, pulled his force back to Sevastopol in a desperate rear-guard action. As the Reds drew the noose tighter around the beleaguered city, the Whites took to the sea in everything that floated to escape the oncoming Bolshevik forces.

Whipple arrived at Sevastopol on the morning of 14 November and reported to Vice Admiral Newton McCully for orders. Hundreds of boats scurried about the harbor, often crammed to the gunwales with fleeing White Russians. In addition to *Whipple*, cruiser *St. Louis* and two destroyers—*Overton* (DD-239) and *Humphreys* (DD-236)—stood by to evacuate selected individuals bearing passes from Admiral McCully.

During the entire time *Whipple* remained at the doomed port, her main battery was trained out and manned. Armed boat crews carried evacuees out to the ship while her landing force stood in readiness. As her last boatload pushed off from shore, Bolshevik troops reached the main square and began firing on the fleeing White Russians; *Whipple* had been just a step ahead of the Reds.

Whipple then towed a barge loaded with wounded White Russian troops out of range of the Bolshevik guns and then turned the tow over to *Humphreys*. As *Whipple* passed *Overton*, Vice Admiral McCully, on the latter's bridge, called out by megaphone: "Well done, *Whipple*." The last American vessel out of Sevastopol, the destroyer headed for Constantinople with her passengers, both topside and below decks. Each carried pitifully few belongings, had no food, and possessed very little money. Many were sick or wounded.

After disembarking the refugees at Constantinople, *Whipple* resumed her station ship and mail carrying duties with the Near Eastern Naval Detachment and continued the task through the end of 1920 and into the spring of 1921. On 2 May 1921, the destroyer, along with her division mates, sailed for the Far East, transiting the Suez Canal and called at Bombay, India; Colombo, Ceylon; Batavia, Java; Singapore, Straits Settlements; and Saigon, French Indochina. She arrived at her new home port, Cavite, Philippine Islands, near Manila, on 29 June. For the next four years, the destroyer served in the Asiatic Fleet, "showing the

flag" and standing ready to protect American lives and property in strife-torn China. She operated out of Cavite in the winter months, conducting tactical exercises in the Philippines until heading north to North China ports in the spring for summer operations out of Tsingtao.

Warfare between local warlords around Shanghai in late 1924 and early 1925 resulted in *Whipple*'s being called upon to serve as a transport. On 15 January 1925, the Marine detachment from *Sacramento* (PG-19) went ashore to protect American property, while about the same time, an expeditionary force of marines, led by Capt. James P. Schwerin, USMC, embarked in *Whipple* and her sisters *Borie* (DD-215) and *Barker* (DD-213). The three destroyers landed the marines on 22 January, relieving the 28-man detachment from the gunboat at that time.

On 18 May 1925, *Whipple* and her division sailed for the United States, via Guam, Midway, and Pearl Harbor, and arrived at San Diego on 17 June. Five days later, the ship got underway for the east coast of the United States; and she arrived at Norfolk on 17 July. She next operated off the east coast from Maine to Florida and cruised to Guantanamo Bay for maneuvers with the Fleet. During this time, *Whipple* put ashore a landing force in Nicaragua to protect American lives and property threatened by the banditry and unrest in that troubled Central American country. On four separate instances, in late 1926 and early 1927, a landing party from the destroyer served on shore, earning the ship the Second Nicaraguan Campaign Medal.

Whipple departed Norfolk on 26 May 1927 to begin a cruise with her division to northern European ports. She then steamed south for a brief tour in the Mediterranean before departing Gibraltar on 29 January 1928 and heading for Cuba. She then conducted operations in the Caribbean out of Guantanamo Bay, until 26 March when she set course for the west coast. She operated in the Pacific out of the Destroyer Base at San Diego, Calif., until 1 August 1929. *Whipple* departed the west coast, bound for the Asiatic Station and her second tour with the Asiatic Fleet.

Whipple spent the next decade with the Asiatic Fleet, watching the rising ascendancy of Japan over China and the Far East. She resumed the usual routine common to ships of her type with the Fleet: winter exercises in the Philippine Islands and summer maneuvers out of Tsingtao, China, with cruises to Chinese coastal ports in the interim.

While on exercises in Subic Bay during the spring of 1936, *Whipple* and *Smith-Thompson* (DD-212) collided on 14 April. The latter suffered such serious damage in the mishap that she had to be scrapped. As a consequence, *Whipple*, whose own bow had been bent around until it faced sternward, received *Smith-Thompson*'s undamaged bow and soon reentered active service.

Meanwhile, tension between China and Japan continued to worsen, particularly in North China. Long-simmering antagonisms erupted in fighting near Peking on 7 July 1937 which soon became an all-out war in the vicinity. Two weeks later, a small squadron of Asiatic Fleet units, incuding *Whipple*, sailed from Chefoo on 24 July. The destroyer—in company with sisters *Alden* (DD-211), *Barker* (DD-213), and *Paul Jones* (DD-230)—rendezvoused with Fleet flagship *Augusta* (CA-31), on the 25th, en route to the coast of Siberia. The five ships arrived at Vladivostok, USSR, on the 28th.

The visit, the first by American men-of-war since the establishment of diplomatic relations with the Soviet Union in 1933, lasted until 1 August when the five ships headed back to China. Within the next fortnight, while the Fleet continued its routine, hostilities broke out between Chinese and Japanese forces at Shanghai; and the undeclared Sino-Japanese War entered a new phase.

The Fleet continued its mission of observing the conflict, standing ready to evacuate Americans from Chinese ports should the occasion arise. By mid-1938, when the war had moved inland and up the Yangtze, the Fleet resumed its former routine. *Whipple* and her division mates, in company with squadron tender *Black Hawk* (AD–9), visited Bangkok, Siam, in June 1938.

As the Japanese war machine continued to devour China, the Nipponese captured most of the major coastal cities and ports and those along the lower Yangtze. Opportunities for trouble multiplied for the western nations still trying to maintain their interests in China. In the spring of 1939, one such occasion came at Amoy, China, where a Chinese gunman shot a Japanese citizen. The Japanese responded by landing Special Naval Landing Force personnel near the International Settlement of Koolangsu. The British and Americans did likewise, landing bluejackets from *Marblehead* (CL–12) and the British light cruiser *Birmingham*. By September 1939, *Whipple* was serving as station ship at Amoy, her landing force ashore and Capt. John T. G. Stapler, Commander, South China Patrol, embarked on board.

At 2355 on 3 September 1939, *Whipple*'s deck log noted that France had declared war on Germany, two days after German troops invaded Poland. World War II had begun in Europe, substantially altering the balance of power in the Orient as Britain pulled out much of her China Station fleet to bolster the Home and Mediterranean Fleets. *Whipple* operated on neutrality patrol off the Philippines into 1941, as Admiral Thomas C. Hart prepared the small Asiatic Fleet for war.

On 25 November 1941—two days in advance of the "war warning" which predicted that hostile Japanese action in the Pacific was imminent—Hart dispatched *Whipple*'s Destroyer Division (DesDiv) 58, along with the tender *Black Hawk*, to Balikpapan, Borneo, to disperse the surface ships of his fleet from their vulnerable position within the confines of Manila Bay. There, *Whipple* awaited the outbreak of war which came on 8 December 1941 (7 December east of the date line) with the Japanese attack on Pearl Harbor.

Originally slated to join a British force based around the battleship HMS *Prince of Wales* and the battlecruiser HMS *Repulse*, *Whipple*'s mission was aborted when Japanese land-based torpedo planes and high-level bombers sank both of these capital ships in the South China Sea off Kuantan, Malaya, on 10 December. *Whipple* arrived at Singapore on 11 December and departed on the 14th, bound for the Netherlands East Indies.

Fighting a desperate rearguard action in the face of a swift-moving and well-organized enemy, the multinational Australian–British–Dutch–American (ABDA) force faced formidable obstacles as they withdrew to the "Malay Barrier." During this time, *Whipple* conducted important escort and patrol duties into February 1942. On 12 February, the destroyer got underway from Prigi Bay, Java, in a dense fog. As she headed for Tjilatjap, on the south coast of Java, she was struck a glancing blow by the Dutch light cruiser *De Ruyter*. As the Dutch ship materialized out of the murk, *Whipple* alertly swung left to avoid a collision, a wise move that undoubtedly averted more serious damage. Drydocked at Tjilatjap on the 13th, *Whipple* ascertained the damage to be minor and rejoined the fleet for active service.

At 1640 on 26 February, *Whipple* and sistership *Edsall* (DD–219) departed Tjilatjap to rendezvous with *Langley* (AV–3) off the south coast of Java. Making contact at 0629, the destroyers took up screening positions to escort the vulnerable auxiliary—carrying a load of aircraft to bolster the sagging defenses of Java—into Tjilatjap. At 1150, lookouts spotted nine high-level bombers approaching from the east. Four minutes later, a stick of bombs splashed around *Langley*—clearly the object of Japanese attention. During a second attack shortly after noon, all three ships put up brisk antiaircraft fire.

At 1212, the Japanese, undaunted by *Langley*'s evasive maneuvers, struck hard. A stick of bombs fell on or near the former aircraft carrier and set her afire.

Whipple broke off firing at 1224 as the attackers veered away in a northeasterly direction. She changed course and closed *Langley* to evaluate that vessel's damage. Shortly thereafter, four Japanese fighter planes dove on the three-ship convoy, but one soon limped off to the east, hit by antiaircraft fire.

Langley was abandoned at 1325, and *Whipple* proceeded close aboard to rescue survivors; using two of the destroyer's life rafts, a cargo net slung over the side, and a number of lines trailed over the side. Staying some 25 yards off the sinking seaplane tender, *Whipple* picked up some 308 men from *Langley*'s crew and embarked Army personnel for the vital P-40 fighters carried on the doomed ship's abbreviated flight deck. At 1358, the task at hand completed, *Whipple* backed off and stood out to destroy the derelict, opening fire at 1429 with her 4-inch main battery. After nine rounds of 4-inch and two torpedoes, *Langley* settled lower and lower but refused stubbornly to sink. Soon, orders arrived directing *Whipple* and her sister ship to clear the area prior to any more bombing attacks.

Whipple accordingly vacated the vicinity and subsequently rendezvoused with *Pecos* (AO–6) in the lee of Christmas Island to transfer the Army pilots to the oiler. At 1020 on 27 February, three Japanese twin-engined bombers attacked Christmas Island. One later singled out *Whipple* and dropped a stick of bombs which missed the rapidly dodging destroyer.

On 28 February, *Whipple* began transferring *Langley* crew members to *Pecos*, completing the task by 0800. While one destroyer transferred personnel, the other circled and maintained an antisubmarine screen. When the job of transferring survivors from the lost seaplane tender had been completed, the two destroyers parted company with the oiler. Changing course in anticipation of orders to retire from Java, *Whipple* prepared to send a message relative to these orders when the destroyer's chief radioman heard a cell for help over the radio—from *Pecos*, then under attack by Japanese bombers near Christmas Island.

Whipple sped to the scene to render assistance if possible. Throughout the afternoon, as the destroyer closed the oiler, all hands on board prepared knotted lines and cargo nets for use in picking up survivors. *Whipple* went to general quarters at 1922 when she sighted several small lights off both bows.

Whipple slowly closed and began picking up survivors of *Pecos*. After interrupting the proceedings to conduct an unsuccessful attack on a submarine lurking in the area, she returned to the task and continued the search until she had received 231 men from the oiler. *Whipple* soon cleared the area, believing that a Japanese aircraft carrier was near. Within a few days, Java fell to the onrushing Japanese who were gradually consolidating their expanding "Greater East Asia Co-Prosperity Sphere." *Whipple* joined the battered remnants of the Asiatic Fleet in Australian waters.

Subsequently sailing to Melbourne, Australia, and arriving on 23 March, *Whipple* operated with Australian and New Zealand Navy warships on convoy escort duties along the Great Barrier Reef until 2 May. She departed Sydney on that day, bound for the New Hebrides Islands, and from there pushed on via American Samoa to Hawaii, arriving at Pearl Harbor on 6 June. Together with sister ship *Alden*, *Whipple* departed Pearl Harbor on 8 June for San Francisco, escorting an eastward-bound convoy to the west coast, arriving off the Golden Gate on the 18th.

During a yard availability at Mare Island, the destroyer's topside weight was cut down as 20-millimeter antiaircraft guns replaced two banks of her torpedo tubes. Thus modified for convoy escort work, *Whipple* put to sea to commence the first of seven round-trip convoy escort missions from the west coast to Hawaii which lasted into the spring of 1943.

Standing out of San Francisco Bay on 11 May 1943, *Whipple* sailed for the Caribbean with a convoy routed through the Panama Canal for Santa Ana Bay, Curacao, Netherlands West Indies. After the cargo ships loaded a petroleum cargo, the convoy pushed on for Cuba and arrived at Guantanamo Bay on 29 May. From Guantanamo, the destroyer escorted a convoy to Trinidad but returned to the Cuban base on 19 June before heading north to the New York Navy Yard for voyage repairs.

Later departing New York on 10 July, *Whipple* escorted a group of ships which rendezvoused with a convoy bound for Casablanca, French Morocco, and Gibraltar. Returning to Charleston, S.C., on 27 August, the destroyer put to sea on 7 September as a unit in a slow tow convoy bound via the Caribbean to Recife, Brazil. *Whipple* headed north soon thereafter, guarding a convoy to Trinidad, and then up the eastern seaboard to Charleston, making port on 19 November.

After another convoy escort run from Norfolk to Guantanamo Bay and the Canal Zone, *Whipple* joined three other destroyers in completing the "hunter-killer" task group based around *Guadalcanal* (CVE–60). Departing Norfolk on 5 January 1944, the group went to sea to hunt German U-boats active in the Atlantic.

On 16 January, aircraft from *Guadalcanal* sighted three U-boats on the surface, fueling, some 300 miles off Flores. Carrier-based Avengers attacked the group and sank *U–544* in the ensuing attack. After replenishing at Casablanca, the group returned to the high seas and searched convoy lanes for signs of German submarines until arriving at Norfolk on 16 February. Detached from the "hunter-killer" group soon thereafter, *Whipple* underwent voyage repairs at the Boston Navy Yard. On 13 March, the destroyer departed the east coast in company with Convoy UGS–36, bound for the Mediterranean.

In the early morning darkness of 1 April, German planes—Dornier 217's and Junkers 88's—came in low and fast to attack the convoy. Keeping up a heavy fire with her 20-millimeter batteries, *Whipple* sent up a substantial part of the tremendous barrage which drove off the 30 German planes and saved the convoy. Arriving at Bizerte, Tunisia, on 3 April, the destroyer subsequently returned to Norfolk on the 30th.

For the remainder of 1944 and into the spring of 1945, *Whipple* performed convoy escort duties off the east coast, across the Atlantic to Casablanca, and occasionally into the Caribbean. Arriving at New London, Conn., on 6 June 1945, *Whipple* was redesignated an auxiliary, AG–117. After acting as a target ship for submarines off New London, the erstwhile destroyer entered the New York Navy Yard on 9 July for conversion to a high-speed target vessel.

On 5 August, *Whipple* departed New York for duty in the Pacific. Transiting the Panama Canal, the target ship proceeded via San Diego to Hawaii and arrived at Pearl Harbor on 30 August. She subsequently served as a target vessel for submarines of the Pacific training command until 21 September.

The need for her services no longer required, *Whipple* departed Pearl Harbor and proceeded to the east coast, arriving at Philadelphia on 18 October. Decommissioned on 9 November 1945, her name was struck from the Navy list on 5 December. Stripped for scrap, the hulk was sold on 30 September 1947 to the Northern Metals Co. of Philadelphia.

Whipple received two battle stars for her World War II service.

III

(DE–1062: dp. 4,064; l. 438'; b. 47'; dr. 25'; s. 27 k.; cpl. 243; a. ASROC, 1 5'', 4 tt.; cl. *Knox*)

The third *Whipple* (DE–1062) was laid down on 24 April 1967 at Seattle, Wash., by the Todd Shipyards Corp.; launched on 12 April 1968; sponsored by Mrs. Kirkland B. Alexander; and commissioned on 22 August 1970, Comdr. Jack Campbell in command.

Whipple conducted sea trials from 24 to 26 September before returning to the Puget Sound Navy Yard, Bremerton, Wash., for fitting-out availability from 27 to 30 September. On 1 October, the escort ship proceeded to Nanoose, British Columbia, for a visit prior to further trials at Carr Inlet, Wash.

On 9 October, the ship got underway for San Diego and made port four days later. *Whipple* departed the west coast on the 16th, bound for her new home port, Pearl Harbor, and duty with the Cruiser-Destroyer Force, Pacific Fleet. Soon after her arrival on the 22d, she commenced local operations in the Hawaiian area which lasted until 20 November when she tied up alongside tender *Bryce Canyon* (AD–36) for availability which ran until 4 December.

Five days later, while engaged in local operations, the destroyer escort investigated an unidentified submarine contact off the Barking Sands Missile Test Range, Kauai. Following that hunt, *Whipple* resumed local cruising through 20 December.

Returning to her home port the following day, the escort ship commenced a holiday upkeep period which lasted through 13 January 1971. She then conducted weapons trials off Hawaii before undergoing preshakedown tests.

On 8 February, *Whipple* commenced shakedown which included underway training exercises and the ship's first battle problem. Termination of the shakedown period on 19 March was soon followed by availability at the Pearl Harbor Naval Shipyard. On 1 April—while undergoing yard work which lasted into July—the escort ship was assigned to newly formed Destroyer Squadron (DesRon) 33.

After sea trials in late August, the ship commenced weapons trials. From 4 to 10 October, the ship performed plane-guard duties for *Constellation* (CVA–64), while additionally conducting antiaircraft and surface gunnery exercises. A dependents' cruise to Lahaina, a Navy Day "open house," and host-ship duties to Australian destroyer HMAS *Hobart* occupied *Whipple* through 25 October, after which time she conducted further trials and gunnery shoots.

Whipple underwent upkeep for the first four days of November before she got underway on 5 November for the filming of the at-sea phase of an "Hawaii Five-O" television episode. From 8 to 18 November, *Whipple* participated in SEATO exercise RIMPAC–4, conducting antisubmarine warfare exercises in company with Australian, New Zealand, Canadian, Japanese, and American units.

Following her return to Hawaiian waters, *Whipple* conducted further trials and began preparations for a Western Pacific (WestPac) deployment. On 27 January 1972, *Whipple* departed Pearl Harbor in company with the rest of DesRon 33 and proceeded via Midway and Guam to the Philippines. The ship's subsequent Manila stopover, where she made port on 13 February, coincided with the initial work-up phase for SEATO exercise "Seahawk." Naval forces of Great Britain, Australia, New Zealand, the Philippines, and Thailand, as well as the United States, participated in these exercises. Accordingly, *Whipple*, in company with Australian carrier HMAS *Melbourne*, took part in the simulated convoy escort operation.

Upon detachment from "Seahawk," *Whipple* stopped at Subic Bay for maintenance prior to proceeding to the Gulf of Tonkin to relieve *Higbee* (DD–806) as Positive Identification and Radar Advisory Zone (PIRAZ) ship. After taking up station on 28 February, *Whipple* performed escort duties besides conducting her regular patrols. Her PIRAZ work during this time was light, as reduced air activity over North Vietnam was accomplished by low visibility and a cancellation of many scheduled flights.

While *Whipple* operated in company with *Parsons* (DDG–33) on PIRAZ duties, the escort ship's electronic "eyes" maintained the air "picture" for the northern half of the Gulf of Tonkin. The destroyer escort next took up plane-guard duties for *Hancock* (CVA–19) before providing gunfire support in Military Region 1 for the South Vietnamese Army's 3d Division. *Whipple*

An SH-3 *Sea King* antisubmarine helicopter hovers over the flight deck of *Whipple* (FF-1062) during fleet exercises, 1978. An SH-2D LAMPS (Light Airborne Multipurpose System) helicopter, designed for operation from cruisers and destroyers, is spotted on *Whipple*'s deck forward of her Sea Sparrow missile launcher. (KN-26918)

conducted 52 missions and expended 2,361 rounds of 5-inch ammunition.

Night harassment and interdiction fire against unobserved area targets comprised the majority of the missions. On some occasions, *Whipple* operated in conjunction with aerial spotters who directed the destroyer escort's fire on enemy troop movements, coastal defense guns, artillery sites, and tanks. During *Whipple*'s first gunfire support assignment on 11 April, the ship twice dueled enemy shore guns, with enemy shells impacting within 150 and 200 yards of the ship. For this action, *Whipple* received the Combat Action Ribbon.

From 20 to 24 April, *Whipple* received repairs to her 5-inch gun from *Hector* (AR-7) and Mobile Technical Unit 13. Moored alongside the repair ship in Danang harbor in the daytime, the ship would patrol off the harbor mouth in the evening. Upon completion of gun repairs, the escort ship joined *Tripoli* (LPH-10) for "Freedom Porch" strikes.

After a brief period planeguarding on "Dixie" and "Yankee" stations for *Hancock*, *Whipple* received a needed upkeep at Danang from 3 to 10 May while *Piedmont* (AD-17) replaced the escort's 5-inch gun. She then returned to "Yankee" Station where she once more operated with *Hancock*, conducting escort and planeguarding operations through June.

Following availability at Subic Bay and a visit to Hong Kong, *Whipple* returned to the line and provided gunfire support in the vicinity of Point "Claudia" for the Republic of Vietnam's 1st and 3d Divisions. From 17 to 25 June, she fired harassment and interdiction missions at night and made runs during daylight hours in which she was aided by OV-1 Mohawks which pinpointed enemy bunker complexes, rocket sites, and supply routes.

On 26 June, *Whipple* moved north to the vicinity of Point "Allison" to provide gunfire support for Operation LAM SON 72. Coastal defense sites in the Demilitarized Zone (DMZ) and point targets in the Cua Viet River region felt the sting of salvos she fired in preparation for a South Vietnamese Marine Corps counteroffensive.

Continuing to provide gunfire support for LAM SON 72, *Whipple* received a call for help at dusk on 5 July. Vietnamese marines—under heavy attack by tank-supported North Vietnamese Army infantry—radioed for immediate assistance. The escort ship—the first ship in the vicinity to do so—soon answered the call. *New-*

port News (CA–148) subsequently opened fire with her 8-inch guns to parry the North Vietnamese thrust.

Whipple returned to planeguarding duties from 9 to 17 July—this time for *Saratoga* (CVA–60)—and continued combat operations in the Gulf of Tonkin. Following this duty, the escort ship returned to Subic Bay on the 18th for upkeep which lasted until 27 July, when the ship departed Philippine waters, bound for Vietnam. En route, heavy seas damaged the fiberglass 5-inch gun shield, forcing a change of plans and a return to Subic Bay.

Following in-port repairs, *Whipple* joined Task Group (TG) 77.6—based around *America* (CVA–66)—bound for Yankee Station. Upon relief by *James E. Kyes* (DD–787) as screen commander, *Whipple* put about for the Philippines and joined her squadron mates for the homeward-bound voyage to Pearl Harbor. After stops en route at Guam and Midway for fuel, the destroyer escort made port at Pearl Harbor on 25 August.

Underway training, convoy and antisubmarine warfare exercises, and testing of the ship's ASROC occupied *Whipple* during October. November and December saw the ship undergo restricted availability at the Pearl Harbor Naval Shipyard.

Whipple conducted post-availability shakedown in January 1973 and commenced a period of routine training and exercises which continued until 14 May when the destroyer escort departed Pearl Harbor for her second WestPac deployment. She proceeded to Japan and arrived at Yokosuka on 24 May. Two days later, *Whipple* sailed for Taiwan and arrived there on 30 May. Availability alongside tender *Prairie* (AD–15) preceded the escort ship's deployment in Vietnamese waters, and she departed Taiwan on 5 June, bound for "Yankee Station."

Deployed as picket-escort from 8 to 30 June in the Gulf of Tonkin, *Whipple* returned to Subic Bay for repairs to her rudder. The destroyer escort conducted sea trials before once more returning to "Yankee Station" as an escort for *Coral Sea* (CVA–43).

Whipple visited Hong Kong from 1 to 8 August and screened *Coral Sea* back to Subic Bay before returning to Tonkin Gulf for picket-escort and PIRAZ duties. This line deployment concluded on 6 September when the vessel departed for upkeep at Singapore.

Following her return to the Philippines, the ship took part in Amphibious Exercise PEGASA II, off Mindoro. At its conclusion on 2 October, *Whipple* headed toward "Yankee Station" for another deployment as picket. During that assignment, typhoons Nora and Opal swirled through the Tonkin Gulf giving *Whipple* plenty of experience in storm evasion.

Following a return to Subic Bay for upkeep, *Whipple* made a 21-day, round-trip voyage to Colombo, Sri Lanka, to "show the flag." On the passage to Colombo, she carried several tons of bulk foodstuffs and miscellaneous supplies for the small American community in Sri Lanka. Once the escort ship arrived at Colombo, she served as central mailing point for Christmas packages from the Americans there to friends and relatives in the United States and elsewhere.

After departing Sri Lanka on 31 October, *Whipple* proceeded to the Philippines and arrived at Subic Bay on 8 November to prepare for a voyage home. She got underway on 20 November; made brief stops at Guam and Midway for refueling; and, in company with her squadron mates, steamed single-file into Pearl Harbor on 7 December. The destroyer escort spent the remainder of the year 1973 in a leave and upkeep standdown period.

Whipple resumed local operations out of Pearl Harbor and engaged in routine exercises, inspections, and maneuvers through August. Early in September 1974, the ship commenced preparations for her third WestPac deployment and, on 1 October, got underway for Subic Bay.

Arriving on the 16th, the destroyer escort conducted type training exercises in the Philippines from 23 to 26 October before receiving orders to make for Ambon, Indonesia, for a "showing-the-flag" and goodwill mission. On 27 October, the ship departed Subic and headed south in the teeth of a typhoon.

Upon making port at Ambon on the morning of 1 November, *Whipple* began carrying out the diplomacy of a goodwill visit. Her crew distributed "Project-Handclasp" material, painted a school, and topped off her visit with an unusual and time-consuming refuelling operation—a three-day, round-the-clock affair—utilizing tanker trucks. Underway again on 4 November, *Whipple* made for Subic Bay once more.

After arriving at the Philippine base on 8 November, the destroyer escort commenced restricted availability which lasted until the 16th when the ship sailed for Kaohsiung, Taiwan.

Whipple undertook ASW operations out of Kaohsiung before proceeding via Subic Bay to Hong Kong. The escort ship arrived at the British Crown Colony on 2 December before once more heading for Philippine waters where she remained for the remainder of the year 1974.

After celebrating New Year's 1975 at Subic Bay, *Whipple* proceeded to Buckner Bay, Okinawa, for local operations which lasted through 10 January. Upon reaching Philippine waters three days later, *Whipple* joined Task Group 77.5, consisting of *Coral Sea*, *Knox* (DE–1052), and *Gridley* (DLG–21), in local Philippine operating areas.

Detached from TG 77.5 on 27 January, *Whipple* conducted ASW exercises with *Reasoner* (DE–1063) before rejoining *Coral Sea* and planeguarding and steaming in company with the carrier through 2 February. After one week in port, *Whipple* steamed out of Subic Bay on 9 February, bound for Pearl Harbor.

Resuming local operations in the Hawaiian area after her return on 22 February, *Whipple* conducted routine exercises and maneuvers through the summer of the year. On 1 July 1975, *Whipple*'s designation was changed to FF–1062 during a Navy-wide reclassification. On August, *Whipple* entered Drydock No. 4 at the Pearl Harbor Naval Shipyard for a major overhaul which was to include reconfiguring her superstructure to accommodate a LAMPS system.

Whipple completed overhaul on 24 March 1976. The ensuing months were spent in refresher training in the Hawaiian area where the ship obtained certification over the full range of her weapons and propulsion systems. The period October to December was spent in preparation for a forthcoming deployment to the western Pacific.

On 3 January 1977, *Whipple* departed on her fourth deployment since commissioning. From that date until her return to Pearl Harbor, the frigate operated as a part of the 7th Fleet in various advanced exercises. Following post-deployment standdown, *Whipple* resumed training operations in the Hawaiian area until December when she entered the Pearl Harbor Naval Shipyard for a restricted availability.

Completing her repair work on 3 February 1978, *Whipple* resumed the pattern of operations out of her home port which she had assumed following the previous deployment. On 3 April, the ship departed Hawaii for a four-nation naval exercise, "RIMPACK '78," which took place in the Central Pacific. She returned on 22 April. Further exercises followed as the ship prepared for another extended deployment to the western Pacific. *Whipple* departed Pearl Harbor on 24 June. During the period 5 to 10 July, *Whipple* made the first visit to Guadalcanal, Solomon Islands, by a United States Navy ship since 1957. For most of the remainder of the year, the ship operated with the 7th Fleet throughout the reaches of the western Pacific. *Whipple* returned to Pearl Harbor on 15 December having met all operational commitments during her deployment.

Whipple received two battle stars for service in Vietnam.

Whippoorwill

A small nocturnal bird common to the eastern United States, so-called for its reiterated cry.

I

(Minesweeper No. 35: dp. 840; l. 187'10''; b. 35'5''; dr. 8'10''; cpl. 66; a. none; cl. *Lapwing*)

The first *Whippoorwill* (Minesweeper No. 35) was laid down on 12 December 1917 at Mobile, Ala., by the Alabama Drydock and Shipbuilding Co.; launched on 4 July 1918; sponsored by Miss M. I. Evans; and commissioned on 1 April 1919, Lt. Birney O. Halliwill in command.

After fitting out, *Whippoorwill* departed Boston on 3 July 1919, bound for Scotland. Operating subsequently from the port of Kirkwall, the minesweeper participated in the clearing of the North Sea Mine Barrage as part of Division 3, Minesweeping Squadron, Atlantic Fleet. Hair-trigger mines and frequent foul weather made sweeping the barrage a difficult and dangerous mission; but, by late in the autumn of 1919, the task was completed by a miscellaneous group of new minesweepers, chartered trawlers, and submarine chasers.

Returning to the United States in November 1919, *Whippporwill* was later assigned to the Pacific Fleet. Having been classified as AM–35 on 17 July 1920, the minesweeper arrived at Pearl Harbor, her new home port, on 1 March 1921. She would operate out of that base for the next 20 years, with brief periods spent as station ship at Pago Pago, Samoa, between 1931 and 1934.

Whippoorwill's prime duty was service to the Fleet. Besides filling the role for which she was designed—sweeping and laying mines—upon occasion she towed targets and plane-guarded. Noteworthy highlights of her Pearl Harbor-based deployment came in the early 1920's, when she participated in surveys of various and sundry Pacific islands. In July 1923, for example, *Whippoorwill*—together with her sistership *Tanager* (AM–5)—accomplished the first survey of Johnston Island in modern times. During that cruise, she carried members of the joint expedition sponsored by the Department of Agriculture and the Bishop Museum of Hawaii. She also carried a Douglas DT–2 floatplane on her fantail, hoisting it into the water so that it could take off for aerial survey and mapping flights over Johnston. A little over a year later, in September 1925, the plane's pilot, Lt. Comdr. John Rodgers, would win fame as a member of the crew of the PN–9 flying boat.

Whippoorwill made other cruises, carrying members of ornithological surveys to islands such as Kingman Reef, Palmyra, Christmas Island, Jarvis Island, Howland Island, and Baker Island. The islands would later assume importance as transpacific air commerce spread its wings toward the Far East and South Pacific.

Ultimately, however, *Whippoorwill*'s Hawaiian idyll ended. Refitted and modernized, the minesweeper departed Pearl Harbor on 5 May 1941, bound for the Asiatic Fleet, as war clouds gathered over the Pacific and Far East. En route, the minecraft plane-guarded at prearranged stations, serving as a direction-finding station for patrol planes winging their way to the Philippines to reinforce the Asiatic Fleet's air wing—Patrol Wing 10.

After touching briefly at Guam, in the Marianas, on 23 May, *Whippoorwill* reached Manila on the 30th. There, she became part of Mine Division 9, Mine Squadron 3, Asiatic Fleet. In the ensuing months, *Whippoorwill* performed a variety of service tasks. She towed targets for the cruisers and destroyers of the Fleet to fire at during battle practices and gunnery shoots, assisted in unmooring and mooring the Fleet's submarine and destroyer tenders from buoys, and conducted similar activities.

That spring, *Whippoorwill* operated with *Canopus*

(AS–9) during maneuvers in the southern Philippines, touching at Zamboanga and steaming in the Sulu Sea, before returning to Cavite and anchoring in Canacao Bay. Soon thereafter, she commenced operations with the Inshore Patrol which carried out a busy slate of operations as the Philippines feverishly prepared for the impending war with Japan. *Whippoorwill* operated on patrol duties and laid mines—laying the field near Caballo Island, near Corregidor, at the entrance to Manila Bay. She and *Tanager* also laid the mine field at Subic Bay while operating out of the section base at Olongapo.

After an overhaul at Cavite and at the Verdadero Dockyard across Canacao Bay from Cavite, *Whippoorwill* took up patrol duties in the late autumn, frequently alternating with the gunboats *Asheville* (PG–21) and *Tulsa* (PG–22). That duty was not without its share of interesting moments. On 22 November, while on patrol station "Cast," she fired four shots across the bow of the sailing vessel *Remedio VIII* before the vessel hove to. She later prevented the Army tug *Harrison* from entering the area and warned off other vessels on the 26th and 28th.

Relieved by *Tulsa* on station on 30 November, *Whippoorwill* returned to Canacao Bay before she got underway on 3 December for sweeping operations out of Cavite. Five days later, on 8 December 1941 (7 December east of the international date line), the Japanese unleashed their onslaught against American, British, and Dutch possessions in the Far East and in the Pacific.

At 0415 on the 8th, *Whippoorwill* received the news of the attack on Pearl Harbor. Lt. Comdr. Charles A. Ferriter, the ship's commanding officer, soon called his crew to quarters and announced the news. Now, after months of escalating tension and feverish preparations for war, the blow had fallen. Within hours, *Whippoorwill* was underway, commencing her first wartime sweeping operations in Manila Bay.

On the following day, 9 December, Japanese bombers caught General Douglas MacArthur's Far Eastern Air Force on the ground at its principal fields of Nichols and Clark Fields, destroying it as a viable retaliatory force. Thus, with little in the way of air cover, Cavite—the small, crowded base of operations for the Asiatic Fleet—lay naked to an attack from the sky.

The Japanese did not wait long to exploit their advantage—at 1230 on 10 December, the air raid alert was broadcast at Cavite. At 1250, *Whippoorwill* weighed anchor and stood out to maneuver in Manila Bay, away from the confining waters near Cavite itself. Soon the enemy's high-level bombers were droning overhead, above the effective range of the navy yard's 3-inch batteries; every ship in the harbor opened up with their antiaircraft batteries. In the ensuing action, *Whippoorwill* claimed assists in splashing two bombers and sending another one crashing on shore nearby. However, the planes that did get through wreaked havoc. Stick after stick of bombs blasted the navy yard—its buildings and docks—explosions reverberated like thunderclaps.

Peary (DD–226)—alongside Central Wharf for an overhaul—was hit by a bomb that struck the foremast, snapping it off above the searchlight platform and sending shards of metal down onto the bridge and fire-control platform, killing or wounding nearly every man there—including the commander and his executive officer. Meanwhile, bombs blasted and set afire the torpedo warehouse across the wharf; warheads exploded and burned.

Comdr. Ferriter saw *Peary*'s predicament and moved his ship through the burning navy yard and eased *Whippoorwill* near the destroyer's stern and passed a towline. Braving the burning firebrands from the blazing warehouse, the destroyermen made fast the line, and the minesweeper commenced backing. The towline stretched taut—only to part! Twice more Ferriter's command closed the immobile destroyer, both ships endangered by warheads detonating nearby. Finally, on the third try, the line held; and, with debris showering upon the minesweeper and her crippled charge, *Whippoorwill* pulled *Peary* free.

Soon thereafter, *Whippoorwill* moored *Peary* to a buoy in Manila Bay and took the destroyer's wounded to the hospital at Sangley Point in her motor launch. Later that evening, the minesweeper unmoored from the destroyer and stood out, anchoring for the night farther out in Manila Bay.

With Philippine waters vulnerable for surface ships, those ships of the Asiatic Fleet that could do so sailed for points south. *Whippoorwill* headed for Borneo on 12 December and arrived at Balikpapan on the 15th. Four days later, the minecraft—in company with *Tulsa, Asheville,* and *Lark* (AM–21)—joined Task Force (TF) 7 and withdrew further south to the Celebes, arriving the next day. Later, *Whippoorwill* screened *Tulsa* as the two ships proceeded for Java.

Arriving at Surabaya, three days before Christmas of 1941, Comdr. Ferriter went ashore and reported for orders to the Dutch naval commander there. Three days later, the minesweeper commenced local patrols and sweeps out of Surabaya and continued that duty into February 1942, often operating in company with Dutch units, before she received orders to move to Tjilatjap, a port on Java's south coast.

Arriving early on 26 February, *Whippoorwill* and *Lark* put to sea at 1400 the next day to search for survivors of the seaplane tender *Langley* (AV–3), reportedly sunk south of Java. Three hours out of Tjilatjap, the minesweeper's lookouts sighted a strange vessel and altered course to close and identify her. The mysterious ship turned out to be *Tulsa,* also searching for *Langley* survivors.

The trio of ships continued their search, the minesweepers steaming independently of the gunboat. At 2229, *Whippoorwill* and *Lark* arrived in the area in which *Langley* had been reported lost, passed a large oil slick, and smelled a strong odor of gasoline and oil —mute testimony to the tragedy that had gone before.

On the following day, the last day of February, the minesweepers abandoned their search and were about to put about to return to Tjilatjap. At 0507, however, lookouts noted a pulsating fire on the horizon; and the minesweepers closed cautiously. The burning vessel turned out to be the British merchantman *City of Manchester*—of the Ellerman Line—that had been torpedoed and gunned by the Japanese submarine *I–153.* *Whippoorwill* lowered a boat at 0550 and rescued the British sailors from their rafts and life boats. Ten injured men were transferred to *Tulsa* which had providentially shown up on the scene of the rescue—the gunboat having a well-equipped sick bay that the minesweepers lacked.

Following that rescue mission, *Whippoorwill* returned to Tjilatjap, arriving on 1 March, only to stand out later that day as Java, too, was becoming more untenable with each passing hour. Retiring in the face of a ruthless enemy drawing tight the noose around Java, *Whippoorwill* crept southward towards Australia. As she proceeded on her anxious voyage, other retiring Asiatic Fleet ships met their doom at the hands of the marauding Japanese—*Asheville, Pecos* (AO–6), and the destroyers *Edsall* (DD–219) and *Pillsbury* (DD–227).

Whippoorwill dropped anchor at Fremantle on 9 March and operated out of Fremantle into May before she shifted to Albany, Australia. The minesweeper conducted local patrols and guardship operations in the shipping channels and harbors there from mid-May to late August when she returned to Fremantle. For the remainder of 1942, *Whippoorwill* operated alternatively at Exmouth Bay, Albany, or Fremantle, patrolling locally and towing targets. On occasion, she acted as reference vessel for submarines of the Southwest Pacific forces on their training cruises. The beginning of 1943 found *Whippoorwill* engaged in local patrol operations out of Exmouth Gulf, and she continued that duty until February, when she made another brief visit to Fremantle. On 18 and 19 February 1943, she engaged in night exercises with American submarines on maneuvers. Six days later, while underway off the coast, she encountered a cyclone which wrenched two 300-pound depth charges from their tracks.

After returning to Exmouth Gulf, she remained there through March 1943 before sailing for Fremantle and a six-day drydocking period. Upon completion of this brief refit, she returned to Exmouth Gulf on 24 April and conducted minesweeping operations in the area. On 15 May, while enroute to Fremantle, she picked

Whippoorwill (AM–35) near Cavite, *circa* June 1941. (19–N–27110)

up an echo with her sonar gear and came to general quarters. She dropped depth charges but lost the contact. Arriving at Fremantle two days later, 17 May, she commenced a series of antisubmarine patrols which lasted into November.

On 1 December, she began an extensive refit. During the yard work, she was reclassified an ocean-going tug and redesignated AT–169 on 1 March 1944. The long overhaul was completed on 5 March, and the ship proceded to Brisbane.

Coming under the operational control of Commander, Service Force, 7th Fleet, *Whippoorwill* arrived at Brisbane on 20 March. For the next 10 days, 21 to 31 March 1944, she underwent final conversion to an ocean-going tug. This involved the removal of her minesweeping gear and the addition of a heavy-duty towing engine which had once been fitted on board *Dobbin* (AD–3).

On 8 April, the newly refitted *Whippoorwill* with *LST–385* under tow, got underway for New Guinea, and arrived at Milne Bay with her charge on 15 April. The tug then served Hollandia and at Mios Woendi; also receiving orders to Seeadler Harbor, in the Admiralty Islands, to serve on "battle-damage standby" duty—prepared to take any battle-damaged ships under tow and out of the front lines.

Whippoorwill was reclassified an ocean-going tug, old, on 15 May 1944 and designated ATO–169. She then continued operations off New Guinea and in the backwater areas of the war in the Pacific until receiving orders to head north for Leyte in February 1945. Later operating at Hollandia and Ulithi, *Whippoorwill* resumed operations in the Philippine Islands on 15 June 1945 and served as a harbor tug in the Manila Bay area through the end of the war.

Touching at Leyte Gulf, Manila Bay, Zamboanga, and Samar, *Whippoorwill* finally rounded out her tour in the Philippine Islands on 20 December, when she departed Samar, bound for the Marshall Islands. Arriving at Eniwetok in company with *Vireo* (ATO–144) and *Rail* (ATO–139), she departed that island on 4 January 1946, bound for Pearl Harbor, arriving at the Pacific base that had once long served as her home port on the 15th. After a 10-day stay, *Whippoorwill* in company with *Rail*, got underway again on 25 January, and headed for San Francisco, Calif.

Arriving there on 5 February 1946, *Whippoorwill* soon began preparation for inactivation and, on 17 April 1946, the stalwart ship was decommissioned at San Francisco. Struck from the Navy list on 10 June 1946, she was turned over to the Maritime Commission for disposal on 6 November 1946.

Whippoorwill was awarded one battle star for her World War II service.

II

(MSC–207: dp. 412; l. 145'; b. 28'; dr. 12'; s. 12.8 k.; cpl. 40; a. 1 20mm., 2 .50-cal. mg., 1 81mm. M.; cl. *Redwing*)

The second *Whippoorwill* (MSC–207) was laid down on 7 January 1954 at Bellingham, Wash., by the Bellingham Shipyards Co. as AMS–207; launched on 13 August 1954; sponsored by Mrs. Walter A. Yatch; reclassified MSC–207 on 7 February 1955; and commissioned at Tacoma, Wash., on 20 October 1955, Lt. (jg.) Tom I. Kolstad in command.

On 7 November, the mine countermeasures ship reported for duty with the Commander, Mine Force, Pacific Fleet. Over the next 10 months, she first conducted shakedown training along the west coast and then began normal duty with the Mine Force out of Long Beach, Calif. That duty lasted until 1 August 1956, when she departed Long Beach for her new home port, Sasebo, Japan. After stops at Oahu and Midway, the coastal minesweeper arrived at Sasebo on 21 August and reported for duty to the Commander, Mine Flotilla 1.

Whippoorwill was based in Japan for the next 14 years; and, during the first eight of those years, her duties centered upon training. She participated in numerous 7th Fleet mine exercises as well as many multinational mine exercises with units of the South Korean, Royal Thai, Japanese, Philippine, and Nationalist Chinese Navies. She also participated in several large amphibous training exercises conducted in Korea, the Philippines, and at Okinawa in the Ryukyus.

Her one brush with less than peaceful duty came in the fall of 1958 when the Chinese communists began and continued their bombardment of Nationalist-held islands—Quemoy, Little Quemoy, and Matsu—located just off the mainland. *Whippoorwill* earned the Armed Forces Expeditionary Medal for her service in the Taiwan Strait during the crisis there that fall. Her service in the Taiwan Strait lasted from 10 September until 4 November when tension in the area finally began to cool. Upon concluding her servce in the Taiwan Strait, she resumed her more peaceful employment in training missions with the 7th Fleet and units of Allied navies.

The year 1964 brought the ship still closer to actual "hot war" operations. From 16 July to 2 August 1964, *Whippoorwill* joined a barrier patrol established in the South China Sea off the coast of South Vietnam to assist the South Vietnamese Navy in preventing waterborne infiltrators and logistics from North Vietnam from reaching the Viet Cong rebels in the south. During that phase of American involvement, the Navy's role remained essentially passive in nature. While American ships such as *Whippoorwill* stopped no craft themselves, they vectored South Vietnamese ships in on suspicious contacts.

Though the barrier patrols were dissolved on 2 August, and *Whippoorwill* resumed her familiar training schedule, events occurred in the Gulf of Tonkin that same day which increased American involvement in the Vietnamese civil war and eventually brought *Whippoorwill* into intimate association with that conflict over the next six years. After nine months of normal 7th Fleet operations, the minesweeper returned to Vietnamese waters on 18 April 1965 as one of the American ships assigned to Operation "Market Time." That operation consisted of continuous patrols along South Vietnamese coasts in an effort to interdict the increasing volume of arms and supplies being smuggled from the north into South Vietnam in support of Viet Cong guerrillas.

In many respects, *Whippoorwill*'s "Market Time" duties resembled the barrier patrols she had conducted the previous summer. However, they differed from those patrols in two major respects. First, as a result of the increasingly direct involvement of American forces in the Vietnam conflict, ships on "Market Time" station actively participated in stop-and-seizure operations rather than limiting themselves to surveillance and passive assistance to the South Vietnamese Navy. Secondly, as a result of the increased communist logistic effort from north to south, "Market Time" operations became a continuous and intensive assignment. Until she returned to the United States in the fall of 1970, *Whippoorwill*'s sole mission in the Vietnam conflict consisted of "Market Time" patrols. She alternated month-long tours on station in Vietnamese waters with assignments of variable duration at other points in the Orient. Most often these missions away from Vietnam consisted of mine warfare exercises, upkeep and liberty calls in Japanese ports, and periodic overhauls. Less frequently, they consisted of port calls at other places in the Far East.

On 1 September 1970, *Whippoorwill* concluded her final tour of duty along the coast of Vietnam. She steamed home—via Sasebo, Subic Bay, and Pearl Harbor—and arrived in Long Beach, Calif., on 12 November. After voyage repairs, she moved to San Francisco where she was decommissioned on 15 December 1970. Decommissioning, however, did not end her active naval service, for she joined *Thrasher* (MSC–203) and *Reaper* (MSO–467) as a reserve training ship in Reserve Mine Division 52. For almost five years, she operated out of Treasure Island Naval Station training naval reservists during their annual active duty periods. On 2 May 1975, *Whippoorwill* moved from San Francisco to the Inactive Ship Facility at Vallejo, Calif., where she was deactivated completely by 30 June 1975. Her name was struck from the Navy list on 1 July 1975, and she was sold to the Republic of Singapore. As of August 1979, she served the Republic of Singapore Navy as RSS *Jupiter*.

Whippoorwill received six battle stars and the Meritorious Unit Commendation for Vietnam service.

Whipstock

(YO–49: dp. 1,731; l. 235'0''; b. 37'0'')

Whipstock (YO–49)—a fuel oil barge constructed in 1941 at Napa, Calif., by the Basalt Rock Co., Inc.—was acquired by the Navy in mid-1942 and was placed in service on 23 September 1942.

Information regarding *Whipstock*'s wartime service is scarce. However, she probably carried fuel from storage areas to various rear-area bases in the western and southwestern Pacific. By May of 1945, she was located at Tulagi in the Solomon Islands. Through the summer, she made voyages to such diverse places as Tarawa, Johnston Island, Pearl Harbor, Midway Island, Saipan, and Okinawa. In October 1945, she moved to Japan where she began service supporting forces occupying Japan and China. She remained in the Far East supporting the occupation from 1946 to 1949. The little surviving information regarding her service thereafter strongly suggests that she remained in the Orient for the remainder of her long Navy career. Her name was finally struck from the Navy list sometime in 1975. One source indicates that the action occurred on 1 January while another places the date sometime in September. She was subsequently sold by the Navy, presumably for scrapping.

Whirlwind

(ScStr.: t. 59 (gross); l. 117'; b. 12'; dr. 3'6'' (mean); s. 20 k.; cpl. 9; a. 1 3-pdr., 1 1-pdr., 1 mg.)

Whirlwind (SP–221)—a wooden-hulled, triple-screw steam yacht, completed in 1909 at Morris Heights, N.Y., by the Charles L. Seabury Co. and the Gas Engine and Power Co.—was acquired by the Navy on 11 May 1917 from Julius Fleischmann of New York; and commissioned at the New York Navy Yard on 26 June 1917, Lt. (jg.) A. S. Johnstone, USNRF, in command.

Whirlwind was outfitted at the Seabury yard and arrived at New Haven, Conn., on 17 August. She soon commercial patrols off the Cornfield Point lightship. Her duties included seeing that passing vessels kept within their designated channels and that other section patrol boats were on their stations. She also escorted Allied ships through the nets that guarded those waters.

Whirlwind continued her daily routine of patrols through the remainder of the month of August. During this time, in the course of one of her normal cruises, she prevented steamer *Noreg*, out of Nova Scotia, from fouling the submarine net during a heavy squall on the 24th. Early the following month, the patrol boat inspected the 11th Division of 3d Naval District local patrol forces on station in Long Island Sound and continued her routine duties of hailing and instructing vessels as to proper channels.

By early September, it had become apparent that the vessel's sea-keeping qualities left much to be desired. Her heavy rolling and pitching caused the Navy to cease using her as an offshore patrol vessel. She arrived at her builder's yard at Morris Heights on 13 September for overhaul. She was then decommissioned

at the Marine Basin, Brooklyn, N.Y., on 8 December 1917.

Reconsidered for naval use in a different nautical environment, *Whirlwind* was recommissioned at Waukegan, Ill., on 29 September 1918. Operating out of the Great Lakes Naval Training Station, Great Lakes, Ill., the yacht cruised to Waukegan and Chicago, Ill., and to Milwaukee, and Manitowoc, Wis., before proceeding to Detroit, Mich., where she was decommissioned on 3 December 1918. During this time, she made three cruises on Lake Michigan with members of the training station commandant's family embarked. The commandant of Great Lakes at that time was Medal of Honor holder Capt. William A. Moffett—who later became Chief of the Bureau of Aeronautics and who perished in lighter-than-air ship *Akron* in April 1933.

Whirlwind was struck from the Navy list on 24 April 1919 and was subsequently sold on 30 June 1919.

Whistler

(MB: t. 20 (gross); l. 50'; b. 11'6''; dr. 3' (mean); s. 25 k.; cpl 7; a. 1 1-pdr., 1 Colt mg.)

Whistler (SP–784)—a wooden-hulled motorboat constructed at Marblehead, Mass., by J. E. Graves, and completed in 1917—was acquired by the Navy from Lawrence F. Percival, of Boston, on 17 May 1917; and commissioned at Boston on 31 July 1917.

Attached to the Boston section of the 1st Naval District, *Whistler* operated from the Commonwealth Pier—the district headquarters—on harbor entrance patrols. On occasion, in line with her employment, she carried dispatches to other vessels and craft of the entrance patrol. One break in her routine came in the spring of 1918, when she stood by as *O–5* (Submarine No. 66) conducted sea and submergence trials in Hingham Bay on 30 May 1918.

Subsequently decommissioned and struck from the Navy list on 19 May 1919, *Whistler* was sold to J. E. Doherty, of Boston, on 20 June 1919.

Whitaker

A Royal Navy name honoring Sir Edward Whitaker (1660–1735), who distinguished himself as captain of HMS *Dorsetshire* in 1704 and attained the rank of vice admiral in 1708.

———————————

(DE–571: dp. 1,300; l. 306'0''; b. 37'0''; dr. 9'0''; s. 26 k.; cpl. 200; a. 3 3'', 1 2-pdr., 2 40mm., 8 20mm., 2 dct., 6 dcp., 1 dcp. (hh.); cl. *Buckley*)

Whitaker (DE–571)—a *Buckley*-class destroyer escort—was laid down on 20 October 1943 at Hingham, Mass., by the Bethlehem-Hingham Shipyard; launched on 12 December 1943; and delivered to the Royal Navy, under lend-lease, on 28 January 1944. Simultaneously commissioned as HMS *Whitaker* (K.580) on that day, the escort vessel (a "Captain"-class frigate in Royal Navy parlance) subsequently performed her duties under the White Ensign into the autumn of 1944, taking part in the Normandy invasion and in escorting convoys—probably in the Western Approaches area and in the English Channel in the wake of the invasion of France in the summer of 1944.

Whitaker was torpedoed by *U–483* at 0210 on 1 November 1944, off the north coast of Ireland. Damage control measures brought the resultant fires under control by 0320 but not before the ship had lost much of her bow. Towed first to Londonderry and then to Belfast, Northern Ireland, *Whitaker* remained inactive for the rest of the war. Struck from the United States Navy list on 19 May 1945, the ship was returned to the custody of the United States Navy on 3 December 1945 but remained in the British Isles for ultimate disposition. She was sold to John Lee, of Belfast, on 9 January 1947 and was subsequently broken up for scrap.

White Marsh

A town in Gloucester County, Va. White Marsh was the birthplace of Dr. Walter Reed, the Army physician, pathologist, and bacteriologist who conquered yellow fever at the turn of the century.

(LSD–8: dp. 9,375 (tl.); l. 457'9"; b. 72'2"; dr. 18'0"; s. 15.4 k.; cpl. 326; a. 1 5", 12 40mm., 16 20mm.; cl. *Ashland*)

White Marsh (LSD–8) was laid down on 7 April 1943 at Oakland, Calif., by the Moore Drydock Co.; launched on 19 July 1943; sponsored by Mrs. William C. Wise, the wife of Col. Wise, USMC; and commissioned on 29 January 1944, Comdr. George H. Eppelman, USNR, in command.

After commissioning, the dock landing ship made two voyages from San Francisco to Morro Bay, Calif., where she delivered two cargoes of LCM's to the boat basin located there before heading to San Diego for shakedown. She completed that training and returned to San Francisco on 15 March. On the 23d, the ship got underway for Hawaii with a load of landing craft and passengers. She arrived at Oahu on 30 March and reported for duty with the 5th Amphibious Force, Pacific Fleet. She made a round-trip voyage to San Francisco and back to Pearl Harbor between 31 March and 15 April. From then until late in May, she conducted amphibious exercises in preparation for the Marianas campaign.

On the 29th, *White Marsh* departed Pearl Harbor in company with Task Group (TG) 52.15, bound for Saipan. After a stop at Eniwetok en route, she and her task unit arrived in the Marianas before dawn of 15 June. Later that morning, *White Marsh* and her companion ships disembarked troops of the 2d and 4th Marine Divisions and the landing went forward. Following the initial assault, the dock landing ship settled into a routine of repair duties for damaged landing craft for a week before departing the Marianas to return to the United States.

After a stop at Pearl Harbor en route, the ship entered San Francisco on 11 July. Following voyage repairs, she loaded cargo and passengers; got underway for Hawaii; arrived back in Oahu on 28 July; and remained there until 12 August, preparing for the invasion of the Palau Islands. She loaded tanks and embarked troops of the Army's 710th Tank Battalion and departed Pearl Harbor on 12 August in company with TG 23.4. Staged through Guadalcanal where she participated in amphibious rehearsals, *White Marsh* arrived off Angaur on 16 September and, after disembarking the 710th Tank Battalion, again started repair work on damaged landing craft. On 21 September, she left the Palaus on her way to the Western Caroline Islands. Following the occupation of Ulithi Atoll, from 23 to 25 September, she departed that atoll and proceeded to New Guinea.

She arrived at Hollandia on 28 September and reported for duty with the 7th Amphibious Force. The next day, she returned to sea, bound for Finschhafen, located farther down the northern coast of New Guinea opposite the island of New Britain. The ship embarked troops, loaded cargo at Finschhafen, resumed her voyage, and arrived at Manus on 2 October. There, she prepared for her third amphibious landing of the war, the invasion of the Philippines.

On the 12th, she departed Manus as a unit of TG 78.2 and set a course for San Pedro Bay, Leyte. *White Marsh* disembarked her troops and unloaded her cargo there on 20 October, the day of the initial landings, and departed the island that same afternoon, bound for New Guinea. The dock landing ship reached Hollandia

on 24 October, loaded troops, and then steamed to Biak Island on the 29th. At Biak, she took on additional soldiers and some cargo before heading back to the Philippines on the 31st. She arrived at Dulag, Leyte, on 5 November, disembarked her passengers, unloaded cargo, and departed the island on the 6th.

During November and December, *White Marsh* continued to make reinforcement and resupply voyages between New Guinea and Leyte to support the campaign to liberate the southern Philippines. That routine ended late in December when she arrived at Aitape, New Guinea, to prepare for the invasion of Luzon.

She departed Aitape on 28 December, bound for northern Luzon in company with a unit of TG 78.1. She arrived off Lingayen on the night of 8 and 9 January and, the following morning, unloaded troops and cargo for the assault. She then served briefly again as a landing craft repair ship but departed Lingayen Gulf on the 10th. En route to Leyte, *White Marsh's* unit suffered a kamikaze attack which resulted in severe damage and considerable casualties on board *Du Page* (APA–41).

The dock landing ship, however, arrived unscathed at Leyte on 13 January, but soon returned to sea as an element of TG 78.2, bound for Wakde Island. She arrived there on 17 January and loaded Luzon-bound troops and equipment. She departed Wakde on the 19th and set a course for Lingayen. En route, her unit again came under aerial attack when a single "Kate" torpedo bomber succeeded in torpedoing *Shadwell* (LSD–15). During the attack, *White Marsh's* antiaircraft battery joined those of her colleagues and brought down the enemy aviator. She arrived back in Lingayen Gulf on 27 January and began landing troops and cargo. That afternoon, she completed the unloading operations, got underway, and returned to Leyte on 30 January.

The ship remained at Leyte until 2 February when she headed for Guadalcanal. En route, she received orders diverting her to Milne Bay, New Guinea, where she arrived on 10 February. After loading 11 LCM's, she departed Milne Bay on the 13th and arrived at Guadalcanal on the 15th. There, she reported for duty with TransRon 18. On 27 February, she departed Guadalcanal, bound for the Russell Islands to conduct amphibious training there with elements of the 1st Marine Division. On 15 March, she departed the Russell Islands, bound ultimately for Okinawa. En route, she stopped at Ulithi for six days before continuing on to the Ryukyus.

White Marsh and her division mates arrived off Okinawa during the night of 31 March and 1 April. Early in the morning, she disembarked her troops for the landings. Once again, after completing the disembarkation process, the dock landing ship anchored and began landing craft repair duty. Throughout her two-month stay at Okinawa, enemy air activity was heavy, but *White Marsh* only engaged Japanese aircraft on three occasions—on 6, 12, and 15 April—and claimed hits on two of the attackers.

On 3 June, the ship departed Okinawa and proceeded to Leyte. She entered San Pedro Bay on 8 June and remained there for three days. On the 11th, the ship moved to Manicani Island where she loaded six motor torpedo boats and their crews for transportation to Okinawa. She left Manicani on 15 June and arrived in Kerama Retto on the 19th. She discharged cargo and personnel during the next two days and began a voyage to the Philippines on the 22d. She arrived at Leyte on 27 June and began a period of tender availability.

White Marsh remained at Leyte until 14 July when she got underway for home. She stopped at Eniwetok on 21 July, loaded cargo and passengers, resumed her voyage, and arrived at Oahu on 29 July. She remained there only overnight and, the next day, got underway for the west coast. The ship reached San Francisco on 29 July and was receiving repairs there when Japan capitulated in mid-August.

White Marsh sailed for the Aleutians on 26 August and arrived at Adak Island on 3 September but departed again the following day, bound for the Japanese island of Honshu. She put into Ominato Ko on 11 September and reported for duty with the logistic support group assigned to the Northern Japan Occupation Force which she served as a small craft repair ship and a floating boat pool until 25 November when she departed Japan to return to the United States.

Steaming via Pearl Harbor, she arrived at San Pedro, Calif., on 15 December. From there, she moved on, via the Panama Canal, to New Orleans for a brief tour of duty with the Atlantic Fleet before being decommissioned at Norfolk in March of 1946 and beginning over four and one-half years in reserve there.

On 8 November 1950—as a part of the Navy's expansion of its active forces to enable it to meet its increased demands during the Korean conflict—*White Marsh* was placed back in commission, Comdr. C. B. Bright in command. During the period from her reactivation to the beginning of 1954, she alternated two deployments to the 6th Fleet with Atlantic Fleet service along the east coast. In January 1954, her home port was changed to San Diego, Calif.; and the ship was reassigned to the Pacific Fleet. Between January 1954 and September of 1956, the dock landing ship made two deployments to the western Pacific during which she conducted amphibious exercises and made port visits to various Far Eastern ports such as Hong Kong and Yokosuka. When not deployed to the Orient, she conducted routine operations out of San Diego.

In September 1956, *White Marsh* was decommissioned once more; but she remained active, serving the Military Sea Transportation Service while manned by a civil service crew. That duty lasted until November of 1960 at which time she was transferred, on loan, to the Taiwan Navy which she served as *Chung Cheng* (LSD-191). In 1977, she was permanently transferred to the Taiwan Navy.

White Marsh earned four battle stars for her World War II service.

White Plains

A city in, and the seat of government for, Westchester County, N.Y. After the Battle of Long Island on 27 August 1776, during the Revolutionary War, George Washington was forced to evacuate Long Island and, later, the entire state of New York. During the retreat through New York and New Jersey, contingents of American soldiers fought a series of sharp rearguard actions which held up the British forces and allowed the Continental Army to escape intact to Pennsylvania. On 28 October 1776, the second of those engagements was fought near White Plains, N.Y. Though the American troops were ultimately driven from the field, they held the British back long enough to allow General Washington's main force to make good its retreat.

I

(CVE-66: dp. 10,400 (f.); l. 512'3''; b. 65'2''; ew. 108'1''; dr. 22'6''; s. 19.3 k. (tl.); cpl. 860; a. 1 5'', 12 40mm., 20 20mm., 24 ac.; cl. *Casablanca*)

White Plains (CVE-66) was laid down on 11 February 1943 at Vancouver, Wash., by the Kaiser Shipbuilding Co., Inc., under a Maritime Commission contract (MC hull 1103) as *Elbour Bay* (ACV-66); renamed *White Plains* on 3 April 1943; redesignated CVE-66 on 15 July 1943; launched on 27 September 1943; sponsored by Mrs. Marc A. Mitscher; delivered to the Navy on 15 November 1943 at Astoria, Oreg.; and commissioned that same day, Capt. Oscar A. Weller in command.

The escort aircraft carrier completed outfitting at Astoria on 4 December 1943 and began shakedown training on the 8th. At the conclusion of her initial cruise, the warship entered San Diego on 21 December. On the 30th, she returned to sea, bound via Pearl Harbor for the Gilbert Islands. She arrived at Tarawa Atoll on 11 January 1944 and unloaded the aircraft she had transported. On the 17th, the ship headed back to Oahu, arriving in Pearl Harbor six days later. Following a four-day turnaround period, *White Plains* again set course for the Central Pacific to provide aircraft logistics support for the Marshall Islands operation. By the time she reached Tarawa on 3 February, Majuro Atoll had been taken unopposed, and Kwajalein's Japanese garrison had been all but subdued. The next day, she got underway for Majuro where she arrived on the 5th. From there, the escort carrier moved on to Kwajalein for a brief visit before heading back to Hawaii. *White Plains* stopped briefly at Oahu before continuing on toward the west coast on 23 February. She arrived in Alameda, Calif., on 3 March.

While on the west coast, *White Plains* conducted operational training for her own ship's company and carrier qualifications for three air squadrons. In April, she embarked her own permanently assigned air unit, Composite Squadron (VC) 4, composed of 16 Wildcat fighters and 12 Avenger torpedo bombers. She departed the west coast at San Diego on 24 April and arrived in Pearl Harbor on 1 May. During the next month, she conducted air operations and amphibious support training out of Pearl Harbor.

At the end of May, she stood out of port in company with units of the task force assembled to invade the Marianas. *White Plains'* portion of the Fleet sortied from Eniwetok Atoll and, during the voyage from there to the Marianas, her aircraft provided antisubmarine and combat air patrol. During the assault on Saipan, her planes continued to cover the Fleet against submarine and air attack, strafed the beaches, and spotted for gunfire support ships. They helped repulse at least three major enemy air attacks. On 17 June, while helping to fight off those raids, her antiaircraft gunners earned their first definite kill. Later VC-4 Avengers successfully torpedoed an enemy transport during a sweep of the island of Rota.

White Plains departed the combat zone on 2 July but, after a week at Eniwetok, returned to the Marianas with her air squadron upgraded to a total of 28 aircraft. During her second tour of duty in the Marianas, the escort carrier supported the Tinian assault late in July. Her planes carried out sortie after sortie in support of the troops ashore and over the ships assembled, but *White Plains* herself suffered no enemy attacks. Her heavy flight schedule proved grueling to air squadron and ship's company alike.

She completed her participation during the first week in August and departed the Marianas and headed for Espiritu Santo in the New Hebrides. She arrived in Segond Channel on 16 August and began preparations for the invasion of the Palau Islands. Those preparations included amphibious support training in the Solomon Islands. *White Plains* and 10 of her sister escort carriers moved into the vicinity of the Palaus during the second week of September. Their planes provided a portion of the prelanding bombardment and support for the troops after the 15 September assault. In contrast to the Marianas campaign and later operations, the Palaus, though extremely difficult on the troops ashore, brought little opposition to the ships in the waters surrounding the islands. No enemy air attacks developed because the Japanese were husbanding their aircraft for the defense of the Philippines, and—as a result of Japan's new strategic concept of defense in depth at some distance from the beaches—few shore batteries were sited near enough to the coast to fire upon ships. On 21 September, *White Plains* joined the forces detached from the Palau operation for the occupation of Ulithi Atoll which, happily, was undefended.

In October, after repairs at Manus in the Admiralty Islands, *White Plains* headed for the invasion of the Philippines at Leyte. The initial assault went forward on the 20th. Aircraft from *White Plains* provided air support for the troops and ASW and combat air patrols for the ships assembled in Leyte Gulf. However, because of the strategic importance of the Philippines which lay athwart their lines of communication with the East Indies, the Japanese chose to oppose the landings with their surface fleet. They launched their surface counterattack in three distinct phases. While a decoy force of planeless carriers under Admiral Ozawa moved south from Japan in an attempt to draw off Halsey's 3d Fleet and the large carriers, the forces under Vice Admirals Nishimura and Shima attempted to force the Surigao Strait from the south, and Vice Admiral Kurita's Center Force tried to sneak through the Central Philippines and transit the hopefully unguarded San Bernardino Strait. The Center Force, by far the strongest of the enemy fleets involved, consisted of five battleships—including the mammoth men-of-war *Yamato* and *Musashi*—11 heavy cruisers, two light cruisers, and 19 destroyers. By the time Kurita's Center Force cleared the San Bernardino Strait on 25 October, it had been reduced by four heavy cruisers and one battleship, *Musashi*. Three cruisers fell prey to submarine attacks in Palawan Passage on the 23d, and *Musashi* and heavy cruiser *Myoko* succumbed to TF 38's air attacks in the Sibuyan Sea the following day. The battlewagon sank while *Myoko* headed back to Brunei Bay, heavily damaged. In addition, on the night of 24 and 25 October, Vice Admiral Oldendorf's old battleships in Leyte Gulf obliterated Nishimura's force and sent Shima's packing.

In the meantime, after Admiral Halsey received information indicating that a battered Center Force had begun retirement, Ozawa's decoy force finally managed to draw the American carriers off to the north. However, Kurita's retrograde movement proved to be only temporary; and he once again reversed course and headed back toward San Bernardino Strait. With Oldendorf regrouping in Leyte Gulf and Halsey off chasing the Japanese carriers, only three task groups—composed of escort carriers, destroyers, and destroyer escorts—remained off Samar between Kurita and Leyte Gulf. *White Plains* was an element of "Taffy 3," the northernmost of the three units and the one which bore the brunt of Kurita's surface onslaught. Rear Admiral Clifton A. F. Sprague's "Taffy 3" first learned of Kurita's presence when, at 0637, a pilot on routine patrol spotted the force and attacked with depth charges. Rear Admiral Sprague was incredulous and demanded identification verification which came disconcertingly enough when the enemy battleships' pagoda masts—unmistakable indicators—loomed over the horizon.

For the next two and one-half hours, the Japanese force chased "Taffy 3" southward and subjected the escort carriers and their counterattacking screen to a murderous, but mercifully and frequently inaccurate, heavy-caliber cannonade. The carriers' aircraft fearlessly fought back, making dummy runs on the Japanese ships to slow their speed of advance after expending all their bombs, torpedoes, and ammunition. During their own suicidal counterattacks, three of the escorts, *Johnston* (DD–557), *Hoel* (DD–533), and *Samuel B. Roberts* (DE–413) were sunk by heavy caliber gunfire. Later, *Gambier Bay* (CVE–73) succumbed to the same fate while *Fanshaw Bay* (CVE–70), *Kalinin Bay* (CVE–68), *Dennis* (DE–405), and *Heermann* (DD–532) suffered heavy damage from the same source. Throughout the surface phase of the action, *White Plains'* leading position in the disposition protected her from any gunfire damage; but, the ship still had an aerial ordeal to endure.

Miraculously, the Japanese surface force broke off its pursuit between 0912 and 0917, and, after milling around in apparent confusion for a time, retired northward to San Bernardino Strait. The retreat by Kurita's surface force, however, did not end the ordeal for *White Plains* and her colleagues. After a 90-minute respite, they suffered harassment from a different quarter. At 1050, a formation of six enemy fighters appeared and began simultaneous kamikaze attacks. Two of them singled out *White Plains* as their victim. Her antiaircraft gunners responded with a hail of gunfire. They scored a hit on one of the intruders, and he immediately changed course and succeeded in fatally crashing into *St. Lo*. His comrade continued on toward *White Plains*, but her antiaircraft guns finally brought him down mere yards astern. His explosion scattered debris all over her deck and sides but caused only 11 relatively minor casualties. In the meantime, *Kitkun Bay* (CVE–71) and *Kalinin Bay* also suffered kamikaze crashes, but neither proved fatal. That attack proved to be her final combat action, not only of the Battle off Samar but also of the war. She steamed to Manus with the other surviving carriers and arrived there on 31 October. After an inspection of the damage, it was decided that the battered escort carrier should return to the United States for complete repairs. Accordingly, she

White Plains (CVE–66) at San Diego, 8 March 1944, with *Wildcat* fighters and *Avenger* torpedo bombers on her deck. She is followed by a *Fletcher-class* destroyer in the pattern camouflage widely used in the Pacific during 1944. (80–G–381865)

departed Manus on 6 November and headed—via Pearl Harbor—to the west coast. She arrived in San Diego on 27 November and imediately began repairs.

Ready for action once more, *White Plains* stood out of San Diego on 19 January 1945. However, for the remainder of the war, she carried out the relatively tame assignment of ferrying replacement aircraft from the United States to bases in the western Pacific. During the last months of the war, she visited such places as Kwajalein, Hollandia, Ulithi, Saipan, Guam, Leyte, and Pearl Harbor. All had been scenes of major combat actions, but, by that time, all had become rear areas. Her closest approach to the fighting after Leyte Gulf came just after the Okinawa landings in April when she steamed to within 100 miles of the island to launch two squadrons of Marine Corps F4U Corsairs for duty there.

The end of hostilities in mid-August found her en route from Pearl Harbor to the west coast. She arrived at San Pedro, Calif., on the 22d but soon moved to San Diego. From there, she headed back to the western Pacific on 6 September to begin "Magic-Carpet" duty bringing American fighting men home from the Orient. Twenty days later, she arrived in Buckner Bay, Okinawa, where she embarked more than 800 passengers for the voyage to the United States. On 28 September, she pointed her bow eastward and set a course, via Pearl Harbor, for San Diego. The escort carrier entered San Diego on 16 December and disembarked her passengers. After nine days in port, she got underway for Pearl Harbor and stopped there only briefly on 1 November before setting out on the return voyage to the west coast. The warship visited San Francisco for five days from 7 to 12 November and then headed across the Pacific once more. She entered port at Guam in the Marianas on 27 November, embarked passengers, and then began the return voyage on 30 November. *White Plains* arrived in Seattle, Wash., on 14 December 1945. She remained there until 30 January 1946, when she embarked upon the voyage, via the Panama Canal and Norfolk, Va., to Boston, Mass. The carrier entered Boston on 17 February 1946 and began preparations for decommissioning.

White Plains was decommissioned on 10 July 1946 and was berthed with the Boston Group, Atlantic Reserve Fleet. She remained with the reserve fleet for 12 years. On 12 June 1955, she was redesignated a utility aircraft carrier (CVU–66). Finally, her name was struck from the Navy list on 1 July 1958. She was sold on 29 July to the Hyman Michaels Co., of Chicago, Ill., for scrapping.

White Plains (CVE–66) earned five battle stars during World War II as well as the Presidential Unit Citation for her part in the Battle off Samar.

II

(AFS–4: dp. 16,100 (f.); l. 581'; b. 79'; dr. 28'; s. 20 k. (tl.); cpl. 486; a. 4 3''; cl. *Mars*)

The second *White Plains* (AFS–4) was laid down on 2 October 1965 by the National Steel & Shipbuilding Co. at San Diego, Calif.; launched on 26 July 1966; sponsored by Mrs. Bob Wilson; and commissioned at the Long Beach Naval Shipyard on 23 November 1968, Capt. Thomas B. Brenner in command.

The combat stores ship spent the first nine months of her commissioned service engaged in a series of routine post-commissioning activities in California waters. In February 1969, she went through a series of qualification trials in preparation for her final contract trials which she passed successfully in mid-March. Shakedown training followed in April, and post-shakedown availability at the San Francisco Bay Naval Shipyard occupied her time during the last half of May and the first three weeks of June. During the second week in July, the ship participated in her first fleet exercise, Operation "Beagle Baron." She spent the last half of the month making preparations for her

first deployment to the western Pacific. On 20 August, *White Plains* stood out of San Francisco Bay and shaped a course for the Far East. On 3 September, she reached her first port of call in the Orient, Yokosuka. While in Japan, she also visited Sasebo before getting underway on 16 September for Subic Bay and thence to the Vietnam combat zone. After topping off her replenishment cargo at Subic Bay, the ship arrived in Vietnamese waters on 23 September. There, she cruised for 14 days engaged in underway replenishment operatons with warships of the 7th Fleet on station off the coast. The deployment lasted for another four months during which she made three more replenishment cruises in the combat zone along the Vietnamese coast. On 11 February 1970, *White Plains* departed Subic Bay on her way home. She stopped at Pearl Harbor near the end of the month and arrived in San Francisco on 5 March.

The combat stores ship remained in the United States only three months. During that time, she took the normal post-deployment standdown break, underwent a restricted availability, and conducted refresher and type training. On 10 July, she headed back to the western Pacific for her second tour of duty in the Vietnam conflict. She reported for duty with the 7th Fleet on 22 July and, between that time and early December, made five different replenishment cruises in the combat zone. On 8 December, the ship departed Yokosuka, Japan, to return to the United States. She arrived back in San Francisco on 18 December and immediately commenced post-deployment standdown. On 15 April 1971, she began her first regular overhaul at Hunters Point Naval Shipyard, and it occupied her until 8 July when she put to sea for post-overhaul trials. Type and refresher training took up the remainder of July as well as August and September. In October, she began preparations for her third deployment to the western Pacific.

On 20 November, *White Plains* stood out of San Francisco Bay on her way to the Far East and, after a two-week voyage, arrived in Subic Bay on 7 December. Again, she made a series of replenishment cruises in the Vietnam combat zone and punctuated them with visits to such ports as Hong Kong; Singapore; Sattahip, Thailand; Kaohsiung, Taiwan; and Subic Bay. She remained in the Far East for over seven months and conducted 10 replenishment cruises to Vietnamese waters. On 8 July 1972, *White Plains* departed Sasebo, Japan, and shaped a course for home. She arrived at Oakland, Calif., on 19 July and remained there until 5 September at which time she moved to Alameda for a restricted availability at the Todd Shipyard. The ship completed repairs on 3 October and began preparations to return to the western Pacific. On 31 October, the combat stores ship got underway from Alameda and set a westerly course. After a two-week voyage, she entered her new home port, Sasebo, on 13 November. There, she immediately began another restricted availability, this time for conversion of her propulsion system to the use of Navy distillate fuel. That conversion took up the remainder of 1972 and the first 15 days of 1973.

White Plains' return to duty coincided with the end of American involvement in the Vietnam war; however, that did not signal an end to duty in Vietnamese waters. Through the first seven months of 1973, she continued to make replenishment cruises in the former combat zone to bring stores to the American ships engaged in Operation "End Sweep," the taking up of mines planted by the Navy in North Vietnamese waters during the war. "End Sweep" came to a conclusion late in July, and *White Plains* began real peacetime duty at that point. For the next two years, she operated out of Sasebo making periodic voyages to provide supplies to units of the Fleet at sea. She also made the usual port calls throughout the Orient and participated in training exercises, notably with units of the Republic of Korea Navy in November of 1974 and January of

1975. On 1 August 1975, she changed home ports from Sasebo to Yokosuka and, on 5 September, began regular overhaul at her new base of operations. That repair period lasted until 15 April 1976 at which time she resumed her replenishment duty with the 7th Fleet.

The year 1976 proved a very active one for *White Plains*. In addition to her normal duty supplying the 7th Fleet, she joined in three non-routine operations. Late in May and early in June, she voyaged to the Mariana Islands where Typhoon Pamela had just wreaked so much havoc. The ship carried supplies to the relief of the storm-battered island of Guam. During the second week of July, she interrupted her normal routine again, this time to rush to the Indian Ocean, via Subic Bay, to resupply the carrier contingency force sent to patrol the eastern coast of Africa during the flare-up between Kenya and Uganda. She remained in the Indian Ocean until 5 August whereupon she headed back to Yokosuka to resume her normal support duties with the 7th Fleet. On 27 September, she departed Yokosuka for another special mission. During the next five weeks, she sailed to Australia, participated in the bilateral amphibious and antisubmarine exercise Operation "Kangaroo II," visited the Australian port of Townsville, and then returned to Yokosuka. She arrived back in her home port on 11 November and resumed her duties keeping the fleet supplied. Since that time, *White Plains* has continued to make replenishment swings from Yokosuka to 7th Fleet units operating in such diverse places as the Philippine Sea, the South China Sea, and the Sea of Japan. In late October and early November of 1977, the ship voyaged to the Indian Ocean again to replenish American warships engaged in Operation "Midlink." Upon concluding that mission, she returned to Yokosuka and resumed her replenishment duties out of that port. As of January 1979, she continued to operate from Yokosuka in support of the 7th Fleet.

White Plains (AFS-4) earned seven battle stars during the Vietnam conflict.

White River

Rivers in Arkansas, Colorado, Indiana, South Dakota, Texas, Vermont, and Washington.

(LSMR-536: dp. 1,084 (f.); l. 206'3"; b. 34'6"; dr. 6'8"; s. 12.6 k. (tl.); cpl. 138; a. 1 5", 4 4.2" M., 10 rk. ln., 4 40mm.; cl. *LSMR-501*)

LSMR-536 was laid down on 9 June 1945 at Houston, Tex., by the Brown Shipbuliding Co.; launched on 14 July 1945; and commissioned on 28 November 1945, Lt. John M. Cates, USNR, in command.

Departing Houston on 3 December, *LSMR-536* made a three-day stop at Galveston before continuing on to Charleston, S.C., where she completed outfitting. She stood out of Charleston on 8 January 1946 to conduct shakedown training at Little Creek, Va. After about a month of training, she headed south to Florida on 7 February, arriving in Green Cove Springs on 10 February. There, she was placed in commission, in reserve, until 31 July at which time she was placed out of commission and was berthed at Green Cove Springs with the Atlantic Reserve Fleet.

Just over four years later, on 16 September 1950, the warship was recommissioned, Lt. Henry O. Bergkamp, USNR, in command. She completed outfitting at Savannah, Ga., and, on 20 November, got underway for shakedown training at Little Creek once again. She completed that evolution and departed the Chesapeake Bay area on 1 March 1951 for duty with the Pacific Fleet. She transited the Panama Canal on 14 March and arrived in San Diego, Calif., 10 days later. There, she became a unit of LSMR Division 3 and spent the next 14 months practicing her amphibious support role at San Clemente Island.

On 12 May 1952, she departed San Diego in company with *LSMR-527* and three large landing support ships.

The formation steamed by way of Pearl Harbor and Midway and arrived in Yokosuka, Japan, on 19 June. Later, she moved to Sasebo to prepare for her first cruise in the combat zone off the Korean coast. She embarked upon that cruise in mid-July and arrived off Cho Do, an island off the western coast of Korea in the southern portion of the Korea Bay, on the 16th. She patrolled on station at that location until 15 August when she headed back to Japan.

After visits to Sasebo and Yokosuka, she conducted landing exercises at Chigasaki late in September. She returned to Yokosuka and Sasebo, between which ports she made runs during October and most of November. On 27 November, the ship departed Sasebo to return to station in the vicinity of Cho Do. That assignment, consisting mostly of night illumination fire, lasted until mid-December when she headed back to Japan. *LSMR-536* remained at Sasebo from 19 December 1952 until 18 January 1953. She returned briefly to Cho Do on 20 January and then began patrolling Taenchong Do, Paengnyong Do, and Kirin Do in addition.

She returned to Yokosuka on 13 February and remained there until the 24th when she got underway to return home. Steaming by way of Midway and Pearl Harbor, the warship arrived in San Diego on 24 March. Following training operations at San Clemente Island, she moved to the San Francisco-Vallejo area for overhaul at the Mare Island Naval Shipyard. All told, she remained on the west coast 11 months, departing from San Diego to return to the western Pacific on 10 February 1954.

After stops at Pearl Harbor and Midway, *LSMR-536* arrived in Yokosuka on 11 March. Though the ship returned to the Korean coast periodically during her second tour of duty with the 7th Fleet, combat operations played no part in her activities, because hostilities had been effectively ended by the armistice of 19 July 1953. She concluded her first peacetime deployment to the Far East when she reentered San Diego on 7 November 1954. She spent the year 1955 engaged in operations out of San Diego, primarily amphibious training maneuvers at San Clemente Island. On 1 October 1955, she was named *White River*.

Early in 1956, the ship deployed briefly to the western Pacific. She departed San Diego on 4 January 1956 and arrived in Yokosuka on 6 February. She participated in a large-scale amphibious maneuver at Iwo Jima later that month and then returned briefly to Yokosuka before heading home on 3 March. *White River* arrived back in San Diego on 31 March and resumed local operations. On 7 September 1956, she was decommissioned and berthed with the San Diego Group, Pacific Reserve Fleet.

In June of 1965, *White River* was moved from San Diego to the Long Beach Naval Shipyard where she underwent extensive modifications in preparation for her return to active service. On 2 October 1965, she was recommissioned, Lt. William C. Carlson in command. She departed Long Beach on 30 October and headed for San Diego whence she conducted shakedown training and shore bombardment drills. On 8 February 1966, she departed San Diego to rejoin the 7th Fleet in the Far East for the first time in a decade. She and her division stopped in the Hawaiian Islands for about two weeks during which they conducted additional shore bombardment drills at Kahoolawe Island before resuming their voyage west on 1 March. She stopped at Midway Island on 5 March and entered Yokosuka 10 days later. Training and port visits in Japan occupied her next eight weeks. On 9 May, she departed Yokosuka, bound for the coast of Vietnam by way of Subic Bay in the Philippines.

She arrived off the I Corps zone of operations on 25 May and immediately began gunfire support missions for Operation "Mobile." Two days later, she concluded her support of "Mobile" and shifted to support for the South Vietnamese Army's 2d Division operating near Quang Ngai. She continued to support that unit intermittently for the next two months, interrupting this duty only to provide gunfire and rockets for three other operations: "Oakland"; "Deckhouse III," an amphibious landing; and "Franklin." At the conclusion of the latter operation, she headed—via Subic Bay and Hong Kong —for Yokosuka where she remained until 16 September.

After another stop at Subic Bay, she returned to the Vietnamese coast at the end of September to continue gunfire support for the troops ashore. During the next two months, she provided call fire in the northern portion of the II Corps operational zone. On 30 November, she terminated her second tour of duty in Vietnamese waters and headed, via Okinawa, to Yokosuka where she spent the remainder of the year in upkeep.

White River departed Japan once more on 23 January. Again, she stopped at Subic Bay, first to load ammunition and then to complete some maintenance work. She returned to the coast of the I Corps tactical zone on 9 February and began delivering gunfire for marines ashore engaged in Operation "Desoto." She concluded that assignment on 11 February, refuelled in Danang, and got underway to support Operation "Deckhouse VI," an amphibious operation which was conducted by the Special Landing Force near Sa Huyen in the southern reaches of the I Corps tactical zone as an extension of the "Desoto" operation which had been temporarily halted during the Tet holidays. She finished her part in the "Desoto-Deckhouse VI" operation on 23 February and headed for Subic Bay where she rearmed and conducted upkeep from 24 February to 2 March. *White River* returned to the Vietnamese coast on 13 March and resumed shore bombardment duties in support of Operation "Beacon Hill," a combined helicopter- and waterborne-amphibious assault conducted near Dong Ha. On 23 March, she was released from the "Beacon Hill" operation to rearm at Camranh Bay whence she proceeded to the III Corps tactical zone to provide gunfire support for operations near Rung Sat.

On 2 April, she was relieved by *Carronade* (IFS-1) and headed toward Yokosuka where she arrived on 17 April after a four-day stop at Keelung, Taiwan. She made necessary repairs at Yokosuka and then headed back to Vietnam on 29 May. Following ammunition replenishment at Subic Bay, the warship arrived off the I Corps tactical zone on 11 June and conducted shore bombardments there and in the II Corps zone until 21 July when she departed Vietnamese waters to return to Subic Bay for upkeep. *White River* arrived back off the Vietnamese coast at the beginning of August and stayed there until 23 August. The ship made a voyage to Yokosuka at the end of the month, arriving there on 8 September and remaining until 16 October for repairs. She began her last 1967 tour of duty off the Vietnamese coast on 31 October. It lasted until 27 December and consisted almost entirely of gunfire support for forces operating in the II Corps tactical zone. At its conclusion, she returned to Subic Bay for upkeep.

During 1968, *White River* continued to operate out of her home port, Yokosuka, and made four deployments to the war zone off Vietnam to render gunfire support for American and South Vietnamese troops operating in that strife-torn republic. In 1969, she served no time in the war zone. Apparently, she participated in maneuvers at Buckner Bay, Okinawa, and made repairs. On 22 May 1970, *White River* was decommissioned at Yokosuka after a highly unfavorable inspection and survey. Her name was struck from the Navy list concurrently, and she was sold in November 1970 to the Nissho-Iwai American Corp. of New York City for scrapping.

White River was awarded two battle stars for her service in the Korean War and seven for her duty during the Vietnam conflict.

White Sands

A region of white (gypsum) sand dunes in Dona Ana County in southern New Mexico.

(ARD-20: l. 291'8"; b. 81'; dr. 32'10" (subm.); cpl. 112; cl. *ARD-12*)

ARD-20, an auxiliary repair dock, was laid down on 20 December 1943 at Alameda, Calif., by the Pacific Bridge Co.; launched early in 1944; and placed in service on 31 March 1944, Lt. Comdr. Gutav Jones, USNR, in command.

After training at the Drydock Training Center located at Tiburon, Calif., she departed San Francisco Bay on 11 June under tow of SS *Stratford Point*. She stopped briefly at Espiritu Santo in the New Hebrides Islands before arriving at her assigned base, Seeadler Harbor, at Manus in the Admiralty Islands, on 12 August. As a unit of the 7th Fleet's Service Squadron 3, *ARD-20* repaired battle-damaged ships at Manus for the next eight months. On 16 April 1945, *ATA-176* towed her out of Seeadler Harbor and set a course for Morotai Island located just north of Halmahera in the northern Moluccas. The two vessels arrived at Morotai on 29 April. She conducted repairs at Morotai until 24 July when she was towed to Manicani Island repair base—located near Samar in the Philippines—where she spent 19 months.

She departed Manicani on 25 February 1947, under tow by SS *Robert Eden*, and arrived in Apra Harbor, Guam, on 9 March. Later in the year, SS *Robert Hartley* towed her by way of Pearl Harbor to San Pedro, Calif., where the two vessels arrived on 11 September. She was placed out of service on 7 October 1947 and berthed with the San Pedro Group, Pacific Reserve Fleet.

Eighteen years later, in October 1965, she was moved to the Long Beach Naval Shipyard where work began on her modernization and conversion. On 14 September 1966, she was placed in service as *ARD(BS)-20*—a bathyscaph support auxiliary repair dock—and assigned to the Submarine Force, Pacific Fleet, to conduct CNO research projects related to deep submergence vehicles and their operation. On 9 March 1968, she was named *White Sands*, and her hull designation was shortened back to ARD-20. From 1968, *White Sands* conducted tests with the deep submergence vehicle *Trieste* in various open ocean environments. Those tests took place near the Undersea Weapons Center near San Clemente Island, Calif. In February 1969, she departed the west coast to participate in the search for the nuclear submarine *Scorpion* (SSN-589) lost near the Azores. She concluded her part in that assignment early in August and returned, via the Panama Canal, to San Diego on 7 October 1969. There, she resumed her research assignment with deep submergence vehicles. On 1 August 1973, *White Sands* was reclassified an auxiliary deep submergence support ship, AGDS-1. She served under that designation until late in the summer of 1974 when she was placed out of service. Her name was struck from the Navy list in September 1974, and she was sold for scrapping.

Whitecap

A wave crest breaking into white foam.

(Tr: t. 303; l. 143'0"; b. 22'8"; dr. 13'5" (aft); s. 11 k.; cpl. 18; a. 1 6-pdr., 1 3")

The trawler *Whitecap* was built in 1916 at Manitowoc, Wis., by the Manitowoc Shipbuilding Co. and, at the time of her acquisition by the Navy on 28 April 1917, was owned by the Bay State Fisheries Co., of South Boston, Mass. Assigned the classification SP-340, *Whitecap* was commissioned on 8 May 1917.

Initially attached to the 1st Naval District, *Whitecap* began operations out of the 2d Naval District in late February of 1918. During her career, *Whitecap* operated primarily out of Newport, R.I., patrolling between that base and New London, Conn. Occasionally, her coastal patrols took her to Nantucket Island, Block Island, and Montauk Point, as well as to New York

City. When not at sea keeping tabs on the coastwise traffic of naval and merchant vessels, *Whitecap* performed local tow and escort service out of Newport.

Decommissioned at Boston, Mass., on 11 March 1919, *Whitecap* was returned to her previous owners on 1 April 1919. Her name was struck from the Navy list, and the ship resumed peacetime fishing pursuits.

Whitefish

A freshwater food fish—closely related to the trout and salmon—found in waters of the Northern Hemisphere.

The name *Whitefish* was assigned to SS–432—a *Balao*-class submarine to be built at Philadelphia, Pa., by the Cramp Shipbuilding Co.—but the contract for her construction was cancelled on 29 July 1944.

Whitehall

A town in Washington County, N.Y., at the southern end of Lake Champlain. Whitehall has been called the birthplace of the United States Navy since that was where Benedict Arnold constructed 16 small ships in 1776 to prevent a British fleet from invading American territory down the Lake Champlain-Hudson River corridor. The American ships were defeated on 11 October 1776 at the Battle of Valcour Island, but they delayed the British advance and then won a great strategic victory by enabling the Americans to have another year in which to strengthen their forces in the area. Thus, a year later, the Americans defeated the British at Saratoga in the pivotal battle of the War for Independence.

I

(SwGbt.: t. 326; l. 126'; b. 28'2''; dr. 8'; a. 2 32-pdr. P.r., 2 32-pdrs.)

Whitehall—a side-wheel gunboat and converted ferry built in 1850 at Brooklyn, N.Y.—was purchased by the Navy there on 10 October 1861 and was commissioned soon thereafter at the New York Navy Yard, Acting Master Francis P. Allen in command.

Assigned to the South Atlantic Blockading Squadron, *Whitehall* sailed for Port Royal, S.C.; but her unseaworthy condition prevented her completing the voyage south. She put in to Philadelphia in early November for emergency repairs and stopped again at Hampton Roads for the same purpose a few days later. *Whitehall* left Newport News for Port Royal on 5 November—only to be forced back to Hampton Roads by high seas on 6 November. On 7 November, carpenters examining *Whitehall* declared her unseaworthy. Nevertheless, she was badly needed at Port Royal and proceeded south towed by *Connecticut* on 12 November 1861. Again *Whitehall* turned back, reentering Hampton Roads on 13 November 1861. That same day, she was ordered to Baltimore for an extensive overhaul.

Whitehall was reassigned to the North Atlantic Blockading Squadron in Hampton Roads on 29 November 1861. She departed the Virginia capes on 6 December 1861, bound for Annapolis, Md., to pick up arms and provisions for the squadron and returned to Hampton Roads. On 29 December 1861, *Whitehall* and eight other steamers engaged CSS *Sea Bird* in the roads shortly after the Confederate steamer had captured a water schooner and attacked the Army steamer, *Express*, which had been towing it. After an action lasting one-half hour, *Sea Bird* withdrew from the battle and retired under the protection of Confederate shore batteries. *Whitehall* and *Morse* covered Union forces as they withdrew.

On 2 January 1862, *Whitehall* got underway for Hatteras Inlet, N.C. However, she immediately became disabled and returned to Hampton Roads. Flag Officer Louis M. Goldsborough, commanding the North Atlantic Blockading Squadron, called *Whitehall* "the worst sea boat of all the ferryboats with which I have had to do, and certainly the most unfortunate." A survey taken of the vessel on 22 February 1862 found both her machinery and hull badly deteriorated.

Whitehall saw her final action on 8 and 9 March 1862 against the Confederate ironclad CSS *Virginia*, the former *Merrimack*. On 8 March, federal gunboats, including *Whitehall*, attempted to draw the Rebel vessel away from Union warships anchored off Newport News. Failing this, *Whitehall* engaged Confederate steamers *Yorktown* and *Jamestown*, inflicting minor damage. During the *Monitor-Virginia* engagement on 9 March 1862, *Whitehall* and the rest of the Union fleet abstained from direct battle, preferring to fire long-range, ineffective shots at *Virginia*. *Whitehall* suffered three casualties and had parts of her upperworks burned by Confederate shot during the two days of activity.

Early on the morning of 10 March 1862 at Old Point Comfort, Va., a flash fire swept and totally destroyed *Whitehall*. There were no casualties.

II

(PCER–856: dp. 850 (tl.) ; l. 184'6''; b. 33'1''; dr. 9'5''; s. 15.7 k. (tl.) ; cpl. 99; a. 1 3'', 6 40mm., 4 dcp., 1 dcp. (hh.), 2 dct.; cl. *PCER–848*)

The second *Whitehall* was laid down on 17 December 1943 at Chicago, Ill., by the Pullman Standard Car Manufacturing Co. as *PCER–856*; launched on 21 April 1944; sponsored by Miss Mary B. Visznecki; and commissioned on 11 November 1944, Lt. Maynard L. Berry, USNR, in command.

PCER–856 remained at Chicago until early December, first for an availability and later to participate in a war bond drive. On 7 December, she departed Chicago and headed for New Orleans by way of the Illinois and Mississippi Rivers. Arriving at her destination on 18 December, she remained there almost two months undergoing repairs to her shaft struts, damaged during the trip from Chicago. At the conclusion of repairs, she got underway for Miami, Fla., whence she completed shakedown training between 17 February and 8 March 1945. After 11 days of repairs and modifications at the Miami Shipyard, the ship headed north to Norfolk, Va., from which port she conducted special trials in Chesapeake Bay for the Bureau of Ships. She departed Norfolk on 2 April and arrived in Key West, Fla., on the 6th. After a brief period of antisubmarine warfare (ASW) training at the Fleet Sound School, *PCER–856* headed for the Canal Zone on 11 April. She transited the canal on the 17th and shaped a course for Hawaii. During that voyage, she made two hedgehog runs on an underwater sound contact later evaluated as non-submarine.

The warship arrived in Pearl Harbor on 5 May but remained only 14 days for repairs before continuing on to the western Pacific. She departed Oahu on 19 May, made stops at Eniwetok, Guam, and Ulithi, and arrived off Okinawa on 18 June. At Okinawa, the ship drew duty with the antisubmarine patrol protecting the auxiliaries in Hagushi anchorage. Additional assignments consisted of escort missions between the several anchorages around the island and the evacuation of battle casualties. On 25 and 26 June, *PCER–856* participated in the unopposed occupation of one of Okinawa's many islets, Kume Shima. She remained at Okinawa for another month after that operation, getting underway for the Philippines on 25 July. She arrived at Leyte on the 30th and began a month of repairs. Halfway through the availability period, she received word that hostilities had ceased, and she joined the other ships at Leyte in one of the most spectacular pyrotechnic displays ever made, in celebration of the war's end. The warship completed repairs early in September and returned to Okinawa on the 9th. On the 13th, she ran aground but 90 minutes later backed off under her own power. Damage proved minimal—she lost only her underwater sound projector. She remained at Okinawa for about a month, safely riding out four typhoons in the process.

On 15 October, *PCER–856* departed the Ryukyus to return to the United States. Further problems with her shaft struts forced her into port at Midway Island where she entered drydock for temporary repairs. She finally reached Pearl Harbor on 6 November but stayed only two days before continuing on to San Diego. Her stay at San Diego, from 18 to 28 November, brought more repairs in preparation for her voyage to Key West. On the 28th, she departed San Diego and, 17 days later, arrived in Key West. There, she completed her inactivation overhaul. On 20 February 1946, she departed Key West and headed north for Norfolk, where she arrived three days later. *PCER–856* remained at Norfolk, inactive, for the next eight months. During that time, on 26 June 1946, she was placed out of commission, in reserve. Though not in commission, she returned to active service that fall as a part of the Naval Reserve training program. Early in November, she moved to Philadelphia where she came under the control of the Commandant, 4th Naval District.

For the remainder of her Navy career, *PCER–856* served in the reserve training program. From November 1946 to April 1960, she was based at Philadelphia and operated along the east coast. She was returned to commissioned status on 18 November 1950 though she remained a Naval Reserve training ship. On 15 February 1956, she was named *Whitehall*. The ship changed home ports in April 1960, leaving Philadelphia late in the month and arriving in Cleveland, Ohio, on 6 May. During the remaining decade of her career, *Whitehall* annually made between eight and twelve fortnight cruises on the Great Lakes and numerous weekend cruises for the purpose of training reservists. During those cruises, she visited all the major ports on the lakes, both American and Canadian. On 15 March 1962, she was redesignated PCE–856. In April 1970, a board of inspection and survey found her to be unfit for further naval service. On 9 May, she departed Cleveland for the last time. After transiting the St. Lawrence Seaway and stopping at Montreal and Halifax, she arrived in Philadelphia on 20 May. *Whitehall* (PCE–856) was decommissioned at Philadelphia on 1 July 1970, and her name was simultaneously struck from the Navy list. On 17 May 1973, she was sold to the R. W. Denny Corp., of Montvale, N.J., for scrapping.

Whitehall earned one battle star for World War II service as *PCER–856*.

Whitehead

(ScGbt: t. 136; l. 93'1½''; b. 19'9''; dr. 8'; s. 8 k.; a. 1 30-pdr. P.r.)

Whitehead—a screw steamer built in 1861 at New Brunswick, N.J.—was purchased by the Navy on 17 October 1861 at New York City from D. B. Martin; and commissioned on 19 November 1861, Acting Master Charles A. French in command.

The following day, *Whitehead* reached Hampton Roads and joined the North Atlantic Blockading Squadron. She sailed for the North Carolina coast on 28 December 1861 and arrived at Hatteras Inlet on 4 January 1862.

During the next few months, the steamer *Whitehead* carried out extensive operations against Confederate vessels and shore installations in the sounds and rivers of North Carolina. On 7 and 8 February, she helped to capture Roanoke Island. On 10 February, *Whitehead* took schooner *M. C. Etheridge* in Pasquotank River, N.C. On 10 April, she made prizes of schooners *Comet* and *J. J. Crittendon* and of sloop *America* in Newbegun Creek. Together with *Lockwood*, *Putnam*, and *Shawsheen*, *Whitehead* blocked the mouth of the Albemarle

and Chesapeake Canal with fill on 23 and 24 April. She captured schooner *Eugenia* in Bennett's Creek on 20 May and took *Ella D* off Keel's Creek two days later.

Late in September, *Whitehead* briefly left North Carolina waters to participate in a Federal assault upon Confederate forces gathered at Franklin. On 3 October, *Commodore Perry*, *Hunchback*, and *Whitehead* entered the Blackwater River and fired on Rebel troops for over six hours before a barricade placed across the channel necessitated retreat.

Whitehead soon returned to Pamlico Sound but was ordered north on 16 November 1862 for repairs at the Washington Navy Yard. At this time, 3-inch iron plate was placed over her guns and around her pilot house. Back in fighting trim, *Whitehead* returned to North Carolina late in December 1862.

Her first noteworthy action came early in the spring of 1863 when she helped to lift the Confederate siege of Washington, N.C., which lasted from 31 March to 16 April. On 6 and 7 July, *Whitehead*, *Commodore Perry*, *Southfield*, and *Valley City* bombarded and occupied Williamston, N.C. *Whitehead* captured several prisoners during an expedition up the Pasquotank River on 14 August 1863 and destroyed a Confederate corn mill on the Roanoke River on 22 February 1864. On 1 and 2 March 1864, *Whitehead* and *Southfield* sailed up the Chowan River and freed *Bombshell* from her encirclement by Confederate shore batteries.

Whitehead encountered the formidable Confederate ram, *Albemarle*, on three occasions. In the early morning hours of 19 April 1864, *Ceres*, *Miami*, *Southfield*, and *Whitehead* engaged the ram in the Roanoke River. All received damage, and *Southfield* was sunk. Darkness prevented *Whitehead* from returning *Albemarle* fire. As a result of this costly Union naval defeat, Plymouth, N.C., fell to Confederate troops the next day.

Union vessels, including *Whitehead*, again fought *Albemarle* on 5 May 1864. This three-hour battle was inconclusive, and the ram withdrew up the Roanoke. *Whitehead* battled *Albemarle* a third time on 24 May 1864. A shell from *Whitehead* exploded near the ram's stern and caused the dreaded Confederate warship to withdraw.

Whitehead resumed routine patrol and reconnaissance duty soon after this. On 12 July 1864, she ascended the Scuppernong River to Columbia, N.C., and burned a bridge used to transport supplies to Southern troops at Plymouth. *Whitehead* and steamers *Thomas Colyer* and *Massasoit* joined in an expedition up the Chowan River, N.C., on 28 July 1864, capturing steamer *Arrow* and a large quantity of cotton and tobacco on 29 July at Gatesville, N.C. *Whitehead* proceeded to the Norfolk Navy Yard for repairs on 20 August 1864. She completed these in time for her to participate in the recapture of Plymouth on 31 October 1864.

For the closing months of the Civil War, *Whitehead*—but for occasional runs to Norfolk for supplies—patrolled the inland waters of North Carolina. She was decommissioned at the Philadelphia Navy Yard on 29 June 1865 and was sold at public auction there on 10 August 1865. Redocumented as *Nevada* on 7 October 1865, the steamer remained in mercantile service until she was destroyed by fire on 1 September 1872 at New London, Conn.

Whitehurst

Henry Purefoy Whitehurst, Jr.—born on 16 February 1920 at New Bern, N.C.—was appointed a midshipman on 14 July 1938 and, because of the exigencies of war, graduated with the Naval Academy's Class of 1942 on 19 December 1941. He reported to the heavy cruiser *Astoria* (CA–34) on the morning of 18 January 1942 at Pearl Harbor, Hawaii.

Whitehurst served as a junior watch and division officer in *Astoria* as that ship took part in the Battles of the Coral Sea and Midway, and was in the cruiser when she participated in the landings on Guadalcanal on 7 August 1942. The next day, *Astoria* screened the vital transports as they unloaded supplies and equipment for the marines ashore, and that evening stood out to a night retirement station off Savo Island.

A little after 0152 on the morning of 9 August, a Japanese force under Vice Admiral Gunichi Mikawa—which had slipped undetected into the waters south of Savo Island—unleashed a devastating night attack on the Southern and Northern Forces. In the former, *Chicago* (CA–29) was damaged and the Australian heavy cruiser HMAS *Canberra* crippled so badly that she later sank.

The Northern Force, unaware of the enemy's presence until too late, soon took staggering punishment. *Vincennes* (CA–44) and *Quincy* (CA–39) sank before daylight, but *Astoria* lingered on while her surviving officers and men labored to save their ship. However, the damage proved too great; and *Astoria*—like her two sister ships—eventually succumbed shortly after noon on 9 August. Among the dead suffered in the Battle of Savo Island was Ensign Whitehurst.

(DE–634: dp. 1,400; l. 305′0′′; b. 37′0′′; dr. 9′5′′ (mean) ; s. 23.5 k.; cpl. 186; a. 3 3′′, 4 1.1′′, 8 20mm., 2 dct., 8 dcp., 1 dcp. (hh.), 3 21′′ tt.; cl. *Buckley*)

Whitehurst (DE–634) was laid down on 21 March 1943 at San Francisco, Calif., by the Bethelehem Steel Co.; launched on 5 September 1943; sponsored by Mrs. Robie S. Whitehurst, the mother of Ensign Whitehurst; and commissioned on 19 November 1943, Lt. Comdr. James R. Grey in command.

Following sea trials, calibration tests, and shakedown off the west coast, *Whitehurst* proceeded to Hawaii, arriving at Pearl Harbor on 4 February 1944. Underway for the Solomons on the 7th, the destroyer escort sailed via Majuro and Funafuti in company with *James E. Craig* (DE–201) and *SC–502*—escorting SS *George Ross*, SS *George Constantine* and SS *Robert Lucas*—and arrived on 23 February at Espiritu Santo in the New Hebrides.

After shifting to Noumea, New Caledonia, and back to Espiritu Santo, *Whitehurst* joined *Osterhaus* (DE–164) and *Acree* (DE–167) on 22 March to escort oilers *Kankakee* (AO–39), *Escambia* (AO–80), and *Atascosa* (AO–66). *Whitehurst* and *Atascosa* were detached from that task unit on 26 March to proceed independently to a rendezvous with other task forces operating in the area. While *Atascosa* refueled ships from Destroyer Squadron 47, an enemy plane appeared. All ships present, including *Whitehurst*, opened fire but scored no hits as the plane climbed upward and out of sight. Once refueling had been completed, *Whitehurst* and the oiler returned to Espiritu Santo.

At the completion of a mission escorting *President Monroe* (AP–104) to Milne Bay, New Guinea, *Whitehurst* remained in waters off New Guinea on local escort duties until 17 May. She then participated in the amphibious operation against Wakde Island, screening the amphibious ships as they landed troops of General Douglas MacArthur's forces. *Whitehurst*, in company with other units of Task Unit (TU) 72.2.9, later escorted echelon S–4 of the invasion force to Humboldt Bay. The destroyer escort subsequently joined *Wilkes* (DD–441), *Swanson* (DD–443), and *Nicholson* (DD–442) to screen echelon H–2 as it steamed toward Bosnic, Biak, in the Schouten Islands, for landings there.

Arriving off Biak on 28 May, *Whitehurst* took up a patrol station off the western entrance to the channel between Owi Island and Biak. While there, she received an urgent message from *LCI–34* which had been taken under fire by Japanese shore batteries. *Whitehurst* arrived on the scene in time to be shelled, herself; but the enemy's rounds fell harmlessly nearby and caused no damage to the ship. The destroyer escort soon was relieved by *Stockton* (DD–646) and *Swanson* in covering *LCI–34*, and then protected *LCT–260* as that landing craft embarked casualties from the beachhead. *Whitehurst* subsequently screened echelon H–2 as it retired from Biak to Humboldt Bay.

Whitehurst performed escort duties and trained through the summer of 1944. The tempo of the war, however, was increasing. With the Japanese being driven from one island after another, American planners looked toward the next rung of the ladder to Tokyo—the Philippine Islands. Accordingly, *Whitehurst*, Lt. Jack C. Horton, USNR, now in command, was placed in the antisubmarine and antiaircraft screen of TU 77.7.1, a group of fleet tankers slated to supply units of the 7th Fleet on its drive into the Philippines. On 27 October—a week after American troops had landed on Leyte—two enemy planes attacked *Whitehurst*; but both were driven off by antiaircraft fire from the ship's guns.

Two days later—on 29 October—*Whitehurst* received word that, on the previous day, *Eversole* (DE–404) had been torpedoed and sunk by a Japanese submarine. While *Bull* (DE–693) picked up survivors from the sunken destroyer escort, *Whitehurst*—detached from TU 77.7.1 to conduct a search—soon picked up a contact. At general quarters, the destroyer escort conducted three attacks without positive results. When *Whitehurst* pressed home a fourth depth charge attack, her efforts were crowned with success. In quick succession, five to seven explosions rumbled up from the depths. Another violent underwater burst soon followed, causing a concussion that damaged *Whitehurst*'s detecting gear.

Bull continued the search after *Whitehurst*—with her damaged sound gear—requested her to do so but found nothing except a stretch of disturbed water. As the waves calmed, lookouts in both ships noticed many pieces of wood and other debris bobbing in a widening oil slick. The Japanese submarine *I–45*—the one that had killed *Eversole*—had been destroyed. While *Bull* continued picking up *Eversole* survivors in the vicinity, *Whitehurst* returned to TU 77.7.1 and with that task unit headed back to Kossol Roads in the Palaus.

Nearly a month later, following another stint of local escort operations, *Whitehurst* again came to grips with the enemy. While escorting a 12-ship convoy from Leyte to New Guinea, *Whitehurst* came under attack by two Japanese "Lilly" medium bombers. One skimmed low and dropped a bomb that fell well clear of the ships. The second started a glide bombing attack, but *Whitehurst*'s guns tumbled that raider into the sea.

After arriving with the convoy at New Guinea on 25 November, *Whitehurst* spent the remainder of 1944 and the first few months of 1945 in escort operations between New Guinea and the Philippines. She did not again engage the enemy until the Okinawa campaign.

When the American landings on Okinawa commenced on 1 April 1945, *Whitehurst* was among the many screening vessels protecting the valuable transports and cargo vessels. On 6 April, while on patrol station off Kerama Retto, the destroyer escort drove off an enemy plane that had attacked the cargo vessel SS *Pierre*. Three days later, the escort vessel was relieved of her escort duties off Kerama Retto, and she shifted to Okinawa to operate off the southwest coast of that island.

Taking up station on the 10th, she was still steaming in that capacity early in the afternoon two days later when a low-flying enemy plane closed the ship only to be driven off by *Whitehurst*'s gunfire. At 1430, four "Val" dive-bombers approached the area from the south; and one detached itself from the group and headed for *Whitehurst*. It circled and soon commenced a steep dive while two of its companions also commenced an attack, one from the starboard beam and one from astern. The latter two planes spun down in flames, destroyed by antiaircraft fire, but the original attacker continued down in spite of the 20-millimeter hits that tore at the plane. This "Val" crashed into the ship's forward superstructure on the port side of the pilot house, penetrating bulkheads and starting fires that enveloped the entire bridge, while the plane's bomb continued through the ship and exploded some 50 feet off her starboard bow.

Whitehurst circled, out of control, while *Vigilance* (AM–324)—patrolling a nearby sector—rang up flank speed and raced toward the burning destroyer escort to render assistance. By the time *Vigilance* finally caught up with *Whitehurst*, the destroyer escort's crew had put out the most serious fires; but the minesweeper proved invaluable in aiding the wounded. The prompt and efficient administering of first aid and the injection of plasma undoubtedly saved many lives—21 of the 23 wounded transferred to *Vigilance* were saved.

With a *Vigilance* signalman on board—*Whitehurst's* signal bridge personnel had been decimated—the damaged destroyer escort limped into Kerama Retto for temporary patching. Then, seaworthy enough for a voyage to Hawaii, *Whitehurst* reached Pearl Harbor on 10 May and was docked for repairs and alterations.

Once the yard work had been completed and the ship had been converted to a floating power station, *Whitehurst* departed Pearl Harbor on 25 July 1945, bound for the Philippine Islands. Soon after she reached Luzon, Japan capitulated. Nevertheless, the ship supplied the city of Manila with power from August through October of 1945. She was scheduled to depart Manila on 1 November, bound for Guam; but a typhoon in the vicinity resulted in a two-day delay. *Whitehurst* eventually reached Guam on the afternoon of 7 November.

Operating as a unit of Escort Division 40, *Whitehurst* supplied electrical power to the dredge *YM-25* into 1946. Returning to the continental United States in April 1946, *Whiehurst* was decommissioned on 27 November 1946 and placed in the Atlantic Reserve Fleet at Green Cove Springs, Fla., in January 1947.

Reactivated in the summer of 1950 as a result of the outbreak of war in Korea, *Whitehurst* was recommissioned on 1 September 1950 and soon sailed for the Far East. The destroyer escort earned three battle stars for her activities during the Korean War between 25 February and 19 September 1951.

She remained in the Far East until 1955, when she returned to Pearl Harbor via Midway. After working locally out of Pearl Harbor for a year, the destroyer escort operated between Hawaii and Guam into 1956. Early in that year, she broadened her duties and itinerary by performing surveillance duties among the islands and atolls assigned the Trust Territories for the Pacific Islands. She also performed search and rescue missions in the Marianas and Carolines, periodically stopping at various islands to provide medical care for the natives and to record population changes.

Departing Guam on 22 February for Yokosuka, Japan, the ship sailed via the northern Marianas, the Bonins, and the Volcano Islands. She spent two weeks in Japanese waters before returning to Guam on 17 March. Returning to the Central Carolines for patrol duties in early April 1956, *Whitehurst* stood by a damaged seaplane at the island of Lamotrek for two weeks before she returned to Guam on 14 April, en route to Pearl Harbor.

After a period of local operations out of Pearl Harbor, *Whitehurst* headed back to the Far East and touched at Guam, Formosa, Hong Kong, and Sasebo, Japan, before representing the United States Navy at the graduation ceremonies of the Republic of Korea Naval Academy on 10 April. She returned to Sasebo before shifting to Yokosuka en route to Midway and Hawaii. Arriving at Pearl Harbor on 30 April 1957, *Whitehurst* underwent four weeks of upkeep and repairs before beginning six weeks of duty with 20th Century Fox during the filming of the World War II adventure movie "The Enemy Below." During that time, she portrayed the destroyer escort USS *Haynes.*

Upon completion of the filming of the movie, *Whitehurst* operated off Oahu until late in September, when she was ordered to Seattle, Wash., for duty as training ship with the 13th Naval District. The veteran destroyer escort trained reservists on weekend drill cruises and, during this time, made one extended cruise to Guaymas, Mexico, in November 1957. After being overhauled at Seattle from February to April 1958, *Whitehurst* returned to active training duties, becoming a Group II ASW reserve ship in July. On 6 December 1958, *Whitehurst* was decommissioned and placed in an "in service" status as a unit of the Select Reserve ASW Force.

Thereafter, into the 1960's, *Whitehurst* cruised one weekend per month and made one two-week cruise per year. During the fiscal year 1961, the destroyer escort placed second in the national competition and the battle efficiency competition among the west coast Group II Naval Reserve destroyer escorts.

Commissioned on 2 October 1961 for duty with the Pacific Fleet, Lt. Comdr. Donald L. MacLane, USNR, in command, *Whitehurst* operated actively with the fleet after being "called to the colors" as a result of the Berlin crisis that autumn. The destroyer escort departed Seattle on the 4th, bound for her new home port of Pearl Harbor, Hawaii.

After a period of training in the Hawaiian area, *Whitehurst* departed Pearl Harbor on 10 February 1962 for a deployment to the Western Pacific (WestPac). During the deployment, she operated with the 7th Fleet out of Subic Bay, Philippines, and made a good-will visit to Sapporo, Japan. The ship also operated in the South China Sea and the Gulf of Siam.

Returning to the United States via Hawaii, *Whitehurst* arrived at Seattle in company with *Charles E. Brannon* (DE-446) on 17 July 1962. Subsequently decommissioned on 1 August 1962 and placed in Group II in-service status as a Naval Reserve training ship, *Whitehurst* resumed operations out of Seattle. During 1963, the ship received two major changes in her configuration when her 40-millimeter mounts and ship-to-shore power reels—the latter items having enabled her to function as a floating power station—were removed.

Whitehurst, in subsequent years, visited San Diego, Calif.; Bellingham, Port Angeles, and Everett, Wash.; and Esquimalt, British Columbia. On 17 January 1965, while operating in the Strait of Juan de Fuca, and steaming in dense fog off the Vancouver narrows, *Whitehurst* collided with the Norwegian freighter SS *Hoyanger*. Both ships then ran aground in shallow water. The destroyer escort suffered a five-foot gash in her stern above the waterline while the freighter got off with three feet of scraped bow plates. The following day, both ships were pulled off by tugs.

Whitehurst operated locally out of Seattle and ranged as far south as San Diego and San Francisco into 1967. One of the highlights for the destroyer escort in 1966 was the visit of astronaut Comdr. Richard F. Gordon, Jr., in November of 1966. The ship transported Gordon and his family from Seattle to his home town of Bremerton on 18 November before she returned to her home port.

Soon *Whitehurst's* home port was shifted to Portland, Oreg., from Seattle. The ship she was to replace, *McGinty* (DD-365), was being deactivated as part of an economy drive. However, *Whitehurst's* days were also numbered, and she, too, was soon deactivated. On 12 July 1969, the destroyer escort was taken out of service and struck from the Navy list. She was eventually taken to sea and sunk as a target by *Trigger* (SS-564) on 28 April 1971.

Whitehurst earned six battle stars for her World War II service and three battle stars for Korean service.

Whiteside

A county in northwestern Illinois.

(AKA-90: dp. 13,910 (tl.); l. 459'2''; b. 63'0''; dr. 26'4'' (lim.); s. 16.5 k. (tl.); cpl. 366; trp. 78; a. 1 5'', 8 40mm., 18 20mm.; cl. *Andromeda*; T. C2-S-B1)

Whiteside (AKA-90) was laid down on 22 April 1944 at Oakland, Calif., by the Moore Drydock Co. under a Maritime Commission contract (MC hull 1190); launched on 12 June 1944; sponsored by Mrs. Miriam C. Becker; delivered to the Navy on 11 September 1944; and commissioned that same day, Comdr. C. P. Woodson in command.

Between 11 September and 7 November, the attack cargo ship fitted out, conducted shakedown training, and underwent post-shakedown availability. She then loaded her first cargo at San Francisco and got underway on the 18th for Hawaii. The ship arrived at Oahu on 24 November and remained in Pearl Harbor until 6 December. On the latter day, she put to sea to participate in Army amphibious exercises at Maui. During a night retirement exercise on the night of 13 and 14 December, *Bayfield* (APA–33) rammed *Whiteside* on her starboard side near her number 2 hold. *Whiteside* returned to Pearl Harbor on 18 December to await repairs which began with drydocking on the 24th. She completed repairs on 12 January 1945 and resumed amphibious training with other ships of Transport Squadron (TransRon) 16 at Maui and Kahoolawe Islands. Those operations lasted until 18 January.

The next day, the ship began loading cargo and passengers in preparation for the Iwo Jima assault. She departed Pearl Harbor on 27 January in convoy, bound for Iwo Jima. She stopped at Eniwetok and Saipan along the way and arrived off the objective early on the morning of 19 February. The attack cargo ship participated in the D-day landings sending supplies and ammunition ashore to the troops struggling to wrest the island from a tenacious foe. She continued to fuel the offensive ashore until 5 March when—with 188 battle casualties embarked—she set a course for Guam in the Marianas, where the casualties disembarked. She then moved on to the New Hebrides.

She arrived at Espiritu Santo on 19 March and began loading cargo the next day for the Army's 27th Division in preparation for the Ryukyus campaign. *Whiteside* steamed out of Segond Channel on 25 March bound—via Ulithi—for Okinawa. The attack cargo ship arrived in the Ryukyus on 9 April, eight days after the landings. She remained there a week conducting unloading operations that were frequently interrupted by enemy air raids. During her stay off Okinawa, *Whiteside* engaged two of the hordes of attacking aircraft but claimed no kills.

On 16 April, she departed Okinawa in company with the other ships of TransRon 16. After stops at Saipan and Guam, the ship arrived at Ulithi on 26 April. On 8 May, the ship stood out of the lagoon and set a course for the southern Solomons. She arrived off Lunga Point, Guadalcanal, on the 14th, loaded cargo, and got underway soon thereafter for Munda on New Georgia. From there, she headed for Finschhafen, New Guinea, where she discharged one Army cargo and took on another, bound for the Philippines.

Whiteside departed Finschhafen on 2 June and arrived at Leyte on the 6th. There, she discharged a portion of her cargo and then moved to Guinan Harbor on Samar to unload a Navy cargo. On 12 June, she set sail for Subic Bay where she arrived two days later and unloaded her remaining cargo. She remained at Subic Bay until 25 June when she put to sea to participate in a month of amphibious exercises at Cebu with units of the Americal Division. She returned to Subic Bay on 26 July and began repairing her boilers, an evolution which lasted until 7 August. On the latter day, she returned to sea for more amphibious training, this time at Luzon with units of the 1st Cavalry Division.

Those exercises ended abruptly on 15 August when Japan capitulated. *Whiteside* returned to Subic Bay on 16 August and remained there until the 20th when she moved to Batangas on Luzon to load elements of the 1st Cavalry Division for occupation duty in Japan. On 24 August, she departed Batangas in company with Task Force (TF) 33, the Tokyo occupation force. After a 48-hour stopover in Subic Bay, occasioned by a typhoon, she arrived at Yokohama, Japan, on 2 September, the day of the formal surrender ceremonies conducted on board *Missouri* (BB–63) in Tokyo Bay. Over the next two days, she unloaded her embarked troops and their attendant cargo and, on the 4th, shaped a course for Leyte.

Whiteside arrived at Leyte on 11 September, fueled and provisioned, and then headed for Mindanao to load troops and cargo of the Army's 41st Infantry Division. She completed her mission at Mindanao on 19 September and departed the island on the 20th, returning to Tacloban on Leyte. On the 22d, the attack cargo ship stood out of Leyte Gulf on her way to Kure, Japan. Diverted to Buckner Bay, Okinawa, en route, the ship did not reach Japan until 5 October. She remained in Japan until 15 October at which time she got underway for Manila in the Philippines to load landing craft for duty in conjunction with the transfer of Nationalist Chinese troops. She arrived in Manila on 21 October and departed again on the 23d. On the 26th, she arrived in Haiphong, French Indochina, and began loading troops and cargo of the 583d Regiment of the Nationalist Chinese Army. The attack cargo ship stood out of Haiphong on 30 October and set a course for Chinwangtao where she arrived on 7 November. She disembarked the Chinese troops on the 7th and departed Chinwangtao the following day, bound for Taku. The ship remained at Taku until early December when she got underway for the United States. She arrived in San Francisco on 27 December.

Whiteside remained at San Francisco until the summer of 1946. On 5 June, she got underway for the Marshall Islands to provide support services for Operation "Crossroads," the large-scale nuclear tests conducted at Bikini Atoll that summer. She reached Kwajalein Atoll on 17 June and remained in the Marshalls assisting the operation until the end of August when she embarked upon a voyage that took her to Okinawa, Guam, Eniwetok, and thence back to Pearl Harbor. The ship remained at Pearl Harbor from the end of October to the latter part of November. On 23 November, she departed Oahu and set a course for the Marshalls. She arrived at Majuro on 30 November, visited Kwajalein during the first week in December, and Eniwetok in mid-month, before beginning a voyage that took her via Guam and Japan to China. She arrived in Yokosuka, Japan, on 16 January 1947 and, for the next six weeks, made port visits to Sasebo, Tsingtao and Shanghai. On 5 March, she departed Tsingtao and shaped a course—via Okinawa and Oahu—for the California coast. She arrived at San Francisco on 28 April and remained there until 15 June when she headed back to the Far East. *Whiteside* reached Tsingtao on 3 July and stayed there until 27 July when she sailed for Shanghai. From there, she moved on to Sasebo and thence to Yokosuka where she lay in port from 10 August to 3 September. The ship visited Okinawa during the second week in September and then spent the rest of the month at Guam in the Marianas. She returned to Tsingtao on 7 October but departed again five days later headed—via Yokosuka—back to the west coast.

Whiteside arrived in San Francisco on 29 October to begin a seven-month tour of duty plying the waters along the west coast of North America. She visited ports ranging south to San Diego and north to Adak and Kodiak in Alaska, though for the most part she remained in California waters. On 10 June 1948, she departed San Francisco to return to the western Pacific. She stopped at Pearl Harbor in mid-June and then continued on to Tsingtao where she arrived on 7 July. She visited Shanghai, Sasebo, and Yokosuka in July and August. Early in September, she stopped at Subic Bay in the Philippines before continuing on to the Marianas where she made port calls at Guam and Saipan. From Saipan, she set a course for Pearl Harbor on 21 September. Following a seven-day stop at Oahu, the attack cargo ship continued her voyage east on 7 October and arrived in Oakland, Calif., on the 12th. She remained there until 26 November when she got underway to return to the Far East. The ship made Yokosuka late in December and visited Kogo Saki,

Sasebo, and Tsingtao before beginning the return voyage late in January 1949.

On her way home, *Whiteside* made a 16-day stopover at Pearl Harbor before continuing on to San Francisco, where she arrived on 27 February. The ship remained there until 7 May when she moved to San Diego. After a pause at the latter port from 8 to 11 May, she departed there on the 11th and steamed, via Pearl Harbor, back to Yokosuka, which port she entered on 9 June. Over the following five weeks, she stopped at Sasebo, Okinawa, Taiwan, and Subic Bay before departing the latter place on 18 July to return home. Following the customary stop at Pearl Harbor from 30 July to 6 August, she resumed her voyage and entered San Francisco Bay on 11 August. In late August and early September, she made a round-trip voyage from the west coast to Pearl Harbor and back before entering the Mare Island Naval Shipyard for a three-month overhaul. She completed repairs on 4 January 1950 and departed Mare Island that same day, bound for the Orient. She enjoyed a month at Oahu, from 10 January to 11 February, and then continued on to Manila where she arrived on 24 February. During March, she visited Subic Bay, Guam, and Saipan before heading home on 6 April. On the night of 25 and 26 April, *Whiteside* shifted to San Francisco where she remained for a month before embarking upon a voyage to the Marshall Islands. That voyage, which lasted from 26 May to 10 July, included both outbound and return voyage stops at Pearl Harbor in addition to visits to Eniwetok and Kwajalein Atolls.

While *Whiteside* completed the return voyage to the west coast, events in the Far East ordained her return to that theater of operations. On 25 June, the armed forces of communist North Korea invaded the Republic of Korea (ROK), and the United States moved rapidly to bolster South Korea. With elements of the 1st Provisional Marine Brigade (Reinforced) embarked, *Whiteside* stood out of San Diego on 14 July, bound for Japan. She made port at Yokosuka on the 30th and, by 2 August, was at Pusan, South Korea, the major port through which United Nations men and materiel were being funneled into the conflict, and landed her marines. She departed Pusan on 5 August and reentered Yokosuka two days later. On the night of 1 and 2 September, she moved to Kobe and, on the 10th, from there to Inchon carrying troops and supplies to assault Inchon and begin the drive on Seoul. She remained at Inchon from the day of the initial landings, 15 September, until D plus 6 at which time she headed back to Japan. She arrived in Sasebo on the 22d but departed there again the next day to return to the United States. The attack cargo ship arrived at San Francisco on 8 October and remained there for three weeks before getting underway to return to the Far East. After a non-stop voyage, she arrived in Sasebo on 17 November. On the 23d, she weighed anchor for Yokosuka where she entered port on the 25th. After a 10-day stay at Yokosuka and a brief stop at Sasebo, *Whiteside* arrived at Inchon on 10 December to participate in the evacuation of United Nations forces on the heels of the massive communist Chinese intervention. The ship returned to Yokosuka on 17 December and headed for home on the 20th. She arrived in San Francisco on 5 January 1951.

Two round-trip voyages between San Francisco and Sasebo occupied her time between February and August 1951. From August to early December, she operated on the west coast and then headed back to the western Pacific. After stops at Sasebo and Yokosuka, *Whiteside* returned to San Francisco on 7 February 1952. The routine, voyages between San Francisco and Japan, occupied her for the remainder of her active career. She completed her last round-trip to the Orient on 28 February 1957 and, after almost a year of west coast operations, was decommissioned at Astoria, Oreg., on 30 January 1958. *Whiteside* remained in reserve with the Pacific Reserve Fleet until the spring of 1971 at which time she was sunk as a target.

Whiteside earned two battle stars for World War II service and four battle stars for service in the Korean conflict.

Whitewood

A species of tree, having a milky white bark, usually found in the south of Florida and in the Bahamas. In the United States, these trees are known as tulip trees, lindens, and cottonwoods.

(AN–63: dp. 1,275; l. 194'6½''; b. 34'7''; dr. 11'8½''; s. 12.1 k.; cpl. 57; a. 1 3''; cl. *Ailanthus*)

YN–84—a wooden-hulled net tender—was laid down

The net layer *Whitewood* (AN–63). (United States Naval Institute)

on 24 October 1942 at Rockland, Maine, by the Snow Shipyard, Inc.; named *Whitewood* on 5 July 1943; reclassified a net laying ship, AN–63, on 1 January 1944; launched on 21 April 1944; sponsored by Mrs. Eben Kenney; and commissioned on 17 July 1944, Lt. John I. Beam, USNR, in command.

Whitewood tended and laid nets and buoys at Boston, Mass., and at Newport and Melville, R.I., through the remainder of 1944 and into 1945. After a drydocking which began at the Boston Navy Yard in March 1945, the net layer shifted to Portland, Maine, in July. There she worked out of the Navy Net Depot at Little Diamond Island through the end of World War II in August 1945. After shifting to Newport, R.I., at the end of the month, she provided services for the naval net depot there and assisted in laying experimental net installations off Block Island.

Although apparently slated for inactivation on 22 October 1945, *Whitewood* apparently remained in commission through the end of the year. Early in 1946, the ship was placed in "deferred disposal" status pending possible future use. On 11 April, she was selected to participate in Operation "Nanook," Arctic exercises slated to take place in the summer of 1946. Taken to the Boston Naval Shipyard, the ship was under conversion for the rest of the spring and into the summer. During this time, on 20 May, a fire broke out on board the ship in one of her after storerooms and caused "Nanook's" planners to fear that the wooden-hulled ship's services would be lost to the pending operation. Fortunately, the fire was put out before major damage occurred; and the shipyard was able to repair the ship enabling her to take part in "Nanook" as scheduled.

The nucleus of the "Nanook" force, Task Force (TF) 68, consisted of *Norton Sound* (AV–11), *Atule* (SS–403), *Northwind* (WAG–282), *Alcona* (AK–157), *Beltrami* (AK–162), and *Whitewood*. On 3 July, *Whitewood* departed Boston to rendezvous with *Northwind* off Greenland.

For the remainder of July and into August, *Whitewood* operated in the Canadian Arctic, off western Greenland. She transited the Davis Strait to the northern part of Baffin Bay in company with *Northwind* and *Atule* and conducted exercises en route. All ships in TF 68 except the two AK's eventually rendezvoused at Melville Bight, Baffin Bay, on 20 July. *Whitewood* and *Atule* subsequently accompanied *Norton Sound* to Thule harbor to recover a PBM Mariner forced down with engine trouble.

From 22 July to 5 August, all activities in "Nanook" centered around Thule; *Norton Sound* remained at anchor there, in North Star Bay, servicing her two PBM's. Meanwhile, *Whitewood* and *Atule* operated from North Star Bay as they conducted exercises and tests in the Smith Sound-Kane Basin area. On 5 August, *Norton Sound* and *Whitewood* headed for Dundas Harbor, Devon Island, to attempt air and surface operations there. Unfortunately, the ships found the harbor iced over, with a belt of pack ice extending out three miles down the coast. *Northwind* later joined the two ships in the vicinity of Dundas Harbor, searching for a suitable anchorage that could accommodate the ships and their attached aircraft. *Whitewood* succeeded in finding a small, ice-free anchorage at Tay Bay, off northwestern Bylot Island.

In the ensuing weeks, *Whitewood* reconnoitered the coastal areas in Lancaster, Eclipse, and Jones Sounds, and Prince Regent, Admiralty, and Navy Board Inlets. Operating on this duty in company with *Northwind*, *Whitewood* landed shore parties that set up positions ashore to obtain terrestrial navigation "fixes" to dovetail with the photographic coverage obtained from the ships and planes of the project's task force.

Eventually, the summer Arctic weather deteriorated to the point where it hindered *Whitewood*'s surveying efforts—especially her terrestrial fixes. Released from the expedition in early September, *Whitewood* received

her sailing orders on 6 September and soon set her course for Boston. She arrived there on 19 September for repairs.

While at Boston, *Whitewood* was reclassified a miscellaneous auxiliary (AG) on 14 January 1947 and was given the alphanumeric hull number AG–129. She conducted refresher training in Chesapeake Bay soon thereafter and returned to Boston on 9 July to prepare for the next round of Arctic operations.

She sailed for the Canadian Arctic in company with the Navy's newest icebreaker, *Edisto* (AG–89), to participate in the successor to Operation "Nanook." The basic missions for TF 68 in this Arctic stint were the resupply of existing weather stations and the establishment of a new one at Melville Harbor, Ville Island.

Whitewood performed reconnaissance and survey work during the expedition, while *Wyandot* (AK–283) completed her assigned task, supplying the weather station at Thule. When *Whitewood* and *Edisto* tried to force their way through the ice to deliver needed supplies to the station at Slidre Fjord, the heavy pack ice damaged *Whitewood*'s bow sheathing, steering engine, and propeller, necessitating her return to Boston for repairs. After transferring her cargo to *Edisto*—which eventually forced her way through the pack ice to Slidre Fjord—*Whitewood* headed home.

Whitewood underwent repairs at Boston between 1 September and 18 October before sailing for Bayonne, N.J., for an overhaul that lasted through the end of October. She headed back northward and operated out of Argentia, Newfoundland; and Grondal and Sondrestromfjord, Greenland; into late 1948 supporting the International Ice Patrol. During the tour, she touched at such ports as Narsarssuak, Grondal, Argentia, and Breton.

On 6 December 1948, while the ship was operating in heavy pack ice, a shifting floe sprung a leak in her port chain locker. A seam opened there, and the ship began to fill uncontrollably. In order to save the ship, her commanding officer, Lt. Comdr. F. E. Clark, ordered her beached. Meanwhile, *Edisto*, which had just completed refresher training in Narragansett Bay, was summoned to join *Hoist* (ARS–40) in assisting *Whitewood* out of her predicament. Eventually, with a patch applied to her side, *Whitewood* made Boston on 8 January 1949—exactly one month after her serious accident. Subsequently cleared for disposal on 12 March, she was decommissioned at Newport on 1 April and struck from the Navy list on 7 June. She was then sold to Walter H. Wimms of Los Angeles, Calif., on 3 March 1950 and scrapped.

Whitfield

A county in northwestern Georgia.

Late in World War II, *Whitfield* (AKA–111)—an *Andromeda*-class attack cargo ship—was scheduled to be built for the Navy under a Maritime Commission contract (MC hull 2898) by the Federal Shipbuilding and Drydock Co., of Kearny, N.J. However, due to the end of the war in the Pacific, the contract for her construction was cancelled on 27 August 1945 before her keel was laid down.

Whitfield County

A county in northwestern Georgia.

(LST–1169: dp. 5,777 (f.); l. 384'0"; b. 56'6"; dr. 16'1" (max.); s. 14.5 k.; cpl. 153; trp. 376; a. 6 3"; cl. *LST–1156*)

LST–1156 was laid down on 26 November 1952 at Sturgeon Bay, Wis., by the Christy Corp.; launched on 22 August 1953; sponsored by Mrs. John L. Clarkson of Lake Forest, Ill.; and commissioned on 14 September 1954, Lt. Comdr. Frank S. Handler in command.

After shakedown training in the Gulf of Mexico, the tank landing ship departed New Orleans on 13 October, bound for her home port, Little Creek, Va. Upon arrival in the Tidewater area, the tank landing ship entered the Norfolk Naval Shipyard for an availability that lasted from 25 October to 4 November. She then joined LST Division 44, Squadron 4, Flotilla 2, Amphibious Force, Atlantic Fleet. For the remainder of 1954, *LST–1169* operated locally in Chesapeake Bay.

Following a short availability at Norfolk, between 5 and 22 January 1955, *LST–1169* made a run to Havana, Cuba, and, upon her return, reentered the shipyard for further work. She cleared Norfolk on 11 April, bound for the Caribbean, and took part in amphibious exercises at Vieques Island, Puerto Rico, with a reconnaissance team embarked. During that deployment, *LST–1169* visited Charlotte Amalie, St. Thomas, Virgin Islands, before heading home on 29 April with units of the 3d Battalion, 10th Marines, embarked. After debarking the marines at Morehead City, N.C., *LST–1169* pressed northward, reaching Norfolk on 6 May. Except for a brief cruise to Boston between 14 and 23 June, the ship remained at Little Creek well into the summer of 1955.

Named *Whitfield County* on 1 July 1955, the tank landing ship remained engaged in local operations into 1956, a year in which she underwent an overhaul at Norfolk between 23 January and 23 May. She then operated in Chesapeake Bay and off the Virginia capes until 13 August, when she got underway for the west coast. After skirting a Caribbean hurricane, she transited the Panama Canal on the 20th. Shortly after leaving the naval station at Rodman, Canal Zone, *Whitfield County* suffered an explosion and fire. The repairs necessitated by that accident delayed the ship's arrival at her new home port, San Diego, Calif., until 5 September.

Upon arrival, *Whitfield County* became flagship for LST Division 12—an assignment that soon changed when she was transferred to Division 11—and she soon commenced a regular slate of divisional and squadron exercises out of San Diego that stretched into August of 1957.

The ship departed San Diego on 13 August to begin her first deployment to the Western Pacific (WestPac). She called at Pearl Harbor between 24 August and 4 September and reached Yokosuka, Japan, on the 16th. A little over a week later, she proceeded to Camp McGill to load vehicles and embark troops for the first of several amphibious exercises. After maneuvers at Okinawa, *Whitfield County* then returned her passengers and cargo to Fukuoka, Japan, before she visited Sasebo en route to Yokosuka.

Three days after her arrival back at Yokosuka on 11 October, *Whitfield County* sailed to Iwakuni to pick up troops for additional landing exercises at Okinawa, returning to Yokosuka on 31 October. She departed Japanese waters on 3 November and reached Son Gap To, South Korea, soon thereafter, beaching on 7 and 8 November to load cargo that she returned to Yokosuka on the 12th. Six days later, after again loading troops and vehicles, *Whitfield County* sailed for Okinawa, offloading her cargo upon arrival and taking on board units of the 12th Regiment, 3d Marine Division.

The tank landing ship arrived at Dingalan Bay, Luzon, on 30 November and served as the base for a reconnaissance team during amphibious exercises that lasted until 10 December. She then joined elements of the 7th Fleet at sea for exercises which kept her busy until she arrived at Subic Bay, Philippines, the day after Christmas.

Whitfield County remained there into 1958 before steaming to Naha, Okinawa, on 4 February, for the first of two voyages lifting marines and their vehicles. She arrived back at Dingalan Bay on 26 February for exercises in which she acted as receiving ship for simulated battle casualties. On 8 March, *Whitfield County* headed for the west coast and reached San Diego on the last day of March.

Between 14 April and 3 May, *Whitfield County* underwent an overhaul at the National Steel and Shipbuilding Corp., San Diego. She then operated off the southern California coast into the summer. Her routine was broken late in July during the crisis in Lebanon, when American armed forces went on alert for a global posture of readiness. During that time, she cruised to Pearl Harbor between 25 July and 20 August, after which time she resumed her regular routine out of San Diego.

Shifting to San Francisco, and later to Mare Island and Alameda, *Whitfield County* underwent an overhaul at the Todd Shipyard Corp. in preparation for the ship's second WestPac deployment. She sailed for the Far East on 23 April 1959, called at Pearl Harbor en route, and reached Yokosuka on the 22d of May. She then visited Hong Kong between 9 and 16 June and returned to Sasebo on the 21st, via Naha, Okinawa. She then lifted LVT's (landing vehicles, tracked), to Chinhae, Korea, between 22 and 28 June before returning to Sasebo.

Subsequently loading elements of the 3d Marine Division at Naha on 6 July, *Whitfield County* transported the marines to Numazu, Japan, arriving there a week later. Shifting to Yokosuka shortly thereafter, the tank landing ship remained there into August, undergoing needed upkeep and conducting local operations.

Underway for Inchon, Korea, on 5 August, *Whitfield County* rendezvoused with other units of Landing Ship Squadron 1 and took part in Operation "Seahorse," a full-scale joint amphibious exercise with embarked units of the American Army's 7th Cavalry Regiment. En route to the maneuver site, *Whitfield County* evaded Typhoon "Ellen." Embarking the elements of the 7th Cavalry at Inchon soon after her arrival on 12 August, the tank landing ship sortied for Pohang Dong, on the coast of Korea, to take part in Operation "Seahorse." *Whitfield County* proved to be the only LST involved, because the other units of Landing Ship Squadron 1 had been unable to reach the area due to typhoon evasion tactics.

Visiting Otaru and Hakodate at the end of August as part of President Dwight D. Eisenhower's "People-to-People" program, *Whitfield County* was en route to Buckner Bay, Okinawa, for routine training evolutions with amphibious tractor units of the 3d Marine Division when she was diverted for contingency loading at Naha, Okinawa. She received those orders in light of the developing crisis in the land-locked kingdom of Laos.

Whitfield County remained in a high state of readiness in the Okinawa area from 7 September to 12 October. She steamed between Naha and Buckner Bay during that time and also conducted routine training evolutions, making one transit of the Taiwan Strait and evading five typhoons. During that period, the ship earned a well-done from Commander, Amphibious Squadron 1 for her contributions to relief efforts for Japanese victims of Typhoon "Vera."

Ordered to Sasebo on 12 October, the ship underwent voyage repairs there; cleared that port on 2 November, bound for the west coast of the United States; and reached San Diego on 24 November. She then remained at her home port in leave and upkeep status for the remainder of the year.

Following local operations out of her home port into the summer of 1960—including participation in Operation "Swandive"—held off Camp Pendleton on 8 and 9 February and Operation "Bigtop," held between 2 and 10 May—*Whitfield County* got underway for her third WestPac tour. After stopping briefly at Pearl Harbor between 22 and 26 June, the tank landing ship joined Landing Ship Squadron 9 in Japan on 1 July.

Homeported then at Yokosuka, Japan, *Whitfield County* would spend the next 13 years in the Far East, supporting American presence in the Orient. Her operating schedule reflected the growing American involvement in the affairs of Southeast Asia—particularly in Vietnam.

Whitfield County spent the better part of August 1960 conducting independent ship exercises and transporting marines between Naha and Numazu and back. She also engaged in the usual typhoon evasions common to operations in that area of the world. In September, the tank landing ship departed Yokosuka for a six-week cruise that was slated to take the ship to Okinawa, Hong Kong, and Subic Bay; but, soon after leaving Okinawa, she received word to report to Subic Bay. There, she rendezvoused with *Windham County* (LST–1170) and set out for Singapore, Federated Malay States, on 26 September.

Reaching Singapore on the 30th, the two tank landing ships embarked 600 Malayan troops and their gear, part of a United Nations (UN) force assigned peacekeeping duties in the turbulent Belgian Congo. Early in July, Belgian troops had gone into action against mutinous Congolese troops, the Congo government appealing to the UN for "military assistance." In the ensuing weeks, much bloody fighting had taken place, and the first UN troops (Tunisians) arrived in mid-July.

Departing Singapore on 3 October, *Whitfield County* and *Windham County* tarried briefly at Port Swettenham, Malayan Republic, to complete the loading and embarkation process begun at Singapore. On 4 October, the two amphibious ships departed Port Swettenham, bound for the port of Matadi, located on the Congo River.

Whitfield County rounded the Cape of Good Hope on 22 October and reached the mouth of the Congo on the 31st. She and her sistership then ascended the river some 82 miles to Matadi. After disembarking the 600 troops and their equipment, the two tank landing ships departed Matadi on 2 November, bound for Yokosuka. They reached their home port five days before Christmas of 1960 and spent the remainder of the year in port.

For the next two years, *Whitfield County* continued her operations out of Sasebo and ranged from Okinawa to Japan, with port visits at Japanese ports and to Hong Kong. She also operated upon occasion at Subic Bay.

In mid-1964, however, the tempo of operations for the tank landing ship began to change—reflecting the increased role that the United States was playing in Vietnam.

On 22 July, *Whitfield County* departed Yokosuka for a routine trip to Okinawa, but was called away for duty off the coast of Vietnam. She remained at sea for 41 days with marines embarked, on station off the coast of South Vietnam and ready for any contingency. During that time, the Tonkin Gulf incident occurred early in August and further escalated tensions between the United States and communist North Vietnam.

Whitfield County—her services apparently not needed at that time—returned to Yokosuka early in October for much-needed leave and upkeep. She next conducted type training, made a troop lift from Numazu to Okinawa, and underwent more upkeep in November and December, before rounding out the year in readiness to operate in South Vietnamese waters once more if the situation demanded it.

With a logistical support load on board, *Whitfield County* departed Okinawa, bound for South Vietnam. She arrived at Danang on 5 January 1965 and offloaded part of the cargo before shifting to Chu Lai to discharge the remainder. She sailed for Subic Bay the following day, 6 January, as part of the Subic-RVN (Republic of Vietnam) shuttle force. Arriving at Subic Bay three days later, the tank landing ship took on a load of cargo earmarked for Vietnamese ports and sailed for Danang on the 16th with another logistical support load on board.

After unloading that cargo at Danang, *Whitfield County* shifted to Camranh Bay to load cargo for transport to Phan Rang and Saigon. Ultimately reaching Saigon on 28 January and unloading the remaining cargo, she took on board cargo to be lifted to Qui Nhon. Subsequently routed onward to Okinawa after loading cargo at Danang, the tank landing ship reached Okinawa on 10 February.

Taking on board elements of the Army's 4th Cavalry Regiment, *Whitfield County* proceeded to Saigon, reaching that port on 20 February. After returning to Okinawa, via Danang, Vietnam, and Keelung, Formosa, *Whitfield County* subsequently steamed back to Vietnamese waters with elements of the 1st Marine Division embarked and put the marines ashore at Chu Lai. The tank landing ship continued her busy pace of operations, carrying return cargo from Danang to Okinawa (arriving at the latter place on 2 April), before she embarked marine elements for maneuvers at Numazu. Reaching her destination on 6 April, she immediately disembarked the marines and returned to Yokosuka for overhaul.

Following that yard work and the ensuing refresher training, *Whitfield County* remained at Yukosuka through much of the summer before sailing for Iwakuni, Japan, and arriving there on 27 August to load equipment and embark men of Marine Air Group (MAG) 13 for transfer to Vietnam. Underway on the 29th, *Whitfield County* reached Chu Lai on 6 September. She then returned to Japan and made a second trip from Iwakuni to Chu Lai, bringing in the second element of MAG–13.

Whitfield County proceeded thence to Danang to embark elements of Marine Battalion Landing Team (BLT) 1/9 for passage to Okinawa. The tank landing ship then proceeded to Naha, where she took on board the men and equipment of the Army's 526th Engineering Detachment. Offloading at Qui Nhon, the ship shifted to Chu Lai and Danang, where she loaded return equipment and sailed for Okinawa. Upon delivering her equipment to Okinawa, she pushed on for Japan and reached Yokosuka on 24 October.

The ship's upkeep period in Japan lasted into November, when she headed for Hong Kong and six days of "R and R" (rest and recreation). Departing the British Crown Colony on 23 November, *Whitfield County* proceeded to Kaohsiung, Taiwan, where she loaded 600 tons of cement slated for transport to South Vietnam. Reaching Phan Rang on the 30th, the tank landing ship offloaded her cargo and departed that port on 1 December, bound for Danang. The normally short trip became a four-day voyage after she ran into heavy weather soon after leaving Phan Rang, but she finally reached Danang on the 5th and took on board equipment for lift to Okinawa. After first offloading the retrograde cargo at Naha, *Whitfield County* reached her home port on 15 December and remained there over Christmas.

She was not to enjoy a New Year's Day in port, though, as she sailed for Vietnamese waters on 29 December, pointing her bow toward Vung Tau and her first deployment with Riverine Forces. Slated to join River Assault Flotilla 1, *Whitfield County* arrived at Cap St. Jacques on 7 January 1967, embarked a river pilot and one River Assault Flotilla liaison officer and proceeded up the muddy Long Tau River to Saigon. She subsequently beached at Newport South Ramp that evening and remained there until the 10th, embarking men and equipment of River Assault Flotilla 1.

Departing Saigon on the 10th, *Whitfield County* arrived at Vung Tau late that same evening. The next day, the tank landing ship began providing messing, berthing, and logistical support for the men of the river assault force and the 1,800 troops from the 9th Army Division who were training with the riverine forces. On 26 February, *Whitfield County* weighed anchor and headed for Yokosuka, arriving there on 9 March. On 5 April, she got underway for Okinawa to load cargo for South Vietnam. A port visit slated for 11 April at Keelung, Taiwan, was cancelled due to the urgent need for tank landing ships for the impending Operation "Oregon." The ship sped to Chu Lai, reached that port on the 15th, and discharged her cargo upon arrival. She then took on board 92 tons of vehicles, 200 officers and men, and the cargo of a Marine Corps headquarters battalion; and proceeded to Danang where she arrived the next day.

Offloading upon her arrival, *Whitfield County* came under the operational control of Naval Support Activities, Danang (NavSuppAct), to support Operation "Oregon" and remained in that status until the 23d. During that time, the tank landing ship conducted two beachings at Chu Lai and transported a total of 1,300 tons of general cargo, bombs, and vehicles.

Released from "Oregon" on 23 April, *Whitfield County* departed Chu Lai and headed toward the Philippines for type training and a visit to Manila. En route, however, the workhorse tank landing ship was ordered to proceed at "all best speed" to Subic Bay. Upon arrival there on the 25th, she loaded cargo from *Seminole* (AKA-104). Then, after picking up additional ammunition, *Whitfield County* got underway on the 27th, bound for South Vietnam.

On the morning of the 30th, *Whitfield County* rendezvoused with Amphibious Ready Group (ARG) "Alfa"—consisting of *Okinawa* (LPH-3), *Bayfield* (APA-33), and *Point Defiance* (LSD-31)—which was then conducting Operation "Beaver Cage." The operation—an over-the-beach landing in quest of one battalion and three companies of local Viet Cong guerrillas and at least one North Vietnamese Army (NVA) battalion—had begun on the 28th.

Assigned an operational area after transferring men and mail brought out from Subic Bay, the tank landing ship steamed in the amphibious objective area until 10 May, when she embarked 100 patients and 100 empty oxygen bottles from *Sanctuary* (AH-17) for transportation to Danang. Reaching her destination the following day, *Whitfield County* returned to ARG "Alfa" on the morning of the 13th, again landed passengers and delivered mail, refilled oxygen bottles, ice cream, and other dairy products to *Sanctuary*. Upon the termination of "Beaver Cage" that afternoon—the enemy having fled—the tank landing ship proceeded to a holding area at sea northeast of Danang and rendezvoused with the other ships of the ARG that evening.

Three days later, in a commanders' conference on board *Okinawa*, the commander of Amphibious Squadron 9 revealed the next operation, "Beau Charger." On the morning of 17 May, the task group rendezvoused with *Regulus* (AF-57) for replenishment and, during the early evening hours, began its approach to the demilitarized zone (DMZ).

The largest concentration of naval gunfire support ships since Korea softened the DMZ prior to ARG "Alfa's" assault that was aimed at destroying enemy forces and supplies and evacuating non-combatants. At 0800, Operation "Beau Charger" commenced as destroyers quickly moved in and blasted the enemy guns. Resistance at the beach was confined to sniper fire and shells from quickly silenced North Vietnamese shore batteries. Pronounced resistance came at helicopter landing zones, however; but despite that, the helo-landed marines linked up with tank units and initiated search and destroy operations that lasted through the next week.

Whitfield County operated in support of "Beau Charger" until 25 May, conducting "Boat Reps" (replenishment via landing craft and boats) of supplies needed ashore with craft from *Point Defiance*. Significantly, "Beau Charger" proved that naval gunfire was highly effective; but also showed that such support was needed farther inland as well. That requirement ultimately resulted in the recommissioning of *New Jersey* (BB-62) for gunfire support duties.

Proceeding to Danang on 25 May, *Whitfield County* reached her destination on the 26th and, after offloading, was detached from ARG "Alfa." She subsequently

transported a load of bombs from Danang to Chu Lai, loading return vehicles there for transportation to Naha, before she returned to Danang to load equipment and embark men of Amphibious Construction Battalion 1, Detachment "B." The tank landing ship departed Vietnamese waters on the morning of 3 June and reached Naha on the 9th. Offloading the vehicles and backloading deadlined generators, *Whitfield County* arrived back at Yokosuka on the 14th.

Whitfield County returned to Vietnamese waters in the summer to resume her support operations for riverine activities in the Mekong Delta region, basing again at Vung Tau. She departed Yokosuka on 28 July and reached her destination—via Hong Kong—on 17 August. Relieving *Vernon County* (LST-1161) of TF 117 support duties on the following day, *Whitfield County* got underway on 20 August for the confluence of the Vam Co and Soirap Rivers to rendezvous with the Mobile Riverine Base (MRB).

From 20 August to 5 September, *Whitfield County* provided "housekeeping" services and support for River Division III, "C" Company, 2d Brigade, 9th Infantry Division, and "A" Company, 9th Battalion. She supplied ammunition, water, and rations to the troops in the field; was the focal point of helicopter support operations; served as combat store warehouse; and provided mortuary services for the killed-in-action (KIA) periodically returned to the ship.

Toward the end of that period, on 3 September, the MRB shifted its base of operations from Soirap-Vam Co area back to Vung Tau to support projected riverine strikes into the Rung Sat special zone. On the 11th, the MRB proceeded to the Mekong River entrance, escorted by various units of the Riverine Division who provided minesweeping, close fire support, and reconnaissance when needed. Subsequently, while located in the Dong Tam area, *Whitfield County* assisted search and destroy operations in the Cam Son secret zone, Dinh Tuong province, Kien Hoa province, and in the Giong Troms district.

On 28 September, the MRB shifted again, this time to the confluence of the Cua Tien and Cua Dai Rivers, to facilitate strike operations into Kien Hoa province. *Whitfield County* worked in that locale until 1 October, when the MRB was shifted back to Dong Tam to support projected strikes into the Western Ben Zong secret zone, Dinh Troung province, to destroy North Vietnamese and Viet Cong forces in that area.

Whitfield County subsequently supported mobile riverine operations at Vung Tau and back at the junction of the Soirap and Vam Co Rivers into late October. While in the latter locale, elements of the riverine forces provided the necessary security during the lower house elections for the Republic of Vietnam's parliament. Returning to Vung Tau on 24 October, *Whitfield County* was there relieved by *Westchester County* (LST-1167) and returned to Japan.

The tank landing ship then underwent a period of upkeep back at Yokosuka before she returned to Vietnamese waters at the end of November. She operated between Danang and Chu Lai through early December, transporting vehicles and other cargo, before she steamed back to Yokosuka. She arrived back at her home port three days before Christmas and remained in port until late in January 1968.

Underway on 22 January with a cargo of two pontoon causeway sections, the vehicles and men of BMU-1, and a CH-46 helicopter, with its accompanying "Sea Van"—an experimental housing seeing its first operational test and evaluation on *Whitfield County*—the tank landing ship headed for Vietnam. Touching at Naha en route, *Whitfield County* reached Danang on 31 January; transferred the "Sea Van" to *Vernon County*; and relieved that ship as support LST for ARG "Bravo." With the relief and transfer of the marines and equipment completed, *Whitfield County* took on board the men and mail to be transported to ARG "Bravo," and got underway on 2 February.

Over the ensuing month and one-half, *Whitfield County* operated with ARG "Bravo" within various operating areas off the DMZ, occasionally returning to Danang for mail, fleet freight, and passengers for delivery to the other units of the ready group. The ship also sailed to Subic Bay as part of the task force for upkeep between 21 and 28 February before she returned to Vietnamese waters. *Terrell County* (LST–1157) relieved *Whitfield County* as support LST at Danang on 14 March.

After a subsequent port call at Hong Kong and a quick run to her home port for restricted availability, *Whitfield County* returned to Vietnamese waters for a resumption of operations with the Mobile Riverine Force, in mid-July 1968, again relieving sistership *Vernon County*, at Dong Tam. During her deployment with TF 117 in ensuing months, *Whitfield County* operated on a nearly non-stop, 24-hour a day basis, supporting the Army's 4/47th Infantry Battalion, 9th Division, and three helicopters of an Army aviation detachment, as well as the boats and men of River Assault Division 92. By the time *Westchester County* relieved *Whitfield County* on 23 September, the latter had travelled over 900 miles within the Mekong Delta, processed over 25,000 hot rations, and handled roughly 4,000 tons of cargo.

Subsequently visiting Bangkok, Thailand, for "R and R," *Whitfield County* then headed for Danang, where she side-loaded tow causeway sections for transportation to Okinawa. She then returned to Yokosuka for repairs before again heading for Vietnam toward the end of November. Touching at Subic Bay en route, the tank landing ship reputedly became the first ship of her type to utilize water-filled causeway sections to serve as armor along the thinly-armored sides of the ship. The causeway sections would provide a water-filled barrier against recoilless rifle projectiles and rockets.

After relieving *Washtenaw County* (LST–1166) at Dong Tam on the last day of November, *Whitfield County* spent the rest of 1968 as support LST for Mobile Riverine Group "Alfa," TG 117.1, one of the two task groups that made up Mobile Riverine Flotilla 1. Other ships of MRG "Alfa" were the barracks ships *Benewah* (APB–35) and *Colleton* (APB–36), the landing craft repair ship *Sphinx* (ARL–24), and *APL*'s *26* and *30*. Embarked in *Whitfield County* were elements of the Army's 9th Infantry and a "Cyclops" aviation detachment, equipped with Hughes CH–6 Cayuse helicopters. The ship herself performed a five-fold role: (1) maintaining a round-the-clock, air- and water-mobile resupply readiness to provide field units with ammunition, rations, fresh water, and fuel; (2) serving as a mobile base for helicopter operations; (3) providing harassment and call-fire when necessary; (4) supplying boat service among the ships of the MRG; and (5) providing subsistence, berthing, and services for embarked personnel.

At 2330 on 9 January 1969, the MRG base at Dong Tam came under enemy rocket and mortar attack. *Whitfield County* went to general quarters and participated in counterbattery fire, hurling 16 rounds of 3-inch projectiles in the direction of the hostile fire. Although securing at midnight, the tank landing ship manned her guns a half-hour later, lobbing three rounds of call fire.

Whitfield County subsequently shifted from Ben Tre to the Song Ham Loung anchorage and returned to Dong Tam at 1100 on 20 January to commence turnover to *Vernon County*, her relief with TG 117.1. That night, communist forces attacked the MRG and the base at Dong Tam with rockets and mortars; *Whitfield County* went to general quarters at 2159 and, between 2250 and 2300, expended 12 rounds against the enemy artillerymen. Between 1 and 22 January, *Whitfield County*'s gunners loosed a total of 78 rounds of call-fire; and the ship held flight quarters for the recovery of Cayuse and UH–1b Huey helicopters 306 times, without mishap. At 2300 on 23 January, the tank landing ship's turnover to *Vernon County* was complete.

However, there was more work for *Whitfield County* before she could clear the muddy Vietnamese waters. At 2321, she headed for Vung Tau. There, she took over from *Tom Green County* (LST–1159) in supporting and resupplying TG 117.2, MRG "Bravo." Her sister ship had recently been damaged in a Viet Cong rocket attack while beached at the Vung Tau ramps.

Late the next day—after loading a tank deck cargo of palletized ammunition and C-rations; and a main-deck load of crated supplies, spare parts, stores and fresh provisions—*Whitfield County* got underway for the mouth of the Bassac River (Cua Tranh De). On the morning of the 26th, *Whitfield County*, escorted by two PBR's, transited the Bassac River without incident and over the ensuing days resupplied and provisioned the ships of TG 117.2—*Satyr* (ARL–26), *Mercer* (APB–39), and *Nueces* (APB–40). The tank landing ship then returned to Vung Tau, where she was relieved as support LST for TG 117.2 by *Iredell County* (LST–839) on 30 January. At noon that day, *Whitfield County* headed for Hong Kong.

The tank landing ship spent six days at the British Crown Colony before she sailed for Okinawa to pick up cargo earmarked for shipment to her home port. After loading vehicles and nine men from Beachmaster Unit 1, WestPac Detachment, at Red Beach 1, Chin Wan, Okinawa, *Whitfield County* proceeded on to Yokosuka, reaching that port on the morning of 17 February.

After upkeep at her home port in late February, *Whitfield County* acted as observer at the Republic of Korea (ROK) Navy amphibious exercise, Phiblex 1–69, at Chinhae, Korea, between 28 March and 2 April. During that time, she also trained ROK naval personnel. The tank landing ship subsequently returned to her home port for more upkeep before she sailed, via Subic Bay, for Vietnamese waters where she loaded side-protection causeway sections.

Arriving at Dong Tam on 8 May, she there relieved sistership *Windham County* as support LST for River Assault Flotilla 1, TF 117. As before, the ship operated alternately at Dong Tam, Song Ham Loung (Ben Tre), and My Tho. At 0205 on 6 June, while the ship was at Dong Tam, four rounds of hostile fire landed between 50 and 300 yards from the ships of the MRF. *Whitfield County* immediately set general quarters; and, in the next 35 minutes, her guns hurled some 140 rounds of 3-inch counterbattery fire at the enemy artillery. The riverine force again came under enemy fire that morning; *Whitfield County* again blasted the enemy positions with 170 more rounds of 3-inch projectiles.

Whitfield County subsequently shifted to Ben Tre but returned to Dong Tam by 13 June. While the ship lay anchored there, Storekeeper 3d Class L. E. Smith, assigned as roving sentry on the port side of the ship, spotted a swimmer in the water at 0100 on the 15th. Since Viet Cong sappers were known to have been active in that area, Storekeeper Smith promptly opened fire. Within a short time, the water around the ship was thoroughly grenaded. Later that morning, a Vietnamese body that had been shot was found floating nearby. For his prompt action, Storekeeper Smith received the recommendation for the Navy Commendation Medal for "effectively thwarting an attempt to mine the ship."

Three days later, rocket fire landed within 50 yards of the ship, at 1405 on 18 June. Unable to return the fire because of the presence of "friendly" forces in the area, *Whitfield County* shifted her anchorage to avoid being hit. Later that afternoon, the riverine force shifted its anchorage back to My Tho.

The LST was relieved by *Tom Green County* on Independence Day, 4 July. Between 8 May and 4 July, *Whitfield County* had expended some 2,982 rounds of 3-inch projectiles on call-fire and counterbattery fire; conducted some 850 helicopter landings; and travelled 394 miles within the Mekong Delta. She had also witnessed the gradual turnover of all River Assault Flotilla 1 assets to the Republic of Vietnam Navy, the beginning of the redeployment of the 9th Infantry Division from the Mekong Delta; and the gradual disbanding of TF 117. When she sailed on 5 July, she left the Delta region for the last time.

Returning to Yokosuka via Keelung, Taiwan, *Whitfield County* soon commenced a badly needed overhaul, one that lasted into the autumn. For the remainder of the year, the tank landing ship operated locally in Japanese waters.

For the next three years, *Whitfield County* worked out of Yokosuka, touching occasionally at Okinawa in the course of amphibious maneuvers and exercises and at Subic Bay in the Philippines. She served three tours with ARG "Bravo" in 1970; two tours as support LST for Operation "Market Time" interdiction operations, out of Vung Tau in 1971; she served one tour of ARG "Alfa" and one with "Market Time" forces in 1972. Highlighting the ship's activities in 1971 were her support activities for the grounded refrigerator ship *Regulus* (AF–57) at Hong Kong. Typhoon "Rose" slammed into the Chinese mainland on 16 August of that year, forcing the auxiliary aground on rocks in the western harbor. During that period in late August 1971, *Whitfield County* provided berthing and messing facilities for *Regulus'* crew.

Reaching Yokosuka two days before Christmas of 1972 after exercising with Marine Corps units at Okinawa, *Whitfield County* remained at her long-time home port into 1973. There, she was decommissioned on 15 March 1973. *Whitfield County* was struck from the Navy list in May 1977 and slated for subsequent sale.

Whatfield County performed services of signal importance during the Vietnam War—services that were important but, due to their nature, largely unsung in the public eye. Nonetheless, the ship earned the Presidential Unit Citation (for her operations with TF 117 from 8 May to 5 July 1969); three Navy Unit Commendations; three Meritorious Unit Commendations; and 12 battle stars.

Whiting

A small European food fish.

The name *Whiting* was assigned to SS–433—a *Balao*-class submarine to be built at Philadelphia, Pa., by the Cramp Shipbuilding Co.—but the contract for her construction was cancelled on 29 July 1944.

Whiting, Kenneth, see *Kenneth Whiting.*

Whitley

Counties in Indiana and Kentucky.

(AKA–91: dp. 13,910 (tl.); l. 459'2''; b. 63'0''; dr. 26'4'' (lim.); s. 16.5 k. (tl.); cpl. 366; a. 1 5'', 8 40mm.; cl. *Andromeda*; T. C2–S–B1)

Whitley (AKA–91) was laid down on 2 May 1944 at Oakland, Calif., by the Moore Drydock Co. under a Maritime Commission contract (MC hull 1191); launched on 22 June 1944; sponsored by Mrs. John R. Reilly; delivered to the Navy on 21 September 1944; and commissioned that same day, Comdr. Albert C. Thompson, USNR, in command.

Following shakedown training out of San Diego, *Whitley* loaded cargo at San Francisco and sailed on 9 November, bound for the Hawaiian Islands. She arrived at Oahu on 27 November and remained in the islands until late January 1945 conducting amphibious training and testing amphibious equipment and techniques. On 27 January, the attack cargo ship departed Pearl Harbor and steamed for the western Pacific. The ship arrived in Eniwetok lagoon on 5 February, took on fuel and supplies, and then continued her voyage on the 7th. She arrived in the Marianas soon thereafter and conducted landing rehearsals at Saipan and Tinian until 16 February when she got underway for the Bonin Islands.

The attack cargo ship arrived off Iwo Jima at dawn on the 19th and began disembarking elements of the 5th Marine Division. She remained in the vicinity of Iwo Jima for eight days in all, but her only brush with combat came on the night of 23 and 24 February when her antiaircraft battery briefly and inconclusively engaged two Japanese planes. In the evening of 27 February, she joined a convoy bound via the New Hebrides for Guadalcanal. The ship stopped at Espiritu Santo on 15 March and embarked members of the Royal New Zealand Air Force for transportation to Guadalcanal. At the latter island, she exchanged the New Zealanders for a complement of Hawaii-bound marines.

Whitley arrived back at Oahu on 16 April. She conducted voyage repairs at Pearl Harbor and then underwent refresher training near Maui until 11 May when she left Hawaii with a convoy bound for San Francisco, where she arrived on 18 May. Two days later, she sailed for Aberdeen, Wash., where she loaded cargo bound for Hawaii. *Whitley* arrived at Oahu on 12 June and, after a 10-day stopover, got underway for the ammunition depot at Bangor, Wash. There, in mid-July, the attack cargo ship took on another cargo for Hawaii, returned to Pearl Harbor later in the month, and remained there through the end of hostilities on 15 August.

USS *Whitley* (AKA–91), August 1952. (80–G–483292)

The ship departed Oahu on 23 August and arrived in Lingayen Gulf in the Philippines on 24 September. There, she embarked troops of the Army's 27th Regimental Combat Team (RCT). On 1 October, she set sail for Japan and arrived off Wakayama on the 7th. After more than a fortnight's wait while minesweepers cleared the mines from Nagoya Channel, she anchored in Ise Bay near Nagoya on 27 October and began unloading her passengers and their equipment.

She departed Nagoya on 1 November and set course for the Marianas. She entered Apra harbor, Guam, on the 8th, embarked Navy officers and men for transportation home; and began her homeward voyage on 17 November. Following stops at Oahu, Panama, and Jacksonville, Fla., *Whitley* arrived at Norfolk on 2 January 1946. Repairs at Norfolk preceded a series of voyages between ports on the east coast—such as Bayonne, N.J., and Norfolk, Va.—and places in the North Atlantic—such as Argentia, Newfoundland; Guantanamo Bay, Cuba; and Narsarssuak, Greenland. In November, she began the first of three round-trip voyages from the east coast to Bremerhaven in Germany. Those four voyages occupied her time completely until August of 1947.

Between August 1947 and May 1949, she made a series of training cruises and supply voyages from Norfolk and Bayonne to various locations in the Caribbean area. In May and June of 1949, she added the Mediterranean Sea to her itinerary with a round-trip voyage from the east coast, via Casablanca, to Naples, Italy, where she embarked detachees from the 6th Fleet for transportation home. She arrived back in Norfolk on 29 June and resumed her passenger and cargo runs to bases in the Caribbean area. That employment occupied her time until the summer of 1950. On 12 July 1950, she embarked upon a voyage which took her to Thule, Greenland, and to Cornwallis Island in the far northern reaches of Canada. She returned to the United States at Boston on 31 August and spent the remainder of 1950 and the entire year of 1951 plying the waters along the Atlantic coast and in the Caribbean engaged in training exercises and transporting people and supplies between various bases. The only exception to that routine came in April and May of 1951 when she made a round-trip voyage from Norfolk to Casablanca, Morocco, and back.

The year 1952 brought with it increased duty in European and African waters. On 16 January, she put to sea from Norfolk, bound, via Casablanca, for Naples and Genoa in Italy. She returned to Norfolk on 5 March; but, after a logistics run to Newfoundland in April, she embarked upon another voyage to the Mediterranean on 10 May. After visiting Golfe Juan and Naples, she headed back to the United States, arriving in Norfolk on 25 June. Two months of local operations ensued. However, on 26 August, the attack cargo ship headed back to Europe—this time to Greenock, Scotland, to participate in a NATO exercise, Operation "Mainbrace," conducted off the coast of Norway. At the conclusion of the exercise, she visited Portsmouth, England, before returning to Norfolk where she arrived on 11 October and resumed local operations and training and supply cruises to the Caribbean area. In November and December of 1953, she made another round-trip voyage to Casablanca and Naples to carry cargo to the 6th Fleet. She returned to Norfolk on 23 December and then conducted local operations until 2 March 1954, when she began another deployment in the Mediterranean with the 6th Fleet. She sailed direct to Naples but, on the homeward voyage, stopped at Casablanca and at Portsmouth, England. She returned to Norfolk on 22 April and resumed her normal routine. Later in the year, she made her final voyage to the Mediterranean and then conducted fleet exercises in the West Indies.

On 29 January 1955, she entered the Monti Marine Shipyard in Brooklyn, N.Y., to begin inactivation overhaul. In April 1955, she moved south to Charleston,

S.C., to complete the inactivation process. *Whitley* was decommissioned at Charleston on 16 August 1955. She remained inactive, berthed with the Charleston Group, Atlantic Reserve Fleet, until 1 July 1960, when her name was struck from the Navy list, and she was transferred to the Maritime Administration for layup. She was reinstated on the Navy list on 1 December 1961 and then transferred to the Italian Navy in February 1962 as a loan. She served as *Etna* (A5328) until 1 May 1973. She was returned to the United States Navy and simultaneously sold to the Italian Navy. Her name was struck from the Navy list for the last time on 1 May 1973.

Whitley earned one battle star during World War II.

Whitman

Robert Scott Whitman, Jr.—born on 1 January 1916 at Johnson City, N.Y.—was appointed a midshipman on 24 August 1935 and graduated from the Naval Academy with the Class of 1939. After sea duty in the heavy cruiser *Quincy* (CA–39) from 26 June 1939 to 1 February 1941, Whitman underwent heavier-than-air instruction at the Naval Air Station at Pensacola, Fla. He won his wings there and then received further instruction at the Transition Training Squadron, Pacific Fleet, before he reported to Patrol Squadron (VP) 44 on 4 November 1941.

Whitman remained with VP–44 into the spring and early summer of 1942. With the reinforcement of Midway Atoll in the face of an impending Japanese thrust, VP–44 was dispatched to that key island base. During the first few days of June 1942, the PBY's based at Midway flew long patrols over the trackless ocean, searching for signs of enemy shipping. Then, on 3 June, came the first surface contact.

One of the searchers on patrol that morning, Whitman's plane was the third to spot the enemy ships and at 0925 radioed a report calling attention to the "main body." After sending back a second message amplifying the data contained in his report of the initial sighting, Whitman brought his plane back to Midway in accordance with instructions.

The following day at 0715, his PBY–5A Catalina was again airborne; he reported that the aircraft was being "opposed by two enemy observation planes." That proved to be the last word heard from Whitman's aircraft, as the enemy planes shot it down in flames.

Records of what happened later are sketchy, but it appears that about half of the plane's crew was lost; six survivors, including the badly wounded Ensign Jack H. Camp, USNR, were picked up by a search PBY on 6 June. Camp later died at 0203 on the 7th.

(DE–24: dp. 1,140; l. 289'5"; b. 35'1"; dr. 8'3" (mean); s. 21 k.; a. 3 3", 4 1.1", 9 20mm., 2 dct., 8 dcp., 1 dcp. (hh.); cl. *Evarts*)

Whitman (BDE–24) was laid down on 7 September 1942 at the Mare Island Navy Yard, Vallejo, Calif., and was initially earmarked for transfer to the Royal Navy under lend-lease. However, the Navy decided to retain the ship for its own use; and she was reclassified to DE–24 on 7 January 1943. She was launched on 19 January 1943; sponsored by Mrs. Josephine P. Whitman, the widow of the late Lt. (jg.) Whitman; and commissioned at Mare Island on 3 July 1943, Lt. Carl E. Bull in command.

After shakedown out of San Diego, and post-shakedown availability, *Whitman* departed San Francisco on 11 September, escorting Convoy 2298, bound for the Hawaiian Islands. Nine days later, she arrived at Pearl Harbor and safely delivered her charges. She then convoyed the seaplane tender *Pocomoke* (AV–9) to Canton and Phoenix Islands in early October before she was detached to return to Pearl Harbor.

In November, she moved to the Central Pacific for her first major operation, the thrust against the Japanese-held Gilbert Islands. With the Commander, Escort Division 10 embarked as concurrent Commander, Task Group (TG) 57.7, *Whitman* patrolled off the entrance to Tarawa lagoon and performed local escort missions into December of 1943.

Returning, via Funafuti in the Ellice Islands, to Hawaii, *Whitman* underwent engine repairs at the Pearl Harbor Navy Yard in January 1944, before she participated in the invasion and occupation of the Marshalls, escorting a group of tankers (designated as Task Unit (TU) 53.8.3) to Majuro on D plus four day. The destroyer escort subsequently performed several convoy escort missions between Hawaii and the Marshalls and then steamed to the west coast in March for a major overhaul at the Mare Island Navy Yard. She returned to Pearl Harbor on 10 May.

Whitman departed the Hawaiian Islands on 27 May to escort TU 16.6.4, a Service Force unit, to the forward areas. The tanker group to which *Whitman* was attached fueled some of the ships of the Fleet participating in the Marianas operation that June. The destroyer escort subsequently performed local escort missions in the Marshalls before heading back to Pearl Harbor in the autumn.

After returning to Hawaiian waters, *Whitman* operated with Pacific Fleet submarines out of Pearl Harbor from October 1944 to May 1945, providing target services to the submariners' training program. In addition, whenever a shortage of escort vessels came up, ships such as *Whitman* were summoned to provide a variety of services, including antisubmarine patrols and planeguarding. While engaged in the latter on 23 February 1945, *Whitman* rescued Lt. (jg.) Ward J. Taylor after he had made a forced landing while the destroyer escort was planeguarding for *Fanshaw Bay* (CVE-70). *Whitman* performed her service speedily and brought Taylor safely on board only five minutes after the accident occurred.

After that stint in Hawaiian waters, the destroyer escort was assigned to TG 96.3 in June 1945 and performed patrol and escort missions to Eniwetok, Johnston Island, Kwajalein, and Ulithi through the summer of 1945.

On 10 August, the day upon which the Japanese indicated a desire to surrender unconditionally to the Allies, *Whitman* departed Eniwetok with Convoy EU-172, bound for Ulithi. She was en route from Ulithi to Eniwetok with Convoy UE-123 when the Japanese capitulated five days later. She was at Eniwetok when the formal surrender was signed on board *Missouri* (BB-63) in Tokyo Bay.

Departing Kwajalein for the last time on 14 September, *Whitman* sailed for Pearl Harbor and arrived there on the 20th. Her stay was brief, however, for she got underway for the west coast the next day. Making port at San Pedro on 27 September, *Whitman* was decommissioned on 1 November and struck from the Navy list on the 16th. Sold to the National Metal and Steel Co. of Terminal Island, Calif., and delivered on 31 January 1947, the ship was scrapped on 20 March 1948.

Whitman (DE-24) earned four battle stars for her World War II service.

Whitney

William Collins Whitney—born on 5 July 1841 in Conway, Mass.—received his higher education at Yale and Harvard and settled in New York City to practice law. As corporation counsel of that city between 1875 and 1882, Whitney completely reorganized and simplified the work of his department, thus saving taxpayers thousands of dollars annually.

After becoming Secretary of the Navy in the cabinet of President Grover Cleveland in 1885, Whitney proved to be a powerful advocate of naval expansion, desiring that the warships of the United States Navy be equal to the best in the world. Under his administration, that service made progress towards becoming the "New Navy."

During his time in office, Congress authorized the battleships *Maine* and *Texas*, one armored cruiser, four gunboats, a practice vessel for the Naval Academy, a ram, a torpedo boat, and the dynamite gun cruiser *Vesuvius*. In addition, Whitney changed the title of the Washington Navy Yard to the Naval Gun Factory and limited its mission to the manufacture of naval ordnance.

After leaving office in March 1889 at the end of the first Cleveland administration, Whitney returned to his long-time home, New York City, where he died on 2 February 1904.

(AD-4: dp. 8,325; l. 483'9½"; b. 61'0"; dr. 17'2" (mean); s. 16 k.; cpl. 416; a. 8 5", 4 3", 2 6-pdrs., 2 21" tt.; cl. *Dobbin*)

Whitney (AD-4) was laid down on 23 April 1921 at

The destroyer tender *Whitney* (AD-4) at San Diego, 7 October 1932. Her boats are alongside, and the masts of four "flushdeck" destroyers can be seen beyond her. (NH 65007)

the Boston Navy Yard; launched on 12 October 1923; sponsored by Mrs. Roderick Tower, the granddaughter of William C. Whitney; and commissioned on 2 September 1924, Capt. R. Drace White in command.

Together with her sistership *Dobbin* (AD–3), the destroyer tender was designed to provide service, supplies, and repairs for three divisions of destroyers for a two-month period under wartime conditions. As such, her facilities included storage capacity for fuel and lubricating oil, fresh water, provisions, spare parts, and repair facilities such as optical and machine shops.

Following her shakedown and trials, *Whitney*—initially based at Boston, Mass.—tended destroyers of the Atlantic Fleet and soon thereafter commenced a routine of following the fleet south for the winter, operating out of such ports as Gonaives, Haiti, and Guantanamo Bay, Cuba. She first visited the Panama Canal Zone in February 1926 and returned to Hampton Roads in the spring. During the more temperate months of the year, *Whitney* operated from ports along the eastern seaboard of the United States.

She followed a steady routine of summer and winter fleet movements until February 1932, when she transited the Panama Canal for the first time, en route to the California ports of San Diego and San Francisco. After operating on the Pacific coast for the next two years, *Whitney* returned to the Caribbean in April 1934 and to Hampton Roads that June. However, her stay in the Atlantic was a brief one, for she was back on the Pacific coast that autumn, reflecting growing American concern about the naval challenge to the United States in the Pacific resulting from the expansionist aspirations of Japan.

After repairs at Mare Island in December 1934, *Whitney* visited Port Angeles, Wash., in May 1935, supporting destroyers taking part in Fleet Problem XVI—the fleet maneuvers conducted that year in the northern Pacific from the coast of Alaska to the vicinity of Hawaii. During Fleet Problem XVI, *Whitney* also visited Dutch Harbor, Alaska, and made her first voyage to Pearl Harbor, Oahu.

Back at San Diego in June, *Whitney* remained on the west coast for a year before heading for the east coast in June 1936, following Fleet Problem XVII. She subsequently tended the Battle Fleet's destroyers at Balboa, Canal Zone, in the autumn and returned to San Diego in November 1936.

With Fleet Problem XVIII during the spring of 1937, *Whitney* joined the fleet train in voyaging directly to Pearl Harbor in April. She remained in Hawaiian waters only a month, though, before she returned to San Diego following the Battle Force-vs.-augmented Scouting Force exercises. The destroyer tender followed the same routine the following year, visiting Pearl Harbor in May 1938, as part of Fleet Problem XIX.

Whitney transited the Panama Canal again in January 1939 and operated briefly out of Limon Bay, Canal Zone. After participating in Fleet Problem XX, *Whitney* returned through the canal to the west coast, reaching San Diego in May.

Following the movement of the fleet to Hawaii that had begun upon conclusion of Fleet Problem XXI in April 1940, *Whitney* made another trip there in the autumn of that year. The destroyer tender performed her vital but unglamorous duties at Pearl Harbor into the summer of 1941. She departed Hawaiian waters on 20 August, proceeded to the west coast, and touched at San Diego and Long Beach before returning to Oahu on 18 September.

Whitney tended the destroyers of the Fleet into the late autumn and early winter, as tensions increased in the Pacific and Admiral Husband E. Kimmel, the Commander in Chief of the Pacific Fleet, kept the fleet working in an intensive training program. His warships followed a routine pattern of movements, but the entire fleet was never allowed in port at any one time, lest the Japanese might attack.

Such a routine was being followed on the weekend of 6 and 7 December 1941 as two carrier task forces were at sea. All the battleships, however, were in port, as well as a number of other ships engaging in routine upkeep and repairs or rest and recreation.

Among the ships in upkeep status were the destroyers *Conyngham* (DD–371), *Case* (DD–370), *Reid* (DD–369), *Tucker* (DD–374), and *Selfridge* (DD–357), moored alongside *Whitney* at berths X–8 and X–8S. The destroyer tender was providing steam, electricity, as well as flushing and fresh water to the five destroyers alongside. Most of the tender's officers and some 90 percent of her enlisted men were on board.

Unbeknownst to the men at Pearl Harbor that Sunday morning, a Japanese carrier task force had approached Oahu undetected and had launched aircraft within 200 miles of the island. As the harbor began to awaken, death and destruction were winging their way toward it. Shortly before 0800, the attack began.

Whitney sailors witnessed the attack's beginning; and, at 0800, the ship went to general quarters. A minute later, the first Japanese plane passed over the *Whitney* nest, strafing as it came. Within five minutes of the general alarm, *Whitney* had unlimbered her .50-caliber machine guns.

At 0809, she began to make preparations to get underway, and began issuing supplies to the ships alongside—most in "coldiron" status with dead machinery plants due to their upkeep status. A minute later, *Whitney*'s heavier antiaircraft guns began firing, her 3-inch guns barking at passing Japanese aircraft, hurling out the first of the 88 rounds she would send up at the Japanese attackers.

Whitney began issuing ammunition and ordnance stores to the destroyers alongside at 0830, securing steam devices to those ships at about the same time. At 1000, shortly after the attack ended, *Reid* and *Selfridge* got underway, followed much later by *Case*, *Tucker*, and *Conyngham*. Although all Japanese planes had cleared the area shortly after 0945, jittery gunners —uncertain of the nationality of any planes appearing overhead—fired accidentally at American aircraft throughout the day, *Whitney* logging firings at 1105 and 2110.

After the Japanese had left, there was plenty to do in the wake of the devastating attack. At 1130, *Whitney* received orders to remain at anchor, which she did. At 1335, the tender sent over five lengths of hose and two submersible pumps to *Raleigh* (CL–7), then fighting for survival where she had been torpedoed alongside Ford Island early in the attack. With no wounded on board, *Whitney*'s doctors assisted in handling casualties on board *Solace* (AH–5), moored nearby.

Comdr. N. M. Pigman, *Whitney*'s commanding officer, subsequently wrote in his after action report that his men had been "calm and unexcited throughout" the attack, manning their battle stations efficiently and carrying out their orders "promptly and without confusion." He gave them the highest praise for their conduct during the engagement that had catapulated the United States into global war.

Over the next few months, *Whitney* performed her vital tender services at Pearl Harbor, before she took on a cargo of ammunition, torpedoes, fuel, and supplies in late April 1942 and departed Hawaiian waters on the 18th of that month bound for the Tonga Islands. Ultimately arriving at Tongatabu on 29 May 1942, *Whitney* operated at that port, providing services to destroyers and other combatant ships through midsummer.

Departing Tongatabu on 16 August—nine days after the start of Operation "Watchtower," the invasion of the Solomons and the first American amphibious assault of the war—*Whitney* arrived in Noumea, New Caledonia, on the 20th. She was based there during the critical period in the Solomons operations and provided battle-damage repairs and tender upkeep services to numerous destroyers, enabling them to return quickly to action and help the United States Navy to gain the upper hand.

Very much in need of an overhaul for herself and rest and recreation for her crew, *Whitney* departed Noumea, headed for Australian waters, and reached Sydney on 23 April for a fortnight's stay.

Returning to Noumea on 8 May, *Whitney* repaired over the next few months and kept in operation many units of the hard-pressed destroyer forces which were fighting for the northern Solomons. Heading for the New Hebrides on 10 September, she arrived at Espiritu Santo on the 12th and conducted her vital labors there until 27 October, when she received orders sending her to Purvis Bay in the Solomons.

From late October 1943 through late May 1944, *Whitney* serviced many types of ships and craft at Purvis Bay, Tulagi, before she returned, via Noumea, to Australian waters on 23 June 1944.

Back in business in early July, *Whitney* reached Manus, in the Admiralties, on 3 July, and remained there for a month, providing tender services. She then shifted to Espiritu Santo, arriving there on 10 August. She subsequently touched at Macquitti Bay, Russell Islands; and Guadalcanal, before returning to Espiritu Santo on 29 August.

After operating again out of Purvis Bay and Manus, *Whitney* arrived at Hollandia, New Guinea, on 23 January 1945. However, her stay in port was brief, for she got underway again in four days, bound for the Philippines.

Reaching San Pedro Bay, off the island of Leyte, on the last day of January 1945, *Whitney* remained in those waters through V–J Day in mid-August. She accomplished repairs on numerous types of ships and craft, receiving special commendation from Commander, Philippine Sea Frontier, for providing repair and upkeep services to destroyer escorts between 1 and 15 April 1945. Underway for Buckner Bay, Okinawa, on 30 August, the destroyer tender stopped there only briefly before pushing on for Korea.

Whitney arrived in Jinsen (now Inchon) harbor on 8 September, and—as a unit of Service Division 101—rendered services to ships and craft engaged in the occupation of Korea until departing from the Far East on 18 November 1945.

After returning to San Diego, *Whitney* was decommissioned on 22 October 1946 and transferred to the custody of the Maritime Commission at Suisun Bay, Calif., on 21 November 1946. Struck from the Navy list on 22 January 1947, the ship—which had given the Fleet more than two decades of continuous service and had prepared for combat the ships staging for amphibi-

ous operations in the Solomons, Marianas, Gilberts, and the Philippines—was sold for scrap to the Dulien Ship Products firm on 18 March 1948.

Whitney received one battle star for her World War II service.

Whittemore, Charles, see *Charles Whittemore.*

Wichita

A city in the state of Kansas.

I

(CA–45: dp. 10,000; l. 608'4''; b. 61'9''; dr. 19'10'' (mean); s. 32.5 k. (max.); cpl. 929; a. 9 8'', 8 5'', 8 .50-cal. mg.; cl. *Wichita*)

The first *Wichita* (CA–45) was laid down on 28 October 1935 at the Philadelphia Navy Yard; launched on 16 November 1937; sponsored by Mrs. William F. Weigester, the daughter of the Honorable W. A. Ayres, chairman of the Federal Trade Commission; and commissioned on 16 February 1939, Capt. Thaddeus A. Thomson in command.

After fitting-out, *Wichita* sailed south for the Gulf of Mexico and arrived at Houston, Tex., on 20 April to take part in a dedicatory and memorial service at the San Jacinto Battle Monument and War Relic Museum. Ten days later, she received a silver service from representatives of the city government of Wichita, Kansas, the cruiser's namesake city. After leaving Houston on 1 May, *Wichita* conducted her shakedown cruise, visiting the Virgin Islands, Cuba, and the Bahamas before she returned north to her builder's yard for post-shakedown repairs.

She was still undergoing availability when war broke out in Poland on 1 September 1939. Less than a month later, on the 25th, *Wichita* reported for duty to the Commander in Chief, United States Fleet and was assigned to Cruiser Division (CruDiv) 7, Atlantic Squadron. She accordingly departed Philadelphia, bound for the Virginia capes, and reached Hampton Roads two days later.

Wichita departed Hampton Roads on 4 October and relieved *Vincennes* (CA–44) on Neutrality Patrol that day. She remained at sea until the 9th, when she returned to Hampton Roads. She then shifted to the Norfolk Navy Yard on the 12th and underwent repairs there until 1 December.

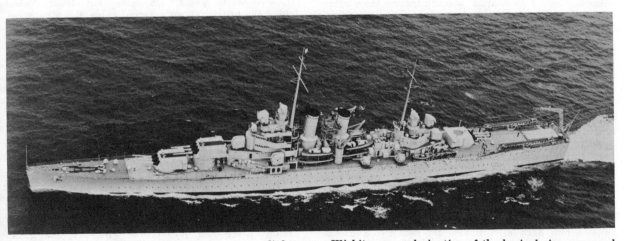

The heavy cruiser *Wichita* (CA–45) in prewar light gray. *Wichita* was a derivative of the basic design prepared for the *Brooklyn* (CL–40)-class, similar in characteristic and appearance but with three 8-inch turrets in lieu of the five 6-inch turrets mounted in the *Brooklyn*s. (80-G-465909)

Three days later, *Wichita* got underway for Cuba and arrived at Guantanamo Bay on the 8th. Upon her arrival there, her commanding officer, Capt. Thomson, assumed command of the newly formed Caribbean Patrol which included: *Wichita* and *Vincennes*; the flush deck destroyers *Borie* (DD–215), *Broome* (DD–210), *Lawrence* (DD–250), *King* (DD–242), and *Truxtun* (DD–229); and patrol plane (VP) squadrons VP–33 and VP–51. All units were based upon Guantanamo Bay or San Juan, Puerto Rico.

Over the ensuing weeks, *Wichita* and her consorts of the Caribbean Patrol exercised out of Guantanamo Bay. Four days before Christmas, the heavy cruiser departed Cuban waters bound for Puerto Rico and reached San Juan two days later. She then visited St. Thomas, Virgin Islands, briefly on 28 and 29 December 1939 before returning to San Juan and remaining there until 2 January 1940.

Arriving back at Guantanamo Bay on the 3d, *Wichita* exercised locally from 8 to 24 January and then departed Cuban waters as flagship of the newly constituted Antilles Detachment, which also included *Vincennes* and Destroyer Squadron (DesRon) 10. Two days later, the force separated, with *Wichita* and Destroyer Division (DesDiv) 82 visiting Willemstad, Curaçao, Netherlands West Indies from 26 to 30 January before getting underway to rendezvous with *Vincennes* and her group of destroyers on 31 January, en route back to Puerto Rican waters.

Wichita conducted exercises in the Guantanamo-Culebra, Puerto Rico, area through late February, when she sailed for Hampton Roads. She arrived at Norfolk on 4 March and spent five days before moving north to Philadelphia, where she remained a fortnight. After returning to Norfolk at the end of March, *Wichita* then operated out of Hampton Roads on exercises well into the spring.

In June, however, the heavy cruiser drew the assignment of "showing the flag" in South American waters to counter German propaganda in some of America's "good neighbors" to the south. As early as mid-May 1940, while the Germans were executing their devastating blitzkrieg against the Low Countries and France, Edwin C. Wilson, the United States Minister to Uruguay, had reported from Montevideo of an upsurge in Nazi propaganda. The State Department and the President himself came to share Wilson's concern over the German effort to extend its influence into the western hemisphere.

Quincy (CA–39) was the first ship dispatched to Uruguay's capital city, Montevideo, reaching that port on 20 June to a tumultuous reception. Ten days later, *Wichita*—with Rear Admiral A. C. Pickens, Commander, CruDiv 7 embarked—joined *Quincy* there after stopping at Rio de Janeiro en route.

The influence of those heavy cruisers, ". . . to furnish a reminder of the strength and the range of action of the armed forces of the United States . . ." continued when *Wichita* and *Quincy* sailed on 3 July. They visited Rio Grande de Sol; Santos; Rio de Janeiro; Bahia; and Pernambuco, Brazil, before they returned to Montevideo on 23 August. The ships then "showed the flag" at Buenos Aires, Argentina, and at Rio de Janeiro again before they returned to Hampton Roads on 22 September.

Wichita stayed at Norfolk for a week before she proceeded to New York City, arriving there on 30 September. During the next three months, *Wichita* served as a training ship for Naval Reserve midshipmen of the V–7 reserve program and conducted gunnery practices, primarily in the vicinity of the Southern Drill Grounds off the Virginia capes.

The heavy cruiser departed Hampton Roads on 7 January 1941, bound for Cuban waters, reaching Guantanamo four days later. During the next two and one-half months, *Wichita* participated in fleet maneuvers in the Caribbean and took part in practice amphibious landings at Puerto Rico. During that time, the ship

called at Portland Bight, Jamaica; Culebra; Guayanilla, Fajardo Roads, and Mayaguez, Puerto Rico, before she arrived at the New York Navy Yard on 23 March.

Wichita sailed for Bermuda on 6 April and reached her destination two days later. Subsequently, in company with *Tuscaloosa* (CA–37), *Wichita* operated in the North Atlantic, sailing to within 800 miles of Ireland; she then returned to the New York Navy Yard on 17 May and went into drydock on 21 June.

After finishing that period of repairs on 2 July, *Wichita* shifted to Newport, R.I., whence she sortied on 27 July and headed for Iceland in the van of Task Force (TF) 16 as part of Operation "Indigo II," the occupation of that strategic island. She arrived at Reykjavik on 6 August but returned to Newport on the 20th. She then shifted to Casco Bay, Maine, from 25 to 27 August before she sailed for Newfoundland, reaching Placentia Bay soon thereafter for a month-long stay. American planners, however, fearing a German response to the United States' increasing role in the Battle of the Atlantic, meanwhile authorized the movement of a task force to Iceland, to base there and sweep into the Denmark Strait. As part of this movement, *Wichita* set sail for Icelandic waters on 23 September—in company with *Wasp* (CV–7), *Mississippi* (BB–41), *Vulcan* (AR–5), and four destroyers—and arrived at Reykjavik on 28 September.

Two days prior to *Wichita*'s arrival, the ships of the Atlantic Fleet received orders to protect all ships engaged in commerce in United States defensive waters. The Navy was authorized to patrol, cover, escort, and report or destroy any German or Italian naval forces encountered. This action came within a week of the first United States Navy-escorted convoy eastbound to Great Britain and within two weeks of President Franklin D. Roosevelt's "shoot-on-sight" orders authorizing American naval units to attack any vessel threatening United States shipping or shipping under American escort.

Wichita—as part of Task Group (TG) 7.5 (nicknamed the "White Patrol")—remained engaged in patrol operations in Icelandic waters through the end of the fateful year 1941, and the ship lay at anchor at Hvalfjordur, Iceland, when the Japanese attack upon Pearl Harbor plunged the United States into World War II on 7 December 1941.

Wichita got underway on 5 January 1942 and made a refresher training and raider sweep into the Denmark Strait before returning to Hvalfjordur on the 10th. Five days later, a hurricane-force storm, with gusts up to 100 knots, hit Iceland. *Wichita* rode out the storm well until the seaplane tender *Albemarle* (AV–5) began to drag her anchors in the gale, as did the nearby merchantman SS *West Nohno*. *Wichita* maneuvered to avoid *Albemarle*, but *West Nohno* fouled the heavy cruiser's anchor cable and struck her side against *Wichita*'s bow. Later *Wichita* collided with a British trawler, before she ran aground at 1641 on an even keel. The cruiser then spent the rest of the night where she was, in the wind, sleet, and rain that resulted in reduced visibility conditions.

The next day, *Wichita* took stock of her condition. Investigation disclosed minor damage from the collisions, some leakage, and "repairable" damage to hull and stem from grounding. After effecting temporary repairs, *Wichita* sailed for the New York Navy Yard and arrived there on 9 February.

After repairs and alterations at the yard, *Wichita* sailed for Newport, R.I., on the 26th, touching briefly there before moving on to Boston the following day. Shifting from thence to Casco Bay "Base Sail," Maine, the heavy cruiser exercised in those waters until 11 March, when she sailed for Boston for ammunition but returned to Casco Bay soon thereafter.

Wichita was then assigned to a task force formed around *Wasp* and *Washington* (BB–56), the group coming under the command of Rear Admiral John W. Wilcox, Jr., embarked in the latter. *Wichita* sortied on 26 March, slated to report to Commander, Naval

Forces, Europe, for duty, in company with *Wasp*, *Washington*, *Tuscaloosa*, and eight destroyers. The next day, the force ran into heavy weather, during which time Admiral Wilcox was washed overboard from his flagship. Despite an intensive search, none of the ships recovered the missing flag officer. Command of the task force thus devolved upon Rear Admiral Robert C. "Ike" Giffen, who flew his flag in *Wichita*.

On 3 April, *Wichita*'s task force rendezvoused with three British light cruisers, HMS *Edinburgh*, HMS *Gambia*, and HMS *Frobisher*. *Edinburgh* then guided the American ships into Scapa Flow, their new base of operations, arriving there on the 4th. Over the weeks that ensued, *Wichita* exercised out of Scapa Flow with units of the British Fleet.

The heavy cruiser, her training and indoctrination with the Royal Navy completed, subsequently put to sea on 28 April to cover the movement of Convoys QP-11 and PQ-15—ships sailing to and coming from the vital lend-lease port of Murmansk. Evidence of German activity soon appeared in the form of reports of shadowing aircraft and lurking U-boats. Moreover, there were problems on the Allied side. On 1 May 1942, the British battleship, HMS *King George V*, rammed and sank the destroyer HMS *Punjabi*, necessitating the former's returning to port for repairs. Her place was taken by sistership HMS *Duke of York*.

After the force had completed its coverage of QP-11, it returned toward Seidisfjord, Iceland. The men-of-war from the United States Navy of the mixed American-British force were detached and put into Hvalfjordur where they arrived on 6 May.

Following almost a week in port, *Wichita* got underway on the 12th and relieved *Tuscaloosa* on patrol in Denmark Strait, between Iceland and Greenland. A week later, she returned to Hvalfjordur only to put to sea as part of a joint American-British covering force protecting one leg of the movement of Murmansk-bound Convoy PQ-16 and eastbound QP-12 before returning to Scapa Flow, her mission accomplished, on the 29th. While at that port, King George VI inspected *Wichita* and other ships of the task force, including *Washington*, on 7 June.

Underway for Hvalfjordur on the 12th and arriving on the 14th, *Wichita* relieved the heavy cruiser HMS *Cumberland* on "White Patrol" in Denmark Strait soon thereafter. While on patrol on the 17th, *Wichita* spotted a Focke-Wulf (FW) 200 "Condor," a four-engined maritime reconnaissance and bomber aircraft, and opened fire, driving off the snooper. Three days later, the heavy cruiser scared off another FW-200.

Enemy activity near the Murmansk convoy routes and in Denmark Strait area did not let up over ensuing days. On the 21st, *Wichita* sighted a submarine periscope and took evasive action—no attack was forthcoming, though, and the cruiser soon resumed her patrolling. The next day, she spotted her third "Condor" but did not fire.

Wichita then proceeded to Hvalfjordur and steamed thence to Seidisfjordur at the end of June. Underway from the latter port on the 30th to cover Convoy PQ-17, the warship sortied as part of the "Cruiser Covering Force" (*Wichita* with three other heavy cruisers and a trio of destroyers). Other support forces included two battleships, a carrier, one heavy and one light cruiser apiece, and nine additional destroyers.

The convoy itself was a large one—36 merchantmen (laden with a variety of war cargo consigned to the Russians under lend-lease) and one "CAM-ship" (a catapult-equipped merchantman with one "Hurricane" fighter for local convoy defense). Unfortunately, an ordeal lay ahead of these Allied ships.

By 1 July, it was evident that the Germans had detected this movement of shipping since direction-finder bearings indicated increasing U-boat activity to the east. One intercepted German message actually told of the convoy's being spotted. *Wichita* sailors noted that the weather was becoming foul. Visibility was poor; ceilings never rose above 200 feet and sometimes closed down completely.

At 2340 on 2 July, German aircraft—long-range "Condors"—radioed the position of the convoy as it headed through the wintry seas toward Russia. The next day, an intercepted message revealed that the Germans were dispatching a strong surface force—built around the vaunted battleship *Tirpitz*, the sistership to the late *Bismarck*—to intercept the convoy. Early in the afternoon, photo reconnaissance of Trondheim (Norway) harbor, confirmed that *Tirpitz*, the heavy cruiser *Admiral Hipper*, and four destroyers were at sea.

U-boats and "Condors" consistently shadowed the ships of PQ-17—an ominous portent. On 4 July, Independence Day, *Wichita* launched two Curtiss SOC Seagull floatplanes, each armed with depth charges, to reconnoiter the fringes of the convoy and attack the shadowing U-boats. The planes returned at 1645 having sighted no enemy submarines but having tangled with some of the enemy's scouting planes.

The feared attacks finally materialized later that day—25 Heinkel (HE) 111 bombers, armed with torpedoes, swarmed against the starboard side of the convoy: three ships took "fish"—they were later abandoned and sunk; one ship had already been torpedoed the previous night. The situation, however, would not get better.

The presence of German heavy units—*Tirpitz* and *Admiral Hipper* with their screen—at sea forced the convoy to change course. At 1923, the convoy received the fateful message: "Owing to threats from surface ships, PQ-17 is to disperse and proceed Russian ports." That order sealed the fate of most of the merchantmen. At 1936, the Admiralty message came through: "Convoy is to scatter."

The pell-mell rush to Murmansk was on, unhelped by the covering force, for on the heels of the orders to "scatter" came the dispatch to the cruiser force at 1944: "Withdraw to westward at high speed." Obeying, *Wichita* and the others came about and, at 2025 on the 4th, increased to 25 knots. The next day, while south of Spitzbergen, the ships were spotted and shadowed by a pair of FW-200's. Both *Wichita* and *Tuscaloosa* opened fire with their antiaircraft guns, but the elusive "Condors" slipped away.

Wichita joined up with the rest of the Fleet on 6 July and proceeded thence to Hvalfjordur, arriving two days later. Within a week, the heavy cruiser again became a flagship, this time for Rear Admiral Giffen once more, for TF 99. Underway for Scapa Flow on the 19th, the ship arrived on the 21st, only to set out the next day for the Admiralty dockyard at Rosyth, Scotland. Arriving on the 23d, *Wichita* was drydocked for repairs on the 24th and remained there until 9 August.

However, the repairs to correct a propeller vibration appeared to be ineffective as the naval attache in London radioed on 12 August that the ship's combat efficiency was seriously lessened at speeds in excess of 20 knots. Accordingly, two days later, *Wichita* received orders to head, via Hvalfjordur, for the United States. As she returned homeward, the cruiser was complimented on her "smartness and efficiency" by Admiral John C. Tovey, Commander in Chief, Home Fleet, who visited the ship prior to her departure and addressed her crew.

After a quick stop at Hvalfjordur, *Wichita* reached New York on 22 August and entered drydock at the New York Navy Yard the same day. Undocked on 5 September, the heavy cruiser underwent post-repair trials before moving down to Hampton Roads within a week. She conducted gunnery exercises in Chesapeake Bay; visited Baltimore from 24 to 28 September; and returned to the Virginia capes operating area to resume exercises and training.

Underway for Casco Bay on 5 October, she reached her destination on the 6th. She then loaded ammunition at Boston and returned to Casco Bay for exercises which lasted into late October, when the cruiser was assigned to TG 34.1. Commanding the task group was Rear Admiral H. Kent Hewitt in *Augusta* (CA–31). Other ships included the new battleship *Massachusetts* (BB–59), *Tuscaloosa*, Cruiser Division 8, and Destroyer Squadrons 8 and 11. Underway on 24 October, *Wichita* set course for North African waters, screening the passage of the invasion convoy slated to carry out Operation "Torch."

On the day of the initial assault, 8 November 1942, *Wichita* went to general quarters at 0540, tasked with neutralizing French shore batteries at Point El Hank and Table d'Aukasha and French warships in Casablanca harbor. Because of the unknown attitude of the French forces toward the landings, *Wichita* and the other ships were ordered not to open fire "unless and until hostile intent" was indicated.

However, the French decided to resist; and they proved stubborn. Ordered to attack at 0623, *Wichita* stood toward the North African coast, her spotting planes—Curtiss SOC's—airborne to spot her fall of shot. French fighters—possibly Dewoitine 520's or American-built Curtiss Hawk 75's—attacked the "Seagulls," and one had to make a forced landing. Its crew was picked up by one of the heavy cruiser's escorts.

At 0704, the guns of the French battleship *Jean Bart* boomed from Casablanca harbor, as did the ones emplaced at El Hank. Although moored to a pier and still incomplete, *Jean Bart* packed a powerful "punch" with her main battery. *Massachusetts* subsequently opened fire in return at 0705; and *Tuscaloosa* did so shortly thereafter.

Wichita's 8-inch battery crashed out at 0706, aimed at El Hank. Checking fire at 0723 when her spotting planes informed her that the French guns appeared to be silenced, the heavy cruiser shifted her 8-inch rifles in the direction of French submarines in Casablanca harbor. Subsequently checking fire at 0740, *Wichita* began blasting the French guns at Table d'Aukasha shortly before 0800.

After resumption of firing on French shipping in Casablanca's harbor, *Wichita* received orders at 0835 to cease fire. At 0919, however, she opened fire again—this time directing her guns at French destroyers in harbor and at the light cruiser *Primauguet*. Later, at 1128, *Wichita* came within range of the French battery at El Hank, and the Vichy gunners scored a hit on the American cruiser. A 194-millimeter shell hit her port side, passed into the second deck near the mainmast, and detonated in a living compartment. Fragments injured 14 men—none seriously—and the resulting fires were quickly extinguished by *Wichita*'s damage control parties.

Torpedoes from a Vichy French submarine caused *Wichita* to take evasive action at 1139. Two "fish" went by a length ahead of the ship, and another passed deep under the bow or slightly ahead. After ceasing fire at 1142, *Wichita* received orders an hour later to attack French ships making for the harbor entrance at Casablanca. Accordingly, the heavy cruiser—aided by improved visibility and air spotting—again battered *Primauguet*, starting fierce fires that gutted a large part of that ship. At 1505, *Wichita* ceased fire; and her guns remained quiet for the rest of the day. That evening, she steamed seaward to avoid nocturnal submarine attacks and, over the ensuing days, patrolled offshore between Casablanca and Fedhala. Ordered to return to the United States, her task with "Torch" completed, *Wichita* sailed for Hampton Roads on 12 November. Diverted to New York while en route, she reached her revised destination on the 19th for repairs.

Soon thereafter, *Wichita* sailed for the Pacific. On 29 January 1943, the heavy cruiser tasted her first action in her new theater during the night torpedo attack by Japanese planes off Rennell Island.

Unidentified aircraft had appeared on *Wichita*'s radar screen throughout the afternoon, circling at 40 to 50 miles, sometimes approaching as close as 20 miles before widening the range. *Wichita* and the other two heavy cruisers in the force, *Louisville* (CA–28) and *Chicago* (CA–29), together with their screen, had zig-zagged after nightfall. At 0842 (Z) time, the Japanese "snoopers" closed enough to strafe the ships before retiring. Intermittent attacks followed. Making radar contact on approaching enemy aircraft at 0843 (Z), *Wichita* opened fire on them a minute later.

Events followed one another in rapid succession. The planes, torpedo-carrying "Betty" bombers, sought out *Chicago* and illuminated her with flares. That cruiser took two torpedo hits within a minute. *Wichita* and *Chicago* nevertheless kept up a heavy barrage in their sector and set two "Betties" ablaze. *Wichita* then took a "Betty" under fire as it passed overhead from the starboard quarter. One torpedo dropped by that plane broached and ran parallel to the ship to starboard; the other "fish" headed directly for the ship. Fortunately for *Wichita*, the enemy's torpedo proved to be a dud.

Chicago was later taken in tow by *Louisville*, and the formation attempted to retire from the area. However, Japanese torpedo planes caught the ships again the next day. *Chicago* took four more torpedoes and went down quickly.

Wichita then trained out of Efate, in the New Hebrides, before sailing for Oahu on 7 April 1943 and arriving at Pearl Harbor a week later. The heavy cruiser's time in Hawaiian climes was short, though, for she was soon underway for the inhospitable Aleutians, heading on 18 April for Adak, Alaska, as flagship for TG 52.10. Reaching her destination six days later, *Wichita* led an offensive sweep to the west and northwest of the island of Attu as flagship of TG 16.14 —*Wichita*, *Louisville*, and four destroyers—before returning to Adak on the 26th.

Subsequently underway for the Attu covering area as flagship of TG 16.7, *Wichita* operated with the battleships *New Mexico* (BB–40) and *Nevada* (BB–36) and their screens from 29 May to 18 June. Later in June, she operated to the north of the Aleutian chain with the battleships. She shelled Kiska on 22 July as flagship of TG 16.21 before steaming southwest of that island and returning to Adak at the end of the month.

Wichita remained in the Aleutian theater through mid-August and then steamed south and entered the Puget Sound Navy Yard, Bremerton, Wash., on 4 September. She underwent repairs and alterations there until 3 December 1943 and, on the following day, sailed for San Francisco. She reached that port on the 6th but sailed for the Hawaiian Islands the next day.

The heavy cruiser trained and exercised in the Hawaiian operating area until she sortied on 16 January 1944 for the invasion of the Marshall Islands. The cruiser was assigned to TG 58.3 which also included one carrier, two light carriers (CVL's), two battleships, and nine destroyers. The group was under the overall command of Rear Admiral Frederick C. Sherman in *Bunker Hill* (CV–17).

While *Wichita* screened the task group, *Bunker Hill* and the two light fleet carriers launched air strikes that pummelled enemy positions on Kwajalein on 29 January. On the 30th and 31st, they struck Eniwetok while American marines and soldiers were landing on Kwajalein and Majuro.

Subsequently arriving at Majuro Atoll on 4 February, *Wichita* sortied for Truk on the 12th, attached to TG 58.2. The carriers launched the first strikes against that strategic Japanese base on the 16th. Enemy ships, shore installations, and aircraft all felt the heavy blows of bombs from the American carrier planes as Vice Admiral Marc A. Mitscher's "pet hate" took a pounding from the aviators of TF 58.

The enemy struck back that night with nocturnal air strikes against the American warships and succeeded in torpedoing *Intrepid* (CV–11) shortly after midnight. *Wichita* was then assigned to Task Unit (TU) 58.2.4, a new task unit formed to escort the crippled carrier back to safety and repairs. The group reached Majuro on the 20th.

A little over a week later, on 28 February, *Wichita* sailed for Hawaii and arrived at Pearl Harbor on 4 March. Becoming the flagship for CruDiv 6 on 9 March, the warship set sail for Majuro on the 15th, arriving there on the 20th. She then supported the fast carriers as their planes hit Japanese installations on Yap, Woleali, and in the Palaus; on 30 March, she catapulted off two of her floatplanes, and picked up the three-man crew of a ditched Grumman TBF Avenger from *Lexington* (CV–16). *Wichita* subsequently remained with the fast carriers as they continued air strikes against the Palaus and Woleali, returning to Majuro each time.

On 13 April, *Wichita* headed for New Guinea to support strikes on Hollandia and Wakde. A little over a week later, her carriers remained north of Hollandia while conducting air strikes on Japanese positions that were neutralized by the afternoon of the 22d. *Wichita* then patrolled off the coast of New Guinea.

Task Group 58.2 returned to the vicinity of Truk and launched more air attacks against the Japanese base there on 29 April. Japanese torpedo planes attacked the formation but scored no hits. Because of her position in the formation, *Wichita* did little firing. Following on the heels of the Truk strike, *Wichita*, together with other cruisers and a screen of destroyers, left the carriers and shelled Japanese targets on Satawan Island in the Nomol group of the Caroline Islands.

Returning to Majuro on 4 May, *Wichita* trained there for a month before shifting to Kwajalein, a staging point for operations against the Japanese-held Mariana Islands. As an element of TU 53.10.8, *Wichita* operated southeast of Saipan, to seaward of the ships shelling the southern part of that island on 14 June. The next day, she, too, added to the destruction wreaked upon Japanese installations ashore, pounding those enemy positions on the south coast of Saipan. That evening, she covered the retirement of empty transports.

The next day, *Wichita* shelled Japanese gun positions on the west coast of Guam before returning to Saipan later that day, the 16th. On the 17th, the heavy cruiser rendezvoused with TG 58.7 west of the Marianas; over the three days that ensued, she patrolled back and forth, east to west, to the westward of the Marianas, in hope of contacting elements of a large Japanese carrier task force known to be approaching that island group.

During the morning and afternoon hours of 19 June, *Wichita* contributed to the antiaircraft barrage which was so effective in warding off enemy air attacks in an action which came to be known as the "Marianas Turkey Shoot," or the Battle of the Philippine Sea. During that engagement, *Wichita*'s gunners claimed assists on two "Kates." In the aftermath of the battle, one of the heavy cruiser's floatplanes rescued an American fighter pilot whose plane had been shot down by the Japanese.

Detached for duty off Saipan, *Wichita* reached that island on the 25th and covered transports that evening. She remained in the vicinity, covering the vital troopships, as well as escort carriers (CVE's), into the first week of July 1944. Later, after her task unit (TU 52.17.8) was redesignated as TU 53.18.1, *Wichita* shelled Japanese installations on the west coast of Guam from the 8th through the 12th. After returning to Saipan from the 13th to the 17th, the heavy cruiser took up close-support bombardment chores off Guam on the 18th—remaining thus engaged into early August.

Departing Guam on 10 August, *Wichita* reached Eniwetok three days later. Underway again on the 29th of that month, the heavy cruiser rendezvoused with TG 38.1 soon thereafter. *Wichita* screened that fast carrier task group as their planes hit Japanese targets in the Palaus, Carolines, Philippines, and Netherlands East Indies, pounding airfields and shipping and extending their operations as far as the Central Philippines. On 12 September, a *Wichita* floatplane picked up a ditched pilot from *Hornet* (CV–12) in the Camotes Sea. Two days later, the cruiser's airmen performed another rescue, saving two pilots and two aircrew from downed planes from *Wasp* (CV–18).

In mid-September, while TG 38.1's planes were providing air support for the unfolding invasion of Morotai, *Wichita* was again screening the carriers. The group covered the Morotai landings until the 20th, when it began a high-speed approach toward the island of Luzon in the Philippines.

On 21 September, the group launched aircraft that proceeded toward the vicinity of Manila, leaving destruction in their wakes. Returning strikes reported "considerable damage to enemy aviation and shipping." Shortly after dawn on the 22d, however, the Japanese attempted to strike back. At 0734, *Wichita* splashed an attacker some 50 yards from her, the plane's bomb falling harmlessly into the sea. The heavy cruiser downed a second plane at 0745, splashing the enemy aircraft into the sea some 8,000 yards on her port quarter.

Wichita continued her screening activities on the 24th, northeast of the island of Samar, while TG 38.1's planes hit Japanese shipping and shore installations on Cebu, Negros, and Coron. On the 25th, the cruiser set course for the Admiralties and reached Manus three days later.

Underway for a raid on Okinawa on 2 October, *Wichita* encountered heavy seas and high winds en route, through the 7th, and began the high speed approach with the fast carriers on the 9th. The following day, the flattops launched strikes against Okinawa. At 1350 on the 10th, a Vought OS2U Kingfisher from *Biloxi* (CL–80) ran out of fuel and made a forced landing near *Wichita*, who obligingly picked her up and repaired the plane.

The next day, the 11th, found *Wichita* northeast of Cape Engano, on Luzon, while the fast carriers' planes hit Aparri, Luzon. On the 12th, the fast carriers launched strikes against Formosa, pounding Japanese airfields and installations there as part of the overall preparation for the upcoming assault against the Philippine island of Leyte. Although the American ships encountered considerable resistance, they shot down many enemy planes and inflicted heavy damage upon Japanese installations ashore.

The fast carriers inflicted considerable damage upon the enemy throughout the following day, but the enemy managed to strike back and cause enough damage of his own, making determined and skillful attacks against the ships of TG 38.1. After *Canberra* (CA–70) took torpedoes that flooded her engine rooms and two fire rooms, *Wichita* took the crippled *Canberra* in town and, screened by three light cruisers and five destroyers, steamed for a point east of Luzon.

The following day, the enemy drew blood again, torpedoing *Houston* (CL–81), forcing that ship to be taken under tow by *Canberra*'s sistership *Boston* (CA–69). On the morning of the 15th, a tug relieved *Wichita* of towing *Canberra*; but, as *Wichita* headed back to rejoin TG 38.1, she was ordered to form part of the screen for the "cripple division" built around *Canberra* and *Houston*.

On the 16th, Japanese planes hit the formation, torpedoing *Houston* again in spite of the heavy concentration of combat air patrol (CAP) fighters from two light carriers. Fortunately, one plane managed to score a hit —the CAP took care of the rest, breaking up the raid before more damage could be inflicted. *Wichita* launched one of her SOC's at 1522 and rescued the pilot of a fighter from *Cabot* (CVL–27) who had ditched during the defense of the crippled cruisers.

After evading a typhoon on the 18th, *Wichita* left the cripples three days later and, after fueling, proceeded for operations in the area west of Luzon. She then turned south toward the waters west of Leyte. The carriers which she was screening launched searches to try to locate enemy ships. Subsequently steaming north in an attempt to close the enemy fleet units, *Wichita* took station with TF 34, battleships under Vice Admiral Willis A. Lee. When the enemy was reported 140 miles north—a force of three carriers, four cruisers and six destroyers—TF 34 received orders to close at 20 knots. Carrier planes found the Japanese and attacked, scoring hits.

Later, TF 34 received orders detaching them to go to the aid of the escort carriers caught by a superior Japanese surface force off Samar. While en route, *Wichita* and *New Orleans* (CA–32) joined a surface striking force to finish off the "cripples" left by the carrier planes to the northward. Some five hours later, the ships sighted a target—the crippled carrier *Chiyoda*. The 8-inch guns of the two heavy cruisers soon spoke and, within one-half hour's time, had reduced the ship to wreckage, observers reporting "great clouds of smoke with intermingling flashes of fire" boiling upward. *Wichita* was the last ship to cease fire at 1642; 13 minutes later, *Chiyoda* sank.

That was not to be the last of Admiral Ozawa's decimated striking force to be dispatched, however, for the cruisers, led to the target by night fighters from *Essex* (CV–9), soon came upon *Hatsuzuki* at 1840, shortly before nightfall. *Hatsuzuki* put up a stubborn fight but only postponed the inevitable—slowed up by torpedo attacks from some of the screening destroyers, the Japanese man-of-war soon came under fire of the heavier guns of the cruisers. *Wichita* commenced firing on her at 1910—ultimately, at 2056, *Hatsuzuki* blew up and sank. She had however, straddled *Wichita* several times, and shell fragments wounded one man, slightly, on board that heavy cruiser.

Wichita resumed her screening operations for fast carriers in the aftermath of the Battle of Leyte Gulf, operating primarily east of Samar before supporting ground troops on Leyte on 28 October. She later fought off a determined air attack on the 30th, although *Franklin* (CV–13) and *Belleau Wood* (CVL–24) were damaged. Heading for Ulithi on the last day of October, *Wichita* reached her destination on 2 November.

Wichita then operated off Leyte and Luzon into mid-November, after her replenishment at Ulithi, before she detected very heavy vibrations in number four engine unit. Investigation revealed that the tail shaft had broken, and the propeller was trailing. It was then considered unsafe for the ship to make high speed. Detached as a consequence, *Wichita* headed for Ulithi on the 18th and reached the Carolines on the 20th.

After Commander, Cruiser Division 6, Rear Admiral C. Turner Joy, shifted his flag from *Wichita* to *San Francisco* (CA–38), the former underwent a brief inspection by divers before she was to head "stateside" for repairs. They found that a strut for number three screw was cracked. With only two shafts, now, *Wichita* sailed for the United States on the 27th. Fueling at Eniwetok and stopping briefly at Pearl Harbor while en route, *Wichita* pushed on for San Pedro, Calif., on the 9th of December. Reaching the west coast six days later, the heavy cruiser entered the Terminal Island Navy Yard soon thereafter. She remained in dockyard hands, undergoing necessary repairs and alterations, until 8 February 1945.

Underway for Pearl Harbor on 28 February, *Wichita* arrived in Hawaiian waters on 6 March, remaining at Pearl Harbor only five days before heading for the Carolines, via the Marshalls, on the 11th. Refueling at Eniwetok, the heavy cruiser arrived at Ulithi on the 20th.

The next day, *Wichita*, as part of TF 54, set sail for Okinawa in the last great invasion of World War II. As an element of TU 54.2.3, *Wichita* covered minesweeping units in fire support sector four on 25 March, retiring to seaward for the night. As part of Fire Support Unit 3 the following day, *Wichita* was off Okinawa when lookouts spotted a periscope to starboard at 0932. Making an emergency turn to starboard, the heavy cruiser evaded the torpedo that was fired.

At 1350, *Wichita* commenced firing with her main battery, shelling Japanese installations on Okinawa, before she ceased fire at 1630 and retired to sea for the night. Soon after dawn the following morning, 27 March, several Japanese planes attacked the formation in which *Wichita* was proceeding; the heavy cruiser's gunners shot down one. That morning and afternoon, *Wichita* again lent the weight of her salvoes to the "softening-up" process; even her SOC joined in, dropping two bombs.

After floating mines—which had been delaying the start of the morning bombardment—had been cleared, *Wichita* resumed her bombardment activities on the 28th. The next day, the 29th, *Wichita* put into Kerama Retto to replenish ammunition. That rocky outcropping near Okinawa had been invaded to provide an advance base for the operations against the island. It was still in the process of being cleared of defenders even as *Wichita* entered the harbor, among the first ships to utilize the newly secured body of water. "You are the first to receive the keys of Kerama Retto," radioed the senior officer present afloat to *Wichita*, "with scenery and sound effects."

When she had replenished her stock of ammunition, *Wichita* resumed her shellings of the Japanese defenders on Okinawa, covering the movement of underwater demolition teams (UDT's). She performed the same covering services for UDT's the next day, 30 March, as well as bombarding selected targets ashore. On the 31st, *Wichita* shelled the beach area to breach the sea wall in preparation for the landings. That evening, the heavy cruiser retired to seaward to cover the approaching transports.

On Easter Sunday, 1 April 1945, the day of the initial assault across the shores of Okinawa, *Wichita* provided neutralization fire on Japanese positions defending the southern beaches. She kept up a rapid, nearly continuous fire with everything from 8-inch to 40-millimeter guns. Near noon, her services temporarily not needed, she replenished ammunition.

After performing a call-fire mission on the 2d, *Wichita* replenished fuel and ammunition at Kerama Retto on the 3d. She subsequently took up a fire support station near Ie Shima and supported the minesweepers operating off that point on the 4th. During the night, *Wichita* fired harassment missions against the Japanese defenders. On the 5th, she was to join TG 51.19 east of Okinawa to carry out a bombardment of Tsugen Shima in company with *Tuscaloosa*, *Maryland* (BB–46), and *Arkansas* (BB–33), but the approach of enemy planes cancelled the mission. That evening, though, *Wichita* shelled Japanese shore batteries at Chiyama Shima which had taken *Nevada* (BB–36) under fire earlier that day.

On 6 April, *Wichita* searched for troop concentrations, tanks, vehicles, and boat revetments on the east coast of Okinawa—targets of opportunity for her batteries. Shortly before sunset, a "Zeke" (Mitsubishi A6M5) came out of the clouds on the port quarter. The encounter was apparently one of mutual surprise, as *Wichita*'s commander later recounted: "We seemed nearly as much of a surprise to the plane as it did to us." As the "Zeke" dove for the heavy cruiser's bridge, antiaircraft fire reached up and tore the plane apart—it disintegrated over the ship and splashed in the sea off the starboard bow. There was no damage to the ship.

The following day, *Wichita* entered Nakagusuku Wan—a body of water later renamed Buckner Bay—during the morning to bombard a pugnacious shore battery. The enemy managed to land several shots "very close aboard the port side" but was ultimately silenced. For the next two days, *Wichita* carried out a similar slate of harassing fire on Japanese shore batteries, pillboxes, and other targets of opportunity. Underway for Kerama Retto on the afternoon of 10 April, the heavy cruiser replenished her ammunition supply that evening and returned to the bombardment areas the following day.

Wichita subsequently served four more tours of duty off Okinawa, her 8-inch guns providing part of the heavy volume of firepower necessary to support the troops advancing ashore against the tenacious Japanese defenders. She hit pillboxes, ammunition dumps, troop concentrations spotted by her observers aloft in one of her SOC's, camouflaged installations and caves, waterfront areas suspected of supporting suicide boat launching ramps and harboring swimmers, as well as trenches and artillery emplacements. During that period of time, she was damaged twice: the first time came when a small caliber shell penetrated a fuel oil tank, five feet below the waterline, on 27 April. After repairs at Kerama Retto on 29 and 30 April (she had spent the 28th firing harassment rounds against Japanese positions ashore and making unsuccessful attempts to patch the hole), *Wichita* provided more harassment and interdiction fire before being hit by "friendly" fire during an air raid on 12 May. A 5-inch shell hit the port catapult, with fragments striking the shield of an antiaircraft director. Twelve men were injured, one so severely that he died that night.

Withdrawn to Leyte for rest and replenishment, *Wichita* returned to Okinawa on 18 June. For the remainder of the war, the heavy cruiser provided surface and air protection for minesweepers operating to the west of Okinawa. She was off the island when, on 15 August 1945, she received word that the war with Japan was over.

Wichita became part of the occupying force in Japanese waters soon thereafter. She sortied from Buckner Bay on 10 September and reached Nagasaki on the following day as part of TG 55.7. During the ship's first stay at Nagasaki, 10,000 ex-prisoners of war (POW's) were repatriated through that port, their long captivity at the hands of the Japanese over at last.

Wichita shifted briefly to Sasebo on the 25th and stayed there for four days before returning to Nagasaki on the 29th. Back to Sasebo shortly thereafter, the heavy cruiser was in port when a severe typhoon struck that area from 9 to 11 October. *Wichita* was not damaged during those storms.

While at Sasebo, *Wichita* inspected harbor installations and ships to monitor Japanese compliance with the terms of surrender. The heavy cruiser later received orders; on 5 November, her first passengers reported on board for transportation back to the United States. Underway on the latter date, the ship fueled at Tokyo before she headed for San Francisco, reaching that port on 24 November 1945.

Drydocking at the Mare Island Naval Shipyard two days later, *Wichita* underwent repairs and alterations in preparation for further "Magic Carpet" duty, before she was undocked on 1 December. Departing the west coast for the Hawaiian Islands on the 6th, *Wichita* reached Pearl Harbor on the 12th, bound, ultimately, for the Marianas. The heavy cruiser brought back homecoming servicemen from Saipan, arriving at San Francisco on 12 January 1946.

Departing "Frisco" on 27 January, *Wichita* transited the Panama Canal Zone between 5 and 9 February and reached Philadelphia on the 14th. Assigned to the 16th Fleet, *Wichita* was placed in reserve on 15 July 1946. Decommissioned on 3 February 1947, the heavy cruiser was laid up at Philadelphia. She was struck from the Navy list on 1 March 1959. Later that year, on 14 August, she was sold for scrapping to the Union Minerals and Alloys Corp.

Wichita was awarded 13 battle stars for her World War II service.

II

(AOR–1: dp. 37,360; l. 659'; b. 96'; dr. 33'; s. 20 k.; cpl. 390; a. 4 3''; cl. *Wichita*)

The second *Wichita* (AOR–1) was laid down on 16 June 1966 at Quincy, Mass., by the General Dynamics Corp.; launched on 16 March 1968; sponsored by Mrs. Howard B. Yeager; and commissioned on 7 June 1969, Capt. Robert R. Deibler in command.

After fitting out in the Boston Naval Shipyard, *Wichita* on 17 June sailed for the west coast. Following stops at San Juan, Puerto Rico, and Guantanamo Bay, Cuba, and after transiting the Panama Canal, she arrived at Long Beach, Calif., her home port, on 19 July. For the next four months, she remained at Long Beach undergoing postconstruction availability. In December, she got underway to conduct standardization trials, followed by shakedown training. In February 1970, the ship began a two-month post-shakedown availability at Long Beach. In April, she began normal operations out of Long Beach, which included type training and damage control training which kept the ship busy until 22 June, when she began her first deployment to the western Pacific. She changed operational control to Commander, 7th Fleet on Independence Day and arrived in Subic Bay on 11 July. After adjusting her load at Subic, she got underway for her first line period in support of the combat ships operating off the coast of Vietnam. During her first deployment to the western Pacific, *Wichita* made five separate line swings to replenish the ships operating on "Yankee Station." She terminated each at Subic Bay and varied her routine with two liberty calls at Hong Kong. The ship concluded her first deployment when she arrived back in Long Beach on 2 February 1971.

Wichita spent the next six months engaged in operations out of her home port. These included refresher training, underway replenishments, and port visits to other American and Canadian ports. She also participated as a support ship in the tests conducted on the new Mark 48 torpedo. On 7 August, she departed Long Beach for her second tour of duty with the 7th Fleet. She arrived in Subic Bay on the 24th and embarked upon her first line swing on the 31st. After two periods on station off Vietnam, *Wichita* visited Sattahip, Thailand, late in October. Two more line periods followed in November and early December. On 10 December, however, she received orders to join a contingency force bound for the Indian Ocean in the wake of the Indo-Pakistani War. She remained in the Indian Ocean until early January 1972 at which time all ships returned to the operating area off the coast of Vietnam. *Wichita*, however, after a very brief tour on station off Vietnam went to Subic Bay for a much-needed upkeep. She made one more line swing to "Yankee Station" in February and then headed back to Long Beach, where she arrived on 31 March. *Wichita* remained in the United States only long enough to allow for the usual month of post-deployment leave and upkeep and to conduct some major repairs at Hunters Point Naval Shipyard.

On 17 July, she again pointed her bow westward and set a course for the Far East. On 4 August, the ship arrived in Subic Bay. During the next six months, *Wichita* made six replenishment voyages to the waters surrounding Vietnam. She also made frequent stops at Subic Bay to load supplies and conduct repairs as well as liberty calls at Hong Kong and at Sattahip in Thailand. She concluded that deployment when she arrived back in Long Beach on 16 March 1973.

The end of that deployment coincided with the end to American involvement in the Vietnamese civil war. While that stopped *Wichita*'s support of combat operations, it did not interrupt her pattern of deployments to the western Pacific. She settled into a more normal routine alternating peacetime operations with the 7th Fleet with routine duties along the west coast of the United States. After six months on the west coast of the United States, the ship embarked upon her fourth tour of duty with the 7th Fleet, her first under peacetime conditions. She provided routine support for the ships of the 7th Fleet and for the ships assigned to

The multipurpose replenishment ship *Wichita* (AOR–1).

a fast carrier task force operating in the Indian Ocean. She returned to Long Beach on 26 March 1974 and, following post-deployment standdown and a brief period of west coast operations, entered the Long Beach Naval Shipyard on 28 June to begin her first regular overhaul. She remained in the shipyard until the following January.

On 24 January 1975, her home port was changed from Long Beach to San Francisco. Four days later, she completed overhaul and got underway for the first time since early in the previous summer. Following trials out of Long Beach, a voyage to Acapulco, Mexico, and refresher training out of San Diego, *Wichita* finally arrived in her new home port on 4 April. After a month of preparations, the ship departed San Francisco on 6 May, bound for a seven-month deployment to the western Pacific. She arrived in Subic Bay on 24 May and began a tour of duty with the 7th Fleet characterized by a full schedule of underway replenishments and port visits to such places as Hong Kong, Sasebo, and Yokosuka in addition to Subic Bay. Her assignment lasted until 26 November at which time she departed Subic Bay to return home. She made a stop at Pearl Harbor early in December and reentered San Francisco on the 15th.

Wichita spent the entire year of 1976 engaged in normal operations out of San Francisco. She participated in type training and in several operational readiness exercises. By the end of the year, she was preparing for her sixth deployment to the western Pacific. That deployment began on 12 April 1977 after a period of refresher training. After a somewhat extended voyage, she arrived in Subic Bay on 4 May. During this deployment, the ship initially operated from Subic Bay; but, after 26 July, she limited her

activities to the East China Sea and the Sea of Japan, operating from the Japanese ports of Sasebo and Yokosuka. Those duties in support of the 7th Fleet continued until 6 November when she departed Yokosuka to return to the United States. She concluded the deployment at Alameda, Calif., on 21 November.

Following post-deployment standdown, *Wichita* resumed normal west coast operations. These included the usual type training and operational readiness exercises as well as port visits to American and Canadian ports. She also helped to train naval reservists. While participating in the initial phases of RIMPAC 78, the ship visited Pearl Harbor on 5 and 6 April 1978 to take on stores and to give her crew a brief liberty. She returned to Pearl Harbor later in the month at the conclusion of her RIMPAC duties. Such activities as these occupied her time until 2 November when she entered the Triple A Shipyard at Hunters Point, Calif., to begin a nine-month overhaul. As of the summer of 1979, she was completing that overhaul.

Wichita earned four battle stars for Vietnam service.

Wickakee

One of the names of the scarlet painted-cup called in Massachusetts "Indian Paintbrush." The term is probably derived from one of the Algonquin dialects.

(YTB–529: dp. 325 (f.); l. 100'; b. 25'; dr. 11'6'' (max.); s. 12 k.; cpl. 8; cl. *Hisada*)

Wickakee (YTB–529) was scheduled to be built by the Gibbs Gas Engine Co., Jacksonville, Fla.; but the contract for her construction was cancelled in October 1945.

Lambert Wickes—born sometime in 1735 in New England—was appointed to the Continental Navy on 22 December 1775 and probably received his commission as a captain in the Navy in early 1776. Designated as number 11 on the Continental Navy's seniority list, Wickes was given command of the 16-gun brig *Reprisal*.

The Committee of Secret Correspondence of Congress, by arrangement with the Marine Committee, issued orders for Capt. Wickes to proceed to the West Indies in *Reprisal* and bring out munitions for use by General Washington's army. In addition, Wickes was to transport William Bingham to his post, the French possession of Martinique, as agent for the American colonies.

Reprisal passed down the Delaware River from Philadelphia during the latter part of June 1776. While en route, *Reprisal* went to the aid of the harried Continental 6-gun brig *Nancy*—bound from St. Croix and St. Thomas with 386 barrels of gunpowder—which was being chased by six British men-of-war. In order to save *Nancy*, her captain ran her aground. *Reprisal* and *Lexington*—the latter under the command of Capt. John Barry—kept boats from HMS *Kingfisher* at bay and succeeded in landing some 200 barrels of the precious powder. In this engagement, Wickes' brother Richard was killed while serving as third lieutenant in *Reprisal*.

Clearing the Delaware capes on 3 July, *Reprisal*, under Wickes' sterling seamanship, captured a number of prizes in the West Indies and had a sharp engagement with HMS *Shark*, beating her off and escaping into port.

On 24 October 1776, Wickes was ordered to France with Benjamin Franklin as passenger. During the voyage, *Reprisal* captured two brigs and reached Nantes on 29 November where the ship's important passenger disembarked. Setting sail in January 1777, Wickes took *Reprisal* to sea on a cruise which took her to the Bay of Biscay and the mouth of the English Channel. On 5 February, his ship captured the British merchantman *Lisbon Packet* after a hard action of 40 minutes duration. During the battle, *Reprisal* suffered two officers seriously wounded and one man killed.

During the remainder of this foray against British shipping, Wickes took five additional prizes and left them at Port Louis. Wickes moved *Reprisal* to L'Orient but was ordered to leave the port in 24 hours by the French government—the port authorities apparently stirred to action by bitter remonstrances from the British government. Wickes, however, claimed that *Reprisal* had sprung a leak and needed to be careened for hull repairs. Wickes proved to be skillful at gaining time; as, on several occasions, he thwarted the intentions of the French government to have him sail.

In April 1777, the Continental vessels *Lexington* and *Dolphin* joined *Reprisal* and constituted a squadron under Wickes' command. Setting sail from St. Auzeau on 28 May, the ships cruised around Ireland in June, July, and August; during one phase of the voyage, the three ships captured 15 ships in five days. On 14 September, Wickes left France in *Reprisal*, in company with *Dolphin*, bound for home. Around 1 October, *Reprisal* foundered off the Grand Banks of Newfoundland, with the loss of all hands except the cook.

Louis H. Bolander, the assistant librarian at the Naval Academy, wrote an article in 1928, entitled "A Forgotten Hero of the American Revolution." Appearing in *Americana*, in April 1928, the article closed with a fitting epitaph for Capt. Lambert Wickes: "Thus closed a career distinguished for patriotism, gallantry and humanity, for not a single charge of cruelty or harshness was ever breathed against him by any one of his many prisoners. Franklin, who knew him well, said of him, 'He was a gallant officer, and a very worthy man.'"

(Destroyer No. 75: dp. 1,247 (f.); l. 314'4½''; b. 30' 11¼''; dr. 9'0'' (mean); s. 35.24 k.; cpl. 100; a. 4 4'', 2 1-pdrs., 12 21'' tt., 2 dct.; cl. *Wickes*)

The first *Wickes* (Destroyer No. 75) was laid down on 26 June 1917 at Bath, Maine, by the Bath Iron Works; launched on 25 June 1918; sponsored by Miss Ann Elizabeth Young Wickes, the daughter of Dr. Walter Wickes, a descendant of Lambert Wickes; and commissioned on 31 July 1918, Lt. Comdr. John S. Barleon in command.

After an abbreviated shakedown, *Wickes* departed Boston on 5 August and arrived at New York on the 8th. Later that day, she sailed for the British Isles, escorting a convoy of a dozen merchantmen. After shepherding her charges across the Atlantic, *Wickes* was detached from the convoy to make a brief stop at Queenstown, Northern Ireland, on 19 August. Underway again the following day, the warship sailed for the Azores to pick up passengers and United States-bound mail at Punta Delgada before continuing on to New York.

Wickes subsequently escorted convoys off the northeast coast of the United States. She departed New York on 7 October, bound for Nova Scotia; but, during the voyage north, her crew was hit by influenza. Soon after the ship's arrival at Halifax, 30 men—including the commanding officer—were hospitalized ashore.

Soon the outbreak of "flu" in *Wickes* abated, but bad luck seemed to dog the destroyer. She departed New York at 1748 on 23 October, screening ahead of the armored cruiser *Pueblo* and escorting a convoy of merchant vessels. At 2104, *Wickes* sighted an unidentified ship to port on a collision course. She immediately changed her course and switched on her lights. When the oncoming ship failed to give way, the destroyer ordered full speed astern and went to general quarters. At 2110, only six minutes after the initial sighting, the unidentified ship's bow smashed into *Wickes'* port billboard. The stem of the stranger cut through the destroyer's keel and caused extensive damage forward. Fortunately, there were no personnel casualties; and the flood was contained by a key bulkhead which held fast. In this case of "hit and run" on the high seas, the assailant remained unknown, since she scraped the destroyer's port side and steamed off into the night. Stopping engines at 2112, *Wickes'* crew took stock of the damage and put about for the New York Navy Yard, where she arrived at 0453 on 24 October.

While the ship was undergoing repairs there, the signing of the armistice on 11 November 1918 stilled the guns of World War I. Now the task of establishing a fair peace for victors and vanquished lay ahead. To take part in forging what was hoped to be a wise and just settlement of issues raised by the war, President Woodrow Wilson sailed for Europe in the transport *George Washington*; and *Wickes* served as part of the escort screen for the President's ship, departing from New York on 4 December 1918, bound for Brest, France.

Wickes subsequently cruised to northern European ports in late 1918—calling at Hamburg and Stettin, Germany; and Harwich, England. During this European cruise, while mooring at Hamburg on 3 March 1919, the destroyer collided with the German merchantman *Ljusne Elf*. After repairs, the destroyer shifted to Brest in June and from there escorted *George Washington* as that transport carried President Wilson back home to the United States.

After celebrating the 4th of July 1919 off the Atlantic coast, *Wickes* and her sisters sailed for the Pacific, transiting the Panama Canal on 24 July 1919 with the mass movement of the ships from Atlantic to Pacific. Later in that year, Commander William F. Halsey took command of the ship, after an overhaul at the Mare Island Navy Yard. Halsey, who would win fame in the second World War, later stated in his memoirs that *Wickes* was "the best ship I ever commanded; she was also the smartest and the cleanest." As flagship for Destroyer Division 10, *Wickes* operated off the west coast into 1922, conducting the usual target practices and exercises. As a wave of peacetime austerity swept over the United States, the Navy felt the "pinch" of decreased expenditures and the widespread antimilitary sentiment which cropped up in the aftermath of World War I. Accordingly, *Wickes* was decommissioned and placed in reserve at San Diego, Calif., on 15 May 1922.

The destroyer lay out of commission for eight years. Recommissioned on 26 April 1930, *Wickes* shifted to the Atlantic and was based at New York. She operated off the eastern seaboard, making training cruises with Naval Reserve detachments from the 3d Naval District embarked. From 3 to 18 February 1931, the ship visited Tampa, Fla., for the Florida State Fair and Gasparilla Carnival, before she shifted to Mobile, Ala., to take part in Mardi Gras observances. In November, the busy destroyer visited Bridgeport, Conn., to participate in the Armistice Day observances on the 11th. In April 1932, two years after being recommissioned, *Wickes* reported for duty with Rotating Reserve Squadron 20 and subsequently shifted back to the Pacific.

From 1933 to 1937, *Wickes* operated out of San Diego. Decommissioned on 6 April 1937, the destroyer remained in reserve only a short time because of the increase of tension in Europe and the Far East. Fighting broke out in Poland on 1 September 1939 as German forces invaded that country and thus triggered British and French assistance to Poland. World War II was on.

President Roosevelt promptly directed that the Navy establish a "Neutrality Patrol" off the eastern seaboard, in the approaches to the Panama Canal and Guantanamo Bay, and at the two entrances to the Gulf of Mexico. To help patrol these stretches of sea, the Navy quickly reactivated 77 destroyers and light minelayers.

Wickes was recommissioned on 30 September 1939, Lt. Comdr. Charles J. Stuart in command. Over the ensuing month, the destroyer was fitted out while moored at the destroyer base alongside *Whitney* (AD-4). Early in November, she shifted to the Mare Island Navy Yard, Vallejo, Calif., for drydocking. After returning to San Diego on the 21st, *Wickes* departed the west coast on the 27th, bound for Panama in company with her division, Destroyer Division (DesDiv) 64. En route, she fueled from *Neches* (AO-5) and arrived at Balboa on 6 December. Transiting the canal on the 7th, the destroyer arrived at the Naval Operating Base (NOB), Key West, Fla., on the 11th and commenced neutrality patrol duty.

Wickes and her sister ships patrolled alternately in the Yucatan Channel between the east coast of Cuba and the Yucatan Peninsula and in the passage between Florida and the west coast of Cuba. They shadowed belligerent merchantmen and warships of the British and Commonwealth navies searching for German freighters or passenger ships caught in or near American coastal waters by the outbreak of war.

On her first patrol, *Wickes* spotted a cruiser—possibly HMAS *Perth* or HMS *Orion* (her log is not specific here)—at 1058 on 14 December. The destroyer shadowed the cruiser, changing courses and speeds to conform with the other ship's movements, until well after nightfall. Anchored off Port Everglades, Fla., just before Christmas of 1939, *Wickes* noted the British destroyer HMS *Hereward* (H.93) maintaining a diligent patrol 12 miles off the Florida coast between 23 and 25 December.

Wickes returned to Key West on 30 December but enjoyed barely enough time to refuel and provision before she got underway again on 2 January 1940. She maintained a patrol off the Yucatan Peninsula for a week

before returning to Key West on the 9th. Shifting to Guantanamo Bay soon thereafter, *Wickes* exercised with larger units of the Atlantic Squadron from 24 to 26 January before proceeding with DesDiv 64 for Puerto Cabello, Venezuela, on the 26th. Arriving the following day, the ships commenced a three-day port visit.

After leaving Puerto Cabello, *Wickes* and her division mates visited St. Thomas, Virgin Islands, before joining DesDiv 65 at St. Eustatius, Dutch West Indies, on 6 February. The next day, these two divisions rendezvoused with *Wichita* (CA-45) and DesDiv 82; together with DesDivs 61 and 83 and the heavy cruiser *Vincennes* (CA-44), these ships formed the "Antilles Detachment" of the Atlantic Squadron. After formation steaming and exercises, *Wickes* arrived back at Guantanamo Bay on 9 February before shifting to NOB Key West on the 14th.

In late February, *Wickes* again patrolled the Florida Straits, visiting the Dry Tortugas in the course of her operations. At the end of March, she sailed on the Yucatan Patrol. Returning to Key West on 8 April *Wickes* maneuvered alongside *Twiggs* (DD-127) at the fuel pier there. The two ships touched and broke off the propeller guard from *Twiggs* which punctured a small hole above *Wickes*' waterline. The damage, fortunately, was minor, and the destroyer returned to sea shortly thereafter to conduct short range battle practice off Key West before undertaking another stint on the Yucatan Patrol in mid-April.

From late April through mid-June, *Wickes* visited San Juan, Puerto Rico, and St. Thomas. She departed from the latter port on 1 July to join *Texas* (BB-35) *Arkansas* (BB-33), and *New York* (BB-34) that afternoon and conducted simulated torpedo attacks upon them at night. *Wickes* then operated out of San Juan for the remainder of the month.

Meanwhile, in Europe, the situation facing the British had materially worsened. The devastating German blitzkrieg had carried the Low Countries before it and knocked France out of the war. British destroyer forces had suffered terribly in the ill-fated Norwegian campaign and in the evacuation from Dunkirk. Moreover German U-boats had taken their toll in their operations against British convoys. With Italy's entry into the war in the summer of 1940, the British were faced with another long lifeline to defend in the Mediterranean.

Prime Minister Winston Churchill appealed to President Roosevelt for assistance; and, during the summer of 1940, an agreement was worked out between the United States and Great Britain. In return for 50 "overage" American destroyers transferred to the Royal Navy, the United States received leases, for a duration of 99 years, on strategic base sites stretching from Newfoundland to British Guiana.

Accordingly, 50 ships were picked for transfer—*Wickes* among them. After her last Caribbean tour, the destroyer returned to Key West on 24 July. She shifted to Galveston, Tex., on 27 July for an overhaul at Todd's Drydock Co. and remained there through August.

Wickes departed Galveston in company with *Evans* (DD-79), on 22 September, touched briefly at Key West and arrived at the Norfolk Navy Yard, Portsmouth Va., on the 26th. On 9 October, *Wickes* departed Hampton Roads with DesDiv 64 and stopped at the Naval Torpedo Station, Newport, R.I., soon thereafter. The ships transited the Cape Cod Canal, en route to Provincetown, Mass., and after stopping there briefly, pushed on for Halifax, Nova Scotia, where they arrived on 16 October.

As part of the fifth group of destroyers transferred to the British and Canadians, *Wickes* was visited by Prime Minister Mackenzie King of Canada and Rear Admiral F. L. Reichmuth, USN, the Commander, Destroyers, Atlantic Fleet, on 19 October, during the indoctrination period for the prospective British crew. On 23 October 1940, *Wickes* was turned over to the Royal

Navy. Her name was struck from the Navy list on 8 January 1941.

Commissioned simultaneously on the 23d under the White Ensign as HMS *Montgomery* (G.95)—Lt. Comdr. W. L. Puxley, RN, in command—the destroyer underwent further fitting out and familiarization before departing Canadian waters on 1 November, bound for the British Isles. En route, *Montgomery* and the other of her sister ships in company swept through the scene of the one-sided naval engagement between the armed merchant cruiser HMS *Jervis Bay* and the German "pocket battleship" *Admiral Scheer*. This action had occurred on 5 November when the German warship attacked a convoy escorted by the erstwhile merchant steamship. *Jervis Bay* had gallantly interspersed herself between the raider and the convoy, allowing the latter to escape while being herself smashed to junk and sunk. *Montgomery* found nothing, however, and after searching briefly for the German "pocket battleship"—with orders to shadow by day and attack by night—arrived at Belfast, Northern Ireland, on 11 November.

Shifting to Plymouth, England, a week later, *Montgomery* was allocated to the Western Approaches command and based at Liverpool. During the course of one of her early patrols, *Montgomery* rescued 39 survivors from the torpedoed motor tanker *Scottish Standard* which had been torpedoed and sunk by *U-96* on 21 February 1941. Disembarking the rescued mariners on the 24th, *Montgomery* resumed her Western Approaches patrols soon thereafter.

The flush-decker underwent repairs at Barrow, Lancashire, from April to September and was later assigned to the 4th Escort Group. Based now at Greenock, Scotland, the destroyer operated between the British Isles and Canadian ports through the end of 1941. On 13 January 1942, the Panamanian-registered steamer SS *Friar Rock* was torpedoed and sunk by *U-130* 100 miles southeast of Cape Race, Newfoundland. Four days later, *Montgomery* picked up seven survivors from that ship.

In February 1942, *Montgomery* came under the aegis of the Western Local Escort Force at Halifax. Later in 1942, the destroyer was loaned to the Royal Canadian Navy before she sailed south and underwent repairs at the Charleston (S.C.) Navy Yard which lasted into the following year 1943. Resuming her coastwise convoy escort operations in February 1943, *Montgomery* rescued survivors of the torpedoed *Manchester Merchant*—sunk by *U-628* on 25 February 1943, 390 miles off Cape Race.

The destroyer remained with the Western Local Escort Force into late 1943, operating out of Halifax. On 12 December 1943, she assisted the Bowater-Lloyd Paper Co. barge *Spruce Lake* and, on the 27th, departed Halifax for the British Isles, carrying the surviving crew members from the torpedoed British destroyer HMS *Hurricane* which had been sunk by *U-415* on Christmas Eve.

Arriving in England soon thereafter, *Montgomery* was placed in reserve in the Tyne River on 23 February 1944. Removed from the "effective list"—the British equivalent of the United States Navy's "Navy list"—the veteran flush-decker was subsequently broken up for scrap in the spring of 1945 shortly before the end of the war in Europe.

II

(DD–578: dp. 2,050; l. 376'1''; b. 39'8''; dr. 13'0''; s. 35 k.; cpl. 273; a. 5 5'', 6 40mm., 7 20mm., 10 21'' tt,. 2 dct., 6 dcp.; cl. *Fletcher*)

The second *Wickes* (DD–578) was laid down on 15 April 1942 at Orange, Tex., by the Consolidated Steel Co.; launched on 13 September 1942; sponsored by Miss Catherine Young Wickes, the great-great-grandniece of Lambert Wickes; and commissioned on 16 June 1943, Lt. Comdr. William Y. Allen, Jr., in command.

Departing New Orleans on 13 July, *Wickes* sailed for Cuban waters and reached Guantanamo Bay three days later. She conducted shakedown training until 11 August, when she set sail for Charleston, S.C., where she commenced her post-shakedown availability.

Wickes then trained into the autumn, ranging from Trinidad, in the British West Indies to Casco Bay, Maine; and from Norfolk, Va., to Argentia, Newfoundland, from 1 September to 6 November. Between drills at sea, the ship underwent brief periods of repair in the navy yards at Boston and Norfolk.

On 6 November, *Wickes* departed the Boston Navy Yard in company with the small aircraft carrier *Cabot* (CVL–28) and sister destroyer *Bell* (DD–587)—their destination: the Canal Zone. Transiting the Panama Canal between 12 and 15 November, the destroyer reached San Diego, Calif., on the 22d, but pushed on for the Hawaiian Islands and reached Pearl Harbor on the 27th. Over the ensuing days, the destroyer exercised in those local waters, conducting antisubmarine and antiaircraft drills. On several occasions during this training, her routine was interrupted by orders to rendezvous with and augment the screens of various task groups returning from the operations which wrested the Gilbert Islands from Japan.

Wickes—in company with sisterships *Charles J. Badger* (DD–657) and *Isherwood* (DD–520)—departed Pearl Harbor on 10 December 1943 and set a course for the Aleutian Islands. Over the next few months, *Wickes* operated in the Aleutians. To her commanding officer and crew, the duties performed seemed "uneventful," their "greatest battles," he recalled were fought against the elements and the "dreary monotony of Aleutian duty."

Such an enervating routine was interrupted by three bombardments conducted by Task Force (TF) 94 against the Kuril Islands, Paramushiro and Matsuwa. The first raid hit Paramushiro on 4 February 1944 and marked the first time that *Wickes* made contact with the enemy. She bombarded Japanese targets in the town of Kurabuzaki on the southern tip of the island.

Early in March, *Wickes*—in company with other units of TF 94—made another sweep into Japan's backyard. On the lookout for Japanese shipping as they steamed through the Sea of Okhotsk, the task force found slim pickings before again shelling targets on Paramushiro on 4 March. Another bombardment was slated to take place there, but unfavorable weather made it impossible.

Two months later, *Wickes'* guns once more joined in a cannonade against Japanese facilities on Paramushiro and at Matsuwa, on 26 May and 13 June, respectively. Darkness and fog presented difficulties for the American forces but did not constitute insurmountable difficulties. On 2 August, while TF 94 was again steaming to shell Matsuwa, *Wickes* made visual contact with a "snooper," a Mitsubishi G4M "Betty" bomber. On van picket station, the destroyer opened fire on the intruder—the ship's first antiaircraft action. Unfortunately, the plane managed to escape and, together with the worsening weather, nullified TF 94's chances of making an undetected approach to Matsuwa. The bombardment was accordingly cancelled.

Wickes' tour in one of the most difficult operating areas on the globe finally ended when she "very happily" departed Adak, Alaska, on 7 August, headed south in company with other units of Destroyer Squadron (DesRon) 49. Reaching San Francisco on 16 August, *Wickes* moored at Pier 36. There, she received minor repairs from the facilities and workmen of the Matson Navigation Co., under the eye of the Assistant Industrial Manager, Mare Island Navy Yard. During the refit, the ship received a "dazzle" camouflage pattern, designed to confuse observers as to the ship's heading and speed.

Underway from the west coast upon completion of repairs and alterations, *Wickes* set a course for Pearl Harbor once more, in company with *Kimberly* (DD–521), *Young* (DD–580), and *William D. Porter* (DD–579)—other units of DesRon 49. Reaching Hawaiian waters, *Wickes* spent the first two weeks of September engaged in supporting landing rehearsals at Lahaina Roads, Maui, "in preparation for forthcoming operations." While in port between exercises at sea, *Wickes* received additional radar gear while alongside *Yosemite* (AD–19), in preparation for the ship's slated role as a fighter-director ship.

Thus newly outfitted, *Wickes* left Pearl Harbor on 15 September, as part of Task Group (TG) 33.2, the group slated to hit the island of Yap. Reaching Eniwetok, in the Marshalls, on the 25th, the destroyer spent the next two days replenishing fuel and provisions. Resuming her voyage on the 28th, *Wickes* reached Manus, in the Admiralties, on 3 October. En route, the ship crossed the equator for the first time.

However, changing operational requirements resulted in the cancellation of the Yap invasion. *Wickes* was thus reassigned to the 7th Fleet and earmarked for participation in the assault on the island of Leyte. She remained at Manus until 14 October, conducting general upkeep and engaging in gunnery and antisubmarine warfare (ASW) training.

Wickes—with a fighter-director team embarked—departed the Admiralties on 14 October. As a screening unit of task group "Baker"—TG 79.4—a transport group, the destroyer reached Leyte Gulf according to plan, on D day, 20 October. She then proceeded to her assigned radar picket station near the center of the gulf and assumed duties as picket and fighter-director ship.

Over the next four days, *Wickes* remained on that station as the invasion—the first step in the liberation of the Philippines—unfolded. She frequently saw Japanese aircraft—particularly in the area where the transports were congregated—but none came within range of her guns. She even made one good sound contact, on the 22d, and dropped an 11-charge pattern but observed no positive results.

Wickes witnessed the Battle of Surigao Strait from a faraway vantage point in the pre-dawn darkness of 25 October. "It is no exaggeration," recorded her historian, "to state that this engagement was exciting even from a distance." During the rest of her time on station, *Wickes*' fighter-director team evaluated the air situation, controlling the protecting combat air patrol (CAP) overhead on the first two days of the landings, 20 and 21 October. During the first afternoon, the *Wickes*-directed CAP splashed a "Zeke" or "Zero" carrier-borne fighter.

Subsequently clearing Leyte Gulf, *Wickes* served as screen commander for a 12-ship group of LST's headed for New Guinea. The group, Task Unit (TU) 79.14.9, reached Hollandia, arriving without incident on 1 November. *Wickes* dropped anchor soon after her arrival and remained there through the 4th.

Wickes subsequently spent most of November in screening operations, escorting a transport group during all phases of its replenishment run to Leyte. Transports and cargo ships, TG 79.15, were screened to Noemfoor Island and during the loading operations that ensued. She then escorted them to Leyte, where they were unloaded on the 18th. She then escorted the auxiliaries back to Seeadler Harbor, Manus, where she arrived on the 25th.

Wickes departed Manus on the 28th, bound for Torokina, Bougainville, in the Solomons, escorting the troopships of Transport Division 38. En route, she touched at Finschhafen on the 29th during the division's stopover to embark troops and reached Torokina on 1 December.

Wickes remained at Torokina, Empress Augusta Bay, until the 15th, patrolling the outskirts of that body of water in company with her sisterships of DesRon 49. The next day, she began the return trip to the Admiralty Islands but stopped in the Huon Gulf for a landing exercise to prepare for her next slated operation. She finally reached Manus on the 21st. The destroyer spent Christmas in port and replenished her logistics requirements until the 27th.

Underway on that day, *Wickes* proceeded to Luzon for the assault at Lingayen. On the approach run, the ship—screening tractor groups "Able and Baker" of TF 79—steamed with TU 79.11.3. Embarked was a new fighter-director team taken on at Manus.

The northbound run proved largely uneventful, except for what the ship's historian called "a moderate amount of heckling" by enemy aircraft day and night. Again, *Wickes* proved exceptionally adept at fighter-direction duties. Her team vectored CAP planes to oncoming enemy planes, and they accordingly splashed four "Tojo" fighters into the waters off Luzon on the morning of 8 January 1945.

The ship herself did not fire upon any enemy planes until reaching Lingayen Gulf itself the following day, 9 January, when she fired at a pair of attacking planes, driving them off but not splashing them. That same evening, *Wickes* departed the coast of Luzon with her charges, screening the unloaded ships as they headed out of the battle area.

About one-half hour before sunrise on the morning of 10 January, a Japanese plane—a single-engined fighter—pushed over in a dive and dropped a bomb which exploded off the destroyer's starboard side, close aboard. Fragments, scything through the air, wounded 15 sailors topside and punctured the ship with a few small holes.

That brush with the enemy, and the light damage inflicted by the attacker, did not keep the ship off the "front lines," for she was soon back in action again, operating on antisubmarine patrols in Leyte Gulf during most of the time between 13 and 25 January.

On 26 January, she sortied as part of TG 78.3 and took station as escort and fighter-director ship for the passage of the task group through the Mindanao and Sulu Seas, en route to Luzon, for landings on the west coast in the vicinity of San Felipe, Zambales Province. The landings themselves took place two days later, meeting no opposition and calling for no bombardment. Friendly natives, happy to see their liberators, came out in *bancas* and other craft to greet the Americans warmly. On the 30th, *Wickes* stood in readiness during another unopposed landing—the one made at Grande Island, in Subic Bay. For the next two weeks, the destroyer was based on Subic Bay, operating in the waters off southwestern Luzon. During that period, she made a short run to Mindoro and back, escorting for convoys of landing craft each way.

Meanwhile, preparations were being made for assaults on Bataan and Corregidor—the scene of the humiliating disasters for the United States and her Filipino allies three years before. Minesweeping operations commenced on 13 February. At sunset that day, *Wickes* joined her sistership *Young* in supporting the thinly armored "sweepers" off Manila Bay, retired with them that night, and returned with them the next morning.

As the ships worked their way into an area between Corregidor and Carabao Islands, Japanese shore batteries emplaced on those islands and on Caballo began to lob shells at the minecraft and their escorts. *Wickes* teamed with *Young* to deliver vigorous counter-battery fire, knocking out the pugnacious guns. Other destroyers and cruisers also participated in the silencing of the enemy emplacements, but *Wickes*' historian modestly recorded, "No claim is made by *Wickes* to have done the job single-handed, but it is certain that this ship's gunfire was accurate and effective, and contributed materially toward the successful result and protection of the minesweepers who were able to proceed with their task unmolested for the remainder of the day." Nevertheless, both *Wickes* and *Young* had some close shaves, as the enemy landed some shells close aboard but fortunately did not hit either ship.

On the morning of the 15th, *Wickes* shelled Japanese positions in Mariveles Harbor, just prior to the landings there. She then stood by to render gunfire support for the troops as they went ashore. However, when no opposition developed, the destroyer took up a patrol station, on watch for submarines. Meanwhile, throughout the day, 7th-Fleet destroyers and cruisers—assisted by planes— continued giving Corregidor a pasting.

Between 0400 and daylight on the 16th, *Wickes* steamed in company with *Picking* and *Young*, to intercept "suicide boats" that had penetrated Mariveles Harbor. Many drifting mines revealed themselves with the wash of dawn—but no suiciders. *Wickes* destroyed one mine with gunfire and was about to destroy others when minesweepers arrived on the scene and relieved the destroyer of that duty.

Wickes then proceeded to conduct another shore bombardment mission—this time against the beaches on Corregidor over which the assault was to pass. Paratroops drifted down and landed on the top of the island as part of the many-faceted attack designed to destroy the enemy units heavily entrenched there. When the troops commenced landing, Japanese guns opened up from caves on the rocky island. *Wickes* replied with counter-battery rounds against Corregidor and Caballo Islands, maneuvering to keep Caballo covered for the remainder of the day.

Late on the afternoon of the 16th, *Wickes*—in company with *Picking* and *Young*—was detached from that duty. "By all standards," recounted the ship's historian when reviewing the Philippine operations, "this operation was the most interesting one the *Wickes* ever took part in." It had afforded the ship the opportunity to observe, closely, the activities of other units: paratroops, heavy bombers, minesweepers, and ground troops alike. "All hands felt that at last the *Wickes* had produced some results and definitely accomplished something after months of more or less routine duties," "Fire from enemy shore batteries," he went on, "added just the right amount of hazard and provided the first real test of the ship under fire."

However, there would be quite enough "hazard," in the ship's future operations. Inexorably, the mighty American Navy bore down upon the shores of Nippon itself. Yet every step that the American armada took closer to the Japanese home islands increased the intensity of the enemy's resistance.

For *Wickes*, upon conclusion of her support of the Corregidor assaults, there was a tender availability awaiting her in Leyte Gulf. After those repairs, *Wickes* —in company with *Luce* (DD–522) and *Charles J. Badger*—escorted the heavy cruisers *Portland* (CA–33) and *Minneapolis* (CA–36) to Ulithi, in the Carolines, departing Philippine waters on 2 March and returning eight days later on the 10th.

Wickes participated in the landing practices in Leyte Gulf for the next operation on the American timetable, the assault on Okinawa Gunto. From 13 to 16 March, the forces slated to take part in that thrust trained and rehearsed for the upcoming event. Activities during those days of training included duty in the tractor group "George" screen—TG 51.7—fire support drills, and ASW patrols around the transport area—all skills that would be very much needed.

After replenishing fuel, ammunition, and provisions and receiving additional fighter-director equipment, *Wickes*—with a new fighter-director team embarked— sortied for Okinawa on 19 March with TG 51.7.

Upon her arrival off Okinawa on the 26th, *Wickes* acted as a fire support vessel, supporting the landings by scheduled bombardments on Yakabi Shima, Kerama Retto; but there was no opposition on that island that required additional naval gunfire. Commencing on 26 March and continuing through 4 May, *Wickes* conducted regular radar-picket and fighter-director duties on the various stations off Okinawa. During that period, the CAP, vectored to the enemy by Lt. (jg.) James R. Baumgartner, USNR, the senior fighter-director officer embarked, engaged 42 enemy aircraft, destroyed eight, and damaged four.

Late on the afternoon of 22 April, the *Wickes*-directed CAP scored their most signal success. On Radar Picket Station 14, about 70 miles northwest of Okinawa,

Wickes vectored Marine fighters from Yontan Field to a large raid approaching from the northward. The flying Leathernecks knocked down 26 Japanese planes, probably splashed another pair, and damaged four.

After later turning over her fighter-director team to *Gainard* (DD–706), on 4 May, *Wickes* alternated duty on the antiaircraft screen protecting the transports off Hagushi beach with antisubmarine patrols. She also supervised underway fueling operations for a day. She then underwent a period of needed upkeep to have her boilers cleaned.

During the 51 days *Wickes* spent off Okinawa, she took enemy aircraft under fire no less than 14 times, and was, four times, the object of attention from kamikazes. Her gunners claimed five "kills" from the suiciders' ranks, and one "probable." Two of the downed enemy aircraft managed to crash close enough to send pieces of themselves onto the ship's fantail—fortunately doing no damage. On one occasion, one of the kamikazes attempted to torpedo the ship, but its "fish" also missed. In addition, *Wickes* may have saved the hospital ship *Relief* (AH–1) from serious damage when she deflected, with her gunfire, a suicider atempting to crash into the ship-of-mercy.

Until 10 April, *Wickes* patrolled her picket stations alone, without support. After that time, a landing craft or another destroyer was always present. Other incidental occurrences that came up during the ship's time off the embattled isle of Okinawa included the rescue of five men from a raft from the fast transport *Dickerson* (APD–21); fishing out a crashed fighter pilot from the fleet carrier *Bennington* (CV–20); and exploding a drifting mine with gunfire. Remarkably, in contrast to some of her sisterships that suffered grievous damage at the hands of the suicidal kamikaze, *Wickes* suffered only three casualties: all wounded when a plane strafed the ship.

Wickes departed the Okinawa area on 15 May, bound for Ulithi, while the campaign continued on. She screened a convoy of auxiliaries and merchantmen to the Western Carolines, reaching her destination on the 21st. She then nested alongside the destroyer tender *Prairie* (AD–15) and received a 10-day availability. The time spent there at the sprawling, busy, advance base was, truly, "a welcome rest" after the long hours of general quarters and alerts that were part and parcel of duty off Okinawa. "Although all hands had gained a great deal of confidence in our ability to handle air attacks," wrote the ship's historian, "it was difficult, after more than a month of picket duty, not to feel like fugitives from the law of averages, as so many other ships had been hit."

Wickes—her availability alongside *Prairie* completed by early June—departed Ulithi on 7 June, escorting another slow convoy. Her destination was again Okinawa. She safely reached there with her charges on the 13th and took on board another fighter-director team. In company with two or three supporting destroyers, *Wickes* then returned to the picket lines. Most enemy air activity then took place nocturnally.

Her second stay at Okinawa proved briefer than the first. The ship headed for Saipan on the 23d of June with a slow convoy but with onward routing approved to Pearl Harbor. Reaching Saipan on the 29th, *Wickes* departed that same day, bound for the Hawaiian Islands in company with *Picking* and *Hall* (DD–583).

Making port at Pearl Harbor on 7 July, *Wickes'* time in Hawaiian waters proved brief; for, on the 8th, she was bound "stateside," her bow "very happily pointed" toward the Golden Gate. She made the last leg of the voyage in company with her old companion, *Picking*, and two other ships, *Sproston* (DD–577) and *Brackett* (DE–41). All ships arrived on the morning of 14 July and proceeded to the Naval Ammunition Depot at Mare Island to unload ammunition. Upon completion of that task, *Wickes* got underway for Hunters Point, tying up at pierside at sunset, with 47 days' availability ahead of her.

Within a day or two after arrival, DesRon 49 was dissolved; and *Wickes* was reassigned to DesRon 58. The war in the Pacific, though, ended before the destroyer completed her scheduled overhaul on 31 August 1945.

With the end of the war, however, it soon became evident that with the massive shipbuilding programs that had come along during hostilities there was a surplus of ships for anticipated postwar needs. Along with the decommissioning and scrapping of many of the older fleet units, some of the newer ships were decommissioned and placed in reserve.

Wickes was among the latter. Completing her overhaul by early September of 1945, the ship conducted refresher training exercises into the autumn and winter. Her service career was growing short. She was placed out of commission, in reserve, on 20 December 1945. She never returned to active duty, even during the Korean War when many of her sisterships were pulled out of mothballs and recommissioned. Struck from the Navy list on 1 November 1972, her hulk was later expended in ordnance tests.

Wickes earned five battle stars for her World War II service.

Wico

Wico—a screw steam tanker of 6,300 tons' displacement built in 1888 at Newcastle, England, by Armstrong Mitchell and Co., Ltd.—was owned by the Standard Oil Co., of New Jersey, prior to World War I. Apparently earmarked by the Navy for use as a depot oiler and designated Id. No. 1278 in 1917 or 1918, the vessel apparently was never taken over for naval service. However, she was armed by a naval crew to man the two 4-inch guns which were mounted on the ship. After the armistice, these guns were removed at New York on 7 February 1919. The ship was broken up for scrap in December 1922.

Wicomico

A county in southeastern Maryland on the eastern shore of the Chesapeake Bay.

(Yard Tug No. 26: t. 152; l. 91'5''; b. 21'; dr. 10'; s. 10 k.; a. 1 3-pdr., 1 1-pdr.)

Wicomico (Yard Tug No. 26)—a steam tug built at Philadelphia by Neafie and Levy as *C. G. Coyle*—was completed in 1892. Acquired by the Navy from W. G. Coyle for service during the Spanish-American War, the tug was renamed *Choctaw* and commissioned on 19 April 1898, Lt. (jg.) Walter O. Hulme in command.

Attached to the Auxiliary Naval Force for patrol duty during the war with Spain, *Choctaw* operated in the Gulf of Mexico through the cessation of hostilities. On 26 August 1898, she was decommissioned at the Pensacola Navy Yard. Recommissioned on 15 June 1899, *Choctaw* sailed for Portsmouth, N.H., with *Monongahela* in tow, before reporting to the naval training station at Newport, R.I., for duty as a yard tug and ferry. Subsequently detached and sent to the Norfolk Navy Yard for repairs, the ship was again placed out of commission on 15 July 1902.

Placed back in active service in 1904, *Choctaw* served at the Washington Navy Yard through World War I. She was renamed *Wicomico* on 20 February 1918 and designated YT–26 on 17 July 1920. Transferred to the Norfolk Navy Yard on 21 April 1921, *Wicomico* served in the 5th Naval District through the outbreak of World War II in September 1939, and into the following year.

On 15 February 1940, *Wicomico* collided with *Goff* (DD–247) in Hampton Roads and sank shortly thereafter. Struck from the Navy list on 27 February 1940, the ship was salvaged and subsequently scrapped.

Widgeon

A fresh water duck.

I

(Minesweeper No. 22: dp. 950; l. 187'10''; b. 35'6''; dr. 9'9½'' (mean); s. 14 k.; cpl. 85; a. 2 3''; cl. *Lapwing*)

Widgeon (Minesweeper No. 22) was laid down on 8 October 1917 at Chester, Pa., by the Sun Shipbuilding Co.; launched on 5 May 1918; sponsored by Miss Mildred Moyer; and commissioned on 27 July 1918, Lt. Comdr. John A. Monroe in command.

Widgeon served with Minesweeping Group 2 of the Atlantic Fleet during the last months of World War I. After the armistice, she was assigned to the North Sea Minesweeping Detachment and departed Boston, Mass., on 28 June 1919, bound for Scotland. Arriving at Kirkwall on 10 July, *Widgeon* operated in the North Sea between Scotland and Norway, sweeping up mines sown by the Allies the year before to deter the German High Seas Fleet. These duties—often difficult and dangerous—kept the minesweeper occupied through the summer of 1919. Following the conclusion of the operation, *Widgeon* headed home—via Brest, France; Punta Delgada, Azores; and Hamilton, Bermuda—and arrived at New York on 19 November 1919.

Widgeon operated off the east coast through 1921. During this period, she was designated AM–22 on 17 July 1920. Selected for conversion to a salvage vessel for duty on the Pacific coast, the minesweeper was decommissioned at Charleston, S.C., on 15 April 1922. She underwent conversion at the Charleston Navy Yard and was recommissioned there on 5 March 1923.

Despite her new equipment, the ship retained her minesweeper designation. In a departmental letter of 21 November 1923, the Navy's Bureau of Construction and Repair specified that *Widgeon*'s equipment be utilized to determine "their exact capabilities in salvage work." Furthermore, "*Widgeon* should be considered available for salvage or rescue work and the Commander, Submarine Divisions, Pacific, is authorized to send . . . *Widgeon* to render such service when needed."

Operating out of Pearl Harbor, Territory of Hawaii, *Widgeon* served as the primary submarine rescue vessel for the Hawaiian area. During this time, she proved her versatility by recovering practice mines or torpedoes and served as a training ship for fleet divers. In 1926, the ship was extensively altered to increase her capabilities as a submarine rescue vessel. The ship was finally reclassified ASR–1 on 22 January 1936, over a decade after she began operating as such.

Widgeon continued her routine operations out of Pearl Harbor into the late 1930's as the world crisis deepened in Europe and the Far East. On 7 December 1941, the submarine rescue vessel lay alongside a berth at the submarine base at Pearl Harbor, when Japanese aircraft swept over the Pacific Fleet's base. When the raid was over later that morning, the Pacific Fleet's battleships ceased to exist as a potential retaliatory force to threaten Japan's massive "southern operation" in the Far East.

Despite keeping up a steady defensive fire with rifles and machine guns during the attack, *Widgeon*'s crewmen did not claim to have downed any of the attackers. Then, soon after the enemy planes disappeared, smoke still boiled into the Pacific skies as *Widgeon* got underway from her berth at the submarine base and set her course for Ford Island to begin salvage operations on the overturned *Oklahoma* (BB–37). When she reached "Battleship Row," she found that burning oil spewing from the shattered tanks on *Arizona* (BB–39) was threatening the ships nested immediately ahead, *Tennessee* (BB–43) and the torpedoed *West Virginia* (BB–48). Accordingly, under orders from the Commander, Battle Force, *Widgeon* assisted *Tern* (AM–31) and *YG–17* in fighting the fires.

Widgeon subsequently took part in salvaging *Nevada* (BB–36), *California* (BB–44), and *Oklahoma*. Her work on *Nevada* earned the ship a commendation from Commander, Battle Force, and her divers conducted many a foray into the darkened and treacherous interiors of the sunken battleships. When this work was well in hand and her service in that capacity was no longer required, *Widgeon* returned to her duties with the submarines of the Pacific Fleet. She towed targets for gunnery exercises and served as a target during torpedo-firing drills. She also recovered practice torpedoes at the conclusion of the day's training activities.

Widgeon operated in this capacity from April 1942 to 7 September 1943, when she got underway for the California coast. Arriving at San Diego on 18 September, the warship operated off the west coast as a torpedo recovery and submarine rescue ship into the spring of 1944, when she was relieved by *Ortolan* (ASR–5). In May, *Widgeon* returned to Pearl Harbor and resumed her operations as the Hawaiian-based submarine rescue vessel. She continued this duty through the end of the war in the Pacific and into November 1945, after which time she completed another tour at San Diego. In the summer of 1946, *Widgeon*—as part of Task Unit 1.2.7, the salvage unit of Joint Task Force 1—supported Operation "Crossroads," the atomic bomb tests at Bikini Atoll.

Subsequently returning to the west coast, *Widgeon* was decommissioned on 5 February 1947 and struck from the Navy list on 23 December 1947. Soon thereafter, she was sold to the Basalt Rock Co., of Napa, Calif., and scrapped.

Widgeon received one battle star for her World War II service.

II

(MSC–208: dp. 412; l. 145'0''; b. 28'0''; dr. 12'0'' (max.); s. 12.8 k.; cpl. 40; a. 1 20mm., 2 .50-cal. mg., 1 81mm. M.; cl. *Redwing*)

The second *Widgeon* (AMS–208) was laid down on 3 May 1954 at Bellingham, Wash., by the Bellingham Shipyards, Inc.; launched on 15 October 1954; sponsored by Mrs. John F. Cushing, the wife of the treasurer of the Bellingham Shipyards; reclassified MSC–208 on 7 February 1955; and commissioned at the naval station at Tacoma, Wash., on 16 November 1955, Lt. Bruce G. Stone in command.

Ready for sea on 15 December 1955, *Widgeon*—a unit of the Pacific Fleet Mine Force—sailed on 3 January 1956 for visits to San Francisco and Long Beach, Calif. The new minesweeper operated out of the latter port until 29 January, at which time she shifted to San Diego to undergo shakedown training. Upon completion of shakedown, the ship underwent a four-week availability at the Long Beach Naval Shipyard.

The ship underwent further trials and alterations before she sailed to the Western Pacific (WestPac) on 1 October 1956. Proceeding in company with Mine Division (MinDiv) 95, *Widgeon* reported to Commander, Naval Forces, Far East (ComNavFE) for duty and was assigned to MinDiv 32, Mine Squadron 3, Mine Flotilla 1.

Homeported at Sasebo, Japan, *Widgeon* operated in the Far East for the next 13 years. During that time, she participated in local operations in Japanese waters, as well as voyages to Korea and Okinawa for exercises. She conducted joint minesweeping operations and exercises with units of the Japanese Maritime Self-Defense Forces, the Republic of Korea (ROK) Navy, Chinese Nationalist Navy, and visited ports such as Kobe, Yokosuka, Nagasaki, Kagoshima, Aburatsu, Beppu, Kochi, Tsushima, Japan; Kaohsiung, Taiwan; Maisuru, Japan; Hong Kong; Buckner Bay; Subic Bay, Philippines; and Pohang and Koje Do, Korea. Interspersed with her active training evolutions, the minesweeper underwent routine periods of upkeep and alterations and repairs at her home port of Sasebo.

Participation in the increasing American involvement in the war in Vietnam, however, highlighted the minesweeper's lengthy WestPac deployment. From the mid-1960's, the ship commenced a regular schedule of deployments on "Market Time" patrol stations in the coastal waters off South Vietnam, on patrol and interdiction to cut off the seaborne flow of supplies to the communist Viet Cong forces inside South Vietnam. During one such cruise in January 1967—while being diverted from a "Market Time" patrol to conduct classified operations in the Gulf of Tonkin—the ship made the national news when she was rammed by a swordfish. Later during that same cruise, while the ship was crossing the South China Sea, she sighted a McDonnell F4–C Phantom crash into the sea. *Widgeon* altered course in time to rescue one man of the two-man crew. The other flier, the pilot, died in the crash. Commander, Naval Forces, Philippines, later cited *Widgeon* for her outstanding performance of duty during the rescue.

Widgeon returned to Sasebo on 17 February 1967, worn and beaten from heavy seas, and was under repairs during March and April. On 1 May, a Navy P–3 Orion patrol plane, with a crew of 12 men on board, crashed in the Tsushima Strait off the southern coast of Korea. *Widgeon* headed for the scene of the crash, transiting the hazardous Hirado Strait for search and rescue (SAR) operations. She searched for two days and recovered numerous bits of debris but was unable to locate any survivors or the fuselage of the plane. The minesweeper ultimately returned to Sasebo on 5 May to commence refresher training.

Widgeon spent the months of July through September on her sixth "Market Time" patrol and a cruise in the South China Sea. Departing Sasebo on 3 July, the minesweeper arrived at Bangkok, Thailand, on the 15th. She later operated with mine countermeasures units of the Royal Thai Navy in the Gulf of Thailand in a SEATO exercise, "Sea Dog," before she operated on "Market Time" stations from 27 July to 12 September. When she arrived at Kaohsiung, Taiwan, on 16 September, the ship's crew had not touched land in 60 days. *Widgeon* subsequently spent the rest of the year engaged in local operations out of Sasebo and Buckner Bay, Okinawa, and made a visit to Hong Kong for rest and recreation.

Over the next two years, *Widgeon* continued her operations in the Far East and Southeast Asian waters. During that time, she conducted two "Market Time" patrols for which she later received the Meritorious Unit Commendation. The award, given the ship on 16 August 1970, was for the period from 1 June 1968 to 13 September 1969. During that time, *Widgeon* served with the Mine Countermeasures Ready Group and Coastal Surveillance Forces in combat operations off the coast of South Vietnam. She maintained a consistently high standard of readiness that enabled her to assume assigned duties early or on very short notice, and she completed three stints on "Market Time" patrol stations. She not only inspected or boarded over 1,100 vessels but, on occasion, returned "hostile" fire from shore and conducted underwater searches. Throughout the repeated patrol extensions, "the continually outstanding performance, high state of morale, preparedness, and ingenuity of the officers and men of *Widgeon* attested to their exceptional team spirit and professionalism. By their exemplary courage and dedication, they contributed significantly to the success of anti-infiltration efforts in the Republic of Vietnam and enhanced the reputation of the Mine Countermeasures Ready Group, thereby reflecting credit upon themselves and the United States Naval Service."

Ultimately, after 13 years of continuous service in WestPac operating areas, *Widgeon* sailed for the United States on 17 August 1969, in company with *Catskill* (MCS–1), *Vireo* (MSC–205), and *Warbler* (MSC–206). Proceeding via Pearl Harbor, she arrived at Long Beach exactly one month later. Later that autumn, on

1 October 1969, *Widgeon* was decommissioned and placed in reserve; she got underway the next day for her new home port, San Diego.

For the next three years, *Widgeon* operated as a Group II Naval Reserve training (NRT) ship. She operated primarily in the San Diego area but twice visited Ensenada, Mexico, once in 1972 and once in 1973. Struck from the Navy list on 2 July 1973, *Widgeon* was sold in January 1974.

Widgeon (MSC–208) earned six engagement stars for her Vietnam service and a Meritorious Unit Commendation.

Wieldrecht

(Tanker: dp. 7,350; l. 340'; b. 47.3'; dr. 20'11" (aft); s. 10 k.; cpl. 95; a. 1 5", 1 3")

Wieldrecht (Id. No. 2519)—a tanker built in 1913 by the *Rotterdamsche Droogdok Maatschappij* at Rotterdam in the Netherlands for Ph. van Ommeren's company *N. V. Maatschappij Stoomschip Wieldrecht*—was seized by United States customs officials at New York City early in 1918 under the right of angary and was commissioned there on 4 April 1918. However, she was soon decommissioned and turned over to the United States Shipping Board (USSB) which operated her until June. She was returned to the Navy and was commissioned again at Montevideo, Uruguay, on 17 June 1918 for service in the Naval Overseas Transportation Service, Comdr. William B. Wells in command.

After refitting at New York, *Wieldrecht* arrived at Norfolk where she took on a cargo of fuel oil and departed that port on the 5th with a convoy bound for France. She reached Brest on 24 July, discharged her cargo, and sailed again with a homeward-bound convoy on the 26th. The tanker entered New York on 20 August and made repairs for the remainder of the month. On 3 September, she headed south to Norfolk to load more fuel oil to join another convoy bound for Europe. She passed between Capes Charles and Henry on 7 September and headed across the Atlantic. The ship entered Brest on 25 September and, the following day, moved to La Pallice, where she discharged her fuel oil. On 8 October, *Wieldrecht* started back across the Atlantice once more. After arriving at New York 16 days later, she made repairs, loaded her third cargo of fuel oil for American forces in France, and got underway on 4 November. She arrived at La Pallice on the 24th and remained there until 17 December when she began her homeward voyage. *Wieldrecht* reached New York on 5 January 1919 and loaded one final cargo for Europe. The tanker exited New York harbor on 12 February and proceeded to Rotterdam in the Netherlands. She arrived early in March, discharged her cargo, and set sail on the return voyage on the 19th. *Wieldrecht* stood into New York harbor on 4 April.

On 8 April 1919, *Wieldrecht* was decommissioned and turned over to the United States Shipping Board at Philadelphia. Two days later, she was returned to her Dutch owners. She served in mercantile service under the Dutch flag until 1930 when her name disappeared from the mercantile lists.

Wieringen

Wieringen—formerly named *Burgemeesters' Jacob*—was a 7,400-ton steel-hulled freighter built at Stockton, England, in 1902, by the firm of Ropner and Son. Inspected by the United States Navy in the 3d Naval District on 30 March 1918 for possible service as a depot collier, she was designated Id. No. 2547.

Although not taken over by the Navy, she was armed on 2 November 1918 and assigned a naval armed guard crew to man the one 4-inch and one 3-inch gun mounted on the vessel. This armament and the attendant gunners were removed on 8 March 1919.

Wilbert A. Edwards

(ScStr: dp. 650; l. 160'0"; b. 23'10"; dr. 10'0" (mean); s. 11.0 k.; cpl. 36; a. 2 3", 2 1-pdrs.)

Wilbert A. Edwards—a wooden-hulled fishing boat built in 1911 at Solomons Island, Md., by M. M. Davis for the W. A. Edwards Corp.—was inspected by the Navy for possible use as a patrol vessel on "distant service." Although Navy General Order No. 314 of 28 July 1917 specified that "scout patrol" vessels having compound names would be known by the surname only (hence, *Wilbert A. Edwards* would become simply *Edwards*), this ship appears to have retained her name for the duration of her service. Her logs, in fact, carry the name *W. A. Edwards*, while the *Ship's Data, U.S. Naval Vessels 1918* carries the full name *Wilbert A. Edwards* on the list of naval vessels.

The ship's deck logs do not commence until 17 September 1917, a little over a month after the ship was commissioned at the Norfolk Navy Yard, Portsmouth, Va., on 10 August. Apparently, Lt. D. C. Kindell, USNRF, was the ship's first commanding officer; he was relieved by Lt. Robert Phillips, NNV, on 17 September, while the ship lay at Gravesend Bay, N.Y. Two days later, *Wilbert A. Edwards* departed Gravesend Bay, bound for Boston; transited the Cape Cod Canal on the morning of the 20th, and arrived at the Boston Navy Yard later that day. After voyage repairs, *Wilbert A. Edwards* sailed for Halifax, Nova Scotia, on 25 September, on what was probably supposed to be the first leg of a voyage to Ponta Delgada in the Azores, to take up patrol duties from that port.

However, the next day, the erstwhile fishing craft suffered an engine casualty and notified the nearby Coast Guard cutter *Algonquin* of her plight. The latter took the disabled ship in tow that afternoon and took her to Halifax, Nova Scotia, where they arrived on the 27th. There, *Wilbert A. Edwards* coaled before getting underway in tow of *Algonquin* on 1 October. The ships ran into a heavy storm on the afternoon of the first day out of port.

Weather conditions had worsened rapidly, and *Wilbert A. Edwards* rolled and labored heavily, shipping much water. By 0500 on the 2d, the chief engineer on board reported to Lt. Phillips that the ship was taking water and that he was unable to keep the flooding under control. Three hours later, the executive officer, Lt. (jg.) Henry J. Porter, USNRF, and the ship's carpenter examined the steering gear and found the quadrant working loose on the rudder, the stuffing box slack in its bed, and all bolts loose in the woodwork. They tried to repair the damage but could not. Meanwhile, as if problems with the rudder were not enough, the flooding continued below decks as the ship rolled and pitched at an alarming rate. By noon, though, the water in the engine room had not gained on the pumps. At last the ship seemed to be holding her own.

Algonquin kept *Wilbert A. Edwards* in tow as she steamed ahead at slow speed, and the two ships eventually returned to Halifax on 4 October.

After ultimately returning to Boston in company with the collier *Mars*, *Wilbert A. Edwards* underwent repairs there. However, the Navy concluded that she would not be fit for "distant service" and, on 2 February 1918, assigned the ship duties in the 1st Naval District. *Wilbert A. Edwards* remained in district service into 1919, spending most of her time under repairs. She was decommissioned at Boston on 21 August 1919 and was struck from the Navy list on 24 September of the same year.

Simultaneously sold to her former owners, the W. A. Edwards Corp., *Wilbert A. Edwards* resumed civilian operations which she continued into the late 1940's.

Wild Cat

I

(Sch.: t. 48; cpl. 31; a. 3 guns)

The first *Wild Cat*, a schooner, was purchased at Baltimore, Md., late in 1822 for service with the "mosquito fleet" formed by Commodore David Porter to suppress the pirates then ravaging seaborne commerce in the West Indies. She was probably outfitted at Norfolk, Va., late in 1822 and commissioned early in 1823, Lt. Charles W. Skinner in command.

Wild Cat was one of eight, shallow-draft Chesapeake Bay schooners acquired to give the West Indies Squadron the capability of pursuing pirates into the shoal waters along the coasts of Cuba and Puerto Rico, where the freebooters sought refuge from justice. On 15 February 1823, she departed Hampton Roads in company with the other ships of Commodore Porter's squadron. After a brief stop at St. Thomas on 4 March, she and her consorts headed for the coast of Puerto Rico the following day. For the next 18 months, she intermittently patrolled the northern coast of Cuba and Puerto Rican waters searching for pirates and escorting convoys of merchantmen.

By the fall of 1823, yellow fever broke out among the crews of the squadron and reached almost epidemic proportions. Key West became untenable as a base, and most of the ships returned north—*Wild Cat* among them. During the remaining months of 1823, she completed repairs and recruited replacements for her decimated crew. Early in 1824—after the yellow fever subsided—she returned south with the squadron and resumed her antipiracy patrols and merchant convoy cruises. She continued that duty until the summer of 1824 when another bout with yellow fever began. Early in June, she was sent ahead of the squadron to carry word to Washington that the dreaded disease had once again forced the squadron to depart its station. *Wild Cat* returned to the West Indies that fall and resumed the campaign against the pirates. However, her return to duty proved brief for, during a storm in October, she sank with all hands.

II

(Sch: t. 30)

The second *Wild Cat*—a wooden-hulled schooner captured by the Federal Navy in 1862—served as a tender to warships of the South Atlantic Blockading Squadron. The vessel was never labeled, and records of her construction and capture have not been found. Her activities and actual duties during that tour are not described in any detail in the available records, but it is known that she operated from St. Helena to Port Royal, S.C.

During that service, she assisted refugees from a plantation attacked by Confederate marauders. On 13 June, *Wild Cat* sailed up to Hutchinson's Island, off St. Helena Sound, in company with the gig from the sloop-of-war *Dale*, Lt. W. T. Truxtun, commanding, to investigate a large fire ashore. Upon arrival in the vicinity. the Union sailors found the burning Marsh Plantation, set afire by a marauding Confederate band. The Southern troops had plundered the belongings of the poor negroes there, wounding some, generally striking terror into the hearts of the inhabitants. As *Wild Cat* sailed up the river, she came in contact with many canoes paddled by panic-stricken former inhabitants of the plantation. Lt. Truxtun soon placed all of the refugees on board *Wild Cat* and had them transported out of the area. A few days later, while reconnoitering the vicinity, *Wild Cat* shelled some Confederate raiders spotted near the Ashepoo River.

Wild Cat continued to operate in South Carolina's coastal waters through March of 1865. After a brief spell as pilot boat at Charleston, S.C., in April, the schooner was transferred to the Army on 15 April 1865. Apparently returned to the Navy within three months time, *Wild Cat* was sold at Charleston on 28 July 1865. Her subsequent fate is unknown.

III

(Freighter: t. 36; l. 64'; b. 15'6''; dr. 6' (mean); s. 9 k.; cpl. 10; a. none)

The third *Wild Cat*—a single-screw, wooden-hulled freight boat built at Milton, Del., by R. T. Potter and completed in 1915—was acquired by the Navy from R. T. Potter on 5 July 1917 and commissioned on 17 July 1917.

Designated SP–879, *Wild Cat* was assigned to the New London section of the 2d Naval District for local freight-carrying duties. On occasion, she served as a dispatch boat and towed ash lighters and coal scows. She also transported garbage, guns, and ordnance materials. In February 1919, when some subchasers were going out of commission at New London, *Wild Cat* assisted in their demobilization by mooring astern of a nest of them and taking on board their depth bombs and "Y" gun charges and transporting these items to magazines on shore.

When the need for her services with the 2d Naval District diminished, *Wild Cat* was turned over to the Coast and Geodetic Survey at the Marine Basin, Brooklyn, N.Y., on 14 April 1919.

Wild Goose

(ScStr.: l. 60'0''; b. 10'0''; dr. 2'6''; s. 19.0 k.; a. 1 1-pdr.)

Wild Goose—a wooden-hulled, screw steamer designed by Charles L. Seabury and built in 1913 by the consolidated firms of the Gas Engine and Power Co. and the Charles L. Seabury Co.—was acquired by the Navy from Charles L. Harding of Boston, Mass.; assigned the classification SP–562; and was taken over on 21 April 1917. After fitting out, she was commissioned on 25 June 1917.

Since no deck logs for this vessel exist, the ship's daily routine remains a mystery. She was initially assigned to the 1st Naval District for section patrol duties and, by November 1918, had been shifted to the 5th Naval District. She was retained by the Navy through the end of World War I and was stationed at the Washington Navy Yard as of 1 October 1919. Loaned to the city of Norfolk, Va., on 21 June 1920, she was subsequently returned to the Navy, placed on the sale list on 24 August 1920, and was sold on 17 November 1920. Her subsequent fate is unknown.

Wild Goose II

(MB: l. 33'6''; b. 10'0''; dr. 2'9''; s. 10.0 k.; a. 1 mg.)

Wild Goose II—a wooden-hulled motor boat—was built at Marblehead, Mass., by W. H. Chamberlain and was acquired by the Navy from Winthrop C. Winslow of Boston, Mass. Assigned the classification SP–891, *Wild Goose II* was delivered to the Navy on 7 July 1917.

There are no deck logs extant for *Wild Goose II* nor any other records indicating whether or not the craft was ever placed in commission. She apparently operated in the 1st Naval District, as the 1 November 1918 issue of the *Navy Directory* lists the ship's post office address as the 1st Naval District. To avoid confusion with *Wild Goose* (SP–562), the Navy took away the vessel's name, *Wild Goose II*, and retained only the designation, SP–891, in accordance with Navy General Order No. 386, dated 11 April 1918. SP–891 was dropped from the Navy list in 1920, and her subsequent fate is a mystery.

Wildcat

(AW–2: dp. 15,425; l. 441'6"; b. 57'0"; dr. 27'9"; s. 11.0 k.; cpl. 148; a. 1 5", 1 3", 12 20mm.; cl. *Stag*; T. Z–ET1–S–C3)

Wildcat (AW–2) was originally projected as the "Victory" tanker *Leon Godchaux*. However, before her construction began, the ship was allocated to the Navy. She was classified as IX–130 and renamed *Wildcat* on 27 October 1943 and acquired by the Navy under a bareboat charter from the War Shipping Administration (WSA). The ship was laid down under a Maritime Commission contract (MCE hull 1934) on 16 November 1943 at New Orleans, La., by the Delta Shipbuilding Co.; launched on 7 January 1944; sponsored by Mrs. Leonie Godchaux Mayer; reclassified AW–2 on 4 February 1944; delivered to the Navy at New Orleans on 16 February; and commissioned the following day, 17 February 1944.

Soon thereafter, the ship was shifted to Tampa, Fla., for hull alterations by the Tampa Shipbuilding Co., and was decommissioned at Key West, Fla., on 10 April 1944. At the naval operating base there, *Wildcat* underwent the balance of the conversion from tanker to water distilling ship into the autumn of 1944.

Recommissioned at Key West on 15 October 1944, Lt. Comdr. George H. Burrows, USNR, in command, *Wildcat* conducted shakedown training in the Gulf of Mexico before she underwent post-shakedown alterations at Todd's Shipbuilding Co., Galveston, Tex.

Wildcat departed Galveston on 5 December, bound via the Panama Canal Zone for the western Pacific. She transited the canal and at Balboa underwent minor repairs from 11 to 21 December to her engineering plant before she got underway on the latter day for the Admiralty Islands. She made port at Manus on 23 January 1945 and, two days later, shifted to Humboldt Bay, New Guinea.

Attached to Service Squadron 9, 7th Fleet, *Wildcat* soon sailed in convoy for the Philippines and, on 6 February, dropped anchor in Leyte Gulf, off the municipality of Dulag, on the eastern coast of Leyte. Two days later, the ship moved to San Pedro Bay, Leyte, where she remained into April, distilling and issuing fresh potable water to small craft and merchant vessels.

She received a tender availability alongside *Whitney* (AD–4) from 11 to 18 April before shifting to Calicoan Island to transfer her deck cargo to SS *Ben Ruffin*. *Wildcat* then returned to San Pedro Bay on 23 April to resume her water distilling and issuing duties there. *Wildcat* got underway for Manila on the morning of the 25th but grounded on a pinnacle near the approach channel to San Pedro Bay at 0855. After she was refloated, she proceeded to Manicani Island, Samar, where she was dry-docked in *ABSD–5* on 31 May for repairs to her damaged hull. She remained there until 4 July, when she shifted to *YFD–21* for the remainder of the repairs. Upon completion of that hull work, *Wildcat* undocked on 19 July; headed for Manila on the 24th; and arrived on the 26th to assume duties there as station ship..

Anchored in Manila Bay when news of Japan's final capitulation came on 15 August 1945, *Wildcat's* sailors witnessed the "riotous celebrations, skyrockets and light displays" which accompanied that welcome news. *Wildcat* later moved to Subic Bay, Luzon, but returned to Manila on 5 September to resume distilling and distributing potable water to the various ships and small craft. The distilling ship remained in Philippine waters through the autumn of 1945 and headed home to the United States in December.

Wildcat was slated to be returned to the WSA for disposal at Norfolk in mid-1946, but the ship was retained for use in Operation "Crossroads"—the atomic bomb tests at Bikini Atoll. *Wildcat* subsequently performed support tasks with Joint Task Force 1 in the summer of 1946. Declared "radiologically cleared," the distilling ship was released from "Crossroads" on 11 September 1946.

Decommissioned at the 13th Naval District on 17 January 1947 and returned to the WSA that day, the erstwhile water distilling ship was struck from the Navy list on 10 June 1947. She was laid up at Olympia, Wash., with the National Defense Maritime Administration Reserve Fleet. *Wildcat* was eventually broken up for scrap sometime in the mid-1970's.

Wilderness

A region in Orange County, Va., south of the Rapidan River, that was the scene of battles during the Civil War in 1863 and 1864.

(SwStr: t. 390; l. 137'; b. 25'; dr. 6'; s. 13 k.; a. 4 24-pdrs.)

B. N. Creary—sometimes spelled *B. N. Crary*—was a wooden-hulled, side-wheel steamer built in 1864 at Brooklyn, N.Y. Acquired by the Union Navy at New York City on 30 May 1864 and simultaneously renamed *Wilderness*, she fitted out at the New York Navy Yard and was commissioned on 20 July 1864.

After arriving at Hampton Roads shortly thereafter, *Wilderness* was assigned immediately to the 2d Division of the North Atlantic Blockading Squadron. She operated between Hampton Roads and various points along the James River through the end of August. While she performed a variety of duties during that time, she operated primarily as a supply ship. She also served as a transport and dispatch vessel when the occasion demanded. On the average, she apparently made two trips upriver from Hampton Roads per week, delivering fresh vegetables and provisions to the crews of naval vessels operating up the James River and to the crews of the lighthouses situated along that waterway.

Occasionally, however, nearby action enlivened her predominately pedestrian duties. On 15 July 1864, when Confederate guns located near Malvern Hill fired on Union ships, *Wilderness* made a night run down the James with casualties embarked, bound for the hospital at Norfolk. On the 27th of that month, *Wilderness* was compelled by the heavy movement of Union troops across two pontoon bridges spanning the James to remain between them. While thus immobile, the sidewheeler observed the gunboats *Agawam* and *Mendota* shelling Confederate positions across nearby Four Mile Creek.

On 25 August, Acting Rear Admiral S. P. Lee, commanding the North Atlantic Blockading Squadron, reported to Secretary of the Navy Gideon Welles that "to promote the efficiency of the blockade of the bars" (off the North Carolina coast) he had directed Capt. Melancton Smith, the commander of naval forces on the James, "to have the *Wilderness* prepared at once for service on the blockade of Wilmington." By 1 September, when Admiral Lee reported the composition of his squadron, he listed *Wilderness* as a "supply steam: ordered to fit out as gunboat and join (the) blockade."

By late October, *Wilderness* had been armed with a battery of four 24-pounders, enabling her to be classed as a gunboat. On 28 October, Rear Admiral David D. Porter, the new commanding officer of the North Atlantic Blockading Squadron, issued orders to Acting Master Henry Arey, commanding the newly converted sidewheeler, to "proceed and report to the senior officer off Eastern Bar (Cape Fear River) for duty on the blockade as a chaser."

Wilderness went into action almost immediately. At 1905 on the evening of 31 October, while patrolling off New Inlet, N.C., she spotted a strange vessel bearing south by west, heading over the bar. *Niphon*, on station nearby, also saw the ship and came about. *Wilderness*, steaming at top speed and firing as she came, ultimately overhauled the strange vessel and captured her at 1945.

The prize turned out to be the British blockaderunner *Annie* and was described by Arey as ". . . a fine steamer, with two propellers, one smokestack and . . . schooner-rigged." Sailors from *Wilderness* boarded the ship, finding her cargo to consist of 540 bales of cotton, 30 tons of pressed tobacco, and 14 casks of "spirits of turpentine." *Niphon* took on board the passengers and crew of the runner while *Wilderness* took charge of the prize. During the transfer of prisoners, Confederate guns at neaby Fort Fisher opened fire on the Union vessels. One shell struck *Wilderness*, passing through her hurricane deck on the starboard side and going through a water tank at the port gangway, where it exploded, damaging the rim of the gunboat's port wheel.

Repaired at Beaufort, N.C., when the ship put into that port for coal, *Wilderness* resumed blockade duties off Wilmington soon thereafter. Shortly before the Union assault on Fort Fisher, the key Confederate stronghold guarding the approaches to the seaport of Wilmington, a daring plan to reduce some of the defenses by using an explosive-laden ship was put into motion. The sidewheel steamer *Louisiana* was stripped and filled with explosives; manned by a volunteer crew commanded by Comdr. A. C. Rhind; and towed into position, first by *Sassacus* and later by *Wilderness*, off the fort. The latter took up the tow on 18 December, but heavy weather delayed the start of the entire operation. In the final attempt, made on 23 December, *Wilderness*—manned by Acting Master Arey, four officers and "enough men to handle the vessel"—took *Lousiana* in close to the walls of Fort Fisher. Rhind and his men lit the fuses, kindled a fire aft, and then escaped in small boats to *Wilderness*.

The fuses set by Rhind failed to detonate the explosives, but the fire aft did. *Louisiana* blew up as planned, but other than to send out a heavy shock wave, had little effect. At dawn the next day, Christmas Eve, the first assault on Fort Fisher began. However, as Admiral Porter subsequently wrote, "I was in hopes I should have been able to present to the nation Fort Fisher and surrounding works as a Christmas offering, but I am sorry to say it has not been taken yet." The expedition failed dismally, due to the temerity exhibited by the Army commander, General Benjamin F. Butler.

During the first attempt to reduce and invest the Confederate stronghold, on 24 and 25 December 1864, *Wilderness* lay in reserve offshore, in the first division. Through much of the action, *Wilderness* served as tender to the flagship *Malvern* and spotted her fall of shot. On the 25th, the side-wheeler took on board the bodies of the sailors who had been killed on *Ticonderoga* and *Juniata* and also received the wounded from those ships.

After transferring these casualties to Fort Jackson, *Wilderness* returned to Beaufort, where she took two coal schooners in tow and pulled them to Wilmington, getting underway on the 28th as Union forces were preparing to make a second attempt to take Fort Fisher. Delivering her tows soon thereafter, the sidewheel steamer supported the landings against the Confederate stronghold on 13 January 1865, taking on board a draft of troops from the transport *Atlantic*. She took the troops to within 500 yards of shore and, while anchored there, transferred the men to boats for the final run to shore.

The following day, *Wilderness* delivered mail among the fleet and took on ammunition; later, she delivered cargo to *New Ironsides*.

Subsequently, *Wilderness* took part in the occupation of former Confederate works at Smithville, N.C., on 19 January, Acting Master Arey and a boat crew from the ship participating directly in the operation. *Wilderness* remained in the vicinity of the mouth of the Cape Fear River into February and then returned to her former operating area, the James River.

Admiral Porter ordered *Wilderness* up the Chickahominy River to try to communicate with General Philip Sheridan. Collaterally, the ship was to gain all the information she could learn about the river itself and Southern forces in the area before returning to Aiken's Landing with any dispatches which needed to be delivered. Subsequently, the side-wheeler received orders to proceed without delay to New Berne, N.C., to cooperate with Army forces of General Sherman in the movement up the Chowan River toward Winton, N.C. Arriving on 2 April with dispatches from Admiral Porter, *Wilderness* resumed her operations in the sounds of North Carolina, performing general utility duties for the North Atlantic Blockading Squadron through the end of the Civil War.

Decommissioned on 10 June 1965, *Wilderness* was acquired by the Treasury Department at the Boston Navy Yard on 6 September 1865 and sailed for Baltimore, Md., on the 17th. There, the side-wheeler was fitted out for her new duties as a revenue cutter and, following repairs and alterations, was ordered to Florida waters on 28 November.

Reaching Key West on 8 December, *Wilderness* operated out of that port for a year, before she shifted up the east coast to Charleston, S.C., on 14 December 1866 for repairs. *Wilderness* subsequently operated in the Gulf of Mexico, ranging from New Orleans to Veracruz, Mexico. She apparently operated out of New Orleans, in the gulf, through the summer of 1872.

Ordered to New York for repairs on 2 September 1872, *Wilderness* reached New York City on the 19th. Records indicate that the ship was to be dismantled. The orders, dated 3 January 1873, are recorded as "carried into effect, January 11." Now, whether or not this means that the name was retained and an entirely new ship was built is not entirely clear. In any event, she is listed as being ordered to New Orleans for duty on 3 July. Sailing on the 7th, she arrived at her new duty station on the 19th.

During the ship's period in a "limbo" of sorts, she was renamed *John A. Dix* on 11 June 1873. She apparently then operated in the Gulf of Mexico, out of New Orleans, through the autumn of 1879, when she was temporarily stationed at Mobile, Ala.

The cutter operated in the Florida Keys in the spring of 1880 and into the early 1880's. Ordered to New York City for replacement of her boilers in the autumn of 1883, she arrived there on 30 October. Ordered back to Florida waters upon completion of those repairs on 1 February 1884, she departed New York City on 13 March and arrived at Key West nine days later. Resuming operations in the Florida Keys, *John A. Dix* cruised the Gulf of Mexico between Florida and Texas, from the Mississippi to the Rio Grande, through the end of the 1880's. Ordered to New Orleans, La., on 28 March 1891, *John A. Dix* arrived there on 7 April. Placed out of commission soon thereafter, the erstwhile side-wheel gunboat was sold on 18 May 1891 at Algiers, La.

Wildwood

A resort city in Cape May County, New Jersey. It is located on a barrier island off the Atlantic coast of the Cape May Peninsula, some 33 miles southwest of Atlantic City. Wildwood was incorporated as a borough in 1895 and became a city in 1911 through consolidation with the borough of Holly Beach City.

(PC–1181: dp. 450 (f.); l. 173'8''; b. 23'; dr. 10'10'' (max.); cpl. 65; s. 20.2 k.; a. 1 3'', 1 40mm., 3 20mm., 4 dcp., 2 dct., 2 dcp. (Mousetrap); cl. PC–461)

Wildwood was laid down as *PC–1181* on 5 October 1942 at Jacksonville, Fla., by the Gibbs Gas Engine Co.; launched on 15 April 1943; and commissioned on

17 September 1943, Lt. Carver J. Peacock, USNR, in command.

PC–1181 was fitted out at the Charleston (S.C.) Navy Yard and then moved to Florida waters for shakedown training out of Miami and sonar and anti-submarine warfare training at the Fleet Sound School at Key West. Then, her skills thus honed, the patrol craft got underway from Kest West on 6 November to escort Convoy KN–275 to New York City and arrived there with her charges on Armistice Day, 11 November.

One week later, *PC–1181* sailed for Cuba with Convoy NG–399. One day out, she developed an oil leak and put into Norfolk, Va., on the 20th. The submarine chaser repaired the damage and got underway on the 22d, overtook the convoy, and completed the voyage to Guantanamo.

Having made port at Guantanamo Bay on 27 November, *PC–1181* sailed for New York with Convoy GN–99 on the 30th, arriving at her destination on 6 December. However, the respite allowed the ship was a short one, for she quickly got underway again, proceeding to sea with Convoy NG–404 and drawing the duty of covering a lagging merchantman. Arriving at Guantanamo on 20 December, the submarine chaser sailed for New York on Christmas Day.

PC–1181 arrived at New York on New Year's Day 1944 but departed that port six days later with Convoy NG–409. Two days out, she was detached to stand by the disabled merchantman SS *Beta*, which had developed engine trouble. Completing her mission as the merchantman repaired her engines, *PC–1181* was en route to rejoin the convoy when her sonar operators picked up a contact at 2132 on 12 January. In the meantime, *PC–618* developed a stronger contact, and the escort commander, soon seeing that *PC–1181*'s contact was somewhat less distinct, ordered that submarine chaser to break off her search and assist *PC–618*. This proved unproductive, however, and the two submarine chasers abandoned the hunt to rejoin the convoy, subsequently arriving at Guantanamo Bay on 15 January.

PC–1181 continued to escort the coastwise convoys into the spring of the year. She operated off the eastern seaboard of the United States as far north as New York and into the Caribbean Sea. Eventually, her area of operations embraced the Gulf of Mexico, as she escorted convoys bound from Guantanamo Bay to the Panama Canal Zone from May of 1944, under the aegis of Commander, Panama Sea Frontier. In the meantime, the Battle of the Atlantic was being won by the Allies as they gained the upper hand over German Admiral Dönitz' U-boat arm. Eventually, the Allied armies on the continent of Europe forced Germany out of the war in the bitter struggle which ended in May 1945.

The convoy system, established to provide protection against the U-boats which occasionally conducted forays into the Gulf of Mexico, was then abolished, and *PC–1181* assumed new duties—this time under the aegis of Commander, Submarine Squadron 3. The submarine chaser served as target vessel for submarines operating in the gulf, out of Panama. She remained operating in the gulf through the end of the war with Japan in August 1945. Shifted to the local defense forces of the Panama Canal, *PC–1181* operated in this capacity, conducting patrols and training operations out of Coco Solo, Canal Zone, until June 1946. Departing Coco Solo on 13 July, *PC–1181* sailed for Florida, arrived at Key West six days later, and was decommissioned there on 18 August 1946.

Placed in the status of a district craft for use by local Naval Reserve training units, *PC–1181* was delivered to St. Petersburg, Fla., soon thereafter. She operated with that area's reserve units embarked between St. Petersburg and Key West until February 1950. Subsequently placed in reserve at Brownsville, Tex., and later shifted to the Atlantic Reserve Fleet's berthing area at Norfolk, Va., *PC–1181* was named *Wildwood* by 15 February 1956. However, she never served actively under that name. She was struck from the Navy list on 1 April 1959 and was sold for scrap soon thereafter.

Wileman

William Wolfe Wileman—born on 4 May 1917 in Ventura County, Cailf.—graduated from the University of California at Berkeley in 1940 and enlisted in the Naval Reserve on 12 February 1941 as a seaman second class. After basic training at Oakland, Calif., he transferred to the Pensacola Naval Air Station for aviation training on 3 April and, the following day, received his appointment as an aviation cadet. He finished the basic course at Pensacola in August and moved to the Miami Naval Air Station on the 31st for advanced training. His flight instruction ended on 4 November; and, on the 5th, Wileman was commissioned an ensign in the Naval Reserve.

The *Navy Directory* for 1942 suggests that Ens. Wileman was assigned to Fighting Squadron (VF) 6 on board *Enterprise*. While he may have served briefly with that unit and on board that ship, he was definitely a member of VF–2 on board *Yorktown* by the time of the Battle of the Coral Sea early in May 1942. During that action in the evening of 7 May, Ens. Wileman earned the Navy Cross for shooting down at least one, and perhaps two, Japanese fighters. Later, he transferred to VF–5 and saw service at various locations in the southwestern Pacific. At the time of his death on 13 September 1942, Ens. Wileman was based ashore on Guadalcanal in the Solomon Islands with a portion of VF–5 assigned to the "Cactus Air Force" at Henderson Field. Further details of Ens. Wileman's death are unavailable, but he was presumed dead as a result of enemy action while defending his base from Japanese air raids.

(DE–22: dp. 1,150; l. 289'5''; b. 35'2''; dr. 11'0''; s. 19½ k.; cpl. 156; a. 3 3'', 4 1.1'', 9 20mm., 8 dcp., 2 dct.; cl. *Evarts*)

Wileman (DE–22) was laid down on 30 April 1942 at the Mare Island Navy Yard as *BDE–22*, a destroyer escort allocated to the United Kingdom under the lend-lease program; launched on 19 December 1942; sponsored by Mrs. Fred Yam; reallocated to the United States Navy and redesignated *DE–22* on 25 January 1942; named *Wileman* on 19 February 1943; and commissioned on 11 June 1943, Lt. Aaron F. Beyer, USNR, in command.

Following shakedown along the west coast, *Wileman* departed San Francisco on 20 August in company with *Fletcher* (DD–445) and a three-ship convoy. The five ships arrived in Pearl Harbor on 27 August, but *Wileman* departed again a week later to escort *Wharton* (AP–7) on a voyage to the South Pacific. Ports of call during the cruise included Tutuila, Samoa; Noumea, New Caledonia; and Suva in the Fiji Islands. *Wharton* and *Wileman* parted company at Suva.

The transport returned to San Francisco while the destroyer escort reported for a month of patrol and escort duty in the Ellice Islands. On 25 October, she departed the Ellice Islands to return to Oahu. The warship entered Pearl Harbor on 2 November and began preparations for her role in the upcoming Gilbert Islands invasion.

After about two weeks at Hawaii, *Wileman* stood out of Pearl Harbor as part of the screen of a convoy carrying garrison troops to the Gilberts. She reached Makin Island at midday on the 24th. As a greeting, the Japanese launched an air attack on Makin from nearby Jaluit and Mili. Three twin-engine "Betty" bombers picked out the *Wileman* convoy and attempted a torpedo attack. *Wileman*, the other destroyer escort, and the ships of the convoy themselves all went to general quarters and opened fire on the intruders. Their gunfire dissuaded two of the Japanese planes from pressing home their attack, and only the third succeeded in making his drop. Neither side, however, drew any blood during the encounter. The single torpedo passed wide of the entire convoy, and American antiaircraft gunners brought down no Japanese planes.

After seeing her charges safely to Makin, *Wileman* began about a month of convoy escort and patrol duty between the islands of the Gilberts, Phoenix, and Ellice groups as part of the Americans' effort to consolidate their position in the Gilberts in preparation for the conquest of the Marshalls, the next hop in the Navy's leapfrog thrust through the Central Pacific toward Japan.

On 8 January 1944, the destroyer escort returned to Pearl Harbor to prepare for her role in Operation "Flintlock," the Marshalls invasion. Twenty days later, she departed Oahu in the screen of a convoy bound for the Central Pacific. As in the case of the Gilberts operation, *Wileman* took no part in the actual assault phase of Operation "Flintlock." Instead, she again escorted the ships carrying part of the garrison troops—the 16th Marine Defense Battalion and a Construction Battalion unit—for Kwajalein Atoll. The assault itself went forward just three days after *Wileman* left Pearl Harbor, and Kwajalein had been secured for three days when she reached the atoll on 10 February. The convoy entered the lagoon upon arrival, and *Wileman* began an uneventful 18 days on antisubmarine patrol in and around the atoll and later at Majuro. The warship departed the Marshalls on 28 February and reentered Pearl Harbor on 8 March.

After three weeks of gunnery drills and sonar exercises, *Wileman* left the Hawaiian Islands on 30 March in an antisubmarine hunter/killer task group built around *Altamaha* (CVE–18). The unit arrived in the eastern Marshalls at the end of the first week in April and began its search for Japanese submarines. The hunting proved less than good. During the voyage from Oahu, a plane from *Altamaha* claimed to have attacked an enemy submarine and took credit for a probable kill. While actually on patrol in the Marshalls, the group's only contact with the enemy almost proved to be a disaster. Just after sunset on 15 April, one of the ships in the screen sighted a torpedo heading straight for the carrier. Warned in time by voice radio, *Altamaha* maneuvered out of the torpedo's path, and it passed harmlessly ahead. The group failed to make contact with the torpedo's launcher—probably a submarine—and continued its patrol.

Later in the month, *Wileman* and her colleagues in the screen traded carriers with Task Group (TG) 11.2 and *Altamaha* headed back to Pearl Harbor with *Coghlan* (DD–606) and *Preble* (DM–20) while her former screen continued the patrol with *Fanshaw Bay* (CVE–70). *Kalinin Bay* (CVE–68) also joined the hunter/killer group just before the conclusion of the operation; but, despite the additional escort carrier, success eluded the unit. The task group concluded its patrol of the eastern Marshalls on 6 May and headed back to Pearl Harbor. The warships arrived at Oahu on 13 May, and the task group was dissolved.

Training exercises occupied the two weeks the destroyer escort spent at Pearl Harbor before her 27 May departure for the Central Pacific. *Wileman* entered the lagoon at Eniwetok on 4 June with her convoy of 11 oilers and one tanker. From there, she moved to Majuro, arriving on the 15th. For the opening phase of the Marianas campaign, *Wileman* again drew escort duty rather than participation in the actual assault. On 18 June, she left Majuro lagoon to escort transports to the anchorage off Saipan. Arriving there on 22 June, she departed again on the 26th to screen a task group back to Eniwetok. She reached the atoll on 30 June and remained in the area for three weeks.

Late in July, she put to sea with a group of oilers operating as a replenishment group for the Fast Carrier Task Force. For the next two months, she cruised between the Marianas and Eniwetok escorting convoys and replenishment groups in support of the Marianas

campaign and the fast carrier sweeps of Japan's inner defense line and logistics routes. On 15 September, her duty in the forward area ended when she headed via Pearl Harbor to San Francisco where she arrived on 6 November.

Less than a week later, the destroyer escort put to sea to return to Oahu with a convoy of six LSM's and three merchant ships. The warship entered Pearl Harbor on 21 November and soon began intensive sound and gunnery training. During her stay in the Hawaiian Islands, she also served a tour as a school ship for gunnery officers and another as a target and adversary for Pacific Fleet submarines undergoing type training.

Wileman began 1945 with a round-trip voyage to Majuro, departing Pearl Harbor on 5 January and returning on the 21st. She remained at Oahu only briefly, getting underway again that same day for the west coast and an overhaul. She arrived at Terminal Island, Calif., on the 29th. She began repairs and modifications on the 31st and completed them in mid-April. On 19 April, the warship shaped a course back to Pearl Harbor, where she arrived on the 25th. There, she resumed duty as a school ship, again training gunnery personnel and acting as target ship and surface opponent for Pacific Fleet submarines. Later, she also served as escort and plane guard for *Corregidor* (CVE–58) and *Tripoli* (CVE–64) during air training operations conducted northeast of Oahu in June 1945.

On 22 June, she stood out of Pearl Harbor to return to the Central Pacific. She arrived at Eniwetok on 30 June and began duty as a unit of the Marshalls and Gilberts Escort and Patrol Force (TG 96.3). For just over a month, she escorted convoys between Eniwetok and Ulithi and conducted antisubmarine patrols in the Marshalls. On 2 and 3 August, the destroyer escort voyaged to Kwajalein where she was assigned hunter/killer and air-sea rescue duty. While at Kwajalein, *Wileman* received word of the Japanese capitulation on 14 August.

However, the destroyer escort continued to operate with TG 96.3 until mid-September. On 14 September, she quit her Eniwetok-Kwajalein-Ulithi circuit and headed for home. She stopped overnight at Pearl Harbor on 20 and 21 September and then continued on to the west coast. The warship arrived in San Pedro, Calif., on 27 September.

The destroyer escort was decommissioned on 16 November 1945 at Terminal Island, and her name was struck from the Navy list on 28 November 1945. In January 1947, she was sold to the Pacific Bridge Co. and was scrapped by that firm on 23 June 1947.

Wileman earned four battle stars during World War II.

Wiley

Besides a few details of his service in the Navy, little is known of the life of William Wiley. He entered the Navy on 2 April 1803 and was assigned to the schooner *Enterprise* in the Mediterranean squadron. After attaining the rates of boatswain, boatswain's mate, and then a reduction to quartermaster, Wiley took part in the daring raid led by Lt. Stephen Decatur, Jr., in the ketch *Intrepid* at Tripoli harbor on 16 February 1804, destroying the frigate *Philadelphia* in the engagement. Quartermaster Wiley was transferred to the brig *Scourge* soon thereafter, and this is where his documentary trail ends.

(DD–597: dp. 2,050; l. 376'4''; b. 39'8''; dr. 17'9'' (mean); s. 35 k.; cpl. 273; a. 5 5'', 10 40mm., 7 20mm., 2 dcp., 6 dct., 10 21'' tt.; cl. *Fletcher*)

Wiley (DD–597) was laid down on 10 August 1943 at Bremerton, Wash., by the Puget Sound Navy Yard; launched on 25 September 1944; sponsored by Mrs. Herbert V. Wiley, wife of Vice Admiral Herbert V.

Wiley, USN (Ret.); and commissioned there on 22 February 1945, Comdr. B. P. Field, Jr., in command.

The destroyer conducted shakedown out of San Diego, Calif., through the end of April 1945; underwent post-shakedown availability at Puget Sound; and then sailed for the Hawaiian Islands, departing Port Angeles on 19 May and arriving at Pearl Harbor on the 26th. She trained in the vicinity of Oahu for three weeks before getting underway on 13 June to escort *Cape Gloucester* (CVE–109) to the Philippines.

Arriving at Leyte on 13 July and in Subic Bay on the 15th, *Wiley* operated out of the Philippines on training exercises through the first week of August. The ship departed Subic Bay on 9 August and escorted a small group of tankers to the Ryukyus. Within a week, Japan capitulated, ending the war in the Pacific.

Wiley subsequently joined the North China force in operations off the coast of Asia, while Chinese communist and Nationalist forces fought for supremacy in the strategic northern provinces once occupied by the Japanese. Over the next three months, this peacekeeping duty took the destroyer to Dairen, Port Arthur, Chefoo, Tsingtao, and Chinwangtao. The ship destroyed floating Japanese mines with gunfire and screened the cruisers of Cruiser Division 6. On 8 September, *Wiley* covered the landings of a peacekeeping force of American troops at Jinsen—now Inchon—Korea.

Detached from this duty with the cruisers, *Wiley* joined a fast carrier task force on 12 October for operations in the Gulf of Pohai. During the latter part of October, the destroyer served in the screen for *Antietam* (CV–36) and *Boxer* (CV–21) and served as plane guard for the carriers while they conducted routine flight operations over the Yellow Sea. Detached from this duty on 18 November, *Wiley* joined *San Francisco* (CA–38) at anchor off Taku. Four days later, *Wiley* shifted to Jinsen, took on board passengers and mail, and proceeded to Shanghai, Tsingtao, and Taku, disembarking some of her passengers at each port before returning to Jinsen on 30 November.

Wiley remained in the Far East into December and then sailed, via Guam, Eniwetok, and Pearl Harbor, for the United States. After arriving at San Francisco, Calif., on 3 January 1946, *Wiley* received her inactivation orders on 11 March and put into San Diego the next day.

Decommissioned and placed in reserve on 15 May 1946, *Wiley* remained berthed at San Diego until struck from the Navy list on 1 May 1968. She was sold to the National Metal and Steel Co., of Terminal Island, Calif., on 2 April 1970 and subsequently scrapped.

Wiley, Henry A., see *Henry A. Wiley*.

Wilhelmina

Wilhelmina—born on 31 August 1880—ascended to the throne of the Netherlands on 23 November 1890 upon the death of her father, William II. After a regency of almost eight years, Wilhelmina was declared of age on 31 August 1898 and was crowned on 6 September. She ruled over a neutral Holland in World War I and, when forced to flee her homeland when it was overrun by the Germans in May 1940, rallied the Dutch government-in-exile until the liberation of the Netherlands. Abdicating in favor of her daughter Juliana in September 1948, Wilhelmina died on 28 November 1962.

(Transport: dp. 13,250; l. 451'2''; b. 54'1''; dr. 26'6'' (mean); s. 16.5 k.; cpl. 274; a. 4 6'', 2 1-pdrs., 4 dc.)

Wilhelmina—a steel-hulled, single-screw, passenger and cargo steamer built at Newport News, Va., by the Newport News Shipbuilding and Drydock Co. for the Matson Navigation Co.—was launched on 18 September 1909 and departed her builders' yard on 7 December of that year. Under the Matson flag, *Wilhelmina* conducted regular runs between San Francisco, Calif., and Honolulu, Hawaii, carrying passengers and cargo between 1910 and 1917.

Inspected by the Navy at the 12th Naval District, San Francisco, on 18 June 1917—two months after the United States entered World War I—the steamship was later taken over by the United States Shipping Board on 1 December 1917. Soon thereafter, she sailed for Chile where she obtained a cargo of nitrates. Delivering that cargo at Norfolk, Va., *Wilhelmina* shifted to New York on 23 January 1918. Given the Id. No. 2168, the ship was then taken over by the Navy and apparently commissioned on 26 January 1918. Lt. Comdr. Joe W. Jory, USNRF, is listed as being in command in February. *Wilhelmina* was diverted to "special duty" and made her first voyage to France soon thereafter, departing New York with a general cargo on 1 February and returning on 26 March. Upon her return, she shifted to the New York Navy Yard, Brooklyn, N.Y., where she was taken in hand and converted to a troopship for service with the Cruiser and Transport Force. When her extant deck logs begin, her commanding officer is listed as Comdr. William T. Tarrant.

On 10 May 1918, *Wilhelmina* sailed out of New York on the first of six wartime voyages to France and back prior to the November armistice. During these passages, *Wilhelmina* carried 11,053 troops "over there" to strengthen the American Expeditionary Force (AEF). The transport's half-dozen trips were all made safely, as far as she was concerned, although not totally without incident.

While in convoy with six other troopships and four destroyers, *Wilhelmina* was present when the transport *Covington* was torpedoed on 1 July. Nearly a month later, on the 30th, one of *Wilhelmina*'s lookouts spotted what he thought to be a submarine periscope at 0730. Going to general quarters, the transport surged ahead and opened fire to drive the submarine away. A short while later, when the periscope reappeared, *Wilhelmina* again fired at it, with the shell falling 50 yards short.

Two weeks later, while *Wilhelmina* and *Pastores* (Id. No. 4540) were steaming under the protection of *Hull* (Destroyer No. 7), the erstwhile Matson steamship again went to general quarters to drive away what looked like a submarine. Shortly after 2000 on 14 August, while *Wilhelmina*'s crew and passengers were holding abandon ship drill, a lookout spotted what looked like a submarine periscope 200 yards from the ship and just forward of the port beam. The captain of the transport ordered the helm put over to starboard soon after the sighting, as the submarine moved away on an opposite course. The one-pounder on the port wing of the signal bridge barked out two shots, both missing. Three shots from the after port 6-inch gun followed, until their angle was masked by the ship's superstructure. The submarine, however, apparently frustrated, submerged. It may have remained in the area to try again, as on the following day, 15 August, a submarine periscope appeared some 200 yards away from the troopship, prompting three salvoes which drove the would-be attacker off.

In company with seven other transports—including *Wilhelmina*—on 23 August, in a convoy escorted by *Huntington* (Armored Cruiser No. 5) and destroyers *Fairfax* and *Hull*, *Pastores* spotted what she took to be a submarine periscope at about 0950. *Hull* rang up full speed and reversed course; *Huntington* and *Fairfax* soon did likewise but found nothing.

Later that day, however, the enemy apparently reappeared. *Pastores*' commander sighted a periscope at 1904; *Hull* sighted the same object five minutes later. The periscope appeared to be about 500 yards distant, three points off *Wilhelmina*'s starboard bow, and running on a course to the right and nearly opposite that of the convoy. *Pastores* went to battle stations and headed for the periscope. *Wilhelmina*, too, turned toward the enemy.

With the 'scope in sight for about 10 seconds, the time allotted the gun crews of the American ships that spotted the enemy was short. *Pastores* got off one round of 4-inch at the swirling water where the object had disappeared. Frustrated by the submarine's going deep, *Wilhelmina*, unable to ram, turned aside to port. *Hull*, rushing to the scene, soon dropped three depth bombs.

Three days later, on the 26th, *Wilhelmina* noticed a suspicious wake five degrees off her port bow, 2,500 yards away and passing from port to starboard. Going to general quarters, *Wilhelmina* fired a shot from one of her forward guns shortly before she loosed three shots in succession from the forward starboard 6-inch battery. Nine rounds came from the after battery on that side; and, as the ship swung, the superstructure masked the forward guns. The wake soon disappeared; both *Pastores* and the Italian transport *Dante Alighieri* also fired several rounds at what was possibly a submersible with no apparent success.

Wilhelmina emerged from World War I unscathed, although near-missed by a torpedo on 1 September. After the armistice, she continued her troop-carrying activities, bringing back part of the AEF from France. She conducted seven postwar, round-trip voyages, returning 11,577 men home to the United States including 2,610 sick and wounded.

These postwar voyages were not made entirely without incident either. A fire broke out in a storeroom where blankets and pillows were kept, a little over six hours after the ship departed Bassens, France, standing down the Gironde River on 25 March 1919. The fire, reported at 2152, was put out by 2210. Slight damage had been caused in the fire.

Wilhelmina subsequently entered the Ambrose Channel on 4 April and docked at Pier 1, Hoboken, N.J., the following day. There, she disembarked the troops and patients carried back from France. She began her last voyage shortly thereafter, returning to New York on 6 August 1919. There, she was decommissioned, struck from the Navy list, and returned to her owners on 16 August 1919.

Wilhelmina remained under the Matson house flag through the 1920's and 1930's. Sold to British interests in 1940, the steamship was sailing with Convoy HX-90, bound for Halifax, Nova Scotia, in the North Atlantic, on 2 December 1940, when *U-94*, part of a group which included *U-47* of Scapa Flow fame, drew a bead on a tanker and the steamer *W. Hendrik*, and fired two torpedoes. Both missed but continued on to strike and sink *Wilhelmina*.

Wilhoite

Thomas Mack Wilhoite—born on 12 February 1921 in Guthrie, Ky.—enlisted in the Naval Reserve on 16 June 1941 at Atlanta, Ga., and received his aviation indoctrination training at the Naval Reserve Air Base, Atlanta, Ga. On 7 August, he reported for flight instruction at the Naval Air Station (NAS), Pensacola, Fla., and was appointed an aviation cadet the following day. Transferred to NAS, Miami, Fla., on 15 January 1942 for further training, he became a naval aviator on 6 February.

Three days later, he was commissioned an ensign and, at the end of February, reported to the Advanced Carrier Training Group, Atlantic Fleet, NAS, Norfolk, Va. There, he joined Fighting Squadron (VF) 9, then fitting out and, in time, became the assistant navigation officer for that squadron.

Operation "Torch"—the invasion of French North Africa—saw VF-9 assigned to the carrier *Ranger* (CV-4). Each section of the squadron drew assigned tasks on 8 November 1942, the first day of the landings; and Wilhoite flew one of five Grumman F4F-4 Wildcats which attacked the French airdrome at Rabat-Sale, the headquarters of the French air forces in Morocco. Despite heavy antiaircraft fire, he pressed

home a determined attack and set three French bombers afire with his guns.

In a second strike directed at the Port Lyautey airdrome later that day, Wilhoite flew as part of the third flight and destroyed one fighter—a Dewoitine 520—by stafing. However, the Vichy ground gunners served their weapons well; and Wilhoite's Wildcat took hits from the intense flak and crashed about one mile from Port Lyautey.

Wilhoite received a Silver Star, posthumously, for displaying "conspicuous gallantry and intrepidity" during the strikes at Rabat-Sale and Port Lyautey. The accompanying citation also cited Wilhoite's "superb airmanship and tenacious devotion to duty" in pressing home his stafing attacks. Although he was killed in action, Wilhoite had played his part in the significant operations of VF-9 in neutralizing Vichy French air power that, if unhindered, could have severely hampered Operation "Torch."

(DE-397: dp. 1,200; l. 306'0''; b. 36'7''; dr. 8'7'' (mean); s. 21 k.; cpl. 186; a. 3 3'', 2 40mm., 10 20mm., 2 dct., 8 dcp., 1 dcp. (hh.); cl. *Edsall*)

Wilhoite (DE-397) was laid down on 4 August 1943 at Houston, Tex., by the Brown Shipbuilding Co.; launched on 5 October 1943; sponsored by Mrs. Corinne M. Wilhoite, the mother of Ensign Wilhoite; and commissioned at Houston on 16 December 1943, Lt. Eli B. Roth in command.

After her shakedown out of Great Sound, Bermuda, from 9 January to 10 February 1944, *Wilhoite* underwent post-shakedown availability at the Charleston (S.C.) Navy Yard from 11 to 21 February. She then got underway for Gibraltar with Convoy UGS (United States to Gibraltar) 34 on 23 February. On two occasions during the voyage, the destroyer escort depth-charged presumed submarine contacts with inconclusive results. After turning the convoy over to British escort vessels once she had passed through the Strait of Gibraltar, *Wilhoite* returned to the United States with Convoy GUS (Gibraltar to the United States) 33 and arrived at New York City on 3 April.

After a 10-day availability at the New York Navy Yard, the destroyer escort operated briefly with submarines and PT boats and conducted antiaircraft firing practice in Block Island Sound, Brooklyn, N.Y., before shifting south to the Tidewater area to pick up Convoy UGS-40 in Hampton Roads late in April.

The transatlantic passage proved largely uneventful; but, as the Allied ships transited the Strait of Gibraltar, the British antiaircraft cruiser HMS *Caledon*, the destroyer *Benson* (DD-421), and two minesweepers equipped with special jamming apparatus, *Steady* (AM-118) and *Sustain* (AM-119), joined the convoy. A recent increase in German air activity had prompted concern over the safety of UGS-40, a large and important convoy consisting of some 80 vessels.

At 2106 on 11 May, *Wilhoite*'s search radar picked up "bogeys" some 18 miles northeast of UGS-40. Two minutes later, the screening ships commenced their barrage. Observers in *Wilhoite* saw the attacking planes, torpedo-carrying Junkers (Ju.) 88's, sheer away from the flak, fly aft along the transport screen to the northward, and then cut across the stern of the convoy, circling. Soon, as the Ju. 88's came around the stern of the convoy, *Wilhoite*—coordinating the defense of that sector—sent up several barrages with her 3-inch, 40- and 20-millimeter guns.

About 2123, one Ju. 88 singled out *Wilhoite* as her target and attacked. The destroyer escort responded by bringing all her guns to bear and fired such a heavy and accurate barrage that the German pilot dropped his torpedo about 2,000 yards from its target. The plane, apparently damaged by the flak, then banked sharply and disappeared in the ship's smokescreen.

The heavy antiaircraft fire from the convoy's escorts and the support by friendly fighters downed an estimated 17 of the enemy torpedo planes. The convoy itself suffered no losses and safely reached its destination, Bizerte, Tunisia. For his part in directing *Wilhoite*'s highly successful sector defense of UGS-40, Lt. Roth, the ship's commanding officer, received a Letter of Commendation.

Wilhoite rested at Bizerte from 13 to 21 May before getting underway to return to the United States with Convoy GUS-40. At 2105 on 29 May, however, *Wilhoite* and *Evarts* (DE-5) were detached from the screen of GUS-40 to go to the aid of Task Group (TG) 21.11 which the German U-boat *U-549* had brazenly attacked northwest of the Canary Islands, torpedoing *Block Island* (CVE-21) and *Barr* (DE-576). The former sank quickly, but the latter remained afloat while *Ahrens* (DE-575) and *Eugene E. Elmore* (DE-686) cooperated in sinking the U-boat. The latter then took the stricken *Barr* in tow.

Wilhoite and *Evarts* arrived on the scene at 1715 on the 30th; soon thereafter, *Robert I. Paine* (DE-578) and *Ahrens* sailed for Casablanca, Morocco. The remaining ships then set course for Casablanca as well, avoiding the track of two homeward-bound U-boats reportedly in the area. On the 31st, the small seaplane tender *Humboldt* (AVP-21) arrived and assumed command over the little force.

At 0930 on 1 June, *Eugene E. Elmore* cast off the tow of *Barr*, and *Wilhoite* picked it up. Moving ahead at eight knots, *Wilhoite* towed the damaged *Barr*, despite the latter's cracked hull which made the task of pulling the ship immeasurably more difficult by causing the damaged ship to yaw. Good damage control in *Barr* later lessened that problem; and, as the convoy neared Casablanca on 5 June, a Dutch tug, HMRT *Antic*, joined and took the damaged destroyer escort in tow, relieving *Wilhoite*. PC-480 then relieved *Wilhoite* and *Evarts* of screening duties as the ships neared the swept channel at their destination.

Upon finishing fueling at Casablanca, *Wilhoite* departed that Moroccan port—her commanding officer, Lt. Roth, having earned a second Letter of Commendation for his ship's performance in towing *Barr* to safety—and sailed to New York with GUS-41. After her arrival there, the ship received repairs at the New York Navy Yard before she sailed on 24 June for battle practices in Casco Bay, Maine. She later acted as a target in training exercises for submarines operating out of New London, Conn., before she once more touched at New York and shifted south to Norfolk where, on 21 July, she joined a hunter-killer task group based around the escort carrier *Bogue* (CVE-9).

Four days after her assignment to *Bogue*'s group, TG 22.3, *Wilhoite* sortied with that carrier and the rest of her screen, *Haverfield* (DE-393), *Swenning* (DE-394), *Willis* (DE-395), and *Janssen* (DE-396), bound for Bermuda. While exercising in that area on antisubmarine warfare (ASW) exercises and night battle practice, *Bogue* and her consorts honed their respective and collective skills in those areas for the rest of July and into the following month.

At 0630 on 3 August, however, a message arrived that abruptly cut short the training. TG 22.3 was to proceed to the vicinity of 46°15′ N, 21°15′ W for offensive operations against a westbound enemy submarine. At 1646 on the next day, *Wilhoite* picked up a sound contact and attacked at 1702; listeners picked up seven detonations but could ascertain no positive results. At 1405 on the 7th, the destroyer escort laid two "hedgehog" projectile patterns and one standard depth charge pattern on a target later evaluated as a school of fish.

Undaunted, the *Bogue* group pressed on with the hunt. Their vigilance and training ultimately paid off. At 0043 on 19 August, night-flying aircraft from *Bogue* attacked a submarine running on the surface. *Wilhoite* was the first ship to hear the transmission and relayed it to *Bogue*. Six minutes later, *Haverfield*,

Janssen, and *Swenning* headed for the scene, detached to take part in the hunt while *Wilhoite* and *Willis* remained with *Bogue* as her screen. Meanwhile, the carrier launched planes, maintaining the start of a continuous air patrol over the area.

Unfortunately, the trio of destroyer escorts returned empty handed at 1225 on the 20th. However, no sooner had they returned, when carrier aircraft reported attacking a submarine that had just surfaced. *Wilhoite*, *Janssen*, *Haverfield*, and *Willis* headed for the scene—a spot some 60 miles distant—hearing a report at 1443 that the submarine (which had apparently submerged but had been damaged and brought to the surface) had again surfaced and was under attack.

Ultimately, the planes from Composite Squadron 42, flying from *Bogue*, inflicted enough damage on the submarine—later identified as *U-1229*—to force the German crew to abandon ship. While *Bogue*'s airmen watched, *U-1229*'s crew went over the side. The submarine—scuttling charges apparently set—exploded and settled into the Atlantic. Later, at 1610, the destroyer escorts arrived on the scene; *Wilhoite* picked up one body of a German sailor, who was summarily buried at sea. *Janssen* picked up *U-1229*'s survivors.

Wilhoite, along with the other units of TG 22.3, later received the Presidential Unit Citation for the group's submarine-hunting activities. *Wilhoite* had been a part of the powerful and sustained offensive during a period of heavy U-boat activity threatening the uninterrupted flow of supplies to the European theater that, since the Allied invasion of France in June of 1944, had assumed great importance. As the citation text concluded: "The gallantry and superb teamwork of the officers and men who fought the embarked planes and who manned *Bogue* and her escort vessels were largely instrumental in forcing the complete withdrawal of enemy submarines from supply routes essential to the maintenance of our established military supremacy."

But, for ships like *Wilhoite*, there was little time to rest on her laurels. Germany was not beaten yet; there would still be more U-boats to fight.

Proceeding to Argentia after TG 22.3's kill of *U-1229*, *Wilhoite* and her consorts again went after enemy submarines reported in that area. Attacks made over a three-day period, 8, 9, and 10 September, were all unsuccessful. *Wilhoite* then patrolled off the Grand Banks before she sailed for the New York Navy Yard at the end of September for voyage repairs.

Upon completion of her yard period on 7 October, *Wilhoite* trained off Montauk Point, Long Island, in ASW tactics before she got underway for Norfolk on 14 October with the remainder of CortDiv 51. Joining *Bogue* at Norfolk and becoming TG 33.3, the ships headed south to Bermuda, arriving there on 23 October. *Wilhoite* and her consorts subsequently trained in ASW tactics out of Great Sound, Bermuda, into November.

Wilhoite returned to New York with TG 33.3 before the unit put to sea for a "barrier patrol" between Brown's Bank and the Nova Scotia entrance to the Gulf of Maine in early December. Detached from *Bogue*'s screen at 1235 on 7 December, *Wilhoite* assisted *Cockrill* (DE-398) in developing a sonar contact until 11 December, when *Wilhoite* headed for Norfolk.

Wilhoite rejoined *Bogue*'s screen and departed Norfolk on the day after Christmas 1944, bound for Bermuda. The destroyer escort patrolled with TG 22.3 out of Port Royal Bay before she returned to New York for repairs on 16 January 1945. *Wilhoite* resumed operations with that illustrious aircraft carrier on 20 January, planeguarding for her as she conducted carrier qualifications (carquals) off Quonset Point, R.I.

Detached from that duty on the 21st, *Wilhoite* sailed for Casco Bay, Maine, where she exercised in ASW and gunnery for a week. She again screened and planeguarded for *Bogue* off Quonset Point into early February, while the carrier once more ran carquals for her embarked air group. The destroyer escort then spent a period of availability at the New York Navy Yard from 8 to 19 February before she engaged in training operations into late March, out of Casco Bay and Portsmouth, N.H.

Wilhoite departed Casco Bay on 28 March and, on the following day, rendezvoused with TG 22.14—the unit assigned the task of hunting a reported southbound U-boat placed by intelligence information at 46°45' N, 41°30' W. At 1139 on 31 March, *Janssen*—part of Task Unit (TU) 22.3.1—made a sound contact. *Wilhoite* picked it up soon thereafter and attacked at 1146, her "hedgehog" hurling a pattern of projectiles six minutes later. She left two deep explosions thereafter but could ascertain no evidence of having scored any hits.

After another brief period of unsuccessful "barrier patrols" between 1 and 6 April, *Wilhoite* trained out of New London in ASW tactics with *Mackerel* (SS-204) and units of *Bogue*'s TG 22.3, before she resumed active U-boat hunting activities. At 2327 on 19 April, *Wilhoite* went to general quarters to investigate a radar contact and, at 2343, illuminated the area with starshell. The object of the attention turned out to be a large, drifting iceberg.

Meanwhile, the war on the European continent had been nearing its end; but the Battle of the Atlantic continued. Soon after the encounter with the iceberg, *Wilhoite* resumed "barrier patrols" with *Bogue*'s TG 22.3. She was screening the carrier when *Bogue*'s planes spotted a U-boat running on the surface at 1300 on 23 April. The aircraft attacked, but the U-boat "pulled the plug" and went deep in time to escape.

The next day, *U-546* torpedoed and sank *Frederick C. Davis* (DE-136)—the last American combatant ship loss in the Battle of the Atlantic. However, the U-boat had little time to savor the victory, for the entire scouting line of desroyer escorts moved swiftly to the scene to rescue their sistership's surivivors and to commence ASW operations. *U-546* was brought to the surface, damaged, and sunk by gunfire from the destroyer escorts, quickly avenging *Frederick C. Davis'* loss.

Over the next few days, *Wilhoite* conducted more "barrier patrols" as part of a group of warships carrying out sweeps in scouting line formation. The ships formed around two escort carriers, *Bogue* and *Card* (CVE-13); the former parolling to the south, the latter to the north.

At 2000 on 7 May, *Wilhoite*, *Haverfield* (DE-398), and *Flaherty* (DE-135) proceeded to the scene of a "disappearing radar contact" that had been made by *Otter* (DE-210). At 2125, *Wilhoite* reached the point of contact and commenced a search in company with *Haverfield*, *Flaherty*, *Otter*, *Swenning*, and *Varian* (DE-798). At 2202, however, the search was cancelled abruptly, and the ships returned to their previous scouting line stations. While the ships had been engaged in their search, Germany—worn down by pressure from the western Allies on the one hand and the ceaseless heavy pressure by the Russians on the other —surrendered at Reims, France, on 7 May. World War II, as far as the European theater was concerned, was over.

Nevertheless, *Wilhoite* remained at sea on "barrier patrol" until 9 May, when she headed for New York City. The destroyer escort was repaired there from 11 to 19 May before she shifted south for more major repairs and alterations at the Charleston (S.C.) Naval Shipyard in preparation for the ship's upcoming deployment to the Pacific—still very much an active theater of war in the spring of 1945.

Wilhoite trained at Guantanamo Bay after her refit at Charleston and then headed for the Pacific, transiting the Panama Canal on 16 July. Arriving at San Diego, Calif., on the 24th, *Wilhoite* sailed for Hawaii with CortDiv 59—*Edsall* (DE-129), *Stewart* (DE-238), and *Moore* (DE-240)—arriving there on 5 August. In ensuing days, *Wilhoite* and her consorts trained in Hawaiian waters.

Wilhoite had arrived too late to participate in active operations, however, because the war in the Pacific ended while she was training in the Hawaiian Islands. On 14 August 1945 (west of the international date line), the Japanese capitulated.

Wilhoite departed Pearl Harbor on 20 August bound for Saipan in the Marianas. After her arrival there, she escorted SS *Sea Sturgeon* to Okinawa in company with the minesweeper *Ptarmigan* (AM-376). While engaged in that local escort duty, *Wilhoite* was forced to reverse course off Okinawa during a typhoon; the ship did not enter Buckner Bay, but proceeded instead back to Saipan.

Meanwhile, the surrender of Japanese garrisons was proceeding apace. In late September, *Wilhoite* sailed for Marcus Island, relieving *Gilmore* (DE-18) there as station ship on 27 September. Anchoring off the south shore of the island, *Wilhoite* supported the small American occupying force in case of any trouble with the garrison of some 2,400 Japanese troops still on the island. By 8 October, the latter was on board the transport *Daikai Maru* and on its way back to Japan. *Wilhoite*, herself, in company with *LCI-336*, departed Marcus on 12 October, bound for Saipan.

Wilhoite subsequently operated on local escort missions to Pagan Island, Agrihan Island, and Iwo Jima and then she supported the American occupation of Japan until 6 January 1946. At that time, the destroyer escort—her task in the Far East completed—sailed for the United States, via Saipan and Pearl Harbor. After touching at San Diego, she proceeded on to New York, via the Panama Canal. Following a complete overhaul at the New York Naval Shipyard, *Wilhoite* shifted south to Green Cove Springs, Fla., where she was decommissioned on 19 June 1946 and placed in the Atlantic Reserve Fleet.

Her sojourn in reserve was to last through the Korean War of 1950 to 1953. Taken out of reserve and reactivated in 1954, *Wilhoite* underwent an extensive conversion to a radar picket ship, receiving sophisticated radar equipment.

Reclassified to DER-397 on 2 September 1954, *Wilhoite* was recommissioned on 29 January 1955 at the Charleston Naval Shipyard, Lt. Comdr. Lambert V. Forde in command, but remained in dockyard hands at Charleston for final installation of equipment and further tests until 22 March. She then proceeded, via Norfolk, Va., to Guantanamo Bay, Cuba, for a rigorous 10-week shakedown. After her post-shakedown availability, *Wilhoite* sailed for the Pacific on 20 July; she officially became part of the Pacific Fleet's Cruiser-Destroyer Force on the 24th.

Upon her arrival at her new home port, Seattle, Wash., on 12 August, *Wilhoite* became a unit of Cort Ron 5 and soon commenced what would become a regular routine of duty as a coastal radar picket ship under the overall direction of Commander, Western Continental Air Defense Command. In the next three years and seven months, *Wilhoite* conducted a total of 30 picket tours before she sailed for Hawaii and her new home port of Pearl Harbor on 4 March 1959.

For the next four years, *Wilhoite* operated out of Pearl Harbor on "barrier patrols" and special operations; ranging as far north as Adak, Alaska, where, on one occasion in December of 1964, a heavy storm with 50-knot winds buffeted the ship against a pier, causing some damage. In 1961, *Wilhoite* took part in Operation "Deep Freeze '61," crossing the Antarctic Circle on 8 February. During that cruise, she visited ports in New Zealand and Australia before she returned to Pearl Harbor via Pago Pago, Samoa.

Besides "special operations" on "barrier patrols" from Pearl Harbor, *Wilhoite* carried out search and rescue (SAR) missions, ready for any eventuality while on station. During her third SAR patrol, in the autumn of 1963, the ship sighted an approaching Japanese fishing vessel, *Kayo Maru*. *Wilhoite* subsequently took on board Eichi Nakata, a man who had been bitten by a shark, and carried him to Midway where he received medical treatment. After that mission of mercy, *Wilhoite* returned to Pearl Harbor on 22 October 1963.

By the mid-1960's, however, further changes were in store for the veteran warship. The growing pace of incursions by North Vietnamese-backed Viet Cong communist guerrillas against South Vietnam had resulted in escalating American support of the latter. *Wilhoite* accordingly was deployed to the Western Pacific (WestPac) in the spring of 1965, beginning a cycle of WestPac tours that lasted into 1969.

Wilhoite conducted intermittent WestPac deployments, with corresponding "Market Time" patrols off the coast of Vietnam, into January of 1969. Her's was unsung duty—long hours of ceaseless patrol, aiding the fledging South Vietnamese Navy in detecting and preventing supplies, weapons, and other materials from being infiltrated into South Vietnam by the Viet Cong and the North Vietnamese. Often assisted by only two small boats, a Coast Guard patrol boat and aircraft, *Wilhoite* upon occasion had the responsibility for patrol over 2,750 square miles of ocean—an ample assignment for a ship with the size and range of a radar picket destroyer escort.

Occasionally, there were periods of excitement to enliven an otherwise tedious duty. On 19 June 1965, *Wilhoite* relieved *Kretschmer* (DER–329) on "Market Time" station and assumed the duties of "mother ship" to two Navy "Swift" (PCF) boats, providing berthing accommodations for extra crew members and supplying them with food, fuel, and fresh water.

At approximately 2000 on 11 July, a "Market Time" patrol aircraft detected a steel-hulled trawler running darkened some 55 miles from the coast of South Vietnam, on a westerly heading. *Wilhoite*, notified by radio of the trawler's course, set hers to close and identify the ship, commencing covert surveillance as soon as she picked up radar contact. The next morning, 12 July, *Wilhoite* closed for identification purposes but later opened the range.

By that point, the trawler had changed course, heading away from the coast; *Wilhoite* accordingly maintained surveillance for three more days. Entering the "Market Time" area, the trawler drew more pursuers —*Gallup* (PGM–85), USCGC *Point Orient* (WPB–82319), and *PCF–79*—all under the command of Comdr. C. R. Stephan, embarked in *Wilhoite*. On 15 July, *Wilhoite* intercepted the unidentified trawler five miles from the beach. Ignoring calls to surrender broadcast by a psychological warfare unit embarked in *Point Orient*, the trawler was soon taken under fire, running aground in flames on a sandbar at the mouth of the River De Say Ky in Quang Ngai province.

Throughout the night, *Wilhoite* and the other ships intermittently fired into the beached trawler; the following morning, a party went on board the wreck to inspect the damage and learn the nature of her cargo. The holds were found jammed with guns, ammunition, and explosives—the largest arms cache captured during the Vietnam War. Ultimately relieved of her "Market Time" patrol duties on 26 July, *Wilhoite* sailed for Hong Kong and a period of recreation.

Alternating the tours of duty on Market Time stations with periods in port at Hong Kong, Sasebo, and Yokosuka, *Wilhoite* periodically returned to such ports as Pearl Harbor and Subic Bay.

Not all of the ship's highlights of "Market Time" operations were combat-oriented ones. On 6 September 1968, for example, *Wilhoite* was called upon to perform an SAR mission, while she was riding out the tail-end of Typhoon "Bess." Assigned to locate a lost Vietnamese Navy PGM, *Wilhoite* centered her search on a point some 30 miles from the port of Danang. Although she never sighted the PGM, however, the radar picket destroyer escort maintained contact via voice radio; and ultimately, the PGM was able to reorient herself and continue on her voyage.

Later, while returning to her patrol station, *Wilhoite*

came across an Army landing craft, *LCU–1481*, which had been adrift and lost for some 48 hours. Typhoon "Bess" had proved a nuisance to the LCU, for it had caused damage that had rendered the craft powerless. *Wilhoite* stood by while another LCU was dispatched from Danang to take the stricken *LCU–1481* in tow and bring her to port safely.

Later that autumn, *Wilhoite* received an availability alongside the veteran destroyer tender *Dixie* (AD–14) at Subic Bay from 25 to 28 September. On the latter day, the radar picket destroyer escort sortied for "Market Time" once more, relieving the Coast Guard cutter *Ingham* (WPG–35) on station. *Wilhoite* later saw her first action of that deployment when she was called upon to deliver gunfire support in an area north of An Thoi. There, *Wilhoite* shelled an area heavily infested with Viet Cong, destroying or damaging several enemy junks that had attempted to infiltrate war materiel from the north.

Wilhoite departed Vietnamese waters on 15 January 1969, bound for Hawaii. She stopped for fuel at Subic Bay and at Apra Harbor, Guam, before she continued on, arriving at Pearl Harbor on 1 February. After a period of tender availability alongside *Isle Royale* (AD–29), from 17 February to 3 March, *Wilhoite* underwent a restricted availability at the Pearl Harbor Naval Shipyard before she conducted her sea trials at the end of May. On 2 June, the radar picket destroyer escort departed the Hawaiian Islands for the west coast; and she arrived at Bremerton, Wash., a week later. There, on 2 July, *Wilhoite* was decommissioned.

Simultaneously struck from the Navy list, *Wilhoite* was sold on 19 July 1972 to General Metals Corp., Tacoma, Wash., and subsequently scrapped.

Wilhoite received the Presidential Unit Citation, a Navy Unit Commendation, and one battle star for World War II service and six battle stars for her duty in Vietnam.

Wilke, Jack W., see *Jack W. Wilke*.

Wilkes

Charles Wilkes—born on 3 April 1798 in New York City—served in merchant ships between 1815 and 1817 before being appointed a midshipman in the United States Navy on New Year's Day 1818. Following initial training in *Independence*, he transferred to *Guerriere* in July 1818 for a cruise in the Baltic and Mediterranean Seas. After a two-month assignment in *Washington* between March and May 1821, Midshipman Wilkes received orders to *Franklin*, in which ship he voyaged to South America. During that cruise, Wilkes briefly commanded *Franklin*'s tender *Waterwitch* before being detached from *Franklin* on 3 March 1823 to command the American merchant ship *Ocain* on her way back to Boston, where he arrived on 15 October. From there, he reported to Washington for duty in conjunction with the court-martial of Capt. Stewart, his former commanding officer in *Franklin*. On 28 April 1827, Wilkes was promoted to lieutenant. Apparently at home awaiting orders between 1826 and 1830, Lt. Wilkes requested surveying duty in March of 1827 but withdrew his application in July 1828 in favor of one for duty with a proposed exploring expedition. Late that fall, he received orders to New York where he set about the task of procuring the necessary instruments for that expedition.

In April 1830, Lt. Wilkes resumed sea duty. Assigned to *Boston*, he made a cruise in her to the Mediterranean. On 15 November, he transferred to *Fairfield* in which ship he served until May 1831 at which time he was detached and ordered home to await orders. Late in the spring of 1832, Wilkes returned to active duty as a member of the team which surveyed Narragansett Bay. In February 1833, he received orders to duty in charge of the Depot of Charts and Instruments (forerunner both of the Naval Oceanographic Office and of the Naval Observatory). In August of 1836, Wilkes briefly took leave of that post when he sailed to Europe to acquire additional equipment for the exploring expedition. He returned to the Depot of Charts and Instruments after that trip; and, in March 1837, Secretary of the Navy Mahlon Dickerson requested Wilkes to take a position in the astronomy department of the exploring expedition. That fall, he participated in an oceanographic survey of the Carolina coast.

The following spring, Wilkes learned that he had been chosen to command the South Seas Exploring Expedition. President Van Buren approved his appointment on 20 April, and Wilkes assumed command of *Vincennes* at Norfolk on 7 July. He received his final orders on 11 August and set sail in *Vincennes*—in company with *Peacock*, *Porpoise*, *Sea Gull*, *Flying Fish*, and *Relief*—on the 18th. After stops at Rio de Janeiro, Brazil, and Tierra del Fuego located at the southern tip of South America, Wilkes took his expedition on its first cruise through Antarctic waters in February and March of 1839. He returned to Tierra del Fuego and then later headed through the south seas to Sydney, Australia, where he arrived on 29 November. On the day after Christmas, he embarked upon his second voyage to the Antarctic. In January 1840, he sighted the actual land mass which constitutes Antarctica, though it took later explorations to vindicate his assertions that the continent existed.

By late spring 1840, the expedition moved north again and began the exploration of the islands of the South Pacific. After surveying the Fiji Islands between May and August, the expedition departed those islands, bound for Hawaii on 11 August. The Hawaiian survey, conducted between 24 September 1840 and 5 April 1841, centered upon a study of the volcanoes, Mauna Loa and Kilauea. Wilkes completed his work in Hawaii in April 1841 and set sail on the 5th for the west coast. After surveys of parts of the coast of the Pacific Northwest during the summer of 1841, he brought his expedition into San Francisco on 14 August. Its arrival back in the United States, however, signaled no end to the work of the expedition. On 1 November, it put to sea once again, this time for a voyage to the western Pacific. During that cruise, Wilkes visited Manila in the Philippines, the British colony at Singapore, and Cape Town on the southern tip of Africa. Wilkes and his command concluded the expedition upon arrival at New York on 10 June 1842.

For almost 19 years, Wilkes worked with the data gathered by his expedition. During that period, he supervised the publication of the results of that exploration in a series of *Narratives* under the auspices of the Navy. He also received two promotions during that time—to commander in 1843 and to captain in 1855. The only break in this duty came in the second half of 1858 when the Secretary of the Navy sent Wilkes on a special mission to evaluate the potential for naval use of the natural resources—primarily iron, coal, and timber—of North Carolina's Deep River region.

The outbreak of the Civil War, however, brought an interruption to his scientific work. On 19 April, he was detached from his duty with the expedition publication program in order to help destroy the Norfolk Navy Yard before Union forces abandoned it to the Confederacy. In May, Capt. Wilkes received orders to take command of the steam-powered frigate *San Jacinto*. He arrived on board his new command on 27 August, at Monrovia, Liberia, just before she set sail to return to the United States. During the voyage home, he took her to the West Indies in search of the Southern commerce raider, CSS *Sumter*, under the command of Capt. Raphael Semmes—later commanding officer of the famous Confederate cruiser CSS *Alabama*. During that mission, his ship stopped at Cienfuegos, Cuba, for coal, and Wilkes learned that the South's commissioners

to England and France, James Mason and John Slidell, had escaped from Charleston on board the fast coastal packet *Theodora* and were then in Havana awaiting transportation to Europe. *San Jacinto* quickly headed for Havana, hoping to catch *Theodora* when she embarked upon her return trip but arrived a day late. He learned, however, that Mason and Slidell were still in Cuba and planned to board the British mail packet *Trent* at St. Thomas for the voyage to Europe.

Thereupon, he concocted a plan to intercept *Trent* in Old Bahama Channel, some 230 miles east of Havana, and capture the two Confederate diplomats. On 8 November, the British ship steamed into sight, and Wilkes coerced her into stopping with two shots across her bow. A boarding party seized Mason and Slidell and their secretaries and then allowed the neutral ship to continue her voyage. *San Jacinto* then headed home with her prisoners. Upon his arrival in Boston, Wilkes was loudly acclaimed for his action, but soon the clouds of war with Great Britain over the incident began to darken the horizon. Ultimately, the dubious legality of Wilkes' action and the threat of war with Britain and France brought a complete disavowal of Wilkes' act by the Federal Government and the release of the prisoners.

On 30 November, Capt. Wilkes was detached from *San Jacinto* and ordered to duty with the Board of Naval Examiners. That assignment lasted until the following summer. He commanded the James River Flotilla briefly in July and August of 1862 and received his promotion to commodore at that time. On 29 August, Wilkes left that post and took over the Potomac River Flotilla. That assignment proved to be of short duration. On 8 September, he received orders to command the West India Squadron. Promoted to acting rear admiral, Wilkes directed the West India Squadron—primarily concerned with hunting down Southern commerce raiders and blockade runners—until the summer of 1863. On 1 June, he was detached from the squadron and, on the 30th, set sail from Havana for the United States in *Roanoke*.

Conflicts with the Navy Department, probably stemming from his treatment during the *Trent* affair negotiations, culminated in Wilkes' court-martial early in 1864 over the publication of a letter he wrote to Gideon Welles castigating the Secretary for statements made against Wilkes in his annual report. On 26 April 1864, Acting Rear Admiral Wilkes was found guilty by court-martial of disobediance of orders, insubordination, and other specifications and was sentenced to receive a public reprimand and suspension from the service for three years. President Lincoln reduced the term of suspension to one year, at the conclusion of which Wilkes retired from the Navy. On 6 August 1866, he was promoted to rear admiral on the retired list and, for the remainder of his life, worked for the completion of publication of the results of the Wilkes Exploring Expedition. He also took time out to do some writing, including an autobiography. On 8 February 1877, Rear Admiral Wilkes died at Washington, D.C. Initially interred at Oak Hill Cemetery in Washington, his body was moved to Arlington National Cemetery in August 1909.

I

(Torpedo Boat No. 35: dp. 165; l. 175'0'' (wl.); b. 17'7⅝''; dr. 4'8'' (mean); s. 25.99 k. (tl.); cpl. 28; a. 3 1-pdr. rf., 3 18'' tt.; cl. *Blakely*)

The first *Wilkes* (Torpedo Boat No. 35) was laid down on 3 June 1899 at Morris Heights, N.Y., by the Gas Engine & Power Co. and the Charles L. Seabury & Co.; launched on 28 September 1901; sponsored by Miss Harriet E. Rankin; and commissioned at the Norfolk Navy Yard on 18 September 1902, Lt. (jg.) Dudley W. Knox in command.

Wilkes spent the bulk of her career in reserve. Soon after her commissioning, she was assigned to the Reserve Torpedo Flotilla based at Norfolk, Va. There, she remained until the winter of 1906 and 1907 when she briefly returned to full commission for service with the 3d Torpedo Flotilla. On 30 May 1907, she was again placed in reserve with the Reserve Torpedo Flotilla at Norfolk. There, she remained until 23 November 1908 when she was recommissioned and assigned to duty with the Atlantic Torpedo Fleet based at Charleston, S.C. On 22 December 1909, she went back into reserve, this time at the Charleston Navy Yard. Apparently in commission, in reserve, while at Charleston, *Wilkes* was decommissioned there on 14 November 1913, and her name was struck from the Navy list on the following day. She was sunk as a target sometime during the summer or fall of 1914.

II

(Destroyer No. 67: dp. 1,110 (n.); l. 315'3''; b. 29'11''; dr. 10'8¼'' (aft); s. 29.58 k.; cpl. 99; a. 4 4'', 2 1-pdrs., 2 .30-cal. mg., 12 21'' tt.; cl. *Sampson*)

The second *Wilkes* (Destroyer No. 67) was laid down on 11 March 1915 at Philadelphia by the William Cramp & Sons Ship & Engine Building Co.; launched on 18 May 1916; sponsored by Miss Carrie McIver Wilkes; and commissioned on 10 November 1916, Lt. Comdr. Julius F. Hellweg in command.

Wilkes spent the winter preceding America's entry into World War I outfitting—first in the Philadelphia Navy Yard and later in the Torpedo Station located at Newport, R.I.—and conducting fleet maneuvers in Cuban waters. She returned from those operations at the height of the crisis over the German declaration of unrestricted submarine warfare, arriving in Norfolk on 7 March 1917. Just one month later, on 6 April, the United States joined the war against the Central Powers. At the end of April, the destroyer escorted the French cruiser *Amiral Auge* from Norfolk to New York. On 15 June, she departed New York in the screen of the first American troop convoy to voyage to Europe. She escorted her charges into Saint Nazaire on 26 June then headed for Portsmouth, England, where she celebrated Independence Day. From there, she continued on to her permanent European base, Queenstown, Ireland, where she arrived on the 6th.

Wilkes operated from the Queenstown base for the duration of World War I. For the most part, she conducted antisubmarine patrols and escorted convoys bound for England on the last leg of their voyage. Occasionally, however, she was called upon to shepherd convoys into port at Brest and Saint Nazaire, France. Although her duties appeared routine, they were strenuous. She spent many arduous days at sea in the stormy Atlantic with only hours or, at most, a day or two in port to provision. Though it appears that she never saw combat with German U-boats, she did witness the results of their depredations once when she rescued 23 survivors of the torpedoed British merchantman SS *Purley* on 25 July 1917. She continued her patrol and escort duties until after Christmas 1918, over a month after the cessation of hostilities. On 26 December, she departed Queenstown and headed for home. On 7 January 1919, she arrived in New York.

Immediately upon her return, *Wilkes* began overhaul at New York. That occupied her time until 1 May when she embarked upon her most noteworthy postwar mission—duty as a picket ship for the first transatlantic flight. Only one of the four Navy-Curtiss (NC) flying boats slated for the mission actually completed the flight. NC–4 reached the Azores at Horta on 17 May, made the hop to Ponta Delgada on the 20th, and departed the Azores for Lisbon, Portugal, on the 27th. *Wilkes* served as a picket on that second leg of the flight as the fourth ship in a line of 14 destroyers between the Azores and the European continent. The NC–4 reached her destination that same day, and *Wilkes'* part in the event was completed. While NC–4 finished the third and last leg of its flight—from Lisbon to Plymouth, England—on 30 and 31 May, *Wilkes* pointed her bow homeward. The destroyer reentered New York harbor on 4 June and resumed peacetime operations along the Atlantic coast. For the next 34 months, she plied the waters off the eastern seaboard in the spring, summer, and fall. Late each fall, she headed south to participate in fleet maneuvers in Cuban waters, the Caribbean, and the Gulf of Mexico. During that time, she was based at three different ports—Newport, R.I.; New York, N.Y.; and Charleston, S.C. On 12 April 1922, *Wilkes* entered the Philadelphia Navy Yard where she was placed out of commission on 5 June 1922.

Wilkes remained inactive at Philadelphia for over four years. In the summer of 1926, she was turned over to the Coast Guard, desperately in need of additional ships to suppress the illegal, but lucrative, traffic in alcoholic beverages spawned by Prohibition. She was commissioned a Coast Guard destroyer at New London,

Wilkes (Destroyer No. 67) on trials, 28 September 1916. She has not yet been armed; weights have been installed in the positions of guns and torpedo tubes. (NR&L(M) 3832)

Conn., on 23 August 1926, Lt. Comdr. M. J. Ryan, USCG, in command. For the next eight years, she patrolled the east coast from New England to Florida. In 1934, the repeal of Prohibition brought an end to the illicit alcohol trade and the "Rum Patrol" as well. *Wilkes* completed her last Coast Guard patrol at Philadelphia on 15 March 1934. There, she was placed out of commission on 29 March and returned to the Navy. On 5 July, her name was struck from the Navy list. She was sold on 22 August 1934 for scrapping under the terms of the London Treaty for the limitation of naval armaments.

III

(DD–441: dp. 1,630; l. 348'3"; b. 35'4"; dr. 10'2"; s. 35 k.; cpl. 239; a. 4 5", 10 21" tt., 2 dct., 1 dcp., 12 .50-cal. mg.; cl. *Gleaves*)

The third *Wilkes* (DD–441) was laid down on 1 November 1939 by the Boston Navy Yard; launched on 31 May 1940; sponsored by Mrs. Bessie Wilkes Styer; and commissioned on 22 April 1941, Lt. Comdr. J. D. Kelsey in command.

Wilkes was ready for sea on 1 June 1941 and then conducted shakedown training off the New England coast. The destroyer arrived in Bermuda on 24 August and helped to screen *North Carolina* (BB–55) and *Washington* (BB–56) on their shakedown cruises in the Caribbean. She departed Bermuda on 9 September and, two days later, arrived back in Boston for a brief availability, setting sail on 25 September for Guantanamo Bay, Cuba, and four days of training. *Wilkes* left Cuban waters and, on 2 October, arrived at Hampton Roads, Va., three days later. During the remainder of October, *Wilkes* visited Gravesend Bay, N.Y.; Casco Bay, Maine; and Provincetown, Mass.

On 2 November, the destroyer arrived at Argentia, Newfoundland, briefly escorted *Yukon* (AF–9), and made rendezvous with *Salinas* (AO–19), which had just survived two torpedo hits, and escorted the damaged oiler to Cape Sable, Nova Scotia.

On 28 November, *Wilkes* departed Cape Sable escorting Convoy HX–162. During the destroyer's passage to Iceland, Japanese naval aircraft attacked the Pacific Fleet's base at Pearl Harbor, pushing the United States into full participation in World War II. The convoy reached its destination the next day, and *Wilkes* spent the rest of December escorting convoys from Argentia, Newfoundland, to Hvalfjordur and Reykjavik, Iceland. *Wilkes* returned to Boston where she refueled, took on provisions, and remained through the holiday season.

On New Year's Day 1942, the destroyer got underway and the following day arrived at Casco Bay, Maine, where she conducted exercise runs. On 5 January, *Wilkes* departed Casco Bay in company with *Madison* (DD–425), *Roper* (DD–147), and *Sturtevant* (DD–240), bound for Argentia, Newfoundland. She arrived two days later and, on the 10th, made rendezvous with Convoy HX–169, accompanying it for the next eight days. On 18 January, she was relieved as escort, and she set course for Ireland with *Madison*, *Roper*, and *Sturtevant*. Three days later, she moored at Londonderry. On 25 January, *Wilkes* got underway and soon made contact with Convoy ON–59, taking station and relieving the British escort vessels. She arrived at Boston on 8 February, requiring docking.

On 12 February 1942, *Wilkes* received orders to depart Boston on 15 February and to proceed to Casco Bay, Maine, on a routine "milk run" in company with *Truxton* (DD–229) and to join *Pollux* (AKS–2) en route. *Truxtun* was delayed, so *Wilkes* went ahead and met *Pollux* according to schedule on 15 February; *Truxtun* joined up the following day.

While en route to Argentia, Newfoundland, at about 0350 on 18 February 1942, *Wilkes'* commanding officer was awakened by the navigator and informed that the ship was believed to be northward of the plotted track. Visibility was poor, and weather conditions prevented

obtaining radio direction finder bearings. Continuous fathometer soundings were taken, and all were in excess of 30 fathoms except one sounding of 15 fathoms which was obtained just prior to grounding. The signal, "Emergency stop," to warn the other vessels was immediately given by searchlight, and the message "*Wilkes* aground do not know which side" was broadcast on the TBS. The words, "*Wilkes* aground," were also broadcast on the distress frequency. However, no message was received from *Pollux* or *Truxtun* until after these ships had also grounded. *Wilkes* found herself stranded to port of *Pollux*; *Truxtun* to starboard. About 0700, *Wilkes* succeeded in backing clear of the beach. After seeing that *Pollux* had received help from *George E. Badger* (DD–196), she left the scene. However, *Pollux* and *Truxtun* were totally lost, along with the 205 men who went down with them. The casualty list from the two lost ships was the Atlantic Fleet's largest list of the war up to that time.

No deaths occurred on *Wilkes*. She remained at Argentia for six days before beginning a voyage to Boston for repairs.

On 1 April 1942, *Wilkes* was assigned to Task Force (TF) 21 at the Boston Navy Yard where she conducted post repair trials and underwent a three-day availability. On 6 April, *Wilkes* got underway for Casco Bay, Maine, escorting *Augusta* (CA–31).

On the 8th, the destroyer sighted the British oil tanker SS *Davila*. One minute later, the two ships collided; *Davila's* bow struck *Wilkes* on the port side, abreast of her number one fireroom. After the two ships separated, the destroyer returned to Boston where she entered the navy yard for restricted availability which continued until 3 June. The next day, she conducted post-repair trials.

Following gunnery and antiaircraft practice and antisubmarine exercises at Casco Bay, *Wilkes* made a short escort mission screening Convoy BX–26. Three days later, she got underway for New York in company with *Buck* (DD–420) and *Swanson* (DD–443), arrived the following day, and anchored at the New York Navy Yard. On 1 July 1942, the destroyer sailed for Little Placentia Harbor, Newfoundland, where she performed escort and patrol duty before returning to New York where she remained until the 12th.

The next day, *Wilkes* got underway and joined Convoy AS–4, nine ships of American, British, Norwegian, and Dutch registry. On the 16th, the second ship of the first column of the convoy, SS *Fairport*, was torpedoed forward and aft and sank. Survivors got clear in four boats and several rafts. *Kearny* (DD–432) made depth charge attacks and rescued the survivors while *Wilkes* continued a sound search and released nine depth charges with no visible results.

At 1600 on 17 July, the destroyer made an underwater sound contact. Three minutes later, she delivered a modified "intermediate depth charge attack." Large amounts of air were seen to emerge at the scene of the attack in the center of which appeared the bow of a submarine, which then rolled over and disappeared, apparently out of control. At 1614, *Wilkes* delivered a deep attack, including three 600-pound charges at the scene of the air blows. More air broke the surface, and the whole area was covered with dark brown liquid and oil.

Three days later, *Wilkes* was detached from the formation and proceeded to Trinidad, where she refueled before sailing for the Virginia capes and arrived at Norfolk on 25 July. The destroyer then made two coastal runs to New York before getting underway from that port on 19 August and steaming for Halifax harbor, Nova Scotia, where she arrived on 21 August. She remained moored off Greenoch until 5 September. At that time, she proceeded to sea to escort USAT *Siboney* to New York. She then spent the remainder of September conducting various exercises in Casco Bay, Maine.

Wilkes sailed for Virginia on 30 September 1942 and, two days later, arrived at Hampton Roads. For the greater part of October, the destroyer conducted various drills and maneuvers, including amphibious operations with TF 33. On 24 October, *Wilkes* got underway from Norfolk and took station in a convoy steaming for North Africa.

On 8 November 1942, *Wilkes* participated in the assault on Fedhala, French Morocco. Operating with TF 34, she was assigned duty as a control vessel during the first phase and as a fire support vessel during the second. The ship made radar contact on the surface, and a short while later her fire control party reported a dark object in the water. *Wilkes* dropped a standard nine-charge pattern. Thereafter, sound conditions were unfavorable due to the depth charge turbulence which was extreme in the shallow water— 40 fathoms. After 15 minutes, the search was abandoned. No casualties or hits resulted from enemy action.

The next day, while steaming off Fedhala Point, *Wilkes* sighted a French destroyer emerging from Casablanca. She left her patrol station and proceeded toward the enemy ship. However, the shore battery on Pointe d'Oukach opened fire, and *Wilkes* was forced to discontinue her chase as the destroyer retreated back to Casablanca.

On 11 November, *Wilkes* received news that Casablanca had capitulated; and the destroyer then resumed patrolling the area around the convoy anchorage. At 1958, a rocket burst near the convoy area; and, one minute later, *Winooski* (AO–38) reported being torpedoed. At 2000, *Joseph Hewes* (AP–50) reported the same fate and sank in less than one hour. *Bristol* (DD–453) illuminated to open fire on a surfaced submarine and also made a depth charge attack with negative results.

The next day, *Wilkes* escorted *Augusta* into Casablanca. She then returned toward the patrol area and resumed patrolling her assigned station. *Wilkes* picked up a submarine contact at 2300 yards and made a shallow depth charge attack, expending four 300-pound and two 600-pound charges without success. *Wilkes* then abandoned her search and continued her patrol. Little more than an hour later, two ships in the convoy anchorage area were torpedoed. A U-boat hit a third ship after 26 more minutes had passed. The convoy was ordered to weigh anchor and proceed to sea. *Wilkes* got underway and took station in the convoy's antisubmarine screen off its starboard bow. The convoy changed base course 20 degrees every 15 minutes for almost two hours to avoid detection.

On 15 November 1942, *Electra* (AK–21), a cargo ship in another convoy, was torpedoed. *Wilkes* made a submarine contact at 1800 yards and made a depth charge attack with negative results. The destroyer then screened the damaged ship as she was being towed into Casablanca.

Two days later, *Wilkes* rejoined the convoy as it steamed homeward and, on 30 November 1942, arrived at Norfolk. She spent the month of December conducting short escort and patrol missions in waters in New York and Casco Bay, Maine.

Wilkes began the new year 1943 with two voyages from New York to Casablanca and back, taking place between 14 January and 14 February and between 6 March and 5 April. The destroyer then made runs between New York and Norfolk through 14 May 1943.

The next day, she got underway escorting a convoy to the Panama Canal and arrived on 21 May at Cristobal, Canal Zone. Four days later, *Wilkes* returned to Hampton Roads. From 29 May through 9 June, the destroyer visited ports along the northeast coast of the United States and then devoted the remainder of 1943 escorting convoys to North Africa, making three round trips from 10 June until Christmas Day when she returned to New York.

On 7 January 1944, *Wilkes* got underway for the Canal Zone—along with *Swanson* (DD–443) and *Marshall* (DD–676)—transited the canal, and arrived at Balboa on 12 January. A week later, *Wilkes*

escorted troop-laden SS *Mormacdove*, via the Galapagos, Bora Bora, and Noumea to Milne Bay, New Guinea, where they arrived on 20 February 1944. Five days later, the destroyer got underway for Cape Gloucester, New Britain, made rendezvous with an LST convoy en route, and escorted them to Borgen Bay, Cape Gloucester, Megin Island, Cape Cretin, and the Tami Islands.

On 1 March 1944, *Wilkes* was anchored in Oro Bay, Buna, New Guinea. Two days later, she embarked American Army troops, complete with equipment, and got underway with eight other destroyers and three high-speed transports and sailed for Los Negros Island of the Admiralty group in order to reinforce elements of the 1st Cavalry Division who were then holding the beachhead.

On 4 March, *Wilkes* arrived off Hayne Harbor, Los Negros Island, and disembarked all troops and equipment without incident. The destroyer remained there to operate as a fire support ship and received on board casualties evacuated from the combat areas. The next day, *Wilkes* bombarded Lemondrol Creek, just south of Momote air strip, and targets on the western end of Hayne Harbor. She continued performing such duty through 7 March when *Wilkes* proceeded to Seeadler Harbor, at Manus Island, Admiralty Group, to assist in the landings there.

After a two-day round trip to Cape Sudest and a brief patrol in Seeadler Harbor, *Wilkes* returned to Cape Sudest on 24 March for availability. On 9 April, she steamed back to Seeadler Harbor to escort a convoy from Los Negros Island to Langemak Bay, New Guinea. On the 11th, the destroyer anchored in Oro Bay and underwent availability.

Wilkes arrived at Cape Cretin on 17 April and took on board Lt. Gen. Walter Krueger, Commander, Sixth Army, and his staff for transportation to combat areas to observe the landings in the Wakde-Sarmi area of New Guinea. Three days later, *Wilkes* made rendezvous with TF 77 and took station as a radar picket. On 22 April 1944, the destroyer participated in the landings at Tanahmerah Bay, New Guinea, and, after the troops had gone ashore, continued operations in that area.

D day for the landings at Wakde Island was 17 May 1944. *Wilkes* contributed fire support and served in the antisubmarine screen. On 26 May, after refueling and repair, the destroyer proceeded toward Biak Island and participated in the landings there.

On 5 June, *Wilkes* helped to escort a convoy consisting of nine LST's, three LCI's, four LCT's and escorts through the dangerous waters between the Schouten Islands. The destroyer then continued operations in the Humboldt Bay area and spent the latter part of June bombarding targets ashore on Aitape and Toem, New Guinea. During July, *Wilkes* participated in the landings at Noemfoor Island on the 1st and at Cape Sansapor on the 30th.

On 19 August, *Wilkes* departed the New Guinea area and set a course for the Marshall Islands, arriving at Eniwetok on 25 August. Three days later, she joined TF 38 and acted as a screen while the mighty flattops launched air strikes on Iwo Jima, Chichi Jima, Saipan, Yap, Ulithi, Peleliu, and Formosa. On 14 October, *Wilkes* accompanied the task force to the Philippines and that day made strikes against Luzon. She also screened them during a raid on Leyte on the 17th and during an attack against Samar Island on the 24th.

The next day, the destroyer—as part of Task Group (TG) 38.4—acted as a communication link between two task groups en route to intercept the Japanese Northern Force off Cape Engaño. On the 26th, *Wilkes* and *Swanson* (DD–443) were detached and proceeded to Ulithi Atoll for upkeep and repairs.

On 3 November, *Wilkes* got underway with *Nicholson* (DD–442) for Apra Harbor, Guam, and arrived there the next day. After a brief round trip to Manus, Admiralty Islands, *Wilkes* and *Nicholson* escorted Convoy GE–29 to Eniwetok, arriving on 26 November.

Wilkes set sail for Pearl Harbor on 1 December and arrived seven days later. On the 15th, the destroyer arrived at the Puget Sound Navy Yard. Two days later, she entered Todd's Pacific Shipbuilding Co. yard at Seattle for an overhaul.

On 28 January 1945—after completing her availability and post-repair trials—*Wilkes* made rendezvous with *Franklin* (CV-13) and proceeded to San Francisco. Three days later, she was underway again with *Franklin* for Pearl Harbor where she arrived on 13 February. She then conducted routine operations and participated in various exercises and drills with *Shangri-La* (CV-38).

On 9 March, *Wilkes* got underway in company with *New Mexico* (BB-40) and *Nicholson* for Ulithi, Caroline Islands. After a brief refueling at Eniwetok, the destroyer arrived on 19 March at Ulithi. Three days later, she formed in the van of *De Grasse* (AP-164) and proceeded to Guam. While en route, *Wilkes* rescued four survivors of a PBM which had run out of fuel. On 26 March, she entered Apra Harbor, Guam, and was drydocked for repairs to the underwater sound equipment. On 1 April, *Wilkes* proceeded singly to Saipan. This was the first of two consecutive trips which lasted until 27 April.

At that time, *Wilkes* received orders to escort a six-ship convoy to Okinawa and arrived at Hagushi anchorage on 1 May. Three days later, she sighted a red flare fired from a downed PBM. *Wilkes* took PBM 93 V464 under tow to Kerama Retto and resumed patrol duty. On 6 May, the destroyer was ordered to return to Kerama Retto for limited availability and logistics. Four days later, she got underway and patrolled off the southern entrance to Kerama Retto. Between 12 and 22 May, *Wilkes* covered carriers for routine flight operations and strikes on Nansei Shoto.

On 22 May 1945, *Wilkes* escorted *Makin Island* (CVE-93) to Kerama Retto for provisions and ammunition replenishment. They departed the following day and, after making mail deliveries, *Wilkes* returned to her patrol station covering the carrier strikes on Nansei Shoto.

On 24 June, *Wilkes* and her task unit set course for Leyte and arrived at San Pedro Bay three days later. That day, she sailed for Ulithi, and she arrived there on 30 June for limited availability.

Wilkes sortied from Ulithi on 9 July 1945 and spent more than a month supporting TF 38. On 15 August, *Wilkes* received an official notice telling her that Japan had capitulated. Five days later, *Wilkes* was anchored at Ulithi Atoll, Caroline Islands, undergoing voyage repairs and routine upkeep. On 24 August, *Wilkes* got underway as part of the autisubmarine screen with Task Unit 30.8.9 patrolling off the Mariana and Bonin Islands.

Wilkes proceeded to Okinawa, arriving on 3 September. She then made rendezvous with TG 70.6 on the 7th in the Yellow Sea. On the 10th, the destroyer set her course for the outer transport anchorage at Jinsen (now Inchon), Korea, and arrived the next day. Three days later, she conducted fueling exercises, then spent the remainder of September and October, through the 20th, in the Ito-Jinsen area, delivering passengers and undergoing availability.

On 21 October 1945, *Wilkes* got underway from Jinsen, bound for the Marianas, and arrived at Saipan on the 27th. That same day, she pushed on toward Hawaii and reached Pearl Harbor on 4 November. Three days later, she headed for the west coast of the United States and arrived at San Diego on the 13th. *Wilkes* departed the west coast on 16 November, transited the Panama Canal, and reached Charleston, S.C., on 2 December.

The destroyer reported for duty in the Inactive Fleet, Atlantic, on 3 December. She was moored in the navy yard from 4 to 31 December undergoing preservation. *Wilkes* was placed out of commission, in reserve, on 4 March 1946. Her name was struck from the Navy list on 16 September 1968, and she was sold to the Southern Scrap Material Co., Ltd., New Orleans, on 29 June 1972.

Wilkes received 10 battle stars for her World War II service.

IV

(T–AGS–33: dp. 2,540 (f.); l. 286'7½''; b. 48'0''; dr. 15'0'' (max.); s. 15 k.; cpl. 49; cl. *Wilkes*)

The fourth *Wilkes* (T–AGS–33)—an oceanographic survey vessel—was laid down on 18 July 1968 at Bay City., Mich., by the Defoe Shipbuilding Co.; launched on 31 July 1969; sponsored by Mrs. Hollis L. Jay, the great grand-daughter of Charles Wilkes; and was accepted by the Military Sealift Command (MSC) at the Boston Naval Shipyard on 16 July 1971. W. B. Nilsen was the ship's first master.

Wilkes was assigned to special projects with MSC Atlantic upon her joining MSC in 1971. Operated by a civil service crew but under the direction of the Oceanographer of the Navy, *Wilkes* conducted oceanographic missions, collecting, processing, and evaluating hydrographic, acoustic, and meteorological data. Inactivated on 20 April 1975 and placed in "ready reserve status," *Wilkes* was returned to active service on 31 March 1976. Assigned to MSC Atlantic, she remained active into 1979.

Wilkes-Barre

A city in Pennsylvania.

Wilkes-Barre (CL-90)—a *Cleveland*-class light cruiser—was laid down on 6 September 1941 at Philadelphia, Pa., by the William Cramp Shipbuilding Co., but was renamed *Astoria* (q.v.) on 16 October 1942.

I

(CL–103: dp. 10,000; l. 610'1''; b. 66'6''; dr. 20'0'' (mean); s. 33 k.; cpl. 992; a. 12 6'', 12 5'', 20 40mm., 10 20mm.; cl. *Cleveland*)

Wilkes-Barre (CL–103) was laid down on 14 December 1942 at Camden, N.J., by the New York Shipbuilding Corp.; launched on 24 December 1943; sponsored by Mrs. Grace Shoemaker Miner, the wife of a prominent Wilkes-Barre doctor; and commissioned at the Philadelphia Navy Yard on 1 July 1944, Capt. Robert L. Porter, Jr., in command.

After fitting-out, *Wilkes-Barre* conducted her shakedown cruise in Chesapeake Bay and in the Gulf of Paria, Trinidad, British West Indies, before she returned to Philadelphia for post-shakedown availability. Getting underway on 23 October, the new light cruiser conducted training over ensuing days as she headed for the Panama Canal and the Pacific. Soon after transiting the isthmian waterway on 27 October, *Wilkes-Barre* arrived at San Diego, Calif., where she loaded provisions and ammunition. Then, following gunnery exercises off San Clemente Island, Calif., the warship headed for Hawaii on 10 November.

Wilkes-Barre reached Pearl Harbor on the 17th and conducted exercises in the Hawaiian operating area between 19 and 24 November and between 2 and 3 December, before she left Oahu in her wake on 14 December, bound for the Carolines. Upon her arrival at Ulithi, *Wilkes-Barre* joined Cruiser Division (CruDiv) 17 and sortied on 30 December as part of a support unit for Vice Admiral John S. McCain's Task Force (TF) 38.

Planes from TF 38 hit targets on Formosa and in the southern Ryukyus and, later, on Japanese targets on Luzon, in support of the landings on that Philippine island. TF 38 delivered a second strike upon Japanese positions on Formosa on 9 January 1945, before it passed through the Bashi Channel on the night of 9 and 10 January 1945 and headed into the South China Sea to counter the threat of enemy surface units opposing the Lingayen Gulf landings. On 12 January—the day that Navy aircraft sank 127,000 tons of merchant and naval shipping in the Indochina area—*Wilkes-Barre* and her sisters in CruDiv 17 were detached from Task Group (TG) 38.2 and became TG 34.5 which was set up to deal with enemy warships reported off Cam-ranh Bay, French Indochina. However, search planes from the cruisers found no trace of the supposed enemy force; and *Wilkes-Barre*, with the rest of CruDiv 17, rejoined TF 38.

On 13 and 14 January, soon after the abortive Cam-ranh Bay sweep, *Wilkes-Barre* and her consorts ran into rough weather—a tropical disturbance which caused stormy weather with intermittent squalls, heavy seas, and strong winds from the northeast. *Wilkes-Barre* rolled as much as 38 degrees to a side as she proceeded on a northeasterly course into the teeth of the gale.

However, the weather soon cleared enough to permit air strikes against Japanese shipping and targets on the coasts of China and French Indochina. Through holes in the thick overcast, American carrier planes bombed Japanese shipping at Takao, Amoy, and Swatow on 15 January and at Hainan Island, Indochina, and Hong Kong on the 16th. Fueling operations for the task group—hampered by the generally bad weather that had prevailed during the period—was finally completed on the 19th, shortly before the ships transited the Balintang Channel.

Strikes against Formosa continued on 21 January, but the enemy drew blood in return, damaging *Langley* (CVL–27) and *Ticonderoga* (CV–14). The next day, almost as if in revenge, Navy planes pounded Japanese targets-of-opportunity on the island of Okinawa, in the final act of the 27-day drama.

On 26 January, TF 38 arrived at Ulithi for replenishment and repairs. At Ulithi, TF 38 became TF 58 when command of the Fast Carrier Task Force passed to Vice Admiral Marc A. Mitscher.

Within two weeks, *Wilkes-Barre* was at sea again, still with CruDiv 17 but attached to TG 58.3, Rear Admiral Frederick C. Sherman, whose flag as commander of the group flew in *Essex* (CV–9). The light cruiser and her consorts appeared off the coast of Honshu, Japan, on 16 February and screened the carriers as their planes bombed Tokyo, the capital of the Japanese empire. The raid served as a diversion for what was taking place to the southward—the invasion of Iwo Jima. Admiral Sherman's planes pounded Japanese airfields and industrial sites near Tokyo in raids that marked the first bombings of their kind since Lt. Col. Doolittle had brought his "Tokyo Raiders" in from *Hornet* (CV–8)—alias "our new secret base at Shangri-La"—in April 1942.

After two days of strikes against the Japanese capital, the task group headed toward Iwo Jima and conducted strikes on Japanese positions on Chichi Jima and Haha Jima en route. On 19 February 1945, marines left their transports and headed toward the black beaches of Iwo Jima.

It soon became evident that the going would be tough against General Tadamichi Kuribayashi's garrison of defenders on Iwo Jima. On 21 February, *Wilkes-Barre* was called in to assist in the shore bombardment. The light cruiser, her fire directed by spotters aloft in her Kingfishers, proceeded to demolish enemy gun positions, pillboxes, fortified caves, and ammunition dumps. On one occasion, her prompt and effective call-fire turned back a Japanese counterattack.

Wilkes-Barre rejoined TG 58.3 on 23 February and screened the group's carriers as their planes hit targets in and near Tokyo on 25 February and on Okinawa on 1 March. Four days after the latter strikes, TG 58.3 put into Ulithi to replenish and refuel.

The light cruiser remained at anchor in Ulithi Lagoon from 5 to 14 March, before she participated in exercises with TF 59 on the 14th and 15th. The latter day, she was reassigned to TG 58.3 and soon thereafter headed for Japan.

Steaming east of Okinawa on the 18th, the carriers hurled their squadrons against Japanese airfields on Kyushu; and—with bombs and rockets, and strafing with machine guns—the American carrier planes continued their attacks on the following day as well. The raids drew retaliatory strikes—met by the combat air patrol (CAP) and gunfire from the screen. On the 19th, *Wilkes-Barre* bagged her first aircraft—a "Judy" dive-bomber.

The Japanese managed to draw blood from the American force, however, as two well-dropped bombs turned the carrier *Franklin* (CV–13) into a floating inferno on the 19th. While the task group subsequently retired toward a fueling rendezvous—moving slowly to protect the "cripples"—Japanese aircraft continued the harassment.

The air strikes continued in ensuing days. Planes from TG 58.3 hit Japanese targets in the Okinawa area on 23 and 24 March. On the latter day, *Wilkes-Barre*'s Kingfisher rescued two downed pilots from the light carrier *Bataan* (CVL–29) off Minami Daito Shima. Three days later, *Wilkes-Barre* returned to waters near Minami Daito and, in company with a destroyer group and the rest of CruDiv 17, shelled the airfield there.

On the 29th, after a high-speed, night approach toward Kyushu, the carriers—screened by *Wilkes-Barre* and her sisterships and destroyers—launched dawn searches and strikes against points along the coasts of Kyushu and the Inland Sea. Again, one of *Wilkes-Barre*'s planes performed a rescue mission, rescuing two fliers from *Bunker Hill* (CV–17) from the waters off Yaku Shima.

On Easter Sunday, 1 April 1945, American troops commenced the invasion of Okinawa. Their accomplishment was one of the most difficult Allied undertakings in the war and the conflict's biggest American amphibious assault. As men and materiel began establishing a beachhead, TF 58, *Wilkes-Barre* included, began its supporting operations.

Beginning on D day, 1 April, the fast carriers flew an extended series of support missions at Okinawa and made neutralizing raids against airfields in Kyushu, Shikoku, and southern Honshu. A key base for Japanese planes turned out to be Sakashima Gunto in the Nansei Shoto group, and that site came under heavy air attacks. Nevertheless, the suiciders, taking off from bases in the Japanese home islands, proved persistent.

Japanese planes attacked TG 58.3 on 11 April; and, from noon until dark, *Wilkes-Barre*'s guns—and those of the other screening ships—put up lethal barrages of antiaircraft fire at the oncoming enemy. She knocked down three Mitsubishi "Zeke" fighters and a "Val" dive-bomber and also scored assists with two more "Zekes."

When TF 58 subsequently headed north to launch strikes against the airfields on southern Kyushu, *Wilkes-Barre* went along. Those bases, thought to be the source of the Japanese air raids upon the joint expeditionary forces on Okinawa, were under attack throughout the 16th. Meanwhile, "flash red" alerts came one after another as the enemy planes—stirred like a nest of angry bees—attempted to penetrate the umbrella of the combat air patrol (CAP). Together with the fighters, *Wilkes-Barre* and the other ships in the screen swung into action. The cruiser herself bagged a bomber at 1854 on 16 April and a "Zeke" at 0939 on the 17th.

Wilkes-Barre's Kingfisher pilots again showed their skill at rescuing downed pilots, picking up two Navy fliers some 30 miles east of Okinawa on 26 April. Over the first 10 days of May 1945, the fast carriers—operating some 60 miles east of Okinawa—continued to launch strikes against that island. On 10 May, CruDiv 17, with escorting "tin cans," was temporarily detached from TG 58.3 for another night shelling of Minami Daito Shima.

"Snoopers," winging near the task group early the following day, sized up the disposition; and thus gave a hint of what was to come: a lightning-like foray. Two kamikazes plunged through the flak-torn skies and crashed into the fleet carrier *Bunker Hill*, enveloping the flattop's after deck in flame. At 1059, *Wilkes-Barre* received orders to stand by the critically injured carrier.

Capt. Robert L. Porter brought his light cruiser alongside *Bunker Hill* at 1115, placing *Wilkes-Barre's* bow hard against the flattop's starboard quarter. The cruiser played 10 streams of water on the persistent fires, while 40 men, trapped astern in *Bunker Hill* scrambled to safety. Destroyers *Stembel* (DD–644), *Charles S. Sperry* (DD–697), and *English* (DD–696) also added their fire hoses to the joint effort to save the stricken carrier.

Wilkes-Barre transferred fire-fighting gear—rescue breathing apparatus and handy-billies—to *Bunker Hill* in exchange for the carrier's injured and dying. At 1534—when the flames finally were well under control and her assistance was no longer needed—*Wilkes-Barre* finally cleared the blackened flattop.

Bunker Hill's captain later praised the ships which had labored bravely and tirelessly to save the carrier. "The *Wilkes-Barre*, the *Sperry*, and *Stembel* and *English* did a magnificent job. They came alongside not knowing whether we were likely to have explosions aboard. The *Wilkes-Barre* evacuated our seriously wounded, and with their able assistance, we got through."

On the 12th, *Wilkes-Barre* held burial services on board for the 13 men from the carrier who had succumbed to their wounds and transferred their surviving shipmates to the hospital ship *Bountiful* (AH–9). That day, TF 58 travelled to Kyushu to launch strikes on the 13th against the network of airfields there. The Japanese air arm responded on the 14th. Commencing at midnight, other task groups came under coordinated assaults; but Japanese planes did not molest *Wilkes-Barre's* group until dawn. Falling shell fragments, possibly from "friendly" guns, hit the ship during that raid, wounding nine men on the after signal bridge. At 0816, the cruiser claimed an assist in splashing a "Zero."

On 28 May, fleet and task force designations were changed to reflect the switch in command when Vice Admiral John S. McCain relieved Vice Admiral Mitscher. *Wilkes-Barre*, her tour off Okinawa and the Japanese home islands completed, left TG 38.3 on 29 May and headed for the Philippines.

Wilkes-Barre remained in the snug anchorage at San Pedro Bay from 1 to 20 June, receiving repairs, upkeep, and replenishment. She then conducted gunnery and tactical exercises off Samar from 20 to 23 June and then returned to anchorage for the remainder of the month.

For the coup de grace administered against Japan's homeland, TF 38 sortied from Leyte Gulf on 1 July. As part of TG 38.3, *Wilkes-Barre* steamed along with her sisters of CruDiv 17. For the first week of July, the ships engaged in intensive aircraft patrol and firing practice.

Carrier planes struck Hokkaido and Honshu on 10 July. Four days later, *Wilkes-Barre* and other ships parted company with the task group and conducted antishipping sweeps off northern Honshu and across Kii Suido.

On the 17th, American planes seared the Tokyo plains with incendiaries and rockets. On the night of 24 and 25 July, *Wilkes-Barre* and other bombardment ships departed the task group and, at 1210, opened fire with their main batteries on the Kushimoto seaplane base and on the Shionomisaki landing field on the south coast of Honshu.

Navy planes struck Kure and Kobe from 24 to 27 July in strikes aimed at ferreting out merchant shipping hidden in the Inland Sea. On the 30th, American planes gutted the manufacturing centers of Tokyo and Nagoya; but, horrible as they were, these raids were only a prelude to the awesome air strikes to come, the dropping of the atomic bombs on Hiroshima and Nagasaki.

Typhoons kept American planes out of the skies for most of the first week of August; but, on 7 August, the ships turned north for further strikes on the Honshu-Hokkaido area. Foul weather prevented attacks on the 8th, but the following two days presented favorable conditions for air strikes which continued apace. During that time, the two atomic bombs, Russia's entry into the Far Eastern war, and then nearly incessant pressure kept on the Japanese by ships and planes of the armada massed off her shores, all combined to force Japan to a decision to surrender. On the 15th, the orders finally came through to cease offensive operations —the war was over.

CruDiv 17 was detached from TG 38.3 on 23 August and, on the 27th, after 59 days at sea, formed part of the 3d Fleet that made its way triumphantly into Sagami Wan, the entrance to Tokyo Bay. *Wilkes-Barre* was among that procession, and her 6-inch guns covered the occupation of the Yokosuka Naval Base. On 3 September, the day after the official surrender of Japan, *Wilkes-Barre* moved into Tokyo Bay proper, over 103,000 miles after her commissioning.

As flagship for demilitarization group, Task Unit (TU) 35.7.2, *Wilkes-Barre* churned out of Tokyo Bay on 9 September and proceeded to Tateyama Wan, anchoring late that afternoon. On the 10th, she covered the seizure of the former midget submarine and suicide boat base there, before she returned to Tokyo Bay.

Subsequent operations in connection with the occupation of the erstwhile enemy's homeland kept *Wilkes-Barre* busy. She anchored off Koajiro Ko, Sagami Wan, between 12 and 14 September to demilitarize the Aburatsubo and Kurihama midget submarine bases on the Sagami peninsula. She next anchored in Tokyo Bay to refuel and take on provisions on the 14th before shifting to Onagawa Wan between the 15th and 17th. She then conducted another demilitarization mission, her guns covering the occupation at Katsuura Wan before turning to Tokyo on 24 September.

From 24 September to 4 October, *Wilkes-Barre* anchored within sight of Mount Fujiyama, Japan's sacred mountain, and held gunnery and tactical exercises between 24 and 28 October. Detached from the 5th Fleet on 5 November, *Wilkes-Barre* set out on the 9th for Korea and reached Jinsen (now Inchon) on the 13th.

On the 16th, *Wilkes-Barre*—in company with destroyers *Hart* (DD–594) and *Bell* (DD–587)—shifted to Tsingtao, China. Further occupation duties kept her at that port until the 19th; but, over the ensuing weeks, she steamed twice to Taku and Chinwangtao, China, before returning to Tsingtao where she spent the remainder of the year 1945.

Finally sailing for the United States on 13 January 1946, *Wilkes-Barre* proceeded, via Pearl Harbor, and reached San Pedro, Calif., on the last day of January. *Wilkes-Barre* got underway on 4 March, bound for the east coast of the United States. Transiting the Panama Canal between 12 and 14 March, the light cruiser put into Philadelphia on the 18th and remained there through the spring and summer of 1946. She got underway for the Gulf of Mexico on 20 October and reached New Orleans in time to celebrate Navy Day on 27 October.

From New Orleans, *Wilkes-Barre* sailed for Guantanamo Bay, Cuba, and a period of refresher training in company with sisterships *Dayton* (CL–105) and *Providence* (CL–82). After returning to Norfolk, Va., on 13 December, *Wilkes-Barre* made a goodwill cruise to England and Norway; underway on 17 February 1947, she reached Plymouth, England, on the 27th. She then operated in the waters of the British Isles throughout March and April and made one trip to Bergen, Norway, before returning to the United States

317

for eventual assignment to the United States Reserve Fleet.

Decommissioned on 9 October 1947, *Wilkes-Barre* was simultaneously placed in reserve at Philadelphia. She remained in "mothballs" at Philadelphia until struck from the Navy list on 15 January 1971—the last light cruiser on the Navy list. Thereafter, the ship was subjected to underwater explosive tests. On 12 May 1972, her battered hulk broke in two. The after section sank of its own accord on that day; the forward section sank on the 13th, as a result of a scuttling charge. Presently off the Florida Keys, the ship continues to serve society, however, as an artificial reef.

Wilkes-Barre received four battle stars for her World War II service.

Wilkinson

Theodore Stark Wilkinson—born on 22 December 1888 at Annapolis, Md.—entered the Naval Academy in 1905 and graduated first in the class of 1909. He served the two years of sea duty, then required by law prior to commissioning, in the battleships *Kansas* and *South Carolina*, before he received his ensign's commission on 5 June 1911. After instruction at George Washington University, Washington, D.C., under the auspices of the Bureau of Ordnance, Wilkinson reported to the battleship *Florida* on 25 July 1913 for sea duty. During his time in that dreadnought, Ens. Wilkinson led *Florida*'s 2d Company in action during the landings on 21 and 22 April 1914 at Veracruz. For his skillful and courageous leadership of that unit of the battleship's landing force and his exhibition of "eminent and conspicuous" conduct, he received the Medal of Honor.

On 4 August, he was transferred to *Tennessee* and two days later sailed eastward in her across the Atlantic. That armored cruiser and *North Carolina* were ordered to European waters to evacuate Americans trapped on the continent by the outbreak of World War I. On 3 September, he became an assistant to the naval attache at Paris and a month later left that post to join *North Carolina* in the Mediterranean. Subsequently, the young officer had tours of sea duty: first as aide, to Commander, 2d Division, Atlantic Fleet, and then as aide to the commander of the 7th Division.

From July 1916 to July 1919, Wilkinson served with distinction as the head of the Experimental Section, Bureau of Ordnance (BuOrd), where he developed ordnance materials and devices, most notable being a noxious gas filler for shells and an "exceptionally satisfactory smoke screen." Additionally, he was deemed largely responsible for the successful design of a depth charge and for the development of the firing mechanism of the Mark VI mine used in the North Sea Mine Barrage.

Following that tour ashore—for which he received a letter of commendation—Wilkinson went to sea, first serving as gunnery officer in the battleship *Kansas* and later as fire control officer in the battleship *Pennsylvania*. In 1921 and 1922, Wilkinson commanded, in succession, the destroyers *Osborne* (DD–295), *Goff* (DD–247), and *Taylor* (DD–94), before he returned to BuOrd's experimental section.

After commanding *King* (DD–242) from January 1925 to December 1926, Wilkinson headed the Records Section of the Bureau of Navigation (BuNav) Officer Personnel Division. In June 1930, he became fleet gunnery officer and aide to Commander, Scouting Fleet (later, Commander, Scouting Force), Rear Admiral A. L. Willard. Detached from that duty in December 1931, he soon assumed the duties of secretary to the Navy's General Board. While in that assignment, Wilkinson had additional duty during the arms limitation talks at Geneva in 1933 and in London in 1934.

From September 1934 to June 1936, Wilkinson served as executive officer of *Indianapolis* (CA–35). Over the next three years, he headed the Planning Division of BuNav and then returned to *Indianapolis*, this time in a staff capacity, as Chief of Staff to Commander, Scouting Force. In January 1941, he fleeted up to command the battleship *Mississippi* (BB–41).

Detached from that duty in September 1941 and promoted to flag rank, Wilkinson—as a rear admiral—became the director of the Office of Naval Intelligence (ONI), in October, a post in which he worked for the next 10 months. Subsequently reporting for duty as Commander, Battleship Division 2, Pacific Fleet, in August 1942, Wilkinson eventually became Deputy Commander, South Pacific Area and South Pacific Force on 30 January 1943 and acted in that capacity until July 1944, when he assumed command of the 3d Amphibious Force, South Pacific.

In that billet, Wilkinson earned the Distinguished Service Medal (DSM), for commanding the forces that supported the New Georgia campaign; took Vella Lavella and the Treasury Islands; and established a "highly important" position on the west coast of Bougainville. Subsequently redesignated as Commander, 3d Amphibious Force, Pacific Fleet, with the rank of vice admiral, on 12 August 1944, Wilkinson won a gold star in lieu of a second DSM for his leadership in the assaults that took Peleliu and Angaur, in the Palaus; and Ulithi, in the Carolines.

Subsequently, Wilkinson earned another gold star in lieu of a third DSM, for commanding Task Force 79 in action in the Philippines between 1 October 1944 and 18 January 1945—operations that included the landings conducted by the Southern Attack Force at Leyte in October 1944 and at Lingayen in January 1945.

Ordered to the Navy Department in September 1945 for temporary duty, Vice Admiral Wilkinson became a member of the Joint Strategic Survey Committee of the Joint Chiefs of Staff in January 1946. He was serving in that capacity when he lost his life on 21 February 1946 in an automobile accident at Norfolk, Va.

(DL–5: dp. 4,730; l. 493'0''; b. 50'0''; dr. 14'0''; s. 30 k.; cpl. 403; a. 2 5'', 4 3'', 8 20mm., 2 rkt. (Weapon "Alfa"), 1 dct.; cl. *Mitscher*)

Wilkinson (DD–930) was laid down on 1 February 1950 at Quincy, Mass., by the Bethlehem Steel Co. Shipbuilding Division; reclassified a destroyer leader, DL–5, on 9 February 1951; launched on 23 April 1952; sponsored by Lady Catherine Moore, the former Mrs. Theodore S. Wilkinson; and commissioned on 3 August 1954, Comdr. Donald G. Dockum in command.

After shakedown training out of Guantanamo Bay, Cuba, and the usual post-shakedown availability, *Wilkinson* departed her home port, Newport, R.I., on 21 February 1955—with Rear Admiral Arleigh Burke, Commander, Destroyer Force, Atlantic Fleet (and soon to become the Chief of Naval Operations) and members of his staff embarked—and carried Admiral Burke on an inspection tour that included visits to San Juan, Puerto Rico; St. Thomas, Virgin Islands; Guantanamo Bay and Havana, Cuba; and Key West, Fla. Upon her return, the destroyer leader became flagship for Commander, Destroyer Flotilla (DesFlot) 2, part of the Atlantic Fleet's antisubmarine forces. For three months thereafter, the ship conducted antisubmarine warfare (ASW) exercises.

On 11 July, *Wilkinson*—with 70 1st and 3d class NROTC midshipmen embarked—departed the east coast for a training cruise. During the ensuing voyage, the warship touched at Edinburgh, Scotland; Copenhagen, Denmark; and Guantanamo Bay, before returning to the United States on 2 September.

Wilkinson departed her home port on 24 October 1955 for air defense exercises in the Gulf of Mexico, with Commander, DesFlot 6 embarked. During that cruise, *Wilkinson* visited New Orleans and Havana, before she arrived back at Newport on 18 November. On 2 December, the ship entered the Boston Naval Shipyard for a five-month overhaul and the installation of improved 3-inch antiaircraft guns.

The frigate *Wilkinson* (DL–5). *Wilkinson* and her sisters were an outgrowth of large-destroyer design studies begun during World War II.

After successfully completing her sea trials for her newly installed 3-inch, 70-caliber battery, *Wilkinson* conducted underway training out of Guantanamo Bay. She later visited Port-au-Prince, Haiti; Charleston, S.C.; and Norfolk, Va.; before taking part in large-scale ASW maneuvers in June. The ship's performance during the fiscal year 1956 earned her the Battle Efficiency "E."

In July 1956, *Wilkinson* departed Newport, bound for San Diego, Calif., and duty with the Pacific Fleet. En route to her new home port, the frigate visited Havana; Balboa, Canal Zone; and Buena Ventura, Colombia; before she became flagship of Commander, Destroyer Squadron (DesRon) 17—the first ship of her type assigned to the Pacific Fleet.

Between August 1956 and March 1957, *Wilkinson* operated locally out of San Diego and took part in ASW, air defense, and amphibious exercises. One highlight of that period occurred on 14 September 1956, when *Wilkinson* headed a veritable "armada" of 70 fighting ships during a 1st Fleet review off Long Beach, in what some called the largest naval parade on the west coast in 22 years.

During March and April 1957, *Wilkinson* operated in the Bering Sea and the Aleutians, visiting Kodiak and Dutch Harbor, Alaska, en route to her operating area. While steaming back to San Diego, she touched at Esquimalt, British Columbia; Seattle, Wash.; and San Francisco. Later, during part of May, Rear Admiral Chester Wood, Commander, Cruiser-Destroyer Force, Pacific Fleet, embarked in *Wilkinson* for air defense and ASW exercises. In June, the warship visited Portland, Oreg., to take part in the annual Rose Festival activities.

Wilkinson's home port was changed from San Diego to Long Beach in July 1957, and the destroyer leader entered the naval shipyard there in February 1958 for extensive modifications to her power plant. Released

from the yard in September, the destroyer leader conducted underway training out of San Diego and operated locally for the remainder of 1958.

In January 1959, *Wilkinson* deployed on her first Western Pacific (WestPac) cruise, visiting Pearl Harbor, Hawaii; Subic Bay, Philippines; Buckner Bay, Okinawa; Kaohsiung, Taiwan; and the Japanese ports of Yokosuka and Kure, before she returned to Long Beach in March, embarking Commander, DesRon 19, upon arrival.

After again operating locally between April and October 1959, she participated in various exercises off the coast of California and in another 1st Fleet review. *Wilkinson* began her second WestPac deployment when she departed Long Beach in October. Coming under the operational control of Commander, 7th Fleet, *Wilkinson* took part in the Taiwan Strait patrol, ASW tactics, and various fast carrier task force operations in the Far East.

Returning to Long Beach in March 1960, *Wilkinson* entered the naval shipyard there for a five-month overhaul. During that period of repairs and alterations, the ship's combat intelligence center (CIC) was enlarged and modified; and a long-range air search radar was added. In addition, a DASH (Destroyer Anti-Submarine Helicopter—sometimes sardonically nicknamed the "Down At Sea Helicopter") system—was installed. This change increased *Wilkinson*'s ASW capacity severalfold.

Following *Wilkinson*'s departure from the shipyard in August 1960, she carried out six weeks of underway training out of San Diego. She operated locally during October and November and, after a month-long leave and upkeep period in December, was deployed to West-Pac for the third time, departing Long Beach on 3 January 1961.

En route to the Far East, *Wilkinson*—a unit of Destroyer Division 191—visited Pearl Harbor; Midway;

and Apra Harbor, Guam. In mid-March 1961, she headed for the South China Sea where an increased American naval presence was required by the Laotian crisis. After operating with a fast carrier task group almost continuously well into the spring, the destroyer leader departed WestPac on 12 May and reached Long Beach on the 27th.

She entered the Long Beach Naval Shipyard in June for the installation of improved sonar equipment, a task that continued into mid-1962. After refresher training, the warship operated in Puget Sound for technical evaluation of her new sonar system and then returned south, down the coast, to work with submarines in the southern California operating area.

Following further local operations, *Wilkinson* departed Long Beach on 17 June 1963 to return to the Atlantic Fleet. Calling at the Mexican ports of Acapulco and Salina Cruz en route, *Wilkinson* transited the Panama Canal on 29 June and arrived at Newport on 5 July.

Within two weeks, *Wilkinson* was underway for sonar evaluation that continued until 8 December. During the operation, the ship visited Bermuda and New York City. The frigate subsequently made another operational evaluation of the sonar system from 1 July 1964 to 20 May 1965, at which time she reported to Commander, Cruiser-Destroyer Force, Atlantic Fleet. During that time, the ship operated in the Gulf of Mexico and the Caribbean and along the continental shelf between Newport and New York. During the cruise, the ship visited Key West, Fla., and conducted type training in the Jacksonville, Fla., operating area while steaming back to Newport.

After a pre-overhaul tender availability, *Wilkinson* visited New York City for four days; off-loaded ammunition subsequently at Earle, N.J.; and proceeded to Boston for an overhaul which lasted until 5 February 1966.

After returning via Earle to Newport a little over a month later, *Wilkinson* sailed south to Cuban waters for refresher training—conducting those evolutions between 11 March and 28 April. While still at Guantanamo, on 8 April, the ship received orders at 0310 to assist a burning freighter. Underway at 0407, *Wilkinson* sped at flank speed to the scene of the disaster and, at 0720, reached the stricken Norwegian passenger-freighter *Viking Princess*. A fire and rescue party from USCGC *Cook Inlet* (W–384) had meanwhile boarded the blazing merchantman to fight her fires. At 0809, *Wilkinson* began closing the Nationalist Chinese merchantman *Chungking Victory* to receive the surviving crew members of *Viking Princess*—a process completed by 0914. The frigate took the 13 survivors back to Guantanamo where she arrived shortly before noon and disembarked the rescued mariners.

After departing Guantanamo Bay on 28 April, *Wilkinson* touched at San Juan, Puerto Rico, and reached Newport on 2 May. She remained in port until departing on the last day of the month, bound for Boston and an availability. During the ensuing overhaul, the ship received a number of repairs and alterations, including the final installation of new sonar equipment then being evaluated by the Navy. Briefly departing Boston on 15 August and again on 30 August, the frigate conducted sea trials and tested her sonar—during cruises lasting but a day or two—before she completed her availability and sailed for Newport on 31 August, reaching her home port the following day.

For the remainder of 1966, *Wilkinson* remained in port at Newport except for three periods of independent steaming exercises (ISE's)—from 6 to 9 September, from 23 to 26 September, and from 2 to 5 December. Underway on 15 January 1967, *Wilkinson* headed south to Argentine waters, subsequently taking part in the Argentinian naval review at Mar del Plata from 4 to 8 February on the occasion of the celebrations commemorating the sesquicentennial of Argentina's independence.

Returning to Newport on 5 March, *Wilkinson* then proceeded to the Bethlehem Steel Shipyard at East Boston, Mass., where she received a data acquisition system for her sonar equipment. She returned—via Stamford, Conn., where she participated in Veteran's Day memorial services—to Newport on 4 May.

Later that month, *Wilkinson* sailed for Montreal, Canada, where she served as part of the United States exhibit during "United States Week," from 21 to 28 May, at the world's fair, Expo 67. Highlighting *Wilkinson*'s stay at Montreal was a surprise visit to the exposition by President Lyndon B. Johnson. During the ceremonies at the United States exhibit, *Wilkinson* men served as Presidential Honor Guard.

Returning to Newport on 1 June, *Wilkinson* continued further sonar evaluations into the summer and fall months of 1967, operating primarily out of Newport but also east of the Bahamas. Between her periods at sea were times in port for tender availabilities and type training in the Narragansett Bay operating area.

The ship put into Port Everglades to take on fuel on 3 October and was standing back out on the 5th when a weak cleat snapped while the motor whaleboat was being secured for sea. The whiplash of the line struck a sailor, injuring both of his legs and requiring immediate medical attention beyond that which the ship could provide. *Wilkinson* immediately headed back to Port Everglades at flank speed, radioing ahead for a boat to pick up the injured seaman. A torpedo retriever boat, sent out by the Naval Ordnance Laboratory and Test Facility, took the man on board to a waiting ambulance at pierside. The seaman was then taken to Homestead Air Force Base hospital where he was treated for fractures of both legs.

After the incident, *Wilkinson* returned to sea and conducted further sonar tests—in company with *Grouper* (AGSS–214)—before the frigate visited Freeport, Grand Bahama, from 11 to 13 October. Proceeding back to Newport soon thereafter, *Wilkinson* reached her home port on the 25th but soon headed south for repairs at the Norfolk Naval Shipyard. She returned to her home port on 21 December.

Beginning 1968 in-port at Newport, *Wilkinson* spent much of the rest of the year conducting further technical evaluation of sonar equipment in the Bahamas, interspersed with type training in the Mayport operating area and in-port periods at Newport. After a pre-overhaul period of availability alongside *Yosemite* (AD–19), *Wilkinson* entered the Boston Naval Shipyard on 13 September for her regular overhaul that rounded out the year and lasted into June 1969.

Following her sea trials, *Wilkinson* got underway for Narragansett Bay for sonar tests, before she set course for Earle, N.J., to load ammunition in preparation for refresher training. Late in July, the frigate visited New York City from 25 to 28 July before she shifted to Newport on the latter date. She remained in her home port for almost a month, conducting a dependents' cruise in Narragansett Bay operating areas on the 22d. It was during that cruise that the ship's commanding officer announced that *Wilkinson* was to be decommissioned as part of a cut back in military expenses.

With the cancellation of all her previous schedules, *Wilkinson* shifted to the South Annex of the Boston Naval Shipyard to commence inactivation on 3 September. Shifting to the Naval Inactive Ship Facility at Philadelphia on the 22d, *Wilkinson* was decommissioned on 19 December 1969 and placed in reserve.

Struck from the Navy list on 1 May 1974, *Wilkinson* was sold to Luria Brothers. She departed Philadelphia under tow on 19 June 1975 to be scrapped.

Will Rogers

Will Rogers—born on 4 November 1879 near the present town of Claremore, Okla.—received sporadic formal education between 1887 and 1898, when he left home to become a cowboy on the Ewing Ranch in Lipscomb County, Tex., near the town of Higgins. After managing his father's ranch from 1899 to 1902, he sailed for South America, where he spent five months with the gauchos of the Argentine pampas. Later in 1902, the still-restless Rogers sailed for South Africa, where he took a job breaking in horses for the British Army. While in South Africa, he began his show business career, where he joined "Texas Jack's Wild West Show," to be billed as "The Cherokee Kid."

Joining the Wirth Brothers' circus in 1903, he toured Australia and New Zealand before returning to the United States the following year to appear at the St. Louis Exposition and receive his first vaudeville bookings in Chicago. He made his first appearance in New York in 1905 and, over the next 10 years, made three trips to Europe and traveled extensively in Canada and his native United States. During this time, he also made the first airplane flight in Atlantic City, N.J., as a passenger.

From 1916 to 1925, Rogers appeared occasionally with the famed Ziegfield Follies; he made his first motion picture in 1918—"Laughing Bill Hyde"—and moved to California in 1919 to work in the Goldwyn studios. The year 1922 proved a landmark one for the cowboy-humorist, as he began a weekly syndicated column which eventually reached a large readership through some 350 newspapers. He maintained this regularly featured column until his death in 1935.

From 1925 to 1928, Rogers traveled the length and breadth of the United States in a "lecture tour." During this time he became the first civilian to fly from coast to coast with pilots flying the mail in early air mail flights. The National Press Club, Washington, D.C., dubbed him "Ambassador at Large of the United States"; and, in 1927, he visited Mexico City with the transatlantic aviation pioneer Charles A. Lindbergh as a guest of Ambassador Dwight Morrow. In subsequent years, Rogers gave numerous after-dinner speeches; became a popular convention speaker; gave benefits for victims of floods, droughts, or earthquakes. After the Great Depression hit the United States, Rogers gave radio talks on "unemployment," with ex-President Coolidge, President Hoover, and former Presidential candidate Al Smith.

He made a trip to the Orient in 1931 and to Central and South America the following year. In 1934 he made a globe-girdling tour and returned to play the lead in Eugene O'Neill's stage play, "Ah Wilderness." Also during the period 1930 to 1935, he made movies for Fox studios and radio broadcasts for the Gulf Oil Company.

Through Rogers' continuing series of columns between 1922 and 1935, as well as in his personal appearances and radio broadcasts, he won the loving admiration of the American people, poking jibes in witty ways at the issues of the day and prominent people—often politicians. He wrote from a non-partisan point of view and became a friend of presidents and a confidant of the great. Loved for his cool mind and warm heart, he was often considered the successor to such greats as Mark Twain (Samuel Clemens) and Artemus Ward.

An avid booster of aviation, Rogers undertook a polar flight with a fellow Oklahoman, Wiley Post, in the summer of 1935. It ended in tragedy. Post's plane crashed at Point Barrow, Alaska, on 15 August 1935, killing Post and his passenger—Will Rogers.

(SSBN–659: dp. 7,320 (surf.), 8,220 (subm.); l. 425'; b. 33'; dr. 31'4''; s. 6 k. (surf.), 20+ k. (subm.); cpl. 140; a. 16 Polaris, 4 21'' tt.; cl. *Benjamin Franklin*)

Will Rogers (SSBN–659)—the 41st and last Polaris submarine—was laid down on 20 March 1965 at Groton, Conn., by the General Dynamics Corporation's Electric Boat Div.; launched on 21 July 1966; sponsored by Mrs. Hubert H. Humphrey, the wife of the Vice President of the United States; and commissioned on 1 April 1967, Capt. R. Y. Kaufman and Comdr. W. J. Cowhill in command of the Blue and Gold crews, respectively.

Following shakedown, *Will Rogers* culminated her initial training and work-up by conducting a successful Polaris missile shot in the Atlantic missile range off Cape Kennedy, Fla., on 31 July 1967. In October of that year, she made her first deterrent deployment.

Will Rogers was based out of Groton, Conn., until 1974 when she shifted to a forward deployment at Rota, Spain. She conducted additional deterrent deployments from Rota over the next four years, into 1978, bringing the total number of patrols made to 35.

Willamette

A river that flows north from its source near Eugene, Oreg., and empties into the Columbia River near Portland.

The contract for the construction of *Willamette*—a projected screw sloop-of-war of the *Contoocook* class—was cancelled in 1866 before her keel was laid.

Willapa

A bay off southwestern Washington state, adjacent to Pacific County.

Willapa (ACV–53)—a "Ruler"-class auxiliary aircraft carrier built for the United Kingdom—was laid down on 21 May 1943 at Seattle, Wash., by the Seattle-Tacoma Shipbuilding Co. and reclassified CVE–53 on 10 June 1943. Launched on 8 November 1943, the ship was transferred under lend-lease to the Royal Navy on 5 February 1944 to be manned by a Canadian crew. Renamed HMCS *Puncher* (D.79), the carrier served the Royal Canadian Navy in the Atlantic and Mediterranean for the duration of hostilities, mainly in a training role.

Decommissioned on 16 February 1946 at Norfolk, Va., and returned to American custody on that day, the escort carrier was struck from the Navy list on 12 March 1946, having never seen active service with the United States Navy.

Initially sold to William B. St. John, of New York City, on 9 January 1947, the carrier was subsequently resold to a British firm on 4 February 1947 and converted for mercantile service. She later served successively as *Muncaster Castle*, *Bardic*, and *Bennevis*, into the 1970's.

Willapa Bay

A bay off the coast of Washington state.

Willapa Bay (CVE–109)—a *Commencement Bay*-class escort carrier—was laid down on 10 January 1944 at Tacoma, Wash., by the Todd-Pacific Shipyards, Inc. However, prior to her launching, the carrier was renamed *Cape Gloucester* (q.v.) on 26 April 1944.

Willard Keith

Willard Woodward Keith, Jr.—born on 13 June 1920 in Berkeley, Calif.—enlisted in the Marine Corps Reserve on 18 April 1939 and served as an enlisted man until he received an honorable discharge on 3 November 1940 to take an appointment as 2d lieutenant in the reserves on the following day. Called to active duty on 20 February 1941, he served "stateside" until his unit was transferred to the South Pacific in the spring of 1942 to build up for the first Allied offensive in that theater—Guadalcanal.

Eventually promoted to captain, Keith led Company "G," 2d Battalion, 5th Marines, from the initial phase of the Guadalcanal campaign. He landed with them at Tulagi on 7 August 1942.

By that autumn, the campaign on Guadalcanal Island was still a hard-fought one. In an offensive aimed against Japanese artillery positions sited beyond the Matanikau River and within range of the important Henderson Field airstrip, the 2d Battalion was assigned the left flank position. Initial elements of the battalion crossed the Matanikau in rubber boats before dawn on 3 November 1942, supported effectively by dive bomber strikes, artillery, and naval gunfire. That afternoon, Capt. Keith led his company against a Japanese strongpoint manned by a platoon not only reinforced with heavy machine guns but concealed by heavy jungle growth and entrenched on commanding high ground. Realizing that neither mortar nor artillery fire could reach the Japanese positions, Keith—determined to evict the Japanese—initiated and led successive bayonet and hand grenade charges in the face of heavy fire. Although the Japanese platoon was annihilated, Capt. Keith was struck in the head by a bullet and killed instantly.

While the 1st Marine Division (Reinforced)—of which the 2d Battalion, 5th Marines was a part—received the Presidential Unit Citation, Capt. Willard W. Keith, Jr., was awarded a Navy Cross posthumously for a "grim determination and aggressive devotion to duty" in keeping with the "highest traditions of the naval service."

The contract for the construction of *Willard Keith* (DE–314)—an *Evarts*-class destroyer escort laid down on 22 January 1944 at Vallejo, Calif., by the Mare Island Navy Yard—was cancelled on 13 March 1944.

The contract for the construction of *Willard Keith* (DE–754)—a *Cannon*-class destroyer escort whose keel had been laid down on 14 September 1943 at San Pedro, Calif., by the Western Pipe and Steel Co.—was cancelled on 2 October 1943.

I

(DD–775: dp. 2,220; l. 376'6''; b. 41'2''; dr. 15'8'' (max.); s. 34 k.; cpl. 336; a. 6 5'', 12 40mm., 11 20mm., 2 dct., 6 dcp., 10 21'' tt.; cl. *Allen M. Sumner*)

Willard Keith (DD–775) was laid down on 5 March 1944 at San Pedro, Calif., by the Bethlehem Steel Co.; launched on 29 August 1944; sponsored by Mrs. Willard W. Keith, the mother of Capt. Keith; and commissioned two days after Christmas of 1944, Comdr. Lewis L. Snyder in command.

After shakedown training out of San Diego, Calif., *Willard Keith* operated temporarily out of the Precommissioning Training Center at San Francisco, Calif., as training ship for engineering personnel. During that time, she made weekly trips from San Francisco to San Clemente Island and back.

Completing that tour of training duty in mid-April 1945, *Willard Keith* sailed for the Western Pacific (WestPac) on 16 April, heading for Pearl Harbor in company with *Atlanta* (CL–104) and *Tillman* (DD–641). After onward routing to the forward area, *Willard Keith* arrived at Okinawa on 29 May. Assigned screening and radar picket duties for the remainder of the Okinawan campaign, *Willard Keith* destroyed two Japanese planes during her tour. Her closest brush with the enemy came on the final day of the campaign when a Japanese torpedo plane winged in low and unobserved and launched her "fish." Fortunately, the warhead proved a dud and only left a dent in *Willard Keith*'s hull.

After her baptism of fire, *Willard Keith* then joined a cruiser-destroyer task force on 24 June for antishipping sweeps into the East China Sea. Due to the losses inflicted upon the once-large Japanese merchant marine, however, the pickings were slim. *Willard Keith* spent the remainder of the war engaged in such largely fruitless operations and, with the coming of the Japanese surrender, drew screening duties with the initial occupying forces in the erstwhile enemy's home waters. That autumn, the destroyer visited the Japanese ports of Wakayama, Yokosuka, Nagoya, and Tokyo, on occasion performing courier service between ports, carrying men and mail.

Chosen as the flagship for Commodore John T. Bottom, Jr., Commander, Task Flotilla 1 and area commander, *Willard Keith* wore the commodore's burgee pennant while remaining at Nagoya from the last part of October until early December. On 5 December, Commodore Bottom's burgee came down, and *Willard Keith* put to sea to rendezvous with her sisterships in Destroyer Squadron (DesRon) 66. She then sailed east, reaching the west coast in time to spend Christmas at San Diego, Calif.

Subsequently, *Willard Keith* proceeded down the west coast; transited the Panama Canal; crossed the Gulf of Mexico and then proceeded around the tip of Florida, bound for New York City. After voyage repairs at the New York Navy Yard, Brooklyn, N.Y., the destroyer stood out of the yard on the last day of January and proceeded up the eastern seaboard to Newport, R.I. She engaged in gunnery exercises out of that port and, upon conclusion of that first phase of her peacetime training program, returned to New York. She made five more short round trips between New York and Newport until 12 July, when she set out for Guantanamo Bay, Cuba.

After operations in the British West Indies area, *Willard Keith* returned to Norfolk, Va., from whence she escorted the veteran battleships *Washington* (BB–56) and *North Carolina* (BB–55) to Culebra, Puerto Rico, for shore bombardment exercises. The destroyer then returned to Norfolk as part of the screen for the battlewagons, before she drew another escort assignment, this time with the aircraft carrier *Philippine Sea* (CV–47). Conducting exercises and maneuvers en route, the carrier and her consorts reached Guantanamo Bay for training before returning northward and putting into Newport.

Christmas and New Year's holidays came and went before the destroyer operated locally between Pensacola and Key West. During her time in those waters, she deviated from her routine once, when she sailed to Mobile, Ala., on 13 February 1947 to serve as one of the Navy's official representatives to the yearly Mardi Gras festivities. For the remainder of the spring months, *Willard Keith* cruised routinely between Newport and Key West, carrying out training duties off the eastern seaboard.

Arriving at Norfolk on 20 June 1947, *Willard Keith* was assigned to the Atlantic Reserve Fleet a short time later. "Mothballed" at Charleston (S.C.) Naval Shipyard, the destroyer remained inactive until the Fleet buildup brought about by the Korean War in 1950.

Recommissioned on 23 October 1950, *Willard Keith* was assigned to the Atlantic Fleet. After her activation was completed on 27 November, the ship departed Charleston, shaping course for Norfolk, Va. Subsequently pushing on to Guantanamo Bay—planeguarding for the Fleet carrier *Intrepid* (CV–11) en route—*Willard Keith* reached her destination on 13 January 1951 to commence her shakedown soon thereafter.

Completing that training phase on Washington's Birthday 1951, *Willard Keith* stopped briefly at Culebra for gunnery exercises before proceeding on to Norfolk and upkeep. After a three-month overhaul, the destroyer returned to the Guantanamo region for further refresher training. She then returned to Norfolk for a tender upkeep.

On 3 September 1951, *Willard Keith* departed the east coast, bound for the Mediterranean and duty with the 6th Fleet. Relieving *Dennis J. Buckley* (DD–808) as a unit of that force on the 22d of the month, *Willard Keith* spent the next six months in the "Med," making operational visits to such ports as Gibraltar; Naples and Trieste, Italy; Augusta Bay, Sicily; Istanbul, Turkey; Leros, Greece; and Suda Bay, Crete.

From November of 1951 to February of 1952, *Willard Keith* operated in company with *John W. Weeks* (DD–701) as a unit of the Northern European Force under the overall command of Real Admiral W. F. Boone. During that period of time, the destroyer visited Plymouth, England; Copenhagen and Bornholm, Denmark; Bremerhaven, Germany; Bordeaux, France; and Londonderry, Northern Ireland. While operating out of the last-named port, she conducted exercises jointly with British destroyers.

While in northern European waters, *Willard Keith* performed rescue and escort duties for a week, assisting the crippled SS *Flying Enterprise* before that ship broke apart and sank in heavy seas. That incident gained the United States Navy international attention at the time. The owners of the lost ship, the Isbrandtsen Lines, later presented a plaque to *Willard Keith* in appreciation for her assistance rendered to their vessel.

Completing her duty in European waters early in February 1952, *Willard Keith* shaped course for home, reaching Norfolk on 6 February for leave and upkeep. Once the needed voyage repairs had been accomplished and both officers and men refreshed after their deployment overseas, the destroyer headed north, departing Norfolk on 21 April 1952. She was bound for Argentia, Newfoundland, with a party of observers from the United States Naval Underwater Sound School embarked on board. From 21 April to 12 May, the destroyer then conducted antisubmarine warfare (ASW) drills for the benefit of the observers.

Upon the ship's return to Norfolk, all hands began to make preparations for a scheduled midshipmen's cruise. In early June, the ship sailed to Annapolis, Md., and embarked 72 officers-to-be, taking them to Norfolk. Subsequently, *Willard Keith* sailed to European waters and then to Guantanamo Bay. Ports visited during the midshipmen's cruise included Torquay, England, and Le Havre, France.

Returning to Norfolk via Guantanamo, *Willard Keith* disembarked her passengers and resumed her routine of training. She conducted two weeks of hunter/killer training in company with the escort carrier *Block Island* (CVE–106), a task group under the command of Rear Admiral D. V. Gallery.

Willard Keith put back into Norfolk at the end of November and spent the remainder of the year there. She departed her home port nine days into the new year, though, setting sail for Pensacola, Fla., assigned as plane guard for the light carrier *Monterey* (CVL–26). En route, however, an urgent message from Commandant, 6th Naval District, directed the ship to proceed to a rendezvous with an LST which had a Marine sergeant on board who was stricken with appendicitis. *Willard Keith* complied and transported the man to Charleston, S.C., where he received medical attention. The ship received a special commendation from the Commandant of the 6th Naval District for her fine work in helping to save the man.

Ultimately completing her assigned duties in company with *Monterey*, *Willard Keith* returned to Norfolk to prepare for a scheduled three and one-half month overhaul. After repairs and alterations at the Philadelphia Naval Shipyard from 11 February to 27 May, *Willard Keith* conducted refresher training out of Guantanamo Bay after first stopping at Norfolk en route. Returning to her home port on 4 August, the destroyer subsequently sailed for the Far East on 25 September in company with the other ships of Destroyer Division (DesDiv) 221.

The division reached Yokosuka, Japan, on 10 November 1953, via Bermuda, Gibraltar, Naples, Port Said, Aden, Colombo, and Manila. *Willard Keith* and her sisterships operated with Naval Forces, Far East, under the overall command of Rear Admiral Robert P. Briscoe. Operating with the hunter/killer group for the initial part of her time in the Far East, the destroyer served with part of the United Nations Blockading and Escort Group. In company with *James C. Owens* (DD–776), *Willard Keith* performed plane guard services for two weeks with the Australian aircraft carrier, HMAS *Sydney*, as that ship conducted flight operations. During the course of the tour, *Willard Keith* visited the ports of Sasebo and Yokosuka, Japan; Inchon, Korea; and Buckner Bay, Okinawa.

Completing her WestPac tour in March 1954, *Willard Keith* and her squadron mates returned to the United States via Midway; Hawaii; San Francisco; Long Beach; the Panama Canal; Havana, Cuba; and Key West, Fla., returning to Norfolk on 1 May and thus completing the ship's circumnavigation of the globe. For the remainder of the year 1954, *Willard Keith* operated from Labrador to the Caribbean, taking part in antisubmarine warfare (ASW) exercises and amphibious exercises interspersed with routine upkeep periods in port.

After spending Christmas, 1954, in her home port, *Willard Keith* departed Norfolk five days into the new year, 1955, bound for the Mediterranean. She paid goodwill calls at the ports of Algiers, Naples, Genoa, and the Azores in the course of her extended deployment, before she returned to Norfolk on 15 March. Then, after a brief upkeep period, *Willard Keith* offloaded stores and ammunition and shifted to the Norfolk Naval Shipyard for a four-month overhaul. Emerging from the shipyard on 8 August, the destroyer conducted refresher training out of the familiar waters of Guantanamo Bay before conducting gunfire support exercises with the rest of her division at Culebra. Returning northward that autumn, she conducted amphibious warfare gunfire support exercises as a fire support unit during Marine Corps amphibious landing exercises off the coast of North Carolina.

For the next seven years, *Willard Keith* remained with DesRon 22, operating from the Atlantic Ocean to the Red Sea and Persian Gulf. She participated in a variety of goodwill missions, midshipmen cruises, and the usual training assignments in gunnery, ASW, and the like. She also participated in the "quarantine" operations in the autumn of 1962 during the Cuban missile crisis. One of the more pleasant highlights of that period occurred during the opening of the St. Lawrence Seaway in 1959—during which time *Willard Keith* escorted the Royal yacht, HMS *Brittania*, the latter having Her Majesty, Queen Elizabeth II, embarked on board.

On 1 October 1963, *Willard Keith* began a new phase of her career. Reporting to DesRon 34 for duty, the warship soon commenced operating as a Naval Reserve training (NRT) ship. For the next nine years, *Willard Keith* operated in that capacity, accomplishing reserve training with monthly drill weekend cruises for the reservists permanently assigned to the ship's reserve crew and undertaking two-week active duty training cruises for reservists getting their annual active sea duty training. She ranged from the eastern seaboard to Guantanamo Bay as an NRT destroyer, providing the platform for training necessary to maintain a skilled pool of reservists ready for any eventuality.

Ultimately considered to have capabilities that were not up to modern Fleet standards, *Willard Keith* was chosen for inactivation and transfer. Decommissioned on 1 July 1972 at Norfolk, Va., *Willard Keith* was transferred to the Navy of the Republic of Colombia. Simultaneously stricken from the Navy list, the destroyer was renamed *Caldes* (DD–02). She served the Colombian Navy until disposed of in 1977.

Willard Keith (DD–775) earned two battle stars for her World War II service.

Willet

A large shore bird of central North America, whose name comes from its call, "pilly-will-willet."

(Minesweeper No. 54: dp. 950; l. 187'10''; b. 35'6''; dr. 9'9½'' (mean); s. 14 k.; cpl. 85; a. none; cl. *Lapwing*)

Willet (Minesweeper No. 54) was laid down on 19 May 1919 at the Philadelphia Navy Yard; launched on 11 September 1919; sponsored by Miss Caroline Chantry, the daughter of Comdr. A. J. Chantry, CC; and commissioned on 29 January 1920, Lt. Albion O. Larsen in command.

After brief service with the Atlantic Fleet Train, *Willet* was decommissioned on 29 May 1920 and simultaneously transferred, on loan, to the United States Shipping Board. She operated with the civilian firm of Merritt, Chapman, and Scott through World War II. During the 1920's and 1930's, she was based at the Merritt, Chapman, and Scott salvage depot in New York before being shifted to Key West, Fla., from which point she operated during World War II. Classified as a salvage vessel on 13 September 1941 and simultaneously redesignated ARS–12, *Willet* operated in the Caribbean and Gulf of Mexico through the end of hostilities. She assisted stranded or grounded vessels, fought fires on burning ships, and escorted coastwise convoy runs.

Declared surplus to naval needs on 1 December 1947, *Willet* was struck from the Navy list on 5 December 1947.

Although listed as "disposed of" as of 6 July 1948, subsequent records indicate that the ship lay berthed at the Navy Net Depot at Melville, R.I., into the late fall of 1948. She was berthed in a shallow water anchorage not normally used by active vessels and served as a breakwater protecting other ships of the Atlantic Reserve Fleet berthed at Melville. On 2 November 1948, the erstwhile minesweeper and salvage vessel was delivered to her purchaser, Joseph Demaso, of Miami, Fla., and scrapped soon thereafter.

Willet Rowe

Willet Rowe—a wooden-hulled, side-wheel steamer built at Brooklyn, N.Y., in 1863—was taken over by the Navy for service as a gunboat and purchased on 16 October 1863. Soon thereafter, she was renamed *Iris* (*q.v.*).

Willett, Kenneth, see Kenneth Willett.

William A. McKenney

(Freighter: dp. 12,800; l. 410'6''; b. 55'1''; dr. 26'5'' (mean); cpl. 62; a. 1 5'', 1 3'')

William A. McKenney—a steel-hull, single screw freighter launched on 28 October 1916 at Newport News, Va., by the Newport News Shipbuilding and Drydock Co., for the Crowell and Thurlow Shipbuilding Co.—was inspected by the Navy for possible use as a depot collier at Norfolk on 12 December 1917. Available records indicate that the ship would be turned over to the War Department by the United States Shipping Board (USSB) about 20 February 1918 for use as a cargo transport. She was to be manned by the Navy on a "bare ship basis" and would be operated for the War Department account.

Transferred to the Navy on 5 June 1918 for operation by the Naval Overseas Transportation Service (NOTS), *William A. McKenny* was assigned Id. No. 2102 and commissioned at Norfolk on the same day. She made two wartime voyages carrying cargo for NOTS, commencing her first voyage at Norfolk on 19 June and her second from Newport News on 7 September. Her ports of call included Brest, St. Nazaire, La Pallice, and Verdon Roads; her cargo included steel rails, trucks, and engine supplies.

After completing her second wartime round-trip crossing of the Atlantic, she was at Norfolk when World War I ended on 11 November 1918. Her only postwar voyage, to La Pallice with Army supplies, began when she departed Norfolk on 22 November. After completing her unloading, *William A. McKenney* departed French waters on Christmas, 1918, and arrived at New York on New Year's Day, 1919.

Decommissioned at New York on 31 January 1919 and simultaneously struck from the Navy list, *William A. McKenney* was turned over to the USSB for return to her owners. Sometime in the mid-1920's, the ship was acquired by the Mystic Steamship Co., Boston, Mass. She operated with that company into the late 1930's and was later owned by the Koppers Coal Co., of Pittsburgh, Pa., but still operated by Mystic.

On 4 October 1942, *William A. McKenney* came under attack by *U–175* in the North Atlantic. The U-boat surfaced and shelled and torpedoed the steel-hulled bulk carrier, sinking her off the coast of British Guiana.

William Ashton

(Tr: t. 433 (f.); lbp. 120'; b. 22'6''; dph. 12'5''; s. 9.5 k.; cl. "Strath")

William Ashton—a steel-hulled, steam screw trawler built in 1918 at Torry Shipbuilding Co., Aberdeen, Scotland, by J. Duthie for the British Admiralty—was leased by the United States Navy for service with the North Sea Minesweeping Detachment on 26 May 1919 and was commissioned that day. No records have been located for this vessel, but it can be assumed that she served in one of the two trawler divisions serving with the Minesweeping Detachment, North Atlantic Fleet, in clearing the North Sea Mine Barrage. Ships of her type were proved to be inadequate to stand up to the harsh demands of minesweeping in the inhospitable North Sea and were returned to the British Admiralty after comparatively short service. *William Ashton* was decommissioned and returned on 5 August 1919.

William B. Preston

Born on 25 November 1805 at Smithfield, Va., William Ballard Preston entered Hampden-Sydney College in 1821, where he was active in literary and forensic activities. Graduating in 1824, Preston studied law at the University of Virginia and was admitted to the bar in 1826.

The young attorney soon entered politics as a Whig and was elected to the Virginia House of Delegates in 1830. During the 1831–1832 session, he took an active part in the campaign to abolish slavery. Then there followed an eight-year hiatus in his political activities during which he returned to the practice of law. In 1840, he was elected to the State Senate, where he served from 1840 to 1844, before returning to the House of Delegates. In 1846, he was elected to the United States House of Representatives.

In March of 1849, President Zachary Taylor appointed the Virginia lawyer and congressman Secretary of the Navy. During Preston's tenure in that office, the United States Navy acquired new duties in the course of America's westward expansion and acquisition of California. Trade and commerce in the Pacific beckoned, and the Stars and Stripes flew from the masts of Navy ships in Chinese waters, while the shores of Japan, then unopened to the west, presented a tantalizing possibility for commercial intercourse. The Navy also was progressing through a technological transition, especially in the area of moving from sails to steam propulsion, and with the improvements in gunnery and

324

naval ordnance. Upon the death of President Taylor, new President Millard Fillmore reorganized the cabinet and appointed another Secretary of the Navy. Preston retired from office and withdrew from politics and public life.

Resuming his private law practice, Preston acquired a reputation for being a fine defense laywer before being sent to France in 1858 to negotiate for the establishment of a line of commercial steamers to operate between Le Havre and Norfolk. The mission to France progressed well, and the project appeared promising until it was brought to nought by the American Civil War.

As states in the lower South seceded from the Union, the pressure mounted upon Virginia to do likewise. Moderate sentiment still held sway through 1860; but, early in 1861, increasing tensions forced Virginians to consider secession. On 13 February 1861, the secession convention met in Richmond and numbered William B. Preston amongst the delegates.

As the Confederacy was established and the United States divided into two hostile camps, both sides moved steadily toward open conflict. A special delegation, composed of William B. Preston, H. H. Stuart, and George W. Randolph, travelled to Washington where they met President Lincoln on 12 April. Finding the President firm in his resolve to hold the Federal forts then in the South, the three men returned to Richmond on the 15th.

With the news of the firing on Fort Sumter in South Carolina on 12 April 1861, conservative and moderate strength in the secessionist convention melted away. On the 16th, convinced that secession was inevitable, William B. Preston submitted, in secret session, an ordinance of secession. Supported 88 to 55, the Preston Resolution passed, and Virginia left the Union.

Elected senator from Virginia in the Confederate States Congress, he served in that legislative body until his death at Smithfield on 16 November 1862.

(Destoyer No. 344: dp. 1,308; l. 314'4''; b. 30'11''; dr. 9'10''; s. 35.0 k.; cpl. 221; a. 4 4'', 1 3'', 12 21'' tt.; cl. *Clemson*)

William B. Preston (Destroyer No. 344) was laid down on 18 November 1918 at the Norfolk Navy Yard, Portsmouth, Va.; launched on 9 August 1919; sponsored by Mrs. William Radford Beale, the eldest daughter of William B. Preston; designated DD–344 on 17 July 1920; and commissioned on 23 August 1920, Lt. James B. Ryan in temporary command. On 7 September 1920, Comdr. William E. Eberle reported on board as commanding officer.

Following commissioning, *William B. Preston* operated with Destroyer Division (DesDiv) 19 and conducted trials and training off the east coast through the end of 1920. She then proceeded south to join the Fleet in Guantanamo Bay, Cuba, for winter maneuvers. After these exercises, she transited the Panama Canal to participate in the Fleet's visit to Callao, Peru, and arrived at that port on 21 January 1921.

The ship next received orders transferring her to DesDiv 45, Destroyer Squadron (DesRon) 14; and she joined the Asiatic Fleet in mid-1922. With her home port at Cavite, near Manila in the Philippines, the destroyer cruised with her division on exercises and maneuvers. In the summer months, the ships would base out of Chefoo on the north coast of Shantung province, China, while moving southward to Philippine waters for the winter exercises. In between, there were visits to China coastal ports such as Amoy, Foochow, and Swatow and occasional tours on the Yangtze between Shanghai and Hankow.

In 1926, civil strife broke out in China which was essentially a struggle between north and south for control of the country. To the southward, the Nationalist, or Kuomingtang, party moved north from its base at Canton to extend its controls over warlord-dominated areas. Led by a young Army officer named Chiang Kai-

shek, the Nationalists had reached Nanking by March 1927.

William B. Preston arrived in the troubled atmosphere surrounding that port on the Yangtze River on 21 March and dropped anchor off the city, joining sister-ship *Noa* (DD–343). Under orders to evacuate Americans, the destroyers took on 175 refugees—102 on *Noa* and 73 on *William B. Preston*.

Gunfire, coming closer to the city, alerted the American destroyermen to the danger posed by the approaching Cantonese. Northern Chinese troops meanwhile melted away from the city that they were supposed to defend, leaving many foreigners endangered by the prospect of undisciplined and looting southerners rampaging through the defenseless city. An armed guard from *Noa* stood by on shore while signal parties from *William B. Preston* and *Noa* wig-wagged the information about the tense conditions in Nanking to the ships anchored in the muddy river.

When the situation had worsened to a point of no return, *Noa* commenced firing with her 4-inch guns; *William B. Preston* joined in with her main battery as well and, in the 10-minute barrage, fired 22 rounds of 4-inch projectiles to scare off the rampaging Cantonese. Bluejackets on both American ships also provided fire with bolt-action Springfield rifles and drumfed Lewis guns. British cruiser HMS *Emerald* and destroyer HMS *Wolsey* added to the din with their guns; and the Chinese, faced by this Anglo-American determination, withdrew.

Four days later, with the situation much quieter in Nanking, *William B. Preston* prepared to leave the area in company with refugee-laden SS *Kungwo* on 25 March. Snipers, firing from concealed positions ashore, sent the destroyer's anchor detail scurrying for cover; and ricocheting bullets whined into the pre-dawn darkness. A Lewis gun on the destroyer soon stopped the annoyance; and the ship, with her civilian charges, was soon underway, headed downriver.

Three hours later, while proceeding between Silver Island and Hsing Shan fort, small arms fire again crackled from the shore, first directed at *Fungwo* and next at *William B. Preston*. Bluejackets on the destroyer promptly broke out their Lewis guns and Springfields to reply, but the situation suddenly worsened when a 3-inch gun at the fort opened fire on the ships.

One shell splashed into the muddy river ahead of the destroyer; another fell in the ship's boiling wake; and the third passed through the fire control platform. The destroyer's number one 4-inch gun was quickly trained around and bellowed a reply—three salvoes which, when accompanied by the rattle of small arms and machine guns from the warship, silenced the harassment from ashore.

Emerging from this gauntlet, *William B. Preston* and her charges joined British gunboat *Cricket* and SS *Wenchow*, 52 miles below Chinkiang. Snipers once again harassed the Anglo-American flotilla, but machine-gun fire from *Cricket* soon forced the Chinese to beat a hasty retreat.

After turning *Kungwo* over to the British gunboat, *William B. Preston* returned to Nanking unhampered by further sniping. On 27 March, with 70 more refugees embarked, the ship cleared Nanking and headed downriver. Lt. Comdr. G. B. Ashe, the ship's commanding officer, recalled that the Chinese had emplaced a fieldpiece at a key river bend and, accordingly, ordered general quarters well in advance.

Cleared for action with guns trained out and the Stars and Stripes streaming from the gaff, *William B. Preston* rounded the bend, ready for a showdown. The Chinese, however, at the sight of the destroyer ready to "breathe fire" like a typical Chinese dragon, allowed the ship to pass unmolested.

Receiving the Yangtze Service Medal for these actions against snipers while convoying American nationals out of the troubled areas, *William B. Preston* returned to routine cruising soon thereafter. She was back in the

USS *William B. Preston* (DD–344) flying a homeward-bound pennant at her main as she heads home from the Asiatic Station in the early 1930s. (NR&L(M) 24832)

United States by 1929, homeported at San Diego, Calif., and assigned to the Battle Force.

To meet the obligations imposed by the naval treaties of the 1920's and 1930's, *William B. Preston* was part of a group of destroyers laid up in reserve at Philadelphia. She was decommissioned there on 15 October 1934.

As America's Navy grew to two-ocean strength in the first months following the outbreak of World War II in Europe, the need for auxiliaries to support the Fleet multiplied accordingly. On 18 November 1939, *William B. Preston* was selected for conversion to a small seaplane tender and redesignated AVP–20. Soon thereafter, the ship entered the New York Navy Yard for conversion.

William B. Preston was recommissioned on 14 June 1940, with Lt. Comdr. Francis J. Bridget in command. On 2 August 1940, the ship was reclassified again, this time to destroyer-seaplane tender, and redesignated AVD–7.

She departed the New York area three days later and arrived at Hampton Roads the following day. On 11 August, she headed for the Caribbean and arrived at Guantanamo Bay, Cuba, four days later. She then steamed to Panama, transited the canal on 24 August, and proceeded on to San Diego, Calif., where she arrived on 5 September for an eight-day pause en route to Hawaii.

After mooring to a Submarine Base pier at Pearl Harbor on 19 September, the ship commenced operations with the Fleet. She engaged in such tasks as tending scout planes, towing targets during fleet exercises, and making routine offshore patrols through 30 September. She then anchored at Palmyra Island to tend PBY Catalinas through 4 October, when she returned to Pearl Harbor.

As patrol plane reinforcements winged their way across the broad, blue Pacific, bound for the Asiatic Fleet, *William B. Preston* served as a plane guard for three days in October and then resumed her routine duties out of Pearl Harbor. On 6 December 1940, the seaplane tender set course for the Philippines and her second tour of duty with the Asiatic Fleet.

En route, she lay to at plane guard station "George," while VP–26 passed overhead on course for the Philippine Islands. On 13 December, she was fueled from *Wright* (AV–1) and then lay to in the lee of Wake Island before proceeding on to Guam. She arrived at Apra Harbor on 17 December but soon pressed onward and completed the last leg of her voyage to the Philip-

pines when she anchored in Canacao Bay, off the Cavite Navy Yard, on 22 December 1940.

After operating in the Manila area through Christmas 1940, the tender took station at Puerto Princessa Harbor, near the island of Palawan, where she tended PBY's to mid-January 1941. Moving on to Tutu Bay, Jolo, on 15 January, she visited Igat Bay and Caldera Bay, both off Mindanao, before returning to Canacao Bay on 8 February.

From February to November 1941, as the situation in the Far East grew more tense with each passing tick of the clock, the Asiatic Fleet continued its preparations for war. While some fleet units, including the majority of the destroyers, were sent south, *William B. Preston* was maintained in readiness in the Philippines for any eventuality. She tended PBY's and occasionally acted as target tug for fleet maneuvers in the southern islands in the Philippine archipelago. After an overhaul at the Cavite Navy Yard in November, she departed the Manila area on 1 December, bound for the southeastern coast of Mindanao.

Upon her arrival in Davao Gulf, the ship dropped anchor in Malalag Bay, where she was joined by a group of PBY's which soon commenced patrols. With war only a matter of days away, the planes reconnoitered several small bays and inlets, looking out for strange ships or for any signs of suspicious activity.

Shortly after 0300 on 8 December 1941, *William B. Preston* picked up the following radio message: "Japan has commenced hostilities. Govern yourselves accordingly."

Japan had indeed commenced hostilities, launching a devastating air strike on Pearl Harbor while their invasion fleets moved southward from Indochina towards the raw-material-rich British and Dutch possessions in Malaya and the East Indies. The Philippines, too, were on the timetable for conquest.

Soon after the receipt of the notification of war, all of the planes tended by the destroyer-seaplane tender were readied for operations. Two remained behind while the rest flew off on their first war patrols over the Celebes Sea. The ship, meanwhile, shifted anchorage away from the two moored Catalinas to lessen the chance of one bomb damaging both ship and planes in one fell swoop. Bluejackets on *William B. Preston* belted ammunition for the ship's antiaircraft defense of four .50-caliber watercooled Browning machine guns and took down the awnings which had shielded the crew from the tropical sun.

Around 0800, the ship's commanding officer, Lt. Comdr. Etheridge Grant, went forward to check the progress of the preparations to slip the anchor chain (should that become necessary). Suddenly a lookout called out, "Aircraft!" Grant sprinted to the bridge while Japanese planes swept around the narrow neck of the land shielding Malalag Bay from the broad Gulf of Davao. Nine "Claudes" and 13 "Vals" from the Japanese carrier *Ryujo* roared in low over the water, their cowl guns winking fire.

Going for the planes first, the "Claudes" made short work of the Catalinas that rode at their mooring buoys like sitting ducks. Within a few short moments, both PBY's had been shot to pieces. Blazing and shattered, the two patrol planes sank into the waters of the bay as the survivors, carrying one dead and one wounded comrade with them, struck out for shore.

Meanwhile, the ship lowered a boat to pick up survivors while she got underway for the open sea. Slipping her anchor chain, *William B. Preston* zigzagged across the bay as both "Claudes" and "Vals" declared "open season" on the fleeing tender. Skillfully evading the bombs, the ship managed to emerge from the attack unscathed and returned to the bay to pick up her boat and the survivors from the two lost planes.

Later that day, upon receipt of orders dispatching her to Moro Gulf, *William B. Preston* got underway to establish another advance base for PBY's at Polloc Bay. Retiring from Davao Gulf, the destroyer-seaplane tender slipped past four Japanese destroyers whose attention was probably focused on bigger game elsewhere. One hour later, a snooping Japanese plane picked up the ship's scent and trailed her for three hours, leading those on board *William B. Preston* to suspect that the Japanese were sending out a second strike to finish the job begun earlier. Steering as close to the shoreline as safe navigation would permit, Lt. Comdr. Grant prepared to beach the ship should that prove necessary, but the plane departed and left the seaplane tender alone.

Arriving off the mouth of Moro Bay in the afternoon, the ship lay to until the following morning, 9 December, when she entered the bay. An explosion ahead of the ship sent the American bluejackets to their general quarters stations before it was discovered that the local fishermen were just out dynamiting for their catch!

The ship found a PBY awaiting her arrival and commenced tending operations. Three more Catalinas arrived later in the afternoon, as well as two OS2U Kingfishers which had been attached to *Heron* (AVP-2) at Balabac. After being informed that Japanese troops had landed north of Gagayan and were marching overland to Polloc, the ship prepared to get underway and dispatched the PBY's on patrol over the Celebes Sea. Leaving word that the planes were to rendezvous with the ship at Tutu Bay, Jolo, *William B. Preston* got underway on 10 December.

The ship arrived at Tutu Bay later that day and found the PBY's awaiting her, after having found no trace of enemy activity during their patrol sweeps. At sunset, a veritable procession of masts and funnels moved across the southern horizon; and the men on the *William B. Preston* could only guess to whom they belonged.

The following day, the planes were again sent out on patrols while the ship upped anchor and proceeded for Tawi Tawi, receiving word en route that the PBY's were to return to Lake Lanao in Mindanao and the OS2U's were to rendezvous with the ship at Tawi Tawi. Although she had never hoisted aboard any aircraft before, *William B. Preston*'s ingenious bluejackets rigged up a rude cradle between the two 50-foot motorboats aft and provided padding for the Kingfisher's center float with mattresses and life jackets. One OS2U was taken aboard and berthed in this fashion while the other was towed astern. Smooth seas and a 15-knot pace facilitated the towing operation, and the two planes arrived safely at Tarakan, Borneo.

Met by two Dutch destroyers, *Kortenaer* and *Witte de With*, the seaplane tender made port at Tarakan but was soon underway again, this time for Balikpapan, Borneo, where she met many "old friends" from the Asiatic Fleet—*Marblehead* (CL-12), *Holland* (AS-3), *Langley* (AV-3), *Gold Star* (AK-12), and *Heron*. Two hours after arrival, the ship received orders to accompany the small fleet to Makassar and got underway on 13 December.

After arriving at Makassar, *William B. Preston* spent three days provisioning and catching up on news of the progress of the war. The picture of the latter looked bleak, as Japanese forces swept southward, sweeping everything before them and forcing Allied naval, air, and ground units southward into the East Indies. The ship arrived at Sourabaya, Java, shortly before Christmas but, after further provisioning and fueling, departed the Dutch naval base there on the 27th.

The ship arrived at Darwin, Australia, on the day after New Year's Day 1942 and soon received orders to provision to capacity and take on large stocks of spare parts, food, and replacement crews for the decimated ranks of personnel in PatWing 10. The ship then proceeded north for Ambon, in the Dutch East Indies, crowded with 100 extra men and much topside freight.

Upon her arrival at Ambon, the destroyer-seaplane tender found sister ship *Childs* (AVD-1) and passed that ship enough fuel to enable her to reach Darwin. After delivering her embarked men and cargo, *William B. Preston* proceeded to Kendari, where she was skillfully camouflaged to blend in with the verdant hillside to which she was moored—in fact, so skillfully hidden that her PBY's had trouble locating her when they returned to their base!

For the remainder of January and into February, the ship continued her tending operations as the forces combatting the Japanese rapidly dwindled. On 12 February 1942, *William B. Preston* dropped anchor at Darwin to commence tending PBY's from that base in northwestern Australia. In about a week, her fuel began running low, forcing Lt. Comdr. Grant to go ashore to arrange for a delivery of much-needed fuel and gasoline for the ship.

At 0955, lookouts called down that "large formations of planes (were) approaching" and the ship went to general quarters. Within minutes, the ship was underway with the executive officer, Lt. Lester O. Wood in command. Zigzagging her way through the crowded harbor, *William B. Preston* made for the open sea as Japanese planes droned closer and closer.

The first wave of planes attacked the town and its nearby fuel dumps and docks; the second wave went after the ships in the harbor, with transports and cargo ships as the primary objectives. Within minutes of each other, transports *Tulagi* and *Meigs* took hits; and ships alongside the docks were heavily hit as bombs rained indiscriminately on the port area.

Four bombs exploded off *William B. Preston*'s bow, breaking bridge windows. Heavy volumes of .30- and .50-caliber antiaircraft fire forced some of the attackers to keep their distance, but others pressed the attack with vigor. *Peary* (DD-226), slower in getting underway, was enveloped in bomb splashes as Japanese accuracy marked the ship for destruction. Heavily hit, the hardluck *Peary* burst into flames and rapidly became an inferno as bomb after bomb tore the ship apart and forced her down by the stern.

The seaplane tender's turn was next, however; and she was hit aft, just forward of the after deckhouse. The ship lost steering control forward; and, in the interim period between regaining control by hand-steering aft, Lt. Wood conned and steered the ship using her engines and, despite a jammed rudder, succeeded in making for an opening in the harbor boom. Negotiating it by "judicious use of engines and slight assistance from the rudder with direct hand steering," *William B. Preston* escaped the inferno that left Darwin shattered and ruined as a base of operations for the Allies.

Heading south down the western coast of Australia, the ship took stock of her damage. Eleven men were killed, two missing, and three wounded by the bomb hit aft. The after living compartment was a mass of wreckage; rivets were popped and seams sprung; the after deck house was riddled with holes; the after 4-inch and machine guns had been put out of action. At about 1445, a Japanese "Mavis" patrol plane (Kawanishi E7K) attacked the ship, but her bombs splashed harmlessly into the ship's wake, and the plane discontinued her attack.

Proceeding to Derby, Australia, *William B. Preston* encountered more bad luck, touching briefly on a shoal as she entered the harbor, and reduced the effective speed of the starboard engine down to eight knots. Meanwhile, the single remaining PBY attached to the ship returned from Darwin with the men who had gone ashore and had been caught away from the ship during the attack, including Lt. Comdr. Grant, who had been blown out of a motorboat while returning to the ship.

On 23 February, the damaged *William B. Preston* proceeded for Broome, Australia, and was soon joined by *Childs* and *Heron*, who both assisted the damaged seaplane tender in making emergency repairs. As Java fell, to the north, three of *William B. Preston*'s planes served in the evacuation of Surabaya and Tjilatjap. Meanwhile, the ship received orders to proceed for Fremantle for repairs.

Upon arrival, however, there were not sufficient facilities available to effect the needed yard work, so the ship was routed on to Sydney. There, on the east coast of Australia, *William B. Preston* received a much-needed overhaul and repair period. Her old 4-inch guns were replaced by 3-inch antiaircraft guns, while 20-millimeter Oerlikons were added as well to augment her close-in antiaircraft capability. Following her availability, the ship proceeded to Fremantle and reported for duty to Commander, Patrol Wing 10, in June 1942.

Java had fallen, as had the Philippines and Malaya. Thus, the Australian sub-continent stood as the last Allied bastion in the southwest Pacific to oppose further Japanese expansion. Operating out of Fremantle, the destroyer-seaplane tender alternated with *Heron* and *Childs* at such advance bases as Exmouth Gulf and Fremantle through the early summer of 1942.

Anchored in the vicinity of Bay of Rest, Exmouth Gulf, Western Australia, *William B. Preston* continued her operations as a seaplane tender through early July, attached to Patrol Wing 10 and servicing two PBY-5 planes. One plane conducted a daily patrol as far as Broome, while the other remained at a buoy near the ship with her crew living on board the tender. The ship's log noted that she was "in all respects ready to slip anchor and get underway instantly—day or night." The calm waters of the bay and the generally perfect flying weather combined to greatly facilitate flight operations.

Relieved by *Heron* on 14 July, the ship cleared Exmouth Gulf, bound for Fremantle for general upkeep. Securing alongside *Isabel* (PY–10) at north dock, Fremantle, she commenced a yard period, taking on fuel, gasoline, and provisions over the next eight days, departing on 26 July. She steamed back to Exmouth Gulf and relieved *Heron* on the 29th.

For the remainder of 1942 and into 1943, *William B. Preston* continued this general routine, exchanging tender duties with *Heron* and *Childs* and undergoing periodic general upkeep at Fremantle. In February 1943, a heavy storm hit Exmouth Gulf, sending two PBY's onto a reef. A third Catalina took off despite the typhoon and made its way through sheets of rain and thick clouds to safely arrive at Geraldton. Within two days, replacement planes had arrived; and *William B. Preston* recommenced tender operations.

On 1 April, the seaplane tender moved to Shark's Bay, Western Australia, to serve as an advance base; she subsequently tended PBY's for a time at West Lewis Island, near Enderby Island, Western Australia. Later, following the month of January 1944, in which the ship received full oveahul and upkeep, *William B. Preston* operated out of Fremantle on submarine exercises serving as a target vessel for the undersea boats operating out of that port. She continued these activities through the spring and summer of 1944.

At Darwin, on 18 August, the ship embarked the Deputy Commander, Fleet Air Wing 10, and other men from that unit for transportation to the Admiralty Islands. After departing Australia, she proceeded to New Guinea, arriving at Milne Bay on 22 August. Pushing on to the Admiralties, the ship dropped anchor at Manus on the 24th, disembarking her passengers and fueling preparatory to heading for the Ellice Islands. The ship made Funafuti on 31 August.

Attached to Service Force, Pacific Fleet, and under orders from Commander, Air, Pacific Fleet (ComAirPac), *William B. Preston* headed for the United States. Stopping briefly at Palmyra Island and Pearl Harbor en route to the west coast, the seaplane tender arrived at San Francisco on 18 September. She then proceeded to San Pedro, Calif., and thence to Terminal Island for overhaul.

From 1 October to 8 November, *William B. Preston* underwent voyage repairs and alterations to her armament. The ship also received a much-needed drydocking for bottom work before getting underway for post-repair trials which concluded on 16 November. Putting out to sea on 21 November, the newly refitted ship rendezvoused with *Ranger* (CV–4) as the carrier engaged in training operations and carrier qualification flights for new pilots.

For the remainder of 1944, the destroyer-seaplane tender operated as plane guard and antisubmarine escort ship out of San Diego. Alternating in company with *Ranger* or *Matanikau* (CVE–101), she kept a sharp eye out for planes forced to "ditch" while in the hands of student pilots learning the nuances of the Grumman F6F Hellcat fighter.

After spending New Year's Day 1945 at San Diego, *William B. Preston* continued plane guarding and screening duties, clearing her home port on 2 January to join *Matanikau* off the California coast. During flight operations on 3 January, a Hellcat crashed while taking off, and the destroyer-seaplane tender sped to the rescue. The ship's whaleboat, soon in the water, rescued the soaked pilot, and *William B. Preston* subsequently returned the aviator to his carrier via highline transfer.

For the remainder of January and into February, the ship's duties continued to be much in the same vein, until she returned to the Bethlehem Steel repair yard at Alameda, Calif., on 14 February, for availability. She remained in dockyard hands until the 21st, after which time she rejoined *Matanikau* during further carrier qualification trials.

After returning to port for a hull inspection at the Naval Repair Base, San Diego, *William B. Preston* operated with a succession of carriers engaged in flight training: *Takanis Bay* (CVE–89), *Thetis Bay* (CVE–90), *Siboney* (CVE–120), and old faithful *Ranger*. On 26 July, a wave caved in the forward port in the ship's office, flooding the radio room and putting it out of commission. Detached from further duty, she returned to San Diego where repairs could be made.

Following completion of work to make good the damage, *William B. Preston* returned to further plane guard activities, alternating with *Ranger* and *Puget Sound* (CVE–113). War's end on 15 August 1945 found the venerable destroyer-seaplane tender at anchor in San Diego harbor.

As newer AVP's joined the Fleet and the end of the war made further expansion unnecessary, the need for older ships like *William B. Preston* diminished. The ship departed the west coast and arrived at Philadelphia on 9 October 1945 for preparation for disposal. On 6 December 1945, the *William B. Preston* was decommissioned; and, on 3 January 1946, her name was struck from the Navy list. On 6 November 1946, the Northern Metals Co., of Philadelphia, purchased the hulk for scrapping.

William B. Preston received one battle star for her World War II service.

William Bacon

(Sch.: t. 183; l. 95'0''; b. 26'0''; dr. 8'10'' (max.); dph. 8'3''; a. 1 13'' M.; 2 32-pdrs.)

William Bacon—a wooden-hulled schooner—was purchased by the Navy on 6 September 1861 from Van Brunt and Slaight and commissioned at the New York Navy Yard, Brooklyn, N.Y., on 3 February 1862, Acting Master William P. Rogers, USN, in command.

Assigned to the mortar flotilla attached to Flag Officer David Glasgow Farragut's West Gulf Blockading Squadron, *William Bacon* departed New York under tow on 6 February and arrived at Key West, Fla., on 18 February. The next day, she shifted to Pilot Town.

Flag Officer Farragut gathered his forces at the mouth of the Mississippi to commence one phase of the move designed to split the Confederacy asunder along that major waterway. Defending the mouth of that key artery were Forts Jackson and St. Philip, mounting between them 115 guns, in addition to a heavy barrier of chained hulks and logs that lay in the river below the forts to obstruct the passage.

The steamer *Westfield* took *William Bacon* under tow on the morning of 11 April and, at 0915, headed upriver; at 1300, the crew on board the mortar schooner began dressing the masts with green bushes in an attempt to camouflage the ship—a standard practice throughout the flotilla as it began to clear for action with the Confederate forces upstream.

William Bacon and the other ships of the mortar flotilla kept up a steady, heavy fire on the two Confederate forts over the next week. Farragut's squadron, meanwhile, battered their way through the barrier and successfully made passage. Three days later, the forts —heavily battered by the shells from the mortar flotilla and surrounded on the landward sides by the Army's expeditionary forces under General Benjamin Butler— surrendered, thus removing a formidable barrier to the Federal operations. *William Bacon,* her task in the reduction of the forts completed, dropped down the river to Southwest Pass, where she awaited further orders.

Because of the enervating climate, however, *William Bacon* did not tarry long at the mouth of the Mississippi. She sailed for Hampton Roads soon thereafter and refitted there into the summer. Briefly assigned to the Potomac Flotilla, *William Bacon* subsequently received orders on 11 December 1862 to report for duty with the North Atlantic Blockading Squadron off Wilmington, N.C. Three days later, she began taking on stores at Hampton Roads for delivery to the ships already off Wilmington and apparently arrived later in the month to take up her duties. Extant records indicate that the blockade had been strengthened with additional ships by 29 December—*William Bacon* included.

William Bacon operated primarily off Wilmington and the sounds of North Carolina into 1863. Relieving *Matthew Vassar* at Little River Inlet on 13 March 1863, she was receiving fresh water from the steamer *Victoria* on 21 March, off the mouth of the Little River, when lookouts sighted a sail to the westward at about 0900. *Victoria,* Acting Volunteer Lieutenant Edward Hooker commanding, immediately got up steam and gave chase. In accordance with orders from Hooker, *William Bacon* slipped her anchor chain and made sail.

Victoria, the faster of the two Union vessels, managed to close the range in the fog and mist prevailing offshore that morning and lobbed a few shots at the stranger, all of which fell close aboard. While *William Bacon* came up rapidly, the unidentified vessel hove

around and stood toward the two blockaders; Acting Master Rogers, commanding *William Bacon,* later reported: "And as we did not know but what there might be some resistance, every man was at the gun ready for immediate action."

While *William Bacon* thus stood by in a posture of readiness, *Victoria* lowered a boat. Soon, the blockaders learned the identity of the strange ship: she was the English steamer *Nicolai I,* bound from Nassau, New Providence, in the Bahamas, for Charleston, S.C., with a cargo of dry goods, arms, and ammunition. *Victoria* consequently took her prize into custody and took her up to the main body of the fleet. *William Bacon* soon returned to the drudgery of coastal patrols.

Records are not clear as to what the ship did next, but it may be presumed that she served in a support capacity for the duration of the Civil War. Ultimately decommissioned at the Washington Navy Yard on 17 June 1865, *William Bacon* was sold at auction to William L. Wall and Co., on 20 July of the same year.

William Badger

William Badger was a New Hampshire shipwright who built the 74-gun ship-of-the-line *Washington* and merchant ships for the West Indies trade. The whaling ship *William Badger* may have been named for him.

(Whaler: t. 334; l. 106'0''; b. 26'0''; dph. 13'3''; a. 1 32-pdr.)

William Badger—a wooden-hulled whaling ship— was purchased by the Navy on 18 May 1861 from Henry F. Thomas, at New Bedford, Mass. Assigned to the North Atlantic Blockading Squadron, *William Badger* served as a stationary supply ship at Hampton Roads, Va., into the summer of 1862. Late in July, *William Badger*—laden with a "goodly supply of provisions, clothing, and stores" for the ships of the Union Navy maintaining the blockade off Confederate-held Wilmington, N.C.—was towed by the steamer *State of Georgia* to the North Atlantic Blockading Squadron base at Beaufort, N.C. She remained there as a supply hulk for the remainder of the Civil War and, on occasion, served as an accommodations vessel.

Sold at auction at Beaufort on 17 October 1865 to a Capt. James Abel, *William Badger* may have been broken up shortly thereafter, as she is not carried on mercantile lists in succeeding years.

William C. Cole

William Carey Cole—born in Chicago, Ill., on 23 August 1868—was appointed a naval cadet on 5 September 1885 and graduated from the Naval Academy on 7 June 1889. At the end of the two years of service at sea then required by law—in *Iroquois* and *Charleston* —Cole received his commission as an ensign on 1 July 1891.

After further sea service in *Nipsic,* Cole headed the branch hydrographic office in Cleveland, Ohio, from 23 October 1894 to 10 September 1896 before he went first to the cruiser *Raleigh* and later to dispatch boat *Dolphin.* After a stint in the hydrographic office in Washington, D.C., and a brief tour at the Washington Navy Yard, Cole reported once more to *Dolphin* and, while in that ship, took part in the Spanish-American War off Santiago, Cuba.

Subsequently serving at the Washington Navy Yard and commanding, in succession, tug *Tecumseh* and yacht *Sylph,* Cole went to the Newport News Shipbuilding and Drydock Co. in the summer of 1905 to familiarize himself with the work of a naval inspector of equipment before assuming that office in the General Electric Co., of Schenectady, N.Y., and later in the New York Shipbuilding Co., Camden, N.J.

On 18 April 1907, Cole—by then a lieutenant commander—became the navigator of the new battleship

Kansas when she was first commissioned. He subsequently became her executive officer before reporting to the Naval Academy. Promoted to commander on 20 October 1910, Cole subsequently assumed simultaneous command of all of the ships at the Naval Academy, including the steam sloop *Hartford* and the cruiser *Olympia*.

Cole next went to the Asiatic Station and reported for duty at Olongapo, Philippine Islands, on 10 March. There, he assumed command of the monitors *Monadnock* and *Monterey* (in first reserve) but was detached from that duty on 4 December. He took command of the gunboat *Helena* two days after Christmas of 1913 and assumed the concurrent duties of Senior Officer, Yangtze Valley.

Detached in the spring of 1915, Cole attended the long course at the Naval War College, Newport, R.I., and then became Inspector of Engineering Material in the Boston District. On 10 April 1917, shortly after the United States entered World War I, Cole took command of the armored cruiser *Frederick* (Armored Cruiser No. 8) and remained in that warship until 23 September when he was given command of *Nevada* (Battleship No. 36). For "exceptionally meritorious service in a duty of great responsibility" commanding *Nevada* during World War I, Cole received the Navy Cross.

After leaving *Nevada* on 7 May 1919, Cole served in London as assistant attache before he went to Washington, D.C., where he became, in time, the Assistant Chief of Naval Operations, remaining in that duty into 1922. Attaining flag rank on 28 January 1922, he was detached from his Assistant CNO duties on 10 March and went to the Panama Canal Zone where he became Commander, Special Service Squadron —a naval force colloquially known as the "Banana Fleet"—on 29 April 1922, hoisting his two-starred flag in the cruiser *Birmingham*.

In the spring of 1923, Cole fleeted up to duty as chief of staff to the Commander in Chief, United States Fleet and remained in that billet for two years before he became Commandant of the Norfolk Navy Yard in the autumn of 1926. Subsequently serving as Commander, Battleship Division 4 from 11 July 1928 to 21 May 1929 and as Commander, Scouting Fleet— with the rank of vice admiral—from 21 June 1929 to 14 June 1930, Cole became Commandant of the 12th Naval District in the summer of 1930. Relieved on 1 June 1932, he briefly served as Inspector of Petroleum Reserves from 28 June to 6 August 1932, before he was retired on 1 September 1932. Cole died at the Naval Hospital, Mare Island Navy Yard, Vallejo, Calif., on 28 May 1935.

William C. Cole (DE–286)—slated for construction at Hingham, Mass., by the Bethlehem Steel Co.—was renamed *Sutton* (q.v.) on 18 September 1943.

I

(DE–641: dp. 1,400; l. 306'0''; b. 37'0''; dr. 9'5''; s. 23.5 k.; cpl. 186; a. 3 3'', 4 1.1'', 10 20mm., 2 dct., 8 dcp., 1 dcp. (hh.); cl. *Buckley*)

William C. Cole (DE–641) was laid down on 5 September 1943 at San Francisco, Calif., by the Bethlehem Steel Co.; launched on 29 December 1943; sponsored by Mrs. William C. Cole, the widow of Admiral Cole; and commissioned on 12 May 1944, Lt. Clay Harrold in command.

Following shakedown in the San Diego area, *William C. Cole* underwent post-shakedown availability at her builder's yard before departing the west coast on 19 July, bound for the Hawaiian Islands. After reaching Oahu, the new destroyer escort trained out of Pearl Harbor for the remainder of the month.

William C. Cole departed Oahu on 1 August in company with *Snyder* (DE–645), as part of the screen for the oilers *Neches* (AO–47) and *Atascosa* (AO–66); the

seaplane tender *Kenneth Whiting* (AV–14); the escort carriers *Bougainville* (CVE–100) and *Admiralty Islands* (CVE–99); the refrigeration ship *Aldebaran* (AF–10); and the merchant freighter SS *Cape Pillar*. After delivering that convoy safety to Majuro in the Marshalls, *William C. Cole* escorted *Admiralty Islands* and *Bougainville* back to Pearl Harbor.

After a five-day availability, *William C. Cole* departed Pearl Harbor with the destroyer escorts *M. R. Nauman* (DE–416) and *Samuel B. Roberts* (DE–413) in the screen for a Marshalls-bound merchant convoy. *William C. Cole* was detached on 28 August and escorted the freighter SS *Cape Page* to Kwajalein before she headed for Hawaii on 1 September. Upon her arrival at Pearl Harbor, the destroyer escort commenced a week's availability.

William C. Cole departed the Hawaiian Islands on 15 September and subsequently convoyed the escort carrier *Copahee* (CVE–12) to Manus, in the Admiralty Islands. On 25 September, *William C. Cole* reported to Commander, South Pacific Forces, for duty.

Underway from Seeadler Harbor, Manus, on 1 October, *William C. Cole* and sistership *Gendreau* (DE–639) sailed for the Solomon Islands. From 4 to 11 October, *William C. Cole* trained out of Purvis Bay with the other ships of Escort Division (CortDiv) 73. One week later, on 18 October, the destroyer escort escorted SS *Cape Johnson* from Lunga Point, Guadalcanal, to Cape Torokina, Bougainville, before returning to Purvis Bay for upkeep and gunnery training that lasted for the remainder of October.

William C. Cole operated out of Purvis Bay into February 1945, performing local escort missions between Guadalcanal, Bougainville, and New Caledonia; ships escorted included SS *Sea Cat*, SS *Sea Snipe*, *General O. H. Ernst* (AP–133), *Wharton* (AP–7), *West Virginia* (BB–48), *General M. M. Patrick* (AP–150), *Windsor* (APA–55), *Ormsby* (APA–49), and *Crescent City* (APA–21).

After gunnery exercises from 3 to 23 February, *William C. Cole* reported by dispatch on the 23d to Commander, 5th Fleet. From 24 February through the first week in March, she performed screening duties off the transport staging area, Lunga Point, Guadalcanal, protecting the transports of Amphibious Squadron (PhibRon) 4 during landing exercises in the vicinity. While the transports of PhibRon 4 loaded at Lunga Point, *William C. Cole* screened them from 10 to 13 March. On the latter day, she received onward routing and proceeded for the Russell Islands.

On the 15th, the destroyer escort headed for Ulithi, in the Western Carolines, in company with *Lang* (DD–399), *Stack* (DD–406), and *Paul G. Baker* (DE–642), escorting various units of PhibRon 4. Detached on the 21st, *William C. Cole* joined *Paul G. Baker* to escort for the attack cargo ships, *Theenim* (AKA–63) and *Lacerta* (AKA–29), to the Marianas. After delivering their charges safely to Saipan, the two destroyer escorts proceeded immediately to Ulithi where they were replenished before sortieing with Carrier Division 22— less *Sangamon* (CVE–29) and *Santee* (CVE–27)—as part of the escort that included the destroyers *Massey* (DD–778), *Drexler* (DD–741), and *Metcalf* (DD–595). Relieved of escort and screening duties for the carriers on 31 March, *William C. Cole* subsequently joined other ships of CortDiv 73 escorting Transport Squadron 18 on its way to Okinawa.

The ships made their final approaches through the western islands off Okinawa and arrived off the beachhead by midday. Light enemy aircraft activity greeted the initial forces—activity that would, in time, become heavy and nearly ceaseless. Between 1 and 4 April, the ship went to general quarters numerous times during the many air raid alerts caused by enemy planes in the vicinity. *William C. Cole* assisted in downing two planes.

Retiring from Okinawa on 5 April as an escort for Transport Division (TransDiv) 42, *William C. Cole* headed for Saipan. Upon arrival, the ship received routing to Ulithi where she took on stores. Underway again on 13 April, *William C. Cole* sailed for Okinawa once more, this time in the screen for ships of TransDiv 56.

Detached from escort duties upon her arrival off the western invasion beaches on 17 April, *William C. Cole* soon commenced her activities as a vessel in the screen. She remained on screening stations until retiring on the 26th in company with *Bunch* (APD–79), *Mullaney* (DD–528), *Charles E. Lawrence* (APD–37), and *Richard W. Suesens* (DE–342), as escort for TransDiv 104. After reaching Ulithi on the 30th, *William C. Cole* underwent four days of availability.

Returning to active duty upon completion of repairs, the destroyer escort steamed on a picket station off the island of Yap before returning to the Western Carolines on 13 May. The following day, in company with *Chase* (APD–54) and as escort for the battleship *West Virginia* and the heavy cruiser *Tuscaloosa* (CA–37), *William C. Cole* got underway to return to Okinawa. Arriving there on the 17th, she reported for screening duties.

While on station, *William C. Cole* observed moderate enemy air action from 19 to 23 May; but, on the 24th, she came under attack herself. Between 1830 on the 24th and 0600 on the 25th, the ship destroyed two enemy aircraft. First, an "Oscar" attempted a suicide run while *Cole* was northeast of Ie Shima and crashed within a few feet of the destroyer escort's starboard beam. The plane passed so close to the ship that one of its wingtips bent a "spoon" of a tube of a torpedo mount which had been trained to starboard. The second plane, a "Tony," came in from the ship's starboard side and was taken under a heavy fire from the ship's 20-millimeter and 40-millimeter guns. This attacker overshot the ship and crashed some thousand yards beyond its target.

On the 30th, *William C. Cole* loaded ammunition at Kerama Retto to replenish her depleted magazines before weighing anchor on the next day to sail to Saipan with a convoy of merchantmen. On 2 June, *Ringness* (APD–100) and *William C. Cole* rendezvoused at sea with a Ulithi-bound convoy, and they arrived at their destination on the 6th having safely delivered their charges. Upon fueling, *William C. Cole* sailed for the Philippines, in company with the destroyer *Shields* (DD–586) and the destroyer escort *Davis* (DE–357), as escorts for a merchant, Leyte-bound convoy.

The convoy reached San Pedro Bay on the 10th, and *Cole* received repairs to the damage she had suffered on the 24th during the kamikaze attack off Okinawa. Subsequently sailing for Luzon in company with *Vammen* (DE–644), *William C. Cole* fueled upon arrival at Lingayen and soon thereafter headed for Okinawa convoying LST group 104. Arriving there on the 24th, the destroyer escort shifted to Kerama Retto the following day where she rendezvoused with *Curtiss* (AV–4), two ATA's (124 and 125), and *LCI–993* to join *Witter* (DE–636) and *Forrest* (DMS–24) in escorting those ships to Saipan, where they arrived on 30 June.

Assigned to a patrol area east of Saipan on 2 July, *William C. Cole* operated on that station until relieved on the 11th by *Fieberling* (DE–640). The destroyer escort remained at Saipan until 22 July, when she shifted to Guam. Once there, she performed patrol work out of Apra Harbor for a week before she returned to Saipan in company with *Austin* (DE–15). *William C. Cole* ended July escorting the attack transport *Logan* (APA–196) to the Marshalls.

After shepherding the attack transport safely to Eniwetok, *William C. Cole* proceeded independently to Saipan, arriving on 8 August. Following training exercises with submarines, antiaircraft firing practices, and a six-day availability, the destroyer escort patrolled off Tinian until relieved on 17 August, two days after Japan capitulated, bringing the long Pacific war to a close.

For *William C. Cole*, however, the end of the war did not mean the end to her activities. She escorted *PC–1587* to Iwo Jima and later operated off that island on air-sea rescue assignments for the remainder of August. *William C. Cole* then operated out of Iwo Jima on air-sea rescue assignments for the entire month of September and into October of 1945 before she returned to Saipan, her base for similar operations until she departed the western Pacific, bound for the west coast of the United States.

After a yard availability at the Puget Sound Navy Yard, Bremerton, Wash., *William C. Cole* returned—via Pearl Harbor and Guam—to the Far East in the spring of 1946 and operated out of Shanghai, Okinawa, and Tsingtao into the summer. She then returned—via Guam, Kwajalein, and Pearl Harbor—to San Diego on 28 July. Following still another tour of duty in the Far East under the aegis of Commander, Naval Forces, Far East from 10 March to 31 August 1947—at Sasebo, Pusan, Yokosuka, Wakayama, and Kagoshima—*William C. Cole* operated locally out of San Diego until she was decommissioned and placed in reserve on 13 March 1948. She was later inactivated on 28 April of that year.

William C. Cole remained in reserve until struck from the Navy list on 1 March 1972. She was then sold to Zidell Explorations, Inc., of Portland, Oreg., on 20 November 1972 and subsequently scrapped.

William C. Cole (DE–641) received one battle star for her participation in the capture and occupation of Okinawa.

William C. Lawe

William Clare Lawe—born on 26 January 1910 at Carson City, Mich.—enlisted in the Navy on 27 April 1928, at Detroit, and attained the rate of aviation metalsmith third class (AM3c). Lawe was assigned to a part of Torpedo Squadron (VT) 8 which received the new Grumman TBF–1 (Avenger) torpedo plane. This detachment from VT–8 temporarily left carrier *Hornet* (CV–8) to train in the TBF's. They eventually arrived at Luke Field, Hawaii, for final training prior to rejoining their squadron mates in *Hornet*.

As American cryptoanalysts found that the Japanese planned an assault on strategic Midway Atoll, preparations proceeded rapidly to prepare the island to repel the expected attack. Accordingly, AM3c Lawe volunteered to participate in a detachment flight to Midway as aircrew in one of the six planes commanded by Lt. Langdon K. Fieberling. Lawe rode as gunner in the Avenger flown by Ens. Charles E. Brannon, USNR.

After arriving at Midway on 1 June 1942, the six-plane detachment spent the next few days in readiness. On 4 June at 0600, Lt. Fieberling's six planes took off, bound for the Japanese fleet. Attacked by Japanese "Zero" fighters within six minutes of their departure, the TBF's evaded their pursuers and climbed to 4,000 feet. At 0700, the airmen sighted the Japanese fleet and applied full throttle as they dove to 150 feet.

The six TBF's roared astern of the Japanese carriers, but suddenly found themselves beset by swarms of "Zeroes". One pilot, his plane shot up badly in the early approach, dropped his torpedo at the nearest target of opportunity—a light cruiser—and then nursed his crippled plane back to Midway. But five other aircraft—including Ens. Brannon's with AM3c Lawe on board—were shot down miles from their objective.

For his part in this brave action, AM3c Lawe received a posthumous Distinguished Fying Cross.

William C. Lawe (DE–313)—an *Evarts*-class (GMT type) destroyer escort—was laid down on 22 January 1944 at Vallejo, Calif., by the Mare Island Navy Yard; but her construction was cancelled on 13 March 1944, and her incomplete hull was scrapped soon thereafter. The name was then assigned to DE–373.

William C. Lawe (DE–373)—a *John C. Butler*-class (WGT type) destroyer escort—was to be built at Orange, Tex., by the Consolidated Steel Co., but the contract for her construction was cancelled on 6 June 1944.

I

(DD–763: dp. 2,425; l. 390'6''; b. 40'10''; dr. 14'; s. 34.6 k.; cpl. 288; a. 6 5'', 12 40mm., 10 20mm., 5 21'' tt., 2 dcp., 6 dct.; cl. *Gearing*)

William C. Lawe (DD–763) was laid down on 12 March 1944 by the Bethlehem Steel Co., San Francisco, Calif.; launched in May 1945; sponsored by Mrs. Nancy Lee Lawe; and commissioned on 18 December 1946, Comdr. George R. Lee in command.

After commissioning, *William C. Lawe* requested an extended fitting-out period due to the failure of the starboard reduction gear. On 29 January 1947, the ship returned to the Bethlehem Steel Co. for repairs. *William C. Lawe* reported to San Diego for shakedown on 28 March 1947 and continued operations in the San Diego and San Francisco areas until 9 October when she set course for Pearl Harbor, Hawaii. The destroyer remained at Pearl Harbor for three months. She then departed on 16 January 1948, together with three other destroyers and aircraft carrier *Valley Forge* (CV–45), for an around-the-world cruise for training and goodwill purposes. The ship returned to San Diego on 12 June 1948 after a five-month cruise in which the ship had steamed over 46,000 miles.

For the next 18 months, *William C. Lawe* conducted local operations in the San Diego area with periods of upkeep and repair at San Francisco. In October 1949, the destroyer received word of assignment to the Atlantic Fleet and, on 5 October, proceeded to her new home port at Newport, R.I., via the Panama Canal. During the same month, she left Newport to join in Second Task Fleet cold weather operations in the Arctic region. *William C. Lawe* returned to Newport, R.I., on 21 November 1949 and remained at her new home port for the remainder of the year.

During January 1950, *William C. Lawe* operated with *Wright* (CVL–49) in antisubmarine exercises off Bermuda; and, during the following month, the destroyer took part in Exercise "Portrex" off Puerto Rico and Vieques Island in the Caribbean. This exercise was cut short when *William C. Lawe* received orders to proceed to Norfolk, Va., and escort President Truman, on board his yacht, *Williamsburg*, to Key West, Fla., arriving there on 16 March. The destroyer returned to Newport on 6 April and occupied the following weeks with local operations.

In May, the ship spent Armed Forces Day in Savannah, Georgia; and, in August, the destroyer went north to Rockland, Maine, to participate in the Maine Lobster Festival. For the remainder of the year, *William C. Lawe* operated out of Newport, R.I., with frequent runs to Norfolk, Va.

On 8 January 1951, *William C. Lawe* set sail for the Mediterranean and a 6th Fleet deployment. During the next several months, she visited ports in France, Italy, Greece, and Turkey. Upon her return to the United States on 16 May, the destroyer spent the summer months at the Boston Naval Shipyard undergoing overhaul, followed by refresher training at Guantanamo Bay, Cuba. Returning to Newport on 23 October, the ship remained in the local area for the Christmas holidays, then celebrated the New Year at Boston.

William C. Lawe conducted cold weather operations in the Atlantic during the early part of 1952. The exercises were interrupted by a visit to Halifax, Nova Scotia, on 6 February. In the spring, the destroyer spent several weeks in antisubmarine operations in the Caribbean; then, on 3 June, the ship departed Newport and, together with *Power* (DD–839), *William C. Lawe* escorted *Oriskany* (CVA–34) around Cape Horn to the Pacific and up the west coast of South America. Off Panama, the carrier proceeded alone, and the two destroyers transited the Panama Canal and returned to Newport on 22 July.

On 26 August 1952, *William C. Lawe* joined in the major NATO Exercise "Mainbrace" which was conducted off Norway and Denmark and took the ship to ports in Scotland, Germany, and England. Upon completion of "Mainbrace," the destroyer spent two weeks operating with units from the British Joint Antisubmarine School at Londonderry, Northern Ireland. She then returned to her home port on 3 November and remained in port until February 1953.

On 9 February 1953, *William C. Lawe*, along with five other destroyers and *Salerno Bay* (CVE–110), headed south for hunter-killer operations in the Caribbean. Continuous operations were interspersed with liberty visits at Trinidad, Puerto Rico, Virgin Islands, Barbados, and the Dominican Republic. Further antisubmarine exercises were conducted off the eastern seaboard throughout the spring of 1953, interrupted by an Armed Forces Day visit to Beaumont, Tex. In June, the ship commenced a three-month overhaul at the Boston Naval Shipyard, followed by refresher training at Guantanamo Bay, Cuba. *William C. Lawe* returned to Newport from the Caribbean in early December and spent the Christmas holidays in her home port.

January through March of 1954 were spent in hunter-killer operations with carrier *Mindoro* (CVE–120). Maneuvers extended south to the Caribbean and back to Newport, ending in late March. In May, the ship weighed anchor once again for the Mediterranean where, in addition to visiting ports in Italy, Spain, and France, she also conducted amphibious landing exercises with units of the Greek and Turkish armies. *William C. Lawe* took part in Exercise "Lantflex" in November, then spent the holiday season at Newport.

The destroyer began the year 1955 with another hunter-killer operation in the Caribbean, this time with carrier *Valley Forge* (CV–45). After visiting Puerto Rico and Jamaica, she returned to Newport, R.I., in early April. *William C. Lawe* conducted two midshipmen cruises and then proceeded to Boston in August for a routine shipyard overhaul. She returned to Newport, R.I., in November for local operations which lasted to the close of the year.

William C. Lawe rang in the new year, 1956, with refresher training at Guantanamo Bay, Cuba, then visited New Orleans, La., for the Mardi Gras celebration. March and April were spent in antiair warfare exercises off the east coast. The destroyer sailed for the Mediterranean on 1 May and spent a month in the eastern Mediterranean visiting ports in Greece, Lebanon, and Turkey. In mid-June, she headed west and made stops at Italy, France, Spain, Sardinia, and Gibraltar. *William C. Lawe* returned to Newport, R.I., on 25 August 1956 and conducted east coast operations until mid-December when she berthed at New London, Conn., for the holidays.

In January 1957, the destroyer returned to Newport for a tender availability; and, on the 28th of that month, *William C. Lawe* pulled up anchor and proceeded to the Mediterranean for a five-month tour of duty. She visited ports in Greece, Sicily, Italy, and France. The ship returned to her home port for May and June, then spent eight weeks on a midshipmen cruise. *William C. Lawe* spent the remainder of 1957 at the Boston Naval Shipyard undergoing overhaul.

During the first half of 1958, the destroyer completed refresher training at Guantanamo Bay, then joined in antisubmarine warfare exercises in the North Atlantic. In early July, a crisis in the Middle East sent *William C. Lawe* to rendezvous with the 2d Fleet. She travelled as far as the Azores before returning to the United States on 8 August. The remainder of the summer was spent preparing for a Mediterranean cruise. *William C. Lawe* got underway on 2 September for the western

William C. Lawe (DD–763) in a high-speed turn.

Mediterranean where she remained for the next several months. The crew enjoyed Christmas and New Year's celebrations on the French Riviera at Cannes, France.

Returning to the United States on 12 March 1959, the ship tied up alongside a destroyer tender for upkeep and repairs. In June, *William C. Lawe*'s home port was changed to Mayport, Fla., where the ship remained in local operations throughout the year.

The first quarter of 1960 was a busy period for the destroyer. *William C. Lawe* served as a rescue destroyer for aircraft carrier operations, a training ship for midshipmen on their annual summer cruise, a school ship for the Fleet Sonar School, and a search and rescue destroyer along the flight route of the President of the United States during his trip to the 1960 summit conference in Europe.

She returned to Mayport, Fla., in September and commenced preparations for a material inspection prior to Mark I FRAM (Fleet Rehabilitation And Modernization) overhaul. On 12 November, *William C. Lawe* departed Mayport for Charleston, S.C., to commence preparations for FRAM conversion. On 5 December

1960, *William C. Lawe* changed status to "In Commission In Reserve" and began FRAM overhaul.

Eleven months later, the destroyer resumed an "In Commission" status; and, on 11 November 1961, she departed Charleston for Mayport, Fla. On 4 December, she departed for Guantanamo Bay, followed by a rest period through the remainder of the year.

On 1 January 1962, the ship became a member of Destroyer Squadron 16, also homeported at Mayport, Fla. In early March, *William C. Lawe* deployed to the Mediterranean where she participated in numerous NATO and 6th Fleet operations. On 2 October 1962, the destroyer returned to Mayport for an anticipated "at home" period after almost seven months at sea. However, the Cuban missile crisis intervened; and, on 22 October, the ship headed for the Caribbean, returning to her home port on 6 December. Minor repairs were made in Rawls Bros. Shipyard, Jacksonville, Fla.

The destroyer completed sea trials during February 1963; and, for the next several months, *William C. Lawe* served as a school ship for the Fleet Sonar School and as a rescue destroyer along the flight route of the

President of the United States during his trip to the 1963 Pan-American conference in Puerto Rico. *William C. Lawe* then deployed to the Mediterranean on 11 August and returned to Mayport on 23 December 1963.

The new year, 1964, began with leave and upkeep. In late February, the destroyer departed for the Caribbean to participate in the annual Operation "Springboard." *William C. Lawe* then proceeded to Annapolis, Md., where she embarked midshipmen for a cruise to northern European ports. The ship returned to Mayport, Fla., on 25 July for a scheduled leave and upkeep period.

From 13 to 24 September, *William C. Lawe* joined the Royal Canadian Navy in a joint antisubmarine exercise, "Canus-Slamex." She then steamed for the month of October with her destroyer squadron as a member of the "Gold Group" in accordance with the new "Blue and Gold" concept for operational readiness. The destroyer returned to Mayport, Fla., in November for inspection and upkeep. On 1 December, *William C. Lawe* moored at Charleston, S.C., for a regular three-month overhaul.

The yard period was completed on 1 April 1965, and the ship commenced refresher training on 25 April at Guantanamo Bay, Cuba. The crisis in the Dominican Republic interrupted this training; and, from 28 April to 8 May, the destroyer supported United States operations in that area.

William C. Lawe returned to Mayport on 25 June. The month of July was spent in upkeep; and, after "Blue-Gold" operations, the ship once again got underway on 26 August for the Dominican Republic where she served as flagship for Task Force (TF) 124. The destroyer departed for Mayport on 17 September and underwent a two-week tender availability before sailing for the Mediterranean on 14 October. The end of November found *William C. Lawe* in the Middle East, and she spent the Christmas holidays at Mombasa, Kenya. She departed Kenya on 29 December for Djibouti, French Somaliland, and celebrated the arrival of the new year, 1966, at sea in the Indian Ocean.

William C. Lawe operated in the Middle East until 29 January 1966 when she rejoined the 6th Fleet. The ship arrived at Mayport, Fla., on 9 March and commenced leave and upkeep. May and June were spent in support of Gemini IX and X. For the next several months, the destroyer served as a school ship for the Fleet Sonar School at Key West, Fla.; joined in "Demolex 1–66" off the coast of North Carolina; and conducted type training exercises. *William C. Lawe* returned to Mayport on 19 November and remained in port for the remainder of the year.

The ship's first 1967 underway period was a three-week "Springboard" operation in the Caribbean during February. Operations with the Bureau of Commercial Fisheries in the Virginia capes area followed. On 1 May, *William C. Lawe* deployed to the Mediterranean. While conducting routine exercises at Villefranche, she received a 24-hour notice to speed to the eastern Mediterranean upon the outbreak of the Arab-Israeli War. She remained in the area for three weeks.

The destroyer remained in the Mediterranean and continued operations until 31 August when she departed for her home port. Upon returning to Mayport, the ship spent the remainder of 1967 serving as a sonar school ship at Key West and undergoing various inspections at her home port.

January, February, and March of 1968 saw *William C. Lawe* conducting exercises in the Caribbean with in-port periods at Mayport. Returning to her home port on 28 March, the ship prepared for an upcoming overhaul. After antisubmarine exercises and a two-week trip to Guantanamo Bay, Cuba, during May, *William C. Lawe* got underway for Charleston, S.C., and overhaul.

After a successful sea trial in October, the destroyer returned to Mayport, Fla., on 5 November. At this time, *William C. Lawe* was placed in "Reduced Operational Status," and she spent the remainder of 1968 in Mayport, Fla.

The ship continued in reduced operational status for the first five months of 1969. On 7 July, *William C. Lawe* left Mayport en route to Newport, R.I., for repairs. She returned to Mayport on 19 July and began preparations for refresher training and inspections in the Caribbean which were completed in early October.

From 7 October to 10 November 1969, the destroyer prepared for deployment to the Middle East. After a refueling stop in Puerto Rico, the ship arrived at Dakar, Senegal, on 22 November. She transited the Cape of Good Hope and arrived at Lourenco Marques, Mozambique, on 11 December. The ship spent Christmas at Mombasa, Kenya, and arrived at Massawa, Ethiopia, on New Year's Day.

William C. Lawe continued her Middle East deployment until 16 May 1970 when she returned to Mayport, Fla. After a month of leave and upkeep, the destroyer travelled to Panama City, Fla., to test stockpiled ASROC's (antisubmarine rockets). This was followed by a midshipman cruise and a tender availability until 26 July. The ship conducted antisubmarine exercises and type training in the Virginia Capes area throughout August. From 3 to 25 September, *William C. Lawe* took part in the surveillance of a Soviet task group in the Caribbean. She returned to Mayport on 26 September and, except for a brief period of planeguard duty with *Franklin D. Roosevelt* (CVA-42), the destroyer remained in her home port for the remainder of the year.

William C. Lawe began the year 1971 with duty as a support ship for *Von Steuben*'s (SSBN-632) Poseidon firing at Cape Kennedy. Two weeks of "Springboard" operations in the Caribbean followed, and the destroyer returned to Mayport on 25 February for tender availability and restricted availability at the Jacksonville Shipyard.

On 21 April 1971, the destroyer deployed to the Middle East. During the five-month deployment, the ship visited ports in Porto Grande, Cape Verde Islands; Massawa, Ethiopia; Djibouti, French Territory of Afars and Issas; Karachi, Pakistan; Cochin, India; Recife, Brazil; and Port of Spain, Trinidad. *William C. Lawe* returned to Mayport, Fla., on 20 September. The remaining days of September and most of October were spent in leave and upkeep status.

On 8 November 1971, *William C. Lawe* put to sea as a member of Destroyer Squadron (DesRon) 16, conducting surveillance of four units of the Soviet Navy which were visiting Cuba. The destroyer returned to her home port on 30 November and prepared for an upcoming restricted availability at the Jacksonville Shipyard. On 13 December, the ship began a tender availability with *Yosemite* (AD-19) which took her through the end of the year.

The new year, 1972, ushered in *William C. Lawe*'s first yard availability of major proportions since 1968; she was assigned restricted overhaul at the Jacksonville Shipyards, Jacksonville, Fla. Upon successful completion of dock trials in late March and refresher training at Guantanamo Bay, Cuba, the destroyer performed a surveillance mission in the Caribbean until early June. The ship spent the remainder of the summer in upkeep; involvement in Operation "Pinklace," a NATO exercise; and a destroyer development group antisubmarine exercise.

In early October, *William C. Lawe* received word of an upcoming Southeast Asian deployment. After a month of preparation, the ship set sail for Pacific waters. On 10 December, *William C. Lawe* experienced her first combat action in 27 years of service during a daring night raid on North Vietnamese coastal defense sites in which she received hostile return fire. The remainder of 1972 was spent as a gunfire support unit off the coast of South Vietnam.

William C. Lawe rang in 1973 with continued gunline duty off Vietnam. After an upkeep period at Subic

Bay, Philippines, from 14 to 25 January, the ship returned to gunfire support duty until a general cease fire went into effect throughout Vietnam on 28 January 1973. The destroyer continued operations in the area as a planeguard for *Enterprise* (CVA-65) and *Coral Sea* (CVA-43). She also conducted activities in support of American prisoners-of-war releases, troop withdrawals, and 7th Fleet operations. *William C. Lawe* left the Gulf of Tonkin on 14 May.

The destroyer arrived at Pearl Harbor, Hawaii, on 28 May, then proceeded to San Diego before transiting the Panama Canal. She arrived at Mayport, Fla., on 14 June and, on 20 August, shifted home port to New Orleans, La. For the remainder of 1973, *William C. Lawe* participated in various training periods at sea as well as hosting over 1,000 visitors in her new home port.

The ship continued training operations during the early months of 1974. On 23 March, *William C. Lawe* departed for Charleston, S.C., and a tender availability which lasted until 10 May. For the next several months, the destroyer operated in her home port area with exercises held at Port Everglades, Fla., and the Charleston-Jacksonville operations areas. On 15 August 1974, *William C. Lawe* commenced regular overhaul at Todd and Avondale Shipyards, New Orleans, La.

William C. Lawe completed sea trials on 15 April 1975 and departed from Charleston, S.C., on 14 May. She conducted various drills and exercises in and out of port. On 16 June, the destroyer sailed for Freeport, Bahamas, for a two-week active duty training cruise with reservists embarked. A restricted availability at Charleston, S.C., followed, and the destroyer returned to New Orleans on 17 August to prepare for an arduous Caribbean deployment.

On 29 August, the ship got underway for Roosevelt Roads, Puerto Rico, the first stop in a series of weapons and gunfire tests. Refresher training was held at Guantanamo Bay, Cuba, prior to returning to New Orleans on 7 October 1975. During a tender availability in Pensacola, Fla., in November, *William C. Lawe* had pictures of the ship and crew taken by many Navy photographers for use in recruiting posters and advertisements. Returning to New Orleans just prior to Thanksgiving, *William C. Lawe* moved to the Avondale Shipyard, Avondale, La., for restricted availability which took her through the remainder of the year.

The destroyer departed for Charleston, S.C., on 21 February 1976 where she conducted gunnery exercises in the Jacksonville operating area. The ship got underway on 3 March for Nassau, Bahamas, and a Bicentennial port visit, returning to New Orleans on 17 March. Two months later, the destroyer returned to Mayport, Fla., for four weeks of tender availability prior to a Caribbean deployment.

On 12 June 1976, *William C. Lawe* got underway for Roosevelt Roads, Puerto Rico, and, after routine exercises, returned to New Orleans, La., on 30 June via Mayport, Fla. The remainder of 1976 was spent conducting local operations and undergoing routine leave and upkeep. Highlights of the year included operations with FS *Jean D'Arc* and FS *Forbin* of the French Navy and Bicentennial port visits to Corpus Christi and Brownsville, Tex.

January and February 1977 were spent in New Orleans preparing for upcoming fleet exercises. *William C. Lawe* joined in Operation "Cleansweep" on 10 March, followed by a visit to Nassau, Bahamas, and tender availability at Pensacola, Fla. The ship departed on 8 May and returned to New Orleans after a brief visit to Gulfport, Miss.

On 17 June, the destroyer set course for Charleston, S.C., where she underwent restricted availability until 21 September when she departed for her home port. Except for a three-day operation with a French destroyer and a French frigate in the Gulf of Mexico, *William C. Lawe* occupied the month of October with preparation for the second major fleet exercise of the year. "Comptuex 1–78" was held in the Caribbean from

3 to 12 November, followed by a port visit at Nassau, Bahamas. Departing the Bahamas on 19 November, *William C. Lawe* stopped briefly at Port Everglades, Fla., before returning to New Orleans on 21 November for the holiday season.

The destroyer arrived at Mayport, Fla., on 17 January 1978 for intermediate maintenance availability. The ship returned to New Orleans on 27 March and spent from March through June in restricted availability.

On 21 June, the destroyer, in company with *Davis* (DD–937) and *Robert A. Owens* (DD–827), departed her home port; and, after off-loading ammunition at the Naval Weapons Station, Charleston, S.C., she set sail for a cruise of the Great Lakes. During this cruise, over 190,000 visitors toured the three destroyers in both United States and Canadian cities. Port visits included Ogdensburg, Oswego, and Buffalo, New York; Erie, Pa.; Toledo and Ashtabula, Ohio; Detroit, Mich.; Montreal, Quebec, Toronto, and Halifax, Canada. *William C. Lawe* returned to New Orleans on 27 September.

On 21 October 1978, the destroyer set her course for Mayport, Fla., for a month-long intermediate maintenance availability, then sailed to the Caribbean for gunnery exercises. *William C. Lawe* returned to New Orleans on 12 December and began preparations for the upcoming Christmas leave period.

A recommendation to strike *William C. Lawe* from the Navy list was rescinded on 27 July 1979, and the destroyer was retained for additional active service.

William C. Lawe received two battle stars for her Vietnam service.

William C. Miller

William Cicero Miller—born on 18 July 1919 in Thomasville, N.C.—enlisted in the Navy as an apprentice seaman at Raleigh, N.C., on 20 October 1937. After instruction at the Naval Training Station, Norfolk, Va., Miller was advanced to the rate of seaman 2d class on 21 February 1938 and joined Scouting Squadron (VS) 6, attached to the aircraft carrier *Enterprise* (CV–6), on 30 September of that year.

Miller remained with VS–6 into 1941 and became the rear-seat man for Lt. Clarence E. Dickinson, Jr., around April of that year. In the ensuing months the two became an efficient pilot/radioman team; and, on the morning of 7 December 1941, they both boarded their aircraft—a Douglas SBD–3 Dauntless—for what was to be a routine scouting flight. They were under orders to proceed to Ford Island and land there to refuel. Their ship, *Enterprise*, together with the rest of Task Force 8, would return later that day.

Dickinson and Miller arrived over Oahu to discover the Japanese attack on Pearl Harbor underway. After one of the section had been shot down by a Japanese fighter, the commander of VS–6, Lt. Comdr. Halstead Hopping, broadcast the word that Pearl Harbor was being attacked. Miller and the other rear-seat men immediately unlimbered their .30-caliber machine guns.

Attacking "Zero" fighters riddled Dickinson's plane, but Miller—already wounded once—downed one and ultimately exhausted his ammunition in the defense of the aircraft until she had been set afire. Dickinson called for Miller to bail out but received no answer. The pilot managed to get out of the falling plane; but Miller—either dead or so severely wounded that he was unable to free himself from the aircraft—remained with it until it crashed into a cane field. For his devotion to duty, despite his wounds, Miller was awarded a posthumonus commendation by the Commander in Chief of the Pacific Fleet.

(DE–259: dp. 1,140; l. 289'5''; b. 35'1''; dr. 8'3'' (mean); s. 21.0 k.; cpl. 156; a. 3 3'', 4 1.1'', 9 20mm., 2 dct., 8 dcp., 1 dcp. (hh.); cl. *Evarts*)

William C. Miller (DE–259) was laid down on 10

January 1943 at Boston, Mass., by the Boston Navy Yard; launched on 22 February 1943; sponsored by Mrs. Melvin B. Miller, the mother of the late Radioman 3d Class Miller; and commissioned on 2 July 1943, Lt. Comdr. Frederick C. Storey, USNR, in command.

William C. Miller got underway on 19 July, bound for Bermuda. There, she conducted her shakedown before returning to Boston for post-shakedown availability and remained in the navy yard until 27 August, when she sailed for Panama. After transiting the Panama Canal between 1 and 3 September, the destroyer escort arrived at San Diego on the 12th and shifted to San Francisco on the 15th, before sailing for Hawaii nine days later in the screen for Convoy 4796. She returned to the west coast early in the fall but departed San Francisco on 19 October, bound for the Gilbert Islands and Operation "Galvanic."

As a unit of Task Group (TG) 54.9, 5th Fleet, *William C. Miller* screened the ships of the Tarawa garrison group and patrolled in area "Longsuit" off the invasion beaches into early December. She then guarded the entrance to the lagoon at Tarawa through the middle of the month before departing the Gilberts on Christmas Eve, bound for the Hawaiian Islands.

Reaching Pearl Harbor on 30 December 1943, *William C. Miller* underwent upkeep alongside the destroyer tender *Black Hawk* (AD–9) and remained in Hawaiian waters into February 1944. That year was to prove a busy one for the destroyer escort. She earned the other six of her seven battle stars in the next year and one-half operating on screening, escorting, and hunter-killer duties with convoys for the remainder of 1944. During that period, *William C. Miller* supported the occupation of Kwajalein and Majuro from 29 January to 8 February 1944; the capture of Eniwetok from 17 February to 2 March; the capture and occupation of Saipan from 26 June to 10 August; and the capture and occupation of Tinian from 24 July to 10 August. It was during the Saipan screening operations, however, that the ship avenged the loss of her namesake.

At 2120 on the evening of 13 July, a patrol plane sighted a Japanese submarine submerging some 78 miles from Rorogattan Point, Saipan, and reported the enemy's position. Accordingly, *William C. Miller* and the other members of a hunter-killer group—*Gilmer* (APD–11) carrying the officer in tactical command (OTC)—altered course and departed the screen for the transport area to track the submersible. At 0022 on the following day, the destroyer escort and her sisters arrived on the scene and commenced searching.

Seven hours later, *William C. Miller* obtained sound contact at a range of 1,700 yards. The destroyer escort approached at 15 knots and dropped a 13-charge pattern at 0726. Opening the range after observing no damage, the escort vessel attacked for the second time, dropping a second pattern at 0752, once again, of 13 charges.

That pattern appears to have proved devastating to Japanese submarine *I–6*. At 0804, *William C. Miller* noted pieces of wood popping to the surface about 500 yards ahead, one point on the starboard bow. One minute later, a "heavy and prolonged underwater explosion"—estimated to be about three times the shock of a depth charge explosion—shook the ship.

Shortly thereafter, observers in *William C. Miller* noted a large "boil" in the water some 50 yards in diameter. At 0806, the destroyer escort laid a third 13-charge pattern that apparently landed atop the submarine, completing whatever devastation had been wreaked by the second salvo. *William C. Miller* closed the oil slick and debris and lowered a boat to investigate. The ship soon recovered small pieces of cork insulating material; fractured wooden decking; and a fur-lined, Japanese seaman's cap. The depth charge barrage had literally torn the submarine apart. A postwar accounting credited *William C. Miller* with the destruction of *I–6*.

After the completion of the Tinian campaign, *William C. Miller* departed that island on 21 August in company with *Indianapolis* (CA–35). The destroyer escort paused briefly at Eniwetok, in the Marshalls, on the 24th before she pushed on for the Hawaiian Islands, arriving at Pearl Harbor on 2 September. *William C. Miller* returned to Eniwetok at the end of October and then shifted to Ulithi, in the Carolines, where she picked up Ulithi-to-Eniwetok Convoy Number 19 on 5 November. After bringing that convoy safely into port five days later, *William C. Miller* departed the Marshall Islands on 13 November with Eniwetok-to-Pearl Harbor Convoy Number 21. Making port at Pearl Harbor on 24 November, the destroyer escort underwent ordnance repairs at the Pearl Harbor Navy Yard into the following year.

William C. Miller sortied from Pearl Harbor on 6 February 1945, as part of Task Unit (TU) 51.6.2 to participate in the assault and occupation of Iwo Jima between 23 February and 16 March. She returned to Pearl Harbor in early April, via Guam and Eniwetok. The destroyer escort subsequently steamed back to the west coast and remained there, first at San Francisco and then at San Diego, until 13 June when she sailed for the Hawaiian Islands in company with *Cabana* (DE–260).

After arriving at Pearl Harbor on 19 June, *William C. Miller* escorted a convoy to Eniwetok which she reached on 6 July. She soon put to sea to operate in the screen of 3d Fleet units in their operations against the Japanese home islands. She performed those duties into mid-August when hostilities with Japan ceased.

William C. Miller arrived at Ulithi on 19 August but soon sailed for Tokyo Bay as part of the initial occupation forces. She arrived at Tokyo Bay on 26 August and was there at the time of the formal Japanese surrender on 2 September.

Later that month, the destroyer escort headed home —via Ulithi, Eniwetok, and Pearl Harbor—and reached San Francisco on 17 October. *William C. Miller* was decommissioned at the Mare Island Naval Shipyard on 21 December and stripped of all usable equipment. On 8 January 1946, *William C. Miller* was struck from the Navy list. Sold to Mr. Fred Perry of New York City on 10 April 1947, her hulk was subsequently scrapped on 19 November 1947.

William C. Miller received seven battle stars for her World War II service.

William Caldwell

(Tr: t. 290; l. 125'; b. 23'6''; dph. 12'7''; dr. 11'6'' (max.); s. 10.5 k.; cpl. 19; a. small arms; cl. "Castle")

William Caldwell—a steel-hulled, coal-burning, screw steam trawler built for the British Admiralty in 1918 at Beverly, England, by Cook, Welton, and Gemmell, Ltd.—was leased to the United States Navy in the spring of 1919 for service with the North Sea Minesweeping Detachment which was established to clear the North Sea Mine Barrage that had been laid during World War I. She was commissioned at Grimsby, England, on 28 May 1919, Ens. Charles A. Ryan, USNRF, in command.

After arriving at Kirkwall, Scotland, the base of the detachment, on 1 June, *William Caldwell* got underway for the minefields on the 10th. She delivered "plunger kites" and sweep wire to the minesweepers engaged in the clearance work, followed them as they cut loose mines from their moorings, and sank the drifting mines with rifle fire. *William Caldwell* returned to Kirkwall on 14 June but later shifted to the port of Thurso to load supplies. Returning to her home base on the 29th to discharge her cargo, the trawler moved to Base 18, Inverness, Scotland, at the end of the following month and remained there from 30 July to 1 August.

She next returned to Kirkwall, tended the minesweepers based there, and performed local towing duties before she towed a barge from Kirkwall to the Shetlands. Upon her arrival at Lerwick, she delivered supplies to the tender *Panther*. Standing out of Lerwick on 16 August, *William Caldwell* ran aground on a reef near North Ronaldsay Firth, Orkney Islands, and suffered slight hull damage. Refloated at 0130 on the 17th with the use of her anchors and sweep wire to "kedge" the ship off the reefs at high tide, the trawler put into Rosyth on the 22d. There, she underwent hull repairs before she returned to Kirkwall on the 27th. *William Caldwell* subsequently performed additional local towing and barge-handling duties and delivered supplies during some of the final mine clearance operations in mid-to-late September.

Departing Kirkwall on 28 September, *William Caldwell* touched at Granton, Scotland, and Harwich, England, before arriving at Brightlingsea, England, on 3 October, in company with the converted yacht *Yankton* and the trawler *Thomas Laundry*. *William Caldwell* was decommissioned on 6 October 1919 and returned to the British Admiralty.

William Darnold

(Tr: t. 290; l. 125'5''; b. 23'5''; dph. 12'7''; s. 10 k.; cpl. 16; a. rifles; cl. "Castle")

William Darnold—a steel-hulled, screw steam trawler built in 1918 at Beverley, England, by Cook, Welton, and Gemmell, Ltd., for the British Admiralty—was leased by the United States Navy in the spring of 1919 for service sweeping the North Sea Mine Barrage and was commissioned on 30 May 1919 at Grimsby, England, Lt. Edmond Delany in command.

William Darnold—assigned to the 2d Trawler Division, Minesweeping Detachment, North Atlantic Fleet—got underway on 31 May for the Orkney Islands, in company with four other trawlers. She arrived at Kirkwall, Scotland—the base of the Minesweeping Detachment—on 2 June. She remained there until 16 June, when she shifted briefly to Ottswick. While returning to Kirkwall two days later, *William Darnold* came across a drifting mine and destroyed it with small arms fire.

After spending a week in local operations out of Kirkwall, streaming sweep wire daily to give her winchman experience in operating the ship's winch, *William Darnold* sailed for the minefields on 7 July to participate in the fourth minesweeping operation undertaken by the Minesweeping Detachment. The tactics employed in the operation involved two-ship sweeps in which a wire was streamed between two minecraft to catch a mine and detonate it or cut it adrift so that it could be exploded with rifle fire. Often, the gear—whether it was a "kite," or "otter," or the wire itself—would become damaged. Repair or replacement of the damaged gear had to be effected to enable the operations to resume.

Operating together on 9 July, *William Darnold* and *John Graham* exploded 22 mines and cut adrift 15 more which were sunk or detonated by gunfire during the day's operations. At 1530, a jarring blast shook *William Darnold*, when a mine—set off by the explosions of four others which she had exploded at that time—exploded beneath the ship's port side, damaging her hull and machinery and causing her to be towed to the anchorage for the night.

During the evening hours, *William Darnold*'s crew effected the necessary repairs, enabling the ship to resume operations the next morning, 10 July. Over the next two days, the trawler worked in the minefield, conducting her sweep operations. On 12 July, the trawler *Richard Bulkeley* accidentally exploded a mine close aboard; the ship sank in four minutes, taking seven men—including Comdr. Frank L. King, the commander of the trawler division—down with her.

William Darnold cut her own wire and proceeded to the scene of the disaster, lowering a boat and searching for survivors. Eventually, *Richard Bulkeley*'s survivors were picked up by other vessels in the vicinity.

Returning to Kirkwall on 13 July, *William Darnold* moored alongside *Prometheus* (Repair Ship No. 3) for "urgent repairs." The trawler then spent the next three weeks awaiting further orders before getting underway for Brightlingsea, England, on 5 August. Touching at Inverness, Scotland, en route, *William Darnold* slightly damaged the entrance lock to the Caledonian Canal during the transit of 5 August.

Making port at Brightlingsea on 10 August, the trawler moored near *Chattanooga* (Cruiser No. 16) to transfer commissary supplies before receiving an inspection from British naval authorities. The following day, on 11 August 1919, *William Darnold* was decommissioned and returned to the British Admiralty.

William Ditter, see J. William Ditter.

William D. Porter

William David Porter—born on 10 March 1808 in New Orleans, La.—spent much of his childhood in Chester, Pa. After an early and unsuccessful attempt to stow away on his uncle's, John Porter's, ship, ship-of-the-line *Franklin*, he signed on *Franklin* at the age of 12. Porter was appointed a midshipman on 1 January 1823 and 11 years later was commissioned a lieutenant. From 1838 to 1840, he served as lighthouse inspector for the portion of the east coast between Norfolk and New York. That duty was followed in 1840 with an assignment at the Washington Navy Yard as ordnance officer. During this assignment, he became interested in the development of an explosive shell suitable for naval use. After leaving Washington, Porter spent the next decade superintending the outfitting of new steam ships for the Navy, commanding supply vessels, and delivering mail and supplies to Navy units abroad.

Following retirement between 1855 and 1859, he was returned to active duty and took command of *St. Mary's*. In that sloop-of-war, he patrolled the Pacific coasts of Mexico and Central America for two years protecting American interests in that area.

The secession of Southern states in 1860 and 1861 caused *St. Mary's* to be recalled to her base at Mare Island, Calif. In the summer of 1861, Porter was relieved of command of the ship and ordered to Washington. In the autumn, he was assigned to special duty in St. Louis, Mo., to assist in establishing the Western Flotilla to seize and control the Mississippi and its tributaries for the Union. On 3 October, he was given the command of a ferryboat-turned-gunboat, *New Era*. Serving under Flag Officer Andrew Foote, he patrolled the Cumberland River, keeping a wary eye upon the growing Confederate defenses along the river. In November, he took his ship to St. Louis for repairs; and, upon his return to the flotilla at Cairo, *New Era* sported a new name, *Essex*, in honor of his father's ship during the War of 1812.

Between January and August 1862, Porter served gallantly up and down the Mississippi. On 10 January, *Essex* and *St. Louis* engaged three Confederate gunboats and forced them to retreat to the protection of Southern shore batteries. The two Union gunboats repeated the feat three days later and succeeded in damaging their opponents. Only Confederate shore batteries prevented the capture of the three steamers.

On 6 February, *Essex* joined the rest of Foote's gunboat squadron in the attack on Fort Henry. Porter's ship, second in line, sustained heavy fire from shore batteries and received at least 15 direct hits. About half an hour into the fray, *Essex* took a 32-pound shot through her bow shield. It pierced her boilers, releasing steam which severely scalded 28 men. Comdr. Porter—himself blinded and scalded—continued to conn his ship until she was clear of the action.

337

Though still severely hampered by his injuries, Porter directed the extensive repair and renovation of *Essex* from his sick bed. At the same time, he also superintended the construction of two other warships, the ironclads *Lafayette* and *Choctaw*.

Porter completed the renovation of *Essex* at St. Louis in July and rejoined the Western Flotilla at Vicksburg later that month. At dawn on the 22d, Porter took *Essex* out to confront the Confederate ironclad ram *Arkansas* which had recently left her refuge in the Yazoo River to seek greater safety under the cover of Vicksburg's shore batteries. In company with the smaller converted riverboat *Queen of the West*, *Essex* moved in toward the Southern warship. During the approach of the two Union ships, Confederate shore batteries subjected them to a withering fire. Finally, *Essex* struck *Arkansas* a jarring blow but at an oblique angle. As a result, she glanced off the Southern ram and ran aground parallel to her adversary. Porter worked furiously to free his ship and, after much difficulty, managed to retire, with *Queen of the West* close behind.

Thereafter, since *Essex* had sustained only minor damage, Porter kept her on station patrolling the lower Mississippi River between Vicksburg and Baton Rouge. On 5 August, his ship and *Sumter* assisted Union Army troops in repelling a Confederate land attack on Baton Rouge. The following morning, he headed north to Vicksburg to confront *Arkansas* once more. He found his quarry on a bend in the river, close to the shore. In the ensuing bombardment, Porter used an incendiary shell which he himself had invented. After about 20 minutes of shelling, *Arkansas* erupted into flames and soon blew up. Evidence suggests that the Confederate crew had set their own ship afire to prevent her capture. Be that as it may, Porter's bold action played no small part in the ram's destruction. Moreover, Congress recognized the role played by Porter and his ship in June 1864 when they belatedly awarded the *Essex* crew $25,000 in prize money.

Porter's last real action in the war occurred in September 1862 when *Essex* conducted a bombardment of Natchez, Miss., and duelled the shore batteries at Port Hudson. Later that month, he returned to New Orleans where new orders awaited him. Promoted to the rank of commodore, Porter was assigned to duty at New York. There, he served in various capacities until hospitalized in April 1864. On 1 May 1864, Commodore Porter died of heart disease at St. Luke's Hospital in New York City. Although he was buried initially at Greenwood Cemetery in New York, he was moved to Philadelphia in June and laid to rest beside his famous father, Commodore David Porter.

(DD–579: dp. 2,050; l. 376′6″; b. 39′4″; dr. 17′9″; s. 35.5 k.; cpl. 273; a. 5 5″, 4 40mm., 4 20mm., 10 21″ tt., 2 dct., 6 dcp.; cl. *Fletcher*)

William D. Porter (DD–579) was laid down on 7 May 1942 at Orange, Tex., by the Consolidated Steel Corp.; launched on 27 September 1942; sponsored by Miss Mary Elizabeth Reeder; and commissioned on 6 July 1943, Lt. Comdr. Wilfred A. Walter in command.

William D. Porter departed Orange shortly after being commissioned. After stops at Galveston, Tex., and Algiers, La., the destroyer headed for Guantanamo Bay, Cuba, on 30 July for shakedown. She completed shakedown a month later and, following a brief stop at Bermuda, continued on to Charleston, S.C., where she arrived on 7 September. *William D. Porter* completed post-shakedown repairs at Charleston and got underway for Norfolk, Va., at the end of the month. For about five weeks, the warship operated from Norfolk conducting battle practice with *Intrepid* (CV–11) and other ships of the Atlantic Fleet.

On 12 November, she departed Norfolk and the following day rendezvoused with *Iowa* (BB–61). That battleship was on her way to North Africa carrying President Franklin D. Roosevelt to the Cairo and Teheran Conferences. During battle drills on the afternoon of the 14th, *William D. Porter* inadvertently fired a live torpedo at *Iowa*. However, the destroyer signalled *Iowa* in plenty of time to allow the battleship to turn hard to starboard, parallel to the torpedo's wake. The torpedo exploded some 3,000 yards astern of the mighty man-of-war. *William D. Porter* completed her part in the mission and steamed west to Bermuda, where she arrived on 16 November.

A week later, she returned to Norfolk and prepared for transfer to the Pacific. She got underway for that duty on 4 December, steamed via Trinidad, and reached the Panama Canal on the 12th. After transiting the canal, the destroyer set a course for San Diego, where she stopped between 19 and 21 December to take on cold weather clothing and other supplies necessary for duty in the Aleutian Islands.

On 29 December, *William D. Porter* arrived in Dutch Harbor, on the island of Unalaska, and joined TF 94. Between 2 and 4 January 1944, she voyaged from Dutch Harbor to Adak, whence she conducted training operations until her departure for Hawaii on the 7th. The warship entered Pearl Harbor on 22 January and remained there until 1 February at which time the destroyer put to sea again to escort *Black Hawk* (AD–9) to Adak. The two ships arrived at their destination nine days later, and *William D. Porter* began four months of relatively uneventful duty with TF 94. She sailed between the various islands in the Aleutians chain, serving primarily as an antisubmarine escort.

On 10 June, the destroyer stood out of Attu and headed for the Kuril Islands. She and the other ships of TF 94 reached their destination early on the morning of the 13th. They started to shell their target, the island of Matsuwa, at 0513. After 20 minutes, *William D. Porter*'s radar picked up an unidentified surface vessel, closing her port quarter at a speed in excess of 55 knots. Her radar personnel tentatively identified the craft as an enemy PT-type boat, and the warship ceased fire on Matsuwa to take the new target under fire. Soon thereafter, the craft's reflection disappeared from the radar screen, presumably the victim of TF 94's gunfire. Not long afterward, the task force completed its mission and retired from the Kurils to refuel at Attu.

On 24 June, the destroyer left Attu with TF 94 for her second mission in the Kurils. Following two days at sea in steadily increasing fog, she arrived off Paramushiro on the 26th. In a dense fog with visibility down to about 200 yards, she delivered her gunfire and then departed with TF 94 to return to the Aleutians. A month of training exercises intervened between her second and third voyages to the Kurils. On 1 August, she cleared Kuluk Bay for her final bombardment of the Kurils. On the second day out, an enemy twin-engine bomber snooped the task force and received a hail of fire from some of the screening destroyers. That proved to be the only noteworthy event of the mission, because the following day the bombardment was cancelled due to poor weather and the enemy reconnaissance plane. *William D. Porter* dropped anchor in Massacre Bay at Attu on 4 August.

After a month of antisubmarine patrol, the warship departed the Aleutians for a brief yard period at San Francisco preparatory to reassignment to the western Pacific. She completed repairs and stood out of San Francisco on 27 September. She reached Oahu on 2 October and spent the ensuing fortnight in training operations out of Pearl Harbor. On the 18th, she resumed her voyage west; and, 12 days later, the warship pulled into Seeadler Harbor at Manus in the Admiralty Islands. She departed Manus early in November to escort *Alshain* (AK–55) via Hollandia to Leyte.

Though *William D. Porter* arrived in the western Pacific too late to participate in the actual invasion at Leyte, combat conditions persisted there after her arrival in San Pedro Bay. Soon after she anchored there, Japanese planes swooped in to attack the ships in the anchorage. The first plane fell to the guns of a nearby destroyer before reaching *William D. Porter*'s effective range. A second intruder appeared, however, and the destroyer's 5-inch guns joined those of the assembled transports in bringing him to a fiery end in mid-air.

For the remainder of the year, *William D. Porter* escorted ships between Leyte, Hollandia, Manus, Bougainville, and Mindoro. On 21 December, while steaming from Leyte to Mindoro, she encountered enemy air power once again. Two planes made steep glides and dropped several bombs near the convoy. The destroyer opened up with her main battery almost as soon as the enemies appeared but to no avail. Their bombs missed their targets by a wide margin, but the two Japanese aircraft apparently suffered no damage and made good their escape. Not long thereafter, four more airborne intruders attacked. *William D. Porter* concentrated her fire on the two nearest her, one of which fell to her antiaircraft fire. The second succumbed to the combined efforts of other nearby destroyers, and the remaining two presumably retired to safety. From then until midnight, enemy aircraft shadowed the convoy, but none displayed temerity enough to attack. Before dawn the following morning, she encountered and destroyed a heavily laden, but abandoned, enemy landing barge. After completing her screening mission to Mindoro, *William D. Porter* returned to San Pedro Bay on 26 December to begin preparations for the invasion of Luzon.

For the Lingayen operation, *William D. Porter* was assigned to the Lingayen Fire Support Group of Vice Admiral Jesse B. Oldendorf's Bombardment and Fire Support Group (TG 77.2). The destroyer departed San Pedro Bay on 2 January 1945 and joined her unit in Leyte Gulf the following day. The entire group then passed south through the Surigao Strait, thence crossed the Mindanao Sea, rounded the southern tip of Negros, and then proceeded generally north along the western coasts of Negros, Panay, Mindoro, and finally, Luzon.

By the time the unit reached the southwestern coast of Luzon, it came within the effective range of Luzon-based aircraft. Beginning on the morning of 5 January, enemy planes—including kamikazes—brought the force under attack. *William D. Porter* saw no action during the first stage of those attacks, because the group's combat air patrol (CAP) provided an effective protective blanket. However, the last raid broke through the CAP umbrella at 1650 and charged to the attack. *William D. Porter* took three of those planes under fire at about 1713, but growing darkness precluded evaluation of the results of that engagement. During that raid, cruiser *Louisville* (CA–28) and escort carrier *Manila Bay* (CVE–61) suffered extensive damage from kamikaze crashes.

Before dawn on the 6th, the destroyer moved into Lingayen Gulf with her unit to begin preinvasion bombardment. Throughout the day, enemy planes made sporadic attacks upon the bombarding ships. That evening, *William D. Porter* began firing on shore batteries guarding the approaches to the landing beaches. At 1738, her attention was diverted to a lone plane; and her antiaircraft battery brought it down handily. Twenty minutes later, a twin-engine "Betty" ran afoul of the destroyer's gunners who splashed this one neatly as well. *William D. Porter* then returned to her primary mission, shore bombardment.

After the 9 January landings, the destroyer's mission changed to call fire and night harassing fire in support of the troops. Then, from 11 to 18 January, she stood off Lingayen Gulf with TG 77.2 to protect the approaches from incursion by enemy surface forces. On the 18th, she reentered the gulf to resume support duty for forces ashore and to contribute to the anchorage's air and antisubmarine defenses. On 3 February, the warship bombarded abandoned enemy barges to assure that they would not be used against the invasion force or as evacuation vehicles. She then resumed her antisubmarine and air defense role until 15 February, when she departed Lingayen Gulf to escort *Lindenwald* (LSD–6) and *Epping Forest* (LSD–4) to Guam.

After returning briefly to Lingayen Gulf, *William D. Porter* moved on to Leyte to prepare for the assault on Okinawa. She remained at Leyte during the first half of March; then joined the gunfire support unit attached to the Western Islands Attack Group for a week of gunnery practice at Cabugan Island. She departed the Philippines on 21 March, reached the Ryukyu Islands on the morning of the 25th, and began supporting the virtually unopposed occupation of Kerama Retto. Between 25 March and 1 April, she provided antiaircraft and antisubmarine protection for the ships in the Kerama roadstead, while performing some fire-support duties in response to what little resistance the troops met ashore on the islets of Kerama Retto.

However, by the time the main assault on Okinawa began on the morning of 1 April, she had been reassigned to TF 54, Rear Admiral Morton L. Deyo's Gunfire and Covering Force. During her association with that task organization, *William D. Porter* rendered fire support for the troops conquering Okinawa, provided antisubmarine and antiaircraft defenses for the larger warships of TF 54, and protected minesweepers during their operations. Between 1 April and 5 May, she expended in excess of 8,500 rounds of 5-inch shells —both at shore targets and at enemy aircraft during the almost incessant aerial attacks on the invasion force. During that period, she added five additional plane kills to her tally.

The constant air raids—launched from Kyushu and Formosa—prompted the Americans to establish a cordon of radar picket ships around Okinawa, and it was to this duty that *William D. Porter* switched in early May. Between 5 May and 9 June, she stood picket duty, warned the fleet of the approach of enemy air raids, and vectored interceptors out to meet the attackers. She brought down another enemy plane with her own guns; and fighters under her direction accounted for seven more.

On 10 June 1945, *William D. Porter* fell victim to a unique—though fatal—kamikaze attack. At 0815 that morning, an obsolete "Val" dive-bomber dropped unheralded out of the clouds and made straight for the warship. The destroyer managed to evade the suicide plane, and it splashed down close aboard her. Somehow, the explosive-laden plane ended up directly beneath *William D. Porter* before it exploded. Suddenly, the warship was lifted out of the water and then dropped back again. She lost power and suffered broken steam lines. A number of fires also broke out. For three hours, her crew struggled courageously to put out the fires, repair the damage, and keep the ship afloat. The crew's efforts, however, availed nought; and, 12 minutes after the order to abandon ship went out, *William D. Porter* heeled over to starboard and sank by the stern. Miraculously, her crew suffered no fatal injuries. The warship's name was struck from the Navy list on 11 July 1945.

Wiliam D. Porter received four battle stars for her service in World War II.

William F. McCauley

(ScStr.: t. 149 (gross); l. 100'0"; b. 21'0"; dr. 12'0" (f.); s. 12.0 k.; cpl. 15; a. none)

William F. McCauley (listed in some contemporary merchant shipping registers as *William F. McCaulley*) —a steel-hulled, screw, steam tug built in 1894 by J. H. Dialogue and Sons of Camden, N.J.—was chartered by the Navy from the Propeller Tow Boat Co., Savannah, Ga., and simultaneously commissioned on 13 April 1918. Designated SP–2360, *William F. McCauley* performed tug services in the 12th Naval District for the duration of World War I. She was returned to her prewar owners about a fortnight after the cessation of hostilities, on 26 November 1918. She was simultaneously struck from the Navy list.

William G. Anderson

(Bark: t. 593; l. 149'7''; b. 30'1''; dph. 14'3''; a. 6 32-pdrs., 1 24-pdr. how.)

William G. Anderson—a fast sailing bark built in 1859 at Boston, Mass., by C. F. and H. D. Gardiner—was initially owned by Edmund Boynton of Boston and acquired at Boston by the Navy on 23 August 1861. *William G. Anderson* was commissioned at the Boston Navy Yard on 2 October 1861, Acting Volunteer Lieutenant William C. Rogers in command.

Standing out to sea on 11 October, *William G. Anderson* joined the West Gulf Blockading Squadron, searching for Confederate privateers in the sea lanes of the West Indies. At daybreak on 12 November, lookouts on the bark made out a sail running before the wind in the Bahama channel and tacked to give chase. When within four miles, those in *William G. Anderson* saw the schooner bear away with the British flag at the main masthead. At 0930, the Union vessel succeeded in bringing the stranger to, and discovered her to be the Confederate privateer *Beauregard*, seven days out of Charleston, S.C. *William G. Anderson* sent over an officer to board the prize, who found that the crew had gotten drunk and was engaged in spiking the privateer's sole 12-pound pivot gun and cutting her rigging and sails. A prize crew took over the erstwhile privateer, and the Confederate crew was placed in irons on board *William G. Anderson*.

After bringing her prize into Key West, Fla., on 19 November, *William G. Anderson* set sail a week later. She cruised off Puerto Rico, Cuba, Bermuda, and the Windward Islands into the spring of the following year. She sighted 210 vessels, boarded 66, and had found Confederate privateers, in her commander's words, "rare during that time." She concluded that cruise at the Boston Navy Yard on 16 April 1862.

William G. Anderson departed Boston on 8 May and joined Rear Admiral David G. Farragut's West Gulf Blockading Squadron at Ship Island, off the mouth of the Mississippi River. On 14 June, Acting Master William Bailey and 30 men left the ship under cover of darkness, crossed Mississippi Sound, and sailed about 15 miles up the Jordan River. Penetrating Confederate territory by night, the Union raiders escaped notice by encamped Confederate cavalry and seized the 60-ton Confederate schooner *Montebello*, a ship used by local forces to transport troops across Mississippi Sound. The raiders managed to tow *Montebello* out into the sound before they were noticed by the Confederate forces in the vicinity.

Departing the Ship Island station on 25 June, the bark patrolled the Southwest Pass of the Mississippi River before she took up a blockade station off Galveston, Tex., on 6 July. At the end of August, while on station off Galveston, *William G. Anderson* bagged her second prize—the English-owned schooner *Lilly*. The cargo manifest for *Lilly* showed that she was apparently carrying only salt, drugs, and quinine. Closer investigation, however, revealed 350 kegs of gunpowder and a consignment letter authorizing the British skipper to turn the material over to the first Confederate Army commander he encountered.

William G. Anderson placed a prize crew of six men, under Acting Master C. W. Harriman, on board *Lilly* and sent her to Key West while the bark resumed her patrols. On 4 September, she intercepted and captured the schooner *Theresa*, laden with cavalry carbines. Two weeks later, the Union bark bagged another blockade runner, the schooner *Reindeer* (ex-*Jeff Davis*) laden with 288 bales of cotton en route to Havana.

William G. Anderson arrived at Pensacola Bay, Fla.,

on 3 October and remained there on station, protecting the navy yard until the next spring. Underway on 10 April 1863, the bark resumed blockade duties off the coast of Texas soon thereafter. On 15 April, she captured the cotton-laden schooner *Royal Yacht* after a six-hour chase. Seven days later, *William G. Anderson* teamed with *Rachel Seaman* to capture the schooner *Nymph* which was attempting to run the Union blockade off Pass Cavallo, Tex.

Just eight days later, *William G. Anderson* spotted a sloop trying to run the blockade and gave chase. About six miles north of the lighthouse at St. Joseph's Island, Tex., the sloop ran aground and was deserted by her crew. The rough seas that day made it impossible for the Union ship to send men to board the prize; but, on 3 May, the weather had abated enough to permit an expedition shoreward.

William G. Anderson sent in her launch, second cutter, and gig to take off the cotton from the prize. Two of the boats were just in the edge of the breakers as the gig's bow grounded on the beach. At that juncture, Confederate soldiers, under the command of Capt. Edward E. Havvy, CSA, charged down the hill nearby, firing as they advanced. The launch and the second cutter managed to clear the beach although hit several times by rifle fire; but the enemy captured the ship's gig and the five men that had been in it. *William G. Anderson* fired five shots from her pivot gun in an attempt to drive off the enemy, but the ship was beyond effective range.

Stationed off Pilot Town, La., between 27 May and 24 June, *William G. Anderson* subsequently resumed her blockading operations off the Texas coast. On 25 August, she captured the schooner *Mack Canfield* laden with 133 bales of cotton—off the mouth of the Rio Grande River. Two days later, the armed Union bark bagged the cotton-laden schooner *America*; and, although the prize capsized while under tow, *William G. Anderson*'s crew retrieved 40 bales of cotton from the sea.

After cruising off Galveston, *William G. Anderson* departed that vicinity on 17 September and took station off New Orleans. She remained there until 30 November, when she sailed back to Galveston and another stint of blockading off the Texas coast. *William G. Anderson* shifted to Pensacola Bay, Fla., on 19 February 1864 and served there protecting the navy yard until 1 April 1865. Entering Mobile Bay on 3 April 1865, *William G. Anderson* was there six days later when Lee surrendered at Appomattox Court House, Va., assuring the speedy end of the Civil War.

William G. Anderson remained in Mobile Bay into the late summer and was then once more stationed at Pensacola Bay, this time from 13 September to 25 November. Alternating between that port and New Orleans until mid-June 1866, the bark set course north from Pensacola on 15 June 1866, bound for the New York Navy Yard.

Arriving there on 30 June, *William G. Anderson* was decommissioned on 21 July 1866. The erstwhile blockade ship was sold at public auction on 28 August 1866 to A. A. Low and Brother; her subsequent fate is unrecorded.

William G. Fargo

The wooden screw steamer *William G. Fargo* was acquired by the Navy on 19 August 1863. She was renamed *Honeysuckle* (q.v.) sometime on or close to the day of her commissioning, 3 December 1863.

William G. Putnam

(ScStr.: t. 149; l. 103'6''; b. 22'0''; dph. 7'2''; s. 7 k.; cpl. 62; a. 1 32-pdr. P.r., 2 24-pdr. sb. how.)

William G. Putnam—a wooden-hulled tug built in

1857 at Brooklyn, N.Y.—was purchased by the Navy on 24 July 1861 at New York City and renamed *General Putnam* soon thereafter.

On 13 September 1861, with Acting Master William J. Hotchkiss in command, *General Putnam* departed New York, bound for Washington, D.C., and arrived at the navy yard there three days later. On the night of the 17th, she headed down river to join the Potomac Flotilla but the next day was ordered on down the Chesapeake Bay and joined the Atlantic Blockading Squadron at Old Point Comfort, Va., on 23 September. Within a few days, the tug was operating off the North Carolina coast where her initial duty was to reconnoiter Okracoke Inlet. She also patrolled off Hatteras Inlet and assisted in the sinking of three stone-laden schooners in an attempt to help to tighten the blockade by impeding navigation and obstructing the inlets in the area. On 29 October 1861, the day on which the Atlantic Squadron was divided into the North and South commands, *General Putnam* was allocated to the newly established North Atlantic Blockading Squadron; but she continued to operate primarily in the waters of North Carolina.

In February 1862, *General Putnam* took part in the expedition which captured Roanoke Island, N.C. On the 7th, at the beginning of the action, *Ceres* and *General Putnam* steamed a mile or so ahead of the main force to reconnoiter and discovered 15 steamers and 10 sailing vessels close inshore between Pork and Weir Points, above the marshes of Croatan Sound. Soon *General Putnam* fired upon a Confederate shore battery in an engagement that lasted all afternoon.

The next morning, she resumed firing in company with *Underwood* and other vessels as they started to pass a cluster of vessels which had been sunk as obstructions. *General Putnam* emerged unscathed from nearly continuous shelling by the enemy guns. Meanwhile, between 1500 and 2400 that day, some 10,000 troops landed on Roanoke Island.

On the 10th, after sister tug *Ceres* ran aground off Elizabeth City, *General Putnam* assisted her to pull free. In addition to helping *Ceres*, *General Putnam* attempted to put out a fire which was raging in a Confederate armed schooner nearby. The blaze proved to be beyond control, but the tug did manage to pick up one man from the water as he swam from the burning ship. In the operation, Union warships captured eight Confederate vessels; opened the obstructed passage to Albemarle Sound; and raised the stars and stripes over Pork Point battery.

Over the ensuing days, *General Putnam*—sometimes referred to in dispatches as simply *Putnam* and sometimes by her former name, *William G. Putnam*—conducted daily reconnaissance in Currituck Sound and missions in the Chesapeake Canal. For the next six months, *General Putnam* carried detachments of Army troops and equipment sent to search out and destroy rebel boats used to carry suplies. While stationed at Plymouth or New Berne, the ship operated in the Pasquotank and Chowan Rivers and the creeks of Dingaderry, Rochahock, and Seems.

In October, *Putnam*, needing repairs, sailed for Hampton Roads and arrived there on 22 October with intelligence data for Rear Admiral S. P. Lee. On 6 November, the screw steam gunboat received orders to remain in Virginia waters and to maintain a "strict and vigorous" blockade of the western shore of the Chesapeake Bay between Fortress Monroe and the south side of the Piankatank River. Proceeding to Yorktown, Va., *Putnam* joined a small flotilla there operating with the Army in an attempt to take Mathews Court House up the East River. Ordered to capture or destroy all Confederate vessels that could be used to run the Union blockade, *Putnam* operated in that capacity until the campaign against Mathews Court House had been successfully accomplished by 23 November.

Subsequently serving as guard vessel in the York River and off neighboring coasts, she cooperated with the Army in landing troops on expeditions up to West Point and also patrolled to check for violations of the blockade until 15 January 1863. By that time, her boilers had become useless, and she was unable to move, having no steam. She nevertheless remained on active service in those waters, stationed so as to enfilade Gloucester Point, until she was towed to Baltimore to receive a new boiler and rifle screening. She returned to her station in June 1863 and resumed duty helping to blockade Chesapeake Bay and its tributaries.

On 11 August, *General Putnam*, *Commodore Jones*, and *Commodore Morris* were operating in the Piankatank River on blockade duties when they sighted a schooner, a canoe, and a launch that had run the blockade. Men from the steamers manned two cutters, two boats, and a gig to give chase but soon encountered heavy sniper fire from Confederate soldiers and guerrillas in the woods. After *Putnam*'s commanding officer, Acting Master Hotchkiss, had been slain in the engagement, the boats then withdrew. Upon Hotchkiss' death, Acting Master Lewis assumed command of *General Putnam;* and the ship shelled the woods for about four miles as she dropped down river.

Subsequently towed to Yorktown, *General Putnam* was stationed at the mouth of Queen's Creek, where she formed an indispensable part of the defense of Yorktown while Major General Foster erected a citadel there. By that time, *General Putnam*—with an "overweight boiler"—had become less useful for blockade duty; but she found profitable employment dragging for torpedoes near Yorktown.

Acting Master H. H. Savage took command of *General Putnam* off Newport News on 16 November 1863; and the tug soon proceeded up Nansemond River, where she later captured a large runner and destroyed a canoe used by the Confederate forces in the area for running mail across the river. *General Putnam* remained on picket duty off the mouth of the Nansemond River to intercept blockade runners until 15 December, when she returned to Newport News.

In February and March of 1864, she patrolled the Back and Poquosin Rivers and joined an expedition on 8 March to head up the Mattapony River, convoying Army transports. She covered the landing of General Kilpatrick's troops at Sheppard's Landing, two miles above West Point, before proceeding to the mouth of the Rappahannock and ascending that river to a point five miles below Urbana. On 13 March, *General Putnam* returned to Yorktown and later resumed her patrols on the Back and Poquosin Rivers.

From mid-April 1864, *General Putnam* operated in joint Army-Navy operations in the James and Nansemond Rivers, covering the landings of troops and, upon occasion, providing covering fire. She moved ahead of Army transports, dragging for torpedoes from Harrison's Bar to one mile above Bermuda Hundred, clearing a channel for the landing of troops at City Point and at Bermuda Hundred. She then operated with General Graham's gunboats, supporting the occupation of Fort Powhatan and Wilson's Wharf.

General Putnam then accompanied Army gunboats up the Appomattox River and anchored at Gilliam's Bar. She then reconnoitered the river below the bar and, by order of General Graham, towed the gunboat *Chamberlain* down into the channel. Informed that Confederate pickets had advanced, in force, as far as Gilliam's Bar, the Union flotilla retreated on 11 May to Point of Rocks and shelled the nearby woods. During the action, *General Putnam* discovered the Confederate battery at Fort Clifton, opened fire on the enemy guns, and soon obtained the range. The battery replied, but a shell from *General Putnam*'s 24-pound howitzer exploded in the embrasure of their rifled gun, causing the Confederate gunners to break and run.

After that engagement, the Union steamer returned down river, only to engage in further combat operations on the Appomattox River almost daily into June, remaining on guard against surprise attacks. Union forces repeated the attack upon Fort Clifton on 9 and 10 June and silenced the enemy battery there.

On 28 July 1864, *General Putnam* was reassigned to the James River and, for the remainder of her naval service, *General Putnam* operated alternately in the James and Appomattox Rivers, and also in Mobjack Bay, until March of 1865 when she returned to Yorktown. Detached from the North Atlantic Blockading Squadron on 18 March 1865, she patrolled the Rappahannock and St. Mary's Rivers.

After the collapse of the Confederacy in April, the tug was ordered to the Washington Navy Yard with 23 other vessels from her division. *General Putnam* arrived there on 14 May and was decommissioned on 2 June 1865. She was subsequently transferred to the Treasury Department for use by the Lighthouse Board. As *Putnam*, she remained in the service of the board until 1885 when she was broken up.

William G. Thomas

William G. Thomas (DE–193)—a *Cannon*-class destroyer escort—was renamed *Garfield Thomas* (q.v.)

on 3 November 1943, before the ship's launching on 12 December 1943.

William H. Bates

William Henry Bates—born on 26 April 1917 at Salem, Mass.,—enlisted in the Navy in July 1940. Commissioned as ensign in the Naval Reserve on 30 January 1941, Bates received instruction at the Naval Reserve Supply Officer's School at the Naval Medical Center, Washington, D.C., before serving successive tours of duty at the Washington Navy Yard and in *Constellation* (IX–20).

Bates remained in the Supply Corps through the end of World War II, participating in the Iwo Jima campaign in the spring of 1945 and eventually becoming the supply officer for the 4th Naval District by 1949. While Bates was stationed there, his father—Representative George J. Bates of the 6th Massachusetts Congressional District—was killed in a plane crash at the Washington (D.C.) National Airport on 1 November 1949.

Bates resigned his reserve commission—he had attained the rank of lieutenant commander by that

The launch of *William H. Bates* (SSN–680).

time—on 14 February 1950, to fill the seat of his late father in the United States House of Representatives. For the nearly two decades preceding his death on 22 June 1969, Bates staunchly advocated a strong military posture for the United States. On the Joint Congressional Committee on Atomic Energy and the House Armed Services Committee, he vigorously supported the development of nuclear-powered naval vessels. He also vigorously backed incentive pay programs and the establishment of better housing facilities for servicemen. He constantly sought means to enhance the training, caliber, and morale of military personnel.

(SSN-680: dp. 3,640 (surf.), 4,640 (subm.); l. 292'3''; b. 31'8''; dr. 27'; s. 15+ k. (surf.), 25+ k. (subm.); cpl. 108; a. 4 tt., SUBROC; cl. *Sturgeon*)

William H. Bates (SSN-680)—originally projected as *Redfish*—was laid down on 4 August 1969 at Pascagoula, Miss., by the Ingalls Nuclear Shipbuilding Div. of Litton Industries; launched on 11 December 1971; sponsored by Mrs. Andrew R. Grainger, the wife of Ens. Andrew R. Grainger and the daughter of Representative Bates; and commissioned on 5 May 1973, Comdr. Glenn N. Arthur in command.

After shakedown, *William H. Bates*—homeported at New London, Conn.,—worked out of the submarine base at Groton. She was deployed to the eastern Atlantic between July and October 1974 and conducted her first patrol mission before visiting Holy Loch, Scotland, and Halifax, Nova Scotia, en route home. However, her respite was brief, for the nuclear attack submarine was again underway on patrol over the Christmas holidays and into January 1975. After voyage repairs at Holy Loch, *William H. Bates* shifted to Faslane, Scotland, for a port visit.

Sailing for home in late January, the submarine was refitted at the Norfolk Naval Shipyard, Portsmouth, Va., before conducting local operations off Ft. Lauderdale, Fla., into the summer of 1975. She was deployed to European waters again soon thereafter, taking part in antisubmarine warfare exercises. In November, the submarine took part in NATO Exercises "Moby Dick" and "Ocean Safari 75," before she returned to New London in December.

William H. Bates conducted her first Mediterranean deployment the following year, departing New London on 5 May 1976. During this tour, she honed her skills in exercises with other ships of the United States Navy and other NATO naval units. During the deployment, she visited Bizerte, Tunisia; Augusta Bay, Sicily; and La Spezia and Naples, Italy. After departing the Mediterranean on 6 September 1976, the submarine took part in Exercise "Ocean Safari 76" in mid-month. On 14 October, the submarine returned to Groton.

William H. Bates underwent voyage repairs and later prepared for another overseas deployment. She departed Groton during the summer of 1977 and completed her assigned mission on 3 October, mooring alongside the tender *Holland* (AS-32) on that day. She subsequently transited the North Sea for a port visit to Bremerhaven, Germany, where she spent five days. *William H. Bates* then took part in Exercise "Ocean Safari 77" with NATO units while returning from European waters to Groton.

From there, *William H. Bates* operated in the Atlantic until moving to San Diego in May 1978 for service in the Pacific Fleet into 1980.

William H. Brown

(SwGbt: t. 800; a. 2 12-pdrs.)

On 30 September 1862, *William H. Brown*, a side-wheel steamer, was transferred to the Navy by the War Department; and she served as a transport and dispatch vessel for the Mississippi Squadron for the duration of the Civil War. The ship carried supplies and messages between the squadron's base at Cairo, Ill., and its ships at various locations on the Mississippi River and its tributaries. Her only recorded engagement came on 13 April 1964 during the Red River expedition when she fired on Confederate shore batteries while assisting the grounded *Chillicothe*. Confederate return fire hit her drum and disabled her so that she had to be towed back to Cairo for repairs.

After hostilities ended, the ship was placed out of commission at Mound City, Ill., on 12 August 1865. Five days later, she was sold at auction to Mr. R. R. Hudson.

William H. Standley

William Harrison Standley—born on 18 December 1872 at Ukiah, Calif.—graduated from the Naval Academy in 1895 and served the two years' sea duty then required by law in the cruiser *Olympia* before he received his commission as an ensign in 1897. During the Spanish-American War, he served in the monitor *Monterey* and later in *Alert*. After the fighting with Spain had ended, he joined the gunboat *Yorktown*, during the Philippine Insurrection. He won a commendation for bravery during a volunteer reconnaissance mission carried out at Baler, Philippine Islands, on 11 April 1899. In conjunction with a feint conducted by Lt. J. C. Gilmore, Standley—then an ensign—bravely ventured into enemy territory to reconnoiter insurgent positions.

Ordered to the gunboat *Marietta* on 29 May 1901, Standley later became Officer in Charge, Branch Hydrographic Office, San Francisco, Calif., in October of the same year. Assigned to the training ship *Pensacola* in June 1902, he later served as engineer in the ship *Adams* and as aide to the Commandant of the Naval Station at Tutuila, Samoa. Designated as the captain of the yard there in 1905, Standley discharged his duties as officer in charge of the native guard and chief customs officer until detached with orders to the United States in October 1906.

Reporting to the receiving ship *Independence* in January 1907, Standley served as executive officer of the cruiser *Albany* from February 1909 to August 1910. From January 1910, he also discharged duties as *Albany*'s navigator as well. Standley then reported to the armored cruiser *Pennsylvania* on 3 November 1910 and was navigator of that ship until becoming aide to the Commandant of the Mare Island Navy Yard at Vallejo, Calif. After three years in that post, Standley became executive officer of the battleship *New Jersey* and later took command of the gunboat *Yorktown* on 15 May 1915.

Returning to the Naval Academy on 14 October 1916 as Assistant to the Superintendent in charge of Building and Grounds, he later served for 11 months as Commandant of Midshipmen. Under his direction, the new seamanship and navigation buildings were constructed, and over four million dollars were expended in enlarging Bancroft Hall to accommodate the increased number of midshipmen appointed during the World War I period. For his "highly meritorious" service in those posts at Annapolis, Standley received a special letter of commendation from the Secretary of the Navy.

Detached from the Naval Academy in July 1919, Standley soon thereafter assumed command of the pre-dreadnought battleship *Virginia* and, a year later, received orders to attend the Naval War College. After completing his studies at Newport, Standley returned to sea, serving as Assistant Chief of Staff to the Commander in Chief, Battle Fleet, from 5 July 1921 to 30 June 1923, before he reported to Washington for duty heading the War Plans Division in the Office of the Chief of Naval Operations (CNO). Completing the latter tour on 1 February 1926, Standley then commanded *California* (BB-44) from 15 February 1926 to 11 October 1927.

He returned to shore duty in Washington, D.C., as Director of the Fleet Training Division, Office of the CNO, and held that post until 14 May 1928. He then served as Assistant CNO until 17 September 1930, when he became Commander, Destroyer Squadrons, Battle Fleet, a title that changed to Commander, Destroyers, Battle Force, U.S. Fleet, on 1 April 1931, with additional duty as Commander, Destroyers, U.S. Fleet. Designated as a member of the Navy Department's Selection Board on 18 November 1931, Standley became Commander, Cruisers, Scouting Forces—with additional duties as Commander, Cruisers, U.S. Fleet, and Commander, Cruiser Division 5—on 16 December of the same year.

Appointed vice admiral on 20 January 1932 while in command of the Battle Force's cruisers, Standley was placed in command of the Battle Force, U.S. Fleet, with the rank of admiral, on 20 May 1933. Breaking his flag in his former command, *California*, the admiral remained at sea until 1 July 1933, when President Franklin D. Roosevelt appointed him CNO.

Before being retired at his own request on 1 January 1937 and handing over the reins of office to Admiral William D. Leahy, Admiral Standley frequently performed the duties of Acting Secretary of the Navy, due to the declining health of Secretary of the Navy Claude A. Swanson. Standley represented the United States as a delegate to the London Naval Conference between 7 December 1935 to 25 March 1936 and signed that accord on behalf of the United States. In addition, during his tenure as CNO, Standley initiated the Vinson-Trammell Naval Bill that provided for establishing, building, and maintaining the United States Navy at treaty strength.

Recalled to active duty on 13 February 1941, Standley served as naval representative on the planning board of the Office of Production Management (OPM) for seven months. After leaving the OPM in the autumn of 1941, Standley served as the American naval member on the Beaverbrook-Harriman Special War Supply Mission to the USSR. Upon his return from Russia, Standley became a member of the Navy Board for Production Awards.

When President Roosevelt established the Roberts Commission to investigate the attack on Pearl Harbor, he selected Admiral Standley as one of the members of that sensitive body which studied the attack into early 1942. In February 1942, Standley was appointed American Ambassador to the USSR, a post he held into the autumn of 1943.

Subsequently recalled to active duty once more, in March 1944, Standley served in the Office of Strategic Services throughout the remaining period of hostilities. Relieved of all active duty on 31 August 1945, Standley lived in retirement at San Diego, Calif., until his death on 25 October 1963.

(DLG–32: dp. 8,150 (f.); l. 547'0''; b. 55'0''; dr. 29'0''; s. 30 k.; cpl. 440; a. 1 5'', 2 3'', LAMPS, Terrier, ASROC, 6 Mk. 32 tt., 2 Mk. 25 tt.; cl. *Belknap*)

William H. Standley (DLG–32) was laid down on 29 July 1963 at Bath, Maine, by the Bath Iron Works; launched on 19 December 1964; sponsored by Mrs. Charles B. Wincote, daughter of the late Admiral Standley; and commissioned on 9 July 1966, Capt. C. F. Moul in command.

Following fitting-out and ship's qualification trials, *William H. Standley* spent the holiday season in Boston before heading for Guantanamo Bay, Cuba, in January 1967. After a two and one-half month shakedown period, *William H. Standley* became flagship for Rear Admiral E. R. Bonner, Commander, Cruiser Destroyer Flotilla 6, during a "Springboard" exercise ·in the Caribbean. After highlighting the cruise with port visits to San Salvador and San Juan, Puerto Rico, the guided-missile frigate returned to Boston in April for post-shakedown availability.

On 12 June 1967, *William H. Standley* departed Boston and spent five weeks on operations with the Operational Test and Evaluation Force. During that voyage, she touched at Santa Cruz de Tenerife, Canary Islands, a spot seldom visited by naval vessels. Subsequently arriving at her first home port, Mayport, Fla., on 14 July 1967, *William H. Standley* became the flagship for Commander, Destroyer Squadron (ComDesRon) 8 the following week.

Following an underway period on the Atlantic Fleet Weapons Range and a visit to Frederikstad, St. Croix, Virgin Islands, *William H. Standley* prepared for her first deployment to the Mediterranean. On 6 October 1967, the guided-missile frigate stood out to sea, leaving Mayport in her wake, bound for the ship's first tour of duty with the 6th Fleet.

Transiting the Atlantic in company with *Goodrich* (DDR–831) and *Turner* (DDR–834), *William H. Standley* joined Task Group (TG) 60.2 as flagship for ComDesRon 8 upon her arrival in the Mediterranean. While attached to the 6th Fleet, the guided-missile frigate witnessed the rapid build-up of Soviet naval strength in the Mediterranean basin and visited the ports of Palma de Majorca, Spain; Valetta, Malta; Naples, Italy; and Suda Bay, Crete.

For the first three months of 1968, *William H. Standley* participated in a bilateral exercise with French naval units, "Phiblex 10–68," and conducted picket duty in the eastern Mediterranean, before she sailed for home late in March 1968.

Arriving back at her home port on the 28th, *William H. Standley* spent a month undergoing post-deployment upkeep, before she conducted planeguard duty for *Intrepid* (CVS–11) in May. Soon thereafter, she responded to an emergency recall and got underway to search for the missing *Scorpion* (SSN–589), the atomic submarine that had disappeared somewhere south of the Azores while en route back to the United States from a Mediterranean deployment.

William H. Standley conducted an Atlantic transit with ComDesRon 8 embarked and, in company with five submarines and four destroyers, took part in the extensive hunt for the missing submarine. The Navy officially declared *Scorpion* as lost on 5 June; and *William H. Standley* returned to Mayport the following day.

Later in June, the guided missile frigate embarked 40 midshipmen and took those officers-to-be on their summer cruise before disembarking them at Norfolk, Va., late in July. *William H. Standley* entered the Charleston (S.C.) Naval Shipyard early in August for restricted availability and received alterations that would permit her to function as a PIRAZ (Positive Identification Radar and Advisory Zone) ship to conduct operations in Southeast Asia.

After sea trials and a final in-port period at Mayport, *William H. Standley* departed her home port on 2 December for her first deployment to the Western Pacific (WestPac) area. After a brief stop at the Atlantic Fleet Weapons Range at San Juan, Puerto Rico, *William H. Standley* proceeded onward, transiting the Panama Canal for the first time on 9 December.

Reaching Hawaii in time for Christmas, *William H. Standley* subsequently departed Pearl Harbor after the Yuletide holidays and reached Subic Bay, Philippines, early in January 1969 to receive new equipment and run sea trials.

Departing Subic Bay on 23 January for the Gulf of Tonkin, *William H. Standley* arrived on station and relieved *Mahan* (DLG–11) as PIRAZ ship. During her month on station, the guided missile frigate maximized the use of her communications systems and her tactical data collection facilities, contributing significantly to 7th Fleet operations off the coast of Vietnam.

Relieved by *Mahan* on 25 February, *William H. Standley* sailed for Japan and reached Sasebo five days later for upkeep and recreation. Departing that Japanese port on 14 March, the guided missile frigate arrived at Subic Bay on the 17th for three days of training.

Resuming her operations in Vietnamese waters on 22 March, *William H. Standley* began a "difficult and demanding line period." Tensions in Korea had erupted, causing the American naval forces in the Far East to go on alert. North Korean and American forces had exchanged fire briefly near the demilitarized zone between the two Koreas on 11 March; and, on 15 April, North Korean fighters downed an EC-121 reconnaissance plane over international waters in the Sea of Japan. The plane, based at Atsugi, Japan, crashed with 31 men on board.

During her 50 days on the "line," *William H. Standley* spent approximately half the time on PIRAZ station and half on the southern Sea Air Rescue (SAR) station. Operational requirements necessitated the southward movement and required the ship to base two helicopters simultaneously. *William H. Standley* met the test, earning a commendatory message from Rear Admiral E. J. Rudd, entitled: "Stellar *Standley*."

Relieved by *King* (DLG–10) on station, *William H. Standley* sailed to Hong Kong for some well-earned rest and recreation, arriving at the British Crown Colony on 18 May. Departing on the 24th, the guided missile frigate sailed for Japanese waters and reached Yokosuka on 28 May.

William H. Standley returned to the "line" after eight days of intensive upkeep, relieving *Sterett* (DLG–31) as southern SAR ship on 9 June. For the next nine days, the guided missile frigate acted as SAR and strike support ship for the aircraft carriers stationed in the Gulf of Tonkin. Relieved by *Chicago* (CG–11) on 18 June, *William H. Standley* reached Pearl Harbor on Independence Day, pushing on for the Galapagos the next day. Transiting the Panama Canal on 16 July, the guided missile frigate reached Mayport on 20 July.

From September through the year's end, *William H. Standley* remained at Mayport, preparing for her second WestPac cruise. Underway on 5 January 1971, the guided missile frigate transited the Panama Canal four days later, and reached Pearl Harbor on the 23d. After four days in Hawaii, the ship took in her lines and headed for the Marianas, arriving at Guam on 5 February for a six-hour fueling stop.

Upon leaving Guam, *William H. Standley* set course for Subic Bay and, after assisting a merchantman in distress, the Philippine freighter *Santa Anna*, reached her destination on 10 February. Two days later, she sailed for the Gulf of Tonkin.

For the next 25 days, *William H. Standley* escorted *Ranger* (CVA–61) on the northern SAR station, before she put into Sasebo for a port visit. After brief patrol duty in the Sea of Japan, the guided missile frigate returned to the Gulf of Tonkin to serve as PIRAZ vessel. She subsequently visited Hong Kong and Subic Bay (effecting rudder repairs at the latter port) and conducted one more PIRAZ tour before beginning her homeward voyage.

Sailing via Sattahip, Thailand; Singapore, Federated Malay States; Victoria, Seychelles; Lourenco Marques; the Cape of Good Hope; Rio de Janeiro, Brazil; and Roosevelt Roads, Puerto Rico, *William H. Standley* reached Mayport on 18 August, having circumnavigated the globe and steamed some 51,000 miles. For the remainder of 1971, the guided missile frigate recuperated from the lengthy voyage, participating in refresher training and conducting local operations off the Florida coast.

Departing Mayport on 19 January 1972, *William H. Standley* took part in Operation "Snowy Beach" before being detached on the 25th to proceed to Yorktown, Va., to take on weapons. Subsequently returning to Mayport on the 28th, the guided missile frigate departed her home port on 17 February to participate in Atlantic Fleet exercises. During the course of this cruise, she visited the port of Nassau, New Providence, Bahamas, and Port Everglades, Fla., before she returned to Mayport on 9 March.

After her post-deployment in-port period, *William H. Standley* exercised in the Caribbean as flagship for Commander, Cruiser-Destroyer Flotilla (CruDesFlot) 6 that autumn, conducting gunnery shoots—with both guns and missiles—at drone targets under wartime conditions. During her time in Caribbean waters, the ship visited San Juan.

As the year drew to a close, the guided missile frigate prepared for her first major overhaul since commissioning. After entering the Charleston (S.C.) Naval Shipyard on 20 November 1969, *William H. Standley* spent the first half of 1970 in shipyard hands.

Upon completion of that period of repairs and alterations, *William H. Standley* conducted missile firings on the Atlantic Fleet Weapons Range and trained at Guantanamo Bay for six weeks, breaking those underway evolutions with visits to San Juan and to Port-au-Prince, Haiti. Called away from her training on 5 August, *William H. Standley* went to the aid of a foundering Panamanian merchantman off the northeastern tip of Hispaniola, an "exacting seamanship evolution" accomplished "very professionally."

Embarking 25 naval reservists on 20 March, *William H. Standley* stood out to sea on that day and operated, for the next nine days, off the eastern seaboard between Jacksonville, Fla., and Charleston, S.C. During that time, she conducted an antisubmarine warfare (ASW) exercise against *Trutta* (SS–421) and conducted LAMPS helicopter work-up, before she returned to her home port and remained there until 30 April.

The guided missile frigate made one more exercise and spent one more period in port before she headed out from Mayport, bound for the Mediterranean and her second tour with the 6th Fleet. Rendezvousing with TG 27.4, *William H. Standley* proceeded across the Atlantic. While she was en route, the guided missile frigate's LAMPS helicopter crashed at sea. Of the crew of four men, all but one were rescued. The fourth man went down with the helicopter.

Reaching Rota, Spain, on 22 June, *William H. Standley* completed turnover procedures with *Harry E. Yarnell* (DLG–17) and then joined Task Force (TF) 60 at sea. During her second deployment with the 6th Fleet, *William H. Standley* participated in Operations "Good Friendship," "Quick Draw," two "National Weeks," and "Bystander." She visited the ports of Livorno, Italy; Cannes and Golfe Juan, France; Palma, Majorca; Athens and Corfu, Greece; Mersin and Izmir, Turkey; and Barcelona, Malaga, and Rota, Spain.

Departing Rota on 9 December, *William H. Standley* transited the Atlantic and arrived at her new home port, Charleston, S.C., a week before Christmas of 1972. In port at Charleston between 18 December 1972 and 17 January 1973, the guided missile frigate then underwent a seven and one-half month overhaul. Following that period of repairs and alterations, *William H. Standley* trained locally and prepared for another Mediterranean deployment.

Departing Charleston on 14 June 1974, *William H. Standley* reached Rota on the 27th and, during the early part of her tour, visited the French ports of St. Tropez and Theoule, where the ship joined in celebrations commemorating the 30th anniversary of the Allied landings during World War II. She then visited the Italian port of Civitavecchia.

From July to September, *William H. Standley* spent many days at sea due to the Greco-Turkish crisis on the island of Cyprus. She underwent a brief tender overhaul at Augusta Bay, Sicily, and followed up the repairs with a full slate of underway activities. Highlighting that period were two events: the tow of *Vreeland* (DE–1068) when that ship developed serious boiler trouble on 4 October; and the surveillance of Soviet warships in the eastern Mediterranean. During the latter, *William H. Standley* discovered a Soviet submarine and maintained sonar contact for over 49 hours, forcing the surfacing of a "Zulu"-class submarine.

For the remainder of the cruise, the guided missile frigate continued her schedule of at-sea periods interspersed with visits to Genoa and San Remo, Italy, and to Rota. Departing the last-named port on 24 November, she arrived back in Charleston on 9 December.

Following the ensuing Christmas leave period, the ship underwent repairs at the Norfolk Naval Shipyard, Portsmouth, Va., and emerged from the yard late in February 1975. On 1 July 1975, *William H. Standley* was redesignated as a guided missile cruiser, CG–32. As the summer wore on, the ship operated out of Guantanamo Bay, Roosevelt Roads, and San Juan. She subsequently sailed for the Mediterranean on 2 October 1975, leaving Charleston in her wake on that day, bound, as before, for Rota.

Taking over from *Luce* (DLG–7), *William H. Standley* operated in the "middle sea" into the winter, spending Christmas at Naples. The guided missile cruiser remained in the Mediterranean into the spring before turning over her duties to *Harry E. Yarnell* at Gibraltar on 25 April 1976 and heading for Charleston on that day.

Between mid-February and late July 1977, *William H. Standley* conducted one more deployment to the 6th Fleet. After returning to Charleston on 1 August, the guided missile cruiser sailed at the end of the month to join the Pacific Fleet. Leaving Charleston behind on the last day of August, *William H. Standley* transited the Panama Canal on 5 and 6 September, reaching her new home port of Bremerton, Wash., on the 29th. En route, she had touched at San Diego and San Francisco, Calif., and rescued a fishing boat adrift off Santa Barbara.

William H. Standley underwent a major overhaul from the autumn of 1977 into the late summer of the following year. She then ran trials and operated locally on training evolutions out of San Diego, spending Christmas holidays in port.

As of 1979, *William H. Standley* remained a vital unit of the United States Pacific Fleet.

William H. Standley was awarded four engagement stars for her Vietnam War service.

William Isom

The vice president of the North American Transportation & Trading Co. just after the turn of the century.

(Tanker: dp. 7,045; lbp. 293'; b. 47'; dr. 23' (aft); s. 10½ k.; cpl. 44; a. 1 5'', 1 3'')

William Isom (Id. No. 1555)—a tanker constructed in 1917 at Baltimore, Md., by the Baltimore Drydock & Shipbuilding Corp.—was taken over by the United States Shipping Board on 24 April 1918 from the Sinclair Gulf Corp. and was commissioned at New York on 1 May 1918, Lt. Comdr. Wenzel Habel, USNRF, in command.

Initially assigned to the Naval Overseas Transportation Service, she was reassigned to the Fleet Train by 1 July as a depot tanker. In that role, she carried fuel and supplies to various American ships and stations. She appears never to have seen service overseas but rather remained close to America's shores throughout her 15 months of naval service. On 21 August 1919, she was decommissioned, transferred to the United States Shipping Board, and returned to her owners, all simultaneously.

Following her brief naval career, *William Isom* resumed mercantile service with the Sinclair Gulf Corp. until 1920 when she was sold to the American Italian Commercial Corp. In the mid-1920's she was sold to the Cuba Distilling Co. In 1930, Edwin B. DeGolia acquired her and the following year renamed her SS *Edwin B. DeGolia*. She served with the Hillcone Steamship Co. under that name until late 1947 or early 1948 when the Artemis Maritime Co., of Panama, acquired her and renamed her SS *Demosthenes*. She continued in mercantile service with that company and under that name until late in 1955 or early in 1956. At that point, all mention of her in mercantile lists ceased.

William J. Pattison

William Joseph Pattison—born on 15 January 1921 at Long Island City, N.Y.—enlisted in the Navy on 23 August 1939 at Indianapolis, Ind. A conscientious sailor, Pattison advanced steadily in rating and, at least once, was meritoriously promoted. By the beginning of 1943, he had reached the rank of signalman 3d class and was serving in *Eberle* (DD–430) in the South Atlantic. On 10 March 1943, his ship encountered the German blockade runner, *Karin*, which was flying the Dutch flag. The task group commander, Rear Admiral O. M. Read, ordered *Eberle* to ignore the ship's Allied flag and board her. Pattison was one of the 14 men chosen from *Eberle*'s complement to board the blockade runner before her crew could scuttle her and was the second American to reach the enemy ship's deck. In spite of rising flames and explosions, Pattison performed his salvage duties—primarily maintaining contact with *Eberle* while his colleagues searched for demolition charges. While executing his duty, Pattison was killed by the explosion of one of the German demolition charges. For his ". . . exemplary conduct and heroic devotion to duty . . .," SM3c Pattison was awarded the Navy Cross, posthumously.

(APD–104: dp. 1,650 (tl.); l. 306'0''; b. 37'0''; dr. 12'7'' (lim.); s. 23.6 k. (tl.); cpl. 204; trp. 162; a. 1 5'', 6 40mm., 6 20mm., 2 dct.; cl. *Crosley*)

William J. Pattison (DE–594) was laid down on 4 January 1944 at Hingham, Mass., by the Bethlehem Shipbuilding Co.; launched on 15 February 1944; sponsored by Miss Sally McKillop; reclassified a high-speed transport and redesignated APD–104 on 17 July 1944; and commissioned at Boston on 27 February 1945, Lt. Comdr. Leslie W. Bennett, USNR, in command.

Following shakedown training out of Guantanamo Bay, Cuba, and amphibious training at Hampton Roads, Va., she conducted post-shakedown repairs at the Portsmouth (N.H.) Navy Yard between 20 and 27 April. On the latter day, the high-speed transport departed Portsmouth, bound for New York. There she rendezvoused with *General William Weigel* (AP–119), and the two ships got underway on 1 May and headed for the West Indies. After a stop at San Juan, Puerto Rico, from 4 to 8 May, the two ships continued on to Panama, where they arrived on the 10th. *William J. Pattison* transited the canal on 12 May and set course for San Diego, Calif. Diverted en route in order to provide emergency medical treatment to an appendicitis victim on board a Liberty ship, she did not reach San Diego until 22 May. The warship remained there only two days before putting to sea on the 24th in company with *Begor* (APD–127) and *Cavallaro* (APD–128). After a six-day voyage filled with gunnery drills and tactical exercises, the three high-speed transports arrived in Pearl Harbor on 30 May. *William J. Pattison* spent the next two weeks in amphibious and underwater demolition team (UDT) training, mostly at Maui.

On 13 June, she embarked 10 officers and 50 enlisted men and got underway for the Marshalls, in company with *Cavallaro* and SS *Cape Meares*. The three ships entered the lagoon at Eniwetok on 21 June; but two days later got underway again with a convoy bound for Ulithi Atoll in the Caroline Islands. She remained at Ulithi from 26 June to 1 July, when she began the two-day voyage to Leyte. After eight days at that island in the Philippines, she headed back to Ulithi on the 12th. In late July and early August, the warship made two voyages from Ulithi to Okinawa. Though both visits were somewhat enlivened by air raid alerts, *William J. Pattison* saw no action. The end of hostilities found the ship on her way from Okinawa to the Marianas. She arrived at Guam on 17 August and embarked UDT 18. On 20 August, she sailed in company with *Begor* and a group of LST's to join the 3d Fleet off Japan. The two high-speed transports soon parted company with the slower LST's and made the rendezvous on the night of 24 and 25 August.

She arrived in Tokyo Bay late in the afternoon of 27 August to begin her part in the postwar occupation of Japan. On the 30th, she supported the marines who occupied Yokosuka Naval Base, and her UDT unit carried out an inspection of the base's harbor facilities. Later, she participated in the demilitarization of captured Japanese warships. For the next month, *William J. Pattison* steamed among various Japanese bases located throughout the Home Islands, reconnoitering to prepare for their occupation by Marine Corps, Army, or Navy men. She also helped with further demilitarization projects.

On 30 September, the ship got underway on the first leg of her journey home. After stops at Guam, Eniwetok, and Pearl Harbor, the warship arrived back in San Diego on 22 October 1945.

William J. Pattison remained active with the Amphibious Forces, Pacific Fleet, into 1946. Early in that year, she moved to Green Cove Springs, Fla., where she was placed out of commission sometime in March. She remained in reserve there until 1 June 1960, when her name was struck from the Navy list. On 18 January 1962, she was sold to the First Steel & Ship Corp., of New York City, for scrapping.

William Johnson

Born sometime in 1715 at Smithtown, County Meath, Ireland, William Johnson came to America as a young man and soon became a prominent agent of the British in dealing with the Indian tribes of New York, particularly the Mohawks. He deserves much of the credit for keeping the Six Nations from supporting the French during King George's War in the mid-1740's. He fought with distinction during the French and Indian War; and, in the decade following the return of peace, he contributed greatly to the smooth transition from French to British rule north of the Ohio River. Johnson died on 11 July 1774 near the sight of the present town of Johnstown, N.Y., while attempting to persuade the leaders of the Six Nations not to become involved in Lord Dunmore's War which had broken out in Virginia.

(Tr: t. 324; l. 138′5″; b. 23′7″; dph. 12′8″; s. 10.5 k.; cpl. 25; a. small arms; cl. "Mersey")

William Johnson—a steel-hulled, screw steam trawler built in 1918 at Selby, England, by Cochrane and Sons, Ltd., for the British Admiralty—was acquired by the United States Navy in the spring of 1919 on loan from the Royal Navy for service with the forces sweeping the North Sea Mine Barrage and was placed in commission on 28 May 1919 at Grimsby, England, Lt. Valerious V. Black, USNRF, in command.

Assigned to Trawler Division 2, Minesweeping Detachment, United States Atlantic Fleet, *William Johnson* shifted to Kirkwall, Scotland—the base of the minesweeping force—on 30 May. She participated in the third sweep made by the detachment between 6 June and 1 July, one of seven trawlers to take part in this operation. *William Johnson* exploded a floating mine on 10 June and destroyed two more the next day. On the 14th, she was rocked by an explosion when a mine detonated under the ship. Fortunately, no damage resulted, and the ship remained on station in the minefields. She destroyed another mine during this sweep—on the 16th—before later returning to Kirkwall.

After voyage repairs and replenishing, *William Johnson* sailed again for the minefields to participate in the fourth sweep operation. While sweeping on 9 July, the trawler exploded a mine close aboard that "shook up the vessel considerably." Again, however, the trawler seemed to bear a charmed life—her log records (probably with a sigh of relief from the sailor who wrote it) "apparently no damage" was done.

A charmed life, though, did not hold for a sister Mersey-class trawler, *Richard Bulkeley*. On 12 July, the latter fouled a mine in her kite; and while her crew was trying to disengage it, accidentally set it off. The resultant explosion shattered the after part of the hull, opening the ship up to the sea; she filled with water quickly and sank within seven minutes. Comdr. Frank R. King, commanding the ill-fated trawler, went down with his ship as he endeavored to make sure that each member of his crew reached safety. *William Johnson* and *John Collins*—another trawler—altered course to close as *Richard Bulkeley* sank, and soon the former had picked up two men. Comdr. Ellis Lando, a classmate of King's, embarked in *William Johnson* as Commander, Trawler Division 2, risked his own life by diving overboard into the North Sea in an attempt to rescue a third sailor from *Richard Bulkeley's* crew. Comdr. Lando managed to get the man aboard, but the sailor's injuries proved fatal, and he was pronounced dead a short time later.

The loss of *Richard Bulkeley*—together with the general fragile construction evidenced in the group of trawlers loaned to the Navy—meant an end for most of the trawler's active minesweeping operations. *William Johnson*, however, appears to have been an exception, as she not only participated in the last two sweep operations but also performed unglamorous support tasks as well. She arrived at Rosyth, Scotland, Navy Yard, on 1 August; loaded a cargo of 14 reels of sweep wire the next day; and transported the cargo to Kirkwall. There, she took on board some minesweeping kites and delivered both kites and wire to other sweepers anchored in the harbor. She then proceeded to the minefields and took part in the sixth minesweeping operation conducted by the detachment.

Shifting to Inverness upon the completion of her operations, *William Johnson* took on a cargo of sweep wire and lubricating oil and delivered them to Kirkwall in mid-September before taking part in the last American minesweeping operation in the North Sea. By 30 September 1919, the commander of the Minesweeping Detachment could report that the Barrage was swept. With the task completed, the remaining trawlers were returned to the Admiralty.

Sailing to Brightlingsea, near Harwich, England, *William Johnson* was decommissioned and simultaneously delivered to the British Admiralty on 8 October 1919.

William Jones

During the American War of Independence from Great Britain, William Jones—born in 1760 at Philadelphia, Pa.—joined a company of volunteer infantry at age 16 and fought in the battles of Trenton and Princeton, N.J. He later served with distinction under Capt. Thomas Truxtun in the Pennsylvania state privateer *St. James*. During this service, Jones was twice wounded and captured by the British.

From 1790 to 1793, Jones made his home in Charleston, S.C., and sailed in the merchant service before he returned to Philadelphia. After establishing himself as a merchant in the shipping trade, Jones entered politics and ran for office. He subsequently served a term in the House of Representatives during the 7th United States Congress, from 1801 to 1803.

On 12 January 1813, Jones accepted the post of Secretary of the Navy in the cabinet of President James Madison, but he resigned on 2 December 1814 to return to private business. Subsequently appointed collector of customs at Philadelphia in 1827, he held this post until retirement in 1829.

William Jones died on 6 September 1831 at Bethlehem, Pa.

(DD–308: dp. 1,215; l. 314′4½″; b. 30′11¼″; dr. 9′4″ (mean); s. 35 k.; cpl. 122; a. 4 4″, 1 3″, 12 21″ tt.; cl. *Clemson*)

William Jones (Destroyer No. 308) was laid down on 2 October 1918 at San Francisco, Calif., by the Bethle-

The destroyer *William Jones* (DD–308). The numerous ships of the "four-stacker" classes formed the bulk of the destroyer force into the years just before World War II. (San Diego, 1920s)

hem Shipbuilding Corp.; launched on 9 April 1919; sponsored by Mrs. Ernest P. McRitchie, the wife of the assistant naval architect at Bethlehem Shipbuilding Corp.; reclassified as DD–308 on 17 July 1920; and commissioned at the Mare Island Navy Yard at Vallejo, Calif., on 30 September 1920, Lt. Comdr. C. E. Rosendahl in temporary command. Lt. Comdr. J. G. B. Gromer took command on 16 November.

Initially assigned to Division 34, Squadron 12, Destroyer Force, Pacific Fleet, *William Jones* operated off the west coast on duty in connection with the Officers' Engineering School until October 1921, cruising as far north as Seattle and as far south as the waters off the Panama Canal Zone. Assigned to Destroyer Squadrons, Battle Fleet, early in 1922, the destroyer operated with this force over the next seven years. Her operations took the ship up and down the west coast from Puget Sound to the Panama Canal. She took part in fleet maneuvers, exercises in torpedo firing and gunnery, and battle practices. In March 1925, she joined the Fleet for Fleet Problem V during which she screened the Battle Fleet units off Baja Calif., as they carried out maneuvers designed to practice protective screening, seizing and occupying a lightly defended position, and fueling at sea.

Later that summer, *William Jones* served as one of the ships plane-guarding for the *PN–9* flying boat flight to Hawaii. Dogged with misfortune throughout the operation, none of the planes actually flew all the way to Hawaii. One, *PN–9* number 3, was forced down by a malfunctioning fuel line. *William Jones* located her and went to her assistance, later towing her into San Francisco harbor on 1 September. *PN–9* number 1, flown by Comdr. John Rodgers, eventually reached Hawaii after an epic voyage in which her intrepid crew stripped the fabric from one wing and used it to fabricate a sail which propelled their fragile craft to Oahu.

From 5 to 15 September, *William Jones* participated in the Diamond Jubilee celebrations at San Francisco before resuming her operations and exercises off the west coast. She worked along the Pacific coast until 3 and 4 March 1926, when she transited the Panama Canal to take part in maneuvers with the Fleet in the Atlantic. She visited a succession of east coast ports and returned to the west coast on 30 June, when she moored again at San Diego.

William Jones conducted a reserve training cruise to Alaskan waters from 7 to 21 July 1928, pausing at Ketchikan, Juneau, and Sitka. After the ship's return to San Diego, she participated in tactical exercises off Balboa and, later, in joint Army-Navy maneuvers off Port Angeles, Wash., in July 1929.

Upon the conclusion of the joint exercises, the destroyer arrived at San Diego late in August 1929 and remained inactive there until decommissioned on 24 May 1930. In accordance with the London treaty for the limitation and reduction of naval armaments, the warship was struck from the Navy list on 13 August 1930 and sold for scrap on 25 February 1932.

William L. Jones

(Sch.)

William L. Jones—a wooden-hulled, Chesapeake-Bay schooner—was purchased by the Navy at Baltimore, Md., on 13 August 1861. Subsequently filled with stones, the schooner was taken to Hampton Roads, Va., in the first contingent of the Union Navy's "stone fleet" slated to block the entrances to the sounds off the coast of North Carolina. Her ultimate disposition is unrecorded, but most of the vessels of that first contingent sank at their moorings at Hampton Roads and thus never reached North Carolina waters.

William Lee

(Ship: t. 418)

William Lee—the last wooden-hulled whaling ship built at Newport, R.I.—was acquired by the Navy on 16 November 1861. Loaded with stones and initially earmarked for use as an obstruction at Savannah, Ga., *William Lee* made a final one-way voyage, southbound, soon thereafter, under Horace A. Lake, master. On the afternoon of 19 December 1861, 16 whalers—*William Lee* included—were ultimately positioned in a controlled checkerboard pattern across the entrance to Charleston, S.C., harbor and sunk in a planned pattern of destruction. As Herman Melville described their fate: "They sunk so slow, they died so hard, but, gurgling, dropped at last;" *William Lee*, regarded by one contemporary newspaper correspondent as having been a "fine old ship" was among those 16 ships that had sunk in their pre-arranged positions by the following day.

William M. Hobby

William Matthews Hobby, Jr.—born on 27 July 1899 in Sylvania, Ga.—was appointed a midshipman from the 1st district of Georgia on 20 June 1919 and graduated in the class of 1923.

After initial sea duty in the battleship *Oklahoma* (BB–37) from June 1923 to April 1925, Hobby underwent brief aviation instruction at Pensacola, Fla.; reported to destroyer *Kidder* (DD–319) on 21 November 1925; and served in that ship as she earned the 2d Nicaraguan campaign ribbon.

Hobby then underwent submarine instruction at the Submarine Base, New London, Conn., from late December 1927 to June of the following year. He then travelled to the Asiatic station, where he reported to the submarine tender *Canopus* (AS–9) on 10 August 1928, prior to his joining the submarine *S–37* (SS–142) 10 days later. After successive tours in *S–41* (SS–146) and *S–30* (SS–135), Hobby returned to the United States for service at the United States Naval Academy from May 1931 to June 1933. He then helped to fit out the submarine *Cachalot* (SS–171) before serving back-to-back tours in battleship *Tennessee* (BB–43) and training ship *Wyoming* (AG–17) into the summer of 1938.

Hobby reported to the Federal Shipbuilding and Dry Dock Co., Kearny, N.J., on 11 May 1939, to supervise the fitting out of the new *Sims*-class destroyer *Anderson* (DD–411) and to become her first commanding officer when she was placed in commission.

Detached on 22 March 1941, Hobby then rejoined the battleship *Oklahoma* four days later as damage control officer and 1st lieutenant. After the battleship capsized and sank in the Japanese attack against Pearl Harbor on 7 December 1941, Hobby served briefly in the 12th Naval District before he joined the new battleship *Washington* (BB–56) on 3 January 1942. He acted as navigator of that battlewagon until he relieved Comdr. Walter E. Moore as executive officer of the light cruiser *Juneau* (CL–52) at Espiritu Santo on 2 November 1942.

Ten days later, *Juneau* was heavily damaged during the Naval Battle of Guadalcanal. The following afternoon, Friday the 13th, while she was returning to Espiritu Santo, the cruiser was literally blown into bits by a torpedo from the Japanese submarine *I–26* which detonated her magazine. Commander Hobby was among those who perished in the cataclysmic blast that tore the ship apart.

(APD–95: dp. 1,650; l. 306'0"; b. 37'0"; dr. 12'7"; s. 23.6 k.; cpl. 201; trp. 162; a. 1 5", 6 40mm., 6 20mm.; 2 dct.; cl. *Charles Lawrence*)

William M. Hobby (DE–236) was laid down on 15 November 1943 at the Charleston (S.C.) Navy Yard. Since she had been constructed in a drydock, there was no launching ceremony *per se*, and she was floated out on 2 February 1944. The ship was redesignated a fast transport, APD–95, on 17 July 1944; and she was completed as such at her builder's yard. She was simultaneously christened and commissioned at Charleston on 4 April 1945. Miss Catherine Hobby, the sister of the late Commander Hobby, sponsored the ship; Lt. Comdr. Frank N. Christiansen, USNR, was her first commanding officer.

Following shakedown training in Guantanamo Bay, Cuba, *William M. Hobby* proceeded to Norfolk, Va. From 16 to 21 May, the new fast transport conducted an "amphibious shakedown," including shore bombardment exercises off Bloodsworth Island in Chesapeake Bay. After post-shakedown repairs at the Norfolk Navy Yard, *William M. Hobby* held additional shakedown gunnery training in Chesapeake Bay before she departed Hampton Roads, Va., on 3 June, bound for Panama in company with her sistership *Amesbury* (APD–46).

William M. Hobby reached Christobal on 8 June, completed the transit of the canal on the 10th, and set course for the California coast immediately thereafter. Arriving at San Diego on the 17th, the fast transport got underway for the Hawaiian Islands in company with *Amesbury* and *O'Reilly* (DE–330) on the 20th.

Making Pearl Harbor on the 27th, *William M. Hobby* trained underwater demolition teams (UDT's) at Maaleea Bay, Maui, Territory of Hawaii, in July before she embarked UDT 29 for transportation to the west coast. Departing the Hawaiian Islands on 2 August, *William M. Hobby* made port at Oceanside, Calif.—near San Diego—one week later.

Shifting briefly to San Pedro, the fast transport returned to Oceanside and disembarked UDT 29 on 13 August. The following day, Japan surrendered, ending the war in the Pacific. On the 16th, *William M. Hobby* sailed for Hawaii.

Reaching Pearl Harbor on the 22d, the fast transport got underway on the 24th for the Marshall Islands, in company with *Ira Jeffrey* (APD–44) and *Blessman* (APD–48), and arrived at Eniwetok on 1 September. Pushing on to the Philippines, she anchored in Manila Bay on the 5th. *William M. Hobby* cruised in the Philippine archipelago—touching at Subic Bay, Zamboanga, Mindanao, Bugo, Macajalar Bay, and San Pedro Bay—until she sailed for Okinawa, and from thence to Japan.

Reaching Wakayama, Japan, on 28 September, *William M. Hobby* soon got underway for Hiro Wan, Honshu, with UDT 5 embarked. Daybreak on 1 October found the fast transport entering the Inland Sea. There, she joined *Tracy* (DM–19), who led the APD to her anchorage at Hiro Wan. That morning, the ship sighted a floating mine off her port bow and destroyed it with 40-millimeter, 20-millimeter, and rifle fire. The ship's embarked UDT reconnoitered beaches and shore installations at Hiro Wan from 2 to 10 October to prepare the way for the arrival of American occupation troops in the Kure area.

On 11 October, *William M. Hobby* got underway for the island of Shikoku and arrived at the port of Mitsuhama later that day. The fast transport disembarked the 15 American Army officers, 18 enlisted men, and two Japanese officers whom she had carried as passengers and remained at anchor off Mitsuhama while UDT 5 reconnoitered the beaches there.

After returning once more to Hiro Wan, *William M. Hobby* got underway for the United States on 14 October. Proceeding via Guam, Eniwetok, Pearl Harbor, San Diego, and the Panama Canal, she arrived at Philadelphia on 9 December. The fast transport subsequently shifted southward via Norfolk to Green Cove Springs, Fla., where she arrived on 6 January 1946. She was decommissioned there and placed in reserve on 6 April 1946.

William M. Hobby remained in reserve until she was struck from the Navy list on 1 May 1967. Transferred to the government of South Korea on a grant-in-aid on 23 July 1967, the fast transport was renamed *Chr Ju* (PG–87). Initially classified as a gunboat (PG), she was later reclassified in Korean service to APD–87 in 1972. She remained in service with the Korean Navy into 1979.

William M. Wood

See *Wood* (DD–317) for the biography of *William M. Wood*.

The contract for the construction of *William M. Wood* (DE–287)—a *Rudderow*-class destroyer escort slated to be built by the Bethlehem-Hingham Shipyard of Hingham, Mass.—was cancelled on 12 March 1944, before her keel was laid.

With the cancellation of the contract for the construc- of DE–287, the name *William M. Wood* was assigned to DE–557, a *John C. Butler*-class destroyer escort slated to be built by the Boston Navy Yard. However, before fabrication of the warship began, the contract for her construction was cancelled on 10 June 1944.

I

(DD–715: dp. 2,425; l. 390'6"; b. 40'10"; dr. 18'6"; s. 34.6 k. (tl.); cpl. 345; a. 6'5", 12 40mm., 4 20mm., 5 21" tt., 6 dcp., 2 dct.; cl. *Gearing*)

William M. Wood (DD–715) was laid down on 2 November 1944 at Newark, N.J., by the Federal Shipbuilding & Drydock Co.; launched on 29 July 1945; sponsored by Mrs. Joseph P. Tracy; and commissioned at the New York Naval Shipyard on 24 November 1945, Comdr. George R. Wilson in command.

Following shakedown out of Guantanamo Bay, Cuba, and type training in the Norfolk area, *William M. Wood* operated in the Caribbean Sea from April to June 1946. In June, she was reassigned to the Pacific Fleet. She arrived in San Diego during the first week in July but departed there a week later, bound for Hawaii. The destroyer operated out of Pearl Harbor from mid-July to late September, when she received orders to duty along the coast of China. The warship arrived in Tsing-tao, China, near the middle of October and began patrolling the Yellow Sea between northern China and Korea in an effort to stem postwar smuggling. That task lasted until February 1947 when she headed back to the United States, arriving in San Diego early in March.

During the following six months, *William M. Wood* conducted type training along the Pacific coast and underwent a three-month overhaul. In October 1947, the destroyer joined Destroyer Division (DesDiv) 131 in screening *Valley Forge* (CV–45) on an extended voyage to the western Pacific. In the ensuing seven months, the ships called at Sydney, Australia; Hong Kong; Shanghai and Tsingtao in China; and Yokosuka, Japan. She returned to San Diego with the unit in May 1948 and resumed normal training and upkeep operations which were broken once by a two-month overhaul at the Mare Island Naval Shipyard.

On 1 April 1949, a new fleet organization was promulgated reassigning *William M. Wood* to the Atlantic Fleet. The destroyer, however, remained on the west coast until 5 October, when she finally sailed for her new home port, Newport, R.I. She reported for duty with the Destroyer Force, Atlantic Fleet (DesLant) on 21 October. The warship served DesLant as a school ship training junior officers in gunnery and engineering. In May 1950, the warship participated in a Navy-Marine Corps amphibious exercise conducted on the North Carolina coast. During the following month, she conducted underway training out of Newport. July brought a brief tour of duty in Caribbean waters with a hunter/killer group and a quick visit to Iceland.

The destroyer returned to Newport in August but put to sea the next month for the first of many deployments with the 6th Fleet in the Mediterranean Sea. After two months of duty, however, *William M. Wood* left the 6th Fleet to resume operations out of United States ports. Following a brief leave and upkeep period at Newport, the destroyer moved south to Pensacola, Fla., where she served for a time as plane guard for *Monterey* (CVL–26) during carrier qualifications.

At the conclusion of that assignment, she returned to normal duty out of Newport. In January 1952, she embarked upon her second Mediterranean cruise. That tour of duty lasted seven months during which time she participated in several NATO multinational exercises. That tour of duty also included visits to ports in the United Kingdom, Belgium, and Germany. She returned to Newport in July and, after a voyage to Halifax in company with *Midway* (CVB–41) late in September, entered the Boston Naval Shipyard to begin conversion to a radar picket destroyer. She was placed out of commission on 2 October 1952 and redesignated DRR–715.

William M. Wood completed her conversion to a radar picket destroyer during the summer of 1953 and was recommissioned on 6 June 1953, Comdr. J. S. Slaughter in command. Following a shakedown cruise to Guantanamo Bay, Cuba, that fall, she began her third tour of duty with the 6th Fleet in November. At the end of several weeks of operations with the 6th Fleet, the radar picket destroyer returned to Norfolk early in February 1954.

The following month, she journeyed south to Pensacola, Fla., where she once again planeguarded for *Monterey* during carrier qualifications. The summer of 1954 brought the ship a two-month midshipman cruise to European waters where she made port calls at Cadiz, Spain, and Rotterdam in the Netherlands. She returned to Norfolk in August and spent the remainder of 1954 engaged in training operations. In January of 1955, she embarked upon her fourth deployment to the Mediterranean. Again, NATO exercises and port visits at various points along the Mediterranean littoral kept the ship busy. She was in port at Volos, Greece, between 19 and 21 April, during which time the city suffered a series of severe earthquakes. She remained there after the disaster and rendered all possible aid to the victims.

Returning to the United States that summer, she entered the Philadelphia Naval Shipyard for a major overhaul. That fall, the warship conducted refresher training and then returned to Norfolk to prepare for her upcoming Mediterranean deployment. That tour of duty began in February 1956 and ended the following June. Between June and October, she operated out of Norfolk along the coasts of the Carolinas, Georgia, and Florida conducting air defense exercises. Mounting tensions in the Middle East precipitated an Israeli invasion of the Egyptian Sinai on 29 October, and *William M. Wood* hastened to the eastern Mediterranean in November to join Task Force (TF) 26 in helping to restore peace and order in that chronically troubled sector of the world. The crisis cooled quickly enabling the warship to return home in time to celebrate the Christmas holidays.

The warship began 1957 with Operation "Springboard," conducted in the West Indies in January and February. In March, she escorted *Canberra* (CA–70) when that cruiser carried President Eisenhower to Bermuda to confer with British Prime Minister Harold Macmillan. *William M. Wood* provided transportation for the members of the press who covered the President's visit. In June, she entered the Norfolk Naval Shipyard for a three-month overhaul.

Following that, she conducted refresher training out of Guantanamo Bay, Cuba, for six weeks. In November, the destroyer resumed normal duty out of Norfolk with the Atlantic Fleet. She began 1958 the same way she began 1957, with "Springboard" exercises in the Caribbean during January and February. Then in June, at the conclusion of three months of normal Atlantic Fleet duty, the warship embarked upon a Mediterranean cruise.

Not long after her arrival in the Mediterranean, fighting erupted in Lebanon. The intensification of the strife prompted the pro-western Lebanese President Chamoun to seek military help from the United States. President Eisenhower responded immediately by sending Marine Corps units ashore in the troubled country and stationing 6th Fleet ships offshore to support them. During the period 14 July and 3 September, *William M. Wood* spent 40 days on station patrolling off the Lebanese coast. Following brief visits to Izmir, Turkey; Naples, Italy; and Gibraltar, she headed back to Norfolk and arrived there on 30 September. Normal Atlantic Fleet operations, including exercises along the coast and in the Caribbean, ensued.

Over the next decade, *William M. Wood* continued to alternate 6th Fleet deployments with duty along the Atlantic coast and in the Caribbean area. In August 1962, she returned to the United States from her 10th Mediterranean assignment and resumed operations out of Norfolk.

That employment, however, was interrupted in October when President John F. Kennedy declared the "quarantine" of Cuba in response to the siting of offensive, nuclear missiles on the island. For 57 days, *William M. Wood* participated in the quasi-blockade patrols conducted around Cuba to prevent the importation of further missiles and to ensure the removal of those already there.

At the successful conclusion of that mission, the warship resumed normal east coast operations. In February 1963, members of Venezuela's communist insurgent group, the FALN, hijacked the Venezuelan freighter, SS *Anzoategui*, and *William M. Wood* joined ships from several navies in an international search for the merchant ship. Their efforts proved to be in vain for the terrorists eluded capture, entered the Brazilian port of Belem, and received political asylum.

Following her return from her 11th Mediterranean deployment in the spring of 1964, *William M. Wood* entered the Philadelphia Naval Shipyard on 18 May 1964 to begin a Fleet Rehabilitation and Modernization (FRAM) overhaul. During that period, she was converted from a radar picket destroyer back to an all-purpose destroyer. She was redesignated DD–715 on 1 July 1964 and completed her FRAM conversion on 11 March 1965 when she headed back to Norfolk to rejoin the Atlantic Fleet.

In the midst of her post-overhaul refresher training, a revolution broke out in the Dominican Republic on 24 April. On the 29th, the destroyer received orders interrupting her refresher training, and she hastened to the scene of the conflict to protect foreign nationals caught in the middle and to support an American, and later, multinational expeditionary force dispatched to the island by the Organization of American States. The situation was soon stabilized, and *William M. Wood* began a coastal patrol and surveillance assignment. While so engaged, she picked up 13 foreigners, including some American citizens, who requested evacuation. These people were transferred to *Pawcatuck* (AO–108) on 7 May; and, the following day, *O'Hare* (DD–889) relieved her on station off the Dominican Republic. *William M. Wood* then resumed refresher training and completed it on 20 May.

On 18 June, after post-refresher availability at Norfolk, the destroyer embarked upon another tour of duty in the Mediterranean with the 6th Fleet and continued alternating such deployments with normal duty out of Norfolk with the Atlantic Fleet. During 1968, she operated with the antisubmarine warfare (ASW) forces attached to the Atlantic Fleet. In May and June of 1968, she participated in the unsuccessful search for the nuclear attack submarine *Scorpion* (SSN–589) reported missing on 27 May. She closed the year in overhaul at Norfolk.

During her last eight years of active service, *William M. Wood* made two more routine Mediterranean cruises and then served there on a three-year extended deployment. During the first of her last two normal Mediterranean deployments, which lasted from 12 November 1969 to 22 May 1970, she shadowed two new Soviet ships, *Moskva* and *Leningrad*, to gather intelligence on the new hermaphrodite cruisers/ASW carriers. The second of the two cruises lasted from 8 February to 23 July 1971 and consisted of more routine 6th Fleet operations, mostly training exercises both multinational and unilateral.

Following almost 13 months of 2d Fleet operations during late 1971 and early 1972, the warship embarked upon an extended assignment to the 6th Fleet on 18 August. Her home port was officially changed to Athens, Greece, from which port she operated for almost three years. The warship spent most of her time during that period engaged in training operations with other units of the 6th Fleet and with elements of Allied navies. She also made several forays into the Black Sea for special operations there. In July and August of 1974, she conducted continuous patrols in the vicinity of Crete during the Turkish invasion of Cyprus.

Her extended deployment with the 6th Fleet ended in June of 1975 when she began a long voyage home. The destroyer visited ports in France, Germany, Denmark, England, and Bermuda before arriving back in Norfolk on 23 July. After six months of normal operations out of Norfolk, *William M. Wood* deployed to the Mediterranean one final time in January of 1976. She returned to the United States that summer and resumed 2d Fleet operations. On 1 December 1976, she was placed out of commission at Norfolk, and her name was struck from the Navy list that same day. She was stripped at Norfolk and sold for scrap sometime in 1977.

William N. Page

William Nelson Page—born on 6 January 1854 in Campbell County, Va.—attended special courses in engineering at the University of Virginia and became a civil and mining engineer. He took part in the construction of the Chesapeake and Ohio (C&O) Railway, directing the location and construction of the New River canyon bridge in 1871 and 1872, of the Mill Creek Canyon (Va.) bridge in 1874. In 1875 and 1876, he led the surveying party charged with mapping out the route of the double-track railway ordered by Congress to extend between the Ohio River and Hampton Roads. He was the general manager of the Hawks Nest Coal Co. between 1877 and 1880; operated the Victoria Blast Furnace at Goshen, Va., from 1880 to 1885; and located and built the Powellton bridge of the C&O Railway between 1885 and 1889.

After developing the Mt. Carbon Collieries, he organized and developed the Gauley Mountain Coal Co. between 1889 and 1917 and became a consulting coal engineer for that organization. Page served as a consulting engineer for other coal-producing firms during that time as well. In addition to his engineering achievements, Page served as a mayor of Anstead, West Virginia, for 10 years and rose to the rank of brigadier inspector general in the West Virginia National Guard. Page died in Washington, D.C., on 7 March 1932.

(Freighter: dp. 12,163; l. 395'1''; b. 55'0''; dph. 34'5''; dr. 27'0''; s. 12.0 k.; cpl. 97; a. 1 4'', 1 3'')

William N. Page—a steel-hulled, single-screw steamship built under a shipping board contract in 1918 at Camden, N.J., by the New York Ship Building and Dry Dock Corp.—was taken over by the Navy for operation by the Naval Overseas Transportation Service (NOTS); assigned Id. No. 3844; and simultaneously commissioned at Camden on 18 December 1918, Lt. H. L. Ertel, USNRF, in command.

After fitting out, *William N. Page* loaded general cargo and locomotives and departed New York on 11 January 1919. She arrived at Brest, France, on the 27th, unloaded her cargo, and sailed, in ballast, for Norfolk on 8 February.

Making arrival at her destination on the 27th, *William N. Page* loaded cargo and underwent voyage repairs before she sailed for La Pallice, France, on 23 March. Arriving there on 8 April, she found the harbor congested and shifted to Verdon-sur-Mer the same day. There, she unloaded and took on board 995 tons of return Army cargo over ensuing days. She ultimately sailed for Norfolk on 10 May.

William N. Page concluded her last voyage for NOTS on 25 May when she arrived at Norfolk and commenced unloading. Six days later, on 31 May 1919, she was decommissioned and struck from the Navy list. Simultaneously returned to the Shipping Board, *William N. Page* remained in active merchant service for nearly three decades. Her successive owners and operators included the Mystic Steamship Co., the Koppers Coal Co., and Eastern Gas and Fuel Associates. She operated with the last-named firm from about 1943 until her name disappeared from period shipping registers after 1947.

William P. Biddle

William Phillips Biddle—born in Philadelphia, Pa., on 17 December 1853—was commissioned a second lieutenant in the Marine Corps on 22 June 1875. After sea duty in *Hartford* and *Powhatan*, he served at the Marine Barracks at Philadelphia and New York before he returned to sea duty in *Kearsarge* in 1882. Promoted to 1st lieutenant two years later and to captain in 1894, Biddle served in the cruiser *Baltimore* in June 1895 and shortly afterwards was transferred to the cruiser *Olympia*, in which he served during the Spanish-American War, and took part in the Battle of Manila Bay in April 1898. He later commanded the marines ashore in the Philippines who had secured the Cavite Navy Yard and established outposts covering the approaches to Manila.

Biddle next served in Marine expeditionary forces in the Boxer Rebellion in 1900 and in pacification operations during the Philippine Insurrection from 1901 to 1903 before he returned to the United States for duty at Headquarters, Marine Corps. Promoted to lieutenant colonel on 23 March 1903, Biddle commanded a reinforcing battalion of marines embarked in the auxiliary cruiser *Dixie* sent to Panama when a revolution broke out there in November 1903. The ship arrived just in time to participate in the celebrations honoring the independence of that country from Colombia.

Later promoted to colonel in 1905, Biddle was chosen commandant of the Marine Corps on 3 February 1911 and served in that post until his retirement on 24 February 1914 with the rank of major general. During his tenure, Biddle emphasized training and established recruit depots at Philadelphia; Port Royal, S.C.; Mare Island, Calif.; and Puget Sound, Wash.

Recalled to active duty during World War I, Biddle served primarily on court-martial duty at San Diego before returning to private life after a second retirement. On 24 February 1923—exactly nine years after his initial retirement, Biddle died at Nice, France. He was buried at Arlington National Cemetery.

I

(AP–15: dp. 14,450; l. 507'0''; b. 56'0''; dr. 25'6''; s. 16.5 k.; a. 1 5'', 4 3'', 4 .50-cal. mg.; cl. *Heywood*)

Initially laid-down for the British government as *War Surf*, the ship that ultimately became known as *William P. Biddle* (AP–15) was completed in 1919 as the single-screw, steel-hulled freighter *Eclipse*. Built by the Bethlehem Shipbuilding Corp. of Alameda, Calif., under a United States Shipping Board contract, the former *War Surf* was requisitioned by the United States government before she was delivered to the United Kingdom and thus never actually carried her British name.

After a period of about 10 years under the ownership of the Shipping Board, *Eclipse* was acquired by the Baltimore Mail Steamship Co., of Baltimore, Md., in about 1930. Reconstructed at the Federal Shipbuilding and Drydock Co., Kearny, N.J., to the lines drawn up by the noted naval architect firm of Gibbs and Cox, Inc., *Eclipse* was lengthened by 46'6''; accommodations were installed for 81 tourist-class passengers; and the ship was reengined to give her a substantial boost in horsepower and speed.

Renamed *City of Hamburg*, the steamship performed passenger, fast freight, and mail service between the terminal ports of Baltimore, Hampton Roads, Le Havre and Hamburg with the Baltimore Mail Steamship Co. from 1938 to 1939, when the United States government refused further subsidies for the firm's international operations. *City of Hamburg* was acquired by the Panama-Pacific Line and renamed *City of San Francisco* in 1939, and she operated between New York and San Francisco until acquired by the Navy on 13 November 1940.

Simultaneously placed in commission "in ordinary" as *William P. Biddle* (AP–15), at Oakland, Calif., with Capt. Campbell D. Edgar in command, the ship was taken in hand for extensive conversion at the Moore Dry Dock Co. of Oakland. Over the ensuing months, the erstwhile passenger-cargo vessel was transformed to a transport, with the dockyard workers sometimes putting in 24-hour shifts. *William P. Biddle*—now sporting the peacetime Navy gray—was ultimately placed in full commission on 3 February 1941. That day, Capt. Frank A. Braisted broke his broad command pennant in the ship as Commander, Troop Transports, Base Force.

Shifted to the Mare Island Navy Yard, Vallejo, Calif., soon thereafter, *William P. Biddle* underwent further alterations there through mid-February. She ran her post-repair trials in San Francisco Bay on the 21st and, two days later, shifted to San Diego, Calif., where she embarked marines of the 7th Defense Battalion, USMC. The transport then departed San Diego on 27 February, bound for the Hawaiian Islands.

After a two-day layover at Pearl Harbor, *William P. Biddle* got underway at 1040 on 9 March. An hour later, she joined the light cruiser *Concord* (CL–10) (with Commander, Cruiser Division 3 embarked)—her escort for the voyage to Samoa. On the 15th, the two ships arrived at Pago Pago, where *William P. Biddle* disembarked 24 officers and 405 enlisted men of the composite infantry-artillery unit that was the first unit of the Fleet Marine Force to serve in the Southern Hemisphere during World War II.

After fueling *Concord* at Pago Pago, *William P. Biddle* and her escort sailed for the Hawaiian Islands on the 20th. The transport then spent three days at Pearl Harbor before pushing on for the west coast, arriving at San Diego on 4 April. She subsequently took part in maneuvers off San Clemente Island, conducting landing exercises at Pyramid Cove, into May.

Meanwhile that spring, plans to reinforce the Fleet Marine Forces of the Atlantic Fleet for the possible occupation of Martinique were proceeding apace. On 24 May, General Thomas Holcomb, the Commandant of the Marine Corps, drew upon the manpower resources of the 2d Marine Division, selecting the 6th Marine Regiment (Col. Leo D. Hermle, USMC, in command) for "temporary shore duty beyond the seas." Brought up to strength by drafts from the 2d and 8th Regiments, and joined by reinforcing tank, artillery, and service elements, the 6th Marine Regiment embarked in *William P. Biddle*, *Heywood* (AP–12), *Fuller* (AP–14), *Manley* (APD–1), *McKean* (APD–5), *Stringham* (APD–6), and *Little* (APD–4). *William P. Biddle* took on board 27 officers and 497 enlisted men from the 6th and 2d Defense Battalions, USMC, while moored at the Long Pier, Destroyer Base, San Diego. At 1826 on Memorial Day 1941, the transport, flying Commodore Braisted's pennant as ComTransBaseFor, departed San Diego, bound for that duty "beyond the seas."

En route, *William P. Biddle* fueled *Little* and arrived at the Pacific entrance to the Panama Canal at 2048 on 9 June. Less than an hour later, *Stringham* transferred five officers and 51 enlisted marines from "K" Company to the transport before she began the transit of the canal. *William P. Biddle* passed through the last set of locks—Pedro Miguel—shortly before midnight on the 9th and moored at Cristobal at 0512 on the 10th to take on fuel.

Slipping out to sea at 2211 from Limon Bay, Cristobal, in company with *Fuller* and *Heywood* and escorted by the venerable "flush-deckers" *Tattnall* (DD–125) and *Barry* (DD–248), *William P. Biddle* sailed for Charleston, S.C., the assembly point for an expeditionary force.

While the ships were en route, however, changes in the ultimate disposition of the troops had occurred. Late that spring, British Prime Minister Winston Churchill had come to President Franklin D. Roosevelt with a request for assistance. Britain, feeling that her back was to the wall, wanted the United States to send troops to Iceland. In response to this request, the President turned to the Navy and discovered that a reinforced infantry regiment, the 6th Marines, earmarked for possible expeditionary duty, was already en route from the west coast—a tailor-made Iceland occupation force!

The most probable mission for these marines had been either the seizure of Martinique or the occupation of the Azores. However, intelligence indicated that Germany was about to invade Russia. As a result, President Roosevelt suspended the planning for the Azores operation and instead decided to assume the guardianship over Iceland.

Meanwhile, *William P. Biddle* and her consorts continued on their voyage from San Diego. The transports cleared the canal and turned north, then passed the western end of Cuba, and arrived at Charleston on 15 June. The next day, the 1st Marine Brigade (Provisional) came into existence, with Brigadier General John Marston in command. Six days later, with the last of the equipment loaded, the convoy sailed for Newfoundland.

William P. Biddle—as part of the convoy now escorted by a strong contingent of escorts ranging from battleships to destroyers—anchored in Placentia Bay, Argentia, on 28 June. On 1 July, the government of Iceland issued an invitation for the United States to land troops; and, by dawn on the 2d, the convoy was en route to conduct the landing on the strategic island in the North Atlantic. *William P. Biddle* arrived at Reykjavik on 7 July and commenced disembarking the 3d Battalion, 6th Marines.

Hitler had ordered his U-boats to spare American shipping; but the Americans—unaware of this German policy—hurried to unload the four transports and two accompanying cargo ships. Since there was little local labor, the marines furnished the working parties. Round-the-clock effort was immeasurably aided by the nearly 24 hours of daylight prevalent at that time of year. The landing was completed by 11 July, and *William P. Biddle* and her consorts soon sailed for home, leaving the 1st Marine Brigade (Provisional) to establish the base that would be their home on the bleak, treeless island for the next eight months.

William P. Biddle arrived at the Norfolk Navy Yard on 22 July for post-voyage repairs and upkeep. She then made one more voyage to Iceland, departing Norfolk on 14 August and arriving at Staten Island, N.Y., the next day. There, she embarked Army troops at the beginning of September and got underway on 5 September, arriving at Reykjavik on the 16th. Departing Iceland on the 25th, *William P. Biddle* arrived at the New York Navy Yard on 6 October.

After repairs there, the transport headed south and arrived at Hampton Roads on 23 October. She operated in Lynnhaven Roads and Hampton Roads, training in amphibious warfare tactics and techniques until 17 January 1942. During that time, tensions in the Pacific had reached their peak when a Japanese carrier force attacked Pearl Harbor on 7 December 1941 and pushed the United States over the brink of a rapidly eroding neutrality into war.

The transport departed Norfolk on 17 January 1942, arrived at the Army docks at New York the next day, and remained in the New York area until shifting back to Norfolk at the end of the month. For the rest of that winter, the ship carried troops—taking marines to San Juan, Puerto Rico, and Army troops to Guantanamo—before entering the Norfolk Navy Yard on 1 March for reconversion.

William P. Biddle received an augmented antiaircraft battery and new davits to accommodate more up-to-date landing craft before she departed the yard on 15 April. She trained in the Chesapeake Bay area from 16 April to 13 October before getting underway for North Africa on 24 October as part of Operation "Torch," the first major American combat landing in the European-African-Middle Eastern Area.

The transport sailed as part of Task Group (TG) 34.9, the "Center Attack Group"—commanded by Capt. Robert Emmett—which consisted of a dozen transports and three cargo ships. Embarked in the transports were the Army's 3d Infantry Division, the 1st Battalion of the 67th Armored Regiment, and assorted special units. There were 19,810 men riding in those ships, along with 79 light M3 "General Stuart" tanks. The task assigned TG 34.9 was a pivotal one, since it was to be launched against the key port of Fedhala, to the northeast of the seaport of Casablanca, on the coast of French Morocco.

William P. Biddle arrived off the Casablanca-Fedhala sector at 0011 on 8 November, heaving-to in the transport area and hoisting out her boats and tank lighters. At 0445, the first troops began storming ashore. By 1513, men in *William P. Biddle* noted that the American flag had been raised over the beachhead. The transport continued her unloading evolutions into the following day, a slow process due to lack of boats and lighters, many of which had become stranded on the beaches by the low tide.

While the ship herself saw little action, four of her landing boats did. Carrying 113 officers and men of a Headquarters Military Police (MP) company, those four craft set out for Beach "Yellow" at about 0400 on the 11th. Two blundered into French waters off Casablanca where a French patrol craft raked the boats with machine gunfire, killing the MP company commander in the fusillade. Both American craft sank, and the survivors were taken prisoner. The other two boats returned to the ship in the forenoon and reported the fate of their less fortunate sisters. The lost landing craft had carried three officers and 84 men. When planes of unknown nationality appeared later that day, the transport group—taking no chances—fired at them; and *William P. Biddle* contributed her share of fire.

Unloading operations proceeded over the ensuing days, until French resistance ceased. On the 11th, French torpedoes struck the USAT *Joseph Hewes*, the oiler *Winooski* (AO–38), and the destroyer *Hambleton* (DD–455). *Joseph Hewes* sank at 2050, and boats from *William P. Biddle* rescued one officer and 12 men, brought them aboard the transport, and berthed and clothed them. The next day, when the Army transports *Hugh L. Scott*, *Edward Rutledge*, and *Tasker H. Bliss* were torpedoed, *William P. Biddle*'s boats again participated in rescue efforts and later landed survivors at Fedhala.

After shifting to the secured port of Casablanca to unload more cargo on the 16th, the transport set course for the United States the next day. Her performance during Operation "Torch" had been impressive, eliciting praise from Commander, Transport Division 1 and Commander TG 34.9. The latter, Capt. R. E. M. Emmet, remarked simply: "The (*William P.*) *Biddle* has developed into a smart ship."

William P. Biddle reached Hampton Roads on 30 November and received repairs and alterations at the Norfolk Navy Yard between 6 and 17 December; fueled at Craney Island, and shifted to local Army embarkation piers on the 18th to embark the men and gear of Construction Battalion 40 (Seabees). Standing out of Hampton Roads two days after Christmas of 1942 as part of TF 39, *William P. Biddle* headed south; transited the Panama Canal on 3 January 1943; and made port at Noumea, New Caledonia, on 27 January. Pushing on two days later, the ship then called at Espiritu Santo in the New Hebrides from 3 to 5 February before she headed for home. During that period, on 1 February, *William P. Biddle* was reclassified an attack transport, APA–8.

William P. Biddle soon headed home. She retransited the Panama Canal on 24 February, steamed north via Norfolk, and arrived back at New York on 11 March. In keeping with her new designation, the ship entered the Todd-Erie Basin Yard, Brooklyn, N.Y., to be overhauled and outfitted as an attack transport. Alterations were made from 12 March to 21 April to the ship's armament and to her boat equipment to enable her to function better in her new role. Departing New York on 24 April, *William P. Biddle* stood into Norfolk harbor the following day, where, in the ensuing days, she embarked Army troops at the Army port of embarkation. Departing Norfolk on 8 June, the attack transport headed once more for the Mediterranean.

William P. Biddle arrived at Oran on 22 June and trained off that port in amphibious exercises on the 24th and 25th. Soon thereafter, she joined the veritable Allied armada bound for Sicily, that strategic island on the "toe" of the Italian "boot."

William P. Biddle, as part of Task Force (TF) 85 under the overall direction of Rear Admiral Alan G. Kirk, formed part of TG 85.2, Attack Group 2, attached to Transport Division 5. Together with *Charles Carroll* (APA–28), *Susan B. Anthony* (AP–72), *Thomas Jefferson* (APA–30), *Procyon* (AKA–2), *Arcturus* (AKA–1), and five LST's, *William P. Biddle* landed troops at landing area "Cent," the easternmost beachhead established on 10 July, and then troops, supported by naval gunfire, pushed inland. By 17 August, when Allied forces entered the city of Messina, Sicily was secured.

William P. Biddle, however, did not see the end of the campaign; she sailed from Scoglitti on 12 July and reached Oran on the 15th. There, she took on board German and Italian prisoners of war for transportation to the United States, departing Oran on the 22d, bound for Newport News, Va.

Making port on 3 August, the attack transport remained in the Tidewater area only briefly before getting underway for the west coast. Embarking Marine Corps units at Guantanamo Bay on 28 August, en route, *William P. Biddle* shifted to Panama on the 30th to pick up Army troops, transited the canal, and arrived at San Diego on 9 September. Then, after taking on stores and provisions at San Francisco between 12 and 20 September, the attack transport headed for the Hawaiian Islands.

After a brief respite in Hawaiian waters, *William P. Biddle* departed Honolulu on 1 October and arrived at Samoa on the 8th. Three days later, the attack transport sailed for New Zealand and arived at Wellington on the 18th. She conducted landing exercises with marines at Hawkes Bay, New Zealand, between 20 and 22 October—to prepare for the upcoming landings at Tarawa—before returning to Wellington.

The attack transport departed that port on 1 November, transporting units of the 2d Marines, bound for Efate, the staging area for the assault on the Gilbert Islands. After staying at Efate from 8 to 13 November, the ship sortied for Tarawa on the 13th as part of TF 53.

William P. Biddle and her sister transports closed the target atoll while the ships that would provide gunfire support for the landings blasted Japanese positions ashore from 16 to 19 November, "softening up" the island for the landings. On 20 November, the first troops began heading ashore with the 2d Marine Division landing on Betio Island in the face of stiff resistance. During the early phase of the landings, at 0550 on the 20th, Japanese shore batteries had opened fire on the transports; five shells had fallen near *William P. Biddle*, shrapnel wounding one man. At 0558, the transports then moved out of range of the guns. After bitter fighting, the marines had established a small beachhead by sundown. By 1130 on the 23d, Betio was secured; five days later, Major General Julian C. Smith announced that the remaining enemy forces on Tarawa had been wiped out. The assault, however, had cost 990 marines killed and 2,296 wounded. The Japanese fought, literally, to the last man: 4,690 men drew their last breath for their emperor on Tarawa.

Soon thereafter, having delivered her mottle-garbed marines to the beaches of Tarawa, *William P. Biddle* departed the Gilberts and paused briefly at Pearl Harbor on 2 December on her way to the west coast. Arriving at San Diego on the 13th, the attack transport

remained in the vicinity of the southern California coast for the remainder of 1943 and into mid-January 1944, embarking elements of the 4th Marine Regiment and dividing her time between a drydocking at San Diego and amphibious exercises off San Clemente Island.

William P. Biddle subsequently embarked marines at San Diego and departed that port on 13 January 1944, bound for Hawaii. She refuelled at Lahaina Roads, off the island of Maui, before she proceeded on to the Marshall Islands. On "D day," 31 January, the attack transport arrived off the beachheads to see the glowing fires set by the shore bombardment of the supporting heavy ships off shore. During the initial stage of Operation "Flintlock," *William P. Biddle* was the first transport to be 100 percent unloaded.

After departing the Marshalls on 4 February, the attack transport went to Funafuti in the Ellice Islands and remained there from 9 to 13 February. Following a rest at anchor off Noumea from 19 February to 8 March, *William P. Biddle* commenced an extended series of movements that ultimately took her to Guadalcanal on 11 March, Tulagi on 12 March, Kwajalein on 4 April; back to Guadalcanal with the marines of the 22d Division embarked on 13 April; to Cape Gloucester, New Britain, on 28 April with Army troops of the 40th Infantry Division; to the Russells with the 1st Marine Division on 3 May; to Tulagi on 4 May; and to Guadalcanal on the 10th. From 10 May to 3 June, *William P. Biddle* conducted exercises in the Solomons, perparing for the upcoming push against Guam.

With the 1st Battalion, 22d Marines, embarked, *William P. Biddle* departed the Solomons on 4 June and arrived at Kwajalein four days later. From that island, the transport sortied on the 12th to serve as a floating reserve for the Saipan operation. When it became evident that her services would not be required in that operation, *William P. Biddle* was released from those duties on 3 July and retired to Eniwetok in the Marshalls.

Departing Eniwetok on 17 July, *William P. Biddle* turned her bow toward the island of Guam. She arrived in the transport area off the town of Agat, Guam, at 0615 on 21 July. She took part in the initial assault landings there, putting ashore a major part of Combat Landing Team 1, 22d Regiment, 1st Provisional Marine Brigade, with their equipment, on Beach "Yellow One," immediately south of Agat, on the west coast of Guam.

She took on board casualties from the fighting ashore on 21 July, later transferring patients to *Leedstown* (APA–56) and *Lafayette* (APA–43) before she departed the transport area on the 25th, bound for Eniwetok where she arrived four days later.

After periods at the Pearl Harbor Navy Yard and at Honolulu, *William P. Biddle* returned again to Eniwetok on 25 September before she ultimately shifted to Manus, in the Admiralties, to prepare for the ship's sixth major combat operation—the return to the Philippines and the invasion of the island of Leyte.

Attached to transport group "Baker" (TG 79.4) of the Southern Attack Force, *William P. Biddle* transported and landed elements and equipment of the Army's XXIV Corps on Beach "Blue One" on the east coast of Leyte. She arrived in her assigned anchorage in the transport area at 0840 on 20 October and soon hoisted out her boats and lowered them. By 0855, all of her boats were waterborne. The ship then assisted other amphibious assault ships in the vicinity—*Clay* (APA–39), *Capricornus* (AKA–57), *Comet* (AP–166), and *Bolivar* (APA–34), lending her boats to assist those ships in unloading. Although two enemy planes had been sighted near the transport area during the frequent air raid alerts, they were out of range and neither the ships nor her boat's guns were fired. The only casualties suffered by the ship were three men wounded by shrapnel and one by wounds suffered when a mortar projectile hit the LCVP in which he was serving.

Leaving Leyte behind on 24 October, *William P. Biddle* shifted to Hollandia, Dutch New Guinea, arriving there four days later. After embarking elements of the 346th Harbor Craft Co. and the Army's 673d Machine Gun Battery at Hollandia, the transport shifted to Morotai, where she spent five days, from 5 to 10 November, loading 304 tons of cargo—rations, organizational gear, and vehicles—and elements of the 310th Bomb Wing, USAAF.

William P. Biddle departed Morotai on the 10th, arrived at Leyte three days later, and anchored off the east coast of the island. A solitary "Jill" had attacked her formation 100 miles east of Leyte Gulf, but gunfire from *Catskill* (LSV–1) splashed the intruder before he could do any damage.

After landing those resupply units in the San Jose, Leyte, area, *William P. Biddle* shifted, in succession, to Manus from 20 to 27 November, Cape Gloucester, New Britain, from 28 November to 10 December, and back to Manus from 11 to 16 December, before she conducted training operations at Lae, New Guinea, from 16 to 21 December. *William P. Biddle* subsequently returned to Manus where she spent the last 10 days of the year.

With troops from the 1st Battalion, 185th Infantry, 40th Division (Reinforced), USA, embarked, *William P. Biddle* sailed from the Admiralties on 31 December 1944, bound once more for the Philippines. This operation would be the last combat operation in which the ship would participate in World War II, the landings at Lingayen Gulf, Luzon.

Arriving in the transport area at 0712 on 9 January 1945, *William P. Biddle* commenced debarkation of her troops at 0745; but, two minutes later, an enemy plane attacked the formation of transports. *William P. Biddle*'s after 40-millimeter Bofors mount flung out 72 rounds; during that time, the surrounding ships opened fire as well. During the attack, two of the ship's crew, in exposed gun stations, were wounded by shrapnel, probably from "friendly" gunfire thrown up at the attacking plane.

William P. Biddle completed debarking her assault waves by 0905 and finished unloading the cargo and troop working parties at 1740. At 1815, the attack transport got underway and retired from the area, bound for Leyte.

William P. Biddle called at Leyte from 6 to 7 February, from Mindoro from 9 to 10 February, and Leyte from 12 to 15 February, before she arrived at Pearl Harbor on 18 March. Her Hawaiian stop was only a brief one for, after 14 months continuous duty outside the continental United States, *William P. Biddle* was San Francisco-bound on 21 March.

After a yard availability at the Moore Dry Dock Co., Oakland, from 29 March to 1 June, *William P. Biddle* conducted refresher training out of San Diego before she returned via San Francisco to Pearl Harbor on 5 July. Shifting to Honolulu on the 6th, the attack transport subsequently got underway within a week, on 12 July, for the Marshalls. After a brief stop at Eniwetok on the 21st, the ship pushed on for Ulithi, arriving there on the 25th, for a one-day layover on her voyage to the Philippines.

Arriving at Leyte on the 28th, *William P. Biddle* departed that island on 4 August, with casualties and patients—both Army and Navy—embarked. Arriving back at Ulithi on 8 August, *William P. Biddle* was at sea when news of the Japanese capitulation came through. She subsequently arrived at San Pedro on 25 August.

William P. Biddle operated between the Philippines and the west coast of the United States into the autumn, transporting Army and Navy replacements, casualties, and separatees, as part of the "Magic-Carpet" fleet. Putting into San Pedro on 13 December 1945, *William P. Biddle* brought her active transport career to a close. On 3 January 1946, after several moves between west coast ports, the veteran attack transport got underway from San Pedro and headed for the east coast. After transiting the Panama Canal soon

thereafter, *William P. Biddle* arrived at Norfolk on 9 February and was placed out of commission there on 9 April 1946.

Struck from the Navy list on 5 June 1946, *William P. Biddle* was turned over to the Maritime Commission at Lee Hall, Va., on 19 July 1946. Placed in the reserve fleet in the James River, *William P. Biddle* remained there until she was towed away and scrapped in 1957.

William P. Biddle earned seven battle stars for her World War II service.

William R. Rush

William Rees Rush—born in Philadelphia on 19 September 1857—took the oath of office as a midshipman on 6 June 1872; graduated from the Naval Academy on 20 June 1877; and was commissioned ensign on 15 October 1881. Between that time and the outbreak of the Spanish-American War in the spring of 1898, Rush served in *Ranger, Bennington, Boston,* and *Albatross.* He also received instruction in ordnance at the Washington Navy Yard; worked in the Hydrographic Office; completed the course of instruction at the Naval Torpedo Station, Newport, R.I.; and attended the Naval War College.

During the war with Spain, Rush served as a turret division commander in the armored cruiser *Brooklyn,* the flagship of Rear Admiral Winfield S. Schley's "Flying Squadron," during blockade operations off Cienfuegos, Cuba, and participated in the Battle of Santiago on 3 July 1898. Detached from *Brooklyn* in October 1899, Rush went to sea in the battleship *Massachusetts* as executive officer; later commanded the gunboat *Marietta;* and served as executive officer in the cruiser *Albany.*

In the ensuing years, Rush again alternated tours of duty afloat with assignments ashore. He served at the Boston Navy Yard in the equipment department; at the Naval War College; and travelled to the Philippines where he became captain of the yard at Cavite in February 1906. In June of 1907, he assumed command of the gunboat *Wilmington,* the first of a series of successive sea commands that included *Ranger, Missouri, Connecticut, Hancock, Washington,* and *Florida,* and the first division of the United States Fleet.

While commanding *Florida* (Battleship No. 30), Rush was given command of the naval brigade that was sent ashore at Veracruz during the landings there in April 1914 at the height of a diplomatic crisis between Mexico and the United States. When Rush led the brigade ashore on the 21st, he and his men met heavy resistance. Rush was wounded in the early fighting but continued to direct the efforts of his brigade. For his conduct during the landings, Capt. Rush was awarded the Medal of Honor. His citation took note of the fact that he was required to be at points of great danger in directing the officers and men of the brigade and that in doing so he exhibited "conspicuous courage, coolness, and skill." "His responsibilities were great," the citation continued, "and he met them in a manner worthy of commendation."

Rush was later given command of the Boston Navy Yard on 6 November 1914, a post he held until he requested retirement on 9 October 1916. With the onset of World War I, however, Rush was recalled to active duty and was awarded the Navy Cross for "exceptionally meritorious services in a duty of great responsibility" as commandant of the Boston Navy Yard during World War I.

Relieved of all active duty on 25 July 1919, Rush subsequently lived, in retirement, in Italy. He died at Pallanza, Italy, on 2 October 1940.

The contract for the construction of *William R. Rush* (DE–288)—a *Rudderow*-class destroyer escort slated to be built at Hingham, Mass., by the Bethlehem-Hingham

Shipyard—was cancelled on 12 March 1944 before her keel had been laid.

The name *William R. Rush* was assigned to DE–556— a *John C. Butler*-class destroyer escort scheduled to be built by the Boston Navy Yard—but the order for the ship's construction was cancelled on 10 June 1944.

I

(DD–714: dp. 2,425; l. 390'6"; b. 41'1"; dr. 18'6" (max.); s. 35.0 k.; cpl. 336; a. 6 5", 12 40mm., 20 20mm., 5 21" tt., 6 dcp., 2 dct.; cl. *Gearing*)

William R. Rush (DD–714) was laid down on 15 October 1944 at Newark, N.J., by the Federal Shipbuilding and Drydock Co.; launched on 8 July 1945; sponsored by Mrs. Dorothy Flagg Biddle, a cousin of Capt. Rush; and commissioned on 21 September 1945, Comdr. Theodore E. Vogeley in command.

After fitting out at the New York Navy Yard and shakedown training out of Guantanamo Bay and Casco Bay, Maine, *William R. Rush* took part in 8th Fleet maneuvers off the eastern seaboard into May of 1946. The destroyer then moved southward, to Pensacola, Fla., where she served as a plane guard for *Ranger* (CV–4) as the veteran carrier conducted flight training operations. Arriving back at Newport, R.I., her home port, on 28 July, *William R. Rush* spent the rest of the year in local operations.

The destroyer departed Newport on 9 February 1947, bound for Europe and her first overseas deployment. She touched at ports of call in England, Ireland, Norway, France, Germany, Denmark, French Morocco, and Gibraltar before returning to Newport in June. For the next two years, *William R. Rush* operated off the eastern seaboard, exercising with submarines and escorting and planeguarding for carriers.

In July 1949, *William R. Rush* sailed for Europe for an extended European and Mediterranean deployment that lasted into the following year. She touched at ports in France, Greece, Crete, Turkey, Gibraltar, England, Scotland, and Belgium, before she returned to Newport. Subsequently overhauled for three months at Boston, the destroyer carried out refresher training in Guantanamo Bay from May into July 1950. Commencing in mid-July, *William R. Rush* conducted a training cruise that took the warship and her embarked midshipmen from Halifax, Nova Scotia, to Guantanamo Bay.

Returning to Newport on 1 September 1950, *William R. Rush* visited Argentia and St. Johns, Newfoundland, during October; spent much of the following month engaged in Operation "Convex I"—a convoy and striking force exercise; and underwent a period of upkeep back in her homeport, preparing for her next extended deployment.

On 3 January 1951, *William R. Rush* sailed for the Far East. Steaming via the Panama Canal, Pearl Harbor, Midway, and Sasebo, Japan, the destroyer subsequently joined Task Force (TF) 77 in Korean waters and conducted her first shore bombardment mission on 7 February, shelling North Korean rail lines along the coast. Bombardment and escort missions kept the ship continuously occupied until 13 June, when she began her voyage to the United States, steaming via the Indian Ocean, the Suez Canal, the Mediterranean, and the North Atlantic.

William R. Rush completed her circumnavigation of the globe when she returned to Newport on 8 August 1951. She spent the rest of 1951 on maneuvers and exercises from her home port before she entered the Boston Naval Shipyard at the end of the year for conversion to a radar picket ship. The ensuing refit—during which she was decommissioned on 21 December 1951—entailed replacing the ship's 40-millimeter Bofors batteries with rapid-fire 3-inch mounts; removing her torpedo tubes; and receiving improved electronic and radar equipment to enable the ship to perform her new picket role, itself

an outgrowth of World War II experience with kamikazes in the Pacific. Reclassified to DDR–714 on 18 July 1952, *William R. Rush* was recommissioned on 3 September 1952, Comdr. N. B. MacIntosh in command.

Returning to Newport from her shakedown cruise as a DDR soon thereafter, *William R. Rush* underwent refresher training in Guantanamo Bay before she called at Mobile Bay, Ala., for the 1953 Mardi Gras festivities.

William R. Rush conducted her second 6th Fleet deployment from April to October and then operated locally out of Newport. She performed varying duties into the summer of the following year, carrying out, in succession: antisubmarine warfare (ASW) exercises; plane-guard duties with carriers; and a tour as engineering school ship for the Atlantic Fleet Destroyer Force. She next embarked 66 NROTC midshipmen and sailed for the British Isles, touching at Irish and British ports before she returned to Guantanamo Bay for training. Disembarking the midshipmen at Norfolk on 3 September 1954, *William R. Rush* soon thereafter shifted to Boston for a three-month overhaul.

Over the next decade, from 1954 to 1964, *William R. Rush* was deployed to the Mediterranean, for tours of duty with the 6th Fleet, on eight occasions, touching at ports that ranged from Gibraltar to Beirut, Lebanon, and including Pollensa Bay and Palma, Majorca; Naples and Leghorn, Italy; Athens and Salonika, Greece; Golfe Juan, France; Barcelona and Rota, Spain. During her service with the 6th Fleet, *William R. Rush* operated as plane guard and radar picket for fast carrier task forces and participated in NATO exercises. There were highlights of the cruises: in 1955, while at Golfe Juan, the destroyer hosted Mrs. James J. Cabot, the daughter of Capt. William R. Rush; and, in 1957, the ship cruised the Mediterranean with Naval Academy midshipmen embarked.

In between the Mediterranean deployments, *William R. Rush* operated from the Arctic Circle to the Caribbean, homeported first at Newport, from 1954 to 1958, and then from Mayport, Fla., from 1958 to 1964. She twice penetrated north of the Arctic Circle, in the autumn of 1957 and late in 1960, both times on NATO exercises.

There were highlights of the ship's closer-to-home deployments as well. In the summer of 1960, the ship embarked 35 Naval Academy midshipmen and took part in operations off the eastern seaboard with the Atlantic Fleet. She visited Quebec, Canada; Hamilton, Bermuda; and Poughkeepsie, N.Y., during the cruise. That autumn, the ship served on "barrier patrol" when Cuban Premier Fidel Castro threatened the Caribbean nations of Nicaragua and Honduras. Two years later, in the fall of 1962, after American reconnaissance planes discovered the presence of Soviet offensive missiles in Cuba, *William R. Rush* returned to the area and operated with TF 135 on the Cuban "quarantine" line from 20 October to 3 December. The ship was at sea continuously during that period, except for an availability alongside the destroyer tender *Yosemite* (AD–19) from 12 to 17 November.

William R. Rush departed Mayport on 22 June 1964 and arrived at the New York Naval Shipyard on the 26th. Once at the shipyard, the ship commenced a 10-month Fleet Rehabilitation and Modernization (FRAM) overhaul, at the completion of which she would resume her old classification, DD–714.

William R. Rush departed New York on 30 April 1965. Homeported back at Newport, the modernized destroyer soon commenced regular operations with the Fleet, following essentially the same sort of schedule that she had pursued since commissioning in 1945.

As a member of Destroyer Squadron (DesRon) 10, she operated off the eastern seaboard between Newport and Key West, Fla., assuming a new role as an antisubmarine warfare ship. Returning to Newport on 27 July 1965 from refresher training out of Guantanamo Bay and a week of providing services to the Fleet Sonar School at Key West, *William R. Rush* embarked 25

NROTC midshipmen for three weeks at sea with Canadian Navy units on exercise "CANUS (Canadian and United States) SILEX 1–65."

The ship then went back to Newport for availability alongside *Yosemite* and then conducted two weeks of type training before moving south to Key West for a month of Sonar School services. A highlight of that deployment to Florida coastal waters came in September, when she rescued seven Cuban nationals who had originally been bound back to Cuba to bring out relatives. Their two boats had developed engine trouble and were in danger of capsizing in heavy seas.

William R. Rush returned to Newport shortly before Thanksgiving of 1965 and spent the remainder of the year in home waters before getting underway on 14 February 1966 for the Mediterranean. Highlighting the ship's 10th Mediterranean deployment were the usual good will stops at ports in Italy, Rhodes, Sicily, and Turkey; ASW exercises with American and Spanish Navy units, including Exercise "Spanex I–66"; and 6th Fleet antiaircraft and ASW maneuvers. Relieved on 21 June at Gibraltar, the destroyer returned to the east coast of the United States.

William R. Rush spent the remainder of 1966 on operations off the eastern seaboard, ranging from Newport to the Virginia capes, pursuing a well-rounded slate of exercises including, among others, such areas as gunfire support and ASW. Early in 1967, the ship enhanced her capabilities as an ASW destroyer by receiving two Destroyer Antisubmarine Helicopters (DASH) and becoming fully qualified in DASH operations.

William R. Rush departed Newport on 1 March 1967 and crossed the Atlantic in company with *Galveston* (CLG–3). The destroyer subsequently called at Gibraltar, Sardinia, and Athens before transiting the Suez Canal on 1 April. She relieved *Steinaker* (DD–863) the following day at Port Suez. *William R. Rush* then set course for Bahrain, a small island in the Persian Gulf off the coast of Saudi Arabia. En route, the destroyer was fueled from the French oiler *Aritrea* at Massawa, Ethiopia, on 6 April.

Arriving at Bahrain on 13 April, *William R. Rush* joined *Valcour* (AGF–1), the flagship of Rear Admiral E. R. Eastwold, Commander, Middle East Forces (MidEastFor). In the ensuing weeks, the destroyer—on her first MidEastFor deployment—visited Al Misirah, a small island off the coast of Oman, where the British Royal Air Force maintained a small logistics airfield; Karachi, Pakistan; and Massawa for a fuel stop. *William R. Rush* returned to Port Suez on 21 May and was relieved there by *Fiske* (DD–842).

The next day, *William R. Rush* transited the Suez Canal on her way back to the Mediterranean. At that time, tension was great in the Suez since the President of the United Arab Republic, Gamal Abdel Nasser, had demanded on 17 May that the United Nations Expeditionary Force (UNEF) be withdrawn from Egypt and the Gaza Strip posthaste. On the 20th, Egypt began patrolling Israel's coast.

The growing aura of uneasiness in the Middle East was noticeable. The destroyer's commanding officer subsequently reported: "As (*William R.*) *Rush* passed through the Canal we could feel an atmosphere of tension all about us; gun emplacements and troops were obvious on both sides of the Canal."

Over the next few days, the situation worsened. Meanwhile, *William R. Rush* moored alongside *Tidewater* (AD–31), where she spent the first few days of June undergoing a tender availability. However, the outbreak of full-scale war between Israel and her Arab neighbors on 5 June meant a hurried deployment seaward.

The destroyer operated with 6th Fleet units as they conducted emergency contingency force operations until the 17th. She subsequently called at Istanbul from 21 to 26 June before serving as plane guard and picket for *America* (CVA–66) south of Crete. The destroyer later touched at Kavalla, Greece, and Sardinia and Rota, homeward bound. She finally reached Newport on 20 July, ending the eventful deployment.

That autumn, *William R. Rush* operated off the coast of Florida, aiding the Fleet Sonar School in training officers and participating in ASW exercises. She then enjoyed a period of leave and upkeep at her home port to round out the year.

Late in January 1968, *William R. Rush* operated out of Newport as school ship for the Naval Destroyer School. In mid-March, she continued her training-oriented activities when she embarked 32 prospective destroyer officers and sailed for the Caribbean in company with *Gainard* (DD–706) and *Glennon* (DD–840). During that cruise, she visited St. Croix, Virgin Islands, and San Juan, Puerto Rico. Soon after the ship returned to her home port, she shifted to the Boston Naval Shipyard for a four-month overhaul.

Over the next 11 years, *William R. Rush* conducted two more Mediterranean deployments, in early 1960 and from the autumn of 1970 to the spring of 1971, in between which she operated, as before, off the eastern seaboard and into the Caribbean. Ports visited with the 6th Fleet included Rota and Barcelona, Spain; Piraeus, Greece; Venice, Genoa and San Remo, Italy; Sfax, Tunisia; and Valetta, Malta. A social highlight of the 1969 deployment was when the officers and men of the ship were hosted royally on three separate occasions by Contessa Catherine Rush Visconti-Prasca—the daughter of the ship's namesake—at her villa.

During that deployment, the ship participated in the usual slate of maneuvers and exercises including stints planeguarding for *Forrestal* (CVA–59) and *John F. Kennedy* (CVA–67), and taking part in NATO Exercise "Dawn Patrol." Returning home, *William R. Rush* visited Liverpool, England, and Oslo, Norway, and then spent a gruelling period in the North Atlantic—operating, on occasion, north of the Arctic Circle again—with a hunter-killer group tasked with perfecting ASW tactics. For her part in that significant evolution—operating in company with *Wasp* (CVS–18)—*William R. Rush* received the Meritorious Unit Commendation.

Highlighting the ship's 1970 and 1971 6th Fleet deployment was a special intelligence mission. On 23 January 1971, *William R. Rush* departed Naples and, over the next 26 days, shadowed the Soviet helicopter carrier *Leningrad* in the Gulf of Sollum, gathering new and noteworthy intelligence data on that ship and her operations. Following that event, the destroyer resumed her other duties, ultimately returning home to Newport on 2 May 1971.

On 5 April 1972, *William R. Rush*—in company with *Charles H. Roan* (DD–853)—departed Newport for her last extended deployment under the Stars and Stripes, bound for the Middle East and Indian Ocean. En route, the ship visited Port-au-Spain, Trinidad; Recife, Brazil; Luanda, Angola; and Lourenco Marques, Mozambique, before arriving at Port Louis, Mauritius, on 11 May. *William R. Rush* subsequently stopped at Moroni, Grand Comoro, Comores Islands; Mombasa, Kenya; Karachi, Pakistan; and Kharg Island, off the coast of Iran. Additionally, the ship spent a two-week upkeep period at the MidEastFor home port, Bahrain, where she was visited by the Honorable William P. Rogers, the Secretary of State, on 3 July. She later called at Dammam, Saudi Arabia, where she embarked 19 Royal Saudi Naval Force officers for underway training from 15 to 19 July.

A Red Sea excursion took *William R. Rush* to Massawa and return visits to Mombasa, Port Louis, and Bahrain. In the course of the deployment and during transits between ports, *William R. Rush* twice conducted surveillance operations at Russian naval anchorages near Socotra Island and Cape Guardafui and once at Coetivy Island.

During the time spent operating under the aegis of Commander, MidEastFor, *William R. Rush* operated primarily as an ambassador of good will, "showing the flag" in an area where the Soviet Union's naval presence was becoming more marked.

Ultimately, after conducting exercises with *Charles H. Roan* and the British frigate HMS *Lowestoft*, *Wil-*

liam R. Rush departed Bahrain. She continued her circumnavigation of the globe with visits to the ports of Karachi, Pakistan; Colombo, Sri Lanka; Singapore; Hong Kong; Yokosuka, Japan; Midway; Pearl Harbor; San Diego; and the Panama Canal before she arrived back at Newport on 31 October 1972.

William R. Rush subsequently operated out of Newport on local operations into March of 1973. Then, after an overhaul at the Boston Naval Shipyard, *William R. Rush* was assigned to DesRon 28 on 2 July 1973 for service as a Naval Reserve training ship.

Homeported at Fort Schuyler, Bronx, N.Y., *William R. Rush* spent the next five years training selected reserve crews and operating between the Virginia capes Operating Area and Halifax, Nova Scotia.

William R. Rush was decommissioned at Fort Schuyler on 1 July 1978 and was simultaneously struck from the Navy list. Transferred that same day to the navy of the Republic of Korea (ROK) under the terms of the Security Assistance Program, the destroyer became ROKS *Kang Won* (DD–922) and operated with the South Korean Navy into 1979.

William Rockefeller

William Rockefeller—the younger brother of John D. Rockefeller—was born on 31 May 1841 at Richford, in Tioga County, N.Y. He entered business at the age of 16, clerking for a miller in Cleveland, Ohio, before he joined his brother John's produce business a year later. When John D. Rockefeller subsequently entered the oil refining industry—going into partnership with Samuel Andrews—and found that it promised to develop into a booming export business, he invited William to take charge of the Rockefeller and Andrews exporting business in New York. In 1867, William Rockefeller and Co. was formed as a subsidiary to Rockefeller and Andrews.

William Rockefeller built up the company's export traffic, which in time became the Standard Oil Co. of New York. Rockefeller remained the firm's president until 1911, when the Standard Oil trust was dissolved as a result of antitrust legislation. Retiring from his once-active role as a captain of industry, William Rockefeller devoted the remainder of his life to his railroad interests and investments until dying of pneumonia at the age of 81 on 24 June 1922 at Tarrytown, N.Y.

(Tanker: dp. 15,500; l. 446′; b. 58′2″; dr. 27′6″; s. 10.5 k.; cpl. 51; a. none)

William Rockefeller—sometimes cited as *William D. Rockefeller*—a steel-hulled tanker built for carrying oil in bulk, was constructed at Philadelphia by William Cramp and Sons for the Standard Oil Co. and completed in December 1916. Acquired by the Navy for duty with the Naval Overseas Transportation Service (NOTS), *William Rockefeller* was commissioned on 9 January 1918, Lt. Comdr. Richard E. Tull, USNRF, in command.

William Rockefeller conducted her maiden voyage for NOTS soon after commissioning, transporting a bulk cargo of oil from Philadelphia to England. After arriving at Sheerness on 18 March, she discharged her cargo and returned to Philadelphia on 9 April. She bunkered, underwent minor repairs, and loaded a full cargo of fuel oil before sailing on 28 April for New York.

The next day, she joined a convoy bound for Scotland and made port at Lamlash on 15 May. Three days later, the bulk oil tanker proceeded on for Rosyth. On 21 May 1918, the German submarine *UC–58* torpedoed *William Rockefeller*, and the latter sank in just 13 minutes. While the tanker's two escorting destroyers subjected the German U-boat to a fierce depth charge attack, *William Rockefeller*'s crew abandoned ship. Eleven men, including Commander Tull, the command-

ing officer, were awarded Navy Crosses for bravery. All but three men of her complement of 51 were saved.

William Seiverling

William Frank Seiverling, Jr., born on 22 September 1920 at Elizabethtown, Pa., enlisted in the United States Marine Corps at Philadelphia, Pa., on 2 February 1942. Attached to the Marine Barracks, Parris Island, S.C., for basic training from 3 February to 12 March, he moved to the base at New River, N.C., on the latter date and served there until 17 May 1942. He began service in the field on 19 June 1942 and, by the following fall, was on Guadalcanal helping to wrest control of that island from the Japanese. Pvt. Seiverling was killed on 1 November 1942 during the enemy attack across the Matanikau River on that island. When the enemy attacked, Seiverling ran down the hill in the face of enemy fire, killing at least one sniper and perhaps several others. Later, he covered the evacuation of wounded marines from his own platoon; and, after hearing that the 2d Platoon was also in trouble, he ran between that unit and the enemy to cover his comrades' withdrawal. Once again, he killed several Japanese before he himself was hit by enemy machine-gun fire. Though wounded, Pvt. Seiverling continued to deliver a withering fire into an enemy position with his automatic rifle. As he started back over the ridge to make his own retirement, he was fatally wounded. For unselfishly giving his life for his comrades and his country, Pvt. Seiverling was awarded the Navy Cross, posthumously.

(DE–411: dp. 1,350; l. 306′0″; b. 36′7″; dr. 13′4″ (mean); s. 24.3 k. (tl.); cpl. 222; a. 2 5″, 4 40mm., 10 20mm., 3 21″ tt., 8 dcp., 1 dcp. (hh.), 2 dct.; cl. *John C. Butler*)

William Seiverling (DE–441) was laid down on 2 December 1943 at Newark, N.J., by the Federal Shipbuilding & Drydock Co., launched on 7 March 1944; sponsored by Mrs. Grace Seiverling; and commissioned at the New York Navy Yard on 1 June 1944, Lt. Comdr. Charles F. Adams, Jr., in command.

Following commissioning, *William Seiverling* conducted shakedown training in the vicinity of Bermuda. She returned to New York on 26 July and began post-shakedown availability at the New York Navy Yard. She completed repairs on 8 August and put to sea on the 9th, bound ultimately for the western Pacific. After several stops along the way, she transited the Panama Canal on 25 August. The warship remained at Balboa until the 30th, at which time she continued her voyage. She stopped at San Diego from 2 to 11 September before getting underway for Pearl Harbor on the latter date. The destroyer escort reached Oahu on 17 September and began a series of missions out of the Pearl Harbor base. For the remainder of September and during the first week in October, those operations consisted of torpedo, surface gunnery, and shore bombardment exercises. After 8 October, *William Seiverling* began antisubmarine warfare duty, first on a training basis and, after 1 November, as a unit of a hunter-killer force built around *Corregidor* (CVE–58). That employment continued until 24 November, when she sortied from Pearl Harbor in company with Task Group (TG) 12.4, a hunter-killer group built around *Tulagi* (CVE–72). That unit steamed via Eniwetok to Ulithi, where it arrived on 2 December.

For the next three months, *William Seiverling* operated with the hunter-killer group from the base at Ulithi. She helped to patrol the sea lanes between various islands in the Central Pacific to keep them clear of Japanese submarines. On 28 December, the destroyer escort departed Ulithi in company with the *Tulagi* group to provide ASW support for the Lingayen landings scheduled for the beginning of the second week in January 1945. She and her unit stopped at

Kossol Roads in the Palau Islands from 29 December 1944 until 1 January 1945. On the latter day, she sortied with the task group and set a course—via the Surigao Strait, the Sulu Sea, and the South China Sea—for Luzon. During the transit, enemy air attacks were frequent, but *William Seiverling* never got into the action until she arrived off Lingayen Gulf on 7 January. On that day, her guns warded off a single attacker whose approach was quite desultory in nature. She patrolled the waters off Lingayen Gulf until 17 January at which time she joined the screen of TG 77.4 and TG 77.3 and headed south. She conducted patrols with elements of the two task groups until 1 February when she began retirement through the Sulu Sea with TG 77.4. On 5 February, the warship reentered the lagoon at Ulithi. Upkeep occupied the next two weeks. On 19 February, the destroyer escort reported for duty with the 5th Fleet as an element of Task Unit (TU) 50.7.3. That same day, she departed Ulithi with that task unit and headed—via Guam—to the vicinity of Iwo Jima to support the battle then in progress for that island. For about a month, she and the other ships of the task unit conducted antisubmarine patrols of the sea lanes between the Marianas and Iwo Jima. On 11 March, she cleared the Iwo Jima area to return to her base at Ulithi where she arrived on 14 March.

William Seiverling remained at Ulithi completing logistics until 21 March at which time she got underway with TG 52.1 to support the assault on and occupation of Okinawa. Her first mission in support of the Ryukyu campaign consisted of antisubmarine protection for escort carriers, the planes of which provided close air support for the troops assaulting Okinawa. That phase of her Okinawa service lasted until 15 April at which time she began another series of antisubmarine patrols along the route between Okinawa and Ulithi with TU 50.7.3, the reconstituted *Tulagi* hunter-killer group. Those patrols occupied her time until 30 April at which time she parted company with the unit to return to Ulithi for repairs to her main propulsion plant. The warship arrived back in the lagoon at Ulithi on the afternoon of 3 May and commenced repairs. She completed repairs on 15 May and stood out of the anchorage on the 16th to escort *Genesee* (AOG-8) back to Okinawa. Upon arrival in the Ryukyus on 20 May, she began duty patrolling on various antisubmarine and antiaircraft defense stations around Okinawa. During that phase of her Okinawa duty, *William Seiverling* came under air attack on numerous occasions—including the 25 May attack when a suicider succeeded in crashing and sinking *Bates* (DE-68)—and she claimed three kills and a number of hits but suffered no damage herself. On 28 May, the destroyer escort received orders to join the screen of TG 30.7 with which she conducted antisubmarine patrols about 400 miles north of Guam. On 5 June, her unit shaped a course via Guam to Ulithi where it arrived on 8 June.

William Seiverling remained at Ulithi for about two weeks conducting repairs and provisioning. On 24 June, she departed the atoll and shaped a course for San Pedro Bay, Leyte, where she and her division mates joined TG 30.8 on 26 June. On the 28th, TG 30.8—with *William Seiverling* in company—departed Leyte to return to Ulithi. The task group reentered Ulithi on 30 June and commenced logistics operations in preparation for its logistics support missions to the 3d Fleet carriers during the summer air strikes on the Japanese home islands. *William Seiverling* served in the screen of the 3d Fleet replenishment group through most of July. On 23 July, she returned to Ulithi for repairs to her sound gear and to take on stores and provisions. She returned to sea on 25 July and rendezvoused with *Salamaua* (CVE-96) on the 28th. She conducted antisubmarine patrols with that escort carrier until 1 August at which time the task unit set a course for Leyte and temporary duty with the 7th Fleet. She and her unit mates arrived in San Pedro Bay on 5 August and remained there until 8 August when they resumed

antisubmarine patrols to the northeast of Luzon. That duty occupied her time until the end of hostilities on 15 August and thereafter.

She continued patrols of that nature, operating from the base on Leyte near San Pedro Bay until 27 August at which time she set a course for Japan and duty in conjunction with the occupation. The warship arrived in Tokyo Bay on 2 September, the day Japan formally surrendered to the Allies. She supported the occupation forces in Japan until 17 October when she departed Yokosuka to escort a convoy of tank landing ships to Manila. She reached her destination on 25 October and remained there for repairs and provisions until 3 December. On the latter day, the warship stood out of Manila Bay to return to the United States. After stops at Guam, Eniwetok, and Pearl Harbor, *William Seiverling* arrived in San Pedro, Calif., on 26 November. The destroyer escort began preparations for inactivation almost immediately upon arrival. *William Seiverling* was placed in commission, in reserve, sometime in December. Though inactive, the warship remained in commission, in reserve, until formally decommissioned on 21 March 1947.

The outbreak of hostilities in Korea during the summer of 1950 brought many warships in the reserve fleet back to active duty. Accordingly, on 27 December 1950, *William Seiverling* was recommissioned at San Diego, Lt. Comdr. Walter C. Cole in command. She spent the first three months of 1951 conducting shakedown training along the California coast. On 16 April, she departed San Diego in company with Escort Squadron (CortRon) 9, bound for the Far East. After stops at Pearl Harbor and Midway, she arrived in Sasebo, Japan, on 14 May. From there, she moved south to Keelung, Taiwan, where she joined the Taiwan Strait patrol. In July, the warship arrived in the Korean war zone. From the 6th to the 12th, she conducted shore bombardment missions near Songjin. When not engaged in shore bombardment, *William Seiverling* patrolled the North Korean coast as a unit of the United Nations Blockading Force. Early in September she joined the naval forces blockading Wonsan harbor. On 8 September, while operating with minesweepers in the inner harbor at Wonsan, the destroyer escort drew fire from an enemy shore battery. She began maneuvering radically and opened counter battery fire. The enemy, however, proved far more accurate than did the American warship. Throughout the brief action, he consistently straddled *William Seiverling* and succeeded in scoring three hits, one of which struck the ship below the waterline at the number 2 fireroom. That hit caused *William Seiverling* to break off the action and retire to Sasebo for repairs. The warship remained at Sasebo for the remainder of that deployment. She returned to the United States on 22 November.

William Seiverling completed repairs and conducted normal operations along the California coast during the first 10 months of 1952. On 17 October 1952, she departed San Diego to return to the Far East. After stops at Pearl Harbor and at Midway Island, she arrived in the western Pacific at Yokosuka on 11 November. By 16 November, the destroyer escort was back on station with the Wonsan blockade. That duty—including shore bombardment missions—lasted until 26 December. After upkeep, she returned to the Korean coast on 5 January 1953. Her western Pacific deployment lasted until late May and included three more tours of duty in the coastal waters around Korea. She departed the Far East on 22 May and reentered San Diego on 9 June. She resumed local operations until January of 1954 at which time the warship entered the Long Beach Naval Shipyard for overhaul. She completed repairs on 26 March and resumed training duty out of San Diego for the next two months. On 20 May, *William Seiverling* stood out of San Diego on her way back to the Orient. The warship arrived in Japan on 8 June but was soon back in Korean waters participating in a landing exercise at Sokcho Ri. Between 29 June and 26 July, the ship made a series of goodwill visits to the Japanese ports of Kobe, Nagoya, Muroran, and Niigata. During the remainder of that deployment, she resumed duty with TF 95. Late in November, she completed her western Pacific assignment and set a course for San Diego. *William Seiverling* arrived back in her home port on 10 December 1954.

The warship's active career lasted just a little over two more years. During that time, she made two more deployments to the western Pacific. During the first 7th Fleet assignment, she operated in the old familiar northwestern Pacific near Japan and Korea. Also during that deployment, she visited Maizuru, Japan, where, in June and July of 1955, she took custody of lend-lease ships being returned to the United States. Her second and final deployment of that period took her to the southwestern Pacific for visits to New Zealand and Australian ports before she headed north for duty on the Taiwan Strait patrol. She returned to San Diego from the last tour of duty in the Far East on 18 February 1957. She resumed normal operations until 15 June at which time she began preparations for decommissioning. *William Seiverling* was placed out of commission at San Diego on 27 September 1957. She remained in the Pacific Reserve Fleet until 1 December 1972 when her name was struck from the Navy list. On 20 September 1973, she was sold to Levin Metals Corp., of San Jose, Calif., for scrapping.

William Seiverling earned four battle stars during World War II and three battle stars during the Korean conflict.

William T. Powell

William Thomas Powell—born on 3 October 1918 in Cincinnati, Ohio—enlisted in the Navy on 4 October 1939 and received training at the Naval Training Station, Newport, R.I., before reporting to the heavy cruiser *San Francisco* (CA–39)—then a unit of the Atlantic Fleet's Neutrality Patrol—on 17 December 1939, at Norfolk, Va.

He advanced through the ranks to attain the rating of gunner's mate, 2d class, on 1 April 1942. *San Francisco*, while Powell served in her, took part in the war in the Pacific from the outset. The ship lay at Pearl Harbor during the Japanese attack of 7 December 1941 and participated in the ensuing operations: the abortive relief expedition to Wake Island; screening Task Force (TF) 17 during the Marshalls-Gilberts raids and *Lexington* (CV–2) in TF 11 during the raid on Rabaul.

San Francisco also took part in the initial American offensive in the South Pacific—the invasion of the Solomon Islands. Guadalcanal remained a bitter battleground from August 1942 to February 1943, and history records the many sharp battles fought in the hotly contested waters of the Solomons. On 12 November 1942, a large formation of Japanese bombers—twin-engined "Betties"—attacked a formation of American transports off Lunga Point. With ample warning, the vital ships got underway, screened by destroyers and cruisers—*San Francisco* included, and the intense antiaircraft fire and superb seamanship on the part of the Americans prevented the enemy from successfully pressing home his attack.

The victory had not been achieved without cost, however, as an already-damaged "Betty" loosed her torpedo off *San Francisco's* starboard quarter. The "fish" passed alongside, but the plane crashed into *San Francisco's* after control station. Gunner's Mate Powell was manning a 20-millimeter Oerlikon on the gun platform at the time. He courageously refused to abandon his post in the face of the oncoming plane, and with cool determination and utter disregard for his own personal safety, maintained a steady fire on the crippled "Betty" until she hit nearby, killing Powell in the fiery explo-

sion that engulfed his position. Fifteen men, including the cruiser's executive officer, were killed and 29 wounded.

For his perseverance and relentless devotion to duty, Gunner's Mate 2d Class Powell received the Purple Heart and Navy Cross posthumously. He also received, posthumously, the Presidential Unit Citation awarded *San Francisco* for her performance at the Battle of Cape Esperance and the Naval Battle of Guadalcanal.

(DE–213: dp. 1,400; l. 306'0''; b. 36'10''; dr. 9'5'' (mean); s. 23.7 k.; cpl. 186; a. 3 3'', 5 1.1'', 8 20mm., 3 21'' tt., 2 dct., 8 dcp., 1 dcp. (hh.); cl. *Buckley*)

William T. Powell (DE–213) was laid down on 26 August 1943 at Charleston, S.C., by the Charleston Navy Yard; launched on 27 November 1943; sponsored by Mrs. Elsie V. Powell, mother of Gunner's Mate Powell; and commissioned on 28 March 1944, Lt. James L. Davenport, USNR, in command.

After fitting out, *William T. Powell* got underway from Charleston on 18 April, flying the command pennant of Comdr. George F. Adams, USNR, Commander, Escort Division (CortDiv) 66, and bound for Bermuda.

At 1541 on 20 April, the ship's search radar disclosed a contact. Seven minutes later, *William T. Powell* went to general quarters as lookouts noted a submarine running on the surface. The destroyer escort charged ahead at flank speed and challenged the submarine, only to be informed that the stranger was *Pomfret* (SS–391), en route from New London, Conn., to Key West, Fla. "All hands very disappointed when sub turned out to be friendly," noted Comdr. Adams in the destroyer escort's war diary as the ship continued on toward Bermuda.

Upon her arrival on the 21st, *William T. Powell* moored alongside *Hamul* (AD–20) and got underway three days later to commence her shakedown. In the ensuing weeks, the new destroyer escort's operations ran the gamut of activities for the ships of her type: exercises with submerged submarines (in her case, the old "R" boat, *R–7* (SS–84); torpedo attack practices; fueling at sea; simulated depth-charge and "hedgehog" attacks; shore bombardments, and the inevitable gunnery drills. She operated out of Great Sound, Bermuda, and normally returned to anchor each evening upon the completion of the day's slate of activities.

Her shakedown completed shortly after the middle of May, *William T. Powell* sailed for Charleston on the 18th. She met SS *Willis A. Slater* off the sea buoy to Great Sound that day and escorted the merchantman on her northward voyage, patrolling 2,000 yards ahead. Leaving *Willis A. Slater* off Charleston, *William T. Powell* put into port on the 23d and, from 24 May to 6 June 1944. underwent post-shakedown availability. During the overhaul, the ship received four 40-millimeter Bofors guns, replacing the bank of torpedo tubes, to give the ship a more potent antiaircraft battery.

Underway for the Canal Zone on 9 June, *William T. Powell* test-fired her new 40-millimeter battery en route and reached Cristobal, Canal Zone, at 1147 on 11 June. She transited the canal two days later and got underway again at 0627 on the 14th for exercises at sea near Taboga Island. She practiced repelling attacks by motor torpedo boats.

William T. Powell subsequently retransited the canal, eastbound on 15 June, and moored at Cristobal at 1818 that day. She joined *Prince William* (CVE–31) on the 17th and escorted the CVE as she headed, via Port Everglades, Fla., for Hampton Roads, Va.

Released from that escort duty on the 24th, *William T. Powell* then operated at Norfolk from 29 June to 9 July as a school ship for destroyer escort crew trainees before she sortied from Hampton Roads on 10 July in the screen of Convoy UGS–48.

At 0029 on 1 August 1944, *William T. Powell* received a TBS message from the task force commander, Capt. C. M. E. Hoffman, in *Moffett* (DD–362), to man battle stations in anticipation of an enemy air attack.

The destroyer escort complied and soon, together with the other escorts of sector 3, began making funnel smoke.

Radar picked up the enemy attackers at 90 miles away; *William T. Powell* and her sisters, meanwhile, continued steaming back and forth at the rear of the convoy, making smoke. The convoy received an additional alert from radio Algiers at 0037 and, 13 minutes later, detected many friendly and enemy planes. The escorts now began making chemical smoke from the CS canisters on the fantail of each ship; with visibility near zero, the ships commenced conning by radar.

HMS *Delhi*—a British antiaircraft cruiser—commenced the action at 0058, firing by radar control. At 0105, lookouts in *William T. Powell* spotted flares close aboard on the port side of the convoy; but the gunners were cautioned not to fire. Ten minutes later, however, with enemy planes within range, the convoy opened up; mount 21 in *William T. Powell* glimpsed an enemy bomber through the eerie murk and fired a four-round burst; the plane, obscured in smoke and clouds, soon disappeared. The firing lasted only a minute; *William T. Powell* ceased fire at 0116, feeling detonations from time to time—believed to be either bombs or torpedoes exploding at the end of their runs.

By 0153, the quartermaster on watch in *William T. Powell* could write: "Things cool off a bit and Condition Easy-One is set." At 0230, the convoy received a white alert (all clear), and the escorts ceased making smoke and took their normal screening stations. Seven minutes later, the destroyer escort secured from general quarters. The defense of UGS–48 was a successful one; the enemy did not claim any of the ships. As Lt. Davenport, the commanding officer of *William T. Powell*, wrote in his subsequent report of the action: "The value of smoke as a protection against Night Air Attack was proved. Visibility was absolutely zero, and flares were useless to the attacking planes."

After seeing all ships of UGS–48 safely to their Mediterranean destination, *William T. Powell* served with TF 62 as it escorted the homeward-bound group, GUS–48, back to the United States before heading north for training in the Casco Bay area. During the night of 14 and 15 September, while en route to Casco Bay, *William T. Powell* rode out a hurricane with no damage.

The destroyer escort shepherded Convoys UGS–55 and GUS–55 to their respective Mediterranean and east coast destinations in September and October, before she became a unit of Task Unit (TU) 27.1.2 based at Argentia, Newfoundland. She operated out of Argentia as part of that antisubmarine, hunter-killer group from 28 November to 24 December 1944 before shifting to Casco Bay and operating from that base from Christmas Eve to New Year's Day.

After TU 27.1.2 was redesignated TG 22.9, *William T. Powell* resumed operations from Argentia on 4 January 1945 and continued them through the end of the month. Following that stint of hunter-killer duty, the destroyer escort exercised with American submarines out of New London, Conn., for almost a month—4 February to 2 March 1945—and trained in Casco Bay from 18 to 21 March.

After the completion of that training period, *William T. Powell* proceeded with TG 22.9, via the Azores, to Liverpool, England. Upon arrival, TG 22.9 was redesignated and reconstituted as TG 120.1 on 4 April; *William T. Powell* operated as "flagship" for that unit's senior officer, Comdr. Vernon A. Isaacs, USNR.

TG 120.1—later redesignated Escort Group 32—subsequently performed antisubmarine hunter-killer group and support unit duties for convoys in the western approaches to the British Isles. During the closing weeks of the European war, *William T. Powell* patrolled shallow water approaches, sank floating and drifting mines, and supported the escorts for 12 convoys in submarine-infested waters. She based on Londonderry, Northern Ireland, from 5 April to 23 May,

through the cessation of hostilities with Germany and, after that enemy's capitulation, helped to accept the surrender of German U-boats.

Released from the 12th Fleet and the Western Approaches Command on 24 May 1945, the destroyer escort soon sailed for home, entering the Brown Shipbuilding Co., Inc., yard in Houston, Tex., on 15 June for conversion to a radar picket ship. However, while she was in the yard for alterations, Japan capitulated in mid-August.

She departed her conversion yard on 22 October 1945 and soon proceeded to Guantanamo Bay, Cuba, for refresher training. Following post-shakedown availability, *William T. Powell* trained in Casco Bay into late January 1946 and underwent a logistics period at Boston. She then sailed to Miami, Fla., where she joined the presidential yacht, *Williamsburg* (AGC–369), from 8 to 13 February before sailing for Norfolk. She later pushed on for Quonset Point, R.I., on 31 March and, in April, plane-guarded for *Salerno Bay* (CVE–110)—in company with *Reuben James* (DE–153)—in Narragansett Bay and off Norfolk and participated in fleet exercises at Guantanamo Bay and Culebra in May.

Departing the latter on 20 May, *William T. Powell* sailed for New York in company with *Mindoro* (CVE–120) and *Reuben James*. The destroyer escort subsequently returned to the Norfolk and Casco Bay operating areas in early June and July before visiting Bar Harbor, Maine, for 4th of July celebrations. Soon thereafter, she resumed training evolutions in Casco Bay before heading south on 19 July for Pensacola, Fla. She served there as temporary relief for *William R. Rush* (DD–714) and plane-guarded for *Ranger* (CV–4) while that venerable carrier was serving as a training vessel.

William T. Powell operated with one of her former World War II cohorts, *Spangenburg* (DE–223), in Casco Bay later that summer and off New London served as a target vessel for submarines from 13 to 30 September. She arrived at Newport, R.I., on 30 September, moored alongside *Yellowstone* (AD–27) for a three-week tender availability, and subsequently departed Newport on 22 October, bound for Casco Bay where she arrived the same day. She conducted Navy Day observances there on the 27th before she transited the Cape Cod canal and arrived at New London on 12 December. She spent the remainder of the year operating on training evolutions with submarines.

For the next 11 years, *William T. Powell* operated off the eastern seaboard of the United States ranging from Casco Bay to Cape Henry to Key West and into the West Indies and Guantanamo Bay. Her ports of call included Newport; Norfolk; Boston; New York City; Port-au-Prince, Haiti; Culebra and San Juan, Puerto Rico; Havana and Santiago, Cuba; St. Thomas, Virgin Islands; and Nassau, Bahamas.

During that period, the ship underwent several changes of status and two reclassifications. On 5 November 1948, she was assigned to the 4th Naval District and homeported at the Philadelphia Naval Shipyard to serve as a Naval Reserve training (NRT) ship. On 18 March 1949, the warship was reclassified DER–213. Decommissioned on 9 December 1949, the vessel was reactivated on 28 November 1950 and resumed the role of an NRT ship. She was reclassified DE–213 on 1 December 1954 and continued training duty until September 1957. *William T. Powell* was placed out of commission, in reserve, at Philadelphia on 17 January 1958.

Struck from the Navy list on 1 November 1965, *William T. Powell* was sold on 3 October 1966 to the North American Smelting Co., Wilmington, Del., and was scrapped.

Although she participated in the defense of Convoy UGS–48 on 1 August 1944, and was in proximity to enemy forces, *William T. Powell* inexplicably received no battle star for that action.

William V. Pratt

William Veazie Pratt—born on 28 February 1869 at Belfast, Maine—was appointed to the Naval Academy from Maine's third congressional district on 9 September 1885. He graduated in 1889 and served two years at sea in the protected cruiser *Atlanta* as a passed midshipman before receiving his ensign's commission on 1 July 1891. Following his commissioning, Pratt served successively in *Chicago, Philadelphia, Petrel, Lancaster,* and *Annapolis*. In 1898, during the Spanish-American War, he did tours of duty on board *Mayflower*, the prize *New Foundland,* and *Newark* (Cruiser No. 19). During his tour of duty in *Mayflower*, Pratt saw service in the blockades of Havana, Santiago de Cuba, and at Puerto Rico. Following the war, he served in *Bennington*, the monitor *Monadnock, Indiana* (Battleship No. 1), and *Kearsarge* (Battleship No. 5). Later, as he moved up the ranks, he served as navigator in *Newark* and then as executive officer in *St. Louis* (Cruiser No. 20) and *California* (Armored Cruiser No. 6). In January of 1911, he began a tour of duty as a student at the Naval War College at Newport, R.I., that lasted until June of 1913. Following that, he served as aide to the Commander, Torpedo Flotilla, Atlantic Fleet, during which service he was in both *Dixie* and *Birmingham* (Light Cruiser No. 2). In 1914 and 1915, he also commanded *Birmingham* as additional duty. In November 1915, Pratt, by then a captain, concluded duty with the Torpedo Flotilla and began a year's assignment in the Panama Canal Zone. In September 1916, Capt. Pratt went to the Army War College for a course of instruction. During that assignment, he also performed temporary additional duty in the Office of the Chief of Naval Operations from February to May 1917. After the United States entered World War I in April of 1917, Capt. Pratt was detached from the Army War College on 19 May and was reassigned permanently to the Office of the Chief of Naval Operations where his major assignment was liaison with the Army over troop movements overseas and coordinating convoy traffic across the ocean. By August 1918, Capt. Pratt had been appointed the first Assistant Chief of Naval Operations.

In January 1919, Capt. Pratt assumed command of *New York* (Battleship No. 34). He commanded the battleship for some 22 months, after which he took over duty as Commander, Destroyer Force, Pacific Fleet, on 1 November 1920. On 21 June 1921, Pratt was selected for rear admiral; and, the following month, he reported for duty with the General Board of the Navy. About three months later, he was formally "frocked" as Rear Admiral Pratt. Through most of his 19 months of service with the General Board, Pratt busied himself with the thorny problems of naval disarmament and a critically reduced naval budget. Detached from duty with the General Board, Rear Admiral Pratt assumed command of Battleship Division 4 on 25 June 1923 at San Francisco on board *Pennsylvania* (BB–38). He served in that capacity until the summer of 1925 when he was called to Washington for temporary duty with the General Board. He concluded that assignment in late August and moved to Newport, R.I., where he became President of the Naval War College. After two years at Newport, Pratt assumed duties as Commander, Battleship Divisions, United States Fleet, on 24 September 1927. He held that position for less than a year. On 26 June 1928, Admiral Pratt broke his four-starred flag on board *California* (BB–44) as Commander, Battle Fleet. On 21 May 1929, Admiral Pratt relieved Admiral Henry A. Wiley as Commander, United States Fleet. He held that office until September 1930. On 17 September, he assumed duty as Chief of Naval Operations. During his tenure in that office, Admiral Pratt also served as advisor to the American delegation to the London Naval Conference. Admiral Pratt served as Chief of Naval Operations until 30 June 1933 at which time he retired from active duty. After eight years of retirement, Admiral Pratt was called back to active duty in January 1941 to help expedite the development of escort carriers for antisubmarine warfare. He went back into retirement once again on 15 July 1941. Admiral Pratt died at Chelsea, Mass., on 25 November 1957.

(DLG–13: dp. 5,709; l. 513′; b. 52′; dr. 18′; s. 33 k.; cpl. 377; a. 1 5″, 4 3″, 1 mis. ln., Terrier, ASROC 6 15.5″ tt., 1 dcp.; cl. *Coontz*)

William V. Pratt (DLG–13) was laid down on 7 March 1958 by the Philadelphia Naval Shipyard; launched on 16 March 1960; sponsored by Mrs. William V. Pratt; and commissioned on 4 November 1961, Comdr. Boyd E. Gustafson in command.

Following shakedown training in the West Indies and post-shakedown availability at Philadelphia, *William V. Pratt* joined Destroyer Squadron (DesRon) 18 as an

USS *William V. Pratt* (DLG–13) off Philadelphia, 14 December 1961.

active unit of the fleet in September 1962. Operating out of Norfolk, Va., she cruised the Atlantic seaboard and the West Indies until 4 August 1963 at which time she departed Norfolk to participate in NATO exercise, Operation "Riptide IV," in European waters. She returned to Norfolk in September and resumed normal 2d Fleet operations. That employment continued until 3 February 1964 when she embarked upon her first tour of duty with the 6th Fleet in the Mediterranean Sea. She returned to Norfolk on 9 August and once again took up her east coast-West Indies routine. In September and October, she visited European waters again to participate in two NATO exercises, Operations "Masterstroke" and "Teamwork." The warship returned to Norfolk on 20 October and resumed 2d Fleet operations. In November, she began her first shipyard overhaul at Norfolk. She completed repairs on 26 March 1965 and put to sea for trials.

On 15 April, she arrived in her new home port, Mayport, Fla. She conducted refresher training in the Guantanamo Bay operating area in May and June and returned to Mayport on 3 July. The warship resumed east coast operations until 27 August, at which time she deployed to the Mediterranean once again. That four-month deployment ended on 17 December when the guided missile frigate reentered Mayport. For the next six months, *William V. Pratt* conducted operations out of Mayport. She voyaged twice to the West Indies and once to the Gulf of Mexico. The warship also operated briefly off the Virginia capes. In July of 1966, she deployed to the Mediterranean for the third time in her career. She conducted operations with the 6th Fleet for the next five months, departing the Mediterranean for home on 10 December. She arrived back in Mayport 10 days later.

Following six months of normal operations along the east coast and in the West Indies, *William V. Pratt* departed Mayport on 20 June 1967 for her only deployment to the western Pacific during the American involvement in the Vietnamese civil war. En route, she transited the Panama Canal and made port calls at San Diego, Pearl Harbor, Midway, and Guam before arriving in Subic Bay in the Philippines on 28 July. Early in August, she reparted the Philippines for the Gulf of Tonkin and duty on the northern sea-air rescue (SAR) station. She relieved *Berkeley* (DDG–15) on 12 August and remained on station in the gulf until early in September. After upkeep in Subic Bay, she headed back to the Gulf of Tonkin late in the month to take up duty on the south SAR station. That tour of duty lasted until the latter part of November at which time she departed the gulf for port visits to Hong Kong and Kaohsiung on the island of Taiwan. She did one more period of duty on the south SAR station before leaving the western Pacific via Yokosuka in Japan, Midway Island, and Pearl Harbor. The warship arrived in San Diego on 31 December. On 2 January 1968, she resumed her voyage back to Mayport. *William V. Pratt* transited the Panama Canal on 10 January and reentered her home port on the 15th.

In February 1968, the warship moved to Charleston to prepare for regular overhaul. On 1 March, she entered the Charleston Naval Shipyard and began a six-month repair period. She departed Charleston on 6 September and arrived back in Mayport two days later. After refresher training in the West Indies, *William V. Pratt* resumed her routine of alternating 2d and 6th Fleet tours of duty. Over the next four years, the guided missile frigate was deployed to European waters once each year. She departed Mayport on 7 January 1969 and set a course for the Mediterranean. She reported for duty with the 6th Fleet on 18 January and, for the next five months, conducted the normal round of port visits and exercises. On 1 June, she arrived in Rota, Spain, for turnover ceremonies before heading north on the 3rd for a series of hunter/killer exercises and visits to northern European ports. She concluded that assignment on 7 July when she departed Portsmouth, England,

to return to the United States. The warship arrived back in Mayport on 15 July and resumed normal 2d Fleet operations. That employment lasted until 30 April when she pointed her bow eastward again and headed for the Mediterranean. In addition to the usual exercises and port visits, that deployment included duty with a special contingency force assembled in the eastern Mediterranean in response to Syrian intervention in the Jordanian civil war on the side of militant, antigovernment, Arab guerrillas. She steamed around off the Levantine coast from early September to early October before the American show of force finally succeeded in securing a Syrian withdrawal. The warship then resumed normal 6th Fleet operations until 1 November when she departed Barcelona, Spain, on her way home.

For the remainder of 1970 and during the first seven months of 1971, *William V. Pratt* operated out of Mayport along the east coast and in the West Indies. Her 1971 deployment began early in August, but it consisted of a cruise to northern European waters for hunter/killer exercises and visits to northern European ports rather than a Mediterranean cruise. She returned to Mayport on 8 October and, on the 29th, began converting her main propulsion plant to the use of Navy distillate fuel. She completed that modification on 17 January 1972 and resumed local operations until 18 February when she got underway for duty with the 6th Fleet. The warship participated in the usual schedule of training evolutions, multiship exercises, and port visits through the spring and early summer. On 28 June, after turnover ceremonies at Rota, the guided missile frigate headed home. She reentered Mayport on 8 July and began post-deployment standdown and preparations for her decommissioning incident to a major modernization overhaul. In September, she moved to Philadelphia for the antiaircraft warfare (AAW) modernization overhaul. *William V. Pratt* was decommissioned at the Philadelphia Naval Shipyard.

William V. Pratt was recommissioned at Philadelphia on 6 October 1973, Comdr. Rodney B. McDaniel in command. On the 23d, she departed Philadelphia, bound for her new home port, Charleston, S.C. She arrived at her destination on the 26th. The guided missile frigate conducted post-overhaul shakedown training in December and resumed 2d Fleet operations early in 1974. Those operations continued until 23 September at which time she departed Charleston to deploy to the Mediterranean once again. She changed operational control to the 6th Fleet at Rota, Spain, on 2 October. The following day, the warship entered the Mediterranean proper and began operations as a unit of the screen for *Independence* (CV–62). For the next five months, *William V. Pratt* conducted exercises with carriers *Independence* and *Saratoga* (CV–60). She ranged the length and breadth of the "middle sea," making port visits and performing the usual training missions. On 8 March 1975, she conducted turnover at Rota and got underway for Charleston. The warship reentered her home port on the 19th and, after about a month of post-deployment standdown for leave and upkeep, she resumed normal 2d Fleet operations. Those missions brought an NROTC midshipman cruise in May and readiness exercises in June. On 1 July 1975, *William V. Pratt* was reclassified a guided missile destroyer and received the designation DDG–44. On 14 August, she departed Charleston to participate in UNITAS XVI, a series of multinational exercises conducted annually with units of various Latin American navies. Those exercises occupied her time for most of what remained of 1975. On 8 December, the warship arrived back in Charleston and began holiday leave and upkeep as well as preparations for a restricted availability.

The ship entered the Charleston Naval Shipyard on 15 December and remained there until 29 March 1976. She returned to Charleston on 7 April and resumed normal 2d Fleet duty. That assignment—broken only by her participation in the International Naval Review held at New York on Independence Day—continued through the summer of 1976. On 4 October, *William V. Pratt* departed Charleston in company with *Jesse L. Brown* (FF–1089), *Julius A. Furer* (FFG–6), and *Valdez* (FF–1096) for another tour of duty with the 6th Fleet in the Mediterranean. The ships arrived in Rota on 14 October, completed turnover briefings, and entered the Mediterranean on the 16th. The warship served in the screen of *Franklin D. Roosevelt* (CV–42) for the bulk of her 6th Fleet assignment. Once again, she visited ports and conducted exercises throughout the Mediterranean. That tour of duty with the 6th Fleet lasted until the beginning of April 1977. After turnover at Rota, the guided missile destroyer got underway on 11 April to return to the United States. She moored at Charleston once again on 21 April and, on the 27th, entered the Charleston Naval Shipyard for a 10-week availability. She completed repairs on 8 July and resumed 2d Fleet training operations out of Charleston. That employment continued through the end of 1977 and into 1978. On 11 July 1978, she departed Charleston for another deployment to South American waters to participate in UNITAS XIX. During that cruise, she completed a circumnavigation of the South American continent while engaged in a series of readiness exercises with Latin American navies. She returned to Charleston on 3 December and spent the remaining days of the year in port.

William V. Pratt earned one battle star during the Vietnam conflict.

William Ward Burrows

William Ward Burrows—born in South Carolina on 16 January 1758—was described by a contemporary, Washington Irving, as a "gentlemen of accomplished mind and polished manner." Burrows served with the state troops of South Carolina in the American Revolution, before he moved to Philadelphia. There, on 12 July 1798, he was made Commandant of the Marine Corps—newly established by President John Adams.

The first Marine Corps units to be organized by the industrious new commandant were those that served in the ships of the fledgling United States Navy. During the first seven months in which Burrows held the office of commandant, the United States embarked on the Quasi-War with the French Republic. At that time, the headquarters of the Corps was at Philadelphia, then the capital of the country. In addition to organizing his headquarters staff and securing a barracks for transient personnel, Burrows established the Marine Band under the original leadership of Drum Major William Farr. On 4 July 1800, that musical organization first appeared in public at Tun Tavern, in probably the last social function attended by marines while they retained their headquarters at Philadelphia.

Burrows reached Washington, D.C., on 15 July, to establish the new Marine Corps headquarters there in the wake of an advance detachment sent down in March to protect the Washington Navy Yard, then under construction. The remainder of the marines in Philadelphia were soon shifted down to Washington, and during that time, Burrows received a promotion to Lieutenant Colonel Commandant.

Although the Quasi-War with France continued into the autumn of 1800, Congressional pressure to reduce the cost of a naval establishment frustrated some of Burrows' efforts to establish the Marine Corps on a solid, permanent footing. Nevertheless, the Corps was able to weather the storm because another armed conflict, the Barbary Wars, highlighted the nation's need for marines.

Burrows resigned his post as Commandant for health reasons on 6 March 1804, and he died exactly one year later, on 6 March 1805. Under his leadership, the United States Marine Corps gained a firm and enduring foundation upon which succeeding leaders built the Corps of later years.

(AP–6: dp. 8,450; l. 386'2¼"; b. 53'0"; dr. 9'6" s. 12.5 k.; cpl. 178; a. 4 3", 5 .50-cal. mg., 4 .30-cal mg.; cl. *William Ward Burrows*)

Santa Rita—a twin-screw, steel-hulled, passenger and cargo motorship launched in May 1929 at Copenhagen, Denmark, by Burmeister and Wain—was built for the Grace Steamship Co., Inc., and operated between New York and ports in South America and on the west coast of the United States, carrying passengers and freight. She was acquired by the Navy on 6 February 1940 and was commissioned "in ordinary" as *William Ward Burrows* (AP–6) on 9 February at Pier 5 of the Norfolk Navy Yard, Portsmouth, Va. Converted to a troop transport at the Norfolk Navy Yard, *William Ward Burrows* was placed in full commission on 15 May 1940, Comdr. Ross A. Dierdorff in command.

After fitting-out, *William Ward Burrows* sailed from Norfolk on her maiden voyage on 6 July and proceeded to Weehawken, N.J., to take on a cargo of structural steel. Departing that port on the 15th, the transport embarked a company of marines as well as a group of women and children—naval dependents—for transportation to Guantanamo Bay, Cuba. After delivering her passengers, she touched at San Juan, Puerto Rico; Cristobal, Canal Zone; transited the Panama Canal; visited Balboa, Canal Zone; and the California ports of San Diego; San Pedro; Vallejo (the Mare Island Navy Yard); and the Naval Air Station at Alameda, before she proceeded on to her ultimate destination of Midway Island, where she dropped anchor on 2 October.

William Ward Burrows began, consequently, what would become a series of voyages that formed part of the belated American attempt to fortify her outposts in the Pacific—islands such as Wake, Midway, and Johnston. *William Ward Burrows* carried the pioneer construction unit—80 men and 2,000 tons of equipment—to Wake Island in January of 1941, departing Honolulu the day before Christmas of 1940 and arriving at its destination late in the afternoon of 9 January 1941.

William Ward Burrows would conduct eight more voyages prior to the outbreak of war in the Pacific, carrying construction employees, sailors, and marines, and the miscellaneous cargo necessary to sustain the outposts of the American defense system in the Pacific. On what proved to be her last pre-war voyage to Wake, the transport took westward a cargo of dynamite, as well as employees of civilian contractors and a sprinkling of Navy and Marine Corps personnel. In addition, she towed *Pan American Airways Barge* (PAB) No. 4, laden with general cargo. She arrived at Wake on 11 November, disembarked her passengers, discharged her cargo, and delivered her tow before she headed back to Hawaii on the 13th.

Soon after arriving, she shifted to Honolulu and embarked 33 marines, 60 sailors, and 55 civilian contractor's employees for transport to Wake on the 28th. She got underway at 0825 on 29 November, towing *PAB–7*. The ship, herself, carried 1,819 tons of cargo—general supplies, lumber, "reefer boxes" (refrigerators), a boat, 10 trailers, and 20 tons of gasoline in tins.

Heavy seas and stormy winds prevailed for the entire passage. *William Ward Burrows*, nevertheless, plowed along at five knots with *PAB–7* in tow; she rendezvoused with *Sonoma* (AT–12) on 5 December and took on board an appendicitis patient from the Hawaii-bound tug for medical attention. As the transport continued on toward Wake Island, the weather—as Commander Dierdorff observed—was "uniformly abominable," but all hands took the rough weather well.

The ship crossed the international date line on 6 December and accordingly set her calendars ahead to compensate. Unbeknownst to the solitary transport, a Japanese carrier task force was proceeding toward Pearl Harbor. On the morning of 7 December 1941 (8 December on the transport's side of the date line), that task force struck Pearl Harbor a devastating blow and plunged the United States into a war in both oceans.

At 0705 on 8 December, *William Ward Burrows* received word of the attack. The crew was called to general quarters; the captain set air and submarine watches; lookouts were alerted, as were the gun crews. Civilian workmen embarked on board immediately volunteered their services "in any capacity."

The next day, 9 December, *William Ward Burrows* received orders to return to Honolulu with her loaded cargo and *PAB-7*. The war news she received was grim. Pearl Harbor had been attacked and Midway shelled (by the Japanese destroyers *Ushio* and *Akebono*). False sightings of Japanese task forces here and there proliferated. Comdr. Dierdorff later recalled: "As reports came in, the general impression we gained was that most of the Nipponese fleet was between us and Hawaii." He was not far from the truth.

On 13 December, the transport received word to take *PAB-7* to Johnston Island. Accordingly, the ship altered course and on 15 December delivered the barge—with her cargo load of "general cargo" and lumber—and embarked passengers for transportation to Hawaii. That day, at 1340, *William Ward Burrows'* rudder touched a 3-fathom coral head—in an area believed to have been dredged to a safe depth of 30 feet. Fortunately, the transport cleared the navigational hazard with only minor damage to the tip of the rudder.

That evening, *William Ward Burrows* remained at anchor to the south of Johnston Island in an anchorage deemed safe from submarine attack. Comdr. Dierdorff posted full submarine lookouts, fully manned the bridge, and put the engine room on five minutes' notice to get underway. Squally weather prevented his using a 40-foot motor launch as picket.

At 1810, Ens. J. A. Peterson, USNR—the officer of the deck—sounded the general alarm; when Comdr. Dierdorff reached the bridge, he saw that enemy ships were shelling Johnston Island from the northward, setting fire to oil storage tanks near the center of the island. One large shell struck 30 yards astern of *William Ward Burrows*, and another passed over the forecastle. Other splashes erupted from the waters between the ship and the island.

Fortunately for *William Ward Burrows* and her 227 passengers—132 of them civilians—the enemy did not see her. Knowing that his 3-inch guns were inadequate for a surface gunfire duel with ships of unknown size, Comdr. Dierdorff wisely decided not to open fire. Favored by darkness and rain squalls, *William Ward Burrows* got underway at 1830 and escaped to the southward. By that time, the bombardment had ceased. At about 2330, Johnston Island reported no casualties and advised *William Ward Burrows* not to return; thus, early the next morning, the transport set course for Honolulu and home.

William Ward Burrows entered drydock on New Year's Day 1942 for repairs to her rudder and nine days later emerged and began loading cargo destined for Midway. After embarking a draft of marines for transportation to that key atoll, the transport got underway on 18 January. She arrived five days later and began working her cargo. Two days later, a Japanese submarine boldly surfaced a mere mile away and began shelling the island. However, about three minutes later, fire from Marine Corps guns ashore drove the submarine away.

The ship soon headed back to Pearl Harbor and arrived there on 3 February. Between early February and mid-March, she made two more round-trip voyages to Midway before she conducted an interisland trip among the islands of the Hawaiian group carrying general cargo and transporting Army troops to Hilo and Maui. She next voyaged to Midway, carrying general cargo, lumber, provisions, "reefer boxes," cable reels, and a two-ton truck while transporting naval and Marine Corps personnel. In mid-May, she returned to the west coast of the United States.

Following an overhaul at the Mare Island Navy Yard, Vallejo, Calif., *William Ward Burrows* loaded to within 90 percent of her capacity, taking on board 1,437 tons of cargo—which included ammunition and lumber—and departed San Francisco at 1053 on 23 July. The transport arrived at Pearl Harbor on the 31st and unloaded. After taking on a different cargo, the ship sailed for the New Hebrides at 1849 on 4 August.

After picking up her escort, *Flusser* (DD–368), later that day, *William Ward Burrows* made Fila Harbor, Efate Island, on 17 August. Underway again from Efate on 26 August, this time escorted by *McFarland* (AVD–14), *William Ward Burrows* headed for the Solomons. *Tracy* (DM–19), *Colhoun* (APD–2), *Little* (APD–4), *Gregory* (APD–3), *Gamble* (DM–15), and SS *Kapara* joined them the next day.

While passing through Indispensable Strait on the 29th, the ships received word from "Cactus"—the code-name for Henderson Field, Guadalcanal—at 1105, that an enemy air raid was imminent. While the APD's and DM's deployed to provide an antiaircraft screen around *William Ward Burrows* and *Kapara*, the transport prepared for action. At 1205—exactly an hour after the alert was broadcast from "Cactus"—a formation of Japanese planes droned overhead at 25,000 feet. Two minutes later, *William Ward Burrows* opened fire with her 3-inch battery and expended 50 rounds. Seven minutes later, lookouts observed two enemy bombers falling in flames, due to the fire from the task group. The surviving enemy aircraft soon fled, having caused no damage.

Shortly thereafter, *William Ward Burrows* proceeded to Lunga Roads, off Kukum Point, Guadalcanal, and dropped anchor. She got underway for Tulagi Harbor that afternoon but ran hard aground on the southeast end of Sylvia Reef at 1750, only five minutes after entering the harbor channel. In an effort to get out of the predicament, *William Ward Burrows* rang down full speed astern at 1752 and attempted to use her stern anchor as a kedge; but the ship refused to budge. *Little* passed a towline to the transport at 1904, but darkness intervened and kept *William Ward Burrows* aground for the night.

The next day, the transport passed a line to *Tracy*. The minecraft began pulling, backing with *William Ward Burrows'* engines running full astern, but the towline parted. Meanwhile, the transport's crew had begun unloading equipment into lighters, in an effort to lighten the ship. At 1458, lookouts spotted 18 Japanese bombers—Mitsubishi G4M "Betties"—at 22,000 feet. Helplessly aground, *William Ward Burrows* was in a bad situation; but, fortunately for her, the Japanese had business elsewhere. They attacked *Colhoun* at 1512—after she had unloaded 17 tons of stores consigned to the Marine Corps garrison on Guadalcanal—and, in two minutes, succeeded in scoring four direct hits. The luckless fast transport sank by the stern at about 1515.

At 2035, 20 wounded men from *Colhoun* were brought on board the transport for medical attention. Reflecting later upon the incident, *William Ward Burrows'* commanding officer, Lt. Comdr. E. I. McQuiston, concluded that, had she not run aground, his ship, too, would have been at Kukum Point and probably would have been the object of the Japanese attack. In that light, perhaps the grounding had been a blessing for the transport.

On the morning of the 31st, *William Ward Burrows* once more ran up her engines at full speed astern in another attempt to free the ship. At 1100, she went to general quarters when she received word of approaching Japanese planes—unable to maneuver and hard aground, the ship was still in a vulnerable position. Again, however, good fortune was with the ship, for the air raid never materialized.

Finally, on 2 September, with the aid of *YP–346* (on the port quarter), *YP–239* (on the starboard), and *Gamble*, *William Ward Burrows* at last floated free. She remained anchored off Sylvia Reef to take stock of the damage and found it light. *Gamble*, however, soon reported a submarine in the immediate vicinity, and the transport got underway to seek safety in the inner harbor at Tulagi. Unfortunately, the ship developed too much way to clear a patch of shoals, and she again grounded—this time on Southern Cross Reef.

Again, *William Ward Burrows* backed engines, but to no avail. Higgins boats pulling on the port quarter and pushing on the starboard side failed to budge her. Fortunately, that time aground was shorter than the first. On the afternoon of 3 September, aided by the trusty *Gamble* and *YP–239*, *William Ward Burrows* pulled free.

After being refloated from Southern Cross Reef, the transport again got underway for Kukum Point to discharge part of her cargo. She then proceeded back to Tulagi to unload the remainder. Upon completing that task, she again headed for Kukum Point at 0545 on the 5th; she hove to at 0756 finding all available boats engaged in picking up the survivors from *Little* and *Gregory*, APD's that had tangled with a detachment of the "Tokyo Express" and been sunk by the gunfire of Japanese destroyers *Yudachi*, *Hatsuyuki*, and *Murakumo* on the night of 4 and 5 September. As those boats passed his ship, Comdr. McQuiston invited them to come alongside and transfer the wounded to the transport. *William Ward Burrows* picked up 27 that morning and an additional 214 later, all for passage to Espiritu Santo. Her task completed at Guadalcanal, *William Ward Burrows*, escorted by *Gamble*, got underway at 1858.

At 0715 on 8 September, the transport dropped anchor at Segond Channel, Espiritu Santo, and later refueled from *Sabine* (AO–25). After disembarking the APD survivors and discharging more of her cargo, *William Ward Burrows* took on passengers and light freight and pushed on independently for New Caledonia on the 12th. Reaching Noumea on the 14th, she continued her voyage through the Pacific war zone to Suva, in the Fiji Islands, in company with USAT *Ernest R. Hinds* and escorted by *Buchanan* (DD–484). There, she brought on board more cargo and mail for delivery to Pearl Harbor.

Again sailing in company with *Ernest R. Hinds* and escorted by *Raleigh* (CL–7), *William Ward Burrows* made port at Pearl Harbor on 28 September. She remained at that point until 4 October loading cargo at both the Hickam Field dock and at the Navy Yard. She sailed for the Fiji Islands at 1400 that day, in company with *Tangier* (AV–8) and escorted by *Woodworth* (DD–460). Upon arrival at Suva on the 15th, the transport worked her cargo and, on the 18th, pushed on for Espiritu Santo where she arrived three days later.

Underway for New Caledona on the 27th, *William Ward Burrows* arrived at Noumea the following day and unloaded her passengers and mail. She tarried there until 14 November, when she pushed on for Samoa. Upon arrival, she discharged passengers and mail; picked up other passengers; and then proceeded back to the Hawaiian Islands, arriving at Pearl Harbor on 27 November.

The transport made one round-trip voyage to Midway and back before she shifted to the west coast of the United States for her second "stateside" visit since the war began. Arriving at San Francisco, Calif., on 2 February 1943, she spent the next few weeks exchanging cargoes and embarking passengers. She sailed for the Hawaiian Islands on 21 February, in company with *Henderson* (AP–1) and escorted by *Bulmer* (DD–222) and *Parrott* (DD–218).

The convoy, designated Task Group 15.6, ran into heavy weather on 25 February and for four days fought through mountainous seas. *William Ward Burrows* occasionally shipped water over both bow and stern and rolled very heavily in the rough seas and heavy swells, but arrived safely at Pearl Harbor on 2 March.

The ship devoted most of 1943 to making interisland transport runs, travelling among the islands of the Central Pacific, especially those of the Hawaiian chain. The most dramatic incident during this period of her service occurred on 6 November as she was approaching Midway toward the end of a run from Pearl Harbor. The ship's steering gear failed, and she was forced to lie to off the channel entrance until repairs could be made. Meanwhile, *PC–598* stood out of Midway to help protect the transport and joined *PC–586* at 1418. At 2034, *PC–598* reported picking up a submarine contact. A minute later, the transport went to general quarters. At 2040, *PC–598* fired a floating flare to illuminate the area; and she commenced dropping depth charges a minute later. *William Ward Burrows*—underway off the coast, with *PC–586* patrolling ahead—later lost contact with *PC–598* as that vessel went off to the hunt.

The next morning, with the danger passed and the steering casualty repaired, the transport entered the lagoon and began discharging her cargo. The ship remained at Midway from 8 to 10 November and soon set her sail for Pearl Harbor, with *PC–586* again as ocean escort. She made one more interisland cargo-carrying voyage before she began her third run to the South Pacific.

Three days before Christmas 1943, *William Ward Burrows*, escorted by *PC–549* and *PC–596*, departed Pearl Harbor with a cargo of ammunition. She traveled via Palmyra and American Samoa—transferring mail to *PC–596* on 30 December to deliver it to the port of Tutuila. The transport ultimately arrived at Havannah Harbor, Efate, at 0847 on 5 January 1944 and moored alongside the battleship *Alabama* (BB–60). After working cargo on board the battleship between 6 and 11 January, she proceeded to Espiritu Santo, where she discharged cargo between the 13th and 15th.

Proceeding thence to Funafuti, in the Ellice Islands, the ship remained at that port for two days before she set her course toward Pearl Harbor and arrived there on 28 January. After repairs, the transport made two more voyages to Midway Island—completing the second on 29 April—before she became the flagship of Service Squadron (ServRon) 12.

ServRon 12—dubbed "the harbor stretchers"—was a harbor development and salvage unit whose job was to clear harbors in the forward areas, making it possible to berth ships and bring supplies to the front-line areas at the earliest possible moment. Commanded by Capt. (later Commodore) Leon S. Fiske, ServRon 12 would play a part in the stepping-stone advance that eventually carried American forces to the Japanese home islands themselves.

Underway on 16 May—in company with *Boreas* (AF–8), *Fortune* (IX–46), *Triumph* (AM–323), and *Vigilance* (AM–324)—*William Ward Burrows* dropped anchor at Majuro lagoon in the Marshalls, on the 25th. Two days later, she shifted to Kwajalein, where she served into mid-July.

The flagship of ServRon 12 departed Kwajalein on 15 July, bound for Eniwetok. She sailed in company with her former running-mate and sister ship *Bowditch* (the erstwhile Grace Liner *Santa Inez*) (AGS–4), and escorted by *Bancroft* (DD–598); their courses set for the Marianas.

On the 21st, lookouts in the ship sighted starshell and heard the sound of heavy gunfire from Saipan—probably the mopping-up operations by the American forces ashore, since organized Japanese resistance on Saipan had ceased on the 9th. *William Ward Burrows* passed near Tinian on the 22d, observing from close-hand the preparatory bombardments paving the way for the landing of Major General Harry Schmidt's marines that would follow two days later. Late on the 23d, *William Ward Burrows* dropped anchor in Tanapag Harbor, Saipan, where she became a base of operations for the harbor development unit and immediately began salvage and harbor development operations, providing water and stores to the various ships assigned to ServRon 12 as well as small craft from other units.

Her stay at Saipan was not without incident. On 30 July, shortly after midnight, a tremendous explosion rocked the area; the concussion from the blast blew in the plywood light shields at the *William Ward Burrows'* hatches facing the island. Japanese infiltrators had detonated a cache of 84 tons of dynamite. Boats from the ship put out to investigate but could only ascertain that damage to the dump had been done and the guards had disappeared, probably killed in the blast.

The following morning, *William Ward Burrows* disembarked a detachment of four officers and 180 enlisted men of Naval Construction Battalion (NCB) ("Seabees") 301 to continue harbor development work at Saipan and stood out of Tanapag Harbor, bound for newly conquered Guam in company with *Vega* (AK–17), *Agenor* (ARL–3), *LST–431*, and escorted by the destroyers *Stockham* (DD–683) and *Tisdale* (DE–33). After a one-day passage, *William Ward Burrows* dropped anchor at Apra Harbor and began unloading salvage equipment. Soon various barges and other salvage craft were operating from alongside the transport which supplied them with water and stores as they worked on local harbor development tasks.

Commodore William M. Quigley, the new Deputy Commander, Forward Area, and his staff reported aboard on 18 August. The ship's force immediately began constructing a wooden addition to the communication office on the promenade deck, port side. In addition, a voice radio and operations office was built on the port side of the gun deck. These alterations were made to help the ship fill her new role as the ship in which the Senior Officer Present, Afloat, (SOPA) was embarked.

William Ward Burrows soon resumed her work as base ship for harbor operations at Apra Harbor. She again supplied various ships and small craft with stores and water, until she detected a leak in one of her fresh water tanks. After patient searching, the ship's force found the affected area and soon repaired it. Shortly thereafter, Commodore Quigley and his staff disembarked and set up shop in the repair ship *Luzon* (ARG–2).

William Ward Burrows next embarked seabees and their equipment and took on board a cargo of dynamite that partially filled one of her holds. She continued the loading evolution until 2 October when she got underway in company with her escort, *Caravan* (AM–157). Soon after they cleared the harbor, the barometer began dropping steadily—a sign of an impending typhoon.

The storm developed throughout the night and struck with full force the next morning. *William Ward Burrows* plunged through the tempest, "like a sailboat between two mountains of water," as the ships' historian later recounted. During the morning, hands in the transport estimated that the wind velocity was at least 85 knots. Fortunately, *William Ward Burrows* suffered little damage—one life raft lost over the side—and she and *Caravan* continued their voyage. On 4 October, they joined *Hydrographer* (AGS–2), *ARD–16*, and *Pakana* (ATF–108).

Altering course toward Ulithi Atoll, *William Ward Burrows* effected the necessary minor repairs to the storm damage suffered in the typhoon before she again got underway on 9 October, bound for her original destination, the Palaus. She hove to off Peleliu and unloaded her cargo into amphibious trucks (DUKW's) and her dynamite cargo into an LCT.

Five days after her arrival, *William Ward Burrows* shifted to a position between the islands of Bairakaseru and Garakayo, where she lay to, while a survey boat from NCB–301 took soundings of a nearby inlet in preparation for anchoring *ARD–16*. The transport eventually moved to a spot between Angaur and Peleliu and hove to for the night. During her stay in the Palaus, several air alerts occurred, giving all hands some anxious hours; but the transport never sighted any enemy aircraft and continued her support duties, transferring navigational gear and buoys to *Papaw* (WLB–308).

Departing Peleliu on 23 October, *William Ward Burrows* headed back to the Marianas to resume her flagship duties for ServRon 12. En route, *Caravan*—again her ocean escort—made a contact on what she believed was an enemy submarine and made one attack. However, she lost the contact and eventually rejoined her charge and shepherded the transport safely back to Guam.

William Ward Burrows operated at Guam into the spring of 1945. Getting underway for the Ryukyus on 30 May, in the wake of the invasion of Okinawa, *William Ward Burrows*—escorted by *Sustain* (AM–119)—reached that island on 3 June and entered Buckner Bay. As she steamed to her assigned anchorage, the transport came under attack from a solitary "Jill" that roared down out of the clouds. Immediately, the ships in the anchorage blanketed the sky with antiaircraft fire and sent the "Jill" crashing about 1,000 yards from *Burrows'* anchorage. This proved to be only the first of almost continuous air raid "flash" alerts that would characterize the ship's sojourn in Okinawan waters. Five days later, she observed a kamikaze crash the fast minelayer *J. William Ditter* (DM–31), four miles away.

At 1908 on 11 June, the transport—at general quarters and "on the lookout for low-flying bogies"—sighted a "Jill" or "Sonia" off her port side at 1,500 feet. The transport and all of the other ships in the area immediately opened fire, "engulfing the plane and vicinity with tracer fire and shell bursts." The plane roared past *William Ward Burrows*, *Bowditch*, an LSD, and a "Liberty" ship, making a banking turn over the nearby Katsuren Hanto peninsula, and crashed at 1911, about 700 yards astern of *Burrows*.

The following day, the transport moved to the Yonabaru anchorage and began unloading equipment for the Seabee unit that had begun to establish camps on the beach. Air alerts continued almost ceaselessly, day or night, but unloading operations proceeded regardless.

After that period of work offshore, *William Ward Burrows* got underway and proceeded to Chimu Wan, an anchorage on the northward side of Buckner Bay, and dropped anchor there on 2 July. However, twice after the ship reached that body of water, typhoons nearby forced her to get underway to seek maneuvering room in the open sea. On 19 July, for example, she sortied with LST group 35—16 LST's and two LCM's—and remained at sea until the morning of the 21st. Air alerts, too, continued to make life hectic almost until the end, but Japan—worn down by ceaseless Allied pressure, particularly from American seapower—indicated a willingness to surrender and accepted the terms of the Potsdam Declaration on 15 August.

But for *William Ward Burrows*, however, the cessation of hostilities did not mean an end to the ship's work. The veteran transport participated in the occupation of the erstwhile enemy's homeland, continuing her vital support role between 2 September 1945 and 26 January 1946. During that time, she successfully weathered another major typhoon in September of 1945 without suffering major damage.

Her task completed in the Far East, *William Ward Burrows* sailed for the United States in the spring of 1946. She reported to Commandant, 13th Naval District, for disposition on 17 March 1946 and was decommissioned on 16 May of the same year. Struck from the Navy list on 15 August 1946, *William Ward Burrows* was delivered to the War Shipping Administration, Maritime Commission, and simultaneously delivered to the Commission's reserve fleet for lay up. She remained in reserve until she was sold in 1957 and scrapped.

William Ward Burrows received four battle stars for her World War II service.

John Foster Williams—born on 12 October 1743 at Boston, Mass.—was appointed a captain in the Navy of Massachusetts and received command of the brig *Hazard* late in 1777. In the following year, he took her to sea in a fruitless search for British West Indiamen; but he and his ship eventually achieved success in 1779. While cruising in the West Indies, *Hazard* fell in with the privateer brigantine *Active* on 16 March. At the end of a "smart action" of 35-minutes' duration, "yard arm to yard arm," *Active* struck her colors and became *Hazard*'s prize, after having suffered 13 killed and 20 wounded out of her 95-man crew. *Hazard* sent the captured brigantine back to Massachusetts under a prize crew and subsequently returned home in April, after taking several other prizes.

In May, *Hazard* returned to sea, this time in company with the brig *Tyrannicide*. At 0830 on 15 June, the two ships fell in with two British ships and—after a short, sharp engagement—forced both enemy vessels to strike their colors. Later that summer, *Hazard*—like the rest of the Massachusetts Navy—took part in the ill-fated Penobscot expedition, an operation which eventually cost the state's navy all of its commissioned vessels.

Williams received command of the new 26-gun frigate *Protector* in the spring of 1780 and took her to sea in June. In accordance with instructions from the Board of War, the new warship cruised in the vicinity of the Newfoundland Banks, on the lookout for British merchantmen. Her vigilance was rewarded early in June.

At 0700 on 9 June 1780, *Protector* spotted a strange ship bearing down on her, flying British colors. At 1100, the Continental frigate, also flying English colors, hailed the stranger and found her to be the 32-gun letter-of-marque *Admiral Duff*, bound for London from St. Kitts. When the enemy's identity had been ascertained, *Protector* hauled down British colors and ran up the Continental flag—opening fire almost simultaneously. The action ensued for the next hour and one-half, until *Admiral Duff* caught fire and exploded, leaving 55 survivors for *Protector* to rescue soon thereafter.

With the coming of peace, Williams returned to his native Boston and died there on 24 June 1814.

George Washington Williams—born in Yorkville, S.C., on 30 July 1869—graduated from the United States Naval Academy in 1890. He served the required two years of sea duty in *Pensacola*, before he was commissioned an ensign on 1 July 1892.

Williams served in a succession of sea and shore billets through the turn of the century: the former in *Essex*, *Columbia*, *Yankee*, *Buffalo*, *Panther*, *Richmond*, and *Monongahela*; the latter at the Naval Torpedo Station, Newport, R.I. In addition, he served on the staff of the Commander in Chief, Asiatic Fleet, in 1899 and commanded the torpedo boat *Bainbridge* in 1903 before commanding the 1st Torpedo Boat Flotilla. Reporting to *Wisconsin* (Battleship No. 9) on 5 April 1905, Williams subsequently joined the protected cruiser *Chicago* for a tour of duty which included participating in relief efforts at San Francisco, Calif., in the wake of the destructive earthquake and fire which destroyed much of that city.

In the years immediately preceding World War I, Williams served as ordnance officer in *Montana* (Armored Cruiser No. 13); commander of the Atlantic Torpedo Fleet; Inspector of Ordnance in Charge at the Naval Torpedo Station; commanding officer of the cruiser *Cleveland* and later of battleship *Oregon*, before he assumed command of *Pueblo* (Armored Cruiser No. 7) on 29 April 1917.

Williams—by that time a captain—was awarded the Navy Cross for "distinguished service in the line of his profession" while commanding *Pueblo* during World War I, as the armored cruiser engaged in the "important, exacting, and hazardous duty of transporting and escorting troops and supplies to European ports through waters infested with enemy submarines and mines."

Detached from *Pueblo* on 6 September 1918, Williams participated in fitting out the new dreadnaught *Idaho* (Battleship No. 42) and later served ashore in the Office of Naval Intelligence. He took the Naval War College course in 1919 and 1920 before commanding the new dreadnaught *New Mexico* (BB–40) from 31 May 1921 to 18 May 1922. After detachment from *New Mexico*, Williams became the senior member of the Pacific Coast section of the Board of Inspection and Survey.

Reaching flag rank on 29 September 1922, Williams served as Chief of Staff to the Commander in Chief, Atlantic Fleet, and later as the Chief of Staff to the Commander in Chief, United States Fleet, when the former command was reorganized. Detached from this duty in the spring of 1923, Williams subsequently served at Charleston, S.C., as the commandant of the 6th Naval District before breaking his two-star flag in *Concord* (CL–10) on 15 September 1924 as Commander, Destroyer Squadrons, Scouting Fleet.

Rear Admiral Williams died on 18 July 1925 at the Naval Hospital, Charleston, S.C.

The second *Williams* (DD–108) commemorates John Foster Williams; the third (DE–372) honors Rear Admiral George Washington Williams.

(ScStr.: t. 97 (gross); l. 90′0″; b. 21′0″; dr. 7′9″ (mean); dph. 9′0″; s. 8.0 k.)

Apparently, sometime in 1917, *E. T. Williams*—a tug built in 1898 by Thomas McCluskey at Baltimore, Md.—was chartered by the Navy and assigned the classification SP–3241. However, records of the vessel's naval career are both sparse and conflicting. Although Navy General Order No. 314, issued on 28 July 1917, had specified that scout patrol vessels bearing compound names should thereafter be known solely by their surnames—in this case *Williams*—the 1918 issue of *Ships Data, U.S. Naval Vessels* listed the tug as *E. T. Williams*. It also reported that she was assigned to the 5th Naval District. The 1919 issue, on the other hand, states that *E. T. Williams* was "... not taken over." No logs or other records have been found to resolve the matter or to delineate the details of the tug's service—if any—in the Navy.

I

(MB: t. 41 (gross); l. 90′0″; b. 12′0″; dr. 5′; dph. 6′; s. 15 k.; cpl. 11; a. 3 3-pdrs., 2 mg.)

Williams—sometimes cited as *Williams '18*—was originally built as *Grayling*. Completed in 1907 at City Island, N.Y., by B. Frank Wood, and designed by the firm of Tams, Lemoine, and Crane, the wooden-hulled, screw steam yacht was owned by Justus Ruperti of New York City in the years preceding World War I.

Acquired by the Navy for inshore patrol duties, *Williams*—assigned the classification SP–498—was commissioned at New York City on 16 March 1918, Boatswain M. T. Moran, USNRF, in command. During the vessel's "unofficial trial trip" on 18 March, the patrol craft suffered a broken propeller shaft and was towed to the Philadelphia Marine Basin for repairs. One month later, while being taken in tow by *Aramis* (SP–418), *Williams* was jammed between *Aramis* and the dock, suffering damage again.

Apparently still without propulsion, *Williams* was towed to an offshore mooring and used for a month as a floating classroom by groups of hydrophone trainees, or "listeners." At the end of each day, she was towed back to port. Drydocked in May and apparently restored to active duty (instead of being towed to her offshore duty station) with a repaired shaft, *Williams* made a trial trip on 14 May.

Ten days later, misfortune again reared its head. *Williams*' propeller struck the bottom while off Sandy Hook and was damaged. After repairs soon thereafter, the motor patrol boat trained "listeners" using "listening tubes" for the remainder of the spring and summer of 1918. During this time, she suffered slight damage in collision with the tug *Relief* on 27 September.

At 1045 on 16 October, *Williams* speedily got underway to reach the area where the British steamer *Port Phillip* was sinking. She arrived and lay to off the ship. There is no indication in the patrol craft's log as to providing assistance for *Port Phillip*, but we can assume that she aided the distressed steamer and its crew.

On 17 October, all listening gear was removed and stored; and the ship was drydocked for repairs at the New York Navy Yard. She apparently remained at the yard into December, after the armistice which ended World War I. All armament, ammunition, and gear were removed during the early part of December, 1918. *Williams* then sailed to Shady Side, N.J., on 18 December 1918, where she was simultaneously decommissioned and returned to her owner. She was apparently struck from the Navy list on the same day.

II

(Destroyer No. 108: dp. 1,191; l. 314'4½''; b. 30'11½''; dr. 9'2'' (mean); s. 34.02 k.; cpl. 113; a. 4 4'', 2 1-pdrs., 12 21'' tt.; cl. *Wickes*)

The second *Williams* (Destroyer No. 108) was laid down on 25 March 1918 at San Francisco, Calif., by the Union Iron Works plant of the Bethlehem Shipbuilding Corp.; launched on 4 July 1918; sponsored by Mrs. H. G. Leopold, the wife of Comdr. H. G. Leopold; and commissioned on 1 March 1919 at the Mare Island Navy Yard, Vallejo, Calif., Comdr. Matthias E. Manly in command.

Following shakedown, *Williams* and *Belknap* (Destroyer No. 251) departed Newport, R.I., on 5 June 1919, bound for the Azores. Arriving at Ponta Delgada on the 11th, *Williams* proceeded to Gibraltar, where she picked up information pertaining to minefields still extant in the Adriatic, for delivery to the Commander, Naval Forces, Eastern Mediterranean. The destroyer's brief tour of duty in this area of the world took her to Spalato, Yugoslavia; Gallipoli, in the Dardanelles; and Trieste, Italy, where she operated as part of the American naval forces keeping watch on the tense local situations there in the aftermath of the World War.

After returning to the United States—via Spalato and Gibraltar—and arriving at New York City on 1 August 1919, *Williams* was eventually assigned to the Pacific Fleet. Classified DD–108 on 17 July 1920, the destroyer operated out of San Diego until decommissioned there on 7 June 1922 and placed in reserve.

The German invasion of Poland on 1 September 1939 began hostilities in Europe, and President Franklin D. Roosevelt immediately declared America's neutrality. To augment the fleet units already engaged in the Neutrality Patrol hurriedly placed off the eastern seaboard and gulf coast of the United States, the Navy recommissioned 77 destroyers and light minelayers.

Williams was accordingly placed in commission at San Diego on 6 November 1939, Lt. Comdr. Louis N. Miller in command. Following a refit at Mare Island, the destroyer operated in the San Diego area until sailing for Panama on 5 February. Transiting the Panama Canal on the 16th, she lay at Balboa for a brief time. During her stay there, the destroyer "manned the rail" in honor of President Roosevelt, who was then engaged in an informal inspection of the Canal Zone's defenses. Underway soon thereafter, *Williams* arrived at the Naval Operating Base (NOB), Key West, Fla., on 27 February.

Over the ensuing months, *Williams* operated with the Atlantic Squadron of the fleet, conducting neutrality patrols as well as training cruises. While conducting her scheduled operations from Key West, the destroyer took part in short-range battle practices and ship-handling drills, while keeping a weather eye on shipping in her vicinity. In March, she conducted an astronomical survey in the Bahamas.

On 9 April, *Williams* transported a survey party to Palmetto Island in the British West Indies before shifting to Guantanamo Bay, Cuba. After moving back to Key West for a time, *Williams* departed Florida's waters on 2 June and arrived at New York on 4 June. She conducted two training cruises for embarked Naval Reserve contingents, which kept her busy into the late summer of 1940. After a final refit at the Boston Navy Yard, she departed Charlestown, Mass., on 18 September, bound for Canadian waters; and reached Halifax, Nova Scotia, two days later.

As one of the 50 flush-deck destroyers transferred to the British under lend-lease—in return for leases on important base sites in the Western Hemisphere—*Williams* was selected as one of the six units slated for the Royal Canadian Navy. Soon after her arrival at Halifax on 20 September 1940, she got underway for a brief familiarization cruise for the Canadian crewmen. *Williams* was decommissioned and turned over to the Canadian government on 24 September; her name was subsequently struck from the Navy list on 8 January 1941.

Renamed HMCS *St. Clair* (I.65)—her name commemorating the river which forms the boundary between Michigan and Ontario—the destroyer was fitted out for convoy escort duties and sailed for the British Isles on 30 November, in company with HMCS *St. Croix* (ex-*McCook*, DD–152) and HMCS *Niagara* (ex-*Thatcher*, DD–162).

Operating with the Clyde Escort force, *St. Clair* escorted convoys in and out of the heavily travelled "western approaches" to the British Isles in the spring of 1941. Late in May, when the powerful German battleship *Bismarck* and the heavy cruiser *Prinz Eugen* slipped through the Denmark Straits, the "flush decker" became involved in the intensive and widespread effort to destroy the German dreadnought. Eventually, a British force located and sank *Bismarck* on 27 May, but not before the tragic loss of the battle cruiser HMS *Hood* on 24 May. The search for the elusive German battlewagon brought some of the British units dangerously close to exhaustion of their fuel supplies. Two "Tribal"-class destroyers, HMS *Mashona* and HMS *Tartar*, were located by German long-rang bombers soon after *Bismarck* had slipped beneath the waves and sunk in devastating attacks. *St. Clair*, near the battle area, became involved in the action when she, too, came under attack. The old destroyer doggedly put up a good defense—shooting down one, and possibly, a second, enemy plane.

St. Clair subsequently joined the Newfoundland Escort Force after this group's establishment in June 1941 and operated on convoy escort missions between Newfoundland and Reykjavik, Iceland, through the end of 1941. *St. Clair* was assigned to the Western Local Escort Force following repairs at St. John, New Brunswick, in early 1942, and operated out of Halifax over the next two years, escorting coastwise convoys until withdrawn from this service in 1943 due to her deteriorating condition.

Operating as a submarine depot ship at Halifax until deemed unfit for further duty "in any capacity" in August 1944, *St. Clair* was used as a fire-fighting and damage control hulk until 1946. Handed over to the War Assets Corp. for disposal, on 6 October 1946, *St. Clair* was subsequently broken up for scrap.

Williams (DE–290)—a *Rudderow*-class destroyer escort—was slated to be built at Hingham, Mass., by the Bethlehem-Hingham Shipyard; but the contract for her was cancelled on 12 March 1944.

III

(DE–372: dp. 1,350; l. 306'; b. 36'8''; dr. 9'5'' (mean); s. 24 k.; cpl. 186; a. 2 5'', 4 40mm., 10 20mm., 2 dct., 8 dcp., 1 dcp. (hh.); cl. *John C. Butler*)

The third *Williams* (DE–372) was laid down on 5

June 1944 at Orange, Tex., by the Consolidated Steel Corp.; launched on 22 August 1944; sponsored by Mrs. E. Willoughby Middleton, the first cousin of Rear Admiral Williams; and commissioned on 11 November 1944, Lt. Comdr. L. F. Loutrel in command.

Following shakedown out of Great Sound, Bermuda, *Williams* underwent post-shakedown availability at Boston before shifting to New London, Conn., on 11 January 1945. Departing on the 19th, she moved to Newport, R.I., to rendezvous with *Riverside* (APA–102), and got underway on the 30th for Panama. *Williams* escorted the attack transport to Balboa, in the Canal Zone, and subsequently sailed for the west coast in company with *Sims* (APD–50), arriving at San Diego on 7 February.

Williams soon steamed independently to Hawaii, arriving at Pearl Harbor on 16 February. Following a period of training and minor repairs, the destroyer escort pushed on for the New Hebrides before escorting a group of LCI's from Espiritu Santo to Lunga Point from 25 to 27 March. Returning via Tulagi to Espiritu Santo on the 30th, *Williams* shifted to Noumea soon thereafter, to rendezvous with *Vulcan* (AR–5) and escort the repair ship to Ulithi where they arrived on 15 April.

After shifting to Manus, in the Admiralties, upon the conclusion of this escort mission, *Williams* convoyed *Long Island* (CVE–1) to Guam which she reached on 25 April, before escorting *Copahee* (CVE–12) to Eniwetok, and eventually returning to Manus on 6 May.

Four days later, the busy escort vessel departed the Admiralties with *Presley* (DE–371), *Ross* (DD–563), and *Howorth* (DD–592), bound for the Philippines escorting Transport Division 11. While en route on the afternoon of 15 May, ships in the group sighted a derelict mine and sank it with gunfire. The escorts delivered their charges at Leyte on 16 May, and *Williams* subsequently sailed for Hollandia and Manus, arriving at the latter on 30 May.

Her respite in the Admiralties ended on 4 June when the warship got underway again and joined sister ship *Presley* in escorting a task unit bound for Tinian with ground forces of the Army Air Force 20th Bomber Command embarked. Completing this mission on the 7th, *Williams* operated between Manus and the Marshalls into the latter part of June when she escorted *Lander* (APA–178) to Eniwetok.

Williams operated out of Manus through the end of the war with Japan in mid-August 1945. During this time, she carried out drills, training exercises, and harbor entrance patrols before spending the first weeks of September in operations with the Ulithi unit of the Western Carolines Patrol and Escort Group.

After a brief visit to Yap and a stint towing a derelict ammunition barge, *Williams* was transferred to the Marianas patrol on 20 September. She escorted *Bougainville* (CVE–100) to Okinawa between 24 and 27 September before getting underway on the latter date to return to Guam.

On the return passage, on the night of 29 September, *Williams* found herself trapped in the path of a severe tropical hurricane. A huge breaking wave pounded into the starboard side of the ship and nearly rolled *Williams* over. One man was swept overboard and out of sight in the stormy sea. Severe structural damage occurred topside, and minor flooding occurred below decks. However, round-the-clock work by damage control parties soon restored the ship to fighting efficiency, and she resumed her passage. Before she reached Guam, she spotted a floating mine and destroyed it with gunfire.

Williams underwent permanent repairs at Guam before she sailed via Pearl Harbor for the west coast of the United States. Decommissioned at San Diego on 4 June 1946, *Williams* was inactivated and placed in reserve on 7 October of the same year. She never saw further service and was struck from the Navy list on 1 July 1967. Stripped to a hulk, the former destroyer

escort was towed to sea from San Diego and sunk as a target by shellfire and missiles launched from both ships and planes on 29 June 1968.

Williams, C. P., see *C. P. Williams.*

Williams, see *Governor Williams.*

Williams, Henry P., see *Henry P. Williams.*

Williamsburg

Middle Plantation—later renamed Williamsburg—was settled in colonial Virginia during 1633 as an offshoot of Jamestown. Renamed about 1699 to honor William III, King of England, the city remained the capital of the colony into the revolutionary years and presently is the seat of James City County.

(PG–56: dp. 1,805 (f.); l. 243'9"; b. 36'0"; dr. 14'0"; s. 13.5 k. (max.); cpl. 81; a. 2 3", 6 .50-cal. mg., 2 .30-cal. Lewis mg., 2 dct., 1 "Y"-gun, 16 rifles, 10 pistols)

Aras—a steel-hulled, diesel-powered yacht—was laid down on 19 March 1930 at Bath, Maine, by the Bath Iron Works Corp.; launched on 8 December 1930; and delivered to the wood-pulp magnate, Hugh J. Chisholm, on 15 January 1931. The Navy acquired *Aras* on 24 April 1941 and renamed her *Williamsburg*. Classified a gunboat, PG–56, the erstwhile pleasure craft entered the Brewer Drydock and Repair Co., Brooklyn, N.Y., her conversion yard, on 23 June.

Commissioned at the New York Navy Yard on 7 October, Lt. Comdr. Frederick S. Hall in command, *Williamsburg* was ordered to the Norfolk Navy Yard to complete fitting-out and arrived there on 5 November. After final alterations, the gunboat departed Norfolk on 2 December, touched briefly at Washington, D.C., and eventually arrived at Halifax, Nova Scotia, on 6 December, the day before Japanese planes attacked Pearl Harbor.

Williamsburg departed Halifax on 8 December, bound for Iceland; proceeded via Hval Fjordur; and reached Reykjavik later in December 1941. She arrived at a time when the newly established Naval Operating Base (NOB), Iceland, was encountering rough sledding. Rear Admiral James L. Kauffman, the first commandant of NOB Iceland, had arrived in Reykjavik in the battleship *Arkansas* (BB–33) shortly after the United States entered the war. He found that no quarters existed ashore, either for himself or for his staff. Moreover, while tentative arrangement had been made to assign a station ship to Reykjavik, the congestion of shipping there and the shortage of space made a permanently pier-moored ship an impossibility. Therefore, it was necessary to have a ship that could be anchored clear of the docks. The problem was solved when Admiral Kauffman transferred his flag from *Arkansas* to *Williamsburg* at Hvalfjordur on 23 December. Since the Army's Port Authority in Iceland at that time was also in need of headquarters, its commanding officer and his staff were also accommodated in *Williamsburg*.

Rear Admiral Kauffman flew his flag in *Williamsburg* into the spring of 1942. By then, the ship had been moored alongside the main quay at Reykjavik. She not only provided Kauffman with a headquarters, but also served as quarters for the communications personnel and the admiral's staff. When Camp Knox—the naval facility on Iceland—was completed in mid-May, Kauffman hauled down his flag and moved ashore to release *Williamsburg* for other duties.

The gunboat got underway on 18 May, with a party of Army officers embarked, for an inspection tour of the island of Iceland. Led by Major General Bonesteel, the

The crew of USS *Williamsburg* (AGC–369) man the rail as President Harry Truman returns on board after fleet maneuvers off the Virginia capes, 1946. (80–G–702503)

party inspected bases at Akureyi, Dalvik, Budareyi, and Reydarfjord. While making the cruise, the ship escorted the British troop and supply vessel SS *Lochnagar* to these ports. With the inspection trip completed by the end of May, *Williamsburg* put to sea to make contact with the disabled merchantman SS *Gemini*, reportedly suffering from a damaged propeller and under tow by the British tug *Jaunty*.

Assisted by a PBY, the gunboat searched for *Gemini* and *Jaunty*. Escorted by *Duane* (WPG–33) and *Babbitt* (DD–128), the tug and merchantman finally hove into sight on 1 June; and *Williamsburg* fell in as additional escort to Reykjavik. Shifting to Hvalfjordur on 4 June, the gunboat underwent tender repairs alongside *Melville* (AD–2) into the middle of the month. Returning to Reykjavik soon thereafter, *Williamsburg* escorted *Pegasus* (AK–48) on a coastwise supply mission to Akureyi. En route, a PBY provided air coverage; and the gunboat sank a drifting mine with machinegun fire. She returned to Reykjavik on 20 June.

After transporting a party of Army officers and nurses to Hvalfjordur and back to Reykjavik for an inspection trip and a visit to the battleship *Washington* (BB–56), *Williamsburg* operated on local patrol and convoy escort during July 1942. On the 12th, in the midst of one such mission escorting SS *Richard Henry Lee*, *Williamsburg* took on board 28 sealed boxes of gold bullion—valued at approximately $1,500,000—at Seydisfjord and transported it to Reykjavik where she turned it over to *Washington*. When the transfer of the precious metallic cargo was completed, *Williamsburg* berthed alongside *Melville* for tender repairs from 14 to 16 July.

Williamsburg next steamed on Weather Station Patrol "Baker" from 18 to 20 July and towed two buoys from Reykjavik to Hvalfjordur before returning to her home port on the 22d to remain there until the end of the month.

Williamsburg again served as a VIP transport the following month, taking a USO troupe—"Command Performance"—to Hvalfjordur, where the entertainers put on two shows on 2 August. Eight days later, the converted yacht got underway for Londonderry, Northern Ireland, for emergency repairs. Underway on the

10th, she joined HMS *Paynter*, HMS *Bredon*, and HMS *Blackfly* in escorting Convoy RU–35 which included nine merchantmen. Detached at the Minches on 14 August, *Williamsburg* proceeded independently through the Irish Sea and arrived at Londonderry later that day. She was then drydocked from mid-August into the second week of September.

Her repairs completed on the 10th, the gunboat conducted antisubmarine practices in company with a British submarine on 13 and 14 September before getting underway on the 15th for Iceland. Proceeding again independently, she battled her way through a gale which sprung both depth charge tracks and tumbled three depth charges into the sea, as she rolled and pitched violently in the fury of the storm. While en route, she received dispatch orders to rendezvous with the merchant vessel *Medina* and screen her at Hofn, during the cargoman's unloading. The gunboat proceeded ahead without sonar (it had developed a casualty en route) and with both depth charge tracks badly sprung. Having no radar, she experienced difficulty finding her charge before she finally made contact with *Medina* at Berusford on the 18th. Both ships started for Reykjanes soon thereafter.

Detached from escorting *Medina* on the 19th, *Williamsburg* rendevoused with *Uranus* (AF–14) and relieved *Leary* (DD–158) as escort the same day. She convoyed the stores ship to Budareyi, where *Uranus* delivered supplies to the Army base there. Underway for Seydisfjord on 22 September, *Williamsburg* spotted an unidentified four-engined bomber overhead at 0830 but, due to the mist and rain, could not identify the plane. Word soon came, however, that the plane was indeed an enemy—possibly a Focke Wulf FW 200 "Condor" used for antishipping and reconnaissance missions by the Luftwaffe. The plane approached again at 0945 and once more failed to identify itself. *Williamsburg* manned her general quarters stations but lost the plane in the swirling mist and fog. The enemy aircraft never came within the gunboat's range.

At Seydisfjord on 24 September, *Williamsburg* took on board 15 survivors from the merchantmen SS *William Hooper* and SS *Daniel Morgan*, both sunk during the ordeal of Convoy PQ–17 at the hands of German planes and submarines. While en route to Reykjavik with these mariners, the gunboat sighted two drifters well inside the fjord at Adelvik and moved closer for a better look. After investigation, *Williamsburg* continued on her way, having found only two Icelandic fishing trawlers. She arrived at Reykjavik on 29 September.

Shifting to Hvalfjordur on the 30th, *Williamsburg* underwent repairs alongside *Melville* from 30 September to 3 October, at last receiving repairs to her damaged depth charge tracks. The gunboat subsequently escorted SS *Lochnagar* on revictualling missions to Budareyi, Seydisfjordur, and Akureyi, before she returned to Reykjavik later in the month.

Following further coastwise convoy escort runs in November and December, *Williamsburg* underwent a tender overhaul and availability alongside *Vulcan* (AR–5) through Christmas of 1942. Upon the completion of these alterations and repairs on 3 January, *Williamsburg* resumed her coastwise convoy escort duties and continued the task through January of 1943. After getting underway for New York Harbor on 7 February, the gunboat touched at St. John's, Newfoundland, en route and was briefly diverted to Argentia to escort *Pontiac* (AF–20). *Williamsburg* eventually arrived at the Bethlehem Steel Co. docks, Hoboken, N.J., on 22 February, to receive an overhaul.

After one month of repairs and alterations, *Williamsburg* sailed for Norfolk where, after her arrival on 31 March, she soon became the flagship for Rear Admiral Donald B. Beary, Commander, Fleet Operational Training Command, Atlantic Fleet. Over the next two years, *Williamsburg* operated primarily in the Hampton Roads-Chesapeake Bay region, occasionally deploying to Newport, R.I.; New York; Florida waters, or Guantanamo Bay, Cuba.

Williamsburg came under the aegis of Commander, Service Force, Atlantic Fleet, on 16 June 1945. On 10 July, she entered the Norfolk Navy Yard for conversion to an amphibious force flagship (AGC). The need for such specialized craft had been realized in the Pacific; and, with the war with Japan not yet over, *Williamsburg* was selected for the metamorphosis. The end of the war with Japan—hastened by atomic bombs at Hiroshima and at Nagasaki—resulted in further work being cancelled. Instead, *Williamsburg*'s new employment was to be that of presidential yacht —to replace *Potomac* (AG–25), the former Coast Guard cutter and long-time favorite of the late President Roosevelt.

Williamsburg remained at Norfolk into November undergoing conversion. The ship then sailed for the Washington Navy Yard where, on 5 November 1945, she relieved *Potomac* as presidential yacht. Five days later, on 10 November 1945, the erstwhile gunboat was redesignated AGC–369.

In the ensuing years, *Williamsburg* served two presidents, Harry S. Truman and Dwight D. Eisenhower. While under the former, she embarked American and foreign notables—including George C. Marshall, Secretary of State; Miguel Aleman, President of Mexico; and two successive British Prime Ministers, Winston Churchill and Clement R. Attlee. During the ship's first tour as presidential yacht, she cruised the Potomac and Chesapeake Bay regions, occasionally venturing into the open sea for cruises to Florida, Bermuda, Cuba, and the Virgin Islands.

President Truman's successor, Dwight D. Eisenhower, made only one cruise in *Williamsburg* before ordering her decommissioning. He came on board at Washington on 14 May 1953 and cruised to Yorktown, Va., where he disembarked to visit the ship's namesake, the colonial city of Williamsburg, Va. Reembarking the Chief Executive at Yorktown later that day, *Williamsburg* touched at Norfolk, Va., and Annapolis, Md., before she returned to the Washington Navy Yard to disembark the President on 18 May.

That proved to be *Williamsburg*'s last cruise as presidential yacht, because President Eisenhower directed that the ship be placed out of commission. Accordingly decommissioned at the Washington Navy Yard on 30 June 1953, she was turned over to the Potomac River Naval Command for maintenance and preservation. Subsequently shifted to Newport, R.I., she remained in "special status" from about 2 April 1959. She was struck from the Navy list on 1 April 1962.

Transferred to the National Science Foundation a little over four months later, on 9 August 1962, *Williamsburg* underwent a change from presidential yacht to oceanographic research vessel at the Woods Hole Oceanographic Institute. During the overhaul, the presidential staterooms and other yacht-like trappings were removed, and special facilities installed.

Among the modifications was a seawater aquarium for preservation of live specimens and a lab equipped with microscopes and other instruments for examining and classifying samples of marine life. Two winches and a small crane were fitted for dredging and deep sea work, while a small side deck platform was added to permit long line fishing. The ship's engines, too, were reconditioned, and her bilge keels were modified to make the ship more stable.

Renamed *Anton Bruun*, in honor of the noted Danish marine biologist, the ship made 10 scientific cruises in the Indian Ocean, conducting broad sample studies of bottom, midwater, and surface life. She caught specimens of plankton; did long line fishing and trolling in deep water; conducted meteorological observations; and periodically obtained water samples. A multinational assemblage of scientists—including those from the United States, India, Thailand, Brazil, and Pakistan—worked on board the ship during this cruise.

Upon the conclusion of the Indian Ocean expedition, *Anton Bruun* returned to the United States in February of 1965. Eight months later, she sailed for the Pacific Ocean to make a series of eight cruises in the Southeastern Pacific Oceanographic Program, conducting biological research in the area of the Humboldt Current and other areas of the southeastern Pacific. *Anton Bruun* subsequently continued her oceanographic voyages until 1968. During that year, while laid up for repairs in a floating drydock, the ship suffered extensive damage when the drydock sank unexpectedly. According to the book, *Oceanographic Ships Fore and Aft*, published by the Oceanographer of the Navy in 1971, *Anton Bruun* was slated to be transferred to the Indian government. Restoration, in view of the apparent damage suffered in the drydock mishap, appeared uneconomical. Offered for sale by the Maritime Administration, the erstwhile gunboat, presidential yacht, and oceanographic vessel was acquired by a commercial concern whose intention was to use the ship as a combination floating hotel-restaurant-museum to be permanently berthed in the Salem River, in New Jersey.

Williamson

William Price Williamson—born in August 1884 in Norfolk, Va.—was appointed midshipman on 29 June 1903 and graduated from the Naval Academy with the class of 1907, in the advanced section of that class, on 12 September 1906. Assigned to *Indiana* (Battleship No. 1), he landed from that ship at Kingston, Jamaica, in January 1907 and was cited by his commanding officer for his efficient work in a rescue party during fires resulting from an earthquake there.

Williamson later joined *Kansas* (Battleship No. 21) and made the globe-girdling cruise of the "Great White Fleet" (1907–1908) in her before he was ordered to Washington, D.C., in March 1909 for "ordnance instruction." From there, he went to *Utah* (Battleship No. 31) in October of 1911. While in that dreadnought, he commanded the gun battery of *Utah*'s landing force during the landings at Veracruz, Mexico, in April 1914.

Wiliamson inspected ordnance at the E. W. Bliss and Co., Brooklyn, N.Y., from 1914 to 1916 before he joined *Galveston* (Cruiser No. 17) on 13 May 1916 for a brief tour of duty. He then journeyed to the Asiatic Station to become the Inspector of Ordnance and Powder at the Naval Magazine and Chemical Laboratory, Olongapo, P.I. (later called the Naval Ammunition Depot, Olongapo) on 7 July 1916.

Returning to the United States in the spring of 1918, he was assigned duty assisting in the fitting out of *Orizaba* (Id. No. 1536) and became the ship's first executive officer when that transport was commissioned. Williamson then worked closely with the ship's commanding officer, Capt. R. Drace White—another ordnance expert—in developing a workable depth charge thrower for use on board transports, in the hope of providing them with some measure of protection of their own. Wiliamson's invention was a modified Lyle gun (one used for line-throwing in rescue operations). In the first test on 16 August 1918, the crude depth charge projector hurled a 50-pound charge approximately 150 feet.

However, before using their creation in actual operations against submarines trailing her convoy, the two officers wanted at least one more test with a larger propellant charge. Accordingly, on 17 August 1918, they commenced another experiment—one that proved to be a disaster.

Williamson fired the gun, but a defective fuse caused the depth charge to explode prematurely, killing him instantly. The blast knocked Capt. White to the deck (with a broken jaw, broken knee, and flesh wounds),

and killed three sailors. In addition, four other officers and 22 other enlisted men were wounded in the tragic explosion. For his work, however, Williamson was awarded the Navy Cross posthumously.

(DD–244: dp. 1,190; l. 314'4''; b. 30'8''; dr. 9'3'' (mean); s. 35 k.; cpl. 122; a. 4 4'', 1 3'', 12 21'' tt.; cl. *Clemson*)

Williamson (Destroyer No. 244) was laid down on 27 March 1919 at Camden, N.J., by the New York Shipbuilding Co.; launched on 16 October 1919; sponsored by Comdr. Williamson's widow; reclassified from Destroyer No. 244 to DD–244 in the Navy's fleet-wide assignment of alphanumeric hull numbers on 17 July 1920; and commissioned at the Philadelphia Navy Yard on 29 October 1920, Lt. Comdr. J. C. Cunningham in command.

The new destroyer was partially fitted out at Philadelphia into mid-December. After calibrating compasses in Delaware Bay, she received the remainder of her torpedo equipment at the Naval Torpedo Station, Newport, R.I., before her fitting-out was completed at the New York Navy Yard.

Williamson departed New York on 3 January 1921, bound for Europe and, after proceeding via Bermuda, arrived at Brest, France, in company with her sistership *Sands* (DD–343), on 16 February. She remained in French and British waters—touching at Cherbourg, France; and Gravesend and Portsmouth, England—into the spring before sailing for the eastern Mediterranean on 23 May.

Assigned to U.S. naval forces in Turkish waters, *Williamson* arrived at Ineboli, Turkey, on 22 June. There, she landed passengers and investigated local political conditions. At intervals in the ensuing months, *Williamson* made cruises from Constantinople to Odessa, Russia; Ghelenjik Bay; Novorossisk; and Theodosia, before returning to Constantinople. She made another cruise to Odessa on 22 June 1922, delivering passengers and serving for a time as station ship there. On 2 July, the destroyer departed that port, bound for Constantinople, and transferred stores en route to her relief, *Bulmer* (DD–222). Six days later, *Williamson* headed for Gibraltar on her way to the United States and arrived back at Philadelphia on 27 July.

After joining the Atlantic Fleet at Hampton Roads, Va., on 6 September, *Williamson* shifted to New York for exercises and gunnery drills before she returned to Hampton Roads on 28 September for further exercises off the Virginia capes in the Southern Drill Grounds. The destroyer operated off the eastern seaboard and at Guantanamo Bay, Cuba, participating in war games and routine battle practices into early 1923. She returned to the New York area in November of that year, engaging, at intervals, in more rehearsals and gunnery drills. She departed New York on 6 May 1924 for maneuvers with the Scouting Fleet.

After returning to New York for voyage repairs, the destroyer sailed for the Southern Drill Grounds on 19 May and arrived at Hampton Roads on the 28th to conduct depth charge practices before she returned to Newport to take part in high speed target and torpedo practice at the Naval Torpedo Station. Later, *Williamson* participated in the search for a life boat missing from the steamer SS *Boston* and made a cruise to Guantanamo Bay in company with sisterships *King* (DD–242), *McFarland* (DD–237), and *James K. Paulding* (DD–238) before returning to New York on 8 December.

Over the next few years, *Williamson*'s routine remained fairly standard for vessels of her type in active service. She cruised off the east coast of the United States and into the Caribbean, operating at intervals out of Guantanamo Bay during the annual Fleet concentrations there. However, there were breaks in this routine. Although *Williamson* operated primarily with Destroyer Squadrons, Scouting Force, she spent a brief period in January and February 1927 in the Special Service Squadron operating off the east coast of Nicaragua during an outbreak of revolutionary violence.

After returning to the New York Navy Yard on 30 June 1927, *Williamson* trained Naval Reserve units off the eastern seaboard. Overhauled in the spring of 1928, the destroyer conducted additional reserve training cruises into 1930. Highlights in the ship's activities during that time were planeguarding for *Lexington* (CV-2) in Guantanamo Bay in May 1930 and an extended reserve cruise that took her to Mayport, Fla.; the Dry Tortugas; Key West; and Rebecca Shoals and Havana, Cuba.

Williamson continued operating off the east coast into mid-1931 as part of Destroyer Division 9, Flotilla 1, Scouting Force, before she shifted to San Diego, Calif., in March 1932, to operate briefly off the west coast in the spring before returning to the east coast. Upon reaching Norfolk on 17 December 1932, *Williamson* was placed in rotating reserve. She subsequently sailed on 1 July 1933 bound, via the Canal Zone, for the west coast. Arriving at San Diego on 21 July, the ship planeguarded for the carrier *Saratoga* (CV-3) during the summer.

Williamson returned to the east coast in the spring of the following year and, in July 1934, was one of the escorts for *Houston* (CA-30) while President Franklin D. Roosevelt was embarked in that heavy cruiser. The destroyer subsequently proceeded to the Washington Navy Yard on 19 July 1934. There, she received an early sonar installation before sailing for the west coast, returning to San Diego in November. She later underwent a rotating reserve overhaul in the summer of 1935 before joining Destroyer Squadron 3.

That summer, *Williamson* cruised to Alaska and, operating from Auke Bay, visited Portage Cove, Skagway, and Juneau, while patrolling coastal waters between 20 July and 31 July. Returning to San Diego on 9 August, *Williamson* conducted battle problems and local operations from that port with the other ships in her division into 1936.

Sailing for Balboa on 9 May 1936 to participate in Fleet Problem XVII in June, *Williamson* later underwent an overhaul at the Norfolk Navy Yard. She subsequently operated in the Gulf of Mexico and proceeded thence via Mobile, Ala., and the Panama Canal to San Diego, where she arrived on 30 October 1936.

Williamson conducted local operations out of that port into the winter and planeguarded for *Ranger* (CV-4) in February 1937 before shifting to Hawaiian waters in the spring. Arriving at Pearl Harbor on 25 April, *Williamson* operated in the Hawaiian Islands with other units of the Destroyer Force of the United States Fleet until she returned to the west coast in June. She operated off the west coast for the remainder of 1937 and returned to Pearl Harbor in January 1938 for an overhaul in the navy yard there. She then took part in Fleet Problem XIX and, upon the conclusion of those exercises, returned to San Diego on 28 April 1938. She then shifted to the east coast, arriving at Philadelphia on 2 June for conversion to a new and special type of auxiliary vessel.

With the increase in patrol plane forces in the Navy at that time, there arose in the Fleet's air wings an urgent need for tenders to support such aircraft. Accordingly, two flushdecked *Clemson*-class destroyers were chosen for conversion to light seaplane tenders (AVP's): *Williamson* and *Childs* (DD-241).

As the conversion work proceeded apace into the autumn, all torpedo gear was removed from both ships, as were two of each ship's 4-inch guns, the 3-inch antiaircraft gun, their depth charge tracks, and the forward two boilers. Additional deckhouse space was added forward. Internal arrangements were changed to accommodate the personnel of a 12-plane patrol plane (VP) squadron and a supply of aviation gasoline. A boat derrick was added to the existing searchlight tower structure to handle a pair of 30-foot motor launches to be used for tending the planes in the water. The ship retained her forward and aftermost 4-inch guns; and four .50-caliber machine guns were added for antiaircraft defense.

As experimental vessels, *Williamson* and *Childs*—simultaneously reclassified on 1 July 1938 to AVP-15 and AVP-14, respectively—would soon prove successful; and, although more ships of their type were added to the Fleet prior to World War II, *Williamson* and *Childs* were the trailblazers.

On the last day of 1938, the metamorphosis was complete. Painted pale gray and wearing the hull number "15" and proudly displaying the red-centered blue and white star which indicated her aviation affiliation, *Williamson* departed Philadelphia on 3 January 1939, bound for Norfolk. There she took on board men and materiel from Patrol Wing (PatWing) 5 and soon headed for the Florida Keys where she provided tender services to VP 15 before returning to Philadelphia on 11 March 1939 for a post-shakedown availability.

After shifting briefly to Newport, *Williamson* sailed for the west coast on 21 April. Proceeding via San Diego, the light seaplane tender made port at Seattle, Wash., and reported to Commander, PatWing 4 for temporary duty. She operated off the California coast from 26 May to 23 August before shifting to Kodiak, Alaska, to service two patrol squadrons, VP-41 and VP-42.

While *Williamson* was tending PBY's in the Pacific northwest, war broke out in eastern Europe on 1 September 1939, when Germany invaded Poland.

That autumn, *Williamson* operated out of Seattle and shifted to the Puget Sound Navy Yard on 5 February 1940 for an overhaul. The light seaplane tender got underway for the Hawaiian Islands on 5 April and participated in Fleet Problem XXI before returning to Seattle on 21 May for a period of local operations and upkeep at Naval Air Station (NAS) Seattle. That summer, on 2 August 1940, she was again reclassified—this time to a seaplane tender (destroyer) AVD-2.

Before the entry of the United States into the war in December 1941, *Williamson* spent the last of her peacetime months engaged in valuable survey work between Acapulco, Mexico, and the Aleutian Islands. In the summer of 1941, the seaplane tenders and planes of PatWing 4, under the direction of Rear Admiral John S. McCain—later to become the famed task force commander—conducted an intensive survey of possible advance seaplane base sites in the Aleutians and along the Alaskan peninsula—work that paid handsome dividends within a year.

December 7, 1941, found *Williamson* under overhaul at the Puget Sound Navy Yard. After temporary duty with Destroyer Squadron (DesRon) 82, she helped to escort bomb-battered *Maryland* (BB-46) into the Puget Sound Navy Yard on 30 December. The tender completed her repairs and took on stores in January 1942 and then shifted to the Aleutians to resume her duties as a tender for the PBY's of PatWing 4. During the early wartime period, the ship performed local escort missions and delivered urgently needed war materials to Army and Navy bases at Cold Bay, Seattle, Dutch Harbor, and Kodiak. *Williamson* and her sister tenders also stocked emergency seaplane bases with vital necessities: buoys, gasoline, lubricating oil, ammunition, and bombs. Those temporary sites provided shelter for PBY's forced down by weather and proved valuable as alternate bases dispersed well enough to prevent a complete disaster if the Japanese attacked the established base sites. In addition, *Williamson* rescued and salvaged PBY's closed out of their havens by the "notorious Alaskan fog."

On 20 May, prior to the Japanese invasion of the Aleutians, *Williamson* rescued Brigadier General Simon Bolivar Buckner from Kiska, when the general and his party were stranded there by 60-knot winds that prevented seaplanes from taking off after completing

The destroyers *Williamson* (DD-244) and *Hovey* (DD-208) in the Panama Canal, followed by two sister ships.

an inspection tour of the Near and Rat Island groups.

Early in June 1942, when the Japanese occupied Kiska and Attu in the Aleutians—as a diversion from the major Japanese thrust directed at the key atoll of Midway in the Central Pacific—*Williamson* lay at Umnak Pass, near the newly established Army airstrip there—the westernmost field in the Aleutian chain. Two Japanese planes from one of the carriers supporting the operation—either *Ryujo* or *Junyo*—strafed the ship and wounded six men. Fortunately, there were no fatalities.

Williamson, in company with *Casco* (AVP-12), later set up an advanced seaplane base at Chernofski and supported the PBY squadron assigned the mission of bombing the Japanese troops on Kiska Island until Army planes could take over the task. On 23 June, after having established the advanced site, the destroyer-seaplane tender left the Aleutians and steamed to Seattle for badly needed repairs.

After returning to Dutch Harbor in August, she proceeded to sea on the 25th to attempt the rescue and salvage of a PBY down at sea in extremely rough weather. During the operation, *Williamson* was attempting to take the damaged Catalina in tow when a wave threw the PBY against one of the tender's propeller guards. The shock of the collision dislodged a pair of depth charges from the plane's wing shackles, and the resultant explosion wounded 16 men and blew one man over the side into the water. Efficient damage control, however, managed to localize the flooding aft, where the most severe damage was located. All hands turned to and bailed out the flooded spaces by an old-fashioned, but effective, method—the "bucket brigade."

While returning to Dutch Harbor, *Williamson* was shadowed by a Japanese patrol plane but made port without further incident. There, Seabees reinforced the damaged hull with "I" beams taken from a dismantled hangar. Yankee ingenuity thus enabled *Williamson* to creep back to Seattle on one engine at nine knots—via Kodiak, Yakutat, and the scenic Alaskan Inside Passage.

By the time *Williamson*'s repairs had been completed, newer, more modern AVP's were entering the Fleet, and the need for *Williamson*'s tending planes was lessening considerably. She was accordingly reclassified an AVD (Escort Type) and, on 3 January 1943, was ordered to support the shakedown training of escort carriers. *Williamson* served as plane guard and escort for carriers operating in the Puget Sound and San Diego operating areas. Those carriers included *Core* (CVE-13), *Card* (CVE-11), *Long Island* (CVE-1), *Barnes* (CVE-20), *Nassau* (CVE-16), *Altamaha* (CVE-18), *Breton* (CVE-23), *Copahee* (CVE-12), *Casablanca* (CVE-55), *Corregidor* (CVE-58), *Coral Sea* (CVE-66), *Tripoli* (CVE-64), and *Natoma Bay* (CVE-62). During that time, *Williamson* picked 14 men from the water after accidental crashes.

Relieved from that shakedown duty in the spring of 1943, *Williamson* supported the invasion and occupation of Kiska and Attu in April and May of 1943. On 15 May 1943, four torpedo wakes—all clean misses—streaked by the ship—her closest call of the campaign and, indeed, her last brush with the Japanese in the Aleutian theater.

Returning to San Diego late in the spring of 1943, *Williamson* briefly trained with submarines and then resumed escorting and planeguarding for carriers on their shakedown cruises. On 1 December 1943, *Williamson* was reclassified from AVD–2 back to her original classification, a destroyer, DD–244.

After repairs at the Mare Island Navy Yard in January 1944, *Williamson* sailed for the Hawaiian Islands on 24 January, arriving six days later. The destroyer departed Pearl Harbor on 7 February, bound for the South Pacific. She proceeded via American Samoa to Espiritu Santo and performed escort duties between Guadalcanal and Funafuti, in the Ellice Islands, until early April, when she joined Task Unit (TU) 34.6.4 for screening operations in the New Guinea area. Refuelling areas included those between Truk, New Ireland, and the Admiralties.

Upon completion of that assignment, *Williamson* proceeded to Purvis Bay, Solomons, where she reported to Commander, Group 3, 5th Amphibious Force (Rear Admiral R. L. Conolly), on 7 May 1944. At that time, the erstwhile seaplane tender was again chosen for special duty.

Gear was installed for underway fueling of scout observation planes from battleships and cruisers to enable the planes to spot gunfire for their parent ships without having to be recovered by them. Rehearsals in the Guadalcanal area proved that *Williamson*'s new rig was suitable for fueling Vought OS2U Kingfisher and Curtis SOC Seagull spotting planes. With her new equipment thus tested, *Williamson* departed for Kwajalein, the final staging point for the Marianas operation, on 1 June. Nine days later, on the 10th, the destroyer got underway for the first operational test of the underway refuelling concept which had been developed by Rear Admiral W. L. Ainsworth.

Upon her arrival at Saipan on 14 June, *Williamson* reported for duty to Admiral Ainsworth—Commander,

Bombardment and Gunfire Support Force—and commenced refuelling battleship and cruiser spotting planes. *Williamson*'s service enabled the ships on the bombardment lines to conduct almost uninterrupted gunfire support for the landings then in progress. On the 16th, she took up her duties fueling the spotter planes of the ships pummelling Japanese positions on Guam.

Williamson soon returned to Saipan, however, as the approach of a Japanese Fleet made a consolidation of American forces desirable. The ensuing Battle of the Philippine Sea resulted in the withdrawal of the enemy force and freed the Americans to resume operations in the Marianas. On 17 June, while conducting screening duties, *Williamson* rescued a Japanese merchant seaman from the water two days after his ship had been sunk. After giving him a bath, medical attention, and food, *Williamson* transferred the man to the flagship *Indianapolis* (CA-35).

The destroyer departed Saipan on 25 June and arrived at Eniwetok on 3 July. Six days later, *Williamson* sailed once more for Guam and in ensuing days again operated as refuelling unit for spotter planes during the invasion and occupation of Guam. Once the landings had been made, *Williamson* acted as a terminal vessel for mail and passenger seaplanes arriving from Eniwetok, until 16 August. During the Guam operation, *Williamson* had a brush with the Japanese—when a shore battery near the town of Agat, on the west coast of the island, opened fire. But, as the ship's commanding officer reported, "Getting underway and opening the range solved this problem."

Williamson departed Guam on 16 August and proceeded to Pearl Harbor, escorting a convoy. She was overhauled at the Pearl Harbor Navy Yard before she operated as plane guard and carrier escort for Carrier Division 11. From the autumn of 1944 until 8 January 1945, the destroyer provided escort and plane guard services for *Ranger* (CV-4), *Saratoga* (CV-3), *Bataan* (CVL-29), *Corregidor* (CVE-58), and *Makassar Strait* (CVE-91). During that time, *Williamson* rescued seven men while on plane guard station.

On 10 January, *Williamson* joined the 5th Fleet and sortied from Pearl Harbor, bound for the Carolines. After upkeep at Ulithi, *Williamson* took part in rehearsal operations at Saipan and Tinian for the impending invasion of Iwo Jima—the next island on the road to Tokyo Bay.

Upon completion of those practice exercises in the Marianas, the Iwo-bound task forces headed for their objective. Again, as at Saipan and Guam, *Williamson* performed her unique services for the bombardment phase of the Iwo Jima operation. In addition, she rescued the survivors of two carrier planes which had "ditched" nearby; provided medical and damage control assistance to a badly damaged LCI; rescued an LCM that had drifted 20 miles from Iwo Jima; kept watch on a damaged PBM patrol plane (carrying members of the press) until the arrival of a seaplane tender group; and transferred one of her own crew to *Nevada* (BB-36) for an emergency appendectomy.

With the completion of the bombardment phase on 26 February, *Williamson* headed for Saipan with a brood of damaged landing craft. On some days making a "speed of advance" of only three knots to allow the landing craft to keep up, the destroyer ultimately reached her destination, where she parted company with her brood and proceeded independently to Ulithi where she prepared for the invasion of Okinawa.

Reaching Okinawa on 25 March, *Williamson* operated as an antisubmarine screening vessel and spotting plane refuelling unit with Fire Support Group 1. On the 28th, the destroyer rescued a fighter pilot whose aircraft had been damaged by antiaircraft fire and forced to "ditch" nearby. Once the invasion forces stormed ashore on 1 April, *Williamson* joined the Seaplane Base Unit in Kerama Retto and refueled ship-based, patrol, and transport float and seaplanes, as well as furnished aviation gasoline to battleship and cruiser aviation units.

After three weeks in the forward area, during which time frequent air raid alerts became the routine, *Williamson* departed the Ryukyus and returned to Guam. She acted as a plane guard and an escort for carriers training in the Marianas. During that period, she made one escort trip to Ulithi and one to Leyte and Samar and provided her services to *Hoggatt Bay* (CVE–75), *Nehenta Bay* (CVE–74), *White Plains* (CVE–66), *Manila Bay* (CVE–61), *Vella Gulf* (CVE–111), *Makin Island* (CVE–93), *Makassar Strait*, and *Casablanca*. While on plane guard station, she rescued three downed aviators.

After operating in that capacity through the cessation of hostilities with Japan in mid-August 1945, *Williamson* headed via Pearl Harbor for the west coast and arrived at San Diego on 25 September 1945. Soon pushing on for the east coast, she transited the Panama Canal on 10 and 11 October and reached Philadelphia on the 16th. Decommissioned on 8 November 1945, the veteran destroyer was struck from the Navy list on 19 December 1945.

Sold through the Navy Disposal Agency on 17 October 1946, her hulk was acquired by the North American Smelting Co., Philadelphia, and removed from Navy custody on 30 October 1946. She was subsequently scrapped on 4 November 1948.

Williamson earned four battle stars for her World War II service.

Williamson, John J., see *John J. Williamson*.

Willimantic

(ScStr.: dp. 10,690 (n.); l. 396'0''; b. 53'0'' (wl.); dr. 24' (aft); s. 10.5 k.; cpl. 52)

Willimantic (Id. No. 3549)—a cargo steamer launched on 29 May 1918 at Seattle, Wash., by the Todd Drydock & Construction Co. for the United States Shipping Board—was delivered to the Navy on 2 November 1918 at Puget Sound and was commissioned that same day, Lt. Comdr. Erik G. Froberg, USNRF, in command.

Assigned to the Naval Overseas Transportation Service, *Willimantic* completed her trials and loaded a cargo of flour and put to sea on 14 December, bound via the Panama Canal for New York where she arrived on 9 January 1919. On the 21st, still loaded with 6,400 tons of flour, she departed New York and set a course for the Mediterranean Sea. The cargoman arrived at Gibraltar on 7 February but remained only briefly since she received orders there to continue her voyage immediately—destination: Fiume on the Adriatic coast. *Willimantic* reached Fiume 11 days later and unloaded her cargo of flour. After almost a month there, she set sail on 12 March to return home. Loaded only with water for ballast, she stopped again at Gibraltar and the Azores on the way and arrived back in New York on 13 April. *Willimantic* was decommissioned at New York on 21 April 1919 and was returned to the United States Shipping Board the same day. She remained on the rolls of the Shipping Board, and later those of the Maritime Commission, through the 1920's and 1930's. Early in 1942, she was transferred to the United Kingdom and served with the British during the remainder of the war. In 1945, her name disappeared from the merchant marine registers.

Willing

Because of the end of World War II, the contract for the construction of *Willing* (ARS–49)—a *Bolster*-class salvage ship scheduled to be built by the Basalt Rock Co., of Napa, Calif.—was cancelled on 12 August 1945.

Willis

Walter Michael Willis—born on 14 January 1917 at Minneapolis, Minn.—enlisted in the Naval Reserve as a seaman 2d class at Minneapolis. Willis received an appointment as reserve aviation cadet on 22 December 1939. Six days later, he reported to Pensacola Naval Air Station for flight instruction and, on 14 August 1940, emerged with his aviator's wings.

Commissioned an ensign on 10 September, Willis soon joined Bombing Squadron (VB) 6, based in *Enterprise* (CV–6), and flew Douglas SBD Dauntless dive bombers until early in December 1941. On the morning of 7 December, as *Enterprise* was returning from Wake Island to Hawaii, the carrier sent up a flight of SBD's to scout the water ahead. Willis took off in one of these bombers for what was intended to be a routine flight to Ford Island, the naval air station at Pearl Harbor. However, instead of enjoying an ordinary scouting mission, these planes ran head-on into a war, for they arrived almost simultaneously with the start of the Japanese attack upon Pearl Harbor. In the ensuing aerial melee, Willis and his gunner were among the Americans shot down.

(DE–395: dp. 1,200; l. 306'; b. 36'7''; dr. 8'7'' (mean); s. 21 k.; cpl. 186; a. 3 3'', 2 40mm., 8 20mm., 2 dct., 8 dcp., 1 dcp. (hh.), 3 21'' tt.; cl. *Edsall*)

Willis (DE–395) was laid down on 17 July 1943 at Houston, Tex., by the Brown Shipbuilding Co.; launched on 14 September 1943; sponsored by Mrs. Marie E. Willis, the mother of the late Ens. Willis; and commissioned on 10 December 1943, Lt. Comdr. G. R. Atterbury, USNR, in command.

After fitting-out at Houston and loading ammunition at the San Jacinto Ordnance Depot, *Willis* departed Galveston, Tex., on 5 January 1944—in company with *Kretchmer* (DE–329)—bound for the British West Indies and reached Bermuda on the 10th.

Following shakedown, *Willis* departed Bermuda on 3 February—in company with *Kretchmer* and *Thomason* (DE–203)—and arrived at Charleston, S.C., on the 6th. The destroyer escort underwent post-shakedown availability in the navy yard there over the ensuing week and sailed on 15 February for the Chesapeake Bay, escorting the merchantman SS *Exanthia* to Hampton Roads where she arrived the next day.

Two days later, *Willis* then proceeded—in company with *Stewart* (DE–238)—to Staten Island, N.Y., and, upon arrival, reported for duty to Commander, Escort Division (CortDiv) 51. Subsequently, *Willis* joined Task Group (TG) 21.11 at Hampton Roads on 26 February, the hunter-killer group formed around the escort carrier *Bogue* (CVE–9).

That day, the task group put to sea for operations in the Central Atlantic that took its ships first to Casablanca—visited from 18 to 22 March—and then to the British West Indies in mid-April. Besides *Bogue* and *Willis*, the group was composed of *Haverfield* (DE–393), *Swenning* (DE–394), *Janssen* (DE–396), and *Hobson* (DD–464). They scored their first success on 13 March when *Hobson* teamed with *Haverfield*, planes from *Bogue*'s Composite Squadron (VC) 95, a Canadian vessel, and British aircraft to sink *U–575*.

Willis continued to operate in *Bogue*'s screen into the summer, calling at Casablanca for a second time from 29 May to 2 June, before TG 22.2 moved to Bermuda. On 24 June, 800 miles southwest of the Azores, TG 22.2 bagged another Axis submersible when planes of *Bogue*'s VC–69 sent the Japanese submarine *I–52* to the bottom. The task group completed that stint of hunter-killer operations on 30 June when it arrived at Port Royal Bay, Bermuda. *Willis* departed Bermuda on 1 July and proceeded to Hampton Roads, where TG 22.2 was dissolved upon its arrival there on the 3d.

The destroyer escort then underwent repairs at Bayonne, N.J., from 4 to 14 July, after which time she joined CortDiv 51 for a period of refresher training out of Casco Bay, Maine. Proceeding back to Hampton Roads upon completion of those training evolutions, *Willis* moored at the Naval Operating Base (NOB), Norfolk, Va., on 22 July.

The next day, the destroyer escort sailed for Bermuda, again as a unit of TG 22.3 and screening *Bogue*. Other ships in the escort carrier's screen included *Haverfield* (with Commander, CortDiv 51 embarked), *Swenning, Janssen,* and *Wilhoite* (DE–397). The group conducted antisubmarine warfare (ASW) training exercises and gunnery drills en route to Bermuda and arrived there on 29 July.

Bogue and her escorts resumed hunter-killer operations on 2 August. Four days later, *Willis* obtained a sonar contact at 1353 and fired a full "hedgehog" pattern which produced no positive results. A little over a week later, the ship participated in a futile search for a lost plane from *Bogue*.

Four days later, however, *Bogue*'s planes scored again: aircraft from VC-42 found and destroyed *U-1229*. *Willis* arrived on the scene in time to take part in the search for possible survivors but obtained only oil samples from the extensive slick covering the waters in the area. Soon after the search for survivors was discontinued at 1730, she rejoined *Bogue*'s screen.

Four days later, TG 22.3 reached the Naval Air Base at Argentia, Newfoundland, for a brief period of inport upkeep. The group subsequently resumed hunter-killer operations soon thereafter; and, during the ensuing patrols, *Willis* obtained a sonar contact at 1147 on 14 September. She fired a pattern of "hedgehogs" and made two depth charge runs before she laid a sonobuoy pattern. *Swenning* joined the search at 1600, and the two destroyer escorts made a coordinated attack. *Willis* and her sistership then combed the area thoroughly throughout the night but finally gave up the hunt at 1906 the following day.

The next day, *Willis* contacted a lost carrier plane and vectored her back to her ship. The radio operator on duty in *Willis* was subsequently commended for his action that enabled a lost aircraft and her crew to reach home safely.

Willis arrived at the New York Navy Yard on 25 September for repairs and got underway again on 7 October, bound for New London, Conn., in company with most of CortDiv 51. The destroyer escorts conducted ASW exercises out of New London for a week before they moved to Norfolk; whence, on 23 October, they joined TG 22.3 and headed for Bermuda, their base for gunnery and ASW exercises from 25 October to 20 November.

Willis proceeded back to New York for an emergency availability period late in November, reaching the navy yard there on the 25th. Shortly before she left the yard to shift to Pier 92, New York, on 28 November 1944, the ship received the Presidential Unit Citation "for outstanding performance in combat as an escort vessel in two task groups with USS *Bogue* during the periods: 26 February to 19 April 1944, and 4 May to 3 July 1944."

The destroyer escort sailed on 4 December for ASW operations with TG 22.3, again formed around the now famous *Bogue*. In ensuing days, the group operated off the northeastern seaboard, running into rough weather over a week after their departure from New York. At 1030 on 13 December, the wheelhouse inclinometer in *Willis* registered one roll of 62 degrees. The ships did not experience good hunting but investigated numerous sonar and radar contacts with negative results. On 16 December, *Willis* moored at the convoy escort piers, Norfolk, where she remained through Christmas.

Underway for the British West Indies on 26 December, *Willis* and the rest of TG 22.3 operated out of Bermuda, conducting ASW exercises from 28 December 1944 to 14 January 1945 before heading north and touching at New York City en route to Casco Bay for gunnery and ASW maneuvers. *Willis* planeguarded for *Bogue* in the carrier qualification areas off Quonset

Point and Narragansett Bay before the destroyer escort put into the New York Navy Yard for availability. She returned north upon completion of those repairs and alterations and resumed her training out of Casco Bay.

After another brief, unscheduled availability—this time at the Boston Navy Yard—*Willis* again resumed training in Casco Bay before she shifted south to conduct ASW exercises out of New London. At the end of March, she became part of Task Unit (TU) 22.3.1 to conduct further training exercises before joining TG 22.14 on the last day of the month.

For most of the first week of April, *Willis* carried out a scouting patrol well off the eastern seaboard before proceeding to Hampton Roads, arriving at Norfolk on 8 April. Underway again two days later, the destroyer escort shifted north, honing her ASW skills in exercises conducted in company with *Bogue* off the coast of Rhode Island, putting into Melville, R.I., in mid-April.

On 16 April, *Willis* cleared Melville as part of TG 22.3 to conduct hunter-killer operations—known as Operation "Teardrop"—on "barrier patrol" to prevent the penetration of U-boats to the east coast of the United States. Four days out of Melville, TG 22.3 rendezvoused with TG 22.4. At 0840 on 24 April, *U-546* torpedoed and sank *Frederick C. Davis* (DE–136), one of the other escort destroyers in combined screen. A search immediately began; and a covey of escorts flushed out the enemy submersible and sank her in a determined attack.

Three days later, *Willis* picked up a sonar contact and decided that it was "a possible enemy submarine." The destroyer escort fired a "hedgehog" pattern and was soon joined by *Cockrill* (DE–398), who likewise fired her "hedgehogs" at 2138. Both ships then began a retiring search in which they were soon joined by *Swenning* and *Janssen*.

At 0040 the next day, the 28th, *Hayter* (DE–212), *Hubbard* (DE–211), and *Otter* (DE–210) joined forces with the four escorts already searching the area, but none of the ships achieved positive results. On 30 April, *Willis*, in company with *Swenning*, TU 22.7.1 and TG 22.8, left the screen of the task group to investigate a disappearing radar contact reported by aircraft from *Core* (CVE–13).

Rejoining TG 22.3 on 1 May, *Willis* suffered minor storm damage when a heavy wave tore loose her number 1 gun shield, ripping a 4-inch hole in the deck; but a damage control party patched the tear as the ship proceeded independently to Bayonne, N.J., for permanent repairs. While the destroyer escort was there, Germany surrendered at Reims, France, on 7 May, ending the war in Europe.

Upon completion of the repairs, *Willis*—now earmarked for service in the Pacific, a theater of war—underwent a month-long availability at the Norfolk Navy Yard before sailing for Guantanamo Bay, Cuba, to conduct refresher training. From 2 to 15 July, the ship carried out those evolutions, after which time she sailed in company with most of the ships in CortDiv 7 for the Canal Zone.

Transiting the Panama Canal between 17 and 19 July, *Willis* reached San Diego, Calif., on 26 July and pushed on toward Hawaii at the end of the month. She arrived at Pearl Harbor on 7 August and reported for duty to the Commander, Destroyers, Pacific Fleet. For *Willis*, however, there were to be no more active combat operations—because a week later, Japan—reeling under the unexpected power of a pair of atomic bombs—capitulated. World War II was over.

Willis trained in the Hawaiian Islands until 20 August and then departed Pearl Harbor, bound for the Marianas as part of TU 12.5.1. She reached Saipan on 30 August but got underway again the next day, escorting *Wharton* (AP-7) to the Marshalls. The ships reached Eniwetok Atoll on 3 September.

Willis subsequently escorted the attack transport *Lycoming* (APA-155) to Saipan between 6 and 9 September and, on 13 September, proceeded from Saipan to Guam, reporting for duty upon arrival to Commander, Submarines, Pacific Fleet. She remained on operations out of Guam, probably as a target vessel for submarines, through the end of the year. She ultimately departed Apra Harbor, Guam, on 10 January, bound for home.

Reaching San Pedro on 28 January, via Pearl Harbor, *Willis* transited the Panama Canal on 19 and 20 February and reached Houston on the 26th. From there, she pushed on to Green Cove Springs, Fla. Decommissioned on 14 June 1946, *Willis* was placed in reserve and berthed at Mayport, Fla.

Willis remained inactive for the next decade in Florida waters until transferred to the Philadelphia group of the Reserve Fleet on 29 August 1957. She remained there into the 1970's. Never modernized, *Willis* was considered "unessential to the defense of the United States" by mid-1972; and, on 1 July of that year, her name was struck from the Navy list. She was stripped and, on 17 August 1973, was sold to Edward O. Sanchez, of New Bedford, Mass., and scrapped.

Willis was awarded one battle star for her World War II service and a Presidential Unit Citation for her work with *Bogue* in the Battle of the Atlantic.

Willis A. Lee

Willis Augustus Lee, Jr.—born on 11 May 1888 in Natlee, Ky.—was appointed to the Naval Academy in 1904 and graduated in 1908. During the summer following his graduation, Lee, a crack shot, served as a member of the Navy rifle team and was assigned to *Idaho* (Battleship No. 24) from October 1908 to May 1909, when he returned to the Navy rifle team for the summer of 1909.

Ordered to duty in the cruiser *New Orleans* that autumn, Lee was assigned in that warship from her recommissioning on 15 November 1909 until May of 1910, when he was transferred to *Helena* (Gunboat No. 8) on the Asiatic Station. Detached in January 1913 to return to the United States, Lee participated in the national rifle match that summer, again as a member of the Navy team. Rejoining *Idaho* in July 1913, he was subsequently transferred to *New Hampshire* (Battleship No. 25) that December for a tour of duty that lasted for two years. During that time, Ens. Lee participated in the occupation of the Mexican seaport of Veracruz in April 1914, as a member of his ship's landing force.

In December 1915, Lee reported for duty as the inspector of ordnance at the Union Tool Co., Chicago, Ill., and held that assignment for three years. In November 1918, Lee went to Queenstown, Ireland, and there joined *O'Brien* (Destroyer No. 51). He subsequently served in *Lea* (Destroyer No. 18) from December 1918 to June 1919 before returning to the United States to participate again in shooting matches as a member of the United States Navy rifle team.

Upon completion of those matches in September 1919, Lee joined *Bushnell* (Submarine Tender No. 2), the flagship for Submarine Division 15, Atlantic Fleet, as her executive officer. In the summer of 1920, Lee was a member of the American rifle team that competed in the Olympic Games at Antwerp, Belgium, winning, with Capt. Cyrus T. Osburn, nine gold, two silver, and two bronze medals, winning personally five firsts, one second, and one third.

Commanding *Fairfax* (DD–93) from September 1920 to June 1921, he assumed command of *William B. Preston* (DD–344) at Newport, R.I., and took her to the Asiatic Station, via the Suez Canal. Detached from that command in July 1924, Lee served a tour of shore duty at the New York Navy Yard from November 1924 to November 1926. He had two more tours of sea duty in the late 1920's—in *Antares* (AG–10) and as commanding officer of *Lardner* (DD–286)—before completing the senior course at the Naval War College in the spring of 1929. From June 1929 to May 1930, Lee was the Inspec-

tor of Ordnance at Naval Ordnance Plant, Baldwin, L.I. Between those tours of duty were shooting matches in which Lee served as captain of the Navy team.

After duty in the Division of Fleet Training, Office of the Chief of Naval Operations, from the fall of 1930 into the spring of 1931, Lee joined *Pennsylvania* (BB–38), the flagship of the United States Fleet, as her navigator, and he later became the battleship's commanding officer. Detached from that duty in June 1933, he returned to Washington to serve as the head of the Gunnery Section, Division of Fleet Training, from 1933 to 1935; and later, from 1935 to 1936, as head of the Tactical Section.

Returning to sea in the fall of 1936, Lee commanded *Concord* (CL–10) until July 1938, when he joined the staff of Rear Admiral Harold R. Stark, Commander, Cruisers, Battle Force, of which *Concord* was flagship. In December of 1938, Lee became Admiral Stark's chief of staff, serving in that capacity until May 1939, when the flag was shifted to *Honolulu* (CL–48).

In June 1939, Lee became the Assistant Director of the Division of Fleet Training and, in January 1941, fleeted up to become the Director of that division. In February 1942, he became assistant chief of staff to the Commander in Chief, United States Fleet (CinCUS), remaining in that assignment until August 1942, when he headed for the Pacific theater to become Commander, Battleship Division 6, with his flag in *Washington* (BB–56). Subsequently, Lee—by that time a rear admiral—commanded the Pacific Fleet's battleships, with additional duty as Commander, Battleship Division 6, and Commander, Battleship Squadron 2.

During his service in the Pacific theater, Rear Admiral Lee commanded a task force that intercepted Japanese forces attempting to recapture positions on Guadalcanal. In an action that occurred on the night of 14 and 15 November 1942, Lee's force sought out and destroyed a more powerful one, sinking the Japanese battleship *Kirishima*; during the engagement, his flagship, *Washington*, performed sterling work, maintaining steady and accurate fire with her 16-inch guns. Despite heavy losses suffered by the American force—heavy damage to *South Dakota* (BB–60) and the loss of two destroyers—they won a decisive victory.

Following the capture of the Gilbert Islands in November 1943, Lee commanded a task force that attacked Nauru Island. Carrier aircraft pounded the island while the battleships subjected it to a heavy bombardment, starting large fires and destroying a number of enemy planes on the ground. In January 1944, battleships under his command screened a carrier task force as it pounded Kavieng, New Ireland, heavily damaging two Japanese cruisers in the process.

Under his command, the fast battleships formed an effective unit of the task forces ranging the Pacific. Although the ships would see little action in their designed role—that of meeting enemy battleships in surface ship engagements—the fast battleships of the American fleet served as fast, powerful, floating antiaircraft batteries, screening the carriers that had displaced them as the kingpins of the fleet.

Lee's battleship forces operated with the Truk striking force in February 1944 and later protected the task forces raiding in the Saipan-Tinian area. From April through June, battleships under his command screened the carriers in numerous engagements. On 1 May, he directed the bombardment of Ponape, heavily damaging the enemy installations there. At the invasion of Saipan, his battleships opened the way for the landing forces. On 19 June 1944, when the American Task Force 38 was subjected to heavy air attack by Japanese carrier-based planes during the Battle of the Philippine Sea, Lee directed the deployment of the battleships in the screen with such great effectiveness that many enemy aircraft were shot down.

For his outstanding service and energetic and inspiring leadership, Lee received the Navy Cross, the Legion of Merit, and the Distinguished Service Medal (DSM) and a gold star in lieu of a second DSM.

Unfortunately, Vice Admiral Lee did not live to see the final surrender of Japan. On 25 August 1945, 10 days after "V–J" day, he succumbed to a fatal heart attack while in his launch, returning to his flagship, *Wyoming* (AG–17), off the coast of Maine. He was buried, with honors, at Arlington National Cemetery.

(DL–4: dp. 4,730; l. 493'0''; b. 50'0''; dr. 14'0''; s. 30 k.; cpl. 403; a. 2 5'',·4 3'', 8 20mm., 2 rkt. (Weapon "Alfa"), 1 dct.; cl. *Mitscher*)

Willis A. Lee (DD–929) was laid down on 1 November 1949 at Quincy, Mass., by the Shipbuilding Division of the Bethlehem Steel Co.; reclassified a destroyer leader, DL–4, on 9 February 1951; launched on 26 January 1952; sponsored by Mrs. Fitzhugh L. Palmer, Jr.—niece of Vice Admiral Lee; and commissioned at the Boston Naval Shipyard on 5 October 1954, Comdr. F. H. Schneider in command.

Following her shakedown at Guantanamo Bay, *Willis A. Lee* returned to her homeport, Newport, R.I., and began a career of operations with the U.S. Atlantic Fleet. She was deployed to the Mediterranean for the first time in July of 1955, cruising with the 6th Fleet—the first ship of her type to operate with that force. Upon the conclusion of her first tour with the 6th Fleet later that year, *Willis A. Lee* returned to the east coast and operated off the eastern seaboard in air defense exercises.

In February 1956, *Willis A. Lee*—reclassified as a frigate in 1955—sailed southward to the Dominican Republic, where she represented the United States in American Day festivities at Ciudad Trujillo, the capital city of that West Indian nation. The frigate then spent considerable time at the Boston Naval Shipyard before resuming active operatons. In November, whle participating in antisubmarine warfare (ASW) exercises, *Willis A. Lee* assisted the distressed fishing vessel, *Agda*, off Montauk Point, Long Island, fighting and extinguishing a blazing oil fire and thus saving several lives.

In February 1957, the ship carried His Majesty, King Ibn Saud, of Saudi Arabia, to New York City during his official visit to the United States. Later that month, she sailed to Washington, D.C., to participate in ceremonies honoring the birthday of George Washington. That spring, *Willis A. Lee* played "movie star," when she was filmed by the Louis de Rochemont studios for a part in the cinerama production, "Windjammer," while she operated on ASW exercises in the North Atlantic. She subsequently participated in the International Naval Review held that summer at Hampton Roads, Va., before becoming part of a large combined NATO fleet that conducted intensive ASW and air defense exercises in the North Atlantic that autumn. During those maneuvers, *Willis A. Lee* crossed the Arctic Circle for the first time on 20 September.

Over the next two years, *Willis A. Lee* was twice deployed to the Mediterranean for operations with the 6th Fleet, separating those tours with local operations out of Newport and in the Caribbean and off the coast of Florida, primarily on ASW and air defense exercises. In the summer of 1959, she participated in Operation "Inland Sea" as flagship for Rear Admiral E. B. Taylor, Commander, Task Force 47, on a cruise on the Great Lakes. During that historic voyage, she transited the newly opened St. Lawrence Seaway and visited the ports of Chicago, Ill.; Milwaukee, Wis.; Detroit, Mich.; Erie, Pa.; and Cleveland, Ohio. That autumn, *Willis A. Lee* returned to her schedule of maneuvers and exercises in the North Atlantic.

Willis A. Lee, with Commander, Destroyer Force, Atlantic Fleet, embarked, conducted an inspection cruise—commencing in February 1960—of Atlantic Fleet ports and installations that took the ship to San Juan, Puerto Rico; St. Thomas, Virgin Islands; and Ciudad Trujillo. Upon the conclusion of that cruise, the warship took part in Operation "Springboard"—an annual exercise in the Caribbean.

In the summer of 1960, *Willis A. Lee* conducted a midshipmen's training cruise while participating in more fleet exercises. She subsequently visited Montreal, Canada, and New York City before she took part in various refueling-at-sea and replenishment exercises as part of LANTFLEX (Atlantic Fleet Exercise) 2–60.

After a brief trip to Charleston, S.C., in August, *Willis A. Lee* participated in Operation "Sword Thrust," a NATO fleet exercise in the North Atlantic which combined the efforts of more than 60 British, French, Norwegian, Canadian, and American warships. While carrying out simulated attacks on the European continent during the course of the maneuvers, *Willis A. Lee* again crossed the Arctic Circle. After calling at Le Havre, France, *Willis A. Lee* returned to Newport. In November, she entered the Boston Naval Shipyard for an extensive overhaul, part of the Fleet Rehabilitation and Modernization (FRAM) program.

An early view of the *Mitscher*-class frigate *Willis A. Lee* (DL–4). Compare this photograph with that of *Wilkinson* (DL–5).

During her FRAM overhaul, *Willis A. Lee* was altered significantly to enable her to perform her designed role more efficiently. When she finally left the yard almost a year later, she displayed a distinctly altered silhouette. She then had a helicopter hangar in place of the after 3-inch twin gun mount to accommodate the DASH helicopter system. She had also received topside antisubmarine torpedo armament. Her two "Weapon Alfa" mounts had been removed. Chief among the new equipment installed in the ship was a bow-mounted sonar dome, utilizing revolutionary new concepts in underwater sound-ranging.

Emerging from the shipyard in September 1960, *Willis A. Lee* participated in a rescue operation soon thereafter, embarking the crew from the storm-endangered Texas Tower No. 2, off the coast of Massachusetts. *Willis A. Lee* then stood guard over the early warning tower, fighting off Hurricane "Esther" as she remained in the vicinity of the abandoned "Texas Tower."

Willis A. Lee spent much of her ensuing career involved in sonar evaluations of her bow-mounted system. She ranged from the mid-Atlantic to the Caribbean, frequently operating with submarines, and upon occasion visited Bermuda. There were highlights, though, of that normally routine duty—such as in the autumn of 1962 when the United States and Soviet Russia stood at the brink of a possible nuclear confrontation over the issue of Soviet missiles in Cuba. *Willis A. Lee* operated on the Cuban "quarantine line" for 10 days, deploying in the Caribbean until President Kennedy called off the operation. She then resumed her sonar evaluations.

After spending January and February of 1963 at the Boston Naval Shipyard for more alterations and improvements on the experimental sonar system, *Willis A. Lee* operated in Haitian waters during March, conducting further sonar evaluations. She varied that duty with a brief in-port visit at Port-au-Prince during the troubled political situation there at that time.

That summer, *Willis A. Lee* was attached to Destroyer Development Group (DesDevGru) 2, a group of ships engaged in experimental work of various kinds, and finished out the year 1963 in the Boston Naval Shipyard undergoing extensive boiler repairs.

With the exception of two brief trips to Newport, *Willis A. Lee* remained at the Boston Naval Shipyard until 29 April 1964, when she returned to her home port to prepare for a southern cruise. Underway on 6 May for type training in Guantanamo Bay, the frigate conducted further sonar evaluations later that month en route back to Newport before returning to her home port on 26 May. *Willis A. Lee* subsequently conducted three more evaluation cruises before she participated in Exercise "Steel Pike," the largest peacetime amphibious exercise in history. During those maneuvers, *Willis A. Lee* served as the flagship for Rear Admiral Mason Freeman, Commander, Cruiser-Destroyer Flotilla 2. To then round out the year, the frigate conducted another sonar evaluation cruise, calling twice at Key West during the voyage. She returned north on 11 December and spent the remainder of the year under restricted availability at the Bethlehem Steel Shipyard, East Boston, Mass.

Willis A. Lee resumed sonar testing operations in 1965 and operated twice in the Bahama area. She subsequently conducted type training off the Virginia capes and in the Narragansett Bay area before arriving at the Boston Naval Shipyard on 30 June to commence a lengthy overhaul to her engineering plant and modifications to her sonar system.

For the remainder of her career, *Willis A. Lee* continued in her routine of sonar development and testing, homeported out of Newport with occasional periods of yard repairs at Boston. During her final years, the frigate operated off the Virginia capes, in the Caribbean, and Narragansett Bay areas, and was deployed to the Mediterranean for the fourth and last time in November 1966. She returned to Newport on 20 May 1967—thus completing her first extended deployment since 1961.

Placed out of commission in December 1969, *Willis A. Lee* was struck from the Navy list on 15 May 1972. She was sold to the Union Minerals and Alloys Corp., of New York City, and taken under tow for her final voyage on 5 June 1973. She was subsequently scrapped.

Willis, John, see *John Willis.*

Willmarth

Kenneth Willmarth—born on 13 February 1914 in Cleveland Township, Chippewa, Wis.—graduated from the State Teacher's College at Eau Claire, Wis., with a BS before he enlisted in the Naval Reserve at Minneapolis, Minn., on 17 June 1941. After receiving instruction as an apprentice seaman in *Prairie State*—the former battleship *Illinois* (BB-7)—from 18 September to 9 October, Willmarth received an honorable discharge on 10 October to accept an appointment as midshipman in the Naval Reserve the following day. After training again in *Prairie State* (IX-15) and receiving a commission as ensign on 17 January 1942, Willmarth joined *Vincennes* (CA-44) while that cruiser lay alongside the east jetty, Navy Yard annex, South Boston, Mass., on 28 February 1942.

Initially a junior watch and division officer in the ship's "M" division, Ens. Willmarth served in *Vincennes* until the predawn darkness of 9 August 1942 in the Solomon Islands when an avalanche of steel unleashed by Vice Admiral Gunichi Mikawa's cruiser force smothered *Vincennes*, *Astoria* (CA-34), and *Quincy* (CA-39) of the northern screening group in some 20 minutes' time. Ens. Willmarth was among those killed in *Vincennes* as his ship took at least 57 known shell hits and possibly absorbed two torpedoes; the battered heavy cruiser sank within an hour of the start of the engagement.

(DE-638: dp. 1,400; l. 306'; b. 37'; dr. 9'5" (mean); s. 23.5 k.; cpl. 205; a. 3 3", 4 1.1", 10 20mm., 3 21" tt., 1 dcp. (hh.), 2 dct., 8 dcp.; cl. *Buckley*)

Willmarth (DE-638) was laid down on 25 June 1943 at San Francisco, Calif., by the Bethlehem Steel Company's Shipbuilding Division; launched on 21 November 1943; sponsored by Mrs. Eva Willmarth, the mother of Ens. Willmarth; and commissioned on 13 March 1944, Lt. Comdr. James G. Thorburn, Jr., USNR, in command.

Following shakedown out of San Diego and post-shakedown availability at her builder's yard, *Willmarth* was assigned to Escort Division (CortDiv) 40. She stood out of San Francisco Bay on 31 May, as screen for the four-ship Convoy 2410 bound for Hawaii, and arrived at Pearl Harbor on 9 June.

On 12 June, together with *Donaldson* (DE-44) and *McCoy Reynolds* (DE-42), *Willmarth* screened the sortie of the Marshall Island-bound Convoy 4212-A. After delivering the convoy safely to Eniwetok nine days later, *Willmarth* proceeded on to the Treasury Islands, anchoring in Blanche Harbor at 1130 on the 26th.

Shifting successively to Tulagi and Purvis Bay, *Willmarth* operated on local escort and patrol missions in the Solomon and Treasury Island groups for the remainder of July. She escorted a small convoy to Dreger Harbor, New Guinea, between 1 and 5 August and then shifted to Milne Bay for repairs on her port propeller.

Underway for the Treasury Islands on 24 August, *Willmarth* made radar contact with an unidentified ship at 0200 on the 25th. *Willmarth* tracked the stranger and challenged her at 0335, when about two miles distant. The latter did not reply, but instead altered course away from the destroyer escort and increased speed. *Willmarth* in turn churned up 18 knots and went to general quarters at 0340.

Willmarth repeated the challenge at 0406 but again received no reply. On the port beam of her target, the escort vessel illuminated the stranger with her searchlight and discovered her to be a freighter of some 8,000 to 10,000 tons. Only 2,500 yards away, *Willmarth's* men could see the freighter's crew manning their guns to challenge the destroyer escort.

Willmarth opened the range to 4,000 yards as the freighter responded with two different call signs, perhaps seeking to confuse the escort vessel. Just as *Willmarth* began to flash a call for recognition signals, the freighter commenced fire with 3-inch guns. The destroyer escort rang down for 20 knots and opened the range to 8,000 yards, refraining from firing because of the stranger's appearance and location, "indicating that it was friendly." With respect to the freighter's fierce—but fortunately ineffective—fire, *Willmarth's* war diarist noted charitably that the ship's "range was excellent, but deflection was off." No shells landed closer than 1,000 yards away.

Willmarth subsequently anchored at Blanche Harbor later on the 25th. Late the next day, she got underway on an escort assignment and convoyed *Stratford* (AP–41) to Green Island, Bougainville, arriving on the 29th to screen the transport as she unloaded. She eventually escorted the troopship to Emirau Island and Torokina, Bougainville, before proceeding independently to the Treasury Islands. She conducted training exercises over the balance of September before she performed local escort missions and the like out of her Treasury Islands' base into October.

Willmarth departed Blanche Harbor on 6 October in company with *Whitehurst* (DE–634), bound for Dutch New Guinea. She arrived three days later and sortied on the 12th with Task Unit (TU) 77.7.1 which included *Ashtabula* (AO–51), *Saranac* (AO–74), *Chepachet* (AO–78), *Salamonie* (AO–26), *Mazama* (AE–9), and merchant ship SS *Pueblo*. Other escorts were *Witter* (DE–636), *Bowers* (DE–637), and *Whitehurst*.

Willmarth operated with TU 77.7.1 until she was released late on the 13th to escort *Chepachet* and SS *Pueblo* to Kossol Passage, in the Palaus. Arriving there at 1821 on the 14th, she remained anchored for two days before beginning to patrol the harbor entrance on the 17th. Relieved of this duty by *Lovelace* (DE–198), *Willmarth* got underway during the forenoon on 20 October to screen the sortie of *Ashtabula*, *Saranac*, *Chepachet*, *Salamonie*, *Mazama*, and SS *Durham Victory* for the Philippines.

Willmarth proceeded north with her convoy, while American troops splashed ashore on the beaches of Leyte to commence the liberation of the Philippines. On the 23d, three days after the main landing began, the destroyer escort anchored off Leyte midway between the northern and southern transport areas while her oilers refueled the ships from Task Group (TG) 77.2. That evening, *Willmarth* steamed eastward toward a night anchorage and, at 1825, observed antiaircraft fire over the northern transport area.

Underway again off Homonhon Island early the next morning, the destroyer escort received a report of enemy aircraft orbiting over the northern transport area. As she steamed along the convoy's flank, she commenced making black smoke at 0844 to lay a protective screen in anticipation of the enemy's arrival. While the radio crackled with reports of ships under attack, *Willmarth* spotted no enemy planes nearby, only many puffs of "flak" splattering the skies to the westward of her screening position in the refueling group.

With the receipt of a "flash white" at 1343, the oilers resumed refueling TG 77.2. *Willmarth* shifted to Samar Island shortly before 1700 before going to general quarters at 1706 upon receipt of a "flash red." After waiting for well over an hour for the enemy to make an appearance, the convoy stopped and prepared to anchor for the night.

At 1843, however, three "Jills" roared in low from the east, torpedoes slung menacingly beneath their bellies. *Willmarth's* guns opened fire on two just before they released their "fish." One torpedo holed *Ashtabula* and forced her to a halt, dead in the water. While the oiler's repair parties controlled the flooding and patched the hole, the convoy passed out of Leyte Gulf and reformed in the wake of the attack. Eventually, *Ashtabula*, repairs effected, rejoined at 2230.

Willmarth and the convoy remained underway throughout the evening, maneuvering on various courses and speeds in Leyte Gulf until the first rays of sunlight streaked the eastern skies. After going to general quarters at 0458, the destroyer escort remained at battle stations throughout the day. Less than an hour after her crew first closed up at action stations, two "Jills" attacked the convoy from the westward. *Willmarth* immediately opened fire with her 3-inch and 1.1-inch batteries. As one "Jill" roared across the stern of the convoy, it was caught by gunfire from *Willmarth* and other ships of the convoy and crashed in flames far astern.

While maneuvering and making smoke to mask the convoy, the destroyer escort spotted a floating mine which she sank with gunfire. Soon thereafter, another "Jill" passed through the area and drew fire from *Willmarth*. Unfortunately, the shells were not observed to hit; and the plane escaped.

The convoy anchored in the fueling area at 1152, three hours after the last attack. *Willmarth* and the other escorts screened the convoy and provided an antisubmarine screen patrol around the valuable auxiliaries. Later that afternoon, *Willmarth* repulsed an attack made by a lone plane which came out of the sun in a glide-bombing attack at 1420. The destroyer escort's gunfire damaged the plane and caused it to spin into the water about five miles away.

The convoy departed the fueling area at 1646. Frequent alerts and enemy planes enlivened the evening hours as the group maneuverd throughout the night in a retirement formation. *Willmarth's* war diarist noted that the Japanese planes seemed loathe to attack ships in the fueling area during daylight, probably because of the heavy concentration of antiaircraft fire that could be directed at an attacker.

The next day, 26 October, saw a repetition of the same routine that had kept the destroyer escort active since her arrival in Leyte Gulf three days earlier. After maneuvering on screening duties through the night, the warship spotted a lone "Val" dive bomber making an attack at 0550; *Willmarth* opened fire from 6,000 yards but failed to score any hits. Within minutes, she and her sister escorts were laying smoke screens to cover the convoy for the next hour. Thereafter, they provided antisubmarine screening protection while the oilers conducted fueling operations.

After following the same routine on the 27th, *Willmarth* departed Leyte Gulf and headed for the Palaus. At 0800 on 28 October, *Willmarth*—escorting the oilers earmarked to refuel the 7th Fleet ships—rendezvoused with the carriers of Task Group 77.4 and screened the refuelling operations for the balance of the day. Detached that afternoon, *Willmarth* screened *Ashtabula* and *Chepachet* as they voyaged to Kossol Roads, in the Palaus. Arriving on 31 October, *Willmarth* refueled from *Mascoma* (AO–83) and anchored, her job done.

The respite afforded the destroyer escort was a brief one, however, for she got underway on 1 November for Hollandia and Seeadler Harbor, escorting a convoy. Entering Humboldt Bay on the 4th, *Willmarth* anchored there over the next two days before proceeding to sea to screen the sortie of TG 78.4—HMS *Ariadne*, 12 LSM's, 4 LCI's, 8 LCI(G)'s, *PC–1122* and *PC–1133*—on the 7th.

For the next three days, *Willmarth* screened the convoy to its destination—Mapia and Asia Islands, near Morotai—before arriving in the invasion area on the 11th. As the convoy neared Morotai, *Willmarth's* lookouts observed antiaircraft fire between 0415 and 0530. Two "bogies" passed within four miles of the convoy; but, as *Wilmarth*'s war diarist recorded, "evidently they either did not sight us or were not interested, as they proceeded directly toward the area from which flak appeared." There was a reason why *Willmarth* did not open fire on the two planes that seemed so close— she carried the only reliable air-warning radar in the entire convoy and to open fire prematurely would have disclosed the position of the little convoy and exposed it to possible air attacks. At 0832, the destroyer escort anchored just off the southern coast of Morotai, near *Ariadne*, while the remainder of the convoy (save the LCM's) proceeded to another part of the island to load for the impending invasion of Mapia and Asia Islands. The mission of the assault group was to establish weather station and LORAN—long range radio aid to navigation—facilities.

On 13 November, with the assault ships having embarked their troops, *Willmarth* got underway in company with TG 78.14, bound for Pegun Island. At 0500, two days later—she was joined by *Shaw* (DD–373) and *Caldwell* (DD–605). *Willmarth*, the two destroyers, and *PC–1122* bombarded the southern part of the island prior to the landings and provoked no return fire from the beach. After a half-hour of firing, HMS *Ariadne* signalled that "H" hour was 0630, meaning that the first wave of LVT(A)'s would hit the reef at that time.

Willmarth remained at her bombardment station for the rest of the morning, ceasing fire as the first assault wave splashed toward the beachhead. The accompanying LCI(G)'s laid their own barrage, thus obviating the need for the destroyers' gunfire. By noon, the island was in American hands. When surrounded, the remaining garrison—only 12 to 14 Japanese soldiers—committed suicide.

Meanwhile, since she was not needed for bombardment, *Willmarth* patrolled to the northward of the invasion beach and came across canoes full of natives to the north. One native, speaking good English, told *Willmarth* that the remainder of the Japanese garrison, about 170 men, had waded across the reef to Bras Island the previous night—thus accounting for the sparse reception given the invasion forces.

While plans were being laid to go after this remnant on Bras Island, *Willmarth* conducted antisubmarine patrol around the unloading assault craft and made abortive attempts to pull several LCI's that had been stranded by low tides off the reefs. At 1730 on the 15th, the destroyer escort succeeded in towing one off after about an hour's time and began operations to free another one of the infantry assault craft. However, the destroyer escort's efforts were frustrated by the line's parting and the near approach of darkness.

Four LCI(G)'s had to be left on the reef—as was one LCI—when the task group headed for Morotai. Arriving on 17 November, *Willmarth* fueled from *Salamonie* before anchoring. Underway again on the 18th, with the Asia Island occupation force, *Willmarth* and two PC's served as escort for *Ariadne*, four LCM's, four LCI's, and four LCI(G)'s. Embarked in the assault craft were 400 troops.

Three-fourths of a mile off Igi Island, *Willmarth*, *Ariadne*, and *PC–1122* conducted shore bombardment from 0542 to 0619 on the 19th. Troops splashed ashore from landing craft eight minutes after the bombardment ceased and met no opposition. An unfortunate result of the shore bombardment was that two natives were wounded and one killed—the Japanese had evacuated the island in the face of imminent invasion the previous evening.

Willmarth subsequently screened the movement of the convoy to the Mapia Islands, where the landing craft loaded troops and unloaded shore personnel and supplies. When the loading was completed at 1800 on the 20th, the convoy shifted to Asia Island, where the destroyer escort screened the landing craft as they embarked more troops on the 21st. *Willmarth* continued her screening duties until arriving in the southern

anchorage near the naval base at Morotai Island at 1238 on 22 November. While there, the escort vessel witnessed an enemy night air raid on the airfield installations on Morotai. The Japanese boldly conducted their attacks despite antiaircraft fire and searchlights. Local port restrictions forbade the use of any antiaircraft batteries larger than 40 millimeter! *Willmarth*'s war diary sadly noted this restriction, recommending that 3-inch gunfire could do very little damage to shore installations in the area.

While the rest of TG 78.14 departed Morotai on the 23d, Willmarth remained behind as *LSM–205* and *LSM–314* loaded equipment for the Asia and Mapia Island forces. She then escorted those craft to Hollandia where they delivered their cargo. Over the next three days, *Willmarth* escorted the two landing craft on their appointed rounds, dropping off supplies at Asia and Mapia Islands. At one point, the arrival of the little convoy at Mapia on the 26th almost went unnoticed.

Willmarth experienced great difficulty contacting anyone on shore: "We finally succeeded in rousing someone by blowing our siren and whistle together." A jeep soon appeared on the beach, its occupants using the headlights to signal. Heavier swells than at Asia Island made unloading through the surf difficult. One of the LSM's was holed several times by scraping on the jagged coral heads of the reef. When unloading was completed at 1130, the diminutive convoy headed for Hollandia.

On 1 December 1944, *Willmarth* and the other ships from CortDiv 40 set sail for Manus, in the Admiralties, for assignment to Service Squadron (ServRon) 4. Arriving at Seeadler Harbor the following day, *Willmarth* spent the next three months operating on local escort missions between Manus, Ulithi, Hollandia, and the Palaus.

On 4 March 1945, *Willmarth* reported to the Commander, 5th Fleet, for duty. Between the 5th and 18th, she conducted antisubmarine patrols in the Palaus before being sent to Ulithi to refuel and replenish. She got underway again on the 21st to screen the sortie of TF 54—the pre-invasion bombardment group—as it got underway for Okinawa.

Assigned to screen TF 54, *Willmarth* operated with Fire Support Unit 2 (TU 54.1.2) built around *Colorado* (BB–45), in Fire Support (FS) areas 4 and 5, off Okinawa. The destroyer escort screened *Colorado* for the entire day on 26 March as the battleship delivered gunfire support for the troops ashore. Over the next two days, the warship screened fire support units and escorted them to night retirement areas. She was refuelled at Kerama Retto on the 30th before returning to screening duties with heavy units off the island.

On 1 April, she was steaming on station 16 of a circular screen around TU 54.3.2, a night retirement group built around *Idaho* (BB–42), when several enemy planes flew near the convoy. Screening destroyers fired upon the intruders who probably did not come to attack the Allied force but merely to keep it awake and permit it little rest.

Detached from this duty to provide a screen for *Arkansas* (BB–33), one of the oldest battleships on active service in the Navy, *Willmarth* operated to seaward as the battleship worked inshore to open fire on Japanese positions holding up the American advance near Naha airport. After commencing this duty at 0630, *Willmarth* had been serving on antisubmarine patrol for over six hours when Japanese shore battery guns boomed out salvoes at *Arkansas*.

Arkansas' main battery trained 'round to reply and quickly commenced counterbattery fire. At the time of the initial firing, *Willmarth* was located about one mile southwestward of the battleship, maintaining her screening position to seaward. At 1323, a Japanese shell hurtled over *Willmarth*'s bridge "painly heard" by all men there. It splashed beyond the ship, 150 yards away. With only one boiler operating (the other had been secured to repair a leaking gasket) the destroyer escort was hampered in getting away, but she headed seaward at her best speed. Soon another shell landed only 15 yards beyond the destroyer escort's starboard quarter. While increasing the range, *Willmarth* turned toward each splash, thus avoiding getting hit by the Japanese guns. *Arkansas*, by this time beyond gun range of the Nipponese guns, did not conduct any further counterbattery fire; *Willmarth* soon emerged from the enemy battery's zone of fire and proceeded to sea unscathed.

After retiring to Kerama Retto soon thereafter for fueling, *Willmarth* operated on screening station A–27 until 6 April, when she returned to Kerama Retto with an appendicitis patient on board for medical treatment. Several bogies flew near the ship while she steamed to the fleet anchorage, and one was downed by a nearby ship at 0200.

At 1525, while still three miles north of Kerama Retto, *Willmarth* spotted three "Val" dive bombers. One peeled off and maneuvered to make an attack. Ten minutes later, it attempted to crash into the ship. Bracketed by flak, the "Val" bore in, apparently intent on crashing into the destroyer escort. Heavy 3-inch and 1.1-inch fire bracketed the plane when she became visible, dodging in and out of the broken clouds overhead. Seven 3-inch bursts rocked the plane as she made her deadly aproach. Lookouts on the destroyer escort noted a thin line of smoke tracking from the suicider's port wing as he went into his dive. The 20-millimeter battery on *Wilmarth* opened fire when the plane's range lessened to 2,000 yards; and, at 800 yards, the Oerlikons seemed to have their effect. Pieces of the "Val's" wing began flying off in the slipstream, indicating that the shells were beginning to hit. Six feet of the port wing soon broke away, shot off by the flak, and the "Val" spun into the sea 20 yards off the ship's port side, slightly abaft her beam.

Willmarth entered Kerama Retto at 1610; and, while preparing to anchor, saw *LST–447* hit by a suicide plane south of the harbor entrance. Flames had engulfed the entire amidships section of the stricken landing ship, and explosions tore holes in the stricken ship's side. The jagged edges in turn ripped gashes in *Willmarth*'s hull at the waterline. One hole, unfortunately, opened up one of the destroyer escort's fuel tanks, and the oil leaking out made further close operations hazardous.

Willmarth stood clear while dense smoke from the burning LST further complicated firefighting. Eventually, the destroyer escort picked up the ship's survivors and later transferred them to *Crescent City* (APA–21). While steaming to the ship's anchorage in the harbor, she took an enemy plane under fire as it approached from the south; and multiple gunfire from all ships present in the habor knocked it down.

Willmarth anchored, transferred her appendicitis patient ashore, and patched the hole in her side caused by the damaged *LST–447* before proceeding on the 7th to screening station "Able–60" near the transport area off the west coast of Okinawa. Following her shift to another screening station on the morning of the 8th, *Willmarth* escorted *Saranac* (AO–74) to Kerama Retto on the 9th. On 10 April, the destroyer escort departed the Okinawa area, bound for Guam in the screen for 12 transports.

Arriving at Guam on the 14th, *Willmarth* developed boiler trouble while there and spent the entire month of May and most of June undergoing repairs. On 28 June, the destroyer escort got underway for Ulithi. En route, she picked up a sonar contact, and in company with *Trippe* (DD–403), over the ensuing two days, conducted an unsuccessful hunt. *Willmarth* then proceeded on to Ulithi where she arrived on the last day of June.

Underway again on 3 July, *Willmarth* stood out of Ulithi lagoon screening the logistics force of the 3d Fleet which would provide the needed supplies for Admiral William F. Halsey's fast carrier task forces as it pounded the Japanese homeland. During the passage north, the destroyer escort planeguarded for *Steamer Bay* (CVE–87) and conducted antisubmarine screening operations. She picked up the crew of a downed TBF Avenger on 20 July. On that occasion, two swimmers from *Willmarth* helped to get the downed airmen on board. However, one of the crewmen died. The two survivors and the body of the dead man were transferred to *Steamer Bay* later that day.

Willmarth subsequently planeguarded for *Gilbert Islands* (CVE–107) in early August, continuing her screening and escort duties with TG–30—the replenishment group for the 3d Fleet. She was at sea when the atomic bombs were dropped upon Hiroshima and Nagasaki on 6 and 9 August, respectively, and when Japan surrendered on the 15th.

Willmarth remained on escort duty off the coast of Japan into September. In mid-September, the ship underwent an availability in Tokyo Bay and rode out a storm there on 18 September. Departing Tokyo Bay on 24 September to return to the United States, *Willmarth* touched at Pearl Harbor, San Diego, and the Panama Canal before undergoing an overhaul at Norfolk which lasted until late in October.

Shifting to the St. John's River, Fla., soon thereafter, *Willmarth* prepared for inactivation with the Florida group of the 16th (Reserve) Fleet. Berthed in the Green Cove Springs facility, *Willmarth* was decommissioned on 26 April 1946 and placed in reserve. She remained there until struck from the Navy list on 1 December 1966. Sold on 1 July 1968 to the North American Smelting Co., of Wilmington, Del., the ship was broken up for scrap soon thereafter.

Willmarth received four battle stars for her participation in World War II.

Willoughby

A bay at Norfolk, Va., an estuary of Hampton Roads, named in 1608 by Capt. John Smith to honor both his birthplace and his close friend Lord Willoughby.

I

(ScStr: t. 147 (gross); l. 104'5''; b. 22'0''; dph. 6'8''; cpl. 17)

The first *Willoughby* (SP–2129)—a wooden-hulled ferry—was originally built in 1903 at South Rondout, N.Y., as *Augustus J. Phillips*. Chartered by the Navy from the Chesapeake Ferry Co. of Portsmouth, Va., for local district patrol duties in World War I, *Willoughby* was assigned the classification SP–2129 and commissioned on 8 February 1918. She operated in the 5th Naval District for the duration of World War I and was ultimately decommissioned and returned to her pre-war owners, the Chesapeake Ferry Co., on 26 September 1919.

II

(AGP–9: dp. 2,592; l. 310'9''; b. 41'1''; dr. 13'6''; s. 18.2 k.; cpl. 340; a. 2 5'', 8 40mm., 8 20mm., 2 dct.; cl. *Oyster Bay*)

The second *Willoughby* (AVP–57) was laid down on 15 March 1943 at Houghton, Wash., by Lake Washington Shipyards; reclassified from a small seaplane tender, AVP–57, to a motor torpedo boat tender, AGP–9, on 11 May 1943; launched on 21 August 1943; sponsored by Mrs. D. R. Lee; and commissioned on 18 June 1944, Lt. Comdr. A. J. Church in command.

After fitting out and undergoing trials, *Willoughby* conducted her shakedown out of San Diego, Calif., exercising in antisubmarine warfare operations, antiaircraft and gunnery drills, and running further speed trials from 9 July to 4 August. Following a post-shakedown availability at Terminal Island, Calif., from 5 to 11 August, the motor torpedo boat tender shifted to

San Francisco where she loaded stores before getting underway on 15 August, bound for Funafuti, in the Ellice Islands.

While she was en route, her destination was changed to Manus, in the Admiralties. *Willoughby* fueled and took on stores at Tulagi on 1 September before she reached her destination, Seeadler Harbor, Manus, on 6 September. Her stay there proved brief, however, for she got underway that day, bound for the Padaido Islands.

The voyage to Mios Woendi proved eventful, as *Willoughby* picked up a sound contact at 1335 on the 7th, distance 1,000 yards. Going to general quarters, the ship commenced a run on what, after the executive officer had reported seeing a torpedo wake pass the ship, she believed to be a submarine. At 1342, the motor torpedo boat tender dropped four depth charges and, although she lost contact with the submarine, continued her search of the area. Regaining a slight sound contact at 1512, *Willoughby* made another run but did not drop depth charges. The ship secured from general quarters at 1632, resumed her voyage, and arrived at Mios Woendi the following day.

Willoughby tended PT boats at Mios Woendi from 9 September to 12 October. During that time, the New Guinea campaign was gradually coming to an end; PT boats operating from that base were finding slimmer pickings to choose from in regard to Japanese barge traffic. All combat patrols from Mios Woendi would finally cease on 16 November when the Japanese evacuation had been completed.

Willoughby was part of the burgeoning force of PT boats and their tenders that had grown as the war in the Southwest Pacific had progressed. So significant had been the role of PT boats in the island-hopping campaigns that they were slated to take part in supporting the initial landings in the Philippines. Moving the boats from New Guinea to the Philippine Islands, however, presented a problem.

Comdr. Selman S. Bowling, commanding Motor Torpedo Boat Squadron (MTBRon) 21, considered the voyage too long to be made "in one hop, even if escorted by tenders." The margin of safety for the ships to operate with, once they arrived in the objective area after the long voyage, was deemed unacceptable. Fuel was critical.

Ultimately, the decision was made to route the boats via the recently secured Palau Islands, sending them along with their tenders. *Willoughby* made up part of this significant movement—"the largest and longest mass movement of PT's under their own power during the war"—that began on Friday, the 13th of October, at Mios Woendi.

On that day, *Willoughby*, in company with *Oyster Bay* (AGP–6)—Commander Bowling's flagship—*Wachapreague* (AGP–8), *Half Moon* (AVP–26), two Army craft, and 45 PT's, sailed for the Palaus on the first leg of their monumental voyage. At Kossol Roads, the PT's fueled from the tenders, while the tenders in turn fueled from accompanying oilers. On the second leg of the trip, the PT's fueled at sea from the tenders, a difficult task but a necessary one if the PT's were to arrive off Leyte with their tanks full and ready to go.

The PT's arrived at Leyte Gulf on the morning of 20 October—the first day of the landings on the western beaches of Leyte proper—and commenced patrols that evening. *Willoughby* steamed to San Pedro Bay, off Leyte, arriving there at 1443 on 21 October, and tended the PT's of MTBRon 7 and MTBRon 21 over the ensuing weeks—weeks that did not lack for excitement! On the 23d, *Willoughby* took on board a man from *PT–325* who had been wounded by shrapnel during enemy air attacks that day. The next day, heavy air attacks upon the invasion forces commenced at 0750; combat air patrol (CAP) fighters splashed four twin-engined "Betty" bombers, one of them attempting a suicide dive into a transport. A few moments later, a formation of "Sally" light bombers came into the area;

and the heavy antiaircraft barrage claimed three of the enemy. CAP fighters and antiaircraft fire combined to down most of another mixed group of Japanese planes—"Nicks," "Vals," and a "Dinah" that attacked subsequently.

Willoughby gunners claimed two planes downed—this was reduced to one the next day—and one of the planes she damaged crashed into and sank a nearby LCI. The motor torpedo boat tender brought on board five of the survivors and saw a kamikaze crash into the ocean-going tug *Sonoma* (ATO–12). During the day, *Willoughby* stood at general quarters at one point for a stretch of six and one-half hours.

Enemy air attacks enlivened the next day, the 25th, as well. During that 24-hour span, *Willoughby* was at general quarters for 11 and one-half hours. She also shot down one Japanese plane.

Meanwhile, major Japanese naval forces were approaching the Philippines from three directions. The enemy's southern force was heading through the Sulu Sea in the direction of Surigao Strait; his central force was crossing the Sibuyan Sea toward the San Bernardino Strait; and a northern force of Japanese carriers was north of Luzon, hoping to lure the American fast carrier task force away from Leyte Gulf.

For the first time since Guadalcanal, the opposing sides arrayed battleships against one another. Rear Admiral Jesse B. Oldendorf deployed his forces across the northern end of Surigao Strait. Thirty-nine of the 45 PT boats that had come from Mios Woendi and made the long voyage via the Palaus deployed in sections of three boats each, strung out through the straits and along the coasts of Mindanao, Leyte, and Bohol, into the Mindanao Sea, to detect and report on the enemy's approach.

In the Battle of Surigao Strait that followed, the PT's played a significant role. "The skill, determination, and courage displayed by the personnel of these small boats is worthy of the highest praise," reported Admiral Chester W. Nimitz subsequently. "Their contact reports," he continued, "as well as the firing and illumination they drew from the enemy, gave ample warning to our own main body; and, while the issue of the later main engagement was never in doubt, the PT's action very probably threw the Japanese command off balance and contributed to the completeness of their subsequent defeat."

All boats attached to *Willoughby* participated in that important encounter, while the tender herself remained at San Pedro Bay. In ensuing days, the motor torpedo boat tender experienced enemy air attacks at odd intervals during the daylight hours. On the morning of the 27th, one of her boats came under attack by Japanese planes, when a "Zeke" dropped a fragmentation bomb off the bow of *PT–132*. Two men died and eight were wounded; the boat subsequently pulled next to *Willoughby* and transferred the dead and wounded to the tender.

Also while at San Pedro Bay, the ship experienced a storm of hurricane intensity on 30 October. During that spell of heavy weather, the storm carried away one of the ship's motor launches, but it was later recovered. The ship herself suffered no damage.

From 31 October to 12 November, *Willoughby* experienced daily air raids. On 5 November, Japanese planes scored a direct hit on *PT–320*, moored off the tender's starboard bow, demolishing it and killing nearly the entire crew. Only one man survived. A week later, on 12 November, a flight of suiciders attacked. While *Willoughby* herself was not touched, she witnessed kamikazes crash into *Egeria* (ARL–8) and *Achilles* (ARL–41).

Willoughby and her sister ship, *Wachapreague*, retired from Leyte on the 13th and arrived at Mios Woendi on the 16th. On the 17th and 18th, the motor torpedo boat tenders loaded stores and supplies. Later, in company with *Pontus* (AGP–20), *Wachapreague*, seven Army crash boats and 41 PT's, *Willoughby* departed New Guinea and proceeded vai Kossol Roads, back to the Philippines, in a repeat performance of the previous mass movement of PT's from New Guinea to that strategic archipelago. After servicing the PT's en route, at Kossol Roads, on 23 November, *Willoughby* steamed into Leyte Gulf, arriving late on the 27th.

The tender manned her general quarters stations when a large American task force nearby—composed of battleships, cruisers, and destroyers—underwent a Japanese air attack. Shells from "friendly" ships fell "perilously near" *Willoughby*, but she emerged unscathed as the force repulsed the enemy raid.

Shifting to Espiritu Santo soon thereafter, *Willoughby* picked up necessary spare parts vital to the continued operation of PT boats in the Philippine Islands on 4 January 1945 and sailed for the Treasury Islands the following day, where she picked up more spare parts after her arrival on the 8th. She continued loading operations at Green Island, Emirau Island, and Manus before returning to the Philippines, anchoring in San Juanico Strait on 18 January.

Over the next three days, *Willoughby* unloaded the vital spares that had been gathered on the recently completed voyage. She then steamed to Mangarin Bay, off Mindoro Island—towing a fuel barge and a small pontoon drydock, and in company with 25 Army tugs escorted by two destroyer escorts—and arrived there on the last day of the month. En route, on 27 January, she spotted an enemy plane; but it did not attack the convoy.

Willoughby's sojourn at Mindoro was brief. Underway soon thereafter, she took the kamikaze-damaged destroyer *Gansevoort* (DD–608) in tow. Since no other vessels were available to tow the crippled destroyer, *Willoughby* drew that special duty and pulled the ship to San Pedro Bay, arriving on 5 February. *Willoughby* then resumed tending PT's at San Pedro Bay the following day.

Willoughby—carrying the personnel of MTBRons 20 and 30—departed Leyte on 19 February in a Mindoro-bound convoy with 25 LST's, 15 LSM's, nine LCI's, seven motor minesweepers (YMS), a PC, an APC, and three subchasers (SC). On the morning of 21 February, the Japanese submarine *RO–43* torpedoed *Renshaw* (DD–499), one of the convoy's escorts. The torpedo struck the destroyer's forward fire room, leaving her dead in the water. *Shaw* (DD–373) stayed behind to protect the crippled *Renshaw* while the convoy proceeded on.

RO–43 slipped away, however, only to meet her doom in less than a week—the victim of planes from the escort carrier *Anzio* (CVE–57) on the 26th. Ultimately, a tug, dispatched from Leyte, brought the crippled *Renshaw* into port.

Willoughby meanwhile arrived at Mangarin Bay, Mindoro, on 23 February to prepare for the imminent invasion of Palawan, in the southern Philippine Islands. On 27 February, the motor torpedo boat tender weighed anchor and set out for Palawan with a convoy of 19 LST's and 21 PT's, escorted by four destroyers. On 28 February, units of the 8th Army went ashore on Palawan, the westernmost major island in the Philippine archipelago. The next day, *Willoughby* and her charges from MTBRons 20 and 23 arrived off that island at Puerta Princessa and began operations. The invading troops of the 8th Army found little opposition awaiting them ashore; and the PT's, patrolling the length of the island, found no enemy forces afloat.

Off the southern tip of Palawan, however, the PT's found a small Japanese garrison on the island of Pandanan. The boats repeatedly strafed the enemy positions, encountering a volume of fire that was initially heavy but that later slackened and finally disappeared. Late in April 1945, a landing party went ashore and discovered the reason for the lack of interest apparently shown them by the enemy ashore—the enemy had evacuated! Thus, at the end of April, the PT's ceased patrols off Palawan.

Relieved by *Mobjack* (AGP–7) at Puerto Princessa on 30 April, *Willoughby* weighed anchor and sailed for Samar, arriving at PT Base 17 on 2 May. She spent the next eight days steaming to various points in Leyte Gulf, taking on stores in preparation for the expected invasion of Brunei Bay in British North Borneo.

Willoughby returned to Mangarin Bay in company with five merchantmen and two destroyer escorts and then spent the period from 13 May to 4 June off Mindoro, tending MTBRons 13 and 16, preparing for the North Borneo operation to come. The tender got underway on 5 June and the following day arrived at Puerto Princessa, where the PT's refueled and underwent minor repairs.

Willoughby weighed anchor on 7 June and headed for Brunei Bay, rendezvousing in Balabac Strait on the 8th with the Brunei assault force, and continued in company with those warships for the remainder of the voyage toward her objective. Meanwhile, on 9 June, four of her boats—*PT–78, –81, –82, and –84*—patrolled the invasion area. The next day, the 9th Australian Division moved ashore at Brunei Bay and pushed inland.

Willoughby arrived at Brunei Bay on 10 June and went to general quarters at 0615 in preparation for the assault phase of the strikes on Labuan Island, Muara Island, and Polompong Point. Shortly thereafter, a lone Japanese plane attacked the formation to which *Willoughby* was attached and dropped two bombs which splashed into the water without causing any damage.

Willoughby tended MTBRons 13 and 16 in Brunei Bay into August 1945. Early in June, the ship experienced several air raid alerts; and three enemy planes actually entered the area on the 14th. In the meantime, ashore, the Australians were encountering heavy resistance from the Japanese on Labuan Island. The PT's supporting the campaign destroyed a 60-foot sailing vessel and six barges during the first phase of the landings and then ran out of targets afloat. They then machinegunned and mortared enemy positions, and at times conducted joint strikes with Royal Australian Air Force planes at Jesselton, Miri, and Kudat—enemy-held oil centers on North Borneo.

During her time at Brunei Bay, *Willoughby* shifted her anchorage on 10 July, moving to a spot off Muara Island, the site of the newly established PT boat base. She remained there for the rest of the war. She lay at Muara Island on 15 August when word reached her that the Japanese had decided to accept the terms of the Potsdam Declaration. Simultaneously, offensive operations by MTBRons 13 and 16 ceased.

On 24 August, *Willoughby* got underway for Mindanao to take on a cargo of diesel fuel and arrived at Zamboanga on the 26th. During her passage, she sighted a Japanese horned-type mine and destroyed it with gunfire. *Willoughby* returned to Muara Island at the end of the month, encountering en route on 28 August and sinking another stray Japanese mine.

From 30 August to 8 September, *Willoughby* tended PT's off Muara Island before she embarked 38 officers and 318 men of the 9th Australian Division and loaded 50 tons of supplies on the 9th, at nearby Labuan Island. She got underway on the following day, bound for Tanjong Po, off the mouth of the Sarawak River. En route, she rendezvoused with six PT's whom she accompanied for the rest of the passage.

Making arrival on the 11th, 180 troops disembarked from *Willoughby* and went on board five of the PT's. The sixth boat embarked Capt. W. C. Jennings, Comdr. J. P. Engle, USNR, and Lt. Comdr. A. W. Fargo, USNR—three American naval officers who had been invited to attend the surrender of Japanese forces in North Borneo. Soon, the six PT's and the Australian corvette HMAS *Kapunda* headed upriver.

Although the surrender ceremonies had been set for 1400 on board *Kapunda*, the Japanese commander, General Yamamura, reported that he was "indisposed" to attend. Ordered to show up, however, the general arrived at 1500. The surrender was signed, and the

Japanese left the surrender ship, *Kapunda*, at 1600. The half.dozen PT's then proceeded on to Kuching on the Sarawak River and put ashore the first Australian occupation troops.

The next morning, 12 September, *Willoughby* disembarked the remaining Australian troops to the PT's and unloaded the 50 tons of stores into two LCT's brought to Tanjong Po for that purpose. On the 13th, 210 former Allied prisoners of war and internees—kept at Kuching—embarked in *Willoughby*. Among the men transferred were two enlisted men who had been captured by the Japanese after their ship, the heavy cruiser *Houston* (CA–30), had been sunk in Sunda Strait on 1 March 1942. Several stretcher cases went on board the Australian hospital ship *Manunda*, anchored off Tanjong Po.

Underway on the afternoon of 13 September, *Willoughby* and her PT's headed for Labuan Island and, upon her arrival there on the evening of the 14th, discharged all evacuees. *Willoughby* subsequently made two additional voyages to Kuching, each time transporting Australian troops and relief supplies on the in-bound passage and taking out former prisoners of war and internees on the return trip. She made her last visit to Tanjong Po on 23 September, returning to Brunei Bay and anchoring at her usual berth off Muara Island late the following day.

Willoughby subsequently returned via the Philippine Islands to the west coast of the United States, arriving at the Mare Island Navy Yard, Vallejo, Calif., in early December 1945 for temporary duty there in connection with the repair of vessels at the yard. She continued that duty into 1946.

In the meantime, the Coast Guard inspected the vessel for suitability as a weather ship; and, after the ship was classified as "not essential to the defense of the U.S.," *Willoughby* was decommissioned on 26 June 1946 and was simultaneously turned over to the Coast Guard at Government Island, Oakland, Calif. Her name was struck from the Navy list on 19 July 1946.

Renamed *Gresham* and classified as WAVP–387, the erstwhile motor torpedo boat tender served with the Coast Guard through the late 1960's. In 1967, with the formation of Coast Guard Squadron 3, *Gresham* operated in conjunction with Navy forces on Operation "Market Time"—the interdiction of communist coastal arms and munitions traffic along the coastline of Vietnam. Later classified as a medium endurance cutter, WMEC–387, *Gresham* was turned over to the Maritime Administration on 21 May 1973 for layup in the James River and was sold on 25 October 1973 to B. V. Intershitra of Rotterdam, Holland.

Willoughby (AGP–9) earned three battle stars for her World War II service.

Willowherb

A purple herb of the evening-Primrose family usually found in marshy areas.

Willowherb—a modified "Flower-class" corvette built at Midland, Ontario, Canada—was originally laid down as *Vitality* (PG–100), under a reverse lend-lease arrangement. She was turned over to the British on 9 September 1943 and was renamed *Willowherb* (K.283). She served with the Royal Navy through the end of World War II.

Returned to the United States and turned over to Navy custody in the early summer of 1946, *Willowherb* retained her British name and was classified as BPG–100. A board of inspection and survey "inspected and found [the ship] beyond economical repair," on 7 June 1946. On 20 December 1946, the Navy authorized the ship for disposal; and she was sold "to a private pur-

chaser" on the day after Christmas of 1946. Her name was struck from the Navy list on 5 March 1947.

Wilmer

(Gy: a. 1 12-pdr. (l.))

Wilmer—a wooden-hulled galley—was built on Lake Champlain in 1808. Few records concerning this craft exist, but it is known that, under the command of Sailing Master Daniel S. Stellwagen, she participated in the Battle of Lake Champlain as part of Commodore Thomas MacDonough's squadron on 11 September 1814. She was sold at Whitehall, N.Y., in July of 1815.

Wilmette

A residential village in Cook County, Ill., some 15 miles north of Chicago.

(Str.: dp. 2,600 (est.); lbp. 265'0''; b. 38'2''; dph. 19'6''; s. 16.5 k. (tl.); cpl. 209; a. 4 4'', 2 3'', 2 1-pdrs.)

Eastland—a twin-screw steamer constructed in 1903 by Jenks Shipbuilding Co. at Port Huron, Mich.—was acquired by the Navy on 21 November 1917 from the Central Trust Co. of Illinois; converted to a gunboat; renamed *Wilmette* on 20 February 1918; and commissioned on 20 September 1918, Capt. William B. Wells in command.

Commissioned late in World War I, *Wilmette* saw no combat service. She trained sailors and engaged in normal upkeep and repairs until placed in ordinary at Chicago, Ill., on 9 July 1919, retaining a 10-man caretaker crew on board. On 29 June 1920, the gunboat was returned to full commission, Capt. Edward A. Evers, USNRF, in command.

For the remainder of her 25-year career, the gunboat served as a training ship for naval reservists in the 9th, 10th, and 11th Naval Districts. She made voyages along the shores of the Great Lakes carrying trainees assigned to her from the Great Lakes Naval Station in Illinois. Not long after her second commissioning, the gunboat participated in the gunfire sinking of the former German submarine *UC–97* on Lake Michigan. *Wilmette* remained in commission, carrying out her reserve training mission until she was placed "out of commission, in service," on 15 February 1940.

Designated IX–29 on 17 February 1941, she resumed training duty at Chicago on 30 March 1942, preparing armed guard crews for duty manning the guns on armed merchantmen. That assignment continued until the end of World War II in Europe obviated measures to protect transatlantic merchant shipping from German U-boats. On 9 April 1945, she was returned to full commission for a brief interval. *Wilmette* was decommissioned on 28 November 1945, and her name was struck from the Navy list on 19 December 1945. Almost a year later, on 31 October 1946, she was sold to the Hyman Michaels Co. for scrapping.

Wilmington

A city in Delaware.

(Gunboat No. 8: dp. 1,571; l. 251'10''; b. 40'2''; dr. 9' (mean); cpl. 212; a. 8 4'', 4 3-pdrs.; cl. *Wilmington*)

Wilmington (Gunboat No. 8) was laid down on 8 October 1894 at Newport News, Va., by the Newport News Shipbuilding Co.; launched on 19 October 1895; sponsored by Mrs. Anne B. Gray; and commissioned on 13 May 1897, Comdr. Chapman C. Todd in command.

USS *Wilmette* at Chicago, *circa* 1918. (19-N-10494)

The new gunboat conducted sea trials and underwent training off the east coast and joined the North Atlantic Squadron at Key West. *Wilmington* trained and underwent exercises in gunnery and tactics in late 1897 and early 1898 as tension between the United States and Spain was rising steadily closer to open hostilities.

On 21 April 1898, two months after the sinking of battleship *Maine* in Havana harbor, Cuba, the United States declared war on Spain. Meanwhile, the Navy had moved its warships into position to attack Spanish possessions in the Far East and in the Caribbean. On 15 July 1898, *Wilmington* arrived off Cape Cruz, near Manzanillo, Cuba, and joined *Wompatuck* on station with the blockading forces.

The following day, *Wilmington* overhauled two small charcoal-burning fishing boats off the harbor mouth and questioned their Cuban crews. From the brief interrogation, the Americans learned that a submarine cable connected Santa Cruz and Jucaro. The gunboat then proceeded to the spot mentioned by the fishermen and lowered a grappling hook. Finding the cable, *Wilmington* cut it and made for Cuarto Reales to join *Helena* (Gunboat No. 9), *Wompatuck*, and *Hist*.

On 17 July, *Wilmington* led the three other ships to El Guayabal, 20 miles north of Manzanillo, Cuba. Upon their arrival at Guayabal, the warships found *Scorpion*, *Hornet*, and *Osceola*. During the afternoon hours, the four commanding officers met in conference and formulated preliminary plans for an expedition to Manzanillo to destroy the Spanish shipping there.

Accordingly, at 0300 on 18 July, the American ships set out from Guayabal and set course for Manzanillo. At 0645, the group split up according to plan: *Wilmington* and *Helena* made for the north channel; *Hist*, *Hornet*, and *Wompatuck* for the south; *Scorpion* and *Osceola* for the central harbor entrance. Fifteen minutes later, the two largest ships entered the harbor with black smoke billowing from their tall funnels and gunners ready at their weapons.

Taking particular care not to damage the city beyond the waterfront, the American gunners directed their gunfire solely at the Spanish ships and took a heavy toll of the steamers congregated there. Spanish supply steamer *Purissima Concepcion* caught fire alongside a dock and sank at her moorings; gunboat *Maria Ponton* blew up when her magazines exploded; gunboats *Estrella* and *Delgado Perrado* also burned and sank while two transports, *Gloria* and *Jose Garcia*, went down as well. Two small gunboats, *Guantanamo* and *Guardian* were driven ashore and shot to pieces.

Beyond the effective range of Spanish shore batteries, the Americans emerged unscathed, leaving columns of smoke to mark the pyres of the enemy's supply and patrol vessels. The twenty-minute engagement ended with the attackers withdrawing to sea to resume routine patrol duties with the North Atlantic Squadron for the duration of hostilities.

Late in the summer, the gunboat headed home and was drydocked at Boston from 24 September to 3 October. Following repairs, the ship departed the Massachusetts coast on 20 October, bound, via Charleston, S.C., for Norfolk. Arriving at Hampton Roads on 31 October, the ship put into the Norfolk Navy Yard on the following day for further repairs, overhaul, and preparation for foreign service.

With the reestablishment of the South Atlantic Squadron, *Wilmington* got underway on Christmas Eve and set her course for Puerto Rico. She arrived at San Juan on 30 December 1898 but resumed her voyage south on 2 January 1899 and proceeded via Port Castries, St. Lucia, to Port-of-Spain, Trinidad, where she made port on the 15th.

Six days later, the gunboat left Trinidad behind and pointed her straight stem toward Venezuela. On the 23d, the ship arrived off Barima Point and stood up the Santa Catalina River, which led to the main branch of the Orinoco. After a brief stop at the town of Las Tablas, *Wilmington* put into Ciudad Bolivar on the

24th where the mayor, the American consul, and a number of city officials came on board the ship for a visit. Diplomatic affairs occupied the officers, with the commanding officer vsiting the provincial governor and collector of customs. The ship was "full-dressed" with flags and appropriate ceremonial trappings on 28 January when she welcomed the citizens of the city on board. Two days later, the gunboat departed Ciudad Bolivar to return to Port-of-Spain.

She was based at Trinidad through February and into March. During this time. she visited Guanta in northern Venezuela; Georgetown, British Guiana; and proceeded up the Surinam River to Paramaibo, Dutch Guiana.

Departing Paramaibo on 6 March, she commenced the initial leg of her cruise up the Amazon River. Navigable for nearly 2,300 miles of its 3,200-mile length during the rainy season, the Amazon and its verdant banks presented the ship's company with interesting and unusual flora and fauna as she proceeded upriver. Calling at Para and Manaos, Brazil, en route, the ship arrived at the Peruvian border at Leticia, Peru, on 11 April. Heaving-to, the gunboat dropped anchor off Leticia to secure permission from Peruvian authorities to proceed further up the Amazon. With permission granted, *Wilmington* again got underway and arrived at Iquitos on 13 April. While numerous official calls were exchanged during the visit, the gunboat also acquired a small menagerie: three monkeys and one tiger cat which were presented to the ship by the Peruvians.

On 18 April, the gunboat departed Iquitos, headed back down stream, and reached Rio de Janeiro on 28 May, completing a 4,600-mile round-trip voyage on the Amazon. On 6 June, *Wilmington* entered the Brazilian government drydock at Rio de Janeiro for routine bottom cleaning and remained there until 4 July when she got underway and cruised south along the coast visiting Brazilian and Uruguayan ports. She arrived at Montevideo on 16 July and spent one month operating out of that port.

On 17 August, the ship departed Montevideo. However, at 1750 the following day, the port propeller shaft failed, resulting in a change of course back to Montevideo. After remaining in the Uruguayan port for the days following her arrival on 22 August, she departed on 3 September, steaming by her starboard engine only, for Buenos Aires.

Arriving on 4 September, *Wilmington* broke the Argentine flag at the main and her saluting guns barked out a 21-gun salute to the Argentine nation as the gunboat entered port. After the usual boarding calls and shore visits by the American officers to the American charge d'affairs and consul, the gunboat entered the drydock at Buenos Aires on 8 September.

Unshipping the port propeller shaft and landing the propeller and a section of the shaft on 16 September, the ship left the drydock the following day with the assistance of two tugs and proceeded to basin number 4 at the Brazilian navy yard.

Wilmington remained incapacitated at the basin until 18 January 1900, when she was moved to Ensenada, Argentina. Eleven days later, cruiser *Chicago* passed a towline to the gunboat, and the two ships set out for Montevideo. On 9 February, steamship *Corunda* arrived with new shafts from the New York Navy Yard. Subsequently, the gunboat returned to Buenos Aires, under tow from gunboat *Montgomery*, and entered drydock on 3 March 1900, nearly six months after having first been crippled by the damaged propeller shaft.

Once the repairs were finally corrected after dockyard overhaul and a trial period, *Wilmington* continued cruising on the South American station through the summer and early fall of 1900. While the ship was en route to Rio de Janeiro on 10 May 1900, her inclinometer recorded 45-degree rolls in each direction while traversing heavy, choppy seas. On 16 October 1900, the ship departed Pernambuco, Brazil, bound for the Far East.

Arriving at Gibraltar on 3 November, the ship pushed on across the Mediterranean and transited the Suez Canal early in December, arriving at Port Said on the 4th. On 21 January 1901, the gunboat made port at Manila, in the Philippines, to commence her Asiatic service.

Departing from Cavite on 10 May, the ship headed for the China coast and called at Hong Kong on the 13th. Still nominally attached to the South Atlantic Fleet, *Wilmington* served in Chinese waters through 1904 on routine cruises showing the stars and stripes along the China coast at ports such as Swatow, Amoy, Foochow, Shanghai, and Hong Kong. On 30 June 1904, the ship was decommissioned at Cavite.

On 2 April 1906, the ship was recommissioned there, with Comdr. William L. Rodgers in command. For the next two years, the ship served off the China coast, carrying out her routine cruising and "showing the flag." On 17 December 1908, the gunboat commenced her river service, on the Yangtze as far as Hankow, with the Yangtze River Patrol. Ordinary activities included the usual calls and port visits to such places as Hong Kong, Canton, and Swatow. She conducted target practice after constructing her own target rafts and laying out a firing area. On one occasion, Chinese fishermen decided that the raft presented a good perch from which to fish. Repeated attempts by the gunboaters to shoo away the fishermen only ended in frustration. Finally, as the ship steamed slowly toward the area, she fired a few blank rounds purposely "over," and the squatters promptly abandoned their erstwhile fishing vantage point.

After repairs while stationed at Hong Kong from 30 June 1912 to 30 June 1914, the ship resumed her routine cruises, attached to the Far Eastern Squadron, Asiatic Fleet, and continued such duty for the next five years.

On 7 April 1917, while at Shanghai, *Wilmington* received a cable informing the ship that Germany and the United States were at war. Events in the Atlantic had resulted in the severing of relations and the commencement of hostilities. In the Far East, the neutral Chinese greeted the news by issuing terms of internment to all belligerent shipping on 5 May. While *Palos* (River Gunboat No. 1), *Monocacy* (River Gunboat No. 2), *Quiros* (Gunboat No. 40), *Samar* (Gunboat No. 41), and *Villalobos* (Gunboat No. 42) were directed to stay and be interned, *Wilmington* got underway on the 6th, within the stated 48-hour limit, and made for the Philippines.

Arriving at Manila on 11 May, the gunboat moored alongside *Brooklyn* (Cruiser No. 3). Proceeding first to Cavite and then to Olongapo, the ship commenced patrol duties in the Philippine Islands, off Corregidor Island's north channel. Operating from Mariveles Bay, the gunboat cruised on patrol duty in the Manila Bay area through the fall of 1917, with occasional overhauls at Cavite. She helped to protect the Philippines for the duration of hostilities, intercepting and escorting various vessels entering Philippine waters while carrying out regular drills and exercises. She remained in the archipelago into February 1919, when she again steamed to Shanghai, China.

The gunboat remained at Shanghai as station ship from 11 February to 24 June, when she got underway for Hankow. Five days later, the ship dropped anchor off the American consulate at that port. On 11 July, after weeks of official calls and routine business, *Wilmington* was fouled by a raft of logs; and two Chinese raftsmen fell overboard into the muddy river. The gunboat rescued the two men while other members of the crew proceeded to cut away the log raft.

The ship continued routine patrol and "flag-showing" duties through 1919 and 1920 and into 1921. On 8 July 1921, the starboard propeller shaft parted, and the propeller was carried away. Proceeding on one engine, the ship finally arrived at Shanghai on 22 July and entered drydock. *Wilmington* operated on the Yangtze through December, when she headed south for duty along the China coast until heading to the Philippines where she operated into the late spring of 1922.

On 2 June of that year, the ship departed Olongapo and set her course for the east coast of the United States. En route, she called at Singapore; Colombo, Ceylon; Bombay and Karachi, India; Aden, Arabia; Port Said, Egypt; Gilbraltar; and Ponta Delgada, in the Azores. On 20 September 1922, the ship dropped anchor off the Portsmouth (N.H.) Navy Yard.

The ship remained there in an unassigned state until July 1923, when she was ordered to join the 3d Regiment, United States Naval Reserve Force, 9th Naval District, for the states of Ohio and Kentucky. After repairs and overhaul, *Wilmington* departed Portsmouth on 19 July, bound for Toledo, Ohio.

The ship anchored off Quebec, Canada, on the 25th and proceeded on toward Montreal on the following day, arriving on 27 July. After passing through the Soulanges and Cornwall Canals, the gunboat proceeded up the St. Lawrence River to Kingston, Canada, before setting course for the Welland Canal. After coaling at Fort Colburn, *Wilmington* entered Lake Erie, stopped briefly at Cleveland, and arrived off Toledo on 1 August 1923.

Wilmington served as a training ship on Lake Erie— operating out of Toledo and calling at Cleveland and Buffalo—well into 1923. On 2 September of that year, the ship became inactive as her men were released from their training period. She remained in this state until 1 June 1924, when a large draft of reservists reported on board for training.

During that month, she operated in company with *Paducah* (Gunboat No. 18), *Dubuque* (PG–17), and the unclassified vessel *Wilmette*. On 10 June, the commanding officer, 7 officers, and 55 men left the ship at Cleveland to participate in a parade in conjunction with the Republican Party's national convention. The following day, Secretary of the Navy Curtis D. Wilbur came on board to inspect the ship.

Wilmington remained as training vessel on the Great Lakes for reservists through the 1930's, occasionally calling at Chicago, as well as her normal ports of call —Toledo, Buffalo, and Cleveland. During the winter months, she was laid up at her home base in preparation for spring and summer cruising.

On 27 January 1941, the gunboat was designated IX–30 and renamed *Dover*. Based at Toledo, Ohio, the ship cruised on Lake Erie between Toledo and Cleveland until the autumn of 1942, when she headed down the St. Lawrence River toward the Atlantic. She arrived at Quebec on 24 November and began voyage repairs and received a 5-inch gun which was installed forward. *Dover* departed Quebec on 17 December and reached the Gut of Canso the next day.

The ship operated in the vicinity of Canso and Gaspe Bay from 18 December and put into Halifax, Nova Scotia, on Christmas Eve. On Christmas Day, 1942, *Dover* escorted Convoy HF–42 out of the harbor, bound for Boston, and arrived with her charges at the Massachusetts port on 27 December.

Following this duty, she put into New York, where she remained until 27 January 1943, at which date she turned her bow south and headed for the warmer climes

The gunboat *Wilmington* as a Naval Reserve training ship. Note her heavy elevated conning tower, designed to protect bridge personnel from bandit sniping in the Chinese rivers.

of the gulf coast. Arriving at Miami on 1 February, she soon departed and made port at Gulfport, Miss., three days later.

Subsequently operating under orders of the Commandant, 8th Naval District, at New Orleans, La., *Dover* served as an armed guard training ship, performing this duty through the remainder of the war.

Decommissioned on 20 December 1945, she was struck from the Navy list on 8 January 1946 and sold for scrap on 30 December 1946.

Wilmington (CL–79) was laid down as a *Cleveland*-class light cruiser on 16 March 1942 at Newport News, Va., by the Newport News Shipbuilding and Drydock Co. Converted to a light aircraft carrier before launching, her name was changed to *Cabot* (q.v.) and the ship was designated CVL–28.

Fargo-class light cruiser *Wilmington* (CL–111) was laid down on 5 March 1945 at Philadelphia, Pa., by William Cramp and Sons. However, construction of the warship was suspended on 12 August 1945; and her unfinished hulk was subsequently scrapped.

Wilmot, R. W., see *R. W. Wilmot*.

Wilrose II

(MB: t. 44 (gross); l. 75′6′′; b. 17′; dr. 4′3′′ (aft); s. 9½ to 10 k.; cpl. 5; a. 1 3-pdr., 3 mg.)

Wilrose II (SP–195)—a motorboat built in 1908 by S. F. Noch at Stamford, Conn.—was acquired by the Navy from R. H. Meyer of Jackonville, Fla., on 3 May 1918 at Jackonville and was placed in service on 8 May 1918.

Wilrose II—variously referred to in Navy records as *Wild Rose*, *Wildrose*, or simply *Wilrose*—served with the section patrol contingent of the 6th Naval District which then included the coasts of South Carolina, Georgia, and Florida as far south as the St. John's River. The motorboat was responsible for patrolling along that coastline and its harbors to protect them against enemy attack—primarily against the U-boat menace. She pursued that duty through November 1918 when the armistice ending hostilities made such patrols unnecessary. However, the end of the war did not terminate her service; she continued to be active in the 6th Naval District at least until the waning months of 1919. In January 1920, she was slated for sale; and she was sold on 10 March to the Charles Dry Dock & Machine Co., of Charleston, S.C. Presumably, her name was struck from the Navy list concurrently with the sale.

Wilson

Charles Wilson—born in Boston, Mass., sometime in 1836—enlisted in the Navy on 15 October 1861, at Chicago, Ill. Assigned to *Carondelet*—commanded by Comdr. Henry Walke—Seaman Wilson served in that gunboat during the operations which captured Forts Henry and Donaldson in February 1862. He exhibited conspicuous courage under fire on the night of 4 April 1862 during the flotilla's passage down the Mississippi River past Island No. 10 to New Madrid. During the passage, Wilson—knee deep in water and exposed to Confederate gunfire—stood on the bow of the gunboat as he took soundings and called out the depths of the river, enabling *Carondelet* to make the passage safely. His soundings were the only significant guide for the gunboat as it threaded its way through the tortuous channel. Walke's running the gauntlet turned out to be a crucial factor in the Union's capture of Island No. 10 and its later operations to the southward.

Later that year, the gallant sailor also served during the capture of rebel batteries opposite Point Pleasant on 6 April and Confederate positions below Madrid on the 7th. He took part in the naval engagement above Fort Pillow on the 10th, in the Battle of Memphis on 6 June, and in the action with the Confederate ram CSS *Arkansas* on 15 July. On 24 January 1863 Walke officially commended Wilson "for the distinguished service." Wilson eventually attained the rank of boatswain.

(DD–408: dp. 1,725; l. 341′4′′; b. 35′6′′; dr. 10′9′′ (mean); s. 38.5 k.; cpl. 184; a. 4 5′′, 4 .50-cal. mg., 16 21′′ tt., 2 dct.; cl. *Benham*)

Wilson (DD–408) was laid down on 22 March 1937 at Bremerton, Wash., by the Puget Sound Navy Yard; launched on 12 April 1939; sponsored by Mrs. Edward B. Fenner, the wife of Rear Admiral Edward B. Fenner, the Commandant of the 13th Naval District; and commissioned on 5 July 1939, Lt. Comdr. Russell G. Sturges in command.

After fitting out, the destroyer sailed for San Francisco, Calif., and arrived there on 16 September. Two days later, she shifted to the Mare Island Navy Yard, Vallejo, Calif., where she loaded torpedoes with exercise warheads. She subsequently operated out of Long Beach, Calif., and between San Diego and the Canal Zone before sailing for South American waters. On her shakedown cruise, *Wilson* visited Guayaquil, Ecuador, and Callao, Peru, and then shifted briefly to Balboa, Canal Zone, en route to Manzanillo Bay, Mexico.

Returning to San Diego on 17 November, *Wilson* later sailed north to her builders' yard for post-shakedown availability, upkeep, and machinery trials. *Wilson* returned to San Diego on 11 February 1940 and was assigned to Destroyer Division (DesDiv) 12, Destroyer Squadron (DesRon) 6. She operated locally in waters off the southern California coast until she departed Long Beach on 2 April, bound for the Hawaiian Islands and participation in the last big prewar fleet problem—Fleet Problem XXI.

En route to Hawaii, *Wilson* planeguarded for *Saratoga* (CV–3) as a unit of the White Fleet striking force and as part of the antisubmarine screen. She arrived at Lahaina Roads, off the island of Maui, Territory of Hawaii, on 10 April. *Wilson* subsequently operated in the Hawaiian area with *Lexington* (CV–2) during another phase of the Fleet Problem which lasted into May 1940. Near the close of the maneuvers, President Franklin D. Roosevelt—alarmed by continuing Japanese aggression in the Far East—ordered the fleet to remain in Hawaiian waters.

Retained in Hawaii with the fleet, *Wilson* patrolled off Honolulu on 25 and 26 May before returning to the west coast for a brief overhaul at the Puget Sound Navy Yard. Late in June, she shifted south to San Diego, arriving there on 28 June. She departed that port on 5 July to screen battleship *Maryland* (BB–46) to Hawaii. Arriving at Pearl Harbor on the 12th, *Wilson* patrolled off Honolulu and subsequently conducted tactical operations in the Hawaiian operating area into November of 1940.

As part of DesDiv 15, DesRon 8, *Wilson* departed Pearl Harbor on 2 December and arrived at San Diego six days later. She remained there until the day after Christmas 1940, when she shifted to the Bethlehem Steel Co. yard at San Pedro, Calif., for an overhaul that lasted into late January of the following year.

Upon completion of her yard period at San Pedro, *Wilson* sailed for the Hawaiian Islands on 20 January, joining Task Force (TF) 3—based around battleships *West Virginia* (BB–48) and *Tennessee* (BB–43)—on the morning of the 21st and reached Pearl Harbor on the 27th. For the remainder of her tour in Hawaiian waters, *Wilson* operated with TF 1.

Meanwhile, as the German U-boat offensive took an increasingly heavy toll of Allied shipping, the Navy needed to strengthen Admiral Ernest F. King's Atlantic Fleet. As one of the measures taken to achieve this end, *Wilson*—together with Sterett (DD–407) and *Lang* (DD–399) and screening *Mississippi* (BB–41) and *Savannah* (CL–43)—secretly departed the Hawaiian operating area on 19 May, ostensibly for local maneuvers. They transited the Panama Canal on the night of 2 and 3 June and arrived at Guantanamo Bay, Cuba, on the 5th.

After a brief in-port period, *Wilson* steamed on antisubmarine patrol off the entrance to Guantanamo Bay on 9 and 10 June before heading north with Task Group (TG) 7.1 (Battleship Division 3) and TG 7.4 (DesRon 8) on the 11th. Arriving at Philadelphia on 15 June, *Wilson* later shifted to the Boston Navy Yard before joining the light cruisers *Philadelphia* (CL–41) and *Savannah* in TF 27 late in June for Neutrality Patrol duties in the Atlantic. She touched briefly at Bermuda from 8 to 15 July before she returned to the Hampton Roads area on the 17th. She underwent a brief overhaul at the Charleston Navy Yard in late July and early August before joining *Lang* and *Sterett* off the Virginia capes on 17 August and heading further north.

Transiting the Cape Cod Canal, the three destroyers arrived at Casco Bay, Maine, on the 19th and conducted exercises there until *Wilson* and *Lang* sailed for Bermuda in early September. From that newly established base, *Wilson* exercised in antiaircraft gunnery practice in company with *Nashville* (CL–43) and *Lang* from 17 to 20 September before making rendezvous at sea with *Philadelphia* on 3 October and escorting her into the Chesapeake Bay.

On 7 October, *Wilson* departed the Tidewater area and operated out of Bermuda into the winter of 1941, serving at various times as screen for such ships as *Wasp* (CV–7), *Nashville*, and *Long Island* (AVG–1), the Navy's first escort carrier.

On 3 December, *Wilson* rendezvoused with *Wasp* and served as plane guard while that carrier's air group flew refresher training exercises, day and night. The two ships then conducted gunnery drills before returning to Grassy Bay, Bermuda, on the 5th. On 7 December, *Wilson* lay at anchor in Bermuda waters while, on the other side of the world, Japanese planes attacked the United States Fleet at Pearl Harbor, sinking or damaging 18 warships and plunging the United States inextricably into World War II.

The United States was now at war in both oceans, with Japan in the Pacific and Germany and Italy in the Atlantic and felt that other nations might attempt to take advantage of the momentary American setback. One situation where such a possibility seemed to be especially strong was created by the presence of Vichy French warships at Martinique. To be certain that the naval units there did not sortie and attempt to return to their Vichy consorts, a task force, *Wasp* and *Brooklyn*, escorted by *Sterett* and *Wilson*, sailed for Martinique. Fortunately, the confrontation between the United States and Vichy France over this matter failed to materialize; and the crisis abated. *Wilson* soon returned to Bermuda and, except for a brief trip to New York, remained there for the rest of 1941.

Wilson operated between Bermuda and New York into February before entering the Norfolk Navy Yard, Portsmouth, Va., in March 1942 for a brief refit. Adjudged "ready for distant service" by 21 March, *Wilson* arrived at Casco Bay on the 24th and joined TF 39 as it assembled prior to crossing the Atlantic to reinforce the British Home Fleet.

At 0748 on 26 March, TF 39—*Wasp*, *Washington* (BB–56), *Wichita* (CA–45), *Tuscaloosa* (CA–37), and eight destroyers (including *Wilson*)—departed Portland harbor, Maine. *Wilson* and the other destroyers screened the sortie of the heavy warships. At 1033 on the following day, as the task force labored through heavy seas, the "man overboard" alarm sounded in the flagship *Washington*. A quick check revealed that the task force commander, Rear Admiral John W. Wilcox, Jr., apparently had been washed over the side. TF 39

quickly reversed course, and *Wasp* launched four Vought SB2U–2 Vindicators to try to spot the missing flag officer from the air. A light snow hampered visibility, particularly for the aviators, but Wilcox' body was spotted floating face down approximately an hour after he had disappeared. However, the gusting winds and heavy seas prevented recovery; and Rear Admiral Robert C. Giffen, in *Wichita*, assumed command of the task force. One of *Wasp*'s scout planes crashed astern of her, adding additional lives to the toll of death that day.

Met on 3 April by the British light cruiser *Edinburgh*, the task force arrived at Scapa Flow the following day. *Wilson* commenced operations off the northern British Isles almost immediately. She conducted training exercises and served in the screen for the heavy covering force formed to protect convoy runs to northern Russia. *Wilson* attacked several submarine sound contacts, but she could not claim any conclusive proof of damage to a U-boat.

Wilson got underway from Hvalfjordur, Iceland, for home on 12 May and, eight days later, was proceeding from New York to Norfolk when she sighted what she thought was an enemy submarine on the surface. The destroyer attempted to ram, but the "enemy" dived quickly, foiling the American warship's attack. Seven depth charges churned the sea. Moments later, a signalman with a long glass reported seeing the "submarine" —"rise, roll over and submerge." In all probability, the submarine was nothing more than a whale, for postwar assessment gives no U-boat sinking to *Wilson* on that day.

Overhauled at the Norfolk Navy Yard from 21 May to 4 June, *Wilson* sailed for the Pacific on 4 June, transited the Panama Canal on the 9th, and arrived at San Diego 10 days later. She operated locally out of that port for the remainder of the month, serving—with *Aaron Ward* (DD–483)—on 23 June as plane guard for *Wasp* as that carrier's air group broke in new aircraft—Grumman TBF–1 Avengers and Douglas SBD3 Dauntlesses—off San Clemente and Catalina Islands.

On 1 July, as part of TF 18, *Wilson* sailed for the South Pacific. While the ship proceeded southwestward, plans were being drawn up for the invasion of Guadalcanal, the key island in the Solomons chain. There, the Japanese were building an airbase that threatened, not only the tenuous Allied hold on the New Caledonia area, but the very lifeline from the United States to Australia and New Zealand as well. After a brief pause at Tongatabu in the Tonga Islands, *Wilson* set a course for the Koro Islands, where the dress rehearsal of the landings on Guadalcanal took place late in July. At the end of the practice invasion, Operation "Watchtower" was slated to commence on 7 August 1942.

Assigned to the screen and fire support detail, *Wilson* arrived off the assigned beachhead in the early morning twilight. During the approach, the heavy cruiser *Quincy* (CA–39), *Vincennes* (CA–44), and *Astoria* (CA–34) shelled Japanese positions on Lunga Point pinpointed by previous intelligence estimates. *Wilson* soon took station in the screening circle to seaward of the transports and, at 0840, followed *Ellet* (DD–398) to her assigned station as control and salvage vessel off "Beach Red."

Wilson conducted a brief shore bombardment of Beach Red before resuming routine screening for the unloading transports. Since the Japanese on Guadalcanal were taken completely by surprise, the morning went by fairly peacefully. By the evening, a beachhead had been established; and, despite heavy resistance on the islands of Tulagi and Tanambogo, Operation "Watchtower" was well on its way.

Wilson continued screening the transports into the next day. While engaged in that duty, she received orders to taken station for repelling an air attack detected coming down from Rabaul, the Japanese air base on New Britain. At 1155, twin-engined "Betty" torpedo bombers roared over the ridge of Florida Island, headed for the center of the formation. The planes, flying at altitudes ranging from 50 to 100 feet, made a massed torpedo attack met with heavy gunfire from the transports and their screening ships. Most of the attackers splashed into the glassy sea, slapped down by the barrage. Targets were so numerous and the fire so heavy that *Wilson*'s executive officer subsequently reported, "Because of the great number of bursts all over the targets it was impossible to tell whether this vessel accounted for any."

However, the Japanese had drawn blood from the transports and their escorts, severely damaging the transport *George F. Elliot* (AP–13) and the destroyer *Jarvis* (DD–393). The former burned into the night, her fires uncontrollable, and the latter, without means of communication, sailed off to the north of Guadalcanal, and to doom the following day at the hands of a swarm of Japanese aircraft that mistook her for a crippled *Achilles*-class cruiser.

Meanwhile, *Wilson* took *Jarvis*' place in the screen of the northern force. At 0145 on 9 August—while steaming at 10 knots as antisubmarine screening vessel off the starboard bow of *Vincennes*, *Quincy*, and *Astoria*— the destroyer spotted two starshells on the port quarter blossoming into the squally night. Word soon crackled over the TBS that enemy ships were in the vicinity.

Searchlights on board the cruisers of Vice Admiral Gunichi Mikawa's attacking force were suddenly snapped on and illuminated the three American cruisers. *Wilson* turned left to bring all guns to bear and opened fire immediately, continuing to turn until her own cruisers fouled the range and momentarily prevented her from keeping up the fire.

Not to be daunted, *Wilson*'s gunners, 12,000 yards from the enemy ships, simply raised the trajectory of their shells and shot over *Quincy*, *Vincennes*, and *Astoria*. Several enemy salvoes burst in the water between *Wilson* and the nearest "friendly" ships, 1,000 yards on the port beam; by that time, all three American heavy cruisers were "completely enveloped in flames."

Turning soon thereafter, *Wilson* noted that enemy searchlights were still on and resumed fire from 9,600 yards. A "friendly" destroyer, however, passed between *Wilson* and the enemy, forcing the former to check fire momentarily. *Wilson* continued firing at the searchlights until the Japanese ceased fire, satisfied that they had destroyed the enemy force opposing them. All told, the Japanese sank four heavy cruisers that night: *Quincy*, *Vincennes*, *Astoria*, and the Australian HMAS *Canberra* and damaged one, *Chicago* (CA–29).

In the wake of the Battle of Savo Island, the Americans regrouped. At 0500, *Wilson* received directions to picked up survivors. At 0640, five miles to the southeast of Savo Island, she commenced bringing some of the water and oil-soaked cruisermen from *Vincennes* and *Quincy* on board. She then began to screen the battered *Astoria*, drifting three miles to the southeast of Savo, with her number 2 turret, conning tower, and lower bridge afire. She soon brought on board 211 of *Astoria*'s officers and men.

Although knowing fully that an explosion might occur in the cruiser's forward magazines—fires still raged deep within the bowels of the ship—Lt. Comdr. W. H. Price, *Wilson*'s commanding officer, unhesitatingly put his ship alongside *Astoria*'s starboard bow "in a most seamanlike manner." Soon, the destroyer began pumping water to fight the fires; a working party assisted the remaining *Astoria* sailors in attempting to save the ship—a valiant but futile effort. *Astoria* clung to life until noon, when she finally succumbed to the massive damage inflicted by Mikawa's cruisers.

Relieved by *Buchanan* (DD–484) at 1135, *Wilson* cleared *Astoria*'s side and headed for the transport area, where she transferred the survivors she had picked up to the transport *Hunter Liggett* (AP–27).

The destroyer then got underway for New Caledonia, steaming in the transport screen.

However, before she reached Noumea, *Wilson* was ordered to screen the oiler *Cimarron* (AO–22). *Dewey* (DD–349), *Monssen* (DD–434), *Buchanan* (DD–484), and *Ellet* helped her in this mission. After refueling TF 61 at sea, the group put into Efate.

After escorting the oiler *Kaskaskia* (AO–27) to Noumea, *Wilson* conducted patrol and escort duties into mid-September and then sailed for Pearl Harbor with TF 11. Mooring alongside the tender *Dixie* (AD–14) on the 21st, *Wilson* was found to need a yard overhaul and sailed for the west coast of the United States and entered the Mare Island Navy Yard, Vallejo, Calif.

Back in top trim, the destroyer sailed on 9 December 1942 for the war zone. After stops at Pearl Harbor and Midway, she headed for a point about 500 miles from enemy-held Wake Island. There, she served as radio direction finder ship, guiding and directing Army B–24 Liberator bombers to their target and return. Upon completion of that task, *Wilson* returned to Midway and, on Christmas Day, got underway for Hawaii, arriving at Pearl Harbor three days later.

Wilson next escorted the light carrier *Copahee* (CVE–12) to the New Hebrides, arriving at Espiritu Santo on 17 January 1943 before she pushed on to Guadalcanal, arriving at Lunga Point amidst a Japanese air raid on nearby Henderson Field. After screening transports off Lunga Point, *Wilson* anchored at Tulagi, but soon thereafter got underway to bombard Japanese positions between the Bonegi River and westward to Cape Esperance.

From Guadalcanal, *Wilson* shifted to Espiritu Santo once more and, on 5 February, joined a task group consisting of *Nashville*, *Helena* (CL–50), *Honolulu* (CL–48), *St. Louis* (CL–49), and six other destroyers. After cruising to Noumea, New Caledonia, with that force, *Wilson* returned to Guadalcanal, where she prepared for the assault on the Japanese-held Russell Islands. During that operation, she acted as a screen and escort ship between Tulagi and the Russells.

Wilson spent much of March in the Solomons, working near Guadalcanal, Purvis Bay, and Tulagi—screening and patrolling—before she proceeded via Espiritu Santo to Havannah harbor for a tender availability. Later, the destroyer operated with the escort carrier *Chenango* (CVE–28) as she ferried planes to Guadalcanal; she remained with that ship as plane guard and escort into late April.

For the rest of the summer, *Wilson* operated out of Guadalcanal, Noumea, Espiritu Santo, and Havannah Harbor, providing cover for convoys going to and from Guadalcanal and conducting training exercises and plane guarding for *Chenango*. After returning to Guadalcanal with a convoy, *Wilson* sortied on the evening of 24 July, in company with six other destroyers, and headed for Munda, New Georgia. There, she shelled Japanese positions ashore before she returned to Purvis Bay the following day.

Over the ensuing days, *Wilson* alternated time at Purvis Bay with patrols off Lunga Point and Kukum beach, Guadalcanal, and escort duty shepherding LST's to Rendova.

While the campaign for the island of Guadalcanal itself had ceased in February, the eviction of the Japanese from the rest of the Solomons continued into the summer. American ships still encountered Japanese counterparts in sharp night engagements; and the latter were finding, much to their chagrin, that the United States Navy was learning how to fight at night.

Early on 10 August, while operating with five other destroyers, *Wilson* located several Japanese barges. Unfortunately, early gun failures—three of the four main battery guns jammed—limited *Wilson*'s role to that of a spectator as the other ships blasted the barges to pieces.

Her gun casualties repaired, *Wilson* soon resumed her patrols off Guadalcanal, screening transports unloading troops and supplies. Such duty was comparatively tame compared to what was to come for the destroyer. At the end of August, she commenced operations with TF 38 but broke her training operations with that force with a cruise to Sydney, Australia. She soon returned to the Noumea-Espiritu Santo area and resumed tactical exercises with TF 38. On 19 October, however, *Wilson* screened a convoy of LST's and LCI's to Vella Lavella less than two weeks after the Japanese had evacuated that island.

On 5 November, while planes from Rear Admiral Frederick C. Sherman's task force were raiding the Japanese base at Rabaul—*Wilson* was back with the carriers and picked up a three-man crew of a ditched Avenger.

Wilson returned to Espiritu Santo following the Rabaul strike but spent only five hours there before leaving again for a return engagement at Rabaul. That strike, again under Rear Admiral Sherman, soon drew an enemy response.

Shortly after noon on 11 November, while TG 50.3 drew near to their objective, "it became apparent that we were in for a battle." A Japanese force estimated at over 70 planes was winging its way toward the carriers and was picked up at a distance of 75 miles. Soon, the initial increment was fighting its way through the carriers' combat air patrol (CAP).

During the five ensuing raids, and a battle that lasted a little under two hours, all of the American ships conducted intense evasive maneuvers. *Wilson* remained near *Bunker Hill* (CV–17), steaming consistently at almost 30 knots, and bagged two of the 12 "Vals" and "Kates" shot down by her part of the formation. The American strike at Rabaul—the second within a week—netted one Japanese destroyer, *Suzunami*, sunk.

Back at Espiritu Santo, *Wilson* was assigned to TG 50.5 on 14 November. Formed around the carriers *Saratoga* and *Princeton*, that group screened the carriers as they launched strikes on the enemy airfields on Nauru Island in the Gilbert Islands. Soon thereafter, TG 50.5 joined two other groups to cover the occupation of Makin and Tarawa Islands in the Gilberts. *Wilson* operated half-way between Makin and Tarawa, providing antisubmarine and antiaircraft screening protection for the vital flattops. After a return strike on Nauru was cancelled, *Wilson* retired to Espiritu Santo and Havannah harbor.

On Christmas Day, *Wilson* stood out of Havannah harbor for exercises in company with the battleships *Washington* (BB–56) and *North Carolina* (BB–55). She then put into Noumea for a drydocking and tender availability before she headed for Kwajalein on 25 January 1944 as a part of a strong force that included *Bunker Hill*, *Cowpens* (CVL–25), and *Monterey* (CVL–26), and the fast battleships *Iowa* (BB–61) and *New Jersey* (BB–62). *Wilson* participated in the strikes against Kwajalein, in a carrier support group, performing her vital but unglamorous function of plane guard and screening vessel.

After a brief in-port period of one day, *Wilson* cleared Majuro headed for Truk, which, according to *Wilson's* commanding officer, "was to be the toughest 'nut' of the Pacific to crack." But the awesomeness of Truk was overcome by carrier strikes which heavily battered the island. *Wilson* supported those operations against Truk; and, while the carriers were retiring, they launched raids against Saipan and Tinian, their first operations against the Marshall Islands. After returning to Majuro, *Wilson* screened TG 50.8 back to Havannah harbor and, while en route, made a sound contact. The destroyer dropped a depth charge pattern but, in the ensuing turbulence created by the explosion of the charges, was unable to regain contact.

After drills and exercises out of Espiritu Santo, *Wilson* participated in the strikes on Kavieng, New Ireland, as part of TG 36.3 formed around the escort carrier *Manila Bay* (CVE–61). The task group then proceeded north of the Solomon Islands, to Emirau,

where *Manila Bay* and her escorts covered convoys operating in that area. After that evolution, *Wilson* returned to Purvis Bay, off Florida Island, where she picked up a convoy and escorted it back to Havannah harbor.

Having performed escort and screening operations almost continuously, *Wilson* received orders to screen battleships *Tennessee* (BB–43) and *Mississippi* (BB–42) to Pearl Harbor. Departing Efate on 7 April, *Wilson* arrived at Pearl Harbor nine days later and was soon underway for Puget Sound, reaching there on the 24th. Shifting down to San Francisco six days later, *Wilson* joined the battleships *Maryland* (BB–46), *Colorado* (BB–45), *Washington*, and *California* (BB–44), and escorted them to the Hawaiian Islands, reaching Pearl Harbor on 10 May.

Subsequently heading west, via Majuro, and resuming her operations with the fast carrier task force, TF 58, in mid-June, *Wilson* took part in the strikes on Saipan as part of TG 58.4. While patrolling west of the Marianas on 19 June, Wilson received reports of enemy aircraft closing the formation at a distance of 100 miles. Going to general quarters, the destroyer awaited the onslaught; but, with the exception of one "Kate," all of the incoming "bogies" were intercepted and the attacks broken up by the CAP.

On the following day, 20 June, the carriers of TF 58 again launched air strikes against Guam and Rota. Detached along with *Sterett* and *Lang* (DD–399), *Wilson* conducted a shipping sweep and heckling mission against those islands, providing the ships the opportunity to "get close enough to see what the beach looked like, plus a little target practice on some sampans and shore bombardment on gun emplacements east of Agana, on the south coast of Guam." *Wilson* later participated in similar missions in the Palaus before she received orders on 4 August sending her, via Pearl Harbor, to the west coast of the United States. The destroyer reached the Puget Sound Navy Yard, Bremerton, on the 20th.

Wilson underwent availability at the Todd-Pacific shipyard, Seattle, Wash., through the end of the summer. Shifting down to Alameda, Calif., soon thereafter, she rendezvoused with *Yorktown* (CV–10) and set out for Pearl Harbor on 13 October. The destroyer subsequently exercised intensively in the Hawaiian operating area for a month before she proceeded, in company with sistership *Sterett*, to the Admiralties. En route, the ships picked up a sound contact and dropped a full shallow pattern. They observed air bubbles near the dropping point but saw no other evidence of having made a successful attack. After *Wilson* and her consort systematically searched the area but could not regain contact, they proceeded on to Manus.

There, *Wilson* steamed to Leyte and, on Christmas Day, headed toward a rendezvous point in Surigao Strait to meet a convoy and escort it to San Pedro Bay. On 27 December, *Wilson* got underway as one of nine destroyers assigned to a resupply echelon escorting a convoy from Leyte Gulf to Mangarin Bay, Mindoro, and back.

Expecting suicide attacks from any of the many airfields within striking distance, *Wilson* set her course southward, bound for the Mindanao Sea. The convoy was a large and important one: 23 LST's, 3 "Liberty"-type merchantmen, a "Liberty"-type tanker, five Army inter-island steamers, 23 LCI's, a motor torpedo boat tender, 30 PT boats, two seaplane tenders (AVP's); a converted LST serving as a PT boat tender, *Orestes* (AGP–10), and 3 "coast boats."

The first intimation of trouble came at 0310 on the 28th, when *Stevens* (DD–479) reported a bogey at 11 miles and closing. *Wilson* went to general quarters soon after receiving that report and prepared for action. However, by 0352, the enemy planes—probably "snoopers"—had disappeared from the radar screens. About sunrise, which came at 0659, *Wilson* received reports that the bad weather over Leyte had prevented a CAP.

The resulting lack of fighter cover would be felt strongly later that morning. On the other hand, the dawn revealed only scattered clouds over the convoy, and visibility was excellent.

Then, at 1013, came the tocsin, "many bogies reported bearing 033, 22 miles." Soon the sky became dotted with flak bursts as the escorts and the ships in the convoy opened up as the enemy planes closed. The first Japanese aircraft came from the starboard quarter and soon was set afire by antiaircraft fire before it crashed into the "Liberty" ship SS *William Sharon* at 1021. A minute later, another attacker crashed into the "Liberty" ship SS *John Burke*. The latter blew up in a thunderclap; and "an enormous white cloud covering an area of several thousand yards" came only seconds after a tremendous flash had occurred. *John Burke* literally disintegrated.

By 1030, the raid was over as quickly as it had begun. *Wilson* altered course at high speed, racing to get to the crippled *William Sharon*, "whose superstructure was by now a raging inferno." At 1043, after passing through the LCI group, the destroyer came alongside the blazing "Liberty" ship and played her hoses on the fire that was consuming the merchantman's superstructure. Then a report of bogies prompted her to clear the side of the burning "Liberty" ship. Although the raid did not develop, the destroyer's leaving *William Sharon*'s side allowed a lifeboat full of men to escape being crushed between the destroyer and the cargo ship.

Wilson circled to port, came back alongside *William Sharon* at 1053, and soon began taking her survivors on board for treatment of wounds and burns. But no sooner had she settled into carrying out that urgent business than the receipt of a "flash red" again forced her to clear the side of the stricken ship. All fire fighters and their hoses and survivors were recalled to the destroyer, and she stood back toward the convoy to prepare to fight off the expected attack.

That raid did not materialize, either, so *Wilson* resumed her fire-fighting chores. At 1205—just as the fire fighters had reboarded the "Liberty" ship—ammunition in ready service boxes on board the blazing ship began to explode forcing the destroyer to withdraw again. Returning once more at 1237, *Wilson* skillfully remained alongside until the fires were out—that not until 1340—more than an hour later.

Then, with *William Sharon*'s survivors embarked, *Wilson* left the ship as a derelict, drifting southeast at a speed of two and one-half knots. While en route to rejoin the convoy, the destroyer sank a damaged LCM with 40-millimeter fire. *Wilson* resumed her position in the screen at 1630, just as an "Oscar" circled the formation and flew away.

The convoy was not yet out of the figurative woods. At 1836, *Pringle* (DD–477) reported a bogey 34 miles away and closing. Seven minutes later, the ships began firing. *Wilson* bent on flank speed and put her rudder over hard left to unmask her starboard antiaircraft battery. The ship's action report succinctly summed up the ensuing situation, "The picture at this point was moving too fast for an accurate analysis."

With almost 20 Japanese planes darting in and diving to the attack, the destroyermen or the sailors on the ships being escorted had little time for analysis either but kept busy fighting off the Japanese planes. When the last Japanese planes had disappeared, four or five of the enemy had been downed in the melee at the cost of one LST sunk.

During the next day, *Wilson* and her consorts came under attack four more times but escaped without damage. Nor did the tempo of attacks decrease on the 29th —almost continuous raids kept *Wilson* at general quarters for most of the day, and she "assisted materially" in splashing two planes that day—one a victim of her 20-millimeter battery.

Arriving at Mangarin Bay on the 30th, the convoy anchored; but *Wilson* and the other ships of the screen maintained patrol stations, circling as necessary. Meanwhile, bogies closing from the northwest came into radar range, and the escorts commenced firing. *Wilson* came right, unmasking her port battery, and 5-inch shells from her guns scored hits on a "Frances" that blew up off the port side of the formation. *Gansevoort* (DD–608) and other ships in the forward part of the screen shared the kill.

Another "Frances" approached from the port quarter. Observed at 0708, the plane circled right and crossed from port to starboard, just ahead of *Wilson*, in an attempt to dive on the convoy. After the destroyer's 5-inch guns had hurled 12 rounds at the intruder, it passed across to the starboard side of the ship. One of the ship's 20-millimeter guns emptied an entire magazine into the "Frances," and it splashed soon thereafter. Such close proximity to enemy planes resulted in some confused shooting. In the heat of a confused engagement, often there was little time to check fire when a "friendly" ship or plane ventured too close; and shrapnel bursts near *Wilson* injured one man.

When the attack abated, *Wilson* transferred the wounded survivors from *William Sharon* to an LCM for further transportation to *LST–734*. Resuming her patrol station off Mangarin Bay two hours later, steaming between *Philip* (DD–498) and *Gansevoort*, *Wilson* went to general quarters at 1540 when *Gansevoort* reported a bogey in the vicinity. Soon thereafter, *Wilson*'s spotters saw a "Zeke," apparently damaged by the heavy antiaircraft barrage laid down by nearby ships, go into a steep dive and level off a few feet above the wavetops, boring in on *Gansevoort*.

While the destroyermen in *Wilson* watched, helplessly, the suicider crashed *Gansevoort*'s port beam between number 2 funnel and the 40-millimeter gun mounts. Although *Wilson* had been out of gun range to aid in her defense, the destroyer sped to *Gansevoort*'s assistance at 25 knots.

As *Wilson* approached, she slowed to avoid running down any of the many men seen swimming in the water —survivors from the stricken destroyer that was now suffering a raging fire amidships. As their ship neared the blazing "tin can," *Wilson*'s men threw lifejackets and rafts over the side to help the struggling men. Although the approach was hampered by *Gansevoort*'s rigged-out 26-foot motor whaleboat, *Wilson* came alongside the starboard side and played 14 hoses on the fire while *Philips* came alongside the port bow of the damaged ship. Meanwhile, the whaleboat was lowered to *Wilson*'s deck and cut loose. At 1640—a little less than three-quarters of an hour after *Wilson* had reached *Gansevoort*—bogies were reported in the area; and a "flash red" sounded. By that time, all fires on *Gansevoort* had been extinguished, so *Wilson* got underway and circled at high speed in the vicinity and later jettisoned *Gansevoort*'s motor whaleboat before she took station, at 1840, in the antiaircraft screen for the reformed convoy.

The day's activities were still far from over for the battle-hardened destroyer. At 2120, *Pringle* reported a bogey in the vicinity. *Wilson* went to general quarters, and, at 2135, opened fire in full radar control. She shot well—her first salvo hit the target. *Philip*, too, joined in, adding her bit to splash the intruder on the port quarter of the group.

After the eventful convoy run had been completed, *Wilson* reentered Leyte Gulf on 1 January 1945. She sortied on the 4th with nine other destroyers, bound for Lingayen Gulf, escorting several patrol craft, transports, an LST flotilla, and an LSM and LCT group. Five days later, *Wilson* and her consorts reached Lingayen Gulf; and she proceeded to her fire support sector to bombard her prescribed area. During her ensuing period on station, *Wilson* experienced several air attacks but escaped without damage as she continued her shore bombardment duties.

Later that day, 9 January, *Wilson* began shepherding many unloaded ships on their voyage toward Leyte.

While en route, the convoy experienced a surprise air attack when a single Japanese plane darted out of the clouds and dropped a bomb near *Wickes* (DD–528)—fortunately only a near miss.

After fueling and rearming at Leyte, *Wilson* proceeded toward Morotai and then back to Leyte. She next returned to Lingayen Gulf, screening a convoy. "Fast on the trigger" on 24 January, *Wilson's* gunners blasted a bogey out of the sky before any of the other ships in the formation had a chance to open fire.

Soon after reporting for duty in Lingayen Gulf, *Wilson* received a fire support sector and, at 1123, commenced firing. She ceased at 1136, "target destroyed"—obtaining results after the fourth salvo. For the remainder of the day, the destroyer continued her vital job of supporting the troops ashore and expended a total of 108 rounds of 5-inch ammunition. Shore spotters reported that she scored many hits on her targets.

Escorting a slow convoy back to Leyte, *Wilson* departed Lingayen Gulf on 31 January, delivered her charges at San Pedro Bay, and headed on to Hollandia, Dutch New Guinea. She sailed thence to Manus and Port Purvis in the Solomons.

On 21 March, *Wilson* arrived back at Ulithi in the screen of the Northern Attack Force, earmarked for participation in the next operation—the Ryukyus. After completing logistic preparations, *Wilson* headed for Okinawa and reached a point off the southwest part of the island at 0100 on Easter Sunday, 1 April 1945—D day for the operation. Greeted by a closing bogey upon arrival, *Wilson* promptly opened fire and forced the plane to turn away and retire.

At 0422, while making a second sweep through the transport area off Hagushi beach, *Wilson* picked up a second bogey at a range of 14,000 yards and immediately opened fire. The enemy aircraft came relentlessly closer, seemingly oblivious to the antiaircraft fire sent up in his path. Finally, the barrage took effect; and the plane crashed some 1,500 yards off *Wilson's* starboard beam.

Over the ensuing days, *Wilson* manned various screening stations near the unloading transports. On 4 March, she received orders to proceed to Guam in company with three other destroyers. En route, however, that directive was changed, and *Wilson* instead received orders to rendezvous with a convoy and escort it back to Okinawa.

Wilson subsequently reached the southern end of Kerama Retto on 16 April and was patrolling as the convoy entered "Wiseman's Cove" when she sighted two planes flying in loose echelon formation at medium altitude off the starboard quarter. *Wilson* immediately increased speed to 20 knots and took the lead plane under fire.

While the gunfire did not knock that plane down, its companion executed a wingover and headed toward *Wilson* in a shallow glide. *Wilson* increased speed again —this time to 25 knots—and put over full left rudder to keep her guns unmasked. Meanwhile, the main and secondary batteries kept up a punishing fire, blackening the sky with puffs of antiaircraft. Soon the 5-inch and 40-millimeter fire took effect, and the plane hit the water about 75 yards off the starboard quarter.

The enemy, however, was not dead yet. The plane bounced off the water and came toward *Wilson*, the propeller striking and lodging into the 40-millimeter gun tub. The plane itself then spun around and passed between 5-inch guns number 3 and 4, and splashed into the sea on the port side, taking with it "a few incidentals such as mooring reels and loose gear." A 250-kilogram bomb carried by the plane passed through the skin of the ship just above the waterline on the starboard side and finally came to rest in an after living compartment. Only the booster charge exploded causing some internal damage to the ship: shrapnel penetrated into adjacent fuel tanks, rupturing the tank bulkheads and the main lead to group three magazines, resulting in minor fires and the flooding of those magazines. Tragically, five men, whose station was in the group three magazine, were killed by drowning and burns as a result of the rupture of the sprinkling system. Three other men were blown overboard at the time the plane hit; and two of them received serious injuries. Fortunately, the ship had been in a turn when she was hit; so she continued on around and managed to pick up her men after completing the circle, bringing them on board for medical treatment. .

In "Wiseman's Cove," *Wilson* underwent repairs (the unexploded bomb being removed in the process) and thereafter remained in operation in the Okinawa area until June. During that time, she performed screening duties for the transports and shore bombardment on targets ranging from Naha to the southern tip of Okinawa. Finally departing Okinawa on 12 June, the destroyer arrived at Pearl Harbor on the 26th, after calls en route at Ulithi and Eniwetok.

Subsequently based at Saipan, *Wilson* performed screening for convoys, patrolling, and coordinating air-sea rescues. She remained engaged in that duty through the cessation of hostilities in mid-August, when Japan capitulated.

In the autumn of 1945, *Wilson* operated at Iwo Jima and Hagushi before shifting to China waters in late October. Subsequently, the veteran destroyer returned to the west coast of the United States, reaching San Diego in late December 1945. Although initially slated to be decommissioned in the Altantic, *Wilson* was later earmarked for use in the atomic tests at Bikini Atoll, reaching there on 31 May 1946. Used as a target during those tests, *Wilson* was decommissioned on 29 August 1946 and apparently remained afloat, at Kwajalein, over the next year and one-half. Late in February 1948, she was authorized for destruction by scuttling. She was sunk in deep water off Kwajalein on 8 March 1948. Her name was struck from the Navy list on 5 April of the same year.

Wilson received 11 battle stars for her service during World War II.

Wilson, Henry B., see *Henry B. Wilson.*

Wilson, Le Ray, see *Le Ray Wilson.*

Wilson, Robert L., see *Robert L. Wilson.*

Wiltsie

Irving Day Wiltsie—born on 14 November 1898 in Hartford, Conn.—graduated in the Naval Academy class of 1921 and then served at sea in a succession of ships—*Arizona* (BB–39), *Wyoming* (BB–32), *Raleigh* (CL–9), and *Cleveland* (CL–21)—before he underwent flight instruction at Pensacola, Fla., from 1925 to 1927. He subsequently served in aviation units based in *Milwaukee* (CL–5), *Memphis* (CL–13), and *Texas* (BB–35) before he returned to Pensacola as an instructor. After another tour of sea duty—in *Louisville* (CA–28)—Wiltsie commanded the Naval Reserve aviation base at Minneapolis, Minn., from 29 June 1935 to 4 June 1937. He later commanded the bombing squadrons attached to *Saratoga* (CV–3) from June 1937 to June 1939, before he served at the naval air station at San Diego, Calif. He subsequently joined *Yorktown* (CV–5) as navigator on 27 June 1941 and received a promotion to commander on 1 July.

Wiltsie remained in *Yorktown* until her loss at the pivotal Battle of Midway from 4 to 6 June 1942. During the early stages of the action, Wiltsie displayed "outstanding professional ability" as he provided complete and accurate navigational information to air plot, thus enabling the carrier's air group to pinpoint their targets.

During the Japanese torpedo attacks on 4 June, when "Kates" from the carrier *Hiryu* located *Yorktown* and carried out a successful attack against her, Wiltsie, on instructions from the captain, conned the ship from his battle station in the conning tower and was later deemed directly responsible for the ship's evading a pair of torpedoes. When injuries sustained during the attack incapacitated the carrier's executive officer, Comdr. Wiltsie assumed these duties and directed the organization of a salvage party which fought valiantly to save the ship.

When *Yorktown* eventually succumbed to her damage and the *coup de grace* administered by Japanese submarine *I–168*, Wiltsie coolly and calmly directed the salvage party and the wounded to rescuing vessels alongside the doomed carrier.

Wiltsie—promoted to captain in September 1942—commanded *Albemarle* (AV–5) from 6 October 1942 to 12 June 1943. After this tour, he supervised the fitting-out of escort carrier *Glacier* (CVE–33) at the Seattle-Tacoma Shipbuilding Co. and went on to supervise the same kind of activities of *Liscome Bay* (CVE–62). Wiltsie would command this escort carrier until the ship's loss off Makin, in the Gilberts, in the autumn of 1943.

In the predawn darkness of 24 November 1943, *I–175* torpedoed *Liscome Bay*—the flagship of Rear Admiral Henry M. Mullinix—and started fires among bombs and ammunition. Fed by aviation gasoline, the flames spread rapidly, and the carrier rocked with explosions. Wiltsie immediately left the bridge and proceeded along the starboard gallery deck level to ascertain the damage to his ship, as communications had been severed early-on. Despite the tremendous structural damage and raging fires, the captain bravely headed aft to determine the full extent of the damage. Damage control efforts failed, however, and the carrier sank soon thereafter, carrying the intrepid Wiltsie, Admiral Mullinix, and 644 officers and men down with her.

The citation for Capt. Wiltsie's posthumous Navy Cross noted his "calm, courageous action and valiant devotion to duty" which inspired the surviving members of the crew.

(DD–716: dp. 2,425; l. 390'6''; b. 41'1''; dr. 18'6''; s. 35 k.; cpl. 336; a. 6 5'', 12 40mm., 20 20mm., 5 21'' tt., 2 dct., 6 dcp.; cl. *Gearing*)

Wiltsie (DD–716) was laid down on 13 March 1945 at Port Newark, N.J., by the Federal Shipbuilding and Drydock Co.; launched on 31 August 1945; sponsored by Mrs. Irving D. Wiltsie, the widow of Capt. Wiltsie; and commissioned on 12 January 1946 at the New York Naval Shipyard, Brooklyn, N.Y., Comdr. Raymond D. Fusselman in command.

Following a shakedown cruise which took the ship to Guantanamo Bay, Cuba, *Wiltsie* transited the Panama Canal on 8 July 1946 and proceeded to San Diego. She spent the fall and winter of 1946 engaged in training exercises before departing the west coast on 6 January 1947, bound for the Far East. She subsequently operated out of Tsingtao, China, on exercises and maneuvers while standing by the American community in that port during rising local tensions between the communist and Nationalist Chinese. *Wiltsie* remained at Tsingtao until June 1947, when she shifted to Sasebo, Japan, for occupation duty. Departing Sasebo on 8 March 1948, the destroyer proceeded to Bremerton, Wash., for an overhaul at the Puget Sound Naval Shipyard.

After training off the west coast, *Wiltsie* sailed once more for the Far East, departing San Diego on 1 October. Late that autumn, she again operated out of Tsingtao during the evacuation of Americans from that port to Yokohama because of the Chinese civil war then raging. During this period of anxiety, *Wiltsie* briefly visited Hong Kong and Okinawa before returning to Tsingtao.

Chinese communist forces meanwhile inexorably rolled southward, crossing the Yangtze at midnight on 20 April 1949. Four days later, Nanking fell. *Wiltsie* arrived at Shanghai on 22 April, to stand by during the evacuation of all foreign nationals from the city. Over the ensuing days, *Wiltsie* watched a veritable parade of merchant vessels of many nationalities—Chinese, Dutch, Norwegian, French, Danish, British, and American—as well as American, British, and Chinese naval vessels. On Thursday, 5 May 1949, 20 days before the fall of the city to the communists, *Wiltsie* departed Chinese waters for the last time, bound for Buckner Bay, Okinawa.

From there, *Wiltsie* soon headed homeward and made port at San Diego on 4 June 1949. She later moved up the coast; embarked NROTC midshipmen at Treasure Island, near San Francisco, on 1 August; and departed the following day for a training cruise to Balboa, Panama, and the Galapagos Islands. Returning to San Diego on 31 August, the destroyer soon sailed for Hawaii, where she participated in Operation "Miki," a mock invasion of the Hawaiian Islands in which Army, Navy, and Air Force units all took part. Returning to the west coast soon thereafter, *Wiltsie* spent the period from December 1949 to April 1950 at the Mare Island Naval Shipyard, Vallejo, Calif., undergoing an overhaul.

On the morning of 25 June 1950, Far Eastern tensions flared into open warfare when 75,000 North Korean troops swarmed across the 38th parallel into South Korea. The communist forces struck at six points along the border and launched amphibious assaults at two places on South Korea's east coast. Later that day, the Security Council of the United Nations (UN) passed a resolution calling for a North Korean withdrawal and a cease-fire. The North Koreans ignored both aspects of the resolution.

In July, *Wiltsie* sailed for the Far East to augment the meager American naval presence in Korean waters; and, when she reached the combat zone, the military picture looked bleak for the hard-pressed UN forces. North Korean troops continued to push the UN troops toward the southern coast of the Korean Peninsula.

For five days in mid-August, the Republic of Korea (ROK) 3d Division, supported from the sea by the Navy's Task Group (TG) 96.51, blocked the enemy's southward advance near Yonghae. Meanwhile, UN forces had established a defensive perimeter north of Pusan. Isolated, the 3d ROK Division faced annihilation.

On the evening of 16 August, the United States Navy came to the rescue when *Helena* (CA–75), with four LST's and escorting destroyers, closed the coast. Capt. J. R. Clark, Commander, Destroyer Division 111, embarked in the recently arrived *Wiltsie*, assumed direction of the embarkation operation for the ROK troops. He ordered the four LST's to beach at a pre-arranged site, guided in by jeep headlights from shore. Before sunrise the next day, 327 officers and 3,480 men of the 3d ROK Division, 1,260 civilians, and 100 vehicles had been loaded in an orderly evacuation accomplished without loss. Comdrs. Malcolm W. Cagle and Frank A. Manson, in their book, *The Sea War in Korea*, cited that evacuation as "the final naval contribution to the salvation of the Pusan perimeter."

The Pusan perimeter held. Meanwhile, General Douglas MacArthur made plans to relieve the heavy pressure on the UN forces in the south by striking deep behind North Korean lines. In a desperate gamble, American forces went ashore at Inchon on 15 September 1950. *Wiltsie* participated in one phase of this assault, screening the fast carriers of Task Force (TF) 77—*Philippine Sea* (CV–47), *Valley Forge* (CV–45), and *Boxer* (CV–21)—as their aircraft hit communist ground targets to support the advance of troops ashore. The Inchon landings stopped the enemy's momentum as he was on the verge of pushing UN forces into the sea. The North Koreans then found themselves outflanked and their supply lines interdicted. For the remainder of the deployment, *Wiltsie* supported UN troops ashore with call-fire support; screened TF 77 as it conducted air strikes against enemy supply lines and troop concentrations; and patrolled in the Taiwan Strait to safeguard Nationalist Chinese neutrality.

Wiltsie returned to San Diego in March of 1951, underwent repairs at Long Beach, and subsequently departed the west coast for her fourth tour of duty in the Far East. In Korean waters, she resumed her

screening, call-fire, and interdiction duties. Highlighting her blockading activities of Wonsan, *Wiltsie* fired retaliatory gunfire missions against troublesome communist shore batteries. In March 1951, those guns kept up an uncomfortable fire upon the American ships engaged in the blockade.

On 13 March, before it was silenced by air strikes from TF 77's planes, one battery landed shells near *Manchester* (CL–83), *Douglas H. Fox* (DD–779), *James E. Kyes* (DD–787), and *McGinty* (DE–365). One week

USS *Wiltsie* (DD–716).

later, enemy guns shelled *Wiltsie* and *Brinkley Bass* (DD–887) as they patrolled their blockade station, fortunately doing no damage.

Wiltsie returned to the west coast late in 1952, but soon found herself back in the Far East for her third Korean War deployment. After leaving the west coast on 2 January 1953, the destroyer patrolled the Formosa Strait for a time and operated off the North Korean coast before shifting to Wonsan. Meanwhile, the stalemated "police action" with the North Koreans and communist Chinese "volunteers" had long before bogged down and would soon be in its third year. The Navy continued it operations to support UN ground troops, interdicted enemy supply lines by air and by surface gunfire, and blockaded the enemy's coasts. By late in April 1953, when truce negotiations had bogged down, the communists resorted to an all-out offensive in an attempt to convert military gain in the field into political gains at the conference table.

Eight days after *Wiltsie* and *Theodore E. Chandler* (DD–717) had destroyed a train near Tanchon on 3 June, communist shore batteries took *Wiltsie* under fire off Wonsan, lobbing 45 105-millimeter shells in her direction, scoring a hit on the destroyer's fantail. Fortunately, the ship suffered no casualties and soon resumed her local patrol operations. On 15 June, *Wiltsie* evacuated 13 Korean civilians from Yo-do Island to Sokcho-ri.

Eventually, a cease-fire in Korea was negotiated, but hostilities continued up to the minute the truce was to take effect. While preparing to abandon the Wonsan seige in accordance with the armistice stipulations, *Wiltsie* screened minesweeping operations and joined in the last-minute shelling of communist ground targets. In company with *Porter* (DD–800) and *Bremerton* (CA–130), *Wiltsie* shelled targets at Wonsan until a few minutes before the 2200 deadline. On 27 July 1953, the Korean armistice finally came into effect. However, *Wiltsie* remained in Korean waters, screening the continuing minesweeping operations between Hungnam and Wonsan until 6 August 1953.

Wiltsie conducted seven WestPac deployments between 1953 and 1961. During each tour, she carried out training and patrol assignments in Far Eastern waters, operating off the coasts of Japan, Korea, and Okinawa; visiting such ports as Yokosuka, Kobe, and Sasebo, Japan; Hong Kong; and Philippine ports such as Olongapo and Manila. Also during this time, she plane-guarded for fast carrier task forces, patrolled the Taiwan Strait to prevent communist Chinese incursions against the Nationalists on Taiwan, and undertook antisubmarine warfare and gunnery training exercises.

Between deployments to WestPac and the Far East, *Wiltsie* underwent regular overhaul and repair periods at the Long Beach Naval Shipyard. In addition, she conducted an NROTC midshipman training cruise; visited Seattle, Wash., and Esquimalt, British Columbia; and visited Melbourne, Australia, in May 1959 to celebrate the anniversary of the key Battle of the Coral Sea.

In November 1961, *Wiltsie* began a 10-month scheduled overhaul at the Pearl Harbor Naval Shipyard, Pearl Harbor, in which she underwent Fleet Rehabilitation and Modernization (FRAM) alterations. She received an enclosed bridge; a helicopter hangar and landing platform; triple-mounted Mk. 32 torpedo tubes; an ASROC launcher; and late model radar and sonar. She also received many improvements in accommodations for both officers and enlisted men. Following this "face lift," *Wiltsie* conducted refresher training and upkeep before becoming flagship of DesDiv 72, homeported in San Diego.

Following sonar calibrations at Puget Sound, *Wiltsie* spent one week off southern California, participating in Exercise "Steel Gate"—an amphibious landing exercise near Camp Pendleton in which the destroyer trained in support evolutions for landings. After the conclusion of this maneuver, *Wiltsie* departed the west coast for the Far East, leaving San Diego on 18 May 1963. Arriving at Yokosuka on 6 June, via Pearl Harbor and Midway, *Wiltsie* soon got underway for a 30-day Taiwan Strait mission. During this time, she visited Keelung and Kaohsiung, Formosa. Her scheduled rest period at Hong Kong at the end of the assignment had to be cancelled because of a typhoon.

Returning to Yokosuka for upkeep on 30 July, *Wiltsie* departed in early August for participation in Exercise "Tire Iron." This large-scale fleet exercise involved three carriers, a guided missile cruiser, and 16 destroyers, as well as a replenishment group of nine ships. The exercise evaluated the effectiveness of task force-type operations; and, at the conclusion of the maneuver, one of the largest underway replenishment evolutions in history took place.

Wiltsie subsequently operated out of Sasebo and Yokosuka into the fall of 1963; she departed Sasebo on 29 October and operated briefly with TG 77.6 until 10 November, when she was detached to return home. After a stop at Pearl Harbor, the destroyer made port at San Diego on 24 November.

In January 1964, *Wiltsie* joined *Ticonderoga* (CVA–14), *Theodore E. Chandler*, and *Henderson* (DD–885) in antiaircraft warfare exercises off the west coast and served as a plane guard for the carrier. She subsequently moved westward to the middle Pacific with *Ticonderoga* and arrived at Pearl Harbor on 18 February. After completing her exercises in Hawaiian waters, she returned to the west coast of the United States in the spring and soon participated in antisubmarine and antiair warfare training with *Yorktown* (CVA–10) and *Coral Sea* (CVA–43).

In June, *Wiltsie* embarked midshipmen for a six-week training program and later underwent 10 days of hull repairs at Long Beach. Later in the month, she participated in exercises in support of Marine Corps units engaged in night reconnaissance and in amphibious and paratroop landing training at San Clemente Island and at Camp Del Mar, Calif.

Drydocked during August and September for hull and sonar dome repair, *Wiltsie* put to sea soon thereafter for tests and trials of her DASH (drone antisubmarine helicopter) qualification system which ended successfully on 3 November. The destroyer subsequently participated in Operation "Union Square," an extensive fleet exercise, before returning to San Diego to prepare for the ship's 14th WestPac deployment.

Wiltsie sailed for the western Pacific on 5 January 1965, in company with the 16 other ships of Cruiser Destroyer Flotilla 7. Originally scheduled to visit Japan in the first part of the cruise, *Wiltsie* was diverted to duty with *Coral Sea* and *Hancock* (CVA–19) during bombing raids on Viet Cong positions in South Vietnam in February.

The destroyer spent 69 of her next 80 days at sea in Vietnamese waters. She served in a variety of roles, including antisubmarine warfare screening ship, plane guard destroyer, and early warning picket ship. In March, before proceeding to Hong Kong, she shadowed a Russian intelligence ship which was gathering information on American task groups.

Upon the completion of her visit to the British Crown Colony, *Wiltsie* again sailed for Vietnam and operated with TG 71.1 on Operation "Market Time," engaged in patrolling the South Vietnamese coastline to interdict the flow of arms and ammunition and infiltration by North Vietnamese into South Vietnam.

In May and June, *Wiltsie* conducted several gunfire support missions against Viet Cong supply depots and troop concentrations in South Vietnam. During this deployment off the coast of Vietnam, *Wiltsie* transferred 64.2 short tons of stores from *Mars* (AFS–1) by the vertical replenishment method, utilizing the capabilities of one of *Mars'* supply helicopters.

Following a visit to Japan in mid-June, *Wiltsie* returned to the United States, arriving at San Diego on

399

2 July. *Wiltsie* next underwent a period of repairs and refresher training which carried over into 1966. After taking part in training evolutions off the west coast in the spring, *Wiltsie* again headed for the Orient on 4 June 1966. While at Guam for a refueling stop, the destroyer suffered slight damage on 22 June when a fuel barge collided with the ship, necessitating repairs which delayed her for 15 hours.

Towers (DDG-9) and *Buck* (DD-761), which had steamed in company with *Wiltsie* since leaving San Diego, proceeded ahead, leaving *Wiltsie* to sail independently. Underway on 23 June, the ship encountered heavy seas which delayed her arrival at Subic Bay until late in the afternoon of the 27th. After two days of upkeep, the destroyer proceeded for Vietnamese waters.

On 2 July, *Wiltsie* commenced duty with TU 70.8.9, a naval gunfire support unit. In the ensuing fortnight, the destroyer fired 1,076 rounds of 5-inch shells at Viet Cong positions in the II, III, and IV Corps areas of South Vietnam. One such mission resulted in the destruction of a 12-man Viet Cong (VC) squad.

After a brief period of upkeep, *Wiltsie* proceeded to the northern search and rescue (SAR) station, approximately 50 miles east of the North Vietnamese port of Haiphong, to stand by with *Towers* ready to recover downed airmen. For two periods—from 31 July to 2 September and from 28 September to 1 November, *Wiltsie* patrolled the northern SAR station. In August and again in October, the destroyer participated in rescues from the waters off the North Vietnamese coast, saving a total of nine men. Moreover, on 207 occasions during two months, the ship acted as a refueling vessel for units of Helicopter Squadron 6, providing some 70,000 gallons of aviation fuel for the thirsty helicopters engaged in rescue duty.

On 9 October, one rescue helo approached the ship, dangerously low on fuel. Although the danger existed of a crash landing as the chopper hovered over the fantail, Electrician's Mate 1st Class Donald J. Adams attached the helicopter's lowered hook to the fuel hose and tended it while it was hoisted up to begin the fueling operation. For his action under these dangerous circumstances, Adams was awarded a special letter of commendation from the Commander in Chief of the Pacific Fleet (CINCPACFLT).

Upon completion of these SAR duties, *Wiltsie* prepared for her homeward voyage. She called at the port of Hualien, Taiwan, on 4 November for a five-day visit. She departed Nationalist Chinese waters on 10 November, made a fuel stop at Okinawa the next day, and arrived at Yokosuka on 14 November.

Wiltsie joined TG 77.8, based around *Constellation* (CVA-64), and stood out of Yokosuka on 22 November, bound for the west coast. Three days out, the task group ran into bad weather which reduced its speed from 22 to 6 knots. High winds prevailed for five days, and all ships suffered moderate storm damage. The heavy seas battered open a seam forward in *Wiltsie*; caused three cracks in the fantail area of the main deck and the loss of two ladders; and ripped two holes in the port bow of the motor whaleboat. Numerous examples of smaller damage were recorded below decks, inside the ship.

An underway replenishment with *Sacramento* (AOE-1) on the evening of 29 November turned out to be a difficult affair. Only after three separate approaches, seven fuel hose separations, and seven hours alongside was the fueling completed. The ship remained blackened by oil on parts of her superstructure and hull sides until after she arrived at San Diego on 3 December. After over 50,000 miles of steaming, *Wiltsie* moored at San Diego for upkeep which would last into the new year, 1967.

Following operations off the southern California coast in the spring and into the summer, *Wiltsie* departed San Diego on 19 September 1967, bound for the Far East. After stopovers at Pearl Harbor and Guam, the destroyer arrived at Subic Bay on 11 October. Shift-

ing to Danang, South Vietnam, soon thereafter, *Wiltsie* moved to the northern SAR station on 21 October and shifted to the southern SAR station five days later. Typhoon "Emma" forced the ship to sortie from Tonkin Gulf on 5 November, before the storm abated enough to allow the ship to resume her operations on the 7th.

During this tour, she assisted in the search for two men lost overboard from *William V. Pratt* (DLG-13). *King* (DLG-10) and *Chevalier* (DD-805) also took part, but 12-foot seas and 30-knot winds hampered search operations and prevented any of the ships from sighting the men.

On 13 November, *Wiltsie* relieved *Buck* (DD-761) on the northern SAR station, only to be relieved in turn by *Rogers* (DD-876) after an uneventful tour. Bad weather had cancelled the air strikes planned against enemy positions ashore. After rest and relaxation at Hong Kong, an upkeep alongside *Klondike* (AD-22), and an in-port period at Subic Bay, *Wiltsie* returned to the SAR station in Tonkin Gulf, operating in company with *King*. During this second deployment, *Wiltsie* participated in six rescues involving 10 men. The first took place at 1420 on 22 December, when an A-7 Corsair II from VA-147 went down at a position some 40 miles northwest of *King*.

An intensive search failed to locate the downed plane's pilot, and all search aircraft were vectored back to their base. *Wiltsie* refueled a helicopter during this period when the chopper approached the ship low on fuel. The Christmas cease-fire which went into effect on 25 December resulted in only photo-reconnaissance flights being run against North Vietnam; no SAR opportunities were thus presented to *Wiltsie* and *King* until 29 December, when an F-4 Phantom of VF-161 (*Coral Sea*) crashed 51 miles from the northern SAR station among some islands off the coast near Haiphong. *King* guided a helicopter to the scene and it picked up both pilots—cold but well—and returned them to their carrier, *Coral Sea*.

Monsoons limited air action over the last few days of 1967 and the first few days of 1968. Two *Oriskany* planes went down on 10 January 1968; *Wiltsie* provided communications relays where necessary and closely plotted aircraft positions, while *King* assumed air control function and direction. The latter's UH-2 helicopter picked up two pilots from one of the planes while a logistics helo plucked the crewman of the second plane from the water. Later in the day, *King* picked up two more downed pilots, giving her a total of four for the day.

After being relieved by *De Haven* (DD-727) and *Reeves* (DLG-24), *King* sailed to Subic Bay and *Wiltsie* to Hong Kong before she, too, headed for Subic Bay, where she arrived on the 23d. Three days later, while at Subic Bay, *Wiltsie* received word of the capture of the American intelligence-gathering vessel *Pueblo* (AGER-2). On the following day, *Wiltsie* and *King* sailed for SAR station to relieve *De Haven* and *Reeves* a day early.

When the SAR station was shifted south, *Wiltsie*, *King*, and the PIRAZ station ship *Belknap* (DLG-26) conducted joint patrols in the heavy weather hanging over the station. *Wiltsie*'s SAR tour was largely uneventful, as monsoon activity curtailed American air strikes over the north, and no opportunities presented themselves to pick up airmen.

Relieved by *Southerland* (DD-743) on station on 17 February, *Wiltsie* sailed to Subic Bay where she off-loaded part of her ammunition in preparation for the cruise home. Departing there on 22 February in company with *Buck* and *King*, *Wiltsie* and her consorts made a fuel stop at Darwin and visited Brisbane from 2 to 7 March before proceeding on to the west coast of the United States.

Following stops at Pago Pago, American Samoa, and Pearl Harbor, for fuel, *Wiltsie* moored at San Diego on 23 March and remained there into May. On 22 May, she became schoolship for an engineering officers' course and performed this duty until 9 June.

Assigned plane guard duties for *Hancock* (CVA–19) during that ship's carrier qualification evolution from 10 to 22 June, *Wiltsie* put her own motor whaleboat in the water on one occasion when one of the carrier's F-8 Crusaders went into the water immediately after take-off. However, *Hancock*'s rescue helo effected the rescue before the destroyer's boat arrived.

On the 26th, *Wiltsie* sailed for San Francisco Bay to undergo an overhaul at the naval shipyard at Vallejo, Calif. Emerging from the yard on 6 November, *Wiltsie* spent the remainder of 1968 in refresher training which continued into the spring of 1969.

Departing San Diego on 16 April 1969, in company with the remainder of DesDiv 72—*Buck, John W. Thomason* (DD-760), and *Perkins* (DD-877)—*Wiltsie* participated in type training evolutions with *Oriskany* before arriving at Pearl Harbor on 24 April. Underway again soon thereafter, bound for the ship's WestPac deployment, *Wiltsie* refueled at Midway, steamed on picket station ahead of *Oriskany*, and arrived at Subic Bay on 10 May.

Underway for Yankee Station soon thereafter, *Wiltsie* arrived there on 16 May and was soon shuffled between three carriers—*Oriskany, Bon Homme Richard* (CVA-31), and *Ticonderoga* (CVA-14)—within a 24-hour span, serving successively as plane guard for each. Returning to Subic Bay in company with *Ticonderoga* on 20 May, *Wiltsie* underwent a tender upkeep alongside *Klondike* (AD-22) before being shifted to Sasebo, Japan. At Sasebo from 29 May to 6 June, *Wiltsie* then deployed to Yankee Station to provide "shotgun" services for *Benjamin Stoddert* (DDG-22). When *Wiltsie*'s evaporators broke down on the 10th, the destroyer was relieved by *Douglas H. Fox* (DD-779) and headed back to Sasebo for repairs.

She subsequently operated in the Sea of Japan escorting *Sterett* (DLG-31) for three weeks before returning to Sasebo on 13 July. Eleven days later, the destroyer departed Japanese waters, bound for the Vietnam war zone.

Wiltsie provided plane guard services for *Bon Homme Richard* until detached to join *Biddle* (DLG-34) and *Chicago* (CG-11) on the south SAR station. After conducting antisubmarine warfare exercises en route, *Wiltsie* spent from 7 to 10 August on south SAR before deploying to the PIRAZ station with *King* on the 10th, 11th, and 12th. Returning to south SAR on the 13th, she remained at sea there for the remainder of August.

After rejoining *Bon Homme Richard*, *Wiltsie* escorted the carrier to Sasebo, Japan, from 2 to 4 September. Following a period of upkeep and recreation there, the destroyer visited Hong Kong en route to her final commitment in the Vietnamese war zone. She was deployed on Yankee Station for the remainder of September, and the destroyer then shifted to Subic Bay. There, she prepared for a gunnery exercise and proceeded to sea on 10 October for operations with *Craig* (DD-885) and *Cochrane* (DDG-21). On that day, *Wiltsie* participated in sinking the after section of the hull of *Frank E. Evans* (DD-754), the destroyer that had been cut in two during a collision with Australian aircraft carrier HMAS *Melbourne* the previous 3 June.

Rendezvousing with *Bon Homme Richard* soon thereafter, *Wiltsie* and the carrier steamed to Japan, arriving at Yokosuka on 15 October. Two days later, with ComDesDiv 72 embarked, *Wiltsie* got underway with the remainder of her division to escort *Bon Homme Richard* back to the United States and arrived at San Diego at the end of a fortnight's voyage. For the remainder of 1969, the destroyer remained in her home port.

Wiltsie conducted an ASW training operation early in January 1970 and returned to San Diego on the 8th. Between that day and 15 April, *Wiltsie* remained in port. During this time, she suffered hull damage while moored alongside *John W. Thomason*. "Exceptionally high winds" buffeted the ships together when a mooring camel between the two ships overturned, opening riveted seams in *Wiltsie*'s hull. On 13 March 1970, *Wiltsie* was drydocked at the San Diego Marine and Shipbuilding Co. and was under repairs there until 7 April.

After operating locally out of San Diego into the summer, *Wiltsie* departed her home port on 27 July 1970, bound for her 18th WestPac deployment. Following stops at Pearl Harbor, Midway, and Guam, she arrived at Subic Bay on 18 August. There, she took on additional .50-caliber machine guns and flak jackets before getting underway on 21 August for the Gulf of Tonkin.

Relieving *Gurke* (DD-783) three days later as picket for *Bainbridge* (DLGN-25) on TF 77's northern SAR/PIRAZ station, *Wiltsie* operated on station until 9 September. During that assignment, the ship provided in-flight refueling services to ship and shore-based helicopters standing ready to rescue downed aircrews. Although the ship originally headed for Kaohsiung for upkeep, the track of Typhoon "Georgia" resulted in a re-routing to Subic Bay.

Departing Luzon on 18 September, *Wiltsie* sailed for regions II and III of South Vietnam to perform 22 days of gunfire support duty to assist operations of the United States 1st Air Cavalry Division; the 1st Australian Task Force, South; and an ARVN battalion. During the deployment on the "gun line"—her first since 1967—*Wiltsie* fired 3,365 rounds of 5-inch ammunition before she departed the station on 11 October and headed for Taiwan for rest and recreation at Keelung.

While there, *Wiltsie* was preparing to move on to Japan when urgent orders arrived on the evening of 19 October to report back to the "gun line." Typhoon "Joan" had damaged another destroyer severely enough to limit her ability to fight, so *Wiltsie* was substituted. Arriving at her station in the Gulf of Thailand on the morning of 23 October, *Wiltsie* supported the ARVN 21st Division with gunfire, shelling communist troop concentrations, gun positions, and supply lines for five days, expending 485 rounds of 5-inch projectiles.

Returning to Subic Bay, she offloaded the special equipment taken on board for the "gunline" deployments—flak jackets, .50-caliber machine guns (for use against possible sappers or small boats), and "pool radio equipment"—and departed the Philippines on 20 January, bound for the United States. After stopping en route at Guam, Midway, and Pearl Harbor, *Wiltsie* arrived at San Diego on 11 February.

During the ensuing year, *Wiltsie* remained on the coast of southern California, for the most part at San Diego. In March and April, she served plane guard duty for *Oriskany* and *Enterprise* (CVA-65); and, in June, she entered the Long Beach Naval Shipyard for an overhaul which lasted until mid-November 1971.

On 19 February 1972, the destroyer was notified that, effective 1 July, she would be assigned to the Naval Reserve Force and based at San Francisco for training duty. While she was in the Hunters Point Naval Shipyard preparing for her new role, however, she received word on 22 May that—instead of beginning reserve duty in July—she would head back to the Far East for her 19th deployment in the western Pacific.

On 25 July, *Wiltsie* sailed for the Orient in company with *Meyerkord* (DE-1058) and *Lang* (DE-1060) and touched at Pearl Harbor, Midway, and Guam before arriving at Subic Bay on 16 August.

Refueling and rearming from *Ashtabula* (AO-51) on the 29th, *Wiltsie* headed north, for Japan, sidestepping Typhoon "Kate" en route. She reduced her speed to 12 knots in the worsening weather conditions before putting into Buckner Bay, Okinawa, to refuel on 2 November before again setting out for Sasebo. The next morning, while underway and approaching the coast of Kyushu, Fire Control Technician 3d Class Bernhardt L. Olsen was swept over the side. *Wiltsie*, joined by *Richard B. Anderson*, and the Japanese Maritime Self Defense Force vessels *Asagunmo, Makiguma,* and *Hickugo,* conducted a day-long search for her missing sailor but came away empty-handed. A few days later, his body was discovered washed up on a nearby island.

Later departing Sasebo on 6 November, she served as screen for *King* as a Peacetime Aerial Reconnaissance Program (PARPRO) picket in the Sea of Japan from the 8th to the 10th, before returning to Sasebo. Shifting to Korean waters for a port visit to Pusan, South Korea, from 27 to 30 November, and replenishing at Sasebo, *Wiltsie* served a second tour as PARPRO picket ship for *Halsey* (DLG–23) from 30 November to 6 December.

Subsequently returning again to Sasebo to replenish, *Wiltsie* refueled at Keelung and spent Christmas at Hong Kong before shifting to the Philippines where she spent the remainder of 1970. Early in 1971, the destroyer returned to Vietnamese coastal waters to render gunfire support for South Vietnamese army units between 4 and 18 January 1971.

Undergoing four days of upkeep and repairs alongside *Jason* (ARH–1), *Wiltsie* prepared for another "gun line" mission off the Vietnamese coast. The destroyer loaded the extra equipment necessary for her specialized support role—flak jackets for exposed personnel, .50-caliber machine guns, and special radio equipment for contacting shore units calling for gunfire support. Ready for action, *Wiltsie* departed Subic Bay on 21 August. While en route to Vietnam, the destroyer spotted a submarine, which quickly submerged when she, in turn, spotted *Wiltsie*. Her sonarmen tracked the submarine for an hour before being informed that the stranger was, in fact, friendly.

On 23 August, *Wiltsie* became part of TG 75.9, operating off the Northern Military Region I. While providing gunfire support for Operation "Lam Son 72," the destroyer fired some 1,803 rounds of 5-inch shells to support the ARVN 147th Brigade in efforts to destroy enemy forces in their area. Typhoon "Elsie," which was approaching near the DMZ, temporarily suspended *Wiltsie*'s gunfire support operations while she sidestepped the tropical disturbance by moving to safer waters. Resuming her operations after three days of typhoon evasion, *Wiltsie* returned to the "gun line" and supported ARVN operations around Quang Tri City. Ordered to proceed south on 6 September, *Wiltsie* departed the waters off northern South Vietnam to fire gunnery missions supporting the 2d ARVN Division in the vicinity of Chu Lai.

Terminating her operations supporting the 2d ARVN Division to shift to interdiction of waterborne logistics craft and surveillance of merchant ships in the Hon La anchorage in North Vietnam, *Wiltsie* found diversified operations and hostile fire in store for her. Her 5-inch guns wreaked havoc on storage dumps, coastal defense sites, radar installations, and supply routes. On 14 September, she spotted a crippled A–7 Corsair plunging into the Gulf of Tonkin and soon thereafter rescued the pilot from the water.

Two days later, she conducted a single-ship raid against a bridge on a major North Vietnamese supply route. During the action, she came under fire from North Vietnamese shore batteries that fired some 70 rounds at the destroyer. This was the only time that the ship came under hostile fire in Vietnam. The next day, *Wiltsie* and two other ships conducted a "reactive strike" on the coastal defense site, pounding it with 5-inch gunfire. Supply route and waterborne supply interdiction continued thereafter until *Wiltsie*, relieved by *Henry W. Tucker* (DD–875), departed the area on the 20th.

Returning to Subic Bay for upkeep on the 21st, the destroyer remained in port until 27 September when she sailed for the Gulf of Thailand for gunnery support duties off the west coast of Vietnam. Between late September and early November, *Wiltsie* operated on station in the Gulf of Thailand. During the gunfire operations, she expended 1,940 rounds of 5-inch into the U Minh forest, supporting the ARVN 21st Division. Gunfire direction was provided by air spotting, but the dense foliage of the U Minh forest often prevented assessment of results.

In addition to her gunfire support duties, *Wiltsie* was given the task of detecting and tracking waterborne supply traffic. Supported in this operation by P–3 Orion patrol planes, *Wiltsie* discouraged the enemy from attempting supply by sea along the western coastline of South Vietnam. *Henry W. Tucker* relieved *Wiltsie* on 2 November.

After a week of upkeep at Singapore, *Wiltsie* resumed gunfire support operations in Military Region I near the DMZ. She spent a week firing round-the-clock gunfire support missions before joining *Saratoga* (CVA–60) with TU 72.0.1, as plane-guard destroyer. Between 21 November and 8 December, she escorted the attack carrier as she launched air strikes against enemy forces ashore. In the predawn hours of 28 November, an A–6 Intruder crashed upon takeoff; and *Wiltsie* proceeded to the scene of the accident, pinpointing the location and vectoring rescue helicopters from *Saratoga* to the point. One of the aircraft's crew was rescued quickly and returned to his carrier, but the other pilot, despite the combined efforts of *Bainbridge* and helicopters from *America* (CVA–66), was never found.

Wiltsie proceeded to Hong Kong for rest and recreation and to Kaohsiung for an upkeep alongside *Bryce Canyon* (AD–36). During this availability, all four of her 5-inch guns were rebarreled due to the excessive wear experienced during her gunfire support deployments. The ship departed Taiwan on 27 December to return to the "gun line."

Arriving on station two days later, she resumed her operations off Quang Tri City, south of the DMZ, and continued these operations until 22 January 1973, when she was detached from TG 75.9 to proceed to Yokosuka. From there, the ship sailed for home, arriving at her new home port, San Francisco, on 16 February.

However, *Wiltsie*'s time on the west coast was comparatively brief for—following a yard period at Willamette Shipyard, Richmond, Calif.—she got underway again for WestPac on 16 June 1973. Arriving at Yokosuka, via Adak, Alaska, on 28 June, the destroyer shifted to Kure before conducting ASWEX 7–73 with Japanese Maritime Self Defense Force units from 9 to 12 July. Moving to Kaohsiung on 22 July, the ship participated in Exercise "Sharkhunt II" with Chinese units before spending an in-port period at Keelung from 28 July to 1 August.

Soon thereafter, *Wiltsie* returned home via Pearl Harbor, arriving at San Francisco on 30 August. She participated in COMPTUEX II–73 in October and served as plane guard for *Coral Sea* in local operations off the California coast in December. The destroyer continued the routine of local operations out of San Francisco for the remainder of her active service, embarking Naval Reserve units for active duty training on cruises off the west coast and to Hawaii and, on occasion, serving as escort vessel for submarines on their sea trials out of Mare Island. Decommissioning preparations began at Alameda in November 1975, and *Wiltsie* was decommissioned there on 23 January 1976. Simultaneously struck from the Navy list, the veteran of Korean War and Vietnam service was transferred, via sale, to Pakistan.

Transferred on 29 April 1977, the destroyer was reactivated and overhauled during 1977. Renamed *Tariq* (D.165), the ship reached Pakistan in mid-1978 to commence her active service with the Pakistani Navy.

Wiltsie (DD–716) received eight battle stars for Korean War service and seven for Vietnam.

Wimbee

(IX–88: dp. 22; l. 59′9″; b. 13′3″; dr. 8′2″; s. 7 k.)

Condor—an auxiliary yawl built in 1938 at Bremen, Germany—was acquired by the Navy from Mr. W. L.

MacFarland of Greenwich, Conn., in August 1942 to serve in what Samuel Eliot Morison has called the "Hooligan Navy," a motley assortment of sailing ships and pleasure craft assembled by the Navy to combat the U-boat menace before America's huge antisubmarine warship production program hit full gear. She was renamed *Wimbee* and was placed in service at Port Everglades, Fla., on 11 September 1942. Assigned to the 7th Naval District, *Wimbee* served only five months in the Navy, for the most part conducting antisubmarine patrols in the Gulf of Mexico. On 17 March 1943, she was placed out of service. Struck from the Navy list on 28 June 1944, she was transferred to the Maritime Commission and sold on 7 February 1945 to Mr. Paul Liskey of Harrisonburg, Va.

Winamac

A Potawatomi Indian chief who assisted General William Henry Harrison in securing the Treaty of Fort Wayne in 1809.

(YTB–394: dp. 345 (f.); l. 100'; b. 25'; dr. 11'; s. 12 k.; cpl. 14; cl. *Sassaba*)

Winamac (YT–394) was laid down on 8 November 1943 at Jacksonville, Fla., by the Gibbs Gas Engine Co.; launched on 7 March 1944; sponsored by Mrs. William F. James, the wife of Lt. (jg.) W. F. James, USNR, assistant superintendent of shipbuilding at Jacksonville; reclassified YTB–394 on 15 May 1944; and placed in service on 12 September 1944.

Winamac operated actively in the 11th Naval District, San Diego, Calif., until she was placed in reserve, in service, in August 1946. She then probably assisted in the berthing of ships in the Pacific Reserve Fleet. However, her time in reserve was comparatively short, for she was placed in active service in August 1947. Reclassified YTM–394 in February 1962, *Winamac* has served in the 11th Naval District since the summer of 1947 and remained there, providing tug and tow services to ships of the Fleet and standing ready to provide pilotage and waterfront fire protection into late 1979.

Winchester

(Steam Yacht: t. 399 (gross); l. 225'; b. 21'; dr. 5'6" aft); s. 31.65 k.; a. 1 3'', 1 6-pdr., 2 mg., 1 Y-gun)

Winchester (SP–156)—a steel-hulled yacht built in 1916 by the Bath Iron Works, at Bath, Maine—was acquired on 30 May 1917 from Mr. Peter W. Rouss and

commissioned on 4 September 1917, Lt. (jg.) R. C. Nickerson, USNRF, in command.

Winchester was initially assigned to section patrol duty in the 2d Naval District. From commissioning to January 1918, she patrolled the coasts of Massachusetts and Connecticut between Chatham and New London. In January 1918, she was reassigned to the 5th Naval District and operated in the Norfolk-Hampton Roads area of Virginia until a month after the end of World War I. Throughout the latter period, she was assigned to special duty with the Bureau of Construction and Repair to test minesweeping equipment. Late in December 1918, she moved once again, this time to City Island, N.Y., but her testing duties continued almost uninterrupted until decommissioning. On 13 April 1919, she returned to the 5th Naval District. *Winchester* operated out of Yorktown, Va., until placed out of commission at Norfolk on 19 December 1919. After several attempts, she was finally sold to Cox & Stevens, of New York City, on 24 March 1921.

Winder

A city in northern Georgia about 20 miles west of Athens and some 40 miles east-northeast of Atlanta. The community is the seat of government for Barrow County.

(PCS–1376: dp. 245 (tl.); l. 136'0"; b. 24'6"; dr. 8'7"; s. 14.1 k. (tl.); cpl. 57; a. 1 3'', 1 40mm., 2 20mm., 2 dct.; cl. *PCS–1376*)

PCS–1376 was laid down on 13 October 1942 at Whitestone, N.Y., by the Wheeler Shipbuilding Corp.; launched on 3 April 1943; sponsored by Mrs. J. E. Flipse; and commissioned on 9 July 1943, Lt. (jg.) J. P. Morgan III, USNR, in command.

Following several days of trials, *PCS–1376* departed Long Island for shakedown training in the vicinity of Cuba. At the conclusion of the cruise in August, she reported for duty as a school ship at the Submarine Chaser School located at Miami, Fla. The warship did double duty until the end of 1943 conducting antisubmarine patrols at night and training submarine chaser nucleus crews in the daytime. On New Year's Day 1944, she discontinued her nightly antisubmarine patrols and concentrated on preparing crews to man new submarine chasers. On 1 October 1944, she also gave up training duty but continued to support the school's mission by acting as an escort for larger ships conducting the actual at-sea training. That type of duty lasted until the cessation of hostilities in August 1945 at which time she resumed actual onboard training.

The fast, destroyerlike yacht *Winchester* (SP–156), armed for Navy service during World War I.

That assignment, however, endured for only two months. On 8 October 1945, she received orders to report for duty with the Atlantic Fleet Operational Training Command at Norfolk, Va. On 29 October, she began an extended availability at the conclusion of which on 21 December the ship headed for Norfolk. By March 1946, the submarine chaser was homeported at Charleston, S.C., engaged in training naval reservists. However, by the beginning of 1947, she had moved back to Norfolk. On 28 February 1947, *PCS–1376* was placed out of commission but remained active with the 5th Naval District Naval Reserve training program. On 10 June 1947, the ship was placed in service and continued her Naval Reserve training duties at Norfolk. On 4 January 1950, she was again placed out of service and was berthed at Norfolk. In May 1950, she was reassigned from the Norfolk Group, Atlantic Reserve Fleet, to the Green Cove Springs (Fla.) Group. There, she remained until the middle of 1957. On 15 February 1956, she was named *Winder*. However, she carried that name only 19 months, because her name was struck from the Navy list on 5 September 1957. She was sold for scrapping on 15 April 1958 to Mr. Fred Irvine of Miami, Fla.

Windham Bay

A bay on the southeastern coast of Alaska off Frederick Sound.

(CVE–92: dp. 10,400 (f.); l. 512'3"; b. 65'2"; ew. 108'1"; dr. 22'6"; s. 19.3 k. (tl.); cpl. 860; ac. 28; a. 1 5", 16 40mm.; cl. *Casablanca*)

Windham Bay (CVE–92) was laid down under a Maritime Commission contract (MC hull 1129) on 5 January 1944 at Vancouver, Wash., by the Kaiser Shipbuilding Co.; launched on 29 March 1944; sponsored by Mrs. Henry M. Cooper; and commissioned on 3 May 1944, Capt. Charles W. Oexle in command.

Following commissioning, *Windham Bay* conducted shakedown training in Puget Sound and then headed for San Diego on 6 June. There, she conducted air qualifications and catapult trials before taking on a load of Hawaii-bound aircraft and passengers. She departed San Diego on 12 June and arrived in Pearl Harbor on the 19th. Trading her cargo of aircraft and passengers for a similar one bound for the Marshall Islands, *Windham Bay* stood out of the harbor on 25 June and arrived at Majuro on 2 July. After unloading her aircraft, she moved on to Kwajalein where she loaded planes and men of Marine Night Fighter Squadron 532 and headed for the Marianas. The marines flew off near Saipan, and *Windham Bay* put into Garapan anchorage to unload the squadron's gear.

Afterward, the escort carrier took on a load of captured Japanese aircraft and other material for transportation back to Hawaii. She arrived in Pearl Harbor on 10 July and remained there for 15 days, getting underway for the west coast on 25 July. The warship arrived in San Diego on 31 July and soon began overhaul at San Pedro.

Repairs took the entire month of August, but she was back at sea on 1 September with a load of aircraft bound for Emirau and Manus. She arrived at Emirau at mid-month and at Manus on the 18th. From there, she voyaged to Espiritu Santo on a passenger run, returning to Manus on 5 October with a load of planes. After a brief visit to Guadalcanal during the second week in October, she got underway for the United States. *Windham Bay* steamed via Espiritu Santo and arrived in San Diego on 20 October. In November, she made another voyage from the west coast to the South Pacific, carrying aircraft to Manus and picking up about 350 casualties from the Palau campaign at Guadalcanal on 24 November for the return voyage to San Diego.

The escort carrier remained at San Diego from 10 December until the 27th when she resumed aircraft

ferrying operations. She arrived in Pearl Harbor on 2 January 1945, unloaded one cargo of aircraft there and took on another made up of F4U Corsairs. She departed Pearl Harbor on 5 January and arrived at Midway Island on the 9th to unload the Corsairs. Departing Midway the next day, *Windham Bay* returned to Oahu on the 13th. On 1 February, the ship stood out of Pearl Harbor on her way to the Central Pacific. Carrying replacement aircraft for the fleet carriers of Task Force 58, she made a stop at Eniwetok on her way to the staging base at Ulithi Atoll in the Western Carolines.

From there, she operated with the 5th Fleet Logistics Group, Task Group 50.8, in support of the fast carrier strikes conducted during the Iwo Jima and Okinawa operations. During the next four months, she visited Guam and the Ryukyu Islands. On 4 to 5 June, while steaming with the logistics group in support of TF 58 and the strikes on Okinawa, the carrier steamed right through the famous typhoon of 1945, suffering lost and damaged planes as well as damage to her flight and hangar decks. On 16 June, she cleared the Marianas en route to Oahu. The warship arrived in Pearl Harbor on the 25th but departed again two days later. She entered port at San Diego on 11 July and immediately began repairs to correct the typhoon damage she had suffered earlier in the month. Those repairs lasted through late August so that she missed the final weeks of the war.

On 26 August, she departed San Diego on her way back to the Central Pacific carrying Marine Fighter Squadron (VMF) 312 to Guam. She stopped briefly at Pearl Harbor and arrived in Apra Harbor on 15 September. After unloading passengers and cargo at Guam, *Windham Bay* headed for Samar in the Philippines where she arrived on 19 September. There, she loaded passengers, planes, and equipment for transportation back to Hawaii. She got underway from Leyte on 24 September, made a stop at Guam on the 27th, and arrived back at Oahu on 7 October. On the 8th, she continued eastward toward the west coast and arrived at San Diego on the 14th.

Five days later, the ship headed back to Pearl Harbor on her way to participate in Operation "Magic Carpet," the return of American servicemen to the United States. After a round-trip voyage to San Pedro, Calif., and back to Pearl Harbor, she set out for the western Pacific once more on 13 November. Arriving at Samar in the Philippines on the 26th, she loaded passengers and then headed east again on the 28th. She stopped at Oahu along the way and arrived in Port Hueneme, Calif., on 17 December. She moved to San Pedro on the 18th and remained there through the New Year.

On 8 January 1946, *Windham Bay* departed San Pedro, headed for Hawaii, and arrived in Pearl Harbor on 14 January. She departed Oahu again on the 15th and arrived in San Pedro on the 21st. Within days, however, she moved north to Tacoma, Wash., where she reported for duty with the Pacfic Reserve Fleet on 25 January 1946. She remained there—in commission, in reserve—until 23 August 1946 when she was placed out of commission.

The escort carrier stayed with the Reserve Fleet until hostilities erupted in Korea during the summer of 1950. On 28 October 1950, she was recommissioned at Bremerton, Wash., Capt. Charles E. Brunton in command. On 20 November, she steamed south to California, visiting San Francisco on the way to San Diego where she arrived on 2 December. After 11 days, the escort carrier returned to San Francisco whence she embarked upon a voyage to Pearl Harbor on the 19th. Returning to the west coast at Alameda on 2 January 1951, the warship headed west again five days later. She arrived in Yokohama, Japan, on the 24th and unloaded a cargo of aircraft for use in the Korean conflict which the United States had entered under the auspices of the United Nations. Departing Japan two days later, she visited Saigon in French Indochina and Manila in the

Philippines before shaping a course back to the United States. *Windham Bay* reentered San Francisco Bay on 24 February.

At this juncture, the escort carrier settled into a routine of transpacific resupply voyages between the United States and Japan. Over the next 20 months, she made nine round-trip voyages, beginning each at either San Francisco or San Diego, stopping always at Yokosuka, and returning always to San Francisco. She broke that nine-voyage routine in October and November 1952 when she visited Takao, Japan, and Bangkok, Thailand, before returning via Japan to the west coast at Alameda on 9 December.

Windham Bay continued her aircraft ferrying voyages between the United States and Japan during 1953. The war in Korea, however, began to subside in intensity at about the same time, and her passages began to take on more of a peacetime character. She began making more stops and side trips in addition to Yokosuka—notably to Hawaii, the Philippines, and at other Japanese ports. French Indochina also returned to her itinerary in May of 1954 and again in February and March of 1955 when she made visits to Saigon, capital of the newly constituted Republic of South Vietnam. On 12 June 1955, she was redesignated CVU–92. In May 1957, she added Naha, Okinawa, to her list of ports of call; and, in December, she made one more stop at Saigon. Otherwise, the remainder of her career consisted of the normal west coast-to-Japan aircraft resupply voyages in support of the fast carriers assigned to the western Pacific.

Her career lasted until the end of 1958. In January 1959, she was decommissioned and was berthed with the San Francisco Group, Pacific Reserve Fleet. Her name was struck from the Navy list on 1 February 1959, and she was subsequently sold to the Hugo Neu Steel Products Corp., of New York City. The ship was scrapped in Japan in February of 1961.

Windham Bay earned three battle stars during World War II.

Windham County

Counties in Connecticut and Vermont.

(LST–1170: dp. 2,590; l. 384'; b. 55'6''; dr. 16'2''; s. 14 k.; cpl. 157; a. 6 3''; cl. *LST–1156*)

LST–1170 was laid down on 21 April 1953 by the Christy Corp., Sturgeon Bay, Wis.; launched on 22 May 1954; sponsored by Mrs. Joseph McCarthy; and commissioned on 15 December 1954, Lt. Comdr. Max Wells in command.

The new tank landing ship joined the Atlantic Fleet at her home port, Little Creek, Va., in January 1955. Following shakedown and type training, the ship was named *Windham County* on 1 July 1955 and spent much of that month and August in more training exercises. She helped to support Operation "Caesar," an underwater surveillance project, which lasted through the end of the year.

On 21 February 1956, the ship reported to the Norfolk Naval Shipyard for overhaul and conversion.

From January to mid-March 1957, LST–1170 operated off the Virginia capes area. On 14 March, after a brief stop at Davisville, R.I., *Windham County* proceeded to the Caribbean for operations off Barbados. Upon returning to Little Creek on 1 April 1957, she operated from home port until 2 May, when she was deployed to the Mediterranean Sea for a tour of duty with the 6th Fleet. During the cruise, she made stops at Tangier, Morocco; Spain; Malta; Italy; and Gibraltar. She returned to Davisville on 1 October; then headed for Little Creek, arriving there on 18 October 1957. She got underway for the Caribbean on 14 November for a fortnight of exercises. After returning to Little Creek on the 26th, she ended the year, 1957, undergoing routine upkeep.

In January 1958, *Windham County* transited the Panama Canal and arrived at San Diego on the 27th. Following some four months of operations on the west coast, she sailed for the Western Pacific (WestPac) on 6 June, touched at Pearl Harbor, and arrived in Yokosuka, Japan, for a six-month deployment. While lifting Marine Corps units and cargo, she visited Kure, Kobe, Yokohama, and Sasebo, Japan; Subic Bay, Philippines; Okinawa; Formosa; Korea; and Hong Kong.

Windham County returned to San Diego on 10 December 1958. The ship engaged in three full-scale amphibious exercises the first half of 1959. She then operated along the southern California coast until 28 November when she headed north and arrived at San Francisco on 1 December 1959.

Following a two-month overhaul, *Windham County* returned to San Diego and spent the late winter and early spring in intensive refresher training. The ship prepared for a change of her home port from San Diego to Yokosuka, where she was to become a unit of LST Division 92 of Landing Ship Squadron 9. On 16 June, the ship departed San Diego; and she arrived at Yokosuka on 19 July. In September, she received notice that she would participate in a United Nations troop lift from Malaya to the Republic of the Congo. On 4 October 1960, the ship arrived at Port Swettenham, Malaya, where she embarked 300 Malayan troops. The ship then steamed for 27 consecutive days before arriving at Matadi, Republic of the Congo, on 31 October, having crossed the Indian Ocean, rounded the Cape of Good Hope, and navigated the Congo River. The ship departed Matadi on 31 October and arrived at Capetown, South Africa, on 11 November. She then visited Singapore and Hong Kong before returning to Yokosuka on 20 December 1960.

On 4 January 1961, *Windham County* stood out to sea to carry Marine Corps troops from Iwakuni, Japan, to Cubi Point, Philippines. During February, the tank landing ship carried another group of marines from Okinawa to Numazu, Japan. On 24 March, she began a period of shuttling marines and equipment between Yokosuka and Okinawa which lasted until early in May. The ship then participated in SEATO Operation "Pony Express" on North Borneo. Upon the completion of this mission, she returned via Subic Bay to Yokosuka where she arrived on 9 June.

On 1 August, the ship entered the Ship Repair Facility, Yokosuka, for an overhaul. Beginning on 23 October, she conducted a three-week underway training period; and, on 20 November, she commenced two weeks of amphibious training with the Japanese Maritime Self-Defense Force; then spent the remainder of the year at Yokosuka undergoing upkeep.

The ship sailed on 25 January 1962 for Numazu, Japan, to take on marines and took them to Okinawa, before visiting Hong Kong and Subic Bay. Shortly thereafter, the ship took part in SEATO Operation "Tunlungan" at Mindoro, Philippines, and then reembarked participating troops for transport to Naha and Iwakuni, Japan.

Windham County visited Bangkok, Thailand, in June 1962 and in late July went to Inchon, Korea, to pick up Army troops bound for Pohang, Korea. Upon completion of that task, she returned to Yokosuka. Runs to Numazu and Naha with troops in October preceded her return to Yokosuka for upkeep. December 1962 brought her independent ship's exercises and marine troop lifts from Numazu to Naha.

On 3 January 1963, *Windham County* got underway for Hong Kong, where she served as a station ship and did much to promote the "People to People" program. She returned to Yokosuka in February but left on 2 March to lift marines to Taiwan and then spent the rest of the month and most of April in upkeep in Yokosuka. From May through September, *Windham County* underwent an overhaul which began in Sasebo and was completed at Yokosuka. October and November were devoted to underway and refresher training. On 5

December 1963, the ship headed for Okinawa for type training and a troop lift back to Japan. After unloading her passengers at Numazu, she returned to Yokosuka on 18 December for an inspection and upkeep holiday period.

Windham County sailed on 2 January 1964 for Korea to participate in Operation "Firehouse," a cold weather amphibious assault conducted at Chumunjin. Late in January she returned to Yokosuka for upkeep and left on 26 February to take part in Operation "Backpack," a joint American-Taiwanese practice amphibious assault which took place at Che Cheng, Taiwan. She returned to Yokosuka on 26 March 1964 and, from April until June, conducted lifts and training exercises which took her to Taiwan; Iwakuni, Japan; Okinawa; and Hong Kong. On 17 June, *Windham County* took on Korean Army students and carried them to Pusan to observe a demonstration of amphibious and beachhead staging techniques.

On 21 July 1964, the ship got underway for operations in Okinawan waters. While these exercises were still in progress, the Gulf of Tonkin incident occurred and necessitated a rapid buildup of Americans in South Vietnam and in nearby waters. The ship loaded marines and proceeded to the South China Sea, where she remained on station from 16 August to 28 September and spent 56 continuous days at sea. *Windham County* returned to Yokosuka on 19 October. She visited Beppu, Japan, from 19 to 23 November and participated in a variety of "People-to-People" activities. The ship proceeded to Iwakuni, Japan, for special operations which kept her busy until shortly before Christmas 1964, when the ship returned to Yokosuka for upkeep.

During January 1965, the LST was in Yokosuka for upkeep and type training. On 6 February, she left for training at Poyang, Korea, but was diverted to Okinawa on 8 February in a general alert of 7th Fleet forces. From March through May, she was involved in shuttles of personnel and cargo from Okinawa to Danang, Vietnam. On 31 May 1965, she returned to Yokosuka for upkeep. *Windham County* departed Yokosuka on 23 June and participated in various lift operations between Okinawa and Vietnam. Beginning on 5 September, she commenced an overhaul at Yokosuka.

Leaving the yard on 12 October 1965, *Windham County* was engaged in personnel- and cargo-carrying missions along the coast of Vietnam before returning to Yokosuka on 10 December for upkeep. *Windham County* departed on 6 January 1966 for Naha, Okinawa, and carried out numerous shuttles along the Vietnam coast. She arrived in Yokosuka on 5 June for hull repairs and, on 1 August, commenced regular yard overhaul in Yokosuka. The ship began sea trials on 7 December 1966 and ended the year with type training and upkeep.

Refresher training occupied January 1967, and the ship sailed on 15 February for almost two months of operations off the coast of Vietnam. On 15 April, *Windham County* headed for Okinawa and arrived at Naha on 20 April. She returned to Yokosuka on 24 April but, after a month of upkeep, got underway again on 26 May to resume transport duties off Vietnam. *Windham County* returned to Yokosuka on 20 July and entered normal upkeep. She departed on 9 August and, during the period of 19 August through 4 September, was involved in Operation "Schoolhouse Lift," delivering prefabricated structures to small villages throughout the Philippines.

On 4 September, the ship departed Manila and proceeded to Danang. Upon completion of several missions, she received upkeep in Subic Bay. After departing that base on 4 October, she returned, via Okinawa, to her home port for a short upkeep period. The ship departed on 29 October and headed back to Vietnam. She stopped briefly at Naha en route and also was diverted from her planned course to evade Typhoon "Emma" but finally reached Danang on 9 November. From the 10th to the 16th, she supported Operation "Badger Hunt" and then moved to Duc Pho to conduct salvage operations for *Clarke County* (LST–601) and *Iredell County* (LST–839). After the latter ship had been pulled free, *Windham County* escorted the damaged LST to Danang. She then returned to Duc Pho to provide a ready helicopter for subsequent operations. During the remainder of her deployment to Vietnam, she spent most of her time carrying troops, equipment, and mail to support operations ashore. On 27 December, she was detached from these duties and proceeded to Japan.

The ship arrived in Yokosuka on 5 January 1968 and commenced a period of upkeep and inspections. *Windham County* got underway for Kaohsiung, Taiwan, on 29 January to support "Former Champ," a joint United States-Chinese amphibious exercise. While in Taiwan, she also participated in amphibious Exercise "Final Round." Upon completing these, she headed for Yokosuka on 5 April and arrived there on 10 April. She promptly began a cycle of upkeep, type training, and inspection.

On 6 June, the ship left Yokosuka to return, via Okinawa, to Vietnam to serve as a support ship for Task Group (TG) 117.2 in the Mekong Delta. She arrived at Wunder Beach, Vietnam, on 17 June and unloaded 152 jeeps there before moving on to Vung Tau which she reached on the 20th and began almost two months of duty supporting riverine operations. On 15 August 1968, she set out for Thailand. After a five-day visit to Bangkok, the ship headed for Japan. However, Typhoon "Wendy" prevented the ship from stopping at Okinawa, and she proceeded to Yokosuka for a period of upkeep, arriving on 24 August. She again departed Yokosuka on 3 October to return to Vietnam. After several months of action, she reported to Subic Bay on 14 November for upkeep. She left the Philippines on 5 December and arrived at Yokosuka on 13 December 1968.

After a period of upkeep and inspections, *Windham County* departed Yokosuka on 10 March 1969 for Vietnam. She spent the remainder of March, April, and the first part of May operating in the Mekong Delta. She departed on the 10th and returned, via Subic Bay and Hong Kong, to Yokosuka on 1 June 1969. She left Japan on 23 July and set a course for Vietnam. *Windham County* began 1970 in preparation for overhaul at Yokosuka. That renewal effort was completed on 7 April. She sailed on the 13th for Korea to take part in Operation "Golden Dragon," a joint American-Korean amphibious exercise. She returned to Yokosuka on 5 May 1970 for upkeep and training. She left Yokosuka on 30 May and proceeded to the Philippines, arriving at Subic Bay on 13 June 1970 to begin exercises and upkeep After a brief trip to Hong Kong, the ship returned to Yokosuka on 20 August 1970. From August through early December, the ship was involved in shuttles between Okinawa and Japan and routine upkeep and inspection. On 12 December, *Windham County* got underway for Vietnam.

She remained in the combat zone for the rest of 1970 through 23 February 1971, when she was relieved and returned to Yokosuka, arriving on 12 March 1971. During the period from 12 March through 29 July, *Windham County* was involved in routine shuttles between Okinawa, Numazu, Subic Bay, and Yokosuka. On 29 July 1971, she arrived back in Vietnam and engaged in various operations off the coast. On 7 September 1971, she was relieved and returned to Yokosuka, arriving there on the 27th to begin a period of restricted availability. Beginning on 9 November, she made several shuttles to Okinawa and Numazu and went to Hong Kong in early November. She was relieved on 17 December and returned to Yokosuka on 23 December 1971 to finish the year in holiday routine.

Windham County departed in early February 1972 to resume her shuttle operations between Japan and Okinawa to Vietnam. In October, she visited Singapore and Bangkok; and, in November, she stopped in Hong Kong and Taiwan and then returned to Yokosuka in December 1972.

The tank landing ship *Windham County* (LST–1170). (USN 1106155)

An intensive period of preparation for transfer to the Turkish Navy began. *Windham County* was decommissioned on 1 June 1973 and turned over to the Turkish Navy. She was renamed TCG (Turkish Republic Ship) *Ertugrul* and assigned Turkish hull number L401.

She is the second ship to bear this name, the first being a Turkish Navy training vessel that was lost at sea with great loss of life in 1889 near Oshima Island, southern Japan, in a violent storm.

Windham County earned 10 battle stars for her service in Vietnam.

Windhover

A small European hawk named for its ability to hover over one spot despite the wind. The windhover is related to the American sparrowhawk.

Windhover (ASR–18)—projected as a *Chanticleer*-class submarine rescue vessel—was to be built at Savannah, Ga., by the Savannah Machine Foundry; but, because of Japan's collapse, the contract for her construction was cancelled on 12 August 1945.

Windigo

An alternate spelling of the Algonquian Indian word "weendigo" which means "cannibal." It refers to a mythical tribe of cannibals said by the Chippewa and Ottawa tribes to inhabit an island in Hudson Bay.

(YTB–421: dp. 345 (f.); l. 100'0"; b. 25'0"; dr. 9'7"; s. 12 k.; cpl. 8; cl. *Sassaba*)

Windigo (YTB–421) was laid down on 17 August 1944 at Curtis Bay, Md., by the Coast Guard Yard; launched on 28 October 1944; sponsored by Mrs. W. G.

Green; completed on 27 March 1945; and delivered to the Navy on 6 April 1945.

Upon being placed in service, *Windigo* was assigned to the Pacific Fleet. After a period of duty with the 1st Fleet, she moved to the western Pacific in the spring of 1946 to join the American naval forces in the Philippines. That summer, she served temporarily at the Leyte-Samar naval operating base before moving on to her base at Subic Bay.

Though she served in the Pacific area for the remainder of her career, sketchy records make it difficult to ascertain exactly where she operated. At first, she was in the Philippines; and, in all probability, she remained there at least until 1965 when her assignment changed from "Advanced Bases, Pacific," to "Pacific Fleet." Even this change in her status does not necessarily indicate a change in location, only in administrative assignment. During that time, she also received a new classification and became a medium harbor tug, YTM–421, effective in February 1962. In any event, it is definitely known that, sometime in October 1971, she was placed out of service, assigned to the Pacific Reserve Fleet, and berthed in Hawaii. Later records indicate that, in 1974, she was berthed at Guam, still with the Pacific Reserve Fleet. The move from the 14th Naval District to Guam probably occurred in 1973, but no documents have been found to confirm this inference. She remained in reserve at Guam until June 1976, when her name was struck from the Navy list. As of the beginning of 1977, *Windigo* was waiting disposal by sale.

Winding Gulf

(Freighter: dp. 12,163; l. 395'1"; b. 55'0"; dph. 34'5"; dr. 27'0" (mean); s. 12.0 k.; cpl. 75; a. 1 5", 1 3")

Winding Gulf—a steel-hulled, single-screw freighter launched on 22 June 1918 at Camden, N.J., by the New

York Shipbuilding Corp. for Castner, Curran, and Bullitt, Inc.—was taken over by the Navy on 19 August 1918 for operation by the Naval Overseas Transportation Service (NOTS); designated Id. No. 3379; and commissioned on the same day, Lt. Comdr. Charles A. Geddes, USNRF, in command.

Winding Gulf departed her builder's yard on 23 August and, two days later, arrived at Pier 5, Bush Docks, New York City. There, she took on board 6,119 tons of locomotives and sailed for France in convoy on 2 September. Arriving first at Verdon Roads, France, on 19 September, *Winding Gulf* shifted successively to La Pallice, Quiberon, and St. Nazaire before she finally unloaded her cargo at the last-named port. After she had completed the discharging process and had gotten underway, *Winding Gulf* struck a concrete pier and damaged four plates and 10 frames in her bow. Following temporary repairs, the freighter shifted to Quiberon on 4 October to await the formation of a homeward-bound convoy.

The ship departed the French coast on 8 October and arrived at New York City on 21 October. After discharging ballast at Pier 5, Bush Docks, the cargo vessel shifted to Shewan's Dry Dock, where repairs were made to the vessel's bridge, bow plates, winches, and main engines. She undocked on 11 November 1918, the day the armistice was signed bringing World War I to a close.

Winding Gulf sailed on 22 November with 6,983 tons of general cargo in her holds but collided with *Edward Luckenbach* (Id. No. 1662) one day out. After returning to port and undergoing repairs, *Winding Gulf* got underway again on 12 December to continue her interrupted voyage and arrived at Verdon Roads on the day after Christmas. Congested port facilities there caused the ship to move to La Pallice. After unloading there, *Winding Gulf* took on ballast and 4,110 tons of return Army cargo. Although the ship was ready to sail on 18 February 1919, damaged lock gates at the harbor basin delayed her departure for another week; and she was unable to get underway for home until the 25th.

After arriving at New York on 13 March 1919, *Winding Gulf* was decommissioned, struck from the Navy list, and turned over to the United States Shipping Board on 26 March 1919. Returned to Castner, Curran, and Bullitt, Inc., Boston, Mass., *Winding Gulf* operated in the freight trade through the 1920's. Acquired by the Mystic Steamship Co., of Boston, in 1926, the steel-hulled cargo vessel was in the hands of the Koppers Coal Co., of Boston, in the 1930's and later operated with the Eastern Gas and Fuel Association until being ultimately broken up for scrap in about 1947.

Windlass

(ARS(D)-4: dp. 1,080 (f.); l. 224'3"; b. 34'0"; dr. 7'1" (lim.); s. 13.2 k.; cpl. 65; a. none; cl. *Gypsy*)

Windlass (ARS(D)-4)—originally conceived as *LSM-552*—was laid down on 27 August 1945 at Houston, Tex., by Brown's Shipbuilding Co., Inc.; launched on 7 December 1945; and commissioned on 9 April 1946 in Houston at the Tennessee Coal and Iron Docks, Lt. Comdr. Rodney F. Snipes, USNR, in command.

Following further alterations and trials, *Windlass* shifted to Galveston, Tex., on 13 December, en route to her home port, Charleston, S.C. The salvage ship operated locally out of Charleston into May 1947 when she shifted to Norfolk in May to conduct a towing exercise with her sister ship, *Salvager* (ARS(D)-3). The two ships departed the tidewater area for Bayonne, N.J., on 18 June, before they shifted to Narragansett Bay to salvage the tug *One Wolf* (YTB-179)—sunk in a collision in December 1946. *Windlass* and *Salvager* pooled their efforts to lift the sunken yard tug from 130 feet of water. One body still on board the sunken tug was recovered and taken ashore for burial.

Windlass and her sister ship returned to Bayonne on 28 July but sailed for Mexico early the next month. Arriving at Veracruz on 15 August, *Windlass* assisted *Salvager* in raising two sunken Mexican barges in a two-week operation. Both salvage vessels then headed northward, bound for Bayonne. After touching at Key West, Fla., and Norfolk, they conducted exercises in Chesapeake Bay before they reached Bayonne early in September.

On 10 September, *Windlass*, in company with *Salvager*, began searching for the sunken *YP-387*. She located the wreck and began salvage operations while *Salvager* returned to Bayonne, apparently to get necessary equipment. *Windlass* apparently shifted briefly to Norfolk, Va., for the same reason before both heavy-lifting salvage vessels returned to the site of the sunken YP off Hereford, N.J., on 1 October. Two days later, they placed demolition charges in the sunken "Yippie boat" and blew her up to prevent her from being a hazard to navigation. *Windlass* and her sister ship then returned to Bayonne.

Later that month, though, *Windlass* and *Salvager* again went to sea via Charleston, S.C., this time to 31°19'N/80°58'W, to search for *YTB-274*. Aided by a blimp, the two salvage vessels streamed sweep wires and eventually located the sunken wreck of the YTB on 21 October. *Windlass* and *Salvager* went into three-point moors over the sunken ship and commenced salvage operations. They recovered one body on 27 October before they blew up the wreck on 2 November to prevent its becoming a navigational menace. After exercises on their return voyage, the two salvage vessels made port at Bayonne on 3 November.

Windlass underwent a regular overhaul at the Charleston Naval Shipyard in April 1948, during which time she received additional radio and electronic gear and heavier anchors. The yard also reinforced the hull and added various engineering features. Upon completion of those alterations, *Windlass* returned to her home berth at Bayonne in June and remained there until 5 August, when she and *Salvager* sailed for Norfolk.

Windlass and *Salvager* assisted in a four-point moor over *U-1105* on 10 August and conducted salvage tests on the former German U-boat—off Piney Point, Md.—until 25 August. Hurricane "Carol" interrupted operations as she swept through the area on 30 and 31 August, but both salvage vessels rode out the storm without damage, despite the force 5 winds. *Windlass* took the almost-submerged *U-1105* under tow, supporting her partially with pontoons, and moored the ship on 28 September. *Windlass* and *Salvager* then performed various moors and salvage operations on the submarine's hulk off Piney Point into mid-November before returning to Bayonne. There, *Windlass* remained into 1949.

Again in company with *Salvager*, *Windlass* moved to Newport, R.I., in early February 1949, for a period of upkeep alongside *Vulcan* (AR-5). Later that month, *Windlass* shifted to Newport and trained there before she returned to Bayonne on 23 March.

Windlass conducted mooring operations with USCG Tug *8188* and *YTB-541* at Little Placentia Harbor, Argentia, Newfoundland, in late May before returning to Bayonne on 1 June. She remained in port there until the 28th, when she got underway for Norfolk, again in company with *Salvager*. *Windlass* remained at Norfolk until 8 July, when she headed for Piney Point, the scene of her earlier experimental salvage evolutions on *U-1105*. From 11 July to 26 September, *Windless* and *Salvager* assisted in the shifting of moorings of *U-1105* while salvage tests were being conducted upon the ship. During that time, a heavy storm—with winds up to 80 knots—passed through the area, forcing *Windlass* to shift her mooring to deeper water where her anchors would hold.

For the remainder of 1949, *Windlass* operated in company with *Salvager*, at Norfolk, Bayonne, and in the Little Creek area, before both ships underwent availability alongside *Amphion* (AR–13) at Charleston. From there, the longstanding partners returned to Bayonne to await their next assignment.

Their opportunity came soon enough; for, late in January 1950, *Missouri* (BB–63) ran aground off the Thimble Shoals Light in Chesapeake Bay. *Windlass* and all other available salvage vessels were called to the scene to assist in one of the largest single salvage efforts since World War II. Various attempts to float the battleship off the shoal proved unsuccessful. That included running a division of destroyers by at high speed (an attempt to dislodge the ship by the wave force from the wakes of the ships) and the off-loading of fuel and ammunition. Still, the big battlewagon refused to budge.

Finally, however, a solution was worked out. With *Windlass* and *Salvager* in keystone positions, the various tugs, salvage ships, and submarine rescue vessels were utilized so as to maximize their pulling power. As a result of that combined effort, *Missouri* finally slid free but nearly ran down several of the salvage ships, including *Windlass*. For her part in that operation, *Windlass* received a commendation.

For the remainder of 1950, *Windlass* performed various salvage tasks off the eastern seaboard and in the British West Indies. She investigated the wreck of SS *Chile* off Cape Henry, ascertaining whether or not the wreck was of sufficient danger to be a hazard to navigation; recovered practice mines; raised an LCVP off Wolf Trap Light; and planted moorings at Bermuda. Early in 1951, the ship continued planting moorings, this time in Lynnhaven Roads. *Windlass*'s divers, requalified early that year, cleared a fouled tug propeller and removed several objects from Norfolk harbor.

After conducting a channel survey at Charleston, S.C., in April, *Windlass* returned to the Hampton Roads area, where she was present when the seaplane tender *Valcour* (AVP–55) caught fire on 14 May 1951. *Windlass* rendered fire fighting assistance, pumped necessary compartments dry, and maintained flooding boundaries while rigging temporary gasoline lines and removing the volatile aviation gas from the seaplane tender's storage tanks. *Windlass*' divers subsequently inspected that ship for underwater damage, and *Windlass* herself received a commendation for her part in averting a near disaster.

Other operations performed by *Windlass* during 1951 included removing channel obstructions, raising an LCM and a small boat, refloating the grounded *PC–572* off Cedar Point, removing the obstruction which had fouled a propeller of *Gearing* (DD–710), righting a target sled, conducting diving school, and mooring the hulk of the former *YC–313* in the Potomac River. *Windlass* arrived at the Charleston Naval Shipyard on 12 November 1951 and remained there until 8 January 1952, undergoing an overhaul. During that time, the ship's hull was again stiffened and her engines overhauled.

After leaving the shipyard, *Windlass* conducted diving operations off Cape Charles before she proceeded to St. Thomas, Virgin Islands, to assist in rigging *YC–1060* for technical tests. On 14 February 1952, *Windlass*, towing *YC–1010*, got underway for Norfolk. Two days later, while the salvage ship and her charge were en route to their destination, an explosion occurred in *Windlass*' port engine crankcase, injuring one man and starting a fire. After the crew extinguished the blaze with no further damage, *Windlass* proceeded the remainder of the way to Norfolk on one engine. After arrival, both of *Windlass*' engines were inspected carefully and again overhauled.

In March, April, and May 1952, *Windlass* operated at Roosevelt Roads, Puerto Rico, rigging test targets for demolition experiments. In addition, she set off the charges and retrieved underwater models before returning to Norfolk, again towing *YC–1010*. The ship continued her association with ordnance-related projects that summer, surveying a mooring site; and mooring underwater explosive barges and *Dorado* (ex-SS–428)

in Chesapeake Bay at the mouth of the Patuxent River for the Naval Ordnance Laboratory (NOL), Solomons, Md. During July and August, the ship set off some of the charges involved in NOL's testing program.

Windlass then sailed to Cape Fear, N.C., later that summer and surveyed the area around the sunken *YSD–68*. A hurricane caused a brief change in plans, however, as the salvage ship shifted briefly to Charleston to avoid it. On 29 September, *Windlass* began dragging the bottom with a "hawk" anchor and, on 6 October, located the self-propelled seaplane wrecking derrick on the bottom, upside down. Despite a period of "unusually adverse weather" and what *Windlass*' command history termed "the usual salvage job setbacks," *Windlass* raised *YSD–68* early in November. The bad weather during that period had meant frequent interruptions to put into the nearest port—Southport, N.C.

Returning to the Norfolk area after salvaging *YSD–68*, *Windlass* conducted local salvage and diving operations for the remainder of 1952. The salvage vessel remained at Norfolk into February of 1953, when she commenced a search for a downed Navy plane on the 5th of the month. Crash boats from NAS, Atlantic City, N.J., assisted *Windlass* in the dragging operations begun that same day and located the plane, minus its tail section, soon thereafter. *Windlass* raised the plane, brought it on board between the two "horns" forward, and returned to Norfolk where the aircraft was removed by a dockside crane. That salvage effort set a precedent for the new and useful application of ships like *Windlass* and her sisters.

After salvaging a target raft at Newport News, Va., *Windlass* pulled the grounded yacht *Boudoin* off the south shore of the Potomac River on 18 February before resuming local operations that carried into the summer of 1953. *Windlass* emerged from her overhaul in early October and proceeded thence to St. Thomas and Roosevelt Roads, where the ship assisted in underwater explosive experiments in November.

Shifting back to Norfolk, *Windlass* served as standby and duty salvage vessel there into the spring of 1954, recovering several practice mines and anchors during that time. She participated in Project "Caesar" out of Shelburne harbor, Nova Scotia, trenching and blasting in the ocean floor off the Nova Scotia coast. At one point during the mission, *Windlass* took shelter in Shelburne harbor from Hurricane "Edna."

In September, *Windlass* returned to Norfolk where she resumed her local operations. Two months later, on 8 November 1954, *Windlass* headed to a point off Cape Henry where she commenced salvage operations trying to raise two sunken planes. One broke up while being raised and could not be recovered. On 13 November, *Windlass* recovered the body of one aviator that had been lost in one of the downed planes.

Windlass operated locally out of Norfolk into 1955. The following summer, she again participated in Project "Caesar" evolutions—in mid-June off Shelburne; in late July off Cape May, N.J.; and in September off Cape Hatteras, N.C. After underway training out of Newport and rest and recreation at New York City, *Windlass* attempted the salvage of the sunken yacht *Turbatross* off Tangier Island in Chesapeake Bay. Although the Navy salvage effort was initially successful in raising the sunken vessel, *Turbatross*' hull worked badly and sank again when a sling strap parted.

Windlass received a summons to assist in refloating the grounded destroyer *Basilone* (DDE–824) off Fort Story, Va. Rough weather hampered the operations which were begun on 5 January 1956, and *Seneca* (ATF–91) also ran aground during the attempt to pull *Basilone* free. Wires snapped on board *Hoist* (ARS–40), and *Windlass* dragged dangerously near the destroyer and the beach but managed to cut loose and steer clear. With ice on her decks and rigging, *Windlass* returned to Norfolk the next day.

When the weather moderated, *Windlass* and *Salvager* returned to the scene of the dual grounding. The former pulled off stranded *Seneca*, and the latter pulled *Basilone* free. *Windlass* remained in the vicinity to pick up beach gear anchors and wires strewn over the bottom, recovering a total of 14 anchors.

For the next 10 years, *Windlass* conducted a regular schedule of operations out of Norfolk or Charleston, performing salvage and diving jobs of many different types. In mid-July 1956, the ship again participated in Project "Caesar"; she pulled a target sled off a beach in Chesapeake Bay in November, and finished the year by pulling *Seagull* (MSF-55) off the beach east of Little Creek. In the spring of 1957, *Windlass* operated for three weeks at Chincoteague, Va., in a Jupiter missile nose cone recovery. That summer, the ship recovered most of the wreckage from two AJ Savage bombers that had collided late in June off Oceanview, Va. She later conducted exercises with *Salvager* before returning to Norfolk for diver qualifications; she was preparing to enjoy Christmas liberty when an emergency work request—to raise the sunken *YSD-56*—came through. On 16 December 1957, the ship put to sea and spent five days engaged in the task, only to admit defeat when the badly wrecked YSD appeared so badly torn and ruptured that refloatation was impossible, and the YSD sank again on 23 December. At 2315 that evening, Commander, Service Force, Atlantic Fleet, sent a dispatch releasing *Windlass* from recovery operations so that all hands could enjoy the Christmas holidays.

Windlass subsequently recovered the wrecks of airplanes, salvaged small landing craft that had sunk during amphibious maneuvers, and participated in other classified projects in locales that ranged from Argentia, Newfoundland, to Chesapeake Bay; from Guantanamo to Assateague Island, Va.; and from San Salvador to Nova Scotia. In addition, the ship cleared navigational channels and, again operating in company with *Salvager*, raised the sunken *YTB-495* in mid-June of 1960. She retrieved the downed airship *KE-5* in mid-July of that year and recovered two destroyer anchors slipped during Hurricane "Donna" in September 1960. The year 1961 was one which held both honor and tragedy for the ship. In May 1961, she received the Ney Award for having the best general mess in ships of her class. The sadness came when one man was killed and one seriously injured during the salvage of *Baldwin* (DD-624) which had run aground under tow off Montauk Point, N.Y.

In July 1965, the ship's home port was changed from Little Creek, Va., to Davisville, R.I. No sooner had she shifted her base northward when she was called to the Mississippi River on salvage alert due to the passage of Hurricane "Betsy." She departed Davisville on 11 September and arrived at New Orleans on 20 September to commence salvage operations on the USNS *Kellar*, sunk in the Mississippi. She moored over *Kellar* on the 23d; commenced salvage rigging; and ultimately righted the MSTS ship on 7 October.

After salvage operations on *Kellar* were completed on 11 November, *Windlass* began preparations for decommissioning. On 23 November 1965, *Windlass* was decommissioned at New Orleans and converted to a non-self-propelled craft over the ensuing months. Reclassified as a medium salvage craft on 16 October 1967 and given the hull number YMLC-4, *Windlass* was placed in service with Advanced Bases, Pacific area, but was used "minimally" in ensuing years. Since replacement craft attained superior lift capability, the need for *Windlass'* services diminished; she was accordingly struck from the Navy list on 1 August 1972 and sold on 6 March 1973 to the Union Minerals and Alloys Corp., N.Y., where she was cut up for scrap.

Windom

William Windom—born in Belmont County, Ohio, on 10 May 1827—studied law at Mount Vernon, Ohio, and gained admission to the Ohio bar in 1850. In 1852, he became prosecuting attorney for Knox County but retained that position only until 1855 when he moved to Minnesota. Windom ran successfully for a seat in the United States House of Representatives in 1858 and represented Minnesota in that body from 1859 to 1869. In 1870, he was appointed to serve out the unexpired term of the late Daniel S. Norton in the United States Senate. Later reelected on his own merits, he served in the Senate until 1881 when, with two years remaining of his current term, he resigned to enter President Garfield's cabinet as Secretary of the Treasury. His tenure, however, proved brief. When Garfield died in September as a result of wounds inflicted by an assassin in July, Windom resigned to allow Chester A. Arthur to choose his own Secretary of the Treasury. The Minnesota legislature thereupon voted to allow Windom to serve out his term in his still-vacant Senate seat.

In 1889, Windom became Secretary of the Treasury in the administration of Benjamin Harrison. During this second term of office, Windom set the military character of the Revenue Marine—later merged with the Lighthouse Service and the Lifesaving Service to form the Coast Guard—by appointing Capt. Leonard G. Shepard, USRM, to replace the civilian who had formerly held the position. That act was the first in a series which ultimately formalized the military nature of the Coast Guard organization. Windom remained in his cabinet post until his death on 29 January 1891.

(Revenue cutter: dp. 525; l. 170'8"; b. 27'0"; dr. 8' 3"; s. 15 k.; a. 1 gun)

Windom, a revenue cutter completed in 1896 at the Iowa Iron Works in Dubuque, Iowa, was accepted by the Treasury Department on 11 May 1896. Partially incomplete, she was moved from Dubuque—via Cairo, Ill., and New Orleans, La.—to Baltimore, Md., where she was completed and placed in commission on 30 June 1896.

For the next 17 months, she operated out of Baltimore making an annual winter cruise of the fishing grounds between the Virginia capes and Cape Hatteras. In March 1898, with war against Spain looming just over the horizon, President McKinley reluctantly began the process of preparing for the fight. On the 24th, he issued the executive order instructing the Revenue Cutter Service to cooperate with the Navy for the duration of the crisis. Two days later, she received orders to report at Norfolk, and there she found herself on 25 April when Congress passed the resolution recognizing that a state of war existed between the United States and Spain.

Five days later, *Windom* departed Hampton Roads on her way to the blockade off Cuba. She stopped at Key West, Fla., for four days and arrived off the Cuban coast on 8 May. She patrolled the southern coast of Cuba near Cienfuegos until the 13th. During that time, she cut the Cienfuegos cable, the Spanish colonial government's only link with the outside world; and, on 12 May, she helped to cover the withdrawal of an ill-starred Navy boat expedition. At a critical point in that action, the cutter closed the enemy shore and silenced the Spanish battery and briefly dispersed their infantry allowing the harassed boats to reach safety. The following day, she withdrew from the area to return to Key West—probably for fuel and provisions. She again got underway for the combat zone on 27 May and took up station off Havana on the 28th. For the remainder of the Spanish-American War, *Windom* participated in the blockade of Havana, returning to Key West on two occasions—once during the last two weeks of June and again during the first week in August.

Hostilities ended on 13 August; *Windom* reverted to Treasury Department control on the 17th; and she returned to Norfolk on the 22d. She remained there until 3 October at which time she headed for New York where she transferred most of her armament to *Gresham* before resuming duty at Baltimore with the Revenue Cutter Service on the 13th. From the fall of 1898 to the summer of 1906, *Windom* operated out of Baltimore, cruising the waters of the Chesapeake Bay and occasionally venturing out into the Atlantic in the vicinity of the Virginia capes. On 13 July 1906, the cutter departed Arundel Cove, Md., to sail—via Key West, Fla., and Mobile, Ala.—to her new base of operations, Galveston, Tex. She arrived there on 6 August and began duty patrolling the gulf coast of the United States. That assignment lasted for five years.

On 1 August 1911, she left Galveston to return to Arundel Cove. She arrived at the station on the shores of the Chesapeake on 1 September and was placed out of commission on the 12th. Her retirement, however, was only a brief one, for she returned to full commission on 1 November. She served at Washington, D.C., from mid-November 1911 until early May 1912. On 7 May, she headed back to the Gulf of Mexico. Initially, she assisted in flood relief at New Orleans; but, in June, she resumed her coastal patrols out of Galveston. She cruised the entire gulf coast from Texas to Key West over the next 18 months. After war broke out in Europe in August 1914, the cutter took on the added responsibility of enforcing America's neutrality laws.

In November 1914, *Windom* headed back to Arundel Cove to be decommissioned again. She arrived at the depot on 3 December but made a short voyage to Washington before going out of service. She returned to Arundel Cove on 13 January 1915; and, on the 15th, she was placed out of commission. On 13 December 1915, near the end of a year of inactivity, *Windom* was renamed *Comanche*. Less than a month later, on 8 January 1916, the cutter went back into service under her new name. On 19 January, she departed the Chesapeake Bay area to return to her old patrol area in the Gulf of Mexico. She arrived at Galveston on 2 February and resumed her old routine.

The United States' declaration of war on the Central Powers once again brought the cutter under Navy Department control on 6 April 1917. *Comanche* continued to patrol the gulf coast even in naval service. Her second period of serivce with the Navy lasted over two years until 28 August 1919 at which time she was returned to the jurisdiction of the Treasury Department. She continued her patrols of the gulf for another seven months and then headed for Key West where she was decommissioned on 17 April 1920 for repairs. Recommissioned in July, the ship relieved *Tallapoosa* at Mobile and rejoined the Gulf Division. Serving successively at Mobile, Key West, and Galveston, she patrolled coastal waters constantly until June of 1930. During that period, she left the Gulf of Mexico only once, in 1923, for repairs at Baltimore and Norfolk. On 2 June 1930, she was detached from the Gulf Division and was ordered back to Arundel Cove. She arrived at her destination on 1 July and was placed out of commission on the 31st. She was sold to Weiss Motor Lines, of Baltimore, on 13 November 1930.

Windsor

A county in the state of Vermont and a city in Connecticut. APA–55 was named for the county; and ARD–22, for the city.

I

(APA–55: dp. 13,143; l. 473'1''; b. 66'0''; dr. 25'0'' (lim.); s. 18.6 k.; cpl. 552; trp. 1,511; a. 2 5'', 4 40mm., 18 20mm.; cl. *Windsor*)

SS *Excelsior*—a steel-hulled, single-crew cargo vessel —was laid down under a Maritime Commission contract (MC hull 589) on 23 July 1942 at Sparrow's Point, Md., by the Bethlehem Sparrow's Point Shipyard, Inc.; renamed *Windsor* and classified a transport, AP–100, on 5 October 1942; launched on 28 December 1942; sponsored

by Miss Patricia Moreell, the daughter of Rear Admiral Ben Moreell, Chief of the Bureau of Yards and Docks; reclassified an attack transport, APA–55, on 16 June 1943; and commissioned at the Norfolk Navy Yard, Port·mouth, Va., on 17 June 1943, Comdr. D. C. Woodward in command.

Windsor began her shakedown on 20 June and conducted eight training cruises in Chesapeake Bay. After post-shakedown availability, the ship departed the east coast of the United States on 9 December, bound for the Pacific. Upon reaching Pearl Harbor, *Windsor* became a unit of Transport Division (TransDiv) 4, 5th Fleet Amphibious Force.

Windsor embarked the men and equipment of the 3d Battalion, 17th Regimental Combat Team, 7th Army Division, and departed the Hawaiian Islands on 22 January 1944, bound for the Marshall Islands as part of Task Force (TF) 52. *Windsor* participated in the assault landing at Kwajalein and, after the island had been secured early in February, sailed for the Ellice Islands.

Reaching Funafuti soon thereafter, *Windsor* there joined the 3d Fleet and was subsequently ordered to Guadalcanal, Solomon Islands, for amphibious training and maneuvers. After shifting to Torokina, Bougainville, on 28 March and to Milne Bay, New Guinea, on 1 April, the attack transport was assigned to the 7th Fleet Amphibious Forces late in April.

Meanwhile, on 22 April, the 7th "Amphibs" had put ashore Army troops at Hollandia and took the Japanese completely by surprise. However, the following evening, a Japanese air raid blew up a captured ammunition dump and ensuing fires destroyed nearly 60 percent of the supplies landed.

As a result, *Windsor*—initially ordered to Tanahmerah Bay—was diverted to Humboldt Bay, Hollandia, as part of the effort to replenish the lost supplies. Upon arriving there on 24 April, she landed troops of the 2d Battalion of the American Army's 34th Infantry Division. Simultaneous with the landings at Tanahmerah and Humboldt Bays, the 7th Amphibious Force also put troops ashore to secure Aitape and its vital airstrip. *Windsor* participated in the Aitape landing, putting ashore various units of the 32d Division on 3 May.

Windsor left New Guinea's waters on 7 May and headed for the Solomons, arriving at Guadalcanal three days later. At the end of May and the beginning of June, the attack transport embarked units of the 3d Marine Division, left the Solomons on 4 June, and headed for the Central Pacific. She anchored first at Eniwetok and later at Kwajalein to prepare for and to await orders to begin her next operation, the occupation of Guam, in the Marianas.

However, the amphibious forces first headed for Saipan—regarded by some as the key to Japan's inner defenses. The assault on that island on 15 June resulted in the Japanese Fleet's challenging the Americans for the first time since the Battle of Midway, two years before. In the ensuing Battle of the Philippine Sea, on 19 and 20 June 1944, the enemy suffered heavily, losing three carriers. In the two-day battle, the Japanese Navy lost nearly 92 percent of its carrier-based aircraft (395 planes) as opposed to 130 planes lost by TF 58, the fast carrier task force under Vice Admiral Marc A. Mitscher.

Meanwhile, the unexpectedly stiff resistance on Saipan and the sortie of the Japanese Fleet had necessitated a delay in the landings on Guam. Finally, as part of Task Group (TG) 53.3, *Windsor* took part in the assault landings on Guam, landing troops of the 2d Battalion, 3d Marine Regiment, 3d Marine Division, on D day, 21 July, following close on the heels of intensive naval gunfire and carrier-based aircraft attacks. The attack transport put ashore her battle-garbed marines on the Asan beaches on the northern shores of Guam.

After the capture of the Marianas, the Navy turned its attention to the Western Caroline Islands. Fast carrier task forces ranged a wide area prior to the landings at Peleliu, Palau Islands, and Morotai, in the Netherlands East Indies, diverting or destroying Japanese forces that might have attempted to interfere with the invasion. Their planes struck Chichi Jima, Iwo Jima, Yap, Palau, and Mindanao, in the Philippines. Three days before the assault troops were slated to go ashore, ships and planes hurled an intensive air and surface bombardment against the Japanese defenses, while minesweepers cleared the waters off Peleliu and Angaur Islands, and underwater demolition teams destroyed beach obstructions. On 15 September, *Windsor* participated in the assault landings at Peleliu, putting ashore various elements of the 1st Marine Division, as part of TF 32.

Following the successful landings on Peleliu, *Windsor* retired to Humboldt Bay and there was assigned to TF 78. A month later, the attack transport sortied as part of TF 78, bound for the Philippine Islands. While the ships proceeded north, the initial assault on Leyte began on 20 October when elements of the Army 10th and 24 Corps went ashore after heavy bombardment had softened up defenses ashore. Two days after D day, 22 October, *Windsor* arrived at Leyte; completed her unloading in record time; and stood out to sea later that day, bound once more for Humboldt Bay.

There, *Windsor* embarked another group of reinforcements and headed back toward Leyte on 9 November, as part of TF 79. One day out of San Pedro Bay, their destination, the task force came under an attack by Japanese planes that lasted for three hours. *Windsor* emerged unscathed and put into San Pedro Bay on the morning of 14 November, commencing her unloading at 0804 and completing it at 1315, having disembarked the troops and equipment of the 32d Division. During that time, Japanese planes attacked the ships at 0900; but antiaircraft fire from the vital auxiliaries and their escorts, coupled with Army fighter planes, drove off the enemy. At the completion of that particular reinforcement operation, *Windsor*'s historian recorded: "The unloading time of five hours and nineteen minutes, averaging 95.9 tons per hour, was a new record for this ship and equalled by very few of the other transports in the Task Force."

Proceeding from San Pedro Bay later on the 14th, *Windsor* steamed to Manus, in the Admiralty Islands, and moved thence to Tulagi, Florida Island, Guadalcanal. Departing Tulagi on 27 November, *Windsor* headed for San Francisco, Calif.

The attack transport subsequently underwent general repairs at Moore's Shipyard, Oakland, Calif., from 13 December 1944 to 16 February 1945. She sailed for Hawaiian waters on 22 February. Routed onward to the western Pacific, *Windsor* departed Pearl Harbor on 20 March, with a contingent of construction battalion ("Seabees") troops embarked, and made calls at Eniwetok, Guam, and Samar, in the Philippines, discharging passengers and cargo in Guiuan roadstead, Samar, on 9 April. The attack transport lay off Samar for nearly two weeks before she received onward routing to return to San Francisco and, on her ensuing voyage, touched at Peleliu, Guam, Saipan, Tinian, and Pearl Harbor to pick up passengers. From San Francisco, *Windsor* headed up the west coast to Seattle, Wash., where she loaded general cargo and troops. She then returned to Pearl Harbor, reaching that port on 11 June and debarking the troops and discharging the cargo.

Shifting to Honolulu, *Windsor* there picked up troops slated for transportation to Okinawa and, as part of Task Unit (TU) 96.6.15, proceeded to Hagushi Beach, where she remained from 25 July to 5 August. During that time, the attack transport, together with other warships in the vicinity, came under almost nightly harassing attacks from Japanese planes but emerged unscathed. *Windsor* then sailed for Ulithi in Convoy OKU–17, reaching her destination on 10 August.

While *Windsor* lay at anchor at Ulithi lagoon, Japan accepted the unconditional surrender terms of the Potsdam Declaration; and hostilities ceased on 14 August.

On 19 August, *Windsor*, as part of TU 94.18.12, proceeded to the Philippines, reaching Leyte on the 23d. From there, she proceeded to the island of Cebu, in the southern Philippines, where she was assigned to Trans Div 53, TF 33.

After embarking troops of the Americal Division and supplies on 31 August, *Windsor* sailed for Japan as part of the Tokyo occupation force. As the initial increments went ashore between 8 and 10 September, within a week of the formal Japanese surrender on 2 September, *Windsor* landed her troops. The attack transport returned to Cebu, loaded equipment, and embarked the troops of the Army's 77th Division, and landed that unit at Hakodate, Hokkaido, in early October.

After the occupation of Japan, *Windsor* served under the aegis of Commander, Service Force, Pacific, reporting for duty with the "Magic Carpet" operation on 19 November. She remained in that duty for the remainder of 1945, participating in the massive sealift of returning sailors, soldiers, and marines to the United States.

After reporting to Commander, Western Sea Frontier, for disposition on 8 January 1946, *Windsor* received onward routing and transited the Panama Canal late in January, bound for the 8th Naval District. Decommissioned on 4 March 1946, *Windsor* was struck from the Navy list on 12 April 1946 and delivered to the War Shipping Administration, at Mobile, Ala., on 1 August 1946, for disposition.

Windsor earned five battle stars for her World War II service.

II

(ARD–22: l. 491'8"; b. 81'0"; dr. 33'3" (subm.); cpl. 112; cl. *ARD–12*)

The second *Windsor* (ARD–22) was laid down as *ARD–22* on 24 January 1944 at Alameda, Calif., by the Pacific Bridge Co. Launched soon thereafter, *ARD–22* was commissioned on 21 April 1944.

Little information is available regarding the wartime career of *ARD–22*. All that is known indicates that she deployed to advanced bases in the western Pacific and that, by 11 May 1945, she was at Kerama Retto in the Ryukyu Islands supporting the Okinawa campaign.

Following the end of the war, *ARD–22* supported the occupation of former Japanese territories, though exactly where she did so remains a mystery. By 1948, she returned to American territorial waters at Old Woman's Bay, Kodiak, Alaska. She remained there assigned to the repair facility until the fall of 1951 when she was towed to Pearl Harbor for alterations and for assignment to the Reserve Fleet.

She remained in reserve until June 1954 when she was recommissioned and assigned to the repair facility located at Subic Bay in the Philippines. She served there for the next 16 years providing repair facilities for the ships of the 7th Fleet. On 9 May 1967, she was named *Windsor*. The auxiliary drydock was decommissioned late in 1970; and, on 1 June 1971, she was leased to Taiwan. She continued to serve the Taiwan Navy on that basis until 19 May 1976 when she was sold and struck from the Navy list at the time of the sale.

Windsor earned one battle star during World War II as *ARD–22*.

Winfield S. Cahill

(ScStr.: t. 299 (gross); l. 150'0"; b. 24'6"; dr. 12'0" (mean); s. 12.0 k.; cpl. 37; a. 1 3", 2 mg.)

Winfield S. Cahill—a wooden-hulled "Menhaden fisherman" built in 1912 by M. M. Davis, of Solomons, Md.—was acquired by the Navy from the Eubank Tankard Co., of Kilmarnock, Va. The contract for purchasing the vessel was signed on 4 June 1917, and she was delivered to the Navy eight days later, on 12 June. While the ship was being fitted out at the Norfolk Navy Yard, Admiral W. S. Benson, the Acting Secretary of the Navy, promulgated General Order No. 314, on 28 July 1917, whereby the compound names of all scout patrol (SP) vessels were shortened to the surname only. Thus, *Winfield S. Cahill* became, officially, simply *Cahill* (SP–493), although she would be, at times in future, referred to indiscriminately as either *Cahill*, *Winfield S. Cahill*, or *W. S. Cahill*.

Commissioned at the Norfolk Navy Yard on 10 August 1917, Lt. (jg.) John B. Will in command, *Cahill* soon sailed for France as part of Squadron 4, Division 10, Patrol Force, Atlantic Fleet. Initially earmarked for escort duty "on distant service," *Cahill* and her sisters proved to be not only inadequate for the task but also unsafe. Originally designed for a very low freeboard to facilitate the commercial fishing trawler operations, the ship was immersed even further by the addition of guns and deckhouses. This increased the ship's tophamper to a point where she became decidedly unstable in heavy seas such as those encountered off Brest—the port from which the "Menhaden fishermen" operated.

After the foundering of *Rehoboth* (SP–384) on 4 October 1917, *Cahill* and her sisters were relegated to minesweeping duties, their previous places as escorts for troopships and supply vessels being taken by other craft. *Cahill* performed minesweeping operations out of Brest for the duration of World War I.

Since it was apparently deemed inadvisable to take the former fishing craft back across the Atlantic, *Cahill* was decommissioned on 8 September 1919 and sold abroad. She is carried on mercantile registers of the time as *Winfield S. Cahill*—her original name—until she was renamed *Eraclea* when acquired by the Genoa, Italy-based firm of *Societa Navagazione & Galligianti* about 1922. She operated under Italian registry, out of Genoa, until about 1927 or 1928, when she was acquired by Demetrios Z. Pandakis of Piraeus, Greece, who subsequently used her as a tug until 1937 or 1938, after which time her name disappeared from shipping registers.

Winged Arrow

(AP–170: dp. 13,910 (tl.); l. 459'2''; b. 63'0''; dr. 23'0'' (lim.); s. 16.5 k. (tl.); cpl. 276; trp. 1,575; a. 1 5'', 4 3'', 12 20mm.; cl. *La Salle*; T. C2–S–B1)

Winged Arrow (AP–170) was laid down on 26 January 1943 at Oakland, Calif., by the Moore Drydock Co. under a Maritime Commission contract (MC hull 1156); launched on 3 April 1943; sponsored by Miss Amy-Ann McGinniss; acquired by the Navy from the War Shipping Administration on 21 April 1944; and commissioned that same day, Comdr. J. E. Shomier in command.

On 30 April, *Winged Arrow* put to sea with a full complement of Army replacement troops, bound for Oahu where she arrived on 6 May. There, she practiced amphibious operations with soldiers from the Army's 27th Division in preparation for the occupation of the Mariana Islands. At the end of May, she departed Pearl Harbor with troops embarked, bound for Kwajalein in the Marshalls where she arrived on 9 June. Since *Winged Arrow*'s embarked troops were assigned to the floating reserve, they were not scheduled to be on hand at Saipan on D day. Therefore, she remained at Kwajalein for several days before departing there on a schedule calculated to put her off Saipan on 17 June, two days after the initial assault. The following day, she transferred her troops to LST's; and they landed at Agingan Point on Saipan. The transport then retired to Eniwetok to prepare for the second phase of the Marianas operation, the landings on Tinian. After a somewhat lengthy wait at Eniwetok occa-

sioned by the unexpectedly difficult task of rooting out the defenders of Saipan, *Winged Arrow* returned to the island on 19 July and retracted units of the 2d Marine Division for the Tinian assault. On the morning of 24 July, she and several other ships carried that division, made up of the 2d and 8th Marine Regiments, around to the southwestern coast of Tinian opposite Tinian Town where they feigned a landing to draw enemy forces from the real objective on the eastern coast. Upon concluding the feint, *Winged Arrow* transported the marines back around to waters off the actual invasion beaches where they remained in the floating reserve. On the 26th, they went ashore to reinforce and support the 4th Marine Division during the reduction of Tinian. *Winged Arrow* then embarked passengers, including 458 Japanese prisoners of war, at Saipan for transportation to Pearl Harbor. After disembarking the passengers at Oahu on 10 August, the transport continued eastward to San Francisco, where she arrived on 19 August.

She completed almost a month's availability at San Francisco and then moved to San Diego on 19 September. There, she embarked a Marine Corps aviation unit for transportation to the Marshalls. She departed San Diego on 21 September and, after stops at Pearl Harbor and Majuro, disembarked her passengers at Roi islet in Kwajalein Atoll on 15 October. She embarked more passengers there and got underway again on 22 October, bound ultimately for Hollandia on the northern coast of New Guinea. After stops at Majuro and Manus in the Admiralty Islands, the transport arrived at Hollandia on 21 November. At the New Guinea base, the ship began preparations for the invasion of Luzon in the Philippines.

Early in January 1945, she embarked troops of the Army's I Corps, probably units of the 158th Regimental Combat Team, and sailed for Lingayen Gulf on the northwestern coast of Luzon as a part of Rear Admiral Richard L. Conolly's Reinforcement Group (Task Group 77.9). She and the other ships of her task group arrived off Lingayen on 11 January, two days after the initial assault. Her troops eventually landed near Mabilao about 15 miles east of the town of Lingayen itself and moved up to support other I Corps troops already engaged with the Japanese. During her stay at Lingayen Gulf, *Winged Arrow* was straddled by bombs and near-misses by a kamikaze who splashed close aboard her bow, but she performed her part in the operation without suffering casualties or damage.

She departed Lingayen on the night of 12 and 13 January, joined a convoy of fast transports, and shaped a course for Leyte Gulf. En route, the convoy suffered another kamikaze attack. One of the intruders succeeded in crashing *Zeilin* (AP–9), but *Winged Arrow* again escaped damage. After about a week at Leyte, the transport carried more reinforcements to Luzon, landing them just north of Subic Bay at La Paz. She returned to Leyte and remained there until 16 February when she got underway with a Ulithi-bound convoy which included her damaged former travelling mate, *Zeilin*. The task unit reached Ulithi on 18 February, but *Winged Arrow* did not remain there long. Continuing her voyage, she stopped at recently invaded Iwo Jima where she embarked units of the 5th Marine Division for transportation to Hawaii. After disembarking the marines at Hilo and spending from 12 to 17 April in the islands, she resumed her voyage to the west coast of the United States and entered San Francisco Bay on the 23d.

Winged Arrow spent almost a month undergoing repairs at San Francisco. She departed that port on 16 May and headed north to Seattle where she arrived on the 19th. She embarked Army replacement troops for the Okinawa campaign and got underway again on 22 May. She made brief stops at Pearl Harbor, Eniwetok, and Ulithi before arriving in the Ryukyus in June. She remained at Okinawa until 8 July when she headed back to Pearl Harbor with 1,056 Japanese prisoners of war embarked. Steaming via Saipan and Eniwetok, she reached Oahu on 22 July. After unloading the prisoners of war, she took on a mixed group of passengers, which included male and female members of the armed forces as well as male and female civilians, for transportation back to the United States. The transport stood out of Pearl Harbor on 24 July and arrived in San Francisco six days later.

The ship underwent a round of voyage repairs at San Francisco before returning to sea on 11 August. En route to the western Pacific, she received word of the Japanese capitulation on 14 August. She made brief calls at Eniwetok and Ulithi before arriving at her destination, Leyte, on the day of the actual surrender ceremony, 2 September 1945.

After a side trip to Tacloban, *Winged Arrow* departed the Philippines on 5 September with 1,500 returning Americans embarked. She made a two-day stop at Ulithi and arrived in San Francisco once again prior to returning to the Far East. She arrived at Saipan in the Marianas in mid-October and picked up more returning troops there and at Guam and Tinian before getting underway on the 27th to transport them back to the United States. The ship entered San Francisco once again on 10 November but departed again for the Orient two weeks later. This time, her destination was Jinsen, Korea, where she arrived on 13 December and probably disembarked occupation troops before heading back to the United States on the 15th. She arrived in Seattle early in January 1946 and remained there until the 28th when she put to sea once again, bound for Asia. The ship arrived at Shanghai, China, on 1 February and remained there until the 17th at which time she headed south to Hong Kong for a two-day visit before heading back to the west coast. *Winged Arrow* left Hong Kong on 22 February; stopped along the way at Guam, Truk, and Wake Island; and reentered Seattle on 29 March.

The transport embarked upon her final voyage for the Navy on 14 April. She made a stop at San Francisco and then shaped a course back to the Philippines on 26 April. *Winged Arrow* stood into Manila Bay on 14 May, moved to Subic Bay on 15 May, and headed for Samar on the 16th. She stopped only briefly at Samar on the 18th and then pointed her bow eastward. She concluded her final transpacific voyage for the Navy at San Francisco on 5 June. On the 27th, she headed north to Seattle and inactivation, arriving there on the 30th. She completed inactivation overhaul and was placed out of commission at Seattle and transferred to the Maritime Commission on 12 August 1946 for disposal. Her name was struck from the Navy list on 28 August 1946. In 1948, she was sold and converted to mercantile service. Between 1948 and 1965, she served several steamship companies under the names *Susan*, *Noordzee*, *Fairhope*, and finally *Green Bay*. Her name disappeared from mercantile lists late in 1965. Presumably she was broken up.

Winged Arrow earned four battle stars during World War II.

Wingfield

John David Wingfield—born in Richmond, Va., on 4 November 1916—enlisted in the United States Naval Reserve at Washington, D.C., on 15 November 1940 and was appointed an aviation cadet on 5 February 1941. Following flight training at Jacksonville and Miami, Fla., he was appointed a naval aviator on 20 August 1941 and was commissioned an ensign in the United States Naval Reserve on 5 September 1941. After further training in the Advanced Carrier Training Group, Pacific Fleet, he reported for duty to Scouting Squadron Two on 28 December 1941. He was awarded the American Defense Service Medal and the Navy Cross: "For extraordinary heroism and valiant disregard for his own personal safety as pilot of a scouting plane in action against enemy Japanese forces in the

Coral Sea on 8 May 1942. With keen determination in pursuing his objective, Ensign Wingfield, when his bomb failed to release during his initial dive on an enemy Japanese carrier, gallantly returned to the scene of attack without protection or support to complete his assigned mission." He failed to return from this mission.

(DE–194: dp. 1,240; l. 306'; b. 36'10"; dr. 10'6"; s. 19.5 k.; cpl. 186; a. 3 3″, 2 40mm., 8 20mm., 2 dct., 8 dcp., 1 dcp. (hh.), 3 21″ tt.; cl. *Cannon*)

Wingfield (DE–194) was laid down on 7 October 1943 at Newark, N.J., by the Federal Shipbuilding and Drydock Corporation; launched on 30 December 1943; sponsored by Mrs. E. E. Wingfield; and commissioned on 28 January 1944, Lt. Comdr. H. E. Purdy in command.

Following shakedown training in Bermuda and refresher training in Casco Bay, Maine, *Wingfield* reported for duty on 1 April 1944 as a training ship for the Destroyer Escort School. She began her primary work on 8 April when she began an escort voyage for a coastal convoy to New York. *Wingfield*, in company with *Thornhill* (DE–195), cleared Norfolk on the 16th for a submarine hunt south of Cape Hatteras, then to Great Sound, Bermuda. She returned to Norfolk on 1 May and became the flagship of Destroyer Escort Division 55.

All ships of this division entered New York harbor on 9 May 1944 and returned to Norfolk the next day with the New York section of Convoy UGS–42, bound for North Africa. This 108-ship convoy sortied from Hampton Roads on 13 May and reached Bizerte, Tunisia, on 1 June. She returned to New York with another convoy on 29 June and got underway from that port on 10 July for refresher training in Casco Bay. Between 24 July and 7 September, she made a second voyage, escorting UGS–49, from Norfolk to Bizerte and back to New York.

After completing voyage repairs in the New York Navy Yard and battle practices at Casco Bay, *Wingfield* cleared New York on 14 October 1944 for the first of five escort voyages to ports in Great Britain. She returned to New York from Plymouth, England, on 9 November. *Wingfield* again sailed from New York to Plymouth and back between 2 December 1944 and 1 January 1945. She made a run from New York to Roath Docks, Cardiff, Wales, and back between 18 January and 18 February; one from Boston to Roath Docks, Cardiff, Wales, and back to New York between 8 March and 4 April; and one from New York to Southampton, England, and back between 24 April and 23 May 1945. She was at Southampton on "V–E Day" and enjoyed the honor of escorting the first peacetime convoy from England to New York.

Despite the presence of aggressive "wolf packs" of U-boats during the later days of the war, not one ship escorted by *Wingfield* was damaged by an enemy submarine. During her service in the North Atlantic, this ship rendered medical aid to merchant vessels in convoy on more than 100 occasions.

After upkeep in the New York Navy Yard and refresher training at Guantanamo Bay, *Wingfield* transited the Panama Canal on 1 July 1945 with units of Escort Division 55. She stopped briefly at San Diego and arrived at Pearl Harbor on 20 July and underwent a five-day upkeep period. The ship then operated in the Hawaiian area training student officers in underway gunnery practices and antisubmarine exercises.

On 8 August 1945, *Wingfield* cleared Pearl Harbor with all other units of Escort Division 55 escorting SS *Empress of Australia* to the safety of the Eniwetok Atoll, Marshall Islands. While at sea on 15 August, the ships received word that Japan had capitulated. The ocean escorts entered Eniwetok lagoon the next day. Between 24 and 29 August, *Wingfield* joined in a vain search for a reported life raft.

On 4 September, Wotje and Maloelap expressed their

willingness to surrender. On that day, *Wingfield* proceeded with *Baron* (DE–166) for the Jaluit Atoll to accept the surrender of the Japanese garrison, then proceeded to Maloelap for the surrender of that atoll. Wotje was formally surrendered on board *Baron* by Rear Admiral Nobukazu Yoshimi, and Maloelap by Rear Admiral Shochi Tamada on board *Wingfield*.

On 6 September, *Wingfield* became the first American warship to enter the Maloelap Atoll. She proceeded to Toroa Anchorage where Admiral Tamada, Imperial Japanese Navy (I.J.N.), Lt. Inabi, I.J.N., and Lt. Aoki, I.J.N., arrived on board, signed the surrender agreement, and departed the ship. The entire event was completed in 25 minutes. All hands were at battle stations in dress whites for the ceremony.

A brief and simple flag raising ceremony was held on 10 September. Capt. H. B. Grow, USNR, in the presence of the Japanese garrison and a landing force from *Wingfield*, read the proclamation; copies written in Japanese were distributed to the Japanese garrison. The United States flag was raised over the atoll and colors were sounded, while a detachment of officers, sailors, and marines stood at attention with the Japanese, who also joined in saluting the flag. *Wingfield* fired a 21-gun salute as the colors reached the top of the flagpole.

During the next six days, *Wingfield* supervised Japanese compliance with the terms of surrender. On 16 September, the ship got underway to a new anchorage off Engenben Island to allow minesweepers to clear Toroa Anchorage. Meanwhile, she continued to receive Japanese arms on board; and, on 26 September, she transported 56 ill Japanese to Mille for evacuation to Japan. The next day, Toroa Anchorage and Enijun Channel were declared free of mines; and *Wingfield* returned to supervise the garrison until 1 November when a Japanese evacuation ship came to anchor and evacuated 163 Japanese Army personnel of the Maloelap garrison.

Wingfield got underway on 2 November, touching at Majuro Atoll to unload medical equipment, and thence proceeded to Kwajalein lagoon where she embarked Navy veterans for transportation to the United States. She put to sea from Kwajalein Atoll on 7 December 1945 and steamed by way of Pearl Harbor and San Diego to arrive in the Boston Naval Shipyard on 25 January 1946. After repairs and dock trials, she stood out of Boston harbor on 17 February and reported to Green Cove Springs, Fla., on 20 February 1946 for inactivation. She was placed out of commission, in reserve, on 15 June 1946 and assigned to the Florida Group of the Atlantic Reserve Fleet.

Wingfield was transferred to the Government of France on 10 September 1950, under terms of the Military Assistance Program. She served the French Navy as *Sakalave* (F–720). She was scrapped in 1960.

Wingina

The principal chief of the Secotan Indians in North Carolina during Sir Walter Raleigh's two expeditions in 1585 and 1586. He was ultimately killed during one of his attempts to resist the coming of the English settlers.

(YTB–395: dp. 345 (f.); l. 100'; b. 25'; dr. 11'; s. 12 k.; cpl. 14; cl. *Sassaba*)

Wingina (YT–395) was laid down on 25 January 1944 at Jacksonville, Fla., by the Gibbs Gas Engine Co.; reclassified YTB–395 on 15 May 1944; launched on 14 July 1944; sponsored by Mrs. Ralph B. Weidner, the wife of Ens. R. B. Weidner, USNR; and completed and placed in service on 15 December 1944.

Initially allocated to the 13th Naval District, *Wingina* was placed in reserve, out of service, in March 1946, and berthed at Astoria, Oreg., with the Columbia River Group of the Reserve Fleet. Reactivated in July

1947, the large harbor tug operated into the late 1970's. In February 1962, she was reclassified a medium harbor tug, YTM–395.

For a brief time—June 1964 to March 1965—*Wingina* was carried on the naval vessel register as being in "active" status, but as a "redesignated activity craft." At the end of that period, she was reclassified back to "active, in service," a status in which she operated in the 13th Naval District, providing pilotage, tug and tow services, and waterfront fire protection, well into 1979.

Winifred

(ScStr: dp. 5,850; l. 290'0"; b. 42'2"; dph. 21'0"; dr. 18'9" (mean); s. 10.0 k.; cpl. 55; a. 2 4", 1 mg.)

Winifred—a steel-hulled, single-screw freighter—was laid down on 31 January 1898 at Bath, Maine, by the Bath Iron Works; launched on 8 July 1898; and delivered to her managing owners, Hiller, Bull, and Knowlton, of New York City, on 1 October 1898. Reputed by some to be the first American "tramp" steamer—a freighter steaming on non-scheduled, cargo-carrying runs between a varying slate of ports—*Winifred* initially operated on the New York to Puerto Rico route.

By late in 1917, *Winifred* was operating under the auspices of the Gulf Refining Co., of Port Arthur, Tex. In the autumn of that year, the ship was armed; and, on 17 October 1917, a Navy armed guard unit under the command of Chief Boatswain's Mate W. A. Moon was placed on board the ship. After docking at Bayonne to take on a cargo of oil, *Winifred* shifted to Hampton Roads, where she joined a convoy. Departing Hampton Roads on 8 November, the steamer reached Dover, England, on the 29th and Gravesend on the 30th. She remained in British waters for the remainder of 1917, touching at Sheerness, Cardiff in Wales, and at Dover.

Winifred operated in European waters into the summer of the following year. Assigned Identification Number 1319, *Winifred* was commissioned as a vessel of the Naval Overseas Transportation Service (NOTS) on 21 June 1918, while in drydock at Liverpool, Lt. J. B. Barneson, USNRF, in command.

Operating primarily from Cardiff, Wales, *Winifred* performed coastwise and cross-channel service, lifting supplies from English to French ports and vice-versa. She operated for NOTS in this vital logistics capacity through the end of World War I.

Winifred departed Liverpool, England, on 12 December 1918; proceeded homeward via the Azores; and arrived at New York on 8 January 1919. Shifting to Philadelphia soon thereafter, the ship was placed out of commission there on 13 March 1919. Simultaneously struck from the Navy list, she was turned over to the United States Shipping Board on the same day for disposal. *Winfield* was returned to her prewar owner, the Gulf Refining Co., and homeported at Port Arthur, Tex., until 1936 when she was abandoned due to age and deterioration.

Winjah

An alternative spelling to Winyah, a bay off the coast of South Carolina which serves as the estuary of the Pee Dee, Black, and Waccamaw Rivers and is located slightly above Georgetown, S.C.

Winjah (ACV–54)—a *Prince William*-class escort carrier—was laid down on 5 June 1943 at Tacoma, Wash., by the Seattle-Tacoma Shipbuilding Co.; assigned to the United Kingdom under lend-lease on 23 June; redesignated CVE–54 on 15 July; launched on 22 November; and delivered to the British on 18 February 1944.

Renamed *Reaper* (D 82), the carrier operated in the Royal Navy for the duration of World War II. After arriving at Norfolk, Va., on 13 May 1946, *Reaper* was decommissioned on 20 May and returned to the United States Government. Authorized for disposal on 14 June, *Winjah* was struck from the Navy list on 8 July and sold to the Waterman Steamship Co., of Mobile, Ala., on 12 February 1947.

Winjah Bay

A bay in Alaska.

Originally projected as *Winjah Bay*, CVE–110 was renamed *Salerno Bay* (*q.v.*) on 6 November 1943, three months before her keel was laid down.

Winnebago

A tribe of Sioux Indians who lived along the banks of the Wisconsin River and on the south side of what is now the city of Green Bay. They joined forces with Tecumseh and fought the Americans at the Battle of Tippecanoe in 1811 and aided the British during the War of 1812. However, in the Black Hawk War of 1832, the Winnebago captured the chief, Black Hawk, and delivered him to the United States government, thus ending the war. The tribe later made a treaty with the United States in September 1832, relinquishing all of their lands south of the Wisconsin River and east of the Mississippi.

I

(Mon: dp. 1,300; l. 229'0''; b. 56'0''; dr. 6'0''; dph. 8'6''; s. 9 k.; cpl. 120; a. 4 11'' D.sb.; cl. *Milwaukee*)

The contract for construction of the first *Winnebago* —a double-turreted, river monitor—was awarded to James B. Eads of St. Louis, Mo., on 27 May 1862; and the hull of the ship was built at Carondelet, Mo., by the Union Iron Works. Launched on 4 July 1863, *Winnebago* was commissioned on 27 April 1864, Acting Master A. S. Megathlin in command.

Assigned to the Mississippi Squadron, *Winnebago* operated on the Mississippi and its tributaries protecting that vital waterway for Union forces during the last year of the Civil War. On 15 June 1864, she dueled Confederate artillery after Rebel guns had fired upon the wooden side-wheeler *General Bragg*, off Como Landing, La. *General Bragg*'s return fire caused the Confederates to move their guns to Ratliff's Landing, whence they began shelling the paddle-wheel steamer *Naiad*. Alerted by the sound of the gunfire, *Winnebago* headed toward the action and soon joined the battle. Eventually, the combined fire from the three Union ships silenced the Confederate battery.

Meanwhile, to the south, Rear Admiral David G. Farragut was preparing to attack the Confederate forts at Mobile, Ala. Accordingly, on 1 July, Rear Admiral David D. Porter reported to Secretary of the Navy Gideon Welles that *Winnebago* and *Chickasaw* had been sent to Farragut's West Gulf Blockading Squadron off Mobile.

In spite of rough weather en route, *Winnebago* made passage without incident, even proceeding on the final part of the voyage independently, without a tow. Her performance impressed Farragut, who was nearly finished with his preparations to attack the Confederate positions at Mobile Bay. Her arrival with *Chickasaw* and that of the monitor *Tecumseh* completed the Union squadron. All was now ready.

At 0530 on 5 August 1864, *Winnebago* got underway as Farragut's squadron moved out for battle. With Comdr. Thomas H. Stevens in command, the double-turreted monitor got underway from her anchorage near Sand Island and proceeded up the bay, "for the purpose of attacking the enemy."

Braving the heavily gunned defenses of Fort Morgan and known Confederate minefields ("torpedoes"), Farragut's squadron of four ironclad monitors and 14 wooden steamships boldly attacked. *Winnebago* steamed third in the column of ironclads, astern of *Tecumseh* and *Manhattan*, while *Chickasaw* brought up the rear. At 0700 that morning, *Winnebago* took station between Fort Morgan and the wooden vessels of the fleet, in line of battle. This formation enabled the armored monitors to draw the fire from the shore guns away from the wooden ships of Farragut's battle line.

The monitors' orders were clear: to neutralize the fire of the Confederate guns that raked the approach of the Union ships and to look out for the Rebel ironclads when Farragut's ships were abreast of the forts. At 0715, *Winnebago* commenced her fire, her Dahlgren smooth-bores hurling grape and canister against the Confederate emplacements of Fort Morgan. Suddenly, about three-quarters of an hour later, *Tecumseh* struck a "torpedo" and sank "instantaneously," within a cable's length of *Winnebago*. Farragut, undaunted, ordered the squadron to proceed. The sinking of *Tecumseh* scarcely checked their passage.

As she steamed past Fort Morgan, engaging the Confederate guns on her starboard hand, *Winnebago* took on board 10 survivors from the ill-fated *Tecumseh* (who had been bravely plucked from the waters of Mobile Bay by a boat from *Metacomet*) and steamed slowly up the bay. That part of the passage had been made with comparatively little damage. The worst part of the battle for the Union squadron lay ahead, when the ships successfully completed passage and the Confederate ironclad ram CSS *Tennessee* attacked.

However, before *Winnebago* could get into position to have a major role in the fighting—which caused more damage to the Union squadron than did the batteries at Fort Morgan—*Tennessee* was forced to surrender to the overwhelmingly more powerful Union squadron.

Winnebago anchored at 1045, her part in the Battle of Mobile Bay over. She had been hit 19 times, three shots penetrating the deck near her after turret, but fortunately had suffered no casualties.

Winnebago subsequently remained in the Mobile Bay area, supporting the ensuing siege of Fort Morgan. On the night of 8 August, the monitor sent a boat crew, 14 men under the command of Acting Ensign Michael Murphy, out on a special mission. Setting out from the ship after moonset, Murphy's men cut the telegraph cable between Fort Morgan and the city of Mobile. The expedition, as Comdr. Stevens later reported, was "one of danger and difficulty . . . neatly performed."

Winnebago, after the Battle of Mobile Bay, periodically shelled Fort Morgan—then under siege from the shoreward side—as did the other warships of the squadron. Ultimately, the superior firepower and overwhelming numbers amassed against Fort Morgan resulted in its surrender on 24 August.

The twin-turreted monitor remained at Mobile Bay into 1865. On 5 January 1865, a boat crew—again under the command of Acting Ensign Murphy—set out from the ship on a foraging mission. They carried out their nocturnal prowl behind enemy lines, returning with copper kettles used for distilling turpentine, 1,300 pounds of copper pipes, and four sloop-rigged boats from Bon Secours Bay, Ala.

On 27 March, joint Army-Navy operations aimed at capturing the city of Mobile commenced. The key objective of the initial thrust centered on Spanish Fort, located near the mouth of the Blakely River and the key to the city's defenses. Six "tinclad" gunboats and supporting heavier units moved up the Blakely River to cut the fort's communications with Mobile while the army began to move on the landward side.

The Confederates had attempted to stymie any waterborne advance on the fort by sowing mines thickly in the river waters. Sweeping operations by the Union forces netted 150 "torpedoes" but unfortunately did not completely clear the river—with disastrous effects.

An "American-primitive" rendition of the Civil War monitor USS *Winnebago*.

While *Winnebago* managed to emerge from the campaign that followed unscathed, her sistership *Milwaukee* did not. On 28 March, that river monitor—while dropping downriver from a point within a mile and one-half of Spanish Fort—fouled a "torpedo." She and *Winnebago* had gone upriver to shell a Confederate transport supposedly carrying supplies to the beleaguered Confederate garrison. After the enemy steamer had beat a hasty retreat, the ironclad gunboats headed downriver, where *Milwaukee*—in an area previously swept—struck a mine on her port side. She sank by the stern, fortunately remaining afloat forward, permitting the crew to escape. No men were lost. Over the ensuing days, two more Union ships fell victim to Confederate "torpedoes" in the Blakely River.

Nevertheless, undaunted, Union riverine forces subsequently cleared the Blakely, thus opening the way upstream. *Winnegago* participated in that operation, destroying Confederate obstructions through the channel.

Winnebago later served on convoy duty after the fall of Selma, Ala., in April of 1865. She protected a convoy carrying some 13,000 troops under Major General Steele, USA, to Selma and Montgomery, Ala. Later, the monitor's task, in company with *Octorora*, was to remain near the junction of the Tombigbee and Alabama Rivers. There, she covered a Union force erecting fortifications above that point to prevent local navigation by Confederate ships and craft.

Ultimately joined by the gunboat *Sebago*, *Winnebago* and *Octorora* blockaded the Rebel ironclad CSS *Nashville* and the gunboat CSS *Morgan* up the Tombigbee River. Their presence kept the Confederate warships within their lair until the end of hostilities.

Winnebago returned to Mobile Bay at the end of the Civil War. Laid up across from New Orleans, on the Algiers side of the Mississippi, on 27 September 1865, *Winnebago* remained there into the early 1870's. She was renamed twice during that time: the first to *Tornado* on 15 June 1869; and then given back her original name *Winnebago* on 10 August 1869. Sold at auction to Nathaniel McKay, at New Orleans, on 12 September 1874, the erstwhile member of the West Gulf Blockading Squadron was sold, by McKay, to the Peruvian Navy, who renamed her *Manco Capac*.

II

(Freighter: dp. 9,625; lbp. 360'7"; b. 48'2"; dr. 24'7"
  (mean); dph. 20'2"; s. 8.75 k.; cpl. 176; a. 1 5",
  1 3")

The second *Winnebago*—a steel-hulled, screw steamer completed in 1900 at Stockton, England, by Craig, Taylor, and Co.—had previously sailed in mercantile service under a succession of names—*Haugarland*, *Hamp-*

ton, and *Heathcraig*—before being inspected by the Navy on 4 February 1918. Taken over on a bare ship basis from the American Transatlantic Co., of New York City on 9 February at Hoboken, N.J., the freighter was given the classification Id. No. 2353 and was commissioned at New York City on 6 March 1918, Lt. Comdr. A. R. Cushing, USNRF, in command.

Assigned to the Naval Overseas Transportation Service (NOTS), *Winnebago* was fitted and armed as a cargo carrier but made only one round-trip voyage for NOTS. She departed New York City on 23 March, arrived at Norfolk two days later, and loaded a cargo of dynamite for the Army. The freighter sailed for France on 31 March and made port at Paulliac, via Brest, on 25 April. There, she discharged her cargo; sailed for the United States on 13 May; and arrived at New York City on the 30th.

While it had originally been intended to transfer the vessel to the Shipping Board, a change of orders resulted in her being returned to her previous owners. Thus, on 11 June 1918, *Winnebago* was turned over to the American Transatlantic Co. for a resumption of merchant service, and her name was struck from the Navy list.

Winnebago was eventually sold to the Albert Jensen *Aktieselskab*, a Danish firm based at Copenhagen, Denmark, sometime in 1923 or 1924. Renamed *Fie Jensen*, the freighter was subsequently renamed *Ontario* in 1926 or 1927 and served under the Danish flag into the late 1920's.

Winnemucca

A city in northwestern Nevada situated on the Humboldt River. Winnemucca is the seat of government for Humboldt County.

I

(PC–1145: dp. 280; l. 173'8"; b. 23'0"; dr. 10'10";
  s. 20.2 k. (tl.); cpl. 65; a. 1 3", 1 40mm., 3 20mm.,
  2 dct., 4 dcp. (K-guns), 2 dcp. (Mousetrap); cl.
  PC–461)

PC–1145 was laid down on 2 June 1943 at Bay City, Mich., by the Defoe Shipbuilding Corp.; launched on 27 October 1943; and commissioned at New Orleans, La., on 1 June 1944, Lt. J. L. Houget, USNR, in command.

PC–1145 completed shakedown training in the Gulf of Mexico on 11 June and reported for duty to the Commander, Gulf Sea Frontier. For the next year, the submarine chaser plied the waters of the Gulf of Mexico and the Atlantic seaboard conducting antisubmarine patrols and escorting coastwise convoys. In the performance of those duties, the little warship ranged as far north as New York City and as far south as the Panama Canal Zone.

Following the victory in Europe, *PC–1145* received orders assigning her to the Pacific Fleet. Early in June 1945, she departed her base at Miami and headed via the Panama Canal for the California coast and underwent repairs at San Diego before continuing west to Hawaii. She departed San Diego on 15 July and arrived in Pearl Harbor on the 21st. She did not resume her westward voyage toward the Marshall Islands until 7 August. The submarine chaser reported for duty upon her arrival at Eniwetok Atoll on the 13th, but hostilities ceased the following day.

Nevertheless, the submarine chaser remained in the western Pacific more than a year. For about a month following her arrival, she performed patrol and escort duty in the Marshalls and the Carolines. On 7 September, she departed Eniwetok for a round-trip voyage to Japan, returning almost a month later, on 5 October. The ship then resumed her patrol and escort duties in the Marshalls and Carolines. After a round-trip voyage to Wake Island late in October, she reported to the atoll commander at Majuro in November for duty as station search and rescue ship. That assignment lasted until mid-February 1946 when she departed Majuro for extensive maintenance at Guam.

She completed repairs on 16 June and departed Guam on an inspection tour of the Western Carolines carrying representatives of the United States Commercial Company, a public corporation charged with responsibility for the economic rehabilitation of the Central Pacific region. For the next four months, *PC–1145* served the United States Military Government administering the Central Pacific islands and worked hand-in-hand with officials of the United States Commercial Company surveying the region in preparation for efforts to reestablish a viable local economy.

In November, she departed the Central Pacific for her first complete overhaul since commissioning. She entered the Pearl Harbor Naval Shipyard on 21 November and remained there until 23 December. On the latter day, she reported to the Commander, Fleet Training Center, Pearl Harbor, under whose auspices she conducted refresher training and made a cruise to Hilo. *PC–1145* departed Pearl Harbor on 27 February 1947 and, on 4 March, arrived at Midway Island where she reported for duty to the Commander, Naval Operating Base, Midway. There, she served as an air search and rescue ship until the end of the second week in May. Relieved by *PC–1172* on the 13th, *PC–1145* headed back to Pearl Harbor. The warship operated out of the Oahu base conducting upkeep and repairs and serving as a training ship until late July. She then returned to Midway and resumed duty as search and rescue vessel. On 15 November, *PCS–1399* relieved her at Midway; and *PC–1145* returned to Pearl Harbor for a restricted availability.

For the remainder of her active career, *PC–1145* alternated between duty out of Pearl Harbor and service as an air search and rescue ship, at first based at Midway but later at Kwajalein, Johnston Island, Guam, and Samoa. After 1950, however, Guam and Samoa ceased to be duty stations for the submarine chaser and her sister ships. Duty in and out of Pearl Harbor consisted of repairs, training, target towing, and antisubmarine warfare operations. *PC–1145* departed Pearl Harbor for the last time on 19 February 1955 and arrived in San Francisco a week later. Following nearly four months of repairs at Treasure Island, she stood out of San Francisco Bay on her way to Astoria, Oregon, and inactivation. On 15 August 1955, the ship was placed out of commission at Astoria and was berthed with the Columbia River Group, Pacific Reserve Fleet. On 15 February 1956, the submarine chaser—still inactive—was named *Winnemucca*. She remained with the reserve fleet until 1 June 1960 when her name was struck from the Navy list. On 1 November, she was transferred to the Navy of the Republic of Korea.

II

(YTB–785: dp. 356 (f.); l. 109'; b. 31'; dr. 14'; s. 12 k. (tl.); cpl. 12; cl. *Natick*)

The second *Winnemucca* (YTB–785) was laid down in September 1965 at Marinette, Wis., by the Marinette Marine Corp.; launched in December 1965; delivered to the Navy in April 1966; and placed in service in June 1966.

Initially assigned to the 5th Naval District, the large harbor tug operated in the Norfolk area until the following spring. Reassigned at that time to Vietnam, she arrived in that country on 10 June and, for the remainder of America's involvement in that conflict, she served with Task Force 117, the Mobile Riverine Force. During her almost six years of combat operations on the rivers and in the swamps of South Vietnam, *Winnemucca* earned two Presidential Unit Citations and four Navy Unit Commendations. At the end of America's participation in that civil war in 1973, the tug was reassigned to the 17th Naval District and operated out of Adak, Alaska. That tour of duty ended late in 1975 when the ship began service at San Francisco, attached to the 12th Naval District. As of 1 January 1979, *Winnemucca* was still active at San Francisco.

Winnemucca earned 13 battle stars during the Vietnam conflict.

Winnetka

(YTB–376: dp. 325; l. 102'2''; b. 24'; dr. 10'; s. 12.5 k.; cl. *Allaquippa*)

Winnetka (YTB–376)—a harbor tug built in 1944 at Port Arthur, Tex., by the Gulfport Boiler & Welding Works, Inc.—was placed in service on 28 June 1944. She departed Galveston, Tex., on 18 July and proceeded via the Panama Canal to the Pacific. The tug served for some time at Pearl Harbor but, by the beginning of 1945, had moved west to the Mariana Islands for operations principally at Guam and Saipan. She was later reassigned to the naval base at Iwo Jima in the Volcano-Bonins chain and served there until January 1946 when she ran aground on Iwo Jima. Damaged beyond economic repair and not economically salvageable, *Winnetka* was abandoned where she lay. Her name was struck from the Navy list on 19 July 1946.

Winnipec

(SwGbt.: t. 1,030; l. 225'0''; b. 35'0''; dph. 12'0''; dr. 5'8'' (aft))

Winnipec—a double-ended, iron-hulled, sidewheel gunboat—was built in 1864 at Boston, Mass., by Harrison Loring. The ship was launched on 20 August 1864, but there is no record of her having been commissioned during the Civil War or any portion of the year 1865. Deck logs exist for her during the period 1 January to 6 October 1866, at which time she was assigned to the Naval Academy as a practice ship. She remained so assigned until late in 1867 when she moved to Norfolk, Va., for repairs. In 1868, she was placed in ordinary at Norfolk and remained in that status until she was sold to Mr. Thomas Clyde on 17 June 1869.

Winona

The chief village of the Kiyuksa band of the Mdewakanton Sioux. It was located on the site occupied by the present town of Winona in Winona County, Minn.

I

(SwGbt: t. 507; l. 158′8″; b. 28′0″; dph. 12′0″; dr. 10′6″; s. 9 k.; a. 1 11″ D.sb., 1 20-pdr. P.r., 2 24-pdr. how.)

The first *Winona*—a sidewheel gunboat constructed in 1861 at New York City by C. & R. Poillon—was launched on 14 September 1861; delivered to the Navy at the New York Navy Yard on 26 November 1861; and commissioned on 11 December 1861, Lt. Comdr. Edward T. Nichols in command.

Ordered to the Gulf Blockading Squadron and allocated to the West Gulf Blockading Squadron when Union naval responsibility in the area was divided early the next year, she served at the mouth of and in the Mississippi River for the next seven months. On 24 April 1862, she attempted to pass Forts Jackson and St. Philip but snagged herself on obstructions while the rest of her unit fought its way past the Confederate forts on the river banks and the South's naval forces. Eventually freeing herself, *Winona* remained below the forts with Comdr. David D. Porter's mortar flotilla while Flag Officer Farragut moved on upriver to capture New Orleans. Four days later, her commanding officer took part in accepting the Confederate capitulation of Fort St. Philip. In May, she moved upstream with the mortar boats to join the investment of the Southern stronghold at Vicksburg.

That siege began in earnest late on the afternoon of 26 June when Farragut's mortar boats began their bombardment. At dawn on the 28th, *Winona* joined the other ships of Farragut's fleet in steaming past the Vicksburg batteries under a hail of fire to unite with the fleet under Flag Officer Davis which had been fighting its way down the river from its base at Cairo, Ill. Once above Vicksburg, *Winona* and her colleagues settled into a more or less routine schedule supporting the first Vicksburg campaign and attempting to blockade the Confederate ironclad, *Arkansas*, in the Yazoo River. On 15 July, however, the Southern warship bested a three-gunboat expedition sent up the

Yazoo after her, disabling *Carondelet* in the river and chasing *Queen of the West* and *Tyler* back down the river. *Arkansas* continued out of the Yazoo and into the Mississippi to begin a bold dash through the 33-ship Union fleet of which *Winona* remained a unit. Firing as she went, the Confederate warship hurtled through the startled Northern squadron, briefly engaging *Winona* as she raced past her. *Winona* responded briefly, but the Confederate ship passed through the gauntlet safely and moored under the protection of the Vicksburg batteries. Soon thereafter, *Winona*, under tow of *Wissahickon*, repassed Vicksburg with the rest of Farragut's force and went back to New Orleans.

By late August, the gunboat had joined the blockade off Mobile, Ala. On 4 September, she was one of three ships on station off that important Confederate port. During the day, she and the gunboat *Cayuga* scampered back and forth investigating ships sighted. At about 1705 that afternoon, the lookout on board *Oneida* spied the third strange vessel of the day. *Winona* received orders to investigate and steamed off toward the stranger. Disregarding the gunboat's hail, the stranger —a barkentine-rigged steamer bearing the unmistakable lines of a British gunboat and flying the red British ensign—bore on toward *Oneida*. *Winona* came about and gave chase. As the intruder approached, *Oneida* loosed a warning shot across her bow at about 1800. The unidentified warship did not even slacken speed. *Oneida* put two more shots across her bow in quick succession and then began firing into the ship itself. At 1805, the stranger hauled down the British colors and raised the Confederate ensign. At that point *Winona* commenced firing at what later proved to be the Confederate commerce raider *Florida*. The chase continued until about 1827 when *Florida* crossed the bar into Mobile Bay and *Winona*, *Oneida*, and *Rachel Seamen* gave up pursuit because of a combination of growing darkness, shallow water, and the guns of Fort Morgan. *Florida* had been severely riddled but Lt. John Newland Maffit had succeeded in his audacious dash through the Union blockade in spite of a skeleton crew laid low for the most part by yellow fever and

A contemporary print depicts the "ninety-day gunboat" *Winona*.

the fact that he was unable to return fire because his guns lacked sponges, rammers, and other necessary equipment. Later, he would repeat the feat on an outward voyage to become a successful commerce raider excelled only by Semmes and Waddell.

Winona, meanwhile, resumed her blockade duty off Mobile. That duty lasted until December when she received orders to return to the Mississippi. On 14 December, while anchored near Profit Island, she was fired upon by a well-concealed Confederate shore battery. Though she returned fire, her's proved ineffective because she had insufficient steam to bring her broadside to bear on the target. After suffering under the deadly accurate Southern fire, she was forced to retire from the engagement.

In April 1863, the gunboat provided support for the campaign against Port Hudson, Miss., one of the two last Confederate strongholds on the river. On 18 June, when a Confederate Army force occupied Plaquemine in Iberville Parish, La., *Winona* drove them out with gunfire and then moved on to the fort at nearby Donaldsonville to warn the Union garrison assigned there about the proximity of a large Southern force. The Confederates did not attack the fort immediately; and, in the meantime, *Winona* steamed up and down the river just in case. On two occasions during the following 10 days, she sighted and bombarded relatively large Southern concentrations ashore. When the Confederates finally attacked the fort at Donaldsonville on 28 June, *Winona*'s guns helped to repulse them. At the conclusion of that action, she returned north to participate in the final stages of the siege of Vicksburg, which finally surrendered on 4 July 1863.

On 25 August, the gunboat arrived in Baltimore, Md., for extensive repairs. She concluded the yard work in February 1864 and departed Baltimore to join the South Atlantic Blockading Squadron off the coasts of South Carolina and Georgia. For the remainder of the Civil War, that coastal region constituted her area of operations. Though stationed principally on the Charleston, S.C., blockade station, she also operated on the Suwanee River where she captured and destroyed a steamer on 25 March 1864. She also participated in attacks on Forts Rosedon and Beaulieu near Savannah, Ga. After the Confederate evacuation and Union occupation of Charleston in February 1865, *Winona* operated on the Combahee River in Georgia until the end of hostilities in April. She was apparently placed out of commission on 9 June 1865. Laid up first at the Portsmouth (N.H.) Navy Yard, she was moved to the New York Navy Yard on 22 November 1865. She was sold at New York on 30 November 1865.

Winooski

A river in north central Vermont which empties into Lake Champlain.

I

(SwGbt.: dp. 1,173; l. 205'0''; b. 35'0''; dph. 11'6''; a. 10 guns)

The first *Winooski*, a double-ended, sidewheel gunboat, was launched on 30 July 1863 at the Boston Navy Yard; towed to Providence, R.I., for the installation of her machinery; completed at the New York Navy Yard; and placed in comission on 27 June 1865, Comdr. George W. Cooper in command.

For the rest of 1865, she conducted tests at New York. Between April and August 1866, the warship cruised the fishing banks along the coast of Maine and in the Gulf of St. Lawrence. She stood out of Portsmouth, N.H., on the last day of August and set course for the West Indies. She patrolled the Caribbean until a yellow fever epidemic forced her to return to Portsmouth and quarantine late in June of 1867. Laid up at the end of the period of quarantine, the

ship remained at Portsmouth until 25 August 1868 when she was sold to Mr. John Mullen.

II

(AO–38: dp. 21,580 (lim.); l. 501'5''; b. 68'0''; dr. 30'9'' (lim.); s. 16.7 k. (tl.); cpl. 249; a. 1 4'', 2 3'', 8 .50-cal. mg.; cl. *Kennebec*; T. T–2)

The second *Winooski* (AO–38) was laid down as *Calusa* on 23 April 1941 at Sparrows Point, Md., by the Bethlehem Steel Co. under a Maritime Commission contract (MC hull 144); launched on 12 November 1941; sponsored by Mrs. Laurence B. Levi; taken over by the Navy on 5 January 1942; renamed *Winooski* (AO–38) on 9 January 1942; and commissioned at Baltimore, Md., on 27 January 1942, Comdr. Walter C. Ansel in command.

Following a brief period of shakedown training in the Chesapeake Bay, *Winooski* embarked upon her first mission in mid-February. She arrived in Baytown, Tex., on 25 February and began loading a cargo of fuel. The oiler departed Baytown on 2 March and arrived in Norfolk on the 7th. The next day, *Winooski* got underway for Newport, R.I., where she remained until the 25th. On that day, the ship got underway in company with *Delta* (AK–29) and *Lea* (DD–118), bound for Iceland. She and her consorts arrived in Reykjavik on 1 April and remained there until the 4th, at which time she returned to sea. The oiler arrived back at Norfolk on 13 April. Four days later, she stood out to sea en route to Baton Rouge, La. She loaded fuel at Baton Rouge from 23 to 25 April and then set a course back to Norfolk in which port she arrived on the 29th. She discharged her cargo at Craney Island and, on 4 May, embarked upon another voyage to Baytown. The oiler loaded fuel at Baytown from 9 to 11 May and stood out to sea on the return voyage. She reentered Norfolk on the 16th. Four days later, the ship steamed out of Chesapeake Bay again, on her way to Argentia, Newfoundland. She arrived at her destination on the 23d and began almost a month of harbor fuelling duty there. On 15 June, *Winooski* cleared Argentia for Norfolk where she arrived on 29 June. After a nine-day availability at the Norfolk Navy Yard, the oiler resumed duty, starting out on a voyage to Deer Park, Tex., on 8 July. She returned to Norfolk from Deer Park on 21 July but, two days later, headed back to Argentia where she resumed duty as station oiler from 26 July to 13 August. She returned to Norfolk on 16 August and remained there until 2 September at which time she got underway for Iceland once again. She stopped at Reykjavik for one week, from 10 to 17 September, and reentered Norfolk on the 25th.

Following a yard availability, *Winooski* began preparations for the amphibious assault on the Moroccan coast. In addition to her cargo of fuel oil, the ship deck-loaded two high-speed fire support boats for use in the invasion. On 24 October, she rendezvoused with the other ships of Task Force (TF) 34 and set a course for North Africa. The fleet arrived off Fedhala early in the morning of 8 November. *Winooski* launched the fire support boats and, while they moved in to assist the troops assaulting the beaches, she proceeded to fuel the ships in the anchorage. She continued fueling operations unmolested until 11 November when the enemy launched a series of submarine counterattacks against the invasion fleet. At about 2000 hours that evening, a torpedo struck the oiler just abaft of the bridge, punching a hole in her number 6 tank and damaging several other compartments as well. *Winooski* listed about eight degrees, but she corrected it almost immediately by shifting cargo and resumed her duties the following day. Further submarine attacks occurred on the 12th, but *Winooski* emerged unscathed and quickly put farther out to sea where she and the other ships maneuvered evasively to avoid submarine attacks. On 15 November, she put into port at Casablanca and resumed fueling operations. She remained in that port until 23 November at which time she got underway for Gibraltar for a three-month repair period.

On 27 February 1943, *Winooski* joined a convoy headed for the United States, GUS-5. After a transatlantic voyage without incident, the oiler arrived back in Norfolk on 11 March. On the 21st, the ship stood out of Chesapeake Bay on her way to Beaumont, Tex. She arrived in Beaumont on 26 March and began loading cargo. *Winooski* returned to Norfolk on 2 April and remained there for five days. On the 8th, she got underway again, bound for Aruba in the Netherlands West Indies. At Aruba on the 13th, the oiler loaded cargo again and headed back to Norfolk, where she arrived on the 18th. After a brief yard period, during which four PT boats were deck-loaded on board her, *Winooski* departed Norfolk on 25 April for New York, there to join a convoy bound for the Mediterranean. The convoy put to sea on 28 April. *Winooski* arrived in Casablanca on 16 May, loaded additional fuel oil—she had refueled escorts on the transatlantic run—and departed Casablanca on the 18th. The following day, she entered port at Oran, Algeria. That evening, her anchorage came under enemy air attack. The oiler brought every gun on board—including the light machineguns on the deck-loaded PT's—to bear on the attackers but failed to score a kill. The enemy, however, did little better, for the harbor suffered very little damage. The oiler remained in North Africa until 22 July, providing distant support for the invasion and occupation of Sicily. She unloaded the PT boats on 22 May; and, on 1 June, she shifted to Mers-el-Kebir. On 21 July, the oiler moved back to Oran where she remained overnight before getting underway for Gibraltar. There, the ship joined up with a convoy and set a course for the United States. She arrived in Hampton Roads on 3 August.

On 12 August, she embarked upon another voyage to Beaumont, Tex., arriving there on the 18th. She loaded cargo and then got underway again on the 20th. The oiler arrived back at Norfolk on 25 August and began preparations for another transatlantic voyage. On 1 September, the ship headed for New York where she arrived on the following day. On 5 September, *Winooski* put to sea with a convoy bound for the British Isles. She provided refueling services to the convoy's escorts along the way and arrived in Belfast Lough, Ireland, on 14 September. After further refueling operations, she moved to Loch Long, Scotland, where she discharged the remainder of her oil to the dock. After a visit to Gourrock, Scotland, the oiler departed the United Kingdom, bound for home. She reentered Norfolk on 1 October and remained there one week before embarking upon another voyage to Aruba. She reached the Dutch colony on 13 October, loaded oil, and headed back to Norfolk on the 14th. She returned to Hampton Roads on the 20th, discharged her cargo at the Standard Oil dock, and entered the Norfolk Navy Yard for a 20-day availability. She exited the yard on 11 November and anchored in Hampton Roads. Between 13 and 26 November, *Winooski* made another round-trip voyage from Norfolk to Texas and back. On 5 December, she rendezvoused with another transatlantic convoy, this time off Cape Henry, Va., and set a course for North Africa. She arrived in Casablanca on 20 December and remained there until the 28th, at which time she joined the homeward-bounty Convoy GUS-25. The oiler reentered Chesapeake Bay on 17 January 1944 and moored at Norfolk.

On 4 February, *Winooski* departed Norfolk with a load of oil bound for Bermuda. She arrived at her destination on 6 February, discharged her cargo and, on 14 February, set a course for Baytown, Tex. She loaded cargo at Baytown between the 20th and the 24th and then shaped a course back to Norfolk, where she arrived on 1 March. From 5 to 19 March, the oiler made another Texas run, this time to Port Arthur and back to Norfolk. Six days after her return, she was on

her way back to Texas. On the return voyage, however, the ship was diverted to Casco Bay, Maine, where she discharged her cargo. The ship entered New York on 9 April and remained there until the 12th at which time she headed back to Texas for another load of oil. *Winooski* reentered New York harbor on the 27th and began preparations for another transatlantic voyage. The convoy stood out of New York on 3 May, and *Winooski* arrived in Avonmouth, England, on the 16th. From there, she moved to Belfast whence she departed on the 19th to return to the United States. The oiler arrived back in New York on 28 May and remained there until 8 June when she stood out to sea with another convoy, bound for Europe. She arrived in Swansea, England, on the 19th. She discharged cargo there and returned to sea on the 22d. After a brief stop at Belfast Lough, *Winooski* departed for home on 24 June and reentered Norfolk on Independence Day 1944.

She remained in the Norfolk area until 14 July when she returned to sea with a convoy bound for the Mediterranean, a part of the force being sent to invade southern France. *Winooski* reached the Strait of Gibraltar on 28 July and put into Mers-el-Kebir on the 30th. On 3 August, she set sail for Palermo, Sicily, and arrived there two days later. The oiler remained at Palermo providing logistics support for the bombardment and fire support units of the invasion fleet until 28 August. On that day she departed Palermo and, after visits to Bizerte and Oran, got underway to return home on 4 September. She entered New York harbor 10 days later. The ship stayed in the New York area until 18 September when she headed back to Norfolk. The ship arrived at her destination on the 19th and entered the navy yard for alterations. She completed modifications on 8 October and, after a series of trials, departed Norfolk on the 14th. The oiler made a stop at Aruba to load oil and aviation gasoline and then set a course for the Panama Canal. She arrived at Cristobal, Canal Zone, on 22 October and transited the canal that same day.

On 23 October, *Winooski*—by then a unit of the Pacific Fleet—embarked upon a long voyage to the Admiralty Islands. She arrived in Seeadler Harbor at Manus on 16 November and remained there for more than a month fueling American warships and conducting underway training. On 23 December, she departed Manus with Task Group (TG) 77.6 and arrived in Leyte Gulf on the 30th. She remained at Leyte until 2 January 1945 at which time she put to sea with TG 77.10, bound for Mindoro where she and the other units of Task Unit (TU) 77.10.5 were to establish a forward logistics base for the forces engaged in the assault and occupation of Luzon. The unit with which *Winooski* steamed came under air attack several times; and, though the oiler herself escaped unscathed, one ship— *Ommaney Bay* (CVE-79)—fell victim to the kamikaze attacks and suffered such severe damage that American ships had to sink her with torpedoes. *Winooski* arrived safely in Mangarin Bay, Mindoro, on 4 January; and, though she and her consorts had to put to sea each night because of the danger of air attacks, they remained in that vicinity until 8 January and provided fuel for the warships engaged in the Lingayen Gulf operation. On the 8th, she left Mindoro to rendezvous with TG 77.9, the Luzon Reinforcement Group, and set a course with that task group for Lingayen Gulf. The ships arrived in Lingayen Gulf on the morning of 11 January, but *Winooski* departed the gulf again that evening to join TG 77.4, the Escort Carrier Group, for several days of refueling operations before returning to the gulf on the 15th. She resumed anchorage fueling duty at Lingayen for the remainder of the month.

On 10 February, *Winooski* moved from Lingayen Gulf to recently captured Subic Bay. She resumed fueling operations at that location and remained there until near the end of the first week in April. She departed Subic Bay on 5 April and headed back to Leyte, arriving in San Pedro Bay on the 8th. There, the oiler loaded provisions, stores, and a cargo of fuel oil before getting underway for Zamboanga where she arrived on the 16th. Two days later, she departed Zamboanga in company with TU 78.2.15 for the landing at Pollac harbor on southern Mindanao. The ship arrived in the landing area on the 19th and conducted fueling operations until 29 April when she set sail for Tawi Tawi in the Sulu Archipelago. She arrived at her destination on the 30th and remained there awaiting the successful conclusion of Allied landings at Tarakan, Borneo. On 1 May, she received word that the landings at Tarakan were proceeding smoothly and got underway for Borneo. The oiler arrived at Tarakan on 2 May and remained there conducting fueling operations until the 7th at which time she headed back to the Philippines. Steaming via Tawi Tawi, *Winooski* arrived back in San Pedro Bay on the 10th and remained there until the 14th when she got underway to return to Tarakan. She resumed harbor fueling duty at Tarakan from 16 May to 1 June. From there, she moved back to Tawi Tawi where she conducted fueling operations for a day or two before sailing on to Zamboanga.

Winooski stayed at Zamboanga, making preparations for the landings at Brunei Bay, Borneo, from 5 to 7 June. On the latter day, she departed Zamboanga and joined TG 78.1. The task group arrived at Brunei Bay on the morning of 10 June. The landings went off smoothly, and the oiler began her usual routine of refueling the ships of the invasion fleet. She carried out those operations until 14 June at which time she headed back to Leyte. She replenished at Leyte on 17 and 18 June and returned to Brunei Bay on the 21st. She remained there until the 29th at which time she headed, via Zamboanga, back to Leyte. *Winooski* replenished at San Pedro Bay from 8 to 12 July and steamed via Guiuan, Samar, back to Brunei Bay. The ship served as station oiler at Brunei Bay from 16 to 19 July and returned to Leyte on the 24th.

For the remaining three weeks of the war and through the first four months of the postwar period, *Winooski* steamed the length and breadth of the Philippine Archipelago delivering fuel to American ships throughout the area. On 17 December, *Monongahela* (AO-42) relieved her of duty as station oiler at Manila. Three days later, *Winooski* began the long voyage home. En route, however, she received a change in orders; and, after a brief stop in Pearl Harbor to disembark passengers and load cargo, she reversed course for Japan on 5 January 1946. The oiler arrived at Yokosuka, Japan, on 17 January, discharged her cargo to ships at the naval base, and got underway for home again on the 24th. She arrived in San Francisco, Calif., on 8 February but remained only nine days. She set sail for Norfolk, Va., on the 17th. The ship transited the Panama Canal on the 26th and arrived in Norfolk early in March. After almost two months of preparations, *Winooski* was placed out of commission at Norfolk on 30 April 1946. She was delivered to the War Shipping Administration for disposal on 1 August 1946, and her name was struck from the Navy list on 8 October 1946.

Winooski earned four battle stars during World War II.

Winslow

John Ancrum Winslow—born in 1811 in Wilmington, N.C.—became a midshipman in 1827. While serving at Tobasco during the Mexican War, he was commended for gallantry in action by Commodore Matthew Perry.

The outbreak of the Civil War found Winslow serving ashore as commanding officer of the 2d Lighthouse District. After Flag Officer A. H. Foote relieved Comdr. John Rodgers in command of the Western Flotilla, he requested that Winslow be sent west to assist him as executive officer. At Cairo, Ill., Winslow labored to fit out and man gunboats for service on the Mississippi and its tributaries. In October 1861, he assumed command of *Benton* at St. Louis. As that deep-draft gunboat was steaming down river to Cairo, she ran aground on a sandbar. While attempting to refloat the ship, Winslow was injured by a flying chain link and forced to return home late in the year to recover. When he was able to return to duty in the summer of 1862, Winslow was given comparatively minor assignments. He contracted malaria, became discontented, and asked to be reassigned to other duty.

Detached from the Mississippi Squadron, Winslow returned to his home in Roxbury, Mass., early in November and was confined to bed there for a month attempting to regain his health. On 5 December, orders arrived directing him to proceed via New York to the Azores where he was to assume command of screw sloop *Kearsarge*. Two days later, he went to New York where he embarked in *Vanderbilt* for passage to Fayal. However, when he reached that island on Christmas Eve, he found that *Kearsarge* had sailed to Spain for repairs; and he was forced to remain at Fayal until spring. When the screw sloop finally returned early in April 1863, he assumed command.

In *Kearsarge*, he cruised among the Azores seeking Confederate commerce raider *Alabama* until autumn when he shifted to European waters. At Ferrol, Spain, Winslow learned that CSS *Florida* was at Brest, France, undergoing overhaul; and he promptly sailed for that port to prevent her from slipping out to sea again. While keeping track of the progress of the repair work on the Southern warship through spies, he also made runs along the coast of western Europe, checking on rumors of other Confederate raiders in the area.

In January 1864, *Kearsarge* returned to Cadiz for naval stores and repairs; and, while she was away from Brest, *Florida* put to sea on 18 February. When *Kearsarge* returned and learned that the quarry had escaped, she shifted to Calais, France, where CSS *Rappahannock* was moored. On 12 June, Winslow received a telegram informing him that *Alabama* was at Cherbourg. He hastened there in *Kearsarge* and, on 19 June, in an epic battle off that port, won a complete victory which gained him promotion to commodore.

Advanced to rear admiral in 1870, Winslow commanded the Pacific Fleet from that year to 1872. Shortly after his retirement, he died at Boston on 29 September 1873.

Cameron McRae Winslow, second counsin of Rear Admiral John A. Winslow, was born in Washington, D.C., on 29 July 1854. After graduating from the United States Naval Academy in 1874 and following extensive sea duty in succeeding years, then-Lieutenant Winslow served on board USS *Nashville* during the Spanish-American War. He was commended for extraordinary heroism when, on 11 May 1898, he commanded a boat expedition from *Nashville* and *Marblehead* which succeeded in cutting two submarine cables off Cienfuegos, Cuba, which linked Cuba with Europe. Despite withering enemy fire from point blank range which resulted in a bullet wound to his hand, Winslow retained command throughout the engagement.

Winslow commanded USS *Charleston* from 1905 to 1907 and battleship *New Hampshire* from 1908 to 1909. Promoted to rear admiral on 14 September 1911, Winslow was Commander in Chief, United States Pacific Fleet, from 13 September 1915 until 29 July 1916 when he was retired due to the statutory age limit. Recalled to active duty in World War I, he served as Inspector of Naval Districts on the Atlantic coast until again retiring on 11 November 1919. Admiral Winslow died in Boston on 2 January 1932.

Winslow (Torpedo Boat No. 5) and *Winslow* (Destroyer No. 53) honored Rear Admiral John Ancrum Winslow, and *Winslow* (DD–359) honored Rear Admiral Cameron McRae Winslow as well.

I

(Torpedo Boat No. 5: dp. 142 (f.); l. 161'6¾''; b. 16'⅜''; dr. 5'0'' (mean); s. 24.82 k. (tl.); cpl. 20; a. 3 1-pdrs., 3 18'' tt.; cl. *Foote*)

The first *Winslow* (Torpedo Boat No. 5) was laid down on 8 May 1896 at Baltimore, Md., by the Columbian Iron Works; launched on 8 May 1897; sponsored by Miss E. H. Hazel; and commissioned on 29 December 1897 at the Norfolk Navy Yard, Lt. John B. Bernadou in command.

On 6 January 1897, *Winslow* departed Norfolk and proceeded via New York to Newport, R.I., where she loaded torpedoes and drilled her crew in torpedo firing before returning to Hampton Roads on the 30th.

During *Winslow*'s seven-week sojourn at Norfolk, the battleship *Maine* sank in Havana Harbor; and the United States began drifting steadily closer to war with Spain. On 11 March, *Winslow* steamed out of Norfolk and headed south to Key West, Fla., a base much nearer the probable theater of operations in the approaching conflict. The warship operated from that port through the remainder of March and the first three weeks in April. On Monday, the 25th, President McKinley reluctantly ratified a joint resolution of Congress which proclaimed that a state of war had existed between the United States and Spain since the previous Thursday.

During the next fortnight, the warship patrolled the northern coast of Cuba near Havana, Cardenas, and Matanzas. Early in the morning of 11 May, *Winslow* left her blockade station off Matanzas and proceeded to Cardenas to replenish her coal bunkers. Upon reporting to *Wilmington* (Gunboat No. 8) for that purpose, she was ordered to take on a Cuban pilot and scout the entrance of Cardenas Bay for mines. *Winslow* then entered the bay in company with the revenue cutter *Hudson*. The two ships conducted a meticulous search of the channel, found no mines, and returned to *Wilmington* around noon to make their report. At this point, the commanding officer of *Wilmington* decided to take his ship—escorted by *Winslow* and *Hudson*—into Cardenas harbor in search of three Spanish gunboats reportedly in port. *Winslow* marked shoal water to *Wilmington*'s portside and, upon reaching a point about 3,000 yards from the city, sighted a small, gray steamer moored alongside the wharf. The torpedo boat received orders to move in closer to determine whether or not the vessel was an enemy warship.

By 1335, *Winslow* reached a point approximately 1,500 yards from her quarry when a white puff of smoke from the Spaniard's bow gun signaled the beginning of an artillery duel which lasted one hour and 20 minutes. *Winslow* immediately responded with her 1-pounders, but enemy batteries ashore then entered the fray. The Spanish concentrated their efforts on little *Winslow*, and she soon received a number of direct hits. The first shot to score on the torpedo boat destroyed both her steam and manual steering gear. While her crew tried to rig some type of auxiliary steering system, *Winslow* used her propellers to keep her bow gun in position to fire. Then, all at once, she swung broadside to the enemy. Almost immediately, a shot pierced her hull near the engine room and knocked the port main engine out of commission. She maneuvered with her remaining engine to evade enemy fire and maintained a steady return fire with her 1-pounders. At this point, *Wilmington* and *Hudson* brought their guns to bear on the Spanish ship and shore batteries, and the combined fire of the three American warships put the Spanish gunboat out of action and caused the shore batteries to slacken fire.

All but disabled, *Winslow* requested *Hudson* to tow her out of action. The revenue cutter approached the stricken torpedo boat and rigged a tow line between the two ships. As *Hudson* began to tow *Winslow* out to sea, one of the last Spanish shells to strike the torpedo boat hit her near the starboard gun and killed Ens. Worth Bagley who had been helping to direct the warship's maneuvers by carrying instructions from the deck to the base of the engine room ladder. Ens. Bagley had the dubious distinction of being the first naval officer killed in the Spanish-American War; and in memory of his sacrifice and devotion to duty, Torpedo Boat No. 24, Destroyer No. 185, and DD–386 each carried the name, *Bagley*.

Badly damaged, *Winslow* was towed clear of the action. Her commanding officer and a number of others in her crew were wounded. Lt. Bernadou saw that the dead and wounded were transferred to *Hudson*, and he then left the ship himself after turning command over to Chief Gunner's Mate George P. Brady, who—along with Chief Gunner's Mate Hans Johnsen and Chief Machinist T. C. Cooney—later received the Medal of Honor and was promoted to warrant officer.

The day following the engagement, *Winslow* arrived at Key West for temporary repairs there and at Mobile, Ala. She returned to Key West for 10 days before sailing north on 16 August. After brief stops at Port Royal, S.C., and at Norfolk, Va., the ship reached New York on 27 August and was placed out of commission at the New York Navy Yard on 7 September 1898 to begin more extensive repairs.

But for a short voyage to Philadelphia in mid-October, *Winslow* remained inactive until early in 1901, first at New York—in a decommissioned status—and later at the Norfolk Navy Yard where she was officially listed as "in reserve." In any event, the torpedo boat had returned to full commission by 30 June 1901 and—assigned to the Naval Torpedo Station at Newport—spent the next three years training naval officers and enlisted men in the techniques of torpedo firing and helping them to polish their skills in gunnery and

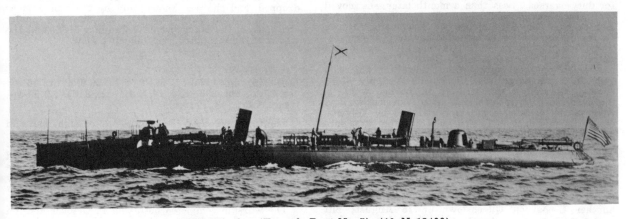

USS *Winslow* (Torpedo Boat No. 5). (19–N–12400)

shipboard engineering. In all probability, she also participated in some of the work done to improve the "automotive" torpedo.

Information on her activities between July 1904 and February 1906 is extremely sketchy, but she probably spent the majority of that time either in reserve or out of commission at New York. Whatever the case, *Winslow* was recommissioned at the New York Navy Yard on 16 February 1906 and steamed south to Norfolk, where she was placed in the Reserve Torpedo Flotilla. Sometime during fiscal year 1909, she was transferred to Charleston, S.C., though she remained in reserve.

On 1 June 1909, the torpedo boat was turned over to the Massachusetts Naval Militia at Charleston. She moved north to Boston where she served as a school ship for volunteer seaman of the local naval militia until the following November. On 2 November 1909, the Massachusetts Naval Militia returned *Winslow* to the Navy, and she was placed in reserve at the Boston Navy Yard until the summer of 1910. On 12 July 1910, *Winslow* was placed out of commission at Boston, and her name was struck from the Navy list. In January 1911, she was sold to H. Hanson of New York City.

II

(Destroyer No. 53: dp. 1,050 (n.); l. 305'3''; b. 30'4'' (wl.); dr. 10'5½'' (aft); s. 29.05 k.; cpl. 106; a. 4 4'', 8 21'' tt.; cl. *O'Brien*)

The second *Winslow* (Destroyer No. 53) was laid down on 1 October 1913 at Philadelphia, Pa., by William Cramp & Sons; launched on 11 February 1915; sponsored by Miss Natalie E. Winslow; and commissioned on 7 August 1915, Lt. Neil E. Nichols in command.

After trials off the upper east coast, *Winslow* joined the 6th Division, Atlantic Fleet Torpedo Flotilla. The destroyer participated in maneuvers in Cuban waters during the winter of 1915 and 1916 and, in the spring, began operations along the eastern seaboard. By October 1916, she was serving in coastal waters near Newport, R.I. During that assignment, the destroyer rendered assistance to the crews of Allied ships captured and sunk by the German submarine *U-53*. At the end of the month, the warship went into the New York Navy Yard and remained there through the end of the year. In January 1917, she steamed south to Cuba, where she joined the rest of the Fleet to participate in annual winter maneuvers. Following the Fleet exercise, *Winslow* returned north to the Chesapeake.

When the United States entered World War I on 6 April 1917, the destroyer rode at anchor in the York River near Yorktown, Va. She had been there guarding the river mouth since February when American relations with Germany began to deteriorate as a result of the latter country's return to unrestricted submarine warfare. Soon after Congress declared war, *Winslow* moved north to the New York Navy Yard to prepare for duty overseas. Less than a month later, she moved to Boston, Mass., from where she got underway for Europe on 7 May with five other destroyers. After a 10-day passage, *Winslow* reported for duty at Queenstown, Ireland, on the 17th. On the 21st, she began patrolling the approaches to the British Isles.

Winslow operated out of Queenstown for almost a year in a campaign to defend Allied supply ships against Germany's unrestricted submarine warfare. She escorted convoys into and out of Queenstown and went to the assistance of ships attacked by U-boats. Just after midnight on 11 June, she spied her first submarine and rushed to the attack. Her target submerged, and the destroyer dropped a series of depth charges. She failed, however, to find any evidence supporting the success of her attack and resumed her patrol. On 30 July, *Winslow* picked up the captain and 12 crewmen from the torpedoed SS *Whitehall* and brought them safely into Queenstown. She sighted another U-boat off Queenstown on 16 August; but heavy weather covered the submarine's tracks when

it submerged; and *Winslow* made no attack. Six weeks later, on 24 September, the warship rushed to the assistance of an American schooner, *Henry Lippett*, being shelled by another submarine. When the destroyer reached the little sailing vessel, she was in flames; and the U-boat had just submerged. *Winslow* delivered a desultory depth charge barrage on what appeared to be the submarine's moving wake; then broke off the attack to assist the schooner's crew.

During the remainder of her assignment at Queenstown, *Winslow* attacked two more submarines, the first on 11 October and the second on 3 January 1918. In both cases, she depth-charged oil slicks which appeared to originate from damaged, submerged U-boats. In neither case did she receive visible confirmation of a sinking; however, during the 3 January attack, one of her depth charges threw a large mass of dark liquid high in the air. From this description, it appears that her depth charge brought up fuel oil from what was believed to be *U-61*. Unfortunately for *Winslow*, lack of more definite proof of this premise precludes crediting her with a sinking.

At the beginning of April 1918, the warship was reassigned to the United States Naval Forces in France. Operating from Brest, she spent the remainder of the war shepherding American troop transports into French ports. Although the destroyer engaged the enemy on at least seven different occasions, in no instance did she score a confirmed sinking. On 8 August, she helped rescue survivors from *Westward Ho*, sunk the preceding day by a submarine. On 5 September, she attacked the submarine that had just torpedoed *Mount Vernon*; but her depth charges—like those of *Conner* (Destroyer No. 72), *Nicholson* (Destroyer No. 52), and *Wainwright* (Destroyer No. 62)—failed to shorten the career of *U-82*. Her final action of the war came slightly over a fortnight later when she depth-bombed a U-boat that attacked the convoy in her care. As in all previous cases, proof of a certain kill eluded her.

Winslow continued her patrols out of Brest through the end of hostilities on 11 November. After the armistice, she continued to operate in French waters and served as one of the escorts for *George Washington* when that ship brought President Woodrow Wilson into the harbor on 13 December. Fifteen days later, the warship departed France to return to the United States. She reached New York on 12 January 1919 and resumed peacetime duty with the Atlantic Fleet. During May, *Winslow* served as one of the rescue pickets stationed along the route across the Atlantic flown by three Navy NC-type seaplanes. After that, the destroyer returned to normal operations along the east coast and annual winter maneuvers in Cuban waters until placed in reduced commission at Philadelphia on 10 December 1919. In June 1921, she returned to active duty along the east coast until the following March. *Winslow* was placed out of commission at the Philadelphia Navy Yard on 5 June 1922. In July 1933, her name was dropped, and she was known only by the hull number assigned her in July 1920, DD-53. She was finally struck from the Navy list on 7 January 1936, and she was sold for scrapping the following June.

III

(DD-359: dp. 1,850; l. 381'0''; b. 36'2''; dr. 16½'; s. 35 k.; cpl. 238; a. 8 5'', 8 21'' tt., 8 1.1'', 2 50-cal. mg., 2 dct.; cl. *Porter*)

The third *Winslow* (DD-359)—one of eight ships in a unique class of heavily armed destroyer squadron leaders—was laid down on 18 December 1933 at Camden, N.J., by the New York Shipbuilding Co.; launched on 21 September 1936; sponsored by Miss Mary Blythe Winslow; and commissioned at the Philadelphia Navy Yard on 17 February 1937, Comdr. Irving R. Chambers in command.

The warship completed outfitting in October and, on the 19th, embarked upon a shakedown cruise which took her to ports in Sweden, England, France, Portugal, and Africa. Upon her return to the western hemisphere, she passed her final acceptance trials off the coast of Maine and was assigned to Battle Force, Destroyers, in the Pacific. Early in 1938, she transited the Panama Canal and joined Destroyer Squadron 9 at San Diego. Over the next three years, *Winslow* conducted operations in the eastern Pacific—generally between Hawaii and the west coast—from her home port at San Diego.

By 1941, events in Europe—where World War II was already in its second year—necessitated the strengthening of American naval forces in the Atlantic. Accordingly, *Winslow* retransited the canal in April and, after visiting Guantanamo Bay in Cuba, reported for duty at Norfolk, Va. That summer, she conducted training operations with submarines off the New England coast. Later, she also participated in neutrality patrols, particularly those directed at keeping watch over the Vichy French ships at Martinique and Guadeloupe in the French Antilles. Early in August, *Winslow* joined *Tuscaloosa* (CA–37) in escorting *Augusta* (CA–31) as that heavy cruiser carried President Franklin D. Roosevelt to Argentia, Newfoundland, to meet British Prime Minister Winston Churchill in the conference which resulted in the Atlantic Charter. Then, after escorting transports carrying reinforcements to Iceland, the destroyer arrived in Halifax, Nova Scotia, early in November and became a unit in the screen of America's first convoy to the Orient. Convoy WS–12X, bound via the Cape of Good Hope for Singapore, departed Halifax on 10 November. Just before the convoy reached Capetown, South Africa, where the destroyers were to part company with the convoy and head for home, word arrived that the Japanese had attacked Pearl Harbor.

After leaving the convoy at Capetown, *Winslow* returned to the United States where she was assigned to Vice Admiral Jonas H. Ingram's 4th Fleet, which had grown out of the South Atlantic neutrality patrols. The warship patrolled the area between Brazil and Africa, hunting German submarines and blockade runners until April 1944. On two occasions during that period, she returned briefly to the United States—in June 1942 and in October 1943—to undergo repairs at Charleston, S.C.

In April 1944, the warship began escorting newly constructed warships from Boston, via Norfolk, to the West Indies. After three such voyages, she began escorting convoys from New York to England and Ireland in August. She made five round-trip voyages across the Atlantic before putting into Charleston again in March 1945 for a four-month overhaul.

While in Charleston for alterations, she lost her torpedo tubes, traded her light, single-purpose, 5-inch guns for five dual-purpose 5-inch guns. In addition, she received 16 40-millimeter and four 20-millimeter antiaircraft guns in preparation for services in the Pacific.

However, by the end of her refresher training out of Casco Bay, Maine, hostilities had ceased. Accordingly, *Winslow* received orders to begin experimental work testing antiaircraft ordnance. On 17 September 1945, the ship was redesignated AG–127. She continued her experimental work with the Operational Development Force until she was decommissioned on 28 June 1950. *Winslow* remained in reserve, berthed with the Charleston Group, Atlantic Reserve Fleet, until declared unfit for further naval service on 5 December 1957. Her name was struck from the Navy list on that same day, and she was sold on 23 February 1959 for scrapping.

Winston

Counties in Alabama and Mississippi.

(AKA–94: dp. 14,200 (lim.); l. 459'2''; b. 63'0''; dr. 26'4'' (lim.); s. 16.5 k. (tl.); cpl. 247; a. 1 5'', 8 40mm.; cl. *Andromeda*; T. C2–S–B1)

Winston (AKA–94) was laid down on 10 July 1944 at Kearny, N.J., by the Federal Shipbuilding & Drydock Co. under a Maritime Commission contract (MC hull 216); launched on 30 November 1944; sponsored by Mrs. Benjamin Fairless; delivered to the Navy on 18 January 1945; and commissioned at the New York Navy Yard on 19 January 1945, Comdr. Morgan C. Wheyland, USNR, in command.

Winston completed her fitting-out at New York and then departed on 3 February, bound for the Virginia capes. She reached Hampton Roads the following day and, for the next nine days, conducted shakedown training in the Chesapeake Bay. Following post-shakedown availability at the Norfolk Navy Yard, she put to sea once again on 1 March, bound for Hawaii. En route, the vessel transited the Panama Canal on 7 March and arrived in Pearl Harbor on the 20th. After discharging her cargo, the attack cargo ship stood out of Pearl Harbor on 29 March, set a course for the west coast, and reached San Francisco on 4 April. There, *Winston* loaded 2,496 tons of cargo bound for the 4th Marine Division, headed back toward Hawaii on 10 April, and arrived at Maui nine days later. She discharged her cargo there and, on 27 April, received orders to conduct amphibious training at Kahoolawe Island. That operation lasted until 1 May. The following day, she stopped briefly at Honolulu before departing Hawaii on her way back to the west coast. She arrived in San Francisco Bay on 9 May, loaded ammunition at Port Chicago, and headed back to Hawaii on the 14th. In June and July, she made two more such round-trip voyages ferrying ammunition between Oahu and San Francisco.

After her return to Pearl Harbor in August, *Winston* resumed duty with the amphibious forces. The war,

USS *Winston* (AKA–94) off South Vietnam, 1967. (K–41458)

however, ended before she saw any combat action. Instead, she drew duty supporting the American postwar occupation in Asia. On 7 September, she stood out of Pearl Harbor to transport the Army's 98th Infantry Division to Japan. She stopped at Saipan from the 19th to the 22d and arrived at Wakayama, Japan, on 27 September. On 1 October, *Winston* got underway for the Philippines and, a week later, entered port at Manila. On the 8th, she moved to Subic Bay where she loaded landing craft to replace those she had left with the occupation forces in Japan. The following day, the ship left Subic Bay and headed—via Lingayen Gulf and Aringay—back to Japan. She reached Hiro Wan on 22 October and remained there for eight days. She put to sea again on the 30th and set a course for Pearl Harbor. *Winston* made a three-day stop at Oahu, from 10 to 13 November, before continuing on toward the United States. She transited the Panama Canal on 29 November and arrived at Norfolk, Va., on 7 December.

For almost two years, the ship plied the waters of the western Atlantic, participating in amphibious maneuvers with marines from the Central American coast in the south to the shores of Greenland in the north. Late in 1947, *Winston* was inactivated briefly at Baltimore; but she returned to active service early in 1948. During that year, she resumed exercises with the marines and travelled the length of the coast of North America. At the beginning of 1949, she embarked units of the 2d Marine Division and sailed on 3 January for a four-month tour of duty in the Mediterranean Sea. On 24 May, the attack cargo ship returned to the United States from her first cruise with the 6th Fleet. After disembarking the marines at Morehead City, N.C., she proceeded to Norfolk and resumed east coast operations out of that port.

On 2 September, she left the Chesapeake Bay on her way to the Pacific Ocean. The ship transited the Panama Canal on the 7th, remained at Balboa until the 10th, and then headed north to the Pacific Northwest. She visited Olympia, Seattle, and Tacoma before moving south to San Diego on 29 September. *Winston* departed that port on 10 October, bound for Hawaii. For the next three weeks, she participated in Operation "Miki," a combined Army, Navy, Air Force, and Marine Corps exercise simulating a massive invasion of the Hawaiian Islands. She returned to the west coast in mid-November and paid visits to Tacoma, Wash., and San Francisco, Calif., before heading south toward Panama on 22 November. She entered the canal on 4 December, set a course back toward the Virginia capes later that day, and arrived in Hampton Roads on 8 December.

For the next seven months, *Winston* made training voyages out of Norfolk and conducted amphibious exercises with marines embarked. However, the eruption of hostilities in the Far East late in June 1950— when communist North Korea invaded South Korea— took the attack cargo ship back to the Orient. On 14 August, *Winston* stood out of Hampton Roads, bound— via the Panama Canal and the California coast—for the western Pacific. She transited the canal on the 19th and arrived in San Diego on the 27th. On 1 September, the ship embarked upon a non-stop voyage to Kobe, Japan, which she reached on the 16th. After two days at Kobe, *Winston* continued her voyage to the combat zone off the coast of Korea. On 26 September, she and the other units of Transport Division (TransDiv) 11 landed reinforcements at Inchon where, only 11 days before, the American Navy had landed troops in a classic combined operation which forced communist forces to withdraw from much of South Korea. She continued participation in that operation for five days before retiring to Sasebo, Japan. Two weeks later, she returned to Inchon to reembark marines for the landings at Wonsan carried out between 25 and 31 October. Completing her part in that operation, the attack cargo ship began a shuttle service between Pusan and the combat areas ferrying fresh troops and supplies—first to Wonsan and, later, to Hungnam.

Late in November, Chinese communist forces entered the conflict and began an all-out drive against United Nations (UN) forces to drive them out of North Korea. By early December, most UN troops were pushed across the 38th parallel into South Korea, but a few held coastal enclaves at Wonsan and Hungnam. *Winston* participated in the evacuation of troops from both areas. That operation occupied most of the final month of 1950. During the first eight months of 1951, the attack cargo ship continued her duty running troops and supplies between various points on the eastern coast of Korea. When UN forces began their push back northward, the naval forces along the eastern coast supported their advance by elaborate feints at amphibious landings far behind enemy lines. *Winston* participated in three of those diversions between April and June. Otherwise, her mission remained one of cargo and troop transportation.

After visits to Sasebo and Hong Kong in June and July, respectively, she departed Hong Kong on 14 July and shaped a course back to the United States. She arrived in San Diego on 1 August and began operations along the California coast. At the beginning of 1952, she left the coast for a voyage to Hawaii and an overhaul at the Pearl Harbor Naval Shipyard. At the conclusion of this refurbishing work, she resumed operations along the west coast out of San Diego.

In November, *Winston* loaded ammunition at San Francisco and, on the 12th, headed out to sea to return to the western Pacific. She arrived in Yokosuka, Japan, on the 29th; but, instead of heading back to the Korean coast immediately, the attack cargo ship made a circuit of port visits, stopping at Sasebo, Hong Kong, Subic Bay, and, returning to Japan, at Naha and Kobe before reentering Yokosuka. Between 12 and 14 February 1953, she made her first return visit to Korea, carrying troops and equipment from Japan to Pusan. From then until the armistice in July, shuttle missions between Japan and Korea remained her sole mission. Then, as the diplomatic offensive replaced military operations, the issue of prisoner exchange came to the fore, and *Winston* was chosen as one of the ships to participate in Operation "Big Switch." She made four trips between Koje Do, Cheju Do, and Pusan repatriating over 3,000 prisoners of war and civilian internees tween August and September of 1953.

She returned to Japan early in September and, after stops at Sasebo and Yokosuka, the ship departed the latter port on 22 September to return to the United States. En route, she made a two-day layover at Pearl Harbor between 3 and 5 October and arrived in San Diego on the 12th. She remained there until 8 December, at which time she put to sea en route to Pearl Harbor and another shipyard overhaul. After completing those repairs in February 1954, she headed home on the 24th and arrived at San Diego on 3 March. Six months of west coast operations under the auspices of the Commander, Amphibious Force, Pacific Fleet, ensued.

In September, she headed back to the western Pacific once more for a five-month deployment during which she participated in 7th Fleet amphibious exercises and transported Marine Corps units between various bases in the Far East. On 17 March 1955, *Winston* arrived back in San Diego to begin another six months with the Pacific Fleet Amphibious Force. Coastal operations, including participation in amphibious exercises at Camp Pendleton, occupied her through the summer.

On 29 August, she stood out of San Diego on her way to the Far East once again. The ship entered Yokosuka on 15 September to begin an eventful tour of duty with the 7th Fleet. She participated in Marine Corps landing exercises at Okinawa in November and, in February 1956, joined in another amphibious operation but this time at Iwo Jima. Late in February, she visited Yokosuka before heading home via Pearl Harbor. She reentered San Diego on 23 March and resumed local operations along the California coast. Those operations included a brief period of service in conjunction with the filming of the movie, "The Good Shepherd." On 1 February 1957, *Winston* was placed out of commission, in reserve, apparently berthed at either San Diego or San Francisco.

After more than 45 months of inactivity, *Winston* was recommissioned at San Francisco on 24 November 1961. For the next year, she conducted operations in the eastern Pacific. In the fall of 1962, she began preparations for a deployment to the western Pacific. She stood out of San Diego on 16 October and stopped at Pearl Harbor at the beginning of November. There, she received orders to carry relief supplies to typhoon-stricken Guam which she did later that month. At Subic Bay for upkeep early in December, *Winston* began her first tour of duty with the 7th Fleet since recommissioning. That tour included a period of service as station ship at Hong Kong and missions training South Korean marines in amphibious operations at Pohang. She also carried an entire United States Marine Corps air group from Yokosuka to Kaohsiung, Taiwan.

On 2 May 1963, the attack cargo ship ended her cruise back at San Diego; and she resumed local operations in the eastern Pacific. Amphibious training occupied her time during the summer, and an overhaul at Portland took care of late September, October, and November. After post-overhaul training early in 1964, the ship voyaged to Hawaii to take part in amphibious exercises.

She returned to the west coast in May and began preparations for another Far Eastern cruise. On 18 June, she stood out of San Diego bound, via Pearl Harbor, for the Orient. During her stop at Pearl Harbor, *Winston* and her boats took part in the filming of Otto Preminger's movie, "In Harm's Way."

By the time the ship arrived at Okinawa, the Tonkin Gulf incident had occurred and revised all 7th Fleet deployment plans. Thus, for the remainder of that tour of duty, *Winston* ranged the South China Sea conducting contingency patrols with combat-loaded Marine Corps units embarked, though her only Vietnam duty came as a result of a natural disaster rather than the civil war in that country. She supported relief efforts in the flood-soaked area around Danang. Near the end of the year, the ship pulled into San Diego to end her second western Pacific deployment since recommissioning.

Winston spent the first five months of 1965 engaged in operations—amphibious exercises for the most part—along the coast of southern California. Late in May, she embarked marines and their equipment for a brief deployment to the Far East. The ship stood out of San Diego on 24 May, made a three-day stop at Pearl Harbor along the way, and arrived in Buckner Bay, Okinawa, on 17 June. Between 21 and 28 June, she made a voyage from Buckner Bay to Sasebo, Japan, and back. During the latter part of the first week in July, *Winston* steamed from Okinawa to South Vietnam, arriving at Danang on the 7th. After a three-day lay-over, *Winston* put to sea, bound for Japan, and arrived at Yokosuka on the 19th where she remained for eight days. On the 27th, she sailed for the United States and, on 11 August, entered port at San Diego. Through the end of September, the ship went "cold iron" there for repairs but resumed operations out of her home port at the beginning of October. Amphibious exercises, independent ship's drills, and upkeep at San Diego occupied her during much of the winter of 1965 and 1966. During the latter half of February 1966, the ship prepared for another tour of duty in the western Pacific.

Winston departed San Diego on 1 March 1966 for the first Far Eastern deployment in which she would conduct major operations in Vietnamese waters. She stopped at Pearl Harbor overnight on 10 and 11 March and arrived at Okinawa on the 26th. There, she unloaded one cargo and took on another—mostly lumber for construction activities at Chu Lai, South Vietnam. She arrived at Chu Lai on the 5th and spent the next four days unloading her cargo. On the 10th, she moved to Danang where she helped *Skagit* (AKA–105) unload her cargo, and she herself loaded elements of the 4th Marines. The following day, she departed Danang for the Colo area near Hue, arriving there on the 12th. Between 13 and 15 April, her boats ferried ammunition and supplies up the Hue River, both banks of which were in enemy hands.

At the completion of that dangerous mission, she reembarked all boats and crewmen and got underway for Hong Kong. Following a week of liberty, she returned to sea, set a course for Japan on 23 April, and arrived at Sasebo on the 27th. She spent three weeks in upkeep there before sailing on 16 May for Okinawa. She held amphibious training exercises in the Okinawa area on 17 and 18 May and, from 19 to 23 May, embarked Regimental Landing Team 5 and its equipment for transportation to Chu Lai. She set out for Vietnam on the 23d and arrived at Chu Lai on the 27th. She unloaded cargo, disembarked passengers; and, after a brief stop at Danang on 2 June, got underway for Taiwan.

She arrived in Keelung on 4 June and remained there until the 7th when she returned to sea bound for Subic Bay in the Philippines. En route, however, she was rerouted to Yokosuka, Japan, where she arrived on 11 June. At the end of almost a month of upkeep at Yokosuka and several days of operations near Okinawa, *Winston* suffered damage to one of her boilers. That casualty forced her into Subic Bay for repairs, and she did not return to sea until 22 July.

On 26 July, after a rough transit which had taken her through the developing Typhoon "Ora," the cargo ship returned to Vietnam at Camranh Bay. The next day, she embarked men and equipment of the Army's 572d Light Equipment Company for transportation north to Tuy Hoa. She anchored there the same day and began unloading. That operation lasted two days and proved difficult and hazardous due to the soft sand beach, large numbers of fishing craft and equipment crowding the area, and large amounts of debris. On the 29th, she headed north from Tuy Hoa to evacuate a South Vietnamese unit from Qui Nhon. That reverse amphibious operation saved the unit the heavy casualties it would have sustained fighting its way south along routes held by strong insurgent forces. *Winston* departed Qui Nhon on 31 July and delivered the South Vietnamese troops to Tuy Hoa that same day. Over the next three days and nights, she completed another difficult unloading operation complicated by the proximity of the enemy and the possibility of hostile fishing craft. She departed the Vietnamese coast on 3 August and, after a stop at Okinawa, arrived at Yokosuka on the 11th. A week later, she headed home, stopped at Pearl Harbor from 27 to 29 August, arrived back in San Diego on 5 September, and resumed local operations along the southern California coast.

On 11 January 1967, *Winston* entered the Long Beach Naval Shipyard and began a three-month overhaul. She completed repairs on 27 April and spent the month of May engaged in refresher training. In June, she conducted amphibious exercises, and July brought preparations for her return to the western Pacific. The ship departed San Diego on 21 July and arrived in Pearl Harbor on the 29th. During the first week in August, she participated in another series of amphibious exercises conducted off Molokai. Two days after completing that training, she exited Pearl Harbor to resume her voyage west.

She arrived in Danang on 2 September and, after three days in port, returned to sea to join Amphibious Ready Group (ARG) Alfa. During her six-week tour of duty with that mobile, self-contained amphibious unit, *Winston* participated in two combat operations. On 9 September, she helped backload marines of Special Landing Force (SLF) Alfa at Danang. On 16 September, she found herself off the Vietnamese coast near Hoi An. During Operation "Ballistic Charge," the Special Landing Force went ashore by both heli-

427

copters and surface assault craft. *Winston* boats participated in the lift and in the backload operation a week later. Almost a month later, she again participated in an amphibious landing, Operation "Bastion Hill," near Quang Tri City. That operation ended on 20 October, and *Winston* served with ARG Alfa just eight more days before heading for Hong Kong and a liberty visit. From Hong Kong, she proceeded to Japan, arriving in Yokosuka on 17 November. After a brief upkeep, she began her homeward voyage on the 21st and entered San Diego on 10 December.

During the early months of 1968, *Winston* made preparations for another deployment to the western Pacific. She spent most of March in the shipyard at Treasure Island undergoing repairs. Late in April, she took part in Operation "Beagle Leash," an amphibious exercise which simulated an attack on the Marine Corps base at Camp Pendleton. Throughout the summer, the ship participated in various single- and multi-ship training exercises honing her amphibious landing skills in preparation for another combat cruise off the coast of Vietnam.

On 31 October, *Winston* stood out of San Diego and set course, via Pearl Harbor, for the Far East. She arrived at Okinawa on 24 November but departed the following day, bound for Vietnam. She arrived in Danang on 29 November, unloaded 300 tons of cargo, and set sail for Subic Bay that same day. The attack cargo ship entered Subic Bay on 2 December and reported for duty with ARG "Alfa." On the 9th, she put to sea to return to the coast of Vietnam.

She arrived at Danang on the 11th and, for about a month, engaged in routine steaming with ARG "Alfa." On 5 January 1969, however, her troops went ashore in the I Corps combat zone for operations against Viet Cong forces in Operation "Valiant Hunt." That action continued until 12 January but proved to be only a preliminary to Operation "Bold Mariner" which she joined on the 13th. "Bold Mariner" was purported to be the largest amphibious operation of the Vietnam conflict to that date, and *Winston* participated in it until 25 January. After a brief stop at Danang on the 26th to unload some cargo, the ship got underway for a liberty call at Singapore which lasted from 1 to 10 February. She arrived back at Danang on St. Valentine's Day. The ship operated off the coast of Vietnam, periodically departing the area for port calls at various places, until May 1969. After a stop at Yokosuka, Japan, near the end of the month, she headed back to the United States. *Winston* arrived back in San Diego on 12 June.

There, she began preparations for inactivation. *Winston* was placed out of commission sometime in November 1969 and, on 17 February 1970, she was transferred to the temporary custody of the Maritime Administration for lay up with the National Defense Reserve Fleet at Suisun Bay, Calif. *Winston* remained berthed at Suisun Bay until 1 September 1976 at which time her name was struck from the Navy list, and her transfer to the Maritime Administration was made permanent.

Winston earned seven battle stars during the Korean War and another seven battle stars for service during the Vietnam conflict.

Winterberry

Any of a variety of American hollies which bear bright red berries during the winter.

(AN–56: dp. 1,275 (tl.) ; l. 194'6''; b. 37'0''; dr. 13'6'' (lim.) ; s. 12.1 k. (tl.); cpl. 56; a. 1 3''; cl. *Ailanthus*)

Winterberry (AN–56)—originally projected as *Tupelo* (YN–75)—was laid down on 17 September 1943

at Stockton, Calif., by the Stockton-Pollock Shipbuilding Co.; reclassified an auxiliary net-laying ship and redesignated AN–56 on 20 January 1944; launched on 22 March 1944; and commissioned on 30 May 1944, Lt. Sheldon E. Aarens in command.

Following preliminary operations along the California coast, *Winterberry* departed San Pedro on 30 July and headed west. The net-laying ship arrived in Pearl Harbor on 10 August and remained there for almost a month. She stood out of Pearl Harbor on 5 September to resume her voyage westward. *Winterberry* stopped briefly at Johnston Island on 9 September and reached Majuro Atoll on the 15th.

Records regarding *Winterberry*'s service between mid-September 1944 and the time of the Okinawa invasion in April 1945 are fragmentary and imprecise. She appears to have served at Majuro, Guam, Ulithi, and in the Palau Islands. In November, she was definitely at Kossol Roads in the Palau group because she reported sighting a submarine at 0858 on the 19th while she was laying tropedo nets at the west entrance to the roadstead. She indicated that the submarine submerged and surfaced three times in the space of two minutes and then moved off before *YMS–33* belatedly got underway to investigate. That submarine probably was *I–37*, which *Conklin* (DE–439) and *McCoy Reynolds* (DE–440) sank later that day about 20 miles north of the west entrance.

While it is conceivable that she was in the neighborhood of the Ryukyu Islands for the preliminary occupation of the roadstead at Kerama Retto, no hard evidence supports the conclusion. In any event, she was off Okinawa on 1 April 1945, D day for the invasion of that bitterly contested island. By the 7th, she had moved to Ulithi. *Winterberry* was back at Okinawa by 28 May. At 0730 that day, an enemy plane attacked the ships assembled in Buckner Bay. *Winterberry* opened fire, but the enemy succeeded in crashing into one of the attack transports. Fifteen minutes later, three more dive bombers raided the anchorage. They dove in from the sun and immediately drew antiaircraft fire. *Winterberry* opened up with her guns and assisted in bringing down two of the three raiders. At the height of that melee, a Japanese "Val" swooped on the anchorage. *Winterberry* could not fire on this enemy because friendly ships were in her line of fire, but the other ships brought him down.

During the early afternoon of 3 June, she again assisted in downing a *kamikaze*. At 1912 on the 11th, she joined the antiaircraft barrage when a single "Val" swooped down out of a heavy cloud cover. Oblivious to the curtain of gunfire, he dove at *LSD–6*. He overshot the dock landing ship, climbed, did a wingover and entered his second suicide dive. This time, he chose a victory ship; but the antiaircraft fire, which he had ignored so contemptuously, cut his mission short. *Winterberry*'s guns combined with those of the other ships in the area to splash the *kamikaze* but a scant few yards short of his intended victim.

During the waning months of World War II, *Winterberry* continued to serve at Okinawa. On 5 August, she departed the Ryukyus, bound for Saipan where she arrived on the 11th. The cessation of hostilities on 15 August found her still at Saipan. However, on the 20th, she got underway for Iwo Jima. The net-layer reached her destination three days later and operated in the Volcano Islands—at Iwo Jima and at Chichi Jima—until late in October. On 24 October, she departed Iwo Jima to return to the United States. After stops at Sapian, Eniwetok, Johnston Island, and Pearl Harbor, she entered San Diego harbor on 29 November and reported to the Commandant, 11th Naval District, for disposal. She was decommissioned at San Diego on 15 February 1946, and her name was struck from the Navy list on 26 February 1946. The former net-layer was subsequently transferred to the Maritime Commission for final disposition. She was sold to Joe

Medina Enterprises, of San Diego, Calif., on 31 March 1947.

Winterberry earned one battle star for World War II.

Winterswijk

A commune in the Gelderland province of the Netherlands.

(ScStr.: t. 3,205 (gross); l. 320'0''; b. 47'6''; dph. 22'10''; dr. 23' (f.); s. 9.0 k.; a. none)

Winterswijk—a steel-hulled screw steamer completed in 1914 at Albasserdam, Holland, by Jan Smit and Co. and operated prior to World War I by the firm of Erhardt and Dekkers of Rotterdam—was taken over by the United States Government on 20 March 1918 under the ancient right of angary which allowed a belligerent nation to use the property of a neutral power when necessary, but subject to full indemnification. *Winterswijk* was assigned to the Naval Overseas Transportation Service (NOTS) and commissioned at Key West on 2 April 1918, Lt. Francis R. Nichols, USNRF, in command.

After loading a cargo of coal, *Winterswijk* sailed for Cuba on 4 April and arrived at Antilla, Cuba, on the 7th. There, she discharged her valuable black, dusty cargo and later loaded a cargo of sugar. Underway again on 15 April, *Winterswijk* arrived at Boston eight days later. After unloading, the steamer was decommissioned and turned over to the United States Shipping Board on 27 April 1918. Simultaneously struck from the Navy list, *Winterswijk* remained under the custody of the Shipping Board until returned to her owner. The veteran of 25 days of service in the United States Navy subsequently resumed postwar operations with Erhardt and Dekkers.

Winthrop

(Tug: t. 58 (gross); l. 80'0''; b. 18'6''; dr. 8'3'' (mean); s. 10 k.)

Winthrop (SP-3297)—a tug constructed in 1883 at Wilmington, Del., by Jackson & Sharp—was taken over by the Navy on 18 October 1918. The sketchy records of *Winthrop*'s service suggest that she was never placed in commission; instead she was probably in service. Her status as a tug lends credence to that conclusion. In any case, the tug served the Navy actively from October 1918 until late in 1919. First, she was assigned to the 2d Naval District, probably operating at Newport, R.I. By 1 May 1919, she had moved to the 3d Naval District and most likely performed tug duties at New York. By 1 October, the ship had returned to New England, this time assigned to the 1st Naval District and, in all likelihood, based at Portsmouth, N.H. The bases and duties suggested in the foregoing are speculative in the absence of hard documentation; but, here again, her designation as a tug makes them highly probable.

Winthrop remained in the 1st Naval District for the remainder of her Navy career. Although, on 30 October 1919, she was ordered sold, she remained in Navy custody for almost two more years. She was sold on 4 June 1921. The records do not indicate to whom she was sold nor to what purpose she was subsequently put.

Wintle

Jack William Wintle—born on 18 April 1908 at Pittsburg, Kan.—was appointed a midshipman at the Naval Academy on 14 June 1928 and graduated on 2 June 1932. He reported for duty in *California* (BB-44) on the 30th and completed a three-year tour of duty in the battleship before being transferred to submarine tender *Bushnell* (AS-2). That assignment lasted 17 months. On 7 August 1936, he reported to the Puget Sound Navy Yard to help supervise the fitting out of *Perkins* (DD-377); and he remained in the destroyer after she went into commission on 18 September 1936. In the summer of 1939, Lt. (jg.) Wintle received postgraduate instruction at the Naval Academy before reporting for duty at the Philadelphia Navy Yard to help prepare *Du Pont* (DD-152) for recommissioning and service on the Neutrality Patrol. His tour of duty in that destroyer—one of the first in the Atlantic Squadrons to be fitted with sonar—ended in August 1940 when he was sent to New Orleans where he served almost two years instructing NROTC midshipmen. Late in April 1942, he reported to the Bureau of Navigation in Washington where he learned that his next assignment was to be aide and flag lieutenant to the Commander, South Pacific Area and South Pacific Force. On 15 June 1942, Wintle received his promotion to lieutenant commander and, four days later, reported for duty in his new assignment in the South Pacific.

Lt. Comdr. Wintle served under Rear Admiral Daniel J. Callaghan, Chief of Staff to the Commander, South Pacific Area and South Pacific Force, through the early months of the bitter struggle for Guadalcanal in late 1942. Late in October 1942, when Rear Admiral Callaghan went to sea as the commander of a cruiser-destroyer force, Wintle joined him in his flagship *San Francisco* (CA-38) as a member of his staff. On the night of 12 and 13 November, Callaghan's force met a Japanese raiding force built around battleships *Hiei* and *Kirishima*. During the confused melee off Savo Island, *San Francisco* suffered a terrific pounding from enemy ships—and briefly lost power completely. At that point, several Japanese salvos scored on her superstructure, obliterating her flag and navigating bridges. All but one member of the admiral's staff were killed, and Lt. Comdr. Wintle was among the casualties. For this sacrifice, Wintle was awarded the Navy Cross, posthumously.

I

(DE-25: dp. 1,140; l. 289'5''; b. 35'2''; dr. 11'0''; s. 21.5 k. (tl.); cpl. 156; a. 3 3'', 4 1.1'', 9 20mm., 8 dcp., 2 dct.; cl. *Evarts*)

Wintle (DE-25) was laid down on 1 October 1942 at the Mare Island Navy Yard as BDE-25, one of the destroyer escorts allocated to the Royal Navy under the lend-lease program; launched on 18 February 1943; sponsor unknown (Lt. Comdr. Wintle's widow sponsored DE-266 which ship carried the name *Wintle* at the time *BDE-25* was launched); reallocated to the United States Navy on 4 June 1943; named *Wintle* on 14 June 1943 when DE-266 was allocated to the Royal Navy as her replacement; and commissioned on 10 July 1943, Lt. Comdr. Leonard W. Bailey, USNR, in command.

Wintle completed shakedown training in late July and early August and returned to the Mare Island Navy Yard for post-shakedown repairs. On 21 September, she put to sea with a Hawaii-bound convoy and arrived at Pearl Harbor on 8 October. She departed Oahu, Hawaii, almost immediately to return home in the screen of another convoy on 17 October. On the 25th, the destroyer escort stood out of San Francisco Bay in the screen for a convoy bound, via Pearl Harbor, to Viti Levu in the Fiji Islands. She delivered her charges at Nandi Harbor on 14 November and, after a three-day stopover, departed Viti Levu on 17 November to escort *Neshanic* (AO-71) to Funafuti in the Ellice Islands. She stopped there for two days before returning to sea on the 21st to escort *Tallulah* (AO-50) to a fueling rendezvous. When she returned to Funafuti the following day, Operation "Galvanic," the Gilbert Islands invasion, was well underway. All the destroyer escort's recent movements and those she made over the following fortnight were undertaken to support the warships participating in that campaign. On 8 December, *Wintle* completed her labors in behalf of "Galvanic" and set a course for Funafuti where she stopped between 9 and 12 December before continuing on toward Oahu in the screen for a convoy.

The warship arrived in Pearl Harbor on 21 December. After several days in port, she began battle practice training in the Hawaiian operating area. On 3 January 1944, *Wintle* and *Dempsey* (DE-26) came alongside one another to practice fueling at sea. After transferring about 1,000 gallons of fuel to *Wintle*, *Dempsey* prepared to leave. Suddenly, she rammed *Wintle* on her starboard side. Her anchor ripped open *Wintle*'s starboard side from the lower platform deck to the main deck at frame 40. *Dempsey*'s anchor also broke *Wintle*'s degaussing coil and severed her return steam line. In her haste to change course, *Dempsey* swerved sharply, colliding with *Wintle* again, this time stern to stern, crushing *Wintle*'s propeller guard against her hull. The damaged destroyer escort's repair party quickly stuffed mattresses into the breach in her hull and shored them up as best they could to prevent serious flooding. *Wintle* was able to make 10 knots without shipping too much water and reached Pearl Harbor the following morning to begin repairs. She completed repairs rapidly and returned to sea to resume exercises on 11 January.

Ten days later, *Wintle* received orders assigning her to the 5th Amphibious Force for Operation "Flintlock," the invasion of the Marshall Islands. She departed Pearl Harbor that same day escorting four tank landing ships to Majuro. *Wintle* and her charges reached that atoll on 1 February to find that the American force had taken it without opposition the previous day. The destroyer escort led the patrol of the entrance of the lagoon on the 2d, then met *Caliente* (AO-53) at sea, and escorted her into the lagoon on the 3d. She then resumed antisubmarine warfare (ASW) patrol off Majuro and contined the task for the next six days. On the 9th and 10th, she escorted *Sangay* (AE-10) to Kwajalein, then headed back to Pearl Harbor, where she arrived on the 23d. *Wintle* remained in the Hawaiian Islands until 2 March, when she got underway with *Stadtfeld* (DE-29) to escort a three-ship convoy to the Gilberts. They saw their charges safely to the Gilberts on 11 March and got underway the following day for the Solomons. Proceeding via Funafuti, the two destroyer escorts arrived off Lunga Point, Guadalcanal, on 18 March and reported for duty with the 3d Fleet. For the next six months, *Wintle* crisscrossed the Southwest Pacific escorting tankers, transports, and cargomen to and from various American bases, most frequently between the Solomons and the Admiralty Islands. When not engaged in escort missions, she honed her ASW skills during exercises with American submarines.

On 19 September, she arrived at Manus Island concluding her last Solomons-Admiralties run. On the 22d, she headed out of Seeadler Harbor for a new theater, the Palau Islands in the Central Pacific. The warship arrived in the anchorage at Kossol Passage three days later. Her stay proved brief because she set course back to Manus that same day. She reached Seeadler Harbor on 5 October and, after a brief availability alongside *Piedmont* (AD-17), headed back to the Palaus where she arrived on 15 October. During the following month, *Wintle* performed patrol and escort duties in the Palaus. On 10 November, she relieved *Buchanan* (DD-484) off Denges Passage and fired starshells over the passage and nearby Ngeregong Island in support of troops embarked in landing craft patrolling against the possibility of enemy reinforcements reaching Peleliu from Ngeregong. That duty lasted until 12 November when she left station to assist *PC-1260*, damaged in a collision with *Kenmore* (AK-221).

The destroyer escort exited Kossol Passage on 15 November and steamed via Ulithi to the Marianas. She entered Apra Harbor, Guam, on the 28th and became a unit of the Saipan Patrol and Escort Force. For about 12 weeks, the warship patrolled the Marianas, primarily between Guam and Saipan. On Christmas night, she helped to repulse a Japanese air raid on Army Air Force installations ashore on Saipan. Two days later, she rescued three survivors from a B-29 bomber that crashed near Nafutan Point. After the excitement of late December, January 1945 was uneventful except for two round-trip voyages to Eniwetok and back.

On 5 February 1945, she received orders transferring her to the Marshalls-Gilberts Escort Force. She arrived at Eniwetok on 10 February and began duty escorting convoys from bases in the Marshalls and Gilberts to forward areas. She made frequent voyages between Guam, Kwajalein, and Eniwetok and cruised with a hunter/killer group in search of Japanese submarines reportedly operating in the Marshalls. On the night of 2 April, *Wintle* exchanged gunfire with Japanese shore batteries on bypassed Wotje Atoll after they opened fire on her while she hunted for a midget submarine. During American air strikes on enemy-held Mili, Jaluit, and Wotje in late April and early May, *Wintle* provided air-sea rescue services; but, fortunately, no aviator needed her assistance. On the night of 5 and 6 May, she covered the evacuation of natives from Japanese-held Jaluit Atoll. On 13 May, *Wintle* departed Eniwetok to screen two merchant ships on a voyage to the Palaus.

Wintle arrived in Kossol Passage on the 18th and, two days later, headed for Ulithi. There, she joined two ships damaged at Okinawa, *Hazelwood* (DD-531) and *Rathburne* (ADP-25), and escorted them on the Ulithi-to-Eniwetok leg of their voyage home. The ships departed Ulithi on 25 May and made Eniwetok on the 29th. There, the destroyer escort resumed patrol and escort duties with the Marshalls-Gilberts Escort Force which she continued to perform until mid-June.

On 17 June, *Wintle* and *Levy* (DE-162) stood out of Eniwetok to take up ASW station on the shipping lanes between Eniwetok and the Marianas. The next day, she responded to a report that *Endymion* (ARL-9) had been torpedoed but, upon reaching the repair ship, found no submarine to attack. After an unsuccessful search, she headed back to Eniwetok. The warship continued intermittent patrols until 1 July when she put to sea from Eniwetok lagoon to rendezvous with a hunter/killer group built around *Kassan Bay* (CVE-69). She searched for Japanese submarines along the Eniwetok-Marianas shipping lanes until relieved by *Snyder* (DE-745) on 8 July. *Wintle* returned to Eniwetok where she took on fuel and supplies in preparation for the long voyage back to the United States. The destroyer escort exited the lagoon on 12 July, visited Pearl Harbor on the 18th and 19th, and entered San Francisco Bay on the 26th.

The ship unloaded ammunition at the Mare Island Navy Yard and entered Hunters Point for repairs that same day. She was in drydock on 15 August when news of the Japanese capitulation arrived; and, on the 18th, most work ceased. Finally, on 15 November 1945, *Wintle* was placed out of commission and was berthed at Mare Island. On 28 November 1945, her name was struck from the Navy list. The former warship was sold for scrap to the Union Minerals & Alloys Corp. on 25 August 1947.

Wintle (DE-25) earned three battle stars during World War II.

DE-266—an *Evarts*-class destroyer escort—was named *Wintle* on 23 February 1943; laid down on 11 March 1943; and, sponsored by Mrs. Mary Clyde Wintle, Lt. Comdr. Wintle's widow, was launched on 22 April 1943. However, on 14 June 1943, the ship was allocated to the United Kingdom; and she was turned over to the Royal Navy on 16 August 1943.

Renamed *Capel* (K. 470) to honor Admiral Sir Thomas Bladen Capel who commanded the frigate *Phoebe* at Trafalgar, the ship served the British primarily in the North Atlantic. She was a part of the naval force which supported the Allied invasion of Normandy in June 1944 and was active in the Atlantic after General Eisenhower's troops had secured a foothold in western Europe. HMS *Capel* was torpedoed by *U-486* on 26 December 1944 and sank in the English Channel.

Wisconsin

The 30th state, admitted to the Union in 1848.

I

(Battleship No. 9: dp. 11,564 (n.); l. 373'10''; b. 72'2.5''; dr. 23'8.1'' (mean); s. 16 k.; cpl. 531; a. 4 13'', 14 6'', 16 6-pdrs., 6 1-pdrs., 4 .30-cal. mg.; cl. *Illinois*)

The first *Wisconsin* (Battleship No. 9) was laid down on 9 February 1897 at San Francisco, Calif., by the Union Iron Works; launched on 26 November 1898; sponsored by Miss Elizabeth Stephenson, the daughter of Senator Isaac Stephenson of Marinette, Wis., and commissioned on 4 February 1901, Capt. George C. Reiter in command.

Departing San Francisco on 12 March 1901, *Wisconsin* conducted general drills and exercises at Magdalena Bay, Mexico, from 17 March to 11 April before she returned to San Francisco on 15 April to be drydocked for repairs. Upon completion of that work, *Wisconsin* headed north along the western seaboard, departing San Francisco on 28 May and reaching Port Orchard, Wash., on 1 June. She remained there for nine days before heading back toward San Francisco.

She next made a voyage—in company with the battleships *Oregon* and *Iowa*, the cruiser *Philadelphia*, and the torpedo-boat destroyer *Farragut*—to the Pacific Northwest, reaching Port Angeles, Wash., on 29 June. She then shifted to Port Whatcom, Wash., on 2 July, and participated in the 4th of July observances there before she returned to Port Angeles the following day to resume her scheduled drills and exercises. Those evolutions kept the ship occupied through mid-July.

Following repairs and alterations at the Puget Sound Navy Yard, Bremerton, Wash., from 23 July to 14 October, *Wisconsin* sailed for the middle and southern reaches of the Pacific, reaching Honolulu, Hawaii, on 23 October. After coaling there, the battleship then got underway for Samoa on the 26th and exercised her main and secondary batteries en route to her destination.

Reaching the naval station at Tutuila on 5 November, *Wisconsin* remained in that vicinity, along with the collier *Abarenda* and the hospital ship *Solace*, for a little over two weeks. Shifting to Apia—the scene of the disastrous hurricane of 1888—*Wisconsin* hosted the Governor of German Samoa before the man-of-war departed that port on the 21st, bound—via Hawaii—for the coastal waters of Central and South America.

Wisconsin reached Acapulco on Christmas Day, 1901, and remained in port for three days. After coaling, the man-of-war twice visited Callao, Peru, and also called at Valparaiso, Chile, before she returned to Acapulco on 26 February 1902.

Wisconsin exercised in Mexican waters—at Pichilinque Bay and Magdalena Bay—from 5 to 22 March, carrying out an intensive and varied slate of exercises that included small-arms drills; day and night main battery target practices; and landing force maneuvers. She conducted further drills of various kinds as she proceeded up the west coast, touching at Coronado, San Francisco, and Port Angeles before she reached the Puget Sound Navy Yard on 4 June.

The battleship underwent repairs and alterations until 11 August. She then conducted gunnery exercises off Tacoma and Seattle, Wash., before she returned to the Puget Sound Navy Yard on 29 August for further work. She remained there until 12 September, when she sailed for San Francisco, en route to Panama.

Wisconsin—as flagship, Pacific Squadron—with Rear Admiral Silas Casey embarked, arrived at Panama, Colombia, on 30 September 1902, to protect American interests and to preserve the integrity of transit across the isthmus. Casey offered his services as a mediator in the crisis that had lasted for three years and invited leaders of both factions—conservatives and liberals—to meet on board *Wisconsin*. Over succeeding weeks, through October and into November, prolonged negotiations ensued. Ultimately, however, the warring sides came to an agreement, and signed a treaty on 21 No-

USS *Wisconsin* (Battleship No. 9) after a 1909 modernization gave her a cage foremast and a new gray finish. (NR&L(0) 4006)

vember 1902. The accord came to be honored, in Colombian circles, as "The Peace of *Wisconsin*." When Rear Admiral Henry Glass, Admiral Casey's successor as Commander in Chief, Pacific Squadron, wrote his report to the Secretary of the Navy for fiscal year 1903, he lauded his predecessor's diplomatic services during the Panama crisis. "The final settlement of the revolutionary disturbance," Glass wrote approvingly, "was largely due to his efforts."

Her task completed, the battleship departed Panama's waters on 22 November and arrived at San Francisco on 5 December to prepare for gunnery exercises. Four days later, Rear Admiral Casey shifted his flag to the armored cruiser *New York*, thus releasing *Wisconsin* from flagship duties for the Pacific Squadron. The battleship consequently carried out her firings until 17 December, when she sailed for Bremerton. Reaching the Puget Sound Navy Yard five days before Christmas of 1902, *Wisconsin* then underwent repairs and alterations until 13 May 1903, when she sailed for the Asiatic Station.

Proceeding via Honolulu, *Wisconsin* arrived at Yokohama, Japan, on 12 June, with Rear Admiral Yates Stirling embarked; three days later, Rear Admiral Stirling exchanged flagships with Rear Admiral P. H. Cooper, who broke his two-starred flag at *Wisconsin*'s main as Commander of the Asiatic Fleet's Northern Squadron while Admiral Stirling hoisted his in the tender *Rainbow*.

Wisconsin operated in the Far East, with the Asiatic Fleet, over the next three years before she returned to the United States in the autumn of 1906. She followed a normal routine of operations in the northern latitudes of the station—China and Japan—in the summer months, because of the oppressive heat of the Philippine Islands that time of year, but in the Philippine Archipelago in the winter. She touched at ports in Japan and China, including Kobe, Yokohama, Nagasaki, and Yokosuka; Amoy, Shanghai, Chefoo, Nanking, and Taku. In addition, she cruised the Yangtze River (as far as Nanking), the Inland Sea, and Nimrod Sound. The battleship conducted assigned fleet maneuvers and exercises off the Chinese and Philippine coasts, intervening those evolutions with regular periods of in-port upkeep and repairs. During that time, she served as Asiatic Fleet flagship, wearing the flag of Rear Admiral Cooper.

The battleship departed Yokohama on 20 September and, after calling at Honolulu en route between 3 and 8 October, arrived at San Francisco on the 18th. After seven days' stay at that port, she headed up the west coast and reached the Puget Sound Navy Yard on 28 October. She was decommissioned there on 15 November 1906.

Recommissioned on 1 April 1908, Capt. Henry Morrell in command, *Wisconsin* was fitted out at the Puget Sound Navy Yard until the end of April. After shifting to Port Angeles from 30 April to 2 May, the battleship proceeded down the western seaboard and reached San Francisco on 6 May to participate in a fleet review at that port. She subsequently returned to Puget Sound to complete the installation of her fire control equipment between 21 May and 22 June.

Soon thereafter, *Wisconsin* retraced her southward course, returning to San Francisco in early July. There, she joined the battleships of the Atlantic Fleet in setting out on the transpacific leg of the momentous circumnavigation of the globe. The cruise of the "Great White Fleet" served as a pointed reminder to Japan of the power of the United States—a dramatic gesture made by President Theodore Roosevelt as signal evidence of his "big stick" policy. *Wisconsin*, during the course of her part of the voyage, called at ports in New Zealand, Australia, the Philippines, Japan, China, Ceylon, and Egypt; transited the Suez Canal; visited Malta, Algiers, and Gibraltar before arriving in Hampton Roads on Washington's Birthday, 1909, and passing in review there before President Roosevelt. The epic voyage had

confounded the doomsayers and critics, having been accomplished without any serious incidents or mishaps.

Wisconsin departed from the Tidewater area on 6 March and arrived at the Portsmouth (N.H.) Navy Yard three days later. The pre-dreadnought battleship there underwent repairs and alterations until 23 June, doffing her bright "white and spar color" and donning a more businesslike gray. The man-of-war joined the Atlantic Fleet in Hampton Roads at the end of June, but she remained in those waters only a short time, for she sailed north to Portland, Maine, arriving there on 2 July in time to take part in the 4th of July festivities in that port.

The battleship next headed down the eastern seaboard, cruising off Rockport and Provincetown, Mass., before she returned, with the fleet, to Hampton Roads on 6 August. Over the ensuing weeks, *Wisconsin* fired target practices in the southern drill grounds, off the Virginia capes, breaking those underway periods with upkeep in Hampton Roads.

Wisconsin steamed with the fleet to New York City—where she anchored in the North River to take part in the Hudson-Fulton celebrations between 22 September and 5 October—before she underwent repairs at the Portsmouth (N.H.) Navy Yard from 7 October to 28 November. She then dropped down to Newport, R.I., upon the conclusion of that yard period, picking up drafts of men for transportation to the Atlantic Fleet at Hampton Roads.

Wisconsin operated with the fleet off the Virginia capes through mid-December, before she headed for New York for the Christmas holidays in port. Subsequently cruising to Cuban waters in early January 1910, the battleship operated out of Guantanamo Bay for a little over two months, from 12 January to 19 March.

The pre-dreadnought battleship then visited Tompkinsville, N.Y., and New Orleans, La., before she discharged ammunition at New York City on 22 April. Later that spring, 1910, she moved to the Portsmouth (N.H.) Navy Yard, where she was placed in reserve. She was moved to Philadelphia in April 1912 and, that autumn, took part in a naval review off Yonkers, New York, before resuming her reserve status with the Atlantic Reserve Fleet. Placed "in ordinary" on 31 October 1913, *Wisconsin* remained in that status until she joined the Naval Academy Practice Squadron in the spring of 1915, assuming training duties along with the battleships *Missouri* and *Ohio*. With that group, she became the third battleship to transit the Panama Canal, making that trip in mid-July 1915 en route to the west coast of the United States with her embarked officers-to-be.

Wisconsin discharged her duties as a midshipman's training ship into 1917 and was moored at the Philadelphia Navy Yard on 6 April of that year, when she received word that the United States had declared war on Germany. Two days later, members of the Naval Militia began reporting on board the battleship for quarters and subsistence.

On 23 April, *Wisconsin*, *Missouri*, and *Ohio* were placed in full commission and assigned to the Coast Battleship Patrol Squadron. Within two weeks, on 2 May, Comdr. (later Admiral) David F. Sellers reported on board and took command. Four days later, the battleship got underway for the Virginia capes; and she arrived at Yorktown, Va., on the 7th.

From early May through early August, *Wisconsin* operated as an engineering school ship on training cruises in the Chesapeake Bay-York River area. She trained recruits as oilers, watertenders, and firemen—who, when qualified, were assigned to the formerly interned merchantmen of the enemy taken over by the United States upon the declaration of war, as well as to submarine chasers and the merchant vessels then building in American yards.

Wisconsin then maneuvered and exercised in company with the battleships *Kearsarge*, *Alabama*, *Illinois*,

Kentucky, Ohio, Missouri, and *Maine* between 13 and 19 August, en route to Port Jefferson, L.I. Over the ensuing weeks, *Wisconsin* continued training and tactical maneuvers based on Port Jefferson, making various training cruises into Long Island Sound.

She subsequently returned to the York River region early in October and resumed her training activities in that locale, operating primarily in the Chesapeake Bay area. *Wisconsin* continued that duty into the spring of 1918, interrupting her training evolutions between 30 October and 18 December 1917 for repairs at the Philadelphia Navy Yard.

After another stint of repairs at Philadelphia from 13 May to 3 June 1918, *Wisconsin* got underway for a cruise to Annapolis but, after passing the Brandywine Shoal Light, received orders to stick close to shore. Those orders were later modified to send *Wisconsin* up the Delaware River as far as Bombay Hook, since an enemy submarine was active off Cape Henlopen. Postwar examination of German records would show that *U–151*—reportedly the first of six enemy submarines to come to the eastern seaboard in 1918—sank three schooners on 23 May and other ships over ensuing days.

Getting underway again on 6 June, *Wisconsin* arrived at Annapolis on the following day. On the next day, the battleship embarked 175 3d class midshipmen and got underway for the York River. The ship conducted training evolutions in the Chesapeake Bay region until 29 August, when she returned to Annapolis and disembarked midshipmen. Underway for Yorktown on the 30th, *Wisconsin* there embarked 217 men for training as firemen, water tenders, engineers, steersmen and signalmen, resumed her training duties, and continued the task through the signing of the armistice on 11 November.

She completed her training activities on 20 December, sailed north, and reached New York City three days before Christmas. *Wisconsin* was among the ships reviewed by Secretary of the Navy Josephus Daniels from the deck of the yacht *Mayflower* and by Assistant Secretary of the Navy Franklin D. Roosevelt from *Aztec* (SP–590) on the day after Christmas, 26 December.

Wisconsin cruised with the fleet in Cuban waters that winter and, in the summer of 1919, made a midshipman training cruise to the Caribbean.

Placed out of commission on 15 May 1920, *Wisconsin* was reclassified BB–9 on 17 July 1920, while awaiting disposition. She was sold for scrap on 26 January 1922 as a result of the Washington Treaty.

II

(BB–64: dp. 45,000; l. 887'3''; b. 108'3''; dr. 28'11'' (mean); s. 33 k.; cpl. 1,921; a. 9 16'', 20 5'', 80 40mm., 49 20mm.; cl. *Iowa*)

The second *Wisconsin* (BB–64) was laid down on 25 January 1941 at the Philadelphia Navy Yard; launched on 7 December 1943; sponsored by Mrs. Walter S. Goodland; and commissioned on 16 April 1944, Capt. Earl E. Stone in command.

After her trials and initial training in the Chesapeake Bay, *Wisconsin* departed Norfolk, Va., on 7 July 1944, bound for the British West Indies. Following her shakedown, conducted out of Trinidad, the third of the *Iowa*-class battleships to join the Fleet returned to her builder's yard for post-shakedown repairs and alterations.

On 24 September 1944, *Wisconsin* sailed for the west coast, transited the Panama Canal, and reported for duty with the Pacific Fleet on 2 October. The battleship later moved to Hawaiian waters for training exercises and then headed for the Western Carolines. Upon reaching Ulithi on 9 December, she joined Admiral William F. Halsey's 3d Fleet.

The powerful new warship had arrived at a time when the reconquest of the Philippines was well underway. As a part of that movement, the planners had envisioned landings on the southwest coast of Mindoro, south of Luzon. From that point, American forces could threaten Japanese shipping lanes through the South China Sea.

The day before the amphibians assaulted Mindoro, the 3d Fleet's Fast Carrier Task Force (TF) 38—supported in part by *Wisconsin*—rendered Japanese facilities at Manila largely useless. Between 14 and 16 December, TF 38's naval aviators secured complete tactical surprise and quickly won complete mastery of the air and sank or destroyed 27 Japanese vessels; damaged 60 more; destroyed 269 planes; and bombed miscellaneous ground installations.

The next day the weather, however, soon turned sour for Halsey's sailors. A furious typhoon struck his fleet, catching many ships refuelling and with little ballast in their nearly dry bunkers. Three destroyers—*Hull* (DD–350), *Monaghan* (DD–354), and *Spence* (DD–512)—capsized and sank. *Wisconsin* proved her seaworthiness as she escaped the storm unscathed.

As heavily contested as they were, the Mindoro operations proved only the introduction to another series of calculated blows aimed at the occupying Japanese in the Philippines. For *Wisconsin*, her next operation was the occupation of Luzon. By-passing the southern beaches, American amphibians went ashore at Lingayen Gulf—the scene of the Japanese landings nearly three years before.

Wisconsin—armed with heavy antiaircraft batteries —performed escort duty for TF 38's fast carriers during air strikes against Formosa, Luzon, and the Nansei Shoto, to neutralize Japanese forces there and to cover the unfolding Lingayen Gulf operations. Those strikes, lasting from 3 to 22 January 1945, included a thrust into the South China Sea, in the hope that major units of the Japanese Navy could be drawn into battle.

Air strikes between Saigon and Camranh Bay, Indochina, on 12 January resulted in severe losses for the enemy. TF 38's warplanes sank 41 ships and damaged 31 in two convoys they encountered. In addition, they heavily damaged docks, storage areas, and aircraft facilities. At least 112 enemy planes would never again see operational service. Formosa, already struck on 3 and 4 January, again fell victim to the marauding American airmen, being smashed again on 9, 15, and 21 January. Soon, Hong Kong, Canton, and Hainan Island felt the brunt of TF 38's power. Besides damaging and sinking Japanese shipping, American planes from the task force set the Canton oil refineries afire and blasted the Hong Kong Naval Station. They also raided Okinawa on 22 January, considerably lessening enemy air activities that could threaten the Luzon landings.

Subsequently assigned to the 5th Fleet—when Admiral Spruance relieved Admiral Halsey as Commander of the Fleet—*Wisconsin* moved northward with the redesignated TF 58 as the carriers headed for the Tokyo area. On 16 February 1945, the task force approached the Japanese coast under cover of adverse weather conditions and achieved complete tactical surprise. As a result, they shot down 322 enemy planes and destroyed 177 more on the ground. Japanese shipping—both naval and merchant—suffered drastically, too, as did hangars and aircraft installations. Moreover, all this damage to the enemy had cost the American Navy only 49 planes.

The task force moved to Iwo Jima on 17 February to provide direct support for the landings slated to take place on that island on the 19th. It revisited Tokyo on the 25th and, the next day, hit the island of Hachino off the coast of Honshu. During these raids, besides causing heavy damage on ground facilities, the American planes sent five small vessels to the bottom and destroyed 158 planes.

On 1 March, reconnaissance planes flew over the island of Okinawa, taking last minute intelligence photographs to be used in planning the assault on that island. The next day, cruisers from TF 58 shelled Okino Daito Shima in training for the forthcoming operation. The force then retired to Ulithi for replenishment.

Wisconsin's task force stood out of Ulithi on 14

March, bound for Japan. The mission of that group was to eliminate airborne resistance from the Japanese homeland to American forces off Okinawa. Enemy fleet units at Kure and Kobe, on southern Honshu, reeled under the impact of the explosive blows delivered by TF 58's airmen. On 18 and 19 March, from a point 100 miles southwest of Kyushu, TF 58 hit enemy airfields on that island. However, the Japanese drew blood during that action when kamikazes crashed into *Franklin* (CV–17) on the 19th and seriously damaged that fleet carrier.

That afternoon, the task force retired from Kyushu, screening the blazing and battered flattop. In doing so, the screen downed 48 attackers. At the conclusion of the operation, the force felt that it had achieved its mission of prohibiting any large-scale resistance from the air to the slated landings on Okinawa.

On the 24th, *Wisconsin* trained her 16-inch rifles on targets ashore on Okinawa. Together with the other battlewagons of the task force, she pounded Japanese positions and installations in preparation for the landings. Although fierce, Japanese resistance was doomed to fail by dwindling numbers of aircraft and trained pilots to man them. In addition, the Japanese fleet, steadily hammered by air attacks from 5th Fleet aircraft, found itself confronted by a growing, powerful, and determined enemy. On 17 April, the undaunted enemy battleship *Yamato*, with her 18.1-inch guns, sortied to attack the American invasion fleet off Okinawa. Met head-on by a swarm of carrier planes, *Yamato*, the light cruiser *Yahagi*, and four destroyers went to the bottom, the victims of massed air power. Never again would the Japanese fleet present a major challenge to the American fleet in the war in the Pacific.

While TF 58's planes were off dispatching *Yamato* and her consorts to the bottom of the South China Sea, enemy aircraft struck back at American surface units. Combat air patrols (CAP) knocked down 15 enemy planes, and ships' gunfire accounted for another three, but not before one kamikaze penetrated the CAP and screen to crash on the flight deck of the fleet carrier *Hancock* (CV–19). On 11 April, the "Divine Wind" renewed its efforts; and only drastic maneuvers and heavy barrages of gunfire saved the task force. None of the fanatical pilots achieved any direct hits, although near-misses, close aboard, managed to cause some minor damage. Combat air patrols bagged 17 planes, and ships' gunfire accounted for an even dozen. The next day, 151 enemy aircraft committed *hara-kiri* into TF 58, but *Wisconsin*, bristling with 5-inch, 40-millimeter and 20-millimeter guns, together with other units of the screens for the vital carriers, kept the enemy at bay or destroyed him before he could reach his targets.

Over the days that ensued, American task force planes hit Japanese facilities and installations in the enemy's homeland. Kamikazes, redoubling their efforts, managed to crash into three carriers on successive days —*Intrepid* (CV–11), *Bunker Hill* (CV–17), and *Enterprise* (CV–6).

By 4 June, a typhoon was swirling through the Fleet. *Wisconsin* rode out the storm unscathed, but three cruisers, two carriers, and a destroyer suffered serious damage. Offensive operations were resumed on 8 June, with a final aerial assault on Kyushu. Japanese aerial response was pitifully small; 29 planes were located and destroyed. On that day, one of *Wisconsin*'s floatplanes landed and rescued a downed pilot from the carrier *Shangri-La* (CV–38).

Wisconsin ultimately put into Leyte Gulf and dropped anchor there on 13 June for repairs and replenishment. Three weeks later, on 1 July, the battleship and her consorts sailed once more for Japanese home waters for carrier air strikes on the enemy's heartland. Nine days later, carrier planes from TF 38 destroyed 72 enemy aircraft on the ground and smashed industrial sites in the Tokyo area. So little was the threat from the dwindling Japanese air arm that the Americans made no attempt whatever to conceal the location of their armada which was operating off her shores with impunity.

On the 15th, *Wisconsin* again unlimbered her main battery, hurling 16-inch shells shoreward at the steel mills and oil refineries at Muroran, Hokkaido. Two days later, she wrecked industrial facilities in the Hitachi Miro area, on the coast of Honshu, northeast of Tokyo itself. During that bombardment, British battleships of the Eastern Fleet contributed their heavy shellfire. By that point in the war, Allied warships were able to shell the Japanese homeland almost at will.

Task Force 38's planes subsequently blasted the Japanese naval base at Yokosuka, and put one of the two remaining Japanese battleships—the former fleet flagship *Nagato*—out of action. On 24 and 25 July, American carrier planes visited the Inland Sea region, blasting enemy sites on Honshu, Kyushu, and Shikoku. Kure then again came under attack. Six major fleet units were located there and badly damaged, marking the virtual end of Japanese sea power.

Over the weeks that ensued, TF 38 continued its raids on Japanese industrial facilities, airfields, and merchant and naval shipping. Admiral Halsey's airmen visited destruction upon the Japanese capital for the last time on 13 August 1945. Two days later, the Japanese capitulated. World War II was over at last.

Wisconsin, as part of the occupying force, arrived at Tokyo Bay on 5 September, three days after the formal surrender occurred on board the battleship *Missouri* (BB–63). During *Wisconsin*'s brief career in World War II, she had steamed 105,831 miles since commissioning; had shot down three enemy planes; had claimed assists on four occasions; and had fueled her screening destroyers on some 250 occasions.

Shifting subsequently to Okinawa, the battleship embarked homeward-bound GI's on 22 September, as part of the "Magic Carpet" operation staged to bring soldiers, sailors, and marines home from the far-flung battlefronts of the Pacific. Departing Okinawa on 23 September, *Wisconsin* reached Pearl Harbor on 4 October, remaining there for five days before she pushed on for the west coast on the last leg of her statesidebound voyage. She reached San Francisco on 15 October.

Heading for the east coast of the United States soon after the start of the new year, 1946, *Wisconsin* transited the Panama Canal between 11 and 13 January, and reached Hampton Roads, Va., on the 18th. Following a cruise south to Guantanamo Bay, Cuba, the battleship entered the Norfolk Naval Shipyard for overhaul. After repairs and alterations that consumed the summer months, *Wisconsin* sailed for South American waters.

Over the weeks that ensued, the battleship visited Valparaiso, Chile, from 1 to 6 November; Callao, Peru, from 9 to 13 November; Balboa, Canal Zone, from 16 to 20 November; and La Guajira, Venezuela, from 22 to 26 November, before returning to Norfolk on 2 December 1946.

Wisconsin spent nearly all of 1947 as a training ship, taking naval reservists on two-week cruises throughout the year. Those voyages commenced at Bayonne, N.J., and saw visits conducted at Guantanamo Bay, Cuba, and the Panama Canal Zone. While underway at sea, the ship would perform various drills and exercises before the cruise would end where it had started, at Bayonne. During June and July of 1947, *Wisconsin* took Naval Academy midshipmen on cruises to northern European waters.

In January 1948, *Wisconsin* joined the Atlantic Reserve Fleet at Norfolk, for inactivation. Placed out of commission, in reserve, on 1 July 1948, *Wisconsin* was assigned to the Norfolk group of the Atlantic Reserve Fleet.

Her sojourn in "mothballs," however, was comparatively brief because of the North Korean invasion of South Korea in late June 1950. *Wisconsin* was recommissioned, on 3 March 1951, Capt. Thomas Burrowes in command. After shakedown training, the revitalized battleship conducted two midshipmen training cruises, taking the officers-to-be to Edinburgh, Scotland; Lisbon, Portugal; Halifax, Nova Scotia; New York City; and Guantanamo Bay, Cuba, before she returned to Norfolk.

Wisconsin departed Norfolk on 25 October 1951, bound for the Pacific. She transited the Panama Canal on the 29th and reached Yokosuka, Japan, on 21 November. There, she relieved *New Jersey* (BB–62) as flagship for Vice Admiral H. M. Martin, Commander, 7th Fleet.

On the 26th, with Vice Admiral Martin and Rear Admiral F. P. Denebrink, Commander, Service Force, Pacific, embarked, *Wisconsin* departed Yokosuka for Korean waters to support the fast carrier operations of TF 77. She left the company of the carrier force on 2 December and, screened by the destroyer *Wiltsie* (DD–716), provided gunfire support for the Republic of Korea (ROK) Corps in the Kasong-Kosong area. After disembarking Admiral Denebrink on 3 December at Kangnung, the battleship resumed station on the Korean "bombline," providing gunfire support for the American 1st Marine Division. *Wisconsin's* shellings accounted for a tank, two gun emplacements, and a building. She continued her gunfire support task for the 1st Marine Division and 1st ROK Corps through 6 December, accounting for enemy bunkers, artillery positions, and troop concentrations. On one occasion during that time, the battleship received a request for call-fire support and provided three starshells for the 1st ROK Corps, illuminating a communist attack that was consequently repulsed with considerable enemy casualties.

After being relieved on the gunline by the heavy cruiser *St. Paul* (CA–73) on 6 December, *Wisconsin* retired only briefly from gunfire support duties. She resumed them, however, in the Kasong-Kosong area on 11 December, screened by the destroyer *Twining* (DD–540). The following day, 12 December, saw the embarkation in *Wisconsin* of Rear Admiral H. R. Thurber, Commander, Battleship Division 2. The admiral came on board via helicopter, incident to his inspection trip in the Far East.

The battleship continued naval gunfire support duties on the "bombline," shelling enemy bunkers, command posts, artillery positions, and trench systems through 14 December. She departed the "bombline" on that day to render special gunfire support duties in the Kojo area, blasting coastal targets in support of United Nations (UN) troops ashore. That same day, she returned to the Kasong-Kosong area. On the 15th, she disembarked Admiral Thurber by helicopter. The next day, *Wisconsin* departed Korean waters, heading for Sasebo to rearm.

Returning to the combat zone on the 17th, *Wisconsin* embarked United States Senator Homer Ferguson of Michigan on the 18th. That day, the battleship supported the 11th ROK division with night illumination fire that enabled the ROK troops to repulse a communist assault with heavy enemy casualties. Departing the "bombline" on the 19th, the battleship later that day transferred her distinguished passenger, Senator Ferguson, by helicopter to the carrier *Valley Forge* (CV–45).

Wisconsin next participated in a coordinated air-surface bombardment of Wonsan to neutralize pre-selected targets. She shifted her bombardment station to the western end of Wonsan harbor, hitting boats and small craft in the inner swept channel during the afternoon. Such activities helped to forestall any communist attempts to assault the friendly-held islands in the Wonsan area. *Wisconsin* then made an anti-boat sweep to the north, utilizing her 5-inch batteries on suspected boat concentrations. She then provided gunfire support to UN troops operating at the "bombline" until three days before Christmas 1951. She then rejoined the carrier task force.

On 28 December, Francis Cardinal Spellman—on a Korean tour over the Christmas holidays—visited the ship, coming on board by helicopter to celebrate Mass for the Catholic members of the crew. The distinguished prelate departed the ship by helicopter off Pohang. Three days later, on the last day of the year, *Wisconsin* put into Yokosuka.

Wisconsin departed that Japanese port on 8 January 1952 and headed for Korean waters once more. She reached Pusan the following day and entertained the President of South Korea, Syngman Rhee, and his wife, on the 10th. President and Mrs. Rhee received full military honors as they came on board, and he reciprocated by awarding Vice Admiral Martin the ROK Order of the Military Merit.

Wisconsin returned to the "bombline" on 11 January and, over the ensuing days, delivered heavy gunfire support for the 1st Marine Division and the 1st ROK Corps. As before, her primary targets were command posts, shelters, bunkers, troop concentrations, and mortar positions. As before, she stood ready to deliver call-fire support as needed. One such occasion occurred on 14 January when she shelled enemy troops in the open at the request of the ROK 1st Corps.

Rearming at Sasebo and once more joining TF 77 off the coast of Korea soon thereafter, *Wisconsin* resumed support at the "bombline" on 23 January. Three days later, she shifted once more to the Kojo region, to participate in a coordinated air and gun strike. That same day, the battleship returned to the "bombline" and shelled the command post and communications center for the 15th North Korean Division during call-fire missions for the 1st Marine Division.

Returning to Wonsan at the end of January, *Wisconsin* bombarded enemy guns at Hodo Pando before she was rearmed at Sasebo. The battleship rejoined TF 77 on 2 February and, the next day, blasted railway buildings and marshalling yards at Hodo Pando and Kojo before rejoining TF 77. After replenishment at Yokosuka a few days later, she returned to the Kosong area and resumed gunfire support. During that time, she destroyed railway bridges and a small shipyard besides conducting callfire missions on enemy command posts, bunkers, and personnel shelters, making numerous cuts on enemy trench lines in the process.

On 25 February, *Wisconsin* arrived at Pusan where Vice Admiral Shon, the ROK Chief of Naval Operations; United States Ambassador J. J. Muccio; and Rear Admiral Scott-Montcrief, Royal Navy, Commander, Task Group 95.12, visited the battleship. Departing that South Korean port the following day, *Wisconsin* reached Yokosuka on 2 March. A week later, she shifted to Sasebo to prepare to return to Korean waters.

Wisconsin arrived off Songjin, Korea, on 15 March 1952 and concentrated her gunfire on enemy railway transport. Early that morning, she destroyed a communist troop train trapped outside of a destroyed tunnel. That afternoon, she received the first direct hit in her history, when one of four shells from a communist 155-millimeter gun battery struck the shield of a starboard 40-millimeter mount. Although little material damage resulted, three men were injured. Almost as if the victim of a personal affront, *Wisconsin* subsequently blasted that battery to oblivion with a 16-inch salvo before continuing her mission. After lending a hand to support once more the 1st Marine Division with her heavy rifles, the battleship returned to Japan on 19 March.

Relieved as flagship of the 7th Fleet on 1 April by sistership *Iowa* (BB–61), *Wisconsin* departed Yokosuka, bound for the United States. En route home, she touched briefly at Guam, where she took part in the successful test of the Navy's largest floating drydock on 4 and 5 April, marking the first time that an *Iowa*-class battleship had ever utilized that type of facility. She continued her homeward-bound voyage, via Pearl Harbor, and arrived at Long Beach, Calif., on 19 April. She then sailed for the east coast; her destination: Norfolk.

Early in June 1952, *Wisconsin* resumed her role as a training ship, taking midshipmen to Greenock, Scotland;

Brest, France; and Guantanamo Bay, Cuba, before returning to Norfolk. She departed Hampton Roads on 25 August and participated in a North Atlantic Treaty Organization (NATO) exercise, Operation "Mainbrace" which commenced at Greenock and extended as far north as Oslo, Norway. After her return to Norfolk, *Wisconsin* underwent an overhaul in the naval shipyard there. She then engaged in local training evolutions until 11 February 1953, when she sailed for Cuban waters for refresher training. She visited Newport, R.I., and New York City before returning to Norfolk late in April.

Following another midshipman's training cruise to Rio de Janeiro, Brazil; Port-of-Spain, Trinidad; and Guantanamo Bay, *Wisconsin* put into the Norfolk Naval Shipyard on 4 August for a brief overhaul. A little over a month later, upon conclusion of that period of repairs and alterations, the battleship departed Norfolk on 9 September, bound for the Far East.

Sailing via the Panama Canal to Japan, *Wisconsin* relieved *New Jersey* (BB–62) as 7th Fleet flagship on 12 October. During the months that followed, *Wisconsin* visited the Japanese ports of Kobe, Sasebo, Yokosuka, Otaru, and Nagasaki. She spent Christmas at Hong Kong and was ultimately relieved of flagship duties on 1 April 1954 and returned to the United States soon thereafter, reaching Norfolk, via Long Beach and the Panama Canal, on 4 May 1954.

The *Iowa*-class battleship *Wisconsin* (BB–64) off Norfolk during the 1950s. (USN 1087641)

Entering the Norfolk Naval Shipyard on 11 June, *Wisconsin* underwent a brief overhaul and commenced a midshipman training cruise on 12 July. After revisiting Greenock, Brest, and Guantanamo Bay, the ship returned to the Norfolk Naval Shipyard for repairs. Shortly thereafter, Wisconsin participated in Atlantic Fleet exercises as flagship for Commander, 2d Fleet. Departing Norfolk in January 1955, *Wisconsin* took part in Operation "Springboard," during which time she visited Port-au-Prince, Haiti. Then, upon returning to Norfolk, the battleship conducted another midshipman's cruise that summer, visiting Edinburgh; Copenhagen, Denmark; and Guantanamo Bay before returning to the United States.

Upon completion of a major overhaul at the New York Naval Shipyard, *Wisconsin* headed south for refresher training in the Caribbean, later taking part in another "Springboard" exercise. During that cruise, she again visited Port-au-Prince and added Tampico, Mexico, and Cartagena, Colombia, to her list of ports of call. She returned to Norfolk on the last day of March 1956 for local operations.

Throughout April and into May, *Wisconsin* operated locally off the Virginia capes. On 6 May, the battleship collided with the destroyer *Eaton* (DDE-510) in a heavy fog. *Wisconsin* put into Norfolk with extensive damage to her bow and, one week later, entered drydock at the Norfolk Naval Shipyard. A novel expedient speeded her repairs and enabled the ship to carry out her scheduled midshipman training cruise that summer. A 120-ton, 68-foot long section of the bow of the uncompleted battleship *Kentucky* was transported, by barge, in one section, from the Newport News Shipbuilding and Drydock Corp., Newport News, Va., across Hampton Roads to the Norfolk Naval Shipyard. Working round-the-clock, *Wisconsin*'s ship's force and shipyard personnel completed the operation which grafted the new bow on the old battleship in a mere 16 days. On 28 June 1956, the ship was ready for sea.

Embarking 700 NROTC midshipmen, representing 52 colleges and universities throughout the United States, *Wisconsin* departed Norfolk on 9 July, bound for Spain. Reaching Barcelona on the 20th, the battleship next called at Greenock and Guantanamo Bay before returning to Norfolk on the last day of August. That autumn, *Wisconsin* participated in Atlantic Fleet exercises off the coast of the Carolinas, returning to port on 8 November 1956. Entering the Norfolk Naval Shipyard a week later, the battleship underwent major repairs that were not finished until 2 January 1957.

After local operations off the Virginia capes from 3 to 4 January and from the 9th to the 11th, *Wisconsin* departed Norfolk on the 15th, reporting to Commander, Fleet Training Group, at Guantanamo Bay. Breaking the two-starred flag of Rear Admiral Henry Crommelin, Commander, Battleship Division 2, *Wisconsin* served as Admiral Crommelin's flagship during the ensuing shore bombardment practices and other exercises held off the isle of Culebra, Puerto Rico, from 2 to 4 February 1957. Sailing for Norfolk upon completion of the training period, the battleship arrived on 7 February.

The warship conducted a brief period of local operations off Norfolk before she sailed, on 27 March, for the Mediterranean. Reaching Gibraltar on 5 April, she pushed on that day to rendezvous with TF 60 in the Aegean Sea. She then proceeded with that force to Xeros Bay, Turkey, arriving there on 11 April for NATO Exercise "Red Pivot."

Departing Xeros Bay on 14 April, she arrived at Naples four days later. After a week's visit—during which she was visited by Italian dignitaries—*Wisconsin* conducted exercises in the eastern Mediterranean. In the course of those operational training evolutions, she rescued a pilot and crewman who survived the crash of a plane from the carrier *Forrestal* (CVA-59). Two days later, Vice Admiral Charles R. Brown, Commander, 6th Fleet, came on board for an official visit by highline and departed via the same method that day. *Wisconsin* reached Valencia, Spain, on 10 May and, three days later, entertained prominent civilian and military officials of the city.

Departing Valencia on the 17th, *Wisconsin* reached Norfolk on 27 May. On that day, Rear Admiral L. S. Parks relieved Rear Admiral Crommelin as Commander, Battleship Division 2. Departing Norfolk on 19 June, the battleship, over the ensuing weeks, conducted a midshipman training cruise through the Panama Canal to South American waters. She transited the canal on 26 June; crossed the equator on the following day; and reached Valparaiso, Chile, on 3 July. Eight days later, the battleship headed back to the Panama Canal and the Atlantic.

After exercises at Guantanamo Bay and off Culebra, *Wisconsin* reached Norfolk on 5 August and conducted local operations that lasted into September. She then participated in NATO exercises which took her across the North Atlantic to the British Isles. She arrived in the Clyde on 14 September and subsequently visited Brest, France, before returning to Norfolk on 22 October.

Wisconsin's days as an active fleet unit were numbered, and she prepared to make her last cruise. On 4 November 1957, she departed Norfolk with a large group of prominent guests on board. Reaching New York City on 6 November, the battleship disembarked her guests and, on the 8th, headed for Bayonne, N.J., to commence pre-inactivation overhaul.

Placed out of commission at Bayonne on 8 March 1958, *Wisconsin* joined the "Mothball Fleet" there, leaving the United States Navy without an active battleship for the first time since 1895. Subsequently taken to the Philadelphia Naval Shipyard, *Wisconsin* remained there with her sistership *Iowa* into 1981.

Wisconsin earned five battle stars for her World War II service and one for Korea.

Wiseman

Osborne Beeman Wiseman—born on 20 February 1915 in Zanesville, Ohio—was appointed to the Naval Academy on 22 June 1934, and graduated on 2 June 1938. After sea duty in *Saratoga* (CV-3) and *Roe* (DD-418), Wiseman was transferred to the Naval Air Station at Pensacola, Fla., for flight training. Detached on 17 March 1941, having won his wings, Wiseman joined Bombing Squadron (VB) 3, embarked in *Saratoga*.

After that carrier was torpedoed by the Japanese submarine *I-25* off Oahu on 11 January 1942 and sent to the Puget Sound Navy Yard, Bremerton, Wash., for repairs and alterations, her aviation units were transferred ashore to operate from Ford Island. When *Yorktown* (CV-5) returned to Pearl Harbor for repair of the damage sustained early in May at the Battle of the Coral Sea, her units were transferred from the ship and replaced by some of *Saratoga*'s old units—Bombing Squadron 3, Torpedo Squadron 3, and Fighting Squadron 3. Wiseman reported on board *Yorktown* in time to take part in the pivotal Battle of Midway.

On the first day of the carrier action, 4 June, Lt. (jg.) Wiseman flew two sorties—one against the carrier *Soryu* that morning and one against *Hiryu* that afternoon. The latter, by that point, was the last of the four enemy flattops afloat, and the strike in which Wiseman participated proved to be the *coup de grace* administered to that ship. Japanese "Zero" fighters, however, swarmed over the Dauntlesses of VB-3 and VB-6, exacting some measure of revenge for the pounding administered to *Hiryu*. In that melee, Wiseman's plane was shot down. Neither he nor his gunner were seen again.

Having played a major part in turning the tide of the war in the Pacific, Lt. (jg.) Wiseman was awarded the Navy Cross, posthumously, for his heroism and devotion to duty.

(DE–667: dp. 1,400; l. 306'; b. 36'10''; dr. 9'5''
(mean); s. 24 k.; cpl. 186; a. 3 3'', 4 1.1'', 8 20mm.,
2 dct., 8 dcp., 1 dcp. (hh.); cl. *Buckley*)

Wiseman (DE–667) was laid down on 26 July 1943
at Pittsburgh, Pa., by the Dravo Corp.; launched on
6 November 1943; sponsored by Mrs. June Holton, the
widow of Lt. (jg.) Wiseman; and commissioned at
Algiers, La., on 4 April 1944, Lt. W. B. McClaran, Jr.,
USNR, in command.

Following shakedown in the Bermuda area and post-
shakedown availability in the Boston Navy Yard, *Wiseman* departed Boston on 24 May 1944 on the first of
three round-trip convoy escort missions that she conducted through the autumn of 1944. Subsequently converted to a floating power station—the necessity for
ship-to-shore electrical facilities having been proved
during earlier phases of the Pacific war—at the
Charleston (S.C.) Navy Yard, *Wiseman* sailed for the
Pacific on 11 January 1945.

Making port at Pearl Harbor on 3 February, the
destroyer escort operated for a month in the Hawaiian
Islands before setting sail for the Philippines on 3
March. Arriving at Manila on the 23d, *Wiseman* commenced furnishing power to that nearly demolished
city on 13 April and, over the next five and one-half
months, provided some 5,806,000 kilowatt-hours of
electricity.

In addition, *Wiseman*'s evaporators furnished
150,000 gallons of drinking water to Army facilities in
the harbor area and to many small craft. Her radios
were also utilized to a great extent. Placed at the disposal of the Navy's port director, the ship's communication outfit was used to handle harbor radio traffic
until the director's equipment arrived and was installed
ashore.

Following her vital service at Manila, *Wiseman*
shifted to Guam, where she provided power for the
Army dredge *Harris* (YM–25) for a period of two
months. She then returned to the United States and
was decommissioned at San Diego on 31 May 1946. She
was inactivated there on 31 January 1947.

Recommissioned in the autumn of 1950, after the
onset of the Korean War that June, *Wiseman*—under
the command of Lt. Comdr. Jay W. Land—rushed to
Korea, reaching the port of Mason, near the mouth of
the Naktong River, at the western anchor-point of the
former beachhead at Pusan. As she had done at Manila
in 1945, *Wiseman* now supplied electricity to a city
unable to generate its own. Later, the ship provided
comforts-of-home to units of the 1st Marine Division
quartered on the nearby pier, providing hot showers,
cigarettes, and hot meals cooked in the ship's galley.
The destroyer escort also provided instruction in seamanship, gunnery, radar, sonar, and damage control
to 80 midshipmen from the Republic of Korea (ROK)
Naval Academy and 120 ROK Navy enlisted men.

Late in 1951, *Wiseman* returned to the United States
and underwent an extensive overhaul at the Mare
Island Naval Shipyard, Vallejo, Calif., before she conducted refresher training out of San Diego through
the spring and summer of 1952. The ship then sailed
again for Korean waters, reaching the combat zone
that autumn.

In her second Western Pacific (WestPac) deployment
since recommissioning, *Wiseman* screened light carrier
task forces off the west coast of Korea; carried out
patrol assignments close inshore; blockaded and bombarded segments of the northeastern Korean coast, and
provided antisubmarine screen and escort services for
replenishment groups. Later in the deployment, she
also participated in hunter-killer operations, trained in
antisubmarine warfare (ASW) evolutions, and served
as division flagship during a goodwill call at Manila.

Over the next few years, *Wiseman* conducted four
more WestPac deployments and spent the interludes
between them in training out of San Diego and upkeep
at Mare Island Naval Shipyard or the San Francisco
Naval Shipyard. Upon occasion, she conducted Naval

Reserve training cruises—one taking her to the Hawaiian Islands. During the overseas deployments,
Wiseman operated with units of SEATO navies—
Australian, New Zealand, British, Philippine, Pakistani, and Thai—and visited ports from Australia to
Japan. Upon completion of her sixth deployment, *Wiseman* was designated as a Group I Naval Reserve Training (NRT) ship. Accordingly, on 16 May 1959, the
ship was decommissioned and turned over to the 11th
Naval District. Lt. W. V. Powell was the first officer-in-
charge.

For the next two years, *Wiseman* operated out of
San Diego on NRT duties. Every third weekend of the
month, a reserve cruise took her to sea for periods of
ASW training; and, during the summers, the destroyer
escort made two-week reserve cruises.

However, in 1961, the Berlin crisis changed the veteran destroy escort's routine after the building of the
Berlin Wall heightened tensions in August of that
year. President John F. Kennedy ordered the activation of reserve units—including the Selected Reserve
Crew and NRT ships. Recommissioned on 2 October
1961, Lt. Comdr. C. V. Wilhoite, Jr., in command,
Wiseman was immediately prepared for duty with the
7th Fleet. Since the repair and overhaul facilities at
San Diego were overworked, *Wiseman* was overhauled
at Long Beach, spending the pre-Christmas holidays
in the Bethlehem shipyards there.

Deploying to WestPac again in January of 1962,
Wiseman conducted patrol operations off the coast of
the troubled country of Vietnam. She received a "well
done" for her performance of duty and in March won
commendation for giving medical aid to a fisherman
with an infected leg on board a South Vietnamese fishing junk. Later that spring, the ship also visited Hong
Kong, Subic Bay, and Japanese ports—including Yokohama, where she hosted celebrations for Armed Forces
Day on 19 and 20 May.

Returning to San Diego on 17 July, via Midway and
Pearl Harbor, *Wiseman* was decommissioned and
placed in service on 1 August, resuming her duties as
NRT ship with the Group II Naval Reserve. Before the
end of 1962, the ship was assigned to Reserve Destroyer
Division 272 of Reserve Destroyer Squadron 27.

Placed in reserve but remaining in service, *Wiseman*
was berthed at San Diego through the remainder of
the 1960's as part of the Pacific Fleet's reserve units.
Struck from the Navy list on 15 April 1973, the veteran
of World War II and Korean service was subsequently
scrapped.

Wiseman (DE–667) received six battle stars for her
Korean War service.

Wissahickon

A small stream in southeastern Pennsylvania which
rises in Montgomery County near Lansdale and flows
south some 40 miles to empty into the Schuylkill River
in Philadelphia.

I

(ScGbt.: t. 507; l. 158'4''; b. 28'0''; dr. 10'8''; dph.
12'0''; s. 10½ k.; a. 1 11'' D. sb., 1 20-pdr., 2 24-pdrs.)

The first *Wissahickon*, a screw gunboat, was built in
1861 at Philadelphia by John Lynn and was delivered
to the Navy on 12 November 1861 at the Philadelphia
Navy Yard where she was placed in commission on 25
November 1861, Lt. A. N. Smith in command.

Assigned to the West Gulf Blockading Squadron,
Wissahickon participated in her first combat action on
24 April 1862 when she passed Forts Jackson and St.
Philip with the squadron commanded by Flag Officer
David Glasgow Farragut. On 9 June, she took part in
the attack on the Confederate works at Grand Gulf,
Miss. Nineteen days later, the gunboat joined in the
dash by the Southern batteries at Vicksburg, Miss. She

remained above the Confederate citadel until 15 July, the day that the powerful Southern ironclad ram *Arkansas* made her successful exit from the Yazoo River and ran through the Union fleet to the protection of Vicksburg's batteries. That evening, *Wissahickon* joined *Iroquois, Oneida, Richmond, Sumter,* and *Hartford* in repassing the Confederate stronghold to carry out an attack on the new Southern warship. However, darkness reduced that action to an inconclusive exchange of broadsides as the Federal ships passed the shore batteries and their well-concealed floating foe. Soon thereafter, *Wissahickon* proceeded downriver to New Orleans and thence to Philadelphia for repairs.

Her yard work began on 5 August and was completed two months later to the day. She departed Philadelphia on 8 October to join the South Atlantic Blockading Squadron and to participate in the blockade off the coast of Georgia. The gunboat participated in the attack on Fort McAllister, located on the shores of the Big Ogeechee River in Georgia, on 27 January 1863. A month and a day later, she helped to destroy the blockade runner *Rattlesnake*—the former CSS *Nashville*—near that same place. On 19 March, *Wissahickon* destroyed the steamer *Georgiana* off Charleston, S.C. The gunboat returned to Philadelphia on 25 April and underwent repairs until 21 May. Returning to the blockade after repairs, the warship participated in the attack on Fort Wagner in July and in the bombardment of Fort Sumter in September. For the remainder of the year, the gunboat patrolled off Port Royal, S.C.

Routine blockade duty occupied most of her time in 1864. However, in November, she participated in an expedition up the Broad River in Georgia in support of Sherman's advancing army. During the last month of 1864 and the first months of 1865, the warship participated in operations against Savannah, Ga.

After the war ended, she entered Port Royal for repairs on 1 May 1865. On 20 June, the ship arrived at the New York Navy Yard where she was placed out of commission on 1 July 1865. *Wissahickon* was sold at auction at New York on 25 October 1865. The steamer was documented as *Adele* on 20 January 1866 and operated comercially out of New York. Her final disposition is unknown.

II

(Yacht: dp. 194; l. 120'; b. 14'2''; dr. 6'; dph. 8'9''; s. 12 k.; cpl. 19; a. 1 3-pdr., 2 mg.)

Valda—a composite hull (iron frame and wood planking), single-screw, steam yacht designed by F. D. Lawley and built in 1899 and 1900 by George Lawley and Son Corp.—was renamed *Wissahickon* in either late 1901 or early 1902. She was owned by Mrs. Charles W. Henry when the United States entered World War I.

Although the evidence on the question is inconclusive, *Wissahickon* may have served in the Naval Militia for the state of Maine before being acquired by the United States. One record source consulted lists the ship as being acquired by the Navy on 13 July 1917. Since the Navy considered the yacht to be too light to stand up to the rigors of "distant service," she was placed in commission with the Naval Reserve Force. There is no record as to when this commissioning occurred, although her log—which does not begin until 20 August 1917—lists the reporting of men on board the vessel as early as April 1917. The first extant log entry states that she was commanded by Lt. (jg.) E. W. Haskell, USNRF. *Ship's Data,* the 1918 volume, states that she was commissioned on 3 October 1917, but no primary source corroborates this date.

In any case, *Wissahickon* served without her name under the designation *SP–852* for the duration of her World War I service. She did not resume her original name, *Wissahickon,* until some time before January 1919. While in the Navy, she conducted coastal patrols in the 1st and 3d Naval Districts. Initially based at the section base at Rockland, Maine, *SP–852* spent most of the winter of 1917 and 1918 moored to a pier at Rockland. In January 1918, all of her officers and men were confined to the ship with colds and sore throats, and the ship herself was quarantined until the bout with illness was finished.

She then returned to patrol duty out of Rockland which continued until mid-summer of 1918. *SP–852* shifted south and arrived at Boston on 20 August. She operated out of the section base at East Boston through the winter of 1918. It appears that the ship resumed her original name in the fall of 1918, probably around September or November. The September 1918 edition of the *Navy Directory* lists the vessel, by name—*Wissahickon*—in its index, while the ship's log referred to her merely as *SP–852* as late as November 1918.

The logs for 1919 commence on 1 January 1919, and the ship bears the name *Wissahickon.* She remained at Boston until late in January, when she shifted to Camden, Maine. Her name was struck from the Navy list on 10 February 1919, and she was decommissioned at Camden on 12 February. Three days later, orders directed that the ship be returned to her owner, Mrs. Charles Henry of Philadelphia.

Wissoe II

(MB: t. 67 (gross); l. 83'6''; b. 16'6''; dr. 4'8'' (aft); s. 10.5 k.; cpl. 11; a. 2 1-pdrs., 1 mg.)

Wissoe II (SP–153)—a wooden-hulled motorboat constructed in 1916 at Morris Heights, N.Y., by the New York Yacht, Launch, & Engine Co.—was acquired on 23 April 1917 from Mr. George L. Carnegie of Fernandina, Fla., and was commissioned on 30 April 1917. Assigned to the section patrol of the 6th Naval District, *Wissoe II* patrolled the southeastern coast of the United States, guarding against enemy submarines and protecting coastwise mercantile traffic from their depredations. She was decommissioned soon after the end of World War I and returned to her owner on 18 January 1918. Her name was struck from the Navy list concurrently with her return.

Wistaria

(MB: l. 52'; b. 11'; dr. 3'7'' (aft); s. 9 k.; a. 1 1-pdr., 1 mg.)

Wistaria (SP–259)—a motor yacht built by the Elco Company—was acquired by the Navy sometime in mid-1917 from Mr. Clifton N. Jelliffe of New York City. She was found to be unsuitable for naval service and was never commissioned, though her name was carried briefly on the Navy list. She was returned to her owner on 10 December 1917, and her name was struck from the Navy list.

Witek

Frank Peter Witek—born in Derby, Conn., on 10 December 1921—enlisted in the United States Marine Corps at Chicago, Ill., on 20 January 1942. After training at the Marine Corps Base, San Diego, and at Camp Pendleton, Oceanside, Calif., Witek was sent to the forward areas on 5 February 1943.

During the campaign for the Marianas, Private 1st Class Witek won a posthumous Medal of Honor "for conspicuous gallantry and intrepidity at the risk of his life, above and beyond the call of duty." When fire from well-camouflaged Japanese positions surprised and halted the advance of his rifle company during the Battle of Lingayen, at Guam, on 3 August 1944, Private Witek daringly remained standing, emptying a full magazine from his automatic rifle into a depression sheltering Japanese troops, killing eight of the enemy and allowing his own men to take cover.

During his platoon's withdrawal to consolidate their lines, Witek remained behind, guarding a severely wounded comrade, courageously returning the Japanese fire until stretcher bearers arrived. He then covered the evacuation with sustained automatic rifle fire as he moved backward toward his own lines.

Later, when his platoon was again pinned down by a Japanese machine gun, Witek, on his own initiative, boldly moved forward ahead of the reinforcing tanks and infantry, alternately throwing hand grenades and firing as he advanced to within five to 10 yards of the enemy position. He destroyed the gun and an additional eight Japanese, before he was hit and killed by a rifleman's bullet.

(DD–848: dp. 2,425; l. 390′6″; b. 41′1″; dr. 18′6″ (max.); s. 35.0 k.; cpl. 369; a. 6 5″, 12 40mm., 10 20mm., 5 21″ tt., 6 dcp., 2 dct.; cl. *Gearing*)

Witek (DD–848) was laid down on 16 July 1945 at Bath, Maine, by the Bath Iron Works; launched on 2 February 1946; sponsored by Mrs. Nora Witek, the mother of Private 1st Class Witek; and commissioned at the Boston Naval Shipyard on 23 April 1946, Comdr. Nels C. Johnson in command.

Witek departed Boston on 27 May, bound for Cuban waters, and reached Guantanamo Bay on 1 June. She conducted shakedown training out of Guantanamo until 2 July, when she headed north, returning to Boston on 6 July for post-shakedown availability. Fitted out for experimental development work in antisubmarine warfare (ASW) systems, *Witek* received the classification of EDD–848. She arrived at New London, Conn., her new home port, on 7 December 1946.

Over the next 20 years, *Witek* operated primarily off the eastern seaboard of the United States from Narragansett Bay to the Virginia capes and to Key West, Fla. She ranged on occasion into the Caribbean and touched at places such as Nassau, Bahamas; Guantanamo Bay and Havana, Cuba; the Panama Canal Zone; St. Croix, Virgin Islands; Bridgetown, Barbados; San Juan, Puerto Rico; Hampton Roads; and Boston. On one occasion, the ship visited the west coast— spending six months in operations out of San Diego, testing the sound gear formerly installed in the German heavy cruiser *Prinz Eugen*—in mid-1948. During those tests, carried out under the supervision of the Naval Electronics Laboratory, *Witek*'s silhouette took on a decidedly different "look" compared to that usually associated with a *Gearing*-class destroyer. Her second twin 5-inch gun mount (mount 52) was removed at the Boston Naval Shipyard, and its place was taken by the "house-trailer full" of former German electronics equipment. That "trailer" was eventually removed at the Norfolk Naval Shipyard in the autumn of 1950. Its place was taken, in turn, by a trainable Mk. 15 "hedgehog" mount.

While at Nassau, Bahamas, in late October 1954, *Witek* went to the aid of the local fire department in the British colony when a serious fire threatened the city. Faced with a bad warehouse fire, 140 men from *Witek* rushed into action with 3,000 feet of fire hose, walkie-talkie radio sets, "smoke-eater" masks, four fog applicators, and two portable pumps on Sunday, 24 October. Working for two hours alongside Nassau police, firemen, and volunteers, *Witek*'s sailors earned a unanimous vote of thanks in "helping stem what might have been the most disastrous fire in the Colony's history."

Due to the nature of *Witek*'s work, her routine was little publicized, and she gained none of the overseas deployment excitement in the course of her more than two decades of experimental work. She made no deployments to the Mediterranean nor any to the western Pacific; in addition, she never visited European waters. Outside of visiting La Guaira, Venezuela, the seaport for Caracas, in January 1948, *Witek* spent most of her underway time off the eastern seaboard and in the western Atlantic—sometimes in the Caribbean—participating in experimental exercises with other units of the Operational Development Force based at New London. She operated primarily with other experimental ships, such as *Maloy* (EDE–791), and submarines, testing ASW electronics installations. On some occasions, when she conducted project work out of New London, she would slip up the coast to Rockland, Maine, or to Portsmouth, N.H. Her local operations in Long Island Sound even earned her the nickname: "The Galloping Ghost of the Long Island Coast."

On occasion, though, outside of her normal independent routine, *Witek* conducted exercises with carrier task forces for ASW maneuvers. During one such evolution in 1955, *Witek* exercised with the fleet carrier *Leyte* (CVS–20) and the atomic submarine *Nautilus* (SSN–571); other carriers with which *Witek* operated included *Antietam* (CVS–36) and *Randolph* (CVA–15).

Besides carrying out operational tests of ASW electronics equipment, *Witek* served as the test-bed for the "pump jet" propulsion system. On 2 July 1958, *Witek* entered Drydock No. 4 at the Boston Naval Shipyard for an "extensive overhaul and installation of the pump jet system." The destroyer remained in drydock at Boston until a little over a week before Christmas, when she emerged with the new system installed. Over the ensuing years, *Witek* tested the system under operational conditions. In 1960, she operated for a time with Task Group "Alfa," the first time in four years since she had operated with the fleet. She conducted extensive ASW operations with that unit until returning to her home port.

Due to the grounding of *Bache* (DD–470) in early 1968, *Witek* was retained in active service. Subsequently decommissioned at Norfolk, Va., on 19 August 1968, the ship's name was struck from the Navy list on 17 September 1968. She was then berthed at the Inactive Ship Facility, Norfolk, to await final disposition.

Witter

Jean Carter Witter—born in San Francisco on 31 January 1921—matriculated at the University of California at Berkeley in September 1938. He graduated in the spring of 1942 and was commissioned an ensign in the United States Naval Reserve on 13 May 1942 as a result of his completion of the NROTC program at the university. On 25 May, he reported to the Commandant, 12th Naval District for temporary duty while awaiting transportation to permanent duty in *San Francisco* (CA–38) then active in the Pacific. Once on board the heavy cruiser, Ens. Witter participated in the assault on Guadalcanal and Tulagi early in August. He was present when *Wasp* (CV–7) was torpedoed, and he fought in the Naval Battle of Guadalcanal. Ens. Witter was killed during the brutal night action off Cape Esperance on the night of 12 and 13 November 1942 as a result of one of the more than 45 shell hits suffered by his ship.

(DE–636: dp. 1,400; l. 306′0″; b. 37′0″; dr. 13′6″; s. 23.6 k. (tl.); cpl. 213; a. 3 3″, 4 1.1″, 8 20mm., 8 dcp., 1 dcp. (hh.), 3 21″ tt.; cl. *Buckley*)

Witter (DE–636) was laid down on 28 April 1943 at San Francisco, Calif., by the Bethlehem Steel Co.; launched on 17 October 1943; sponsored by Mrs. Jean C. Witter; and commissioned on 29 December 1943, Comdr. Alan C. Davis, USNR, in command.

Witter departed San Francisco on 18 January 1944 and began her shakedown training. During that cruise, she visited San Diego and then underwent post-shakedown repairs at the Mare Island Navy Yard before returning to San Francisco at the end of February. On 8 March, she stood out of San Francisco and steamed, via Pearl Harbor, to the Gilbert Islands, arriving in Majuro lagoon on the 22d. She departed Majuro on 26 March and—after side visits to Makin, Tarawa, and Abemama in the Gilberts—she arrived in Espiritu Santo on 3 April. There, she remained for 12 days escorting ships into and out of the harbor at Espiritu Santo. On the 15th, the destroyer escort stood out of Segond Channel to rendezvous at sea with SS *William Charlie Yeager* and escort that ship to the southern Solomons. They reached Tulagi on the 21st; and, while the merchantman put into Tulagi, *Witter* moved on to Purvis Bay at Florida Island.

On 25 April, *Witter* departed the southern Solomons in company with Task Unit (TU) 34.9.6, bound for Cape Gloucester on the island of New Britain in the Bismarck Archipelago. She arrived in Borgen Bay near Cape Gloucester on 28 April and remained until 1 May when she accompanied TU 34.9.6 to the Russell Islands subgroup of the Solomons. She arrived in the Russells on 3 May but departed that same day for her primary theater of operations for the next 10 weeks, the island of New Guinea. On 5 May, she entered Milne Bay at the southeastern tip of New Guinea. By the time *Witter* reached that port, American forces had already made almost simultaneous landings at Aitape, Tanahmerah Bay, and Humboldt Bay, in actions known collectively as the Hollandia operation. Thus, for the next several weeks, *Witter* drew duty escorting resupply and reinforcement convoys to the three landing areas, making stops at such intermediary places as Cape Cretin and Cape Sudest. After the 17 May assault on the Toem-Wakde-Sarmi area located a little farther up the northern coast of New Guinea, she added that region to her itinerary. At the end of the first week in July, Biak Island—located off the northern coast of New Guinea, opposite the large bay which separates the Vogelkop from the rest of the island—came within *Witter*'s sphere of operations.

In mid-month, however, the destroyer escort left New Guinea for a new field of endeavor, the northern Solomons. She departed Humboldt Bay on 15 July and, after a brief stop at Cape Cretin, arrived in the northern Solomons at Empress Augusta Bay, Bougainville, on the 18th. On the 20th, she departed Empress Augusta Bay and, that same afternoon, arrived in the Treasury Islands subgroup. For almost three weeks, she remained in the vicinity of Blanche Harbor in the Treasuries, conducting antiair and antisubmarine warfare exercises.

Between 9 and 12 August, she voyaged back to New Guinea, stopping at Finschhaven and Langemak Bay before returning to Blanche Harbor on the 12th and resuming her exercise schedule in the Treasuries. On 21 August, she began a move farther north in the Solomons, arriving in the Green Islands subgroup that same day. Three days later, she moved on again, this time to Manus in the Admiralty Islands where she stopped overnight on the 26th and 27th. On the latter day, the warship made the brief voyage from Manus to Emirau Island. She remained there for almost a month, putting to sea only once during that period—between 19 and 22 September—to rescue the crew of a downed PBJ (the Navy version of the Army's B-25 Mitchell bomber).

After returning the rescued aircrewmen to Emirau on the 22d, she returned to sea that same day on her way back to Manus. From there, she continued her voyage toward Milne Bay on 24 September. On the 26th, she paused near Porlock and Cape Nelson to help SS *Richard H. Dana*, aground on Curtis Reef. While her boats assisted in the transfer of Army troops from the merchantman to *Stratford* (AP-41), *Witter* patrolled to seaward to protect against possible enemy submarine attack. On the 27th, she resumed her voyage and arrived in Milne Bay that same day.

Between 29 September and 6 October, *Witter* made a roundabout voyage from Milne Bay via Treasuries and back to New Guinea at Humboldt Bay. At Humboldt Bay, she reported for duty to TU 77.7.1 for the Leyte

operation. Her task unit, a part of the 7th Fleet Service Force, departed Humboldt Bay on 12 October to take up replenishment station at sea some 180 miles west of the already-invested Palau Islands. At mid-month, the oilers she escorted refueled the Leyte invasion force at sea and, on the 18th, headed for the anchorage at Kossol Passage in the Palaus. After two days in the Palaus, *Witter* and her charges got underway to join the main force in Leyte Gulf. They arrived in the gulf three days after the 20 October assault.

The warship's visit to Leyte proved to be lively. Air attacks by the Japanese abounded. During one attack in the early evening of the 24th, a Japanese torpedo bomber started a run on *Witter* from almost dead ahead while she was maneuvering to change anchorages just south of Samar Island. Though he appeared to be hit by her 20-millimeter fire, the plane traversed her entire length to starboard and finally burst into flames some 300 to 400 yards astern.

The air attacks continued intermittently the following day, and *Witter* observed many bogeys and picked up others on her radar but contributed no more downed aircraft to the American tally. For the remainder of her stay in Leyte Gulf, *Witter* and the oilers she screened continued underway to avoid numerous air attacks and conduct refueling operations.

On the 27th, she escorted the unit out of Leyte Gulf en route to a position about 120 miles east of Leyte. Sporadic air attacks continued but diminished as Leyte receded astern. On the 28th, her charges began refueling TG 77.4 and, just before noon the following day, completed those operations and set course for Kossol Passage. They arrived in the Palaus late on 31 October but, after the oilers refueled that night and the following morning, headed back to Leyte early in the afternoon of 1 November. On the 3d, however, they reversed course on orders and reentered Kossol Passage the following day. The stay proved brief. She and her charges set sail again that evening and arrived in San Pedro Bay, Leyte, on the 7th. She remained there—harrassed by alerts but not by attacks—until the 11th when she departed, escorting her precious oilers. On 14 November, *Witter* and her charges arrived back in Humboldt Bay.

She was anchored in Humboldt Bay until 2 December when she got underway in the escort of a convoy bound for Seeadler Harbor at Manus. *Witter* and her charges entered the harbor the following day, and the destroyer escort remained there until mid-month, conducting tactical exercises in the vicinity until her departure. Between the 15th and the 23d, she made a round-trip voyage from Manus to Ulithi and back. Following an availability and more exercises at Manus during the last week of 1944 and the first week of 1945, she repeated her voyage to Ulithi and back between 6 and 14 January 1945. Another such run late in the month was followed by an availability at Manus which included a period in drydock. During February, she made two voyages from Manus, one to Majuro between 5 and 20 February and the other to Humboldt Bay between the 21st and the 23d.

On 28 February, *Witter* stood out of Seeadler Harbor, bound for the Central Pacific. Steaming first to Ulithi, where she joined a convoy headed for the Marianas, the warship arrived at Guam on 7 March. After three days of patrols around Guam and Saipan, she departed the Marianas to return to Ulithi to prepare for the invasion of Okinawa. The destroyer escort entered the lagoon at Ulithi on the 11th and spent the next 10 days patrolling the anchorage and its entrances. On 21 March, she stood out of Ulithi with Task Force (TF) 54, bound for the Ryukyu Islands and the last great amphibious operation of World War II. On the 25th, she rendezvoused with a minesweeping unit about six miles south of Okinawa and began screening it as well as the heavy units of Admiral Oldendorf's bombardment group while both performed their preliminary functions.

For the next 12 days, *Witter* performed her antisubmarine screening duties for various units of the fleet off Okinawa. Though subjected to intermittent air attack and forced to witness several suicide attacks, she escaped unscathed until 6 April. Her primary duty throughout the period remained antisubmarine patrols at various points around the island of Okinawa. During that time, she made several sonar contacts but made no depth charge attacks.

At about 1611 on the afternoon of 6 April, while off the southeastern coast of Okinawa, she sighted two enemy aircraft about eight miles distant approaching her from the south-southwest. The warship went to general quarters, rang up 23 knots, and began radical maneuvers to evade them. Within five minutes, both Japanese planes showed smoke, evidence of hits registered by her guns. One of the intruders splashed into the sea, but his colleague pressed home his own attack and crashed into *Witter* at the waterline on the starboard side at frame number 57. His bomb exploded in the number 1 fireroom, opening that and several other compartments to the sea.

Witter lost control briefly but restored it again almost as quickly. Damage control took the situation well in hand, and soon *Witter* was proceeding under her own power at 10 knots. With the assistance of *Morris* (DD–417), *Richard P. Leary* (DD–664), *Gregory* (DD–802), and *Arikara* (ATF–98), the destroyer escort limped toward Kerama Retto. *Morris* left the formation at 1715 and, at 1819, also suffered a suicide crash. *Richard P. Leary* then also dropped out of the group to assist *Morris* while *Arikara* and *Gregory* continued on with *Witter*. The little flotilla entered the anchorage at Kerama Retto at a little after 2130, and *Arikara* towed the damaged destroyer escort to a waiting berth.

Witter remained at Kerama Retto until late June, undergoing temporary repairs and dodging sporadic air attacks by constantly shifting from anchorage to anchorage—a process which slowed repairs considerably. Finally, on 25 June, she appeared seaworthy enough to attempt the voyage home and departed the Ryukyu Islands. Steaming by way of Saipan, Eniwetok, and Pearl Harbor, she arrived in San Diego, Calif., on 24 July. Two days later, she resumed her travels and headed, by way of the Panama Canal, for the east coast of the United States. The warship arrived in the Philadelphia Navy Yard on 16 August, shortly following the cessation of hostilities. She immediately began permanent repairs and conversion to a fast transport, which she had been so designated the day before her arrival. The end of the war, however, brought a quick halt to her conversion. On 22 August, the work, hardly begun, was ordered stopped. She was assigned to the Atlantic Reserve Fleet at Philadelphia on 1 September and was decommissioned there on 22 October 1945. Her name was struck from the Navy list on 16 November 1945, and —almost 13 months later on 2 December 1946—her hulk was sold to the Northern Metals Co., of Philadelphia.

Witter earned two battle stars during World War II.

Wiwoka

(MB: t. 25; l. 62'; b. 11'6''; dr. 4' (aft); s. 10 k.; cpl. 10; a. 1 1-pdr., 1 mg.)

Wiwoka (SP–250)—a motorboat built in 1912 at South Boston, Mass., by Murray & Tregurtha—was acquired from Mr. Joseph V. Gallagher of New York on 25 July 1917 and was commissioned on 11 September 1917. *Wiwoka* patrolled the coastline around New York as a unit of the Section Patrol for the duration of World War I. Shortly after hostilities ceased in November 1918, she was decommissioned—probably in December 1918 since her battery was removed on the 18th —and the motorboat was returned to her owner on 17 January 1919. Her name was struck from the Navy list that same day.

Woban

A Natick Indian word meaning "wind."

(YT–138: dp. 325 (f.); l. 100'0''; b. 25'0''; dr. 11'5'' (max.); s. 13 k.; cpl. 11; a. 2 .50-cal. mg.; cl. *Woban*)

Woban (YT–138) was laid down on 25 September 1939 at Bremerton, Wash., by the Puget Sound Navy Yard; launched on 6 November 1939; and completed on 14 February 1940.

Assigned to the 13th Naval District upon completion and delivery, *Woban* operated out of the Puget Sound Navy Yard, performing local tug and tow services for ships of the Pacific Fleet well into World War II. By the end of hostilities, the harbor tug had been assigned to the 17th Naval District and operated in Alaskan waters until March 1946, when she returned to the 13th Naval District. During her World War II career, the ship was reclassified a large harbor tug, YTB–138, on 15 May 1944.

Woban conducted her harbor operations out of Puget Sound through the end of the 1940's and was reassigned to the 17th Naval District by 1953. She later operated out of San Diego, performing district tug and tow services in the 11th Naval District for the remainder of her career. During that time, she was reclassified again to a medium harbor tug, YTM–138, in February 1962.

Taken out of service in early 1967, *Woban* was struck from the Navy list on 1 February 1967 and sold soon thereafter.

Wolcott, Oliver, see *Oliver Wolcott*.

Wolf, Alfred. See *Alfred Wolf*, to be included in the forthcoming revised edition of Vol. I.

Wolf, Donald W., see *Donald W. Wolf*.

Wolffish

A fish, any of several large marine blennies, with strong teeth and great ferocity.

The name *Wolffish* was assigned to SS–434, a *Balao*-class submarine to be built by the Cramp Shipbuilding Co., Philadelphia, Pa., but the contract for her construction was cancelled on 29 July 1944.

Wolverine

An American mammal found mostly in the northern United States. The state of Michigan is known as the "Wolverine State."

I

Michigan (q.v.), the Navy's first iron-hulled warship, was renamed *Wolverine* on 17 June 1905 to clear the name *Michigan* for Battleship No. 27. On 17 July 1920, *Wolverine* was designated IX–31.

II

(SwStr: dp. 7,200; l. 500'0''; b. 58'1''; dr. 15'6''; s. 18.0 k.; cpl. 325; a. none)

The second *Wolverine* (IX–64)—a side-wheel excursion steamer built in 1913—was originally named *Seeandbee*, a euphonious name based upon her owners' company name—the Cleveland and Buffalo Transit Co. She was constructed by the American Shipbuilding Co. of Wyandotte, Mich. The Navy acquired the sidewheeler on 12 March 1942 and designated her an unclassified miscellaneous auxiliary, IX–64. Conversion to

The iron sidewheeler *Michigan*, renamed *Wolverine* late in her life to allow her original name to be given to a new battleship (Battleship No. 27).

a training aircraft carrier began on 6 May 1942; and the name *Wolverine*, commemorating the first ship of the name, was approved on 2 August. *Wolverine* was commissioned at Buffalo, N.Y., on 12 August 1942, Comdr. George R. Fairlamb in command.

As the Navy's first side-wheeled aircraft carrier, *Wolverine* was equipped to handle plane take-offs and landings, a vital duty that she performed for the duration of World War II. She contributed to the winning war effort in World War II by training hundreds of pilots in basic carrier operations. During an inspection conducted by the admiral on 27 October 1942, she briefly flew the four-starred flag of the Commander in Chief of the United States Fleet and Chief of Naval Operations, Admiral Ernest J. King.

Her task completed and the war over in the summer of 1945, *Wolverine* was decommissioned on 7 November 1945 and struck from the Navy list on 28 November. The ship was transferred to the War Shipping Administration on 26 November 1947 and sold later that same year for scrapping.

Wompatuck

A variant spelling of Wampatuck. See *Wampatuck* for biography.

(Tug: dp. 323; l. 130'; b. 25'6''; dr. 12' (mean); cpl. 28; a. 3 3-pdrs., 2 6-pdrs.)

Atlas—an iron-hulled, screw tug completed in 1886 at Wilmington, Del., by Harlan and Hollingsworth—was acquired by the Navy from the Standard Oil Co. on 4 April 1898; simultaneously renamed *Wompatuck*; outfitted at the New York Navy Yard; and commissioned on 6 April 1898, Lt. Charles W. Jungen in command.

Assigned to the North Atlantic Squadron, *Wompatuck* departed New York on 16 April and proceeded—via Norfolk, Va., Port Royal, S.C., and Key West, Fla.—to the Caribbean. She arrived off Havana, Cuba, on 30 April, bearing dispatches and mail for the ships of the North Atlantic Squadron blockading Cuba.

On 12 May, Capt. Charles F. Goodrich, the commanding officer of the auxiliary cruiser *St. Louis*, embarked in *Wompatuck* with Lt. A. W. Catlin, USMC, eight marines, and 11 volunteer sailors. The tug then headed for the mouth of the harbor at Santiago, Cuba, to attempt to cut the undersea telegraph cable linking Cuba with Jamaica. Unluckily for the Americans, a Spanish patrol craft sighted them; and Goodrich ordered a hasty retirement, "not knowing what might be the resources of the defense in guns and search lights."

At daybreak of 18 May, *St. Louis* and *Wompatuck* slowly closed the Santiago harbor entrance in a second attempt to locate and destroy the cable. The cruiser's grapnel soon snagged on the telegraph cable; but, almost simultaneously, the Spanish batteries ashore opened fire on the two American warships. Although neither *Wompatuck* nor *St. Louis* was well-suited for a slugging match with coast defense batteries, both stayed on station until communications between Jamaica and Cuba had been broken. In his subsequent action report, Capt. Goodrich lauded Lt. Jungen's "praiseworthy display of coolness and pluck in battle."

The next day, *St. Louis* and *Wompatuck* endeavored to cut Spanish cable connections at Guantanamo Bay. The tug proceeded into the harbor and dragged her hook along the bottom while the auxiliary cruiser lay-to outside, her main battery at the ready. Spanish shore batteries soon opened fire and eventually drove the American ships out to sea.

After a brief period of repairs at Key West, *Wompatuck* returned to the blockade. She later took part in the landings of Army troops at Daiquiri to relieve pressure on the marines entrenched at Guantanamo.

During the Daiquiri operation, *Wompatuck* screened Army transports on the voyage to the landing zone and later towed 18 launches, whaleboats, and cutters towards the shore to help land the troops from the transports. After she had pointed the first landing parties toward the beaches, she shelled Spanish defense positions to prevent the Spanish defenders from launching a counterattack against the American force ashore.

Eight days later, *Wompatuck* joined the armed steamer *Hist* and the armed yacht *Hornet* in reconnoitering the port of Manzanillo, Cuba. Second in column, the tug followed *Hist*'s lead and opened fire on the Spanish ships—one torpedo boat and three "gun vessels" each mounting two guns—as soon as she reached firing range.

During the ensuing 55-minute duel—in which the Spanish torpedo boat was sunk—*Wompatuck* was forced to maneuver out of column formation in order to bring her after battery to bear. Her forward 3-pounder had fired only seven rounds before the stress sheared off rivets at the base of the mount, rendering it useless. Jungen ordered the helm put over to starboard and thus permitted his vessel to maintain a "brisk . . . and well-directed" fire.

An enemy shell—part of an intense fusillade—meanwhile struck *Hornet* and severed a steam line. Escaping steam scalded three men. *Wompatuck*, seeing *Hornet* in distress, stopped, backed down, and passed the yacht a tow line which had been laid out with foresight earlier that afternoon as the ship had cleared for action.

After her first attempt to pull *Hornet* out of danger failed, *Wompatuck* came alongside to make certain that the towing hawser was securely fastened. Meanwhile, the Spanish had noticed that *Hornet* was disabled. The two-ship "nest" provided too good a target to pass up, and the Spaniards concentrated their gunfire on *Wompatuck* and *Hornet*. A "hot and uncomfortable" fire from cannon, mortars, and small arms soon fell around the two American warships. *Wompatuck* took three minor caliber hits, one of which holed her port whaleboat and passed four feet from Lt. Jungen.

As the two American vessels crept out of danger, a sloop full of Spanish soldiers approached them from their disengaged side, hoping that the *yanquis* were too busy to notice them. However, *Hornet*'s alert gunners were not to be fooled and got off a well-placed 6-pounder shell which sank the sloop—soldiers and all.

While *Wompatuck* licked her wounds, the American fleet routed their Spanish enemies in battle at Santiago on 3 July, ending Spanish hope for a victory. *Wompatuck* subsequently assisted *Hist* and *Hornet* in breaking Spanish cables between Media Luna and Quizaro.

One week later, on 18 July, *Wompatuck* formed part of the American squadron that conducted a bold and devastating three-pronged raid on Manzanillo. The American warships—which also included *Wilmington* (Gunboat No. 8), *Helena* (Gunboat No. 9), the tug *Osceola*, *Hist*, and *Hornet*—approached the enemy from three directions through the various shipping channels and destroyed four Spanish gunboats, three transports, and a store ship with a withering fusillade. The Americans, having caught the enemy unawares, succeeded in emerging from the counterbattery fire unscathed.

Following the Manzanillo action, *Wompatuck* underwent repairs at Key West. One of her 3-pounders had been put out of action when the rivets holding the base of its mount failed under the stress of firing.

The conclusion of what Theodore Roosevelt called a "Splendid Little War" that summer meant that the Fleet would soon return to its peacetime pursuits. *Wompatuck* departed Guantanamo Bay on 14 August, convoying *Rodgers* (Torpedo Boat No. 4) to Key West before proceeding north with *Morris* (Torpedo Boat No. 14) in tow and arriving at New York on 26 August. After repairs, the tug proceeded on to Boston, which she visited from 2 to 9 September. After towing the monitor *Wyandotte* to Philadelphia for decommissioning, *Wompatuck* returned to New York on 15 September and was decommissioned at the New York Navy Yard on 15 October 1898.

Recommissioned at New York on 12 November 1900, *Wompatuck* departed New York on 10 December and rendezvoused in Hampton Roads with *Annapolis* (Gunboat No. 10), the yacht *Frolic*, and the screw tug *Piscataqua*. Underway for the Far East on 30 December, the ships proceeded to the Philippines—via the Mediterranean, the Suez Canal, Colombo, and Singapore—arriving at Cavite on 24 April 1901.

For the next few years, *Wompatuck* participated in operations to restore order during the Philippine Insurrection, as the United States sought to establish sovereignty in a part of its newly won empire. Based out of Cavite during this time, the tug performed a wide variety of duties. She cooperated with Army units at Lubang, Tilig, and Luk Bay, Philippines, in the spring of 1901 and subsequently provisioned lighthouses at Kapones Island, Subig, and Olongapo; transported men and mail; and assisted vessels in distress. She carried out regular transportation services between Cavite and Olongapo into the spring of 1903 and later sailed for Chinese waters to take part in the Fleet's summer target practices at Chefoo.

Assigned to the naval station at Cavite in 1904, *Wompatuck* performed yeoman service until decommissioned on 31 July 1931. During her tour at Cavite, she was designated YT–27 on 17 July 1920, when the Navy adopted its modern, alphanumeric system of hull designations.

Wompatuck's name was struck from the Navy list on 11 February 1938. She apparently was laid up at Cavite for more than three years, awaiting disposal. However, she was withdrawn from the sale list on 9 July 1941 and converted to a self-propelled, diesel oil barge. The erstwhile tug was redesignated *YO–64* on 9 October 1941 and served until the Philippines fell to the Japanese. While no records have been found delineating her fate after Pearl Harbor, it can be assumed that she was either captured by the Japanese when they took Cavite on 2 January 1942 or was scuttled by American or Filipino forces to prevent her capture.

YO–64 was struck from the Navy list on 21 April 1944.

Wood

William Maxwell Wood—born in about 1809 in Baltimore, Md.—was appointed assistant surgeon on 16 May 1829 and, between 1830 and 1838, served with the West Indies and Home Squadrons, as well as with the Army during the Seminole wars.

He became fleet surgeon with the Pacific Squadron in 1844 and, upon completion of his tour, was about to return to the United States when relations between that country and Mexico became decidedly strained. The commander of the Navy's Pacific Squadron, Commodore John D. Sloat, consequently entrusted certain dispatches to Wood to carry back to the United States with him. Wood volunteered to travel through Mexico and report upon conditions there. Accompanied by the American consul from Mazatlan, Mexico, the former fleet surgeon commenced his journey across Mexico.

Arriving at Guadalajara on 10 May, Wood and his companion found the town "in a high state of agitation" owing to the reception there of the news of the battles between American and Mexican forces at Palo Alto and Resaca de la Palma, on the Rio Grande River. The surgeon immediately wrote a dispatch to Sloat at Mazatlan, and it was delivered in five days—an exceptional occurrence in those days. His message that hostilities with Mexico had actually commenced was the first tidings of that nature that Sloat had received.

Wood meanwhile continued on his journey across Mexico and subsequently arrived at Mexico City to be "startled and shocked by hearing newsboys crying through the streets 'Grand victory over the North Americans.'" He later learned through a trusted friend of the Mexican minister of war that General Zachary Taylor's men had, in fact, annihilated the Mexican Army's choice regiment. Surgeon Wood remained in Mexico City not less than a week and gathered more information which he sent off to Commodore Sloat, apprising him of the situation, via Guadalajara.

Wood continued his mission, as he had since the beginning of it, in civilian clothes—running the risk of being apprehended as a spy—and, while posing as an Englishman, inspected the defenses of the castle at Chapultepec. Continuing on to Veracruz, the surgeon carefully took notes on Mexico, its condition and resources. Ultimately, the physician reached a neutral man-of-war and was taken to the flagship of the American blockading squadron. Sailing on a vessel especially detached for the purpose, Wood carried the vital intelligence information to Washington.

Meanwhile, Commodore Sloat took action. As he later recorded in a letter to Wood, "The information you furnished me at Mazatlan from the City of Mexico, via Guadalajara, (at the risk of your life) was the only reliable information I received of that event, and which induced me to proceed immediately to California, and upon my own responsibility to take possession of that country, which I did on the 7th of July, 1846."

Sloat considered the performance of Wood's journey through Mexico "as an extraordinary feat, requiring great courage, presence of mind, and address. How you escaped from the heart of an enemy's country . . . has always been a wonder to me."

Following the Mexican War, Wood served in the receiving ship at Baltimore and later went to the steamer *Michigan*, operating on the Great Lakes. He again served as fleet surgeon—this time with the East India Squadron—from 1856 to 1858, and took part in Commodore Andrew H. Foote's attack upon the Chinese Barrier Forts—of "enormous strength . . . built of large blocks of granite . . . heavily armed."—at Canton, China, in response to Chinese attacks upon American shipping.

Wood subsequently served a second tour in *Michigan* before he became fleet surgeon for the North Atlantic Blockading Squadron. While thus serving, Wood witnessed the historic battle of the ironclads USS *Monitor* and CSS *Virginia* (the former USS *Merrimack*) in Hampton Roads; and later took part in the assault and capture of Sewall's Point.

After the Civil War, Wood served at Baltimore in 1866 and 1867 and was President of the Naval Examining Board in 1868 before he became Chief of the Bureau of Medicine and Surgery in 1870. Appointed medical director on 3 March 1871, Wood retired later that same year and died in Baltimore on 1 March 1880.

I

(DD–317: dp. 1,215; l. 314'5''; b. 31'8''; dr. 9'4'' (mean); s. 35.0 k.; cpl. 95; a. 4 4'', 1 3'', 12 21'' tt.; cl. *Clemson*)

Wood (Destroyer No. 317) was laid down on 23 January 1919 at San Francisco, Calif., by the Union Iron Works plant of the Bethlehem Shipbuilding Corp; launched on 28 May 1919; sponsored by Mrs. George Kirkland Smith, the granddaughter of William Maxwell Wood; reclassified DD–317 on 17 July 1920; and commissioned at the Mare Island Navy Yard, Vallejo, Calif., on 28 January 1921, Lt. Comdr. Paul M. Bates in command.

Following commissioning, *Wood* underwent her trials before mooring at the Santa Fe docks, San Diego, Calif., where she remained as part of the "rotating reserve" into the summer of 1921. The new destroyer then spent the ensuing months, into the late spring of 1922, operating off the coast of southern California on drills and exercises, off the port of San Pedro, and the Coronado Islands.

At the end of that period of activity in June of 1922, *Wood* shifted northward and reached Seattle, Wash., on 1 July 1922. She spent the 4th of July there before visiting Port Angeles, Wash., with the fleet, for exercises and maneuvers. She then conducted tactical drills and exercises in the Pacific Northwest, touching at Tacoma, Port Angeles, Bellingham, and Seattle before departing Port Angeles on 2 September, bound for Mare Island.

After taking on board ammunition at Mare Island on 5 and 6 September, *Wood* put to sea, bound for San Diego, Calif., for a machinery overhaul. Upon completion of those repairs, the destroyer rejoined the fleet for rehearsals for shortrange battle practices. She then operated on various trials into November.

Over the next nine and one-half years, *Wood* operated with the Battle Fleet in an active role, while many of her sisters lay in "Red Lead Row" awaiting the call to active service. Breaking her local operations off the west coast, *Wood* participated in Fleet Problems I through IX—the large scale fleet exercises that were held once a year (except in 1924, when three were held) involving most of the Fleet's active units. During the course of those maneuvers, she ranged from the Caribbean to the Panama Canal and from Hawaii to the coast of Central America. She also ventured as far north as the coast of Alaska.

Highlighting *Wood*'s service in the autumn of 1925 was the cruise with the fleet to Australia as part of Destroyer Division 34. The destroyer subsequently took part in the search for the downed *PN–9* flying boat. In March 1927, during one of the phases of Fleet Problem VII, *Wood* participated in the search for survivors from the lost German steamship *Albatros* and later that same year, from 27 June to 16 July, *Wood* supported American peace-keeping forces ashore on Nicaragua.

Decommissioned at San Diego on 31 March 1930, *Wood* was struck from the Navy list on 22 July. Her hulk was then sold for scrap on 14 November 1930.

Exchequer was laid down under a Maritime Commission contract (MC hull 590) on 26 August 1942 at Sparrows Point, Md., by the Bethlehem Steel Co.; renamed *Wood* and classified APA–101 on 5 October 1942; reclassified to AP–56 on 1 February 1943; and launched on 13 February 1943.

However, prior to commissioning, *Wood* was renamed *Leedstown* (q.v.) on 17 March 1943.

Wood County

Counties in Ohio, Texas, West Virginia, and Wisconsin.

(LST–1178: dp. 7,804; l. 442'; b. 62'; dr. 17'; s. 17.2 k.; cp. 174; trp. 540; a. 6 3''; cl. *De Soto County*)

Wood County (LST–1178) was laid down on 1 October 1956 at Lorain, Ohio, by the American Shipbuilding Co.; launched on 14 December 1957; sponsored by Miss Margaret Ackerman, the daughter of the president of the American Shipbuilding Co.; and commissioned on 5 August 1959 at the Norfolk Naval Shipyard, Portsmouth, Va., Comdr. Maxton M. Midgett in command.

Following her shakedown and initial operations on the Atlantic seaboard, *Wood County* was deployed to the Mediterranean for the first time in the summer of 1960, as part of Amphibious Squadron (PhibRon) 2. She subsequently conducted her second deployment to the 6th Fleet in the autumn of 1961 after escorting a division of ocean minesweepers from the east coast to the Mediterranean. During that deployment, the tank landing ship visited Polensa Bay, Majorca, Spain; and the British Crown Colony of Malta, where she embarked a detachment of British commandoes that she eventually landed at Bomba, Libya, during an exercise. In addition, the ship also visited Valencia, Rota, and Barcelona, Spain; Messina and La Spezia, Italy; Cannes, France; and Pilos and Athens, Greece, before she returned to Little Creek, Va., her home port, in February 1962.

On 1 April 1962, *Wood County* was transferred to PhibRon 12. Later that month, the tank landing ship participated in a large scale demonstration exercise off Little Creek—an evolution witnessed by President John F. Kennedy and the Shah of Iran. Immediately thereafter, *Wood County* proceeded to Vieques, Puerto Rico, where she participated in Atlantic Fleet Amphibious Exercise 1–62.

Wood County underwent a regular overhaul at Newport News, Va., from June to August 1962, before she stood out to sea for trials and refresher training. The tank landing ship deployed to the Caribbean to take part in amphibious brigade exercises and then to become part of the "Caribbean Ready Squadron." In the autumn of 1962, after American aerial reconnaissance disclosed the presence of Soviet offensive missiles in Cuba, President Kennedy insisted that the missiles be withdrawn and imposed a "quarantine" on Cuba. *Wood*

County participated in that operation off the Cuban coast which ended after the Soviet Union removed the missiles.

The warship began the new year 1963 in the familiar tropical climes of the Caribbean but soon sailed for the Mediterranean. During this deployment, she served as part of the 6th Fleet's amphibious strike force and visited Italian, French, and Spanish ports during the course of her tour. She participated in Operation "Southtrap"—a NATO exercise in which she embarked and landed 1,000 Turkish troops with their vehicles. Other landing exercises were held with NATO forces in Turkey, Sardinia, Mallorca, and Greece. She returned home to Little Creek on 19 October 1963.

Following upkeep and type training evolutions, *Wood County* shifted to Davisville, R.I., to load Mobile Construction Battalion (CB or Sea Bee) 4. She transported the Sea Bees to Guantanamo Bay, Cuba, and carried Mobile CB Battalion 1 from Guantanamo back to Davisville on the return voyage. The following month, the tank landing ship took part in routine Caribbean exercises and, upon completion, took part in a pair of successive Atlantic Fleet amphibious exercises. That summer, in August, *Wood County* participated in a special balloon-launch in a joint Navy-Air Force project before undergoing overhaul and upkeep at Charleston and Jacksonville, respectively.

After a lengthy in-port period, *Wood County* departed Little Creek in April 1965 for what promised to be a routine Caribbean deployment. Exercise "Quick Kick VII" took place soon thereafter, before the ship put in to San Juan, Puerto Rico, to allow the crew liberty. Departing San Juan shortly thereafter, the tank landing ship received urgent orders to sail for the Dominican Republic.

There, a coup to return the ousted former President, Juan Bosch, to power, had developed into a bloody civil war when communist elements took control of the pro-Bosch movement to turn it toward their own ends. Heavy fighting developed in and around the capital city of Santo Domingo, prompting President Lyndon B. Johnson to order American marines to the Caribbean isle to halt the coup and protect American lives.

Wood County's task was to evacuate American nationals threatened by the strife in the capital city. To do this, the tank landing ship put in to Puerto de Haina —nine miles from the center of Santo Domingo—and took on board 415 passengers for passage to Puerto Rico. *Wood County* disembarked the refugees at San Juan and returned to the Dominican Republic with marines and a few newspapermen embarked. En route, the ship transferred the newsmen to *Boxer* (LPH–4) before she landed the marines in an amphibious operation near Santo Domingo. Moving to Puerto de Haina for the second time, *Wood County* embarked 1,013 more refugees and ferried them to San Juan. Upon completion of this task, *Wood County* remained in the vicinity, on patrol duty in a stand-by status, until she returned north and put in to Little Creek on 30 June.

Wood County operated locally off the Virginia capes into February of 1966. She later transported an engineering battalion to Vieques before commencing a restricted availability in April. During July, the tank landing ship operated between Santo Domingo and San Juan. In September and October, the ship prepared for an impending Mediterranean deployment.

Wood County lifted the 3d Battalion, 8th Engineers, to Rota, Spain, before she participated in a combined amphibious assault with French units at Lovo Santo, Corsica, in November 1966. The tank landing ship took part in an amphibious exercise off Sardinia in January of 1967 and in two more during March before undertaking a role in a joint amphibious evolution with ships of the Italian Navy at Tagliamento, Italy, and another exercise off Sardinia in April.

On her return voyage to the United States in May 1967, *Wood County* escorted an ocean minesweeper division back from its 6th Fleet deployment and then entered the Norfolk Naval Shipyard for an overhaul which lasted from June 1967 to September 1968. The tank landing ship then was placed in reserve operating status to be effective until January 1970.

During this reserve period, *Wood County* operated in a restricted operating status and with a reduced manning level, due to the problems asesociated with the ship's main propulsion system—the six Cooper-Bessemer diesel engines. While *Wood County* remained pierside at Little Creek for the greater part of 1969, her crew labored to preserve and maintain the ship and conducted training on board and on shore. The tank landing ship was also used as a demonstration ship for the amphibious school—a stationary training aid—through the summer of 1969. Groups of students from the school came on board periodically to tour the LST-type vessel.

On 2 September 1969, *Wood County* proceeded to the Horne Brothers Shipyard, Newport News, Va., to have the six Cooper-Bessemer engines replaced by a like number of Fairbanks-Morse diesels. The work progressed well into the spring of 1970. On 15 June, the tank landing ship successfully completed her sea trials and, on the 19th, officially competed her yard period at Newport News. On the 20th, she set out on her two-week shakedown cruise.

On Sunday, 21 June, *Wood County* sighted a red flare and atered course to investigate. She found that the 36-foot sailboat *Hiro* had been adrift for three days due to a rudder casualty, and she rescued the two occupants. Six days later, *Wood County* performed her second rescue of the week when she hauled on board two men from a small fishing boat which had been the object of a massive search by Coast Guard ships and planes for the past three days.

From August to October 1970, *Wood County* underwent shakedown and amphibious refresher training under the auspices of the Atlantic Fleet Amphibious Operational Training Unit. From 16 to 26 October, the tank landing ship provided transportation and berthing for representatives of many amphibious type commands at the Philadelphia Naval Base for participation in a fire-fighting school conducted there at the time.

Wood County underwent type training, acting as control ship for drone aircraft used in various gunnery exercises by the ships in PhibRon 6. Returning to port, *Wood County* soon commenced a tender availability in preparation for the ship's first Mediterranean deployment in four years. By 16 January 1971, the ship's cargo—two PCF Swift boats and a pair of Ammi pontoons—were secured and ready for sea. This was the first instance of Ammi pontoons being side-loaded on a tank landing ship for a transoceanic voyage. *Wood County* stood out of Little Creek on 19 January, bound for Malta and Crete.

The tank landing ship made port at Valetta, Malta, on 6 February and off-loaded the two Swift patrol craft. Those boats were to be used by the Maltese government to combat smuggling off the island's coasts. Departing the same day, *Wood County* pressed on for Crete and arrived two days later. There, she turned the two 54-ton Ammi pontoons over to the Royal Hellenic Navy for use in extending a pier in the harbor at Souda Bay.

Departing Souda Bay on 9 February, *Wood County* returned home via Barcelona, Spain, and Gibraltar and arrived at Little Creek on 28 February.

However, soon after returning to her home port, *Wood County* began preparations to return to the Mediterranean. The coming deployment would be especially significant, as *Wood County* had been assigned the task of support ship to the product of the Navy's newest developments in hydrofoil technology, the gunboat *Tucumcari* (PGH-2). On 22 March 1971, *Tucumcari* was deck-loaded piggyback on board *Wood County*; and, three days later, the tank landing ship sailed from Little Creek, bound for the first stop on the special demonstration deployment.

Over the ensuing months, *Wood County* and *Tucumcari* visited seven NATO nations and 16 ports—Copenhagen and Frederickshaven, Denmark; Kiel and Olpenitz, Germany; Portsmouth and Portland, England; and Rendsburg, Germany. Then, after a transit of the Kiel Canal, she stopped at Rosyth, Scotland; Brest and Toulon, France; Naples, Brindisi, La Spezia, and Augusta, Italy; Athens, Greece; and Golcuk, Turkey. *Tucumcari* was demonstrated in hopes that NATO would develop a guided-missile hydrofoil weapons system. In addition to providing a base of operations and facilities for briefings and discussions between United States liaison officers and foreign representatives, *Wood County* provided logistics support, messing and berthing facilities, and engaged in numerous public relations efforts to promote international goodwill. The performance of *Wood County* and *Tucumcari* both elicited praise from the Chief of Naval Operations; Commander Amphibious Force, U.S. Atlantic Fleet; the United States NATO Mission; Commander in Chief, United States Naval Forces Europe, and others.

Upon *Wood County*'s return, she offloaded *Tucumcari* and began preparations for a Board of Inspection and Survey inspection in November. Following that, *Wood County* was placed out of commission, in reserve, on 15 February 1972. On 1 May 1972, *Wood County* was decommissioned.

Wood County was berthed in the James River, as part of the National Defense Reserve Fleet, in temporary custody of the Maritime Administration, from 1972 to July 1977. After that date, the tank landing ship was shifted to the Portsmouth, Va., berthing area, where she remained into 1978.

Wood, Leonard, see *Leonard Wood*.

Wood, Maria A., see *Maria A. Wood*.

Wood, Sallie, see *Sallie Wood*.

Woodbine

A vine native to North America also known as honeysuckle, Virginia creeper, and American ivy.

(Launch: dp. 85; l. 95'0''; b. 16'0''; dr. 5'2'' (mean); dph. 7'0''; cpl. 6)

Woodbine—a wooden-hulled launch—was built in 1913 at New Brighton, N.Y., for the United States Lighthouse Service—initially served as a lighthouse tender at Baltimore until she was shifted to Philadelphia in about 1915. The Navy took over the ship during World War I for use as a section patrol craft and operated her in the 4th Naval District (Philadelphia) into 1919. She was returned to the Lighthouse Service on 1 July 1919 and was struck from the Navy list the same day. *Woodbine* remained in operation with the Lighthouse Service until about 1935.

Woodbury

Levi Woodbury—born in Francestown, N.H., on 22 December 1789—graduated from Dartmouth College at Hanover, N.H., in 1809. He studied law in offices in Litchfield, Conn.; Boston, Mass.; and Exeter, N.H., before being admitted to the New Hampshire bar in 1812. He practiced law in Francestown until 1816 when he received an appointment to the New Hampshire bench as judge of the superior court. In 1819, while still a New Hampshire judge, he moved his residence to Portsmouth. In 1822, he gave up his judgeship in a successful bid for the governorship of New Hampshire in which office he served until 1824. After a term in the lower house of the state legislature, he was elected to the United States Senate for the term beginninng on 4 March 1825.

At the conuclusion of that term in 1831, he declined a nomination to the New Hampshire state senate to remain active in national politics. In May 1831, Woodbury accepted the post of Secretary of the Navy in President Andrew Jackson's cabinet. Well suited to the office by virtue of service on the Senate naval committee, Woodbury revised the rules of conduct and procedure within the nation's naval establishment. Woodbury held his office as Secretary of the Navy until 30 June 1834 at which time he assumed the duties of the Secretary of the Treasury. In that role, he opposed the rechartering of the United States Bank and supported Jackson's fiscal policy. He liked the independent treasury and hard currency and warned against the danger of inflation in 1836. During the Panic of 1837, he devised a scheme whereby those who held Federal obligations suffered no loss as a result of the depreciated paper currency.

When the new administration assumed the reins of power, Woodbury gave up his duties as Secretary of the Treasury. Again declining a proffered state office—that of Chief Justice of the superior court of New Hampshire—in favor of national political office, he won another term in the United States Senate. Woodbury took his seat in the Senate on 4 March 1841 and served until 20 November 1845 at which time he resigned to accept a seat on the United States Supreme Court vacated by the death of Joseph Story. He served on the Supreme Court until his death at Portsmouth, N.H., on 4 September 1851.

I

(Sch: t. 115; a. 4 12-pdrs., 1 6-pdr.)

The first *Woodbury*—a schooner-rigged revenue cutter sometimes referred to as *Levi Woodbury*—was authorized on 8 November 1826. Exactly a week later, Capt. H. D. Hunter, of the United States Revenue Cutter Service, was designated to superintend construction of the vessel. Referred to as *Woodbury* on 7 February 1837, the revenue cutter was launched on 27 March 1837 at Baltimore, Md., by L. H. Duncan, shipbuilder.

When ready for sea, *Woodbury* proceeded southward to New Orleans, slated to relieve the revenue cutter *Campbell* at that port; and arrived at her destination on 21 June. Little is recorded of the vessel's activities in 1837; but records indicate that, as of 28 March 1838, *Woodbury* was operating in the Gulf of Mexico in cooperation with the United States Navy, protecting American commerce from the Mexican privateers.

During the state of emergency incident to tension between Mexico and the United States, *Woodbury* was placed under naval control. Her orders, from the Collector of Customs at New Orleans to her commanding officer, were specific: "You will proceed to sea forthwith, taking your cruising ground from Chandalier Islands to the mouth of the Sabine River, and in the event of any vessel sailing under our flag, being in your presence unlawfully attacked, by an armed force, you will render such aid and protection as may be in your power."

At the time *Woodbury* was dispatched to Mexican waters, France and Mexico were engaged in the brief "Pastry War" over alleged mistreatment of French nationals by the Mexican government. In the summer of 1838, the French had established a blockade off the key seaport of Veracruz, Mexico, and retained it there into the autumn. *Woodbury* was brought-to off Veracruz by a French warship and collided with her; the French graciously allowed *Woodbury* to proceed to Veracruz for repairs. Apparently detained in port by the French admiral, *Woodbury* witnessed the French bombardment of the fortress at San Juan de Ulua that compelled its surrender on 28 November. The following day, with the French apparently in command of the

situation at Veracruz, *Woodbury* sailed for New Orleans.

Records of what the ship did next are sketchy, but indicate that she may have proceeded to Savannah, Ga., for repairs soon thereafter. She later moved to Belize, Honduras, where she apparently operated under naval orders before returning to Florida. Records show that she was in Pensacola Bay, Fla., in early June of 1839. Ordered to Baltimore for repairs, *Woodbury* arrived there on 26 August 1839.

Returning to the Gulf of Mexico, *Woodbury* sailed for New Orleans on 23 September, following her refit at Baltimore. She probably remained in the gulf into mid-1841 before again returning to Baltimore in July of that year for repairs.

Woodbury conveyed bearers of dispatches to Veracruz and back in April and December of 1842 and, in May of 1844, was dispatched to Veracruz to receive and carry to New Orleans the fourth installment of the indemnity fund established by the arbitration board as a result of the claims convention between Mexico and the United States in 1839.

However, war between Mexico and the United States over the question of Texas' annexation was only a matter of time, and *Woodbury* participated in the conflict in a vital support role. During the tense period preceding hostilities, the revenue cutter served as a dispatch boat in the Gulf of Mexico, touching at Corpus Christi and Galveston, Tex., and ranging as far as the mouth of the Mississippi.

On 2 March 1846, *Woodbury*, commanded by Capt. Winslow Foster, arrived at Aransas Pass, Tex., to support General Zachary Taylor's move southward. Taylor had moved into Texas, basing at Corpus Christi, in July of 1845. Meanwhile, tensions between the United States and Mexico had increased markedly; and Taylor was planning to move to the Rio Grande. He advanced prior to his receiving promised naval support and was forced to use what forces he had at hand.

Woodbury's arrival was timed perfectly. Capt. Foster promptly placed his ship at Taylor's disposal—something later praised by the general in subsequent dispatches—and the revenue cutter convoyed the transports bearing Taylor's troops to Point Isabel, just north of the mouth of the Rio Grande. Taylor's army soon moved into an encampment across from Matamoros; and *Woodbury*, her task completed, sailed for Galveston. Taylor later conveyed his gratitude to Capt. Foster on 26 March, expressing his "thanks for the handsome manner in which you have extended your assistance and that of your vessel to the operations of the Army. . . ."

Although that service had been rendered independent of the Navy, *Woodbury* later received orders directing her to cooperate with both services—Army and Navy—that spring. The revenue cutter returned to New Orleans and then sailed back to the mouth of the Rio Grande. There, on 12 June, the ship was given orders to "remain off the Rio Grande or Brazos Santiago and assist the naval vessel or vessels on the station in covering the depot (established by Taylor there) and the public stores. It is expected you will without waiting for orders, cooperate with the naval force when necessary."

Sailing from Brazos Santiago on 25 June 1846, *Woodbury* arrived at Belize on 6 July. On 8 July, although regarded as "entirely unfit for duty and unseaworthy," *Woodbury* was ordered to report to General Taylor or Commodore David F. Stockton. However, those orders were changed the following day, when she was sent to New York for repairs. Accordingly, the revenue cutter sailed on the 11th and arrived at Brazos Santiago on the 21st.

Five days later, while *Woodbury* lay at that port, troops on board the transport *Middlesex* mutinied. Lt. McClane, of *Woodbury*, accordingly went on board the transport, restored order, and landed the troops before returning to the cutter.

Woodbury later sailed to Belize in early August and, "after a tedious passage of 18 days," reached the Staten Island Quarantine Ground on 7 September. Later apparently seen to be unfit for further service, *Woodbury* was slated to be dismantled by orders dated 14 September 1846. She was sold on 1 June 1847 and subsequently was broken up.

II

(RC: dp. 370; l. 130'; b. 27'; dr. 5'4'' (aft); a. 7 guns)

Mahoning—a steam-powered revenue cutter built in 1863 and 1864 at Philadelphia, Pa., by J. W. Lynn & Sons—was placed in commission in the Revenue Cutter Service (alternatively called the Revenue Marine) on 18 July 1864. She patrolled the American coastline from Massachusetts to Maine for the major portion of her active career. On 5 June 1873, she was renamed *Levi Woodbury*. She continued her patrols of the New England coast through the last quarter of the 19th century.

Soon after the war with Spain broke out in April of 1898, the revenue cutter began operations with the Navy. Ordered to duty with the North Atlantic Fleet on 24 March, two days later, she received orders to report to Norfolk, Va., and arrived there on 2 April. Known simply as *Woodbury* in Navy records, the revenue cutter conducted operations with the North Atlantic Fleet from 8 May to the end of hostilities in August. Though she may have participated in troop convoys to Cuba, the cutter's primary duty consisted of blockading the port of Havana. She took no prizes during her brief naval career and appears to have been involved in no engagements.

Control of the cutter was returned to the Treasury Department on 17 August 1898, and she returned to her former base at Portland, Maine, on 16 November to resume patrols of the New England coast. That routine occupied her for the next 17 years. On 19 July 1915, the revenue cutter was placed out of commission at Portland. She was sold on 10 August to Thomas Butler & Co., of Boston, Mass.

III

(DD-309: dp. 1,308; l. 314'4½''; b. 30'11½''; dr. 9'4'' (mean); s. 33.46 k.; cpl. 122; a. 4 4'', 1 3'', 12 21'' tt., 2 dct.; cl. *Clemson*)

The third *Woodbury* (Destroyer No. 309) was laid down on 3 October 1918 at San Francisco, Calif., by the Union Iron Works plant of the Bethlehem Shipbuilding Corp.; launched on 6 February 1919; sponsored by Miss Catherine Muhlenberg Chapin, the daughter of newspaper publisher W. W. Chapin; reclassified DD-309 on 17 July 1920; and commissioned at the Mare Island Navy Yard, Vallejo, Calif., on 20 October 1920, Lt. Comdr. Frank L. Lowe in command.

Woodbury departed San Francisco on 22 November and reached San Diego, her assigned home port, the following day. *Woodbury* moored at the Reserve Docks, where she remained into 1921. The destroyer—like many of her numerous sisters begun during World War I—had entered service at a time when the post-World War I cutbacks in funds and personnel had seriously curtailed American peacetime naval operations. Accordingly, she was placed in a "rotating reserve" established by the Navy to maintain a "force in readiness." In operation, the system required that one-third of a given force remain pierside, maintained by only the minimum number of officers and men, while another third was to be half-manned as it remained berthed at a buoy in the harbor. The last third was fully manned and remained at buoys in the harbor but for periodic operations underway at sea.

Woodbury departed her mooring at the Reserve Docks on 1 February 1921 and, over the next few days, conducted torpedo practices and made a 30-knot speed run off the southern California coast. During that brief underway period, the destroyer conducted her operations during the day and returned to her mooring buoy in the evenings. She remained largely port-bound from March to May, but moved to San Pedro, Calif., on 14 June. There, her crew assisted in preservation and maintenance work on *William Jones* (DD-308) while she lay in drydock at the Los Angeles Ship Building and Dry Dock Co., San Pedro. *Woodbury* then underwent a drydocking herself for the application of anticorrosive and antifouling paint to her bottom. *Woodbury* later returned to San Diego and, but for a run, via Los Angeles harbor, to Seattle, Wash., stayed there for the remainder of 1921.

Underway on the morning of 14 January 1922, *Woodbury* led *Nicholas* (DD-311), *S. P. Lee* (DD-310), and *Young* (DD-312) to sea. She arrived off Goat Island, near San Francisco, at 0820 the following day and lay to, embarking passengers for transportation to the Puget Sound Navy Yard, Bremerton, Wash., before she resumed her cruise up the Pacific coast. The destroyer reached Puget Sound on the afternoon of the 18th, discharged her passengers, and soon commenced her scheduled overhaul.

Woodbury remained at Puget Sound through March 1922. She got underway for San Diego on 3 April but put into Port Angeles, Wash., when *Nicholas* developed a machinery casualty. Upon completion of *Nicholas'* repairs, *Woodbury* resumed her passage southward and reached San Diego on 8 April.

The destroyer lay at berth 35, San Diego harbor, into the summer, again as part of the inactive arm of the "rotating reserve." From early July to late September, *Woodbury* provided essential maintenance and upkeep services to her sisterships in the decommissioned Destroyer Division 17 moored alongside. There were only two breaks in the ship's routine during that time: a tender upkeep period alongside *Melville* (AD-2) and her participation in the funeral of the late Rear Admiral Uriel Sebree, USN (Ret.), on 8 August, for which she sent a party ashore to form part of the naval escort for the casket.

Woodbury got underway on 26 September 1922 and conducted gunnery exercises in company with *Young* and *Nicholas*. After another period of upkeep alongside *Melville*, the destroyer participated in an intensive slate of gunnery and torpedo drills. Then, late in October, she also performed torpedo recovery chores for the battleships *Idaho* (BB-40) and *New Mexico* (BB-42).

After spending the remainder of 1922 in San Diego waters, *Woodbury* stood out of San Diego harbor on 6 February 1923, in company with Destroyer Squadrons 11 and 12 and the tender *Melville*, all ships bound for Mexico, and, ultimately, for Panama. Arriving at Magdalena Bay on the 8th, *Woodbury* refueled from *Kanawha* (AO-1) before she pushed on for Panamanian waters on the 11th. That afternoon, she rendezvoused with the dreadnoughts of Battleship Divisions 3, 4, and 5 and conducted exercises with them en route to Panama.

Over the ensuing weeks, *Woodbury* took part in the first of the Navy's large scale fleet maneuvers, Fleet Problem I. Held in the vicinity of the strategic Panama Canal Zone, Fleet Problem I was designed to ascertain the defensive condition of that isthmian waterway, to allow for the formulation of the "estimate of the situation," and to facilitate the study of war plans. *Woodbury* took part in the exercises as part of the "attacking" forces built around the Battle Fleet. The opposing forces consisted of the Scouting Fleet, augmented by a division of battleships.

During one phase of the operation, while the ships lay anchored at Panama Bay, *Henderson* (AP-1)—bearing the Secretary of the Navy, Edwin A. Denby, and the Chief of Naval Operations, Admiral Robert E. Coontz—stood through the fleet. Later, *Woodbury* resumed her operations with the Battle Fleet—conducting gunnery drills, antisubmarine screening, protective screening for the battleships—and serving as a target for Battleship Division 4 during its long-range battle practices.

Returning to San Diego on 11 April, *Woodbury* remained there into the summer. Departing her home port on 25 June, however, she sailed for the Pacific Northwest and reached Tacoma, Wash., via San Francisco, on 2 July. There, her landing force participated in the Independence Day parade at Tacoma.

Woodbury departed Tacoma on 9 July and reached Port Angeles the same day. For nearly two weeks, the destroyer operated out of that port, conducting exercises, tactical maneuvers, and short range battle practices. After that stint of operations, she shifted to Bellingham, Wash., and, later, to Seattle.

Underway at 0405 on 27 July, *Woodbury* departed the fleet's anchorage off Admiralty Head, near Seattle, in company with Destroyer Divisions 32 and 33 to escort *Henderson* in which the President of the United States, Warren G. Harding, was embarked. *Woodbury* consequently formed part of the presidential escort as the transport sailed through the fleet.

Once her duties in connection with the Presidential review were completed, *Woodbury* returned to the routine of exercises, acting as a target for the gunnery drills carried out by Battleship Division 4. She later conducted tactical exercises while screening the battleships of that division, before she put in to Lake Washington, via the Lake Washington Ship Canal, on 4 August. She remained there for a little over a week before she got underway on the 13th for Port Townsend.

After torpedo-firing and gunnery evolutions out of Port Townsend in company with *William Jones*, *Woodbury* got underway for Keyport, Wash., en route back to Seattle and Puget Sound. Reaching the navy yard on the 20th, she embarked the Commander in Chief, United States Fleet (CinCUS), Admiral Robert E. Coontz, his staff, and a party of congressmen at 0840 on the 22d. With the CinCUS' four-starred flag at her main, *Woodbury* cast off from Pier 5, Puget Sound Navy Yard, and sailed for Keyport. There, Admiral Coontz disembarked with his staff and the congressmen and inspected the naval torpedo station.

The admiral and his party then reembarked in the destroyer, and she returned them to the navy yard, where they left the ship at 1110. At noon, however, the CinCUS returned on board. *Woodbury* subsequently arrived at Seattle's Bell Street Dock at 1310 and disembarked the admiral. The next day, the destroyer carried Admiral Coontz to his flagship, the armored cruiser *Seattle* (CA–11). Over the ensuing days, *Woodbury* also carried, as passengers, Rear Admiral William C. Cole, chief of staff for the CinCUS, and Rear Admiral Luther E. Gregory, CEC, the Chief of the Bureau of Yards and Docks.

After completing her tour in the waters off the Pacific Northwest coast of the United States, *Woodbury* departed Port Angeles and headed south. She conducted tactical maneuvers and exercises with battleships en route and stood into San Francisco Bay on 31 August.

Woodbury remained at San Francisco for a week. She got underway on the morning of 8 September 1923 with other destroyers of Squadron 11, bound for San Diego, and while skirting the coast over the ensuing hours, conducted tactical exercises and maneuvers. In addition, the ships were making a 20-knot speed run. Led by the leader, *Delphy* (DD–261), the squadron steamed into the worsening weather. Later that evening, *Delphy*—unfortunately basing her movements on an inaccurate navigational bearing—made a fateful turn, believing she was heading into the Santa Barbara Channel. In fact, she was headed—as were all of the ships astern of her in follow-the-leader fashion—for jagged rock pinnacles and reefs off Point Arguello.

Shortly after 2105, tragedy struck Squadron 11's ships, one by one. Seven ships, led by *Delphy* and including *Woodbury*, ran hard aground. Some of the de-

stroyers farther astern saw what was happening and managed to avoid disaster by quick-thinking seamanship.

Woodbury came to rest alongside a small island—later nicknamed "Woodbury Rock"—that she used as a permanent anchor. Volunteers took across four lines and rigged them across the gap of tumbling surf between the destroyer and the rock that would later bear her name. Meanwhile, although water was pouring into the forward boiler room and engine room spaces, Comdr. Louis P. Davis, the ship's commanding officer, ordered full speed astern. Ens. Horatio Ridout, the engineer officer, and his men worked with great courage to try to produce the horsepower necessary to get the ship out of her predicament; but their efforts were brought to nought when all power failed, due to the flooding, at 2230.

As the floodwaters below engulfed and drowned out her power supply and it became impossible to move the ship, Comdr. Davis turned to his reserve plan. While *Woodbury* settled astern, the thundering breakers struck her full force, causing her bow to rise and fall rythmically. The hawsers tenuously connecting the ship with "Woodbury Rock" stretched taut and then sagged with the movement of ship and sea. Nevertheless, one by one, *Woodbury*'s crew clambered across the chasm, monkey-fashion, in a well-organized abandon ship operation. Later, men from the stranded sistership *Fuller* (DD–297) reached "Woodbury Rock."

Ultimately, all of *Woodbury*'s crew reached safety, some taken off to *Percival* (DD–298) by the fishing boat *Bueno Amor de Roma*, under the command of a Captain Noceti. The rough log entry for *Woodbury*, dated 9 September 1923, sums up the ship's status as of that date: "*Woodbury* on rocks off Point Arguello, Calif., abandoned by all hands and under supervision of a salvage party composed of men from various 11th squadron ships."

Officially placed out of commission on 26 October 1923, the ship was struck from the Navy list on 20 November of the same year. She was simultaneously ordered sold as a hulk, but a subsequent sale, on 6 February 1924 to a Santa Monica (Calif.)-based salvage firm, the Fryn Salvage Co., was never consummated. Yet another sale, to a Robert J. Smith of Oakland, Calif., is recorded as having been awarded on 19 October 1925, but whether or not the hulk was scrapped is not recorded.

IV

(CGC: dp. 220; l. 125'0''; b. 23'6''; dr. 6'9'' (mean); s. 13.0 k.; cpl. 38; a. 1 3''; cl. *Active*)

The fourth *Woodbury*—a twin-screw, diesel-powered, steel-hulled Coast Guard cutter—was built in 1927 at Camden, N.J., by the American Brown Boveri Electric Corp., for the United States Coast Guard, and was fitted out to service navigational aids. Initially homeported at Norfolk, Va., *Woodbury* served at a succession of other ports prior to the entry of the United States into World War II: St. Petersburg, Fla., from 1929 to 1934; Gulfport, Miss., in 1935 and 1936; Corpus Christi, Tex., in 1936 and 1937; and Galveston from 1937 to 1941. In the summer of 1941, when the Coast Guard was taken into the Navy for service during the national emergency, *Woodbury* was serving at Galveston.

Either late in 1941 or early in 1942, *Woodbury* was classified as a submarine chaser, WSC–155, and somewhat later was shifted to patrol and escort duties in the Chesapeake Bay region to strengthen Allied antisubmarine warfare forces in that area where German U-boats had recently been taking a heavy toll of American coastwise shipping.

On the night of 16 February 1942, *Woodbury* was patrolling off the entrance to Chesapeake Bay in a dense fog. Shortly after 2145, lookouts on board the cutter heard two explosions in quick succession; and the ship's radioman soon picked up distress signals from a torpedoed vessel out in the murk. *Woodbury* accordingly altered course to pick up survivors.

The stricken vessel turned out to be the tanker *E. H. Blum*, and *Woodbury* rescued her entire crew of 40 men by 2245.

Shortly thereafter, *Woodbury* was transferred to the 8th Naval District. After brief inshore patrol work, the ship underwent an overhaul in which her armament was increased and then was placed under the direct operational control of Commander, 8th Naval District, for convoy escort duties between the Mississippi Passes and her old home port, Galveston.

While thus engaged, *Woodbury* picked up a sound contact at 1815 on 8 August 1942, 30 miles south of the Mississippi delta. She delivered a depth charge attack and noted a large oil slick, but could not confirm her "kill." As *Woodbury* patrolled the vicinity the following day, she noted that the waters were covered with diesel and lube oil and pieces of granulated cork over an area two miles long. Whether or not the Coast Guard cutter had actually destroyed a U-boat was never determined when the Allies investigated German records after the war.

Woodbury performed convoy escort work in the Gulf of Mexico, escorting coastwise shipping between ports on the gulf coast from Florida to Texas. She again delivered a depth charge attack on a suspected enemy submarine on 13 November 1942; but, since she was the sole escort for the convoy, she soon returned to her escort duties.

Her available records only span the time period from February to December of 1942, but it is reasonable to assume that she performed similar duties—convoy escort and inshore patrol—for the remainder of World War II. Apparently decommissioned and sold in 1948, *Woodbury* was renamed *Humble AC-3*, and, under the aegis of the Humble Oil and Refining Co., served as a tug through the late 1950's. Later acquired by the firm of Caribbean Towing Inc., she was renamed *Challenge* in about 1963. She is listed in the 1979 American Bureau of Shipping register as still serving, as a tug, with that firm.

Woodbury, Levi, see *Levi Woodbury*.

Woodcliff Bay

Woodcliff Bay (CVE-93)—a *Casablanca*-class escort aircraft carrier—was renamed *Makin Island* (q.v.) on 17 December 1943 to commemorate the recent capture of that island in the Gilbert group by American amphibious forces.

Woodcock

A game bird that frequents wooded areas.

(Minesweeper No. 14: dp. 950 (n.); l. 187'10''; b. 35'6''; dr. 9'9½'' (mean); s. 14.0 k.; cpl. 85; a. 2 3''; cl. *Lapwing*)

Woodcock (Minesweeper No. 14) was laid down on 19 October 1917 at Chester, Pa., by the Chester Shipbuilding Co.; launched on 12 May 1918; sponsored by Mrs. Lewis T. Kniskern; and commissioned at the Philadelphia Navy Yard on 19 February 1919, Lt. (jg.) W. J. Fanger in command.

After performing experimental minesweeping work at Newport, R.I., and tending lightships at New York, *Woodcock* sailed for the Orkney Islands and reached Kirkwall, Scotland, on 10 July 1919. Over the ensuing months, the ship operated in the North Sea on minesweeping duties with the Atlantic Fleet's minesweeping detachment. During that time, *Woodcock* spent 54 days in the minefields and 28 in port for needed upkeep and

voyage repairs occasioned by the heavy weather often encountered by the ships of the detachment.

Upon conclusion of the sweeping operations, the ship returned to the east coast of the United States and operated with Mine Squadron 1, Mine Division 5, Atlantic Fleet, until she was decommissioned at the Portsmouth (N.H.) Navy Yard on 5 May 1922. Meanwhile, she had been classified as AM-14 on 17 July 1920.

Woodcock remained in reserve at Portsmouth until recommissioned there on 21 February 1924. She then became station ship at Port-au-Prince, Haiti, to support Marine Corps peace-keeping forces there. As such, *Woodcock* was one of the three *Lapwing*-class ships recommissioned for service as gunboats. Her sisterships, *Penguin* (AM-33) and *Pigeon* (AM-47), were sent to the Asiatic Fleet for duty with the Yangtze Patrol.

Outside of yearly return voyages to a navy yard in the United States such as that of Charleston, S.C., for repairs and alterations, *Woodcock* remained in Haitian waters, based on Port-au-Prince, through the spring of 1934. That summer, when President Franklin D. Roosevelt decided to pull the Marine Corps occupation force —a veritable fixture in Haitian history since August 1915—out of Haiti, *Woodcock* took part in that important troop lift. On 15 August 1934, amidst impressive shoreside ceremonies and "most friendly feelings displayed by the populace," *Woodcock*—in company with *Bridge* (AF-1), *Argonne* (AS-10), and Army transport *Chateau Thierry*—embarked 79 officers and 747 enlisted men of the 1st Marine Brigade, the last of the occupation troops, and eventually took them back to the United States, thus closing a colorful chapter in Marine Corps history.

Soon thereafter, the minesweeper—or quasi-gunboat —shifted to Guantanamo Bay, Cuba. She served as a district craft—occasionally exercising with the fleet during its winter maneuvers and participating in some of the Fleet's amphibious exercises under the aegis of the Commandant, 15th Naval District, through the outbreak of war in Europe in the autumn of 1939.

During World War II, *Woodcock* operated under the auspices of the Panama Sea Frontier command, working between the Canal Zone and New Orleans. While performing towing, salvage, and local escort duties, she assisted vessels in distress and stood by to protect them until help arrived. During her service in gulf waters, the ship was twice reclassified—first becoming an ocean-going tug, AT-145, on 1 June 1942; then an ocean-going tug (old), ATO-145, on 15 May 1944.

Following the war, *Woodcock* continued local operations out of Cristobal and called at the Galapagos Islands in the spring of 1946. Retained until the arrival of *Recovery* (ARS-43), *Woodcock* performed her final towing service that summer. She took *YR-64* from Cristobal to New York, reaching the latter port on 27 August 1946. After getting underway the following day, *Woodcock* headed south; arrived at Charleston on 31 August; and reported to Commandant, 6th Naval District, for disposition.

Decommissioned at Charleston on 30 September 1946, *Woodcock* was struck from the Navy list on 23 April 1947 and transferred to the Maritime Commission on 4 August of the same year. She was sold to the Potomac Shipwrecking Co., Inc., of Pope's Creek, Md., on 19 December 1947.

Woodford

Counties in Illinois and Kentucky.

(AKA-86: dp. 13,910; l. 459'2''; b. 63'0''; dr. 26'4'' (lim.); s. 16.5 k.; cpl. 425; a. 1 5'', 8 40mm., 16 20mm.; cl. *Tolland*; T. C2-S-AJ3)

Woodford (AKA-89) was laid down under a Maritime Commission contract (MC hull 1399) on 17 July 1944 at Wilmington, N.C., by the North Carolina

Shipbuilding Co.; launched on 5 October 1944; sponsored by Mrs. Ruth E. McInnis, the wife of J. Frank McInnis who was in charge of the construction of all Maritime Commission ships built on the east coast; and placed in service on 19 October. The merchant tug *Rescue* towed *Woodford* to Hoboken, N.J., to be converted at the Todd Shipyard Corp. for Navy service. She was commissioned at the Todd Shipyard on 3 March 1945, Capt. Winston P. Folk in command.

After initial trials in Long Island Sound, shakedown in Chesapeake Bay, post-shakedown availability at the Norfolk Navy Yard, further shakedown trials, and another availability, *Woodford* reported at the Naval Operating Base (NOB), Norfolk, on 19 April to take on her first cargo. When loaded, the attack cargo ship got underway on 28 April and headed for the Panama Canal, on the first leg of her voyage to the Pacific.

Woodford's passage, in company with her escort, the high-speed transport *Runels* (APD–85), was uneventful until early on 1 May, when *Runels* made a sound contact. While her escort sought to develop the contact, the attack cargo ship went to general quarters and commenced evasive action. Later, both ships stood down from quarters when *Runels* lost the contact and could not regain it.

Woodford transited the isthmian waterway on 3 May and spent two days at Balboa before heading for Pearl Harbor in company with *Runner* (SS–476), *Moray* (SS–300), and *Carp* (SS–338). While en route, the ships conducted joint exercises, exchanging officers between the ships at various intervals to enable them to each observe the drills from a different perspective.

Also, while en route, the ships received the news that President Harry S. Truman had declared 8 May 1945 as "V-E Day," marking the victorious conclusion of the war with Germany. As *Woodford's* commanding officer recounted, "While the stirring news was received on board *Woodford* with joy, the joy was tinged with the thought that, after all, a terrific job lay ahead."

The attack cargo ship ultimately reached Pearl Harbor on 20 May where she discharged her cargo. A week later, she shifted to Honolulu where she took on a cargo tabbed as "high priority"—ammunition earmarked for the 10th Army at Okinawa. Once loaded, *Woodford* set out independently for the Marshalls on 2 June but, en route, was rerouted to the Carolines.

Reaching Ulithi on 14 June, *Woodford* subsequently joined Convoy UOK–27 headed for Okinawa, but was again rerouted—this time to Kerama Retto, to await orders for discharge of her "high priority" cargo. For three weeks, from 24 June to 15 July, the attack cargo ship—her ammunition cargo still in her holds—lay in the roadstead of that group of small islands. During her stay, she went to general quarters 21 times because of alerts or actual enemy attacks—an uncomfortable situation for a ship laden with ammunition.

Finally, orders came—but not to unload at either Okinawa or Kerama Retto. Instead, *Woodford* was directed to retire to the Marianas and unload at Guam. The attack cargo ship weighed anchor at Kerama Retto on 15 July and proceeded toward the Marianas with Convoy OKS–14. Reaching Saipan on the 21st, *Woodford* proceeded independently toward Guam one week later and anchored in Agana Bay on the 29th. There, transferring her ammunition into amphibious trucks (DUKW's), *Woodford* at long last discharged her dangerous cargo.

Upon completion of the unloading, the attack cargo ship immediately returned to Saipan to await further orders. There, at 0900 on 15 August, *Woodford* received word that the Japanese had capitulated. Pandemonium then reigned in the anchorage. *Woodford's* commanding officer recounted that "whistles and sirens sounded in blasts of raucous joy, drowning out the glad shouts that went up from thousands of men."

Two days after the capitulation, *Woodford* sailed for the Philippines and reached Leyte on the 20th. There, she joined Transport Squadron (TransRon) 13, Transport Division (TransDiv) 53. Shifting to Cebu soon thereafter, TransRon 13 loaded the men and equipment of the Americal Division—part of the force slated to occupy the erstwhile enemy's capital.

Woodford and her consorts subsequently sailed for Tokyo Bay, reaching that body of water on 8 September 1945—six days after the formal Japanese surrender ceremony on board the battleship *Missouri* (BB–62). The attack cargo ship disembarked her troops and discharged her cargo before she returned to the Philippines with TransDiv 53. Upon arriving back at Leyte on 16 September, the ship detached her first group of homeward-bound sailors eligible for discharges before getting underway to proceed independently to Cebu to commence taking on board troops before the arrival of the rest of TransDiv 53.

Combat-loaded with the men and equipment of the Army's 77th Division, *Woodford* returned to Japanese waters with TransDiv 53 and carried those troops and their equipment to Otaru, on the island of Hokkaido, arriving there on 5 October. Upon completion of that operation, she returned to the Philippines.

Woodford remained in the Far East into December. Between 27 October and 4 November, she lifted rear elements of the 3d Amphibious Corps—the 30th Construction Battalion (SeaBees) and the 32d Special Construction Battalion from San Pedro Bay—from San Pedro Bay, Leyte, to Taku, China, in company with TransDiv 37, before proceeding singly to Guam to discharge cargo. From there, on 4 December, she proceeded to Sasebo, on the island of Kyushu, Japan.

Steaming into Sasebo harbor on 8 December, the ship anchored there until the 10th, when she went alongside a dock. There, she embarked elements of the 5th Marine Division and their equipment to be transported to the west coast of the United States. The ship's departure from the Far East, however, was not without elements of a "Hollywood thriller." Intelligence officers had uncovered what they thought to be Japanese sabotage plans which had tabbed *Woodford* with destruction after midnight on 13 December. Taking no chances that the discovery was a hoax, *Woodford* accordingly doubled the watch, manned her guns and searchlights, and broke out carbines and Thompson submachine guns. As the ship's commanding officer later reported: "The cost of the all-night vigil was happily no more, however, then a loss of sleep for all hands; not a shot was fired nor a saboteur discovered."

At 1100 on 14 December, with a homeward-bound pennnant at the gaff, *Woodford* stood out to sea to begin the 6,047-mile passage to San Diego; and she reached her destination on the last day of 1945. After discharging cargo and disembarking her passengers, the attack cargo ship underwent voyage repairs at San Francisco into February 1946 before she sailed for the east coast of the United States.

Making port at Norfolk, via the Panama Canal, on 25 February, *Woodford* shifted briefly to New York before she returned to Norfolk on 7 March to be inactivated in the 5th Naval District. Accordingly, on 1 May 1946, *Woodford* was decommissioned; one week later, on 8 May, her name was struck from the Navy list on 10 May; and she was returned to the War Shipping Administration (WSA) of the Maritime Commission.

The erstwhile attack cargo ship was acquired from the WSA by the A. H. Bull Steamship Co., of New York City, in 1947 and renamed *Suzanne*. Subsequently acquired by the Westmount Shipping Co., also of New York, and renamed *Rappahannock*, the ship performed general cargo-carrying services into 1973. Her name disappears from the *Record of the American Bureau of Shipping* in 1974.

Woodford, Sgt. Howard E.,
see *Sgt. Howard E. Woodford.*

Woodpecker

A bird of strongly contrasting colors, black and white or green and yellow, with red markings about the head. It is of solitary habits and wide distribution but found chiefly in warm climates.

(MSC–209: dp. 320; l. 144'; b. 28'; dr. 9'; s. 13 k.; cpl. 50; a. 1 40mm.; cl. *Redwing*)

Woodpecker (MSC–209) was laid down as AM–209 on 23 June 1954 by the Bellingham Shipyards Co., Bellingham, Wash.; reclassified MSC–209 on 7 February 1955; launched on 7 January 1955; sponsored by Mrs. John L. Thomas; and commissioned on 3 February 1956, Lt. Roy M. Malone in command.

During trials and training at Long Beach, Calif., *Woodpecker* joined the Mine Force, Pacific Fleet, and prepared—by a trip to San Diego for underway training and two short yard periods in May and August at Wilmington Boat Works, Wilmington, Calif.—for duty in the Far East.

On 1 October 1956, *Woodpecker* sailed for Japan via Pearl Harbor and Midway. Upon completion of voyage repairs in Yokosuka, she moved to Sasebo, her new home port, arriving there in early November 1956.

The minesweeper spent the year 1957 conducting various exercises in Taiwan, Korea, Japan, Saipan, and Dingalan Bay, Philippines. The year 1958 began with *Woodpecker* conducting minesweeping exercises with the Republic of Korea Navy at Koji Do, Korea. During the year, the ship conducted two good-will tours in Japan: the first from 23 to 27 January; and the second from 28 May to 15 June. The latter encompassed eight Japanese cities. *Woodpecker* took part in combined minesweeping operations with the Republic of Korea and the Japanese Maritime Self Defense Forces. Due to tension between communist China on the mainland and Nationalist Chinese on Taiwan, *Woodpecker* served in the Formosa Strait area from September to November. Upon her return to Sasebo on 8 November, she underwent availability and interim dry-docking throughout November. She finished out the year 1958 by searching for and locating a downed Air Force plane off Fukuoka, Japan.

Woodpecker spent the early part of 1959 conducting exercises at Taiwan and at Subic Bay and Manila in the Philippines. On 22 March, the ship departed Sasebo for a brief trip to Yosu Hae, Korea. *Woodpecker* sailed for Okinawa on 8 April and remained at Buckner Bay through the 27th of that month. She then returned to Sasebo and prepared for a voyage to Korea. *Woodpecker* arrived at Pusan, Korea, on 1 June and operated between Pusan and Pohang for nine days before returning to Maizuru, Japan.

Woodpecker spent the period from 9 June through 30 September visiting Maizuru, Sasebo, and Yokosuka, Japan. The ship arrived at Kaohsiung, Taiwan, on 30 September and operated between that port and Sasebo through 26 October. *Woodpecker* then spent the remainder of 1959 visiting Hong Kong and in port at Sasebo.

The new year, 1960, found *Woodpecker* at Sasebo. On 25 January, she began searching for a downed aircraft in waters near Iwakuni and Imabari, Japan. The search continued into February and ended on 4 February when the ship returned to Sasebo and remained there until 28 March when she sailed for Okinawa. Departing Buckner Bay on 13 April, *Woodpecker* returned to Sasebo to join in fleet exercises before going into dry-dock on 21 April and was under repairs until 31 May.

Woodpecker arrived at Pusan, Korea, on 9 June 1960 for "Phiblex" operations off Pohang, South Korea, and spent the remainder of June conducting exercises at Yongil Mon and San Chon Po, Korea, and Miko Wan, Japan.

On 1 July, the minesweeper got underway for Sasebo where she remained until 18 July when she departed for Minamata, Japan. *Woodpecker* spent four days at Minamata and five days at Yokosuka before returning to Sasebo on 1 August. She remained at her home port until 9 September when she began a two-day round-trip voyage to Pohang, Korea.

Woodpecker departed Sasebo on 13 October, bound for Hong Kong. On 29 October, she set course for Okinawa and remained at Buckner Bay until 6 November when she sailed for her home port. During December, *Woodpecker* visited Kure and Hiroshima, Japan, before returning to Sasebo on 11 December for the remainder of 1960.

The ship spent the first part of 1961 undergoing various inspections, overhaul, and refresher training at Yokosuka. From 18 to 25 July, *Woodpecker* made a "People-to-People" visit to Maizuru and Tsuruga Wan, Japan. During August and September, the ship took part in exercises with the Republic of Korea Navy and the Japanese Maritime Self Defense Force. This was followed by a rest and rehabilitation run to Hong Kong and a period in dry dock ending on 30 November. *Woodpecker* finished the year 1961 in the area of Fukuoka Wan and Iwakuni, Japan, conducting two plane hunts, with one success.

Woodpecker spent 1962 in much the same manner as the previous year. During January, she transported an explosive ordnance disposal (EOD) team to Ikishima, Japan. A period of exercises and inspections followed, along with a "People-to-People" visit to Tokuyama and Shimonoseki, Japan, in July. From October through December, *Woodpecker* underwent an overhaul at Sasebo followed by mine countermeasures refresher training.

An exciting episode in *Woodpecker*'s career occurred on 24 February 1962 in Japan's Inland Sea. A fire fighting team from the ship joined one from *Widgeon* (MSC–208) in fighting and extinguishing a raging fire in the engine room of *Daiyu Maru*.

From 2 through 25 January 1963, *Woodpecker* conducted refresher training at Yokosuka, Japan. She closed the month with a "People-to-People" visit to Kobe, Japan. The ship spent February and March participating in combined operations "Minex" with the navies of Korea and Japan. After several inspections and port visits, *Woodpecker* entered drydock in mid-September at Sasebo. On 1 November, the ship took part in Operation "Yellow Bird" in Lingayen Gulf, off Luzon in the Philippines. Following a rest and recreation at Hong Kong, *Woodpecker* joined in Operation "Big Dipper" in Taiwanese waters which kept her busy through the end of the year.

Woodpecker began 1964 by taking part in Operation "Polar Bear" at Chinhae, Korea, and then participated in Exercise "Back Pack" at Taiwan from 28 February to 8 March. She devoted the remainder of the year to several inspections, upkeep, and overhaul at Subic Bay, Philippines, and at Sasebo, Japan.

Overhaul and refresher training filled the months of January and February 1965 for the minesweeper. After making port visits at Manila, Philippines, and Bangkok, Thailand, the ship conducted Operation "Jungle Drum" —a joint United States-Thai operation which lasted from 14 to 30 March—in the Gulf of Siam.

After a brief upkeep period at Subic Bay, *Woodpecker* was ordered to South Vietnam when the Navy began coastal surveillance operations to combat communist infiltration from the north. This first deployment to Operation "Market Time" patrols was conducted during September and October 1965 and for the periods in 1966 from March through April and from July through August. During these operations, *Woodpecker* functioned as a patrol vessel: monitoring coastal traffic, boarding suspicious junks, and participating in naval gunfire support missions.

About this time, *Woodpecker* underwent a series of modifications which increased her capabilities and fitted her to carry out challenging operations in Southeast Asia. A series of ship alterations in 1965 and 1966 modernized the ship's communications facilities. In

October 1966, she became the first coastal minesweeper in the Western Pacific (WestPac) to operate an on-line cryptographic facility. *Woodpecker* returned to her "Market Time" patrol off the coast of South Vietnam for April and May 1967, then again in December of that year.

The 1st of January 1968 found *Woodpecker* on "Market Time" duty off South Vietnam. She completed that assignment on 12 January and proceeded via Subic Bay to Sasebo where she underwent availability.

On 26 March 1968, *Woodpecker* got underway for Okinawa and a month of exericses. The ship sailed on 27 April for Exercise "Tarawa" held at Manila with minesweepers from the Philippines, Australia, and Great Britain. The exercise ended on 24 May 1968; and, a month later, she took part in "Reftrex 3–68" and underwent her annual operational readiness inspection.

"Market Time" patrol duty in Vietnam occupied *Woodpecker* until 7 September when she moved to Subic Bay for repairs which lasted through 27 October and then spent the remainder of 1968 at Sasebo.

The year 1969 began with a two-week fleet service mine test at Buckner Bay. After an upkeep period in Sasebo, *Woodpecker* returned to sea for a joint exercise with the Japanese Maritime Self Defense Force. On 3 March 1969, the ship commenced her regularly scheduled overhaul. Sea trials, refresher training, and two inspections followed. *Woodpecker* sailed for Vietnam on 13 July and began "Market Time" patrol. Her duties included search and rescue missions, illumination firing, plus harassment and interdiction fire. The ship returned to Sasebo on 1 October. Mine countermeasures refresher training at Buckner Bay from 10 to 22 October was followed by a brief stay at Sasebo. From 3 to 13 November, *Woodpecker* joined in a mine countermeasure exercise with the Korean and British navies. Then, a dependents' cruise and a port visit to Kagoshima, Japan, ensued. The remainder of the year was spent in leave and upkeep status at Sasebo, Japan.

For the first three months of 1970, *Woodpecker* conducted operations in Subic Bay, Philippines; Buckner Bay, Okinawa; and Vietnam. She returned to Sasebo on 22 April and remained there through 29 June, except for a period of refresher training at Yokosuka. On 7 July, *Woodpecker* left Sasebo and proceeded to Kaohsiung for a "Minex" exercise with elements of the Taiwanese Navy. This was followed early in August by exercises with units of the Japanese fleet at Mutsuwan, Japan. The ship returned to Sasebo on 21 August and made preparations for her return to the United States. *Woodpecker* returned to Pearl Harbor on 31 October and reached Long Beach, Calif., on 11 November. After a short upkeep period, she departed for Seattle, Wash., and inactivation. On 15 December 1970, *Woodpecker* was decommissioned and converted to a Naval Reserve training vessel. She was stricken from the Navy list on 1 July 1975 and sold to Singapore.

Woodrow R. Thompson

Woodrow Reginald Thompson—born on 12 March 1919 at Belva, W. Va.—enlisted in the United States Marine Corps on 12 January 1940 at Charleston, W. Va. He went through "boot camp" at Parris Island, S.C., and served at Quantico, Va.; Guantanamo Bay, Cuba; and Parris Island, attaining promotions to private, first class, on 20 September 1940; to corporal on 1 September 1941; and to sergeant on 1 July 1942.

When his unit, the 1st Marine Division (reinforced), was sent to Guadalcanal, Sergeant Thompson sailed with them. There, his platoon took part in operations designed to drive the Japanese 4th Infantry from a bridgehead at the mouth of the Matanikau River. On the evening of 8 October 1942, the marines dug in for the night in the steaming jungle. Soon the Japanese launched a desperate counter-attack against the hastily prepared marine positions, charging against the thinly held right flank of the American lines.

Fierce fighting ensued. Small arms, automatic weapons, and grenades were the principal weapons. Desperate hand-to-hand combat took place in the night as the Japanese sought to escape envelopment. Sergeant Thompson refused to be dislodged from his position and gave his life early on 9 October, "after exacting a tremendous toll on the enemy." For his devotion to duty and "extraordinary heroism," Thompson received a posthumous Navy Cross. The 1st Marines subsequently received a Presidential Unit Citation.

Woodrow R. Thompson (DE–451)—a *John C. Butler*-class destroyer escort—was scheduled to be built at Newark, N.J., by the Federal Shipbuilding and Drydock Co.; but the contract for her construction was cancelled on 6 June 1944.

Woodrow R. Thompson (DD–721)—a *Gearing*-class destroyer—was laid down on 1 August 1945 at Newark, N.J., by the Federal Shipbuilding and Drydock Co. The contract for her construction was cancelled on 12 December 1945, but it was decided to reinstate the award of the contract early in 1946—but to suspend work on the ship. Accordingly, the ship was launched, as planned, on 16 March 1946, and sponsored by Mrs. Robert L. Thompson, the mother of Sergeant Thompson. Delivered in a partially completed state to the 3d Naval District, New York, N.Y., for maintenance and preservation, on 31 July 1946, *Woodrow R. Thompson* was struck from the Navy list on 2 November 1954. She was sold for scrap on 29 August 1955.

Woodrow Wilson

Thomas Woodrow Wilson—born on 28 December 1856 at Staunton, Va.—graduated from Princeton University in 1879 before attending University of Virginia Law School. He subsequently earned a doctorate at Johns Hopkins and then taught at Bryn Mawr and Wesleyan before accepting a teaching post at Princeton, his alma mater. He became president of Princeton in 1902 and brought the university to national prominence. In 1910, Wilson was elected governor of New Jersey and served a two-year term in which he effected several key progressive reforms.

After becoming the Democratic Party's presidential candidate in the 1912 elections, Wilson defeated a badly split Republican Party and was inaugurated president on 4 March 1913. Wilson's first term in the White House was marked by liberal reforms which were popularized under the label, the "New Freedom." Upon the outbreak of World War I in Europe, Wilson tried to keep the United States neutral. While patiently insisting on American rights as a neutral, he successfully guided the country through the *Lusitania* crisis in the spring of 1915.

While abstaining from intervention in Europe's affairs for a time, the United States, under Wilson's leadership, moved decisively in Latin America and the Caribbean when it saw American rights threatened. American naval or military units landed in Mexico, Santo Domingo, Haiti, and Nicaragua to restore order and to establish benevolent American protection for its own nationals as well as for the nationals of the troubled countries.

Eventually, pressures to enter the war—despite the 1916 campaign slogan "He kept us out of war"—proved too great. In April 1917, the United States joined the Allied and Associated Powers in the war against the Central Powers. Exercising his powers as Commander in Chief, Wilson was well aware of the Navy's role in the "war to end wars" and "to make the world safe for democracy." In a speech to the officers of the Atlantic Fleet on 11 August 1917, the President said: ". . . the officers of this Navy . . . have the distinction of saying how this war is going to be won."

With the Navy guarding the sea lanes to Europe, the United States eventually sent substantial numbers of troops "over there," to join the battle on the Western Front. On 11 November 1918, the armistice was signed, ending World War I.

Between 1914 and 1917, Wilson had based his appeals for peace upon the formula, "peace without victory." After the United States entered the conflict, the President continued to strive for the ideal of a peace wherein there would be no victor—none vanquished. Instead, he urged the recognition of the rights of smaller nations and freedom of the seas. His "Fourteen Points" attempted to apply these broad ideals to specific problem areas of the peaceful postwar settlement. Incorporating these fourteen points of international ethics into a comprehensive plan, Wilson broke precedent by leading the American delegation to the Peace Conference at Paris. Once there, however, he found to his dismay that European leaders were not as ready as he to make high ideals the foundation of a postwar settlement that would be fair and just for all. As a result, negotiations were weakened by many compromises with Wilson's ideals, and the treaty, with its provision for a League of Nations, was rejected by the Republican-controlled Senate. Taking his fight to the people, Wilson embarked upon a strenuous speaking tour, valiantly fighting to convince the American people that only collective security could keep the United States out of future wars. In September 1919, worn out by the struggle for his League of Nations, Wilson broke, physically, and remained ill throughout the remainder of his second term. Never fully recovered, he lived quietly in Washington after Warren G. Harding won the 1920 elections and brought "normalcy" to the United States; Wilson died in Washington on 3 February 1924.

(SSBN–624: dp. 7,250 (surf.), 8,220 (subm.); l. 425'; b. 33'; dr. 31'4''; s. 16 k. (surf.), 20+ (subm.); cpl. 140; a. 16 Polaris mis., 4 tt.; cl. *Lafayette*)

Woodrow Wilson (SSBN–624) was laid down on 16 September 1961 at Vallejo, Calif., by the Mare Island Naval Shipyard; launched on 22 February 1963; sponsored by Miss Eleanor A. Sayre, the granddaughter of President Wilson; and commissioned on 27 December 1963, Comdr. C. N. Mitchell and Comdr. W. N. Dietzen in command of the Blue and Gold crews, respectively.

Woodrow Wilson departed Vallejo, Calif., on 9 January 1964, bound for the east coast on a route which would take her through the Panama Canal. After stopping briefly at San Diego, the submarine proceeded on to Panama, arriving on 19 January at the west coast end of the canal. Violent anti-American demonstrations and riots over a recent flag-displaying incident had resulted in an extremely tense atmosphere. As a result, the submarine transited the canal in a record seven hours and ten minutes while combat-ready marines and soldiers guarded the locks.

Making port at Charleston, S.C., on 5 February, the *Woodrow Wilson* conducted shakedown off the lower eastern seaboard into March and underwent her post-shakedown availability into April. She put to sea at the end of May upon the conclusion of these repairs and alterations and commenced her first deterrent patrol out of Charleston in June.

Woodrow Wilson subsequently operated in the Atlantic until the autumn of 1969 conducting her patrols from forward bases at Rota, Spain, and Holy Loch, Scotland. She was then transferred to the Pacific and arrived at Pearl Harbor on 19 November, via Charleston and the Panama Canal. The fleet ballistic missile submarine continued toward the western Pacific to be based at Guam. She conducted deterrent patrols from Apra Harbor through 1972. In that year, she shifted back to the Atlantic and served with the Atlantic Fleet into 1978. Between 1964 and 1977, the ship performed 37 deterrent patrols.

Woods, Don O., see *Don O. Woods*.

Woodson

Jeff Davis Woodson—born in Autman, Tex., on 10 June 1908—enlisted in the United States Navy on 23 June 1926 at Little Rock, Ark. Earning his first rating as a fireman third class in four months, he served in *Aroostook* (CM–3) and advanced to the rating of fireman second class on 1 January 1929. That summer, he transferred to an aviation squadron, VJ–1B, and began training as an aviation machinist's mate. In April 1929, he took a reduction in rank to enter the aviation field and became an aviation machinist's mate third class. However, after training at the Naval Air Station, San Diego, and pilot training at the Naval Air Station, Pensacola, he was advanced to the rating of aviation pilot first class.

During the 1930's he served in various patrol and scouting squadrons and even served a tour of duty in *Lexington* (CV–2). By the late spring of 1937, Woodson had advanced to the rating of chief aviation machinist's mate. During 1940 and 1941, he served successively in VU–1, the destroyer *Benham* (DD–397), and at the naval air stations located at Norfolk and Pensacola. On 2 September 1941, he joined Torpedo Squadron 8 attached to *Hornet* (CV–8). For the next few months, he and his ship conducted training out of Norfolk. That routine continued after the attack on Pearl Harbor on 7 December.

On 4 March 1942, his ship put to sea and headed for San Diego, Calif., where she arrived on the 20th. With his TBD stored below decks with the rest of the carrier's own aircraft complement, Chief Woodson departed the west coast in *Hornet* on 2 April with her deck loaded with 16 Army B–25 bombers—the celebrated Halsey-Doolittle Tokyo raiders. Five days out to sea, Chief Woodson was temporarily promoted to the rank of lieutenant (junior grade). Six days after that, *Hornet* launched her extra flock for their raid against Tokyo and headed for Oahu. A week later, he rode *Hornet* into Pearl Harbor.

On 30 April, his carrier departed Pearl Harbor in an effort to join *Yorktown* (CV–5) and *Lexington* in the Battle of the Coral Sea. The naval air battle which stopped Japan's southward advance, however, ended before *Hornet* could arrive. She turned around and reentered Pearl Harbor on 26 May. Unknown to Lt. (jg.) Woodson and his colleagues, an even greater struggle loomed on the immediate horizon. Two days later, *Hornet* returned to sea in company with *Enterprise* as the first contingent of the American force sent to stop Japan's attempt to capture Midway Island. Soon joined by battered, but quickly repaired, *Yorktown*, the force lay in wait for an immense Japanese invasion fleet built around four of the six aircraft carriers that had struck Pearl Harbor the previous December.

After days of anxious waiting, patrol planes from Midway finally sighted the Japanese carriers early on the morning of 4 June. After more tense waiting, the decision was finally made to launch strikes against the enemy despite the rather hazy information regarding his position. Aircraft rose from all three carriers and many, including Lt. (jg.) Woodson's Torpedo Squadron 8, missed the rendezvous with their fighter cover. Pressing on in spite of the lack of escorts, Torpedo Squadron 8 made first contact with the enemy. Disregarding overwhelming odds, inadequate defenses, and lack of fighter support, Woodson and his comrades gallantly pressed home their attacks. All Japanese fighters swooped in on the almost-defenseless torpedo bombers and literally massacred them. Lt. (jg.) Woodson was killed in a valiant effort to sink one of the perpetrators of the Pearl Harbor attack.

His sacrifice, though, was not in vain. Since all their fighter cover was down near the surface shooting up Woodson and his colleagues, the enemy carriers were sitting ducks when the American dive-bombers and fighters finally made contact. Three enemy carriers, *Akagi*, *Kaga*, and *Soryu*, rapidly sustained mortal injury and *Hiryu* received only brief respite due to her location far ahead of the other three. In due time, she, too, took fatal hits; and, with all four of their carriers gone, the Japanese were forced to retire and give up any idea of an assault on Midway.

For his "extraordinary heroism and distinguished service beyond the call of duty . . ." and in recognition of the fact that his sacrifice ". . . was a determining factor in the defeat of the enemy forces . . .," Lt. (jg.) Woodson was awarded the Navy Cross posthumously.

(DE–359: dp. 1,350; l. 306'0''; b. 36'7''; dr. 13'4''; s. 24.3 k. (tl.); cpl. 222; a. 2 5'', 4 40mm., 10 20mm., 8 dcp., 1 dcp. (hh.), 2 dct., 3 21'' tt.; cl. *John C. Butler*)

Woodson (DE–359) was laid down on 7 March 1944 at Orange, Tex., by the Consolidated Steel Corp., Ltd.; launched on 29 April 1944; sponsored by Mrs. Joyce M. Woodson; and commissioned on 24 August 1944, Lt. Comdr. J. L. Foley in command.

After fitting out at Galveston, Tex., the destroyer escort embarked upon her shakedown cruise on 11 September. En route to her training area in the vicinity of Bermuda, she assisted the survivors of *Warrington* (DD–383) which had sunk off the east coast during a hurricane. *Woodson* rescued a number of survivors, carried them to Norfolk, Va., and then resumed shakedown training around Bermuda. The warship completed that training and arrived in Boston, Mass., on 25 October. After two weeks of post-shakedown availability, she stood out of Boston on 6 November, bound for Norfolk where she spent the remainder of the month serving as a school ship for the Operational Training Command, Atlantic Fleet.

On the last day of November, she departed Norfolk and shaped a course for the Pacific Ocean and duty with the 7th Fleet in the southwestern Pacific. Steaming via the Panama Canal, the Galapagos Islands, and Bora Bora in the Society Islands, she arrived at Hollandia on the northern coast of New Guinea on 3 January 1945. Upon her arrival, the destroyer escort was assigned to convoy duty between New Guinea and the Philippines, primarily on the Hollandia-to-Leyte run. Early in April, however, she dropped her runs to New Guinea and limited her operations to escort missions among major ports in the Philippines such as Leyte, Lingayen Gulf, and Manila Bay. That duty lasted until 25 May when she reported to the Commander, Task Group (TG) 71.5 at Subic Bay for duty escorting submarines to and from their war patrol release points. When not engaged in her primary duty, *Woodson* participated in post-refit exercises with submarines and conducted antisubmarine patrols. Such activities occupied her through the end of hostilities and until the end of August.

On the 31st, she was detached from TG 71.5 and departed Subic Bay, bound for the Ryukyus. At Okinawa on 4 September, she became an element of TG 70.3, the escort group for the occupation forces headed for northern China and Korea. On 5 October, she left Okinawa and steamed to Shanghai where she arrived late the following day. She next returned to Leyte and remained there until 22 October when she headed back to Okinawa where she joined another China occupation convoy which sailed in early November. At Hong Kong at mid-month, the destroyer escort departed again on the 21st and shaped a course for Okinawa where she arrived on 24 November. Two days later, she began her voyage home.

Stopping at Pearl Harbor en route, *Woodson* arrived in San Pedro, Calif., on 16 December to begin inactivation overhaul. On 16 May 1946, the was placed in commission, in reserve, and remained so until 15 January 1947 at which time she was decommissioned. Except for a brief period during the winter of 1948 and 1949 when she made a round-trip run under tow to Long Beach for an overhaul, she remained at San Diego until the spring of 1951. On 19 May 1951, *Woodson* was recommissioned at San Diego, Lt. Comdr. A. Dennett in command.

The warship spent most of the summer of 1951 conducting shakedown training and other local operations along the coast of southern California. On 4 September, she got underway from San Diego on her way to the east coast. Steaming via the Panama Canal, *Woodson* arrived in Newport, R.I., in mid-September and began local operations. On 19 October, the warship departed the Newport area to participate in the annual Atlantic Fleet exercises held in the vicinity of Puerto Rico. She returned to Newport on 17 November and remained there through the end of the year.

On 16 January 1952, the destroyer escort headed for Philadelphia where she arrived two days later. There, she began a three-month overhaul at the Philadelphia Naval Shipyard. *Woodson* completed repairs on 22 April and headed back to Newport but under tow given by *Atakapa* (YTB–49).

She reentered Newport on 25 April but remained there less than two weeks, departing again on 7 May. She reached Guantanamo Bay, Cuba, four days later and began six weeks of refresher training. The destroyer escort completed that assignment on 20 June and set course—via Ciudad Trujillo, Dominican Republic—for Newport. The warship reentered her home port on 28 June. Two days later, she became an element of the newly formed Hunter/Killer Group, Atlantic Fleet, under the overall command of Rear Admiral Daniel V. Gallery, the captor of *U–505* during World War II.

For the next five years, *Woodson* ranged the length of the Atlantic coast of the United States from Newport in the north to Cuba and the West Indies in the south. Her activities consisted mostly of type training and independent ship's exercises. Frequently, however, she served as target ship for submarines engaged in training and as school ship for the Fleet Sonar School located at Key West. Fleet exercises, special projects, and periodic overhauls also added further variety to her schedule of operations. During June 1957, she also participated in the International Fleet Review held at Norfolk. That same month, her home port was changed from Newport, R.I., to Key West, Fla. Summer brought a midshipman cruise down the St. Lawrence to Quebec, Canada, and thence back to Boston and finally to Norfolk. On 16 August, she finally entered her new home port for the first time since her reassignment.

Her stay there proved brief for, on 30 August, she embarked upon her first voyage to the Mediterranean Sea in company with Escort Squadron (CortRon) 12. She arrived at Naples, Italy, on 14 September and, soon thereafter, began a full round of NATO exercises, highlighted by amphibious assault training at Soudha Bay, Crete. At the conclusion of her Mediterranean assignment on 6 November, she departed Gibraltar and headed via the Azores to Key West. Upon her arrival in Key West on 20 November, *Woodson* saw CortRon 12 broken up and parcelled out ship by ship to various ports to support the training of Naval Reserve units.

She got underway on 2 December; headed for her own new home port, New Orleans, La.; and arrived there two days later. For the remainder of her active career, *Woodson* cruised the waters of the Gulf of Mexico and the West Indies training New Orleans-based naval reservists. On 16 May 1959, her status was reduced from in commission to in service, though her mission, Naval Reserve training, remained the same. She helped naval reservists polish their skills both at dockside at New Orleans and underway in the Gulf of Mexico until 11 August 1962 when she was placed in reserve. Following inspection and survey in June 1965, her name was struck from the Navy list on 1 July 1965. She was sold for scrapping to the Boston Metals Co., of Baltimore, Md., on 16 August 1966.

Woodstock

A city in northern Illinois which serves as the seat of McHenry County and a town in Vermont.

(PC–1180: dp. 450 (f.); l. 173'8''; b. 23'; dr. 10'10'' (max.); cpl. 65; s. 20.2 k.; a. 1 3'', 1 40mm., 6 20mm., 4 dcp., 2 dct., 2 dcp. (Mousetrap); cl. PC–461)

Woodstock (PC–1180) was originally laid down as PC–1180 on 5 October 1943 at Sturgeon Bay, Wis., by the Leathem D. Smith Shipbuilding Co.; launched on 27 November 1943; sponsored by Mrs. Sue Wallen, the first Gold Star mother in the city of Green Bay, Wis.; and commissioned at New Orleans, La., on 10 February 1944, Lt. Philip H. Tomlinson, USNR, in command.

PC–1180 departed New Orleans on 20 February, bound for Miami, Fla., to conduct training out of the Submarine Chaser Training Center there. On 20 March, she departed Key West as part of the screen for Convoy KN–303 and put into New York nine days later after an uneventful passage. The submarine chaser then proceeded south and joined the Cuba-bound Convoy NG–427. All 36 ships of this group arrived safely at Guantanamo Bay on 13 April.

PC–1180 weighed anchor four days later and rendezvoused with the Trinidad section of Convoy GN–127, bound for New York. Delivering her charges safely to their destination on 24 April, the vessel sailed south on 1 May as part of the screen of Convoy NG–432, again bound for Cuba. On 7 May, four hours out of Guantanamo Bay, PC–1180 rescued a French merchant sailor who had fallen overboard from the merchantman SS *Sagittaire*.

The escort vessel subsequently made one more round-trip from Guantanamo Bay to New York City—with Convoys GN–132 and NG–430 on the northward and southward runs, respectively—before escorting Convoy GZ–72 from Guantanamo Bay to the Panama Canal Zone from 13 to 17 June. Transiting the Panama Canal on the 19th, PC–1180 proceeded northward to the California coast in company with PC–470 and arrived at San Diego on 28 June. After taking on provisions and ammunition there, she departed San Diego on 8 July, bound for Hawaii, and arrived at Pearl Harbor eight days later in company with PC–1251 and PC–1260.

PC–1180 spent just shy of a month in Hawaiian waters before she headed across the Pacific for Guadalcanal, sailing from Pearl Harbor on 13 August. She then conducted amphibious assault practice with Army troops and marines rehearsing for the assault and occupation of the southern Palaus.

The subchaser operated as screen for the ships involved in the strike on Angaur Island—the southernmost isle in the Palaus and the most valuable because of its phosphate deposits. American planners, however, were less interested in its minerals than they were for another reason. They slated the island for use as a bomber strip. The American strikes against the island began with pre-invasion bombardments by *Tennessee* (BB–43) and *Pennsylvania* (BB–38), four light cruisers and five destroyers. This bombardment continued for five days, while carrier planes carried out air strikes, and minecraft swept the approaches. Meanwhile, underwater demolition teams swam ashore to destroy obstacles on the landing beaches themselves.

On 17 September 1944, the first marines went ashore to begin the actual occupation on Angaur. During this time, PC–1180 served as mine-disposal vessel, detonating swept mines with gunfire, in Kossol Passage. On the 19th, two days after the strikes against Angaur began, YMS–19 fouled a Japanese mine and sank soon thereafter. PC–1180 closed the sinking vessel, lowered a boat and life rafts, and picked up the survivors.

PC–1180 subsequently escorted convoys locally in the waters between Ulithi and the Palaus until late in 1944. After escorting local convoys between Ulithi and Eniwetok early in 1945, she supported the assault on Okinawa in the spring of 1945.

The subchaser performed local escort operations as a unit of the 9th Fleet, in the Okinawa area, into the summer of 1945. She departed Ora Wan, Okinawa, on 19 July, escorting LST Flotilla 35 to Buckner Bay. On 25 July, in company with PC–1127, PC–1180 got underway for the Philippines, escorting LST Group 104.

Arriving on 13 August 1945 at San Pedro Bay, four days after the atomic bomb devastated Nagasaki, PC–1180 lay at anchor in San Pedro on the day Japan capitulated—15 August—and remained there until the 27th when she shifted to Manila before sailing for Japan from Batangas Bay on 3 September.

Escorting LST Flotilla 25, PC–1180 picked up a contact—suspected to be a submarine—on 9 September. With conditions in the Far East still tense, even after the Japanese surrender in Tokyo Bay, escorts were especially alert, lest a Japanese submarine which failed to hear that the war was over attack any Allied warships. PC–1180 went to general quarters, challenged the suspected submarine and received no reply, and sped to conduct a depth charge attack at 0749—16 minutes after the initial contact. Although the crow's nest observer, several men in the crew, and at least one officer topside reported air bubbles appearing on the surface and the water turning a dense black immediately after the explosion, no evidence came to the fore that the contact had actually been a maverick submarine. Once contact was lost, PC–1180 returned to the convoy screen. On 12 September, PC–1180 entered Tokyo Bay.

Shifting to Yokosuka on 19 September and to Yokohama the following day, the submarine chaser departed for Aomori, Japan, on the 21st. She delivered mail upon her arrival there three days later, before she conducted survey operations of Aomori Wan harbor. With the American landings at Aomori on the 24th, a Lt. C. H. Wheatley came on board to act as control officer in PC–1180. The submarine chaser served as control vessel for these occupation landings.

On 1 October, PC–1180 shifted to Hakodate Ko and to Otaru, Hokkaido, the following day. Capt. R. T. Strong, USNR, boarded the ship on 3 October for temporary duty in connection with the landings at Otaru.

The vessel remained in Japanese waters until departing Yokohama on 4 December for Guam. Arriving at Apra Harbor on the 8th, PC–1180 stayed at Guam until 9 January 1946, when she got underway and proceeded via Ulithi to Yap in the Caroline Islands. Returning to Apra Harbor on 24 January, she stayed in port until 9 February, when she sailed for the Marshalls.

Reaching Majuro on 15 February, she put to sea three days later on an air-sea rescue patrol station off Dalap Island, Majuro Atoll. She conducted two such air-sea rescue patrols, one in late February and one in March, before she returned to Guam on 25 March. In company with PC–1086, PC–1180 sailed for the United States on 10 May 1946, bound for Astoria, Oreg., via Eniwetok, Johnston Island, and Pearl Harbor.

Making port at Astoria on 6 June 1946, the subchaser initially anchored in the Columbia River before shifting to Swan Island at Portland, Oreg., on the 11th and, soon thereafter, to the conversion dock of the Willamette Iron and Steel Co. to prepare for decommissioning.

Decommissioned at the Willamette Iron and Steel Co. on 15 November 1946, PC–1180 was berthed with the Columbia River Group of the Pacific Reserve Fleet. While she was laid up, the patrol vessel was named *Woodstock* on 15 February 1956.

Struck from the Navy list on 1 July 1960, *Woodstock* was subsequently sold for scrap in 1961.

PC–1180 received two battle stars for her World War II service.

Selim E. Woodworth was born circa the year 1824 in New York State. Appointed a midshipman on 16 June 1838, he was ordered to duty with the Wilkes Exploring Expedition. However, the order was sent to Norfolk and was not forwarded to him. When he finally reported in response to a duplicate order, the expedition had already sailed. As a result, he was sent on 20 November to the Mediterranean for duty in the ship of the line *Ohio.* On 3 August, he was detached from *Ohio* for a three-month leave; he requested and received an additional leave of three months to visit Milano, Italy. On 24 December, Woodworth was ordered to *Falmouth,* fitting out at New York.

While he was serving in *Falmouth,* news reached him at Pensacola, Fla., of the death of his father. He obtained leave, returned to New York, and became attached to the receiving ship, *North Carolina.* He next served on *Lawrence* in September before entering the Naval School in Philadelphia on the 29th of that month. On 20 May 1844, Selim Woodworth was warranted a passed midshipman. After a leave of six months, he reported to the new sloop-of-war *Jamestown* and served in her on the coast of Africa, helping to suppress the slave trade. He was transferred to *Truxtun,* detached on 24 November 1845, and granted a three-month leave.

At that time, Woodworth requested permission to cross the United States to join his squadron on the Pacific Coast. He arrived at West Port, Missouri, where he joined a party consisting of approximately 1,800 persons, including women and children, which was to travel in 560 wagons drawn by oxen. After a long and difficult journey across the North American continent—once long interrupted when he left the main party to lead an expedition to rescue a group of Americans who were in grave distress in the Rocky Mountains— Woodworth reported on board sloop-of-war *Warren* at Monterey Bay, Calif., on 17 May 1847. On 8 October, he requested a leave of absence in order to make a trip across the southern part of South America with permission to join the squadron on the coast of Brazil or in the United States. Permission was to be granted whenever he could be spared. He left *Warren* on 16 February 1848 to take command of the bark *Anita.* From 5 June 1848 until 1850, naval registers carry him as attached to the Pacific Squadron; however, no record of him has ever been found.

On 11 February 1850, Selim E. Woodworth resigned. For a little more than a decade, he lived in San Francisco and took a prominent part in the development of the state of California. He and his brother were among the organizers of the vigilance committee, and Selim Woodworth was the group's first president.

After the outbreak of the Civil War, Woodworth returned to the east coast and reentered the Navy on 10 September 1861 as an acting lieutenant. On 13 January 1862, he assumed command of *John P. Jackson,* a former ferry boat, converted to a steam gunboat. This vessel was assigned to the Mortar Flotilla raised by Comdr. David D. Porter to support Flag Officer Farragut's conquest of New Orleans and the lower Mississippi River. While in command, he assisted in the capture of Forts Jackson and St. Philip in April and participated in operations around Vicksburg in June and July. Porter commended Woodworth for these services, and President Lincoln recommended him to Congress for special thanks. On 29 September 1862, at his own request, he was detached from command of *John P. Jackson* and allowed to return to the North. Later that autumn, he was assigned to the Mississippi Squadron and reported at Cairo, Ill., for duty.

On 1 January 1863, he was given command of the "tinclad," stern-wheel steamer, *Glide.* On 24 January, Porter—now a Rear Admiral—recommended Woodworth for appointment to the regular Navy. Woodworth was commissioned a commander in April 1863, to date from 16 July 1862. After *Glide* was burned, he commanded the ram *General Price* from 7 February 1863

through August. After months of commendable fighting up and down the Mississippi River, Comdr. Woodworth was detached from *General Price* and sent to the Pacific where he took command of the bark *Narragansett* on 7 October 1863. After having brought *Narragansett* around the Horn, he arrived in New York on 18 March 1865. *Monocacy,* a double-ended gunboat, was his last command, which he assumed on 30 November 1865. Comdr. Selim E. Woodworth resigned from the Navy on 2 March 1866 and resided with his family in Europe until 1871 or 1872. During the siege of the Franco-Prussian War, he was in Paris and cleverly escaped through the Prussian lines by way of that city's famous sewers. He then returned to San Francisco in 1872 and died there in 1873.

(DD–460: dp. 1,620; l. 347'9''; b. 36'1''; dr. 17'4''; s. 37.6 k.; cpl. 276; a. 4 5'', 1 1.1'' quad., 5 20mm., 2 dct., 6 dcp., 5 21'' tt.; cl. *Benson*)

Woodworth (DD–460) was laid down on 30 April 1941 at San Francisco, Calif., by the Bethlehem Steel Company; launched on 29 November 1941; sponsored by Mrs. Selim E. Woodworth, niece and daughter-in-law of Comdr. Woodworth; and commissioned on 30 April 1942, Lt. Comdr. R. C. Webb, Jr., in command.

After four months spent in fitting out and shakedown, *Woodworth* spent the remainder of 1942 performing escort duty in the Southwest Pacific area. She stopped at many ports between Australia and Guadalcanal. *Woodworth* was attached to Task Force (TF) 65 in January 1943, conducting patrols and exercises at the western entrance to Espiritu Santo, New Herbrides.

On 2 February, *Woodworth* passed to the control of Vice Admiral Leary who commanded TF 69 from his flagship, *New Mexico* (BB–40). Two days later, that formation was merged with TF 18 consisting of *Wichita* (CA–45), two carriers, three light cruisers, and four destroyers. An oiler and another destroyer also joined the force on the 5th. The month of February was devoted to patrolling and escorting transports in waters between the Solomons and the New Hebrides. After escorting transports to the Fiji Islands on 1 March, *Woodworth* returned to Espiritu Santo on the 13th and joined TF 15 organized around the carrier *Enterprise* (CV–6). *Woodworth* entered port at Espiritu Santo on 21 March and the following day commenced tender availability. On 3 April, she headed back to the Solomons, arriving at Tulagi on the 5th for entrance patrol. The next day, *Woodworth* escorted *Tappahannock* (AO–43) to Kukum and then resumed her patrol.

On the 7th, while escorting oiler *Tappahannock* in the Solomons area, *Woodworth* came under enemy air attack by six planes north of Rua Sura Island. Four bombs dropped close aboard *Tappahannock.* Two struck the sea on the starboard side and threw considerable water over the ship. The attack, which lasted about four minutes, caused no personnel casualties and only minor material damage. *Woodworth* spent the remainder of April and early May in tactical training exercises, escort, and patrol in waters between the New Hebrides and New Caledonia. From 8 May to 29 June, *Woodworth* escorted transports carrying reinforcements to Guadalcanal and helped to screen TF 10—consisting of two carriers, three battleships, one cruiser, and several destroyers—to Noumea. *Woodworth* continued on to Aukland, New Zealand, where she underwent restricted availability before escorting oiler *Tallulah* (AO–50) to Noumea. *Woodworth* then screened transports steaming from Espiritu Santo to Guadalcanal.

On 30 June—while escorting amphibious forces to Rendova Island, Solomon Islands—*Woodworth* came under air attack by 12 low-flying Japanese torpedo bombers. *Woodworth*'s successful maneuvers enabled her to avoid the torpedoes, and she suffered only one personnel casualty and mere superficial damage from three machine gun hits. The majority of the enemy aircraft fell in flames, and none was seen to escape.

On 2 July 1943, *Woodworth* and *Jenkins* (DD–447)

bombarded Japanese positions on Wickham Island, Vonguna, New Georgia, to assist the advance of troops ashore. The next day, *Woodworth* sailed for Tulagi, touched at Port Purvis and Rendova Harbor, and arrived off Rice Anchorage on 5 July 1943 to participate in the first landing operations there. Later that day, she headed for Port Purvis. On 11 July, *Woodworth*—with fast transports *Kilty* (DD–137), *Crosby* (DD–164), and *Schley* (DD–103)—took part in the second landing operations at Rice Anchorage. While returning to Guadalcanal the following morning, *Taylor* (DD–468) fired on, depth charged, but failed to sink a Japanese submarine—*I–25.*

On 13 July, as part of Task Group (TG) 36.1, *Woodworth* took part in the Battle of Kolombangara, one of a series of naval engagements for control of waters between Vella La Vella and Kolombangara to the south and Choiseul to the north. The enemy force consisted of one cruiser and five destroyers. *Woodworth* fired four torpedoes, and a fifth misfired. During the action, she was struck a glancing blow to the stern by destroyer *Buchanan* (DD–484) causing some flooding and light damage, but she continued to screen cruiser *St. Louis* (CL–49) which was hit by a torpedo. *Gwin* (DD–433) was also hit and exploded. Nothing could be seen of that destroyer but a 300-foot-high column of smoke. Damage control efforts for *Gwin* were futile, and she was scuttled. *Woodworth* suffered no personnel casualties.

Woodworth conducted patrol and escort operations between Espiritu Santo and Guadalcanal until 7 October when she joined TF 38. Following training exercises, she departed Espiritu Santo on 29 October with TF 38 organized around carriers *Saratoga* (CV–3) and *Princeton* (CV–23). They launched air attacks on Buka, Shortland Islands, on 1 and 2 November 1943 and conducted raids on Rabaul on 5 and again on 11 November before becoming detached from TF 38 on the 14th.

Woodworth sailed for Guadalcanal on 16 November in the escort of transport *Pinckney* (APH–2); then took part in patrol operations in the Solomon area until late December as part of TG 36.1. On 26 December, *Woodworth* departed Espiritu Santo to carry a deck cargo of 1,500 rounds of 5-inch projectiles and 1,500 rounds of 5-inch powder charges to Port Purvis near Tulagi.

On the evening of 8 January 1944, *Woodworth* took part in the bombardment of the Shortland Islands and encountered ineffective return fire from the shore. She conducted escort and patrol operations between the northern Solomons and the Bismarck Archipelago until 13 January when she joined Destroyer Squadron (Des Ron) 12 and—with *Farenholt* (DD–491), *Lansdowne* (DD–486), and *Buchanan* (DD–484)—conducted a bombardment of shore installations, barge concentrations, and staging points on the northeast coast of Bougainville, Baniu Harbor, and Ruri Bay, Solomon Islands; but she encountered no return fire and no air or surface opposition. While transiting Bougainville Strait, *Woodworth* fired five salvoes at a Japanese tent camp on the northwest tip of Choiseul Island. She then spent the remainder of January and February, through the 13th, in escort and training exercises to Torokina, barge-hunting off Bougainville, escort to Port Purvis, and escort and training exercises at Sidney, Australia.

On 13 February, *Woodworth*, in the company of TF 38, covered the advance of the assault on Green Island. The following day, the task force was attacked by a group of six enemy dive bombers. *St. Louis* (CL–49) was hit and suffered the loss of 23 men. Several snoopers later approached the task force and were taken under fire, *Woodworth*'s guns accounted for one while she and her sister ships sustained no casualties or damage. On 14 and 15 February, *Woodworth*—with *Farenholt, Buchanan, Lansdowne,* and *Lardner* (DD–487)—conducted an antishipping sweep of St. George's Channel north of Rabaul, New Britain, but encountered no Japanese vessels. On 17 and 18 February, the same destroyers bombarded Rabaul and shore batteries on Praed Point. *Woodworth* fired torpedoes at two ships leaving Simpson Harbor and later at large groups of ships in Kervia Bay. She also fired her guns at targets near Timber Point and Cape Gazelle. On 24 February, while conducting an antishipping sweep along Truk-Kavieng, New Ireland, shipping lanes about 60 miles northwest of Kavieng, she made radar contact with a Japanese merchant vessel and a large, heavily laden tanker. *Woodworth* fired 38 rounds of 5″/38-caliber at the merchant vessel which was closed and sunk by DesDiv 24. *Woodworth* fishtailed at various times to avoid shells from the shore batteries. Two enemy ships were sunk in the harbor, and one other was damaged and left burning. The American warship also set numerous barges afire in Steffen Strait and engaged Japanese shore batteries. *Woodworth* arrived at Port Purvis, Florida Island, on 26 February.

From 1 through 21 March, *Woodworth* conducted training exercises, escort missions, antisubmarine searches, and barge-hunting operations throughout the Solomon Islands. She fired at enemy positions and encountered no opposition. *Woodworth* departed Port Purvis with *Buchanan* on 22 March, bound for Pearl Harbor. She joined TG 35.6 with a merchant convoy of five ships off Guadalcanal and proceeded to Hawaii with it. On 9 April, *Woodworth* cleared Pearl Harbor and steamed to San Francisco. She was drydocked at the Mare Island Navy Yard on 15 April 1944.

The destroyer underwent an overhaul and refresher training exercises until 21 July when she joined TG 12.1 and steamed to Hawaii on a presidential cruise with *Dunlap* (DD–384), *Cummings* (DD–365), *Fanning* (DD–385), and *Baltimore* (CA–68). That cruiser was carrying President Franklin D. Roosevelt to Pearl Harbor to discuss future strategy in the Pacific with Admiral Nimitz and General MacArthur. Following the historic conference, the task force took the President north to Alaska and the Aleutian Islands. Mr. Roosevelt left *Baltimore* at Kodiak on 8 August and proceeded to Bremerton, Wash., on destroyer *Cummings*. *Woodworth* arrived at San Francisco on 14 August 1944 but sailed the following day for Pearl Harbor where she arrived on 20 August for more than one month of training exercises. On 30 September, she entered Ulithi Atoll for antisubmarine patrol; and, on 7 October, she joined TG 38.1.

The carriers of *Woodworth*'s task group launched an air strike on Okinawa on 10 October, and the planes later raided Japanese installations at Aparri, northern Luzon. On 12 October, the first strikes on Formosa were launched. *Woodworth* was on a picket station 12 miles east of the formation when she was attacked by Japanese torpedo planes at 1815. She fired at several planes but failed to score any hits. The ship sustained heavy weather damage and expended 160 rounds of 5-inch ammunition, 100 rounds of 40-millimeter, and 320 rounds of 20-millimeter. The following day, five Japanese twin-engine, land-based planes attacked the formation. *Woodworth* shot down one plane which crashed in flames after passing over the fantail. During the action, *Canberra* (CA–70) was hit by a torpedo and sustained heavy damage. A third day of strikes against Formosa on the 14th summoned three waves of air attacks by the Japanese. Friendly fighters intercepted and repelled the first two strikes. The third wave consisted of eight or nine enemy aircraft; *Woodworth* claimed to have shot down three: "Two planes were seen to burst into flames. It was a pretty sight." All the planes destroyed were credited to the use of Mk 32 projectiles of which the *Woodworth* used 75 percent. Unfortunately, in this action, *Houston* (CL–81) was torpedoed and heavily damaged.

On 15 October, TG 38.1 began preparations for attacks on Japanese installations in the Philippines. The first of these occurred on 18 October at Luzon, Philippine Islands. These attacks continued through the end of the month to support the first phase of General MacArthur's liberation of the Philippines. *Woodworth* was then detached from TG 38.1 and steamed to Leyte Gulf to join TG 30.3 before it sailed for Ulithi.

Woodworth spent November in screening exercises, antisubmarine patrol at Eniwetok, and escorted a convoy to the Palau Islands. She spent December patrolling off Peleliu and Angaur Island in the Palau group; conducting independent antisubmarine patrol; and escorting a convoy to Leyte Gulf. *Woodworth* and *McCalla* (DD–488) then screened a five-ship convoy to Ulithi on 2 January 1945. There, *Woodworth* underwent tender availability until 11 January. The next day, she assisted in the rescue of *LCI–600* and participated in hunter-killer operations with *McCalla*.

Woodworth got underway as TU 94.18.12 on 15 January for gunnery practice. She was boarded by Capt. W. P. Burford and staff and served as a station ship for gunnery practice off Kossol Roads, Palau, throughout February. On 12 March, Capt. Burford relieved Comdr. D. E. Brown as CTU 94.6.21. Thus, *Woodworth* became the station ship for the Ulithi Surface Patrol and Escort Group and participated in search and rescue operations for the remainder of March. *Woodworth* next underwent tender availability and took patrol station off Mugai Channel at the entrance to Ulithi Harbor on 25 April. She took part in escort and gunnery exercises with *Enterprise* and *Hubbard* (DD–748) until 5 May.

Woodworth patrolled the transport anchorage area southwest of Okinawa on 9 May; the following day, she escorted *Makin Island* (CVE–93) to Kerama Retto harbor and there joined a task unit consisting of six CVE's and nine escorts. From 10 May through 28 May, *Woodworth* took part in daily air strikes on Okinawa. On 28 May, she and *Henley* (DD–553) escorted *Natoma Bay* (CVE–62) to Kerama Retto, Okinawa Shima, where *Woodworth* underwent repairs until 6 June. The following day, while conducting air strikes on Miyako Retto of Sakishimo Gunto, two undetected enemy planes closed the formation and made suicide dives on the CVE's. One crashed into *Natoma Bay* and the other into the sea.

Woodworth supported air strikes on Okinawa; Kyushu, Japan; and various islands of the Ryukyus from 8 June until 21 June when she rescued a crashed pilot from *Steamer Bay* (CVE–87). She spent 22 and 23 June on radar picket duty off Okinawa and departed the Ryukyus on 24 June, bound for Leyte Gulf. She underwent tender availability from 1 to 10 July when she turned her attention to screening the fueling and replenishing of TF 38 (Fast Carrier Force) and devoted the remainder of July to assisting logistic operations for the Fast Carrier Force during strikes on the main islands of Japan.

On 2 August, *Woodworth* escorted oiler *Neshanic* (AO–71) via Guam to Ulithi. On the 12th, *Woodworth* joined in an attempt to rescue a downed pilot, but he was dead when help arrived. On 14 August, *Woodworth* was ordered to proceed independently to Iwo Jima to pick up mail and passengers for the Fast Carrier Force. She joined in the refueling and replenishment of the flattops on 18 August. On 22 August, she was then assigned to a task unit organized around Rear Admiral Thomas L. Sprague in *Ticonderoga* (CVA–14) which was charged with providing air coverage for the first occupation force to go to the Japanese homeland. On 5 September, *Woodworth* took part in firing practices and replenishment until 10 September when she anchored in Tokyo Bay. But for brief training and escort periods at sea, she remained there through the end of the month.

On 1 October, *Woodworth* got underway for Okinawa and left that island on 6 October, bound for home with 50 men and eight officers embarked as passengers for the voyage. She arrived in Portland, Oreg., on 19 October and, 10 days later, headed south for San Pedro, Calif.

Woodworth was transferred to the Atlantic Fleet in November and proceeded through the Panama Canal to Charleston, S.C. After inactivation overhaul there,

the destroyer was placed out of commission, in reserve, on 11 April 1946. She was placed in service on 30 January 1947 for Naval Reserve training duty. Placed in full commission on 21 November 1950, the ship was briefly assigned to the 3d Naval District before she was decommissioned at the New York Naval Shipyard on 14 January 1951 and overhauled to prepare her for transfer to the Government of Italy. Her name was struck from the Navy list on 22 January 1951, and she was turned over to the Italian Navy on 11 June 1951. She served Italy as *Artigilere* (D–553)—operating as a command ship for motor torpedo boat flotillas—until struck from the Italian Naval Vessel Register in January 1971 and scrapped.

Woodworth received seven battle stars for her service in World War II.

***Woodworth, J. M.**, see J. M. Woodworth.*

***Wooley, James**, see James Wooley.*

Woolsey

Melancthon Taylor Woolsey was born in 1782 near Plattsburg, N.Y. After studying law for a time, he entered the Navy as a midshipman on 9 April 1800. His first assignment was the frigate *Adams* in which he made a cruise to the West Indies in 1800 and 1801. He served briefly in the Tripolitan War just before its end in 1805. In 1807, newly promoted Lt. Woolsey received orders to Washington, D.C., where he developed a code of signals for the Navy. From there, he was ordered to the shores of Lake Ontario in 1808 for the purpose of supervising the construction of *Oneida*. At the same time, he received a concurrent assignment as the commanding officer of the shore facilities located there. When the United States went to war with Great Britain in 1812, he was still in command of *Oneida* and the shore station at Sackett's Harbor. On 19 July 1812, a British squadron of five ships appeared. Woolsey attempted to escape to open water with *Oneida*, but the enemy squadron sealed off that avenue. Instead, he returned to Sackett's Harbor, landed half his battery, and repelled the British convincingly after a sharp two-hour exchange.

Early in October, Commodore Isaac Chauncey arrived on the scene and assumed overall command of American naval activities on the Great Lakes. Woolsey stayed on as second in command and remained commanding officer of *Oneida*. During the fall of 1812, Woolsey concentrated upon the construction, purchase, and outfitting of additional war vessels. Throughout the entire war, a construction race caused naval dominance on Lake Ontario to alternate between the British and Americans. Woolsey enabled America to grab the lead in the fall of 1812 by acquiring eight schooners to augment *Oneida* and the three-gun *Julia*. On 8 November, he commanded *Oneida* when the 19-gun warship and four of the newly acquired schooners encountered HMS *Royal George*—a large, 24-gun, ship-rigged sloop-of-war off Kingston and chased her into that port. Later, they followed her in and subjected her to bombardment. In May 1813, Woolsey commanded *Oneida* as her guns supported the capture of York (Toronto) and the assault on Fort George.

Woolsey was promoted to master commandant in July 1813 and by August was in the new schooner *Sylph*. Late in September 1813, he commanded his ship in a running fight between the American lake flotilla and Commodore Yeo's British force. That series of skirmishes resulted in another period of American dominance of Lake Ontario. On 5 October, his ship participated in the capture of the enemy cutter *Drummond* and the sloops-of-war *Elizabeth*, *Mary Ann*, and *Lady Gore* off False Ducks. In May 1814, after a winter of feverish preparation for the third summer of campaigning, Woolsey went to the supply depot at Oswego to pick up guns, cables, and other supplies needed at Sackett's Harbor. While he was there, the British squadron appeared off Oswego. By spreading false intelligence about his destination, Woolsey was able to take advantage of a dark night and make good his escape. The British learned of their mistake and sought to overhaul him which they did at Sandy Creek. Woolsey, however, had prepared an ambush in concert with Maj. Daniel Appling and his 150-man contingent of the United States Rifle Regiment. The British landing force was soundly trounced by Appling's riflemen and 200 Indian allies. Woolsey, in turn, brought his guns to bear on the squadron itself. The Americans defeated the enemy convincingly, killing 10, wounding 52, and capturing the rest. Woolsey then proceeded to Sackett's Harbor with his ordnance and supplies. Soon thereafter, he assumed command of the new brig, *Jones*, and retained that command until the end of the war in 1815.

After the war, Master Commandant Woolsey remained at Lake Ontario in command of the naval station at Sacketts' Harbor. In 1816, he was promoted to captain. He left Sackett's Harbor in 1824 to assume command of the frigate, *Constellation*, which he took on a West Indies cruise until June of 1827. He took command of the navy yard at Pensacola, Fla., late in 1827 and held the position until 1831. Between 1832 and 1834, Woolsey served as commodore in command of the Brazilian Station. His last active duty took him to the Chesapeake Bay where he supervised surveys from 1836 until his health began to decline in 1837. Commodore Woolsey died at Utica, N.Y., on 18 May 1838.

Melancthon Brooks Woolsey, the son of Commodore Melancthon Taylor Woolsey, was born at Sackett's Harbor, N.Y., on 11 August 1817. He entered the Navy as a midshipman on 24 September 1832. After duty at sea and a tour at the Naval School, Woolsey became a passed midshipman on 16 July 1840. He progressed through the rank of master to that of lieutenant by 1847. It was in that rank that he was placed on the reserve list by the retiring board in September 1855. Lt. Woolsey returned to active duty in 1861 as a result of the Civil War. Assigned initially to the receiving ship at New York, Woolsey had assumed command of the steamer *Ellen* by late 1861 and began patrol duty with the South Atlantic Blockading Squadron. During that tour, his ship fought Confederate forces on three separate occasions. In May 1862, he engaged Fort Pemberton at Wapper Creek, S.C. On 1 June, his ship repelled a Confederate cavalry attack at Secessionville. Three days later, he commanded *Ellen* during the attack on James Island.

In July 1862, he was promoted to commander and placed in command of the sloop *Vandalia*. That duty lasted until early 1863, at which time he was transferred to command of the steamer *Princess Royal*. That ship was assigned to the West Gulf Blockading Squadron and patrolled the coasts of Louisiana and Texas. On 28 June 1863, *Princess Royal* helped to defend the town of Donaldsville, La., against a determined Southern attack, and Comdr. Woolsey received high commendation from his superiors for his ship's contribution to the successful defense of the town. He remained with the blockade through the end of the war and, by July 1866, saw his name returned to the active list in the rank of captain.

Following the Civil War, Capt. Woolsey commanded the sloop-of-war *Pawnee* on the South Atlantic Station in 1867 and 1868. In 1869, he took command of the South Atlantic Station flagship *Guerriere*. In 1871, Woolsey was promoted to commodore, probably as flag officer in charge of the South Atlantic Station. His last tour of duty came in March 1873, when he took over as commandant of the navy yard at Pensacola, Fla. Commodore Woolsey received orders detaching him from command of the navy yard in the summer of 1874. At the time, an epidemic of yellow fever raged at Pensacola, and Woolsey deemed it necessary to remain at his post to prevent panic. As a result of his devotion to duty, Commodore Woolsey contracted the disease and died at Pensacola on 2 October 1874.

The first *Woolsey* (Destroyer No. 77) was named in honor of Commodore Melancthon Taylor Woolsey, and the second *Woolsey* (DD–437) commemorated both him and his son, Commodore Melancthon Brooks Woolsey.

I

(Destroyer No. 77: dp. 1,154 (n.); l. 314'4½''; b. 30'11¼'' (wl.); dr. 9'8½'' (aft); s. 35.33 k.; cpl. 131; a. 4 4'', 2 1-pdrs., 12 21'' tt., 2 dct., 1 Y-gun; cl. *Wickes*)

The first *Woolsey* (Destroyer No. 77) was laid down on 1 November 1917 at Bath, Maine, by the Bath Iron Works; launched on 17 September 1918; sponsored by Mrs. Elise Campau Wells; and commissioned on 30 September 1918, Lt. Comdr. Frederick V. McNair in command.

After trials out of Bath and outfitting at the Boston Navy Yard and the Newport Torpedo Station, *Woolsey* headed for New York on 9 October to join *Virginia* (Battleship No. 13) before sailing for Europe. On 13 October, she and the battleship departed New York harbor in the screen of Convoy HX–52. After a relatively uneventful voyage, the convoy was turned over to a British escort force on the 22d. *Woolsey* then set course for Buncrana, located in the far northern portion of Ireland, and arrived there on 23 October. Two days later, she departed Buncrana and stood down the Irish Sea en route to Ponta Delgada in the Azores. After fueling at Ponta Delgada on the 30th, the destroyer continued her voyage home and reentered New York on 5 November. After about a month at New York, during which time hostilities ended under the armistice of 11 November, *Woolsey* left New York on her way back to Europe to join the American naval contingent assigned there for postwar duty. She arrived in Brest, France, on 20 December and reported for duty to the Commander, Naval Forces Europe.

For the next seven months, she performed various missions for America's naval establishment in Europe. Her primary mission consisted of runs between Brest and ports in southern England—notably Plymouth and Southampton—transporting passengers and mail. On 11 March 1919, she was one of the four American destroyers to escort *George Washington* into Brest, France, when that ship arrived with President Woodrow Wilson embarked. After a four-month return to cross-channel runs between England and France, *Woolsey* was honored a second time when she was assigned duty as one of *George Washington's* escorts for President Wilson's return voyage to the United States from the Versailles peace conference. She departed Brest late in June 1919 in company with *George Washington* and arrived in Hampton Roads on 8 July.

Ten days later, *Woolsey* put to sea again bound for a new assignment—the Pacific Fleet. She reached Panama on the 24th, transited the canal, and headed for maneuvers in the Hawaiian Islands. At the completion of those maneuvers, she returned to the continental United States at San Diego. On 31 May 1920, the destroyer was placed out of commission at the Mare Island Navy Yard—probably for an extensive overhaul because she was recommissioned again on 20 October 1920. For the remainder of her relatively brief career, *Woolsey* operated with the Pacific Fleet along the western coast of North America. While operating off the Pacific coast of Panama near Coiba Island early on the morning of 26 February 1921, *Woolsey* was cut in half during a collision with the merchant vessel, SS *Steel Inventor*, and sank.

461

(DD–437: dp. 1,630; l. 347'7''; b. 35'6''; dr. 12'6''; s. 35 k.; cpl. 234; a. 4 5'', 10 21'' tt., 2 dct.; cl. *Gleaves*)

The second *Woolsey* (DD–437) was laid down on 9 October 1939 at Bath, Maine, by the Bath Iron Works; launched on Lincoln's Birthday 1941; sponsored by Mrs. Irving Spencer; and commissioned on 7 May 1941, Lt. Comdr. William H. Von Dreele in command.

Following a shakedown cruise in the Caribbean Sea, *Woolsey* joined the Atlantic Fleet at the beginning of the second week in September. Initially, she served on the Neutrality Patrol, established by President Franklin D. Roosevelt to keep the war in Europe from spreading to the western hemisphere. For a time, she also served as a unit in the screen of the newly commissioned battleship *North Carolina* (BB–55). As the year 1941 waned and the United States approached closer and closer to active belligerency, *Woolsey* began escorting convoys between the United States and Iceland.

The attack on Pearl Harbor and America's entry into World War II found the destroyer in Iceland completing the first leg of one such round-trip voyage. War brought a change to *Woolsey*'s range of duties. Her convoy escort work was broadened to include voyages to the British Isles and Puerto Rico. That duty occupied her energies until the fall of 1942 when she participated in her first invasion operation.

For Operation "Torch," the invasion of Vichy French-controlled North Africa, *Woolsey* was assigned to Destroyer Squadron (DesRon) 13 which served as antisubmarine screen for the Center Attack Group, the Fedhala landing force. That task organization sortied from Hampton Roads, Va., on 24 October and, four days later, rendezvoused with the other units which comprised Task Force (TF) 34. After a meandering and mercifully uneventful crossing, the ships reached the vicinity of the Moroccan coast, and each of the three task groups went their separate ways. *Woolsey* arrived off Fedhala with the Center Attack Force just before midnight on 7 November. Between 0500 and 0600 the next morning, the troops landed at Fedhala and consolidated their beachhead quickly. Resistance soon dissipated, and *Woolsey* seems not to have participated actively in this phase of the operation other than to conduct antisubmarine patrols against a menace which, at that juncture, failed to materialize.

Later, however, the German Navy belatedly took a hand in the fracas. U-boats began attacking the transports. On the 11th, *U–173* sank *Joseph Hewes* (AP–50). Between then and the 15th, several other attacks occurred. On the 16th, *U–173* returned to the area and probably was the German submarine responsible for torpedoing *Electra* (AK–21). That time though, the U-boat failed to make good her escape. *Woolsey*, still on antisubmarine patrol, caught the submarine's reflection with her sonar and, joined by *Swanson* (DD–443) and *Quick* (DD–490), charged to the attack. The three destroyers made a coordinated depth-charge assault that sent *U–173* to oblivion. The following day, *Woolsey* departed the Moroccan coast to return to Hampton Roads, where she arrived on the 30th.

After a series of training operations along the eastern seaboard—primarily off the New England coast—the destroyer began duty escorting transatlantic convoys in mid-January 1943. On the 14th, she departed New York with Convoy UGF–4. The convoy reached Casablanca on the 25th; and, after a week in port, *Woolsey* escorted the return convoy, GUF–4, back to New York, arriving there on 13 February. At the beginning of March, she helped shepherd Convoy UGF–6 to Casablanca; then made a brief round-trip voyage from Casablanca to Gibraltar and back before returning to the east coast with GUF–6 early in April. The warship then plied the waters of the eastern seaboard until mid-May, conducting antisubmarine patrols and screening coastwise convoys between Norfolk and New

York. On 14 May, *Woolsey* put to sea from New York with her last transatlantic convoy, UGS–8. She and her charges reached Casablanca on 1 June, and the destroyer remained there a fortnight. On the 15th, she departed Morocco; but, instead of returning to the United States as she had done in the past, she headed via Gibraltar to Algiers on the Mediterranean coast of North Africa.

When *Woolsey* reached Gibraltar the next day, an Atlantic phase of her wartime career ended, and the Mediterranean phase began. She reported for duty with the 8th Fleet just in time to participate in the invasion of Sicily, and operations in Italian waters consumed the bulk of her time and energy during the ensuing eight months. For the Sicily assault, she drew duty as a fire-support ship for one of three sectors into which the Licata landing beaches were divided. Save for one brief round-trip voyage to Algiers in mid-July, *Woolsey* provided gunfire support for the Army operating ashore on Sicily and helped to defend Allied shipping from German air attacks. Though she appears not to have accounted for any *Luftwaffe* aircraft, she did succeed in destroying an enemy railroad battery with gunfire.

By mid-August, with Sicily secured, she began preparations for the landings on the Italian mainland at Salerno. For that invasion, the destroyer was assigned to the Southern Attack Force fire support group which consisted of five cruisers—four American and one British—and the four destroyers of *Woolsey*'s DesRon 13. In that capacity, she supported the landings on the southern sector of the Gulf of Salerno shoreline. During the assault on 9 September, however, she received only one call for fire support. That event occurred just after 1630 when her shore fire-control party called upon her to join *Bristol* (DD–453) in shooting up an enemy tank formation.

After completing her mission at Salerno the next day, *Woolsey* returned to more routine missions. She made voyages between Naples and North African ports escorting supply echelons to the expanding Italian campaign. While operating outside of Oran, Algeria, on 16 December, she encountered the German submarine *U–73*. After forcing the U-boat to surface with a full pattern of depth charges, *Woolsey*'s gunners went to work and completed the destruction of *U–73*. The destroyer rescued and made prisoners of the U-boat's 23 survivors.

Late in January 1944, the destroyer returned to amphibious operations, this time as a unit of the Fire Support Group for the Anzio landings. Arriving off the beachhead on 22 January 1944, she delivered call fire support for the troops as they landed. The relative ease experienced during the opening phase at Anzio, however, belied the actual complexion of the campaign. Failing to break out of the beachhead early, the Army forces were soon surrounded on three sides by German forces which threatened to push them into the sea. The dogged determination of American infantrymen and the yeoman-like support provided them by the Navy enabled the troops ashore to hold on until a link-up was made with the Salerno forces in May. During the first month of that desperate struggle, *Woolsey* provided gunfire support for the troops ashore and protected the ships which constituted their lifeline to the outside world. Late in February, however, she departed the Italian campaign to return to the United States for necessary repairs. After a stop at Gibraltar on 17 February, she headed via Horta in the Azores to Boston, Mass., where she arrived on the 25th.

Completing her repairs at Boston in mid-March, she conducted refresher training at Casco Bay, Maine, before heading back to the Mediterranean at the end of the third week in April. She stopped at Gibraltar on the last day of that month and arrived at Oran on May Day. The ensuing three months saw her operating out of Oran conducting antisubmarine patrols of the approaches to that port. While operating with a hunting group composed of *Benson* (DD–421), *Ludlow*

(DD–438), and *Niblack* (DD–424) in mid-May, *Woolsey* experienced her third and last encounter with a German U-boat. A report of torpedo tracks from a newcomer to the Mediterranean, *U–960*, brought DesDiv 25 to the area between Oran and Cartagena early on the 17th to commence a two-day search and destroy mission. During the night of 18 and 19 May, the four destroyers split themselves into two search groups and began searching a possible submarine track 10 miles to each side of it. About an hour and 40 minutes into the mid-watch, the four warships received word that a plane had spotted the submarine some 10 miles ahead of *Niblack* and *Ludlow*. Those two ships charged to the attack; and, by the time *Woolsey* arrived on the scene with *Benson* and *Madison* (DD–425), the two destroyers had succeeded in forcing the U-boat to surface after delivering 11 depth charge attacks over the space of four hours. Immediately, all five destroyers opened fire on the submarine while a British Wellington bomber shifted through the melee at low altitude to drop depth bombs near *U–960*. The German ship suffered a number of 5-inch hits before submerging again. *Niblack* responded with more depth charges. That attack evidently rung the death knell for *U–960*, for she immediately resurfaced, and her crew scrambled off just as she made her final plunge at about 0715 on the 19th. The destroyers picked up the U-boat's captain and 21 of her crew. While *Niblack* and *Ludlow* received official credit for sinking the enemy submarine—no doubt a fair assessment considering their four-hour attack and the fact that *Niblack* probably delivered the coup de grace—*Woolsey*'s 5-inch gunfire probably contributed significantly to the enemy's destruction.

Following that action, *Woolsey* continued relatively routine patrols until the end of July when she began preparations for the invasion of southern France. For that operation, *Woolsey* was assigned to the Bombardment Group attached to Camel Force. In that capacity, she supported the landings on the right flank of the assault area—near St. Raphael. During the 15 August invasion, her guns knocked out two German tanks; but, though the Camel area assault proved to be the most heavily contested thrust, the entire southern France operation constituted little more than a walkover.

Consequently, very soon after the initial invasion, *Woolsey* shifted to supporting the 1st Airborne Division's drive along the coast toward Italy. She fired upon enemy lines of communication along the coast—particularly roads—and supported the liberation of Cannes on 24 August. The destroyer continued her operations along the Franco-Italian coast until late October. At that time, she headed for Naples for a visit before returning to Oran, where she arrived on 29 November. The warship was back off the southern coast of France in mid-December and resumed her interdiction duties until mid-January 1945. At that time, she bade farewell to the Mediterranean and the 8th Fleet. Following a brief tour of duty patrolling in the Azores, *Woolsey* returned to the United States, arriving in New York on 23 February.

After operating along the New England coast until late April and escorting a convoy to Great Britain in May, the warship returned home to receive a reinforced antiaircraft battery preparatory to her impending transfer to the war in the Pacific. Late in June, she steamed south to conduct refresher training out of Guantanamo Bay, Cuba. Completing that duty on 7 July, she transited the Panama Canal two days later and reported for duty with the Pacific Fleet. She stopped at San Diego, Calif., from 18 July to 3 August. A week later, while she was still at Pearl Harbor, Japan capitulated. Late in August, she escorted a convoy carrying occupation troops to Japan. She stopped at Sasebo until 26 September and then began a voyage during which she made a series of port visits—at Manila, Shanghai, Okinawa, and Saipan.

From the last-named place, *Woolsey* got underway on 3 November to return home. After stops at Pearl Harbor and San Diego, the destroyer ended her brief interlude with the Pacific Fleet on 29 November when she retransited the Panama Canal. She arrived in Charleston, S.C., on 4 December and began preparations for inactivation. On 8 March 1946, the destroyer was placed in commission, in reserve. Eleven months later, on 6 February 1947, she was placed out of commission. Berthed with the Charleston Group, Atlantic Reserve Fleet, for 10 years, *Woolsey* was towed to Boston in late October of 1957. Her name was struck from the Navy list on 1 July 1971, and she was sold to Andy International, Inc., for scrapping on 29 May 1974.

Woolsey (DD–437) earned seven battle stars during World War II.

Woonsocket

A town in southeastern Rhode Island that in turn takes its name from an Indian word that meant "at the place of the mist."

I

(PF–32: dp. 2,415; l. 303'11"; b. 37'6"; dr. 13'8"; s. 20.3 k.; cpl. 176; a. 3 3", 4 40 mm., 4 20 mm., 2 dct., 1 dcp. (hh.); cl. *Tacoma*; T. S2–S2–AQ1)

The first *Woonsocket* (PF–32)—originally PG–140 and redesignated PF–32 on 25 June 1943—was laid down under a Maritime Commission contract (MC hull 1443) on 12 August 1943 at Superior, Wisc., by Walter Butler Shipbuilders, Inc.; launched on 27 September 1943; sponsored by Mrs. Ernest E. Dupre, wife of the mayor of Woonsocket, R. I.; ferried to the Boston Navy Yard for completion; accepted by the Navy on 27 July 1944; and commissioned with a Coast Guard crew on 1 September 1944, Comdr. William J. Conley, USCG, in command.

Following shakedown off Bermuda, *Woonsocket* returned to Boston for conversion to a weather ship before proceeding to Newfoundland—arriving at Argentia on 30 October—for meteorological charting duties off Newfoundland through the end of World War II and into the early months of 1946. She was decommissioned by the Navy on 16 March 1946 and recommissioned simultaneously by the Coast Guard on a loan basis. *Woonsocket* served with the Coast Guard until her final decommissioning on 18 September 1946 at New Orleans, La.

Struck from the Navy list on 14 May 1947, the *Tacoma*-class frigate was subsequently transferred to the Government of Peru. She served the Peruvian Navy first as *Teniente Galvez* and later simply as *Galvez* into the 1960's.

II

(YTM–754: dp. 390 (f.); l. 107'; b. 27'; dr. 13'; s. 12 k. (tl.); cpl. 16; cl. *Chicopee*)

The second *Woonsocket* (YTM–754), a medium harbor tug, was acquired by the Navy in 1964 from the Army which she had served as *LT–1965*. Renamed *Woonsocket* and designated YTM–754, she was placed in service in September 1964 and was assigned to the 1st Naval District. She plied waters in the vicinity of Boston until April of 1968 when she was reassigned to the 5th Naval District at Norfolk, Va. She served there until September of 1975 at which time she was placed out of service. Her name was concurrently struck from the Navy list, and she was subsequently sold.

Worcester

The county seat of Worcester County, Mass., first settled in 1713. Called Quinsigamond Plantation until renamed for the English industrial and educational center, Worcester became a town in 1722, a county seat in 1731, and received its city charter in 1848.

I

(SlpW: dp. 3,050; l. 296'10''; b. 41'; dr. 9'9''; s. 13 k.; cpl. 153; a. 4 12-pdrs.; cl. Contoocook)

Manitou—a bark-rigged screw steam sloop-of-war built of unseasoned white oak timbers—was laid down in 1863 at Boston, Mass., by the Boston Navy Yard and was launched on 25 August 1866. Renamed *Worcester* on 15 May 1869, she was apparently placed in commission on 27 February 1871, Comdr. William D. Whiting in command. Among the ship's officers at the time of her commissioning was the naval strategist and author, Lt. Comdr. Alfred T. Mahan.

After an abbreviated fitting out, *Worcester* loaded a cargo of supplies to be delivered to the suffering victims of the Franco-Prussian War. Although she had never conducted sea trials, she departed Boston on 5 March 1871 with a heavy cargo in her holds. Heavy weather sprang up soon after she left port, and Comdr. Whiting was obliged to use caution in using the ship's spread of canvas until he felt sure of the ship's seakeeping qualities. Three days out, on 8 March, the port forward boiler burst, sending clouds of steam into the forward part of the ship and severely scalding 10 men —four of whom later died. A subsequent court finding revealed that the explosion had been due to defective tubes.

For most of the remainder of the voyage, the ship weathered heavy gales that lasted from two to three days at a stretch. But for the explosion, the ship performed well on her maiden voyage and carried a good spread of canvas for the remainder of the trip to England. Making port at Plymouth, England, on 4 April, *Worcester* eventually discharged her cargo at London. The plan to sell the cargo to raise money to purchase relief supplies for the French fell through. It seemed that the French really did not need help after all, and those who did could not afford to pay the cost of transporting the supplies from the French coast to their districts.

Worcester concluded her business at London, sailed to Liverpool where she received on board some ordnance before returning to Boston. There, she remained until January 1872. Made flagship of the North Atlantic Squadron under Rear Admiral S. P. Lee, *Worcester* served in that capacity until 1875. She was placed in ordinary in 1876 and laid up at the Norfolk Navy Yard, Portsmouth, Va., the following year. Made receiving ship at Norfolk in 1878, with Capt. Walter W. Queen in command, *Worcester* was laid up at the Norfolk Navy Yard during 1879 and 1880. Eventually, the ship's hull rotted, and it was found unfit for repair in 1881. On 27 September 1883, the sloop-of-war was sold and was presumably broken up soon thereafter.

———

Worcester (PF–62)—a *Tacoma-class* frigate—was renamed *Gladwyne* (q.v.) on 18 August 1944.

II

(CL–144: dp. 14,700; l. 680'; b. 71'; dr. 26'; s. 33.0 k.; cpl. 1,070; a. 12 6'', 22 3'', 24 20mm.; cl. Worcester)

The second *Worcester* (CL–144) was laid down on 29 January 1945 at Camden, N.J., by the New York Shipbuilding and Drydock Corp.; launched on 4 February 1947; sponsored by Miss Gloria Ann Sullivan, the daughter of Mayor and Mrs. F. G. Sullivan of Worcester, Mass.; and commissioned at the Philadelphia Naval Base on 26 June 1948, Capt. T. B. Dugan in command.

Combining destroyer maneuverability with cruiser size and given a main battery that could deal not only with surface targets but with aircraft as well, *Worcester* embodied many of the lessons learned during World War II. She and her sister ship, *Roanoke* (CL–145), epitomized the hard-hitting dual-purpose cruiser.

Worcester—assigned to Cruiser Division (CruDiv) 10—spent the first year of her commissioned service

The steam sloop-of-war *Worcester*. (NR&L(0) 8161)

completing her fitting out, conducting shakedown training off the eastern seaboard of the United States, and undergoing availability and type training. In the summer of 1949, she participated in her first large-scale training exercises in Guantanamo Bay and visited Kingston, Jamaica. Late in the summer, she sailed for the Mediterranean, departing Newport, R.I., on 6 September 1949 and reaching Gibraltar 10 days later. She made her first deployment with the 6th Fleet in the ensuing months, visiting Malta; Bizerte, Tunisia; Golfe-Juan, France; Argostoli and Phaleron Bay, Greece; Iskenderum, Turkey; Trieste and Venice, Italy; and Gibraltar. During that 6th Fleet deployment, she engaged in exercises and maneuvers with fast carrier task forces, including the carrier *Leyte* (CV-32) and the heavy cruiser *Des Moines* (CA-134). She returned to Norfolk on 10 December.

Worcester operated off the eastern seaboard, ranging from Newport to Norfolk and south to Puerto Rico, with visits in between to Philadelphia, before she began her second 6th Fleet deployment in the spring of 1950. She departed Norfolk on 3 May, arrived at Lisbon on the 13th, and entered the Mediterranean soon thereafter.

In between her cycles of drills and exercises in the "Med," *Worcester* visited Augusta, Sicily; Bizerte; Genoa and La Spezia, Italy; and Golfe Juan, on the southern coast of France, before she put into Phaleron Bay on 20 July. However, she was there only a week before she received orders to sail for the Far East. While the light cruiser and her consorts had been operating in the Mediterranean, war had broken out in Korea on 25 June. Accordingly, *Worcester* departed Phaleron Bay on 27 July, in company with Destroyer Division (DesDiv) 21—*Fred T. Berry* (DDE-858), *Keppler* (DDE-765), *Norris* (DDE-959), and *McCaffrey* (DDE-860). Reaching Port Said, Egypt, on the morning of the 29th, *Worcester* transited the Suez Canal that afternoon.

Reaching Colombo for provisions and fuel, *Worcester* and her escorts tarried there from 7 to 9 August before pushing on toward the Malacca Strait. They then proceeded through the Bashi Channel to Buckner Bay, Okinawa, where they arrived on 19 August. En route, the American warships had been diverted through the Bashi Channel to be available to counter any invasion attempt by the communist Chinese of Formosa.

After fueling from *Navasota* (AO-106), *Worcester* departed Buckner Bay on the 20th and set a course for Keelung, Formosa, to join the Formosa Patrol.

Joining that force on the 21st, *Worcester* remained at anchor at Keelung from the 22d through the 26th. She got underway on the 27th to add her potentially powerful antiaircraft "punch" to the screen of Task Force (TF) 77—the fast carrier task force consisting of *Philippine Sea* (CV-47) and *Valley Forge* (CV-45), then operating in the Yellow Sea off the coast of Korea.

The following day, the light cruiser—steaming in company with *Norris* (DDE-859)—joined TF 77 and proceeded into the Yellow Sea for operations against enemy targets located in central and southwestern Korea. Each day in ensuing days, the carriers launched their strikes against North Korean ground targets while the screen provided protection in case of any attempts by the communist North Korean air forces to interrupt the operation. Her helicopter also performed plane-guard duty, standing by in the air to rescue any ditched pilots from the waters nearby.

On 4 September, *Worcester*'s radar picked up an unidentified contact at 1331. The combat air patrol—four Vought F4U Corsairs from *Valley Forge*—soon reported the stranger as being a twin-engined bomber with a pointed nose, a single tailfin, and high inverted gull wings. It also bore red star markings. At 1345, the 4FU's vectored to the "bogey" by *Fletcher* (DDE-445), unceremoniously splashed the stranger 49 miles away.

The following day, *Worcester* went to general quarters at 1108 and commenced maneuvering at 20 knots to avoid possible attack when her radar picked up an unidentified plane closing the formation from the east. Three minutes later, the cruiser fired three rounds of 6-inch projectiles in the direction of the intruder to warn her—it turned out to be a British Short "Sunderland" flying boat on patrol. At 2143, *Worcester* secured from battle stations and resumed her cruising with TF 77.

There was one more day of flight operations off the Korean coast, 6 September, before *Worcester* transferred her helicopter to *Philippine Sea* to clear the ship for a practice antiaircraft firing. The cruiser later recovered the "chopper" before heading for Sasebo, Japan, for replenishment of fuel, ammunition, stores, and provisions.

Worcester remained at Sasebo from 7 to 10 September and got underway at 0532 on 11 September, again with TF 77, and proceeded to the operation area in the Yellow Sea to support a large-scale amphibious assault by United Nations (UN) forces against enemy forces in the Inchon and Seoul areas of Korea.

Worcester subsequently supported the Inchon landing —the daring stroke aimed at outflanking the North Korean invaders by a strategic landing behind their lines in South Korea masterminded by General Douglas MacArthur. *Worcester* screened the fast carrier task forces as their planes dropped lethal loads on North Korean targets ashore until she was detached on the 20th to conduct a shore bombardment mission as part of TG 95.2 in the vicinity of Pohang Dong. Proceeding to the objective via the straits north of the Quelpart Islands and west of Tsushima, the light cruiser rendezvoused with *Helena* (CA-75) three miles off the east coast of Korea and 12 miles north of Pohang Dong.

Over the ensuing days, *Worcester* patrolled off the coast with TG 95.2. She relieved *Helena* in her fire support duties at 0600 on the 24th, freeing the heavy cruiser to proceed to Sasebo. While her own helicopter was aloft providing antisubmarine screening, *Worcester* commenced firing at 0805, shelling nine North Korean troop concentrations ashore. Directed by Korean Military Advisory Group (KMAG) personnel ashore, *Worcester* delivered call-fire throughout the day with pinpoint accuracy at troop concentrations and command posts. Relieved by *Samuel N. Moore* (DD-747) as fire support ship, *Worcester* patrolled in company with *Brush* (DD-745) to seaward of the fire support area for the night.

Worcester returned the following day and resumed her fire support duties, adding to the troubles of the already beaten and retreating North Korean forces. Throughout the 25th, *Worcester*—using KMAG spotting from shore—delivered fire support for the advancing UN forces, breaking up communist troop concentrations with her precise 6-inch fire. As the ship's war diary at one point recorded: "Spotter reported troops dispersed. KMAG reported that all firing has been very effective and instrumental in enemy retreat."

Worcester spent the night hours on the 25th and into the 26th patrolling eight miles of a stretch of coast between Yonghae and Utchin. The rapid advance of the UN forces on the 26th obviated fire support from *Worcester*'s guns; but the cruiser received word that *Brush* had hit a mine off Tanchon, North Korea, at 1220. While *Samuel N. Moore* took over the on-call fire support duties in the vicinity, *Worcester* bent on 27 knots and went to *Brush*'s aid.

The cruisermen found *Brush* down by the bow with a 3-degree port list. There were five dead and 30 injured. At 0101 on the 27th, *Worcester* commenced taking on board the more seriously wounded of the destroyer's company via highline transfer, eventually receiving 15 stretcher cases—all men suffering from burns—by 0228. The cruiser then altered course for Japan and, later that day, took on board four more stretcher patients, six ambulatory patients, and a corpse. At that time, two hospitalmen—who had been transferred from *Worcester* to *Brush* to tend the wounded on the destroyer—returned to the cruiser.

Proceeding in company with the crippled *Brush*, *Bolster* (ARS–38), and *De Haven* (DD–727), *Worcester* headed for Sasebo and reached port late on the afternoon of the 29th. As she was being made fast to her buoy in Sasebo harbor, *Worcester* received a warm message from the destroyer that she had aided: "With us you are not only big league but world champions. The kindness consideration and eagerness to help of *Worcester*'s ship's company will never be forgotten by the *Brush*."

The stay in Sasebo, however, proved a short one for *Worcester*, because she got underway on the 30th to return to Korean waters to resume her fire support and interdiction duties. At 0600 on 1 October, *Worcester* joined the blockading force off the east coast of Korea, south of the 41st parallel, ready to render gunfire support for UN troops advancing against North Korean forces. As she patrolled off the coast, *Worcester* launched her helicopter to conduct antisubmarine and antimine patrols and frequently stationed lookouts in the bows of the ship, their eyes peeled for mines. Periodically, the screening destroyers found and destroyed mines drifting nearby. Recent encounters with the horned spheres had resulted in all operations being carried on at the 100-fathom curve, which meant maximum gun range for the ships if call-fire was required.

Worcester—having served as flagship for TG 95.2, Rear Admiral C. C. Hartman embarked—arrived back at Sasebo for replenishment on 8 October and fueled there before disembarking Rear Admiral Hartman. While still at Sasebo, *Worcester* became a flagship again the next day when Rear Admiral Allan E. Smith, Commander, TF 95, came on board with his staff and broke his flag in the light cruiser. At 1248 on the 10th, *Worcester* got underway to return to the east coast of Korea—this time to screen minesweeping operations at the important port of Wonsan and to support the advance of the 3d Republic of Korea (ROK) Army Division.

Early on the 11th, the operation became truly an international one, when the British destroyer HMS *Cockade*, the Australian destroyer HMAS *Warramunga*, and the Canadian destroyer HMCS *Athabaskan* joined *Worcester*'s group which already included the British light cruiser HMS *Ceylon* and the heavy cruiser *Helena* besides the American warships *Rochester* (CA–124), *Harold J. Thomas* (DDR–833), and *Maddox* (DD–731). On the 12th, the battleship *Missouri* (BB–63) joined, bringing her heavy guns to the unit.

While *Missouri*'s helicopter searched the projected bombardment track for mines, the UN force formed up for battle. At 1150, when a shell from an unobserved shore battery fell 5,000 yards short of the group, it apparently signalled the beginning. *Worcester* hoisted the blue and white UN flag to the foretruck and commenced firing at exactly noon on 12 October. For almost the next 90-odd minutes, *Worcester*'s 6-inch guns hammered at iron works and railroad tunnels in the vicinity. The next day, she extended her target list to include railroad marshalling yards, tearing up sections of track and blasting rolling stock.

Over the next few days, *Worcester* and the ships in company with her proceeded to rain destruction on targets of opportunity near Wonsan—targets that ranged from railroad marshalling yards to rolling stock and adjacent warehouse areas. Also, on 16 October, in an action reminiscent of the "Battle of the Pips" in World War II, *Worcester*, *Helena*, and accompanying destroyers fired at unidentified radar contacts—"blips" on the radar screens that approached from the northward. They (the contacts) were probably two flocks of geese.

After returning to Sasebo, *Worcester* returned briefly to Wonsan to transfer mail, passengers, and her helicopter unit to *Rochester* on 21 October, before she sailed from Wonsan at 1723 on that day, in company with *Helena* and screened by *Southerland* (DD–743) and *English* (DD–696). Joined later by *Collett* (DD–730), *Worcester* parted company with the others and, escorted only by *Collett*, headed for Sasebo where, upon arrival, Rear Admiral Smith disembarked and shifted his flag to the destroyer tender *Dixie* (AD–14).

Worcester completed the transfer of helicopter personnel, spares, and equipment to Fleet Activities, Sasebo, and, at 1701 on 23 October, headed for Yokosuka. She reached that port at 0823 on the 25th. After replenishment, liberty for her crew, and the cleaning of two boilers, the light cruiser left the Far East on 27 October, bound for Pearl Harbor. The day after she sailed, *Worcester* received a dispatch from Admiral C. Turner Joy, Commander, Naval Forces, Far East, which said: "Upon the *Worcester*'s departure from the Far East I wish to extend a hearty 'well done' to the entire ship's company. Your rapid deployment from the European station to the Far East, followed by your immediate and most effective participation in the Korean effort, clearly demonstrates that your status of war readiness was excellent."

Returning to Philadelphia on 21 November—via Pearl Harbor and the Panama Canal—*Worcester* later spent six days at Norfolk, 23 to 29 November, before she was overhauled at the Boston Naval Shipyard from 1 December 1950 to 20 March 1951. After another brief period at Norfolk from 22 to 30 March, the light cruiser operated at Guantanamo Bay, Cuba, on refresher training for nearly a month before she headed back to Norfolk. Departing that port on 15 May, *Worcester* headed for the Mediterranean and her third deployment to the 6th Fleet.

Worcester conducted four more 6th Fleet "Med" deployments into the mid-1950's and twice visited northern European ports. During that time, she participated in fleet maneuvers and exercises and paid good-will calls on many ports—ranging from Bergen, Norway; to Copenhagen, Denmark; to Dublin, Ireland; and Portsmouth, England. Between her foreign deployments were operations closer to home: local operations out of eastern seaboard ports like Boston and Norfolk. In addition, the ship also plied the warmer waters of the Caribbean and West Indies, ranging from Guantanamo Bay to Kingston, Jamaica.

Transferred from the Atlantic to the Pacific Fleet in January of 1956, *Worcester* made two more deployments to operate with the 7th Fleet, visiting such highly frequented ports as Sasebo and Yokosuka, Japan; Hong Kong; Manila; as well as the Japanese ports of Hakodate, Nagaski, Shimoda, Yokohama, and Kobe. Returning each time to her home port at Long Beach, Calif., the ship conducted local operations between her cruises in Oriental waters.

On 2 September 1958, *Worcester* departed Long Beach and steamed for the Mare Island Naval Shipyard to commence the inactivation process. Decommissioned at Mare Island on 19 December 1958 and simultaneously placed in reserve, *Worcester* was subsequently berthed at San Francisco and, later, at Bremerton, Wash., before she was struck from the Navy list on 1 December 1970. Sold to Zidell Explorations, Inc., of Portland, Oreg., on 5 July 1972, the revolutionary light cruiser that never had a chance to prove herself in her designed role was subsequently broken up for scrap.

Worcester was awarded two battle stars for her Korean War service.

Worden

John Lorimer Worden—born on 12 March 1818 in Westchester County, N.Y.—was appointed midshipman in the Navy on 10 January 1834. He served his first three years in the sloop-of-war *Erie* on the Brazilian Station. Following that, he was briefly assigned to the sloop *Cyane* before reporting to the Naval School at

Philadelphia for seven months of instruction. He returned to sea in July 1840 for two years with the Pacific Squadron. Between 1844 and 1846, Worden was stationed at the Naval Observatory in Washington, D.C. During the Mexican War, he cruised the west coast, primarily in the store ship *Southampton*, but in other ships as well. In 1850, he returned to the Naval Observatory for another two-year tour of duty. The ensuing nine years were filled with sea duty which took Worden on several cruises in the Caribbean and Mediterranean Seas.

Brought to Washington early in 1861, he received orders in April to carry secret dispatches—regarding the reinforcement of Fort Pickens—south to the warships at Pensacola. During the return journey north, Worden was arrested near Montgomery, Ala., and was held prisoner until exchanged about seven months later. Though still ill as a result of his imprisonment, Comdr. Worden accepted orders to command the new ironclad *Monitor* on 16 January 1862. He reported to her building site at Greenpoint on Long Island and supervised her completion. He placed the new warship in commission at the New York Navy Yard on 25 February and two days later sailed for Hampton Roads. However, steering failure forced the ironclad back to New York for repairs. On 6 March, she headed south again, this time under tow by *Seth Low*. On the afternoon of 8 March, Worden's command approached Cape Henry, Va., while inside Hampton Roads, the Confederacy's own ironclad, CSS *Virginia*, wreaked havoc with the Union Navy's wooden blockading fleet. During that engagement, the Southern warship sank the sloop *Cumberland* and severely damaged *Congress* and *Minnesota* before retiring behind Sewell's Point. Arriving on the scene too late to participate in the engagement, Worden and his command set about assisting the grounded *Minnesota*.

At daybreak on the 9th, *Virginia* emerged once more from behind Sewell's Point to complete her reduction of the Federal fleet at Hampton Roads. As the Confederate ironclad approached *Minnesota*, Worden maneuvered *Monitor* out from the grounded ship's shadow to engage *Virginia* in the battle that revolutionized naval warfare. For four hours, the two iron-plated ships slugged it out as they maneuvered in the narrow channel of Hampton Roads, pouring shot and shell at one another to almost no visible effect. Three hours into the slug fest, Worden received facial wounds when a Confederate shell exploded just outside the pilot house. He relinquished command to his first officer, Samuel D. Green. About an hour later, *Monitor* withdrew from the battle temporarily and, upon her return to the scene, found that *Virginia*, too, had withdrawn. The first battle between steam-driven, armored ships had ended in a draw.

After the battle, Worden moved ashore to convalesce from his wounds. During that recuperative period, he received the accolade of a grateful nation and the official thanks of Congress. Late in 1862, he took command of the ironclad monitor *Montauk* and placed her in commission at New York on 14 December 1862. Later in the month, Worden took his new ship south to join the South Atlantic Blockading Squadron off Port Royal, S.C. On 27 January 1863, he led his ship in the bombardment of Fort McAlister. A month later, newly promoted Capt. Worden took his ship into the Ogeechee River, found the Confederate privateer *Rattlesnake* (formerly CSS *Nashville*), and destroyed her with five well-placed shots. His last action came of 7 April 1863, when *Montauk* participated in an attack on Charleston, S.C.

Not long after the Charleston attack, Capt. Worden received orders to shore duty in conjunction with the construction of ironclads at New York. That assignment lasted until the late 1860's. In 1869, he began a five-year tour as Superintendent of the Naval Academy during which he was promoted to rear admiral. During the late 1870's, he commanded the European Squadron, visiting ports in northern Europe and patrolling the

eastern Mediterranean during the Russo-Turkish War of 1877–78. He returned ashore and concluded his naval career as a member of the Examining Board and as President of the Retiring Board. When he retired on 23 December 1886, Congress voted him full sea pay in his grade for life. Rear Admiral Worden resided in Washington, D.C., until his death from pneumonia on 19 October 1897. After funeral services at Washington's St. John's Episcopal Church, he was buried at Pawling, N.Y.

I

(Torpedo Boat Destroyer No. 16: dp. 605 (f.); l. 248'0'' (wl.); b. 23'1¼''; dr. 10'11''; s. 29.86 k. (tl.); cpl. 72; a. 2 3'' rf., 6 6-pdr. rf., 2 18'' tt.; cl. *Truxtun*)

The first *Worden* (Torpedo Boat Destroyer No. 16) was laid down at Sparrows Point, Md., on 13 November 1899 by the Maryland Steel Co.; launched on 15 August 1901; sponsored by Mrs. Daniel F. Worden, the daughter-in-law of Rear Admiral Worden; and commissioned on St. Patrick's Day 1903, Lt. Benjamin B. McCormick in command.

Worden passed her final acceptance test on 18 July and began duty with the 2d Torpedo Flotilla, based at Norfolk, Va. For more than four years, she remained a unit of the 2d Torpedo Flotilla and conducted operations along the eastern seaboard from Maine south to the Caribbean and the Gulf of Mexico. Annually, she participated in the Fleet maneuvers held in the warm waters of the Caribbean.

On 18 November 1907, the warship was placed in reserve at the Norfolk Navy Yard. As a unit of the Reserve Torpedo Flotilla, she was berthed first at Norfolk and, later, at Charleston, S.C. Save for a six-month interlude from May to November of 1909 when she was returned to full commission, *Worden* remained inactive until 1912. Then, though still in reserve, she was loaned to the Pennsylvania Naval Militia for training purposes and was stationed at Philadelphia until returned to Charleston and the Reserve Torpedo Flotilla the following year.

Sometime in 1914, the torpedo-boat destroyer became a tender to the Atlantic Fleet Submarine Force and continued to operate in support of submarines until sometime in March 1917 when she was sent to New York on special duty in connection with a recruiting campaign necessitated by the probability that the United States would enter World War I. In June, she was reassigned back to her own type command as a unit of Division B, Destroyer Force; however, she continued her recruiting duty at New York through the end of the year.

On 16 January 1918, *Worden* got underway for Europe in company with *Hopkins* (Coast Torpedo Vessel No. 6), *Macdonough* (Coast Torpedo Vessel No. 9), *Paul Jones* (Coast Torpedo Vessel No. 10), and *Stewart* (Coast Torpedo Vessel No. 13). She steamed with them, via Bermuda, to Ponta Delgada in the Azores, where she arrived on 29 January. There, *Worden* and *Stewart* parted company with the other three warships and put to sea again on 4 February to continue on to the French coast. They reached Brest on the 9th and soon thereafter began escorting coastal convoys and hunting for enemy U-boats. During the remaining nine months of World War I, *Worden* maintained a grueling schedule escorting convoys between ports on the French coast.

On 18 December, about five weeks after the 11 November armistice, she stood out of Brest in company with *Flusser* (Destroyer No. 20), *Stewart*, and *Whipple* (Coast Torpedo Vessel No. 15) to return home. Following refueling and provisioning stops in the Azores and at Bermuda, she and her traveling companions arrived at Philadelphia on 3 January 1919. She remained in commission for a little over six months, probably at Philadelphia. In any event, *Worden* was placed out of commission there on 13 July 1919, and her name was struck from the Navy list on 15 September 1919. In 1920, on the first anniversary of her return home, 3 January, she was sold to Joseph G. Hitner, of Philadelphia, for conversion to mercantile service.

II

(Destroyer No. 288: dp. 1,215 (n.); b. 314'4½''; b. 30'11½''; dr. 9'9¾'' (aft) (f.); s. 34.47 k. (tl.); cpl. 120; a. 4 4'', 1 3'', 12 21'' tt.; cl. *Clemson*)

The second *Worden* (Destroyer No. 288) was laid down on 30 June 1919 at Squantum, Mass., by the Bethlehem Shipbuilding Corp.; launched on 24 October 1919; sponsored by Mrs. Emilie Neilson Worden; and commissioned on 24 February 1920 at the Boston Navy Yard, Lt. Comdr. David H. Stuart in command.

The destroyer spent the first four years of her decade of active service in operations along the Atlantic coast of the United States. After fitting out, she departed Boston, loaded torpedoes and spare parts at Newport, and embarked upon her shakedown cruise to Key West and Cuban waters. She completed that voyage at New York on 1 May and joined Destroyer Division 42, 3d Squadron, Atlantic Fleet. From May to July, she conducted operations along the length of the Atlantic seaboard, from Key West to Newport. On 21 July, she arrived in Charleston and remained there until the following summer. On 25 June 1921, she departed Charleston for a 4th of July visit to New York and gunnery practice off Block Island. In August, she made a voyage to Guantanamo Bay, Cuba, with Naval Academy midshipmen embarked, returning them to Annapolis, Md., on the 22d.

Worden stopped briefly at Hampton Roads, then headed via New York to Boston for repairs at the navy yard which she completed early in November. On the 16th, she loaded torpedoes at Newport and headed south to Charleston, where she arrived on the 18th. She remained there until the spring of 1922. On 29 May of that year, she got underway for a voyage which took her up the coast to Philadelphia; thence to Yorktown, a temporary base for battle practice and gunnery drills. Late in July, *Worden* made a brief cruise to New York and then returned to the southern drill grounds located off the Virginia capes.

During August, September, and October, she conducted battle practice off the capes, departing the area periodically for visits to New York; Beaufort, N.C.; and Newport. On 21 November, the destroyer entered port at Boston for a repair period which lasted until the end of 1922. Shen then left Boston and loaded torpedoes at Newport on New Year's Day 1923. On 5 January, she arrived at Lynnhaven Roads, Va., but, soon thereafter, continued south to Guantanamo Bay, Cuba, where she resumed gun and torpedo drills through the end of the month. On 12 February, she transited the Panama Canal with the Scouting Fleet for Fleet Problem I, the first set of combined maneuvers with Battle Fleet, conducted in the Gulf of Panama. She retransited the canal on 27 March and resumed training in the Guantanamo Bay area until late April. After visits to several gulf coast ports—Galveston, Tex.; New Orleans, La.; Tampa, Fla.; and Key West, Fla.—she returned to Newport on 15 May. Early in June, she visited Washington, D.C., and, by mid-month, had entered the Philadelphia Navy Yard for repairs. *Worden* left Philadelphia on 12 October and resumed gunnery drills and battle practice at the southern drill grounds off the Virginia capes. Those drills, punctuated by visits to Fall River, Mass., and to Baltimore, Md., occupied her time until mid-November, at which time she entered the Philadelphia Navy Yard for repairs to a ruptured boiler.

On 3 January 1924, *Worden* departed Philadelphia and, after a brief stop at Lynnhaven Roads, Va., rendezvoused with Scouting Fleet as a unit of its screen. Conducting drills and exercises along the way,

Scouting Fleet headed for Colon, Panama, where the warships refueled before continuing on to Culebra Island with the combined United States Fleet (Scouting Fleet and Battle Fleet). *Worden* participated in the annual spring exercises in the West Indies until late spring. On 4 May, she arrived back in Philadelphia to prepare for her first and only deployment outside the western hemisphere. After a brief repair period at Boston and a visit to Newport, she headed across the Atlantic in mid-June. On the 27th, she passed through the Strait of Gibraltar to begin a year of duty with the United States Naval Forces in Europe. During the early portion of that tour, *Worden* called at Palermo, Sicily, and then headed for the Adriatic Sea.

Her tour in the Adriatic was prompted no doubt by the murder of two Americans in the newly established state of Albania and the internal strife which followed and which resulted in the brief ouster of Prime Minister Ahmed Zogu and his temporary replacement by a provisional government under Bishop Fan Stylian Noli. During her stay in the Adriatic, *Worden* visited Pola and Venice in Italy and Spalato in Yugoslavia as well as Durazzo in troubled Albania.

Later in the year, the destroyer left the Mediterranean for visits to Gravesend, England; Cherbourg, France; Leith, Scotland; and Amsterdam in the Netherlands. At the conclusion of that circuit, she returned to the Mediterranean and continued her tour of duty with Naval Forces, Europe, until the summer of 1925.

She returned to New York on 16 July of that year and resumed her former schedule of operations with the Scouting Fleet. On 13 September, she entered the Philadelphia Navy Yard for repairs. The destroyer did not leave the yard until December. On the 7th, she headed south to join in the annual winter maneuvers held in the West Indies and in Panama Bay on the Pacific side of the isthmus. Scouting Fleet transited the canal on 4 and 5 February 1926 to join Battle Fleet for Fleet Problem VI in Panama Bay. In March, *Worden* returned to the Caribbean with Scouting Fleet and resumed battle practice, gunnery drills, and torpedo exercises in the West Indies. She completed that phase of her 1926 training schedule late in the spring and arrived back in Philadelphia on 5 May. During the early part of the summer, the warship continued her training schedule, this time off the New England coast near Narragansett Bay. On 2 July, she entered the Philadelphia Navy Yard for a three-month repair period.

On 11 October, *Worden* stood out of Philadelphia on her way south once more. After a brief stop at Hampton Roads, the destroyer continued on her way and arrived in Guantanamo Bay, Cuba, on the 16th. For the next month, she conducted engineering trials and battle practice near Haiti in the Gulf of Gonaives. Returning north in mid-November, she visited the Naval Academy for a time before heading back to Philadelphia where she arrived on 15 December. The warship bade farewell to Philadelphia once again on 5 January 1927 and pointed her bow southward for a stop at Yorktown followed by the 1927 edition of the annual winter maneuvers. She reached Guantanamo Bay on 12 January and commenced gunnery and battle practice with Scouting Fleet in preparation for the annual Fleet problem.

In contrast to the previous fleet problems in which she had participated, Fleet Problem VII brought Battle Fleet to the Caribbean instead of taking Scouting Fleet to the Pacific. The exercise was staged in March; and, by late April, *Worden* had returned north, this time to New York City. During the summer of 1927, she conducted normal training exercises off the Atlantic coast and participated in the Fleet Review conducted off Cape Henry, Va., in June for President Calvin Coolidge. On 11 September, she entered the Philadelphia Navy Yard and remained there for the rest of the year.

On 7 January 1928, she started south from Philadelphia. This time, however, she participated only in the preliminary drills and exercises for the annual fleet problem. She headed back to Philadelphia in April and arrived there on the 14th. Meanwhile, Scouting Fleet and Battle Fleet joined and executed Fleet Problem VIII in the broad expanse of the Pacific between San Francisco, Calif., and the Hawaiian Islands. A month later, *Worden* returned to sea for her usual round of operations along the Atlantic seaboard. That duty lasted until late in October at which time her base of operations changed to Charleston, S.C. Local operations out of that port occupied her time until early December when she returned north to Philadelphia for a month. In January 1929, she moved to Norfolk for repairs to her turbines; and, after post-repair trials in the Chesapeake Bay in February, she headed south for winter maneuvers. The destroyer arrived at Guantanamo Bay on 28 February. She concluded her part in those exercises later in the spring and returned north, arriving in New York on 2 May. During the summer, she conducted normal operations along the northeastern coast. On 21 September, *Worden* arrived in Philadelphia. The warship remained there until she was decommissioned on 1 May 1930. Her name was struck from the Navy list on 22 October 1930, and she was sold for scrapping on 17 January 1931.

III

(DD–352: dp. 1,726; l. 341'3''; b. 34'2''; dr. 8'10''; s. 36.5 k.; cpl. 186; a. 5 5'', 4 .30-cal. mg., 8 21'' tt., 2 dct.; cl. *Farragut*)

The third *Worden* (DD–352) was laid down on 29 December 1932 at the Puget Sound Navy Yard; launched on 27 October 1934; sponsored by Mrs. Katrina L. Halligan, the wife of Rear Admiral John Halligan, Commander, Aircraft, Battle Force; and commissioned on 15 January 1935, Comdr. Robert E. Kerr in command.

After fitting out, *Worden* departed Puget Sound on 1 April 1935 for her shakedown cruise that took her first to San Diego, Calif., and thence along the coast of Lower California and Mexico to San Jose, Guatemala, and Punta Arenas, Costa Rica. The new destroyer then transited the Panama Canal on 6 May and steamed north to Washington, D.C., where on 17 May she embarked Rear Admiral Joseph K. Taussig, Assistant Chief of Naval Operations, along with a congressional party, for a cruise down the Potomac River to Mount Vernon.

Worden subsequently returned to the Washington Navy Yard where her guns were disassembled for alterations. She then shifted south on 21 May to the Norfolk Navy Yard. In the ensuing weeks, the ship underwent voyage repairs at Norfolk. The yard work was broken once by trials and tests off Rockland, Maine, and completed in the early summer. She ultimately left the Norfolk Navy Yard on 1 July and spent the weekend of the 4th at New Bedford, Mass., before setting her course for the west coast. After proceeding via Guantanamo Bay and the Panama Canal, she arrived back at the Puget Sound Navy Yard on 3 August.

After a post-shakedown refit at her builders' yard, *Worden* shifted south to San Diego, reaching that port on 19 September, and commenced four years of operations from there as a unit of Destroyer Squadrons, Scouting Force. She performed valuable duty as a training ship for the Fleet Sound School, San Diego, and conducted the usual tactics and type training evolutions in local waters and in maneuvers that took her from Seward, Alaska, to Callao, Peru. She also participated in regularly scheduled fleet problems and battle tactics with combined forces of the United States Fleet in the Caribbean Sea and in the Hawaiian Islands. One of the highlights of her operations during that time came in the autumn of 1939. In mid-September—*Worden*, in company with *Hull* (DD–350) and escorting the aircraft carrier *Ranger* (CV–4)—voyaged to Callao, Peru, for a visit that coincided with the Inter-

American Technical Aviation Conference at Lima. While *Ranger* proceeded independently homeward upon conclusion of her visit, the destroyers paused at Balboa, Canal Zone, before returning to San Diego.

The coming of war in Europe on 1 September 1939 altered *Worden*'s somewhat idyllic pattern of operations out of San Diego. Five days after hostilities began in Poland, the Navy commenced its Neutrality Patrol duties on 6 September. On 22 September, the Chief of Naval Operations directed the Commander in Chief of the United States Fleet to transfer, temporarily, to the Hawaiian area two heavy cruiser divisions, a destroyer flotilla flagship (a light cruiser), two destroyer squadrons, one destroyer tender, an aircraft carrier, and base force units necessary for servicing those ships. That dispatch marked the establishment of the Hawaiian Detachment—the forerunner of the ultimate basing of the Fleet at Pearl Harbor.

Worden was attached to this new force, commanded by Vice Admiral Adolphus Andrews, whose flag flew in the heavy cruiser *Indianapolis* (CA–35). On 5 October 1939, she sailed for Pearl Harbor with Andrews and his large "detachment."

Worden worked primarily in the Hawaiian Islands over the next two years, interspersing her time at Pearl Harbor and its environs with regular periods of upkeep on the west coast. Intensive type-training and tactical evolutions in task force exercises and maneuvers kept the Hawaiian detachment busy while the world watched Japan continue a bloody undeclared war in China. Upon the conclusion of Fleet Problem XXI in the Spring of 1940, the entire Fleet was based in Hawaiian waters.

On the morning of 7 December 1941, *Worden* lay in a nest alongside destroyer tender *Dobbin* (AD–3), receiving upkeep. She suffered no damage in the attack made by Japanese carrier-based planes that occurred on the "date that will live in infamy," but one of her gunners, Quartermaster 3d Class Raymond H. Brubaker, trained his .50-caliber Browning machine gun on a low-flying bomber and sent it splashing into the waters nearby. Within two hours of the commencement of the attack, *Worden* had gotten underway and was proceeding to the open sea.

Although, in the operational plans for the attack, Japanese submarines were supposed to pick off American ships as they emerged from Pearl Harbor, their attempts to carry out the mission failed dismally. The danger of enemy submarines, however, did exist; and purported submarine sightings proliferated. Thus, many depth charges churned the sea that December day and killed a great number of unfortunate fish.

Worden picked up a submarine contact at 1240—well over three hours after the attack by the enemy aircraft had been completed—and dropped seven depth charges. That afternoon, the destroyer joined a task force built around the light cruiser *Detroit* (CL–8), the flagship of Rear Admiral Milo Draemel. Searching the seas southwest of Oahu, *Worden* rendezvoused with the fleet oiler *Neosho* (AO–23) and escorted her to a fueling rendezvous with Admiral Aubrey W. Fitch's Task Force (TF) 11 built around the aircraft carrier *Lexington* (CV–2).

While *Neosho* fueled the ships of TF 11 on the morning of 11 December, *Worden* assumed a screening station on *Lexington*'s bow and the next night escorted *Neosho* away from danger when *Dewey* (DD–349) discovered what looked like a surfaced enemy submarine and went on the offensive. After having seen *Neosho* to a safe haven at Pearl Harbor, *Worden* returned to the open sea on 14 December as part of the covering force moving toward beleaguered Wake Island. Hampered by the indecision attendant upon an unexpected change of command at the top of the Pacific Fleet, the Wake Island Relief Expedition was recalled on the morning of 22 December; and the island fell two days before Christmas.

Worden returned to patrol and escort operations in the Hawaiian Islands; and, while thus engaged with the *Lexington* task force, twice dropped depth charges on suspected enemy submarine contacts off Oahu on 16 January 1942 and again six days later.

Detached from TF 11 on the last day of the month, *Worden* left Pearl Harbor on 5 February to escort the seaplane tender *Curtiss* (AV-4) and the fleet oiler *Platte* (AO-24), via Samoa and the Fiji Islands, to New Caledonia, and reached Noumea on 21 February. Three days later, when the merchantman SS *Snark* struck a mine in Bulari Passage, *Worden* went to her assistance, passing a tow line to the sinking ship and pulling her clear of the channel entrance. *Worden*'s medical department tended six injured men, and the ship brought the crew safely to port.

Departing Noumea on 7 March, *Worden*—in company with *Curtiss*—set course for Pearl Harbor and reached that port on the 19th. That day, the destroyer entered the navy yard there and, after her repairs had been finished, joined TF 11 on 14 April.

Worden headed out to sea on the 15th, in company with the *Lexington* task force, bound for a rendezvous area southwest of the New Hebrides Islands, where, on 1 May, they joined Rear Admiral Frank Jack Fletcher's TF 17, built around the carrier *Yorktown* (CV-5). On the 2d, after the two carrier task forces had fueled, *Worden* was detached to escort the fleet oiler *Tippecanoe* (AO-21) to Noumea. In her absence, the American carriers—in the Battle of the Coral Sea —blunted a powerful Japanese thrust toward Australia and the tenuous Allied supply lines and turned it away from strategic Port Moresby.

On 12 May—two days after she reached Noumea— *Worden* was joined in that port by the cruisers and destroyers of the former *Lexington* task force. "Lady Lex" had succumbed to massive internal explosions and fires started during the battle. As part of that group, *Worden* put to sea on the 13th and, the following day, rendezvoused with TF 16 off Efate in the New Hebrides. Formed around the carriers *Enterprise* (CV-6) and *Hornet* (CV-8), this force was commanded by Vice Admiral William F. Halsey.

TF 16 reached Pearl Harbor on the 26th to fuel and replenish stores on the eve of what seemed to be shaping up as a critical battle. American intelligence men had cracked enough of the Japanese fleet's naval code to be able to determine the enemy's future course of action and had picked up information which indicated that Japan planned a major thrust centering on Midway and including a diversionary strike in the Aleutians. Accordingly, Admiral Chester W. Nimitz, Commander in Chief, Pacific Fleet, took decisive action and prepared for what history would record as the turning point of the war in the Pacific—the Battle of Midway.

Worden sailed on 28 May with TF 16—the force now under the command of Rear Admiral Raymond A. Spruance, who had replaced Halsey. Later, TF 17— formed around the hurriedly repaired and replenished *Yorktown*—rendezvoused with Spruance's force to the north of Midway.

Worden screened *Enterprise* and *Hornet* throughout the Battle of Midway as planes from those carriers and from *Yorktown* turned back the Japanese armada from 4 to 6 June 1942. *Worden* returned to Pearl Harbor on the 13th and was soon assigned to the screen of a revitalized TF 11, built around the newly repaired *Saratoga* (CV-3). The destroyer escorted *Saratoga* as she sailed to Midway and flew off reinforcement groups of Army and Marine Corps aircraft before returning to the Hawaiian Islands for training.

On 9 July, *Worden* headed for the South Pacific with *Saratoga*'s task force but was temporarily detached on the 21st to escort *Platte* to Noumea, reaching that port four days later. While *Platte* took on her vital cargo to replenish ships of the carrier task force, *Worden* patrolled the harbor entrance. On the 28th, *Worden* and *Platte* got underway to rejoin *Saratoga*. En route on the first night out, *Worden* sighted

signal lights in the darkness. She soon took on board 36 survivors of the sunken Army transport *Tjinegara* which had been torpedoed on the 25th by the Japanese submarine *I-169* and sunk about 75 miles southwest of Noumea.

Worden returned to the *Saratoga* group to the south of the Fiji Islands on the following day, when the carrier forces joined marine-laden troop transports that had sailed from Wellington, New Zealand, for the invasion of the Solomon Islands. Her stay with the carrier was brief, for the destroyer was soon detached to escort the fleet oiler *Cimarron* (AO-22) to Noumea, where she landed the *Tjinegara*'s survivors on 1 August.

Worden caught up with TF 16 on 3 August and, shortly before daybreak on the 7th, was screening *Saratoga* as the carrier launched air strikes against Japanese positions on Guadalcanal and Tulagi preparatory to the landings. Their efforts, together with those of the cruisers and destroyers, provided the coordinated shore bombardment which covered the 20,000 marines who went ashore to begin the campaign that would— after six months of the fiercest fighting of the war— evict the Japanese from Guadalcanal the following February.

For the next two weeks, *Worden* operated with *Saratoga* south of the Solomons protecting supply and communication lines leading to Guadalcanal. During the Battle of the Eastern Solomons, *Worden* screened the flattop as she launched air strikes in company with *Enterprise* to sink the Japanese carrier *Ryujo* and damage the seaplane tender *Chitose*. Less than a week later, however, Japanese submarine *I-26* torpedoed *Saratoga* and put her out of action, necessitating a trip to the mainland United States for repairs.

Worden screened *Saratoga*'s retirement via Tongatabu in the Tonga Islands to Pearl Harbor, arriving there on 23 September. Five days later, she sailed with two other destroyers—screening the battleships *Idaho* (BB-42) and *Pennsylvania* (BB-38)—for the west coast of the United States. She reached San Francisco on 4 October but departed again a week later with *Gansevoort* (DD-608) to accompany *Idaho* to Puget Sound where they arrived on the 14th. *Worden* soon returned south to San Francisco and later joined *Dewey* in screening *Nevada* during her post-repair trials in the San Pedro-San Diego area.

Two days after Christmas 1942, *Worden* sailed from San Francisco to support the occupation of Amchitka Island in the Aleutians. She reached Dutch Harbor, Alaska, on New Year's Day 1943 and, on 12 January, was guarding the transport *Arthur Middleton* (AP-55) as that transport put the preliminary Army security unit on the shores of Constantine Harbor, Amchitka Island. The destroyer maneuvered into the rock-edged harbor and stayed there until the last men had landed and then turned to the ticklish business of clearing the harbor.

A strong current, however, swept *Worden* onto a pinnacle that tore into her hull beneath her engine room and caused a complete loss of power. *Dewey* passed a towline to her stricken sister and attempted to tow her free, but the cable parted, and the heavy seas began moving *Worden*—totally without power— inexorably toward the rocky shore. The destroyer then broached and began breaking up in the surf; Comdr. William G. Pogue, the stricken destroyer's commanding officer, ordered abandon ship; and, as he was directing that effort, was swept overboard into the wintry seas by a heavy wave that broke over the ship.

Pogue was among the fortunate ones, however, because he was hauled, unconscious, out of the sea. Fourteen of his crew drowned. *Worden*, herself, was a total loss. Her name was struck from the Navy list on 22 December 1944.

Worden (DD-352) earned four battle stars for her World War II service.

IV

(DLG–18: dp. 7,903; l. 533'; b. 53'; dr. 24'6''; s. 34 k.; cpl. 400; a. 4 3'', 6 12.75'' tt., 1 ASROC, 2 Terrier mis. ln.; cl. *Leahy*)

The fourth *Worden* was laid down on 19 September 1961 by Bath Iron Works Corp., Bath, Maine; launched on 2 June 1962; sponsored by Mrs. William R. Smedberg III; and commissioned at Boston on 3 August 1963, Capt. Scott Lothrop in command.

Following her commissioning, *Worden* spent a two-month fitting-out period at the Boston Naval Shipyard. The guided missile frigate departed Boston on 12 October, bound for Bermuda for shakedown training. She then proceeded to Hampton Roads and sailed from Norfolk on 28 October for her home port, San Diego, Calif., arriving there on 13 November. Following a trip to Dabob Bay and Seattle for sonar measurements, *Worden* became the flagship of her squadron.

In January 1964, *Worden* fired a series of missiles at the Pacific Missile Range for systems qualifications tests. She continued operations in the San Diego area until she entered the Long Beach Naval Shipyard in March for a post-shakedown availability which was completed in early May.

From 18 May to 26 June, the ship participated in underway training at San Diego. *Worden*'s first fleet exercise took place from 10 to 17 July, a major antiair warfare exercise. On 11 August 1964, the frigate sailed for the western Pacific for a Far East deployment. After refueling at Midway and Guam, the ship arrived in Subic Bay, Philippines, on 30 August and became an active participant in 7th Fleet activities. *Worden*

visited Yokosuka, Japan, in late October and early November, then continued operations in Southeast Asia until the end of 1964.

On New Year's Day, 1965, *Worden* entered the port of Hong Kong for a period of rest and recreation. After a brief visit to Yokosuka, Japan, the frigate set course for the United States on 24 January. The ship arrived at her home port on 17 February and remained in port through 5 March when the ship commenced a three-month restricted availability at the Long Beach Naval Shipyard.

On 2 June 1965, *Worden* returned to San Diego for evaluation of a newly installed radar system. She continued to operate in her home port area and participated in Fleet Exercise "Range Bush" off the coast of southern California during the period 18 through 24 November 1965. She ended the year making preparations for deployment to the western Pacific.

The frigate departed her home port on 7 January 1966 for Subic Bay, Philippines, via Pearl Harbor and Guam. She arrived at the Philippines on 30 January and, the following day, set course for the Gulf of Tonkin and operations with the 7th Fleet. On 4 February, *Worden* assumed "Tomcat" duties west of Hainan Island. After an eight-day visit to Sasebo, Japan, *Worden* departed on 1 March and returned to the Gulf of Tonkin to assume plane-guard duties for *Ranger* (CVA–61).

On 19 March, the frigate received a helicopter detachment on board; and, the following day, a rescue helicopter from *Worden* pulled a downed Phantom pilot from the water three miles from the beach, saving him from certain capture by North Vietnamese junks

USS *Worden* (DLG–18) at high speed.

converging on the area. Another such rescue was effected on 23 May. *Worden* conducted operations in the Gulf of Tonkin until 17 June when she completed her commitment and proceeded to Yokosuka, Japan, for a short upkeep period prior to the return trip to California.

The frigate arrived at San Diego, Calif., on 10 July. During the period 11 September to 21 October, the ship fired a series of missiles at the Pacific Missile Range, Pt. Mugu, Calif., as part of a missile test project. As of 31 December 1966, *Worden* was moored at the Naval Station, San Diego, preparing for future operations involving the project.

January 1967 was spent providing services for continued missile tests, and the frigate remained in port during February, training and preparing for an upcoming deployment. On 13 March, *Worden* took part in the second "Comtuex" of the year, then returned to San Diego.

Worden began a six-month deployment to the western Pacific on 8 April when she sailed for Japan via Pearl Harbor. On 26 April, the frigate arrived at Yokosuka, Japan. May began with *Worden* en route to Subic Bay via the Okinawa missile range. On 14 May, the ship reached Danang, South Vietnam, and served on a search and rescue station until mid-September with intermittent periods of upkeep and liberty at Subic Bay, Hong Kong, Sasebo, and Yokosuka. During a visit to Hong Kong on 13 August, a Greek freighter lost control and rammed *Worden* on the starboard side inflicting minor damage. As the frigate departed Hong Kong for Subic Bay, she sighted and rescued a dugout canoe with three Philippine nationals who had been adrift for three days.

On 14 September 1967, *Worden* departed the search and rescue station the last time for Yokosuka via Subic Bay. The ship departed Japan on 23 September for Pearl Harbor, thence to San Diego, arriving on 6 October. *Worden* remained in port until 16 November when she conducted local operations and type training. With the exception of a dependent's cruise and an off-load of ammunition at Seal Beach, *Worden* remained in port at San Diego for the month of December and thus ended the year.

The early days of 1968 found *Worden* at San Diego, Calif., completing plans and preparations for yard overhaul, her first since commissioning. On 9 January, the frigate sailed to the San Francisco Bay Naval Shipyard where she entered drydock. The major shipyard jobs were completed toward the middle of April. On 6 May, the ship began sea trials, and the overhaul was officially completed on 13 May 1968.

Upon returning to San Diego two days later, *Worden* conducted various exercises and evaluations in preparation for an upcoming western Pacific deployment. On the 1st of July, the frigate commenced six weeks of refresher training. The 16th day of August marked the end of refresher training and the beginning of a period of logistics and material pre-deployment preparations. The ship spent the month of September conducting missile firings and antisubmarine warfare exercises. During the period 1 to 10 October, *Worden* joined in Exercise "Beat Cadence," a simulation of the Tonkin Gulf task organization.

After a brief tender availability, *Worden* departed San Diego en route to Subic Bay, Philippines, via Pearl Harbor, arriving on 22 November. Three days later, the ship departed Subic Bay and became involved in a search and rescue (SAR) incident when a helicopter with nine Navy men on board ditched in the approach to the harbor. All of the men were rescued, and the helicopter was towed by boat to a nearby beach.

Worden then steamed to Danang, South Vietnam, for SAR briefings and anti-PT boat exercises before assuming duties as commander of the task unit at the northern SAR station. The frigate shifted to the southern SAR station on 5 December and remained on station without incident until 29 December when *Coontz* (DLG-9) relieved the ship. *Worden* then proceeded to

Kaohsiung, Taiwan, for an overnight logistics stop en route to Sasebo, Japan, for repairs and a well-earned rest.

The New Year, 1969, found *Worden* en route to Sasebo, Japan. After stopping at Keelung, Taiwan; and Subic Bay, Philippines; the ship returned to the northern SAR station, Danang, South Vietnam, on 25 January 1969. She remained on station through 18 February when she departed for Subic Bay; then to Singapore and Hong Kong. The frigate returned to her station on 14 March for a week of service before departing the last time for Subic Bay, arriving on 23 March. For the remainder of the month, she conducted task group operations.

Worden returned to Subic Bay on 4 April, then began a cruise which took her to Sydney, Australia (14 to 21 April); Wellington, New Zealand (25 to 27 April); and Pago Pago, American Samoa (1 May). The ship arrived at San Diego, Calif., on 8 June and conducted a Secretary of the Navy guest cruise and a materiel inspection through 30 June.

The frigate conducted local operations throughout July and August. On 22 September, she set sail for Acapulco, then transited the Panama Canal. *Worden*'s ultimate destination was Bath, Maine, where, on 10 November 1969, she was decommissioned at Bath Iron Works Corp.

The lengthy yard period which followed was the product of a Navy-wide program to enhance the anti-air warfare capability of all guided missile frigates which included the installation of the Navy Tactical Data System (NTDS) and two Terrier missile directors.

Worden was recommissioned at the Bath Iron Works 18 months later on 16 January 1971. On 6 February, the ship departed for the transit to her new home port of Long Beach, Calif. After a period of refresher training at Guantanamo Bay, Cuba, and liberty at Acapulco, *Worden* arrived at Long Beach on 19 March 1971. During the next two months, the ship underwent an intensive training period off the southern California coast in connection with the modernization program.

On 7 July 1971, the frigate entered the Long Beach Naval Shipyard for an eight-week period of postshakedown availability. The ship began preparations for her fourth overseas deployment beginning on 7 September following her departure from the shipyard. In late August, *Worden* crew members learned the ship was to be permanently assigned to the 7th Fleet with a home port change to Yokosuka, Japan. This major policy decision alleviated the burden of long family separations.

Worden got underway on 20 October 1971 for her new home port. She stopped briefly at Pearl Harbor before arriving at Yokosuka on 11 November. During the last six weeks of the year, *Worden* conducted special operations in the Sea of Japan and enjoyed a month-long holiday rest.

The frigate sailed from Yokosuka on the 3d of January 1972 for special operations in the Sea of Japan. Returning to Yokosuka on 17 January, the ship prepared for the first cruise in three years to the Gulf of Tonkin. These preparations took her to Buckner Bay, Okinawa, and Subic Bay, Philippines.

On 6 February, *Worden* left the Philippines and proceeded west to assume duties in the Gulf of Tonkin. The frigate operated on the northern SAR station, then moved closer to the North Vietnamese coast off Thanh Hoa until 11 March when she proceeded back to her home port, Yokosuka, Japan. After a month of operations off Japan and Okinawa in connection with amphibious Exercise "Golden Dragon," *Worden* moved south to help counter a North Vietnamese major offensive. She assumed duties as an escort for *Coral Sea* (CVA-43).

The first major air strike on Haiphong since 1968 took place on the 15th of April. During the strike, *Worden* was damaged by two anti-radiation missiles inadvertently fired by United States support aircraft.

One crew member was killed, and nine others were seriously injured; they were airlifted by helicopter to the carrier *Tripoli* (CVU–64) for treatment. *Worden* proceeded to Subic Bay for a 10-day repair period. The frigate returned to the Gulf of Tonkin until 11 May and operated as an escort for *Kitty Hawk* (CVA–63). She took a break from 8 to 11 May and assumed a search and rescue station off Thanh Hoa during the first mine-laying strikes on North Vietnam.

On 16 May 1972, *Worden* began a restricted availability at Yokosuka, Japan, followed by missile tests at Okinawa. On 20 June, she returned to duties at the southern SAR station, operating off Cape Mui Ron for the next month. After a brief visit to Yokosuka, *Worden* returned to the Gulf of Tonkin on 9 August and served as escort for *Midway* (CVA–41) and *Kitty Hawk*.

Worden moved to the middle search and rescue station off Vinh on the 1st of October, then to the southern station shortly after. On 17 October, *Worden* departed for Hachinohe, Japan, and Navy Day festivities. The ship went into drydock at Yokosuka on the 25th of October for replacement of both propellers. *Worden* again returned to the Gulf of Tonkin on 18 November where she operated until 5 December. After a visit to Taiwan, the frigate finished out the year at Yokosuka, Japan, in a much-needed standdown period.

Operations in the Gulf of Tonkin and in-port periods characterized *Worden*'s employments during 1973. Support of Task Force (TF) 77 and TF 78 was interspersed with needed repair availabilities in Yokosuka, Japan, and Subic Bay, Philippines, and relaxing port visits to Hong Kong and Taiwan.

On 28 January 1973, the Vietnam cease fire was announced, and *Worden* joined TF 78 at Subic Bay. During the sweeping of Haiphong harbor, she functioned as Rear Admiral McCauley's flagship as well as the helicopter support platform, the repair and logistic facility for the minesweeping units, and task force antiair warfare and surface defense. For later operations, the frigate served on antiair picket station and as the Positive Identification and Radar Advisory Zone (PIRAZ) station. Besides the inherent responsibility for aircraft control and identification and air surveillance, *Worden* functioned as search and rescue asset coordinator and platform for the pre-positioned helicopter.

After the combat and post-hostility period had ended, *Worden* began stressing new phases of operations: antisubmarine warfare and engineering readiness. The last underway period of the year, 30 November to 3 December, was spent conducting ship antisubmarine tactics with *Bausell* (DD–845) and *Darter* (SS–576). *Worden* returned to Yokosuka to a Christmas holiday upkeep period and a rest from the activities of the past year.

Worden's first exercise of the new year 1974 was "Aswex 3–74" (Taeknando III) with the Republic of Korea Navy, conducted from 14 to 17 January. After a brief return to Yokosuka, she participated in joint Exercise "Fly-A-Way" off Okinawa, returning to her home port on 8 February.

The ship remained in Yokosuka until 25 February in upkeep status, then sailed for Subic Bay, Philippines, for surface missile exercises. The missile exercises marked the first multi-ship missile exercise in the western Pacific of the post-Vietnam era. *Worden* followed these exercises with a port visit to Keelung, Taiwan, and tender availability at Sasebo, Japan. On 29 March, the frigate departed Sasebo for operations with *Midway* (CVA–41) in the Sea of Japan. She also joined *Parsons* (DDG–33) in a search and rescue exercise simulating a North Korean surface unit. *Worden* returned to Yokosuka on 7 April to begin a lengthy upkeep period in preparation for her representation of the United States at the Shimoda Black Ship Festival on 15 May. On 10 May 1974, a major earthquake occurred on the Izu Peninsula causing extensive damage to the Shimoda area. As a result, the Black Ship

Festival was cancelled, and *Worden* continued upkeep with a brief underway period for type training.

The ship got underway on 25 May and joined *Midway* (CVA–41) and the task group to conduct air operations in the Yokosuka and northern Japan operations areas. While underway, *Worden* joined the Japanese Maritime Self Defense Force in joint Exercise "Aswex 5–74." On 4 June, *Worden* was detached from *Midway* and proceeded independently to the Okinawa missile range to conduct missile firing tests followed by a port visit to Keelung, Taiwan. While in port, eight first class NROTC midshipmen embarked in *Worden* to participate in the six-week "Westpactramid 1–74."

On 27 June, *Worden* returned to Yokosuka to begin a short upkeep period to prepare for the American-Japanese midshipmen exchange cruise. The frigate sailed from Yokosuka on 17 July in company with *Midway* and the task group for air operations off northern Japan. After a brief stop in Yokosuka, *Worden* departed on 22 July for Kure, Japan, to participate in the midshipmen exchange cruise. The final phase of the cruise took place in port at Yokosuka on 30 and 31 July and included spirits and social events. *Worden* remained in Yokosuka until 2 August, when she sailed for task group operations along the northern coast of Japan. On 15 August, she began a period in port at Yokosuka and, in late August, sailed for the eastern Pacific, nearer the United States than she had been since deploying to the Pacific in October of 1971. During this period, *Worden* remained in the company of *Kanin*, a Kynda II-Class Soviet cruiser.

Worden departed the area on 4 September for Hong Kong, thence to Yokosuka, Japan. Upon arrival on 25 September, *Worden* underwent upkeep, then sailed to Sasebo to embark Japanese officers for training. *Worden* made rendezvous with *Midway* and conducted an operational readiness inspection en route to Yokosuka. Arriving in port on 11 October, the ship began an upkeep period and was drydocked on the 25th. Three days of underway training late in November signaled the approaching end of the upkeep period. Following a Thanksgiving celebration, the ship got underway for Manila, Philippines, arriving there on 4 December. Four days later, she joined *Midway* and steamed for northern Japan, conducting Operation "Command Diamond," a major Air Force and Navy exercise off Okinawa on 16 December. *Worden* arrived in Yokosuka on 19 December and entered a holiday period which closed the year 1974.

The frigate departed the naval ship repair facility at Yokosuka on 13 January 1975 en route to Subic Bay, Philippines. During this two-week at-sea period, she conducted antiaircraft and antisubmarine warfare operations with *Midway*. The ship arrived on 27 January for a week at Subic Bay and participated in Operation "Readex" before returning to Yokosuka on 19 February. Upon arrival, she commenced a 20-day availability period; and, on 11 March, she got underway for 10 days of routine flight operations off Okinawa. She then returned to Yokosuka where she commenced upkeep and preparation for an upcoming cruise. On 25 March, *Worden* got underway for Pusan, Korea, for a port visit, thence to Subic Bay for operations. After completing operations, *Worden* headed for Thailand and a much awaited port visit.

The frigate, as part of the 7th Fleet, assisted in the evacuation of Americans from Vietnam as part of Operation "Frequent Wind." As the operation came to a close on 3 May, *Worden* returned to Thailand to resume her port visit. However, the capture of the SS *Mayaquez* by the Cambodians on 13 May interrupted her stay; and she sailed for Hong Kong. The *Mayaquez* was freed before *Worden* reached the British crown colony, so she proceeded to Yokosuka, arriving there on 20 May.

After various inspections, *Worden* operated with *Midway* for 11 days in mid-June; followed by a dependents' cruise. By directive from the Secretary of the Navy, dated 30 June 1975, *Worden*'s designator was changed from a guided missile frigate (DLG) to a guided missile cruiser (CG). Following an at-sea period from 8 to 21 July with *Midway*, *Worden* conducted a midshipmen cruise with the Japanese Maritime Self Defense Force. August saw operations in ocean areas between Japan and Okinawa with *Midway* in preparation for "Midlink–75," a CENTO exercise in the Indian Ocean. *Worden* and *Midway* arrived in Yokosuka on 22 August for a lengthy upkeep period.

On 4 October 1975, the cruiser got underway for "Midlink-75," the first stop being Subic Bay, Philippines. En route, she participated in Exercise "Cape Diamond." Departing Subic Bay on 14 October, she joined Exercise "Merlion" with the Royal Singapore Navy and Air Force off the coast of Malaysia. On 30 October, she arrived at Colombo, Sri Lanka. On 3 November, the cruiser got underway for Bandar Abbas, Iran, conducting naval maneuvers and training exercises en route. On 11 and 12 November, elements of the Pakistan Navy joined *Worden* and conducted training before she arrived at Bandar Abbas. After a week in Iran attending conferences and meetings to plan the at-sea operations, the cruiser departed on 19 November to Exercise "Midlink-75." Ten days later, *Worden* departed for her home port of Yokosuka, Japan, via Subic Bay, Philippines. During her brief stay at Subic Bay, the cruiser enjoyed the honor of a visit by the Honorable J. William Middendorf II, Secretary of the Navy. The ship entered Yokosuka harbor on 19 December and celebrated the holiday season at her home port.

Worden entered the bicentennial year moored at the Yokosuka Naval Base, Yokosuka, Japan. On 3 January 1976, the cruiser sailed from Yokosuka, making port visits to Hong Kong; Okinawa; Pusan, Korea; and Sasebo, Japan; with exercises and task group operations held en route. The ship returned to her home port on 2 February and began a pre-overhaul restricted availability. *Worden* went into drydock from 20 February until 22 June, and the regular overhaul came to a close on 6 December. On 13 December, *Worden* went to sea for five days of independent steaming exercises; then the cruiser returned to Yokosuka on 17 December and spent the holiday season in port.

During the first six months of 1977, *Worden* conducted comprehensive post-overhaul training and inspections in the areas of Yokosuka, Japan; and Subic Bay, Philippines. Operations commenced on 18 June at Subic Bay with "Multiplex" exercises. After a port visit to Singapore, *Worden* arrived at Yokosuka on 14 July and remained in port through 23 July when she set sail for Subic Bay. The cruiser conducted underway replenishment drills and "Missilex" exercises before arriving in Hong Kong on the morning of 13 August.

On 2 September, *Worden* returned to her home port of Yokosuka and began preparing for an upcoming deployment. This deployment commenced on 27 September when *Worden* sailed for Subic Bay, thence to Victoria Quay, Fremantle, Australia, for a month-long visit. The ship then visited Bandar Abbas, Iran, from 9 to 21 November and Singapore from 5 to 11 December. *Worden* arrived at Yokosuka, Japan, on 21 December and enjoyed a period of leave and liberty for the holiday season.

From 14 to 21 January 1978, *Worden* cruised to Chinhae, South Korea. After briefly returning to Yokosuka on 25 January, the cruiser left again for operations with *Midway* and the task group. On 13 February, *Worden* and *Midway* rendezvoused with TF 77 and conducted "Readex 78," maneuvering to avoid detection by "enemy" ships and land-based aircraft from Okinawa while positioning for a simulated assault on the island of Okinawa. On 19 February, *Worden* got underway for Yokosuka, via Chinhae, South Korea. She arrived there on 27 February and began an in-port period.

Worden's in-port period was marked by several inspections, an open house, plus visits from staff members of the 7th Fleet and officers of the Japanese Maritime Self Defense Force. On 23 March, the ship departed for Chinhae and conducted antisubmarine warfare training en route. Once anchored, she completed the final phase of a Navy technical proficiency inspection. She returned to her home port on 28 March and conducted operations with *Midway* from 11 to 23 April. Preparations for a material inspection continued throughout April and May. *Worden* spent May in an upkeep period in Yokosuka with support from the destroyer tender *Prairie* (AD–15) and the Yokosuka repair facility.

On 30 May, the cruiser departed for Keelung, Taiwan, her first liberty port in 1978. *Worden* returned to Yokosuka on 9 June for a brief four-day visit before joining carrier task group activities in the northern Philippine Sea. She returned to Yokosuka, Japan, on 28 June for an in-port period which ended on 19 July with a three-week transit to Subic Bay with the *Midway* task group. Having detached from task group operations and traveled to Buckner Bay, Okinawa, *Worden* commenced "Missilex 4–78" on the morning of 1 August. Due to three successive unsuccessful launch attempts by the Japanese antiaircraft training ship *Azuma*, the exercise was cancelled, and *Worden* headed back to Subic Bay, Philippines, and a week of upkeep.

After successfully completing a missile shoot on 12 August, the cruiser returned to Yokosuka briefly before taking part in task group operations on 22 August. On 1 September, she paid Chinhae, Korea, a port visit, then returned to her home port one week later. From 19 September to 2 October, *Worden* operated with *Midway*, after which time she conducted a two-day, combined antisubmarine warfare exercise with elements of the Republic of Korea Navy. The cruiser continued operations with *Midway*, then returned to Yokosuka for an in-port period.

On 6 November 1978, *Worden* got underway from Yokosuka for underway tests and evaluations. She took part in "Maulex 1–79," an amphibious exercise involving units of the United States and Republic of Korea Navies, then celebrated Thanksgiving at Hong Kong. On 3 December, the ship entered Subic Bay, Philippines, for various tests and then made rendezvous with *Midway* and returned to Yokosuka, Japan, on 22 December for the duration of the holiday season.

Worden spent the year 1979 operating out of Yokosuka, Japan, and was still homeported there as of early 1980.

Worden earned nine battle stars for her Vietnam service.

Worland

A town in Bates County, Mo., and the county seat of Washakie County, Wyo.

(PCE–845: dp. 903 (f.); l. 184′6″; b. 33′1″; dr. 9′5″; s. 15.4 k.; cpl. 99; a. 1 3″, 6 40mm., 2 dct.; cl. *PCE–842*)

PCE–845 was laid down on 24 July 1943 at Chicago, Ill., by the Pullman Standard Car Manufacturing Co.; launched on 1 December 1943; and commissioned on 1 March 1944 at New Orleans, Lt. Glenn W. Morrow, USNR, in command.

Following shakedown, *PCE–845* departed Miami, Fla., on 18 April, bound for Port-of-Spain, Trinidad, British West Indies. The patrol escort operated with Admiral Jonas I. Ingram's 4th Fleet, escorting coastal convoys between Port-of-Spain and Brazilian ports such as Recife, Bahia, Belem, and Rio de Janeiro until December. Departing Trinidad on the 7th, *PCE–845* shaped a course for the Florida keys and a stint of training operations before departing Key West on 21 January 1945 and heading for the Pacific.

The escort vessel arrived at Hollandia, New Guinea,

USS *Worland* (PCE–845). (NH 85418)

on 2 March, whence she was routed onward to the Philippines. Operating out of Mangarin Bay, Mindoro, she conducted escort missions and antisubmarine patrols to the western and southwestern islands of the Philippine Archipelago. In July, she began patrolling Leyte Gulf and continued the mission until V–J Day in mid-August.

Departing San Pedro Bay, Leyte, on the 15th, *PCE–845* escorted the kamikaze-damaged destroyer *Hugh W. Hadley* (DD–774) to Hawaii, arriving at Pearl Harbor on 24 August. For the next two years, the escort vessel operated out of that base on air-sea rescue and weather patrols as a unit of Service Squadron 7.

On 30 August 1947, the small ship sailed for the mainland of the United States. Proceeding via San Diego and the Panama Canal, *PCE–845* arrived at Algiers, La., on 2 October and was subsequently decommissioned at Galveston, Tex., on 22 December and laid up.

Reactivated three years later for service as a naval district training ship, she initially operated out of New Orleans, attached to the 8th Naval District. In this role, her mission occasionally took her to the Mexican port of Veracruz. Then, after proceeding up the Mississippi River late in 1950, *PCE–845* was recommissioned at Chicago, Ill., on 11 December, for service on the Great Lakes for the 9th Naval District.

Over the next 14 years, the patrol craft made regular reserve training cruises on Lakes Superior and Michigan. On 15 February 1956, the ship was named *Worland*.

She departed Chicago on 6 April 1964, bound for the eastern seaboard. En route, she called at Milwaukee, Detroit, and Quebec before arriving at Philadelphia on 28 April. Decommissioned on 25 May 1964, *Worland* was assigned to the Philadelphia Group of the Atlantic Reserve Fleet.

Struck from the Navy list on 1 June 1964, *Worland* was subsequently acquired on 6 August 1964 by the Cape Fear Technical Institute of Wilmington, N.C., and renamed *Advance II*, commemorating the Confederate blockade runner *Advance* of Civil War days. She serves as a training and research ship in the marine technology program of the Cape Fear Technical Institute.

Worthington

Cities in Minnesota and Ohio and a town in Indiana.

(PC–1137: dp. 280; l. 173'8''; b. 23'0''; dr. 10'10'';
s. 20.2 k. (tl.); cpl. 65; a. 1 3'', 1 40mm., 5 20mm.,
2 dct., 2 K-guns, 2 dcp. (mousetrap); cl. PC–461)

PC–1137 was laid down on 29 December 1942 at Bay
City, Mich., by the Defoe Shipbuilding Co.; launched
on 29 March 1943; towed down the Mississippi River
to New Orleans for outfitting and acceptance trials;
and commissioned there on 23 October 1943, Lt. George
D. Lewis, USNR, in command.

After shakedown training out of the Submarine
Chaser Training Center at Miami, Fla., PC–1137 headed for the southwestern Pacific late in November. She
transited the Panama Canal on 5 and 6 December and
arrived at Guadalcanal in the Solomon Islands on 18
February 1944. Assigned to Task Group (TG) 35.6, the
ship spent the next five months escorting convoys
among various American bases in the southwestern
Pacific and conducting antisubmarine patrols from
bases throughout the Solomons chain. On 26 July, she
concluded that duty and began training to prepare for
the invasion of the Western Carolines. Those preparations lasted until 4 September, at which time she departed Guadalcanal in the screen for LST Flotilla 13,
bound for the Palaus.

During the initial assault on Peleliu between 14 and
16 September, she served as forward control and reference ship for the landings on Orange Beach 3. On the
16th, she completed that assignment and began screening the operational area against Japanese submarine
attack. She remained so occupied until 15 November
when she received orders assigning her to TG 96.3 at
Eniwetok Atoll and signaling a return to convoy escort
duty. Between 23 November 1944 and 3 March 1945, the
warship travelled the circuit between Eniwetok, Ulithi,
Guam, and Saipan, screening supply and reinforcement
convoys.

On 4 March, PC–1137 set a course for Pearl Harbor.
She arrived at Oahu on 13 March and began a seven-
week repair period during which she was converted to
a combat communications control ship. She completed
repairs and conversion near the end of the first week in
May and then spent the following week in amphibious
training exercises at Maui. On 21 May, PC–1137 put
to sea with LST Flotilla 35 en route to the Mariana
Islands. She arrived at Saipan on 10 June and reported
for duty as a convoy escort. For the remainder of the
war, she made the convoy run between the Marianas
and Okinawa in support of the final campaign of World
War II and conducted antisubmarine patrols out of
Apra Harbor, Guam. On 20 August, five days after the
cessation of hostilities, she was officially reclassified a
combat communications control ship, PCC–1137. After a
repair period in late August and early September, the
ship departed Guam on 20 September, bound for Japan
and duty in the occupation forces there.

She arrived in Tokyo Bay on 25 September and
joined TG 53.4. The submarine chaser operated in Japanese waters with the occupation forces until the beginning of 1946. After several months service in the
Central Pacific—notably at Truk, Eniwetok, and Guam
—she departed Eniwetok to return to the United States.

The ship made a six-day stopover at Pearl Harbor
and then continued on to the west coast, arriving in
Astoria, Oreg., on 27 May. She began the inactivation
process immediately and was decommissioned on 10
August. Berthed with the Columbia River Group,
Pacific Reserve Fleet, PCC–1137 lay idle during the remaining 12 years and six months of her Navy career.
On 15 February 1956, she received the name Worthington, one she wore for only three years. On 29 May
1959, her name was struck from the Navy list; and,
presumably, she was sold for scrapping.

Worthington earned one battle star during World
War II as PC–1137.

Wovoka

A Paiute Indian—born in about 1856 in the Mason
Valley of Nevada—who while in a delirium, during or
near 1888, had a dream that he described as a revelation from the Great Spirit. As a result of this experience, he became a prophet, foretelling of the return to
the old way of life for the Indians, and instituted a
"ghost dance" that became widespread among his fol-
lowers. However, when his prophecies failed to materialize, his popularity diminished, especially in view of
the Sioux uprisings in 1890 and 1891. He gradually lost
his adherents and died, relatively unnoticed, in 1932. He
was buried on the shore of Walker Lake, Nevada.

(YTB–396: dp. 345 (f.); l. 100'0''; b. 25'0''; dr.
11'0''; s. 12 k.; cpl. 14; cl. Sassaba)

Wovoka (YT–396) was laid down on 10 March 1944
at Jacksonville, Fla., by Gibbs Gas Engine Co.; reclassified YTB–396 on 15 May 1944; launched on 28
July 1944; sponsored by Mrs. Ruth J. Martin; and
delivered to the Navy on 2 March 1945.

After intial service in the 12th Naval District, San
Francisco, Calif., Wovoka was inactivated and placed
out of service in March of 1946. Her stay in the reserve
fleet, berthed at Seattle, Wash., was a comparatively
short one, for she was reactivated in September of 1950
during the fleet-wide expansion caused by the Korean
War. Soon thereafter, she resumed her unsung but vital
tasks as a harbor tug at San Francisco and provided
tug and tow services in the 12th Naval District into the
early 1970's. Reclassified a medium harbor tug, YTM–
396, in February of 1962, with the advent of larger,
more powerful tugs, Wovoka was ultimately placed out
of service. Struck from the Navy list on 1 June 1974,
she was sold in October 1974.

Woyot

The dialect spoken by the Mission Indians of southern California; also, one of their gods who, according
to legend, died and returned to life as the moon.

(YT–150: dp. 325 (f.); l. 100'0''; b. 25'0''; dr. 9'7''
(f.); s. 12 k.; cl. Woban)

Woyot (YT–150) was laid down on 3 October 1940
at Bay City, Mich., by the Defoe Bridge & Metal
Works; launched on 18 April 1941; completed and delivered to the Navy on 3 June 1941 and placed in
service on 7 June 1941.

The harbor tug soon began duty in the 5th Naval
District and served in the vicinity of Norfolk and
Hampton Roads through the end of World War II. On
15 May 1944, Woyot was reclassified a large harbor tug
and was redesignated YTB–150. Sometime between 1
March and 1 July 1946, she was placed out of service,
in reserve, and was berthed at Green Cove Springs
with the Florida Group, Atlantic Reserve Fleet.

She was laid up until September 1950 when she was
reactivated in response to the increased need for ships
occasioned by the outbrak of war in Korea. Initially,
the tug was assigned to the 6th Naval District; but,
by 1 January 1953, she had returned to the 5th Naval
District and Norfolk, Va. There, she spent the remaining 16 years of her Navy career. In February 1962,
Woyot changed classifications again, this time to be a
medium harbor tug, YTM–150. On 1 July 1969, after a
career which spanned almost three decades, Woyot was
placed out of service and her name struck from the
Navy list. On 7 May 1970, the tug was sold to a private
citizen.

Wrangell

A volanic mountain in southeastern Alaska, near the Yukon territory.

(AE–12: dp. 11,295; l. 459'2''; b. 63'0''; dr. 28'3''; s. 16.4 k.; cpl. 267; a. 1 5'', 4 3'', 4 40mm., 10 20mm.; cl. *Mount Hood*; T. C2–S–AJ1)

Wrangell (AE–12) was laid down under a Maritime Commission contract (MC hull 1375) as SS *Midnight* on February 1944 at Wilmington, N.C., by the North Carolina Shipbuilding Corp.; launched on 14 April 1944; sponsored by Mrs. G. T. Cambell; delivered to the Navy, incomplete, on 28 May 1944; moved to Hampton Roads, Va.; converted to an ammunition ship by the Norfolk Shipbuilding and Drydock Co.; and commissioned on 10 October 1944 at the Norfolk Navy Yard, Comdr. Haskell C. Todd in command.

Following shakedown in Hampton Roads, *Wrangell* sailed on 13 November for the Naval Ammunition Depot, Earle, N.J., to load ammunition. Escorted by the destroyer *Borie* (DD–704), she stood out to sea on the last day of the month and headed for the Panama Canal. The ammunition ship transited the isthmian waterway on 7 December; and, although initially ordered to proceed directly to the Marshall Islands, was rerouted to Hawaii.

Wrangell arrived at Pearl Harbor on 21 December, but got underway again on Christmas Eve, bound for the Marshalls. Arriving at Eniwetok on the last day of 1944, the ammunition ship joined a Ulithi-bound convoy (number 31) that day and pushed on for the Carolines. *Wrangell* dropped anchor in Ulithi Lagoon on 5 January and reported for duty to Commander, Service Squadron 10. Over the next five months, *Wrangell* operated from Ulithi supporting the Fleet's operations against Iwo Jima, Okinawa, and the Japanese home islands. In those months, she transferred over, 10,000 tons of all types of ammunition to combatant ships steaming alongside while underway and would frequently serve two ships at a time: heavy ships (battleships, aircraft carriers, and heavy cruisers) alongside to port and light units (light cruisers and destroyers) alongside to starboard.

On her first operation, *Wrangell* reached Iwo Jima on 22 February and supplied bombardment forces there with ammunition over the next six days until she re-

tired from the area on the 28th. The nature of operations at Iwo, coupled with the deep waters relatively close inshore, prevented the ship's anchoring and necessitated conducting cargo operations while either drifting or underway at slow speed.

After retiring from Iwo Jima on 28 February, *Wrangell* proceeded to the Marianas and arrived at Saipan on 3 March. From that island, she proceeded independently to Ulithi where she anchored three days later. On the 13th, the ammunition ship sortied with Task Group (TG) 58.8 and supported Task Force (TF) 58 over the ensuing days as it attacked enemy shore installations and shipping in preparation for the invasion of the Ryukyus and hit Okinawa itself when troops finally landed on that island on 1 April.

Between 22 March and 18 April, *Wrangell* rearmed over 50 combatant ships. On the 19th, in company with Task Unit (TU) 50.8.6, the ship was detached from TG 50.8 at sea and proceeded south to Ulithi, arriving there on 22 April.

However, with the Okinawa campaign at its height, her respite from operations proved to be a short one. Admiral Mitscher's task force was daily striking the Japanese-held islands of the Nansei Shoto and along the coast of the Japanese home islands, and required replenishment. Thus, after 10 days of round-the-clock reloading, *Wrangell* departed Ulithi on 2 May and, three days later, rendezvoused with TG 50.8 southeast of Okinawa. From 6 May to 1 June, *Wrangell* passed ammunition "to all comers"—rearming as many as a dozen ships a day—and she filled the magazines of over 50 in the three-week period.

She then retired to San Pedro Bay, Leyte, in the Philippines, for upkeep and repairs. *Wrangell* subsequently returned to the open sea on 8 July and rendezvoused with TG 30.8 (the redesignated TG 50.8) on the 17th. From 20 July to 1 August, she rearmed 35 ships and hit a high point of transferring 700 tons of ammunition in a single day.

Wrangell was detached from TG 30.8 on 2 August and headed south for the Philippines. Arriving at San Pedro Bay on 6 August, the ship immediately commenced replenishing her stocks of ammunition. Work was interrupted on 10 August, though, when the fleet received the news that Japan was willing to surrender. Cargo operations were secured that night, as all hands eagerly awaited news about Japan's future actions.

The ammunition ship *Wrangell* (AE–12) in the South China Sea, 1966.

After Japan capitulated, *Wrangell* paused briefly in Tokyo Bay to take part in the initial phase of the occupation of the erstwhile enemy's home islands, before she pushed on for the Philippines and, ultimately, home, that autumn. Departing Philippine waters on 25 October, *Wrangell* steamed via Pearl Harbor, reached the coast of Panama on 21 November, and transited the canal later that day. She subsequently unloaded ammunition and ordnance supplies at Earle, N.J., and headed for the Gulf of Mexico on 16 January 1946. She arrived at Orange, Tex., five days later, and was ultimately placed in reserve on 17 May. She was decommissioned and laid up at Orange on 19 November 1946.

The outbreak of war in Korea in the summer of 1950 prompted the Navy to recall many inactive ships from the "mothball" fleet. *Wrangell* was one of them and was recommissioned on 14 November 1951 at Orange, Capt. Olin P. Thomas in command. The ammunition ship shifted to New York, her new home port, and arrived there on 21 December. She soon headed south to Norfolk for an administrative inspection and repairs alongside a tender.

Wrangell loaded ammunition at Earle, N.J., between 23 May and 18 June after operating out of Boston and Newport, R.I., for a time, and in June, once more conducting underway training evolutions out of Newport. In the summer, she participated in exercises at Onslow Beach, N.C., and at Newport before taking part in Operation "Noramex" in the North Atlantic. These replenishment exercises conducted off the coast of Labrador were her first since World War II.

Wrangell made her first deployment to the Mediterranean between January and June 1953, touching at ports that ranged from Gibraltar to Bizerte, Tunisia; Marseille to Golfe Juan, France; from Augusta, Sicily, to Bari, Italy; and from Oran, French Morocco, to Taranto, Italy, before she returned to New York on 10 July, via Gibraltar.

After local operations and repairs, *Wrangell* sailed for her second Mediterranean deployment in the autumn. At 1014 on 4 October 1953—while en route from Reykjavik, Iceland, to Bizerte, Tunisia, in company with the oiler *Aucilla* (AO–56)—the ammunition ship sighted a fishing vessel flying international distress signals. *Wrangell* maneuvered near the drifting vessel and lowered a boat with a boarding party, Ens. P. R. Frosell in charge. *Wrangell*'s men found the fishing boat, *Jules Verne* (registered at Douarnenez, France), to have wreckage strewn about topside and two feet of water in her engine compartment. The investigation also revealed the only living occupant of the craft to be a dog; the boarding party also found the corpse of a man estimated to have been dead for five days.

Leaving food and water for the dog, the boarding party soon returned to the ship, and *Wrangell* took *Jules Verne* under tow. At 1403 the next day, 5 October, *Jules Verne* began to founder, however, and sank eight minutes later; the dog, swimming in the water, was hauled on board *Wrangell*, whose crew adopted the animal and made him the ship's mascot.

Ultimately arriving at Bizerte on 9 October, *Wrangell* operated with the 6th Fleet only briefly, touching at Cagliari, Sardinia; Taranto, Italy; Suda Bay, Crete; Phaleron Bay, Greece; and Naples, Italy, before returning via Gibraltar to New York and the naval ammunition depot at Earle.

Wrangell conducted three more Mediterranean deployments into the late 1950's, supplying 6th Fleet warships with ammunition. There were notable highlights during those deployments: in the autumn of 1956, during the Suez crisis, *Wrangell* supported the units of the 6th Fleet evacuating American nationals from the troubled area.

In mid-July 1958, President Dwight D. Eisenhower ordered marines to land in Lebanon to protect American lives and property. During the intervention, *Wrangell* participated in the 6th Fleet's operations, visiting Beirut four times in August and September, after

which time the ship proceeded to Naples, arriving there on 15 September.

In between Mediterranean deployments, *Wrangell*'s area of operations ranged from Charleston, S.C., to Holy Loch, Scotland; and from the Virginia capes to Guantanamo Bay, Cuba. During her operations, she conducted underway rearming experiments with a number of ships, including the then-new aircraft carrier *Forrestal* (CVA–59) and the guided missile cruiser *Boston* (CAG–1).

Wrangell continued alternating local operations off the eastern seaboard with Caribbean and Mediterranean deployments into the late 1960's. The ship's first replenishment of a nuclear-powered warship came on 17 August 1962, when she rearmed the nuclear-powered aircraft carrier *Enterprise* (CVAN–65).

In the autumn of 1962, after the discovery by reconnaissance aircraft of Soviet missiles in Cuba, President John F. Kennedy instituted a naval blockade of Cuba to turn back Russian ships that attempted to deliver more missiles and their support equipment to Cuban ports. During the crisis, *Wrangell* spent 35 days in the Caribbean, arming and rearming various units of the blockade force. Ultimately, the Russians removed the missiles from Cuba and thus eased the tension.

Wrangell conducted three more Mediterranean deployments in the first half of the 1960's and, between those deployments, conducted local operations on the eastern seaboard and into the Caribbean. After successive home-port changes over the years—from New York to Naples to Norfolk to Charleston—*Wrangell* was preparing for her 10th Mediterranean deployment when orders came directing her to sail for the Far East and her first service in the Pacific since World War II. She had been loading ammunition at Earle, N.J., for a week when the message arrived on 28 August rerouting her from the Mediterranean to the Pacific. The ship departed Charleston on 27 September 1965 in response to the critical need in the Southeast Asian area for ammunition ships, in keeping with the escalating nature of the war in Vietnam.

Transiting the Panama Canal on 2 October, *Wrangell* arrived at Pearl Harbor on the 19th, where she loaded additional ammunition. She soon sailed for Southeast Asian waters and, operating out of Subic Bay, Philippines, and making seven stints to the "line," provided ammunition for ships operating on both the "Yankee" and "Dixie" stations into the spring of 1966. During her five months in WestPac, *Wrangell* transferred over 6,800 tons of ammunition in 74 underway replenishments. In addition, besides ammunition, the ship delivered fleet freight, mail, transient personnel, movies, and, on two occasions, fresh water and provisions. Arriving back at Subic Bay after her seventh mission on the "line," *Wrangell* departed Philippine waters on 2 May.

On 21 June, *Wrangell* arrived back at Charleston, via Singapore; Bombay, India; the Suez Canal; Beirut, Lebanon; and Barcelona, Spain; thus completing a circumnavigation of the globe. *Wrangell* remained in the vicinity of Charleston for the remainder of the year, entering the Charleston division of the Jacksonville Shipyard Co. on 10 October 1966 for a major overhaul.

On 15 May 1967, *Wrangell* departed Charleston, bound again for the Mediterranean—arriving to "inchop" to the 6th Fleet at about the time of the outbreak of the Arab-Israeli War of 1967. She supported the 6th Fleet during that crisis situation and, after the abatement of the conflict, resumed routine operations—underway replenishments, alternated with port visits, "showing the flag" at ports like Corfu, Greece; Suda Bay, Crete; Ismir, Turkey; and Palma, Majorca.

Wrangell left the Mediterranean on 13 January, departing Rota, Spain, on that day and sailing for the east coast of the United States. Arriving back at Charleston 10 days later, the ammunition ship provided services that spring and exercised in various phases of training or upkeep. After short periods at the Naval Weapons Stations at Charleston, S.C., and Yorktown, Va.—where ammunition was transferred and the crew was indoctrinated to the special elements of weapons handling—*Wrangell* spent much time in drills and exercises to implement inport training.

Following upkeep and repair periods at the Charleston Naval Shipyard during April and May 1967, *Wrangell* prepared for her upcoming WestPac deployment. On 4 September 1967, the ammunition ship got underway; transited the Panama Canal; spent five days at Pearl Harbor; and, after evading Typhoon "Faye" off Wake Island, arrived at Subic Bay on 16 October. She soon departed Subic Bay for the coast of North Vietnam and employment on the "Yankee Station."

Wrangell finished out the year with three operating periods off the coast of Vietnam and in the Tonkin Gulf. The largest underway replenishments were conducted with such men-of-war as the battleship *New Jersey* (BB-62) and the carriers *Constellation* (CVA-60) and *Ranger* (CVA-61). In addition, she armed many smaller units—destroyers, guided missile destroyers, and Coast Guard cutters. One of the latter, *Winnebago* (WHEC-40), sent her whaleboat across to *Wrangell* on 21 November while off the Mekong Delta in what *Wrangell's* command history termed "what may well be history's smallest rearming." *Winnebago's* request: five rounds of 5-inch ammunition!

Only two days later, on 23 November, *Wrangell* and other American and South Vietnamese naval vessels took part in a search and rescue mission in the South China Sea. Despite the winds and heavy seas of Typhoon "Mamie," the ammunition ship located the Indian vessel *Laxmi Jayanti*, helpless due to a steering casualty. Ultimately, after making temporary repairs, the Indian ship resumed her voyage, under escort, to Saigon. *Wrangell*, her part in the search completed, headed for Subic Bay.

While en route back from Subic Bay to "Yankee Station," the ship received the nod for another mercy mission. On 3 December, *Wrangell* reversed course on orders from Commander, Naval Forces, Philippines, and rendezvoused with the freighter SS *American Pilot*, sending over a corpsman in the ship's motor whaleboat to assist a sailor who had suffered an arm wound that was bleeding profusely. After her corpsman had stanched the bleeding and given sufficient help to enable the man to be safely transferred to a shore facility for further treatment, *Wrangell* continued on for "Yankee Station." She subsequently spent Christmas in Hong Kong and later returned to the waters off the coast of Vietnam. There, she engaged in nearly continuous rearmings of a host of ships, including the attack carriers, *Ranger*, *Constellation*, and the veteran *Hancock* (CV-19), with Task Force 77. These operations were part of the ship's regular routine that alternated load-in operations at Subic Bay with replenishment work during line deployments in the South China Sea and Tonkin Gulf.

The end of January 1970 found the ship enjoying a temporary pause in her hectic schedule, undergoing a period of tender overhaul alongside the repair ship *Ajax* (AR-15) at Sasebo, Japan. Returning to Subic Bay soon thereafter, *Wrangell* loaded ammunition to return to the "line," in February.

After a series of routine rearmings near the demilitarized zone (DMZ), rough weather and high seas frustrated several attempts by the destroyer *George K. MacKenzie* (DD-836) to come alongside. Since the destroyer's magazines were low, the need to replenish her stocks was urgent; so *Wrangell* and *George K. MacKenzie* anchored inside the sheltered lee of Camranh Bay to effect the transfer. While nearby patrol craft periodically dropped antiswimmer charges and kept a lookout for possible Viet Cong interference in the operation, the job was completed in two hours. As the ship's history for the year stated: "For *Wrangell*,

the Camranh Bay episode was the closest she had ever brought her thousands of tons of ammunition to hostile fire. All hands breathed a sigh of relief when the exciting, risky rearming of the *MacKenzie* was over."

Back in Subic Bay on 10 April, *Wrangell* turned over ammunition ship duties to *Mazama* (AE-9) and headed for home two days later. However, before she coud complete the voyage, North Korean MiG fighters shot down an EC-121 reconnaissance plane over the Sea of Japan. The resulting crisis saw a show of American naval force in that area—a presence that *Wrangell* supported.

Wrangell transported ammunition from Sasebo to Yokosuka to Sasebo again before heading for Pearl Harbor on 3 May. During her recently completed deployment, she had supplied ammunition to ships ranging from the battleship *New Jersey* to the Coast Guard cutter *Ingham* (WMEC-35), transferring nearly 12,000 tons of that necessary commodity. Port visits included Subic Bay, Hong Kong, Singapore, Sasebo, Yokosuka, Pearl Harbor, Acapulco, and the Panama Canal before the ship eventually arrived back at her home port, Charleston, on 10 June 1969.

After repairs and underway training evolutions during the summer, *Wrangell* departed Charleston on 6 October, standing down the Cooper River, bound for what proved to be the ship's last Mediterranean deployment. Subsequently returning to the east coast, the veteran ammunition ship was decommissioned at Norfolk on 21 December 1970. Initially placed in reserve at Charleston, *Wrangell* was transferred to the Inactive Ship Facility at Norfolk in late February 1971 and was subsequently placed in the National Defense Reserve Fleet, James River berthing area, in the temporary custody of the Maritime Administration, on 29 April 1971. *Wrangell* was struck from the Navy list on 1 October 1976 and was awaiting final disposition in June 1979.

Wrangell earned three battle stars for her World War II service and a further five for her performance in the Vietnam war.

Wren

Solomon Wren—born in 1780 in Loudoun County, Va.—enlisted in the Marine Corps at Alexandria, Va., on 1 April 1799. Assigned to the schooner *Enterprise*, Wren rose in rank and, by the end of 1803, had been promoted to sergeant. In February 1804, Sgt. Wren volunteered for the expedition mounted to destroy the frigate *Philadelphia*, captured by the Tripolitan pirates on 31 October 1803 after grounding on an uncharted reef off Tripoli. Under the command of Lt. Stephen Decatur, Jr., Wren and 68 other sailors and marines entered Tripoli harbor on the night of 16 February in the ketch *Intrepid* and succeeded in setting fire to the former American ship. Later that year, on 3 August, Sgt. Wren was slightly wounded while assigned to *Gunboat No. 4* during another attack on Tripoli. On 20 September, he transferred to the frigate *John Adams* and returned home. He was detached from the Marine Corps on 24 March 1805, and no further record of his life has been found.

(DD-568: dp. 2,050; l. 376'6"; b. 39'8"; dr. 17'9"; s. 35 k.; cpl. 273; a. 5 5", 10 40mm., 7 20mm., 10 21" tt., 6 dcp., 3 dct.; cl. *Fletcher*)

Wren (DD-568) was laid down on 24 April 1943 at Seattle, Wash., by the Seattle-Tacoma Shipbuilding Corp.; launched on 29 January 1944; sponsored by Mrs. Jeanne F. Dockweiler; and commissioned on 20 May 1944, Comdr. Edwin A. McDonald in command.

Following commissioning, *Wren* operated out of San Diego conducting shakedown training. In August, she reported for duty with the Northern Pacific Force in the Aleutian Islands; and her duties there consisted largely of patrol and escort work between the islands of the Aleutian chain. She did, however, participate in four shore bombardment missions against the Japanese Kuril Islands with Task Force (TF) 92 between November 1944 and April 1945. Her first action occurred on 21 November 1944 when she participated in the shelling of Matsuwa. Her second and third bombardment missions took her to Paramushiro on 5 January and 18 February 1945, respectively. Her final bombardment of the Kurils took place on 15 March 1945, and Matsuwa again served as the target.

On 19 April, she stood out of Kulsk Bay, bound for Hawaii. The destroyer arrived at Pearl Harbor on the 25th but soon continued her voyage to the Western Carolines. She stopped at Ulithi Atoll until 17 May at which time she left the lagoon on her way to join in the six-week old Okinawa campaign. The ship served in the Ryukyus from 21 May to 18 June, performing antisubmarine patrols and standing antiaircraft radar picket watch. She came under air attack on several occasions but sustained no major hits while ending the careers of at least four of her airborne attackers.

Departing Okinawa on 18 June, she arrived at Leyte in the Philippines three days later and remained there until 1 July when she joined units of TF 38 for the final series of carrier-based aerial attacks on Japan. *Wren* spent the remaining weeks of the war at sea with TF 38 supporting the carriers while their planes struck the Japanese homeland.

On 26 August, *Wren* entered Tokyo Bay with other elements of the 3d Fleet to begin the occupation of Japan and to prepare for the formal surrender ceremony at which she was present on 2 September. She departed Japan that same day and, during the next month, visited Iwo Jima and Eniwetok. The warship returned to Tokyo on 13 October for a visit of just over a month. She departed Japan on 18 November and arrived at Oahu on the 28th. Resuming her voyage east on 1 December, she entered San Diego on the 7th. After a two-day visit, she headed—by way of the Panama Canal—for the Philadelphia Naval Shipyard where she arrived on 23 December. After an inactivation overhaul at Philadelphia, *Wren* moved to Charleston, S.C., late in March 1946. On 13 July 1946, the destroyer was placed out of commission at Charleston.

A little over five years later, on 7 September 1951, *Wren* was placed back in commission at Charleston, Comdr. George M. Hagerman in command. For the next two years, she operated along the eastern seaboard and in the West Indies. During the latter months of 1951, she conducted standardization and vibration tests under the auspices of the Bureau of Ships and its research facility at Carderock, Md., the so-called David Taylor Model Basin. She returned to Charleston in December and, throughout 1952 and for the first eight months of 1953, performed normal operations and training in the western Atlantic.

In August 1953, *Wren* was reassigned to Destroyer Division (DesDiv) 61 for deployment to the Far East. She stood out of Norfolk on 28 August and transited the Panama Canal on 2 September. After stops at San Diego, Pearl Harbor, and Midway, she arrived in Yokosuka on 3 October. A week later, she put to sea to join Task Force (TF) 77 in the Sea of Japan. The fast carriers conducted air operations there and in the Yellow Sea, and *Wren* provided screen and plane-guard services to them between 10 October and 26 November. Following that assignment, she joined the Australian carrier HMAS *Sydney* and provided similar services until mid-December when she returned to Japan at Sasebo for the Christmas holidays.

The destroyed rejoined TF 77 on 3 January 1954 and cruised with the carriers until the 17th when she became a unit of TF 95. She served along the Korean coast carrying out cease-fire surveillance missions with TF 95 until 1 February, when she returned to Sasebo to prepare for the voyage home. She departed Japan on 11 February and, taking a westward route through the Indian and Atlantic Oceans, completed a circum-

navigation of the globe when she arrived in Norfolk on 9 April.

For the remainder of her active career, *Wren* operated out of Norfolk periodically making overseas deployments. Among her 2d Fleet activities were midshipman summer cruises, some to northern European ports and others to West Indian and American ports. She also served with the 6th Fleet in the Mediterranean Sea on several occasions. Annual "Springboard" exercises took her to Puerto Rico, Cuba, and Panama each spring. During her 1957 Mediterranean deployment, the ship served with the Mid East Force in the Indian Ocean and participated in Operation "Crescent" with units of the Pakistani Navy. In December 1963, after almost a decade of duty with the Atlantic Fleet, *Wren* was placed out of commission, in reserve. She spent the next 11 years in the reserve fleet, berthed at Philadelphia. Her name was struck from the Navy list in December 1974. On 22 October 1975, she was sold to the North American Smelting Co., Wilmington, Del., for scrapping.

Wren earned three battle stars during World War II.

Wright

The first *Wright* (AZ-1) was named for Orville Wright; the second, CVL-49, honored both Wright brothers: Orville and Wilbur.

I

(AZ-1: dp. 11,500 (f.); l. 448'; b. 58'; dr. 23'4⅜'' (mean); s. 15 k. (max.); cpl. 288; a. 2 5'', 2 3'', 2 mg.; cl. *Wright*)

The first *Wright* (AZ-1) was originally the unnamed "hull no. 680" laid down at Hog Island, Pa., by the American International Shipbuilding Corp. under a United States Shipping Board contract. Named *Wright* on 20 April 1920, the ship was launched on 28 April. A little over two months later, the Navy signed a contract with the Tietjen and Lang Dry Dock Co. of Hoboken, N.J., to convert the ship to a unique type of auxiliary vessel—a "lighter-than-air aircraft tender." On 17 July 1920, the ship received that classification and was designated AZ-1.

Wright (AZ-1) was commissioned at the New York Navy Yard on 16 December 1921. Her first commanding officer was Capt. (later Admiral) Alfred W. Johnson, who also discharged the collateral duties of Commander, Air Squadrons, Atlantic Fleet. Johnson was the first of a long line of commanding officers for the ship, some of whom later distinguished themselves—men such as John Rodgers, Ernest J. King, Aubrey W. Fitch, P. N. L. Bellinger, and Marc A. Mitscher.

From the New York Navy Yard, *Wright* sailed for the Philadelphia Navy Yard and reached there on 22 February 1922. After installation of her armament, the lighter-than-air aircraft tender departed Philadelphia on 2 March, touching at Hampton Roads, Va., and Charleston, S.C., en route to the Florida coast. Arriving at Key West on the 11th, *Wright* reported for special duty with the first division of Scouting Squadron 1 —a unit that included the seaplane *NC-10* piloted by Lt. Clifton A. F. Sprague and a half-dozen F5L seaplanes. Three days later, the tender put to sea for operations with Scouting Division 1 out of Guantanamo Bay, Cuba. There, she was later joined by the six planes of Division 2 and two planes of Division 3.

Wright—fitted out with a unique "balloon well" built into the ship's hull, aft, to enable her to tend a kite balloon assigned to the ship for experimental operations—departed Guantanamo Bay on 10 April and—while en route back to Key West—conducted maneuvers to experiment with the kite observation balloon.

A few weeks after *Wright* reached her destination, the NC-10 flying boat had her bottom sucked out while she attempted to take off and began to sink in seven feet of water. A rescue and repair party salvaged the

The seaplane tender *Wright* (AV–1). (80–G–463531)

hull and other parts of the seaplane and brought them on board the tender. Two days later, *Wright* sailed for the Philadelphia Navy Yard and, after brief stops at Norfolk and Charleston en route, arrived there on 8 May.

Following repairs and alterations at Philadelphia between 8 May and 21 June, *Wright* headed south and conducted tending operations from Norfolk to Pensacola, Fla., and back. While in Hampton Roads on 16 July, *Wright* sent up her kite balloon for the last time before transferring it ashore to be based at the Hampton Roads Naval Air Station (NAS).

Later that summer, *Wright* visited New York City and then shifted to Newport, R.I., arriving there on 7 August. The ship tended seaplanes in that vicinity, as they engaged in formation bombing exercises on stationary and towed targets. *Wright* and her brood subsequently operated off Solomons Island, Md., where the seaplanes conducted battle practice and bombing rehearsals. From 15 to 24 September, she tended the 13 F5L seaplanes from Scouting Squadron 1 as they conducted bombing practice on towed targets in the Chesapeake Bay region. Later that autumn, *Wright* visited Baltimore.

Following her visit to that port, *Wright* cruised down the eastern seaboard for training operations out of Key West. On 28 January 1923, *Wright* departed Florida waters in company with the converted minesweepers *Sandpiper* (AM–51) and *Teal* (AM–23) and supported the 18 patrol planes of Scouting Squadron 1 in combined fleet tactics in waters ranging from Cuba and Honduras to the Panama Canal.

Between 18 and 22 February, *Wright*'s planes participated in Fleet Problem I—a phase of which tested the defenses of the Panama Canal. Assigned to the "Blue" fleet, *Wright* and the two sister "Bird-boats" (*Sandpiper* and *Teal*) tended the planes from Scouting Squadron 1 that assisted that force as well as Army coastal and air units in defending the Panama Canal against air attack. The attacking "Black" fleet used two battleships as substitutes for "aircraft carriers" which it did not possess. On 21 February, one of those simulated flattops, *Oklahoma* (BB–37), launched a single plane to scout ahead of the "Black" fleet, and, the following morning, sent a single plane aloft. That aircraft—which took off from Naranyas Cay—represented a carrier air group, and made her approach to the canal undetected. It dropped 10 miniature bombs and theoretically "destroyed" the Gatun spillway.

After returning to Key West on 11 April, *Wright* spent the next two years off the eastern seaboard of the United States, operating out of Hampton Roads and Newport in waters that ranged from the Virginia capes to the Virgin Islands.

Wright ultimately departed Hampton Roads on 21 January 1925 as "flagship" for Capt. Harry E. Yarnell, Commander, Air Squadrons, Scouting Fleet, bound for the Pacific Ocean. After transiting the Panama Canal, the tender reached Pearl Harbor on 25 February and operated in the Hawaiian area until 8 June when she proceeded back to the east coast of the United States, reaching Norfolk on 18 July.

Soon after *Wright*'s return to the eastern seaboard, work began to convert the ship to a heavier-than-air aircraft tender; and, by 1 December, the work was complete. Reclassified AV–1, the tender continued to support the seaplanes of the Scouting Fleet, operating out of Hampton Roads and Newport, to ports of Florida, Cuba, and Panama. As flagship for Commander, Aircraft Squadrons, Scouting Force—reclassified to Commander, Aircraft, Scouting Force in 1932—*Wright* usually spent four months of each winter in operations out of Guantanamo Bay in waters reaching from Panama to the Virgin Islands. For the remainder of the year, she worked in the Narragansett and Chesapeake Bay areas, operating, as before, out of Hampton Roads and Newport with periodic cruises to the warmer climes of Florida or port visits to New York City.

Wright's tending duties along the eastern seaboard and into the Caribbean continued until 3 February 1932. Varying her duties as tender were several assignments for special service.

When the Coast Guard destroyer *Paulding* rammed and sank the submarine *S–4* (SS–109) on the afternoon of 17 December 1927 off Provincetown, Mass., *Wright* immediately loaded six salvage pontoons at the Norfolk Navy Yard and set out for the scene of the disaster. Although delayed by strong Atlantic gales, *Wright* reached Provincetown, via Boston, on the afternoon of 21 December.

Meanwhile, on the day that *Wright* departed Norfolk, her commanding officer, specially detached, Capt. Ernest J. King, took the train from Norfolk to New York and proceeded thence by plane to Provincetown. Arriving on board *Falcon* (AM–28) at 1315 on 18 December, Capt. King became senior aide to Rear Admiral F. H. Brumby and took direct charge of the salvage operations. *S–4* was finally brought to the surface on St. Patrick's Day 1928 and subsequently taken to the Boston Navy Yard.

Meanwhile, *Wright* had been detached from the operation two days after Christmas 1927 and returned to Norfolk. The following year, the ship's routine was broken by transporting building materials to the hurricane-devastated island of St. Croix; and, in 1929, she carried marines to Cuba when trouble threatened in Haiti.

Wright stood out of Hampton Roads on 5 January 1932 and supported air patrol squadron tactical evolutions ranging from Cuba and Jamaica to Coco Solo, Canal Zone. Arriving at the latter port on 1 February, the tender transited the isthmian waterway two days later, accompanying and tending the planes from Patrol Squadrons (VP) 2 and 5. After tactical evolutions off Acapulco and at Magdalena Bay, Mexico, *Wright* made port at NAS, North Island, San Diego, on 20 February.

From the time of her arrival at NAS, North Island, on 20 February 1932 until 10 September 1939, *Wright* made 14 extended cruises in support of naval seaplane squadrons. The first of those began when she departed San Diego on 1 May 1933 for an aviation transport run that included an inspection by Rear Admiral John Halligan, Commander, Aircraft Squadrons, Battle Force, of the Fleet Air Base (FAB) at Pearl Harbor. After returning to San Diego on 4 June, *Wright* operated along the west coast, followed by a cruise to Panama and the Caribbean, between 31 August and 14 October, tending the planes from VP-2F, VP-5F, VP-10, and Utility Patrol Squadron 3.

Wright sailed again for Hawaiian waters on 5 January 1934; and—in operations that took her from Hilo Bay, Hawaii, to Midway Island and French Frigate Shoals—tended 32 seaplanes. She then returned to San Diego on 30 May and departed again on 18 July for her first voyage to Alaskan waters. Steaming by way of Seattle, Wash., the tender visited Ketchikan and Juneau in early August before she tended two squadrons of seaplanes in waters near Seward and Sitka, Alaska. Proceeding via Vancouver, Briitsh Columbia, and San Francisco, *Wright* arrived back in San Diego on 6 September 1934 and remained in nearby waters for the rest of the year.

On 4 January 1935, *Wright* departed San Diego for tender operations off Panama; Cartagena, Colombia; Curaçao, Netherlands West Indies; Trinidad, British West Indies; and the Dominican Republic and Haiti. Upon completion of those exercises, she returned to San Diego on 1 March but soon sailed again for northern climes to operate between Dutch Harbor and Sitka from 29 April to 28 May before resuming her local tending operations along the coast of California.

Wright departed San Diego on 10 October and took up a plane guard station off Las Tres Marias, Mexico, soon thereafter, covering one leg of the flight of the Consolidated XP3Y which took off from Cristobal harbar, Canal Zone, on 14 October for a non-stop flight to Alameda, Calif. Commanded by Lt. Comdr. Knefler "Sock" McGinnis who was assisted by Lt. (jg.) J. K. Averill, Naval Aviation Pilot T. P. Wilkinson, and a crew of three—the plane passed abeam of *Wright* at 2210 on 14 October. That XP3Y reached Alameda in 24 hours and 45 minutes—thus establishing a new world's record for Class C seaplanes of 3,281.383 miles airline distance and 3,443.225 miles broken-line distance.

Returning to San Diego from her planeguard station on 17 October, *Wright* spent only a short period in port and sailed again four days later, for Palmyra Island. Reaching that point on the last day of October, *Wright* supported the planes photographing the island and served as "home" for the survey party sent ashore. Setting course for Pearl Harbor on 2 November, she later embarked men of VP-6F for transport to French Frigate Shoals. She then tended three squadrons of seaplanes off East Island while her diving party engaged in reef-blasting operations for the seaplane base being established there.

Terminating that support duty on 12 November, *Wright* headed for the west coast, reaching San Diego on 28 November. For the remainder of 1935, *Wright* operated locally. Her coastwise duties were interrupted

between 16 January and 28 February 1936 by an aviation support cruise to Post Office Bay, Galapagos Islands; Santa Elena, Ecuador; and Balboa, Canal Zone. *Wright* then participated in fleet problems off Lower California and cruised to Sitka Sound, Alaska, where she tended a utility plane wing (two squadrons) and a patrol wing of five squadrons, between 22 August and 28 September.

After repairs at the Mare Island Navy Yard, Vallejo, Calif., *Wright* departed San Diego on 10 October 1936 for Pearl Harbor and thence sailed once more to French Frigate Shoals, reaching there on 25 October. She then landed a camp detachment to establish a base on East Island, and tended seaplanes from VP-1, VP-3, VP-4, and VP-10 until 6 November.

After returning to the west coast, *Wright* subsequently made a winter training cruise to the Caribbean between 2 February and 26 March 1937 and then, after her return to San Diego, departed the west coast on 18 April in company with *Langley* (CV-1) for fleet problems that stretched to the Hawaiian Islands. Following her return to San Diego on 3 June, *Wright* spent the next year in coastal operations that took her as far south as Lower California. She made a cruise to Kodiak and Sitka Sound between 20 June and 5 August 1938. On 20 October of that year, Commander, Aircraft, Scouting Force, was detached from the ship; and *Wright* became flagship for Commander, Patrol Wing (PatWing) 1, Aircraft, Scouting Fleet.

The tender departed San Diego on 2 January 1939 to participate in winter maneuvers in the Caribbean with her aviation units and took part in Fleet Problem XX. Reaching Norfolk from Puerto Rico on 14 March, the seaplane tender returned to the west coast soon thereafter, as part of the general movement of the fleet from Atlantic to Pacific. Back at San Diego on 16 May, *Wright* operated out of that port until 10 September, when she sailed for the Hawaiian Islands to become flagship for PatWing 2, based at Pearl Harbor.

Arriving there on 19 September—less than three weeks after the outbreak of war in Europe—*Wright* spent the next two years supporting the establishment of aviation bases on Midway, Canton, Johnston, Palmyra, and Wake Islands. She transported marines and aviation personnel, as well as construction workers and contractors, between those valuable bases, time and again landing cargo that ranged from construction materials to gasoline and ordnance supplies and other advance base gear. In September 1941, *Wright* was selected as the flagship of PatWing 1, Aircraft, Scouting Force.

Wright departed Pearl Harbor on 20 November, bound for Wake Island, arrived at that advanced base on the 28th, and landed Comdr. Winfield S. Cunningham, who took command of the naval activities on the vulnerable isle. Other passengers who went ashore from the seaplane tender included asphalt technicians, other construction workers, and Marine Corps officers. The ship also delivered 63,000 gallons of gasoline to Wake's storage tanks before setting course for Midway. There, she delivered a cargo that included ammunition and disembarked passengers that included men reporting for duty at the NAS and with other Marine Corps ground units. Then, with military and civilian passengers embarked, *Wright* departed Midway on 4 December and headed for Pearl Harbor.

While en route, she received the electrifying news that the Japanese had attacked Pearl Harbor on the morning of 7 December. Word of the attack arrived shortly after 0800 that day, and *Wright* cleared for action and manned her battle stations. Fortunately for her, she never crossed the path of the Japanese striking force.

After reaching Pearl Harbor the day after the Japanese attack, *Wright* got underway on 19 December to transport 126 marines of the 4th Defense Battalion, with their gear, to Midway. She returned to Pearl Harbor on the day after Christmas with 205 civilians embarked. *Wright* then underwent voyage repairs, loaded stores and cargo, embarked passengers, and set sail for the South Seas.

Departing Pearl Harbor on 2 April, *Wright* touched at Tutuila, Samoa; the Fiji Islands; Espiritu Santo, in the New Hebrides—where she debarked men of VP–72—and Noumea, New Caledonia, before she reached Sydney, Australia, on 26 April. After visiting Melbourne and Fremantle, *Wright* headed for the Hawaiian Islands, retracing her course, and reached Pearl Harbor on 16 June. For the next five and one-half months, *Wright* shuttled military passengers, arms, gasoline, and other equipment to Midway and other defense bases of the Hawaiian Sea Frontier.

Leaving Oahu on 1 December, *Wright* headed for the South Pacific carrying, as passengers, the officers and men of Marine Scout Bomber Squadron (VMSB) 233 and VMSB–234, along with other passengers and logistic support cargo. The seaplane tender debarked the personnel from VMSB–233 at Espiritu Santo and those from VMSB–234 at Noumea before she returned to Pearl Harbor on 17 January 1943. She sailed thence to Midway, transporting a group of passengers that included 205 marines, and from there shifted to the Fiji Islands where she disembarked the 7 officers and 254 enlisted men of FAB Unit 13 who were put ashore with their gear and logistic cargo.

Departing the Fijis on 9 March, *Wright* sailed by way of Pearl Harbor, reaching Oakland, Calif., for an overhaul at the Moore Dry Dock Co. Following repairs and alterations, the tender put to sea on 20 July, bound for the Hawaiian Islands, and debarked the men of Marine Fighter Squadron (VMF) 223 at Pearl Harbor a week later.

Wright sailed again for the Fijis at the end of July, arriving there on 12 August; and landed the 46 officers and 399 men of VMF–222 and VMSB–236. She next proceeded to Rendova harbor, Rendova Island, and tended the planes of VP–14 until 17 January 1944. She then shifted to Hawthorn Sound, New Georgia, to tend that squadron along with those from VP–71 until 18 April.

Upon arriving at Gavutu harbor, Florida Island, in the Solomons, on 20 April, *Wright* loaded aviation stores before she proceeded to Espiritu Santo for repairs that lasted through the end of May. Underway on 1 June, *Wright* transported eight naval officers and 256 Army passengers to Tulagi harbor before she steamed to Blanche harbor on 5 June. A week later, eight planes—along with 26 officers and 52 men—from VP–101 arrived and operated from *Wright* until 17 June.

Heading for Seeadler Harbor on that day, *Wright* embarked passengers and loaded bombs and 170 bundles of cots for transportation to New Guinea. Reaching Humboldt Bay on 23 June, the ship tended the planes and housed the 30 officers and 54 men of VP–33 until 16 July, when she put to sea for Mios Woendi, in the Padiado Islands, Dutch New Guinea, arriving on the 17th. She then based five planes from VP–52—and supported the 36 officers and 66 enlisted men attached to the squadron—and three patrol planes from Royal Australian Air Force No. 20 Squadron from 19 to 26 July.

Rear Admiral Frank D. Wagner, Commander, Aircraft, 7th Fleet, broke his flag in *Wright* on 27 July and used the tender as his temporary flagship. That same day, VP–11 arrived at Mios Woendi and operated from *Wright*. VP–52 left for duty elsewhere on 3 August, the same day that the tender stood out of the Mios Woendi anchorage that had been her "home" for over a month, bound via Edema Island, British New Guinea, for the Admiralties. Returning to Mios Woendi on 27 August after safely delivering her cargo and passengers of Fleet Air Wing 17, *Wright* embarked the officers and men of Patrol Aircraft Service Unit 1–12 for transportation back to Seeadler Harbor, Manus, where she arrived on 3 September.

Departing Manus the following day, *Wright* sailed

for Milne Bay, New Guinea, where she debarked men from a construction battalion, and then proceeded with Pacific Service Force passengers, general cargo, and hospital patients to Brisbane, Australia. There, on 26 October, *Wright* embarked Rear Admiral Robert O. Glover, Commander, Service Force, 7th Fleet—along with his staff of 64 officers and 204 men—and became the flagship for Service Squadron 7, Service Force, Pacific Fleet. Reclassified as headquarters ship effective 1 October 1944, *Wright*'s designation was changed from AV–1 to AG–79.

Proceeding from Brisbane via New Guinea, *Wright* reached Seeadler Harbor on 5 January 1945, for repairs that lasted until the 14th. She then proceeded via Humboldt Bay to San Pedro Bay, Leyte, reaching Philippine waters on 3 February 1945. During her passage, the ship was renamed *San Clemente* on 1 February 1945, to clear the name *Wright* for the light fleet carrier, CVL–49, then under construction.

San Clemente remained as flagship for ServRon 7 and the nerve center of the Pacific Fleet Service Force, based on San Pedro, Subic, and Manila Bays, through the end of hostilities with Japan in mid-August of 1945 and the formal Japanese surrender on 2 September. She departed Manila on 3 January 1946, bound for the China coast; reached Shanghai soon thereafter; and became flagship for Service Division 101—Commodore E. E. Duval, commanding—on 5 February. *San Clemente* remained at Shanghai in support of the Navy occupation forces there until 7 April, when she was relieved by *Holland* (ARG–18) as flagship of ServRon 101. With hundreds of veterans embarked as passengers, *San Clemente* departed Chinese waters on 8 April, bound—via Yokosuka, Japan, and Pearl Harbor—for home.

Reaching San Francisco on 2 May, *San Clemente* got underway again eight days later and headed for the east coast of the United States. Reaching the New York Naval Shipyard (the old New York Navy Yard) on 29 May, she commenced inactivation proceedings and was decommissioned on 21 June 1946. Struck from the Navy list on 1 July 1946, the illustrious tender was transferred to the Maritime Commission for disposal on 21 September 1946. She was sold for scrap on 19 August 1948.

Wright (AV–1) earned two battle stars for her World War II service.

Wright (CV–47)—an *Essex*-class carrier laid down on 19 August 1944 at Quincy, Mass., by the Bethlehem Steel Company's Fore River plant—was renamed *Philippine Sea* (q.v.) on 13 February 1945, prior to the ship's launching.

II

(CVL–49: dp. 14,500; l. 684'; b. 76'9''; ew. 115'; dr. 28'; s. 33 k.; cpl. 1,787; a. 40 40mm.; ac. 50+; cl. *Saipan*)

The second *Wright* (CVL–49) was laid down on 21 August 1944 at Camden, N.J., by the New York Shipbuilding Corp.; launched on 1 September 1945 (the day before the formal Japanese surrender ceremony on board the battleship *Missouri* (BB–63) in Tokyo Bay); sponsored by Mrs. Harold S. Miller, a niece of the Wright brothers; and commissioned at the Philadelphia Naval Shipyard on 9 February 1947, Capt. Frank T. Ward in command.

Wright departed Philadelphia on 18 March 1947 and stopped briefly at Norfolk, Va., en route to the Naval Air Training Base at Pensacola, Fla. After her arrival there on 31 March, *Wright* soon commenced a rigorous schedule of air defense drills and gunnery practice while acting as a qualification carrier for hundreds of student pilots at the Naval Air Training Base, conducting 40 operational cruises—each of between one and four days' duration off the Florida coast. In addition,

483

the carrier embarked a total of 1,081 naval reservists and trained them in a series of three two-week duty tours.

On 3 September 1947, *Wright* embarked 48 midshipmen for temporary training duty and later welcomed 62 Army officers when she stood out to sea on 15 October in company with *Forrest Royal* (DD–872) to let her guests observe flight operations in the Pensacola area. The exercises included the catapulting of a Grumman F6F-type aircraft for rocket-firing operations.

That exercise was her last prior to her departure from Pensacola on 24 October to return north. She arrived at the Philadelphia Naval Shipyard soon thereafter and, from 1 November to 17 December, underwent post-shakedown repairs and alterations before she returned to Pensacola two days before Christmas where she resumed her regular schedule of pilot qualification training under the operational control of the Chief of Naval Air Training, Commander Air Atlantic. *Wright* spent the year 1948 engaged in those pilot carrier qualification operations, before she put into the Norfolk Naval Shipyard on 26 January 1949 to commence a four-month overhaul.

Following refresher training in Cuban waters, *Wright* returned to Norfolk on 1 August 1949 and four days later shifted to Newport, R.I., for two weeks of antisubmarine warfare (ASW) training in the Narragansett Bay area with submarines and destroyers. She also visited New York City before taking up a steady schedule of carrier qualifications, air defense tactics and exercises out of Quonset Point, R.I.; Key West and Pensacola, Fla. But for 10 days of maneuvers with the 2d Task Fleet from 21 to 31 October 1949, she continued that duty until 7 January 1951, when she embarked the last increment of personnel from Fighter Squadron (VF) 14 for temporary duty.

Wright then sailed from Norfolk on 11 January with a fast carrier task group and reached Gibraltar on the 21st for her first tour of duty with the 6th Fleet in the Mediterranean. *Wright*'s first Mediterranean deployment took her from Gibraltar to Oran, Algeria. She proceeded thence to Augusta Bay, Sicily; Suda Bay, Crete; Beirut, Lebanon; and Golfe Juan, France—her replenishment and liberty ports during the never-ending cycle of fleet training and readiness exercises with the 6th Fleet.

Departing Golfe Juan on 19 March, *Wright* made port at Newport on the 31st. The carrier later entered the Norfolk Naval Shipyard and underwent an overhaul there before she took part in Atlantic Fleet maneuvers out of Guantanamo Bay, Cuba; engaged in ASW tactics and carrier operations in Narragansett Bay; received further repairs at the Boston Naval Shipyard; and participated in a convoy exercise that ran from 25 February to 21 March 1952; and ranged from Newport to waters of the Panama Canal Zone and Trinidad in the British West Indies.

As flagship for Carrier Division (CarDiv) 14, *Wright* sailed on 9 June 1952 in company with four destroyers, forming Task Group (TG) 81.4 for ASW operations along the Atlantic seaboard until the 27th, when the ships arrived at New York City. Returning to Quonset Point on 1 July, *Wright* trained units of the organized naval reserves concurrently with hunter-killer tactics and pilot training in operations out of Narragansett Bay until 26 August. On that day, she set course from Quonset Point and later rendezvoused with Vice Admiral Felix B. Stump's 2d Task Fleet en route to northern Europe for combined defense exercises and maneuvers with naval units of other North Atlantic Treaty Organization (NATO) navies.

En route, *Wright*, escorted by *Forrest Royal*, was detached to ferry men and gear of Marine Night Fighter Squadron (VMF(N)) 114 to Port Lyautey, French Morocco, an operation she completed on 4 September. Two days later, *Wright* and her escort rejoined the task force; and they reached the Firth of Clyde, Scotland, on the 10th.

Three days later, *Wright* put to sea with two British destroyers acting as her plane guard for NATO Operation "Mainbrace." She conducted air defense maneuvers and tactics evolutions with the British carriers HMS *Illustrious* (R–87) and HMS *Eagle* (R–05) en route to Rotterdam, Holland, where the force arrived on the 25th. On 29 September, *Wright* departed Rotterdam, bound for the United States, and arrived at Newport on 9 October.

That day, she embarked Rear Admiral W. L. Erdman, Commander, Carrier Division 4, and spent the next few months engaged in carrier qualification duties in waters ranging from Newport to the Virgina capes, before she began her second deployment to the Mediterranean. She reached Golfe Juan on 21 February 1953 and operated with the 6th Fleet until 31 March, when she sailed for home, via the Azores.

Wright returned to Newport and, after a rigorous schedule of training in Narragansett Bay, sailed on 5 May for the Gulf of Mexico. During that training cruise, she visited Houston, Tex., where she hosted some 14,000 visitors on 16 and 17 May. Returning to Quonset Point on 28 May, *Wright* operated locally for another month before shifting south for a stint of operations out of Mayport, Fla.

Wright was overhauled at the Philadelphia Naval Shipyard from 31 July to 21 November and then conducted refresher training in Cuban waters from 4 January to 16 February 1954. Next, after departing Davisville, R.I., on 5 April, *Wright* sailed for the Far East—via the Panama Canal; San Diego, Calif.; and Pearl Harbor—and reached Yokosuka, Japan, on 28 May. The carrier, with Marine Attack Squadron 211 embarked, operated with the 7th Fleet off both coasts of Korea and also off Okinawa before she visited Hong Kong from 24 to 30 September. Departing Yokosuka on 15 October, *Wright* arrived at San Diego on the last day of October and entered the Long Beach Naval Shipyard where she remained until 23 February 1955.

At that point, *Wright* was attached to CarDiv 17, Pacific Fleet, and operated locally out of San Diego until 3 May, when she put to sea as part of TG 7.3—formed around the flagship *Mount McKinley* (AGC–27)—for the atomic test, Operation "Wigwam," carried out in Pacific waters. Returning to the west coast on 20 May, *Wright* subsequently cruised to Pearl Harbor briefly before she entered the Mare Island Naval Shipyard on 14 July to commence preparation for inactivation. After shifting to the Puget Sound Naval Shipyard, Bremerton, Wash., on 17 October, for the final phase of preservation for inactivation, *Wright* was decommissioned at Puget Sound on 15 March 1956 and assigned to the Bremerton group of the Pacific Reserve Fleet.

During her time in reserve, *Wright* was reclassified on 15 May 1959 an auxiliary aircraft transport, AVT–7. However, she never served in that role; but remained inactive until 15 March 1962, when she was taken to the Puget Sound Naval Shipyard for conversion to a command ship and reclassified as CC–2. The conversion—which lasted a year—included extensive alterations to enable the ship to function as a fully equipped mobile command post afloat for top echelon commands and staff for strategic direction of area or world-wide military operations. Facilities were built into the ship for world-wide communications and rapid, automatic exchange, processing, storage, and display of command data. A portion of the former hangar deck space was utilized for special command spaces and the extensive electronics equipment required, while a major portion of the flight deck was utilized for specially designed communications antenna arrays. In addition, facilities were provided to enable the ship to operate three helicopters.

Recommissioned at Puget Sound on 11 May 1963, Capt. John L. Arrington, II, in command, *Wright* (CC–2) operated locally on trials and training evolutions in the waters off the Pacific Northwest until 3

September, when she departed Seattle and proceeded to San Diego which she reached three days later. For the next three weeks, the ship trained in nearby waters before she returned to Puget Sound on 30 September to commence her post-shakedown availability.

Following those repairs and alterations—which took up all of the month of October and most of November—*Wright* prepared to shift to her new home port, Norfolk. She departed Seattle on 26 November, stopped briefly at San Diego three days later to embark civilian engineers and personnel who were to conduct surveys of communications and air conditioning equipment, and was steaming south off the coast of northern Mexico when she picked up a distress message from the Israeli merchantman SS *Velos* on 1 December. *Wright* altered course and rendezvoused with *Velos* later that same day. The command ship's medical officer was flown across to the Israeli ship and treated a seaman suffering from kidney stones. Upon completion of that mission of mercy, *Wright* resumed her voyage to Balboa.

Transiting the Panama Canal on 7 and 8 December, *Wright* steamed via St. Thomas, Virgin Islands, and moored at the Hampton Roads Army Terminal on 18 December. After a subsequent brief operational period off the Virginia capes, *Wright* entered port on 21 December and remained there through Christmas and New Year's.

For the next six years, *Wright* operated out of Norfolk, training to perform her assigned mission as an emergency command post afloat. Regular overhauls performed at the Norfolk Naval Shipyard saw the ship receiving the repairs and alterations that continually improved her capabilities to carry out her task. She operated primarily off the Virginia capes, but ranged as far north as Bar Harbor, Maine, and as far south as Rio de Janeiro, Brazil, and Punta del Este, Uruguay. Her other ports of call included Newport; Fort Lauderdale and Port Everglades, Fla.; Boston; New York City; Annapolis; Philadelphia; Norfolk; and Guantanamo Bay, Cuba. On occasion, she alternated on "alert" status with *Northampton* (CC–1).

There were highlights and breaks from the cycle of

The command ship *Wright* (CC–2) shows off her massive array of communications antennas. (KN–5885)

485

periods in port and at sea. From 11 to 14 April 1967, *Wright* lay at anchor off the coast of Uruguay, providing a world-wide communications capability in support of President Lyndon B. Johnson as he attended the Latin American summit conference at Punta del Este. On 8 May 1968, *Wright* went to the aid of *Guadalcanal* (LPH–7) after that amphibious assault ship had suffered a machinery failure and had gone dead in the water 180 miles south of Norfolk. She towed the helpless assault ship 84 miles before other ships arrived on the scene to help out. Later that same year, *Wright* received the coveted Ney award in the large mess afloat category. That award is given annually to the ship that maintains the highest food standards. During the *Pueblo* (AGER–2) crisis in February 1969, *Wright*—while en route to Port Everglades, Fla.—was hurriedly recalled to Norfolk and, upon her arrival there, stood by, on alert.

Ultimately decommissioned on 27 May 1970, *Wright* was placed in reserve at the Philadelphia Naval Shipyard. As of 28 June 1979, she was still there.

Wyalusing

An Indian word which means "at the dwelling of the ancient warrior." It refers to the site of Wyalusing in Bradford County, Pa., the former site of a Munsee and Iroquois Indian settlement.

(SwGbt: dp. 1,173; t. 974; l. 205'0''; b. 35'0''; dr. 9'0''; dph. 11'6''; s. 14 k.; cpl. 154; a. 2 100-pdr. P.r., 4 9'' D.sb., 4 24-pdr. how., 2 9-pdr. r., 2 heavy 12-pdr. sb.)

Wyalusing—a double-end, side-wheel gunboat built at Philadelphia by C. H. & W. H. Cramp—was launched on 12 May 1863 and commissioned at the navy yard there on 8 February 1864, Lt. Comdr. Walter W. Queen in command.

Assigned to the North Atlantic Blockading Squadron, *Wyalusing* joined the contingent of that force stationed in Albemarle Sound, N.C., on 29 April. Just 10 days before her arrival, the Confederate ironclad ram *Albemarle* had made her long-awaited appearance in battle, ramming two of the blockading Union gunboats in the process. As a result of her support, Confederate land forces recaptured Plymouth, N.C., on 20 April. *Wyalusing* had her first scrape with the formidable Confederate warship on 5 May. *Albemarle* steamed out of her haven on the Roanoke River that afternoon accompanied by steamers *Bombshell* and *Cotton Plant* to try to wreak more havoc on the blockaders. The Union picket boats stationed at the mouth of the Roanoke retired to raise the alarm. Gunboats *Mattabesset*, *Sassacus*, *Whitehead*, and *Wyalusing* immediately formed a line of battle supported by *Miami*, *Commodore Hull*, and *Ceres*. When the Southern ram appeared, *Mattabesset*, *Whitehead*, and *Wyalusing* opened fire almost simultaneously. *Wyalusing* passed *Albemarle* at about 150 yards distance, rounded her, and headed to attack *Bombshell*. The latter Confederate, however, had already surrendered, so *Wyalusing* backed clear of her and renewed the attack on the more formidable foe, *Albemarle*. A heavy, but inconclusive, gun action ensued. Impending darkness brought the fighting to a close; and *Albemarle* headed back up the Roanoke.

Wyalusing and her consorts resumed blockade station in the sound, but all efforts were made over the next fire months to destroy the Confederate ironclad, The first of those missions was concocted and attempted by five *Wyalusing* sailors on 26 May. They rowed up Middle River that afternoon carrying two 100-pound torpedoes and then carried them by stretcher across the swampland separating the Middle and Roanoke Rivers to a point just above and opposite *Albemarle*'s mooring place at Plymouth. Two of the sailors then swam across the river with a towline attached to the explosive devices and then hauled them across. The torpedoes were

then joined together by a bridle, and one of the sailors guided them down toward the ram hoping to place the bridle across her prow with a torpedo making contact with either side of her hull. He was then to swim clear before another man stationed across the river detonated the torpedoes electrically. Unfortunately, the Confederates caught sight of both swimmer and torpedoes when they were just a few yards short of their goal. A hail of musketry from the shore followed soon after a sentry's hail. The swimmer quickly cut the guide line, retired, and then swam back across the river. The five Union sailors scattered. Three returned to *Wyalusing* on the evening of 28 May. The remaining two rejoined their ship the following night after rescue by *Commodore Hull*. All five ultimately received the Medal of Honor for their daring attempt.

During the ensuing months, while *Wyalusing* remained on station in the sound, more unsuccessful plans to destroy the Confederate ram were developed. It was not until the night of 27 and 28 October that Lt. William B. Cushing accomplished *Albemarle*'s destruction in a steam launch outfitted with a spar torpedo. That event opened the way for the recapture of Plymouth and for further offensive action on the Roanoke and Middle Rivers. On 29 October, *Wyalusing*, in company with other gunboats, steamed up the Roanoke toward Plymouth; but, just below the objective, impassable barriers barred the way. Undaunted, the warships crossed over to Middle River, journeyed to another crossover point above Plymouth, and then steamed downriver toward the goal. The next day, the gunboats exchanged shot and shell with Confederate shore batteries and rifle pits protecting Plymouth. The Confederates fought stubbornly but the heavy-caliber Union cannonade eventually prevailed and forced the Southerners to abandon their fortifications. A landing party from *Wyalusing* took possession of Fort Williams, captured prisoners, and helped to retake Plymouth.

On 9 December, an expedition, of which *Wyalusing* was a part, moved farther up the Roanoke to capture Rainbow Bluff and another Confederate ram, rumored to be under construction at Halifax, N.C. While anchoring near Jamesville, N.C., *Ostego*, another gunboat, struck two torpedoes (mines) and sank up to her gun deck. *Basely*, a tug, moved alongside *Ostego* to offer assistance; but she, too, struck a torpedo and sank immediately. *Wyalusing* and the remainder of the expedition left the two partially sunken ships under the protection of their own unsubmerged guns and headed upriver cautiously dragging for torpedoes as they went. By the time they had reached the point of attack, the Confederate positions at Rainbow Bluff had been so well reinforced and the approaches so heavily strewn with torpedoes that the Union ships had to abandon the enterprise. *Wyalusing* and her consorts returned to Plymouth on 28 December 1864 and resumed blockade and amphibious support duties. On 9 January 1865, she captured the schooner *Triumph*, laden with salt, at the mouth of the Perquimans River. She also helped to clear the various rivers and streams along the sound of obstructions and torpedoes and managed to capture a Confederate schooner in the process. She continued duty in the Albemarle Sound and Cape Hatteras areas until a month after Lee's surrender at Appomattox on 9 April. She arrived in New York on 21 May and was decommissioned there on 10 June 1865. Later transferred to Philadelphia, she was sold there on 15 October 1867.

Wyandance

(MB: t. 21; l. 60'11''; b. 11'7''; dph. 5'7''; dr. 1'11'' (forward); s. 14¼ k.; cpl. 5; a. 2 1-pdrs.)

Wyandance (SP–359)—a motorboat built in 1905 at Bayonne, N.J., by the Electric Boat Co.—was acquired from Mr. M. S. Burrill of Jericho, Long Island, N.Y., on 19 June 1917 and was commissioned on 24 August 1917 at New York. She served the Navy only briefly—a little more than five months—as a patrol boat with the section patrol in the 3d Naval District. *Wyandance* was decommissioned early in 1918; and her name was struck from the Navy list on 2 February 1918, the day on which she was returned to her owner.

Wyandank

Probably a variant spelling of Wyandance.

(SwStr: t. 400; l. 132'5''; b. 31'5''; dph. 10'10''; a. 2 12-pdrs.)

Wyandank—a wooden-hulled, sidewheel ferry built at New York City in 1847 and sometimes documented as *Wyandanck*—was acquired by the Navy on 12 September 1861 from the Union Ferry Co. of Brooklyn, N.Y., and used during the Civil War as storeship for the Potomac Flotilla. After hostilities ended, *Wyandank* served at Annapolis, Md., into the 1870's as a floating barracks for marines assigned to the United States Naval Academy. She was broken up there in 1879.

Wyandot

A county in Ohio.

(AKA–92: dp. 13,910; l. 459'3''; b. 63'0''; dr. 26'4'' (lim.); s. 18.6 k.; cpl. 368; a. 1 5'', 8 40mm., 18 20mm.; cl. *Andromeda*; T. C2–S–B1)

Wyandot (AKA–92) was laid down on 6 May 1944 under a Maritime Commission contract (MC hull 1192) at Oakland, Calif., by the Moore Dry Dock Co.; launched on 28 June 1944; acquired by the Navy and simultaneously commissioned on 30 September 1944, Comdr. E. G. Howard in command.

Following her shakedown, *Wyandot* departed San Francisco on 25 November 1944, bound for the Hawaiian Islands. She made port at Pearl Harbor on 2 December and, after loading cargo earmarked for the Marshalls and Marianas, headed for Eniwetok and Guam. After delivering her cargo to those western Pacific bases, the attack cargo ship returned to the Hawaiian Islands.

Wyandot departed Pearl Harbor on 26 January 1945 and proceeded thence via Eniwetok to Tacloban where she joined the forces massing for the assault on Okinawa. Assigned to a support role with the amphibious forces, *Wyandot*—partially unloaded—was returning from a night retirement alert about 0400 on 29 March when a Japanese horizontal bomber, probably on a night heckler mission, came in off *Wyandot*'s starboard quarter and dropped a pair of bombs, one of which hit close aboard the ship's starboard quarter, sprinkling her stern with what appeared to be picric acid.

The second bomb plunged into the water near the attack cargo ship's starboard side and scored an underwater hit, making two large cracks in her hull. The two forward holds and the forward magazine flooded quickly, and *Wyandot* listed slightly to starboard. Putting the remainder of her landing craft and boats in the water, the vessel painfully made her way to an advanced repair base, down by the bow and steaming slowly, but still afloat.

Within a short time, the ship's force, aided by the salvage experts of the repair unit, had made the necessary temporary repairs; *Wyandot* consequently returned to her place off the beaches of Okinawa and continued discharging ammunition, vehicles, gasoline, provisions, and special equipment earmarked for the American 10th Army on Okinawa.

Wyandot, her mission at Okinawa completed, sailed for the west coast of the United States, via Pearl Harbor, for permanent repairs and reached the Naval Dry Docks at Terminal Island, San Pedro, Calif., on

6 June. After brief periods at San Diego, and later San Francisco, *Wyandot* headed for Pearl Harbor once more—but too late to participate in any further combat operations. She arrived at Pearl Harbor on 28 August.

Wyandot subsequently visited the Far East that autumn, departing Pearl Harbor on 7 October and visiting, in succession, Okinawa; Tientsin, China; Guam; Eniwetok; and Kwajalein before returning to Pearl Harbor on 27 November. The next day, the cargo ship got underway for the Atlantic; steamed via the Panama Canal; and arrived at Norfolk, Va., on 19 December.

Wyandot operated out of Norfolk for the next two years. Early in 1947, she departed the Hampton Roads area and took part in the 1947 Atlantic Fleet exercises—maneuvers that took the ship as far as Trinidad in the British West Indies. Departing Trinidad on 8 March, the attack cargo ship took part in further exercises before she made a transatlantic passage to Casablanca, French Morocco. Staying at Casablanca from 24 to 30 March, *Wyandot* returned via New Orleans to Norfolk on 30 April.

Again operating off the eastern seaboard early that summer, *Wyandot* subsequently headed for her first deployment in Arctic waters, departing Boston on 16 July 1947 for Thule, Greenland, and the Devon and Cornwallis Islands. Returning to Boston on 25 September, *Wyandot* spent the next year operating along the eastern seaboard and gulf coast of the United States, as well as making two cruises to the Caribbean and one to Panama.

On 16 July 1948, *Wyandot* departed Boston, visiting the Arctic again as part of the Navy's annual cold-weather exercises in those climes. She revisited the bases she had called upon the previous year and returned to Boston on 18 September, en route to Norfolk.

Over the next two years, *Wyandot* operated out of Norfolk and made her first Mediterranean deployment, visiting ports in Italy and French Morocco; the island of Crete; Great Britain; Cuba; Puerto Rico; the Virgin Islands; Haiti; Newfoundland; Bermuda; Nova Scotia; the Panama Canal Zone; and Curaçao, Netherlands West Indies.

Early in 1951, *Wyandot* was selected to participate in Operation "Bluejay"—transporting construction materials to the northern part of Greenland—and was busy in that mission from May to September of that year. She returned to that area in 1952 as part of Operation "SuNAC" (Supply Northern Atlantic Construction). The following year, *Wyandot* conducted logistical support missions in the Caribbean and later participated in the joint United States and Canadian resupply operations with Arctic weather stations. *Wyandot* again deployed to the Mediterranean and Caribbean areas between 1953 and 1955, winning the coveted Battle Efficiency Award for 1955.

In the spring of 1955, *Wyandot* joined Task Force 43 for Operation "Deepfreeze I" in the Antarctic. After a brief yard availability, the ship loaded supplies and equipment at Davisville, R.I., and shifted to Norfolk, from whence she departed on 14 November. Sailing via the Panama Canal and Port Lyttleton, New Zealand, *Wyandot* arrived at McMurdo Sound, Antarctica, on 27 December. While in those cold southern latitudes, she served as the flagship for Rear Admiral Richard E. Byrd, officer-in-charge of the Antarctic programs.

After establishing the base at "Little America," *Wyandot* returned home and operated with the Atlantic Fleet into the late 1950's. Decommissioned on 10 July 1959 and struck from the Navy list on 1 July 1960, the ship was reinstated on the list because of the increased east-west tension over the crisis situation in Berlin.

Recommissioned in November 1961, *Wyandot* was transferred to the Military Sea Transportation Service (MSTS) in March 1963 and reclassified as T–AKA–92. Later reclassified as T–AK–283, *Wyandot* served with MSTS, Atlantic, through the 1960's and was shifted to MSTS' successor organization, the Military Sealift Command (MSC) by October 1973, and to MSC, Pacific, by 1 July 1974. On 31 October 1975, *Wyandot* was placed in the Maritime Administration Reserve Fleet.

Wyandot (AKA–92) was awarded one battle star for her World War II service.

Wyandotte

A city in Wayne County, Michigan, on the Detroit River, 11 miles southwest of Detroit, and a county in Kansas. Both are named for the Wyandotte Indians. The county was established on 29 January 1859 and was the location of the constitutional convention in July of that year which framed the antislavery constitution under which Kansas was admitted to the Union on 25 January 1861.

I

(ScStr: t. 464; s. 7 k.; a. 4 32-pdrs., 1 24-pdr. D. how.)

The first *Wyandotte*—a former merchant steamer built at Philadelphia in 1853 as *Western Port*—was chartered by the Navy Department in the autumn of 1858 to participate in an American naval expedition up the Parana River to Asuncion, Paraguay. After the vessel had been fitted out as a gunboat, she was commissioned under her original name on 27 October 1858, Comdr. Thomas T. Hunter in command.

Western Port soon sailed for South American waters and—at Montevideo, Uruguay—joined the task force commanded by Flag Officer William Branford Shubrick which had been assembled to support the negotiations of United States Commissioner to Paraguay, James Butler Bowlin. President Buchanan had appointed Bowlin to seek redress for the shelling of United States Steamer *Water Witch* in 1855 which had resulted in the death of the American ship's helmsman. Shubrick's fleet got underway from Montevideo on 30 December 1858 and ascended the Rio de la Plata and the Parana and the Paraguay Rivers. It arrived off Asuncion on 25 January 1859, and Bowlin went ashore to conduct negotiations which succeeded in winning an apology for the United States and a large indemnity for survivors of the dead helmsman. Bowling also signed a new commercial treaty between the United States and Paraguay.

After the conclusion of the negotiations, *Western Port* returned to the United States and was decommissioned on 28 May 1859. She was purchased by the Navy Department on 6 June 1859 and renamed *Wyandotte*.

After repairs, *Wyandotte* was recommissioned on 19 September 1859 and assigned to the home squadron. She spent much of the next year cruising—for the most part in the Caribbean—in an effort to suppress the slave trade. On 9 May 1860, she captured the barque *William*—a slave ship carrying 570 Africans at the time of her capture—off the Isle of Pines near the south coast of Cuba. She took her prize to Florida and arrived at Key West on the 12th. The ship landed the Blacks on the 16th, turned the prize over to a United States marshall on the 22d, and soon resumed her cruising.

During the first weeks of the secession in the mid- and late autumn of 1860, *Wyandotte* guarded and reprovisioned Federal military installations along the gulf coast. On 16 November 1860, she was ordered to protect Fort Taylor, Key West, Fla., while *Mohawk* watched Fort Jefferson. These actions saved Key West for the Union, permitting its wartime use as the home port of the Gulf Blockading Squadron.

In mid-December, *Wyandotte* sailed for Pensacola and entered the dry dock in the navy yard there to have her fouled bottom scraped and to receive minor repairs. She was refloated on 9 January 1861 and

refused to surrender when Confederate forces took over the Pensacola Navy Yard three days later. Instead, she towed *Supply* out to sea.

Wyandotte remained in Pensacola Bay performing valuable observation and communication duty. She transported troops from Fort Barrancas, Fla., to Fort Pickens on 10 February 1861 and regularly patrolled the inner shore of Santa Rosa Island to prevent Confederate soldiers from attacking Fort Pickens by land. The vessel took part in the daring nighttime reinforcement of Fort Pickens on 12 April 1861, the day of the firing upon Fort Sumter, S.C. With the outbreak of hostilities, *Wyandotte* joined the Gulf Blockading Squadron on 17 May 1861. After carrying out patrol and transport assignments, she proceeded to the New York Navy Yard for major repairs on 23 August 1861.

On 5 December 1861, *Wyandotte* departed New York, bound for Port Royal, S.C., and duty with the South Atlantic Blockading Squadron. There, she was dispatched to Tybee Island, Ga., for reconnaissance work on 19 December 1861 and then was transferred to the blockade off Wassaw Sound, Ga., on 23 February 1862. *Wyandotte* returned to Port Royal in late April 1862 and proceeded to the blockade off Mosquito Inlet, Fla., on 12 May 1862. She returned to Port Royal in July, sailing to New York a second time for extensive repairs on 25 July 1862.

Wyandotte left the navy yard on 1 September 1862 for duty in the Potomac River with the Potomac Flotilla. She was reassigned to the North Atlantic Blockading Squadron at Hampton Roads on 7 October 1862, deploying off Fort Monroe, Va., as a guard vessel. On detail, *Wyandotte* salvaged valuable supplies from the schooner *Marie Banks*, wrecked off Cape Henry light, Va., on 10 February 1863. She was repaired at the Norfolk Navy Yard and got underway again on 11 April 1863 to resume blockade duty. However, badly strained, the vessel could no longer withstand rolling seas and was condemned as fit for guard duty only on 3 October 1863. She spent the remainder of the war off Norfolk.

Wyandotte was decommissioned at the New York Navy Yard on 3 June 1865 and was sold at auction there on 12 July 1865. She was redocumented for merchant service on 23 September 1865 but was stranded when she ran aground off Duxbury, Mass., on 26 January 1866 and damaged beyond economical repair.

II

(Mon.: dp. 2,100; l. 224'0''; b. 43'0''; dr. 11'6''; s. 13 k.; cpl. 100; a. 2 15'' D. sb.; cl. *Canonicus*)

Tippecanoe—a *Canonicus*-class monitor constructed by Miles Greenwood at the shipyard of John Litherbury at Cincinnati, Ohio—was laid down on 28 September 1862; and launched on 22 December 1864. However, she was not completed until 1866 when she was laid up at New Orleans. In the year 1869, she was twice renamed: to *Vesuvius* on 15 June and to *Wyandotte* on 10 August.

Between the years 1870 and 1872, the monitor was laid up at Key West, Fla., and at the Philadelphia Navy Yard. In 1873 and 1874, *Wyandotte* underwent extensive repairs by John Roach at Chester, Pa. On 24 January 1876, the warship was commissioned, with Lt. Thomas C. Terrell in command.

Wyandotte operated with the North Atlantic Squadron off the east coast into 1879, on exercises and training cruises, basing for a time out of Hampton Roads, Va. She later served as station ship at Washington, D.C., before being laid up in 1885 and placed in ordinary—first at Richmond and then at Norfolk, Va.

Transferred to the Connecticut state militia in 1896, she was serving in this capacity when, at the opening of the Spanish-American War, some Americans along the eastern seaboard felt apprehensive, lest the Spanish

Navy attack American cities. Their anxiety was fed by the fact that the major warships of the United States Fleet had gathered around Key West far from the major metropolitan centers to the north. This uneasiness swept over the east coast and produced a clamor for the Navy to take steps to protect the "endangered" cities.

As a result, the Navy reactivated old ships—for the most part, of Civil War vintage—for local defense. Recommissioned on 30 April 1898, with Lt. John B. Milton in command, *Wyandotte* sailed from New Haven, Conn., on 17 May, to guard Boston. The venerable warship remained on station from 19 May to 5 September, but no Spanish armada ever appeared.

After hostilities ended, *Wyandotte* steamed to Philadelphia, where she arrived on 9 September. She was decommissioned there on 20 September and later sold for scrap on 17 January 1899.

Wyffels

Lawrence Edward Wyffels—born on 20 January 1915 in Marshall, Minn.—enlisted in the United States Navy on 17 March 1936. He served in *Enterprise* (CV–6); and was advanced to carpenter on 25 June 1942. He was killed in enemy action on 26 October 1942 when *Enterprise* suffered bomb damage during the Battle of Santa Cruz Island. Disregarding his own safety, Carpenter Wyffels courageously fought the blaze ignited by bombs and repeatedly entered burning compartments to rescue the wounded trapped inside. Carpenter Wyffels was posthumously awarded the Silver Star for his intrepid devotion to duty.

(DE–6: dp. 1,140; l. 289'5''; b. 35'1''; dr. 8'3'' (mean); s. 19½ k.; cpl. 198; a. 3 3'', 4 1.1'', 2 40mm., 9 20mm., 3 dct., 8 dcp., 1 dcp. (hh.); cl. *Evarts*)

Wyffels (DE–6), intended for transfer to Great Britain, was laid down as BDE–6 on 17 October 1942 at Charlestown, Mass., by the Boston Navy Yard; launched on 7 December 1942; retained by the United States and redesignated DE–6 on 25 January 1943; renamed *Wyffels* on 19 February 1943; and commissioned on 15 April 1943, Lt. Robert Messigner Hinckley, Jr., in command.

Following sea trials in April, the destroyer escort got underway from Boston on 8 May 1943 and for the remainder of the month conducted exercises out of Bermuda. In June, she alternated operations out of Norfolk with drydock periods. On 27 June 1943, she departed from Hampton Roads on the first of 11 wartime voyages escorting convoys across the treacherous Atlantic to Mediterranean ports. Her first voyage proved uneventful, although the return from Casablanca was enlivened by the investigation of sound contacts. On 29 July, the destroyer escort left her station to guard a tanker, SS *British Pride*, which had fallen behind due to engine failure. Long, anxious hours ensued as *Wyffels* circled the disabled ship while repairs were being made; she then escorted the straggler back to her convoy.

Between August 1943 and April 1945, *Wyffels*, with occasional interruptions for exercises off the New England coast, conducted 10 more successful circuit voyages escorting convoys to and from North Africa. On her Atlantic crossings, the ship acted as a versatile and valuable part of the Atlantic convoy system, marshalling reluctant merchantmen, protecting stragglers, and searching for the source of each sound contact which might, at any time, turn out to be a predatory German submarine. In winter, stormy weather and heavy seas slowed the awkward merchant ships and increased the number of stragglers, complicating the task of the escort vessels.

On 11 May 1944, *Wyffels* was escorting UGS–40, a convoy of 56 merchant ships bound for Bizerte, when

Evarts-class destroyer escorts such as *Wyffels* (DE–6), seen here on 26 April 1943, were built to a British Admiralty specification and called "short-hull" escorts, in contrast to their larger American-designed contemporaries of other classes.

she experienced her most perilous moments. Shortly after sunset, a task force order to go to general quarters jolted *Wyffels* from the normal routine of convoy duty. Ships of the escort began laying smoke, and soon *Wyffels'* radar picked up a group of approaching planes. After a tense, six-minute wait, the ominous calm of the Mediterranean night was broken as first *Benson* (DD–421) and then *Evarts* (DE–5) opened fire.

Moments later, seamen in *Wyffels* spotted the first wave of attacking planes as they came into view low over the water, some four miles away. Three of the aircraft veered off to make a run on the convoy at an altitude of about 200 feet. *Wyffels* opened fire as the planes passed down her port side and sped off toward the convoy's port quarter. Moments passed as the destroyer escort patrolled at full speed, her guns silent. An aerial attacker appeared out of the smoke, dropped an ill-aimed torpedo, and disappeared. Then, at 2124, *Wyffels* engaged a clearly visible Junkers bomber which approached the ship's starboard bow at an altitude of 100 feet. Amidst a telling crossfire from *Wyffels* and other members of the escort, the plane banked to the right, missing the forward part of the ship. Smoke poured from the attacker as it rapidly lost altitude and disappeared in a burst of black smoke.

Soon after, *Wyffels* took under fire another plane which emerged from the convoy's barrage and passed directly over the ship's forecastle and along her starboard side. The aircraft then continued on its way, apparently without having suffered serious damage. Other ships continued to fire for 10 minutes, but the raiders had departed without scoring a single hit on the convoy or its escort.

Through the final year of the war in Europe, *Wyffels* continued her protection of Atlantic convoys. On 13 April 1945, as *Wyffels* was en route home from what was to be her last wartime Atlantic convoy, the destroyer escort received word that President Franklin D. Roosevelt had died, and she lowered her colors to half mast. After repairs at Charleston later that month, she arrived at Miami on 11 May. In the following months, she operated off Florida and in the Bahamas, serving as a school ship training student crews in basic gunnery and antisubmarine warfare.

On 28 August 1945, she was decommissioned and leased to the Republic of China, which she served as *T'ai Kang*. *Wyffels* was permanently transferred to the Republic of China in February 1948 and was struck from the Navy list on 12 March 1948.

Wyffels received one battle star for World War II service.

Wyman

Eldon P. Wyman—born in Portland, Oreg., on 11 January 1917—attended the University of Oregon from 1936 to 1940 before he enlisted in the Naval Reserve as an apprentice seaman on 22 August 1940 at Portland. After training in *Tuscaloosa* (CA–37), he accepted an appointment as midshipman in the Naval Reserve on 17 March 1941.

Attending the Naval Reserve Midshipman's School at Northwestern University, Chicago, Ill., Wyman was commissioned ensign on 12 June and reported to *Oklahoma* (BB–37) on 19 July. That battleship subsequently operated out of Pearl Harbor as a unit of Battleship Division 1 on exercises in the Hawaiian operating area and off the west coast as tensions increased in the Pacific and in the Far East. By early in December 1941, Wyman was serving as junior watch officer of the ship's "F" (fire control) division. Moored outboard of *Maryland* (BB–46) on that "day of infamy," *Oklahoma* took four aerial torpedoes and

rolled over at her berth; among those trapped within the doomed ship's hull was Ensign Eldon P. Wyman.

Robert H. Wyman—born at Portsmouth, N.H., on 12 July 1822—was appointed midshipman on 11 March 1837 and served initially in the razee *Independence* on the Brazil station. After sea duty in the sloops-of-war *Fairfield* and *John Adams*—the latter commanded by his father—he was appointed passed midshipman in 1843. Over the next three years, Wyman served in South American waters in the schooner *On-ka-hy-e*, the brig *Perry*, and the frigate *Brandywine* before participating in the Mexican War in Commodore Conner's Home Squadron—first in the steamer *Princeton* and later in the brig *Porpoise* and the sloop *Albany*. During that time, he took part in the expeditions against Tampico during November 1864 and Veracruz in March 1847.

Passed Midshipman Wyman spent a tour of duty ashore at the Naval Observatory, Washington, D.C., before reporting to the receiving ship at Boston, *Franklin*, and subsequently being promoted to lieutenant on 16 July 1850. Over the next decade, he served at sea; and the outbreak of the Civil War in April 1861 found him in command of *Richmond* on the Mediterranean station.

Early in July, soon after he brought that steam sloop-of-war home for wartime duty, he took command of *Yankee*. In September, Wyman assumed command of *Pocahontas*. That ship, as part of the Potomac River Flotilla, helped to keep open the Union's vital waterway communications with Washington while cutting off Southern forces from their sympathizers in southern Maryland.

Commanding the steamer *Pawnee* from October 1861, Wyman took part in Flag Officer DuPont's capture of the key seaport of Port Royal, S.C. After that operation, Wyman returned north and took command of the Potomac River Flotilla on 6 December 1861. He held this important post until the end of June 1862. During his time in the Potomac, he was active in maintaining Union control of that vital river and of much of the Rappahannock during General McClellan's Peninsular Campaign. His ships destroyed Southern bridges, captured nine Confederate ships, and burned 40 schooners.

Promoted to commander on 16 July 1862, Wyman was ordered to command the gunboat *Sonoma* on the James River. Transferred to the West Indian Squadron the following October, he commanded the steam sloop *Wachusett* and the paddle steamer *Santiago de Cuba*, and captured the blockade runners *Brittania* and *Lizzie*. During the last two years of the War Between the States, Wyman served on special duty in the Navy Department in Washington.

After the Civil War, Wyman commanded *Colorado*, the flagship for the European Squadron, and was promoted to captain on 25 July 1866 and took command of the steam sloop *Ticonderoga* the following year. After that tour of sea duty, Wyman headed the Navy's Hydrographic Office for eight years, receiving promotions to commodore on 19 July 1872 and to rear admiral on 26 April 1878. His leadership of the Hydrographic Office proved to be of great importance to the Navy and seafaring men in general. Through the Civil War, the United States Navy had relied upon foreign sources—principally British—for their navigational charts, doing little of their own hydrographic work. Under Wyman's direction, the office began a systematic and sustained program of world-wide charting and surveying, the precursor of the Navy's present globe-girdling oceanographic research effort.

Following his promotion to flag rank in the spring of 1878, Wyman was given command of the North Atlantic Squadron. Subsequently becoming chairman of the Lighthouse Board, Rear Admiral Wyman died in Washington, D.C., on 2 December 1882.

The first *Wyman* (DE–38) honors Ensign Eldon P.

Wyman; the second *Wyman* (T–AGS–34) honors Rear Admiral Robert H. Wyman.

I

(DE–38: dp. 1,140; l. 289′5″; b. 35′1″; dr. 8′3″; s. 21 k.; cpl. 156; a. 3 3″, 4 1.1″, 9 20mm., 8 dcp., 2 dct., 1 dcp. (hh.); cl. *Evarts*)

The first *Wyman* (DE–38) was originally laid down as *BDE–38* on 7 September 1942 at Bremerton, Wash., by the Puget Sound Navy Yard for the Royal Navy; launched on 3 June 1943; and sponsored by Mrs. Joe L. Aprill. However, the ship's transfer to the United Kingdom was canceled. The destroyer escort was designated DE–38 on 16 June; named *Wyman* on the 23d; and was commissioned at the Puget Sound Navy Yard on 1 September 1943, Lt. Comdr. Robert W. Copeland, USNR, in command.

Following shakedown, *Wyman* departed Puget Sound on 7 November, bound for Hawaii, and arrived at Pearl Harbor on the 14th. Assigned to duty with Submarines, Pacific Fleet, the destroyer escort operated out of Pearl Harbor on submarine exercises from 1 December 1943 through the spring of 1944.

Detached from this duty on 22 June 1944, *Wyman* sailed for the Marshall Islands and began antisubmarine warfare (ASW) operations in the American convoy routes between Eniwetok and Saipan. Joining Task Group (TG) 12.2, based around *Hoggatt Bay* (CVE–75), *Wyman* departed Eniwetok on 5 July and headed for the ASW operating area. En route, she left her formation to investigate a submarine contact which had been developed and depth-charged by *Lake* (DE–301). *Wyman* fired one barrage of depth bombs from her "hedgehog" but did not come up with evidence that she had either damaged or destroyed her enemy.

The destroyer escort arrived in her patrol zone on 9 July and refueled from *Guadalupe* (AO–32) on the 11th. She remained in the area from 12 to 18 July before proceeding to investigate a surface radar contact at 0024 on the 19th. The destroyer escort closed the range until she lost radar contact at 0045 and switched immediately to her sonar. *Wyman* picked up a strong metallic echo and, at 0051, fired a full pattern of "hedgehog" projectiles, with negative results. She reloaded, opened the range, and then closed for a second attack, as *Reynolds* (DE–42) closed in the meantime.

At 0125, *Wyman* launched a second full pattern from her "hedgehog"—dead on the target. A series of violent explosions rocked the destroyer escort, as the depth bombs blew the submarine apart. *Wyman* circled to starboard and passed through her own firing point in order to regain contact but picked up only a "mush" echo—indicative that her contact had been destroyed. Remaining on the scene of the action, *Wyman* lowered a motor whaleboat to recover oil samples from the water and to fish out debris. In the large, spreading, oil slick, men in the boat picked up two five-gallon oil cans, one small gasoline can, and a piece of teak wood. As it was gathering this materiel, *Wyman*'s motor whaler was strafed by two planes from *Hoggatt Bay*, whose pilots had mistaken the boat for a surfaced submarine. Fortunately, there were no fatalities; and the injured men were soon transferred to *Hoggatt Bay* for medical treatment.

Oil from the sunken submarine—later identified by a postwar examination of Japanese records as *RO–48*—continued to bubble up in copious quantities into the next day. Satisfied that the kill was definite, *Wyman* rejoined TG 12.2 and arrived at Eniwetok on 22 July.

Her respite was short, however, for she again got underway on 26 July. Two days later, at 1733, lookouts in *Hoggatt Bay* and *Wyman* simultaneously spotted a Japanese submarine, *I–55*, running on the surface. *Wyman* and *Reynolds* charged after the enemy submersible as she went deep in an effort to escape. *Wyman* picked up the fleeing I-boat by sonar at 1805. Eight minutes later, the destroyer escort fired a "hedgehog"

pattern which struck its target with deadly accuracy. *Wyman*'s sound operators heard the sounds of heavy explosions from beneath the sea as *I–55* began to blow apart. While opening the range at 1819, a further set of explosions rocked the sea, sounding the death knell for the enemy I-boat. *Reynolds* then added a "hedgehog" pattern, but her target had already perished. Large quantities of debris and oil, visible evidence of *Wyman*'s second "kill," soon came to the surface.

With the dissolution of TG 12.2 on 9 August, *Wyman* joined TG 57.3 for escort duty in waters between the Marshalls and Marianas. On 31 August, the destroyer escort escorted fuel ships of Task Unit 30.8.10 to a rendezvous with TG 38.4 and back to link up with TG 38.2 and Task Force 34. After completing this mission on 20 October 1944, the day of the first landings in the Philippine Islands, *Wyman* resumed escort operations between the Marshalls and Marianas and also participated in hunter-killer operations into early 1945, supporting the invasion of the strategic island of Iwo Jima.

She departed from Ulithi on 13 March 1945 and proceeded to the fueling area for TG 50.8 for duty as escort with the Logistics Support Group for the invasion of Okinawa. During this tour of duty, which lasted into the spring of 1945, she sank three floating Japanese mines by gunfire.

The destroyer escort remained with the 5th Fleet until 10 June, continuing her unglamorous but vital role, screening the important convoys bringing men and munitions to the war zone for the drive against the Japanese homeland. After a stop at Guam, *Wyman* headed for the United States, proceeding via Pearl Harbor and Eniwetok, and arrived at San Francisco on 15 July.

The end of the war changed the Navy's plans for the ship. On 17 August—while in the midst of her scheduled 42-day overhaul during which she was to receive her "ultimate approved armament"—all work on the ship "except that necessary to place the ship in safe and habitable condition" was halted. Declared surplus to the needs of the postwar Navy, *Wyman* was decommissioned on 17 December 1945 and struck from the Navy list on 8 January 1946.

Having been stripped prior to her decommissioning, the ship's hulk was sold to the National Steel and Metal Company, of Terminal Island, Calif., on 16 April 1947 for scrapping—a process which was completed by 14 March 1948.

Wyman received six battle stars for her service on convoy-escort and hunter-killer operations.

II

(T–AGS–34: dp. 2,596 (f.); l. 286′7½″; b. 48′0″; dr. 15′0″; s. 15.5 k.; cpl. 43; cl. *Wilkes*)

The second *Wyman* (T–AGS–34)—an oceanographic survey vessel—was laid down on 18 July 1968 at Bay City, Mich., by the Defoe Shipbuilding Co.; launched on 30 October 1969; sponsored by Mrs. Francis J. Blouin, wife of the Deputy Chief of Naval Operations, Vice Admiral F. J. Blouin; and was accepted by the Military Sealift Command (MSC) on 19 November 1971 at the Boston Naval Shipyard. J. H. Blythe was the ship's first civil service master.

Wyman, designed and built to conduct hydrographic and oceanographic studies and operated by a civilian crew, serves with MSC under the technical direction of the Oceanographer of the Navy. Initially assigned to MSC Atlantic, *Wyman* was transferred to MSC Pacific on 16 November 1974 for a brief tour of duty that lasted into the summer of 1975. She was returned to MSC Atlantic at Port Canaveral, Fla., on 21 August 1975 and remained active with that fleet into 1979.

Wyoming

The first *Wyoming* was named for the valley in Luzerne County, eastern Pennsylvania, that runs along the Susquehanna River; the second and third commemorate the state of Wyoming, the 44th to join the Union.

I

(ScSlp: dp. 1,457; lbp. 198'6"; b. 33'2"; dr. 14'10" (max.); s. 11.0 k.; cpl. 198; a. 2 11" D.sb., 1 60-pdr. P.r., 3 32-pdrs.; cl. *Wyoming*)

The first *Wyoming*—a wooden-hulled screw sloop-of-war—was laid down at the Philadelphia Navy Yard in July 1858; launched on 19 January 1859; sponsored by Miss Mary Florida Grice; and commissioned in October 1859, Comdr. John K. Mitchell in command.

Wyoming soon sailed via Cape Horn for the Pacific and arrived off the coast of Nicaragua in April 1860. There, she relieved *Levant* and operated along the Pacific coast of the United States and Central America into the spring of 1861. During that time, she participated in the search for the sloop *Levant* when that warship disappeared in the late autumn of 1860.

The outbreak of the Civil War found *Wyoming* at San Francisco, Calif., preparing for another cruise. She was instructed to remain in the vicinity of the Golden Gate to protect mail steamers operating off the California coast, but Comdr. Mitchell—a naval officer of Southern origin and persuasion—defied his orders and took his ship to Panama instead.

Mitchell's flagrant disobedience cost him his command and also resulted in his dismissal from the service. As a result, *Wyoming* came under the temporary command of her executive officer, Lt. Francis K. Murray, on 4 July 1861. While returning to Monterey, Calif., *Wyoming* was plagued by mishaps. First, her bottom struck a coral head off La Paz, Mexico, and was pulled free only after three days aground during which she lost her false keel. She then ran short of coal and arrived at Monterey with empty bunkers.

Wyoming subsequently shifted to San Francisco where, on 9 August, she received a new commanding officer, Comdr. David Stockton McDougal. The warship

then proceeded to the coast of Lower California to protect American whaling interests against possible incursions by Confederate cruisers. After that service, she operated in South American waters into 1862.

Following repairs at Mare Island, *Wyoming* received orders—dated 16 June 1862—to proceed immediately to the Far East in search of "armed piratical cruisers fitted out by the rebels" and soon headed west, bound for the Orient.

Word of the Union ship's subsequent appearance in Far Eastern waters spread fast and far. In the Strait of Sunda, off Java, Capt. Raphael Semmes, the commanding officer of Confederate cruiser *Alabama*, learned from an English brig of *Wyoming*'s arrival in the East Indies; and a Dutch trader later confirmed this report. On 26 October, Semmes wrote confidently in his journal that "*Wyoming* is a good match for this ship," and "I have resolved to give her battle. She is reported to be cruising under sail—probably with banked fires—and anchors, no doubt, under Krakatoa every night, and I hope to surprise her, the moon being near its full."

Although in their search for each other, *Wyoming* and *Alabama* unknowingly came close to each other, they never met; and it would be up to another Union warship, the sloop *Kearsarge*, to destroy the elusive Confederate raider. Yet, despite being unsuccessful in tracking down Confederate cruisers, *Wyoming* did render important service to uphold the honor of the American flag in the Far East the following year, 1863.

Ordered to Philadelphia that spring—after what had been a largely fruitless cruise—*Wyoming* was in the midst of preparations to leave the East Indies Station when an event occurred that changed her plans.

In May 1863, *Wyoming* had "showed the flag" to Yokohama, standing by to protect American lives and property during an outbreak of anti-foreign agitation in Japan. Nevertheless, that agitation continued into the early summer months, as the Japanese began to resent all foreigners in their country. Urged by his

The steam sloop *Wyoming*. Black hulls with narrow white streaks were characteristic of post-Civil War American seagoing warships.

advisors, the Japanese Mikado had set 25 June 1863 as the date for the expulsion of all aliens.

Although he was largely powerless to force compliance with his directive, some officials took it literally and tried to impement it. One attempt of this kind was made by the powerful local ruler of the clan of Choshiu, the Prince of Nagato.

That clan, the most warlike in Japan and the one which could be said to have been the forerunner of the modern Japanese Army, threw down the gauntlet to western nations on 26 June. At one o'clock that morning, two armed vessels—illegally flying the flag of the Japanese central government, or shogunate, attacked the American merchantman *Pembroke*, bound for Nagasaki and Shanghai, as she lay anchored in the Strait of Shimonoseki. Fortunately, *Pembroke* suffered no casualties; got underway; and moved out of danger, escaping via Bungo Strait and continuing her voyage for Shanghai, post-haste, without making her scheduled stop at Nagasaki.

Word of the incident did not reach Yokohama from Japanese sources until 10 July. That evening, mail from Shanghai brought "authentic information" confirming the Japanese report. The United States Minister in Japan, Robert H. Pruyn, sent for the Minister of Foreign Affairs for the Japanese government and informed him—in the presence of Comdr. McDougal—of the gravity of the situation, stressing that an insult to the American flag was a serious matter. After being told by Pruyn that the United States government would demand satisfaction and expect a statement from the Japanese concerning the offense, the Japanese diplomat begged that the Americans do nothing until his government at Yedo (later named Tokyo) would take action.

After the Japanese left, McDougal told Pruyn that he had decided to proceed instantly to the Shimonoseki Strait to seize and, if necessary, to destroy, the offending vessels. The two men agreed that failure to punish the outrage properly would encourage further antiforeign incidents.

Accordingly, *Wyoming* prepared for sea. At 4:45 a.m. on 13 July, Comdr. McDougal called all hands; and the sloop got underway 15 minutes later, bound for the strait. After a two-day voyage, *Wyoming* arrived off the island of Hime Shima on the evening of 15 July and anchored off the south side of that island.

At five o'clock the following morning, *Wyoming* weighed anchor and steamed toward the Strait of Shimonoseki. She went to general quarters at nine, loaded her pivot guns with shell, and cleared for action. The warship entered the strait at 10:45 and beat to quarters. Soon, three signal guns boomed from the landward, alerting the batteries and ships of the *daimyo* Choshiu of *Wyoming*'s arrival.

At about 11:15, after being fired upon from the shore batteries, *Wyoming* hoisted her colors and replied with her 11-inch pivot guns. Momentarily ignoring the batteries, McDougal ordered *Wyoming* to continue steaming toward a bark, a steamer, and a brig at anchor off the town of Shimonoseki. Meanwhile, four shore batteries took the warship under fire. *Wyoming* answered the Japanese cannon "as fast as the guns could be brought to bear" while shells from the shore guns passed through her rigging.

Wyoming then passed between the brig and the bark on the starboard hand and the steamer on the port, steaming within a pistol shot's range. One shot from either the bark or brig struck near *Wyoming*'s forward broadside gun, killing two men and wounding four. Elsewhere on the ship, a marine was struck dead by a piece of shrapnel.

Wyoming, in hostile territory, then grounded in uncharted waters shortly after she had made one run past the forts. The Japanese steamer, in the meantime, had slipped her cable and headed directly for *Wyoming* —possibly to attempt a boarding. The American man-of-war, however, managed to work free of the mud and then unleashed her 11-inch Dahlgrens on the enemy ship, hulling and damaging her severely. Two well-directed shots exploded her boilers and, as she began to sink, her crew abandoned the ship.

Wyoming then passed the bark and the brig, firing into them steadily and methodically. Some shells were "overs" and landed in the town ashore. As Comdr. McDougal wrote in his report to Gideon Welles on 23 July, "the punishment inflicted (upon the *daimyo*) and in store for him will, I trust, teach him a lesson that will not soon be forgotten."

After having been under fire for a little over an hour, *Wyoming* returned to Yokohama. She had been hulled 11 times, with considerable damage to her smokestack and rigging. Her casualties had been comparatively light: four men killed and seven wounded—one of whom later died. Significantly, *Wyoming* had been the first foreign warship to take the offensive to uphold treaty rights in Japan.

However, the ship's projected return to Philadelphia did not materialize due to the supposed continued presence of *Alabama* in Far Eastern waters. She repaired her damages, resumed the search and sailed to the Dutch East Indies. She subsequently voyaged to Christmas Island, examining it to determine whether or not it was used as a supply base for "the use of rebel cruisers." Finding the island uninhabited and the report of its use as a supply base unfounded, *Wyoming* returned to Anjer, Java, where McDougal found out, to his surprise, that *Alabama* had passed the Sunda Strait on 10 November—only a day after *Wyoming* had sailed for Christmas Island. At noon that day, *Alabama* and *Wyoming* had been only 25 miles apart.

Writing from Batavia on 22 November, McDougal later reported that *Wyoming* had scoured the waters of the East Indies, visiting "every place in this neighborhood where she (*Alabama*) would likely lay in case she intended to remain in this region." Although acknowledging that the condition of *Wyoming*'s boilers prevented a heavy pressure of steam from being carried, McDougal promised to make every effort in his power to find and capture *Alabama*.

Wyoming then cruised to Singapore in search of the Confederate raider, but found nothing, and continued on to the Dutch settlement of Rhio, near Sunda Strait. She subsequently sailed north, putting into Cavite, Luzon, in the Philippine Islands, on Christmas Eve. There, through the courtesy of the Spanish Navy, *Wyoming* underwent much-needed boiler repairs and coaled. She then sailed for Hong Kong and Whampoa, China.

Wyoming continued her search for the elusive *Alabama* into February of 1864. She sailed to Foochow, China, to protect American interests and proceeded thence, via Hong Kong, to the East Indies. When the sloop-of-war reached Batavia, however, Comdr. McDougal found that there was now no alternative but to return to the United States for repairs, because the ship's boilers were in such poor condition. Accordingly, *Wyoming* began her long-delayed return voyage to the United States, via Anjer, the Cape of Good Hope, St. Helena, and St. Thomas. After a voyage of almost three months, she arrived at the Philadelphia Navy Yard on 13 July 1864; having completed a circumnavigation of the globe begun when she left that port following her commissioning.

The presence of CSS *Florida* off the east coast, however, meant another change in plans for the weary *Wyoming*. Commodore C. K. Stribling, commandant of the Philadelphia Navy Yard, ordered the newly arrived screw sloop to sea to search for *Florida*. "It is with regret that I send you on this service," Stribling wrote McDougal, "After so long a cruise, and one in which you have rendered such important service, yourself, officers and crew, were entitled to a respite from active service; but the great importance of capturing the rebel privateer will, I hope, be an incentive to all under your command cheerfully to perform this service."

Although *Wyoming* required extensive repairs, she nevertheless sailed. As events proved, however, *Wyo-*

ming's machinery—so long from repairs in an American navy yard—proved unequal to the strain. For five days, the ship attempted to carry out the orders given her—contending with fresh northeast winds and a head sea—but returned to Philadelphia on 19 July, due to a leaky boiler. She was decommissioned on 23 July for a complete overhaul.

Recommissioned on 11 April 1865, Comdr. John P. Bankhead in command, *Wyoming* proceeded to the East Indies Station, via Cape Horn, and reached Singapore on 25 September 1865, in time to participate in the search for CSS *Shenandoah*, a Confederate raider which remained at sea for one month after the end of the Civil War. Following service on the East Indies Station into 1866, the screw sloop-of-war was made part of the Asiatic Squadron with that unit's establishment in 1867.

Sailing from Yokohama on 28 April 1867, *Wyoming* headed for the island of Formosa. On 13 June, she participated in a punitive expedition against Formosan natives who had murdered the crew of the American merchant bark *Rover* that had been wrecked off the coast of Formosa a short time before. During that action, she sent a landing party ashore in company with one from the sloop *Hartford*.

Subsequently returning to the United States having performed her last service in the Far East, *Wyoming* was decommissioned on 10 February 1868 and placed "in ordinary" at Boston, Mass. After extensive repairs at Portsmouth, N.H., Navy Yard, during 1870 and into 1871, *Wyoming* was recommissioned on 14 November 1871, Comdr. John L. Davis in command.

From 1872 to 1874, *Wyoming* operated on the North Atlantic Station. Her ports of call included Havana, Cuba; Key West, Fla.; Aspinwall, Panama; Santiago, Cuba; Kingston, Jamaica; San Juan, Puerto Rico; Key West, Fla.; Hampton Roads, Va.; and New Bedford, Mass. After that tour of duty, cruising and "showing the flag" in the West Indies and Gulf of Mexico, *Wyoming* was decommissioned at the Washington Navy Yard on 30 April 1874 and remained laid up there for the next two years.

The veteran screw sloop-of-war became the receiving ship at Washington in 1877 and apparently served in that capacity into early the following year. Recommissioned on 20 November 1877, *Wyoming* left Washington, loaded articles for the Paris Exposition, and departed the east coast of the United States on 6 April 1878, bound for France. After discharging the cargo at Le Havre, France, the ship visited Rouen, France, and Southampton, England, before she departed the latter port on 25 June and headed for the United States. She reached Norfolk on 22 August, shifted to Washington in mid-September, and to New York in early November, before she sailed on 26 November for the European Station.

Wyoming reached Villefranche, France, near the port of Nice, on Christmas Eve 1878 and remained there into 1879 before getting underway for Smyrna on 24 January 1879. *Wyoming* remained in the Mediterranean into November of 1880, touching at many of the more famous ports in that historic body of water—and in the Black Sea—before heading home late in 1880.

Wyoming returned to the United States in early 1881, arriving at Hampton Roads on 21 May. She sailed for Beaufort, S.C., on 15 June and thence proceeded to Annapolis, Md. Decommissioned on 30 October 1882 and turned over to the Superintendent of the Naval Academy, *Wyoming* spent the next decade employed as a practice ship for midshipmen. Later taken to Norfolk, Va., she was sold at the port on 9 May 1892 to E. J. Butler, of Arlington, Mass.

II

(Monitor No. 10: dp. 3,225; l. 255'1''; b. 50'0''; dr. 12'6'' (mean); a. 2 12'' blr., 4 4'', 2 6-pdrs.; cl. *Arkansas*)

The second *Wyoming* (Monitor No. 10) was laid down on 11 April 1898 at San Francisco, Calif., by the Union Iron Works; launched on 8 September 1900; sponsored by Miss Hattie Warren, daughter of Senator Francis E. Warren of Wyoming; and commissioned at the Mare Island Navy Yard, Vallejo, Calif., on 8 December 1902, Comdr. V. L. Cottman in command.

After fitting out at Mare Island, *Wyoming* ran her trials and exercises in San Pablo and San Francisco Bays and conducted exercises and target practice off the southern California coast through the summer of 1903 before she headed south in the autumn, reaching Acapulco, Mexico, on 31 October. She subsequently shifted further south, to Colombia, where a civil war threatened American lives and interests. The monitor accordingly arrived in Panamanian waters on 13 November and sailed up the Tuira River in company with the protected cruiser *Boston*, with a company of marines under Lt. S. A. M. Patterson, USMC, and Lt. C. B. Taylor, USMC, embarked, to land at "Yariza" and observe the movements of Colombian troops.

The presence of American armed might there and elsewhere ultimately resulted in independence for the Panamanians. During that time, *Wyoming* anchored at the Bay of San Miguel on 15 December. The following day, a boat with 11 marines embarked left for the port of La Palma, under sail. While *Boston* departed the scene on the 17th, *Wyoming* shifted to La Palma on the following day. There, Lt. Patterson, USMC, with a detachment of 25 marines, commandeered the steamer *Tuira* and took her upriver. While the marines were gone, a party of evacuated American nationals came out to the monitor in her gig.

Meanwhile, Patterson's marines had joined the ship's landing force at the village of Real to keep an eye on American interests there. Back at La Palma, *Wyoming* continued to take on board American nationals fleeing from the troubled land and kept up a steady stream of supplies to her landing party of bluejackets and marines at Real. Ultimately, when the need for them had passed, the landing party returned to the ship on Christmas Eve.

Wyoming remained in Panamanian waters into the spring of 1904 keeping a figurative eye on local conditions before she departed Panama Bay on 19 April, bound for Acapulco. After remaining at that port from 27 to 29 April, *Wyoming* visited Pichilinque, Mexico, from 3 to 9 May. She subsequently reached San Diego on the 14th for a nine-day stay.

For the remainder of 1904, *Wyoming* operated off the west coast, ranging from Brighton Beach and Ventura, Calif., to Bellingham, Wash., and Portland, Oreg. She attended a regatta at Astoria, Oreg., from 22 to 27 August and later took part in ceremonies at the "unveiling of monuments" at Griffin Bay, San Juan Islands, and Roche Harbor before she entered the Puget Sound Navy Yard, Bremerton, Wash., on 22 October.

Wyoming was overhauled there into the following year. She departed the Pacific Northwest on 26 January 1905 and steamed via San Francisco to Magdalena Bay, Mexico, for target practice. Later cruising to Acapulco and Panamanian waters, *Wyoming* also operated off San Salvador and Port Harford, Calif., before she returned to Mare Island on 30 July to be decommissioned on 29 August 1905.

Recommissioned on 8 October 1908, Comdr. John J. Knapp in command, *Wyoming* spent over two months at Mare Island refitting. Converted to oil fuel—the first ship to do so in the United States Navy—she underwent tests for her oil-burning installation at San Francisco, Santa Barbara, and San Diego into March 1909.

During those tests, *Wyoming* was renamed *Cheyenne* on 1 January 1909, in order to clear the name *Wyoming* for the projected Battleship No. 32. The ship consequently underwent more tests on her oil-burning equipment at Santa Barbara, San Pedro, and San Diego before she was placed in reserve at Mare Island on 8 June. She was decommissioned on 13 November of the same year.

Recommissioned, in reserve, on 11 July 1910, Lt. Comdr. C. T. Owens in command, *Cheyenne* was assigned to the Washington (state) Naval Militia in 1911 and operated in an "in commission, in reserve" status into 1913. Shifting to the Puget Sound Navy Yard early in February of 1913, *Cheyenne* was fitted out as a submarine tender over the ensuing months. Finally, on 20 August 1913, *Cheyenne* was placed in "full commission," Lt. Kenneth Heron in command.

The newly converted submarine tender operated in the Puget Sound region until 11 December, when she sailed for San Francisco. In the ensuing months, *Cheyenne* tender the submarines of the 2d Submarine Division, Pacific Torpedo Flotilla, at Mare Island, San Francisco, and San Pedro, into April of 1914. Later that spring, when troubled conditions in Mexico threatened American lives and property, *Cheyenne* interrupted her submarine tending duties twice, once in late April and once in mid-May, to embark refugees at Ensenada and San Quentin, Mexico, transporting them both times to San Diego.

Cheyenne then resumed her submarine tending operations on the west coast, continuing them into 1917. On 10 April of that year, four days after the United States entered World War I—she proceeded to Port Angeles, Wash., the designated point of mobilization for the Pacific Fleet, in company with the submarines *H-1* (Submarine No. 28) and *H-2* (Submarine No. 29), arriving there on the 16th. Subsequently shifting to the Puget Sound Navy Yard, *Cheyenne* remained at that port for most of a month, taking on stores and provisions, loading ammunition, and receiving men on board to fill the vacancies in her complement. On 28 April, *Cheyenne* guarded *N-1* (Submarine No. 35) as she ran trials off Port Townsend, Wash. On 4 May, the warship returned to Puget Sound for drydock and yard work. Completing that refit late in May, *Cheyenne* shifted southward to San Pedro, Calif., where she established a submarine base and training camp for personnel for submarine duty.

Cheyenne subsequently joined the Atlantic Fleet, serving as flagship and tender for Division 3, Flotilla 1, Submarine Force, Atlantic Fleet. On 17 December 1918, the ship was transferred to Division 1, American Patrol Detachment. While with that force, *Cheyenne* lay at Tampico, Mexico, protecting American lives and property from 15 January to 9 October 1919. Proceeding north soon thereafter, the warship arrived at the Philadelphia Navy Yard on 23 October 1919, where she was decommissioned on 3 January 1920.

While inactive at Philadelphia, the ship was classified as a miscellaneous auxiliary, IX-4, in the fleet-wide designation of alphanumeric hull numbers of 17 July 1920. Subsequently recommissioned at Philadelphia on 22 September of the same year, *Cheyenne* was towed to Baltimore, Md., by the tug *Lykens* (AT-56).

Based there, *Cheyenne* was assigned to training duty with Naval Reserve Force (USNRF) personnel of subdistrict "A," 5th Naval District, and trained USNRF reservists through 1925. Basing at Baltimore, she occasionally visited Hampton Roads during her cruises. On 21 January 1926, the minesweeper *Owl* (AM-2) took *Cheyenne* in tow and took her to Norfolk and thence to Philadelphia where she arrived on 27 January for inactivation.

Decommissioned on 1 June 1926, *Cheyenne* was struck from the Navy list on 25 January 1937, and her stripped-down hulk was sold for scrap on 20 April 1939.

III

(Battleship No. 32: dp. 27,243 (f.); l. 562'0''; b. 93'2½''; dr. 28'6'' (mean); s. 21.22 k. (tl.); cpl. 1,063; a. 12 12'', 21 5'', 2 3'', 2 21'' tt.; cl. *Wyoming*)

The third *Wyoming* (Battleship No. 32) was laid down on 9 February 1910 at Philadelphia, Pa., by William Cramp and Sons; launched on 25 May 1911; sponsored by Miss Dorothy Eunice Knight, the daughter of former Chief Justice Jesse Knight of the Wyoming Supreme Court; and commissioned at the Philadelphia Navy Yard on 25 September 1912, Capt. Frederick L. Chapin in command.

Wyoming departed Philadelphia on 6 October and completed the fitting-out process at the New York Navy Yard, Brooklyn, N.Y., before she joined the fleet in Hampton Roads, Va. Reaching the Tidewater area on 30 December 1912, she became the flagship of Rear Admiral Charles J. Badger, Commander, United States Atlantic Fleet, soon thereafter. Sailing on 6 January 1913, the new battleship visited the soon to be completed Panama Canal and then conducted winter fleet maneuvesr off Cuba before she returned to Chesapeake Bay on 4 March.

After gunnery practice off the Virginia capes, on the southern drill grounds, *Wyoming* underwent repairs and alterations at the New York Navy Yard between 18 April and 7 May. She participated in war games off Block Island between 7 and 24 May—a period of activity broken by repairs to her machinery, carried out at Newport, R.I., between 9 and 19 May—before she underwent more repairs at Newport. She then visited New York City from 28 to 31 May for the festivities surrounding the dedication of the monument honoring the battleship *Maine*, destroyed in Havana harbor on 15 February 1898.

Shifting to Annapolis, Md., on 4 June, *Wyoming* embarked a contingent of Naval Academy midshipmen and took the young officers-to-be on a summer cruise off the coast of New England that lasted into late August. Disembarking the "middies" at Annapolis on 24 and 25 August, *Wyoming* then conducted torpedo and target practices in the southern drill grounds, out of Hampton Roads, into the late autumn. She was docked at New York for repairs between 16 September and 2 October and then ran a full-power trial as she headed south to Norfolk to resume exercises off the Virginia capes before sailing for Europe on 25 October.

Reaching Valetta, Malta, on 8 November, the dreadnought-type battleship visited Naples, Italy, and Villefranche, France, during the course of her Mediterranean cruise. The battleship then left French waters astern on the last day of November and reached New York on 15 December.

Wyoming then underwent voyage repairs at the New York Navy Yard, remaining there through the end of 1913. Getting underway on 6 January 1914, the battleship reached Hampton Roads on the morrow and spent the next three days coaling to prepare for the annual fleet exercises in the warmer Caribbean climes.

Wyoming exercised with the fleet, out of Guantanamo Bay and Guacanayabo Bay, Cuba, between 26 January and 15 March, before setting her course northward for Cape Henry, Va. She then ranged with the fleet from the southern drill grounds, off the Virginia capes, to Tangier Sound, for gunnery drills and practices. She remained engaged in that routine until 3 April, when she headed for the New York Navy Yard and an overhaul.

After that period of repairs, which lasted from 4 April to 9 May, *Wyoming* subsequently embarked a draft of men for transport to the fleet, departed Hampton Roads on 13 May, and headed for Mexican waters. She reached Veracruz on 18 May—less than a month after American sailors and marines had occupied that Mexican port.

Wyoming remained at Vera Cruz over the months that ensued, into the late autumn of 1914, before she returned northward. After conducting exercises off the Virginia capes en route, she put into the New York Navy Yard on 6 October and then underwent repairs and alterations which lasted until 17 January 1915.

Shifting down the coast upon completion of that yard period, *Wyoming* left Hampton Roads in her wake on 21 January for the annual exercises in Cuban waters and in the Caribbean. Returning to the Tidewater area on 7 April, the battleship carried out tactical exercises and maneuvers along the eastern seaboard—primarily off Block Island and the southern drill grounds—into the late autumn, when she again entered the New York Navy Yard for an overhaul.

After repairs lasting from 20 December 1915 to 6 January 1916, *Wyoming* got underway on the latter day, bound for war games in the southern drill grounds. She subsequently headed farther south, reaching Culebra, Puerto Rico, on 16 January. After visiting Port-au-Prince, Haiti, on 27 January, *Wyoming* put into Guantanamo Bay on the 28th and then operated in Cuban waters—off Guantanamo and Guacanayabo Bays and the port of Manzanillo—until 10 April, when she sailed for New York.

Wyoming remained in the New York Navy Yard from 16 April to 26 June, undergoing repairs; she then operated off the New England coast, out of Newport, and off the Virgina capes through the remainder of 1916. Departing New York on 9 January 1917, *Wyoming* then conducted routine maneuvers in the Guantanamo Bay region through mid-March. She departed the Caribbean on 27 March and was off Yorktown, Va., when the United States entered World War I on 6 April 1917.

Over the months that ensued, *Wyoming* served in the Chasepeake Bay region as an engineering ship until until 13 November 1917. On that day, Rear Admiral Hugh Rodman broke his flag in *New York* (Battleship No. 34) as Commander, Battleship Division 9. After preparations for "distant service," *Wyoming*, *New York*, *Delaware* (Battleship No. 28), and *Florida* (Battleship No. 30) sailed for the British Isles on 25 November and reached Scapa Flow, Orkney Islands, on 7 December 1917. Although retaining their American designation as Battleship Division 9, those four dreadnoughts became the 6th Battle Squadron of the British Grand Fleet upon arrival in British waters.

Wyoming carried out maneuvers and tactical exercises with the units of the British Grand Fleet until 6 February 1918. On that day, she got underway with the other ships of the 6th Battle Squadron and eight British destroyers to guard a convoy routed to Stavanger, Norway. En route, *Wyoming* dodged torpedo wakes off Stavanger, on 8 February but reached Scapa Flow safely two days later. In the following months, *Wyoming* continued to patrol off the British Isles, guarding the coastwise sea lanes against the danger posed by the still-powerful German High Seas Fleet.

Between 30 June and 2 July 1918, *Wyoming* operated with the 6th Battle Squadron and a division of British destroyers, guarding Allied minelayers as they planted the North Sea Mine Barrage. Later, *Wyoming* returned to the Firth of Forth, where she was inspected by the King of England, His Majesty George V, along with other units of the Grand Fleet.

Although American and German capital ships never met in combat on the high seas, they nevertheless made rendezvous. On 21 November 1918—10 days after the armistice ended World War I—*Wyoming*, *New York*, *Texas* (Battleship No. 35), and *Arkansas* (Battleship No. 33) joined the Grand Fleet as it escorted the German High Seas Fleet into the Firth of Forth to be interned following the cessation of hostilities.

Later, *Wyoming*, hoisting the flag of Rear Admiral William S. Sims, Commander, Battleship Division 9, sailed on 12 December 1918 from Portland, England, bound for France. The following morning, she and other battleships rendezvoused with *George Washington* (Id. No. 3018) off Brest, France. Embarked in the transport was the President of the United States, Woodrow Wilson, enroute to the Paris Peace Conference.

After serving in the honor escort for the President and his party, *Wyoming* returned Admiral Sims to Plymouth, England, along with the newly appointed ambassador to Great Britain. Debarking her distinguished passengers on 14 December, the battleship loaded 381 bags of mail and, within a few hours, sailed for the United States. Reaching New York City on Christmas Day 1918, she remained there through New Year's Day 1919. On 13 January 1919, she became the flagship of Battleship Division 7, 3d Squadron, and broke the flag of Rear Admiral Robert E. Coontz.

Wyoming departed New York on 1 February and, following winter maneuvers in Cuban waters, returned north, reaching New York on 14 April. However, she stood out to sea soon thereafter, getting underway on 12 May to serve as a link in the chain of ships stretching across the Atlantic to guide the NC-boats on their flight across that ocean. After completing her duty as plane guard and meteorological station, *Wyoming* returned to Hampton Roads on the last day of May.

Later embarking midshipmen and taking them on their southern cruise in the Chesapeake Bay-Virginia capes area, *Wyoming* entered the Norfolk Navy Yard on 1 July to prepare for service in the Pacific. On that day, she became a unit of the newly designated Pacific Fleet, assigned the duty as flagship for Battleship Division 6, Squadron 4. On the morning of 19 July, the fleet, led by flagship *New Mexico* (Battleship No. 40), got underway for the Pacific. Transiting the Panama Canal soon thereafter, the fleet reached San Diego, Calif., on 6 August.

Shifting to San Pedro, Calif., three days later, *Wyoming* operated out of that port into the autumn. After an overhaul at the Puget Sound Navy Yard, Bremerton, Wash., from 15 September 1919 to 19 April 1920, *Wyoming* returned to her base at San Pedro on 4 May. Over the next few months, the battleship exercised off the southern California coast. During that time, she was reclassified BB–32 on 17 July 1920.

Departing San Diego on the last day of August 1920, *Wyoming* sailed for Hawaiian waters and conducted exercises and maneuvers there through September. Returning to San Diego on 3 October, *Wyoming* subsequently conducted tactical evolutions off the western seaboard, ranging north to Seattle. Departing San Francisco, Calif., on 5 January 1921, *Wyoming*, over the ensuing weeks, conducted further drills, exercises, and maneuvers reaching from Panama Bay to Valparaiso, Chile, and was reviewed by the President of Chile on 3 February. Returning north via Panama Bay and San Pedro, *Wyoming* arrived at the Puget Sound Navy Yard on 18 March and remained there into the summer.

Upon completion of repairs, *Wyoming* headed south and, on 2 August, reached Balboa, Canal Zone, where she embarked Rear Admiral Hugh Rodman and members of the commission to Peru for transportation to New York City. Reaching her destination on 19 August, she disembarked her passengers and, that afternoon, broke the flag of Admiral Hilary P. Jones, the Commander in Chief, United States Atlantic Fleet.

Over the next 41 months, *Wyoming* operated primarily in the Atlantic, off the eastern seaboard of the United States, participating in Atlantic Fleet exercises, ranging from the coast of New England to the Virginia capes. She took part in the routine winter maneuvers of the fleet in Caribbean and Cuban waters, serving at various times as flagship for Vice Admiral John D. McDonald, Commander, Battleship Force; and, later, Commander, Scouting Fleet, and his successors, Vice Admiral Newton A. McCully and Vice Admiral Josiah S. McKean. During that time, the ship received routine repairs and alterations at the New York Navy Yard and conducted a midshipman's training cruise in the summer of 1924, cruising to Torbay, England; Rotterdam, Holland; Gibraltar; and the Azores.

Departing New York on 26 January 1925, the battleship conducted battle practice in Cuban waters, out of Guantanamo Bay, and then transited the Panama Canal on 14 February to join the Battle Fleet for exercises along the coast of California. *Wyoming* next sailed for

Hawaiian waters and operated in those climes from late April to early June. After a visit to San Diego from 18 to 22 June, the battleship returned to the east coast, via the Panama Canal, and arrived back at New York City on 17 July to resume operations off the coast of New England. Following those training evolutions with a cruise to Cuba and Haiti, *Wyoming* underwent an overhaul at the New York Navy Yard from 23 November 1925 to 26 January 1926. During her yard period, Comdr. William F. Halsey, Jr., reported on board as the battleship's executive officer. The future fleet admiral served in *Wyoming* until 4 January 1927.

Wyoming subsequently took part in the Fleet's annual winter maneuvers in the Caribbean and then returned northward, reaching Annapolis on 29 May to embark midshipmen for their summer training cruise. After touching at Newport, R.I.; Marblehead, Mass.; Portland, Maine; Charleston, S.C.; and Guantanamo Bay, *Wyoming* returned to Annapolis on 27 August, disembarking the officers-to-be upon arrival. The ship then put into the Philadelphia Navy Yard for modernization.

Converted from a coal burner to an oil burner, *Wyoming* also received new turbines, blisters for added underwater protection against torpedoes, and other alterations. Completing the overhaul on 2 November 1927 and heading south for Norfolk, *Wyoming* then underwent a post-modernization shakedown cruise to Cuba and the Virgin Islands before returning to Philadelphia on 7 December. Two days later, she hoisted the flag of Commander, Scouting Fleet, Vice Admiral Ashley H. Robertson.

Over the next few years, *Wyoming* operated out of Norfolk, New York, and Boston, making training cruises for the Naval Reserve Officers' Training Corps (NROTC) units hailing from Yale, Harvard, Georgia Tech, and Northwestern. That duty took her from the Gulf of Mexico to Nova Scotia and into the Caribbean, as well as to the Azores. During the course of that duty, she departed Hampton Roads on 12 November 1928; and, on the night of 13 and 14 November, picked up eight survivors of the sunken British merchant steamship *Vestris*; and landed them at Norfolk the following day, 15 November.

Relieved as flagship of the Scouting Force on 19 September 1930, *Wyoming* then became the flagship of Rear Admiral Wat T. Cluverius, Commander, Battleship Division 2, and performed that duty until 4 November. After then hoisting the flag of Rear Admiral H. H. Christy, Commander, Training Squadron, Scouting Fleet, the battleship conducted a training cruise into the Gulf of Mexico, during which she visited New Orleans.

Returning north after that cruise, *Wyoming* was placed in reduced commission at the Philadelphia Navy Yard on 1 January 1931 to prepare for demilitarization and conversion to a training ship in accordance with the 1930 London Treaty for the limitation and reduction of naval armaments. During that process, *Wyoming* lost her blisters, side armor, and the removal of guns and turret machinery from three of her six main battery turrets. On 21 May 1931, *Wyoming* was relieved of her duties as flagship for the Scouting Force by *Augusta* (CA–31) and by *Arkansas* (BB–33) as flagship of the Training Squadron.

Wyoming subsequently visited Annapolis upon the completion of her demilitarization and, between 29 May and 5 June 1931, embarked Naval Academy midshipmen for a cruise to European waters. Sailing on 5 June, the ship was in the mid-Atlantic 10 days later, when she went to the aid of the foundering ice-cutting submarine *Nautilus*, commanded by the famed British Arctic explorer, Sir Hubert Wilkins. *Wyoming* took the disabled submersible in tow and took her to Queenstown, Northern Ireland. Later in the course of the cruise, the former battleship visited Copenhagen, Denmark; Greenock, Scotland; Cadiz, Spain; and Gibraltar, before she returned to Hampton Roads on 13 August. During her

cruise, she had been redesignated from a battleship, BB–32, to a miscellaneous auxiliary, AG–17, on 1 July 1931.

Over the next four years, *Wyoming* continued summer practice cruises for Naval Academy midshipmen and training cruises for NROTC midshipmen with units from various universities. Her service took her throughout the Caribbean and the Gulf of Mexico, as well as to northern European ports and into the Mediterranean.

However, there were new jobs for the old campaigner. On 18 January 1935, she embarked men of the 2d Battalion, 4th Marine Regiment, at Norfolk, for the winter-spring landing assault practices at Puerto Rico and the Panama Canal Zone. In almost every succeeding year, *Wyoming* took part in amphibious assault exercises, as the elements of the Fleet Marine Force and Navy developed tactics for use in possible conflicts of the future.

Departing Norfolk on 5 January 1937, *Wyoming* transited the Panama Canal; headed for San Diego soon thereafter; and spent the following weeks engaged in assault landing exercises and gunnery drills at San Clemente Island, off the coast of California. On 18 February 1937, during the culminating phase of a multi-faceted (land, sea, and air) exercise, a shrapnel shell exploded prematurely as it was being rammed into one of the ship's 5-inch broadside guns. Six marines were killed, and 11 were wounded. Immediately after the explosion, *Wyoming* sped to San Pedro, where she transferred the wounded marines to the hospital ship *Relief* (AH–1).

Completing her slate of exercises and war games off the California coast on 3 March, *Wyoming* stood out of Los Angeles harbor on that day and headed back to the east coast. Returning to Norfolk on the 23d of the same month, the ship served as temporary flagship for Rear Admiral Wilson Brown, Commander, Training Squadron, from 15 April to 3 June, during the preparations for the upcoming Naval Academy practice cruise. Putting to sea on 4 June from Hampton Roads, *Wyoming* reached Kiel, Germany, on 21 June 1937, where she was visited by officers from the ill-fated German "pocket battleship" *Admiral Graf Spee*. Her embarked midshipmen subsequently toured Berlin before *Wyoming* sailed for home on 29 June, touching at Torbay, England, and Funchal, Madeira, before returning to Norfolk on 3 August.

After local exercises, *Wyoming* disembarked her midshipmen at Annapolis on 26 August. For the next few months, *Wyoming* continued in her role as training ship —first for Naval Reserve units and then for Merchant Marine Reserve units, ranging from Boston to the Virgin Islands and from New York to Cuba, respectively, before she underwent an overhaul at the Norfolk Navy Yard between 16 October 1937 and 14 January 1938.

For the next three years, *Wyoming* continued her operations out of Norfolk, Boston, and New York, visiting Cuban waters, as well as Puerto Rico and New Orleans. In addition, she conducted a Naval Academy midshipman's practice cruise to European waters in 1938, visiting Le Havre, France; Copenhagen; and Portsmouth, England. Ultimately, on 2 January 1941, *Wyoming* became the flagship for Rear Admiral Randall Jacobs, Commander, Training, Patrol Force, and continued in her training ship duties into the autumn months.

In November 1941, *Wyoming* embarked on yet another phase of her career—that of a gunnery training ship. She departed Norfolk on 25 November 1941 for gunnery training runs out of Newport, R.I., and was off Platt's Bank when the Japanese attacked Pearl Harbor, Territory of Hawaii, on 7 December 1941.

Putting into Norfolk on 28 January 1942, *Wyoming* sailed out into the lower reaches of Chesapeake Bay on 5 February to begin a countless chain of gunnery training drills in that area that would carry her through World War II. So familiar was her appearance in that

The former battleship *Wyoming*, demilitarized under the London Treaty, served as a gunnery training ship during World War II. In this view, an assortment of modern antiaircraft guns and directors contrast a bit oddly with her original cage foremast. (19–N–68181)

area that *Wyoming* earned the nickname of the "Chesapeake Raider." Assigned to the Operational Training Command, United States Atlantic Fleet, the former dreadnought battleship provided the platform on which thousands of gunners trained in guns, ranging from 5-inch to .50-caliber.

Refitted at Norfolk between 12 January and 3 April 1944, *Wyoming* took on a different silhouette upon emerging from that yard period; the rest of her 12-inch turrets were removed, and replaced with twin-mount 5-inch guns; in addition, newer models of fire control radars were installed. She resumed her gunnery training activities on 10 April 1944, operating in the Chesapeake Bay region. The extent of her operations can be seen from a random sampling of figures; in a single month, November 1944, *Wyoming* trained 133 officers and 1,329 men in antiaircraft gunnery. During that month, she fired 3,033 5-inch shells, 849 3-inch; 10,076 40-millimeter; 32,231 20-millimeter; 66,270 .30-caliber; and 360 1.1-inch ammunition. She claimed the distinction

of firing off more ammunition than any other ship in the fleet, training an estimated 35,000 gunners on some seven different types of guns.

On 30 June 1945, *Wyoming* completed her career as "Chesapeake Raider" when she departed Norfolk for the New York Navy Yard and alterations. Leaving the yard on 13 July 1945, she entered Casco Bay soon thereafter, reporting for duty to Vice Admiral Willis A. Lee, Commander, Composite Task Force 69. She fired her first experimental gunnery practice at towed sleeves, drone aircraft, and radio-controlled targets, as the largest operating unit of the force established to study methods and tactics for dealing with the Japanese *kamikazes*. Subsequently, Composite Task Force 69 became the Operational Development Force, United States Fleet, on 31 August 1945. Upon the death of Admiral Lee, the reins of command passed to Rear Admiral R. P. Briscoe.

Even after the broadening of the scope of the work of the force to cover all the operational testing of new devices of fire control, *Wyoming* remained the backbone of the unit through 1946. On 11 July 1947, *Wyoming* entered the Norfolk Naval Shipyard and was decommissioned on 1 August 1947. Her men and materiel were then transferred to *Mississippi* (AG–128) (ex-BB–41).

Wyoming's name was struck from the Navy list on 16 September 1947, and her hulk was sold for scrapping on 30 October 1947. She was then delivered to her purchaser, Lipsett, Inc., of New York City, on 5 December 1947.

Wythe

A county in southwestern Virginia.

(LST–575: dp. 2,080 (f.); l. 328'0''; b. 50'0''; dr. 11'2''; s. 10.0 k.; cpl. 151; trp. 340; a. 8 40mm., 8 20mm.; cl. *LST–542*)

LST–575 was laid down on 3 May 1944 at Evansville, Ind., by the Missouri Valley Bridge and Iron Co.; launched on 9 June 1944; sponsored by Mrs. E. L. Cochrane; and commissioned at New Orleans on 30 June 1944, Lt. Patrick R. Shea, USNR, in command.

On 5 July, *LST–575* got underway for St. Andrews Bay, Fla. The new tank landing ship conducted her shakedown there, in the ensuing fortnight—two weeks of "beaching, retracting, firing, towing, and fueling"—before she moved to Gulfport, Miss., where she took on board a tank deck cargo of quonset hut sections and iron pipe. Returning to New Orleans soon thereafter, *LST–575* underwent some structural modifications and received a coat of "moonlight" camouflage like that used in the Pacific. Then, after loading *LCT–793* on her main deck, *LST–575* set out for Cuba, on 7 August, and reached Guantanamo Bay a week later.

On the 17th, *LST–575* sailed for the Canal Zone in Convoy GS (Guantanamo to Canal Zone) 85 and transited the Panama Canal on 23 August. While most of the original convoy pushed on for Pearl Harbor, the LST, with Army Air Force personnel embarked, turned northward and arrived at San Diego on 5 September.

After provisioning and receiving voyage repairs, *LST–575*, accompanied by *LST–677*, got underway on the 9th for the Hawaiian Islands. Arriving at Pearl Harbor eight days later, *LST–575* discharged her tank deck cargo before she shifted to West Loch one week later, where she shifted her ballast until she listed enough to slip *LCT–793* into the water.

Having safely launched her landing craft, *LST–575* spent the ensuing weeks conducting several training exercises, including a three-day cruise to Maui. Later in the training, the LST practiced loading LVT's (landing vehicle, tracked) and troops.

However, it soon became evident that changes were afoot for the ship and her crew, once she moored back at the Waipio Point Amphibious Base and began conversion to a new, special type of support ship—a self-propelled floating barracks—a "mother ship" for small ships and craft utilized in amphibious operations.

As part of the metamorphosis, two quonset huts were erected on the main deck, one for officers' quarters and the other for a bakery. Large showers and heads were installed on the former tank deck for the use of transient personnel. Four shore-type salt-water evaporators were installed forward on the main deck to distill the tons of water required by small craft and ships. In addition, bunks were mounted in tiers of four on the after end of the tank deck—accommodation for 196 men —and additional bunks were added to the crew's quarters, while on the forward part of the tank deck, 16 shore-type refrigeration units were installed for storing fresh and frozen provisions. In short, the ship was equipped with all of the necessities to enable the ship to function as a tender to small craft.

The idea—converting LST's to floating barrack-type vessels—came from Capt. Stanley Leith, operations officer on the staff of Vice Admiral Richmond Kelly Turner, Commander, Amphibious Forces, Pacific, who had suggested it to the admiral. To many, the ships' initial designation—LST(M), or, simply, a modified LST—came to stand for "mother ship." It was perhaps that concept that caused the crew of *LST–575* to give her the nickname "Mammy Yokum" after a famous cartoon character of the day.

By 15 January 1945, *LST(M)–575* had completed her conversion and emerged with her nickname boldly painted on her conning tower. She immediately entered the floating drydock *ARD–3* where dock workers scraped her bottom and gave her a coat of camouflage paint. In the ensuing week, she took on board provisions and ammunition and embarked the men and equipment of Standard Landing Craft Unit (SLCU) 40. As if that were not enough, two army pigeon lofts—complete with feathered and cooing occupants and their caretakers— were placed on board. With loading completed late on the afternoon of 27 January, *LST(M)–575* sailed for the Philippines. After a 29-day passage, via Eniwetok, Ulithi, and Kossol Roads, the LST made port at Leyte on 25 February.

Occasional air raid alerts at Leyte interrupted the ship's loading of fuel and provisions, but eventually the task was completed, as the ship prepared for her first major operation. She departed Leyte with a large convoy on 19 March, bound for Okinawa.

During the voyage, while underway in spite of roughening seas, *LST(M)–575* fueled and watered PC's, PCS's, and SC's. On the morning of 26 March, the convoy arrived at Kerama Retto—a group of islands 15 miles southwest of Okinawa itself. Throughout that day—the first day of the landings—*LST(M)–575* stood by while boats and LVT's churned shoreward under the protecting guns of the supporting heavy units. As the Army troops captured the important outlying islands of Kerama Retto, *LST(M)–575* stood out to sea on night-retirement, but returned with the daylight and anchored within the southwestern edge of the island circle. Using the modified LST as a base, SLCU–40 commenced operations of a boat pool for that area.

On the morning of the 28th, *LST(M)–575* sailed around Kerama Retto and anchored inside the northern entrance to the anchorage there, being among the first ships to enter and, according to the ship's commanding officer, the first to assume permanent anchorage. The ship would remain at Kerama Retto for the next three and one-half months, providing fuel, water and provisions, and even medical assistance, to ships ranging from escort carriers to submarine chasers. On occasion, the ship handled as many as 28 landing craft per day, and the ship's supply department dispensed between 250 and 350 tons of fresh and dry provisions monthly. The ship loaded similar tonnage from refrigerator ships at night. All this work took place despite frequent "flash red" alerts and kamikaze attacks on ships in the Kerama Retto area.

In the early weeks of the campaign, the ship's berthing capacities were taxed to the limit. The SLCU–40 boat pool remained on board for the entire time, a group frequently enlarged by boat crews from other ships in the anchorage. Moreover, ships whose galleys had been destroyed or damaged by kamikaze attacks sent parties of their men on board *LST(M)–575* for the priceless privilege of eating a hot meal. Sometimes, the ship's cooks fed as many as 750 men daily.

While the ship was performing her vital service function at Kerama Retto, she was reclassified from LST(M)–575 to APB–41 and given the name *Wythe*, effective 31 March 1945. Ultimately, in mid-July, *Wythe* shifted to Buckner Bay, Okinawa, and SLCU–40 went ashore to base. The barracks ship functioned in her original capacity there—an existence hampered by two typhoons: one in late July and one in early August— through the end of the war with Japan in mid-August.

After serving as administrative flagship for Commander, Naval Forces, Ryukyus—berthing and messing

140 men into late August 1945—*Wythe* sailed for Jinsen (now Inchon), Korea, to serve as part of the occupation forces in that area, taking part in Operation "Campus." Dropping anchor in Jinsen harbor on 12 September, *Wythe* supported the 7th Amphibious Force beach party and spent two weeks in that port before she shifted to Taku, China, where she berthed and fed the men from a boat pool there.

Wythe subsequently shifted to Tsingtao, China, and performed similar, but vital, support duties into the spring of 1946, alternating her duties at Tsingtao and Jinsen. On 14 April 1946, in company with her sistership *Yavapai* (APB–42), she sailed for Panama and, proceeding via Okinawa and Pearl Harbor, transited the Panama Canal between 9 and 11 June. *Wythe* ultimately arrived at New Orleans on the 16th.

Wythe's active days were numbered. She reported to Commander, Texas Group, 16th Fleet, on 14 October 1946, and was subsequently inactivated. Placed in reserve at Orange, Tex., on 29 May 1947, and simultaneously decommissioned there, *Wythe* remained in reserve until she was struck from the Navy list on 1 May 1959. Her stripped hulk was sold for scrap to the Marlene Blouse Corp. on 10 September 1959.

LST(M)–575 earned one battle star for her World War II service during the Okinawa campaign.

X

X–1

(X–1: dp. 36.3 (subm.), 31.5 (surf.); l. 49'7''; b. 7'0''; dr. 6'2'' (mean); cpl. 10)

X–1—the Navy's only midget submarine—was laid down on 8 June 1954 at Deer Park, Long Island, N.Y., by the Engine Division of Fairchild Engine and Airplane Corp.; launched on 7 September 1955 at Oyster Bay, Long Island, by Jakobson's Shipyard; delivered to the Navy on 6 October at New London, Conn.; and placed in service on 7 October 1955, Lt. K. Hanlon in command.

X–1 served in a research capacity in rigorous and extensive tests to assist the Navy to evaluate its ability to defend harbors against very small submarines. Further tests conducted with the *X–1* helped to determine the offensive capabilities and limitations of this type of submersible.

Originally powered by a hydrogen peroxide/diesel engine and battery system, an explosion of her hydrogen peroxide supply on 20 May 1957 resulted in the craft's modification to diesel-electric drive. On 2 December 1957, *X–1* was taken out of service and inactivated at Philadelphia, Pa.

Towed to Annapolis in December 1960, *X–1* was reactivated and attached to Submarine Squadron 6 and based at the Small Craft Facility of the Severn River Command for experimental duties in Chesapeake Bay. In tests conducted under the auspices of the Naval Research Laboratory, *X–1* performed for scientists who observed her operations from a platform suspended beneath the Bay Bridge, to learn more about the properties and actions of sea water.

Remaining in an active, in service, status through January 1973, *X–1* was again taken out of service on 16 February 1973 and, on 26 April, was transferred to the Naval Ship Research and Development Center, Annapolis. On 9 July 1974, the submersible was slated for use as a historical exhibit; and she was subsequently placed on display on the grounds of the Naval Station complex, North Severn, near Annapolis.

The experimental submersible *X–1*, 15 September 1955.

Xanthus

In Greek mythology, Achilles' horse who spoke with a human voice.

(AR–19: dp. 10,920 (f); l. 441'6''; b. 56'11''; dr. 22'0''; s. 12.5 k.; cpl. 525; a. 1 5'', 3 3'', 4 40mm., 12 20mm.; cl. Xanthus; T. EC2–S–C1)

Xanthus (AR–19) was laid down under Maritime Commission contract (MCE hull 2664) as Hecla on 6 June 1944 at Baltimore, Md., by the Bethlehem-Fairfield Shipyard, Inc.; launched on 31 July 1944; sponsored by Mrs. J.W.A. Waller; delivered to the Navy on a loan basis on 16 August 1944; renamed Xanthus and designated AR–19 on 6 December 1944; and commissioned on 9 May 1945, Comdr. Stanley G. Nichols in command.

Following training operations and a transit of the Panama Canal, Xanthus arrived at Pearl Harbor on 20 July to serve there as a repair ship. On 11 August, she sailed for Adak, Alaska, to join forces massing there for the projected assaults on the Kurils and northern Japan. The Japanese capitulation, however, obviated such operations. Instead of an invasion—there was now an occupation.

As part of Task Group (TG) 40.2, Xanthus proceeded to Japan and arrived at Ominato on 9 September—the same date that Japanese forces there surrendered to Vice Admiral Frank Jack Fletcher. The ship remained at Ominato through 21 November, serving as flagship for the commander of TG 56.2, the repair and logistics group. Subsequently reporting for duty with Service Squadron 104, the ship operated out of Okinawa through late January 1946.

On 10 February 1946, Xanthus sailed for Tsingtao, China, and helped to stabilize troubled conditions there in the wake of the Japanese withdrawal. As Communist and Nationalist Chinese jockeyed for position in the volatile situation in their country, Xanthus supported American naval activities in that port until sailing for home on 8 April 1946.

Subsequently arriving at Norfolk, Va., in the spring of that year, the repair ship was laid up at the Maritime Commission facility in the James River, Va., in an "on hand" status, through 1961. On 1 September 1962, the ship was struck from the Navy list.

Xarifa

(Yacht: t. 378; l. 192'0''; b. 26'8''; dph. 15'5''; dr. 15'0''; s. 11 k.; cpl. 71; a. 2 3-pdrs., 2 mg.)

Xarifa—a wooden-hulled, seagoing, sailing yacht equipped with an auxiliary steam engine—was built in 1896 at Cowes, Isle of Wight, England, by John S. White & Co., Ltd. Apparently completed as Xarifa, she served for a time as Ophelie before she was purchased by C. N. Nelson in, or sometime before, 1911. She then resumed the name Xarifa and operated out of Port Washington, Long Island, N.Y.

After the outbreak of World War I, the Navy acquired the graceful yacht on 9 August 1917 for service in European waters and designated her SP–581. However, while the ship was being fitted out, she was found to be unsuitable for "distant service" and was prepared for duty on section patrol.

Assigned to the 3d Naval District, Xarifa was commissioned at the New York Navy Yard on 23 February 1918, Lt. (jg.) F. J. Littlefield, USNRF, in command; and patrolled the approaches to New York harbor through the armistice. She was decommissioned on 31 March 1919 and returned to her owner on 4 May 1919.

Xenia

Minor planet number 625, which was discovered by August Kopff in Heidelburg, Germany, on 11 February 1907. The word Xenia is a Greek term for hospitality or present. Shortly after the ship was commissioned, the town of Xenia—in Greene County, Ohio—demonstrated how well it deserved the name which it shares with the planet and the warship by offering to adopt the attack cargo ship.

(AKA–51: dp. 4,087; l. 426'0''; b. 58'0''; dr. 15'6''; s. 16.9 k.; cpl. 303; a. 1 5'', 8 40mm., 10 20mm.; cl. Artemis; T. S4–SE2–BE1)

Xenia (AKA–51) was laid down under Maritime Commission contract (MC hull 1912) on 4 May 1945 at Providence, R.I., by the Walsh-Kaiser Co., Inc.; launched on 27 June 1945; sponsored by Mrs. Roger W. Armstrong; and commissioned at the Boston Navy Yard on 28 July 1945, Lt. Comdr. G. B. Service, USNR, in command.

Following shakedown, Xenia operated off the east coast with Service Force, Atlantic Fleet, from September 1945 until 17 April 1946, when she reported to the Commandant, 3d Naval District, New York, N.Y., for disposal. Decommissioned on 13 May 1946, Xenia was struck from the Navy list on 30 November 1946 and subsequently transferred to the government of Chile. Renamed Presidente Errazuriz, she served the Chilean Navy, for a time serving as fleet flagship, until 1962.

Y

Yacal

A Philippine timber tree having a heavy, hard, wood. Yacal herself was built principally of this wood.

(YFB–688: dp. 66; l. 71'0'; b. 13'0''; dr. 8'0'')

Yacal (YFB–688)—a small ferryboat constructed in the Philippine Islands by the Cavite Navy Yard—was launched on 15 September 1932. Completed on 11 November 1932, the small, wood-constructed coal-burner performed yard duties at Cavite for almost a decade. Following up their devastating attack on Pearl Harbor, Japanese forces struck at the Philippines in December 1941 and scored lightning-quick successes. In the destructive deluge which engulfed the Philippines, Yacal met her end on 2 January 1942. Records do not indicate whether she was destroyed by her own forces to prevent capture or by the Japanese. In any event, she was struck from the Navy list on 24 July 1942.

Yacona

A misspelling of Yocona, a river in the state of Mississippi that flows westward from Pontotoc and Lafayette Counties to join the Tallahatchie River in Quitman County.

I

(ScStr: t. 527 (gross); l. 211'0''; b. 27'3''; dph. 15'9''; dr. 13'9''; s. 10.0 k.; cpl. 67; a. 2 3'', 2 .30-cal. Colt mg.; 10 Mk. I dc.)

The first Yacona—a steel-hulled screw steam yacht formerly named Cem and Amelia—was built in 1898 at Kinghorn, Scotland, by John Scott and Co., shipwrights, and was purchased around 1906 by the noted financier and oil industry pioneer, H. Clay Pierce, of New York City. The Navy acquired the graceful yacht at New York City on 29 September 1917 for service during World War I. Yacona was fitted out at the

Boston Navy Yard; assigned the designation SP-617; and commissioned on 10 December 1917, Lt. Comdr. John W. Wilcox, Jr., in command.

Following operations in coastal waters as far south as New York, *Yacona*—now commanded by Lt. Comdr. George A. Alexander—departed Newport, R.I., on 24 February, bound for Bermuda. The voyage was uneventful until 26 February, when, at 1130, heavy seas smashed in the ports on the starboard side of the deck house in *Yacona*, flooding her pay office and radio room and carrying away part of the bulwarks on the starboard bow. Later that day, the ship developed a leak that inundated some of her bunker spaces and flooded the fireroom to a depth of one foot. Reducing speed accordingly, the yacht nevertheless performed a service for *SC-256* the following day, taking the 110-foot craft in tow during the afternoon. *Yacona*'s log noted that during the 1200 to 1600 watch, all hands were engaged in removing water from the fireroom bilges.

Arriving at Bermuda on 1 March, *Yacona* remained there into April, undergoing voyage repairs. She departed Bermuda's waters on the morning of 8 April to escort a convoy that consisted of two Army tugs, *Cadmus* and *Seminole*; the tanker *Chestnut Hill* (SP-2526); the destroyer tender *Leonidas*; and six subchasers: SC's *143, 147, 179, 227, 338,* and *95*. En route to the Azores, *Yacona* conducted gunnery and general quarters drills and made part of the passage under sail to conserve coal. *Yacona* and her convoy arrived at Ponta Delgada on the morning of 22 April and moored alongside the Russian bark *Montrosa*. After coaling ship, *Yacona* headed for Bermuda on 4 May, in company with *Wadena* and the fuel ship *Arethusa*, and made port at Hamilton 10 days later.

The yacht made one more round-trip voyage to Ponta Delgada and back, escorting a group of six subchasers, the cruiser *Salem* and the destroyer *Connelly* eastbound and returning west-bound in company with the tugs *Arctic* (SP-1158), *Goliah, Undaunted,* and *Wadena* on 20 June. After engine repairs at the British dockyard there and having her hull painted, *Yacona* departed Bermuda on 9 July in company with the minesweeper *Comber* (SP-344) and the tug *Mojave* (SP-15) and headed for New London. On the voyage to the Connecticut coast, the converted yacht carried the American vice consul to Switzerland, Louis Lombard, and his son as passengers.

The ship reached New London on the afternoon of 12 July and spent almost two months on the east coast undergoing repairs. On 6 September, she departed Charleston, S.C., escorting a convoy—consisting of three 110-foot subchasers assigned to the French Navy: SC-*365, 366,* and *367*—and headed for Bermuda.

Yacona, in company with the cruiser *Chicago*, escorted one more convoy to the Azores between 15 and 27 September. While *Yacona*'s crew was heaving in her port anchor as she was departing Ponta Delgada on 2 October, it fouled the mooring gear. To "expedite matters and join the convoy" then sortieing for Hamilton, *Yacona* slipped the anchor and 15 fathoms of chain. At 1622 on the afternoon of 9 October, *Yacona* spotted a suspicious object on the surface; went to general quarters; commenced firing three minutes later; but, after identifying the target as a drifting buoy, ceased fire.

Yacona arrived back at St. George's Harbor, Bermuda, on the 12th; departed those waters at 1620 on 5 November, bound for New York; and arrived at the New York Navy Yard on 11 November 1918, the day that the armistice ended World War I.

Next attached to Division 3, Battleship Force 1, United States Atlantic Fleet, *Yacona* departed Boston on 10 December and anchored off the mouth of the York River, Va., on the 13th. The following day, she shifted her anchorage up the river and, on the 15th, briefly flew the flag of Rear Admiral Thomas Washington. After moving to Hampton Roads the day after Christmas of 1918, *Yacona* sailed for New York, N.Y., and arrived at Tompkinsville, Staten Island, on the 13th. *Yacona* did not tarry long, however, for she sailed for New London on the 15th, arriving there the following day.

Placed in reserve in January 1919, *Yacona* remained at New London into June. *Yacona* departed New London on 13 June and arrived at the New York Navy Yard on the 16th to unload her ammunition and have her ordnance removed. On 26 June 1919, *Yacona* was decommissioned and placed in reserve.

The ship apparently languished inactive at the New York Navy Yard until the autumn of 1920. On 22 April 1920, the Navy decided to sell the vessel but, on 14 September, cancelled the sale order. Instead, *Yacona* was taken out of reserve and recommissioned on 11 October 1920, Lt. Comdr. Ralph E. Simpson, USN, in command.

The yacht remained at the navy yard into February

Yacona (SP-617) in wartime camouflage at Boston, with the converted yacht *Isabel* and two local passenger steamers in the background.

1921, being prepared for a long voyage to the Far East. Upon completion of her overhaul, *Yacona* departed New York on 1 March and proceeded to Bermuda, utilizing sails once more in order to conserve precious coal. After calling at Hamilton from 5 to 14 March, *Yacona* pressed on across the Atlantic, visiting Ponta Delgada from 24 to 29 March before reaching Gibraltar on 3 April.

She remained at that British bastion for almost a month, weighing anchor on the 28th and heading for Malta on the next leg of her passage to the Orient. While at Malta from 3 to 8 May, *Yacona* full-dressed ship in honor of the anniversary of the accession of King George V to the throne of England and, along with all other ships and batteries in the harbor, fired a 21-gun national salute at noon that day to celebrate the event.

Yacona got underway again on 8 May, bound for the entrance to the Suez Canal. After taking on supplies at Port Said, *Yacona* transited the canal on the 13th and proceeded to Aden, Arabia. There, *Yacona* took on fresh water and coal and resumed her eastward voyage on the 23d and arrived at Bombay, India, on 1 June. There, she once again dressed-ship, this time for the King's Birthday on the 3d. The ship departed that port on the 4th. After calling at Colombo, Ceylon, from 9 to 24 June and at Singapore from 3 to 7 July, *Yacona* stood into Manila Bay on 14 July, her long odyssey from the eastern seaboard of the United States completed. There, *Yacona* was decommissioned on 27 July 1921 and turned over to representatives of the Insular Government. Records of her service for the Philippines apparently have not survived.

II

(AOG–45: dp. 2,300; l. 221'0''; b. 37'0''; dph. 15'0''; s. 15.0 k.; cpl. 58; a. 1 3'', 6 20mm.; cl. *Mettawee*; T. T1–M–A2)

The second *Yacona* (AOG–45) was laid down under a Maritime Commission contract (MC hull 2071) on 23 November 1944 at Bayonne, N.J., by the East Coast Shipyard, Inc.; launched on 14 January 1945; sponsored by Mrs. Amy Gilhardt; and commissioned on 7 February 1945, Lt. Richard A. Urquhart, USNR, in command.

Following shakedown in Chesapeake Bay, *Yacona* sailed for Miami, Fla., on 19 April. On the 25th, she departed for temporary duty at the Naval Training Station at Miami and operated out of there on training duties into the fall of 1945. A three-day port visit to Havana, Cuba, from 31 July to 3 August, punctuated her duty in Florida's coastal waters. *Yacona* departed Miami on 4 November, bound for Hampton Roads; and was decommissioned at Norfolk on 20 December 1945. Struck from the Navy list on 8 January 1946, the gasoline tanker was delivered to the War Shipping Administration, Maritime Commission, on 25 July 1946.

Acquired by the Gulf Oil Co., of Philadelphia, Pa., in 1947, *Yacona* served this petroleum concern until late in 1976, when she was purchased by the *Sociedad Compañia de Navegacion Dormar, Ltd.* She served under the Colombian flag, homeported at Isla de San Andres, Colombia, carrying oil to vessels in Colombia's lakes, bays, and sounds.

Yahara

A river which rises at a small lake in Dane County, Wis., and flows south and southeast past Madison to empty into the Rock River about nine miles northwest of Janesville.

(AOG–37: dp. 2,700; l. 220'6''; b. 37'0''; dr. 13'1''; s. 10 k.; cpl. 62; a. 1 3'', 2 40mm.; cl. *Sequatchie*; T. T1–M–A2)

Yahara (AOG–37) was laid down under a Maritime Commission contract (MC hull 1800) on 6 June 1944 at Bayonne, N.J., by the East Coast Shipyard, Inc.; launched on 30 July 1944; sponsored by Miss Cynthia Tenety; converted for naval service at Brooklyn, N.Y., by the Marine Basin Co.; and commissioned at the New York Navy Yard on 29 September 1944, Lt. N. Clark Biggs, USNR, in command.

The new gasoline tanker got underway for Norfolk, Va., on 30 October. Following shakedown in Chesapeake Bay, *Yahara* sailed for the Netherlands West Indies on 22 November to take on a cargo of aviation gasoline and diesel oil at Aruba. Loaded to capacity, she sailed on 1 December for the west coast; transited the Panama Canal on the 6th; and proceeded via San Diego, Calif., to Hawaii.

Upon her arrival at Pearl Harbor on 2 January 1945, the ship joined Service Squadron (ServRon) 8. Departing Pearl Harbor on 5 January for the Phoenix group, she delivered her cargo of aviation gas and oil to Canton Island on the 13th and returned to Pearl Harbor two days later.

She continued her fuel shuttle operations in the Hawaiian chain through most of February, making runs to Johnston Island and Maui. The tanker sailed for the Marshalls on the 25th as part of Task Unit 16.8.13. En route, she delivered a cargo of aviation gasoline to the naval air station at Johnston Island for use by planes engaged in the search for Lt. Gen. Millard F. Harmon, whose plane had been lost at sea. The ship arrived at Eniwetok on 13 March and, after waiting four days for a convoy bound for the Western Carolines, got underway on St. Patrick's Day and proceeded independently to Ulithi.

Joining ServRon 10 a week later, she took on a cargo of gasoline, diesel oil, and lubricating oil. However, she stood by at Ulithi, awaiting instructions through all of April and the first half of May before the long-awaited orders arrived and directed her to join Task Force 51.

On 19 May, *Yahara* got underway for Kerama Retto, in company with Convoy UOK 16. Rerouted en route, to the beachhead at Hagushi, the tanker arrived off Okinawa on 28 May. She remained in the Okinawa area through the cessation of hostilities in August, at Naha, Ie Shima, Chimu Wan, and Buckner Bay. During this period, she provided shuttle tanker services, transporting fuel from large tankers offshore to shore installations, and served as a small craft fueling center. In the course of her operations, she weathered three typhoons (19 to 21 July; 1 to 3 August; 16 to 18 September) and, after the September "blow," was forced to assume emergency harbor duty, as all of the smaller yard oilers had been driven aground by the fury of the storm. A fourth typhoon struck on 9 October; and *Yahara*, while riding it out, lost her starboard anchor when its chain parted. The ship dragged her port anchor some three miles while winds in excess of 125 knots lashed Buckner Bay.

Her duty completed and the war over, *Yahara* sailed for home on 14 December, in company with sistership *Ponchatoula* (AOG–38). Arriving at Pearl Harbor on 5 January 1946, *Yahara* resumed her voyage to the west coast on the 9th and arrived at San Francisco on the 20th. She spent the remainder of the month on the California seaboard before heading for the Panama Canal and the east coast.

From 4 March to 25 April, *Yahara* served the 16th Fleet (the Atlantic Fleet Reserve), providing diesel oil to ships on reserve duty at Lake Charles, La., and Jacksonville, Fla. Decommissioned at New Orleans on 21 May, *Yahara* was struck from the Navy list on 19 July 1946 and transferred to the War Shipping Administration, Maritime Commission, on 5 November 1946.

Late in 1947, *Yahara* was acquired by the Texas Oil Co. and renamed *El Caribe*. She subsequently operated under a succession of flags—Norwegian, British, and French—into the 1950's before her documentary trail becomes cloudy. Homeported at Oslo, Norway, from 1947 to 1952, she served the Texas Oil Company's Norwegian subsidiary and then sailed under the British flag with first the Verbomilia Steamship Co. and later with the Cousotanker Co., Ltd. (both of London) in 1953 and 1954. Her last recorded registry was French; and, still as *El Caribe*, she homeported at Marseilles, France, from 1954 to 1958, with the *Societé Meridionale d'Armement*. Renamed *Crysanthi P*, she is carried on the American Bureau of Shipping's *Record* from 1958 to 1960 under this name but without any clue as to her nationality or ownership. Thereafter, all trace of the ship seems to have disappeared.

Yahara received one battle star for World War II service.

Yakutat

A bay on the southern coast of Alaska.

(AVP–32: dp. 2,411 (f.); l. 310'9''; b. 41'2''; dr. 11'11''; s. 18.5 k.; cpl. 367; a. 2 5'', 8 40mm., 6 20mm., 2 dct.; cl. *Barnegat*)

Yakutat (AVP–32) was laid down on 1 April 1942 at Seattle, Wash., by Associated Shipbuilders, Inc.; launched on 2 July 1942; sponsored by Mrs. Peter Barber, a mother who had lost three sons when the battleship *Oklahoma* (BB–37) was sunk on 7 December 1941 at Pearl Harbor; and commissioned on 31 March 1944, Comdr. George K. Fraser in command.

After her shakedown in the San Diego, Calif., area, *Yakutat* got underway on 25 May and arrived at San Pedro, Calif., late the following day. Following postshakedown availability in the West Coast Shipbuilders' yard at San Pedro, the small seaplane tender sailed for Pearl Harbor, Hawaii, on 17 June; she reached Ford Island one week later.

Underway at 0700 on 28 June, *Yakutat* steamed for the Marshalls as an escort for *Makin Island* (CVE–93). Arriving at Kwajalein on 6 July, she shifted to Eniwetok within a week, where she embarked officers and men of a patrol service unit and took on board a cargo of 5-inch illuminating ammunition. She sailed for Saipan on 14 July.

Reaching recently secured Tanapag Harbor on 17 July, *Yakutat* began setting up a seaplane base there and immediately commenced servicing seaplanes, providing subsistence and quarters for the aviators and aircrews attached to those aircraft. The tender provided the aircraft with gasoline and oil via bowser fueling boats and commenced servicing planes by the over-the-stern method as well.

Yakutat remained at Tanapag Harbor for the rest of July, all of August, and into September. After shifting to the Garapan anchorage, Saipan, on 8 September, *Yakutat* transferred all plane personnel to *Coos Bay* (AVP–25) and sailed for the Palaus on the 12th. In company with *Chandeleur* (AV–10), *Pocomoke* (AV–9), *Onslow* (AVP–48), and *Mackinac* (AVP–13), *Yakutat* reached Kossol Passage on 16 September, the day after the initial landings on Pelelieu.

Proceeding to the seaplane operation area via a "comparatively well-marked channel" and "while sweeping operations went on continuously" nearby, *Yakutat* soon commenced laying out a seaplane anchorage. The following day, the tender serviced the first plane of Patrol Bomber Squadron (VPB) 216, furnishing fuel and boat service.

With nine planes operational, VPB 216 was based on *Yakutat*, conducting long-range patrols and antisubmarine sweeps daily. During that time, the tender also served as secondary fighter director unit and experienced air alerts on six occasions. Enemy planes remained in the vicinity for varying lengths of time and occasionally dropped bombs in the lagoon area.

Yakutat serviced the Martin PBM patrol planes into early November 1944. On 9 November, the ship got underway for Ulithi and arrived there the following day. *Yakutat* tended planes there from 13 to 26 November before she underwent a drydocking for a routine bottom cleaning and hull repairs. She then sailed for Guam on the 29th.

Reaching Apra Harbor on the 30th, *Yakutat* loaded spare parts for Martin PBM Mariner flying boats before she got underway on the 2d to return to Saipan. She arrived later the same day; completed the discharge of her cargo two days later and, on the 5th, took on board 13 officers and 30 men of VPB 216 for temporary subsistence.

Yakutat tended planes of VPB 16 and VPB 17 at Saipan through mid-January of 1945. She departed Tanapag harbor on the morning of 17 January, steamed independently for Guam, and reached her destination later that day. However, she remained there only a short time, for she sailed on the 19th for the Palaus and reached Kossol Roads on the 21st. *Yakutat* discharged cargo there and fueled seaplanes until 6 February, when she sailed in company with *St. George* (AV–16) and escorted by *PC–1130*, bound for the Carolines.

Anchoring at Ulithi on the 7th, *Yakutat* tended seaplanes there for most of February; highlighting that brief tour was the ship's going to the vicinity of a crashed Vought OS2U Kingfisher floatplane on the 10th. After salvaging equipment from the plane—the aircraft apparently too badly damaged to warrant repair—*Yakutat* sank the plane with gunfire and returned to her anchorage in the seaplane operating area.

On 25 February, *Yakutat* sailed for the Marianas in company with *St. George* and reached Garapan harbor two days later. She tended seaplanes there for a little less than a month before sailing for Okinawa on the 23d to take part in Operation "Iceberg," the conquest of the Ryukyus.

Yakutat tended the PBM Mariners of VPB 27 for the rest of the war. The seaplane tender established seadrome operations at Kerama Retto on the 28th and spent the rest of the important Okinawa campaign engaged in her vital but unsung task. The presence of enemy aircraft in the vicinity on numerous occasions meant many hours spent at general quarters stations, lookouts' eyes and radar alert for any sign of approaching enemy planes. *Yakutat* provided quarters and subsistence for the crews of the Mariners and furnished the planes with gas, lube oil, and JATO (jet-assisted take-off) units. The twin-engined Martin flying boats conducted antisubmarine and air-sea rescue ("Dumbo") duties locally, as well as offensive patrols that ranged as far as the coast of Korea.

Although the ship received a dispatch on 21 June to the effect that all "organized resistance on Okinawa has ceased," her routine remained busy. A week later, for example, a Consolidated PB2Y Coronado crashed on take-off and sank approximately 500 yards off the starboard beam of the ship. *Yakutat* dispatched two boats to the scene and rescued eight men. Boats from another ship rescued the remaining trio of survivors from the Coronado. All men were brought on board *Yakutat*, where they were examined and returned to their squadron, VPB 13.

On 15 July, *Yakutat* sailed for Chimu Wan, Okinawa —in company with *Norton Sound* (AV–11), *Chandeleur*, *Onslow*, *Shelikof* (AVP–52), and *Bering Strait* (AVP–34)—but returned to port due to a typhoon in the vicinity. However, she got underway again the following day and reached Chimu Wan the same date. She remained there, tending seaplanes, largely anchored but occasionally moving to open water to be free to maneuver when typhoons swirled by. On one occasion, while returning to Chimu Wan after a typhoon evacuation, *Yakutat* made sonar contact on a suspected submarine, on 3 August. The seaplane tender made one attack, dropping depth charges from her stern-mounted tracks, but lost the contact soon thereafter.

Yakutat was at Chimu Wan when Japan capitulated and hostilities ended on 15 August. With the officers and men of the crew assembled aft, the ship's commanding officer, Lt. Comdr. W. I. Darnell humbly led his crew in offering thanks to God "for being kept afloat to see the final day of this war."

Although V–J Day meant that offensive operations against the Japanese ceased, it only meant the beginning of the long occupation of the erstwhile enemy's homeland and possessions. *Yakutat* remained at Chimu Wan for the rest of August and for most of September, before she sailed for Japanese home waters on 20 September, in company with *St. George*.

En route, the two seaplane tenders caught up with Vice Admiral Jesse B. Oldendorf's Task Unit 56.4.3 formed around the battleships *Tennessee* (BB–43) and *California* (BB–44) and became units of Task Force 56, and later, when redesignated, as Task Force 51.

Yakutat reached Wakanoura Wan, Honshu, on the 22d, finding *Floyds Bay* (AVP–40) already there and operating as tender for seaplanes. *Yakutat* underwent a brief availability alongside *Cascade* (AD–26) before she commenced her tending operations at Wakanoura Wan. She operated as tender for seaplanes using that port until 12 October, when she shifted to Hiro Wan where she performed seaplane tender operations and seadrome control duties for a little over a month.

Underway on 14 November, *Yakutat* arrived at Sasebo on the 15th, stayed there until the 19th, and then set sail for the United States with 58 officers and 141 enlisted men embarked as passengers. After stopping at Midway for fuel on the 27th, the small seaplane tender continued on, bound for the Pacific Northwest.

Reaching Port Townsend, Wash., on 6 December, *Yakutat* transferred all passengers to *LCI–957* for further transportation and then shifted to Sinclair Inlet, Wash., where she offloaded all bombs and ammunition before reporting on the 7th to the Bremerton Group of the Pacific Reserve (19th) Fleet.

Yakutat subsequently shifted south to the naval air station at Alameda, Calif., where she was decommissioned on 29 July 1946. Transferred on loan to the Coast Guard on 31 August 1948, the erstwhile small seaplane tender was towed to the Hunters Point Naval Shipyard in September, where she was fitted out into the winter months. She was recommissioned at San Francisco on 23 November 1948 as USCGC *Yakutat* (WAVP–380).

Proceeding via the Panama Canal and Kingston, Jamaica, *Yakutat* eventually commenced weather patrol duties in the North Atlantic out of Portland, Maine, in late January 1949. Homeported at New Bedford, Mass.,

in 1949, *Yakutat* operated out of that port over the next 11 years, always ready to perform her assigned missions of search and rescue, ocean station patrol, and providing meteorological and oceanographic services. Periodically, the ship conducted refresher training in company with naval units out of Guantanamo Bay, Cuba.

During the course of her operations, *Yakutat* proceeded, in February 1952, to the scene of an unusual maritime disaster that occurred off Cape Cod. Two tankers—SS *Fort Mercer* and SS *Pendleton*—each broke in two and foundered, almost simultaneously. *Yakutat*, as ship in tactical command of the rescue efforts, consequently picked up men from both ships and directed the rescue efforts by other participating vessels in the vicinity. Later that year, in December, *Yakutat* rescued survivors of a plane crash off the entrance to St. George's Harbor, Bermuda, with her small boats.

Participating in Coast Guard operations as part of Operation "Market Time" off the coast of Vietnam in 1967 and again in 1970 and 1971, *Yakutat* was also redesignated as a medium endurance cutter and given the alphanumeric hull number WHEC–380. Returned to the Navy in 1970, *Yakutat* was transferred to the Navy of the Republic of South Vietnam on 10 January 1971.

Renamed *Tran Nhat Duat* (HQ–03), the former seaplane tender and weather ship cooperated with units of the United States Navy on coastal patrol and counterinsurgency missions off the coast of embattled South Vietnam until the collapse of that country in the spring of 1975.

Fleeing to the Philippines, *Tran Nhat Duat* and her five sisterships of the former South Vietnamese Navy lay moored in Subic Bay awaiting disposition—ships without a country. The Philippine government, however, acquired the ships in 1975, and title was formally transferred on 5 April 1976. *Tran Nhat Duat* and her sistership *Tran Quac Toan* (HQ–06) (ex-*Cook Inlet*, WHEC–384 and AVP–36) were acquired only to be cannibalized for spare parts to keep the other four units of the class in operating condition.

Yakutat (AVP–32) received four battle stars for her World War II service. She also received one award of the Navy Unit Commendation, one award of the Meritorious Unit Commendation, and four battle stars for Vietnam service while assigned to the United States Coast Guard.

Yakutat (AVP–32) as a Coast Guard cutter (WHEC–380), in the gray finish used on cutters operating in Vietnam.

Yale

I

(Str: dp. 10,669 (gross); l. 527'6"; b. 63'2"; dr. 23' (mean); s. 21.8 k.; cpl. 436; a. 4 6-pdrs., 4 3-pdrs.)

SS *Paris*—a steamship built in 1888 and 1889 by J. & G. Thompson at Glasgow, Scotland—was acquired by the Navy on 27 April 1898 under charter from the International Navigation Co.; renamed *Yale*; and commissioned on 2 May 1898, Capt. W. C. Wise in command.

That same day, she put to sea from New York bound for Puerto Rico to patrol and help locate Admiral Cervera's Spanish fleet. On 8 May, two days after her arrival off Puerto Rico, *Yale* encountered and captured the Spanish cargo ship *Rita*, installed a prize crew in her, and sent her into Charleston, S.C.

The following day, she had another brief encounter with the enemy off San Juan when a Spanish armed transport came out and fired a few shots. *Yale*, possessing armament greatly inferior to the enemy ship, was forced to retire from the scene. She returned to San Juan the following day, and a shore battery fired two poorly aimed shots at her, both of which fell far short.

Pursuant to her orders, *Yale* patrolled off Puerto Rico until 13 May at which time she cleared the area for St. Thomas in the Danish West Indies (Virgin Islands) to telegraph her report to Washington. She returned briefly to Puerto Rico on 16 and 17 May, then headed for Cape Haitien, Haiti, in company with *St. Paul*. She remained at Cape Haitien until 21 May, then headed for waters off Santiago de Cuba where the Spanish fleet had been discovered. *Yale* remained there while the United States fleet assembled off Santiago to blockade Cervera's ships in that port. On the 28th, she quit the area; stopped briefly at Port Antonio, Jamaica; and then set a course for Newport News, Va. The ship spent 20 days at Newport News, heading back to Cuba on 23 June. She arrived off Santiago on 27 June but remained there only two days. On the 29th, she got underway for Key West, Fla., stopping there overnight on 3 and 4 July before continuing on to Charleston. *Yale* returned to Santiago on 11 July and remained in Cuban waters until the 17th. After a stop at Guanica, Puerto Rico, she set a course for New York on 26 July. She spent most of the first two weeks of August in New York and returned to Cuba on the 15th. Remaining only briefly, she embarked troops for the return voyage to New York.

Yale arrived back in New York on 23 August and remained there until decommissioned on 2 September 1898. Though returned to her owners after decommissioning, *Yale* was not struck from the Navy list until 3 July 1899. She returned to merchant service—first under the name SS *City of Paris* and later as SS *Philadelphia*—and operated out of New York until the mid-1920's, at which time all reference to her in merchant registers ceased.

II

ScStr: dp. 5,200 (n.); l. 403'; b. 63'; dr. 19' (mean); s. 22.4 k.; cpl. 213)

The second *Yale* (Id. No. 1672)—a screw steamer built in 1906 by the Delaware River Steamboat Co.—was purchased by the Navy on 13 March 1918 and commissioned at the Mare Island Navy Yard on 25 March 1918, Lt. Comdr. Richard C. Brennan, USNRF, in command.

After being fitted out for naval service at the Mare Island Navy Yard, *Yale* put to sea on 20 May, bound for Nicaragua carrying a detachment of marines to duty at the legation at Managua. Steaming via Acapulco, Mexico, she arrived at Corinto, Nicaragua, on the 27th, landed the marines and some mail, and then headed on to the Panama Canal. She transited the canal on 30 May and continued her voyage to Norfolk, where she arrived on 3 June. She operated in the Chesapeake Bay area until 10 July when she departed Newport News, Va., in a convoy bound for Europe. On 21 July, the convoy arrived in Brest, France; and *Yale* was assigned duty as a cross-channel transport. During the war, she made 31 uneventful, round-trip voyages carrying troops between Southampton, England, and the French ports of Brest and Le Havre. She continued that service after the end of hostilities on 11 November and made another 54 round-trip voyages carrying passengers and supplies.

On 6 May 1919, she departed Brest for the last time and set a course—via the Azores—to the United States. She anchored off Weehawken, N.J., on 22 May and disembarked passengers. Through the summer of 1919, she steamed up and down the east coast shuttling passengers between Norfolk and Hoboken, N.J. On 3 September, she moored in Back Channel at Philadelphia and remained there until sold. *Yale* was decommissioned on 10 June 1920. She was subsequently sold to the Harvard-Yale Syndicate which reconditioned her and put her in passenger service between San Pedro and San Francisco.

After 15 years of fast passenger service along the west coast, *Yale* was laid up in 1935; in 1940, she was moved to Sitka, Alaska, where she served as a worker's dormitory. She was again acquired by the Navy on 30 April 1943 and commissioned on 8 August 1943, Lt. Comdr. W. N. VanDenbrugh in command. She was renamed *Greyhound* (IX–106) on 19 August 1943. After brief service, *Greyhound* was decommissioned on 31 March 1944 and began duty as a floating barracks for personnel at various Puget Sound training schools. She was placed out of service on 9 March 1948, and her name was struck from the Navy list on 18 June 1948. She was turned over to the Maritime Commission on 12 November 1948 and placed with the National Defense Reserve Fleet at Olympia, Wash., until 5 June 1949 when she was sold for scrapping.

Yamacraw

Trapper (ACM–9) (q.v.) was transferred to the Coast Guard in 1948 and was renamed *Yamacraw* (WARC–333). In 1959, she was returned to the Navy and was commissioned as *Yamacraw* (ARC–5).

Yanaba

A Navajo Indian word that means "she meets the enemy."

(YTB–547: dp. 325 (f.); l. 100'; b. 25'; dr. 11'6" (max.); s. 12 k.; cpl. 8; cl. *Hisada*)

Yanaba (YTB–547) was laid down on 19 October 1944 at Brooklyn, N.Y., by Ira S. Bushey and Sons; launched on 21 May 1945; and completed and placed in service on 17 November 1945.

Placed out of service, in reserve, in March 1946 with the Florida group of the Reserve Fleet, *Yanaba* was reactivated for service with the 7th Naval District in May 1947. Shifted to the 6th Naval District, Charleston, S.C., in 1950, *Yanaba* remained active in that district well into 1979, providing tug and tow service, pilotage, and standing ready to provide waterfront fire protection. She operated as a medium harbor tug, YTM–395, having been reclassified as such in February 1962.

Yancey

A county in western North Carolina established in 1833 and named for Bartlett Yancey, born in Caswell County, N.C., on 19 February 1785, who represented

The Coast Guard cable ship *Yamacraw* (WARC–333), formerly the Navy minelayer *Trapper* (ACM–9). She was originally built to plant and tend controlled defensive minefields for the Army's Coast Artillery Corps, which was responsible for such mine operations until the function was transferred to the Navy in 1949.

that state in Congress from 1813 to 1817. He died on 30 August 1828.

(AKA–93: dp. 13,910; l. 459'3''; b. 63'0''; dr. 26'4'' (lim.) ; s. 16.5 k.; cpl. 368; a. 1 5'', 8 40mm., 18 20mm.; cl. *Andromeda*; T. C2–S–B1)

Yancey (AKA–93) was laid down under a Maritime Commission contract (MC hull 1193) on 22 May 1944 at Oakland, Calif., by the Moore Dry Dock Co.; launched on 8 July 1944; sponsored by Miss Beverly Bartlett; and commissioned on 11 October 1944, Comdr. Edward R. Rice, USNR, in command.

After fitting out at San Francisco, Calif., the attack cargo ship received her boat group of 26 landing craft and conducted an intensive shakedown out of San Pedro, Calif. She underwent post-shakedown alterations and repairs at San Diego, Calif., before she shifted back to San Francisco. There, she loaded cargo from 18 to 24 November and sailed the next day for the Hawaiian Islands.

Yancey reached Pearl Harbor on 2 December and, upon arrival, was assigned to Transport Division (TransDiv) 47, Transport Squadron (TransRon) 16. The attack cargo ship remained at Pearl Harbor through mid-January 1945, unloading cargo and preparing for the impending invasion of Iwo Jima in the Volcano Islands. Finally, on 27 January 1945, *Yancey* stood out of Hawaiian waters, bound for the Marianas with elements and cargo of the 5th Marine Division as part of Task Group (TG) 51.12.

En route, *Yancey* stopped at Eniwetok, in the Mar-

shalls, for supplies and fuel. At Saipan, she later transferred her passengers to LST's and at Tinian rehearsed for the Iwo Jima operation. Finally, *Yancey* arrived off Iwo Jima at 0624 on 19 February, D day for the initial landing. During her time off the invasion beaches, the ship lost two landing craft (LCVP's)—one to mortar fire and the other to broaching in the heavy surf. For the first four days of the operation, *Yancey*'s boats and landing craft were in almost constant use—carrying troops and cargo and evacuating wounded. The ship also transferred 8-inch ammunition to the heavy cruiser *Pensacola* (CA–24), a process that had to be carried out by boat due to unfavorable weather and to damage which *Yancey* suffered when the two ships banged hard together.

Due to the tactical situation ashore, *Yancey* did not begin discharging general cargo until the morning of the 27th, when she anchored off "Red" beach. There, bad weather and unfavorable beach conditions made unloading slow, and nightly air raids interrupted the process several times. Much of the time, landing craft could not be used due to the high surf, so cargo had to be carried ashore by LST's, LSM's, and LCT's.

During that unloading period, *Yancey* received her baptism of fire in the form of a long-range mortar shell. The ship, however, did not suffer any casualties and continued her duties offshore, embarking casualties. Thirty of the wounded were kept on board for evacuation, while others were transferred to nearby hospital ships. *Yancey* finally completed the unloading procedure on 2 March and, screened by a pair of destroyers, got

507

underway for Saipan in company with three other transports.

After discharging casualties and fueling at Saipan, *Yancey* proceeded via Tulagi to Espiritu Santo where she joined the rest of her squadron and embarked units of the Army's 27th Division.

On 25 March, *Yancey* sortied for the Ryukyus as part of TG 51.3, the group earmarked as the mobile reserve. En route, via a scheduled stop in the Carolines, *Yancey* towed a disabled LSM to Ulithi.

On Easter Sunday, 1 April 1945, American forces started going ashore at Okinawa, beginning the long and bloody battle for that island. Eight days later, *Yancey* reached Kerama Retto with the rest of Trans-Div 47, which had been detached from TG 51.3. She soon received orders sending her to battle and got underway on 11 April for the Hagushi beaches.

Yancey anchored off the beach on the 12th and commenced discharging her cargo that night. There, she started a routine of working hatches, securing to man all antiaircraft batteries, and at night making smoke. "Smoke boats"—landing craft equipped with smoke-laying equipment—from the attack cargo ship and picket boats—with armed sailors—were furnished ships in the outer anchorage. This measure improved security, but it prevented the boats so employed from unloading the ships.

Air raids caused further problems. *Yancey*'s commanding officer estimated that while *Yancey* was off Okinawa, she lost 15 hours and 13 minutes due to the enemy airmen. Fortunately, her gunners were good and her fire control discipline excellent. On the evening of the 15th, her number four 40-millimeter mount registered hits on a Nakajima Ki. 43 "Oscar" and claimed a "sure assist" as the plane crashed some 3,000 yards from the ship.

The ship, the first AKA of her group to complete the unloading, finally put to sea on the 16th and headed independently for the Marianas. During the Okinawa campaign, *Yancey* had fortunately suffered only three casualties: two men were wounded by shrapnel and a third suffered a broken arm. No boats were lost, and there were no accidents on board ship.

After a brief stop at Guam to draw replacement boats and to allow her officers and men to get ashore for some rest and recreation, *Yancey* rejoined her squadron at Ulithi on 27 April and underwent 14 days of upkeep and logistics. In addition, she received much-needed boiler repairs and conducted intensive antiaircraft training during which her crew won numerous five-case "beer prizes" for shooting down target sleeves.

On 8 May, *Yancey* received orders for detached duty in connection with the movement of men and materiel from rear area bases. Over the next two months, while the fighting continued on Okinawa and Allied forces moved inexorably closer to Japan, raiding her shores with near impunity, *Yancey* touched at Manus in the Admiralties; Finschhafen, New Guinea; Tulagi; Hollandia, Dutch New Guinea; and finally Guiuan, on the island of Samar, in the Philippines.

After reporting back to TransDiv 47, TransRon 16, at San Pedro Bay, Leyte Gulf, on 16 July, *Yancey* proceeded with the rest of the division to Iloilo, on the island of Panay, to conduct amphibious training exercises with the Army's 43d Division which included landing on Negros Island.

On 15 August 1945, the attack cargo ship was in the Philippines loading equipment for slated exercises when Japan capitulated. The next day, the training exercises were cancelled, and the troops disembarked. TransDiv 47 provisioned at Iloilo and sailed for Batangas, Luzon, Philippines, to join the rest of TransRon 16. There, she commenced loading elements of the 1st Cavalry Division for the occupation of Japan.

Completing the loading process on the 23d, *Yancey* weighed anchor on the 25th as a member of Task Force (TF) 33. However, the ships had to turn back because of a tropical storm in the vicinity. The typhoon delayed the task force for only a day, as the ships weathered the fringes of the storm at Subic Bay before again getting underway soon thereafter.

Yancey entered Tokyo Bay on the morning of 2 September, the day Japan signed the formal articles of surrender on the deck of the battleship *Missouri* (BB–63), anchored there. Shortly after the conclusion of those ceremonies, the attack cargo ship headed into Yokohama harbor, the third ship in her squadron to enter that port and the first to start unloading. The ship completed her unloading in 19 hours and then proceeded to an anchorage off Yokohama.

TransRon 16 proceeded to sea on 4 September and steamed via Leyte Gulf to Zamboanga. There, they commenced loading elements of the Army's 41st Infantry Division on the 16th. Completing that process on the 18th, *Yancey* and her sisters shifted soon thereafter to Bugo, Mindanao, where she picked up Army LCM's. Ultimately, TG 54.28, of which *Yancey* was a part, assembled in Leyte Gulf on the 21st. The following day, all ships weighed anchor and headed for the Inland Sea of Japan.

Due to minesweeping difficulties, however, the landings scheduled for the Kure-Hiroshima area were postponed; and the task group sailed instead for Buckner Bay, Okinawa. On 28 September, the ship put to sea to evade a typhoon. On 1 October, she returned and anchored in Buckner Bay. Two days later, *Yancey* again headed for Japanese waters and entered Bungo Suido on the 5th, beginning the long, difficult passage up the Inland Sea along the channel swept through the mine-fields. The next morning—after spending the night anchored in the cleared channel—*Yancey* headed for Hiro Wan, where the landings were made.

The ship completed her unloading in 48 hours. On 9 October, she was detached from TransRon 16 and reported to CinCPac for assignment. The following day, *Yancey* rode out a typhoon with 130 fathoms of chain on deck, a second anchor ready to go, and steam at the throttle. On the 11th, the rest of her squadron hoisted "homeward bound" pennants and headed for home, leaving *Yancey* to celebrate the first anniversary of her commissioning anchored in Hiro Wan, Japan, "waiting orders."

On 15 October, *Yancey* got underway for the Philippines. She drew replacement boats at Subic Bay and stopped at Manila for logistics before she sailed for French Indochina. En route to Haiphong, the ship's force readied the attack cargo vessel to receive her next passengers, Chinese troops.

Assigned to Task Unit (TU) 78.6.7, *Yancey* reached Doson, French Indochina, on 2 November. However, embarkation of the men of the 471st Regiment, 62d Chinese Army, did not begin for 11 days. The delay permitted both officers and men from *Yancey* to see the local sights ashore. On the 13th, *Yancey* brought on board by boat 1,027 officers and men—and one interpreter. The next day, the task unit—three attack transports (APA's) and *Yancey* stood out for Takao, Formosa.

The trip, as recorded by *Yancey* commanders, was uneventful, except for rough weather which caused the Chinese to suffer numerous cases of seasickness. Regular Chinese Army rations—tea and rice—were served twice a day, augmented by that staple, the "C" ration. North of Takao, on the 18th, TU 78.6.7 dropped anchor. By 1700 that day, the disembarking was complete. The Chinese had cooperated fully during the trip, and one *Yancey* sailor observed that they seemed "most appreciative of what little could be done to make them comfortable."

The following day, 18 November, *Yancey* proceeded to Manila to await further orders. On 25 November—exactly one year after the ship had left the United States and headed for the war zone—the attack cargo ship received her orders to proceed to the east coast of the United States for duty with the Service Force, Atlantic Fleet. The ship's captain, Comdr. Rice, had the orders read over the ship's public address system. As a Yancey sailor recorded: "the response left no doubt that all hands were satisfied."

After embarking a capacity load of Army and Navy men returning to the United States for discharge, *Yancey* left Manila harbor on 27 November. Streaming a homeward-bound pennant 310 feet long and adorned with 27 stars, *Yancey* headed for home.

Reaching Balboa, Panama Canal Zone, on the last day of the year—via Pearl Harbor (where the ship fueled and received boiler repairs) and with Navy passengers embarked (the Army had been put ashore at Pearl Harbor)—*Yancey* was the last ship to transit the Panama Canal in 1945.

Six days into the new year, 1946, *Yancey* cleared Cristobal, Canal Zone, bound for Louisiana. After a brief stop at New Orleans, the attack cargo ship proceeded on, via Jacksonville, Fla., to Norfolk, where she arrived on 29 January. Less than a month later, on 27 February, *Yancey* sailed farther north and reached the Philadelphia Naval Shipyard the following day.

Over the next few months, *Yancey* underwent a regular overhaul there and then operated off the eastern seaboard and into the western Atlantic. During that time, she called at Bayonne, N.J.; Bermuda; San Juan, Puerto Rico; Guantanamo Bay, Cuba; Balboa, Canal Zone; Jacksonville, Fla.; and made return calls at Norfolk, Bayonne, and Bermuda. In addition, the ship visited the New York Naval Shipyard and Davisville, R.I., before being assigned tentatively to TF 68 effective on 9 November.

In compliance with her new orders, *Yancey* proceeded back to the west coast, sailing via Cristobal and the Panama Canal. Ultimately arriving at San Pedro, Calif., *Yancey* reported for duty to Commander, TF 68.

Yancey was reassigned to Service Force, Pacific Fleet, and homeported at San Francisco, Calif., on 11 November. The next day, she shifted to Port Hueneme, Calif., where she began loading cargo for Operation "Highjump."

Departing Port Hueneme on 2 December, *Yancey* pressed southward, headed for Antarctica, and spent Christmas at sea. Two days later, she saw her first icebergs—visible evidence that she was entering the polar latitudes. She sighted the northern limit of the Antarctic pack ice on the 28th and spent the next two days investigating ice conditions. She fueled from *Canisteo* (AO–99) 10 miles south of Scott Island, Antarctica, purportedly becoming the first ship to conduct an underway refueling below the Antarctic Circle.

After threading her way through the pack ice over the ensuing weeks, *Yancey* finally arrived at Bay of Whales, Antarctica, mooring at the shelf ice on 18 January 1947. Subsequently departing that "port" on 6 February for the area to the north of the ice floes, the attack cargo ship entered the pack ice on the 9th. Over the next three days, she pressed through the floes that extended for a width of almost 275 miles.

On 13 February, *Yancey* joined TU 68.1.2 which also included the Coast Guard icebreaker, USCGC *Northwind*, towing the attack cargo ship *Merrick* (AKA–97). Within a week, the ships were riding out a fierce storm that justified—at least to *Yancey* sailors—the Antarctic's title as "The World's Stormiest Sea."

Yancey reached Port Chalmers, New Zealand, on 22 February and departed that port on 5 March, bound for Samoa. Subsequently departing Pago Pago on 27 March bound for Hawaii with *YTL–153* in tow, the attack cargo ship arrived at Pearl Harbor on 14 April. She soon got underway for the west coast of the United States and reached Port Hueneme on 2 May 1947. There, *Yancey* disembarked a unit of a construction battalion ("Seabees") and discharged TF 68 cargo. Her duty with TF 68 thus completed on 15 May, *Yancey* reported for duty to Commander, Service Division (ServDiv) 12.

Shortly thereafter, *Yancey* shifted to San Pedro before heading to Terminal Island, Calif., for restricted availability on 20 May. After that period of repairs and alterations, *Yancey* returned to Port Hueneme to load cargo earmarked for shipment to Pearl Harbor and Guam.

Over the next decade, *Yancey* operated between west coast ports and advanced bases in the Western Pacific (WestPac), including ports in Japan, Korea, and the Philippines. During that period, she also supported United Nations (UN) actions in Korea, operating in support of the initial attempts to fight the North Korean aggressors; in the first UN counter-offensives in early 1951; and in the final phases of activity that preceded the armistice in the summer of 1953. Finally, after having served continuously since 1944, *Yancey* was deactivated at San Francisco in December 1957 and placed out of commission in March 1958.

Her sojourn in reserve, however, proved short. On 17 November 1961, as part of President John F. Kennedy's bid to build up the United States Navy, *Yancey* was recommissioned at Portland, Oreg., Capt. Gordon R. Keating in command.

Soon to join the Atlantic Fleet, *Yancey* departed San Diego on 12 January 1962 and reached Norfolk, her new assigned home port, on 2 February, there becoming the newest member of Amphibious Squadron (PhibRon) 12. Over the ensuing months, *Yancey* took part in a varied slate of exercises and maneuvers.

Yancey participated in Operation "Phiblex" in the spring of 1962, operating off Roosevelt Roads and Vieques, Puerto Rico. She later paid a port call at Charlotte Amalie, St. Thomas, Virgin Islands, before she returned to Roosevelt Roads and reloaded equipment and embarked marines slated to return to Morehead City, N.C. Subsequently returning to Norfolk on 2 May, *Yancey* touched briefly at Charleston, S.C., to take on additional landing craft before returning to the Tidewater region to spend the remainder of May.

Subsequently visiting Boston, Mass., and Rockland, Maine, *Yancey* participated in amphibious boat exercises at Provincetown, Mass., before she got underway on 24 July for Davisville, R.I. There, she loaded a Seabee unit and their equipment and headed eastward, bound for Rota, Spain.

Offloading one Seabee unit and onloading another, *Yancey* then paused briefly at Gibraltar before touching at Lisbon on the return leg of her voyage to the United States. Disembarking the seabees and unloading their equipment at Davisville, *Yancey* headed back to Norfolk, reaching her home port on 18 August 1962.

On 17 October, *Yancey* again sailed from Norfolk and proceeded to Morehead City, N.C., to load marines and equipment for Operation "PhiBrigLex" (Amphibious Brigade Exercises) slated for Vieques, Puerto Rico. Upon arrival, the attack cargo ship loaded immediately and set out to join the rest of the ships in the squadron. She soon was fighting her way through Hurricane "Ella" which caused her to alter her course to avoid the most severe part of the storm.

Meanwhile, a crisis was brewing in the Caribbean. American reconnaissance had disclosed the presence of Soviet offensive missiles on Cuban soil. Accordingly, on 23 October 1962, President Kennedy ordered a naval quarantine of Cuba to make sure that no more offensive weapons were taken to that island. *Yancey* supported the ensuing naval operations in waters near Cuba as the United States and the Soviet Union stood, in Secretary of State Dean Rusk's words, "eyeball to eyeball."

After the removal of the offensive missiles, tension relaxed, and *Yancey* resumed her former routine of operations along the eastern seaboard and into the Caribbean. Over the next eight years, *Yancey* deployed regularly to the Mediterranean, where she joined in multilateral NATO exercises and supported the United States 6th Fleet's presence in that area of the world.

Once again, however, *Yancey* was called upon to perform her vital support duties during a time of crisis. In the early spring of 1965, she was on a routine training mission when civil strife erupted into warfare in the

The attack cargo ship *Yancey* (AKA–93) at San Francisco, 17 July 1956.

turbulent Dominican Republic. Commander, Caribbean Sea Frontier. ordered the attack cargo ship to proceed at once to the troubled area, just as she was preparing to enter San Juan harbor for liberty.

On Friday, 30 April, the sixth day of the crisis, *Yancey* arrived off Santo Domingo, the strife-torn capital city. Incorporated into the Caribbean Force already on the scene, the attack cargo ship took on board 593 evacuees representing some 21 nations. Included in the group were the daughter of the United States ambassador to the Dominican Republic, the wife of the United States naval attache, the Belgian ambassador, 16 nuns from the Dominican Order; and several seven- or eight person families. Among the 21 countries represented were Italy, France, Germany, Hungary, Colombia, Mexico, Chile, Switzerland, Canada, Lebanon, and the United States.

Upon their arrival on board the ship, the evacuees received information folders in Spanish and English, blankets, fresh fruit and milk, and various other items. In addition, nurseries, rest areas, information booths, infirmaries, and various other makeshift stations proliferated on board. Everything from baby bottles and diapers to canes and crutches were provided the people whose routine had been so unceremoniously uprooted by open warfare.

Women and children evacuees slept in the officers and crews' quarters, respectively, while *Yancey*'s men and the male evacuees slept "under the stars." Sacrifices made by the ship's company included missing a few meals to ensure that the embarked refugees had enough to eat and abstaining from showers in order to conserve

water—despite the almost constant 100-degree temperatures during the day. Her crew worked nearly around the clock in order to care for the sick, injured, elderly, and the children. Highlighting the voyage back to San Juan, between 30 April and 1 May, was a birth—the ship's doctor, Lt. Ben Passmore, MC, delivered Stephen Yancey Paez, the son of Mr. and Mrs. Rodolfo Paez, at sea on 1 May. A ship-wide ceremony ensued, with a cake-cutting and the traditional passing out of cigars.

Representatives of the Red Cross; the Commander, Caribbean Sea Frontier; and several hundred relatives greeted *Yancey*'s arrival at San Juan on 1 May, and the 594 evacuees (the new arrival included) disembarked swiftly. There was more work in store for the attack cargo ship; and, in response to urgent requests from the marines landed at Santo Domingo, the ship loaded hundreds of tons of gasoline, oil, and ammunition before she returned to the Dominican Republic.

Soon after the ship's arrival back in Santo Domingo on 2 May, *Yancey*'s sailors worked round-the-clock shifts getting the vitally needed materiel ashore to the marines. On the 3d, the ship received 150 evacuees; and, on the following day, an additional 300 more displaced persons came up the gangways. Again, the ship's crew responded, in her commander's words, "magnificently." Once again the ship inaugurated nurseries, infirmaries, "kiddie" watches, and other special arrangements to take care of her guests. Newspapers were printed in Spanish and English, and interpreters were constantly on duty and in demand. Although there were inconveniences to those civilians unaccustomed, as they were, to shipboard life, the evacuation itself was pref-

510

erable to lying flat on the ground, listening to the whine of bullets overhead back in Santo Domingo.

Ultimately, *Yancey* disembarked the second contingent of refugees, having carried well over one-fourth of the total number of people evacuated from the Dominican Republic. She returned to Norfolk soon thereafter, soon to commence preparations for resumption of training and cruising off the eastern seaboard and into the Caribbean basin.

Toward the end of her career, *Yancey* made headlines. On 21 January 1970, *Yancey*, at anchor near one stretch of the Chesapeake Bay Bridge-Tunnel near Norfolk, dragged her anchors in a snowy gale and, driven by the winds that gusted up to 50 miles an hour, drifted inexorably toward the span. The collision between the attack cargo ship and the bridge put the later out of service "for at least three weeks." The Navy started up a free shuttle service for commuters that normally utilized the bridge-tunnel, using helicopters and LCU's. Fortunately, there were no vehicles on the bridge, and no one was injured.

Subsequently, *Yancey* deployed once more to the Mediterranean in the spring of 1970. She returned to the United States that summer and entered inactive status at Norfolk on 1 October of that year. Placed out of commission, in reserve, there on 20 January 1971, *Yancey* was towed to the James River berthing area for the National Defense Reserve Fleet on 18 March 1971. She remained there until her name was struck from the Navy list sometime between 1 October and 31 December 1976. Presumably she was sold for scrap.

Yancey earned two battle stars for her operations in World War II and three for her Korean service.

Yanegua

Yanegua was a late 18th century Cherokee chief, prominent in tribal relations with white settlers, who lived near the present site of Bryson City, N.C. The term Yanegua means "Big Bear."

(YTB–397: dp. 345 (f.); l. 100'0''; b. 25'0''; dr. 11'0''; s. 12.0 k.; cpl. 14; a. none; cl. *Sassaba*)

Yanegua (YT–397) was laid down on 24 April 1944 at Jacksonville, Fla., by the Gibbs Gas Engine and Power Co.; reclassified YTB–397 on 15 May 1944; launched on 14 September 1944; sponsored by Mrs. Bette M. Keating; and completed and delivered to the Navy on 23 March 1945.

After service in the 12th Naval District, the large harbor tug was placed in reserve at Astoria, Oreg., in the Columbia River Reserve Group of the 19th (Reserve) Fleet. She was later shifted to San Diego, Calif. Apparently reactivated in response to the Navy's expansion during the Korean conflict, *Yanegua* was placed in service during March 1951 in the 11th Naval District at San Diego and performed her vital tow and tug services in that district through the 1970's, a task she still performed as of early 1979. During the ship's tour at San Diego, she was reclassified a medium harbor tug, YTM–397, in February 1962.

Yank

(MB: l. 60'1½''; b. 10'; dr. 3' (aft); s. 21 mph.; cpl. 10; a. 1 1-pdr., 1 .30-cal. mg.)

Yank (SP–908)—a motorboat built in 1917 by Julius Peterson at Nyack, N.Y.—was acquired by the Navy on 8 October 1917 from Mr. N. Ackerman of New York City and commissioned on 10 October 1917. Assigned to the 3d Naval District, *Yank* patrolled the coast of Rhode Island and Connecticut throughout America's participation in World War I. She briefly remained on the Navy list after the armistice but was finally returned to her former owner on St. Valentine's Day

1919. Her name was simultaneously struck from the Navy list.

Yankee
I

(SwStr.: t. 328; l. 146'; b. 25'7''; a. 2 32-pdrs.)

The first *Yankee*—a side-wheel steamer built in 1860 at New York City—was one of three steam tugs chartered early in April 1861 at New York City for use on the expedition to provision Fort Sumter, S.C. She departed New York on 8 April and arrived off Charleston Bar on the 15th, a few hours after Major Robert Anderson's command had evacuated the fort and embarked in Federal transport *Baltic*. On the 20th, *Yankee* assisted in the evacuation of the Norfolk Navy Yard, Norfolk, Va., towing *Cumberland* to safety. She then returned to the New York Navy Yard.

Yankee left the navy yard on the 26th for duty as a dispatch and escort vessel between Annapolis and Havre de Grace, Md. On 30 April 1861, she received orders to Hampton Roads for reconnaissance duty between the Rip Raps and Cape Henry, Va. Confederate batteries at Gloucester Point, Va., fired upon *Yankee* on 8 May 1861, doing little damage. After further reconnaissance duty along the eastern shore of Virginia and the James River, *Yankee* proceeded to the Washington Navy Yard on the 25th to deliver prize schooners *General Knox* and *Georgeanna*. She sailed for Hampton Roads on the last day of May and arrived on 2 June but was sent north a week later for major repairs at the Philadelphia Navy Yard.

On 2 July 1861, *Yankee* departed Philadelphia bound via the Washington Navy Yard for Hampton Roads. However, Confederate activity along the Potomac River necessitated that the vessel remain at Washington; and she was formally attached to the Potomac Flotilla on the 9th.

In ensuing months, *Yankee* was busy operating against Confederate vessels in the Potomac and Southern forces along its banks. On 18 July 1861, she captured the Confederate schooner *Favorite* in the Yeocomico River, Va. On 29 July, she and *Reliance* engaged a Confederate battery at Marlborough Point, Va. *Yankee* destroyed the sloops *T. W. Riley* and *Jane Wright* near Smith's Island, Va., on 16 August 1861 and captured the schooner *Remittance* near Piney Point, Md., on 28 August. A landing party from *Anacostia* and *Yankee* destroyed abandoned Confederate entrenchments and batteries at Cockpit Point and Evansport, Va., on 9 March 1862, the day of the engagement between the Union ironclad *Monitor* and the Confederate armored ram *Virginia*.

During brief service with the James River Flotilla supporting General McClellan's beleaguered army at Harrison's Landing in July and August 1862, *Yankee* assisted in the capture on 27 July of *J. W. Sturges* in Chippoak Creek, Va. She returned to the Potomac Flotilla on 30 August 1862 and guarded the water approaches to the Federal capital until the following spring.

Coeur de Lion, *Primrose*, *Teaser*, and *Yankee* left the Potomac Flotilla for Hampton Roads and duty with the North Atlantic Blockading Squadron in April 1863. *Yankee* participated in the capture of the strong Confederate position at Hill's Point, Va., on the Nansemond River on 20 April, even though the armed tug's length and draft impaired her maneuverability. She returned to the Rappahannock River on 1 May 1863.

During duty on the Rappahannock, *Yankee* captured the schooner *Cassandra* and her cargo of whiskey and soda on 11 July 1863. She took the schooner *Nanjemoy* in the Coan River, Va., on 15 July; and captured the sloop *Clara Ann* on 1 August 1863. *Yankee* assisted in landing Union cavalry and infantry under General Gilman Marston on the Potomac-Rappahannock peninsula on 12 January 1864 and helped destroy a Confederate encampment under construction at Carter's Creek, Va., on 29 April 1864.

Yankee's last major operation of the war occurred on 7 March 1865, when the tug joined *Commodore Read*, *Delaware*, *Heliotrope* and Army troops in a raid upon Hamilton's Crossing near Fredericksburg, Va. The force destroyed a train depot, a railroad bridge, 28 loaded freight cars, and a Confederate army wagon train. Moreover, she made prisoners of 30 Confederates as well.

On 5 May 1865, *Yankee* sailed to the Washington Navy Yard. *Yankee* was decommissioned there on 16 May 1865 and was sold at public auction on 15 September 1865 to George B. Collier.

II

(ScStr.: dp. 6,225 (f.); l. 406'1½''; b. 48'4½''; dr. 21'1'' (aft); s. 14.5 k.; cpl. 282; a. 10 5'', 6 6-pdrs., 2 Colt mg.)

El Norte—a steamer built in 1892 at Newport News, Va., by the Newport News Shipbuilding & Drydock Co. —was acquired by the Navy from the Southern Pacific Company on 6 April 1898; renamed *Yankee*; and commissioned at New York on 14 April 1898, Comdr. Willard H. Brownson in command.

After fitting out as an auxiliary cruiser, the ship patrolled the coastal waters between Block Island and Cape Henlopen until 27 May. That day, *Yankee* stopped at Tompkinsville, N.Y., to coal ship. On the 29th, she returned to sea and shaped a southerly course to join the fleet off Cuba. En route, she touched briefly at St. Nicholas Mole, Haiti, on the evening of 2 June and then continued on toward Cuba. Early the following morning, *Yankee* joined the blockade off Santiago de Cuba and conducted patrols there for the next five days. On the morning of the 6th, she dueled shore batteries

briefly and, near Santiago on the 7th, joined *Marblehead* and *St. Louis* for a cable cutting incursion into Guantanamo Bay. While *St. Louis* dragged for and cut the three cables, *Yankee* and *Marblehead* covered her activities by engaging the Spanish gunboats *Alvarado* and *Sandoval*. After putting the Spanish gunboats to flight, the two American warships turned their attention toward the fort at Caimanera which had been making a nuisance of itself with its single large-caliber gun—a venerable, smooth-bore muzzleloader. As *Yankee* and *Marblehead* silenced their last adversary, *St. Louis* completed her cable-cutting mission; and the three ships exited the bay.

Yankee then briefly resumed blockade duty off Santiago but, on the 8th, got underway for St. Nicholas Mole with dispatches. On 9 June, just before she arrived at her destination, the auxiliary cruiser stopped two merchantmen and inspected them. They turned out to be the Norwegian SS *Norse* and the British SS *Ely*, so *Yankee* allowed them to proceed on their way. She completed her mission at Haiti and returned to Santiago early the following morning. At about noon on the 10th, *Yankee* set a course for Port Antonio, Jamaica, to deliver dispatches and to search for the suspected blockade runner SS *Purissima Concepcion*. After delivering the dispatches at Port Antonio on the 10th and visiting Montego Bay in search of *Purissima Concepcion*, the warship returned to the Santiago area on the 12th. That same day, however, she received orders to move again. This time to Cienfuegos, about halfway up the southern coast of Cuba from Santiago, to stand guard there against *Purissima Concepcion*'s expected run.

The auxiliary cruiser arrived off Cienfuegos on 13 June and began patrolling the approaches to the harbor. At about 13:15 that afternoon, she spied a steamer standing out of the port toward her. Identifying the stranger as the Spanish gunboat *Diego Velazquez*, *Yankee* cleared for action and closed the enemy. At

Yankee as a training ship in the early 1900s, in peacetime white-and-buff with auxiliary sail rig. Her 5-inch battery is carried in broadside hull casemates.

about 1,500 yards range, the American ship put her helm over, unmasked her port battery, and opened fire. The Spanish gunboat, markedly inferior to *Yankee* in armament, opted for a running fight in which she presented the smallest possible target and in which *Yankee* could bring only one or two of her guns to bear without turning away from her target's course. Consequently, *Diego Velazquez* came about and headed back toward Cienfuegos, firing as she went. *Yankee* followed, shooting her port forecastle gun constantly and periodically turning to starboard to unmask her entire port battery. Ultimately, *Diego Velazquez* reached safety under the protection of Sabanilla Battery; and the gunboat *Lince* came out to join her in the fray. *Yankee* continued to fire her port battery as she passed the two gunboats and shore battery abeam at about 4,000 yards range. She completed one pass and then put the helm to port and came about for another pass, this time bringing her starboard battery into action for the first time. During *Yankee*'s second pass, *Diego Velazquez* and *Lince* abandoned the fight and sought refuge in Cienfuegos harbor. *Yankee* continued firing on Sabanilla Battery until 1500 hours and then withdrew to her blockade station off the harbor.

Yankee remained off Cienfuegos for two days. On the 14th, there was a brief moment of anxiety when a large man-of-war started out of the harbor. *Yankee* cleared for action and stood in toward the warship, but all hands breathed a sigh of relief when the newcomer was identified as the neutral German SMS *Geier*. The following afternoon, the auxiliary cruiser gave up her vigil for *Purissima Concepcion* off Cienfuegos and set a course back to the eastern end of Cuba. She rejoined the Santiago blockade on the 16th but put into the anchorage at Guantanamo Bay the following day to take on coal. Late on the 18th, the ship returned to sea bound once more for blockade duty off Cienfuegos. On the 19th, during the passage from Guantanamo Bay to Cienfuegos, *Yankee* stopped and inspected two sailing vessels—a British schooner and a Norwegian bark—and a steamer, the British SS *Adula*. All three had their papers in order, and the auxiliary cruiser allowed them to proceed unmolested. That evening, she arrived off Cienfuegos and began cruising on blockade station between that port and Casilda.

At about 0830 on the morning of 20 June, *Yankee* sighted a steamer lying in Casilda harbor closely fitting the description of *Purissima Concepcion*. The American ship stood in as close to the shoals as she dared and then fired a shot across the steamer's bow in an unsuccessful effort to make her show her colors. Instead, the merchantman began preparations for getting underway. *Yankee* responded by opening a steady fire at extreme range. As the supposed Spanish steamer moved farther into shoal water and disappeared behind some islets, *Yankee* shifted fire to an enemy gunboat and a floating battery, both of which had opened an ineffective fire upon her. The extreme range—in excess of 5,000 yards —made the gunfire from both sides so ineffective that *Yankee* broke off the engagement and resumed her patrols between Casilda and Cienfuegos. The auxiliary cruiser continued her blockade of that stretch of the Cuban coast until 24 June when her dwindling supply of coal forced her to head for Key West. En route to that base, she visited the Isle of Pines where she captured and destroyed five Spanish fishing vessels on the 25th.

Yankee arrived in Key West on 27 June and began taking on coal. She completed her refueling operation and departed Key West on 3 July, bound for New York, where she arrived on the 5th. She remained at New York until the 12th, taking on ammunition for transportation to the Eastern Squadron on the Cuban blockade. On the 13th, she reached Norfolk where she spent another four days taking on additional ammunition for the ships of the blockading squadron. *Yankee* left Hampton Roads on 17 July and arrived in Guantanamo Bay four days later. There, she began the tedious, but

dangerous, job of transferring her cargo of ammunition to the various warships in the anchorage. The ship remained at Guantanamo Bay until 11 August, on which day she resumed blockade duty, patrolling initially in search of the armed merchant ship *Montserrat*. Three days later, while she cruised the northern coast of Cuba, *Yankee* received word of the cessation of hostilities in response to Spain's suit for peace. She reentered Guantanamo Bay on the afternoon of 15 August and remained there until the 24th when she headed home.

Yankee stopped briefly at Tompkinsville, N.Y., at the end of August and then made a round-trip voyage to League Island, Pa., and back to Tompkinsville at the beginning of September. She returned to League Island on the 19th. There, her crew of New York Naval Militia reservists left the ship to return home via train for mustering out. Though she remained in commission technically until decommissioned on 16 March 1899, *Yankee* spent the interim at League Island. That location also remained her home for the more than three years she spent in reserve. Her inactivity ended when she was placed back in commission on 1 May 1903, Comdr. G. P. Colvocoressee in command.

Following recommissioning, *Yankee* served along the east coast between Chesapeake Bay and the Maine coast training landsmen in the ways of the sea. Early in December 1903, she headed south for winter maneuvers and gunnery drills with the North Atlantic Fleet in the gulf and the Caribbean. After visiting a number of West Indian ports in conjunction with the exercises, she returned north late in March 1904 and, on 6 April, was moored to a pier at League Island where she remained until October. On the 16th, she got underway for Newport News to embark 400 landsmen there before resuming her training schedule.

In December, *Yankee* made a round-trip voyage to Panama to exchange marine garrisons in the Canal Zone. She disembarked some of the returning marines at Hampton Roads on 31 December 1904 and on New Year's Day 1905 pushed on toward Tompkinsville to deliver the remainder. After a return voyage to Newport News, she headed for League Island where she entered the navy yard for repairs on 13 January.

The ship completed those repairs on 9 March and loaded men, stores, and ammunition at Tompkinsville on the 10th, 11th, and 12th before getting underway for the West Indies. For the next 17 months, the island of Hispaniola, Cuba's neighbor to the east, became her center of operations. Successive coups since assassination of the dictator Heureaux in 1899 had added civil strife and anarchy to the list of woes of a country already racked by desperate financial problems. *Yankee* served as one of the ships sent to support American forces ashore in Santo Domingo to restore and help to straighten out the country's financial muddle. She spent most of her time in Dominican waters and ports, departing infrequently for replenishment stops at such American bases as Key West and Guantanamo Bay and made one voyage back to New York in July 1905 for repairs at the New York Navy Yard.

The ship, by then classified as a transport, left Santo Domingo on 21 August 1906 and after participating in the Presidential Naval Review held at Oyster Bay, N.Y., between 2 and 4 September, she unloaded stores at New York in preparation for inactivation. On 25 September, *Yankee* was again placed out of commission at Portsmouth, N.H. Sometime during the next two years, she was moved to the Boston Navy Yard, for it was at that location that she was once again commissioned on 15 June 1908, Comdr. Charles C. Marsh in command.

After shakedown early in July, the ship resumed a familiar duty—training. With naval militia reservists or Naval Academy midshipmen embarked, she spent the summer of 1908 cruising the Atlantic coast between Boston and Chesapeake Bay. On 23 September 1908, during one such training exercise, *Yankee* ran aground on Spindle Rock near Hen and Chickens lightship. She remained there until refloated on 4 December. Her reprieve however, was short-lived. While being towed to New Bedford, she sank in Buzzard's Bay. *Yankee*'s name was finally struck from the Navy list on 17 April 1912.

Yankton

A county and its seat in southeastern South Dakota. They are located on the Missouri River.

(Yacht: dp. 975 (est.); l. 185'0" (wl.); b. 27'6"; dr. 13'10" (mean); s. 14 k.; cpl. 78; a. 6 3-pdrs., 2 Colt mg.)

Penelope—a steel-hulled schooner built in 1893 at Leith, Scotland, by Ramage & Ferguson—was acquired by the Navy in May 1898; renamed *Yankton*; and commissioned on 16 May 1898 at Norfolk, Va., Lt. Comdr. James D. Adams in command.

Purchased to augment the Navy for the Spanish-American War, *Yankton* remained at Norfolk until 18 June when she exited the Chesapeake Bay, bound for Cuba. She arrived off Santiago de Cuba on the 25th and reported for duty with Rear Admiral William T. Sampson's North Atlantic Fleet. Two days later, she took up blockade station off the southern coast of Cuba, near Cienfuegos. During three weeks of patrolling that station, she encountered the enemy on three occasions. First, as she was steaming to Casilda at about 0845 on 25 June, she observed sister yacht *Eagle* engaging a Spanish shore battery on Cape Muño. *Yankton* closed the shore to assist her and opened fire at 0850. Twenty minutes later, after learning that one of her shells had landed in the midst of the enemy battery, she ceased fire. That afternoon, she joined *Dixie* in shelling several Spanish gunboats lying behind the reef at Casilda. Three days later, at about 1600, she sighted smoke on the southwestern horizon, apparently made by a ship steering generally for Cienfuegos. *Yankton* chased the intruder for about two hours, but her quarry apparently enjoyed a three-knot advantage over the yacht. *Yankton*'s commanding officer broke off the chase after tentatively identifying the fleeing vessel as the Spanish auxiliary cruiser *Alfonso XII*. However, he cited no evidence to corroborate that identification.

Following that encounter, the converted yacht resumed her blockade duty and continued the uneventful routine until 21 July. On that day, she got underway for Guantanamo Bay, where she remained for nine days —probably for upkeep and replenishment. On 30 July, she stood out of Guantanamo Bay and, the following day, resumed station off Cienfuegos. She remained there until three days after signing the armistice protocol of 12 August, when she departed Cuban waters. After a two-day stop at Key West, Fla., she continued her voyage north to Hampton Roads where she arrived on 22 August.

Yankton remained in the Virginia capes-Norfolk area until the beginning of 1899. On 15 January, she stood out of Chesapeake Bay and headed south to Cuba. After a one-night stop at Palm Beach, Fla., the yacht reached Guantanamo Bay on the 24th. She returned to the newly independent country to perform coastal survey work and to participate in the four-year, postwar occupation of Cuba. Once each year, she returned north to Portsmouth, N.H., for an annual overhaul of two to three months' duration before resuming her duties in Cuban waters. During that period, *Yankton* called most frequently at Santiago de Cuba and at the newly leased American naval base on the shores of Guantanamo Bay. Later, her duties took *Yankton* to Nipe Bay, Levisa Bay, and Gibara—all located in Oriente province along the northeastern shore of the island. By early 1902, she had moved round the island to the area of Cienfuegos and the Isle of Pines—both in the area of her old wartime blockade station off the southern coast of central Cuba. About that time, her area of operations was expanded to include Puerto Rico, a former Spanish possession acquired by the United States at the settlement of the Spanish-American War.

In June of 1903, *Yankton* completed her share of the Cuban survey work and departed Santa Cruz Del Sur on the 17th. After a six-day layover at San Antonio, Jamaica, to take on coal and provisions, she resumed her homeward voyage on 24 June and arrived in Port Royal, S.C., on the 29th. Later, she moved farther north to Norfolk, Va., where she became tender to *Franklin*, the receiving ship at the naval station there. That duty lasted through 1904. By 1905, the yacht was tender to the Atlantic Fleet flagship, *Maine* (Battleship No. 10). In the summer of 1906, she became simply a tender for the Atlantic Fleet and operated as such along the New England coast with the Fleet into the fall. Late in December, *Yankton* moved to Cuban waters, when the Fleet headed south for spring maneuvers, and supported American warships during exercises which lasted from January to April. During the second week in April, she returned to Norfolk and resumed tending duties out of that port until late in 1907.

On 16 December 1907, *Yankton* departed Hampton Roads to accompany the "Great White Fleet" on its round-the-world cruise. She visited Trinidad in the British West Indies and Rio de Janeiro, Brazil, on her way around Cape Horn. During the passage up the western coast of South America, the warship made six stops in Chilean ports—most notably Punta Arenas and Valparaiso—and one at Callao, Peru. After a short side trip to the Galapagos Islands during the first week in March and stops at Acapulco and Magdalena Bay in Mexico, she reached San Diego, Calif., on the 31st. She remained on the west coast until 30 June, when the fleet departed San Francisco, bound for Honolulu, Hawaii. From there, the yacht moved on to Tutuila, Samoa, and thence to New Zealand. After a visit to Auckland from 10 to 16 August, she steamed on to Australia where she made stops at Sydney and at Thursday Island.

On 9 September, *Yankton* set a course for the Philippine Islands and reached Manila Bay on the 18th and remained in the Philippines through the first week in October. While there, the yacht visited Cavite, Manila, and Olongapo several times each. On 9 October, she cleared Olongapo and joined the rest of the Fleet for the voyage to Japan. On 18 October, she arrived in Yokohama and provided services to the Fleet during a nine-day goodwill visit to Japan. After that, the Fleet returned to the Philippines for a month. On 29 November, she departed the Philippines to return to the United States via the Indian Ocean and the Mediterranean Sea. En route, she stopped at Singapore and Colombo, Ceylon, before transiting the Suez Canal early in January 1909. During her passage through the Mediterranean, the yacht stopped at Messina, Sicily, from 9 to 14 January, to assist the victims of an earthquake that had recently struck that island. From there, the ship continued her voyage—via Villefranche, France; Gibraltar; and Funchal in the Madeira Islands—and arrived at Fort Monroe, Va., on 17 February 1909.

Between 1909 and 1917, *Yankton* continued her routine as tender to the Atlantic Fleet. At the beginning of each year, she left the northeastern coast of the United States to support the Fleet during maneuvers and exercises out of Guantanamo Bay, Cuba. The lone exception to that east coast-Caribbean schedule came in the late fall of 1912 when she visited Hispaniola to investigate conditions and to protect American interests during political unrest in the Dominican Republic. She remained in the vicinity of that island from 6 November 1912 until 4 January 1913, steaming between and visiting the port towns of Monte Christi and Puerto Plata. Following that mission, she moved on to winter maneuvers in Cuban waters and generally resumed her previous routine.

During the first few months of 1917, *Yankton* patrolled the waters around Cuba, helping to protect the flow of trade to and from Cuba and other Latin American nations. War came early in the spring, less than two months after the German Empire announced its resumption of unrestricted submarine warfare. A month after the 6 April declaration of war, the converted yacht began duty with the newly organized Patrol Force. Her initial assignment sent her to the waters along the coast of northern New England. Late in August, *Yankton* headed for Gibraltar to join a section of the Patrol Force protecting Allied shipping in the approaches to the coasts of England and France from German U-boats.

The converted yacht served at the Gibraltar station until mid-August 1918. Besides the Atlantic approaches to the strait, she patrolled portions of the western Mediterranean. In addition to carrying out offensive patrols against enemy submarines, she joined the screens which escorted convoys on the final legs of their voyages to Europe and North Africa and shepherded Allied ships in the western Mediterranean. Her logs indicate several brushes with U-boats which, unfortunately, could not be confirmed by other sources.

On the other hand, the brief scrape with *U-38* unquestionably did occur in May 1918. On the 5th, *Yankton* was steaming in company with a convoy bound from Bizerte, Tunis, to Gibraltar when she sighted the U-boat to port. As other ships opened fire, the yacht rang up full speed and charged to the attack. About that time, a tremendous explosion occurred, and *Yankton* crewmen spied a large geyser of water near the Italian steamer SS *Alberto Treves*. *Yankton* fired her guns at the culprit and, after the submarine submerged, dropped depth charges in the vicinity of its last known position. *Alberto Treves* had suffered a single, non-fatal torpedo hit and managed to make port at Marseilles—only to be sunk in the Atlantic five months later by a torpedo from *U-155*.

Through the remainder of the war, *Yankton* engaged no other enemy submarines, but she did assist torpedoed merchantmen. On 29 May, she helped to rescue the crew of another Italian steamer, SS *Piero Maroncelli*. On Independence Day 1918, the German Navy treated *Yankton* to a 4th of July display when a U-boat torpedoed the British ship SS *Merida*. Fortunately, the torpedo failed to sink *Merida*, and she reached port under her own power. The warship continued to patrol and escort convoys until 19 August when she received orders to return to the United States for repairs. Steaming via Lisbon, Portugal, and Ponta Delgada in the Azores, she reached the New York Navy Yard on 5 September. *Yankton* was operating with the Atlantic Fleet when the armistice was signed on 11 November 1918. Just less than a month later, she received orders directing her to return to European waters.

The ship arrived in Plymouth, England, on 16 January 1919, but departed soon thereafter to carry two naval officers to Murmansk, Russia, where they were to serve as American port officers. She reached her destination in turbulent northern Russia on 8 February. When Rear Admiral N. A. McCully arrived to take command of American forces in northern Russia on 23 February, he took up residence in the converted yacht. Later, he abandoned her for a more suitable flagship, *Des Moines* (Cruiser No. 15). *Yankton* and the other American ships assigned to northern Russia took no active part in the military operations conducted against Bolshevik forces located nearby, though they did, on occasion, provide some measure of support for the forces of other Allied nations. The yacht contented herself with patrols, with duty as radio ship at Murmansk, and with service as a military passenger transport between Murmansk and Arkhangelsk. In June, she served temporarily both as port officer and radio ship for Murmansk. On 9 July, after bringing passengers from

A peacetime view of the converted yacht *Yankton*. (NR&L(0)3966).

Arkhangelsk to Murmansk, she departed the latter port —in company with *SC-95*, *SC-256*, and *SC-354*—and headed back to England.

She remained in European waters until near the end of 1919. On 7 December, she received orders to return to the United States and arrived in New York sometime in January 1920. She was decommissioned at New York on 27 February 1920 and remained there until sold on 20 October 1921. Presumably, her name was struck from the Navy list sometime between decommissioning and sale, probably about the time her sale was ordered on 5 June 1920. Following her sale, *Yankton* was converted to mercantile service, but she turned up in government records once again two years after her sale when she was seized in New York laden with illegal rum. After extensive litigation, she returned to merchant service—honest merchant service, this time —until broken up at Boston during the summer of 1930.

Yantic

A river in the state of Connecticut.

(ScGbt: dp. 836; lbp. 179'0''; b. 30'; dr. 13'9'' (max.); s. 9.5 k.; cpl. 154; a. 1 100-pdr. P.r., 1 30-pdr. P.r., 2 9'' D.sb., 2 24-pdr. how., 2 12-pdrs.; cl. *Nipsic*)

Yantic—a wooden-hulled screw gunboat built at the Philadelphia Navy Yard—was launched on 19 March 1864 and commissioned on 12 August 1864, Lt. Comdr. Thomas C. Harris in command.

The next day, *Yantic*—in company with the tugs *Aster* and *Moccasin*—sailed in pursuit of the Confederate "pirate" CSS *Tallahassee*. The gunboat went to the northward and eastward of Nantucket during her cruise but, as her commanding officer reported, "obtained no information to justify a longer search for the piratical vessel." Consequently, after a week at sea, *Yantic* returned to the Philadelphia Navy Yard and commenced her post-trial repairs.

Meanwhile, CSS *Tallahassee* had left Halifax, Nova Scotia, at 1300 on 20 August, before any Federal warships could arrive, setting in motion a search. Agitation in Washington over *Tallahassee* resulted in Secretary of the Navy Gideon Welles' sending identical telegrams to the commandants of the navy yards at New York and Philadelphia on the 20th, each asking what vessels were ready for sea.

Yantic subsequently received orders directing her to proceed to Wood's Hole, Mass., where she was to await further orders. She arrived there at 1000 on 13 September. *Yantic* later operated off the eastern seaboard between Hampton Roads and New York and, on 1 November, visited Halifax—a port swarming with "secessionists and other sympathizers"—to obtain information on the activities of CSS *Olustee* (as the Confederates had renamed *Tallahassee*).

After the Confederate ship had managed to elude her pursuers, *Yantic* joined the North Atlantic Blockading Squadron off Wilmington, N.C. During the Union's first attempt to take Fort Fisher, N.C., on Christmas Eve 1864, the screw gunboat suffered her first casualties. At 1500 that afternoon, during the bombardment phase of the action, the ship's 100-pounder rifled gun burst, mortally wounding the division officer, the gun captain, and four men. On his own initiative, Comdr. Harris—thinking his ship "badly shattered" and not knowing the extent of the damage —ordered his ship hauled out of line. After obtaining medical assistance from the steamer *Fort Jackson* and reporting the assessed damage to the flagship *Malvern*, Harris took *Yantic* back into action, opening fire with his remaining effective guns, the 30-pounder rifle and a 9-inch Dahlgren.

On Christmas Day 1864, *Yantic* assisted in the debarking of the troops of General Benjamin Butler and covered the landing operations. At 1400, on the 25th, as Lt. Comdr. Harris later reported, the troops landed "amidst deafening and encouraging cheers from the men-of-war and from the troops still aborad the transports, cheers which were echoed by the fleet by a fire that elicited but a feeble response from the fort." General Butler, however, "to the surprise and mortification of all" (as Harris later recounted), recalled the troops; and the landing operation ceased.

The first Union attempt to reduce and take Fort Fisher thus proved to be a dismal failure; but, before another attempt was made, General Butler was replaced by a more dynamic and aggressive man, Major General Alfred H. Terry. *Yantic* provided a landing party and gunfire support for the second amphibious attack that commenced on 13 January 1865. In the action—a bloody one in which the sailors and marines of the naval landing force charged on the run into withering Confederate gunfire and suffered accordingly grievous casualties in the frontal assault—Fort Fisher was finally taken on 15 January. During the battle, *Yantic* lost three men—two on 15 January and one, who had been wounded mortally on the 15th, who died on the 20th.

The next month, *Yantic* participated in the capture of Fort Anderson, N.C., between 17 and 19 February, in her second major landing operation in a little over a month. For the remainder of the Civil War, *Yantic* served on blockade duties, as part of the successful Union interdiction operation, preventing trade by sea with the Confederacy.

For a little over three more decades, *Yantic* "showed the flag" of the United States in the West Indies, in South American waters, and in the Far East—as well as along the eastern seaboard of the United States. After operating fairly close to home from 1865 to 1872, she then cruised to the Asiatic Station, where she operated for the next four years, 1873 to 1877.

During that particular tour of duty, *Yantic* stood ready to provide assistance for Americans and protection for their property. While operating with the Asiatic Squadron—precursor of the Asiatic Fleet and the 7th Fleet—the gunboat put ashore her landing force at Shanghai, China, on 3 May 1874, in company with the landing party from the sidewheeler *Ashuelot* to aid in quelling a riot by the local natives.

At other times during that Asiatic Squadron deployment, *Yantic* conducted a regular routine of cruises to ports ranging from Canton, Borneo, the Philippine Islands, and Hong Kong. In late 1874, when the Pacific Mail Steamer *Japan* foundered, *Yantic* searched for her. In the spring of 1875, the gunboat later protected the salvagers of *Japan*'s cargo from pirates.

Subsequently, *Yantic*'s crew took part in celebrations attending the unveiling of the statue of Admiral David G. Farragut in Washington, D.C., on 25 April 1881, before sailing later that spring to Mexican waters. In June, at Progreso, Yucatan, she investigated the detention of the American bark *Acacia* before returning northward to familiar waters off the eastern seaboard of the United States. In October 1881, *Yantic* also took part in observances commemorating the centennial of the Battle of Groton Heights and in festivities celebrating the centennial of the American victory at Yorktown, Va.

In June of 1883, *Yantic* headed for the coasts of Greenland, Comdr. Frank Wildes in command, as tender for the steamer *Proteus*, the latter carrying the men of the second relief party sent out to search for the exploration party led by Lt. A. W. Greely, USA. After touching at Disco, Upernavik, and Littleton Island, *Yantic* returned to New York on 29 September 1883. She carried back with her the men of the relief party, led by Lt. Garlington, and also the officers and men of *Proteus*, which had been crushed in heavy ice on 23 July 1883. Unfortunately, neither ship found any trace of the ill-fated Greely expedition.

Yantic "showed the flag" along the eastern seaboard and into the waters of South America and the West Indies from 1884 to 1897. In 1898, she was then loaned

USS *Yantic* in full dress during her service as a training ship. Her hull is painted black, relieved only by a narrow white streak above her gun ports, which have been fitted with glass panes.

to the naval militia of the state of Michigan and served as training ship on the Great Lakes until 1917.

With America's entry into World War I, the Navy expanded. Accordingly, the Civil-War gunboat was recommissioned in 1917 and assigned as a training ship at the Naval Training Station, Great Lakes, Ill. After the armistice, she was struck from the Navy list on 24 July 1919 and ordered sold. However, the venerable *Yantic* was withdrawn from the sale list on 31 December of the same year and again assigned duty as a training ship—this time with the Naval Reserve Forces of the 9th, 10th, and 11th Naval Districts. Commissioned on 15 May 1921, *Yantic*—designated IX–32—operated out of Cleveland, Ohio, until 30 June 1926, when she was decommissioned and again loaned to the state of Michigan.

Yantic suddenly sank alongside the dock at the foot of Townsend Ave., Detroit, Mich., on 22 October 1929. Subsequent investigation revealed that the sinking had been caused by structural weakening, owing to "natural deterioration." She was struck from the Navy list on 9 May 1930.

Yapashi

The generic name of fetishes, representing human forms, found in a prehistoric pueblo above Cochiti, New Mexico.

(YTB–531: dp. 218; l. 100'0''; b. 25'0''; dr. 9'7'' (f.); s. 12.0 k.; cpl. 16; cl. *Hisada*)

On 23 March 1945, the name *Yapashi* was assigned to YTB–531, a *Hisada*-class large harbor tug slated to be built at Jacksonville, Fla., by the Gibbs Gas Engine Co. However, the contract for the construction of the yardcraft was cancelled in October 1945.

Yaquima

A noted female Indian chief whose name was later taken by the Yaquima Indians, a small tribe that lived in what is now the western part of the state of Oregon.

(YT–171: l. 113'0''; b. 25'0''; dr. 13'8'' (max.); a. 2 .30-cal. mg.)

Dauntless No. 14—a steel-hulled, single-screw, diesel-powered tug—was built in 1940 by the Jacobson Shipyards of Oyster Bay, Long Island, N.Y., for the Dauntless Towing Line, Inc., of New York City. Acquired by the Navy on 6 January 1941, *Dauntless No. 14* was renamed *Yaquima* and classified as YT–171—a harbor tug—on 9 January. Converted for naval service at the Portsmouth (N.H.) Navy Yard, *Yaquima* either was placed "in service" or was ready for service on 9 March. Other records indicate another "in service" date, 18 April 1941, which was probably the day that the vessel actually began her operations in the 1st Naval District.

She served a brief tour of duty at New London, Conn., from 15 July to 11 August and then resumed service at Portsmouth. The ship was equipped with a decompression chamber and minor diving equipment at that time, so it is likely that the craft was used as a back-up submarine rescue vessel. In any event, *Yaquima* performed tug and tow service at Portsmouth for the duration of World War II. During that time, she was reclassified a large harbor tug, YTB–171, on 15 May 1944.

Subsequently placed out of service at the Boston Naval Shipyard on 3 December 1945, *Yaquima* was struck from the Navy list on 8 May 1946 and turned over to the War Shipping Administration for further disposition on 7 June of the same year.

Yarborough

George Hampton Yarborough, Jr.—born on 14 October 1895 at Roxboro, N.C.—enrolled in class no. 4, Marine Corps Reserve, on 7 April 1917, the day after the United States entered World War I, and was given the provisional rank of second lieutenant. After instruction at the Marine Barracks, Parris Island, S.C., he reported to the Marine Barracks at Philadelphia on 4 June 1917 for duty with the 16th Company, 5th Regiment of Marines. Taken to New York in *Seattle* (Armored Cruiser No. 11), Yarborough embarked in *Henderson* (Transport No. 1) on 14 June; sailed for France that day; and reached St. Nazaire on the 27th.

Yarborough, promoted to first lieutenant on 11 August 1917, served two tours of detached duty while assigned to the 5th Regiment, first at Cosne, France, between 8 December 1917 and 4 January 1918, and then at Gondrecourt, France, between 22 February and 23 April 1918.

On 23 June 1918, the height of the battle for Belleau Wood, Lt. Yarborough arrived on the front lines. The next day, intense enemy fire from skillfully placed machine guns pinned down Yarborough's unit—a platoon in a support position in the American lines. The young lieutenant dashed from one shell hole to another, in the open, steadying his men, until a burst of machine gun fire hit him. Severely wounded, he refused aid until other wounded men in his unit received medical attention. Finally moved to shelter, he succumbed to his severe gunshot wounds on 26 June. Cited for his bravery, First Lieutenant Yarborough received the Distinguished Service Cross and Navy Cross, posthumously.

(DD–314: dp. 1,308; l. 314′4½″; b. 30′11½″; dr. 9′4″ (mean); s. 35.0 k.; cpl. 122; a. 4 4″, 1 3″, 12 21″ tt.; cl. *Clemson*)

Yarborough (Destroyer No. 314) was laid down on 27 February 1919 at San Francisco, Calif., by the Bethlehem Shipbuilding Corporation's Union Iron Works plant; launched on 20 June 1919; sponsored by Miss Kate Burch, the fiancee of the late Lt. Yarborough; designated DD–314 on 17 July 1920; and commissioned at the Mare Island Navy Yard, Vallejo, Calif., on 31 December 1920, Lt. Comdr. C. E. Rosendahl—later the Navy's pre-eminent authority on airships—in command.

Following commissioning, *Yarborough* was fitted out at Mare Island into late January 1921 and departed the yard on the 25th, bound for Port Richmond, Calif., where she fueled. After trials in San Francisco Bay, Monterey Bay, and San Pedro Bay, the new destroyer tied up at the Reserve Dock at San Diego, Calif., on 2 February. Outside of a trip to San Pedro with liberty parties embarked, the ship remained pierside through mid-April.

Destroyers like *Yarborough* entered service in the midst of post-World War I cutbacks in operating funds and personnel, forcing the adoption of a "rotating reserve" system. One third of the ships in a given large unit would be fully manned and would lie at anchor in harbor; another third would only be half-manned and lie at anchor; and the last segment would be manned by only a bare maintenance crew, necessary to keep the ship in basic operating condition, alongside a pier.

One event highlighted the ship's largely port-bound routine in 1921. She embarked Marine detachments

from the cruisers *Charleston* (CA–19) and *Salem* (CL–3), both units under the command of 1st Lt. J. K. Martensteen, USMC, and transported them to Santa Catalina Island on 18 April. Underway from San Diego at 0615 on the 18th, she stood into Isthmus Cove, Santa Catalina Island at 1145, anchoring at 1205. After landing the marines, she got underway and hove to briefly to embark a passenger—Capt. Franck T. Evans, the chief of staff to Commander, Destroyer Force, Pacific Fleet and the son of the famous admiral Robley D. ("Fighting Bob") Evans—before she resumed her passage. Unfortunately, *Yarborough* collided with a buoy at the entrance to San Pedro harbor—an embarassing occurrence in view of the ship's high-ranking passenger. Fortunately, the ship sustained only minor damage to a propeller blade, and no disciplinary action was taken.

Yarborough remained alongside the Santa Fe dock at San Diego until 30 June, when she headed for the Mare Island Navy Yard. After a drydocking, the destroyer ran trials off the southern California coast, during which she shipped heavy seas over the forecastle that caused some damage to her bridge on 11 July. Visiting San Francisco briefly, the destroyer returned to San Diego on the 13th, where she remained into mid-October.

Yarborough subsequently ran gunnery exercises and drills in company with her sistership *Wood* (DD–317) late in October, after receiving on board a large draft of men from *Jacob Jones* (DD–130). *Yarborough* apparently joined the operating segment of the "rotating reserves" at that point because the rest of her career was largely one of operational activity.

She spent the majority of 1922 operating from San Diego, touching at ports in the Pacific Northwest like Port Angeles and Seattle, Wash., and familiar California ports like San Diego and San Pedro. Upon occasion, she operated with the battleship forces and conducted drills and exercises in antisubmarine screening, torpedo firings, and, of course, the staple, gunnery.

The following year, however, *Yarborough* began her voyages beyond what had become the usual west coast routine. After maneuvers out of San Pedro with the Battle Fleet, *Yarborough* departed that port on 9 February 1923, bound for Magdalena Bay, Mexico. Arriving there on the 6th—in company with Destroyer Squadrons 11 and 12 and the destroyer tender *Melville* (AD–2)—she was underway again two days later, this time bound for Panama.

In the succeeding days that February, *Yarborough* took part in the first of the large United States Fleet exercises—Fleet Problem I. Staged off the coast of Panama, Fleet Problem I pitted the Battle Fleet against an augmented Scouting Fleet. *Yarborough* screened the Battle Fleet's dreadnoughts, often serving as a picket in a special defensive screen arrangement ahead of the heavy units. The exercise continued into March; and, during a lull in the maneuvers, Secretary of the Navy Edwin Denby, embarked in *Henderson* (AP–1), reviewed the assembled forces on 14 March.

After further exercises, *Yarborough* departed the Panama area on 31 March as part of the screen for the northward-bound battleships. She arrived at San Diego on 11 April. For the remainder of the year, her schedule remained routine, operations within the vicinity of either San Diego, San Francisco, or San Pedro, with a period under repairs at Mare Island and drydocked on a marine railway at San Diego.

On 2 January 1924, *Yarborough* got underway for Panama to participate in the next series of fleet exercises—Fleet Problems II, III, and IV—conducted concurrently. Problem II simulated the first leg of a westward advance across the Pacific; Problem III tested the Caribbean defenses and the transit facilities of the Panama Canal; and Problem IV simulated the movement from a main base in the western Pacific to the Japanese home islands—represented in that case by islands, cities, and countries surrounding the Caribbean.

Yarborough's role in the maneuvers was similar to those she had performed before. However, there was one exception because, during one phase of the exercises, she operated with *Langley* (CV-1)—the Navy's first aircraft carrier. She screened *Langley* on 25 January and witnessed an air attack upon the ship by planes of the "black" fleet. The destroyer also performed those tasks for which she had been designed—torpedo attacks and screening maneuvers—both with and against battleships. *Yarborough* and her sisterships participated in the intensive exercises through late February, after which the destroyer paid a brief call upon New Orleans, La.—her only visit ever to that port—between 1 and 11 March.

After further exercises off Puerto Rico, *Yarborough* headed for home; transited the Panama Canal on 8 April; and arrived at San Diego on the 22d. For the remainder of the year, she operated in and around her home port.

The Scouting Fleet once more "battled" the Battle Fleet in March of 1925, in Fleet Problem V, off the coast of Baja, Calif. After that series of exercises which trained the Fleet in protective screening, seizing and occupying an unfortified anchorage, fueling at sea, and conducting submarine attacks, the Fleet set its course westward.

Yarborough departed San Francisco as part of this movement on 15 April 1925. Her log noted: "underway in company with the United States Fleet to engage in joint Army and Navy Problem No. 3 and proceed to the Hawaiian Islands." Screening Battleship Division 5, as a unit of Destroyer Division 34—she proceeded via Mamala Bay, Oahu, and arrived at Pearl Harbor, Hawaii, on 28 April. When the Fleet later concentrated in Lahaina Roads, Maui, *Yarborough* served a brief tour as guardship, patrolling off the entrance to the Fleet anchorage.

During subsequent maneuvers out of Lahaina, *Yarborough* and her mates performed as "Cruiser Division 1" for the sake of the exercise, acting in that guise from 19 to 29 May, before returning to Pearl Harbor for upkeep.

After visiting Hilo, *Yarborough* departed Pearl Harbor on 1 July 1925, bound for the South Pacific as part of the Fleet's Australasian cruise. *Yarborough* subsequently visited Pago Pago, Samoa, from 10 to 11 July; Melbourne, Australia, from 23 to 30 July; Lyttleton, New Zealand, from 11 to 21 August; and Wellington, New Zealand, from 22 to 24 August. Returning via Pago Pago, *Yarborough* and her division mates were pressed into service on 7 September as part of the dragnet searching for the downed *PN-9* No. 1—a flying boat which attempted to make a flight from the west coast to Hawaii. Destroyer Division 34's ships steamed at eight-mile intervals in a scouting line and searched over the next three days before word reached them that *PN-9* No. 1 had been found, her lower wings stripped to make a sail that had taken them close to Oahu.

Yarborough eventually returned via Pearl Harbor to San Diego on 19 September and remained in the vicinity of her home port for the remainder of 1925. Early the following year, 1926, she took part in Fleet Problem VI, off the west coast of Central America, operating with the Battle Fleet and its train convoy against the "enemy" forces as represented by the Scouting Fleet and Control Force. *Yarborough* later visited Port Aberdeen, Port Angeles, Washington, and the Puget Sound Navy Yard before she rounded out the year operating locally from San Diego.

The year 1927 proved to be a busy one for *Yarborough*, one that she began, as usual, at San Diego. Departing that port on 17 February, the destroyer transited the Panama Canal on 5 March, Atlantic-bound. The loss of the German steamship *Albatross*, however, forced a change in plans. *Yarborough* retransited the canal four days later, on 9 March, and headed for the Galapagos Islands in company with the rest of Destroyer Division 34. Forming a scouting line, the flush-deckers combed the seas for survivors of the *Albatross*. During the search, *Yarborough* often operated in sight of her sisterships *Sloat* (DD-316) and *Shirk* (DD-318)—but found nothing. Abandoning the search on the 13th, the ship retransited the canal and rejoined the Fleet.

Participating in Fleet Problem VII later that month, *Yarborough* operated off Gonaives, Haiti, and visited Staten Island and New York late in May and early in June. While in the New York area, the destroyer participated in the presidential review, when President Calvin Coolidge inspected the Fleet from the decks of his presidential yacht, *Mayflower*, on 4 June.

Yarborough subsequently headed for Panama, arriving at Colon on 9 June. She shifted to Puerto Cabezas, Nicaragua, soon thereafter, due to an outbreak of unrest there. She joined *Denver* (PG-28) and *Robert Smith* (DD-324) in guarding American interests in that port before heading back to Colon, retransiting the Panama Canal, and undergoing a drydocking at Balboa. She returned to Puerto Cabezas on 9 July and found *Tulsa* (PG-22) and *Shirk* in port.

Yarborough remained at Puerto Cabezas into early August, drilling her landing force in light marching order early in the deployment to be ready for any emergency. The destroyer sailed for the Panama Canal on 5 August, transited the canal on the 7th, and arrived at San Diego on the 23d. She exercised out of San Diego and off San Clemente Island for the rest of 1927.

The following spring, *Yarborough* again operated in Hawaiian waters, taking part in Fleet Problem VIII which was staged between San Francisco and Honolulu. Returning to the west coast upon completion of that group of maneuvers, the destroyer continued her regular schedule of operations in tactics and gunnery out of Port Angeles, San Diego, and San Pedro.

Yarborough participated in her final large-scale maneuvers in January 1929, operating between San Diego and the westward side of the Panama Canal Zone, in Fleet Problem IX. That problem—significant in that the new aircraft carrier *Lexington* (CV-2) participated in the Fleet's war games for the first time—pitted the Battle Fleet (less submarines and *Lexington*) against a combination of forces—including the Scouting Force (augmented by *Lexington*), the Control Forces, Train Squadron 1, and 15th Naval District and local Army defense forces. The scenario studied the effects of an attack upon the Panama Canal and conducted the operations necessary to carry out such an eventuality. As before, *Yarborough*'s role was with the Battle Fleet, screening the dreadnoughts of the battle line.

After alternating periods in port and operating locally, *Yarborough* was moored at the Destroyer Base at San Diego that autumn and prepared for decommissioning. Simultaneously, she participated in the reactivation of ships that had been in reserve during the past few years. Two of those ships were *Upshur* (DD-144) and *Tarbell* (DD-143). *Yarborough* was decommissioned on 29 May 1930; and, on 3 November 1930, her name was struck from the Navy list. Scrapped on 20 December of the same year, her remains were sold as scrap metal on 25 February 1932.

Yarnall

John Joliffe Yarnall—born in Wheeling, Va. (now W.Va.) in 1786—was appointed midshipman in the Navy on 11 January 1809. Between 1809 and 1812, Yarnall cruised the coastal waters of the United States in *Chesapeake* and *Revenge* performing duty that was tantamount to blockading his own country to enforce President Madison's embargo on trade with the European adversaries during the Napoleonic Wars. In 1813, he was transferred to Oliver Hazard Perry's command on the Great Lakes and became the first lieutenant on board Perry's flagship, *Lawrence*. He participated in the decisive Battle of Lake Erie on 10 September 1813 and, though wounded, refused to leave his post during the engagement. When Perry shifted his flag to *Niagara* during the battle, Lt. Yarnall assumed command of *Lawrence*. After the battle, he took the squadron's wounded on board and carried them back to Erie for medical attention. For his gallantry in the battle, Yarnall earned Perry's commendation as well as a medal expressing the gratitude of Congress and the country.

In the spring of 1815, Yarnall sailed from New York with Stephen Decatur in the frigate *Guerriere* for the Mediterranean Sea. On 17 June, off the Algerian coast, his ship encountered and captured *Meshuda*, the flagship of the Algerine "Navy." While defending his country's honor and rights during that engagement, the valiant Yarnall again suffered wounds. Probably because of his wounds, Lt. Yarnall was chosen as the bearer of dispatches from Decatur's squadron to the government in Washington. In July 1815, he embarked in the sloop-of-war *Epervier* for the voyage home. The warship was last seen on 14 July 1815 as she passed through the Strait of Gibraltar and into the Atlantic. Presumably, Yarnall and all others on board went down with her during the transatlantic voyage.

I

(Destroyer No. 143: dp. 1,154 (n.); l. 314′4½″; b. 30′11¼″; dr. 9′10¼″ (aft) (f.); s. 35.12 k. (tl.); cpl. 122; a. 4 4″, 2 3″, 12 21″ tt., 2 .30-cal. mg., 2 dct.; cl. *Wickes*)

The first *Yarnall* (Destroyer No. 143) was laid down on 12 February 1918 at Philadelphia, Pa., by William Cramp & Sons Ship & Engine Building Co.; launched on 19 June 1918; sponsored by Mrs. Marie H. Bagley; and commissioned on 29 November 1918, Comdr. William F. Halsey, Jr., in command.

Assigned to Division 15, Destroyer Force, *Yarnall* served briefly with United States naval forces in France during 1919. By 1 January 1920, her division had been reassigned to Flotilla 5, Destroyer Squadron 4, Pacific Fleet, and operated out of the San Diego destroyer base. Her division—redesignated Division 13 in February—received orders in April to proceed to the Asiatic station; but she apparently did not begin that assignment until late the following fall. *Yarnall* returned from the Far East to the United States late in the summer of 1921 and began repairs at Puget Sound. In December, she was reassigned to Division 11 and again operated out of San Diego until 29 May 1922 when she was decommissioned there and placed in reserve.

After almost eight years of inactivity, the destroyer was recommissioned at San Diego on 19 April 1930, Comdr. John F. McClain in command. Assigned initially to Division 11, Squadron 10, Battle Fleet Destroyer Squadrons, *Yarnall* operated briefly on the west coast before being transferred to the east coast sometime late in 1930. By New Year's Day, 1931, her home port had been changed to Charleston, S.C. In March, she joined the Scouting Force as a unit of Destroyer Division 3 but retained Charleston as her home port. The destroyer operated out of that base until late in the summer of 1934 when, though still a unit of Scouting Force Destroyers, she returned to the west coast. Based at San Diego, the warship remained active along the California coast until late in 1936. She then returned to the east coast and, on 30 December 1936, was placed out of commission at Philadelphia and berthed there with the reserve fleet.

As a part of President Roosevelt's program to bolster the minuscule Atlantic Squadron after war broke out in Europe in September 1939, *Yarnall* ended her 21-month, second retirement on 4 October 1939 when she was recommissioned at Philadelphia, Lt. Comdr. John G. Winn in command. She became a unit of Destroyer Squadron 11 of the Atlantic Squadron, the small fleet assigned the enormous task of keeping war out of the western hemisphere. She operated out of Norfolk in the Neutrality Patrol until the fall of 1940 when the United States concluded the destroyers-for-bases deal with the United Kingdom.

Yarnall was one of the 50 overage destroyers chosen to be turned over to the Royal Navy in return for the right to establish American bases on British territory in the western hemisphere. She proceeded to St. John's, Newfoundland, where she was decommissioned by the United States Navy on 23 October 1940; and, that same day, the Royal Navy commissioned her as HMS *Lincoln* (G.42), Comdr. G. B. Sayer, RN, in command.

The veteran destroyer departed St. John's on 3 November and arrived in Belfast, Northern Island, on the 9th. *Lincoln* moved from there to Londonderry where she was assigned to the First Escort Group, Western Approaches Command. For almost a year, she met troop transport and cargo convoys in mid-ocean and escorted them into ports in the British Isles. Between September 1941 and February 1942, the destroyer was refitted at Woolwich, England. At the conclusion of that overhaul, she was turned over to an expatriate Norwegian crew and was sent back across the ocean to serve with the Western Local Escort Force, operating along the Newfoundland coast between Halifax and St. John's. In July 1942, HMS *Lincoln* became HMCS *Lincoln* when she was transferred from the Royal Navy to the Royal Canadian Navy—though still manned by Norwegians. Her duty in Canadian waters continued until the end of 1943, at which time she recrossed the Atlantic. She departed Halifax on 19 December and arrived back in Londonderry on Christmas Day. Early in 1944, the venerable warship was placed in reserve in the Tyne River. Her service to the Allied cause, however, had not quite ended. On 26 August 1944, she was transferred to the Soviet Navy to be cannibalized to provide spare parts for eight of her sisters previously given to the Russians. Her name had already been struck from the United States Navy list on 8 January 1941—soon after her transfer to the Royal Navy.

II

(DD–541: dp. 2,050; l. 376′5″; b. 39′7″; dr. 17′9″; s. 35.2 k. (tl.); cpl. 329; a. 5 5″, 10 40mm., 7 20mm., 10 21″ tt., 6 dcp., 2 dct.; cl. *Fletcher*)

The second *Yarnall* (DD–541) was laid down on 5 December 1942 at San Francisco, Calif., by the Bethlehem Steel Co.; launched on 25 July 1943; sponsored by Mrs. Earl Groves; and commissioned on 30 December 1943, Comdr. Benjamin F. Tompkins in command.

The destroyer spent the first two months of 1944 conducting her shakedown cruise and other training exercises in the San Diego operating area. She departed the west coast early in March and arrived at Oahu on the 19th. For the next 10 weeks, *Yarnall* carried out additional tactical exercises in the Hawaiian Islands.

On 31 May, the warship stood out of Pearl Harbor with Task Group (TG) 52.17 and set a course—via Kwajalein in the Marshall Islands—for the invasion of Saipan in the Marianas. For that operation, *Yarnall* was assigned to Fire Support Group 1 under Rear Admiral Jesse B. Oldendorf. When her task group began its prelanding bombardment of Saipan on 14 June, *Yarnall* screened *Cleveland* (CL–55) and *Montpelier* (CL–57) and managed to add 148 rounds of 5-inch shell of her own to the effort. On 15 June, the day of the assault, she continued to screen *Cleveland* and, on the following day, carried out her first call fire mission—a dual-purpose action to help repulse an enemy counterattack and to destory a bothersome pillbox.

On the 17th, as a result of the submarine sightings of the Japanese fleet moving toward the Marianas, *Yarnall* and 20 other destroyers were detached from direct support for the invasion and ordered to screen the fast carriers. *Yarnall* joined TG 58.7, Rear Admiral Willis A. Lee's hastily composed battle line, in preparation for what would be the Battle of the Philippine Sea. She tasted her first antiaircraft combat at 0515 on 19 June when a "Zeke" tried to bomb *Stockham* (DD–683) and then began a strafing run on *Yarnall*. Three guns of her main battery quickly took the intruder under fire and began scoring hits on him. As the plane closed the destroyer's port quarter, it exploded and splashed into the sea to give *Yarnall* her first victory over the enemy.

About five hours after that attack, the ship received word of the first of the four large air raids launched by the Japanese Mobile Fleet to attempt to break up the American invasion force off Saipan. At about 1045, *Yarnall* and *Stockham* encountered the first carrier-based air of the battle when five "Val" dive bombers peeled off to attack the two picket destroyers. *Yarnall*'s guns opened up on them and splashed one before the remaining four flew off to attack the larger ships of the American fleet. Word of the approach of the second raid arrived at 1110; and, 35 minutes later, about 20 enemy planes managed to break through the reception committee of F6F Hellcats vectored out to intercept them. *Yarnall* took seven of those planes under fire and splashed one. That was her last combat of the day. Though the Japanese mounted two more raids, they approached Task Force (TF) 58 from directions which did not bring them in close proximity to *Yarnall*.

On the 20th, no enemy planes attacked TF 58. Instead, the Japanese began their retirement toward Japan. American carrier search planes found the enemy late in the day, and TF 58 launched air strikes from extreme range. After darkness fell that evening, *Yarnall*'s searchlights helped to guide the returning airmen to their carriers. The following day, the destroyer returned to the coast of Saipan to resume call fire missions supporting the troops fighting ashore. She continued her labors in the Marianas until 8 July, when the warship left in the screen of a convoy bound for the Marshalls. After arriving at Eniwetok on the 12th, she took on ammunition, provisions, and fuel and headed back to the Marianas on the 15th. There, she resumed patrol and antisubmarine screening duties and kept at such tasks until the 25th when she moved inshore to provide gunfire support for the troops occupying Tinian.

The warship alternated screening and bombardment missions in the Marianas until 16 August when she again sailed for the Marshalls. *Yarnall* remained at Eniwetok from 20 to 29 August. On the latter day, she left the anchorage in company with TG 38.2 for an aerial sweep of the Philippine Islands in preparation for the invasion of the archipelago at Leyte. Following those raids, the carriers and their escorts rested at Ulithi Atoll between 1 and 6 October.

On the latter day, Yarnall sortied with the entire Fast Carrier Task Force for a three-day aerial sweep of Japanese air bases on Formosa. During that operation, *Yarnall* provided aircrew rescue services and performed antiaircraft and antisubmarine screening duties. During the first day of that attack, the destroyer fired on 15 enemy planes and splashed two of them. The following evening, she barely evaded a bomb which exploded close astern. She emerged unscathed from another bombing attack on the 14th.

Following the Formosa raid, *Yarnall*'s unit steamed south to operate off Luzon. She screened the carriers while their planes suppressed Japanese land-based airpower in the vicinity during the landings at Leyte. During the three-phased Battle for Leyte Gulf which thwarted the Japanese attempt to break up the American liberation of Leyte, *Yarnall* continued to screen the carriers as they raced northward to destroy Admiral Ozawa's decoy force built around planeless aircraft carriers. After successfully completing that mission, TF 38 made a fueling rendezvous on 30 and 31 October and then resumed its duty pounding enemy installations on Luzon.

At the end of the first week in November, the carriers

and their escorts once again retired to Ulithi. The destroyer returned to sea on 14 November to screen TF 38 during further aerial attacks on Japanese installations in the Philippines. On 23 November, she headed back to Ulithi with TG 38.1 for logistics. In December, she returned to the Philippines with TG 38.1 to support the landings on the island of Mindoro and to continue the pressure on Japanese air forces based on Luzon. During that mission, she successfully weathered the famous typhoon on 17 December 1944 which claimed destroyers *Hull* (DD–350), *Monaghan* (DD–354), and *Spence* (DD–512). She returned to Ulithi on 24 December and remained there until January 1945.

On New Year's Day, TG 38.1 stood out of Ulithi to provide air support for landings on Luzon at Lingayen Gulf. The planes hit Formosa on the 3d and 4th, pounded airfields on Luzon on the 6th and 7th, and returned to Formosa installations on the day of the landings, 9 January. That night, *Yarnall* accompanied the fast carriers through Bashi Channel into the South China Sea to begin a series of raids on Japan's inner defense line. Unopposed by the Japanese Fleet, TF 38 sent planes against bases at Camranh Bay and Saigon in Indochina, then against Formosa on 15 January. Fighters attacked Amoy, Swatow, and Hong Kong in China as well as Hainan Island in the Gulf of Tonkin. On the 16th, they returned to Hong Kong and Hainan for a repeat performance and for good measure made a sweep of Canton. The task force exited the South China Sea via Balintang Channel and then hit Formosa and the Nansei Shoto on 21 January. Okinawa felt the carriers' punch on the 22d; and, two days later, TF 38 set a course back to Ulithi.

On 10 February, *Yarnall* left Ulithi with TF 38 to attack the Japanese home islands for the first time since the Halsey-Doolittle raid and to provide strategic cover for the assault on Iwo Jima. For two days, 16 and 17 February, the skies over Tokyo rained death and destruction. On the 18th, *Yarnall* steamed south with the carriers to lend the marines a hand during the Iwo Jima landings. While TF 38 planes supported the assault, *Yarnall* protected their floating bases from enemy air and submarine attacks. She remained in the vicinity of the Volcano Islands until the 22d when she and the carriers again headed toward the Japanese home islands for another swipe at Tokyo on the 25th. Then, after rendezvousing with TG 50.8, the logistics group, TF 38, sent its planes to strike Okinawa on 1 March.

On 3 March, *Yarnall* received orders transferring her from TG 58.2 to TG 59.6 for a practice attack on the main body of TF 59. While closing the objective on the night of 4 and 5 March, she collided with *Ringgold* (DD–500). *Ringgold* suffered a sheared off bow while *Yarnall* also suffered one man killed and six others injured. Towed to Ulithi by *Molala* (ATF–106), she reached the anchorage on 7 March. On the 8th, her bow broke off and sank. While at Ulithi, she had a false bow fitted for the voyage back to the United States for permanent repairs. She stood out of Ulithi on 5 April and steamed via Pearl Harbor to the Mare Island Navy Yard where she underwent repairs until 2 July.

The warship returned to Pearl Harbor in July and conducted training operations in the Hawaiian Islands through the end of the war. Two days after the cessation of hostilities, *Yarnall* set a course for Tokyo, Japan, to participate in the postwar occupation. She was present in Tokyo Bay on 2 September when Japanese officials signed the surrender document on board *Missouri* (BB–63) and remained in the Far East supporting minesweeping operations until the end of October. On the 31st, she put to sea and shaped a course for San Diego, Calif., where, though she remained in commission, she was placed in an inactive status. Berthed at San Diego with the Pacific Reserve Fleet, *Yarnall* was finally placed out of commission on 15 January 1947.

The outbreak of the Korean conflict in June 1950 brought many ships out of the "mothball fleet." *Yarnall* was ordered back into active service on 31 August 1950, and she was recommissioned at San Diego on 28 February 1951. She reported for duty with the Pacific Fleet on 20 March and conducted shakedown training and other exercises along the west coast until mid-May. On 15 May, *Yarnall* departed San Diego for Japan. Steaming via Pearl Harbor, she arrived in Yokosuka on 7 June and, three days later, got underway for her first tour of combat duty in Korean waters. For the most part, *Yarnall* served in the screen of TF 77, the carrier task force, though on occasion she did close the coast of Korea to provide gunfire support for the United Nations troops operating ashore. Her first Korean War deployment was punctuated by periodic port calls, mostly at Yokosuka, but also at Okinawa and at Keelung, Taiwan. In August, she served briefly with the Taiwan Strait patrol before returning to the Korean combat zone in September.

Her first Korean War deployment lasted until December. On 8 December, the destroyer departed Yokosuka and steamed via Midway and Pearl Harbor to San Diego where she arrived on the 21st. From there, she moved to Long Beach early in 1952 for an overhaul. The warship completed repairs early that summer and returned to San Diego on 11 June. A month and a day later, she departed San Diego; set a course via Pearl Harbor and Midway for the western Pacific; and arrived in Yokosuka on 6 August. On the 8th, she again got underway and, after an overnight stop at Sasebo on 10 and 11 August, headed for the Korean operating area. Again, her duties consisted of screening TF 77 carriers and providing bombardment services, frequently at the besieged port city of Wonsan. As during the previous deployment, she alternated tours of duty in Korean waters with port calls at Japanese ports for repairs, upkeep, rest, and relaxation. Later, in November, she returned to the Taiwan Strait patrol before resuming her tours of duty with TF 77 and on the bombline. On 30 January 1953, she concluded her second Korean War deployment by departing Sasebo for the United States. Steaming via Midway and Pearl Harbor, *Yarnall* arrived in San Diego on 16 February.

While *Yarnall* enjoyed her stateside rotation, hostilities in Korea ceased when an armistice was finally signed on 27 July 1953. The warship, however, continued to make annual deployments to the Far East and frequently operated in Korean waters with TF 77. She continued to alternate deployments to the Orient with periods of normal operations out of San Diego until September of 1958 when she was decommissioned.

Berthed at Stockton, Calif., *Yarnall* remained inactive for almost a decade. On 10 June 1968, she was transferred, on a loan basis, to the Taiwanese Navy which she served as *Kun Yang* (DD–8). She was returned to the United States Navy in 1974 for disposal. Her name was struck from the Navy list on 25 January 1974, and she was retransferred back to Taiwan by sale. As of early 1980, *Kun Yang* remained active with the Taiwan Navy.

Yarnall (DD–541) earned seven battle stars during World War II and two battle stars during the Korean conflict.

Yarnell, Harry E., see *Harry E. Yarnell*.

Yarrow

(MB: t. 29 (gross); l. 65′; b. 13′; dr. 5′ (forward); s. 13 mph.; cpl. 8; a. 1 3-pdr., 2 mg.)

Yarrow (SP–1010)—a wooden-hulled motorboat constructed in 1913 by Kargard of Chicago, Ill.—was formally acquired by the Navy on free lease on 27 August 1917 from Mr. K. D. Clark, exactly a month after she was commissioned on 27 July 1917. *Yarrow* served as a section patrol craft in the 9th Naval Dis-

trict cruising the waters of Lake Michigan during World War I. Her naval career continued after the armistice, and she was not returned to her owner until 7 March 1919. Simultaneously with the return, her name was struck from the Navy list.

Yatanocas

One of nine villages of the Natchez Indians in the 17th and early 18th centuries. It was located near the site of the present-day city of Natchez, Miss.

(YTB–544: dp. 218; l. 100′0″; b. 25′0″; dr. 9′7″ (f.); s. 12 k. (tl.); cl. *Hisada*)

Yatanocas (YTB–544) was laid down on 12 April 1945 at Morris Heights, N.Y., by the Consolidated Shipbuilding Corp.; launched on 9 July 1945; delivered to the Navy and placed in service on 14 December 1945.

The large harbor tug served briefly in the 3d Naval District before being placed out of service, in reserve, in March 1946. She was berthed with the Florida Group, Atlantic Reserve Fleet, at Green Cove Springs until May 1947 at which time she was placed back in service. Since that time, *Yatanocas* has served the Commandant, 6th Naval District and has operated at Charleston, S.C., for her entire active career. In February 1962, she was redesignated a medium harbor tug, YTM–544. As of 1 January 1979, she was still active at Charleston.

Yaupon

An Indian term designating a type of holly tree.

(ATA–218: dp. 1,275 (tl.); l. 194′6″; b. 34′7″; dr. 14′1″ (f.); s. 12.1 k.; cpl. 57; a. 2 40mm.; cl. *ATA–214*)

ATA–218 was laid down as *Yaupon* (AN–72) on 29 January 1944 at Slidell, La., by the Canulette Shipbuilding Co. Her name was cancelled on 12 August 1944, and she was designated *ATA–218*. She was launched on 16 September 1944 and commissioned on 10 March 1945.

Information regarding *ATA–218*'s brief Navy career is almost totally lacking. Even her decommissioning date is unknown. Her name was struck from the Navy list on 17 April 1946, and she was sold through the War Shipping Administration on 3 January 1947. Presumably, she was scrapped.

Yavapai

A county in central Arizona, established on 21 December 1864 and named for the Yavapai Indians of the Yuma language group. The name itself means "people of the sun."

(LST–676: dp. 3,960 (tl.); l. 328′0″; b. 50′0″; dr. 11′2″; s. 10.0 k.; cpl. 151; a. 7 40mm., 12 20mm.; cl. *LST–542*)

LST–676 was laid down on 22 April 1944 at Ambridge, Pa., by the American Bridge and Iron Co.; launched on 6 June 1944; sponsored by Mrs. C. F. Goodrich; and commissioned, at New Orleans, La., on 30 June 1944, Lt. Pat Munroe, USNR, in command.

LST–676 departed New Orleans on 7 July for Florida and conducted shakedown training out of St. Andrews Bay—two weeks filled with drills of every description ranging from firefighting to abandon ship and from gunnery to beaching exercises. Returning to New Orleans following her shakedown, *LST–676* took *LCT–900* on board on her main deck and sailed on 2 August for Cuba, arriving at Guantanamo Bay on the 9th, en route to Panama.

Reaching Colon on 16 August, *LST-676* took on board 105 army passengers for transportation to the west coast and transited the Panama Canal that day. After discharging her passengers at San Pedro, Calif., on 1 September, *LST-676* sailed for Hawaii and arrived at Pearl Harbor on the 14th.

While at Pearl Harbor, *LST-676* received word that she had been selected for conversion to a logistics vessel for landing craft, a self-propelled barracks ship. The need for large numbers of small craft in the amphibious operations of the American campaign in the Pacific—craft and ships such as LCI's, LCT's, SC's, PC's, PCS's and YMS's—meant logistics headaches. Those vessels needed fuel, water, and provisions just like the larger ships; and thus specialized ships for supporting them were needed, too.

Still another large group of small craft needing support were the LCM's and LCVP's left behind when their transports sortied on night retirements from the beaches. The idea of a barracks ship came, apparently, from Capt. Stanley Leith, operations officer for Commander, Amphibious Forces, Pacific Fleet, Vice Admiral Richmond K. Turner. When Leith suggested to Turner that LST's be converted to serve as "mother ships," the admiral readily agreed, and a program to make these changes was promptly launched.

However, before her conversion, *LST-676* was to perform one more duty as a true LST, lifting a detachment of marines and their equipment to Hilo, Hawaii. She returned to Pearl Harbor on 2 October to moor at the Waipio Amphibious Operating Base at West Loch.

There the landing ship underwent the conversion to a self-propelled barracks ship of the *Benewah* (APB-35) class. Sixteen large refrigeration units were installed, as was stowage for dry provisions. Berthing space was provided at the after end of the former tank deck. One quonset hut was added topside to provide a wardroom and quarters for transient officers and another was erected for a bakery and galley. Besides those main deck structures, the ship received portable distilling tanks to produce fresh water and several storage tanks for it.

Thus equipped to furnish fuel, water, fresh and dry provisions, the ship—reclassified as a modified LST, *LST(M)-676*—conducted her shakedown at Hilo before she put into the Supply Depot at Pearl Harbor. There, she loaded 385 tons of fresh, frozen, and dry provisions, and, in addition, embarked 8 officers and 198 men from a boat pool for transportation. On 24 January 1945, *LST(M)-676* departed Pearl Harbor, via Eniwetok and Guam, bound for Iwo Jima.

The Iwo Jima campaign marked the first time that LST(M)'s were utilized in operations. On the D-plus-one day at Iwo Jima, 20 February 1945, *LST(M)-676* proceeded to an anchorage about one-half mile south of Mount Suribachi—the scene of the famous flag-raising —and soon began tending the assault boats carrying men and equipment to "Green" and "Yellow" beaches.

During the ensuing 10 days of the operation to capture Iwo Jima, the converted LST fed 3,499 men and berthed 2,307; LCI's, SC's, and LST's took on a total of 75,527 pounds of fresh and dry provisions, 37,250 gallons of water; and 89,334 gallons of fuel oil. Even after the island was considered secured, *LST(M)-676* remained in the vicinity, taking part in the occupation and garrisoning of the island and furnishing logistics support for the ships and landing craft in the area.

LST(M)-676 remained at Iwo Jima until 27 April. During the time she spent there supporting the invasion and occupation of that key island, she fed 27,823 officers and men and berthed 12,350. She transferred some 561 tons of fresh and dry provisions between 275 ships ranging in size from destroyers to LCT's. In addition, 203 ships received some 305,884 gallons of water between them, and 95 ships took on 324,030 gallons of fuel.

Retiring to Guam after the successful conclusion of the Iwo Jima operation, the ship there received word

that she had been given the name *Yavapai and* redesignated APB–42, effective on 1 May 1945. She effected repairs at Guam before she departed that island in late June, bound for Okinawa.

Yavapai arrived at Okinawa almost at the height of the campaign. Called upon to take over the function of provisioning small craft, *Yavapai* anchored off the Hagushi beachhead to proceed with her vital duties. During daylight hours, the ship provided logistics support to ships and small craft; at night, she manned the antiaircraft batteries against the almost ever-present Japanese raiding aircraft.

Some 556 ships came alongside during the days *Yavapai* spent at Okinawa and, when the end of the war came in mid-August 1945, she was still at Okinawa, performing her "over the counter" logistics function there. She subsequently participated in Operation "Campus," the occupation of the southern half of Korea. Arriving at Jinsen, Korea (later known as Inchon), on 12 September, *Yavapai* provided food, fuel, and water; "mothered" a 300-man boat pool; and acted as station ship for their activities.

The barracks ship remained in the Far East into the spring of 1946. She served two tours at Jinsen (from 12 September 1945 to 31 January 1946 and from 21 February 1946 to 8 April 1946) and two at Tsingtao, China (from 1 to 20 February 1946 and from 9 to 14 April 1946), before she sailed for the United States. After proceeding via Okinawa and Pearl Harbor, *Yavapai* transited the Panama Canal on 11 June and arrived at the Charleston Naval Shipyard, Charleston, S.C., on 20 June.

Decommissioned there on 3 December 1946, *Yavapai* was placed in reserve and remained in that status into the late 1950's before being struck from the Navy list.

LST(M)-676 received one battle star for her World War II service.

Yazoo

A river formed by the joining of the Tallahatchie and Yalobusha Rivers in Leflore County in northwestern Mississippi. It winds southward across flat, fertile farm land and prime forested acreage before emptying into the Mississippi River at Vicksburg.

(Mon: dp. 1,175; l. 225'; b. 45'; dr. 6'; s. 9 k.; a. 2 11" D. sb.; cl. *Casco*)

Yazoo—a single-turreted, twin-screw monitor—was laid down in March 1863 by Merrick & Sons, Philadelphia, Pa.; launched on 8 May 1865; and completed on 15 December 1865.

Yazoo was a *Casco*-class monitor intended for service in the shallow bays, sounds, rivers, and inlets of the Confederacy. These warships sacrificed armor plate for a shallow draft and were fitted with a ballast compartment designed to enable them to ride exceptionally low in the water during battle. However, design changes and contract disputes delayed the first launching of a ship of the class until the spring of 1864. It was then discovered that the monitors had only three inches freeboard, even without turret, guns, and stores.

As a consequence of this revelation, the Navy Department ordered the contractor on 24 June 1864 to raise the deck of *Yazoo* 22 inches to give her sufficient freeboard. The ship was laid up at the Philadelphia Navy Yard on 20 December 1865, and she saw no commissioned service.

Her name was twice changed: first to *Tartar* on 15 June 1869 and then back to *Yazoo* on 10 August 1869. *Yazoo* was sold at Philadelphia on 5 September 1874 to A. Purvis & Son.

The side-wheel steamer *St. Mary*—captured by the Union Navy at Yazoo City, Miss., on 13 July 1863—

was renamed *Yazoo* but was again renamed *Alexandria* (*q.v.*) in December 1863.

I

(AN–92: dp. 775 (f.); l. 168'6''; b. 33'10''; dr. 10'9''; s. 12.0 k.; cpl. 46; a. 1 3''; cl. *Cohoes*)

Yazoo (AN–92) was laid down on 6 July 1944 at Duluth, Minn., by the Zenith Dredge Co.; launched on 18 October 1944; sponsored by Mrs. S. H. Griffin, the wife of Colonel S. H. Griffin, USA; and commissioned on 31 May 1945, Lt. Lionel Krisel, USNR, in command.

Yazoo departed Duluth on 15 June, bound for the Atlantic; travelling via the Great Lakes and the St. Lawrence Seaway; and arrived at the Boston Navy Yard to commence fiting out. After shakedown training out of Melville, R.I., she underwent post-shakedown alterations at Boston. She conducted net defense evolutions at Melville before beginning net-laying operations which she carried out in the vicinities of Newport, R.I., New York City, and Boston during the next 18 months.

Yazoo departed Newport on 13 May 1947 and laid fleet moorings at Argentia, Newfoundland, before returning from that cruise on 18 August to resume local operations. She operated out of Newport into 1948. In January of that year, her duties included ice-breaking in the channels of Narragansett Bay after the severe winter weather had frozen the water there.

That spring, *Yazoo* pulled a large Navy cargo vessel off the beach at Davisville between 22 and 25 April 1948 and then made a cruise to Terceina, in the Azores, during September and October of that year, to lay a fleet mooring there. She spent much of the year following her return to the eastern seaboard serving as a target ship for submarines and towing targets for surface battle practices. She conducted similar operations in 1950, with time out in June of that year for laying a light indicator net during Operation "Martex."

After an overhaul at the Charleston (S.C.) Naval Shipyard from July to September 1950, *Yazoo* trained out of Norfolk, Va., before she resumed extensive work with nets off Newport. During March 1951, *Yazoo* took part in Atlantic Fleet mining exercises out of Key West, Fla., and then spent the remainder of the year performing mine tests and exercises out of Charleston. Between February and April 1952, *Yazoo* laid nets off Cape Henry during exercises in the Chesapeake Bay.

In January 1953, semi-permanent mine tracks were installed on the net-layer, enabling the ship to lay 24 moored-type mines. On 9 January, the ship's home port was changed to Key West, Fla., to enable her to commence a schedule of tests and exercises under the auspices of the Operational Development Force. She participated in Operation "Hardex" off the Virginia capes in June and July of that year before she resumed duty out of Key West later that summer. She performed services for the Mine Evaluation Detachment from April to August of the following year and—after salvage operations off Key Largo, Fla.—joined in Atlantic Fleet exercises that extended along the eastern seaboard of the United States during October 1954.

Yazoo continued her routine of local operations out of Key West into 1955. During most of March of that year, the ship took part in one of the largest fleet mine exercises ever held. In one phase of the operation, she planted Coast Guard buoys marking a channel; and she was one of the final ships to clear the area after the resultant clean-up operation. In April 1955, the ship's home port was again changed—this time back to Charleston—and she took part in a joint United States–Canadian exercise, Operation "Canminus" in which *Yazoo* operated as principal minelaying and recovery ship.

During the summer of 1955, *Yazoo* conducted mine exercises out of Key West, Port Everglades, and Charleston with the Atlantic Fleet Mine Force. She spent September and November in company with *Orleans Parish* (LST–1069) and *Peregrine* (EMSF–373), carrying out a special project off the coast of Fedhala, French Morocco, the site of the original American landings in North Africa in November 1942. On her return voyage, *Yazoo* called at Gibraltar, the Azores, and Bermuda, and reached Charleston on 9 December 1955. She entered the naval shipyard there on 6 January 1956 for an overhaul and, later that spring, carried out refresher training out of Norfolk and two weeks of net-tending training at the Harbor Defense Unit, Little Creek, Va.

Yazoo joined *Exultant* (MSO–441) and *Fidelity* (MSO–443), on 18 June 1956, in carrying out a special mine project off the coast of Charleston and Cape Romain, S.C., that lasted until 23 July. After that task, *Yazoo* again operated out of Key West, providing services to the Mine Warfare Evaluation Detachment in a Mine Force special project. Later, during Atlantic Fleet mining exercises between 29 October and 24 November, *Yazoo* laid two large Coast Guard buoys; assisted *Gwin* (DM–33) in establishing a 10-mile exercise channel with Coast Guard lighted buoys and dan buoys; laid surface minefields; delivered triangulation data to the umpiring group during aerial minelaying; and participated in the mine recovery and clean-up phase. She then proceeded to Key West, where she conducted a Mine Force special project in company with *Observer* (MSO–461) and *Salute* (MSO–470).

In the spring of 1957, *Yazoo* cruised in the Caribbean with the Mine Force and called at San Juan, Puerto Rico; Charlotte Amalie, St. Thomas, Virgin Islands; and Ciudad Trujillo, Dominican Republic. Upon her return to Charleston, the ship carried out several special mine projects in local areas and spent a fortnight operating with the Mine Warfare Evaluation Detachment at Key West. After an overhaul in the Norfolk Naval Shipyard from July to August 1957, *Yazoo* conducted refresher training out of Charleston and participated in a service mine test.

The ship spent the first three weeks of 1958 training with the Harbor Defense Unit at Norfolk before she shifted southward to Charleston to participate in Atlantic Fleet amphibious exercises. During July and August of that year, *Yazoo* participated in Exercise "Sweep Clear III," a NATO minesweeping exercise near Sydney, Nova Scotia. During the cruise—on 26 July 1958—the net layer visited Louisburg, Nova Scotia, and recovered a cannon from a French man-of-war that sank on 26 July 1758—two hundred years earlier!

Following her return to Charleston on 15 August, *Yazoo* took part in fleet service mine tests and trained foreign mine warfare officers in the Charleston vicinity. She spent the remainder of 1958 in operations out of Charleston and off the Virginia capes.

Overhauled at the Charleston Naval Shipyard between February and May 1959, *Yazoo* conducted refresher training and then took part in Exercise "Clear Sweep IV" off Charleston. Among the ship's duties performed in that vicinity were conducting net training and type training, planting buoys, and laying practice mines for mine warfare schools. During September of 1959, *Yazoo* carried out sweep gear evaluation for the Bureau of Ships in the Charleston area before she returned to active operations as a minelaying and recovery unit during Fleet exercises off the Virginia capes and at Onslow Bay, N.C.

Yazoo again took part in amphibious exercises at Onslow Bay in January of 1960, before she carried out service mine tests out of Charleston that lasted into the spring. In July 1960, *Yazoo* received the battle efficiency competition award for the fiscal year 1960. That autumn, *Yazoo* distinguished herself while participating in Operation "Clear Sweep V" off Nova Scotia. On 12 October, *Yazoo* received special praise for towing *Hummingbird* (MSC–192) 35 miles to port after that minecraft had suffered a materiel casualty. Three days later, on the 15th, when the Canadian escort maintenance ship HMCS *Cape Scott* (ARE–101) suffered a casualty, *Yazoo* came to the rescue and towed the ship out of dangerous waters, saving her from almost certain grounding in the shoals of Shelburne Harbor.

After returning southward, *Yazoo* underwent a lengthy overhaul at Charleston from November 1960 to February of 1961. She operated again with the Mine Force in the Caribbean from February to March 1961, taking part in Fleet amphibious warfare exercises before completing a service mine test off Charleston. That spring, she again participated in exercises off Charleston with Canadian minesweeping and minelaying units and then underwent harbor net training at Norfolk. In July, *Yazoo* cruised off the coast of Maine, detonating underwater explosions under the auspices of the Office of Naval Research for the Carnegie Institute of Washington, D.C., and received commendations for a job well done from both agencies.

Yazoo underwent repairs at Charleston from late July 1961 into September, before she resumed her schedule of mining exercises and net training out of Charleston and Norfolk. After a year of such duty, she was decommissioned on 28 August 1962. Assigned to the Norfolk group of the Atlantic Reserve Fleet, *Yazoo* was struck from the Navy list on 1 July 1963 and transferred to the Maritime Administration (MarAd) for lay up in the James River. She remained in MarAd custody until sometime between 1973 and 1975.

Yeaton

(WPC–156: dp. 220; l. 125′; b. 23′6″; dr. 9′; s. 11 k.; cpl. 38; a. 1 3″; cl. *Active*)

Yeaton—a 125-foot steel-hulled, diesel-powered Coast Guard cutter—was completed in 1927 at Camden, N.J., by the American Brown Boveri Electric Corp.—and commissioned into Coast Guard service soon thereafter. She initially served at Norfolk, Va., in 1928; and successively at St. Petersburg, Fla., from 1929 to 1931; at Pascagoula, Miss., in 1932 and 1933; back at St. Petersburg in 1934; at Gulfport, Miss., from 1935 to 1938; at Stapleton, N.Y., in 1939; and at Gallups Island, Mass., in 1940. When the Coast Guard came under Navy control in 1941, *Yeaton* most probably operated on patrol duties. No records of the ship's wartime service have been found, however, leaving one only to conjecture. Sometime in 1942, the ship was classified as a patrol craft and given the hull number WPC–156.

After World War II, *Yeaton* resumed operation with the Coast Guard, out of New London, Conn. In the 1960's, the Coast Guard reclassified the ship as a medium endurance cutter (WMEC) and gave her the identification WMEC–156. *Yeaton* was eventually decommissioned and laid up in 1970.

Yellowstone

I

(Freighter: dp. 12,570; l. 416′6″; b. 53′0″; dr. 26′3″ (mean); dph. 34′6″; s. 10.0 k.; cpl. 79; a. none)

The first *Yellowstone* was a steel-hulled, single-screw freighter launched as *War Boy* on 9 December 1917 by the Moore and Scott Shipbuilding Co. of Oakland, Calif., and was completed in 1918. Inspected by the Navy in the 12th Naval District, with an eye toward utilizing the ship as a depot collier, and assigned Id. No. 2657, the freighter sailed from the west coast to the eastern seaboard, and was taken over by the Navy at Philadelphia for operation with the Naval Overseas Transportation Service (NOTS). She was commissioned at Cramps' Shipbuilding Co. yard on 21 September 1918, Lt. Comdr. Lawrence Dodd, USNRF, in command.

Soon thereafter, *Yellowstone* moved to New York where she arrived on the 24th. She underwent repairs at the Morse Drydock and Repair Co. yards, Brooklyn, and suffered damage in a minor sideswiping collision

with the British-registry *Moorish Prince* on 13 October. Shifting to Pier 5, Bush Terminal, Brooklyn, on the morning of the 15th, after repairs from her brush with *Moorish Prince*, the vessel took on board 6,672 tons of general cargo—including automobiles and locomotives—earmarked for American forces in France, over the next few days. On 27 October, *Yellowstone* got underway, in convoy, for France, "proceeding under confidential orders on Army transport duty to port of debarkation," St. Nazaire.

The war ended on 11 November while *Yellowstone* was en route to France and, three days later, the ship arrived at Quiberon Bay. She remained at anchor there until she received onward routing to St. Nazaire. There, she discharged her cargo and began taking on "return" cargo for transport to the United States. That load included "aeroplane parts." After shifting briefly to the St. Nazaire roadstead, *Yellowstone* departed the French coast, proceeding independently, on 27 November.

On 15 December, and when only two days from New York, *Yellowstone* sighted a derelict three-masted schooner and altered course to close. She discovered the water-logged *Joseph P. Cooper* of Mobile, Ala., abandoned with her decks and cabin awash and with the forerigging gone and the forecastle smashed in. She looked like she had been adrift from 6 to 8 weeks.

After leaving the derelict, *Yellowstone* continued her passage and arrived at Pier 5, Bush Terminal, Brooklyn, N.Y., on the 17th. Shifting to Pier 1 at the end of December, she spent a week at anchor off the Statue of Liberty before returning to Bush Terminal and, later, shifting to the Army docks at Brooklyn. There, from 17 to 25 January, the cargo vessel took on board 5,150 tons of supplies and, on the latter day, got underway for France.

During the crossing, she ran into a heavy gale on 4 February. The ship rolled considerably at the outset, shipping water and spray amidships, and labored heavily in the raging tempest. Five days later, with the storm still giving no signs of abating, *Yellowstone*'s steering gear went out of commission. Soon both auxiliary systems—steam and hand-powered—also did likewise. Pumping oil through waste pipes in an attempt to break the force of the waves, *Yellowstone* wallowed through the storm while her engineers worked mightily to repair the casualty. By the 12th, the situation was well in hand, and the ship was once again able to utilize her steering gear effectively; and *Yellowstone* anchored at Quiberon Bay at 0953 on 14 February.

The ship's troubles were not over, however, as she grazed the jetty wall while entering the locks at St. Nazaire. At 0545, the engineer officer reported to the captain that two boilers were under water and the steam was cut off. As the ship moored alongside the nearby quay, *Yellowstone*'s crew broke out a tarpaulin and collision mat. Soon thereafter, the freighter, still with way on, nudged into the bridge walk of the lock. By 0630, under tow by a French tug, *Yellowstone* reached a safe basin, where she dropped both anchors and began to take stock of the situation.

Divers examining the damage reported that a hole, six inches in width, had been opened up in the ship's side, extending from a point 10 feet beneath the waterline and about six feet in length. Drydocked on 11 March, *Yellowstone* grazed SS *Alesia* that morning, causing minor damage to that vessel's railings on her promenade and boat decks.

Undocked upon completion of the hull repairs on 6 April, *Yellowstone* loaded a return cargo of structural iron (ballast), barbed wire, and 6-inch artillery pieces. On 19 April, the ship shifted from St. Nazaire to Brest and got underway the next day for the United States.

Mooring at Pier 3, Bush Terminal, Brooklyn, on 7 May, *Yellowstone* unloaded through mid-month. At noon on 24 May, a Shipping Board crew reported on board; and, at 1247, *Yellowstone* was decommissioned. Simultaneously struck from the Navy list and returned to the Shipping Board, *Yellowstone*'s subsequent career proved to be a short one. On 10 December 1920, she ran hard aground off St. Michael's, in the Azores. Although the ship was listed as "stranded," and a total loss, her entire crew of 45 men was saved.

II

(AD–27: dp. 16,880 (f.); l. 492'0"; b. 70'0"; dr. 28'0" (max.); s. 18.0 k.; cpl. 962; a. 2 5", 8 40mm., 22 20mm.; cl. *Shenandoah*)

The second *Yellowstone* (AD–27) was laid down on 16 October 1944 at Tacoma, Wash., by the Seattle Division of the Todd-Pacific Shipyards, Inc.; launched on 12 April 1945; sponsored by Mrs. F. A. Zeusler, the wife of Capt. F. A. Zeusler, USCG, the District Coast Guard Officer of the 13th Naval District; and commissioned on 16 January 1946, Capt. J. A. Ferrall, Jr., in command.

After shakedown training out of San Diego and repairs at Puget Sound Naval Shipyard to correct minor deficiencies which appeared during her initial cruise, *Yellowstone* operated in the Seattle area into March 1946. She departed Seattle on the last day of the month, transited the Panama Canal on 11 April, and arrived at Newport, R.I., on the 20th to take up her duties tending destroyers of the Atlantic Fleet.

Yellowstone performed faithful service to the Fleet for the next 28 years, providing repair, supply, and auxiliary services (power and fresh water, etc.) not only to destroyers (the purpose for which she was designed) but also to aircraft carriers and submarines. In time, this valuable adjunct to the fleet earned a reputation for reliability and dependability that caused some to nickname her "Old Faithful," after the famous geyser in Yellowstone National Park. The destroyer tender also earned the coveted battle efficiency "E" award 10 times.

Yellowstone was deployed to the Mediterranean 11 times between 1947 and 1968. Her ports of operation ranged from Izmir, Turkey, to Naples, Italy; from Venice to Taranto; from Suda Bay, Crete, to Gibraltar; and included cities in Spain, France, Italy, and Greece. In between her deployments with the 6th Fleet, the destroyer tender operated out of Boston, Newport, Norfolk, or Bermuda.

Her tasks were performed mostly unheralded and from from the public eye but were necessary to maintain the ships of the Fleet in operational trim. In Octo-

ber 1969, she performed a noteworthy repair job when she relaced 1,162 tubes in the number one propulsion boiler of *Forrest Royal* (DD–872) as that ship was preparing to deploy to the Mediterranean. Working against the destroyer's deadline, *Yellowstone*'s skilled artisans accomplished the task in only 12 days and thus allowed her to get underway on time.

Soon thereafter, *Yellowstone* deployed to the Mediterranean for the 12th and last time. She arrived at Naples on 9 December 1969 and, before long, found herself with another difficult, major repair task ahead of her. She replaced the starboard propeller of *Sampson* (DDG–10)—a job that normally required a dry-docking. Repair, supply, and deck divisions of both ships participated in the evolution that earned *Yellowstone* a commendation.

A little more than a month later, the tender's talent was once again subjected to a rigorous test. On 10 February 1970 at Naples, the Greek registry freighter *Mautric* collided with *Yellowstone* and the tender's nest of destroyers. *Semmes* (DDG–18), *Samuel B. Roberts* (DD–823), and *Charles F. Adams* (DDG–2) all suffered extensive hull and structural damage, but *Yellowstone* worked nearly 24-hour shifts from 13 to 22 February and effected the necessary repairs. Capt. R. D. Wood, commanding *Yellowstone*, and Senior Chief Ship Fitter William S. Burman received Navy commendation medals for heading the exemplary repair work that soon had all ships back in operational condition.

After a brief in-port period at Piraeus, Greece, from 18 March to 5 April, *Yellowstone* returned to Naples, where she subsequently performed her second underwater propeller replacement of the deployment—on *Corry* (DD–817). The repair ship sailed for home in mid-May and arrived at Mayport, Fla., on 1 June. One month later, on 1 July, the ship's home port was changed from Mayport to Charleston, S.C.

The destroyer tender provided services to ships of Cruiser-Destroyer Flotilla (CruDesFlot) 6 into January of 1971. At the end of that month, she sailed for Puerto Rico and took part in "Springboard" exercises before returning to Charleston on 16 February. That spring, when the Commander, CruDesFlot 6, embarked in *America* (CVA–66) to deploy to the 6th Fleet, *Yellowstone*'s commanding officer became the administrative deputy to the Charleston representative of Commander, CruDesFlot 6. In that role, he coordinated local pier assignments; arranged for tug and tow services; made military guardship and pier sentry assign-

The destroyer tender *Yellowstone* (AD–27).

ments; scheduled ship tours; provided information and assistance to dependents; and represented the destroyer force at meetings of numerous naval station, base, and district advisory boards and committees.

Yellowstone remained in port at Charleston into 1973. Among the noteworthy events that occurred that year was the ship's nomination to receive the Ney award, recognizing the ship's outstanding food service mess, as the nominee of the Commander, Cruiser Destroyer Force, Atlantic Fleet.

After 28 years of continuous service to the Fleet—the last few years of which were spent along the eastern seaboard of the United States—*Yellowstone* was decommissioned on 11 September 1974. Struck from the Navy list the next day and subsequently transferred to the Maritime Administration for disposal, the veteran auxiliary was sold in September 1975.

III

(AD–41: dp. 21,916; l. 641'10''; b. 85'0''; dr. 24'0''; s. 20.0 k.; cpl. 1,500; a. 1 5''; cl. *Samuel Gompers*)

The third *Yellowstone* (AD–41) was laid down on 2 June 1977 at San Diego, Calif., by the National Steel and Shipbuilding Co.; launched on 27 January 1979; and sponsored by Mrs. Donald C. Davis, the wife of Admiral Donald C. Davis, the Commander in Chief of the Pacific Fleet. *Yellowstone* is slated to be delivered to the Navy in mid-January of 1980 and should join the fleet in the middle of the year.

Yew

An evergreen tree and shrub that yields valuable timbers for cabinet-making and archery.

(YN–37: dp. 560 (l.); l. 163'2''; b. 30'6''; dr. 11'8''; s. 12.5 k.; cpl. 48; a. 1 3''; cl. *Aloe*)

Yew (YN–37) was laid down on 22 May 1941 at Camden, N.J., by the John H. Mathis Co.; launched on 4 October 1941; sponsored by Miss Alice E. Morgan, daughter of Comdr. A. L. Morgan, USN (Ret.); and placed in service on 1 July 1942.

Records for *Yew*'s service are practically non-existent. The The fragmentary evidence available shows that the ship was reclassified AN–37 on 1 January 1944. The net tender was ultimately decommissioned at Oran, Algeria, on 30 November 1944 and simultaneously transferred to the French Navy under lend-lease. She served as *Scorpion* (A–728) until she was nominally returned by the French on 21 March 1949 but was sold outright to the French on the same day. Her American name, *Yew*, was struck from the Navy list on 28 April 1949.

Scorpion served the French Navy into the mid-1970's before she was disposed of.

Yo Ho

(MB: l. 46'4''; b. 10'0''; dr. 2'8½'' (mean); s. 9 k.; cpl. 4; a. 2 mg.)

Yo Ho (SP–463)—a motor boat built in 1910 at Bath, Maine, by the Bath Marine Construction Co.—was acquired by the Navy from H. D. Bacon, of Bath, and commissioned on 12 May 1917, Boatswain T. H. Barber, USNRF, in command. Operating in an unattached status from the 2d Naval District, *Yo Ho* served through the armistice which ended World War I on 11 November 1918. She was sold for junk on 2 June 1919 to G. F. Blackburn of New York, N.Y.

Yokes

William John Yokes—born on 15 November 1918 in Franklin, Pa.—enlisted in the Navy at Cleveland, Ohio,

on 3 January 1942 and ultimately advanced to the rating of seaman 2d class.

Attached to the armed guard detachment in SS *Steel Navigator*, Yokes was killed in action on 19 October 1942 when his ship—a straggler from Convoy ON–137 —was attacked by the German submarine *U–610*. For several days prior to the engagement, heavy seas and high winds had caused a dangerous shift in ballast in the merchantman. Yokes acted beyond the scope of his duty when he and his shipmates volunteered to go below and perform the physically exhausting task of shifting ballast to trim the ship. That they did for some 30 hours without rest. On 19 October 1942, lookouts spotted the periscope of *U–610*, and the armed guard unit swiftly manned their guns. Soon the gunfire registered several near-misses to the enemy's periscope, and he withdrew temporarily.

Later that day, *U–610* returned and torpedoed the hapless merchantman, sinking her immediately. Among the dead, Yokes was commended posthumously by the Chief of Naval Personnel, who cited the seaman's "courageous and unfailing devotion to duty . . . fortitude, skill and bravery" in conduct "in keeping with the highest traditions of the naval service."

(ADP–69: dp. 1,650; l. 306'0''; b. 37'0''; dr. 12'7'' (lim.); s. 23.6 k.; cpl. 205; trp. 162; a. 1 5'', 6 40mm., 6 20mm., 2 dct.; cl. *Charles Lawrence*)

Yokes (DE–668) was laid down on 22 August 1943 at Orange, Tex., by the Consolidated Steel Co.; launched on 27 November 1943; sponsored by Mrs. Charlotte Yokes, the widow of Seaman Yokes; reclassified from DE–668 to a high-speed transport, APD–69, on 27 June 1944; and commissioned on 18 December 1944, Lt. Comdr. Paul E. Warfield, USNR, in command.

Following her shakedown training out of Bermuda and post-shakedown availability at the Norfolk Navy Yard, *Yokes* shifted to the west coast, via the Panama Canal, and arrived at San Diego, Calif., on 14 March 1945. After further training, *Yokes* departed San Diego on 19 March, bound for the Hawaiian Islands. She made port at Pearl Harbor on the 26th and trained at Maui with underwater demolition teams (UDT's) for one week before she sailed for the western Pacific.

Arriving at Okinawa on 1 May 1945, *Yokes* operated in that vicinity through June, serving as an antisubmarine screening vessel, a rescue ship, and as an escort ship. On 10 May, her gunners claimed a "Zeke."

The ship shifted to the Marianas in July, escorting LST Flotilla 36 from Okinawa to Saipan between 4 and 10 July and then briefly anchoring at Apra Harbor, Guam, before heading for the west coast of the United States. Proceeding via Pearl Harbor, where the ship took on board the 14 officers and 79 men of UDT–28 on 25 July, *Yokes* reached Oceanside, Calif., on 2 August. Transferring UDT–28 to *LCT–395* upon her arrival, the high-speed transport sailed for San Diego that same day.

Shifting to the Western Pipe and Steel Co. yard at San Pedro on 5 August, *Yokes* underwent a 15-day yard availability before she conducted a brief stint of training off the coast of southern California. She departed San Diego on 5 September to return to the Far East, touching at Manila Bay, Subic Bay, Tacloban, Samar, Buckner Bay, Guam, Manus, and Shanghai on transport operations into the winter. Departing Manila Bay on 23 January 1946, *Yokes* steamed via Pearl Harbor for the west coast of the United States, making port at San Diego on 15 February and remaining there under repairs through the summer.

Decommissioned at San Diego on 19 August 1946, *Yokes* was berthed there, in reserve, until struck from the Navy list on 1 April 1964. Sold to the National Metal and Steel Corp. of Terminal Island, Calif., the hulk of the former high-speed transport subsequently was scrapped.

Yokes received one battle star for her World War II service.

Yolo

A county in central California, established in 1850. The name itself is apparently a linguistic corruption of Yo Doy, the name of a small Indian tribe of that region.

(LST-677: dp. 3,960; l. 328'0"; b. 50'0"; dr. 11'2"; s. 10.0 k.; cpl. 151; trp. 340; a. 8 40mm.; cl. *LST-542*)

LST-677 was laid down on 25 April 1944 at Ambridge, Pa., by the American Bridge and Iron Co.; launched on 16 June 1944; sponsored by Mrs. Lee S. Kreeger; ferried down the Mississippi River to New Orleans; and commissioned there on 3 July 1944, Lt. Charles R. Bast, USNR, in command.

LST-677 conducted her shakedown training out of Panama City, Fla., and then loaded naval construction battalion (SeaBee) equipment at Gulfport, Miss., before embarking men of the staff of LST Flotilla 6 for transport to combat staging areas. She put to sea from New Orleans on the morning of 8 August 1944, with a convoy bound for Cuba, and then proceeded by way of the Panama Canal and San Diego to the Hawaiian Islands.

She reached Pearl Harbor on 19 September and, in the ensuing weeks, conducted amphibious warfare exercises at Maui with Army amphibious teams and their embarked tracked landing vehicles. That duty came to an end on 19 October when she moored at the amphibious repair dock at Waipio Point, Pearl Harbor, for conversion to a highly specialized type of support ship for amphibious operations.

LST-677's conversion to a landing craft tender, or self-propelled barracks ship, was completed by 21 January 1945. The ship—reclassified initially to *LST(M)-677*—spent the following days taking on 406 tons of fresh, frozen, and dry provisions and embarking 315 officers and men of a boat pool for transportation to the Solomon Islands. She left Hawaii astern on the morning of 2 February with an amphibious task group that carried out battle rehearsals in the Solomons before proceeding by way of the Carolines to Okinawa. During the voyage to the next stop on the island-hopping campaign toward the Japanese home islands, *LST(M)-677* was reclassified a self-propelled barracks ship, APB-43, and given the name *Yolo*, effective on 31 March.

Yolo arrived off Okinawa on 1 April—D day for that strongly held island—and added to the gunfire that drove away enemy bombers that threatened the formation in which she was steaming. The following day, she opened fire on a suicide plane, joining the other ships nearby in putting up a devastating antiaircraft barrage that literally blew the plane to bits. That same day, she became the headquarters ship for the 70th Naval SeaBee Pontoon Barge detachment and commenced tender duties that, in the ensuing weeks, saw her service or provision small craft alongside on 915 occasions.

Yolo dispensed a grand total of 991 tons of issues—including 514 tons of dry provisions and 477 tons of frozen foods; delivered nearly 200,000 gallons of fuel to small craft; handled more than 12,000 communications and brought on board several casualties from shore for emergency treatment while they were waiting to be transferred to hospital ships. Under day and night threat of enemy suicide planes and bombers, she shot down one aircraft, assisted in the downing of three others; and witnessed the destruction of more than 50 enemy planes in the vicinity of her anchorage.

Yolo's duties at Okinawa terminated on 28 June when she sailed for the Philippines with a convoy of amphibious vessels that reached San Pedro Bay, Leyte, on 3 July. Upon her arrival, she reported for duty to Service Squadron 10 and was assigned to Service Division (ServDiv) 101. On 22 July, she sailed for Subic Bay with fresh provisions for an attack transport and two attack cargo ships. She then embarked a draft of 50 men for passage back to Leyte. With the cessation of hostilities with Japan in mid-August 1945, *Yolo* became "home" for 235 men of ServDiv 101 awaiting occupation service in Japan. She headed out to sea on 3 September; joined a troop convoy off Batangas, Luzon; and proceeded thence to Tokyo Bay where she anchored on 15 September—less than a fortnight after the formal Japanese surrender in Tokyo Bay.

Assigned to the Yokohama area, she provisioned small craft on an emergency basis and provided living quarters for men from various naval units until permanent facilities were established ashore. When *Yolo*'s occupation service in the Far East came to an end, she was routed by way of the Panama Canal to Norfolk, Va., where she was decommissioned on 9 August 1946. Assigned to the Norfolk Group of the Reserve Fleet, *Yolo* remained in reserve until struck from the Navy list on 1 May 1959. She was removed from Navy custody on 5 February 1960 and sold to the J. C. Berkwit Co., of New York City, and subsequently scrapped.

Yolo (APB-43) earned one battle star for her World War II service.

Yonaguska

One of the most prominent chiefs of the East Cherokees during the first half of the 19th century. Yonaguska fostered peace but steadfastly refused to agree to the removal of his portion of the tribe to the west. Later in life, he led his people in a successful abolition of the use of alcohol.

(YT-195: dp. 218; l. 100'0"; b. 25'0"; dr. 9'7" (f.); s. 12 k. (tl.); cl. *Woban*)

Yonaguska (YT-195) was laid down on 21 July 1942 at the Pearl Harbor Navy Yard; launched on 17 August 1943; completed and placed in service on 22 February 1944.

Yonaguska spent her entire career in the Hawaiian Islands. She was first assigned to the Commandant, 14th Naval District and served at Pearl Harbor for the remainder of World War II. On 15 May 1944, she was redesignated a large harbor tug and received the hull number, YTB-195. She continued to serve the 14th Naval District after the war.

Sometime in 1949, however, she went out of service, for she was loaned to the United States Coast Guard on 3 August 1949. Presumably, she did her Coast Guard service in the Hawaiian Islands as well because when she was returned to the Navy in June 1954 she was returned to the custody of the 14th Naval District. Upon her return, she was placed in reserve and remained inactive until January 1958 when she returned to active duty in the 14th Naval District. In February 1962, *Yonaguska* was redesignated a medium harbor tug and was reclassified YTM-195. The tug served at Pearl Harbor for the next 12 years. In August 1974, she was placed out of service, and her name was struck from the Navy list. Soon thereafter, she was sold for scrapping.

York

An industrial city—the seat of government of a county of the same name—in southern Pennsylvania, some 23 miles south of Harrisburg.

Chester (CL-1) (*q.v.*) was renamed *York* on 10 July 1928 to free the name *Chester* for heavy cruiser CA-27.

York County

Counties in Maine, Nebraska, Pennsylvania, South Carolina and Virginia.

(LST–1175: dp. 3,560; l. 445'; b. 62'; dr. 18'; s. 17 k.; cpl. 170; trp. 410; a. 6 3"; cl. *Suffolk County*)

York County (LST–1175) was laid down on 4 June 1956 at Newport News, Va., by the Newport News Shipbuilding and Drydock Co.; launched on 5 March 1957; sponsored by Mrs. William C. France; and commissioned on 8 November 1957, Lt. Comdr. Warren M. Schofer in command.

The new tank landing ship then was fitted out and underwent ready-for-sea trials at Port Everglades, Fla., and conducted shakedown training out of her home port, Little Creek, Va., which she completed on 17 May 1958. She conducted various operations in the Virginia area until 15 July when all training was cancelled due to the crisis in Lebanon; and *York County* prepared for extended operations. However, the Lebanon crisis lessened; and the ship proceeded to Vieques Island, Puerto Rico, for amphibious exercises.

On 7 August, *York County* returned to her home port and began preparations for a regularly scheduled deployment to the Mediterranean. She arrived at Gibraltar in late September 1958; then visited Greece, Turkey, Lebanon, and Italy. She returned to Little Creek on 25 March 1959. However, the ship recrossed the Atlantic to hold leading roles in two major amphibious exercises, "Tralex 3–59" and "Tralex 4–59" which were conducted off the coast of Spain.

In November, *York County* entered the Norfolk Shipbuilding and Drydock Co. for maintenance and upkeep. She next departed the east coast of the United States on 11 January 1960 for her second Mediterranean deployment. Following her arrival back at her home port on 15 June, *York County* participated in "Tralex 1–60" and "Lantphibex 500/61" in the area of Vieques, Puerto Rico. In July, she proceeded to Baltimore for an overhaul by the Maryland Shipbuilding and Drydock Co.

Upon emerging from the yard, the ship conducted refresher training before deploying to the Caribbean towards the end of November for training operations with other amphibious ships. She returned to Little Creek on 19 January 1961. The next major exercise, "Solant Amity III," started on 17 April and took *York County* 27,000 miles in an effort to establish greater understanding between the peoples of the United States and southern Africa. The ship cruised along both the Atlantic and the Indian Ocean coasts of Africa and visited 12 ports in 10 countries and received some 23,000 visitors.

After a short midshipman cruise in early November 1961, *York County* headed for the Caribbean where she participated in Exercise "Phiblex 4–61" before returning to Little Creek in January 1962 for leave and upkeep. On 26 February, she conducted a two-week reserve cruise off the coast of Florida.

On 15 May, *York County* sailed for the Mediterranean where she conducted practice and demonstration landings and participated in the Navy's "People to People" program. *York County* returned home on 19 October and made a one-day turnaround to take part in the Cuban blockade. It was not until 5 December 1962 that the ship finally returned to the Hampton Roads area for leave and upkeep, followed by a four-month yard and drydock period at Jacksonville, Fla., and six weeks of selected underway training exercises.

In July of 1963, *York County* revisited the Caribbean and transported the highly publicized Puerto Rican National Guard from Ponce, Puerto Rico, to Isla de Vieques. While in the West Indies, she also patrolled off Haiti, ready to evacuate American civilians if the civil disorders in that island required such action. Fortunately, tension eased, and *York County* returned to Little Creek on 4 October.

A visit to Portland, Maine, from 9 to 11 November, preceded a short trip to Roosevelt Roads, Puerto Rico, to transport the men and equipment of Military Construction Battalion 7. *York County* returned on 25 November and finished the year undergoing tender availability and upkeep.

For the early part of 1964, *York County* worked at Vieques, Puerto Rico, and Onslow Beach, N.C. She took part in the Naval Academy's Memorial Day ceremonies at Annapolis, Md. During June and July, *York County* received alterations at the Norfolk Naval Shipyard. On 13 August, the ship lifted the 3d LAAM Battalion to Vieques and reembarked the unit on 17 September for the return passage. Ten days later, she returned to Little Creek and commenced preparations for an overseas exercise.

On 7 October 1964, *York County* got underway to join in Operation "Steel Pike I," the largest joint amphibious operation held since World War II. The ship returned home on 28 November 1964 and operated locally into the following spring.

On 30 April 1965, *York County* sailed for the Dominican Republic and transported marines and equipment to Port Haina. She conducted surveillance duties during the crisis in that nation before returning to Norfolk on 7 June and remaining in the Virginia capes-Hampton Roads area for most of the summer.

From September until December 1965, *York County* was deployed to the Caribbean and participated in numerous amphibious assault exercises and a major fleet exercise, "Phibaswex/Meblex 2–65."

York County was in her home port from 1 January 1966 until 24 January for leave and upkeep. She transported general cargo to Roosevelt Roads, Puerto Rico, then embarked marines and equipment for delivery to Cherry Point, N.C., before returning to Little Creek on 9 February.

From 18 February through 18 April 1966, *York County* underwent preparations for overhaul and tender availability. Following this, she traveled to New York City for independent ship exercises, returning home on 26 April. In May, the ship hosted the Swedish ambassador and the Inter-Allied Confederation of Reserve Officers. *York County* received her overhaul in two parts. The first was accomplished at the Key Highway floating drydock of Bethlehem Steel Corp., Baltimore, Md.; the second part was completed on 30 September at Horne Bros. Shipyard, Newport News, Va.

On 13 October 1966, the ship reloaded ammunition and received refresher training out of Little Creek until 16 November. During the remainder of the month, the ship received new cryptographic equipment and was refuelled prior to deployment. *York County* sailed for the West Indies on 28 November and conducted amphibious exercises and training in the Caribbean for five months. She returned to Little Creek, Va., on 6 May 1967 and underwent tender availability.

In June, the ship successfully passed a nuclear technical proficiency inspection; acted as a setting for a training film; and transported a Marine Corps engineering company to Vieques Island and back. From 5 to 21 July, *York County* participated in the antisubmarine Exercise "Plumb Bob III."

During August, *York County* supported LVT training for Marine Corps reservists and provided control ship duty for drones. She spent September and October in restricted availability and on standby duty, ready to support NASA operations. On 31 October, *York County* got underway for the middle Atlantic where she served as a recovery ship for the Apollo IV space shot. On 15 December 1967, the ship underwent tender availability which lasted through the end of the year.

On 17 January 1968, *York County* got underway from Little Creek; stopped briefly at Morehead City, N.C., later that day; and then headed for the Caribbean. While in the West Indies, she visited Vieques, Puerto Rico; Kingston, Jamaica; and St. Croix, Virgin Islands. The ship returned to Little Creek on 15 February, resumed operations in the Virginia capes area, and took part in the Apollo VI recovery training exercises.

On 13 June 1968, *York County* departed Onslow Beach, N.C., for exercises in waters off Puerto Rico. During the cruise, she visited Vieques Island, Puerto Rico; Guantanamo Bay, Cuba; St. Croix, Virgin Islands; and San Juan and Roosevelt Roads, Puerto Rico. *York County* arrived back at Little Creek on 3 August and conducted various exercises and operations in the Virginia area into the autumn.

On 25 October 1968, *York County* got underway for a deployment in the Caribbean which lasted into February 1969. She returned to Little Creek on the 19th of that month and began a period in port which lasted into May. On 12 May, the ship began another brief Caribbean cruise to take part in Exercise "Exotic Dancer." After stops at Ponce and Roosevelt Roads, Puerto Rico, and at St. Croix, Virgin Islands, she participated in a simulated blockade in her part of the exercise. She returned home via San Juan, Roosevelt Roads, and Ponce, Puerto Rico, and reached Little Creek on 9 June. But for a special amphibious exercise at Onslow Beach, N.C., from the 23d to the 28th, the ship spent the remainder of June and most of July at Little Creek.

On 22 July, *York County* departed Little Creek; crossed the Atlantic; and joined the Mediterranean Ready Amphibious Force. After making several successful landings throughout the Mediterranean and enjoying liberty in many ports, *York County* returned to Little Creek on 12 December 1969.

York County entered the Norfolk Shipbuilding and Drydock Company's yard on 20 January 1970 for an overhaul. By 10 August, the ship was ready for sea. She conducted various exercises in the South Carolina operating area. Then, from 2 to 17 September, she prepared for a deployment with the 6th Fleet.

The next day, the ship sailed for the Mediterranean, and she transited the Strait of Gibraltar on 29 September. On 9 October, *York County* conducted Exercise "Deep Express" at Alexandroupolis, Greece. She visited several ports in Greece and Spain before returning to Little Creek on 17 November. The ship finished out the year 1970 at Little Creek undergoing tender availability.

On 18 January 1971, the ship got underway for Vieques Island, Puerto Rico, to participate in the "Firex" exercise. She continued to operate in the Caribbean until 22 February when she arrived at Miami for two days of liberty. The ship returned to Little Creek on 27 February and immediately went alongside *Amphion* (AR–13) for tender availability which lasted until 17 March.

After completing fire-fighting training in Philadelphia, *York County* remained at Little Creek until 25 April except for loading ammunition and gasoline at Craney Island, Va. During this time, the crew prepared the ship for Exercise "Exotic Dancer," which commenced on 26 April and lasted through 14 May 1971. Upon her return home, *York County* operated in the Virginia coastal area and got ready for a month-long cruise in the Caribbean.

York County returned to Virginia on 6 August for tender availability followed by type training exercises. On 9 September, the ship was again deployed to the Caribbean and returned to Little Creek on 28 October where she spent the rest of 1971.

She spent January 1972 preparing for an upcoming Caribbean and eastern Pacific cruise. On the last day of the month, *York County* got underway for the Canal Zone. She left Cristobal on 8 February and, for the first time in her history, transited the Panama Canal and entered the Pacific.

Following operations off the coast of Panama, *York County* reentered the Atlantic; proceeded to Guantanamo Bay, Cuba; spent two days there; then moved to the Bahamas to onload dredging equipment at Andros Island before returning to Little Creek on 20 March 1972. She remained at Little Creek until 12

April when she sailed to Wilmington, N.C., for the annual Azalea Festival.

From 18 April to 8 May 1972, the ship remained in port at Little Creek; and, on 9 May, she got underway for Exercise "Exotic Dancer V." She returned to her home port on 24 May. *York County* was decommissioned there on 17 July 1972 and transferred to the Italian government. She served the Italian Navy as *Nave Caorle* (L–9891) into 1979.

Yorktown

A town in Virginia where the climactic battle of the American Revolution was fought in the autumn of 1781.

I

(Slp: dp. 566; lbp. 117'8''; b. 32'11''; dph. 15'0''; dr. 15'6''; cpl. 150; a. 16 32-pdrs.)

The first *Yorktown*—laid down in 1838 by the Norfolk Navy Yard and launched in 1839—was commissioned on 15 November 1840, Comdr. John H. Aulick in command.

Yorktown departed Hampton Roads on 13 December, bound for the Pacific. After calling at Rio de Janeiro from 23 January to 5 February 1841, the sloop rounded Cape Horn and arrived at Valparaiso, Chile, on 20 March.

The ship operated along the Pacific coast of South America until 26 May, when she sailed from Callao, Peru, bound for the Pacific isles. Looking after the interests of the American whaling industry and of the nation's ocean commerce, she called at the Marquesas, the Society Islands, New Zealand, and the Hawaiian Islands. After completing her mission in the South and Central Pacific, she departed Honolulu on 6 November and headed for the coast of Mexico.

Yorktown called at Mazatlan before heading south to resume operations along the coast of South America. She continued her cruising—primarily out of Callao and Valparaiso—through the early fall of 1842, when she departed Callao on 23 September, bound for San Francisco, where she arrived on 27 October.

Shifting to Monterey on 11 November, the sloop called again at Mazatlan on the 22d before she proceeded to Valparaiso. *Yorktown* remained at that port until she got underway on 2 May 1843 for the east coast of the United States. After rounding Cape Horn and calling at Rio de Janeiro, she arrived at New York on 5 August. Six days later, the sloop was decommissioned.

Placed in active service once more, on 7 August 1844, with Comdr. Charles H. Bell in command, *Yorktown* departed New York on 11 October, bound for Funchal, Madeira. After proceeding thence to Porto Praya, the sloop joined the Africa Squadron on 27 November.

Yorktown ranged up and down the west coast of Africa, going as far south as Capetown, Cape Colony, as she labored to curtail the slave trade. In the course of her patrols, the vigilant sloop captured slave-ships *Pons*, *Panther*, and *Patuxent*.

On 2 May 1846, *Yorktown* departed Porto Praya and returned to the east coast of the United States, reaching Boston on the 29th. There, on 9 June, the sloop was once again decommissioned.

Subsequently recommissioned at Boston, she sailed on 22 November 1848 for her second deployment with the African Squadron. Still engaged in hunting down slave ships, *Yorktown* cruised along the African coast, carefully observing each ship she encountered for any sign of the illicit traffic in human flesh. On 6 September 1850, she struck an uncharted reef at Isle de Mayo in the Cape Verde Islands. Although the ship broke up in a very short time, not a life was lost in the wreck.

II

(Gunboat No. 1: dp. 1,910; l. 244′5″; b. 36′0″; dr. 14′0″ (mean); s. 16.14 k.; cpl. 191; a. 6 6″, 4 3-pdrs., 4 1-pdrs., 2 30-cal. mg.; cl. *Yorktown*)

The second *Yorktown* (Gunboat No. 1)—a steel-hulled, twin-screw gunboat protected by a then armored deck—was laid down on 14 May 1887 at Philadelphia, Pa., by the William Cramp and Sons' shipyard; launched on 28 April 1888; sponsored by Miss Mary Cameron, the daughter of United States Senator Don Cameron; and commissioned at the League Island (Philadelphia) Navy Yard on 23 April 1889, Comdr. French E. Chadwick in command.

Yorktown conducted final sea trials before being assigned to the "Squadron of Evolution" in the autumn of 1889. *Yorktown* operated with that unit as it developed tactical maneuvers for use by the new steel-hulled naval vessels then coming into service in the United States Navy.

After this duty, *Yorktown* departed the east coast of the United States on 7 December 1889, bound for European waters; stopped briefly at Fayal in the Azores; and arrived at Lisbon, Portugal, two days before Christmas. The ship subsequently cruised the Mediterranean into the early spring of the following year, calling at ports in Spain, Morocco, France, Italy, Greece, and Malta. Following her return to the United States on 17 June 1890, the warship entered drydock at the New York Navy Yard on 1 July for repairs that lasted until 8 August. Upon the completion of these alterations, *Yorktown* took part in the ceremonies marking the embarkation of the remains of the noted inventor, John Ericsson—of *Monitor* fame—for transportation back to his native Sweden for burial.

Yorktown next again operated in the Squadron of Evolution—sometimes referred to as the "White Squadron"—off the eastern seaboard and into the Gulf of Mexico into the summer of 1891. Under Acting Rear Admiral John G. Walker, the squadron normally cruised in the Gulf of Mexico from January to April and off the east coast from May to October. While in the gulf, the ships called at Galveston, Tex., New Orleans, La., and Pensacola, Fla., and carried out target practice in Tampa Bay. Later, the squadron conducted small arms practice at Yorktown, Va., after arriving at Hampton Roads. In July 1891, the squadron carried out exercises and maneuvers in connection with the naval militias of New York and Massachusetts during which it added torpedo attacks upon the Fleet to the usual target practices. In addition, it conducted drills and landing exercises—the precursors of the amphibious landing operations of World War II over five decades later.

The Secretary of the Navy's report for the fiscal year 1891 noted with pride that "useful experience" had been gained by the Squadron of Evolution in the training of commanding, navigating, and watch officers in skillfully and safely maneuvering vessels in formation and in restricted waters. In addition, engineers were trained in regulating and maintaining economical coal consumption.

On 8 October 1891, *Yorktown*, under the command of Comdr. Robley D. Evans, departed New York to join the Pacific Squadron. The gunboat put in to Charlotte Amalie, Virgin Islands, to "coal ship" on 14 October. While the ship was engaged in this grimy, dusty duty, an incident occurred on the other side of the South American continent that would directly affect *Yorktown*'s future employment. A revolution in Chile had caused deep division in the country. The victors charged the United States with favoritism when it sheltered some of the losing side's leaders in the American consulate at Valparaiso. A mob of Chileans, wielding knives and clubs and throwing rocks, set upon a liberty party from the cruiser *Baltimore*. In the ensuing riot, two bluejackets were killed and 18 wounded. Thirty-six American sailors were arrested by the local authorities and incarcerated in Chilean jails. War fever ran high in both Chile and the United States.

After getting underway on 17 October, *Yorktown* made few stops en route to the troubled Chilean seaport and weathered fierce gales in transiting the Strait of Magellan. In the days before rapid communication had shrunk distances and had allowed quick transmission of orders and news, the passage of time was critical. War between the United States and Chile could have broken out at any time during *Yorktown*'s hurried voyage 'round the Horn.

The gunboat eventually arrived at Valparaiso on 30 November. Less than two weeks later, *Baltimore*—her presence now no longer advisable—departed, leaving American interests in the hands of Comdr. Evans. Over the ensuing weeks, Chile and the United States teetered on the brink of war; but cooler heads prevailed. Locally, Evans' patience was "dangerously tested," but it held in spite of various provocations by the Chileans. One inflammatory incident occurred when Chilean torpedo boats bore down on Evans' ship, turning their helms hard over at the last possible instant to avoid a collision. On another occasion, a group of sullen locals threw rocks at Evans and his gig as it lay at the foot of a jetty.

After a month of "showing the flag," *Yorktown* embarked refugees from the American, Spanish, and Italian legations in mid-January 1892. She got underway on the 19th and arrived at Callao, Peru, on the 25th. While *Yorktown* lay anchored there, tension between the United States and Chile relaxed and the crisis abated. *Yorktown* may have looked "none too potent" at Valparaiso, but her visit—as Evans' biographer Edwin A. Folk later wrote, ". . . sufficed to make the natvies realize that she flew a battleship-size flag and was commanded by an officer who knew how to defend it." *Yorktown* had proved her mettle in a struggle of nerves in which one misstep could cause a war. The Chilean government made amends, provided gold for the families of the slain American bluejackets, and restored the American minister, who had been declared *persona non grata* during the incident.

Yorktown stood out of Callao on 4 March, steamed northward via San Diego and San Francisco, and eventually arrived at the Mare Island Navy Yard, Vallejo, Calif. The gunboat subsequently underwent repairs there until late in the following month. Having weathered one diplomatic storm and international incident, Comdr. Evans and his trim white-and-buff-painted command soon set sail on another mission that, if handled wrongly, could have caused ill-feeling with the British.

That spring, *Yorktown*—along with two other naval vessels and a trio of revenue cutters—headed toward Arctic waters on 27 April to protect the great herds of seals in the Bering Sea from vicious poachers. Traveling along the west coast of the United States, the gunboat and her crew "braced," in Evans' words, "at the prospect of doing something." As at Valparaiso, Evans faced the possibility of becoming involved in an international incident arising from possible confrontations with Canadian sealers. Operating under the protection of the British crown, the latter had taken particularly heavy catches. Many American vessels put to sea under the British flag in an attempt to evade prosecution by their own government. Fortunately for Evans and unfortunately for the law-breakers, the British agreed to help put an end to the heedless slaughter of seals and decided upon joint action with the United States in prosecuting the poachers.

About 110 schooners, large and small, made up the sealing fleet. They were "armed" with double-barrelled shotguns for killing the animals and Winchester rifles for dealing with any humans who attempted to interfere with their brutal, but lucrative, trade. The fact that the great majority of seals killed had been female—still with young in many cases—almost doubled the toll of slain seals. As Evans noted: "the slaughter in the North Pacific was fearful."

Arriving at Port Townsend, Wash., on 30 April, Yorktown put to sea on 13 May, arriving at Iliuliuk, Unalaska, one week later. Coaling there, the gunboat skirted the ice floes near the seal rookeries at Pribilof Island, reconnoitering the vicinity for sealers. Assisted by a revenue cutter, Yorktown guarded the passes to the Bering Sea. The crews of the patrolling American ships lacked fresh provisions but carried on in spite of the hardships imposed by both diet and climate. Fresh fish, however, proved abundant. Codfish was the staple with an occasional gourmet treat of salmon.

Besides the patrols made during this deployment in northwestern waters, Yorktown conducted routine operations such as target practices. Among the officers assigned to the ship at that time was Lt. Bradley Fiske, a bright and creative young officer who had invented and constructed a practical telescopic gunsight.

Fiske's sight had been tested in Baltimore and had favorably impressed that ship's officers—including her commander, Capt. W. S. Schley. Evans, however, had not taken a liking to Fiske's newfangled gadget but nevertheless consented to allow a second test on board Yorktown (the first one had failed miserably, much to the inventor's chagrin). On the afternoon of 22 September 1892, during scheduled target practice, Fiske's invention worked as designed and elicited begrudging praise from Evans. As Fiske himself later wrote in the Naval Institute Proceedings, modern naval gunnery had its birth not in the British Navy but in the American—off Unalaska on 22 September 1892, in Yorktown.

This event went largely unnoticed by the world at large, and the gunboat continued her unsung but important task of protecting the seals in Alaskan waters. She continued this thankless task until 21 September when she departed Unalaska for the Mare Island Navy Yard. From 11 to 24 October, the ship underwent repairs there before proceeding on to the east coast via Cape Horn. Yorktown eventually arrived at Norfolk, Va., on 24 February 1893.

After repairs at the New York Navy Yard from 25 April to 26 July, Yorktown retraced her route south and sailed again around Cape Horn into the Pacific. She then moved north to resume patrolling the Bering Sea. She protected seal rookeries into 1894 before returning to Mare Island for repairs which lasted into mid-September.

On 24 September 1894, Yorktown sailed for the western Pacific and duty on the Asiatic Station. Sailing via Honolulu, Hawaii, she reached Yokohama, Japan, on 8 December 1894 and spent the next three years touching at the principal ports-of-call along the coasts of China and Japan, "showing the flag" in the Far East. She departed Yokohama early in the autumn of 1897 and made port at Mare Island on 18 November 1897. Subsequently laid up at Mare Island and decommissioned on 8 December, the gunboat remained inactive there through the Spanish-American War in 1898.

Recommissioned on 17 November 1898, Comdr. Charles S. Sperry in command, Yorktown sailed again for the Far East on 7 January 1899. Rumors of German machinations in Samoa lengthened Yorktown's stay at Hawaii from a few days to a few weeks; but, when the anticipated trouble failed to materialize, Yorktown resumed her voyage to the Philippine Islands. She arrived at Cavite Navy Yard, near Manila, on 23 February.

There, Yorktown was assigned the task of keeping a seaborne lookout for gun-runners who were thought to be supplying guns and ammunition to the "Insurrectos," Filipinos who were fighting for independence. Initial Filipino-American cooperation had been replaced by open warfare when what the former regarded as promises of independence in return for assistance against the Spanish had turned to apparent overlordship by the United States.

At one point, rumors flew concerning possible German gun-running activities; and Yorktown patrolled off the entrance to Subic Bay and from thence to Lingayen to keep a lookout for the "filibusters." She continued coastal patrol work over the next three years, cooperating with the Army, transporting and convoying troops and patrolling wide areas of often badly charted waters. Upon occasion, Yorktown served as "mother ship" to smaller gunboats, providing officers and men to man those patrol craft. Among the junior officers who served in Yorktown at this time were future Admirals (then ensigns) William H. Standley and Harry E. Yarnell, and the future naval historian and archivist, Dudley W. Knox.

Yorktown stood in to Baler Bay, on the west coast of Luzon, on 11 April 1899, on a mission to relieve a dwindling but brave Spanish garrison that had been under siege by Insurrectos for nine months. Lt. James C. Gillmore and a party of sailors in the ship's whaleboat provided a decoy, ostensibly taking soundings of a nearby river. Meanwhile, Ensign Standley and an enlisted man landed further up the coast to reconnoiter. The next day, Gillmore and his boat crew drifted into a trap, running aground too far from the river's mouth and out of sight of Yorktown. Filipino guerillas, hidden in the jungle-covered banks, raked the boat with a murderous fusillade of rifle fire. Two American sailors were killed; two were mortally wounded; and the remainder, including Gillmore, were slightly wounded. The survivors were taken prisoner and endured months of privation until finally freed by Army troops. Ensign Standley completed his mission and, together with the enlisted signalman, made it back to the ship.

In the spring of 1900, the situation in China worsened until it culminated in the famed "Boxer Rebellion." Some Chinese Imperial troops, supporting the "Society of Righteous Harmonious Fists" (the "Boxers") besieged the foreign legations at Peking and at Tientsin. An international relief force was sent to relieve the siege; Yorktown was withdrawn from her patrol duties in the northern Philippines to provide assistance to the operations off the coast of North China. She departed Manila on 3 April 1900, bound for China; and, after she reached the mainland, her landing force served ashore at Taku. In June of 1900, she assisted Oregon (Battleship No. 3) back off a reef near that Chinese port.

The gunboat departed Shanghai on 10 September 1900 and reached Cavite on the 17th. In the Philippines, she resumed her cooperation with Army forces, still engaged in pacification operations, and continued these duties for the next two years. In between pacification missions, she performed survey work: at Guam in November 1901 and at Dumanquillas Bay, Philippines, in February 1903. Yorktown departed the Far East in early 1903 and returned to Mare Island on 3 June. Two weeks later, on the 17th, she was decommissioned.

Recommissioned at Mare Island on 1 October 1906, Comdr. Richard T. Mulligan in command, Yorktown was fitted out there until 9 November. Underway on that day, she operated off the west coasts of Mexico, Honduras, and Nicaragua into the following summer, ready to protect American lives and property. After repairs at San Francisco and Mare Island, Yorktown conducted target practice at Magdalena Bay, Mexico, and relieved Albany as station ship at Acapulco. She then cruised with the 2d Squadron of the Pacific Fleet to Magdalena Bay and San Francisco.

Over the ensuing months, Yorktown continued her regular local operations; she took part in the reception for the United States Atlantic Fleet—en route to wield President Theodore Roosevelt's "Big Stick" in the Far East—at San Francisco on 1 May, and participated in festivities for the Rose Festival at Portland, Oreg., on the 30th of that month. From June to September, Yorktown conducted seal patrols in Alaskan waters, out of Nome, Unalaska, and Sitka, and between 15 and 19 September, established a site for a wireless station at Valdez, Alaska.

After that stint of independent duty, Yorktown sailed south to rejoin the Pacific Fleet, conducting battle practices between 19 November and 1 December at Magdalena Bay. She later joined the armored cruisers West Virginia and Colorado and the tender

Glacier at Acajutla, Salvador, before sailing for Corinto, Nicaragua, in March of 1909 to protect American interests there.

After more target practices at Magdalena Bay, *Yorktown* was repaired at Mare Island in June and into July before shifting to Seattle, Wash., to participate in festivities for the Seattle Exposition. Later in July, the ship visited Esquimalt, British Columbia, Canada. She subsequently cruised off the Pacific coast and participated in the Portola festival at San Francisco in October.

From 13 December 1909 to 27 March 1910, *Yorktown* operated off Corinto, Nicaragua, with the Nicaraguan Expeditionary Squadron, protecting American interests. She then pursued a schedule of exercises and maneuvers, operating between California and British Columbia through June and July. She returned to a posture of readiness off Corinto and San Juan del Sur between 13 August and 7 September. She then operated off Ecuadorian, Colombian, and Peruvian ports, with the United States Consul General at Large embarked, between 19 September and 16 October before putting into Panama for coal and stores. She subsequently protected American interests at Amapala, Honduras, and the familiar Corinto for most of November and December. She spent Christmas at Corinto before shifting to Amapala, en route to San Francisco and Mare Island.

From March to July of 1911, *Yorktown* cruised off the west coasts of Mexico, Nicaragua, and Honduras. On 29 May, she rescued the survivors from the foundered steamer *Taboga*, of Panamanian registry. Another period of repairs and upkeep in the late summer of 1911 proceeded the ship's resuming her "show the flag" duties off the Pacific coasts of South and Central America. She returned to Mare Island in May of 1912, and was decommissioned there for alterations on 15 July.

Recommissioned on 1 April 1913, Comdr. George B. Bradshaw in command, *Yorktown* operated out of San Diego on shakedown into mid-April. She was soon back at Corinto, however, remaining in Nicaragua until 5 June, protecting American interests in that perennially troubled country. After a brief period of operations off the coast, she returned to Corinto on 21 June and remained there for over a month before departing on 31 July to coal at Salina Cruz, Mexico. She moved to Mazatlan on 10 August and there picked up mail, delivering it to the port of Topolobampo, Mexico, on the 11th. *Yorktown* remained there, protecting American interests, until mid-September.

For the remainder of 1913, *Yorktown* conducted local operations out of San Diego and San Francisco. In January 1914, though, the gunboat returned to Mexican waters and investigated local conditions at Ensenada between 3 and 6 January before moving, in subsequent months, to a succession of ports: Mazatlan, San Blas, Miramir, Topolobampo, and La Paz to extend protection to American citizens and their interests should Mexican civil unrest warrant armed intervention or a show of force.

Following an overhaul at Mare Island from 24 June to 2 September 1914, *Yorktown* served in Mexican waters again into June 1915. From that point until the entry of the United States into World War I in April 1917, *Yorktown* continued her routine of patrols off Mexican, Nicaraguan, and Honduran ports, investigating local conditions and varying that extension of diplomacy with repairs at Mare Island and maneuvers out of San Diego.

After the United States joined the Allied and Associated Powers, *Yorktown* operated off the coast of Mexico until August of 1917, when she paused briefly at San Diego. She then cruised off the west coasts of Central and South America into 1918. After a refit at Mare Island, *Yorktown* sailed for the east coast on 28 April 1918, transiting the Panama Canal en route, and arrived at New York on 20 August. The gunboat escorted a coastal convoy to Halifax, Nova Scotia, soon thereafter before returning to New York. She performed local coastwise escort duties through the end of World War I. After a period of upkeep at the New York Navy Yard in December, she departed the east coast on 2 January 1919 on her last voyage to California.

Arriving at San Diego on 15 February 1919, *Yorktown* was placed out of commission at Mare Island on 12 June 1919. The veteran steel-hulled gunboat was sold to the Union Hide Co., Oakland, Calif., on 30 September 1921.

III

(CV–5: dp. 19,800; l. 809'6''; b. 83'1''; dr. 28'0''; s. 32.5 k.; cpl. 2,919; a. 8 5'', 22 .50-cal. mg., ac. 81–85; cl. *Yorktown*)

The third *Yorktown* (CV–5) was laid down on 21 May 1934 at Newport News, Va., by the Newport News Shipbuilding and Drydock Co.; launched on 4 April 1936; sponsored by Mrs. Franklin D. Roosevelt; and commissioned at the Naval Operating Base (NOB),

Yorktown (CV–5) lies dead in the water as her crew repairs battle damage at Midway. Her guns and directors are manned, and a number of Grumman FAF–4 *Wildcat* fighters are clustered at the forward end of the flight deck.

Norfolk, Va., on 30 September 1937, Capt. Ernest D. McWhorter in command.

After fitting out, the aircraft carrier trained in Hampton Roads and in the southern drill grounds off the Virginia capes into January of 1938, conducting carrier qualifications for her newly embarked air group.

Yorktown sailed for the Caribbean on 8 January 1938 and arrived at Culebra, Puerto Rico, on 13 January. Over the ensuing month, the carrier conducted her shakedown, touching at Charlotte Amalie, St. Thomas, Virgin Islands; Gonaives, Haiti; Guantanamo Bay, Cuba; and Cristobal, Panama Canal Zone. Departing Colon Bay, Cristobal, on 1 March, *Yorktown* sailed for Hampton Roads and arrived there on the 6th and shifted to the Norfolk Navy Yard the next day for post-shakedown availability.

After undergoing repairs through the early autumn of 1938, *Yorktown* shifted from the navy yard to NOB Norfolk on 17 October and soon headed for the Southern Drill Grounds for training.

Yorktown operated off the eastern seaboard, ranging from Chesapeake Bay to Guantanamo Bay, into 1939. As flagship for Carrier Division (CarDiv) 2, she participated in her first war game—Fleet Problem XX—along with her sistership *Enterprise* (CV–6) in February 1939. The scenario for the exercise called for one fleet to control the sea lanes in the Caribbean against the incursion of a foreign European power while maintaining sufficient naval strength to protect vital American interests in the Pacific. The maneuvers were witnessed, in part, by President Roosevelt, embarked in the heavy cruiser *Houston* (CA–30).

The critique of the operation revealed that carrier operations—a part of the scenarios for the annual exercises since the entry of *Langley* (CV–1) into the war games in 1925—had achieved a new peak of efficiency. Despite the inexperience of *Yorktown* and *Enterprise*—comparative newcomers to the Fleet—both carriers made significant contributions to the success of the problem. The planners had studied the employment of carriers and their embarked air groups in connection with convoy escort, antisubmarine defense, and various attack measures against surface ships and shore installations. In short, they worked to develop the tactics that would be used when war actually came.

Following Fleet Problem XX, *Yorktown* returned briefly to Hampton Roads before sailing for the Pacific on 20 April. Transiting the Panama Canal a week later, *Yorktown* soon commenced a regular routine of operations with the Pacific Fleet. Operating out of San Diego into 1940, the carrier participated in Fleet Problem XXI that April.

Fleet Problem XXI—a two-part exercise—included some of the operations that would characterize future warfare in the Pacific. The first part of the exercise was devoted to training in making plans and estimates; in screening and scouting; in coordination of combatant units; and in employing fleet and standard dispositions. The second phase included training in convoy protection, the seizure of advanced bases, and, ultimately, the decisive engagement between the opposing fleets. The last pre-war exercise of its type, Fleet Problem XXI, contained two exercises (comparatively minor at the time) where air operations played a major role. Fleet Joint Air Exercise 114A prophetically pointed out the need to coordinate Army and Navy defense plans for the Hawaiian Islands, and Fleet Exercise 114 proved that aircraft could be used for high altitude tracking of surface forces—a significant role for planes that would be fully realized in the war to come.

With the retention of the Fleet in Hawaiian waters after the conclusion of Fleet Problem XXI, *Yorktown* operated in the Pacific off the west coast of the United States and in Hawaiian waters until the following spring, when the success of German U-boats preying upon British shipping in the Atlantic required a shift of American naval strength. Thus, to reinforce the Atlantic Fleet, the Navy transferred a substantial force from the Pacific including *Yorktown*, a battleship division, and accompanying cruisers and destroyers.

Yorktown departed Pearl Harbor on 20 April 1941 in company with *Warrington* (DD–383), *Somers* (DD–381), and *Jouett* (DD–396); headed southeast; transited the Panama Canal on the night of 6 and 7 May; and arrived at Bermuda on the 12th. From that time to the entry of the United States into the war, *Yorktown* conducted four patrols in the Atlantic, ranging from Newfoundland to Bermuda and logging 17,642 miles steamed while enforcing American neutrality.

Although Adolph Hitler had forbidden his submarines to attack American ships, the men who manned the American naval vessels were not aware of this policy and operated on a wartime footing in the Atlantic.

On 28 October, while *Yorktown*, battleship *New Mexico* (BB–41), and other American warships were screening a convoy, a destroyer picked up a submarine contact and dropped depth charges while the convoy itself made an emergency starboard turn, the first of the convoy's three emergency changes of course. Late that afternoon, engine repairs to one of the ships in the convoy, *Empire Pintail*, reduced the convoy's speed to 11 knots.

During the night, the American ships intercepted strong German radio signals, indicating submarines probably in the vicinity reporting the group. Rear Admiral H. Kent Hewitt, commanding the escort force, sent a destroyer to sweep astern of the convoy to destroy the U-boat or at least to drive him under.

The next day, while cruiser scoutplanes patrolled overhead, *Yorktown* and *Savannah* (CL–42) fueled their escorting destroyers, finishing the task just at dusk. On the 30th, *Yorktown* was preparing to fuel three destroyers when other escorts made sound contacts. The convoy subsequently made 10 emergency turns while *Morris* (DD–417) and *Anderson* (DD–411) dropped depth charges, and *Hughes* (DD–410) assisted in developing the contact. *Anderson* later made two more depth charge attacks, noticing "considerable oil with slick spreading but no wreckage."

The short-of-war period was becoming more like the real thing as each day went on. Elsewhere on 30 October and more than a month before Japanese planes attacked Pearl Harbor, *U–562* torpedoed the destroyer *Reuben James* (DD–245), sinking her with a heavy loss of life—the first loss of an American warship in World War II.

After another Neutrality Patrol stint in November, *Yorktown* put into Norfolk on 2 December and was there five days later when American fighting men in Hawaii were rudely awakened to find their country at war.

The early news from the Pacific was bleak: the Pacific Fleet had taken a beating. With the battle line crippled, the unhurt American carriers assumed great importance. There were, on 7 December, only three in the Pacific: *Enterprise*, *Lexington* (CV–2), and *Saratoga* (CV–3). While *Ranger* (CV–4), *Wasp* (CV–7), and the recently commissioned *Hornet* (CV–8) remained in the Atlantic, *Yorktown* departed Norfolk on 16 December 1941 and sailed for the Pacific, her secondary gun galleries studded with new 20-millimeter Oerlikon machine guns. She reached San Diego, Calif., on 30 December 1941 and soon became flagship for Rear Admiral Frank Jack Fletcher's newly formed Task Force (TF) 17.

The carrier's first mission in her new theater was to escort a convoy carrying Marine reinforcements to American Samoa. Departing San Diego on 6 January 1942, *Yorktown* and her consorts covered the movement of marines to Tutuila and Pago Pago to augment the garrison already there.

Having safely covered that troop movement, *Yorktown*, in company with sistership *Enterprise*, departed Samoan waters on 25 January. Six days later, TF 8, built around *Enterprise*, and TF 17, built around *Yorktown*, parted company. The former headed for the

Marshall Islands, the latter for the Gilberts—each bound to take part in the first American offensive of the war, the Marshalls-Gilberts raids.

At 0517, *Yorktown*—screened by *Louisville* (CA–28) and *St. Louis* (CL–49) and four destroyers—launched 11 torpedo planes (Douglas TBD–1 Devastators) and 17 scout bombers (Douglas SBD–3 Dauntlesses) under the command of Comdr. Curtis W. Smiley. Those planes hit what Japanese shore installations and shipping they could find at Jaluit; but adverse weather conditions hampered the mission in which six planes were lost. Other *Yorktown* planes attacked Japanese installations and ships at Makin and Mili Atolls.

The attack by TF 17 on the Gilberts had apparently been a complete surprise since the American force encountered no enemy surface ships. A single, four-engined, Kawanishi E7K "Mavis," patrol-bomber seaplane attempted to attack American destroyers that had been sent astern in hope of recovering planes overdue from the Jaluit mission. Antiaircraft fire from the destroyers drove off the intruder before he could cause any damage.

Later, another "Mavis"—or possibly the same one that had attacked the destroyers—came out of low clouds 15,000 yards from *Yorktown*. The carrier withheld her antiaircraft fire in order not to interfere with the combat air patrol (CAP) fighters. Presently, the "Mavis," pursued by two Wildcats, disappeared behind a cloud. Within five minutes, the enemy patrol plane fell out of the clouds and crashed in the water.

Although TF 17 was slated to make a second attack on Jaluit, it was cancelled because of heavy rainstorms and the approach of darkness. Therefore, the *Yorktown* force retired from the area.

Admiral Chester W. Nimitz later called the Marshalls-Gilberts raids "well conceived, well planned, and brilliantly executed." The results obtained by TF's 8 and 17 were noteworthy, Nimitz continued in his subsequent report, because the task forces had been obliged to make their attacks somewhat blindly, due to lack of hard intelligence data on the Japanese-mandated islands.

Yorktown subsequently returned to Pearl Harbor and replenished there before she put to sea on 14 February, bound for the Coral Sea. On 6 March, she rendezvoused with TF 11—formed around *Lexington* and under the command of Rear Admiral Wilson Brown—and headed towards Rabaul and Gasmata to attack Japanese shipping there in an effort to check the Japanese advance and to cover the landing of Allied troops at Noumea, New Caledonia. However, as the two flattops—screened by a powerful force of eight heavy cruisers (including the Australian HMAS *Australia*) and 14 destroyers—steamed toward New Guinea, the Japanese continued their advance toward Australia with a landing on 7 March at the Huon Gulf, in the Salamaua-Lae area on the eastern end of New Guinea.

Word of the Japanese operation prompted Admiral Brown to change the objective of TF 11's strike from Rabaul to the Salamaua-Lae sector. On the morning of 10 March 1942, American carriers launched aircraft from the Gulf of Papua. *Lexington* flew off her air group commencing at 0749 and, 21 minutes later, *Yorktown* followed suit. While the choice of the gulf as the launch point for the strike meant that the planes would have to fly some 125 miles across the Owen Stanley mountains—a range not known for the best flying conditions—that approach provided security for the task force and ensured surprise.

In the attacks that followed, *Lexington*'s SBD's from Scouting Squadron (VS) 2 commenced dive-bombing Japanese ships at Lae at 0922. The carrier's Torpedo Squadron (VT) 2 and Bombing Squadron (VB) 2 attacked shipping at Salamaua at 0938. Her fighters from Fighter Squadron (VF) 2 split up into four-plane attack groups: one strafed Lae and the other, Salamaua. *Yorktown*'s planes followed on the heels of those from "Lady Lex." VB–5 and VT–5 at-

tacked Japanese ships in the Salamaua area at 0950, while VS–5 went after auxiliaries moored close in shore at Lae. The fighters of VF–42 flew over Salamaua on CAP until they determined that there was no air opposition and then strafed surface objectives and small boats in the harbor.

After carrying out their missions, the American planes returned to their carriers; and 103 planes of the 104 launched were back safely on board by noon. One SB3–2 of VS–2 had been downed by Japanese antiaircraft fire. The raid on Salamaua and Lae was the first attack by many pilots of both carriers; and, while the resultant torpedo and bombing accuracy was inferior to that achieved in later actions, the operation gave the fliers invaluable experience which enabled them to do so well in the Battle of the Coral Sea and the Battle of Midway.

Task Force 11 retired at 20 knots on a southeasterly course until dark, when the ships steered eastward at 15 knots and made rendezvous with Task Group (TG) 11.7 (four heavy cruisers and four destroyers) under Rear Admiral John G. Crace, Royal Navy—the group that had provided cover for the carriers on their approach to New Guinea.

Yorktown resumed her patrols in the Coral Sea area, remaining at sea into April, out of reach of Japanese land-based aircraft and ready to carry out offensive operations whenever the opportunity presented itself. After the Lae-Salamaua raid, the situation in the South Pacific seemed temporarily stabilized, and *Yorktown* and her consorts in TF 17 put in to the undeveloped harbor at Tongatabu, in the Tonga Islands, for needed upkeep, having been at sea continuously since departing from Pearl Harbor on 14 February.

However, the enemy was soon on the move. To Admiral Nimitz, there seemed to be "excellent indications that the Japanese intended to make a seaborne attack on Port Moresby the first week in May." *Yorktown* accordingly departed Tongatabu on 27 April, bound once more for the Coral Sea. TF 11—commanded by Rear Admiral Aubrey W. Fitch, who had relieved Brown in *Lexington*—departed Pearl Harbor to join Fletcher's TF 17 and arrived in the vicinity of *Yorktown*'s group, southwest of the New Hebrides Islands, on 1 May.

At 1517 the next afternoon, two Dauntlesses from VS–5 sighted a Japanese submarine, running on the surface. Three Devastators took off from *Yorktown*, sped to the scene, and carried out an attack that only succeeded in driving the submarine under.

On the morning of the 3d, TF 11 and TF 17 were some 100 miles apart, engaged in fueling operations. Shortly before midnight, Fletcher received word from Australian-based aircraft that Japanese transports were disembarking troops and equipment at Tulagi in the Solomon Islands. Arriving soon after the Australians had evacuated the place, the Japanese landed to commence construction of a seaplane base there to support their southward thrust.

Yorktown accordingly set course northward at 27 knots. By daybreak on 4 May, she was within striking distance of the newly established Japanese beachhead and launched her first strike at 0701—18 F4F–3's of VF–42, 12 TBD's of VT–5, and 28 SBD's from VS and BV–5. *Yorktown*'s air group made three consecutive attacks on enemy ships and shore installations at Tulagi and Gavutu on the south coast of Florida Island in the Solomons. Expending 22 torpedoes and 76 1,000-pound bombs in the three attacks, *Yorktown*'s planes sank a destroyer (*Kikuzuki*), three minecraft, and four barges. In addition, Air Group 5 destroyed five enemy seaplanes, all at the cost of two F4F's lost (the pilots were recovered) and one TBD (whose crew was lost).

Meanwhile, that same day, TF 44, a cruiser-destroyer force under Rear Admiral Crace (RN), joined *Lexington*'s TF 11, thus completing the composition of the Allied force on the eve of the crucial Battle of the Coral Sea.

Elsewhere, to the northward, the enemy was on his

way. Eleven troop-laden transports—escorted by destroyers and covered by the light carrier *Shoho*, four heavy cruisers, and a destroyer—steamed toward Port Moresby. In addition, another Japanese task force—formed around the two Pearl Harbor veterans, carriers *Shokaku* and *Zuikaku*, and screened by two heavy cruisers and six destroyers—provided additional air cover.

On the morning of the 6th, Fletcher gathered all Allied forces under his tactical command as TF 17. At daybreak on the 7th, he dispatched Crace, with the cruisers and destroyers under his command, toward the Louisiade archipelago to intercept any enemy attempt to move toward Port Moresby.

Meanwhile, while Fletcher moved northward with his two flattops and their screens in search of the enemy, Japanese search planes located the oiler *Neosho* (AO–23) and her escort, *Sims* (DD–409) and identified the former as a "carrier." Two waves of Japanese planes—first high level bombers and then dive bombers—attacked the two ships. *Sims*—her antiaircraft battery crippled by gun failures—took three direct hits and sank quickly with a heavy loss of life. *Neosho* was more fortunate in that, even after seven direct hits and eight near-misses, she remained afloat until, on the 11th, her survivors were picked up by *Henley* (DD–391) and her hulk sunk by the rescuing destroyer.

In their tribulation, *Neosho* and *Sims* had performed a valuable service, drawing off the planes that might otherwise have hit Fletcher's carriers. Meanwhile, *Yorktown* and *Lexington*'s planes found *Shoho* and punished that Japanese light carrier unmercifully, sending her to the bottom. One of *Lexington*'s pilots reported this victory with the radio message, "Scratch one flattop."

That afternoon, *Shokaku* and *Zuikaku*—still unlocated by Fletcher's forces—launched 27 bombers and torpedo planes to search for the American ships. Their flight proved uneventful until they ran into fighters from *Yorktown* and *Lexington*, who proceeded to down nine enemy planes in the ensuing dogfight.

Near twilight, three Japanese planes incredibly mistook *Yorktown* for their own carrier and attempted to land. The ship's gunfire, though, drove them off; and the enemy planes crossed *Yorktown*'s bow and turned away out of range. Twenty minutes later, when three more enemy pilots made the mistake of trying to get into *Yorktown*'s landing circle, the carrier's gunners splashed one of the trio.

However, the Battle of the Coral Sea was far from over. The next morning, 8 May, a *Lexington* search plane spotted Admiral Takagi's carrier striking force—including *Zuikaku* and *Shokaku*, the flattops that had proved so elusive the day before. *Yorktown* planes scored two bomb hits on *Shokaku*, damaging her flight deck and thus preventing her from launching aircraft; in addition, the bombs set off explosions in gasoline storage tanks and destroyed an engine repair workshop. *Lexington*'s Dauntlesses added another hit. Between the two American air groups, the hits scored killed 108 Japanese sailors and wounded 40 more.

While the American planes were bedeviling the Japanese flattops, however, *Yorktown* and *Lexington*—alerted by an intercepted message which indicated that the Japanese knew of their whereabouts—were preparing to fight off a retaliatory strike. Sure enough, shortly after 1100, that attack came.

American CAP Wildcats slashed into the Japanese formations, downing 17 planes. Some, though, managed to slip through the fighters; and the "Kates" that did so managed to launch torpedoes from both sides of *Lexington*'s bows. Two "fish" tore into "Lady Lex" on the port side; dive bombers—"Vals"—added to the destruction with three bomb hits. *Lexington* developed a list with three partially-flooded engineering spaces. Several fires raged belowdecks, and the carrier's elevators were out of commission.

Meanwhile, *Yorktown* was having problems of her own. Skillfully maneuvered by Capt. Elliott Buckmaster, her commanding officer, the carrier dodged eight torpedoes. Attacked then by "Vals," the ship managed to evade all but one bomb. That one, however, penetrated the flight deck and exploded belowdecks, killing or seriously injuring 66 men.

Yorktown's damage control parties brought the fires under control; and, despite her wounds, the ship was still able to continue her flight operations. The air battle itself ended shortly before noon on the 8th; and, within an hour, "Lady Lex" was on an even keel, although slightly down by the bow. Her damage control parties had already extinguished three out of the four fires below. In addition, she was making 25 knots and was recovering her air group.

At 1247, however, disaster struck *Lexington*, when a heavy explosion, caused by the ignition of gasoline vapors, rocked the ship. The flames raced through the ship, and further internal explosions tore the ship apart inside. *Lexington* battled for survival; but, despite the valiant efforts of her crew, she had to be abandoned. Capt. Frederick C. Sherman sadly ordered "abandon ship" at 1707. Her men went over the side in an orderly fashion and were picked up by the cruisers and destroyers of the carrier's screen. Torpedoes fired by *Phelps* (DD–361) hastened the end of "Lady Lex."

As *Yorktown* and her consorts retired from Coral Sea to lick their wounds, the situation in the Pacific stood altered. The Japanese had won a tactical victory, inflicting comparatively heavy losses on the Allied force; but the Allies, in stemming the tide of Japan's conquests in the South and Southwest Pacific, had achieved a strategic victory. They had blunted the drive toward strategic Port Moresby and had saved the tenuous lifeline between America and Australia.

Yorktown had not achieved her part in the victory without cost, but had suffered enough damage to cause experts to estimate that at least three months in a yard would be required to put her back in fighting trim. Unfortunately, there was little time for repairs, because Allied intelligence—most notably the cryptographic unit at Pearl Harbor—had gained enough information from decoded Japanese naval messages to estimate that the Japanese were on the threshold of a major operation aimed at the northwestern tip of the Hawaiian chain—two islets in a low coral atoll known as Midway.

Thus armed with this intelligence, Admiral Nimitz began methodically planning Midway's defense, rushing all possible reinforcement in the way of men, planes, and guns to Midway. In addition, he began gathering his naval forces—comparatively meager as they were—to meet the enemy at sea. As part of those preparations, he recalled TF 16, *Enterprise* and *Hornet* (CV–8), to Pearl Harbor for a quick replenishment.

Yorktown, too, received orders to return to Hawaii; and she arrived at Pearl Harbor on 27 May. Miraculously, yard workers there—laboring around the clock—made enough repairs to enable the ship to put to sea. Her air group—for the most part experienced but weary—was augmented by planes and flyers from *Saratoga* (CV–3) which was then headed for Hawaiian waters after her modernization on the west coast. Ready for battle, *Yorktown* sailed as the central ship of TF 17 on 30 May.

Northeast of Midway, *Yorktown*, flying Rear Admiral Fletcher's flag, rendezvoused with TF 16 under Rear Admiral Raymond A. Spruance and maintained a position 10 miles to the northward of the latter. Over the days that ensued, as the ships proceeded toward a date with destiny, few men realized that within the next few days the pivotal battle of the war in the Pacific would be fought.

Patrols, both from Midway itself and from the carriers, proceeded apace during those days in early June. On the morning of the 4th, as dawn began to streak the eastern sky, *Yorktown* launched a 10-plane group of Dauntlesses from VB–5 which searched a northern semicircle for a distance of 100 miles out but found nothing.

Meanwhile, PBY's flying from Midway had sighted

the approaching Japanese and broadcast what turned out to be the alarm for the American forces defending the key atoll. Admiral Fletcher, in tactical command, ordered Admiral Spruance, with TF 16, to locate the enemy carrier force and strike them as soon as they were found.

Yorktown's search group returned at 0830, landing soon after the last of the six-plane CAP had left the deck. When the last of the Dauntlesses had landed, a flight deck ballet took place in which the deck was spotted for the launch of the ship's attack group—17 Dauntlesses from VB–3; 12 Devastators from VT–3, and six Wildcats from "Fighting Three." *Enterprise* and *Hornet*, meanwhile, launched their attack groups.

The torpedo planes from the three American flattops located the Japanese carrier striking force but met disaster. Of the 41 planes from VT–8, VT–6, and VT–3, only six returned to *Enterprise* and *Yorktown*, collectively. None made it back to *Hornet*.

The destruction of the torpedo planes, however, had served a purpose. The Japanese CAP had broken off their high-altitude cover for their carriers and had concentrated on the Devastators, flying low "on the deck." The skies above were thus left open for Dauntlesses arriving from *Yorktown* and *Enterprise*. Virtually unopposed, the SBD's dove to the attack. The results were spectacular.

Yorktown's dive-bombers pummeled *Soryu*, making three lethal hits with 1,000-pound bombs that turned the ship into a flaming inferno. *Enterprise*'s planes, meanwhile, hit *Akagi* and *Kaga*—turning them, too, into wrecks within a very short time. The bombs from the Dauntlesses caught all of the Japanese carriers in the midst of refueling and rearming operations, and the combination of bombs and gasoline proved explosive and disastrous to the Japanese.

Three Japanese carriers had been lost. A fourth, however, still roamed at large—*Hiryu*. Separated from her sisters, that ship had launched a striking force of 18 "Vals" that soon located *Yorktown*.

As soon as the attackers had been picked up on *Yorktown*'s radar at about 1329, she discontinued the fueling of her CAP fighters on deck and swiftly cleared for action. Her returning dive bombers were moved from the landing circle to open the area for antiaircraft fire. The Dauntlesses were ordered aloft to form a CAP. An auxiliary gasoline tank—of 800 gallons capacity—was pushed over the carrier's fantail, eliminating one fire hazard. The crew drained fuel lines and closed and secured all compartments.

All of *Yorktown*'s fighters were vectored out to intercept the oncoming Japanese aircraft, and did so some 15 to 20 miles out. The Wildcats attacked vigorously, breaking up what appeared to be an organized attack by some 18 "Vals" and 18 "Zeroes." "Planes were flying in every direction," wrote Capt. Buckmaster after the action, "and many were falling in flames."

Yorktown and her escorts went to full speed and, as the Japanese raiders attacked, began maneuvering radically. Intense antiaircraft fire greeted the "Vals" and "Kates" as they approached their release points.

Despite the barrage, though, three "Vals" scored hits. Two of them were shot down soon after releasing their bomb loads; the third went out of control just as his bomb left the rack. It tumbled in flight and hit just abaft number two elevator on the starboard side, exploding on contact and blasting a hole about 10 feet square in the flight deck. Splinters from the exploding bomb decimated the crews of the two 1.1-inch gun mounts aft of the island and on the flight deck below. Fragments piercing the flight deck hit three planes on the hangar deck, starting fires. One of the aircraft, a *Yorktown* Dauntless, was fully fueled and carrying a 1,000-pound bomb. Prompt action by Lt. A. C. Emerson, the hangar deck officer, prevented a serious conflagration by releasing the sprinkler system and quickly extinguishing the fire.

The second bomb to hit the ship came from the port side, pierced the flight deck, and exploded in the lower part of the funnel. It ruptured the uptakes for three boilers, disabled two boilers themselves, and extinguished the fires in five boilers. Smoke and gases began filling the firerooms of six boilers. The men at number one boiler, however, remained at their post despite their danger and discomfort and kept its fire going, maintaining enough steam pressure to allow the auxiliary steam systems to function.

A third bomb hit the carrier from the starboard side, pierced the side of number one elevator and exploded on the fourth deck, starting a persistent fire in the rag storage space, adjacent to the forward gasoline stowage and the magazines. The prior precaution of smothering the gasoline system with CO_2 undoubtedly prevented the gasoline's igniting.

While the ship recovered from the damage inflicted by the dive-bombing attack, her speed dropped to six knots; and then—at 1440, about 20 minutes after the bomb hit that had shut down most of the boilers—*Yorktown* slowed to a stop, dead in the water.

At about 1540, *Yorktown* prepared to get underway again; and, at 1550, the engine room force reported that they were ready to make 20 knots or better. The ship was not yet out of the fight.

Simultaneously, with the fires controlled sufficiently to warrant the resumption of fueling operations, *Yorktown* began fueling the gasoline tanks of the fighters then on deck. Fueling had just commenced when the ship's radar picked up an incoming air group at a distance of 33 miles away. While the ship prepared for battle—again smothering gasoline systems and stopping the fueling of the planes on her flight deck—she vectored four of the six fighters of the CAP in the air to intercept the incoming raiders. Of the 10 fighters on board, eight had as much as 23 gallons of fuel in their tanks. They accordingly were launched as the remaining pair of fighters of the CAP headed out to intercept the Japanese planes.

At 1600, *Yorktown* churned forward, making 20 knots. The fighters she had launched and vectored out to intercept had meanwhile made contact; *Yorktown* received reports that the planes were "Kates." The Wildcats downed at least three of the attacking torpedo planes, but the rest began their approach in the teeth of a heavy antiaircraft barrage from the carrier and her escorts.

Yorktown maneuvered radically, avoiding at least two torpedoes before two "fish" tore into her port side within minutes of each other. The first hit at 1620. The carrier had been mortally wounded; she lost power and went dead in the water with a jammed rudder and an increasing list to port.

As the list progressed, Comdr. C. E. Aldrich, the damage control officer, reported from central station that, without power, controlling the flooding looked impossible. The engineering officer, Lt. Comdr. J. F. Delaney, soon reported that all fires were out; all power was lost; and. worse yet, it was impossible to correct the list. Faced with that situation, Capt. Buckmaster ordered Aldrich, Delaney, and their men to secure and lay up on deck to put on life jackets.

The list, meanwhile, continued to increase. When it reached 26 degrees, Buckmaster and Aldrich agreed that the ship's capsizing was only a matter of minutes. "In order to save as many of the ship's company as possible," the captain wrote later, he "ordered the ship to be abandoned."

Over the minutes that ensued, the crew left ship, lowering the wounded to life rafts and striking out for the nearby destroyers and cruisers to be picked up by boats from those ships. After the evacuation of all wounded, the executive officer, Comdr. I. D. Wiltsie, left the ship down a line on the starboard side. Capt. Buckmaster, meanwhile, toured the ship for one last time, inspecting her to see if any men remained. After finding no "live personnel," Buckmaster lowered himself into the water by means of a line over the stern. By that point, water was lapping the port side of the hangar deck.

Picked up by the destroyer *Hammann* (DD–412), Buckmaster was transferred to *Astoria* (CA–34) soon thereafter and reported to Rear Admiral Fletcher, who had shifted his flag to the heavy cruiser after the first dive-bombing attack. The two men agreed that a salvage party should attempt to save the ship since she had stubbornly remained afloat despite the heavy list and imminent danger of capsizing.

Interestingly enough, while the efforts to save *Yorktown* had been proceeding apace, her planes were still in action, joining those from *Enterprise* in striking the last Japanese carrier—*Hiryu*—late that afternoon. Taking four direct hits, the Japanese flattop was soon helpless. She was abandoned by her crew and left to drift out of control and manned only by her dead. *Yorktown* had been avenged.

Yorktown, as it turned out, floated through the night; two men were still alive on board her—one attracted attention by firing a machine gun that was heard by the sole attending destroyer, *Hughes*. The escort picked up the men, one of whom later died.

Meanwhile, Buckmaster had selected 29 officers and 141 men to return to the ship in an attempt to save her. Five destroyers formed an antisubmarine screen while the salvage party boarded the listing carrier, the fire in the rag storage still smoldering on the morning of the 6th. *Vireo* (AT–144), summoned from Pearl and Hermes Reef, soon commenced towing the ship. Progress, though, was painfully slow.

Yorktown's repair party went on board with a carefully predetermined plan of action to be carried out by men from each department—damage control, gunnery, air, engineering, navigation, communication, supply, and medical. To assist in the work, Lt. Comdr. Arnold E. True brought his ship, *Hammann*, alongside to starboard, aft, furnishing pumps and electric power.

By mid-afternoon, it looked as if the gamble to save the ship was paying off. The process of reducing topside weight was proceeding well—one 5-inch gun had been dropped over the side, and a second was ready to be cast loose; planes had been pushed over the side; the submersible pumps (powered by electricity provided by *Hammann*) had pumped out considerable quantities of water from the engineering spaces. The efforts of the salvage crew had reduced the list about two degrees.

Unbeknownst to *Yorktown* and the six nearby destroyers, the Japanese submarine *I–158* had achieved a favorable firing position. Remarkably—but perhaps understandable in light of the debris and wreckage in the water in the vicinity—none of the destroyers picked up the approaching I-boat. Suddenly, at 1536, lookouts spotted a salvo of four torpedoes churning toward the ship from the starboard beam.

Hammann went to general quarters, a 20-millimeter gun going into action in an attempt to explode the "fish" in the water. One torpedo hit *Hammann*—her screws churning the water beneath her fantail as she tried to get underway—directly amidships and broke her back. The destroyer jackknifed and went down rapidly.

Two torpedoes struck *Yorktown* just below the turn of the bilge at the after end of the island structure. The fourth torpedo passed just astern of the carrier.

Approximately a minute after *Hammann*'s stern disappeared beneath the waves, an explosion rumbled up from the depths—possibly caused by the destroyer's depth charges going off. The blast killed many of *Hammann*'s and a few of *Yorktown*'s men who had been thrown into the water. The concussion battered the already-damaged carrier's hull and caused tremendous shocks that carried away *Yorktown*'s auxiliary generator; sent numerous fixtures from the hangar deck overhead crashing to the deck below; sheared rivets in the starboard leg of the foremast; and threw men in every direction, causing broken bones and several minor injuries.

Prospects for immediate resumption of salvage work looked grim, since all destroyers immediately commenced searches for the enemy submarine (which escaped) and commenced rescuing men from *Hammann* and *Yorktown*. Capt. Buckmaster decided to postpone further attempts at salvage until the following day.

Vireo cut the towline and doubled back to *Yorktown* to pick up survivors, taking on board many men of the salvage crew while picking up men from the water. The little ship endured a terrific pounding from the larger ship but nevertheless stayed alongside to carry out her rescue mission. Later, while on board the tug, Capt. Buckmaster conducted a burial service; two officers and an enlisted man from *Hammann* were committed to the deep.

The second attempt at salvage, however, would never be made. Throughout the night of the 6th and into the morning of the 7th, *Yorktown* remained stubbornly afloat. By 0530 on the 7th, however, the men in the ships nearby noted that the carrier's list was rapidly increasing to port. As if tired, the valiant flattop turned over at 0701 on her port side and sank in 3,000 fathoms of water, her battle flags flying.

Yorktown (CV–5) earned three battle stars for her World War II service; two of them being for the significant part she had played in stopping Japanese expansion and turning the tide of the war at Coral Sea and at Midway.

IV

(CV–10: dp. 27,100; l. 872'0''; b. 93'0''; e.w. 147'6''; dr. 28'7''; s. 32.7 k. (tl.); cpl. 3,448; a. 12 5'', 32 40mm., 46 20mm., ac. 80+; cl. *Essex*)

The fourth *Yorktown* (CV–10) was laid down on 1 December 1941 at Newport News, Va., by the Newport News Shipbuilding & Drydock Co. as *Bon Homme Richard*; renamed *Yorktown* on 26 September 1942; launched on 21 January 1943; sponsored by Mrs. Eleanor Roosevelt; and commissioned on 15 April 1943 at the Norfolk Navy Yard, Capt. Joseph J. ("Jocko") Clark in command.

Yorktown remained in the Norfolk area until 21 May at which time she got underway for shakedown training in the vicinity of Trinidad. She returned to Norfolk on 17 June and began post-shakedown availability. The aircraft carrier completed repairs on 1 July and began air operations out of Norfolk until the 6th. On the latter day, she exited Chesapeake Bay on her way to the Pacific Ocean. She transited the Panama Canal on 11 July and departed Balboa on the 12th. The warship arrived in Pearl Harbor on 24 July and began a month of exercises in the Hawaiian Islands. On 22 August, she stood out of Pearl Harbor, bound for her first combat of the war. Her task force, TF 15, arrived at the launching point about 128 miles from Marcus Island early on the morning of 31 August. She spent most of that day launching fighter and bomber strikes on Marcus Island before beginning the retirement to Hawaii that evening. The aircraft carrier reentered Pearl Harbor on 7 September and remained there for two days.

On the 9th, she stood out to sea, bound for the west coast of the United States. She arrived in San Francisco on 13 September, loaded aircraft and supplies, and returned to sea on the 15th. Four days later, the aircraft carrier reentered Pearl Harbor. After 10 days in the Hawaiian Islands, *Yorktown* returned to sea to conduct combat operations on the 29th. Early on the morning of 5 October, she began two days of air strikes on Japanese installations on Wake Island. After retiring to the east for the night, she resumed those air raids early on the morning of the 6th and continued them through most of the day. That evening, the task group began its retirement to Hawaii. *Yorktown* arrived at Oahu on 11 October and, for the next month, conducted air training operations out of Pearl Harbor.

On 10 November, *Yorktown* departed Pearl Harbor in company with Task Force (TF) 50—the Fast Carrier Forces, Pacific Fleet—to participate in her first major assault operation, the occupation of certain of the Gilbert Islands. On the 19th, she arrived at the launch point near Jaluit and Mili and, early that morning, launched the first of a series of raids to suppress enemy airpower during the amphibious assaults on Tarawa, Abemama, and Makin. On the 20th, she not only sent raids back to the airfield at Jaluit, but some of her planes also supported the troops wresting Makin from the Japanese. On 22 November, her air group concentrated upon installations and planes at Mili once again. Before returning to Pearl Harbor, the aircraft carrier made passing raids on the installations at Wotje and Kwajalein Atolls on 4 December. The warship reentered Pearl Harbor on 9 December and began a month of air training operations in the Hawaiian Islands.

On 16 January 1944, the warship exited Pearl Harbor once again to support an amphibious assault—Operation "Flintlock," the Marshall Islands operation. Her task group, Task Group (TG) 58.1, arrived at its launching point early on the morning of 29 January, and its carriers—Yorktown, Lexington (CV-16), and Cowpens (CVL-25)—began sending air strikes aloft at about 0520 for attacks on Taroa airfield located on Maloelap Atoll. Throughout the day, her aircraft hit Maloelap in preparation for the assaults on Majuro and Kwajalein scheduled for the 31st. On the 30th, Yorktown and her sister carriers shifted targets to Kwajalein to begin softening up one of the targets itself. When the troops stormed ashore on the 31st, Yorktown aviators continued their strikes on Kwajalein in support of the troops attacking that atoll. The same employment occupied the Yorktown air group during the first three days in February. On the 4th, however, the task group retired to the Fleet anchorage at recently secured Majuro Atoll.

Over the next four months, Yorktown participated in a series of raids in which she ranged from the Marianas in the north to New Guinea in the south. After eight days at Majuro, she sortied with her task group on 12 February to conduct air strikes on the main Japanese anchorage at Truk Atoll. Those highly sucessessful raids occurred on 16 and 17 February. On the 18th, the carrier set a course for the Marianas and, on the 22d, conducted a single day of raids on enemy airfields and installations on Saipan. That same day, she cleared the area on her way back to Majuro. The warship arrived in Majuro lagoon on 26 February and remained there, resting and replenishing until 8 March. On the latter day, the carrier stood out of Majuro, rendezvoused with the rest of TF 58, and shaped a course for Espiritu Santo in the New Hebrides. She reached her destination on 13 March and remained there for 10 days before getting underway for another series of raids on the Japanese middle defense line. On 30 and 31 March, she launched air strikes on enemy installations located in the Palau Islands; and, on 1 April, her aviators went after the island of Woleai. Five days later, she returned to her base at Majuro for a week of replenishment and recreation.

On 13 April, Yorktown returned to sea once more. On this occasion, however, she laid in a course for the northern coast of New Guinea. On 21 April, she began launching raids in support of General Douglas MacArthur's assault on the Hollandia area. That day, her aviators attacked installations in the Wakde-Sarmi area of northern New Guinea. On the 22d and 23d, they shifted to the landing areas at Hollandia themselves and began providing direct support for the assault troops. After those attacks, she retired from the New Guinea coast for another raid on Truk lagoon, which her aircraft carried out on 29 and 30 April. The aircraft carrier retuned to Majuro on 4 May; however, two days later she got underway again, bound for Oahu. The warship entered Pearl Harbor on 11 May and, for the next 18 days, conducted training operations in the Hawaiian Islands. On 29 May, she headed back to the Central Pacific. Yorktown entered Majuro lagoon again on 3 June and began preparations for her next major amphibious support operation—the assault on the Marianas.

On 6 June, the aircraft carrier stood out of Majuro with TF 58 and set a course for the Mariana Islands. After five days steaming, she reached the launch point and began sending planes aloft for the preliminary softening up of targets in preparation for the invasion of Saipan. Yorktown aircrews concentrated primarily upon airfields located on Guam. Those raids continued until the 13th when Yorktown, with two of the task groups of TF 58, steamed north to hit targets in the Bonin Islands. That movement resulted in a one-day raid on the 16th before the two task groups headed back to the Marianas to join in the Battle of the Philippine Sea. Task Force 58 reunited on 18 June and began a short wait for the approaching Japanese Fleet and its aircraft.

On the morning of 19 June, Yorktown aircraft began strikes on Japanese air bases on Guam in order to deny them to their approaching carrier-based air and to keep the land-based planes out of the fray. Duels with Guam-based aircraft continued until mid-morning. At about 1017, however, she got her first indication of the carrier plane attacks when a large bogey appeared on her radar screen. At that point she divided her attention, sending part of her air group back to Guam and another portion of it out to meet the raid closing from the west. Throughout the battle, Yorktown's planes continued both to strike the Guam airfields and intercept the carrier raids. During the first day of the Battle of the Philippine Sea, Yorktown aircraft claimed 37 enemy planes destroyed and dropped 21 tons of bombs on the Guam air bases.

On the morning of the 20th Yorktown steamed generally west with TF 58 while search planes groped for the fleeing enemy task force. Contact was not made with the enemy until about 1540 that afternoon when a Hornet (CV-12) pilot spotted the retiring Combined Fleet units. Yorktown launched a 40-plane strike between 1623 and 1643 and sent it winging after the Japanese. Her planes found Admiral Ozawa's force at about 1840 and began a 20-minute attack during which they went after Zuikaku on whom they succeeded in scoring some hits. They, however, failed to sink that carrier. They also attacked several other ships in the Japanese force though no records show a confirmed sinking to the credit of the Yorktown air group. On 21 June, the carrier joined in the futile stern chase on the enemy carried out by TF 58 but gave up that evening when air searches failed to contact the Japanese. Yorktown returned to the Marianas area and resumed air strikes on Pagan on the 22d and 23d. On the 24th, she launched another series of raids on Iwo Jima. On 25 June, she laid in a course for Eniwetok and arrived there two days later. On the 30th, the aircraft carrier headed back to the Marianas and the Bonins. She renewed combat operations on 3 and 4 July with a series of attacks on Iwo Jima and Chichi Jima. On the 6th, the warship resumed strikes in the Marianas and continued them for the next 17 days. On 23 July, she headed off to the west for a series of raids on Yap, Ulithi, and the Palaus. She carried out those attacks on 25 July and arrived back in the Marianas on the 29th.

On the 31st, she cleared the Mariana Islands and headed—via Eniwetok and Pearl Harbor—back to the United States. Yorktown arrived in the Puget Sound Navy Yard on 17 August and began a two-month overhaul. She completed repairs on 6 October and departed Puget Sound on the 9th. She stopped at the Alameda Naval Air Station from 11 to 13 October to load planes and supplies and then set a course back to the western Pacific. After a stop at Pearl Harbor from the 18th to the 24th, Yorktown arrived back in Eniwetok on 31 October. She departed the lagoon on 1 November and arrived at Ulithi on the 3d. There, she reported for duty with TG 38.4. That task group left Ulithi on 5 November, and Yorktown departed with it.

On 7 November, the aircraft carrier changed operational control to TG 38.1 and, for the next two weeks, launched air strikes on targets in the Philippines in support of the Leyte invasion. Detached from the task force on 23 November, *Yorktown* arrived back in Ulithi on the 24th. She remained there until 10 December at which time she put to sea to rejoin TF 38. She rendezvoused with the other carriers on 13 December and began launching air strikes on targets on the island of Luzon in preparation for the invasion of that island scheduled for the second week in January. On the 17th, the task force began its retirement from the Luzon strikes. During that retirement, TF 38 steamed through the center of the famous typhoon of December 1944. That storm sank three destroyers—*Spence* (DD–512), *Hull* (DD–350), and *Monaghan* (DD–354)—and *Yorktown* participated in some of the rescue operations for the survivors of those three destroyers. She did not finally clear the vicinity of Luzon until the 23d. The warship arrived back in Ulithi on 24 December.

The aircraft carrier fueled and provisioned at Ulithi until 30 December at which time she returned to sea to join TF 38 on strikes at targets in the Philippines in support of the landings at Lingayen. The carriers opened the show on 3 January 1945 with raids on airfields on the island of Formosa. Those raids continued on the 4th, but a fueling rendezvous occupied *Yorktown*'s time on the 5th. She sent her planes against Luzon targets and on antishipping strikes on the 6th and 7th. The 8th brought another fueling rendezvous; and, on the 9th, she conducted her last attack—on Formosa—in direct support of the Lingayen operation. On 10 January, *Yorktown* and the rest of TF 38 entered the South China Sea via Bashi Channel to begin a series of raids on Japan's inner defenses. On 12 January, her planes visited the vicinity of Saigon and Tourane Bay, Indochina, in hopes of catching major units of the Japanese fleet. Though foiled in their primary desire, TF 38 aviators still managed to rack up a stupendous score—44 enemy ships of which 15 were combatants. She fueled on the 13th and, on the 15th, launched raids on Formosa and Canton in China. The following day, her aviators struck at Canton again and paid a visit to Hong Kong. Fueling took up her time on 17, 18, and 19 January; and, on the 20th, she exited the South China Sea with TF 38 via Balintang Channel. She participated in a raid on Formosa on the 21st and another on Okinawa on the 22d before clearing the area for Ulithi. On the morning of 26 January, she reentered Ulithi lagoon with TF 38.

Yorktown remained at Ulithi arming, provisioning, and conducting upkeep until 10 February. At that time, she sortied with TF 58, the 3d Fleet becoming the 5th Fleet when Spruance relieved Halsey, on a series of raids on the Japanese and thence to support the assault on and occupation of Iwo Jima. On the morning of 16 February, the aircraft carrier began launching strikes on the Tokyo area of Honshu. On the 17th, she repeated those strikes before heading toward the Bonins. Her aviators bombed and strafed installations on Chichi Jima on the 18th. The landings on Iwo Jima went forward on 19 February, and *Yorktown* aircraft began support missions over the island on the 20th. Those missions continued until the 23d at which time *Yorktown* cleared the Bonins to resume strikes on Japan proper. She arrived at the launch point on the 25th and sent two raids aloft to bomb and strife airfields in the vicinity of Tokyo. On the 26th, *Yorktown* aircrewmen conducted a single sweep of installations on Kyushu before TG 58.4 began its retirement to Ulithi. *Yorktown* reentered the anchorage at Ulithi on 1 March.

She remained in the anchorage for about two weeks. On 14 March, the aircraft carrier departed the lagoon on her way to resume raids on Japan and to begin preliminary support work for the Okinawa operations scheduled for 1 April. On 18 March, she arrived in the operating area off Japan and began launching strikes on airfields on Kyushu, Honshu, and Shikoku. The task group came under air attack almost as soon as operations began. At about 0800, a twin-engine bomber, probably a "Frances," attacked from her port side. The ship opened fire almost immediately and began scoring hits quickly. The plane began to burn but continued his run passing over *Yorktown*'s bow and splashing in the water on her starboard side. Just seven minutes later, another "Frances" tried his luck; but he, too, went down, a victim of the combined fire of the formation. No further attacks developed until that afternoon; and, in the meantime, *Yorktown* continued air operations. That afternoon, three "Judy's" launched attacks on the carrier. The first two failed in their attacks and were shot down for their trouble. The third succeeded in planting his bomb on the signal bridge. It passed through the first deck and exploded near the ship's hull. It punched two large holes through her side, killed five men, and wounded another 26. *Yorktown*, however, remained fully operational, and her antiaircraft gunners brought the offender down. She continued air operations against the three southernmost islands of Japan on the 19th but retired for fueling operations on the 20th.

On the 21st, she headed for Okinawa, on which island she began softening-up strikes on the 23d. Those attacks continued until the 28th when she started back to Japanese waters for an additional strike on the home islands. On the 29th, the carrier put two raids and one photographic reconnaissance mission into the air over Kyushu. That afternoon, at about 1410, a single "Judy" made an apparent suicide dive on *Yorktown*. Her antiaircraft gunners opened up on him and scored numerous hits. He passed over the ship, very near to her "island," and splashed about 60 feet from her portside.

On 30 March, *Yorktown* and the other carriers of her task group began to concentrate solely on the island of Okinawa and its surrounding islets. For two days, the 30th and 31st, they pounded the island in softening-up strikes. On 1 April, the assault troops stormed ashore; and, for almost six weeks, she sent her planes to the island to provide direct support for the troops operating ashore. About every three days, she retired to the east to conduct fueling rendezvous or to rearm and reprovision. The only exception to that routine came on 7 April when it was discovered that a Japanese task force built around the elusive battleship, *Yamato*, was steaming south for one last, desperate, offensive. *Yorktown* and the other carriers quickly launched strikes to attack that valued target. Air Group 9 aviators claimed several torpedo hits on *Yamato* herself just before the battleship exploded and sank as well as at least three 500-pound bomb hits on light cruiser *Yahagi* before that warship followed her big sister to the bottom. The pilots also made strafing runs on the escorting destroyers and claimed to have left one afire in a sinking condition. At the conclusion of that action, *Yorktown* and her planes resumed their support for the troops on Okinawa. On 11 April, she came under air attack again when a single-engine plane sped in on her. *Yorktown*'s antiaircraft gunners proved equal to the test, however, and splashed him just inside 2,000 yards' range. Sporadic air attacks continued until her 11 May departure from the Ryukyus, but *Yorktown* sustained no additional damage and claimed only one further kill with her antiaircraft battery. On 11 May, TG 58.4 was detached to proceed to Ulithi for upkeep, rest, and relaxation.

Yorktown entered the lagoon at Ulithi on 14 May and remained there until 24 May at which time she sortied with TG 58.4 to rejoin the forces off Okinawa. On 28 May, TG 58.4 became TG 38.4 when Halsey relieved Spruance and 5th Fleet again became 3d Fleet. That same day, the carrier resumed air support missions over Okinawa. That routine lasted until the beginning of June when she moved off with TF 38 to resume strikes on the Japanese homeland. On 3 June, her aircraft made four different sweeps of airfields. The following day, she returned to Okinawa for a day of additional support missions before steaming off to evade a typhoon. On the 6th and 7th, she resumed Okinawa strikes. She sent her aviators back to the Kyushu airfields and, on the 9th, launched them on the first of two days of raids on Minami Daito Shima. After the second day's strikes on the 10th, *Yorktown* began retirement with TG 38.4 toward Leyte. She arrived in San Pedro Bay at Leyte on 13 June and began replenishment, upkeep, rest, and relaxation.

The warship remained at Leyte until 1 July when she and TG 38.4 got underway to join the rest of the fast carriers in the final series of raids on the Japanese home islands. By 10 July, she was off the coast of Japan launching air strikes on the Tokyo area of Honshu. After a fueling rendezvous on the 11th and 12th, she resumed strikes on Japan, this on the southern portion of the northernmost island—Hokkaido. Those strikes lasted from the 13th to the 15th. A fueling retirement and heavy weather precluded air operations until the 18th at which time her aviators returned to the Tokyo area. From the 19th to the 22d, she made a fueling and underway replenishment retirement and then, on the 24th, resumed air attacks on Japan. For two days, planes of her air group pounded installations around the Kure naval base. Another fueling retirement came on the 26th, but the 27th and 28th found her planes in the air above Kure again. On the 29th and 30th, she shifted targets back to the Tokyo area before another fueling retirement and another typhoon took her out of action until the beginning of the first week in August. On 8 and 9 August, the carrier launched her planes at northern Honshu and southern Hokkaido. On the 10th, she sent them back to Tokyo. The 11th and 12th brought another fueling retirement and a typhoon evasion; but, on the 13th, her aircraft hit Tokyo for the last time. On the 14th, she retired to fuel destroyers again; and, on the 15th, Japan agreed to capitulate so that all strikes planned for that day were cancelled.

From 16 to 23 August, *Yorktown* and the other carriers of TF 58 steamed around more or less aimlessly in waters to the east of Japan awaiting instructions while peace negotiations continued. Then, on the 23d, she received orders to head for waters east of Honshu where her aircraft were to provide cover for the forces occupying Japan. She began providing that air cover on the 25th and continued to do so until mid-September. After the formal surrender on board *Missouri* (BB–63) on 2 September, the aircraft carrier also began air-dropping supplies to Allied prisoners of war still living in their prison camps. On 16 September, *Yorktown* entered Tokyo Bay with TG 38.1. She remained there, engaged in upkeep and crew recreation, through the end of the month. On 1 October, the carrier stood out of Tokyo Bay on her way to Okinawa. She arrived in Buckner Bay on 4 October, loaded passengers on the 5th, and got underway for the United States on the 6th.

After a non-stop voyage, *Yorktown* entered San Francisco Bay on 20 October, moored at the Alameda Naval Air Station, and began discharging passengers. She remained at the air station until 31 October at which time she shifted to Hunters Point Navy Yard to complete minor repairs. On 2 November, while still at the navy yard, she reported to the Service Force, Pacific Fleet, for duty in conjunction with the return of American servicemen to the United States. That same day, she stood out of San Francisco Bay, bound for Guam on just such a mission. She arrived in Apra Harbor on 15 November and, two days later, got underway with a load of passengers. She arrived back in San Francisco on 30 November and remained there until 8 December. On the latter day, the warship headed back to the Far East. Initially routed to Samar in the Philippines, she was diverted to Manila en route. She arrived in Manila on 26 December and departed there on the 29th. She reached San Francisco again on 13 January 1946. Later that month, she moved north to Bremerton, Wash., where she was placed in commission, in reserve, on 21 June. She remained there in that status through the end of the year. On 9 January 1947, *Yorktown* was placed out of commission and was berthed with the Bremerton Group, Pacific Reserve Fleet.

Yorktown remained in reserve for almost five years. In June of 1952, she was ordered reactivated, and work began on her at Puget Sound. On 15 December 1952, she was placed in commission, in reserve, at Bremerton. Her conversion continued into 1953 and she conducted post-conversion trials late in January. On 20 February 1953, *Yorktown* was placed in full commission, Capt. William M. Nation in command. The aircraft carrier conducted normal operations along the west coast through most of the summer of 1953. On 3 August, she departed San Francisco on her way to the Far East. She arrived in Pearl Harbor and remained there until the 27th at which time she continued her voyage west. On 5 September, the carrier arrived in Yokosuka, Japan. She put to sea again on the 11th to join TF 77 in the Sea of Japan. The Korean War armistice had been signed two months earlier; and, therefore, the carrier conducted training operations rather than combat missions. She served with TF 77 until 18 February 1954 at which time she stood out of Yokosuka on her way home. She made a stop at Pearl Harbor along the way and then moored at Alameda once more on 3 March. After a brief repair period at Hunters Point Naval Shipyard, *Yorktown* put to sea to serve as a platform for the filming of the movie "Jet Carrier." She conducted further, more routine, operations along the west coast until 1 July at which time she headed

The modernized *Yorktown* as an antisubmarine carrier (CVS–10) in 1968, with S–2 *Trackers*, E–1 *Tracer* early-warning planes, and an SH–3 *Sea King* ASW helicopter on her flight deck. (USN 1129551)

back to the Orient. She stopped at Pearl Harbor from 8 to 28 July before continuing on to Manila, where she arrived on 4 August.

Yorktown operated out of the Manila-Subic Bay area, conducting 7th Fleet maneuvers, for the duration of the deployment. She did, however, take periodic breaks from that schedule to make frequent port visits to Yokosuka; and, during the Christmas holidays, she made a liberty call at Hong Kong on the Chinese coast. In January of 1955, she was called upon to help cover the evacuation of Nationalist Chinese from the Tachen Islands located near the communist-controlled mainland. *Yorktown* entered Yokosuka for the last time on 16 February 1955 but departed again on the 18th to return home. After an overnight stop at Pearl Harbor on 23 and 24 February, she resumed her voyage east and arrived in Alameda on 28 February. On 21 March 1955, she was placed in commission, in reserve, at the Puget Sound Naval Shipyard where she was to receive extensive modifications—most significantly, an angled flight deck to increase her jet aircraft launching capability. She completed her conversion that fall and, on 14 October, was placed back in full commission.

The aircraft carrier resumed normal operations along the west coast soon after recommissioning. That assignment lasted until mid-March 1956. On the 19th, she stood out of San Francisco Bay on her way to her third tour of duty with the 7th Fleet since her reactivation in 1953. *Yorktown* stopped at Pearl Harbor from 24 March to 9 April and then continued her voyage west. She arrived in Yokosuka, Japan, on 18 April and departed again on the 29th. The warship operated with the 7th Fleet for the next five months. During that time, she conducted operations in the Sea of Japan, the East China Sea, and the South China Sea. She also visited such places as Sasebo, Manila, Subic Bay, and Buckner Bay at Okinawa. On 7 September, the aircraft carrier stood out of Yokosuka and pointed her bow to the east. After a non-stop voyage, she arrived back at Alameda on 13 September. She resumed west coast operations for about two months. On 13 November, she embarked upon a round-trip to Pearl Harbor, from which she returned to Alameda on 11 December. *Yorktown* resumed normal operations out of Alameda upon her return and remained so employed until March of 1957. On 9 March, she departed Alameda for yet another tour of duty in the Far East. She made stops at Oahu and Guam along the way and arrived at Yokosuka on 19 April. She put to sea to join TF 77 on 25 April and served with that task force for the next three months. On 13 August, the warship departed Yokosuka for the last time, made a brief pause at Pearl Harbor, and arrived in Alameda on the 25th.

On 1 September, her home port was changed from Alameda to Long Beach, and she was reclassified an antisubmarine warfare (ASW) aircraft carrier with the new designation CVS-10. On the 23d, she departed Alameda and, four days later, entered the Puget Sound Naval Shipyard for overhaul and for modification to an ASW carrier. That yard period lasted until the beginning of February 1958. She departed the naval ammunition depot at Bangor, Wash., on 7 February and entered Long Beach five days later. For the next eight months, *Yorktown* conducted normal operations along the west coast. On 1 November, she departed San Diego to return to the western Pacific. After a stop at Pearl Harbor from the 8th to the 17th, *Yorktown* continued her voyage west and arrived in Yokosuka on the 25th. During that deployment, the aircraft carrier qualified for the Armed Forces Expeditionary Medal on three occasions. The first time came on 31 December and 1 January 1959 when she participated in an American show of strength in response to the communist Chinese shelling of the offshore islands, Quemoy and Matsu, held by Nationalist Chinese forces. During January, she also joined contingency forces off Vietnam during internal disorders caused by communist guerrillas in the southern portion of that country. That month also saw her earn the expeditionary medal for

service in the Taiwan Strait. The remainder of the deployment—save for another visit to Vietnamese waters late in March—consisted of a normal round of training evolutions and port visits. She concluded that tour of duty at San Diego on 21 May. The warship resumed normal operations along the west coast, and that duty consumed the remainder of 1959.

In January of 1960, *Yorktown* headed back to the Far East via Pearl Harbor. During that deployment, she earned additional stars for her Armed Forces Expeditionary Medal for duty in Vietnamese waters at various times in March, April, May, and June. She returned to the west coast late in the summer and, late in September, began a four-month overhaul at the Puget Sound Naval Shipyard.

Yorktown emerged from the shipyard in January 1961 and returned to Long Beach on the 27th. She conducted refresher training and then resumed normal west coast operations until late July. On 29 July, the aircraft carrier stood out of Long Beach, bound once again for the Orient. She made an extended stopover in the Hawaiian Islands in August and, consequently, did not arrive in Yokosuka until 4 September. That tour of duty in the Far East consisted of a normal schedule of antiair and antisubmarine warfare exercises as well as the usual round of port visits. She concluded the deployment at Long Beach on 2 March 1962. Normal west coast operations occupied her time through the summer and into the fall. On 26 October, the warship left Long Beach in her wake and set a course for the Far East. During that deployment, she served as flagship for Carrier Division (CarDiv) 19. She participated in a number of ASW and AAW exercises, including the SEATO ASW exercise, Operation "Sea Serpent." The deployment lasted until 6 June 1963 at which time the carrier set a course back to Long Beach.

Yorktown arrived back in her home port on 18 June and resumed normal operations for the remainder of the year. Those operations continued throughout most of 1964 as well. However, on 22 October, she pointed her bow westward again and set out for a tour of duty with the 7th Fleet. Another period of operations in the Hawaiian Islands delayed her arrival in Japan until 3 December. The 1964 and 1965 deployment brought *Yorktown* her first real involvement in the Vietnamese civil war. In February, March, and April, she conducted a series of special operations in the South China Sea in waters near Vietnam—presumably ASW services for the fast carriers conducting air strikes against targets in Vietnam in support of the increased American involvement in the civil war in that country. She concluded her tour of duty in the Far East on 7 May 1965 when she departed Yokosuka to return to the United States. The carrier arrived in Long Beach on 17 May.

For the remainder of her active career, *Yorktown*'s involvement in combat operations in Vietnam proved a dominant feature of her activities. After seven months of normal operations out of Long Beach, she got underway for the western Pacific again on 5 January 1966. She arrived in Yokosuka on 17 February and joined TF 77 on Yankee Station later that month. Over the next five months, the aircraft carrier spent three extended tours of duty on Yankee Station providing ASW and sea-air rescue services for the carriers of TF 77. She also participated in several ASW exercises, including the major SEATO exercise, Operation "Sea Imp." The warship concluded her last tour of duty on Yankee Station early in July and, after a stop at Yokosuka, headed home on the 15th. She disembarked her air group at San Diego on 27 July and reentered Long Beach that same day. She resumed normal operations—carrier qualifications and ASW exercises—for the remainder of the year and during the first two months of 1967.

On 24 February 1967, *Yorktown* entered the Long Beach Naval Shipyard for a seven-month overhaul. She completed repairs early in October and, after refresher training, resumed normal west coast operations for most of what remained of 1967. On 28 December, she stood out of Long Beach, bound for her last tour of duty in the western Pacific. After a stop at Pearl Harbor, she arrived in the Far East late in January. Instead of putting in at a Japanese port for turnover, *Yorktown* headed directly to the Sea of Japan to provide ASW and search and rescue (SAR) support for the contingency force assembled in the wake of the North Korean capture of *Pueblo* (AGER-2). She remained on that assignment for 30 days. On 1 March, she was released from that duty, and the warship headed for Subic Bay in the Philippines. During the remainder of the deployment, the aircraft carrier did another three tours of duty with TF 77 on Yankee Station. In each instance, she provided ASW and SAR support for the fast carriers launching air strikes on targets in Vietnam. She concluded her last tour of duty in Vietnamese waters on 16 June and set a course for Yokosuka where she stopped from 19 to 21 June before heading back to the United States.

Yorktown arrived back in Long Beach on 5 July and entered the Long Beach Naval Shipyard that same day for almost three months of repairs. She completed repairs on 30 September and resumed normal operations. Late in November and early in December, she served as a platform for the filming of another movie, "Tora! Tora! Tora!," which recreated the Japanese attack on Pearl Harbor. In December, she served as one of the recovery ships for the Apollo 8 space shot. The two unique missions mentioned above were conducted out of Pearl Harbor. She departed Pearl Harbor of 2 January 1969 and, after a two-week stop in Long Beach, continued her voyage to join the Atlantic Fleet. Steaming all the way around South America, the aircraft carrier arrived in her new home port—Norfolk, Va.—on 28 February. She conducted operations along the east coast and in the West Indies until late summer. On 2 September, *Yorktown* departed Norfolk for a northern European cruise and participation in the major fleet exercise Operation "Peacekeeper." During the exercise, she provided ASW and SAR support for the task force. The exercise ended on 23 September, and *Yorktown* began a series of visits to northern European ports. After a visit each to Brest, France, and Rotterdam in the Netherlands, *Yorktown* put to sea for a series of hunter/killer ASW exercises between 18 October and 11 November. She resumed her itinerary of port visits on 11 November at Kiel, Germany. After that, she stopped at Copenhagen, Denmark, and at Portsmouth, England, before getting underway for home on 1 December. She reentered Norfolk on 11 December and began her holiday leave period.

During the first half of 1970, *Yorktown* operated out of Norfolk and began preparations for inactivation. On 27 June 1970, *Yorktown* was decommissioned at Philadelphia, Pa., and was berthed with the Philadelphia Group, Atlantic Reserve Fleet. She remained there almost three years before her name was struck from the Navy list on 1 June 1973. During 1974, the Navy Department approved the donation of *Yorktown* to the Patriot's Point Development Authority, Charleston, S.C. She was towed from Bayonne, N.J., to Charleston, S.C., in June of 1975. She was formally dedicated as a memorial on the 200th anniversary of the Navy, 13 October 1975. As of April 1980, she was still on display at Patriot's Point, S.C.

Yorktown (CV-10) earned 11 battle stars and the Presidential Unit Citation during World War II and five battle stars for Vietnam service.

Yosemite

A valley in east central California on the western slope of the Sierra Nevada mountains. It is now the site of Yosemite National Park.

I

(Auxiliary cruiser: dp. 6,179; l. 389'2''; b. 48'0''; dr. 20'1'' (mean); s. 16 k.; cpl. 285; a. 2 5'', 6 6-pdrs., 2 Colt mg.)

At the begining of the Spanish-American War, *El Sud*—a merchant steamer built in 1892 by the Newport News Shipbuilding & Drydock Co.—was acquired by the Navy from the Southern Pacific Co. on 6 April 1898. The ship was renamed *Yosemite* and placed in commission on 13 April 1898, Comdr. William H. Emory in command.

After fitting out as an auxiliary cruiser at League Island, Pa., and at Newport News, Va., *Yosemite* departed Hampton Roads on 30 May for duty with the Eastern Squadron off the coast of Cuba. She stopped at Key West, Fla., for five days and then headed for Havana on 7 June, arriving there the same day. *Yosemite*, however, kept on the move. She left Havana the next day; visited Santiago and Guantanamo Bay on the 10th; and then, after a brief return to Santiago, headed for Kingston, Jamaica, on the 12th. The auxiliary cruiser spent the night of 16 and 17 June at Kingston and returned to Cuban waters on the 19th. On 23 June, she cleared the Guantanamo Bay area for San Juan, Puerto Rico. She arrived off San Juan on the 25th to participate in the blockade of that port.

Soon after her arrival, *Yosemite* intercepted the Spanish steamer SS *Antonio Lopez* when the latter tried to run into San Juan. In spite of heavy covering fire from enemy shore batteries and gunboats *Alfonso III* and *Isabella II*, *Yosemite* attacked the blockade runner and succeeded in pounding her almost to pieces. At the conclusion of that encounter, the auxiliary cruiser pulled back out of range of the gunboats and their protecting shore batteries to resume her blockade station. She concluded that assignment on 15 July and, after a three-day visit to St. Thomas in the Danish West Indies (Virgin Islands), headed back toward the Virginia capes on the 18th.

Yosemite arrived at Hampton Roads on 22 July and remained there until 15 August, two days after hostilities ceased. For almost a month, she operated along the Atlantic coast. Then, between 8 and 19 September, the auxiliary made a voyage to Haiti and then resumed east coast operations briefly before putting in at League Island on 23 September—apparently for repairs because she remained until late in December. *Yosemite* departed League Island on 29 December and arrived in Norfolk on the 30th. The ship remained there until 8 April 1899 at which time she got underway for New York. Following a month-long stay, the auxiliary cruiser departed New York on 10 May for duty in the Mediterranean Sea, the Suez Canal, and the Indian Ocean. She arrived in the Mariana Islands—at San Luis d'Apra on Guam—on 7 August.

She spent the next eight months at Guam surveying the harbor and serving as station ship. On 17 April 1900, *Yosemite* departed Guam for a voyage to Japan where she underwent repairs at Yokohama and Uraga. Following a brief visit to Nagasaki on 7 and 8 June, the ship headed for the Philippines on the 9th. She arrived in Cavite on the 14th and began additional repairs. On 30 June, *Yosemite* completed repairs and set a course for Guam. She reached the harbor at San Luis d'Apra on 6 July and resumed duty as station ship. Between 2 and 29 August, she made a round-trip voyage back to Cavite to pick up stores for Guam. Upon her return to Guam, *Yosemite* resumed station-ship duties.

On 13 November 1900, the former auxiliary cruiser was blown from her anchorage by a particularly violent hurricane—first ashore and then out to sea from Apra harbor. For two days, her crew fought heroically to save their ship, but she shipped water badly and, due to a damaged screw, made only two knots headway even after the storm passed. Finally, after the weather abated completely, her crew was taken off by the Navy collier *Justin*, and *Yosemite* was scuttled.

II

(ScStr.: dp. 2,069 (n.); l. 256'0''; b. 33'0''; dr. 17'3''
(mean); s. 16.00 k. (tl.); a. 2 6-pdrs.)

SS *Clearwater*—a screw steamer built in 1894 by
Wigham Richardson & Co. at Newcastle, England—was
acquired by the War Department sometime during the
latter half of 1899 and renamed *Ingalls.* She was used
by the Army as a transport until 23 December 1910
when she was transferred to the Navy. Renamed
Yosemite, she was placed in commission, in reserve,
on 11 November 1911 at the Norfolk Navy Yard, Ens.
Alfred H. Miles in command.

Based at Norfolk, *Yosemite* served the Navy only
very briefly, working as tender to Submarine Division
3, Atlantic Torpedo Fleet. On 23 January 1912, just
over two months after her commissioning, she was
decommissioned at Norfolk. Her name was struck from
the Navy list on 1 March 1912, and she was sold to the
Boston Iron & Metal Works on 10 June 1912 for
scrapping.

On 1 January 1931, *San Francisco* (CM-2) (*q.v.*)
was renamed *Yosemite* (CM-2) to free the name *San
Francisco* for the projected heavy cruiser CA-38.

III

(AD-19: dp. 14,037 (tl.); l. 530'6''; b. 73'4''; dr. 25'6''
(lim.); s. 19.6 k. (tl.); cpl. 1,076; a. 4 5'', 8 40mm.,
23 20mm.; cl. *Dixie*)

The third *Yosemite* (AD-19) was laid down on 19
January 1942 by the Tampa Shipbuilding Co., Inc., at
Tampa, Fla.; launched on 16 May 1943; sponsored by
Mrs. Melville W. Powers; and commissioned on 25
March 1944, Capt. George C. Towner in command.

Between late March and mid-June, the destroyer
tender was fitted out at Tampa. On 21 June, she got
underway for the Virginia capes, steamed via Key
West, and arrived at Hampton Roads on the 26th. For
the next 10 days, the destroyer tender conducted shakedown training in Chesapeake Bay and then put into
Norfolk for additional outfitting and some modifications to her below-deck spaces. Early in August, she
made a voyage to Fort Pond Bay, N.Y., to load torpedoes. On the 6th, she headed south to Guantanamo Bay
and thence proceeded to the Canal Zone, transited the
Panama Canal, and arrived at Balboa on the 13th.
From there, the ship continued her voyage west to
Hawaii and arrived in Pearl Harbor on 29 August.

As soon as she moored, *Yosemite* went to work. For
the next six months, the ship's company made repairs
on over 200 ships. She remained at Oahu until February
of 1945. On the 15th, she exited the harbor and set a
course for Eniwetok Atoll in the Caroline Islands.
She arrived there on the 22d but remained for only five
days before moving farther westward to the forward
base at Ulithi Atoll. She entered the Ulithi anchorage
on 3 March, and her crew set again to work repairing
the veteran ships of the war in the Pacific. On 25 May,
Yosemite departed Ulithi in a convoy bound for Leyte
Gulf in the Philippines. She arrived in San Pedro Bay
on the 28th and resumed her work supporting the Fleet
in its march toward Japan. She remained at Leyte
through the end of the war but, soon thereafter, got
underway for Japan.

The destroyer tender arrived in Sasebo on 22 September and began tending ships assigned to the occupation forces in the Far East. That assignment lasted
until March 1946. On the 15th, she stood out of
Yokosuka on her way home. *Yosemite* transited the
Panama Canal in mid-April and arrived in New York
on the 22d.

Soon after her arrival back in the United States,
Yosemite became the flagship for the Commander, Destroyers, Atlantic Fleet. Except for several brief
interruptions for shipyard overhauls, she served in
that capacity from 17 June 1946 until the spring of
1962. During that 16-year period, she spent most of her
time in port at Newport, R.I., though on occasion she
did make voyages to the West Indies. In addition, near
the end of that stretch of time, the destroyer tender
made two overseas deployments. In June 1958, she
voyaged to northern Europe for the purpose of tending
ships engaged in an exercise in the North Atlantic.
Later, on 17 March 1959, she again departed Newport
for a brief tour of duty tending the ships of the 6th
Fleet. She concluded that assignment when she returned

The destroyer tender *Yosemite* (AD-19).

to Newport on 24 July and resumed duty as tender to the Atlantic Fleet destroyers and as flagship for their type commander.

On 1 April 1962, *Yosemite*'s role changed somewhat when the Atlantic Fleet cruisers and destroyers were brought together into a single type command. At that time, she became flagship for the new command, Cruiser-Destroyer Force, Atlantic Fleet. Late that fall, during the Cuban missile crisis and the American quarantine of the island, *Yosemite* departed Newport for a time and headed south via Norfolk to Kingston, Jamaica, where she tended the ships engaged in that operation. In December, she returned to Newport and resumed her normal schedule. Over the next six years, the destroyer tender remained at Newport except for occasional overhauls and for short voyages to the West Indies early each year to tend Atlantic Fleet ships participating in the annual "Springboard" exercise.

In 1969, the complexion of her operations changed somewhat. In April, she resumed overseas deployments after a hiatus of 10 years. She departed Newport on 7 April and arrived in Naples on the 19th. During that tour of duty in the Mediterranean, she served as flagship for the Commander, Service Force, 6th Fleet. *Grand Canyon* (AR-28) relieved her of tender duties on 14 August, the Service Force commander shifted his flag to *Mississinewa* (AO-144), and *Yosemite* sailed for the United States on the 15th. On the voyage home, she took on board a badly burned West German seaman from SS *Sinclair Venezuela* and transported him to the naval hospital at Newport. On 24 October, *Yosemite*'s home port was changed from Newport, R.I., to Mayport, Fla.; and the destroyer tender got underway for that city three days later. The ship arrived at Mayport on the 30th and began tending ships.

Since that time, *Yosemite* has been based at Mayport. She has served as flagship for various units of the Cruiser-Destroyer Force, Atlantic Fleet—notably Cruiser-Destroyer Flotilla 2 and Cruiser Destroyer Group 12. She has also made two additional deployments to the Mediterranean, one from July to December 1974 and the second from September 1977 to March 1978. She resumed tender duties at Mayport on 12 March 1978 and, as of October 1978, was engaged in those duties.

Young

John Young—born *circa* 1740—began his seafaring career at an early age in the colonial merchant marine and, at the start of the American Revolution, was commissioned 23d on the list of captains in the Continental Navy. On 20 September 1776, the Continental Congress directed Young to take the sloop-of-war *Independence* to Martinique to protect American mercantile shipping in the West Indies. Collaterally, *Independence* was to raid British shipping whenever the opportunity arose.

On 5 July 1777, Young was ordered to Nantes, France, and subsequently arrived at Lorient with two prizes. On 17 February 1778, while in French waters, he sailed through the French Fleet, saluting that nation's government with a 13-gun salute. In return he received a nine-gun salute, one of the earliest salutes rendered by the French government to the fledgling American government. At the time, John Paul Jones was on board *Independence*.

Young returned to America in the spring of 1778 and successively commanded two Pennsylvania privateers, *Buckskin* and *Impertinent*, before he was given command of the sloop-of-war *Saratoga*—then fitting out at Philadelphia, Pa.—in May 1780. Young took her to sea on 13 August 1780 and, in the course of the ship's first cruise, captured one prize before she returned to port for repairs and alterations.

Subsequent cruises were more successful, as Young commanded *Saratoga* on three more sweeps at sea in which he took a total of eight more prizes. Young proved himself a daring and resourceful commander. On one occasion, he took *Saratoga* between two British ships and captured both. Largely as a result of his dedication and emphasis on training, *Saratoga* compiled a distinguished, but altogether brief, record before her untimely—and still unexplained—loss.

Saratoga set sail from Cap Francais, in what is now the Dominican Republic, on 15 March 1781. After taking a prize three days later, the sloop-of-war became separated from her later that day when a strong gale swept through the area, the high winds nearly swamping the prize commanded by Midshipman Penfield. After the storm passed by, *Saratoga* was nowhere to be seen, having vanished without a trace.

Lucien Young—born in Lexington, Ky., on 31 March 1852—was appointed a midshipman on 21 June 1869 and served in the practice ships *Dale*, *Savannah*, and *Constellation* before graduating from the Naval Academy on 31 May 1873. Ordered to *Alaska* on 23 July 1873, Young, as a passed midshipman, was commended for extraordinary heroism when he saved the life of a seaman who had been knocked overboard.

Young was detached from *Alaska* at Lisbon, Portugal, and soon joined *Hartford*. Commissioned ensign on 16 July 1874, he joined *Powhatan*—on the North Atlantic Station—on 10 December of the following year. Subsequently ordered to *Huron*, he served in that ship until her tragic grounding off Nag's Head, N.C., on 24 November 1877. The ship, en route to Cuban waters for survey duty, foundered shortly after 0100 on the 24th. Ensign Young and an enlisted man—Seaman Antonio Williams—struggled ashore through the tumbling surf and gained the beach. Not receiving much assistance from an apparently apathetic group of bystanders, Young sent a horseman off at a gallop for a life-saving depot seven miles away while he, himself, although bruised and barefoot, walked four miles to yet another station, and, apparently finding it unmanned, broke in and got out mortar lines and powder for a Lyle gun. The sheriff of the locality then took Williams and Young to a point abreast the wreck. By the time they arrived, however, the 34 survivors had already reached shore. For his indefatigable efforts, Young received a commendation from the Secretary of the Navy; was awarded a gold medal by act of Congress from the Life-Saving service of the United States; was made an honorary member of the Kentucky legislature; and received advancement to the rate of master.

Ordered to *Portsmouth* on 17 March 1878, he arrived in Le Havre, France, in time to take charge of a detail of men to serve at the Universal Exposition in Paris, France. Following that duty, he served in *Portsmouth* with the Training Squadron until he was detached from that ship on 5 April 1880.

Young's next tour of duty was ashore in the Bureau of Equipment and Recruiting; and, while there, he served for a time as naval aide to the Secretary of the Navy. Master Young then served successive tours of sea duty in the monitor *Montauk* and the training ship *Minnesota*. Next came service as executive officer of *Onward* and, finally, a tour holding the same office in *Shenandoah*. While in the latter, Young took part in the landings in Panama to protect American interests in the spring of 1885.

A series of assignments ashore followed: Naval Torpedo Station, Newport, R.I.; at the Naval War College at Newport; at the Bureau of Navigation, and at the office of Naval War Records—the activity then compiling the monumental documentary collection, the *Official Records of the Union and Confederate Navies*. Young next returned to sea, serving successive tours in *Detroit*, *Boston*, *Yorktown*, and *Alert*.

Given command of *Hist*, Lt. Young placed that ship in commission and, during the Spanish-American War, took part in two engagements off Manzanillo, Cuba, and in the cutting of the cable between Cape Cruz and Manzanillo from late June 1898 to mid-August. Relieved of command of *Hist* in February 1899, Young received promotion to lieutenant commander on 3 March and became Captain of the Port of Havana on 22 August of the same year. In the spring of 1900, he became Commandant, Naval Station, Havana.

Following his duty in Cuba, Young became lighthouse inspector in the 9th Naval District and served in that capacity into 1904. In March 1904, he was given command of *Bennington* (Gunboat No. 4) and was in command of that ship at the time of her boiler explosion in the summer of the following year. At San Diego on 21 July 1905, *Bennington* was preparing to get underway for sea; Commander Young and the ship's surgeon, F. E. Peck, were returning to the ship in a boat and were not far from the anchorage when the explosion occurred at 1030. Young hurried back to the ship, took command, ordered her watertight compartments closed and her magazines flooded, and then secured the services of an Army tug nearby.

Young later was assigned to duty at the Mare Island Navy Yard and ultimately became Captain of the Yard there before becoming Commandant of the Naval Station, Pensacola, and of the 8th Naval District. His area of command was later extended to include the 7th Naval District.

Rear Admiral Young died at New York, N.Y., on 2 October 1912.

The first *Young* (DD–312) commemorated Capt. John Young, the Revolutionary War captain; the second ship of the name, *Young* (DD–580), honored Rear Admiral Lucien Young.

I

(DD–312: dp. 1,190; l. 314'5"; b. 31'8"; dr. 9'3" (mean); s. 35.0 k.; cpl. 95; a. 4 4", 1 3", 12 21" tt.; cl. *Clemson*)

The first *Young* (DD–312) was laid down on 28 January 1919 at San Francisco, Calif., by the Union Iron Works Plant of the Bethlehem Shipbuilding Corp.; launched on 8 May 1919; sponsored by Mrs. John R. Nolan; designated DD–312 on 17 July 1920; and commissioned on 29 November 1920, Lt. H. J. Ray in command.

Young fitted out at the Mare Island Navy Yard into December. Assigned to Division 34, Squadron 2, Pacific Fleet Destroyer Force, the destroyer remained inactive in the San Diego area through the end of 1921. Shortages—in both personnel and funds—meant curtailed and reduced operations for the large number of destroyers that the Navy found itself with in the period immediately following World War I. The "rotating reserve" system kept the ships and their comparatively skeleton crews occupied. One third of a unit would lie alongside a pier, manned by only a bare maintenance crew; one third of the ships would lie in the stream at San Diego harbor in a half-manned status; while the last third would be fully manned but would remain in harbor most of the time. The destroyers were moved from one status to the other periodically; and, in spite of the reduced-manning and operations schedule, the ships maintained a high state of readiness.

Young departed San Diego on 14 January 1922, bound for Bremerton, Wash., and, proceeding via San Francisco, Calif., reached the Puget Sound Navy Yard on the 18th. Overhauled at Puget Sound, the destroyer departed the yard on 3 April and arrived at her home port, San Diego, on the 8th. The remainder of the year passed fairly uneventfully, with the destroyer continuing her largely anchored existence in San Diego harbor. However, she did fire short-range battle practices, operated briefly off the Mexican Coronados Islands, and recovered torpedoes for *Idaho* (BB–42) during the autumn of the year 1922.

The in-port routine changed the following year, when *Young* departed San Diego on 6 February 1923 and headed for Panama. En route, she stopped briefly at Magdalena Bay—the traditional target practice grounds for the Pacific Fleet—and fueled from *Cuyama*

(AO–3) before proceeding on south to the Pacific side of the Panama Canal Zone.

Young participated in Fleet Problem I over the ensuing weeks. In this, the first Fleet Problem held by the United States Navy, the Battle Fleet was pitted against the Scouting Fleet—the later augmented by a division of battleships. During the war games, *Young* performed antisubmarine screening for the dreadnoughts of the Battle Fleet and, when the scenario of exercises called for it, dashed in and made simulated torpedo attacks on the "enemy" battlewagons of the augmented Scouting Fleet. Upon completion of one phase of the exercises, she was present in Panama Bay when Secretary of the Navy Edwin Denby, accompanied by a party of congressmen embarked in the transport *Henderson* (AP–1), reviewed the Fleet on 14 March.

Young later departed Panamanian waters on 31 March and arrived back at San Diego on 11 April. She remained there until 25 June, when she headed north. She called at San Francisco from the 27th to the 29th and arrived at Tacoma, Wash., on 2 July. Two days later, in keeping with the occasion, *Young* sent her landing force ashore to march in Tacoma's Independence Day parade.

After shifting to Seattle, *Young* underwent a period of upkeep alongside *Melville* (AD–2) between 16 July and 17 August. During that time, on 23 July, President Warren G. Harding, on a cruise to Alaska in *Henderson*, reviewed the Fleet—one of his last official acts before his death a short time later.

After spending a few days at Lake Washington following her upkeep period alongside *Melville*, *Young* underwent a brief yard period at the Puget Sound Navy Yard before she sailed south, escorting Battle Division 4 to San Francisco Bay at the end of August. En route, *Young* practiced torpedo attacks through smoke screens as part of the slate of tactical exercises.

Following a brief period moored at Pier 15, San Francisco, Division 11 got underway to return to San Diego on the morning of 8 September. As the ships made passage down the California coast, they conducted tactical and gunnery exercises in the course of what was also a competitive speed run of 20 knots. Ultimately, when the weather worsened, the ships formed column on the squadron leader, *Delphy* (DD–261). Unfortunately, through an error in navigation, the column swung east at about 2100, unaware of the danger that lurked in the fog-shrouded reefs dead ahead of them.

At 2105, *Delphy*—still steaming at 20 knots—ran hard aground off Padernales Point, followed, in succession, by the other ships steaming in follow-the-leader fashion. Only quick action by the ships farthest astern prevented the total loss of the entire group.

Young, however, became one of the casualties. Her hull torn by a jagged pinnacle, she swiftly capsized, heeling over on her starboard side within a minute and a half, trapping many of her engine and fire room personnel below. Lt. Comdr. William L. Calhoon, *Young*'s commanding officer, knew that there was no time to launch boats or rafts as the ship's list increased alarmingly following the grounding. Calhoun accordingly passed the word, through his executive officer, Lt. E. C. Herzinger, and Chief Boatswain's Mate Arthur Peterson, to make for the port side, to stick with the ship, and to not jump.

While the survivors clung tenaciously to their precarious, oily, surf-battered refuge, Boatswain's Mate Peterson proposed to swim 100 yards to a rocky outcropping to the eastward known as Bridge Rock. Before he could do so, however, *Chauncey* (DD–296) providentially grounded between *Young* and Bridge Rock, shortening the escape route. The two ships were about 75 yards apart.

At that juncture, Peterson unhesitatingly risked his life, diving into the swirling sea and swimming through the tumbling surf with a line to the nearby *Chauncey* —also aground but in a far better predicament since she had remained on a comparatively even keel. Eager hands from *Chauncey* hauled Peterson aboard and made the line fast. Soon, a seven-man life raft from the sistership was on its way to *Young* as a makeshift ferry. The raft ultimately made 11 trips bringing the 70 *Young* survivors to safety. By 2330, the last men of the crew were on board *Chauncey*; at that point, Lt. Comdr. Calhoun and Lt. Herzinger (the latter having returned to the ship after having been in the first raft across) left *Young's* battered hull.

In the subsequent investigation of the "Point Honda Disaster" the Board of Investigation commended Lt. Comdr. Calhoun for his "coolness, intelligence, and seamanlike ability" that was directly responsible for the "greatly reduced loss of life." The Board also cited Boatswain's Mate Peterson for his "extraordinary heroism" in swimming through the turbulent seas with a line to *Chauncey*; Lt. Herzinger drew praise for his "especially meritorious conduct" in helping to save the majority of the ship's crew.

Rear Admiral S. E. W. Kittelle, Commander, Destroyer Squadrons, subsequently cited Lt. Comdr. Calhoun's display of leadership and personality that saved "three-quarters of the crew of the *Young*" and Lt. Herzinger for his "Coolness and great assistance in the face of grave danger." Also commended by the admiral was Fireman First Class J. T. Scott, who attempted to close off the master oil valve to prevent a boiler explosion, volunteering to go below to the fireroom and go below the floor plates. The water, rapidly rising through the gashes in the ship's hull, however, prevented Scott from completing the task. He survived.

Twenty men were lost in *Young*, the highest death-toll of any of the ships lost in the disaster at Point Honda. Decommissioned on 26 October 1923, *Young* was stricken from the Navy list on 20 November 1923 and ordered sold as a hulk.

II

(DD–580: dp. 2,050; l. 376'; b. 39'8''; dr. 17'9''; s. 35 k.; cpl. 273; a. 5 5'', 10 40mm., 7 20mm., 10 21'' tt., 6 dcp., 2 dct.; cl. *Fletcher*)

The second *Young* (DD–580) was laid down on 7 May 1942 at Orange, Tex., by the Consolidated Steel Corp.; launched on 15 October 1942; sponsored by Mrs. J. M. Schelling; and commissioned on 31 July 1943, Lt. Comdr. George B. Madden in command.

Following shakedown in the Gulf of Mexico and the Caribbean Sea, *Young* briefly operated out of Guantanamo Bay, Cuba. During that assignment, she formed part of the escort for *Iowa* (BB–61) when that battleship carried President Franklin D. Roosevelt across the Atlantic on the first leg of his journey to the Teheran Conference of November 1943. In the midst of that voyage, the destroyer received orders instructing her to head for the Pacific theater. She transited the Panama Canal on 24 November and reported for duty with the Pacific Fleet. She arrived in Pearl Harbor early in December and received orders assigning her to the 9th Fleet in the northern Pacific. *Young* remained at Pearl Harbor for several weeks and then headed for the Aleutian Islands where she arrived in mid-January 1944.

Her arrival in Alaskan waters, however, came some three months after the Aleutians campaign ended. Her duties for the next eight months, therefore, consisted of escort and patrol missions spiced with an occasional bombardment of Japanese installations in the Kuril Islands. She was an element of Rear Admiral Wilder D. Baker's striking force on 2 February 1944 when that unit conducted the first bombardment of Japanese home territory in the Kurils. She twice returned to those islands in June, shelling Matsuwa on the 13th and Paramushiro on the 26th. Otherwise, her only enemy during the first eight months of 1944 proved to be the foul Aleutians weather.

During September, she returned to the United States for an overhaul. Upon completing repairs, the destroyer departed San Francisco Bay on 6 October, bound for the western Pacific. Reporting in at Manus in the Admiralty Islands late in the month, she received orders to join the escort of a supply convoy bound for the newly invaded Philippines. She reached Leyte on 18 November in the midst of an enemy air attack on the invasion fleet. She and her colleagues in the convoy screen combined to splash three of the attacking aircraft.

On 19 December, *Young* departed Leyte with 10 other destroyers in the screen of the first Mindoro resupply echelon. The unit came under enemy air attack early in the morning of the 21st but encountered no concerted air opposition until near dusk. At about 1718, a raid of five kamikazes broke through the combat air patrol, and three of the suicide planes succeeded in their missions, hitting *LST–460*, *LST–479*, and Liberty ship SS *Juan de Fuca*. Both LST's had to be abandoned, but SS *Juan de Fuca* carried on and reached Mindoro safely with the convoy on the 22d. During the return voyage, enemy planes returned to harass the convoy but failed to inflict damage. During the approach to and the retirement from Mindoro, *Young* claimed a total of five unassisted splashes and two assists.

Young's first amphibious assault came during the invasion of Luzon in January 1945. During the main landing on the 9th, she served as a unit of the screen for the landing craft of Attack Group "Baker" and covered part of the landings at Lingayen itself. The assault went off practically unopposed, an example of the new Japanese tactic of fighting an amphibious force inland with conventional infantry tactics rather than trying to smash it at the beach. Since the American troops encountered no real resistance until they had advanced inland well beyond the range of destroyer guns, *Young* and her colleagues had little to do at Lingayen.

That pattern repeated itself at Zambales later in the month when *Young*, in reconnoitering the landing area, encountered a small boat embarking a Filippino guerrilla lieutenant who informed the destroyer that the area had already been secured by his forces. The Zambales landing went off without a shot being fired.

During operations around Subic and Manila Bays, the warship joined *Nicholas* (DD–449) in destroying two Japanese 17-foot suicide boats sent in from Corregidor to break up the Mariveles occupation force on 14 February. Two days later, she participated in the reduction and capture of the source of those boats—Corregidor. She bombarded the "Rock" before the assault and then helped silence enemy batteries on Caballo Island when they opened up on the landing craft. Later that morning, she threaded her way through mine-infested waters to provide gunfire support for the troops taking the island fortress.

During the following weeks, the destroyer conducted patrols out of Subic Bay. In April, she supported the Army's landing on Mindanao, but that operation, thanks to strong Moro guerrilla activity, proved to be another walkover. She continued her patrol operations in the Philippines until the end of the third week in May at which time she received orders to return to the United States for repairs. Steaming via Eniwetok and Pearl Harbor, she arrived in San Francisco Bay on 12 June and began a 47-day overhaul at the Mare Island Navy Yard.

Late in July, she completed her post-overhaul trials and, early in August, headed back toward Pearl Harbor. However, by the time of her arrival, hostilities had already ceased. Instead of continuing west, she began operations in the Hawaii area as escort and plane guard for *Saratoga* (CV–3). On 25 September, she departed Hawaii in company with various units of the 3d Fleet en route to the east coast for the 1945 Navy Day celebration. On 27 October, she arrived in New York where President Harry Truman reviewed the assembled ships.

Young remained in New York until 1 November when she got underway for Charleston, S.C., where she was placed in reserve on 31 January 1946. Finally decommissioned sometime in January 1947, the destroyer remained in reserve until 1 May 1968 at which time her name was struck from the Navy list. On 6 March 1970, she was sunk as a target off the midatlantic coast.

Young (DD–580) earned five battle stars during World War II.

Young, Cassin, see *Cassin Young*.

Young, Stephen, see *Stephen Young*.

Young America

(ScTug: t. 173; dr. 10'6''; a. 1 30-pdr. P.r., 1 32-pdr., 1 12-pdr. r.)

On 24 April 1861, Union sloop-of-war *Cumberland* captured *Young America* in Hampton Roads, Va., as that Confederate tug attempted to help blockade-running schooner *George M. Smith* enter the James River laden with munitions for the Confederacy. *Cumberland* armed the prize—a screw steamer built in 1855 at New York City—and used her as a tender. However, early in June, *Young America* was ordered to the Washington Navy Yard for repairs to her machinery. She broke down while en route and was towed up the Potomac by Union steamer *Resolute*. Repairs completed, the tug departed Washington late in July, bound for Hampton Roads and duty with the North Atlantic Blockading Squadron. After patrol and reconnaissance assignments, *Young America* proceeded to the Baltimore Navy Yard on 13 October 1861 for further repairs and returned to duty in Hampton Roads late in November. On 26 February 1862, the vessel briefly left the Virginia capes area for Currituck Inlet, N.C., to rescue crewmen and stores threatened with capture when Union screw steamer *R. B. Forbes* grounded on 25 February.

Young America performed invaluable service to the squadron during engagements with CSS *Virginia* (the former Federal screw frigate *Merrimack*) on 8 and 9 March 1862. On 8 March, *Young America* towed USS *Roanoke* to an anchorage off Sewell's Point, Va., enabling the frigate to bombard Confederate batteries ashore. On 9 March, she refloated the grounded Union frigate, *St. Lawrence*, and jockeyed the vessel into firing position against *Virginia*. Later, *Young America* rescued the crew of Union gunboat *Whitehall* when fire destroyed that vessel on 10 March 1862. She also rescued personnel on board *Henry Adams*, grounded at Nag's Head, N.C., on 26 August 1862. *Young America* left for repairs at the Baltimore Navy Yard in September.

Young America returned to Hampton Roads in mid-October 1862, resuming duties as an armed guard tug. On 30 November 1862, *Zouave* and *Young America* towed monitor *Passaic* to the Washington Navy Yard for repairs but returned to Newport News early in December and, but for occasional runs north, operated in the vicinity of Hampton Roads and the James River through the end of the Civil War. On 7 January 1864, the tug was finally purchased by the Navy from the Boston prize court.

Young America was assigned to captured Confederate ram CSS *Atlanta* for use as a tug on 9 April 1864 and assisted troops under General Wild in repulsing a Confederate attack upon Wilson's Wharf, James River, Va., on 24 May 1864. She remained with the James River Squadron, Fourth Division, until the end of the war.

Young America was decommissioned on 9 June 1865 at the Norfolk Navy Yard and was sold at public auction at New York City on 12 July 1865 to Camden & Amboy Railroad Co.

Young Rover

(AuxStr: t. 418; l. 141'; b. 28'1''; dr. 11' (f.); s. 13 k.; a. 1 12-pdr. Sawyer r., 4 32-pdrs.)

Young Rover, a bark with auxiliary steam propulsion, was purchased by the Navy at Boston on 27 July 1861; converted to naval service at the Boston Navy Yard; and commissioned there on 10 September 1861, Acting Master I. B. Studley in command.

On 6 September, the warship received orders to report for duty with the Atlantic Blockading Squadron. She arrived in Hampton Roads, Va., on the 17th and was soon dispatched to blockade duty off the Carolinas. On 1 November, she brought help and stood by during the rescue of a Marine Corps battalion and the ship's company of the chartered steamer *Governor* which soon thereafter sank in a heavy gale off the southern Atlantic coast. Later that month, she returned to Hampton Roads and blockaded the mouth of the York River. The warship operated out of Hampton Roads into the spring of 1862 serving as a unit of the North Atlantic Blockading Squadron which was laboring to seal off the Confederate coast. On 17 April 1862, *Young Rover* was reassigned to the Potomac River Flotilla to guard against the traffic in supplies to the South between Maryland and Virginia.

That assignment lasted less than a month. On 14 May 1862, she received orders to join the East Gulf Blockading Squadron at Key West, Fla. She served briefly off the South Pass at the mouth of the Apalachicola River in far northwestern Florida and then settled down to a summer's worth of duty blockading St. Marks on Apalachee Bay where the gulf coast of Florida begins its southward turn, and the Florida panhandle becomes a peninsula. She returned to Key West early in October and, on the 11th, received orders to proceed to Philadelphia for repairs. At the conclusion of the yard work, she resumed duty along the Atlantic coast from the base at Hampton Roads and remained so employed during the winter of 1862 and 1863.

After repairs at Baltimore in April and May of 1863, she returned to Hampton Roads where she began duty as guardship as a consequence of her deteriorating sailing and her almost nonexistent steaming abilities. That assignment, conducted at various locations in the southern Chesapeake Bay—Fortress Monroe, Hampton Roads, and at the mouths of the James and York Rivers—occupied her until the fall of 1864. On 20 November 1864, she received orders to proceed to the Delaware breakwater, there to protect American shipping entering and leaving the Delaware. She departed Hampton Roads on 1 December and arrived at the mouth of the Delaware several days later. For the remainder of the war, she served on the Delaware River under the cognizance of the Commandant, Philadelphia Navy Yard. Following the collapse of the Confederacy, *Young Rover* was sold at auction at the Boston Navy Yard on 22 June 1865.

Youngstown

A city in northwestern Ohio, the seat of Mahoning County.

Youngstown (CL–94)—a *Cleveland*-class light cruiser —was laid down on 4 September 1944 at Philadelphia, Pa., by the Cramp Shipbuilding Co.; but because of the end of hostilities in the Pacific, the contract for her construction was cancelled on 12 August 1945, when the ship had been 54.1 percent completed. On 21 January 1946, the Navy approved the cancellation of the contract and the disposition of the ship, and the unfinished ship was subsequently scrapped on the ways.

Yourasovski

(Former Russian torpedo-boat destroyer: dp. 350; l. 202½'; b. 22'4''; dr. 7'6''; s. 27 k.; cpl. 64; a. 2 11-pdrs., 2 mg., 2 tt.; cl. *Bestrashi*)

Yourasovski, or more properly *Kapitan Yourasovski*—a torpedo-boat destroyer built in 1899 for the Imperial Russian Navy at the Schichau yard in Danzig, Germany—was placed in commission in the Imperial Russian Navy soon thereafter and was assigned to the Siberian Flotilla, probably based at Vladivostok. She served with that unit at least until the beginning of World War I.

Not long after the outbreak of war, she and most of her sisters were transferred to the Russian Baltic Fleet with which she served until the Treaty of Brest-Litovsk ended hostilities on the Eastern Front in March 1918. Sometime before Germany's collapse on the Western Front, *Kapitan Yourasovski* was again transferred, this time to the fleet operating out of Murmansk.

When American forces moved into northern Russia in the spring of 1918, they found the Russian warship in a dilapidated, but repairable, condition. Craftsmen attached to *Olympia* (Cruiser No. 6) set about the task of reconditioning her for service with the Allied interventionist forces. With a crew of 50 from *Olympia's* company, *Kapitan Yourasovski* was placed in service in the summer of 1918. She served as a patrol vessel and a home for 50 American sailors until late 1918 or early 1919 at which time she was placed out of service.

The disposition of the former Imperial Russian torpedo-boat destroyer is not known; however, she does not appear on any postwar Soviet Navy listings. Presumably, she was eventually scrapped.

Yucca

I

(Gunboat: t. 373; l. 145'7''; b. 23'7''; dph. 11'3''; a. 1 30-pdr. Parrott rifle, 1 12-pdr. sb.)

Yucca—a wooden-hulled screw steamer built in 1864 by Donald McKay at East Boston, Mass.—was purchased by the Navy on 25 February 1865 and was commissioned at Boston on 3 April 1865, Acting Master Henry C. Wade in command.

Commissioned just six days before General Lee surrendered the Army of Northern Virginia effectively ending the Civil War, *Yucca* saw no combat in that or any other conflict. Her period of active service covered only three years, most of which she spent on the Gulf Station. By 1868, she had moved to Portsmouth, N.H., where she was placed in ordinary. On 26 August 1868, she was sold at Portsmouth to Mr. R. M. Funkhauser.

Before her keel was laid down on 5 March 1919, Tug No. 32, originally named *Yucca*, was renamed *Napa* (q.v.).

II

(IX–214: dp. 10,749 (dwt.); l. 453'; b. 56'; s. 10 k.; cpl. 70; a. 1 4'', 1 3'', 8 20mm.)

The second *Yucca* (IX–214)—a tanker constructed in 1920 by the Bethlehem Steel Co. at Alameda, Calif., and formerly named SS *Utacarbon*—was acquired from the War Shipping Administration in February 1945; renamed *Yucca* on 9 March 1945; converted to naval use at San Francisco, Calif., and placed in commission on 9 July 1945.

Yucca missed the war entirely. She did not make it to Pearl Harbor until late in August and departed that port on her way to duty in the Central Pacific on 3 September. She stopped at Ulithi Atoll in the Western Carolines on the 22d but continued her voyage that same day, arriving at Buckner Bay, Okinawa, on the

29th. The mobile storage tanker remained there only four days before getting underway for Japan on 3 October. She arrived in Nagoya on the 6th but returned to the Ryukyus later that month. On 11 November, the tanker began her voyage back to the United States. Steaming via Eniwetok in the Marshall Islands and Pearl Harbor, she arrived in the Panama Canal Zone on 6 January 1946, transited the canal and departed the western terminus on 8 January. She arrived in Mobile, Ala., on the 15th and changed operational control to the Commandant, 8th Naval District, for inactivation preparations. *Yucca* was placed out of commission at Mobile on 19 February 1946, and she was returned to the War Shipping Administration for disposal. Her name was struck from the Navy list on 12 March 1946, and she was sold on 24 January 1947 to the Pinto Island Metals Co. for scrapping.

Yukon

A river which rises in the Yukon territory of Canada, then crosses the border into Alaska, and flows on to empty in the Bering Sea.

I

(AF–9: dp. 12,546 (f.); l. 416'10''; b. 53'10''; dr. 25'9'' (f.); s. 12.3 k.; cpl. 229)

The first *Yukon* (AF–9)—a steamer constructed in 1920 as SS *Mehanno* by the Moore Shipbuilding Co. at Oakland, Calif., for the United States Shipping Board—was acquired by the Navy on 14 November 1921; renamed *Yukon*; converted to a stores ship; designated AF–9; and commissioned on 6 December 1921, Comdr. Leo Sahm in command. *Yukon* served briefly as a unit of the Train, Pacific Fleet; however, on 14 April 1922, she was decommissioned and placed in reserve at Philadelphia. She remained there until late in 1939 when she was moved to New York for a partial conversion and preparations for her return to active service. *Yukon* was recommissioned at Brooklyn, N.Y., on 19 January 1940, Comdr. Mays L. Lewis in command.

Following shakedown, *Yukon* was assigned to the Service Force, Atlantic Fleet. During the first two years of her resumed service, the ship made 13 round-trip voyages between the United States and the West Indies. In December 1941, however, her zone of operations was changed to the North Atlantic, and she made a voyage to Reykjavik, Iceland. While returning to the United States from Iceland on 23 January 1942, *Yukon* suffered partial disability when her main air compressor went out. Two days later, USCGC *Alexander Hamilton* came to her aid and took the ship in tow for Reykjavik. On the 29th, *Alexander Hamilton* turned her charge over to the British tug *Frisky* and took up escort station. About an hour later, a torpedo struck the Coast Guard cutter, and *Yukon* went to general quarters. About one-half hour after that, the enemy submarine attacked *Yukon*; but her torpedo missed its mark, passing some 250 yards astern. The cutter remained afloat for about a day before being sunk by American gunfire. *Yukon* arrived safely at Reykjavik where she completed repairs before heading back to the United States. The ship resumed her voyages between the United States and American bases in the Atlantic, visiting such diverse places as Bermuda, Nova Scotia, Iceland, Trinidad, and Newfoundland. On 23 July 1943, while steaming in convoy a few hours out of Sydney, Nova Scotia, SS *El Mirlo* struck *Yukon*, damaging her portside considerably. Nevertheless, the stores ship succeeded in keeping up with the convoy and safely made Argentia, Newfoundland. She made temporary repairs at Argentia, returned to the United States at Boston on 5 August, and began permanent repairs.

Yukon returned to active service in the fall of 1943. Between that time and the summer of 1944, she made four voyages, all to either Bermuda or the West Indies. In July, her itinerary changed. She departed New York on the 11th and anchored in Hampton Roads the following evening. On the morning of 14 July, she passed between Capes Charles and Henry with a 120-ship convoy, UGS 48, bound for the Mediterranean Sea. Upon entering the "middle sea," *Yukon* and two men-of-war, a destroyer and a destroyer escort, parted company with the convoy and set course for Oran, Algeria. She arrived in the North African port on 30 July, discharged some fresh provisions, and took on some cargo bound for Naples. The following day, the stores ship stood out of Oran and headed for the Italian peninsula. She arrived in Naples on 3 August but the following morning received orders to move immediately to Castellamare Bay to provision the fleet preparing for the invasion of southern France. *Yukon* left the Naples area on 5 August and set a course via Palermo on the southern coast of Sicily for Bizerte in Tunisia. The ship entered the North African port on 8 August and, the following day, sailed with a west-bound convoy, GUS–48. On 28 August, after crossing half the Mediterranean and the entire Atlantic, she entered port at Boston.

After upkeep at Boston, she put to sea on 5 September to carry supplies to an Army base located at Ikateg Fjord, Greenland. Steaming via Argentia in Newfoundland and Angmagssalik on the eastern coast of Greenland, she made one false start and then, on her second attempt, successfully navigated Angmagssalik, Ikerrasak, and Ikateg fjords to arrive at the Army airstrip. She began unloading her cargo, an operation made doubly hazardous by large quantities of floating ice. In spite of the danger, *Yukon*'s crew completed the unloading successfully, allowing the ship to leave before the imminent closing of the fjord by ice. She continued her voyage east, bound for Reykjavik, Iceland.

On the afternoon of 22 September, she steamed into the swept channel in the approaches to Reykjavik in company with *Babbitt* (DD–128). At about 1551, she recorded an underwater shock of undetermined origin and reported it to her escort. As *Babbitt* began searching the area, *Yukon* registered another underwater shock of lesser intensity and went to general quarters. Two minutes later at 1552, lookouts observed a torpedo pass astern of the ship and explode about 1,500 yards to her portside. The stores ship began making emergency turns to evade the enemy torpedoes; but, at 1557, one struck her on the starboard side about 50 feet from the stem.

The ship made an emergency turn to starboard and rang up full speed, just in case circumstances forced her to beach. Down by the bow, *Yukon* transferred fuel oil aft and pumped about 60,000 gallons more overboard to correct the problem. Far more serious, her entire bow was blown open from the stem aft to some 60 feet, the outer shell of her double bottom was ruptured to port and starboard, and a dangerous crack appeared across the vessel amidships. Such was her condition when she began limping back to Reykjavik that many on board doubted her ability to make it the short distance into the Icelandic port.

At 1808, after about two hours steaming at barely three knots, Yukon met two tugs sent out from Reykjavik in response to her SOS. She took on board the pilot she had requested and, with the aid of the tugs, moved into the port. Circumstances, however, forced her to ground on the soft mud inshore until the following day when the ship moved into her designated berth.

Yukon completed temporary repairs at Reykjavik and then got underway in company with *O'Toole* (DE–527) and *Abnaki* (ATF–96). After nine days at sea, *Yukon* put into Argentia, Newfoundland, to weather a severe storm. The storm passed, and the ship resumed her voyage to Norfolk, Va., where she arrived on 5 December. She immediately entered the Norfolk Navy Yard and began permanent repairs. She returned to sea in mid-February 1945 and voyaged to New York where she loaded cargo for the West Indies. She stood

out of New York on 18 February, steamed by way of Bermuda to San Juan, Puerto Rico, and returned to Norfolk on 7 March.

Eight days later, the ship passed between Capes Charles and Henry out into the Atlantic on her way to the Pacific. She transited the Panama Canal and continued on to Pearl Harbor. From there, she resumed her voyage west and on 5 May entered the lagoon at Ulithi Atoll in the Western Carolines. Following a 12-day layover, during which she unloaded her cargo, *Yukon* departed Ulithi on the 17th and set a course for the southwestern Pacific. She made an overnight stop at Manus in the Admiralty group on the 21st and 22d and arrived in Auckland, New Zealand, on 4 June. On the 12th, *Yukon* stood out of Auckland and laid a course for Hawaii, arriving in Pearl Harbor on the 28th.

The store ship unloaded her cargo at Pearl, took on a partial one bound for the South Pacific, and got underway again on 8 July. After stops at Espiritu Santo and Noumea, the ship arrived back in Auckland, New Zealand, at the end of the month. *Yukon* departed Auckland on 11 August; and, while the ship steamed toward Hawaii, Japan capitulated. She arrived in Pearl Harbor on the 27th and, after a three-week layover in Hawaii, headed back to the southwestern Pacific, where she made a stop each at Manus in the Admiralty Islands and at Samar in the Philippines.

Departing Samar on 4 November 1945, she steamed back to Pearl Harbor where she stopped for over a month before continuing on to the Panama Canal. She transited the canal sometime between 21 and 24 January 1946 and departed the Canal Zone on the latter day. *Yukon* arrived in Norfolk on the last day of January and began preparations for inactivation. She was decommissioned at Norfolk on 18 March 1946. Her name was struck from the Navy list on 17 April 1946, and she was turned over to the Maritime Commission for custody pending disposal on 1 July 1946. On 29 July, she was sold to the Boston Metals Co., of Baltimore, Md., for scrapping.

II

(AO–152: dp. 32,953 (f.); l. 620'; b. 83.5'; dr. 32'; s. 18.9 k.; cpl. 44; cl. *Maumee*; T. T5–S–12a)

The second *Yukon* (AO–152) was laid down on 16 May 1955 at Pascagoula, Miss., by the Ingalls Shipbuilding Corp.; launched on 16 March 1956; sponsored by Mrs. John P. Womble, Jr.; and placed in service with the Military Sea Transportation Service in May of 1957.

Since then, *Yukon* has been operated by a civilian crew on a contract basis with the Military Sea Transportation Service (now the Military Sealift Command). In so doing, she has carried petroleum products from gulf coast ports and such oil-producing areas as Venezuela and the Persian Gulf to American military bases throughout the world. Those operations have taken her into every ocean and many seas. As of 1979, she continued to operate with the Military Sealift Command carrying oil to American installations abroad.

Yuma

One of the major tribes of Indians who lived on land on both sides of the lower Colorado River, near the present site of what is now Yuma, Arizona.

(Mon: dp. 1,175; l. 225'; b. 45'; dph. 9'1''; s. 9 k.; cpl. 60; a. 2 11'' D. sb.; cl. *Casco*)

Yuma—a twin-screw, shallow-draft, single-turreted river monitor—was laid down at Cincinnati, Ohio, by Alexander Swift and Co., and launched on 30 May 1865. Due to a miscalculation in the displacement of ships of the *Casco*-class, *Yuma*—as originally designed—was unseaworthy. Alterations were accordingly carried out on the vessel during the spring of 1866 to remedy the shortcoming in design, but the ship never saw active service. Laid up from 1866 to 1874, *Yuma* was twice renamed during this time period: first, to *Tempest* on 15 June 1869 and, second, back to *Yuma* on 10 August 1869.

The monitor was subsequently sold at auction to Theodore Allen, at New Orleans, La., on 12 September 1874.

I

(ScTug: t. 136; l. 92'; b. 21'; dr. 10'3'' (mean); cpl. 22)

Asher J. Hudson, later renamed *Yuma*—a tug built at Camden, N.J., by John H. Dialogue and Son and completed between 1888 and 1891—was inspected by the Navy at New Orleans, La., on 1 July 1918 and taken over from the Alabama Coal Transportation Co., of New Orleans, soon thereafter.

Given the classification of SP-3104, *Asher J. Hudson* was commissioned at New Orleans on 1 August 1918. She operated locally out of New Orleans for the duration of the war. The tug was classified YT-37 on 17 July 1920 and subsequently renamed *Yuma.* She was eventually decommissioned and sold on 5 August 1921 to the Crown Towing Co., of New Orleans, La.

II

(AT-94: dp. 1,589 (tl.); l. 205'0''; b. 38'6''; dr. 15'4'' (f.); s. 16.5 k. (tl.); cpl. 85; a. 1 3'', 2 40mm.; cl. *Navajo*)

The second *Yuma* (AT-94) was laid down on 13 February 1943 at Portland, Oreg., by the Commercial Iron Works; launched on 17 July 1943; sponsored by Mrs. W. J. Jones; and commissioned on 31 August 1943, Lt. W. R. J. Hayes in command.

Following shakedown in September and about 10 weeks of operations along the west coast, the tug departed San Francisco on 12 December 1943, bound for the southwestern Pacific. She arrived at Melbourne, Australia, on 1 February 1944 and operated in Australian waters for the next three months, also visiting the ports of Sydney, Fremantle, and Brisbane as a unit of the 7th Fleet. At the end of April, the ship was reassigned to the 3d Fleet and moved to Noumea, New Caledonia. On 4 June, she returned to 7th Fleet jurisdiction at Milne Bay, New Guinea, to prepare for the landings on Noemfoor Island and at Cape Sansapor, both of which she supported in July. In August, she returned to the South Pacific area for duty in the Solomon and New Hebrides Islands. That assignment lasted until February 1945 when she headed for the Marianas and service in support of the 5th Fleet.

She arrived at Saipan on 11 February and remained there until sailing for the invasion of the Ryukyus as a part of the Western Islands Attack Group, Task Group (TG) 51.1, during the third week in March. Attached to the unit assigned to the conquest of Kerama Retto for use as a forward base, she moved into that anchorage almost a week before the initial assault on Okinawa itself on 1 April and remained there until mid-May, supporting the forces afloat around the island. She towed several battle-damaged and kamikaze-crashed ships, including *Hinsdale* (APA-120), crashed by a suicide plane on 1 April during a feigned landing operation along the island's southern coast.

At mid-May, the fleet tug concluded her six-week tour of duty at the Okinawa inferno and set course, via Guam, for Ulithi where she arrived on the 24th. On 7 June, she stood out of Ulithi for a month of duty at Leyte which ended on 18 July with her departure for the Marshalls. She arrived at Eniwetok on 24 July and remained until the beginning of the second week in September. At that time, she departed the Philippines for occupation duty in Japan.

Arriving in Tokyo Bay on 18 September, she provided support services for American forces in Japan until the first week in April 1946. On the 5th, the tug left Japan, bound for Hawaii. She arrived at Oahu on 18 April and remained there until 26 August, when she headed back to the Far East. She arrived in Yokosuka, Japan, on 10 September and resumed duty with American occupation forces in Asia. Over the next six months, she provided towing services in Japan, Korea, the Philippines, China, and the Ryukyus.

Yuma left the Far East again in May 1947, departing from Samar in the Philippines. She stopped at Pearl Harbor briefly in June and continued on to San Francisco, Calif., where she arrived on 10 June. In July, the tug voyaged to Pearl Harbor before returning to the west coast at Puget Sound on the 28th. From that time until February of 1948, she operated along the western coast of the United States, visiting ports in Washington, Oregon, and California. Late in February 1948, she sailed to Pearl Harbor and thence proceeded to the Aleutian Islands where she operated until late August. In September, she steamed to Tsingtao, China, making one round-trip run between Tsingtao and Yokosuka before departing the former port, bound for Oahu on 29 November. The tug entered port at Pearl Harbor on 27 December and remained there until 7 January 1949 at which time she got underway to return to the west coast. She spent February and March engaged in normal west coast operations and in April returned to the Aleutians where she served until late August. The tug resumed duty along the California coast upon her arrival in San Francisco on 27 August. In December, she made a round-trip voyage to Pearl Harbor and back to the west coast.

On 9 February 1950, *Yuma* departed San Diego for Oahu and arrived in Pearl Harbor 10 days later. After almost two months of duty at Pearl Harbor, the tug got underway on 10 April for a mission in the Pacific Trust Territories. Based at Guam, she performed duty at Taongi Atoll and Kusaie Island in the Carolines, at Koror in the Palaus, and at Saipan. On 9 July, she departed Guam and, four days later, arrived in Yokosuka, Japan. That move, however, did not presage her early participation in the war which had broken out in Korea just two weeks earlier for, after visits to Sasebo in Japan and to Subic Bay in the Philippines, she returned to Guam on 2 August and resumed duty in the Pacific Trust Territories for another year. During that 12-month period, she visited Japanese ports and, no doubt, performed missions in distant support for the United Nations forces fighting in Korea. She also made several voyages to Pearl Harbor and operated at various islands—notably Kwajalein, Eniwetok, and Guam—in the Trust Territories. In September 1951, she returned to Japan, arriving at Sasebo on the 17th. With that arrival, *Yuma* began her seven months of duty in the combat zone. She made numerous voyages between Japanese ports and Wonsan, Korea, in support of the troops and ships fighting in and around Korea.

She concluded her brief interlude with the Korean conflict on 22 April 1952 when she departed Sasebo, bound for Pearl Harbor. She arrived in Oahu on 5 May and, for most of the year, made voyages from Pearl Harbor to Eniwetok and Kwajalein in the Marshalls in support of the nuclear testing in progress at those islands. She completed that service in November, returning to Pearl Harbor on the 21st. In January and February 1953, she operated at Midway Island with *Current* (ARS-22) during the salvage of a grounded civilian ship, SS *Quartette.* Following overhaul at Pearl Harbor during the spring and summer of 1953, she returned to the Aleutians once more for duty and, for the next 18 months, alternated between Alaskan and Hawaiian waters.

In February 1955, the tug returned to the west coast where she operated until decommissioned on 11 November 1955. *Yuma* was berthed at Astoria, Oreg., until 17 January 1958 at which time she was placed in service. She cruised the coasts of Washington, Oregon, and California for most of the year. On 3 December, she departed Astoria and headed—via Pearl Harbor and Midway—for the Far East. She arrived in Yokosuka on 16 January 1959, at Hong Kong on 3 February, Singapore on 20 February, Ceylon on 27 February, Bombay on 7 March, and finally at Karachi, Pakistan, on 11 March. There, she was placed out of service and turned over to Pakistan on loan. Her name was struck from the Navy list on 25 March 1959.

Yuma earned two battle stars during World War II and another pair during the Korean War.

III

(YTM–748: dp. 310 (f.); l. 107′; b. 27′; dr. 12′; s. 12 k. (tl.); cpl. 16; cl. *Chicopee*)

The third *Yuma*, a medium harbor tug, was acquired by the Navy in September 1964 from the Army, which she had served as *LT–2078*. Named *Yuma* and designated YTM–748, she was assigned to the 12th Naval District and served as a harbor tug at San Francisco, Calif., until placed out of service in August 1976. She was then assigned to the Pacific Reserve Fleet and was berthed at Bremerton, Wash., where she remained as of 1979.

Yurok

An Indian tribe which inhabited the lower reaches of the Klamath River in far northern California.

On 7 November 1945, while still on the ways, *Yurok* (ATF–164)—laid down as an *Abnaki*-class fleet tug—was reclassified a submarine rescue vessel, redesignated ASR–19, and renamed *Bluebird* (q.v.).

Yustaga

An American Indian tribe which occupied the area of northern Florida surrounding the upper reaches of the Suwannee during the 16th century.

(ASR–20: dp. 1,735 (f.); l. 205′0″; b. 39′3″; dr. 15′6″ (lim.); s. 16 k.; cpl. 106; cl. *Penguin*)

Yustaga (ATF–165) was laid down in July 1945 at Charleston, S.C., by the Charleston Shipbuilding & Drydock Co.; redesignated a submarine rescue vessel on 11 October 1945; assigned the hull designation ASR–20 on 13 November 1945; renamed *Skylark* on 5 December 1945; launched on 19 March 1946; sponsored by Mrs. H. C. Weatherly; and was placed in the Atlantic Reserve Fleet, berthed first at Charleston and later at New London, Conn., until 1 March 1951 at which time she was finally commissioned, Lt. Comdr. Romolo Cousins in command.

Following restricted availability at the Portsmouth (N.H.) Naval Shipyard, *Skylark* conducted her shakedown cruise and training out of Norfolk, Va., during July. The ship then returned to New London and operated out of that base, practicing submarine rescues and serving as a target recovery ship for submarines conducting torpedo-firing drills. In April 1952, the ship temporarily moved south to relieve *Petrel* (ASR–14) as rescue vessel at Key West, Fla., while the latter ship underwent an overhaul. In June, she returned north to New London to resume her former duties. During January and February 1953, *Skylark* was overhauled at the Philadelphia Naval Shipyard; and, after refresher training at Newport, R.I., during March and April, she spent May at Norfolk filling in for *Kittiwake* (ASR–13) while the latter ship went into the shipyard for overhaul. In June, she returned to New London and carried out her training schedule until October when she again headed back to Norfolk to substitute for *Kittiwake*, while the latter participated in Operation "Springboard." Upon the conclusion of that brief assignment, she resumed her New London-based routine. In February and March of 1954, *Skylark* engaged in her own share of Operation "Springboard" exercises,

providing services to Atlantic Fleet submarines during the annual training evolution. She returned to New London late in March and resumed her usual duties. In September, the ship entered the Boston Naval Shipyard for a two-month overhaul.

Until the beginning of 1962, *Skylark* continued the pattern of duties described above. She operated out of New London the majority of the time but, periodically, did temporary duty elsewhere, notably at Norfolk and Key West, taking over briefly the duties of *Kittiwake* or *Petrel* when either ship was incapacitated due to repairs. She also operated regularly in the West Indies during the annual "Springboard" exercises. The one notable exception to that pattern occurred in January and February of 1955 when she assisted *Nautilus* (SSN–571), the Navy's first nuclear-powered submarine, in completing her builders' trials.

At the beginning of 1962, the submarine rescue vessel began a new phase of her career when regular deployments to the 6th Fleet in the Mediterranean became a normal aspect of her activities and continued to be for the remainder of her naval service. She embarked upon the first such cruise on 8 January 1962. During that assignment, she served as flagship of Task Force (TF) 69 and participated in the search for an Air Force jet fighter which crashed at sea near Malaga, Spain. On 7 May 1962, she returned to New London and resumed her duties with the Atlantic Fleet. In April of 1963, she was one of the first ships to answer the distress call sent by *Thresher* (SSN–593) before she sank during diving tests. *Skylark* also participated in the unsuccessful search for the submarine which was conducted for several days after the loss. In July 1963, she was deployed to the Mediterranean once more and again served as flagship of TF 69. That cruise lasted until late October, and *Skylark* reentered New London on 2 November. Nineteen months of duty out of her home port, along the Atlantic coast of the United States, followed her return home.

On 7 July 1965, the submarine rescue vessel stood out of New London once more, bound for the Mediterreanean and duty in support of 6th Fleet submarines. During the latter portion of that cruise, *Skylark* served for several weeks at the ballistic missile submarine base located in Holy Loch, Scotland, before returning home to New London on 29 October. During the remaining eight years of her Navy career, the ship alternated duty along the Atlantic coast of the United States with deployments to the Mediterranean and to the submarine base at Holy Loch. In the spring of 1968, she participated in the unsuccessful rescue attempt and search for *Scorpion* (SSN–589), the second American nuclear-powered submarine to be lost at sea. Her only other major departure from her routine came in June of 1972 when she participated in NATO Exercise "Pink Lace" before beginning a scheduled deployment to Holy Loch and the Mediterranean in July. She returned to New London on 18 November 1972, completing the last deployment of her career. On 30 June 1973, *Skylark* was decommissioned, and her name was struck from the Navy list. On that same day, she was sold to the Brazilian Navy and commissioned as *Gastao Moutinho* (K. 10). As of 1979, she was still an active unit of the Brazilian Fleet.

Z

Zaanland

A river in tne Netherlands which flows past Amsterdam and into the Zuider Zee.

(Freighter: t. 5,417 (gross); l. 389′4″; b. 51′1″; dr. 23′6″ (mean); s. 9 k.; cpl. 81)

Zaanland—a steel-hulled, single-screw cargo vessel

completed in 1900 at Port Glasgow, Scotland, by Russell and Co.—was owned by the *Koninklijke Hollandsche Lloyd* line at the outbreak of World War I. The ship sought security at Hampton Roads, Va., lest, at sea, she fall prey to warships of the Royal Navy. Acquired by the Navy for use by the Naval Overseas Transportation Service (NOTS) on 25 March 1918, the cargo ship was assigned the identification number (Id. No.) 2746 and commissioned at Hampton Roads on 29 March 1918, Lt. Comdr. Daniel Brown, USNRF, in command.

Zaanland was repaired and fitted out at Newport News, Va., by the Newport News Shipbuilding and Drydock Co., before sailing for the Gulf of Mexico on 4 April. Arriving at New Orleans, La., on the 11th, she simultaneously underwent further repairs and conversion work and loaded 4,946 tons of general cargo consigned by the Army Quartermaster Corps. She later departed from New Orleans on 20 April and arrived back at Hampton Roads five days later.

Zaanland sailed from Norfolk on 30 April in Convoy HN–67, bound for La Pallice, France. During the voyage, in a heavy mist at 2026 on 12 May, she apparently suffered a rudder casualty and was rammed by the tanker *Hisko* (Id. No. 1953). The collision tore a jagged, 15-foot hole in the cargo ship's starboard side, amidships between her bridge and fireroom. *Zaanland* soon assumed a heavy list and began to sink by the bow. At 2040, all hands were called topside as boats were launched. Within an hour, all of *Zaanland*'s crew were safely aboard the Army transport *Munalbro*.

Although settling deeper in the water with each passing hour, the cargo ship remained afloat into the next day. At 0400, Lt. Comdr. Brown reboarded *Zaanland* and inspected the ship. He found that there was no hope of towing the vessel to port and predicted that she probably would sink within a few hours. His observation proved to be correct, for *Zaanland* sank, bow first, at 0710 on 13 May 1918.

Munalbro, while endeavoring to overtake the convoy, soon met SS *Minnesota* en route, and transferred *Zaanland*'s crew to the west-bound vessel for passage back to the United States.

Zaca

Probably a Chumash Indian word meaning "village," or "chief."

I

(Freighter: dp. 12,600; l. 416'6''; b. 53'; dr. 26'5¼'' (mean); s. 10 k.; cpl. 70; a. none)

The first *Zaca*—a steel-hulled, single-screw freighter built under a United States Shipping Board contract and completed in 1918 at Oakland, Calif., by the Moore Shipbuilding Co.—was acquired by the Navy for duty with the Naval Overseas Transportation Service (NOTS); designated Id. No. 3792, and commissioned on 30 December 1918 at her builder's yard, Lt. Comdr. James J. Carey, USNRF, in command.

Following sea trials, *Zaca* loaded 7,446 tons of flour at the Sperry Mills Dock, Vallejo, Calif., and got underway from San Francisco Bay on 12 January 1919, bound for the east coast. While in the Canal Zone, the freighter took on board 41 passengers for transportation to Norfolk and transited the Panama Canal on the 30th. She arrived in Hampton Roads on 8 February.

Zaca spent a week at Norfolk replenishing and undergoing minor repairs before sailing for European waters on 15 February with her cargo of flour which had been consigned by the United States Food Administration for the relief of the hungry people of war-torn Europe. After arriving at the free city of Danzig on 19 March, she discharged her cargo and sailed for the United States on 4 April.

Proceeding via Rotterdam, Netherlands, and Plymouth, England, *Zaca* arrived at New York City on 29 April, unloaded her ballast, and was decommissioned on 12 May 1919. Simultaneously returned to the Shipping Board and struck from the Navy list on that same day, *Zaca* operated under the flag of the United States Shipping Board until the latter half of 1925, when her name disappears from shipping registers.

II

(Sch: t. 122 (gross); l. 118'; b. 23'9''; dr. 14'; dph. 11'; s. 9 k.; cpl. 10)

The second *Zaca*—a wooden-hulled, schooner-rigged yacht with an auxiliary engine—was designed by Garland Rotch and completed in 1930 at Sausalito, Calif., by Nunes Bros. Due to the need for local patrol and rescue craft in the busy waters in the San Francisco area during World War II, the schooner was acquired by the Navy from Templeton Crocker on 12 June 1942. Placed in service on 19 June 1942 and assigned to the Western Sea Frontier, *Zaca*—classified a miscellaneous auxiliary and designated IX–73—operated as a plane-guard ship, standing ready to rescue the crews of any planes downed nearby.

Eventually relieved by the frigates (PF's) of Escort Squadron 41, *Zaca* was placed out of service at Treasure Island, Calif., on 6 October 1944; and her name was struck from the Navy list on 13 November 1944. Turned over to the War Shipping Administration on 21 May 1945, *Zaca* was acquired in 1946 by Errol Flynn, an actor famed for his "swashbuckling" roles in numerous movies. Flynn owned the yacht until his death in 1959.

Zafiro

(Collier: t. 1,062 (gross); l. 213'8½''; b. 31'9½''; dr. 15.6'; s. 10.5 k. (tl.); cpl. 1 (1898), 45 (1900); a. 2 37mm. revolving cannons (1900))

Zafiro—a collier constructed in 1884 at Aberdeen, Scotland, by Hall Russell & Co.—was purchased for the Navy by Admiral Dewey at Hong Kong on 9 April 1898 just before his squadron sailed for the Philippines. Though the *Secretary of the Navy's Report* for 1900 indicates that she was placed in commission on 10 April 1898, her role as a commissioned ship must have been unique indeed for her complement showed only one Navy man, her commanding officer. Her status in the Navy from 1898 to 1900 is further complicated by the fact that there are no deck logs extant for her during the period. Her first log begins on 20 September 1900. Finally, after her service in the Spanish-American War, she had no naval complement on board until Ens. L. A. Cotten reported on board to assume command on 10 May 1900. Thus, the date upon which she was placed in commission cannot be established with any precision.

In any event, she sailed from Hong Kong with Dewey's Fleet and served with it as a collier and supply ship during the Battle of Manila Bay and the ensuing Philippines campaign. The lack of documents covering her activities in 1898 and the first half of 1899 precludes any detailed narrative for that period. Presumably, she plied the waters of the Philippine Islands carrying troops, supplies, and dispatches between points in the archipelago. Based at Cavite on Luzon, she is known to have performed such missions during the period from July 1899 to June 1904. Those movements —in support of the Army's suppression of the Philippine insurrection and campaigns against the Moslem Moro tribesmen—took her to a host of exotic places, and length and breadth of the islands. On 10 June 1904, *Zafiro* was placed out of commission at Cavite. Her name was struck from the Navy list on 15 January 1906; and, on 21 October 1910, she was sold to Mr. J. W. Zeeve of Seattle, Wash.

Zahma

(Ketch: t. 75 (gross); l. 93'; b. 20'7''; dph. 9'10''; dr. 7'9'' (mean); s. 8 k.; cpl. 6)

Zahma—a wooden-hulled ketch with an auxiliary engine—was designed by B. B. Crowninshield and completed in 1915 at Neponset, Mass., by George Lawley and Son, Corp., for John H. Cromwell of Cold Spring Harbor, Long Island, N.Y. Inspected by the Navy at the entry of the United States into World War I for possible service as a patrol craft, the vessel was rejected as "unsuitable for naval use."

A quarter of a century later, the exigencies of war changed the Navy's evaluation of the graceful craft, as she was again inspected—this time at the 11th Naval District—in early 1942. Acquired by the Port Director of San Diego from R. J. Rheem on 13 February, *Zahma* was placed in service on 26 February 1942. Classified as a miscellaneous axiliary and designated IX–63, *Zahma* was based at San Diego and operated as a local patrol craft into the spring of 1943. Placed out of service on 13 April 1943, *Zahma's* name was struck from the Navy list on 18 July 1944.

Zane

Randolph Talcott Zane—born on 12 August 1887 in Philadelphia—was appointed a second lieutenant in the United States Marine Corps on 6 January 1909 and, a month later, reported for duty to the Headquarters, United States Marine Corps in Washington, D.C. After instruction at the Marine Officers' School, Port Royal, S.C., Zane joined the Marine detachment in battleship *New Hampshire* at Guantanamo Bay, Cuba, on 27 December 1909.

Detached from *New Hampshire* in the summer of 1911, Zane next served ashore at the Naval Prison, Portsmouth, N.H., until December. Reporting to the Marine Barracks at Washington, D.C., on Christmas Day, 1911, Zane became post quartermaster on 1 January 1912 and held the post until 15 February 1913.

Zane then saw temporary expeditionary service in early 1913, sailing from Norfolk, Va., with Company "I," 2d Regiment, 2d Provisional Brigade of Marines, on board auxiliary cruiser *Prairie* and disembarked at Guantanamo Bay on 27 February. Reembarked in *Prairie* exactly three months later, Zane returned to Washington on 2 June.

After subsequent shore duty at the Marine Barracks at Puget Sound, Wash., and at Mare Island, Calif., and sea duty in the armored cruisers *South Dakota* and *West Virginia*, Zane joined the 4th Marine Regiment at San Diego, Calif., on 29 December 1914. He next served two more tours ashore—at Pearl Harbor, Territory of Hawaii, and at Quantico, Va., before he embarked in the transport *Henderson* on 19 January 1918, bound for France.

By that point a major, Zane served his first tour of duty "over there" in the Bourmont, France, training area, with the 6th Marine Regiment. Then, he went to the front lines, southeast of the famous battlefield at Verdun, where he remained from mid-March to mid-May. After moving with his unit to Vitry-le-François and then to Gisors-Chaumont-en-Vexin, Zane and his companions received urgent orders sending them to the Chateau-Thierry sector.

Maj. Zane participated in the fighting in the vicinity of Belleau Wood, when the untried marines came up against the 461st Imperial German Infantry, a unit that Colonel Robert D. Heinl called "the largest single body of combat-seasoned regular troops which Marines had confronted since Bladensburg." Zane took part in the second phase of the assault, when the 2d and 3d Battalions, 6th Marines, entered the wood, and remained in action through the entire period of fighting. Tragically, Zane was wounded and shell-shocked on

26 June. He never recoovered from his injuries and died on 24 October 1918.

(DD–337: dp. 1,215 (n.); l. 314'4½''; b. 30'11½''; dr. 9'4'' (mean); s. 35.0 k.; cpl. 122; a. 4 4'', 1 3'', 12 21'' tt.; cl. *Clemson*)

Zane (Destroyer No. 337) was laid down on 15 January 1919 at the Mare Island Navy Yard, Vallejo, Calif.; launched on 12 August 1919; sponsored by Miss Marjorie Zane, the daughter of Major R. T. Zane; reclassified DD–337 on 17 July 1920; and commissioned at Mare Island on 15 February 1921, Lt. Comdr. P. Seymour in command.

After fitting out and shakedown, *Zane* fueled at Port Costa, Calif., late in June 1921 and sailed northward to the Puget Sound Navy Yard, Bremerton, Wash., for stores. Returning south to Mare Island once more, *Zane* joined Destroyer Division 14 at San Francisco, Calif., on 22 June and departed that port the following day, bound for the Asiatic Station.

Sailing via Pearl Harbor, Midway, and Guam, *Zane* reached Cavite, Philippine Islands, on 24 August. The destroyer then operated in the Philippines—out of Cavite, Manila, Olongapo, and Lingayen Gulf—on maneuvers and exercises through the spring of 1922. She departed Manila on 3 June 1922, bound for Chinese waters.

Zane reached the Yangtze estuary on 6 June and, while steaming to the mouth of the Whangpoo River, en route to Shanghai, spotted the Chinese river steamer *Tse Kiang* approaching from the starboard quarter. Apparently, the latter knew very little about the rules of the nautical road, as she maintained course and speed, doing nothing to avoid a collision. *Zane* attempted to avoid a fouling when that seemed imminent—but too late. At 1158, *Tse Kiang* rammed the destroyer aft.

Fortunately, the damage was minor; and *Zane* proceeded on her way, reaching Shanghai two and one-half hours later and moored alongside sistership *Rathburne* (DD–113) at the American buoys. *Zane* entered the Yangtsepoo drydock on 15 June for repairs and was undocked on the following day.

Underway for Chefoo on 5 July, *Zane* reached that North China port on the 7th and remained there until the 30th, when she shifted to Chinwangtao, the seaport at the base of the Great Wall of China, to send leave parties to Peking. She lay at Chinwangtao from 31 July to 5 Augst, when she got underway to return to Chefoo on the latter day.

Zane set sail from Chefoo, homeward bound, on 25 August and visited Nagasaki, Japan, on the first leg of her voyage back to the west coast of the United States. Subsequently touching at Midway and Pearl Harbor, the destroyer reached San Francisco on 2 October. Shifting to the Mare Island Navy Yard on 9 October, *Zane* turned in all torpedoes, torpedo gear, and landing force equipment over the three days that ensued. She then fueled at Martinez, Calif., before reaching San Diego and San Pedro. Decommissioned at San Diego on 1 February 1923, *Zane* remained on "Red Lead Row" for seven years.

Recommissioned on 25 February 1930, Lt. Comdr. C. J. Parrish in command, *Zane* operated actively as a unit of the Battle Force for the next decade, except for one brief period during which time she was attached to Rotating Reserve Squadron 20 in late 1934. Initially assigned to Destroyer Division 10, Destroyer Squadron 4, Destroyers, Battle Force, Destroyer Flotilla 2, the ship served through the 1930's in a variety of squadrons, but all within the 2d Destroyer Flotilla.

She participated in some of the inter-war fleet problems—the large-scale fleet maneuvers instituted in the early 1920's that saw the development of equipment and tactics which were used during World War II. She ranged from the west coast of the United States into the Caribbean and western Atlantic Ocean, as well as off the Canal Zone.

However, with the new destroyer construction programs turning out more modern, faster, more heavily armed ships, the need to retain the old "flush-deckers" in the destroyer role diminished. At the same time, there grew a need for high-speed minesweepers, fast minelayers, seaplane tenders, and the like to meet the ever-growing demands on the Navy.

Converted to a high-speed minesweeper at the Pearl Harbor Navy Yard and reclassified as DMS–14 on 19 November 1940, *Zane* operated primarily in Hawaiian waters on the eve of World War II. On the morning of 7 December 1941, she was moored off Pearl City in a nest with her three sisterships of Mine Division 4—*Trever* (DMS–16), *Wasmuth* (DMS–15), and *Perry* (DMS–17).

The crew was just finishing breakfast when, at 0757, a signalman on watch topside observed a single plane drop a bomb on the southern end of Ford Island after a long gliding approach from the northward. Only then did the men topside realize it was a Japanese plane.

With 10 percent of her enlisted men and 25 percent of the officers ashore, *Zane* went to general quarters and, within three minutes of the initial explosion, had manned her .50-caliber antiaircraft machine gun battery. Her commanding officer, Lt. Comdr. L. M. LeHardy, was senior officer afloat in the division and reported: "0800 Observed Japanese plane gliding low over Ford Island, enemy character now positive. This was not a drill."

Commencing fire at "any and all planes which passed within a reasonable distance of the nest," *Zane* began preparations at 0803 for getting underway, as belting and ammunition supply parties turned to. At 0830, *Zane* spotted a "strange submarine" 200 yards astern of *Medusa* (AR–1), anchored in nearby berth K–23. *Zane*'s position in the nest, however, rendered her incapable of opening fire with her after 4-inch gun—her aim was fouled by *Perry* (DMS–17), moored outboard. However, *Monaghan* (DD–354) soon made the whole problem academic at 0840, when she charged down upon the Japanese type "A" midget submarine and destroyed her by ramming and with depth charges.

Meanwhile, the fleet gradually began to fight back and, by the time the second wave of Japanese planes arrived, the enemy found a decidedly hot reception. Gunfire from a nearby ship—possibly *Medusa*—brought down one Japanese plane, whose bomb burst in the water near *Perry*. The enemy aircraft exploded into flames on the way down and crashed on shore near the recently completed deperming station to the loud cheers of all hands topside in *Zane*.

Subsequently, the ships of MinDiv 4 got underway individually and stood out to take up patrol offshore. *Zane* had suffered no damage from the enemy during the raid, but the melee of "friendly" antiaircraft fire from a number of ships nearby—including some in the nest itself—had severed a number of strands of rigging and antennae.

At 1410, *Zane* and *Wasmuth* rigged up a twin-ship, moored-mine sweep with 400 fathoms of wire between them and entered the Pearl Harbor entrance channel at 1547, sweeping up to the vicinity of the gate vessel before the sweep wire parted. Subsequently returning to sea, *Zane* resumed antisubmarine patrols, carrying them out at a time when submarine sightings—most of them fictitious—proliferated.

Zane operated locally out of Pearl Harbor into the spring of 1942. She departed the Hawaiian Islands on 5 April, escorting an 8-knot convoy (number 4079) to San Pedro, Calif. The high-speed minesweeper then underwent repairs and alterations at the Mare Island Navy Yard before she returned to Pearl Harbor in early June.

Meanwhile, the tide of war was beginning to turn. Eight months after Pearl Harbor, the United States Navy was ready to launch its first amphibious operation—codenamed "Watchtower." The target: the Japanese-held Solomon Islands. The jump-off date: 7 August 1942.

American intelligence knew that numerous unmined areas existed off the objective beachheads, but invasion planners thought it best to at least determine the exact boundaries of any minefields that existed in the areas. Accordingly, *Zane* and four of her sisterships—*Hopkins* (DMS–13), *Southard* (DMS–10), *Hovey* (DMS–11), and *Trever*—were to sweep an area extending from the 100-fathom curve toward Port Purvis in the Gavutu Island area before splitting into two groups to head simultaneously toward beach "Red," clearing a 1,000-yard wide stretch through Lengo Channel toward Indispensable Strait. Japanese shore batteries opened up on the ships, but their fire was erratic, and the enemy did no damage. By 1550 on D day, 7 August, the area had been thoroughly swept. No mines were found.

Over the ensuing weeks, the battle for Guadalcanal waxed hot, with the Japanese stubbornly maintaining themselves on the island. The Americans were compelled to bring in their reinforcements during the daylight hours when they controlled the skies. At night, the Japanese—with their superior night-fighting capabilities—ruled the roost in the Solomons. *Zane* worked off Tulagi and Guadalcanal, breaking her sweep and patrol operations with periodic upkeep at Noumea, New Caledonia. On 8 September, during one such sweep operation, the minesweeper watched waves of high flying Japanese planes heading toward Guadalcanal.

Into the autumn, as the fighting ashore became more desperate, the need for supplies—particularly aviation gasoline to keep the "Cactus Air Force" in the air—multiplied. At Espiritu Santo, *Zane* and her sistership *Trever* piled drums of aviation gasoline on their decks, together with torpedoes, ammunition and stores, and—each with two motor torpedo (PT) boats in tow—set sail for Guadalcanal. They reached Tulagi Harbor at 0530 on 25 October 1942.

Trever completed her unloading by 0700. At 0809, the general air raid alarm sounded from ashore. *Trever* cast off and stood into the harbor itself; *Zane* got underway about the same time and lay to about 700 yards ahead of *Trever* in the shelter of Tulagi, Kokotambu, and Songoangona Islands.

At 0955, the signal station at Tulagi informed both ships that three enemy ships had been sighted in the straits between Savo and Florida Islands, entering "Iron Bottom Bay." *Trever*'s commanding officer, the task group commander, Comdr. D. M. Agnew, took a dim view of the recommendation that his ships seek shelter up the Maliala River. Not wanting to be, in his words, "trapped like rats," Agnew elected to run.

Zane and *Trever*—their old engines throbbing—stood out at maximum speed and cleared the channel leading out of Tulagi at 1014. Lookouts noted the stacks and mast-tops of three ships almost simultaneously—21,000 yards distant and bearing 250 degrees, steering a slightly converging course. Within five minutes, the American lookouts noted that the trio of enemy ships had altered course to close.

The three enemy ships—the destroyers *Akatsuki*, *Ikazuchi*, and *Shiratsuyu*—comprised the 1st Attack Unit, dispatched to provide naval gunfire support during the day to Japanese land forces who had hoped to capture Henderson Field. Each of the Japanese ships—with their six 5-inch guns—outgunned their American counterparts who carried but five.

At 1020, the enemy formation changed course again to close the range still further and bring their heavier batteries to bear. *Zane* and *Trever*, meanwhile, skirted the shoal waters on course for Sealark Channel. Ten minutes later, with the range at approximately 9,200 yards, the Japanese destroyers opened fire, and the running sea fight was on.

The Japanese—in view of their slated mission—were using bombardment ammunition instead of armor-piercing shells. Soon shells began landing disturbingly close to the zig-zagging *Trever* and *Zane*. The latter for example, observed one shell land just forward of her bow and one apiece on each side of the forecastle, off the bows. One enemy shell scored a direct hit on *Zane*, hitting the minesweeper's number one 3-inch mount, forward, killing three men instantly. Other shells cut away rigging, antennae, and every halyard except the one to the gaff. That one appropriately flew the national ensign.

Providentially, at 1040, the Japanese ships turned away to engage *Seminole* (AT-65) and a small patrol craft off Lunga Point. The respite offered the two high-speed minesweepers proved fatal to the fleet tug and the YP—the Japanese ships sank them summarily before retiring, harried by American planes from Henderson Field. *Trever* and *Zane*, meanwhile, continued to retire to the eastward. At 1055, the two minecraft changed course to the south and west of San Cristobal Island.

Zane remained in the forward areas of the Southwest Pacific theater through the end of 1942. Again in company with *Trever*, the high-speed minesweeper towed PT boats of Motor Torpedo Boat Squadron 2 from Noumea to Espiritu Santo in mid-November. *Zane* later escorted a convoy from the New Hebrides to Tulagi and Guadalcanal before being sent to Sydney, Australia, in January 1943 for repairs and a well-deserved rest for her crew.

While at Sydney, *Zane* was called upon to perform a rescue mission. On 22 January 1943, the Japanese submarine *I-21*—a craft with an impressive record of "kills" since scoring her first on Christmas Eve 1941—torpedoed and disabled the American steamship *Peter H. Burnett*. The next day, *Zane* received orders to proceed to the last reported position of the crippled steamer.

At 1255 on 25 January, *Zane* spotted a Royal Australian Air Force (RAAF) Catalina flying boat. She, in turn, led the minesweeper to the location of *Peter H. Burnett*'s lifeboat number three. Apparently, the steamer's crew and passengers had thought the ship would sink as a result of the torpedo damage aft and abandoned her; their ship, however, was still afloat.

Zane took on board 14 men—12 crewmembers (including the Master, Charles Darling) and two U.S. Army passengers—at 1330 and altered course to head for the last reported position of the ship from which the men had come. The RAAF Catalina then helpfully radioed the position of the derelict, enabling *Zane* to reach the scene at 1735. She then transferred, via motor whaleboat, 13 of the men back to their ship; one man had been retained on board *Zane* under medical treatment for his injuries suffered when the steamer had been torpedoed. The minesweeper then took *Peter H. Burnett* in tow and pulled her to Sydney, where they both arrived safely on the 27th.

Zane returned to Guadalcanal in late February. In her absence, there had been a change in the situation on that once bitterly contested isle—the Japanese had evacuated it on 7 and 8 February, leaving it in American hands at last.

There was more work to be done, however, in the wake of "Watchtower." With Guadalcanal finally secured, American planners looked toward the Russells —60 miles west northwest of Guadalcanal—isles chiefly remembered by visitors for "rain, mud, and magnificent coconuts." The operation code-named "Cleanslate," was the first forward island-jumping movement made in the South Pacific.

Zane, as part of Task Unit (TU) 61.1.3, towed four landing craft—two LCVP's, one LCV and an LCM—to the objective area. As part of the "Spit Kit Expeditionary Force," the minesweeper thus put into action part of the troops slated to occupy the Russells. On 21 February 1943, Operation "Cleanslate" commenced but encountered no opposition from the enemy, who had only recently evacuated the islands. As Vice Admiral George C. Dyer wrote in his biography of Admiral Richmond K. Turner, *The Amphibians Came to Conquer*, " 'Cleanslate' went off with precision, but without fanfare or publicity."

Dyer has also written that the amphibious forces

"had an excellent opportunity to put together the dozens of suggestions arising out of 'Watchtower' for the improvement of amphibious operations and test them under conditions far more rugged than any rear area rehearsal could provide. The Russells added not only skill but confidence to the amphibians." Upon the wrap-up of "Cleanslate," Admiral Turner himself reported that the operation had developed the technique for moving troops without the benefit of attack cargo ships (AKA's) or attack transports (APA's). Turner expected that that experience would prove useful in planning future offensives.

For *Zane*, her next amphibious operation was "Toenails"—the assault and occupation of New Georgia. *Zane* and *Talbot* (APD-7) comprised TU 31.1.1, the "Onaiavisi Occupation Unit." Each picked up a company of the Army's 169th Infantry Regiment and an LCVP in the Russells on 29 June and headed for their objective, the two small islands guarding the most direct approach to Zanana Beach on New Georgia Island. That beach was slated to be the jump-off point for the flanking attack on strategic Munda airfield.

Bad weather—low ceilings, moderate showers with corresponding poor visibility, shifting and gusty winds, and choppy seas—hampered "Toenails" from the start; but *Zane* and *Talbot* reached the Onaiavisi channel entrance at around 0225 on 30 June to begin their task. However, shortly before 0300, *Zane* grounded during a heavy rain squall while disembarking her troops. Nevertheless, the mishap did not hamper the landing process; for both *Zane* and *Talbot* succeeded in putting both companies of the 169th Regiment ashore without loss on Dume (now known as Sasavele Island) and Baraulu Islands to hold the Onaiavisi entrance until the shore-to-shore movement could commence to Zanana Beach.

Zane remained aground forward until 0523, when she finally managed to back free. However, the high-speed minesweeper grounded aft almost immediately, damaging her propellers. Again she tried using her own power to get free but, despite aid by *Talbot*, could not do so. *Zane*'s predicament was far from good: she was a sitting duck, only five miles from Japanese-held Munda airstrip. Providentially, as Admiral Dyer recounts, "no alert Japanese artillery man hauled up a battery to take *Zane* under fire."

Rail (AT-139)—having received the summons at 0942—finally pulled *Zane* off the rocks at 1419. The fleet tug (a former minesweeper herself) then took *Zane* back to the Solomons for repairs, arriving at Tulagi on 2 July.

After enough temporary patching to permit the ship to leave Guadalcanal under her own power, *Zane* headed via Espiritu Santo and Pearl Harbor to the Mare Island Navy Yard for permanent repairs and alterations. The high-speed minesweeper again sailed westward on 23 September, departing Mare Island, bound for Pearl Harbor. Reaching Oahu on 30 September, she remained in the Hawaiian operating area for the rest of the year 1943 and through mid-January 1944.

Departing Pearl Harbor on 22 January 1944, *Zane* subsequently took part in Operation "Flintlock"—the invasion of the Marshalls. As part of the Southern Attack Force, *Zane* was assigned escort duties in the Southern Transport Screen, TU 52.7.1, in company with sistership *Perry*, four destroyers, and two subchasers (SC's). She screened transports during the Kwajalein phase of "Flintlock" and subsequently served as "sweep" ship and mine disposal vessel during the invasion and occupation of Eniwetok. In that part of the operation, she suffered minor damage from exploding mines, some of which exploded within 100 yards of the ship.

After returning to Pearl Harbor in March for availability, *Zane* during the summer participated in her last major operation, "Forager." Again working as mine disposal vessel, *Zane* was part of Task Group 12.13, the Minesweeping and Hydrographic Survey

Group. Unit 2, to which the ship was attached, included three of her sisterships: *Chandler* (DMS-9), *Palmer* (DMS-5), and *Howard* (DMS-7).

During the landing phases of "Forager"—which commenced on 15 June when Vice Admiral Turner's Task Force 52 (the Northern Attack Force) began sending ashore the marines under the command of Lieutenant General H. M. "Howlin' Mad" Smith, USMC —*Zane* laid dan buoys and destroyed drifting mines with gunfire, working once more as an mine-destruction vessel. She spotted several planes attacking the beachheads, but all were beyond the range of her guns.

Subsequently, when marines and Army troops under Major General R. S. Geiger went ashore on Guam on 22 July under the covering gunfire of Rear Admiral H. W. Hill's task force, *Zane* worked as an antisubmarine escort vessel, steaming in the vanguard of a reserve transport group, TG 53.19. Significantly, the Guam operation proved to be the last front-line tour for the veteran high-speed minesweeper; for, after remaining in the Marianas until 8 August, she reported to Commander, Service Squadron (ServRon) 10, at Ulithi, in the Carolines, for duty as a target-towing vessel.

Zane performed target-towing and local escort duties for the remainder of the war, touching in the Palaus, Marianas, Carolines, and Philippines before V-J Day in mid-August 1945 found her at anchor in San Pedro Bay, off Leyte. During those vital but unglamorous duties, she had been reclassified from a high-speed minesweeper to a miscellaneous auxiliary, AG-109, on 5 June 1945.

The war-weary ship departed the western Pacific in October, beginning her long homeward voyage from Leyte on the 13th. After touching at Eniwetok, Pearl Harbor, and San Diego en route, *Zane* transited the Panama Canal on 25 November and ultimately reached Norfolk, Va., on 29 November. She was decommissioned there on 14 December 1945.

Struck from the Navy list on 8 January 1946, the ship was delivered to Luria Brothers and Co., Inc., on 22 October 1946; her hulk was scrapped on 3 March 1947.

Zane (DMS-14) received six battle stars for her World War II service from Pearl Harbor to the Marianas. In addition, she received the Navy Unit Commendation for her services at Guadalcanal in 1942 and 1943.

Zaniah

A star of the fourth magnitude in the constellation Virgo.

(AG-70: dp. 14,350; l. 441'6''; b. 56'; dr. 23'; s. 12.5 k.; cpl. 181; a. 1 5'', 4 40mm., 12 20mm.; cl. *Basilan*; T. EC2-S-C1)

SS *Anthony F. Lucas*—a "Liberty" ship—was laid down under a Maritime Commission contract (MCE hull 2422) on 29 October 1943 at Houston, Tex., by the Todd-Houston Shipbuilding Corp.; acquired by the Navy under a bareboat charter on 2 November 1943; renamed *Zaniah* and classified as a cargo ship, AK-120, on 13 November; launched on 12 December; sponsored by Mrs. LeRoy Bembry; and accepted by the Navy and commissioned on 22 December 1943, for ferrying to the Alabama Drydock and Shipbuilding Company's yard at Mobile, Ala., for conversion.

Arriving at Mobile on the day after Christmas, *Zaniah* soon entered dockyard hands and was decommissioned on 28 December. Meanwhile, during the conversion, the Navy broadened *Zaniah*'s mission to that of a special stores-barracks-distilling ship and redesignated her AG-70 on 14 March 1944. Before she was completed, a distilling plant capable of producing 80,000 gallons of fresh water was installed in the ship; and she was commissioned on 2 September 1944, Lt. Comdr. Henry Mayfield, USNR, in command.

Zaniah departed Mobile on 17 September, bound—via Key West, Fla.—for Hampton Roads. Arriving at Key West on the 20th, the auxiliary vessel joined a coastwise convoy—KN-339—passing up the eastern seaboard from the 21st to the 24th, before steaming independently for Hampton Roads. *Zaniah* conducted her shakedown training in the Chesapeake Bay before shifting to New York City.

Getting underway again on 23 October, *Zaniah* sailed southward, transited the Panama Canal on 4 November, and arrived at Pearl Harbor on the 22d. *Zaniah* underwent further conversion at the Pearl Harbor Navy Yard—receiving additional office spaces and living quarters to accommodate the staff of a fleet service division. In addition, the ship's force joined yard workmen in installing a large electronics repair and supply department and additional water condensers to enable the ship to furnish fresh water to ships in forward areas of the South Pacific.

Zaniah—thus outfitted for her special operations—departed Pearl Harbor on 10 January 1945 bound for Manus, in the Admiralties. Arriving on the 26th at Seeadler Harbor, she operated for a time with *Sierra* (AD-18) in repairing battle-damaged ships which put into Manus. *Houston* (CL-81) was among the warships which benefited from her services.

Zaniah soon shifted to the Solomons, providing water and repair services at Purvis Bay, Florida Island, from the day of her arrival, Washington's Birthday 1945. She returned to Manus on 19 March before sailing for Hollandia, New Guinea, to join a Philippine-bound convoy, GI-18, on the 29th. *Zaniah* arrived at San Pedro Bay, off Leyte, on 4 April and discharged her much-needed electronics and machinery parts before sailing for the Carolines.

The auxiliary ship operated at Ulithi from 13 to 24 April, providing repair services to ships damaged during the conquest of the Ryukyus. *Zaniah*, herself, sailed for Okinawa on the 24th and arrived on 1 May—one month after the first landings on the embattled island. The first ship of her type in the area, she arrived at a critical time, as her commanding officer wrote: "when damage was at its height and repair facilities and personnel were scarce."

Zaniah's boats soon began a 24-hour schedule of transporting repairmen, in shifts, to damaged vessels. Initially, many men found themselves working 18-hour stints; and, despite daily air attacks and alerts, repair work progressed well. Salvage units from *Zaniah* cleared debris and made damaged hulls seaworthy until more permanent repairs could be made; others restored electrical plants and propulsion machinery; still others performed repairs on the vital and delicate radars and electronics installations on ships. *Zaniah* bore a charmed life—she was never attacked by Japanese planes during her sojourn off Okinawa. On 22 June, two ships were struck nearby—LST-534 and *Ellyson* (DMS-19)—the closest that the vital auxiliary came to being attacked.

Zaniah shifted to Buckner Bay on 10 July and performed her services as a repair and water-distilling ship through the end of the war with Japan in mid-August. She suffered some damage in a typhoon which struck the Fleet's anchorage on 16 September, when *Ocelot* (IX-110) dragged her anchor in the tempest and brushed heavily against *Zaniah*, smashing a motor whaleboat and demolishing some bulwarks and stanchions on board the repair vessel.

That autumn, *Zaniah* later operated out of Tokyo Bay until sailing on 1 December for the United States. Arriving at Seattle, Wash., on Christmas Day, 1945, *Zaniah* shifted to Hawaii, arriving at Pearl Harbor on 11 March 1946. Records are unclear at this point but suggest that the ship may have participated in explosive tests in the 14th Naval District. Decommissioned at Pearl Harbor on 29 April 1946, *Zaniah* was towed to the west coast; reached Suisun Bay, Calif., on 14 May 1947; and was turned over to the Maritime Commission the following day. She was struck from the Navy list on 22 May 1947 and was laid up in the National Defense Reserve Fleet through the 1960's. In November 1972, *Zaniah* was towed to Seattle-Tacoma, Wash., and broken up for scrap.

Zaniah received one battle star for her World War II service.

Zanzibar

A former British protectorate located off the east coast of Africa and comprised of Zanzibar and Pemba Islands. It became a sultanate on 10 December 1963 and attained independence on 12 January 1964—uniting with Tanganyika the same year to form Tanzania.

Zanzibar (PF-92)—a *Tacoma*-class frigate originally classified PG-200—was laid down at Provincetown, Mass., by the Kaiser-Walsh Co., Inc., on 20 October 1943. Completed for the United Kingdom, the warship was turned over to the Royal Navy at Newport, R.I., on 21 June 1944.

Retaining the name *Zanzibar* but given the pendant number K.596, the frigate operated out of Londonderry and Greenock on convoy escort missions into the western Atlantic as far as Boston. In addition, she served as a weather ship on Ocean Station No. 19 in the spring of 1945, a duty which she again performed in the spring of 1946.

Returned to the United States Navy at Brooklyn, N.Y., on 21 May 1946, *Zanzibar* was struck from the Navy list on 29 October 1946 and subsequently was sold for scrap on 17 June 1947.

Zara

(Steam Yacht: t. 184 (gross); l. 152'0''; b. 21'6''; dr. 11' (aft); s. 10 k.; cpl. 62; a. 2 6-pdrs., 2 mg.)

Zara (SP-133)—a steam yacht built in 1891 by Fleming & Ferguson at Paisley, Scotland—was purchased by the Navy from Mr. David H. Friedman of New York on 27 April 1917 and commissioned at New York on 22 May 1917. Assigned to the section patrol in the 3d Naval District, she cruised the waters of Long Island Sound for almost a year. She was placed out of commission on 13 April 1918 and put up for sale. Though her name was struck from the Navy list on 1 May 1918, *Zara* was retained to serve as guard vessel at White Stone near the western entrance to Long Island Sound. She was finally sold on 13 September 1919 to an unrecorded buyer.

Zaurak

(AK-117: dp. 12,350 (lim.); l. 441'6''; b. 56'11''; dr. 26'4'' (lim.); s. 12.8 k. (est.); cpl. 202; trp. 1,052; a. 1 5'', 1 3'', 8 20mm.; cl. *Crater*; T. EC2-S-C1)

Zaurak (AK-117) was laid down on 7 October 1943 at Houston, Tex., by the Todd-Houston Shipbuilding Corp. under a Maritime Commission contract (MCE hull 1964) as *Hugh Young*; renamed *Zaurak* on 13 November 1943; launched on 18 November 1943; sponsored by Miss Betsy Colston Young; delivered to the Navy on 27 November; moved to New Orleans where she underwent conversion for naval use at the Todd Johnson yard; and commissioned on 17 March 1944, Lt. Comdr. John S. Kapuscinski, USNR, in command.

The new cargo ship departed New Orleans on 5 April and arrived in Norfolk on the 13th. After shakedown training in the Chesapeake Bay, she loaded cargo, provisions, and stores at Norfolk and embarked passengers for a voyage to the South Pacific. She stood out of the Chesapeake Bay on 3 May, bound for New York, whence she departed on the 5th. After a stop at Guan-

tanamo Bay, Cuba, she transited the Panama Canal on 19 May and headed independently toward Espiritu Santo in the New Hebrides Islands. Almost a month later, on 14 June, she steamed into Segond Channel. The ship disembarked passengers immediately but remained at Espiritu Santo for three weeks, during which time American forces invaded the Mariana Islands. On 2 July, *Zaurak* departed Espiritu Santo to steam via Noumea, New Caledonia, to Eniwetok and thence to join in the Marianas campaign. She arrived at Eniwetok on the 18th and departed there three days later with a convoy bound for Saipan. She arrived in the anchorage between Saipan and Tinian on 25 July and remained there for 17 days. On 9 August, she embarked 812 battle-weary officers and men of the Army's 27th Infantry Division and, two days later, departed the Marianas bound, via Eniwetok, for Espiritu Santo. The cargo ship arrived back in Segond Channel on 24 August and disembarked her passengers.

For the next two months, *Zaurak* made a series of voyages between various islands in the Southwestern Pacific, visiting several of the Solomon Islands, New Guinea, Emirau, Manus, and New Caledonia. On 23 October, she departed Bougainville in the Solomons with a convoy of 31 ships bound for the Philippines with reinforcements and supplies for the forces that had just invaded Leyte. She steamed into Leyte Gulf at the head of the convoy on 29 October and anchored in San Pedro Bay.

During her 11 days there, *Zaurak* received her baptism of fire. Initially, conditions in the San Pedro Bay anchorage were quiet enough; but, when she moved to the San Juanico Strait anchorage on the 31st, enemy air activity—occasioned by the proximity of Tacloban airfield—rose markedly. On 1 and 2 November, she fired her first shots at enemy planes attacking the airstrip ashore but, due to darkness and extreme range, scored no hits. On the 3d and 4th, Japanese began attacking the ships in the anchorage as secondary targets.

The ship claimed her first enemy plane on the latter morning when a plane attacking the airfield veered out of a searchlight beam and away from shore-based antiaircraft fire to attack the ships in the anchorage. *Zaurak*'s secondary battery opened fire, but the plane flew right through her field of fire to crash into SS *Matthew P. Deady* in the vicinity of that merchant ship's number 1 hatch. Almost immediately, volunteers from *Zaurak* went to the stricken merchantman's aid, rescuing over 20 men from the water around the blazing ship. A little later that same morning, another Japanese plane ran afoul of *Zaurak*'s guns and fell in flames into the water. Soon thereafter, two more intruders approached the ship but never came close enough to become a good target. Though she claimed hits on both, neither plane went down.

During her final five days at Leyte, she experienced several more air attacks, but her guns downed no more planes. On 8 November, the ship had to get underway to ride out a heavy tropical storm which approached in typhoon force. The following day, *Zaurak* embarked passengers and departed Leyte Gulf in a convoy of 20 ships, bound for Hollandia, New Guinea.

After three months of voyages between such places as Guadalcanal, Espiritu Santo, New Caledonia, Bougainville, Green Island, Oro Bay, and Finschhafen, she voyaged to Munda in March 1945 to embark reinforcements for the Iwo Jima operation then in progress. She delivered elements of the 147th Infantry to Iwo Jima on 29 March and remained there for a week, embarking units of the 3d Marine Division on the 27th.

Two days later, she sailed from the Marshalls and, on 1 April, arrived at Guam where the marines disembarked. From there, she headed for Pavuvu in the Solomons, where she embarked Marine Corps and Navy men for passage back to Hawaii. Upon her arrival in Pearl Harbor on 3 May, she learned that most of the marines embarked were needed at Okinawa. She therefore departed Oahu on 6 May and set a course via

Eniwetok and Ulithi for the Ryukyus. She arrived off Okinawa on 13 June and remained there for six days disembarking troops and unloading cargo. On 19 June, she got underway for Ulithi, on the first leg of the voyage back to the United States. After additional stops at Eniwetok, Kwajalein, and Pearl Harbor, she arrived in Seattle on 10 August. Three days later, she entered the Todd Shipyard for her first major overhaul.

While she was in the yard, Japan capitulated. *Zaurak*'s repairs were completed in mid-September; and, after embarking passengers, the ship departed Seattle on 21 September. Steaming via Pearl Harbor and Ulithi, she arrived in Buckner Bay, Okinawa, on 25 October. From there, she moved to Shanghai, China, where she traded replacement troops for men returning home to the United States. From there, she proceeded to Jinsen, Korea, to make a similar personnel trade. Following that, the ship made a stop at Taku in North China and a return visit to Shanghai before getting underway on 1 December to return home. Following a non-stop voyage across the expanse of the Pacific, *Zaurak* entered San Francisco Bay on 20 December. She remained at San Francisco until decommissioned on 12 March 1946. She was transferred to the Maritime Commission that same day for layup at Suisun Bay, Calif., with the National Defense Reserve Fleet. Her name was struck from the Navy list on 28 March 1946.

Zaurak earned one battle star for service in World War II.

Zeal

(AM–131: dp. 890; l. 221'2''; b. 32'0''; dr. 10'9'' (mean); s. 18.1 k. (tl.); cpl. 105; a. 1 3'', 2 40mm.; cl. *Auk*)

Zeal (AM–131) was laid down on 12 January 1942 at Chickasaw, Ala., by the Gulf Shipbuilding Co.; launched on 15 September 1942; sponsored by Mrs. John M. Hughes; and commissioned on 9 July 1943, Lt. Comdr. H. M. Jones, USNR, in command.

After a visit to New Orleans for deperming, *Zeal* got underway late in July for shakedown training en route to Norfolk, Va. During that cruise, she con-

ducted type training out of Key West, Fla. Between 9 and 30 August, post-shakedown availability at the Norfolk Navy Yard occupied her time. On 3 September, she received orders to proceed via Guantanamo Bay to the Panama Canal. She arrived in Guantanamo Bay on 8 September and, after loading supplies, got underway the following day for the Canal Zone. She reached Coco Solo on 12 September and operated from there for the next month. On 12 October, she departed the Pacific terminus of the canal, bound for the southwestern Pacific. En route, the minesweeper made stops at the Galapagos Islands, Bora Bora, and Tutuila. At Suva in the Fiji Islands, she received orders detaching her from her unit to serve as escort for the tanker SS *Pacific Sun* on a voyage from Suva to the New Hebrides Islands. She arrived at Espiritu Santo on 2 November and, three days later, departed on another convoy escort mission.

That mission set the pattern for her first 11 months in the western Pacific. She escorted convoys between the islands of the southwestern Pacific which by that time were becoming increasingly more of a rear area. She also conducted antisubmarine patrols. For the most part, the Solomon Islands, the New Hebrides Islands, Fiji Islands, and the Marshall Islands constituted her zone of operations.

In August 1944, however, she began training for her first amphibious operation. Operating from Tulagi and Florida Island, she practiced minesweeping maneuvers, drilled at gunnery, and participated in rehearsal landings. On 8 September, she got underway with the other units of Mine Division (MinDiv) 14 for the Palau Islands. She arirved off Angaur in the Palaus on the morning of 15 September and spent the next two days sweeping the approaches to the invasion beaches. The sweeps of Angaur, however, netted her no mines. On the 17th, she moved north to Kossol Roads and began screening the fleet anchorage located there against submarine attack.

Soon thereafter, she received orders to proceed to Ulithi Atoll. She arrived there on 21 September and began running sweeps of the lagoon. Here, *Zeal* finally succeeded in fulfilling the mission for which she had originally been built, sweeping eight mines during the anchorage clearing operation. She remained at Ulithi until 25 September at which time she departed the atoll

The steel-hulled minesweeper *Zeal* (MSF–131) in the Far East, 4 August 1955, moored to a buoy alongside a sister ship. The increasing threat of magnetic mines, first used early in World War II, led to the eventual replacement of these ships by newer wooden-hulled sweepers. (NH 68593)

in company with a convoy of LST's bound for Hollandia, New Guinea, where she made a brief stop on the 29th. From there, the ship continued on to Finschhafen and thence to Seeadler Harbor on Manus Island, where she arrived on 2 October.

Zeal remained at Manus for eight days. On 10 October, she got underway with a convoy of minecraft, bound for Leyte Gulf. During the first few days of the transit, weather caused no problems; but, during the latter part, it steadily worsened. By the time *Zeal* arrived in Leyte Gulf, a storm approaching typhoon proportions had worked itself up. On 17 October, the minesweeper began the preinvasion sweep of the Leyte assault beaches on schedule. The storm, however, reached the typhoon stage at that point and forced her to retire from the area.

The typhoon abated that evening; and, on the morning of the 18th, *Zeal* returned to resume her sweep. That day brought the warship her first contact with the Japanese. After she had cut a few moored mines, a "Val" dive-bomber flew over and dropped two bombs which missed nearby *Velocity* (AM–128) by about 200 yards. The Japanese plane made its attack and retired before any gun crews could man their battle stations. Over the next few days, *Zeal* sighted several enemy planes; but the attack on the 18th remained her only close contact with the enemy until after she completed her minesweeping chores on the 23d and moved farther into the gulf near Dulag to join the fire support group there.

During her stay in the gulf, *Zeal* missed the Battle for Leyte Gulf but participated in some engagements with enemy land-based aircraft. One particularly intense air attack came on 25 October when Japanese planes were attacking the ships from almost every angle. A twin engine "Betty" bomber flew up *Zeal*'s starboard side and drew the combined fire of her 3-inch and 20-millimeter batteries. A few seconds later, that intruder burst into flames and splashed into the sea. *Zeal* escaped the air raids with little or no damage, and her crew suffered only one slight casualty. On 28 October, she stood out of Leyte Gulf on her way back to Manus. The minesweeper entered Seeadler Harbor on 5 November.

Nine days later, she began the first leg of a voyage back to the United States. Steaming via Pearl Harbor, she arrived in Portland, Oreg., on 4 December. She was overhauled there at the Albina Shipyards during December and the first two months of 1945. She completed repairs and departed Portland on 4 March, bound for refresher and minesweeping training along the coast of California. That employment occupied her for about a month.

On 2 April 1945, she departed the west coast to return to the war in the western Pacific. After stops at Pearl Harbor and at Eniwetok Atoll, the minesweeper arrived at Kerama Retto in the Ryukyus on 21 May to join in the last campaign of World War II—the seven-week old assault on Okinawa. During her tour of duty at Okinawa, *Zeal* served on the radar picket stations situated around the island and at some distance from which to provide early warning of air attack from enemy bases on Kyushu and Formosa.

Though she witnessed a number of kamikaze and conventional air attacks on other ships, she suffered only one such scrape herself. On the night of 27 May, a Japanese float plane started a run on her, but her antiaircraft batteries quickly discouraged him.

Zeal remained at Okinawa until the beginning of July at which time she embarked upon some large-scale minesweeping operations. The first, designated Operation "Juneau," was conducted in a 60-mile rectangle in the East China Sea. She returned to Okinawa late in July to conduct an availability in preparation for a similar operation, code-named "Skagway." On 15 August, while she was still undergoing repairs, Japan capitulated.

A week later, she departed Okinawa on her way to the "Skagway" area, but the mission was postponed because of the more pressing need of sweeping Japanese home waters for the occupation forces. By late August, she was on her way to northern Honshu and, on 6 September, reported for duty at Ominato Naval Base. She swept mines at that location until 19 October, at which time she received orders to head for Sasebo. She arrived in Sasebo on 24 October but departed two days later to participate in Operation "Klondike"—another major minesweep conducted in the East China Sea. "Klondike" lasted until 8 November, on which date she returned to Sasebo to begin repairs.

Zeal completed repairs on 25 November and departed Sasebo for another series of sweeps at various locations. These she conducted in the vicinity of Formosa and the Pescadores Islands, operating out of Kiirun, Formosa. At the conclusion of that assignment, she spent the holidays at Shanghai, China. She departed Shanghai on 3 January 1946 and arrived in Sasebo on the 5th. Ten days later, she began the first leg of her homeward voyage.

After stops at Eniwetok and Pearl Harbor, she entered San Diego on 9 February. Assigned to the San Diego Group, Pacific Reserve Fleet, *Zeal* was placed out of commission on 4 June 1946. She remained inactive until 19 December 1951 when she was recommissioned at San Diego.

The minesweeper remained on the west coast until 19 May 1952 when she got underway for the western Pacific. After a stop at Pearl Harbor late in May, *Zeal* continued her voyage west and arrived in Sasebo on 18 June. On the 27th, she departed Sasebo for Korean waters and minesweeping operations near Wonsan, Hungnam, and Chongjin. During those operations, she came under fire of enemy shore batteries several times but sustained no damage. In August, she participated in the rescue of 26 of *Sarsi*'s (ATF–111) crewmen after that tug had hit a mine and sunk. She served in the Korean combat zone until the fall of 1952. She departed Sasebo on 19 October and, after stops at Midway and Oahu, arrived in Long Beach on 15 November.

For more than two years, *Zeal* conducted operations—almost exclusively training evolutions—out of Long Beach, San Diego, and other west coast ports. On 21 January 1955, she departed Long Beach and embarked upon another deployment with the 7th Fleet. En route she was redesignated MSF–131. She reached Sasebo on 15 February and, for the next six months, conducted operations off the western coast of Korea as well as in the Sea of Japan. *Zeal* departed Yokosuka on 10 August and, after stops at Midway and Oahu, arrived in Long Beach on 5 September. She conducted west coast operations until decommissioning the following summer on 6 July 1956. She remained with the Pacific Reserve Fleet for just over a decade. Her name was struck from the Navy list on 1 December 1966, and her stripped hull was sunk as a target on 9 January 1967.

Zeal earned four battle stars during World War II and an additional four for her postwar minesweeping service. During the Korean conflict, she earned one battle star.

Zebra

Any of several fleet African mammals related to the horse and distinctively patterned in stripes of black or brown and white or buff.

(AKN–5: dp. 14,350 (tl.); l. 441'6"; b. 56'11"; dr. 28'4"; s. 12.5 k. (tl.); cpl. 228; a. 1 5", 4 40mm.; cl. *Indus*; T. EC2–S–C1)

SS *Matthew Lyon*—a "Liberty" ship built by the Permanente Metals Corp. at Richmond, Calif.—was laid down on 18 March 1943 under a Maritime Commission contract (MCE hull 535); launched on 11 April 1943; sponsored by Mrs. Harry H. Feldhahn; and delivered to the War Shipping Administration (WSA) on 26 April 1943. Operated for the WSA by a civilian contractor, Dichmann W. & P., the ship plied the waters of the Pacific during the summer of 1943. On 12 August, while voyaging to Espiritu Santo in the New Hebrides, she received severe damage as the result of a torpedo fired by the Japanese submarine *I-11*. Several days later, the freighter limped into Espiritu Santo and languished there in Segond Channel for several weeks, apparently headed for scrapping.

Late in September, a naval officer recognized her potential for emergency service as a net cargo ship; and, on 1 October 1943, she was placed in service as *Zebra* (IX-107). Her susbequent success in that role prompted her complete conversion to a net cargo ship and her total rehabilitation to operable status. On 15 February 1944, the ship was redesignated AKN-5, and *Zebra* was placed in commission on 27 February 1944, while in drydock at Espiritu Santo, Lt. Comdr. Robert D. Abernethy, USNR, in command.

During the first three months of her commissioned service, *Zebra* remained at Espiritu Santo completing her partial conversion to a net cargo ship. She began her first mission on 1 June, when she started loading a cargo of reclaimed net material and put to sea on the 8th, bound for New Caledonia. The ship arrived in Noumea on the 11th, unloaded her net material, and took on a general cargo destined for the Fiji Islands. She departed Noumea on 19 June, arrived at Suva three days later, unloaded, and began taking on reclaimed net material. On the 27th, she moved to the other side of the island where she began loading material salvaged from the Nandi net installations. The ship completed loading on 5 July and headed back to New Caledonia that same day. *Zebra* entered Noumea on 8 July and discharged her load of salvaged net gear. Following 10 days at Noumea, the net cargo ship embarked upon a circuit of various South Pacific islands to collect nets and equipment salvaged from the harbor defense installations. Through the remainder of the summer, the ship visited Tongatabu; Bora Bora; Tutuila and Upolu, Samoa; and Funafuti. At each island, she stopped long enough to unload part of the general cargo she had taken on at Noumea and pick up each installation's salvaged net gear. She departed her last port of call on that voyage, Funafuti in the Ellice Islands, on 23 August and returned to Noumea five days later.

Zebra remained at Noumea until 15 September. On that day, she embarked upon a voyage which took her closer to war and which brought her first actual netlaying mission. The ship arrived in Eniwetok lagoon on 24 September and remained there until 3 October when she continued on toward the Western Carolines. Reaching Ulithi Atoll on 8 October, the net cargo ship immediately began installing net gear around the anchorage with two of her sister ships, *Sagittarius* (AKN-2) and *Tuscana* (AKN-3). They completed their mission by 10 November, and *Zebra* loaded the unused material for transportation to the Palaus. She departed Ulithi that same day and entered Barnum Bay near Peleliu two days later. While the fighting on Peleliu continued, the net cargo ship assembled a net installation for the protection of a wharf about to be constructed at the island. She concluded that portion of her mission on 14 November and headed north in company with two net tenders to the anchorage at Kossol Roads. There, she spent 11 days assembling over two miles of net and supporting equipment. At the conclusion of that assignment, *Zebra* received orders to Pearl Harbor. She departed the Palaus on 25 November, stopped at Eniwetok briefly on 4 December, and arrived in Hawaii on the 15th. At Pearl Harbor, she underwent 20 days of repairs and modifications before loading net gear in preparation for her next mission.

She remained at Pearl Harbor through the end of January 1945 awaiting sailing orders. Finally, the ship got underway on 5 February, bound for Iwo Jima. She stopped at Eniwetok between 16 and 21 February and then continued her voyage. Two days out of Eniwetok,

Zebra's convoy received orders changing its destination from Iwo Jima to Saipan in the Marianas. *Zebra*, two net tenders, and a destroyer, however, received instructions to continue on to their original destination as a result of battle damage to her sister ship *Keokuk* (AKN-4). The little task unit arrived off Iwo Jima on 28 February, and *Zebra* immediately began double duty, laying nets and serving as flagship for all minecraft in the vicinity. She stayed at Iwo Jima for 42 days, laying nets in spite of adverse weather, heavy seas, and fire from the doomed but stubborn enemy garrison. She also superintended the laying of ship moorings and performed several salvage jobs including pulling *Zuni* (ATF-95) and *LST-727* off the Iwo Jima beach.

Zebra concluded her tour of duty at Iwo Jima on 11 April and shaped a course back to Eniwetok, where she arrived on the 18th. Continuing east, the ship entered Pearl Harbor again on 28 April for a four-day layover before resuming her voyage to the west coast. On 11 May, the net cargo ship arrived in San Francisco, Calif., to complete her conversion to a net cargo ship. She entered the Oakland yard of the Moore Drydock Co. on 14 May. Work continued until mid-July when she received orders to participate in net laying experiments at Tiburon, Calif. Though speeded up, her conversion had not been completed when she slipped her moorings on 25 July to join the operations up the bay at Tiburon. That duty lasted until 3 August at which time the ship returned to Moore Drydock Co. to complete the remaining conversion work. On 26 August, she made her post-conversion, full power trial run and, soon thereafter, received orders assigning her to the Administrative Command, Minecraft, located at Pearl Harbor.

The ship stood out of San Francisco Bay on 31 August and arrived in Pearl Harbor on 8 September. She remained in Hawaii only 12 days. On 20 September, she headed back to the western Pacific to collect salvaged net equipment. Carrying a small cargo of mine gear for the Marshall Islands command, she steamed to Kwajalein where she arrived on 30 September and unloaded her cargo before proceeding on to Iwo Jima. *Zebra* arrived at the latter island on 9 October, loaded net gear, and then headed for the Marianas on the 29th. The ship made port at Saipan on 1 November, unloaded the salvaged net equipment at the Saipan stockpile, and began loading passengers and equipment for return to the United States.

She departed Saipan on 15 November and stopped at Guam on the 16th. There, she unloaded some minesweeping gear before resuming the voyage on the 29th. Steaming by way of Pearl Harbor, *Zebra* arrived in the Canal Zone on the last day of 1945. Routed on to Norfolk, Va., she reported to the Commandant, 5th Naval District, on 8 January 1946. *Zebra* was decommissioned at Norfolk on 21 January 1946 and simultaneously returned to the War Shipping Administration. Her name was struck from the Navy list on 7 February 1946.

Zebra was awarded one battle star for service during World War II.

Zeelandia

(ScStr: dp. 11,500 (n.); l. 440' (reg.); b. 55.7'; dr. 27'; dph. 34'; s. 15 k.; cpl. 322; a. 4 6", 2 1-pdrs., 2 mg.)

Zeelandia (Id. No. 2507)—a steamer constructed in 1910 by A. Stephens & Sons, Ltd., at Glasgow, Scotland—was operated in transatlantic service by the *Koninklijke Hollandsche Lloyd* lines until March 1918 when she was chartered by the Navy. The ship was placed in commission at New York on 3 April 1918, Comdr. Robert Henderson in command.

Assigned to the Newport News Division of the Transport Force, *Zeelandia* carried troops across the Atlantic during the remaining months of World War I. She made five round-trip voyages to French ports between commissioning and Armistice Day, 11 November 1918. During those voyages, she carried a total of 8,349 passengers—mostly troops—to Europe. Though she claimed to have sighted and engaged German U-boats on several occasions during her wartime service, only one encounter was verified as definitely submarine. That event occurred at dusk on 31 August when a submarine surfaced to attack the convoy in which she cruised. The attacker, however, could not press home his attack because of zigzag tactics and a moderately strong escort.

The steamer remained in naval service between 11 November 1918 and 31 July 1919, making seven voyages between Europe and America returning troops home after the war. During those voyages, she repatriated 15,737 American soldiers and carried 3,170 passengers to Europe. On 31 July 1919, she was transferred to the custody of the Commandant, 3d Naval District for disposal. She was finally placed out of commission on 6 October 1919, was struck from the Navy list the same day, and was simultaneously returned to her owner.

Zeilin

Jacob Zeilin—born in Philadelphia, Pa., on 16 July 1806—entered the Marine Corps as a 2d lieutenant on 1 October 1831 after several years of study at the Military Academy at West Point. By 1836, he reached the rank of 1st lieutenant. Between 1845 and 1848, Lt. Zeilin cruised in *Columbus* and *Congress*. During the Mexican War, he commanded the Marine detachment embarked in *Congress*, which ship was attached to Commodore Robert F. Stockton's force. He took part in the conquest of California and was brevetted to the rank of major for gallantry during the action at the San Gabriel River crossing on 9 January 1847. Later, he took part in the capture of Los Angeles and in the Battle of La Mesa. In 1847, Zeilin served as military commandant at San Diego and, in September, served with the forces that captured Guaymas and those that met the enemy at San Jose on the 30th. For the remainder of the war, Mazatlan was his center of activity, and he fought in several skirmishes with the Mexicans in that area.

After the Mexican War, Zeilin served with the Marine detachment in *Mississippi* in which ship he cruised to Japan with Commodore Matthew C. Perry's expedition. Following that duty, various assignments ashore occupied his time until the outbreak of the Civil War. On 21 July 1861, Zeilin commanded a company of marines during the First Battle of Manassas and received a slight wound. Later, he went to sea again, serving with the South Atlantic Blockading Squadron under Rear Admiral Dahlgren. In 1864, Zeilin assumed command of the Marine Barracks at Portsmouth, N.H. That June, he was appointed Commandant of the Marine Corps in the rank of colonel. In 1874, Zeilin became the Marine Corps' first general officer when he was promoted to brigadier general. Brigadier General Zeilin retired from the Marine Corps on 1 November 1876. Four years later, on 18 November 1880, he died at Washington, D.C.

I

(DD–313: dp. 1,215 (n.); l. 314'4½''; b. 30'1½''; dr. 9'9¾'' (aft); s. 33 k.; cpl. 95; a. 4 4'', 1 3'', 12 21'' tt., cl. *Clemson*)

The first *Zeilin* (DD–313) was laid down on 20 February 1919 at the Bethlehem Shipbuilding Corp. yard in San Francisco, Calif.; launched on 28 May 1919; sponsored by Mrs. William P. Lindley; and commissioned on 10 December 1920 at the Mare Island Navy Yard, Lt. Comdr. James D. Moore in command.

Following shakedown, *Zeilin* reported for duty with Division 33, Squadron 11, Destroyers, Battle Force, based at San Diego, Calif. For the next nine years, she operated out of that port, conducting maneuvers with

the fleet and training with independent ships. In July 1923, she suffered damage in a collision with *Henderson* (AP–1) in Puget Sound but, after repairs, resumed duty with the Battle Force Destroyers. On 22 January 1930, *Zeilin* was decommissioned at San Diego. Her name was struck from the Navy list on 8 July 1930, and she was subsequently scrapped by the Navy.

II

(AP–9: dp. 21,900 (lim.); l. 535'2''; b. 72'6''; dr. 31'3'' (lim.); s. 18.0 k.; cpl. 724; trp. 2,077; a. 4 3'')

The second *Zeilin* (AP–9)—started by the Newport News Shipbuilding & Drydock Co. near the end of World War I as an Army troop transport but completed as SS *Silver State*, a combination passenger liner and cargo carrier for mercantile service—served during the 1920's and 1930's on the West Coast-to-Far East circuit, first with the Pacific Steamship Line, then with the Admiral Orient Line, and finally with the Dollar Line. Renamed SS *President Jackson* on 23 June 1922, she served under that name until acquired by the Navy in July 1940. Renamed *Zeilin* and designated AP–9, she was converted back to a troop transport at Todd-Seattle Drydock Co. and was commissioned on 3 January 1942, Capt. Pat Buchanan in command.

Following shakedown training along the west coast, *Zeilin* made a round-trip voyage from San Diego to Samoa and back between 13 April and 17 June to carry garrison troops to those islands. On 8 July, she again departed the west coast and steamed via Pearl Harbor to the Fiji Islands. At Suva, she prepared for the invasion of the Solomon Islands. Early on the morning of 7 August, she arrived off Guadalcanal with Task Force (TF) 62, the South Pacific Amphibious Force. However, her troops did not land on the first day of the invasion; and, when they did, it was not on Guadalcanal. On the 8th, she sent the marines of the 3d Defense Battalion ashore to help the 2d Marines root out small, but stubborn, enemy defense forces from Tulagi, Gavutu, and Tanambogo. Upon completing her disembarkation, the transport got underway for Noumea, New Caledonia.

For the next two months, she made the circuit between Noumea, New Caledonia; Espiritu Santo, New Hebrides; and Wellington, New Zealand. On 9 October, she departed Noumea to carry troops and supplies to the Solomons. Arriving off Guadalcanal on the 11th, *Zeilin* began unloading off Lunga Point. Still there on the 13th, she witnessed successive enemy air raids on Henderson Field, but she and the other transports escaped attack because the Japanese airmen seemed to feel that the airfield was the only important target. However, the enemy ashore thought otherwise; for, that same day, a shore battery dropped several salvoes around *Zeilin*; but she escaped damage. She returned to Noumea on 17 October and proceeded from there to Espiritu Santo. From the latter port, *Zeilin* set a course back to Guadalcanal on 9 November and arrived off Lunga Point two days later.

This time, Japanese airmen found her more attractive. She began unloading early that morning; and, while she did so, five enemy dive bombers plunged down toward her. During the brief encounter, the transport suffered three damaging near misses, one of which made a glancing hit on her starboard side but exploded some 20 to 25 feet below the surface. As a result of these blows, *Zeilin* shipped a considerable amount of water and suffered cracked plates and a broken propeller shaft. Though damaged and listing, the ship remained in the area performing her duties until later that month. On 26 November 1942, the ship was redesignated an attack transport APA–3. She carried casualties to Espiritu Santo and then sailed via Tutuila, Samoa, back to the United States. She arrived in San Pedro, Calif., on 22 December to begin repairs at the Terminal Island Navy Yard.

Zeilin completed repairs early in March 1943 and

began operations along the west coast. On 17 April, she departed San Diego for Alaskan waters. After a six-day stop at San Francisco, she continued on and arrived in Cold Bay, the rendezvous point for the Attu invasion force, on 1 May. By 11 May, she was off the southern coast of Attu, ready to put her troops ashore at Massacre Bay. After the initial landings, slow progress ashore held up the transport's unloading operations, and Zeilin was forced to remain off Attu until the 16th. The next day, she put into Adak for a five-day layover before heading back to San Diego, where she arrived on 31 May.

Through the summer months of 1943, she operated along the west coast—mostly between San Diego and San Francisco. In August, she returned to Adak, arriving there on the 5th and remaining until the 26th. She returned to San Diego on 2 September and prepared to head back to the southwestern Pacific. Departing the west coast near mid-month, Zeilin steamed to Pearl Harbor, where she stopped for five days before continuing on—via Funafuti and Espiritu Santo—to Wellington, New Zealand. The attack transport remained there from 17 October to 1 November, at which time she moved to Efate where the Tarawa attack force concentrated and practiced for Operation "Galvanic."

On 13 November, Zeilin departed Efate in company with the task force and set course for the Gilbert Islands. She arrived off Betio—the islet of Tarawa Atoll that was the first and primary objective of the assault—during the night of 18 and 19 November. Early the following morning, she began unloading her marines, members of the 2d Battalion, 2d Marines, into landing craft for their assault on Beach Red 2. At about 0615, while she was still transferring troops to the boats, they received a foretaste of the mauling in store for them when a shore battery straddled Zeilin and her assault craft with shells. Neither ship nor troops suffered any injury; but, while Zeilin maintained that clean record during the operation, her passengers were soon to be cut to ribbons as they waded the 700 yards across ankle- to knee-deep foul ground between the edge of the reef and the actual shore.

Zeilin returned to Pearl Harbor at the beginning of December to reload for the Kwajalein phase of the Marshall Islands assault. She got underway again on 22 January 1944 in company with the Southern Attack Force with elements of the Army's 7th Division—old friends from Zeilin's Aleutians service—embarked. On the night of 30 and 31 January, Southern and Northern Attack Forces separated—the northern unit headed for its objectives, Roi and Namur Islands up north, while the southern force zeroed in on Kwajalein Island and nearby islets.

Zeilin and her colleagues reached the transport area off boomerang-shaped Kwajalein Island at about 0545 on the morning of 31 January. The invasion force, however, passed up the main objective on 31 January, preferring instead to take and consolidate positions on the islets located to the west in order to support the main effort scheduled for 1 February. While Zeilin and the other attack transports sent some of their troops against Ennylabegan and Enubuj, high-speed transports Manley (APD–1) and Overton (APD–23) landed the 7th Division Reconnaissance Troop on the islets, Gehh and Ninni. Encountering only light resistance, the troops secured all their first-day objectives by early afteroon and began preparations—in particular the landing of divisional artillery on Enubuj—for the main assault the next morning. During the afternoon and evening of 31 January, Zeilin and the other transports transferred soldiers to LST's for the assault itself and, during the night, moved to their assigned stations some 7,500 yards west of Kwajalein Island.

At 0900, troop-laden landing craft charged the beaches on the western end of the island. For a time, they delayed about 200 yards from shore to allow naval gunfire to lay down one last barrage and then resumed their advance, reaching the beaches at 0930. Soon after the assault force charged ashore, the unloading of their equipment and supplies began. After initial success, the troops ashore advanced slowly, but Zeilin unloaded rapidly and, by the evening of 2 February, had just about completed the task. During the succeeding 36 hours, the 7th Division pushed the Japanese into shrinking pockets of resistance; and, though the island had not been completely subdued, no doubt existed as to the final outcome. Thus, Zeilin set a course for Funafuti, where she arrived on 8 February.

For the next three months, the southwestern Pacific once again became her theater of operations. She carried troops and supplies for units operating in the Solomon Islands and for MacArthur's forces, then leapfrogging up the back of the New Guinea bird. During those months, she visited Guadalcanal and Bougainville in the Solomons, Espiritu Santo, Milne Bay and Cape Sudest on New Guinea, and the newly conquered Admiralty Islands. On 10 May, she returned to Guadalcanal to prepare for the invasion of the Mariana Islands.

Zeilin departed the Solomons on 4 June as a unit of the Southern Attack Force (TF 53) whose specific target was to be Guam. The transport—with marines of the 1st Provisional Brigade embarked—arrived near the Marianas at mid-month and waited in an area 150 to 300 miles east of Guam for its assault scheduled for the 18th, three days following initial landings on Saipan. The operation, however, suffered two postponements: the first caused by the Battle of the Philippine Sea and the second by the unexpectedly bitter opposition which the Americans encountered on Saipan and Tinian. Part of the force was dispatched to Eniwetok to await the arrival of the 77th Division from Hawaii to bolster the Guam force. Zeilin and her marines, however, remained in the Marianas area for another five days as a floating reserve.

When it became apparent that the 1st Provisional Brigade was not needed to bolster the Saipan force, those transports too headed for Eniwetok, departing the Marianas area on 30 June and entering the lagoon at Eniwetok on 3 July. Fifteen days later, Zeilin left the lagoon, rendezvoused with the transports carrying the troops from Hawaii, and shaped a course for the Marianas. Zeilin arrived off Guam on 22 July, the day after the initial assault on that island. She remained in the area only four days—unloading marines, equipment, and supplies—and then departed the Marianas. After an overnight stop at Eniwetok on 29 and 30 July, she continued on to Pearl Harbor where she arrived on 7 August. The attack transport remained at the Hawaiian base for three days, then headed for the west coast. On the 18th, she arrived in San Francisco where a three-month's overhaul restored her to top fighting trim by the begining of the last week in October.

On 21 October, the attack transport stood out of San Francisco to return to the war in the western Pacific. She entered the port of Finschhafen—located on the northeastern coast of New Guinea almost directly across the Dampier Strait from New Britain—on 6 November. She briefly plied the waters off the New Guinea coast, visiting Langemak and Hollandia before heading for Noumea, where she arrived on the 22d. At Noumea, she began preparations for the invasion of Luzon. There, she loaded elements of the Army's 25th Infantry Division and headed for Guadalcanal where, during December, soldiers and ships rehearsed the impending landings. She and her sister ships completed those exercises just before Christmas and, on Christmas Day, headed for Manus in the Admiralty Islands. Zeilin and her consorts remained there from 29 December 1944 until 2 January 1945, at which time they got underway for Luzon. Zeilin's embarked troops formed a part of the first reinforcement echelon for the San Fabian phase of the invasion rather than of the initial assault force. She arrived off the San Fabian beachhead on 11 January, two days after the initial landings.

Her out-bound voyage proved more exciting. *Zeilin* completed the disembarking of troops and the unloading of their attendant supplies and equipment by the evening of the 12th. That night, she formed up with a fast transport convoy and headed for Leyte. The next morning, just after the beginning of the forenoon watch, a single Japanese plane pounced on the convoy. Swooping down from a low cloud, the kamikaze bore in on *Zeilin*'s port quarter. He feigned a bank at *Mount Olympus* (AGC–8) steaming astern of *Zeilin*, but quickly resumed his original course. Surprise and the feint at *Mount Olympus* rewarded the suicide pilot with success. He made it through the fire of *Zeilin*'s after 40-millimeter mount, his "right wing struck the port kingpost and boom serving No. 6 hatch . . ." while the fuselage ". . . swung inboard under the radio antenna and crashed the starboard side of the housetop." At that point, his payload—a cache of incendiary missiles constructed out of ¾-inch gas pipe—showered the decks and started a number of scattered, but small, fires. Damage topside was extensive at the point of impact. The superstructure deck was blown away, deck framing was bent and buckled, and several staterooms were completely destroyed. The plane's engine pierced the superstructure deck and the outboard bulkhead and ended up in one of the landing boats. Worst of all, the attack cost the ship seven men killed outright, three declared missing, and 30 injured. The damage, however extensive, was not fatal, and *Zeilin* continued on her way with the convoy.

After temporary repairs at Leyte, she got underway for Ulithi on 16 February and entered the lagoon on the 18th. She participated in the Iwo Jima campaign briefly in early March, making a voyage to that island between 9 and 16 March to bring in reinforcements to that island. Later that month, she departed the western Pacific to return to the Unied States for permanent repairs. Afer five days at Hawaii, from 12 to 17 April, she continued on to San Francisco where she arrived on the 23d.

Following a two-month repair period, *Zeilin* departed San Francisco on 30 June. She spent the week of 1 to 8 July at San Diego and then headed north to Seattle. On the 23d, she departed the west coast to return to the western Pacific. The attack transport stopped at Eniwetok on 4 to 7 Augst then moved on to Ulithi. Hostilities in the Far East ceased on 15 August; and *Zeilin* exited Ulithi lagoon two days later, bound for Okinawa. At Okinawa from the 21st, she got underway again on the 29th, bound for Leyte, and spent most of the month of September transporting passengers and cargo between points in the Philippine Islands. In October, she carried the Army's 106th Regimental Combat Team to occupation duty at Jinsen, Korea. From there, she headed back to the United States.

Following stops at Ulithi and Guam, she arrived in San Francisco on 14 November. Shuttle voyages along the west coast between the ports of San Diego, San Francisco, San Pedro, Bremerton, and Seattle occupied her for the remainder of 1945 and during January 1946. On 4 February 1946, she departed San Pedro and set her course for the east coast. After transiting the Panama Canal on the 14th, she resumed her voyage on the 15th and arrived in Hampton Roads, Va., on the 21st. On 19 April 1946, *Zeilin* was decommissioned at Portsmouth, Va. Her name was struck from the Navy list on 5 June 1946. She was transferred to the Maritime Commission on 3 July 1946 for disposal but was not sold until 4 May 1948 when she was delivered to American Shipbreakers, Inc., for scrapping.

Zeilin earned eight battle stars for her World War II service.

Zelima

A minor planet in a solar system discovered in 1907 by the German astronomer August Kopff.

(AF–49: dp. 15,500 (f.); l. 459′2″; b. 63′0″; dr. 28′0″; s. 16.0 k.; cpl. 292; cl. *Alstede*; T. R2–S–BU1)

Zelima (AF–49) was laid down on 5 December 1944

USS *Zelima* (AF–49) replenishes *Basilone* (DD–824) and *Ticonderoga* (CVA–34) in the western Pacific.

at Oakland, Calif., by the Moore Drydock Co. under Maritime Commission contract (MC hull 1212) as *Golden Rocket*; launched on 2 March 1945; sponsored by Mrs. J. W. Greenslade; and delivered to the War Shipping Administration on 16 July 1945. She was operated by the United Fruit Co. under a contract with the War Shipping Administration for almost a year. Turned over to the Navy in the summer of 1946, she was renamed *Zelima*; converted to a stores ship at the Mare Island Naval Shipyard; and commissioned on 27 July 1946.

With her home port at San Francisco, *Zelima* spent her first four years of active service carrying provisions and other supplies from the west coast to Japan and other points in the Pacific occupied by American forces. On the return voyages, she often carried servicemen returning home after service in the Far East. The eruption of hostilities in Korea during the summer of 1950 brought an increase in workload for all ships in the Pacific Fleet Service Force, and *Zelima* was no exception. She saw constant duty in the combat zone carrying thousands of tons of food and other supplies to the ships of the 7th Fleet operating off the Korean coast as well as to Army men and Marine Corps units ashore and to Air Force squadrons flying daily sorties from the islands surrounding the Korean peninsula.

With the winding down of the Korean conflict in 1953, *Zelima* resumed her peacetime chores of supplying the American bases spread throughout the Pacific Ocean. However, periodic crises brought her back into potentially dangerous situations. During the waning months of 1958—when the Chinese communists brought their guns to bear on the Nationalist Chinese-held, offshore islands, Quemoy and Matsu—*Zelima* replenished units of the 7th Fleet patrolling the Taiwan Strait and delivered badly needed supplies to Americans stationed on Taiwan itself. Later, in the fall of 1961, she operated off the coast of Vietnam servicing fleet units sent there as a result of an intensification of guerrilla activity in that strife-torn land. A year later, she moved clear across the Pacific to the western coast of Panama where she replenished ships headed toward the Panama Canal on their way to join the "quarantine" of Cuba imposed by President John F. Kennedy in his successful gesture to secure the removal of Russian missiles from that island.

The spring of 1963 saw her return to the Far East and, more specifically, to the waters off troubled Vietnam. Though American involvement remained small at that time, further intensified guerrilla activity in that country brought increasing numbers of American servicemen to Vietnam and warships to their support. *Zelima* provided logistic support to the latter. Following that visit in April and May, she resumed her normal routine for about 16 months. After the Gulf of Tonkin incident spurred an even more rapid acceleration in American involvement, *Zelima*'s visits to the combat zone around the Indochinese peninsula became more regularized and frequent. By the latter 1960's, she made two, sometimes as many as three or four, replenishment visits per year to the ports and coastal waters of Vietnam bringing supplies to both ships at sea and men ashore.

The war in Vietnam dominated the remainder of her career, for she went out of service almost three years before the conflict ended early in 1973. Her last tour of duty off the Vietnamese coast came in May and June of 1969. Following a couple of months of active service, *Zelima* was decommissioned at the Mare Island Naval Shipyard in September 1969. She was turned over to the Maritime Administration for berthing in its National Defense Reserve Fleet group at Suisun Bay, Calif., in June 1970. Her name was struck from the Navy list near the end of 1976, and ownership of the ship was transferred to the Maritime Administration. As of January 1979, she remained in the custody of the Maritime Administration.

Zelima earned one battle star during the Korean War and six battle stars for Vietnamese service.

Zellars

Thomas Edward Zellars—born on 11 August 1898 in Grantville, Ga.—was appointed a midshipman at the Naval Academy on 13 June 1917 and graduated on 3 June 1920, a year early as the result of the wartime shortening of the Academy's course of instruction. On 9 July 1920, he reported for duty in *Mississippi* (Battleship No. 41). Zellars served his entire, brief Navy career in *Mississippi*, rising to the rank of lieutenant (junior grade) and attaining the position of turret commander in *Mississippi*'s No. 2 14-inch turret. On 12 June 1924, while the battleship was engaged in gunnery practice off San Pedro, Calif., an explosion and fire engulfed his turret. Lt. (jg.) Zellars and 47 others were asphyxiated almost immediately but not before he turned on the flood valve which extinguished a burning powder train—an act which undoubtedly saved the ship and many of his shipmates from destruction.

(DD-777: dp. 2,200; l. 376'6''; b. 40'10''; dr. 15'8''; s. 34.2 k. (tl.); cpl. 345; a. 6 5'', 12 40mm., 11 20mm., 10 21'' tt., 6 dcp., 2 dct.; cl. *Allen M. Sumner*)

Zellars (DD-777) was laid down on 24 December 1943 at Seattle, Wash., by the Todd-Pacific Shipyards, Inc.; launched on 19 July 1944; sponsored by Mrs. Thomas M. Zellars; and commissioned on 25 October 1944, Comdr. Blinn Van Mater in command.

After six weeks of shakedown training out of San Diego, Calif., *Zellars* returned north to Bremerton, Wash., for post-shakedown availability. She spent Christmas 1944 in Bremerton but, soon thereafter, got underway for Pearl Harbor and the second phase of training preparatory to her entry into combat. That training lasted until mid-March 1945 at which time she put to sea with a portion of the Okinawa invasion force. She was assigned to Task Group (TG) 54.3, a part of Rear Admiral Morton L. Deyo's Gunfire and Covering Force built around the old battleships. Staged through Ulithi in the Western Carolines, *Zellars* and her consorts arrived in the Ryukyus on 25 March. For the next week, she joined the battleships and cruisers of TF 54, first in supporting the occupation of the roadstead at Kerama Retto and then in subjecting Okinawa itself to a systematic, long-duration, preinvasion bombardment. Because most of the targets on Okinawa were located well inland in accordance with Japan's relatively new strategy of defense in depth, *Zellars*' 5-inch guns usually deferred to the larger caliber batteries on board the battleships and cruisers while she provided them with antisubmarine and antiaircraft protection.

After the 1 April amphibious assault on Okinawa, she continued to screen the larger ships of TG 54.3 and provided call fire in support of the troops ashore. Her combat service, however, proved extremely short; less than a month, in fact. On the afternoon of 2 April, she was screening *Tennessee* (BB-43) when three Japanese "Jills" made a coordinated attack on her. They came at the destroyer's port quarter from an altitude of about 15 feet above water. *Zellars* rang up 25 knots to unmask all batteries and opened fire. She splashed the lead attacker at a range of 1,800 yards and caught the second some 3,000 yards away. The destroyer then shifted fire to the third intruder and began scoring 40-millimeter hits on him. The Japanese pilot, however, pressed home his attack with fanatical courage and crashed into *Zellar*'s port side, forward of the bridge in her number 2 handling room. His 500-kilogram bomb tore through several light bulkheads before exploding on the starboard side of the ship in the scullery. She temporarily lost all power, and the fireroom had to be secured. Meanwhile, the after 20-millimeter guns continued to ward off additional tormentors and assisted in splashing another plane. That evening, she limped into Kerama

Retto with extensive damage. After temporary patching, the destroyer headed back toward the United States and arrived at Terminal Island, Calif., on 1 June.

During some two and one-half months in which the ship underwent repairs and overhaul, World War II ended. *Zellars* conducted refresher training out of San Diego in September, transited the Panama Canal on 8 October, and entered the New York Naval Shipyard on the 16th. Following availability, the destroyer made a cruise—in company with *Midway* (CVB–41)—down the Atlantic coast to Guantanamo Bay, Cuba, and thence to Culebra Island where the destroyer conducted shore bombardment practice. Upon her return to the United States, the warship received orders directing her to escort *Franklin D. Roosevelt* (CVB–42) on her shakedown voyage during January and February of 1946. The highlight of the voyage was an early February visit to Rio de Janeiro, Brazil, from 1 to 11 February. On the return trip, *Zellars* received orders detaching her from the big new carrier and sending her to Pensacola, Fla. She served there until 22 April when she got underway for Earle, N.J. There, Naval Academy midshipmen came on board for a summer cruise that lasted until August.

Following routine repairs and post-availability shakedown at Casco Bay, Maine, the destroyer reported for duty with the Submarine Force, Atlantic Fleet, on 4 October. During the next three months, she served as a target ship for submarines conducting torpedo training. In January and February of 1947, she participated in the first major fleet tactical exercise since Fleet Problem XXI in 1940. The warship returned to Norfolk on 17 March and, for the next four months, operated along the middle Atlantic and New England coasts.

On 21 July, *Zellars* departed Norfolk on a deployment to European waters. She arrived in Plymouth, England, 10 days later and, for the next month, made the rounds to various British ports. Early in September, she transited the Strait of Gibraltar to begin a three-month cruise in the Mediterranean Sea. She visited Soudha Bay at Crete; Taranto, Naples, Venice, Salerno, and Trieste in Italy; and Tangiers on the North African coast. *Zellars* concluded her first 6th Fleet deployment upon her arrival at Boston on 1 December 1947 and entered the Boston Naval Shipyard that same day for a three-month overhaul. Following repairs, she conducted a five-week refresher cruise out of the base at Guantanamo Bay, Cuba. *Zellars* reentered Norfolk again on 20 April 1948 and remained there for six weeks preparing to deploy once more to the 6th Fleet. On 1 June, the destroyer set sail from Norfolk and shaped a course for the Mediterranean. Her second tour of duty with the 6th Fleet proved brief, for she returned to Norfolk early in October. For almost two years, she conducted normal 2d Fleet operations out of Norfolk.

Late in June of 1950, communist forces from North Korea moved south and invaded the Republic of Korea. As a result of this breach of the peace, *Zellars* departed Norfolk in August in company with the other destroyers of Destroyer Division (DesDiv) 162 and headed for the Far East. She and her division mates arrived in Yokosuka, Japan, early in October; provisioned, and set sail for Korean waters. The destroyer remained in the Korean combat zone for nine months. During that time, her primary missions were gunfire support for United Nations troops ashore and coastal surveillance as well as antisubmarine protection for the larger American warships against an underwater threat that never materialized.

As soon as she arrived on station in October 1950, she took part in the opening of Wonsan harbor. Late in November, the communist Chinese intervened in the conflict driving the United Nations troops into a southward retreat. *Zellars* initially supported the retirement of a South Korean division down the east coast and then provided gunfire support to the marines in the defensive perimeter around Wonsan while the Army's 3d Infantry Division was evacuated by sea. In mid-December, the warship moved north from Wonsan to Hungnam to provide gunfire support during the evacuation of another coastal enclave held by retreating United Nations forces. She remained in Korean waters for another six months after the November-December evacuations and ranged both coasts of Korea delivering gunfire in support of the ground troops and interdicting coastal logistics.

The destroyer returned to the United States in July 1951 and resumed duty with the Atlantic Fleet. Upon her return, she concentrated increasingly upon honing her antisubmarine warfare (ASW) capability. Over the next eight years, training in ASW tactics was emphasized on five extended cruises to European and Mediterranean waters and in exercises in the western Atlantic and in the Caribbean Sea.

Late in 1959, *Zellars* entered the Norfolk Naval Shipyard and began Mark II Fleet Rehabilitation and Modernization overhaul and alterations. The addition of more up-to-date equipment added years to her projected service life and greatly enhanced her ASW capability. The most noticeable change was the addition of a flight deck and stowage area for an ASW helicopter. These modifications were completed in June of 1960; and the ship moved south to a new home port—Mayport, Fla. Between June 1960 and December 1965, *Zellars* made five deployments to European waters. Four of those assignments consisted of duty in the Mediterranean with the 6th Fleet and the remaining one involved a midshipman summer cruise to northern European ports. Her duties with the 2d Fleet in the western Atlantic and Caribbean consisted for the most part of training and yard overhauls but were highlighted by participation in operations enforcing the Cuban quarantine in the fall of 1962 and occasional duty supporting the Polaris missile test program.

In 1966, she remained in the western Atlantic for the entire year, breaking her training routine between mid-May and mid-September for regular overhaul at the Boston Naval Shipyard. More than half of 1967 was taken up by the NATO exercise Operation "Matchmaker III," an experiment designed to determine what problems might arise from combined operations of ships of various nations and to test solutions to those problems. The operation began in mid-January 1967 and lasted until mid-August. It took her first to the West Indies, thence across the Atlantic to the waters around northern Europe, and finally to the coasts of New England and Canada.

In September 1967, she resumed 2d Fleet operations along the eastern seaboard. After completing the annual "Springboard" operation in February and preparing at Newport, R.I., for overseas movement, *Zellars* sailed for the Mediterranean once again, putting to sea from Newport on 4 April 1968. That deployment, consisting of the usual unilateral and multinational training exercises and goodwill port visits, lasted until 27 September when she tied up at Newport once again. Following eight months of operations out of Newport, the destroyer embarked upon the last Mediterranean cruise of her career on 9 April 1969. The usual Mediterranean training and port visit routine occupied her time for the next six months.

The warship returned to Newport on 10 October and, one month later, moved to New York where she became a Naval Reserve training ship. That duty constituted her mission for the remaining 16 months of her active career. *Zellars* was decommissioned on 19 March 1971, and her name was struck from the Navy list. Set aside for sale to the Iranian government, she was moved to the Philadelphia Naval Shipyard where she underwent extensive modification over the next 20 months. Renamed *Babr* (DDG–7), she was commissioned in the Iranian Navy on 12 October 1973 at the Philadelphia Naval Shipyard. As of September 1979, she remained active with the Iranian Navy.

Zellars earned one battle star during World War II and four battle stars during the Korean War.

Zenda

(MB: l. 48'; b. 10'; dr. 3'7'' (mean); s. 10.0 k.; cpl. 6; a. 1 Lewis mg.)

Zenda (SP–688)—a wooden-hulled motorboat built in 1912 at Neponset, Mass., by George Lawley & Sons—was acquired by the Navy on 19 May 1917 from Mr. Francis S. Eaton for service with the section patrol. Commissioned on 25 June 1917, she served in the 1st Naval District as a district patrol craft for the duration of World War I. Decommissioned soon after the armistice, she was returned to her owner on 30 January 1919; and her name was struck from the Navy list that same day.

Zenith

(MB: dp. 19; l. 73'3''; b. 11'8½''; dr. 3' 10'' (aft); s. 27 k.; cpl. 12; a. 1 3-pdr., 2 mg.)

Zenith (SP–61)—a motorboat constructed in 1917 at Camden, N.J., by the Mathis Yacht Building Co.—was acquired by the Navy on 21 April 1917 at Philadelphia from Charles Longstreet of that city and commissioned there on 23 April 1917. Assigned to section-patrol duty, *Zenith* conducted surveillance patrols to protect the harbors and estuaries of the 4th Naval District coastline from enemy incursion—primarily against submarine and mining operations. She served until hostilities had ended. She was decommissioned on 21 November 1918 just 10 days after the armistice. That same day, her name was struck from the Navy list; and *Zenith* was returned to her owner.

Zenobia

Minor planet no. 840; the name itself is derived from the Greek word meaning "having life from Zeus." It was also the name of the Queen of Palmyra who reigned from 267 to 272 A.D.

(AKA–52: dp. 7,000; l. 426'0''; b. 58'0''; dr. 16'0''; s. 16.9 k.; cpl. 303; a. 1 5''', 8 40mm., 10 20mm.; cl. *Artemis*; T. S4–SE2–BE1)

Zenobia (AKA–52) was laid down under a Maritime Commission contract (MC hull 1913) on 12 May 1945 at Providence, R.I., by the Kaiser-Walsh Co.; launched on 6 July 1945; sponsored by Mrs. Lillian V. MacDonald; and commissioned at the Boston Navy Yard on 6 August 1945, Lt. Comdr. F. C. Rice in command.

Following her shakedown, *Zenobia* relieved *Vermilion* (AKA–107) as a training ship with the Atlantic Fleet's Operational Training Command on 19 August. She served briefly in that role before she was reassigned to Service Force, Atlantic Fleet (ServLant), on 11 September. She operated with ServLant into 1946.

Although allocated to the Amphibious Force of the Atlantic Fleet on 1 April 1946, *Zenobia*'s days as a United States naval vessel were numbered. She reported to the Commandant, 3d Naval District, on 7 April and was decommissioned exactly one month later, on 7 May, at Brooklyn, N.Y. Struck from the Navy list on 30 November 1946, *Zenobia* was transferred at Brooklyn to the government of the Republic of Chile on 9 December 1946.

Renamed *Presidente Pinto*, the erstwhile Navy attack cargo ship served the Chilean Navy as a transport through the late 1960's and ended her active career as a training ship for midshipmen. She was transferred to "harbor duties" in 1968—probably serving as a floating barracks or accommodation ship—and was replaced as training ship by the four-masted schooner *Esmeralda*. *Presidente Pinto* was probably scrapped in about 1974.

Zeppelin

(ScStr.: dp. 21,753; lbp. 550'; b. 67.2; dr. 26'6''; s. 15.5 k.)

Zeppelin—a steamer constructed in 1914 by *Bremer Vulkan* at Vegesack, Germany, for the North German Lloyd Line—was seized by United States officials at New York soon after the country's entry into World War I and turned over to the Emergency Fleet Corp. The Navy did not acquire her until the spring of 1919, well after the end of the war. She was placed in commission at New York on 5 March 1919, Comdr. William W. Galbraith in command.

Assigned to the New York Division of the Transport Force (not to be confused with the Naval Overseas

Zenith (SP–61) in a light gray finish, her hull number in small white characters at her bow, and a rapid-firing 3-pounder gun on her forecastle. This yacht was designed with the possibility of naval service in mind.

Transportation Service), *Zeppelin* made two round-trip voyages between the United States and Europe, returning 15,800 American soldiers back home. Her third voyage took her back to Europe. However, she did not return to the United States. Instead, she was decommissioned on 25 November 1919 and returned to the United States Shipping Board which, in turn, transferred her to the British on 27 December 1919. Acquired by the Orient Steam Navigation Co., Ltd., in 1920, *Zeppelin* was renamed SS *Ormuz* and served under that name until the latter half of the 1920's. By 1927, her name had disappeared from mercantile lists.

Zeta

The 6th letter of the Greek alphabet.

(ScStr.: t. 60; l. 58'; b. 13'; dph. 5'; s. 8 k.; a. 8 Enfield muskets, 1 "torpedo")

J. G. Loane—a small wooden steamer built at Philadelphia, Pa., in 1844—was purchased by the Navy on 3 June 1864 at Philadelphia from William S. Mason. Renamed *Tug No. 6* and commissioned on 8 June 1864, Acting Ensign Frederick W. Mintzer in command, this small craft was sometimes referred to as *Picket Boat No. 6* in dispatches. Renamed *Zeta* in the following November, she served as a torpedo tug in the James River until April of 1865. Transferred in that month to the Potomac flotilla of Comdr. Foxhall A. Parker, *Zeta* guarded the Bush River (Md.) Bridge until sent to the Washington Navy Yard in May. Her services no longer required, *Zeta* was sold to C. Vanderwerken on 24 June 1865.

Zeus

The king of the Greek gods.

(ARB–4: dp. 3,960 (lim.); l. 328'0''; b. 50'0''; dr. 11'2'' (lim.); s. 11.6 k. (tl.); cpl. 254; a. 1 3'', 8 40mm; cl. *Aristaeus*)

Zeus (ARB–4)—originally projected as *LST–132*—was laid down on 17 June 1943 at Seneca, Ill., by the Chicago Bridge & Iron Co.; launched on 26 October 1943; sponsored by Mrs. C. A. Brown; converted to a battle damage repair ship by the Maryland Drydock Co. at Baltimore, Md.; and commissioned at Norfolk, Va., on 11 April 1944.

Zeus departed Hampton Roads on 16 May and, after a stop at Guantanamo Bay, Cuba, arrived in the Canal Zone on 28 May. She transited the canal on 28 and 29 May and continued her voyage, via San Diego, to Pearl Harbor. The ship arrived in the Hawaiian Islands on 23 June and reported to the Commander, Service Force, Pacific Fleet, for duty. *Zeus* spent the remainder of World War II repairing damaged ships at intermediate bases such as Eniwetok Atoll. After continued service in the Far East, she returned to San Pedro, Calif., in the spring of 1946. On 30 August 1946, she was placed out of commission and was berthed at San Diego with the Pacific Reserve Fleet. *Zeus* remained in reserve until 1 June 1973 at which time her name was struck from the Navy list. Her final disposition remains unknown, but she was probably sold and broken up for scrap.

Zigzag

(MB: l. 44'0''; b. 8'6''; dr. 2'10'' (mean); s. 21.0 k.; a. 1 .30-cal. mg.)

Zigzag—a wooden-hulled motorboat completed in May 1916 by the A. E. Luders Construction Co., of Stamford, Conn.—was acquired by the Navy from T. J. Backman of Bradenton, Fla., and delivered on 27 June 1917.

Assigned the classification SP–106, *Zigzag* was placed in commission on 8 August 1917.

Assigned to the 7th Naval District, she operated on local section patrol duties for the duration of World War I and probably until the cessation of all defensive patrols on 24 November 1918. She was subsequently anchored in the North Beach Basin, Key West, Fla., awaiting disposition when a hurricane battered the Florida Keys on 9 September 1919 and swept through the yacht basin with disastrous results.

The next day, eight SP boats, including *Zigzag*, were found completely wrecked, literally dashed to pieces on the seawall. Salvage crews later hauled the tangled wreckage from the water and burned it, retaining only the machinery to survey it for future disposal. *Zigzag* was struck from the Navy list on 4 October 1919.

Zillah

(MB: t. 16.8; l. 58'8''; b. 11'8''; s. 12.0 k.)

Zillah (SP–2804)—a wooden-hulled motorboat built in 1903 by Charles Clarke & Co. at Galveston, Tex., and rebuilt in 1913 by the same firm—was acquired by the Navy from that same company in June 1918. Though there is no record of the date on which the motorboat was commissioned, she was assigned to the 8th Naval District and served with the naval port guard at Galveston for the remainder of World War I. *Zillah* was placed out of commission on 13 December 1918. Her name was struck from the Navy list on that same day, and she was simultaneously returned to her owner.

Zipalong

(MB: t. 30 (gross); l. 78'0''; b. 11'2''; dr. 4'0'' (mean); s. 15.0 k.; cpl. 8; a. 1 mg.)

Gansetta—a wooden-hulled motorboat built in 1907 at Boston, Mass., by George Lawley and Sons—was subsequently renamed *Zipalong* and was acquired by the Navy in the spring of 1917 from Albert and Leonard Schwarz and W. W. Miller.

Assigned the classification SP–3, *Zipalong* was commissioned on 13 June 1917 at the Philadelphia Navy Yard, Ens. Frank A. Snow, USNRF, in command. With her section base at Cape May, N.J., *Zipalong* conducted local section patrols within the 4th Naval District into the autumn of 1917. Decommissioned on 27 November 1917 at Philadelphia, *Zipalong* was returned to her owners in early 1918 and resumed civilian pursuits.

Zircon

A semi-precious gemstone derived from the mineral, zirconium silicate.

(PY–16: dp. 1,220 (est.); l. 235'4''; b. 34'; dr. 13' (mean); s. 14 k.; cpl. 108; a. 2 3'', 6 .30-cal. mg., 2 dct.)

Nakhoda—a yacht built in 1929 by the Pusey & Jones Corp. at Wilmington, Del.—was acquired by the Navy from automobile body manufacturer, Mr. Fred J. Fisher, of Detroit, Mich., on 9 December 1940; renamed *Zircon* (PY–16); outfitted at the Brooklyn Navy Yard; and commissioned on 25 March 1941, Lt. Comdr. Cornelius M. Sullivan in command.

Though assigned to New London, Conn., as an antiaircraft gunnery school ship specializing in machine-gun training for officer trainees, *Zircon* also conducted inshore patrols and visited ports from New York to Casco Bay, Maine. Those duties continued until the fall of 1941, at which time she began making mail and dispatch runs between Portland, Maine, and Argentia, Newfoundland. In mid-February 1942, she was reassigned to the Eastern Sea Frontier and initially conducted patrols along the coast of New Jersey. Following extensive repairs in June, the converted yacht reported for duty with the Commander, Caribbean Sea Frontier, under whose auspices she escorted convoys between Guantanamo Bay, Cuba, and New York City. *Zircon* steamed back and forth between Cuba and New York—occasionally calling at some of the islands of the West Indies, notably Trinidad and San Salvador—until 1 March 1944. At that juncture, she received a temporary assignment to the Coast Guard's weather patrol. Between March and November 1944, she operated out of Boston and plied the waters of the North Atlantic with the weather patrol. However, she continued to participate to some extent in the protection of New York-Guantanamo Bay convoys and of other mercantile traffic along the North American coast.

On 16 November 1944, *Zircon* reported for duty with the Commander, DD–DE Shakedown Task Group. That duty lasted until 7 December, when she was designated relief flagship for the Commander in Chief, Atlantic Fleet, based at Philadelphia. She served in that capacity through the end of World War II. In September 1945, she received orders to report to the Commandant, 6th Naval District at Charleston, S.C., to prepare for decommissioning and disposal. On 10 May 1946, *Zircon* was decommissioned at Charleston. Her name was struck from the Navy list on 5 June 1946, and she was turned over to the Maritime Commission for disposal on 17 October 1946. She was sold by the War Shipping Administration on 24 April 1947.

Zirkel

(ScStr: dp. 12,700; l. 416'6''; b. 53'; dr. 27'6'' (aft); s. 10 k.; cpl. 62)

Zirkel (Id. No. 3407)—a cargoman built in 1918 at Oakland, Calif., for the United States Shipping Board by the Moore Shipbuilding Co.—was acquired by the Navy on 27 September 1918 for duty with the Naval Overseas Transportation Service and was commissioned that same day at San Francisco, Lt. Comdr. David R. Williams, USNRF, in command.

Zirkel got underway for the Gulf of Mexico with a cargo of nitrates. Steaming via the Panama Canal, she arrived at New Orleans on 30 January 1919 and unloaded her cargo. Following repairs to her turbines, the ship filled her holds with cotton, coffee, and steel and put to sea on 6 February. After a 21-day voyage, *Zirkel* entered port at Liverpool, England, and began unloading her cargo. She then took on about 800 tons of iron ore and headed back to the United States on 13 March. On the 29th, the freighter arrived in Philadelphia and, after unloading, began preparations for demobilization. On 3 May 1919, she was placed out of commission and was returned to the custody of the United States Shipping Board. The Shipping Board retained her until 1930 at which time her name ceased to appear in merchant vessel registers.

Zita

(MB: dp. 7; l. 40'0''; b. 11'0''; dr. 2'4½'' (mean); s. 11.0 k.; cpl. 6; a. 1 1-pdr.)

Zita—a wooden-hulled motorboat built in 1916 at Brooklyn, N.Y., by Charles Johnson—was owned by H. E. Boucher, of Brooklyn, in 1917 at the time of her inspection by the Navy in the 3d Naval District. Records concerning this craft are sparse, but they show that the Navy gave the classification SP-21 to the boat and assigned her to district patrol duties in the 3d Naval District. However, the extant records do not reveal either the length or the character of her service nor do they tell whether or not *Zita* was ever commissioned.

Zizania

The wild, or Indian, rice native to North America.

(Lighthouse tender: dp. 575; l. 161.0'; b. 27.0'; dph. 12.0''; dr. 6'9'' (mean); cpl. 27)

Zizania—a lighthouse tender built at Baltimore in 1888 for the United States Lighthouse Service—was transferred to the War Depatment by an executive order dated 24 April 1917. Subsequently reassigned to the Navy, *Zizania* served during World War I as a tender to section patrol craft operating in the 1st Naval District. When control over the Lighthouse Service on 1 July 1919 reverted to the Department of Commerce, *Zizania*'s name was struck from the Navy list. Based at Portland, Maine, she resumed duty tending lighthouses along the New England coast and remained so employed until 1925 when her name was dropped from the list of Lighthouse Service vessels.

Zoraya

(Yacht: t. 129 (gross); l. 135'; b. 18'; dr. 7'6'' (aft); s. 12 k.; cpl. 33; a. 2 3-pdrs.)

Zoraya (SP-235)—a wooden-hulled yacht constructed in 1901 by J. M. Bayles & Sons at Port Jefferson, N.Y.—was acquired by the Navy from Mr. William Biel for service with the section patrol on 16 August 1917 and commissioned at New York on 17 December 1917. For the duration of the war, *Zoraya* served under the command of the Commandant, 3d Naval District, and patrolled the coasts of New York and New Jersey. On 8 February 1919, some three months after the end of hostilities, the yacht was returned to her owner.

Zouave

An infantry corps recruited in Algeria after the French conquest in 1830. The corps—originally composed of native Algerians of the Zwawa tribe—was noted for its distinctive drill formation and native dress. French soldiers replaced the Algerians by 1840.

At the beginning of the Civil War, Elmer Ephraim Ellsworth, an American lawyer and friend of Abraham Lincoln, organized several regiments of volunteers called Zouaves. These regiments were so-called as they adopted the uniforms and style of drill of the French Zouaves. Other Zouave regiments were organized during the war, though their distinctive uniforms proved to be unsuitable for battle and were abandoned.

(ScTug: t. 127; dr. 9'; s. 10 k.; a. 2 30-pdr. P.r.)

Zouave—a screw steamer built in 1861 at Albany, N.Y.—was purchased by the Navy on 20 December 1861 at New York City and soon therafter was delivered to the Navy at Hampton Roads, Va., for duty in the North Atlantic Blockading Squadron. On 1 February 1862, she was placed in commission, Acting Master Henry Reaney in command—and assigned the tasks of patrolling the mouth of the James River at night and serving as a tender for frigates *Congress* and *Cumberland* during daylight hours.

Shortly after noon on 8 March, the tug was moored to a wharf at Newport News when the quartermaster spotted some black smoke near the mouth of the Elizabeth River. *Zouave* got underway and headed across Hampton Roads to investigate. Soon observers on the tug could make out "what to all appearances looked like the roof of a very big barn belching forth smoke as from a chimney on fire." After a Confederate flag came in view, the men on *Zouave* concluded that the strong looking craft was the long expected Southern ironclad *Virginia*—the rebuilt *Merrimack*—finally emerging to challenge the Union blockaders. *Zouave* then opened up with her 30-pounder Parrott rifle and fired about a half-dozen rounds before she was recalled by a signal hoisted on board *Cumberland*.

By this time, the Union warships in Hampton Roads and batteries at Newport News had also opened fire on the Southern ironclad. When *Virginia* reached a position abreast of *Congress*, she fired a broadside into that Union frigate and headed straight for *Cumberland*.

At this point, *Zouave* was in between the fire of *Virginia*, that of her escorts *Patrick Henry* and *Jamestown*, and the "friendly" Union guns based ashore at Newport News and Fort Monroe. She kept firing at the Southern ships until she was signaled by *Congress* to come alongside. The tug quickly obeyed and began the difficult process of taking the blazing frigate in tow. As *Zouave* was attempting to pull *Congress* into shoal water where she might be safe from further attacks, *Virginia* pulled astern of the retreating Union ships and subjected them to broadside after broadside. When *Congress* grounded, she hoisted a white flag to indicate her surrender.

Zouave cut her towlines; backed up; and, upon pulling free, resumed her firing. Lookouts on the tug thus spotted a signal on *Minnesota*—which had also grounded but was still in the fight—asking for assistance. While the tug was heading for that plucky Union blockader, she was hit "by a shot which carried away our rudder-post and one of the blades of her propeller wheel." Unable to steer and moving straight toward *Virginia*, *Zouave* backed up and used her hawser "over our port quarter" to keep moving toward *Minnesota*. During the passage, *Whitehall* arrived on the scene and assisted *Zouave* to her destination. The battle-damaged tug lay alongside *Minnesota* throughout the night, ready to assist the Union ships insofar as she was able.

The next day, *Zouave* was upstaged by the newly arrived *Monitor* during that novel ironclad's epic battle with *Virginia*. On 11 March, she proceeded, in tow, to the Baltimore Navy Yard for repairs.

Zouave returned to Hampton Roads on 3 May 1862. She spent the next six months deployed in Hampton Roads and surrounding waters on guard duty as an armed tug. She also carried out picket and dispatch assignments. On 26 October 1862, *Zouave* received instructions to hail *Delaware*, then cruising between the Piankatank and York Rivers, Va., and ordering her to report to Hampton Roads to prepare for duty in the North Carolina sounds. On 29 October 1862 at Rip Raps, Va., after *Delaware* failed to acknowledge *Zouave*'s recognition signal, *Zouave* mistakenly fired on *Delaware*, taking the steamer for a Confederate blockade runner.

Returning to Hampton Roads, *Zouave* and *Young America* towed monitor *Passaic* to the Washington Navy Yard for repairs on 30 November 1862. On 18 January 1863, *Zouave* captured the small schooner *J. C. McCabe* and six prisoners in the James River; and, on the night of 11 and 12 April 1863, she participated in a reconnaissance of Jamestown Island in the James. She served as part of the Union force capturing the formidable Confederate position at Hill's Point on the Nansemond River, Va., on 20 April 1863. This relieved Union army positions near Suffolk, Va., of Southern pressure. *Zouave* steamed to Baltimore for repairs in May 1863.

Zouave deteriorated steadily during the remaining two years of the war. On 29 February 1864, she was detailed to *Atlanta* to guard against possible attacks by Confederate torpedo boats. In April 1864, *Zouave* sailed to Baltimore for repairs. She soon returned to Hampton Roads, only to be ordered to the Norfolk Navy Yard for more repairs on 4 August 1864. *Zouave* remained in the yard through early December 1864, then was deployed in the James River until the war's end. After a final round of repairs at Norfolk, the tug proceeded to the New York Navy Yard on 1 June 1865.

Zouave was decommissioned at New York on 14 June 1865 and was sold at public auction there to M. O. Roberts on 12 July 1865.

Zrinyi

(Battleship: dp. 14,500; l. 456'0''; b. 82'0''; dr. 26'6'' (mean) ; s. 20.0 k.: cpl. 880; a. 4 12'', 8 9.4'', 20 3.9'', 6 11-pdrs., 2 11-pdrs. (AA), 3 17.7'' tt.; cl. *Radetzky*)

Zrinyi—an Austro-Hungarian, pre-dreadnought battleship—was laid down on 15 November 1908 at the *Stabilimento Tecnico* of Trieste; launched on 12 April 1910; and completed in July 1911.

During World War I, *Zrinyi* served with the 2d Division of the Austro-Hungarian Navy's battleships and took part in the bombardment of the key seaport of Ancona, Italy, on 24 May 1915. However, Allied control of the Strait of Otranto meant that the Austro-Hungarian Navy was, for all intent and purposes, effectively bottled up in the Adriatic. Nonetheless, their presence tied down a substantial force of Allied ships.

After the Hapsburg Empire collapsed in 1918, the Austrians wanted to turn the fleet over to the newly created state of Yugoslavia to prevent the Italians from getting their hands on the ships. However, the victorious Allies refused to acknowledge the conversations between the Austrians and Yugoslavians and, in due course, reallocated the ships.

Zrinyi had apparently been turned over to the Yugoslavs, as it was a Yugoslavian naval officer, *Korvettenkapitän* Marijan Polic who turned over the ship to representatives of the United States Navy at Spalato, Dalmatia, on the afternoon of 22 November 1919. Simultaneously the pre-dreadnought was commissioned as USS *Zrinyi*; and Lt. E. E. Hazlett, USN, assumed command. The initial American complement consisted of four officers and 174 enlisted men—the latter entirely composed of United States Naval Reserve Force personnel.

Zrinyi remained at anchor at Spalato for nearly a year while the negotiations that would determine her ultimate fate dragged on. Only once, in fact, did she apparently turn her engines over; and that occurred during a severe gale that struck Spalato on 9 February 1920.

On the morning of 7 November 1920, *Zrinyi* was decommissioned; *Chattanooga* (C–16) took her in tow and, assisted by *Brooks* (DD–232) and *Hovey* (DD–208), pulled the battleship to Papaja, Italy. Under the terms of the treaties of Versailles and St. Germain, *Zrinyi* was ultimately turned over to the Italian government at Venice. The pre-dreadnought was later broken up for scrap.

Zuiderdijk

(ScStr: dp. 11,500; l. 412'; b. 53.5'; dr. 24'1''; s. 12 k.; cpl. 124; a. 1 4'')

Zuiderdijk (Id. No. 2724)—a freighter built in 1912 by William Gray & Co. Ltd. at Hartlepool, England—was operated by the Holland-America Line until 1918 at which time the pressing need of the United States for ships to transport men and material to the front in Europe forced President Woodrow Wilson to order the seizure of Dutch ships in American ports under international law's rule of angary. Customs officials at San Juan, Puerto Rico, took possession of her on 21 March 1918 and turned her over to the Navy which placed her in commission on 23 March 1918, Lt. W. F. Keefer, USNRF, in command.

After preliminary refitting, *Zuiderdijk* departed San Juan on 29 March and shaped a course for the Canal Zone. She remained at Cristobal for nearly a month before getting underway on 25 April and steaming north. The ship entered New York harbor on 4 May, unloaded the Panama Railroad Co. cargo she had picked up at Cristobal, and replaced it with Army supplies destined for Europe. She departed the east coast in convoy on 17 May and entered Le Havre, France, on 1 June. After discharging her cargo and taking on ballast, *Zuiderdijk* stood out of Le Havre on 12 June and headed home. She concluded a 20-day crossing when she moored in New York again on 2 July. Eleven days of repairs and cargo loading preceded the ship's second departure for France on 13 July. Arriving at Gironde on the 28th, *Zuiderdijk* pulled into St. Nazaire the following day. She remained there until mid-August, trading the incoming cargo for one bound for New York. The cargo ship left St. Nazaire on 18 August and returned to New York on the last day of the month. During the ensuing two weeks, she went into drydock for repairs, took on fuel, and loaded cargo for France. On 14 September, the ship stood out of New York on her third and final wartime voyage to Europe. Arriving at Brest on 29 September, she moved to Verdon the next day and began discharging her cargo. Upon completion of that operation, *Zuiderdijk* loaded ballast and set sail for the United States on 15 October.

The ship arrived in New York on 28 October. While she was there preparing for the return crossing, the armistice of 11 November ended hostilities. On the 12th, she departed New York on the first of two postwar voyages to Europe. The ship reached Quiberon on 25 November, unloaded her burden, and replaced it with a mixed load of 700 tons of rails for ballast and 500 tons of general cargo for return to the United States. She departed the French coast on 6 December and entered New York harbor on Christmas Eve. After minor repairs, she moved south to Norfolk, Va., where she loaded a cargo belonging to the United States Shipping Board. Late in January 1919, she transported that cargo via the Panama Canal to Guayaquil in Ecuador, loaded a cargo of cocoa and, on 12 February, headed for the canal once again. On 10 March, the ship arrived at St. Thomas in the Virgin Islands where she received orders to continue immediately on to France. *Zuiderdijk* entered Le Havre, France, on 27 March and remained there almost a month before heading back to the United States on 24 April.

Arriving in New York on 7 May, she began loading a Shipping Board cargo for her last voyage as a ship of the United States Navy. She stood out of New York on 17 June, discharged her cargo at London during the first two weeks of July, and continued on to Rotterdam. She reached her destination on 17 July; and, on the 21st, she was simultaneously decommissioned, struck from the Navy list, and returned to her former owners. She resumed mercantile service, first under the Dutch flag with the Holland-America Line and, after 1923, with T. Law & Co. as SS *Misty Law*. Her name disappeared from mercantile records in the early 1930's.

Zumbrota

(MB: t. 34 (gross); l. 70'0''; b. 14'6''; dr. 2'1''; s. 12.5 k.; cpl. 7; a. 1 3-pdr., 2 mg.)

Zumbrota—a motor boat built in 1914 at Port Clinton, Ohio, by the Matthews Boat Co.—was acquired by the Navy on 11 August 1917 from circus entrepreneur, C. E. Ringling, of Sarasota, Fla., for service as a section patrol boat and was designated SP–93.

Commissioned on 11 August, *Zumbrota* was assigned to the 7th Naval District and operated out of Key West, Fla. She conducted local patrols for the duration of the war. Redesignated YP–93 in 1920, she continued her operations in the Florida waters of the 7th Naval District until decommissioned on 5 November 1926. Struck from the Navy list three days later, the boat was sold to the Thompson Fish Co., of Key West, on 3 May 1927.

Zuni

The popular name given to a tribe of Pueblo Indians indigenous to the area around the Zuni River in central New Mexico near the Arizona state line.

(AT–95: dp. 1,589 (tl.); l. 205'0''; b. 38'6''; dr. 15'4''

(f.); s. 16.5 k. (tl.); cpl. 85; a. 1 3'', 2 40mm.; cl. *Navajo*)

Zuni (AT–95) was laid down on 8 March 1943 at Portland, Oreg., by the Commercial Iron Works; launched on 31 July 1943; sponsored by Mrs. J. J. O'Donnell; and commissioned on 9 October 1943, Lt. Ray E. Chance in command.

Zuni completed shakedown training late in October and on the 28th reported for duty with the Western Sea Frontier. The following day, she departed Puget Sound, bound for Kodiak, Alaska. On 10 November, she stood out of the harbor at Kodiak with two barges in tow. In extremely heavy weather during the voyage south, the towlines to both barges parted; and *Zuni* experienced great difficulty in keeping herself afloat. Though she managed to maintain contact with the second barge after it broke loose, she ultimately received orders to abandon it and make for Seattle, Wash.

On 1 December, the tug was reassigned to Service Squadron (ServRon) 2 and departed Seattle that same day with a barge in tow, bound for Oakland, Calif. After repairs at Oakland, the tug headed west for the New Hebrides on 27 December 1943, in company with four cargo ships, and arrived in Espiritu Santo at the end of January 1944. Early in February, the tug left Espiritu Santo, set her course for Hawaii, and arrived in Pearl Harbor on 17 February. She performed routine missions at Oahu for about a month, getting underway on 21 March for a round-trip voyage to Canton Island. She returned to Oahu on 9 April towing two barges from Canton Island. On 20 April, she stood out of Pearl Harbor, pulling three barges bound for Majuro Atoll, and returned to Hawaii on 11 May. On 15 May 1944, she was redesignated ATF–95.

A week later, she began an extended tour of duty in the Central Pacific. Towing *ARD–16*, the tug arrived in Kwajalein lagoon on 2 June. Reassigned to ServRon 12, *Zuni* served as a harbor tug at Kwajalein until mid-July when she again took *ARD–16* in tow and got underway for the Mariana Islands. There, she participated briefly in the 24 July assault on Tinian before settling into a routine of shuttle voyages between Eniwetok and the Marianas. Late in September, she towed *ARD–17* to the Palau Islands where, during the first 18 days of October, she provided support services to the combined forces invading Peleliu. At that point, she received urgent orders to rendezvous with *Houston* (CL–81) after that light cruiser had been damaged by two torpedoes during a Japanese aerial blitz to answer TF 38's raids on Okinawa and Formosa. She relieved *Pawnee* (ATF–74) of the light cruiser and towed the battered warship into Ulithi lagoon on 27 October. After serving at the anchorage there for five days, the tug returned to sea with a group of oilers. Soon another set of urgent orders sent her to aid another light cruiser, *Reno* (CL–96), which had been torpedoed in the Philippines, off the San Bernardino Strait, on 3 November by Japanese submarine *I–41*. Though the cruiser nearly capsized, *Zuni*'s and *Reno*'s ships' companies combined marvelously to meet the threat; and the tug succeeded in towing the cruiser 1,500 miles back to Ulithi.

The tug remained in Ulithi for the rest of November and throughout most of December. During the latter month, she towed the disabled merchantman SS *John B. Floyd* into Ulithi and conducted a solitary cruise to eastward of the Philippines. On 29 December, *Zuni* put to sea with TG 30.8, the replenishment group for TF 38, and cruised for almost a month off Luzon. She returned to Ulithi on 28 January for engine repairs.

She moved back out to sea in February and arrived off Iwo Jima three days after the initial assault. For 31 days, she performed yeoman service for the warships in the area. She pulled a transport off a sand bar. She deliberately ran herself aground alongside a disabled LST to help that ship land ammunition. More routine missions consisted of assisting broached landing craft and laying submerged fuel pipes.

Work in the shallows, however, was as dangerous to her as to others. While attempting to salve *LST–727* on 23 March 1945, she was stranded on Yellow Beach when a broken towline fouled her anchor and propeller. She lost two crewmen in the disaster and suffered a broken keel and holed sides. She was pulled off the beach, temporarily repaired, and towed to Saipan. After further temporary repairs, *Zuni* was towed to Pearl Harbor where she arrived at the end of May. During the more than 14 weeks of repairs she underwent there, World War II ended.

Zuni resumed active duty on 15 September and served with the Pacific Fleet until early in 1946, when she was transferred to the Atlantic Fleet. She served in the 8th Naval District until she was decommissioned on 29 June 1946 and transferred to the United States Coast Guard. Her name was struck from the Navy list on 19 July 1946.

Zuni earned four battle stars for her World War II service.

GUIDE TO THE SERIES

BIBLIOGRAPHY

Previous volumes of this series contain bibliographies of the widely varied historical literature of the United States Navy useful in fleshing out the condensed ship histories they contained. Rather than repeat these lists, this bibliography is restricted to more recently published books and earlier works which were used extensively in the research effort. It also lists the source materials which proved to be especially valuable in producing this new volume.

Readers who desire broader bibliographic assistance may refer to the Naval Historical Center's *United States Naval History: A Bibliography* which may be obtained through the Superintendent of Documents, Government Printing Office, Washington, D.C. 20402.

Unpublished Primary Sources

U.S. Coast Guard. *Records of the United States Coast Guard, 1789 to 1947.* Record Group 26, National Archives.

U.S. Navy. *Action Reports, 1941 to 1945 and 1950 to 1953.* Operational Archives Branch, Naval Historical Center, Washington, D.C.

————. *Area File, 1775 to 1910.* Record Group 45, National Archives. Miscellaneous naval documents arranged by date and geographical area.

————. *Cruising Reports 1898 to 1940.* Record Group 24, National Archives.

————. *Operation Plans, 1941 to 1945 and 1950 to 1953.* Operational Archives Branch, Naval Historical Center, Washington, D.C.

————. *Ships' Logs, 1801 to 1945.* Record Group 24, National Archives.

————. *Ships' Logs, 1945 to the present.* Washington National Records Center, Suitland, Maryland. Logs less than one year are held by the Office of the Chief of Naval Operations.

————. *Subject File 1775 to 1910.* Record Group 45, National Archives. Miscellaneous naval documents arranged by subject matter.

————. *War Diaries, 1941 to 1945 and 1950 to 1953.* Operational Archives Branch, Naval Historical Center, Washington, D.C.

————. *Records of the Board of Naval Commissioners, 1815 to 1842.* Record Group 45, National Archives.

————. *General Correspondence of the Bureau of Construction and Repair, 1850 to 1940.* Record Group 19, National Archives.

————. *Ships' Plans, 1794 to 1940.* Record Group 19, National Archives.

————. *Ship Source File, ca. 1920 to the present.* Ships' Histories Branch, Naval Historical Center, Washington, D.C.

————. *Letters of the Secretary of the Navy to Naval Officers, Men of War, 1798 to 1886.* Record Group 45, National Archives.

————. *Letters from Naval Officers, 1802 to 1886.* Record Group 45, National Archives.

————. *Records of the Immediate Office of the Secretary of the Navy, 1804 to 1946.* Record Group 80, National Archives.

Unpublished Secondary Sources

Clephane, L. P. *History of the Submarine Chasers in the World War.* Record Group 45, Subject File 1911 to 1927, ZOD, Box 802E, 168 pp., National Archives.

Stegmann, George H. *Statistical History of the Vessels of the U.S. Navy.* Ships' Histories Branch, Naval Historical Center, Washington, D.C.

Published Primary Sources

American States Papers: Naval Affairs. 4 vols. Washington: Gales and Seaton, 1834 to 1861. Contains early reports of the Secretaries of the Navy and other important documents.

U.S. Coast Guard. *Record of Movements, Vessels of the U.S. Coast Guard.* 2 vols. Washington: Government Printing Office, 1935. Covers the period from 1790 to 1933.

————. *Register of Commissioned and Warrant Officers.* Washington: Government Printing Office, published annually from 1917 to the present [title varies].

U.S. Congress. *Statutes at Large of the United States, Concurrent Resolutions, Recent Treaties, Conventions and Executive Proclamations* [title varies]. Boston and Washington: various publishers, 1845 to the present.

U.S. Navy. *Annual Report of the Secretary of the Navy.* Washington: various publishers, 1836 to the present. Reports prior to 1836 may be found in *American State Papers.*

————. *Navy and Marine Corps Awards Manual* (NAVPERS 15790). Revised ed. Washington: Government Printing Office, 1953.

————. *Navy Directory.* Washington: Government Printing Office, 1908 to 1942. Issued monthly 1908 to 1920; bimonthly and quarterly thereafter.

————. *Navy Register.* Washington: various publishers, 1800 to the present. Issued annually.

————. *Navy Yearbook.* Washington: Government Printing Office, 1903 to 1921.

————. *Ships' Data, U.S. Naval Vessels.* Washington: various publishers, 1911 to the present. Issued periodically.

————. *Movements of U.S. Vessels.* Washington: Government Printing Office, 1916. Covers 1866 to 1916.

Secondary Sources

Barbey, Daniel E. *MacArthur's Amphibious Navy.* Annapolis: United States Naval Institute, 1969.

Bauer, K. Jack. *Ships of the Navy, 1775 to 1969.* Troy, N.Y.: Rensselaer Polytechnic Institute, 1970.

Benham, Edith W., and Hall, Anne M. *Ships of the U.S. Navy and Their Sponsors, 1797 to 1913.* Norwood, Mass.: Plimpton Press, 1913.

————. *Ships of the U.S. Navy and Their Sponsors, 1913 to 1923.* Norwood, Mass.: Plimpton Press, 1925.

Breyer, Siegfried. *Battleships and Battle Cruisers, 1905–1970.* Garden City, N.Y.: Doubleday, 1973. 480 pp., illus., biblio.

Callahan, Edward W. *List of Officers of the Navy of the United States.* New York: L. R. Hammersley & Co., 1901.

Chapelle, Howard I. *The History of the American Sailing Navy: the Ships and Their Development.* New York: W. W. Norton, 1949.

Dulin, Robert O., Jr., & William H. Garzke, Jr. *Battleships; United States Battleships in World War II.* Annapolis: Naval Institute Press, 1976. 267 pp., illus., biblio.

Dyer, George C. *The Amphibians Came to Conquer.* Washington: United States Government Printing Office, 1972.

Elliott, Peter. *Allied Escort Ships of World War II: A Complete Survey.* Annapolis, Md.: Naval Institute Press, 1977. 575 pp., illus., appendices.

Emmons, George Fox. *The Navy of the United States from Commencement.* Washington: Gideon & Co., 1853.

Hooper, Edwin Bickford. *Mobility, Support, Endurance: A Story of Naval Operational Logistics in the Vietnam War.* Washington: Naval Nistory Division, 1972.

Jane, Fred T., *et. al.* (eds.). *Jane's Fighting Ships* [title varies]. London and New York: various publishers, 1897 to the present.

Lenton, H. T. *American Gunboats and Minesweepers* (World War II Fact Files series). New York: Arco Publishing Co., 1974. 64 pp., illus.

Liddell-Hart, Basil Henry. *History of the Second World War.* New York: G. P. Putnam's Sons, 1971.

Lytle, William M. *Merchant Steam Vessels of the United States 1807 to 1868.* Mystic, Conn.: The Steamship Historical Society of America, Pub. No. 6, 1952.

Naval Engineers Journal. Washington: American Society of Naval Engineers, 1889 to the present. Formerly the Society's *Journal.*

Neeser, Robert W. *Ship Names of the U.S. Navy.* New York: Moffat, Yard & Co., 1921.

————. *Statistical and Chronological History of the United States Navy.* 2 vols. New York: Macmillan Co., 1909.

Polmar, Norman. *Aircraft Carriers: A Graphic History of Carrier Aviation and Its Influence on World Events.* Garden City, N.Y.: Doubleday, 1969.

Preston, Anthony. *Battleships of World War I.* Harrisburg, Pa.: Stackpole Books, 1972.

Reilly, John C., Jr. *The American Destroyer, 1934–1945.* New York: Sterling, 1980.

Reilly, John C., Jr., & Robert L. Scheina. *American Predreadnought Battleships, 1886–1921; An Illustrated History.* Annapolis, Md.: Naval Institute Press, 1980.

Silverstone, Paul H. *U.S. Warships of World War I.* Garden City, N.Y.: Doubleday, 1970.

Watts, Anthony J. *Allied Submarines* (World War 2 Fact Files series), Arco, 1977. 64 pp., illus.

DEPARTMENT OF THE NAVY
NAVAL HISTORICAL CENTER
Washington Navy Yard
Washington, D. C. 20374

IN REPLY REFER TO

EPILOGUE

Now that the DANFS staff has completed its voyage
through the alphabet, we are turning our attention to
the problem of keeping the <u>Dictionary</u> up-to-date. Our
first step in this direction is to be the preparation
of the manuscript for a completely revised and updated
edition of Volume I which first appeared in print over
two decades ago. The new version will bring forward
the stories of the ships that were still in service in
1959 and will contain histories of those "A" and "B"
ships that, for one reason or another, were originally
omitted, including those recently constructed. It will
also contain revised and expanded narratives of many
men-of-war which received somewhat skimpy coverage in
the volume's first edition. Finally, hundreds of illus-
trations--which were virtually absent before--will be
added.

Meanwhile, during our work on the new Volume I, we
shall try to devise a permanent system for winning the
<u>Dictionary</u>'s battle against obsolescence. We are now
considering several different approaches to solving the
problem. The thoughts and suggestions of our readers
will aid us in selecting a method which will be satisfactory to most students of naval history.

RICHARD T. SPEER

JAMES L. MOONEY